The Junior Classic Series

Junior Classic Spanish Dictionary

SPANISH-ENGLISH and ENGLISH-SPANISH

By

WESSELY AND GIRONES

REVISED EDITION

FOLLETT PUBLISHING COMPANY
CHICAGO ILLINOIS
1946

PREFACE

In the compilation of the first edition of the Junior Classic Series of Foreign Language Dictionaries the endeavor of the authors was to produce efficient texts in the smallest possible compass.

That they were successful is testified to by the fact that thousands upon thousands of copies of these volumes are now used daily by students, travelers, and business men all over the civilized world.

Since the publishing of the first edition, however, there has come into current use many words of a somewhat special nature that were not included in the original texts.

Many of these new words or new meanings of old words and phrases have been inserted in their proper place in the body of the dictionary. Some, because of certain typographical difficulties, have been set off to themselves in A List of Popular Words to be found just before the dictionary proper.

It is hoped that these new words will add considerably to the value of these dictionaries and make them even more useful than they have been.

Inasmuch as the aim of the work is to include the largest number of words in the smallest possible space, the translations are necessarily brief and to the point.

Supplementing the general vocabularies themselves are valuable appendixes on pronunciation, proper names, and verb forms.

It is hoped that the many changes, additions, and revisions will add considerably to the everyday usefulness of these volumes and that the new edition will be given an even better reception than that so generously accorded the first.

THE PUBLISHERS.

Key to the Spanish Pronunciation.

ã sounds as *a* in *paper, tame*.
ä » » *a* » *far, lark*.
í » » *e* » *here, we*.
ĩ » » *e* » *hell, tell*.
ĭ » » *i* » *kill, big*.
õ » » *o* » *globe, pope*.
ŏ » » *o* » *not, spot*.
ũ » » *u* » *rule, true*.
ŭ » » *u* » *bull, full*.
y (as vowel) sounds as *i*.

c (before *e* and *i*) sounds as *th* in *thank*.
d' is to be pronounced very much lisped, as if followed by *h*; similar to *dh* in Gaelic *dhú*.
f sounds as *h* very harshly aspirated.
h if heard at all, is to be pronounced with a very slight aspiration.
'h is to be pronounced very harshly aspirated.
z sounds as *th* in *thank*.

Abbreviations.

Abreviaciones usadas en este diccionario.

a. == adjective, *adjetivo*.
ad. == adverb, *adverbio*.
am. == Americanism, *americanismo*.
ar. == arithmetic, *aritmética*.
art. == article, *artículo*.
bot. == botany, *botánica*.
c. == conjunction, *conjunción*.
cant. == cant term, *jerigonza*.
chem. == chemistry, *química*.
com. == commerce, *comercio*.
fam. == familiarly, *familiarmente*.
fig. == figuratively, *metafóricamente*.
gr. == grammatically, *gramática*.
in comp. == in compounds, *usado en palabras compuestas*.
law == law term, *jurisprudencia*.
mar. == marine, *marina*.
med. == medicine, *arte médica*.

mil. == military art, *milicia, guerra*.
mus. == music, *música*.
p. == participle, *participio*.
pl. == plural number, *plural*.
poet. == poetical word, *poéticamente*.
pn. == pronoun, *pronombre*.
pr. == preposition, *preposición*.
rail. == railway, *ferrocarril*.
sf. == feminine substantive, *sustantivo femenino*. |[masculino.
sm. == masculine substantive, *sustantivo*
v. a. == verb active, *verbo activo*.
v. def. == verb defective, *verbo defectivo*.
v. imp. == verb impersonal, *verbo impersonal*.
v. n. == verb neuter, *verbo neutro*.
v. r. == verb reflective, *verbo recíproco*.
vulg. == vulgarly, *vulgarmente*.

UNA LISTA DE PALABRAS POPULARES

SPANISH–ENGLISH

acelerador, m. accelerator
aeródromo, m. airdrome
aerograma, m. wireless message
aeronauta, m. aeronaut, airman
aeronave, f. airship, dirigible
aeroplano, m. aeroplane
alerón, m. aileron
álgebra, f. algebra
altímetro, m. altimeter
altoparlante, m. loudspeaker (radio)
amperaje, m. amperage
amperímetro, m. ammeter
amperio, m. ampere
anfibio, a. amphibian (aeroplane)
antena, f. aerial
ascensor, m. elevator
automóvil, m. automobile
aviación, f. aviation
aviador, m. aviator

biela, f. connecting rod
biplano, m. biplane
bujía, f. sparkplug

calorífero, m. radiator, heater
carburador, m. carburetor
chasis, m. chassis
cigüeñal, m. crank shaft
cinematógrafo, m. moving-picture
circuito, m. hook-up (radio)
condensador, m. condenser [tion
consolidación, f. merger, consolida-

deslizador, m. glider
deslizamiento, m. gliding
detector, m. detector
dínamo, f. dynamo

enfriadero, m. cold storage

farol trasero, m. tail light (of auto-
freno, m. brake   [mobile
freno neumático, air brake
fuselaje, m. fuselage

garaje, m. garage
gasolina, f. gasoline
generador, m. generator (electrical)

hangar, m. hangar (for aeroplane)
hidroavión, m. hydroplane, seaplane
hidroplano, m. hydroplane, seaplane
  (see hidroavión)

kilometraje, m. mileage
kilovatio, m. kilowatt

linterna delantera, f. headlight (of
  automobile)   [tomobile)
linterna trasera, f. tail light (of au-

magneto, m. magneto
marca de fábrica, f. trade-mark
monoplano, m. monoplane
moratoria, f. moratorium
motocicleta, f. motorcycle

neón, m. neon

parabrisa, m. windshield (automo-
paracaídas, m. parachute   [bile
parachoques, m. bumper (of automobile)
perifonear, v. a. to broadcast (radio)
perifonía, f. broadcasting (radio)

radiador, m. radiator (automobile
  and heating)
radio, s. radium (chem.)
radiocomunicación, f. radio, wireless
radiograma, m. radiogram
radioteléfono, m. radiotelephone
radiotelegrafista, n. wireless operator
radiotelegrama, m. radiogram
radiotelegraphía, f. radiotelegraphy,
  wireless
radiotransmisor, m. radio transmitter

sóviet, m. soviet

tenis, m. tennis
tractor, m. tractor
tractor oruga, m. caterpillar tractor
tranvía, m. street-car

vagón tanque, m. tank car
volante de dirección, m. steering
  wheel (automobile)

See page 256 *for* ENGLISH-SPANISH *of A List of Popular Words.*

Clave para la pronunciación de la lengua inglesa.

ǎ se pronuncia como *e* en *ébano, hé.*

á » » » *a* » *ala.*

â sonido propio de la lengua inglesa, participando de *a* y *o,* muy parecido al sonido de *por.*

ã se pronuncia como *a* en *ana,* pero breve y de golpe.

é » » » » *i* » *ídolo, mí.*

ê » » » » *e* » *editor, escampar,* pero breve y de golpe.

i » » » » *ai* » *aislar, maizal,* pero pronunciando ambas letras aun más unidas.

ï » » » » *i* » *igual,* breve y de golpe.

ó » » » » *o* » *cobre, mote.*

õ » » » » *u* » *ubre, único.*

ô » » » » *o* » *por,* pero más participando de *e* que en castellano.

ö » » » » *o* » *dado,* breve y de golpe.

ú » » » » *iu* » *viuda,* pero de golpe.

û sonido propio de la lengua inglesa, muy parecido al de *eu* en la lengua francesa, pero siempre breve y de golpe.

ü se pronuncia como la *u* española, pero breve y de golpe.

ŏŏ, ŏî se pronuncian como *oy* en *hoy,* pero pronunciando ambas letras aun más unidas.

ŏã se pronuncia como *au* en *aula.*

j » » » *ch* » *chapa,* pero así como si estuviera escrita esta voz: *dzchapa.*

sh » » » *ch* » francés.

th » » alguna vez como *z* muy suave *(th):* youth; otra vez *(th)* como *s* silbada: father, that, there.

Los sonidos *j, sh, th,* propios de la lengua inglesa, requieren la viva voz, por no hallarse análogos en el idioma castellano.

SPANISH AND ENGLISH.

A.

á, ã, pr. to. in, at, according to, on, by, for, of.

ababa, *ãbã bã,* sf. red poppy, corn-rose.

abacería, *–thĕrĕ á,* sf. grocery.

abacero, *–thẽ′rõ,* sm. grocer.

bacial, *–thãl′,* a. abbatial.

ábaco, *ã′bãkõ,* sm. abacus (of a column); multiplication-table.

abad, *ãbãd″,* sm. abbot.

abada, *ãbã dã,* sf. female rhinoceros.

abadejo, *–dẽ′h′õ,* sm. codfish; yellow wren; Spanish fly.

abadengo, ga, *–dẽn′gõ,* a. abbatial.

abades, *ãbã′dẽs,* sm. pl. cantharides.

abadesa, *–dẽ′ã,* sf. abbess.

abadía, *–dẽ′ã,* sf. abbey; abbacy.

abajo, *ãbã′h′õ,* ad. under, underneath; below. [flow.

abalanzar, *–lãnthãr′,* v. a. to balance, to counterpoise; to dart; to impel; –, v. n. to rush on with impetuosity; to venture.

abalear, *–lẽãr′,* v. a. to fan or winnow corn.

abalorio, *–lõ′rĕõ,* sm. glass-bead. [cable.

aballestar, *–lyẽstãr′,* v. a. (mar.) to haul a

abanderado, *ãbãndẽrã′dõ,* sm. (mil.) ensign; standard-bearer.

abanderizador, ra, *–rĕthãdõr′,* sm. ringleader, complotter.

abanderizar, *–rĕthãr′,* v. a. to band together. [abandonment.

abandonamiento, *ãbãndõnãmĕẽn′tõ,* sm.

abandonar, *–nãr′,* v. a. to abandon; –se, to despond, to despair; to give one's self up to. [forlornness; debauchery.

abandono, *ãbãndõ′nõ,* sm. abandonment.

abanicar, *ãbãnĕkãr′,* v. a. to fan.

abanico, *–nẽ′kõ,* sm. fan.

abaniquero, *–nĕkẽ′rõ,* sm. fan-maker.

abanto, *ãbãn′tõ,* sm. dwarf-hawk.

abaratar, *ãbãrãtãr′,* v. a. to abate the price. [worn by Spanish peasants.

abarca, *ãbãr′kã,* sf. shoe of coarse leather,

abarcadura, *–dõ′rã,* sf. abarcamiento, *–mĕẽn′tõ,* sm. embrace.

abarcar, *ãbãrkãr′,* v. a. to clasp, to embrace; to contain.

abarcón, *–kõn′,* sm. iron ring, hoop.

abarquillar, *–kĕlyãr′,* v. a. to shape like a boat; –se, to curl up; to be cocked.

abarracarse, *ãbãrrãkãr′sẽ,* v. r. to withdraw into barracks.

abarraganamiento, *ãbãrrãgãnãmĕẽn′tõ,* sm. concubinage.

abarraganarse, *–nãr′sẽ,* v. r. to live in

abarrancadero, *ãbãrrãnkãdẽ′rõ,* sm. boggy place; precipice; difficult business.

abarrancamiento, *–mĕẽn′tõ,* sm. fall into a pit or trap; embarrassment.

abarrancar, *–kãr′,* v. a. to dig holes; –se, to become embarrassed.

abarrotar, *ãbãrrõtãr′,* v. a. to tie down; (mar.) to stow the cargo.

abarrote, *–rõ′tẽ,* sm. (mar.) small stowage.

abastecedor, ra, *ãbãstẽthẽdõr′,* sm. & f. purveyor, caterer.

abastecer, *–thẽr′,* v. a. to purvey.

abastecimiento, *–thẽmĕẽn′tõ,* sm. provision; provisions, pl. [with bastions.

abastionar, *ãbãstĕõnãr′,* v. a. to fortify

abasto, *ãbãs′tõ,* sm. supply of provisions.

abatanar, *ãbãtãnãr′,* v. a. to full cloth.

abate, *ãbã′tẽ,* sm. abbé.

¡abate, *ã′bãtẽ,* I take care!

abatido, da, *ãbãtĕ′dõ,* a. dejected, low-spirited, faint; abject, mean.

abatimiento, *–mĕẽn′tõ,* sm. low spirits, depression.

abatir, *–tĕr′,* v. a. to throw down; to humble; –, v. n. to descend, to stoop.

abdicación, *ãbdĕkãthĕõn′,* sf. abdication.

abdicar, *–dĕkãr′,* v. a. to abdicate.

abdomen, *ãbdõ′mẽn,* sm. abdomen.

abdominal, *ãbdõmĕnãl′,* a. abdominal, abdominous.

abecé, *ãbẽthẽ′,* sm. alphabet.

abecedario, *–thẽdã′rĕõ,* sm. spelling-book, primer.

abedul, *ãbẽdõl′,* sm. birch-tree.

abeja, *ãbẽ′h′ã,* sf. bee; – maestra ó madre, queen-bee.

abejar, *ãbẽh′ãr′,* sm. bee-hive.

abejarrón, *ãbẽ′hãrrõn′,* sm. horse-fly.

abejero, *ãbẽ′hẽ′rõ,* sm. bee-master.

abejón, *ãbẽ′hõn′,* sm. drone; hornet.

abellacarse, *ãbẽlyãkãr′sẽ,* v. r. to degrade one's self.

aberración, *ãbẽrrãthĕõn′,* sf. aberration.

abertal, *ãbẽrtãl′,* a. full of clefts.

abertura, *–tõ′rã,* sf. aperture, chink, cleft; (fig.) plain dealing; (mus.) overture.

abestiar, *ãbẽstĕãr′,* v. a. to stupefy.

abeto, *ãbẽ′tõ,* sm. fir-tree.

abetunado, da, *ãbẽtõnã′dõ,* a. bituminous.

abierto, ta, *ãbĕẽr′tõ,* a. open; sincere; frank.

abigarrar, *ăbǐgârrâr'*, v. a. to variegate, to dapple, to chequer; to diversify.

abigeato, *ăbǐgěâ'tŏ*, sm. cattle-theft.

abigeo, *ăbǐgě'ŏ*, sm. cattle-thief.

abigotado, da, *ăbǐgŏtä'dŏ*, a. (person) wearing long whiskers.

ab intestato, *ăb ǐntěstä'tŏ*, a. intestate.

abismal, *ăbǐsmâl'*, a. abysmal; —aa, s. pl. clasp-nails.

abismar, —*mâr'*, v.a. to depress, to humble.

abismo, *ăbǐs'mŏ*, sm. abyss; gulf; hell.

abitaque, *ăbǐtä'kě*, sm. rafter.   [like.

abizoochado,da, *ăbǐskŏtshä'dŏ*, a. biscuit-

abjuración, *ăbʹhûrăthǐŏn'*, sf. abjuration.

abjurar, —*ʹhûrâr'*, v. a. to abjure, to recant upon oath.   [lification.

ablandamiento, *ăblăndâmǐěn'tŏ*,sm. mollification.

ablandar, —*dâr'*, v. a. & n. to mollify.

ablandativo,va,—*dătǐ'vŏ*,a. mollificative.

ablativo, *ăblătǐ'vŏ*, sm. (gr.) ablative.

ablución, *ăblûthǐŏn'*, sf. ablution, lotion.

abnegación, *ăbněgăthǐŏn'*, sf. abnegation.

abnegar, —*gâr'*, v. a. to renounce.

abobado, da, *ăbŏbä'dŏ*,a. stultified, silly.

abobamiento, —*mǐěn'tŏ*, sm. stupefaction.

abobar, —*bâr'*, v. a. to stupefy.

abocado, da, —*kä'dŏ*, a. light (wine).

abocamiento, —*mǐěn'tŏ*, sm. meeting, interview.

abocar, —*kâr'*, v. a. to seize with the mouth; —se, to meet by agreement.

abocardado,da,—*dä'dŏ*, a. wide-mouthed.

abocinado, da, *ăbŏthǐnä'dŏ*, a. trumpet-like.   [face.

abocinar, —*nâr'*, v. n. to fall upon one's

abochornar, *ăbŏtshŏrnâr'*,v.a. to swelter; to provoke; —se, to be angry with; to blush.

abofellar, *ăbŏfěllâr'*, v. n. to puff, to pant.

abofetear, *ăbŏfětěâr'*, v. a. to slap or box someone's ears.

abogacia, *ăgăthě'ă*, sf. advocateship.

abogada, —*gä'dă*, sf. mediatrix.

abogado, —*dŏ*, sm. advocate; mediator.

abogar, *ăbŏgâr'*, v. n. to advocate; to intercede.   [swollen.

abohetado, da, —*hětä'dŏ*, a. inflated,

abolengo, —*lěn'gŏ*, sm. ancestry; inheritance from ancestors.   [tion.

abolición, —*lǐthǐŏn'*, sf. abolition, abrogation.

abolir, —*lǐr'*, v. a. to abolish.

abolorio, —*lŏ'rǐŏ*, sm. ancestry.

abolsado, da, *ăbŏlsä'dŏ*,a. puckered.

abolladura, *ăbŏlyädû'râ*, sf. indent; relief.

abollar, —*lyâr'*, v. a. to emboss; to confound; to tire, to bore.

abollonar, —*lyŏnâr'*, v. a. to emboss.

abominable, —*mǐnä'blě*, a. abominable, cursed.   [tion, cursedness.

abominación, —*mǐnäthǐŏn'*, sf. abomination.

abominar, —*nâr'*, v. n. to detest.

abonado, da, *ăbŏnä'dŏ*, a. creditable, rich; fit for.   [bail for another.

abonador, —*dŏr'*, sm. & f. person who is

abonamiento, —*mǐěn'tŏ*, sm. surety, bail.

abonanzar, *ăbŏnânthâr'*, v. n. to clear up.

abonar, *ăbŏnâr'*, v. a. to bail; to insure; to improve; to make good an assertion;

to manure; to give one credit; —se, to subscribe to; —, v. n. to clear up.

abonaré, *ăbŏnărě'*, sm. (com.) cheque.

abono, *ăbŏ'nŏ*, sm. approbation; subscription; surety, bail; dung, manure; — de pasaje, (rail.) season-ticket.   [truder.

abordador, *ăbŏrdădŏr'*, sm. boarder; inabordaje,*dăʹh'ě*,sm.act of boarding a ship.

abordar, —*dâr'*, v. a. (mar.) to board.

abordo, —*dŏ*, sm. act of boarding a ship.

aborrachado, da, *ăbŏrrătshä'dŏ*, a. high coloured.   [stormy; to get tipsy.

aborrascarse, *ăbŏrrăskär'sě*, v. r. to grow

aborrecer, *ăbŏrrěthěr'*, v. a. to hate, to abhor; to desert (of birds).   [able.

aborrecible, —*thě'blě*, a. hateful, detestable.

aborrecimiento, —*ăbŏrrěthǐmǐěn'tŏ*, sm. abborrence, hatred.   [tion.

abortamiento, *ăbŏrtămǐěn'tŏ*, sm. abortion.

abortar, —*târ'*, v. n. to miscarry, to have an abortion.

abortivo, va, —*tě'vŏ*, a. abortive.

aborto, —*tŏ*, sm. abortion; monster.

abortón, —*tŏn'*, sm. abortion of a quadruped.   [up.

aborujarse,*ăbŏrû'hâr'sě*,v.r.to be muffled

abotagarse, —*tăgär'sě*, v. r. to be swollen.

abotinado, da, —*tǐnä'dŏ*, a. in the form of Bluchers, half-boots.   [to bud.

abotonar, —*tŏnâr'*, v. a. to button; —, v. n.

abovedar, —*věbêr'*, v. a. to arch, to vault.

aboyar, —*yâr'*, v. a. (mar.) to lay down buoys.   [mountain-canyon.

abra, *â'brä*, sf. bay; mountain-gorge,

abracijo, —*thě'h'ŏ*, sm. embrace, hug.

abrasador,ra, *ăbrăsădŏr'*, sm.&f. burner.

abrasamiento, —*sămǐěn'tŏ*, sm. burning.

abrasar, —*sâr'*, v. a. to burn; to parch the ground; to squander; —se, to be agitated by a violent passion.

abrasilado, da, —*sǐlä'dŏ*, a. of the colour of Brazil-wood.

abrazadera, *ăbrăthădě'râ*, sf. cramp-iron, clasp, hasp, ferule.   [thief-taker.

abrazador, ra, —*dŏr'*, sm. & f. embracer;

abrazamiento, —*mǐěn'tŏ*, sm. embracing.

abrazar, —*thâr'*, v. a. to embrace; to surround; to give into; to contain.

abrazo, —*thŏ*, sm. embrace.

ábrego, *ăb'rěgŏ*, sm. south-west wind.

abrevadero, *ăbrěvădě'rŏ*, sm. watering-place for cattle.

abrevar, —*vâr'*, v. a. to water cattle.

abreviación, *ăbrěvǐăthǐŏn'*, sf. abbreviation, abridgment; shortening.

abreviador, ra, —*dŏr'*, sm. & f. abridger.

abreviar, —*vǐâr'*, v. a. to abridge, to cut short; to accelerate.   [abbreviature.

abreviatura, —*vǐtû'ra*, sf. abbreviation,

abribonarse, *ăbrǐbŏnâr'sě*, v. r. to act the scoundrel.   [peach.

abridero, —*dě'rŏ*, sm. nectarine, hasty

abridor, —*dŏr'*, sm. nectarine-tree; opener; plaiting-iron; —de láminas, engraver; — en hueco, die-sinker.

abrigar, —*gǐ—'*, v. a. to shelter; to protect; —se, to take shelter; (mar.) to becalm.

abrigo, ăbrē'gŏ, sm. shelter; protection, aid;
abril, ăbrēl', sm. April.   [mantle.
abrillantador, ăbrēlyăntădŏr', sm. diamond-cutter.   [mond into facets.
abrillantar, -tăr', v. a. to put a dia-
abrimiento, ăbrēmēēn'tŏ, sm. opening.
abrir, ăbrēr', v. a. to open; to unlock; to
be open; to disclose a secret.   [hook.
abrochador, ăyrŏtshădŏr', sm. button-
abrochar, -tshăr', v. a. to button on, to
clasp on.
abrogación, ăbrŏgăthēŏn', sf. abrogation.
abrogar, -găr', v. a. to abrogate.
abrojo, ăbrŏ'h'ŏ, sm. (bot.) caltrop; -s,
pl. dangerous cliffs.
abromado, da, ăbrŏmă'dŏ, a. hazy, foggy.
abromarse, -sĕ, v. r. (mar.) to be worm-
eaten.
abroquelarse, ăbrŏkĕlăr'sĕ, v. r. to interpose shield or buckler; to use defensive
weapons.   [wood.
abrótano, ăbrŏ'tănŏ, sm. (bot.) southern-
abrumador, ra, ăbrŭmădŏr', a. troublesome, annoying.   [cause trouble.
abrumar, -măr', v. a. to overwhelm; to
abrutado, da, ăbrŭtă'dŏ, a. brutish.
absceso, ăbsthĕ'sŏ, sm. abscess.
absolución, ăbsŏlŭthēŏn', sf. forgiveness;
absolution.
absoluto, ta, ăbsŏlŭ'tŏ, a. absolute, independent; unconditional; imperious.
absolutorio, -tŏ'rēŏ, a. absolutory.
absolver, ăbsŏlvĕr', v. a. to absolve.
absorbencia, ăbsŏrbĕn'thēă, sf. absorption.   [sorbent.
absorbente, -tĕ, sm. & a. (med.) ab-
absorber, -bĕr', v. a. to absorb; (also fig.);
-se, v. r. to be astonished.
absorto, ăbsŏr'tŏ, a. amazed.
abstenerse, ăbstĕnĕr'sĕ, v. r. to abstain.
abstinencia, ăbstēnĕn'thēă, sf. abstinence.
abstinente, -tĕ, a. abstinent, abstemious.
abstracción, ăbstrăkthēŏn', sf. abstraction; retirement.
abstractivo, va, -tē'vŏ, a. abstractive.
abstracto, ta, -tŏ, a. abstract.
abstraer, ăbstrăĕr', v. a. to abstract; to
pass over in silence; to become lost in
thought.
abstraído, ăbstrăē'dŏ, a. retired.
abstruso, sa, ăbstrŏ'sŏ, a. abstruse.
absurdidad, ăbsŭrdēdăd', sf. absurdo,
-sŭr'dŏ, sm. absurdity.
absurdo, da, -sŭr'dŏ, a. absurd.
abubilla, ăbŭbēl'yă, sf. hoopoop.
abuela, ăbŏĕ'lă, sf. grandmother.
abuelo, -lŏ, sm. grandfather; ancestor.
abultado, da, ăbŭltă'dŏ, a. bulky, large,
massive.   [-, v. n. to be bulky.
abultar, -tăr', v. a. to increase, to enlarge;
abundancia, ăbŭndăn'thēă, sf. abundance.
abundante, -tĕ, a. abundant, copious.
abundar, ăbŭndăr', v. n. to abound.
aburrido, da, ăbŭrrē'dŏ, a. weary.
aburrimiento, -mēĕn'tŏ, sm. tediousness.
aburrir, -rēr', v. a. to vex, to weary; to
hazard; to relinquish.   [heap together.
aburujar, ăbŭrŭ'hăr', v. a. to press or

aburujonarse, -'hŏnăr'sĕ, v. r. to clot.
abusar, ăbŭsăr', v. a. to abuse.
abusivo, va, -sē'vŏ, a. abusive.
abuso, ăbŏ'sŏ, sm. ill-usage, misuse.
abyección, ăbyĕkthēŏn', sf. abjectness.
acá, ăkă', ad. here, hither. [plished; old.
acabado, da, ăkăbă'dŏ, a. perfect, accom-
acaballar, -băllăr', v. a. to complete.
acaballadero, -băllyădĕ'rŏ, sm. covering-
season, covering-place of horses and mares.
acaballar, -băllyăr', v. a. to cover a
mare.   [manlike.
acaballerado, da, -băllyĕră'dŏ, a. gentle-
acaballerar, -băllyĕrăr', v. a. to render
genteel.
acabar, -băr', v. a. & n. to finish, to complete; to achieve; to terminate in anything;
to die, to expire; -se, to grow feeble.
acabildar, -bēldăr', v. a. to put to the
acacia, ăkă'thēă, sf. acacia.   [vote.
academia, -dă'mēă, sf. academy; literary
society.   [-, a. academical.
académico, -dă'mēkŏ, sm. academician;
acaecedero, ra, -ĕthĕdĕ'rŏ, a. incidental.
acaecer, -thĕr', v. n. to happen.
acaecimiento, -ĕthēmēĕn'tŏ, sm. event,
incident.
acal, ăkăl', sm. canoe.
acalenturarse, ăkălĕntŭrăr'sĕ, v. r. to be
feverish.
acalia, ăkă'lēă, sf. (bot.) marsh-mallows.
acallar, ăkăllyăr', v. a. to quiet, to hush;
to soften, to assuage, to appease.
acamado, da, ăkămă'dŏ, a. laid flat (of
corn).   [encampment.
acampamento, ăkămpămĕn'tŏ, sm. (mil.)
acampar, -păr', v. a. (mil.) to encamp.
acampo, -pŏ, sm. common pasture.
acanalado, da, ăkănălă'dŏ, a. striated,
fluted.
acanalador, -dŏr', sm. chamfering-plane.
acanalar, -lăr', v. a. to make a channel;
to flute, to chamfer.
acandilado, da, ăkăndēlă'dŏ, a. peaked,
pointed (of hats).   [mon colour.
acanelado, da, ăkănĕlă'dŏ, a. of a cinna-
acanillado, da, ăkănēlyă'dŏ, a. ribbed
(applied to cloth).   [the quart.
acantarar, ăkăntărăr', v. a. to measure by
acanto, -tŏ, sm. (bot.) brankursi, e.
acantonamiento, ăkăntŏnămēĕn'tŏ, sm.
cantonment.   [into cantons.
acantonar, -năr', v. a. (mil.) to divide
acañonear, ăkănyŏnĕăr', v. a. to cannonade.   [pe as coloured.
acaparrosado, da, ăkăpărrŏsă'dŏ, a. cop-
acaponado, da, -pŏnă'dŏ, a. capon-like,
effeminate.
acardenalar, ăkărdĕnălăr', v. a. to beat
black and blue; -se, to be covered with
livid spots.   [caress.
acariciar, ăkărēthēăr', v. a. to fondle, to
ácaro, ă'kărŏ, sm. cheese-mite.
acarreador, ăkărrĕădŏr', sm. carrier.
acarrear, -rĕăr', v. a. to convey in a cart
to occasion.
acarreo, -rĕ'ŏ, sm. carriage, portage.
acaso, ăkă'sŏ, sm. chance, hap, hazard;
-, ad. by chance.

1*

acastorado, da, *ăkăstŏrăˊdŏ*, a. beavered.

acatarrarse, *ăkătărrărˊsĕ*, v. r. to catch cold. [wealthy.

acandalado, da, *ăkăldălăˊdŏ*, a. rich,

acaudalar, -*lărˊ*, v.a. to hoard up riches.

acaudillador, *ăkădăˊilyădŏrˊ*, sm. commander of troops. [troops.

acaudillar, -*lyărˊ*, v. a. to command

acayoiba, *ăkăyŏˊĭbă*, sf. mahogany.

acceder, *ăkthĕdĕrˊ*, v. n. to accede.

accesible, *ăkthĕsˊĭblĕ*, a. attainable; of easy access. [munication.

acceso, *ăkthĕsˊŏ*, sm. access; carnal com-

accesorias, -*sŏˊrĭăs*, sf. pl. out-buildings.

accesorio, ria, -*sŏˊrĭŏ*, a. accessory, additional. [casual.

accidental, *ăkthĭdĕntăl*, a. accidental,

accidentarse, -*tărˊsĕ*, v. r. to have a fit.

accidente, *ăkthĕdĕnˊtĕ*, sm. accident; hap-hazard.

acción, *ăkthĭŏnˊ*, sf. action, operation; battle; position, posture; (com.) share.

accionar, *ăkthĭŏnărˊ*, v. n. to gesticulate.

accionista, -*ĭsˊtă*, sm. actionary, share-holder. [holder.

acebo, *ăthĕˊbŏ*, sm. holly-tree.

acebuche, *ăthĕbŭshˊĕ*, sm. wild olive-tree.

acebuchina, -*tshĕˊnă*, sf. wild olive.

acechador, *ăthĕthădŏrˊ*, sm. listener.

acechar, *ăthĕtshărˊ*, v. a. to lie in ambush, to lurk.

aceche, *ăthĕtshˊĕ*, sm. copperas.

acecho, *ăthĕtshˊŏ*, sm. lying in ambush, waylaying.

acecinar, *ăthĕthĭnărˊ*, v.a. to salt meat and smoke it; -se, to wither.

acedar, *ăthĕdărˊ*, v. a. to sour; to displease, to disquiet.

acedera, -*dĕˊră*, sf. (bot.) sorrel.

acedía, -*dĕˊă*, sf. acidity; squeamishness; roughness; asperity of address.

acedo, da, *ăthĕˊdŏ*, a. acid, acetous.

aceitar, *ăthĕĭtărˊ*, v. a. to oil.

aceite, *ăthĕˊĭtĕ*, sm. oil.

aceitera, *ăthĕĭtĕˊră*, sf. oil-cruet.

aceitería, -*tĕrĕˊă*, sf. oilshop; oil-mill.

aceitero, -*tĕˊrŏ*, sm. oil-seller; oil-cruet.

aceitoso, sa, -*tŏˊsŏ*, a. oily.

aceitunado, da, -*tŭnăˊdŏ*, a. olive-green.

aceitunero, -*tŭnĕˊrŏ*, sm. olive-seller.

aceituno, -*tŭˊnŏ*, sm. olive-tree. [tion.

aceleración, *ăthĕlĕrăthĭŏnˊ*, s. accelera-

aceleradamente, -*dămĕnˊtĕ*, ad. swiftly, hastily. [hurry.

acelerar, -*rărˊ*, v. a. to accelerate; to

acelga, *ăthĕlˊgă*, sf. (bot.) beet.

acémila, *ăthĕˊmĭlă*, sf. beast of burden.

acemilar, -*mĭlărˊ*, a. belonging to mules and muleteers.

acemilería, -*mĭlĕrĕˊă*, sf. mule-stable.

acemilero, -*mĭlĕˊrŏ*, sm. muleteer.

acemita, -*mĭˊtă*, sf. Graham bread.

acemite, *ăthĕmĭˊtĕ*, sm. fine bran; grits.

acendrar, *ăthĕndrărˊ*, v. a. to refine metals; to free from blemish.

acensuar, -*săărˊ*, v. a. to impose a tax.

acento, *ăthĕnˊtŏ*, sm. accent. [tion.

acentuación, *ăthĕntŭăthĭŏnˊ*, sf. accentua-

acentuar, -*tăărˊ*, v. a. to accentuate.

aceña, *ăthĕnˊyă*, sf. water-mill.

aceñero, *ăthĕnyăˊrŏ*, sm. keeper of a water-mill.

acepar, *ăthĕpărˊ*, v. n. to take root.

acepción, *ăthĕpthĭŏnˊ*, sf. acceptation.

acepilladura, *ăthĕpĭlyădŏˊră*, sf. smoothing with a plane; chips, pl.

acepillar, -*yărˊ*, v. a. to plane; to brush.

aceptable, *ăthĕptăˊblĕ*, a. acceptable; worthy of acceptance.

aceptación, -*tăthĭŏnˊ*, sf. acceptation; approbation; acceptance (of a bill).

aceptador, ra, -*tădŏrˊ*, s. acceptor.

aceptar, -*tărˊ*, v. a. to accept, to admit.

acepto, to, *ăthĕpˊtŏ*, a. agreeable.

acequia, *ăthĕˊkĭă*, sf. canal, channel, drain; mill-trench. [drains or cisterns.

acequiar, -*kĭărˊ*, v. a. to construct canals.

acequiero, -*kĭĕˊrŏ*, sm. inspector of canals. [(am.) side-walk.

acera, *ăthĕˊră*, sf. flag-way, pavement;

acerado, da, *ăthĕrăˊdŏ*, a. steeled, made

acerar, *ăthĕrărˊ*, v. a. to steel. [of steel.

acerbidad, -*bĭdăd*, sf. acerbity, rigour.

acerbo, ba, *ăthĕrˊbŏ*, a. rigorous, harsh, rude; cruel.

acerca, *ăthĕrˊkă*, pr. about, relating to.

acercar, -*kărˊ*, v. a. to approach; -se, to accost.

acerico, *ăthĕrĭˊkŏ*, acerillo, -*rĭlˊyŏ*, sm. pin-cushion; small bed-pillow.

acerina, na, -*rĕˊnă*, sf. made of steel.

acero, *ăthĕˊrŏ*, sm. steel; edged small arms; (fig.) courage. [uous, very vigorous.

acérrimo, ma, *ăthĕrˊrĭmŏ*, a. most stren-

acertado, da, *ăthĕrtăˊdŏ*, a. fit, proper; prudent. [true prophet.

acertador, ra, -*tădŏrˊ*, sm. & f. dead-shot.

acertajo, -*tăˊhŏ*, sm. riddle.

acertar, -*tărˊ*, v. a. to hit the mark; to conjecture right; to turn out true; -, v. n. to happen unexpectedly; to take root.

acertijo, -*tĭˊhŏ*, sm. riddle.

aceruelo, *ăthĕrŭĕˊlŏ*, sm. small pack-saddle for riding.

acervar, -*vărˊ*, v. a. to accumulate.

acervo, *ăthĕrˊvŏ*, sm. heap, pile; totality of tithes. [measure.

acetábulo, *ăthĕtăˊbŭlŏ*, sm. apothecary's

acetato, -*tŏˊ*, sm. (chem.) acetate.

acetosa, *ăthĕtŏˊsă*, sf. (bot.) sorrel.

acetre, *ăthĕˊtrĕ*, sm. small bucket; holy-water-fount.

aciago, ga, *ăthĭăˊgŏ*, a. unlucky, ominous

acial, *ăthĭălˊ*, sm. barnacle.

aciano, *ăthĭăˊnŏ*, sm. corn-flower.

acíbar, *ăthĭˊbăr*, sm. aloes-tree; (fig.) bitterness, displeasure.

acibarar, -*bărărˊ*, v. a. to add juice o[r] aloes; to gall; to imbitter.

acicalador, *ăthĭkălădŏrˊ*, sm. polisher; burnisher, burnishing-stick.

acicaladura, -*dŏˊ*ră, sf., acicalamiento, -*mĭĕnˊtŏ*, sm. burnishing.

acicalar, -*lărˊ*, v. n. to polish, to furbish; -se, to dress in style; to paint one's face.

acidez, *ăthĭdĕthˊ*, sf. acidity. [sour.

ácido, *ăˊthĭdŏ*, sm. acid; -, da, a. acid,

acidular, -dûlâr, v. a. to acidulate.
acídulo, a, áthê dêlô, a. aciduous.
acierto, áihtêr tô, sm. act and effect of hitting; dexterity, chance, casualty.
acijado, da, -'hâ dô, a. copperas coloured.
acije, áiht'h'ê, sm. copperas.
acimboga, áthímbô'gâ, sf. citron-tree.
ación, áthíôn', sf. stirrup-leather.
acipado, da, áihêpâ dô, a. well milled (of broadcloth). [boundaries].
acirate, -rê'tê, sm. landmark (to show acitara, -tâ'râ, s. rails of a bridge; partition-wall.
acitrón, -trôn', sm. candied lemon.
aclamación, áklâmáthíôn, sf. acclamation.
aclamar, -mâr', v. a. to applaud, to huzza; to cry up.
aclarar, áklárâr', v.a. to clear; to brighten; to explain; to clarify; —se, to clear up.
aclimatar, áklímâtâr', v. a. to acclimatize.
aclocarse, áklôkâr sê, v. r. to brood.
acobardar, ákôbârdâr', v. a. to intimidate.
acoceador, ra, ákôthêâdôr, sm. & f. kicking horse. [(of horses).
acocear, -thêâr', v. a. to kick; to wince
acocharse, -tshâr sê, v. r. to squat, to stoop down. [to injure sorely.
acochinar, -tshínâr', v. a. to assassinate.
acodar, -dâr', v. a. to lean the elbow upon; to lay layers of vines. [angle.
acodillar, -dîlyâr', v. a. to bend at an acodo, ákô dô, sm. (bot.) layer, scion, shoot.
acogedizo, za, ákô'hêdî thô, a. gathered promiscuously.
acogedor, ra, -'hêdôr', sm.& f. harbourer.
acoger, -'hêr', v. a. to receive; to protect; to harbour; —se, to resort to.
acogida, -'hí'd á, sf. reception; asylum; confluence.
acogimiento, -'hímíên'tô, sm. asylum.
acogollar, -gôlyâr', v. a. to cover delicate plants with straw; —se, to cabbage.
acogombrar, -gômbrâr', v. a. to dig up the ground about plants; to cover plants with earth. [on the head.
acogotar, -gôtâr', v. a. to kill by a blow
acolchar, ákôltshâr', v.a.to quilt; to cotton.
acólito, ákô lítô, sm. acolyte; assistant.
acollarar, ákôlyârâr', v. a. to yoke horses &c.; to couple hounds. [gressor.
acometedor, ra, ákômêtêdôr', sm.& f. ag-
acometer, -têr', v. a. to attack; to undertake; to overtake; to steal over one (sleep).
acometida, -tíd á, sf., acometimiento, ákômêtímíên'tô, sm. attack, assault.
acomodadizo, ákômôdâdê'thô, a. accommodable.
acomodado, da, -dâ'dô, a. commodious; suitable, convenient, fit; wealthy.
acomodamiento, -míên'tô, sm. accommodation.
acomodar, -dâr', v. a. to accommodate, to arrange; —, v. n. to fit, to suit; —se, to condescend, to comply.
acomodaticio, cia, -dâtê thô, a. figurative, metaphorical.

acomodo, -mô'dô, sm. accommodation; employment.
acompañador, ra, ákômpânyâdôr', sm.& f. companion; (mus.) accompanist.
acompañamiento, -míên'tô, sm. attendance; (mus.) accompaniment.
acompañar, -yâr', v. a. to accompany; to join; (mus.) to accompany; —se, to consult with others.
acompasado, da, ákômpâsâ'dô, a. measured by the compass; well-proportioned.
acomplexionado, da, -plêksíôn á'dô, a. of a (good or bad) complexion.
aconchar, ákôntshâr', v. a. to accommodate; (mar.) to embay.
acondicionado, da, ákôndíthíôná'dô, a. conditioned, of a (good or bad) disposition.
acondicionar, -thíôn á r', v. a. to dispose; —se, to acquire a certain position.
acongojar, ákôngô'hâr', v. a. to oppress, to afflict. [monk's hood.
acónito, ákô'nítô, sm. (bot.) aconite,
aconsejable, ákônsê'hâ blê, a. advisable.
aconsejador, ra, -'hâdôr', sm. adviser, counsellor. [to take advice.
aconsejar, -'hâr', v. a. to advise; —se,
aconsonantar, ákônsônántâr', v. a. to use false rhymes.
acontecedero, ra, ákôntêthêdê'rô, a. that which may happen.
acontecer, -thêr', v. imp. to happen.
acontecimiento, -thímíên'tô, sm. event, incident. [bell-shaped.
acopado, da, ákôpâ'dô, a. cup-shaped,
acopar, -pâr', v. n. (mar.) to bend or arch boards.
acopiamiento, -píâmíên'tô, acopio, ákô'píô, sm. gathering, storing.
acopiar, -píâr', v. a. to gather, to store up.
acoplar, -plâr', v. a. to couple; to adjust or fit pieces of timber-work.
acoquinar, -kínâr', v. a. to intimidate.
acorazonado, -râthôná'dô, a. heart-shaped. [shrivel (of fruits).
acorcharse, -tshâr sê, v. r. to dry up and
acordado, da, ákôrdâ'dô, a. deliberate.
acordar, -dâr', v. a. to concert; to tune musical instruments; —, v. n. to agree; —se, to come to an agreement; to remember. [—, s. accord.
acorde, ákôr dê, a. conformable, accordant; acordonar, ákôrdônâr', v. a. (mil.) to form a cordon. [horns.
acornear, -nêâr', v. a. to gore with the
acoro, á kôrô, sm. (bot.) sweet cane, sweet grass.
acorralar, ákôrrâlâr', v. a. to shut up cattle or sheep in pens; to intimidate.
acorrucarse, ákôrrúkâr sê, v. r. to squat.
acortar, ákôrtâr', v. a. to abridge, to shorten; —se, to be perplexed.
acorullar, ákôrûlyâr', v. a. to ship oars.
acosar, ákôsâr', v. a. to pursue close; to molest. [down; accosted.
acostado, da, ákôstâ'dô, a. stretched, laid
acostar, -stâr', v. a. to put to bed; —se, to incline to one side (of buildings); (mar.) to lie along.

acostumbradamente, ăkŏstŭmbrădă-mĕn'tĕ, ad. customarily.

acostumbrar, –brâr', v. a. to accustom; –, v. n. to be accustomed.

acotación, ăkŏtăthĭŏn', sf. setting bounds; quotation in the margin.

acotar, –târ', v. a. to set bounds; to quote; –se, to take to one's heels.

acotillo, –tĭl'yŏ, sm. large sledge-hammer.

acoyundar, –yŭndâr', v.a. to inspan oxen.

acre, ă'krĕ, a. acid; sharp; –, s. acre.

acrecencia, ăkrĕthĕn'thĭă, sf., acrecentamiento, –tămĭĕn'tŏ, sm. increase, augmentation, augment.

acrecentar, –târ', acrecer, ăkrĕthĕr', v. a. to increase, to augment.

acreditar, ăkrĕdĭtâr', v.a. to assure, to affirm; to give credit; –se, to gain credit.

acreedor, ăkrĕĕdŏr', sm. creditor.

acribadura, ăkrĭbădŭ'ră, sf. sifting.

acribar, –bâr', v. a. to sift; to pierce like a sieve. [sieve; to molest, to torment.

acribillar, –bĭlyâr', v. a. to pierce like a sieve.

acriminación, ăkrĭmĭnăthĭŏn', sf. crimination.

acriminador, ra, –dŏr', sm. & f. accuser.

acriminar, –nâr', v. a. to exaggerate a fault; to accuse. [ity.

acrimonia, –mŏ'nĭă, sf. acrimony; asperity.

acrisolar, –sŏlâr', v. a. to refine, to purify.

acristianar, –stĭănâr', v. a. to christen, to baptize.

acritud, ăkrĭtŭd', sf. acrimony.

acromático, ea, ăkrŏmă'tĭkŏ, a. achromatic.

acta, ăk'tă, sf. act; –s, pl. acts, records, pl.

actitud, ăktĭtŭd'', sf. attitude, posture.

actividad, ăktĭvĭdăd'', sf. activity; liveliness.

activo, va, ăktĭ'vŏ, a. active, diligent.

acto, ăk'tŏ, sm. act, action; act of a play: thesis; carnal communication. [ney.

actor, ăktŏr', sm. player, comedian; attor-Actos, ăk'tŏs, spl. Acts of the Apostles.

actriz, ăktrĭth', sf. actress. [tion.

actuación, ăktŭăthĭŏn', sf. actuation, operactuado, da, –tŭă'dŏ, a. actuated; experienced.

actual, ăktŭăl', a. actual, present. [ced.

actualidad, ăktŭălĭdăd'', sf. actuality.

actuante, ăktŭăn'tĕ, a. college-exponent.

actuar, ăktŭăr', v. a. to digest; to proceed; to support a thesis; –se, to instruct one's self.

actuario, ăktŭă'rĭŏ, sm. actuary. [self.

acuario, ăkŭă'rĭŏ, sm. tank.

Acuario, – sm. Aquarius, Waterman (sign of the zodiac). [quartering of troops.

acuartelamiento, ăkŭărtĕlămĭĕn'tŏ, sm.

acuartelar, –târ', v. a. (mil.) to quarter troops; (mar.) to furl sails.

acuartillar, ăkŭărtĭlyâr', v. n. to knock or bend one's knees in walking; to interfere (of horses).

acuático, ca, ăkŭă'tĭkŏ, a. aquatic.

acuátil, –tĭl, a. aquatic.

acubado, da, ăkŭbă'dŏ, a. resembling a pail or bucket.

acucharado, da, –tshără'dŏ, a. spoonlike.

acuchillado, da, –tshĭlyă'dŏ, a. experienced, skilful. [some person, bully.

acuchillador, ra, –tshĭlyădŏr', s. quarreler.

acuchillar, –tshĭlyâr', v. a. to cut with a sabre; –se, to fight with knives.

acudimiento, –dĭmĭĕn'tŏ, sm. aid, assistance. [to be docile.

acudir, –dĭr', v. n. to assist, to succour; to be docile.

acueducto, ăkŭĕdŭk'tŏ, sm. aqueduct.

ácueo, ea, ă'kŭĕŏ, a. watery.

acuerdo, ăkŭĕr'dŏ, sm. deliberation; resolution; tribunal; consent; de –, unanimously.

aculebrar, ăkŭlĕbrâr', v. n. to meander.

acullá, ăkŭlyă', ad. on the other side, yonder. [to heap together; to impute.

acumular, ăkŭmŭlâr', v. a. to accumulate.

acumulativamente, –mŭlătĭvămĕn'tĕ, ad. (law) by way of precaution; jointly.

acuñación, ăkŭnyăthĭŏn', sf. coining.

acuñador, –dŏr', sm. coiner, minter.

acuñar, –yâr', v. a. to coin, to mint; to wedge in, to fasten with wedges.

acuosidad, ăkŭŏsĭdăd'', sf. wateriness.

acuoso, sa, ăkŭŏ'sŏ, a. watery.

acurrucarse, ăkŭrrŭkăr'sĕ, v. r. to muffle one's self up; to squat.

acusación, ăkŭsăthĭŏn', sf. accusation.

acusador, ra, –dŏr', sm. & f. accuser.

acusar, ăkŭsâr', v. a. to accuse; to reproach; –se, to acknowledge sins to a confessor.

acusativo, ăkŭsătĭ'vŏ, sm. (gr.)accusative.

acusatorio, ria, –tŏ'rĭŏ, a. accusatory.

acuse, ăkŭ'sĕ, sm. declaring (at cards).

acústica, ăkŭs'tĭkă, sf. acoustics, pl.

acústico, ca, –ŏ, a. acoustic.

acutángulo, ăkŭtăn'gŭlŏ, sm. acute angle.

achacar, ătshăkâr', v. a. to impute.

achacoso, sa, –kŏ'sŏ, a. sickly, unhealthy.

achaparrarse, –părrâr'sĕ, v. r. to grow stunted.

achaque, ătshă'kĕ, sm. habitual indisposition; monthly courses; excuse; vice; subject, matter.

achaquiento, ta, –kĭĕn'tŏ, a. sickly.

acharolar, –rŏlâr', v. a. to japan.

achicado, da, ătshĭkă'dŏ, a. childish.

achicador, –kădŏr', sm. scoop for baling boats. [duction.

achicadura, –kădŭ'ră, sf. diminution, reachicar, ătshĭkâr', v. a. to diminish; to bale a boat. [too much; to over-heat.

achicharrar, –tshărrâr', v. a. to fry meat.

achicoria, –kŏ'rĭă, sf. (bot.) succory.

achinar, –nâr', v. a. to intimidate.

achisparse, –spăr'sĕ, v. r. to get tipsy.

achocar, ătshŏkâr', v. a. to knock asunder; to hoard money; –se, to become a dotard.

achuchar, ătshŭtshâr', v. a. to crush with a blow. [frolicsome.

achulado, da, ătshŭlă'dŏ, a. waggish.

adagio, ădă'hĭŏ, sm. adage, proverb; (mus.) adagio.

adala, –lă, sf. (mar.) pump-dale.

adalid, ădălĭd', sm. chief, commander.

adamado, da, –mă'dŏ, a. girl-like; effeminate.

adamantino, na, –mäntä'nö, a. adamantine; adamantean.   [like.

adamascado, da, –mäskä'dö, a. damask-

adaptable, ädäptä'blä, a. adaptable.

adaptar, –tär', v. a. to adapt.

adaraja, ädärä'h'ä, sf. projecting-stones left to continue a wall.

adarga, ädär'gä, sf. oval shield.

adargar, –gär', v. a. to shield.

adarve, ädär'vä, sm. flat top of a wall.

adatar, ädätär', v. a. to book an expense.

adecenar, ädäthänär', v. a. to divide troops into companies of ten.

adecuación, ädäküäth'ön', sf. fitness.

adecuado, da, –kä'dö, a. adequate, fit.

adecuar, –küär', v. a. to fit, to accommodate, to proportion.

adefesio, –fä'sĭö, sm. folly, nonsense.

adefueras, –fä'räs, sf. pl. suburbs.

adehala, ädä'lä, sf. gratuity.

adehesar, –äsär', v. a. to convert land into pasture.   [pated; onward, bold.

adelantado, da, ädäläntä'dö, a. antici-

adelantamiento, –mĭen'tö, sm. progress, improvement, advancement.

adelantar, –tär', v. a. & n. to advance, to accelerate; to pay beforehand; to ameliorate, to improve; –se, to take the lead; to outdo.   [ward; henceforth.

adelante, ädälän'tä, ad. farther off; on-

adelfa, ädäl'fä, sf. (bot.) rose-bay.

adelgazar, ädälgäthär', v. a. to make thin or slender; to discuss with subtlety.

ademán, ädämän', sm. gesture; attitude.

ademar, –mär', v. a. to line the sides of mines with planks.

además, –mäs', ad. moreover, besides.

adentellar, ädäntĕlyär', v. a. to bite; to indent; – una pared, to leave bricks to continue a wall.

adentro, ädän'trö, ad. within; inwardly.

aderezar, ädäräthär', v. a. to dress, to adorn; to prepare; to clean, to repair.

aderezo, –rä'thö, sm. adorning; finery; arrangement; – de caballo, trappings.

ad(i)estrador, äd(ĭ)ästrädör', sm. & t. instructor, teacher.

ad(i)estrar, –trär', v. a. to guide; to teach, to instruct; –se, to practise.

adeudado, da, ädäüdä'dö, a. indebted.

adeudar, –där', v. a. to pay duty; to contract debts; –se, to be indebted.

adeudo, ädäü'dö, s. duty; (rail.) freight.

adherencia, ädärän'thĭä, sf. adhesion, cohesion; alliance, kindred.

adherente, –tä, a. adherent, cohesive.

adherir, –rĭr', v. n. to adhere to a sect; to espouse a cause; –, v.n. to hold; to cling.

adhesión, ädäsĭön', sf. adhesion; cohesion.

adiado, da, ädĭä'dö, a. día –, sm. the day appointed.   [mantine.

adiamantado, da, –mäntä'dö, a. ada-

adición, ädĭthĭön', sf. addition; (law) entry into an inheritance.   [tions.

adicionar, –thĭönär', v. a. to make additions.

adicto, ta, ädĭk'tö, a. addicted, devoted to.

adietar, ädĭĕtär', v. a. to put on a diet.

adinerado, da, ädĭnärä'dö, a. moneyed, rich.

adir, ädĭr', v. a. to inherit a legacy.   [rich.

aditamento, ädĭtämän'tö, sm. addition.

adiva, ädĭ'vä, sf., adive, –vä, sm. jackal.

adivinación, ädĭvĭnäthĭön', sf. divination.

adivinador, ra, –dör', sm. & f. diviner, soothsayer.   [tion.

adivinanza, –nän'thä, sf. enigma; divina-

adivinar, –när', v. a. to foretell; to conjecture.   [sayer; fortune-teller.

adivino, na, –vä'nö, sm. & f. diviner, soothsayer.

adjetivar, ädʾhĕtĭvär', v. a. to make the adjective agree with the substantive.

adjetivo, –tä'vö, sm. adjective.   [cation.

adjudicación, ädʾhüdĭkäthĭön', sf. adjudi-

adjudicar, –kär', v. a. to adjudge; –se, to appropriate to one's self.

adjunta, ädʾhün'tä, sf. enclosure.

adjunto, ta, –tö, a. united, joined, annexed; –, s. annex; (gr.) adjective.

adminicular, ädmĭnĭkülär', v. a. to support with legal proof.   [evidence.

adminículo, –nä'külö, sm. legal proof or

administración, ädmĭnĭsträthĭön', sf. administration.   [ministrator.

administrador, ra, –dör', sm. & f. ad-

administrar, –trär', v. a. to administer.

administrativo, va, –trä'vö, a. administrative.   [vellous.

admirable, ädmĭrä'blä, a. admirable, mar-

admiración, ädmĭräthĭön', sf. admiration; wonder; (gr.) note of exclamation.

admirar, –rär', v. a. to admire; to cause admiration.

admisible, ädmĭsĭ'blä, a. admissible.

admisión, ädmĭsĭön', sf. admission, acceptance.   [to concede; to permit.

admitir, ädmĭtĭr', v. a. to receive, to let in;

adobado, ädöbä'dö, sm. pickled pork.

adobar, –bär', v. a. to dress; to pickle; to stew; to tan hides.   [tomer.

adobasillas, –bäsĭl'yäs, sm. chair-bot-

adobe, ädö'bä, sm. adobe, sun-dried brick.

adobería, ädöbärĭ'ä, sf. brick-field; tanyard.

adobo, ädö'bö, sm. repairing, mending; pickle-sauce; paint for ladies; ingredients for dressing leather or cloth.

adocenado, da, ädöthänä'dö, a. very common, ordinary; by the dozen.

adocenar, –när', v. a. to count, sell or make by dozens; to despise.   [illness.

adolecer, ädöläthär', v. n. to be seized with

adolescencia, ädölĕsän'thĭä, sf. adolescence.

adolescente, –tä, a. adolescent, young.

¿ adónde ? ädön'dä, ad. whither ? where ?

adopción, ädöpthĭön', sf. adoption.

adoptador, ra, –tädör', sm. & f. adopter.

adoptar, –tär', v. a. to adopt.

adoptivo, va, –tä'vö, a. adoptive.   [ship.

adoración, ädöräthĭön', sf. adoration, worship.

adorador, ra, –dör', sm. & f. adorer.

adorar, –rär', v. a. to adore; to love exceedingly.   [(in America).

adoratorio, –rätö'rĭö, sm. temple of idols

adormecer, ädörmäthär', v. r. to fall asleep.

adormecimiento, –thĭmĭen'tö, sm. drowsiness, sleepiness.

adormidera, *—mĭdd'rä,* sf. (bot.) poppy.

adornar, *—när',* v. a. to embellish, to ornament. [ments.

adornista, *—nĭś'tä,* sm. painter of ornaments.

adorno, *ädōr'nō,* sm. adornment; ornament, decoration.

adquirir, *ädkīrīr',* v. a. to acquire.

adquisición, *ädkīsīthōn',* sf. acquisition.

adra, *ä'drä,* sf. turn, successive order.

adragante, *ädrägän'tĕ,* sm. gum tragacanth.

adrales, *ädrä'lĕs,* sm. pl. cart-rack.

adrede, *ädrĕ'dĕ,* ad. purposely.

adscribir, *ädskrībīr',* v. a. to appoint a person to a post.

aduana, *ädūä'nä,* sf. custom-house.

aduanar, *—när',* v. a. to enter goods at the custom-house; to pay duty.

aduanero, *—nä'rō,* sm. custom-house officer. [Arabs; horde of gypsies.

adnar, *ädär',* sm. nomadic village of Arabs.

aduendado, da, *ädŭĕndä'dä,* a. ghostly.

adufe, *ädŭ'fĕ,* sm. tambourine.

adufero, *—ä'rō,* sm. tambourine-player.

aduja, *ädŭ'h'ä,* sf. (mar.) coiled cable.

adujar, *—h'är',* v. a. (mar.) to coil a cable.

adulación, *ädŭläthōn',* sf. adulation.

adulador, ra, *—dōr',* s. flatterer; fawner.

adular, *—lär',* v. a. to flatter; to fawn.

adulear, *—lĕär',* v. n. to bawl, to cry out.

adulero, *—lĕ'rō,* sm. driver of horses (or mules). [terate; to commit adultery.

adulterar, *ädŭltĕrär',* v. a. & n. to adulterate.

adulterino, na, *—rē'nō,* a. begotten in adultery; misborn; falsified.

adulterio, *—tĕ'rĭō,* sm. adultery. [adulteress.

adúltero, ra, *ädŭl'tĕrō,* sm. & f. adulterer.

adulto, ta, *ädŭl'tō,* a. adult, grown-up.

adunar, *ädŭnär',* v. a. to unite, to join.

adustión, *ädŭstiōn',* sf. (med.) burning.

adusto, ta, *ädŭs'tō,* a. gloomy, intractable.

advenedizo, za, *ädvĕnĕdē'thō,* a. exotic, foreign. [Advent.

advenimiento, *—mĭĕn'tō,* sm. arrival;

adventicio, cia, *ädvĕntē'thĭō,* a. adventitious; accidental.

adverbio, *ädvĕr'bĭō,* sm. adverb.

adversario, *—sä'rĭō,* sm. adversary; antagonist. [lamity.

adversidad, *—sĭdäd',* sf. adversity, calamity.

adverso, sa, *ädvĕr'sō,* a. adverse, calamitous. [attention to; advice.

advertencia, *—tĕn'thĭä,* sf. advertence;

advertido, da, *—tē'dō,* a. skilful, intelligent.

advertir, *—tīr',* v. a. to advert, to take notice of, to give heed; to mark.

Adviento, *ädvĭĕn'tō,* sm. Advent.

adyacente, *ädyäthĕn'tĕ,* a. adjacent.

aechar, *äĕchär',* v. a. to winnow, to sift.

aecho, *äĕ'chō,* sm. winnowing.

aéreo, rea, *äĕ'rĕō,* a. aerial; airy, fantastic.

aeronauta, *äĕrōnä'ŭtä,* sm. aeronaut.

aerostática, *—stä'tĭkä,* sf. aerostatics.

afabilidad, *äfäbĭlĭdäd',* sf. affability.

afable, *äfä'blĕ,* a. affable, complacent.

afaca, *äfä'kä,* sf. yellow vetch.

afán, *äfän'.* sm. anxiety, solicitude.

afanar, *—är',* v. n. & r. to toil; to be over-solicitous. [taking.

afanoso, sa, *—nō'sō,* a. solicitous; painstaking.

afascalar, *äfäskälär',* v. a. to build ricks of corn, to stack corn.

afear, *äfĕär',* v. a. to deform; to misshape.

afección, *äfĕkthōn',* sf. affection; fondness, attachment.

afectación, *—täthōn',* sf. affectation.

afectadamente, *—tädämĕn'tĕ,* ad. affectedly; for appearance's sake.

afectar, *—tär',* v. a. to affect; to feign.

afectivo, va, *—tē'vō,* a. fond, tender.

afecto, *äfĕk'tō,* sm. affection; passion; disease; —, ta, a. affectionate; disposed; reserved. [moving; tender.

afectuoso, sa, *—tŭō'sō,* a. affectionate;

afeitar, *äfĕitär',* v. a. to shave; to paint.

afeite, *äfĕi'tĕ,* sm. paint, rouge. [the face.

afelpado, da, *äfĕlpä'dō,* a. shaggy.

afeminado, da, *äfĕmĭnä'dō,* a. effeminate.

afeminar, *—när',* v. a. to effeminate.

aferrar, *äfĕrrär',* v. a. to grapple, to grasp, to seize. [wavy pattern.

afestonado, *äfĕstōnä'dō,* a. worked in a

afianzar, *äfĭänthär',* v. a. to bail, to guarantee; to prop. [ing.

afición, *äfĭthōn',* sf. affection; fancy, liking.

aficionado, da, *—nä'dō,* sm. & f. lover, devotee.

aficionar, *—när',* v. a. to inspire affection; —se, to give one's mind to.

afijo, ja, *äfē'h'ō,* a. (gr.) affix.

afiladera, *äfĭlädĕ'rä,* sf. whetstone.

afilado, *äfĭlä'dō,* a. sharp.

afilar, *—lär',* v. a. to whet, to sharpen, to grind. [like.

afiligranado, da, *—lĭgränä'dō,* a. filigree-like.

afilón, *—lōn',* sm. whetstone.

afilosofado, *—lōsōfä'dō,* sm. person who plays the philosopher.

afín, *äfēn',* sm. relation by affinity.

afinación, *äfĭnäthōn',* sf. completion; refining; tuning of instruments.

afinar, *äfĭnär',* v. a. to complete; to tune musical instruments; to refine.

afinidad, *—nĭdäd',* sf. affinity; analogy.

afirmación, *äfĭrmäthōn',* sf. affirmation.

afirmado, *—mä'dō,* sm. macadamization.

afirmar, *—mär',* v. a. to secure, to fasten; to affirm, to assure.

afirmativa, *—mätē'vä,* sf. affirmation.

afirmativo, va, *—tē'vō,* a. affirmative.

aflicción, *äflĭkthōn',* sf. affliction, grief, heart-ache, painfulness.

aflictivo, va, *—tē'vō,* a. afflictive.

afligir, *äflē'h'īr',* v. a. to afflict, to grieve, to torment. [incombustible.

aflogisticar, *äflō'hĭstĭkär',* v. a. to render

aflojar, *äflō'h'är',* v. a. to loosen, to slacken, to relax; to relent; —, v. n. to grow weak; to abate; to grow cool in fervour.

afluente, *äflŭĕn'tĕ,* a. affluent, abundant; loquacious.

afollar, *äfōlyär',* v. a. to blow with bellows.

afondar, *äfōndär',* v. a. to put under water; (mar.) to sink; —, v. n. to go to the bottom.

aforar, *ăfŏrár'*, v.a. to gauge; to measure; to calculate the duty on goods.

aforismo, *ăfŏrĭs'mŏ*, sm. aphorism.

aforístico, ca, *—rĭs'tĭkŏ*, a. aphoristical.

aforo, *ăfŏ'rŏ*, sm. gauging; custom-house examination of goods or luggage.

aforrar, *ăfŏrrár'*, v.a. to line (clothes); (mar.) to sheathe.

aforro, *ăfŏr'rŏ*, sm. lining; sheathing.

afortunado, da, *ăfŏrtŭnă'dŏ*, a. fortunate; happy.

afosarse, *ăfŏsăr'sĕ*, v.r. (mil.) to entrench one's self.

afrancesar, *ăfrănthĕsár'*, v.a. to frenchify.

afrenta, *ăfrĕn'tă*, sf. outrage; insult; infamy.

afrentar, *ăfrĕntár'*, v.a. to affront; to insult.

afrentoso, sa, *—tŏ'sŏ*, a. ignominious; insulting; free from wood-worms.

afretar, *ăfrĕtár'*, v.a. (mar.) to scour; to frenchify.

afrontar, *ăfrŏntár'*, v.a. to confront; to reproach one to one's face with a crime.

afuera, *ăfŭĕ'ră*, ad. abroad; outward; besides, moreover; ¡—! stand out of the way!

afueras, *—s*, sm. pl. environs of a place.

afufar(se), *ăfŭfár'(sĕ)*, v.n. & r. to run away, to escape.

afuste, *ăfŭs'tĕ*, sm. gun-carriage.

agabachado, da, *ăgăbătshă'dŏ*, a. frenchified.

agachadiza, *—tshădĭ'thă*, sf. snipe.

agacharse, *—tshăr'sĕ*, v.r. to stoop, to squat.

agalla, *ăgăl'yă*, sf. gall-nut; —s, pl. glands of the throat; wind-galls of horses; gills of fishes.

agallado, da, *—lyă'dŏ*, a. steeped in an infusion of galls.

agallón, *—lyŏn'*, sm. large gall-nut; —es, pl. strings of large silver beads; wooden beads used for rosaries.

agamuzado, da, *ăgămŭthă'dŏ*, a. chamois coloured.

agarbanzar, *ăgărbănthár'*, v.n. to bud.

agarbarse, *—băr'sĕ*, v.r. to cower, to squat.

agárico, *ăgă'rĭkŏ*, sm. (bot.) agaric (fungous excrescence on the trunks of trees).

agarradero, *ăgărră'dĕ'rŏ*, sm. anchoring-ground; hold, haft.

agarrado, da, *—ră'dŏ*, a. miserable, stingy.

agarrafar, *—răfár'*, v.a. to grapple hard in a scuffle.

agarrar, *ăgărrár'*, v.a. to grasp, to seize; to gripe.

agarro, *ăgăr'rŏ*, sm. grasp.

agarrotar, *ăgărrŏtár'*, v.a. to tie down.

agasajador, ra, *ăgăsă'hădŏr'*, a. officious, complacent.

agasajar, *—hár'*, v.a. to receive and treat kindly; to regale.

agasajo, *ăgăsă'h'ŏ*, sm. graceful reception; kindness; friendly present.

ágata, *ă'gătă*, sf. agate.

agavillar, *ăgăvĭlyár'*, v.a. to tie up corn in sheaves; —se, to associate with a gang of sharpers.

agazapar, *—thăpár'*, v.a. to catch a person; —se, to hide one's self.

agencia, *ăhĕn'thĭă*, sf. agency.

agenciar, *—thĭár'*, v.a. to solicit, to endeavour, to obtain a thing.

agencioso, sa, *—thĭŏ'sŏ*, a. diligent, active; officious.

agente, *ăhĕn'tĕ*, sm. agent, actor; attorney.

agestado, da, *ăhĕstă'dŏ*, (bien ó mal-), good- or bad-looking.

agibílibus, *ă'hĭbĭlĭbŭs*, sm. application, industry.

agilidad, *ăhĭlĭdăd'*, sf. agility, nimbleness.

agilitar, *—tár'*, v.a. to render nimble, to make active.

agio, *ă'hĭŏ*, sm. agio.

agiotador, *—tădŏr'*, agiotista, *—tĭs'tă*, sm. money-changer, bill-broker, stock-broker.

agiotaje, *—tă'h'ĕ*, sm. stock-jobbing.

agitación, *ăhĭtăthĭŏn'*, sf. agitation.

agitanado, da, *—tănă'dŏ*, a. gipsy-like.

agitar, *—tár'*, v.a. to agitate, to move.

aglomerar, *ăglŏmĕrár'*, v.a. to agglomerate, to conglomerate.

agnación, *ăgnăthĭŏn'*, sf. consanguinity.

agnado, da, *—nă'dŏ*, agnaticio, cia, *—nătĭ'thĭŏ*, a. consanguineous.

agnición, *ăgnĭthĭŏn'*, sf. agnition, recognition.

agobiar, *ăgŏbĭár'*, v.a. to bend down to the ground; to oppress.

agolparse, *ăgŏlpăr'sĕ*, v.a. to assemble in crowds.

agone, *ăgŏ'nĕ* (in —), ad. in the struggle of death.

agonía, *ăgŏnĭ'ă*, sf. agony.

agonizar, *—nĭthár'*, v.a. to assist dying persons; —, v.n. to be in the agony of death, to agonise.

agorar, *ăgŏrár'*, v.a. to divine; to augur.

agorero, *ăgŏrĕ'rŏ*, sm. augurer; diviner.

agorgojarse, *ăgŏrgŏ'hár'sĕ*, v.r. to be destroyed by grubs (corn).

agostar, *ăgŏstár'*, v.a. to be parched with heat; —, v.n. to pasture cattle on stubbles in summer.

agostero, *—tĕ'rŏ*, sm. harvester; religious mendicant (who begs corn in August).

agostizo, za, *—tĭ'thŏ*, a. born in August.

agosto, *ăgŏs'tŏ*, sm. August (month); harvest-time.

agotar, *ăgŏtár'*, v.a. to misspend; to exhaust.

agoticado, *—tĭkă'dŏ*, a. Gothic; genteel.

agraciado, da, *ăgrăthĭă'dŏ*, a. graceful.

agraciar, *—thĭár'*, v.a. to embellish; to grace; to give an employment.

agradable, *—dă'blĕ*, a. agreeable; lovely.

agradar, *—dár'*, v.a. to please, to gratify.

agradecer, *—dĕthĕr'*, v.a. to acknowledge a favour.

agradecido, da, *—thĕ'dŏ*, a. thankful.

agradecimiento, *—thĭmĭĕn'tŏ*, sm. gratitude, gratefulness, thankfulness.

agrado, *ăgră'dŏ*, sm. agreeableness, courteousness; will, pleasure; liking.

agramadera, *ăgrămădĕ'ră*, sf. brake (for dressing flax or hemp).

agramar, *—már'*, v.a. to dress flax or hemp with a brake; fuse of hemp.

agramiza, *—mĭ'thă*, sf. stalk of hemp; residue.

agrandar, *ăgrăndár'*, v.a. to enlarge, to extend; to aggrandize.

agranujado, da, *ăgrănŭ'hă'dŏ*, a. grained.

agrario, ria, *ăgră'rĭŏ*, a. agrarian.

agravación, *ăgrăvăthĭŏn'*, sf. aggravation.

agravar, ăgrăvăr', v. a. to oppress; to aggrieve; to aggravate; to exaggerate.

agravatorio, ria, –văto'ryŏ, a. compulsory, aggravating.   [fender.

agraviador, ra, –vlădŏr', s. injurer, offender.

agraviar, –văr', v. a. to wrong, to injure; –se, to be aggrieved; to be piqued.

agravio, ăgră'vĭŏ, sm. offence, injury.

agras, ăgrăth', sm. verjuice; unripe grape; en –, unseasonably.   [gooseberry bush.

agrasón, ăgrăthŏn', sm. wild grape;

agregación, ăgrĕgăthŏn', sf. aggregation.

agregado, –gă'dŏ, sm. aggregate.

agregar, –găr', v. a. to aggregate, to heap together; to collate; to muster.

agresión, ăgrĕsĭŏn', sf. aggression, attack.

agresor, ăgrĕsŏr', sm. aggressor, assaulter.

agreste, ăgrĕs'tĕ, a. rustic; produced by nature without cultivation.

agrete, ăgrĕ'tĕ, a. bitter-sweet.

agriar, ăgrĭăr', v. a. to sour, to acidify; to exasperate.

agricultura, –kŭltōō'ră, sf. agriculture.

agridulce, –dŭl'thĕ, a. half sweet and half sour.   [the taste.

agrillo, lla, ăgrĭl'yŏ, a. sourish, sharp to

agrimensor, ăgrĭmĕnsŏr', sm. land-surveyor, surveyor.

agrimensura, –sōō'ră, sf. land-surveying.

agrimonia, ăgrĭmŏ'nĭă, sf. (bot.) agrimony.

agrio, ă grĭŏ, a. sour, acrid; rough, craggy; sharp, rude, unpleasant; –, sm. acidity of the juice of certain fruits.

agrumarse, ăgrōōmăr'sĕ, v. r. to clog.

agrupar, –păr', v. a. to group (in a picture); to cluster, to crowd.

agrura, ăgrōō'ră, sf. acidity.

agua, ă gwă, sf. water; lustre of diamonds; –llovediza, rain-water; –fuerte, aqua fortis; – bendita, holy water; –s, pl. mineral waters; cloudings in silk.

aguacero, –thă'rŏ, sm. short heavy shower of rain.

aguachirle, –tshĭr'lĕ, sf. slip-slop.

aguada, ăgwă'dă, sf. fresh-water hold or supply on board ship; water-colour; painting in water-colours.

aguaderas, ăgwădĕ'răs, sf. pl. wooden framework for the carriage of jars of water by mules.   [cattle, horse-pond.

aguadero, –dĕ'rŏ, sm. watering-place for

aguado, ăgwă'dŏ, sm. water-drinker.

aguador, –dŏr', sm. water-carrier.

aguaje, ăgwă'hĕ, sm. rapid current of sea-water; (mar.) spring-tide.

aguamanil, ăgwămănĭl', sm. earthen or metal water-jug for the wash-hand stand.

aguamanos, –mă'nŏs, sm. water for washing the hands.   [precious stone).

aguamarina, –mărē'nă, sf. aqua marina

aguamiel, –mĭĕl', sf. hydromel.

aguanieve, –nĭĕ'vĕ, sf. sleet; lap-wing.

aguanoso, sa, –nŏ'sŏ, a. aqueous.

aguantar, ăgwăntăr', v. a. to sustain, to suffer.

aguante, ăgwăn'tĕ, sm. firmness; patience.

aguapié, ăgwăpĭĕ', sm. small wine.

aguar, ăgwăr', v. a. to mix water with wine; –se, to be submerged.

aguardar, ăgwărdăr', v. a. to expect, to wait for; to grant time.   [shop.

aguardentería, –dĕntĕrē'ă, sf. brandy-

aguardentero, –dĕntĕ'rŏ, sm. keeper of a liquor-shop.

aguardiente, –dĭĕn'tĕ, sm. brandy.

aguardo, ăgwăr'dŏ, sm. place where a sportsman waits to fire at the game, stand.

aguarrás, –răs', sf. spirit of turpentine.

aguatocha, ăgwătŏ'tshă, sf. fire-engine.

aguaza, ăgwă'thă, sf. juice extracted from trees by incision.   [boggy or marshy.

aguazarse, –thăr'sĕ, v. r. to become

aguazo, ăgwă'thŏ, sm. painting in gouache.

agudeza, ăgŭdĕ'thă, sf. keenness, sharpness; acuteness; acidity; smartness.

agudo, da, ăgŏ'dŏ, a. sharp-pointed; keen-edged; smart; fine; acute, witty; brisk.

aguijada, ăgĭ'hă'dă, sf. spur, goad.

aguijar, –hăr', v. a. to prick, to spur, to goad; to stimulate.   [&c.; stimulation.

aguijón, –hŏn', sm. sting of a bee, wasp,

aguijonear, ăgĭ'hŏnĕăr', v. a. to prick, to spur; to stimulate.

águila, ă gĭlă, sf. eagle; a gold coin.

aguileño, ña, ăgĭlĕ'nyŏ, a. aquiline; hawk-nosed.

aguilucho, –lŏ'tshŏ, sm. eaglet.

aguinaldo, –năl'dŏ, sm. Christmas-box.

aguja, ăgŏ'hă, sf. needle; bodkin; magnetic needle; (rail.) switch, siding; – de coser, sewing-needle; – de marear, mariner's compass; – de hacer media, knitting-needle.

agujar, –hăr', v. a. to prick with a needle; to sew, to stitch; to knit.

agujazo, –hă'thŏ, sm. prick with a needle.

agujerear, –hĕrĕăr', v. a. to pierce, to bore.

agujero, –hĕ'rŏ, sm. hole in clothes; needle-maker; needle-seller.

agujeta, –hĕ'tă, sf. leather-strap; lace; –s, pl. pour-boire given to post-boys; pains from fatigue.   [shop.

agujetería, –hĕtĕrē'ă, sf. haberdasher's

aguosidad, ăgwŏsĭdăd', sf. lymph.

aguoso, sa, ăgwŏ'sŏ, a. aqueous.

agusanarse, ăgŭsănăr'sĕ, v. r. to be worm-eaten.

agustiniano, ăgŭstĭnĭă'nŏ, agustino, ăgŭstĭ'nŏ, sm. monk of the order of St. Augustin.

aguzadera, ăgŭthădĕ'ră, sf. whetstone.

aguzanieve, –nĭĕ'vĕ, sf. wagtail.

aguzar, ăgŭthăr', v. a. to whet, to sharpen; to stimulate.   [for irons.

aherrojar, ăĕrrŏ'hăr', v. a. to put in chains

ahí, ăē', ad. there.   [like, noble.

ahidalgado, da, ăēdălgă'dŏ, a. gentleman-

ahijada, ăē'hă'dă, sf. goddaughter.

ahijado, –dŏ, sm. godson.

ahijar, ăē'hăr', v. a. to adopt as one's child; –, v. n. to bring forth young; to bud.

ahilarse, ăēlăr'sĕ, v. r. to grow faint for want of nourishment; to grow ropy (of wine).

ahilo, ă*ʾ lŏ, sm. faintness for want of food, inanition

ahinco, ă*n´kŏ, sm. earnestness, eagerness.

ahitar, ah*tar´, v. a. to surfeit; to cloy.

ahogar, ăhŏgăr´, v. a. to throttle, to smother; to drown, to suffocate; to oppress; to quench.

ahogo, ăhŏ´gŏ, sm. anguish, pain. [trees.

ahojar, ăhŏ´jăr´, v. n. to eat the leaves of

ahondar, ăhŏndăr´, v.a. to sink, to deepen; —, v. n. to penetrate far into a thing.

ahora, ăhŏ´ră, ad. now, at present; — —, just now; —, c. whether, or.

ahorcajarse, ăhŏrkă´hăr´ sĕ, v. r. to sit astride. [very angry.

ahorcar, —kăr´, v. a. to hang; —se, to be

ahormar, —măr´, v. a. to fit or adjust a form.

ahorquillado, da, —kĭlyă´dŏ, a. forked.

ahorquillar, —kĭlyăr´, v. a. to prop up with forks.

ahorrar, ăhŏrrăr´, v. a. to enfranchise, to emancipate; to economize; to shun labour.

ahorrativo, va, ăhŏrrătĕ´vŏ, a. frugal, thrifty, saving; niggardly, stingy.

ahorro, ăhŏr´rŏ, sm. parsimony; saving; thrift. [trees.

ahoyar, ăhŏyăr´, v. a. to dig holes for

ahuchar, ăhătshăr´, v. a. to hoard up.

ahuecar, ăhŏĕkăr´, v. a. to hollow, to scoop out; —se, to grow haughty.

ahumar, ăhămăr´, v. a. to smoke, to cure in smoke.

ahusar, ăhăsăr´, v. a. to make a thing as slender as a spindle; —se, to taper. [flight.

ahuyentar, ăhăyĕntăr´, v. a. to put to

aijada, ă*ʾhă´ dă, sf. goad; pungency.

airarse, ărăr´sĕ, v. r. to grow angry.

airazo, ără´thŏ, sm. violent gust of wind.

aire, ă*ʾĕrĕ, sm. air; wind; gracefulness of manners; aspect, countenance; musical composition; en —, in a good humour.

airearse, ărĕăr´sĕ, v. a. to take the air.

airón, ărŏn´, sm. violent gale.

airoso, sa, ărŏ´sŏ, a. airy; windy; graceful, genteel; successful.

aislado, da, ăslă´dŏ, a. insulated, isolated.

aislar, ăslăr´, v. a. to surround with water; to isolate.

ajar, ăhăr´, sm. garlic-field; —, v. a. to spoil, to tarnish; to abuse.

aje, ă*ʾhĕ, sm. habitual complaint.

ajedrez, ăhĕdrĕth´, sm. chess (game); netting, grating.

ajedrezado, da, —thă´dŏ, a. chequered.

ajenabe, ăhĕnă´bĕ, sm. wild mustard.

ajenjo, ăhĕn´hŏ, sm. wormwood, absinthium.

ajeno, na, ă*ʾhă´nŏ, a. foreign, strange; insane; contrary to; ignorant; improper.

ajenuz, ăhĕnŭth´, sm. fennel-flower.

ajetrearse, ăhĕtrĕăr´ sĕ, v.a. to exert one's self; to bustle; to toil; to fidget.

ajetreo, ăhĕtrĕ´ŏ, sm. activity; bustling disposition.

aji, ă*ʾhĕ, sm. red Indian dwarf-pepper.

ajicola, —kŏ´lă, sf. glue made of scraps of leather boiled with garlic.

ajimez, —mĕth´, sm. arched window with a pillar in the centre to support it.

ajipuerro, —pŭĕr´rŏ, sm. (bot.) leek.

ajo, ă*ʾhŏ, sm. garlic; garlic-sauce; paint for ladies; discreditable transaction takes part in by several persons.

ajobar, ăhŏbăr´, v. a. to carry heavy loads upon one's back. [garlic.

ajolio, ăʾhŏ´lĭŏ, sm. sauce made of oil and

ajonje, ăʾhŏn´ʾhĕ, sm. bird-lime.

ajoqueso, ăʾhŏkă´sŏ, sm. dish made of garlic and cheese.

ajorca, ăʾhŏr´kă, sf. gold and silver anklets worn by Moorish women.

ajordar, —dăr´, v. a. to bawl, to cry out.

ajornalar, —nălăr´, v. a. to hire by the day.

ajuar, ăʾhŭăr´, sm. household furniture.

ajudiado, da, ăʾhŭdĭă´dŏ, a. jewish.

ajuiciado, da, ăʾhŭĭthĭă´dŏ, a. judicious, prudent, sensible.

ajustar, ăʾhŭstăr´, v.a. to regulate, to adjust; to concert; to settle a balance.

ajuste, —tĕ, sm. agreement, pact; accommodation. [malefactor.

ajusticiar, —tĭthĭăr´, v. a. to execute a

al, dl, art. for á el.

ala, ă*ʾlă, sf. wing; aisle; row, file; brim of the hat; auricle; —s, pl. (mar.) upper-studding sails; protection.

alabandina, ălăbăndĕ´nă, sf. manganese.

alabanza, —thă, sf. praise, applause.

alabar, ălăbăr´, v. a. to praise, to applaud.

alabarda, —dă, sf. halberd.

alabardero, —dă´rŏ, sm. halberdier.

alabastrado, da, ălăbăstră´dŏ, a. resembling alabaster.

alabastrino, na, —trĕ´nŏ, a. of alabaster.

alabastro, —trŏ, sm. alabaster; gypsum.

álabe, ă*ʾlăbĕ, sm. drooping branch of an olive-tree; flier of a water-mill; fan-wheel.

alabearse, ălăbĕăr´ sĕ, v. r. to warp.

alabeo, —bĕ´ŏ, sm. warp, warping.

alacena, —thĕ´nă, sf. cupboard, small cupboard in the wall; wainscot-chest.

alacrán, —krăn´, sm. scorpion; ring of the mouth-piece of a bridle; stop, hook.

alacranado, da, —nă´dŏ, a. bitten by a scorpion; infected.

alada, ălă´dă, sf. fluttering of the wings.

aladares, —dă´rĕs, sm. pl. love-curls.

alado, ga, —dŏ, a. winged.

álaga, ă*ʾlăgă, sf. (bot.) spelt.

alama, ălă´mă, sf. gold or silver cloth.

alambicado, da, ălămbĭkă´dŏ, a. given sparingly, grudgingly.

alambicar, —kăr´, v. a. to distil; to investigate closely.

alambique, —bĕ´kĕ, sm. alambic; still.

alambre, ălăm´brĕ, sm. copper; copperwire; sheep-bells.

alambrera, —brĕ´ră, sf. wire-cage.

alameda, ălămă´dă, sf. poplar-avenue.

álamo, ă*ʾlămŏ, sm. poplar, poplar-tree; — temblón, aspen-tree.

alamparse, ălămpăr´ sĕ, v. r. to long, to wish earnestly. [a gate.

alamud, ălămŭd´´, sm. door-bolt; bar of

alancear, ălănthĕăr', v. a. to dart, to spear; to wound with a lance.

alano, ălă'nŏ, sm. boar-hound.

alar, ălăr', sm. birdsnare, noose.

alarbe, —bĕ, sm. Arabian; unmannerly person. [—, to boast.

alarde, —dĕ, sm. military review; hacer [—, to boast.

alargar, ălărgăr', v. a. to lengthen; to ex- [tend.

alarida, ălărē'dă, sf. hue and cry. [tend.

alarido, —dŏ, sm. outcry, shout; dar —s. [to howl.

alarife, ălărē'fĕ, sm. architect. [to howl.

alarma, ălăr'mă, sf. (mil.) alarm.

alarmar, —măr', v. a. to alarm, to call to [arms.

alarmista, —mĭs'tă, sm. alarmist. [arms.

alatón, ălătŏn', sm. latten, brass.

alazán,ana, —thăn' a. sorrel-coloured (of horses).

alazo, ălă'thŏ, sm. blow with the wings.

alba, ăl'bă, sf. dawn of day, dayspring; alb, surplice. [cutor.

albacea, —thă'ă, sm. testamentary exe- [cutor.

albaceazgo, —thăăth'gŏ, sm. office of a testamentary executor.

albada, —dă, sf. morning-serenade.

albahaca, —ă'kă, sf. (bot.) sweet basil.

albalá, ălbălă', sm. & f. quittance, certi- ficate; passport.

albanega, —nĕ'gă, sf. hair-net.

albañal, —nyăl', albañar, —nyăr', sm. common sewer; gully-hole.

albañil, —nyĭl', sm. mason, bricklayer.

albañilería, —nyĭlĕrē'ă, sf. masonry.

albar, ălbăr', a. white, whitish.

albarán, ălbărăn', sm. bill or placard for letting a house.

albarazado, da, ălbărăthă'dŏ, a. affected with the white leprosy; pallid, pale.

albarazo, —thŏ, sm. white leprosy.

albarcoquero, ălbărkŏkŏ'rŏ, sm. apricot- tree. [beasts of burden; slice of bacon.

albarda, ălbăr'dă, sf. pack-saddle for [beasts of burden; slice of bacon.

albardar, —dăr', v. a. to saddle with a pack-saddle.

albardilla, —dĭl'yă, sf. small pack-saddle; coping; ridge; mother-wool.

albaricoque, ălbărĭkŏ'kĕ, sm. apricot.

albaricoquero, —kŏkŏ'rŏ, sm. apricot-tree

albarillo, ălbărĭl'yŏ, sm. country-dance tune for the guitar; small kind of apricot.

albarrada, ălbărră'dă, sf. dry wall; trench.

albayalde, ălbăyăl'dĕ, sm. white-lead, ceruse. [nut colour.

albazano, na, —thă'nŏ, a. of a dark chest- [nut colour.

albear, ălbĕăr', v. a. to whiten.

albedrío, —drē'ŏ, sm. free-will, freedom of will; arbitrament. [surgeon.

albéitar, ălbē'ĭtăr, sm. farrier, veterinary [surgeon.

albeitería, ălbēĭtĕrē'ă, sf. farriery.

albengala, ălbĕngă'lă, sf. muslin.

albentola, —tŏ'lă, sf. fine bag-net.

alberca, ălbĕr'kă, sf. reservoir, cistern.

albérchiga, —chĭgă, sf. peach.

albergar, —găr', v. a. to lodge, to har- bour; —se, to take a lodging.

albergue, —gĕ, sm. lodging-house, har- bour; charity-school for orphans.

albina, ălbē'nă, sf. marshy ground inun- dated with sea-water.

albo, ba, ăl'bŏ, a. white.

albogue, ălbŏ'gĕ, sm. bagpipe; cymbal.

albohol, ălbŏŏl', sm. bind-weed; poppy.

albóndiga, ălbŏn'dĭgă, sf. forcemeat-ball

albor, ălbŏr', sm. (poet.) dawn.

alborada, ălbŏră'dă, sf. first dawn of day; (mil.) action fought at the dawn of day; morning-watch.

alborear, ălbŏrĕăr', v. n. to dawn.

alborga, ălbŏr'gă, sf. mat-weed sandal.

albornía, ălbŏrnē'ă, sf. large glazed jug.

albornoz, —nŏth', sm. coarse woollen stuff; moorish cloak. [clusion of a bargain.

alboroque, ălbŏrŏ'kĕ, sm. treat at the con- [clusion of a bargain.

alborotadizo, za, —tădē'thŏ, alboro- tado, da, ălbŏrŏtă'dŏ, a. restless, turbu- lent.

alborotapueblos, —pŭĕ'blŏs, s. disturber.

alborotar, ălbŏrŏtăr', v. a. to make a dis- turbance. [tumult, riot.

alboroto, —rŏ'tŏ, sm. noise, disturbance, [tumult, riot.

alborozar, —rŏthăr', v. a. to exhilarate.

alborozo, —ŏ'thŏ, sm. joy, gaiety.

albricias, ălbrē'thăs, sf. pl. reward given for good news; ¡—! joy! joy!

albufera, ălbŭfĕ'ră, sf. lagoon. [nous.

albugíneo, nea, ălbŭ'hĕnĕŏ, a. albumi- [nous.

albugo, ălbŭ'gŏ, sm. albugo (eye-disease).

albur, ălbŭr', sm. dace (pez).

albura, ălbŭ'ră, sf. whiteness.

alcabala, ălkăbă'lă, sf. commerce-excise.

alcacel, —thĕl', alcacer, —thĕr', sm. meslin, mash.

alcachofa, —chŏ'fă, sf. artichoke.

alcahaz, —ăth', sm. large bird-cage.

alcahazar, —thăr', v. a. to cage birds.

alcahuete, ta, —hŭĕ'tĕ, sm. & f. pimp, bawd.

alcahuetear, —hŭĕtĕăr', v. a. to bawd.

alcahuetería, —hŭĕtĕrē'ă, sf. bawdry.

alcaide, ălkă'ĭdĕ, sm. governor of a castle; jailor, warden. [nor or jailor.

alcaidesa, ălkăĭdĕ'să, sf. wife of a gover- [nor or jailor.

alcaidía, —dē'ă, sf. governorship; gover- nor's district. [ringleader.

alcalde, ălkăl'dĕ, sm. justice of the peace;

alcaldía, —dē'ă, sf. office and jurisdiction of an alcalde.

alcalino, na, ălkălē'nŏ, a. alkaline.

alcamonías, —mŏnē'ăs, sf. pl. various kinds of aromatic seeds.

alcance, ălkăn'thĕ, sm. balance of an ac- count; arm's length; range of fire-arms; capacity, ability; fathom; hit; compass.

alcancía, —thē'ă, sf. money-box; (mil.) hand-grenade.

alcanfor, —fŏr', sm. camphor.

alcanforado, da, —fŏră'dŏ, a. camphorated.

alcantarilla, —tărē'yă, sm. small bridge; drain; conduit under ground.

alcanzado, da, —thă'dŏ, a. necessitous, wanting.

alcanzar, —thăr', v. a. to overtake, to come up with; to reach; to get, to obtain; to be a creditor; —, v. n. to suffice; to reach.

alcaparra, ălkăpăr'ră, sf., alcaparro, —rŏ, sm. caper-bush; caper.

alcaraván, ălkărăvăn′, sm. bittern.

alcaravea, —vā′ā, sf. caraway-seed.

alcartas, ălkărtăth′, sm. paper-bag.

alcatifa, ălkătē′fă, sf. fine carpet.

alcatraz, —trăth′, sm. pelican. [staple.

alcayata, —yā′tă, sf. hook; clothes-hook;

alcózar, —thār′ sm. castle, fortress.

aleazuz, —thŭth′, sm. liquorice.

alce, ăl′thĕ, sm. the cut (at cards).

alcedón, ălthĕăōn′, sm. alción, —thēōn′, sm.

alcoba, —kō′bă, sf. alcove. [halcyon.

alcohol, —kōōl′, sm. antimony; alcohol.

alcoholar, —kōōlăr′, v. a. to paint with
antimony; to rectify spirits; to reduce to
an impalpable powder.

alcorán, —kōrăn′, sm. Alcoran, Koran.

alcoranista, —ēs′tă, sm. expounder of the
Koran. [son of uncouth manners.

alcornoque, —kōrnō′kĕ, sm. cork-tree; per-

alcrebite, —krēbē′tĕ, sm. sulphur, brimstone.

alcribis, —krē′bĭs, sm. tewel, tewel-iron.

alcuza, —kō′thă, sf. oil-bottle. [bar.

aldaba, —dā′bă, sf. knocker; clapper; cross-

aldabada, —dă, sf. rap with a knocker; sudden fear. [knocker.

aldabazo, —thō, sm. violent rap with the

aldabear, ăldăbĕăr′, v. n. to knock at the
door with the knocker.

aldea, ăldā′ă, sf. hamlet; large farm.

aldeana, ăldĕā′nă, sf. countrywoman; lass.

aldeano, —nō, sm. villager; —, a. rustic.

aleación, ălĕăthĭōn′, sf. art of alloying
metals. [alloy.

alear, —ăr′, v. n. to flutter; —, v. a. to

alegación, ălĕgăthĭōn′, sf. allegation.

alegar, —găr′, v. a. to allege, to quote.

alegato, —gā′tō, sm. allegation; (law) plaintiff's deposition.

alegoría, —gōrē′ă, sf. allegory.

alegórico, ca, —gō′rĭkō, a. allegorical.

alegorizar, —gōrĭthăr′, v. a. to allegorise.

alegrar, —grăr′, v. a. to gladden; to lighten;
to exhilarate; to enliven; to beautify;
—se, to rejoice; to grow merry with drinking. [— de cascos, tipsy.

alegre, ăld′grĕ, a. merry, joyful, content;

alegría, ălĕgrē′ă, sf. mirth, gaiety; (bot.)
oily-grain; public festivals, pl.

alegro, ăld′grō, sm. (mus.) allegro.

alegrón, —grōn′, sm. sudden joy; sudden
flicker. [removal.

alejamiento, —′hămĭĕn′tō, sm. elongation;

alejar, —′hăr′, v. a. to remove to a greater
distance.

alelarse, —lăr′ĕ, v. r. to become stupid.

alelí, —ē′, sm. (bot.) winter gilliflower.

aleluya, —lō′yă, sf. allelujah; easter-time.

alemán, ălĕmăn′, sm. German language.

alemana, ălĕmā′nă, sf. (old) Spanish dance.

alentar, ălĕntăr′, v. n. to respire, to breathe;
—, v. a. to animate.

alepín, ălĕpĭn′, sm. a kind of bombasine.

alerce, ălĕr′thĕ, sm. larch-tree.

alero, ăld′rō, sm. gable-end; eaves.

alerta, dĭĕr′tă, sf. (mil.) watch-word.

alerta, —, alertamente, —mĕn′tĕ, ad.
vigilantly, attentively, on the watch,

alertar, ălĕrtăr′, v. a. to render vigilant.

alesna, dăs′nă, sf. awl.

alesnado, da, —nā′dō, a. awl-shaped.

aleta, ăld′tă, sf. fin.

aletargarse, —tărgăr′ĕ, v. r. to fall into
a lethargic state; to sink to sleep.

aletazo, —ă′thō, sm. blow from a wing.

aletear, ălĕtĕăr′, v. n. to flutter, to flit, to
flicker. [tering.

aleteo, —tā′ŏ, sm. flapping of wings; flut-

aleve, ăld′vĕ, a. treacherous, perfidious.

alevosía, ălĕvōsē′ă, sf. treachery, perfidy.

alevoso, sa, —vō′sō, a. treacherous, perfidious. [alphabetically.

alfabéticamente, ălfăbĕ′tĭkămĕn′tĕ, ad.

alfabético, ca, —tĭkō, a. alphabetical.

alfabeto, —tō, sm. alphabet; abecedary.

alfahaya, ălfăhā′yă, sf. floss-silk.

alfajor, —′hōr′, sm. gingerbread.

alfalfa, ălfăl′fă, sf. (bot.) lucern.

alfanjazo, —′hā′thō, sm. cutlass-wound.

alfanje, ălfăn′′hĕ, sm. hanger, cutlass.

alfaquí, ălfăkē′, sm. fakir.

alfar, —făr′, sm. pottery; potter's clay.

alfarería, —fărĕrē′ă, sf. potter's art.

alfarero, —rā′rō, sm. potter. [cate.

alfeñicado, ălfĕnyĭkā′dō, a. sugared; deli-

alfeñique, —kĕ, sm. sugar-paste; weakling.

alferecía, ălfĕrĕthē′ă, sf. epilepsy.

alfil, —fĭl′, sm. bishop (at chess).

alfiler, —fĭlĕr′, sm. pin (to fasten clothes);
—es, pl. pin-money.

alfilerazo, —fĭlĕră′thō, sm. prick of a pin.

alfolí, —fōlē′, sm. granary; salt warehouse.

alfolí(n)ero, —fōlĭ(n)ā′rō, sm. keeper of a
granary or magazine.

alfombra, —fōm′bră, sf. carpet; (poet.) field
adorned with flowers.

alfombrar, —fōmbrăr′, v. a. to carpet.

alfombrero, —fōmbrā′rō, sm. carpet-maker.

alfombrilla, —fōmbrē′yă, sf. small carpet;
(med.) scarlatine. [or nut).

alfóncigo, —fōn′thĭgō, sm. pistachio (tree

alforja, —fōr′hă, sf. saddle-bag, knapsack.

alforjero, —fōr′hā′rō, sm. maker or seller
of saddle-bags.

alga, —gă, sf. (bot.) sea-weed.

algaida, —gā′ĭdă, sf. sand-dune.

algalia, —gā′lĭă, sf. civet; civet-cat.

algarabía, —gărăbē′ă, sf. Arabic tongue;
gabble, gibberish.

algarada, —gărā′dă, sf. loud cry.

algarroba, —gărrō′bă, sf. (bot.) carob.

algarrobera, —gărrōbā′ră, sf., alga-
rrobo, —gărrō′bō, sm. (bot.) carob-tree.

algazara, —găthā′ră, sf. huzza (cry of
Moors); hubbub of a multitude.

álgebra, ăl′′hĕbră, sf. algebra.

algebrista, ăl′hĕbrĭs′tă, sm. algebraist.

algo, ăl′gō, pn. somewhat, something;
ought; —, ad. somewhat.

algodón, ălgōdōn′, sm. cotton; cotton-
plant; cotton-wool. [cotton.

algodonado, da, —dōnā′dō, a. filled with

algodonal, —dōnăl′, sm. cotton-plantation.

algodonero, —dōnā′rō, sm. cotton-plant;
dealer in cotton, cotton-broker.

algoso, za, *algó'só*, a. full of sea-weed.
alguacil, *algwáthil'*, sm. bum-bailiff;
  market-clerk; high constable; watchman.
alguien, *ál'gïen*, pn. somebody.
algún, na, *-gún'*, a. anyone; — poco ó
  tanto, ad. a little, rather.
alhaja, *ala'ha*, sf. furniture; jewel.
alhajar, *-á'har*, v. a. to supply with furniture.   [tion.
alharaca, *-ará'ka*, sf. clamour, vocifera-
alheña, *alen'ya*, sf. (bot.) common privet,
  dogwood; corn-blight.
alhoja, *-ó'ha*, sf. lark.
alhóndiga, *-ón'dïga*, sf. public granary.
alhondiguero, *-ondïgá'ró*, sm. keeper of
  a public granary.
alhucema, *aluthá'ma*, sf. lavender.
aliacanado, da, *alïákaná'dó*, a. jaun-
aliado, da, *alïá'dó*, a. allied.   [diced.
alianza, *alïán'tha*, sf. alliance, league.
aliarse, *alïár'sé*, v. r. to be allied.
alias, *á'lïás*, ad. otherwise.
alicaído, da, *alïkáï'dó*, a. lame-winged;
  weak, extenuated; uncocked.
alicantina, *-kántï'na*, sf. artifice, stratagem, cunning.
alicates, *-ká'tés*, sm. pl. pincers, nippers.
aliciente, *-thïén'té*, sm. attraction, incitement.   [ber).
alicuanta, *-kwán'ta*, a. f. aliquant (num-
alicuota, *-kwó'ta*, a. f. aliquot (quantity).
aliento, *alïén'tó*, sm. breath, respiration;
  courageousness.
alifafe, *alïfá'fé*, sm. tumour (on a horse's
  hock); habitual ailment.
aligación, *-gathïón'*, sf. allegation.
aligador, *-gádór'*, sm. alligator.
aligar, *alïgár'*, v. a. to tie, to unite.
aligeramiento, *-'héraméïén'tó*, sm. alleviation.   [viate; to hasten.
aligerar, *-'héyár'*, v. a. to lighten; to alle-
alijador, *-hádór'*, sm. (mar.) lighter.
alijar, *-hár'*, v. a. (mar.) to lighten, to
  lighter; —, sm. uncultivated ground.
alijo, *ali'hó*, sm. lightening of a ship;
  alleviation.
alimentación, *alïméntáthïón'*, sf. alimentation, maintenance, nourishment.
alimentar, *-tár'*, v. a. to feed, to nourish.
alimenticio, cia, *-tï'thïó*, a. nutritious,
  nutritive.   [sioner.
alimentista, *-tïs'ta*, sm. boarder, pen-
alimento, *alïmén'tó*, sm. aliment, food;
  —s, s. pl. alimony.   [delimitate.
alindar, *alïndár'*, v. a. to fix limits; to
alineación, *alïnéáthïón'*, sm. delimitation.
alinear, *-neár'*, v. a. to measure by line,
  to arrange in line.
aliñar, *alïnyár'*, v. a. to adorn; to season.
aliño, *alïn'yó*, sm. dress, ornament, decoration; apparatus.   [feet; swift-footed.
alípede, *alï'pédé*, a. (poet.) with winged
aliquebrado, da, *-kébrá'dó*, a. broken-
  winged; dejected, low-spirited.
alisadura, *-sádú'ra*, sf. planing, smoothing, polishing; —s, s. pl. shavings, cuttings.

alisar, *alïsár'*, v. a. to plane, to polish;
  to smoothe; to mangle.
aliseda, *alïsé'dá*, sf. plantation of alder-
aliso, *alï'só*, sm. alder-tree.   [trees.
alistado, da, *alïstá'dó*, a. striped.
alistador, *-dór'*, sm. accountant; one
  who enlists.   [conscription, levy.
alistamiento, *-mïén'tó*, sm. enrolment.
alistar, *alïstár'*, v. a. to enlist, to enrol.
aliviador, *alïvïádór'*, sm. assistant.
aliviar, *-vïár'*, v. a. to lighten; to ease,
  to relieve; to mollify.   [comfort.
alivio, *alï'vïó*, sm. alleviation, mitigation;
aljaba, *al'há'bá*, sf. quiver.
aljez, *-héth'*, crude gypsum.
aljibe, *-'hï'bé*, sm. cistern.
aljofaina, *-hófáï'na*, sf. earthen jug;
  wash-hand basin.
aljófar, *-'hófár'*, sm. misshapen pearl;
  (poet.) drop of dew; tear.   [pearls.
aljofarar, *-'hófárár'*, v. a. to adorn with
aljor, *-'hór'*, sm. crude gypsum.
aljuba, *al'hú'bá*, sf. a moorish garment.
alma, *ál'má*, sf. soul; human being;
  principal part of a thing; conscience;
  energy; mould for casting statues.
almacén, *álmáthén'*, sm. warehouse, store,
  magazine.   [rent; housage.
almacenaje, *-théná'h'é*, sm. warehouse
almacenar, *-thénár'*, v. a. to store, to
  lay up.   [keeper.
almacenero, *-théné'ró*, sm. warehouse-
almáciga, *álmá'thïgá*, sf. mastich; nursery.
almadén, *álmádén'*, sm. mine.
almadía, *álmádï'á*, sf. Indian canoe; raft.
almadraba, *-drá'bá*, sf. tunny-fishery.
almadreña, *-drén'yá*, sf. wooden shoe.
almaganeta, *-gáné'tá*, sf. sledge-hammer.
almagrar, *álmágrár'*, v. a. to tinge with
  red ochre, to ruddle.
almagre, *álmá'gré*, sm. red ochre, ruddle.
almanaque, *álmáná'ké*, sm. almanac.
almanaquero, *-ká'ró*, almanaquista,
  -kïs'tá, sm. maker or vender of almanacs.
almáraco, *álmá'rákó*, sm. (bot.) marjoram.
almargo, *álmár'gó*, sm. (bot.) glass-wort.
almarjal, *álmár'hár'*, sm. plantation of
  glass-wort; low marshy ground.   [halter.
almártaga, *-tágá*, sf. litharge; a sort of
almástiga, *álmá'stïgá*, sf. mastich.
almastigado, da, *-gá'dó*, a. containing
  mastich.
almazara, *álmáthá'rá*, sf. oil-mill.
almazarero, *-thá'ró*, sm. oil-miller.
almazarrón, *-thárrón'*, sm. ruddle.
almena, *álmé'ná*, sf. battlement.
almenado, da, *-má'dó*, a. embattled.
almenaje, *-ná'hé*, sm. series of turrets
  around a rampart.   [with battlements.
almenar, *-nár'*, v. a. to crown a rampart
almendra, *álmén'drá*, sf. almond.
almendrada, *-drá'dá*, sf. almond-milk;
almendrado, da, *-drá'dó*, a. almond-like;
  —, sm. macaroon.
almendrera, *álméndré'rá*, sf. almen-
  drero, *-ó*, almendro, *álmén'dró*, sm.
  green almond.   [tree.
almez(o), *álméth'(ó)*, sm. nettle-tree, lotus.

almeza, –thă, sf. lotus-berry.

almiar, ălmĕăr, sm. stack of hay.

almíbar, ălmĕ´băr, sm. syrup; treacle; –es, pl. preserved fruit.

almibarar, ălmĕbărăr, v. a. to preserve fruit in sugar; to conciliate with soft and endearing words.

almidón, –dŏn, sm. starch.

almidonado, da, –dŏnă´dŏ, a. starched; affected; spruce.

almidonar, –dŏnăr, v. a. to starch.

almilla, ălmĭl´yă, sf. under waistcoat; short military jacket: pork-chop.

alminar, ălmĭnăr, sm. minaret.

almiranta, ălmĭrăn´tă, sf. flag-ship; the admiral's wife. [admiral's dues.

almirantazgo, –tăth´gŏ, sm. admiralty.

almirante, ălmĭrăn´tĕ, sm. admiral; swimming-master.

almirez, ălmĭrĕth´, sm. brass mortar.

almizclar, ălmĭthklăr´, v. a. to musk.

almizcle, ălmĭth´klĕ, sm. musk.

almizcleña, –klĕn´yă, sf. grape-hyacinth.

almizcleño, ña, –ŏ, a. musky.

almizclera, ălmĭthklĕ´ră, sf. musk-rat.

almo, ma, ăl´mŏ, a. supporting; nourishing; (poet.) venerable, holy. [hoe.

almocafre, ălmŏkă´frĕ, sm. gardener's

almodrote, –drŏ´tĕ, sm. sauce for mad-apples; hodge-podge.

almofía, –fĕ´ă, sf. wash-hand basin.

almofrej, –frĕh´, sm. pillow-case.

almohada, –ă´dă, sf. pillow, bolster; coach-box; cushion. [working-case.

almohadilla, –ădĭl´yă, sf. small pillow;

almohadón, –ădŏn´, sm. large cushion.

almohaza, –ă´thă, sf. curry-comb.

almohazador, –thădŏr´, sm. groom, stable-boy, ostler.

almohazar, –thăr´, v. a. to curry.

almojábana, –hă´bănă, sf. cheese-cake.

almoneda, –nă´dă, sf. auction.

almonedear, –nĕdĕăr´, v. a. to sell by auction. [joram.

almoraduj, ălmŏrădŭh´, sm. sweet mar-

almorí, ălmŏrĕ´, sm. sweetmeat-cake.

almorranas, ălmŏrră´năs, sf. pl. hemorrhoids. [floor.

almorrefa, ălmŏrră´fă, sf. mosaic-tile

almorta, ălmŏr´tă, sf. chickling vetch.

almorzada, –thă´dă, sf. double-handful of grain &c. [fasted.

almorzado, da, –dŏ, a. one who has break-

almorzar ălmŏrthăr´, v. a. to breakfast.

almotacén, ălmŏtăthĕn´, sm. inspector of weights and measures.

almotacenazgo, –năth´gŏ, sm. office of an inspector of weights and measures.

almozárabe, ălmŏthă´răbĕ, sm. christian who lived under the Moors.

almud, ălmŭd´´, sm. measure of grain (the twelfth part of a fanega).

almudada, ălmŭdă´dă, sf. piece of ground which it takes half a fanega of grain to sow. [(of grain, fruits &c.).

almuerza, ălmŭĕr´thă, sf. double-handful

almuerzo, –ŏ, sm. breakfast; cupboard.

alobadado, da, ălŏbădă´dŏ, a. bitten by a wolf; plague-sore (of animals).

alobunado, da,–bŭnă´dŏ, a. wolf-coloured.

alocado, da, –kă´dŏ, a. crack-brained; foolish, inconsiderate.

alocución, –kŭthŏn´, sf. allocution.

alodio, ălŏ´dĭŏ, sm. allodium.

áloe, ă´lŏĕ, sm. (bot.) aloes.

aloja, ălŏ´hă, sf. metheglin.

alojamiento, ălŏ´hămĭĕn´tŏ, sm. lodging; (mar.) steerage. [side in lodgings.

alojar, –´hăr, v. a. to lodge; –se, to re-

alojería, –hĕrĕ´ă, sf. place where metheglin is prepared and sold.

alojero, –´hĕ´rŏ, sm. seller of metheglin; box near the pit in some theatres of Spain.

alomado, da, –mă´dŏ, a. crook-backed (of horses).

alomar, –măr´, v. a. to distribute equally the strength of a horse; –, v. n. to grow strong and vigorous.

alón, ălŏn´, sm. wing of a bird stripped of its feathers; ¡ – ! let us go! [opium.

alondra, ălŏn´dră, sf. lark.

alopiado, da, ălŏpĭă´dŏ, a. composed of opium.

aloque, ălŏ´kĕ, a. light-red (wine).

alosa, ălŏ´să, sf. shad (pez).

alpañata, ălpănyă´tă, sf. piece of leather for smoothing pottery.

alpargata, ălpărgă´tă, sf. hempen shoe.

alpargatar, –tăr´, v. a. to make hempen shoes. [hempen shoes

alpargatero, –tă´rŏ, sm. manufacturer of

alpargatilla, –tĭl´yă, sm. crafty fellow, wheedler.

alpiste, ălpĭs´tĕ, sm. canary-seed.

alpistela, ălpĭstĕ´lă, alpistera, –ră, sf. cake made of flour, eggs, sesamum and honey. [canary-seed.

alpistero, –tĕ´rŏ, sm. sieve for sifting

alquería, ălkĕrĕ´ă, sf. grange, farm-house.

alquifol, ălkĕfŏl´, sm. aquifou, potter's ore.

alquiladizo, za, ălkĭlădĕ´thŏ, a. for hire.

alquilador, ra, –lădŏr´, sm. (& f.) hirer, tenant.

alquilar, –lăr´, v. a. to let, to hire. [rent.

alquiler, –lĕr´, sm. wages, hire; house-

alquimia, ălkĕ´mĭă, sf. alchemy.

alquímico, ca, –mĕkŏ, a. alchemical.

alquimista, –mĕs´tă, sm. alchemist.

alquitara, –tă´ră, sf. alembic.

alquitarar, –tărăr´, v. a. to distil.

alquitrán, –trăn´, sm. tar, liquid pitch.

alquitranado, –trănă´dŏ, sm. (mar.) tar-paulin.

alquitranar, –trănăr´, v. a. to tar.

alrededor, ălrĕdĕdŏr´ ad. around.

alrededores, –ĕs, sm. pl. environs.

alta, ăl´tă, sf. (mil.) discharge-ticket from hospital.

altanería, ăltănĕrĕ´ă, sf. haughtiness.

altanero, ra, ăltănĕ´rŏ, a. haughty, arrogant, vain, proud.

altar, ăltăr´, sm. altar; – de ánima, altar of indulgence; – mayor, high-altar.

altarero, ăltărĕ´rŏ, sm. decorator of altars for festivals.

altea, *ălté̆'ă̆*, sf. (bot.) marsh-mallow.

alterabilidad, *ăltĕ̆ră̆bĭlĭdăd'*, sf. alterableness; mutability.

alterable, *-rá̆'blĕ̆*, a. alterable, mutable.

alteración, *-thŏ̆n'*, sf. alteration, mutation; strong emotion; disturbance, tumult.

alterar, *ăltĕ̆ră̆r'*, v. a. to alter, to change; to disturb; —se, to fling.

altercación, *ăltĕ̆rkăthŏ̆n'*, sf., altercado, *ăltĕ̆rkă̆'dŏ̆*, sm. altercation, controversy; quarrel, contest, strife.

altercador, ra, *-dŏ̆r'*, sm. (& f.) wrangler.

altercar, *-kă̆r'*, v. a. to dispute, to altercate, to quarrel.

alternación, *ăltĕ̆rnăthŏ̆n'*, sf. alternation.

alternar, *ăltĕ̆rnă̆r'*, v. a. & n. to alternate.

alternativa, *ăltĕ̆rnă̆tĭ'vă̆*, sf. alternative.

alternativo, va, *-vŏ̆*, a. alternate.

alteza, *ăltĕ̆'thă̆*, sf. height, elevation.

Alteza, *-*, sf. Highness (title).

altibajo, *ăltĭbă̆'hŏ̆*, sm. downright blow in fencing; uneven ground; —s, pl. vicissitudes of human affairs, ups and downs.

altillo, *ăltĭl'yŏ̆*, sm. hillock.

altísimo, ma, *ăltĭ̆s'ĭmŏ̆*, a. extremely high, highmost; —, sm. the Most High, God.

altisonante, *ăltĭsŏ̆nă̆n'tĕ̆*, altísono, na, *ăltĭ'sŏ̆nŏ̆*, a. high-sounding, pompous, fustian. [ing, high-sounding.

altitonante, *-tŏ̆nă̆n'tĕ̆*, a. (poet.) thunder-

altivez, *ăltĭvĕ̆th'*, sf. haughtiness, huff.

altivo, va, *ăltĭ'vŏ̆*, a. haughty, proud, high-flown.

alto, ta, *ăl'tŏ̆*, a. high, elevated; arduous, difficult; eminent; enormous, atrocious; —, sm. height; storey; highland; (mil.) halt; (mus.) tenor, tenor-notes; —! , —! ahí! stop there! — de aquí! move off!

altramuz, *ăltră̆mŭ̆th'*, sm. (bot.) lupine.

altura, *ăltŭ̆'ră̆*, sf. height; highness; mountain summit; altitude; —s, pl. the heavens.

alubia, *ălŭ̆'bĭă̆*, sf. kidney-bean.

alucinación, *ălŭ̆thĭnăthŏ̆n'*, sf., alucinamiento, *-nămĭĕ̆n'tŏ̆*, sm. hallucination.

alucinar, *-nă̆r'*, v. a. to blind, to deceive; —se, to deceive oneself, to labour under a delusion.

aludir, *ălŭ̆dĭr'*, v. n. to allude.

alumbrado, da, *ălŭ̆mbră̆'dŏ̆*, a. aluminous; a little tipsy; —, sm. illumination; —por el gas, gas-lighting.

alumbramiento, *-mĭĕ̆n'tŏ̆*, sm. illumination; illusion, deceit; child-birth.

alumbrar, *ălŭ̆mbră̆r'*, v. a. to light; to enlighten, to instruct; to soak in alum-water; —se, to be intoxicated.

alumbre, *ălŭ̆m'brĕ̆*, sm. alum.

alumbrera, *-bră̆'ră̆*, sf. alum-mine.

aluminado, da, *ălŭ̆mĭnă̆'dŏ̆*, a. impregnated with alum.

aluminio, *ălŭ̆mĭ'nĭŏ̆*, sm. aluminium.

aluminoso, sa, *-nŏ̆'sŏ̆*, a. aluminous.

alumno, na, *ălŭ̆m'nŏ̆*, sm. foster-child; disciple, pupil. [modic; long-tusked.

alunado, da, *ălŭ̆nă̆'dŏ̆*, a. lunatic; spas-

alusión, *ălŭ̆sĭŏ̆n'*, sf. allusion, hint.

alusivo, va, *ălŭ̆sĭ'vŏ̆*, a. allusive.

alustrar, *ălŭ̆stră̆r'*, v. a. to give lustre, to polish. [brought to light by washing.

afutación, *ăfŭ̆tăthŏ̆n'*, sf. grains of gold.

aluvión, *ălŭ̆vĭŏ̆n'*, sf. alluvion.

álveo, *ăl'vĕ̆ŏ̆*, sm. bed of a river.

alvéolo, *ălvĕ̆'ŏ̆lŏ̆*, sm. socket of a tooth; cell of a honey-comb. [ware.

alvidriar, *ălvĭdrĭă̆r'*, v. a. to glaze earthen-

alvitana, *ălvĭtă̆'nă̆*, sf. shelter.

alza, *ăl'thă̆*, sf. advance in price; lift.

alzacuello, *-kŭ̆ĕ̆l'yŏ̆*, sm. gorget; pad.

alzadamente, *-dă̆mĕ̆n'tĕ̆*, ad. wholesale.

alzado, *ălthă̆'dŏ̆*, sm. plan of a building showing front elevation; —s, pl. spare stores; —, da, a. fraudulent (of a bankrupt). [rupt).

alzadura, *-dŏ̆'ră̆*, sf. elevation.

alzamiento, *-mĭĕ̆n'tŏ̆*, sm. raise; elevation; higher bid.

alzaprima, *-prĭ'mă̆*, sf. lever.

alzaprimar, *-prĭmă̆r'*, v. a. to lever; (fig.) to excite. [of a mute servant.

alzapuertas, *-pŭ̆ĕ̆r'tă̆s*, sm. part or rôle

alzar, *ălthă̆r'*, v. a. to raise, to lift up, to heave; to construct, to build; to hide; to lock up; to cut cards; to plough for the first time; —se, to rise in rebellion; —se á mayores, to be petulant; —se con algo, to encroach.

allá, *ălyă̆'*, ad. there; thither; in other times.

allanar, *ălyă̆nă̆r'*, v. a. to level, to flatten; to overcome difficulties; to pacify; to subdue; —se, to submit; to tumble down.

allegadizo, za, *ălyĕ̆gă̆dĭ'thŏ̆*, a. swept or scraped together. [conjunct, follower.

allegado, da, *ălyĕ̆gă̆'dŏ̆*, a. near, proximate,

allegar, *ălyĕ̆gă̆r'*, v. a. to collect, to gather; to approach.

allende, *ălyĕ̆n'dĕ̆*, ad. on the other side.

allí, *ălyĭ̆'*, ad. there, in that place.

alloza, *ălyŏ̆'thă̆*, sf. green almond.

allozo, *ălyŏ̆'thŏ̆*, sm. wild almond-tree.

ama, *ă'mă̆*, sf. mistress, house-wife; —de llaves, house-keeper; —de leche, nurse.

amabilidad, *ămă̆bĭlĭdăd'*, sf. amiability, loveliness.

amable, *ămă̆'blĕ̆*, a. amiable, lovely.

amador, ra, *ămă̆dŏ̆r'*, sm. & f. lover, sweetheart. [berry-like.

amadroñado, da, *-drŏ̆nyă̆'dŏ̆*, a. straw-

amaestrado, da, *-ĕ̆stră̆'dŏ̆*, a. taught; artfully contrived. [struct.

amaestrar, *-ĕ̆stră̆r'*, v. a. to teach, to in-

amagar, *-gă̆r'*, v. a. to threaten; to shake one's fist. [symptom.

amago, *ămă̆'gŏ̆*, sm. threat; indication;

amainar, *ămă̆ĭnă̆r'*, v. a. (mar.) to lower a sail; to give up, to withdraw from.

amajadar, *ămă̆hă̆dă̆r'*, v. n. to pen sheep.

amalgama, *ămă̆lgă̆mă̆'*, sf. amalgam.

amalgamación, *ămă̆lgă̆măthŏ̆n'*, sf. amalgamation. [gamate.

amalgamar, *ămă̆lgă̆mă̆r'*, v. a. to amal-

amamantar, *ămă̆mă̆ntă̆r'*, v. a. to suckle.

amancebamiento, *ămă̆nthĕ̆bă̆mĭĕ̆n'tŏ̆*, sm. concubinage. [cubinage.

amancebarse, *-bă̆r'sĕ̆*, v. r. to live in con-

amancillar, *ămănsĭlyăr'*, v. a. to stain, to defile; to injure; to tarnish one's reputation. [—, at day-break.

amanecer, *ămănĕthĕr'*, v. n. to dawn; al

amanojar, *ămănŏhăr'*, v. a. to gather by handfuls. [tamer, subduer; soother.

amansador, ra, *ămănsădŏr'*, sm. & f.

amansamiento, *—mĭĕn'tŏ*, sm. taming.

amansar, *ămănsăr'*, v. a. to tame, to domesticate; to soften, to meeken.

amantar, *ămăntăr'*, v. a. to cover with a

amante, *ămăn'tĕ*, sm. lover. [blanket.

amanuense, *ămănŭĕn'sĕ*, sm. amanuensis, clerk, copyist.

amañar, *ămănyăr'*, v. a. to do a thing cleverly; —se, to accustom one's self to do things cleverly.

amaño, *ămăn'yŏ*, sm. skill, dexterity; —s, s. pl. tools; implements; intrigue.

amapola, *ămăpŏ'lă*, sf. (bot.) poppy.

amar, *ămăr'*, v. a. to love; to fancy.

amaranto, *ămărăn'tŏ*, sm.(bot.) amaranth.

amargar, *ămărgăr'*, v. a. to make bitter; to exasperate; —, v. n. to be bitter.

amargo, ga, *ămăr'gŏ*, a. bitter, acrid; painful; —, sm. bitterness; sweet-meat made of bitter almonds; —s, pl. bitters.

amargón, *ămărgŏn'*, sm. (bot.) dandelion.

amargor, *—gŏr'*, sm. bitterness; sorrow, vexation, distress.

amargoso, sa, *—gŏ'sŏ*, a. bitter.

amargura, *—gŏŏ'ră*, sf. bitterness; sorrow.

amaricado, da, *ămărĭkă'dŏ*, a. effeminate.

amarillazo, za, *ămărĭlyă'thŏ*, a. pale yellow.

amarillear, *—yĕăr'*, v. n. to turn yellow.

amarillejo, ja, *ămărĭlyĕ'hŏ*, amarillento, ta, *—yĕn'tŏ*, a. yellowish.

amarillez, *—yĕth'*, sf. yellowness of the skin. [sm. jaundice.

amarillo, lla, *ămărĭl'yŏ*, a. yellow; —,

amarinar, *ămărĭnăr'*, v. a. (mar.) to man, to equip.

amarra, *ămăr'ră*, sf. cable; martingale.

amarradero, *ămăr'rădĕro*, sm. a post to make fast to; (mar.) mooring-berth.

amarrar, *ămărrăr'*, v. a. to tie, to fasten.

amarrazones, *ămărrăthŏ'nĕs*, sm. pl. (mar.) ground-tackle.

amartelar, *ămărtĕlăr'*, v. a. to court, to make love; —se, to fall in love with.

amartillar, *—tĭlyăr'*, v. a. to hammer; to cock a gun or pistol. [trough.

amasadera, *ămăsădĕ'ră*, sf kneading-

amasadijo, *—dĭ'hŏ*, sm. bread-dough.

amasadura, *—dŏ'ră*, sf. kneading.

amasar, *ămăsăr'*, v. a. to knead; (fig.) to arrange, to prepare, to settle.

amasijo, *ămăsĭ'hŏ*, sm. dough; mixed mortar; bread-dough; medley.

amatista, *ămătĭs'tă*, sf. amethyst.

amatorio, ria, *—tŏ'rĭŏ*, a. relating to love.

amazona, *ămăthŏ'nă*, sf. amazon; masculine woman.

ámbar, *ăm'băr*, sm. amber. [line woman.

ambarino, na, *ămbărĕ'nŏ*, a. amber.

ambición, *ămbĭthĭŏn'*, sf. ambition; covetousness. [to covet.

ambicionar, *ămbĭthĭŏnăr'*, v. a. to crave,

ambicioso, ga, *—thĭ'ŏsŏ*, a. ambitious.

ambiente, *ămbĭĕn'tŏ*, sm. surrounding atmosphere.

ambigú, *ămbĭgŏ'*, sm. ambigu.

ambigüedad, *—gŏĕdăd'*, sf. ambiguity.

ambiguo, gua, *ămbĭ'gŏŏ*, a. ambiguous, doubtful, equivocal.

ámbito, *ăm'bĭtŏ*, sm. circuit, circumference.

ambo, *ăm'bŏ*, sm. double lottery prize.

ambos, bas, *ăm'bŏs*, pn. both.

ambrosia, *ămbrŏ'sĭă*, sf. ambrosia; any delicious liquor; (bot.) buck-thorn.

ambulante, *ămbŏlăn'tĕ*, a. ambulatory; —s, sm. pl. railway post-office.

ambulativo, va, *—lătĕ'vŏ*, a. of a roving disposition. [to terrify, to intimidate.

amedrentar, *ămĕdrĕntăr'*, v. a. to frighten,

amelga, *ămĕl'gă*, sf. ridge between two furrows. [the plough.

amelgar, *—găr'*, v. a. to open furrows with

amelonado, da, *ămĕlŏnă'dŏ*, a. melon-shaped.

amen, *ămĕn'*, sm. amen, so be it; sacristán de —, one who blindly adheres to the opinion of another; — de, besides; except.

amenaza, *ămĕnă'thă*, sf. threat, menace.

amenazar, *—thăr'*, v. a. to threaten, to menace. [ant; to adorn a speech.

amenizar, *ămĕnĭthăr'*, v. a. to render pleas-

ameno, na, *ămĕ'nŏ*, a. pleasant, delicious; flowery (of language). [spoken.

amerengado, *ămĕrĕngă'dŏ*, a. (fig.) fair-

ametalado, da, *ămĕtălă'dŏ*, a. brass-coloured.

amicísimo, *ămĭthĭ'sĭmŏ*, a. most friendly.

amiento, *ămĭĕn'tŏ*, sm. stay of a helmet.

amiga, *ămĕ'gă*, sf. female friend; concubine; school-mistress. [suitable.

amigable, *ămĭgă'blĕ*, a. amicable; friendly;

amigo, *ămĕ'gŏ*, sm. friend; comrade; lover; —, ga, a. friendly. [terrify.

amilanar, *ămĭlănăr'*, v. a. to frighten, to

amillaramiento, *ămĭlyărămĭĕn'tŏ*, sm. tax-assessment.

amillarar, *ămĭlyărăr'*, v. a. to assess a tax.

amillonado, da, *ămĭlyŏnă'dŏ*, a. liable to pay a certain tax, called millones.

amistad, *ămĭstăd'*, sf. friendship; juncture; gallantry; civility, favour; desire.

amistar, *ămĭstăr'*, v. a. & r. to reconcile.

amistoso, sa, *ămĭstŏ'sŏ*, a. friendly; coramito, *ămĕ'tŏ*, sm. amice. [dial.

amnistia, *ămnĭstĭă*, sf. amnesty.

amo, *ă'mŏ*, sm. master of a house; proprietor, owner; foster-father; overseer.

amoblar, *ămŏblăr'*, v. a. to furnish.

amodorrarse, *ămŏdŏrrăr'sĕ*, v. r. to grow sleepy. [mouldy.

amohecerse, *—ĕthĕr'sĕ*, v. r. to grow

amohinar, *—ĕnăr'*, v. a. to put out of humour. [gre.

amojamado, da, *—'hămă'dŏ*, a. dry, meaamojonar, *—'hŏnăr'*, v. a. to set landmarks.

amoladera, *—lădĕ'ră*, sf. whetstone, grind-stone. [coachman; unskilful artist.

amolador, *—lădŏr'*, sm. grinder; unskilful

amoladura, *—lădŏ'ră*, sf. whetting, grinding, sharpening.

amolar, –lắr′, v. a. to whet, to grind, to sharpen.

amoldar, ămŏldăr′, v.a. to mould; to bring one to his duty. [shaped.

amolletado, da, ămŏlyĕtă′dŏ, a. loaf-

amomo, ămŏ′mŏ, sm. (bot.) Guinea-grains.

amonedar, ămŏnĕdăr′, v. a. to coin.

amonestación, ămŏnĕstăthŏn′, sf. advice, admonition; publication of marriage-bans.

amonestar, –nĕstăr′, v. a. to advise, to admonish; to publish bans of marriage.

amoniaco, ămŏn′ăkŏ, sm. ammoniac.

amontarse, ămŏntăr′sĕ, v. r. to take to the woods. [to accumulate.

amontonar, –tŏnăr′, v. a. to heap together,

amor, ămŏr′, sm. love; fancy; flame; the object of love; – mío, mis –es, my love; por – de Dios, for God's sake; – propio, self-love; –es, pl. gallantry; amours, criminal love.

amoratado, da, ămŏrătă′dŏ, a. livid.

amorcillo, –thĭl′yŏ, sm. flirtation.

amoroso, sa, –rŏ′sŏ, a. affectionate, loving; lovely. [head.

amorrar, ămŏrrăr′, v. n. to hang one's

amorronar, –rŏnăr′, v. a. to hoist or fly a flag. [corpse.

amortajar, –tă′hăr′, v. a. to shroud a

amortecen, –tĕthĕn′, sm. pay-master.

amortiguar, –tĭgwăr′, v. a. to mortify, to deaden; to temper.

amortización, –tĭthăthŏn′, sf. mortmain.

amortizar, –tĭthăr′, v. a. to entail an estate, to render it inalienable; to pay, to liquidate, to discharge a debt.

amoscar, ămŏskăr′, v. a. to whisk flies; –se, to drive off flies with the tail (of animals); to fly into a passion at nothing.

amostachado, ămŏstătshă′dŏ, a. moustachioed.

amotinador, ămŏtĭnădŏr′, a. mutineer.

amotinamiento, –nămĭĕn′tŏ, sm. mutiny.

amotinar, ămŏtĭnăr′, v. a. to excite rebellion; –se, to mutiny.

amovible, ămŏvē′blĕ, a. removable.

ampara, ămpă′ră, sf. (law) distraint.

amparar, ămpărăr′, v. a. to shelter, to favour, to protect; to sequestrate; –se, to claim protection.

amparo, ămpă′rŏ, sm. protection, help, support; sequestration; refuge, asylum.

ampelita, ămpēlē′tă, sf. cannel-coal.

ampliación, ămplĭăthŏn′, sf. amplification, enlargement.

ampliar, ămplĭăr′, v. a. to amplify, to enlarge, to extend, to expand. [ing.

ampliativo, va, ămplĭătē′vŏ, a. amplify-

amplificar, ămplĭfĭkăr′, v. a. to amplify.

amplio, lia, ăm′plĭŏ, a. ample, extensive.

amplitud, ămplĭtŭd′, sf. amplitude, extension, largeness.

ampo (de la nieve), ăm′pŏ, sm. whiteness.

ampolla, ămpŏl′yă, sf. blister (on the cuticle); phial, cruet.

ampollar, ămpŏlyăr′, v.a. to raise blisters; –se, to rise in bubbles; –, a. bubble-shaped.

ampolleta, –yĕ′tă, sf. small phial; hourglass, – de arena, powder-box.

amprar, ămprăr′, v. n. to borrow. [tion.

amputación, ămpŭtăthŏn′, sf. amputa-

amputar, ămpŭtăr′, v. n. to amputate.

amuchachado, da, ămŭtshătshă′dŏ, a. boyish, childish.

amueblar, ămŏĕblăr′, v. a. to furnish.

amugronar, ămŭgrŏnăr′, v. a. to provine.

amujerado, da, ămŭhĕră′dŏ, a. effeminate.

amuleto, ămŭlē′tŏ, sm. amulet.

amunicionar, ămŭnĭthŏnăr′, v. a. to supply with ammunition. [with walls.

amurallar, ămŭrălyăr′, v. a. to surround

amurcar, ămŭrkăr′, v. a. to gore.

amurco, ămŭr′kŏ, sm. blow with the horns.

amusco, ămŭs′kŏ, a. dark-brown.

amusgar, ămŭsgăr′, v. a. to lay back the ears; to half-close one's eyes to see better.

ana, ă′nă, sf. ell, (–measure).

anabaptista, ănăbăptĭs′tă, sm. anabaptist.

anacoreta, –kŏrē′tă, sm. anchorite, hermit.

anacorético, ca, –kŏrē′tĭkŏ, a. relating to a hermit. [nism.

anacronismo, –krŏnĭs′mŏ, sm. anachro-

ánade, ă′nădĕ, sm. & f. duck.

anadear, ănădĕăr′, v. n. to waddle.

anadeja, –dē′hă, sf. duckling.

anadino, na, –dē′nŏ, sm. & f. young duck.

anadón, –dŏn′, sm. & f. duck.

anafaya, –fă′yă, sf. thick-corded silk-stuff.

anafe, ănă′fĕ, sm. portable stove.

anagálida, –gă′lĭdă, sf. (bot.) pimpernel.

anagrama, –gră′mă, sf. anagram.

anales, ănă′lĕs, sm. pl. annals.

análisis, ănă′lĭsĭs, sf. analysis.

analista, –lĭs′tă, sm. writer of annals.

analítico, ca, –lē′tĭkŏ, a. analytical.

analizar, –lĭthăr′, v. a. to analyse.

analogía, –lŏhē′ă, sf. analogy.

analógico, ca, –lŏ′hĭkŏ, análogo, ga, ănă′lŏgŏ, a. analogous.

anana, ănă′nă, sm. pine-apple.

anaquel, –kĕl′, sm. shelf in a book-case.

anaranjado, da, –răn′hă′dŏ, a. orange-coloured.

anarquía, ănărkē′ă, sf. anarchy.

anárquico, ca, ănăr′kĭkŏ, a. anarchical, confused.

anascote, ănăskŏ′tĕ, sm. serge.

anata, ănă′tă, sf. annats.

anatema, –tē′mă, sf. anathema.

anatematizar, –tĕmătĭthăr′, v. a. to anathematize.

anatomía, –tŏmē′ă, sf. anatomy.

anatómico, ca, –tŏ′mĭkŏ, a. anatomical.

anatomista, –tŏmĭs′tă, sm. anatomist.

anatomizar, –tŏmĭthăr′, v. a. to anatomize, to dissect.

anca, ăn′kă, sf. buttocks of a horse.

ancianar, ăn′thĭănăr′, v. n. (poet.) to grow old. [antiquity.

ancianidad, ănthĭănĭdăd′, sf. old age;

anciano, na, ănthĭă′nŏ, a. old, stricken in years. [sheet-anchor.

ancla, ăn′klă, sf. anchor; –de esperanza,

anclaje, ănklă′h′ĕ, sm. act of anchoring; anchor-ground; anchorage.

anclar, ánklár', v. n. to anchor.   [nel.
anclote, ánklô'tê, sm. stream-anchor, grapanco, án'kô, sm. roof made of lead.
ancón, ánkôn', sm. anconada, ánkônâ'dâ, sf. bay.   [ground.
ancorage, ánkôrâ'hê, sm. anchoringancorar, ánkôrâr', v. a. to cast anchor.
ancorero, ánkôrê'rô, sm. anchor-smith.
ancho, cha, án'tshô, a. broad, wide, large; —, sm. breadth, width.
anchoa, ántshô'â, sf. anchovy.
anchura, ántshô'râ, sf. width, breadth.
andadero, ra, ándâdê'rô, a. accessible.
andado, ándâ'dô, sm. step-son, —, da, a. beaten, much frequented; threadbare.
andador, —dôr', sm. stroller; leading string; alley or small walk in a garden; —, ra, a. fast-going.
andadura, —dô'râ, sf. walk; pace; amble.
andana, ándâ'nâ, sf. row, rank, line; tier of guns; volley; (mar.) broadside; llamarse —, to unsay, to retract.
andanada, —nâ'dâ, sf. (mar.) broadside.
andanillo, —nîn'yô, sm. go-cart in which children learn to walk.
andar, ándâr', v. n. to go, to walk; to fare; to act, to proceed, to behave, to transact; to elapse; to move (machines); ¡—I well! never mind!
andaraje, ándârâ'hê, sm. wheel of a well.
andarín, ándârîn', sm. fast walker.
andas, án'dâs, sf. pl. hand-barrow, bier with shafts.
andén, ándên', sm. shelf; pavement; (am.) side-walk; (rail.) platform, horse-path round the draw-well.   [building.
ándito, án'dîtô, sm. gallery around a
andorrear, ándôrrêâr', v. a. to stroll.
andorrera, —râ'râ, sf. street-walker.
andrajo, ándrâ'hô, sm. rag (of worn clothes).
andrajoso, sa, —hô'sô, a. ragged.   [dite.
andrógino, ándrô'hînô, sm. hermaphroandrómina, —mînâ, sf. trick, fraud, artifice.   [timbrel.
andullo, ándûl'yô, sm. roll of tobacco;
andurriales, ándûrriâ'lês, sm. pl. byways.
aneaje, ánêâ'hê, sm. alnage, ell-measure.
anear, ánêâr', v. a. to measure by the ell.
aneblar, ánêblâr', v. a. to cloud, to darken.
anécdota, ánêk'dôtâ, sf. anecdote.
anegadizo, za, ánêgâdê'thô, a. easily inundated.   [merge.
anegar, ánêgâr', v. a. to inundate, to subanexar, ánêksâr', v. a. to annex, to join.
anexidades, —sîdâ'dês, sf. pl. appertinent rights.
anexión, ánêksîôn', sf. annexation.
anexo, xa, ánêk'sô, a. annexed.
anfibio, bia, ánfî'bîô, a. amphibious; —, sm. amphibium.   [double meaning.
anfibología, ánfîbôlô'hîâ, sf. words of
anfion, ánfî'ôn, sm. opium.
anfiteatro, ánfîtêâ'trô, sm. amphitheatre.
angarillas, ángârî'yâs, sf. pl. handbarrow; cruet-stand.

ángaro, án'gârô, sm. signal-smoke.
ángol, án'hôl, sm. angel; barshot.
angelical, án'hêlîkâl', a. angelical, heavenborn.
angelote, án'hêlô'tê, sm. large figure of an angel (on altars); fat, goodnatured child.
angina, án'hê'nâ, sf. quinsy.
angla, án'glâ, sf. cape.
anglicismo, ánglîthîs'mô, sm. anglicism.
angostar, ángôstâr', v. a. to narrow, to contract.   [strait.
angosto, ta, ángôs'tô, a. narrow, close.
angostura, ángôstô'râ, sf. narrowness narrow passage.
angra, án'grâ, sf. small bay.
anguarina, ángwârî'nâ, sf. loose coat hanging down to the knees.
anguila, ángê'lâ, sf. eel.
angular, ángûlâr', a. angular: piedra —, sf. corner-stone.   [fulsome flattery.
angulema, —lê'mâ, sf. tow-linen, —s, pl.
ángulo, án'gûlô, sm. angle, corner.
anguloso, sa, —lô'sô, a. angled, cornered.
angustia, ángûs'tîâ, sf. anguish; heart-ache.
angustiar, ángûstîâr', v. a. to cause anguish; [ficulty; to wish eagerly.
anhelar, ánêlâr', v. n. to breathe with difanhelo, ánê'lô, sm. vehement desire, longing.   [rous.
anheloso, sa, ánêlô'sô, a. very desianidar, ánîdâr', v. n. to nestle, to make a nest; to dwell, to inhabit.
anillo, ánîl'yô, sm. gold or silver ring.
ánima, á'nîmâ, sf. soul; diameter of the chase of a gun; —s, pl. bell-ringing at sunset; á las —s, at sunset.
animal, ánîmâl', sm. & a. animal.
animalazo, —â'thô, sm. big animal.
animalejo, —â'hô, sm. small animal, animalcule.   [animal.
animalucho, —lûtsh'ô, sm. ugly, hideous
animar, ánîmâr', v. a. to animate, to enliven, to abet, to comfort, to revive.
ánimo, á'nîmô, sm. soul; courage; mind, intention, meaning, will; thought; ¡—I come on!   [rage; boldness.
animosidad, ánîmôsîdâd', sf. valour, couanimoso, sa, ánîmô'sô, a. courageous, spirited.   [ish manner.
aniñarse, ánînyâr'sê, v. r. to act in a childaniquilar, ánîkîlâr', v. a. to annihilate, to destroy; —se, to decline, to decay; to humble, to consume.
anís, ánîs', sm. (bot.) anise.
anisar, ánîsâr', v. a. to tincture with anise.
anisete, —sê'tê, sm. anisette.
aniversario, ria, ánîvêrsâ'rîô, a. annual; ano, á'nô, sm. anus. [—, sm. anniversary.
anoche, ánôtsh'ê, ad. last night.
anochecer, ánôtshêthêr', v. n. to grow dark.
anodinar, ánôdînâr', v. a. to apply an anodyne.
anodino, na, —dê'nô, a. (med.) anodyne
anomalía, ánômâlî'â, sf. anomaly.
anómalo, la, ánô'mâlô, a. anomalous.
anonadar, ánônâdâr', v. a. to annihilate; to lessen; —se, to humble one's self.
anónimo, ma, ánô'nîmô, a. anonymous;

2*

anotación, *ănŏtăthĭŏn'*, sf. annotation, note.
anotar, *ănŏtăr'*, v. a. to comment, to note.
ánsar, *ăn'săr*, sm. goose. [fare reared.
ansarería, *ănsărĕrē'ă*, sf. place where geese
ansarero, *ănsărĕ'rŏ*, sm. goose-herd.
ansia, *ăn'sĭă*, sf. anxiety, eagerness, hankering. [ingly.
ansiar, *ănsĭăr'*, v. a. to desire exceedingly.
ansioso, sa, *ănsĭŏ'sŏ*, a. anxious, eager.
anta, *ăn'tă*, sf. tapir, antes (pillar).
antagonista, *ăntăgŏnĭs'tă*, sm. antagonist.
antaño, *ăntăn'yŏ*, ad. last year.
antártico, ca, *ăntăr'tĭkŏ*, a. antarctic.
ante, *ăn'tĕ*, sm. dressed buffalo skin; first course of dishes, —, pr. before; in the presence of.
anteado, da, *ăntĕă'dŏ*, a. buff-coloured.
anteanoche, *ăntĕănŏtsh'ĕ*, ad. three nights ago. [ago.
anteanteayer, *ăntĕăyĕr'* ad. three days
antebrazo, *ăntĕbră'thŏ*, sm. fore-arm.
antecama, *ăntĕkă'mă*, sf. bed-carpet.
antecámara, *ăntĕkă'mără*, sf. antechamber.
antecamarilla, *ăntĕkămărĭl'yă*, sf. room leading to the king's antechamber.
antecedente, *ăntĕthĕdĕn'tĕ*, sm. & a. antecedent. [forego.
anteceder, *ăntĕthĕdĕr'* v. a. to precede, to
antecesor, ra, *ăntĕthĕsŏr'*, sm. & f. predecessor, forefather.
antecoger, *ăntĕkŏhĕr'*, v. a. to bring any person or thing before one; to gather in fruit before the due time.
antecristo, *ăntĕkrĭs'tŏ*, sm. antichrist.
antedata, *ăntĕdă'tă*, sf. antedate.
antedatar, *ăntĕdătăr'* v. a. to antedate.
antediluviano, na, *ăntĕdĭlūvĭă'nŏ*, a. antediluvian.
anteespolón, *ăntĕĕspŏlŏn'*, sm. ice-breaker.
antelación, *ăntĕlăthĭŏn'* sf. preference.
antemano, *ăntĕmă'nŏ*, ad. de —, beforehand.
antemeridiano, na, *ăntĕmĕrĭdĭă'nŏ*, a. antemeridian. [fortress-wall.
antemural, *ăntĕmūrăl'*, sm. (mil.) outworks,
antemuralla, *ăntĕmūrăl'yă*, sf. antemuro —*mō'rŏ*, sm. (mil.) rampart, parapet.
antena, *ăntĕ'nă*, sf. feeler, antenna.
antenallas, *ăntĕnăl'yăs*, sf. pl. pincers.
antenoche, *ăntĕnŏtsh'ĕ*, ad. the night before last.
antenombre, *ăntĕnŏm'brĕ*, sm. title prefixed to a proper name (as Don, San, &c.).
anteojo, *ăntĕŏ'hŏ*, sm. spy-glass, eye-glass; — de larga vista, telescope; — de puño, opera-glass, —s, pl. spectacles.
antepagar, *ăntĕpăgăr'*, v. a. to pay in advance.
antepasado, da, *ăntĕpăsă'dŏ*, a. passed, elapsed, —s, sm. pl. ancestors.
antepecho, *ăntĕpĕtsh'ŏ*, sm. (mil.) breastwork, parapet, footstep of a coach, harness.
antepenúltimo, ma, *ăntĕpĕnūl'tĭmŏ*, a. antepenultimate.
anteponer, *ăntĕpŏnĕr'*, v. a. to prefer.
antepuerta, *ăntĕpwĕr'tă*, sf. door-hangings.
antera, *ăntĕ'ră*, sf. (bot.) anther.
anterior, *ăntĕrĭŏr'*, a. anterior, fore, former.
anterioridad, *ăntĕrĭŏrĭdăd'*, sf. anteriority, priority; preference.

antes, *ăn'tĕs*, pr. before, —, ad. first, rather, better.
antesala, *ăntĕsă'lă*, sf. antechamber; hacer —, to wait in an antechamber.
antestatura, *ăntĕstătū'ră*, sf. light, hasty entrenchment of palisadoes and sand-bags.
antevíspera, *ăntĕvĭs'pĕră*, sf. day before yesterday. [tion.
anticipación, *ăntĭthĭpăthĭŏn'*, sf. anticipa-
anticipar, *ăntĭthĭpăr'*, v. a. to anticipate; to forestall.
anticuado, da, *ăntĭkŭă'dŏ*, a. antiquated.
anticuar, *ăntĭkŭăr'*, v. a. to antiquate, to outdate. [antiquarian.
anticuario, *ăntĭkŭă'rĭŏ*, sm. antiquary.
antídoto, *ăntĭ'dŏtŏ*, sm. antidote.
antífona, *ăntĭ'fŏnă*, sf. antiphony, anthem.
antigualla, *ăntĭgŭăl'yă*, sf. monument of antiquity, antique. [ly, of old.
antiguamente, *ăntĭgŭămĕn'tĕ*, ad. ancient-
antigüedad, *ăntĭgŭĕdăd'*, sf. antiquity, oldness, the times of yore; the ancients.
antiguo, gua, *ăntĭ'gŭŏ*, a. antique, old, ancient, —, sm. senior. [antimonarchic.
antimonárquico, ca, *ăntĭmŏnăr'kĭkŏ*, a.
antimonio, *ăntĭmŏ'nĭŏ*, sm. antimony
antinacional, *ăntĭnăthĭŏnăl'*, a. antinational.
antipapa, *ăntĭpă'pă*, sm. anti-pope.
antipara, *ăntĭpă'ră*, sf. screen, gaiter.
antipatía, *ăntĭpătē'ă*, sf. antipathy.
antipático, ca, *ăntĭpă'tĭkŏ*, a. antipathetical.
antípodas, *ăntĭ'pŏdăs*, sm. pl. antipodes.
antítesis, *ăntĭ'tĕsĭs*, sf. (gr.) antithesis.
antojadizo, za, *ăntŏhădĭ'thŏ*, a. capricious, fanciful. [earnestly; to itch.
antojarse, *ăntŏhăr'sĕ*, v. r. to long, to desire
antojera, *ăntŏhĕ'ră*, sf. spectacle-case; blinker (of horses).
antojo, *ăntŏ'hŏ*, sm. whim; longing, fancy.
antor, *ăntŏr'*, sm. seller of stolen goods.
antorcha, *ăntŏr'tshă*, sf. torch, taper
antro, *ăn'trŏ*, sm. (poet.) cavern, den, grotto.
antropófago, *ăntrŏpŏ'făgŏ*, sm. man-eater, cannibal [logy.
antropología, *ăntrŏpŏlŏhē'ă*, sf. anthropology.
antruejar, *ăntrŭĕhăr'*, v. a. to wet with water, or play some joke at a carnival.
antruejo, *ăntrŭĕ'hŏ*, sm. the three days of the carnival. [attack.
antuvión, *ăntūvĭŏn'*, sm. sudden stroke or
anual, *ănŭăl'*, a. annual. [rence.
anualidad, *ănŭălĭdăd'*, sf. yearly recur-
anubarrado, da, *ănūbărră'dŏ*, a. clouded (of linens and silks).
anublar, *ănūblăr'*, v. a. to cloud, to obscure; —se, to become clouded; to miscarry
anudar, *ănūdăr'*, v. a. to knot, to join; —se, to waste away [compliance.
anuencia, *ănŭĕn'thĭă*, sf. condescension,
anuente, *ănŭĕn'tĕ*, a. condescending, courteous.
anulación, *ănŭlăthĭŏn'*, sf. abrogation.
anular, *ănŭlăr'*, v. a. to annul; —, a. annular.
anulativo, va, *ănŭlătĭ'vŏ*, a. derogatory.
anunciar, *ănŭnthĭăr'*, v. a. to announce.
anuncio, *ănŭn'thĭŏ*, sm. advertisement.
anverso, *ănvĕr'sŏ*, sm. obverse (in coins).

anzuelo, *ănthŭăd′ lŏ*, sm. fish-hook; allurement; kind of fritters.

aña, *ăn′yŏ*, sf. stink-fox.

añadidura, *ănyădădŏ′ră*, sf. addition.

añadir, —*dēr′*, v. a. to add.

añafea, —*fĕ′ă*, sf. brown paper.

añafil, —*fēl′*, sm. Moorish trumpet.

añagaza, —*gă′thă*, sf. bird-call.

añal, *ănyăl′*, a. annual.   [manac.

añalejo, —*lĕ′h′ŏ*, sm. ecclesiastical al-

añascar, *ănyăskăr′*, v. a. to collect lumber or odds and ends.

añejar, *ănyĕ′hăr′*, v. a. to make old; —se, to grow old; to become stale.

añejo, ja, *ănyĕ′h′ŏ*, a. old, stale, musty.

añicos, *ănyĕ′kŏs*, sm. pl. bits, small pieces: hacerse —, to overheat one's self.

añil, *ănyēl′*, sm. indigo plant; indigo.

añino, *ănyē′nŏ*, sm. yearling lamb; fleece of a yearling lamb.

año, *ăn′yŏ*, sm. year; —s, pl. birth-day.

añojal, *ănyŏ′hăl′*, sm. fallow land.

añojo, *ănyŏ′h′ŏ*, sm. a yearling calf.

añudar, *ănyădăr′*, v. a. to make fast; to unite.   [to fascinate.

aojar, *ăŏ′hăr′*, v. a. to charm, to bewitch.

aojo, *ăŏ′h′ŏ*, sm. witchery, fascination.

aorta, *ăŏr′tă*, sf. aorta (the great artery).

aovar, *ăŏvăr′*, v. a. to lay eggs.

apabilar, *ăpăbēlăr′*, v. a. to prepare the wick of a wax-candle; —se, to expire.

apacentadero, *ăpăthĕntădĕ′rŏ*, sm. pasture, grazing-ground.   [cattle.

apacentar, —*tăr′*, v. a. to tend grazing

apacible, *ăpăthē′blĕ*, a. affable, gentle, placid, quiet.   [to pacify, to calm.

apaciguar, *ăpăthēgŭăr′*, v. a. to appease.

apacheta, *ăpăchă′tă*, sf. mile-stone.

apadrinar, *ăpădrēnăr′*, v. a. to support, to favour, to patronise.   [fire-engine.

apagaincendios, *ăpăgăēnthēn′dĭŏs*, sm.

apagar, *ăpăgăr′*, v. a. to quench, to extinguish; to damp; to destroy; to soften.

apalabrar, *ăpălăbrăr′*, v. a. to appoint a meeting; to bespeak.   [lever.

apalancar, *ăpălănkăr′*, v. a. to lift with a

apalear, *ăpălĕăr′*, v. a. to cane, to drub; to shovel grain (to prevent its being spoiled).

apancora, *ăpănkŏ′ră*, sf. common crab.

apandillar, *ăpăndēlyăr′*, v. a. to form a faction.   [of stagnant water

apantanar, *ăpăntănăr′*, v. a. to make a pool

apantuflado, da, *ăpăntăflă′dŏ*, a. slipper-like.

apañado, da, *ăpănyă′dŏ*, a. cloth-like.

apañar, *ăpănyăr′*, v. a. to grasp; to pilfer; to patch; —se, to get ready.

apaño, *ăpăn′yŏ*, sm. grasp; seizure; patch.

apañuscar, *ăpănyăskăr′*, v. a. to rumple; to crush.   [like.

apapagayado, da, *ăpăpăgăyă′dŏ*, a. parrot-

aparador, *ăpărădŏr′*, sm. buffet, sideboard; workshop of an artizan; estar de —, to be dressed for receiving visitors.

aparar, *ăpărăr′*, v. a. to stretch out the hands or skirts of clothes for catching any-

thing thrown by another; to dig and heap the earth round plants.

aparato, *ăpără′tŏ*, sm. apparatus; preparation, ostentation, show, circumstance.

aparcería, *ăpărthĕrē′ă*, sf. partnership in a farm (or other business).

aparcero, —*thĕ′rŏ*, sm. partner; associate.

aparear, *ăpărĕăr′*, v. a. to match, to accouple; —se, to be paired off by twos.

aparecer, *ăpărĕthĕr′*, v. n. to appear.

aparecido, —*thĕ′dŏ*, sm. ghost.

aparejar, *ăpărĕhăr′*, v. a. to prepare; to harness horses; to rig a ship.

aparejo, *ăpărĕ′h′ŏ*, sm. preparation; harness, gear; sizing of a piece of linen on which something is to be painted; (mar.) tackle, rigging, —s, pl. tools, implements.

aparentar, *ăpărĕntăr′*, v. a. to make a false show; to pretend, to deceive.

aparente, —*rĕn′tĕ*, a. apparent; convenient.

aparición, *ăpărēthĭŏn′*, sf. apparition.

apariencia, *ăpărĕn′thĭă*, sf. appearance, outside.   [to trees and plants].

aparrado, da, *ăpăr′ră dŏ*, a. crooked (applied

aparroquiar, *ăpărrŏkēăr′*, v. a. to bring customers to a shop.

apartadero, *ăpărtădă′rŏ*, sm. parting-place, siding, cross-roads.

apartadijo, —*dē′h′ŏ*, sm. small part; adjoining closet.   [apartment.

apartado, —*tă′dŏ*, sm. detached or private

apartar, *ăpărtăr′*, v. a. to separate, to divide, to dissuade; to remove; to sort; —se, to withdraw; to be divorced; to desist.

aparte, *ăpăr′tĕ*, sm. break in a line; —, ad. apart, separately; aside on the stage.

aparvar, *ăpărvăr′*, v. a. to arrange the corn for being threshed.

apasionado, da, *ăpăsĭŏnă′dŏ*, a. passionate; suffering, devoted to; fond.

apasionar, —*năr′*, v. a. to excite a passion.

apatía, *ăpătē′ă*, sf. apathy.   [different.

apático, ca, *ăpă′tĭkŏ*, a. apathetic, inapea, *ăpĕ′ă*, sf. tether.

apeadero, *ăpĕădĕ′rŏ*, sm. horse-block; house of accommodation.

apeador, —*dŏr′*, sm. land-surveyor.

apear, *ăpĕăr′*, v. a. to dismount; to measure lands; to take a thing; to dissuade.

apechugar, *ăpĕchăgăr′*, v. a. to push with the breast; to undertake a thing with spirit and boldness.

apedreado, da, *ăpĕdrĕă′dŏ*, a. pelted; cara —a, face pitted with the small-pox.

apedrear, —*drĕăr′*, v. a. to throw stones; to lapidate; —, v. n. to hail; to talk in a rude, uncouth manner.

apego, *ăpĕ′gŏ*, sm. attachment, fondness.

apelación, *ăpĕlăthĭŏn′*, sf. appeal.

apelado, da, —*dă*, a. of the same colour.

apelambrar, *ăpĕlămbrăr′*, v. a. to steep hides in pits of lime-water.

apelante, *ăpĕlăn′tĕ*, sm. appellant.

apelar, *ăpĕlăr′*, v. n. to appeal; to have recourse to; to be of the same colour.

apelativo, *ăpĕlătē′vŏ*, a. (gr.) nombre —, sm. generic name.

apelmazar, *ăpălmăthăr´,* v. a. to compress.
apellar, *ăpĕlyăr´,* v. a. to dress leather.
apellidar, *ăpĕlyĭdăr´,* v. a. to call by name, to proclaim. [name; epithet.
apellido, *ăpĕlyĕ´dŏ,* sm. surname, family-
apenas, *ăpā´năs,* ad. scarcely, hardly.
apéndice, *ăpĕn´dĭthĕ,* sm. appendix, supplement. [to crush.
apeñuscar, *ăpĕnyŭskăr´,* v. a. to rumple.
apeo, *ăpā´ŏ,* sm. survey, mensuration of land, props and stays for underpinning a building.
apeonar, *—năr´,* v. a. to run swiftly.
aperador, *ăpĕrădŏr´,* sm. wheel-wright.
aperar, *ăpĕrăr´,* v. a. to carry on the trade of a cartwright. [ready.
apercibido, da, *ăpĕrthĭbĕ´dŏ,* a. provided;
apercibir, *—thĭbĭr´,* v. a. to prepare; to provide; to warn, to advise.
apercollar, *—kŏlyăr´,* v. a. to seize by the collar; to snatch away secretly; to assassinate [toasted.
aperdigado, da, *—dĭgă´dŏ,* a. broiled,
apernar, *—năr´,* v. a. to seize by the bough or ham [ments; sheep-fold.
apero, *ăpā´rŏ,* sm. agricultural imple-
aperreado, da, *ăpĕrrĕă´dŏ,* a. harassed, dog-weary.
aperrear, *—rĕăr´,* v. a. to throw to the dogs to be torn to pieces, to molest; -se, to worry one's self to death.
apertura, *—tŭ´ră,* sf. aperture, opening, chink, cleft.
apesadumbrar, *ăpĕsădŭmbrăr´,* v. a. to cause trouble and affliction.
apesgar, *ăpĕsgăr´,* v. a. to overload, to press down.
apestar, *ăpĕstăr´,* v. a. to infect with the pestilence; to produce an offensive smell.
apetecer, *ăpĕtĕthĕr´,* v. a. to long, to hanker.
apetecible, *—thĭ´blĕ,* a. desirable.
apetitivo, va, *ăpĕtĭtĕ´vŏ,* a. appetising.
apetito, *ăpĕtĕ´tŏ,* sm. appetite, that which excites desire. [taste, appetising.
apetitoso, sa, *—tŏ´sŏ,* a. pleasing to the
apezuñar, *ăpĕthŭnyăr´,* v. n. to tread heavily (of horses). [knavish.
apicarado, da, *ăpĭkără´dŏ,* a. roguish,
ápice, *ă´pĭthĕ,* sm. summit, point; smallest part of a thing.
apilar, *ăpĭlăr´,* v. a. to pile up.
apimpollarse, *ăpĭmpŏlyăr´sĕ,* v. r. to shoot, to germinate. [pine-shaped.
apiñado, da, *ăpĭnyă´dŏ,* a. pyramidal;
apiñar, *—nyăr´,* v. a. to press things close together; -se, to clog, to crowd.
apio, *ă´pĭŏ,* sm. (bot.) celery.
apiolar, *ăpĭŏlăr´,* v. a. to gyve a hawk; to seize, to kill. [earth.
apisonar, *ăpĭsŏnăr´,* v. a. to ram down
apitonar, *ăpĭtŏnăr´,* v. n. to put forth shoots; to bud. -, v. a. to pick (as hens do their eggs). -se, to rail at each other.
aplacable, *ăplăkă´blĕ,* a. appeasable.
aplacar, *ăplăkăr´,* v. a. to appease, to pacify.

aplanadera, *ăplănădā´ră,* sf. roller for levelling the ground.
aplanar, *ăplănăr´,* v. a. to level, to flatten; to astonish, -se, to fall to the ground.
aplanchado, da, *ăplăntshă´dŏ,* a. ironed, smoothed; —, sm. parcel of linen to be ironed; ironing linen.
aplanchadora, *—dŏ´ră,* sf. ironer.
aplanchar, *—tshăr´,* v. a. to iron linen.
aplantillar, *ăplăntĭlyăr´,* v. a. to adjust or fit a stone, a piece of timber or a board, according to model.
aplastar, *ăplăstăr´,* v. a. to flatten, to crush, to confound. [extol.
aplaudir, *ăplăŭdĭr´,* v. a. to applaud; to
aplauso, *ăplăŭ´sŏ,* sm. applause, approbation, praise. [to invest; to regulate.
aplazar, *ăplăthăr´,* v. a. to call together;
aplicable, *ăplĭkă´blĕ,* a. applicable.
aplicación, *ăplĭkăthĭŏn´,* sf. application, attention. [dustrious.
aplicado, da, *—kă´dŏ,* a. studious, in-
aplicar, *ăplĭkăr´,* v. a. to apply; to clasp; to attribute; -se, to devote one's self to anything; to earn a living.
aplomado, da, *ăplŏmă´dŏ,* a. lead-coloured; leaden; heavy, dull.
aplomar, *—măr´,* v. n. to plumb; -se, to tumble, to fall to the ground.
apocado, da, *ăpŏkă´dŏ,* a. pusillanimous; narrow-hoofed.
Apocalipsis, *ăpŏkălĭp´sĭs,* sm. Apocalypse.
apocar, *ăpŏkăr´,* v. a. to lessen, to diminish; to contract [fabulous.
apócrifo, fa, *ăpŏ´krĭfŏ,* a. apocryphal;
apodar, *ăpŏdăr´,* v. a. to give nick-names.
apoderado, da, *—dĕră´dŏ,* a. powerful; —, sm. proxy, attorney.
apoderarse, *—dĕră´sĕ,* v. r. to take possession of a thing [cal.
apodíctico, ca, *ăpŏdĭk´tĭkŏ,* a. apodicti-
apodo, *ăpŏ´dŏ,* sm. nick-name, sobriquet.
apolillar, *ăpŏlĭlyăr´,* v. a. to gnaw or eat clothes, -se, to be moth-eaten.
apología, *ăpŏlŏ´hĕ̆ă,* sf. apology.
apoltronarse, *ăpŏltrŏnăr´sĕ,* v. r. to grow lazy, to loiter.
apomazar, *ăpŏmăthăr´,* v. a. to glaze printed linens with pumice-stone.
apoplejía, *—plĕ´hĕ̆ă,* sf. apoplexy.
apoplético, ca, *—plā´tĭkŏ,* a. apoplectic.
aporcar, *ăpŏrkăr´,* v. a. to cover plants with earth.
aporrar, *ăpŏrrăr´,* v. n. to stand mute, to remain silent. -se, to become importunate.
aporrear, *ăpŏrrĕăr´,* v. a. to cudgel, to knock, -se, to have a fight; to drudge.
aportadera, *ăpŏrtădā´ră,* sf. provision-chest for portage by mules.
aportadero, *—rŏ,* sm. landing-place.
aportar, *ăpŏrtăr´,* v. n. to arrive at a port.
aportillar, *—tĭlyăr´,* v. a. to make a breach in a wall, to break down, to break open.
aposentar, *ăpŏsĕntăr´,* v. a. to harbour; to house.
aposento, *ăpŏsĕn´tŏ,* sm. room, apartment; inn, a temporary habitation; opera-box.

aposesionar, *ăpŏsĕsĭŏnăr'*, v. a. to give possession.

aposición, *ăpŏsĭthĭŏn'*, sf. (gr.) apposition.

apósito, *ăpŏ'sĭtŏ*, sm. external medicinal application.

aposta, *ăpŏs'tă*, ad. on purpose.

apostadero, *-dĕ'rŏ*, sm. stand, station; (mar) station, dock-yard.

apostar, *ăpŏstăr'*, v. a. to bet, to lay a wager, to post soldiers.

apostasia, *ăpŏstăsĕ'ă*, sf. apostasy.

apóstata, *ăpŏs'tătă*, sm. apostate.

apostatar, *-tăr'*, v. n. to apostatize.

apostema, *ăpŏstĕ'mă*, sf. abscess, tumor.

apostilla, *ăpŏstĭl'yă*, sf. marginal note; postscript.

apóstol, *ăpŏs'tŏl*, sm. apostle.

apostolado, *-lă'dŏ*, sm. apostleship.

apostólico, ca, *-tŏ'lĭkŏ*, a. apostolical.

apostrofar, *ăpŏstrŏfăr'*, v. a. to apostrophise.

apóstrofe, *ăpŏs'trŏfĕ*, sf. apostrophe.

apóstrofo, *ăpŏs'trŏfŏ*, sm. (gr.) apostrophe.

apoteosis, *ăpŏtĕŏ'sĭs*, sf. apotheosis.

apoyar, *ăpŏyăr'*, v. a. to favour, to patronize, to support, to found, —, v. n. to rest on, to lie, —se, to lean upon.

apoyo, *-yŏ*, sm. prop, stay, support; protection.   [valuable, respectable.

apreciable, *ăprĕthĭă'blĕ*, a. appreciable,

apreciar, *-thĭăr'*, v. a. to appreciate, to estimate, to value.

aprecio, *-thĭŏ*, sm. appreciation, esteem.

aprehender, *ăprĕĕndĕr'*, v. a. to apprehend, to seize, to fancy, to conceive.

aprehensión, *-ĕnsĭŏn'*, sf. apprehension, seizure, perception, ready and witty saying.   [sive, quick to understand; fearful.

aprehensivo, va, *-ĕnsĭ'vŏ*, a. apprehensive.

apremiar, *ăprĕmĭăr'*, v. a. to press, to compel.   [tion; judicial compulsion.

apremio, *ăprĕ'mĭŏ*, sm. pressure, constriction.

aprender, *ăprĕndĕr'*, v. a. to learn; — de memoria, to learn by heart.

aprendiz, *-dĭth'*, sm. apprentice.

aprendizaje, *-thă'hĕ*, sm. apprenticeship.

apronsar, *ăprŏnsăr'*, v. a. to press, to calender.   [to capture an enemy's ship.

apresar, *ăprĕsăr'*, v. a. to seize, to grasp;

aprestar, *ăprĕstăr'*, v. a. to prepare, to make ready

apresto, *ăprĕs'tŏ*, sm. preparation.

apresurar, *ăprĕsŭrăr'*, v. a. to accelerate, to hasten, to expedite.

apretadillo, lla, *ăprĕtădĭl'yŏ*, a. somewhat constrained, rather hard put to it.

apretado, da, *ăprĕtă'dŏ*, a. mean, miserable, closehanded, hard, difficult.

apretadura, *-dŭ'ră*, sf. compression.

apretar, *-tăr'*, v. a. to compress, to tighten, to constrain, to distress, to urge

apretón, *-tŏn'*, sm. pressure.   [earnestly.

apretura, *-tŭ'ră*, sf. crowd.

apriesa, *ăprĭĕ'să*, ad. in a hurry.

aprieto, *ăprĭĕ'tŏ*, sm. crowd, conflict; exigence.

aprisa, *ăprĭ'să*, ad. swiftly, promptly.

aprisco, *ăprĭs'kŏ*, sm. sheep-fold, sheep-cot.

aprisionar, *ăprĭsĭŏnăr'*, v. a. to imprison.

aproar, *ăprŏăr'*, v. n. (mar.) to bring a ship's head to the wind.

aprobación, *ăprŏbăthĭŏn'*, sf. approbation.

aprobar, *-băr'*, v. a. to approve.

aproches, *ăprŏtshĕs*, sm. pl. approaches.

aprontar, *ăprŏntăr'*, v. a. to prepare hastily, to get ready.   [paration.

apronto, *ăprŏn'tŏ*, sm. expeditious preparation,

apropiación, *ăprŏpĭăthĭŏn'*, sf. appropriation, assumption.

apropiar, *-pĭăr'*, v. a. to appropriate.

aprovechable, *ăprŏvĕtshă'blĕ*, a. profitable.   [utility, progress.

aprovechamiento, *-mĭĕn'tŏ*, sm. profit,

aprovechar, *-tshăr'*, v. n. to make progress, —, v. a. to profit by a thing.

aproximar, *ăprŏksĭmăr'*, v. a. to approach.

aptitud, *ăptĭtŭd'*, sf. aptitude, fitness, ability.

apto, ta, *ăp'tŏ*, a. apt, fit, able, clever.

apuesta, *ăpŭĕs'tă*, sf. bet, wager.

apulgarar, *ăpŭlgărăr'*, v. a. to press with the thumb.   [musical note, sign.

apuntación, *ăpŭntăthĭŏn'*, sf. annotation;

apuntado, da, *-tă'dŏ*, a. pointed.

apuntador, *-tădŏr'*, sm. prompter; billiard-marker   [to shore a vessel.

apuntalar, *-tălăr'*, v. a. to prop, (mar.)

apuntar, *ăpŭntăr'*, v. a. to aim, to level, to point out; to mark, to begin to appear or show itself; to prompt (theatre), —se, to begin to turn, to be pricked (of wine).

apunte, *ăpŭn'tĕ*, sm. annotation, stage-prompting.   [the fist.

apuñetear, *ăpŭnyĕtĕăr'*, v. a. to strike with

apurado, da, *ăpŭră'dŏ*, a. poor, destitute of means, exhausted.

apurar, *ăpŭrăr'*, v. a. to purify, to clear up, to verify, to exhaust, to tease and perplex.   [affliction.

apuro, *ăpŏ'rŏ*, sm. want, indigence; pain, **aquejar,** *ăkĕhăr'*, v. a. to fatigue, to afflict.

aquel, *ăkĕl'*, — la, —lyă, — lo, —lyŏ, pn. that, he, she; — los, — las, pl. those.

aquerenciarse, *ăkĕrĕnthĭăr'sĕ*, v. r. to be fond of a place (applied to cattle).

aquese, sa, so, *ăkĕ'să*, pn. that.

aqueste, ta, to, *ăkĕs'tĕ*, pn. this, that.

aquí, *ăkĭ'*, ad. here, in this place; — de Dios! God help me!

aquiescencia, *ăkĭĕsthĕn'thĭă*, sf. consent.

aquietar, *ăkĭĕtăr'*, v. a. to quiet, to appease, to lull.   [and silver.

aquilatar, *ăkĭlătăr'*, v. a. to assay gold

aquilea, *ăkĭlĕ'ă*, sf. (bot.) milfoil.

aquilino, na, *-lĭ'nŏ*, a. aquiline.

aquilón, *ăkĭlŏn'*, sm. north wind.

ara, *ă'ră*, sf. altar.

arabesco, *ărăbĕs'kŏ*, sm. arabesque.

arado, *ără'dŏ*, sm. plough.

arador, *ărădŏr'*, sm. plough-man.

arancel, *ărănthĕl'*, sm. fixed price of provisions; tariff.   [berry.

arándano, *ărăn'dănŏ*, sm. bilberry, cran-

arandela, ărăndĕ'lă, sf. pan of the socket of a candlestick ; ruffles of shirts.

aranzada, ărănthă'dă, sf. a measure of land. [chandelier, lustre.

araña, ărăn'yă, sf. spider ; sea-spider ;

arañar, ărănyăr', v. a. to scratch ; to scrape ; to corrode.

araño, ărăn'yŏ, sm. scratch, slight wound.

arar, ărăr', v. a. to plough the land.

arbellón, ărbĕlyŏn', sm. gutter.

arbitrar, ărbĭtrăr', v. a. to arbitrate.

arbitrariedad, ărbĭtrărĕdăd', sf. arbitrariness [va, -trăĭ'vŏ, a. arbitrary.

arbitrario, ria, -tră'rĭŏ, arbitrativo,

arbitrio, ărbĭ'trĭŏ, sm. free-will ; means, expedient, way ; arbitration, arbitrament ; compromise ; [jector, contriver

arbitrista, ărbĭtrĭs'tă, sm. schemer, projector.

árbitro, ăr'bĭtrŏ, sm. arbiter, arbitrator.

árbol, ăr'bŏl, sm. tree ; (mar.) mast.

arbolado, da, ărbŏlă'dŏ, a. forested, wooded. -, sm. wood-land.

arboladura, -dŭ'ră, sf. masting, masts.

arbolar, ărbŏlăr', v. a. to hoist, to set up right. [fastening lime-twigs.

arbolete, -lĕ'tĕ, sm. branch of a tree for

arbolista, -lĭs'tă, sm. arborist.

arbollón, ărbŏlyŏn', sm. flood-gate, sluice.

arbóreo, rea, ărbŏ'rĕŏ, a. arboreous.

arbusto, ărbŭs'tŏ, sm. shrub.

arca, ăr'kă, sf. chest, wooden box ; sepulchral urn. — del Testamento. — féderis, ark of the Covenant.

arcabucería, -bŭthĕrĕ'ă, sf. number of cross-bows ; manufactory of arquebuses.

arcabucero, -bŭthă'rŏ, sm. arquebusier, gunsmith.

arcabuz, -bŭth', sm. arquebuse.

arcada, ărkă'dă, sf. rising of the stomach before vomiting, arcade.

arcaduz, -dŭth', sm. conduit or pipe for conveying water ; draw-well bucket.

arcaísmo, ărkăĭs'mŏ, sm. archaism.

arcángel, ărkăn'hĕl, sm. archangel.

arcano, ărkă'nŏ, sm. arcanum.

arce, ăr'thĕ, sm. maple-tree.

arcilla, ărthĭl'yă, sf. argil, clay.

arcilloso, sa, ărthĭlyŏ'sŏ, a. clayey, argillaceous.

arcipreste, ărthĭprĕs'tĕ, sm. archpriest.

arco, ăr'kŏ, sm. arc, arch ; fiddle-bow, hoop. — del cielo, rainbow.

archiducado, ărtchĭdŭkă'dŏ, sm. archdukedom.

archiducal, -dŭkăl', a. archducal.

archiduque, -dŭ'kĕ, sm. archduke.

archiduquesa, -dŭkĕ'ă, sf. archduchess.

archipiélago, -pĭĕ'lăgŏ, sm. archipelago.

archivar, -văr', v. a. to deposit among archives. [sm. keeper of the records.

archivero, -vĕ'rŏ, archivista, -vĭs'tă,

archivo, ărtchĭ'vŏ, sm. archives.

arder, ărdĕr', v. n. to burn, to blaze.

ardid, ărdĭd', sm. stratagem, artifice, cunning.

ardido, da, ărdĭ'dŏ, a. heated (of grain, tobacco, &c.) ; in a state of fermentation.

ardiente, ărdĭĕn'tĕ, a. ardent, flagrant, burning, passionate ; active, fervid, fiery.

ardilla, ărdĭl'yă, sf. squirrel.

ardor, ărdŏr', sm. great heat ; valour, vivacity, fieriness, fervour.

ardoroso, sa, ărdŏrŏ'sŏ, a. fiery, restless.

arduo, dua, ăr'dŭŏ, a. arduous, difficult ; high.

área, ă'rĕă, sf. area (of a building).

arena, ărĕ'nă, sf. sand ; grit ; arena.

arenal, ărĕnăl', sm. sandy ground.

arenga, ărĕn'gă, sf. harangue, speech.

arengar, -găr', v. n. to harangue.

arenisco, ca, ărĕnĭs'kŏ, arenoso, sa, ărĕnŏ'sŏ, a. sandy, arenaceous.

arenque, ărĕn'kĕ, sm. herring ; — ahumado, red-herring.

areómetro, ărĕŏ'mĕtrŏ, sm. aerometer.

argadijo, ărgădĭ'hŏ, argadillo, ărgădĭl'yŏ, sm. reel ; restless person ; osier-basket.

argado, ărgă'dŏ, sm. prank, trick, artifice.

argamandijo, -măndĭ'hŏ, sm. small cleaning-implements. [building.

argamasa, -mă'să, sf. mortar, cement for

argamasar, -măsăr', v. a. to make mortar.

árgana, ăr'gănă, sf. crane (machine) ; -s, pl. horse-baskets, paniers.

argentado, da, ărhĕntă'dŏ, a. silver-like.

argentar, -tăr', v. a. to silverplate ; to colour [broidery.

argentería, -tĕrĕ'ă, sf. gold or silver embroidery.

argentura, -tŭ'ră, sf. whiteness of silver.

argolla, ărgŏl'yă, sf. large iron-ring ; pillory.

argucia, ărgŭ'thĭă, sf. subtlety.

argüe, ăr'gŭĕ, sm. windlass. [to oppose.

argüir, ărgŭĭr', v. n. to argue, to dispute,

argumentación, ărgŭmĕntăthĭŏn', sf. argumentation. [pute ; to conclude.

argumentar, -tăr', v. n. to argue, to dis-

argumento, ărgŭmĕn'tŏ, sm. argument.

aria, ă'rĭă, sf. (mus.) aria, tune, air.

aridez, ărĭdĕth', sf. drought, want of rain.

árido, da, ă'rĭdŏ, a. dry ; barren.

Aries, ă'rĭĕs, sm. Aries, the Ram (sign of the zodiac).

ariete, ărĭĕ'tĕ, sm. battering-ram.

arijo, ja, ărĭ'hŏ, a. easily tilled (applied to soil).

arillo, ărĭl'yŏ, sm. a small hoop ; ear-ring.

armatoste, ărĭmătĕk', sf. projecting part of a building. [tractable.

arisco, ca, ărĭs'kŏ, a. fierce, rude, unaristarco, ărĭstăr'kŏ, sm. severe censurer of another's writings.

aristocracia, ărĭstŏkră'thĭă, sf. aristocracy.

aristócrata, ărĭstŏ'krătă, sm. aristocrat.

aristocrático, ca, -kră'tĭkŏ, a. aristocratical.

aritmética, ărĭtmĕ'tĭkă, sf. arithmetic.

aritmético, ca, -tĭkŏ, a. arithmetical.

arlequín, ărlĕkĭn', sm. harlequin, buffoon.

arma, ăr'mă, sf. weapon, arms ; — falsa, false alarm.

armada, ărmă'dă, sf. fleet, armada.

armadía, ărmădĕ'ă, sf. raft.

armador, -dŏr', sm. ship-owner ; privateer, cruiser ; jacket, jerkin.

armadura, –dŏ´rā, sf. armour; roof-frame.

armamento, –men´tŏ, sm. warlike preparation, armament.

armar, ärm´r´, v. a. to furnish with arms; to man; to arm, to fit up. – la, to cheat at cards. [board

armario, ärmä´rĭŏ, sm. clothes-press; cupboard.

armatoste, ärmätŏs´tĕ, sm. hulk, lumber, frame. [hulk of a ship, fishing-tackle.

armazón, ärmäthŏn´, sf. wooden frame.

armelina, ärmĕlĭ´nā, sf. ermine-skin.

armería, ärmĕrĭ´ā, sf. arsenal; heraldry, art of armour-making. [of arms.

armero, ärmĕ´rŏ, sm. armourer; keeper of arms.

armilla, ärmĭl´yā, sf. bracelet.

armiño, ärmĭn´yŏ, sm. ermine.

armipotente, ärmĭpŏten´tĕ, a. (poet.) mighty in war.

armisticio, –stĭ´thĭŏ, sm. armistice.

armonía, ärmŏnĭ´ā, sf. harmony.

armónico, ca, ärmŏ´nĭkŏ, a. harmonical.

armonioso, sa, ärmŏnĭŏ´sŏ, a. harmonious.

arna, är´nā, sf. bee-hive.

arnés, ärnĕs´, sm. harness, gear, trapping.

arnilla, ärnĭl´yā, sf. small bee-hive.

aro, ä´rŏ, sm. hoop of wood, iron-staple.

aroca, ärŏ´kā, sf. Portuguese linen.

aroma, ärŏ´mā, sm. & f. aroma; fragrance.

aromático, ca, ärŏmä´tĭkŏ, a. aromatic.

aromatizar, –tĭthär´, v. a. to aromatize.

arpa, är´pä, sf. harp. [to perfume.

arpado, da, ärpä´dŏ, a. serrated, toothed.

arpar, ärpär´, v. a. to tear to pieces, to rend.

arpegio, ärpĕ´k´ĭŏ, sm. (mus.) arpeggio.

arpeo, ärpĕ´ŏ, sm. grappling-iron.

arpía, ärpĭ´ā, sf. (poet.) harpy.

arpillera, ärpĭlyä´rä, sf. sack-cloth.

arpista, ärpĭs´tä, sm. harper.

arpón, ärpŏn´, sm. harpoon. [poon.

arponado, da, ärpŏnä´dŏ, a. like a harpoon.

arponar, ärpŏnär´, v. a. to harpoon.

arponero, ärpŏnĕ´rŏ, sm. harpooner.

arqueada, ärkĕä´dä, sf. (mus.) stroke or movement of the violin-bow.

arqueado, da, –dŏ, a. arched, vaulted.

arquear, ärkĕär´, v. a. to arch, to gauge the dimensions of ships. [a ship.

arqueo, ärkĕ´ŏ, sm. arcuation; gauging of

arqueología, ärkĕŏlŏ´hĕ´ā, sf. archæology.

arquería, ärkĕrĭ´ā, sf. arcade.

arquero, ärkĕ´rŏ, sm. hoop-maker; cashier.

arqueta, –tä, sf. small trunk.

arquilla, ärkĭl´yä, sf. little chest.

arquitecto, ärkĭtĕk´tŏ, sm. architect.

arquitectónico, ca, –tĕktŏ´nĭkŏ, a. architectonic.

arquitectura, –tĕktŏ´rä, sf. architecture.

arquitrabe, –trä´bĕ, sm. architrave.

arrabalero, ärräbälĕ´rŏ, sm. suburban; very common person, churl.

arrabio, ärrä´bĭŏ, sm. cast-iron.

arracada, ärräkä´dä, sf. ear-ring.

arracimarse, ärräthĭmär´sĕ, v. r. to cluster. [ship.

arráez, ärrä´ĕth, sm. captain of a Moorish

arraigar, ärräĭgär´, v. n. to fix the root; to establish.

arraigo, ärrä´ĭgŏ, sm. landed property.

arramblar, ärrämblär´, v. a. to cover with sand (of torrents), to sweep away.

arrancadera, ärränkädĕ´rä, sf. bell of the bell-wether.

arrancar, ärränkär´, v. a. to pull up by the roots, to force out; to wrest, to draw out a tooth.

arrancasiega, ärränkäsĭĕ´gä, sf. mowing of stunted corn; altercation, dispute.

arranque, ärrän´kĕ, sm. extirpation; sudden and violent fit of passion.

arrapiezo, ärräpĭĕ´thŏ, arrapo, ärrä´pŏ, sm. tatter, rag.

arras, är´räs, sf. pl. dowry; earnest-money.

arrasar, ärräsär´, v. a. to demolish, to destroy; –, v. n. to clear up.

arrastrado, da, ärrästrä´dŏ, a. miserable, painstaking.

arrastrar, –rär´, v. a. & n. to creep, to crawl; to drag along the ground; to lead a trump at cards.

arrastre, ärräs´trĕ, sm. lead of a trump at cards; knocking-mill.

arrayán, ärräyän´, sm. myrtle.

¡arre! ärrĕ, gee!, geho!, go on!

arrear, ärrĕär´, v. a. to drive horses, mules &c. [gether, to pick up.

arrebañar, ärrĕbänyär´, v. a. to scrape together.

arrebatado, da, –bätä´dŏ, a. rapid, violent, impetuous, rash, inconsiderate.

arrebatar, –bätär´, v. a. to carry off, to snatch with hurry and precipitation; to enrapture, to dry up.

arrebatiña, –bätĭn´yä, sf. carrying off a thing precipitately out of a crowd.

arrebato, –bä´tŏ, sm. surprise.

arrebol, ärrĕbŏl´, sm. red appearance of the sky; rouge. [rouge.

arrebolar, –bŏlär´, v. a. to paint red; to

arrebozarse, –bŏthär´sĕ, v. r. to swarm (of bees, &c.). [wrap up.

arrebujar, –bŭ´här´, v. a. to crumple, to

arrecafe, –kä´fĕ, sm. (bot.) cardoon; share-wort.

arrecife, –thĕ´fĕ, sm. causeway; reef.

arrecirse, ärrĕthĭr´sĕ, v. r. to grow stiff with cold. [greater distance; to terrify.

arredrar, –drär´, v. a. to remove to a greater distance.

arredro, ärrĕ´drŏ, ad. backwards.

arregazado, da, –gäthä´dŏ, a. turned up; cocked [tuck up the skirts of clothes.

arregazar, –gäthär´, v. a. to truss, to

arreglado, ärrĕglä´dŏ, a. regular, moderate. [adjust.

arreglar, ärrĕglär´, v. a. to regulate; to

arreglo, ärrĕ´glŏ, sm. rule, order; con – á, according to.

arregostarse, ärrĕgŏstär´sĕ, v. r. to relish.

arrejacar, ärrĕhäkär´, v. a. to weed out.

arrejaco, ärrĕhä´kŏ, sm. swift martlet (ave). [fork, trident.

arrejaque, ärrĕhä´kĕ, sm. three-pronged

arrollanarse, ärrŏlyänär´sĕ, v. r. to sit at ease; to make one's self comfortable.

arremangar, ärrĕmängär´, v. a. to tuck up one's sleeves or petticoats.

arremango, _ărrĕmăn'gŏ,_ sm. tucking up of clothes.   [tack; to seize suddenly.

arremeter, _-mĕtĕr',_ v. a. to assail, to attack, assault.

arremetida, _-mĕtĕ'dă,_ sf. attack, assault.

arrendadero, _ărrĕndădĕ'rŏ,_ sm. stable-ring for tying horses.

arrendado, da, _-dă'dŏ,_ a. manageable, tractable (of horses).

arrendador, _-dădŏr',_ sm. tenant, lessee; lessor, hirer.   [mimic, buffoon.

arrendajo, _ărrĕndăh'ŏ,_ sm. mocking-bird,

arrendamiento, _-dămiĕn'tŏ,_ sm. lease

arrendar, _ărrĕndăr',_ v. a. to rent, to let out, to lease, to tie a horse by the reins; to imitate.   [tenant, lessee, farmer

arrendatario, ria, _-dătă'riŏ,_ sm. & f.

arreo, _ărrĕ'ŏ,_ sm. dress, ornament, -s, pl. dependencies, -, ad. successively, uninterruptedly.   [or bun.

arrepápalo, _ărrĕpă'pălŏ,_ sm. sort of fritter

arrepentido, da, _-pĕntĕ'dŏ,_ a. repentant.

arrepentimiento, _-pĕntĕmiĕn'tŏ,_ sm. repentance, penitence

arrepentirse, _-pĕntĕr'sĕ,_ v. r. to repent.

arrepistar, _-pĕstăr',_ v. a. to grind or pound rags into a fine pulp (in paper-mills).

arrequives, _-kĕ'vĕs,_ sm. pl. ornaments; circumstances of a case; requisites.

arrestado, da, _ărrĕstă'dŏ,_ a. intrepid, bold.

arrestar, _-tăr',_ v. a. to arrest, to imprison; -se, to be bold and enterprising.

arresto, _ărrĕs'tŏ,_ sm. boldness in undertaking an enterprise; prison, arrest.

arrezafe, _ărrĕthă'fĕ,_ sm. place full of thistles, brushwood, and brambles.

arriada, _ărriă'dă,_ sf. flood, overflowing.

arriar, _ărriăr',_ v. a. (mar.) to lower, to strike.

arriata, _ărriă'tă,_ sf., **arriate,** _ărriă'tĕ,_ sm. hot-bed, shelving-bed, causeway

arriba, _ărrĕ'bă,_ ad. above, over, up, high, on high, overhead, aloft.

arribada, _-bă'dă,_ sf. arrival of a vessel in port.   [harbour; to fall off to leeward

arribar, _ărrĕbăr',_ v. n. (mar.) to put into a

arribo, _ărrĕ'bŏ,_ sm. arrival

arricete, _ărrĕthĕ'tĕ,_ sm. shoal, sand-bank.

arriendo, _ărriĕn'dŏ,_ sm. lease, farm rent.

arriería, _ărriĕrĕ'ă,_ sf. mule-driver's trade.

arriero, _ărriĕ'rŏ,_ sm. muleteer.

arriesgar, _ărriĕsgăr',_ v. a. to risk, to hazard, to expose to danger

arrimadero, _ărrĕmădĕ'rŏ,_ sm. scaffold; stick or support to lean upon.

arrimadillo, _-mădĕ'yŏ,_ sm. silk wainscoting, pannelling.

arrimadizo, _-mădĕ'thŏ,_ a. sustaining, sustainable; -, sm. parasite, sponger.

arrimador, _-mădŏr',_ sm. back-log in a fire-place.

arrimar, _ărrĕmăr',_ v. a. to approach, to draw near; (mar.) to stow the cargo; to lay aside, to give up a command; to displace, to dismiss.

arrinconar, _ărrĕnkŏnăr',_ v. a. to put a thing in a corner; to lay aside; to drive from office; -se, to retire, to withdraw.

arriscado, da, _ărrĕskă'dŏ,_ a. forward, bold, audacious, impudent; brisk.

arriscador, _-kădŏr',_ sm. olive gleaner.

arrizar, _ărrĕthăr',_ v. a. (mar.) to reef; to tie or lash.

arroba, _ărrŏ'bă,_ sf. weight of twenty-five pounds; measure (thirty-two pints); por -s, by wholesale.   [ecstasy.

arrobadizo, za, _-bădĕ'thŏ,_ a. feigning

arrobamiento, _-miĕn'tŏ,_ sm. rapture; amazement, rapturous admiration.

arrobarse, _ărrŏbăr'sĕ,_ v. r. to be intensely amazed, to be out of one's senses.

arrocero, _ărrŏthĕ'rŏ,_ sm. rice-grower; rice-merchant.

arrocinado, da, _-thĕnă'dŏ,_ a. stupid, asinine; ass-like (applied to horses).

arrocinarse, _-thĕnăr'sĕ,_ v. r. to become dull and stupid.   [knee; -se, to kneel.

arrodillar, _-dĕlyăr',_ v. n. to bend the

arrodrigar, _-drĕgăr',_ **arrodrigonar,** _-drĕgŏnăr',_ v. a. to prop vines.

arrogación, _ărrŏgăthiŏn',_ sf. arrogation; adoption.   [haughtiness.

arrogancia, _ărrŏgăn'thiă,_ sf. arrogance,

arrogante, _-găn'tĕ,_ a. haughty, proud, assuming; valiant, stout: **caballo -,** mettlesome, spirited horse.

arrogar, _ărrŏgăr',_ v. a. to arrogate; to appropriate to one's self.   [or thrown.

arrojadizo, za, _-hădĕ'thŏ,_ a. easily cast

arrojado, da, _-hă'dŏ,_ a. rash, inconsiderate; bold, fearless.

arrojar, _-hăr',_ v. a. to dart, to fling, to jet; to dash; to shed a fragrance; to emit light; to shoot, to sprout.   [fearlessness.

arrojo, _ărrŏ'hŏ,_ sm. boldness, intrepidity,

arrollar, _ărrŏlyăr',_ v. a. to roll up, to revolve, to enwrap; to sweep away; to confound an opponent.   [catch cold.

arromadizarse, _-mădĕthăr'sĕ,_ v. r. to

arromar, _ărrŏmăr',_ v. a. to blunt.

arrompido, _ărrŏmpĕ'dŏ,_ sm. broken ground.

arropar, _ărrŏpăr',_ v. a. to clothe, to dress.

arrope, _ărrŏ'pĕ,_ sm. must (new wine boiled until it is as dense as a syrup).

arropea, _-pĕ'ă,_ sf. irons, fetters, pl.

arrostrar, _ărrŏstrăr',_ v. a. to perform in a cheerful manner; to encounter dangers

arroyada, _ărrŏyă'dă,_ sf. torrent.

arroyar, _ărrŏyăr',_ v. a. to overflow sown

arroyo, _ărrŏy'ŏ,_ sm. rivulet.   [ground.

arroz, _ărrŏth',_ sm. rice.

arrozal, _ărrŏthăl',_ sm. rice-field.   [boar.

arruar, _ărruăr',_ v. n. to grunt like a wild

arrufar, _ărrufăr',_ v. a. to incurvate.

arrufianado, da, _ărrufiănă'dŏ,_ a. impudent; like a ruffian.

arruga, _ărrŭ'gă,_ sf. wrinkle; rumple.

arrugar, _ărrŭgăr',_ v. a. to wrinkle; to rumple, to fold; **- la frente,** to knit the brow; **-se,** to shrivel; to die

arruinar, _ărruĕnăr',_ v. a. to demolish; to ruin.   [cajoling.

arrullador, ra, _ărrŭlyădŏr',_ a. flattering,

arrullar, _ărrŭlyăr',_ v. a. to lull to rest; to court, to bill and coo.   [lullaby.

arrullo, _ărrŭl'yŏ,_ sm. cooing of pigeons;

arrumaco, *ărrŭmă'kŏ*, sm. caress, curl of the lips.

arruinaje, *-mă'h'ĕ*, sm. cargo-stowage.

arrumar, *ărrŭmăr'*, v a. to stow cargo.

arrumazón, *-măthŏn'*, sm (mar.) stowing; cloudy horizon.

arrumbar, *ărrŭmbăr'*, v. a. to set aside as useless lumber; to refute or silence in conversation; to decant wine. -se, (mar) to steer the proper course.

arrunflarse, *ărrŭnflăr'sĕ*, v r to have a "flush" at cards.

arsenal, *ărsĕnăl'*, sm. arsenal; dock-yard

arsénico, *ărsĕ'nĭkŏ*. sm arsenic

arte, *ăr'tĕ*, sm. & f art; skill. artfulness; rudiments of grammar

artefacto, *ărtĕfăk'tŏ*, sm manufacture.

artejo, *ărtĕ'h ŏ*, sm. finger-joint.

arteria, *ărtĕ'rĭă*, sf. artery [artful.

artero, ra, *ărtĕ'rŏ*, a. dexterous, cunning,

artesa, *ărtĕ'să*, sf. kneading-trough; wooden bowl [man.

artesano, *ărtĕsă'nŏ*, sm. artisan, work-

artético, ca, *ărtĕ'tĭkŏ*, a. arthritical, gouty

ártico, ca, *ăr'tĭkŏ* a, arctic, northern.

articulación, *ărtĭkŭlăthŏn'*, sf. articulation, clear and distinct pronunciation.

articular, *ărtĭkŭlăr'*, v a. to articulate, to pronounce distinctly.

artículo, *ărtĭ'kŭlŏ*, sm. article; clause; point; (gr) article, condition

artífice, *ărtĭ'fĭthĕ*, sm. artisan, artist.

artificial, *ărtĭfĭthĭăl'*, a. artificial.

artificio, *ărtĭfĭ'thĭŏ*, sm. workmanship, craft; artifice, cunning, trick.

artificioso, sa, *-thĭŏ'sŏ*, a. skilful, ingenious; artful, cunning.

artillar, *ărtĭlyăr'*, v. a. to mount cannon.

artillería, *ărtĭlyĕrĕ'ă*, sf gunnery, artillery.

artillero, *ărtĭlyĕ'rŏ*, sm artillery-man.

artista, *ărtĭs'tă*, sm, artist, craftsman.

arúspice, *ărŭs'pĭthĕ*, sm augurer, soothsayer.

arveja, *ărvĕ'h'ă*, sf. (bot.) vetch [sayer.

arvejo, *-vĕ'hŏ*, sm (bot.) bastard chick-pea.

arzobispado, *ărthŏbĭspă'dŏ*, sm archbishopric.

arzobispal, *-bĭspăl'*, a. archiepiscopal.

arzobispo, *-bĭs'pŏ*, sm. archbishop.

arzón, *ărthŏn'*, sm. bow of a saddle.

as, *ăs*, sm. ace; roman copper coin.

asa, *ă'să*, sf handle, haft, hold.

asado, *ăsă'dŏ*, sm roast-meat.

asador, *ăsădŏr'*, sm. turn-spit.

asadura, *-dŏ'ră*, sf chitterlings; toll paid for cattle. [satiny.

asaetinado, da, *ăsăĕtĭnă'dŏ*, a. silky,

asalariar, *ăsălărĭăr'*, v. a. to give a fixed salary. [to assail, to fall upon.

asaltar, *ăsăltăr'*, v. a. to storm a position;

asalto, *ăsăl'tŏ*, sm. assault, storm against a place. [ing.

asamblea, *ăsămblĕ'ă*, sf assembly, meeting.

asar, *ăsăr'*, v a. to roast.

asargado, da, *ăsărgă'dŏ*, a. serge-like.

asativo, va, *ăsătĭ'vŏ*, a. boiled in its own juice.

asbestino, na, *ăsbĕstĭ'nŏ*, a. asbestine.

asbesto, *ăsbĕs'tŏ*, sm. asbestos.

ascalonia, *ăskălŏ'nĭă*, sf (bot.) shallot.

ascendencia, *ăsthĕndĕn'thĭă*, sf. ascending line; line of descent.

ascendente, *-dĕn'tĕ*, a. ascending; (rail) tren -, s. up-train

ascender, *-dĕr'*, v n. to be promoted to a higher dignity

ascendiente, *-dĭĕn'tĕ*, sm. ascendant, forefather; influence.

Ascensión, *-sĭŏn'*, sf. feast of Ascension.

ascenso, *ăsthĕn'sŏ*, sm. promotion to a higher dignity or station.

ascensor, *-sŏr'*, sm. lift.

asceta, *ăsthĕ'tă*, sm. ascetic.

ascético, ca, *ăsthĕ'tĭkŏ*, a. ascetic.

asco, *ăs'kŏ*, sm. nausea, loathing.

ascua, *ăs'kŭă*, sf red hot coal.

¡ascuas! *-s*, bow it hurts! good heavens!

aseado, Ca, *ăsĕă'dŏ*, a. clean, elegant, neat.

asear, *ăsĕăr'*, v. a. to set off, to adorn.

asedado, da, *ăsĕdă'dŏ*, a. silky.

asediar, *ăsĕdĭăr'*, v. a. to besiege

asedio, *ăsĕ'dĭŏ*, sm. siege. [one's self.

aseglararse, *ăsĕglără'rsĕ*, v r to secularize

asegundar, *-gŭndăr'*, v a. to repeat.

aseguración, *-gŭră'thĭŏn'*, sf insurance.

asegurador, *-gŭrădŏr'*, sm insurer.

asegurar, *-gŭrăr'*, v. a. to secure, to insure; to affirm to bail

asemejar, *ăsĕmĕ'hăr'*, v a. to assimilate, to make alike [to force one's way.

asenderear, *ăsĕndĕrĕăr'*, v a. to persecute;

asenso, *ăsĕn'sŏ*, sm. assent, consent

asentaderas, *ăsĕntădĕ'răs*, sf pl buttocks.

asentadillas, *-dĭl'yăs*, ad. (á -) sitting on horseback like a woman

asentar, *-tăr'*, v a. to place on a chair or other seat; to suppose; to affirm, to assure, to adjust, to note; -, v n. to sit down; to settle, to sit (of clothes). -se, to settle (of liquids). [concede.

asentir, *ăsĕntĭr'*, v a. to acquiesce, to

asentista, *-tĭs'tă*, sm. purveyor, contractor.

aseo, *ăsĕ'ŏ*, sm. cleanliness, neatness.

asequible, *ăsĕkĕ'blĕ*, a. attainable, obtainable. [mation.

aserción, *ăsĕrthĭŏn'*, sf. assertion, affirmation.

aserradero, *ăsĕrrădĕ'rŏ*, sm. saw-mill.

aserraduras, *-dŏ'răs*, sf. pl. saw-dust.

aserrar, *ăsĕrrăr'*, v. a. to saw, to scrape (upon a fiddle).

asertivo, va, *ăsĕrtĭ'vŏ*, a. affirmative.

asesar, *ăsĕsăr'*, v. n. to become prudent.

asesinar, *-sĭnăr'*, v. a. to assassinate.

asesinato, *-sĭnă'tŏ*, sm. assassination.

asesino, *-sĕ'nŏ*, sm. assassin; impostor, cheat.

asesor, *ăsĕsŏr'*, sm. counsellor, assessor.

asesorarse, *-sŏră'sĕ*, v. r. to employ counsel.

asestar, *ăsĕstăr'*, v. a. to aim, to point.

aseverar, *ăsĕvĕrăr'*, v. ? ? asseverate, to solemnly affirm.

asfalto, *ăsfăl'tŏ*, sm. asphaltum.

así, *ăsĕ'*, ad. so, thus, in this manner; therefore, so that; also; - bien, as well; - que, so that, therefore; así, así, so, so;

tniddling; – que –, whether this or that
way; como –, even so, just so.

asidero, ăsĭdā´rō, sm. handle; hold; occasion, pretext. [tached.

asido, da, ăsē´dŏ, a. fastened, tied, attached.

asiduo, dua, ăsē´dŭŏ, a. assiduous.

asiento, ăsĭĕn´tŏ, sm. chair, bench, stool; seat; contract; entry, residence; – común, privy. [destination.

asignación, ăsĭgnăthĭŏn´, sf. assignation;

asignar, ăsĭgnăr´, v. a. to assign; to attribute.

asignatura, ăsĭgnătū´ră, sf. catalogue of university lectures for one year.

asilla, ăsĭl´yă, sf. small handle; slight pretext; clavicle.

asilo, ăsē´lŏ, sm. asylum, refuge.

asimilar, ăsĭmĭlăr´, v. n. to resemble; –, v. a. to assimilate. [same manner.

asimismo, ăsĭmĭs´mŏ, ad. similarly, in the

asimplado, da, ăsĭmplă´dŏ, a. silly.

asir, ăsēr´, v. a. & n. to grasp, to seize; to hold, to grip, to take root.

asistencia, ăsĭstĕn´thĭă, sf. actual presence; assistance; help; – de Sevilla, magistrate of Seville. [maid at court.

asistenta, –tĕn´tă, sf. hand-maid; servant-

asistente, –tĕn´tĕ, sm. assistant, helper; chief officer of justice at Seville; officer's servant, orderly.

asistir, ăsĭstēr´, v. n. to be present, to assist, –, v. a. to help, to minister, to further; to attend a sick person.

asma, ăs´mă, sf. asthma.

asmático, ca, ăsmă´tĭkŏ, a. asthmatic.

asna, ăs´nă, sf. she-ass, jenny-ass.

asnada, ăsnă´dă, sf. foolish action.

asnal, ăsnăl´, a. asinine.

asnallo, ăsnăl´yŏ, sm. worm-seed.

asnazo, ăsnă´thŏ, sm. a large jack-ass.

asnería, ăsnērē´ă, sf. stud of asses; egregious blunder. [andiron.

asnico, ca, ăsnē´kŏ, sm. & f. little ass;

asnillo, lla, ăsnēl´yŏ, sm. & f. little ass; grass-hopper; field-cricket.

asno, ăs´nŏ, sm. ass, stupid fellow.

asobarcar, ăsŏbărkăr´, v. a. to pick up and put under one's arm. [crafty.

asocarronado, ăsŏkărrŏnă´dŏ, a. waggish;

asociación, ăsŏthĭăthĭŏn´, sf. association; co-partnership.

asociado, –thĭă´dŏ, sm. associate.

asociar, –thĭăr´, v. a. to associate.

asolanar, ăsŏlănăr´, v. a. to parch, to dry up (of easterly winds).

asolar, ăsŏlăr´, v. a. to destroy, to devastate; –se, to settle, to clear (of liquids).

asolear, ăsŏlĕăr´, v. a. to expose to the sun; –se, to be sun-burnt.

asolvarse, ăsŏlvăr´sĕ, v. r. to be stopped (of pipes, canals). [apparition.

asomada, ăsŏmă´dă, sf. sudden appearance.

asomar, ăsŏmăr´, v. n. to begin to appear; –se, to be flustered with wine.

asombradizo, za, ăsŏmbrădĭs´thŏ, a. fearful, timid, easily frightened.

asombrar, ăsŏmbrăr´, v. a. to frighten, to

amaze; to astonish; (poet.) to obscure, to overshadow. [tonishment.

asombro, ăsŏm´brŏ, sm. dread; terror; astonishment.

asombroso, sa, –brŏ´sŏ, a. astonishing, marvellous. [tion, conjecture.

asomo, ăsŏ´mŏ, sm. mark, token, indication, conjecture.

asonancia, ăsŏnăn´thĭă, sf. assonance; harmony,

asortir, ăsŏrtēr´, v. a. to assort.

asotanar, ăsŏtănăr´, v. a. to build arched cellars.

aspa, ăs´pă, sf. reel. [cellars.

aspar, ăspăr´, v. a. to reel; to crucify; to vex, to mortify; –se á gritos, to cry out loudly, to yell. [ment; exclamation.

aspaviento, ăspăvĭĕn´tŏ, sm. astonish-

aspecto, ăspĕk´tŏ, sm. appearance, aspect.

aspereza, ăspĕrĕ´thă, sf. asperity, acerbity.

asperges, ăspĕr´hĕs, sm. sprinkling with holy-water; quedarse –, to be disappointed. [ripe fruit.

asperillo, ăspĕrĭl´yŏ, sm. bitterness of unripe fruit.

áspero, ra, ăs´pĕrŏ, a. rough, rugged; craggy, hirsute, knotty; horrid; harsh, hard; crabbed, severe, austere, gruff.

asperón, ăspĕrŏn´, sm. grindstone.

aspersión, ăspĕrsĭŏn´, sf. aspersion, sprinkling.

aspersorio, –sŏ´rĭŏ, sm. water-sprinkler.

áspid, ăs´pĭd, sm. aspic. [inspiration.

aspiración, ăspĭrăthĭŏn´, sf. aspiration;

aspirante, –răn´tĕ, sm. aspirant, aspirer.

aspirar, ăspĭrăr´, v. a. to inspire the air; to aspire; (gr.) to aspirate. [squeamish.

asqueroso, sa, ăskĕrŏ´sŏ, a. loathsome,

asta, ăs´tă, sf. lance; horn; handle of a pencil, brush.

astaco, ăstă´kŏ, sm. lobster.

asterisco, ăstĕrĭs´kŏ, sm. asterisk.

asterismo, –rĭs´mŏ, sm. constellation.

astil, ăstĭl´, sm. handle, shaft.

astilla, ăstĭl´yă, sf. chip of wood, splinter of timber.

astillar, ăstĭlyăr´, v. a. to chip.

astillazo, –yă´thŏ, sm. crack (produced by a splinter being torn from a block); damage which results from an enterprise to those who have not been its principal authors.

astillero, –yă´rŏ, sm. holdfast for soldiers' arms; dockyard, ship-wright's yard.

astral, ăstrăl´, a. astral.

astricción, ăstrĭkthĭŏn´, sf. astriction.

astrictivo, va, –tē´vŏ, a astrictive, styptic.

astricto, ta, ăstrĭk´tŏ, a. contracted, compressed.

astringente, ăstrĭn´hĕn´tĕ, a. astringent.

astringir, –hĭr´, a. to astringe; to contract.

astro, ăs´trŏ, sm. star. [tract.

astrología, ăstrŏlŏ´hē´ă, sf. astrology.

astrológico, ca, ăstrŏlŏ´hĭkŏ, a. astrological.

astrólogo, ăstrŏ´lŏgŏ, sm. astrologer.

astronomía, ăstrŏnŏmē´ă, sf. astronomy.

astronómico, ca, ăstrŏnŏmĭkŏ, a. astronomical.

astrónomo, ăstrŏ´nŏmŏ, sm. astronomer.

astroso, sa, ăstrŏ´sŏ, a. indecent, sordid.

astucia, ăstŏ´thĭă, sf. cunning, slyness.

asturión, ăstŭriŏn´, sm. pony.

astuto, ta, ăstŏˀtŏ, a. cunning, sly, astute.

asueto, ăsŭˀtŏ, sm. holidays, vacation.

Asunción, ăsŭnthiŏn´, sf. ascent of the Holy Virgin to heaven.

asunto, ăsŭn´tŏ, sm. subject, matter treated upon; affair, business.

asurarse, ăsŭrār´sĕ, v. r. to be burnt in cooking (applied to meat).

asurcar, ăsŭrkăr´, v. a. to furrow sown land for the purpose of rooting out the weeds. [to be frightened.

asustar, ăsŭstăr´, v. a. to frighten; —se, atabacado, da, ătăbăkă´dŏ, a. tobacco-coloured.

atabal, ătăbăl´, sm. kettle-drum.

atabalear, —ăr´, v. n. to make a noise like kettle-drums.

atabalero, —d´rŏ, sm. kettle-drummer.

atabe, ătă´bĕ, sm. small vent left in water-pipes. [taverns.

atabernado, da, —bĕrnă´dŏ, a. retailed in atabladera, —blădĕ´ră, sf. roller to level land sown with corn. [with corn.

atablar, ătăblăr´, v. a. to level land sown

atacado, da, ătăkă´dŏ, a. irresolute; narrow-minded. [poniard.

atacador, —kădŏr´, sm. aggressor; ramrod;

atacar, —kăr´, v. a. to fit clothes tight to the body; to force the charge into fire-arms with a ramrod; to attack, to onset.

atado, ătă´dŏ, sm. bundle, parcel; —, da. a. pusillanimous, easily embarrassed; attached.

atador, —dŏr´, sm. sheaves-binder.

atafagar, —făgăr´, v. a. to stupefy, to take away one's breath; to tease.

atafetanado, da, —fĕtănă´dŏ, a. resembling tiffany. [pack-saddle.

ataharre, ătăăr´rĕ, sm. broad crupper of a

atahorma, —ŏr´mă, sf. osprey (ave).

ataire, ătă´irĕ, sm. moulding in the pannels and frames of doors and windows.

atajadizo, ătă´hădĕˀthŏ, sm. partition-wall.

atajar, ătă´hăr´, v a. to cut off part of the road; to intercept, to stop, to obstruct; —se, to be confounded with dread.

atajasolaces, —hăsŏlă´thĕs, sm. kill-joy.

atajea, —hă´ă, atajía, —hĕ´ă, sf. sewer.

atajo, ătă´hˀŏ, sm. cross-path, by-path.

atalaya, —lă´yă, sf. watch-tower; —, sm. guard in a watch-tower.

atalayar, —lăyăr´, v. a. to overlook the country and sea-coast from a watch-tower; to spy into the action of others. [silk.

atanquía, ătănkĕ´ă, sf. depilatory; refuse of

ataque, ătă´kĕ, sm. attack; trenches; fit of the palsy, &c.; verbal dispute.

ataquizar, —kĭthăr´, v. a. to provine.

atar, ătăr´, v. a. to tie, to bind, to fasten; to stop; —se, to be embarrassed or perplexed. [work.

ataracea, ătărăthă´ă, sf. marquetry, checker-

ataracear, —thăăr´, v. a. to checker, to inlay. [tarantula; surprised, amazed.

atarantado, da, ătărăntă´dŏ, a. bitten by a

atarazana, ătărăthă´nă, sf. arsenal; shed in rope-walks.

atarazar, —thăr´, v. a to bite.

atarear, ătărĕăr´, v. a. to impose a task; —se, to overdo one's self.

atarjea, ătăr´hĕˀă, sf. protecting vault over the pipes of an aqueduct; small drain.

atarquinar, —kĭnăr´, v. a. to bemire.

atarugar, ătărŭgăr´, v. a. to wedge; to silence; —se, to be perplexed.

atasajar, ătăsă´hăr´, v. a. to cut meat into small pieces, and dry it in the sun.

atascar, ătăskăr´, v. a. to stop a leak; to throw an obstacle in the way; —se, to become bogged.

ataúd, ătăŭd´, sm. coffin.

ataujía, ătăŭhĕ´ă, sf. damaskeen.

ataujiado, da, —´hĭă´dŏ, a. worked in a damaskeen fashion. [to adorn.

ataviar, ătăvĭăr´, v. a. to dress out, to trim,

atavío, —vĕ´ŏ, sm. dress, ornament, finery.

atediar, ătĕdĭăr´, v. a. to disgust; —se, to be tired.

ateísmo, ătĕˀĭsˀmŏ, sm. atheism.

ateísta, ătĕˀĭsˀtă, sm. atheist.

atemorizar, ătĕmŏrĭthăr´, v. a. to strike with terror, to daunt. [tion.

atemperación, ătĕmpĕrăthĭŏn´, sf. moderation

atemperar, —pĕrăr´, v. a. to temper, to soften, to assuage; to accommodate.

atenaz(e)ar, ătĕnăth(ĕ)ăr´, v. a. to tear off the flesh with pincers.

atención, ătĕnthĭŏn´, sf. attention, heedfulness; civility, complaisance; observance, consideration; en —, attending; in consideration of; as regards.

atender, —dĕr´, v. n. to be attentive; to heed, to hearken, to expect, to wait for; to look at.

atentado, da, —tă´dŏ, a. discreet, prudent, moderate; noiseless; —, sm. attempt, transgression, offence.

atentar, —tăr´, v. a. to attempt crime; to go about a thing deliberately.

atento, ta, ătĕn´tŏ, a. attentive; heedful; observing; mindful; polite, courteous, mannerly; compliant; notable; —, pr. in consideration. [maceration.

atenuación, ătĕnŭăthĭŏn´, sf. attenuation;

atenuar, ătĕnŭăr´, v. a. to diminish, to macerate, to mince.

atercianado, da, ătĕrthĭănă´dŏ, a. afflicted with the tertian fever.

aterciopelado, da, —thĭŏpĕlă´dŏ, a. velvet-like. [cold.

aterirse, ătĕrĭr´sĕ, v r. to grow stiff with

aternerado, da, ătĕrnĕră´dŏ, a. calf-like.

aterrar, ătĕrrăr´, v. a. to prostrate; to terrify; —se, to be terrified.

aterronar, ătĕrrŏnăr´, v. a. to clod, to coagulate. [to terrify.

aterrorizar, ătĕrrŏrĭthăr´, v. a. to frighten;

atesorar, ătĕsŏrăr´, v. a. to treasure or hoard up riches. [dence.

atestación, ătĕstăthĭŏn´, sf. testimony, evidence

atestado, da, —tă´dŏ, a. stubborn; —, sm. certificate.

atestar. —tăr´, v. a. to cram, to stuff; to

overstock; to attest, to witness; **—se**, to overeat one's self.   [attest.

atestiguar, *–tēgăr'*, v. a. to witness, to

atetado, da, *ătĕtă'dō*, a. mammiform.

atetar, *ătĕtăr'*, y a. to suckle.

atetillar, *–tēlyăr'*, v. a. to lay bare the roots of trees.

atezado, da, *–thĕ'dō*, a. black.

atezar, *–thăr'*, v a. to blacken; **—se**, to grow black.   [wool, &c.; to eat one's fill.

atiborrar, *ătĭbŏrrăr'*, v a. to stuff with

aticismo, *–thĭs'mō*, sm. atticism.

atigrado, da, *–grā'dō*, a. tiger-coloured.

atildar, *ătĭldăr'*, v a. to punctuate, to underline, to censure; to deck, to dress, to adorn.

atinar, *ătĭnăr'*, v. n. to touch the mark, to reach the point, to hit; to guess.

atiriciarse, *ătĭrĭthĭăr'sĕ*, v. r. to grow jaundiced, to get the jaundice.

atisbadero, *ătĭsbădă'rō*, sm. peep-hole.

atisbar, *ătĭsbăr'*, v. a. to pry, to examine closely.

atisuado, da, *ătĭsŭă'dō*, a. tissue-like.

atizar, *ătĭhăr'*, v a. to stir the fire with a poker ; to stir up.

atizonar, *ătĭthŏnăr'*, v. a. to fill up the chinks in a wall; **—se,** to be smutted.

atlántico, ca, *ătlăn'tĭkō*, adj. atlantic.

atlas, *ăt'lăs*, sm. atlas (collection of maps); kind of rich silk.

atleta, *ătlĕ'tă*, sm. wrestler.

atlético, ca, *ătlĕ'tĭkō*, a. athletic.

atmósfera, *ătmŏs'fĕrā*, sf. atmosphere.

atmosférico, ca, *ătmŏsfĕ'rĭkō*, a. atmospherical.

atoar, *ătŏăr'*, v a. to tow a vessel.

atocinar, *ătŏthĭnăr'*, v. a. to cut up a pig for salting.   [gorse.

atocha, *ătŏtsh'ă*, sf. (bot.) broom, furze,

atolondramiento, *ătŏlŏndrămĭĕn'tō*, sm. stupefaction, consternation.

atolondrar, *–drăr'*, v. a. to stun, to stupefy ; **—se,** to be stupefied.

atolladero, *ătŏlyădă'rō*, sm. bog; obstacle, impediment.

atollar, *–lyăr'*, v n. to stick in the mire.

atomismo, *ătŏmĭs'mō*, sm. atomical philosophy.

átomo, *ă'tŏmō*, sm. atom ; mote.   [sophy.

atondar, *ătŏndăr'*, v. a. to spur a horse.

atonía, *ătŏnĕ'ă*, sf (med.) weakness, debility.

atónito, ta, *ătŏ'nĭtō*, a. astonished, amazed.

atontar, *ătŏnăr'*, v. a. to stun, to stupefy; **—se,** to grow stupid.

atorarse, *ătŏrăr'sĕ*, v.r. to stick in the mire.

atormentadamente, *ătŏrmĕntădămĕn'tĕ*, ad. anxiously   [to give pain.

atormentar, *–mĕntăr'*, v. a. to torment,

atorozonarse, *ătŏrŏthŏnăr'sĕ*,v.r.to suffer from gripes or colic.

atortolar, *ătŏrtŏlăr'*, v. a. to intimidate.

atosigar, *ătŏsĭgăr'*, v a. to poison ; to harass, to oppress.

atrabancar, *ătrăbănkăr'*, v. a. to huddle.

atracadero, *–kădă'rō*, sm. landing-place.

atracar, *ătrăkăr'*, v a. to overhaul a ship; to glut, to pamper.

atracción, *ătrăkthĭŏn'*, sf. attraction.

atractivo, va, *–tĭ'vŏ*, a. attractive; **magnetic;** **—**, sm. charm, grace.

atraer, *ătrăĕr'*, v. a. to attract, to allure.

atrafagado, da, *ătrăfăgă'dō*, a. over-busy, overworked.   [self.

atrafagar, *–făgăr'*, v n. to exhaust one's

atragantarse, *–găntăr'sĕ*, v. r. to stick in the throat, to choke; to stick fast in conversation.   [ous.

atraidorado, da, *ătrăĭdŏră'dō*, a.treacher-

atraillar, *ătrăĭlyăr'*, y a. to leash.

atramparse, *ătrămpăr'sĕ*,v.r. to be caught in a snare; to be stopped or blocked up; to be involved in difficulties.

atrancar, *ătrănkăr'*, v. a. to bar a door; to take long steps; to read so fast as to skip over passages.   [to deceive.

atrapar, *ătrăpăr'*, v a. to overtake, to nab;

atrás, *ătrăs'*, ad. backwards; past; **hacia —,** quite the contrary.

atrasado, da, *ătrăsă'dō*, a. in arrear.

atrasar, *ătrăsăr'*, v a. to outstrip, to leave behind ; to hinder another's fortune; to postpone; **— el reloj,** to put back a watch.   [fortune, arrears of money.

atraso, *ătră'sō*, sm. backwardness; loss of

atravesado, da, *ătrăvĕsă'dō*, a. squint-eyed ; oblique ; cross-grained, perverse; mongrel, degenerate.

atravesaño, *–săn'yŏ*, sm. cross-timber.

atravesar, *–săr'*, v. a. to lay a beam of timber across a place; to run through with a sword, to cross, to pass over; to trump a trick ; **—se,** to get in the way; to thwart one's purpose.

atreguado, *ătrĕgwă'dō*,a.rash,precipitate.

atresnalar, *ătrĕsnălăr'*, v. a. to collect sheaves of corn into heaps.   [ture.

atreverse, *ătrĕvĕr'sĕ*, v. r. to dare, to ven-

atrevido, da, *–vĕ'dō*, a. bold, audacious, daring.   [audacity.

atrevimiento, *–vĭmĭĕn'tō*, sm. boldness,

atribución, *ătrĭbŭthĭŏn'*, sf. attribution, imputation.   [ascribe; to impute.

atribuir, *ătrĭbŭĕr'*, v.a. to attribute, to

atribular, *–bŭlăr'*, v. a. to vex, to afflict.

atributivo, va, *–bŭtĭ'vŏ*, a. attributive.

atributo, *–bŏ'tō*, sm. attribute.

atrición, *–thĭŏn'*, sf. attrition.

atril, *ătrĭl'*, sm. mass-book desk.

atrincheramiento, *ătrĭntshĕrămĭĕn'tō*, sm. (mil.) intrenchment.

atrincherar, *–tshĕrăr'*, v. a. to intrench.

atrio, *ă'trĭō*, sm. porch; portico.

atrito, ta, *ătrĕ'tō*, a. contrite, penitent.

atro, ra, *ă'trō*, a. (poet.) black.

atrocidad, *ătrŏthĭdăd''*, sf. atrocity.

atrochar, *ătrŏtshăr'*,v.n. to take by-paths.

atrochemoche, *ătrŏtshĕmŏtsh'ĕ*, ad. criss-cross.

atrofia, *ătrŏfĕ'ă*, sf. atrophy, body.

atrófico, ca, *ătrŏ'fĭkō*, a. affected with atrophy.   [pet-like.

atrompetado, da, *ătrŏmpĕtă'dō*, a. trum-

atronado, da, *ătrŏnă'dō*, a. unadvised, thoughtless, rash.   [struck.

atronarse, *–năr'sĕ*, v. r. to be thunder-

atronerar, *-nĕrăr'*, v. a. to make embrasures in a wall.

atropado, da, *-pă' dŏ*, a. grouped, clumped.

atropar, *-păr'*, v. a. to assemble in groups.

atropellado, da, *-pĕlyă' dŏ*, a. hasty, precipitate.

atropellar, *-pĕlyăr'*, v. a. to trample; to run down; to hurry, to flurry; **-se,** to hurry one's self too much.

atroz, *ătrŏth'*, a. atrocious, heinous, cruel.

atrozar, *ătrŏthăr'*, v. a. to truss a yard to the mast.

atufar, *ătŭfăr'*, v. a. to vex, to plague; **-se,** to be on the fret (applied to wine); to be angry.

atún, *ătŭn'*, sm. tunny-fish. [to be angry.

atunara, *ătŭnă' ră*, sf. tunny-fishery.

aturdido, da, *ătŭrdē' dŏ*, a. hare-brained.

aturdimiento, *ătŭrdĭmĭen' tŏ*, sm. stupefaction; astonishment; dulness.

aturdir, *-dīr'*, v. a. to perturbate, to confuse; to stupefy. [shear.

atusar, *ătŭsăr'*, v. a. to cut the hair; to

auca, *ă' kă*, sf. goose.

audacia, *ăwdă' thĭă*, sf. audacity, boldness.

audaz, *ăwdăth'*, a. audacious, bold.

audiencia, *ăwdĭen' thĭă*, sf. audience; audience-chamber; a court of oyer and terminer. [tory.

auditivo, va, *ăwdĭtē' vŏ*, a. auditive, auditory.

auditorio, *-tŏ' rĭŏ*, sm. auditory.

auge, *ă' whĕ*, sm. the pinnacle of power; apogee of a planet.

augur, *ăgŭr'*, sm. augurer.

augusto, ta, *ăgŭs' tŏ*, a. august, majestic.

aula, *ă' ŭlă*, sf. auditory, lecture-room.

aullar, *ăŭlyăr'*, v. n. to howl. [ing.

aullido, *-yē' dŏ*, **aullo,** *ăŭl' yŏ*, sm. howl-

aumentar, *ăŭmĕntăr'*, v. a. to augment, to increase; **-,** v. n. to grow larger.

aumentativo, va, *-tătē' vŏ*, a. increasing, enlarging.

aumento, *ăŭmĕn' tŏ*, sm. augmentation, increase; promotion, advancement.

aun, *ăŭn'*, ad. yet, as yet, nevertheless; still, farther, even, further.

aunar, *ăŭnăr'*, v. a. to unite, to assemble.

aunque, *ăŭnkĕ'*, ad. though, notwithstanding!. [standing.

¡aupa! *ăŭ' pă*, up, up! up!

aura, *ăŭ' ră*, sf. gentle breeze; **-popular,** popularity.

áureo, rea, *ăŭ' rĕŏ*, a. golden, gilt; **-,** sm. doubloon; apothecary's weight of 4 scruples.

aureola, *ăŭrĕ' ŏlă*, sf. glory; nimbus.

aurícula, *ăŭrē' kŭlă*, sf. (bot.) bear's-ear.

auricular, *-kŭlăr'*, a. within hearing.

aurífero, ra, *ăŭrē' fĕrŏ*, a. (poet.) containing gold.

aurora, *ăŭrŏ' ră*, sf. first dawn of day; (poet.) origin or first appearance of a thing; **- boreal,** north-light.

aurragado, da, *ăŭrrăgă' dŏ*, a. badly tilled.

ausencia, *ăŭsĕn' thĭă*, sf. absence. [self.

ausentarse, *-tăr' sĕ*, v. r. to absent one's

ausente, *ăŭsĕn' tĕ*, a. absent.

auspicio, *ăŭspē' thĭŏ*, sm. auspice; prediction; protection. [crabbed.

austero, ra, *ăŭstĕ' rŏ*, a. austere, severe;

austral, *ăŭstrăl'*, **austrino, na,** *-trē' nŏ*, a. austral, southern.

austro, *ăŭs' trŏ*, sm. south wind.

auténtica, *ăŭtĕn' tĭkă*, sf. certificate.

autenticar, *-tĭkăr'*, v. a. to authenticate.

autenticidad, *-tĭthĭdăd'*, sf. authenticity.

auténtico, ca, *ăŭtĕn' tĭkŏ*, a. authentic.

autillo, *ăŭtēl' yŏ*, sm. horned owl; secret auto-da-fe.

auto, *ăŭ' tŏ*, sm. judicial sentence; warrant, edict, ordinance; **- de fe,** auto-da-fe, sentence given by the Inquisition.

autocracia, *ăŭtŏkră' thĭă*, sf. autocracy.

autócrata, *ăŭtŏkră' tă*, sm. autocrat.

autógrafo, *ăŭtŏ' grăfŏ*, sm. autograph.

autómato, *-mă' tŏ*, sm. automaton.

autonomía, *ăŭtŏnŏmē' ă*, sf. autonomy.

autopsia, *-psē' ă*, sf. autopsy.

autor, *ăŭtŏr'*, sm. author; maker; writer.

autora, *ăŭtŏ' ră*, sf. authoress.

autorcillo, *ăŭtŏrthēl' yŏ*, sm. bad writer.

autoría, *ăŭtŏrē' ă*, sf. managership of a theatre.

autoridad, *ăŭtŏrĭdăd'*, sf. authority.

autoritativo, va, *-tătē' vŏ*, a. authoritative. [sation.

autorización, *ăŭtŏrĭthăthĭŏn'*, sf. authorization.

autorizar, *-thăr'*, v. a. to authorise.

autorzuelo, *ăŭtŏrthŭĕ' lŏ*, sm. scribbler.

auxiliar, *ăŭksēlĭăr'*, v. a. to aid, to help, to assist, to attend a dying person; **-,** a. auxiliary.

auxilio, *ăŭksē' lĭŏ*, sm. aid, help, assistance.

avadarse, *ăvădăr' sĕ*, v. r. to become fordable. [vainly boasting.

avalentado, da, *ăvălĕntă' dŏ*, a. bragging,

avalo, *ăvă' lŏ*, sm. slight shock; earthquake.

avalorar, *ăvălŏrăr'*, v. a. to estimate, to value; to heighten the value of a thing; to inspirit, to animate.

avambrazo, *ărămbră' thŏ*, sm. fore-arm.

avance, *ăvăn' thĕ*, sm. (mil.) advance, attack.

avantrén, *ăvăntrĕn'*, sm. (mil.) limbers of a gun-carriage.

avanzada, *-thă' dă*, sf. (mil.) vanguard.

avanzar, *-thăr'*, v. a. & n. to advance.

avanzo, *ăvăn' thŏ*, sm. (com.) balance.

avaricia, *ăvărē' thĭă*, sf. avarice.

avariento, ta, *-rĭen' tŏ*, a. avaricious, covetous.

avaro, ra, *ăvă' rŏ*, a. avaricious, miserly.

avasallar, *ăvăsălyăr'*, v. a. to subdue, to enslave.

ave, *ă' vĕ*, sf. bird; fowl. [enslave.

avechucho, *-tshŭtsh' ŏ*, sm. sparrow-hawk; ragamuffin.

avecindar, *ăvĕthĭndăr'*, v. a. to admit to the privileges of a citizen; **-se,** to approach, to join. [than one's age.

avejentar, *-hĕntăr'*, v. n. to look more

avejigar, *-hĭgăr'*, v. a. to blister

avellana, *ăvĕlyă' nă*, sf. filbert, hazel-nut.

avellanar, *ăvĕlyănăr'*, sm. plantation of hazels. [grow as dry as a nut.

avellanarse, *-năr' sĕ*, v. r. to shrivel, to

avellano, *ăvĕlyă' nŏ*, sm. hazel-nut tree.

Ave María, *ăvĕ mărē' ă*, sf. Ave, the angelic salutation of the Holy Virgin.

avena, ăvē'nă, sf. oats.
avenamiento, -měen'tŏ, sm. drainage.
avenar, ăvěnăr', v. a. to drain or draw off
avenate, -nă'tě, sm. water-gruel. [water.
avenencia, -něn'thiă, sf. agreement, bargain; union, concord.
aveníceo, cea, -nē'theŏ, a. oaten.
avenida, ăvěnē'dă, sf. flood, inundation; concurrence of several things.
avenido, da, -ně'dŏ, a. agreed.
avenir, -nĭr', v. a. to reconcile; to accommodate; to get reconciled; to join, to consent. [fire-fan.
aventador, ăvěntădŏr', sm. winnower; fan;
aventadura, -dō'ră, sf. wind-gall.
aventajado, da, -hă'dŏ, a. advantageous, profitable; beautiful, excellent.
aventajar, -hăr', v. a. to surpass, to excel. [to be puffed up.
aventar, ăvěntăr', v. a. to fan; to expel; -se,
aventura, -tō'ră, sf. adventure, event, incident; chance. [risk.
aventurar, -tŭrăr', v. a. to venture, to adventure.
aventurero, ra, -tŭră'rŏ, a. adventurous.
avergonzar, ăvěrgŏnthăr', v. a. to shame, to abash; -se, to be ashamed.
avería, ăvěrē'ă, sf. (mar.) average, damage by sea; aviary. [sea-water.
averiado, da, ăvěrĭă'dŏ, a. damaged by
averiarse, ăvěrĭăr'sě, v. r. to suffer damage at sea. [gation.
averiguación, ăvěrĭgŭăthiŏn', sf. investi-
averiguar, -găr', v. a. to inquire, to investigate, to explore. [of birds.
averío, ăvěrē'ŏ, sm. beast of burden; flight
averno, ăvěr'nŏ, sm. (poet.) hell.
aversión, ăvěrsiŏn', sf. aversion, dislike; abhorrence.
avestruz, ăvěstrūth', sm. ostrich.
aviar, ăvĭăr', v. a. to provision, to provide for a journey; to accoutre; to hasten the execution of a thing; -se, to get ready.
avidez, ăvĭděth', sf. covetousness. [ous.
ávido, da, ă'vĭdŏ, a. (poet.) greedy, covet-
aviejarse, ăvĭě'hăr'sě, v. r. to grow old.
aviento, ăvĭěn'tŏ, sm. winnowing-fork.
avieso, sa, ăvĭě'sŏ, a. irregular, out of the way; mischievous, perverse.
avigorar, ăvĭgŏrăr', v. a. to inspire with vigour and spirit. [ness.
avilantez, -lăntěth', sf. forwardness, bold-
avillanado, da, ăvĭlyănă'dŏ, a. clownish, mean, vile, base. [debase.
avillanar, -yănăr', v. a. to villainise, to
avinado, da, ăvĭnă'dŏ, a. tasting or smelling of wine. [peevish, bad-tempered.
avinagrado, da, -gră'dŏ, a. crabbed,
avinagrar, -grăr', v. a. to acidify.
avío, ăvē'ŏ, sm. preparation, provision.
avión, ăvĭŏn', sm. house-swallow.
avisado, da, ăvĭsă'dŏ, a. prudent, cautious; sagacious, skilful; mal —, ill advised, injudicious. [notice; to admonish.
avisar, -săr', v. a. to inform, to give
aviso, ăvē'sŏ, sm. information, intelligence, notice; warning, hint; prudence; care; [counsel.
avispa, ăvĭs'pă, sf. wasp.

avispado, da, -pă'dŏ, a. lively, brisk, vivacious. [peevish.
avispar, -păr', v. a. to spur; -se, to be
avispero, -pě'rŏ, sm. wasps' nest.
avispón, -pŏn', sm. hornet.
avistar, ăvĭstăr', v. a. to descry at a distance; to have an interview, to transact business. [victual.
avituallar, ăvĭtŭălyăr', v. a. (mil.) to
avivar, ăvĭvăr', v. a. to quicken, to enliven, to encourage. [narrowly.
avizorar, ăvĭthŏrăr', v. a. to spy, to search
avocar, ăvŏkăr', v. a. to carry a law-suit into a superior court.
avucasta, ăvŭkăs'tă, sf. widgeon (ave).
avutarda, -tăr'dă, sf. bustard, wild turkey.
axioma, ăksĭŏ'mă, sm. axiom, maxim.
¡ay! ăĭ, alas! ¡— de mí! alas! poor me!
aya, ă'yă, sf. governess, instructress.
ayer, ăyěr', ad. yesterday; lately.
ayo, ă'yŏ, sm. tutor, governor.
ayuda, ăyō'dă, sf. help, aid; support; syringe; —, sm. deputy, assistant.
ayudante, ăyŭdăn'tě, sm. (mil.) adjutant, aid-de-camp. [sist, to further.
ayudar, ăyŭdăr', v. a. to tojaid, to help, to as-
ayunar, -năr', v. a. to fast, to abstain from food. [out knowledge.
ayunas, ăyō'năs, (en), ad. fastingly; with-
ayuno, ăyō'nŏ, sm. fast, abstinence from food; —, na, a. fasting.
ayunque, ăyŭn'kě, sm. anvil.
ayuntamiento, ăyŭntămĭěn'tŏ, sm. Spanish town-council.
ayustar, ăyŭstăr', v. a. (mar.) to bend two ends of a cable. [black.
azabachado, da, ăthăbătshă'dŏ, a. jet-
azabache, -bătsh'ě, sm jet.
azacán, -kăn', sm. water-carrier.
azacaya, -kă'yă, sf. water-pipe.
azada, ăthă'dă, sf. spade, hoe.
azadón, -dŏn', sm. pick-axe, grub-axe.
azafata, -fă'tă, sf. queen's waiting-woman.
azafrán, -frăn', sm. saffron.
azafranar, -frănăr', v. a. to dye with saffron.
azagador, -gădŏr', sm. cattle-path.
azahar, -hăr', sm. orange or lemon flower.
azainadamente, ăthăĭnădăměn'tě, ad. perfidiously; viciously.
azar, ăthăr', sm. unforeseen disaster, unexpected accident; unfortunate card or throw at dice; disappointment; impediment.
azarbe, ăthăr'bě, sm. irrigation-trench.
azarja, ăthăr'hă, sf. silk-reel.
azaroso, sa, -rŏ'sŏ, a. unlucky, ominous.
azaya, ăthă'yă, sf. silk-reel.
aznallo, ăthnăl'yŏ, sm. Scotch fir.
azoe, ă'thŏě, sm. (chem.) nitrogen.
azófar, ăthŏ'făr, sm. latten-brass.
azogadamente, ăthŏgădăměn'tě, ad. in a quick and restless manner
azogar, ăthŏgăr', v. a. to overlay with quick-silver; — la cal, to slake lime; -se, to suffer from quick-silver poisoning; to be in a state of agitation.

azogue, *ăthŏʹgĕ*, sm. quick-silver; –s, pl. ships which carry quick-silver. [works.

azoguería, *–gĕrĕʹă*, sf. amalgamating-

azolar, *ăthŏlărʹ*, v. a. to cut timber with a hatchet.

azor, *ăthŏrʹ*, sm. goshawk. [be agitated.

azorar, *–rārʹ*, v. a. to frighten, to terrify; to

azorrarse, *ăthŏrrārʹsĕ*, v. r. to feel a heaviness in the head.

azotacalles, *–tăkălʹyĕs*, sm. lounger, loafer; (am.) bummer. [flogging.

azotaina, *–tăʹĭnă*, sf. drubbing, sound

azotar, *–tārʹ*, v. a. to whip, to lash; to horsewhip. [a whip; calamity.

azote, *ăthŏʹtĕ*, sm. whip, lash given with

azotea, *ăthŏtĕʹă*, sf. platform, flat roof of a house.

azúcar, *ăthŏʹkăr*, sm. sugar; – de pilón, loaf-sugar; – piedra ó cande, sugar-candy; – terciado ó moreno, brown sugar. [fectioner.

azucarado, da, *ăthăkărăʹdŏ*, a. sugared;

azucarar, *–kărărʹ*, v. a. to sugar, to sweeten. [fectioner.

azucarero, *–kărĕʹrŏ*, sm. sugar-basin; con-

azucena, *ăthŭthĕʹna*, sf. white lily.

azud, *ăthŭdʹ*, sf. dam with a sluice or flood-gate. [tion.

azuda, *ăthŏʹdă*, sf. water-works for irriga-

azuela, *ăthŏĕʹlă*, sf. chip-axe.

azufaifa, *ăthŏfăiʹfă*, sf. jujube.

azufaifo, *–fŏ*, sm. jujube-tree.

azufrado, da, *ăthŏfrăʹdŏ*, a. whitened with sulphur; sulphurous. [phur.

azufrar, *–frărʹ*, v. a. to fumigate with sul-

azufre, *ăthŏʹfrĕ*, sm. sulphur, brimstone.

azufroso, sa, *–frŏʹsŏ*, a. sulphureous.

azul, *ăthŏlʹ*, a. blue; – celeste, sky blue; – subido, bright blue; – turquí, Turkish or deep blue.

azulado, da, *–lăʹdŏ*, a. azure, bluish.

azular, *–lărʹ*, v. a. to dye blue.

azulear, *–lĕărʹ*, v. n. to have a bluish tint.

azulejo, *–lĕʹhŏ*, sm. Dutch glazed tile painted with various colours.

azulenco, *–lĕnʹkŏ*, a. bluish.

azumbre, *ăthŭmʹbrĕ*, sf. liquid measure (half a gallon).

azutero, *ăthŏtĕʹrŏ*, sm. sluice-master.

azuzador, ra, *–thădŏrʹ*, sm. & f. instigator.

azuzar, *–thărʹ*, v. a. to set on dogs; to irritate, to stir up.

B.

baba, *băʹbă*, sf. drivel, slaver.

babada, *băbăʹdă*, sf. thigh-bone.

babadero, *–dăʹrŏ*, babador, *băbădŏrʹ*, sm. bib, chin-cloth. [from the mouth.

babaza, *băbăʹthă*, sf. slime; foam or froth

babear, *băbĕărʹ*, v. n. to drivel, to slaver.

babera, *–bĕʹră*, sf. chin-piece of a helmet; foolish, silly fellow.

babero, *–rŏ*, sm. chin-cloth.

babia, *băʹbĭă*, sf. estar en –, to be absent-minded or dreaming. [fellow.

babieca, *băbĭĕʹkă*, sm. ignorant, stupid

babilonia, *băbĭlŏʹnĭă*, sf. es una –, it is all uproar and confusion.

babosa, *băbŏʹsă*, sf. slug.

babosear, *băbŏsĕărʹ*, v. a. to beslaver.

baboso, sa, *băbŏʹsŏ*, a. drivelling, slavering.

babucha, *băbŏʹtshă*, sf. oriental slipper.

bacallao, *băkălyăʹŏ*, sm. ling, poor jack, cod-fish.

bacanales, *băkănăʹlĕs*, sf. pl. bacchanals.

bacante, *băkănʹtĕ*, sf. bacchant.

bacía, *băthĕʹă*, sf. basin; barber's basin.

bacinica, *băthĭnĕʹkă*, sf. chamber-pot for children.

báculo, *băʹkŭlŏ*, sm. walking-stick; support; – pastoral, bishop's crosier.

bachiller, *bătshĭlyĕrʹ*, sm. bachelor; –, a. garrulous, loquacious. [to prattle.

bachillerear, *bătshĭlyĕrĕărʹ*, v. n. to babble,

badajo, *bădăʹhŏ*, sm. clapper of a bell.

badana, *bădăʹnă*, sf. dressed sheep-skin.

badil, *bădĭlʹ*, badila, *bădĕʹlă*, sf. fire-shovel.

badulaque, *bădŭlăʹkĕ*, sm. stupid fellow.

bagaje, *băgăʹhĕ*, sm. beast of burden; army-baggage. [burden.

bagajero, *–hĕʹrŏ*, sm. driver of beasts of

bagatela, *–tĕʹlă*, sf. bagatelle, trifle.

bagazo, *băgăʹthŏ*, sm. sediment of grapes.

bahía, *băĕʹă*, sf. bay. [olives, palms, &c.

bailador, ra, *băĭlădŏrʹ*, sm. & f. dancer.

bailar, *–lărʹ*, v. n. to dance.

bailarín, ina, *–lărĕnʹ*, sm. & f. dancer.

baile, *băĭʹlĕ*, sm. dance, ball; bailiff.

bajá, *băhăʹ*, sm. bashaw, pacha.

baja, *băʹhă*, sf. fall, diminution; (mil.) ticket of admission into a hospital; (mil.) head of casualties in a muster-roll.

bajada, *băhăʹdă*, sf. descent; inclination.

bajamar, *băhămărʹ*, sf. low water.

bajar, *băhărʹ*, v. a. to lower, to let down; to abate (the price); to lessen; to humble; to bend downwards; –, v. n. to descend; to grow less; –se, to crouch, to lessen.

bajel, *băhĕlʹ*, sm. vessel, ship. [master.

bajelero, *–lĕʹrŏ*, sm. ship-owner, ship-

bajete, *băʹhătĕʹ*, sm. (mus.) barytone.

bajeza, *băʹhăʹthă*, sf. meanness, abject-ness; littleness; lowliness, fawningness.

bajío, *băʹhĕʹŏ*, sm. shoal, sand-bank, decline.

bajo, ja, *băʹhʹŏ*, a. low; abject, despicable; faint; common; dull (of colours); bent; –, pr. under, underneath, below; –, ad. low (of the voice); –, sm. (mus.) base; low place; –s, pl. under-petticoats of

bajón, *băʹhŏnʹ*, sm. bassoon. [women.

bajonero, *băʹhŏnăʹrŏ*, sm. player on the bassoon.

bala, *băʹlă*, sf. ball, bullet, shot; bale of paper; printer's inking-ball. [less.

baladí, *–dĕʹ*, a. mean, despicable, worth-

baladre, *băládʹrĕ*, sm. rose-bay.

baladrón, *–drŏnʹ*, sm. boaster, bully.

baladronada, *–drŏnăʹdă*, sf. boast, brag, bravado.

baladronear, -drōnēǎr, v. n. to boast, to brag.

bálago, bǎ'lǎgŏ, sm. hay-rick; soap-suds.

balance, bǎlǎn'thĕ, sm. fluctuation; equipoise; balance of accounts; rolling of a ship.

balancear, -thēǎr, v. a. & n. to balance; to roll; to hold in equipoise; to waver.

balancilla, -thĭl'yǎ, sf. gold-weights.

balancín, -thĭn', sm. swing-bar of a cart; minting-mill; rope-dancer's pole.

balandra, bǎlǎn'dra, sf. (mar.) bilander, sloop. [comparative estimate.

balanza, -thǎ, sf. scale; pair of scales;

balanzario, -thǎ'rĭŏ, sm. balancer.

balar, bǎlǎr', v. n. to bleat as a sheep.

balaustrada, bǎlǎūstrǎ'dǎ, sf. balustrade.

balaustre, bǎlǎūs'trĕ, sm. baluster.

balazo, bǎlǎ'thŏ, sm. shot. [stuttering.

balbuciente, bǎlbǎthĭěn'tĕ, a. stammering.

balcón, bǎlkŏn', sm. balcony. [conies.

balconaje, -kŏnǎ'h'ĕ, sm. range of balconies.

baldar, -dǎr', v. a. to cripple.

balde, bǎl'dĕ, sm. bucket; de -, ad. gratis, for nothing; en -, in vain.

baldés, bǎldĕs', sm. piece of dressed skin.

baldío, dia, -dē'ŏ, a. untilled, uncultivated.

baldón, -dŏn', sm. reproach, insult.

baldosa, -dŏ'sǎ, sf. fine square tile.

balería, bǎlĕrē'ǎ, sf. pile of balls or bullets.

balido, bǎlē'dŏ, sm. bleating, bleat.

balija, bǎlē'hǎ, sm. portmanteau, mail; post. [postman.

balijero, -'hǎ'rŏ, sm. country or local postman.

balín, bǎlĭn', sm. buck-shot. [goods.

balón, bǎlŏn', sm. large foot-ball; bale of goods.

baloncita, bǎlŏnthē'tǎ, sf. save-all.

balota, bǎlŏ'tǎ, sf. ballot.

balotada, -tǎ'dǎ, sf. ballotade (leap of a horse in which he shows the shoes of his hinder feet).

balsa, bǎl'sǎ, sf. pool; raft, float; ferry.

balsámico, ca, bǎlsǎ'mĭkŏ, a. balmy.

bálsamo, bǎl'sǎmŏ, sm. balsam, balm.

balsear, bǎlsēǎr', v. a. to cross rivers on ferries or floats.

balsero, bǎlsē'rŏ, sm. ferry-man.

balsopeto, bǎlsŏpǎ'tŏ, sm. large pouch carried near the breast; bosom.

baluarte, bǎlǔǎr'tĕ, sm. bastion; bulwark.

balumbo, bǎlǔm'bŏ, sm. bulk of things heaped together.

ballena, bǎlyǎ'nǎ, sf. whale; whale-bone.

ballenato, -nǎ'tŏ, sm. cub of a whale.

ballenero, bǎlyĕnē'rŏ, sm. (mar.) whaler.

ballesta, bǎlyĕs'tǎ, sf. crossbow; á tiro de -, at a great distance. [bow.

ballestada, -tǎ'dǎ, sf. shot from a crossbow.

ballestear, -tēǎr', v. a. to shoot with a crossbow. [hole.

ballestera, bǎlyĕstē'rǎ, sf. (mil.) loop-

ballestería, -tērĕ'ǎ, sf. archery; crossbows; crossbow-men.

ballestero, -tē'rŏ, sm. archer; crossbow-maker; king's armourer. [bow.

ballestilla, bǎlyĕstĭl'yǎ, sf. small cross-

bamba, bǎm'bǎ, sf. riding-chair.

bambalina, -lē'nǎ, sf. soffits of a theatre.

bambolear, bǎmbŏlēǎr', v. n. to reel.

bamboleo, -lē'ŏ, sm. reeling, staggering.

bambolla, bǎmbŏl'yǎ, sf. ostentation, vain show. [boo.

bambú, bǎmbŏ', **bambuo,** -k', sm. bamboo.

banana, bǎnǎ'nǎ, sf. banana, plantain.

banano, bǎnǎ'nŏ, sm. plantain-tree.

banasta, bǎnǎs'tǎ, sf. large basket.

banastero, -tǎ'rŏ, sm. basket-maker.

banasto, bǎnǎs'tŏ, sm. large round basket.

banca, bǎn'kǎ, sf. bench; washing-box.

bancal, bǎnkǎl', sm. garden-bed, parterre; carpet.

bancarrota, bǎnkǎrrŏ'tǎ, sf. bankruptcy.

banco, bǎn'kŏ, sm. bench; carpenter's bench; bench of rowers; bank.

banda, bǎn'dǎ, sf. sash; ribbon; band of troops; party; gang; crew; covey; bank.

bandada, -dǎ'dǎ, sf. covey. [border.

bandearse, -dēǎr'sĕ, v. r. to shift for one's

bandeja, -dē'h'ǎ, sf. salver. [self.

bandera, -dǎ'rǎ, sf. banner, standard, flag.

banderilla, bǎndĕrĭl'yǎ, sf. small decorated dart used at a bull-fight.

banderillear, -rĭlyēǎr', v. a. to plant banderillas in a bull's neck or shoulder.

banderillero, -rĭlyǎ'rŏ, sm. thrower of banderillas.

banderín, -rĭn', sm. cockade.

banderizo, za, -rē'thŏ, a. factious.

banderola, -rŏ'lǎ, sf. bannerol. [man.

bandido, bǎndē'dŏ, sm. bandit, highway-

bando, bǎn'dŏ, sm. faction, party.

bandolera, -lē'rǎ, sf. bandeleer.

bandolero, -lē'rŏ, sm. highwayman.

bandolín, -lĭn', sm. (mus.) mandolin.

bandullo, bǎndǔl'yŏ, sm. belly.

bandurria, -dǔr'rĭǎ, sf. bandore (musical instrument resembling a fiddle).

banquero, -kē'rŏ, sm. banker.

banqueta, -kē'tǎ, sf. three-legged stool.

banquete, -kē'tĕ, sm. banquet.

baña, bǎn'yǎ, sf., **bañadero,** -dǎ'rŏ, sm. pool, puddle (in which wild boars wallow).

bañar, bǎnyǎr', v. a. to bathe; to tub; to water, to irrigate; to candy; to wash over a painting with a second coat of transparent colours.

bañero, -yǎ'rŏ, sm. bath-keeper.

baño, bǎn'yŏ, sm. bath; bathing-place; bathing-tub; varnish; crust of sugar; coat of paint put over another.

baqueta, bǎkě'tǎ, sf. ramrod, gun-stick; drumstick; (mil.) gantlet. [falling body.

baquetazo, -tǎ'thŏ, sm. heavy thud of a

baqueteado, da, -tēǎ'dŏ, a. inured, habituated.

báquico, ca, bǎ'kĭkŏ, a. bacchanal.

baraja, bǎrǎ'h'ǎ, sf. complete pack of cards.

barajadura, -dŏ'rǎ, sf. shuffling of cards.

barajar, bǎrǎ'hǎr', v. a. to shuffle cards; to entangle. [trade, small railing.

barandilla, bǎrǎndĭl'yǎ, sf. small balus-

baratero, bǎrǎtě'rŏ, sm. card-sharper, black-leg.

baratijas, -tĭ'h'ǎs, sf. pl. trifles, toys.

baratillero, -tĭlyǎ'rŏ, sm. fripperer.

baratillo, —tīl'yŏ, sm. frippery.

barato, ta, bārā'tŏ, a. cheap; de —, gratis; —, sm. cheapness, low price; money given by the winners at a gaming-table to the by-standers as part of the gain.

baratura, —tō'rā, sf. cheapness.

baraúnda, bārāūn'dā, sf. noise, hurly-burly.

barba, bār'bā, sf. chin; beard; — á —, face to face; —, sm. actor who personates old men.

barbacana, —kā'nā, sf. (mil.) barbican.

barbada, —bā'dā, sf. beard of a horse; dab (fish).

barbar, bārbār', v. n. to grow a beard; to rear or keep bees; to take root.

barbaridad, —rīdād', sf. barbarity, barbarism; rashness; rudeness.

barbarie, —rīē, sf. barbarism; rusticity.

barbarismo, —rīs'mŏ, sm. barbarism (form of speech); (poet.) crowd of barbarians.

bárbaro, ra, bār'bārŏ, a. barbarous; rash, bold, daring; rude, unpolished.

barbechar, bārbētshār', v. a. to plough.

barbechera, —tshā'rā, sf. series of successive ploughings.   [fallow.

barbecho, bārbētsh'ŏ, sm. first ploughing.

barbería, bārbērē'ā, sf. barber's shop.

barbero, —bā'rŏ, sm. barber.   [rope.

barbeta, —bā'tā, sf. (mar.) rackline; ring-

barbiblanco, ca, bārbīblān'kŏ, a. white-bearded.

barbicano, na, —kā'nŏ, a. grey-beard.

barbihecho, —ētsh'ŏ, a. fresh shaved.

barbilampiño, ña, —lāmpīn'yŏ, a. thin bearded.

barbilucio, cia, —lō'thĭŏ, a. pretty, genteel.

barbilla, bārbĭl'yā, sf. chin-point.

barbinegro, gra, bārbīnā'grŏ, a. black-bearded.

barbirrubio, bia, —rō'bĭŏ, a. red-bearded.

barbo, bār'bŏ, sm. barbel.   [strong beard.

barbón, bārbŏn', sm. man with a thick,

barbosa, bārbō'sā, sf. layer, provine.

barbote, bārbō'tē, sm. chin-cloth.

barbudo, da, bārbū'dŏ, a. long-bearded.

barbulla, bārbŭl'yā, sf. confused noise.

barbullar, —lyār', v. a. to paint badly; to dirty; to talk confusedly and disorderly.

barbullón, ona, —lyŏn', a. loud talking; babel of tongues.

barca, bār'kā, sf. boat, barge.

barcada, bārkā'dā, sf. passage in a ferry-boat; boat full of persons or goods.

barcaje, bārkā'h'ē, sm. fare.

barco, bār'kŏ, sm. boat, barge; bark.

barda, bār'dā, sf. bard.

bardal, bārdāl', sm. mud-wall, covered at the top with straw, brush or fence-wood.

bardana, bārdā'nā, sf. common burdock.

bardar, bārdār', v. a. to cover the top of walls with straw or brushwood.

barga, bār'gā, sf. steepest part of a declivity.

baritono, bārē'tŏnŏ, sm. (mus.) baritone.

barloar, bārlŏār', v. n. (mar.) to grapple for the purpose of boarding.

barloventear, bārlŏvēntēār', v. n. (mar.) to tack, to tack about.   [gage.

barlovento, —vēn'tŏ, sm. (mar.) weather-

barniz, bārnĭth', sm. varnish; Japan paint; printer's ink.

barnizar, —nĭthār', v. a. to varnish.

barómetro, bārō'mētrŏ, sm. barometer.

barón, bārŏn', sm. baron.

baronesa, bārŏnē'ā, sf. baroness.

baronía, bārŏnē'ā, sf. barony; baronage.

barquear, bārkēār', v. n. to cross in a boat.

barquero, bārkā'rŏ, sm. bargeman.

barquilla, bārkĭl'yā, sf. (mar.) log; thin boat-formed pastry-cake.

barquillero, —yā'rŏ, sm. wafer-baker.

barquillo, —yŏ, sm. wafer.

barquín, bārkĭn', sm. large bellows for furnaces.   [body.

barquinazo, —ā'thŏ, sm. thud of a falling

barquino, bārkē'nŏ, sm. wine-bag.

barra, bār'rā, sm. crowbar, lever; ingot of gold, silver, &c.; rock, sandbank; de — á —, from place to place.   [trigue.

barrabasada, —bāsā'dā, sf. trick, plot, in-

barraca, bārrā'kā, sf. hut (for soldiers or for fishermen).   [timber.

barraganete, bārrāgānā'tē, sm. top-

barranca, bārrān'kā, sf. deep break made by mountain-floods; cleft, glen.

barranco, —rān'kŏ, sm. gill; (fig.) great difficulty, embarrassment.

barrancoso, sa, bārrānkŏ'sŏ, a. full of breaks and holes.

barrar, bārrār', **barrear,** bārrēār', v. a. to barricade, to fortify.   [turn-pike.

barreda, bārrā'dā, **barrera,** bārrā'rā, sf.

barredero, —dā'rŏ, sm. mop.

barreduras, bārrēdō'rās, s. pl. sweepings; remains, residue.

barrena, bārrā'nā, sf. borer, gimlet, auger.

barrenar, —nār', v. a. to bore; (fig.) to frustrate one's designs.   [dust-man.

barrendero, bārrēndā'rŏ, sm. sweeper,

barreno, bārrā'nŏ, sm. large borer; hole made with a borer or auger.

barreño, bārrēn'yŏ, sm. earthen pan; tub.

barrer, bārrēr', v. a. to sweep; to carry off the whole.   [turn-pike.

barrera, bārrā'rā, sf. clay-pit; barrier;

barrero, —rā'rŏ, sm. potter; clay-pit.

barretear, —tēār', v. a. to bar; to line the inside of shoes.

barretero, bārrētā'rŏ, sm. one who works with a crowbar, wedge or pick (in mines).

barriada, bārrĭā'dā, sf. suburb, ward of a city.

barrica, bārrē'kā, sf. keg, small barrel.

barricada, —kā'dā, sf. barricade.

barrido, —rē'dŏ, sm. sweep

barriga, —rē'gā, sf. abdomen, belly; pregnancy; (mar.) middle part of a vessel.

barrigudo, da, —gō'dŏ, a. big-bellied.

barril, bārrĭl', sm. barrel, jug.

barrilame, bārrĭlā'mē, sm., **barrilería,** bārrĭlērē'ā, sf. number of barrels collected in one place.

barrilero, bārrĭlā'rŏ, sm. cooper.

barrilete, —ā'tē, sm. (mar.) mouse; keg; holdfast.   [rilla.

barrilla, —rĭl'yā, sf. (bot.) salt-wort, ba-

barrillar, —yār', sm. barrilla-pits.

barrillón, -yŏn', sm. brine-prover.

barrio, bār'rĭō, sm. district of a town.

barrizal, bārrĭhāl', sm. clay-pit.

barro, bār'rŏ, sm. clay, mud.

barroso, sa, bārrŏ'sŏ, a. muddy.

barrote, bārrŏ'tĕ, sm. iron-work of doors, windows, tables; ledge of timber.

barrueco, bārrŭā'kŏ, sm. pearl of irregular shape. [turer.

barruntador, bārrŭntādŏr', sm. conjec-

barruntamiento, -mĭĕn'tŏ, sm. conjecture, guess. [jecture.

barruntar, -tār', v. a. to foresee, to con-

barrunto, -rŭn'tŏ, sm. conjecture. [ness.

bártulos, bār'tŭlŏs, sm. pl. affairs, busi-

barzón, bārthŏn', sm. idle walk.

barzonear, bārthŏnĕār', v. n. to loiter.

basa, bā'sā, sf. basis, base.

basada, bāsā'dā, sf. crane, derrick.

basalto, bāsāl'tŏ, sm basalt, basaltes.

basca, bās'kā, sf. squeamishness, nausea.

bascosidad, bāskŏsĭdād'', sf. nastiness, filth.

base, bā'sĕ, sf. base, basis.

basílica, bāsĭ'lĭkā, sf. basilica (cathedral).

basilisco, bāsĭlĭs'kŏ, sm. basilisk, cockatrice.

basquear, bāskĕār', v. n. to be squeamish.

basquiña, bāskĭn'yā, sf. upper petticoat worn by Spanish women.

basta, bās'tā, sf. basting.

bastante, bāstān'tĕ, a. sufficient, enough.

bastar, bāstār', v. n. to suffice, to be proportioned to something, to be enough.

bastarda, bāstār'dā, sf. bastard-file, italic (type). [bastardize.

bastardear, -dĕār', v. n. to degenerate, to

bastardía, -dē'ā, sf. bastardy; meanness.

bastardo, da, -tār'dŏ, a. bastard, spurious; -, sm. bastard. [sew slightly.

bastear, bāstĕār', v. a. to stitch loosely, to

bastero, bāstĕ'rŏ, sm. maker and seller of pack-saddles.

bastidor, bāstĭdŏr', sm. embroidery-frame; side-scene; -es, pl. scenery (on the stage).

bastilla, bāstĭl'yā, sf. hem, seam.

bastimentar, bāstĭmĕntār', v. a. to supply with provisions.

bastimentero, -tĕ'rŏ, sm. purveyor.

bastimento, -mĕn'tŏ, sm. supply of provisions; (mar.) vessel.

bastión, bāstĭŏn', sm. (mil.) bastion.

basto, bās'tŏ, sm. pack-saddle for beasts of burden; -, ta, a. coarse, rude, unpolished.

bastón, bāstŏn', sm. cane, stick; truncheon; staff of command; military command.

bastonazo, bāstŏnā'thŏ, sm. bastinado.

bastoncillo, -thĭl'yŏ, sm. narrow lace.

bastonear, -nĕār', v. a. to stir must with a stick to prevent its becoming ropy.

bastonero, -nĕ'rŏ, sm. marshal or manager of a ball, steward of a feast; assistant jail-keeper. [four suits at cards.

bastos, bās'tŏs, sm. pl. clubs, one of the

basura, bāsŏ'rā, sf. sweepings; dung, ordure.

basurero, -rĕ'rŏ, sm. dustman; dung-hill.

bata, bā'tā, sf. morning-gown; refuse of silk.

batacazo, -kā'thŏ, sm. noise of a fall.

batahola, bataola, -ŏ'lā, sf. hurly-burly, bustle. [agitation of the mind.

batalla, bātāl'yā, sf. battle, combat, fight;

batallador, bātālyādŏr', sm. combatant, warrior. [to fence with foils; to dispute.

batallar, -yār', v. n. to battle, to fight;

batallón, -yŏn', sm. (mil.) battalion.

batán, bātān', sm. fulling-mill.

batanar, -nār', v. a. to full cloth.

batanear, -nĕār', v. a. to beat, to handle roughly.

batanero, -nĕ'rŏ, sm. fuller. [roughly.

batata, bātā'tā, sf. Spanish potato.

batea, bātĕ'ā, sf. painted tray or hamper of japanned wood; washing-trough.

batería, bātĕrē'ā, sm. battery; impression made on the mind or body.

batera, bātĕ'rā, sf. mantua-maker.

batida, bātē'dā, sf. battue (chase).

batidera, bātĭdĕ'rā, sf. beater (instrument for beating and mixing mortar.)

batidero, -dĕ'rŏ, sm. clashing of one thing against another; collision; uneven ground.

batido, da, bātē'dŏ, a. changeable (applied to silks); benten (as roads), -, sm. batter of flour and water for making the host; wafers, biscuits.

batidor, -dŏr', sm. scout; ranger; outrider; one of the life-guards, who rides before a royal coach; - de oro, gold-beater.

batiente, bātĭĕn'tĕ, sm. jamb or post of a door.

batihoja, bātĭŏ'k'ā, sm. gold-beater; artisan who works iron and other metal into sheets; warp of cloth.

batir, bātĭr', v. a. to beat, to dash; to clash, to clap; to demolish; to move in a violent manner; to strike (of the sun).

batista, bātĭs'tā, sf. batiste, cambric.

baturrillo, bātŭrrĭl'yŏ, sm. hotch-potch, salmagundi.

baúl, bāŭl', sm. trunk; belly.

bauprés, bāŭprĕs', sm. (mar.) bow-sprit.

bausán, ana, bāŭsān', sm. & f. guy; fool; idiot.

bautismal, bāŭtĭsmāl', a. baptismal.

bautismo, bāŭtĭs'mŏ, sm. baptism.

bautisterio, -tĕ'rĭŏ, sm. baptistery.

bautizar, bāŭtĭthār', v. a. to baptise, to christen.

bautizo, bāŭtĭ'thŏ, sm. baptism.

baya, bā'yā, sf. berry; busk, cod.

bayeta, bāyĕ'tā, sf. baize (kind of cloth).

bayetón, -tŏn', sm. coating.

bayo, ya, bā'yŏ, a. bay (of a horse).

bayoneta, bāyŏnĕ'tā, sf. bayonet.

bayonetazo, -nĕtā'thŏ, sm. thrust with a bayonet.

baza, bā'thā, sf. card-trick. [bayonet.

bazo, bā'thŏ, sm. spleen, milt. [wash.

bazofia, bāthŏ'fĭā, sf. offal; refuse; hog-

bazucar, bāthŭkār', v. a. to stir liquids by shaking. [by shaking.

bazuqueo, -kĕ'ŏ, sm. stirring of liquids

be, bĕ, baa (cry of sheep). [methodist.

beata, bĕā'tā, sf. sister of charity; rank

beatería, bĕātĕrē'ā, sf. bigotry.

beaterio, -tā'rĭŏ, sm. house of sisters of charity. [tion.
beatificación, -tĭfĭkáthĭŏn', sf. beatifica-
beatificar, -tĭfĭkár', v. a. to beatify; to hallow, to sanctify, to make blessed.
beatífico, ca, -tĭfĭkŏ, a. beatific.
beatilla, -tĭl'yă, sf. French lawn.
beatísimo, ma, -tĭsĭmŏ, a. most holy; - padre, sm. most holy father (the pope).
beatitud, -tĭtŭd', sf. beatitude, blessedness.
beato, ta, bĕá'tŏ, a. happy, blessed; devout; -, sm. religionist; pious person.
bebedero, bĕbĕdā'rŏ, sm. drinking-trough; place where birds resort to drink.
bebedizo, za, -dē'thŏ, a. drinkable.
bebedizo, -, sm. love-potion.
bebedor, ra, bĕbĕdŏr', sm. & f. tippler.
bobor, bĕbŏr', v. a. to drink. [drunkard.
bebida, bĕbē'dă, sf. drink, beverage.
bebido, da, -dŏ, bien -, drunk.
bebistrajo, bĕbĭstră'h'ŏ, sm. bad drink, cat-lap, washy stuff, water bewitched.
beborretear, bĕbŏrrĕtēár', v. a. to sip.
beca, bā'kă, sf. part of a collegian's dress in the shape of an oar, which is worn over the gown; fellowship; allowance, scholarship; -s, pl. strips of velvet, &c. with which the forepart of cloaks is lined by way of ornament.
becabunga, -bŭn'gă, sf. (bot.) brook-lime.
becada, bĕkă'dă, sf. wood-cock.
becafigo, -fē'gŏ, sm. fig-pecker.
becerra, bĕthĕr'ră, sm. (bot.) snap-dragon.
becerrillo, -rĭl'yŏ, sm. calf; dressed calf-skin.
becerro, -thĕr'rŏ, sm. yearling calf; calf-skin; register in which are entered the privileges and appurtenances of cathedral churches and convents; the Golden Book of the Castilian nobility at Simancas; - marino, sea-calf.
bedel, bĕdĕl', sm. beadle.
bedelia, bĕdĕl'ĭ ă, sf. beadleship.
bederre, bĕdĕr'rĕ, sm. (cant) hangman.
bedija, bĕdĭ'h'ă, sf. flock of wool.
bedilla, bĕdĭl'yă, sf. woollen bed-cloth.
befa, bĕ'fă, sf. jeer, scoff, mock; garland.
befar, bĕfár', v. a. to mock, to ridicule.
befo, fa, bā'fŏ, a. blubber-lipped.
bejucal, bĕ'hŭkăl', sm. reed-plot, reed-bank. [India).
bejuco, -h'ŏ'kŏ, sm. reed (growing in India).
bejuquillo, -'hăkĭl'yŏ, sm. small gold chain. [chain.
beldad, bĕldăd', sf. beauty.
beleño, bĕlĕn'yŏ, sm. (bot.) hen-bane.
bélico, ca, bĕ'lĭkŏ, a. warlike, martial.
belicoso, sa, -kŏ'sŏ, a. martial, pugnacious.
beligerante, -'hĕrăn'tĕ, a. belligerent.
bellacamente, bĕlyăkămĕn'tĕ, ad. knavishly, roguishly. [ning, roguish.
bellaco, ca, -yă'kŏ, a. artful, sly, cunning, roguish.
belladama, -dă'mă, belladona, -dŏ'nă, sf. (bot.) deadly night-shade.
bellaquear, -kĕár', v. a. to cheat, to play roguish tricks.
bellaquería, -kĕr'ĭ ă, sf. knavery, roguery.
belleza, bĕlyă'thă, sf. beauty.

bello, lla, bĕl'yŏ, a. beautiful, handsome, fair, fine; perfect.
bellota, bĕlyŏ'tă, sf. acorn; smelling-bottle (in the shape of an acorn).
bellote, -tĕ, sm. large round-headed nail.
bellotear, -tĕár', v. n. to feed on acorns (applied to swine).
bellotera, -tă'ră, sf. acorn season.
bemol, bĕmŏl', sm. (mus.) b-flat.
bendecir, bĕndĕthĭr', v. a. to consecrate; to praise, to exalt.
bendición, -dĭthĭŏn', sf. benediction.
bendito, ta, -dĕ'tŏ, a. saint, blessed; simple, silly.
bendicite, bĕndĕ'thĭtĕ, sm. grace at meals; clergyman's leave of absence.
benedictino, bĕnĕdĭktē'nŏ, benito, bĕnē'tŏ, sm. Benedictine.
beneficencia, -fĭthĕn'thĭă, sf. beneficence.
beneficiado, -fĭthĭá'dŏ, sm. incumbent of a benefice, beneficiary.
beneficiador, -fĭthĭădŏr', sm. benefactor; improver, careful administrator.
beneficiar, -fĭthĭár', v. a. to benefit; to work and improve mines.
beneficiario, -fĭthĭá'rĭŏ, sm. beneficiary.
beneficio, -fē'thĭŏ, sm. benefit, favour, kindness, labour, culture; profit, benefit-night, - curado, benefice to which a curacy is attached.
benéfico, ca, bĕnĕ'fĭkŏ, a. beneficent, kind.
benemérito, ta, bĕnĕmĕ'rĭtŏ, a. meritorious. [approbation.
beneplácito, -plă'thĭtŏ, sm. good-will, approbation.
benevolencia, -vŏlĕn'thĭă, sf. benevolence, well-wishing.
benévolo, la, bĕnĕ'vŏlŏ, a. benevolent, favourable, kind-hearted.
benignidad, bĕnĭgnĭdăd'', sf. benignity; mildness of the weather. [mild.
benigno, na, bĕnĭg'nŏ, a. benign; kind, mild.
beodo, da, bĕŏ'dŏ, a. drunk, drunken.
berberis, bĕrbĕrĭs', sm. barberry, berberry.
Bercebú, bĕrthĕbŏ', sm. (fam.) the devil.
bergamota, -gămŏ'tă, sf. bergamot (sort of pear). [mŏ'tĕ, sm. bergamot-tree.
bergamote, -gămŏ'tĕ, bergamoto, -gă-
bergante, -găn'tĕ, sm. brazen-faced villain, ruffian.
bergantín, -găntĭn', sm. (mar.) brig.
beril, bĕrĭl', sm. beryl, a precious stone.
berlina, -lē'nă, sf. landau, berlin.
bermejear, -mĕ'hĕár', v. n. to incline to red.
bermejizo, za, -mĕ'hē'thŏ, a. reddish.
bermejo, ja, -mĕ'h'ŏ, a. crimson.
bermejura, -mĕ'hŭ'ră, sf. crimson.
bermellón, -mĕlyŏn', sm. vermilion.
bernardinas, -nărdē'năs, sf. pl. fanfaronade, false boasts.
bernardo, -năr'dŏ, sm. Bernardine monk.
berra, bĕr'ră, sf. coarse water-cress plant.
berrear, -rĕár', v. n. to low, to bellow.
berrenchín, -rĕntshĭn', sm. crying of angry children. [different colours.
berrendo, da, -rĕn'dŏ, a. tinged with two different colours.
berrido, -rē'dŏ, sm. bellowing of a calf.
berrín, -rĭn', sm. child in a violent passion.

berrinche, -rīn'tshě, sm. anger, passion, sulkiness (applied to children).

berrizal, -rĭthăl', sm. place full of water-cress.

berro, bĕr'rō, sm. water-cress. [cress.

berroqueño, ña, bĕrrōkĕn'yō, a. granite-like; piedra - a, granite.

berruga, bĕrrō gā, sf. wart.

berza, -thā, sf cabbage.

besamanos, bĕsāmā'nōs, sm. kissing of hands; levee; court-day.

besar, bĕsăr', v a. to kiss; to knock up against one another; -se, to knock one's head against another's.

beso, bĕ'sō, sm. kiss; collision of persons or things. [idiot.

bestia, bĕs'tiā, sf. beast; animal; dunce.

bestiaje, bĕstiā'h'ĕ, sm. herd of beasts of burden.

bestial, bĕstiăl', a. bestial, brutal.

bestialidad, -lidăd'', sf. bestiality.

besugo, bĕsō'gō, sm. sea-bream.

besuqueo, bĕsōkĕ'ō, sm. repeated kisses.

betún, bĕtūn', sm. bitumen.

bezar, bĕthăr', sf. bezoar (stone).

bezo, bĕ'thō, sm. blubber-lip; proud flesh in a wound

biazas, biā'thās, sf pl. leather-saddlebags.

Biblia, bē'bliā, sf. Bible.

bíblico, ca, bĕ'blĭkō, a. biblical. [worm.

bibliófilo, bĭblĭō'fĭlō, sm book-lover, book-

bibliografía, bĭblĭōgrăfĭ'ā, sf. bibliography. [graphical.

bibliográfico, ca, -grā'fĭkō, a. biblio-

bibliógrafo, bĭblĭō'grăfō, sm. biblio-grapher

bibliómano, na, -mā'nō, a. bibliomaniac.

biblioteca, -lĕ'kā, sf. library.

bibliotecario, -tĕkā'rĭō, sm. librarian

bicoca, bĭkō'kā, sf. sentry-box; small borough or village; thing of little value.

bicho, bĭ'tshō, sm. vermin, hop o' my thumb; mal -, mischievous urchin.

bichón, bĭtshōn', sm. lap-dog.

bielda, bĭĕl'dā, sf. pitchfork with six or seven prongs.

bieldar, -dăr', v. a. to winnow corn.

bieldo, bĭĕl'dō, bielgo, bĭĕl'gō, sm. win-nowing-fork

bien, bĭĕn', sm. good, utility, benefit; welfare; -es, pl. property, riches, land; —, ad. well, right; very; willingly, heartily; - que, although; - está, very well.

bienal, bĭĕnăl', a. biennial. [ity, success.

bienandanza, bĭĕnăndān'thā, sf prosper-

bienaventurado, da, -āvĕntūrā'dō, a. blessed, happy, fortunate, simple, silly.

bienaventuranza, -āvĕntūrăn'thā, sf beatitude; prosperity; -s, pl. the eight beatitudes of heaven mentioned in the Scriptures.

bienestar, -ĕstăr', sm. well-being.

bienhablado, da, -āblā'dō, a. well and civilly spoken.

bienhadado, da, -ādā'dō, a. lucky, happy.

bienhecho, cha, -ĕtsh'ō, a. well-shaped.

bienhechor, ra, -ĕtshōr', sm. & f. bene-factor.

bienio, bĭĕ'nĭō, sm. space of two years.

bienquisto, ta, bĭĕnkĭs'tō, a. generally esteemed and beloved.

bienvenida, -vĕnĭ'dā, sf. welcome.

bigamia, bĭgā'mĭā, sf. bigamy.

bígamo, bĕ'gāmō, sm. bigamist. [tiously.

bigardear, bĭgārdĕăr', v n. to live licen-

bigardía, -dĕ'ā, sf. dissoluteness; trick, turn, jest. [morals; lubber.

bigardo, bĭgăr'dō, sm. friar of loose

bigornia, bĭgōr'nĭā, sf anvil.

bigote, bĭgō'tĕ, sm. whisker, mustachio; tener -s, to be firm and undaunted.

bilioso, sa, bĭlĭō'sō, a. bilious.

bilis, bĕ'lĭs, sf. bile.

bilorta, bĭlōr'tā, sm. ring of twisted willow; cricket (among country people).

billar, bĭl'yăr', sm. billiards, pl.

billear, bĭlyĕăr', v. a. to make cannons (at billiards).

billero, bĭlyă'rō, sm. billiard-player

billete, bĭlyĕ'tĕ, sm. billet, label, esquela, (rail.) ticket, railway-ticket; - directo, through-ticket; - de ida y vuelta, return-ticket.

bimestre, bĭmĕs'trĕ, a. of two months' duration; —, sm. two months leave of absence. [ground for the second time.

binar, bĭnăr', v. a. to plough a piece of

binario, bĭnā'rĭō, sm. binary

binazón, bĭnăthōn', sf ploughing.

binóculo, bĭnō'kŭlō, sm. opera-glass.

biografía, bĭōgrăfĭ'ā, sf. biography.

biógrafo, bĭō'grăfō, sm. biographer.

biombo, bĭōm'bō, sm. screen.

bípedo, bĕ'pĕdō, sm biped.

biricú, bĕrĭkō', sm. sword-belt.

birla, bĭr'lā, sf. bowl for playing.

birlar, -lăr', v. n. to knock down at one blow (at nine-pins); to dispossess.

birlocha, -lōtsh'ā, sf paper-kite.

birlocho, -lōtsh'ō, sm. barouche.

birreta, bĭrrĕ'tā, sf cardinal's red cap.

birretina, bĭrrĕtĭ'nā, sf. grenadier's cap.

bisabuela, -bisăbū'lā, sf. great-grandmother. [father.

bisabuelo, -bisăbū'lō, sm. great-grand-

bisagra, -ā'grā, sf. hinge; shoemaker's polisher. [year.

bisiesto, bisĭĕs't'ō, a. bissextile; año -, leap-

bisojo, ja, bĭsō'h'ā, a. squint-eyed.

bisoñada, bĭsōnyā'dā, bisoñería, -yĕr'ā'ā, sf. inconsiderate speech or action.

bisoño, ña, bĭsōn'yō, a. raw, undisciplined; [novice.

bisonte, bĭsōn'tĕ, sm. bison

bitor, bĭtōr', sm. rail, king of the quails (ave). [nous.

bituminoso, sa, bĭtūmĭnō'sō, a. bitumi-

bivac, bĭvăk', sm. (mil) bivouac.

bivacar, bĭvăkăr', v. a. (mil) to bivouac.

bizarramente, bĭthărāmĕn'tĕ, ad coura, geously, gallantly. [and gallant manner.

bizarrear, -rĕăr', v. n. to act in a spirited

bizarría, -rĕ'ā, sf. gallantry, valour, liberality, generosity

bizarro, rra, bĭthăr'rō, a. brave, gallant; high-spirited, generous

bizco, ca, bĭth'kō, a. squint-eyed.

bizcochero, bĭthkŏtshā'rŏ, sm. biscuit-cask; maker or seller of biscuits.

bizcocho, bĭthkŏtsh'ŏ, sm. biscuit, sea-biscuit; whiting.

bizma, bĭth'mä, sf. cataplasm, poultice.

bizmar, –mä´, v. a. to apply a poultice.

biznieta, –nid'tä, sf. great-granddaughter.

biz8nieto, –nid'tŏ, sm. great-grandson.

bizquear, –kĕä´, v. n. to squint.

blanca, blän'kä, sf. half a maravedi; (mus). minim; magpie.

blanco, ca, –kŏ, a. white, blank; –, sm. first form, prime (printing); blank, mark (to shoot at); – a ropa, linen, linen-cloth; en –, in vain.

blancura, blänkö'rä, sf. whiteness; hoariness.

blandear, bländĕä´, v. n. to soften; to make one change his opinion; –, v. n. to yield; –se, to sway, to waver.

blandir, –dĭr´, v. a. to brandish a sword, lance, &c.; –se, to quiver.

blando, da, blän'dŏ, soft, smooth; cotton-like; mellowy; lithe; mild, gentle.

blandón, –dŏn', sm. wax-taper; church-candlestick.   [loose, insecure.

blanducho, cha, –dŭtsh'ŏ, a. flabby,

blandura, –dö'rä, sf. softness; daintiness, delicacy; gentleness of temper; mild temperature.   [bleacher.

blanqueador, ra, blänkĕädŏr', sm. & f.

blanqueadura, –dö'rä, sf. bleaching; whitening.

blanquear, blänkĕä´, v. a. to bleach; to whitewash; to give coarse wax to bees in winter; –, v. n. to show whiteness.

blanquecer, –kĕthĕr', v. a. to blanch metal.

blanquecino, na, –thĕ'nŏ, a. whitish.

blanqueo, –kä'ŏ, sm. whitening; white-wash.

blanquete, –kä'tĕ, sm. white rouge.

blanquición, blänkĭthĭŏn', sf. blanching (of metals).   [liquid.

blanquimiento, –mĭĕn'tŏ, sm. bleaching

blanquizco, ca, blänkĭth'kŏ, a. whitish.

blasfemable, bläsfĕmä'blĕ, a. blamable.

blasfemador, ra, –mädŏr', sm. & f. blasphemer.   [phemously.

blasfemamente, –mämĕn'tĕ, ad. blas-

blasfemar, bläsfĕmä´, v. n. to blaspheme.

blasfematorio, ria, bläsfĕmätŏ'rĭŏ, a. blasphemous.   [verbal insult.

blasfemia, bläsfĕ'mĭä, sf blasphemy; gross

blasfemo, ma, –mŏ, a. blasphemous; –, sm blasphemer.   [honour, glory.

blasón, bläsŏn', sm. heraldry, blazonry;

blasonador, ra, bläsŏnädŏr', sm. & f. boaster, braggart.

blasonar, bläsŏnä´, v a. to blazon; to blow one's own trumpet.

bledo, blĕ'dŏ, sm. (bot.) wild amaranth; no me importa un –, I don't care a straw.

blonda, blŏn'dä, sf. lace, blonde.

blondo, da, –dŏ, a. light-haired; fair.

bloquear, blŏkĕä´, v. a. to blockade.

bloqueo, blŏkä'ŏ, sm. blockade.   [show.

boato, bŏä'tŏ, sm. ostentation, pompous

bobada, bŏbä'dä, sf. folly, foolishness.

bobático, ca, bŏbä'tĭkŏ, a. silly, stupid.

bobear, bŏbĕä´, v. a. to act or talk in a stupid manner; to dally; to loiter about.

bobería, bŏbĕrĭ'ä, sf. folly, foolishness.

bóbilis, bŏ'bĭlĭs, ad. de – –, without more

bobinas, bŏbĕ'näs, sf. pl. bobbins.   [ado.

bobo, ba, bŏ'bŏ, sm. & f. dunce; stage-buffoon; –, ba, a. stupid, silly; large, ample.

boca, bŏ'kä, sf. mouth; entrance, opening; mouth of a river; – á –, ad. by word of mouth; á pedir de –, to one's heart's content.   [buckram.

bocací, bŏkäthĕ', bocacín, bŏkäthĕn',sm.

bocadillo, –dĕl'yŏ, sm. luncheon given to labourers in the field.

bocado, –kä'dŏ, sm. morsel, mouthful.

bocaje, bŏkä'hĕ, sm. boscage.

bocal, bŏkäl', sm. pitcher; mouth-piece of a trumpet.

bocamanga, bŏkämän'gä, sf. sleeve-wrist.

bocana da, –nä'dä, sf. mouthful of liquor.

bocarte, bŏkär'tĕ, sm. crushing-mill.

bocatejas, bŏkätĕ'h'äs, sf. pl. ridge-tiles.

bocel, bŏthĕl', sm. fluting-plane.

bocina, bŏthĕ'nä, sf. bugle-horn; speaking-trumpet.

bocinero, bŏthĕnĕ'rŏ, sm. horn-blower.

bocón, bŏkŏn', sm. wide-mouthed person; braggart.   [scorching heat; blush.

bochorno, bŏtshŏr'nŏ, sm. sultry weather,

bochornoso, sa, bŏtshŏrnŏ'sŏ, a. shameful, reproachful.

boda, bŏ'dä, sf. nuptials, pl.

bodega, bŏdĕ'gä, sf. wine-cellar; growth of wine; warehouse.

bodegón, bŏdĕgŏn', sm. chop-house, eating-house; tippling-house.

bodegonear, –gŏnĕä´, v. a. to frequent mean eating-houses.   [keeper.

bodegonero, –gŏnĕ'rŏ, sm. eating-house

bodigo, bŏdĕ'gŏ, sm. small loaf of finest flour.

bodijo, bŏdĕ'h'ŏ, sm. hedge-marriage.

bodoque, bŏdŏ'kĕ, sm. pellet; dunce, idiot.

bodoquero, bŏdŏkĕ'rŏ, sm. (am.) smuggler.

bodorrio, bŏdŏr'rĭŏ, sm. hedge-marriage

bodrio, bŏ'drĭŏ, sm. poor soup made of leavings; hodge-podge.

bofes, bŏ'fĕs, sm. pl. lungs, lights.

bofetada, bŏfĕtä'dä, sf. slap, box on the ear.

bofetón, –tŏn', sm. box on the ear; folding-doors on the stage.

boga, bŏ'gä, sf. ox-eyed cackerel; rowing; rower; estar en –, to be fashionable.

bogada, bŏgä'dä, sf. stroke at rowing.

bogador, –gŏr', sm. rower.

bogar, bŏgär', v. n. to row, to paddle.

bohemio, bŏä'mĭŏ, sm. short cloak formerly worn by the guard of archers; gipsy.

boj, bŏ'h, sm. box, box-tree.

boja, bŏ'h'ä, sf. mug-wood, southern-wood.

bojar, bŏ'här', bojear, bŏ'hĕär', v. a. to sail round an island or cape, and measure the coast-line thereof; to scrape off the rough integuments of leather; –, v. n. to measure around.   [trees.

bojedal, bŏ'hĕdäl', sf. plantation of box-

bojeo, *bŏ'hā'ŏ,* sm. circumnavigation; doubling of a cape.

bola, *bŏ'lä,* sf. ball; globe; bolus; game of bowls; (fam.) lie, fib; **escurrir la —,** to take French leave, to run away.

bolazo, *bŏlä'thŏ,* sm. blow of a bowl.

bolear, *bŏleär',* v. n. to knock the balls about (billiards); to throw wooden balls for a wager. [green.

boleo, *bŏlä'ŏ,* sm. Spanish dance; bowling-

bolero, *bŏlä'rŏ,* sm Spanish dancer; runaway child. [dier's billet.

boleta, *bŏlä'tä,* sf. entrance-ticket, sol-

boletero, *-tä'rŏ,* sm. ticket-collector.

boletín, *-tēn',* sm. warrant given for the payment of money; ticket for the quartering of soldiers; bulletin.

boliche, *bŏlētsh'ē,* sm king-ball at bowls; small fish caught in a drag-net near the shore, drag-net. [hole table.

bolichero, *-tshä'rŏ,* sm. keeper of a pigeon-

bolillo, *bŏlēl'yŏ,* sm. small bowl; bobbin; starching-frame, **—s,** pl. starched cuffs worn by counsellors of state, paste-nuts.

bolina, *bŏlē'nä,* sf. noise, scuffle; (mar.) bowline; **ir á la —,** to sail on a wind.

bolo, *bŏ'lŏ,* sm. one of the nine-pins; notch-board of a winding-staircase.

bolsa, *bŏl'sä,* sf purse, purse-net; money, exchange; richest vein of gold in a gold-mine.

bolsería, *-sä'rē'ä,* sf. purse-manufactory.

bolsillo, *-sēl'yŏ,* sm. pocket; money, fortune; the king's private purse.

bolsista, *-sēs'tä,* sm. speculator on change.

bolso, *bŏl'sŏ,* sm. purse of money.

bolsor, *bŏlsŏr',* sm. key-stone.

bollero, *bŏlyä'rŏ,* sm. pastry-cook.

bollo, *bŏl'yŏ,* sm. small Spanish cake.

bollón, *bŏlyŏn',* sm. brass-headed nail.

bollonado, da, *bŏlyŏnä'dŏ,* a. adorned with brass-headed nails.

bomba, *bŏm'bä,* sf. pump; bomb; **dar á la —,** to pump; **— de fuego ó de vaho,** steam-engine; **— de apagar incendios,** fire-engine.

bombarda, *bŏmbär'dä,* sf. bomb-ketch.

bombardear, *bŏmbärdeär',* v. a. to bombard.

bombardeo, *-dä'ŏ,* sm. bombardment.

bombardero, *-dä'rŏ,* sm. bombardier.

bombasí, *bŏmbäsē',* sm. bombasine, dimity

bombazo, *bŏmbä'thŏ,* sm. report of a bursting bomb.

bombo, *bŏm'bŏ,* sm. large drum.

bonachón, *bŏnätshŏn',* sm. good-natured person.

bonancible, *ŏnänthē'blē,* a. calm, fair, serene (applied to the weather at sea).

bonanza, *bŏnän'thä,* sf. fair weather at sea; prosperity. [kind.

bonazo, za, *bŏnä'thŏ,* a. good-natured,

bondad, *bŏndäd',* sf. goodness; suavity; kindness, courtesy; excellence, healthfulness.

bondadoso, sa, *bŏndädŏ'sŏ,* a. bountiful.

bonetada, *bŏnētä'dä,* sf. salutation made by raising the hat,

bonete, *bŏnä'tē,* sm. clerical hat; college-cap; secular clergyman.

bonetería, *bŏnētärē'ä,* sf. hatter.

bonetero, *-tä'rŏ,* sm. cap-maker.

bonico, ca, *bŏnē'kŏ,* a. pretty good, passable; **andar á las bonicas,** to take things easily.

bonito, ta, *bŏnē'tŏ,* a. pretty good, passable; affecting elegance and neatness; graceful, minion; effeminate.

boñiga, *bŏnyē'gä,* sf. cow-dung.

boqueada, *bŏkēä'dä,* sf. act of opening the mouth; **la última —,** the last gasp.

boquear, *-är',* v. n. to gape, to gasp; to breathe one's last, **—,** v. a. to pronounce, to utter a word.

boquera, *bŏkä'rä,* sf. sluice in an irrigating canal; eruption at the corners of the mouth. [hole.

boquerón, *-kērŏn',* sm. anchovy; large

boquete, *bŏkä'tē,* sm gap, narrow entrance.

boquiabierto, ta, *bŏkäbēěr'tŏ,* a. with the mouth open, gaping.

boquiancho, cha, *-än'tshŏ,* a. wide-mouthed. [mouthed.

boquiangosto, ta, *-ängŏs'tŏ,* a. narrow-

boquiduro, ra, *-dŏ'rŏ,* a. hard-mouthed (of horses). [(applied to horses).

boquifresco, ca, *-frēs'kŏ,* a. fresh-mouthed

boquifruncido, da, *-frŭnthē'dŏ,* a. having the mouth contracted.

boquihundido, da, *-hŭndē'dŏ,* a. having the mouth sunk in from age or want of teeth.

boquilla, *bŏkēl'yä,* sf. little mouth; mouth-piece of a musical instrument or a pipe.

boquirroto, ta, *bŏkīrrŏ'tŏ,* a. loquacious, garrulous. [easily imposed upon.

boquirrubio, bia, *-rŏ'bĭä,* a. (fig.) simple,

boquiseco, ca, *-sēk'ŏ,* a. dry-mouthed.

boquituerto, ta, *-tŭěr'tŏ,* a. wry-mouthed.

borbollar, *bŏrbŏlyär',* v. n. to bubble out.

borbollón, *-lyŏn',* borbotón, *-tŏn',* sm. bubbling; **á borbollones,** in hurry and confusion. [boot.

borceguí, *bŏrthēgē',* sm. buskin, half-

borda, *bŏr'dä,* sf. (mar.) board; hut.

bordado, *bŏrdä'dŏ,* sm. embroidery.

bordadora, *-dŏ'rä,* sf. embroiderer.

bordadura, *-dŏ'rä,* sf. embroidery.

bordaje, *bŏrdä'h'ē,* sm. side-planks of a ship. [anything artistically.

bordar, *bŏrdär',* v. a. to embroider; to do

borde, *bŏr'dē,* sm. border; margin; (mar.) board. [windward.

bordear, *bŏrdeär',* v. n. (mar.) to ply to

bordo, *bŏr'dŏ,* sm. board of a ship.

bordón, *bŏrdŏn',* sm. pilgrim's staff; base of a stringed musical instrument.

bordura, *bŏrdŏ'rä,* sf. embroidery.

boreal, *bŏrēäl',* a. boreal, northern.

Bóreas, *bŏ'rēäs,* sm. Boreas, north-wind.

borgoña, *bŏrgŏn'yä,* sf. Burgundy wine.

borla, *bŏr'lä,* sf. tassel; tuft; doctor's bonnet. [twist.

bornear, *bŏrneär',* v. a. to bend, to turn or

borni, *bōrnĕ*, sm. merlin, dwarf-falcon.

borona, *bōrō'nă*, sf. millet; maize.

borra, *bōr'rā*, sf. yearling ewe; goat's hair; nap raised on cloth by shearers; hairy wool. [wine.

borracha, *bōrrätsh'ă*, sf. leather-bag for

borrachear, *-tshĕăr'*, v. n. to be drunk; to get drunk habitually.

borrachera, *-tshā'ră*, sf. drunkenness; hard-drinking; revelry, madness.

borrachez, *-tshĕth'*, sf. intoxication.

borracho, cha, *bōrrätsh'ō*, a. drunk, intoxicated, inflamed by passion. [tippler

borrachón, *-tshōn'*, sm. great drinker.

borrachuela, *-tshŭă'lă*, sf. (bot.) ray-grass.

borrador, *-dōr'*, sm. foul copy; wastebook, blotting-book.

borraja, *bōrrä'h'ă*, sf. (bot.) borage.

borrajear, *-'hĕăr'*, v. a. to scribble.

borrar, *bōrrä'*, v. a. to blot or efface a writing; to blur, to cloud, to obscure.

borrasca, *bōrräs'kă*, sf. storm, violent squall of wind, hazard, danger.

borrascoso, sa, *-kō'sŏ*, a. stormy.

borrasquero, *-kā'rŏ*, sm. reveller.

borregada, *bōrrĕgă'dă*, sf. large flock of sheep or lambs, [simpleton, blockhead.

borrego, ga, *bōr-ĕ'gŏ*, sm yearling lamb,

borreguero, *-rĕgă'rŏ*, sm. shepherd who tends lambs.

borren, *bōrrĕn'*, sm. panel of a saddle.

borrica, *bōrrē'kă*, sf. she-ass, jenny-ass.

borricada, *-kă'dă*, sf. drove of asses; cavalcade on asses, foolish action.

borrico, *bōrrē'kŏ*, sm. ass, jack-ass, blockhead. [fruit.

borrilla, *bōrrēl'yă*, sf. down or bloom on

borriqueño, ña, *bōrrēkēn'yŏ*, a. asinine.

borriquero, *-kē'rŏ*, sm. ass-driver.

borro, *bōr'rŏ*, sm. wether under two years old; dolt.

borrón, *bōrrōn'*, sm. ink-blot, blur; rough draft of a writing; first sketch of a painting; stain, tarnish; unworthy action.

borronear, *-ĕăr'*, v. a. to sketch.

boscaje, *bōskă'h'ĕ*, sm. boscage; landscape (in painting).

bosque, *bōs'kĕ*, sm. forest, grove.

bosquejar, *bōskĕ'hăr'*, v.a.to make a sketch of a painting; to explain a thought rather obscurely; to make a rough model of a figure. [ing; unfinished work.

bosquejo, *bōskĕ'h'ŏ*, sm. sketch of a painting.

bostezar, *bōstĕthăr'*, v.n. to yawn; to gape.

bostezo, *-thă'thŏ*, sm. yawn, yawning.

bota, *bō'tă*, sf. wine-bag; boat.

botabala, *-bă'lă*, sf. ramrod, gun-stick.

botador, *-dōr'*, sm. driver; punch (tool); crow's bill.

botafuego, *-fūĕ'gŏ*, sm. linstock.

botana, *bōtă'nă*, sf. plug, stopple.

botánica, *bōtă'nīkă*, sf. botany.

botánico, ca, *-nīkŏ*, a. botanic. [nist.

botánico, — botanista, *-nīs'tă*, sm. botanist.

botar, *bōtăr'*, v. a. to cast, to fling, to launch. [person.

botarate, *-ră'tĕ*, sm. mad-cap, blustering

botarga, *bōtăr'gă*, sf. gaskins; harlequin's costume; harlequin; motley dress of a harlequin; buffoon.

botasilla, *bōtăsīl'yă*, sf. (mil.) signal given with a trumpet for the cavalry to saddle.

botavante, *-văn'tĕ*, sm. (mar.) grappling-iron. [boat.

bote, *bō'tĕ*, sm. thrust with a pike or lance;

botecillo, *-thēl'yŏ*, sm. small colour-pan;

botella, *bōtĕl'yă*, sf. bottle, flask. [skiff.

botequin, *bōtēkīn'*, sm. small boat.

botica, *bōtē'kă*, sf. apothecary's shop.

boticario, *-kă'rīŏ*, sm. apothecary.

botiga, *bōtē'gă*, sf. shop.

botija, *bōtē'kă*, sf. earthen jar with a short and narrow neck. [little child.

botijo, *-ŏ*, botijón, *bōtē'hōn'*, sm. plump

botilla, *bōtēl'yă*, sf. small wine-bag.

botillería, *-yĕrē'ă*, sf. ice-house.

botillero, *-yēl'rŏ*, sm. preparer or seller of iced liquids. [dash; gaiter; booty.

botin, *bōtēn'*, sm. buskin, half-boot; spatter-

botinero, *bōtīnă'rŏ*, sm. (mil.) booty guard; one who makes or sells gaiters. [chest.

botiquin, *bōtēkīn'*, sm. travelling medicine-

botivoléo, *-vōlē'ŏ*, sm. catching of a ball at the rebound.

botón, *bōtōn'*, sm. button; (bot.) bud.

botonadura, *bōtōnădŏ'ră*, sf. set of buttons for a suit of clothes. [a foil.

botonazo, *-nă'thŏ*, sm. thrust given with a

botonero, ra, *-nă'rŏ*, sm. & f. button-maker; button-seller.

bóveda, *bō'vĕdă*, sf. arch, vault; crypt.

boya, *bō'yă*, sf. (mar.) buoy; piece of cork fastened to a fishing-net.

boyada, *bōyă'dă*, sf. drove of oxen.

boyante, *-yăn'tĕ*, p. & a. buoyant, floating; sailing well; fortunate, successful.

boyar, *bōyăr'*, v. n. (fig.) to buoy, to be boyardo, *-dŏ*, sm. boyar. [afloat.

boyera, *bōyă'ră*, boyeriza, *bōyĕrē'thă*, sf. ox-stall, ox-house.

boyero, *bōyă'rŏ*, sm. ox-herd.

boyezuelo, *bōyĕthŭĕ'lŏ*, sm. young ox.

boyuno, na, *bōyŏ'nŏ*, a. belonging to cattle.

bozal, *bōthăl'*, sm. muzzle; —, a. novice, inexperienced in business.

bozo, *bō'thŏ*, sm. down which precedes the beard; headstall of a horse.

brabante, *brăbăn'tĕ*, sm. Brabant linen.

braceada, *brăthĕă'dă*, sf. violent movement of the arms. [money.

braceaje, *-ā'h'ĕ*, sm. coinage; coining of

bracear, *-ăr'*, v. n. to swing the arms; —, v. a. (mar.) to brace.

bracero, *brăthā'rŏ*, sm. day-labourer; strong-armed man.

bracman, *brăkmăn'*, sm. Brahmin.

braco, ca, *brä'kŏ*, a. flat-nosed; —, s. pointer (dog). [breeches.

braga, *brä'gă*, sf. child's clout; —s, pl.

bragadura, *-dŏ'ră*, sf. fork of the body; fork of a pair of breeches.

bragazas, *brăgă'thăs*, sf. pl. wide breeches; —, sm. one who is easily persuaded.

braguero, *brăgă'rŏ*, sm. truss, braces.

bragueta, -tă, sf. cod-piece.

braguillas, brăgŭ'yăs, sm. child breeched for the first time; dwarfish person.

brama, brā'mă, sf. rut.

bramadera, -dě'ră, sf. rattle.

bramadero, -dě'ro, sm. rutting-place.

bramante, brămăn'tě, sm. pack-thread; bramant linen; roaring.

bramar, brămăr', v. n. to roar, to bellow; to storm, to bluster; to be in a passion.

bramido, brămē'dŏ, sm. cry uttered by wild beasts; clamour of persons enraged; roaring of the elements.   [net.

brancada, brănkă'dă, sf. drag-net, sweep.

brasa, brā'să, sf. live coal; estar hecho unas -s, to be all in a blaze.

brasero, brăsě'ro, sm. brazier.

brasil, brăsĭl', sm. Brazil-wood; rouge.

brasilado, da, -lă'dŏ, a. ruddy.   [ziletto.

brasilete, -lě'tě, sm. Jamaica-wood, bra-

bravamente, brăvămĕn'tě, ad. bravely, gallantly, cruelly; finely, extremely well.

bravata, brăvă'tă, sf. bravado, boast, braggadocio.

braveador, ra, brăvěădŏr', sm. & f. bully.

bravear, -văr', v. n. to bully, to hector.

braveza, brăvě'thă, sf. fury of the elements.

bravío, vía, brăvē'ŏ, a. ferocious, savage, wild; coarse; -, sm. fierceness, savageness.

bravo, va, brā'vŏ, a. brave, valiant; bullying; savage, fierce; rude, unpolished; sumptuous; excellent, fine; ! — ! bravo!

bravura, brăvŭ'ră, sf. ferocity; courage; bravado, boast.

braza, brā'thă, sf. fathom.   [arm-full.

brazada, -thă'dă, sf. extension of the arms;

brazado, -thă'dŏ, sm. arm-full.

brazaje, -thă'h'ě, sm. (mar.) number of fathoms, depth of water.

brazal, brăthăl', sm. bracer (piece of armour); biceps; arm pad of wood or leather (at ball-play).

brazalete, brăthălě'tě, sm. bracelet.

brazo, brā'thŏ, sm. arm; branch of a tree; valour, strength, power; — á —, man to man; á — partido, locked in each other's arms.

brazuelo, brăthŭě'lŏ, sm. small arm; foreleg of beasts; branch of the mouth-bit of a bridle.   [for wrapping up wares.

brea, brě'ă, sf. pitch; tar; coarse canvas

brear, brěăr', v. a. to pitch; to tar; to vex, to plague; to play a joke upon.

brebaje, brěbă'h'ě, sm. beverage.

brecha, brětsh'ă, sf. (mil.) breach; impression made upon the mind; batir en —, (mil.) to make a breach; to persecute.

brega, brě'gă, sf. strife, contest; pun, jest, trick.

bregar, brěgăr', v.n. to contend, to struggle; to struggle with difficulties; —, v. a. to work up dough on a board with a rolling-pin.   [full of brakes and brambles.

breña, brěn'yă, sf. craggy, broken ground

breñal, brěnyăl', breñar, -yăr', sm. briars, underwood.   [bled.

breñoso, sa, -yŏ'sŏ, a. craggy and bram-

brete, brě'tě, sm. fetters, shackles; (fig.) perplexity; difficulties, pl.

bretel, brětěl', sm. brace (for trowsers).

breva, brě'vă, sf. early-fig; early large acorn.

breval, brěvăl', sm. early fig-tree.

breve, brě'vě, sm. apostolic brief; (mus.) brief; —, a. brief, short; en —, shortly.

brevedad, -dăd', sf. brevity, shortness, conciseness.

breviario, brěvĭă'rĭŏ, sm. breviary; brevier (small letter used in printing).

brezal, brěthăl', sm. heath.   [fling.

brezo, brě'thŏ, sm. (bot.) heath, heather,

briaga, brĭă'gă, sf. rope made of bass-weed.

briba, brē'bă, sf. truancy, idleness.

bribón, ona, brĭbŏn', a. vagrant; knavish, rascally.   [ous trick.

bribonada, -nă'dă, sf. knavery, mischiev-

bribonear, brĭbŏněăr', v. n. to rove; to lead a vagabond's life.   [beggar's trade.

bribonería, -mrě'ă, sf. life of a vagabond;

bricho, brĭtsh'ŏ, sm. spangle.

brida, brē'dă, sf. bridle; horsemanship; (fig.) restraint, check, curb.

bridar, -dăr', v. a. to bridle; to curb.

brigada, brĭgă'dă, sf. brigade.

brigadier, -dĭr', sm. brigadier.   [diant.

brillador, ra, brĭlyădŏr', a. brilliant, ra-

brillante, -yăn'tě, a. brilliant; bright, shining; -, sm. brilliant.

brillar, brĭlyăr', v. n. to shine; to sparkle, to glisten; to outshine in talents or merits.

brillo, brē'lyŏ, sm. brilliancy, brightness.

brincador, ra, brĭnkădŏr', sm. & f. jumper, leaper.

brincar, -kăr', v. n. to leap, to jump, to gambol; to omit something; 'o fly into a passion.   [gambol.

brinco, brĭn'kŏ, sm. leap, jump, bounce;

brindar, brĭndăr', v. n. to drink one's health, to toast; -, v. a. to invite; to allure.

brindis, brĭn'dĭs, sf. health, toast.

brío, brē'ŏ, sm. strength, vigour; spirit, courage.   [courageously.

briosamente, brĭŏsămĕn'tě, ad. spiritedly,

brioso, sa, brĭŏ'sŏ, a. vigorous, full of spirit; courageous, lively.

brisa, brē'să, sf. breeze.

brisca, brĭs'kă, sf. a game at cards.

briscar, -kăr', v. a. to embroider with gold or silver twist mixed with silk.

broca, brŏ'kă, sf. reel for twist; drill; shoe-maker's tack.

brocado, brŏkă'dŏ, sm. gold or silver brocade; -, da, a. embroidered, like brocade.

brocal, brŏkăl', sm. kerb-stone; metal rim of the scabbard of a sword.   [and silk.

brocatel, -tĕl', sm. stuff made of hemp

bróculi, brŏ'kŭlĭ, sm. broccoli.

brocha, brŏtsh'ă, sf. painter's brush, pencil.

brochada, -tshă'dă, sf. stroke with a pencil.

brochado, -tshă'dŏ, a. figured (of stuffs).   [decoration worked into cloth.

brochadura, -tshădŏ'ră, sf. ornaments or

broche, brŏtsh'ě, sm. clasp; brooch.

brochón, -tshŏn', sm. large brush; plasterers' brush.   [jest.

broma, brŏ'mă, sf. clatter, noise; joke,

bromear, *—meár',* v. n. to jest; to bore with dull talking. [companion.

bromista, *—mis'tá,* sm. merry fellow; jolly

bronce, *brŏn'thé,* sm. bronze, brass; (poet.) trumpet.

bronceado, *—theá'dŏ,* sm. bronzing.

broncear, *—theár',* v. a. to bronze. [ware.

broncería, *—theré'á,* sf. brass-works, brass-

broncista, *—this'tá,* sm. worker in bronze.

bronco, ca, *brŏn'kŏ,* a. rough, coarse; crusty; crabbed; rude, hoarse; harsh (to the ear). [pers; unmalleability.

bronquedad, *—kédá'ð,* sf. rudeness of man-

broquel, *brŏkĕl',* sm. shield, buckler; (fig.) support, protection; **rajar —es,** to bully, to swagger.

brotadura, *brŏtádŏ'rá,* sf. budding.

brotar, *brŏtár',* v. n. to bud, to germinate; to gush, to rush out; to break out, to appear (applied to the small-pox, &c.).

broza, *brŏ'thá,* sf. bark; vegetable rubbish; brush-wood; farrago; printer's brush.

brozar, *brŏthár',* v. a. to brush type.

brucero, *brŭthé'rŏ,* sm. brush-maker.

bruces, *brŏ'thĕs,* sf. pl. lips; **á —, de —,** face downwards.

brueta, *brŭĕ'tá,* sf. wheel-barrow.

bruja, *brŭ'h'á,* sf. witch, hag. [craft.

brujear, *—heár',* v. n. to practise witch-

brujería, *—heré'á,* sf. witchcraft.

brujidor, *brŭhídór',* sm. glaziers' nippers.

brujir, *—hír',* v. a. to pare off the corners and edges of panes of glass.

brujo, *brŭ'h'ŏ,* sm. sorcerer.

brújula, *brŏ'hŭlá,* sf. sea-compass.

brujulear, *—hŭleár',* v. a. to turn up one card after another; to discover by deduction; to conjecture.

brujuleo, *—hŭlé'ŏ,* sm. exposure of cards (at card games); close examination; con-

brulote, *brŭlŏ'tĕ,* sm. fire-ship. [jecture.

bruma, *mrŭ,* sf. (mar.) haziness.

brumal, *brŭmál',* a. wintry.

brunella, *brŭnĕl'á,* sf. prunello.

bruñido, *brŭnyé'dŏ,* sm. polish, burnish.

bruñidor, *—yídór',* sm. burnisher (person and instrument). [to put on rouge.

bruñir, *—yír',* v. a. to burnish; to polish;

bruñola, *—yŏ'lá,* sf. prunello. [ward.

brusco, ca, *brŭs'kŏ,* a. rude, peevish, for-

brutal, *brŭtál',* a. brutal, brutish; **—,** sm. brute, rude person. [brutal action.

brutalidad, *brŭtálídá'ð,* sf. brutality.

bruto, *brŏ'tŏ,* sm. brute; rude, immoral person; **—, ta,** a. coarse, unpolished, in a rough state. [children into silence.

bu, *bŏ,* sm. word used by nurses to frighten

buba, *bŏ'bá,* sf. pustule; **—s,** pl. venereal disease. [the venereal disease.

bubático, ca, *bŭbá'tíkŏ,* a. infected with

bubón, *bŭbón',* sm. large morbid tumour, full of matter. [pustules.

buboso, sa, *bŭbŏ'sŏ,* a. afflicted with

bucear, *bŭtheár',* v. n. to dive. [to a hound.

buceo, *bŭthé'ŏ,* sm. diving.

bucero, *bŭthé'rŏ,* a. black-nosed (applied

bucle, *bŏ'klĕ,* sm. curl. [(fam.) food

bucólica, *bŭkŏ'líká,* sf. pastoral poetry;

buchada, *bŭtshá'dá,* sf. draught or mouthful of liquor.

buche, *bŭtsh'é,* sm. craw, crop, stomach of quadrupeds; mouthful, sucking ass; pucker or crease in clothes; (fig.) girl's bosom.

buchete, *bŭtshá'tĕ,* sm. blown-out cheek.

buen, *bŭĕn',* a. good. [modiously.

buenamente, *bŭĕnámĕn'tĕ,* ad. easily, com-

buenaventura, *—vĕntŏ'rá,* sf. fortune, good luck.

bueno, na, *bŭĕ'nŏ,* a. good, perfect, fair, plain; fit, proper, sociable, agreeable; strong; sound, healthy; useful. **¿ de dónde —?** where do you come from? **de buenas á buenas,** freely, willingly; **—,** ad. enough, sufficiently; **— está,** enough, no more. [subsistence.

buenpasar, *bŭĕnpásár',* sm. comfortable

buey, *bŭĕ'é,* sm. ox, bullock.

¡ buf! *bŭf,* pooh, pooh!

bufa, *bŏ'fá,* sf. jeer, scoff, taunt, mock.

búfala, *bŏ'fálá,* sf. female buffalo.

bufalino, na, *bŭfálé'nŏ,* a. belonging to buffalo, *bŏ'fálŏ,* sm. buffalo. [buffaloes.

bufar, *bŭfár',* v. n. to choke with anger; to huff; to snort.

bufete, *bŭfá'tĕ,* sm. desk, writing-table.

bufido, *bŭfé'dŏ,* sm. blowing of an animal; snorting of a horse; huff.

bufo, *bŏ'fŏ,* sm buffoon on the stage; **—, fa,** a. comic; **ópera —a,** sf. comic opera.

bufón, *bŭfón',* sm. buffoon, merry Andrew; jester; **—, ona,** a. funny, comical.

bufonada, *—ná'dá,* sf. buffoonery, raillery, sarcastic taunt. [make fun of.

bufonearse, *—neár'sĕ,* v. r. to jest, to

bufonería, *—neré'á,* sf. buffoonery

buhera, *bŭá'rá,* sf. embrasure, loop-hole.

buhero, *—rŏ,* sm. owl-keeper

buho, *bŏ'ŏ,* sm. owl; an unsocial man.

buhonería, *bŭŏnĕré'á,* sf. pedlar's box.

buhonero, *—ná'rŏ,* sm. pedlar, hawker.

buitre, *bŭé'trĕ,* sm. vulture.

buitrero, *bŭétrŏ'rŏ,* sm. vulture-fowler; **—, ra,** a. vulturine.

bujarrón, *bŭhárrón',* sm. Sodomite.

bujería, *bŭhéré'á,* sf. gewgaw, bauble, knick-knack. [perfume-box.

bujeta, *bŭhá'tá,* sf. box made of box-wood;

bujía, *bŭhé'á,* sf. wax-candle.

bula, *bŏ'lá,* sf. papal bull.

bulbo, *bŭl'bŏ,* sm. (bot.) bulb.

bulboso, sa, *bŭlbŏ'sŏ,* a. bulbous.

bulero, *bŭlá'rŏ,* sm. one who is charged with distributing bulls of crusades, and collecting the alms of charity given for

buleto, *—tŏ,* sm. apostolic letter. [them.

bulto, *bŭl'tŏ,* sm. bulk; tumour, swelling; bust, luggage; (am) baggage; **—s á la mano,** pl. (rail.) small luggage; **á —,** indistinctly, confusedly; **en —,** by the lump.

bulla, *bŭl'yá,* sf. confused noise, clatter; crowd; meter **—,** to make a noise.

bullaje, *bŭlyá'h'ĕ,* sm. crowd.

bullanguero, *bŭlyángŏ'rŏ,* sm. rioter.

bullebulle, *bŭlyĕbŭl'yĕ,* sm. busy body.

bullicio, *bŭlyŏ'thĭŏ,* sm. bustle; tumult, uproar.

bullicioso, sa, *—thĭŏ'sŏ,* a. lively, restless, noisy, clamorous, busy; turbulent; boisterous

bullidor, ra, *bŭlyĭdŏr',* a. noisy, turbulent.

bullir, *bŭlyĭr',* v.n. to boil; (fig.) to bustle, to fluster; —, v. a. to manage a business.

bullón, *bŭlyŏn',* sm. making of a decoction; dyeing-mixture.

buñolero, ra, *bŭnyŏlā'rŏ,* sm. & f. maker or seller of buns. [fritter.

buñuelo, *bŭnyŏā'lŏ,* sm. bun; pan-cake.

buque, *bŏ'kĕ,* sm. bulk, capacity of a ship; hull of a ship; vessel, ship.

burdel, *bŭrdĕl',* sm. brothel.

burdo, da, *bŭr'dŏ,* a. coarse (of stuffs).

bureo, *bŭrā'ŏ,* sm. amusement, diversion.

bureocracia, *bŭrĕŏkrā'thĭā,* sf. bureaucracy.

bureocrático, —*krā'tĭkŏ,* a. bureaucratic.

burga, *bŭr'gā,* sf. thermal waters, pl.

burgomaestre, *bŭrgŏmāĕs'trĕ,* sm. burgomaster.

buril, *bŭrĭl',* sm. burine, graver. [master.

burilada, *bŭrĭlā'dā,* sf. stroke of a burine.

buriladura, —*dŏ'rā,* sf. engraving.

burilar, *bŭrĭlār',* v. a. to engrave.

burla, *bŭr'lā,* sf. scoff, mockery, sneer; trick, slight deceit; hoax; de —s, in jest.

burlar, *bŭrlār',* v. a. to mock, to scoff; to hoax, to abuse, to play tricks, to deceive, to frustrate; —se, to jest, to laugh at.

burlesco, ca, —*lĕs'kŏ,* a. burlesque, comical, funny. [ad. de —, in jest.

burlicas, *bŭrlĭ'kās,* **burlitas,** *bŭrlĭ'tās,*

burlón, ona, *bŭrlŏn',* sm. & f. great wag, rantry.

burra, *bŭr'rā,* sf. she-ass. [jack-pudding.

burrada, *bŭrrā'dā,* sf. drove of asses; stupid action. [fuel.

burrajo, —*rā'hŏ,* sm. dry stable-dung for

burrero, *bŭrrā'rŏ,* sm. ass-keeper who sells asses' milk.

burro, *bŭr'rŏ,* sm. ass, donkey; stupid fellow; jack, saw-horse. [olives.

burujo, *bŭrū'hŏ,* sm. dregs of pressed

busca, *bŭs'kā,* sf. search, examination.

buscada, *bŭskā'dā,* sf. research, inquiry.

buscador, ra, —*dŏr',* sm. & f. searcher, investigator.

buscapié, —*pĭā',* sm. (fig.) feeler.

buscapiés, —*s',* sm. crackers (fireworks).

buscar, *bŭskār',* v. a. to seek, to search; to look for or after; to hunt after.

buscarruidos, *bŭskārrŭĭ'dŏs,* sm.quarrelsome fellow. [spy, busybody.

buscavidas, —*vē'dās,* sm. prying person.

buscón, *bŭskŏn',* sm. searcher; cheat, pilferer, petty robber.

busilis, *bŭsĭ'lĭs,* sm. point in question; main point of an argument.

busola, *bŭsŏ'lā,* sf. sea-compass.

busto, *bŭs'tŏ,* sm. bust.

butifarra, *bŭtĭfār'rā,* sf. sausage made in Catalonia; gaskins. [or pay respect to.

bus, *bŭth,* sm. hacer el —, to do homage

buzo, *bŏ'thŏ,* sm. diver.

buzón, *bŭthŏn',* sm. conduit, canal; letter-box; post-box (am.); cover of a cistern, pond, jar, &c.

C.

cabal, *kābāl',* a. just, exact; perfect, complete, accomplished. [intrigue.

cábala, *kā'bālā,* sf. cabala(mystical science);

cabalgada, *kābālgā'dā,* sf. horseback excursion; cavalcade; (mil.) foray

cabalgador, —*dŏr',* sm. rider; horseman.

cabalgadura, —*dŏ'rā,* sf. sumpter-mule, sumpter-horse, beast of burden.

cabalgar, *kābālgār'* v. n. to parade on horseback; to take part in a cavalcade; to spring to horse.

cabalista, *kābālĭs'tā,* sm. cabalist.

cabalístico, ca, —*lĭs'tĭkŏ,* a. cabalistic.

caballa, *kābāl'yā,* sf. horse-mackerel (fish).

caballaje, —*lyā'hĕ,* sm. place where mares and she-asses are served by stallions; money paid for that service.

caballar, —*lyār',* a. belonging to or resembling horses.

caballejo, —*lyā'hŏ,* sm. trave, wooden frame for shoeing unruly horses.

caballerear, —*lyĕrĕār',* v. n. to set up for a gentleman. [chivalrous.

caballeresco, ca, —*lyĕrĕs'kŏ,* a. knightly;

caballerete, —*lyĕrā'tĕ,* sm. spruce young gentleman.

caballería, —*lyĕrā'ā,* sf. cavalry; cavalry-horse; chivalry; knighthood; knight-errantry.

caballeriza, —*lyĕrā'thā,* sf. stable; number of horses, mules, &c. standing in a stable.

caballerizo, —*lyĕrā'thŏ,* sm. head-groom of a stable.

caballero, —*lyā'rŏ,* sm. knight; cavalier; gentleman; rider; horseman; horse-soldier; — andante, knight-errant.

caballeroso, sa, —*lyĕrŏ'sŏ,* a. noble, gentlemanlike. [polished gentleman.

caballerote, —*lyĕrŏ'tĕ,* sm. graceless, un-

caballete, —*lyā'tĕ,* sm. ridge of a house forming an acute angle; horse (instrument of torture); painter's easel; hemp-brake; trestle. [ing-horse.

caballico, —*lyĭ'kŏ,* sm. hobby-horse, rock-

caballo, *kābāl'yŏ,* sm. horse; (at chess) knight; á —, on horseback. [torture).

caballote, —*lyŏ'tĕ,* sm. wooden horse (for

caballuno, na, —*lyŏ'nŏ,* a. belonging to a horse.

cabaña, *kābān'yā,* sf. shepherd's hut, cottage; hovel; flock of ewes; drove of asses for carrying corn; line drawn on a billiard-table, within which the players must play.

cabañal, *kābānyāl',* sm. mule or sheep track (of travelling or migratory herds).

cabañero, ra, —*yā'rŏ,* a. belonging to the droves of travelling mules and asses.

cabañil, —*yĭl',* sm. keeper of asses for carrying corn.

cabecear, *kābĕthĕār',* v. n. to nod with sleep; to shake one's head; (mar.) to pitch.

cabeceo, —*thā'ŏ,* sm. nod, shaking of the head. [bed-pillow; vignette.

cabecera, —*thā'rā,* sf. upper end of a hall;

cabecilla, -thǐľ yǎ, sm. ringleader.

cabecita, -thǐľ ǎ, sf. wrong-headed person.

cabellera, kǎbělyǎ'rǎ, sf. long hair spread over the shoulders; wig; tail of a comet.

cabello, kǎběľ yǒ, sm, hair of the head.

cabelludo, da, -lyǒ'dǒ, a. hairy, overgrown with hair.   [contain, to include.

caber, kǎběr', v. a. & n. to comprehend; to

cabestraje, kǎběstrǎ'h'ě, sm. halter; bridle-money; money paid to a driver for conducting cattle to market.

cabestrar, -trǎr', v. a. to halter; —, v. n. to fowl with a stalking-ox.

cabestrear, -strěǎr', v. n. to be led easily by the halter.

cabestrillo, -trǐľ yǒ, sm. sling, splint; necklace; gold chain.

cabestro, kǎběs'trǒ, sm. halter; bell-ox.

cabeza, kǎběhǎ'dǎ, sf. head; top; end; chief; leader; beginning of a thing.

cabezada, kǎběhǎ'dǎ, sf. head-shake; head-stall of a bridle; head-band of a book; instep of a boot.   [post of a door.

cabezal, -thǎl', sm. pillow; compress;

cabezo, kǎbě'thǒ, sm. summit of a hill.

cabezón, -thǒn', sm. collar of a shirt; opening in a garment for the passage of the head; nose-band.   [tioned head.

cabezorro, -thǒr'rǒ, sm. large disproportioned head.

cabezudo, da, -thǒ'dǒ, a. large-headed; thick-headed; head-strong, obstinate.

cabezuela, -thǔě'lǎ, sf. small head; simpleton; coarse flour; rose-bud.

cabida, kǎbǐ'dǎ, sf. content, capacity; tener - con una persona, to be in high favour with one.

cabildada, kǎbǐldǎ'dǎ, sf. hasty, illgrounded resolution of a chapter or council.

cabildo, kǎbǐľ dǒ, sm. chapter (of a cathedral or collegiate church); meeting of a chapter; corporation of a town.

cabizbajo, ja, kǎbǐthbǎ'h'ǒ, cabizcaído, da, -kǎǐ'dǒ, a. crestfallen; pensive; thoughtful.   [hypocritical.

cabiztuerto, ta, -tǔěr'tǒ, sm. wry-headed;

cable, kǎ'blě, sm. (mar.) cable.

cabo, kǎ'bǒ, sm. extremity; cape, head-land.

cabotaje, -tǎ'h'ě, sm. coasting-trade; pilot-

cabra, kǎ'brǎ, sf. goat.   [age.

cabrahigo, -hě'gǒ, sm. wild fig-tree.

cabrería, kǎbrěrě'ǎ, sf. place where goats' milk is sold.

cabrero, kǎbrě'rǒ, sm. goat-herd.   [stan.

cabrestante, kǎbrěstǎn'tě, sm. (mar.) cap-

cabrilla, kǎbrǐ'yǎ, sf. prawn; —s, pl. Pleiades (constellation); heat-marks on the legs.   [chevron.

cabrio, kǎ'brǐǒ, sm. rafter, roof-spar;

cabrío, kǎbrǐ'ǒ, sm. flock of goats.

cabriola, kǎbrǐǒ'lǎ, sf. caper; gambol.

cabriol(e)ar, -l(ě)ǎr', v. n. to cut capers; to curvet.

cabriolé, -lě', sm. cabriolet, gig.

cabrita, kǎbrǐ'tǎ, sf. small female kid; kid-skin.   [seller of kid-skins.

cabritero, kǎbrǐtě'rǒ, sm. dealer in kids;

cabritilla, kǎbrǐtǐ'yǎ, sf. dressed kid-skin.

cabrito, kǎbrǐ'tǒ, sm. kid.

cabrón, kǎbrǒn', sm. buck, he-goat; one who consents to the adultery of his wife.

cabronada, -ǎ'dǎ, sf. infamous action which a man permits against his own honour.   [tutes his own wife.

cabronazo, -ǎ'thǒ, sm. one who prosti-

cabroncillo, -thǐľ yǒ, sm. easy husband.

cabruno, na, kǎbrǒ'nǒ, a. goatish.

cacahual, kǎkǎhǔǎl', cacaotal, kǎkǎǒtǎl', sm. plantation of chocolate-trees.

cacao, kǎkǎ'ǒ, sm. (bot.) smooth-leaved chocolate nut-tree; cocoa.

cacareador, ra, kǎkǎrěǎdǒr', sm. & f. crowing cock; cackling hen; cackler; braggart.   [to brag, to boast.

cacarear, -rěǎr', v. n. to crow, to cackle;

cacareo, -rě'ǒ, sm. crowing of a cock, cackling of a hen; boast, brag.

cacera, kǎthě'rǎ, sf. canal, channel, conduit.

cacería, kǎthěrě'ǎ, sf. hunting-party.

cacerina, -rě'nǎ, sf. cartridge-box.

cacerola, -rǒ'lǎ, sf. stewing-pan.

caceta, kǎthě'tǎ, sf. small pan used by apothecaries.

cacique, kǎthě'kě, sm. Cazique (prince or nobleman among the Indians).

caco, kǎ'kǒ, sm. pickpocket; coward.

cacofonía, -fǒně'ǎ, sf. harsh unharmonious sound.

cacha, kǎtsh'ǎ, sf. handle of a knife.

cachalote, -lǒ'tě, sm. sperm-whale.

cachamarín, -mǎrěn', sm. (mar.) lugger.

cachar, kǎtshǎr', v. a. to break in pieces.

cacharpalla, kǎtshǎrpǎľyǎ, sf. (am.) farewell-dinner.

cacharro, kǎtshǎr'rǒ, sm. coarse earthen pot; sherd.   [ness.

cachaza, kǎtshǎ'thǎ, sf. inactivity; tardi-

cachemira, kǎtshěmě'rǎ, sf. cashmere.

cachera, kǎtshě'rǎ, sf. coarse, shaggy cloth.   [the fist.

cachete, kǎtshě'tě, sm. check; blow with

cachetero, -tě'rǒ, sm short, broad, sharppointed knife; bull-fighter who kills the bulls with the cachetero.

cachetudo, da, -tě'dǒ, a. chubby-cheeked.

cachicán, kǎtshǐkǎn', sm. farm-overseer.

cachidiablo, -dǐǎ'blǒ, sm. hobgoblin.

cachigordete, -gǒrdě'tě, a. thick and

cachiporra, -pǒr'rǎ, sf. cudgel.   [short

cachivache, -vǎtsh'ě, sm. broken crockery-ware, old trumpery; despicable fellow.

cacho, kǎtsh'ǒ, sm. slice, piece (applied to lemons, oranges, &c.); game of chance at cards.   [(of female beasts).

cachonda, kǎtshǒn'dǎ, a. ruttish, proud

cachorrillo, kǎtshǒrrǐľ yǒ, sm. pocketpistol.

cachorro, ra, kǎtshǒr'rǒ, sm. & f. grown whelp or puppy; cub (of any animal).

cachucha, kǎtshǔtsh'ǎ, sf. Spanish dance and its tune.

cachuela, kǎtshǔě'lǎ, sf. fricassee made of the livers and lights of rabbits.

cachupín, kǎtshǔpǐn', sm. Spanish settler in America.

cada, kǎ'dǎ, pn. every; every one; each.

cadalso, kǎdǎľ sǒ, sm. scaffold.

cadarzo, kạdạr'thọ, sm. floss-silk.
cadáver, kādāvēr, sm. corpse, cadaver.
cadavérico, ca, kādāvá'rīkọ, a. cadaverous.
cadena, kādā'nā, sf. chain; series, link.
cadencia, kādēn'thīā, sf. cadence.
cadente, -tē, a. declining; harmonious, mellifluous (of declamation).
cadera, kādā'rā, sf. hip.
caderillas, kāderīl'yās, sf. pl. crinoline.
cadete, kādē'tē, sm. (mil.) cadet.
caducar, kādūkār', v. n. to dote; to lapse (of a legacy, etc.). [staff.
caduceo, kādūthē'ọ, sm. caduceus; herald's
caducidad, kādūthīdād', sf. caducity; decrepitude.
caduco, ca, kādū'kọ, a. worn out; enfeebled by age, decrepit; perishable; mal —, sm. epilepsy.
caedizo, za, kāēdē'thọ, a. tottering, frail.
caedura, -dū'rā, sf. loose threads dropping from the loom in weaving.
caer, kāēr', v. n. to fall; to tumble down; to lapse; to befall, to happen, to come to pass; to die. [house.
café, kāfē', sm. coffee-tree; coffee; coffee-
cafetera, kāfētā'rā, sf. coffee-pot.
cafetero, -rọ, sm. coffee-tree; coffee-house keeper, coffee-man.
cáfila, kā'fīlā, sm. multitude of people, animals or other things; caravan. [civil.
cafre, kā'frē, a. savage, inhuman; rude, un-
cagafierro, kāgāfīēr'rọ, sm. scoria, dross of iron.
cagajón, -hōn', sm. horse-dung.
cagalar, -lār', sm. rectum.
cagalera, -lā'rā, sf. looseness, diarrhœa.
cagarruta, -rrō'tā, sf. dung of sheep, goats and mice.
cagatinta, -tīn'tā, sm. term of contempt for attorney's clerks.
cagón, ona, kāgōn', sm. &f. person afflicted with diarrhœa; cowardly person.
cahiz, kāīth', sm. measure of corn (about 12 English bushels).
cahizada, -thā'dā, sf. tract of land which requires about one cahiz of grain to be properly sown. [descent.
caída, kāē'dā, sf. fall, falling; declivity,
caídos, -dọs, sm. pl. rents due but unpaid; arrears of taxes. [cunning man.
caimán, kāīmān', sm. caiman, alligator;
caimiento, -mīēn'tọ, sm. low spirits; languidness; fall.
caja, kā'hā, sf. box, case, coffin; chest in which money is kept; libro de -, cash-book.
cajero, kā'hā'rọ, sm. cashier, cash-keeper.
cajeta, kā'hā'tā, sf. snuff-box, poor-box.
cajetín, kā'hētīn', sm. very small box.
cajista, kā'hīs'tā, sm. compositor, composer. [book-case.
cajón, kā'hōn', sm. chest of drawers; locker;
cal, kāl, sf. burnt lime-stone; - viva, quick lime.
cala, kā'lā, sf. creek, small bay; small piece of melon, &c.; hole made in a wall to judge of its thickness.

calabacera, -bāthā'rā, sf. pumpkin.
calabacero, -bāthā'rọ, sm. retailer of pumpkins. [tender pumpkin.
calabacín, -bāthīn', sm. small, young,
calabacino, -bāthē'nọ, sm. wine-gourd.
calabaza, -bā'thā, sf. pumpkin or gourd; - vinatera, bottle-calabash. [head.
calabazada, -bāthā'dā, sf. blow with the
calabazate, -bāthā'tē, sm. preserved pumpkin.
calabozo, -bō'thọ, sm. dungeon. [kin.
calada, kālā'dā, sf. rapid flight of birds of prey. [wood or linen.
calado, kālā'dọ, sm. open work in metal,
calador, -dōr', sm. probe (surgeon's instrument).
calafate, -fā'tē, sm. (mar.) calker.
calafatear, -fātēār', v a. (mar.) to calk.
calafateo, -fātē'ọ, sm. (mar.) calking.
calafatería, -fātērē'ā, sf. (mar.) calking.
calambre, kālām'brē, sm. spasm. cramp.
calamidad, kālāmīdād', sf. misfortune, calamity, misery [fortunate.
calamitoso, sa, -tō'sọ, a. calamitous, un-
cálamo, kā'lāmọ, sm. (bot.) sweet flag; pen; shepherd's flute; currente -, offhand. [be somewhat fuddled.
calamocano, -kā'nọ, a. estar ó ir -, to
calandrajo, kālāndrā'họ, sm. rag hanging down from a garment; ragamuffin.
calandria, kālān'drīā, sf. calendar-lark.
calaña, kālān'yā, sf. character, quality.
calar, kālār', v a. to penetrate, to pierce; to discover a design; to put, to place; las cubas, to gage a barrel; -se, to introduce one's self; to insinuate one's self into; to stoop. [fellow.
calavera, kālāvā'rā, sf. skull; hot-brained
calaverada, -vērā'dā, sf. ridiculous, foolish action.
calaverear, -vērēār', v. n. to act foolishly.
calcañar, kālkānyār', sm. heel-bone.
calcar, kālkār', v a. to counter-draw; to trample on.
calcáreo, rea, kālkā'rēọ, a. calcareous.
calce, kāl'thē, sm. tire of a wheel.
calceta, kālthā'tā, sf. under-stocking.
calcetería, -tērē'ā, sf. trade of a hosier.
calcetero, ra, -tā'rọ, sm. one who makes, mends or sells thread-stockings; knitter.
calcillas, kālthīl'yās, sm. little coward.
calcina, kālthā'nā, sf. mortar.
calcinar, kālthīnār', v a. to calcine.
calco, kāl'kọ, sm. counter-drawing.
calcografía, -grāfē'ā, sf. art of engraving.
calculable, kālkūlā'blē, a. calculable.
calculación, -lāthōn', sf. calculation, computation. [puter.
calculador, -lādọr', sm. calculator, com-
calcular, -lār', v a. to calculate, to reckon, to compute.
cálculo, kāl'kūlọ, sm. calcule, calculation, computation; (med.) gravel.
calda, kāl'dā, sf. warmth, heat; warming or heating, -s, pl. hot baths.
caldear, kāldēār', v a. to weld iron; to warm, to heat.
caldera, kāldā'rā, sf. caldron, kettle, boiler; las -s de Pero Botero, (fam.) hell.

calderada, –rä´dä, sf. a caldron-full.

calderería, –rĕrĕ´ä, sf. brazier's shop.

calderero, –rä´rŏ, sm. brazier, copper-smith.

caldereta, –rä´tä, sf. small caldron; – de agua bendita, holy-water fount.

calderilla, –rĭl´yä, sf. holy water fount; copper-coin. [dron.

caldero, käldĕ´rŏ, sm. bucket-shaped cal-

calderón, käldĕrŏn´, sm. copper, large caldron; paragraph; (mus.) fermata-sign.

calderuela, kälderä´lä, sf. dark lantern (used by sportsmen to drive partridges into the net). [liquors.

caldo, käl´dŏ, sm. broth; –s, pl. spirituous

caldoso, sa, käldŏ´sŏ, a. having too much broth or gravy. [day of every month.

calendas, kälĕn´däs, sf. pl. calends, first

calendario, –dä´rĭŏ, sm. almanac, calendar. [large, clumsy watch.

calentador, –tädŏr´, sm. warming-pan;

calentar, –tär´, v. a. to warm, to heat, to be ruttish or proud (of beasts); –se, to grow hot, to dispute warmly.

calentura, kälĕntŏ´rä, sf. fever.

calenturiento, ta, –tärĭĕn´tŏ, a. feverish; fever-sick.

calera, kälĕ´rä, sf. lime-kiln.

calería, –rĕ´ä, sf. lime-kiln.

calero, kälĕ´rŏ, sm. lime-burner.

calesa, kälĕ´sä, sf. calash, cab. [cabman.

calesero, kälĕsĕ´rŏ, sm. driver of a calash,

calesín, kälĕsín´, sm. single horse-chaise.

caletre, kälĕ´trĕ, sm. understanding, judgment, discernment. [kind.

calibre, kälĭ´brĕ, sm. calibre; (fig.) sort,

calidad, kälĭdäd´´, sf. quality, condition, character; kind.

cálido, da, kä´lĭdŏ, a. hot, calid; fiery, vehemently, en–, on the spot, immediately.

caliente, kälĭĕn´tĕ, a. hot, calid; fiery, vehemently, en–, on the spot, immediately.

califa, käl´ĭfä, sm. caliph.

califato, –fä´tŏ, sm. caliphate.

calificación, kälĭfĭkäthŏn´, sf. qualification; judgment, censure; proof.

calificar, –fĭkär´, v. a. to qualify; to authorise; to attest; to ennoble, –se, to prove one's noble birth.

caligrafía, kälĭgräfĭ´ä, sf. calligraphy.

caligrafo, kälĭ´gräfŏ, sm. one who writes a beautiful hand.

cáliz, kä´lĭth, sm. chalice; flower-cup.

calizo, za, kälĭ´thŏ, a. calcareous. [sea.

calma, käl´mä, sf. calm; calmness, smooth

calmante, kälmän´tĕ, sm. (med.) anodyne.

calmar, kälmär´, v. a. to calm, to quiet, to pacify; –, v. n. to be becalmed.

calmoso, sa, kälmŏ´sŏ, a. calm, tranquil.

calofriarse, kälŏfrĭär´sĕ, v. r. to shiver with cold.

calofrío, –frĕ´ŏ, sm. shivering with cold.

calor, kälŏr´, sm. heat, hotness, ardour, fieriness.

calórico, kälŏ´rĭkŏ, sm. caloric.

calumnia, kälŭm´nĭä, sf. calumny.

calumniador, ra, –nĭädŏr´, sm. & f. calumniator, slanderer. [to slander.

calumniar, –nĭär´, v. a. to calumniate,

calumnioso, sa, –nĭŏ´sŏ, a. calumnious, slanderous. [lively.

caluroso, sa, kälŭrŏ´sŏ, a. warm, hot;

calva, käl´vä, sf. bald pate; a children's game played with stones. [calva.

calvar, kälvär´, v. a. to hit a stone (at

calvario, kälvä´rĭŏ, sm. Calvary; (fig.) debts. [(of the whole head).

calvatrueno, kälväträ´nŏ, sm. baldness

calvicie, kälvĕ´thĭĕ, sf. baldness.

calvinismo, kälvĭnĭs´mŏ, sm. Calvinism.

calvinista, –nĭs´tä, sm. Calvinist.

calvo, va, käl´vŏ, a. bald; barren. [pl.

calza, käl´thä, sf. trousers, pl., stockings,

calzada, kälthä´dä, sf. causeway, highway.

calzado, –dŏ, sm. any kind of shoe or foot-covering.

calzador, kälthädŏr´, sm. shoeing-horn.

calzadura, –dŏ´rä, sf. putting on of shoes; felloe of a cart-wheel.

calzar, kälthär´, v. a. to put on shoes; to strengthen with iron or wood; to stop a wheel; to carry a ball of a certain size (of fire-arms).

calzón, kälthŏn´, sm. breeches, pl.

calzonazo, kälthŏnä´thŏ, sm. big pair of breeches; es un –, he is a weak fellow.

calzoncillos, –thĭl´yŏs, sm. pl. drawers.

calla callando, käl´yä kälyän´dŏ, ad. privately, secretly.

callada, kälyä´dä, sf. dish of tripe; de –, á las –s, ad. without noise, privately.

callado, da, –yä´dŏ, a. silent, reserved, noiseless. [voice; silently.

callandico, kälyändĭ´kŏ, ad. in a low

callar, kälyär´, v. n. to keep silence, to be silent, to hold one's tongue; to conceal, to hush.

calle, käl´yĕ, sf. street; lane; alley; ¡–! strange!, wonderful!, mightily!

callear, kälyĕär´, v. a. to clear the walks in a vineyard of loose branches.

calleja, kälyĕ´h´ä, sf. lane, narrow passage.

callejear, –hĕär´, v. a. to loiter about the streets. [bling.

callejero, ra, –hĕ´rŏ, a. loitering, ram-

callejón, –hŏn´, sm. narrow pass.

callejuela, –hŭĕ´lä, sf. lane, narrow passage; subterfuge, shift. [pl. tripe.

callo, käl´yŏ, sm. corn; wen; callus; –s,

callosidad, kälyŏsĭdäd´, sf. callosity.

calloso, sa, kälyŏ´sŏ, a. callous; horny.

cama, kä´mä, sf. bed, couch; litter; hacer la –, to make up the bed.

camachuelo, –tshŭĕ´lŏ, sm. linnet.

camada, kämä´dä, sf. brood of young animals; – de ladrones, nest of rogues.

camafeo, –fĕ´ŏ, sm. cameo.

camal, kämäl´, sm. halter.

camaleón, kämälĕŏn´, sm. chameleon.

camaleopardo, kämälĕŏpär´dŏ, sm. camoleopard.

camamila, kämämĭ´lä, st. camomile.

camándula, kämän´dŭlä, sf. rosary of one or three decades.

camandulería, kämändŭlĕr´ĕ´ä, sf. hypocrisy, insincerity, dissimulation.

camandulero, -lă´rŏ, a. full of tricks, hypocritical. [king's court.

cámara, kăm´ără, sf. hall; chamber;

camarada, -ră´dă, sm. comrade, companion.

camaranchón, -rănt̃shŏn´, sm. garret.

camarera, -ră´ră, sf. head waiting-maid in great houses.

camarero, -ră´rŏ, sm. valet de chambre.

camariento, ta, -riĕn´tă, a. troubled with diarrhœa. [advisers of the king.

camarilla, -ril´yă, sf. coterie of private

camarín, -rĭn´, sm. shrine behind an altar where the images are kept with their ornaments; closet.

camarista, -ris´tă, sm. a member of the supreme council of la Cámara; –, sf. maid of honour of the queen of Spain.

camarlengo, kămărlĕn´gŏ, sm. lord of the bed-chamber of the king.

camarote, kămărŏ´tĕ, sm. berth, cabin.

camasquince, kămăskin´thĕ, sm. nickname jocularly applied to a meddlesome person. [low.

camastrón, kămăstrŏn´, sm. cunning fellow

cambalache, kămbălă´tshĕ, sm. traffic by exchange, barter.

cambalachear, -tsheăr´, v. a. to barter.

cambalachero, -tshă´rŏ, sm. barterer.

cambiable, kămbĭ´blĕ, a. fit to be exchanged.

cambiar, kămbĭăr´, v. a. to barter, to exchange; to change; to alter; to give or take money on bills.

cambija, kămbĭ´hă, sf. basin of water.

cambio, kăm´bĭŏ, sm. barter, exchange; course of exchange; bank; alteration, change.

cambista, kămbĭs´tă, sm. banker.

cambray, kămbră´ĕ, sm. cambric, fine linen. [horn.

cambrón, kămbrŏn´, sm. common buck-

cambronal, -năl´, sm. thicket of briers, brambles and thorns.

cambronera, -nă´ră, sf. box-thorn.

camella, kămĕl´yă, sf. she-camel; milk-pail. [camels.

camellero, kămĕlyă´rŏ, sm. driver of

camello, kămĕl´yŏ, sm. camel.

camellón, kămĕlyŏn´, sm. ridge turned up by the plough; flower-bed.

camilla, kămil´yă, sf. pallet; bed for women after child-birth; clothes-horse.

caminador, kămĭnădŏr´, sm. good walker.

caminante, -năn´tĕ, sm. traveller, walker.

caminar, -năr´, v. n. to travel; to walk, to march.

caminata, -nă´tă, sf. long walk.

camino, kămĭ´nŏ, sm. highroad; way; – real, highway; de –, in one's way, going along.

camisa, kămĕ´să, sf. shirt; shift, chemise.

camisola, kămĭsŏ´lă, sf. ruffled shirt.

camisolín, kămĭsŏlĭn´, sm. shirt-front.

camisote, kămĭsŏ´tĕ, sm. coat of mail.

camorra, kămŏr´ră, sf. quarrel, dispute.

camorrista, kămŏrris´tă, sm. & f. quarrelsome person.

campamento, kămpămĕn´tŏ, sm. (mil.) encampment, camp, lager.

campana, kămpă´nă, sf. bell; – de chimenea, funnel of a chimney.

campanada, -nă´dă, sf. sound of a bell; (fig.) scandal.

campanario, -rĭŏ, sm. belfry.

campanear, -neăr´, v. a. to ring the bell frequently; to divulge.

campanela, kămpănĕ´lă, sf. rapid rotation upon one foot in a Spanish dance.

campaneo, -nă´ŏ, sm. bell-ringing, chime; affected manner of walking.

campanero, -nă´rŏ, sm. bell-founder; bell-man. [uvula.

campanilla, kămpănĭl´yă, sf. hand-bell;

campanillazo, -lyă´thŏ, sm. signal given with a bell. [small bell often.

campanillear, -lyeăr´, v. a. to ring a

campante, kămpăn´tĕ, p. & a. excelling, surpassing.

campanudo, da, kămpănŏ´dŏ, a. wide, puffed up; pompous, high-sounding.

campánula, kămpă´nŭlă, sf. bell-flower.

campaña, kămpăn´yă, sf. campaign, level country; (mil.) campaign.

campar, kămpăr´, v. n. to encamp; to excel.

campeador, kămpeădŏr´, sm. warrior; surname of the Cid.

campear, kămpeăr´, v. n. to be in the field; to frisk about in the fields; to excel.

campeche, kămpĕtsh´ĕ, sm. Campeachy-wood, camwood.

campeón, kămpeŏn´, sm. champion.

campesino, na, kămpĕsĕ´nŏ, **campestre,** kămpĕs´trĕ, a. rural. [land, campaign.

campiña, kămpĭn´yă, sf. flat tract of arable

campo, kăm´pŏ, sm. country; field; camp;

camuesa, kămŭĕ´să, sf. pippin. [ground.

camueso, -sŏ, sm. pippin-tree; simpleton.

can, kăn´, sm. dog; (poet.) dog-star.

cana, kă´nă, sf. measure (= two ells); –s, pl. grey hair; **peinar** –s, to grow old.

canal, kănăl´, sm. channel, canal.

canalizar, kănălĭthăr´, v. a. to canalise.

canalizo, kănălĭ´thŏ, sm. narrow channel, strait.

canalón, kănălŏn´, sm. large gutter.

canalla, kănăl´yă, sf. mob, rabble, populace, kănă´nă, sf. cartridge-box. [lace.

canana, kănă´nă, sf. cartridge-box.

canapé, kănăpĕ´, sf. canopy, sofa.

canario, kănă´rĭŏ, sm. canary-bird.

canasta, kănăs´tă, sf. basket, hamper.

canastilla, kănăstĭl´yă, sf. small basket.

canasto, kănăs´tŏ, sm. large basket.

cancamusa, kănkămŏ´să, sf. trick, fraud.

cancel, kănthĕl´, sm. screen (at church-doors); royal box in the castle-church.

cancelación, kănthĕlăthĭŏn´, **cancela-dura,** -lădŏ´ră, sf. cancellation, erasion.

cancelar, -lăr´, v. a. to cancel, to expunge; to efface from the memory.

cancelaría, -lără´ă, sf. papal chancery, place where grants and licences are expedited.

cancelario, -lă´rĭŏ, sm. chancellor.

cáncer, kăn´thĕr, sm. cancer (ulcer).

Cáncer, —, sm. Cancer, Crab (sign of the zodiac); [flicted with a cancer.
cancerarse, kǎnthěrǎr sě, v. r. to be af-
canceroso, sa, kǎnthěrṓ sō, a. cancerous.
canciller, kǎnthǐlěr', sm. chancellor.
canción, kǎnthǐṓn', sf. song.
cancionero, kǎnthǐǒněrṓ, sm. song-book.
candado, kǎndǎ'dṓ, sm. padlock.
candela, kǎndě'lǎ, sf. candle.
candelabro, kǎndělǎ'brṓ, sm. candlestick.
Candelaria, —lǎ'rǐǎ, sf. Candlemas.
candelero, —lě'rṓ, sm. candlestick; chandelier.
candelizas, kǎndělě'thǎs, sf. pl. (mar.)
candente, kǎnděn'tě, a. red-hot.
candidato, kǎndǐdǎ'tṓ, sm. candidate.
cándido, da, kǎn'dǐdō, a. white, snowy; candid; simple. [lamp.
candil, kǎndǐl', sm. kitchen- or stable-
candilada, kǎndǐlǎ'dǎ, sf. oil or grease spot.
candileja, kǎndǐlě'hǎ, sf. (bot.) willow.
candonga, kǎndǒn'gǎ, sf. servile civility (intended to deceive); old mule no longer fit for service. [ing.
candongo, ga, —dǒn'gṓ, a. cajoling, fawn-
candonguear, —gěǎr', v. a. to jeer, to sneer.
candor, kǎndǒr', sm. candour, ingenuousness. [ness.
canela, kǎně'lǎ, sf. cinnamon. [ness.
canelo, kǎně'lṓ, sm. cinnamon-tree.
canelón, kǎnělṓn', sm. icicle (hanging from the eaves); sugar-stick with a slice of cinnamon. [sail.
cangreja, kǎngrě'hǎ, sf. brig-sail, gaff-
cangrejo, —ō, sm. cray-fish, crab.
cangrena, kǎngrě'nǎ, sf. gangrene.
cangrenarse, —nǎr'sě, v. r. to be afflicted with gangrene.
cangrenoso, sa, —nō'sō, a. gangrenous.
canguro, kǎngō'rṓ, sm. kangaroo.
caníbal, kǎně'bǎl, sm. cannibal, man-eater.
canícula, kǎně'kūlǎ, sf. dog-days.
canijo, ja, kǎně'hṓ, a. weak, sickly.
canilla, kǎně'lyǎ, sf. shin-bone; tap of a cask; spool.
caninez, kǎněně'th', sf. canine appetite.
canino, na, kǎně'nō, a. canine; hambre —a, sf. canine appetite.
caniquí, kǎně'kě', sf. fine muslin (from the East Indies). [prisoners of war.
canje, kǎn'hě, sm. (mil.) exchange of
canjear, kǎn'hěǎr', v. a. (mil.) to exchange prisoners of war.
canjilón, kǎn'hǐlṓn', sm. earthen pitcher.
cano, na, kǎ'nō, a. hoary, gray-headed.
canoa, kǎnṓ'ǎ, sf. canoe. [canoe.
canoero, kǎnṓě'rṓ, sm. one who steers a
canon, kǎ'nṓn, sm. canon; catalogue, list; canon, a large sort of type; (mus.) canon; —es, pl. canonical law.
canonesa, kǎnṓně'sǎ, sf. canoness.
canongía, kǎnṓn'hě'ǎ, sf., canonicato, kǎnṓnǐkǎ'tṓ, sm. canonry; canonicate.
canónico, ca, kǎnṓ'nǐkō, a. canonical.
canónigo, —nǐgō, sm. canon, prebendary.
canonista, —nǐs'tǎ, sm. canonist.
canonización, kǎnṓnǐthǎthǐṓn', sf. canonisation.

canonizar, —thǎr', v. a. to canonise.
canoro, ra, kǎnṓ'rō, a. canorous, tuneful.
canoso, sa, kǎnṓ'sō, a. hoary, gray-headed.
cansado, da, kǎnsǎ'dō, a. weary, wearied, tired; tedious, tiresome. [fatigue.
cansancio, kǎnsǎn'thǐṓ, sm. lassitude,
cansar, kǎnsǎr', v. a. to weary, to fatigue; to harass, to molest; —se, to grow weary.
cantable, kǎntǎ'blě, a. tunable.
cantada, —dǎ, sf. (mus.) cantata.
cantaleta, —lě'tǎ, sf. pun, jest, joke.
cantar, kǎntǎr', sm. song; —es, pl. Solomon's Song; —, v. a. to sing; to creak; (at cards) to call out the score.
cántara, kǎn'tǎrǎ, sf. pitcher; wine-measure (containing about 32 pints). [cantharis.
cantárida, kǎntǎ'rǐdǎ, sf. Spanish fly.
cantarín, kǎntǎrǐn', sm. opera-singer; fellow who is always singing.
cantarina, —rě'nǎ, sf. opera-singer.
cántaro, kǎn'tǎrō, sm. pitcher; ballot-box; llover á —s, to rain heavily, to pour.
cantatriz, kǎntǎtrǐth', sf. songstress.
cantera, kǎntě'rǎ, sf. quarry.
cantería, kǎntěrě'ǎ, sf. trade of a stone-cutter.
cantero, kǎntě'rō, sm. stone-cutter.
cántico, —kṓ, sm. canticle; —de los —s, the song of Solomon.
cantidad, —tǐdǎd', sf. quantity; number.
cantimplora, —tǐmplṓ'rǎ, sf. syphon; vessel for cooling liquors.
cantina, —tě'nǎ, sf. cellar; canteen.
cantinela, —tǐně'lǎ, sf. short song; irksome repetition of a subject.
cantinero, —ně'rō, sm. butler.
cantizal, —tǐthǎl', sm. stony ground.
canto, kǎn'tō, sm. stone; singing; edge; canto (poet.).
cantón, kǎntṓn', sm. corner; canton.
cantonearse, kǎntṓněǎr'sě, v. r. to walk affectedly.
cantonera, kǎntṓně'rǎ, sf. corner-clips.
cantor, ra, kǎntṓr', sm. & f. singer; songstress. [stores.
cantorral, kǎntṓrrǎl', sm. place full of
canturía, kǎntūrě'ǎ, sf. vocal music.
canutillo, kǎnūtǐl'yō, sm. stalk of a straw.
caña, kǎn'yǎ, sf. cane, reed; staik; — dulce, sugar-cane.
cañada, kǎnyǎ'dǎ, sf. dale (between two mountains); sheep-walk.
cañal, kǎnyǎl', sm. pond-grate; fish-garth.
cañamar, kǎnyǎmǎr', sm. hemp-field.
cañamiel, —mǐěl', sm. sugar-cane. [cloth.
cáñamo, kǎn'yǎmō, sm. hemp; hempen
cañamón, —mṓn', sm. hemp-seed.
cañavera, —vě'rǎ, sf. common reed-grass.
cañaveral, —věrǎl', sm. reed-plot, reed-bank.
cañazo, kǎnyǎ'thō, sm. blow with a cane.
cañería, kǎnyěrě'ǎ, sf. conduit of water, water-pipe. [limbed (of horses).
cañilavado, da, kǎnyǐlǎvǎ'dō, a. small
cañiza, kǎnyě'thǎ, sf. kind of coarse linen.
cañizo, —thō, sm. hurdle.
caño, kǎn'yō, sm. tube, pipe; sewer.
cañón, kǎnyṓn', sm. tube, pipe; cannon.

cañonazo, -nŏ'thŏ, sm. cannon-shot.
cañonear, -nĕăr', v. a. to cannonade.
cañoneo, -nŏ'ŏ, sm. cannonade.
cañonera, -nŏ'rā, sf. embrasure.
cañonería, -rē'ā, sf. pipes of an organ.
cañutillo, kănyūtil'yŏ, sm. bugle (small glass tubes). [phalange; pipe, tube.
cañuto, kănyū'tŏ, sm. internode of a cane.
caoba, kăŏ'bā, sf. mahogany-tree.
caos, kă'ŏs, sm. chaos; confusion.
capa, kă'pā, sf. cloak; mantle; layer, stratum; cover; pretext; de — y gorra, in a plain manner.
capacidad, -thādăd', sf. capacity; extent; talent.
capachero, -tshā'rŏ, sm. basket-maker.
capacho, kăpătsh'ŏ, sm. hamper; frail; bricklayer's-hod; barn-owl.
capada, kăpā'dā, sf. anything portable in a person's cloak. [whistle.
capador, -dŏr', sm. sow-gelder; gelder's
capadura, -dŏ'rā, sf. castration, gelding.
capar, kăpăr', v. a. to geld; (fig.) to castrate, to curtail.
caparazón, kăpārăthŏn', sm. caparison.
caparra, kăpăr'rā, sf. earnest-money.
caparrosa, kăpărrŏ'sā, s. copperas.
capataz, kăpătăth', sm. overseer; warden of the mint.
capaz, kăpăth', a. capacious, capable, spacious, roomy; fit, apt; ingenious, clever.
capazo, kăpă'thŏ, sm. rush-basket, frail.
capcionar, kăpthiŏnăr', v. a. to seize, to arrest.
capcioso, sa, kăₚthiŏ'sŏ, a. captious.
capeador, kăpĕădŏr', a. cloak-stealer.
capear, kăpĕăr', v. a. to rob a passenger of his cloak; to flourish one's cloak before a bull; -, v. n. (mar.) to try or lay to.
capelo, kăpĕ'lŏ, sm. dues received in ancient times by bishops from their clergy; red hat (of a cardinal). [shoe.
capellada, kăpĕlyā'dā, sf. toe-piece of a
capellán, kăpĕlyăn', sm. chaplain; almoner.
capellanía, kăpĕlyănē'ā, sf. chaplainship.
capellar, kăpĕlyăr', sm. moorish cloak.
capellina, kăpĕlyĕ'nā, sf. (mil.) spike-helmet; hood worn by country-people.
capeo, kăpĕ'ŏ, sm. challenging of a bull with a cloak.
capero, kăpĕ'rŏ, sm. priest who carries the cope or pluvial in churches.
caperuza, -rŏ'thā, sf. hood.
capialzado, kăpiālthā'dŏ, a. sloping on the outside and indented on the inside.
capiello, kăpiĕl'yŏ, sm. biggin.
capigorrista, kăpĭgŏrrēs'tā, capigorrón, -gŏrrŏn', sm. vagabond; parasite.
capilar, kăpĭlăr', a. capillary.
capilla, kăpĭl'yā, sf. hood; cowl; chapel.
capilleja, kăpĭlyĕ'h'ā, sf. small chapel.
capillejo, -ŏ, sm. small hood; skein of silk for sewing. [warden.
capiller(o), -lyĕ'r(ŏ), sm. sexton, church-
capillo, kăpĭl'yŏ, sm. child's cap; hood of a hawk. [a monk's cowl.
capilludo, da, kăpĭlyŏ'dŏ, a. resembling

capirotada, kăpĭrŏtā'dā, sf. American paste made up of herbs, eggs, garlic and
capirotazo, -tā'thŏ, sm. fillip. [spice.
capirote, kăpĭrŏ'tĕ, sm. hood.
capisayo, kăpĭsă'yŏ, sm. garment which serves both as a cloak and riding-coat.
capiscol, kăpĭskŏl', sm. precentor.
capitación, kăpĭtăthiŏn', sf. poll-tax.
capital, kăpĭtăl', sm. stock; sum of money put out at interest; fortune of a husband at the time of his marriage; capital-stock of a merchant; -, sf. capital, metropolis; -, a. capital; principal.
capitalista, kăpĭtălĭs'tā, sm. capitalist.
capitalizar, kăpĭtălĭthăr', v. a. to capitalize.
capitán, kăpĭtăn', sm. captain. [talize.
capitana, -tā'nā, sf. admiral's ship.
capitanazo, -nŏ'thŏ, sm. able general.
capitanear, kăpĭtănĕăr', v. a. to have the command in chief of an army; to head a troop of people. [captainry.
capitanía, kăpĭtănē'ā, sf. captainship.
capitel, kăpĭtĕl', sm. spire over the dome of a church; capital (of a column).
capitolio, kăpĭtŏ'liŏ, sm. capitol.
capitón, kăpĭtŏn', sm. pollard, chub.
capítula, kăpē'tŭlā, sf. part of the prayers read at divine service.
capitulación, kăpĭtŭlāthiŏn', sf. capitulation; agreement; -ones, pl. matrimonial contract.
capitular, -lăr', v. a. to conclude an agreement; (mil.) to capitulate; to accuse by public authority; -, v. n. to sing prayers at divine service; -, sm. capitular; -, a. capitulary. [antiphoner.
capitulario, kăpĭtŭlā'riŏ, sm. antiphonal.
capítulo, kăpē'tŭlŏ, sm. chapter of a cathedral; assembly of the prelates of religious orders; chapter (section of a book).
capolar, kăpŏlăr', v.a. to mince; to behead.
capón, kăpŏn', sm. eunuch; gelding; capon; anchor-stopper.
caponar, kăpŏnăr', v. a. to geld; to curtail; to tie up vine-branches.
caponera, kăpŏnĕ'rā, sf. coop (for capons).
caporal, kăpŏrăl', sm. chief, ringleader; (mil.) corporal. [thistle.
capota, kăpŏ'tā, sf. head of the fuller's
capote, -tĕ, sm. rain-cloak; austere look or mien.
capotillo, kăpŏtĭl'yŏ, sm. mantelet.
capotón, kăpŏtŏn', sm. large wide coat.
capotudo, da, kăpŏtŏ'dŏ, a. frowning.
capricornio, kăprĭkŏr'niŏ, sm. wood-bob, wood-beetle; cuckold. [the zodiac).
Capricornio, -, sm. Capricorn (sign of
capricho, kăprēsh'ŏ, sm. caprice, whim, fancy; (mus.) irregular but pleasing composition. [whimsical; obstinate.
caprichoso, sa, -tshŏ'sŏ, a. capricious,
caprichudo, da, -tshŏ'dŏ, a. stubborn, capricious.
caprino, na, kăprē'nŏ, a. goatish.
cápsula, kăp'sŭlā, sf. (bot.) capsule.
capsular, -lăr', a. capsular, capsulary.
captar, kăptăr', v. a. to captivate.

captura, kăptŏ'ră, sf. capture, seizure.

capucha, kăpŭtsh'ă, sf. circumflex; cap, fur-cap, cowl, hood of a woman's cloak; monk's hood.

Capuchina, kăpŭtshĕ'nă, sf. Capuchin nun; (bot.) great Indian cress.

Capuchino, –tshĕ'nŏ, sm. Capuchin monk; –, na, a. appertaining to Capuchin friars or nuns.

capucho, kăpŭtsh'ŏ, sm. cowl or hood forming part of a monk's dress.

Capullo, kăpŭl'yŏ, sm. pod of a silk-worm; rose-bud; coarse stuff made of spun silk.

Cara, kă'ră, sf. face, visage; – á –, face to face.

carabina, kărăbĕ'nă, sf. carbine, carabine.

carabinero, –bĭnă'rŏ, sm. carabinier.

cárabo, kă'răbŏ, sm. horned owl; earth-beetle; chub.

caracol, kărăkŏl', sm. snail; winding stair-case.

caracolear, –kŏlĕăr', v. n. to caracole.

carácter, kărăk'tĕr, sm. character; quality; condition; hand-writing.

característico, ca, –ktĕrĭs'tĭkŏ, a. characteristical.

caracterizar, kărăktĕrĭthăr', v. a. to characterize.

caramanchón, kărămăntshŏn', sm. garret.

carámbano, kărăm'bănŏ, sm. icicle; flake of ice.

carambola, kărămbŏ'lă, sf. cannon (at billiards); trick.

carambolear, –bŏlĕăr', v. n. to cannon (at billiards).

caramelo, kărămă'lŏ, sm. caramel.

caramente, –mĕn'tĕ, ad. dearly.

caramillo, –mĭl'yŏ, sm. small flute; tale-carrying.

carantamaula, kărăntămă'ŭlă, sf. hideous mask.

carantoña, kărăntŏn'yă, sf. hideous mask; vulgar old woman who paints and dresses stylishly or gaudily; –s, pl. caresses.

Carantoñero, kărăntŏnyă'rŏ, sm. wheedler, cajoler.

carátula, kără'tŭlă, sf. pasteboard-mask.

caratulero, –tŭlă'rŏ, sm. dealer in masks.

caravana, kărăvă'nă, sf. caravan.

caravanera, –vănă'ră, sf. caravansary.

caray, kără'ĕ, sm. tortoise-shell.

carbón, kărbŏn', sm. charcoal.

carbonada, kărbŏnă'dă, sf. grillade; kind of pancake.

Carboncillo, –thĭl'yŏ, sm. charcoal-pencil.

carbonear, –nĕăr', v. n. to make coal out of wood.

carbonera, –nă'ră, sf. coal-pit, coal-mine.

carbonería, –nĕrĕ'ă, sf. coal-yard; coal-shed; coal-mine.

carbonero, –nă'rŏ, sm. charcoal-burner.

carbónico, ca, kărbŏ'nĭkŏ, a. carbonic.

carbonilla, kărbŏnĭl'yă, sf. coal-dust.

carbonizar, kărbŏnĭthăr', v. a. to carbonise.

carbono, kărbŏ'nŏ, sm. (chem.) carbon.

carbunclo, kărbŭn'klŏ, carbunco, kărbŭn'kŏ, sm. carbuncle; red pustule.

carcaj, kărkăh', sm. quiver.

carcajada, kărkăhă'dă, sf. horse-laugh.

carcamal, kărkămăl', sm. nick-name for old people.

carcaño, kărkăn'yŏ, sm. heel-bone; screw-clamp, vice.

cárcel, kăr'thĕl, sf. prison; gaol, jail.

carcelaje, –lă'hĕ, sm. prison-fees.

carcelería, –lĕrĕ'ă, sf. imprisonment.

carcelero, –lă'rŏ, sm. jailor.

cárcola, kăr'kŏlă, sf. treadle.

carcoma, kărkŏ'mă, sf. wood-louse; dust made by the wood-louse; grief; anxious concern.

carcomer, –mĕr', v. a. to gnaw, to corrode; –se, to grow worm-eaten.

carcomido, da, –mĕ'dŏ, a. worm-eaten.

carda, kăr'dă, sf. teazel; teasel; card; severe reprimand, wigging, jobation.

cardador, –dŏr', sm. carder, comber.

cardadura, –dŏ'ră, sf. carding.

cardar, –dăr', v. a. to card wool; to raise the wool on cloth with a teasel.

cardenal, kărdănăl', sm. cardinal; Virginian nightingale; livid tumour.

cardenalato, –lă'tŏ, sm. cardinalate.

cardenalicio, cia, –lĕ'thĭŏ, a. belonging to a cardinal.

cardencha, kărdĕn'tshă, sf. teasel; card.

cardenillo, kărdĕnĭl'yŏ, sm. rust of copper; verdigris.

cárdeno, na, kăr'dĕnŏ, a. livid.

cardero, kărdă'rŏ, sm. card-maker.

cardico, kărdĕ'kŏ, sm. small thistle.

cardillo, kărdĭl'yŏ, sm. golden thistle.

cardinal kărdĕnăl', a. cardinal, principal.

cardo, kăr'dŏ, sm. thistle.

cardón, kărdŏn', sm. (bot.) teasel.

carduncha, kărdŭntsh'ă, sf. large iron comb for combing wool.

carduzador, kărdŭthădŏr', sm. carder.

carduzar, –thăr', v. a. to card or comb wool.

carear, kără'ĕ, v. a. to confront criminals; to compare; to tend a drove of cattle; –se, to assemble for business.

carecer, kără'thĕr', v. n. to want.

carena, kără'nă, sf. careening; careen; ship.

carenar, –năr', v. a. to careen a ship.

careo, kără'ŏ, sm. (law) confrontation.

carero, ra, kără'rŏ, a. in the habit of selling things dear.

carestía, kărĕstĕ'ă, sf. scarcity, want; famine; dearness.

careca, kără'tă, sf. pasteboard-mask.

careto, ta, –tŏ, a. blazed (applied to horses).

carga, kăr'gă, sf. load, freight, pack; cargo; charge (of a fire-arm); impost, tax; (fig.) burden of the mind, heaviness.

cargadas, kărgă'dăs, sf. pl. a game at cards.

cargadero, –dă'rŏ, sm. loading-place.

cargadilla, –dĭl'yă, sf. increase of a debt newly contracted.

cargador, –dŏr', sm. freighter; loader; rammer.

cargamento, –mĕn'tŏ, sm. (mar.) cargo.

cargar, kărgăr', v. a. to load, to burden, to freight; to attack the enemy; to charge a gun; to clog; to impose taxes; to impeach; heaviness of the head.

cargazón, kărgăthŏn', sf. cargo (of a ship);

cargo, kär'gô, sm. burden, loading; employment, dignity; office; charge, care; obligation; accusation. [dize.

carguío, kärgē'ô, sm. cargo of merchandise.

cariaguileño, ña, kärīāgīlēn'yô, a. long-faced and crook-nosed.

carialegre, -ālā'grē, a. pleased-looking.

cariampollado, -āmpōlyā'dô, a. round-faced. [chubby.

cariancho, cha, -ān'tshä, a. broad-faced.

cariarse, kärīär'sē, v. r. to grow carious.

caribe, kär'ē bē, sm. cannibal.

caricatura, kärīkätū'rä, sf. caricature.

caricia, kärē'thiä, sf. caress. [ing.

caricioso, sa, -thiä'sō, a. fondling, caress-

caricuerdo, da, -kūēr'dô, a. having a composed look. [alms, pl.

caridad, -dād'', sf. charity; benevolence;

caridoliente, -dōlīēn'tē, a. sad-faced.

caries, kä'rīēs, sf. caries, cariosity.

cariescrito, kärīēskrī'tô, a. corrugated, shrivelled. [a wrinkled face.

carifruncido, da, -frūnthī'dô, a. having

carigordo, da, -gōr'dô, a. full-faced.

carilargo, ga, -lär'gô, a. long-visaged.

carilucio, cia, -lō'thiô, a. smooth-faced.

carilla, kärīl'yä, sf. little face; mask used by bee-keepers.

carilleno, na, kärīlyē'nô, a. full-faced.

carinegro, gra, kärinā'grô, a. swarthy-complexioned. [endearing expression.

cariño, kärin'yô, sm. fondness, tenderness;

cariñoso, sa, -yô'sô, a. affectionate, endearing; loving.

cariota, kärīô'tä, sf. wild carrot.

carirraído, da, -rä'ī dô, a. brazen-faced, impudent. [faced.

carirredondo, da, -rēdōn'dô, a. round-

carita, kärī'tä, sf. lovely face of a woman.

caritativo, va, -tätē'vô, a. charitable.

carlán, kärlän', sm. justice of the peace, J.P.

carlanca, kärlän'kä, sf. training-collar.

carlancón, -kōn', sm. sly-boots, dodger.

carmelina, kärmēlī'nä, sf. paco-wool.

carmelita, -lē'tä, sf. Carmelite.

carmen, kär'mēn, sm. country-house; Carmelite order.

carmenador, kärmēnädōr', sm. teaser.

carmenar, -när', v. a. to card wool; to pull out the hair of the head; to cheat at [play.

carmes, kär'mēs, sm. kermes.

carmesí, kärmēsī', sm. cochineal powder; crimson; purple.

carmín, kärmīn', sm. & a. carmine.

carnada, kärnä'dä, sf. bait, lure.

carnaje, -nä'h'ē, sm. salt beef.

carnal, kärnäl', a. carnal, fleshy; sensual; —, sm. time of the year in which meat may be eaten. [liness.

carnalidad, -lidäd'', sf. lustfulness, flesh-

carnaval, kärnäväl', sm. carnival.

carnaza, kärnä'thä, sf. fleshy part of a hide; abundance of meat.

carne, kär'nē, sf. flesh; meat; pulp (of fruit). [runcle.

carnecilla, -thīl'yä, sf. carnosity, ca-

carnerada, -rä'dä, sf. flock of sheep.

carneraje, -rä'h'ē, sm. tax laid on sheep.

carnerear, -rēär', v. a. to fine the proprietor of sheep which have done damage.

carnerero, -nä'rô, sm. shepherd.

carneril, -rīl', sm. sheep-walk.

carnero, kärnä'rô, sm. sheep, mutton; family-vault. [sheep.

carneruno, na, -rō'nô, a. belonging to

carnestolendas, kärnēstōlēn'däs, sf. pl. shrovetide, shrove-Tuesday.

carnicería, kärnīthērē'ä, sf. shambles, slaughter-house; carnage, slaughter.

carnicero, -thē'rô, sm. butcher; —, ra, a. carnivorous. [animals.

carnicol, -kōl', sm. hoof of cloven-footed

carnificarse, -fīkär'sē, v. r. to carnify, to breed flesh.

carnívoro, ra, kärnē'vôrô, a. carnivorous.

carniza, kärnē'thä, sf. refuse of meat.

carnosidad, kärnōsīdäd', sf. proud flesh; fatness; fleshiness.

carnoso, sa, kärnō'sô, **carnudo**, -nō'dô, a. fleshy; marrowy; pulpous.

caro, ra, kä'rô, a. dear, costly; beloved, affectionate; —, ad. dearly.

caroca, kärō'kä, sm. caress.

carocha, -rōtsh'ä, sf. eggs of the queen-bee.

carochar, -rōtshär', v. a. to lay and hatch eggs (applied to the queen-bee).

caromomia, kärōmō'miä, sf. dry flesh of a mummy.

carona, kärō'nä, sf. padding of a saddle; part of the animal's back on which the **caroña**, kärōn'yä, sf. jade. [saddle lies.

caroquero, kärōkē'rô, sm. wheedler, flatterer.

carótida, kärō'tīdä, sf. the carotid artery.

carozo, kärō'thô, sm. core of a pomegranate.

carpa, kär'pä, sf. carp (fish); part torn off a bunch of grapes. [folio.

carpeta, kärpē'tä, sf. table-carpet; port-

carpintear, kärpīntēär', v. a. to carpenter.

carpintería, -rē'ä, sf. carpentry; carpenter's shop.

carpintero, -tē'rô, sm. carpenter; — de blanco, joiner; — de carretas, cartwright; — de obras de afuera, carpenter who timbers or roofs houses; — de ribera, ship-wright.

carpo, kär'pô, sm. wrist, carpus.

carraca, kärrä'kä, sf. carack (ship); rattle.

carral, kärräl', sm. barrel, butt, vat.

carraleja, -lē'h'ä, sf. black-beetle.

carralero, -lē'rô, sm. cooper.

carrasca, kärräs'kä, sf. evergreen oak, **carrasco**, -kô, sm. evergreen oak. [wine.

carraspada, kärräspä'dä, sf. negus, mulled

carraspante, -pän'tē, a. acrid, strong (of wine).

carraspera, -pē'rä, sf. hoarseness.

carrasqueño, ña, -kēn'yô, a. harsh, sharp; belonging to the evergreen oak.

carrera, kärrā'rä, sf. career, course, race; race-ground; high-road; alley; row, line; course of life; á - abierta, at full speed.

carreta, kärrā'tä, sf. long narrow cart.

carretada, kärrētä'dä, sf. cart-load; great quantity; á -s, in abundance.

carretaje, –*tā'h'ĕ*, sm. cartage.

carrete, *kărrĕ'tĕ*, sm. small reel for winding off silk, &c.; fishing-pulley.

carretear, –*tĕăr'*, v. a. to cart; to drive a cart; –se, to draw unevenly.

carretela, –*tĕ'lā*, sf. light coach.

carretera, –*tĕ'rā*, sf. high-road.

carretería, –*tĕrē'ā*, sf. number of carts; trade of a carman; cart-wright's yard.

carretero, –*tĕ'rŏ*, sm. cart-wright; carman.

carretilla, –*tĕl'yā*, sf. go-cart; squib, cracker; wheel-barrow.

carretón, –*tŏn'*, sm. go-cart (for children).

carriego, *kărrē'gŏ*, sm. osier fish-basket.

carril, *kărrĭl'*, sm. cart-way; cart-rut; furrow. [box on the ears.

carrillada, *kărrĭlyā'dā*, sf. hog's cheek;

carrillo, *kărrĭl'yŏ*, sm. cheek; tackle.

carrilludo, da, –*yŏ'dā*, a. chub-cheeked.

carriola, *kărrĭŏ'lā*, sf. truckle-bed; small chariot; curricle.

carrizo, *kărrē'thŏ*, sm. common reed-grass.

carro, *kăr'rŏ*, sm. cart.

Carro, –, sm. Charles' Wain.

carrocín, *kărrŏthĭn'*, sm. chaise, curricle.

carromatero, –*mātĕ'rŏ*, sm. charioteer, carman. [cart.

carromato, –*mā'tŏ*, sm. two-wheeled tilted

carroña, *kărrŏn'yā*, sf. carrion.

carroñar, *kărrŏnyăr'*, v.a. to infect sheep with the scab.

carroño, ña, *kărrŏn'yŏ*, a. putrid, rotten.

carroza, *kărrŏ'thā*, sf. state-coach; (mar.) awning. [riages or vehicles.

carruaje, *kărrŭā'h'ĕ*, sm. all sorts of car-

carruajero, –*hĕ'rŏ*, sm. carrier, carter, waggoner. [mountainous countries.

carruco, *kărrŏ'kŏ*, sm. small cart used in

carta, *kăr'tā*, sf. letter; map; – blanca, carte-blanche; – credencial ó de creencia, credentials, pl.; – certificada, registered letter; – de vuelta, dead letter; – en lista, letter "to be kept till called for", letter addressed "Post-Office"; – con valores declarados, money-letter.

cartabón, –*bŏn'*, sm. square (tool).

cartapacio, –*pā'thĭŏ*, sm. memorandum-book; scholar's portfolio. [party.

cartapartida, –*părtē'dā*, sf. (mar.) charter-

cartazo, –*thŏ*, sm. insulting, accusing letter.

cartear, *kărtĕăr'*, v. n. to play low cards, to see how the cards lie; –se, to keep up a correspondence by letter.

cartel, *kărtĕl'*, sm. placard; hand-bill; – de comedia, play-bill.

cartela, *kărtĕ'lā*, sf. slip of paper; cornice.

cartera, –*rā*, sf. portfolio, pocket-book; letter-case; flap of a pocket.

cartero, –*rŏ*, sm. letter-carrier, postman.

cartilaginoso, sa, *kărtĭlă hĭnŏ'sŏ*, a. cartilaginous.

cartílago, *kărtē'lăgŏ*, sm. cartilage.

cartilla, *kărtĭl'yā*, sf. short letter; primer.

cartón, *kărtŏn'*, sm. pasteboard; metal ornament; cartoon. [maker.

cartonero, *kărtŏnĕ'rŏ*, sm. pasteboard-

cartuchera, *kărtŭtshĕ'rā*, sf. (mil.) cartridge-box; cartridge-pouch.

cartucho, *kărtŭtsh'ŏ*, sm. cartouch.

cartuja, *kărtŭ'h'ā*, sm. Carthusian order.

cartujo, –*ŏ*, sm. Carthusian monk.

cartulario, *kărtŭlă'rĭŏ*, sm. cartulary.

cartulina, –*lē'nā*, sf. card, visiting-card.

carúncula, *kărŭn'kŭlā*, sf. caruncle.

carvi, *kăr'vĭ*, sm. common caraway.

casa, *kă'sā*, sf. house; home; – de campo, country-house; – de locos, mad-house; – de moneda, mint; – de posada, lodging-house.

casaca, *kăsā'kā*, sf. coat.

casación, –*thĭŏn'*, sf. abrogation.

casadero, ra, –*dĕ'rŏ*, a. marriageable.

casamata, –*mā'tā*, sf. (mil.) casemate.

casamentero, ra, –*mĕntĕ'rŏ*, sm. & f. marriage-maker. [made on cards.

casamiento, –*mĭĕn'tŏ*, sm. marriage; bet

casapuerta, –*pŭĕr'tā*, sf. porch.

casaquilla, –*kĭl'yā*, sf. short and loose jacket.

casar, *kăsăr'*, v. a. to marry; to consort; to couple; to adjust; to abrogate; to annul; –se, to marry. [shop.

casatienda, *kăsătĭĕn'dā*, sf. tradesman's

casca, *kăs'kā*, sf. husks of grapes; bark for tanning leather. [bell; rattle-snake.

cascabel, *kăskăbĕl'*, sm. rattle, little round

cascabelada, –*lā'dā*, sf. jingling of small bells; inconsiderate speech or action.

cascabelear, –*lĕăr'*, v. a. to feed one with vain hopes; –, v. n. to act with levity.

cascaciruelas, *kăskăthĭrŭĕ'lăs*, sm. mean, despicable fellow.

cascada, –*kă'dā*, sf. cascade, water-fall.

cascajal, –*kă'hăl'*, sm. place full of pebbles.

cascajo, –*kă'h'ŏ*, sm. gravel; fragments of broken vessels; rubbish; copper coin.

cascajoso, sa, –*hŏ'sŏ*, a. gravelly.

cascamajar, –*mā'hăr'*, v. a. to pound a thing to bits.

cascanoquí, –*nŏkē'*, sm. Jesuit's bark.

cascanueces, –*nŭĕ'thĕs*, sm. nut-cracker.

cascapiñones, –*pĭnyŏ'nĕs*, sm. (fig.) poor wretch.

cascar, *kăskăr'*, v. a. to crack, to break into pieces; to lick, to beat; –se, to be broken open.

cáscara, *kăs'kărā*, sf. rind, peel, husk; bark. | cáscaras ! –s, zounds ! [Jesuit's bark.

cascarilla, *kăskărĭl'yā*, sf. Peruvian bark.

cascarón, –*rŏn'*, sm. egg-shell; niche for the sacrament. [rude.

cascarrón, na, *kăskărrŏn'*, a. rough, harsh,

cascarudo, da, *kăskărŏ'dŏ*, a. thick-skinned, thick-peeled.

casco, *kăs'kŏ*, sm. skull, cranium; fragments of a pot; helmet; hulk of a ship; crown of a hat, hoof of a horse.

cascote, *kăskŏ'tĕ*, sm. rubbish, fragments of material used in building.

cascudo, da, *kăskŏ'dŏ*, a. large-hoofed.

caseoso, sa, *kăsĕ'ŏsŏ*, a. caseous, cheesy.

casera, *kăsĕ'rā*, sf. bachelor's housekeeper.

casería, *kăsĕrē'ā*, sf. messuage; economical management of a house.

caserío, –*ŏ*, sm. series of houses; village.

caserna, *kăsĕr'nā*, sf. (mil.) barracks.

casero, *kăsă'rŏ*, sm. landlord; –, ra, a. domestic; familiar; house-keeping.

casi, *kă'sĭ*, ad. almost, nearly; – que, – –, very nearly.

casia, *kă'sĭă*, sf. bastard cinnamon.

casillas, *kăsĭl'yăs*, sf. pl. place where backgammon is played; checkers (for backgammon).

casiller, *kăsĭlyĕr'*, sm. cleanser of the close-stools in the royal palace.

casillo, *kăsĭl'yŏ*, sm. trifling cause.

casimiro, *kăsĭmē'rŏ*, sm. kerseymere.

casino, *kăsē'nŏ*, sm. club, club-house.

caso, *kă'sŏ*, sm. case, occurrence, event; hap, casualty; occasion; (gr.) case; en – de eso, in that case; en todo –, at all events; – que, in case; –, sa, a. null and void.   [riage.

casorio, *kăsŏ'rĭŏ*, sm. inconsiderate marriage.

caspa, *kăs'pă*, sf. dandriff; scurf.

¡cáspita! *kăs'pĭtă*, wonderful!

casquetazo, *kăskĕtă'thŏ*, sm. blow with the head.   [cataplasm.

casquete, *kăskă'tĕ*, sm. helmet, casque;

casquiblando, da, *kăskĭblăn'dŏ*, a. soft-hoofed.   [wide-hoofed.

casquiderramado, da, *–dĕrrămă'dŏ*, a.

casquijo, *kăskĭ'hŏ*, sm. gravel.

casquilucio, cia, *kăskĭlŭ'thĭŏ*, a. gay, frolicsome.   [bee.

casquilla, *kăskĭl'yă*, sf. cell of the queen-

casquillo, *kăskĭl'yŏ*, sm. iron socket with which a spear is shod; point of an arrow.

casquimulcño, ña, *–mŭlĕn'yŏ*, a. narrow-hoofed (like mules).   [kind, quality.

casta, *kăs'tă*, sf. cast, race, lineage; breed;

castaña, *kăstăn'yă*, sf. chestnut; jug in the shape of a chestnut; club of hair; – pilonga, dried chestnut.

castañal, *kăstănyăl'*, **castañar**, *–yăr'*, sm. chestnut-grove.

castañeta, *kăstănyē'tă*, sf. castanet.

castañetear, *kăstănyĕtĕăr'*, v. n. to rattle the castanets in dancing.

castaño, *kăstăn'yŏ*, sm. chestnut-tree; –, ña, a. hazelly.

castañuela, *–yŭĕ'lă*, sf. castanet.

castañuelo, la, *–lŏ*, a. chestnut-coloured.

castelán, *kăstĕlyăn'*, sm. governor of a castle.   [district belonging to a castle.

castellanía, *kăstĕlyănē'ă*, sf. castellany,

castellano, *kăstĕlyă'nŏ*, sm. Castilian language, Spanish.

castidad, *kăstĭdăd''*, sf. chastity.

castigar, *–găr'*, v. a. to chastise, to punish; to afflict.   [ishment; correction.

castigo, *kăstĭ'gŏ*, sm. chastisement, pun-

castillejo, *kăstĭlyĕ'hŏ*, sm. castlet; go-cart (for little children).

castillete, *–yĕ'tĕ*, sm. small castle.

castillo, *kăstĭl'yŏ*, sm. castle; cell of the queen-bee.   [scent; pure, uncorrupt.

castizo, za, *kăstē'thŏ*, a. of a noble descent.

casto, ta, *kăs'tŏ*, a. pure, chaste.

castor, *kăstŏr'*, sm. beaver.

castoreo, *kăstŏ'rĕŏ*, sm. castoreum.

castra, *kăs'tră*, sf. pruning [of plants and trees.

castradera, *–dă'ră*, sf. knife for cutting the hives.

castrar, *kăstrăr'*, v. a. to geld, to castrate; to prune; to cut the honey-combs out of bee-hives.   [combs out of hives.

castrazón, *kăstrăthŏn'*, sf. cutting honey-

casual, *kăsŭăl'*, a. casual, accidental.

casualidad, *kăsŭălĭdăd''*, sf. casualty, accident.

casucha, *kăsŭtsh'ă*, sf. miserable hut.

casuísta, *kăsŭĭs'tă*, sm. casuist.

casulla, *kăsŭl'yă*, sf. chasuble.

cata, *kă'tă*, sf. tasting.

catábulo, *kătă'bŭlŏ*, sm. stable.

catacumbas, *–kŭm'băs*, sf. pl. catacombs.

catadura, *–dŭ'ră*, sf. face, countenance.

catafalco, *–făl'kŏ*, sm. funeral canopy over a bier.

catalejo, *–lĕ'hŏ*, sm. telescope.

catálogo, *kătă'lŏgŏ*, sm. catalogue.

cataplasma, *–plăs'mă*, sf. cataplasm. poultice.

catapulta, *–pŭl'tă*, sf. catapult.

catar, *kătăr'*, v. a. to taste; to inspect, to examine; to judge; to esteem.

catarata, *kătără'tă*, sf. cataract (disc se of the eye); water-fall, cascade.

catarral, *kătărrăl'*, a. catarrhal.

catarriento, ta, *kătărrĭĕn'tŏ*, a. catarrhal.

catarro, *kătăr'rŏ*, sm. catarrh.

catarroso, sa, *kătărrŏ'sŏ*, a. catarrhal, catarrhous.   [purging.

catártico, ca, *kătăr'tĭkŏ*, a. cathartic.

catastro, *kătăs'trŏ*, sm. general tax on land.

catástrofe, *kătăs'trŏfĕ*, sf. catastrophe.

catavino, *kătăvē'nŏ*, sm. small cup for tasting wine; –, sm. wine-taster; tippler.

catecismo, *kătĕthĭs'mŏ*, sm. catechism.

cátedra, *kă'tĕdră*, sf. professor's chair.

catedral, *kătĕdrăl'*, a. & sf. cathedral.

catedrático, *–dră'tĭkŏ*, sm. professor of a university.

categoría, *–gŏrē'ă*, sf. category; rank.

categórico, ca, *–gŏ'rĭkŏ*, a. categorical, decisive.

catequismo, *–kĭs'mŏ*, sm. catechism.

catequista, *–kĭs'tă*, sm. catechist.

catequizar, *–kĭthăr'*, v. a. to catechise.

caterva, *kătĕr'vă*, sf. mob.

cato, *kă'tŏ*, sm. Japan earth.   [cism.

catolicismo, *kăthŏlĭthĭs'mŏ*, sm. catholi-

católico, ca, *kătŏ'lĭkŏ*, a. & sm. catholic.

catorcena, *kătŏrthă'nă*, sf. conjunction of fourteen unities.

catorceno, na, *–nŏ*, a. fourteenth.

catre, *kă'trĕ*, sm. field-bed.

catricofre, *kătrĭkŏ'frĕ*, sm. bed-closet.

cauce, *kă'ŭthĕ*, sm. drain.   [guaranty.

caución, *kăŭthĭŏn'*, sf. caution, security,

caucionar, *–thĭŏnăr'*, v. a. to guarantee.

caucho, *kă'ŭtshŏ*, sm. (am.) caoutchouc.

cauda, *kă'ŭdă*, sf. train of a bishop's robe.

caudal, *kăŭdăl'*, sm. property, fortune, wealth; fund, stock; plenty.

caudaloso, sa, *kăŭdălŏ'sŏ*, a. carrying much water (speaking of rivers).

caudatario, *–tă'rĭŏ*, sm. train-bearer of a cardinal.

causa, *kā'ŭsā*, sf. cause; occasion; motive, reason; law-suit; á — de, considering.
causal, *kŭŭsāl'*, a. causal.   [because of.
causante, *kŭŭsăn'tā*, sm. constituent.
causar, *kŭŭsăr'*, v. a. to cause, to produce; to occasion.   [law-suits.
causídico, ca, *kŭŭs'dĭkŏ*, a. belonging to law-suits.
causón, *kŭŭsŏn'*, sm. burning fever which lasts only some hours.
cáustico, *kā'ŭstĭkŏ*, sm. (med.) caustic; —, ca, a. caustic.   [heedfulness.
cautela, *kŭŭtě'lā*, sf. caution, prudence;
cautelar, -*tělār'*, v. a. to take necessary precautions.   [ful.
cauteloso, sa, -*lŏ'sŏ*, a. cautious, heed-
cauterio, *kŭŭtě'rĭŏ*, sm. cautery.
cauterizar, -*rĭthăr'*, v. a. to cauterize; to reproach with severity.
cautivar, *kŏŭtĭvăr'*, v. a. to take prisoner in war; to captivate, to charm.
cautiverio, -*vě'rĭŏ*, sm. captivity; confinement.
cautivo, va, *kŭŭtě'vŏ*, sm. & f. captive.
cauto, ta, *kŭŭ'tŏ*, a. cautious, wary.
cava, *kā'vā*, sf. digging and earthing of vines; wine-cellar.
cavar, *kăvăr'*, v. a. to dig up, to excavate; —, v. n. to penetrate far into a thing; to think profoundly; to paw (of horses).
caverna, *kăvěr'nā*, sf. cavern, cave.
cavernoso, sa, *kăvěrnŏ'sŏ*, a. cavernous.
cavidad, *kăvĭdăd'*, sf. cavity, hollow.
cavilación, *kăvĭlăthĭŏn'*, sf. cavillation.
cavilar, -*lăr'*, v. a. to cavil.
caviloso, sa, -*lŏ'sŏ*, a. captious, cavillous.
cayada, *kăyă'dā*, sf., cayado, -*dŏ*, sm. shepherd's hook.
cayo, *kā'yŏ*, sm. rock, shoal.
caz, *kăth*, sm. canal, trench.
caza, *kā'thā*, sf, chase; game.
cazadero, *kăthădě'rŏ*, sm. hunting-ground.
cazador, -*dŏr'*, sm. hunter, huntsman; —, furtivo, poacher.
cazamoscas, -*mŏs'kăs*, sm. fly-catcher, gnat-snapper (bird).
cazar, *kăthăr'*, v. a. to chase, to hunt.
cazcalear, *kăthkălěăr'*, v. n. to fidget.   [pl.
cazcarria, -*kăr'rĭā*, sf. splashings of dirt.
cazo, *kā'thŏ*, sm. copper saucepan with an iron handle; ladle.
cazolero, ra, -*lě'rŏ*, a. too officious.
cazudo, da, *kăthŏ'dŏ*, a. thick-backed (of knives).
cazuela, *kăthŏě'lā*, sf. stewing-pan.
cazumbrón, *kăthŭmbrŏn'*, sm. cooper.
cazurro, rra, *kăthŏ'rŏ*, a. silent, taciturn.
¡ce! *thě*, hark!, come hither!
cea, *thā'ā*, sf. thigh-bone.
ceática, *thěā'tĭkā*, sf. (med.) sciatica.
ceba, *thā'bā*, sf. sea-weed.
cebada, *thěbā'dā*, sf. barley.
cebadazo, za, -*dā'thŏ*, a. of barley.
cebadera, -*dě'rā*, sf. fodder-bag; nose-bag (for horses).
cebadero, -*dě'rŏ*, sm. place where game or fowls are fed; bell-mule.
cebadura, -*dŏ'rā*, sf. feeding fowls.

cebar, *thěbăr'*, v. a. & n. to feed animals, to fatten; to keep up a fire; to grapple; to prime; to let off a rocket.   [skin.
cebellina, *thěbělyē'nā*, sf. sable; sable-skin.
cebo, *thā'bŏ*, sm. food; bait, lure; priming.
cebolla, *thěbŏl'yā*, sf. onion; bulb of the onion.
cebolleta, -*yā'tā*, sf. tender onion.
cebollino, -*yě'nŏ*, sm. onion-seed.
cebolludo, da, -*yŏ'dŏ*, a. bulbous.
cebón, *thěbŏn'*, sm. fat bullock or hog.
cebra, *thā'brā*, sf. zebra.
cebruno, *thěbrŏ'nŏ*, a. reddish brown.
cecear, *thěthěăr'*, v. a. to pronounce the s in the same manner as the c; to call one by ,,ce-ce''; to lisp.
cecial, *thěthĭăl'*, sm. cod (fish).
cecilia, *thěthě'lĭā*, sf. blind-worm.
cecina, -*nā*, sf. hung beef, salt beef.
cedacero, *thědăthā'rŏ*, sm. sieve-maker.
cedazo, *thědā'thŏ*, sm. hair-sieve, strainer.
ceder, *thěděr'*, v. a. to grant, to resign, to yield, to give up; —, v. n. to submit, to comply, to give in; to abate, to grow less.
cedrella, *thědrěl'yā* sf. cedar-wood.
cedrino, na, *thědrē'nŏ*, a. cedrine.
cedro, *thā'drŏ*, sm. cedar.
cedronela, *thědrŏně'lā*, sf. cider.
cédula, *thā'dŭlā*, sf. slip of paper; bill; decree; schedule; — de cambio, bill of exchange.
céfalo, *thā'fălŏ*, sm. mullet.
céfiro, *thā'fĭrŏ*, sm. zephyr.
cegar, *thěgăr'*, v. n. to grow blind; —, v. a. to deprive of sight; to darken; to shut.
cegarrita, *thěgărrē'tā*, sm. short-sighted person; á -s, with shut eyes.
cegarro, *thěgăr'rŏ*, cegato, ta, *thěgā'tŏ*, a. short-sighted.
ceguedad, *thěgědăd'*, sf. blindness.
ceja, *thě'hā*, sf. eye-brow, edging of clothes; (mus.) bridge of a stringed instrument; summit of a mountain.
cejar, *thě'hăr'*, v. n. to go backward; to slacken, to give in.
cejo, *thě'hŏ*, sm. thick mist or fog which usually arises from rivers.
celada, *thělā'dā*, sf. Burgundy helmet; ambush; artful trick.
celaje, *thělā'h'ě*, sm. colour of the clouds.
celar, *thělăr'*, v. n. & a. to fulfil the duties of an office with care; to watch over; to conceal; to engrave.
celda, *thěl'dā*, sf. cell.
celdilla, *thěldĭl'yā*, sf. cellule.
celebérrimo, ma, *thělěběr'rĭmŏ*, a. most celebrated.   [praise.
celebración, *thělěbrăthĭŏn'*, sf. celebration;
celebrar, -*brăr'*, v. a. to celebrate; to praise; — misa, to say mass.
célebre, *thā'lěbrě*, a. famous, renowned; gay; agreeable in conversation.   [fame.
celebridad, *thělěbrĭdăd'*, sf. celebrity.
celebro, *thělā'brŏ*, sm. skull; brain; fancy.
celemín, *thělěmĭn'*, sm. dry measure (the 12th part of a fanega).   [locity.
celeridad, *thělěrĭdăd'*, sf. celerity, ve-
celeste, *thělěs'tě*, a. heavenly; sky-blue.

celestial, thĕlĕstiál', a. heavenly; perfect; excellent.

celibato, thĕlĕbá'tŏ, sm. celibacy.

célibe, thĕ'lĭbĕ, sm. bachelor.

celo, thá'lŏ, sm. zeal; rut (in animals).

celosía, thĕlŏsĕ'á, sf. lattice of a window.

celoso, sa, thĕlŏ'sŏ, a. zealous; jealous.

célula, thĕ'lŭlá, sf. cellule.

celular, thĕlŭlár', a. cellular.

cementar, thĕmĕntár', v. a. to cement.

cena, thá'ná, sf. supper.

cenáculo, —ná'kŭlŏ, sm. cenatory hall in which our Lord administered the last supper to his disciples.

cenacho, thĕnátsh'ŏ, sm. market-basket.

cenador, —dŏr', sm. one who sups; arbour.

cenagal, —gál', sm. quagmire.

cenagoso, sa, —gŏ'sŏ, a. miry, marshy.

cenar, thĕnár', v. a. to sup. [slender.

cenceño, ña, thĕnthĕn'yŏ, a. lean, thin,

cencerrada, thĕnthĕrrá'dá, sf. rough music, hubbub, clatter, Dutch concert.

cencerrear, —rĕár', v. n. to jingle continually; to play badly; to make a dreadful noise.

cencerro, thĕnthĕr'rŏ, sm. bell worn by the leading-mule; ill-tuned guitar; á —s tapados, privately, by stealth.

cencerrón, —rŏn', sm. grape which remains after the vintage.

cendal, thĕndál', sm. crape; furbelow; (poet.) garter. [potash for cleaning silver.

cendra, thĕn'drá, sf. paste made of boiled

cenefa, thĕnĕ'fá, sf. picture-frame; fringes, pl.; (poet.) bank of a river, brim of a pond.

cenicero, thĕnĭthĕ'rŏ, sm. ash-hole.

ceniciento, ta, —thĭen'tŏ, a. ash-coloured.

cenit, thĕnĭt', sm. zenith.

ceniza, thĕnĕ'thá, sf. ashes, pl.; miércoles de —, Ash-Wednesday.

cenojil, thĕnŏ'hĭl', sm. garter.

censatario, thĕnsátá'rĭŏ, sm. copyholder.

censo, thĕn'sŏ, sm. quit-rent; censual roll; poll-tax. [critic; censorious person.

censor, thĕnsŏr', sm. censor, reviewer,

censual, thĕnsŭál', a. belonging to a quit-rent. [copyholder.

censualista, —lĭs'tá, sm. life-annuitant;

censura, —sŏ'rá, sf. critical review; censure, blame.

censurar, —sŭrár', v. a. to review, to criticise; to censure, to blame.

centauro, thĕntá'ŏrŏ, sm. Centaur.

centella, —tĕl'yá, sf. lightning; spark.

centellar, —tĕlyár', centellear, —tĕlyĕár', v. n. to sparkle.

centena, —tá'ná, sf. hundred. [dreds.

centenadas, —tĕná'dás, ad. á —, by hun-

centenal, —tĕnál', sm. field sown with rye. [secular; —, sm. centennial.

centenario, ia, —ná'rĭŏ, a. centenary;

centeno, —tá'nŏ, sm. common rye; —á, hundredth. [hundredth.

centésimo, ma, —tá'sĭmŏ, a. centesimal,

céntimo, thĕn'tĭmŏ, sm. French copper coin.

centinela, —tĭnĕ'lá, sf. sentry, sentinel; — avanzada, advanced guard; — perdida, forlorn hope; — á caballo, vedette.

centón, —tŏn', sm. cento (literary composition formed by joining scraps from other authors). [central, centric.

central, —trál', a. centrical, —trĭkál', a.

centralizar, —trálĭthár', v. a. to centralize.

céntrico, thĕn'trĭkŏ, a. focal. [fugal.

centrífugo, ga, thĕntrĕ'fŭgŏ, a. centri-

centrípeto, ta, —pĕtŏ, a. centripetal.

centro, thĕn'trŏ, sm. centre; principal object. [cate.

centuplicar, —tŭplĭkár', v. a. to centupli-

céntuplo, pla, thĕn'tŭplŏ, a. centuple, hundredfold.

centuria, —tŏ'rĭá, sf. century.

cenzalo, —thá'lŏ, sm. gnat.

ceñido, da, thĕnyĭ'dŏ, a. moderate; encircled with rings.

ceñidor, thĕnyĭdŏr', sm. belt, girdle.

ceñir, thĕnyĭr', v. n. to gird, to surround, to circle; to environ; to reduce, to abbreviate, to abridge.

ceño, thĕn'yŏ, sm. frown; ferrule.

ceñudo, da, thĕnyŏ'dŏ, a. frowning, grimly.

cepa, thĕ'pá, sf. stock of a vine; origin of a family.

cepacaballo, —kábál'yŏ, sm. cardoon.

copejón, thĕpĕ'hŏn', sm. largest branch of a tree torn from the trunk. [shavings.

cepilladuras, thĕpĭlyádŏ'rás, sf. pl. wood-

cepillo, thĕpĭl'yŏ, sm. plane; brush.

cepo, thĕ'pŏ, sm. block; trap, snare; poor-box; (fig.) entanglement.

ceporro, thĕpŏr'rŏ, sm. old vine.

cequí, sĕkĭ', cequin, sĕkĭn', sm. Venetian gold coin of about 9s.

cera, thá'rá, sf. wax; wax-taper, wax-candle; side-walk; —s, pl. the cells of wax and honey formed by bees.

cerafolio, thĕrá'fŏ'lĭŏ, sm. (bot.) common

corato, thĕrá'tŏ, sm. cerate. [chervil.

cerbatana, thĕrbátá'ná, sf. pea-shooter; acoustic trumpet.

cerca, thĕr'ká, sf. inclosure; fence; —s, pl. objects placed in the foreground of a painting; —, ad. near, at hand, close by; — de, close, near.

cercano, na, thĕrká'nŏ, a. near, close by, neighbour, adjoining.

cercar, —kár', v. a. to inclose, to environ, to circle; to fence.

cercenar, —thĕnár', v. a. to pare; to retrench, to clip; to lop off; to reduce, to lessen; to curtail, to cut away; to abridge.

cercera, —thá'rá, sf. air-tube.

cerceta, —tá'á, sf. widgeon.

cercillo, —thĭl'yŏ, sm. tendril of the vine.

cerciorar, thĕrthĭŏrár', v. a. to assure, to ascertain, to affirm. [circle.

cerco, thĕr'kŏ, sm. blocade of a place;

cerda, —dá, sf. strong hair growing in a horse's tail or mane; bristle.

cerdear, —dĕár', v. n. to be weak in the fore-quarter; to emit a harsh sound; to decline a request by subterfuges.

cerdo, thĕr'dŏ, sm. hog, pig.

cerdoso, sa, —dŏ'sŏ, cerdudo, da, —dŭ'dŏ, a. bristly. [brain.

cerebelo, thĕrĕbá'lŏ, sm. cerebel, the little

ceremonia, _–mō'nlä,_ sf. ceremony.
ceremonial, _–montäl',_ a. &sm. ceremonial.
ceremonioso, sa, _–mōnlō'sō,_ a. ceremonious.
cerería, _thērēr'ā,_ sf. wax-chandler's shop.
cerero, _thērē'rō,_ sm. wax-chandler; idle [vagrant.
cereza, _thērē'thā,_ sf. cherry.
cerezo, _–thō,_ sm. cherry-tree.
cerilla, _thērīl'yä,_ sf. wax-stand; wax-tablet; ear-wax; -s, pl. matches, safety-matches.
cerillera, _thērīlyā'rä,_ sf. little candlestick.
cermeña, _thērmēn'yä,_ sf. muscadine pear.
cernada, _–nä'dä,_ sf. leached ashes.
cerneja, _–nē'hā,_ sf. fetlock.
cerner, _thērner',_ v. a. to sift, to bolt; -,
  v. n. to bud and blossom; to drizzle;
  -se, to waddle.
cernido, _–nē'dō,_ sm. sifting.
cernidura, _–nīd'rä,_ sf. siftings, pl.
cero, _thā'rō,_ sm. zero.
cerollo, lla, _thērōl'yä,_ a. (applied to grain)
  reaped rather green and soft.
cerón, _thērōn',_ sm. dregs of pressed wax
  formed into a cake.
ceroso, _thērō'sō,_ a. waxy. [panic, fear.
cerote, _thērō'tē,_ sm. shoemaker's wax; (fig.)
ceroto, _–tō,_ sm. soft cerate. [monk.
cerquillo, _thērkīl'yō,_ sm. tonsure of a
cerquita, _–kē'tä,_ ad. at a small distance.
cerrada, _thērā'dä,_ sf. backbone-hide of
  an animal.
cerradero, _–dā'rō,_ sm. staple of a lock;
  -, ra, a. serving for locking. [be locked.
cerradizo, za, _–dē'thō,_ a. that which may
cerrado, da, _–dō,_ a. close, reserved; concealed; thick-grown.
cerradura, _–dō'rä,_ sf. locking-up; lock;
  - de golpe, spring-lock.
cerrajear, _thērā'hēär',_ v. n. to do locksmith's work. [smith; locksmith's shop.
cerrajería, _–hēr'ā,_ sf. trade of a lock-
cerrajero, _thērā'hē'rō,_ sm. locksmith.
cerramiento, _–mīēn'tō,_ sm. stopping-up;
  inclosure; finishing of the roof of a building; (rail.) - de vía, block-up.
cerrar, _thērār',_ v. a. & n. to close, to
  shut; to obstruct a passage; to lock; to
  engage the enemy; - la cuenta, to close
  an account; -se, to be shut up; to be
  cicatrized; to grow dark.
cerrazón, _thērāthōn',_ sf. dark and cloudy
  weather which precedes tempests.
cerrero, ra, _thērā'rō,_ a. running wild
  from one hill or eminence to another;
  caballo –, an unbroken horse.
cerril, _thērīl',_ a. mountainous, rough;
  wild, untamed.
cerrión, _thērīōn',_ sm. icicle.
cerro, _thē'rō,_ sm. hill; neck of an animal;
  backbone; combed flax or hemp; en –,
  nakedly, barely.
cerrojo, _thērō'h'ō,_ sm. bolt of a door.
certamen, _thērtä'mēn,_ sm. literary controversy. [shot.
certero, ra, _thērtā'rō,_ a. an excellent
certeza, _thērtē'thä,_ certidumbre, _thēr-
  tīdům'brē,_ sf. certainty.

certificación, _thērtīfīkäthlōn',_ sf. certificate; return of a writ.
certificado, _–fīkä'dō,_ sm. certificate; -,
  da, a. registered (of a letter).
certificar, _–fīkär',_ v.a. to certify, to affirm
certificatorio, ria, _–fīkätō'rīō,_ a. authen-
  ticating. [blue.
cerúleo, lea, _thērü'lēō,_ a. ceruleous, sky-
ceryal, _thērväl',_ cervario, ria, _thērvä'-
  rīō,_ a. belonging to a deer or resembling it.
cervatillo, _thērvätīl'yō,_ sm. small deer.
cervato, _–vä'tō,_ sm. fawn. [brewery.
cervecería, _thērvēthēr'ā,_ sf. brew-house,
cervecero, _–thā'rō,_ sm. brewer.
cerveza, _thērvē'thä,_ sm. beer, ale.
cervicabra, _thērvīkä'brä,_ sf. gazelle.
cerviguillo, _–gīl'yō,_ sm. big nape.
cerviz, _thērvīth',_ sf. nape.
cervuno, na, _thērvü'nō,_ a. deer-coloured.
cesación, _thēsäthlōn',_ sf. cessation, ceasing,
  pause, discontinuation.
cesar, _thēsär',_ v. n. to cease, to desist.
César, _thē'sär,_ sm. Roman emperor.
cesáreo, rea, _thēsä'rēō,_ a. imperial.
cesible, _thēsē'blē,_ a. that which may be
  ceded.
cesión, _thēsīōn',_ sf. cession, transfer.
cesionario, _thēsīōnä'rīō,_ sm. cessionary.
césped, _thēs'pēd,_ sm. sod, turf covered with
  grass; grass-plot. [sods are cut.
cespedera, _–dā'rä,_ sf. field where green
cesta, _thēs'tä,_ sf. basket, pannier.
cestada, _thēstä'dä,_ sf. basket-full.
cestería, _thēstēr'ā,_ sf. basket-shop; basket-
  stand.
cestero, _thēstā'rō,_ sm. basket-maker.
cesto, _thēs'tō,_ sm. hand-basket, hutch.
cetrino, na, _thētrē'nō,_ a. citrine, lemon-
  coloured; jaundiced, melancholic.
cetro, _thā'trō,_ sm. sceptre.
cía, _thē'ä,_ sf. hip-bone.
ciar, _thīär',_ v. a. to rein back; (mar.) to
  backwater; (fig.) to slacken in the pursuit
  of an affair.
ciática, _thīä'tīkä,_ sf. sciatica, hip-gout.
ciático, ca, _–tīkä,_ a. sciatical.
cibera, _thībā'rä,_ sf. mill-hopper; grist put
  at once in the hopper; all seeds or grains;
  husks, grounds.
cibla, _thē'blä,_ sf. shooting at a popinjay.
cicatear, _thīkätēär',_ v. n. to be niggardly.
cicatería, _–tērē'ä,_ sf. niggardliness.
cicatero, ra, _–tā'rō,_ a. niggardly, sordid.
cicatriz, _thīkätrīth',_ sf. cicatrice; gash.
cicatrizar, _–trīthär',_ v. a. to cicatrise.
cicle, _thē'klō,_ sm. cycle. [Cyclops.
cíclope, _thē'klōpē,_ cíclope, _thīklō'pē,_ sm.
cicuta, _thīkü'tä,_ sf. (bot.) hemlock.
cidra, _thē'drä,_ sf. citron.
cidro, _–drō,_ sm. citron-tree.
ciegamente, _thlēgämēn'tē,_ ad. blindly.
ciego, ga, _thlā'gō,_ a. blind.
cielo, _thlā'lō,_ sm. heaven; atmosphere;
  climate; - de la cama, tester of a bed;
  - de coche, roof of a coach; - de la
  boca, roof of the palate.
cien, _thlēn',_ a. one hundred.

ciencia, *thĭĕn'thĭă*, sf. science.
cieno, *thĭä'nō*, sm. mud, mire.
científico, ca, *thĭĕntē'fĭkō*, a. scientific.
ciento, *thĭĕn'tō*, a. one hundred; —, sm.
  a hundred; juego de los —s, piquet
  (game at cards).   [louse, centipede.
cientopiés, —*pĭĕs'*, sm. wood-louse, hog-
cierna, *thĭĕr'nă*, sf. blossom of vines,
  corn, &c.   [to be in its infancy.
cierne, —*nĕ*, en—, in blossom; estar en—,
¡ Cierra España ! *thĭĕr'ră ĕspän'yă*, the
  war-whoop of the ancient Spaniards.
cierro, *thĭĕr'rō*, sm. enclosure.
cierto, ta, *thĭĕr'tō*, a. certain, doubtless;
  por —, certainly.
cierva, *thĭĕr'vă*, sf. hind.
ciervo, *thĭĕr'vō*, sm. deer, hart, stag; —
  volante, stag-beetle.
cierzo, *thĭĕr'thō*, sm. cold northerly wind.
cifra, *thē'fră*, sf. cipher; abbreviation.
cifrar, *thĭfrăr'*, v. a. to write in ciphers;
  to abridge.
cigarra, *thĭgăr'ră*, sf. grass-hopper.
cigarro, —*rō*, sm. cigar.
cigarrero, —*rā'rō*, sm. cigar-seller.
cigarrista, —*rĭs'tă*, sm. one who smokes
  many cigars.
cigarrillo, —*rĭl'yō*, cigarrito, —*rĭ'tō*, sm.
  cigarette.   [well.
cigoñal, *thĭgōnyăl'*, sm. swipe of a draw-
ciguato, ta, *thĭgwă'tō*, a. jaundiced.
cigüeña, *thĭgŭĕn'yă*, sf. stork; crank of a
cigüeño, —*yō*, sm. male stork. [bell.
cilicio, *thĭlĭ'thĭō*, sm. hair-shirt.
cilíndrico, ca, *thĭlĭn'drĭkō*, a. cylindric.
cilindro, —*drō*, sm. cylinder.
cilla, *thĭl'yă*, sf. granary.
cillazgo, *thĭlyăth'gō*, sm. store-house fees
  paid for the tithes kept in a granary.
cillerero, *thĭlyĕrā'rō*, sm. cellarist, butler.
cilleriza, —*rē'thă*, sf. stewardess in a nunnery.
cillero, *thĭlyā'rō*, sm. keeper of a granary;
cima, *thē'mă*, sf. summit; nap; top of
  trees.
cimbalillo, *thĭmbălĭl'yō*, sm. small bell.
címbalo, *thĭm'bălō*, sm. cymbal.
cimbel, —*bĕl'*, sm. decoy-pigeon.
cimborio, —*bō'rĭō*, cimborrio, —*bōr'rĭō*,
  sm. cupola.
cimbra, *thĭm'bră*, sf. centring of an arch.
cimbrado, —*bră'dō*, sm. quick movement
  in a Spanish dance.
cimbr(e)ar, —*br(ĕ)ăr'*, v. a. to brandish a
  rod or wand; — á alguno, to give one a
  drubbing; —, v. n. to bend, to vibrate.
cimbreño, ña, —*brĕn'yō*, a. pliant, flexible.
cimbronazo, —*brōnă'thō*, sm. thrust of
  a foil.   [gold.
cimentado, *thĭmĕntă'dō*, sm. refinement of
cimentar, —*tăr'*, v. a. to lay the foundation of a building; to ground; to establish
  the fundamental principles of religion,
  morals and sciences; to refine metals.
cimenterio, —*tā'rĭō*, sm. cemetery, church-
cimento, *thĭmĕn'tō*, sm. cement. [yard.
cimera, *thĭmā'ră*, sf. crest of a helmet.

cimero, ra, —*rō*, a. uppermost; at the
  very top.   [of a building; basis, origin.
cimiento, *thĭmĭĕn'tō*, sm. ground-work
cimitarra, *thĭmĭtăr'ră*, sf. cimeter, falchion.
cimorra, *thĭmōr'ră*, sf. glanders, pl.
cinabrio, *thĭnă'brĭō*, sm. cinnabar; vermilion.
cinamomo, —*mō'mō*, sm. bead-tree.
cinca, *thĭn'kă*, sf. hacer —, to gain five
  points in the game of nine-pins.
cincel, *thĭnthĕl'*, sm. chisel.   [tor.
cincelador, —*thĕlădŏr'*, sm. engraver, sculp-
cincelar, —*thĕlăr'*, v. a. to chisel, engrave.
cinco, *thĭn'kō*, a. & sm. five.
cincuenta, *thĭnkŭĕn'tă*, sm. fifty.
cincuenteno, na, —*tā'nō*, a. a fiftieth.
cincha, *thĭn'tshă*, girth, cingle.
cinchar, —*tshăr'*, v. a. to girth.
cinchera, —*tshā'ră*, sf. girth-place.
cincho, *thĭn'tshō*, sm. belt used by labourers
  to keep their bodies warm.
cíngaro, ra, *thĭn'gărō*, s. gipsy.
cíngulo, —*gŭlō*, sm. girdle; band, wreath.
cínico, ca, *thĭ'nĭkō*, a. cynical.
Cinosura, *thĭnōsō'ră*, sf. Cynosure, the
  Lesser Bear.
cinqueño, *thĭnkĕn'yō*, cinquillo, —*kĭl'yō*,
  sm. game at cards played among five persons.   [be with child.
cinta, *thĭn'tă*, sf. ribbon; estar en —, to
cintadero, —*tădā'rō*, sm. notch in the
  crossbow to which the string is fastened.
cintagorda, —*gŏr'dă*, sf. coarse hempen
  net for the tunny-fishery. [ribands.
cinteado, da, *thĭntĕă'dō*, a. adorned with
cintero, *thĭntā'rō*, sm. riband-weaver.
cintillo, *thĭntĭl'yō*, sm. hat-band.
cinto, *thĭn'tō*, sm. belt, girdle; (poet.) zodiac.
cintura, *thĭntō'ră*, sf. girdle; waist.
cinturón, —*tŭrōn'*, sm. broad-sword belt.
ciprés, *thĭprĕs'*, sm. cypress-tree.
cipresal, *thĭprĕsăl'*, sm. grove of cypress-
  trees.   [belonging to cypress.
cipresino, na, —*sē'nō*, a. resembling or
circo, *thĭr'kō*, sm. circus.   [circle.
circuir, *thĭrkŭĭr'*, v. a. to surround, to en-
circuito, *thĭrkō'ĭtō*, sm. circuit; circumference.   [currency.
circulación, *thĭrkŭlăthĭōn'*, sf. circulation;
circular, —*kŭlăr'*, a. circular, circulatory;
  —, v. n. to circulate.
círculo, *thĭr'kŭlō*, sm. circle; circumference; district; orb; compasses. [pole.
circumpolar, *thĭrkŭmpōlăr'*, a. near the
circuncidar, *thĭrkŭnthĭdăr'*, v. a. to circumcise.
circuncisión, —*thĭsĭōn'*, sf. circumcision.
circundar, —*dăr'*, v. a. to surround, to
  encircle.
circunferencia, —*fĕrĕn'thĭă*, sf. circum-
circunferencial, —*fĕrĕnthĭăl'*, a. circum-
  ferential, surrounding.
circunflejo, ja, —*flā'h'ō*, a. acento —,
  sm. circumflex.
circunloquio, —*lō'kĭō*, sm. circumlocution.
circunscribir, —*skrĭbĭr'*, v. a. to circumscribe.   [scription.
circunscripción, —*skrĭpthĭōn'*, sf. circum-

circunspección, *-spĕkthiŏn'*, sf. circumspection. [spect, cautious.
circunspecto, ta, *-spĕk'tŏ*, a. circumstance. [circumstantial, minute.
circunstancia, *-stăn'thiă*, sf. circumstance. [circumstantial, minute.
circunstanciado, da, *-stănthiă'dŏ*, a. [to circumvallate.
circunstantes, *-stăn'tĕs*, sm. pl. bystanders. [to circumvallate.
circunvalar, *-vălăr'*, v. a. to surround;
circunvecino, na, *-vĕthĕ'nŏ*, a. neighbouring, adjacent.
cirial, *thĭriăl'*, sm. large candlestick.
cirineo, *thĭrĭnĕ'ŏ*, sm. mate, assistant.
cirio, *thĕ'riŏ*, sm. wax-candle.
cirro, *thĕr'rŏ*, sm. indurated gland; tuft of horse-mane.
ciruela, *thĭrŭĕ'lă*, sf. plum, prune.
ciruelo, *-lŏ*, sm. plum-tree.
cirugía, *thĭrŭ'hĕ'ă*, sf. surgery.
cirujano, *-hă'nŏ*, sm. surgeon.
ciscar, *thĭskăr'*, v. a. to make dirty; **-se,** to ease nature.
cisco, *thĭs'kŏ*, sm. coal-dust.
cisión, *thĭsiŏn'*, sf. incision.
cisma, *thĭs'mă*, sm. & f. schism; disturbance.
cismático, ca, *-mă'tĭkŏ*, a. schismatic.
cisne, *thĭs'nĕ*, sm. swan; (fig.) an eminent musician.
cisquero, *thĭskĕ'rŏ*, sm. pouncing-bag.
cister, *thĭstĕr'*, sm. Cistertian order.
cisterna, *thĭstĕr'nă*, sf. cistern.
cisura, *thĭsŏ'ră*, sf. incisure, incision.
cita, *thĕ'tă*, sf. citation, quotation; rendezvous. [mons.
citación, *thĭtăthiŏn'*, sf. quotation; summons.
citano, *thĭtă'nŏ*, sm. such a one.
citar, *thĭtăr'*, v. a. to make an appointment to meet a person; to convoke; to cite; to quote; to summon; to give judicial notice.
cítara, *thĕ'tără*, sf. (mus.) cithern; partition-wall of the thickness of a common brick.
citarista, *-rĭs'tă*, s. cithern-player.
citatorio, ria, *thĭtătŏ'riŏ*, a. (law) citatory.
citerior, *thĭtĕriŏr'*, ad. hither, nearer.
cito, *thĕ'tŏ*, a. word used to call dogs.
cítola, *thĕ'tŏlă*, sf. mill-clapper.
ciudad, *thiŭdăd'*, sf. city; civic body.
ciudadano, *-dădă'nŏ*, sm. citizen; **-, na,** a. civil; citizen-like.
ciudadela, *-dădĕ'lă*, sf. citadel.
cívico, ca, *thĕ'vĭkŏ*, a. civic.
civil, *thĭvĭl'*, a. civil; polite, courteous; (law) not criminal. [tion.
civilización, *thĭvĭlĭthăthiŏn'*, sf. civilisation.
civilizar, *-thăr'*, v. a. to civilise.
civismo, *thĭvĭs'mŏ*, sm. patriotism.
cizalla, *thĭthăl'yă*, sf. fragments or filings of gold, silver or other metal.
cizallar, *-yăr'*, v. a. to clip money.
clamar, *klămăr'*, v. a. to cry out in a mournful tone; to show a want of something.
clamor, *klămŏr'*, sm. clamour, outcry; exclamation; peal of passing-bells.
clamorear, *klămŏrĕăr'*, v. a. to clamour; **-,** v. n. to toll the passing-bell.
clamoreo, *-rĕ'ŏ*, sm. knell.

clamoroso, sa, *-rŏ'sŏ*, a. clamorous.
clandestino, na, *klăndĕstĕ'nŏ*, a. clandestine, secret, concealed.
clara, *klă'ră*, sf. short interval of fair weather on a rainy day; white of an egg.
claraboya, *-bŏ'yă*, sf. sky-light.
clarea, *klărĕ'ă*, sf. mulled wine.
clarear, *-rĕăr'*, v. n. to dawn; **-se,** to be transparent; to clear up.
clarete, *klăr'tĕ*, a. vino **-,** sm. claret.
claridad, *klărĭdăd'*, sf. brightness, clearness. [clarify.
clarificar, *klărĭfĭkăr'*, v. a. to brighten; to
clarificativo, va, *-fĭkătĭ'vŏ*, a. purificatory, clarifying.
clarín, *klărĭn'*, sm. trumpet; trumpeter.
clarinero, *-nă'rŏ*, sm. trumpeter.
clarinete, *-nă'tĕ*, sm. clarinet; player on the clarinet.
claro, ra, *klă'rŏ*, a. clear, bright; intelligible; evident, manifest; **-,** sm. skylight; opening or space between the columns of a building. [(in painting).
claroscuro, *klărŏskŏ'rŏ*, a. light and shade
clase, *klă'sĕ*, sf. class, rank; order.
clásico, ca, *klă'sĭkŏ*, a. classical.
clasificación, *klăsĭfĭkăthiŏn'*, sf. classification.
clasificar, *-fĭkăr'*, v. a. to classify.
claudicar, *klăŭdĭkăr'*, v. n. to halt, to limp.
claustral, *klăŭstrăl'*, a. claustral.
claustro, *klăŭs'trŏ*, sm. cloister; assembly of the principal members of a university; womb, uterus.
cláusula, *klă'ŭsŭlă*, sf. period; clause.
clausular, *klăŭsŭlăr'*, v. a. to close a period.
clausura, *klăŭsŏ'ră*, sf. clausure, confinement. [scupper-hole.
clava, *klă'vă*, sf. club, heavy stick; (mar.)
clavado, da, *klăvă'dŏ*, a. exact, precise; furnished with nails.
clavar, *klăvăr'*, v. a. to nail; to fasten in, to force in; to drive into; to drive a wedge; (fig.) to cheat, to deceive; **-se,** to run one's self through.
clavazón, *klăvăthŏn'*, sf. set of nails.
clave, *klă'vĕ*, sf. key-stone; (mus.) clef.
clave, **-,** sm. harpsichord, pianoforte.
clavel, *klăvĕl'*, sm. (bot.) common pink.
clavera, *klăvă'ră*, sf. mould for nail-heads; hole in a horse-shoe.
clavero, *-rŏ*, sm. aromatic clove-tree.
clavetear, *klăvĕtĕăr'*, v. a. to garnish with nails.
clavicordio, *klăvĭkŏr'diŏ*, sm. harpsichord.
clavícula, *klăvĕ'kŏlă*, sf. clavicle.
clavija, *klăvĕ'h'ă*, sf. pin, peg. [clove.
clavo, *klă'vŏ*, sm. nail; corn (on the feet);
clemencia, *klĕmĕn'thiă*, sf. clemency.
clemente, *klĕmĕn'tĕ*, a. clement, merciful.
clerecía, *klĕrĕthĕ'ă*, sf. clergy.
clerical, *klĕrĭkăl'*, a. clergical.
clericato, *-kă'tŏ*, sm. state and dignity of a clergyman. [tempt).
clerigalla, *-găl'yă*, sf. priesthood (in contempt).
clérigo, *klĕ'rĭgŏ*, sm. clergyman.
clero, *klĕ'rŏ*, sm. clergy.
cliente, *klĭĕn'tĕ*, sm. client.

clientela, *klĭĕntä´lä*, sf. clientship.

clima, *klē´mä*, sm. climate.

clin, *klĭn*, sf. mane (of a horse). [hospital.

clinica, *klē´nĭkä*, sf. clinical surgery *or*

clínico, ca, *–nĭkŏ*, a. clinical.

clisaje, *klĭsä´h´ĕ*, sm. stereotyping.

clisar, *klĭsär´*, v. a. to stereotype.

clister, *klĭstĕr´*, sm. clyster.

clivoso, sa, *klĭvŏ´sŏ*, a. (poet.) declivous.

clo-clo, *klŏ´klŏ*, sm. clucking of a hen.

cloaca, *klŏä´kä*, sf. sewer.

cloque, *klŏ´kĕ*, sm. grapnel; harpoon.

cloquear, *klŏkĕär´*, v. a. to cluck.

cloqueo, *klŏkä´ŏ*, sm. chuck.

cloquera, *klŏkä´rä*, sf. hatching of fowls;
brooding-time. [fishery.

cloquero, *–rŏ*, sm. harpooner in the tunny-

clorosis, *klŏrŏ´sĭs*, sf. green-sickness.

clueca, *klŭä´kä*, a. clucking and hatching

clueco, ca, *–kŏ*, a. decrepit. [(of a hen).

coacción, *kŏäkthĭŏn´*, sf. coaction, compulsion. [cive.

coactivo, va, *–tĕ´vŏ*, a. coactive, coer-

coadjutor, *kŏäd´hätŏr´*, sm. coadjutor,
assistant. [helper, assistant.

coadyuvador, *–yŭvädŏr´*, sm. fellow-

coadyuvar, *–yŭvär´*, v.a. to help, to assist.

coagular, *kŏägŭlär´*, v. a. to congulate,
to curd.

coágulo, *kŏä´gŭlŏ*, sm. coagulated blood.

coalición, *kŏälĭthĭŏn´*, sf. coalition, confederacy.

coarrendador, *kŏärrĕndädŏr´*, sm. joint
partner in the rent of a property; co-lessor.

coartación, *kŏärthäthĭŏn´*, sf. obligation
of the holder of a benefice, *or* its recipient,
to receive ordination.

coartada, *–tä´dä*, sf. (law) alibi.

coartar, *–tär´*, v. a. to limit, to restrain.

cobalto, *kŏbäl´tŏ*, sm. cobalt. [to restrain.

cobanillo, *kŏbänĭl´yŏ*, sm. basket for
vintage.

cobarde, *kŏbär´dĕ*, a. coward, timid.

cobardía, *–dĕ´ä*, sf. cowardice.

cobertera, *kŏbĕrtä´rä*, sf. pot-lid; procuress.

cobertizo, *–tĕ´thŏ*, sm. small shed; hovel.

cobertura, *–tŏ´rä*, sf. coverlet; covercle;
prerogative of the Spanish grandees to
appear with covered head before their
sovereign.

cobija, *kŏbĭ´h´ä*, sf. gutter-tile.

cobijar, *kŏbĭ´här´*, v. a. to cover, to shelter.

cobradero,ra, *kŏbrädä´rŏ*, a. recoverable.

cobrador, *–dŏr´*, sm. collector of rents.

cobranza, *kŏbrän´thä*, sf. recovery *or* collection of money. [to come to one's self.

cobrar, *kŏbrär´*, v. a. to recover; –se,

cobre, *kŏ´brĕ*, sm. copper; kitchen-furniture.

cobrizo, za, *kŏbrĕ´thŏ*, a. coppery.

cobro, *kŏ´brŏ*, sm. encashment. [coax.

cocar, *kŏkär´*, v. a. to make grimaces; to

cocarar, *kŏkärär´*, v. a. to gather.

coccíneo, nea, *kŏkthĕ´nĕŏ*, a. of a purple
colour.

cocción, *kŏkthĭŏn´*, sf. coction, concoction.

coceador, ra, *kŏthĕädŏr´*, a. kicking (of
horses).

cocear, *kŏthĕär´*, v. a. to kick, to fling out;
(fig.) to repugn, to resist.

cocedero, ra, *kŏthĕdä´rŏ*, a. easily cooked;
–, sm. bake-house.

cocedizo, za, *–dĕ´thŏ*, a. easily boiled.

cocer, *kŏthĕr´*, v. a. to boil; to bake
(bricks, &c.); to digest; –, v. n. to boil;
to ferment; –se, to suffer intense pain.

cocido, da, *kŏthĕ´dŏ*, a. boiled; (fig.)
skilled, experienced; –, sm. oglio, a dish
made of boiled meat and vegetables.

cocimiento, *–mĭĕn´tŏ*, sm. decoction;
dyer's bath.

cocina, *kŏthĕ´nä*, sf. kitchen.

cocinar, *kŏthĭnär´*, v. a. to cook.

cocinera, *–nä´rä*, sf. cook-maid, female

cocinero, *–rŏ*, sm. cook. [cook.

cocle, *kŏ´klĕ*, sm. grapnel.

coclea, *kŏ´klĕä*, sf. endless screw.

coclear, *kŏklĕär´*, v. a. to catch with a harpoon; –, v. n. to cluck. [bug-bear.

coco, *kŏ´kŏ*, sm. cocoa-tree; cocoa-nut;

cocodrilo, *kŏkŏdrĕ´lŏ*, sm. crocodile; (fig.)
false, faithless person.

cocoso, sa, *kŏkŏ´sŏ*, a. worm-eaten.

cochambre, *kŏtshäm´brĕ*, sm. dirty, stinking object. [and filthy objects.

cochambrería, *–brĕrĕ´ä*, sf. heap of nasty

cochambroso, sa, *–brŏ´sŏ*, a. nasty, filthy,
stinking.

cocharro, *kŏtshär´rŏ*, sm. wooden cup.

cochastro, *kŏtshäs´trŏ*, sm. little sucking
wild boar. [– cama, sleeping-car.

coche, *kŏtsh´ĕ*, sm. coach, carriage; (rail.)

cochear, *kŏtshĕär´*, v. n. to drive a coach.

cochera, *kŏtshä´rä*, sf. coach-house.

cocheril, *–rĭl´*, a. belonging to coachmen.

cochero, *kŏtshä´rŏ*, sm. coachman.

cochifrito, *kŏtshĭfrĕ´tŏ*, sm. fricassee.

cochina, *kŏtshĕ´nä*, sf. sow.

cochinería, *–nĕrĕ´ä*, sf. dirtiness, foulness.

cochinilla, *kŏtshĭnĭl´yä*, sf. wood-louse;
cochineal. [filthy; –, sm. pig.

cochino, na, *kŏtshĕ´nŏ*, a. dirty, nasty,

cochiquera, *kŏtshĭkä´rä*, sf. pig-sty.

codaste, *kŏdäs´tĕ*, sm. (mar.) stern-post.

codazo, *kŏdä´thŏ*, sm. blow given with the

codear, *kŏdĕär´*, v. a. to elbow. [elbow.

códice, *kŏ´dĭthĕ*, sm. old manuscript.

codicia, *kŏdĕ´thĭä*, sm. covetousness,
cupidity, greediness.

codiciable, *–thĭä´blĕ*, a. covetable.

codiciar, *–thĭär´*, v. a. to covet, to desire
eagerly. [codicil.

codicilar, *–thĭlär´*, a. pertaining to a

codicilo, *–thĕ´lŏ*, sm. (law) codicil.

codicioso, sa, *–thĭŏ´sŏ*, a. greedy, covetous; diligent, laborious.

código, *kŏ´dĭgŏ*, sm. code of laws.

codillo, *kŏdĭl´yŏ*, sm. knee of horses and
other quadrupeds; angle; crotch of a tree;
codille, a term at hombre.

codo, *kŏ´dŏ*, sm. elbow.

codoña, *kŏdŏn´yä*, sf. quince.

codoñero, *kŏdŏnyä´rŏ*, sm. quince-tree.

codorniz, *kŏdŏrnĭth´*, sf. quail.

coerción, *kŏĕrthĭŏn´*, sf. coercion, restraint.

coercitivo, va, *–thĕ´vŏ*, a. coercive.

coetáneo, nea, *kŏĕtă'nĕŏ*, a. contemporary.

coeterno, na, *kŏĕtĕr'nŏ*, a. coeternal.

coevo, va, *kŏĕ'vŏ*, a. coeval. [tence.

coexistencia, *kŏĕksĭstĕn'thĭă*, sf. coexis-

coexistente, *–tĕ*, a. coexistent.

coexistir, *kŏĕksĭstĭr'*, v. n. to coexist.

cofia, *kŏ'fĭă*, sf. coif; silken hair-net; head-gear.

cofin, *kŏfĭn'*, sm. small basket for fruit.

cofrade, *kŏfră'dĕ*, sm. colleague.

cofradía, *kŏfrădĭ'ă*, sf. confraternity.

cofre, *kŏ'frĕ*, sm. trunk.

cofrero, *kŏfrĕ'rŏ*, sm. trunk-maker.

cogedera, *kŏhĕdĕ'ră*, sf. hive used to gather an escaped swarm of bees.

cogedizo, za, *–dĕ'thŏ*, a. gatherable.

cogedor, *–dŏr'*, sm. collector, gatherer; dust-box.

cogedura, *–dŏ'ră*, sf. gathering.

coger, *kŏ'hĕr'*, v. a. to catch, to lay hold of, to occupy, to take up; to surprise.

cogitabundo, da, *kŏ'hĭtăbŭn'dŏ*, a. pensive, thoughtful. [tate.

cogitar, *–tăr'*, v. a. to reflect, to medi-

cogite, *kŏ'hĕ'tĕ*, (fam.) I have caught you.

cognoscitivo, va, *kŏgnŏsthĭtĕ'vŏ*, a. cognitive. [cabbage, &c.; shoot of a plant.

cogollo, *kŏgŏl'yŏ*, sm. heart of a lettuce.

cogote, *kŏgŏ'tĕ*, sm. occiput.

cogujada, *kŏgŭ'hă'dă*, sf. crested lark.

cogujón, *–'hŏn'*, sm. corner of a mattress or bolster.

cogulla, *kŏgŭl'yă*, sf. cowl, monk's hood.

cohabitar, *kŏăbĭtăr'*, v. n. to cohabit, to live together. [suborn.

cohechar, *kŏĕtshăr'*, v. a. to bribe, to

cohecho, *kŏĕtsh'ŏ*, sm. bribery; season for ploughing the ground.

coheredera, *kŏĕrĕdĕ'ră*, sf. co-heiress.

coheredero, *–rŏ*, sm. co-heir, joint-heir.

coherencia, *kŏĕrĕn'thĭă*, sf. coherence.

coherente, *–tĕ*, a. coherent, cohesive.

cohete, *kŏĕ'tĕ*, sm. sky-rocket.

cohetero, *–tĕ'rŏ*, sm. rocket-maker.

cohibir, *kŏĭbĭr'*, v.a. to prohibit, to restrain.

cohombral, *kŏŏmbrăl'*, sm. cucumber-bed.

cohombro, *kŏŏm'brŏ*, sm. cucumber.

cohonestar, *kŏŏnĕstăr'*, v. a. to give an honest appearance to an action.

cohorte, *kŏŏr'tĕ*, sm. cohort. [cidence.

coincidencia, *kŏĭnthĭdĕn'thĭă*, sf. coin-

coincidente, *–tĕ*, a. coincident.

coincidir, *kŏĭnthĭdĭr'*, v. n. to coincide.

coito, *kŏ'ĭtŏ*, sm. coition, cohabitation.

cojear, *kŏ'hĕăr'*, v. n. to halt, to hobble; to deviate from virtue.

cojera, *kŏ'hĕ'ră*, sf. lameness, halting.

cojijoso, sa, *kŏ'hĕ'hŏ'sŏ*, a. peevish, irritable. [table.

cojín, *kŏ'hĕn'*, sm. cushion.

cojo, ja, *kŏ'h'ŏ*, a. lame, cripple, halt.

cojudo, da, *kŏ'hŏ'dă*, a. entire, not gelt, not castrated.

col, *kŏl*, sf. cabbage.

cola, *kŏ'lă*, sf. tail; train (of a gown); glue; de la–, behind, backwards.

colación, *kŏlăthĭŏn'*, sf. collation (luncheon); collation (bestowing an ecclesiastical benefice).

colacionar, *–thĭŏnăr'*, v. a. to collate, to compare.

colada, *kŏlă'dă*, sf. bucking of linen with lie made of ashes; linen itself thus bucked.

coladera, *–dĕ'ră*, sf. strainer, colander.

coladero, *–rŏ*, sm. colander; narrow passage.

colador, *–dŏr'*, sm. colander. [sage.

coladura, *dŏ'ră*, sf. straining, filtering.

colanilla, *–nĭl'yă*, sf. small bolt.

colapez, *–pĕth'*, colapiscis, *–pĭs'thĭs*, sf. isinglass.

colar, *kŏlăr'*, v. a. & n. to strain, to filter; to confer ecclesiastical benefices; to pass through a strait place; to drink wine; –se, to be filtered.

colateral, *kŏlătĕrăl'*, a. collateral.

colcha, *kŏl'tshă*, sf. coverlet, counterpane.

colchadura, *–dŏ'ră*, sf. quilting.

colchar, *kŏltshăr'*, v. a. to quilt.

colchero, *kŏltshĕ'rŏ*, sm. quilt-maker.

colchón, *kŏltshŏn'*, sm. mattress. [maker.

colchonero, *kŏltshŏnĕ'rŏ*, sm. mattress-

coleada, *kŏlĕă'dă*, sf. wagging of an animal's tail.

colear, *kŏlĕăr'*, v. n. to wag the tail.

colección, *kŏlĕkthĭŏn'*, sf. collection.

colecta, *kŏlĕk'tă*, sf. distribution of a tax levied on a town; collect (an oration of the mass).

colectar, *–tăr'*, v. a. to collect taxes.

colecticio, cia, *–tĕ'thĭŏ*, a. collectitious, assembled together without discipline (of troops).

colectivo, va, *–tĕ'vŏ*, a. collective.

colector, *–tŏr'*, sm. collector, gatherer. ..

colega, *kŏlĕ'gă*, sm. colleague. [gatary.

colegatario, ria, *–tă'rĭŏ*, sm. & f. colle-

colegial, *kŏlĕ'hĭăl'*, sm. collegian; –, a. collegial; iglesia–, sf. collegiate church.

colegiala, *kŏlĕ'hĭălă'*, sf. female member of a seminary or college.

colegiata, *–tă*, sf. collegiate church.

colegio, *kŏlĕ'hĭŏ*, sm. college.

colegir, *kŏlĕ'hĭr'*, v. a. to collect; to deduce; to infer.

cólera, *kŏ'lĕră*, sf. bile; anger, fury, rage.

coléricamente, *kŏlĕ'rĭkămĕntĕ*, ad. in a rage. [sionate.

colérico, ca, *kŏlĕ'rĭkŏ*, a. choleric; pas-

coleta, *kŏlĕ'tă*, sf. cue; short addition to a discourse or writing. [maker.

coletero, *kŏlĕtĕ'rŏ*, sm. buff-breeches

coleto, *kŏlĕ'tŏ*, sm. doublet, jacket.

colgadero, *kŏlgădĕ'rŏ*, sm. hook to hang things upon; –, ra, a. fit to be hung up.

colgadizo, *–dĕ'thŏ*, sm. shed; –, za, a. pendent, suspended. [niture.

colgadura, *–dŏ'ră*, sf. tapestry; bed-fur-

colgajo, *kŏlgă'h'ŏ*, sm. tatter, rag.

colgar, *kŏlgăr'*, v. a. to hang; to suspend; to adorn with tapestry; –, v. n. to be suspended. [bri.

colibrí, *kŏlĭbrĕ'*, sm. humming-bird, coli-

cólica, *kŏ'lĭkă*, sf. colic. [hair in the tail.

colicano, na, *kŏlĭkă'nŏ*, a. having grey

cólico, *kŏ'lĭkŏ*, sm. colic.

colicorto, *kŏlĭkŏr'tŏ*, a. short-tailed (of animals).

colicuar, *kŏlĕkwär'*, v. a. to colliquate, to melt, to dissolve; -se, to become liquid.

coliflor, *kŏlĭflŏr'*, sm. cauliflower.

coligación, *kŏlĭgäthŏn'*, sf. connexion, union, alliance.

colilla, *kŏlĭl'yä*, sf. end or stump of a cigar.

colina, *kŏlĕ'nä*, sf. hill, hillock.

colinabo, *kŏlĭnä'bŏ*, sm. turnip.

coliseo, *kŏlĭsä'ŏ*, sm. opera-house, theatre.

colisión, *kŏlĭsĭŏn'*, sf. collision; friction.

colitigante, *kŏlĭtĭgän'tĕ*,sm. litigant; party to a law-suit.

colmar, *kŏlmär'*, v. a. to heap up.

colmena, *kŏlmä'nä*, sf. hive, bee-hive.

colmenar, *-när'*, sm. bee-hive stand, bee-house.

colmenero, *-nä'rŏ*, sm. bee-master.

colmenilla, *-nĭl'yä*, sf. morel, moril (mushroom).

colmillo, *kŏlmĭl'yŏ*, sm. eye-tooth.

colmilludo, **da**, *-yŏ'dŏ*, a. having eye-teeth; (fig.) sagacious, quick-sighted.

colmo, *kŏl'mŏ*. sm. heap; completion; crown; full; height; á —, plentifully.

colocación, *kŏlŏkäthŏn'*, sf. employment; arrangement; situation.

colocar, *kŏlŏkär'*, v. a. to arrange, to place; to provide with an employment.

colodra, *kŏlŏ'drä*, sf. milking-pail; wooden can with which wine is measured. [head.

colodrillo, *kŏlŏdrĭl'yŏ*, sm. back of the

colofonia, *kŏlŏfŏ'nĭä*, sm. colophony.

colon, *kŏ'lŏn*, sm. (gr.) two points (:); colon, the largest of the intestines.

colonia, *kŏlŏ'nĭä*, sf. colony; silk ribbon two fingers' wide.

colonial, *kŏlŏnĭäl'*, a. colonial.

colonizar, *kŏlŏnĭthär'*, v. a. to colonise.

colono, *kŏlŏ'nŏ*, sm. colonist; farmer.

coloquio, *kŏlŏ'kĭŏ*, sm. colloquy.

color, *kŏlŏr'*, sm. colour, hue, dye; rouge; pretext; **so** —, on pretence, under pretext.

coloración, *kŏlŏräthŏn'*, sf. colouring, coloration.

colorado, **da**, *kŏlŏrä'dŏ*, a. ruddy.

colorar, *kŏlŏrär'*, v. a. to colour; to make plausible; -, v. n. to blush with shame.

colorativo, **va**, *kŏlŏrätĕ'vŏ*, a. colorific.

colorear, *kŏlŏräär'*, v. a. to colour; to palliate, to excuse; -, v. n. to grow red.

colorete, *kŏlŏrä'tĕ*, sm. rouge (paint).

colorido, *kŏlŏrĕ'dŏ*, sm. colouring; pretext, pretence.

colorín, *kŏlŏrĕn'*, sm. linnet; vivid colour.

colorir, *kŏlŏrĭr'*, v. a. to colour.

colorista, *kŏlŏrĭs'tä*, sm. colourist.

colosal, *kŏlŏsäl'*, a. colossal.

coloso, *kŏlŏ'sŏ*, sm. colossus.

columbrar, *kŏlŭmbrär'*, v. a. to discern at a distance; to guess.

columna, *kŏlŭm'nä*, sf. column.

columnata, *-nä'tä*, sf. colonnade. [fro.

columpiar, *-pär'*, v. a. to swing to and

columpio, *kŏlŭm'pĭŏ*, sm. swing, see-saw.

coluna, *kŏlŏ'nä*, sf. column.

colusión, *kŏlŭsĭŏn'*, sf. collusion.

colusorio, **ria**, *kŏlŭsŏ'rĭŏ*, a. collusive.

colza, *kŏl'thä*, sf. rape, rape-seed.

collado, *kŏlyä'dŏ*, sm. hill.

collar, *kŏlyär'*, sm. necklace, necklet.

collera, *kŏlyä'rä*, sf. collar; gang of con-victs chained together.

collón, *kŏlyŏn'*, sm. coward.

collonería, *kŏlyŏnĕrĕ'ä*, sf. cowardice.

coma, *kŏ'mä*, sf. (gr.) comma. [mother.

comadre, *kŏmä'drĕ*, sf. midwife; god-

comadreja, *-drĕ'h'ä*, sf. weasel.

comadrería, *-drĕrĕ'ä*, sf. gossiping.

comadrero, **ra**, *-drä'rŏ*, a. idle and gos-siping.

comadrón, *-drŏn'*, sm. man-midwife.

comandancia, *kŏmändän'thĭä*, sf. com-mand.

comandante, *-dän'tĕ*, sm. commander.

comandar, *kŏmändär'*, v. a. to command.

comarca, *kŏmär'kä*, sf. territory, district; boundary, limit [bordering upon.

comarcano, **na**, *-kä'nŏ*, a. neighbouring,

comarcar, *-kär'*, v. a. to plant trees in a straight line; -, v. n. to border, to con-fine upon.

comaya, *kŏmä'yä*, sf. large basket, pannier.

comba, *kŏm'bä*, sf. curvature (of timber when warped); convexity. [warp.

combar, *kŏmbär'*, v. a. to bend; -se, to

combate, *kŏmbä'tĕ*, sm. combat, conflict; fighting; - singular, duel.

combatidor, *-tĭdŏr'*, sm. combatant.

combatir, *kŏmbätĭr'*, v. a. & n. to combat, to fight; to attack; to contradict. [tion.

combinación, *kŏmbĭnäthŏn'*, sf. combina-

combinar, *kŏmbĭnär'*, v. n. to combine.

combo, **ba**, *kŏm'bŏ*, a. bent, crooked, warped; -s, sm. pl. stand for casks; gawn-tree. [-, sm. combustible; fuel.

combustible, *kŏmbŭstĕ'blĕ*,a. combustible;

comedero, *kŏmĕdä'rŏ*, sm. dining-room.

comedero, *-rŏ*, a. eatable.

comedia, *kŏmä'dĭä*, sf. comedy.

comediante, *-dĭän'tĕ*, sm. player, actor, comedian. [shares.

comediar, *-dĭär'*, v. a. to divide into equal

comedido, **da**, *-dĕ'dŏ*, a. polite, gentle.

comedir, *-dĭr'*, v. a. to commit; -se, to govern one's self. [-, sm. dining-room.

comedor, **ra**, *-dŏr'*, sm. & f. eater; feeder;

comendador, *kŏmĕndädŏr'*, sm. knight commander of a military order.

comendadora, *-dŏ'rä*, sf. mother superior of a nunnery.

comendaticio, **cia**, *-tĕ'thĭŏ*, comenda-torio, ria, *-tŏ'rĭŏ*, a. recommending, introductory (of letters). [expound.

comentar, *kŏmĕntär'*, v. a. to comment, to

comentario, *kŏmĕntä'rĭŏ*, sm. commen-comento, *kŏmĕn'tŏ*, sm. comment [tary.

comenzar, *kŏmĕnthär'*, v. n. to commence, to begin.

comer, *kŏmär'*, v. a. to eat, to chew; to dine; to consume; to take a piece at chess.

comerciable, *kŏmĕrthĭä'blĕ*, a. market-able; sociable.

comercial, *-thĭäl'*, a. commercial.

comerciante, *-thĭän'tĕ*, sm. trader, mer-chant, tradesman.

comerciar, _-thïär'_, v. a. to trade, to commerce; to have intercourse with.

comercio, _kŏmĕr'thïŏ_, sm. trade, commerce; communication, intercourse; company of merchants.

comestible, _kŏmĕstï'blĕ_, a. eatable; _-s, s._ pl. all sorts of provisions.

cometa, _kŏmä'tä_, sm. comet; _-_, sf. kite.

cometer, _kŏmĕtĕr'_, v. a. to commit, to charge; to intrust; to attempt.

comezón, _-thŏn'_, sf. itch; ardent desire.

cómica, _kŏ'mïkä_, sf. actress.

cómico, ca, _-mïkŏ_, a. comic, comical.

comida, _kŏmĕ'dä_, sf. eating, food; dinner.

comilón, ona, _kŏmïlŏn'_, sm. & f. great eater, glutton.

comino, _kŏmē'nŏ_, sm. cumin (plant or seed).

comisaría, _kŏmïsärē'ä_, sf. commissaryship; commissariat.

comisario, _kŏmïsä'rïŏ_, sm. commissary.

comisión, _kŏmïsïŏn'_, sf. trust, commission; mandate; committee.

comisionado, _kŏmïsïŏnä'dŏ_, sm. commissionary; commissioner.

comisionar, _kŏmïsïŏnär'_, v. a. to commission; to depute.

comisionista, _kŏmïsïŏnïs'tä_, sm. commissioner.

comiso, _kŏmē'sŏ_, sm. confiscation.

comistrajo, _kŏmïsträ'hŏ_, sm. hodge-podge.

comitiva, _kŏmïtē'vä_, sf. suite, retinue, followers.

cómitre, _kŏ'mïtrĕ_, sm. boatswain on board a galley.

como, _kŏ'mŏ_, ad. how, in what manner; as; why; in such a manner; in what manner; like; _- quiera_, however.

cómoda, _kŏ'mŏdä_, sf. chest of drawers.

comodatario, _-dätä'rïŏ_, sm. (law) borrower; pawn-broker.

comodato, _-dä'tŏ_, sm. (law) loan.

comodidad, _kŏmŏdïdäd'_, sf. comfort; convenience; profit, interest; _-es_, pl. wealth, estate.

cómodo, da, _kŏ'mŏdŏ_, a. convenient, commodious; comfortable; _-_, sm. utility, profit, benefit.

compacto, ta, _kŏmpäk'tŏ_, a. compact, close, dense.

compadecerse, _-pädĕthĕr'sĕ_, v. r. to pity; to agree with each other.

compadrar, _-pädrär'_, v. n. to become a godfather.

compadrazgo, _-pädräth'gŏ_, sm. godfather-ship.

compadre, _-pä'drĕ_, sm. godfather; compeer, friend.

compadrería, _-pädrĕrē'ä_, sf. friendly intercourse between friends or companions.

compaginar, _-pä'hïnär'_, v. a. to join, to couple.

compañero, ra, _-pänyĕ'rŏ_, sm. & f. companion, friend; compeer, comrade; partner.

compañía, _-pänyē'ä_, sf. company, society; partnership; conference, conferring.

comparación, _-päräthïŏn'_, sf. comparison.

comparar, _-pärär'_, v. a. to compare, to confront.

comparativo, va, _-pärätē'vŏ_, a. comparative.

comparecer, _-pärĕthĕr'_, v. n. to appear before a judge.

comparendo, _-pärĕn'dŏ_, sm. summons.

comparición, _-pärïthïŏn'_, sf. (law) appearance.

comparsa, _-pär'sä_, sm. & f. super.

comparte, _-pär'tĕ_, sm. joint party in a law-suit.

compartir, _-pärtïr'_, v. a. to divide into equal parts.

compás, _-päs'_, sm. pair of compasses; (mus.) measure; rule of life; pattern.

compasar, _-päsär'_, v. a. to measure with a compass.

compasión, _-päsïŏn'_, sf. compassion, commiseration.

compasivo, va, _-päsē'vŏ_, a. compassionate.

compatible, _-pätē'blĕ_, a. compatible, consistent with.

compatriota, _-pätrïŏ'tä_, sm. & f. countryman; countrywoman; fellow-citizen.

compeler, _-pĕlĕr'_, v. a. to compel, to constrain.

compendiar, _-pĕndïär'_, v. a. to epitomize, to abridge.

compendio, _-pĕn'dïŏ_, sm. epitome, abridgment, summary.

compendioso, sa, _-pĕndïŏ'sŏ_, a. brief, abridged, compendious.

compensación, _-pĕnsäthïŏn'_, sf. compensation; recompense.

compensar, _-pĕnsär'_, v. a. & n. to compensate; to make amends; to recompense.

competencia, _-pĕtĕn'thïä_, sf. competition, rivalry; competence.

competente, _-pĕtĕn'tĕ_, a. competent, sufficient.

competer, _-pĕtĕr'_, v. n. to be one's due.

competición, _pĕtïthïŏn'_, sf. competition.

competidor, _-pĕtïdŏr'_, sm. competitor, rival.

competir, _-pĕtïr'_, v. n. to vie; to compete with, to rival.

compilación, _-pïläthïŏn'_, sf. compilation.

compilador, _-pïlädŏr'_, sm. compiler.

compilar, _-pïlär'_, v. a. to compile.

compinche, _-pïn'tshĕ_, sm. comrade, confidant, crony.

complacencia, _-pläthĕn'thïä_, sf. pleasure; compliance.

complacer, _-pläthĕr'_, v. a. to please another; _-se_, to be pleased with.

complaciente, _-pläthïĕn'tĕ_, a. pleasing.

complemento, _-plĕmĕn'tŏ_, sm. complement, completion.

completar, _-plĕtär'_, v. a. to complete.

completo, ta, _-plĕ'tŏ_, a. complete, perfect.

complexión, _-plĕksïŏn'_, sf. complexion, temperature of the body.

complexionado, da, _-plĕksïŏnä'dŏ_, a. complexioned; bien ó mal _-_, of a good or bad complexion.

complexo, _-plĕk'sŏ_, sm. complex.

complicar, _-plïkär'_, v. a. to complicate.

cómplice, _kŏm'plïthĕ_, sm. & f. accomplice.

complicidad, _-plïthïdäd'_, sf. complicity.

complotar, _-plŏtär'_, v. a. to conspire, to plot; author; compositor.

componedor, _-pŏnĕdŏr'_, sm. composer.

componer, _-pŏnĕr'_, v. a. to compose; to compound; to construct; to mend, to repair; to strengthen, to restore; to garnish; to adjust; to reconcile; to compose, to calm.

comportable, _-pŏrtä'blĕ_, a. supportable, tolerable, sufferable.

comportar, _-pŏrtär'_, v. a. to suffer, to

tolerate; **–se**, to comport, to behave one's self.

composición, –*pŏsĭthĭŏn'*, sf. composition; composure, making; adjustment; agreement; musical *or* literary composition; modest appearance.   [compositor.

compositor, –*pŏsĭtŏr'*, sm. composer;

compostura, –*pŏstŏ'rä*, sf. composition, composure; mending, repairing; neatness of dress; accommodation, adjustment; modesty, demureness.

compota, –*pŏ'tä*, sf. conserve of fruit.

compotera, –*pŏtä'rä*, sf. vessel in which jams are served.

compra, *kŏm'prä*, sf. purchase; necessaries bought for the daily use of the house,   [buyer; caterer.

comprador, ra, *kŏmprädŏr'*, sm. & f.

comprar, *kŏmprär'*, v. a. to buy, to purchase.

comprender, *kŏmprĕndĕr'*, v. a. to include, to contain; to comprehend, to understand.   [sible.

comprensible, –*prĕnsĕ'blĕ*, a. comprehen-

comprensión, –*prĕnsĭŏn'*, s. comprehension, understanding.   [prehensive.

comprensivo, va, –*prĕnsĕ'vŏ*, a. com-

compresible, –*prĕsĕ'blĕ*, a. compressible.

compresión, –*prĕsĭŏn'*, s. compression, compressure.   [sive.

compresivo, va, –*prĕsĕ'vŏ*, a. compres-

comprimir, –*prĭmĭr'*, v. a. to compress; to repress, to restrain; **–se**, to subdue one's passion.   [confirm; to prove.

comprobar, –*prŏbär'*, v. a. to verify, to

comprometer, –*prŏmĕtĕr'*, v. a. to compromise; to render one answerable for; to put in danger.   [bitrator, umpire.

compromisario, –*prŏmĭsä'rĭŏ*, sm. ar-

compromiso, –*prŏmĭs'ŏ*, sm. compromise.

compuerta, –*pŭĕr'tä*, sf. half door; sluice.

compuesto, –*pŭĕs'tŏ*, sm. compound; **–, ta**, a. composed, compounded; made up.

compulsa, –*pŭl'sä*, sf. attested copy of an instrument.   [authentic copy.

compulsar, –*pŭlsär'*, v. a. to make an

compulsivo, va, –*pŭlsĕ'vŏ*, a. compulsive.

compulsorio, ria, –*pŭlsŏ'rĭŏ*, a. compulsory; ordering an authentic copy to be made.   [contrition.

compunción, –*pŭnthĭŏn'*, sf. compunction.

compungirse, –*pŭn'hĭr'sĕ*, v. r. to feel compunction.

compungivo, va, –*pŭn'hĕ'vŏ*, a. pricking, stimulating.   [tion.

computación, –*pŭtäthĭŏn'*, sf. computa-

computar, –*pŭtär'*, v. a. to compute.

cómputo, *kŏm'pŭtŏ*, sm. compute, calculation.

comulgar, *kŏmŭlgär'*, v. a. & n. to administer the sacrament; to communicate.

común, *kŏmŭn'*, a. common, usual, general, **–**, sm. community; public: **en –**, conjointly.

comunal, *kŏmŭnäl'*, sm. commonalty.

comunero, ra, *kŏmŭnĕ'rŏ*, a. popular; **–**, sm. joint holder of a tenure of lands.

comunicación, *kŏmŭnĭkäthĭŏn'*, sf. communication.

comunicar, *kŏmŭnĭkär'*, v. a. to communicate; **–se**, to have intercourse; t. correspond; to be united.

comunicativo va, *kŏmŭnĭkätĕ'vŏ*, a. communicative.

comunidad, *kŏmŭnĭdäd'*, sf. commonness; commonalty; community.

comunión, *kŏmŭnĭŏn'*, sf. communion; fellowship; common possession.

comuña, *kŏmŭn'yä*, s. meslin; **–s**, pl. seeds.   [fore.

con, *kŏn*, pr. with; by; **– que**, then, there.

conato, *kŏnä'tŏ*, sm. endeavour, effort; crime attempted but not executed.

cóncava, *kŏn'kävä*, **concavidad**, *kŏn-kävĭdäd'*, sf. concavity.

cóncavo, va, *kŏn'kävŏ*, a. concave.

concebir, *kŏnthĕbĭr'*, v. a. & n. to conceive; to become pregnant.

conceder, –*thĕdĕr'*, v. a. to give; to grant; to concede, to allow.   [council.

concejal, –*thĕ'häl'*, sm. member of a

concejil, –*thĕ'hĭl'*, a. relating to public boards.

concejo, –*thĕ'h'ŏ*, sm. civic body of a small town; town-hall.   [centration.

concentración, –*thĕnträthĭŏn'*, sf. con-

concentrar, –*thĕnträr'*, v. a. to concentrate.

concéntrico, ca, –*thĕn'trĭkŏ*, a. concentric.

concepción, –*thĕpthĭŏn'*, sf. conception; idea, conceit.   [witty sayings.

conceptear, –*thĕptĕär'*, v. n. to abound in

conceptible, –*thĕptĭ'blĕ*, a. conceivable.

conceptista, –*thĕptĭs'tä*, sm. man of genius, wit.   [judgment, opinion.

concepto, –*thĕp'tŏ*, sm. conceit, thought;

conceptuar, –*thĕptŭär'*, v. a. to conceive, to judge, to think.

conceptuoso, sa, –*thĕptŭŏ'sŏ*, a. sharp, witty; sententious.   [relating.

concerniente, –*thĕrnĭĕn'tĕ*, a. concerning,

concernir, –*thĕrnĭr'*, v. imp. to regard, to concern.

concertar, –*thĕrtär'*, v. a. to concert, to settle; to adjust; to conclude an agreement; to compose differences; **–**, v. n. to agree, to accord.

concesión, –*thĕsĭŏn'*, sf. concession.

conciencia, –*thĕn'thĭä*, sf. conscience.

concierto, –*thĕr'tŏ*, sm. concert; agreement; accommodation; (mus.) concert; **de –**, according to agreement.

conciliación, –*thĭlĭäthĭŏn'*, sf. conciliation, reconciliation.

conciliar, –*thĭlĭär'*, v. a. to conciliate, to reconcile; **–**, a. belonging to councils.

conciliativo, va, –*thĭlĭätĕ'vŏ*, a. conciliatory.   [of bishops.

concilio, –*thĕ'lĭŏ*, sm. council; assembly

concinidad, –*thĭnĭdäd'*, sf. harmony.

concisión, –*thĭsĭŏn'*, sf. conciseness.

conciso, sa, –*thĕ'sŏ*, a. concise, brief.

concitar, –*thĭtär'*, v. a. to excite; to stir up commotions.

conciudadanía, –*thĭüdädänĕ'ä*, sf. joint-citizenship; the burgesses.

conciudadano, –*thĭüdädä'nŏ*, sm. fellow-citizen; countryman.

cónclave, *kŏn′ klăvĕ,* conclave, *kŏn-klă′vĕ,* sm. conclave.

concluir, *kŏnklŭĭr′,* v. a. to conclude, to end, to complete; to convince; to infer, to deduce; to disarm an adversary by grasping the hilt of his sword.

conclusión, *−klŭsĭŏn′,* sf. conclusion, end; consequence. [conclusive.

concluyente, *−klŭyĕn′tĕ,* a. concludent.

concolega, *−kŏlĕ′gă,* sm. fellow-collegian.

concomerse, *−kŏmĕr′sĕ,* v. r. to shrug the shoulders, to give a shrug.

concomitante, *−kŏmĭtăn′tĕ,* a. concomitant, accompanying.

concordancia, *−kŏrdăn′thĭă,* sf. concordance, concord; harmony.

concordar, *−kŏrdăr′,* v. a. to accord; −, v. a. to agree, to concord.

concordato, *−kŏrdă′tŏ,* sm. concordate.

concorde, *−kŏr′dĕ,* a. concordant, agreeing.

concordia, *−kŏr′dĭă,* sf. conformity, union, harmony; de −, by common consent.

concreción, *−krĕthĭŏn′,* sf. concretion.

concretar, *−krĕtăr′,* v. a. to combine, to concrete.

concreto, ta, *−krĕ′tŏ,* a. concrete. [tress.

concubina, *−kŏbĭ′nă,* sf. concubine, mistress.

concubinato, *−kŏbĭnă′tŏ,* sm. concubinage.

concúbito, *−kŏ′bĭtŏ,* sm. coition.

conculcar, *−kŭlkăr′,* v. a. to trample under foot. [cupiscence, lust.

concupiscencia, *−kŭpĭsthĕn′thĭă,* sf. concurrencia, *−kŭrrĕn′thĭă,* sf. convention of persons; concurrence; coincidence; confluence.

concurrir, *−kŭrrĭr′,* v.n. to concur; to contribute; to coincide; to convent; to fall in.

concurso, *−kŭr′sŏ,* sm. concourse; crowd.

concusión, *−kŭsĭŏn′,* sf. concussion; shaking. [tortoise-shell.

concha, *kŏn′tshă,* sf. shell; conch; oyster; conchabanza, *−kŏntshăbăn′thă,* sf. the making of one's self easy and comfortable; plotting, conspiracy.

conchabar, *−băr′,* v. a. to join, to unite; −se, to plot, to conspire.

conchado, da, *kŏntshă′dŏ,* a. scaly, covered with shells.

conchil, *kŏntshĭl′,* sm. rock-shell.

conchudo, da, *kŏntshŭ′dŏ,* a. scaly, crustaceous; cunning, crafty.

condado, *kŏndă′dŏ,* sm. earldom, county.

condal, *kŏndăl′,* a. relating to an earl.

conde, *kŏn′dĕ,* sm. earl, count; chief of gypsies. [fit, proper.

condecente, *kŏndĕthĕn′tĕ,* a. convenient, condecorar, *−dĕkŏrăr′,* v. a. to adorn, to embellish.

condenable, *−dĕnă′blĕ,* a. damnable.

condenación, *−dĕnăthĭŏn′,* condena, −dă′nă, sf. condemnation.

condenar, *−dĕnăr′,* v. a. to condemn; to refute; to disapprove; −se, to condemn or blame one's self. [demnatory.

condenatorio, ria, *−dĕnătŏ′rĭŏ,* a. condensatoria.

condensación, *−dĕnsăthĭŏn′,* sf. condensation.

condensar, *−dĕnsăr′,* v. a. to condense, to thicken. [densible, condensive.

condensativo, va, *−dĕnsătĭ′vŏ,* a. condensa, *−dĕn′să,* sf. countess.

condesado, *−dĕsă′dŏ,* sm. earldom.

condescendencia, *−dĕsthĕndĕn′thĭă,* sf. condescendence, condescension, compliance. [descend; to yield, to comply.

condescender, *−dĕsthĕndĕr′,* v. a. to condestable, *−dĕstă′blĕ,* sm. constable; condestablía, *−dĕstăblĕ′ă,* sf. constableship.

condición, *−dĭthĭŏn′,* sf. condition, quality; state, footing; rank; clause, stipulation. [ditioned.

condicionado, da, *−dĭthĭŏnă′dŏ,* a. condicional, *−dĭthĭŏnăl′,* a. conditional, not absolute. [to accord; to condition.

condicionar, *−dĭthĭŏnăr′,* v. n. to agree, condignidad, *−dĭgnĭdăd′,* sf. condignness; condignity.

condigno, *−dĭg′nŏ,* a. condign.

condimentar, *−dĭmĕntăr′,* v. a. to condite, to season. [seasoning.

condimento, *−dĭmĕn′tŏ,* sm. condiment, condiscípulo, *−dĭsthĕ′pŭlŏ,* sm. fellow-disciple, fellow-scholar.

condolecerse, *−dŏlĕthĕr′sĕ,* condolerse, *−dŏlĕr′sĕ,* v. r. to condole; to condole. [forgiving.

condonación, *−dŏnăthĭŏn′,* sf. pardoning, condonar, *−dŏnăr′,* v. a. to pardon, to forgive.

conducción, *−dŭkthĭŏn′,* sf. conveyance; carriage (the act); conduct; payment for conducting. [factory.

conducente, *−dŭthĕn′tĕ,* a. suitable, satisfactory.

conducir, *−dŭthĭr′,* v. a. & n. to convey, to conduct; −, v. n. to be serviceable; −se, to conduct one's self.

conducta, *−dŭk′tă,* sf. conduct; behaviour; conveyance. [conductory.

conductivo, va, *−dŭktĭ′vŏ,* a. conducive, conducto, *−dŭk′tŏ,* sm. conduit, sewer, drain.

conductor, *−dŭktŏr′,* sm. conductor, guide; (rail.) guard, conductor.

conejal, *kŏnĕ′hăl,* conejar, *kŏnĕh′ăr,* sm. rabbit-warren.

conejera, *kŏnĕh′ă′ră,* sf. warren, coney-burrow; cavern inhabited by poor people.

conejero, *−rŏ,* sm. warrener; −, ra, a. trained to hunt rabbits.

conejo, ja, *kŏnĕ′hŏ,* sm. & f. rabbit.

conejuna, *kŏnĕh′ŏ′nă,* sf. rabbit fur.

conejuno, na, *−nŏ,* a. belonging to rabbits; rabbit-like.

conexidades, *kŏnĕksĭdă′dĕs,* sf. pl. (law) all matters pertinent to the principal subject. [junction.

conexión, *kŏnĕksĭŏn′,* sf. connection, conexo, xa, *kŏnĕk′sŏ,* a. connected, united.

confabular, *kŏnfăbŭlăr′,* v. a. to confabulate. [standard.

confalón, *−fălŏn′,* sm. gonfalon, banner, confección, *−fĕkthĭŏn′,* sf. electuary.

confeccionado, *−fĕkthĭŏnă′dŏ,* sm. confectioner. [up into conserves.

confeccionar, *−fĕkthĭŏnăr′,* v. a. to make

confederación, -fĕdĕrăthiŏn', sf. confederacy.

confederado, -fĕdĕră dŏ, a. confederate.

confederar, -fĕdĕrăr', v. a. -se, to confederate.

conferencia, -fĕrĕn'thĭă, sf. conference.

conferenciar, -fĕrĕnthĭăr', v. a. to hold a conference.

conferir, -fĕrĭr', v. a. to confer.

confesado, da, -fĕsă dŏ, a. penitent.

confesar, -fĕsăr', v.a. to confess; to avow.

confesión, -fĕsiŏn', sf. confession, avowal.

confesionario, -fĕsiŏnă'riŏ, sm. treatise on hearing confessions; confessional.

confesionista, -fĕsiŏnĭs'tă, sm. Lutheran.

confeso, sa, -fĕs'ŏ, a. (law) confessed.

confesonario, -fĕsŏnă'riŏ, s. m. confessional.

confesor, -fĕsŏr', sm. confessor.

confiado, da, -fiă'dŏ, a. confident; arrogant, forward.

confiador, -fiădŏr', sm. (law) joint surety.

confianza, -fiăn'thă, sf. confidence; boldness; assurance; en -, confidential; traje de -, sm. undress.

confiar, -fiăr', v. a. & n. to confide, to trust in; to feed with hope.

confidencia, -fidĕn'thĭă, sf. confidence.

confidencial, -fidĕnthĭăl', a. confidential.

confidente, -fidĕn'tĕ, sm. confidant; -, a. true, faithful, trusty.

configurar, -figurăr', v. a. to configure.

confín, -fin', sm. limit, boundary.

confinar, -finăr', v. a. & n. to exile; to confine; to border upon.

confirmación, -firmăthiŏn', sf. confirmation.

confirmar, -firmăr', v. a. to confirm; to corroborate.

confiscación, -fiskăthiŏn', sf. confiscation.

confiscar, -fiskăr', v. a. to confiscate.

confitar, -fităr', v. a. to confect; to preserve, to candy.

confite, -fĭ'tĕ, sm. comfit, confect; -s, pl. whipping given to children.

confitera, -fitĕ'ră, sf. sugar-plum box.

confitería, -fitĕrĭ'ă, s. confectioner's shop.

confitero, -fitĕ'rŏ, sm. confectioner.

confitura, -fitŏ'ră, sf. preserved or potted fruit; jam.

conflación, -flăthiŏn', sf. melting metals.

conflagración, -flăgrăthiŏn', sf. conflagration.

conflicto, -flĭk'tŏ, sm. conflict.

confluencia, -flŏĕn'thĭă, sf. confluence.

confluir, -flŏĭr', v. n. to join (applied to rivers and sea-currents).

conformar, -formăr', v. a. to conform, to fit; -, v. n. to suit, to fit; -se, to submit, to accommodate.

conforme, -fŏr'mĕ, a. conformable, suitable; -, ad. according to.

conformidad, -formidăd', sf. conformity; patience, resignation; de -, by common consent; in company, consolation.

confortación, -fŏrtăthiŏn', sf. comfort.

confortar, -fŏrtăr', v. a. to comfort; to strengthen; to console.

confortativo, va, -fŏrtătĕ vŏ, a. comfortable, cordial.

confracción, -frăkthiŏn', sf. fraction.

confraternidad, -frătĕrnidăd', sf. confraternity; frontation.

confrontación, -frŏntăthiŏn', sf. confrontation.

confrontar, -frŏntăr', v. a. to confront.

confundir, -fŭndĭr', v. a. to confound, to jumble; to perplex; to huddle; to throw into confusion. fly.

confusamente, -fŭsămĕn'tĕ, ad. confusedly.

confusión, -fŭsiŏn', sf. confusion, disorder; tumultuous medley; perplexity, perturbation; obscurity; humiliation.

confuso, sa, -fŏ'sŏ, a. confused, confounded; obscure; perplexed.

confutación, -fŭtăthiŏn', sf. confutation, conviction.

confutar, -fŭtăr', v. a. to confute.

congelación, -hĕlăthiŏn', sf. congelation.

congelar, -hĕlăr', v. a. to congeal.

congeniar, -hĕniăr', v. n. to be congenial.

congerie, -hĕ'riĕ, sf. congeries. tion.

congestión, -hĕstiŏn', sf. (med.) congestion.

conglutinar, -glŏtinăr', v. a. to conglutinate. breaking.

congoja, -gŏ'h'ă, sf. anguish, pang, heartcongojoso, sa, -gŏ'hŏ'sŏ, a. afflictive, painful. to flatter.

congraciar, -grăthĭăr', v. a. to ingratiate.

congratulación, -grătŭlăthiŏn', sf. congratulation. tulate.

congratular, -grătŭlăr', v. a. to congregation, assembly.

congregación, -grĕgăthiŏn', sf. congregation, assembly. meet, to collect.

congregar, -grĕgăr', v. a. to assemble, to congreso, -grĕs'ŏ, sm. congress.

congrua, kŏn'grŭă, sf. a competent sustenance for a priest.

congruamente, kŏngrŭămĕn'tĕ, ad. conveniently, becomingly.

congruencia, -grŭĕn'thĭă, sf. convenience, opportunity, congruency.

congruente, -grŭĕn'tĕ, a. congruent; corresponding. venient, suitable.

congruo, ua, kŏn'grŭŏ, a. congruous, conicónico, ca, kŏ'nĭkă, a. conical.

conjetura, kŏn'hĕtŏ'ră, sf. conjecture.

conjetural, -hĕtŏrăl', a. conjectural.

conjeturar, -hĕtŏrăr', v. a. to conjecture.

conjugación, -hăgăthiŏn', sf. (gr.) conjugation.

conjugar, -hăgăr', v. a. (gr.) to conjugate.

conjunción, -hŭnthiŏn', sf. conjunction.

conjuntamente, -hŭntămĕn'tĕ, ad. together.

conjunto, ta, -hŭn'tŏ, a. united, conjunct; allied by kindred; -, sm. conjunctness, gross. plot.

conjuración, -hŭrăthiŏn', sf. conspiracy.

conjurado, -hŭră'dŏ, sm. conspirator.

conjurador, -hŭrădŏr', sm. conjurer; exorcist.

conjuramentar, -hŭrămĕntăr', v. a. to bind by an oath; to administer an oath.

conjurar, -hŭrăr', v. n. to conjure; to conspire, to plot. orcism.

conjuro, -hŏ'rŏ, sm. conjuration, ex-

conmemoración, –mĕmŏrāthĭŏn', sf. remembrance; commemoration; requiem.

conmemorar, –mĕmŏrār', v. a. to commemorate. [messmate.

conmensal, –mĕnsăl', sm. commensal,

conmensuración, –mĕnsŭrāthĭŏn', sf. commensuration. [mensurate.

conmensurar, –mĕnsŭrār', v. a. to commensurate.

conmigo, –mē'gŏ, pn. with me, with myself. [fellow-soldier.

conmilitón, –mĭlĭtŏn', sm. comrade,

conminación, –mĭnāthĭŏn', sf. commination, threat.

conminar, –mĭnār', v. a. to threaten; to threaten a criminal with punishment.

conminatorio, ria, –mĭnātŏ'rĭŏ, a. comminatory, threatening.

conmiseración, –mĭsĕrāthĭŏn', sf. commiseration, pity, compassion.

conmoción, –mŏthĭŏn', sf. commotion; concussion; fretting; tumult, disturbance.

conmover, –mŏvēr', v. a. to move; to disturb. [tion, exchange.

conmutación, –mŭtāthĭŏn', sf. commuta-

conmutar, –mŭtār', v. a. to commute; to barter, to exchange. [cording to nature.

connatural, –nātŭrăl', a. natural; according to nature.

connaturalizar, –nātŭrălĭthār', v. a. to naturalise; –se, to accustom one's self to.

connivencia, –nĭvĕn'thĭă, sf. connivance.

connotación, –nŏtāthĭŏn', sf. connection; distant relation.

connotado, –nŏtā'dŏ, sm. relationship.

connotar, –nŏtār', v. a. to imply.

connubio, –nŏ'bĭŏ, sm. (poet.) matrimony, cono, kŏ'nŏ, sm. cone. [wedlock.

conocedor, ra, kŏnŏthĕdŏr', sm. & f. connoisseur.

conocer, kŏnŏthĕr', v. a. to know, to understand; –se, to know one another.

conocido, da, kŏnŏthē'dŏ, sm. & f. acquaintance, acquaintant.

conocimiento, –thĭmĭĕn'tŏ, sm. knowledge, understanding; connoisseurship; cognition; acquaintance; (mar.) bill of landing.

conque, kŏnkĕ', sm. condition. [tion.

conquista, –kĭs'tă, sf. conquest; acquisi-

conquistador, –kĭstădŏr', sm. conqueror.

conquistar, –kĭstār', v. a. to conquer.

conreinar, –rēĭnār', v. n. to reign at the same time with another.

consabido, da, –săbē'dŏ, a. already known; above-mentioned. [tion.

consagración, –săgrăthĭŏn', sf. consecra-

consagrar, –săgrār', v. a. to consecrate.

consanguíneo, nea, –săngŭē'nĕŏ, a. consanguineous. [sanguinity.

consanguinidad, –sănginĭdăd', sf. con-

conscripto, –skrĭp'tŏ, a. conscript.

consecución, –sĕkŭthĭŏn', sf. attainment.

consecuencia, –sĕkŭĕn'thĭă, sf. consequence; conclusion; por –, therefore.

consecuente, –sĕkŭĕn'tĕ, a. sm. consequent, consequence.

consecutivo, va, –sĕkŭtē'vŏ, a. consecutive; consequential. [to obtain.

conseguir, –sĕgēr', v. a. to attain, to get,

conseja, –sĕ'k'ă, sf. fable, feigned story.

consejero, –sĕ'hă'rŏ, sm. counsellor.

consejil, –sĕ'hĭl', sf. (cant) public woman.

consejo, –sĕh'ŏ, sm. counsel, advice; council; council-house; (cant) crafty sharper. [children).

consentido, –sĕntē'dŏ, a. spoiled (of

consentir, –sĕntĭr', v. a. to consent, to agree; to comply, to acquiesce; to rely.

conserje, –sĕr'hĕ, sm. warden of a royal castle.

conserva, –sĕr'vă, sf. conserve;

conservación, –sĕrvāthĭŏn', sf. conservation. [guard; to candy fruit.

conservar, –sĕrvār', v. a. to conserve; to

conservativo, va, –sĕrvătē'vŏ, a. conservative.

conservatorio, –sĕrvātŏ'rĭŏ, sm. conservatory; –, ria, a. conservatory, preservative. [great, large.

considerable, –sĭdĕrā'blĕ, a. considerable;

consideración, –sĭdĕrāthĭŏn', sf. consideration, notice, sake, account; reflection.

consideradamente, –sĭdĕrādămĕn'tĕ, ad. considerately. [siderate.

considerado, –sĭdĕrā'dŏ, a. prudent, con-

considerar, –sĭdĕrār', v. a. to consider.

consigna, –sĭg'nă, sf. (mil.) watch-word.

consignación, –sĭgnāthĭŏn', sf. consignation; consignment.

consignador, –sĭgnādŏr', sm. one who consigns goods to a foreign correspondent.

consignar, –sĭgnār', v. a. to consign; to deposit; to forward goods to a correspondent, to be sold for account of the consigners. [consignee.

consignatario, –sĭgnătā'rĭŏ, sm. trustee;

consigo, –sē'gŏ, pn. with one's self.

consiguiente, –sĭgĭĕn'tĕ, a. consequent, consecutive. [stability; solidity.

consistencia, –sĭstĕn'thĭă, sf. consistence,

consistente, –sĭstĕn'tĕ, a. consistent, firm, solid. [contained; to be composed.

consistir, –sĭstĭr', v. n. to consist; to be

consistorio, –sĭstŏ'rĭŏ, sm. consistory; town-house. [nion.

consocio, –sŏ'thĭŏ, sm. partner, compa-

consolación, –sŏlāthĭŏn', sf. consolation.

consolador, ra, –sŏlădŏr', a. consolatory, comfortable. [fort, to cheer.

consolar, –sŏlār', v. a. to console, to com-

consolidar, –sŏlĭdār', a. a. to consolidate, –se, (law) to tie up interest with principal.

consolidativo, va, –sŏlĭdătē'vŏ, a. consolidant, healing. [congruence.

consonancia, –sŏnăn'thĭă, sf. consonance;

consonante, –sŏnăn'tĕ, sm. rhyme; –, sf. (gr.) consonant; –, a. consonant, conformable. [ciety.

consorcio, –sŏr'thĭŏ, sm. partnership, society.

consorte, –sŏr'tĕ, sm. consort, companion, partner; accomplice. [plot.

conspiración, –spĭrāthĭŏn', sf. conspiracy, conspirador, –spĭrādŏr', sm. conspirator, plotter. [plot.

conspirar, –spĭrār', v. n. to conspire, to

constancia, –stăn'thĭă, sf. constancy, steadiness, immutability. [alterable.

constante, –stăn'tĕ, a. constant, firm, un-

5.*

constar, *-stăr',* v. imp. to be evident, certain; to be composed of, to consist of.

constelación, *-stělăthĭŏn',* sf. constellation.   [nation.

consternación, *-stěrnăthĭŏn',* sf. consternation.

consternar, *-stěrnăr',* v. a. to strike with amazement, to confound;   [tiveness.

constipación, *-stĭpăthĭŏn',* sf. cold; costiveness.

constipar, *-stĭpăr',* v. a. to cause a cold; to constipate.   [(in all senses).

constitución, *-stĭtŭthĭŏn',* sf. constitution

constitucional, *-stĭtŭthĭŏnăl',* a. constitutional.   [establish; to appoint.

constituir, *-stĭtŭĭr',* v. a. to constitute; to

constitutivo, va, *-stĭtŭtĭvŏ,* a. constitutive, essential.   [stituent.

constituyente, *-stĭtŭyěn'tě,* sm. constituent.

constreñimiento, *-strěnyĭmĭěn'tŏ,* sm. constraint.

constreñir, *-strěnyěr',* v. a. to constrain, to force; (med.) to constipate.

constricción, *-strĭkthĭŏn',* sf. constriction, contraction.   [gent.

constrictivo, va, *-strĭktĭvŏ,* a. astringent.

construcción, *-strŭkthĭŏn',* sf. construction.   [to construct; to construe.

construir, *-strŭĭr',* v. a. to form, to build,

construpar, *-strŭpăr',* v. a. to deflour.

consuegro, gra, *-sŭě'grŏ,* sm. & f. parents of two children who marry; fathers *or* mothers who marry their children together.   [fort; joy, merriment.

consuelo, *-sŭě'lŏ,* sm. consolation, comfort, joy, merriment.

cónsul, *kŏn'sŭl,* sm. consul; member of the tribunal of commerce.

consulado, *-sŭlă'dŏ,* sm. consulate; tribunal of commerce.

consular, *-sŭlăr',* a. consular.

consulta, *-sŭl'tă,* sf. consult, consultation.

consultación, *-sŭltăthĭŏn',* sf. consultation.   [advice; to give advice.

consultar, *-sŭltăr',* v. a. to consult, to ask

consultivo, va, *-sŭltĭvŏ,* a. consultative.

consultor, ra, *-sŭltŏr',* sm. & f. adviser, counsel.

consumación, *-sŭmăthĭŏn',* sf. consummation, perfection, finishing.

consumado, da, *-sŭmă'dŏ,* a. consummate, complete, perfect, accomplished, exquisite; —, sm. jelly-broth.

consumar, *-sŭmăr',* v. a. to consummate, to finish, to perfect.

consumir, *-sŭmĭr',* v. a. to consume, to destroy; to waste, to exhaust; —se, to waste away, to languish.

consumo, *-sŏ'mŏ,* sm. consumption of provisions and merchandise.

consunción, *-sŭnthĭŏn',* sf. (med.) consumption; wasting.   [stancial.

consustancial, *-sŭstănthăl',* a. consubstancial.

contabilidad, *-tăbĭlĭdăd',* sf. accounts; book-keeping.

contacto, *-tăk'tŏ,* sm. contact.

contadero, ra, *-tădě'rŏ,* a. countable.

contado, da, *-tă'dŏ,* a. scarce, rare; de —, instantly; in hand; al —, cash, ready money.

contador, *-tădŏr',* n. computer, reckoner;

accountant; counter (table); counter (for games).

contaduría, *-tădŭrě'ă,* sf. accountant's office at the exchequer; auditorship.

contagiar, *-tă'hĭăr',* v. a. to infect.

contagio, *-tă'h'ĭŏ,* sm. contagion.

contagioso, sa, *-tă'hĭŏ'sŏ,* a. contagious.

contaminación, *-tămĭnăthĭŏn',* sf. contamination, pollution.

contaminar, *-tămĭnăr',* v. a. to contaminate; to infect by contagion; to corrupt.

contante, *-tăn'tě,* sm. ready money.

contar, *-tăr',* v. a. to count, to reckon, to compute, to calculate; — con, to rely upon.

contemplación, *-těmplăthĭŏn',* sf. contemplation.

contemplar, *-těmplăr',* v. a. to contemplate, to consider, to study; to meditate; to flatter; to condescend.   [templative.

contemplativo, va, *-těmplătĭvŏ,* a. contemporary, coeval.   [temporise.

contemporáneo, nea, *-těmpŏră'něŏ,* a. contemporary, coeval.

contemporizar, *-těmpŏrĭthăr',* v. n. to contemporise.

contencioso, sa, *-těnthĭŏ'sŏ,* a. contentious; quarrelsome.

contender, *-těnděr',* v. n. to contend, to strive; to contest, to debate.

contendiente, *-těndĭěn'tě,* sm. competitor.

contener, *-těněr',* v. a. to contain, to comprehend; to refrain; to repress.

contenido, da, *-těnĭ'dŏ,* a. moderate, temperate, modest; —, sm. tenour, contents.

contentadizo, za, *-těntădĭ'thŏ,* a. bien —, easily contented; mal —, hard to please.

contentar, *-těntăr',* v. a. to content, to satisfy, to please; —se, to be pleased *or* satisfied.

contento, ta, *-těn'tŏ,* a. glad; pleased; content; —, sm. contentment; receipt.

contestación, *-těstăthĭŏn',* sf. answer, reply; debate, disputation.

contestar, *-těstăr',* v. a. to prove, to attest; to answer, to reply; —, v. n. to agree; to accord.   [dence of another.

conteste, *-těs'tě,* a. confirming the evidence of another.

contexto, *-těks'tŏ,* sm. intertexture.

contienda, *-těn'dă,* sf. contest, dispute, debate.

contigo, *-tĭ'gŏ,* pn. with thee.

contigüidad, *-tĭgŭĭdăd',* sf. contiguity.

contiguo, gua, *-tĭ'gŭŏ,* a. contiguous, close.   [abstinence, moderation.

continencia, *-tĭněn'thĭă,* sf. continence, moderation.

continental, *-tĭněntăl',* a. continental.

continente, *-tĭněn'tě,* sm. abstinence; countenance; continent, mainland; —, a. abstinent, moderate.

contingencia, *-tĭn'hěn'thĭă,* sf. accidental possibility, contingent.

contingente, *-tĭn'hěn'tě,* a. fortuitous, accidental; —, sm. contingent.

continuación, *-tĭnŭăthĭŏn',* sf. continuation, lengthening; continuity.

continuar, *-tĭnŭăr',* v. a. & n. to continue.

continuo, nua, *-tĭ'nŭŏ,* a. continuous, ceaseless.   [an affected manner.

contonearse, *-tŏněăr'sě,* v. r. to walk in an affected manner.

contoneo, *-tŏně'ŏ,* sm. affected manner of walking.

contorno, –tŏr′nŏ, sm. environs, pl.; contour, outline; en –, round about.

contorsión, –tŏrsiŏn′, sf. contortion, wry motion. [opposite to.

contra, kŏn′trä, pr. against, contrary to,

contrabajo, –bä′h′ŏ, sm. counter-bass; bass-viol. [counterbalance.

contrabalanzear, –bälänthëär′, v. a. to

contrabandista, –bändis′tä, sm. smuggler, contrabandist. [trade, smuggling.

contrabando, –bän′dŏ, sm. contraband

contrabatería, –bäterë′ä, sf. (mil.) counter-battery.

contracambio, –käm′bĭŏ, sm. re-exchange.

contracarril, –kärrïl′, sm. (rail.) counter-rail. [tion.

contracción, kŏnträkthĭŏn′, sf. contrac-

contradanza, kŏnträdän′thä, sf. country-dance. [to gainsay.

contradecir, –dethĭr′, v. a. to contradict,

contradicción, –dĭkthĭŏn′, sf. contradiction verbal opposition.

contradictorio, ria, –dĭktŏ′rĭŏ, a. contradictory, opposite to.

contradique, –dĭ′kĕ, sm. counter-dike.

contraer, kŏnträĕr′, v. a. & n. to contract, to shrink; to make a bargain; –se, to shrink up. [counter-scarp.

contraescarpa, kŏnträĕskär′pä, sf. (mil.)

contraescritura, –ĕskrĭtŏ′rä, sf. counter-deed. [a countermanding decree.

contrafirmar, –fĭrmär′, v. a. (law) to obtain

contrafoso, –fŏ′sŏ, sm. outer ditch of a fortress. [privilege.

contrafuero, –fwĕ′rŏ, sm. violation of a

contrafuerte, –fwĕr′tĕ, sm. counter-fort.

contraguardia, –gwär′dĭä, sf. counter-guard.

contrahacer, –äthĕr′, v. a. to counterfeit, to falsify; to pirate the works of an author.

contrahaz, –äth′, sm. wrong side of cloth.

contrahecho, cha, –ĕtsh′ŏ, a. deformed, miscreated; counterfeited, feint.

contralor, kŏnträlŏr′, sm. controller, inspector.

contralto, kŏnträl′tŏ, sm. (mus.) contralto.

contramaestre, kŏnträmäĕs′trĕ, sm. (mar.) boatswain; overseer of a manufactory. [catching fish.

contramalla, –mäl′yä, sf. double net for

contramallar, –mälyär′, v. a. to make nets with double meshes. [mand.

contramandar, –mändär′, v. a. to counter-

contramarca, –mär′kä, sf. countermark; customs stamp duty.

contramarco, –mär′kŏ, sm. counter-frame of a glass window. [march.

contramarcha, –mär′tshä, sf. counter-

contramarchar, –märtshär′, v. a. to counter-march. [tide, spring-tide.

contramarea, –märĕ′ä, sf. (mar.) counter-

contramesana, –mĕsä′nä, sf. mizen-mast.

contramina, –mĕ′nä, sf. countermine.

contraminar, –mĭnär′, v. a. to counter-mine; to counter-work. [raye.

contramuralla, –mŏ′räl′yä, sf. fausse-

contramuro, –mŏ′rŏ, sm. countermure.

contraorden, –ŏr′dĕn, sm. countermand.

contraordenar, –ŏrdĕnär′, v. a. to counter-mand. [opposite party.

contrapasar, –päsär′, v. n. to join the

contrapaso, –pä′sŏ, sm. back step.

contrapechar, –pĕtshär′, v. a. to strike breast against breast (applied to horses in tournaments.

contrapelo, –pä′lŏ, ad. against the grain.

contrapesar, –pĕsär′, v. n. to counterpoise.

contrapeso, –pä′sŏ, sm. counterpoise; rope-dancer's pole. [pilaster.

contrapilastra, –pĭläs′trä, sf. counter-

contraponer, –pŏnĕr′, v. a. to compare, to oppose.

contraposición, –pŏsĭthĭŏn′, sf. counter-view, contrast; clair-obscure.

contraprueba, –prŏĕ′bä, sf. counterproof.

contrapuerta, –pwĕr′tä, sf. inner hall-door of a house.

contrapuntearse, –pŏntĕär′sĕ, v. r. to quarrel with abusive language. [point.

contrapunto, –pŏn′tŏ, sm. (mus.) counter-

contrapunzón, –pŏnthŏn′, v. a. to counter-punch; gunsmith's counter-mark.

contraquilla, –kĭl′yä, sf. (mar.) false keel.

contrariar, kŏnträrĭär′, v. a. to contradict, to oppose, to counteract.

contrariedad, –trärĭĕdäd′, sf. contrariety, opposition.

contrario, –trä′rĭŏ, sm. opponent, antagonist; contrary; –, ria, a. contrary, opposite; adverse, abhorrent; por el –, on the contrary; en –, against.

contrarrestar, kŏnträrrĕstär′, v. a. to strike back a ball; (fig.) to resist, to oppose.

contrarresto, –rĕs′tŏ, sm. player who is to strike back the ball; opposition, contradiction. [counter-revolution.

contrarrevolución, –rĕvŏlŭthĭŏn′, sf.

contrarronda, –rŏn′dä, sf. (mil.) counter-round. [organ.

contras, kŏn′träs, sf. pl. bass-pipes of an

contrasellar, –sĕlyär′, v. a. to counterseal.

contraseña, –sĕn′yä, sf. countersign; (mil.) watch-word.

contrastar, kŏnträstär′, v. a. to contrast, to oppose; to resist, to contradict; to assay metals; to examine measures and weights.

contraste, kŏnträ′tĕ, sm. assayer of the mint; assayer's office; assayer of weights and measures; contrast; opposition, strife; (mar.) sudden change of the wind.

contrata, kŏnträ′tä, sf. contract. [merce.

contratación, –träthĭŏn′, sf. trade, com-

contratante, –trätän′tĕ, sm. contractor; trader. [fig.; to contract, to stipulate.

contratar, –trätär′, v. a. to trade, to trade,

contratiempo, –trätĭĕmpŏ, sm. disappointment, misfortune.

contratista, –trätĭs′tä, sm. conventionist.

contrato, –trä′tŏ, sm. contract, pact.

contratreta, kŏnträtrĕ′tä, s. counterplot.

contratrinchera, –trĭntshĕr′ä, s. counter-trench. [of contravallation.

contravalar, –välär′, v. a. to form a line

contravención, –vĕnthĭŏn′, sf. contravention.

contraveneno, -vĕnă'nŏ, sm. counterpoison.

contravenir, -vĕnīr', v. n. to contravene, to transgress; to oppose. [shutter.

contraventana, -vĕntă'nă, sf. windowcontraventor, ra, -vĕntōr', sm. & f. offender, transgressor

contravidriera, -vīdrĭ'ră, sf. second glass window. [bution; tax.

contribución, kŏntrĭbŭthĭŏn', sf. contricontribuir, -trĭbŭīr', v. a. to contribute.

contributario, -trĭbŭtă'rĭŏ, sm. contributor, payer of taxes.

contribuyente, -trĭbŭyĕn'tĕ, v. a. contributing; contributory. [tence.

contrición, -trĭthĭŏn', sf. contrition, penicontrincante, -trĭnkăn'tĕ, sm. competitor.

contristar, -trĭstăr', v. a. to afflict, to sadden.

contrito, ta, -trī'tŏ, a. contrite, penitent.

controversia, -trŏvĕr'sĭă, sf. controversy, dispute. [versialist.

controversista, -trŏvĕrsĭs'tă, sm. controcontrovertir, -trŏvĕrtīr', v. a. to controvert, to dispute.

contumacia, -tŭmă'thĭă, sf. obstinacy, stubbornness; (law) contumacy.

contumaz, -tŭmăth', a. obstinate, stubborn; (law) contumacious. [abuse.

contumelia, -tŭmĕ'lĭă, sf. contumely.

contumelioso, sa, -tŭmĕlĭŏ'sŏ, a. contumelious.

contundir, -tŭndīr', v. a. to beat together; to bruise; to cause a contusion.

conturbación, -tŭrbăthĭŏn', sf. perturbation. [to disquiet.

conturbar, -tŭrbăr', v. a. to perturbate.

contusión, -tŭsĭŏn', sf. contusion.

convalecencia, -vălĕthĕn'thĭă, sf. convalescence, recovery from disease.

convalecer, -vălĕthĕr', v. n. to recover from sickness; to recover lost prosperity or power. [ing.

convecino, na, -vĕthĕ'nŏ, a. neighbour.

convencer, -vĕnthĕr', v. a. to convince.

convencimiento, -vĕnthĭmĭĕn'tŏ, sm. conviction. [pact.

convención, -vĕnthĭŏn', sf. convention.

convencional, -vĕnthĭŏnăl', a. conventional, agreed upon by compact.

conveniencia, -vĕnĭĕn'thĭă, sf. utility, profit; convenience; ease, commodity.

conveniente, -vĕnĭĕn'tĕ, a. useful, convenable, conformable.

convenio, -vĕ'nĭŏ, sm. convention, contract, accordance.

convenir, -vĕnīr', v. n. to agree, to coincide; to compromise; to fit, to suit, to correspond; to assemble.

conventículo, -vĕntĭ'kŭlŏ, sm. conventicle.

convento, -vĕn'tŏ, sm. convent, monastery, nunnery.

conventual, -vĕntŭăl', a. monastic.

convergencia, -vĕr'hĕn'thĭă, sf. convergence. [sociable.

conversable, -vĕrsă'blĕ, a. conversable.

conversación, -vĕrsăthĭŏn', sf. conversation, easy talk; communication.

conversar, -vĕrsăr', v. n. to converse; to live together. [change.

conversión, -vĕrsĭŏn', sf. conversion.

converso, -vĕr'sŏ, sm. convert. [vert.

convertir, -vĕrtīr', v. a. -se, v. r. to conconvexidad, -vĕksĭdăd', sf. convexity.

convexo, xa, -vĕks'ŏ, a. convex.

convicción, -vĭkthĭŏn', sf. conviction.

convicto, ta, -vĭk'tŏ, a. convicted (found guilty).

convidar, -vĭdăr', v. a. to invite, to bid; to allure, to persuade; -se, to offer one's service spontaneously.

convincente, -vĭnthĕn'tĕ, a. convincing.

convite, -vĕ'tĕ, sm. invitation; feast to which persons are invited. [semble.

convocar, -vŏkăr', v. a. to convoke, to asconvocatorio, ria, -vŏkătŏ'rĭŏ, a. that which convokes. [vulus.

convólvulo, -vŏl'vŭlŏ, sm. (bot.) convolconvoy, -vŏī', sm. convoy, conduct, escort, retinue, suit. [escort.

convoyar, -vŏyăr', v. a. to convoy, to convulsión, -vŭlsĭŏn', sf. convulsion.

convulsivo, va, -vŭlsī'vŏ, a. convulsive.

conyugal, -yŭgăl', a. conjugal, connubial.

cónyuges, kŏn'yŭ'hĕs, sm. pl. married couple, husband and wife. [tion.

cooperación, -ŏpĕrăthĭŏn', sf. cooperacooperador, ra, -dŏr', sm. & f. cooperator.

cooperar, -ŏŏpĕrăr', v. a. to cooperate.

cooperativo, va, -ŏŏpĕrătī'vŏ, a. cooperative.

coopositor, -ŏŏpŏsĭtŏr', sm. competitor.

coordinar, -ŏŏrdĭnăr', v. a. to arrange, to classify.

copa, kŏ'pă, sf. cup; top of a tree; crown of a hat; brazier; -s, pl. hearts (at cards).

copado, da, kŏpă'dŏ, a. tufted, copped.

copera, kŏpĕ'ră, sf. cupboard.

copero, -rŏ, sm. cup-bearer.

copete, -tĕ, sm. toupee; crown-work of a looking-glass frame; top of a shoe; top, summit.

copetudo, da, -tŏ'dŏ, a. copped; supercilious on account of one's noble descent.

copia, kŏ'pĭă, sf. plenty, abundance; copy, transcript; portrait taken from original design; copy of a picture; (gr.) list of nouns and verbs. [libro -, copy-book.

copiador, kŏpĭădŏr', sm. copyist; copier.

copiar, kŏpĭăr', v. a. to copy; to imitate, to draw from life; (poet.) to describe, to depict. [dant, plentiful.

copioso, sa, kŏpĭŏ'sŏ, a. copious, abun-

copista, kŏpĭs'tă, sm. copyist. [mark.

copla, kŏ'plă, sf. couplet; sarcastic recoplear, kŏplĕăr', v. n. to make couplets.

coplero, kŏplĕ'rŏ, sm. poetaster; balladseller.

copo, kŏ'pŏ, sm. small bundle of cotton, flax &c., put on the distaff to be spun; flake of snow. [Catholic churches).

copón, kŏpŏn', sm. cibary (cup used in copudo, kŏpŭ'dŏ, a. tufted, tufty, bushy.

cópula, kŏ'pŭlă, sf. joining of two things together; cupola; (gr.) copula.

copulativo, va, kŏpŭlătĕ' vŏ, a. copulative.

coqueta, kŏkĕ'tă, sf. coquette, flirt.

coquetear, —tĕăr' v. n. to coquet.

coquetería, —tĕrĕ'ă, sf. coquetry, flirtation.

coquillo, kŏkĭl'yŏ, sm. cocoa-nut (of the Indian palm-tree).   [amuse children.

coquito, kŏkĕ'tŏ, sm. grimace made to

coracero, kŏrăthĕ'rŏ, sm. cuirassier.

coracha, kŏrătsh'ă, sf. leather sack, used for the transport of cocoa, tobacco, &c., from America.   [sion.

coraje, kŏră'h'ĕ, sm. courage; anger, pas-

corajudo, da, —'hŏ'dŏ, a. angry, passionate.   [of corals; —, a. choral.

coral, kŏrăl', sm. coral; —es, pl. strings

coralero, kŏrălĕ'rŏ, sm. worker or dealer in corals.

coralina, kŏrălĕ'nă, sf. sea-coralline.

corambre, kŏrăm'brĕ, sf. all hides and skins of animals, dressed or undressed.

corambrero, —brĕ'rŏ, sm. dealer in hides.

coramvobis, —vŏ'bĭs, sm. outward appearance, gravity.

coraza, kŏră'thă, sf. cuirass; cuirassier.

corazón, kŏrăthŏn', sm. heart; core; benevolence; courage; centre; pith of a tree; de —, heartily.

corazonada, kŏrăthŏnă'dă, sf. inspiration; quick decision; presentiment.

corbachada, kŏrbătshă'dă, sf. lash given with a hunting-crop.

corbacho, kŏrbătsh'ŏ, sm. hunting-crop.

corbato, kŏrbă'tă, sf. cravat, neckerchief.

corbatín, —tĭn', sm. cravat with a clasp.

corbato, kŏrbă'tŏ, sm. cooler.

corbeta, kŏrbĕ'tă, sf. corvet (light vessel with three masts and square sails).

corcel, kŏrthĕl', sm. steady horse, charger.

corcino, kŏrthĕ'nŏ, sm. small deer.

corcova, kŏrkŏ'vă, sf. hump; protuberance.   [backed, crooked.

corcovado, da, kŏrkŏvă'dŏ, a. hump-

corcovear, —vĕăr', v. n. to curvet, to cut capers.

corcovo, kŏrkŏ'vŏ, sm. curvet; caper.

corchea, kŏrtshĕ'ă, sf. (mus.) crotchet.

corchera, kŏrtshĕ'ră, sf. vessel made of pitched cork to cool liquor.

corcheta, —tă, sf. eye of a hook or clasp.

corchete, —tĕ, sm. clasp; locket; catchpoll; bench-hook of a carpenter's bench.

corcho, kŏrtsh'ŏ, sm. cork; bee-hive; cork-stopple.

cordaje, kŏrdă'h'ĕ, sm. (mar.) cordage.

cordal, kŏrdăl', sm. double-tooth.

cordel, kŏrdĕl', sm. cord, rope; (mar.) line.

cordelazo, kŏrdĕlă'thŏ, sm. lash given with a rope.

cordelería, —lĕrĕ'ă, sf. rope-walk.

cordelero, —lĕ'rŏ, sm. rope-maker.

corderillo, kŏrdĕrĭl'yŏ, sm. dressed lamb-skin.   [lamb-skin; meek, gentle man.

cordero, kŏrdĕ'rŏ, sm. lamb; dressed

cordial, kŏrdĭăl', a. cordial, affectionate; —, sm. cordial.

cordialidad, kŏrdĭălĭdăd', sf. cordiality.

cordillera, kŏrdĭlyĕ'ră, sf. range of mountains.

cordobán, kŏrdŏbăn', sm. cordovan, cordwain.   [lace; military cordon.

cordón, kŏrdŏn', sm. cord, string; twisted

cordonería, kŏrdŏnĕrĕ'ă, sf. lace-making.

cordonero, —nĕ'rŏ, sm. lace-maker; rope-maker.   [wisdom; judgment.

cordura, kŏrdŭ'ră, sf. prudence, practical

coreo, kŏrĕ'ŏ, sm. harmonious melting of musical chords.   [small leather hide.

corezuelo, kŏrĕthĕ'lŏ, sm. sucking-pig;

corifeo, kŏrĭfĕ'ŏ, sm. coryphoeus.

corista, kŏrĭs'tă, sm. chorister.

coriza, kŏrĕ'thă, sf. coryza, dry catarrh; peasant's strap-shoe.

corladura, kŏrlădŭ'ră, sf. gold-varnish.

cornada, kŏrnă'dă, sf. thrust with a bull's horn.

cornadura, kŏrnădŭ'ră, sf. horns, pl.

cornamenta, —mĕn'tă, sf. horns of an animal, pl.   [of rustic flute.

cornamusa, —mŭ'să, sf. cornemuse; sort

córnea, kŏr'nĕă, sf. cornea (second integument of the eye).   [horns.

cornear, —nĕăr', v. n. to butt with the

corneja, kŏrnĕ'h'ă, sf. crow.

córneo, ea, kŏr'nĕŏ, a. horny.

cornerina, —nĕrĕ'nă, sf. onyx.

corneta, —nĕ'tă, sf. cornet; hunting-horn; cornet (ensign).   [bleeding horses.

cornezuelo, —nĕthŭĕ'lŏ, sm. instrument for

cornijal, —nĭ'hăl', sm. corner of a building.

cornisa, —nĭ'să, sf. cornice.   [ling.

corno, kŏr'nŏ, sm. cornelian cherry-tree.

cornucopia, —nŭkŏ'pĭă, sf. cornucopia, horn of plenty; branched candlestick.

cornudo, da, —nŏ'dŏ, a. horned.

coro, kŏr'ŏ, sm. choir, quire; chorus; (poet.) summer solstitial wind.

corógrafo, kŏrŏ'grăfŏ, sm. chorographer.

corolario, kŏrŏlă'rĭŏ, sm. corollary.

corona, kŏrŏ'nă, sf. crown; coronet; top of the head; clerical tonsure; crown (English silver coin); regal power; monarchy; honour, splendour, decoration; halo.

coronación, kŏrŏnăthĭŏn', sf. coronation.

coronar, năr', v. a. to crown; to complete, to perfect; to ornament the top of a building.   [crown; (bot.) coronary.

coronario, ria, —nă'rĭŏ, a. relating to a

coronel, —nĕl', sm. (mil.) colonel.

coronela, kŏrŏnĕ'lă, sf. colonel's lady.

coronilla, —nĭl'yă, sf. crown of the head.

coroza, kŏrŏ'thă, sf. coronet of pasteboard, worn as a mark of infamy.

corozo, —thŏ, sm. bactris (a palm-tree).

corpanchón, kŏrpăntshŏn', sm. huge carcass.

corpezuelo, kŏrpĕthŭĕ'lŏ, corpiño, kŏrpĭn'yŏ, sm. waistcoat; bodice.

corporación, kŏrpŏrăthĭŏn', sf. corporation, guild.   [altar linen.

corporal, kŏrpŏrăl', a. corporal; —es, s. pl.

corporalidad, —rălĭdăd', sf. corporality, corporeity.

corpóreo, rea, kŏrpŏ'rĕŏ, a. corporeal.

corporificar, kŏrpŏrĭfĭkăr', v. a. to embody.

corpudo, da, kŏrpŏ'dŏ, a. corpulent, bulky.

corpulencia, *kŏrpŭlĕn'thĭă*, sf. corpulence.

corpulento, ta, *—tŏ*, a corpulent, bulky.

Corpus, *kŏr'pŭs*, sm. Corpus-Christi day.

corpúsculo, *kŏrpŭs'kŭlŏ*, sm. corpuscle.

corral, *kŏrrāl'*, sm. yard ; a poultry-yard ; play-house ; blank space in notebooks of students who have neglected a lecture.

corralero, *—lā'rŏ*, sm. keeper of a dung-yard.   [flexibility.

correa, *kŏrrā'ă*, sf. leather strap, thong ;

correaje, *—ā'h'ĕ*, sm. heap of leather straps.

correar, *kŏrrĕār'*, v. a. to draw out wool and prepare it for use.

corrección, *kŏrrĕkthŏn'*, sf. correction ; reprehension ; amendment.

correctivo, va, *—tĕ'vŏ*, a. corrective.

correcto, ta, *kŏrrĕk'tŏ*, a. exact, correct.

corrector, *—tŏr'*, sm. corrector ; proof-reader.   [upper grinding-stone.

corredera, *kŏrrĕdā'ră*, sf. race-ground ;

corredizo, za, *—dē'thŏ*, a. easy to be untied.

corredor, *—dŏr'*, sm. runner ; race-horse ; corridor ; broker ; —a, sf. procuress.

corredura, *—dō'ră*, sf. liquor which flows over the brim of a vessel.   [brokerage.

correduría, *—dŭrē'ă*, sf. trade of a broker ;

correería, *—ĕrē'ă*, sf. trade of a strap-maker.

correero, *—ā'rŏ*, sm. strap-maker.

corregencia, *kŏrrĕ'hĕn'thĭă*, sf. coregency.

corregente, *—rĕ'hĕn'tĕ*, sm. coregent.

corregidor, *—'hĭdŏr'*, sm. corregidor (Spanish magistrate).   [regidor.

corregidora, *—'hĭdō'ră*, sf. wife of a cor-

corregir, *—'hĭr'*, v. a. to correct, to amend ; to reprehend ; to mitigate.

correjel, *—hĕl'*, sm. English sole-leather.

correlación, *kŏrrĕlăthŏn'*, sf. correlation.

correlativo, va, *—rĕlătĕ'vŏ*, a. correlative.

correncia, *—rĕn'thĭă*, sf. looseness of the belly.

correo, *—rā'ŏ*, sm. express, courier ; post-boy ; post-office ; bag of letters ; (law) ac-complice ; á vuelta de —, by return of post ; en la casa de —s, "Post-Office," to be kept till called for (applied to letters arrived).   [leathery.

correoso, sa, *—rĕ'sŏ*, a. ductile, flexible,

correr, *kŏrrĕr'*, v. a. & n. to run ; to flow ; to blow (applied to the wind) ; to pass away ; to take the proper course ; to act heedlessly ; —se, to be ashamed ; to fly into a passion.   [strap.

correría, *—rĕrē'ă*, sf. incursion ; leather

correspondencia, *—rĕspŏndĕn'thĭă*, sf. correspondence ; relation ; intercourse, re-ciprocal intelligence ; proportion.

corresponder, *—rĕspŏndĕr'*, v. a. to make a suitable return ; to correspond, to an-swer ; to regard ; to agree, to be congruent ; —se, to correspond ; to esteem one another.

correspondiente, *—rĕspŏndĭĕn'tĕ*, a. cor-respondent, conformable, suitable ; —, sm. correspondent.   [dent.

corresponsal, *—rĕspŏnsăl'*, sm. correspon-

corretaje, *—rĕtā'h'ĕ*, sm. brokerage ; money paid to a pimp.

corretear, *—rĕtĕār'*, v. a. to rove, to ramble.

correvedile, *—rĕvĕdē'lĕ*, sm. tale-bearer ; procurer, pimp.   [at full speed.

corrida, *—rē'dă*, sf. course, race ; de —,

corrido, da, *—rē'dă*, a. expert ; artful ; ashamed.

corriente, *—rĭĕn'tĕ*, sf. course of rivers ; current ; course, progression ; —alterna-tiva ó inversa, alternative or inverse electric fluid ; —, a. current ; easy ; gener-ally received ; common, general ; fluent ; running ; marketable.

corrillero, *—rĭlyā'rŏ*, sm. braggadocio.

corrillo, *—rē'lyŏ*, sm. circle of persons ; —s, pl. town-talk.

corro, *kŏr'rŏ*, sm. circle formed by people who meet to talk or see a show ; round (a dance).   [rate, to strengthen.

corroborar, *—rŏbŏrār'*, v. a. to corrobo-

corroer, *—rŏĕr'*, v. a. to corrode.

corromper, *—rŏmpĕr'*, v. a. to corrupt ; to alter the form of a thing ; to seduce a woman ; to bribe, to suborn ; —, v. n. to stink ; —se, to rot, to putrify.

corrosión, *—rŏsĭŏn'*, sf. corrosion.

corrosivo, va, *—rŏsē'vŏ*, a. corrosive.

corrupción, *—rŭpthĭŏn'*, sf. corruption, putrefaction ; spurious alteration in a book or writing ; depravity.   [abuse.

corruptela, *—rŭptĕ'lă*, sf. corruption ; (law)

corruptible, *—rŭptē'blĕ*, a. susceptible of corruption.

corruptivo, va, *—rŭptē'vŏ*, a. corruptive.

corrupto, ta, *—rŭp'tŏ*, a. corrupted, corrupt.

corruptor, *—rŭptŏr'*, sm. corruptor, mis-leader.

corrusco, *—rŭs'kŏ*, sm. offal, broken bread.

corsario, *kŏrsā'rĭŏ*, sm. corsair, privateer ; —, ria, a. cruising.

corsé, *kŏrsā'*, sf. corset, bodice, stays.

corta, *kŏr'tă*, sf. felling of wood.

cortabolsas, *—bŏl'săs*, sm. pick-pocket.

cortadera, *—dā'ră*, sf. chisel for cutting hot iron ; knife for extracting honey-combs.

cortadillo, *—dē'lyŏ*, sm. small drinking-glass ; echar —s, to speak in an affected manner ; to drink wine.

cortador, *—dŏr'*, sm. butcher ; —es, pl. incisors ; —, ra, a. cutting.

cortadura, *—dō'ră*, sf. cut ; cutting ; in-cision ; fissure ; —s, pl. shreds, cuttings, parings.   [cold iron.

cortafrío, *—frē'ŏ*, sm. chisel for cutting

cortafuego, *—fŭā'gŏ*, sm. fire-proof wall.

cortapicos y callares, *—pē'kŏs ĭ kălyā'-rĕs*, hold your tongue !   [legs in fencing.

cortapiés, *—pĭĕs'*, sm. thrust made at the

cortaplumas, *—plō'măs*, sm. pen-knife.

cortar, *kŏrtār'*, v. a. to cut, to cut off, to curtail ; to separate, to hew, to chop ; (mil.) to cut off part of the enemy's army ; to cut (at cards) ; to interrupt ; to abridge ; —se, to be ashamed or confounded ; to coagulate.

corte, *kŏr'tĕ*, sm. edge of knife, &c. ; abscis-sion, cutting ; cut ; felling of trees ; ex-pedient ; —, sf. court, residence town ; the tribunal of chancery ; retinue, suits ; yard ; courtship, flattery ; —s, sf. pl. cortes, as-sembly of the states of the realm in Spain.

cortedad, kŏrtĕdăd', sf. smallness, littleness; stupidity; pusillanimity.
cortejante, -'hăn'tĕ, a. courtier, gallant.
cortejar, -'hăr', v. a. to make love; to
court; to accompany.
cortejo, -tĕ'h'ŏ, sm. homage; courtship;
gift, present; gallant; wooer.
cortés, kŏrtĕs', a. courteous, genteel, polite.
cortesana, -tĕsă'nă, sf. courtesan.
cortesanazo, za, -nă'thŏ, a. awkwardly
civil.   [ness.
cortesanía, -nĕ'ă, sf. courtesy, polite-
cortesano, na, -să'nŏ, a. court-like;
courteous, gentle.
cortesano, -, sm. courtier, courtling.
cortesía, kŏrtĕsĕ'ă, sf. courtesy, good manners, pl.; polite form of speech in a letter.
corteza, kŏrtĕ'thă, sf. bark; peel; crust;
outward appearance; rusticity.
cortezudo, da, kŏrtĕthŏ'dŏ, a. barky;
rustic, unmannerly.
cortina, kŏrtĕ'nă, sf. curtain.   [a house.
cortinaje, -tĕnă'h'ĕ, sm. set of curtains for
corto, ta, kŏr'tŏ, a. short; scanty, narrow,
small, little; stupid; pusillanimous, fearful; concise; defective; á la -a ó á la
larga, sooner or later.   [mouse.
cortón, kŏrtŏn', sm. ring-worm; field-
corusco, ca, kŏrŭs'kŏ, a. (poet.) brilliant.
corva, kŏr'vă, sf. ham; curb (disease in
horses' knees).   [of an arch.
corvadura, -dŭ'ră, sf. curvature; bend
corvaza, kŏrvă'thă, sf. curb (disease).
corvejón, kŏrvĕ'hŏn', sm. hough; spur
of a cock.
corveta, kŏrvĕ'tă, sf. curvet, bound of a
horse; (mar.) corvet, sloop of war.
corvetear, -vĕtĕăr', v. n. to curvet.
corvo, va, kŏr'vŏ, a. bent, crooked.
corzo, za, kŏr'thŏ, sm. & f. roe-deer, fallow-
deer.
corzuelo, kŏrthŭĕ'lŏ, sm. wheat which has
been left in the husks by the thrashers.
cosa, kŏ'să, sf. thing; - de entidad, important thing; no es -, it does not matter; no hay tal -, no such thing; -, ad.
about, little more or less.
cosaco, kŏsă'kŏ, sm. cossack.   [shoulders.
coscarse, kŏskăr'sĕ, v. r. to shrug the
coscoja, -kŏ'h'ă, sf. scarlet-oak; dry leaves
of the kermes-oak; knob on the cross-bit
of a bridle.
coscojo, -kŏ'h'ŏ, sm. kermes-grain.
cosecha, kŏsĕtsh'ă, sf. harvest; harvest-
time; de su -, of one's own invention.
cosechar, kŏsĕtshăr', v. a. to crop, to reap.
cosechero, kŏsĕtshă'rŏ, sm. husbandman;
vintager.   [woman.
cosedera, kŏsĕdĕ'ră, sf. seamstress, needle-
coser, kŏsĕr', v. a. to sew; to join.
cosicosa, kŏsĭkŏ'să, sf. riddle.
cosido, kŏsĭ'dŏ, sm. stitching, sewing;
clothes for the wash; - de cama, quilts
and blankets of a bed.
cosmético, kŏsmĕ'tĭkŏ, sm. cosmetic.
cosmopolita, -mŏpŏlĕ'tă, sra. cosmopolite,
cosmopolitan.   [agitation; inquietude.
cosquillas, -kĭl'yăs, sf. pl. tickling; (fig.)

cosquilloso, sa, -kĭlyŏ'sŏ, a. ticklish;
easily offended.
costa, kŏs'tă, sf. cost, price; charge, expense; fatigue, labour; coast, shore; á
toda -, at all events.   [side of a ship.
costado, kŏstă'dŏ, sm. side; (mil.) flank;
costal, kŏstăl', sm. sack, large bag; rammer, beetle.   [ground.
costalada, kŏstălă'dă, sf. fall flat on the
costalero, -lă'rŏ, sm. porter (who carries
goods).   [pl.
costaneras, -nă'răs, sf. pl. rafters, timbers,
costanero, ra, -nă'rŏ, a. declivous.
costar, kŏstăr', v. n. to cost; to suffer detriment or loss.   [tas, at first cost.
coste, kŏs'tĕ, sm. cost, expense; á- y cos-
costear, kŏstĕăr', v. a. to pay the cost; -,
v. n. to sail along the coast.
costera, kŏstĕ'ră, sf. side of a bale of goods;
fisherman's basket; outside quire of a ream
of paper.   [ing.
costero, ra, -rŏ, a. outward; (mar.) coast-
costilla, kŏstĭl'yă, sf. rib; (fig.) wife; slave;
wealth; -s, pl. ribs of a ship.
costillaje, -yă'h'ĕ, costillar, -yăr', sm.
human ribs.
costo, kŏs'tŏ, sm. cost, price, expense.
costoso, sa, kŏstŏ'sŏ, a. costly, dear, expensive.   [given to the galley-slaves.
costra, kŏs'tră, sf. crust; broken biscuit.
costrada, kŏstră'dă, sf. Spanish seed-cake.
costroso, sa, kŏstrŏ'sŏ, a. crusty.
costumbre, kŏstŭm'brĕ, sf. custom, habit;
established manner.   [splicing of a rope.
costura, kŏstŭ'ră, sf. seam; needle-work;
costurera, kŏstŭră'ră, sf. seamstress.
cota, kŏ'tă, sf. coat of mail.   [woman.
cotarrera, kŏtărrĕ'ră, sf. a gadding
cotarro, kŏtăr'rŏ, sm. charity-hut for the
reception of beggars.   [front.
cotejar, kŏtĕ'hăr', v. a. to compare; to con-
cotejo, -tĕ'h'ŏ, sm. comparison, collation.
cotí, kŏtĭ', sm. ticking used for mattresses.
cotidiano, na, kŏtĭdĭă'nŏ, a. daily.
cotilla, kŏtĭl'yă, sf. stays, pl.
cotillero, -yă'rŏ, sm. stay-maker.
cotillón, kŏtĭl'yŏn, sm. cotilion (dance).
coto, kŏ'tŏ, sm. inclosure of pasture-
grounds; district; land-mark.
cotón, kŏtŏn', sm. printed cotton.
cotonada, kŏtŏnă'dă, sf. calico, print,
printed calico, prints.
cotonía, kŏtŏnĭ'ă, sf. dimity.
cotorra, kŏtŏr'ră, sf. magpie; small
parrot; loquacious woman.
cotorrera, kŏtŏrră'ră, sf. hen-parrot;
prattling woman.
cotorrería, -rĕrĕ'ă, sf. loquacity.
coturno, kŏtŭr'nŏ, sm. cothurnus; buskin.
covacha, kŏvătsh'ă, sf. small cave, grotto.
covachuela, -tshŭĕ'lă, sf. office of secretary of state.
covachuelista, -tshŭĕlĭs'tă, sm. clerk in
the secretary of state's office.
cavanillo, kŏvănĭl'yŏ, sm. basket for
gathering grapes.
coyunda, -yŭn'dă, sf. strap with which
oxen are tied to the yoke.

coyuntura, *-yŭntŏ͞'rä*, sf. joint, articulation; conjuncture.

coz, *kŏth*, sf. kick; recoil of a gun; flowing back of a flood; á coces, by dint of crabrón, *krăbrŏn'*, sm. hornet. [kicking.

cráneo, *krä'nĕŏ*, sm. skull, head-pan.

crápula, *krä'pŭlä*, sf. intoxication.

crasitud, *krăsĭtŭd''*, sf. grease, fat; corpulency.

craso, sa, *krä͞s'ŏ*, a. fat, greasy, thick.

cráter, *krä'tĕr*, sm. cratera, *krä'tĕ'rä*, sf. crater of a volcano.

creación, *krĕăthĭŏn'*, sf. creation.

creador, *-dŏr'*, sm. the Creator, God.

crear, *krĕär'*, v. a. to create, to make; to establish.   [to raise the price.

crecer, *krĕthĕr'*, v. n. to grow, to increase; creces, *krä'thĕs*, sf. pl. augmentation, increase; additional quantity of corn paid by a farmer to a public granary, besides what he borrowed from it.

crecida, *krĕthĭ'dä*, sf. swell of rivers.

crecido, da, *-dŏ*, a. grown, increased; grave, important; -s, sm. pl. widening stitches in knitting.

creciente, *krĕthĭĕn'tĕ*, sf. swell; leaven; crescent (moon); (mar.) flood-tide.

crecimiento, *-mĭĕn'tŏ*, sm. increase; increase of the price.   [an altar.

credencia, *krĕdĕn'thĭä*, sf. side-board of credencial, *-thĭäl'*, a. credential.

credibilidad, *krĕdĭbĭlĭdäd'*, sf. credibility.

creditiva, *-dĭtĭ'vä*, sf. credentials, pl.

crédito, *krä'dĭtŏ*, sm. credit; belief, faith; reputation; note, bill.

credo, *krä'dŏ*, sm. creed.

credulidad, *krĕdŭlĭdäd'*, sf. credulity.

crédulo, la, *-dŭlŏ*, a. credulous.

creencia, *krĕĕn'thĭä*, sf. credence, belief; persuasion.   [credit.

creer, *krĕĕr'*, v. a. to believe; to think; to creible, *krĕĕ'blĕ*, a. credible, believable.

crema, *krä'mä*, sf. cream; custard; (gr.) crémor, *krä'mŏr*, sm. cremor.   [diæresis.

crencha, *krĕn'tshä*, f. parting of the hair.

crepúsculo, *-pŭs'kŭlŏ*, sm. crepuscule.

cresa, *krä'sä*, sf. maggot.   [twilight.

crespo, pa, *krĕs'pŏ*, a. crisp, curled; obscure and bombastic; angry, displeased.

crespón, *krĕspŏn'*, sm. crape. [some birds.

cresta, *krĕs'tä*, sf. cock's-comb; crest of crestado, da, *-tä'dŏ*, a. crested.

crestón, *-tŏn'*, sm. crest of a helmet.

creta, *krä'tä*, sf. chalk.

cría, *krä'ä*, sf. breed or brood of animals; hatch; suckling; child reared by a nurse.

criada, *krä'dä*, sf. maid-servant, handmaid.

criadero, *-dä'rŏ*, sm. nursery for trees; breeding-place; -, ra, a. fruitful, prolific.

criadilla, *-dĭl'yä*, sf. testicle; small loaf in the form of a testicle; truffle.

criado, *krä'dŏ*, sm. servant; -, da, a. educated, instructed, bred.

criador, *-dŏr'*, sm. Creator; breeder; -, ra, a. fruitful, fecund.

crianza, *krĭän'thä*, sf. breeding, education.

criar, *krĭär'*, v. a. to create, to produce;

to breed, to procreate; to nurse; to suckle; to foster.   [significations).

criatura, *krĭätŏ͞'rä*, sf. creature (in all its criba, *krĕ'bä*, sf. sieve; riddle.

cribadero, *krĭbädä'rŏ*, sm. sieve-maker.

cribar, *krĭbär'*, v. a. to sift.

cribo, *krä'bŏ*, sm. sieve.

crimen, *krĕ'mĕn*, sm. crime, guilt.

criminal, *krĭmĭnäl'*, a. criminal.

criminalidad, *-däd'*, sf. criminality.

criminalista, *-lĭs'tä*, sm. author who has written on criminal matters.

orin, *krĭn*, sf. mane, horse-hair.

criollo, lla, *krĭŏl'yŏ*, sm. & f. Creole.

cripta, *krĭp'tä*, sf. crypt.

crisis, *krä'sĭs*, sf. crisis; (med.) acme; judgment passed after a mature deliberation.

crisma, *krĭs'mä*, sm. & f. chrism.

crismera, *-mä'rä*, sf. chrismatory.

crisol, *krĭsŏl'*, sm. crucible; cruset.

crisolada, *krĭsŏlä'dä*, sf. crucible full of metal.

cristal, *krĭstäl'*, sm. crystal; crystal-glass; looking-glass; (poet.) water.

cristalino, na, *krĭstälĭ'nŏ*, a. crystalline.

cristalización, *-thäthĭŏn'*, sf. crystallisation.   [lise.

cristalizar, *krĭstälĭthär'*, v. a. to crystal-cristiandad, *krĭstĭändäd'*, sf. christianity; observance of the law of Christ.

cristianismo, *-nĭs'mŏ*, sm. Christianism, Christendom,   [tianize.

cristianizar, *-nĭ'thär'*, v. a. to chris-cristiano, na, *krĭstĭä'nŏ*, a. & sm. & f. Cristo, *krĭs'tŏ*, sm. Christ.   [Christian.

cristus, *krĭs'tŭs*, sm. criss-cross-row, alcriterio, *krĭtĕ'rĭŏ*, sm. criterion. [phabet.

crítica, *krĭt'ĭkä*, sf. critic.

criticador, *-dŏr'*, sm. critic, censurer.

criticar, *-kär'*, v. a. to criticise.

crítico, *krĭt'ĭkŏ*, sm. critic, censurer; affected refiner of style and language; -, ca, a. critical.

crónica, *krŏ'nĭkä*, sf. chronicle.   [ness.

cronicidad, *krŏnĭthĭdäd'*, sf. chronical-crónico, ca, *krŏ'nĭkŏ*, a. chronic, chronical.

cronista, *krŏnĭs'tä*, sm. chronicler.

cronología, *krŏnŏlŏ'hĕä*, sf. chronology.

cronológico, ca, *-lŏ'hĭkŏ*, a. chronological.   [meter.

cronómetro, *krŏnŏ'mĕtrŏ*, sm. chrono-cruce de trenes, *krŏthä dä trä'nĕs*, sm. (rail.) crossing of trains.

crucera, *krŏthä'rä*, sf. withers of a horse.

crucero, *-rŏ*, sm. cross-vault of a church under the dome; cross-bearer; piece of timber which lies across the rafters in a building; crick of a mill; (mar.) cruising-station; cruiser; Cross (southern constellation).   [to molest, to torment.

crucificar, *krŏthĭfĭkär'*, v. a. to crucify; crucifijo, *krŏthĭfĭ'h'ŏ*, sm. crucifix.

crudeza, *krŏdä'thä*, sf. unripeness; rudeness; cruelty; vain boasting; indigestion.

crudo, da, *krŏ'dŏ*, a. raw, crude; green, unripe; rude, cruel; unfinished, immature; hard of digestion; blustering, boasting; immature (of tumours).

cruel, *krŭĕl'*, a. cruel; (fig.) insufferable; severe, hard; bloody, violent.

crueldad, *—dăd'*, sf. cruelty, inhumanity, savageness.

cruento, ta, *krŭĕn'tŏ*, a. bloody, cruel.

crujido, *krŭ'hĕ'dŏ*, sm. crack, creak, clash, crackling.

crujir, *krŭ'hĕr'*, v. n. to crackle, to rustle.

crustáceo, cea, *krŭstă'thĕŏ*, a. crustaceous.

cruz, *krŭth*, sf. cross (as instrument, order, ensign of the Christian religion, line); (fig.) trial of patience, &c.

cruzada, *krŭthă'dă*, sf. crusade; indulgences granted to those who support the crusade.

cruzado, *—dŏ*, sm. cruzado (old Spanish coin); crusader; *—*, da, a. cruel, transverse.

cruzamiento, *—mĕĕn'tŏ*, sm. crossing; — de nivel, (rail.) crossing-road; — de vía, (rail.) junction.

cruzar, *krŭthăr'*, v. a. to cross; to cross a road; (mar.) to cruise; *—se*, to be knighted; to cross and trip, to stumble along (of horses).

cuácaro, ra, *kwă'kărŏ*, sm. & f. quaker.

cuaderna, *kwădĕr'nă*, sf. fourth part; (mar.) timber-work forming the ribs of a ship. [of paper; log (of a vessel).

cuadernillo, *—dĕrnĕl'yŏ*, sm. small parcel

cuaderno, *—dĕr'nŏ*, sm. parcel of paper stitched together; small memorandum book; four pages of printed matter; punishment of students. [stable.

cuadra, *kwă'dră*, sf. hall; drawing-room;

cuadrado, da, *kwădră'dŏ*, a. square, quadrate; perfect; *—*, sm. square, quadrate; clock (in stockings); gusset of a shirt sleeve; de *—*, in front, face to face; squared.

cuadragenario, ria, *—'hĕnă'rĕŏ*, a. forty years old. [gesimal, lenten.

cuadragesimal, *—'hĕstmăl'*, a. quadacuadragésimo, ma, *—'hă'sĕmŏ*, a. fortieth. [gular, fourcornered.

cuadrangular, *—'răngŭlăr'*, a. quadrancuadrángulo, *—'răn'gŭlŏ*, sm. quadrangle.

cuadrante, *—drăn'tĕ*, sm. quadrant; dialplate of a sun-dial; square board put up in churches, pointing out the order of masses to be celebrated.

cuadrar, *kwădrăr'*, v. a. & n. to square; to square timbers; to multiply a number by itself; to fit, to suit, to correspond.

cuadratura, *—drătŏ'ră*, sf. quadrature.

cuadricular, *—drĕkŭlăr'*, v. a. to copy by means of squares.

cuadriforme, *—fŏr'mĕ*, a. fourfaced.

cuadrilátero, ra, *—lă'tĕrŏ*, a. quadrilateral. [lar, oblong.

cuadrilongo, ga, *—lŏn'gŏ*, a. quadrangu-

cuadrilla, *kwădrĕl'yă*, sf. gang, crew, troop; any one of the four divisions of sheep-masters which form the board of Mesta; band of armed men, sent in pursuit of highwaymen.

cuadrillero, *—yĕ'rŏ*, sm. member of the court of La Santa Hermandad; commander of an armed band employed by that court. [fold.

cuádriple, *kwă'drĕplĕ*, a. quadruple, fourcuadriplicado, da, *—drĕplĭkă'dŏ*, a. quadrupled. [syllabic.

cuadrisílabo, ba, *—drĭsĭl'ăbŏ*, a. quadricuadriyugo, *—drĭyŏ'gŏ*, sm. cart with four horses.

cuadro, *kwă'drŏ*, sm. square; picture; picture-frame; window-frame; parterre in a garden; (mil.) square body of troops.

cuadrúpedo, da, *kwădrŏ'pĕdŏ*, a. quadruped. [quadruplicate.

cuadruplicar, *kwădrŏplĭkăr'*, v. a. to

cuádruplo, pla, *kwă'drŏplŏ*, a. quadruple, fourfold.

cuajada, *kwă'hă'dă*, sf. butter, curd, coagulated fat. [goose-grass.

cuajaleche, *—lĕtsh'ĕ*, a. (bot.) yellow

cuajamiento, *—mĕĕn'tŏ*, sm. coagulation.

cuajar, *kwă'hăr'*, sm. runnet-bag (of ruminants).

cuajar, *—*, v. a. to coagulate; to ornament too much; *—*, v. n. to succeed; to please; *—se*, to coagulate, to curdle.

cuajarón, *kwă'hărŏn'*, sm. grume, clot, gore. [coagulation.

cuajo, *kwă'h'ŏ*, sm. runnet, rennet;

cual, *kwăl*, a. which; he who; same, like, such; one, other, partly; *—*, ad. as; how.

cualidad, *kwălĭdăd'*, sf. quality.

cualquier, *kwălkĕr'*, a. anyone.

cualquiera, *—ă*, a. anyone, someone, anybody, somebody. [nouns).

cuan, *kwăn*, ad. how, as (used only before

cuando, *kwăn'dŏ*, ad. when; in case that; if; although; even; sometimes; de — en —, from time to time; —más, —mucho, at most, at best; — menos, at least; ¿ de cuándo acá? since when? [tinction.

cuantía, *kwăntĕ'ă*, sf. quantity; rank, dis-

cuantidad, *kwăntĭdăd'*, sf. quantity.

cuantioso, sa, *—tĕŏ'sŏ*, a. numerous, copious.

cuantitativo, va, *—tĭtă'vŏ*, a. quantitive.

cuanto, ta, *kwăn'tŏ*, a. containing, consisting of; as many as, as much as, all, whatever; ¿ cuánto? how much? ¿ cuántos? how many?; *—*, ad. respecting, whilst; —más, moreover, the more as; en — á, with regard to; in the mean time; por —, inasmuch as.

cuarenta, *kwărĕn'tă*, a. forty.

cuarentena, *—tă'nă*, sf. space of forty days; Lent; (mar.) quarantine.

cuaresma, *kwărĕs'mă*, sf. Lent; collection of Lent sermons.

cuaresmal, *kwărĕsmăl'*, a. lenten.

cuarta, *kwăr'tă*, sf. quarter; sequence of four cards in the game of piquet; quadrant (of a circle); (mar.) quarter (point of the compass). [quarter (dry measure).

cuartal, *kwăr'tăl'*, sm. quartern loaf;

cuartana, *—tă'nă*, sf. (med.) quartan.

cuartanal, *—tănăl'*, a. intermittent (of fever). [under a quartan.

cuartanario, ria, *—tănă'rĕŏ*, a. labouring

cuartear, *kwărtĕăr'*, v. a. to quarter, to

divide into four parts; to bid a fourth more at public sales; to make a fourth person at a game; —se, to split into pieces.

cuartel, *kwårtĕl'*, sm. quarter, fourth part; district of a city; place where soldiers are lodged; duty imposed on villages for the quartering of soldiers; dwelling, home; (mar.) hatch.

cuartelero, *—tĕlā'rŏ*, sm. soldier in each company who keeps their apartment clean.

cuarterón, *—tĕrŏn'*, sm. quartern, quarter; upper part of windows, quarteroon.

cuarteta, *—tā'tă*, sf. (poet.) quatrain.

cuartilla, *—tĭl'yă*, sf. fourth part of an arroba, *or* sixteenth part of a quintal; fourth part of a sheet of paper; pastern of horses.

cuartillo, *—tĭl'yŏ*, sf. pint; fourth part of a peck in grain; fourth part of a real.

cuarto, *kwår'tŏ*, sm. fourth part; quarter; dwelling, room, apartment; copper coin worth four maravedís; pedigree; —s, pl. cash, money; —, ta, a. fourth.

cuartón, *—tŏn'*, sm. large joist.

cuarzo, *kwår'thŏ*, sm. quartz.

cuasi, *kwå'sĭ*, ad. almost, nearly.

Cuasimodo, *—mŏ'dŏ*, sm. first Sunday after Easter.   [white feet (horses).

cuatralbo, ba, *kwåtrål'bŏ*, a. having four

cuatrero, *—trā'rŏ*, sm. horse-thief.

cuatrinca, *—trĭn'kă*, sf. union of four persons *or* things; four cards of the same suit.   [four; (mus.) quartet.

cuatro, *kwå'trŏ*, a. four; —, sm. figure

cuatrocientos, tas, *kwåtrŏthĭĕn'tŏs*, a. four hundred.

cuatropea, *—pā'ă*, sf. horse-tax.

cuatropeado, *—pĕå'dŏ*, sm. step in dancing.

cuatropear, *—pĕår'*, v. n. to run on all fours.

cuatrotanto, *—tån'tŏ*, sm. fine amounting to four times the value of the sum *or* object embezzled.   [tub.

cuba, *kŏ'bă*, sf. task; (fig.) toper, drunkard;

cubero, *kŏbā'rŏ*, sm. cooper.

cubertura, *kŏbĕrtŏ'ră*, sf. cover, covering.

cubeta, *kŏbā'tă*, sf. small barrel; bucket.

cubeto, *—tŏ*, sm. small barrel.

cubicar, *kŏbĭkår'*, v. a. to cube a number.

cúbico, ca, *kŏ'bĭkŏ*, a. cubic.

cubierta, *kŏbĭĕr'tă*, sf. cover, covert; pretext; deck of a ship.

cubierto, *—tŏ*, sm. dish-cover; shelter; allowance of a soldier in a house; course of dishes.

cubil, *kŏbĭl'*, sm. lair of wild beasts.

cubilete, *kŏbĭlā'tĕ*, sm. copper pan for baking pies &c.; tumbler; dice-box; small pie stuffed with mince meat.

cubito, *kŏ'bĭtŏ*, sm. ulna.   [nave.

cubo, *kŏ'bŏ*, sm. cube; pail; mill-pool;

cubrepán, *kŏbrĕpån'*, sm. fire-shovel, used by shepherds.

cubrir, *kŏbrĭr'*, v. a. to cover; to palliate; to disguise; to cover a post; to roof a building; to cover a mare; —se, to put on one's hat.   [wicked person.

cuca, *kŏ'kă*, sf. edible cyperus; **mala —,**

cucaña, *kŏkån'yă*, sf. any thing acquired with little trouble and at other people's expense.

cucañero, *—yā'rŏ*, sm. parasite.

cucaracha, *—råtsh'å*, sf. wood-louse.

cucarda, *kŏkår'dă*, sf. cockade.

cuclillas, *kŏklĭl'yăs*, **(en —,)** ad. in a cowering manner.   [cuckold.

cuclillo, *kŏklĭl'yŏ*, sm. cuckoo; (fig.)

cucurucho, *kŏkŏrŏtsh'ŏ*, sm. paper-cornet.

cuchara, *kŏtshå'ră*, sf. spoon.

cucharada, *—rå'dă*, sf. spoonful, ladleful.

cucharón, *—rŏn'*, sm. ladle; large spoon.

cuchichear, *kŏtshĭtshĕår'*, v. n. to whisper.

cuchicheo, *—tshĕ'ŏ*, sm. whispering.

cuchichero, ra, *kŏtshĭtshā'rŏ*, sm. & f. whisperer.

cuchilla, *kŏtshĭl'yă*, sf. large kitchen-knife; chopping-knife; ancient poniard; (poet.) sword; bookbinder's knife.

cuchillada, *—yå'dă*, sf. cut with a knife; gash; —s, pl. wrangles, quarrels.

cuchillería, *—yĕrē'ă*, sf. cutler's shop; place (*or* street) where there are many cutlers' shops.

cuchillero, *—yā'rŏ*, sm. cutler.

cuchillo, *kŏtshĭl'yŏ*, sm. knife; triangular gore, gusset of a garment.

cuchufleta, *kŏtshŏflā'tă*, sf. joke, jest, fun.

cuelga, *kŏĕl'gă*, sf. cluster of grapes hung up for use; birth-day present.

cuello, *kŏĕl'yŏ*, sm. neck; neck of a bottle; collar of a priest's garment; small end of a wax-candle; shirt-collar.   [of the eye.

cuenca, *kŏĕn'kă*, sm. earthen bowl; socket

cuenco, *—kŏ*, sm. earthen bowl.

cuenta, *kŏĕn'tă*, sf. computation, calculation; account; narrative; bead of a rosary; reason, satisfaction.

cuentagarbanxos, *kŏĕntăgårbån'thŏs*, sm. niggardly person.

cuentista, *kŏĕntĭs'tă*, sm. tale-bearer.

cuento, *kŏĕn'tŏ*, sm. a million; butt-end of a spear, &c.; prop, support; fable; tale, story, narrative.

cuerda, *kŏĕr'dă*, sf. cord; string for musical instruments; match for firing a gun; chain of a watch *or* clock; Spanish measure of about 8 ells.   [in his senses.

cuerdo, da, *—dŏ*, a. prudent, judicious;

cuerna, *kŏĕr'nă*, sf. horn vessel into which cows &c. are milked; stag's horn; hunting-horn.

cuerno, *—nŏ*, sm. horn; corn.

cuero, *kŏĕ'rŏ*, sm. hide, skin, leather; (fig.) great drinker.

cuerpo, *kŏĕr'pŏ*, sm. body; cadaver, corpse.

cuerva, *kŏĕr'vă*, sf. crow.

cuervo, *—vŏ*, sm. raven.

cuesco, *kŏĕs'kŏ*, sm. kernel; stone (of fruits); mill-stone of an oil-mill.

cuesta, *kŏĕs'tă*, sf. hill; rising ground with a slope; quest, charity; **ir — abajo,** to go down hill; **— arriba,** with great trouble and difficulty.

cuestión, *kŏĕstĭŏn'*, sf. question; dispute; quarrel; problem.   [able, problematical.

cuestionable, *kŏĕstĭŏnå'blĕ*, a. question-

cuestionar, *kŭěstĭōnăr'*, v. a. to question, to dispute. [gatherer.
cuestor, *kŭěstŏr'*, sm. questor; alms-
cuestura, *kŭěstŏ'rā*, sf. questorship.
cueva, *kŭā'vā*, sf. cave, grotto, den.
cuévano, *kŭā'vănŏ*, sm. great basket for carrying grapes to the wine-press.
cuezo, *kŭā'thŏ*, sm. hod.
cugujada, *kŏgŭ'hä'dā*, sf. sky-lark.
cugulla, *kŏgŭl'yā*, sf. cowl, monk's hood.
cuidado, *kŭĭdä'dŏ*, sm. care, heed, solicitude; fear; custody, charge.
cuidadoso, sa, *—dŏ'sŏ*, a. careful, heedful, vigilant. [mind, to look after.
cuidar, *kŭĭdăr'*, v. a. to heed, to care; to
cuita, *kŭĭ'tā*, sf. grief, affliction, trouble.
cuitado, da, *kŭĭtä'dŏ*, a. anxious, wretched, miserable; timid.
cuja, *kŭ'h'ā*, sf. leather bag.
culada, *kŭlä'dā*, sf. fall on one's backside; -s, pl. rolling of a ship.
culantrillo, *kŭlántrĭl'yŏ*, sm.(bot.) maidenhair, fern.
culantro, *kŭlăn'trŏ*, sm. (bot.) coriander.
culata, *kŭlä'tā*, sf. breech of a gun; screwpin; back part of any thing.
culcusido, *kŭlkŭsī'dŏ*, sm. botch-work.
culebra, *kŭlā'brā*, sf. snake.
culebrear, *kŭlěbrěär'*, v. n. to crankle.
culebrina, *—brě'nā*, sf. (mil.) culverin.
culera, *kŭlā'rā*, sf. stain of urine in the swaddling-clothes of children.
culero, *—rŏ*, sm. clout; disease in birds; -, ra, a. slothful, lazy.
culo, *kŏ'lŏ*, sm. breech, backside; bottom, socket. [ableness; guilt.
culpa, *kŭl'pā*, sf. misdemeanour, culpableness; culpa; a culpable; guilty.
culpable, *kŭlpā'blě*, a. culpable; guilty.
culpado, da, *—dŏ*, sm. & f. transgressor.
culpar, *kŭlpăr'*, v. a. to accuse, to blame.
cultivación, *kŭltĭvāthĭŏn'*, sf. cultivation, culture.
cultivador, *—dŏr'*, sm. cultivator.
cultivar, *kŭltĭvăr'*, v. a. to cultivate.
cultivo, *kŭltĭ'vŏ*, sm. cultivation; improvement; culture of the mind and manners.
culto, ta, *kŭl'tŏ*, a. pure, elegant, correct; polished; enlightened, civilised; -, sm. culture; worship. [style.
cultura, *kŭltŏ'rā*, sf. culture; elegance of
cumbre, *kŭm'brě*, sf. top, summit; greatest height of favour, fortune, &c.
cumpleaños, *kŭmplěăn'yŏs*, sm. birth-day.
cumplido, da, *kŭmplī'dŏ*, a. large, plentiful; faultless; polished, polite, courteous; -, sm. compliment. [compliment.
cumplimentar, *kŭmplĭměntăr'*, v. a. to compliment; complaisant.
cumplimentero, ra, *—tä'rŏ*, a. full of compliments; complaisant.
cumplimiento, *kŭmplĭmĭěn'tŏ*, sm. compliment; accomplishment; perfection; abundance.
cumplir, *kŭmplīr'*, v. a. to execute; to provide; to fulfil; -, v. n. to be convenient; to suffice; —se, to be realized.
cumquibus, *kŭmkě'bŭs*, sm. (fam.) money.
cúmulo, *kŏ'mŭlŏ*, sm. heap, pile; (fig.) press of business.

cuna, *kŏ'nā*, sf. cradle; (fig.) native country; family, lineage; origin; —de viento, hanging cradle.
cundir, *kŭndīr'*, v. n. to spread (of stains); to grow, to increase; to propagate.
cuña, *kŭn'yā*, sf. wedge; (fig.) artifice, slyness. [sister-in-law.
cuñado, da, *kŭnyä'dŏ*, sm. & f. brother- or
cuño, *kŭn'yŏ*, sm. die for coining money; impression made by the die.
cuociente, *kŭŏthĭěn'tě*, sm. (ar.) quotient.
cuota, *kŭŏ'tā*, sf. quote.
cupé, *kŭpā'*, sm. landau. [ticket.
cupo, *kŏ'pŏ*, cupón, *kŭpŏn'*, sm. interest-
cúpula, *kŏ'pŭlā*, sf. cupola, dome.
cupulino, *kŭpŭlī'nŏ*, sm. lantern (small cupola raised upon another). [fretter.
cuquillo, *kŭkĭl'yŏ*, sm. cuckoo; vine-
cura, *kŏ'rā*, sm. parson; -, sf. care, healing.
curable, *kŭrä'blě*, a. curable, healable.
curación, *—thĭŏn'*, sf. cure, healing.
curador, *—dŏr'*, sm. overseer; guardian; curator, administrator.
curadora, *—dŏ'rā*, sf. female guardian.
curaduría, *kŭrädŭrī'ā*, sf. guardianship.
curandero, *kŭrăndā'rŏ*, sm. quack, medicaster.
curar, *kŭrăr'*, v. a. to cure, to heal; to prescribe the regimen of a patient.
curatela, *kŭrätā'lā*, sf. tutorship.
curativo, va, *—tī'vŏ*, a. curative, healing.
curato, *kŭrä'tŏ*, sm. rectory, parsonage; parish; —anejo, chapel at ease.
cureña, *kŭrěn'yā*, sf. gun-carriage; stay of a cross-bow; á—rasa, (mil.) without a breast-work (applied to a barbet-battery); without shelter.
curia, *kŏ'rĭā*, sf. ecclesiastical court where church affairs are examined and decided in Rome; care and skill.
curial, *kŭrĭăl'*, a. belonging to the Roman curia; -, sm. member of the Roman curia; subaltern in the courts of justice.
curiosidad, *kŭrĭŏsĭdăd'*, sf. curiosity; neatness; object of curiosity, rarity.
curioso, sa, *kŭrĭŏ'sŏ*, a. curious; neat, fine, beautiful; careful, attentive, diligent.
curruca, *kŭrrŏ'kā*, sf. babbling warbler.
currutaco, *—tä'kŏ*, sm. beau, fop; -, a. beauish; affected.
cursado, da, *kŭrsä'dŏ*, a. skilled; versed.
cursante, *kŭrsän'tě*, a. frequenting; assiduous; -, sm. student, scholar.
cursar, *kŭrsăr'*, v. a. to frequent a place; to do a thing often.
cursillo, *kŭrsĭl'yŏ*, sm. short course of lectures (in a university).
cursivo, va, *kŭrsē'vŏ*, a. italic (type).
curso, *kŭr'sŏ*, sm. course, direction; course of lectures. [dresser.
curtidor, *kŭrtĭdŏr'*, sm. tanner, leather-
curtidos, *kŭrtī'dŏs*, sm. pl. tanned leather.
curtiduría, *—dŭrī'ā*, sf. tan-yard.
curtir, *kŭrtīr'*, v. a. to tan leather; to sunbrown; to inure to hardships.
curva, *kŭr'vā*, sf. curved line; (mar.) knee.
curvatura, *—tŭ'rā*, sf. curvature, of any piece of timber employed in ship-building.

curvilíneo, nea, *kŭrvĭlĭ'nĕā*, a. curvilinear.
curvo, va, *kŭr'vŏ*, curved, bent. [linear.
cusourro, *kŭskŭr'rŏ*, sm. little crust of
cúspide, *kŭs'pĭdĕ*, sf. cuspis. [bread.
custodia, *kŭstŏ'dĭā*, sf. custody, keeping, hold; guard, escort; monstrance; reliquary in Catholic churches. [man.
custodio, —*dĭŏ*, sm. guard, keeper, watch-
cutáneo, nea, *kŭtā'nĕŏ*, a. cutaneous.
cúter, *kŏ'tĕr*, sm. (mar.) cutter.
cutí, *kŭtĭ'*, sm. ticking, tick.
cutícula, *kŭtĭ'kŭlā*, sf. cuticle.
cutir, *kŭtĭr'*, v. a. to knock one thing against another.
cutis, *kŏ'tĭs*, sm. & f. skin.
cuyo, ya, *kŏŏ'yŏ*, pn. of which, of whom, whose, whereof.

Ch.

cha, *tshā*, sf. tea (in Mexico).
chabacanada, *tshābākānā'dā*, sf. very vulgar word or observation.
chabacano, na, —*kā'nŏ*, a. coarse, unpolished; bungling.
chabeta, *tshābĕ'tā*, sf. forelock-key; perder la —, to lose one's senses.
chacolí, *tshākŏlĭ'*, sm. light red wine of a sourish taste.
chacota, *tshākŏ'tā*, sf. noisy mirth.
chacotear, —*kŏtĕār'*, v. n. to indulge in noisy mirth. [sing the merry-Andrew.
chacotero, ra, —*kŏtā'rŏ*, a. waggish, act-
cháchara, *tshā'tshārā*, sf. chit-chat, chatter, idle talk. [purpose.
chacharear, —*rĕār'*, v. n. to talk to no
chacharería, —*rĕrĭ'ā*, sf. verbiage, garrulity.
chacharero, —*rā'rŏ*, sm. prater.
achacho, *tshātsh'ŏ*, sm. stake at the game of hombre. [ment.
chafaldita, *tshāfāldĭ'tā*, sf. teasing, merri-
chafalditero, —*fāldĭtĕ'rŏ*, sm. teaser.
chafallar, —*fālyār'*, v. a. to botch, to mend.
chafallo, —*fāl'yŏ*, sm. coarse patch.
chafallón, ona, —*fālyŏn'*, sm. & f. botcher.
chafar, —*fār'*, v. a. to mat down the pile of velvet; to cut one short in his discourse.
chafarote, —*fārŏ'tĕ*, sm. short broad Turkish sword. [in clothes &c.
chafarrinada, —*fārrĭnā'dā*, sf. blot or stain
chafarrinar, —*fārrĭnār'*, v. a. to blot, to stain.
chafarrinón, —*fārrĭnŏn'*, sm. blot, stain.
chaflán, *tshāflān'*, sm. blaze of a horse;
chal, *tshāl*, sm. shawl. [slope.
chalán, *tshālān'*, sm. hawker, huckster; who is very clever in selling things; horse-dealer. [fully; to deal in horses.
chalanear, —*nĕār'*, v. a. to sell things art-
chalanería, —*nĕrĭ'ā*, sf. artifice and cunning used by dealers in buying and selling.
chaleco, *tshālĕ'kŏ*, sm. waistcoat.
chalote, *tshālŏ'tĕ*, sm. shallot-garlic.
chalupa, *tshālŭ'pā*, sf. (mar.) sloop.
chamarra, *tshāmār'rā*, sf. garment made of sheep-skins or of very coarse frieze.

chamarreta, —*mārrĕ'tā*, sf. short loose jacket. [uncocked (applied to a hat).
chambergo, ga, *tshāmbĕr'gŏ*, a. slouched,
chambón, —*bŏn'*, sm. unskilful person or gamester. [gown.
chambra, *tshām'brā*, sf. woman's nightcap.
chamelote, *tshāmĕlŏ'tĕ*, sm. camlot.
chamorra, *tshāmŏr'rā*, sf. shorn head.
chamorro, —*mŏr'rŏ*, sm. (bot.) beardless wheat. [liquors; to speak gibberish.
champurrar, *tshāmpŭrrār'*, v. a. to mix
chamuscado, da, *tshāmŭskā'dŏ*, a. tipsy, flustered with wine; addicted to some vice.
chamuscar, —*mŭskār'*, v. a. to singe, to scorch. [(fig.) scolding, wrangling.
chamusquina, —*mŭskĭ'nā*, sf. scorching;
chancero, ra, *tshānthĕ'rŏ*, a. jocose, sportive, merry; —, sm. (cant) young thief.
canciller, —*thĭlyĕr'*, sm. chancellor.
chancillería, —*thĭlyĕrĭ'ā*, sf. chancery.
chancleta, *tshānklĕ'tā*, sf. slipper.
chanclo, *tshān'klŏ*, sm. patten, clog, galosh.
chanfaina, *tshānfā'ĭnā*, sf. ragout of livers and lights; worthless thing.
chanflón, ona, —*flŏn'*, a. made in a bungling manner; —, sm. money beaten out to appear larger.
chantre, *tshān'trĕ*, sm. precentor.
chantría, —*trĭ'ā*, sf. office of a precentor.
chanza, *tshān'thā*, sf. joke, jest, fun.
chanzoneta, —*thŏnĕ'tā*, sf. joke, jest; merry chansonnette.
chapa, *tshā'pā*, sf. thin metal plate which serves to strengthen or adorn the work it covers; rouge. [roof.
chaparra, *tshāpār'rā*, sf. coach with a low
chaparro, —*rŏ*, sm. evergreen oak-tree.
chaparrón, —*rŏn'*, sm. violent shower of rain. [metal plates.
chapear, *tshāpĕār'*, v. a. to garnish with
chapería, *tshāpĕrĭ'ā*, sf. ornament consisting of a number of metal plates.
chapín, *tshāpĭn'*, sm. clog with a cork-sole lined with morocco leather.
chapitel, *tshāpĭtĕl'*, sm. capital of a column.
chaple, *tshā'plĕ*, sm. graver, tool used in engraving. [branches of trees.
chapodar, *tshāpŏdār'*, v. a. to lop off the
chapotear, —*tĕār'*, v. a. to wet with a spunge; —, v. n. to paddle in the water; to dab. [to bungle.
chapucear, *tshāpŭthĕār'*, v. a. to botch,
chapucería, —*thĕrĭ'ā*, sf. clumsy performance, bungling work.
chapucero, —*thĕ'rŏ*, sm. blacksmith; nailer; bungler; —, ra, a. clumsy, rude.
chapurrar, *tshāpŭrrār'*, v. a. to speak gibberish; to mix liquors.
chapuz, *tshāpŭth'*, sm. act of ducking or sousing. [to dive; to souse.
chapuzar, *tshāpŭthār'*, v. a. & r. to duck;
chaqueta, *tshākĕ'tā*, sf. jacket.
chaquete, —*tĕ*, sm. game resembling backgammon. [icing.
charca, *tshār'kā*, sf. pool of water for
charco, —*kŏ*, sm. pool of standing water.
charla, *tshār'lā*, sf. idle chit-chat, prattle.

charlador, ra, *tshärlädór'*, sm. & f. prater, garrulous person.
charladuría, *—dúrĕä*, sf. garrulity, gossip.
charlatín, *—tín'*, sm. mean prattler.
charlar, *—lär'*, v. n. to prattle, to chatter.
charlatán, *tshärlätän'*, sm. prater, idle talker; quack, mountebank. [quackery.
charlatanería, *—tänĕrĕä*, sf. garrulity;
charnela, *tshärnĕlä*, sf. hinge, joint.
charol, *tshäróš'*, sm. varnish; Japan.
charolar, *tshärólär'*, v. a. to varnish; to japan. [japanner.
charolista, *tshäróšís'tä*, sm. varnisher,
charpa, *tshär'pä*, sf. holster.
charrada, *tshärrä'dä*, sf. speech or action of a clown; a dance; any work made in a tasteless manner; tinsel, tawdriness.
charretera, *tshärrĕtä'rä*, sf. epaulet.
charro, *tshär'ró*, sm. churl; —, rra, a. gaudy.
chasco, *tshäs'kó*, sm. fun, joke, jest; lash.
chasquear, *tshäskĕär'*, v. a. to crack a whip; —, v. n. to play tricks; to disappoint; to cheat. [runner (in Peru).
chasqui, *tshäskĕ'*, sm. foot-messenger,
chasquido, *—kĕ'dó*, sm. crack of a whip; crack. [playing tricks.
chasquista, *—kĕs'tä*, sm. person fond of
chata, *tshä'tä*, sf. flat-bottomed boat.
chato, ta, *—tä*, a. flat, flattish; flatnosed.
chaza, *tshä'thä*, sf. point where the ball is driven back or stops, in a game at balls; berth on board ship.
chazador, *tshäthädór'*, sm. person employed to stop the ball and mark the game.
chazar, *tshäthär'*, v.a. to stop the ball before it reaches the winning point; to mark the point whence the ball was driven back.
chelín, *tshĕlín'*, sm. shilling.
chiba, *tshĕbä*, sf. kid.
chibalete, *—lä'tĕ*, sm. chest of drawers with a desk for writing.
chibato, *—bä'tó*, sm. kid between six and twelve months old; he-goat.
chibetero, *tshĕbĕtĕ'ró*, sm. fold for kids.
chibo, *tshĕ'bó*, sm. kid.
chibor, *—bór'*, sm. baboon.
chicada, *tshĕkä'dä*, sf. herd of sickly kids.
chicarrero, *—kärä'ró*, sm. shoemaker who makes pumps.
chico, ca, *tshĕ'kó*, a. little, small; —, sm. little boy. [gallantry.
chicolear, *—kólĕär'*, v. a. to joke, to jest in
chicoleo, *—kólä'ó*, sm. jest in gallantry, joke. [applied to children).
chicorrotín, *—kórrotín'*, a. very small
chicote, ta, *—kó'tĕ*, sm. end of a cable.
chicha, *tshĕtsh'ä*, sf. meat (used only in speaking to children). [vest-fly.
chicharra, *—tshär'rä*, sf. froth-worm, han-
chicharrero, *—tshärrĕ'ró*, sm. hot place or climate. [fish; horse-mackerel.
chicharro, *—tshär'ró*, sm. young tunny-
chicharrón, *—tshärrón'*, sm. crackling, morsel of fried lard left in the pan.
chichisvear, *—tshĕsvĕär'*, v. a. to woo, to court.

chichisveo, *—tshĕsvä'ó*, sm. attendance paid to a lady; gallant, attendant on a lady. [occasioned by a blow.
chichón, *—tshón'*, sm. lump on the head
chichonera, *—tshónä'rä*, sf. tumbling-cap (for children)
chifla, *tshĕ'flä*, sf. whistle; paring-knife.
chifladera, *—flädĕ'rä*, sf. whistle.
chiflar, *—flär'*, v. n. to whistle; to mock, to jest; to tipple.
chifle, *tshĕ'flĕ*, sm. whistle, call.
chiflete, *—flä'tĕ*, chiflo, *tshĕ'fló*, sm. whistle.
chiflido, *—flĕ'dó*, sm. sound of a whistle.
chilindrina, *tshĕlíndrĕnä*, sf. trifle.
chilindrón, *—líndrón'*, sm. game at cards; cut in the head.
chilla, *tshĕl'yä*, sf. call for foxes, &c.; clavo de —, tack; tablas de —, thin boards.
chillar, *—yär'*, v. n. to scream, to shriek; to crackle, to creak; to hiss in frying.
chillido, *—yĕ'dó*, sm. squeak, shriek.
chillón, *—yón'*, sm. bawler; common crier; nail, tack.
chimenea, *tshĕmĕnä'ä*, sf. chimney.
china, *tshĕ'nä*, sf. pebble; porcelain; chinaware; china silk.
chinarro, *—när'ró*, sm. large pebble.
chinazo, *—nä'thó*, sm. blow with a pebble.
chincharrazo, *tshĕntshärrä'thó*, sm. thrust with a sword in an affray.
chincharrero, *—tshärrä'ró*, sm. nasty place infested by vermin.
chinche, *tshĕn'tshĕ*, sf. bug.
chinchorrería, *—tshórrĕrĕ'ä*, sf. mischievous tale. [drag-net.
chinchorro, *—tshór'ró*, sm. fishing-boat;
chinchoso, sa, *—tshŏ'só*, a. peevish, fastidious.
chinela, *tshĕnĕ'lä*, sf. slipper.
chingarse, *tshĕngär'sĕ*, v.r. to get drunk; to cut one's self.
chino, *tshĕ'nó*, sm. chinese language.
chiquero, *tshĕkĕ'ró*, sm. hog-sty.
chiquichaque, *tshĕkĕtshä'kĕ*, sm. sawyer; noise made by things rubbing against each other.
chiquirritín, *—kĕrrĕtín'*, sm. little boy.
chiribitil, *tshĕrĕbĕtĕl'*, sm. crib; small room. [clarion-player.
chirimía, *tshĕrĕmĕ'ä*, sf. clarion; —, sm.
chirinola, *—rĕnŏ'lä*, sf. game played by boys; trifle.
chiripa, *tshĕrĕ'pä*, sf. fortunate chance.
chiripear, *—rĕpĕär'*, v. a. to be fortunate in a game, in spite of not understanding it well. [at games of chance.
chiripero, *—rĕpĕ'ró*, sm. one who is lucky
chirivía, *—rĕvĕ'ä*, sf. (bot.) parsnip; wagtail.
chirla, *tshĕr'lä*, sf. mussel. [tail.
chirlador, ra, *—dór'*, sm. & f. clamorous prattler.
chirlar, *tshĕrlär'*, v. n. to prattle.
chirlo, *tshĕr'ló*, sm. large wound in the face.
chirriar, *tshĕrrĕär'*, v. n. to hiss; to creak; to chirp.
chirrido, *tshĕrrĕ'dó*, sm. chirping of birds.

chirrio, *tshĭrrŏ'ŏ,* sm. creaking noise made by the wheels of a cart.   [(on a violin).
chirrión, *tshĭrrŏn',* sm. tumbrel; scraper
chirrionero, *tshĭrrĭŏnŏ'rŏ,* sm. scavenger.
chirumbela, *tshĭrŭmbŏ'lā,* sf. shawm, cornet.   [swords or other arms.
chis-chás, *tshĭstshās',* sm. clashing of
chisgarabís, *tshĭsgārăbĭs',* sm. superficial meddler.   [of wine.
chisguete, *tshĭsgŏ'tĕ,* sm. small draught
chisme, *tshĭs'mĕ,* sm. misreport; lumber.
chismear, *—mĕār',* v. a. to tattle, to carry tales, to misreport.   [bearing.
chismoso, sa, *—mŏ'sŏ,* a. tattling, tale-
chispa, *tshĭs'pā,* sf. spark; very small diamond; short gun; small particle; slight intoxication; |—s| fire and tow!
chispazo, *—pā'thŏ,* sm. the flying off of a spark from the fire, and the damage it does; tale mischievously circulated.
chispear, *—pĕār',* v. n. to sparkle; to drizzle.   [ber of sparks.
chispero, ra, *—pā'rŏ,* a. emitting a num-
chisporrotear, *—pŏrrŏtĕār',* v. n. to sparkle, to hiss (of liquids).
chisposo, sa, *—pŏ'sŏ,* a. sparkling.
chistar, *—tār',* v. a. to mumble, to mutter.
chiste, *tshĭs'tĕ,* sm. fine witty saying; joke, jest.   [funny.
chistoso, sa, *—tŏ'sŏ,* a. gay, cheerful; |chite! *tshĭt'ĕ,* silence! hush!
chiticalla, *tshĭtĭkăl'yă,* sm. discreet and silent person.   [not to make a noise.
chiticallar, *—yār',* v. a. to keep silence; |chito! *tshĭt'ŏ,* |chitón! *tshĭtŏn',* hush! mum! mum!
|**cho!** *tshŏ,* word used by the drivers of mules or horses to make them stop.
chocar, *tshŏkār',* v. n. to strike, to knock; to encounter, to rush against each other; to fight, to combat; —, v. a. to provoke.
chocarrear, *tshŏkārrĕār',* v. n. to act the buffoon.
chocarrería, *—rĕrĕ'ā,* sf. buffoonery.
chocarrero, *—rŏ'rŏ,* sm. buffoon; —, ra, a. scurrilous, buffoon-like.
chocolate, *tshŏkŏlā'tĕ,* sm. chocolate.
chocolatera, *—lā'rā,* sf. chocolate-pot.
chocolatero, *—rŏ,* sm. chocolate-manufacturer.
chochear, *tshŏtshĕār',* v. n. to dote.
chocho, *tshŏtsh'ŏ,* a. doting.
chofes, *tshŏ'fĕs,* sm. pl. lungs, pl.
chofeta, *tshŏfĕ'tā,* sf. chafing-dish.
chofista, *—fĭs'tā,* sm. a poor fellow who lives upon livers and lights.
cholla, *tshŏl'yā,* sf. skull; (fig.) powers of the mind, judgment.
chopo, *tshŏ'pŏ,* sm. black poplar-tree.
choque, *—kĕ,* sm. shock, collision; (mil.) skirmish; dispute, contest; jar.
choquezuela, *tshŏkĕthŭĕ'lā,* sf. knee-pan, patella, rotula.   [maker or -seller.
chorícero, *tshŏrĭthĕ'rŏ,* sm. sausage-
chorizo, *tshŏrĕ'thŏ,* sm. pork-sausage.
chorlito, *tshŏrlĕ'tŏ,* sm. curlew, gray plover.
chorrear, *tshŏrrĕār',* v. n. to drop from a spout, to gush, to drip; to come successively.

chorrera, *tshŏrrĕ'rā,* sf. spout or place from whence liquids drop; mark left by water or other liquids; frill of the breast of a shirt.   [liquid) rushing from a spout.
chorretada, *—tā'dā,* sf. water (or other
chorrillo, *tshŏrrĭl'yŏ,* sm. the continual coming-in and out-going of money.
chorro, *tshŏr'rŏ,* sm. gush; á—s, abundantly.
chorrón, *tshŏrrŏn',* sm. dressed hemp.
chotacabras, *tshŏtŏkā'brās,* sf. goat-sucker.
choto, *tshŏ'tŏ,* sm. sucking-kid.   [sucker.
chotuno, na, *tshŏtŏ'nŏ,* a. sucking.
choya, *tshŏ'yā,* sf. jack-daw.
choza, *tshŏ'thā,* sf. hut, shepherd's cottage.
chozil, *tshŏthĭl',* sm. hut, hovel.
chozuela, *—thŏ'lā,* sf. small hut.
chubasco, *tshŭbās'kŏ,* sm. squall.
chucero, *—thĕ'rŏ,* sm. (mil.) pikeman.
chuchear, *tshŭtshĕār',* v. a. to fowl with calls, gins and nets; to whisper.   [toy.
chuchería, *—tshĕrĕ'ā,* sf. gewgaw, bauble;
chuchero, *—tshĕ'rŏ,* sm. bird catcher.
chucho, *tshŭtsh'ŏ,* sm. dog; whip, scourge (in Cuba); word used to call a dog.
chuchumeco, *tshŭtshŭmĕ'kŏ,* sm. a sorry, contemptible little fellow.   [to pound.
chuchurrar, *—tshŭrrār',* v. a. to bruise.
chuecazo, *tshŭĕkā'thŏ,* sm. stroke (at ball play).
chufeta, *tshŭfĕ'tā,* sf. jest, joke; coal-pan.
chufleta, *—flĕ'tā,* sf. taunt, jeer.
chufletear, *—flĕtĕār',* v. n. to sneer, to taunt.   [sneering.
chufletero, ra, *—flĕtĕ'rŏ,* a. taunting,
chulada, *tshŭlā'dā,* sf. droll speech or action.
chulear, *—lĕār',* v. a. to jest, to joke.
chuleta, *—lĕ'tā,* sf. chop.
chulo, la, *tshŏ'lŏ,* sm. & f. punster, jester, merry-Andrew; bull-fighter's assistant.
chunga, *tshŭn'gā,* sf. jest, joke; estar de —, to be in good humour.   [humour.
chunguear, *—gĕār',* v. n. to be in good
chupa, *tshŏ'pā,* sf. waistcoat; jacket.
chupadero, ra, *tshŭpādĕ'rŏ,* a. sucking.
**chupador, —rŏ',* sm. sucking-bottle.
chupar, *tshŭpār',* v. a. to suck; (fig.) to sponge upon.
chupetear, *—pĕtĕār',* v. a. to suck gently.
chupetín, *—pĕtĭn',* sm. doublet.
**chupón, —pŏn',* sm. sucker (twig); —, ona, sm. & f. swindler, sponger.
chupona, *tshŭpŏ'nā,* sf. mean, blood-sucking strumpet.
churdón, *tshŭrdŏn',* sm. raspberry-jam.
churre, *tshŏr'rĕ,* sm. thick dirty grease.
churriburri, *tshŭrrĭbŭr'rĕ,* sm. low-fellow; rabble.
churriento, ta, *—ĕn'tŏ,* a. greasy.
churro, ra, *tshŏr'rŏ,* a. applied to sheep that have coarse wool.   [scorched.
churruscarse, *tshŭrrŭskār'sĕ,* v. r. to be
churrusco, *tshŭrrŭs'kŏ,* sm. over-toasted bread.
churumbela, *tshŭrŭmbĕ'lā,* sf. shawm.
chuscada, *tshŭskā'dā,* sf. pleasantry, drollery.

chusco, ca, *tshǎs'kǒ,* a. pleasant, droll.
chusma, —*mǎ,* sf. rabble, mob. [merry.
chus ni mus, *tshǔs nǐ mǔs,* ad. (fam.)
(no decir —, not to say a word.
chuzo, *tshŏ'thǒ,* sm. little spear or pike;
llover á —**s,** to pour heavily.

D.

dable, *dǎ'blě,* a. easy, possible.
dádiva, *dǎ'dívǎ,* sf. gift, present.
dadivoso, sa, *dǎdivǒ'sǒ,* a. generous,
open-handed.
dado, *dǎ'dǒ,* sm. die (pl. dice).
daga, *dǎ'gǎ,* sf. dagger.
dala, *dǎ'lǎ,* sf. pump-dale of a ship.
‡ **dale !** *dǎ'lě,* word used to express displeasure at another's obstinacy.
dalmática, *dǎlmǎ'tǐkǎ,* sf. dalmatica,
vestment worn by the deacons of the Roman Catholic church in the performance
of divine service.
dallador, *dǎlyǎdǒr',* sm. mower.
dallar, —*yǎr',* v. a. to mow grass.
dalle, *dǎl'yě,* sm. scythe.
dama, *dǎ'mǎ,* sf. lady, gentlewoman; mistress; queen (in the game of draughts);
actress who performs the principal parts.
damascado, da, *dǎmǎskǎ'dǒ,* a. damask-
like. [damson (plum).
damasco, *dǎmǎs'kǒ,* sm. damask (stuff).
damasina, *dǎmǎsǐ'nǎ,* sf. light silk stuff
resembling damask. [maskeened.
damasquino, na, *dǎmǎskǐ'nǒ,* a. da-
damería, *dǎměrě'ǎ,* sf. prudery; scruples.
damero, *dǎmǎ'rǒ,* sm. draught-board.
damisela, *dǎmǐsěl'ǎ,* sf. young gentlewoman; girl about town.
damnificar, *dǎmnǐfǐkǎr',* v. a. to hurt,
to damage, to injure.
danza, *dǎn'thǎ,* sf. dance.
danzador, ra, *dǎnthǎdǒr',* sm. & f. dancer.
danzante, *dǎnthǎn'tě,* sm. dancer; fickle,
airy person.
danzar, *dǎnthǎr',* v.n. to dance; to meddle;
sacar á —, to engage a lady to dance.
danzarin, *dǎnthǎrǐn',* sm. fine dancer;
meddling person. [to injure.
dañar, *dǎnyǎr',* v. a. to hurt, to damage;
dañino, na, *dǎnyě'nǒ,* a. noxious; mischievous.
daño, *dǎn'yǒ,* sm. damage, prejudice, loss.
dañoso, sa, *dǎnǒ'sǒ,* a. hurtful, noxious.
dar, *dǎr',* v. a. to give; to supply, to minister,
to afford; to deliver; to bestow; to strike,
to beat, to knock; to communicate; —**se,**
to conform to the will of another; to give
one's self up to; —**se priesa,** to make
haste. [baste.
dardo, *dǎr'dǒ,* sm. dart.
data, *dǎ'tǎ,* sf. date; article put down in
an account; condition, quality.
datar, *dǎtǎr',* v. a. to date.
dataría, *dǎtǎrě'ǎ,* sf. Datary (office where
the pope's bulls are expedited).
datario, *dǎtǎ'rǐǒ,* sm. principal officer of
dátil, *dǎ'tǐl,* sm. (bot.) date. [the Datary.

datilado, da, *dǎtǐlǎ'dǒ,* a. resembling a
dativo, *dǎtě'vǒ,* sm. (gr.) dative. [date.
dato, *dǎ'tǒ,* sm. datum.
dauco, *dǎ'ǔkǒ,* sm. carrot.
de, *dě,* pr. of; from; for; by; on; to; with.
deán, *děǎn',* sm. dean.
deanato, *děǎnǎ'tǒ,* sm. deanship.
debajo, *děbǎ'h'ǒ,* a. under, underneath,
below. [contest, altercation.
debate, *děbǎ'tě,* sm. debate, discussion,
debatir, *děbǎtǐr',* v. a. to debate, to argue,
to discuss. [debit and credit.
debe, *dě'bě,* sm. (com.) debit; — **y haber.**
deber, *děběr',* sm. obligation, duty; debt;
—, v. a. to owe; to be obliged.
debidamente, *děbǐdǎměn'tě,* ad. justly;
duly, exactly, perfectly.
débil, *dě'bǐl,* a. feeble, weak; sickly;
frail; pusillanimous.
debilidad, *děbǐlǐdǎd',* sf. debility, weakness. [weaken.
debilitar, —*tǎr',* v. a. to debilitate, to
débito, *dě'bǐtǒ,* sm. debt; duty.
década, *dě'kǎdǎ,* sf. decade. [cline.
decadencia, *děkǎděn'thǎ,* sf. decay, de-
decaer, *děkǎěr',* v. n. to decay, to decline,
to fade. [decline.
decaimiento, *děkǎǐměn'tǒ,* sm. decay.
decálogo, *děkǎ'lǒgǒ,* sm. the Decalogue.
decampar, *děkǎmpǎr',* v. n. to decamp.
decanato, *děkǎnǎ'tǒ,* sm. seniority.
decano, *děkǎ'nǒ,* sm. senior. [to decant.
decantar, *děkǎntǎr',* v.a. to cry up, to puff;
decapitación, *děkǎpǐtǎthǒn',* sf. decapitation, beheading.
decapitar, —*tǎr',* v. a. to behead.
decena, *děthě'nǎ,* sf. denary.
decenal, *děthěnǎl',* a. decennial.
decenario, ria, —*nǎ'rǐǒ,* a. decennary.
decencia, *děthěn'thǎ,* sf. decency.
deceno, na, *děthě'nǒ,* a. tenth.
decentar, *děthěntǎr',* v. a. to use for the
first time; —**se,** to injure the skin or body.
decente, *děthěn'tě,* a. decent, honest.
decible, *děthě'blě,* a. expressible.
decidir, *děthǐdǐr',* v. a. to decide, to determine. [stanza of ten verses; tithe.
décima, *dě'thǐmǎ,* sf. (poet.) a Spanish
decimal, *děthǐmǎl',* a. decimal; belonging
to tithes.
décimo, ma, *dě'thǐmǒ,* a. tenth.
décimoctavo, va, *děthǐmǒktǎ'vǒ,* decio-
cheno, na, *děthǐǒtshǎ'nǒ,* a. eighteenth.
décimocuarto, ta, —*kwǎr'tǒ,* a. fourteenth.
décimonono, na, —*nǒ'nǒ,* a. nineteenth.
décimoquinto, ta, —*kǐn'tǒ,* a. fifteenth.
décimoséptimo, ma, —*sěp'tǐmǒ,* a. seventeenth.
décimosexto, to, —*sěks'tǒ,* a. sixteenth.
décimotercio, cia, —*těr'thǒ,* a. thirteenth.
decir, *děthǐr',* v. a. to say, to tell, to speak;
to name; — **de repente,** to make impromptu verses; — **de sí,** to affirm any
thing. [mination, resolution; sentence.
decisión, *děthǐsǒn',* sf. decision, deter-
decisivo, va, —*sě'vǒ,* a. decisive, final.

declamación, děklămăthǐŏn', sf. declamation, discourse, oration; oratorical invective; declamatory style of reading.

declamador, ra, –dōr', sm. & f. declaimer.   [harangue.

declamar, děklămăr', v. n. to declaim, to

declaración, děklărăthǐŏn', sf. declaration, explanation; interpretation; manifest; (law) deposition.

declarar, děklărăr', v. a. to declare, to manifest; to expound; to explain; (law) to decide; –se, to declare one's opinion.

declaratorio, ria, děklărătǒ'rǐŏ, a. declaratory, explanatory.

declinable, děklǐnă'blě, a. (gr.) declinable.

declinación, –thǐŏn', sf. declination, descent; decline; (gr.) declination.

declinar, děklǐnăr', v. n. to decline; to decay, to degenerate; –, v. a. (gr.) to decline.

declinatoria, děklǐnătǒ'rǐă, sf. plea which attacks the competency of a judge.

declive, děklǐ'vě, sm. declivity.

decocción, děkǒkthǐŏn', sf. decoction.

decomiso, sa, děkǒmǐ'sǒ, a. confiscate.

decoración, děkǒrăthǐŏn', sf. decoration.

decorar, děkǒrăr', v. a. to decorate; to adorn; to illustrate.

decoro, děkǒ'rǒ, sm. honour, respect; circumspection; honesty; decency.

decoroso, sa, děkǒrǒ'sǒ, a. decorous, decent.   [diminution.

decremento, děkrěměn'tǒ, sm. decrease,

decrepitar, děkrěpǐtăr', v. n. to decrepitate; to crackle in the fire.

decrépito, ta, děkră'pǐtǒ, a. decrepit, crazy, worn out with age.

decrepitud, děkrěpǐtŭd', sf. decrepitude.

decretal, děkrětăl', sf. letter of the pope which decides a question of ecclesiastical law; –, a. decretal.

decretar, děkrětăr', v. a. to decree, to determine; to give a decree in a suit.

decreto, děkră'tǒ, sm. decree, decision; judicial decree.

decuplo, pla, dǎ'kăplǒ, a. decuple, tenfold.

decuria, děkǔ'rǐă, sf. ten Roman soldiers under a decurion; assembly of ten students to take their lessons.

decurión, děkǔrǐŏn', sm. decurion; student who has the care of ten other students.

decursas, děkǔr'săs, sf. pl. arrears of rent.

decurso, –sǒ, sm. course of time.

dechado, dětshă'dǒ, sm. sample, pattern; sampler; model of virtue and perfection.

dedada, dědă'dă, sf. a pinch (of anything), a finger-full.   [drinking-glass.

dedal, dědăl', sm. thimble; very small

dedalera, dědălě'ră, sf. (bot.) fox-glove.

dedicación, dědǐkăthǐŏn', sf. dedication; consecration.

dedicar, dědǐkăr', v. a. to dedicate, to devote, to consecrate, –se, to apply one's self to.

dedicatoria, dědǐkătǒrě'ă, sf. dedication.

dedo, dǎ'dǒ, sm. finger; toe; the forty-eighth part of a Spanish yard; hand of a clock; finger's breadth, small bit; – meñique,

little finger; – pulgar, thumb; – del corazón, middle-finger; – anular, ring-finger.   [derivation, consequence.

deducción, dědăkthǐŏn', sf. deduction,

deducir, dědŭthǐr', v. a. to deduce, to infer; to allege in pleading; to subtract.

defección, děfěkthǐŏn', sf. defection, apostasy.

defectible, –tǐ'blě, a. imperfect, deficient.

defectivo, va, –tǐ'vǒ, a. defective.

defecto, děfěk'tǒ, sm. defect, defectiveness; maimedness.   [perfect, faulty.

defectuoso, sa, –tŭǒ'sǒ, a. defective, im-

defender, děfěnděr', v. a. to defend, to protect; to justify, to assert, to maintain; to prohibit, to forbid; to resist, to oppose.

defensa, děfěn'să, sf. defence, justification, apology; guard, shelter, protection, fence; (mil.) flanking defences.

defensiva, –sǐ'vă, sf. defensive.

defensivo, –sǐ'vǒ, sm. defence, safeguard; –, va, a. defensive.

defensor, ra, děfěnsǒr', sm. & f. defender, protector; lawyer, counsel.   [yielding.

deferente, děfěrěn'tě, a. pliant, docile,

deferir, děfěrǐr', v. n. to defer; to yield to another's opinion; –, v. a. to communicate.

definición, děfǐnǐthǐŏn', sf. definition; decision.

definir, děfǐnǐr', v. a. to define, to describe, to explain; to decide.   [positive.

definitivo, va, děfǐnǐtǐ'vǒ, a. definitive,

deforme, děfǒr'mě, a. deformed, ugly.

deformidad, děfǒrmǐdăd', sf. deformity, ugliness; gross error.   [usurpation.

defraudación, děfrăŭdăthǐŏn', s. fraud,

defraudador, –dǒr', sm. defrauder, usurper.

defraudar, děfrăŭdăr', v. a. to defraud, to cheat; to usurp; to disturb.   [wardly.

defuera, děfǔǎ'ră, ad. externally, out-

defunción, děfŭnthǐŏn', sf. death; funeral.

degeneración, dǎ'hěněrăthǐŏn', sf. degeneracy.

degenerar, dǎ'hěněrăr', v. n. to degenerate.

degollación, děgǒlyăthǐŏn', sf. decollation, beheading.

degolladero, –dǎ'rǒ, sm. throttle; abattoir; seat near the orchestra (in theatres).

degollador, –dǒr', sm. headsman, executioner.   [destroy, to ruin.

degollar, děgǒlyăr', v. a. to behead; to

degradación, děgrădăthǐŏn', sf. degradation.

degradar, děgrădăr', v. a. to degrade; –se, to degrade or demean one's self.

degüello, děgǔě'lyǒ, sm. decollation; neck of a bottle.

degustar, děgŭstăr', v. a. to taste liquors.

dehesa, děhǎ'să, sf. pasture-ground.

dehesar, děhěsăr', v. a. to turn arable land into pasture-ground.

dehesero, děhěsǎ'rǒ, sm. keeper of a pasture-ground.   [Christ.

deicidio, děǐthǐ'dǐǒ, sm. deicide, murder of

deidad, dědăd'', sf. deity, divinity; goddess.

deificación, –fǐkăthǐǒn', sf. deification.

deificar, –fĭkä´, v. a. to deify.
deifico, dĕĭ´fĭkŏ, a. divine.
deismo, dĕĭs´mŏ, sm. deism.
deista, dĕĭs´tä, sm. deist.
dejadez, dĕhädĕth´, s. slovenliness, neglect, lassitude, (dolent; dejected.
dejado, da, dĕhä´dŏ, a. slovenly, idle, indolent,
dejar, dĕ´här, v. a. to leave, to let, to quit; to omit; to permit, to allow; to leave, to forsake; to bequeath; to pardon; –se, to abandon one's self (to).
dejo, dĕ´h´ŏ, sm. end, termination; negligence, laziness; after-taste, tang; effect of a passion; particular accentuation on the last syllable of words.
del, dĕl, a. of the (contraction of de el).
delación, dĕläthĭŏn´, sf. accusation, impeachment.
delantal, dĕläntäl´, sm. apron.
delante, dĕlän´tĕ, ad. before (in the front of; preceding in time; in preference to).
delantera, –tä´rä, sf. forefront, forepart of something; advantage.
delantero, ra, –tä´rŏ, a. foremost; –, sm. one who takes the lead; out-rider.
delastrar, dĕlästrär´, v. a. to unballast.
delatable, dĕlätä´blĕ, a. accusable, blamable. (nounce.
delatar, dĕlätär´, v. a. to accuse, to denounce.
delator, –tŏr´, sm. accuser, informer, denouncer, delator.
delectación, dĕlĕktäthĭŏn´, sf. pleasure, delight; – morosa, deliberate indulgence of some sensual pleasure, that is contrary to good manners, (substitution.
delegación, dĕlĕgäthĭŏn´, sf. delegation,
delegado, dĕlĕgä´dŏ, sm. delegate, deputy.
delegar, dĕlĕgär´, v. a. to delegate, to substitute.
deleitable, dĕlĕĭtä´blĕ, a. delightful.
deleitar, dĕlĕĭtär´, v. a. to delight.
deleite, dĕlĕĭ´tĕ, sm. pleasure, delight; lust. (ful.
deleitoso, sa, –tŏ´sŏ, a. pleasing, delightful.
deletrear, dĕlĕtrĕär´, v. a. to spell; to examine; to conjecture.
delfín, dĕlfĭn´, sm. dolphin; dauphin.
delgado, da, dĕlgä´dŏ, a. thin, delicate, light; slender, lean; acute, fine, ingenious; little, scanty; –, sm. strait place.
deliberación, dĕlĭbĕräthĭŏn´, sf. deliberation; resolution. (liberately.
deliberadamente, –dämĕn´tĕ, ad. deliberate,
deliberar, dĕlĭbĕrär´, v. n. to consider, to deliberate; to consult. (tive.
deliberativo, va, –rätĭ´vŏ, a. deliberative.
delicadeza, dĕlĭkädĕth´ä, sf. tenderness, softness; exquisiteness; delicacy, daintiness; subtlety.
delicado, da, dĕlĭkä´dŏ, a. delicate, tender; faint; finical, minion; exquisite; delicious, dainty; slender, subtle.
delicia, dĕlĭ´thĭä, sf. delight, pleasure.
delicioso, sa, –thĭŏ´sŏ, a. delicious, delightful.
delincuente, dĕlĭnkŭĕn´tĕ, sm. delinquent.
delineación, dĕlĭnĕäthĭŏn´, sf. delineation; sketch.

delinear, dĕlĭnĕär´, v. a. to delineate, to sketch; to describe.
delinquir, dĕlĭnkĭr´, v. n. to transgress the law. (to talk nonsense.
delirar, dĕlĭrär´, v. n. to delirate, to rave;
delirio, dĕlĭ´rĭŏ, sm. delirium; dotage; nonsense. (crime.
delito, dĕlĭ´tŏ, sm. transgression of a law,
della, dello, dĕl´yä, dĕl´yŏ, contractions of the words de ella, de ello, of her, of it.
demagogia, dĕmägŏh´hĕä, sf. demagogy.
demagogo, dĕmägŏ´gŏ, sm. demagogue.
demanda, dĕmän´dä, sf. demand, claim; pretension, complaint; challenge; request; charity-box; – y respuestas, haggling between sellers and buyers before they come to a price.
demandadero, ra, –dädĕ´rŏ, sm. & f. servant of a nunnery or a jail. (ant.
demandado, da, –dä´dŏ, sm. & f. defendant;
demandador, –dädŏr´, sm. petitioner for charity for pious uses; plaintiff, demandant; claimant; suitor, wooer.
demandar, –där´, v. a. to demand, to ask, to petition; to claim; to covet.
demarcación, dĕmärkäthĭŏn´, sf. demarcation; boundary-line.
demarcar, –kär´, v. a. to mark out limits.
demás, dĕmäs´, a. the rest, the others; y así de lo –, and so on; estar –, to be over and above; to be useless or superfluous; por –, in vain, to no purpose.
demasía, dĕmäsĭ´ä, sf. excess in the price; overmuch; arduous enterprise; rudeness; want of respect; abundance, plenty; en –, excessively.
demasiado, da, –sĭä´dŏ, a. excessive, overmuch; bold, daring; useless; –, ad. enough, too.
demencia, dĕmĕn´thĭä, sf. madness.
demente, dĕmĕn´tĕ, a. mad, insane.
demérito, dĕmĕ´rĭtŏ, sm. demerit.
demeritorio, ria, dĕmĕrĭtŏ´rĭŏ, a. without merit.
democracia, dĕmŏkrä´thĭä, sf. democracy.
demócrata, dĕmŏ´krätä, sm. democrat.
democrático, ca, –krä´tĭkŏ, a. democratical. (destroy.
demoler, dĕmŏlĕr´, v. a. to demolish; to
demolición, dĕmŏlĭthĭŏn´, sf. demolition.
demonio, dĕmŏ´nĭŏ, sm. demon.
demora, dĕmŏ´rä, sf. delay; demurrage.
demorar, dĕmŏrär´, v. n. to remain.
demostrable, dĕmŏsträ´blĕ, a. demonstrable. (tion; manifestation.
demostración, –thĭŏn´, sf. demonstra-
demostrar, dĕmŏsträr´, v. a. to prove, to demonstrate, to manifest. (monstrative.
demostrativo, va, –strätĭ´vŏ, a. demonstrative.
denegación, dĕnĕgäthĭŏn´, sf. denial, refusal.
denegar, dĕnĕgär´, v. a. to deny, to refuse.
dengue, dĕn´gĕ, sm. prudery; short veil.
denigración, dĕnĭgräthĭŏn´, sf. defamation, stigma, disgrace.
denigrar, dĕnĭgrär´, v. a. to blacken; to calumniate.

6 *

denodado, da, *děnŏdǎ'dŏ*, a. bold, intrepid, audacious.

denominación, *děnŏmĭnǎthĭon'*, sf. denomination, distinct appellation.

denominar, *děnŏmĭnǎr'*, v. a. to surname.

denotar, *děnŏtǎr'*, v. a. to denote, to express. [ity.

densidad, *děnsĭdǎd''*, sf. density; obscurdenso, sa, *děn'sŏ*, a. dense, thick; compact. [indented.

dentado, da, *děntǎ'dŏ*, a. dentated, toothed;

dentadura, *děntǎdŏ'rǎ*, sf. set of teeth.

dental, *děntǎl'*, sm. plough-share bed; dentist's pelican; wooden fork.

dentar, *děntǎr'*, v. a. & n. to tooth; to indent; to teeth, to cut teeth.

dentellada, *děntĕlyǎ'dǎ*, sf. gnashing of the teeth; nip; pinch with the teeth; —s, snappishly, peevishly.

dentellado, da, *—yǎ'dŏ*, a. denticulated.

dentellear, *—yĕǎr'*, v. a. to bite.

dentera, *děntĕ'rǎ*, sf. setting on edge of teeth; (fig.) jealousy. [ing.

dentición, *děntĭthĭon'*, sf. dentition, teething.

denticular, *děntĭkŭlǎr'*, a. like teeth, toothed.

dentista, *děntĭs'tǎ*, sm. dentist.

dentro, *děn'trŏ*, ad. within.

dentudo, da, *děntŏ'dŏ*, a. uneven-toothed.

denuedo, *děnŏĕ'dŏ*, sm. boldness, intrepidity.

denuesto, *děnŏĕs'tŏ*, sm. affront, insult.

denuncia, *děnŏn'thĭǎ*, sf. denunciation.

denunciable, *—thĭǎ'blĕ*, a. capable of being denounced. [tion.

denunciación, *—thĭǎthĭon'*, sf. denunciation.

denunciador, *—thĭǎdŏr'*, sm. denunciator, accuser. [nounce; to prognosticate.

denunciar, *—thĭǎr'*, v. a. to advise; to denunciatory, ria, *—thĭǎtŏ'rĭŏ*, a. denunciatory. [sent.

deparar, *děpǎrǎr'*, v. a. to offer, to predepartamento, *děpǎrtǎměn'tŏ*, sm. department; (rail.) compartment.

dependencia, *děpěndĕn'thĭǎ*, sf. dependency, relation, affinity; business, affair.

depender, *děpěndĕr'*, v. n. to depend, to be dependent on.

dependiente, *děpěndĭěn'tĕ*, sm. dependant, client, follower; hanger-on; clerk.

deplorable, *děplŏrǎ'blĕ*, a. deplorable, lamentable.

deplorar, *děplŏrǎr'*, v. a. to deplore.

deponer, *děpŏněr'*, v. a. to depose, to declare; to displace; to deposit. [tion.

deportación, *děpŏrtǎthĭon'*, sf. deportation.

deportar, *děpŏrtǎr'*, v. a. to transport.

deposición, *děpŏsĭthĭon'*, sf. deposition; assertion, affirmation; (law) deposition upon oath.

depositar, *—tǎr'*, v. a. to deposit, to confide; to put in any place to be kept safe.

depositaría, *—tǎrē'ǎ*, sf. depository.

depositario, *—tǎ'rĭŏ*, sm. depositary, deposito, *děpŏ'sĭtŏ*, sm. deposit. [trustee.

depravación, *děprǎvǎthĭon'*, sf. depravity.

depravar, *děprǎvǎr'*, v. a. to deprave, to vitiate, to corrupt. [earnest entreaty.

deprecación, *děprěkǎthĭon'*, sf. petition;

depresión, *děprěsĭon'*, sf. depression, abasement. [bumble, to deject.

deprimir, *děprĭmĭr'*, v. a. to depress, to

depuración, *děpŭrǎthĭon'*, sf. purification.

depurar, *děpŭrǎr'*, v. a. to cleanse, to purify, to filter.

derecha, *děrětsh'ǎ*, sf. right hand, right side; á —s, right; well done.

derechamente, *—měn'tĕ*, ad. directly, straight; rightly, prudently.

derechera, *děrětshǎ'rǎ*, sf. direct road.

derecho, cha, *děrětsh'ŏ*, a. right; straight; just; perfect; certain; —, sm. right, justice, law; just claim; tax, duty; fee.

derechura, *děrětshŏ'rǎ*, sf. rectitude, right way. [source; origin.

derivación, *děrĭvǎthĭon'*, sf. derivation;

derivar, *děrĭvǎr'*, v. a. & n. to derive; (mar.) to deflect from the course.

derivativo, va, *—vǎtē'vŏ*, a. derivative.

derogación, *děrŏgǎthĭon'*, sf. derogation, abolition; deterioration; diminution.

derogar, *—gǎr'*, v. a. to derogate, to abolish; to reform.

derogatorio, ria, *—gǎtŏ'rĭŏ*, a. derogatory.

derrama, *děrrǎ'mǎ*, sf. assessment of a tax or impost. [thrift.

derramador, *—dŏr'*, sm. prodigal, spend-

derramamiento, *—mĭĕn'tŏ*, sm. effusion, waste; dispersion.

derramar, *děrrǎmǎr'*, v. a. to drain off water; to spread; to spill, to scatter, to waste, to shed; —se, to be spread, to fly abroad. [marjoy.

derramasolaces, *děrrǎmǎsŏlǎ'thěs*, sm.

derrame, *děrrǎ'mĕ*, sm. loss in measuring; leakage.

derredor, *děrrědŏr'*, sm. circumference, circuit; al —, en —, round about.

derrengado, da, *děrrěngǎ'dŏ*, a. bent, crooked. [to abominate, to detest.

derrengar, *—gǎr'*, v. a. to sprain the hip;

derretimiento, *děrrětĭmĭĕn'tŏ*, sm. liquefaction, fusion.

derretir, *—tĭr'*, v. n. to melt; to consume, to expend; —se, to fall in love very easily; to be melted.

derribar, *děrrĭbǎr'*, v. a. to demolish; to flatten; —se, to throw one's self down on the ground. [a demolished building.

derribo, *děrrē'bŏ*, sm. demolition; ruins of

derrocar, *děrrŏkǎr'*, v. a. to pull down, to demolish.

derrochador, *děrrŏtshǎdŏr'*, sm. prodigal.

derrochar, *—tshǎr'*, v. a. to dissipate.

derrota, *děrrŏ'tǎ*, sf. ship's course; road, path; defeat of an army.

derrotar, *děrrŏtǎr'*, v. a. (mar.) to cause to fall off; to destroy; to defeat.

derrotero, *—tĕ'rŏ*, sm. collection of sea-charts; ship's course; (fig.) course, way.

derruir, *děrrŭĭr'*, v. a. to demolish.

derrumbadero, *děrrŭmbǎdĕ'rŏ*, sm. precipice; thorny or arduous affair; risk.

derrumbar, *—bǎr'*, v. a. to precipitate.

desabarrancar, *děsăbărrănkăr'*, v. a. to drag; to extricate from difficulties.

desabastecer, *–ăbăstěthěr'*, v. a. to cut off supplies from.

desabillé, *–ăbīly̆'*, sm. dishabille, undress.

desabollar, *–ăbŏlyăr'*, v. a. to take bulges out of pewter dishes, &c.

desabonarse, *–ăbŏnăr'sě*, v. r. to withdraw one's subscription.

desabotonar, *–ăbŏtŏnăr'*, v. a. to unbutton; –se, to blossom. [sipid; peevish.

desabrido, da, *–ăbrě'dŏ*, a. tasteless, in-

desabrigado, da, *–ăbrĭgă'dŏ*, a. uncovered; shelterless.

desabrigar, *–ăbrĭgăr'*, v. a. to uncover, to deprive of clothes or shelter.

desabrigo, *–ăbrě'gŏ*, sm. nakedness; destitution.

desabrimiento, *–ăbrĭmĭěn'tŏ*, sm. insipidity; asperity of temper; dejection.

desabrir, *–ăbrĭr'*, v. a. to vex, to plague; to harass; –se, to be angry.

desabrochar, *–ăbrŏtchăr'*, v. a. to unclasp; –se, to unbosom.

desacabalar, *–ăkăbălăr'*, v. a. to pilfer.

desacalorarse, *–ăkălŏrăr'sě*, v. r. to take the fresh air; to cool one's-self. [respect.

desacatamiento, *–ăkătămĭěn'tŏ*, sm. disrespect.

desacatar, *–ăkătăr'*, v. a. to treat in a disrespectful manner.

desacato, *–ăkă'tŏ*, sm. disrespect, incivility.

desacertado, da, *–ăthěrtă'dŏ*, a. inconsiderate. [mit a mistake.

desacertar, *–ăthěrtăr'*, v. a. to err, to com-

desacierto, *–ăthĭěr'tŏ*, sm. error, gross mistake, blunder. [spire courage.

desacobardar, *–ăkŏbărdăr'*, v. a. to in-

desacomodado, da, *–ăkŏmŏdă'dŏ*, a. destitute of the conveniences of life; out of service; incommodious.

desacomodamiento, *–ăkŏmŏdămĭěn'tŏ*, sm. incommodity, trouble.

desacomodar, *–ăkŏmŏdăr'*, v. a. to incommode, to molest; –se, to lose one's place. [tŏ, sm. want of company.

desacompañamiento, *–ăkŏmpănyămĭěn'-*

desacompañar, *–ăkŏmpănyăr'*, v. a. to leave the company.

desaconsejado, da, *–ăkŏnsě'hă'dŏ*, a. inconsiderate, ill-advised.

desacordado, da, *–ăkŏrdă'dŏ*, a. discordant (applied to colours).

desacordar, *–ăkŏrdăr'*, v. a. to untune; –se, to be forgetful; to be at variance.

desacorde, *–ăkŏr'dě*, a. discordant.

desacorrolar, *–ăkŏrrŏlăr'*, v. a. to let the flock or cattle out of the penfold.

desacostumbrado, da, *–ăkŏstŭmbrŭ'dŏ*, a. unusual. [disuse.

desacostumbrar, *–ăkŏstŭmbrăr'*, v. a. to

desacotar, *–ăkŏtăr'*, v. a. to lay open a pasture-ground; to withdraw a prohibition.

desacreditar, *–ăkrědĭtăr'*, v. a. to discredit.

desacuerdo, *–ăkŭěr'dŏ*, sm. derangement of mental faculties; discordance, disagreement, disunion. [to disorder.

desaderezar, *–ăděrěthăr'*, v. a. to undress;

desadeudar, *–ăděŭdăr'*, v. a. to pay one's debts, to get out of debt.

desadorar, *–ădŏrăr'*, v. a. to cease to love.

desadormecer, *–ădŏrměthěr'*, v. a. to wake, to rouse from sleep; to rouse from mental stupor.

desadornar, *–ădŏrnăr'*, v. a. to divest of ornaments or decorations.

desadorno, *–ădŏr'nŏ*, sm. want of embellishments or charms. [affectedness.

desafecto, *–ăfěk'tŏ*, sm. disaffection, dis-

desaferrar, *–ăfěrrăr'*, v. a. to weigh anchor; to loosen; –se, to let go one's hold; to give up.

desafiador, *–ăfĭădŏr'*, sm. challenger.

desafiar, *–ăfĭăr'*, v. a. to challenge, to call out (to fight a duel).

desaficionar, *–ăfĭthĭŏnăr'*, v. a. to destroy one's affection for anything.

desafinar, *–ăfĭnăr'*, v. a. to untune.

desafío, *–ăfĭ'ŏ*, sm. challenge; struggle, contest, combat.

desaforado, da, *–ăfŏră'dŏ*, a. huge; disorderly, lawless, impudent.

desaforar, *–ăfŏrăr'*, v. a. to encroach upon one's rights; (mil.) to cashier; –se, to relinquish one's rights; to be outrageous.

desaforrar, *–ăfŏrrăr'*, v. a. to take the lining from anything.

desafortunado, da, *–ăfŏrtŭnă'dŏ*, a. unfortunate, unlucky. [excess.

desafuero, *–ăfŭě'rŏ*, sm. act of injustice;

desagarrar, *–ăgărrăr'*, v. a. to release.

desagraciado, da, *–ăgrăthĭă'dŏ*, a. ungraceful, inelegant. [to disfigure.

desagraciar, *–ăgrăthĭăr'*, v. a. to deform.

desagradable, *–ăgrădă'blě*, a. disagreeable, unpleasant.

desagradar, *–ăgrădăr'*, v. a. to displease.

desagradecido, da, *–ăgrăděthĭ'dŏ*, a. ungrateful. [sm. ingratitude.

desagradecimiento, *–ăgrăděthĭmĭěn'tŏ*,

desagrado, *–ăgră'dŏ*, sm. asperity, harshness; displeasure.

desagraviar, *–ăgrăvĭăr'*, v. a. to make amends for an injury. [faction.

desagravio, *–ăgră'vĭŏ*, sm. relief, satis-

desagregar, *–ăgrěgăr'*, v. a. to disjoin, to separate. [drain.

desaguadero, *–ăgŭădě'rŏ*, sm. channel,

desaguador, *–ăgŭădŏr'*, sm. channel for carrying off water.

desaguar, *–ăgŭăr'*, v. a. to draw off water; –, v. n. to empty or to flow into the sea.

desaguazar, *–ăgŭăthăr'*, v. a. to drain or draw off the water from a thing.

desagüe, *–ăgŭě'*, sm. channel, drain; extraordinary expense.

desahijar, *děsăhĭhăr'*, v. a. to wean; –se, to swarm (of bees).

desahitarse, *–ăhĭtăr'sě*, v. r. to relieve indigestion. [impudent.

desahogado, da, *–ăhŏgă'dŏ*, a. petulant.

desahogar, *–ăhŏgăr'*, v. a. to ease pain; –se, to recover; to unbosom.

desahogo, *–ăhŏ'gŏ*, sm. ease, alleviation from pain; freedom of speech.

desahuciar, –ăhŭthĭăr´, v. a. to despair; to give up; to dismiss a tenant.

desahucio, –ăhŏˈthĭŏ, sm. dismissing of a tenant or driving away cattle from a pasture-ground (at the expiration of the stipulated time). [smoke.

desahumar, –ăhŭmăr´, v. a. to free from

desairado, da, –ătrăˈdŏ, a. disregarded, slighted. [take no notice.

desairar, –ăˈrăr´, v. a. to disregard, to

desaire, –ăˈĭrĕ, sm. disdain, disrespect; frown of fortune.

desajustar, –ăˈhŭstăr´, v. a. to disproportion; –se, to withdraw from an agreement.

desajuste, –ăˈhŭsˈtĕ, sm. disturbance of proper or regular conditions.

desalar, –ălăr´, v. a. to cut off the wings; to take the salt out of fish, salt meat, &c. by steeping it in fresh water; –se, to run to meet someone with open arms.

desalentar, –ălĕntăr´, v. a. to put out of breath; to discourage. [carpet.

desalfombrar, –ălfŏmbrăr´, v. a. to un-

desaliento, –ălĕˈn´tŏ, sm. dismay, desertion of mind.

desaliñar, –ălĭnyăr´, v. a. to discompose.

desaliño, –ălĭnˈyŏ, sm. slovenliness; carelessness. [human, impious.

desalmado, da, –ălmăˈdŏ, a. cruel, in-

desalmarse, –ălmăr´ sĕ, v. r. to desire very ardently. [turrets.

desalmenado, da, –ălmĕnăˈdŏ, a. without

desalojar, –ălŏˈhăr´, v. a. to dislodge the enemy's troops; –, v. n. to move to other lodgings. [a. suage, to settle.

desalterar, –ăltĕrăr´, v. a. to allay, to

desalumbrado, da, –ălŭmbrăˈdŏ, a. dazzled; groping in the dark.

desamarrar, –ămărăr´, v. a. to unmoor a ship; to untie, to remove.

desamoldar, –ămŏldăr´, v. a. to unmould; to change the proportion or symmetry of anything. [dull, silent person like.

desamorrar, –ămŏrăr´, v. a. to make a

desamotinarse, –ămŏtĭnăr´ sĕ, v. r. to withdraw from mutiny.

desamparar, –ămpărăr´, v. a. to forsake, to abandon; to relinquish; to desist.

desamparo, –ămpăˈrŏ, sm. abandonment; helplessness; dereliction. [furnish.

desamueblar, –ămŏˈĕblăr´, v. a. to un-

desancorar, –ănkŏrăr´, v. a. (mar.) to weigh anchor.

desandar, –ăndăr´, v. a. to retrograde, to go back the same road by which one came.

desandrajado, da, –ăndrăˈhăˈdŏ, a. ragged, in tatters.

desangrar, –ăsăngrăr´, v. a. to bleed one to excess; to drain a pond; (fig.) to exhaust one's means.

desanidar, –ăsănĭdăr´, v. n. to forsake the nest; –, v. a. to dislodge from a post.

desanimar, –ănĭmăr´, v. a. to discourage.

desanudar, –ănŭdăr´, v. a. to untie; to extricate, to disentangle.

desapacibilidad, –ăpăthĭbĭlĭdăˈd´, sf. rudeness, churlishness, peevishness.

desapacible, –ăpăthĕˈ bĭˈ, a. disagreeable, unpleasant, harsh. [prove, to contradict.

desapadrinar, –ăpădrĭnăr´, v. a. to dis-

desaparear, –ăpărĕăr´, v. a. to unmatch.

desaparecer, –ăpărĕthĕr´, v. a. to remove out of sight; –, v. n. –se, to disappear.

desaparejar, –ăpărĕˈhăr´, v. a. to unharness beasts; (mar.) to unrig a ship.

desapasionar, –ăpăsĭŏnăr´, v. a. to root out a passion.

desapego, –ăpăˈgŏ, sm. alienation of affection; coolness; disinterestedness.

desapercibido, da, –ăpĕrthĭbĭˈdŏ, a. unprovided. [sm. unpreparedness.

desapercibimiento, –ăpĕrthĭbĭmĭĕnˈtŏ,

desapestar, –ăpĕstăr´, v. a. to cure persons infected with the plague. [merciless.

desapiadado, da, –ăpĭădăˈdŏ, a. impious,

desaplicación, –ăplĭkăthĭŏn´, sf. want of application. [careless, neglectful.

desaplicado, da, –ăplĭkăˈdŏ, a. indolent,

desapoderar, –ăpŏdĕrăr´, v. a. to dispossess; to repeal a power of attorney.

desapolillar, –ăpŏlĭlyăr´, v. a. to free from moths; to take the air when it is cold and sharp.

desaposentar, –ăpŏsĕntăr´, v. a. to turn someone out of his lodgings.

desaposesionar, –ăpŏsĕsĭŏnăr´, v. a. to dispossess.

desapoyar, –ăpŏyăr´, v. a. to cut the ground from beneath one's feet.

desapreciar, –ăprĕthĭăr´, v. a. to depreciate, to undervalue.

desaprender, –ăprĕndĕr´, v. a. to unlearn. [to loosen.

desapretar, –ăprĕˈtăr´, v. a. to slacken,

desaprisionar, –ăprĭsĭŏnăr´, v. a. to release from confinement; –se, to extricate one's self from difficulties.

desaprobación, –ăprŏbăthĭŏn´, sf. disapprobation. [prove, to reprove.

desaprobar, –ăprŏbăr´, v. a. to disap-

desapropiamiento, –ăprŏpĭămĭĕnˈtŏ, sm. alienation. [alienate.

desapropiarse, –ăprŏpĭăr´ sĕ, v. r. to

desaprovechado, da, –ăprŏvĕtshăˈdŏ, a. useless, unprofitable; backward.

desaprovechamiento, –ăprŏvĕtshămĭĕnˈtŏ, sm. backwardness.

desaprovechar, –ăprŏvĕtshăr´, v. a. to misspend, to turn to a bad use.

desapuntalar, –ăpŭntălăr´, v. a. to take away the props.

desapuntar, –ăpŭntăr´, v. a. to unstitch; to lose one's aim, to aim fire-arms badly.

desarbolar, –ărbŏlăr´, v. a. to unmast a ship; to lay up a ship in ordinary.

desarbolo, –ărbŏˈlŏ, sm. unmasting a ship.

desarenar, –ărĕnăr´, v. a. to clear a place of sand.

desarmadura, –ărmădŏˈră, sf. disarming.

desarmar, –ărmăr´, v. a. to disarm; to disband troops; to dismount (a cross-bow, a cannon); (fig.) to pacify.

desarme, –ar´mĕ, sm. disarmament of ships; breaking up of an army.

desarraigar, –ārrāigār', v. a. to root out; to extirpate.

desarraigo, –ārrā'igŏ, sm. eradication.

desarrapado, da, –ārrāpā'dŏ, a. ragged.

desarrebozar, –ārrĕbŏthār', v. a. to unmuffle; to manifest, to discover.

desarrebujar, –ārrĕbŏŏhār', v. a. to unfold, to spread out. [ad. disorderly.

desarregladamente, –ārrĕglādāmĕn'tĕ, adv. disorderly.

desarreglado, da, –ārrĕglā'dŏ, a. immoderate in eating, drinking, &c.

desarreglar, –ārrĕglār', v. a. to disorder, to derange.

desarreglo, –ārrā'glŏ, sm. disorder, derangement; licentiousness. [to dissuade.

desarrimar, –ārrĭmār', v. a. to remove;

desarrollar, –ārrŏlyār', v. a. to unroll, to unfold; –se, to be unfolded, to open.

desarropar, –ārrŏpār', v. a. to undress.

desarrugar, –ārrŏgār', v. a. to take out wrinkles. [a ship.

desarrumar, –ārrŏmār', v. a. to unload

desasear, –āsĕār', v. a. to make dirty; to discompose.

desaseo, –āsĕ'ŏ, sm. disorder.

desasimiento, –āsĭmĭĕn'tŏ, sm. letting loose; disinterestedness.

desasir, –āsĭr', v. a. to loosen, to disentangle; –se, to extricate one's self.

desasnar, –āsnār', v. a. (fig.) to polish one's manners. [quiet, to disturb.

desasosegar, –āsŏsĕgār', v. a. to disasosiego, –āsŏsĭĕ'gŏ, sm. restlessness, feverishness. [miserable; ragged.

desastrado, da, –āstrā'dŏ, a. wretched,

desastre, –ās'trĕ, sm. disaster; misfortune.

desatacar, –ātākār', v. a. to loosen, to untie; – una escopeta, to draw the charge out of a gun.

desatar, –ātār', v. a. to untie, to loose; to separate; to unriddle; –se, to give rein to one's tongue; to lose all reserve.

desatascar, –ātāskār', v. a. to draw out of the mire; to extricate one from difficulties.

desataviar, –ātāvĭār', v. a. to strip of decorations. [ness in dress.

desatavío, –ātāvĭ'ŏ, sm. want of neatness.

desatención, –ātĕnthĭŏn', sf. want of attention, absence of mind; want of politeness.

desatender, –ātĕndĕr', v. a. to pay no attention; to disregard; to contemn.

desatentado, da, –ātĕntā'dŏ, a. inconsiderate; thoughtless; excessive.

desatento, ta, –ātĕn'tŏ, a. inattentive, careless; rude, uncivil. [treasure.

desatesorar, –ātĕsŏrār', v. a. to spend a

desatinado, da, –ātĭnā'dŏ, a. extravagant; –, sm. fool, madman.

desatinar, –ātĭnār', v. a. & n. to derange one's mind; to throw into a violent passion; to talk nonsense; to reel, to stagger.

desatino, –ātĭ'nŏ, sm. extravagance; staggering; nonsense. [the mire.

desatollar, –ātŏlyār', v. a. to pull out of

desatolondrar, –ātŏlŏndrār', v. a. to bring someone to himself; –se, to recover one's senses, to come to one's self.

desatontarse, –ātŏntār'sĕ, v. r. to come to one's self (from a faint, &c.)

desatracar, –ātrākār', v. a. (mar.) to sheer off. [to clean a well.

desatrancar, –ātrānkār', v. a. to unbar;

desatufarse, –ātŏfār'sĕ, v. a. to grow calm.

desaturdir, –ātŏrdĭr', v. a. to rouse from a state of dizziness or stupor. [authorise.

desautorisar, –āōtŏrĭsār', v. a. to dis-

desavecindado, da, –āvĕthĭndā'dŏ, a. deserted, unpeopled.

desavecindarse, –āvĕthĭndār'sĕ, v. r. to change one's domicile. [disagreement.

desavenencia, –āvĕnĕn'thĭā, sf. discord,

desavenido, da, –āvĕnĭ'dŏ, a. discordant, disagreeing.

desavenir, –āvĕnĭr', v. a. to discompose, to disconcert; –, v. n. to quarrel.

desaventajado, da, –āvĕntāhā'dŏ, a. disadvantageous, unprofitable.

desaviar, –āvĭār', v. a. to deviate from the high road; to strip of necessaries.

desavío, –āvĭ'ŏ, sm. going astray; want of the necessary means.

desavisado, da, –āvĭsā'dŏ, a. ill-advised.

desavisar, –āvĭsār', v. a. to countermand.

desayunar, –āyŏnār', v. a. to give the first intelligence of news; –se, to breakfast. [fast.

desayuno, āyŏ'nŏ, sm. breakfast.

desazogar, –āthŏgār', v. a. to take off the quicksilver from a looking-glass.

desazón, dĕsāthŏn', sf. insipidity; disgust; uneasiness; unfitness of a soil for agricultural purposes.

desazonado, da, –āthŏnā'dŏ, a. illadapted; ill-humoured.

desazonar, –āthŏnār', v. a. to render tasteless; to disgust; –se, to become indisposed. [portmanteau or its contents.

desbalijar, –bālĭhār', v. a. to steal a

desbancar, –bānkār', v. a. to clear a room of the benches; to break the bank (in gambling); (fig.) to supplant.

desbandarse, –bāndār'sĕ, v. r. to disband.

desbaratado, da, –bārātā'dŏ, a. debauched, lewd.

desbaratar, –bārātār', v. a. to destroy; to defeat an army; to dissipate; – la paz, to break the peace; –, v. n. to talk nonsense; –se, to be confounded. [tion.

desbarato, –bārā'tŏ, sm. defeat; dissipa-

desbarbado, –bārbā'dŏ, a. beardless.

desbarbillar, –bārbĭlyār', v. a. to prune the roots of young vines.

desbardar, –bārdār', v. a. to uncover a wall or fence. [beyond limits.

desbarrar, –bārrār', v. n. to slip, to go

desbarretar, –bārrĕtār', v. a. to unbar, to unbolt, to take off the bars and bolts.

desbarrigado, da, –bārrĭgā'dŏ, a. littlebellied. [to open the belly.

desbarrigar, –bārrĭgār', v. a. to rip up,

desbarro, –bār'rŏ, sm. slipping; (fig.) nonsense, extravagance; frenzy.

desbastar, –bāstār', v. a. to smooth; to polish; to waste; to purify one's morals and manners.

desbaste, –bǎs'tě, sm. hewing, smoothing.

desbastecido, da, –bǎstěthě dǒ, a. without sufficient provisions.

desbautizarse, –bǎutǐthǎr'sě, v. r. (fig.) to be irritated.

desbecerrar, –běthěrrǎr', v. a. to wean (animals).

desblanquecido, da, –blǎnkěthě dǒ, a. blanched.

desbocado, da, –bǒkǎ dǒ, a. open-mouthed (applied to a cannon); wild (applied to a horse); foul-mouthed, indecent.

desbocar, –bǒkǎr', v. a. to break the brim of a jar or other vessel; –, v. n. to disembogue; –se, to be insensible of the bridle; to use abusive language.

desboquillar, –bǒkǐl'yǎr', v. a. to break the mouth of a vessel.

desborrar, –bǒrrǎr', v. a. to cut off the loose threads of stuff, when it comes out of the loom; to lop off, breeches.

desbragado, da, –brǎgǎ dǒ, a. without breeches.

desbraguetado, da, –brǎgětǎ dǒ, a. having the forepart of the breeches unbuttoned. rate.

desbrevarse, –brěvǎr'sě, v. r. to evaporate.

desbrozar, –brǒthǎr', v. a. to clear away rubbish. rubbish.

desbrozo, –brǒ'thǒ, sm. clearing away

desbuchar, –bǔtshǎr', v. a. to disclose one's secrets; to ease the stomach (applied to birds of prey).

descabal, –kǎbǎl', a. incomplete.

descabalar, –kǎbǎlǎr', v. a. to make incomplete, to unmatch; to pilfer; to impair.

descabalgar, –kǎbǎlgǎr', v. n. to alight from a horse; –, v. a. to dismount.

descabellado, da, –kǎbělyǎ dǒ, a. dishevelled; disorderly; wild, unrestrained; disproportional; violent. the hair.

descabellar, –kǎbělyǎr', v. a. to disorder

descabezado, da, –kǎběthǎ dǒ, a. beheaded; lightheaded, giddy.

descabezar, –kǎběthǎr', v. a. to behead; to lop off; –se, to puzzle one's brains.

descabullirse, –kǎbǔlyǐr'sě, v. r. to steal away, to scamper; to elude difficulties cleverly.

descaderar, –kǎděrǎr', v. a. to sprain the hip. decay.

descaecer, –kǎěthěr', v. n. to decline, to

descaecimiento, –kǎěthǐmǐěn'tǒ, sm. weakness; languor.

descalabazarse, –kǎlǎbǎthǎr'sě, v. r. to puzzle one's brains.

descalabrado, da, –kǎlǎbrǎ dǒ, a. wounded on the head; imprudent.

descalabradura, –kǎlǎbrǎdǒ'rǎ, sf. contusion or wound in the head.

descalabrar, –kǎlǎbrǎr', v. a. to break or wound the head; to attack one's character.

descalabro, –kǎlǎ'brǒ, sm. calamitous event, considerable loss.

descalcez, –kǎlthěth', sf. nudity of the feet; barefootedness of monks.

descalificar, –kǎlǐfǐkǎr', v. a. to disqualify.

descalzar, –kǎlthǎr', v. a. –se, to pull off the shoes and stockings.

descalzo, za, –kǎl'thǒ, a. barefooted.

descaminar, –kǎmǐnǎr', v. a. to misguide, to lead astray. less; very poor.

descamisado, da, –kǎmǐsǎ dǒ, a. shirtless; very poor.

descampado, da, –kǎmpǎ dǒ, a. disengaged, free, open. working.

descampar, –kǎmpǎr', v. n. to leave off working.

descansado, da, –kǎnsǎ dǒ, a. reposing; rested, refreshed; quiet.

descansar, –kǎnsǎr', v. n. to rest from labour and fatigue; to pause in the execution of a thing; to repose, to sleep; – las tierras, to lie fallow or at rest.

descanso, –kǎn'sǒ, sm. rest, repose.

descanterar, –kǎntěrǎr', v. a. to cut the crust off bread. to lessen.

descantillar, –kǎntǐlyǎr', v. a. to pare off;

descañonar, –kǎnyǒnǎr', v. a. to pluck out the feathers; (fig.) to trick one out of his money. cover the head.

descaperuzar, –kǎpěrǔthǎr', v. a. to uncover the head.

descapillar, –kǎpǐlyǎr', v. a. to take off the hood. the hood.

descapirotar, –kǎpǐrǒtǎr', v. a. to take off the hood.

descarado, da, –kǎrǎ dǒ, a. impudent, barefaced. solently.

descararse, –kǎrǎr'sě, v. r. to behave insolently.

descarga, –kǎr'gǎ, sf. disburdening, unloading; volley, discharge.

descargadero, –kǎrgǎdě'rǒ, sm. wharf.

descargador, –kǎrgǎdǒr', sm. unloader.

descargar, –kǎrgǎr', v. a. to unload, to discharge; –se, to give a plea to an accusation. justification.

descargo, –kǎr'gǒ, sm. discharge, acquittal,

descargue, –kǎr'gě, sm. alleviation from any burden. of affection.

descariño, –kǎrǐn'yǒ, sm. coolness, loss of affection.

descarnar, –kǎrnǎr', v. a. to strip off the flesh; to clean away the flesh from; –se, to dissipate, to squander one's wealth.

descaro, –kǎ'rǒ, sm. impudence.

descarriar, –kǎrrǐǎr', v. a. to lead astray; to separate cattle from one another; –se, to deviate from justice or reason.

descarrilamiento, –kǎrrǐlǎmǐěn'tǒ, sm. (rail.) running off the rails.

descarrilar, –kǎrrǐlǎr', v. n. (rail.) to leave or run off the rails.

descarrillar, –kǎrrǐlyǎr', v. a. to tear the jaws asunder. way.

descarrío, –kǎrrě'ǒ, sm. losing of one's

descartar, –kǎrtǎr', v. a. to discard; to dismiss; –se, to excuse one's self.

descarte, –kǎr'tě, sm. cards discarded; discarding; evasion, subterfuge.

descasar, –kǎsǎr', v. a. to separate a husband and wife.

descascarar, –kǎskǎrǎr', v. a. to decorticate, to husk; –se, to fall off.

descaspar, –kǎspǎr', v. a. to remove dandriff from the head.

descasque, –kǎs'kě, sm. decortication.

descastado, –kǎstǎ dǒ, a. degenerate; ungrateful. arms.

descebar, –thěbǎr', v. a. to unprime firearms.

descendencia, –thěnděn'thǐǎ, sf. descent, offspring.

descendente, –thĕndĕn'tĕ, a. descending; (rail.) tren –, sm. down-train.

descender, –thĕndĕr', v. n. to descend, to walk downward; to flow; to be derived from. [cending; descendant.

descendiente, –thĕndĕn'tĕ, a. & sm. descension, –thĕnsiŏn', sf. descent, descending. [tion.

descenso, –thĕn'sŏ, sm. descent; degradaceñir, –thĕnÿir', v. a. to ungird.

descepar, –thĕpär', v. a. to uproot, to root up; to clear a wood.

descerar, –thĕrär', v. a. to take the empty combs from a bee-hive. [fortified.

descercado, da, –thĕrkä'dŏ, a. open, undescercar, –thĕrkär', v. a. to destroy or pull down a wall.

descerrajar, –thĕrrä'här', v. a. to take off the lock of a door, &c.; to discharge fire-arms. [unravel.

descifrar, –thĭfrär', v. a. to decipher; to descinchar, –thĭntshär', v. a. to ungirth a horse. [claw-hammer.

desclavador, –klävädŏr', sm. nail-claw, desclavar, –klävär', v. a. to draw out nails. [solve.

descoagular, –kŏägŭlär', v. a. to disdescobajar, –kŏbä'här', v. a. to pull the stem from a grape.

descobijar, –kŏbĭ'här', v. a. to uncover, to undress. [pudent.

descocado, da, –kŏkä'dŏ, a. bold, imdescocar, –kŏkär', v. a. to free trees from insects; –se, to be impudent. [ness.

descoco, –kŏ'kŏ, sm. impudence, saucidescoger, –kŏ'hĕr', v. a. to unfold, to expand. [plants.

descogollar, –kŏgŏlyär', v. n. to prune descogotado, da, –kŏgŏtä'dŏ, a. barenecked.

descogotar, –kŏgŏtär', v. a. to knock off the horns of a stag at one blow.

descolar, –kŏlär', v. a. to dock.

descolchar, –kŏltshär', v. a. to untwist a cable.

descolgar, –kŏlgär', v. a. to unhang; –se, to come down gently; to glide; to run (of streams). [out the eye-teeth.

descolmillar, –kŏlmĭlyär', v. a. to draw descolorar, –kŏlŏrär', v. a. to discolour.

descolorido, da, –kŏlŏrĭ'dŏ, a. pale, colourless. [excel, to surpass.

descollar, –kŏlyär', v. n. to overtop, to descomedido, da, –kŏmĕdĭ'dŏ, a. impudent, insolent; huge.

descomedirse, –kŏmĕdĭr'sĕ, v. r. to be rude or disrespectful.

descompasado, da, –kŏmpäsä'dŏ, a. excessive; disproportionate.

descompasarse, –kŏmpäsär'sĕ, v. r. to exceed all rule and measure.

descomponer, –kŏmpŏnĕr', v. a. to discompose, to set at odds, to disconcert; (chem.) to decompose; –, v. n. to be out of temper; to be indisposed; to change for the worse (of the weather).

descomposición, –kŏmpŏsĭthĭŏn', sf. disagreement, discomposure; decomposition.

descompostura, –kŏmpŏstŏ'rä, sf. disagreement; disorder, confusion; want of modesty.

descompuesto, ta, –kŏmpŭĕs'tŏ, a. impudent, insolent.

descomunal, –kŏmŭnäl', a. uncommon; beyond all measure. [discredit.

desconceptuar, –kŏnthĕptŭär', v. a. to desconcertado, da, –kŏnthĕrtä'dŏ, a. disorderly, slovenly.

desconcertar, –kŏnthĕrtär', v. a. to disturb; to confound; to disconcert; –se, to disagree; to exceed the limits of prudence and judgment; to be indisposed with a looseness of the body; to be out of joint.

desconchar, –kŏntshär', v. a. to unscale.

desconcierto, –kŏnthĭĕr'tŏ, sm. discomposure; disorder, confusion; indolence, negligence; sprain.

desconfiado, da, –kŏnfĭä'dŏ, a. diffident, mistrustful. [jealousy.

desconfianza, –kŏnfĭän'thä, sf. diffidence; desconfiar, –kŏnfĭär', v. n. to mistrust, to suspect. [contrary; unequal, unlike.

desconforme, –kŏnfŏr'mĕ, a. discordant, desconformidad, –kŏnfŏrmĭdäd', sf. disagreement, opposition; inequality, unlikeness, dissimilitude.

desconocer, –kŏnŏthĕr', v. a. to disown, to disavow; to be totally ignorant of a thing; not to know a person; not to acknowledge (a favour received).

desconocido, da, –kŏnŏthĭ'dŏ, a. ungrateful; disguised; unknown.

desconsiderado, da, –kŏnsĭdĕrä'dŏ, a. inconsiderate, imprudent.

desconsolado, da, –kŏnsŏlä'dŏ, a. comfortless, painful; sick with indigestion.

desconsolar, –kŏnsŏlär', v. a. to afflict.

desconsuelo, –kŏnsŭĕ'lŏ, sm. affliction, trouble; disorder of the digestive organs.

descontar, –kŏntär', v. a. to discount; to abate, to diminish.

descontentadizo, za, –kŏntĕntädĭ'thŏ, a. squeamish, easily disgusted.

descontentar, –kŏntĕntär', v. a. to discontent, to displease. [tion, disgust.

descontento, –kŏntĕn'tŏ, sm. dissatisfacdesconvenible, –kŏnvĕnĭ'blĕ, a. discordant, disagreeing, dissimilar.

desconveniencia, –kŏnvĕnĭĕn'thĭä, sf. incommodity, inconvenience; discord, disunion; dissimilitude.

desconveniente, –kŏnvĕnĭĕn'tĕ, a. inconvenient; incongruous. [not to suit.

desconvenir, –kŏnvĕnĭr', v.n. to disagree; descopar, –kŏpär', v. a. to lop off the branches of a tree.

descorazonar, –kŏräthŏnär', v. a. to pull out the heart; to dishearten, to discourage; to smite with love.

descorchar, –kŏrtshär', v. a. to strip off the bark; to break a bee hive to steal the honey; to break open a chest or trunk.

descordar, –kŏrdär', v. a. to unstring an instrument. [horns of an anima...

descornar, –kŏrnär', v. a. to knock off the

descorrear, –kōrrěǎr', v. n. to loosen the skin that covers the tenderlings of a deer.

descorrer, –kōrrěr', v. n. to run, to flow; –, v. a. to retrograde: – **la cortina,** to draw the curtain.

descortés, –kōrtěth', a. impolite, uncivil.

descortesía, –kōrtěsě'ǎ, sf. incivility, want of politeness.

descortezar, –kōrtěthǎr', v. a. to descorticate; to flay; (fig.) to polish. [a seam.

descosedura, –kōsědū'rǎ, sf. unseaming

descoser, –kōsěr', v. a. to unseam; to separate; –se, to give rein to one's tongue.

descosido, –kōsī'dō, sm. idle talker.

descostillar, –kōstīlyǎr', v. a. to break the ribs; –se, to fall with great violence on one's back. [off.

descostrarse, –kōstrǎr'sě, v. r. to scale

descotar, –kōtǎr', v. a. to remove the restrictions against the use of a path or road.

descoyuntamiento, –kōyūntǎmiěn'tō, sm. dislocation; pain from overexertion.

descoyuntar, –kōyūntǎr', v. a. to lux or disjoint bones; to vex, to molest.

descrédito, –krě'dītō, sm. discredit.

descreer, –krěěr', v. a. to disbelieve.

describir, děskrībīr', v. a. to draw, to delineate; to describe.

descripción, děskrīpthiōn', sf. delineation; description; inventory. [tive.

descriptivo, va, děskrīptě'vō, a. descrip-

descruzar, –krūthǎr', v. a. to uncross.

descuadernar, –kǔǎděrnǎr', v. a. to unbind; to disorder.

descuajar, –kǔǎ'hǎr', v. a. to dissolve, to liquefy; to pluck up weeds; to frighten.

descuajo, –kǔǎ'hō, sm. eradication.

descuartizar, –kǔǎrtīthǎr', v. a. to quarter (to divide the body into four parts); to carve. [nition; á la –, openly, clearly.

descubierta, –kǔbiěr'tǎ, sf. (mil.) recog-

descubierto, –tō, sm. solemn exposition of the sacrament; deficit.

descubridor, ra, děskǔbrīdōr', sm. & f. discoverer, descrier; investigator; (mil.) scout; vessel on a voyage of discovery.

descubrimiento, –kǔbrīmiěn'tō, sm. discovery, country lately discovered.

descubrir, –kǔbrīr', v. a. to discover, to disclose; to uncover; to reveal; (mil.) to overlook any place in a fortification.

descuello, –kǔěl'yō, sm. excessive stature; pre-eminence; haughtiness.

descuento, –kǔěn'tō, sm. sum paid in part payment of a debt; discount; satisfaction; diminution, decrease.

descuerno, –kǔěr'nō, sm. contempt; affront. [negligent.

descuidado, da, –kǔīdǎ'dō, a. careless,

descuidar, –kǔīdǎr', v. a. & n. to neglect, to relieve from care; to render careless.

descuido, –kǔī'dō, sm. indolence, carelessness, negligence, forgetfulness; want of attention, incivility; improper action; al –, affectedly careless.

descular, –kǔlǎr', v. a. to break the bottom or end of a thing.

desde, děs'dě, pr. since, after, from; – luego, thereupon; – entonces, since then.

desdecir, –děthīr', v. a. to disavow; –, v. n. to degenerate; to differ, to disagree; to tumble down; –se, to gainsay; to retract. [tempt; al –, affectedly careless.

desdén, –děn', sm. disdain, scorn, con-

desdentado, da, –děntǎ'dō, a. toothless.

desdentar, –děntǎr', v. a. to draw out teeth. [despicable.

desdeñable, –děnyǎ'blě, a. contemptible,

desdeñar, –děnyǎr', v. a. to disdain, to scorn; –se, to be disdainful.

desdeñoso, sa, –děnyō'sō, a. disdainful; contemptuous. [a clew.

desdevanar, –děvǎnǎr', v. a. to develop

desdicha, –dīsh'ǎ, sf. misfortune, calamity; great poverty.

desdichado, da, –dīshǎ'dō, a. unfortunate, wretched, miserable.

desdoblar, –dōblǎr', v. a. to unfold, to spread open.

desdorar, –dōrǎr', v. a. to take off the gilding; to tarnish one's reputation.

desdoro, –dō'rō, sm. dishonour, blot on one's reputation.

deseable, děsěǎ'blě, a. desirable.

desear, děsěǎr', v. a. to desire, to wish; to require, to demand.

desecación, děsěkǎthiōn', sf. desiccation.

desecar, děsěkǎr', v. a. to dry.

desechar, děsěthǎr', v. a. to depreciate; to reject, to reprove; to refuse; to exclude, to reprobate; to lay aside.

desecho, děsěsh'ō, sm. residue, remainder; refuse, offal; contempt.

desedificar, –dīfīkǎr', v. a. to scandalise.

desejecutar, –ě'hěkǔtǎr', v. a. (law) to raise a sequestration.

desellar, děsělyǎr', v. a. to unseal.

desembalar, –ěmbǎlǎr', v. a. to unpack.

desembanastar, –ěmbǎnǎstǎr', v. a. to take out of a basket; to talk at random; –se, to break out (of a person confined).

desembarazar, –ěmbǎrǎthǎr', v. a. to disembarrass; to clear; to disencumber; –se, to be extricated from difficulties.

desembarazo, –ěmbǎrǎ'thō, sm. disembarrassment; liberty to do a thing.

desembarcadero, –ěmbǎrkǎdē'rō, sm. landing-place.

desembarcar, –ěmbǎrkǎr', v. a. to unship, to disembark; –, v. n. to disembark, to land.

desembarco, –ěmbǎr'kō, sm. landing; unshipment; landing of stairs; descent, hostile landing. [an embargo.

desembargar, –ěmbǎrgǎr', v. a. to raise

desembargo, –ěmbǎr'gō, sm. (law) raising an embargo.

desembarque, –ěmbǎr'kě, sm. landing.

desembaular, –ěmbǎǔlǎr', v. a. to empty a trunk; to disclose one's secret thoughts.

desembelesarse, –ěmbělěsǎr'sě, v. r. to recover from amazement.

desembocadero, –ěmbōkǎdē'rō, sm. mouth of a river or canal.

desembocar, _ĕmbŏkăr′_, v. n. to disembogue.

desembojar, _ĕmbŏ′hăr′_, v. a. to remove the silk-pods from the southern-wood.

desembolsar, _ĕmbŏlsăr′_, v. a. to empty a purse; to disburse.

desembolso, _ĕmbŏl′sŏ_, sm. disbursement, expenditure.

desemborrachar, _ĕmbŏrrătshăr′_, v. a. to sober; —, v. n. to grow sober.

desembocarse, _ĕmbŏkăr′sĕ_, v. r. to get out of the woods; to get clear of an ambuscade. [muffle.

desembozar, _ĕmbŏthăr′_, v. a. to unbosom. [different.

desemboxo, _ĕmbŏ′thŏ_, sm. uncovering of the face. [tame, to domesticate.

desembravecer, _ĕmbrăvĕthĕr′_, v. a. to

desembriagar, _ĕmbrĭăgăr′_, v. a. & r. to sober; to recover from drunkenness.

desembrollar, _ĕmbrŏlyăr′_, v. a. to disentangle, to disembroil.

desembuchar, _ĕmbŭtshăr′_, v. a. to disgorge; to unbosom. [different.

desemejante, _dĕsĕmĕ′hăn′tĕ_, a. dissimilar.

desemejanza, _thă_, sf. dissimilitude, unlikeness. [similar.

desemejar, _dĕsĕmĕ′hăr_, v. n. to be dissimilar.

desempalagar, _ĕmpălăgăr′_, v. a. to clean one's palate, to restore the appetite; to clear a mill of stagnant water.

desempañar, _ĕmpănyăr′_, v. a. to unswathe; to clean a tarnished looking-glass.

desempapelar, _ĕmpăpĕlăr′_, v. a. to unwrap. [unpack.

desempaquetar, _ĕmpăkĕtăr′_, v. a. to

desemparejar, _ĕmpărĕ′hăr′_, v. a. to unmatch. [the thrashed corn in heaps.

desemparvar, _ĕmpărvăr′_, v. a. to pile

desempatar, _ĕmpătăr′_, v. a. to make unequal. [pave.

desempedrar, _ĕmpĕdrăr′_, v. a. to unpave.

desempeñar, _ĕmpĕnyăr′_, v. a. to redeem; to extricate from debt; to fulfil any duty or promise; to acquit.

desempeño, _ĕmpĕn′yŏ_, sm. redeeming a pledge; proof of an account; performance of an obligation; perfection, completion.

desemperezar, _ĕmpĕrĕthăr′_, v. n. to relinquish habits of laziness and indolence.

desempolvorar, _ĕmpŏlvŏrăr′_, v. a. to free from dust.

desemponzoñar, _ĕmpŏnthŏnyăr′_, v. a. to expel poison; to cure a disordinate passion. [a bow.

desempulgar, _ĕmpŭlgăr′_, v. a. to unbend

desenalbardar, _ĕnălbărdăr′_, v. a. to take off a pack-saddle. [love.

desenamorar, _ĕnămŏrăr′_, v. a. to destroy

desencabalgar, _ĕnkăbălgăr′_, v. a. (mil.) to dismount cannon.

desencabestrar, _ĕnkăbĕstrăr′_, v. a. to disentangle a beast from the halter.

desencadenar, _ĕnkădĕnăr′_, v. a. to unchain; to dissolve all connection or obligation. [thing out of its place.

desencajar, _ĕnkă′hăr′_, v. a. to take a (lesencajonar, _ĕnkă′hŏnăr′_, v. a. to take out of a box.

desencalabrinar, _ĕnkălăbrĭnăr′_, v. a. to remove dizziness. [stranded vessel.

desencallar, _ĕnkălyăr′_, v. a. to float a

desencaminar, _ĕnkămĭnăr′_, v. a. to lose one's way, to go astray. [chant.

desencantar, _ĕnkăntăr′_, v. a. to disenchant

desencantarar, _ĕnkăntărăr′_, v. a. to draw by lot the names of persons for office. [ment.

desencanto, _ĕnkăn′tŏ_, sm. disenchant-

desencapotar, _ĕnkăpŏtăr′_, v. a. to strip of one's cloak; to uncover; to make manifest; to raise and keep up the head of a horse; —se, to put on a pleasing expression. [dissuade from prejudice.

desencaprichar, _ĕnkăprĭtshăr′_, v. a. to

desencerrar, _ĕnthĕrrăr′_, v. a. to free from confinement; to open, to unclose.

desenclavar, _ĕnklăvăr′_, v. a. to draw out nails; to tear from its place.

desenclavijar, _ĕnklăvĭ′hăr′_, v. a. to take out the pegs of a musical instrument.

desencoger, _ĕnkŏ′hĕr′_, v. a. to unfold; —se, to grow bold.

desencolar, _ĕnkŏlăr′_, v. a. to unglue.

desencolerizarse, _ĕnkŏlĕrĭthăr′sĕ_, v. r. to grow calm or appeased.

desenconar, _ĕnkŏnăr′_, v. a. to cure an inflammation; to appease one's passion; —se, to become milder.

desencono, _ĕnkŏ′nŏ_, sm. cooling of anger or passion. [string.

desencordar, _ĕnkŏrdăr′_, v. a. to un-

desencordelar, _ĕnkŏrdĕlăr′_, v. a. to untie, to take away ropes. [straighten.

desencorvar, _ĕnkŏrvăr′_, v. a. to

desendemoniar, _ĕndĕmŏnĭăr′_, desendiablar, _ĕndĭăblăr′_, v. a. to exorcise.

desenfadado, da, _ĕnfădă′dŏ_, a. free, unembarrassed; gay; wide, spacious.

desenfadar, _ĕnfădăr′_, v. a. to assuage anger; to appease passion.

desenfado, _ĕnfă′dŏ_, sm. ease; facility; calmness, relaxation.

desenfaldar, _ĕnfăldăr′_, v. a. to let fall the train of a gown.

desenfangar, _ĕnfăngăr′_, v. a. to clear from mud or filth.

desenfardar, _ĕnfărdăr′_, desenfardelar, _ĕnfărdĕlăr′_, v. a. to open bales of goods. [the monastic life.

desenfrailar, _ĕnfrăĭlăr′_, v. n. to leave

desenfrenado, da, _ĕnfrĕnă′dŏ_, a. outrageous; ungovernable.

desenfrenar, _ĕnfrĕnăr′_, v. a. to unbridle; —se, to give full play to one's passions; to fly into a violent passion.

desenfreno, _ĕnfrĕ′nŏ_, sm. licentiousness.

desenfundar, _ĕnfŭndăr′_, v. a. to take out of a bag, pillow-case.

desenfurecerse, _ĕnfŭrĕthĕr′sĕ_, v. r. to grow calm; to lay aside anger and passion. [hook.

desenganchar, _ĕngăntshăr′_, v. a. to un-

desengañado, da, _ĕngănyă′dŏ_, a. undeceived; despicable, ill-executed.

desengañar, –ĕngănyăr', |v. a. to unde-ceive, to free from error, to disabuse, to free from a mistake, to set right.

desengaño, –ĕngăn'yŏ, sm. undeception; naked truth; reproach, upbraiding.

desengarzar, –ĕngărthăr', v.a. to unravel.

desengastar, –ĕngăstăr', v. a. to take a diamond out of a ring [out the grease.

desengrasar, –ĕngrăsăr', v. a. to take

desengrosar, –ĕngrŏsăr', v. a. to ex-tenuate, to make lean. [off the paste.

desengrudar, –ĕngrŭdăr', v. a. to scrape

desenhebrar, –ĕnhĕbrăr', v. a. to un-thread; to unravel. [harness horses.

desenjaezar, –ĕn'hăĕthăr', v. a. to un-

desenjalmar, –ĕn'hălmăr', v. a. to take off a pack-saddle from a beast of burden.

desenjaular, –ĕnjăŭlăr', v. a. to let loose out of a cage. [chain, to unlink.

desenlabonar, –ĕnlăbŏnăr', v. a. to un-

desenlace, –ĕnlă'thĕ, sm. climax of a dramatic poem; end of an affair.

desenladrillar, –ĕnlădrĭlyăr', v.a. to take up floor-tiles. [to distinguish.

desenlazar, –ĕnlăthăr', v. a. to unlace;

desenlosar, –ĕnlŏsăr', v. a. to unpave.

desenlutar, –ĕnlŭtăr', v. a. to leave off mourning; to banish sorrow.

desenmarañar, –ĕnmărănyăr', v. a. to disentangle.

desenmudecer, –ĕnmŭdĕthĕr', v. a. to re-move an impediment of speech; to break a long silence.

desenojar, –ĕnŏ'hăr', v. a. to appease; –se, to amuse one's self. [anger.

desenojo, –ĕnŏ'hŏ, sm. abatement of

desenredar, –ĕnrĕdăr', v.a.to disentangle; –se, to extricate one's self.

desenrizar, –ĕnrĭthăr', v. a. to uncurl.

desenrollar, –ĕnrŏlyăr', v. a. to unroll.

desenroscar, –ĕnrŏskăr', v. a. to untwist, to unroll. [to unravel.

desensartar, –ĕnsărtăr', v.a. to unthread;

desensillar, –ĕnsĭlyăr', v. a. to unsaddle.

desensoberbecerse, –ĕnsŏbĕrbĕthĕr'sĕ, v. r. to moderate one's pride. [of joint.

desensortijado, da, –ĕnsŏrtĭhă'dŏ,a.out

desentablar, –ĕntăblăr', v. a. to rip off planks; to disturb; to embroil; to inter-rupt a friendly intercourse.

desentenderse, –ĕntĕndĕr'sĕ, v. r. to feign not to understand; to pass by without noticing. [disinterment.

desenterramiento, –ĕntĕrrămĭĕn'tŏ, sm.

desenterrar, –ĕntĕrrăr', v. a. to disinter, to unbury; to recall to memory things for-gotten.

desentoldar, –ĕntŏldăr', v. a. to take away an awning; to strip a thing of its ornaments. [nance.

desentonación, –ĕntŏnăthĭŏn', sf. disso-

desentonar, –ĕntŏnăr', v.a.&n.to humble; to be out of tune; –se, to raise the voice disrespectfully.

desentono, –ĕntŏ'nŏ, sm. disharmony; rude tone of voice. [screw.

desentornillar, –ĕntŏrnĭlyăr', v. a. to un-

desentorpecer, –ĕntŏrpĕthĕr', v. a. to free from torpor; –se, to become lively, smart or pert.

desentrañar, –ĕntrănyăr', v. a. to gut, to eviscerate; to go into a matter very deeply; –se, to give away all one's fortune for love.

desentristecer, –ĕntrĭstĕthĕr', v. a. to banish sadness and grief.

desentronizar, –ĕntrŏnĭthăr', v. a. to de-throne; to deprive of authority.

desentumecer, –ĕntŭmĕthĕr', v. a. to re-store motion to torpid limbs.

desenvainar, –ĕnvăĭnăr', v. a. to un-sheath; to bring to light; to stretch out the claws. [from poison.

desenvenenar, –ĕnvĕnĕnăr', v. a. to cure

desenvergar, –ĕnvĕrgăr', v. a. to unbend a sail.

desenvoltura, –ĕnvŏltŭ'ră, sf. sprightli-ness; cheerfulness; impudence, boldness; lewd posture or gesture; graceful, easy delivery of one's sentiments and thoughts.

desenvolver, –ĕnvŏlvĕr', v. a. to unfold, to unroll; to decipher, to unravel; –se, to be forward. [licentious.

desenvuelto, ta, –ĕnvŭĕl'tŏ, a. forward;

deseo, dĕsĕ'ŏ, sm. desire, wish.

deseoso, sa, dĕsĕŏ'sŏ, a. desirous.

deserción, dĕsĕrthĭŏn', sf. desertion.

desertar, dĕsĕrtăr', v. a. to desert, to for-sake one's colours or post; (law) to aban-don a cause.

desertor, dĕsĕrtŏr', sm. deserter, fugitive.

deservicio, dĕsĕrvĭ'thĭŏ, sm. disservice.

deservir, dĕsĕrvĭr', v. a. to disserve, not to perform one's duty.

deseslabonar, dĕsĕslăbŏnăr', v. a. to cut the links of a chain.

desesperación, dĕsĕspĕrăthĭŏn', sf. despair, desperation; anger, fury, [hopeless.

desesperado, da, –ĕspĕră'dŏ, a. desperate,

desesperanzar, –ĕspĕrănthăr', v. a. to de-prive of hope; to make desperate.

desesperar, –ĕspĕrăr', v. n. to despair; –, v. a. to make desperate.

desestera, –ĕstĕră', v. a. to take away the mats from a room.

desestimación, –ĕstĭmăthĭŏn', sf. dis-esteem, crying down. [to contemn.

desestimar, –ĕstĭmăr', v. a. to disregard,

desfajar, –făjăr', v. a. to ungird.

desfalcar, –fălkăr', v. a. to cut off, to lop off; to dissuade from an undertaking.

desfalco, –făl'kŏ, sm. diminution, deduc-tion. [fall away; –, v. a. to weaken.

desfallecer, –fălyĕthĕr', v. n. to pine, to

desfallecimiento, –fălyĕthĭmĭĕn'tŏ, sm. languor, fainting.

desfavorecer, –făvŏrĕthĕr', v. a. to dis-favour; to contemn; to injure, to hurt; to contradict, to oppose.

desfigurar, –fĭgŭrăr', v. a. to disfigure, to deform; to disguise; –se, to be dis-figured by passion. [move.

desfijar, –fĭhăr', v. a. to unsettle, to re-

desfilar, –fĭlăr', v. n. (mil.) to defile.

desflemar, –flĕmăr', v. a. to clear from phlegm.

desfloración, –flŏrăthĭŏn', sf. defloration.

desflorar, *—flŏrăr,* v. a. to pull or pluck the flowers in a garden; to deflower; to tarnish.

desflorecer, *—flŏrĕthĕr,* v. n. to wither.

desfogar, *—fŏgăr,* v. a. to make an opening for the fire; to give vent to the violence of passion; to moderate passion or desire; —se, to give vent to one's passion or anger.

desfogue, *—fŏ'gĕ,* sm. venting of one's passion.

desfondar, *—fŏndăr,* v. a. to break the bottom of any vessel; to penetrate the bottom of a ship.

desfortalecer, *—fŏrtălĕthĕr,* v. a. to demolish the works of a fortress.

desgajar, *—gă'hăr,* v. a. to lop off the branches of trees; to break in pieces; —se, to be separated; to be torn in pieces.

desgalgadero, *—gălgădĕ'rŏ,* sm. rugged declivitous place.

desgalgar, *—gălgăr,* v. a. to precipitate.

desgana, *—gă'nă,* sf. disgust, want of appetite; aversion, reluctance.

desganar, *—gănăr,* v. a. to deprive of the pleasure of doing something; —se, to lose all pleasure in doing a thing; to lose one's appetite.   [branches of trees.

desganchar, *—gănthăr,* v. a. to lop off

desgañifarse, *—gănyĭfăr'sĕ,* **desgañitarse,** *—tăr'sĕ,* v. r. to scream, to bawl.

desgargantarse, *—gărgăntăr'sĕ,* v. r. to become hoarse by bawling.

desgargolar, *—gărgŏlăr,* v. a. to shed the seed.   [the course.

desgaritar, *—gărĭtăr,* v. n. (mar.) to lose

desgarrado, da, *—gărră'dŏ,* a. licentious, dissolute.

desgarrar, *—gărrăr,* v. a. to rend, to tear; —se, to withdraw, to retire.

desgarro, *—găr'rŏ,* sm. rent, breach; impudence; idle boast; ogling.

desgarrón, *—gărrŏn',* sm. large rent; piece of cloth torn off.

desgastar, *—găstăr,* v. a. to consume, to waste; to corrode; —se, to weaken one's self.   [scream.

desgaznatarse, *—găthnătăr'sĕ,* v. r. to

desglosar, *—glŏsăr,* v. a. to scratch out MS. notes or remarks.   [comment.

desglose, *—glŏ'sĕ,* sm. erasure of a note or

desgobernar, *—gŏbĕrnăr,* v. a. to disturb the order of government; to misgovern; to dislocate; to bar a vein on a horse's leg; to steer an unsteady course; —se, to affect ridiculous motions in dancing.

desgobierno, *—gŏbĭĕr'nŏ,* sm. misgovernment, mismanagement.

desgonzar, *—gŏnthăr,* v. a. to separate; to unhinge; to disjoint.

desgoznar, *—gŏthnăr,* v. a. to unhinge; —se, to distort the body with violent motions.   [grace; enmity; unpleasantness.

desgracia, *—gră'thĭă,* sf. misfortune, disgrace; ungrateful.

desgraciado, da, *—grăthĭă'dŏ,* a. unfortunate, unhappy, miserable; out of favour; disagreeable; ungrateful.

desgraciarse, *—grăthĭăr'sĕ,* v. r. to fall out with; to be out of order; to degenerate.

desgramar, *—grămăr,* v. a. to pluck up grasses; to husk.

desgranar, *—grănăr,* v. a. to shake out the grain from the ears of corn; to scatter about; —se, to wear away (of the touchhole of a fire-arm).   [hair; to disorder.

desgreñar, *—grĕnyăr,* v. a. to dishevel the

desguarnecer, *—gŭărnĕthĕr,* v. a. to strip clothes of trimmings and other ornaments; to deprive a thing of its strength; to disgarnish.   [timber.

desguazar, *—gŭăthăr,* v. a. to cut asunder

desguindar, *—gĭndăr,* v. a. (mar.) to take and bring down; —se, to slide down by a rope.   [in paper-mills.

desguinzar, *—gĭnthăr,* v. a. to cut rags

deshabitado, da, *—ăbĭtă'dŏ,* a. deserted, uninhabited, desolate.

deshabitar, *—ăbĭtăr,* v. a. to quit one's habitation; to unpeople.

deshabituar, *—ăbĭtŭăr,* v. a. to disaccustom.   [vios, avenger of injuries.

deshacedor, *—ăthĕdŏr,* sm. — de agra-

deshacer, *—ăthĕr,* v. a. to undo, to destroy; to cancel, to efface; to rout an army; to spend profusely; to melt; to cut up, to divide; to dissolve in a liquid; to violate a treaty; to diminish; to disband troops; —se, to grieve, to mourn; to excuse one's self; to disappear; to do a thing with vehemence; to mollify; to grow feeble or meagre.

deshalajar, *—ălă'hăr,* v. a. to unfurnish.

desharrapado, da, *—ărră̆pă'dŏ,* a. shabby, ragged, in tatters.

deshebillar, *—ĕbĭlyăr,* v. a. to unbuckle.

deshebrar, *—ĕbrăr,* v. a. to unthread; to divide into filaments; (fig.) to shed a flood of tears.

deshecha, *—ĕtsh'ă,* sf. simulation, fiction; genteel farewell; burden of a song.

deshechizar, *—ĕtshĭthăr,* v. a. to disenchant.   [ment.

deshechizo, *—ĕtshĭ'thŏ,* sm. disenchant-

deshecho, cha, *—ĕtsh'ŏ,* a. undone, destroyed, wasted; melted, in pieces; perfectly mixed (of colours); borrasca -a, violent tempest.   [thaw, to melt.

deshelar, *—ĕlăr,* v. a. to thaw; —se, to

desherbar, *—ĕrbăr,* v. a. to weed.

desheredamiento, *—ĕrĕdămĭĕn'tŏ,* sm. disinheriting.   [—se, to degenerate.

desheredar, *—ĕrĕdăr,* v. a. to disinherit;

deshermanar, *—ĕrmănăr,* v. a. to remove the likeness or similarity of things; —se, to fall out or quarrel with one's brother.

desherrar, *—ĕrrăr,* v. a. to unchain; to rip off the shoes of horses.

deshielo, *—ĭĕ'lŏ,* sm. thaw.   [unweave.

deshilachar, *—ĭlătshăr,* v. a. to ravel, to

deshilado, *—ĭlă'dŏ,* sm. open-work; —, da, a. marching in file.

deshilar, *—ĭlăr,* v. a. to ravel; to convert into lint; to distract bees in order to get them into a new hive.

deshilo, *—ĭsĕ'lŏ,* sm. obstructing the communication of bees, to get them into a new hive.

deshincar, –ĭnkăr´, v. a. to draw out a nail; to tear up what is nailed fast.

deshinchar, –ĭntshăr´, v. a. to reduce a swelling; to explain the cause of one's displeasure; –se, to be removed (applied to a swelling); to abate presumption.

deshojar, –ŏ´hăr´, v. a. to strip off the leaves.   [pare.

deshollejar, –ŏlyĕ´hăr´, v. a. to peel, to

deshollinador, –ŏlyĭnădŏr´, sm. chimney-sweeper, sweep; scraper for sweeping chimneys; (fig.) a careful examiner.

deshollinar, –ŏlyĭnăr´, v. a. to sweep chimneys; to clean what is dirty; to change clothes; to view and examine with careful attention.

deshonestidad, –ŏnĕstĭdăd´, sf. immodesty, indecency; lewdness.

deshonesto, ta, –nĕs´tŏ, a. immodest; lewd; unreasonable.

deshonor, –ŏnŏr´, sm. dishonour; insult.

deshonorar, –ŏnŏrăr´, v. a. to deprive of an office or employ.   [tion of a woman.

deshonra, dĕsŏn´ră, sf. dishonour; seduc-

deshonrabuenos, –ŏnrăbŭĕ´nŏs, sm. calumniator, libeller; he who degenerates from his ancestors.

deshonrar, –ŏnrăr´, v. a. to affront, to insult, to defame; to dishonour; to deflower a woman.   [able, indecent.

deshonroso, sa, –ŏnrŏ´sŏ, a. dishonour-

deshora, dĕsŏ´ră, sf. unseasonable time.

deshuesar, –hŭĕsăr´, v. a. to rid of bones.

deshumedecer, –ŭmĕdĕthĕr´, v. a. to deprive of humidity; –se, to grow dry.

desidia, dĕsĭ´dĭă, sf. idleness, indolence.

desidioso, sa, –sĭ´ŏsŏ, a. lazy, idle.

desierto, ta, dĕsĭĕr´tŏ, a. deserted, solitary; –, sm. desert, wilderness.   [tion.

designación, –sĭgnăthĭŏn´, sf. designa-

designar, –sĭgnăr´, v. a. to design, to intend; to appoint; to express, to name.

designio, dĕsĭg´nĭŏ, sm. design, purpose, road, course,   [uneven, craggy, cliffy.

desigual, dĕsĭgăăl´, a. unequal, unlike;

desigualar, –găălăr´, v. a. to make unequal or dissimilar; –se, to excel, to surpass.

desigualdad, –ĭgăăldăd´, sf. inequality, dissimilitude; inconstancy; knottiness, unevenness.   [undeceive.

desimpresionar, –ĭmprĕsĭŏnăr´, v. a. to

desinclinar, –ĭnklĭnăr´, v. a. to desincline.

desinfección, –ĭnfĕkthĭŏn´, sf. disinfection.   [infect.

desinficionar, –ĭnfĭthĭŏnăr´, v. a. to dis-

desinflamar, –ĭnflămăr´, v. a. to cure an inflammation.   [ness.

desinterés, –ĭntĕrĕs´, sm. disinterested-

desinteresado, da, –ĭntĕrĕsă´dŏ, a. disinterested.

desistir, dĕsĭstĭr´, v. n. to desist, to cease.

desjarretadera, dĕs´hărrĕtădĕ´ră, sf. hooked knife for houghing cattle.

desjarretar, –hărrĕtăr´, v. a. to hough, to hamstring; to deprive one of the means of making a fortune; to bleed to excess.

deslamar, –lămăr´, v. a. to clear of mud.

deslastrar, –lăstrăr´, v. a. to unballast a ship.   [barefaced.

deslavado, da, –lăvă´dŏ, a. impudent,

deslavadura, –lăvădŏ´ră, sf. washing.

deslavar, –lăvăr´, v. a. to wash superficially.

deslazar, –lăthăr´, v. a. to unlace.

desleal, –lĕăl´, a. disloyal; perfidious.

deslealtad, –lĕăltăd´, sf. disloyalty, breach of faith.   [the branches of vines.

deslechugar, –lĕtshŭgăr´, v. a. to prune

desleir, –lĕĭr´, v. a. to dilute, to dissolve.

deslenguado, da, –lĕngŭă´dŏ, a. foulmouthed, free-tongued.

deslenguar, –lĕngăr´, v. a. to cut out the tongue; –se, to slander.

desliar, –lĭăr´, v. a. to untie.

desligar, –lĭgăr´, v. a. to loosen, to unbind; (fig.) to explain.   [limits.

deslindar, –lĭndăr´, v. a. to mark the

deslinde, –lĭn´dĕ, sm. demarcation.

desliz, –lĭth´, sm. slip, sliding; (fig.) slip, weakness.   [place.

deslizadero, –lĭthădĕ´rŏ, sm. slippery

deslizadizo, za, –lĭthădĭ´thŏ, a. slippery, slippy, glib; lubricous.

deslizar, –lĭthăr´, v. n. to slip, to slide; to speak carelessly, to go too far in conversation.

deslomar, –lŏmăr´, v. a. to break the back, to distort the loins, to chine.

deslucimiento, –lŭthĭmĭĕn´tŏ, sm. disgrace, dishonour.

deslucir, –lŭthĭr´, v. a. to tarnish the lustre; to obscure one's merit.

deslumbramiento, –lŭmbrămĭĕn´tŏ,

deslumbre, –lŭm´brĕ, sm. overpowering lustre; dazzling.   [to puzzle.

deslumbrar, –lŭmbrăr´, v. a. to dazzle;

deslustrar, –lŭstrăr´, v. a. to tarnish; to obscure; to blast one's reputation.

deslustre, dĕslŭs´trĕ, sm. spot which obscures the lustre; disgrace, ignominy.

deslustroso, sa, –lŭstrŏ´sŏ, a. unbecoming, ugly.   [sm. languishment.

desmadejamiento, –mădĕhămĭĕn´tŏ,

desmadejar, –mădĕhăr´, v. a. to enervate, to produce languor.   [misconduct.

desmán, dĕsmăn´, sm. misfortune, disaster;

desmandar, –măndăr´, v. a. to countermand; to revoke a legacy; –se, to disband; to stray from the flock.

desmangar, –măngăr´, v. a. to take off the handle of any thing.

desmanotado, da, –mănŏtă´dŏ, a. unhandy, awkward.   [ruinous, dilapidated.

desmantelado, da, –măntĕlă´dŏ, a.

desmantelar, –măntĕlăr´, v. a. to dismantle; to abandon, to forsake; (mar.) to unmast.   [tangle.

desmarañar, –mărănyăr´, v. a. to disen-

desmayado, da, –măyă´dŏ, a. pale, wan; dismayed, appalled.

desmayar, –măyăr´, v. n. to be dispirited or faint-hearted; –, v. a. to dismay, to dispirit; –se, to faint.

desmayo, —ma'yŏ, sm. swoon; dismay.

desmedido, da, —mĕdĭ'dŏ, a. unproportionable. [all measure.

desmedirse, —mĕdĭr'sĕ, v. r. to be beyond

desmedrar, —mĕdrăr', v. n. to decrease, to decay; —, v. a. to deteriorate.

desmejorar, —mĕ'hŏrăr', v. a. to debase, to make worse.

desmelenar, —mĕlĕnăr', v. a. to dishevel.

desmembración, —mĕmbrăthĭŏn', sf. dismemberment.

desmembrar, —mĕmbrăr', v. a. to dismember; to curtail; to separate.

desmentida, —mĕntĭ'dă, sf. giving the lie.

desmentir, —mĕntĭr', v. a. to give the lie.

desmenuzar, —mĕnŭthăr', v. a. to crumble, to chip, to fritter; to examine minutely.

desmeollar, —mĕŏlyăr', v. a. to take out the marrow.

desmerecer, —mĕrĕthĕr', v. a. to demerit.

desmerecimiento, —mĕrĕthĭmĭĕn'tŏ, sm. demerit, ill desert.

desmesurado, da, —mĕsŭră'dŏ, a. excessive; huge; immeasurable.

desmesurar, —mĕsŭrăr', v. a. to perturbate, to put out; to put out of order; —se, to talk impudently, to forget one's self. [to break into bits.

desmigajar, —mĭgă'hăr', v. a. to crumble.

desmigar, —mĭgăr', v. a. to crumble bread into small pieces. [mutilate.

desmochar, —mŏtshăr', v. a. to lop; to

desmoche, —mŏtsh'ĕ, sm. mutilation.

desmontar, —mŏntăr', v. a. to cut down wood; to remove a heap of rubbish; to uncock fire-arms; to dismount a troop of horse; to dismount cannon; —, v. n. to dismount, to alight from a horse, &c.

desmonte, —mŏn'tĕ, sm. felling; clearing a wood. [demoralisation.

desmoralización, —mŏrălĭthăthĭŏn', sf.

desmoralizar, —mŏrălĭthăr', v. a. to demoralise.

desmoronadizo, za, —mŏrŏnădĭ'thŏ, a. delapidated, ruinous, rickety.

desmoronar, —mŏrŏnăr', v. a. to destroy little by little.

desmullir, —mŭlyĭr', v. a. to press together a loose object. [less.

desnarigado, da, —nărĭgă'dŏ, a. nose-

desnarigar, —nărĭgăr', v. a. to cut off the nose. [to take the choicest part.

desnatar, —nătăr', v. a. to skim milk;

desnaturalizar, —nătŭrălĭthăr', v. a. to divest of naturalisation rights; —se, to forsake one's country. [solve.

desnevar, —nĕvăr', v. a. to thaw, to dis-

desnivel, —nĭvĕl', sm. unevenness of the ground. [neck.

desnucar, —nŭkăr', v. a. to break one's

desnudar, —nŭdăr', v. a. to denude, to strip of clothes; to discover, to reveal; —se, to undress.

desnudez, —nŭdĕth', sf. nakedness.

desnudo, da, —nŏ'dŏ, a. naked, bare, uncovered; ill clothed; (fig.) plain, evident.

desobedecer, —ŏbĕĭĕthĕr', v. a. to disobey.

desobediencia, —ŏbĕdĭĕn'thĭă, sf. disobedience; insubordination.

desobediente, —ŏbĕdĭĕn'tĕ, a. disobedient.

desocupación, —ŏkŭpăthĭŏn', sf. leisure, want of occupation.

desocupar, —ŏkŭpăr', v. a. to quit, to empty; —se, to retire from a business; to withdraw from an arrangement.

desoir, —ŏĭr', v. a. to pretend not to hear.

desojar, —ŏ'hăr', v. a. to break the eye of a needle &c.; —se, to strain the sight by looking steadfastly at a thing.

desolación, dĕsŏlăthĭŏn', sf. destruction; affliction. [consolate.

desolado, da, —sŏlă'dŏ, a. desolate, disolar, —sŏlăr', v. a. to lay waste; to harass.

desoldar, —sŏldăr', v. a. to unsolder.

desollada, —sŏlyă'dă, sf. strumpet.

desolladero, —sŏlyădĕ'rŏ, sm. slaughterhouse. [insolent, saucy.

desollado, da, —sŏlyă'dŏ, a. impudent,

desollar, —sŏlyăr', v. a. to flay, to skin; (fig.) to extort an immoderate price.

desorden, dĕsŏr'dĕn, sm. disorder, confusion. [orderly, disordinate.

desordenado, da, —ŏrdĕnă'dŏ, a. disordenar, —ŏrdĕnăr', v. a. to disorder; —se, to get out of order.

desorejar, —ŏrĕ'hăr', v. a. to crop the ears.

desorganización, —ŏrgănĭthăthĭŏn', sf. disorganization. [organize.

desorganizar, —ŏrgănĭthăr', v. a. to disorillar, —ŏrĭlyăr', v. a. to cut off the selvage of cloth.

desovar, —ŏvăr', v. n. to spawn.

desove, dĕsŏ'vĕ, sm. spawning; spawn.

desovillar, —ŏvĭlyăr', v. a. to follow or develop a clew. [snuffers.

despabiladeras, dĕspăbĭlădĕ'răs, sf. pl.

despabilado, da, —păbĭlă'dŏ, a. watchful, vigilant (in the time for sleeping).

despabilador, —păbĭlădŏr', sm. candlesnuffer. [the candle,

despabiladura, —păbĭlădŭ'ră, sf. snuff of

despabilar, —păbĭlăr', v. a. to snuff a candle; (fig.) to despatch briefly; —se, to rouse.

despacio, dĕspă'thĭŏ, ad. slowly, leisurely; little by little; ¡—! softly! gently!

despacito, —păthĭ'tŏ, ad. gently, leisurely; ¡—! wait a bit!

despachaderas, —pătshădĕ'răs, sf. pl. surly words in answer.

despachar, —pătshăr', v. a. to despatch; to expedite; —se, to make haste.

despacho, dĕspătsh'ŏ, sm. despatch, expedition; cabinet; office; counting-house; commission; warrant, patent; expedient; a smart answer.

despachurrar, —tshŭrrăr', v. a. to squash, to crush; to mangle a speech.

despaldillar, dĕspăldĭlyăr', v. a. to dislocate the shoulder.

despalmante, dĕspălmăn'tĕ, sm. (cant) [robber.

despalmar, —pălmăr', v. a. to clean and calk the bottoms of ships; to pare off a horse's hoof.

despampanar, –pămpănăr´, v. a. to prune the shoots of vines; (fig.) to uubosom.

desparejar, –părĕ´hăr´, v. a. to make unequal or uneven.

desparpajar, –părpă´hăr´, v. a. to undo in a disorderly manner; to prattle at random.   [speech or action.

desparpajo, –părpă´h´ŏ, sm. pertness of

desparramar, –părrămăr´, v. a. to disseminate, to overspread; to squander, to lavish; –se, to be dissipated.

despartir, –părtĭr´, v. a. to divide; to conciliate.

desparvar, –părvăr´, v. a. to take the sheaves of corn out of the stack to be thrashed.

despatarrarse, –pătărrăr´sĕ, v. r. to fall on the ground with the legs wide spread.

despavesar, –păvĕsăr´, v. a. to snuff the candle.

despavorido, –păvŏrĭ´dŏ, a. frightened.

despeadura, –pĕădŏ´ră, sf. foundering.

despear, –pĕăr´, v. a. to founder; –se, v. n. to surbate.

despechar, –pĕtshăr´, v. a. to enrage, to excite indignation; to overwhelm with taxes; –se, to despair.

despecho, dĕspĕtsh´ŏ, sm. indignation, displeasure; wrath; harshness of temper; despite, spite; dismay, despair; disrespect, insolence; deceit; derision, scorn; á –, in spite of.

despechugar, –pĕtshăgăr´, v. a. to cut off the breast of a fowl; –se, to uncover the breast; to walk with the breast open.

despedazar, –pĕdăthăr´, v. a. to tear into pieces, to cut asunder; to mangle; –se de risa, to burst into fits of laughter.

despedida, –pĕdĕ´dă, sf. farewell.

despedir, –pĕdĭr´, v. a. to discharge, to dart; to dismiss from office; –se, to take leave.   [sour of temper.

despegado, da, –pĕgă´dŏ, a. rough, sullen.

despegar, –pĕgăr´, v. a. to unglue; –se, to withdraw one's affection.

despego, dĕspĕ´gŏ, sm. asperity; want of love, coolness.   [hair.

despeinar, –pĕĭnăr´, v. a. to entangle the

despejado, da, –pĕ´hă´dŏ, a. sprightly, quick, sagacious; clear.

despejar, –pĕ´hăr´, v. a. to clear away obstructions; –se, to cheer up; to amuse one's self; to become clear weather.

despejo, dĕspĕ´h´ŏ, sm. removal of obstacles; sprightliness; grace.

despeluzar, –pĕlŭthăr´, v. a. to make the hair stand on end; –se, to stand erect.

despellejar, –pĕlyĕ´hăr´, v. a. to skin.

despensa, dĕspĕn´să, sf. pantry, larder; provisions, pl.

despensero, ra, –pĕnsă´rŏ, sm. & f. butler, caterer; steward on board ship; distributer.

despeñadero, –pĕnyădă´rŏ, sm. precipice; (fig.) bold and dangerous undertaking.

despeñar, –pĕnyăr´, v. a. to precipitate; –se, to throw one's self headlong.

despeño, dĕspĕn´yŏ, sm. precipitate fall; flux of the belly.

despepitarse, –pĕpĭtăr´sĕ, v. r. to vociferate; to act imprudently.

desperdiciador, ra, –pĕrdĕthăădŏr´, sm. & f. spendthrift, squanderer.   [squander.

desperdiciar, –pĕrdĭthăăr´, v. a. to squander.

desperdicio, –pĕrdă´thĭŏ, sm. prodigality, profusion; residuum, remains.

desperdigar, –pĕrdĭgăr´, v. a. to separate, to scatter.

desperezarse, –pĕrĕthăr´sĕ, v. r. to stretch oneself on being roused from sleep.

despernado, da, –pĕrnă´dŏ, a. weary, tired.   [legs.

despernar, –pĕrnăr´, v. a. to break one's

despertar, –pĕrtăr´, v. a. to awaken, to rouse from sleep; to excite; –, v. n. to wake up; to grow lively or sprightly.

despierto, ta, dĕspĭer´tŏ, a. awake; vigilant; fierce; brisk, sprightly.

despilfarrar, –pĭlfărrăr´, v. a. to waste through slovenliness.

despilfarro, –pĭlfăr´rŏ, sm. slovenliness; waste; mismanagement.

despintar, –pĭntăr´, v. a. to efface a painting; to obscure things; to mislead; –, v. n. to degenerate; –se, to be deceived by mistaking one card for another.

despinzar, –pĭnthăr´, v. a. to nap cloth.

despinzas, dĕspĭn´thăs, sf. pl. tweezers, pincers.   [to relieve from misery.

despiojar, –pĭŏ´hăr´, v. a. to louse; (fig.)

despique, dĕspĕ´kĕ, sm. vengeance, revenge.

desplantar, –plăntăr´, v. a. to eradicate; to transplant; –se, to lose one's erect posture (in fencing or dancing).

desplante, dĕsplăn´tĕ, sm. oblique posture in fencing.   [tion, unfolding.

desplegadura, –plĕgădŏ´ră, sf. explica-

desplegar, –plĕgăr´, v. a. to unfold, to display; to explain; to elucidate; (mar.) to unfurl; –se, to blow, to open.

desplomar, –plŏmăr´, v. a. to make a wall bulge out; –se, to bulge out; to fall flat to the ground.   [wall.

desplomo, dĕsplŏ´mŏ, sm. jutting out of a

desplumar, –plŭmăr´, v. a. to deplume, to strip off feathers; (fig.) to despoil of one's property.   [lation.

despoblación, –pŏblăthĭŏn´, sf. depopu-

despoblado, –pŏblă´dŏ, sm. desert.

despoblar, –pŏblăr´, v. a. to depopulate; to desolate; –se, to become depopulated.

despojar, –pŏ´hăr´, v. a. to despoil; to deprive of; –se, to undress.

despojo, dĕspŏ´h´ŏ, sm. spoliation; plunder; slough; –s, pl. giblets, wings, neck, heart, and gizzard of fowls; remains; offal.

despolvar, –pŏlvăr´, v. a. to dust.

despolvorear, –pŏlvŏrĕăr´, v. a. to brush, to dust, to beat (carpets, etc.).

desportillar, –pŏrtĭlyăr´, v. a. to break the neck of a bottle, pot.

desposado, da, –pŏsă´dŏ, a. hand-cuffed.

desposar, –pŏsăr´, v. a. to marry, to betroth; –se, to be betrothed or married.

desposeer, –pŏsĕĕr´, v. a. to dispossess.

desposeimiento, –pŏsĕĭmĭen´tŏ, sm. dispossession.

desposorio, _pōsō'rĭō_, sm. mutual promise to contract marriage.

déspota, _dĕs'pŏtä_, sm. despot.

despotado, _dĕspŏtä'dŏ_, sm. despotic government. [despotical.

despótico, ca, _dĕspŏ'tĭkŏ_, a. despotic.

despotismo, _dĕspŏtĭs'mŏ_, sm. despotism.

despreciable, _prĕthĭä'blĕ_, a. contemptible, despicable. [to despise.

despreciar, _prĕthĭär'_, v. a. to depreciate.

desprecio, _prä'thĭō_, sm. scorn, contempt.

desprender, _prĕndĕr'_, v. a. to unfasten, to loosen, to separate; -se, to give way, to fall down; to extricate oneself.

desprendimiento, _prĕndĭmĭĕn'tŏ_, sm. alienation, disinterestedness.

despreocupar, _prĕōkŭpär'_, v. a. to free from prejudice.

desprevenido, da, _prĕvĕnĭ'dŏ_, a. unprovided, unprepared.

desproporción, _prŏpōrthĭōn'_, sf. disproportion. [a. to disproportion.

desproporcionar, _prŏpōrthĭōnär'_, v.

despropósito, _prŏpō'sĭtŏ_, sm. absurdity.

desproveer, _prŏvĕĕr'_, v. a. to deprive of provisions; (mil.) to deprive of ammunition.

desprovisto, ta, _prŏvĭs'tŏ_, a. unprovided.

después, _dĕspŭĕs'_, ad. after, afterwards.

despumar, _pŭmär'_, v. a. to skim.

despuntar, _pŭntär'_, v. a. to blunt; (mar.) to double a cape; ¬ v. n. to manifest wit and genius; al — del día, at break of day. [discompose, to disorder.

desquiciar, _kĭthĭär'_, v. a. to unhinge; to desquijarar, _kĭhärär'_, v. a. to break the jaws.

desquitar, _kĭtär'_, v. a. to retrieve a loss; -se, to win one's money back again; to return by giving like for like; to take revenge. [revenge, retaliation.

desquite, _kĕ'tĕ_, sm. recovery of a loss.

desreglado, da, _rĕglä'dŏ_, a. disorderly, irregular. [lar, to be ungovernable.

desreglarse, _rĕglär'sĕ_, v. r. to be irregular.

desrizar, _rĭthär'_, v. a. to uncurl.

destacamento, _tākämĕn'tŏ_, sm. (mil.) detachment. [body of troops.

destacar, _tākär'_, v. a. (mil.) to detach (a destajar, _tähär'_, v. a. to hire or undertake work by the piece or job, to do taskwork.

destajero, _tähä'rŏ_, sm. task-worker, one who undertakes work by the job.

destajo, _tä'h'ŏ_, sm. job, undertaking work by the job. [horses' hoofs.

destalonar, _tälōnär'_, v. a. to level

destapar, _täpär'_, v. a. to uncover; -se, to be uncovered. [mud-walls.

destapiar, _täpĭär'_, v. a. to pull down

destaponar, _täpōnär'_, v. a. to uncork a bottle.

destazar, _täthär'_, v. a. to cut to pieces.

deste, ta, to, _dĕs'tĕ_, pn. contraction for de este, de esta, de esto.

destejar, _tĕhär'_, v. a. to untile; to leave a thing defenceless. [ravel.

destejer, _tĕ'hĕr'_, v. a. to unweave, to

destello, _dĕstĕl'yŏ_, sm. flowing out drop by drop; sparkle.

destemplado, da, _tĕmplä'dŏ_, a. inharmonious, incongruous (applied to paintings); intemperate.

destemplanza, _tĕmplän'thä_, sf. intemperateness; unsteadiness of the weather; disorder; alteration in the pulse.

destemplar, _tĕmplär'_, v. a. to distemper, to alter, to disconcert; to dissolve; to untune; -se, to be ruffled; to be ill with a fever; to grow blunt; to act improperly.

destemple, _tĕm'plĕ_, sm. discordance; disorder; intemperance, distemper.

desteñir, _tĕnyĭr'_, v. a. to discolour.

desterrar, _tĕrrär'_, v. a. to banish; to expel, to drive away. [wilderness.

desterradero, _tĕrrädĕ'rŏ_, sm. desert.

desterronar, _tĕrrōnär'_, v. n. to break the clods in the fields with a harrow or spade. [tate.

destetar, _tĕtär'_, v. a. to wean, to ablac-

destete, _tä'tĕ_, sm. ablactation.

destierro, _tĭĕr'rŏ_, sm. exile, banishment.

destilación, _dĕstĭläthĭōn'_, sf. distillation.

destiladera, _dĕstĭlädĕ'rä_, sf. still, alembic, filtering-stone; alembic.

destilador, _dĕstĭlädŏr'_, sm. distiller;

destilar, _dĕstĭlär'_, v. a. & n. to distil.

destilatorio, _dĕstĭlätō'rĭō_, sm. distillery; alembic. [intend for.

destinar, _dĕstĭnär'_, v. a. to destine for, to

destino, _dĕstĭ'nŏ_, sm. destiny; fate, doom; destination; office. [abandonment.

destitución, _dĕstĭtŭthĭōn'_, sf. destitution.

destituir, _dĕstĭtŭĭr'_, v. a. to deprive.

destocar, _tōkär'_, v. a. to uncoif; to uncover the head.

destorcer, _tōrthĕr'_, v. a. to untwist; to uncurl; (fig.) to arrange, to put in order; -se, (mar.) to deviate from one's course.

destornillador, _tōrnĭlyädŏr'_, sm. screwdriver. [(fig.) to act or speak rashly.

destornillar, _tōrnĭlyär'_, v. a. to unscrew;

destrabar, _trähär'_, v. a. to unfetter; (fig.) to separate.

destramar, _trämär'_, v. a. to unweave; to break off an intrigue. [tress of hair.

destrenzar, _trĕnthär'_, v. a. to undo a

destreza, _dĕstrĕ'thä_, sf. dexterity, cleverness, cunning, expertness, skill.

destripar, _trĭpär'_, v. a. to unbowel; to disembowel; to trample.

destripaterrones, _trĭpätĕrrō'nĕs_, sm. day-labourer, harrower, clod-beater.

destripular, _trĭpŭlär'_, v. a. to unrig a ship. [all the trumps at cards.

destriunfar, _trĭŭnfär'_, v. a. to extract

destrocar, _trōkär'_, v. a. to return a thing bartered.

destrón, _dĕstrōn'_, sm. blind man's guide.

destronamiento, _trōnämĭĕn'tŏ_, sm. dethronement.

destronar, _trōnär'_, v. a. to dethrone.

destroncar, _trōnkär'_, v. a. to lop, to cut short; to maim, to cut to pieces; (fig.) to ruin, to frustrate.

destrozar, _trōthär'_, v. a. to destroy, to break into pieces; (mil.) to defeat.

destrozo, –trŏ'thŏ, sm. destruction; (mil.) defeat, massacre. [ruin.

destrucción, –trŭkthŏn', sf. destruction.

destructivo, va, –trŭktŏ'vŏ, a. destructive.

destrueque, –trŭŭ'kĕ, sm. mutual restitution of things bartered or exchanged.

destruir, –trŭŏr', v. a. to destroy.

desuellacaras, dĕsŭĕllăkă'răs, sm. impudent, wicked person.

desuello, –sŭĕ'yŏ, sm. (fam.) flaying; impudence; exorbitant price.

desuncir, dĕsŭnthŏr', v. a. to unyoke.

desunión, –ŭnŏn', sf. separation, disjunction; discord, dissension.

desunir, –ŭnŏr', v. a. to separate, to disunite; to occasion discord.

desurdir, –ŭrdŏr', v. a. to unweave cloth.

desusar, –ŏsăr', v. a. to disuse.

desuso, dĕsŏ'sŏ, sm. disuse; obsoleteness.

desvahar, –văăr', v. a. to trim off the withered part of a plant. [less.

desvaído, da, –vă-ĕ'dŏ, a. tall and graceless.

desvalido, da, –vălĕ'dŏ, a. helpless, destitute.

desván, dĕsvăn', sm. garret. [stitute.

desvanecer, –vănĕthĕr', v. n. to divide into imperceptible parts; to cause to vanish; to undo, to remove; to swell with pride; –se, to grow vapid, to become insipid; to vanish; to be affected with giddiness.

desvanecido, –vănĕthĕ'dŏ, a. giddy; proud.

desvanecimiento, –vănĕthĭmĭĕn'tŏ, sm. pride, haughtiness; giddiness; swoon.

desvarío, –vărĕ'ŏ, sm. delirium; giddiness; inconstancy, caprice; extravagance.

desvedar, –vĕdăr', v. a. to revoke a prohibition against a thing.

desvelar, –vĕlăr', v. a. to keep awake; –se, to be watchful. [watchfulness.

desvelo, dĕsvĕ'lŏ, sm. want of sleep;

desvenar, –vĕnăr', v. a. to clear the veins of flesh; to extract from the veins of mines.

desvencijar, –vĕnthĭ-hăr', v. a. to disunite, to weaken, to divide; –se, to be ruptured; to be relaxed. [bandage.

desvendar, –vĕndăr', v. a. to take off a bandage.

desventaja, –vĕntă'hă, sf. disadvantage, damage. [calamity.

desventura, –vĕntŏ'ră, sf. misfortune.

desventurado, da, –vĕntŏră'dŏ, a. unfortunate, calamitous.

desvergonzado, da, –vĕrgŏnthă'dŏ, a. impudent, shameless.

desvergonzarse, –vĕrgŏnthăr'sĕ, v. r. to speak in an impudent manner.

desvergüenza, –vĕrgŭĕn'thă, sf. impudence; shameless word.

desviar, –vĭăr', v. a. to divert from the right way; to dissuade; to parry (at fencing).

desvío, dĕsvĕ'ŏ, sm. turning away, going astray; aversion; disdain; indifference.

desvirar, –vĭrăr', v. a. to pare off the superfluous part of a sole.

desvirtuar, –vĭrtŏăr', v. a. to rob of virtue or strength.

detal, dĕtăl', (en –), ad. in detail; minutely.

detallar, dĕtăllăr', v. a. to detail, to relate minutely.

detalle, dĕtăl'yĕ, sm. detail.

detallista, –yĭs'tă, sm. retailer. [delay.

detención, dĕtĕnthŏn', sf. detention;

detener, dĕtĕnĕr', v. a. to stop, to detain; to arrest; to keep back; to reserve; to withhold; –se, to tarry, to stay.

detenido, da, dĕtĕnĕ'dŏ, a. sparing, niggardly; slow, inactive.

detentar, dĕtĕntăr', v. a. to detain.

deterioración, dĕtĕrĭŏrăthŏn', sf. deterioration, damage.

deteriorar, dĕtĕrĭŏrăr', v. a. to deteriorate.

deterioro, dĕtĕrĭŏ'rŏ, sm. deterioration.

determinación, dĕtĕrmĭnăthŏn', sf. determination, resolution; boldness.

determinado, da, –nă'dŏ, a. determinate; resolute. [mine.

determinar, dĕtĕrmĭnăr', v. a. to determine.

determinativo, va, –nătĕ'vŏ, a. determinative. [crable.

detestable, dĕtĕstă'blĕ, a. detestable, execrable.

detestación, dĕtĕstăthŏn', sf. detestation, abomination. [hor.

detestar, dĕtĕstăr', v. a. to detest, to abhor.

detonación, dĕtŏnăthŏn', sf. detonation.

detractar, dĕtrăktăr', v. a. to detract, to defame, to slander.

detractor, –tŏr', sm. slanderer, detracter.

detractora, –tŏ'ră, sf. detractress.

detrás, dĕtrăs', ad. behind; behind one's back, in the absence of.

detrimento, dĕtrĭmĕn'tŏ, sm. detriment, damage, loss.

deuda, dĕ'ŏdă, sf. debt; fault; offence.

deudo, da, dĕ'ŏdŏ, a. parent; kindred.

deudor, ra, dĕŏdŏr', sm. & f. debtor.

Deuteronomio, dĕŏtĕrŏnŏ'mĭŏ, sm. Deuteronomy.

devanadera, dĕvănădă'ră, sf. reel; movable decoration on the stage.

devanador, ra, –dŏr', sm. & f. winder; quill, bit of paper or other thing, on which yarn is wound into a clew. [up.

devanar, dĕvănăr', v. a. to reel; to wrap

devanear, dĕvănĕăr', v. n. to rave, to talk nonsense; to dote. [pursuit.

devaneo, dĕvănĕ'ŏ, sm. delirium; idle pursuit.

devantal, dĕvăntăl', sm. apron.

devastación, dĕvăstăthŏn', sf. devastation, desolation.

devastador, –dŏr', a. desolater, devastator, harasser, spoiler. [waste.

devastar, dĕvăstăr', v. a. to desolate, to waste.

devengar, dĕvĕngăr', v. a. to deserve.

devoción, dĕvŏthŏn', sf. devotion, piety; strong affection, ardent love. [book.

devocionario, dĕvŏthĭŏnă'rĭŏ, sm. prayer-book.

devolución, dĕvŏlŭthŏn', sf. (law) devolution. [devolutive.

devolutivo, –tĕ'vŏ, a. (law) transferable, devolutive.

devolver, dĕvŏlvĕr', v. a. (law) to return a cause to an inferior court to be tried anew; to restore a thing to its former possessor.

devorar, *dĕvŏrär',* v. a. to devour, to swallow up.

devotero, *—tĕ'rŏ,* sm. pilgrim.

devoto, ta, *dĕvŏ'tŏ,* a. devout, pious, devotional; strongly attached.

dezmar, *dĕthmär',* v. a. to tithe.

dia, *dē'ä,* sm. day; — de años, birth-day.

diabla (á la —), *dĭä'blä,* ad. carelessly; rudely. [man.

diablillo, *dĭäbĭl'yŏ,* sm. acute, clever

diablo, *dĭä'blŏ,* sm. devil, Satan; person of a perverse temper; ugly, cunning or subtle person. [taking; devilishness.

diablura, *dĭäblŏ'rä,* sf. diabolical undertaking; devilishness.

diabólico, ca, *dĭäbŏ'lĭkŏ,* a. diabolical. devilish. [served in sugar.

diacitrón, *—thĭtrŏn',* sm. lemon-peel preserved in sugar.

diaconato, *dĭäkŏnä'tŏ,* sm. deaconship.

diaconisa, *dĭäkŏnĭs'ä,* sm. deaconess.

diácono, *dĭä'kŏnŏ,* sm. deacon. [halo.

diadema, *dĭädä'mä,* sm. & f. diadem;

diafanidad, *—fänĭdäd',* sf. transparency, pellucidness.

diáfano, na, *dĭä'fänŏ,* a. diaphanous, transparent, pellucid. [mid-riff.

diafragma, *dĭäfräg'mä,* sm. diaphragm,

diagnóstico, *dĭägnŏs'tĭkŏ,* sm. diagnosis; —, ca, a. diagnostic.

diagonal, *dĭägŏnäl',* a. diagonal.

dialéctica, *dĭälĕk'tĭkä,* sf. logic, dialectic.

dialéctico, *dĭälĕk'tĭkŏ,* sm. logician; —, ca, a. dialectical, logical.

dialecto, *dĭälĕk'tŏ,* sm. dialect.

dialogismo, *—lŏ'hĭs'mŏ,* sm. dialogism.

diálogo, *dĭä'lŏgŏ,* sm. dialogue.

diamante, *dĭämän'tĕ,* sm. diamond; hardness, resistance; — tabla, diamond cut into angles.

diamantino, na, *—mäntĭ'nŏ,* a. adamantine.

diamantista, *—mäntĭs'tä,* sm. lapidary.

diametral, *dĭä'mĕträl',* a. diametrical, diametral.

diámetro, *dĭä'mĕtrŏ,* sm. diameter.

diana, *dĭä'nä,* sf. (mil.) reveille, the beating of the drum at day-break.

diantre, *dĭän'trĕ,* sm. deuce, devil.

diapasón, *dĭäpäsŏn',* sm. (mus.) diapason, octave.

diario, *dĭä'rĭŏ,* sm. journal, diary; daily newspaper; daily expense; —, ria, a. daily.

diarista, *—rĭs'tä,* sm. journalist.

diarrea, *dĭärrĕ'ä,* sf. diarrhœa.

diatónico, *dĭätŏ'nĭkŏ,* a. (mus.) diatonic.

diatriba, *dĭätrĕ'bä,* sf. diatribe.

dibujador, ra, *dĭbŏ'hädŏr',* a. designer.

dibujar, *—'här',* v. a. to draw, to design; to paint any passion of the mind.

dibujo, *dĭbŏ'hŏ,* sm. drawing, sketch, draught; description. [pression.

dicción, *dĭkthĭŏn',* sf. diction, style, expression.

diccionario, *dĭkthŏnä'rĭŏ,* sm. dictionary.

diciembre, *dĭthĭĕm'brĕ,* sm. December.

dictado, *dĭktä'dŏ,* sm. a title of dignity or honour.

dictador, *dĭktädŏr',* sm. dictator.

dictadura, *—dŏ'rä,* sf. dictatorship.

dictamen, *dĭktä'mĕn,* sm. opinion, notion; suggestion, insinuation.

dictar, *dĭktär',* v. a. to dictate. [insult.

dicterio, *dĭktĕ'rĭŏ,* sm. sarcasm, taunt,

dicha, *dĭtsh'ä,* sf. happiness, good fortune; por —, á —, by chance. [sion.

dicharacho, *—rätsh'ŏ,* sm. vulgar expression.

dicho, *dĭtsh'ŏ,* sm. saying, sentence; declaration; promise of marriage; —, cha, a. said. [ous.

dichoso, sa, *dĭtshŏ'sŏ,* a. happy, prosperous.

diente, *dĭĕn'tĕ,* sm. tooth; fang, tusk; jag.

diestra, *dĭĕs'trä,* sf. right hand; (fig.) favour, support, protection.

diestro, tra, *dĭĕs'trŏ,* a. right; dexterous, skilful, clever; sagacious, prudent; sly, cunning; favourable, propitious; —, sm. skilful fencer; halter, bridle.

dieta, *dĭä'tä,* sf. diet, regimen; diet, assembly; daily salary of judges; —, pl. cattle put on board a fleet to furnish fresh provisions for the sick.

diez, *dĭĕth',* a. & sm. ten; — de rosario, each tenth bead of a rosary.

diezmar, *dĭĕthmär',* v. a. to decimate; to tithe; to take the tenth.

diezmero, *—mĕ'rŏ,* sm. tithe-payer. [old.

diezmesino, na, *—mĕsĕ'nŏ,* a. ten months

diezmo, *dĭĕth'mŏ,* sm. tithe; —, ma, a. tenth.

difamación, *dĭfämäthĭŏn',* sf. defamation.

difamar, *dĭfämär',* v. a. to defame, to libel

difamatorio, ria, *dĭfämätŏ'rĭŏ,* a. defamatory, calumnious.

diferencia, *dĭfĕrĕn'thĭä,* sf. difference; á —, with the difference; —s, pl. controversies, disputes. [ent.

diferencial, *—thĭäl',* a. differential, differ-

diferenciar, *—thĭär',* v. a. to differ, to differenciate; —se, to differ, to distinguish oneself.

diferente, *dĭfĕrĕn'tĕ,* a. different, unlike.

diferir, *dĭfĕrĭr',* v. a. to defer, to put off;

difícil, *dĭfĭ'thĭl,* a. difficult. [to differ.

dificultad, *dĭfĭkŭltäd',* sf. difficulty.

dificultar, *—kŭltär',* v. a. to raise difficulties; to render difficult. [painful.

dificultoso, sa, *—kŭltŏ'sŏ,* a. difficult;

difidencia, *dĭfĭdĕn'thĭä,* sf. diffidence.

difidente, *—tĕ,* a. diffident, disloyal.

difundir, *dĭfŭndĭr',* v. a. to diffuse, to outspread; to divulge. [late.

difunto, ta, *dĭfŭn'tŏ,* a. dead, deceased;

difusión, *dĭfŭsĭŏn',* sf. diffusion.

difusivo, va, *dĭfŭsĕ'vŏ,* a. diffusive.

difuso, sa, *dĭfŏ'sŏ,* a. diffusive, copious; large; prolix, circumstantial.

digerible, *dĭ'hĕrĕ'blĕ,* a. digestible.

digerir, *dĭ'hĕrĭr',* v. a. to digest; to bear with patience; to adjust, to arrange; (chem.) to digest.

digestible, *dĭ'hĕs'tĕ'blĕ,* a. digestible.

digestión, *dĭ'hĕstĭŏn',* sf. digestion, concoction.

digestivo, va, *dĭ'hĕstĕ'vŏ,* a. digestive.

dignación, *dĭgnäthĭŏn',* sf. condescension.

dignarse, *dĭgnär'sĕ,* v. r. to condescend, to deign.

dignidad, *dǐgnǐdǎd'*, sf. dignity, rank; grandeur of mien; prebend of a cathedral superior to a simple canonry, and the dignitary who possesses it.

digno, na, *dǐg'nō*, a. meritorious, worthy; suitable, correspondent.

digresión, *dǐgrēsōn'*, sf. digression; departure of a planet from the equinoctial line.

dij, *dē'h*, **dije,** *dē'hē*, sm. relic; trinket fastened to children's clothes; —es, pl. toys.

dilacerar, *dǐlǎthěrǎr'*, v. a. to dilacerate.

dilación, *dǐlǎthōn'*, sf. delay.

dilapidar, *dǐlǎpǐdǎr'*, v. a. to dilapidate.

dilatable, *dǐlǎtǎ'blē*, a. dilatable.

dilatación, *dǐlǎtǎthōn'*, sf. dilatation, extension; greatness of mind; calmness.

dilatado, da, *dǐlǎtǎ'dō*, a. large, numerous; prolix; spacious, extensive.

dilatar, *dǐlǎtǎr'*, v. a. to dilate, to expand; to spread out; to defer, to protract; to comfort, to cheer up; —se, to expatiate; to speak largely and copiously. [dilates.

dilatativo, va, *–tǎtǐ'vō*, a. that which dilates.

dilatorio, ria, *–tō'rǐō*, a. dilatory.

dilección, *dǐlěkthōn'*, sf. dilection, love, affection, good will.

dilecto, ta, *dǐlěk'tō*, a. loved, beloved.

dilema, *dǐlě'mǎ*, sm. dilemma.

diligencia, *dǐlǐhěn'thǐǎ*, sf. diligence; affair, business; call to ease nature; stage-coach. [self, to endeavour.

diligenciar, *–thǐǎr'*, v. a. to exert one-self, to endeavour.

diligenciero, *–thǐǎ'rō*, sm. agent; apparitor. [prompt, swift.

diligente, *dǐlǐhěn'tē*, a. diligent, assiduous.

dilucidación, *dǐlǔthǐdǎthōn'*, sf. explanation, illustration. [plain.

dilucidar, *–dǎr'*, v. a. to elucidate, to explain.

dilucidario, *–dǎ'rǐō*, sm. explanatory writing.

diluviano, *dǐlǔvǐǎ'nō*, a. diluvian.

diluviar, *dǐlǔvǐǎr'*, v. n. imp. to rain like a deluge. [vast abundance.

diluvio, *dǐlǔ'vǐō*, sm. deluge, inundation; to originate, to flow.

dimanación, *dǐmǎnǎthōn'*, sf. emanation.

dimanar, *dǐmǎnǎr'*, v. n. to spring from; to originate, to flow.

dimensión, *dǐměnsōn'*, sf. dimension; dimensity, extent, capacity, bulk.

dimes, *dē'měs*, sm. pl. **andar en — y diretes,** to use ifs and ands, to contend.

diminución, *dǐmǐnǔthōn'*, sf. diminution; contraction of the diameter of a column as it ascends. [tively; by retail.

diminutamente, *–tǎměn'tē*, ad. diminutively; by retail.

diminutivo, va, *–tǐ'vō*, a. diminutive.

diminuto, ta, *dǐmǐnǔ'tō*, a. defective, faulty, small.

dimisión, *dǐmǐsōn'*, sf. dimission.

dimisorias, *dǐmǐsō'rǐǎs*, sf. pl. dimissory letters. [dicate.

dimitir, *dǐmǐtǐr'*, v. a. to give up, to abdicate.

dinámica, *dǐnǎ'mǐkǎ*, sf. dynamics.

dinamo, *dǐnǎ'mō*, sm. dynamo (electric engine).

dinastía, *dǐnǎstǐ'ǎ*, sf. dynasty. [engine).

dineral, *dǐněrǎl'*, sm. large sum of money.

dinero, *dǐně'rō*, sm. coin, money, coinage.

dingolondangos, *dǐngōlōndǎn'gōs*, sm. pl. showy ornaments on women.

diocesano, na, *dǐōthěsǎ'nō*, a. diocesan.

diócesis, *dǐō'thěsǐs*, sf. diocese.

Dios, *dǐōs'*, sm. God; any person or thing passionately beloved or adored; á —, farewell, adieu; á — y á ventura, at all risks.

diosa, *dǐō'sǎ*, sf. goddess. [risks.

diploma, *dǐplō'mǎ*, sm. diploma, patent.

diplomacia, *dǐplōmǎ'thǐǎ*, diplomática, *dǐplōmǎ'tǐkǎ*, sf. diplomacy.

diplomático, ca, *–mǎ'tǐkō*, a. diplomatic.

diplomatizar, *–mǎtǐhǎr'*, v. a. to act the diplomatist.

diptongo, *dǐptōn'gō*, sm. diphthong.

diputación, *dǐpǔtǎthōn'*, sf. deputation; object of a deputation.

diputado, *–tǎ'dō*, sm. deputy. [stitute.

diputar, *dǐpǔtǎr'*, v. a. to depute; to constitute.

dique, *dē'kē*, sm. dike, dam, mole.

dirección, *dǐrěkthōn'*, sf. direction; guidance, administration.

directivo, va, *–tǐ'vō*, a. directive.

directo, ta, *dǐrěk'tō*, a. direct, straight; apparent, evident.

director, *dǐrěktōr'*, sm. director; conductor; president; manager.

directora, *–tō'rǎ*, sf. directress, governess.

directorio, ria, *–tō'rǐō*, a. directive, directorial; —, sm. directory.

dirigir, *dǐrǐhǐr'*, v. a. to direct; to conduct; to dedicate a work; to regulate, to govern; —se, to address oneself.

dirimente, *dǐrǐměn'tē*, a. breaking off, dissolving.

dirimir, *dǐrǐmǐr'*, v. a. to dissolve, to separate; to accommodate differences.

discernimiento, *dǐsthěrnǐměn'tō*, sm. discernment; appointment of a guardian by the proper magistrates.

discernir, *dǐsthěrnǐr'*, v. a. to discern, to distinguish; to appoint a guardian.

disciplina, *dǐsthǐplǐ'nǎ*, sf. discipline.

disciplinante, *–plǐnǎn'tē*, sm. flagellator.

disciplinar, *–plǐnǎr'*, v. a. to discipline.

discípulo, *dǐsthǐ'pǔlō*, sm. disciple, scholar.

disco, *dǐs'kō*, sm. disk; face of the sun or moon; lens of a telescope; (rail.) disk, signal-disk. [peevish.

díscolo, la, *dǐs'kōlō*, a. ungovernable.

discordancia, *dǐskōrdǎn'thǐǎ*, sf. disagreement, discordance. [cordant.

discordante, *–dǎn'tē*, a. dissonant, discordant.

discordar, *–kōrdǎr'*, v. n. to discord, to disagree. [dissonant

discorde, *dǐskōr'dē*, a. discordant; (mus.)

discordia, *dǐskōr'dǐǎ*, sf. discord, disagreement; contrariety of opinion.

discreción, *dǐskrěthōn'*, sf. discretion; acuteness of mind, sharpness of wit; á —, at the will of another.

discrepar, *–krěpǎr'*, v. n. to differ.

discreto, ta, *dǐskrě'tō*, a. discreet; ingenious, witty, eloquent.

disculpa, *dǐskǔl'pǎ*, sf. apology, excuse.

disculpar, *dǐskǔlpǎr'*, v. a. to exculpate, to excuse, to acquit, to absolve.

discurrir, –*kŭrrĭr'*, v. n. to ramble about, to run to and fro; to discourse upon a subject; to discuss; –, v. a. to invent, to contrive; to meditate. [contemplative.

discursivo, va, –*kŭrsĕ'vŏ*, a. discursive;

discurso, –*kŭr'sŏ*, sm. discourse; ratiocination; discourse, conversation; dissertation; space of time.

discusión, *dĭskŭsĭŏn'*, sf. discussion.

discutir, –*kŭtĭr'*, v. a. to discuss.

disecar, *dĭsĕkar'*, v. a. to dissect. [tomy.

disección, –*sĕkthĭŏn'*, sf. dissection, ana-

disector, –*sĕktŏr'*, sm. dissector, anatomist.

diseminar, *dĭsĕmĭnar'*, v. a. to scatter as seed; to disseminate, to propagate.

disensión, *dĭsĕnsĭŏn'*, sf. dissension, misunderstanding, contest, strife; cause of dissension.

disentería, *dĭsĕntĕrē'ă*, sf. dysentery.

disentimiento, *dĭsĕntĭmĭĕn'tŏ*, sm. dissent, disagreement. [agree.

disentir, *dĭsĕntĭr'*, v. n. to dissent, to dis-

diseñador, *dĭsĕnyădŏr'*, sm. designer.

diseñar, *dĭsĕnyar'*, v. a. to draw, to design.

diseño, *dĭsĕn'yŏ*, sm. design, draught; description; picture. [discussion.

disertación, *dĭsĕrtăthĭŏn'*, sf. dissertation.

disertar, *dĭsĕrtar'*, v. a. to dispute, to debate, to argue. [favour.

disfavor, –*favor'*, sm. disregard, want of

disforme, –*fŏr'mĕ*, a. ugly, monstrous, formless; huge. [querade; dissimulation.

disfraz, –*frath'*, sm. mask, disguise; mas-

disfrazar, –*frăthar'*, v. a. to disguise, to conceal; to cloak, to dissemble.

disfrutar, –*frŭtar'*, v. a. to enjoy.

disfrute, –*frŏ'tĕ*, sm. enjoyment.

disgustar, –*gŭstar'*, v. a. to disgust; to offend; –se, to be displeased, to fall out.

disgusto, *dĭsgŭs'tŏ*, sm. disgust, aversion; ill-humour; grief, sorrow; á –, in spite of.

disidente, *dĭsĭdĕn'tĕ*, a. & s. dissident, dissenter. [lation; hypocrisy.

disimulación, *dĭsĭmŭlăthĭŏn'*, sf. dissimu-

disimulado, da, –*mŭlă'dŏ*, a. reserved, dissembled; á lo –, dissemblingly; reservedly. [cloak; to hide; to tolerate.

disimular, –*mŭlar'*, v. a. to dissemble; to

disimulo, *dĭsĭmŏ'lŏ*, sm. dissimulation.

disipación, *dĭsĭpăthĭŏn'*, sf. dissipation; (chem.) resolution into component parts; resolution into vapour.

disipado, da, –*pă'dŏ*, a. prodigal, lavish.

disipador, ra, –*pădŏr'*, sm. & f. spendthrift. [perse, to scatter; to lavish.

disipar, *dĭsĭpar'*, v. a. to dissipate, to dis-

dislate, *dĭslă'tĕ*, sm. nonsense, absurdity.

dislocación, –*lŏkăthĭŏn'*, sf. dislocation.

dislocarse, –*lŏkar'sĕ*, v. r. to be dislocated or put out of joint.

disminuir, –*mĭnŭĭr'*, v. a. to diminish.

disoluble, –*sŏlŭ'blĕ*, a. dissoluble.

disolución, –*sŏlŭthĭŏn'*, sf. dissolution; lewdness, licentiousness.

disolutivo, va, –*sŏlŭtĕ'vŏ*, a. dissolvent.

disoluto, ta, –*sŏlŭ'tŏ*, a. dissolute, licentious, lewd.

disolver, –*sŏlvĕr'*, v. a. to loosen, to untie; to dissolve, to disunite; to melt, to liquefy; to interrupt. [disagreement, discord.

disonancia, –*sŏnăn'thĭă*, sf. dissonance;

disonante, –*sŏnăn'tĕ*, a. dissonant, inharmonious; (fig.) discordant.

disonar, –*sŏnar'*, v. n. to disagree in sound; to disagree; to be repugnant.

dísono, na, *dĭ'sŏnŏ*, a. dissonant.

dispar, *dĭspar'*, a. unlike, unequal, different.

disparador, –*părădŏr'*, sm. shooter; trigger of a gun-lock.

disparar, –*parar'*, v. a. & n. to shoot, to discharge, to fire; to let off; to throw with violence; to talk nonsense; –se, to run headlong; to stoop, to dart down upon a prey. [sistent, absurd, extravagant.

disparatado, da, –*parătă'dŏ*, a. incon-

disparatar, –*parătar'*, v. n. to extravagate; to talk nonsense. [dity, extravagance.

disparate, –*para'tĕ*, sm. nonsense, absur-

disparidad, –*parĭdăd'*, sf. disparity, inequality.

disparo, –*pa'rŏ*, sm. discharge, explosion.

dispasto(s), –*pas'tŏ(s)*, sm. pulley, tackle-block.

dispendio, –*pĕn'dĭŏ*, sm. extravagant expense; voluntary loss of life, honour or fame.

dispendioso, sa, –*pĕndĭŏ'sŏ*, a. costly, expensive. [granting a dispensation.

dispensa, –*pĕn'să*, sf. dispense; diploma.

dispensable, –*pĕnsă'blĕ*, a. dispensable.

dispensación, –*pĕnsăthĭŏn'*, sf. dispensation, exemption. [distributer.

dispensador, –*pĕnsădŏr'*, sm. dispenser;

dispensar, –*pĕnsar'*, v. a. to dispense; to excuse, to dispense with; to distribute.

dispersión, –*pĕrsĭŏn'*, sf. dispersion.

disperso, sa, *dĭspĕr'sŏ*, a. dispersed.

displicencia, –*plĭthĕn'thĭă*, sf. displeasure, dislike. [offensive; angry, fretful.

displicente, –*plĭthĕn'tĕ*, a. displeasing.

disponer, –*pŏnĕr'*, v. a. & n. to arrange; to dispose, to prepare; to dispose of; to resolve.

disponible, –*pŏnĕ'blĕ*, a. disposable.

disposición, –*pŏsĭthĭŏn'*, sf. disposition, ordering; proportion; resolution; command; power, authority.

dispositivo, va, –*pŏsĭtĕ'vŏ*, a. dispositive.

dispuesto, ta, *dĭspŭĕs'tŏ*, a. disposed, fit, ready; bien –, quite well; mal –, indisposed, ill.

disputa, *dĭspŏ'tă*, sf. dispute, controversy.

disputable, –*pŭtă'blĕ*, a. disputable, controvertible.

disputador, –*dŏr'*, sm. disputant, disputer.

disputar, *dĭspŭtar'*, v. a. & n. to dispute, to controvert, to question; to debate, to argue.

distancia, *dĭstăn'thĭă*, sf. distance, interval; difference.

distante, *dĭstăn'tĕ*, a. distant, far off.

distar, *dĭstar'*, v. n. to be distant; to be different. [different.

dístico, *dĭs'tĭkŏ*, sm. distich.

distinción, *dĭstĭnthĭŏn'*, sf. distinction; difference; prerogative; á –, in contradistinction.

distinguido, da, *-tĭngŭ'dŏ*, a. distinguished, conspicuous.

distinguir, *-tĭngĭr'*, v. a. to distinguish; to see clearly and at a distance; to discern, to set a peculiar value on things or persons; —se, to distinguish oneself.

distintivo, *-tĭntĭ'vŏ*, sm. distinctive mark; particular attribute.   [clear.

distinto, ta, *-tĭn'tŏ*, a. distinct, different;

distracción, *-trăkthĭŏn'*, sf. distraction, want of attention.

distraer, *-trăĕr'*, v. a. to distract; —se, to be absent-minded, to be inattentive.

distraído, da, *-trăĭ'dŏ*, a. absent, inattentive; dissolute, licentious.

distribución, *-trĭbŭthĭŏn'*, sf. distribution, division, separation; arrangement.

distribuidor, *-trĭbŭĭdŏr'*, sm. distributer.

distribuir, *-trĭbŭĭr'*, v. a. to distribute, to dispose; to distribute type.   [tive.

distributivo, va, *-trĭbŭtĭ'vŏ*, a. distributive.

distrito, *dĭstrĭ'tŏ*, sm. district; territory.

disturbar, *-tŭrbăr'*, v. a. to disturb, to interrupt.   [interruption.

disturbio, *-tŭr'bĭŏ*, sm. disturbance,

disuadir, *dĭsŭădĭr'*, v. a. to dissuade.

disuasión, *dĭsŭăsĭŏn'*, sf. dissuasion.

disyunción, *-yŭnthĭŏn'*, sf. disjunction; (gr.) disjunctive particle.   [key.

disyunta, *-yŭn'tă*, sf. (mus.) change of

disyuntivo, va, *-yŭntĭ'vŏ*, a. disjunctive.

diurno, na, *dĭŭr'nŏ*, a. diurnal; daily; —, sm. prayer-book.

diuturnidad, *dĭŭtŭrnĭdăd'*, sf. diuturnity.   [ing.

diuturno, na, *-tŭr'nŏ*, a. diuturnal, last-

diva, *dĭ'vă*, sf. a celebrated songstress.

diván, *dĭvăn'*, sm. Divan (supreme council among the Turks).   [gence.

divergencia, *dĭvĕr'hĕn'thĭă*, sf. divergence.

divergente, *-'hĕn'tĕ*, a. divergent.

diversidad, *-vĕrsĭdăd'*, sf. diversity; variety of things.   [sify, to vary.

diversificar, *-sĭfĭkăr'*, v. a. to diver-

diversión, *-vĕrsĭŏn'*, sf. diversion · sport, amusement; (mil.) diversion.

diverso, sa, *-vĕr'sŏ*, a. diverse, different; several, sundry.   [ing.

divertido, da, *-tĭ'dŏ*, a. amused; amus-

divertimiento, *-tĭmĭĕn'tŏ*, sm. diversion, amusement, pastime, sport.

divertir, *dĭvĕrtĭr'*, v. a. to divert (the attention); to amuse, to entertain; (mil.) to draw the enemy off from some design; —se, to sport, to dally.   [dividend.

dividendo, *dĭvĭdĕn'dŏ*, sm. (ar. & com.)

dividir, *dĭvĭdĭr'*, v. a. to divide, to disunite, to separate; —se, to break up a friendship.

divieso, *dĭvĭĕ'sŏ*, sm. (med.) furuncle.

divinidad, *-vĭnĭdăd'*, sf. divinity; Supreme Being; false god; woman of exquisite beauty.   [sanctify.

divinizar, *-nĭthăr'*, ℵ. a. to deify; to

divino, na, *dĭvĭ'nŏ*, a. divine, heavenly; excellent.

divisa, *dĭvĭ'să*, sf. posy, motto, device.

divisar, *dĭvĭsăr'*, v. n. to perceive indistinctly; to vary.

divisible, *-sĭ'blĕ*, a. divisible.

división, *-sĭŏn'*, sf. division; partition; separation; difference; (gr.) hyphen.

divisor, *-sŏr'*, sm. (ar.) divisor.

divisorio, ria, *-sŏ'rĭŏ*, a. divisive.

divorciar, *dĭvŏrthĭăr'*, v. a. to pronounce a sentence of divorce; to divorce, to separate; —se, to be divorced.

divorcio, *dĭvŏr'thĭŏ*, sm. divorce; separation, disunion.   [tion, publication.

divulgación, *dĭvŭlgăthĭŏn'*, sf. divulga-

divulgar, *-găr'*, v. a. to publish, to divulge.

dobela, *dŏbă'lă*, sf. key-stone.

dobladillo, lla, *dŏblădĭl'yŏ*, a. squat and broad; —, sm. hem.

doblado, *dŏblă'dŏ*, sm. measure of the fold in cloth; —, da, a. robust, thickset; deceitful, dissembling.

dobladura, *-dŏ'ră*, sf. fold.

doblar, *dŏblăr'*, v. a. & n. to double, to fold; to bend; to ring the passing-bell; —se, to bend, to bow, to submit.

doble, *dŏ'blĕ*, a. double; thick and short, robust; artful, deceitful; al —, doubly; —, sm. passing-bell.   [curvate.

doblegar, *dŏblĕgăr'*, v. a. to bend, to in-

doblete, *dŏblĕ'tĕ*, a. false jewel; double taffety.   [& f. duplicity.

doblez, *dŏblĕth'*, sm. crease; fold; —, sm.

doblón, *dŏblŏn'*, sm. doubloon.

doce, *dŏ'thĕ*, a. & sm. twelve.

docena, *dŏthĕ'nă*, sf. dozen.

docenal, *dŏthĕnăl'*, a. sold by the dozen.

doceno, na, *dŏthĕ'nŏ*, a. twelfth.

dócil, *dŏth'ĭl*, a. docile, tractable.

docilidad, *dŏthĭlĭdăd'*, sf. docility, compliance, gentleness.

docto, ta, *dŏk'tŏ*, a. learned.

doctor, *dŏktŏr'*, sm. doctor; physician.

doctora, *-tŏ'ră*, sf. doctoress; wife of a physician or doctor.   [ship.

doctorado, *-ră'dŏ*, sm. doctorate, doctor-

doctoral, *-răl'*, a. doctoral; —, sf. canonry called doctoral in the Spanish cathedrals; —, sm. canon of the doctoral.

doctorando, *-răn'dŏ*, sm. one who is on the point of taking out his degrees as doctor.   [doctor.

doctorear, *dŏktŏrĕăr'*, v. n. to play the

doctrina, *dŏktrĭ'nă*, sf. doctrine, instruction; science; discourse on the tenets of the Christan faith.   [doctrinal.

doctrinal, *-trĭnăl'*, sm. catechism; —, a.

doctrinar, *-trĭnăr'*, v. a. to teach, to instruct.   [muniment, record.

documento, *dŏkŭmĕn'tŏ*, sm. document;

dogal, *dŏgăl'*, sm. rope tied round the neck of asses, mules, &c.

dogma, *dŏg'mă*, sm. dogma.

dogmático, ca, *dŏgmă'tĭkŏ*, a. dogmatical.

dogmatista, *-tĭs'tă*, sm. dogmatist.

dogmatizador, *-tĭthădŏr'*, dogmatizante, *-tĭthăn'tĕ*, sm. dogmatizer, dogmatist.

dogmatizar, *-tĭthăr'*, v. a. to dogmatize.

dogo, *dŏ'gŏ*, sm. terrier.

dolencia, dŏlĕn'thĭă, sf. disease, affliction.

doler, dŏlĕr', v. a. to feel pain; to ache; to be repugnant; to be sorry; to repent; to feel for the sufferings of others; to complain. [ful.

doliente, dŏlĭĕn'tĕ, a. suffering; sorrow-

dolo, dŏ'lŏ, sm. fraud, deceit. [fliction.

dolor, dŏlŏr', sm. pain, aching, ache; af-

dolorido, da, dŏlŏrĭ'dŏ, a. afflicted, painful, heart-sick; —, sm. chief mourner, the nearest relation of a person deceased.

doloroso, sa, dŏlŏrŏ'sŏ, a. sorrowful, afflicted, dolorous, dismal; painful.

doloso, sa, dŏlŏ'sŏ, a. deceitful, knavish.

domable, dŏmă'blĕ, a. tameable.

domador, ra, dŏmădŏr', sm. & f. tamer; subduer; horsebreaker.

domadura, —dŏ'ră, sf. taming, subduing.

domar, dŏmăr', v. a. to tame; to subdue, to master. [able, to tame.

domeñar, dŏmĕnyăr', v. a. to make tract-

domesticable, dŏmĕstĭkă'blĕ, a. tameable.

domesticar, —tĭkăr', v. a. to domesticate.

domesticidad, —tĭlĭdăd', sf. domesticity; affability; servants, domestics, pl.

doméstico, ca, dŏmĕs'tĭkŏ, a. domestical; —, sm. domestic, menial. [ciliated.

domiciliado, da, dŏmĭthĭlĭă'dŏ, a. domi-

domiciliarse, —lĭăr'sĕ, v. r. to establish oneself in a residence.

domicilio, dŏmĭthĭ'lĭŏ, sm. habitation, domicile, home, abode.

dominación, dŏmĭnăthĭŏn', sf. dominion, authority, power; —ones, pl. dominations (some angelic beings).

dominador, —nădŏr', sm. dominator.

dominante, —năn'tĕ, a. dominant, domineering. [moderate one's passions.

dominar, dŏmĭnăr', v. a. to domineer; to

dómine, dŏ'mĭnĕ, sm. grammarian.

domingo, dŏmĭn'gŏ, sm. Sunday.

dominguero, ra, —gĕ'rŏ, a. done or worn on Sunday.

dominguillo, —gĭl'yŏ, sm. figure of a boy made of straw, and used at bullfights to frighten the bulls.

dominica, dŏmĭ'nĭkă, sf. Sunday (in ecclesiastical language).

dominical, —nĭkăl', a. manorial; dominical. [of Saint Dominic.

dominico, —nĕ'kŏ, sm. friar of the order

dominio, dŏmĭ'nĭŏ, sm. dominion, domination, power, authority; domain.

dominó, dŏmĭnŏ' sm. domino (a masquerade garment). [gentleman.]

Don, dŏn, sm. Don (the Spanish title for a

donación, dŏnăthĭŏn', sf. donation, gift.

donado, da, dŏnă'dŏ, sm. & f. lay-brother; lay-sister. [stower, giver.

donador, ra, —dŏr', sm. & f. donor, be-

donaire, dŏnă'ĭrĕ, sm. grace, elegance; witty saying.

donar, dŏnăr', v. a. to make free gifts, to bestow. [pient.

donatario, dŏnătă'rĭŏ, sm. donee, reci-

donativo, —tĕ'vŏ, sm. free contribution.

doncel, dŏnthĕl', sm. king's page.

doncella, —thĕl'yă, sf. virgin, maiden; lady's-maid. [maidenhood.

doncellez, —thĕlyĕth', sf. virginity.

donde, dŏn'dĕ, ad. where; - quiera, anywhere; ¿ de dónde ? whence? ¿ por dónde ? by what way ? for what reason ?

dondiego de noche, dŏndĭă'gŏ dĕ nŏtch'ĕ, sm. (bot.) jalap.

donillero, dŏnĭlyĕ'rŏ, sm. swindler, sharper; cheat. [comely.

donoso, dŏnŏ'sŏ, a. gay, witty; pleasant,

doña, dŏn'yă, sf. lady, mistress.

doquier, dŏkĭĕr', doquiera, dŏkĭă'ră, ad. anywhere.

dorada, dŏră'dă, doradilla, —dĭl'yă, sf. gilt-head, gilt-poll (fish).

doradillo, —dĭl'yŏ, sm. fine brass wire; wagtail.

dorado, da, dŏră'dŏ, a. gilt; —, sm. gilding.

dorador, —dŏr', sm. gilder.

doradura, —dŏ'ră, sf. gilding.

dorar, dŏrăr', v. a. to gild; (fig.) to palliate

dórico, ca, dŏ'rĭkŏ, a. Doric.

dormidero, ra, dŏrmĭdĕ'rŏ, a. sleepy, soporific; —, sm. place where cattle repose.

dormidor, —dŏr', sm. great sleeper.

dormilón, ona, —lŏn', sm. dull, sleepy person. [fall asleep.

dormir, dŏrmĭr', v. n. to sleep; -se, to

dormitar, dŏrmĭtăr', v. n. to doze, to be half asleep.

dormitorio, —tŏ'rĭŏ, sm. dormitory.

dorsal, dŏrsăl', a. dorsal.

dorso, dŏr'sŏ, sm. back.

dos, dŏs, a. & sm. two. [hundred.

doscientos, tas, dŏsthĭĕn'tŏs, a. pl. two

dosel, dŏsĕl', sm. canopy.

doselera, dŏsĕlĕ'ră, sf. valance.

dosis, dŏ'sĭs, sf. dose, dosis.

dospuntos, dŏspŭn'tŏs, sm. (gr.) colon.

dotación, dŏtăthĭŏn', sf. donation, endowment. [donor; institutor.

dotador, ra, —dŏr', sm. one who endows;

dotal, dŏtăl', a. dotal. [to gift.

dotar, dŏtăr', v. a. to endow with a fortune,

dote, dŏ'tĕ, sm. & f. dower, dowry; -s, pl. gifts of nature; endowments. [curves.

dovelar, dŏvĕlăr', v. a. to hew a stone in

dovelas, dŏvĕ'lăs, sf. pl. curved sides of the key-stone of an arch.

dozavo, va, dŏthă'vŏ, sm. twelfth part.

dracma, drăk'mă, sf. drachm.

drago, dră'gŏ, sm. dragon-tree.

dragón, drăgŏn', sm. a dragon; (mil) dragoon; white spots in the pupils of horses' eyes. [dragon.

dragona, —gŏ'nă, sf. shoulder-knot; female

drama, dră'mă, sm. drama.

dramática, drămă'tĭkă, sf. dramatic art.

dramático, ca, —tĭkŏ, a. dramatic.

dramatizar, —tĭthăr', v. a. to dramatize.

dríada, drĭ'ădă, dríade, —ădĕ, sf. dryad.

droga, drŏ'gă, sf. drug; stratagem, artifice, deceit. [drug-trade.

droguería, drŏgĕrĕ'ă, sf. druggist's shop;

droguero, drŏgă'rŏ, sm. druggist.

droguista, drŏgĭs'tă, sm. druggist; cheat, impostor.

dromedario, *drŏmĕdă'rĭŏ,* sm. dromedary.
drops, *drŏps,* sm. (rail.) dead level.
dubitativo, va, *dŭbĭtătī'vŏ,* a. doubtful, dubious (applied to conjunctions).
ducado, *dŭkă'dŏ,* sm. duchy, dukedom; ducat.
ducal, *dŭkăl',* a. ducal. [customed.
ducho, cha, *dŭtsh'ŏ,* a. dexterous; accustomed.
ducientos, tas, *dŭthĭĕn'tŏs,* a. two hundred. [tion.
duda, *dŏ'dă,* sf. doubt, suspense, hesitation.
dudable, *dŭdă'blĕ,* a. dubitable, dubious.
dudar, *dŭdăr',* v. a. to doubt. [doubtful.
dudoso, sa, *dŭdŏ'sŏ,* a. doubtful, dubious.
duela, *dŭĕ'lă,* sf. stave. [uncertain.
duelista, *dŭĕlĭs'tă,* sm. duellist, dueller; quarreller.
duelo, *dŭĕ'lŏ,* sm. duel; grief; affliction; mourning, funeral; –s, pl. troubles; afflictions.
duende, *dŭĕn'dĕ,* sm. elf, hobgoblin.
dueña, *dŭĕn'yă,* sf. married lady; single woman who has lost her virginity.
dueño, *dŭĕn'yŏ,* sm. owner; master.
dulce, *dŭl'thĕ,* a. sweet; pleasing to the taste; mild, soft, gentle, meek; –, sm. comfiture; sweetness.
dulcificante, *dŭlthĭfĭkăn'tĕ,* a. sweetening.
dulcificar, *dŭlthĭfĭkăr',* v. a. to sweeten.
dulzaina, *dŭlthaĭ'nă,* sf. German flute.
dulzaino, –*nŏ,* a. excessively sweet.
dulzura, *dŭlthŏ'ră,* sf. sweetness; gentleness, graciousness; pleasant manner in speaking or writing. [corate.
dulzurar, –*răr',* v. a. (chem.) to edulcorate.
duo, *dŏ'ŏ,* sm. (mus.) duo, duet.
duodécimo, ma, *dŭŏdĕ'thĭmŏ,* a. twelfth.
duplicación, *dŭplĭkăthĭŏn',* sf. duplication.
duplicado, –*kă'dŏ,* sm. duplicate. [tion.
duplicar, –*kăr',* v. a. to double, to duplicate; to repeat. [ness.
duplicidad, –*thĭdăd',* sf. duplicity; falseness.
duplo, *dŭ'plŏ,* sm. double.
duque, *dŭ'kĕ,* sm. duke.
duquesa, *dŭkĕ'să,* sf. duchess.
dura, *dŏ'ră,* sf. duration, continuance.
durable, *dŭră'blĕ,* a. durable, lasting.
duración, –*thĭŏn',* sf. duration.
duradero, ra, –*dĕ'rŏ,* a. lasting, durable.
durante, *dŭrăn'tĕ,* p. & a. during.
durar, *dŭrăr',* v. n. to last, to continue.
durazno, *dŭrăth'nŏ,* sm. peach.
durazno, –, **duraznero,** *dŭrăthnĕ'rŏ,* sm. peach-tree.
dureza, *dŭrĕ'thă,* sf. hardness, solidity, firmness; acerbity; steadiness; want of softness in paintings; tumour, callosity; – de vientre, costiveness; – de oído, hardness of hearing.
durillo, *dŭrĭl'yŏ,* a. rather hard.
durlin, *dŭrlĭn',* sm. (cant) sbirro, bailiff, constable.
durmiente, *dŭrmĭĕn'tĕ,* p. & a. sleeping; –, sm. dormer, dormant; –s, pl. (mar.) clamps, sleepers.
duro, ra, *dŏ'rŏ,* a. hard, solid; unjust; oppressive, rigorous, cruel; stubborn; ava-

ricious; rude, harsh, peevish, rough; –, sm. dollar.
duunvir, *dŭŭnvĭr',* sm. one of the duumviri.
duunvirato, –*vĭră'tŏ,* sm. duumvirate.
dux, *dŭks,* sm. doge (of Venice and Genoa).

E.

e, *ĕ,* c. and.
ea, *ĕ'ă,* a kind of aspiration used to awaken attention; ¡– pues! well then! let us see! [ebonist.
ebanista, *ĕbănĭs'tă,* sm. cabinet-maker.
ébano, *ĕ'bănŏ,* sm. ebony.
ebullición, *ĕbŭlyĭthĭŏn',* sf. ebullition, boiling over.
Eccehomo, *ĕkthĕŏ'mŏ,* sm. Ecce Homo.
eclesiástico, *ĕklĕsĭăs'tĭkŏ,* sm. clergyman, ecclesiastic; –, ca, a. ecclesiastical.
Eclesiástico, –, sm. Ecclesiasticus.
eclipsable, *ĕklĭpsă'blĕ,* a. that may be eclipsed. [shine.
eclipsar, *ĕklĭpsăr',* v. a. to eclipse, to outshine, *ĕklĭp'sĕ,* sm. eclipse.
eclipse, *ĕklĭp'sĕ,* sm. eclipse.
eclíptica, *ĕklĭp'tĭkă,* sf. ecliptic.
eco, *ĕk'ŏ,* sm. echo.
economía, *ĕkŏnŏmĭ'ă,* sf. economy.
económico, ca, –*nŏ'mĭkŏ,* a. economical, avaricious.
económo, *ĕkŏ'nŏmŏ,* sm. economist.
ecuación, *ĕkŭăthĭŏn',* sf. equation.
ecuador, *ĕkŭădŏr',* sm. equator.
ecuestre, *ĕkŭĕs'trĕ,* a. equestrian.
eculeo, *ĕkŭlĕ'ŏ,* sm. wooden horse (for torture). [cal, universal.
ecuménico, ca, *ĕkŭmĕ'nĭkŏ,* a. œcumenical.
echadizo, za, *ĕtshădĭ'thŏ,* a. fit to be thrown away; suborned to pry into other people's actions; supposititious; –, sm. foundling.
echar, *ĕtshăr',* v. a. to cast, to throw, to dart, to jet; to cast away; to shoot, to bud; to impose a tax; –se, to lie, to rest, to stretch oneself at full length.
edad, *ĕdăd',* sf. age.
edecán, *ĕdĕkăn',* sm. (mil.) aide-de-camp.
edición, *ĕdĭthĭŏn',* sf. edition; published book.
edicto, *ĕdĭk'tŏ,* sm. edict. [book.
edificación, *ĕdĭfĭkăthĭŏn',* sf. construction; (fig.) good example.
edificar, –*fĭkăr',* v. a. to build; to fabricate; to construct a building; to set a good example. [instructive.
edificativo, va, –*kătī'vŏ,* a. exemplary, instructive.
edificio, *ĕdĭfĭ'thĭŏ,* sm. building, structure.
editor, *ĕdĭtŏr',* sm. editor, publisher.
educación, *ĕdŭkăthĭŏn',* sf. education.
educador, ra, –*kădŏr',* sm. & f. instructor, educator. [scholar.
educando, da, –*kăn'dŏ,* sm. & f. pupil.
educar, *ĕdŭkăr',* v. a. to educate, to instruct.
educción, *ĕdŭkthĭŏn',* sf. drawing forth, eduction, extraction. [to bring out.
educir, *ĕdŭthĭr',* v. a. to educe, to extract.
efectivamente, *ĕfĕktĭvămĕn'tĕ,* ad. effectually, powerfully; certainly.

efectivo, va, –*tĕ'vŏ*, a. effective, true, certain.

efecto, *ĕfĕk'tŏ,* sm. effect; consequence; purpose; **–s,** pl. effects, goods; **en –,** in fact, in truth.

efectuar, –*tŭăr',* v. a. to effectuate.

efemérides, *ĕfĕmĕr'ĕdĕs,* sf. pl. ephemeris.

efervescencia, *ĕfĕrvĕsthĕn'thĭă,* sf. effervescence, ebullition.

eficacia, *ĕfĭkă'thĭă,* sf. efficacy.

eficaz, –*kăth',* a. efficacious, effective.

eficiente, *ĕfĭthĭĕn'tĕ,* a. efficient, effective.

efigie, *ĕfĭ'hĭ'lĕ,* sf. effigy, image.

efímero, ra, *ĕfĭ'mĕrŏ,* a. ephemeral.

efluvio, *ĕflŭ'vĭŏ,* sm. effluvium.

efugio, *ĕfŭ'hĭŏ,* sm. subterfuge.

efusión, *ĕfŭsĭŏn',* sf. effusion.

égida, *ĕ'hĭdă,* sf. (fig.) protection.

égloga, *ĕ'glŏgă,* sf. eclogue.

egoísmo, *ĕgŏĭs'mŏ,* sm. selfishness.

egoísta, –*ĭs'tă,* sm. self-seeker.

egregio, gia, *ĕgrĕ'hĭŏ,* a. egregious, eminent, remarkable.

eje, *ĕ'hĕ,* sm. axle-tree.

ejecución, *ĕ'hĕkŭthĭŏn',* sf. execution.

ejecutable, –*tă'blĕ,* a. performable.

ejecutar, –*tăr',* v. a. to execute, to perform; to put to death; (law) to distrain, to seize.

ejecutivo, va, –*tĕ'vŏ,* a. executive.

ejecutor, ra, –*tŏr',* sm. & f. executor; (law) distrainer.

ejecutoria, –*tŏ'rĭă,* sf. (law) writ of execution.

ejecutorial, –*tŏrĭăl',* a. applied to the execution of the sentence of an ecclesiastical tribunal.

ejecutoriar, –*tŏrĭăr',* v. a. to obtain a verdict in one's favour; to make the truth of a thing evident.

ejecutorio, ria, –*tŏ'rĭŏ,* a. (law) executory.

ejemplar, *ĕ'hĕmplăr',* sm. exemplar; example; **–,** a. exemplary.

ejemplificar, *ĕ'hĕmplĭfĭkăr',* v. a. to exemplify.

ejemplo, *ĕ'hĕm'plŏ,* sm. example; comparison; pattern, copy; **por –,** for instance.

ejercer, *ĕ'hĕrthĕr',* v. a. to exercise.

ejercicio, –*thĕ'thĭŏ,* sm. exercise.

ejercitación, –*thĭtăthĭŏn',* sf. exercise, practice.

ejercitar, –*thĭtăr',* v. a. to exercise; **–se,** to apply oneself to the functions of an office.

ejército, *ĕ'hĕr'thĭtŏ,* sm. army.

el, *ĕl,* art. m. the.

él, *ĕl',* ella, –*ya,* ello, –*yŏ,* pn. he, she, it.

elaboración, *ĕlăbŏrăthĭŏn',* sf. elaboration.

elaborado, da, –*ră'dŏ,* a. elaborate.

elaborar, *ĕlăbŏrăr',* v. a. to elaborate.

elami, *ĕlămĭ',* sf. the sixth ascending note in the scale of music.

elasticidad, *ĕlăstĭthĭdăd',* sf. elasticity.

elástico, ca, *ĕlăs'tĭkŏ,* a. elastic.

elección, *ĕlĕkthĭŏn',* sf. election, discernment, choice.

electivo, va, –*tĕ'vŏ,* a. elective.

electo, *ĕlĕk'tŏ,* sm. elect.

elector, *ĕlĕktŏr',* sm. elector.

electorado, –*tŏră'dŏ,* sm. electorate.

electoral, –*tŏrăl',* a. electoral.

electricidad, –*trĭthĭdăd',* sf. electricity.

eléctrico, ca, *ĕlĕk'trĭkŏ,* a. electric, electrical.

electrización, –*trĭthăthĭŏn',* sf. electrification.

electrizar, –*trĭthăr',* v. a. to electrify.

electuario, –*tŭă'rĭŏ,* sm. electuary.

elefante, *ĕlĕfăn'tĕ,* sm. elephant.

elegancia, *ĕlĕgăn'thĭă,* sf. elegance.

elegante, –*găn'tĕ,* a. elegant, fine.

elegía, *ĕlĕhĕ'ă,* sf. elegy.

elegible, *ĕlĕ'hĕ'blĕ,* a. eligible.

elegidos, –*'hĕ'dŏs,* sm. pl. the elect, the blessed.

elegir, *ĕlĕ'hĭr',* v. a. to choose, to elect.

elemental, *ĕlĕmĕntăl',* a. elemental.

elemento, –*mĕn'tŏ,* sm. element; **–s,** pl. elements, rudiments, first principles.

elevación, –*văthĭŏn',* sf. elevation; highness; exaltation, dignity; ecstasy, rapture; haughtiness, pride, height; altitude.

elevar, –*văr',* v. a. to raise; to elevate; to heave; **–se,** to be enraptured; to be puffed up, to be conceited.

élice, *ĕ'lĭthĕ,* sf. screw.

elidir, *ĕlĭdĭr',* v. a. to weaken, to enervate.

elipse, *ĕlĭp'sĕ,* sf. (geom.) ellipse.

elipsis, *ĕlĭp'sĭs,* sf. (gr.) ellipsis.

Elíseo, *ĕlĭ'sĕŏ,* **Elisio,** –*sĭŏ,* sm. Elysian fields, pl.

elixir, *ĕlĭksĭr',* sm. elixir.

elocución, *ĕlŏkŭthĭŏn',* sf. elocution.

elocuencia, *ĕlŏkŭĕn'thĭă,* sf. eloquence.

elocuente, –*tĕ,* a. eloquent.

elogiador, *ĕlŏ'hĭădŏr',* sm. eulogist, praiser, eulogise.

elogiar, *ĕlŏ'hĭăr',* v. a. to praise, to eulogise.

elogio, *ĕlŏ'hĭŏ,* sm. eulogy, praise.

elucidación, *ĕlŭthĭdăthĭŏn',* sf. elucidation, explanation.

eludir, *ĕlŭdĭr',* v. a. to elude, to escape by stratagem.

emanación, *ĕmănăthĭŏn',* sf. emanation.

emanar, *ĕmănăr',* v. n. to emanate.

emancipación, *ĕmănthĭpăthĭŏn',* sf. emancipation, to set free.

emancipar, –*thĭpăr',* v. a. to emancipate.

embadurnar, *ĕmbădŭrnăr',* v. a. to besmear, to bedaub.

embajada, *ĕmbă'hă'dă,* sf. embassy.

embajador, *ĕmbă'hădŏr',* sm. ambassador.

embalaje, *ĕmbălă'hĕ,* sm. packing, package, in bales.

embalar, *ĕmbălăr',* v. a. to bale, to pack into bales.

embaldosado, *ĕmbăldŏsă'dŏ,* sm. tile-floor.

embaldosar, –*săr',* v. a. to pave with flags.

embalijar, *ĕmbălĭ'hăr',* v. a. to pack into a portmanteau.

emballestarse, *ĕmbălyĕstăr'sĕ,* v. r. to be on the point of discharging a cross-bow.

embalsadero, *ĕmbălsădĕ'rŏ,* sm. pool of stagnant rain-water.

embalsamador, –*mădŏr',* sm. embalmer.

embalsamar, –*măr',* v. a. to embalm.

embanastar, *ĕmbănăstăr',* v. a. to put into a basket.

embarazada, *ĕmbărăthă'dă,* sf. woman with child.

embarazar, –*thăr',* v. a. to embarrass; **–se,** to become intricate.

embarazo, *ĕmbără'thŏ,* sm. embarrassment; obstacle; pregnancy.

embarazoso, sa, _–thŏ'sŏ,_ a. difficult, intricate, entangled.

embarbecer, _ĕmbārbĕthĕr',_ v. n. to appear, to begin to show (of one's beard); to be getting a beard.

embarcación, _ĕmbārkāthŏn',_ sf. embarkation; navigation; any vessel or ship.

embarcadero, _–dā'rŏ,_ sm. quay, wharf; port; harbour.

embarcar, _ĕmbārkār',_ v. a. to embark; –se, to go on shipboard; (fig.) to engage in any affair. [embarkment.

embarco, _ĕmbār'kŏ,_ sm. embarkation,

embargar, _ĕmbārgār',_ v. a. to lay on an embargo; to impede, to restrain.

embargo, _ĕmbār'gŏ,_ sm. embargo on shipping, sequestration; sin–, notwithstanding.

embarnizador, _–nĭthādŏr',_ sm. varnisher.

embarnizadura, _–nĭthādŏ'rā,_ sf. varnishing. [(fig.) to set off.

embarnizar, _–nĭthār',_ v. a. to varnish

embarque, _ĕmbār'kĕ,_ sm. embarkation.

embarrador, _ĕmbārrādŏr',_ sm. plasterer.

embarradura, _–dŏ'rā,_ sf. plastering (of walls, etc.), laying on of mortar.

embarrancarse, _ĕmbārrānkār'sĕ,_ v. r. to bemire oneself.

embarrar, _ĕmbārrār',_ v. a. to overlay with plaster; to parget; –se, to take to the trees (of frightened birds, etc.).

embarrilar, _ĕmbārrĭlār',_ v. a. to pack in barrels. [sew roughly.

embastar, _ĕmbāstār',_ v. a. to baste, to

embate, _ĕmbā'tĕ,_ sm. breakers, pl., surf, surge; impetuous attack. [impostor.

embaucador, _ĕmbāŭkādŏr',_ sm. sharper,

embaucamiento, _–mĭĕn'tŏ,_ sm. deception, illusion. [pose upon.

embaucar, _–kār',_ v. a. to deceive, to im-

embaular, _ĕmbāŭlār',_ v. a. to pack up in a trunk; to cram, to fill with food beyond satiety.

embazar, _ĕmbāthār',_ v. a. to tinge, to shade; (fig.) to astonish; to impede, to stop, to check; –, v. n. to be amazed; –se, to become tired; to be ashamed.

embebecer, _ĕmbĕbĕthĕr',_ v. a. to astonish, to stupefy; to amuse; –se, to be struck with amazement.

embebecimiento, _ĕmbĕbĕthĭmĭĕn'tŏ,_ sm. amazement, astonishment.

embeber, _ĕmbĕbĕr',_ v. a. to imbibe; to soak; to case, to include; to squeeze, to press; –, v. n. to shrink; –se, to be enraptured; to retain firmly in the mind.

embelecar, _ĕmbĕlĕkār',_ v. a. to impose upon, to deceive.

embeleco, _ĕmbĕlē'kŏ,_ sm. fraud, delusion, imposition. [rapture.

embelesamiento, _ĕmbĕlĕsāmĭĕn'tŏ,_ sm.

embelesar, _–sār',_ v. a. to amaze, to astonish. [ravishment.

embeleso, _ĕmbĕlē'sŏ,_ sm. amazement.

embellecer, _ĕmbĕlyĕthĕr',_ v. a. to embellish, to adorn.

emberrincharse, _ĕmbĕrrĭntshār'sĕ,_ v. r. to fly into a violent passion (of children).

embestida, _ĕmbĕstĭ'dā,_ sf. assault, violent attack. [tack.

embestir, _ĕmbĕstĭr',_ v. a. to assail, to at-

embetunar, _ĕmbĕtŭnār',_ v. a. to cover with gum-resin or bitumen.

emblanquecer, _ĕmblānkĕthĕr',_ v. a. to whiten; –se, to grow white. [enamel.

emblema, _ĕmblē'mā,_ sm. emblem; inlay,

embobamiento, _ĕmbŏbāmĭĕn'tŏ,_ sm. astonishment; stupefaction.

embobar, _ĕmbŏbār',_ v. a. to amuse, to divert from, to distract; –se, to be in suspense, to stand gaping.

embobecer, _ĕmbŏbĕthĕr',_ v. a. to stultify, to stupefy; –se, to become stupefied or stultified. [faction.

embobecimiento, _–thĭmĭĕn'tŏ,_ sm. stupe-

embocadero, _ĕmbŏkādĕ'rŏ,_ sm. mouth of a channel or of a river.

embocadura, _–dŏ'rā,_ sf. mouth-piece.

embocar, _ĕmbŏkār',_ v. a. to put into one's mouth; to put one's mouth to; to swallow in haste; to enter by a pass; (fig.) to take hold of, to seize upon; to deceive.

embodegar, _–bŏdĕgār',_ v. a. to warehouse.

embolar, _–bŏlār',_ v. a. to put balls on the ends of bull's horns.

embolismador, ra, _–bŏlĭsmādŏr',_ sm. & f. detracter, reviler.

embolismar, _–bŏlĭsmār',_ v. a. to propagate malicious rumours.

embolismo, _–bŏlĭs'mŏ,_ sm. imbroglio; confusion. [a pump.

émbolo, _ĕm'bŏlŏ,_ sm. embolus, sucker of

embolsar, _–bŏlsār',_ v. a. to put money into a purse; to reimburse.

embolso, _–bŏl'sŏ,_ sm. putting of money into a purse, repayment.

emboque, _–bŏ'kĕ,_ sm. passage of a ball through a ring, etc. (at games).

emborrachar, _–bŏrrātshār',_ v. a. to intoxicate, to inebriate.

emborrar, _–bŏrrār',_ v. a. to stuff with goat's hair; to comb the wool a second time; to swallow victuals hastily, to cram.

emborrascar, _–bŏrrāskār',_ v. a. to provoke, to enrage. [stupefied.

emborricarse, _–bŏrrĭkār'sĕ,_ v. r. to be

emborrizar, _–bŏrrĭthār',_ v. a. to give the first combing to wool. [(mil.) ambush.

emboscada, _–bŏskā'dā,_ sf. ambuscade;

emboscar, _–bŏskār',_ v. a. (mil.) to post in ambush; –se, to retire into the thickest part of a forest; (mil.) to lie in ambush.

embotadura, _–bŏtādŏ'rā,_ sf. bluntness.

embotar, _–bŏtār',_ v. a. to blunt; (fig.) to enervate, to debilitate. [wine.

embotellar, _–bŏtĕlyār',_ v. a. to embottle

embotijar, _–bŏtĭhār',_ v. a. to lay a stratum of small earthen jars, before the flooring is put down, to keep out the damp; –se, to swell; to be in a passion.

embozado, da, _–bŏthā'dŏ,_ a. covered; involved.

embozar, _–bŏthār',_ v. a. to muffle the greater part of the face; (fig.) to cloak, to dissemble.

embozo, –bŏ'thŏ, sm. part of a cloak, veil or any other thing with which the face is muffled: muffling of one's face.

embravecer, –brăvĕthĕr', v. a. to enrage, to irritate: –, v. n. to grow strong and healthy (of plants).

embravecimiento, –brăvĕthĭmĭĕn'tŏ, sm. fury, rage, passion. [shield.

embrazar, –brăthăr', v. a. to clasp a

embreadura, –brĕădŏ'ră, sf. pitching or tarring of a ship.

embrear, –brĕăr', v. a. to pitch a ship.

embriagar, –brĭăgăr', v. a. to intoxicate, to inebriate: to transport, to enrapture.

embriaguez, –brĭăgĕth', sf. intoxication, drunkenness; rapture, transport of mind.

embridar, –brĭdăr', v. n. to bridle.

embrión, ĕmbrĭŏn', sm. embryo.

embrocar, –brŏkăr', v. a. to pour out of one vessel into another, to decanter.

embrollador, ra, –brŏlyădŏr', sm. & f. entangler, confounder. [embroil.

embrollar, –brŏlyăr', v. a. to entangle, to

embrollo, –brŏl'yŏ, sm. imposture; entangler, broiling. [bearer, impostor; entangler.

embrollón, ona, –brŏlyŏn', sm. & f. tale-

embromado, da, –brŏmă'dŏ, a. misty, hazy, foggy; chaffed. [wheedle.

embromar, –brŏmăr', v. a. to cajole, to

embrujar, –brū'hăr', v. a. to bewitch.

embrutecer, –brūtĭthĕr', v. a. to stupefy.

embuchado, –bŭtshă'dŏ, sm. large sausages made of pork, minced very small.

embuchar, –bŭtshăr', v. a. to cram the maw of animals; to swallow victuals without chewing them.

embudar, –bŭdăr', v. a. to put through a funnel; to insnare. [fice.

embudo, ĕmbŏ'dŏ, sm. funnel; fraud, arti-

embuste, ĕmbŏŏs'tĭ, sm. fraud, imposition; pleasing quibble of children; –s, pl. gewgaws, trinkets. [cheat.

embustero, ra, –tĕ'rŏ, sm. & f. impostor.

embutido, ĕmbŏŏtĭ'dŏ, sm. inlaid work.

embutir, –tĭr', v. a. to inlay; to enchase one thing in another; to mix confusedly; to cram, to eat too much.

emendar, ĕmĕndăr', v. a. to correct, to emérito, ĕmă'rĭtŏ, a. emerited. [amend.

emético, ca, ĕmă'tĭkŏ, a. emetic.

emigración, ĕmĭgrăthĭŏn', sf. emigration, migration. [emigrant (m. & f.).

emigrado, da, –gră'dŏ, a. & s. emigrated;

emigrar, –grăr', v. n. to emigrate.

eminencia, –nĕn'thĭă, sf. eminence.

eminente, –nĕn'tĕ, a. eminent, high; excellent, conspicuous.

emisario, –să'rĭŏ, sm. emissary.

emitir, ĕmĭtĭr', v. a. to emit, to send forth; to let go, to let fly. [ing.

emoliente, ĕmŏlĭĕn'tĕ, a. emollient, soften-

emolumento, ĕmŏlŭmĕn'tŏ, sm. emolument, fee, profit, advantage.

empachar, ĕmpătshăr', v. a. to impede, to embarrass; to cram, to surfeit; –se, to be ashamed, to be confounded.

empacho, ĕmpătsh'ŏ, sm. bashfulness, timidity; embarrassment.

empachoso, sa, –tshŏ'sŏ, a. embarrassing; bashful, timid.

empadronamiento, ĕmpădrŏnămĭĕn'tŏ, sm. register of excisable persons.

empadronar, –pădrŏnăr', v. a. to enter in a register the names of those who are liable to pay certain taxes.

empalagamiento, –pălăgămĭĕn'tŏ, sm. surfeiting, surfeit, disgust; to trouble.

empalagar, –pălăgăr', v. a. to loathe; to

empalago, –pălă'gŏ, sm. disgust, nausea.

empalagoso, –gŏ'sŏ, a. squeamish, loathsome; fastidious, troublesome.

empalar, ĕmpălăr', v. a. to empale.

empalizada, –pălĭză'dă, sf. (mil.) palisade or palisado.

empalizar, –pălĭzăr', v. a. to palisade.

empalmadura, –pălmădŏ'ră, sf. joining of two pieces of wood; welding of metals.

empalmar, –pălmăr', v. a. to join the ends of two pieces of timber.

empalme, –păl'mĕ, sm. (rail.) junction.

empanada, –pănă'dă, sf. meat-pie.

empanar, –pănăr', v. a. to cover with paste.

empantanar, –păntănăr', v. a. to submerge; to drag in the mire; to complicate a matter. [of children.

empañadura, –pănyădŏ'ră, sf. swaddling

empañar, –pănyăr', v. a. to swaddle, to swathe; to tarnish a glass with one's breath; to impeach one's reputation; –se, to grow dull.

empapar, –păpăr', v. a. to imbibe; –se, to imbibe; to go deeply into a matter.

empapelar, –păpĕlăr', v. a. to wrap up in paper. [into bales.

empaquetar, –păkĕtăr', v. a. to pack goods

emparedamiento, –părĕdămĭĕn'tŏ, sm. confinement; cloister. [immure.

emparedar, –dăr', v. n. to confine, to

emparejadura, –hădŏ'ră, sf. equalisation. [match, to fit, to equalise.

emparejar, –hăr', v. a. to level; to

emparentar, ĕmpărĕntăr', v. n. to be related by marriage.

emparrado, –părră'dŏ, sm. vine-arbour.

emparrar, –părrăr', v. a. to embower.

emparvar, –părvăr', v. a. to put grain in order to be thrashed.

empastar, –păstăr', v. a. to paste; to cover plentifully with colours. [pension.

empatadera, –pătădă'ră, sf. check; sus-

empatar, –pătăr', v. a. to equal; to check, to suspend; to cut short a speech.

empate, ĕmpă'tĕ, sm. equality of votes; stop, suspension.

empavesar, –păvĕsăr', v. a. to deck out with flags; (mar.) to dress a ship.

empecatado, da, –pĕkătă'dŏ, a. turbulent.

empedernir, –pĕdĕrnĭr', v. a. to harden; –se, to petrify; to be inflexible.

empedrado, –pĕdră'dŏ, sm. pavement.

empedrador, –pĕdrădŏr', sm. paver, pavier, pavior.

empedrar, –pĕdrăr', v. a. to pave.

empega, *empĕ'gă*, sf. varnish of pitch; mark of pitch.

empegado, *-pĕgă'dō*, sm. (mar.) tarpaulin.

empegadura, *-pĕgădō'ră*, sf. varnish of pitch put on vessels.

empegar, *-pĕgăr'*, v. a. to pitch.

empeine, *-pă'ĭnĕ*, sm. groin; instep; hoof of a beast.   [with skins.

empellejar, *-pĕlyĕ'hăr*, v. a. to cover with skins.

empellón, *-pĕlyōn'*, sm. push, heavy blow; á –ones, rudely.   [with plumes.

empenachar, *-pĕnăchăr'*, v. a. to adorn with plumes.

empeñar, *-pĕnyăr'*, v. a. to pawn, to pledge; to engage, to oblige; –se, to bind oneself to pay debts contracted; to persist in a resolution; to intercede.

empeño, *-pĕn'yō*, sm. obligation; engagement; courage; perseverance; protection.

empeorar, *-pĕōrăr'*, v. a. to make worse; –, v. n. to grow worse.

emperador, *-pĕrădōr'*, sm. emperor.

emperatriz, *-pĕrătrĭth'*, sf. empress.

emperejilar, *-pĕrĕ'hĭlăr'*, v. a. to trick out.   [or indolent.

emperezar, *-pĕrĕthăr'*, v.n. & f. to be lazy

emperifollarse, *-pĕrĭfōlyăr'sĕ*, v. a. to overdress oneself.

empero, *empĕ'rō*, c. yet, however.

emperrarse, *-pĕrrăr'sĕ*, v. r. to grow mad.

empezar, *-pĕthăr'*, v. a. to begin, to commence.   [alted, raised to a high dignity.

empinado, da, *-pĭnă'dō*, a. elevated, exempinadura, *-pĭnădō'ră*, sf. elevation, raising.

empinar, *-pĭnăr'*, v. a. to raise; to exalt; to drink much; –se, to stand on tiptoe; to rise high.   [of hawks with jesses.

empiolar, *-pĭōlăr'*, v. a. to tie the legs

empíreo, *empĕ'rĕō*, sm. empyrean (the highest heaven); –, rea, a. celestial.

empírico, *-pĕ'rĭkō*, sm. quack, empiric; –, ca, a. empirical.

empirismo, *-pĭrĭs'mō*, sm. empiricism.

empizarrado, *-pĭthărră'dō*, sm. slate-roofing.   [to roof with slate.

empizarrar, *-pĭthărrăr'*, v. a. to slate,

emplastadura, *-plăstădō'ră*, sf. plastering.

emplastar, *-plăstăr'*, v. a. to apply plasters; to paint the face; to check the course of an affair; –se, to bedaub one's hands or feet.

emplasto, *-plăs'tō*, sm. plaster.

emplazador, *-plăthădōr'*, sm. (law) summoner, apparitor.   [mons, citation.

emplazamiento, *-plăthămĭen'tō*, sm.sum-

emplazar, *-plăthăr'*, v. a. to summon.

empleado, *-plĕă'dō*, sm. official.

emplear, *-plĕăr'*, v. a. to employ; to occupy; to commission.   [occupation.

empleo, *emplĕ'ō*, sm. employ, employment;

emplomador, *-plōmădōr'*, sm. plumber.

emplomar, *-plōmăr'*, v. a. to lead.

emplumar, *-plūmăr'*, v. a. to adorn with feathers; –se, to get feathers.

emplumecer, *-plūmĕthĕr'*, v. n. to begin to get feathers

empobrecer, *-pōbrĕthĕr'*, v. a. to reduce to poverty; –, v. n. to become poor.

empobrecimiento, *-pōbrĕthĭmĭen'tō*, sm. impoverishing.   [–, v. n. to putrify.

empodrecer, *-pōdrĕthĕr'*, v. a. to corrupt;

empolvar, *-pōlvăr'* v. a. to powder, to sprinkle powder.

empolladura, *-pōlyădō'ră*, sf. brood, hatch, covey (of birds); brood (of bees).

empollar, *-pōlyăr'*, v. a. to brook, to hatch.

emponzoñador, ra, *-pōnthōnyădōr'*, sm. & f. poisoner.   [ing.

emponzoñamiento, *-mĭen'tō*, sm. poisonemponzoñar, *-pōnthōnyăr'*, v. a. to poison; to taint, to corrupt.

emporcar, *-pōrkăr'*, v. a. to soil, to dirty.

emporio, *empō'rĭō*, sm. emporium.

empotrar, *-pōtrăr'*, v. a. to join with a mortise; to scarf, to splice.

emprendedor, *-prĕndĕdōr'*, sm. enterpriser; undertaker.   [to undertake.

emprender, *-prĕndĕr'*, v. a. to enterprise,

empreñar, *-prĕnyăr'*, v. a. to impregnate; –se, to beget.

empresa, *emprĕ' să*, sf. symbol, motto; enterprise, undertaking; design, purpose.

empresario, *-prĕsă'rĭō*, sm. manager of a theatre.   [loan.

empréstito, *-prĕs'tĭtō*, sm. lending money;

empringar, *-prĭngăr'*, v. a. to grease.

empujar, *-pŭ'hăr'*, v. a. to push, to press forward.   [pulse, pushing.

empuje, *empŭ'hĕ*, sm. impulsion, impempujón, *-pŭ'hōn'*, sm. impulse, push; á –ones, pushingly, rudely.   [sword.

empuñadura, *-pŭnyădō'ră*, sf. hilt of a

empuñar, *-pŭnyăr'*, v. a. to clinch, to clutch, to gripe with the fist.

emulación, *ĕmŭlăthĭōn'*, sf. emulation, corrivalship.

emular, *ĕmŭlăr'*, v. a. to emulate, to rival.

émulo, *ĕ'mŭlō*, sm. competitor, rival.

emulsión, *ĕmŭlsĭōn'*, sf. emulsion.

en, *ĕn*, pr. in; for; on, upon.

enaguas, *ĕnă'gŭăs*, sf. pl. petticoat.

enajenación, *-ă'hĕnăthĭōn'*, sf. alienation; absence of mind.

enajenamiento, *-mĭen'tō*, sm. change of affection; rapture, astonishment.

enajenar, *-ă'hĕnăr'*, v. a. to alienate; to rapture; –se, to fall out.

enalbardar, *-ălbărdăr'*, v. a. to lay a pack-saddle on beasts of burden; to cover with a batter of eggs, flour, and sugar.

enamoradamente, *-ămōră'dămĕn'tĕ*, ad. lovingly.   [to love.

enamoradizo, za, *-ămōră'dĕ'thō*,a.inclined

enamorado, da, *-ămōră'dō*, a. in love, enamoured, lovesick.   [wooer.

enamorador, *-ămōrădōr'*, sm. lover.

enamoramiento, *-ămōrămĭen'tō*, sm. enamouring, love-suit.

enamorar, *-ămōrăr'*, v. a. to inspire love; –se, to fall in love.   [slightly in love.

enamoricarse, *-ămōrĭkăr'sĕ*, v. r. to be

enano, na, *ĕnă'nō*, a. dwarfish; –, sm. dwarf.   [high.

enarbolar, *-ărbōlăr'*, v. a. to hoist, to raise

enardecer, –ārdĕthĕr', v. a. to fire with passion, to inflame.

enarenar, –ārĕnār', v. a. to fill with sand.

enarrar, ĕnārrār', v. a. to narrate.

enastar, ĕnāstār', v. a. to put a handle to.

encabalgar, –kābālgār', v. a. to provide horses, to horse.

encabestrar, –kābĕstrār', v. a. to guide by a halter; –se, to be entangled in the halter.

encabezamiento, –kābĕthāmĭĕn'tŏ, sm. register of persons liable to pay a tax; tax, tribute.

encabezar, –kābĕthār', v. a. to make up the tax-roll; –se, to compound for taxes.

encabritarse, –kābrītār'sĕ, v. r. to rear (of horses).   [nails].

encachar, –kāt'shār, v. a. to drive in (of nails).

encadenamiento, –kādĕnāmĭĕn'tŏ, sm. linking together, chaining.

encadenar, –kādĕnār', v. a. to chain, to link together; to connect, to unite.

encajador, –kā'hādŏr, sm. enchasing-tool.

encajadura, –kā'hādŏ'rā, sf. enchasing.

encajar, –kā'hār', v. a. to enchase, to drive in, to foist; to introduce something with craft and cunning; –se, to thrust oneself into some narrow place.

encaje, ĕnkā'h'ĕ, sm. enchasing; joining together; lace; inlaid work.

encajera, –kā'hā'rā, sf. lacewoman.

encajonado, –kā'hŏnā'dŏ, sm. mud-wall supported by pillars of bricks.

encajonamiento, –mĭĕn'tŏ, sm. packing into boxes, etc.

encajonar, –kā'hŏnār', v. a. to pack up in a box, to lay in a chest.

encalabrinar, –kālābrīnār', v. a. to make confused; –se, to become obstinate.

encaladura, –kālādŏ'rā, sf. whitening, whitewash.

encalar, –kālār', v. a. to whitewash.

encallar, kālyār', v. n. (mar.) to run aground; to be checked in the progress of some enterprise.

encallecer, –kālyĕthĕr', v. n. to get corns.

encamarse, –kāmār'sĕ, v. r. to lie abed or a-bed; to go to bed.

encaminar, –kāmīnār', v. a. to guide, to show the way; –se, to take a road.

encandecer, –kāndĕthĕr', v. a. to heat to a white heat.   [to grow old.

encanecer, –kānĕthĕr', v. n. to grow grey;

encanillar, –kānīlyār', v. a. to wind silk, wool or linen on a quill of cane.

encantador, –kāntādŏr', sm. enchanter, sorcerer, magician.   [chantress.

encantadora, –dō'rā, sf. sorceress, en-

encantamiento, –mĭĕn'tŏ, sm. enchantment, charming.   [charm.

encantar, –kāntār', v. a. to enchant, to

encantarar, –kāntārār', v. a. to put into a jar or a pitcher.   [charm.

encanto, ĕnkān'tŏ, sm. enchantment, spell.

encañado, –kānyā'dŏ, sm. conduit of water; hedge of canes or reeds.

encañar, –kānyār', v. a. to enclose with a hedge of cane; to convey water through conduits.

encañizada, –kānyīthā'dā, sf. weir made of cane and reeds for catching mullets.

encañonar, –kānyŏnār', v. a. & n. to begin to grow fledged; to plait, to fold; to introduce.   [plait.

encañutar, –kānyūtār', v. a. to flute; to

encapado, da, –kāpā'dŏ, a. cloaked.

encaperuzarse, –kāpĕrūthār'sĕ, v. r. to cover one's head with a hood.

encapillar, –kāpīlyār', v. a. to cover the head with a hood, &c.

encapotar, –kāpŏtār', v. a. to cover with a cloak; –se, to be clouded; to look sullen.

encapricharse, –kāprītshār'sĕ, v. r. to become stubborn.

encapuchar, –kāpūtshār', v. a. to cover any thing with a hood.   [extol.

encaramar, –kārāmār', v. a. to raise; to

encarar, –kārār', v. n. to face, to come face to face.   [ceration.

encarcelación, –kārthĕlāthĭŏn', sf. incar-

encarcelar, –kārthĕlār', v. a. to imprison.

encarecer, –kārĕthĕr', v. a. to raise the price; (fig.) to enhance, to exaggerate.

encarecimiento, –thīmĭĕn'tŏ, sm. enhancement; exaggeration; con–, ardently.

encargar, –kārgār', v. a. to charge, to commission.   [office, employ.

encargo, ĕnkār'gŏ, sm. charge, commission.

encarnación, –kārnāthĭŏn', sf. incarnation; carnation.

encarnado, da, –kārnā'dŏ, a. incarnate; dyed flesh-colour; –, sm. flesh-colour.

encarnamiento, –mĭĕn'tŏ, sm. (med.) incarnation.

encarnar, –kārnār', v. n. to incarnate, to breed flesh; –, v. a. to give a flesh-colour to pieces of sculpture; to pierce the flesh; –se, to incorporate one thing with an other.

encarnativo, –kārnātĭ'vŏ, a. incarnative.

encarnizado, da, –kārnīthā'dŏ, a. fleshed; blood-shot, inflamed.

encarnizar, –kārnīthār', v. a. to satiate with flesh; to provoke, to irritate; –se, to be glutted with flesh; to be cruelly minded towards.   [lawry, proscription.

encartamiento, –kārtāmĭĕn'tŏ, sm. out-

encartar, –kārtār', v. a. to proscribe; to involve in an unpleasant affair; to enter in the register of taxes; –se, to receive a card which spoils a game.

encarte, ĕnkār'tĕ, sm. cards laid out.

encasquetar, –kāskĕtār', v. a. to cram a hat on to one's head; (fig.) to induce one to adopt or espouse an opinion; –se, to be headstrong.

encastar, –kāstār', v. a. to improve a race of animals; to procreate, to generate.

encastillar, –kāstīlyār', v. a. to fortify with castles; –, v. n. to make the cell of the queen-bee; –se, to shut oneself up for defence in a castle; to be ready.

encebadar, –thĕbādār', v. a. to surfeit with oats and water drunk immediately after (applied to horses); –se, to be surfeited by drinking water immediately after eating oats.

encebollado, –thĕbŏlyă′dŏ, sm. fricassee of beef or mutton and onions, seasoned with spice. [cheese in a wattle.

encellar, –thĕlyar′, v. a. to mould curds or **encenagado, da,** –thĕnăga′dŏ, a. mixed with mud. [ing in dirt or mire.

encenagamiento, –mĭen′tŏ, sm. wallow**encenagar,** v. a. –se, –thĕnăgar′, to wallow in dirt or mire; (fig.) to wallow in vices.

encender, ĕnthĕndĕr′, v. a. to kindle, to light, to set on fire; to inflame, to incite; to foment a party; –se, to fire, to take fire; to fly into a passion. [coloured.

encendido, da, –dī′dŏ, a. inflamed; high **encendimiento,** –dīmĭen′tŏ, sm. inflamation; glow. [blind; sticking-plaster.

encerado, –thĕră′dŏ, sm. oil-cloth; window**encerar,** –thĕrar′, v. a. to wax; to fill or stiffen with wax.

encerotar, –thĕrŏtar′, v. a. to wax thread.

encerrar, –thĕrrar′, v. a. to shut up, to confine; to contain; –se, to withdraw from the world.

encespedar, –thĕspĕdar′, v. a. to turf.

encía, ĕnthĕ′ă, sf. gum (of the teeth).

encíclica, ĕnthē′klĭkă, sf. encyclical epistle.

enciclopedia, –thĭklŏpĕ′dĭă, sf. cyclopædia, encyclopedia. [clopædian.

enciclopédico, ca, –thĭklŏpĕ′dĭkŏ, a. ency**encierro,** –thĭer′rŏ, sm. confinement, enclosure; cloister; prison; driving bulls into the pen-fold for the bull-feasts.

encima, –thē′mă, ad. above, over; at the top; over and above, besides.

encina, –thē′nă, sf. evergreen oak.

encinar, –thĭnar′, sm. evergreen oakwood; evergreen oak-grove. [ribbons.

encintar, –thĭntar′, v. a. to garnish with **enclaustrado, da,** –klăŭstra′dŏ, a. shut up in cloisters.

enclavadura, –klăvădŏ′ră, sf. groove.

enclavar, –klăvar′, v. a. to nail.

enclavijar, –klăvī′har′, v. a. to join closely; to put pegs in a musical instrument.

enclenque, –klĕn′kĕ, sm. weakling.

encobertado, –kŏbĕrtă′dŏ, a. wrapped up.

encoger, –kŏ′hĕr′, v. a. to contract, to shorten; to shrink; –se, to be low spirited; to humble oneself.

encogidamente, –kŏ′hĭdămĕn′tĕ, ad. meanly, abjectly. [timid, narrow-minded.

encogido, da, –kŏ′hī′dŏ, a. pusillanimous, **encogimiento,** –kŏ′hĭmĭen′tŏ, sm. contraction; constriction; pusillanimity.

encohetar, –kŏĕtar′, v. a. to throw squibs at bulls (at bull-fights).

encojar, –kŏ′har′, v. a. to cripple, to lame; –se, to grow lame; to feign sickness.

encoladura, –kŏlădŏ′ră, sf. gluing.

encolar, –kŏlar′, v. a. to glue.

encolerizar, –kŏlĕrĭthar′, v. a. to provoke, to irritate.

encomendar, –kŏmĕndar′, v. a. to recommend; –se, to commit oneself to another's protection.

encomienda, –kŏmĭen′dă, sm. commission, charge; message; (mil.) comman

dery; patronage, protection; –s, pl. compliments. [commendation.

encomio, ĕnkŏ′mĭŏ, sm. encomium, praise, **enconar,** –kŏnar′, v. a. to inflame, to irritate.

encono, ĕnkŏ′nŏ, sm. malevolence, rancour.

enconoso, sa, –kŏnŏ′sŏ, a. hurtful, prejudicial; malevolent.

encontradizo, za, –kŏntrădē′thŏ, a. that which may be met on the way. [in front.

encontrado, da, –kŏntră′dŏ, a. opposite, **encontrar,** –kŏntrar′, v. a. & n. to meet, to encounter; to assemble, to come together; –se, to encounter in an hostile manner, to clash; to be of contrary opinions. [tuous, boastful.

encopetado, da, –kŏpĕtă′dŏ, a. presump**encorajar,** –kŏră′har′, v. a. to give courage, to inflame; –se, to be in a rage.

encorchar, –kŏrtshar′, v. a. to hive bees.

encordar, –kŏrdar′, v. a. to chord musical instruments. [cords; to cord a bed.

encordelar, –kŏrdĕlar′, v. a. to tie with **encorvadura,** –kŏrvădŏ′ră, sf. act of bending; crookedness.

encorvar, –kŏrvar′, v. a. to bend, to crook.

encostrar, –kŏstrar′, v. a. to crust, to incrust; to rough-cast.

encrespar, –krĕspar′, v. a. to curl, to frizzle; –se, to become boisterous; to be involved in quarrels. [haughty, lofty.

encrestado, da, –krĕstă′dŏ, a. (fig.) **encrestarse,** –krĕstar′sĕ, v. r. to get the crest (applied to a young cock).

encrucijada, –krŏthĕ′hă′dă, sf. cross-way.

encrudecer, –krŏdĕthĕr′, v. a. to make a wound worse; to exasperate, to irritate.

encuadernación, –kŭădĕrnăthĭŏn′, sf. binding books. [binder.

encuadernador, –kŭădĕrnădŏr′, sm. book**encuadernar,** –kŭădĕrnar′, v. a. to bind books; to reconcile. [casks.

encubar, –kŭbar′, v. a. to put liquids into **encubiertamente,** –kŭbĭertămĕn′tĕ, ad. secretly; deceitfully. [cealed.

encubierto, ta, –kŭbĭer′tŏ, a. hidden, con**encubridor, ra,** –kŭbrĭdŏr′, sm. & f. concealer, harbourer; receiver of stolen goods.

encubrimiento, –mĭen′tŏ, sm. concealment, hiding. [ceal.

encubrir, –kŭbrīr′, v. a. to hide, to con**encuentro,** –kŭĕn′trŏ, sm. shock, justle; encounter. [elevated.

encumbrado, da, –kŭmbra′dŏ, a. high, **encumbramiento,** –mĭen′tŏ, sm. elevating; height.

encumbrar, –kŭmbrar′, v. a. to raise, to elevate; to mount, to ascend a height; –se, to be raised.

encureñado, da, –kŭrĕnyă′dŏ, a. put into the carriage or stock. [or vinegar.

encurtir, –kŭrtīr′, v. a. to souse in pickle **enchapar,** –tshăpar′, v. a. to veneer.

encharcarse, –tshărkăr′sĕ, v. r. to be inundated.

endeble, ĕndĕ′blĕ, a. feeble, weak.

endecasílabo, ba, –dĕkăs′lăbŏ, a. consisting of eleven syllables.

endecha, –dĕtsh′ă, sf. dirge.

endechar, –dĕtshär´, v. a. to sing funeral songs in honour and praise of the dead; **–se**, to grieve, to mourn.

endemoniado, da, –dĕmōnĭä´dō, a. possessed with the devil; devilish.

endemoniar, –dĕmōnĭar´, v. a. to possess with the devil; to irritate, to provoke.

enderezadamente, –dĕrĕthädämĕn´tĕ, ad. justly, rightly; directly. [direction.

enderezamiento, –mĭĕn´tō, sm. guidance.

enderezar, –dĕrĕthär´, v. a. to rectify, to set right; to address; **–se**, to stand upright.

endiablada, –dĭäblä´dä, sf. mummery.

endiablado, da, –dĭäblä´dō, a. devilish, diabolical; ugly.

endiosar, –dĭōsär´, v. a. to deify; **–se**, to be puffed up with pride.

endosante, –dōsän´tĕ, sm. endorser.

endosar, –dōsär´, v. a. to endorse a bill of exchange.

endosatario, –dōsätä´rĭō, sm. endorsee.

endoso, ĕndō´sō, sm. endorsement of a bill of exchange.

endrina, –drē´nä, sf. sloe. [tree.

endrino, –drē´nō, sm. black-thorn, sloe-tree.

endulzar, –dŭlthär´, v. a. to sweeten; **–se**, to soften.

endurecer, –dŭrĕthĕr´, v. a. to harden, to indurate; **–se**, to become cruel, to grow hard. [pertinaciously.

endurecidamente, ĕndŭrĕthĭdämĕn´tĕ, ad.

endurecimiento, –thĭmĭĕn´tō, sm. hardness; obstinacy; hardness of heart.

enebro, ĕnĕ´brō, sm. (bot.) common juniper. [tile; –, sm. fiend.

enemigo, ga, ĕnĕmē´gō, a. inimical, hostile; –, sm. fiend.

enemistad, –mĭstäd´, sf. enmity, hatred.

enemistar, –mĭstär´, v. a. to make an enemy; –, v. n. to become an enemy.

energia, ĕnĕr´hē´ä, sf. energy, power, vigour; strength of will. [pressive.

energico, ca, ĕnĕr´hĭcō, a. energetic; expressive.

energúmeno, na, ĕnĕrgō´mĕnō, sm. & f. demoniac, one possessed.

enero, ĕnĕ´rō, sm. January.

enervar, ĕnĕrvär´, v. a. to enervate.

enfadadizo, za, ĕnfädädē´thō, a. irritable, irascible. [to trouble.

enfadar, –fädär´, v. a. to vex, to molest, to trouble.

enfado, –fä´dō, sm. trouble, vexation.

enfadoso, sa, –fädō´sō, a. vexatious, troublesome.

enfaldar, –fäldär´, v. a. to lop off the lower branches of trees; **–se**, to tuck up one's clothes.

enfardar, –färdär´, v. a. to pack, to bale goods. [into bales.

enfardelar, –färdĕlär´, v. a. to make up goods.

énfasis, ĕn´fäsĭs, sm. & f. emphasis.

enfático, ca, ĕnfä´tĭkō, a. emphatic.

enfermar, –fĕrmär´, v. n. to fall ill; v. a. to make sick; to weaken.

enfermedad, –fĕrmĕdäd´´, sf. indisposition, illness.

enfermería, –fĕrmĕrē´ä, sf. infirmary.

enfermero, ra, –fĕrmĕ´rō, sm. & f. sick-nurse; hospital nurse or attendant.

enfermizo, za, –fĕrmē´thō, a. infirm, sickly. [indisposed.

enfermo, ma, ĕnfĕr´mō, a. sick, diseased.

enfervorizar, –fĕrvōrĭthär´, v. a. to heat, to inflame, to incite.

enfeudar, –fĕüdär´, v. a. to enfeoff.

enfilar, –fĭlär´, v. a. to put in a row; (mil.) to put in closed ranks; to enfilade.

enfiteusis, –fĭtĕ´üsĭs, sf. emphyteusia, copyhold, alienation of the usufruct.

enfiteuta, –fĭtĕü´tä, sm. emphyteuta, copyholder. [teutic.

enfitéutico, ca, –fĭtĕ´ütĭkō, a. emphyteutic.

enflaquecer, –fläkĕthĕr´, v. a. to weaken, to thin; **–se**, to fall away.

enflaquecimiento, –thĭmĭĕn´tō, sm. extenuation, maceration.

enfoscado, da, ĕnfōskä´dō, a. brow-beaten; confused, entangled.

enfoscarse, –fōskär´sĕ, v. r. to be troubled or perplexed; to be immersed in business; to be cloudy.

enfrascar, –fräskär´, v. a. to pour liquid into a flask; **–se**, to be entangled in brambles and briers; to be involved in difficulties. [to restrain.

enfrenar, –frĕnär´, v. a. to bridle; to curb, to restrain.

enfrente, –frĕn´tĕ, ad. over against, opposite, in front of the house.

enfriadera, –frĭädĕ´rä, sf. cooler, refrigerator. [ration.

enfriamiento, –frĭämĭĕn´tō, sm. refrigeration.

enfriar, –frĭär´, v. a. to cool, to refrigerate; **–se**, to cool down.

enfurecer, –fŭrĕthĕr´, v. a. to irritate, to enrage; **–se**, to grow boisterous or furious (of the wind and sea); to become furious or enraged.

enfurruñarse, –fŭrrūnyär´sĕ, v. r. to grow angry, to frown. [deck.

engalanar, –gälänär´, v. a. to adorn, to deck.

engallado, da, –gälyä´dō, a. erect, upright.

engalladura, –gälyädō´rä, sf. tread, the cock's sperm in the egg. [thigh.

engallarse, –gälyär´sĕ, v. r. to carry it high.

enganchador, –gänshädōr´, sm. (mil.) recruiter.

enganchar, –gänshär´, v. a. to hook, to accroach; to ensnare; to decoy into the military service. [footrap.

engañabobos, –gänyäbō´bōs, sm. impostor, footrap.

engañadizo, za, –gänyädē´thō, a. deceivable, easily deceived. [postor, deceiver.

engañador, –gänyädōr´, sm. cheat, impostor, deceiver.

engañar, –gänyär´, v. a. to deceive, to cheat; **–se**, to be deceived; to make a mistake.

engañifa, –gänyē´fä, sf. deceit, trick.

engaño, ĕngän´yō, sm. mistake, misunderstanding, deceit, fraud. [artful, false.

engañoso, sa, –gänyō´sō, a. deceitful, artful, false.

engarabatar, –gäräbätär´, v. a. to hook; **–se**, to grow crooked.

engarabitarse, –gäräbĭtär´sĕ, v. r. to climb, to mount.

engaritar, –gärĭtär´, v. a. to place sentryboxes; to deceive in a dexterous manner.

engarzar, -gärthär', v. a. to enchain, to link; to curl.

engastar, -gästär', v. a. to enchase.

engaste, ĕngäs'tĕ, sm. enchasing.

engastrimismo, -gästrĭmĭs'mŏ, sm. ventriloquism. [loquist.

engastrimita, -gästrĭmē'tä, sm. ventriloquist.

engatar, -gätär', v. a. to cheat in a dexterous manner. [a cramp-iron.

engatillar, -gätĭlyär', v. a. to bind with

engatusamiento, -gätŭsämēén'tŏ, sm. deception, cheat, coaxing.

engatusar, -gätŭsär', v. a. to coax.

engazar, -gäthär', v. a. to enchain, to link; to splice an end of a rope in a circular form about a block; to dye cloth in the piece. [engender, to produce.

engendrar, -hĕndrär', v. a. to beget, to

engendro, ĕn'hĕn'drŏ, sm. fœtus, embryo; mal—, low breed; a perverse youth.

engolfar, -gŏlfär', v. n. to enter a gulf; —se, to be engaged in arduous undertakings or difficult affairs.

engolillado, -gŏlĭlyä'dŏ, a. wearing the collar which is worn by lawyers in Spain.

engolosinar, -gŏlŏsĭnär', v. a. to give a taste for; —se, to find delight in.

engomadura, -gŏmädŭ'rä, sf. gumming.

engomar, -gŏmär', v. a. to gum.

engordar, -gŏrdär', v. a. to fatten; —se, to grow fat; to grow rich.

engorro, ĕngŏr'rŏ, sm. (fam.) embarrassment, obstacle. [cumbrous.

engorroso, sa, -gŏrrŏ'sŏ, a. troublesome,

engrandecer, -gründĕthĕr', v. a. to augment, to aggrandise; to exaggerate.

engrandecimiento, -thĭmēĕn'tŏ, sm. increase, aggrandisement; exaggeration.

engrasar, ĕngräsär', v. a. to grease, to oil, to fat. [sumption, vanity.

engreimiento, -grēĭmēén'tŏ, sm. presumption, vanity.

engreir, -grēĭr', v. a. to make proud; —se, to grow proud.

engrescar, -grĕskär', v. a. & n. to goad into quarrelling or fighting. [displeased.

engrifarse, -grĭfär'sĕ, v. r. to tiff, to be

engrosar, -grŏsär', v. a. to make fat; —, v. n. to increase in bulk. [ing; gluing.

engrudamiento, -grŭdämēén'tŏ, sm. pasting.

engrudar, -grŭdär', v. a. to paste.

engrudo, ĕngrŭ'dŏ, sm. paste.

engualdrapar, -gŭäldräpär', v. a. to caparison a horse. [with pebbles.

enguijarrar, -gēhärrär', v. a. to pave

engullidor, ra, -gŭlyĭdŏr', sm. & f. devourer; gobbler. [gobble, to glut.

engullir, -gŭlyĭr', v. a. to swallow, to

enharinar, -ärĭnär', v. a. to cover or besprinkle with flour. [rows in a quiver.

enhastillar, -ästĭlyär', v. a. to put arrows in a quiver.

enhebrar, -ĕbrär', v. a. to thread a needle.

enhestar, -ĕstär', v. a. to erect, to set up.

enhilar, -ĭlär', v. a. to thread. [right.

enhorabuena, -ŏräbŭĕ'nä, sf. congratulation; felicitation; —, ad. well and good.

enhoramala, -mä'lä, ad. in an evil hour.

enigma, ĕnĭg'mä, sm. enigma, riddle.

enigmático, ca, ĕnĭgmä'tĭkŏ, a. enigmatical, dark, obscure. [ing.

enjabonadura, ĕn'häbŏnädŭ'rä, sf. soaping.

enjabonar, -häbŏnär', v. a. to soap; to insult with foul language and blows.

enjaezar, -häĕthär', v. a. to caparison a horse.

enjalbegar, -hälbĕgär', v. a. to whitewash the walls of a building.

enjalma, ĕn'häl'mä, sf. pack-saddle.

enjalmero, -hälmĕ'rŏ, sm. pack-saddle maker.

enjambradero, 'hämbrädĕ'rŏ, sm. place where bees swarm to form their hives.

enjambrar, -hämbrär', v. a. to gather a scattered swarm of bees; —, v. n. to swarm; to multiply. [ing of bees.

enjambrazón, -hämbräthŏn', sf. swarming.

enjambre, -häm'brĕ, sm. swarm of bees; crowd, multitude. [cage; to imprison.

enjaular, -häŭlär', v. a. to shut up in a

enjebar, -hĕbär', v. a. to steep in lye.

enjebe, -hĕ'bĕ, sm. lye-steeping; bucking.

enjergar, -hĕrgär', v. a. to set about a business. [trees.

enjertal, -hĕrtäl', sm. nursery of grafted

enjoyar, -hŏyär', v. a. to adorn with jewels; to set a ring with precious stones; to heighten the brilliancy of a thing.

enjuagadura, -hŭägädŭ'rä, sf. rinsing of the mouth.

enjuagar, -hŭägär', v. a. to rinse the mouth and teeth; to rinse clothes.

enjuague, -hŭä'gĕ, sm. water used to rinse the mouth; intrigue.

enjugador, ra, -hŭgädŏr', sm. & f. one who dries; clothes-horse.

enjugar, -hŭgär', v. a. to dry; to wipe off; —se, to dry up; to grow lean.

enjuiciar, -hŭĭthēär', v. a. to prepare a law-suit for judgment; to pass judgment.

enjuncar, -hŭnkär', v. a. to tie with rush ropes. [of fowls.

enjundia, ĕn'hŭn'dēä, sf. fat in the inside

enjutar, -hŭtär', v. a. to dry.

enjutez, -hŭtĕth', sf. dryness.

enjuto, ta, -hŭ'tŏ, a. dried.

enlace, ĕnlä'thĕ, sm. connection, coherence; link; kindred, affinity; flourish.

enladrillado, -lädrĭlyä'dŏ, sm. pavement of brick. [layer.

enladrillador, -lädrĭlyädŏr', sm. bricklayer.

enladrillar, -lädrĭlyär', v. a. to pave a floor with bricks. [grease, to baste.

enlardar, -lärdär', v. a. to rub with

enlazable, -läthä'blĕ, a. which can be fastened together. [knit, to lace.

enlazar, -läthär', v. a. to join, to unite; to

enlodar, -lŏdär', v. a. to bemire.

enloquecer, -lŏkĕthĕr', v. a. to madden, to make mad.

enloquecimiento, -lŏkĕthĭmēĕn'tŏ, sm. enraging, maddening. [flags.

enlosar, -lŏsär', v. a. to lay a floor with

enlozanarse, -lŏthänär'sĕ, v. r. to boast of one's dexterity or strength.

enlutar, -lŭtär', v. a. to put into mourning; —se, to go into mourning.

enmaderar, –mădĕrắr, v. a. to roof a house with timber.

enmarañar, –mărănyăr, v. a. to entangle, to involve in difficulties; to puzzle.

enmarillecerse, –mărĭlyĕthĕr´sĕ, v. r. to become pale or yellow.

enmaromar, –mărŏmăr, v. a. to tie with a rope.

enmascarar, –măskărăr, v. a. to mask; –se, to go in disguise, to masquerade.

enmendación, –mĕndăthĭŏn´, sf. emendation, correction.

enmendar, ĕnmĕndăr, v. a. to correct, to reform; to repair, to compensate; to abrogate.

enmienda, ĕnmĭĕn´dă, sf. correction, amendment; emendation; reward; compensation; parliamentary amendment.

enmohecer, –mŏĕthĕr, v. a. to mould, to must; –se, to grow mouldy or musty; to rust.

enmudecer, –mŭdĕthĕr, v. n. to grow dumb; to be silent; –, v. a. to impose silence.

ennegrecer, –nĕgrĕthĕr, v. a. to blacken; to darken, to obscure.

ennoblecer, –nŏblĕthĕr, v. a. to ennoble.

ennoblecimiento, –thĭmĭĕn´tŏ, sm. ennoblement, nobilitation.

enojadizo, za, ĕnŏ´hădĕ´thŏ, a. fretful, peevish.

enojar, ĕnŏ´hăr, v. a. to irritate, to make angry; to teaze; to molest; to offend; –se, to be boisterous.

enojo, ĕnŏ´h´ŏ, sm. peevishness; anger, choler, passion.

enojoso, sa, –´hŏ´sŏ, a. offensive, vexatious. horrible; wicked beyond measure.

enorme, ĕnŏr´mĕ, a. enormous, vast, huge; monstruosity.

enormidad, ĕnŏrmĭdăd´, sf. enormity, monstruosity.

enramada, –rămă´dă, sf. hut covered with the branches of trees; shed; pent-house; ramification. branches of trees.

enramar, –rămăr, v. a. to cover with the branches of trees.

enranciarse, –rănthĭăr´sĕ, v. r. to grow rancid. rarefy.

enrarecer, –rărĕthĕr, v. a. to thin, to

enredadera, –rĕdădĕ´ră, sf. climbing plant; bind-weed.

enredador, ra, –dŏr´, sm. & f. entangler; tattler, tale-bearer; busybody.

enredar, ĕnrĕdăr´, v. a. to entangle, to ensnare; to confound, to perplex; to puzzle; to sow discord; –se, to fall in love (of unlawful love).

enredo, ĕnrĕ´dŏ, sm. entanglement; perplexity, embarrassment; imposition; mischievous lie; plot of a play.

enredoso, sa, –rĕdŏ´sŏ, a. full of snares and difficulties. open-work embroidery.

enrejado, –rĕ´hă´dŏ, sm. trellis-work;

enrejar, –rĕ´hăr, v. a. to fix a grating to a window; to grate, to lattice.

enriar, –rĭăr, v. a. to steep hemp and flax in water.

enriquecer, –rĭkĕthĕr, v. a. to enrich; to adorn; –, v. n. to grow rich. craggy.

enriscado, da, –rĭskă´dŏ, a. mountainous,

enriscamiento, –mĭĕn´tŏ, sm. taking refuge among rocks.

enriscar, ĕnrĭskăr, v. a. to place on the

top of mountains or rocks; –se, to take refuge among rocks.

enristrar, –rĭstrăr, v. a. to couch the lance; to range, to file; (fig.) to meet a difficulty.

enristre, ĕnrĭs´trĕ, sm. couching a lance.

enrizar, –rĭthăr, v. a. to curl.

enrobustecer, –ĕnrŏbŭstĕthĕr, v. a. to make robust. wheel.

enrodar, –rŏdăr, v. a. to break on the

enrodrigonar, –rŏdrĭgŏnăr, v. a. to prop vines with stakes. hot.

enrojecer, –rŏ´hĕthĕr, v. a. to make red-

enronquecer, –ŏnkĕthĕr, v. a. to make hoarse; –, v. n. to grow hoarse.

enroscadura, –rŏskădŏ´ră, sf. act of twisting. to curl or roll up.

enroscar, –rŏskăr, v. a. to twist; –se,

ensalada, –sălă´dă, sf. salad; hodge-podge, medley.

ensaladera, –dĕ´ră, sf. salad-bowl.

ensalmar, ĕnsălmăr, v. a. to set dislocated bones; to heal by spells.

ensalmo, ĕnsăl´mŏ, sm. enchantment, spell.

ensalobrarse, –sălŏbrăr´sĕ, v. r. to become putrid, as stagnant water.

ensalzar, –sălthăr, v. a. to exalt, to aggrandize; to exaggerate; –se, to boast.

ensamblador, –sămblădŏr´, sm. joiner.

ensanchar, –sănchăr, v. a. to widen, to extend, to enlarge; –se, to assume an air of importance.

ensancho, ĕnsăn´tchŏ, sm. dilation, augmentation; widening; goar.

ensangrentar, –săngrĕntăr, v. a. to stain with blood; –se, to be overzealous in the pursuit of a thing; to proceed in a cruel and barbarous manner.

ensañado, –sănyă´dŏ, a. courageous.

ensañar, –sănyăr, v. a. to irritate, to enrage.

ensartar, –sărtăr, v. a. to string (beads, etc.) (fig.) to go through a long story.

ensayar, –săyăr, v. a. to assay precious metals; to rehearse; to examine, to prove; –se, to exercise oneself.

ensayo, ĕnsă´yŏ, sm. assay, trial, proof; rehearsal of a play.

ensebar, –sĕbăr, v. a. to grease.

ensenada, –sĕnă´dă, sf. creek.

enseña, ĕnsĕn´yă, sf. colours, pl., standard.

enseñanza, –yănthă, sf. teaching, instruction.

enseñar, ĕnsĕnyăr, v. a. to teach, to instruct; –se, to accustom oneself.

enserar, –sĕrăr, v. a. to cover with bass-

enseres, –sĕ´rĕs, sm. pl. chattels, pl. weed.

ensillado, da, –sĭlyă´dŏ, a. hollow-backed.

ensilladura, –dŏ´ră, sf. saddle of a horse's or mule's back.

ensillar, ĕnsĭlyăr, v. a. to saddle.

ensoberbecer, –sŏbĕrbĕthĕr, v. a. to make proud; –se, to become proud; to become boisterous.

ensordecer, –sŏrdĕthĕr, v. a. to deafen; –, v. n. to grow deaf; to become silent.

ensordecimiento, –thĭmĭĕn´tŏ, sm. deafness.

ensortijamiento, –sŏrtĭ'hămĭĕn'tŏ, sm. curling the hair.

ensortijar,–sŏrtĭ'hăr', v. a. to form into a ring; to curl.

ensuciar, –sŭthĭăr', v. a. to stain, to soil; to pollute with vicious habits; –se, to dirty one's bed, &c.; to allow oneself to be bribed by presents.   [boards.

entablado, –tăblă'dŏ, sm. floor made of boards.

entablar, –tăblăr', v. a. to cover or floor with boards.   [small boards.

entablillar, –tăblĭlyăr', v. a. to secure with small boards.

entallador, –tălyădŏr', sm. sculptor; engraver.   [graving.

entalladura, –dŏ'ră, sf. sculpture; engraving.

entallar, –tălyăr', v. a. to sculpture, to carve; to engrave; –, v. n. to cut or shape a thing so as to fit it to the body.

entallecer, –tălyĕthĕr', v. n. to shoot, to sprout (of plants).   [tapestry.

entapizar, –tăpĭthăr', v. a. to hang with tapestry.

entarimar, –tărĭmăr', v. a. to cover a floor with boards.   [man.

ente, ĕn'tĕ, sm. entity, being; ridiculous man.

entenada, –tĕnă'dă, sf. daughter by a former marriage.   [marriage.

entenado, –tĕnă'dŏ, sm. son by a former marriage.

entendederas, –tĕndĕdĕ'răs, sf. pl. understanding, judgment.

entender, –tĕndĕr', v. a. & n. to understand, to comprehend; to remark, to take notice of; to reason, to think; á mi –, in my opinion; –se, to understand each other.   [prudent, knowing.

entendido, da, –tĕndĭ'dŏ, a. wise, learned, prudent, knowing.

entendimiento, –dĭmĭĕn'tŏ, sm. understanding, knowledge, judgment.

enteramente, –tĕrămĕn'tĕ, ad. entirely, completely.   [to instruct.

enterar, –tĕrăr', v. a. to inform thoroughly; to instruct.

entereza, –tĕrĕ'thă, sf. entireness, integrity; uprightness; perfection; firmness of mind.

enterizo, za, –tĕrĕ'thŏ, a. entire, complete.

enternecer, –tĕrnĕthĕr', v. a. to soften; to move to compassion; –, v. n. to pity, to commiserate.

enternecimiento, –thĭmĭĕn'tŏ, sm. compassion, pity, melting.

entero, ra, ĕntă'rŏ, a. entire; perfect, complete; sound; just, right; pure, uncorrupted; strong, robust; uncastrated; por –, entirely, completely.

enterrador, –tĕrrădŏr', sm. grave-digger.

enterrar, –tĕrrăr', v. a. to inter, to bury.

entibiar, –tĭbĭăr', v. a. to cool.

entidad, –tĭdăd', sf. entity, real being; (fig.) consideration, importance.

entierro, ĕntĭĕ'rrŏ, sm. burial; tomb, grave.

entimema, –tĭmĕ'mă, sf. enthymem.

entiznar, –tĭthnăr', v. a. to revile, to defame, to slander.

entoldar, –tŏldăr', v. a. to cover with an awning; to hang the walls with clothes; –se, to dress pompously.

entonación, –tŏnăthĭŏn', sf. modulation; intonation; blowing of the bellows of an organ; (fig.) presumption, pride.

entonador, –dŏr', sm. organ-blower; player of the first verse of a psalm.

entonar, –tŏnăr', v. a. to tune, to intonate; to blow the bellows of an organ; –se, to be puffed up with pride.

entonces, ĕntŏn'thĕs, ad. then, at that time.

entonelar, –tŏnĕlăr', v. a. to barrel.

entontecer, –tŏntĕthĕr', v. a. to mope, to fool; –, v. n., –se, to grow stupid.

entontecimiento, –thĭmĭĕn'tŏ, sm. growing stupid.

entorchado, –tŏrtshă'dŏ, sm. twisted cord which serves for embroideries.

entorchar, –tŏrtshăr', v. a. to twist a cord; to cover cords for musical instruments with wire.

entornar, –tŏrnăr', v. a. to turn.

entornillar, –tŏrnĭlyăr', v. a. to make anything in the form of a screw or ring.

entorpecer, –tŏrpĕthĕr', v. a. to benumb; to stupefy.

entorpecimiento, –thĭmĭĕn'tŏ, sm. torpor, numbness, stupefaction.   [out an eye.

entortar, –tŏrtăr', v. a. to bend; to pull out an eye.

entrada, ĕntră'dă, sf. entrance, entry; –s, pl. temporal angles, pl.

entrambos, bas, ĕntrăm'bŏs, pn. pl. both.

entrampar, –trămpăr', v. a. to entrap, to ensnare; to involve in difficulties; to deceive; to encumber an estate with debts; –se, to become indebted.   [tionate.

entrañable, –trănyă'blĕ, a. intimate, affectionate.

entrañas, ĕntrăn'yăs, sf. pl. entrails, intestines, pl.   [in; to commence.

entrar, ĕntrăr', v. a. & n. to enter, to go in; to commence.

entre, ĕn'trĕ, pr. between; in; –año, in the course of the year; –manos, in hand.

entreabrir, –ŭrĭr', v. a. to half open a door, to leave it ajar.   [greyish.

entrecano, na, –kă'nŏ, a. grey-black, greyish.

entrecejo, –thĕ'hŏ, sm. the space between the eye-brows; frowning supercilious look.

entrecoger, –kŏhĕr', v. a. to catch, to intercept.   [between-decks.

entrecubiertas, –kŭbĭĕr'tăs, sf. pl. (mar.) between-decks.

entredicho, –dĭtsh'ŏ, sm. prohibition; ecclesiastical interdict.   [and fine.

entrefino, na, –fĕ'nŏ, a. between coarse and fine.

entrega, ĕntrĕ'gă, sf. delivery; conveyance.

entregar, ĕntrĕgăr', v. a. to deliver; to restore; –se, to deliver oneself up into the hands of another; to abandon oneself to vice.

entrelazar, –lăthăr', v. a. to interlace.

entrelistado, da, –lĭstă'dŏ, a. striped, variegated.   [time.

entremedias, –mĕd'dĭăs, ad. in the mean time.

entremés, –mĕs', sm. interlude.

entremeter, –mĕtĕr', v. a. to put one thing between others; to intermeddle; to unswathe children.

entremetido, –mĕtĭ'dŏ, sm. meddler, obtruder; –, da, a. meddling.

entremetimiento, –mĕtĭmĭĕn'tŏ, sm. interposition; meddling.

entreoir, –ŏĭr', v. a. to hear without perfectly understanding what is said.

entrepalmadura, -pâlmädö'rä, sf. disease in horses' hoofs.

entrepaño, -pän'yö, sm. panel.

entrepiernas, -piĕr'nâs, sf. pl. opening between the legs; pieces put into the fork of a pair of breeches.

entrepuentes, -pŭĕn'tĕs, sm. pl. (mar.) between-decks.   [sf. interlineal note.

entrerrenglonadura, |-rĕnglönädö'rä,
entrerrenglonar, -rĕglönär', v. a. to write between lines.

entresaca, -sä'kä, sf. cutting down trees, in order to thin a wood.   [to separate.

entresacar, -säkär', v. a. to garble, to sift,

entresuelo, -sŭĕ'lö, sm. entresol.

entretalladura, -tälyädö'rä, sf. sculpture in bass-relief.

entretallar, -tälyär', v. a. to sculpture in bass-relief; to slash, to mangle.

entretejer, -tĕ'hĕr', v. a. to tissue, to interweave.   [strong linen.

entretela, -tĕ'lä, sf. buckram, stiff or

entretelar, -tĕlär', v. a. to put buckram or strong linen between the lining and cloth.

entretener, -tĕnĕr', v. a. to amuse; to entertain, to divert; to allay pain; -se, to amuse oneself.

entretenido, da, -tĕnĕ'dö, a. pleasant, amusing; doing business in an office, in hopes of obtaining a place.

entretenimiento, -tĕnĭmĭĕn'tö, sm. amusement, entertainment.

entrever, -vĕr', v. a. to have a glimpse of, to see imperfectly.

entreverado, da, -vĕrä'dö, a. interlined with fat and lean.   [mix together.

entreverar, -vĕrär', v. a. to intermix, to

entrevista, -vĭs'tä, sf. interview.

entripado, da, ĕntrĭpä'dö, a. contained in the entrails.   [to afflict.

entristecer, -trĭstĕthĕr', v. a. to sadden,

entrojar, -trö'här', v. a. to put up grain in barns.   [the same family.

entroncar, -trönkär', v. n. to belong to

entronización, -trönĭthäthĭön', sf. elevation to a throne.

entronizar, -trönĭthär', v. a. to enthrone.

entronque, ĕntrön'kĕ, sm. relationship with the chief of a family.

entruchada, -trŭchä'dä, sf. clandestine operation, underhand business.

entruchar, -trŭchär', v. a. to decoy, to lure into a snare.

entumecer, -tŭmĕthĕr', v. a. to swell; to benumb; -, v. n. to swell, to surge.

entumecimiento, -thĭmĕn'tö, sm. swelling; torpor.

enturbiar, -tŭrbiär', v. a. to make turbid; to obscure, to confound; -se, to disorder or derange any thing.

entusiasmar, -tŭsĭäsmär', v. a. to transport, to enrapture.

entusiasmo, -tŭsĭäs'mö, sm. enthusiasm.

entusiasta, -tŭsĭäs'tä, sm. enthusiast.

enumeración, ĕnŭmĕräthĭön', sf. enumeration, counting over.

enumerar, ĕnŭmĕrär', v. a. to enumerate.

enunciación, ĕnŭnthĭäthĭön,' sf. enunciation, declaration.   [declare.

enunciar, ĕnŭnthĭär', v. a. to enunciate, to

enunciativo, va, ĕnŭnthĭätĭ'vö, a. enunciative.   [sheath.

envainar, ĕnväĭnär', v. a. to sheathe, to

envalentonar, -välĕntönär', v. a. to encourage, to inspirit.

envanecer, -vänĕthĕr', v. a. to make vain; to swell with pride; -se, to become proud.   [ness, numbness.

envaramiento, -värämĭĕn'tö, sm. stiff-

envarar, -värär', v. a. to benumb.

envasador, -väsädör', sm. funnel.

envasar, -väsär', v. a. to tun, to barrel; to drink to excess.

envejecer, -vĕ'hĕthĕr', v. a. to make old; -, v. n. to grow old.

envejecido, da, -vĕ'hĕthĭ'dö, a. grown old; looking old.   [poisoner.

envenenador, ra, -vĕnĕnädör', sm. & f.

envenenar, -vĕnĕnär', v. a. to envenom, to poison, to despatch.   [ing.

envenenamiento, -mĭĕn'tö, sm. poison-

envestidura, -vĕstĭdö'rä, sf. investiture.

envestir, -vĕstĭr', v. a. to invest; to illuminate, to enlighten; to cover; -se, to accustom oneself.

enviado, -vĭä'dö, sm. envoy, messenger.

enviar, -vĭär', v. a. to send, to transmit, to convey, to despatch.

enviciar, -vĭthĭär', v. a. to vitiate, to corrupt; -se, to be excessively fond of.

envidar, -vĭdär', v. a. to open the game by staking a certain sum.

envidia, ĕnvĭ'dĭa, sf. envy; emulation.

envidiable, -vĭdĭä'blĕ, a. enviable.

envidiar, -vĭdĭär', v. n. to envy, to grudge.   [vidious, jealous.

envidioso, sa, -vĭdĭö'sö, a. envious; in-

envilecer, -vĭlĕthĕr', v. a. to vilify, to debase; -se, to degrade oneself.

envinagrar, -vĭnägrär', v. a. to put vinegar into anything.   [goods.

envío, ĕnvĭ'ö, sm. (com.) remittance of

envirar, -vĭrär', v. a. to clasp together cork-wood to form a bee-hive.

enviscar, -vĭskär', v. a. to glue; to irritate, to anger; -se, to be glued with bird-lime.

envite, ĕnvĭ'tĕ, sm. opening the game by staking a certain sum; invitation.

enviudar, -vĭŭdär', v. n. to become a widower or widow.   [clothes.

envoltorio, -völtö'rĭö, sm. bundle of

envolturas, -tö'räs, sf. pl. swaddling- or swathing-clothes, pl.

envolver, -völvĕr', v. a. to involve; to wrap up; -se, to be implicated in an affair.   [with gypsum.

enyesadura, -yĕsädö'rä, sf. plastering

enyesar, -yĕsär', v. a. to plaster, to parget.

enyugar, -yögär', v. a. to yoke cattle.

enzainarse, -thäĭnär'sĕ, v. r. to squint, to have a cast in one's eye.

enzamarrado, da, -thämärrä'dö, a. dressed in a shepherd's great-coat made of sheep-skins, with the wool on.

8*

enzarzado, da, _–thărthă'dŏ,_ a. curled, matted.

enzarzar, _–thărthăr',_ v. a. to throw among brambles and briers; to sow discord; **–se,** to be entangled among brambles and briers; to be involved in difficulties.

epacta, _ĕpăk'tă,_ sf. epact.

epactilla, _ĕpăktĭl'yă,_ sf. small calendar for the performance of divine service.

épico, ca, _ĕ'pĭkŏ,_ a. epic.

epicúreo, rea, _ĕpĭkū'rĕŏ,_ a. epicurean.

epidemia, _ĕpĭdĕ'mĭă,_ sf. epidemic disease.

epidémico, ca, _–dĕ'mĭkŏ,_ a. epidemic.

epidermis, _ĕpĭdĕr'mĭs,_ sf. epidermis, cuticle.

Epifania, _ĕpĭfănĕ'ă,_ sf. Epiphany.

epigrafe, _ĕpĭ'grăfĕ,_ sf. epigraph, inscription; motto; device, posy.

epigrama, _ĕpĭgră'mă,_ sm. epigram.

epilepsia, _ĕpĭlĕp'sĭă,_ sf. epilepsy.

epilogar, _ĕpĭlŏgăr',_ v. a. to recapitulate, to sum up.

epílogo, _ĕpĕ'lŏgŏ,_ sm. epilogue.

epiqueya, _ĕpĭkĕ'yă,_ sf. mild and prudent interpretation of the law. [bishopric.

episcopado, _ĕpĭskŏpă'dŏ,_ sm. episcopacy;

episcopal, _–păl',_ a. episcopal.

episódico, ca, _ĕpĭsŏ'dĭkŏ,_ a. episodical.

episodio, _–sŏ'dĭŏ,_ sm. episode.

epístola, _ĕpĭs'tŏlă,_ sf. epistle, letter; subdeaconship.

epistolar, _ĕpĭstŏlăr',_ a. epistolary.

epistolario, _–lă'rĭŏ,_ sm. collection of epistles which are read or sung at mass; guide for letter-writing.

epitafio, _ĕpĭtă'fĭŏ,_ sm. epitaph.

epitalamio, _ĕpĭtălă'mĭŏ,_ sm. nuptial song.

epíteto, _ĕpĕ'tĕtŏ,_ sm. epithet.

epitomar, _ĕpĭtŏmăr',_ v. a. to epitomize.

epítome, _ĕpĕ'tŏmĕ,_ sm. epitome, compendium. [dium.

época, _ĕ'pŏkă,_ sf. epoch.

epopeya, _ĕpŏpĕ'yă,_ sf. epopee.

equidad, _ĕkĭdăd'',_ sf. equity, honesty; cheapness; impartiality, justice.

equidistar, _–dĭstăr',_ v. n. to be equidistant.

equilátero, ra, _–lă'tĕrŏ,_ a. equilateral, having all sides equal.

equilibrar, _–lĭbrăr',_ v. a. to equilibrate; to counterpoise, to counterbalance.

equilibrio, _–lĕ'brĭŏ,_ sm. equilibrium.

equinoccial, _–nŏkthĭăl',_ a. equinoctial.

equinoccio, _–nŏk'thĭŏ,_ sm. equinox.

equipaje, _–pă'h'ĕ,_ sm. luggage; equipment; (mar.) crew of a ship; **–s,** pl. (rail.) luggage-office.

equipar, _–păr',_ v. a. to fit out, to equip, to furnish, to accoutre.

equitación, _–tăthĭŏn',_ sf. horsemanship.

equitativo, va, _–tăĭ'vŏ,_ a. equitable; just.

equivalencia, _–vălĕn'thĭă,_ sf. equivalence, compensation.

equivalente, _–vălĕn'tĕ,_ a. equivalent.

equivaler, _–vălĕr',_ v. n. to be of equal value. [error, misunderstanding.

equivocación, _–vŏkăthĭŏn',_ sf. mistake,

equivocar, _–vŏkăr',_ v. a. to mistake, to misconceive, to misunderstand.

equívoco, ca, _ĕkĕ'vŏkŏ,_ a. equivocal, ambiguous; **–,** sm. equivocation, quibble.

era, _ĕ'ră,_ sf. era, æra; thrashing-floor; plot in a garden.

eral, _ĕrăl',_ sm. two-year old ox.

erario, _ĕră'rĭŏ,_ sm. Exchequer, public treasury\ fisc.

erección, _ĕrĕkthĭŏn',_ sf. foundation, establishment; erection, elevation. [solitary.

eremítico, ca, _ĕrĕmĕ'tĭkŏ,_ a. hermitlike,

ergotear, _ĕrgŏtĕăr',_ v. n. to argue, to debate without reason.

erguir, _ĕrgĭr',_ v. a. to erect, to raise up straight; **–se,** to be elated with pride.

erial, _ĕrĭăl',_ a. untilled, uncultivated.

erigir, _ĕrĭhĭr',_ v. a. to erect, to raise, to build; to establish.

erisipela, _ĕrĭsĭpĕ'lă,_ sf. (med.) erysipelas.

erisipelar, _–pĕlăr',_ v. a. to cause erysipelas. [on end (of hair, etc.).

erizamiento, _ĕrĭthămĭĕn'tŏ,_ sm. standing

erizar, _ĕrĭthăr',_ v. a. & r. to bristle.

erizo, _ĕrĕ'thŏ,_ sm. hedgehog.

ermita, _ĕrmĕ'tă,_ sf. hermitage.

ermitaño, _–tăn'yŏ,_ sm. hermit.

erradizo, za, _ĕrrădĕ'thŏ,_ a. wandering to and fro. [roving.

errante, _ĕrrăn'tĕ,_ p. & a. errant, erring.

errar, _ĕrrăr',_ v. a. to err, to commit errors; to mistake; **–,** v. n. to go astray.

errata, _ĕrră'tă,_ sf. error in printing.

erre, _ĕr'rĕ,_ **– que –,** ad. pertinaciously, obstinately.

erróneo, nea, _ĕrrŏ'nĕŏ,_ a. erroneous.

error, _ĕrrŏr',_ sm. error, mistake, fault.

eructar, _ĕrŭktăr',_ v. n. to belch, to eructate.

eructo, _ĕrŭk'tŏ,_ sm. belch, eructation.

erudición, _ĕrŭdĭthĭŏn',_ sf. erudition, learning.

erudito, ta, _–dĕ'tŏ,_ a. learned, lettered.

erupción, _ĕrŭpthĭŏn',_ sf. eruption, outbreak. [belching.

erutación, _ĕrŭtăthĭŏn',_ sf. eructation,

esbelto, ta, _ĕsbĕl'tŏ,_ a. tall, genteel, well-shaped.

esbirro, _ĕsbĕr'rŏ,_ sm. bailiff, apparitor.

escabechar, _ĕskăbĕchăr',_ v. a. to souse, to pickle. [pickled fish.

escabeche, _–bĕtshĕ',_ sm. souse, pickle;

escabel, _ĕskăbĕl',_ sm. foot-stool.

escabrosidad, _–brŏsĭdăd'',_ sf. unevenness, roughness; asperity.

escabroso, sa, _–brŏ'sŏ,_ a. rough, uneven; craggy, crabbed; rude, unpolished.

escabullirse, _–bŭlyĕr'sĕ,_ v. r. to escape, to evade; to slip through one's fingers.

escala, _ĕskă'lă,_ sf. ladder; (mus.) scale.

escalada, _ĕskălă'dă,_ sf. scalade, escalade; **– á escala vista,** a day-light escalade.

escalador, _–lădŏr',_ sm. climber, he who scales walls. [suspicious, wary.

escaldado, da, _ĕskăldă'dŏ,_ a. cautious,

escaldar, _–dăr',_ v. a. to scald.

escalera, _ĕskălĕ'ră,_ sf. staircase; ladder.

escalfador, _ĕskălfădŏr',_ sm. barber's pan for keeping water warm; chafing-dish.

escalfar, -får', v. a. to boil eggs; to scorch. [degree of dignity.

escalón, ĕskălŏn', sm. step of a stair;

escama, ĕskă mă, sf. fish-scale.

escamado, da, ĕskămă dŏ, a. tutored by experience. [broidery.

escamadura, -dŏ ră, sf. scale-like em-

escamar, ĕskămar', v. a. to take off the scales; -, v. n. to embroider scale or shell fashion; -se, to resent, to take ill.

escamoso, sa, ĕskămŏ sŏ, a. scaly.

escamotar, -mŏtar', v. a. to make a thing disappear from one's hands (in conjuring).

escampar, ĕskămpar', v. n. to cease rain-ing; -, v. a. to clean a place.

escanciador, ra, ĕskănthiădŏr', sm. & f. cup-bearer.

escanciar, -thiar', v. a. to pour wine from one vessel into another to drink.

escanda, ĕskăn dă, sf. (bot.) spelt-wheat.

escandalizador, -dălĭthădŏr', sm. scan-dal-monger. [-se, to be scandalised.

escandalizar, -tthar', v. a. to scandalise;

escándalo, ĕskăn dălŏ, sm. scandal.

escandaloso, sa, -dălŏ sŏ, a. scandalous; turbulent.

escaño, ĕskăn yŏ, sm. bench with a back.

escapada, ĕskăpă dă, sf. escape, flight.

escapar, ĕskăpar', v. a. to liberate from danger; to slip one's memory; -, v. n. to escape. [cupboard (in Havannah).

escaparate, ĕskăpără tĕ, sm. shop-front;

escapatoria, -tŏ rĭă, sf. escape, flight; excuse.

escape, ĕskă pĕ, sm. escape, flight; escape-ment (part of a watch); á todo -, with the utmost velocity.

escapulario, ĕskăpŭlă rĭŏ, sm. scapulary.

escarabajear, ĕskărăbăhĕar', v. n. to crawl to and fro like insects; to scribble; to sting, to give pain. [short, ill-shaped person.

escarabajo, ĕskărăbă hŏ, sm. black-beetle;

escaramuza, -mŏ thă, sf. skirmish; dis-pute, quarrel. [misher; disputer.

escaramuzador, -măthădŏr', sm. skir-

escaramuzar, -măthar', v. a. to skirmish.

escarapela, -pă lă, sf. cockade.

escarbadientes, ĕskărbădĭen tĕs, sm. tooth-pick. [scratching.

escarbadura, -dŏ ră, sf. act and effect of

escarbaorejas, -ŏrĕ'h'ăs, sm. ear-pick.

escarbar, ĕskărbar', v. a. to scratch the earth (as fowls do); to inquire minutely into.

escarcha, ĕskărtsh'ă, sf. white frost.

escarchar, -tshar', v. n. to be frozen.

escardadera, -dădĕ ră, sf. woman em-ployed to clear corn-fields of weeds.

escardador, -dŏr', sm. weeder.

escardar, -dar', v. a. to weed. [hook.

escardillo, -dĕl yŏ, sm. small weeding-

escarlata, -lă tă, sf. scarlet (colour); scarlet (cloth); kermes.

escarlatín, -tĭn', sm. coarse kind of scarlet.

escarlatina, -tĕ nă, sf. scarlet-fever, scar-latina. [pick wool.

escarmenar, -mĕnar', v. a. to comb, to

escarmentar, -mĕntar', v. n. to be tu-tored by experience; to take warning; -, v. a. to punish severely.

escarmiento, -mĭen tŏ, sm. warning, cau-tion; chastisement. [to ridicule.

escarnecer, ĕskărnĕthĕr', v. a. to mock,

escarnio, ĕskăr nĭŏ, sm. scoff, contemp-tuous ridicule. [frill round the neck.

escarola, ĕskărŏ lă, sf. (bot.) endive; plaited

escarolado, da, -lă dŏ, a. of the colour of endive, pale yellowish; curly.

escarpa, ĕskăr pă, sf. declivity; scarp.

escarpado, da, -pă dŏ, a. sloped, craggy.

escarpar, -par', v. a. to scarf timbers; (mil.) to escarp, to slope down.

escarpia, ĕskăr pĭă, sf. tenter.

escarpidor, -pĭdŏr', sm. wide, large-toothed comb.

escarpín, -pĭn', sm. sock; pump (shoe).

escasear, ĕskăsĕar', v. a. to give sparingly and with reluctance; to spare; -, v. n. to grow less, to decrease. [liness.

escasez, ĕskăsĕth', sf. scantiness, niggard-

escaso, sa, ĕskă sŏ, a. small, short, little; sparing, niggardly; scanty, defective.

escatimar, ĕskătĭmar', v. a. to curtail, to lessen; to haggle; to corrupt the sense and meaning of words.

escena, ĕsthĕ nă, sf. stage; scene; bed and shepherd's hut made of branches.

escénico, ca, ĕsthĕ nĭkŏ, a. scenic. [cism.

escepticismo, ĕsthĕptĭthĭs mŏ, sm. scepti-

escéptico, ca, ĕsthĕp tĭkŏ, a. sceptic, scep-tical. [tical.

eschelin, ĕsthĕlĭn', sm. shilling.

esclarecer, ĕsklărĕthĕr', v. a. to lighten; to illuminate; to illustrate; -, v. n. to dawn. [noble.

esclarecido, da, -thĕ' dŏ, a. illustrious,

esclarecimiento, -thĭmĭen' tŏ, sm. dawn; illustriousness.

esclavina, ĕsklăvĕ nă, sf. pilgrim's pall; collar worn by priests in Spain; pelerine, fur-cape.

esclavitud, -vĭtŭd', sf. slavery, servitude.

esclavo, va, ĕsklă vŏ, sm. & f. slave, captive.

esclusa, ĕsklŏ să, sf. sluice, flood-gate.

escoba, ĕskŏ bă, sf. broom, besom.

escobada, ĕskŏbă dă, sf. sweeping slightly.

escobajo, -bă'h'ŏ, sm. remains of an old broom; stalk of a bunch of grapes (with-out the fruit). [broom.

escobazo, -bă thŏ, sm. blow given with a

escobilla, -bĭl yă, sf. brush; small broom.

escobillón, -yŏn', sm. artillery-sponge.

escocer, ĕskŏthĕr', v. a. to cause a sharp lively pain; to irritate, to provoke; -se, to smart. [of gauze, &c.

escofieta, -fĭĕ tă, sf. women's head-dress

escofina, -fĕ nă, sf. rasp.

escofinar, -fĕnar', v. a. to rasp.

escoger, -hĕr', v. a. to choose, to select.

escogidamente, -'hĭdămĕn' tĕ, ad. choice-ly, selectly. [scholastic.

escolar, ĕskŏlar', sm. scholar, student; -, a.

escolástico, ca, -lăs'tĭkŏ, a. scholastic; -, sm. professor of theology.

escolio, ĕskŏ lĭŏ, sm. scholion, comment.

escollo, ĕskŏl yŏ, sm. sunken rocks, pl.

escolta, *ĕskŏl'tă,* sf. (mil.) escort, convoy.

escoltar, *–tăr',* v. a. to escort.

escombrar, *ĕskŏmbrăr',* v. a. to remove obstacles; to purify.   [mackerel.

escombro, *ĕskŏm'brŏ,* sm. rubbish.

esconce, *ĕskŏn'thĕ,* sm. corner, angle.

escondedero, *–dĕdĕ'rŏ,* sm. lurking-place.

esconder, *ĕskŏndĕr',* v. a. to hide, to conceal; to dissemble; to contain; –se, to lie hid.

escondidas, –dĭ'dăs, escondidillas, *–dĭl'yăs* (ά–), ad, in a secret manner.

escondite, *–dĭ'tĕ,* sm. concealment; hiding; **juego de –,** hide and seek.

escondrijo, *–drĭ'h'ŏ,* sm. hiding-place.

esconzado, da, *–thă'dŏ,* a. oblique, wry.

escopeta, *ĕskŏpĕ'tă,* sf. firelock, gun; **á tira de –,** within gun-shot.

escopetazo, *–tă'thŏ,* sm. gun-shot; gun-shot wound.

escopetear, *–tĕăr',* v. a. to discharge a gun repeatedly; –se, to discharge firelocks at each other; to insult each other with foul language.   [arms.

escopeta, *–tă'ŏ,* sm. discharge of fire-

escopetero, *–tĕ'rŏ,* sm. musketeer.

escopleadura, *–plĕădŏ'ră,* sf. mortise-hole made in timber.

escoplear, *–plĕăr',* v. a. to chisel out.

escoplo, *ĕskŏ'plŏ,* sm. chisel.

escorbútico, ca, *ĕskŏrbŏ'tĭkŏ,* a. scorbutic.

escorbuto, *–bŏ'tŏ,* sm. scurvy.   [thing.

escoria, *ĕskŏ'rĭă,* sf. dross; lee; worthless

escoriación, *ĕskŏrĭăthĭŏn',* sf. incrustation.

escorial, *ĕskŏrĭăl',* sm. dross-heap.

Escorial, –, sm. Escurial, pleasure-seat near Madrid.

escoriarse, *–rĭăr'sĕ,* v. r. to get skinned.

Escorpio, *ĕskŏr'pĭŏ,* sm. Scorpio, Scorpion (sign of the zodiac).

escorpión, *ĕskŏrpĭŏn',* sm. scorpion.

escorzonera, *–thŏnĕ'ră,* sf. viper-grass.

escotadura, *ĕskŏtădŏ'ră,* sf. curve of a jacket *or* corset.

escotar, *–tăr',* v. a. to cut out a garment about the neck; to slope; to pay one's share of scot and taxes.

escote, *ĕskŏ'tĕ,* sm. slope of a garment; tucker; one's share of a reckoning at a club.

escotero, ra, *–tĕ'rŏ,* a. free, disengaged.

escotilla, *–tĭl'yă,* sf. (mar.) hatchway.

escotillón, *–tĭlyŏn',* sm. trap-door; drop, slot (in theatres).

escozor, *–thŏr',* sm. smart pungent pain; lively sensation *or* perception of the mind.

escriba, *ĕskrĕ'bă,* sm. scribe (among the Hebrews).   [notary; escritoire.

escribanía, *ĕskrĭbănĕ'ă,* sf. office of a

escribano, *–bă'nŏ,* sm. notary, scrivener.

escribiente, *–bĭĕn'tĕ,* sm. amanuensis.

escribir, *ĕskrĭbĭr',* v. a. to write; to compose literary works.   [(law) libel.

escrito, *ĕskrĭ'tŏ,* sm. literary composition;

escritor, *–tŏr',* sm. writer, author.

escritorio, *–tŏ'rĭŏ,* sm. cupboard adorned with inlaid ivory; counting-house; escritoire, writing-desk; office, study.   [ture.

escritura, *–tŏ'ră,* sf. writing; deed; Scrip-

escriturar, *–tŭrăr',* v. a. to bind oneself legally.   [lous.

escrofuloso, sa, *ĕskrŏfŭlŏ'sŏ,* a. scrofu-

escrupulizar, *ĕskrŭpŭlĭthăr',* v. n. to scruple, to doubt.

escrúpulo, *ĕskrŏ'pŭlŏ,* sm. doubt, scruple, scrupulousness; minute on a graduated sphere.   [losity.

escrupulosidad, *–lŏsĭdăd'',* sf. scrupu-

escrupuloso, sa, *–lŏ'sŏ,* a. scrupulous; exact.   [quiry.

escrutinio, *ĕskrŭtĭ'nĭŏ,* sm. scrutiny, en-

escrutiñador, *–tĭnyădŏr',* sm. scrutiniser, enquirer.

escuadra, *ĕskŭă'dră,* sf. square; squadron.

escuadrar, *ĕskŭădrăr',* v. a. to square.

escuadrón, *–drŏn',* sm. squadron, troop of horse.   [in squadrons.

escuadronar, *–drŏnăr',* v. a. to form troops

escuadronista, *–drŏnĭs'tă,* sm. clever cavalry leader.   [scout.

escucha, *ĕskŭtsh'ă,* sf. sentinel, sentry;

escuchar, *–tshăr',* v. a. to listen, to hearken.

escudar, *ĕskŭdăr',* v. a. to shield; to guard from danger; –se, to depend on some means of evading danger.   [office.

escudería, *–dĕrĕ'ă,* sf. shield-bearer's

escuderil, *–dĕrĭl',* a. belonging to the office of a shield-bearer.   [page.

escudero, *–dĕ'rŏ,* sm. shield-bearer; lady's

escudilla, *–dĭl'yă,* sf. porringer.

escudillar, *–yăr',* v. a. to pour out broth into porringers.

escudo, *ĕskŏ'dŏ,* sm. shield, buckler; scutcheon of a lock; Crown (gold coin).

escudriñamiento, *ĕskŭdrĭnyămĭĕn'tŏ,* sm. investigation, scrutiny.

escudriñar, *–yăr',* v. a. to search, to pry into; to examine into.

escuela, *ĕskŭĕ'lă,* sf. school.

esculpir, *ĕskŭlpĭr',* v. a. to sculpture.

escultor, *–tŏr',* sm. sculptor, carver.

escultura, *–tŏ'ră,* sf. sculpture; work of a sculptor.

escupidera, *ĕskŭpĭdĕ'ră,* sf. spittoon.

escupidero, *–dĕ'rŏ,* sm. spitting-place.

escupidura, *–dŏ'ră,* sf. spittle.

escupir, *ĕskŭpĭr',* v. a. to spit.   [lees.

escupiduras, *ĕskŭrrĭdŏ'răs,* sf. pl. dregs,

escurrir, *ĕskŭrrĭr',* v. a. to drain to the dregs; –, v. n. to drop; to slip, to slide; to glide slowly; –se, to slip away.

esdrújulo, *ĕsdrŭ'h'ŭlŏ,* sm. a Spanish word of more than two syllables, the last two of which are short; –, la, a. belonging to the words called **esdrújulos.**

[ese | ŏ'sĕ, | esa | ŏ'să, eso, ŏ'sŏ, that.

esencia, *ĕsĕn'thĭă,* sf. essence.

esencial, *–thĭăl',* a. essential; principal.

esfera, *ĕsfĕ'ră,* sf. sphere; globe.

esférico, ca, *ĕsfĕ'rĭkŏ,* a. spherical.

esferoide, *ĕsfĕrŏ'ĭdĕ,* sf. spheroid.

esfinge, *ĕsfĭn'h'ĕ,* sm. sphinx.

esforzado, da, *ĕsfŏrthă'dŏ,* a. strong, vigorous, valiant.

esforzar, *–thăr',* v. a. to strengthen; –se,

to exert oneself, to make an effort; to be confident. [vigour; effort.

esfuerzo, *ĕsfŭĕr'thŏ*, sm. courage, spirit.

esgrima, *ĕsgrē'mā*, sf. fencing; maestro de –, fencing-master. [fencing-master.

esgrimador, *ĕsgrīmādŏr'*, sm. fencer;

esgrimir, *ĕsgrīmīr'*, v. a. to fence.

eslabón, *ĕslăbŏn'*, sm. link of a chain; steel for striking fire.

eslabonar, *–bōnăr'*, v. a. to link; to unite.

esmaltado, *ĕsmăltădŏr'*, sm. enameller.

esmaltar, *ĕsmăltăr'*, v. a. to enamel.

esmalte, *ĕsmăl'tĕ*, sm. enamel.

esmerado, da, *ĕsmĕrā'dŏ*, a. high-finished.

esmeralda, *–rāl'dā*, sm. emerald. [nice.

esmerar, *–răr'*, v. a. to polish; –se, to endeavour to attain eminence or superior excellence.

esmeril, *–rēl'*, sm. emery. [emery.

esmerilar, *–rīlăr'*, v. a. to polish with an

esmero, *ĕsmā'rŏ*, sm. careful attention, elaborate effort.

esófago, *ĕsŏ'făgŏ*, sm. gullet; throat.

esotro, tra, *ĕsŏ'trŏ*, a. this or that other.

espabiladeras, *ĕspăblĭădā'răs*, sf. pl. snuffers, pl., candle-snuffer.

espabilar, *–bĭlăr'*, v. a. to snuff a candle.

espaciar, *–thĭăr'*, v. a. to extend, to dilate, to spread; to insert spaces (print.); –se, to walk to and fro; to cheer up.

espacio, *ĕspā'thĭŏ*, sm. space, capacity; distance; slowness. [ness, capacity.

espaciosidad, *–thĭōsĭdād'*, sf. spaciousness.

espacioso, sa, *–thĭŏ'sŏ*, a. spacious, roomy; slow.

espada, *ĕspā'dā*, sf. sword; ace of spades; –, m. bull-fighter.

espadachín, *–dāthēn'*, sm. bully. [tail.

espadaña, *–dăn'yā*, sf. (bot.) great cat's-

espadar, *–dăr'*, v. a. to break hemp or flax with a swing-staff.

espadería, *–dĕrē'ā*, sf. sword-cutler's shop.

espadero, *–dā'rŏ*, sm. sword-cutler.

espadilla, *–dīl'yā*, sf. scotching-handle; ace of spades.

espadín, *–dēn'*, sm. small short sword.

espalda, *ĕspăl'dā*, sf. shoulder; shoulder of a bastion: back, back-part.

espaldar, *–dăr'*, sm. back-piece of a suit of armour; back-board; espalier in gardens.

espaldilla, *–dīl'yā*, sf. shoulder-blade.

espalmar, *–măr'*, v. a. to pare a horse's hoof for shoeing.

espantable, *ĕspăntă'blĕ*, a. frightful, horrid, terrible; marvellous, wonderful.

espantadizo, za, *–tādī'thŏ*, a. timid, easily frightened. [bear.

espantajo, *–tā'hŏ*, sm. scarecrow; bug-

espantar, *–tăr'*, v. a. to frighten, to daunt; to chase or drive away.

espanto, *ĕspăn'tŏ*, sm. fright; menace, threat; wonder, surprise.

espantoso, sa, *–tŏ'sŏ*, a. frightful, dreadful; wonderful.

español, *ĕspănyŏl'*, sm. Spanish language.

españoleta, *–yŏlā'tā*, sf. ancient Spanish dance.

esparaván, *ĕspărăvăn'*, sm. malanders, pl.; sparrow-hawk.

esparavel, *–vĕl'*, sm. casting-net, drag-net.

esparcir, *ĕspărthīr'*, v. a. to scatter; to divulge; –se, to amuse oneself.

espartería, *ĕspărtĕrē'ā*, sf. place where mats of esparto are made or sold.

espartero, *–tā'rŏ*, sm. maker and seller of esparto-work. [feather-grass.

esparto, *ĕspăr'tŏ*, sm. (bot.) esparto,

espárrago, *ĕspăr'răgŏ*, sm. asparagus.

espasmo, *ĕspăs'mŏ*, sm. spasm.

espátula, *ĕspă'tŭlă*, sf. spatula.

especería, *ĕspĕthĕrē'ā*, sf. grocer's shop, grocery; spices. [cinal drugs.

especia, *ĕspā'thĭā*, sf. spice; –s, pl. medi-

especial, *ĕspĕthĭăl'*, a. special, particular; en –, specially.

especialidad, *–lĭdād'*, sf. speciality.

especie, *ĕspā'thĭĕ*, sf. species; matter; motive.

especiero, *ĕspĕthĭā'rŏ*, sm. dealer in spices and aromatic drugs. [tion.

especificación, *–fĭkăthĭŏn'*, sf. specifica-

especificar, *–fĭkăr'*, v. a. to specify.

específico, ca, *ĕspĕthĭfĭkŏ*, a. specific, specifical.

especioso, sa, *–thĭŏ'sŏ*, a. neat, beautiful, finished with care; specious.

espectáculo, *ĕspĕktā'kŭlŏ*, sm. spectacle.

espectador, *–dŏr'*, sm. spectator.

espectro, *ĕspĕk'trŏ*, sm. spectre, phantom, ghost, apparition.

especulación, *ĕspĕkŭlăthĭŏn'*, sf. speculation, contemplation; commercial scheme.

especulador, ra, *–dŏr'*, sm. & f. speculator.

especular, *ĕspĕkŭlăr'*, v. a. to speculate.

especulativa, *ĕspĕkŭlătĭvā'*, sf. faculty of speculating. [thoughtful.

especulativo, ya, *–tĭ'vŏ*, a. speculative;

espejismo, *ĕspĕhēs'mŏ*, sm. mirage.

espejo, *ĕspā'hŏ*, sm. looking-glass, mirror.

espera, *ĕspā'rā*, sf. stay, waiting; (law) respite, adjournment, delay.

esperanza, *ĕspĕrăn'thā*, sf. hope; (mar.) áncora de –, sheet-anchor.

esperanzar, *–thăr'*, v. a. to give hope.

esperar, *ĕspĕrăr'*, v. a. to hope; to expect, to wait for.

esperma, *ĕspĕr'mā*, sf. sperm.

espermático, *–mă'tĭkŏ*, a. spermatic.

espernancado, *–nănkā'dŏ*, a. with wide-spread legs.

espesar, *ĕspĕsăr'*, v. a. to thicken, to condense; –se, to grow thick, to solidify.

espeso, sa, *ĕspā'sŏ*, a. thick, dense.

espesor, *ĕspĕsŏr'*, sm. thickness.

espesura, *–sŭ'rā*, sf. thickness, density, solidity.

espetar, *ĕspĕtăr'*, v. a. to spit; to transfix; –se, to be stiff and stately.

espetera, *–tĕ'rā*, sf. kitchen-furniture.

espetón, *ĕspĕtŏn'*, sm. spit; large pin;

espía, *ĕspē'ā*, sm. & f. spy. [sea-pike.

espiar, *ĕspĭăr'*, v. a. to spy, to lurk.

espiga, *espē'gă*, sf. ear (of corn); fusee of a bomb; sail of a galley.

espigadora, *espēgădō'ră*, sf. gleaner.

espigar, *espēgăr'*, v. n. to shoot into ears; to grow, to increase; –, v. a. to glean.

espigón, *–gōn'*, sm. ear of corn; sting.

espina, *espē'nă*, sf. thorn; fish-bone; woolly-cotton thistle.

espinaca, *espĭnă'kă*, sf. (bot.) spinage.

espinar, *–năr'*, v. a. to prick with thorns; –, sm. place full of thorn-bushes, brambles &c.; arduous undertaking.

espinazo, *–nă'thŏ*, sm. spine, back-bone.

espingarda, *espĭngăr'dă*, sf. small piece of ordnance.

espinilla, *espĭnĭl'yă*, sf. shin-bone.

espino, *espē'nŏ*, sm. thorn, prickly tree.

espinoso, sa, *espĭnō'sŏ*, a. thorny, arduous, dangerous.

espión, *espĭōn'*, sm. spy.

espiral, *espĭră'l*, a. spiral; –, sf. spiral line.

espirar, *espĭrăr'*, v. a. to exhale.

espiritar, *espĭrĭtăr'*, v. a. to possess with the devil; to wish someone to the devil; to irritate, to agitate; –se, to be possessed with an evil spirit.

espíritu, *espē'rĭtŭ*, sm. spirit, soul; genius; ardour, courage; el – Santo, the Holy Ghost; –s, pl. demons, hobgoblins. mpl.

espiritual, *espĭrĭtŭăl'*, a. spiritual; ghostly.

espiritualidad, *espĭrĭtŭălĭdăd'*, sf. spirituality; principle and effect of what is spiritual.

espiritualizar, *–thăr'*, v. a. to spiritualize, to refine the intellect.

espirituoso, sa, *espĭrĭtŭō'sŏ*, a. spirituous; vivid, lively.

espitar, *espĭtăr'*, v. a. to put a faucet in.

esplendente, *esplĕndĕn'tĕ*, pa.(poet.) shining, resplendent.

esplendidez, *–dĭdĕth'*, sf. splendour.

espléndido, da, *esplĕn'dĭdŏ*, a. splendid, magnificent; brilliant.

esplendor, *–dōr'*, sm. splendour.

espliego, *esplĭĕ'gŏ*, sm. (bot.) lavender.

espolazo, *espŏlă'thŏ*, sm. violent prick with a spur.

espolear, *–ăr'*, v. a. to spur, to instigate, to incite.

espoleta, *–lĕ'tă*, sf. fusee of a bomb.

espolín, *–lĭn'*, sm. small spool for raising flowers on stuff.

espolique, *espŏlĭ'kĕ*, espolista, *–stă*, sm. running footman.

espolón, *espŏlōn'*, sm. spur of a cock; ice-breaker; (mar.) beakhead of a galley; (mil.) salient angle of a fortification; chilblain, kibe.

espondeo, *espŏndĕ'ŏ*, sm. spondee.

esponja, *espŏn'hă*, sf. sponge.

esponjadura, *–dō'ră*, sf. act of sponging.

esponjar, *espŏn'hăr'*, v. a. to sponge; –se, to be puffed up with pride.

esponjoso, sa, *–hŏ'sŏ*, a. spongy.

esponsales, *–să'lĕs*, sm. pl. espousals, pl.

espontaneidad, *–tănĕĭdăd'*, sf. spontaneity.

espontáneo, nea, *–tă'nĕŏ*, a. spontaneous.

esportillero, *espŏrtĭlyĕ'rŏ*, sm. porter.

esportillo, *–tĭl'yŏ*, sm. pannier, market-basket.

esposas, *espō'săs*, sf. pl. manacles, handcuffs, pl.

esposo, *–sŏ*, sm. husband.

espuela, *espŭĕ'lă*, sf. spur; stimulus; (bot.) larkspur.

espuerta, *espŭĕr'tă*, sf. pannier, basket.

espulgar, *espŭlgăr'*, v. a. to louse; to flea; to examine closely.

espulgo, *espŭl'gŏ*, sm. cleaning from lice or fleas.

espuma, *espō'mă*, sf. froth, spume.

espumadera, *espŭmădĕ'ră*, sf. skimmer.

espumajear, *–hĕăr'*, v. n. to froth at the mouth.

espumajoso, sa, *–hŏ'sŏ*, a. foamy, frothy, full of spume.

espumar, *espŭmăr'*, v. a. to skim, to take off the scum. (from the mouth).

espumarajo, *–mără'hŏ*, sm. foam, froth.

espumoso, sa, *–mŏ'sŏ*, a. spumous, frothy, foamy.

espurio, ria, *espō'rĭŏ*, a. spurious; adulterated, corrupted.

espurrir, *espŭrrĭr'*, v. n. to stretch out the legs.

esputo, *espō'tŏ*, sm. spittle, saliva. per.

esquela, *ĕskĕ'lă*, sf. billet, note, slip of paper.

esqueleto, *ĕskĕlĕ'tŏ*, sm. skeleton.

esquife, *ĕskĕ'fĕ*, sm. skiff, small boat.

esquilador, *ĕskĭlădōr'*, sm. sheep-shearer.

esquilar, *–lăr'*, v. a. to shear sheep.

esquileo, *–lĕ'ŏ*, sm. sheep-shearing.

esquilmar, *ĕskĭlmăr'*, v. a. to gather and get in the harvest.

esquilmo, *ĕskĭl'mŏ*, sm. harvest-corn inned; produce of vines, cattle.

esquilón, *ĕskĭlōn'*, sm. small bell, bell worn by cattle.

esquina, *ĕskĕ'nă*, sf. corner, angle.

esquinado, da, *ĕskĭnă'dŏ*, a. cornered, angled. angle.

esquinar, *–năr'*, v. a. to form into an angle.

esquinazo, *–nă'thŏ*, sm. corner, angle.

esquivar, *ĕskĭvăr'*, v. a. to shun, to avoid, to evade; –se, to disdain, to scorn.

esquivez, *ĕskĭvĕth'*, sf. disdain, scorn.

esquivo, va, *ĕskĕ'vŏ*, a. scornful; shy, reserved.

estabilidad, *ĕstăbĭlĭdăd'*, sf. stability.

estable, *ĕstă'blĕ*, a. stable.

establecer, *ĕstăblĕthĕr'*, v. a. to establish.

establo, *ĕstă'blŏ*, sm. stable.

estaca, *ĕstă'kă*, sf. stake; stick, cudgel.

estacada, *–kă'dă*, sf. (mil.) palisade; paling.

estacar, *–kăr'*, v. a. to enclose with stakes.

estacazo, *–kă'thŏ*, sm. blow given with a stake.

estación, *ĕstăthĭōn'*, sf. state; situation; season of the year; station; railway-station, terminus. seasons.

estacional, *–năl'*, a. belonging to the seasons.

estacionario, ria, *–nă'rĭŏ*, a. stationary.

estadio, *ĕstă'dĭŏ*, sm. race-course; furlong.

estadista, *–dĭs'tă*, sm. statesman.

estadística, *–dĭs'tĭkă*, sf. statistics.

estadístico, ca, *–dĭs'tĭkŏ*, a. statistical.

estado, *ĕstă'dŏ*, sm. state, condition.

estafa, *–fă*, sf. trick, imposition.

estafador, *–fădŏr'*, sm. impostor, swindler.

estafar, -fár´, v. a. to deceive, to defraud.

estafermo, -fér´mŏ, sm. wooden movable figure of an armed man; idle fellow who affects dignity and importance.

estafeta, -fĕ´tã, sf. courier, express; general post-office for letters.

estafetero, -fĕtĕ´rŏ, sm. post-master.

estallar, ĕstãlyár´, v. n. to crack, to burst; to break out into fury. [crash.

estallido, -yĕ´dŏ, sm. crack, crackling.

estambre, ĕstãm´brĕ, sm. fine wool; stamen of flowers.

estamento, ĕstãmĕn´tŏ, sm. name given to each of the three estates of Spain, composing the Cortes.

estameña, -mĕn´yã, sf. serge.

estampa, ĕstãm´pã, sf. print, stamp; pattern, model.

estampador, -dŏr´, sm. printer.

estampar, ĕstãmpár´, v. a. to print.

estampería, -pĕrĕ´ã, sf. office for printing or selling prints. [sells stamps.

estampero, -pĕ´rŏ, sm. he who makes or

estampido, -pĕ´dŏ, sm. report of a gun, &c.; crack.

estampilla, -pĕl´yã, sf. signet.

estancar, ĕstãnkár´, v.a. to check a current; to monopolise; to prohibit, to suspend.

estancia, ĕstãn´thlã, sf. stay, sojourn; mansion, (am.) cattle-ranche; bed-room; (poet.) stanza.

estanco, ĕstãn´kŏ, sm. forestalling, monopoly; place where only monopoly goods are sold; —, ca, a. water-fast.

estandarte, -dãr´tĕ, sm. banner, standard.

estanque, ĕstãn´kĕ, sm. pond, basin.

estanquillero, -kĕlyĕ´rŏ, sm. tobacconist.

estanquillo, -kĕl´yŏ, sm. tobacconist's shop. [pl. props of the cross-beams.

estante, ĕstãn´tĕ, sm. shelf (for books); —s,

estañador, ĕstãnyãdŏr´, sm. tinman.

estañadura, -dŏ´rã, sf. tinning.

estañar, ĕstãnyár´, v. a. to tin.

estaño, ĕstãn´yŏ, sm. tin.

estar, ĕstár´, v. n. to be; to be in a place.

estática, ĕstã´tĭkã, sf. statics.

estatua, ĕstã´tũã, sf. statue.

estatuario, -tũã´rĭŏ, sm. statuary.

estatura, -tŏ´rã, sf. stature.

estatuto, -tŏ´tŏ, sm. statute, law.

este, ĕs´tĕ, sm. east; —, ta, to, pp. this.

estera, ĕstĕ´rã, sf. mat.

esterar, ĕstĕrár´, v. a. to cover with mats.

estercoladura, ĕstĕrkŏlãdŏ´rã, sf. stercoration.

estercolar, -lár´, v. a. to dung, to manure; —, v. n. to void the excrements.

estercolero, -lĕ´rŏ, sm. dung-hill; dung-pit, lay-stall. [type.

estereotipar, ĕstĕrĕŏtĭpár´, v. a. to stereo-

estereotipia, -tĭ´pĭã, sf. stereotypography.

esterero, ĕstĕrĕ´rŏ, sm. mat-maker.

estéril, ĕstĕ´rĭl, a. sterile, barren.

esterilidad, -lĭdãd´, sf. sterility, barrenness. [gold or silver.

esterilla, -yã, sf. ferret lace made of

esterlino, na, -lĕ´nŏ, a. sterling, genuine, lawful. [stick.

esteva, ĕstĕ´vã, sf. plough-handle; long

estevado, da, ĕstĕvã´dŏ, a. bow-legged; hump-backed.

estiércol, ĕstĭĕr´kŏl, sm. dung; excrement.

estigio, gia, ĕstĕ´hĭŏ, a. Stygian.

estilar, ĕstĭlár´, v. a. & n. to use, to be accustomed.

estilo, ĕstĕ´lŏ, sm. style; use, custom.

estima, ĕstĕ´mã, sf. esteem. [of esteem.

estimable, ĕstĭmã´blĕ, a. estimable, worthy

estimación, -mãthĭŏn´, sf. estimation, valuation, account.

estimar, -már´, v. a. to estimate, to value; to esteem; to judge; to thank, to acknowledge. [stimulate, to excite, to goad.

estimular, -mũlár´, v. a. to sting, to

estimulo, ĕstĕ´mũlŏ, sm. sting, stimulus.

estio, ĕstĕ´ŏ, sm. summer. [diary.

estipendiario, ĕstĭpĕndĭã´rĭŏ, sm. stipendiary.

estipendio, -pĕn´dĭŏ, sm. stipend, salary.

estipulación, -pũlãthĭŏn´, sf. stipulation.

estipular, -pũlár´, v. a. to stipulate.

estirar, -rár´, v. a. to dilate, to stretch out; to extend a discourse.

estirón, -rŏn´, sm. pulling; hauling; dar un —, to grow rapidly.

estirpe, ĕstĕr´pĕ, sf. race, origin, stock.

estocada, ĕstŏkã´dã, sf. stab.

estofa, ĕstŏ´fã, sf. quilted stuff; quality.

estofado, da, ĕstŏfã´dŏ, a. quilted; stewed.

estofar, -fár´, v. a. to quilt; to stew meat.

estola, ĕstŏ´lã, sf. stole.

estolidez, ĕstŏlĭdĕth´, sf. stupidity.

estólido, da, ĕstŏ´lĭdŏ, a. stupid.

estomacal, ĕstŏmãkãl´, a. stomachic.

estomagar, -mãgár´, v. a. to stomach, to resent; to enrage.

estómago, ĕstŏ´mãgŏ, sm. stomach.

estopa, ĕstŏ´pã, sf. tow.

estopilla, ĕstŏpĕl´yã, sf. fine spinning-flax; long-lawn (tissue).

estopín, -pĕn´, sm. quick-match.

estopón, -pŏn´, sm. coarse tow.

estoposo, sa, -pŏ´sŏ, a. filamentous.

estoque, ĕstŏ´kĕ, sm. tuck (long narrow sword). [ment.

estorbo, ĕstŏr´bŏ, sm. hindrance, impedi-

estornudar, -nũdár´, v. n. to sneeze.

estornudo, -nŏ´dŏ, sm. sternutation, sneeze. [otro, this other.

estotro, tra, ĕstŏ´trŏ, contraction for este

estrada, ĕstrã´dã, sf. causeway.

estrado, -dŏ, sm. drawing-room; —s, pl. law-court.

estrafalario, ria, -fãlã´rĭŏ, a. slovenly, uncleanly dressed; extravagant. [rupt.

estragar, -gár´, v. a. to deprave, to cor-

estrago, ĕstrã´gŏ, sm. ravage; havoc.

estrambótico, ca, ĕstrãmbŏ´tĭkŏ, a. extravagant, irregular. [trick.

estratagema, ĕstrãtãhĕ´mã, sf. stratagem.

estrategia, -tĕ´hĭã, sf. strategy.

estratégico, ca, -tĕ´hĭkŏ, a. strategical.

estraza, ĕstrã´thã, sf. rag; papel de —, brown paper.

estrechar, ĕstrĕchár´, v. a. to tighten; to

contract, to constringe; to compress; —se, to bind oneself strictly; to reduce one's expenses; to communicate in confidence; to be intimate with.

estrechez, —*těhěth*, sf. straitness, narrowness; intimate union; poverty.

estrecho, *ěstrětsh'ŏ*, sm. strait; narrow passage between two mountains; —, cha, a. narrow, close; strait, tight; intimate; rigid, austere; exact; poor, indigent.

estregadura, —*gădŏ'rǎ*, sf. friction, rubbing.   [against another.

estregar, —*gǎr'*, v. a. to rub one thing

estrella, *ěstrěl'yǎ*, sf. star.

estrellado, da, —*yǎ'dŏ*, a. starry; **huevos** —s, poached eggs.   [to make ashamed.

estrellar, —*yǎr'*, v. a. to dash to pieces;

estremecer, *ěstrěměthěr'*, v. a. to shake, to make tremble; —se, to shake, to tremble.

estremecimiento, —*thǐmǐěn'tŏ*, sm. trembling, shaking.   [Year's gift; handsel.

estrena, estrenas, *ěstrě'nǎ(s)*, sf. New-

estrenar, *ěstrěnǎr'*, v. a. to handsel; to regale; —se, to use for the first time; to begin.   [tion; costiveness.

estreñimiento, —*yǐmǐěn'tŏ*, sm. obstruc-

estreñir, —*yǐr'*, v. a. to restrain; —se, to restrain oneself.

estrépito, *ěstrě'pǐtŏ*, sm. noise, clamour, bustle, noisiness, obstreperousness.

estrepitoso, sa, *ěstrěpǐtŏ'sŏ*, a. noisy.

estribar, *ěstrǐbǎr'*, v. n. to prop; to found; to be supported.   [empty.

estribillo, —*bǐl'yŏ*, sm. burden of a song.

estribo, *ěstrě'bŏ*, sm. buttress; stirrup; step on the side of a coach; **perder los** —s, to lose courage.   [severe.

estricto, ta, *ěstrǐk'tŏ*, a. strict, exact;

estrofa, *ěstrŏ'fǎ*, sf. strophe.

estropajear, *ěstrŏpǎ'hěǎr'*, v. a. to clean a wall with a dry brush.

estropajo, —*pǎ'hŏ*, sm. dish-clout.

estropajoso, sa, —*pǎ'hŏsŏ*, a. ragged; despicable; mean; stammering.

estropear, —*pěǎr'*, v. a. to maim, to cripple.

estructura, *ěstrŭktŏ'rǎ*, sf. structure.

estruendo, —*ěn'dŏ*, sm. clamour, noise; confusion, bustle; pomp, ostentation.

estrujadura, —*hǎdŏ'rǎ*, sf. pressure, compressing.

estrujar, —*hǎr'*, v. a. to press, to squeeze.

estrujón, —*hŏn'*, sm. last pressing of grapes; pressing, squeezing.

estuche, *ěstŭtsh'ě*, sm. case (for scissors &c.); etui; (fig.) a clever fellow.

estudiante, *ěstŭdǐǎn'tě*, sm. scholar, student.   [the manner of students.

estudiantina, —*tě'nǎ*, (á la —), ad. in

estudiar, *ěstŭdǐǎr'*, v. a. to study.

estudio, *ěstŏ'dǐŏ*, sm. study; (also as apartment); — general, university.

estudioso, sa, *ěstŭdǐŏ'sŏ*, a. studious.

estufa, *ěstŏ'fǎ*, sf. stove; hot-house.

estufador, *ěstŭfǎdŏr'*, sm. stewing-pan.

estufero, —*fě'rŏ*, sm. stove-maker.

estufilla, —*fǐl'yǎ*, sf. muff; small brasier.

estupefacción, *ěstŭpěfǎkthǐŏn'*, sf. stupefaction.

estupefacto, —*fǎk'tŏ*, a. petrified with astonishment; stupefied.

estupendo, da, —*pěn'dŏ*, a. stupendous, marvellous.

estupidez, —*pǐděth'*, sf. stupidity.

estúpido, da, *ěstŏ'pǐdŏ*, a. stupid.

estupor, *ěstŭpŏr'*, sm. stupor; astonishment.   [flourer.

estuprador, —*prǎdŏr'*, sm. ravisher, de-

estuprar, —*prǎr'*, v. a. to violate, to deflour.

estupro, *ěstŏ'prŏ*, sm. ravishment, rape.

etapa, *ětǎ'pǎ*, sf. (mil.) rations.   [on.

etcétera, *ětthě'těrǎ*, adv. et cetera, and so

éter, *d'těr*, sm. ether.

etéreo, rea, *ětě'rěŏ*, a. ethereal.

eternidad, *ětěrnǐdǎd'*, sf. eternity, everlasting.   [perpetuate.

eternizar, —*thǎr'*, v. a. to eternalize, to

eterno, na, *ětěr'nŏ*, a. eternal.

ética, *d'ǐtkǎ*, sf. ethics.

ético, ca, *d'ǐtkŏ*, a. ethical, moral.

etimología, *ětǐmŏlŏ'hǐǎ*, sf. etymology.

etimológico, ca, —*lŏ'hǐkŏ*, a. etymological.

etiqueta, *ětǐkě'tǎ*, sf. etiquette, formality.

Eucaristía, *ěǔkǎrǐstǐ'ǎ*, sf. Lord's Supper.

eucarístico, ca, —*rǐs'tǐkŏ*, a. eucharistical.

eufonía, *ěǔfŏnǐ'ǎ*, sf. euphony.

eufónico, ca, *ěǔfŏ'nǐkŏ*, a. euphonious.

Euro, *ěǔ'rŏ*, sm. Eurus, the east-wind.

evacuación, *ěvǎkǔǎthǐŏn'*, sf. evacuation; issue.   [empty.

evacuar, —*kǔǎr'*, v. a. to evacuate, to

evadir, *ěvǎdǐr'*, v. a. to evade, to escape.

evangélico, ca, *ěvǎn'hǎ'lǐkŏ*, a. evangelic.

evangelio, —*hǎ'lǐŏ*, sm. gospel.   [lical.

evangelista, —*lěs'tǎ*, sm. evangelist; gospeller.   [gelize.

evangelizar, —*lěthǎr'*, v. a. to evan-

evaporar, *ěvǎpŏrǎr'*, v. a. to evaporate; —, v. n. to pass away; to grow vapid.

evasión, *ěvǎsǐŏn'*, sf. evasion, escape; subterfuge, poor excuse.

eventual, *ěvěntǔǎl'*, a. eventual, fortuitous.

evidencia, *ěvǐděn'thǐǎ*, sf. evidence, manifestation.   [fest.

evidente, *ěvǐděn'tě*, a. evident, clear, mani-

evitable, *ěvǐtǎ'blě*, a. avoidable.

evitar, *ěvǐtǎr'*, v. a. to avoid.

evocación, *ěvŏkǎthǐŏn'*, sf. evocation; pagan invocation.

evocar, *ěvŏkǎr'*, v. a. to call out; to invoke.

evolución, *ěvŏlǔthǐŏn'*, sf. (mil.) evolution.

exacción, *ěksǎkthǐŏn'*, sf. exaction; impost; contribution.   [to irritate.

exacerbar, —*thěrbǎr'*, v. a. to exasperate.

exactitud, —*ǎktǐtǔd'*, sf. exactness, exactitude.   [assiduous.

exacto, ta, *ěksǎk'tŏ*, a. exact, punctual,

exageración, —*ǎ'hěrǎthǐŏn'*, sf. exaggeration.   [one that exaggerates.

exagerador, ra, —*dŏr'*, sm. & f. amplifier,

exagerar, —*ǎ'hěrǎr'*, v. a. to exaggerate, to amplify.   [elevation.

exaltación, —*ǎltǎthǐŏn'*, sf. exaltation,

exaltar, —*ǎltǎr'*, v. a. to exalt, to elevate; to praise, to extol; —se la cólera, to worry oneself, to get angry.

examen, *ĕksă'mĕn*, sm. examen, examination, trial, inquiry.

exámetro, *ĕksă'mĕtrŏ*, sm. hexameter (verse). [nation.

examinación, *ĕksămĭnăthĭŏn'*, sf. examination.

examinador, *-dŏr'*, sm. examiner.

examinando, *-nān'dŏ*, sm. examinant.

examinar, *-ămĭnăr'*, v. a. to examine.

exánime, *ĕksă'nĭmĕ*, a. spiritless, weak, dead. [ration.

exasperación, *-ăspĕrăthĭŏn'*, sf. exasperation.

exasperar, *-ăspĕrăr'*, v. a. to exasperate, to irritate.

excavación, *-kăvăthĭŏn'*, sf. excavation.

excavar, *-kăvăr'*, v. a. to excavate, to dig out. [ceeding.

excedente, *-thĕdĕn'tĕ*, a. excessive, exceeding.

exceder, *-thĕdĕr'*, v. a. to exceed, to surpass, to excel, to outdo.

excelencia, *-thĕlĕn'thĭă*, sf. excellence.

Excelencia, *-thĕlĕn'thĭă*, sf. Excellency (title).

excelente, *-lĕn'tĕ*, a. excellent.

excelso, **sa**, *ĕksthĕl'sŏ*, a. elevated, sublime, lofty. [tricity.

excentricidad, *-thĕntrĭthĭdăd'*, sf. eccentricity.

excéntrico, **ca**, *-thĕn'trĭkŏ*, a. eccentric.

excepción, *-thĕpthĭŏn'*, sf. exception.

excepto, *ĕksthĕp'tŏ*, ad. except that, excepting. [exempt.

exceptuar, *-tăăr'*, v. a. to except, to excesivo, va, *-thĕsĭ'vŏ*, a. excessive.

exceso, *ĕksthĕ'sŏ*, sm. excess.

excitar, *-thĭtăr'*, v. a. to excite. [tion.

exclamación, *-klămăthĭŏn'*, sf. exclamation.

exclamar, *-klămăr'*, v. a. to exclaim, to cry out.

excluir, *-klŏĭr'*, v. a. to exclude. [cry out.

exclusión, *-klŏsĭŏn'*, sf. exclusion.

exclusivamente, *-klŏsĭvămĕn'tĕ*, ex-clusive, *-klŏsĭ'vŏ*, ad. exclusively.

exclusivo, va, *-sĭ'vŏ*, a. exclusive.

excogitable, *-kŏ'hĭtă'blĕ*, a. imaginable.

excogitar, *-kŏ'hĭtăr'*, v. a. to excogitate, to strike out by thinking. [municate.

excomulgar, *-kŏmŭlgăr'*, v. a. to excommunicate.

excomunión, *-kŏmŭnĭŏn'*, sf. excommunication. [tion, flaying.

excoriación, *-kŏrĭăthĭŏn'*, sf. excoriation.

excoriar, *-kŏrĭăr'*, v. a. to excoriate, to flay. [flay.

excremento, *-krĕmĕn'tŏ*, sm. excrement.

excursión, *-kŭrsĭŏn'*, sf. excursion; liquidation of the estate of a debtor for paying off his debts.

excusa, *ĕksko'să*, sf. excuse, apology, plea.

excusable, *-kŭsă'blĕ*, a. excusable.

excusado, da, *-kŭsă'dŏ*, a. superfluous, useless; preserved; exempted, privileged; —, sm. subsidy from the clergy of Spain for carrying on the war against the infidels; privy, water-closet, W. C.

excusali, *-kŭsălĭ'*, sm. apron, pinafore.

excusar, *-kŭsăr'*, v. a. to excuse; to exempt from taxes; to shun, to avoid; —se, to decline a request.

execrable, *-ĕkră'blĕ*, a. execrable, accursed. [curse.

execración, *-ĕkrăthĭŏn'*, sf. execration.

execrar, *-ĕkrăr'*, v. a. to execrate, to curse.

exención, *-ĕnthĭŏn'*, sf. exemption, immunity, privilege. [vilege.

exentar, *-ĕntăr'*, v. a. to exempt, to prevent, ta, *ĕksĕn'tŏ*, a. exempt, free; —, sm. officer in the Spanish life-guards who holds the rank and brevet of a colonel in the army. [obsequies.

exequias, *ĕksĕ'kĭăs*, sf. pl. funeral rites, obsequies.

exhalación, *-ălăthĭŏn'*, sf. exhalation; velocity. [to evaporate.

exhalar, *-ălăr'*, v. a. to exhale; —se,

exhausto, ta, *-hăgs'tŏ*, a. exhausted.

exhibición, *-ĭbĭthĭŏn'*, sf. exhibition.

exhibir, *-ĭbĭr'*, v. a. to exhibit.

exhortación, *-ŏrtăthĭŏn'*, sf. exhortation.

exhortar, *-ŏrtăr'*, v. a. to exhort.

exhorto, *ĕksŏr'tŏ*, sm. letters requisitorial sent by one judge to another.

exhumación, *-ămăthĭŏn'*, sf. exhumation.

exhumar, *-ămăr'*, v. a. to disinter, to unbury. [want.

exigencia, *-ĭ'hĕn'thĭă*, sf. exigence, exigible, *-hĭ'blĕ*, a. requirable.

exigir, *-hĭr'*, v. a. to demand, to require.

exiguo, gua, *ĕksĭ'gŭŏ*, a. exiguous, small.

eximio, mia, *ĕksĭ'mĭŏ*, a. eximious, famous, very eminent. [vilege.

eximir, *-ĭmĭr'*, v. a. to exempt, to privilege.

existencia, *-ĭstĕn'thĭă*, sf. existence, existency, being.

existente, *-ĭstĕn'tĕ*, a. existing, existent.

existir, *-ĭstĭr'*, v. n. to exist, to be.

éxito, *ĕksĭ'tŏ*, sm. end, termination, issue.

Éxodo, *ĕksŏ'dŏ*, sm. Exodus. [tion.

exoneración, *-ŏnĕrăthĭŏn'*, sf. exoneration.

exonerar, *-ŏnĕrăr'*, v. a. to exonerate, to unload. [ance.

exorbitancia, *-ŏrbĭtăn'thĭă*, sf. exorbitance.

exorbitante, *-ŏrbĭtăn'tĕ*, a. exorbitant, excessive, immoderate.

exorcismo, *-ŏrthĭs'mŏ*, sm. exorcism.

exorcista, *-ŏrthĭs'tă*, sm. exorciser, exorcist.

exorcizar, *-ŏrthĭthăr'*, v. a. to exorcise.

exordio, *ĕksŏr'dĭŏ*, sm. exordium.

exótico, ca, *ĕksŏ'tĭkŏ*, a. exotic. [tension.

expansión, *-pănsĭŏn'*, sf. expansion, expansivo, va, *-pănsĭ'vŏ*, a. expansive.

expatriarse, *-pătrĭăr'sĕ*, v. r. to be exiled; to emigrate. [tion.

expectación, *-pĕktăthĭŏn'*, sf. expectation.

expectativa, *-tătĭ'vŏ*, sf. right or claim respecting some future thing; hope of obtaining a reward.

expectoración, *-pĕktŏrăthĭŏn'*, sf. expectoration. [rate.

expectorar, *-tŏrăr'*, v. a. to expectorate.

expedición, *-pĕdĭthĭŏn'*, sf. expedition; speed, activity. [peditionary.

expedicionario, *-thĭŏnă'rĭŏ*, a. expeditionary.

expediente, *-pĕdĭĕn'tĕ*, sm. affair of easy discussion and despatch; expedient; pretext; provision. [patch.

expedir, *-pĕdĭr'*, v. a. to expedite, to despatch.

expeditivo, va, *-dĭtĭ'vŏ*, a. expeditive, expeditious. [tious, speedy.

expedito, ta, *-dĭ'tŏ*, a. prompt, expedi-

expeler, -pēlēr', v. a. to expel.   [out.
expender, -pēndēr', v. a. to spend, to lay
expensas, ěkspěn'săs, sf. pl. expenses,
charges.   [trial.
experiencia,-pěrīěn'thīă, sf. experience;
experimentado, da, -pěrīměntā'dŏ, a.
experienced, expert.
experimental, -měntăl', a. experimental.
experimentar, -měntăr', v. a. to experience; to experiment.   [trial.
experimento, -měn'tŏ, sm. experiment.
experto, ta, ěkspěr'tŏ, a. expert, experienced.   [purification.
expiación, -pĭăthĭŏn', sf. expiation;
expiar, ěkspĭăr', v. a. to atone for; to
purify.
expiatorio, ria, -pĭătŏ'rĭŏ, a. expiatory.
expirar, ěkspĭrăr', v. n. to expire, to
breathe the last.
explanada, -plănā'dă, sf. esplanade.
explanar, -plănăr', v. a. to explain.
explayar, -plăyăr', v. a. to extend, to
dilate.   [tion, explication.
explicación, -plĭkăthĭŏn', sf. explana-
explicaderas, -dě'răs, sf. pl. manner
in which anything is explained; facility
of explaining.
explicar, -plĭkăr', v. a. to explain, to
expound; -se, to speak plainly; to explain oneself.   [clear, distinct.
explícito, ta, ěksplĭ'thĭtŏ, a. explicit,
exploración, -plŏrăthĭŏn', sf. exploration.   [plorer.
explorador, ra, -rădŏr', sm. & f. ex-
explorar, -plŏrăr', v. a. to explore.
explosión, -plŏsĭŏn', sf. explosion.
exponente, -pŏněn'tě, sm. (ar.) exponent
exponer, -pŏněr', v. a. to expose; to explain.
exposición, -pŏsĭthĭŏn', sf. exposition.
expósito, ta, ěkspŏ'sĭtŏ, a. exposed.
expresar, -prěsăr', v. a. to express.
expresión, -prěsĭŏn', sf. expression.
expresivo, va, -sĭ'vŏ, a. expressive;
energetic.
expreso, sa, -prě'ŏ, a. expressed; express, clear, manifest, not dubious; -, sm.
express, courier.
express, -prěs', m. (rail.) express-train.
exprimir, -prĭmĭr', v. a. to squeeze out;
to express.   [purpose.
ex profeso, -prŏfě'sŏ, ad. avowedly, on
expuesto, ta, -pŭěs'tŏ, a. exposed.   [out.
expulsar, -pŭlsăr', v. a. to expel, to drive
expulsión, -sĭŏn', sf. expulsion.
expulso, sa, ěkspŭl'sŏ, a. expelled; outcast.   [tion, purification.
expurgación, -pŭrgăthĭŏn', sf. expurga-
expurgar, -pŭrgăr', v. a. to expurge, to
purify.   [summate, excellent.
exquisito, ta, -kĭ'sĭtŏ, a. exquisite, con-
éxtasi, éxtasis, ěks'tăsĭ(s), sm. ecstacy,
enthusiasm.
extático, ca, ěkstă'tĭkŏ, a. ecstatical.
extender, -těnděr', v. a. to extend, to
stretch out; -se, to be extended; to increase in bulk; to swell; to be elated with
pride.

extensión, -sĭŏn', sf. extension; extent.
extensivo, va, -sĭ'vŏ, a. extensive.
extenso, sa, ěkstěn'sŏ, a. extensive.
extenuación, -těnŭăthĭŏn', sf. extenuation, feebleness, debility.
extenuar, -těnŭăr', v. a. to extenuate, to
debilitate.
exterior, ěkstěrĭŏr', a. exterior, external;
-, sm. exterior, outward appearance.
exterioridad, -rĭdăd', sf. exteriority;
outward appearance; outside; superficies;
pomp, ostentation.
exteriormente, -měn'tě, ad. externally.
exterminador, -těrmĭnădŏr', sm. ex-
terminator.   [to root out.
exterminar, -năr', v. a. to exterminate,
exterminio, -mě'nĭŏ, sm. extermination,
extirpation.   [ward; foreign.
externo, na, ěkstěr'nŏ, a. external, out-
ex testamento, ěks těstăměn'tŏ, ad. by
will or testament.
extinción, ěkstĭnthĭŏn', sf. extinction.
extinguible, -gĭ'blě, a. extinguishable.
extinguir, -gĭr', v. a. to quench; to extinguish.
extirpación, -sĭrpăthĭŏn', sf. extirpation,
extermination.
extirpar, -păr', v. a. to extirpate, to root
extorsión, -tŏrsĭŏn', sf. extortion.   [out.
extra, ěks'tră, pr. out, without, besides.
extracción, -trăkthĭŏn', sf. exportation;
extraction.
extractar, -tăr', v. n. to extract, to abridge.
extracto, -trăk'tŏ, sm. extract.   [port.
extraer, ěkstrăěr', v. a. to extract; to ex-
extrajudicial, -hŭdĭthĭăl', a. extrajudicial.   [walls.
extramuros, -mŭ'rŏs, a. without the
extranjero, ra, ěkstrăn'hă'rŏ, sm. & f.
stranger, foreigner; -, a. foreign, outlandish.
extrañar, ěkstrănyăr', v. a. to alienate; to
admire; to reprimand.
extraño, ña, ěkstrăn'yŏ, a. foreign; rare;
singular, strange, odd.
extraordinario, ria, -ŏrdĭnā'rĭŏ, a.
extraordinary, uncommon, odd.
extratémpora, -těm'pŏră, sf. dispensation for receiving orders out of the time
specified by the church.
extravagancia, -văgăn'thĭă, sf. extravagance.
extravagante, -văgăn'tě, a. & f. extravagant.   [to lose one's way.
extraviar, -vĭăr', v. a. to mislead; -se,
extravío, -vě'ŏ, sm. deviation; irregularity; misguidance.
extremado, da, ěkstrěmā'dŏ, a. extreme;
accomplished.
extremaunción, -ănthĭŏn', sf. extreme
unction.   [brim of any thing
extremidad, ěkstrěmĭdăd', sf. extremity.
extremo, ma, ěkstrě'mŏ, a. extreme, last;
-, sm. extreme, highest degree; en -
por -, extremely.   [external
extrínseco, ca, ěkstrĭn'sěkŏ, a. extrinsic,
exuberancia,-ŭběrăn'thĭă,sf.exuberance,
luxuriance.

F.

fábrica, *fă´brĭkă*, sf. fabrication; fabric.
fabricante, *făbrĭkăn´tĕ*, sm. fabricator, manufacturer.
fabricar, *–kăr´*, v. a. to build, to construct; to fabricate, to manufacture.
fabril, *făbrĭl´*, a. belonging to manufacturers or workmen.
fabuco, *făbŏŏ´kŏ*, sm. beech-nut.
fábula, *fă´bŭlă*, sf. fable; fiction; rumour, common talk.
fabulista, *făbŭlĭs´tă*, sm. fabulist. [tious.
fabuloso, sa, *–lŏ´sŏ*, a. fabulous, fictifacción, *făkthĭŏn´*, sf. military exploit; faction; feature. [bulent.
faccioso, sa, *–thĭŏ´sŏ*, a. factious, turfacie ecclesiae, (in –), *făthĭĕ ĕkĭd´sĭĕ*, a. legally married.
fácil, *fă´thĭl*, a. facile, easy.
facilidad, *făthĭlĭdăd´*, sf. facility, easiness.
facilitar, *–tăr´*, v. a. to facilitate.
facineroso, *–nĕrŏ´sŏ*, a. wicked, detestably bad.
facistol, *–stŏl´*, sm. chorister's desk.
factible, *făktĭ´blĕ*, a. feasible, practicable.
facticio, cia, *făktĭ´thĭŏ*, a. a factitious.
factor, *făktŏr´*, sm. performer; (ar.) factor; (com.) factor, agent.
factoría, *–rĭ´ă*, sf. factory; factorage.
factura, *făktŏ´ră*, sf. invoice.
facultad, *făkŭltăd´*, sf. faculty.
facultativo, va, *–tĭ´vŏ*, optional; –, sm. master of a science or art. [face.
facha, *făt´să*, sf. appearance, aspect, mien.
fachada, *făt´să´dă*, sf. façade, face, front.
fachenda, *făt´shĕn´dă*, a. vain, ostentatious; –, sm. busybody.
fachendear, *–dĕăr´*, v. a. to pretend to have important business on hand.
faena, *făĕ´nă*, sf. work, labour, fatigue; work on shipboard.
fagina, *făhĭ´nă*, sf. fascine; fagot.
faja, *fă´hă*, sf. band, fillet; border (line); bajo –, by book-post, under open cover.
fajar, *făhăr´*, v. a. to swathe; to fillet.
fajero, *făhă´rŏ*, sm. knitted swaddling-band for children.
falacia, *fălă´thĭă*, sf. fallacy, fraud.
falange, *fălăn´hĕ*, sf. phalanx. [lacious.
falaz, *fălăth´*, a. deceitful, fraudulent; falfalda, *făl´dă*, sf. skirt; lap; flap; train; brow of a hill; perrillo de –, lap-dog.
faldellín, *–dĕlyĭn´*, sm. short under-petticoat.
faldero, ra, *–dĕ´rŏ*, a. belonging to the lap; fond of being constantly among women; perrillo –, lap-dog. [a jacket.
faldillas, *–dĭl´yăs*, sf. pl. small skirts of
faldón, *–dŏn´*, sm. long flowing skirt;
falible, *fălĭ´blĕ*, a. fallible. [bandelet.
falsamente, *fălsămĕn´tĕ*, ad. falsely.
falsario, ria, *fălsă´rĭŏ*, a. falsifying, forging; accustomed to tell falsehoods.
falsear, *fălsĕăr´*, v. a. to falsify, to counter-

feit; –, v. n. to slacken; not to agree in sound. [tib.
falsedad, *–dăd´*, sf. falsehood; untruth.
falsete, *fălsĕ´tĕ*, sm. spigot. [tion.
falsificación, *fălsĭfĭkăthĭŏn´*, sf. falsificafalsificador, *–kădŏr´*, sm. falsifier.
falsificar, *–kăr´*, v. a. to falsify, to forge, to counterfeit. [ful; feint.
falso, sa, *făl´sŏ*, a. false, untrue; deceitfalta, *făl´tă*, sf. fault, defect, want; slight crime, failure, flaw.
faltar, *făltăr´*, v. n. to be wanting; to fail; not to fulfil one's promise; to need; to die.
falto, ta, *făl´tŏ*, a. wanting, defective; jejune; miserable, wretched; mad.
faltriquera, *făltrĭkĕ´ră*, sf. pocket.
falúa, *fălŏ´ă*, sf. (mar.) felucca.
fallar, *fălyăr´*, v. a. to give sentence, to judge; to trump (at cards).
fallecer, *fălyĕthĕr´*, v. n. to die. [death.
fallecimiento, *–thĭmĭĕn´tŏ*, sm. decease.
fallido, da, *fălyĭ´dŏ*, a. disappointed, frustrated; bankrupt. [nounce (at cards).
fallo, *făl´yŏ*, sm. judgment, sentence; refama, *fă´mă*, sf. fame; reputation, name.
familia, *fămĭ´lĭă*, sf. family.
familiar, *fămĭlĭăr´*, a. familiar, domestic; frequent; agreeable; –, sm. domestic; college-servant.
familiaridad, *–dăd´*, sf. familiarity.
familiarizar, *–thăr´*, v. a. to familiarise; –se, to become familiar. [noted.
famoso, sa, *fămŏ´sŏ*, a. famous, renowned;
fámulo, *fă´mŭlŏ*, sm. servant of a college.
fanal, *fănăl´*, sm. poop-lantern of a commodore's ship. [thusiastic.
fanático, ca, *fănă´tĭkŏ*, a. fanatical; enfandango, *făndăn´gŏ*, sm. fandango (lively Spanish dance).
fanega, *fănĕ´gă*, sf. a dry measure of about an English bushel.
fanfarria, *fănfăr´rĭă*, sf. empty brag.
fanfarrón, *–rŏn´*, sm. bully, hector.
fanfarronada, *–nă´dă*, sf. fanfaronade, boast, brag. [brag.
fanfarronear, *–nĕăr´*, v. n. to bully, to fanfarronería, *–nĕrĭ´ă*, sf. fanfaronade.
fango, *făn´gŏ*, sm. mire, mud. [brag.
fangoso, sa, *făngŏ´sŏ*, a. muddy, miry.
fantasía, *făntăsĭ´ă*, sf. fancy; phantasy; caprice; presumption.
fantasma, *făntăs´mă*, sf. phantom.
fantasmagoría, *–gŏrĭ´ă*, sf. phantasmagoria. [whimsical; presumptuous.
fantástico, ca, *făntăs´tĭkŏ*, a. fantastic, faquín, *făkĭn´*, sm. porter, carrier.
faramalla, *fărămăl´yă*, sf. imposition, artful trick; prattling; –, sm. treacherous man. [man.
faramallón, *–yŏn´*, sm. tattling, deceitful farándula, *fărăn´dŭlă*, sf. profession of a low comedian; artful trick.
farandulero, *–lĕ´rŏ*, sm. actor, player; idle tattler, deceitful talker.
faraón, *fărăŏn´*, sm. game at cards.
faraute, *fără´ŭtĕ*, sm. messenger; interpreter; principal manager; meddling fellow.

fardel, *fărdĕl'*, sm. fardel, bag, knapsack.
fardo, *făr'dŏ*, sm. bale of goods, parcel.
farfantón, *fărfăntŏn'*, sm. boasting babbler.
farfantonada, *-tŏnä'dä*, sf. idle boast.
farfulla, *fărfŭl'yä*, sm. stammering person.
farfullar, *-yär'*, v. a. to talk stammeringly; to do in a hurry and confusion.
farisaico, ca, *fărĭsä'ĭkŏ*, a. pharisaical.
farisaismo, *-sä-ĭs'mŏ*, sm. pharisaism.
fariseo, *fărĭsä'ŏ*, sm. pharisee; very tall, ugly person.
farmacéutico, ca, *fărmäthä'ŭtĭkŏ*, a. pharmaceutical.
farmacia, *fărmä'thĭä*, sf. pharmacy.
faro, *fä'rŏ*, sm. (mar.) light-house.
farol, *fărŏl'*, sm. lantern. [body.
farolear, *fărŏleär'*, v. n. to act the busy-body.
farolero, *-lä'rŏ*, sm. lantern-maker; lamp-lighter.
fárrago, *făr'răgŏ*, sm. farrago, medley.
farsa, *făr'sä*, sf. farce; company of players.
farsante, *fărsän'tĕ*, sm. actor, player; mountebank. [ad. justly or unjustly.
fas (por) ó por nefas, *făs ŏ pŏr nä'fäs*,
fascinación, *făsthĭnäthĭŏn'*, sf. fascination; imposition, deceit.
fascinar, *-när'*, v. a. to fascinate; to enchant; to deceive. [planet.
fase, *fä'sĕ*, sf. phasis (of the moon or
fastidiar, *făstĭdĭär'*, v. a. to excite disgust; to grate, to offend. [gust.
fastidio, *făstĭ'dĭŏ*, sm. squeamishness; disgust.
fastidioso, sa, *-dĭŏ'sŏ*, a. fastidious; nauseous; tedious.
fastoso, *făstŏ'sŏ*, a. proud, ostentatious.
fatal, *fätäl'*, a. fatal; mortal; unfortunate.
fatalidad, *fätälĭdäd'*, sf. fatality, mischance, ill luck.
fatalismo, *fätälĭs'mŏ*, sm. fatalism.
fatalista, *fätälĭs'tä*, sm. fatalist.
fatiga, *fätĭ'gä*, sf. toil, fatigue. [harass.
fatigar, *fätĭgär'*, v. a. to fatigue, to tire, to
fatigoso, sa, *-gŏ'sŏ*, a. tiresome, troublesome. [ness, silliness.
fatuidad, *fätŭĭdäd'*, sf. fatuity, foolishness.
fatuo, tua, *fä'tŭŏ*, a. fatuous, stupid, foolish, silly, trifling.
fauces, *fä'ŭthĕs*, sf. pl. fauces, gullet.
fausto, ta, *fä'ŭstŏ*, a. happy, fortunate; —, sm. splendour, pomp. [ostentatious.
faustoso, sa, *-tŏ'sŏ*, a. fastuous, haughty.
fautor, *fäŭtŏr'*, sm. fautor.
fautora, *-tŏ'rä*, sf. fautress.
favor, *făvŏr'*, sm. favour, favor, protection, good graces. [geous, propitious.
favorable, *-ä'blĕ*, a. favourable, advantageous.
favorecer, *-rēthĕr'*, v. a. to favour, to protect. [loved.
favorito, ta, *făvŏrĭ'tŏ*, a. favourite, beloved.
faz, *fäth*, sf. face. [my honour.
fe, *fĕ*, sf. faith, belief; **á — mia,** upon my honour.
fealdad, *fĕäldäd'*, sf. ugliness; turpitude, dishonesty.
Febo, *fä'bŏ*, sm. (poet.) Phœbus (the sun).
febrero, *fĕbrä'rŏ*, sm. February.
febril, *fĕbrĭl'*, a. febrile.
fecal, *fĕkäl'*, a. feculent.
fecundar, *fĕkŭndär'*, v. a. to fertilise.
fecundidad, *-dĭdäd'*, sf. fecundity, fertility.

fecundo, da, *fĕkŭn'dŏ*, a. fruitful, fertile, larga —, great age.
fecha, *fĕtsh'ä*, sf. date (of a letter, &c.);
fechar, *fĕtshär'*, v. a. to date.
fechoría, *fĕtshŏrē'ä*, sf. action, exploit.
felicidad, *fĕlĭthĭdäd'*, sf. felicity, happiness. [to felicitate.
felicitar, *-thĭtär'*, v. a. to congratulate.
feligrés, esa, *-grĕs'*, sm. & f. parishioner.
feligresía, *-grĕsē'ä*, sf. district of a parish.
feliz, *fĕlĭth'*, a. happy, fortunate.
felonía, *fĕlŏnē'ä*, sf. treachery, felony.
felpa, *fĕl'pä*, sf. plush; a good drubbing.
felpilla, *-pĭl'yä*, sf. corded silk for embroidering.
felpudo, da, *-pä'dŏ*, a. shaggy.
femenil, *fĕmĕnĭl'*, a. feminine, womanly.
femenino, na, *-nē'nŏ*, a. feminine, female.
fementido, da, *fĕmĕntĭ'dŏ*, a. false, unfaithful. [clude.
fenecer, *fĕnĕthĕr'*, v. a. to finish, to conclude.
fenecimiento, *-thĭmĭĕn'tŏ*, sm. termination, end.
fenómeno, *fĕnŏ'mĕnŏ*, sm. phenomenon.
feo, ea, *fä'ŏ*, a. ugly, deformed.
feracidad, *fĕräthĭdäd'*, sf. feracity, fertility.
feraz, *fĕräth'*, a. fertile, fruitful. [lity.
féretro, *fä'rĕtrŏ*, sm. bier, coffin, hearse.
feria, *fä'rĭä*, sf. week-day (not Saturday or Sunday); fair, market-day.
ferial, *fĕrĭäl'*, a. ferial.
feriar, *fĕrĭär'*, v. a. to sell, to buy; to give fairings; to suspend. [station.
fermentación, *fĕrmĕntäthĭŏn'*, sf. fermentation.
fermentar, *-tär'*, v. n. to ferment.
fermento, *fĕrmĕn'tŏ*, sm. ferment; leaven.
ferocidad, *fĕrŏthĭdäd'*, sf. ferocity, wildness; cruelty.
feroz, *fĕrŏth'*, a. ferocious, cruel, savage.
ferruginoso, sa, *fĕrrŭ'hĭnŏ'sŏ*, a. ferruginous. [ous.
fértil, *fĕr'tĭl*, a. fertile, fruitful.
fertilidad, *fĕrtĭlĭdäd'*, sf. fertility, fecundity, fruitfulness.
fertilizar, *-thär'*, v. a. to fertilise.
férula, *fä'rŭlä*, sf. ferula, ferule.
ferviente, *fĕrvĭĕn'tĕ*, a. fervent, ardent.
fervor, *fĕrvŏr'*, sm. fervour, zeal, ardour.
fervoroso, sa, *-rŏ'sŏ*, a. fervent, ardent, fervid, passionate. [to woo.
festejar, *fĕstĕhär'*, v. a. to feast; to court.
festejo, *fĕstĕ'hŏ*, sm. courtship; feast.
festín, *fĕstĭn'*, sm. feast.
festividad, *fĕstĭvĭdäd'*, sf. festivity; solemnization of some occurrence.
festivo, va, *-tĭ'vŏ*, a. festive, gay, merry; **día —,** holiday.
festón, *fĕstŏn'*, sm. garland; festoon.
festonear, *fĕstŏneär'*, v. a. to ornament with festoons.
fétido, da, *fä'tĭdŏ*, a. fetid, stinking.
feto, *fä'tŏ*, sm. fœtus.
feudal, *fĕŭdäl'*, a. feudal.
feudalidad, *-lĭdäd'*, sf. feudality.
feudatario, *-tä'rĭŏ*, sm. & a. feudatary.
feudo, *fä'ŭdŏ*, sm. fief; tribute paid to a feudal lord.

fiado, da, *fīă'dŏ,* a. confident; **al —,** upon trust; **en —,** upon bail.

fiador, *fēădŏr',* sm. surety (person); loop of a cloak; (fam.) backside; dog of a musket-lock; staple which supports a gutter.

fiambre, *fēăm'brĕ,* a. cold (applied to meat).

fiambrera, *—brē'rā,* sf. pannier (for carrying cold meat).

fianza, *fēăn'thā,* sf. caution, security.

fiar, *fēăr',* v. a. to bail; to sell on trust; to commit to another, to credit; **—,** v. n. to confide.

fiat, *fē'āt,* sm. consent; (law) fiat.

fibra, *fē'brā,* sf. fibre.

fibroso, sa, *fēbrŏ'sŏ,* a. fibrous.

ficción, *fĭkthĭŏn',* sf. fiction.

ficticio, cia, *fĭktē'thĭŏ,* a. fictitious, fictive.

ficha, *fēsh'ā,* sf. counter (at games).

fidedigno, na, *fĭdēdēg'nŏ,* a. worthy of credit, deserving of belief. [trustee.

fideicomisario, *fĭdēĭkŏmēsā'rĭŏ,* sm.

fideicomiso, *fĭdēĭkŏmē's ŏ,* sf. feoffment in trust. [punctuality.

fidelidad, *fĭdēlĭdād',* sf. fidelity; loyalty;

fideos, *fēdē'ŏs,* sm. pl. vermicelli.

fiebre, *fē'brĕ,* sf. fever.

fiel, *fēĕl',* a. faithful, loyal; **—,** sm. clerk of the market; needle of a balance.

fielazgo, *fēĕlăth'gŏ,* sm. office of the town-clerk.

fieltro, *fēĕl'trŏ,* sm. felt; rain-cloak.

fiera, *fēĕ'rā,* sf. wild beast.

fierabrás, *fēĕrăbrăs',* sm. bully, braggart.

fiereza, *—rē'thā,* sf. fierceness, cruelty, ferocity. [rough, rude.

fiero, ra, *fēĕ'rŏ,* a. fierce, cruel, ferocious;

fiesta, *fēĕs'tā,* sf. feast; festivity; **—s,** pl. holidays, vacations.

figón, *fēgŏn',* sm. eating-house, chop-house.

figonero, *—nā'rŏ,* sm. eating-house keeper.

figura, *fēgŏ'rā,* sf. figure, shape.

figurable, *fēgŏrā'blĕ,* a. figurable, that which may be figured.

figurado, da, *—rā'dŏ,* a. figurative.

figurar, *—rār',* v. a. to figure; **—se,** to fancy, to imagine.

figurativo, va, *—rātē'vŏ,* a. figurative.

figurero, *—rā'rŏ,* sm. mimic, ludicrous imitator.

figurilla, *—rēl'yā,* sf. ridiculous little figure.

figurón, *—rŏn',* sm. low-bred person assuming an air of dignity and importance.

fijacarteles, *fēhăkărtā'lĕs,* sm. billsticker.

fijar, *fēhăr',* v. a. to fix, to fasten; **—se,** to fix or settle itself in a place.

fijo, ja, *fē'hŏ,* a. fixed, firm; settled, permanent; attentive. [in a line, in a row.

fila, *fē'lā,* sf. row, line of soldiers; **en —,**

filamento, *fĭlămĕn'tŏ,* sm. filament.

filantropía, *fĭlăntrŏpē'ā,* sf. philanthropy, good-nature. [**—s,** pl. burdock.

filántropo, *fĭlăn'trŏpŏ,* sm. philanthropist;

filete, *fēlē'tĕ,* sm. fillet; hem; small roasting-spit. [fillets.

filetear, *fēlētār',* v. a. to adorn with

filiación, *fēlĭăthĭŏn',* sf. filiation; regimental register of a soldier's height, age,

filial, *fēlĭăl',* a. filial. [&c.

filiar, *fēlĭăr',* v. n. to prove one's descent.

filibustero, *fēlĭbŭstā'rŏ,* sm. freebooter.

filigrana, *—grā'nā,* sf. filigree.

filisteo, tea, *—stē'ŏ,* a. tall, gigantic.

filo, *fē'lŏ,* sm. edge (of a sword, &c.).

filología, *fēlŏlŏ'hē'ā,* sf. philology.

filológico, ca, *—lŏ'hĭkŏ,* a. philological.

filólogo, *fēlŏ'lŏgŏ,* sm. philologist.

filosofar, *fēlŏsŏfăr',* v. a. to philosophize.

filosofía, *—sŏfē'ā,* sf. philosophy.

filosófico, ca, *—sŏ'fĭkŏ,* a. philosophical.

filosofismo, *—sŏfĭs'mŏ,* sm. philosophism.

filósofo, *fēlŏ'sŏfŏ,* sm. philosopher.

filtración, *fēltrăthĭŏn',* sf. filtration.

filtrar, *fēltrăr',* v. a. to filter, to strain.

filtro, *fēl'trŏ,* sm. filter; love-potion.

fin, *fēn,* sm. end, termination, conclusion; **al —,** at last; **en —, por —,** finally, lastly.

final, *fēnāl',* a. final; **—,** sm. end, termination, conclusion.

finalizar, *fēnālēthăr',* v. a. to finish, to conclude; **—,** v. n. to be finished.

finalmente, *—mĕn'tĕ,* ad. finally, at last.

finca, *fēn'kā,* sf. land or house property.

fineza, *fēnē'thā,* sf. fineness, perfection; expression of love; delicacy, beauty; friendly zeal; small, friendly gift.

fingido, da, *fēn'hē'dŏ,* a. feigned, dissembled, sham.

fingimiento, *fēn'hēmĕn'tŏ,* sm. simulation, pretence, false appearance.

fingir, *fēn'hēr',* v. a. to feign, to dissemble; to imitate.

finiquito, *fēnēkē'tŏ,* sm. close of an account; final receipt or discharge.

finito, ta, *fēnē'tŏ,* a. finite, limited, bounded.

fino, na, *fē'nŏ,* a. fine, perfect, pure; delicate, nice; acute, sagacious.

finura, *fēnŏ'rā,* sf. fineness.

firma, *fēr'mā,* sf. signature, subscription.

firmamento, *fērmămĕn'tŏ,* sm. firmament, sky, heaven.

firmar, *fērmăr',* v. a. to sign, to subscribe.

firme, *fēr'mĕ,* a. firm, stable, strong, secure; constant, resolute.

firmeza, *fērmē'thā,* sf. firmness, stability, constancy. [prosecutor; fiscal.

fiscal, *fĭskăl',* sm. attorney-general, public

fiscalía, *fĭskălē'ā,* sf. office and business of the fiscal. [criminal offence.

fiscalizar, *—lēthăr',* v. a. to accuse of a

fisco, *fēs'kŏ,* sm. fisc, fiscal, exchequer.

fisga, *fēs'gā,* sf. three-pronged harpoon; grimace; raillery, scoff. [jeer.

fisgar, *fēsgăr',* v. a. to mock, to scoff, to

fisgón, *fēsgŏn',* sm. punster, buffoon.

física, *fē'sĭkā,* sf. physics.

físico, ca, *fē'sĭkŏ,* a. physical; real; **—,** sm. naturalist; physician.

fisonomía, *fēsŏnŏmē'ā,* sf. physiognomy.

fisonomista, *—mĭs'tā,* sm. physiognomist.

fístola, *fēs'tŏlā,* sf. fistula. [languid.

flaco, ca, *flă'kŏ,* a. lean, meagre; feeble,

flacura, *flăkŏ'rā,* sf. meagreness.

flagelación, *flå'hělåthǐŏn'*, sf. flagellation.

flagelante, *flå'hělån'tě,* sm. flagellant.

flagrante, *flågrän'tě,* a. flagrant; **en –,** in the act, red-handed.

flagrar, *flågrår',* v. n. to glow, to flame.

flamante, *flåmän'tě,* a. flaming, bright.

flanco, *flän'kŏ,* sm. flank. [quite new.

flanquear, *flänkĕår',* v. a. (mil.) to flank.

flaquear, *flåkĕår',* v. n. to flag; to grow spiritless; to slacken.

flaqueza, *flåkĕ'thå,* sf. leanness, extenuation, meagreness, feebleness, weakness.

flato, *flå'tŏ,* sm. flatulency; gust of wind.

flatulento, ta, *flåtǔlĕn'tŏ,* a. flatulent.

flauta, *flåǔ'tå,* sf. (mus.) flute.

flautado, da, *flåǔtå'dŏ,* a. resembling a flute; **–,** sm. stop of an organ.

flautero, *–tě'rŏ,* sm. flute-maker.

flautista, *–tǐs'tå,* sm. flute-player, flutist.

flecha, *flěĭshå',* sf. arrow.

flechero, *flětshå'rŏ,* sm. archer, bowman.

flema, *flěm'å,* sf. phlegm. [bow-maker.

flemático, ca, *flěmå'tǐkŏ,* a. phlegmatic.

flemón, *flěmŏ'n',* sm. furuncle; ulcer in the gums.

flemoso, sa, *flěmŏ'sŏ,* a. pituitous.

flemudo, da, *flěmŏ'då,* a. dull, sluggish.

flotar, *flětår',* v. a. to freight a ship.

flete, *flě'tě,* sm. (mar.) freight. [ity.

flexibilidad, *flěksǐbǐlǐdåd',* sf. flexibility.

flexible, *flěksěblě,* a. flexible, pliant, docile. [laziness, negligence.

flojedad, *flŏ'hědåd',* sf. feebleness, laxity.

flojo, ja, *flŏ'h'ŏ,* a. flexible, lax, slack; insipid, feeble; lazy. [ficial flowers.

flor, *flŏr',* sf. flower; **–es de mano,** artificial.

florear, *flŏrĕår',* v. a. to adorn with flowers; to flourish (of swords); (mus.) to flourish.

florecer, *flŏrěthěr',* v. n. to blossom.

florero, *flŏrě'rŏ,* sm. flower-pot.

floresta, *flŏrěs'tå,* sf. forest, thicket, grove; fine delightful place.

florete, *flŏrě'tě,* sm. fencing-foil.

floretista, *flŏrětǐs'tå,* sm. fencer.

florido, da, *flŏrǐ'dŏ,* a. florid; choice, excellent.

florín, *flŏrǐn',* sm. florin. [cellent.

florista, *flŏrǐs'tå,* sm. florist.

florón, *flŏrŏn',* sm. flower-work.

flota, *flŏ'tå,* sf. fleet. [with the hand.

flotadura, *flŏtådǔ'rå,* sf. gentle rubbing

flotante, *flŏtän'tě,* a. floating.

flotar, *flŏtår',* v. n. to float.

flote, *flŏ'tě,* sm. floating; **á –,** buoyant.

flotilla, *flŏtǐl'yå,* sf. small fleet, flotilla.

fluctuación, *flǔktǔåthǐŏn',* sf. fluctuation; uncertainty. [irresolute.

fluctuar, *–tǔår',* v. n. to fluctuate; to be

fluidez, *flǔǐděth',* sf. fluidity, liquidness.

fluido, da, *flǔ'ǐdŏ,* a. fluid; (fig.) fluent;

fluir, *flǔǐr',* v. n. to flow. [–, sm. fluid.

flujo, *flǔ'h'ŏ,* sm. (med.) flux; flowing; **– de vientre,** diarrhœa.

fluvial, *flǔvǐål',* a. fluviatic.

fluxión, *flǔksǐŏn',* sf. flowing, fluction.

foco, *fŏ'kŏ,* sm. focus; centre; flash of fire-arms; mortise; (mar.) main-sail of a bilander.

fofo, fa, *fŏ'fŏ,* a. spongy, soft, bland.

fogata, *fŏgå'tå,* sf. blaze; heat caused by the fumes of wine. [a gun.

fogón, *fŏgŏn',* sm. hearth; touch-hole of

fogonazo, *fŏgŏnå'thŏ,* sm. flame of the priming of a gun. [city, fieriness.

fogosidad, *fŏgŏsǐdåd',* sf. excessive vivacity.

fogoso, sa, *fŏgŏ'sŏ,* a. fiery, ardent, fervent; impetuous, boisterous.

foguear, *fŏgĕår',* v. a. to accustom soldiers or horses to stand fire; to clean fire-arms by firing off a small quantity of gunpowder in them. [books).

foliación, *fŏlǐåthǐŏn',* sf. pagination (of

foliar, *fŏlǐår',* v. a. to page.

foliatura, *fŏlǐåtǔ'rå,* sf. numbering the pages of a book; pagination.

follados, *fŏlyå'dŏs,* sm. pl. old-fashioned trunk-hose.

follaje, *fŏlyå'h'ě,* sm. foliage.

follero, *fŏlyě'rŏ,* sm. one who makes or sells bellows.

folletista, *fŏlyětǐs'tå,* sm. pamphleteer.

folleto, *fŏlyě'tŏ,* sm. pamphlet; small manuscript newspaper. [tation.

fomentación, *fŏměntåthǐŏn',* sf. fomentation.

fomentar, *–tår',* v. a. to foment; to patronise; to excite. [patronage.

fomento, *fŏměn'tŏ,* sm. fomentation; fuel;

fonda, *fŏn'då,* sf. hotel, inn, lodging-house.

fondeadero, *fŏndĕådě'rŏ,* sm. anchoring-ground, anchorage.

fondear, *fŏndĕår',* v. a. to sound; to search a ship; **–,** v. n. to cast anchor.

fondista, *fŏndǐs'tå,* sm. innkeeper.

fondo, *fŏn'dŏ,* sm. bottom; ground; space occupied by files of soldiers; **–s,** pl. intrinsic brilliancy of a diamond; stock, fund, capital; **dar –,** to cast anchor; **á –,** perfectly, completely; **–, da,** a. profound.

fontanería, *fŏntånĕrǐ'å,* sf. art of making water-works; conduit-pipes, water-duct.

fontanero, *–nå'rŏ,* sm. conduit-maker; turncock.

forajido, da, *fŏrå'hǐ'dŏ,* a. highway robbing; wicked, villanous (also used substantively). [of a country.

foral, *fŏrål',* a. belonging to the statute law

forastero, ra, *fŏråstě'rŏ,* a. strange, exotic; **–,** sm. stranger.

forcejar, *fŏrthě'hår',* v. n. to struggle, to strive, to oppose.

forcejudo, da, *–hŏ'dŏ,* a. strong, robust.

forense, *fŏrěn'sě,* a. forensic.

forjador, *fŏr'hådŏr',* sm. framer, forger.

forjadura, *–dŏ'rå,* sf. forging.

forjar, *fŏr'hår',* v. a. to forge; to frame; to invent.

forma, *fŏr'må,* sf. form, shape, fashion; handwriting; host to be consecrated by a priest; **de – que,** in such a manner that.

formación, *fŏrmåthǐŏn',* sf. formation; form, figure; twisted cord of silk, gold, silver, &c. used by embroiderers.

formal, *fŏrmål',* a. formal; proper, genuine; serious, grave.

formalidad, *fŏrmålǐdåd',* sf. formality; punctuality; gravity.

formalizar, *-lĭthár',* v. a. to form; *-se,* to grow formal, to affect gravity.

formar, *formár',* y. a. to form, to shape.

formero, *formĕ'rŏ,* sm. centring of an arch.

formidable, *formĭdă'blĕ,* a. formidable, dreadful, terrific.

formón, *formŏn',* sm. paring-chisel; punch.

fórmula, *fŏr'mŭlă,* sf. formule.

formulario, *formŭlă'rĭŏ,* sm. formulary.

fornicación, *fornĭkăthĭŏn',* sf. fornication.

fornicador, *-dŏr',* sm. fornicator.

fornicar, ria, *fornĭkár',* v. n. to commit fornication. [fornication.

fornicario, ria, *-kă'rĭŏ,* a. relating to fornication.

fornitura, *fornĭtŭ'ră,* sf. leather straps worn by soldiers. [ground of the stage.

foro, *fŏ'rŏ,* sm. court of justice; bar; back-

forradora, *forrădŏ'ră,* sf. lining (of clothes).

forraje, *forrá'hĕ,* sm. forage.

forrajeador, *-hĕădŏr',* sm. forager.

forrajear, *forră'hĕár',* v. a. to forage.

forrar, *forrár',* v. a. to line.

forro, *fŏr'rŏ,* sm. lining.

fortalecer, *fortălĕthér',* v. a. to fortify, to strengthen, to encourage.

fortaleza, *-lĕ'thă,* sf. fortitude, valour, courage; strength, vigour; (mil.) fortress, stronghold.

fortepiano, *fortĕpĭă'nŏ,* sm. piano-forte.

fortificación, *fortĭfĭkăthĭŏn',* sf. fortification. [comfort; to fortify a place.

fortificar, *-kár',* v. a. to strengthen, to

fortín, *fortĭn',* sm. (mil.) small fort.

fortuito, ta, *fortĭ'tŏ,* a. fortuitous.

fortuna, *fortŏ'nă,* sf. fortune.

forzado, *forthă'dŏ,* sm. criminal sentenced to the galleys.

forzar, *forthár',* v. a. to force.

forzosa, *forthŏ'să,* sf. decisive move at the game of draughts; necessity.

forzoso, sa, *-thŏ'sŏ,* a. indispensable, necessary.

forzudo, da, *-thŏ'dŏ,* a. strong, vigorous.

fosfórico, ca, *fosfŏ'rĭkŏ,* a. phosphoric.

fósforo, *fŏs'fŏrŏ,* sm. phosphorus; *-s,* pl.

fósil, *fŏs'ĭl,* a. & sm. fossil. [matches.

foso, *fŏ'sŏ,* sm. pit; moat, ditch, fosse.

frac, *frák,* sm. evening-coat, dress-coat.

fracasar, *frăkăsár',* v. n. to crumble, to break into pieces. [struction.

fracaso, *-kă'sŏ,* sm. downfall, ruin, de-

fracción, *frăkthĭŏn',* sf. fraction.

fractura, *-tŏ'ră,* sf. fracture.

fracturar, *-tŭrár',* v. a. to break a bone.

fragancia, *frăgăn'thĭă,* sf. fragrance, sweetness of smell.

fragante, *-găn'tĕ,* a. fragrant, odoriferous; **en —,** in the act itself, red-handed.

fragata, *frăgă'tă,* sf. (mar.) frigate.

frágil, *frá'hĭl,* a. brittle, frail.

fragilidad, *-lĭdăd',* sf. fragility, brittleness; infirmity.

fragmento, *frăgmĕn'tŏ,* sm. fragment.

fragosidad, *frăgŏsĭdăd',* sf. roughness of the road; imperviousness of a forest.

fragoso, sa, *frăgŏ'sŏ,* a. craggy, rough, uneven. [(fig.) reputation for virtue.

fragrancia, *frăgrăn'thĭă,* sf. fragrance;

fragrante, *-grăn'tĕ,* a. fragrant, odoriferous.

fragua, *frá'gŭă,* sf. forge. [ferous.

fraguar, *frăgŭár',* v. a. to forge; to contrive; *—,* v. n. to solidify, to harden (of mortar, clay, &c.).

fraile, *frá'ĭlĕ,* sm. friar, monk.

framasón, *frămăsŏn',* sm. freemason.

frambuesa, *frămbŏĕ'să,* sf. raspberry.

frambueso, *-sŏ,* sm. raspberry-bramble.

francachela, *frănkăchă'lă,* ad. frankly.

francés, *frănthĕ's,* sm. French language.

francesilla, *frănthĕsĭl'yă,* sf. (bot.) common yard crow-foot.

franco, *frăn'kŏ,* sm. frank (coin); *—,* ca, a. frank; generous, liberal.

francolín, *frănkŏlĭn',* sm. Indian partridge.

franela, *frănĕ'lă,* sf. flannel.

franja, *frăn'hă,* sf. fringe.

franquear, *frănkĕár',* v. a. to exempt; to franchise; to disengage; to stamp letters; *-se,* to give oneself up to the service of others; to unbosom oneself.

franqueza, *frănkĕ'thă,* sf. freedom, liberty; generosity. [taxes.

franquicia, *frănkĕ'thĭă,* sf. immunity from

frasco, *frăs'kŏ,* sm. flask; powder-horn.

frase, *frá'sĕ,* sf. phrase. [case.

frasquera, *frăskĕ'ră,* sf. bottle-case, liquor-

frasqueta, *frăskĕ'tă,* sf. frisket of a printing-press.

fraternal, *frătĕrnál',* a. fraternal, brotherly.

fraternidad, *-nĭdăd',* sf. fraternity, brotherhood. [(murderer of a brother).

fratricida, *frătrĭthĭ'dă,* sm. & f. fratricide

fratricidio, *-thĭ'dĭŏ,* sm. fratricide (murder of a brother).

fraude, *frá'ŭdĕ,* sm. fraud, deceit, cheat.

fraudulento, ta, *-dŭlĕn'tŏ,* a. fraudulent, deceitful.

frecuencia, *frĕkŭĕn'thĭă,* sf. frequency.

frecuentación, *-tăthĭŏn',* sf. frequentation.

frecuentar, *-tár',* v. a. to frequent.

frecuente, *frĕkŭĕn'tĕ,* a. frequent.

fregadero, *frĕgădĕ'rŏ,* sm. scullery.

fregado, *frĕgă'dŏ,* sm. scouring of kitchen utensils; (fig.) intrigue; underhand work.

fregador, *-dŏr',* sm. dish-clout. [scour.

fregar, *frĕgár',* v. a. to rub; to cleanse, to

fregona, *frĕgŏ'nă,* sf. kitchen-maid.

freidura, *frĕĭdŏ'ră,* sf. frying.

freír, *frĕĭr',* v. a. to fry. [caprice.

frenesí, *frĕnĕsĭ',* sm. frenzy; extravagant

frenético, ca, *frĕnĕ'tĭkŏ,* a. mad, lunatic, insane. [tongue.

frenillo, *frĕnĭl'yŏ,* sm. impediment of the

freno, *frĕ'nŏ,* sm. bridle; (rail.) brake.

frente, *frĕn'tĕ,* sf. front; face; *— á —,* face to face; **en —,** opposite; (mil.) front rank of a body of troops.

fresa, *frĕ'să,* sf. strawberry.

fresal, *frĕsál',* sm. strawberry-plant; ground bearing strawberry plants.

frescachón, ona, *frĕskăchŏn',* a. good-looking and stout.

fresco, ca, *frĕs'kŏ,* a. fresh, coolish; new; recent; plump, ruddy; brisk, gay; *—,* sm. refreshing air.

9

frescura, frĕskŏ'rä, sf. freshness; frankness; smart repartee; carelessness.

fresno, frĕs'nŏ, sm. ash-tree.

frialdad, frĭäldäd', sf. frigidity, coldness; indifference.

fricación, frĭkäthĭŏn', sf. friction.

fricandó, frĭkändŏ', sm. Scotch collop.

fricción, frĭkthĭŏn', sf. friction.

friega, frĭĕ'gä, sf. friction with flannel.

frígido, da, frĭ'hĭdŏ, a. (poet.) cold.

frío, fria, frĭ'ŏ, a. cold, frigid; indifferent; —, sm. cold; fresh air; shivering.

friolento, ta, frĭŏlĕn'tŏ, a. chilly.

friolera, —lĕ'rä, sf. trifle. [or shagging.

frisadura, frĭsädŏ'rä, sf. act of frizzling

frisar, frĭsär', v. a. to frizzle; to rub against the grain; —, v. n. to resemble; to approach.

friso, frĭ'sŏ, sm. frieze; wainscot.

frisón, frĭsŏn', sm. large draught-horse.

fritada, frĭtä'dä, sf. dish of fried meat or

frito, ta, frĭ'tŏ, p. & a. fried. [fish.

frivolidad, frĭvŏlĭdäd', sf. frivolity.

frívolo, la, frĭ'vŏlŏ, a. frivolous, trifling.

frondosidad, frŏndŏsĭdäd', sf. foliage, tuft of leaves. [ing with leaves.

frondoso, sa, frŏndŏ'sŏ, a. leafy, abound-

frontal, frŏntäl', sm. front-ornament of an altar.

frontera, frŏntä'rä, sf. frontier.

fronterizo, za, frŏntĕrĭ'thŏ, a. limitaneous; opposite, over-against.

frontis, frŏn'tĭs, sm. face, façade. [piece.

frontispicio, frŏntĭspĕ'thĭŏ, sm. frontis-

frontón, frŏntŏn', sm. wall for playing at fives.

frotación, frŏtäthĭŏn', frotadura, frŏtädŏ'rä, sf. friction, rubbing.

frotar, frŏtär', v. a. to rub. [fruitful.

fructífero, ra, frŭktĕ'fĕrŏ, a. fructiferous,

fructificar, —tĭfĭkär', v. a. to fructify, to fertilize.

fructuoso, sa, —tŏŏ'sŏ, a. fruitful; useful.

frugal, frŭgäl', a. frugal, sparing.

frugalidad, frŭgälĭdäd', sf. frugality, parsimony.

fruncidor, frŭnthĭdŏr', sm. plaiter, folder.

fruncimiento, —mĭĕn'tŏ, sm. wrinkling, corrugation; imposture.

fruncir, frŭnthĭr', v. a. to plait; to knit; to reduce to a smaller size; to conceal the truth; —las cejas, to knit the eyebrows; —los labios, to curl the lips.

fruslería, frŭslĕrĕ'ä, sf. trifle, futility.

frustrar, frŭsträr', v. a. to frustrate; to disappoint; —se, to miscarry

fruta, frŭ'tä, sf. fruit; —del tiempo, fruit in season.

frutal, frŭtäl', sm. fruit-tree. [fresh fruit.

frutera, frŭtä'rä, sf. fruit-woman.

frutero, —rŏ, sm. fruiterer; fruit-basket.

frutilla, frŭtĭl'yä, sf. strawberry in Peru; round shell of which rosaries are made.

fruto, frŭ'tŏ, sm. fruit; benefit, profit.

¡fu! fŭ, fy! shame! faugh!

fuego, fŭĕ'gŏ, sm. fire; ¡—! bless me! what is this!

fuelle, fŭĕl'yĕ, sm. bellows; tale-bearer.

fuente, fŭĕn'tĕ, sf. fountain; original, first principle; source; issue, fontanel.

fuera, fŭĕ'rä, ad. without; from outward; over and above; ¡—! out of the way!

fuero, —rŏ, sm. statute-law of a country; jurisdiction; privileges granted to a province.

fuerte, fŭĕr'tĕ, sm. fortification, fort; —, a. vigorous, stout; strong; —, ad. strongly.

fuerza, fŭĕr'thä, sf. force, strength, vigour; valour, courage; violence, coercion; á—de, by dint of; —s, pl. troops.

fuga, fŭ'gä, sf. flight, escape.

fugarse, fŭgär'sĕ, v. r. to escape, to fly.

fugaz, fŭgäth', a. a fugitive; volatile; perishable. [fugitive.

fugitivo, va, fŭ'hĭtĕvŏ, a. & sm. & f. fugitive.

fulano, na, fŭlä'nŏ, sm. & f. such a one.

fulgente, fŭl'hĕn'tĕ, a. (poet.) brilliant.

fulgurar, fŭlgŭrär', v. n. to emit flashes of light. [sharping; cogging, fallacy.

fullería, fŭlyĕrĕ'ä, sf. cheating, card-

fullero, fŭlyĕ'rŏ, sm. card-sharper, cheat.

fulminación, fŭlmĭnäthĭŏn', sf. flash; report; thundering. [n. to rave.

fulminar, —när', v. a. to fulminate; —, v.

fumada, fŭmä'dä, sf. whiff.

fumadero, —dĕ'rŏ, sm. smoking-room.

fumar, fŭmär', v. a. & n. to smoke.

fumarada, fŭmärä'dä, sf. blast of smoke; a pipeful of tobacco.

fumigación, fŭmĭgäthĭŏn', sf. fumigation.

fumigatorio, ria, —gätŏ'rĭŏ, a. fumigatory.

fumosidad, fŭmŏsĭdäd', sf. smokiness.

fumoso, sa, fŭmŏ'sŏ, a. full of smoke or fume, fumid, smoky.

funámbulo, fŭnäm'bŭlŏ, sm. rope-dancer.

función, fŭnthĭŏn', sf. function; solemnity, festival; fight, battle.

funda, fŭn'dä, sf. case, sheath; —de almohada, pillow-case. [groundwork.

fundación, fŭndäthĭŏn', sf. foundation;

fundador, —dŏr', sm. founder.

fundamental, —mĕntäl', a. fundamental.

fundamento, —mĕn'tŏ, sm. foundation, groundwork; reason, cause.

fundar, fŭn'där', v. a. to found; to establish, to ground.

fundible, fŭndĕ'blĕ, a. fusible.

fundición, fŭndĭthĭŏn', sf. fusion; foundry.

fundidor, —dŏr', sm. founder.

fundir, fŭndĭr', v. a. to melt metals.

fúnebre, fŏ'nĕbrĕ, a. mournful, sad; funereal.

funeral, fŭnĕräl', a. funeral; á la —a, manner in which soldiers carry arms during the holy week and at funerals; —es, sm. pl. funeral, obsequies.

funerario, ria, —rä'rĭŏ, a. funeral, funereal.

funesto, ta, fŭnĕs'tŏ, a. funereal, mournful, sad, dismal.

furia, fŏ'rĭä, sf. fury, rage; á toda —, ad. with the utmost speed. [furylike.

furibundo, da, fŭrĭbŭn'dŏ, a. furious,

furioso, sa, fŭrĭŏ'sŏ, a. furious.

furor, fŭrŏr', sm. fury.

furrier, fŭrrĭĕr', sm. quarter-master.

furtivamente, *fŭrtĭvǎmĕn'tĕ*, ad. by
furtivo, va, *-ĭt'vŏ*, a. furtive. [stealth.
fusil, *fŭsĭl'*, sm. fusil, firelock; — que se
  carga por la recámara, breech-loader.
fusilazo, *-lā'thŏ*, sm. musket-shot.
fusilería, *-lĕr'ă'ă*, sf. body of fusileers.
fusilero, *-lĕr'ŏ*, sm. fusileer.
fusión, *fŭsĭŏn'*, sf. fusion.
fusique, *fŭsĕ'kĕ*, sm. kind of snuff-box.
fuste, *fŭs'tĕ*, sm. tree and bows of a saddle;
  shaft of a lance; fust of a column.
fútil, *fŏ'tĭl*, a. futile, trifling.
futilidad, *fŭtĭlĭdād'*, sf. futility.
futuro, ra, *fŭtō'rŏ*, a. & sm. future.

G.

gabacho, cha, *găbătsh'ŏ*, a. applied to the
  natives of some places at the foot of the
  Pyrenees; used also in derision to the
  French. [verano, dust-coat.
gabán, *găbăn'*, sm. great-coat; sack; — de
gabardina, *găbărdē'nă*, sf. cassock.
gabarra, *găbăr'ră*, sf. (mar.) lighter (boat).
gabela, *găbĕ'lă*, sf. gabel, tax, duty.
gabinete, *găbĭnĕ'tĕ*, sm. cabinet.
gaceta, *găthĕ'tă*, sf. newspaper.
gacetero, *găthĕtĕ'rŏ*, sm. gazetteer, news-
  writer; newsvender.
gacetilla, *-tĭl'yă*, sf. news, tidings.
gacetista, *-tĭs'tă*, sm. newsmonger.
gachas, *gătsh'ăs*, sf. pl. any sort of soft
  pap; á —, on all fours; ¡ánimo á las
  — I cheer up! courage! go ahead!
gacho, cha, *gătsh'ŏ*, a. curvated, bent
  downwards. [tacles.
gafa, *gă'fă*, sf. kind of hook; —s, pl. spec-
gaita, *gă'ĭtă*, sf. bagpipe; flageolet; cornemuse.
gaitería, *găĭtĕr'ă'ă*, sf. gay and gaudy dress.
gaitero, *-tĕ'rŏ*, sm. bag-piper, bag-pipe
  player; —, ra, a. gay, gaudy, showy.
gaje, *gă'h'ĕ*, sm. salary, wages; —s, pl. fees.
gajo, *gă'h'ŏ*, sm. branch of a tree broke
  off; part torn off a bunch of grapes.
gala, *gă'lă*, sf. court-dress; día de —,
  court-day; holiday; graceful, pleasing address; parade; hacer —, to glory in having done a thing. [ning rogue.
galafate, *gălăfă'tĕ*, sm. artful thief; cun-
galán, *gălăn'*, sm. gallant, gentleman in
  full dress; courtier; lover; actors who
  perform serious characters in plays, are
  distinguished in order as first, second, &c.
galán; —, ana, a. gallant, fine, neat,
  elegant.
galante, *gălăn'tĕ*, a. gallant, courtly;
  brave, generous, liberal; elegant.
galanteador, *-tĕădŏr'*, sm. wooer, lover.
galantear, *-tĕăr'*, v. a. to court, to woo.
galanteo, *-tă'ŏ*, sm. gallantry, courtship.
galantería, *-tĕr'ă'ă*, sf. gallantry, elegance; liberality, generosity.
galápago, *gălă'păgŏ*, sm. fresh-water tor-

toise; (fig.) cunning man; —s, pl. (mar.)
  cleats, pl. [pense.
galardón, *gălărdŏn'*, sm. reward, recom-
galardonar, *-dŏnăr'*, v. a. to reward, to
  recompense. [indolence.
galbana, *gălbă'nă*, sf. laziness, idleness,
galbanero, ra, *-nă'rŏ*, a. lazy, indolent.
galenismo, *gălĕnĭs'mŏ*, sm. doctrine of
  Galen.
galeón, *gălĕŏn'*, sm. (mar.) galleon.
galeota, *gălĕŏ'tă*, sf. (mar.) galliot.
galeote, *gălĕŏ'tĕ*, sm. galley-slave.
galera, *gălĕ'ră*, sf. (mar.) galley; wagon;
  gally, type-gally; reformatory for lewd
galería, *gălĕr'ă'ă*, sf. gallery. [women.
galga, *găl'gă*, sf. greyhound bitch.
galgo, *găl'gŏ*, sm. greyhound.
gálico, *gă'lĭkŏ*, sm. venereal disease.
galicoso, sa, *gălĭkŏ'sŏ*, a. syphilitic.
galocha, *gălŏtsh'ă*, sf. clog, golosh.
galón, *gălŏn'*, sm. galloon; gallon.
galoneadura, *-nĕădŏ'ră*, sf. garnishing
  with galloons.
galonear, *gălŏnĕăr'*, v. a. to lace.
galope, *gălŏ'pĕ*, sm. gallop; hasty execution of a thing.
galopear, *gălŏpĕăr'*, v. n. to gallop.
galopín, *-pĭn'*, sm. swabber; cabin-boy;
  scullion; boy meanly dressed.
galvánico, oa, *gălvă'nĭkŏ*, a. galvanic.
galvanismo, *gălvănĭs'mŏ*, sm. galvanism.
galladura, *gălyădŏ'ră*, sf. tread (in an egg).
gallarda, *gălyăr'dă*, sf. a Spanish dance.
gallardear, *-dĕăr'*, v. n. to do anything
  gracefully or elegantly. [streamer.
gallardete, *-dĕ'tĕ*, sm. (mar.) pendant;
gallardía, *-dĕ'ă*, sf. genteelness, elegance,
  gracefulness; activity, briskness; liberality.
gallardo, da, *gălyăr'dŏ*, a. gay, graceful,
  elegant, genteel; magnanimous; generous;
  brave, daring.
gallear, *gălyĕăr'*, v. a. to tread (as birds);
  to assume an air of importance; —, v. n.
  to raise the voice menacingly.
galleta, *gălyĕ'tă*, sf. sea-biscuit.
gallillo, *-yĭl'yŏ*, sm. uvula.
gallina, *-yē'nă*, sf. hen; (fig.) coward; —
  ciega, blindman's buff.
gallinaza, *-yĭnă'thă*, sf. hen-dung.
gallinero, ra, *-yĭnĕ'rŏ*, a. preying or
  feeding upon fowls; —, sm. poulterer;
  cock-loft, hen-roost; women's gallery of
  a Spanish theatre.
gallineta, *-yĭnĕ'tă*, sf. sand-piper (bird).
gallipavo, *-pă'vŏ*, sm. turkey.
gallito, *gălyĕ'tŏ*, sm. beau, coxcomb.
gallo, *găl'yŏ*, sm. cock; chief of a village.
gama, *gă'mă*, sf. (mus.) gamut; doe, she-
  deer. [dancing.
gambeta, *gămbĕ'tă*, sf. cross-caper in
gamela, *gămĕ'lă*, sf. hamper, dosser.
gamella, *gămĕl'yă*, sf. yoke for oxen and
  mules; large wooden trough.
gamo, *gă'mŏ*, sm. buck of the fallow deer.
gana, *gă'nă*, sf. appetite; healthy disposition; desire, mind, list; de buena —,

9*

with pleasure, voluntarily; **de mala –**, unwillingly, with reluctance.

ganadería, *gănădĕr'ă*, sf. breeding or feeding of cattle. 　　　[in cattle.

ganadero, *-dā'rŏ*, sm. cattle-owner; dealer

ganado, *gănă'dŏ*, sm. cattle; **– mayor,** black-cattle, mules; **– menor,** sheep, asses; **– merino,** merino sheep; **– de cerda,** swine. 　　　　　[lucre.

ganancia, *gănăn'thiă*, sf. gain, profit,

ganancial, *-thiăl'*, a. lucrative.

gananoioso, sa, *-thiŏ'sŏ*, a. gainful.

ganapán, *gănăpăn'*, sm. porter, carrier.

ganar, *gănăr'*, v. a. to gain, to win.

gancho, *găn'tshŏ*, sm. hook; crook.

ganga, *găn'gă*, sf. little pin-tailed grouse; gangue, bed of minerals; any valuable thing or profit acquired with little trouble or ado.

gangoso, sa, *găngŏ'sŏ*, a. snuffling.

gangrena, *găngrā'nă*, sf. gangrene.

gangrenarse, *-nār'sĕ*, v. r. to become gangrenous.

gangrenoso, sa, *-nŏ'sŏ*, a. gangrenous.

ganguear, *găngĕăr'*, v. n. to snuffle, to speak through the nose.

gangueo, *găngă'ŏ*, sm. snuffling.

gansarón, *gănsărŏn'*, sm. gosling; tall, thin man. 　　　[tall slender person.

ganso, sa, *găn'sŏ*, sm. & f. gander; goose.

gañote, *gănyŏ'tĕ*, sm. wind-pipe; kind of fritters.

garabatear, *gărăbătĕăr'*, v. a. to catch with a hook; to scrawl, to scribble.

garabato, *-bă'tŏ*, sm. pot-hook; attractive deportment; **–s,** pl. scrawling letters or characters; improper gestures or movements of the hands and fingers.

garante, *gărăn'tĕ*, sm. guarantee.

garantía, *-tĕ'ă*, sf. warranty, guaranty.

garantir, *-tĕr'*, v. a. to guarantee.

garañón, *gărănyŏn'*, sm. jack-ass.

garapiña, *gărăpĕn'yă*, sf. ice, ice-cream; the congealed particles of any liquid; kind of black lace.

garapiñar, *-pĭnyăr'*, v. a. to ice.

garapiñera, *-pĭnyĕ'ră*, sf. ice-safe.

garbanzal, *gărbănthăl'*, sm. piece of ground sown with chick-peas.

garbanzo, *-băn'thŏ*, sm. chick-pea.

garbanzuelo, *-thŭā'lŏ*, sm. spavin (foot-disease in horses).

garbear, *gărbĕăr'*, v. n. to affect elegance or fineness. 　　　　[sieve).

garbillo, *-bĭl'yŏ*, sm. riddle (coarse

garbo, *găr'bŏ*, sm. gracefulness, elegance of manner; generosity; cleverness.

garboso, sa, *-bŏ'sŏ*, a. genteel, graceful; liberal, generous. 　　　　[marten.

garduña, *gărdŭn'yă*, sf. pole-cat, house-

garfiña, *gărfĭn'yă*, sf. (cant) stealth.

garfiñar, *-yăr'*, v. a. to steal. 　　[spit.

gargajear, *gărgăhĕăr'*, v. n. to spawl, to

gargajo, *gărgă'hŏ*, sm. phlegm, spittle.

garganta, *gărgăn'tă*, sf. throat, gullet; instep; mountain-flood, torrent; narrow pass between mountains or rivers.

gargantilla, *-tĭl'yă*, sf. women's necklace.

gárgara, *găr'gără*, sf. noise made by gargling. 　　　　　[gargle.

gargarismo, *-rĭs'mŏ*, sm. gargling.

gargarizar, *-rĭthăr'*, v. a. to gargle.

garguero, *gărgŭā'rŏ*, sm. gullet; wind-pipe. 　　　　[line-keeper's lodge.

garita, *gărĕ'tă*, sf. (mil.) sentry-box; (rail.)

garitero, *-tā'rŏ*, sm. master of a gaming-house; gamester.

garlito, *gărlĕ'tŏ*, sm. weel; snare.

garnacha, *gărnătsh'ă*, sf. counsellor's robe.

garra, *găr'ră*, sf. claw, talon, paw; clutch, hand (in contempt).

garrafa, *gărră'fă*, sf. decanter.

garrafal, *-făl'*, a. great, vast, huge.

garrapata, *-pă'tă*, sf. tick (insect); bum-bailiff. 　　　　[to scrawl.

garrapatear, *-pătĕăr'*, v. n. to scribble,

garrapato, *-pă'tŏ*, sm. clothes-moth; **–s,** pl. pot-hooks. 　　　[herd's prick.

garrocha, *gărrŏtsh'ă*, sf. drover's or neat-

garrotazo, *gărrŏtă'thŏ*, sm. blow with a cudgel.

garrote, *gărrŏ'tĕ*, sm. cudgel; capital punishment in Spain, performed by strangling with an iron collar.

garrotillo, *-tĭl'yŏ*, sm. quinsy.

garrucha, *gărrŭtsh'ă*, sf. pulley.

gárrulo, la, *găr'rŭlŏ*, a. chirping; chattering, prattling.

garulla, *gărŭl'yă*, sf. ripe grapes which remain in the basket; (fig.) rabble.

garza, *găr'thă*, sf. heron (bird).

garzo, *găr'thŏ*, sm. agaric; **–, za,** a. blue-eyed. 　　　[age; crest of a helmet.

garzota, *gărthŏ'tă*, sf. night-heron; plum-

gas, *găs*, sm. gas.

gasa, *gă'să*, sf. gauze.

gasconada, *găskŏnă'dă*, sf. gasconade.

gasómetro, *găsŏ'mĕtrŏ*, sm. gasometer.

gastador, *găstădŏr'*, sm. spendthrift, prodigal; corrupter; (mil.) pioneer.

gastar, *găstăr'*, v. a. to expend; to waste; to plunder; to digest; **–se,** to become rotten.

gasto, *găs'tŏ*, sm. expense, cost. 　[rotten.

gastronomía, *găstrŏnŏmĕ'ă*, sf. gastronomy. 　　　　　[fours.

gata, *gă'tă*, sf. she-cat; **á –s,** on all

gatada, *gătă'dă*, sf. clawing; robbery effected in an artful manner; artful action.

gatear, *gătĕăr'*, v. n. to climb up; **–,** v. a. to scratch or claw; to steal.

gatera, *gătă'ră*, sf. cat's hole.

gatesco, ca, *gătĕs'kŏ*, a. feline, catlike.

gatillazo, *gătĭlyă'thŏ*, sm. click of the trigger in firing. 　　　　[of a gun.

gatillo, *gătĭl'yŏ*, sm. tooth-pincer; trigger

gato, *gă'tŏ*, sm. cat; hand-screw; **– de algalia,** civet-cat.

gatuno, na, *gătŭ'nŏ*, a. catlike, feline.

gaudeamus, *găudĕă'mŭs*, sm. feast, entertainment, merry-making. 　　[locker.

gaveta, *găvĕ'tă*, sf. drawer of a desk,

gavia, *gă'vĭă*, sf. (mar.) top, crow's nest; pit into which a tree is transplanted with its roots; cell for mad persons; —s, pl. top-sails of the main and fore-mast. [(ave).

gavilán, *gavilán'*, sm. sparrow-hawk

gavilla, *gavíl'yä*, sf. sheaf of corn; gang of suspicious persons.

gavota, *gävõ'tä*, sf. gavotte (French dance).

gazapera, *gäthäpä'rä*, sf. warren.

gazapo, *gäthä'põ*, sm. young rabbit; artful knave; great lie.

gazmoñada, *gäthmönyä'dä*, **gazmoñería,** —*nyëré'ä*, sf. prudery, hypocrisy.

gazmoñero, ra, —*mönyä'rõ*, **gazmoño, na,** —*mön'yõ*, a, hypocritical. [throttle.

gaznatada, —*nätä'dä*, sf. blow on the

gaznate, —*nä'tě*, sm. throttle, wind-pipe.

gazpacho, —*pätsh'õ*, sm. a Spanish refreshing dish for labourers.

gazuza, *gäthö'thä*, sf. keenness of stomach.

gemelo, la, *hemä'lõ*, sm. & f. twin.

gemido, *hemï'dõ*, sm. groan, moan, howl.

Géminis, *hé'minis*, sm. Gemini, Twins (sign of the zodiac).

gemir, *hemïr'*, v. n. to groan, to moan.

genciana, *hẽnthïä'nä*, sf. (bot.) gentian.

gendarma, *hẽndär'mä*, sm. gendarme.

gendarmería, —*mẽrë'ä*, sf. gendarmery.

genealogía, *hẽnëälõ'hé'ä*, sf. genealogy.

genealógico, ca, —*lõ'hïkõ*, a, genealogical. [progeny, race.

generación, *hẽnẽräthïõn'*, sf. generation;

general, *hẽnẽräl'*, sm. general; —, a. general; en —, gencrally, in general.

generala, —*rä'lä*, sf. (mil.) general (a beat of the drum).

generalato, —*rälä'tõ*, sm. generalship.

generalidad, —*rälidäd'*, sf. generality.

generalísimo, —*räti'simõ*, sm. generalissimo.

generalizar, —*räithär'*, v. a. to generalize.

genérico, ca, —*hẽnë'rïkõ*, a. generic.

género, *hẽn'ẽrõ*, sm. genus; sex, gender; —s, pl. goods, commodities.

generosidad, —*räsïdäd'*, sf. generosity.

generoso, sa, —*rõ'sõ*, a. noble, generous.

Génesis, *hé'nẽsis*, sf. Genesis, first book of the Pentateuch.

genial, *hẽnïäl'*, a. genial.

genio, *hä'nïõ*, sm. genius. [tals.

genital, *hẽnïtäl'*, a. genital; —es, pl. genitals.

genitivo, —*tï'võ*, sm. (gr.) genitive case.

genízaro, ra, *hẽnë'thärõ*, a. begotten by parents of different nations; composed of different species; —, sm. janizary.

gente, *hẽn'tě*, sf. people; nation; family; army, troops.

gentecilla, —*thïl'yä*, sf. mob, rabble.

gentil, *hẽntïl'*, sm. pagan, heathen; —, a. genteel, elegant, excellent.

gentileza, —*lë'thä*, sf. genteelness, elegance of behaviour; politeness.

gentilhombre, —*õm'brě*, sm. gentleman.

gentílico, ca, *hẽntï'ïkõ*, a, pagan, heathenish.

gentilidad, *hẽntïlïdäd'*, sf. **gentilismo,** *hẽntïlïs'mõ*, sm. heathenism.

gentío, *hẽntï'õ*, sm. crowd, multitude.

gentualla, —*tüär'yä*, sf. rabble, mob.

genuflexión, *hẽnüflẽksïõn'*, sf. genuflection.

genuino, na, *hẽnüï'nõ*, a. genuine, pure.

geografía, *hẽõgräfé'ä*, sf. geography.

geográfico, ca, —*grä'fïkõ*, a. geographical

geógrafo, *hẽõ'gräfõ*, sm. geographer.

geología, *hẽõlõ'hé'ä*, sf. geology.

geómetra, *hẽõ'mẽträ*, sm. geometrician.

geometría, *hẽõmẽtré'ä*, sf. geometry.

geométrico, ca, —*mä'trïkõ*, a. geometrical, geometric.

geranio, *hẽrä'nïõ*, sm. (bot.) crane's bill.

germen, *hẽr'mẽn*, sm. germ, bud; source, original cause. [to bud.

germinar, *hẽrmïnär'*, v. n. to germinate,

gerundio, *hẽrün'dïõ*, sm. (gr.) gerund.

gesolreut, *hẽsõlrẽüt'*, sm. (mus.) the first sign or clef to music.

gesticular, *hẽstïkülär'*, v. a. to gesticulate.

gesto, *hẽs'tõ*, sm. face, visage; grimace; aspect, appearance; resemblance.

giganta, *hïgän'tä*, sf. giantess.

gigante, —*tě*, sm. giant; —, a. gigantic.

gigantesco, ca, —*tẽs'kõ*, a. gigantic, giant.

gigantilla, —*tïl'yä*, sf. figure made of paste or pasteboard, with a very large head. [corpulence.

gijas, *hé'häs*, sf. pl. strength; vigour;

gimnasio, *hïmnä'sïõ*, sm. gymnasium; school, academy.

gimnástica, —*näs'tïkä*, sf. gymnastics.

gimnástico, ca, —*näs'tïkõ*, a. gymnastic.

ginebra, *hïnä'brä*, sf. rattle; gin, Geneva.

gineta, *hïnä'tä*, sf. genet (kind of weasel).

girafa, *hïrä'fä*, sf. camelooard.

giralda, *hïräl'dä*, sf. weathercock in the form of a statue.

girándula, *hïrän'dülä*, sf. girandole.

girar, *hïrär'*, v. n. to turn round; to remit by bills of exchange from one place to another. [other.

girasol, *hïräsõl'*, sm. sun-flower.

giro, *hé'rõ*, sm. turning round; circulation of bills of exchange. [rag.

girón, *hïrõn'*, sm. facing of a garment;

gitanada, *hïtänä'dä*, sf. wheedling (like gipsies). [wheedle.

gitanear, *hïtänẽär'*, v. a. to flatter, to

gitanería, —*rë'ä*, sf. wheedling, flattery.

gitanesco, ca, —*nẽs'kõ*, a. gipsy-like.

gitano, na, *hïtä'nõ*, sm. & f. gipsy; sly fellow; person of a genteel, pleasing address. [dress.

glacial, *gläthïäl'*, a. icy.

glacis, *glä'this*, sm. sloping bank, glacis.

gladiator, *glädïätõr'*, sm. gladiator, prizefighter. [fighter.

glándula, *glän'dülä*, sf. gland.

glanduloso, sa, —*lõ'sõ*, a. glandulous.

globo, *glõ'bõ*, sm. globe; sphere; orb; en —, by the lump; — aerostático, air-balloon.

globoso, sa, *glõbõ'sõ*, a. globular.

glóbulo, *glõ'bülõ*, sm. globule. [taffety.

gloria, *glõ'rïä*, sf. glory; sort of light thin

gloriarse, *glõrïär'sě*, v. r. to glory, to pride in; to take delight in.

glorieta, *glõrïä'tä*, sf. bower, arbour.

glorificación, —*fïkäthïõn'*, sf. glorification; praise.

glorificador, –dŏr′, sm. glorifier.
glorificar, –kär′, v. a. to glorify; –se, to boast.
glorioso, sa, glŏrĕ′sŏ, a. glorious.
glosa, glŏs′ä, sf. gloss. [glosser.
glosador, glŏsädŏr′, sm. commentator,
glosar, glŏsär′, v. a. to gloss.
glotón, ona, glŏtŏn′, sm. & f. glutton.
glotonería, glŏtŏnĕrĕ′ä, sf. gluttony.
glutinoso, sa, glŭtĭnŏ′sŏ, a. glutinous, viscous. [ment.
gobernación, gŏbĕrnäthĭŏn′, sf. govern-
gobernador, –dŏr′, sm. governor.
gobernalle, –när′yĕ, sm. rudder, helm.
gobernar, –när′, v. a. to govern; to re-gulate; to direct.
gobierno, gŏbĭĕr′nŏ, sm. government.
goce, gŏ′thĕ, sm. enjoyment, fruition; pos-
goleta, gŏlĕ′tä, sf. schooner. [session.
golfo, gŏl′fŏ, sm. gulf, bay.
golilla, gŏlĭl′yä, sf. Spanish collar; magis-trate who wears the golilla.
golondrina, gŏlŏndrĕ′nä, sf. swallow.
golosina, gŏlŏsĕ′nä, sf. dainty, titbit; cu-pidity, desire. [tonous.
goloso, sa, gŏlŏ′sŏ, a. lickerish; glut-
golpe, gŏl′pĕ, sm. blow, stroke, hit; knock; unfortunate accident; de –, all at once.
golpear, gŏlpĕär′, v. a. to beat, to knock; to give blows; to bruise.
goma, gŏ′mä, sf. gum. [viscosity.
gomosidad, gŏmŏsĭdäd′, sf. gumminess,
gomoso, sa, gŏmŏ′sŏ, a. gummy, viscous.
góndola, gŏn′dŏlä, sf. gondola.
gondolero, gŏndŏlĕ′rŏ, sm. gondolier.
gordiflón, ona, gŏrdĭflŏn′, sm. & f. very corpulent person. [big-bellied.
gordo, da, gŏr′dŏ, a. fat, corpulent, plump,
gordura, gŏrdŏˈrä, sf. grease; fatness, cor-pulence, obesity.
gorgojo, gŏrgŏˈhˈŏ, sm. grub, weevil.
gorgojoso, sa, gŏrgŏˈhŏˈsŏ, a. full of grubs or weevils.
gorgorita, –rĕ′tä, sf. bubble formed on water by the fall of rain.
gorgoritear, –rĭtĕär′, v. n. to warble, to quiver the voice. [voice.
gorgoritos, –rĭˈtŏs, sm. pl. quivers of the
gorigori, gŏrĭgŏˈrĭ, sm. song with which children mimic the clerk's chant at funerals.
gorjear, gŏrˈhĕär′, v. n. to warble; (mus.) to trill, to quaver, to shake. [chirping.
gorjeo, gŏrˈhĕˈŏ, sm. trilling; quaver;
gorra, gŏrˈrä, sf. cap, bonnet.
gorrión, gŏrrĭŏn′, sm. sparrow.
gorrista, gŏrrĭsˈtä, sm. parasite, sponger.
gorro, gŏrˈrŏ, sm. round cap.
gota, gŏ′tä, sf. drop; – coral ó caduca, falling-sickness; – serena, amaurosis.
gotear, gŏtĕär′, v. a. to fall drop by drop.
gotera, gŏtĕˈrä, sf. gutter; fringe of bed-hangings.
gótico, ca, gŏ′tĭkŏ, a. Gothic.
gotoso, sa, gŏtŏ′sŏ, a. gouty.
gozar, gŏthär′, v. a. to enjoy, to have pos-session or fruition of; –se, to rejoice.

gozne, gŏthˈnĕ, sm. hinge.
gozo, gŏ′thŏ, sm. joy, pleasure.
gozoso, sa, gŏthŏ′sŏ, a. joyful, cheerful, content, glad, merry, pleased.
grabado, gräbä′dŏ, sm. engraving.
grabador, –dŏr′, sm. engraver.
grabar, gräbär′, v. a. to engrave; – al agua fuerte, to etch.
gracejo, gräthĕˈhˈŏ, sm. joke, jest, mirth; graceful deliverance.
gracia, grä′thĭä, sf. grace; favour; affabi-lity; benevolence; pardon.
graciosidad, –thĭŏsĭdäd′, sf. graceful-ness, beauty, perfection.
gracioso, sa, –thĭŏ′sŏ, a. graceful, beauti-ful; funny, pleasing; benevolent; gra-tuitous; –, sm. merry-Andrew, buffoon.
grada, grä′dä, sf. step of a staircase; har-row; gradual; –s, pl. (law) bar; seats of an amphitheatre. [steps.
gradería, grädĕrĕ′ä, sf. series of seats or
gradilla, grädĭl′yä, sf. tile-mould.
grado, grä′dŏ, sm. step; degree; will, pleasure. [(mil.) rank.
graduación, grädäthĭŏn′, sf. graduation.
gradual, grädäl′, a. gradual; –, sm. a verse read between the epistle and gospel at the celebration of mass.
graduando, grädäˈdŏ, sm. graduate, candidate for academical degrees.
graduar, grädär′, v. a. to graduate.
graja, grä′hˈä, sf. jay (bird).
grajo, grä′hˈŏ, sm. jack-daw (bird).
grama, grä′mä, sf. dog's grass.
gramática, grämä′tĭkä, sf. grammar.
gramatical, –tĭkäl′, a. grammatical.
gramático, grämä′tĭkŏ, sm. grammarian.
gran, grän′ a. for grande, great.
grana, grä′nä, sf. grain; cochineal; scarlet grain; fine scarlet cloth. [granate.
granada, gränä′dä, sf.(mil.)grenade; pome-
granadero, –dĕˈrŏ, sm. (mil.) grenadier.
granadilla, –dĭl′yä, sf. passion-flower.
granado, da, gränä′dŏ, a. large, remark-able; illustrious; –, sm. pomegranate tree.
granar, gränär′, v. a. to run to seed.
granate, gränä′tĕ, sm. garnet (precious stone).
granazón, –thŏn′, sf. seeding. [stone).
grande, grän′dĕ, a. great; –, sm. grandee (Spanish nobleman).
grandeza, grändĕ′thä, sf. greatness; gran-deur; grandeeship; body of grandees.
grandiosidad, grändĭŏsĭdäd′, sf. great-ness, grandeur; magnificence. [ficent.
grandioso, sa, –dĭŏ′sŏ, a. grand, magni-
grandor, grändŏr′, sm. size, bigness, ex-tent, magnitude.
granear, gränĕär′, v. a. to sow grain in the earth; to engrave; to grain leather.
granero, gränĕ′rŏ, sm. granary.
granito, gränĕ′tŏ, sm. granite.
granizada, gränĭthä′dä, sf. copious fall of hail; multitude of things which fall in abundance.
granizar, –thär′, v. n. to hail. [eyes.
granizo, gränĕ′thŏ, sm. hail; web in the

granja, grăn'h'ă, sf. farm; summer resort.

grano, grā'nŏ, sm. grain.

granoso, sa, –nŏ'sŏ, a. grainy; granulary.

grasa, grās'ă, sf. suet, fat; grease.

grasiento, ta, grăsiĕn'tŏ, a. greasy; rusty, filthy. [gum sandarach.

grasilla, grăsĕl'yă, sf. powder made of

gratificación, grătĭfĭkăthĭŏn', sf. gratification, recompense.

gratificar, grătĭfĭkăr', v. a. to gratify, to reward, to recompense.

gratis, grā'tĭs, a. gratis, for nothing.

gratitud, grătĭtŭd', sf. gratitude, gratefulness. [fulness.

grato, ta, grā'tŏ, a. grateful;

gratuito, ta, grătŭĭ'tŏ, a. gratuitous.

gravamen, grăvā'mĕn, sm. charge, obligation; nuisance. [press, to molest.

gravar, grăvăr', v. a. to burden, to oppress;

grave, grā'vĕ, a. weighty, heavy; grave, important; haughty; troublesome, grievous. [vanity, pride.

gravedad, –dăd', sf. gravity; graveness.

gravemente, –mĕn'tĕ, ad. gravely, seriously. [tion.

gravitación, grăvĭtăthĭŏn', sf. gravitation;

gravitar, grăvĭtăr', v. n. to gravitate; to weigh down. [able.

gravoso, sa, grăvŏ'sŏ, a. onerous, unbearable.

graznar, grăthnăr', v. n. to croak; to cackle; to gaggle.

graznido, –nĭ'dŏ, sm. croak, cackle.

greda, grē'dă, sf. chalk, marl.

greguería, grĕgĕrĭ'ă, sf. outcry, confused clamour. [pany, guild, corporation.

gremio, grē'mĭŏ, sm. lap; society; com-

greña, grēn'yă, sf. entangled, clotted hair.

greñudo, da, grĕn'yŭ'dŏ, a. dishevelled.

gresca, grĕs'kă, sf. clatter, tumult, outcry, confusion; wrangle, quarrel.

grey, grā'ĭ, sf. flock (of sheep and goats); congregation of the faithful. [fire.

griego, ga, grĭē'gŏ, a. fuego –, grecian fire.

grieta, grĭē'tă, sf. crevice, crack, chink.

grifo, grī'fŏ, sm. griffin.

grifón, grĭfŏn', sm. cock for water.

grilletes, grĭlyĕt'ĕs, sm. pl. shackles, fetters. [irons.

grillo, grĭl'yŏ, sm. cricket; –s, pl. fetters,

grima, grī'mă, sf. fright, horror.

gris, grĭs, sm. grizzle, gray; meniver (russian squirrel); cold sharp air or weather. [bawler.

gritador, ra, grĭtădŏr', sm. & f. clamourer,

gritar, grĭtăr', v. n. to cry out, to clamour, to bawl. [confused cry of many voices.

gritería, grĭtĕrĭ'ă, sf. outcry, clamour.

grito, grē'tŏ, sm. cry, scream; á – herido, with a clamorous cry. [currant.

grosella, grŏsĕl'yă, sf. fruit of the red

grosellero, grŏsĕlyĕr'ŏ, sm. currant-bush.

grosería, grŏsĕrĭ'ă, sf. coarseness, illbreeding. [polished.

grosero, ra, grŏsĕr'ŏ, a. coarse, rude, un-

grosura, grŏsŭ'ră, sf. suet, tallow.

grotesco, ca, grŏtĕs'kŏ, a. grotesque.

grúa, grū'ă, sf. crane (machine).

gruesa, grŭĕ'sŏ, sf. gross (twelve dozen); chief part of a prebend.

grueso, sa, –sŏ, a. bulky, gross; large; coarse; –, sm. corpulence.

grulla, grŭl'yă, sf. crane (bird).

grumo, grŏ'mŏ, sm. clod; curd; cluster, bunch; pith of trees.

grumoso, sa, grŭmŏ'sŏ, a. clotted.

gruñido, grŭnyĭ'dŏ, sm. grunt, grunting; growl. [mumbler.

gruñidor, ra, –dŏr', sm. & f. grunter,

gruñir, grŭnyĭr', v. n. to grunt; to creak (of hinges, &c.).

grupa, grŭ'pă, sf. crupper, buttock.

grupera, grŭpĕr'ă, sf. crupper.

grupo, grŭ'pŏ, sm. group.

gruta, grŭ'tă, sf. grotto, grot.

grutesco, grŭtĕs'kŏ, sm. grotesque.

guadaña, gŭădăn'yă, sf. scythe.

guadañero, –yĕr'ŏ, sm. mower. [art.

gualderas, gŭăldĕr'ăs, sf. pl. sides; cheeks or brackets of a gun-carriage.

gualdrapa, gŭăldră'pă, sf. horse-cloth; tatter, rag.

guantada, gŭăntă'dă, sf. slap given with the palm of the hand. [boire.

guante, gŭăn'tĕ, sm. glove; –s, pl. pour-

guantería, –rĭ'ă, sf. glover's shop; glover's

guantero, gŭăntĕr'ŏ, sm. glover. [art.

guapear, gŭăpĕăr', v. n. to boast of one's courage; to take a pride in fine dress.

guapeza, gŭăpĕ'thă, sf. courage; ostentation in dress.

guapo, pa, gŭă'pŏ, a. stout, courageous; valiant, bold; spruce, neat; ostentatious; gay, sprightly.

guarda, gŭăr'dă, sm. & f. guard, keeper; –, sf. custody, wardship, keeping.

guardaaguja, –ăgū'h'ă, sm. (rail.) switchman, pointsman. [keeper.

guardaalmacén, –ălmăthĕn', sm. storeguardabarreras, –bărrĕr'ăs, sm. (rail.) line-keeper. [forest.

guardabosque, –bŏs'kĕ, sm. keeper of a

guardacantón, –kăntŏn', sf. corner-stone.

guardacostas, –kŏs'tăs, sm. guard-ship, cruiser.

guardafuegos, –fŭĕ'gŏs, sm. fender.

guardamonte, –mŏn'tĕ, sm. guard of a gunlock, sword, &c. [petticoat.

guardapiés, –pĭĕs', sm. women's black

guardapolvo, –pŏl'vŏ, sm. any cloth or leather article worn on account of the dust; dust-cont; piece of leather attached to the instep of spatterdashes.

guardar, gŭărdăr', v. a. to keep, to preserve; to guard; –se, to be upon one's guard, to avoid, to abstain from.

guardarropa, gŭărdărŏ'pă, sf. wardrobe; –, sm. keeper of a wardrobe.

guardasellos, –sĕl'yŏs, sm. Keeper of the Seal; – del rey, Lord Privy-Seal.

guardavía, –vĭ'ă, sm. (rail.) line-keeper.

guardia, gŭăr'dĭă, sf. guard; (mar.) watch; –, sm. guardsman (soldier).

guardián, ana, gŭărdĭăn', sm. & f. keeper; guardian. [ship.

guardianía, gŭărdĭănĭ'ă, sf. guardian-

guardilla, gŭărdĭl'yă, sf. garret; skylight.

guarecer, *gŭărĕthĕr'*, v. a. to aid, to succour; to guard; to cure; **-se**, to take refuge.

guarida, *gŭărĕdă*, sf. den, couch of a wild beast; shelter; lurking-place.

guarismo, *gŭăris̄mō*, sm. cipher.

guarnecer, *gŭărnĕthĕr'*, v. a. to garnish; to set (in gold, &c.); to adorn.

guarnición, *gŭărnĭthĭŏn'*, sf. flounce, furbelow; gold setting; sword-guard; garniture; (mil.) garrison.   [maker.

guarnicionero, *—nă'rō*, sm. harness-maker.

guasón, *gŭăṣŏn'*, sm. joker, jester.

guedeja, *gĕdĕ'kʹă*, sf. ear-lock; lion's mane.

guerra, *gĕ'ră*, sf. war; hostility.

guerreador, ra, *gĕrrĕădŏr'*, a. warlike.

guerrear, *gĕrrĕăr'*, v. a. to war, to wage war.   [martial, warlike.

guerrero, *gĕrrĕ'rō*, sm. warrior; —, ra, a.

guerrilla, *—rĭl'yă*, sf. war of partisans; body of skirmishers or light horsemen.

guía, *gĕ'ă*, sm. & f. guide.

guiar, *gĕăr'*, v. a. to guide.

guija, *gĕ'kʹă*, sf. pebble, pebble-stone.

guijarral, *gĭ'hărrăl'*, sm. place abounding in pebbles.   [pebble.

guijarrazo, *—ră'thō*, sm. blow with a

guijarro, *gĭ'hăr'rō*, sm. pebble.

guijarroso, sa, *—·ō'ṣō*, a. pebbly.

guillotina, *gĭlyŏtĕ'nă*, sf. guillotine.

guillotinar, *gĭlyŏtĕnăr'*, v. a. to guillotine.

guinda, *gĭn'dă*, sf. cherry.

guindal, *gĭndăl'*, sm. cherry-tree.

guindilla, *gĭndĭl'yă*, sf. capsicum; nick-name of the Spanish police established in 1843.

guinea, *gĭnĕ'ă*, sf. guinea (gold coin).

guiñada, *gĭnyĕ'dă*, sf. wink, hint.

guiñapo, *—yă'pō*, sm. tatter, rag.

guiñar, *—yăr'*, v. a. to wink, to hint.

guión, *gĭŏn'*, sm. royal standard; hyphen (in writing).   [language.

guirigay, *gĭrĭgăʹĭ*, sm. gibberish, confused tale.

guirindola, *gĭrĭndŏ'lă*, sf. frill.

guirnalda, *gĭrnăl'dă*, sf. garland, wreath.

guisado, *gĭsă'dō*, sm. ragout, fricassee.

guisandero, ra, *gĭsăndĕ'rō*, sm. & f. cook.

guisante, *gĭsăn'tĕ*, sm. (bot.) pea.

guisar, *gĭsăr'*, v. a. to dress victuals.

guiso, *gĕ'ṣō*, sm. seasoning of a dish; condiment.   [country-fashion.

guisote, *gĭṣŏ'tĕ*, sm. dish of meat dressed

guitarra, *gĭtăr'ră*, sf. guitar.

guitarrero, *—ră'rō*, sm. guitar-maker; guitar-player.

guitarrista, *—rĭs'tă*, sm. guitar-player.

gula, *gŏ'lă*, sf. gluttony.

gusano, *gŭsă'nŏ*, sm. maggot, worm.

gusarapo, *gŭsără'pō*, sm. water-worm.

gustar, *gŭstăr'*, v. a. to taste, to gust; to like, to love; to experience, to examine; to take pleasure or delight in a thing.

gusto, *gŭs'tō*, sm. taste; gust, pleasure, delight; liking, mind; election, choice.

gustosamente, *gŭstŏsămĕn'tĕ*, ad. tastefully; very desirously.

gustoso, sa, *gŭstŏ'ṣō*, a. gustable, dainty, lickerish; tasty.

gutagamba, *gŭtăgăm'bă*, sf. gamboge

gutural, *gŭtŭrăl'*, a. guttural.

H.

¡ha! *ă*, **¡ha!** ah! alas!

haba, *ă'bă*, sf. (bot.) bean.

haber, *ăbĕr'*, v. a. to have; to possess; —, v. imp. to happen; to exist; to fall out; to befall; **-se**, to behave; —, sm. property, goods and chattels; (com.) credit.

habichuela, *ăbĭtshŭĕ'lă*, sf. kidney-bean.

hábil, *ă'bĭl*, a. able, clever, skilful, dexterous, apt.

habilidad, *ăbĭlĭdăd'*, sf. ability, ableness, dexterity, aptitude.   [qualification.

habilitación, *—tăthĭŏn'*, sf. habilitation,

habilitado, *—tă'dō*, sm. officer who is charged in every Spanish regiment with the agency of his regiment.   [enable.

habilitar, *ăbĭlĭtăr'*, v. a. to qualify, to

habitable, *ăbĭtă'blĕ*, a. habitable, lodgeable.

habitación, *—thĭŏn'*, sf. habitation, abode, lodging, dwelling, residence.   [dweller.

habitante, *ăbĭtăn'tĕ*, sm. inhabitant,

habitar, *ăbĭtăr'*, v. a. to inhabit, to reside.

hábito, *ă'bĭtō*, sm. dress, habit; habitude, customariness, custom.

habitual, *ăbĭtŭăl'*, a. habitual, customary.

habituar, *ăbĭtŭăr'*, v. a. to accustom; **-se**, to accustom oneself.

habitud, *ăbĭtŭd'*, sf. habitude.

habla, *ă'blă*, sf. speech; language; discourse; talk, conversation.

hablador, ra, *ăblădŏr'*, sm. & f. prattler.

habladuría, *—dŭrĕ'ă*, sf. impertinent speech.

hablar, *ăblăr'*, v. a. to speak; to talk; to reason, to converse; to harangue.

habilla, *ăblĭ'yă*, sf. rumour, report; little tale.   [ticable.

hacedero, ra, *ăthĕdĕ'rō*, a. feasible, prac-

hacedor, ra, *—dŏr'*, sm. & f. maker, author; factor; able performer.

hacendado, *ăthĕndă'dō*, sm. man of property; —, da, a. landed.

hacer, *ăthĕr'*, v. a. & n. to make, to do, to practise; to perform; to effect; to correspond; to matter; to fit, to suit; **-se**, to become.   [hitherward.

hacia, *ă'thĭă*, ad. towards; about; — acá,

hacienda, *ăthĭĕn'dă*, sf. landed property; estate, fortune, wealth; domestic work.

hacina, *ăthĕ'nă*, sf. stack, rick.   [maker.

hacinador, ra, *ăthĭnădŏr'*, sm. & f. stack-

hacinar, *ăthĭnăr'*, v. a. to stack or pile up sheaves of corn; to hoard.

hacha, *ătsh'ă*, sf. large taper; axe, hatchet; — de viento, flambeau.

hachazo, *ătshă'thō*, sm. blow with an axe.

hachero, *ătshă'rō*, sm. torch-stand; (mil.) pioneer.   [bass and pitch.

hachón, *ătshŏn'*, sm. large torch made of

hado, *ă'dō*, sm. fate, destiny.

halagar, *ălăgăr'*, v. a. to cajole, to flatter.

halago, *ălă'gŏ*, sm. cajolery, caress.

halagüeño, ña, *ălăgüĕn'yŏ*, a. attractive,

halcón, *ălkŏn'*, sm. falcon. [flattering.

halconero, *ălkŏnĕ'rŏ*, sm. falconer.

hálito, *ă'lĭtŏ*, sm. breath; gentle breeze.

hallar, *ălyăr'*, v. a. to find; to meet with;
to discover; to mean; –se, to happen to
find; to be pleased with a place; to find
himself, to be.

hallazgo, *ălyăth'gŏ*, sm. finding, discovery; reward given for finding.

hambre, *ăm'brĕ*, sf. hunger; famine; eagerness, desire, greediness.

hambrear, *ămbrĕăr'*, v. n. to be hungry.

hambriento, ta, *ămbrĭĕn'tŏ*, a. hungry;
starved; greedy, eager. [loiterer.

haragán, ana, *ărăgăn'*, sm. & f. idler,

haraganear, *ărăgănĕăr'*, v. n. to lead an
idle life, to loiter. [ness.

haraganería, *–nĕrĭ'ă*, sf. idleness, lazi-

harapo, *ără'pŏ*, sm. rag, tatter.

haraposo, *ărăpŏ'sŏ*, a. ragged.

harina, *ără'nă*, sf. flour; powder, dust.

harinero, *ărĭnĕ'rŏ*, sm. meal-man; meal-
box; –, ra, a. made of flour.

harinoso, sa, *ărĭnŏ'sŏ*, a. mealy.

harnero, *ărnĕ'rŏ*, sm. sieve. [disgust.

hartar, *ărtăr'*, v. a. to cloy, to satiate; to

harto, ta, *ăr'tŏ*, a. satiated; sufficient; –,
ad. enough. [dance.

hartura, *ărtŭ'ră*, sf. satiety; plenty, abun-

hasta, *ăs'tă*, ad. until, as far as; also, even.

hastío, *ăstĕ'ŏ*, sm. loathing; disgust.

hatajo, *ătă'hŏ*, sm. small herd of cattle;
assemblage, collection.

hato, *ă'tŏ*, sm. clothes, wearing-apparel;
herd of cattle, flock of sheep; provisions
for shepherds; heap, cluster; crowd, mul-
haya, *ă'yă*, sf. beech-tree. [titude.

haz, *ăth*, sm. fagot, bundle of brush-wood;
–, sf. right side of cloth; surface of the
ground.

hazaña, *ăthăn'yă*, sf. exploit, achievement.

hazmerreir, *ăthmĕrrĕĭr'*, sm. ridiculous
person, laughing-stock.

he, *ĕ*, ad. behold, look here.

hebilla, *ĕbĭl'yă*, sf. buckle. [buckles.

hebillaje, *ĕbĭlyă'hĕ*, sm. collection of

hebra, *ĕ'bră*, sf. needleful; vein of minerals
or metals; filament. [Hebrews.

hebraico, ca, *ĕbră'ĭkŏ*, a. belonging to the

hebraísmo, *ĕbrăĭs'mŏ*, sm. Hebraism.

hebreo, *ĕbrĕ'ŏ*, sm. Hebrew; Hebrew
language; (fig.) merchant; –, ea, a.
Hebraic, Judaical. [charm.

hechicería, *ĕtshĭthĕrĭ'ă*, sf. witchcraft;

hechicero, ra, *–thă'rŏ*, a. charming, be-
witching. [enchant; to charm.

hechizar, *–thăr'*, v. a. to bewitch; to

hechizo, *ĕtshĕ'thŏ*, sm. bewitchment, enchantment; –, za, a. done on purpose.

hecho, cha, *ĕtsh'ŏ*, a. made, done; accustomed; –, sm. action; act, feat; point
contested.

hechura, *ĕtshŭ'ră*, sf. form, shape, fashion;
making; workmanship; creature; client.

heder, *ĕdĕr'*, v. a. to stink, to smell badly.

hediondez, *ĕdĭŏndăth'*, sf. strong stench.

hediondo, da, *ĕdĭŏn'dŏ*, a. fetid, stinking.

hedor, *ĕdŏr'*, sm. stench, stink.

helada, *ĕlă'dă*, sf. frost; nip.

helado, da, *–dŏ*, a. frozen; glacial, icy;
astonished; astounded; –, sm. ice-cream.

helar, *ĕlăr'*, v. a. & n. to congeal; to freeze;
to astonish, to amaze; –se, to be frozen;
to turn into ice; to congeal.

hélice, *ĕ'lĭthĕ*, sf. helix, helical line.

Hélice, –, sf. Great Bear (constellation).

hembra, *ĕm'bră*, sf. female.

hemina, *ĕmĕ'nă*, sf. measure containing
the third part of a fanega.

hemisferio, *ĕmĭsfĕ'rĭŏ*, sm. hemisphere.

hemorragia, *ĕmŏrră'hĭă*, sf. hemorrhage.

henchir, *ĕntshĭr'*, v. a. to fill up; –se,
to fill or gorge oneself. [crevice.

hendedura, *ĕndĕdŭ'ră*, sf. fissure, chink,

hender, *ĕndĕr'*, v. a. to chink, to split; to
go through; to open a passage.

heno, *d'nŏ*, sm. hay.

heraldo, *ĕrăl'dŏ*, sm. herald.

herbaje, *ĕrbă'hĕ*, sf. herbage, pasture.

herbolario, *ĕrbŏlă'rĭŏ*, sm. herbalist;
ridiculous, extravagant man.

herborizar, *–rĭthăr'*, v. n. to botanise.

heredad, *ĕrĕdăd'*, sf. patrimony, inherited
property; fruitful ground.

heredar, *ĕrĕdăr'*, v. a. to inherit.

heredera, *ĕrĕdĕ'ră*, sf. heiress.

heredero, *ĕrĕdĕ'rŏ*, sm. heir.

hereditario, ria, *ĕrĕdĭtă'rĭŏ*, a. hereditary.

hereje, *ĕrĕ'hĕ*, sm. & f. heretic.

herejía, *ĕrĕhĕ'ă*, sf. heresy.

herencia, *ĕrĕn'thĭă*, sf. inheritance, heri-
tage, hereditament; heirship.

herida, *ĕrĕ'dă*, sf. wound, hurt.

herido, da, *ĕrĕ'dŏ*, a. wounded, hurt.

herir, *ĕrĭr'*, v. a. to wound; to hurt; to
affect, to touch, to move; to offend.

hermafrodita, *ĕrmăfrŏdĕ'tă*, sm. herma-
phrodite, androgyne.

hermana, *ĕrmă'nă*, sf. sister; – de la
caridad, sister of charity.

hermanar, *–năr'*, v. a. to match, to suit,
to acknowledge as a brother; –, v. n. to
fraternise. [half-sister.

hermanastra, *–năs'tră*, sf. step-sister,

hermanastro, *–trŏ*, sm. step-brother,
half-brother. [conformity; brotherhood.

hermandad, *ĕrmăndăd'*, sf. fraternity,

hermano, *ĕrmă'nŏ*, sm. brother; –, na, a.
matched; resembling. [chemical.

hermético, ca, *ĕrmĕ'tĭkŏ*, a. hermetical,

hermosear, *ĕrmŏsĕăr'*, v. a. to beautify,
to embellish, to adorn. [some.

hermoso, sa, *ĕrmŏ'sŏ*, a. beautiful, hand-

hermosura, *ĕrmŏsŭ'ră*, sf. beauty.

hernia, *ĕr'nĭă*, sf. hernia, rupture.

héroe, *d'rŏĕ*, sm. hero.

heroicidad, *ĕrŏĭthĭdăd'*, sf. heroism,
heroic courage or virtue.

heroico, ca, *ĕrŏ'ĭkŏ*, a. heroic.

heroína, *ĕrŏĕ'nă*, sf. heroine.

heroísmo, *ĕrŏĭs'mŏ*, sm. heroism.

herpe, *ĕr'pĕ*, sm. herpes, tetters, pl.

herrada, *ĕrră'dă*, sf. well-bucket.

herrador, *ĕrrădŏr'*, sm. farrier.

herradura, ḗrrădō̆'rā, sf. horse-shoe.

herraje, ḗrră'h'ĕ, sm. iron-work.

herramienta, —mĭĕn'tā, sf. set of tools for workmen; iron-work; (fig.) teeth, grinders.

herrar, ḗrrăr', v. a. to shoe horses.

herrería, ḗrrĕrĕ'ā, sf. iron-works; forge; clamour, confused noise.

herrero, ḗrră'rō, sm. smith. [quantity.

hervidero, ḗrvĭdă'rō, sm. ebullition; great

hervir, ḗrvĭr', v. n. to boil; to be fervent.

hervor, ḗrvŏr', sm. ebullition.

heterogeneidad, ḗtĕrō̆'hĕnĕĭdăd', sf. heterogeneousness. [neous.

heterogéneo, nea, —'hă'nĕō, a. heteroge-

hética, ă'tĭkā, sf. phthisis. hectic.

hético, ca, ă'tĭkō, a. hectic, hectical.

hexámetro, ĕksă'mĕtrō, sm. hexameter.

hez, ĕth, sf. lee, dregs; dross.

hidalgo, ga, ĭdăl'gō, sm. & f. hidalgo; hidalga (nobleman or noblewoman).

hidalguía, ĭdălgĭ'ā, sf. nobility.

hidra, ĕ'drā, sf. hydra.

hidráulica, ĭdră'ŭlĭkā, sf. hydraulics.

hidráulico, ca, —lĭkō, a. hydraulic.

hidrofobia, ĭdrŏfŏ'bĭā, sf. hydrophobia.

hidrógeno, ĭdrŏ'hĕnō, sm. (chem.) hydrogen.

hidropesía, ĭdrŏpĕsĕ'ā, sf. dropsy.

hidrópico, ca, ĭdrŏ'pĭkō, a. hydropical.

hiedra, ĭĕ'drā, sf. ivy.

hiel, ĭĕl', sf. gall, bile.

hielo, ĭĕ'lō, sm. frost, ice.

hiena, ĭĕ'nā, sf. hyæna. [fetters.

hierro, ĭĕr'rō, sm. iron; —s, pl. irons,

hígado, ĕ'gădō, sm. liver; (fig.) courage, [valour.

higo, ĕ'gō, sm. fig.

higuera, ĭgă'rā, sf. fig-tree.

hijastro, tra, ĭ'hăs'trō, sm. & f. step-child.

hijo, ja, ĭ'h'ō, sm. & f. son; daughter; child; young of animals.

hijodalgo, ĭ'hŏdăl'gō, sm. nobleman.

hijuela, ĭ'hŭă'lā, sf. patch; eking-piece; a small drain; inventory of the distributive shares of a succession; rural postman.

hila, ĕ'lā, sf. row, line; lint to lay on sores.

hilacha, ĭlătsh'ā, sf. filament or threads ravelled out of cloth. [riband.

hiladillo, —dĭl'yō, sm. ferret silk; narrow

hilado, ĭlă'dō, sm. spun flax, wool, &c.

hilador, ra, —dŏr', sm. & f. spinner, spinster. [ning-room.

hilandero, ĭlăndă'rō, sm. spinner; spin-

hilar, ĭlăr', v. a. to spin.

hilera, ĭlă'rā, sf. row, line, file.

hilo, ĕ'lō, sm. thread; wire.

hilván, ĭlvăn', sm. basting.

hilvanar, ĭlvănăr', v. a. to baste, to sew slightly; to perform in a hurry.

himeneo, ĭmĕnă'ō, sm. (poet.) marriage.

himno, ĭm'nō, sm. hymn.

hin, ĭn, sm. neighing. [one's foot.

hincapié, ĭnkăpĭĕ', sm. firm planting of

hincar, ĭnkăr', v. a. to thrust in, to drive into. [arrogant.

hinchado, da, ĭntshă'dō, a. swollen; vain,

hinchar, ĭntshăr', v. a. to swell; —se, to swell; to be elated with arrogance.

hinchazón, ĭntshăthŏn', sf. swelling, tumid inflammation; ostentation, vanity.

hinojo, ĭnŏ'h'ō, sm. knee; (bot.) fennel.

hipar, ĭpăr', v. n. to hiccough; to pant.

hipérbola, ĭpĕr'bŏlā, sf. hyperbola, section of a cone. [tion.

hipérbole, —bŏlĕ, sf. hyperbole, exaggera-

hiperbólico, ca, ĭpĕrbŏ'lĭkō, a. hyperbolical. [Virgin Mary.

hiperdulía, —dŭlĭ'ā, sf. worship of the

hipo, ĕ'pō, sm. hiccough. [dria.

hipocondría, ĭpŏkŏndrĭ'ā, sf. hypochon-

hipocóndrico, ca, —kŏn'drĭkō, a. hypochondriac.

hipocresía, —krĕsĕ'ā, sf. hypocrisy.

hipócrita, ĭpŏ'krĭtā, a. & sm. hypocritical; hypocrite. [circus.

hipódromo, —drŏmŏ, sm. hippodrome,

hipopótamo, ĭpŏpŏ'tămŏ, sm. hippopotamus. [cal.

hipostático, ca, —stă'tĭkŏ, a. hypostati-

hipoteca, —tă'kā, sf. mortgage.

hipotecar, —tĕkăr', v. a. to mortgage.

hipotecario, ria, —tĕkă'rĭŏ, a. belonging to a mortgage.

hipótesis, ĭpŏ'tĕsĭs, sf. hypothesis.

hipotético, ca, ĭpŏtĕ'tĭkŏ, a. hypothetical.

hisopear, ĭsŏpĕăr', v. a. to sprinkle water about with a water-sprinkler. [sprinkler.

hisopo, ĭsŏ'pŏ, sm. (bot.) hyssop; water-

hispano, na, ĭspă'nŏ, a. (poet.) Spanish.

histérico, ĭstă'rĭkŏ, sm. hysterics; —, ca, a. hysterical.

historia, ĭstŏ'rĭā, sf. history; tale, story.

historiador, ora, ĭstŏrĭădŏr', sm. & f. historian, historiographer.

historiar, —rĭăr', v. a. to record in history; to represent historical events in painting. [toric; —, sm. historian.

histórico, ca, ĭstŏ'rĭkŏ, a. historical, his-

historieta, ĭstŏrĭĕ'tā, sf. short story, short novel. [to shoot at; á —, fixedly.

hito, ĕ'tŏ, sm. landmark; guide-post; mark

hocicar, ŏthĭkăr', v. a. to break up the ground with the snout; —, v. n. to fall headlong with the face to the ground.

hocico, ŏthĭ'kŏ, sm. snout; flap-mouthed man; (fig.) face; meter el — en todo, to meddle in everything.

hocicudo, da, ŏthĭkŏ'dō, a. long-snouted; blubber-lipped; flap-mouthed.

hogar, ŏgăr', sm. hearth, fire-place; (fig.) house, residence, home. [bread.

hogaza, ŏgă'thā, sf. large loaf of household

hoguera, ŏgă'rā, sf. bonfire; blaze.

hoja, ŏ'h'ā, sf. leaf; blade of a sword; half of each of the principal parts of a coat, &c.; — de lata, tin.

hojalatero, ŏ'hălătă'rō, sm. tin-man.

hojaldrar, ŏ'hăldrăr', v. a. to make a pastry of puff-paste.

hojaldre, ŏ'hăl'drĕ, sf. puff-paste.

hojaldrista, —drĭs'tā, sm. pastry-cook.

hojarasca, ŏ'hărăs'kā, sf. redundancy of leaves; foliage; useless trifles. [a book.

hojear, ŏ'hăr', v. a. to turn the leaves of

hojuela, ŏ'hŭă'lā, sf. puff-paste; skins of olives after pressing.

¡hola! *ŏl'ă*, holla!

holgado, da, *ŏlgă'dŏ*, a. loose, wide, broad; at leisure; in easy circumstances.

holganza, *ŏlgăn'thă*, sf. ease, tranquillity of mind; recreation, amusement.

holgar, *ŏlgăr'*, v. n. to rest; —se, to sport, to be pleased with. [loiterer, vagabond.

holgazán, ana, *ŏlgăthăn'*, sm. & f. idler,

holgazanear, —*năr'*, v. n. to idle, to loiter, to lounge. [dolence.

holgazanería, —*nĕrĕ'ă*, sf. idleness, in-

holgura, *ŏlgŭ'ră*, sf. country-feast; width, breadth; ease, repose.

hollejo, *ŏlyĕh'ŏ*, sm. pellicle, peel.

hollín, *ŏlyĭn'*, sm. soot.

holliniento, ta, *ŏlyĭnĭĕn'tŏ*, a. sooty.

holocausto, *ŏlŏkăŭs'tŏ*, sm. holocaust.

hombre, *ŏm'brĕ*, sm. man; human being; ombre (game at cards).

hombrera, *ŏmbră'ră*, sf. piece of ancient armour for the shoulders.

hombría de bien, *ŏmbrĕ'ă dĕ bĭĕn'*, sf.

hombro, *ŏm'brŏ*, sm. shoulder. [probity.

hombruno, na, *ŏmbrŭ'nŏ*, a. manlike, virile, manly.

homenaje, *ŏmĕnă'hĕ*, sm. homage.

homicida, *ŏmĭthĕ'dă*, sm. & f. murderer;

—, a. homicidal, murderous.

homicidio, —*thĕ'dĭŏ*, sm. murder.

homilía, *ŏmĭlĕ'ă*, sf. homily. [geneity.

homogeneidad, *ŏmŏ'hĕnĕĭdăd'*, sf. homo-

homogéneo, nea, —*hĕ'nĕŏ*, a. homogeneous. [synonymous.

homólogo, ga, *ŏmŏ'lŏgŏ*, a. homologous;

honda, *ŏn'dă*, sf. sling. [sling.

hondazo, *ŏndă'thŏ*, sm. throw with a

hondero, *ŏndĕ'rŏ*, sm. slinger.

hondillo, *ŏndĭ'lyŏ*, sm. any of the pieces of cloth which form the seats of breeches.

hondo, da, *ŏn'dŏ*, a. profound, deep; dif-

hondonada, *ŏndŏnă'dă*, sf. dale. [ficult.

hondura, *ŏndŭ'ră*, sf. depth, profundity.

honestidad, *ŏnĕstĭdăd'*, sf. honesty, modesty; urbanity.

honesto, ta, *ŏnĕs'tŏ*, a. honest; modest.

hongo, *ŏn'gŏ*, sm. mushroom; fungus.

honor, *ŏnŏr'*, sm. honour.

honorable, *ŏnŏră'blĕ*, a. honourable.

honorario, ria, —*ră'rĭŏ*, a. honorary; —, sm. salary. [honourable.

honorífico, ca, —*rĕ'fĭkŏ*, a. creditable.

honra, *ŏn'ră*, sf. honour, reverence; reputation; chastity (in women); —s, pl. funeral honours.

honradez, *ŏnrădĕth'*, sf. honesty, probity.

honrado, da, *ŏnră'dŏ*, a. honest, honourable, reputable. [to caress.

honrar, *ŏnrăr'*, v. a. to honour; to cajole,

honrilla, *ŏnrĭ'lyă*, sf. nice point of honour.

honroso, sa, *ŏnrŏ'să*, a. honourable; honest.

hopalanda, *ŏpălăn'dă*, sf. fur cloak.

hora, *ŏ'ră*, sf. hour; —s, pl. canonical hours; devotional book, prayer-book.

horadar, *ŏrădăr'*, v. a. to bore from side to side.

horario, ria, *ŏră'rĭŏ*, a. horary, horal.

horca, *ŏr'kă*, sf. gallows; pitchfork.

horcajadas, *ŏrkă'hă'dăs*, horcajadillas, —*'hădĭ'yăs*, (á —), ad. astride.

horcajadura, —*hădŭ'ră*, sf. fork formed by the two thighs.

horchata, *ŏrtshă'tă*, sf. orgeat.

horizontal, *ŏrĭthŏntăl'*, a. horizontal.

horizonte, *ŏrĭthŏn'tĕ*, sm. horizon.

horma, *ŏr'mă*, sf. mould.

hormero, *ŏrmĕ'rŏ*, sm. last-maker.

hormiga, *ŏrmĕ'gă*, sf. ant, pismire.

hormigueamiento, *ŏrmĭgĕămĭĕn'tŏ*, sm. formication. [about like ants.

hormiguear, —*gĕăr'*, v. n. to itch; to run

hormiguero, —*gĕ'rŏ*, sm. ant-hill; place where there is a crowd of people moving.

hormiguillo, —*gĭ'lyŏ*, sm. scarf of the hoof; work-people ranged in line, who pass the working materials from hand to hand.

hornacho, *ŏrnătsh'ŏ*, sm. shaft of a mine.

hornada, *ŏrnă'dă*, sf. batch.

hornaza, —*nă'thă*, sf. goldsmith's furnace.

hornazo, *ŏrnă'thŏ*, sm. Easter-cake.

hornero, *ŏrnĕ'rŏ*, sm. baker.

hornilla, *ŏrnĭ'lyă*, sf. stew-hole.

horno, *ŏr'nŏ*, sm. oven; furnace.

horóscopo, *ŏrŏs'kŏpŏ*, sm. horoscope.

horquilla, *ŏrkĭ'lyă*, sf. forked stick.

horrendo, da, *ŏrrĕn'dŏ*, a. horrible; extra-

hórreo, *ŏr'rĕŏ*, sm. granary. [ordinary.

horrible, *ŏrrĕ'blĕ*, a. horrid, horrible.

horrísono, na, *ŏrrĕ'sŏnŏ*, a. (poet.) dread-ful-sounding.

horror, *ŏrrŏr'*, sm. horror, fright.

horrorizar, *ŏrrŏrĭthăr'*, v. a. to cause horror; —se, to be terrified.

horroroso, sa, —*rŏ'sŏ*, a. horrid, hideous, frightful. [pot-herb.

hortaliza, *ŏrtălĕ'thă*, sf. garden-stuff,

hortelano, *ŏrtĕlă'nŏ*, sm. gardener, horti-culturist; ortolan (bird).

hortera, *ŏrtĕ'ră*, sf. wooden bowl; —, sm. nickname of shop-boys in Madrid.

hospedador, ra, *ŏspĕdă'dŏr*, sm. & f. one who kindly receives and entertains guests and strangers, entertainer.

hospedaje, —*dă'hĕ*, sm. kind reception of guests and strangers.

hospedar, —*dăr'*, v. a. to lodge and enter-tain strangers and travellers.

hospedería, —*dĕrĕ'*, sf. a hospitium.

hospedero, —*dĕ'rŏ*, sm. one who kindly receives guests and strangers; hospitaller.

hospicio, *ŏspĕ'thĭŏ*, sm. house of charity.

hospital, *ŏspĭtăl'*, sm. hospital.

hospitalario, ria, *ŏspĭtălă'rĭŏ*, a. applied to the religious communities which keep hospitals.

hospitalero, ra, —*lă'rŏ*, sm. & f. warden of a hospital. [lity.

hospitalidad, *ŏspĭtălĭdăd'*, sf. hospital-

hostería, *ŏstĕrĕ'ă*, sf. inn, tavern, hostelry.

hostia, *ŏs'tĭă*, sf. host; wafer.

hostiario, *ŏstĭă'rĭŏ*, sm. wafer-box.

hostigar, *ŏstĭgăr'*, v. a. to trouble, to molest, to gall, to tire.

hostil, *ŏstĭl'*, a. hostile, adverse.

hostilidad, *ŏstĭlĭdád'*, sf. hostility.

hostilizar, *–thár'*, v. n. to commit hostilities.

hoy, *ŏ'ĭ*, ad. to-day, this day; **de — en adelante,** henceforth, henceforward.

hoya, *ŏ'yä*, sf. hole, pit; sepulture.

hoyo, *ŏ'yŏ*, sm. hole, pit, excavation.

hoyoso, sa, *ŏyŏ'sŏ*, a. full of holes.

hoz, *ŏth*, sf. sickle, reaping-hook.

hozar, *ŏthár'*, v. a. to grub.

hucha, *ŏtsh'ä*, sf. large chest in which labouring people keep their clothes, money, and other valuable articles; money-box.

huebra, *ŏŏ'brä*, sf. day's work; extent of ground which a yoke of oxen can plough in a day; pair of mules with a ploughman let out for a day's work. [a spindle.

hueca, ca, *ŏŏ'kä*, sf. notch at the small end of

hueco, ca, *ŏŏ'kŏ*, a. hollow, concave; empty, vain, ostentatious; —, sm. interval; gap, hole; office vacant, vacancy.

huelga, *ŏŏl'gä*, sf. rest, repose; recreation; fallow ground; strike of workmen; lockout of employers.

huella, *ŏŏl'yä*, sf. track, footstep.

huérfano, na, *ŏŏr'fänŏ*, sm. & f. & a. orphan.

huero, ra, *ŏŏ'rŏ*, a. empty, addle.

huerta, *ŏŏr'tä*, sf. orchard, kitchen-garden.

huerto, *ŏŏr'tŏ*, sm. walled garden, kitchen-garden.

huesa, *ŏŏ'sä*, sf. grave, sepulture.

hueso, *ŏŏ'sŏ*, sm. bone; stone, core.

huesoso, sa, *ŏŏsŏ'sŏ*, a. bony.

huésped, da, *ŏŏs'pĕd*, sm. & f. guest, lodger; inn-keeper; stranger.

hueste, *ŏŏs'tĕ*, sf. army in campaign.

huesudo, da, *ŏŏsŏ'dŏ*, a. bony.

huevar, *ŏŏvár'*, v. n. to lay eggs.

huevera, *ŏŏvā'rä*, sf. ovary of birds; egg-stand; egg-cup.

huevero, ra, *–rŏ*, sm. & f. dealer in eggs.

huevo, *ŏŏ'vŏ*, sm. egg; spawn.

huida, *ŏŏ'dä*, sf. flight, escape.

huir, *ŏŏr'*, v. n. to fly, to escape.

hule, *ŏ'lĕ*, sm. oil-cloth.

humanarse, *ŏŏmänär'sĕ*, v. r. to become man (applied to the Son of God); to become humane or meek.

humanidad, *ŏŏmänĭdád'*, sf. humanity; benevolence; corpulence; —es, pl. humanities, pl., human learning. [kind.

humano, na, *ŏŏmä'nŏ*, a. human; humane

humareda, *–rā'dä*, sf. great deal of smoke; confusion, perplexity.

humeante, *ŏŏmĕän'tĕ*, a. smoking, steaming (of blood, &c.).

humear, *ŏŏmĕár'*, v. n. to smoke.

humedad, *ŏŏmĕdád'*, sf. humidity, moisture, wetness. [wet, to soak.

humedecer, *–dĕthĕr'*, v. a. to moisten, to

húmedo, da, *ŏ'mĕdŏ*, a. humid, wet, moist, damp. [shaft of a chimney.

humero, *ŏŏmĕ'rŏ*, sm. tunnel, funnel.

humildad, *ŏŏmĭldád'*, sf. humility, humbleness; meanness; submission.

humilde, *ŏŏmĭl'dĕ*, a. humble.

humillación, *ŏŏmĭlyäthĭŏn'*, sf. humiliation, submission.

humilladero, *–dá'rŏ*, sm. small chapel in the roads and near the villages.

humillar, *ŏŏmĭlyár'*, v. a. to humble; to subdue; **–se,** to humble oneself.

humo, *ŏ'mŏ*, sm. smoke; fume.

humor, *ŏŏmŏr'*, sm. humor, humour.

humorada, *–rä'dä*, sf. graceful sprightliness. [well- or ill-disposed.

humorado, da, *–dŏ*, a. full of humours;

humoroso, sa, *ŏŏmŏrŏ'sŏ*, a. humorous.

humoso, sa, *ŏŏmŏ'sŏ*, a. smoky.

hundir, *ŏŏndir'*, v. n. to submerge; to sink, to overwhelm; to confound; **–se,** to sink, to go the bottom; to hide, to lie hid.

huracán, *ŏŏräkán'*, sm. hurricane.

hurgar, *ŏŏrgár'*, v. a. to stir; to excite quarrels.

hurón, *ŏŏrŏn'*, sm. ferret; ferreter.

huronear, *ŏŏrŏnĕár'*, v. a. to ferret.

huronera, *ŏŏrŏnā'rä*, sf. ferret-hole; lurking-place.

hurraca, *ŏŏrrä'kä*, sf. magpie.

hurtadillas, (á), *ŏŏrtädĭl'yäs*, ad. by stealth.

hurtar, *ŏŏrtár'*, v. a. to steal, to rob.

hurto, *ŏŏr'tŏ*, sm. theft, robbery.

husar, *ŏŏsár'*, sm. husar. [drains.

husillo, *ŏŏsĭl'yŏ*, sm. clamp-screw; **–s,** pl.

husma, *ŏŏs'mä*, ar. dar á la —, to pry into a thing, to spy out a secret. [to peep.

husmear, *ŏŏsmĕár'*, v. a. to scent; to pry,

huso, *ŏŏ'sŏ*, sm. spindle.

huta, *ŏŏ'tä*, sf. hut.

I.

ictericia, *ĭktĕrĭ'thĭä*, sf. jaundice.

ida, *ĕ'dä*, sf. departure; sally; **–s,** pl. frequent visits; **–s y venidas,** coming and going.

idea, *ĭdā'ä*, sf. idea; scheme.

ideal, *ĭdĕál'*, a. ideal.

idealmente, *–mĕn'tĕ*, ad. ideally.

idear, *ĭdĕár'*, v. a. to conceive; to think, to contrive.

ídem, *ĕ'dĕm*, pn. item, the same.

idéntico, ca, *ĭdĕn'tĭkŏ*, a. identical.

identidad, *ĭdĕntĭdád'*, sf. identity.

identificar, *–fĭkár'*, v. a. to identify.

idilio, *ĭdĭ'lĭŏ*, sm. idyl.

idioma, *ĭdĭŏ'mä*, sm. idiom. [syncrasy.

idiosincrasia, *ĭdĭŏsĭnkrä'sĭä*, sf. idio-

idiota, *ĭdĭŏ'tä*, sm. idiot. [ance.

idiotismo, *–tĭs'mŏ*, sm. idiotism; ignor-

idólatra, *ĭdŏ'läträ*, sm. idolater.

idolatrar, *ĭdŏlätrár'*, v. a. to idolize; to love with excessive fondness.

idolatría, *–trĕ'ä*, sf. idolatry.

ídolo, *ĕ'dŏlŏ*, sm. idol.

idoneidad, *ĭdŏnĕĭdád'*, sf. aptitude, fitness. [suitable.

idóneo, nea, *ĭdŏ'nĕŏ*, a. idoneous, fit,

iglesia, *ĭglā'sĭä*, sf. church.

ignominia, *ĭgnŏmĕ'nĭä*, sf. ignominy, infamy. [nious.

ignominioso, sa, *–mĭnĭŏ'sŏ*, a. ignomi-

ignorancia, ĭgnŏrăn'thĭă, sf. ignorance.

ignorante, -răn'tĕ, a. ignorant, stupid.

ignorar, -răr', v. a. to be ignorant of, not to know. [equally.

igual, ĭgŭăl' a. equal, similar; al -,

igualar, ĭgŭălăr', v. a. to equalize, to equal; to match; -, v. n. to be equal; -se, to level; to agree.

igualdad, -dăd', sf. equality.

igualmente, -mĕn'tĕ, ad. equally.

ijada, ĭ'hă'dă, sf. flank; side of pork or bacon; pork. [pitate.

ijadear, ĭ'hădĕăr', v. n. to pant, to pal-

ijar, ĭ'hăr', sm. flanks, pl.

ilación, ĭlăthŏn', sf. inference, deduction.

ilegal, ĭlĕgăl', a. illegal, unlawful.

ilegalidad, ĭlĕgălĭdăd', sf. illegality.

ilegitimar, ĭlĕ'hĭtĭmăr', v. a. to render illegitimate.

ilegitimidad, -mĭdăd', sf. illegitimacy.

ilegítimo, ma, -hĭ'ĭmŏ, a. illegal; illegitimate.

ileso, sa, ĭlĕ'sŏ, a. unhurt.

ilícito, ta, ĭlĭ'thĭtŏ, a. illicit, unlawful.

ilimitado, da, ĭlĭmĭtă'dŏ, a. unlimited.

iluminación, ĭlŭmĭnăthŏn', sf. illumination. [illuminate, to enlighten.

iluminar, -năr', v. a. to illumine, to

ilusión, ĭlŭsĭŏn', sf. illusion.

ilusivo, va, ĭlŭsĕ'vŏ, a. illusive.

iluso, sa, ĭlŭ'sŏ, a. deceived; fanatical; visionary.

ilusorio, ria, ĭlŭsŏ'rĭŏ, a. illusory.

ilustración, ĭlŭstrăthŏn', sf. illustration; explication. [spire.

ilustrar, -trăr', v. a. to illustrate; to in-

ilustre, ĭlŭs'trĕ, a. illustrious, celebrated.

imagen, ĭmă'hĕn, sf. image.

imaginable, ĭmă'hĭnă'blĕ, a. imaginable.

imaginación, -năthŏn', sf. imagination; fancy; conceit, idea.

imaginar, -'hĭnăr', v. n. to imagine.

imaginaria, -nă'rĭă, sf. (mil.) reserve guard.

imán, ĭmăn', sm. loadstone, magnet.

imbécil, ĭmbĕ'thĭl, a. weak, feeble, imbecile.

imbecilidad, -thĭlĭdăd', sf. imbecility.

imbuir, ĭmbŭĭr', v. a. to imbue; to infuse into the mind.

imitable, ĭmĭtă'blĕ, a. imitable.

imitación, -tăthŏn', sf. imitation; á -, in imitation of.

imitador, ra, -tădŏr', sm. & f. imitator.

imitar, -tăr', v. a. to imitate, to copy; to counterfeit. [tience.

impaciencia, ĭmpăthĭĕn'thĭă, sf. impa-

impacientar, -thĭĕntăr', v. a. to put one out of all patience.

impaciente, -thĭĕn'tĕ, a. impatient.

impar, ĭmpăr', a. unequal, odd; uneven.

imparcial, ĭmpărthĭăl', a. impartial.

imparcialidad, -lĭdăd', sf. impartiality.

impasibilidad, ĭmpăsĭbĭlĭdăd', sf. impassibility.

impasible, -sĭ'blĕ, a. impassible.

impavidez, ĭmpăvĭdĕth', sf. intrepidity.

impávido, da, ĭmpă'vĭdŏ, a. dauntless, intrepid. [ment, obstacle.

impedimento, ĭmpĕdĭmĕn'tŏ, sf. impedi-

impedir, -pĕdĭr', v. a. to impede, to hinder. [to stimulate.

impeler, -pĕlĕr', v. a. to impel; to incite,

impenetrable, -pĕnĕtră'blĕ, a. impenetrable, impervious; incomprehensible.

impenitencia, -pĕnĭtĕn'thĭă, sf. impenitence.

impenitente, -tĕn'tĕ, a. impenitent.

impensado, da, -pĕnsă'dŏ, a. unexpected, unforeseen. [perative.

imperativo, va, -pĕrătĭ'vŏ, a. & sm. im-

imperatorio, ria, -tŏ'rĭŏ, a. imperial.

imperceptible, -pĕrthĕptĭ'blĕ, a. imperceptible. [fection.

imperfección, -pĕrfĕkthŏn', sf. imper-

imperfecto, ta, ĭmpĕrfĕk'tŏ, a. imperfect.

imperial, ĭmpĕrĭăl', sm. roof of a coach; -, a. imperial. [rience.

impericia, -pĕrĭ'thĭă, sf. want of expe-

imperio, ĭmpĕ'rĭŏ, sm. empire.

imperioso, sa, -pĕrĭŏ'sŏ, a. imperious; arrogant, haughty. [skilled.

imperito, to, -pĕrĭ'tŏ, a. unlearned, un-

impermeable, -pĕrmĕă'blĕ, a. impermeable. [able.

impermutable, -pĕrmŭtă'blĕ, a. immut-

impersonal, -pĕrsŏnăl', a. impersonal.

impertérrito, ta, ĭmpĕrtĕr'rĭtŏ, a. intrepid, unterrified.

impertinencia, -pĕrtĭnĕn'thĭă, sf. impertinence; troublesomeness.

impertinente, -tĭnĕn'tĕ, a. impertinent; importunate. [turbable.

imperturbable, -tŭrbă'blĕ, a. imper-

impetración, ĭmpĕtrăthŏn', sf. impetration.

impetrar, -trăr', v. a. to impetrate.

ímpetu, ĭm'pĕtŭ, sm. impetus; impetuosity.

impetuoso, sa, -pĕtŭŏ'sŏ, a. impetuous.

impiedad, -pĭĕdăd', sf. impiety; cruelty.

impío, pía, ĭmpĭ'ŏ, a. impious.

implacable, -plăkă'blĕ, a. implacable, inexorable.

implicación, -plĭkăthŏn', sf. implication.

implicar, -plĭkăr', v. a. to implicate, to involve; to entangle.

implícito, ta, -plĭ'thĭtŏ, a. implicit.

implorar, -plŏrăr', v. a. to implore.

impolítica, ĭmpŏlĭ'tĭkă, sf. incivility; impolicy. [polite.

impolítico, ca, -tĭkŏ, a. impolitic; im-

imponderable, ĭmpŏndĕră'blĕ, a. inexpressible, unutterable.

imponer, -pŏnĕr', v. a. to impose a tax; to impute falsely; to advise; to impose upon. [tion.

importación, -pŏrtăthŏn', sf. importa-

importancia, -pŏrtăn'thĭă, sf. importance, import. [siderable.

importante, -pŏrtăn'tĕ, a. important, con-

importar, -pŏrtăr', v. imp. to be important, to matter. [amount, value.

importe, ĭmpŏr'tĕ, sm. amount or gross

importunación, *–tŭnáthiŏn',* sf. importunity.

importunar, *–tŭnár',* y. a. to importune.

importunidad, *–tŭnĭdád',* sf. importunity, annoyance.   [unreasonable.

importuno, na, *–tŏ'nŏ,* a. importunate

imposibilidad, *ĭmpŏsĭbĭlĭdád',* sf. impossibility.   [possible.

imposibilitar, *–tár',* v. a. to render impossible.

imposible, *ĭmpŏsĕ'blĕ,* a. impossible; extremely difficult.   [impost.

imposición, *–pŏsĭthiŏn',* sf. imposition.

impostor, *–pŏstŏr',* sm. impostor, cheater.

impostura, *–pŏstŏ'rá,* sf. false imputation; imposture, deceit, cheat.

impotencia, *–pŏtĕn'thiá,* sf. impotence.

impotente, *–pŏtĕn'tĕ,* a. impotent.

impracticable, *–práktĭká'blĕ,* a. impracticable, unfeasible.   [tion, curse.

imprecación, *–prĕkáthiŏn',* sf. imprecation.

imprecar, *–prĕkár',* v. a. to imprecate, to curse.

imprecatorio, ria, *–prĕkátŏ'riŏ,* a. containing curses, full of evil wishes.

impregnarse, *–prĕgnár'sĕ,* v. r. to be impregnated.   [office.

imprenta, *–prĕn'tá,* sf. printing; printing-office.

imprescindible, *–prĕsthĭndĕ'blĕ,* a. that which cannot be prescinded *or* put aside.

imprescriptible, *–prĕskrĭptĕ'blĕ,* a. imprescriptible.

impresión, *–prĕsiŏn',* sf. impression; stamp; print; impression, edition; efficacious agency, influence.

impresionar, *–prĕsiŏnár',* v. a. to imprint, to fix on the mind.   [treatise.

impreso, *–prĕ'sŏ,* sm. small book, short

impresor, *–prĕsŏr',* sm. printer.

imprevisto, ta, *–prĕvĭs'tŏ,* a. unforeseen; unprovided against.   [print; to stamp.

imprimir, *–prĭmír',* v. a. to print; to imprint.

improbable, *–prŏbá'blĕ,* a. improbable, unlikely.   [laborious, painful.

improbo, ba, *ĭm'prŏbŏ,* a. corrupt, wicked;

improperar, *–prŏpĕrár',* v. a. to upbraid, to taunt, to chide, to abuse.

improperio, *–prŏpĕ'riŏ,* sm. contemptuous reproach, injurious censure.

impropiedad, *–prŏpiĕdád',* sf. impropriety.   [unfit; misbecoming.

impropio, pia, *ĭmprŏ'piŏ,* a. improper;

improrrogable, *–prŏrrŏgá'blĕ,* a. that which cannot be prorogued.

improvisar, *–prŏvĭsár',* v. a. to extemporize, to improvise.

improviso, sa, *–prŏvĕ'sŏ,* a. improvised, unforeseen; not provided against; de –, unexpectedly.   [dence.

imprudencia, *–prŭdĕn'thiá,* sf. imprudence.

imprudente, *–prŭdĕn'tĕ,* a. imprudent.

impudencia, *–pŭdĕn'thiá,* sf. impudence.

impudente, *–pŭdĕn'tĕ,* a. impudent, shameless, descarado, desfachatado.

impúdico, ca, *–pŏ'dĭkŏ,* a. unchaste; shameless, brazen-faced.

impuesto, *–pŭĕs'tŏ,* sm. tax, impost, duty.

impugnación, *–pŭgnáthiŏn',* sf. opposition, contradiction.

impugnar, *–pŭgnár',* v. a. to impugn, to oppose.

impulsivo, va, *–pŭlsĕ'vŏ,* a. impulsive.

impulso, *–pŭl'sŏ,* sm. impulsion.

impune, *ĭmpŏ'nĕ,* a. unpunished.

impunidad, *–pŭnĭdád',* sf. impunity; guiltlessness.

impureza, *–pŭrĕ'thá,* sf. impurity.

impuro, ra, *ĭmpŏ'rŏ,* a. impure, foul.

imputable, *–pŭtá'blĕ,* a. imputable, chargeable.

imputar, *–pŭtár',* v. a. to impute.   [able.

inaccesible, *ĭnáktĕsĕ'blĕ,* a. inaccessible; (fig.) incomprehensible.   [labour.

inacción, *–ákthiŏn',* sf. cessation from

inadmisible, *–ádmĭsĕ'blĕ,* a. inadmissible.

inadvertencia, *ĭnádvĕrtĕn'thiá,* sf. carelessness, inattention.   [inconsiderate.

inadvertido, da, *–tĭ'dŏ,* a. inadvertent.

inagotable, *ĭnágŏtá'blĕ,* a. inexhaustible.

inaguantable, *–ágŭántá'blĕ,* a. insupportable, insufferable, intolerable.

inajenable, *–á'hĕná'blĕ,* a. inalienable.

inalterable, *–áltĕrá'blĕ,* a. unalterable.

inapelable, *–ápĕlá'blĕ,* a. without appeal.

inapreciable, *–áprĕthiá'blĕ,* a. inappreciable, invaluable.

inaudito, ta, *–ăŭdĕ'tŏ,* a. unheard of.

inauguración, *–áŭgŭráthiŏn',* sf. inauguration, consecration.

inaugurar, *–áŭgŭrár',* v. a. to inaugurate.

incansable, *–kánsá'blĕ,* a. indefatigable.

incapacidad, *–kápáthĭdád',* sf. incapacity, inability; stupidity.

incapaz, *–kápáth',* a. incapable, unable.

incauto, ta, *–kă'ŭtŏ,* a. incautious, unwary, heedless.   [set on fire.

incendiar, *–thĕndiár',* v. a. to kindle, to

incendiario, ria, *–thĕndiá'riŏ,* sm. & a. incendiary.   [tion; combustion.

incendio, *–thĕn'diŏ,* sm. fire, conflagration.

incensar, *–thĕnsár',* v. a. to perfume, to incense.   [censer.

incensario, *–thĕnsá'riŏ,* sm. incensory.

incentivo, *–thĕntĕ'vŏ,* sm. incitement, spur.   [certitude, uncertainty.

incertidumbre, *–thĕrtĭdŭm'brĕ,* sf. incertitude.

incesante, *–thĕsán'tĕ,* a. incessant, continual.

incesto, *–thĕs'tŏ,* sm. incest.   [tinual.

incestuoso, sa, *–thĕstŭŏ'sŏ,* a. incestuous.

incidencia, *–thĭdĕn'thiá,* sf. incidence; accident.   [dent.

incidente, *–thĭdĕn'tĕ,* sm. incident, accident.

incidir, *–thĭdír',* v. n. to fall upon, to meet with.

incienso, *ĭnthiĕn'sŏ,* sm. incense.

incierto, ta, *ĭnthiĕr'tŏ,* a. uncertain, doubtful.

incisión, *–thĭsiŏn',* sf. incision, cut.

incisivo, va, *–thĭsĕ'vŏ,* a. incisive.

inciso, *–thĭ'sŏ,* sm. (gr.) comma.

incitación, *–thĭtáthiŏn',* sf. incitement.

incitar, *–thĭtár',* v. a. to incite, to excite.

incitativo, va, *–thĭtátĕ'vŏ,* a. inciting.

incivil, *–thĭvíl',* a. unpolished, rude.

inclemencia, *–klĕmĕn'thiá,* sf. inclemency, severity; & la –, openly, without shelter.

inclinación, *–klĭnáthiŏn',* sf. inclination.

inclinar, –klīnăr´, v. a. to incline; –, v. n. to resemble; to incline; to be favourably disposed to.

Inclito, ta, ĭn´klĭtŏ, a. famous, illustrious.

incluir, –klŭĭr´, v. a. to include, to comprise; to allow one a share in a business.

inclusa, –klŏ´să", sf. foundling-hospital.

inclusion, –klŭsĭŏn´, sf. inclusion.

inclusive, –klŭsē´vě, ad. inclusively.

incluso, sa, ĭnklŏ´sŏ, a. inclosed.

incoativo, va, –kŏătē´vŏ, a. inchoative, beginning.

incobrable, –kŏbră´blě, a. irrecoverable.

incógnito, ta, ĭnkŏg´nĭtŏ, a. unknown; de –, incognito.   [ence.

incoherencia, ĭnkŏhĕrĕn´thĭă, sf. incoher-

incoherente, –tě, a. incoherent.

incombustible, ĭnkŏmbŭstĭ´blě, a. incombustible.   [mode.

incomodar, –kŏmŏdăr´, v. a. to incommode.

incomodidad, –kŏmŏdĭdăd´, sf. incommodity; indisposition.

incómodo, da, ĭnkŏm´ŏdŏ, a. incommodious, inconvenient.

incomparable, ĭnkŏmpără´blě, a. incomparable, matchless.

incompatibilidad, –pătĭbĭlĭdăd´, sf. incompatibility.

incompatible, –pătĭ´blě, a. incompatible.

incompetencia, –pětěn´thĭă, sf. incompetency.

incompetente, –pětěn´tě, a. incompetent.

incompleto, ta, –plē´tŏ, a. incomplete.

incomplexo, xa, –plěk´sŏ, a. simple, simplex.   [hensible.

incomprensible, –prěnsē´blě, a. incomprehensible.

incomunicación, ĭnkŏmŭnĭkăthĭŏn´, sf. want of communication.

incomunicado, da, –kă´dŏ, a. without communication.   [ceivable.

inconcebible, ĭnkŏnthěbē´blě, a. inconceivable.

inconexo, xa, –kŏněk´sŏ, a. unconnected, incoherent; independent.

incongruencia, –kŏngrŭěn´thĭă, a. incongruity, incongruence.

incongruo, grua, ĭnkŏn´grŭŏ, a. incongruous, disproportionate.

inconmensurable, ĭnkŏnměnsŭră´blě, a. immeasurable.   [able.

inconmutable, –mŭtă´blě, a. incommutable.

inconquistable, –kĭstă´blě, a. unconquerable.   [sequence.

inconsecuencia, –sěkŭěn´thĭă, sf. inconsequence.

inconsiderado, da, –sĭděră´dŏ, a. inconsiderate, heedless.

inconsolable, –sŏlă´blě, a. inconsolable.

inconstancia, –stăn´thĭă, sf. inconstancy, unsteadiness, levity.   [able, fickle.

inconstante, –stăn´tě, a. inconstant, variable.

incontestable, –těstă´blě, a. indisputable, incontrovertible, incontestable.

incontinencia, –tĭněn´thĭă, sf. incontinence, incontinency; unchastity.

incontinente, –tĭněn´tě, a. incontinent.

incontrastable, –trăstă´blě, a. insurmountable.

inconveniencia, –věnĭěn´thĭă, sf. inconvenience, incommodity; unsuitableness.

inconveniente, –věnĭěn´tě, a. inconvenient, incommodious.   [the groin).

inoordio, ĭnkŏr´dĭŏ, sm. bubo (tumour in

incorporación, –pŏrăthĭŏn´, sf. incorporation, annexation.

incorporar, –pŏrăr´, v. a. to incorporate; –se, to become incorporated.

incorpóreo, rea, –pŏ´rěŏ, a. incorporeal, immaterial.

incorrecto, ta, –rěk´tŏ, a. incorrect.

incorregible, –rěhē´blě, a. incorrigible.

incorruptible, –rŭptĭ´blě, a. incorruptible.

increado, da, ĭnkrěă´dŏ, a. uncreated.

incredulidad, –krědŭlĭdăd´, sf. incredulity, incredulousness.

incrédulo, la, –krě´dŭlŏ, a. incredulous.

increible, –krěē´blě, a. incredible.

incremento, –krěměn´tŏ, sm. increment, increase; growth; cause of growth.

increpación, –krěpăthĭŏn´, sf. reprehension.   [tend, to scold.

increpar, –krěpăr´, v. a. to chide, to reprehend, to scold.

incruento, ta, –krŭěn´tŏ, a. unstained with blood.

inculcar, –kŭlkăr´, v. a. to inculcate.

inculpable, –kŭlpă´blě, a. inculpable, unblamable.

inculpar, –kŭlpăr´, v. a. to accuse, to blame.

inculto, ta, –kŭl´tŏ, a. uncultivated, uneducated.   [bency; duty.

incumbencia, –kŭmběn´thĭă, sf. incumbency, duty.

incumbir, –kŭmbĭr´, v. n. to be incumbent upon one.   [diable.

incurable, –kŭră´blě, a. incurable; irremediable.

incuria, –kŭ´rĭă, sf. negligence.

incurrir, –kŭrrĭr´, v. n. to incur.

incursión, –kŭrsĭŏn´, sf. incursion, incurring.   [quiry.

indagación, –dăgăthĭŏn´, sf. search, inquiry.

indagar, –dăgăr´, v. a. to search, to inquire.

indebido, da, –děbē´dŏ, a. undue, illegal, unlawful.

indecencia, –děthěn´thĭă, sf. indecency.

indecente, –děthěn´tě, a. indecent.

indecible, –děthē´blě, a. inexpressible, unutterable.   [indecision.

indecisión, –děthĭsĭŏn´, sf. irresolution, indecision.

indeciso, sa, –děthē´sŏ, a. irresolute; undecided.

indeclinable, –děklĭnă´blě, a. firm, unshaken; (gr.) indeclinable.

indecoroso, sa, –děkŏrŏ´sŏ, a. indecent, unbecoming, indecorous.

indefectible, –děfěktĭ´blě, a. unfailing.

indefenso, sa, –děfěn´sŏ, a. defenceless.

indefinible, –děfĭnē´blě, a. indefinable.

indefinido, da, –děfĭnē´dŏ, a. indefinite.

indeleble, –dělě´blě, a. indelible.

indeliberado, da, –dělĭběră´dŏ, a. indeliberate, unpremeditated.

indemnización, –děmnĭthăthĭŏn´, sf. indemnification.

indemnizar, –thăr´, v. a. to indemnify.

independencia, –děpěnděn´thĭă, sf. independence.

independiente, –děn´tě, a. independent.

indestructible, ĭnděstrŭktĭ´blě, a. indestructible.

indeterminado, da, –*détérmínä'dö*, a. indeterminate; indetermined, irresolute.

indevoto, ta, –*dévö'tö*, a. not devout, impious, irreligious.

indiana, *índiä'nä*, sf. chintz, printed cotton.

indiano, –*nö*, sm. Nabob.

indicación, –*índíkäthión'*, sf. indication.

indicar, –*kär'*, v. a. to indicate. [cative.

indicativo, va, –*käti'vö*, a. & sm. indi-

índice, *ín'díthé*, sm. mark, sign; hand of a watch or clock; index, table of contents; forefinger, index.

indicio, *índí'thíö*, sm. indication, mark; sign, token. [unconcern.

indiferencia, –*díférén'thiä*, sf. indifference,

indiferente, –*té*, a. indifferent.

indígena *índí'hénä*, a. indigenous, native.

indigencia, –*dí'hén'thiä*, sf. indigence, poverty, need. [want.

indigente, –*té*, a. indigent, poor, in

indigestión, *índí'héstión'*, sf. indigestion.

indigesto, ta, –*dí'hés'tö*, a. undigested; indigestible; not properly thought or worked out. [anger.

indignación, –*dígnäthión'*, sf. indignation.

indignar, –*dígnär'*, v. a. to irritate, to provoke, to tease. [meanness.

indignidad, –*dígnídäd'*, sf. indignity;

indigno, na, *índíg'nö*, a. unworthy, indign, disgraceful.

índigo, *ín'dígö*, sm. indigo-plant; indigo.

indirecta, –*dírék'tä*, sf. innuendo, hint,

indirecto, ta, –*tö*, a. indirect. [cue.

indisciplinado, da, *índísthíplínä'dö*, a. undisciplined. [imprudence.

indiscreción, –*kréthión'*, sf. indiscretion,

indiscreto, ta, –*krä'tö*, a. indiscreet, inconsiderate.

indisculpable, –*kúlpä'blé*, a. inexcusable.

indisoluble, *índísölü'blé*, a. indissoluble.

indispensable, –*díspénsä'blé*, a. indispensable. [indispose.

indisponer, –*díspönér'*, v. a. to disable; to

indisposición, –*díspösíthión'*, sf. indisposition, slight disorder.

indispuesto, ta, –*díspués'tö*, a. indisposed.

indisputable, –*díspútä'blé*, a. indisputable, incontrovertible.

indistinto, ta, –*dístín'tö*, a. indistinct.

individual, –*dívídüäl'*, a. individual.

individualidad, –*lídäd'*, sf. individuality. [individually.

individualizar, –*líthär'*, v. a. to specify

individuo, *índívü'dúö*, sm. individual.

indivisible, –*dívísé'blé*, a. indivisible.

indócil, *índö'thíl*, a. indocile; headstrong.

indocilidad, –*thílídäd'*, sf. indocility.

índole, *ín'dölé*, sf. disposition, temper, peculiar genius. [difference.

indolencia, –*dölén'thiä*, sf. indolence, in-

indolente, –*té*, a. indolent, indifferent.

indómito, ta, *índö'mítö*, a. untamed, ungoverned. [suasion.

inducción, –*dükthión'*, sf. induction, per-

inducir, –*düthír'*, v. a. to induce, to abet.

inductivo, va, –*düktí'vö*, a. inductive.

indulgencia, –*dúl'hén'thiä*, sf. indulgence, forgiveness.

indulgente, –*té*, a. indulgent.

indultar, *índültär'*, v. a. to pardon; to exempt. [privilege, exemption.

indulto, *índül'tö*, sm. pardon, amnesty;

industria, *índüs'triä*, sf. industry.

industrial, –*düstriäl'*, a. belonging to industry. [struct.

industriar, –*triär'*, v. a. to teach, to in-

industrioso, sa, –*irió'sö*, a. industrious; ingenious. [unedited.

inédito, ta, *ín'dí'dítö*, a. not published.

inefable, *ínéfä'blé*, a. ineffable, unspeakable, unutterable.

ineficacia, –*fíkä'thiä*, sf. inefficacy.

ineficaz, –*fíkäth'*, a. inefficacious.

ineptitud, –*éptítüd'*, sf. inability, unfitness, ineptitude.

inepto, ta, *ínép'tö*, a. inept, unfit, useless.

inercia, *ínér'thiä*, sf. inertia; inactivity.

inerme, *ínér'mé*, a. disarmed, without arms.

inerte, *ínér'té*, a. inert, dull, sluggish; unskilful, awkward.

inescrutable, –*éskrütä'blé*, a. unscrutable.

inesperado, da, –*éspérä'dö*, a. unexpected, unforeseen.

inestimable, –*éstímä'blé*, a. inestimable.

inevitable, –*ítä'blé*, a. unavoidable.

inexactitud, –*éksäktítüd'*, sf. inaccuracy, want of exactness.

inexacto, ta, –*éksäk'tö*, a. not exact.

inexorable, –*éksörä'blé*, a. inexorable.

infalibilidad, –*fälíbílídäd'*, sf. infallibility.

infalible, –*fälé'blé*, a. infallible. [bility.

infamante, –*fämän'té*, a. defamatory, opprobrious, disgraceful.

infamar, –*fämär'*, v. a. to defame.

infame, *ínfä'mé*, a. infamous.

infamia, *ínfä'miä*, sf. infamy.

infancia, *ínfän'thiä*, sf. infancy.

infando, da, *ínfän'dö*, a. infamous, unspeakably abominable.

infanta, *ínfän'tä*, sf. infanta (princess of the royal blood of Spain); infant (female child under seven years old).

infante, *ínfän'té*, sm. infant; infantryman, foot-soldier.

infantería, –*téré'ä*, sf. infantry.

infanticida, –*títhé'dä*, sm. infanticide (person). [(murder).

infanticidio, –*títhé'díö*, sm. infanticide

infantil, –*fäntíl'*, a. infantile, infantine.

infanzón, –*fänthön'*, sm. nobleman.

infatigable, –*fätígä'blé*, a. indefatigable.

infausto, ta, –*fä'üstö*, a. unlucky, unfortunate, luckless, fatal.

infección, –*fékthión'*, sf. infection.

infectar, –*féktär'*, v. a. to infect.

infecto, ta, –*fék'tö*, a. infected.

infelicidad, –*félthídäd'*, sf. misfortune, infelicity.

infeliz, –*féth'*, a. unhappy, unfortunate.

inferior, –*férior'*, a. inferior.

inferioridad, –*féríórídäd'*, sf. inferiority.

inferir, –*férír'*, v. a. to infer.

infernal, –*férnäl'*, a. infernal, hellish.

infestar, –*féstär'*, v. a. to overrun, to harass, to annoy an enemy by incursions; to infect.

inficionar, —fithiŏnâr', v. a. to infect; to corrupt.
infidelidad, —fidĕilâdâd', sf. infidelity; treachery. [godless.
infiel, —fiĕl', a. infidel; faithless; disloyal;
infierno, —fiĕr'nŏ, sm. hell. [filtration.
infiltración, —filtrãthiŏn', sf. (med.) in-
infiltrarse, —filtrâr'sĕ, v. r. to infiltrate.
infimo, ma, in'fimŏ, a. lowest, lowermost.
infinidad, —finidâd', sf. infinity, immensity.
infinitivo, —finitĭ'vŏ, sm. (gr.) infinitive.
infinito, ta, —fini'tŏ, a. infinite, immense;
—, ad. infinitely, immensely.
inflamable, —flamâ'blĕ, a. inflammable.
inflamación, —mãthiŏn', sf. inflammation; fervour. [desires.
inflamar, —mâr', v. a. to inflame; to kindle
inflamatorio, ria, —mâtŏ'riŏ, a. inflammatory. [with wind.
inflar, inflâr', v. a. to inflate, to swell
inflexibilidad, —flĕksibilidâd', sf. inflexibility.
inflexible, —flĕksĭ'blĕ, a. inflexible.
influencia, —flŭĕn'thiâ, sf. influence.
influir, —flŭir', v. a. to influence, to
prevail upon.
influjo, influ'hŏ, sm. influx, influence.
información, —fŏrmãthiŏn', sf. information; intelligence given; instruction,
judicial inquiry. [lished forms.
informal, —fŏrmâl', a. contrary to estab-
informalidad, —mãlidâd', sf. informality.
informar, —mâr', v. a. to inform.
informe, infŏr'mĕ, sm. information, account; —, a. shapeless, formless. [luck.
infortunio, —fŏrtŏ'niŏ, sm. misfortune, ill
infracción, —frãkthiŏn', sf. infraction;
breach, contravention, violation, trespass.
infractor, —tŏr', sm. violator.
infrascripto, infrãskrip'tŏ, a. under-
written, undersigned.
infructífero, ra, —frŭktĭ'fĕrŏ, a. unfruitful; useless.
infructuoso, sa, —frŭktŭŏ'sŏ, a. fruitless,
unproductive, unprofitable.
infundado, da, —fŭndâ'dŏ, a. groundless.
infundios, —fŭn'diŏs, sm. pl. jobbing in
joint-stock companies. [spire with.
infundir, —fŭndir', v. a. to infuse, to in-
infusión, —fŭsiŏn', sf. infusion.
infuso, sa, infŭ'sŏ, a. infused, introduced.
ingeniar, in'hĕniâr', v. a. to conceive; to
contrive; —se, to work in the mind, to
endeavour to find out.
ingeniero, —hĕniĕ'rŏ, sm. engineer.
ingenio, in'hĕ'niŏ, sm. genius; engine;
means, expedient; — de azúcar, sugar-
mill.
ingenioso, sa, —hĕniŏ'sŏ, a. ingenious.
ingenuidad, —hĕnŭidâd', sf. ingenious-
ness; candour, frankness.
ingenuo, nua, in'hĕ'nŭŏ, a. ingenuous.
ingerir, —hĕrir', v. a. to insert; to introduce, to inclose; —se, to interfere offi-
ingle, in'glĕ, sf. groin. [ciously.
inglés, esa, inglĕs', a. English, English
language.

ingratitud, —grãtitŭd', sf. ingratitude,
unthankfulness. [less; disagreeable.
ingrato, ta, ingrâ'tŏ, a. ungrateful, thank-
ingrediente, —grĕdiĕn'tĕ, sm. ingredient.
inhábil, inâ'bil, a. unable, incapable; awkward. [to disable.
inhabilitar, —âbilitâr', v. a. to disqualify;
inhabitable, —âbitâ'blĕ, a. uninhabitable.
inherente, —hĕrĕn'tĕ, a. inherent.
inhibición, —ibithiŏn', sf. inhibition, prohibition.
inhibir, —ibir', v. a. to inhibit, to prohibit.
inhibitorio, ria, —ibitŏ'riŏ, a. prohibitory.
inhumanidad, —ŭmânidâd', sf. inhuman-
inhumano, na, —ŭmâ'nŏ, a. inhuman. [ity.
inicial, —ithiâl', a. initial.
iniciar, —ithiâr', v. a. to initiate; —se, to
receive the first orders. [tiatory.
iniciativa, va, —tĭ'vŏ, a. initiating, in-
inicuo, cua, inĭ'kŭŏ, a. iniquitous, unjust.
inimaginable, —imâ'hinâ'blĕ, a. unimaginable, inconceivable.
inimitable, —imitâ'blĕ, a. inimitable.
ininteligible, —intĕli'hĕ'blĕ, a. unintelligible. [justice.
iniquidad, —ĭkidâd', sf. iniquity, in-
injertar, in'hĕrtâr', v. a. to ingraft a tree.
injerto, —'hĕr'tŏ, sm. tree ingrafted.
injuria, —'hŏ'riâ, sf. injury.
injuriador, ra, —'hŭriâdŏr', sm. & f. injurer, wrong-doer.
injuriar, —'hŭriâr', v. a. to injure. [sive.
injurioso, sa, —' riŏ'sŏ, a. injurious; offen-
injusticia, —'hŭstĭ'thiâ, sf. injustice.
injusto, ta, —'hŏs'tŏ, a. unjust.
inmaculado, da, —mâkŭlâ'dŏ, a. immaculate. [fading.
inmarcesible, —mârthĕsĭ'blĕ, a. never-
inmediatamente, —mĕdiâtâmĕn'tĕ, ad.
immediately, forthwith.
inmediato, ta, —mĕdiâ'tŏ, a. immediate.
inmemorial, —mĕmŏriâl', a. immemorial,
past time.
inmensidad, —mĕnsidâd', sf. immensity.
inmenso, sa, —mĕn'sŏ, a. immense, infinite. [surable.
inmensurable, —mĕnsŭrâ'blĕ, a. immen-
inminente, —minĕn'tĕ, a. imminent.
inmoble, inmŏ'blĕ, a. immovable; constant. [derate.
inmoderado, da, —mŏdĕrâ'dŏ, a. immo-
inmodesto, ta, —mŏdĕs'tŏ, a. immodest.
inmolar, —mŏlâr', v. a. to sacrifice.
inmortal, —mŏrtâl', a. immortal. [tality.
inmortalidad, —mŏrtâlidâd', sf. immor-
inmortalizar, —lithâr', v. a. to immor-
talize.
inmóvil, inmŏ'vil, a. immovable.
inmovilidad, —mŏvilidâd', sf. immobility.
inmueble, inmŭĕ'blĕ, a. immovable.
inmundicia, —mŭndĭ'thiâ, sf. nastiness,
filth. [obscene.
inmundo, da, inmŭn'dŏ, a. filthy, dirty;
inmune, inmŭ'nĕ, a. free, exempt.
inmunidad, —mŭnidâd', sf. immunity,
privilege. [tability.
inmutabilidad, —mŭtâbilidâd', sf. immu-
inmutable, —tâ'blĕ, a. immutable.

inmutar, -mûtár', v. a. to change, to alter.
innato, ta, -nä'tŏ, a. inborn, natural.
innegable, -négä'blä, a. incontestable, incontrovertible.
innoble, -nŏ'blä, a. ignoble; mean of birth.
innovación, -nŏváthŏn', sf. innovation.
innovador, ra, -dŏr', sm. & f. innovator.
innovar, -vár', v. a. to innovate.
innumerable, -númérä'blä, a. innumerable, numberless.   [dience.
inobediencia, -ŏbédĭén'thĭä, sf. disobe-
inobediente, -tä, a. disobedient.
inobservancia, -ŏbsérvän'thĭä, sf. inad-
  vertency; inobservance.
inocencia, inŏthén'thĭä, sf. innocence.
inocentada, -théntä'dä, sf. harmless
inocente, -tä, a. innocent.   [speech.
inoculación, -ŏkúláthŏn', sf. inoculation.
inocular, -lár', v. a. to inoculate.
inoficioso, sa, -ŏfĭthĭŏ'sŏ, a. inofficious.
inopinado, da, -ŏpĭnä'dŏ, a. unexpected,
  unforeseen, sudden.   [disturb.
inquietar, -kĭétár', v. a. to disquiet, to
inquieto, ta, -kĭé'tŏ, a. restless, unquiet.
inquietud, -kĭétúd', sf. inquietude, anxiety.
inquilino, na, -kĭlĭ'nŏ, sm. & f. tenant;
  lodger.
inquirir, -kĭrĭr', v. a. to inquire.
inquisición, -kĭsĭthŏn', sf. inquisition;
  judicial inquiry.
inquisidor, -dŏr', sm. inquirer; inquisitor.
insaciable, -säthĭä'blä, a. insatiable.
insalubre, -sälú'brä, a. insalubrious.
insalubridad, -sälúbrĭdäd', sf. insalubrity.
insano, na, insä'nŏ, a. insane, mad.
inscribir, -skrĭbĭr', v. a. to inscribe.
inscripción, -skrĭpthŏn', sf. inscription.
insecto, insék'tŏ, sm. insect.
insensatez, -sénsätéth', sf. insensateness,
  stupidity, folly.   [mad.
insensato, ta, -sä'tŏ, a. insensate, stupid,
insensibilidad, -sénsĭbĭlĭdäd', sf. insensibility.   [perceptible.
insensible, -sénsĭ'blä, a. insensible; im-
insensiblemente, -mén'tä, ad. by degrees.
inseparable, -sépärä'blä, a. inseparable.
inserción, -sérthŏn', sf. insertion.
insertar, -sértár', v. a. to insert.
inservible, -sérvĭ'blä, a. unserviceable.
insidioso, sa, -sĭdĭŏ'sŏ, a. insidious.
insigne, insĭg'nä, a. notable.   [signia.
insignia, insĭg'nĭä, sf. badge; -s, pl. in-
insinuación, -sĭnúáthŏn', sf. insinuation.
insinuar, -sĭnúár', v. a. to insinuate; to
  steal into imperceptibly.
insipidez, -sĭpĭdéth', sf. insipidity.
insípido, da, insĭ'pĭdŏ, a. insipid.
insistencia, -sĭstén'thĭä, sf. persistence,
  steadiness.
insistir, -sĭstĭr', v. n. to insist.
insociable, -sŏthĭä'blä, a. unsociable.
insoldable, -sŏldä'blä, a. that cannot be
  soldered; irreparable.
insolencia, -sŏlén'thĭä, sf. insolence, impudence, effrontery.
insolente, -tä, a. insolent, impudent.
insólidum, insŏ'lĭdúm, ad. (law) jointly.
insolvencia, -sŏlvén'thĭä, sf. insolvency.

insolvente, -tä, a. insolvent.
insondable, -sŏndä'blä, a. unfathomable;
  inscrutable.   [able.
insoportable, -sŏpŏrtä'blä, a. insuppor-
inspección, -spékthŏn', sf. inspection,
  survey, control.   [to oversee.
inspeccionar, -thĭŏnár', v. a. to inspect,
inspector, -tŏr', sm. inspector, superintendent.
inspiración, -spĭráthŏn', sf. inspiration.
inspirar, -spĭrár', v. a. to inspire.
instabilidad, -stäbĭlĭdäd', sf. instability,
  inconstancy, fickleness, mutability, fugi-
  tiveness, fugacity, fragility; giddiness.
instable, instä'blä, a. instable, inconstant,
  changing, mutable, fickle, fugacious.
instalación, -stäläthŏn', sf. installation.
instalar, -lár', v. a. to install.
instancia, instän'thĭä, sf. instance.
instantáneo, nea, -tä'néŏ, a. instantaneous.   [mediately, instantly.
instante, instän'tä, sm. instant; al-, im-
instar, instár', v. a. to press, to urge a request or petition; to impugn the solution
  of a question; -, v. n. to be pressing or
  urgent; to be near (of danger, &c.); to
  argue necessity for prompt action.
instigación, -stĭgáthŏn', sf. incitement,
  impulse, instigation.
instigar, -gár', v. a. to instigate.
instinto, instĭn'tŏ, sm. instinct.
institución, -stĭtúthŏn', sf. institution;
  -ones, pl. elements of a science; lesson-
  book.
instituir, -stĭtúĭr', v. a. to institute.
instituto, -stĭtú'tŏ, sm. institute.
instrucción, -strúkthŏn', sf. instruction.
instructivo, va, -tĭ'vŏ, a. instructive,
  conveying knowledge.
instructor, -tŏr', sm. instructor, teacher.
instruir, -strúĭr', v. a. to instruct, to
  teach.   [mental.
instrumental, -strúméntäl', a. instru-
instrumentista, -tĭs'tä, sm. musical
  player.   [machine; means, expedient.
instrumento, -mén'tŏ, sm. instrument;
insubsistencia, -sŭbsĭstén'thĭä, sf. instability, inconstancy.   [unstable.
insubsistente, -tä, a. unable to subsist;
insuficiencia, -sŭfĭthĭén'thĭä, sf. insufficiency, inadequateness.   [quate.
insuficiente, -tä, a. insufficient, inade-
insufrible, -sŭfrĭ'blä, a. insufferable, insupportable.
insulsez, -sŭlséth', sf. insipidity, flatness.
insulso, sa, -sŭl'sŏ, a. insipid; dull,
  heavy; flat; cold.
insultar, -sŭltár', v. a. to insult.
insulto, -sŭl'tŏ, sm. insult; sudden and
  violent attack.   [insurmountable.
insuperable, -sŭpérä'blä, a. insuperable,
insurgente, -sŭr'hén'tä, sm. insurgent.
insurrección, -rékthŏn', sf. insurrection.
intacto, ta, intäk'tŏ, a. untouched; entire;
  intact.
integral, -tégräl', a. integral, whole.
integridad, -tégrĭdäd', sf. integrity; un-
  corruptedness.

íntegro, gra, *ĭn'tĕgrŏ,* a. integral, entire.
intelectual, *–tĕlĕktŭăl',* a. intellectual.
inteligencia, *–ĭnt'hĕn'thĭă,* sf. intelligence; understanding.
inteligente, *–tĕ,* a. intelligent.
inteligible, *–ĭnt'hĕ'blĕ,* a. intelligible.
intemperancia, *–tĕmpĕrăn'thĭă,* sf. intemperance. [ness.
intemperie, *–tĕmpĕ'rĭĕ,* sf. intemperate.
intempestivo, va, *–tĕmpĕstĕ'vŏ,* a. unseasonable. [sign, meaning, view.
intención, *–tĕnthĭŏn',* sf. intention, design.
intencionado, da, *–thĭŏnă'dŏ,* a. inclined, disposed.
intendencia, *–tĕndĕn'thĭă,* sf. administration; employment of an intendant.
intendente, *–tĕ,* sm. intendant.
intensión, *–tĕnsĭŏn',* sf. tension, ardency.
intenso, sa, *ĭntĕn'sŏ,* a. intense, ardent.
intentar, *–tĕntăr',* v. a. to try; to intend, to design. [sign.
intento, *ĭntĕn'tŏ,* sm. intent, purpose, design.
intentona, *ĭntĕntŏ'nă,* sf. extravagant design; chimerical attempt.
intercadencia, *ĭntĕrkădĕn'thĭă,* sf. interruption; inconstancy; intermission of the pulse. [variable.
intercadente, *–kădĕn'tĕ,* a. changeable,
intercalación, *–kălăthĭŏn',* sf. intercalation, insertion. [to insert.
intercalar, *–kălăr',* v. a. to intercalate,
interceder, *–thĕdĕr',* v. n. to intercede.
interceptar, *–thĕptăr',* v. a. to intercept.
intercesión, *–thĕsĭŏn',* sf. intercession, mediation, entreaty. [cessor, mediator.
intercesor, ra, *–thĕsŏr',* sm. & f. intercessor.
interés, *ĭntĕrĕs',* sm. interest; concern, advantage; profit.
interesado, da, *–să'dŏ,* a. interested.
interesante, *–săn'tĕ,* a. interesting, useful, convenient.
interesar, *–săr',* v. n. & r. to be concerned or interested in; *–,* v. a. to interest; to concern, to give a share in. [mean time.
ínterin, *ĭn'tĕrĭn,* ad. in the interim, in the
interinidad, *–nĭdăd',* sf. temporary holding of office. [an employ or office).
interino, na, *ĭntĕrĕ'nŏ,* a. provisional (of interior, *–tĕrĭŏr',* a. interior, internal; *–,* sm. interior, inside; *–es,* pl. entrails, intestines.
interioridad, *–ĭdăd',* sf. inside, interior.
interjección, *–'hĕkthĭŏn',* sf. (gr.) interjection.
interlineal, *–lĭnĕăl',* a. interlineal.
interlocución, *–lŏkŭthĭŏn',* sf. interlocution, dialogue. [locutory.
interlocutorio, ria, *–lŏkŭtŏ'rĭŏ,* a. interlocutory.
intermediar, *–mĕdĭăr',* v. a. to interpose.
intermedio, dia, *–mĕ'dĭŏ,* a. intermediate, intermedial; *–,* sm. interval, intermedium; interlude. [endless.
interminable, *–mĭnă'blĕ,* a. interminable.
intermisión, *–mĭsĭŏn',* sf. intermission, interruption.
intermitente, *–mĭtĕn'tĕ,* a. intermittent.
internar, *ĭntĕrnăr',* v. a. to pierce; to penetrate; *–se,* to insinuate; to wheedle.

interno, *ĭntĕr'nŏ,* a. interior, internal.
interpelación, *ĭntĕrpĕlăthĭŏn',* sf. interpellation.
interpelar, *–pĕlăr',* v. a. to appeal to.
interpolación, *–pŏlăthĭŏn',* sf. interpolation; interruption. [to interrupt.
interpolar, *–pŏlăr',* v. a. to interpolate;
interponer, *–pŏnĕr',* v. a. to interpose.
interposición, *–pŏsĭthĭŏn',* sf. interposition; mediation. [tation.
interpretación, *–prĕtăthĭŏn',* sf. interpretation.
interpretar, *–prĕtăr',* v. a. to interpret, to explain; to translate.
intérprete, *ĭntĕr'prĕtĕ,* sm. interpreter.
interregno, *ĭntĕrrĕg'nŏ,* sm. interreign.
interrogación, *–rŏgăthĭŏn',* sf. interrogation, a question put.
interrogante, *–rŏgăn'tĕ,* a. interrogative.
interrogar, *–rŏgăr',* v. a. to interrogate.
interrogatorio, *–rŏgătŏ'rĭŏ,* sm. interrogatory.
interrumpir, *–rŭmpĭr',* v. a. to interrupt.
interrupción, *–rŭpthĭŏn',* sf. interruption, discontinuance.
intersección, *–sĕkthĭŏn',* sf. intersection.
intervalo, *–vă'lŏ,* sm. interval.
intervención, *–vĕnthĭŏn',* sf. intervention, mediation. [mediate.
intervenir, *–vĕnĭr',* v. n. to intervene, to
interventor, ra, *–vĕntŏr',* sm. & f. intervener; controller.
intestado, da, *ĭntĕstă'dŏ,* a. intestate.
intestino, na, *–tĕstĕ'nŏ,* a. intestine, internal, interior. [hint.
intimación, *–tĭmăthĭŏn',* sf. intimation.
intimar, *–tĭmăr',* v. a. to intimate.
intimidad, *–tĭmĭdăd',* sf. intimacy.
intimidar, *–dăr',* v. a. to intimidate.
íntimo, ma, *ĭn'tĭmŏ,* a. internal, innermost; intimate, familiar.
intitular, *–tĭtŭlăr',* v. a. to entitle.
intolerable, *–tŏlĕră'blĕ,* a. intolerable, insufferable.
intolerancia, *–tŏlĕrăn'thĭă,* sf. intolerance.
intolerante, *–tĕ,* a. intolerant.
intramuros, *ĭntrămŭ'rŏs,* a. within the walls. [able, impenetrable.
intransitable, *ĭntrănsĭtă'blĕ,* a. impassintransitivo, va, *–trănsĭtĕ'vŏ,* a. (gr.) intransitive. [governable.
intratable, *–tră'blĕ,* a. intractable, unintrepidez, *–trĕpĭdăth',* sf. intrepidity; temerity. [daring.
intrépido, da, *ĭntrĕ'pĭdŏ,* a. intrepid,
intriga, *ĭntrĕ'gă,* sf. intrigue.
intrigante, *–trĭgăn'tĕ,* sm. intriguer.
intrigar, *–trĭgăr',* v. n. to intrigue.
intrincar, *–trĭnkăr',* v. a. to intricate, to entangle, to involve; to confound.
intrínseco, ca, *–trĭn'sĕkŏ,* a. intrinsic, internal; judicial. [duction.
introducción, *ĭntrŏdŭkthĭŏn',* sf. introduction.
introducir, *–dŭthĭr',* v. a. to introduce; *–se,* to insinuate.
introductor, *–dŭktŏr',* sm. introducer.
introito, *ĭntrŏ'ĭtŏ,* sm. entrance, entry.
intrusión, *–trŭsĭŏn',* sf. intrusion, obtrusion.

intruso, sa, *întrŏ´ sŏ*, a. intrusive, obtrusive.
intuición, –*tŭîthĭŏn´*, sf. intuition.
intuitivo, va, –*tŏ´ vŏ*, a. intuitive.
inundación, –*ŭndăthĭŏn´*, sf. inundation,
    deluge.   [flow.
inundar, –*dăr´*, v. a. to inundate, to over-
inusitado, da, –*ăsîtă´ dŏ*, a. unusual.
inútil, *înŏ´ tîl*, a. useless.
inutilidad, –*ĭlîdăd´*, sf. uselessness.
inutilizar, –*thăr´*, v. a. to render useless.
invadir, –*vădîr´*, v. a. to invade, to attack
    a country.   [render null and void.
invalidar, –*vălîdăr´*, v. a. to invalidate, to
inválido, da, *ĭnvă´ lîdŏ*, a. invalid, null;
    –, sm. (mil.) invalid.
invariable, –*vărĭă´ blĕ*, a. invariable.
invasión, –*văsĭŏn´*, sf. invasion.
invasor, ra, –*văsŏr´*, sm. & f. invader.
invectiva, –*vĕktî´ vă*, a. invective.
invencible, –*vĕnthĭ´ blĕ*, a. invincible.
invención, –*vĕnthĭŏn´*, sf. invention.
inventar, –*vĕntăr´*, v. a. to invent.
inventariar, –*tărĭăr´*, v. a. to make an
    inventory.
inventario, –*tă´ rĭŏ*, sm. inventory.
invento, *învĕn´ tŏ*, sm. invention.
inventor, –*vĕntŏr´*, sm. inventor.
inverisimil, –*vĕrĭsĕ´ mîl*, a. unlike, im-
    probable.   [hood, improbability.
inverisimilitud, –*mĭlîtŭd´*, sf. unlikeli-
invernadero, –*vĕrnădă´ rŏ*, sm. (mil.)
    winter-quarters; green-house.
invernar, –*vĕrnăr´*, v. n. to pass the
    winter; to be the winter season.
invernizo, sa, –*vĕrnî´ thŏ*, a. winterly.
inversión, –*vĕrsĭŏn´*, sf. inversion.
inverso, sa, *învĕr´ sŏ*, a. inverted, reciprocal.
invertir, –*vĕrtîr´*, v. a. to invert.
investidura, –*vĕstîdŏ´ ră*, sf. investiture.
investigación, –*vĕstîgăthĭŏn´*, sf. investi-
    gation, research; inquest.
investigar, –*vĕstîgăr´*, v. a. to investigate,
    to search out.
investir, –*vĕstîr´*, v. a. to invest.
inveterarse, –*vĕtĕrăr´ sĕ*, v. r. to become
    antiquated, to grow old.
invicto, ta, *învîk´ tŏ*, a. unconquerable.
invierno, *învĭĕr´ nŏ*, sm. winter.
inviolabilidad, –*vĭŏlăbîlîdăd´*, sf. in-
    violability.
inviolable, –*vĭŏlă´ blĕ*, a. inviolable.
invisible, –*vîsĕ´ blĕ*, a. invisible.
invocación, –*vŏkăthĭŏn´*, sf. invocation.
invocar, –*vŏkăr´*, v. a. to invoke.
involuntario, ria, –*vŏlŭntă´ rĭŏ*, a. in-
    voluntary.   [able.
invulnerable, –*vŭlnĕră´ blĕ*, a. invulner-
ipso facto, *îp´ sŏ făk´ tŏ*, ad. (law) imme-
    diately, without delay.   [away, to depart.
ir, *îr*, v. n. to go, to walk; –se, to go
ira, *ĕ´ ră*, sf. anger, wrath.   [enraged.
iracundo, da, –*răkŭn´ dŏ*, a. passionate,
iris, *ĕ´ rîs*, sf. rainbow; iris (of the eye);
    water-lily, nenuphar; peace-maker.
ironía, *îrŏnĕ´ ă*, sf. irony.
irónico, ca, *îrŏ´ nîkŏ*, a. ironical.
irracional, *îrrăthĭŏnăl´*, a. irrational.
irradiación, –*rădĭăthĭŏn´*, sf. irradiation.

irrazonable, –*răthŏnă´ blĕ*, a. unreason-
    able.   [concileable.
irreconciliable, –*rĕkŏnthîlĭă´ blĕ*, a. irre-
irrecusable, –*rĕkŭsă´ blĕ*, a. not to be re-
    fused; inevitable.   [consideration.
irreflexión, –*rĕflĕkthĭŏn´*, sf. rashness, in-
irrefragable, –*rĕfrăgă´ blĕ*, a. irrefragable,
    irrefutable.   [normal.
irregular, –*rĕgŭlăr´*, a. irregular, ab-
irregularidad, –*rĕgŭlărîdăd´*, sf. irregu-
    larity, anomaly.
irreligioso, sa, –*rĕlî´ hĭŏ´ sŏ*, a. irre-
    ligious, impious.   [able, helpless.
irremediable, –*rĕmĕdĭă´ blĕ*, a. irremedi-
irremisible, –*rĕmîsĕ´ blĕ*, a. irremissible,
    unpardonable.   [irretrievable.
irreparable, –*rĕpără´ blĕ*, a. irreparable,
irreprensible, –*rĕprĕnsĕ´ blĕ*, a. irre-
    prehensible.
irresistible, –*rĕsîstĕ´ blĕ*, a. irresistible.
irresolución, –*rĕsŏlŭthĭŏn´*, sf. irresolu-
    tion.
irresoluto, ta, –*rĕsŏlŭ´ tŏ*, a. irresolute.
irreverencia, –*rĕvĕrĕn´ thĭă*, sf. irre-
    verence, want of reverence, respect or
    veneration.
irreverente, –*rĕvĕrĕn´ tĕ*, a. irreverent.
irrevocable, –*rĕvŏkă´ blĕ*, a. irrevocable.
irrisible, –*rîsĕ´ blĕ*, a. laughable.
irrisión, –*rîsĭŏn´*, sf. mockery, mocking
    laughter.   [able.
irrisorio, ria, –*rîsŏ´ rĭŏ*, a. risible, laugh-
irritación, –*rîtăthĭŏn´*, sf. irritation;
    wrath.   [to exasperate.
irritar, –*rîtăr´*, v. a. to annul; to irritate,
irrupción, –*rŭpthĭŏn´*, sf. irruption, in-
    isla, *îs´ lă*, sf. isle, island.   [road.
isleño, ña, *îslĕn´ yŏ*, sm. & f. islander.
isleta, *îslĕ´ tă*, sf. islet.
islote, *îslŏ´ tĕ*, sm. small barren island.
israelita, *îsrăĕlî´ tă*, sm. Israelite, Jew.
istmo, *îst´ mŏ*, sm. isthmus.
italiano, *îtălĭă´ nŏ*, sm. Italian language.
ítem, *ĕ´ tĕm*, sm. item, another article; –,
    ad. also.
itinerario, *îtĭnĕră´ rĭŏ*, a. & sm. itinerary.
izar, *îthăr´*, v. a. (mar.) to hoist.   [handed.
izquierdo, da, *îthkĭĕr´ dŏ*, a. left; left-

J.

jabalí, *hăbălĕ´*, sm. wild boar.
jabalina, –*lĕ´ nă*, sf. wild sow; javelin.
jabón, *hăbŏn´*, sm. soap.
jabonado, *hăbŏnă´ dŏ*, sm. washing with
    soap; parcel of linen washed with soap.
jabonadura, –*nădŏ´ ră*, sf. soap-suds;
jabonar, –*năr´*, v. a. to soap.   [lather.
jabonería, –*nĕrĕ´ ă*, sm. soap-house.
jabonero, –*nĕ´ rŏ*, sm. soap-boiler.
jaca, *hă´ kă*, sf. nag, pony.
jácara, *hă´ kără*, sf. country song or
    dance tune.
jacarear, *hăkărĕăr´*, v. n. to sing jácaras.
jacinto, *hăthîn´ tŏ*, sm. hyacinth.

jaco, 'hǎ'kŏ, sm. nag, pony; ash-coloured parrot.

jactancia, 'hǎktǎn'thĭǎ, sf. boasting.

jactancioso, sa, –thĭŏ'sŏ, a. boastful, vain-glorious.

jactarse, 'hǎktǎr'sě, v. r. to boast.

jaculatoria, 'hǎkŭlǎtŏ'rĭǎ, sf. ejaculatory prayer, short and hurried prayer.

jaez, 'hǎěth', sm. harness.

jalapa, 'hǎlǎ'pǎ, sf. jalap.

jalea, 'hǎlě'ǎ, sf. jelly.   [the chase.

jalear, 'hǎlěǎr', v. a. to egg on hounds to

jaleo, 'hǎlě'ŏ, sm. halloo.

jaletina, 'hǎlětě'nǎ, sf. fruit jelly; gelatine.

jamás, 'hǎmǎs', ad. never; para siempre –, for ever.

jamón, 'hǎmŏn', sm. ham, gammon.

jándalo, la, 'hǎn'dǎlŏ, a. having the gait and dialect of an Andalusian.

jaque, 'hǎ'kě, sm. check (at the game of chess); – y mate, check-mate.

jaquear, 'hǎkěǎr', v. a. to check.

jaqueca, 'hǎkě'kǎ, sf. megrim.

jarabe, 'hǎrǎ'bě, sm. syrup.

jarana, 'hǎrǎ'nǎ, sf. merry clatter, outcry.

jarcia, 'hǎr'thǐǎ, sf. bundle, packet; bundle or heap of odds and ends; (mar.) tackle.

jardín, 'hǎrdǐn', sm. garden.   [tackle.

jardinería, 'hǎrdǐněrǐ'ǎ, sf. gardening.

jardinero, ra, –něr'ŏ, sm. & f. gardener.

jareta, 'hǎrě'tǎ, sf. lacing-seam.

jaropar, 'hǎrŏpǎr', v. a. to medicine.

jarope, 'hǎrŏ'pě, sm. medical draught.

jarra, 'hǎr'rǎ, sf. jug, jar, pitcher; en – de –s, with arms placed akimbo; with hands to the sides.

jarrete, 'hǎr rě'tě, sm. hock, hough.

jarretera, 'hǎrrětě'rǎ, sf. garter.

jarro, 'hǎr'rŏ, sm. pot with one handle.

jarrón, 'hǎrrŏn', sm. large jug, urn.

jaspe, 'hǎs'pě, sm. jasper.   [speckle.

jaspear, 'hǎspěǎr', v. a. to marble, to speckle.

jaula, 'hǎ'ŭlǎ, sf. cage; cell for mad persons; (rail.) cattle-van.

jauría, 'hǎŭrǐ'ǎ, sf. pack of hounds.

jazmín, 'hǎthmǐn', sm. jessamine.

jefe, 'hě'fě, sm. chief, head, leader; (rail.) – de tren, guard, conductor.

jengibre, 'hěn'hǐ'brě, sm. (bot.) ginger.

jerarquía, 'hěrǎrkǐ'ǎ, sf. hierarchy.

jerárquico, 'hěrǎr'kǐkŏ, a. hierarchical.

jerga, 'hěr'gǎ, sf. coarse frieze, any coarse cloth; jargon; large sack.

jergón, 'hěrgŏn', sm. coarse mattress.

jerife, 'hěrǐ'fě, sm. Moorish title of honour.

jerigonza, 'hěrǐgŏn'thǎ, sf. jargon, gibberish.

jeringa, 'hěrǐn'gǎ, sf. syringe.   [berish.

jeringar, –gǎr', v. a. to syringe, to squirt.

jeringazo, –gǎ'thŏ, sm. clyster.

jeroglífico, 'hěrŏglǐ'fǐkŏ, a. hieroglyphical; –, sm. hieroglyph, hieroglyphic.

Jesucristo, 'hěsŭkrǐs'tŏ, sm. Jesus Christ.

jesuíta, 'hěsŭǐ'tǎ, sm. Jesuit.

jesuítico, oa, –ǐ'tǐkŏ, a. jesuitical.

jiba, 'hě'bǎ, sf. hump-back.

jibado, 'hǐbǎ'dŏ, a. hump-backed.

jibia, 'hǐ'bǐǎ, sf. cuttle-fish.

jícara, 'hě'kǎrǎ, sf. chocolate-cup.

jigote, 'hǐgŏ'tě, sm. minced meat.

jilguero, 'hǐlgě'rŏ, sm. linnet.

jinete, 'hǐně'tě, sm. cavalier.

jocoserio, ria, 'hŏkŏsě'rǐŏ, a. jocoserious.

jocosidad, –sǐdǎd', sf. jocosity.

jocoso, sa, 'hŏkŏ'sŏ, a. waggish, good-humoured.

jornada, 'hŏrnǎ'dǎ, sf. journey; military expedition; act (of a Spanish play); – rompida, fight, battle.

jornal, 'hŏrnǎl', sm. day-work; journal; á –, by the day.

jornalero, –lě'rŏ, sm. day-labourer.

joroba, 'hŏrŏ'bǎ, sf. hump.

jorobado, da, 'hŏrŏbǎ'dŏ, a. hump-backed.

jorobar, 'hŏrŏbǎr', v. a. to importune, to tease.

jota, 'hŏ'tǎ, sf. jot, tittle; Spanish dance.

joven, 'hŏ'věn, a. young; –, sm. & f. youth; young woman.

jovial, 'hŏvǐǎl', a. jovial, gay, merry.

jovialidad, –lǐdǎd', sf. joviality, gaiety.

joya, 'hŏ'yǎ, sf. jewel; present, gift.

joyería, 'hŏyěrǐ'ǎ, sf. jeweller's shop.

joyero, 'hŏyě'rŏ, sm. jeweller.

juanete, 'hŭǎně'tě, sm. knuckle-bone of the great toe.

jubilación, 'hŭbǐlǎthǐŏn', sf. festivity.

jubilar, 'hŭbǐlǎr', v. a. to pension off; to superannuate; to lay aside as useless; –, v. n. to become a pensioner on retiring or leaving office.

jubileo, 'hŭbǐlě'ŏ, sm. jubilee.

júbilo, 'hŏ'bǐlŏ, sm. joy, merriment, festivity.

jubón, 'hŭbŏn', sm. doublet, jacket.

judaico, oa, 'hŭdǎ'ǐkŏ, a. Judaical, Jewish.

judaísmo, –ǐs'mŏ, sm. Judaism, Jewish religion.

judaizar, –ǐthǎr', v. a. to judaize.

Judas, 'hŏ'dǎs, sm. (fig.) traitor.

judía, 'hŭdǐ'ǎ, sf. French bean, kidney-bean.

judicatura, 'hŭdǐkǎtŭ'rǎ, sf. judicature; dignity of a judge.

judicial, 'hŭdǐthǐǎl', a. judicial, juridical.

judío, día, 'hŭdǐ'ŏ, a. Jewish; –, sm. Jew; word of contempt used in anger.

juego, 'hŭě'gŏ, sm. play, amusement, diversion, sport; game, gambling; –s, pl. public games of the ancients.

jueves, 'hŭě'věs, sm. Thursday.

juez, 'hŭěth', sm. judge.

jugada, 'hŭgǎ'dǎ, sf. playing of a card.

jugador, ra, –dŏr', sm. & f. player; gamester.

jugar, 'hŭgǎr', v. a. & n. to play, to sport, to trifle, to toy; to gamble, to game; to intervene; to mock.   [playing.

jugarreta, –rě'tǎ, sf. bad play, unskilful playing.

jugo, 'hŭ'gŏ, sm. sap, juice.

jugoso, sa, 'hŭgŏ'sŏ, a. juicy, succulent.

juguete, 'hŭgě'tě, sm. toy, play-thing, gew-gaw, trinket.

juguetear, –těǎr', v. n. to trifle, to fool.

juguetón, ona, –tŏn', a. playful.

juicio, hŭǐ'thǐŏ, sm. judgment.

juicioso, sa, 'hŭǐthǐŏ'sŏ, a. judicious, prudent.

julepe, 'hŭlě'pě, sm. julap.   [prudent.

julio, *hŏ'lēŏ*, sm. July (month).

jumenta, *hămĕn'tă*, sf. female ass.

jumento, *–tŏ*, sm. beast of burden; ass; stupid person. [Chinese ship].

junco, *hŭn'kŏ*, sm. (bot.) rush; junk (small

juncoso, sa, *hŭnkō'sŏ*, a. full of rushes.

junio, *hŏ'nĭŏ*, sm. June (month).

junta, *hŭn'tă*, sf. congress, assembly, council, meeting. [same time.

juntamente, *–mĕn'tĕ*, ad. jointly; at the

juntar, *hŭntăr'*, v. a. to join, to unite; –se, to meet, to assemble; to be closely united.

junto, *hŭn'tŏ*, ad. near, close to; (de) por –, by the bulk, in the lump.

juntura, *hŭntō'ră*, sf. juncture; joint.

Júpiter, *hŏ'pĭtĕr*, sm. Jupiter (planet); (chem.) tin.

jura, *hŏ'ră*, sf. oath of allegiance.

jurado, ra, *hŏră'dŏ*, sm. jury; juror, jury-man; jurat.

jurador, ra, *–dŏr'*, sm. & f. swearer.

juramentar, *–mĕntăr'*, v. a. to swear; –se, to bind oneself by an oath.

juramento, *–mĕn'tŏ*, sm. oath.

jurar, *hŏrăr'*, v. a. to swear, to make oath; to curse.

jurídico, ca, *hŏrē'dĭkŏ*, a. lawful, legal, juridical; done according to law.

jurisconsulto, *hŏrĭskŏnsŏl'tŏ*, sm. lawyer, jurist. [legal authority.

jurisdicción, *–dĭkthĭŏn'*, sf. jurisdiction.

jurisperito, *–pĕrē'tŏ*, sm. professor of jurisprudence. [prudence.

jurisprudencia, *–prŏdĕn'thĭă*, sf. juris-

jurista, *hŏrĭs'tă*, sm. jurist, lawyer.

juro, *hŏ'rŏ*, sm. right of perpetual pro-perty; de –, certainly.

justa, *hŏs'tă*, sf. joust, tilt, tournament.

justamente, *–mĕn'tĕ*, ad. justly, just.

justicia, *hŏstē'thĭă*, sf. justice; equity.

justiciero, ra, *hŏstĭthĭĕ'rŏ*, sm. & f. ad-ministrator of justice.

justificación, *–fĭkăthĭŏn'*, sf. justifica-tion; adjustment of lines of type.

justificado, da, *–fĭkă'dŏ*, a. equal, justi-fied; conformable to justice.

justificar, *–fĭkăr'*, v. a. to justify; to ad-just lines of type. [ficatory.

justificativo, va, *–fĭkătē'vŏ*, a. a justi-

justillo, *hŏstĭl'yŏ*, sm. sleeveless jacket.

justipreciar, *hŏstĭprĕthĭăr'*, v. a. to estimate anything.

justo, ta, *hŏs'tă*, a. just; lawful; honour-able; –, sm. just and pious man; al –, ad. fitly, duly; punctually.

juvenil, *hŏvĕnēl'*, a. juvenile, youthful.

juventud, *hŏvĕntŭd'*, sf. youthfulness, youth. [cature.

juzgado, *hŏthgă'dŏ*, sm. tribunal; judi-

juzgar, *hŏthgăr'*, v. a. & n. to judge.

K.

kaleidoscopio, *kălēĭdŏskŏ'pĭŏ*, sm. kalei-doscope.

kan, *kăn*, sm. Khan, Khane, oriental prince; call-house for journeymen in the Orient. [ingredients of china.

kaolin, *kăŏlēn'*, sm. kaolin, one of the two

kepis, *kĕ'pĭs*, sm. military cap.

kermes, *kĕr'mĕs*, sm. church-ale, annual fair, fairing.

kilogramo, *kĭlŏgră'mŏ*, sm. kilogram.

kilómetro, *kĭlŏ'mĕtrŏ*, sm. kilometre.

kiosco, *kĭŏs'kŏ*, sm. kiosk. [brandy.

kirs, *kĭrs*, kirsváser, *–ăăs'ĕr*, sm. cherry-

L.

la, *lă*, art. f. the.

laberinto, *lăbĕrēn'tŏ*, sm. labyrinth.

labia, *lă'bĭă*, sf. (fam.) winning eloquence.

labio, *lă'bĭŏ*, sm. lip; edge of anything.

labor, *lăbŏr'*, sf. labour, task; needle-work; husbandry, tillage.

laboratorio, *lăbŏrătŏ'rĭŏ*, sm. laboratory.

laboriosidad, *lăbŏrĭŏsĭdăd'*, sf. laborious-ness, assidulty.

laborioso, sa, *lăbŏrĭŏ'sŏ*, a. laborious.

labrado, da, *lăbră'dŏ*, a. worked (applied to figured cloth); –, sm. cultivated land.

labrador, ra, *–dŏr'*, sm. & f. labourer; cultivator, farmer; peasant.

labrantío, tía, *lăbrăntē'ŏ*, a. arable.

labranza, *lăbrăn'thă*, sf. tillage; hus-bandry; tilled land.

labrar, *lăbrăr'*, v. a. to work; to labour; to cultivate the ground; to build.

labriego, *lăbrĭĕ'gŏ*, sm. peasant.

lacayo, *lăkă'yŏ*, sm. lackey, foot-man.

lacerar, *lăthĕrăr'*, v. a. to tear to pieces, to lacerate. [wretchedness.

lacería, *lăthĕrē'ă*, sf. misery, poverty.

lacio, cia, *lă'thĭŏ*, a. faded, withered; languid. [cise.

lacónico, ca, *lăkŏ'nĭkŏ*, a. laconic, con-

laconismo, *lăkŏnĭs'mŏ*, sm. laconism.

lacra, *lă'kră*, sf. mark left by a wound; fault, vice. [to damage financially.

lacrar, *lăkrăr'*, v. a. to injure one's health; [suck.

lacre, *lă'krĕ*, sm. sealing-wax. [giving

lactancia, *lăktăn'thĭă*, sf. time of

lacticinio, *lăktĭthē'nĭŏ*, sm. milk-pottage.

ladear, *lădĕăr'*, v. a. to move to one side; to incline; –, v. n. to incline to one side; –se, to incline to an opinion or party.

ladera, *lădĕ'ră*, sf. declivity.

ladilla, *lădĭl'yă*, sf. crablouse. [crafty.

ladino, na, *lădē'nŏ*, a. sagacious, cunning,

lado, *lă'dŏ*, sm. side; party; companion; ¡á un –! clear the way!

ladrar, *lădrăr'*, v. n. to bark. [tion.

ladrido, *lădrē'dŏ*, sm. barking; vocifera-

ladrillal, *lădrĭlyăl'*, ladrillar, *–yăr'*, sm. brick-kiln.

ladrillo, *lădrĭl'yŏ*, sm. brick. [wayman.

ladrón, *lădrŏn'*, sm. thief, robber, high-

ladronera, *–nĕ'ră*, sf. den of robbers.

ladronicio, *–nē'thĭŏ*, sm. larceny, theft, robbery. [ness.

lagaña, *lăgăn'yă*, sf. lippitude, bleared-

lagañoso, sa, _-yŏ' sŏ,_ a. blear-eyed.
lagar, _lăgăr',_ v. a. press-house; wine-press.
lagarero, _lăgărŏ'rŏ,_ sm. wine-presser; one employed in olive-pressing.
lagartija, _lăgărtî'h'ă,_ sf. eft, newt.
lagarto, _lăgăr'tŏ,_ sm. lizard; sly artful person, [of lions.
lago, _lă'gŏ,_ sm, lake; - de leones, den
lágrima, _lă'grîmă,_ sf. tear.
lagrimal, _lăgrîmăl',_ sm. lachrymary bag.
lagrimoso, sa, _-mŏ'sŏ,_ a. weeping, shedding tears, [ficiency.
laguna, _lăgŏ'nă,_ sf. lake; lagoon; de-
lagunoso, sa, _lăgŏnŏ'sŏ,_ a. marshy, fenny.
laical, _lăîkăl',_ a. lay, laical. [country.
lama, _lă'mă,_ sf. mud, slime, ooze; flat even
lamedor, ra, _lămĕdŏr',_ sm. & f. licker; loch (medicine); enticement, allurement.
lamedura, _lămĕdŏ'ră,_ sf. act of licking.
lamentable, _lămĕntă'blĕ,_ a. lamentable, deplorable, pitiable.
lamentación, _-tăthŏn',_ sf. lamentation.
lamentar, _-tăr',_ v. a. to lament, to bewail; -, v. n., -se, to lament, to complain, to cry.
lamento, _lămĕn'tŏ,_ sm. lamentation.
lamer, _lămĕr',_ v. a. to lick, to lap.
lámina, _lă'mînă,_ sf. plate, sheet of metal; copper-plate, engraving, print.
lámpara, _lăm'pără,_ sf. lamp.
lamparero, _-părŏ'rŏ,_ sm. lamp-lighter.
lamparilla, _-părî'l'yă,_ sf. night-light.
lamparón, _-părŏn',_ sm. king's evil.
lampiño, ña, _-pîn'yŏ,_ a. beardless.
lampión, _lămpîŏn',_ sm. large lantern.
lamprea, _lămprŏ'ă,_ sf. lamprey (fish).
lana, _lă'nă,_ sf. wool.
lanar, _lănăr',_ a. woolly.
lance, _lăn'thĕ,_ sm. cast, throw; favourable opportunity; chance, hap-hazard; sudden quarrel; - de teatro, clap-trap.
lancear, _lănthĕăr',_ v. a. to wound with a lance.
lancero, _lănthĕ'rŏ,_ sm. pikeman, lancer.
lanceta, _lănthĕ'tă,_ sf. lancet. [lancet.
lancetada, _-tă'dă,_ sf. lancing, cut of a
lancha, _lăn'tshă,_ sf. barge, lighter; launch.
lanchón, _lăntshŏn',_ sm. (mar.) lighter.
langosta, _lăngŏs'tă,_ sf. locust; lobster; sharper, swindler.
langostin, _lăngŏstîn',_ sm. small locust.
languidez, _lăngîdĕth',_ sf. languidness.
lánguido, da, _lăn'gîdŏ,_ a. languid, faint, weak; langorous, languishing.
lanudo, da, _lănŏ'dŏ,_ a. woolly, fleecy.
lanza, _lăn'thă,_ sf. lance, spear; pole of a coach; -s, pl. duty paid by the nobility of the realm (in lieu of military services).
lanzada, _-thă'dă,_ sf. stroke with a lance.
lanzadera, _-dā'ră,_ sf. shuttle.
lanzar, _lănthăr',_ v. a. to throw, to dart, to launch, to fling; (law) to eject.
lapicero, _lăpîthĕ'rŏ,_ sm. metal pencil-case.
lápida, _lă'pîdă,_ sf. flat stone, on which inscriptions are engraved [dary.
lapidario, _lăpîdă'rîŏ,_ sm. -, ria, a. lapi-
lápiz, _lă'pîth,_ sm. lead-pencil; black chalk used in drawing; black lead.

lapizar, _lăpîthăr',_ v. a. to pencil.
lardar, _lărdăr',_ v. a. to baste; to beat with a stick.
lardoso, sa, _lărdŏ'sŏ,_ a. greasy, fatty.
lares, _lă'rĕs,_ sm. pl. household-gods of the ancient Romans; home.
larga, _lăr'gă,_ sf. delay, adjournment.
largamente, _-mĕn'tĕ,_ ad. for a long time.
largar, _lărgăr',_ v. a. to loosen, to slacken; to let go; -se, to set sail.
largo, ga, _lăr'gŏ,_ a. long; large, generous, liberal; copious; á la -a, at length, extensively; -, ad. largely, profusely.
largueza, _lărgŏ'thă,_ sf. length, largeness; liberality, generosity.
largura, _lărgŏ'ră,_ sf. length, longitude.
lascivia, _lăsthĕ'vîă,_ sf. lasciviousness; lewdness.
lascivo, ya, _-vŏ,_ a. lascivious; lewd.
lasitud, _lăsîtŏd',_ sf. lassitude, weariness.
lástima, _lăs'tîmă,_ sf. compassion, pity; object of pity.
lastimar, _lăstîmăr',_ v. a. to hurt; to wound; to move to compassion; -se, to be moved to compassion; to grieve.
lastimero, ra, _-mă'rŏ,_ a. sad, mournful; lamentable. [mournful.
lastimoso, sa, _-mŏ'sŏ,_ a. grievous, grievous.
lastrar, _lăstrăr',_ v. a. to ballast a ship.
lastre, _lăs'trĕ,_ sm. ballast; motive.
lateral, _lătĕrăl',_ a. lateral.
latido, _lătî'dŏ,_ sm. pant, palpitation.
latigazo, _lătîgă'thŏ,_ sm. lash, crack of a whip.
látigo, _lă'tîgŏ,_ sm. thong of a whip.
latin, _lătîn',_ sm. Latin tongue.
latinajo, _lătînă'h'ŏ,_ sm. Latin jargon.
latinidad, _lătînîdăd',_ sf. Latinity, Latin tongue.
latinizar, _-thăr',_ v. a. to latinize.
latino, na, _lătî'nŏ,_ a. Latin.
latir, _lătîr',_ v. n. to palpitate. [tude.
latitud, _lătîtŏd',_ sf. breadth; width; lati-
lato, ta, _lă'tŏ,_ a. ample, large, diffuse, extensive.
latón, _lătŏn',_ sm. brass, latten.
latonero, _lătŏnŏ'rŏ,_ sm. brazier.
latria, _lătrî'ă,_ sf. worship, adoration due to God only. [theft, robbery.
latrocinio, _lătrŏthî'nîŏ,_ sm. larceny,
laud, _lăăd',_ sf. lute (musical instrument).
laudable, _lăădă'blĕ,_ a. laudable, praiseworthy.
láudano, _lă'ădănŏ,_ sm. laudanum.
laude, _lă'ădĕ,_ sf. tombstone with an epitaph engraved on it; -s, pl. Lauds.
laurear, _lăărĕăr',_ v. [a. to crown with laurel; to graduate; (fig.) to reward.
laurel, _lăărĕl',_ sm. (bot.) laurel; laurel-crown as a reward.
lauréola, _lăărŏ'ŏlă,_ sf. crown of laurel.
lavacaras, _lăvăkă'răs,_ sm. (fig. & fam.) mean flatterer. [laundry.
lavadero, _-dĕ'rŏ,_ sm. washing-place;
lavadura, _-dŏ'ră,_ sf. wash, washing.
lavamanos, _-mă'nŏs,_ sm. washing-stand (in a sacristy).
lavandera, _lăvăndă'ră,_ sf. laundress.

lavar, *lăvăr'*, v. a. to wash; to whitewash.

lavativa, *lăvătē'vă*, sf. clyster.

lavatorio, *-tō'rĭŏ*, sm. act of washing; medicinal lotion; ceremony of washing the feet on Holy Thursday.

laxante, *lăksăn'tĕ*, sm. (med.) laxative.

laxar, *lăksăr'*, v. a. to loosen, to soften.

laxitud, *lăksĭtŭd'*, sf. laxity; laxness; weariness.

laxo, xą, *lăk'sŏ*, a. lax, slack; (fig.) vague.

layar, *lăyăr'*, v. a. to turn up the ground with a two-pronged instrument.

lazada, *lăthă'dă*, sf. running knot.

lazareto, *-rā'tŏ*, sm. lazaretto, lazaret.

lazarillo, *-rĭl'yŏ*, sm. boy who guides a blind man; [tie; bond.

lazo, *lă'thŏ*, sm. slip-knot; snare, trick;

le, *lĕ*, pn. him, her; and dative of the feminine ella, she.

leal, *lĕăl'*, a. loyal; faithful.

lealtad, *lĕăltăd'*, sf. loyalty.

lebrel, *lĕbrĕl'*, sm. greyhound. [pan.

lebrillo, *lĕbrĭl'yŏ*, sm. glazed earthen-ware

lección, *lĕkthĭŏn'*, sf. reading; lesson; lecture; lection.

lector, *lĕktŏr'*, sm. reader, lecturer.

lectoría, *lĕktŏrē'ă*, sf. lectureship.

lectura, *lĕktŏ'ră*, sf. reading, lecture.

leche, *lĕtsh'ĕ*, sf. milk. [maid.

lechera, *lĕtshā'ră*, sf. milkwoman, dairy-

lechería, *-rē'ă*, sf. cow-house, dairy.

lecho, *lĕtsh'ŏ*, sm. bed; litter. [fellow.

lechón, *lĕtshŏn'*, sm. sucking pig; dirty

lechuga, *lĕtshō'gă*, sf. lettuce.

lechugado, da, *-gă'dŏ*, a. having leaves like lettuce. [lettuces.

lechuguino, *-gē'nŏ*, sm. bed of small

lechuza, *lĕtshō'thă*, sf. owl.

leer, *lĕĕr'*, v. a. to read; to lecture.

lega, *lā'gă*, sf. lay-sister.

legacía, *lĕgăthē'ă*, sf. embassy, legation.

legado, *lĕgă'dŏ*, sm. deputy; legate; legacy.

legajo, *lĕgă'h'ŏ*, sm. bundle of loose papers tied together.

legal, *lĕgăl'*, a. legal; loyal, faithful.

legalidad, *lĕgălĭdăd'*, sf. legality, fidelity.

legalización, *lĕgălĭthăthĭŏn'*, sf. legalization.

legalizar, *-thăr'*, v. a. to legalize.

legar, *lĕgăr'*, v. a. to depute; to bequeath.

legatario, *lĕgătă'rĭŏ*, sm. legatee.

legible, *lĕhē'blĕ*, a. legible.

legión, *lĕhĭŏn'*, sf. legion.

legionario, ria, *-nă'rĭŏ*, a. legionary.

legislación, *lĕhĭslăthĭŏn'*, sf. legislation.

legislador, *-dŏr'*, sm. legislator, lawgiver.

legislar, *lĕhĭslăr'*, v. a. to legislate.

legislativo, va, *-lătē'vŏ*, a. legislative, lawgiving.

legislatura, *-tō'ră*, sf. legislature.

legista, *lĕhĭs'tă*, sm. legist.

legítima, *lĕhē'tĭmă*, sf. (law) legitimate portion of the paternal or maternal estate.

legitimación, *-măthĭŏn'*, sf. legitimation.

legitimar, *-măr'*, v. a. to legitimate.

legitimidad, *-mĭdăd'*, sf. legitimacy.

legítimo, ma, *lĕhē'tĭmŏ*, a. legitimate, lawful.

lego, *lā'gŏ*, sm. lay-brother.

legua, *lā'gŭă*, sf. league. [stuff.

legumbre, *lĕgŭm'brĕ*, sf. pot-herbs, garden-

leído, da, *lĕē'dŏ*, a. well-read.

lejano, na, *lĕhă'nŏ*, a. distant, remote, far.

lejía, *lĕhē'ă*, sf. lie, lye.

lejos, *lĕh'ŏs*, ad. at a great distance, far off; -, sm. perspective, distant prospect.

lelo, la, *lĕ'lŏ*, a. stupid, ignorant.

lema, *lā'mă*, sm. argument of a poem explained in the title; lemma.

lencería, *lĕnthĕrē'ă*, sf. sortment of linen of different sorts; linen-draper's shop.

lendroso, sa, *lĕndrŏ'sŏ*, a. lousy, nitty.

lengua, *lĕn'gŭă*, sf. tongue; language, tongue.

lenguaje, *-gŭă'h'ĕ*, sm. language.

lenidad, *lĕnĭdăd'*, sf. lenity, mildness.

lenitivo, va, *-tē'vŏ*, a. lenient, mitigant; -, sm. emollient.

lente, *lĕn'tĕ*, sm. & f. lens. [lentil.

lenteja, *lĕntē'h'ă*, sf. (bot.) lentil.

lentitud, *lĕntĭtŭd'*, sf. slowness.

lento, ta, *lĕn'tŏ*, a. slow, tardy, lazy.

leña, *lĕn'yă*, sf. wood, timber. [cutter.

leñador, *-yădŏr'*, sm. woodman, wood-

leñera, *-yă'ră*, sf. place for fire-wood.

leñero, *-yă'rŏ*, sm. timber-merchant.

leño, *lĕn'yŏ*, sm. block, log; trunk of a tree.

leñoso, sa, *-yŏ'sŏ*, a. woody. [tree.

Leo, *lā'ŏ*, Leo (sign of the zodiac).

león, *lĕŏn'*, sm. lion; beau, masher, dandy.

leona, *lĕŏ'nă*, sf. lioness.

leonado, da, *-nă'dŏ*, a. lion-coloured, tawny; fallow.

leonera, *-nă'ră*, sf. lion-cage.

leonero, *-nă'rŏ*, sm. keeper of lions.

leopardo, *-păr'dŏ*, sm. leopard.

lepra, *lā'pră*, sf. leprosy.

leproso, sa, *lĕprŏ'sŏ*, a. leprous.

lerdo, da, *lĕr'dŏ*, a. slow, heavy; dull of comprehension. [injury.

lesión, *lĕsĭŏn'*, sf. hurt, damage, wound;

lesna, *lĕs'nă*, sf. awl.

letal, *lĕtăl'*, a. mortal, deadly.

letanía, *lĕtănē'ă*, sf. litany; -s, pl. supplicatory processions.

letárgico, ca, *lĕtăr'hĭkŏ*, a. lethargic.

letargo, *lĕtăr'gŏ*, sm. lethargy.

letra, *lĕt'ră*, sf. letter; handwriting; printing-type; words of a song; bill of exchange; -s, pl. letters, learning.

letrado, da, *-ră'dŏ*, a. learned, lettered; -, sm. lawyer; professor of law.

letrero, *lĕtrā'rŏ*, sm. inscription.

letrilla, *lĕtrĭl'yă*, sf. short poem, generally written to be sung to music.

letrina, *lĕtrē'nă*, sf. privy, W.C.

leva, *lā'vă*, sf. act of weighing anchor; (mil.) levy; (mar.) press.

levadizo, za, *lĕvădē'thŏ*, a. that can be lifted or raised; puente -, draw-bridge.

levantamiento, *lĕvăntămĭĕn'tŏ*, sm. elevation; insurrection.

levantar, *-tăr'*, v. a. to raise, to lift up; to heave; to build up; to impute falsely; to elevate, to promote; -se, to rise; to get up from bed; to stand up; to start.

levante, *-tĕ*, sm. Levant; east; east-wind.

leve, *lā'vĕ*, a. light; trifling.

levita, *lěvĭ'tă*, sm. levite; —, sf. great-coat, frock-coat.

Levítico, *lěvĭ'tĭkŏ*, sm. book of Leviticus.

ley, *lā'ĭ*, sf. law; loyalty; —es, pl. collection of laws.

leyenda, *lěyěn'dă*, sf. reading, lecture.

lía, *lě'ă*, sf. thin bass-rope.

liar, *lĭăr'*, v. a. to tie, to bind, to fagot.

libación, *lĭbăthĭŏn'*, sf. libation.

libelo, *lĭbě'lŏ*, sm. petition; written charge against a prisoner; lampoon, libel.

liberal, *lĭběrăl'*, a. liberal, generous.

liberalidad, *—lĭdăd'*, sf. liberality, generosity.   [independence; freeness.

libertad, *lĭběrtăd'*, sf. liberty, freedom;

libertador, **ra**, *—tă'dŏr*, sm. & f. deliverer, liberator.

libertar, *—tăr'*, v. a. to free, to set at liberty; to exempt, to clear from an obligation *or* debt.   [licentiousness.

libertinaje, *—tĭnă'h'ĕ*, sm. libertinism,

libertino, **na**, *—tě'nŏ*, sm. & f. dissolute, licentious, lewd.

liberto, *lĭběr'tŏ*, sm. freed man.

líbitum, *lě'bĭtŭm*, (ad —), ad at will.

libra, *lě'bră*, sf. pound; — carnicera, flesh-pound of thirty-six ounces; — esterlina, a pound sterling.

Libra, —, sf. Libra, Balance (sign of the zodiac).

librar, *lĭbrăr'*, v. a. to free, to deliver; to give an order for paying a certain sum; to dispatch, to expedite; — bien *ó* mal, to get over a thing well *or* ill; —se, to escape.

libre, *lě'brě*, a, free; exempt; innocent.

librea, *lĭbrě'ă*, sf. livery.

librejo, *lĭbrě'h'ŏ*, sm. little book, pamphlet.

libremente, *lĭbrěměn'tě*, ad. freely; boldly; audaciously, impudently.

librería, *—rě'ă*, sf. book-seller's shop; library; — de alquiler, circulating-library.   [lero, stationer.

librero, *lĭbrě'rŏ*, sm. book-seller; — pape-

libreta, *lĭbrě'tă*, sf. loaf of bread which weighs sixteen ounces; small memorandum-book.   [memorandum-book.

libro, *lě'brŏ*, sm. book; — de memoria,

licencia, *lĭthěn'thĭă*, sf. permission, license; licentiousness.

licenciado, *—thĭă'dŏ*, sm. licentiate.

licenciamiento, *—thĭămĭěn'tŏ*, sm. taking of the degree of licentiate.

licenciar, *—thĭăr'*, v. a. to permit, to allow; to license.   [dissolute.

licencioso, **sa**, *—thĭŏ'sŏ*, a. licentious,

liceo, *lĭthě'ŏ*, sm. lyceum.   [licitly.

lícitamente, *lě'thĭtămĕntě*, ad. lawfully,

lícito, **ta**, *lě'thĭtŏ*, a. lawful, licit.

licor, *lĭkŏr'*, sm. liquor.

lid, *lĭd*, sm. contest, fight; dispute.

lidiador, *lĭdĭădŏr'*, sm. combatant.

liebre, *lĭě'brě*, sf. hare.

liendre, *lĭěn'drě*, sf. louse, nit.

lienzo, *lĭěn'thŏ*, sf. linen; face *or* front of building.   [coalition; alloy.

liga, *lě'yă*, sf. garter; bird-lime; league,

ligadura, *lĭgădŏ'ră*, sf. ligature, binding.

ligar, *lĭgăr'*, v. a. to tie, to bind, to fasten; to allay; to confederate; —se, to league; to be allied; to bind oneself to the performance of a contract.

ligazón, *—thŏn'*, sf. union, connection.

ligereza, *lĭ'hěrě'thă*, sf. lightness; levity.

ligero, **ra**, *lĭ'hă'rŏ*, a. light, swift, easy.

lija, *lĭ'h'ă*, sf. angel-fish; fish-skin.

lijar, *lĭ'hăr'*, v. a. to smooth, to polish.

lila, *lě'lă*, sf. lilac-tree; lilac-flower; came-

lima, *lě'mă*, sf. file.   [lot of Lisle.

limadura, *lĭmădŏ'ră*, sf. filing.

limar, *lĭmăr'*, v. a. to file; to polish.

limbo, *lĭm'bŏ*, sm. limbo (a region assigned to the departed souls of children).

limitación, *lĭmĭtăthĭŏn'*, sf. limitation, restriction.

limitado, **da**, *—tă'dŏ*, a. limited.

limitar, *—tăr'*, v. a. to limit; to restrain.

límite, *lě'mĭtě*, sm. limit, boundary.

limítrofe, *lĭmě'trŏfě*, a. limiting, border-

limo, *lě'mŏ*, sm. slime, mud.   [ing.

limón, *lĭmŏn'*, sm. lemon.

limonada, *lĭmŏnă'dă*, sf. lemonade.

limonar, *—năr'*, sm. plantation of lime-trees.

limosna, *lĭmŏ'snă*, sf. alms, charity.

limosnero, *lĭmŏsně'rŏ*, sm. almoner; —, ra, a. charitable.   [pick.

limpiadientes, *lĭmpĭădĭěn'tĕs*, sm. tooth-

limpiador, *—dŏr'*, sm. cleanser, scourer.

limpiar, *lĭmpĭăr'*, v. a. to scour, to cleanse, to clear, to purify.

limpieza, *lĭmpĭě'thă*, sf. cleanliness, neatness; chastity; integrity; purity of blood.

limpio, **pia**, *lĭm'pĭŏ*, a. clean; limpid, neat; pure.

limpión, *lĭmpĭŏn'*, sm. cleansing, cleaning.

linaje, *lĭnă'h'ě*, sm. lineage, race, descent.

linar, *lĭnăr'*, sm. flax-field.

linaza, *lĭnă'thă*, sf. linseed.

lince, *lĭn'thě*, sm. lynx.

lindar, *lĭndăr'*, v. n. to be contiguous.

linde, *lĭn'dě*, sm. landmark, boundary.

lindero, *lĭndě'rŏ*, sm. landmark, boundary.

lindeza, *lĭndě'thă*, sf. neatness, elegance.

lindo, **da**, *lĭn'dŏ*, a. neat, handsome, pretty.

línea, *lě'něă*, sf. line; boundary, limit.

lineal, *lĭněăl'*, a. lineal.

linear, *lĭněăr'*, v. a. to draw lines.

linfa, *lĭn'fă*, sf. lymph.

linfático, **ca**, *lĭnfă'tĭkŏ*, a. lymphatic.

lino, *lě'nŏ*, sm. flax.

linterna, *lĭntěr'nă*, sf. lantern.

lío, *lě'ŏ*, sm. bundle, parcel.

liquidación, *lĭkĭădthĭŏn'*, sf. liquidation.

liquidar, *lĭkĭdăr'*, v.a. to liquefy, to melt; to clear accounts.

líquido, **da**, *lě'kĭdŏ*, a. liquid.

lira, *lě'ră*, sf. lyre.

lirio, *lě'rĭŏ*, sm. (bot.) iris.

lis, *lĭs*, sf. fleur-de-lis.

lisiar, *lĭsĭăr'*, v. a. to lame; to hurt a limb.

liso, **sa**, *lě'sŏ*, a. plain, even, flat, smooth.

lisonja, *lĭsŏn'h'ă*, sf. adulation, flattery.

lisonjear, -'hĕăr', v. a. to flatter.
lisonjero, -'hă'rŏ, sm. mean flatterer;
—, ra, a. fawning; flattering; pleasing.
lista, lĭs'tă, sf. slip of paper, shred of
linen; list, catalogue; — grande, list of
drawers in a lottery; en —, en — de
correos, "Post-office," "to be kept till
called for" (address for letters where the
private address is unknown).
listo, ta, lĭs'tŏ, a. ready, prompt, active.
listón, lĭstŏn', sm. large shred; ferret
(narrow silk riband).   [candour.
lisura, lĭsŏ'ră, sf. smoothness; sincerity,
litera, lĭtĕ'ră, sf. litter.
literal, lĭtĕrăl', a. literal.
literario, ria, lĭtĕră'rĭŏ, a. literary.
literato, ta, lĭtĕră'tŏ, a. learned, lettered;
—, sm. literary man; —s, pl. literati, the
learned.
literatura, lĭtĕrătŏ'ră, sf. literature.
litigante, lĭtĭgăn'tĕ, sm. litigant.
litigar, -găr', v. a. to litigate, to carry on
litigio, lĭtĭ'h'ĭŏ, sm. law-suit.   [a cause.
litigioso, sa, lĭtĭ'hĭŏ'sŏ, a. litigious.
litografía, lĭtŏgră'fĭă, sf. lithography.
litográfico, ca, -gră'fĭkŏ, a. lithographic.
litografiar, -grĭăr', v. a. to lithograph.
litógrafo, lĭtŏ'gră'fŏ, sm. lithographer.
litoral, lĭtŏrăl', a. littoral.
litro, lĭ'trŏ, sm. litre (measure).
liturgia, lĭtŏr'hĭă, sf. liturgy.
litúrgico, ca, lĭtŏr'hĭkŏ, a. liturgical.
liviandad, lĭvĭăndăd', sf. lightness;
levity, imprudence; incontinence.
liviano, na, lĭvĭă'nŏ, a. light; imprudent;
unchaste; —s, sm. pl. lungs.
lívido, dá, lĭ'vĭdŏ, a. livid.
lo, lŏ, pn. it; —, art. neutr. the.
loable, lŏă'blĕ, a. laudable.
loar, lŏăr', v. a. to praise; to approve.
loba, lŏ'bă, sf. she-wolf.
lobanillo, lŏbănĭl'yŏ, sm. wen, chafe.
lobato, lŏbă'tŏ, sm. young wolf.
lobo, lŏ'bŏ, sm. wolf.   [sad.
lóbrego, ga, lŏ'brĕgŏ, a. murky, obscure,
lobreguez, lŏbrĕgĕth', sf. obscurity, dark-
lobuno, na, lŏbŏ'nŏ, a. wolfish.   [ness.
local, lŏkăl', a. local.
localidad, lŏkălĭdăd', sf. locality.
localizar, -thăr', v. a. to localize.
loco, ca, lŏ'kŏ, a. mad, crack-brained.
locuacidad, lŏkŏăthĭdăd', sf. loquacity.
locuaz, lŏkŏăth', a. loquacious, garrulous.
locución, lŏkŏthĭŏn', sf. locution.
locura, lŏkŏ'ră, sf. madness, frenzy, folly;
absurdity.
locutorio, lŏkŭtŏ'rĭŏ, sm. parlour.
lodazal, lŏdăthăl', sm. muddy place.
lodo, lŏ'dŏ, sm. mud, mire.
lodoso, sa, lŏdŏ'sŏ, a. muddy, miry; lu-
tulent; lutarious.
logaritmo, lŏgărĭt'mŏ, sm. logarithm.
lógica, lŏ'hĭkă, sf. logic.   [logician.
lógico, ca, lŏ'hĭkŏ, a. logical; —, sm.
lograr, lŏgrăr', v. a. to gain, to obtain.
logrear, lŏgrĕăr', v. n. to lend on interest.
logrero, lŏgrĕ'rŏ, sm. usurer.

logro, lŏ'grŏ, sm. gain, benefit; interest;
loma, lŏ'mă, sf. hillock.   [usury.
lombarda, lŏmbăr'dă, sf. red cabbage.
lombriz, lŏmbrĭth', sf. dew-worm.
lomillo, lŏmĭl'yŏ, sm. small loin; cross-
stitch (needle-work).
lomo, lŏ'mŏ, sm. loin; back of a book;
double of any cloth; ridge between two
furrows; llevar ó traer —, to carry on
lona, lŏ'nă, sf. canvas.   [the back.
lóndiga, lŏn'dĭgă, sf. lark.
longanimidad, lŏngănĭmĭdăd', sf. long-
sufferance, patience.   [(best kind).
longaniza, -nĕ'thă, sf. German sausage
longitud, lŏn'hĭtŭd', sf. length; longitude.
lonja, lŏn'hă, sf. exchange; grocer's shop;
warehouse; slice of ham.
lonjista, lŏn'hĭs'tă, sm. grocer who sells
cocoa-nuts, spices, &c.
loor, lŏŏr', sf. (poet.) praise.
loquear, lŏkĕăr', v. n. to play the fool; to
rejoice, to revel.   [house.
loquero, lŏkĕ'rŏ, sm. keeper of a mad-
loro, lŏ'rŏ, sm. parrot.
lorri, lŏr'rĭ, sm. (rail.) lowry.
losa, lŏ'să, sf. flag-stone.
lote, lŏ'tĕ, sm. lot.
lotería, lŏtĕrĭ'ă, sf. lottery.
loza, lŏ'thă, sf. delft, crockery.
lozanear, lŏthănĕăr', v. n. to act and
speak in a pompous, ostentatious fashion.
lozanía, -nĕ'ă, sf. verdure, exuberant
growth of plants; vigour; vivacity.
lozano, na, lŏthă'nŏ, a. luxuriant; sprightly.
lucero, lŏthĕ'rŏ, sm. morning-star, day-star.
lúcido, da, lŏ'thĭdŏ, a. shining, magnificent, splendid.
luciérnaga, lŏthĕr'năgă, sf. glow-worm.
lucimiento, lŏthĭmĭĕn'tŏ, sm. splendour,
lustre, applause; brightness.
lucio, cia, lŏ'thĭŏ, a. lucid, bright.
lucir, lŏthĭr', v. n., -se, to shine, to be
brilliant; to dress to advantage; to outshine.
lucrativo, va, lŏkrătĭ'vŏ, a. lucrative.
lucro, lŏ'krŏ, sm. gain, profit, lucre.
lucha, lŏtch'ă, sf. struggle, strife.
luchador, lŏtchădŏr', sm. wrestler.
luchar, lŏtchăr', v. a. to wrestle, to struggle.
ludibrio, lŏdĕ'brĭŏ, sm. mockery, derision.
luego, lŏĕ'gŏ, ad. presently, immediately;
soon afterwards.
lugar, lŏgăr', sm. place, spot; village;
employment, office; dignity; cause; motive; en — de, instead of, in lieu of.
lugareño, ña, lŏgărĕn'yŏ, a. & sm. & f.
belonging to a village; inhabitant of a
village.   [tenant.
lugarteniente, lŏgărtĕnĭĕn'tĕ, sm. lieu-
lúgubre, lŏ'gŏbrĕ, a. sad, gloomy; lugubrious, dismal.   [dresses, fare.
lujo, lŏ'hŏ, sm. profuseness in pomp,
lujoso, sa, lŏ'hŏ'sŏ, a. showy, profuse,
lavish, sumptuous.
lujuria, lŏ'hŏ'rĭă, sf. lewdness; luxury.
lujurioso, sa, -rĭŏ'sŏ, a. luxurious, voluptuous, lewd.

lumbre, *lŭm'brĕ*, sf. fire; spark. [light.
lumbrera, *lŭmbrā'rä*, sf. luminary; sky-
uminaria, *lŭmīnā'rĭä*, sf. illumination;
perpetual lamp in catholic churches.
luminoso, sa, *–nō'sŏ*, a. luminous, lucid.
luna, *lŏ'nä*, sf. moon; glass plate for mir-
rors. [–, a. lunar.
lunar, *lŭnär'*, sm. mole; stain of infamy;
lunático, ca, *lŭnä'tĭkŏ*, à. lunatic, moon-
lunes, *lŏ'nĕs*, sm. Monday. [struck.
luneta, *lŭnā'tä*, sf. stall (in a play-house);
eye-glass.
lupanar, *lŭpänär'*, sm. brothel.
lupia, *lŏ'pĭä*, sf. encysted tumour.
lustre, *lŭs'trĕ*, sm. gloss, lustre; splendour.
lustro, *lŭs'trŏ*, sm. lustrum (space of five
years).
lustroso, sa, *lŭstrŏ'sŏ*, a. bright, brilliant.
luteranismo, *lŭtĕränĭs'mŏ*, sm. Luther-
anism.
luterano, na, *–rä'nŏ*, sm. & f. Lutheran.
luto, *lŏ'tŏ*, sm. mourning (dress).
luz, *lŭth'*, sf. light; candle; day; notice,
information, hint; luces, pl., windows;
lanterns; knowledge, science.

Ll.

llaga, *lyä'gä*, sf. wound, sore.
llagar, *lyägär'*, v. a. to wound, to hurt.
llama, *lyä'mä*, sf. flame; lama (animal).
llamada, *lyämä'dä*, sf. call; (mil.) beat
of the drum to summon troops; (mil.)
chamade.
llamador, *lyämädŏr'*, sm. door-knocker.
llamamiento, *–mĭĕn'tŏ*, sm. calling; convocation.
llamar, *lyämär'*, v. a. to call; to summon,
to cite; to invoke; to knock at the door.
llamarada, *–rä'dä*, sf. sudden blaze of
fire; sudden burst of merriment.
llana, *lyä'nä*, sf. trowel; page (of a book, &c.).
llanada, *–nä'dä*, sf. wide tract of level
ground; plain.
llano, na, *lyä'nŏ*, a. plain, even, level,
smooth; meek, affable; plain, clear, evident; unmannerly; –, sm. level field.
llanto, *lyän'tŏ*, sm. flood of tears, cry.
llanura, *lyänŏ'rä*, sf. evenness, level;
vast tract of level ground.
llares, *lyä'rĕs*, sm. pl. pot-hanger. [key.
llave, *lyä'vĕ*, sf. key; –maestra, master-
llavero, *lyävā'rŏ*, sm. keeper of the keys
of a place; key-ring; bunch of keys.
llegada, *lyĕgä'dä*, sf. arrival, coming.
llegar, *lyĕgär'*, v. a. to arrive; to reach;
–se, to proceed to some neighbouring
place; to unite.
llena, *lyā'nä*, sf. alluvion, overflow.
llenar, *lyĕnär'*, v. a. to fill, to stuff, to
gorge; to overwhelm (with compliments,
kindness, &c.), –se, to feed gluttonously;
to lose patience.
lleno, na, *lyā'nŏ*, a. full, replete; complete; de –, entirely, fully.

llevadero, ra, *lyĕvädā'rŏ*, a. tolerable.
llevar, *lyĕvär'*, v. a. to carry, to convey,
to transport; to bear; to introduce.
lloraduelos, *lyŏrädŭĕ'lŏs*, sm. weeper.
llorar, *lyŏrär'*, v. a. & n. to weep, to cry;
to bewail.
lloriquear, *lyŏrĭkĕär'*, v. n. to whine.
lloro, *lyŏ'rŏ*, sm. weeping, crying.
llorón, *lyŏrŏn'*, sm. weeper. [tears.
lloroso, sa, *lyŏrŏ'sŏ*, a. mournful, full of
llovediza (agua –), *lyŏvĕdĭ'thä*, sf. rain-
llover, *lyŏvĕr'*, v. imp. to rain. [water.
llovisnar, *lyŏvĭsnär'*, v. imp. to drizzle.
lluvia, *lyŏ'vĭä*, sf. rain.
lluvioso, sa, *lyŭvĭŏ'sŏ*, a. rainy.

M.

macareno, na, *mäkärā'nŏ*, s. bragging,
boasting. [roni.
macarrones, *mäkärrŏ'nĕs*, sm. pl. maca-
macarse, *mäkär'sĕ*, v. r. to rot (of fruit).
macear, *mäthĕär'*, v. a. to pound with a
mallet; to knock. [soften.
macerar, *mäthĕrär'*, v. a. to macerate, to
macero, *mäthĕ'rŏ*, sm. mace-bearer.
maceta, *mäthā'tä*, sf. flower-pot.
macilento, ta, *mäthĭlĕn'tŏ*, a. lean, extenuated; withered.
maciso, sa, *mäthē'thŏ*, a. massive, solid.
machaca, *mätshä'kä*, sm. & f. ignorant,
tiresome person.
machacar, *mätshäkär'*, v. a. to pound, to
crush; –, v. n. to importune, to molest.
machacón, ona, *–kŏn'*, a. heavy, importunate, tedious. [stupidity.
machada, *mätshä'dä*, sf. flock of he-goats;
machete, *mätshā'tĕ*, sm. cutlass.
macho, *mätsh'ŏ*, sm. male animal; he-
mule; he-goat; pillar; hook to catch hold
in an eye; –, a. masculine, male; vigorous.
machón, *mätshŏn'*, sm. buttress.
machorra, *mätshŏr'rä*, sf. barren woman.
machucadura, *mätshükädŏ'rä*, sf. pounding, bruising.
machucar, *–kär'*, v. a. to pound, to bruise.
machucho, cha, *mätshŭtsh'ŏ*, a. mature,
ripe; judicious.
madama, *mädä'mä*, sf. madam.
madeja, *mädĕh'ä*, sf. skein of thread;
lock of hair.
madera, *mädā'rä*, sf. timber, wood.
maderería, *–rĕrē'ä*, sf. timber-yard.
madero, *mädā'rŏ*, sm. beam of timber.
madrastra, *mädräs'trä*, sf. step-mother.
madraza, *mädrä'thä*, sf. very fond mother.
madre, *mä'drĕ*, sf. mother; womb, matrix;
bed of a river.
madreperla, *–pĕr'lä*, sf. mother of pearl.
madreselva, *–sĕl'vä*, sf. honey-suckle.
madrigal, *mädrĭgäl'*, sm. madrigal.
madriguera, *–gä'rä*, sf. burrow; den,
lurking-place.
madrina, *mädrē'nä*, sf. godmother.
madrona, *mädrŏ'nä*, sf. mother who spoils
her children by over-indulgence.

madroño, *mådrön'yŏ,* sm. strawberry, strawberry-plant. [at break of day.

madrugada, *mådrügå'då,* sf. dawn; de –,

madrugador, ra, *–gådör',* sm. & f. early riser. [to anticipate, to be beforehand.

madrugar, *–går',* v. n. to get up early;

madurar, *mådürår',* v. a. to ripen; –, v. n. to ripen, to grow ripe; to arrive at maturity.

madurativo, va, *mådürätĭ'vŏ,* a. matura-tive, ripening. [wisdom.

madurez, *–rĕth',* sf. maturity; prudence;

maduro, ra, *mådö'rŏ,* a. ripe, mature; prudent, judicious.

maestra, *måĕs'trå,* sf. mistress; school-mistress; master's wife.

maestrante, *måĕstrån'tĕ,* sm. academician.

maestranza, *–trän'thå,* sf. equestrian club; dock-yard; ship-building.

maestrazgo, *–träth'gŏ,* sm. grand-master-ship of a military order.

maestre, *måĕs'trĕ,* sm. grand-master of a military order; ship-master.

maestresala, *–så'lå,* sm. chief waiter at a nobleman's table in Spain.

maestría, *måĕstrĕ'å,* sf. mastership.

maestro, *måĕs'trŏ,* sm. master; –, tra, a. masterly, principal.

magia, *må'hĭå,* sf. magic. [magician.

mágico, ca, *–'hĭkŏ,* a. magical; –, sm.

magisterio, *måhĭstĕ'rĭŏ,* sm. mastery; mastership. [magistracy.

magistrado, *–trå'dŏ,* sm. magistrate;

magistral, *–trål',* a. magisterial; –, sm. person who enjoys a prebend.

magistratura, *–trätö'rå,* sf. magistracy.

magnanimidad, *mågnånĭmĭdåd',* sf. mag-nanimity. [nimous.

magnánimo, ma, *mågnå'nĭmŏ,* a. magna-

magnate, *–tĕ,* sm. magnate.

magnesia, *mågnĕ'sĭå,* sf. magnesia.

magnético, ca, *–ĭĭkŏ,* a. magnetic.

magnetismo, *–ĭĭs'mŏ,* sm. magnetism.

magnetizar, *–tĭthår',* v. a. to magnetize.

magníficat, *mågnĭ'fĭkåt,* sm. the Magnificat.

magnificencia, *–fĭthĕn'thĭå,* sf. magni-ficence, splendour.

magnífico, ca, *mågnĭ'fĭkŏ,* a. magnificent, splendid. [greatness, grandeur.

magnitud, *mågnĭtöd',* sf. magnitude;

magno, na, *måg'nŏ,* a. great.

mago, ga, *må'gŏ,* sm. & f. magician.

magra, *må'grå,* sf. rasher, slice of pork.

magro, gra, *–grŏ,* a. meagre.

magulladura, *mågülyådö'rå,* sf. bruise, contusion.

magullar, *–yår',* v. a. to bruise, to contuse.

mahometano, *måŏmĕtå'nŏ,* s. & a. Moham-medan. [medanism.

mahometanismo, *–nĭs'mŏ,* sm. Moham-

mahómon, *måŏn',* sm. nankeen.

maitines, *måtĭ'nĕs,* sm. pl. matins.

maíz, *måĭth',* sm. maize, Indian corn.

maizal, *–thål',* sm. field sown with Indian corn. [corn.

majada, *måhå'då,* sf. sheep-fold.

majadería, *–dĕrĭ'å,* sf. absurd speech; insult. [blockish; –, sm. gawk.

majadero, ra, *–dĕ'rŏ,* a. dull, silly,

majadura, *–dö'rå,* sf. pounding, bruising.

majar, *måhår',* v. a. to pound.

majestad, *måhĕståd',* sf. majesty.

majestuoso, *måhĕstöö'sŏ,* a. majestic(al).

majo, *må'h ŏ,* sm. boaster; gallant.

majuela, *måhöĕ'lå,* sf. fruit of the white hawthorn. [thorn.

majuelo, *–lŏ,* sm. vine newly planted; haw-

mal, *mål,* sm. evil, hurt, injury; illness; –, a. (used only before masculine sub-stantives) bad; –, malamente, ad. badly.

mala, *må'lå,* sf. mail.

malandrín, *målåndrĭn',* sm. highwayman; –, a. malign. [some.

malavenido, da, *–åvĕnĭ'dŏ,* a. quarrel-

malaventura, *–åvĕntö'rå,* sf. calamity, misfortune. [fortunate.

malaventurado, da, *–åvĕntörå'dŏ,* a. un-

malbaratador, ra, *–bårätådör',* sm. spend-thrift, lavisher.

malcontento, *–kŏntĕn'tŏ,* sm. game at cards; –, ta, a. discontented, malcontent.

malcriado, da, *–krĭå'dŏ,* a. ill-bred, ill-behaved, unmannerly; naughty.

maldad, *måldåd',* sf. wickedness.

maldición, *–dĭthĭŏn',* sf. malediction, cursing. [damned, cursed.

maldito, ta, *måldĭ'tŏ,* a. perverse, wicked;

malear, *målĕår',* v. a. to prevent, to cor-rupt. [calumny.

maledicencia, *målĕdĭthĕn'thĭå,* sf. slander,

maleficiar, *–fĭthĭår',* v. a. to adulterate, to corrupt; to bewitch.

maleficio, *–fĭ'thĭŏ,* sm. witchcraft, en-chantment. [maleficent.

maléfico, ca, *målĕ'fĭkŏ,* a. mischievous,

maleta, *målĕ'tå,* sf. portmanteau.

malevolencia, *–vŏlĕn'thĭå,* sf. malevolence.

malévolo, la, *målĕ'vŏlŏ,* a. malevolent.

maleza, *målĕ'thå,* sf. wickedness, malice; brambles, briers, pl. [lavish.

malgastar, *–gåstår',* v. a. to waste, to

malhablado, da, *–åblå'dŏ,* a. foul-mouthed.

malhecho, *–ĕtsh'ŏ,* sm. flagitious action, wrong. [factor.

malhechor, ra, *–ĕtshŏr',* sm. & f. male-

malhumorado, da, *–ümörå'dŏ,* a. ill-humoured, peevish.

malicia, *målĭ'thĭå,* sf. malice, perversity; suspicion; cunning, artifice.

maliciar, *–thĭår',* v. a. to corrupt, to adulterate; –, v. n. to suspect maliciously.

malicioso, sa, *–thĭö'sŏ,* a. malicious, wicked, malign. [malice.

malignidad, *målĭgnĭdåd',* sf. malignity.

maligno, na, *målĭg'nŏ,* a. malignant, malicious. [cards like whist).

malilla, *målĭl'yå,* sf. manilla (game at

malmandado, da, *–måndå'dŏ,* a. disobe-dient. [t – I so much the worse!

malo, la, *må'lŏ,* a. bad, ill, wicked; sickly;

malograr, *målŏgrår',* v. a. to disappoint; –se, to fail of success. [miscarriage.

malogro, *målŏ'grŏ,* sm. disappointment,

malparado, da, *–pårå'dŏ,* a. ill condi-tioned, hurt. [had a miscarriage.

malparida, *–pårĭ'då,* sf. woman who has

malparir, _-pâr̃er̃'_, v. n. to miscarry.
malparto, _-pär̃'tô_, sm. abortion.
malquistar, _-kistär̃'_, v. a. to excite quarrels.
malquisto, ta, _-kis'tô_, a. hated, detested.
malrotar, _-rôtär̃'_, v. a. to misspend, to lavish. [some.
malsano, na, _-sä'nô_, a. sickly; unwhole-
maltratamiento, _-trätämĭen'tô_, sm. ill treatment. [abuse, to maltreat.
maltratar, _-trätär̃'_, v. a. to treat ill, to
malva, _mäl'vä_, sf. (bot.) mallows.
malvabisco, _-bis'kô_, sm. marsh-mallows.
malvado, da, _-vä'dô_, a. wicked, very perverse.
malvasia, _-väsĭ'ä_, sf. malmsey (wine).
malversación, _-versäthĭon'_, sf. malversa-
tion. [son who misapplies property.
malversador, ra, _-versädôr̃'_, sm. & f. per-
malversar, _-versär̃'_, v. a. to misapply.
malvís, _mälvis'_, sm. red-wing (pájaro).
malla, _mäl'yä_, sf. mesh, mash; coat of mail.
mallo, _-yô_, sm. mall; mallet.
mama, _mämä'_, sf. mamma.
mamadera, _-dä'rä_, sf. breast-pump.
mamaluco, _-lä'kô_, sm. dolt, simpleton.
mamar, _mämär̃'_, v. a. to suck; to cram.
mamarrachada, _-rätshä'dä_, sf. collection of rude or ridiculous pictures; foolish action or speech.
mamarrachista, _-rätshĭs'tä_, sm. dauber.
mamarracho, _-rätsh'ô_, sm. daub; grotesque ornament.
mameluco, _mämĕlü'kô_, sm. Mameluke.
mamola, _mämô'lä_, sf. chuck under the chin.
mamón, ona, _mämôn'_, sm. & f. sucking animal; child who is suckled for a long time. [book.
mamotreto, _-trä'tô_, sm. memorandum-
mampara, _mämpä'rä_, sf. screen.
mampostería, _-pôstĕr̃ĭ'ä_, sf. rubble-work.
maná, _mänä'_, sm. manna.
manada, _mänä'dä_, sf. flock, drove of cattle; crowd, multitude. [origin.
manantial, _mänäntĭäl'_, sm. source, spring;
manar, _mänär̃'_, v. n. to spring from; to distil from; to issue; to abound.
manceba, _-thä'bä_, sf. concubine.
mancebo, _-bô_, sm. youth; companion.
mancilla, _-thĭl'yä_, sf. spot, blemish.
manco, ca, _män'kô_, a. handless; one-
handed; maimed, faulty.
mancomún, _-kômün'_, de -, ad. jointly, by common consent.
mancomunar, _-kômünär̃'_, v.a.to associate, to unite; to make two or more persons pay jointly the costs of a law-suit; -se, to act together, to join in the execution of a thing. [fellowship.
mancomunidad, _-kômünĭdäd'_, sf. union,
mancha, _män'tshä_, sf. stain, spot.
manchado, da, _-tshä'dô_, a. spotted.
manchar, _-tshär̃'_, v. a. to stain, to soil.
manda, _män'dä_, sf. offer, proposal; legacy.
mandado, _-dä'dô_, sm. mandate; command; errand, message.
mandamiento, _-mĭen'tô_, sm. mandate; commandment.

mandar, _mändär̃'_, v. a. to command, to order; to offer; to bequeath; to send.
mandarín, _mändär̃in'_, sm. mandarin.
mandatario, _-tä'rĭô_, sm. a mandatory.
mandato, _-dä'tô_, sm. mandate, order; ec-
clesiastical ceremony of washing twelve persons' feet on Maundy Thursday.
mandíbula, _mändĭ'bülä_, sf. jaw-bone.
mandil, _mändĭl'_, sm. coarse apron.
mando, _män'dô_, sm. command, authority, power; mandamus.
mandón, ona, _-dôn'_, a. imperious, domineering; -, sm. imperious, haughty person.
manecilla, _mänĕthĭl'yä_, sf. small hand; book-clasp.
manejable, _-hä'blä_, a. manageable.
manejar, _-här̃'_, v. a. to manage; -se, to be able to move after having been de-
prived of motion.
manejo, _mänĕ'h'ô_, sm. managery, administration; horsemanship, manége.
manera, _mänĕ'rä_, sf. manner, mode; kind.
manes, _mä'nes_, sm. pl. manes, pl. (souls of the dead).
manga, _män'gä_, sf. sleeve; hurricane; cloak-bag; straining-bag; body of troops in a line.
mango, _män'gô_, sm. handle, haft.
mangonear, _-gônĕär̃'_, v. n. to rove idly.
mangoto, _mängô'tô_, sm. wide sleeve.
manguito, _mängĭ'tô_, sm. muff.
manía, _mänĭ'ä_, sf. frenzy, madness.
maniatar, _mänĭätär̃'_, v. a. to manacle, to hand-cuff. [frantic.
maniático, ca, _-ä'tĭkô_, a. maniac, mad.
manifactura, _-fäktü'rä_, sf. manufacture.
manifestación, _-festäthĭon'_, sf. manifestation. [declare.
manifestar, _-festär̃'_, v. a. to manifest, to
manifiesto, ta, _-fĭes'tô_, a. manifest, open, clear; -, sm. act of exposing the Holy Sacrament to the public adoration; mani-
festo. [manacle.
manilla, _mänĭl'yä_, sf. bracelet; hand-cuff.
maniobra, _-ô'brä_, sf. handiwork; handling; cleverness in handling; (mil.) manœuvre.
maniobrar, _-ôbrär̃'_, v. a. to work with the hands; to work a ship; (mil.) to manœuvre troops; to intrigue.
maniota, _-ô'tä_, sf. shackles, hand-cuffs, pl.
manipulación, _-püläthĭon'_, sf. manipulation. [late.
manipular, _-pülär̃'_, v.a.(fam.) to manipu-
manípulo, _mänĭ'pülô_, sm. maniple.
maniqueismo, _-keĭs'mô_, sm. Manicheism.
maniqueo, a, _mänĭkä'ô_, a. Manichean.
maniquí, _mänĭkĭ'_, sm. mannikin.
manir, _mänir̃'_, v. a. to keep meat until it grows tender. [liberal.
manirroto, ta, _-rô'tô_, a. wasteful, too
manjar, _män'här̃'_, sm. food, victuals.
mano, _mä'nô_, sf. hand; hand of a clock or watch; first hand at play; á -, at hand; with the hand; á -s llenas, liberally, abundantly; -á-, in company, familiarly.
manojo, _mänô'h'ô_, sm. bundle of herbs, &c.

manopla, mănŏ'plă, sf. gauntlet; coachman's whip.
manosear, mănŏsĕăr', v. a. to handle.
manoseo, -sĕ'ŏ, sm. handling.
manotada, -tă'dă, sf. blow with the hand.
manoteo, -tĕ'ŏ, sm. manual gesticulation.
mansedumbre, mănsĕdŭm'brĕ, sf. meekness, gentleness. [abode, home.
mansión, mănsĭŏn', sf. sojourn, residence;
manso, sa, măn'sŏ, a. tame; gentle, soft; —, sm. leading male in a flock of goats, sheep or black-cattle. [drubbing.
manta, măn'tă, sf. blanket; thrashing,
manteamiento, măntĕămĭn'tŏ, sm. tossing in a blanket.
mantear, -tĕăr', v. a. to toss in a blanket.
manteca, -tă'kă, sf. pomatum; butter.
mantecada, -tĕkă'dă, sf. toast.
mantecado, -tĕkă'dŏ, sm. butter-cake.
mantecoso, sa, -tĕkŏ'sŏ, a. buttery.
mantel, măntĕl', sm. table-cloth.
mantelería, -lĕrĕ'ă, sf. table-linen.
manteleta, -lĕ'tă, sf. mantelet.
mantellina, măntĕlyĕ'nă, sf. woman's mantle.
mantener, -tĕnĕr', v. a. to maintain, to support; to nourish; -se, to support oneself. [tenance; subsistence.
mantenimiento, -tĕnĭmĭĕn'tŏ, sm. mainmanteo, măntĕ'ŏ, sm. long cloak worn by priests and students.
mantequera, măntĕkĕ'ră, sf. churn.
mantequero, -rŏ, sm. butter-man.
mantequilla, măntĕkĭl'yă, sf. butter-cake.
mantilla, măntĭl'yă, sf. head-covering for women; cloak; mantle of state; housing, horsecloth; -s, pl. swaddling-clothes.
manto, măn'tŏ, sm. mantle; cloak, robe.
mantón, măntŏn', sm. large veil. [able.
manuable, mănŭă'blĕ, a. tractable, manageable.
manual, mănŭăl', a. manual, handy; easily performed with the hand; —, sm. manual.
manufactura, -făktŏ'ră, sf. manufacture.
manufacturar, -făktŭrăr', v. a. to manufacture. [slavery.
manumitir, -mĭtĭr', v. a. to release from
manuscrito, -skrĭ'tŏ, sm. manuscript; —, a. written. [maintenance.
manutención, -tĕnthĭŏn', sf. maintaining;
manzana, mănthă'nă, sf. apple.
manzanal, -thănăl', manzanar, -thănăr', sm. orchard. [chamomile.
manzanilla, mănthănĭl'yă, sf. common
manzano, mănthă'nă, sm. apple-tree.
maña, măn'yă, sf. handiness, dexterity, cleverness, cunning, artifice; evil habit or custom. [—, ad. to-morrow.
mañana, -yă'nă, sf. morning, morrow;
mañoso, sa, -yŏ'sŏ, a. skilful, handy.
mapa, mă'pă, sm. map. [cunning.
mapamundi, -măn'dĭ, sf. map of the world.
maquilar, măkĭlăr', v. a. to measure and take the miller's dues for grinding corn; to retrench, to clip.
máquina, mă'kĭnă, sf. machine. [tion.
maquinación, măkĭnăthĭŏn', sf. machina-

maquinador, ra, măkĭnădŏr', sm. & f. schemer, machinator. [nically.
maquinalmente, -nălmĕn'tĕ, ad. mechanically.
maquinar, -năr', v. a. to machinate; to conspire.
maquinaria, -nă'rĭă, sf. mechanics.
maquinista, -nĭs'tă, sm. machinist, mechanician.
mar, măr, sm. & f, sea.
maraña, mărăn'yă, sf. shrub, thicket; perplexity, puzzle; knot of a play. [mus.
marasmo, mărăs'mŏ, sm. (med.) marasmaravedí, mărăvĕdĭ', sm. maravedi (smallest Spanish coin).
maravilla, -vĭl'yă, sf. wonder; á las -s, uncommonly well; exquisitely; á -, marvellously.
maravillar, -vĭlyăr', v. a. to admire; -se, to wonder, to be astonished.
maravilloso, sa, -vĭlyŏ'sŏ, a. wonderful, marvellous.
marca, măr'kă, sf. frontier province; due measure or weight of anything; mark.
marcador, -dŏr', sm. marker, assay-master.
marcar, mărkăr', v. a. to mark; to observe, to note, to designate.
marcial, mărthĭăl', a. martial, warlike.
marcialidad, -lĭdăd', sf. freedom, assumed familiarity.
marco, măr'kŏ, sm. door-case, window-case; picture-frame; mark (weight of eight ounces); branding-iron; measure of ground which may be sown with a fanega of grain.
márcola, măr'kŏlă, sf. pruning-hook.
marcha, măr'tshă, sf. march.
marchamar, -măr', v. a. to put a mark on goods at the custom-house.
marchamo, mărtshă'mŏ, sm. mark put on goods at the custom-house. [to march.
marchar, mărtshăr', v. n. to go; to go off;
marchitable, mărtshĭtă'blĕ, a. perishable.
marchitar, -tăr', v. a. to wither; to fade; to deprive of vigour.
marchito, ta, mărchĭ'tŏ, a. faded, withered.
marea, mărĕ'ă, sf. tide. [a ship.
mareaje, mărĕă'hĕ, sm. art of navigating
marear, mărĕăr', v. a. to work a ship; to molest; -se, to be sea-sick.
marejada, mărĕhă'dă, sf. sea-swell, headsea, main, main-sea, surge.
mareo, mărĕ'ŏ, sm. sea-sickness.
marfil, mărfĭl', sm. ivory.
margarita, mărgărĕ'tă, sf. pearl; common daisy; periwinkle.
margen, măr'hĕn, sm. & f. margin; border.
marginal, măr'hĭnăl', a. marginal.
marginar, -năr', v. a. to make annotations on the margin.
margrave, mărgră'vĕ, sm. margrave.
marica, mărĕ'kă, sf. magpie; milksop.
maricón, mărĭkŏn', sm. coward, poltroon.
maridable, -dă'blĕ, a. matrimonial.
maridillo, -dĭl'yŏ, sm. small brazier, foot-bottle (for women).
marido, mărĭ'dŏ, sm. husband.
marimacho, -mătsh'ŏ, sm. virago.
marimanta, -măn'tă, sf. bugbear.
marimorena, -mŏră'nă, sf. dispute, quarrel.

marina, _mărē'nă_, sf. navy.   [sailors, pl.
marinaje, _mărĭnā'h'ĕ_, sm. seamanship;
marinar, _năr'_, v. a. to salt fish.
marinería, _nĕrē'ă_, sf. seamanship; body
of seamen.
marinero, _ndĭ'rŏ_, sm. mariner.
marinesco, ca, _nĕs'kŏ_, a. nautical.
marino, na, _mărē'nŏ_, a. marine; —, sm.
mariner, seaman.   [flight.
mariposa, _mărĭpŏ'să_, sf. butterfly; rush-
mariscal, _mărĭskăl'_, sm. marshal; farrier;
blacksmith.
marisco, _mărĭs'kŏ_, sm. sea-shell.
marital, _mărĭtăl'_, a. marital.   [marine.
maritimo, na, _mărĭ'tĭmŏ_, a. maritime,
Maritornes, _tŏr'nĕs_, sf. ill-shaped, awkward woman.   [ridge-pot.
marmita, _m..mē'tă_, sf. flesh-pot, por-
marmitón, _mŭbn'_, sm. scullion.
mármol, _măr'mŏl_, sm. marble.
marmolista, _lĭs'tă_, sm. worker in marble.
marmóreo, ea, _mărmŏ'rĕŏ_, a. marbled.
marmota, _tă_, sf. marmot.   [marble.
maroma, _mărŏ'mă_, sf. rope.
marqués, _mărkĕs'_, sm. marquis.
marquesa, _mărkĕ'să_, sf. marchioness.
marquesado, _sā'dŏ_, sm. marquisate.
marrajo, _mărrā'h'ŏ_, sm. white shark; —,
ja, a. sly, cunning.
marrana, _mărră'nă_, sf. sow.
marrano, _nŏ_, sm. pig, hog.
marras, _măr'răs_, ad. long ago, long since.
marro, _măr'rŏ_, sm. quoits (game); disappointment, failure.
marrón, _mărrŏn'_, sm. quoit, pitcher.
marrullería, _mărrŭlyĕrē'ă_, sf. knavery,
cunning; prank, trick.
marrullero, ra, _yā'rŏ_, a. crafty, cunning.
marsellés, _mărsĕlyĕs'_, sm. shooting-jacket.
marsopla, _mărsŏ'plă_, sf. spermaceti-whale.
marta, _măr'tă_, sf. marten, martern,
marto, _măr'tĕ_, sm. iron.
martes, _măr'tĕs_, sm. Tuesday.
martillada, _mărtĭlyā'dă_, sf. blow with a
hammer.
martillar, _yăr'_, v. a. to hammer.
martillo, _mărtĭl'yŏ_, sm. hammer.
martinete, _mărtĭnĕ'tĕ_, sm. sand-martin;
hammer in copper-works; copper-mill.
mártir, _măr'tĭr_, sm. & f. martyr.
martirio, _mărtĭ'rĭŏ_, sm. martyrdom.
martirizar, _mărtĭrĭthăr'_, v. a. to martyr.
martirologio, _rŏlŏ'hĭŏ_, sm. martyrology.
marzo, _măr'thŏ_, sm. March.
mas, _măs_, ad. but, yet.
más, —, ad. more; besides, moreover; á -
tardar, at latest; de — á -, more and
more; sin - ni -, without more ado.
masa, _mă'să_, sf. dough, paste; mortar;
mass.
mascadura, _măskăd'ră_, sf. mastication.
mascar, _măskăr'_, v. a. to chew.
máscara, _măs'kără_, sm. & f. mask; masker,
masquerader; pretext.
mascarada, _măskără'dă_, sf. masquerade.
mascarilla, _rĭl'yă_, sf. small mask.
mascarón, _rŏn'_, sm. carved satyr's faces
for fountains and buildings.

mascujar, _-kŭ'hăr'_, v. n. to masticate
with difficulty; to pronounce with difficulty.
masculino, _-kŭlĭ'nŏ_, a. masculine, male.
mascullar, _-kŭlyăr'_, v. a. to falter in
speaking.
masera, _măsĕ'ră_, sf. kneading-trough.
masticación, _măstĭkăthĭŏn'_, sf. mastication.   [chew.
masticar, _-kăr'_, v. a. to masticate, to
mástil, _măs'tĭl_, sm. (mar.) top-mast.
mastín, _măstĭn'_, sm. mastiff.   [cress.
mastuerzo, _-tŭĕr'thŏ_, sm. (bot.) common
mata, _mă'tă_, sf. shrub; sprig, blade; coppice; lock of matted hair.   [guisher.
matacandelas, _mătăkăndĕ'lăs_, sf. extin-
matachín, _-tshĭn'_, sm. merry-Andrew;
dance performed by grotesque figures.
matadero, _-dĕ'rŏ_, sm. slaughter-house.
matador, _-dŏr'_, sm. murderer.
matadura, _-dŏ'ră_, sf. saddle-gall.
matanza, _mătăn'thă_, sf. slaughtering;
cattle to be slaughtered; massacre.
matar, _mătăr'_, v. a. to kill; to execute; to
murder; to quench, to extinguish fire; to
slack lime; to gall a horse; -se, to kill
oneself, to commit suicide.
matasanos, _mătăsă'nŏs_, sm. quack, charlatan, empiric.
matasiete, _-sĭĕ'tĕ_, sm. bully, braggadocio.
mate, _mă'tĕ_, sm. check-mate; —, a. unpolished.
matemática, _mătĕmă'tĭkă_, sf. mathematics.
matemático, ca, _-tĭkŏ_, a. mathematical;
—, sm. mathematician.
materia, _mătĕ'rĭă_, sm. matter, materials;
subject; matter (pus).
material, _mătĕrĭăl'_, a. material, corporal;
rude; uncouth; —, sm. ingredient, materials, pl.   [rudeness, coarseness.
materialidad, _-lĭdăd'_, sf. materiality;
materialismo, _-lĭs'mŏ_, sm. materialism.
materialista, _-lĭs'tă_, sm. materialist.
maternal, _mătĕrnăl'_, a. maternal, motherly.
maternidad, _-nĭdăd'_, sf. motherhood,
motherliness.   [motherly.
materno, na, _mătĕr'nŏ_, a. maternal,
matiz, _mătĭh'_, sm. shade of colour; shading.
matizar, _mătĭthăr'_, v. a. to mix colours
well; to beautify.
matón, _mătŏn'_, sm. bully.
matorral, _mătŏrrăl'_, sm. shrub, thicket.
matraca, _mătră'kă_, sf. wooden rattle; jest,
contemptuous joke; coxcomb.
matraquear, _-kăr'_, v. a. to jest, to scoff,
to mock, to ridicule.
matricida, _mătrĭthĕ'dă_, sm. & f. matricide
(person).   [der).
matricidio, _-thĭ'dĭŏ_, sm. matricide (mur-
matrícula, _mătrĕ'kălă_, sf. register, list.
matricular, _mătrĭkŭlăr'_, v. a. to matriculate.   [connubial.
matrimonial, _-mŏnĭăl'_, a. matrimonial,
matrimonio, _-mŏ'nĭŏ_, sm. marriage,
matrimony.   [form.
matriz, _mătrĭth'_, sf. matrix, womb; mould,
matrona, _mătrŏ'nă_, sf. matron.
matutino, na, _mătŭtĭ'nŏ_, a. matutinal.

maula, *mä'ŭlä*, sf. object found in the street; deceitful tricks, imposition; —, sm. cheat, bad payer. [swindler.

maulero, *mäŭlä'rŏ*, sm. impostor, cheat.

maullador, ra, *—yädŏr'*, a. cat which is always mewing.

maullar, *—yär'*, v. a. to mew.

maullido, *—yê'dŏ*, sm. mew, cry of a cat.

mausoleo, *mäŭsěŏ'lŏ*, mausoleo, *—sŏlä'ŏ*, sm. mausoleum.

máxima, *mäk'simä*, sf. maxim.

máxime, *—mě*, ad. principally.

máximo, ma, *—mŏ*, a. chief, principal; very great.

mayo, *mä'yŏ*, sm. May; May-pole.

mayor, *mäyŏr'*, a. greater, larger; elder; —, sm. superior; major; —, sf. first proposition in a syllogism; por—, wholesale; —es, sm. pl. forefathers.

mayoral, *—räl'*, sm. head-shepherd; leader.

mayorazgo, *—räth'gŏ*, sm. first-born son with the right of primogeniture, son-and-heir; family estate entailed on the eldest son. [tration, stewardship.

mayordomía, *mäyŏrdŏmě'ä*, sf. administ-

mayordomo, *—dŏ'mŏ*, sm. steward.

mayoría, *mäyŏrě'ä*, sf. advantage, excellence, superiority; majority.

mayorista, *—rǐs'tä*, sm. student of the highest classes in grammar-schools.

mayormente, *mäyŏrměn'tě*, ad. principally, chiefly.

mayúscula, *mäyŭs'kŭlä*, sf. capital letter.

maza, *mä'thä*, sf. club; mace; importunate, troublesome fellow.

mazada, *mäthä'dä*, sf. blow with a mallet.

mazapán, *—pän'*, sm. marchpane.

mazmorra, *mäthmŏr'rä*, sf. Moorish dungeon.

mazo, *mä'thŏ*, sm. mallet; bundle of ribands; importunate, tiresome person.

mazorca, *mäthŏr'kä*, sf. spindle full of thread; ear of corn.

me, *mě*, pn. me. [thread; ear of corn.

mea, *mä'ä*, sf. term used by children to express their want to make water.

meada, *mě'ä'dä*, sf. quantity of urine made at one time.

meadero, *—ä'rŏ*, sm. urinal.

meados, *mě'ä'dŏs*, sm. pl. urine, piss.

mear, *měär'*, v. n. to make water; to pump ship.

mecánica, *měkä'nĭkä*, sf. mechanics; mean, despicable thing; management of soldiers, affairs. [mechanician.

mecánico, ca, *—kŏ*, a. mechanical; —, sm.

mecanismo, *měkänĭs'mŏ*, sm. mechanism.

mecer, *měthěr'*, v. a. to stir, to agitate; to rock; to dandle a child to rest.

mecha, *mětsh'ä*, sf. wick; bacon with which fowls and meat are larded.

mechar, *mětshär'*, v. a. to lard.

mechero, *mětshä'rŏ*, sm. nozzle of a lamp; socket of a candlestick; — de gas, burner.

mechinal, *mětshǐnäl'*, sm. square stones left projecting in a wall to be continued.

mechón, *mětshŏn'*, sm. large lock of hair; large bundle of threads or fibres.

medalla, *mědäl'yä*, sf. medal; gold coin weighing an ounce.

medallón, *—yŏn'*, sm. medallion.

media, *mä'dĭä*, sf. stocking.

mediación, *mědĭäthĭŏn'*, sf. mediation, intervention. [between.

mediador, *mědĭädŏr'*, sm. mediator; go-

medianería, *—něrě'ä*, sf. bounds or limits of contiguous things; partition-wall.

medianero, ra, *—nä'rŏ*, a. mediating, interceding. [crity.

medianía, *—ně'ä*, sf. moderation; medio-

medianista, *—nĭs'tä*, sm. student of the fourth class in grammar.

mediano, na, *mědĭä'nŏ*, a. moderate, middling; mediocre.

mediante, *mědĭän'tě*, ad. by means of.

mediar, *mědĭär'*, v. n. to be in the middle; to intercede for another; to mediate.

mediator, *mědĭätŏr'*, sm. ombre (game).

medicina, *mědĭthĭ'nä*, sf. physic; medicine.

medicinal, *—thĭnäl'*, a. medicinal. [cine.

medicinar, *—thĭnär'*, v. a. to medicine.

médico, *mä'dĭkŏ*, sm. physician; —, ca, a.

medida, *mědĭ'dä*, sf. measure. [medical.

medidor, *mědĭdŏr'*, sm. measurer.

mediero, *mědĭä'rŏ*, sm. hosier.

medio, día, *mä'dĭŏ*, a. half; á medias, by halves; —, sm. middle; expedient; way, mean; medium; mexican coin.

mediocre, *mědĭŏ'krě*, a. middling, moderate, mediocre. [crity.

mediocridad, *mědĭŏkrĭdäd'*, sf. medio-

mediodía, *—ä'ä*, sm. noon, mid-day.

mediopaño, *—pän'yŏ*, sm. thin woollen cloth. [moderate.

medir, *mědĭr'*, v. a. to measure; —se, to be

meditación, *mědĭtäthĭŏn'*, sf. meditation.

meditar, *mědĭtär'*, v. a. to meditate.

mediterráneo, nea, *—těrrä'něŏ*, a. mediterranean. [improvement.

medra, *mä'drä*, sf. progress, melioration.

medrar, *mědrär'*, v. n. to thrive, to prosper; to improve. [ous; terrible.

medroso, sa, *mědrŏ'sŏ*, a. fearful, timorous.

medula, *mědŭ'lä*, médula, *mä'dŭlä*, sf. marrow; principal substance; (fig.) pith.

meduloso, sa, *mědŭlŏ'sŏ*, a. full of marrow, marrowy.

mejido, da, *mě'hě'dŏ*, a. beaten up with sugar and water (of eggs).

mejilla, *mě'hĭl'yä*, sf. cheek.

mejor, *mě'hŏr'*, a. & ad. better.

mejora, *mě'hŏrä*, sf. improvement, melioration, growth.

mejorar, *mě'hŏrär'*, v. a. to improve, to meliorate, to heighten; to cultivate; to mend; —, v. n. to recover, to grow well from a disease or calamity; —se, to improve, to grow better.

mejoría, *—rě'ä*, sf. improvement, melioration; mending; repairs; improvement in health; advantage; superiority.

melada, *mělä'dä*, sf. slice of toasted bread steeped in honey.

melancolía, *mělänkŏlě'ä*, sf. melancholy.

melancólico, ca, *—kŏ'lĭkŏ*, a. melancholy, sad, gloomy.

melena, *mĕlā'nă*, sf. dishevelled hair hanging loose over the eyes; fore-top hair or mane. [hair.

melenudo, da, *mĕlēnōͦ dŏ*, a. having bushy

melífero, ra, *mĕlē'fĕrŏ*, a. productive of honey. [flowing with honey.

melifluo, flua, *—flōͦ*, a. honey-mouthed;

melindre, *mĕlin'drĕ*, sf. fritters made of honey and flour; prudery.

melindrear, *—drēăr'*, v. n. to act the prude.

melindroso, sa, *—drō'sŏ*, a. prudish, finical. [peach.

melocotón, *mĕlŏkŏtŏn'*, sm. (bot.) common

melodía, *mĕlŏdē'ă*, sf. melody.

melodioso, sa, *—dĭō'sŏ*, a. melodious.

melodrama, *—drā'mă*, sf. melodrama.

melón, *mĕlŏn'*, sm. melon.

melonar, *—năr'*, sm. bed of melons.

melosidad, *mĕlŏsĭdăd'*, sf. sweetness.

meloso, sa, *mĕlŏ'sŏ*, a. honied; mellow:

melote, *—tĕ'*, sm. molasses, treacle.

mella, *mĕl'yă*, sf. notch in edged tools; gap.

mellado, da, *—yā'dŏ*, a. gap-toothed.

mellar, *—yăr'*, v. a. to notch; to deprive of lustre and splendour.

mellizo, za, *—yĕ'thŏ*, a. twin.

membrana, *mĕmbrā'nă*, sf. membrane.

membranoso, sa, *—nŏ'sŏ*, a. membranous, filmy.

membrete, *—brĕ'tĕ*, sm. memorandum, note; line of a letter containing the name of the addressee; invitation card.

membrillo, *—brīl'yŏ*, sm. quince-tree; fruit of the quince-tree. [membered.

membrudo, da, *—brō'dŏ*, a. strong, robust;

mementos, *mĕmĕn'tŏs*, sm. pl. two prayers at mass for the quick and the dead.

memorable, *mĕmŏrā'blĕ*, a. memorable.

memoria, *mĕmŏ'rĭă*, sf. memory; memoir; —s, pl. compliments.

memorial, *mĕmŏrĭăl'*, sm. memorandum-book; memorial, brief.

memorialista, *—lĭs'tă*, sm. amanuensis; writer of petitions for others.

mención, *mĕnthŏn'*, sf. mention.

mencionar, *—năr'*, v. a. to mention.

mendicante, *mĕndĭkăn'tĕ*, a. mendicant, begging; —, sm. mendicant. [to beg.

mendigar, *—găr'*, v. a. to ask charity,

mendigo, *mĕndē'gŏ*, sm. beggar.

mendiguez, *mĕndĭgĕth'*, sf. beggary.

mendrugo, *—drŏ'gŏ*, sm. broken bread given to beggars.

menear, *mĕnăr'*, v. a. to move from place to place; to manage; —se, to be brisk and active, to stir about. [body.

meneo, *mĕnă'ŏ*, sm. waddling motion of the

menester, *mĕnĕstĕr'*, sm. necessity, need, want; —es, pl. natural necessities, pl.

menesteroso, sa, *—rŏ'sŏ*, a. needy, necessitous. [different pulse and roots.

menestra, *mĕnĕs'tră*, sf. pottage made of

menestral, *—trăl'*, sm. tradesman, handicraftsman. [poverty; disgrace.

mengua, *mĕn'gŭă*, sf. decay, decline;

menguado, da, *—gŭā'dŏ*, a. cowardly; foolish; avaricious; hora —a, fatal

moment; —s, sm. pl. stitches picked up in knitting, pl. [water; decline.

menguante, *—gŭăn'tĕ*, sf. ebb-tide, low-

menguar, *—gŭăr'*, v. n. to decay, to fall off; to fail, to diminish.

menjurje, *mĕn'hŭr'hĕ*, sm. hodge-podge.

menor, *mĕnŏr'*, sm. & f. minor (one under age); minor (second proposition in the syllogism); —, a. less, smaller, minor; por —, by retail, in small parts; minutely.

menoría, *—rē'ă*, sf. inferiority; nonage.

menorista, *—rĭs'tă*, sm. third-class student of grammar.

menos, *mā'nŏs*, ad. less; with exception of; á lo —, ó por lo —, at least, however.

menoscabar, *—kăbăr'*, v. a. to lessen; to make worse; to reduce. [terioration, loss.

menoscabo, *—kā'bŏ*, sm. diminution, de-

menospreciar, *—prĕthĭăr'*, v. a. to under-value; to despise, to contemn. [scorn.

menosprecio, *—prĕ'thĭŏ*, sm. contempt;

mensaje, *mĕnsā'h'ĕ*, sm. message, errand.

mensajero, *—hā'rŏ*, sm. messenger.

menstruación, *mĕnstrūăthĭŏn'*, sf. menstruation.

mensual, *mĕnsūăl'*, a. monthly. [nowned.

mentado, da, *mĕntā'dŏ*, a. famous, re-

mental, *mĕntăl'*, a. mental, intellectual.

mentar, *mĕntăr'*, v. a. to mention.

mente, *mĕn'tĕ*, sf. mind, understanding; sense, meaning. [brained.

mentecato, ta, *—kā'tŏ*, a. silly, crack-

mentidero, *mĕntĭdā'rŏ*, sm. talking-corner.

mentir, *mĕntĭr'*, v. a. to lie.

mentira, *mĕntē'ră*, sf. lie, falsehood.

mentiroso, sa, *mĕntĭrŏ'sŏ*, a. lying.

mentís, *mĕntĭs'*, you lie.

menudear, *mĕnŭdăr'*, v. a. to repeat, to detail minutely.

menudencia, *—dĕn'thĭă*, sf. trifle; minuteness; —s, pl. small matters. [fowls.

menudillos, *—dīl'yŏs*, sm. pl. giblets of

menudo, da, *mĕnŏ'dŏ*, a. small; minute; of no moment; á —, repeatedly, often; por —, minutely; by retail; —s, sm. pl. copper coin.

meñique, *mĕnyĕ'kĕ*, sm. little finger.

meollo, *mĕŏl'yŏ*, sm. marrow.

meón, ona, *mĕŏn'*, a. continually making water. [noisy, fellow.

mequetrefe, *mĕkĕtrā'fĕ*, sm. insignificant,

meramente, *mĕrāmĕn'tĕ*, ad. merely, solely.

mercader, *mĕrkădĕr'*, sm. dealer, trader.

mercadería, *—dĕrē'ă*, sf. commodity, merchandise; trade. [place.

mercado, *mĕrkā'dŏ*, sm. market; market-

mercancía, *mĕrkănthē'ă*, sf. trade, traffic; saleable goods. [cantile.

mercantil, *—tīl'*, a. commercial, mer-

merced, *mĕrthĕd'*, sf. wages, favour, grace, mercy; will, pleasure; religious military order, whose chief object is to redeem captives; estar á —, to live at another's expense. [labourer; —, a. mercenary.

mercenario, *mĕrthĕnā'rĭŏ*, sm. &c.

mercería, *mĕrthĕrē'ă*, sf. mercery

mercero, *mĕrthă'rŏ*, sm. haberdasher.
mercurial, *mĕrkŭriăl'*, sm. (bot.) all-good, mercury goose-foot; —, a. mercurial.
mercurio, *mĕrkŏ'riŏ*, sm. mercury, quick-silver.
merecedor, ra, *mĕrĕthĕdŏr'*, a. deserving.
merecer, *–thĕr'*, v. n. to deserve, to merit.
merecido, da, *–thĕ'dŏ*, a. meritorious.
merendar, *mĕrĕndăr'*, v. n. to take a collation between dinner and supper.
merengue, *mĕrĕn'gĕ*, sm. meringues, pl.
mergo, *mĕr'gŏ*, sm. plungeon (bird).
meridiano, *mĕridiă'nŏ*, sm. meridian; —, a. meridional.
meridional, *–diŏnăl'*, a. southern, meridional.   [dional.
merienda, *mĕriĕn'dă*, sf. luncheon.
merino, *mĕrĭ'nŏ*, sm. royal judge and inspector of sheep-walks; shepherd of merino sheep; —, na, a. moving from pasture to pasture.
mérito, *mĕ'ritŏ*, sm. merit, desert.
meritorio, ria, *mĕritŏ'riŏ*, a. meritorious.
merluza, *mĕrlŏ'thă*, a. cod.
merma, *mĕr'mă*, sf. waste, leakage.
mermar, *mĕrmăr'*, v.n. to waste, to diminish.
mermelada, *mĕrmĕlă'dă*, sf. marmelade.
mero, *mĕ'rŏ*, sm. pollack; —, ra, a. mere, pure.   [marauder.
merodeador, *mĕrŏdĕădŏr'*, sm. (mil.)
merodear, *–dĕăr'*, v. n. to pillage, to go   [marauding.
mes, *mĕs*, sm. month.
mesa, *mĕ'să*, sf. table; landing-place (of a stair-case); — redonda, table d'hôte, ordinary; — de trucos, Spanish truck-table.
mesada, *–să'dă*, sf. monthly pay or wages.
mesana, *–să'nă*, sf. (mar.) mizen-mast.
mesar, *–săr'*, v. a. to tear one's hair out.
meseta, *–sĕ'tă*, sf. landing (of a staircase).
Mesías, *mĕsĕ'ăs*, sm. Messiah.
mesón, *mĕsŏn'*, sm. inn, hostelry.
mesonero, *–nĕ'rŏ*, sm. inn-keeper.
Mesta, *mĕs'tă*, sf. proprietors of black-cattle and sheep considered as a body; annual meeting of owners of flocks.
mestizo, za, *mĕstĭ'thŏ*, a. of a mongrel breed.   [politeness; moderation.
mesura, *mĕsŏ'ră*, sf. grave deportment.
mesurado, da, *–ră'dŏ*, a. moderate; modest; gentle; prudent.
mesurar, *–răr'*, v. a. to assume a serious countenance.
metafísica, *mĕtăfĕ'sĕkă*, sf. metaphysics.
metafísico, ca, *–sĭkŏ*, a. metaphysical; —, sm. metaphysician.
metáfora, *mĕtă'fŏră*, sf. metaphor.
metafórico, ca, *mĕtăfŏ'rikŏ*, a. metaphorical.
metal, *mĕtăl'*, sm. metal; brass, latten; compass or strength of the voice.
metálico, ca, *mĕtă'lĭkŏ*, a. metallic.
metalurgia, *–lŭr'hĕă*, sf. metallurgy.
metamorfósis, *–mŏrfŏ'sĭs*, sf. metamorphosis, transformation.   [position.
metátesis, *mĕtă'tĕsĭs*, sf. metathesis, transmetéoro, *mĕtĕ'ŏrŏ*, sm. meteor.   [rology.
meteorología, *mĕtĕŏrŏlŏ'hĕ'ă*, sf. meteorometer, *mĕtĕr'*, v. a. to place, to put; to

smuggle goods into the country; to occasion; —se, to intermeddle, to interfere.
metódico, ca, *mĕtŏ'dĭkŏ*, a. methodical.
método, *mĕ'tŏdŏ*, sm. method.
metonimia, *mĕtŏnĕ'mĕă*, sf. metonymy.
metralla, *mĕtrăl'yă*, sf. grape-shot.
métrico, ca, *mĕ'trĭkŏ*, a. metrical.
metro, *mĕ'trŏ*, sm. metre; verse.
metrópoli, *mĕtrŏ'pŏlĕ*, sf. metropolis, the chief or principal city of a country; archiepiscopal church.   [metropolitan.
metropolitano, *mĕtrŏpŏlĭtă'nŏ*, sm.
mezcla, *mĕth'klă*, sf. mixture, medley.
mezclar, *mĕthklăr'*, v.a. to mix, to mingle; —se, to mix; to marry a person of inferior rank.   [of colours.
mezcolanza, *–kŏlăn'thă*, sf. bad mixture
mezquindad, *–kĭndăd'*, sf. penury, poverty; avarice.   [avaricious, covetous.
mezquino, na, *–kĕ'nŏ*, a. poor, indigent;
mezquita, *–kĕ'tă*, sf. mosque.
mf, *mĕ*, pn. oblique case of the pronoun yo;
miaja, *mĭă'h'ă*, sf. crumb.   [—, pn. my.
mico, *mĕ'kŏ*, sm. monkey.
microscópico, ca, *mĭkrŏskŏ'pĭkŏ*, a. microscopical.
microscopio, *–kŏ'pĭŏ*, sm. microscope.
miedo, *mĭă'dŏ*, sm. fear, dread.
miel, *mĭĕl'*, sf. honey.   [dog-fish; rake.
mielga, *mĭĕl'gă*, sf. (bot.) lucern; small
miembro, *mĭĕm'brŏ*, sm. member.
mientras, *mĭĕn'trăs*, ad. in the mean time.
miércoles, *mĭĕr'kŏlĕs*, sm. Wednesday.
mierda, *mĭĕr'dă*, sf. excrement, ordure.
mies, *mĭĕs*, sf. harvest.
miga, *mĕ'gă*, sf. crumb; —s, pl. fried bread-crumbs.   [particle.
migaja, *mĭgă'h'ă*, sf. scrap, crumb, small
migajón, *–hŏn'*, sm. crumb without crust.
migar, *mĭgăr'*, v. a. to crumble.
mijo, *mĕ'h'ŏ*, sm. (bot.) millet.
mil, *mĭl*, sm. one thousand.
milagro, *mĭlă'grŏ*, sm. miracle, wonder; offering of wax or any other substance, hung up in churches in commemoration of a miracle.
milagroso, sa, *–grŏ'sŏ*, a. miraculous.
milano, *mĭlă'nŏ*, sm. kite, glede (bird.)
milésimo, ma, *mĭlĕ'sĭmŏ*, a. thousandth.
milicia, *mĭlĕ'thĕă*, sf. militia.
miliciano, *mĭlĭthĭă'nŏ*, sm. militia-man; —, na, a. military.   [serve in the army.
militar, *mĭlĭtăr'*, a. military; —, v. n. to
milla, *mĭl'yă*, sf. mile.
millar, *mĭlyăr'*, sm. thousand.
millón, *mĭlyŏn'*, sm. million.
millonario, *–nă'rĭŏ*, sm. millionaire.
mimar, *mĭmăr'*, v. a. to coax, to wheedle, to flatter; to fondle, to caress.
mimbre, *mĭm'brĕ*, sm. twig of an osier.
mímico, ca, *mĕ'mĭkŏ*, a. mimic.
mimo, *mĕ'mŏ*, sm. buffoon, merry-Andrew; mime; prudery, delicacy.
mimoso, sa, *mĕmŏ'sŏ*, a. delicate, fond
mina, *mĕ'nă*, sf. conduit, subterraneous canal; mine; source of water.
minador, *mĭnădŏr'*, sm. miner.

minar, *mĭnăr'*, v.a. to undermine, to mine.
mineral, *mĭnĕrăl'*, sm. mineral; spring of water; —, a. mineral.
mineralogía, *—lŏ'hĕ'ă*, sf. mineralogy.
mineralógico, ca, *—lŏ'hĭkŏ*, a. belonging to mineralogy.
minero, *mĭnĕ'rŏ*, sm. miner.
miniatura, *mĭnĭătŏ'ră*, sf. miniature.
mínima, *mĕ'nĭmă*, sf. (mus.) minim.
mínimo, ma, *—mŏ*, s. least, smallest; —s, sm. pl. second class in grammar-schools.
minio, *mĕ'nĭŏ*, sm. minium, red-lead.
ministerio, *mĭnĭstĕ'rĭŏ*, sm. ministry (office); [of justice; minstrel.
ministril, *—trĭl'*, sm. tipstaff; petty officer
ministro, *mĭnĭs'trŏ*, sm. minister of state; petty officer of justice. [diminish.
minorar, *mĭnŏrăr'*, v. a. to lessen, to
minoridad, *mĭnŏrĭdăd'*, sf. minority.
minucioso, sa, *mĭnŭthĭŏ'sŏ*, a. superfluously exact; [to letters.
minúscula, *mĭnŭs'kŭlă*, a. small (applied
minuta, *mĭnŭ'tă*, sf. minute, first draught of an agreement in writing.
minutero, *mĭnŭtĕ'rŏ*, sm. minute-hand of a watch or clock.
minuto, *mĭnŭ'tŏ*, sm. minute.
mío, *mĕ'ŏ*, mía, *mĕ'ă*, a. my, mine.
miope, *mĭŏ'pĕ*, sm. one near-sighted.
mira, *mĕ'ră*, sf. sight of a gun; needle or point in mathematical instruments for directing the sight; estar á la —, to be on the look-out.
mirada, *mĭră'dă*, sf. glance; gaze.
mirador, ra, *—dŏr'*, sm. & f. spectator, looker-on; belvedere, gazebo.
miramiento, *—mĭĕn'tŏ*, sm. consideration; circumspection.
mirar, *mĭrăr'*, v. a. to behold, to look; to observe, to spy; —, v. imp. to concern; por lo que mira á, as to, concerning; —se, to look at oneself; to look at one
mirlo, *mĭr'lŏ*, sm. blackbird. [another.
mirón, ona, *mĭrŏn'*, sm. & f. spectator, looker-on, by-stander; prier, one who inquires with too much curiosity and officiousness, gazer.
mirra, *mĭr'ră*, sf. myrrh.
mirto, *mĭr'tŏ*, sm. myrtle.
misa, *mĭs'ă*, sf. mass; - del gallo; midmisal, *mĭsăl'*, sm. missal. [night mass.
misantropía, *mĭsăntrŏpĕ'ă*, sf. misanthropy. [thropist.
misántropo, *—ăn'trŏpŏ*, sm. misanmiscelánea, *—thĕlă'nĕă*, sf. miscellany.
miserable, *mĭsĕră'blĕ*, a. miserable, wretched, unhappy; exhausted; avaricious. [(med.) miserere.
miserere, *mĭsĕrĕ'rĕ*, sm. the Miserere;
miseria, *mĭsĕ'rĭă*, sf. misery; niggardliness; trifle. [clemency.
misericordia, *mĭsĕrĭkŏr'dĭă*, sf. mercy;
misericordioso, sa, *—kŏrdĭŏ'sŏ*, a. merciful, clement.
misión, *mĭsĭŏn'*, sf. mission.
misionero, *—nĕ'rŏ*, sm. missionary.
mismo, ma, *mĭs'mŏ*, a. same, similar, equal.
misterio, *mĭstĕ'rĭŏ*, sm. mystery.

misterioso, sa, *—rĭŏ'sŏ*, a. mysterious, mystical.
mística, *mĭs'tĭkă*, sf. mysticalness.
místico, ca, *—tĭkŏ*, a. mystic, mystical.
mitad, *mĭtăd'*, sf. moiety, half.
mitigación, *mĭtĭgăthĭŏn'*, sf. mitigation.
mitigar, *—găr'*, v. a. to mitigate.
mitología, *mĭtŏlŏ'hĕ'ă*, sf. mythology.
mitológico, ca, *—lŏ'hĭkŏ*, a. mythological.
mitones, *mĭtŏ'nĕs*, sm. pl. mittens.
mitra, *mĕ'tră*, sf. mitre.
mitrado, *mĭtră'dŏ*, a. mitred.
mixtión, *mĭkstĭŏn'*, sf. mixing, mixture.
mixto, ta, *mĭks'tŏ*, misto, ta, *mĭs'tŏ*, a. mixed, mingled.
mixtura, *mĭkstŭ'ră*, sf. mixture.
mocadero, *mŏkădĕ'rŏ*, sm. pocket-handkerchief.
mocedad, *mŏthĕdăd'*, sf. youthfulness.
moción, *mŏthĭŏn'*, sf. motion.
moco, *mŏ'kŏ*, sm. snot; snuff of a candle.
mocosidad, *mŏkŏsĭdăd'*, sf. mucosity.
mocoso, sa, *mŏkŏ'sŏ*, a. snotty, snivelly; mucous.
mochila, *mŏtshĕ'lă*, sf. knapsack.
mocho, cha, *mŏtsh'ŏ*, a. dishorned, having the horns cut off; cropped, shorn; lopped, having the branches cut off; maimed, mutilated.
mochuelo, *mŏtshŭĕ'lŏ*, sm. red owl.
moda, *mŏ'dă*, sf. fashion, mode.
modelar, *mŏdĕlăr'*, v.a. to model, to form.
modelo, *mŏdĕ'lŏ*, sm. model, pattern.
moderación, *mŏdĕrăthĭŏn'*, sf. moderation; temperance. [temperate.
moderado, da, *—ră'dŏ*, a. moderate,
moderar, *mŏdĕrăr'*, v. a. to moderate.
moderno, na, *mŏdĕr'nŏ*, a. modern.
modestia, *mŏdĕs'tĭă*, sf. modesty, decency.
modesto, ta, *mŏdĕs'tŏ*, a. modest.
modificación, *mŏdĭfĭkăthĭŏn'*, sf. modification; limitation. [moderate.
modificar, *—kăr'*, v. a. to modify; to
modificativo, va, *—kătĭ'vŏ*, sm. & a. modificative. [dress; —, sf. milliner.
modista, *mŏdĭs'tă*, a. person fond of modo, *mŏ'dŏ*, sm. mode, method, manner; moderation; mood. [ness.
modorra, *mŏdŏr'ră*, sf. drowsiness, doziness
modorrar, *—răr'*, v. a. to render heavy with sleep; —se, to become flabby.
modorro, rra, *mŏdŏr'rŏ*, a. drowsy, sleepy.
modrego, *mŏdrĕ'gŏ*, sm. dunce, dolt.
modulación, *mŏdŭlăthĭŏn'*, sf. modulation.
modular, *mŏdŭlăr'*, v. a. to modulate.
mofa, *mŏ'fă*, sf. mockery. [scorner.
mofador, ra, *mŏfădŏr'*, sm. & f. scoffer,
mofar, *—făr'*, v. a. & r. to deride; to mock; to scoff.
moflete, *—flĕ'tĕ*, sm. chub-cheek, blub-cheek.
mogollón, *—gŏlyŏn'*, sm. hanger-on, parasite, sponger. [with moss.
mohecer, *—ĕthĕr'*, v. a. to moss, to cover
mohína, *—ĕ'nă*, sf. animosity, desire of revenge, resentment, grudge.
mohíno, na, *—ŏ'nă*, a. fretful, peevish.
moho, *mŏ'ŏ*, sm. (bot.) moss. [mossy.
mohoso, sa, *mŏŏ'sŏ*, a. mouldy, musty;

11*

mojadura, _mŏ'hădŏ'rä_, sf. act of moisten-
ing or wetting. [meddle, to interfere.
mojar, _mŏ'hăr'_, v. a. to wet, to moisten; to
moje, _mŏ'hě'_, sm. fricassee, ragout.
mojicón, _mŏ'hĭkŏn'_, sm. cuff, punch.
mojiganza, _-găn'thä_, sf. masquerade;
mummery.
mojigato, _-găto_, a. hypocritical.
mojón, _mŏ'hŏn'_, sm. land-mark.
mola, _mŏ'lä_, sf. mole.
moldar, _mŏldăr'_, v. a. to mould.
molde, _mŏl'dě_, sm. mould; model.
moldura, _mŏldŏ'rä_, sf. moulding.
mole, _mŏ'lě_, a. soft, mild; —, sf. vast size
or quantity; massiness.
molécula, _mŏlě'kŭlä_, sf. molecule.
moledor, _mŏlědŏr'_, sm. grinder; tiresome
fellow, bore.
moler, _mŏlěr'_, v. a. to grind, to pound; to
vex, to molest; to waste, to consume by use.
molestar, _mŏlěstăr'_, v. a. to vex, to molest,
to trouble.
molestia, _mŏlěs'tĭä_, sf. injury, molestation.
molesto, ta, _-tŏ_, a. molest, vexatious.
moletón, _mŏlětŏn'_, sm. milled flannel.
molicie, _mŏlĭ'thĭě_, sf. tenderness, softness.
molienda, _mŏlĭěn'dä_, sf. act of grinding
or pounding; fatigue, lassitude.
molinero, _mŏlĭně'rŏ_, sm. miller.
molinete, _-nă'tě_, sm. windlass; turnstile.
molinillo, _-nĭl'yŏ_, sm. hand-mill; choco-
molino, _mŏlĭ'nŏ_, sm. mill. [late-mill.
mollar, _mŏlyăr'_, a. soft, pappy, pulpous;
credulous.
molleja, _mŏlyě'hä_, sf. gland; gizzard.
mollera, _-yěrä_, sf. crown or top of the
mollete, _-yě'tě_, sm. French roll. [head.
molletudo, da, _mŏlyětŏ'dŏ_, a. chub-faced.
momentáneo, nea, _mŏměntäně'ŏ_, a.
momentaneous.
momento, _mŏměn'tŏ_, sm. moment.
momería, _mŏměrě'ä_, sf. mummery.
momio, mia, _mŏ'mĭŏ_, a. meagre, lean.
momia, _mŏ'mĭä_, sf. mummy.
momo, _mŏ'mŏ_, sm. buffoonery, grimaces.
mona, _mŏ'nä_, sf. female monkey; ludicrous
imitator; drunkenness; drunkard.
monacal, _mŏnäkăl'_, a. monachal, monkish.
monacillo, _-thĭl'yŏ_, sm. acolyte.
monada, _mŏnä'dä_, sf. grimace.
monago, _mŏnä'gŏ_, monaguillo, _-gŭl'yŏ_,
sm. acolyte.
monarca, _mŏnär'kä_, sm. monarch.
monarquía, _-kě'ä_, sf. monarchy.
monárquico, ca, _mŏnär'kĭkŏ_, a. monar-
chical. [cloister.
monasterio, _mŏnästě'rĭŏ_, sm. monastery.
monástico, ca, _mŏnäs'tĭkŏ_, a. monastic.
monda, _mŏn'dä_, sf. pruning of trees.
mondadientes, _-dĭěn'těs_, sm. toothpick.
mondadura, _-dŏ'rä_, sf. cleaning, cleansing; —s, pl. parings, peelings.
mondar, _mŏndăr'_, v. a. to clean, to cleanse;
to husk, to peel; to deprive of money.
mondo, da, _mŏn'dŏ_, a. neat, clean, pure;
— y lirondo, without any admixture.
mondongo, _-dŏn'gŏ_, sm. paunch, tripe.
moneda, _mŏně'dä_, sf. money, coinage.

moned(e)ar, _mŏněd(ĕ)är'_, v. a. to coin.
monedero, _mŏnědě'rŏ_, sm. coiner.
monería, _-rĕ'ä_, sf. grimace, mimicry;
trifle, gewgaw. [coins.
monetario, _-tě'rĭŏ_, sm. cabinet of ancient
monición, _mŏnĭthŏn'_, sf. admonition;
publication of the banns (of marriage).
monises, _mŏnĭ'sěs_, sm. pl. (vulg.) money.
monita, _mŏ'nĭtä_, sf. cunning, craft.
monitor, _mŏnĭtŏr'_, sm. admonisher; (mar.)
monitor, turret-ship. [nun.
monje, _mŏn'hě_, sm. monja, _-hä_, sf. monk;
mono, na, _mŏ'nŏ_, a. neat, pretty, nice; —,
sm. monkey, ape.
monólogo, _mŏnŏ'lŏgŏ_, sm. monologue.
monopolio, _mŏnŏpŏ'lĭŏ_, sm. monopoly.
monopolista, _-pŏlĭs'tä_, sm. monopolist,
monopoliser.
monosílabo, ba, _-sĭ'läbŏ_, a. monosylla-
bical; —, sm. monosyllable.
monotonía, _-tŏně'ä_, sf. monotony. [nous.
monótono, na, _mŏnŏ'tŏnŏ_, v. n. monoto-
monstruo, _mŏn'strŏŏ_, sm. monster.
monstruosidad, _-sĭdäd'_, sf. monstruosity.
monstruoso, sa, _-ŏ'sŏ_, a. monstrous.
monta, _mŏn'tä_, sf. amount, sum total.
montaje, _mŏntä'hě_, sm. mounting of
artillery; —s, pl. carriage or bed of a
cannon. [in fencing.
montante, _mŏntän'tě_, sm. broadsword used
montaña, _mŏntän'yä_, sf. mountain.
montañés, esa, _-yěs'_, a. pertaining to
the mountains; mountainous; —, s.
mountaineer.
montañoso, sa, _-yŏ'sŏ_, a. mountainous.
montar, _mŏntăr'_, v. n. to mount (on horseback); to amount to. [untamed.
montaraz, _-răth'_, a. mountainous; wild,
montazgo, _mŏntäth'gŏ_, sm. toll to be paid
for cattle passing from one province into
another.
monte, _mŏn'tě_, sm. mountain; wood, forest;
difficulty; — alto, lofty grove; — bajo,
copse, coppice, brush-wood.
montera, _mŏntě'rä_, sf. peasant's cap.
montería, _-rě'ä_, sf. hunting, chase.
montero, _mŏntě'rŏ_, sm. huntsman, hunter.
montés, esa, _mŏntěs'_, montesino, na,
_-sĭ'nŏ_, a. bred or found in a forest or
mountain.
montón, _mŏntŏn'_, sm. heap, pile; mass,
cluster; á -ones, abundantly, by heaps.
montuoso, sa, _mŏntŏŏ'sŏ_, a. mountainous,
hilly. [intended for the saddle.
montura, _mŏntŏ'rä_, sf. horses and mules
monumento, _mŏnŏměn'tŏ_, sm. monument;
altar raised in churches on Holy Thursday
to resemble a sepulchre; —s, pl. monu-
ments or remains of antiquity.
monzón, _mŏnthŏn'_, sm. monsoon. [ness.
moña, _mŏn'yä_, sf. doll; (fam.) drunken-
moño, _-yŏ_, sm. hair on the crown of the
head tied together; tuft of feathers on the
heads of some birds.
moquear, _mŏkěär'_, v. n. to blow the nose.
moquero, _mŏkä'rŏ_, sm. pocket-handkerchief. [or nose.
moquete, _mŏkä'tě_, sm. blow on the face

moquillo, _-kil′yō_, sm. pip (disease in
moquita, _-kē′tä_, sf. snivel.   [fowls].
morada, _mōrä′dä_, sf. habitation, abode,
residence.   [coloured.
morado, da, _-dō_, a. violet, mulberry-
morador, _-dōr′_, sm. inhabitant, lodger.
moral, _mōräl′_, sm. mulberry-tree; —, sf.
morals, ethics; —, a. moral.
moralidad, _mōrälidäd′_, sf. morality.
moralista, _mōrälis′tä_, sm. moralist.
moralizar, _mōrälithär′_, v. n. to moralise.
moralmente, _mōrälmen′te_, ad. morally.
morar, _mōrär′_, v. n. to inhabit, to dwell.
moratoria, _mōrätō′riä_, sf. letter of license
granted to a debtor.   [soft, mellow.
mórbido, da, _mōr′bidō_, a. morbid, diseased;
morboso, sa, _mōrbō′sō_, a. diseased, morbid.
morcilla, _-thil′yä_, sf. black-pudding.
mordacidad, _-däthidäd′_, sf. mordacity.
mordaz, _mōrdäth′_, a. corrosive, biting;
sarcastic; mordacious.
mordaza, _-dä′thä_, sf. gag.
mordedura, _-dēdō′rä_, sf. bite.
morder, _mōrder′_, v. a. to bite.
mordiscar, _-diskär′_, v. a. to gnaw, to nibble.
mordisco, _-dis′kō_, mordiscón, _-dis-
kōn′_, sm. bite.
morena, _mōrä′nä_, sf. brown bread; sea-eel.
moreno, na, _-nō_, a. brown, swarthy.
morga, _mōr′gä_, sf. dregs of oil.
moribundo, da, _mōribūn′dō_, a. dying.
morigeración, _-′herathiōn′_, sf. temperance.
morigerar, _mōriherär′_, v. a. to moderate.
morillo, _mōril′yō_, sm. andiron.
morir, _mōrir′_, v. n. to die, to expire; —se,
to go out, to be extinguished; to be be-
numbed.
morisco, ca, _mōris′kä_, a. Moorish; —, sm.
name given to the Moors who remained
in Spain after its restoration.
morisma, _-mä_, sf. Mohammedan sect;
multitude of Moors.
morisqueta, _-kē′tä_, sf. Moorish trick.
moriaco, ca, _mōriä′kō_, a. affecting ignorance and stupidity.
moro, ra, _mō′rō_, a. Moorish.   [podge.
morondanga, _mōröndän′gä_, sf. hodge-
morondo, da, _mōrōn′dō_, a. bald; leafless.
morosidad, _mōrōsidäd′_, sf. slowness,
delay, tardiness, dilatoriness.
moroso, sa, _mōrō′sō_, a. slow, tardy, heavy.
morrada, _mōrrä′dä_, sf. butting with the
heads between two people.
morral, _mōrräl′_, sm. fodder-bag, nose-bag;
sportsman's-bag.
morralla, _mōrräl′yä_, sf. hotch-potch.
morrillo, _-ril′yō_, sm. pebble; fat of the
nape of a sheep.   [melancholy.
morriña, _-rin′yä_, sf. murrain; sadness,
morrión, _mōrriōn′_, sm. morion, spike-
helmet.   [object; overhanging lip.
morro, _mōr′rō_, sm. any round skull-like
morrudo, da, _-rō′dō_, a. blubber-lipped.
mortaja, _mōrtä′h′ä_, sf. shroud, winding-
sheet; mortise.
mortal, _mōrtäl′_, a. mortal; fatal, deadly.
mortalidad, _-lidäd′_, sf. mortality.

mortandad, _-tändäd′_, sf. mortality, epidemic disease.   [firing at festivities.
morterete, _-tērē′te_, sm. small mortar for
mortero, _mōrtē′rō_, sm. mortar (cannon).
mortífero, ra, _mōrtē′ferō_, a. mortiferous,
fatal.   [cation; vexation, trouble.
mortificación, _mōrtifikäthiōn′_, sf. mortifi-
mortificar, _-fikär′_, v. a. to mortify; to
afflict, to vex.   [—, a. mortuary.
mortuorio, _mōrtüō′riō_, sm. burial, funeral;
moruno, na, _mōrō′nō_, a. Moorish.
mosaico, ca, _mōsä′ikō_, a. Mosaic.
mosca, _mōs′kä_, sf. fly.
moscardón, _mōskärdōn′_, sm. large gad-
fly; importuning, sly fellow.
moscatel, _-kätel′_, a. muscadine or mus-
catel grape.   [deceitful fellow.
moscón, _mōskōn′_, sm. large fly; crafty,
mosquero, _mōskē′rō_, sm. fly-trap.
mosquetería, _mōskētēri′ä_, sf. body of
musketeers; musketry.
mosquetero, _-tē′rō_, sm. musketeer.
mosquitero, _mōskitē′rō_, sm. mosquito-net.
mosquito, _mōskē′tō_, sm. gnat, mosquito;
tippler, toper, fuddler.
mostachón, _mōstächōn′_, sm. marchpane.
mostaza, _mōstä′thä_, sf. mustard; mustard-
seed; hail-shot.   [and mustard.
mostillo, _-til′yō_, sm. sauce made of must
mosto, _mōs′tō_, sm. must, new wine.
mostrador, _-trädōr′_, sm. counter; shop-
front.
mostrar, _-trär′_, v. a. to show, to exhibit;
—se, to appear, to show oneself.
mostrenco, ca, _-tren′kō_, a. strayed,
ownerless; vagabond, vagrant; ignorant,
stupid.
mota, _mō′tä_, sf. bit of thread, &c., sticking to cloth; slight defect or fault.
mote, _mō′te_, sm. nickname.   [ridicule.
motejar, _mōte′här′_, v. a. to censure, to
motilar, _mōtilär′_, v. a. to cut off the hair.
motín, _mōtin′_, sm. mutiny.   [to crop.
motivar, _mōtivär′_, v. a. to give a reason,
to assign a motive.
motivo, _mōtē′vō_, sm. motive, cause, reason.
motor, _mōtōr′_, sm. mover, motor; —, a.
movable.
motriz, _mōtrith′_, a. motory, motive.
movedizo, za, _mōvēdē′thō_, a. movable;
variable, inconstant.
mover, _mōver′_, v. a. to move; to touch
pathetically; to stir up; to excite.
movible, _mōvē′ble_, a. movable.
móvil, _mō′vil_, a. movable.   [constancy.
movilidad, _mōvilidäd′_, sf. mobility; in-
movimiento, _-mien′tō_, sm. movement,
motion; sedition.
moza, _mō′thä_, sf. girl, lass; maid-servant;
last or conquering game.
mozo, za, _mō′thō_, a. young; —, sm. youth,
lad; man-servant.   [officiating bishop.
muceta, _mūthē′tä_, sf. mantlet worn by an
muchacha, _mütshätsh′ä_, sf. girl; lass.
muchachada, _-tshä′dä_, sf. boyish trick.
muchacho, _-tshō_, sm. boy; lad; —, cha,
a. boyish, girlish.   [tude, plenty.
muchedumbre, _mütshēdüm′bre_, sf. multi-

mucho, cha, *mătsh'ŏ,* a. much, abundant; —, ad. much. [moulting.

muda, *mŏ'dă,* sf. change, alteration; act of moulting.

mudable, *mŭdă'blĕ,* a. changeable, variable, mutable. [tion; inconstancy.

mudanza, *mŭdăn'thă,* sf. change; mutation; inconstancy.

mudar, *mŭdăr',* v. a. to change; to mew, to moult; to change one's voice; —se, to change; to change sentiments and manners; to shift; to change house.

mudez, *mŭdĕth',* sf. dumbness.

mudo, da, *mŏ'dŏ,* a. dumb; silent, mute.

mueca, *mŭĕ'kă,* sf. grimace, wry face.

muela, *mŭĕ'lă,* sf. upper mill-stone; grindstone; mill-dam; hillock; —s, pl. grinders, molar-teeth.

muelle, *mŭĕl'yĕ,* a. tender, delicate, soft; —, sm. spring; regulator; quay, wharf.

muérdago, *mŭĕr'dăgŏ,* sm. (bot.) mistletoe.

muermo, *mŭĕr'mŏ,* sm. glanders.

muerte, *mŭĕr'tĕ,* sf. death.

muerto, —*tŏ,* sm. corpse; —, ta, a. dead.

muesca, *mŭĕs'kă,* sf. notch, groove.

muestra, *mŭĕs'tră,* sf. pattern; fag-end of a piece of stuff; copy written to be imitated by boys; indicative sign; specimen, design, model; (mil.) muster-roll; dial, clock which does not strike; watch.

mugido, *mŭ'pĭ'dŏ,* sm. lowing of an ox.

mugir, *mŭ'hĭr',* v. n. to low; to bellow.

mugre, *mŏ'grĕ,* sm. dirt sticking to clothes, &c; [filthy.

mugriento, ta, *mŭgrĭĕn'tŏ,* a. greasy, dirty.

mujer, *mŭ'hĕr',* sf. woman.

mujeril, *mŭ'hĕrĭl',* a. womanish, womanly.

mula, *mŏ'lă,* sf. she-mule; [very dirty.

muladar, *mŭlădăr',* sm. laystall; anything.

mular, *mŭlăr',* a. belonging to mules.

mulatero, *mŭlătĕ'rŏ,* sm. muleteer.

mulato, *mŭlă'tŏ,* a. mulatto.

muleta, *mŭlĕ'tă,* sf. crutch.

mulo, *mŏ'lŏ,* sm. mule.

multa, *mŭl'tă,* sf. mulct, fine, penalty.

multar, *mŭltăr',* v. a. to impose a pecuniary penalty; [tiplication.

multiplicación, *mŭltĭplĭkăthĭŏn',* sf. multiplicador, ra, —*kădŏr',* sm. & f. multiplier; (ar.) multiplicator; [plicand.

multiplicando, —*kăn'dŏ,* sm. (ar.) multiplicar, —*kăr',* v. a. to multiply.

multiplice, *mŭltĭ'plĭthĕ,* a. multiple; multiplicious; [plicity.

multiplicidad, *mŭltĭplĭthĭdăd',* sf. multitude, great number; [up.

multitud, *mŭltĭtŭd',* sf. multitude, great number; [up.

mullir, *mŭlyĭr',* v. a. to beat up, to shake worldly.

mundano, na, *mŭndă'nŏ,* a. mundane;

mundinovi, *mŭndĭnŏ'vĭ,* mundinuevo, —*năĕ'vŏ,* sm. raree-show, magic-lantern.

mundo, *mŭn'dŏ,* sm. world.

munición, *mŭnĭthĭŏn',* sf. ammunition.

municionar, —*năr',* v. a. to munition.

municipal, *mŭnĭthĭpăl',* a. municipal.

munificencia, —*fĭthĕn'thĭă,* sf. munificence, liberality.

muñeca, *mŭnyă'kă,* sf. wrist; child's doll.

muñeco, —*kŏ,* sm. puppet; effeminate fellow; [poration; messenger.

muñidor, *mŭnyĭdŏr',* sm. beadle of a corporation;

muñón, *mŭnyŏn',* sm. brawn; stump of an amputated limb.

muralla, *mŭrăl'yă,* sf. rampart, wall.

murciélago, *mŭrthĭĕ'lăgŏ,* sm. bat.

murmullo, *mŭrmŭl'yŏ,* sm. murmur, mutter; [privy calumny.

murmuración, —*mŭrăthĭŏn',* sf. backbiting.

murmurador, ra, —*rădŏr',* sm. & f. detractor, backbiter.

murmurar, —*răr',* v. a. to murmur, to purl; to backbite; [stream.

murmurio, —*mŭr'rĭŏ,* sm. murmuring of a muro, *mŏ'rŏ,* sm. wall.

murria, *mŭr'rĭă,* sf. heaviness of the head.

musa, *mŏ'să,* sf. Muse.

musaraña, *mŭsără'nyă,* sf. shrew-mouse; hobgoblin; vermin.

muscular, *mŭskŭlăr',* a. muscular.

músculo, *mŭs'kŭlŏ,* sm. muscle.

muselina, *mŭsĕlĭ'nă,* sf. muslin.

museo, *mŭsĕ'ŏ,* sm. museum.

musgo, *mŭs'gŏ,* sm. moss.

música, *mŏ'sĭkă,* sf. music.

musical, *mŭsĭkăl',* a. musical. [musical.

músico, ca, *mŏ'sĭkŏ,* s. musician; —, a.

muslo, *mŭs'lŏ,* sm. thigh.

mustiamente, *mŭstĭămĕn'tĕ,* ad. sadly, in a melancholy manner.

mustio, tia, *mŭs'tĭŏ,* a. parched, withered; sad, sorrowful; musty. [inconstancy.

mutabilidad, *mŭtăbĭlĭdăd',* sf. mutability.

mutación, —*thĭŏn',* sf. mutation, change.

mutilación, *mŭtĭlăthĭŏn',* sf. mutilation.

mutilar, —*lăr',* v. a. to mutilate, to maim.

mutual, *mŭtŭăl',* mutuo, tua, *mŏ'tŭŏ,* a. mutual, reciprocal. [most illustrious.

muy, *mŭĭ',* ad. very; greatly; — ilustre,

N.

nabal, *năbăl',* nabar, —*băr'* sm. turnipfield; —, a. made of turnips.

nabo, *nă'bŏ,* sm. rape, colewort.

nácar, *nă'kăr,* sm. mother of pearl, nacre.

nacarado, da, —*ră'dŏ,* a. set with mother of pearl; pearl-coloured.

nacer, *năthĕr',* v. n. to be born, to bud; to shoot (of plants); to rise; to grow; —se, to be propagated by nature (as grass).

nacido, da, *năthĭ'dŏ,* a. proper, apt, fit; inborn; —, sm. tumour, abscess; —s, pl. all men born. [ity.

nacimiento, —*mĭĕn'tŏ,* sm. birth; Nativ-

nación, *năthĭŏn',* sf. nation.

nacional, —*năl',* a. national.

nacionalidad, —*nălĭdăd',* sf. national customs, nationality. [by no means.

nada, *nă'dă,* sf. nothing; —, ad. in no way,

nadaderas, —*dĕ'răs,* sf. pl. swimming bladders (for learning to swim).

nadadero, —*dĕ'rŏ,* sm. swimming-place.

nadador, ra, —*dŏr',* sm. & f. swimmer.

nadar, *nădăr',* v. n. to swim.

nadie, *nä´dlē*, sm. nobody, no one.

nado, *nä´dŏ*, á –, ad. afloat.

naipe, *nä´i-ē*, sm. playing-card.

nalga, *näl´gä*, sf. buttock, rump.

nao, *nä´ŏ*, sf. ship, vessel.

naranja, *närän´hä*, sf. orange.

naranjada, –*hä´dä*, sf. conserve of oranges; orange-water.

naranjado, do, –*dŏ*, a. orange-coloured.

naranjal, *närän´häl*, sm. orangery.

naranjazo, *´hä´thŏ*, sm. blow with an orange.   [orange-tree.

naranjero, –*´hä´rŏ*, sm. orange-seller.

naranjo, *närän´´hŏ*, sm. orange-tree.

narciso, *närthē´ŏ*, sm. (bot.) daffodil; narcissus flower; precious stone of the colour of daffodil; fop, coxcomb.

narcótico, ca, *närkŏ´itkŏ*, a. narcotic.

nardo, *när´dŏ*, sm. spikenard.

narigón, *närĭgŏn´*, sm. large nose; –, ona, a. big-nosed.

narigudo, da, –*gŏ´dŏ*, a. big-nosed.

nariz, *närĭth´*, sf. nose; sense of smelling.

narración, *närräthŏn´*, sf. narration.

narrar, *närär´*, v. a. to narrate, to tell.

narrativa, *närrätĭvä*, sf. narrative, relation; talent for narration.

nasa, *nä´sä*, sf. osier lobster-pot.

nata, *nä´tä*, sf. cream.

natal, *nätäl´*, a. natal, native.

natalicio, cia, *nätälĭthĭŏ*, a. natal.

natillas, *nätĭl´yäs*, sf. pl. cream made of boiled flour, eggs and sugar.

natividad, *nätĭvĭdäd´*, sf. nativity.

nativo, va, *nätĭ´vŏ*, a. native.

natural, *nätŭräl´*, sm. temper, natural disposition; –, a. natural, native; common, usual; ingenuous, unaffected; al –, unaffectedly.

naturaleza, –*lĕ´thä*, sf. nature.

naturalidad, –*lĭdäd´*, sf. birth-right; naturalness; ingenuity, candour.

naturalista, –*lĭ´stä*, sm. naturalist.

naturalizar, –*lĭthär´*, v. n. to naturalize; –se, to become accustomed.

naufragar, *näŭfrägär´*, v. n. to be shipwrecked, to suffer wreck; to suffer ruin in one's affairs.

naufragio, *näŭfrä´hĭŏ*, sm. shipwreck.

náufrago, ga, *nä´ŭfrägŏ*, a. relating to shipwreck.

náusea, *nä´ŭsĕä*, sf. nauseousness, nausea.

náutica, *nä´ŭtĭkä*, sf. art of navigating.

navaja, *nävä´h´ä*, sf. clasp-knife; razor.

navajada, –*hä´dä*, sf. gash given with a knife.   [shaving-towel.

navajero, –*´hä´rŏ*, sm. razor-case;

naval, *nävä̆l´*, a. naval.

nave, *nä´vĕ*, sf. ship; nave.

navegable, *nävĕgä´blĕ*, a. navigable.

navegación, –*gäthŏn´*, sf. navigation.

navegador, –*gädŏr´*, navegante, –*gän´tĕ*, sm. navigator.

navegar, *nävĕgär´*, v. n. to navigate.

naveta, *nävĕ´tä*, sf. censer.

navidad, *nävĭdäd´*, sf. nativity.

navío, *nävĕ´ŏ*, sm. ship.

náyade, *nä´yädĕ*, sf. naiad, water-nymph.

neblina, *nĕblĕ´nä*, sf. mist, fine rain, drizzle.

nebuloso, sa, *nĕbŭlŏ´sŏ*, a. misty, cloudy, nebulous, foggy, hazy, drizzling.

necear, *nĕthĕär´*, v. n. to talk nonsense.

necedad, –*däd´*, sf. gross ignorance, stupidity; imprudence.

necesaria, –*sä´rĭä*, sf. privy, water-closet.

necesario, ria, –*sä´rĭŏ*, a. necessary.

necesidad, –*sĭdäd´*, sf. necessity, need, want.   [needy.

necesitado, da, –*sĭtä´dŏ*, a. necessitous,

necesitar, –*sĭtär´*, v. a. to necessitate; –, v. n. to want, to need.

necio, cia, *nĕ´thĭŏ*, a. ignorant, stupid, foolish; imprudent.

necrología, *nĕkrŏlŏ´hĕ´ä*, sf. necrology, an account of persons deceased.   [tuary.

necrologio, –*lŏ´hĕŏ*, sm. necrology, mortuary.

néctar, *nĕk´tär*, sm. nectar.   [abominable.

nefando, da, *nĕfän´dŏ*, a. base, nefarious,

nefario, ria, *nĕfä´rĭŏ*, a. nefarious, abominable.   [or wrong.

nefas, *nĕ´fäs*, ad. por fas ó por –, right

negación, *nĕgäthŏn´*, sf. negation.

negado, *nĕgä´dŏ*, a. incapable, unfit.

negar, *nĕgär´*, v. a. to deny, to abnegate; to refuse; –se, to decline to do a thing.

negativa, –*tĕ´vä*, sf. negation; repulse; negative.

negativo, va, –*tĕ´vŏ*, a. negative.

negligencia, *nĕglĭ´hĕn´thĭä*, sf. negligence.

negligente, –*hĕn´tĕ*, a. negligent, careless, heedless.

negociación, *nĕgŏthĭäthŏn´*, sf. negotiation; commerce.   [dealer.

negociante, –*thĭän´tĕ*, sm. & f. trader,

negociar, –*thĭär´*, v. n. to negotiate (bills of exchange, political affairs).

negocio, *nĕgŏ´thĭŏ*, sm. business, affair; negotiation.   [appear black.

negrear, *nĕgrĕär´*, v. n. to grow black, to

negrillo, *nĕgrĭl´yŏ*, sm. black poplar.

negro, gra, *nĕ´grŏ*, a. black; jetty; –, sm. negro, blackamoor.

negrura, *nĕgrŏ´rä*, sf. blackness.

negruzco, ca, *nĕgrŭth´kŏ*, a. blackish.

némine discrepante, *nĕ´mĭnĕ dĭskrĕpän´tĕ*, ad. unanimously.

nene, *nĕ´nĕ*, sm., nena, *nĕ´nä*, sf. baby.

neófito, *nĕŏ´fĭtŏ*, sm. neophyte.

nervio, *nĕr´vĭŏ*, sm. nerve.

nervoso, sa, *nĕrvŏ´sŏ*, a. nervous.

nervudo, –*vŏ´dŏ*, a. nervous, vigorous.

nesga, *nĕs´gä*, sf. gore (of a gown).

neto, ta, *nĕ´tŏ*, a. neat, pure, net.

neutral, *nĕŭträl´*, a. neutral, neuter.

neutralidad, –*ĭdäd´*, sf. neutrality.

neutralizar, –*ĭthär´*, v. a. (chem.) to neutralize.

neutro, tra, *nĕ´ŭtrŏ*, a. neutral, neuter.

nevada, *nĕvä´dä*, sf. heavy fall of snow.

nevar, *nĕvär´*, v. n. to snow.

nevera, *nĕvä´rä*, nevería, –*rĕ´ä*, sf. [ice-house.

ni, *nĭ*, c. neither, nor.

nicho, *nítsh'ŏ*, sm. niche.
nido, *nē'dŏ*, sm. nest; habitation.
niebla, *nē'blā*, sf. fog, mist.
nieta, *nē'tā*, sf. granddaughter.
nieto, *nē'tŏ*, sm. grandson.
nieve, *nē'vĕ*, sf. snow.
nigromancia, *nĭgrŏmān'thĭā*, sf. necro- [mancy.
nigromante, *—mān'tĕ*, sm. necromancer.
nigromántico, ca, *—mān'tĭkŏ*, a. necro-
mantic.
nimiamente, *nĭ'mĭāmĕntĕ*, ad. excessively.
nimiedad, *nĭmĭĕdād'*, sf. excess; extravagant nicety.
nimio, mia, *nĭ'mĭŏ*, a. excessive, too little.
ninfa, *nĭn'fā*, sf. nymph.
ningún, *nĭngūn'*, a. none, not one.
ninguno, na, *nĭngŏ'nŏ*, a. none, not one,
neither. [of the eye.
niña, *nĭn'yā*, sf. little girl; pupil, apple
niñada, *—yā'dā*, sf. puerility, childishness.
niñear, *—yĕār'*, v. n. to act like a child.
niñera, *—yā'rā*, sf. nursemaid. [action.
niñería, *—yĕrē'ā*, sf. puerility, childish
niñero, ra, *—yā'rŏ*, a. fond of children.
niñez, *—yĕth'*, sf. childhood.
niño, ña, *nĭn'yŏ*, a. childish; —, sm. child,
infant; desde —, from infancy, from a
níspera, *nĭs'pĕrā*, sf. medlar. [child.
níspero, *nĭs'pĕrŏ*, sm. medlar-tree.
nitrato, *nĭtrā'tŏ*, sm. (chem.) nitrate.
nitro, *nē'trŏ*, sm. nitre, saltpetre.
nivel, *nĭvĕl'*, sm. level, plane; á —, perfectly level.
nivelador, *nĭvĕlādŏr'*, sm. leveller.
nivelar, *nĭvĕlār'*, v. a. to level.
no, *nŏ*, ad. no; not.
noble, *nŏ'blĕ*, a. noble, illustrious, generous.
nobleza, *nŏblĕ'thā*, sf. nobleness, nobility.
noción, *nŏthĭŏn'*, sf. notion, idea.
nocivo, va, *nŏthĭ'vŏ*, a. noxious, hurtful.
nocturno, na, *nŏktūr'nŏ*, a. nocturnal,
nightly; —, sm. nocturn.
noche, *nŏtsh'ĕ*, sf. night; —buena, Christmas eve; ¡buenas —s! good night!
nodriza, *nŏdrē'thā*, sf. nurse.
nogal, *nŏgāl'*, sm. common walnut-tree.
nómade, *nŏ'mādĕ*, a. nomad, nomadic.
nombradía, *nŏmbrādē'ā*, sf. fame, reputa-
tation. [tion; appointment.
nombramiento, *—mĭĕn'tŏ*, sm. nomina-
nombrar, *—brār'*, v. a. to name; to nominate, to appoint. [tion.
nombre, *nŏm'brĕ*, sm. name; title; reputa-
nomenclatura, *nŏmĕnklātŏ'rā*, sf. nomenclature; catalogue.
nómina, *nŏ'mĭnā*, sf. catalogue.
nominador, *—nādŏr'*, sm. nominator.
nominal, *—nāl'*, a. nominal. [native.
nominativo, *—nātĭ'vŏ*, sm. (gr.) nomi-
nomparelle, *nŏmpārĕl'yĕ*, sf. nonpareil
non, *nŏn*, a. odd, uneven. [(type.)
nona, *nŏ'nā*, sf. none.
nonada, *nŏnā'dā*, sf. trifle.
nonagenario, ria, *—'hĕnā'rĭŏ*, a. ninety
years old; —, sm. & f. nonagenarian.
nonagésimo, ma, *—'hĕ'sĭmŏ*, a. ninetieth.
nonato, ta, *nŏnā'tŏ*, a. applied to one who
has not been naturally born, but dragged

out of the mother's womb by means of
the cesarean section.
nono, na, *nŏ'nŏ*, a. ninth.
no obstante, *nŏ ŏbstān'tĕ*, ad. nevertheless, notwithstanding.
nord, *nŏrd*, sm. north wind.
nordest(e), *—ĕs'tĕ*, sm. north-east.
noria, *nŏ'rĭā*, sf. chain-pump; draw-well.
norma, *nŏr'mā*, sf. square (tool); rule to
guide and govern all operations.
norte, *nŏr'tĕ*, sm. north; rule, guide.
nos, *nŏs*, pn. we.
nosotros, tras, *—ŏ'trŏs*, pn. we, ourselves.
nostalgia, *nŏstāl'hĭā*, sf. home-sickness.
nota, *nŏ'tā*, sf. note, notice, remark.
notable, *nŏtā'blĕ*, a. notable, remarkable;
—, sm. introductory observation.
notar, *nŏtār'*, v. a. to note, to mark; to
remark. [tary; notary's office.
notaría, *nŏtārē'ā*, sf. profession of a no-
notario, *nŏtā'rĭŏ*, sm. notary.
noticia, *nŏtĭ'thĭā*, sf. notice, knowledge,
information, note; news.
noticiar, *nŏtĭthĭār'*, v. a. to give notice.
noticioso, sa, *—thĭŏ'sŏ*, a. informed;
learned.
notificación, *—fĭkāthĭŏn'*, sf. notification.
notificar, *—fĭkār'*, v. a. to notify, to inform.
notoriedad, *nŏtŏrĭĕdād'*, sf. notoriety.
notorio, ria, *nŏtŏ'rĭŏ*, a. notorious.
novación, *nŏvāthĭŏn'*, sf. renovation of an
obligation formerly contracted.
noval, *nŏvāl'*, a. grown on newly broken
up ground; newly broken up ground, and
the fruits it produces. [in anything.
novato, ta, *nŏvā'tŏ*, a. new, commencing
novator, *—tŏr'*, sm. innovator.
novecientos, tas, *nŏvĕthĭĕn'tŏs*, a. nine
hundred.
novedad, *nŏvĕdād'*, sf. novelty, modern-
ness; admiration excited by novelties.
novela, *nŏvĕ'lā*, sf. novel, falsehood, fiction.
novelero, ra, *nŏvĕlā'rŏ*, a. fond of novels;
fond of hearing and telling news; new-
fangled; inconstant; —, sm. newsmonger.
novena, *nŏvĕ'nā*, sf. term of nine days ap-
propriated to some special worship.
novenario, *nŏvĕnā'rĭŏ*, sm. novenary.
noveno, na, *nŏvĕ'nŏ*, a. ninth.
noventa, *nŏvĕn'tā*, sm. ninety.
novia, *nŏ'vĭā*, sf. bride; woman betrothed.
noviciado, *nŏvĭthĭā'dŏ*, sm. novitiate.
novicio, *nŏvĭ'thĭŏ*, sm. novice.
noviembre, *nŏvĭĕm'brĕ*, sm. November.
novilunio, *nŏvĭlŏ'nĭŏ*, sm. new-moon.
novilla, *nŏvĭl'yā*, sf. heifer.
novillada, *—yā'dā*, sf. drove of young
bulls; fight of young bulls.
novillo, *nŏvĭl'yŏ*, sm. young bull or ox.
novio, *nŏ'vĭŏ*, sm. bridegroom.
novísimo, ma, *nŏvĭ'sĭmŏ*, a. newest; —,
sm. either of the four last events of man
(death, judgment, heaven and hell).
nubada, *nŏbā'dā*, sf. shower of rain; plenty.
nublado, da, *—dā*, a. clouded (of stuffs).
nubarrón, *nŏbārrŏn'*, sm. heavy shower
of rain, large cloud.
nube, *nŏ'bĕ*, sf. cloud; film.

nublado, *nūblā'dŏ*, sm. clouds announcing a storm. [to be clouded.
nublarse, *nūblār'sĕ*, v. r. to be afflicted,
nuca, *nŏ'kā*, sf. nape, scruff of the neck.
núcleo, *nŏ'klĕŏ*, sm. kernel of a nut.
nudillo, *nūdĭl'yŏ*, sm. knuckle; small knot made in stockings.
nudo, *nŏ'dŏ*, sm. knot; knuckle.
nudoso, sa, *nūdŏ'sŏ*, a. knotty.
nuera, *nūĕ'rā*, sf. daughter-in-law.
nuestro, tra, *nūĕs'trŏ*, a. our.
nueva, *nūĕ'vā*, sf. news.
nueve, *nūĕ'vĕ*, sm. & a. nine.
nuevo, va, *–vŏ*, a. new, modern, fresh; ¿ qué hay de –? is there any news? what news?
nuez, *nūĕth'*, sf. walnut; Adam's apple; apretar á uno la –, to strangle; – moscada ó de especia, nutmeg.
nulidad, *nūlĭdād'*, sf. nullity.
nulo, la, *nū'lŏ*, a. null. [genius.
numen, *nŏ'mĕn*, sm. divinity; poetical
numeración, *nūmĕrāthĭōn'*, sf. numeration.
numerador, *nūmĕrādŏr'*, sm. numerator.
numeral, *nūmĕrāl'*, a. numeral.
numerar, *–rār'*, v. a. to number, to numerate, to count.
numerario, ria, *rā'rĭŏ*, a. numerary; –, sm. hard cash, coin.
numérico, ca, *nūmĕ'rĭkŏ*, a. numerical.
número, *nū'mĕrŏ*, sm. number; cipher.
Números, *–s*, sm. pl. the book of Numbers.
numeroso, sa, *nūmĕrŏ'sŏ*, a. numerous.
nunca, *nūn'kā*, ad. never.
nunciatura, *nūnthĭātŏ'rā*, sf. nunciature.
nuncio, *nūn'thĭŏ*, sm. messenger; nuncio.
nuncupativo, va, *nūnkŭpātĭ'vŏ*, a. nominal; verbally pronounced.
nupcial, *nūpthĭāl'*, a. nuptial. [ding.
nupcias, *nūp'thĭās*, sf. pl. nuptials, wednutra, *nŏ'trā*, nutria, *–trĭā*, sf. otter.
nutrición, *nūtrĭthĭōn'*, sf. nutrition.
nutrimento, *–mĕn'tŏ*, sm. food, aliment, nourishment; nutrition.
nutrir, *nūtrĭr'*, v. a. to nourish.
nutritivo, va, *nūtrĭtĭ'vŏ*, a. nutritive.
nutriz, *nūtrĭth'*, sf. nurse. [nourishing.

Ñ.

ñagaza, *nyāgā'thā*, sf. bird-call.
ñañaros, *nyānyā'rŏs*, sm. pl. speaking puppet-show.
ñaque, *nyā'kĕ*, sm. hodge-podge.
ñoclos, *nyŏ'klŏs*, sm. pl. kind of macaroons.
ñoño, ña, *nyŏ'nyŏ*, a. decrepit, impaired by age.
ñoñería, *nyŏnyĕrĕā'*, sf. dotage.

O.

ó, *ŏ*, c. or; either.
¡ o ! *ŏ*, interj. oh!
obcecación, *ŏbthĕkāthĭōn'*, sf. obduracy.
obcecar, *ŏbthĕkār'*, v. a. to blind, to darken.
obedecer, *ŏbĕdĕthĕr'*, v. a. to obey.

obediencia, *ŏbĕdĭĕn'thĭā*, sf. obedience; á la –, at your service, your most obedient.
obediente, *–tĕ*, a. obedient.
obelisco, *ŏbĕlĭs'kŏ*, sm. obelisk. [pl.
obenques, *ŏbĕn'kĕs*, sm. pl. (mar.) shrouds,
obertura, *ŏbĕrtŏ'rā*, sf. (mus.) overture.
obesidad, *ŏbĕsĭdād'*, sf. obesity.
obeso, sa, *ŏbĕ'sŏ*, a. obese, fat.
óbice, *ŏ'bĭthĕ*, sm. obstacle. [copate.
obispado, *ŏbĭspā'dŏ*, sm. bishopric; episobispillo, *–pĭl'yŏ*, sm. boy-bishop; large black-pudding; croup of a fowl.
obispo, *ŏbĭs'pŏ*, sm. bishop; – de anillo, bishop in partibus.
objeción, *ŏbhĕthĭōn'*, sf. objection, opposition, exception. [pose.
objetar, *ŏbhĕtār'*, v. a. to object, to opobjetivo, va, *–tĭ'vŏ*, a. objective.
objeto, *ŏbhĕ'tŏ*, sm. object.
oblación, *ŏblāthĭōn'*, sf. oblation, offering.
oblada, *ŏblā'dā*, sf. funeral offering.
oblata, *–tā*, sf. money given to the church to defray the expenses of celebrating mass; host and chalice offered before being consecrated in the celebration of mass.
oblea, *ŏblĕ'ā*, sf. wafer.
oblicuidad, *ŏblĭkŭĭdād'*, sf. obliquity.
oblicuo, cua, *ŏblĭ'kŭŏ*, a. oblique.
obligación, *ŏblĭgāthĭōn'*, sf. obligation; –ones, pl. character and integrity.
obligado, *–gā'dŏ*, sm. public contractor; (law) obligee.
obligar, *ŏblĭgār'*, v. a. to oblige.
obligatorio, ria, *–tŏ'rĭŏ*, a. obligatory.
oblongo, ga, *ŏblŏn'gŏ*, a. oblong.
oboe, *ŏbŏ'ĕ*, sm. hautboy, oboe.
óbolo, *ŏ'bŏlŏ*, sm. obolus; obole.
obra, *ŏ'brā*, sf. work; means, virtue, power; toil, work, labour, employment; poner por –, to set to work.
obrada, *ŏbrā'dā*, sf. as much ground as two mules or oxen can plough in a day.
obrador, ra, *–dŏr'*, sm. & f. workman, workwoman; artificer; work-shop.
obrar, *ŏbrār'*, v. a. to work; to operate, to act; to put into practice.
obrepción, *ŏbrĕpthĭōn'*, sf. obreption.
obrepticio, cia, *–tĭ'thĭŏ*, a. obreptitious.
obrero, ra, *ŏbrĕ'rŏ*, sm. & f. workman; day-labourer.
obscenidad, *ŏbsthĕnĭdād'*, sf. obscenity.
obsceno, na, *ŏbsthĕ'nŏ*, a. obscene.
obscurecer, *ŏbskŭrĕthĕr'*, v. a. to obscure, to darken; –, v. imp. to grow dark; –se, to disappear.
obscuridad, *ŏbskŭrĭdād'*, sf. obscurity; darkness.
obscuro, ra, *ŏbskŭ'rŏ*, a. obscure, dark.
obsequiar, *ŏbsĕkĭār'*, v. a. to court.
obsequio, *–sĕ'kĭŏ*, sm. obsequiousness, compliance. [compliant, officious.
obsequioso, sa, *–sĕkĭŏ'sŏ*, a. obsequious,
observación, *ŏbsĕrvāthĭōn'*, sf. observation; remark. [tor.
observador, *–dŏr'*, sm. observer, observaobservancia, *ŏbsĕrvān'thĭā*, sf. observance; ceremonial reverence.
observar, *ŏbsĕrvār'*, v. a. to observe.

observatorio, *-servătŏ'rĭŏ*, sm. observatory. [pediment, hindrance.
obstáculo, *ŏbstä'kŭlŏ*, sm. obstacle, impediment.
obstar, *ŏbstär'*, v. n. to oppose, to obstruct, to hinder. [stubbornness.
obstinación, *ŏbstĭnäthĭŏn'*, sf. obstinacy,
obstinado, *-nä'dŏ*, a. obstinate.
obstinarse, *-när'sĕ*, v. r. to be obstinate.
obstrucción, *ŏbstrŭkthĭŏn'*, sf. (med.) obstruction.
obstruir, *ŏbstrŭĕr'*, v. a. to obstruct; -se, to be blocked up, to be obstructed.
obtener, *ŏbtĕnĕr'*, v. a. to obtain.
obtuso, sa, *-tŭ'sŏ*, a. obtuse, blunt.
obué, *ŏbŭĕ'*, sm. (mus.) hautboy.
obús, *ŏbŭs'*, sm. (mil.) howitzer.
obvención, *ŏbvĕnthĭŏn'*, sf. casual profit.
obviar, *-vĭär'*, v. a. to obviate, to prevent.
obvio, via, *ŏb'vĭŏ*, a. obvious, evident.
ocasión, *ŏkäsĭŏn'*, sf. occasion, opportunity, danger, risk.
ocasional, *ŏkäsĭŏnäl'*, a. occasional.
ocasionar, *-när'*, v. a. to cause, to occasion; to move, to excite.
ocaso, *ŏkä'sŏ*, sm. occident. [western.
occidental, *ŏkthĭdĕntäl'*, a. occidental.
occidente, *-dĕn'tĕ*, sm. occident, west.
occipucio, *-pў'thĭŏ*, sm. occiput.
océano, *ŏthĕ'änŏ*, sm. ocean.
ocio, *ŏ'thĭŏ*, sm. leisure; pastime.
ociosidad, *ŏthĭŏsĭdäd'*, sf. idleness, leisure.
ocioso, sa, *ŏthĭŏ'sŏ*, a. idle; vacant; procre, *ŏ'krĕ*, sm. ochre. [fitable.
octava, *ŏktä'vä*, sf. octave.
octavario, *-vä'rĭŏ*, sm. eight days' festival.
octavo, va, *ŏktä'vŏ*, a. eight; libro en —, octavo volume.
octubre, *ŏktŏ'brĕ*, sm. October.
ocular, *ŏkŭlär'*, a. ocular; -, sm. eye-glass.
oculista, *-lĭs'tä*, sm. oculist.
ocultación, *ŏkŭltäthĭŏn'*, sf. concealment
ocultar, *-tär'*, v. a. to hide, to conceal.
oculto, ta, *ŏkŭl'tŏ*, a. hidden, concealed, secret. [business, employment.
ocupación, *ŏkăpäthĭŏn'*, sf. occupation;
ocupar, *-pär'*, v. a. to occupy, to hold an office; -se, to occupy, to follow a business.
ocurrencia, *ŏkŭrrĕn'thĭä*, sf. occurrence, accident; idea occurring to the mind.
ocurrir, *ŏkŭrrĕr'*, v. n. to meet; to occur, to happen. [eight-sided.
ochavado, da, *ŏtshävä'dŏ*, a. octagonal.
ochavar, *-vär'*, v. a. to form an octagon.
ochavo, *ŏtshä'vŏ*, sm. small Spanish brass coin, valued at two maravedíes.
ochenta, *ŏtshĕn'tä*, a. eighty.
ocho, *ŏtsh'ŏ*, sm. & a. eight.
ochocientos, *-thĭĕn'tŏs*, a. eight hundred.
oda, *ŏ'dä*, sf. ode.
odiar, *ŏdĭär'*, v. a. to hate; -se, to hate one another.
odio, *ŏ'dĭŏ*, sm. hatred. [one another.
odioso, sa, *ŏdĭŏ'sŏ*, a. odious, hateful.
odorífero, ra, *ŏdŏrĕ'fĕrŏ*, a. odoriferous, fragrant.
odre, *ŏ'drĕ*, sm. wine-bag; drunkard.
oeste, *ŏĕs'tĕ*, sm. west-wind.

ofender, *ŏfĕndĕr'*, v. a. to offend, to injure; -se, to be vexed; to take offence.
ofensa, *ŏfĕn'sä*, sf. offence, injury.
ofensivo, va, *-sĕ'vŏ*, a. offensive, injurious.
ofensor, *-sŏr'*, sm. offender.
oferta, *ŏfĕr'tä*, sf. offer; offering.
ofertorio, *-tŏ'rĭŏ*, sm. offertory.
oficial, *ŏfĭthĭäl'*, sm. workman, artificer; officer; clerk in a public office.
oficiala, *-thĭä'lä*, sf. work-woman.
oficiar, *-thĭär'*, v. a. to officiate, to minister (of clergymen, &c.).
oficina, *ŏfĭthĕ'nä*, sf. work-shop; office, counting-house, business-room; -s, pl. lower apartments in houses.
oficio, *ŏfĕ'thĭŏ*, sm. office, employ, occupation, ministry; function; official letter; trade, business; notary's office; -s, pl. divine service.
oficiosidad, *ŏfĭthĭŏsĭdäd'*, sf. diligence; officiousness; importunity.
oficioso, sa, *-thĭŏ'sŏ*, a. officious, diligent; meddling.
ofrecer, *ŏfrĕthĕr'*, v. a. to offer; to present; to exhibit; -se, to offer, to occur, to present itself. [promise.
ofrecimiento, *-thĕmĭĕn'tŏ*, sm. offer,
ofrenda, *ŏfrĕn'dä*, sf. offering, oblation.
ofrendar, *-där'*, v. a. to present offerings to God. [sight; obfuscation.
ofuscación, *ŏfŭskäthĭŏn'*, sf. dimness of
ofuscar, *-kär'*, v. a. to darken, to render obscure.
oídas, *ŏĕ'däs*, de ó por -, by hearsay.
oí', *ŏĕ'dŏ*, sm. hearing; ear; touch-hole.
oidor, *ŏĕdŏr'*, sm. hearer; judge appointed to hear pleadings and decide law-suits.
oír, *ŏĕr'*, v. a. to hear; to listen; to understand.
ojal, *ŏhäl'*, sm. button-hole. [stand.
¡ojalá! *ŏ'hälä'*, would to God! God grant!
ojaladura, *-dŏ'rä*, sf. the set of button-holes in a suit of clothes.
ojalar, *ŏ'hälär'*, v. a. to make button-holes
ojeada, *ŏ'hĕä'dä*, sf. eye-glance, ogle.
ojear, *ŏ'hĕär'*, v. a. to eye, to view; to glance; to rouse or put up game by hallooing. [the chase by hallooing.
ojeo, *ŏ'hĕ'ŏ*, sm. putting up of game for
ojera, *ŏ'hĕ'rä*, sf. bluish circle under the lower eyelid, indicative of indisposition.
ojeriza, *ŏ'hĕrĕ'thä*, sf. spite, grudge, ill-will. [(fam.) anus.
ojete, *ŏ'hĕ'tĕ*, sm. eyelet-hole in clothes;
ojimel, *ŏ'hĕmĕl'*, sm. oxymel.
ojo, *ŏ'k'ŏ*, sm. eye; sight; eye of a needle;
ola, *ŏ'lä*, sf. wave. [arch of a bridge.
olaje, *ŏlä'hĕ*, sm. succession of waves, sea-swell.
oleada, *ŏlĕä'dä*, sf. surge; violent emotion.
olear, *ŏlĕär'*, v. a. to administer extreme unction. [oil.
óleo, *ŏ'lĕŏ*, sm. oil; extreme unction; holy
oler, *ŏlĕr'*, v. a. to smell, to scent; -, v. n. to smell; to smack of.
olfato, *ŏlfä'tŏ*, sm. smell; scent
oligarquía, *ŏlĭgärkĕ'ä*, sf. oligarchy.
oligárquico, ca, *-gär'kĭkŏ*, a. oligarchical.
olímpico, ca, *ŏlĕm'pĭkŏ*, a. olympic.

Olimpo, ŏlĭm'pŏ, sm. (poet.) heaven.
oliva, ŏlĕ'vä, sf. olive; olive-tree; owl.
olivar, ŏlĭvär', sm. olive-grove.
olivo, ŏlĕ'vŏ, sm. olive-tree.
olmo, ŏl'mŏ, sm. elm-tree.
olor, ŏlŏr', sm. odour, scent.
oloroso, sa, ŏlŏrŏ'sŏ, a. fragrant, odorous.
olvidadizo, za, ŏlvĭdädĕ'thŏ, a. forgetful.
olvidar, ŏlvĭdär', v. a. to forget.
olvido, ŏlvĕ'dŏ, sm. forgetfulness.
olla, ŏl'yä, sf. round earthen pot; oglio; — podrida, dish composed of different boiled meats and vegetables; —s, pl. gulf.
ollería, ŏlyĕrē'ä, sf. pottery.
ollero, ŏlyĕ'rŏ, sm. potter.
ombligo, ŏmblē'gŏ, sm. navel.
ominoso, sa, ŏmĭnŏ'sŏ, a. ominous.
omisión, ŏmĭsĭŏn', sf. omission.
omitir, ŏmĭtĭr', v. a. to omit.
omnipotencia, ŏmnĭpŏtĕn'thĭä, sf. omnipotence, almightiness. [almighty.
omnipotente, —pŏtĕn'tĕ, a. omnipotent,
omniscio, scia, ŏmnĭs'thĭŏ, a. all-knowing.
once, ŏn'thĕ, sm. & a. eleven.
onceno, na, ŏnthĕ'nŏ, a. eleventh.
onda, ŏn'dä, sf. wave.
ondear, ŏndär', v. a. to undulate; to fluctuate; —se, to see-saw.
oneroso, sa, ŏnĕrŏ'sŏ, a. burdensome.
ontología, ŏntŏlŏhē'ä, sf. ontology.
onza, ŏn'thä, sf. ounce; linx.
onzavo, va, —thä'vŏ, a. eleventh; —, sm. eleventh part. [darkness.
opacidad, ŏpäthĭdäd', sf. opacity, gloom,
opaco, ca, ŏpä'kŏ, a. opaque, dark; melancholy, gloomy.
opción, ŏpthĭŏn', sf. option, choice.
ópera, ŏ'pĕrä, sf. opera.
operación, ŏpĕräthĭŏn', sf. operation.
operar, ŏpĕrär', v. n. to operate, to act.
operario, —rē'rĭŏ, sm. operator, labourer.
opiata, ŏpĭä'tä, sf. opiate.
opilación, ŏpĭläthĭŏn', sf. obstruction of the body; stoppage of menstruation.
opilar, ŏpĭlär', v. a. to oppilate, to obstruct.
ópimo, ma, ŏ'pĭmŏ, a. rich, fruitful.
opinable, ŏpĭnä'blĕ, a. problematical.
opinión, ŏpĭnĭŏn', sf. opinion.
opio, ŏ'pĭŏ, sm. opium.
opíparo, ra, ŏpē'pärŏ, a. sumptuous.
oponer, ŏpŏnĕr', v. a. to oppose; —se, to oppose, to be opposite. [nity.
oportunidad, ŏpŏrtŭnĭdäd', sf. opportu-
oportuno, na, —tŏ'nŏ, a. seasonable, opportune. [competition of skill.
oposición, ŏpŏsĭthĭŏn', sf. opposition;
opositor, —tŏr', sm. opposer, opponent.
opresión, ŏprĕsĭŏn', sf. oppression.
opresivo, va, —sĕ'vŏ, a. oppressive.
opresor, —sŏr', sm. oppressor.
oprimir, ŏprĭmĭr', v. a. to oppress; to crush, to press, to squeeze. [miny.
oprobio, ŏprŏ'bĭŏ, sm. opprobrium, igno-
optar, ŏptär', v. a. to choose, to elect.
optativo, ŏptätē'vŏ, sm. (gr.) optative.
óptica, ŏp'tĭkä, sf. optics. [tician.
óptico, ca, —tĭkŏ, a. optical; —, sm. op-

optimista, —mĭs'tä, sm. optimist.
óptimo, ma, ŏp'tĭmŏ, a. best. [adverse.
opuesto, ta, ŏpŭĕs'tŏ, a. opposite, contrary.
opulencia, ŏpŭlĕn'thĭä, sf. wealth, riches.
opulento, ta, —lĕn'tŏ, a. opulent, wealthy.
opúsculo, ŏpŭs'kŭlŏ, sm. opuscule.
oración, ŏräthĭŏn', sf. oration, speech; prayer; —ones, pl. prayers at sunset.
oráculo, ŏrä'kŭlŏ, sm. oracle.
orador, ŏrädŏr', sm. orator.
orar, ŏrär', v. n. to harangue; to pray.
orate, ŏrä'tĕ, sm. & f. lunatic, madcap.
oratoria, ŏrätŏ'rĭä, sf. oratory, rhetorical skill. [—, ria, a. rhetorical.
oratorio, —rĭŏ, sm. oratory; oratorio;
orbe, ŏr'bĕ, sm. orb, sphere, the earth; celestial body.
órbita, ŏr'bĭtä, sf. orbit.
orden, ŏr'dĕn, sm. & f. order (in all its meanings); — del día, order of the day.
ordenación, —näthĭŏn', sf. arrangement; ordination; edict, ordinance.
ordenando, —nän'dŏ, sm. candidate for holy orders. [ordinance; ordination.
ordenanza, —nän'thä, sf. order; statute.
ordenar, —när', v. a. to arrange; to order; to ordain; —se, to take holy orders.
ordeñar, —nyär', v. a. to milk.
ordinal, ŏrdĭnäl', a. ordinal.
ordinario, ria, —nä'rĭŏ, a. ordinary, common; —, sm. ordinary; established judge of ecclesiastical cases; carrier, carman; de —, regularly, commonly, ordinarily.
orear, ŏrĕär', v. a. to cool, to refresh; to air; —se, to take the air.
orégano, ŏrĕ'gänŏ, sm. wild marjoram.
oreja, ŏrĕ'hä, sf. ear; auricle.
orejera, —hĕ'rä, sf. covering for the ears to defend them from cold; pot-ear.
orejón, —hŏn', sm. preserved peach; young nobleman of the ancient nobility of Peru.
oreo, ŏrĕ'ŏ, sm. breeze, fresh air.
orfandad, ŏrfändäd', sf. orphanage.
organero, ŏrgänĕ'rŏ, sm. organ-builder.
orgánico, ca, ŏrgä'nĭkŏ, a. organic; harmonious.
organista, —nĭs'tä, sm. organist.
organización, —nĭthäthĭŏn', sf. organization; arrangement.
organizar, —nĭthär', v. a. to organize.
órgano, ŏr'gänŏ, sm. organ.
orgullo, ŏrgŭl'yŏ, sm. pride, haughtiness.
orgulloso, sa, —yŏ'sŏ, a. proud, haughty.
oriental, ŏrĭĕntäl', a. oriental, eastern.
oriente, ŏrĭĕn'tĕ, sm. orient. [aperture.
orificio, ŏrĭfē'thĭŏ, sm. orifice, mouth,
origen, ŏrē'hĕn, sm. origin, source; natal country; family, extraction.
original, ŏrĭhĭnäl', a. original, primitive; —, sm. original, first copy.
originalidad, —nälĭdäd', sf. originality.
originar, —när', v. a. & n. to originate.
originario, ria, —nä'rĭŏ, a. originary.
orilla, ŏrĭl'yä, sf. limit, border, margin; edge of cloth; foot-path in a street; shore.
orillar, —yär', v. n. & a. to approach the shore; to arrange, to order.
orillo, ŏrĭl'yŏ, sm. list, selvage.

orin, *ŏrĭn'*, sm. rust; urine.
orina, *ŏrē'nă*, sf. urine.
orinal, *ŏrĭnăl'*, sm. chamber-pot.
orinar, *-năr'*, v. n. to pass or make water.
oriundo, da, *ŏrĭŭn'dŏ*, a. derived from.
orla, *ŏr'lă*, sf. list, selvage, border.
orladura, *ŏrlădŏŏ'ră*, sf. border, edging, list.
orlar, *ŏrlăr'*, v. a. to border, to edge.
ornamento, *ŏrnămĕn'tŏ*, sm. ornament,
     embellishment; [decoration.
ornato, *ŏrnă'tŏ*, sm. apparel, ornament,
oro, *ŏ'rŏ*, sm. gold; -s, pl. diamonds (at
oropel, *ŏrŏpĕl'*, sm. tinsel; [cards).
orquesta, *ŏrkĕs'tă*, sf. orchestre, orchestra.
ortiga, *ŏrtē'gă*, sf. (bot.) nettle.
ortodoxia, *ŏrtŏdŏk'sĭă*, sf. orthodoxy.
ortodoxo, xa, *-dŏk'sŏ*, a. orthodox.
ortografía, *-grăf'ă*, sf. orthography.
ortográfico, ca, *-gră'fĭkŏ*, a. orthogra-
     phical.
oruga, *ŏrŏŏ'gă*, sf. (bot.) rocket; caterpillar.
orujo, *ŏrŏŏ'hŏ*, sm. peel of pressed grapes.
orza, *ŏr'thă*, sf. gallipot, crock.
os, *ŏs*, pn. you.
osa, *ŏ'să*, sf. she-bear. [daringly.
osadamente, *ŏsădămĕn'tĕ*, ad. boldly,
osadía, *-dē'ă*, sf. boldness, intrepidity;
     zeal, fervour.
osamenta, *-mĕn'tă*, sf. skeleton.
osar, *ŏsăr'*, v. n. to dare, to venture.
osario, *ŏsă'rĭŏ*, sm. charnel-house.
oscilación, *ŏsthĭlăthĭŏn'*, sf. oscillation.
oscilar, *-lăr'*, v. n. to oscillate.
ósculo, *ŏs'kŭlŏ*, sm. kiss.
osificarse, *ŏsĭfĭkăr'sĕ*, v. r. to ossify.
oso, *ŏ'sŏ*, sm. bear; - blanco, polar bear.
ostensible, *ŏstĕnsē'blĕ*, a. ostensible, ap-
     parent. [manifestation.
ostensión, *-sĭŏn'*, sf. show, exhibition,
ostensivo, va, *-sē'vŏ*, a. ostensive.
ostentación, *-tăthĭŏn'*, sf. ostentation,
     ambitious display, vain show.
ostentar, *-tăr'*, v. a. to show; -, v. n. to
     boast, to brag. [tatious.
ostentoso, sa, *-tŏ'sŏ*, a. sumptuous, osten-
ostiario, *ŏstĭă'rĭŏ*, sm. ostiary, door-keeper.
ostiatim, *ŏstĭă'tĭm*, ad. from door to door.
ostra, *ŏs'tră*, sf. oyster. [woman.
ostrera, *ŏstrĕ'ră*, sf. oyster-bed; oyster-
ostrogodo, da, *ŏstrŏgŏ'dŏ*, a. ostrogothic.
osudo, da, *ŏsŏŏ'dŏ*, a. bony, full of bones.
otoñal, *ŏtŏnyăl'*, a. autumnal.
otoñar, *ŏtŏnyăr'*, v. n. to spend the autumn-
     season; to grow in autumn; -se, to be
     seasoned, to be tempered (applied to earth
otoño, *ŏtŏ'nyŏ*, sm. autumn. [after rain).
otorgamiento, *ŏtŏrgămĕn'tŏ*, sm. grant,
     licence, license; contract.
otorgar, *-găr'*, v. a. to consent, to stipulate.
otro, tra, *ŏ'trŏ*, a. another, other.
otrosí, *ŏtrŏsē'*, ad. besides, moreover; -,
     sm. item; (law) every petition made after
     the principal.
ovación, *ŏvăthĭŏn'*, sf. ovation.
ovalado, da, *ŏvălă'dŏ*, a. oval-formed.
óvalo, *ŏ'vălŏ*, sm. oval.
ovar, *ŏvăr'*, v. n. to lay eggs.
ovario, *ŏvă'rĭŏ*, sm. ovary.

oveja, *ŏvĕ'hʹă*, sf. ewe; -s, pl. white spume
     or froth of waves which break against
ovejero, *-hă'rŏ*, sm. shepherd. [rocks.
ovejuno, na, *-hŏŏ'nŏ*, a. relating to ewes.
ovillar, *ŏvĭlyăr'*, v. n. to wind off from a
     reel, to reel off; to coil up; -se, to double
ovillo, *ŏvĭl'yŏ*, sm. clew. [oneself up.
ovíparo, ra, *ŏvĕ'părŏ*, a. oviparous, egg-
     bearing.
ovoso, sa, *ŏvŏ'sŏ*, a. full of sea-weeds.
óxido, *ŏk'sĭdŏ*, sf. (chem.) oxide.
oxígeno, *ŏksē'hĕnŏ*, sm. (chem.) oxygen.
¡oxte! *ŏks'tĕ*, keep off! begone!
oyente, *ŏyĕn'tĕ*, a. & sm. & f. hearing;
     auditor, hearer.

P.

pabellón, *păbĕlyŏn'*, sm. pavilion; sum-
     mer-house.
pábilo, *pă'bĭlŏ*, sm. wick; snuff of a candle.
pábulo, *pă'bŭlŏ*, sm. food, provender;
     aliment. [bundle.
paca, *pă'kă*, sf. spotted agouti; bale,
pacato, ta, *păkă'tŏ*, a. pacific, quiet, mild,
     gentle, tender, peaceable.
pacer, *păthĕr'*, v. a. to pasture, to graze.
paciencia, *păthĕn'thĭă*, sf. patience.
paciente, *-tĕ*, a. & sm. patient.
pacificación, *păthĭfĭkăthĭŏn'*, sf. pacifica-
     tion; peace of mind.
pacificar, *păthĭfĭkăr'*, v. a. to pacify, to
     appease; -, v. n. to treat for peace. [ful.
pacífico, ca, *păthē'fĭkŏ*, a. pacific, peace-
pacotilla, *păkŏtĭl'yă*, sf. freight, portage;
     (mar.) adventure. [to stipulate.
pactar, *păktăr'*, v. a. to convent, to contract,
pacto, *păk'tŏ*, sm. contract, pact.
pachorra, *pătshŏr'ră*, sf. sluggishness.
padecer, *pădĕthĕr'*, v. a. to suffer any
     bodily affliction; to sustain an injury; to
     be liable to.
padecimiento, *-thĕmĕn'tŏ*, sm. suffering,
     sufferance. [agnail (on the finger).
padrastro, *pădrăs'trŏ*, sm. step-father;
padrazo, *pădră'thŏ*, sm. over-indulgent
     father.
padre, *pă'drĕ*, sm. father; -s, pl. parents;
     ancestors; all the members of a religious
     congregation taken as a body. [nity.
padrinazgo, *pădrĭnăth'gŏ*, sm. compater-
padrino, *pădrē'nŏ*, sm. god-father; second;
     protector, assistant. [pattern, model.
padrón, *pădrŏn'*, sm. poll; indulgent parent;
paga, *pă'gă*, sf. payment, fee.
pagadero, ra, *păgădĕ'rŏ*, a. payable.
pagador, *-dŏr'*, sm. payer; paymaster.
pagaduría, *-dŭrē'ă*, sf. paymaster's office.
paganismo, *păgănĭs'mŏ*, sm. paganism,
     heathenism.
pagano, *păgă'nŏ*, sm. heathen, pagan; one
     who pays or contributes his share; -, na,
     a. heathenish; pagan.
pagar, *păgăr'*, v. a. to pay; to requite;
     -se, to be pleased with oneself.

pagaré, *păgărĕ'*, sm. bond, note of hand, promissory note, I. O. U. (I owe you).

página, *pă'hĭnă*, sf. page of a book.

pago, *pă'gŏ*, sm. payment; reward.

pais, *pă̆is*, sm. country, region.

paisaje, *păĭsă'hĕ*, sm. landscape.

paisanaje, *–sănă'hĕ*, sm. peasantry, lay inhabitants of a country.

paisáno, na, *–să'nŏ*, a. of the same country; –, sm. countryman.

paja, *pă'hă*, sf. straw; echar –s, to draw lots with straws.

pajar, *pă'hăr*, sm. straw-loft.

pajarear, *–ĕăr*, v. a. to go bird-catching; to loiter about.

pajarera, *–rĕ'ră*, sf. aviary.

pajarero, *–rĕ'rŏ*, sm. bird-catcher. [low.

pájaro, *pă'hărŏ*, sm. bird; sly, acute fellow.

pajarota, *–rŏ'tă*, pajarotada, *–rŏtă'dă*, sf. false, idle report.

pajarraco, *–ră'kŏ*, pajarruco, *–rŏ'kŏ*, sm. large bird; cunning fellow.

paje, *pă'hĕ*, sm. page.

pajera, *pă'hĕ'ră*, sf. stack of straw.

pajero, *–rŏ*, sm. dealer in straw.

pajizo, za, *pă'hĭ'thŏ*, a. made of straw; thatched with straw; straw-coloured.

pajuela, *pă'hŏ̆ĕ'lă*, sf. match.

pala, *pă'lă*, sf. shovel; fire-shovel.

palabra, *pălă'bră*, sf. word; á media –, at the least hint; de –, by word of mouth.

palabrada, *–bră'dă*, sf. low language.

palabrita, *–brĭ'tă*, sf. short word; word full of meaning.

palaciego, ga, *–thĭĕ'gŏ*, a. pertaining or relating to the palace; –, sm. courtier.

palacio, *pălă'thĭŏ*, sm. palace.

palada, *–dă*, sf. a shovel-full.

paladar, *pălădăr*, sm. palate; taste, relish.

paladín, *–dĭn*, sm. paladin.

paladino, na, *–dĭ'nŏ*, a. manifest, clear, public.

palafrén, *–frĕn*, sm. palfrey.

palafrenero, *–frĕnĕ'rŏ*, groom.

palanca, *pălăn'kă*, sf. lever.

palancada, *–kă'dă*, sf. leverage.

palancana, *–kă'nă*, palangana, *–gă'nă*, sf. basin. [with stakes.

palanquera, *–kĕ'ră*, sf. enclosure made with stakes.

palanqueta, *–kĕ'tă*, sf. bar-shot; small lever. [clash.

palatinado, *pălătĭnă'dŏ*, sm. palatinate.

palatino, na, *–tĭ'nŏ*, a. belonging to the palace or courtiers; –, sm. Palatin.

palco, *păl'kŏ*, sm. box in a play-house; – de proscenio, stage-box.

palenque, *pălĕn'kĕ*, sm. passage from the pit to the stage in a play-house.

palestra, *pălĕs'tră*, sf. inclosure, palisade; palestra; art of wrestling. [trowel.

paleta, *pălĕ'tă*, sf. fire-shovel; palette.

paletada, *pălĕtă'dă*, sf. trowel-full.

paleto, *pălĕ'tŏ*, sm. fallow deer; clown, rustic.

palia, *pă'lĭă*, sf. altar-cloth; square.

paliar, *pălĭăr*, v. a. to palliate, to excuse; to cloak.

paliativo, va, *–tĭ'vŏ*, a. palliative.

palidez, *pălĭdĕth'*, sf. paleness, wanness.

pálido, da, *pă'lĭdŏ*, a. pallid, pale.

palillero, *pălĭlyĕ'rŏ*, sm. one who makes or sells tooth-picks; tooth-pick case.

palillo, *pălĭ'lyŏ*, sm. knitting-needle case; rolling-pin; tooth-pick; –s, pl. bobbins; drumsticks. [tation.

palinodia, *pălĭnŏ'dĭă*, sf. palinody, recantation.

palio, *pă'lĭŏ*, sm. cloak; pall.

palique, *pălĭ'kĕ*, sm. trifling conversation.

palitroque, *pălĭtrŏ'kĕ*, sm. rough, ill-shaped stick. [with a stick.

paliza, *pălĭ'thă*, sf. cudgelling, drubbing

palizada, *pălĭthă'dă*, sf. palisade.

palma, *păl'mă*, sf. date palm-tree; palm of the hand; palm-leaf.

palmada, *pălmă'dă*, sf. slap given with the palm of the hand, clap; –s, pl. clapping of hands. [winder.

palmatoria, *–tŏ'rĭă*, sf. wax-stand, wax-palmear, *pălmĕăr*, v. a. to slap with the open hand; to clap.

palmera, *pălmĕ'ră*, sf. palm-tree.

palmeta, *–mĕ'tă*, sf. ferule.

palmito, *–mĭ'tŏ*, sm. dwarf fan-palm.

palmo, *păl'mŏ*, sm. palm. [the open hand.

palmotear, *pălmŏtĕăr*, v. a. to slap with

palmoteo, *–tĕ'ŏ*, sm. clapping of hands.

palo, *pă'lŏ*, sm. stick; cudgel; blow given with a stick; execution on the gallows; suit at cards; –s, pl. masting.

paloma, *pălŏ'mă*, sf. pigeon, dove; – torcaz, ring-dove; – zorita, wood-pigeon.

palomar, *pălŏmăr*, sm. pigeon-house.

palomera, *–mĕ'ră*, sf. bleak place, much exposed to the wind.

palomilla, *–mĭ'lyă*, sf. young pigeon; back-bone of a horse; chrysalis; horse of a milk-white colour. [fumitory.

palomina, *–mĕ'nă*, sf. pigeon-dung; (bot.)

palomino, *–nŏ*, sm. young pigeon; stain of excrement upon the tail of a shirt.

palomo, *pălŏ'mŏ*, sm. cock-pigeon.

palotada, *pălŏtă'dă*, sf. stroke with a battledore.

palote, *pălŏ'tĕ*, sm. stick of a middling size; drum-stick; –s, pl. thick lines copied by children learning to write. [clash.

paloteo, *pălŏtĕ'ŏ*, sm. fight with sticks.

palpable, *pălpă'blĕ*, a. palpable, evident.

palpar, *–păr*, v. a. to feel, to touch, to grope. [panting.

palpitación, *pălpĭtăthĭŏn*, sf. palpitation.

palpitar, *–tăr*, v. n. to palpitate.

palude, *pălŏ'dĕ*, sf. lake, pool. [rude.

palurdo, da, *pălŏr'dŏ*, a. rustic, clownish.

pampana, *păm'pănă*, sf. vine-leaf.

pampanilla, *pămpănĭ'lyă*, sf. loin-cloth of leaves worn by the Indians.

pámpano, *păm'pănŏ*, sm. young vine-branch or tendril. [tendrils.

pampanoso, sa, *–pănŏ'sŏ*, a. abounding in

pampirolada, *–pĭrŏlă'dă*, sf. (fig. & fam.) impertinence.

pamplina, *–plĕ'nă*, sf. toasted bread steeped in gravy; duck-weed; futility, trifle.

pampringada, *–pringá'dă,* sf. frivolous thing. [wheat; gold-leaf, silver-leaf.

pan, *păn,* sm. bread; loaf; food in general;

pana, *pă'nă,* sf. velvet, plush. [medicine.

panacea, *pănăthé'ă,* sf. panacea, universal

panadería, *–deré'ă,* sf. trade of a baker; bakehouse.

panadero, *–dă'rŏ,* sm. baker.

panadizo, *–dĕ'thŏ,* sm. whitlow; pale-faced, sickly person. [(in Havannah).

panal, *pănăl',* sm. honey-comb; sweet-rusk

panarra, *pănăr'ră,* sm. dolt, simpleton.

pandero, *pănd'ro,* sm. timbrel.

pandilla, *–dĭl'yă,* sf. plot, league.

pando, da, *păn'dŏ,* a. bulging, convex.

pandorga, *–dŏr'gă,* sf. fat, bulky woman.

panegírico, ca, *pănĕhé'rĭkŏ,* a. panegyrical; —, sm. eulogy.

panegirista, *–hĭrĭs'tă,* sm. panegyrist.

panera, *pănă'ră,* sf. granary.

pánfilo, *păn'flŏ,* sm. slow, sluggish, heavy person.

paniaguado, *pănĭăgŭă'dŏ,* sm. table-fellow; comrade.

pánico, ca, *pă'nĭkŏ,* a. panic.

paniego, ga, *pănĭé'gŏ,* a. eating or yielding much bread.

panilla, *pănĭl'yă,* sf. small measure of oil.

panizo, *pănĭ'thŏ,* sm. panic-grass.

panoja, *pănŏ'hă,* sf. (bot.) pannicle.

panorama, *pănŏră'mă,* sm. panorama.

pantalón, *păntălŏn',* sm. pantaloon; – de media pierna, breeches, small-clothes.

pantalla, *–tăl'yă,* sf. candle-screen, lamp-shade; (fig.) man of straw.

pantano, *–tă'nŏ,* sm. pool of stagnant wa-ter; morass; obstacle, difficulty.

pantanoso, sa, *–tănŏ'sŏ,* a. marshy, fenny,

panteísta, *–tĕĭs'tă,* sf. pantheist. [boggy.

panteón, *–tĕŏn',* sm. Pantheon.

pantera, *–tĕ'ră,* sf. panther.

pantomima, *–tŏmé'mă,* sf. pantomime.

pantomímico, ca, *–tŏmé'mĭkŏ,* a. panto-mimical. [leg).

pantorrilla, *–tŏrrĭl'yă,* sf. calf (of the

pantorrilludo, da, *–tŏrrĭlyŏ'dŏ,* a. hav-ing very large or thick calves.

pantuflo, *păntŭ'flŏ,* sm. slipper, shoe.

panza, *păn'thă,* sf. belly, paunch.

panzada, *pănthă'dă,* sf. belly-full of food.

panzudo, da, *–thŏ'dŏ,* a. big-bellied.

pañal, *pănyăl',* sm. swaddling-cloth; cloth in which anything is wrapped up; tail of a shirt. [clothier.

pañero, *pănyă'rŏ,* sm. woollen-draper.

paño, *păn'yŏ,* sm. cloth; breadth of cloth.

pañuelo, *pănyŭé'lŏ,* sm. handkerchief.

papa, *pă'pă,* sm. pope; pap; –s, pl. pota-

papá, *păpă',* sm. papa. [toes.

papada, *păpă'dă,* sf. double-chin.

papadilla, *–dĭl'yă,* sf. the fleshy part under the chin.

papado, *păpă'dŏ,* sm. popedom, papacy.

papagayo, *–gă'yŏ,* sm. parrot.

papal, *păpăl',* a. papal, papistical.

papalina, *păpălĕ'nă,* sf. cap with ear-flaps.

papamoscas, *–mŏs'kăs,* sm. gnat-snapper.

papanatas, *–nă'tăs,* sm. oaf, simpleton, ninny. [tinence.

paparrucha, *–rŭtsh'ă,* sf. folly, imper-

papel, *păpĕl',* sm. paper; writing; part acted in a play; – de estraza, brown paper; – sellado, stamped paper.

papelera, *–lă'ră,* sf. writing-desk, paper-case. [papers without order.

papelería, *–lĕré'ă,* sf. large bundle of

papelero, *–lă'rŏ,* sm. paper-manufacturer.

papeleta, *–lă'tă,* sf. slip of paper on which something is written.

papelón, *–lŏn',* sm. large piece of paper; prolix writing; cartoon; pamphlet.

papera, *păpă'ră,* sf. wen on the throat.

papilla, *păpĭl'yă,* sf. pap; guile, deceit.

papirotada, *păpĭrŏtă'dă,* sf. fillip on the neck or face; rap on the nose.

papirote, *–rŏ'tĕ,* sm. fillip.

papista, *păpĭs'tă,* sm. papist.

papo, *pă'pŏ,* sm. double-chin, under-chin.

papudo, da, *păpŭ'dŏ,* a. double-chinned.

paquebot, *păkĕbŏt',* sm. packetboat.

paquete, *păkĕ'tĕ,* sm. small packet, bundle.

par, *păr,* a. equal, alike, even; sin –, matchless; –, sm. pair; Peer.

para, *pă'ră,* pr. for, to, in order to, towards, to the end that.

parabién, *părăbĭén',* sm. congratulation; felicitation; event.

parábola, *pără'bŏlă,* sf. parable; parabola.

parabólico, ca, *–bŏ'lĭkŏ,* a. parabolical.

paracleto, *–klĕ'tŏ,* sm. Paraclete (name given to the Holy Ghost). [buffers.

parachoques, *–tshŏ'kĕs,* sm. pl. (rail.)

parada, *pără'dă,* sf. halt; suspension; pause; relay; dam, bank; stake, set, bet; (mil.) parade. [end.

paradero, *–dă'rŏ,* sm. halting-place; term,

parado, da, *pără'dŏ,* a. remiss, careless, in-

paradoja, *–dŏ'h'ă,* sf. paradox. [dolent.

parador, *–dŏr',* sm. one who stops or halts; inn.

parafrasear, *–frăsĕăr',* v.a. to paraphrase.

paráfrasi, *pără'frăsĭ,* sf. paraphrase.

paragoge, *părăgŏ'h'ĕ,* sf. addition of a letter or syllable at the end of a word.

paraguas, *pără'gŭăs,* sm. umbrella.

paraíso, *părăĕ'sŏ,* sm. Paradise.

paraje, *pără'h'ĕ,* sm. place, residence; condition; disposition.

paralelo, la, *–lĕ'lŏ,* a. & sm. & f. parallel.

paralelógramo, *–lĕlŏ'grămŏ,* sm. paral-lelogram, oblong; –, ma, a. parallelo-gramic. [sied.

paralítico, ca, *–lĕ'tĭkŏ,* a. paralytic, pal-

paralogismo, *–lŏ'hĭs'mŏ,* sm. paralogism, false reasoning.

páramo, *pă'rămŏ,* sm. desert, wilderness; any place extremely cold.

parangón, *părăngŏn',* sm. paragon, model, comparison. [to parallel.

parangonar, *–gŏnăr',* v. a. to compare,

parapeto, *–pĕ'tŏ,* sm. parapet, breast-work.

parar, *părăr',* v. n. to stop, to halt; –, v. a. to stop, to detain; to treat ill; to stake at cards; — **en mal,** to have a bad end; **sin —,** instantly, without delay; **—se,** to stop, to halt; **—,** sm. lansquenet (game at cards). [conductor.

pararrayo, -*rā'yŏ,* sm. lightning-rod.

parasismo, -*sīs'mŏ,* sm. paroxysm, fit.

parásito, *pār'ă stŏ,* sm. parasite, sponger.

parasol, *pārăsŏl',* sm. parasol.

parca, *pār'kă,* sf. (poet.) Fate, Fatal Sister. [given to grammar-scholars.

parce, *pār'thě,* sm. schedule of pardon

parcial, *pārthĭăl',* a. partial.

parcialidad, -*lĭdăd',* sf. partiality; sociability; party, faction.

parco, ca, *pār'kŏ,* a. sparing, scanty; sober, moderate. [(fig.) deception, jest.

parchazo, *pārtshā'thŏ,* sm. large plaster.

parche, *pār'tshě,* sm. plaster; drum-skin.

pardal, *pārdăl',* a. clownish, rustic; cunning; **—,** sm. grey sand-piper.

pardear, *pārdĕăr',* v. n. to grow grey or brownish; to become dusky. [oath.

pardiez, *pārdĭēth',* jocular affirmation or

pardillo, *pārdĭl'yŏ,* sm. linnet.

pardo, da, *pār'dŏ,* a. grey.

pardusco, ca, -*dūs'kŏ,* a. grayish, grizzly.

parear, *pārĕăr',* v. a. to match, to pair, to couple.

parecer, *pārĕthĕr',* sm. opinion, advice, counsel; countenance, air, mien; **—,** v. n. to appear; to seem; **—se,** to present oneself to view; to resemble.

parecido, da, -*thĭ'dŏ,* a. resembling, like.

pared, *pārĕd',* sf. wall; **— medianera,** party-wall.

paredón, *pārĕdŏn',* sm. thick wall.

pareja, *pārĕ'kă,* sf. pair, couple, brace; accouplement. [dred.

parentela, *pārĕntĕ'lă,* sf. parentage, kin-

parentesco, -*tĕs'kŏ,* sm. cognation, kindred; union, chain, link.

paréntesis, *pārĕn'tĕsĭs,* sm. parenthesis.

pares y nones, *pā'rĕs ī nŏ'nĕs,* sm. pl. even or odd. [in the East-Indies.

paria, *pā'rĭă,* sm. pariah, the lowest caste

parias, *pā'rĭăs,* sf. pl. tribute paid by one prince to another as an acknowledgment of superiority; placenta, after-birth.

parida, *pārĕ'dă,* sf. woman lately delivered.

paridad, *pārĭdăd',* sf. parity, equality.

pariente, ta, *pārĭĕn'tă,* sm. & f. kinsman; kinswoman.

parihuela, *pārĭhŭĕ'lă,* sf. barrow.

parir, *pārĭr',* v. a. to bring forth; to produce; to lie in; to lay eggs. [gossip.

parla, *pār'lă,* sf. easy delivery, loquacity,

parlador, ra, -*dŏr',* sm. & f. prater.

parlamental, -*mĕntăl',* a. parliamentary.

parlamentar, -*mĕntăr',* v. n. to talk, to converse; to parley.

parlamentario, -*mĕntă'rĭŏ,* sm. member of parliament; **—,** a. parliamentary.

parlamento, -*mĕn'tŏ,* sm. harangue delivered in a public assembly; parliament.

parlanchín, na, *pārlăntshĭn',* a. & sm. & f. chatterer, jabberer.

parlar, *pārlăr',* v. a. to chatter, to talk.

parleta, *pārlĕ'tă,* sf. conversation on trifling subjects. [chatter, to gossip.

parlotear, *pārlŏtĕăr',* v. n. to prate, to

Parnaso, *pārnă'sŏ,* sm. (poet.) Parnassus.

parodia, *pārŏ'dĭă,* sf. parody.

parola, *pārŏ'lă,* sf. eloquence; chatter.

parpadear, *pārpădĕăr',* v. n. to twinkle.

párpado, *pār'pădŏ,* sm. eye-lid.

parque, *pār'kĕ,* sm. park; (mil.) park of artillery. [nailed to a wall.

parra, *pār'ră,* sf. vine raised on stakes or

párrafo, *pār'răfŏ,* sm. paragraph; a mark in printing. [earthen jar.

parral, *pārrăl',* sm. vine-arbour; a large

parricida, *pārrĭthĕ'dă,* sm. & f. parricide (person).

parricidio, -*thĕ'dĭŏ,* sm. parricide (murder).

parrillas, *pārrĭl'yăs,* sf. pl. gridiron.

parro, *pār'rŏ,* sm. gander, goose.

párroco, *pār'rŏkŏ,* sm. parson.

parroquia, *pārrŏ'kĭă,* sf. parish.

parroquial, *pārrŏkĭăl',* a. parochial.

parroquiano, -*kĭă'nŏ,* sm. parishioner; customer; **—,** a. parochial.

parsimonia, *pārsĭmŏ'nĭă,* sf. parsimony.

parte, *pār'tě,* sf. part; side; party; **de ocho días á esta —,** within these last eight days; **de —á —,** from side to side, through.

partear, *pārtĕăr',* v. a. to deliver, to deliver a woman of a child.

partera, *pārtĕ'ră,* sf. midwife.

partero, *pārtĕ'rŏ,* sm. man-midwife.

partible, *pārtĕ'blĕ,* a. divisible, partible.

partición, *pārtĭthĭŏn',* sf. partition, division. [pation.

participación, -*thĭpăthĭŏn',* sf. partici-

participar, -*thĭpăr',* v. a. & n. to participate, to partake. [sharing.

participe, *pārtĕthĭpĕ,* a. participant.

participio, *pārtĭthĕ'pĭŏ,* sm. participle.

partícula, *pārtĕ'kŭlă,* sf. particle.

particular, *pārtĕkŭlăr',* a. particular, special; **—,** sm. private gentleman; peculiar matter or subject treated upon.

particularidad, -*lărĭdăd',* sf. particularity; friendship, intimacy.

particularizar, -*lărĭthăr',* v. a. & r. to particularize.

partida, *pārtĕ'dă,* sf. departure; party of soldiers; item in an account; parcel; game at play; **—s,** pl. parts, talents, accomplishments; the laws of Castile.

partidario, *pārtĭdă'rĭŏ,* sm. partisan.

partido, *pārtĕ'dŏ,* sm. party; district.

partidor, *pārtĭdŏr',* sm. parter, divider.

partija, *pārtĕ'kă,* sf. partition, division.

partir, *pārtĭr',* v. a. to part, to divide, to separate, to cut, to cleave; to break; **—,** v. n. to depart; **—se,** to differ in opinion.

partitivo, va, *pārtĭtĕ'vŏ,* a. (gr.) partitive.

parto, *pār'tŏ,* sm. child-birth.

parva, *pār'vă,* sf. unthrashed corn laid in heaps to be thrashed; multitude. [ness.

parvidad, *pārvĭdăd',* sf. littleness, minute-

parvo, va, *pār'vŏ,* a. small, little.

párvulo, la, *pár'vŭlŏ,* a. very small; innocent; –, sm. child.

pasa, *pá'să,* sf. raisin.

pasada, *păsă'dă,* sf. passage; pace, step; manner, behaviour; **de –,** on the way, in passing.

pasadera, *păsădě'ră,* sf. stepping-stone.

pasadero, ra, *–dě'rŏ,* a. supportable, sufferable; passable; –, sm. stepping-stone.

pasadizo, *păsădě'thŏ,* sm. narrow passage; narrow, covered way, subway.

pasado, *păsá'dŏ,* sm. (gr.) past time; **–s,** pl. ancestors.

pasador, *păsădŏr',* sm. smuggler; sharp-pointed arrow from a crossbow; bolt of a lock; woman's brooch.

pasaje, *păsă'h'ĕ,* sm. passage.

pasajero, ra, *–hă'rŏ,* a. transient, transitory, fugitive; –, sm. & f. traveller, passenger.

pasalicor, *–lĭkŏr',* sm. hydrometer, test-liquor.

pasamanería, *–mănĕr'ĕ'ă,* sf. lace-making.

pasamano, *–mă'nŏ,* sm. balustrade.

pasante, *păsăn'tĕ,* sm. assistant of a physician or lawyer; student who acts the teacher or lecturer to beginners.

pasantía, *–tě'ă,* sf. profession of a law-student who practises under the direction of a professor of the faculty.

pasapasa, *păsăpa'să,* sm. legerdemain.

pasaporte, *–pŏr'tĕ,* sm. passport; (mil.) furlough.

pasar, *păsăr',* v. a. to pass; to surpass; to suffer; to strain; to dissemble; –, v. n. to pass; –, v. imp. to happen; **–se,** to go over to another party; to become corrupt or putrid.

pasatiempo, *–tĭĕm'pŏ,* sm. pastime, amusement.

pasavolante, *–vŏlăn'tĕ,* sm. inconsiderate speech or action; seaman entered in the muster-book, but not actually existing.

Pascua, *păs'kŭă,* sf. Passover; Easter.

pascual, *păskŭăl',* a. paschal.

pase, *pá'sĕ,* sm. pass-bill; permit, cocket.

paseante, *păsĕăn'tĕ,* sm. walker; **– en corte,** one who has neither office nor employ.

pasear, *păsĕăr',* v. a. & n. to walk; to be at the walk; to walk about; **–se,** to walk for exercise or amusement; to loiter, to gape about.

paseo, *păsĕ'ŏ,* sm. walk.

pasibilidad, *păsĭbĭlĭdăd',* sf. passibleness.

pasible, *păsĭ'blĕ,* a. passible.

pasillo, *păsĭl'yŏ,* sm. small narrow passage.

pasión, *păsĭŏn',* sf. passion.

pasionaria, *–nă'rĭă,* sf. passion-flower.

pasito, *păsĭ'tŏ,* ad. gently, softly.

pasiva, *păsĭ'vă,* sf. (gr.) passive.

pasivo, va, *păsĭ'vŏ,* a. passive.

pasmar, *păsmăr',* v. a. to cause a spasm; to benumb; to chill; –, v. n. to marvel, to wonder; **–se,** to suffer spasms; to be astonished.

pasmo, *păs'mŏ,* sm. spasm, convulsion; astonishment, amazement.

pasmoso, sa, *păsmŏ'sŏ,* a. marvellous, wonderful.

paso, *pá'sŏ,* sm. pace, step; passage; manner of walking; flight of steps; accident; (rail.) – **á nivel,** railway-crossing; **al –,** on the way, in passing.

paspié, *păspĭĕ',* sm. a Breton merry dance.

pasquín, *păskĭn',* sm. pasquinade, pasquil, lampoon.

pasta, *păs'tă,* sf. paste; excessive meekness or mildness.

pastar, *păstăr',* v. a. to pasture, to graze.

pastel, *păstĕl',* sm. pie; crayon for drawing.

pastelería, *–lĕr'ĕ'ă,* sf. pastrycook's shop; pastry.

pastelero, ra, *–lĕ'rŏ,* sm. pastrycook.

pastilla, *păstĭl'yă,* sf. lozenge.

pasto, *păs'tŏ,* sm. pasture; pasture-ground; **á –,** abundantly.

pastor, *păstŏr',* sm. shepherd; pastor.

pastoral, *–răl',* a. pastoral, rural.

pastorela, *–rĕ'lă,* sf. pastoral.

pastoril, *–rĭl',* a. pastoral.

pastoso, sa, *păstŏ'sŏ,* a. mellow, doughy.

pastura, *păstŏ'ră,* sf. pasture; pasture-ground.

pasturaje, *păstŭră'h'ĕ,* sm. pasturage.

pata, *pá'tă,* sf. foot and leg of an animal; duck; **–** de cabra, unforeseen impediment; **á la – coja,** Scotch hoppers (children's play); **á –,** on foot.

patada, *pătă'dă,* sf. kick; step, pace; tract.

patagalana, *–ydlă'nă,* sf. limping; halt.

patagón, *–gŏn',* sm. large clumsy foot.

patalear, *–lĕăr',* v. n. to kick about violently.

pataleo, *–lĕ'ŏ,* sm. act of stamping one's foot.

pataleta, *–lĕ'tă,* sf. fainting-fit; swoon.

patán, *pătăn',* sm. clown, churl, country-man.

patarata, *pătără'tă,* sf. fiction, false story; kickshaw.

patata, *pătă'tă,* sf. potato.

patatús, *–tŏs',* sm. swoon, fainting-fit.

patear, *pătĕăr',* v. a. to kick.

patena, *pătĕ'nă,* sf. patine.

patente, *pătĕn'tĕ,* a. patent, manifest, evident; –, sf. patent; warrant; letters of marque.

paternal, *pătĕrnăl',* a. paternal, fatherly.

paternidad, *–nĭdăd',* sf. paternity, fatherhood.

paterno, na, *pătĕr'nŏ,* a. paternal, fatherly.

pateta, *pătĕ'tă,* sm. nickname given to a lame person.

patético, ca, *pătĕ'tĭkŏ,* a. pathetic.

patíbulo, *pătĭ'bŭlŏ,* sm. gibbet, gallows.

paticojo, ja, *pătĭkŏ'h'ŏ,* a. lame, crippled.

patilla, *pătĭl'yă,* sf. whiskers; **–s,** pl. (vulg.) devil.

patín, *pătĭn',* sm. skate, ice-spur.

patio, *pă'tĭŏ,* sm. court behind a house; pit in play-houses.

patitieso, sa, *pătĭtĭĕ'sŏ,* a. stupefied, surprised.

patituerto, ta, *–tŭĕr'tŏ,* a. crook-legged.

patizambo, ba, *–thăm'bŏ,* a. bandy-legged.

pato, ta, *pă'tŏ,* a. equal, similar; –, sm. **–a,** sf. duck.

patochada, *–tŏhă'dă,* sf. blunder, nonsense, folly.

patología, *–lŏ'hĕ'ă,* sf. pathology.

patológico, ca, *–lŏ'hĭkŏ,* a. patologic.

patraña, *patrăn'yă*, sf. fabulous story.
patria, *pä'trĕä*, sf. native country.
patriarca, *pätrĭä'kä*, sm. patriarch.
patriarcado, *–kä'dŏ*, sm. patriarchate.
patriarcal, *–kăl'*, a. patriarchal.
patricio, *pätrē'thĭŏ*, sm. patrician; –, a. native, national.
patrimonial, *pätrĭmŏnĭăl'*, a. patrimonial.
patrimonio, *–mŏ'nĭŏ*, sm. patrimony.
patrio, tria, *pä'trĭŏ*, a. native, paternal.
patriota, *pätrĭŏ'tă*, sm. & f. patriot.
patriótico, ca, *pätrĭŏ'tĭkŏ*, a. patriotic.
patriotismo, *–tĭs'mŏ*, sm. patriotism.
patrocinar, *pätrŏthĭnăr'*, v. a. to favour, to patronise, to protect. [tronage.
patrocinio, *–thĕ'nĭŏ*, sm. protection, patrón, *pätrŏn'*, sm. patron, protector; master of a trading vessel; landlord of a house or inn; guardian saint of a country, town, &c.
patrona, *pätrŏ'nă*, sf. patroness.
patronado, da, *pätrŏnä'dŏ*, a. having a patron. [sm. patronage.
patronato, *–nä'tŏ*, patronazgo, *–năth'gŏ*,
patronímico, *–nĕ'mĭkŏ*, sm. patronymic.
patrono, *pätrŏ'nŏ*, sm. lord of the manor.
patrulla, *pätrūl'yä*, sf. (mil.) patrol.
patrullar, *–yăr'*, v. n. to patrol, camp or garrison.
patudo, da, *pätŏ'dä*, a. club-footed.
paulatino, na, *päŭlätĕ'nŏ*, a. slowly, by degrees. [munication; reproof, chiding.
paulina, *päŭlĕ'nä*, sf. decree of excommunica.
pausa, *päŭsä*, sf. pause; repose; á–s, by intervals. [ate; calm, quiet, paused.
pausado, da, *päŭsä'dŏ*, a. slow, deliberate.
pausar, *päŭsăr'*, v. n. to pause.
pauta, *päŭtä*, sf. ruler made out of a board with cat-gut strings.
pava, *pä'vä*, sf. turkey-hen; pea-hen.
pavoro, *pävŏ'rŏ*, sm. & f. one who feeds turkey-fowls. [remains, relics.
pavesa, *pävĕ'sä*, sf. embers, hot cinders;
pavía, *pävĭ'ä*, sf. peach with hard stones.
pávido, da, *pä'vĭdŏ*, a. timid, fearful.
pavimento, *pävĭmĕn'tŏ*, sm. pavement.
pavipollo, *–pŏl'yŏ*, sm. young turkey.
pavo, *pä'vŏ*, sm. turkey; – real, peacock.
pavón, *pävŏn'*, sm. peacock, peafowl.
pavonar, *pävŏnăr'*, v. n. to give iron or steel á bluish colour.
pavonear, *–năr'*, v. n. to strut, to walk with affected dignity. [able.
pavoroso, sa, *–rŏ'sŏ*, a. awful, formidpavura, *pävŏ'rä*, sf. fear, dread, terror.
payo, *pä'yŏ*, sm. clown, churl.
paz, *päth*, sf. peace; tranquillity, ease; ¡–! peace! hush! [ning to end.
pe, *pĕ*, ad. de – á –, entirely, from beginpeaje, *pĕä'hĕ*, sm. bridge-toll; ferriage.
peal, *pĕäl'*, sm. sock; worthless person.
peana, *pĕä'nä*, sf. pedestal; foot-stool, footboard.
peatón, *pĕätŏn'*, sm. rural postman.
peazgo, *pĕäth'gŏ*, sm. bridge-toll; ferriage.
pebete, *pĕbĕ'tĕ*, sf. pastil for fumigation; fusee, match.

pebetero, *pĕbĕtĕ'rŏ*, sm. censer.
peca, *pä'kä*, sf. freckle, spot.
pecado, *pĕkä'dŏ*, sm. sin.
pecador, ra, *–dŏr'*, sm. & f. sinner.
pecaminoso, sa, *–mĭnŏ'sŏ*, a. sinful.
pecar, *pĕkăr'*, v. n. to sin.
pecina, *pĕthĕ'nä*, sf. fish-pond. [knave.
pécora, *pä'kŏrä*, sf. sheep; cunning fellow,
pecoso, sa, *pĕkŏ'sŏ*, a. freckled.
pectoral, *pĕktŏräl'*, a. pectoral; –, sm. cross worn by bishops on the breast.
peculiar, *pĕkŭlĭăr'*, a. peculiar, special.
peculio, *pĕkŏ'lĭŏ*, sm. private fortune; capital allowed to a minor.
pecunia, *pĕkŏ'nĭä*, sf. hard cash, specie.
pecuniario, ria, *–nĭä'rĭŏ*, a. pecuniary,
pechar, *pĕtshăr'*, v. n. to pay taxes.
pechera, *pĕtshĕ'rä*, sf. stomacher; frill.
pechero, ra, *–rŏ*, a. liable to pay taxes; –, sm. commoner, plebeian; bib.
pecho, *pĕtsh'ŏ*, sm. breast; teat; bosom; courage, valour; tax, contribution; dar el –, to suckle; tener –, to have patience; tomar á –s, to take to heart.
pechuga, *pĕtshŏ'gä*, sf. breast of a fowl; bosom. [hoarseness.
pechuguera, *pĕtshŏgĕ'rä*, sf. cough,
pedagogia, *pĕdägŏ'hĭä*, sf. pedagogism.
pedagógico, ca, *–gŏ'hĭkŏ*, a. pedagogic.
pedagogo, *–gŏ'gŏ*, sm. pedagogue.
pedáneo, *pĕdä'nĕŏ*, a. petty, inferior (of law-courts).
pedante, *pĕdän'tĕ*, sm. pedant.
pedantear, *–tĕăr'*, v. n. to play the pedant.
pedantería, *–tĕrē'ä*, sf. pedantry.
pedantesco, ca, *–tĕs'kŏ*, a. pedantic.
pedantismo, *–tĭs'mŏ*, sm. pedantry.
pedazo, *pĕdä'thŏ*, sm. piece, bit.
pedernal, *pĕdĕrnäl'*, sm. flint.
pedestal, *pĕdĕstäl'*, sm. pedestal, foot.
pedicular, *pĕdĭkŭlăr'*, a. lousy.
pedido, *pĕdē'dŏ*, sm. voluntary contribution, which is called for by government in urgent necessities of the State; request.
pedigüeña, *–gŭĕn'yä*, a. craving, demanding, beggary.
pediluvios, *–lŏ'vĭŏs*, sm. foot-bath.
pedimento, *–mĕn'tŏ*, sm. petition.
pedir, *pĕdĭr'*, v. a. to petition, to beg, to supplicate, to solicit.
pedo, *pä'dŏ*, sm. wind from the bowels.
pedorreras, *pĕdŏrrĕ'räs*, sf. flatulency.
pedorrero, ra, *–rŏ*, a. flatulent.
pedrada, *pĕdrä'dä*, sf. throw of a stone.
pedrea, *pĕdrĕ'ä*, sf. conflict of boys belonging to different wards or districts fighting with stones; lapidation.
pedregal, *pĕdrĕgäl'*, sm. shingle; place full of stones.
pedregoso, sa, *–gŏ'sŏ*, a. stony.
pedrera, *pĕdrĕ'rä*, sf. quarry, stone-pit.
pedrería, *pĕdrĕrē'ä*, sf. collection of precious stones. [lapidary.
pedrero, *pĕdrĕ'rŏ*, sm. stone-cutter; slinger,
pedrisco, *pĕdrĭs'kŏ*, sm. hail-stone.
pedrusco, *pĕdrŏs'kŏ*, sm. rough piece of marble.
peer, *pĕĕr'*, v. n. to break wind. [marble.

pega, pá'gä, sf. pitch; glue.

pegadizo, za, pégädé thö, a. clammy, viscous; contagious. [plasm.

pegado, pégä'dö, sm. sticking-plaster, cataplasm.

pegadura, -dö'rä, sf. pitching.

pegajoso, sa, -'hö'sö, a. sticky, viscous; contagious; attractive.

pegar, pégär', v. a. to cement; to join, to unite; to beat; – **fuego,** to set fire to; –, v. n. to take root; –se, to intrude, to steal in.

Pegaso, pégä'sö, sm. Pegasus.

pegote, pégö'tä, sm. pitch-plaster; impertinent intruder, hanger-on, sponger.

peguntar, pégän'tär', v. a. to brand cattle with melted pitch.

peinado, peiná'dö, sm. hair combed, dressed and curled. [ing-gown.

peinador, -dör', sm. hair-dresser; dress-

peinar, peiná'r', v. a. to comb the hair.

peine, peí'nä, sm. comb.

peinería, peïnerë'ä, sf. shop where combs are made and sold.

peinero, -nä'rö, sm. & f. comb-maker.

peineta, -nä'tä, sf. convex comb for women.

peladilla, pëlädïl'yä, sf. sugared almond, burnt almond; small pebble.

peladura, -dö'rä, sf. plucking.

pelafustán, -füstän', sm. ragamuffin.

pelagallos, -gäl'yös, sm. common people out of work. [pocket.

pelagatos, -gä'tös, sm. cutpurse, pick-

pelaje, pëlä'hä, sm. colour or tint of animals' hair.

pelandusca, pëländüs'kä, sf. strumpet.

pelar, pëlär', v. a. to pull out the hair; to strip off the feathers. [of stairs.

peldaño, pëldän'yö, sm. step of a flight

pelea, pëlä'ä, sf. battle, fight; quarrel.

pelear, pëlëär', v. a. to fight, to combat; –se, to scuffle. [ficant fellow.

pelele, pëlä'lä, sm. man of straw; insigni-

peletería, pëlëtërë'ä, sf. trade of a furrier; fellmonger's shop.

peletero, -tä'rö, sm. furrier.

peliagudo, da, pëliägö'dö, a. downy, furry; arduous, difficult; ingenious, dexterous.

pelícano, pëlë'känö, sm. pelican; – peüká'nö, a. gray-haired; hoary.

pelicorto, ta, pëlïkör'tö, a. short-haired.

película, pëlë'külä, sf. pellicle. [risk.

peligrar, pëlïgrär', v. n. to be in danger; to

peligro, pëlë'grö, sm. danger, risk, peril.

peligroso, sa, pëlïgrö'sö, a. dangerous, perilous. [trifle.

pelillo, pëlïl'yö, sm. short, tender hair;

pelma, pël'mä, sf. **pelmazo,** pëlmä'thö, sm. heavy paste or cake; food which lies heavy on the stomach.

pelo, pä'lö, sm. hair; pile; flaw (in precious stones); á –, to the purpose, timely.

pelón, ona, pëlön', a. hairless, bald.

pelota, pëlö'tä, sf. ball; – **de viento,** foot-ball.

pelotazo, pëlötä'thö, sm. blow with a ball.

pelote, pëlö'tä, sm. goat's hair.

pelotear, pëlötëär', v. n. to play at ball; to argue, to dispute.

pelotera, -tä'rä, sf. women's quarrel.

pelotero, -tä'rö, sm. ball-maker.

pelotón, -tön', sm. large ball; (mil.) platoon.

peltre, pël'trä, sm. pewter. [toon.

peltrero, pëlträ'rö, sm. pewterer. [proof.

peluca, pëlü'kä, sf. periwig, peruke; re-

peludo, da, -dö, a. hairy; –, sm. bass-mat of an oval shape.

peluquería, -kërë'ä, sf. shop where wigs are made and sold.

peluquero, -kä'rö, sm. peruke-maker.

pelusa, pëlö'sä, sf. bloom on fruit; fluff rubbed off from clothes in wear.

pella, pël'yä, sf. ball; clew; mass of metal in its crude state; lard in the state in which it is taken from hogs; heron (bird).

pellada, pëlyä'dä, sf. gentle blow.

pelleja, pëlyë'h'ä, sf. skin stripped from an animal; female toper.

pellejería, -'hër'ë'ä, sf. fellmonger's shop.

pellejero, -'hä'rö, sm. fellmonger, leather-dresser.

pellejo, pëlë'h'ö, sm. skin, hide; pelt; peel; wine-skin, leather-bag for wine; oil-skin; tippler, drunkard, fuddler.

pellejudo, da, -'hü'dö, a. thick-skinned.

pellica, pëlyë'kä, sf. coverlet of fine furs.

pellico, -kö, sm. dress made of skins or

pelliza, pëlyë'thä, sf. pelisse. [furs.

pellizcar, pëlyïthkär', v. a. to pinch.

pellizco, pëlyïth'kö, sm. pinch; nip; small bit; (fig.) remorse.

pena, pä'nä, sf. punishment, pain; á **duras** –s, with great difficulty or trouble.

penacho, pënätsh'ö, sm. tuft on the heads of some birds; crest; pride, haughtiness.

penal, pënäl', a. penal.

penalidad, -lïdäd', sf. suffering, trouble; hardship; penalty; punishableness.

penar, pënär', v. n. to suffer pain; –, v. a. to chastise; –se, to grieve, to mourn.

penates, pënä'tës, sm. pl. Penates, household-gods, pl.

penca, pën'kä, sf. prickly leaf of a plant; scourge, lash.

pendanga, -dän'gä, sf. common prostitute.

pendencia, -dën'thïä, sf. quarrel, dispute.

pendenciero, ra, pëndënthïä'rö, a. quarrelsome.

pender, pëndër', v. n. to impend, to hang over; to depend; to be irresolute.

pendiente, -dïën'tä, sm. & f. slope, declivity; –s, pl. ear-rings, ear-drops, pl.

péndola, pën'dölä, sf. pendulum.

pendolista, -lïs'tä, sm. penman.

pendón, pëndön', sm. standard; banner.

péndulo, la, pën'dülö, a. pendent, hanging; –, sm. pendulum.

penetrable, pënëträ'blä, a. penetrable; comprehensible. [complete intelligence.

penetración, -thïön', sf. ; penetration;

penetrar, -trär', v. a. to penetrate; –se, to coexist as two bodies in the same place.

península, pënïn'sülä, sf. peninsula.

penitencia, pënïtën'thïä, sf. penitence; penalty, fine.

penitencial, –thǐál', a. penitential.
penitenciar, –thǐár', v. a. to impose a penance for a fault committed.
penitenciaría, –thǐárě ǎ, sf. office of a penitentiary.
penitenciario, –thǐǎ rǐ ǒ, sm. penitentiary.
penitenta, peníten'tǎ, sf. female penitent.
penitente, –tě, a. penitent, repentant; –, sm. penitent.
penoso, sa, penǒ'sǒ, a. painful.
pensado, pensǎ dǒ, de –, sm. on purpose.
pensamiento, –mǐěn'tǒ, sm. thought.
pensar, pensǎr', v. n. to think. [thinking.
pensativo, va, –tǐ vǒ, a. pensive, thought-
pensión, pěnsǐǒn', sf. pension; toil. [ful.
pensionado, da, –nǎ dǒ, sm. & f. pensioner, pensionary.
pensionar, –nǎr', v. a. to impose pensions.
pensionario, –nǎ rǐǒ, sm. pensionary.
pensionista, –nǐs tǎ, sm. & f. pensioner, pensionary; boarder. [teuch.
Pentatéuco, pěntǎtǎ ǎkǒ, sm. the Penta-
Pentecostés, pěntěkǒstěs, sm. Pentecost, Whitsuntide. [last but one.
penúltimo, ma, penǔl tǐmǒ, a. penultimate.
penuria, pěnǒ rǐǎ, sf. penury, poverty, indigence, neediness, extreme want.
peña, pěn yǎ, sf. rock, large stone.
peñascal, –yǎskǎl', sm. rocky hill or mountain. [rough cloth.
peñasco, –yǎs kǒ, sm. large rock; strong,
peñascoso, sa, –yǎskǒ sǒ, a. rocky, mountainous.
peñón, pěnyǒn', sm. rocky mountain.
peón, pěǒn', sm. pedestrian; day-labourer; foot-soldier; gig, humming-top; pawn (at chess); hive of bees.
peonía, pěǒně ǎ, sf. (bot.) peony.
peonza, pěǒn'thǎ, sf. whip-top; noisy little fellow. [worse.
peor, pěǒr', a. & ad. worse; worse and
peoría, pěǒrě ǎ, sf. deterioration, detriment.
pepinar, pěpǐnǎr', sm. cucumber-field.
pepino, pěpǐ nǒ, sm. cucumber.
pepita, pěpǐ tǎ, sf. kernel; pip.
pepitoria, –tǒ rǐǎ, sf. fricassee made of giblets, livers and lights.
pequeñez, pěkěnyěth', sf. littleness.
pequeño, ña, pěkěn yǒ, a. little, small;
pera, pǎ rǎ, sf. pear. [young.
perada, pěrǎ dǎ, sf. conserve of pears.
peral, pěrǎl', sm. pear-tree.
percance, pěrkǎn'thě, sm. perquisite; bad luck, non-success.
percepción, pěrthěpthǐǒn', sf. perception, notion. [ceivable.
perceptible, –tě blě, a. perceptible, per-
percibir, pěrthǐbǐr', v. a. to receive; to perceive, to comprehend.
percusión, –kǔsǐǒn', sf. percussion.
percha, pěrtch'ǎ, sf. perch.
perder, pěrděr', v. a. to lose; –se, to go astray; to be lost; to be spoiled.
perdición, –dǐthǐǒn', sf. losing of a thing; perdition, ruin, loss. [lost.
pérdida, pěr dǐdǎ, sf. loss, damage; object
perdidizo, za, –dǐdě thǒ, a. lost on purpose.

perdido, da, pěrdě dǒ, a. lost, strayed.
perdigar, –dǐgǎr', v. a. to broil partridges slightly before they are roasted; to stew larded meat in an earthen pan.
perdigón, –dǐgǒn', sm. partridge trained to decoy others; –ones, pl. hail-shot.
perdiguero, ra, –dǐgǎ rǒ, a. setting, pointing (of dogs).
perdiz, pěrdǐth', sf. partridge.
perdón, pěrdǒn', sm. pardon.
perdonable, –dǒnǎ blě, a. pardonable.
perdonar, –dǒnǎr', v. a. to pardon, to forgive.
perdulario, ria, –dǔlǎ rǐǎ, a. extremely careless with regard to one's own interest.
perdurable, –dǔrǎ blě, a. perpetual, everlasting.
perecedero, ra, pěrěthědǎ rǒ, a. perishable; –, sm. misery, extreme want.
perecer, pěrěthěr', v. n. to perish, to die; to perish for want of the necessaries of life; –se, to die of love or envy. [age.
peregrinación, –grǐnǎthǐǒn', sf. pilgrim-
peregrinamente, –měn'tě, ad. rarely, curiously. [pilgrimage.
peregrinar, pěrěgrǐnǎr', v. a. to go on a pilgrimage.
peregrino, na, –grě nǒ, a. foreign, travelling; going on a pilgrimage; strange; –, sm. pilgrim.
perejil, pěrěhǐl', sm. parsley.
perendengues, pěrěnděn'gěs, sm. pl. ear-drops, ear-rings, pl.
perenne, pěrěn'ně, a. perennial, perpetual.
perentorio, ria, –tǒ rǐǒ, a. peremptory, decisive.
pereza, pěrě thǎ, sf. laziness, idleness.
perezoso, sa, –thǒ sǒ, a. lazy, idle.
perfección, pěrfěkthǐǒn', sf. perfection.
perfeccionar, –thǐǒnǎr', v. a. to perfect, to complete, to finish.
perfecto, ta, –fěk tǒ, a. perfect, complete.
perfidia, pěrfě dǐǎ, sf. perfidy.
pérfido, da, pěr fǐdǒ, a. perfidious.
perfil, pěrfǐl', sm. profile.
perfilado, da, –lǎ dǒ, a. well-formed, delicate (of features).
perfiladura, –lǎdǒ rǎ, sf. art of profile-drawing; sketching of outlines.
perfilar, –lǎr', v. a. to draw profiles; to sketch outlines; –se, to incline.
perfumador, pěrfǔmǎdǒr', sm. perfumer; perfuming-pan.
perfumar, –fǔmǎr', v. a. to perfume.
perfume, –fǒ'mě, sm. perfume.
perfumería, –fǔměrě ǎ, sf. perfumer's shop.
pergamino, –gǎmě nǒ, sm. skin dressed for writing, parchment.
pericia, pěrě thǐǎ, sf. skill, knowledge, connoisseurship.
pericón, pěrǐkǒn', sm. large fan.
perifollo, –fǒl yǒ, sm. common chervil; ribbon or other women's ornament.
perifrasear, –frǎsěǎr', v. a. to periphrase.
perifrasis, pěrě frǎsǐs, sf. periphrasis, circumlocution.
perigallo, pěrǐgǎl yǒ, sm. little double-chin of lean persons; tall, lean, lank person; sling made of twine.

12*

perihelio, –*hd'lĕŏ*, sm. perihelium.

perilla, *pĕrĭl'yă*, sf. small pear; pear-shaped ornament; pommel; de –s, at the proper time.   [vagrant.

perillán, ana, –*yăn'*, a. artful, knavish.

perímetro, *pĕrĕ'mĕtrŏ*, sm. circumference, compass.   [neat little woman.

perinola, *pĕrĭnŏ'lă*, sf. die with four facets;

periódico, ca, *pĕrĭŏ'dĭkŏ*, a. periodical; –, sm. newspaper.   [periodical;

periodista, *pĕrĭŏdĭs'tă*, sm. editor of a periodical.   [periodical.

período, *pĕrĕ'ŏdŏ*, sm. period.

peripatético, *pĕrĭpătĕ'tĭkŏ*, sm. peri-patetic.   [drama).

peripecia, –*pă'thĭă*, sf. peripetia (in a

peripuesto, ta, –*pŭĕs'tŏ*, a. tricked up, very spruce in dress.

periquito, –*kĕ'tŏ*, sm. parroquet.

peristilo, –*stĕ'lŏ*, sm. peristyle.

perito, ta, *pĕrĕ'tŏ*, a. skilful, experienced.

perjudicar, *pĕr'hŏdĭkār'*, v. a. to preju-dice, to injure, to hurt, to damage.

perjudicial, –*dĭthĭăl'*, a. prejudicial, da-maging.   [jury.

perjuicio, *pĕr'hŏŏ'thĭŏ*, sm. prejudice, in-

perjurar, –*hŏrăr'*, v. n. to forswear, to swear falsely; to swear; –se, to perjure oneself.

perjurio, –*hŏ'rĭŏ*, sm. perjury, false oath.

perjuro, ra, –*hŏ'rŏ*, a. perjured, forsworn.

perla, *pĕr'lă*, sf. pearl; de –s, much to the purpose; eminently fine.   [palsied.

perlático, ca, *pĕrlă'tĭkŏ*, a. paralytic,

perlesía, *pĕrlĕsĕ'ă*, sf. paralysis, palsy.

permanecer, *pĕrmănĕthĕr'*, v. n. to persist.

permanencia, –*nĕn'thĭă*, sf. permanence, perseverance.

permanente, –*nĕn'tĕ*, a. permanent.

permisión, *pĕrmĭsĭŏn'*, sf. permission, leave.   [licence.

permiso, –*mĕ'sŏ*, sm. permission, leave,

permitir, –*mĭtĕr'*, v. a. to permit, to give leave.   [change.

permuta, –*mŏ'tă*, sf. permutation, ex-

permutar, –*mŏtăr'*, v. a. to exchange, to permute.

pernada, –*nŏ'dă*, sf. kick with the foot.

pernear, *pĕrnĕăr'*, v. n. to kick, to shake the legs; to fret.   [legged.

pernetas, *pĕrnĕ'tăs* (en –), ad. bare-

pernicioso, sa, *pĕrnĭthĭŏ'sŏ*, a. pernicious, destructive.

pernil, *pĕrnĕl'*, sm. ham, gammon.

pernio, *pĕr'nĭŏ*, sm. hinge for doors and windows.

perniquebrar, *pĕrnĭkĕbrăr'*, v. a. to break the legs; –se, to break one's leg.

pernoctar, –*nŏktăr'*, v. n. to pass the night; to be awake the whole night. [yet.

pero, *pĕ'rŏ*, sm. kind of apple; –, c. but,

perogrullada, –*grŭlyă'dă*, sf. truth of no moment and universally known.

perol, *pĕrŏl'*, sm. boiler, kettle.

peroración, *pĕrŏrăthĭŏn'*, sf. peroration, the conclusion of an oration.

perorar, –*răr'*, v. a. to put an end to a speech; to make an harangue.

perorata, –*ră'tă*, sf. harangue, speech.

perpendicular, *pĕrpĕndĭkŭlăr'*, a. per-pendicular.   [plummet, pendulum.

perpendículo, –*dĭ'kŭlŏ*, sm. plumb,

perpetrar, *pĕrpĕtrăr'*, v. a. to perpetrate, to commit a crime.   [xeranthemum.

perpetua, –*pĕ'tŭă*, sf. everlasting flower,

perpetuar, –*pĕtŭăr'*, v. a. to perpetuate.

perpetuidad, –*pĕtŭĭdăd'*, sf. perpetuity.

perpetuo, tua, –*pĕ'tŭŏ*, a. perpetual.

perplejidad, –*plĕhĭdăd'*, sf. perplexity.

perplejo, ja, –*plĕ'hŏ*, a. perplexed.

perra, *pĕr'ră*, sf. bitch; drunkenness, in-toxication.   [master.

perrera, *pĕrră'ră*, sf. kennel; bad pay-

perrería, *pĕrrĕrĕ'ă*, sf. pack of dogs; drudgery.   [dogs out of the church.

perrero, *pĕrrĕ'rŏ*, sm. beadle who drives – de falda, lap-dog.

perrillo, –*rĕl'yŏ*, sm. little dog; trigger;

perro, *pĕr'rŏ*, sm. dog; obstinate person; – de aguas, water-dog; – de muestra, pointer; – de presa, bull-dog; – de ayuda, Newfoundland-dog; – lebrel, greyhound.

persecución, *pĕrsĕkŭthĭŏn'*, sf. persecu-tion; toil, trouble, fatigue.

perseguidor, –*sĕgĭdŏr'*, sm. persecutor.

perseguir, –*sĕgĭr'*, v. a. to pursue a fugitive; to dun; to persecute.

perseverancia, *pĕrsĕvĕrăn'thĭă*, sf. per-severance, constancy.

perseverante, –*tĕ*, a. perseverant.

perseverar, *pĕrsĕvĕrăr'*, v. n. to per-severe, to persist.

persiana, *pĕrsĭă'nă*, sf. Venetian blind.

persignarse, –*sĭgnăr'sĕ*, v. r. to make the sign of the cross.   [steadiness.

persistencia, –*sĭstĕn'thĭă*, sf. persistence,

persistir, –*sĭstĕr'*, v. n. to persist.

persona, *pĕrsŏ'nă*, sf. person; de – á –, from man to man; hacer de –, to boast, to brag.

personaje, –*sŏnă'hĕ*, sm. personage.

personal, –*sŏnăl'*, a. personal.

personalidad, –*sŏnălĭdăd'*, sf. personality.

personero, –*sŏnĕ'rŏ*, sm. deputy, agent, attorney.   [sonify.

personificar, –*sŏnĭfĭkăr'*, v. a. to per-

perspectiva, –*spĕktĭ'vă*, sf. perspective; false, deceitful appearance.

perspicacia, –*spĭkă'thĭă*, sf. perspicacity, clear-sightedness.

perspicaz, –*spĭkăth'*, a. perspicacious, quick-sighted; sagacious.

persuadir, –*sŭădĕr'*, v. a. to persuade; –se, to be persuaded.

persuasión, –*sŭăsĭŏn'*, sf. persuasion.

persuasiva, –*sŭăsĕ'vă*, sf. persuasiveness.

persuasivo, va, –*sŭăsĕ'vŏ*, a. persuasive.

pertenecer, –*tĕnĕthĕr'*, v. n. to belong to, to appertain, to concern.

pertenencia, –*tĕnĕn'thĭă*, sf. right of pro-perty; appurtenance, dependence.

pértiga, *pĕr'tĭgă*, sf. long pole or rod.

pertiguería, –*gĕrĕ'ă*, sf. office or employ-ment of a verger.

pertiguero, –*gĕ'rŏ*, sm. verger.

pertinacia, —nă'thiă, sf. pertinacity, obstinacy, stubbornness.

pertinaz,—nàth', a. pertinacious, obstinate.

pertrechar, —pertrětshăr', v. a. to supply a place with ammunition and other warlike stores; to dispose, to arrange, to prepare; —se, to be provided with the necessary defensive stores and arms.

pertrechos, —trětsh'ŏs, sm. pl. tools, instruments; ammunition, warlike stores.

perturbación, —tŭrbăthiŏn', sf. perturbation, disquiet of mind.

perturbador, —tŭrbădŏr', sm. perturbator, disturber. [disturb.

perturbar, —tŭrbăr', v. a. to perturb, to perversidad, —věrsĭdăd', sf. perversity, malignity. [pravation, corruption.

perversión, —věrsĭŏn', sf. perversion; depperverso, sa, —věr'sŏ, a. perverse, extremely wicked. [corrupt.

pervertir, —vertĭr', v. a. to pervert, to pesa, pā'eă, sf. weight.

pesadez, pěsăděth', sf. heaviness; gravity, weight; slowness; peevishness, fretfulness; trouble, fatigue.

pesadilla, —dĭl'yă, sf. nightmare.

pesado, da, pěsă'dŏ, a. peevish, troublesome, cumbersome; tedious, injurious; heavy, weighty.

pesadumbre, —dŭm'brě, sf. weightiness, gravity; quarrel, dispute; grief, trouble.

pésame, pě'sămě, sm. message of condolence.

pesantez, pěsăntěth', sf. heaviness.

pesar, pěsăr', sm. sorrow, grief; repentance; á — ad. in spite of, notwithstanding; —, v. n. to weigh, to be of weight; to repent; —, v. a. to weigh.

pesaroso, sa, pěsărŏ'sŏ, a. sorrowful, full of repentance; restless, uneasy.

pesca, pěs'kă, sf. fishing, fishery.

pescadería, —děrĭ'ă, sf. fish-market.

pescado, pěskă'dŏ, sm. fish (in general).

pescador, —dŏr', sm. fisher, fisherman.

pescante, pěskăn'tě, sm. crane; coach-box.

pescar, —kăr', v. a. to fish, to catch fish.

pescozón, —kŏthŏn', sm. slap on the neck with the open hand.

pescuezo, —kŭěthŏ, sm. neck.

pesebre, pěsě'brě, sm. crib, manger.

pesebrera, pěsěbrě'ră, sf. row of mangers in a stable.

pesebrón, —brŏn', sm. boot of a coach.

peseta, pěsě'tă, sf. piece of two reales de plata. [weighing gold or silver coin.

pesillo, pěsĭl'yŏ, sm. small scales for pesimista, pěsĭmĭs'tă, sm. pessimist.

pésimo, ma, pěs'ĭmŏ, a. very bad.

peso, pě'sŏ, sm. weight, heaviness; balance-scales; Spanish dollar, piaster.

pespuntar, pěspŭntăr', v.a. to back-stitch.

pespunte, —pŭn'tě, sm. back-stitching.

pesquera, pěskě'ră, sf. fishery. [tion.

pesquisa, pěskě'să, sf. inquiry, examina-

pesquisar, pěskĭsăr', v. a. to inquire.

pesquisidor, —sĭdŏr', sm. examiner, inquirer; magistrate appointed to inquire

into the causes and circumstances of a violent death.

pestaña, pěstăn'yă, sf. eye-lash.

pestañear, —yěăr', v. a. to move the eye-lashes or eye-lids. [lids or eye-lashes.

pestañeo, —yě'ŏ, sm. moving of the eye-

peste, pěs'tě, sf. pest, plague, pestilence.

pestífero, ra, pěstĭ'fěrŏ, a. pestilential.

pestilencia, pěstĭlěn'thiă, sf. pestilence.

pestillo, pěstĭl'yŏ, sm. bolt.

pesuña, pěsŭn'yă, s. solid hoof.

petaca, pětă'kă, sf. covered hamper; tobacco-pouch.

petar, pětăr', v. a. to please, to content.

petardear, pětărděăr', v. a. to beat down a door with petards; —, v. n. to cheat.

petardista, —dĭs'tă, sm. & f. deceiver, cheat. [fraud, imposition.

petardo, —pětăr'dŏ, sm. petard; cheat,

petate, pětă'tě, sm. straw-bed; (am.) sleeping-mat of the Indians; (mar.) sailors' beddings on board; (mar.) passengers' luggage; poor fellow.

petición, pětĭthiŏn', sf. petition, demand.

petímetre, —mă'trě, sm. fop, coxcomb, beau.

petitorio, ria, —tŏ'riŏ, a. petitory, petitionary; —, sm. impertinent and repeated petition.

peto, pě'tŏ, sm. breast-plate; plastron.

petrificación, pětrĭfĭkăthiŏn', sf. petrification, petrifaction.

petrificar, —kăr', —se, y. r. to petrify.

petulancia, pětŭlăn'thiă, sf. petulance, insolence.

petulante, —lăn'tě, a. a petulant, insolent.

pez, pěth, sm. fish; —, sf. rosin, pitch; meconium; — griega, colophony.

pezón, pěthŏn', sm. leaf-stalk; nipple.

pezonera, —ně'ră, sf. linch-pin; breast-glass, breast-pump; round piece of lead, or pewter used by suckling women, to form the nipples.

pezuña, pěthŭn'yă, sf. solid hoof.

piada, piă'dă, sf. chirping of birds; pulling of chickens. [merciful; moderate.

piadoso, sa, piădŏ'sŏ, a. pious, mild,

pian piano, piăn piă'nŏ, ad. gently, softly.

piar, piăr', v. n. to squeak, to pule, to chirp. [ewes.

piara, piă'ră, sf. herd of swine; flock of

piastra, piăs'tră, sf. piaster; Turkish

pica, pě'kă, sf. pike. [silver coin.

picacho, pĭkătsh'ŏ, sm. sharp point.

picada, pĭkă'dă, sf. puncture.

picadero, —dě'rŏ, sm. riding-school; —s, pl. blocks of wood put under the keel of a ship, while she is building.

picadillo, —dĭl'yŏ, sm. minced meat, hash.

picador, —dŏr', sm. riding-master; pricker.

picadura, —dŏ'ră, sf. prick; puncture; gusset in clothes. [quant.

picante, pĭkăn'tě, sm. piquancy; —, a. pi-

picapedrero, —pědrě'rŏ, sm. stone-cutter.

picaporte, —pŏr'tě, sm. picklock.

picar, pĭkăr', v. a. to prick; to sting, to mince; to nibble; to pursue an enemy; to itch; —se, to be piqued; to be moth-eaten; to begin to rot.

picardear, _-deár',_ v. n. to play the knave.
picardía, _-dí'ă,_ sf. knavery, roguery; deceit, malice; lewdness. [knavish.
picaresco, ca, _-pĭkáres'kŏ,_ a. roguish,
pícaro, ra, _pĭ'kărŏ,_ a. knavish, roguish; mischievous, malicious; sly; merry, gay; -, sm. & f. rogue, knave.
picarote, _-rŏ'tĕ,_ sm. notorious villaïn, great impostor. [displeasure.
picazón, _-thŏn',_ sf. itching, prurience.
pico, _pĕ'kŏ,_ sm. beak; bill, nib; peak; loquacity; **perder por el** -, to lose by too much chattering. [small pox.
picoso, sa, _pĭkŏ'sŏ,_ a. pitted with the
picotazo, _pĭkŏtá'thŏ,_ sm. peck of a bird.
picote, _pĭkŏ'tĕ,_ sm. coarse stuff made of goat's hair; glossy silk stuff.
picotear, _-teár',_ v. a. to peck (of birds); -, v. n. to prattle, to chatter; -se, to wrangle (applied to women).
picotero, ra, _-tá'rŏ,_ a. wrangling, chattering, prattling. [pointed.
picudo, da, _pĭkŏ'dŏ,_ a. beaked; sharp-
pichón, _pĭtshŏn',_ sm. young pigeon.
pie, _pĭ'ĕ,_ sm. foot; leg; basis; trunk (of trees); foundation; occasion; **á** -, on foot; **á** - **enjuto,** without labour or pain; dry-shod.
piedad, _pĭĕdád',_ sf. piety; mercy, pity.
piedra, _pĭĕ'dră,_ sf. stone; gravel; hail; -s, pl. playing-counters.
piel, _pĭĕl',_ sf. skin; hide; peel.
piélago, _pĭĕ'lăgŏ,_ sm. high sea; great plenty, numberlessness.
pienso, _pĭĕn'sŏ,_ sm. common daily allowance given to horses or mules.
pierna, _pĭĕr'nă,_ sf. leg; leg of mutton; stroke; hanger (in writing); cheek of a printing-press; **- de sábana,** one of the breadths of a sheet.
pieza, _pĭĕ'thă,_ sf. piece; piece of furniture.
pífano, _pĭ'fănŏ,_ sm. fife; fife-player, piper.
pifia, _pĭ'fĭă,_ sf. sound of a rebounding billiard ball. [dwarfish.
pigmeo, mea, _pĭgmĭ'ŏ,_ sm. & a. dwarf;
pila, _pĭ'lă,_ sf. trough for water, in which cattle drink; font; pile, heap; holy-water basin; **nombre de** -, Christian name; **sacar de** -, to stand godfather or godmother. [at once; pile, heap.
pilada, _pĭlá'dă,_ sf. quantity of mortar made
pilar, _pĭlár',_ sm. large water-basin of a fountain; pillar.
pilastra, _pĭlás'tră,_ sf. pilaster.
píldora, _pĭl'dŏră,_ sf. pill.
pilón, _pĭlŏn',_ sm. large water-basin, drinking-trough; loaf of sugar.
pilongo, ga, _pĭlŏn'gŏ,_ a. lean, meagre.
pilotaje, _pĭlŏtá'h'ĕ,_ sm. pilotage.
piloto, _pĭlŏ'tŏ,_ sm. pilot; **- práctico,** coast-pilot. [is nearly all skin.
piltrafa, _pĭltrá'fă,_ sf. piece of meat that
pillada, _pĭlyá'dă,_ sf. knavish trick.
pillaje, _pĭlyá'h'ĕ,_ sm. pillage, plunder.
pillar, _pĭlyár',_ v. a. to pillage, to plunder, to forey, to seize; to chop at.

pillería, _-yĕrĕ'ă,_ sf. gang of vagabonds or rogues; knavish trick or sham.
pillo, lla, _pĭl'yŏ,_ a. marauding, good-for-nothing. [ground.
pimental, _pĭmĕntál',_ sm. pepper-bearing
pimentero, _-tá'rŏ,_ sm. pepper-box; pepper-plant. [pepper plant.
pimentón, _-tŏn',_ sm. ground fruit of the
pimienta, _pĭmĭĕn'tă,_ sf. pepper.
pimiento, _-tŏ,_ sm. (bot.) capsicum.
pimpín, _pĭmpĭn',_ sm. children's play.
pimpollo, _pĭmpŏl'yŏ,_ sm. sucker; bud.
piña, _pĕ'nă,_ sf. landmark in the form of a cone; jaunt, felloe of a wheel.
pináculo, _pĭná'kŭlŏ,_ sm. pinnacle.
pinar, _pĭnár',_ sm. grove of pines.
pincel, _pĭnthĕl',_ sm. pencil. [touch.
pincelada, _-lá'dă,_ sf. dash with a pencil;
pinchadura, _pĭntshădŏ'ră,_ sf. puncture.
pinchar, _pĭntshár',_ v. a. to prick.
pincho, _pĭn'tshŏ,_ sm. thorn. [about.
pindonguear, _pĭndŏngeár',_ v. n. to gad
pingajo, _-gá'h'ŏ,_ sm. rag, tatter.
pingüe, _pĭn'güĕ,_ a. fat, greasy; fertile.
pino, _pĕ'nŏ,_ sm. (bot.) pine; **á** -, upright.
pinta, _pĭn'tă,_ sf. spot, blemish, scar; mark on playing cards; pint.
pintado, da, _pĭntá'dŏ,_ a. painted, mottled; **venir** -, to fit exactly. [dauber.
pintamonas, _-mŏ'năs,_ sm. bad painter.
pintar, _pĭntár',_ v. a. to paint, to picture; to limn, to describe; to exaggerate; -, v. n. to begin to ripen; to show, to give signs of; -se, to paint one's face.
pintarrajar, _-rá'hár',_ v. a. to variegate.
pintarrajo, _-rá'h'ŏ,_ sm. daub.
pintiparado, da, _pĭntĭpará'dŏ,_ a. exactly like, closely resembling.
pintiparar, _-párár',_ v. a. to compare.
pintor, _pĭntŏr',_ sm. painter.
pintoresco, ca, _-rĕs'kŏ,_ a. picturesque.
pintorrear, _-reár',_ v. a. to daub.
pintura, _pĭntŏ'ră,_ sf. painting; picture.
pinzas, _pĭn'thăs,_ sf. pl. nippers, small pincers.
pinzón, _pĭnthŏn',_ sm. chaffinch.
piña, _pĭn'yă,_ sf. pine-apple; fir-cone; mass of silver in the shape of a pine-apple.
piñón, _pĭnyŏn',_ sm. pine-apple seed; pinion; spring-nut of a gun. [monds.
piñonata, _-yŏná'tă,_ sf. conserve of al-
piñonate, _-ná'tĕ,_ sm. paste made of almonds and sugar.
pío, pía, _pĕ'ŏ,_ a. pious, devout; mild, merciful; -, sm. cry of chickens.
piocha, _pĭŏ'tshă,_ sf. ornament for women's head-dresses.
piojería, _pĭŏ'hĕrĕ'ă,_ sf. lousiness; misery.
piojo, _pĭŏ'h'ŏ,_ sm. louse; troublesome hanger-on. [stingy.
piojoso, sa, _-hŏ'sŏ,_ a. lousy; miserable,
pipa, _pĕ'pă,_ sf. wine-cask; pipe (liquid measure); tobacco-pipe; pipe which children make of the stalks of corn; reed of a clarion; fusee of a bomb.
pipero, _pĭpá'rŏ,_ sm. cooper.
pipiar, _pĭpĭár',_ v. n. to pule, to chirp.

pipote, *pipŏ'tă*, sm. keg.

pique, *pĕ'kĕ*, sm. pique, offence taken; echar á —, to sink a ship; á —, in danger, on the point of; steep (shore).

piquera, *pĭkĕ'ră*, sf. bung-hole of a barrel.

piquete, *pĭkĕ'tĕ*, sm. slight prick or sting; tracing-picket; (mil.) picket.

pira, *pĕ'ră*, sf. funeral pile.

piramidal, *pĭrămĭdăl'*, a. pyramidal.

pirámide, *pĭrā'mĭdĕ*, sf. pyramid.

pirata, *pĕrā'tă*, sm. pirate; cruel wretch.

piratear, *-tĕăr'*, v. n. to pirate.

piratería, *-tĕrĕ'ă*, sf. piracy.

piropo, *pĭrŏ'pŏ*, sm. 'carbuncle; (fig.) affectation of purity in speech.

pirotécnica, *pĭrŏtĕk'nĭkă*, sf. pyrotechny.

pirueta, *pĕrŭĕ'tă*, sf. pirouette.

pisada, *pĭsă'dă*, sf. foot-step; kick.

pisar, *pĭsăr'*, v. a. to tread, to trample; to stamp on the ground; to hammer down paving-stones; to despise.

pisaverde, *pĭsăvĕr'dĕ*, sm. fop, coxcomb, jackanapes.

piscina, *pĭsthĕ'nă*, sf. fish-pond.

Piscis, *pĭs'thĭs*, sm. Piscis, Fishes (sign of the zodiac). [pavement; floor, storey.

piso, *pĕ'sŏ*, sm. tread, trampling; floor, pisón, *pĭsŏn'*, sm. rammer. [under foot.

pisotear, *pĭsŏtĕăr'*, v. a. to trample, to tread

pista, *pĕs'tă*, sf. trace, foot-print.

pisto, *pĭs'tŏ*, sm. thick broth; á —s, little

pistola, *pĭstŏ'lă*, sf. pistol. [by little.

pistolera, *pĭstŏlĕ'ră*, sf. pistol-holster.

pistoletazo, *-lĕtă'thŏ*, sm. pistol-shot.

pistolete, *-lĕ'tĕ*, sm. pocket-pistol.

pita, *pĕ'tă*, sf. (bot.) agave; term used to call hens.

pitagórico, ca, *pĭtăgŏ'rĭkŏ*, a. Pythagorean.

pitanza, *pĭtăn'thă*, sf. pittance, daily allowance; price.

pitirrojo, *pĭtĭrrŏ'hŏ*, sm. robin red-breast.

pito, *pĕ'tŏ*, sm. pipe; play among boys.

pitón, *pĭtŏn'*, sm. tenderling; sprig, young shoot of a tree. [ress.

pitonisa, *pĭtŏnĭ'să*, sf. sorceress, enchantpitorra, *pĭtŏ'rră*, sf. wood-cock.

pizarra, *pĭthăr'ră*, sf. slate. [slate-pit.

pizarral, *pĭthărrăl'*, sm. slate-quarry.

pizca, *pĭth'kă*, sf. mite; pinch.

pizpereta, *-pĕrĕ'tă*, a. sharp, brisk, lively (applied to women).

pizpirigaña, *-pĭrĭgăn'yă*, sf. play among boys, in which they pinch one another's hands.

placa, *plă'kă*, sf. clasp of a broadsword belt; star, insignia of an order of knighthood. [congratulation.

pláceme, *plă'thĕmĕ*, sm. compliment of

placentero, ra, *plăthĕntĕ'rŏ*, a. joyful, merry. [v. imp. to please.

placer, *plăthĕr'*, sm. pleasure, delight; —,

plaga, *plă'gă*, sf. plague.

plagar, *plăgăr'*, v. a. to plague, to torment.

plagiario, ria, *plă'hĭă'rĭŏ*, a. & sm. plagiarising, plagiarist.

plagio, *plă'hĭŏ*, sm. plagiarism.

plan, *plăn*, sm. plan; desigu, plot.

plana, *plă'nă*, sf. trowel; page (of a book); level; — mayor, (mil.) staff-office.

plancha, *plăn'tshă*, sf. plate; ironing-iron.

planchar, *-tshăr'*, v. a. to iron linen.

planchear, *-tshĕăr'*, v. a. to plate, to sheath.

planeta, *plănĕ'tă*, sm. planet.

planetario, *plănĕtă'rĭŏ*, a. planetary.

planisferio, *plănĭsfĕ'rĭŏ*, sm. planisphere.

plano, na, *plă'nŏ*, a. plain, level, flat; —, sm. plan, ground-plot; (rail.) — inclinado, dead level. [—s, pl. brag, boast.

planta, *plăn'tă*, sf. plant; plantation.

plantación, *-tăthĭŏn'*, sf. plantation.

plantador, *-dŏr'*, sm. planter.

plántano, *plăn'tănŏ*, sm. plantain-tree.

plantar, *plăntăr'*, v. a. to plant; to fix upright; to strike or hit a blow; to found, to establish; —se, to stand upright.

plantear, *-tĕăr'*, v. a. to plan, to trace.

plantel, *plăntĕl'*, sm. nursery-garden.

plantificar, *-tĭfĭkăr'*, v. a. to plant; to beat; to box, to kick.

plantilla, *-tĭl'yă*, sf. young plant; first sole of a shoe; vamp; plate of a gun-lock.

plantillar, *-tĭlyăr'*, v. a. to vamp or sole shoes or stockings.

plantío, tia, *plăntĕ'ŏ*, a. planted; ready to be planted; —, sm. planting; nursery.

plantón, *plăntŏn'*, sm. scion, sprout; (mil.) sentry punished with extra duty.

plañidera, *plănyĭdĕ'ră*, sf. weepingwoman. [to bewail.

plañir, *plănyĭr'*, v. n. to lament, to grieve,

plasta, *plăs'tă*, sf. paste, soft clay.

plata, *plă'tă*, sf. silver; plate (wrought silver); en —, briefly.

plataforma, *-fŏr'mă*, sf. platform; (rail.) — giratoria, turn-plate, turn-table.

plátano, *plă'tănŏ*, sm. plane-tree.

plateado, da, *plătĕă'dŏ*, a. silvered; plated.

plateadura, *-dŏ'ră*, sf. silvering.

platear, *plătĕăr'*, v. a. to silver.

platería, *plătĕrĕ'ă*, sf. silversmith's shop; trade of a silversmith.

platero, *plătĕ'rŏ*, sm. silversmith.

plática, *plă'tĭkă*, sf. discourse, conversation. [practise.

platicar, *plătĭkăr'*, v. a. to converse, to

platillas, *plătĭl'yăs*, sf. pl. fine French linen.

platina, *plătĭ'nă*, sf. platina. [linen.

plato, *plă'tŏ*, sm. dish; mess.

platónico, ca, *plătŏ'nĭkŏ*, a. platonic.

plausible, *plăŭsĕ'blĕ*, a. plausible.

playa, *plă'yă*, sf. shore, strand.

plaza, *plă'thă*, sf. square, place; fortified place; office, public employment; enrolling of soldiers.

plazo, *plă'thŏ*, sm. term; tilt-yard.

pleamar, *plĕămăr'*, sf. (mar.) high water.

plebe, *plĕ'bĕ*, sf. common people, populace.

plebeyo, ya, *plĕbĕ'yŏ*, a. plebeian; —, sm. commoner.

plectro, *plĕk'trŏ*, sm. (poet.) plectrum.

plegable, *plĕgă'blĕ*, a. pliable.

plegadera, *-dĕ'ră*, sf. folding-stick.

plegador, *-dŏr*, sm. folding instrument; plaiter.

plegadura, _-dō'rā,_ sf. fold, plaiting.

plegar, _plĕgăr',_ v. a. to fold, to plait; **—,** v. imp. to please; **plegue á Dios que,** God grant that.

plegaria, _plĕgă'rĭā,_ sf. public prayer.

pleita, _plĕĭ'tā,_ sf. plaited strand of bass.

pleiteador, _-tĕădōr',_ sm. pleader; wrangler.

pleitear, _-tĕăr',_ v. a. to plead, to litigate.

pleitista, _-tĭs'tā,_ sm. litigious person.

pleito, _plă'ĭtŏ,_ sm. contract, bargain; dispute, controversy, debate; law-suit.

plenamente, _plĕnămĕn'tĕ,_ ad. fully, completely.

plenario, ria, _-nă'rĭŏ,_ a. complete, full.

plenilunio, _plĕnĭlŏ'nĭŏ,_ sm. full-moon, full-faced moon. [plenipotentiary.

plenipotenciario, _-pŏtĕnthĭă'rĭŏ,_ sm.

plenitud, _-tŭd',_ sf. fulness, abundance.

pleonasmo, _plĕŏnăs'mŏ,_ sm. pleonasm.

pliego, _plĭĕ'gŏ,_ sm. sheet of paper.

pliegue, _plĭĕ'gĕ,_ sm. fold, plait; plight; ruff.

plomar, _plŏmăr',_ v. a. to mark with a black-lead pencil; to stop teeth with lead.

plomero, _plŏmĕ'rŏ,_ sm. plumber.

plomizo, za, _plŏmĕ'thŏ,_ a. leaden.

plomo, _plŏ'mŏ,_ sm. lead; **á —,** perpendicularly.

pluma, _plŏ'mā,_ sf. feather, plume. [larly.

plumada, _plŏmă'dā,_ sf. dash with a pen.

plumaje, _plŏmă'k'ĕ,_ sm. plumage; plume.

plumero, _-mĕ'rŏ,_ sm. bunch of feathers; feather-broom. [notary.

plumista, _-mĭs'tā,_ sm. petty scrivener.

plural, _plŏrăl',_ a. (gr.) plural.

pluralidad, _-lĭdăd',_ sf. plurality.

pluvial, _plŏvĭăl',_ a. rainy. [matic.

pneumático, ca, _pnĕŭmă'tĭkŏ,_ a. pneu-

poblacho, _pŏblă'chŏ,_ sm. populace, rabble.

población, _-lăthĭŏn',_ sf. population.

poblado, _-lă'dŏ,_ sm. town, village, inhabited place.

poblador, _-dŏr',_ sm. populator, founder.

poblar, _pŏblăr',_ v. a. to populate, to people; to fill, to occupy; to bud, to get leaves.

pobre, _pŏ'brĕ,_ a. poor, indigent.

pobrete, _pŏbrĕ'tĕ,_ sm. poor, unfortunate man; useless person. [avarice.

pobretería, _-tĕrĕ'ā,_ sf. poor people;

pobreza, _pŏbrĕth'ā,_ sf. poverty, poorness.

pocero, _pŏthĕ'rŏ,_ sm. well-digger; nightman. [dirty place.

pocilga, _pŏthĕl'gā,_ sf. pig-sty; any nasty,

pócima, _pŏ'thĭmā,_ sf. potion.

poco, ca, _pŏ'kŏ,_ a. little, scanty; few; **—,** ad. little; **— ha que,** lately, latterly; **— á —,** gently, little by little; **—,** sm. a small part.

poda, _pŏ'dā,_ sf. pruning of trees.

podadera, _pŏdădĕ'rā,_ sf. pruning-knife.

podar, _pŏdăr',_ v. a. to prune.

podenco, _pŏdĕn'kŏ,_ sm. hound.

poder, _pŏdĕr',_ sm. power, authority; command; force; **—,** v. n. to be able; to possess the power of doing or performing; **—,** v. imp. to be possible.

poderhabiente, _-ăbĭĕn'tĕ,_ sm. attorney.

poderío, _pŏdĕrĕ'ŏ,_ sm. power, authority; wealth, riches. [nent, excellent.

poderoso, sa, _-rŏ'sŏ,_ a. powerful; emi-

podre, _pŏ'drĕ,_ sf. pus, matter.

podredumbre, _pŏdrĕdŭm'brĕ,_ sf. putrid matter; grief.

podrir, _pŏdrĭr',_ v. n. to rot, to putrefy.

poema, _pŏĕ'mā,_ sm. poem.

poesía, _pŏĕsĕ'ā,_ sf. poetry; poesy.

poeta, _pŏĕ'tā,_ sm. poet.

poética, _pŏĕ'tĭkā,_ sf. poetry, poetics.

poético, ca, _-tĭkŏ,_ a. poetical.

poetisa, _-tĭs'ā,_ sf. poetess.

poetizar, _-tĭthăr',_ v. a. to poetize.

polaca, _pŏlă'kā,_ sf. tongue of a shoe.

polaina, _pŏlă'ĭnā,_ sf. spatterdashes.

polar, _pŏlăr',_ a. polar. [block.

polea, _pŏlĕ'ā,_ sf. pulley; (mar.) tackle-

polémica, _pŏlĕ'mĭkā,_ sf. polemics.

polémico, ca, _-mĭkŏ,_ a. polemical.

policía, _pŏlĭthĕ'ā,_ sf. police; politeness; neatness.

poligamia, _pŏlĭgă'mĭā,_ sf. polygamy.

polígamo, _pŏlĕ'gămŏ,_ sm. polygamist.

polígono, _-gŏnŏ,_ sm. polygon; **—, na,** a. [polygonal.

polilla, _pŏlĭl'yā,_ sf. moth.

pólipo, _pŏ'lĭpŏ,_ sm. polypus.

polisílabo, ba, _pŏlĭsĕ'lăbŏ,_ a. polysyllabic.

politécnico, _-tĕk'nĭkŏ,_ a. polytechnical.

politeísmo, _-tĕĭs'mŏ,_ sm. polytheism.

política, _pŏlĕ'tĭkā,_ sf. politics; politeness.

político, ca, _-tĭkŏ,_ a. political; polite; **—,** sm. politician.

poliza, _pŏlĕ'thā,_ sf. written order to receive or recover a sum of money; policy; passport.

polo, _pŏ'lŏ,_ sm. pole. [port.

poltrón, ona, _pŏltrŏn',_ a. idle, lazy; commodious, easy; **silla -ona,** elbow-chair; **—,** sm. poltroon. [ness, indolence.

poltronería, _-nĕrĕ'ā,_ sf. idleness, laziness.

polución, _pŏlŭthĭŏn',_ sf. pollution.

polvareda, _pŏlvărĕ'dā,_ sf. cloud of dust.

polvo, _pŏl'vŏ,_ sm. powder, dust; **un —,** a pinch of snuff. [fireworks, pl.

pólvora, _-vŏrā,_ sf. gun-powder; artificial

polvorear, _pŏlvŏrĕăr',_ v. a. to powder.

polvoriento, ta, _-rĭĕn'tŏ,_ a. dusty.

polvorín, _-rĭn',_ sm. powder reduced to the finest dust; powder-flask.

polvorista, _-rĭs'tā,_ sm. manufacturer of gun-powder. [to powder.

polvorizar, _-rĭthăr',_ v. a. to pulverize;

polvoroso, sa, _-rŏ'sŏ,_ a. dusty; **poner pies en —,** to scamper away.

polla, _pŏl'yā,_ sf. pullet; money staked at cards; pool. [hatch, covey.

pollada, _-yă'dā,_ sf. flock of young fowls;

pollera, _-yă'rā,_ hen-coop; go-cart.

pollería, _-yĕrĕ'ā,_ sf. poultry-market.

pollero, _-yĕ'rŏ,_ sm. poulterer.

pollino, _-yĕ'nŏ,_ sm. young, untamed ass; dull, stupid, heavy fellow. [nestling.

pollo, _pŏl'yŏ,_ sm. chicken just hatched,

pomada, _pŏmă'dā,_ sf. pomatum, pomade.

pómez, _pŏ'mĕth,_ sf. pumice-stone.

pomo, _pŏ'mŏ,_ sm. fruit in general; apple; pommel.

pompa, *pŏm'pă,* sf. pomp; bubble.

pomposo, sa, *pŏmpŏ'sŏ,* a. pompous.

ponche, *pŏn'tshĕ,* sm. punch.

ponchera, *pŏntshĕ'ră,* sf. punchbowl.

poncho, cha, *pŏn'tshŏ,* a. soft, mild; —, sm. (am.) sleeveless frock.

poncil, *pŏnthĭl',* a. bitter orange or lemon.

ponderable, *pŏndĕră'blĕ,* a. ponderable; measurable by scales; wonderful.

ponderación, *-dĕrăthĭŏn',* sf. pondering, considering; exaggeration.

ponderar, *-dĕrăr',* v. a. to ponder, to weigh; to exaggerate, fing, hyperbolical.

ponderativo, va, *-dĕrătĕ'vŏ,* a. exaggerat-

ponedero, ra, *pŏnĕdĕ'rŏ,* a. egg-laying; capable of being laid or placed; —, sm. nest; nest-egg; covey.

poner, *pŏnĕr',* v. a. to put, to place; to impose; to lay eggs; —se, to oppose; to set (of stars); to become.

poniente, *pŏnĭĕn'tĕ,* sm. west; west wind.

pontaje, *pŏntă'hĕ,* **pontazgo,** *-tăth'gŏ,* sm. bridge-toll.

pontificado, *pŏntĭfĭkă'dŏ,* sm. pontificate.

pontifical, *-fĭkăl',* a. & sm. pontifical.

pontifice, *pŏn'tĭfĭthĕ,* sm. Pope, pontiff.

pontificio, cia, *-fĭthĭŏ,* a. pontifical.

pontón, *pŏntŏn',* sm. pontoon.

ponzoña, *pŏnthŏn'yă,* sf. poison.

ponzoñoso, sa, *-thŏnyŏ'sŏ,* a. poisonous.

popa, *pŏ'pă,* sf. (mar.) poop, stern.

populacho, *pŏpŭlătsh'ŏ,* sm. populace, mob.

población, *-lăthĭŏn',* sf. population.

popular, *-lăr',* a. popular.

popularidad, *-lărĭdăd',* sf. popularity.

populoso, sa, *-lŏ'sŏ,* a. populous.

poquedad, *pŏkĕdăd',* sf. paucity, littleness; cowardice.   [through; on account of

por, *pŏr,* pr. for, by, about; by means of;

porcelana, *pŏrthĕlă'nă,* sf. porcelain, china.

porción, *pŏrthĭŏn',* sf. part, portion; lot.

porciuncula, *-thĭŭn'kŭlă,* sf. small por-   [tion.

porcuno, na, *pŏrkŭ'nŏ,* a. hoggish.

pordiosear, *-dĭŏsĕăr',* v. a. to beg alms.

pordiosería, *-sĕrĕ'ă,* sf. beggary.

pordiosero, ra, *-sĕ'rŏ,* sm. & f. beggar.

porfía, *pŏrfĕ'ă,* sf. obstinate quarrel; stubbornness; importunity; á —, emulously; with strife and contention.   [born.

porfiado, da, *-fĭă'dŏ,* a. obstinate, stub-

porfiador, ra, *-fĭădŏr',* sm. & f. disputer, wrangler.   [to persist in a pursuit.

porfiar, *-fĭăr',* v. a. to dispute obstinately;

pórfido, *pŏr'fĭdŏ,* sm. porphyry.

pormenor, *pŏrmĕnŏr',* sf. detail.

poro, *pŏ'rŏ,* sm. pore.

porosidad, *pŏrŏsĭdăd',* sf. porosity.

poroso, sa, *pŏrŏ'sŏ,* a. porous.

porque, *pŏrkĕ',* c. because; why.

porqué, *-,* sm. cause, reason.

porquería, *pŏrkĕrĕ'ă,* sf. nastiness, foulness; brutishness, rudeness; trifle; dirty action.

porqueriza, *-rĕ'thă,* sf. pig-sty.

porquero, *pŏrkĕ'rŏ,* sm. swine-herd.

porra, *pŏr'ră,* sf. cudgel.

porrazo, *pŏrră'thŏ,* sm. blow with a cudgel.

porrería, *pŏrrĕrĕ'ă,* sf. stupidity, folly, silliness.   [en —, stark-naked.

porreta, *pŏrrĕ'tă,* sf. green leaf of leek;

porrillo, *-rĭl'yŏ,* (á —,) ad copiously, abundantly.   [water.

porrón, *-rŏn',* sm. earthen pitcher for

portabandera, *pŏrtăbăndă'ră,* sf. colour-sheath.

portacartas, *-kăr'tăs,* sm. mail; postman.

portada, *pŏrtă'dă,* sf. portal, porch; frontispiece.

portador, *-dŏr',* sm. carrier, porter.

portaestandarte, *-ĕstandăr'tĕ,* sm. (mil.) standard-bearer; cornet.   [musket.

portafusil, *-fŭsĭl',* sm. (mil.) sling of a

portaguión, *-gĭŏn',* sm. standard-bearer of cavalry.

portal, *pŏrtăl',* sm. porch; portico, piazza.

portamanteo, *-măntă'ŏ,* sm. portmanteau, cloak-bag.   [plate.

portapaz, *-păth',* sm. & f. the image-

portarse, *pŏrtăr'sĕ,* v. r. to behave, to comport.

portátil, *pŏrtă'tĭl,* a. portable.   [comport.

portazgo, *-tăth'gŏ,* sm. toll, turnpike-duty.

portazguero, *-tăthgŏ'rŏ,* sm. toll-gatherer.

portazo, *pŏrtă'thŏ,* sm. bang of a door; banging a door in one's face.

porte, *pŏr'tĕ,* sm. porterage, portage; deportment, demeanour, conduct.

portento, *pŏrtĕn'tŏ,* sm. prodigy, portent.

portentoso, sa, *-tŏ'sŏ,* a. prodigious, marvellous, strange.

portería, *pŏrtĕrĕ'ă,* sf. principal door of a convent; porter's office.

portero, *pŏrtĕ'rŏ,* sm. porter, gate-keeper.

portezuela, *-thŭĕ'lă,* sf. little door.

pórtico, *pŏr'tĭkŏ,* sm. portico, porch, lobby.

portillo, *-tĭl'yŏ,* sm. aperture in a wall; gap, breach; —s, pl. small gates of a town, through which nothing dutiable is allowed to pass.

portón, *-tŏn',* sm. inner door of a house.

porvida! *pŏrvĭ'dă,* sf. by the living God!

pos, *pŏs',* en —, ad. after, behind; in pursuit of.

posa, *pŏ'să,* sf. passing-bell; stops made by the clergy who conduct a funeral, to-sing a responsary.

posada, *pŏsă'dă,* sf. lodging-house, inn, hotel; pocket-case, containing a knife, spoon, and fork; —s, pl. apartments for the ladies in waiting in the royal palace.

posaderas, *-dĕ'răs,* sf. pl. buttocks.

posadero, *-dĕ'rŏ,* sm. inn-keeper; back-side, bottom.

posar, *pŏsăr',* v. n. to lodge; to sit down, to repose; —, v. a. to lay down a burden.

posdata, *pŏsdă'tă,* sf. postcript.

poseer, *pŏsĕĕr',* v. a. to hold, to possess.

poseído, da, *pŏsĕĭ'dŏ,* a. possessed with the devil.

posesión, *pŏsĕsĭŏn',* sf. possession.

posesivo, va, *-sĕ'vŏ,* a. (gr.) possessive.

posesor, ra, *-sŏr',* sm. & f. possessor.

posesorio, ria, *-sŏ'rĭŏ,* a. possessory

posibilidad, *posibilidad'*, sf. possibility; wealth, riches.

posible, *pos'blē*, a. possible. [situation.

posición, *posithión'*, sf. position; posture;

positivo, va, *-tē'vō*, a. positive.

pósito, *pō'stō*, sm. public granary; **-pío,** granary for charity.

poso, *pō'sō*, sm. sediment, dregs, lees.

posponer, *posponer'*, v. a. to postpone.

posta, *pōs'tā*, sf. post; post-house; post-stage; **-,** sm. person who travels post.

poste, *pōs'tē*, sm. post, pillar.

poste restante, **-** *restān'tē*, a. to be kept till called for (of letters).

postema, *postē'mā*, sm. abscess, tumour; dull, troublesome person.

postergación, *postergathión'*, sf. missing out, putting back, passing over.

postergar, *-gār'*, v. a. to leave behind.

posteridad, *posteridad'*, sf. posterity.

posterior, *posterior'*, a. posterior.

posterioridad, *-ridad'*, sf. posteriority.

postigo, *postē'gō*, sm. wicket; postern; pane or sash of a window.

postillón, *postilyón'*, sm. postillion.

postilloso, sa, *-yō'sō*, a. scabby, pustulous. [natural; **-,** sm. false hair.

postizo, za, *postē'thō*, a. artificial (not natural).

postor, *postōr'*, sm. bidder at a public sale; bettor.

postración, *postrathión'*, sf. prostration.

postrar, *postrār'*, v. a. to humble, to humiliate; **-se,** to prostrate oneself.

postre, *pōs'trē*, a. last in order; **á la -,** at last; **-,** sm. dessert.

postrer, *postrēr'*, postrero, ra, *-rā'rō*, a. last in order, hindermost.

postrimería, *postrimerē'ā*, sf. last portion or last years of life.

postrimero, ra, *-mā'rō*, a. hindermost.

póstumo, ma, *pōs'tūmō*, a. posthumous.

postura, *postō'rā*, sf. posture, position; tax on eatables; price asked or offered; bet, wager; agreement, convention.

potable, *pōtā'blē*, a. potable, drinkable.

potaje, *pōtā'h'ē*, sm. pottage; drink made up of several ingredients; medley of various useless things.

potar, *pōtār'*, v. a. to equalize and mark weights and measures.

potasa, *pōtā'sā*, sf. potash.

pote, *pō'tē*, sm. pot, jar; flower-pot; standard measure or weight.

potencia, *pōtēn'thiā*, sf. power; mightiness.

potentado, *-tā'dō*, sm. potentate, prince.

potente, *pōtēn'tē*, a. potent, powerful, mighty.

poterna, *pōtēr'nā*, sf. postern, sally-port.

potestad, *pōtestād'*, sf. power, dominion; jurisdiction.

potra, *pō'trā*, sf. rupture, hernia.

potro, ra, *pō'trō*, sm. & f. colt; foal.

potroso, sa, *pōtrō'sō*, a. afflicted with a rupture; fortunate, lucky. [door).

poyo, *pō'yō*, sm. bench (near the street-door).

poza, *pō'thā*, sf. puddle; hole.

pozal, *pōthāl'*, sm. bucket, pail.

pozo, *pō'thō*, sm. well; **- de nieve,** ice-house, ice-cellar; snow-pit.

práctica, *prāk'tikā*, sf. practice.

practicable, *-kā'blē*, a. practicable, feasible.

practicante, *-kān'tē*, sm. practiser; practitioner in surgery and medicine under a distinguished master.

practicar, *-kār'*, v. a. to practise.

práctico, ca, *prāk'tikō*, a. practical; skilful, experienced; **-,** sm. practiser, practitioner. [sf. meadow, mead.

pradera, *prādē'rā*, pradería, *prādērē'ā*,

prado, *prā'dō*, sm. lawn, meadow.

Prado, **-,** sm. a public walk in Madrid.

pragmática, *prāgmā'tikā*, sf. royal edict.

prasio, *prā'siō*, sm. prase, a precious stone.

preámbulo, *preām'bulō*, sm. preamble; circumlocution.

prebenda, *prebēn'dā*, sf. prebend.

prebendado, *-dā'dō*, sm. prebendary.

prebendar, *-dār'*, v. a. to give prebend.

preboste, *prebōs'tē*, sm. provost.

precario, ria, *-kā'riō*, a. precarious.

precaución, *-kāuthión'*, sf. precaution.

precaver, *-kāver'*, v. a. to prevent, to guard against. [preference; superiority.

precedencia, *-thēdēn'thiā*, sf. precedence;

precedente, *-thēdēn'tē*, p. & a. precedent, foregoing. [before.

preceder, *-thēdēr'*, v. a. to precede, to go

precepto, *prethēp'tō*, sm. precept, order.

preceptor, *-thēptōr'*, sm. master, teacher, preceptor. [votions.

preces, *prā'thēs*, sf. pl. prayers; devotions.

preciado, da, *prethiā'dō*, a. proud, presumptuous. [pride in.

preciarse, *-thiār'sē*, v. a. to boast, to take

precio, *prā'thiō*, sm. price, value.

preciosidad, *prethiōsidad'*, sf. excellence, preciousness.

precioso, sa, *-thiō'sō*, a. precious.

precipicio, *-thipē'thiō*, sm. precipice; violent, sudden fall; ruin, destruction.

precipitación, *-thipitathión'*, sf. precipitation, inconsiderate haste.

precipitado, da, *-tā'dō*, a. precipitate, headlong, hasty.

precipitar, *-tār'*, v. a. to precipitate; **-se,** to run headlong to one's destruction.

precisar, *prethisār'*, v. a. to compel, to oblige, to necessitate.

precisión, *-thisión'*, sf. necessity, compulsion; preciseness.

preciso, sa, *prethē'sō*, a. necessary, requisite; precise, exact; abstracted.

precocidad, *-kōthidad'*, sf. precocity.

preconizar, *-kōnithār'*, v. a. to proclaim.

precoz, *prekōth'*, a. precocious.

precursor, ra, *-kūrsōr'*, sm. & f. harbinger, fore-runner.

predecesor, ra, *-dēthesōr'*, sm. & f. predecessor, antecessor, runner.

predecir, *-dēthir'*, v. a. to foretell.

predestinación, *-destināthión'*, sf. predestination.

predestinar, *-destinār'*, v. a. to predestine.

predial, *prědiǎl'*, a. consisting in landed property *or* relating to it.
predicable, *prědikǎ'blě*, a. fit to be preached; predicable. [sermon.
predicación, *-kǎthiǒn'*, sf. preaching, predicado, *-kǎ'tǒ*, sm. predicate.
predicador, *-kǎdǒr'*, sm. preacher.
predicamento, *-kǎmēn'tǒ*, sm. predicament.
predicar, *-kǎr'*, v. a. to publish; to preach.
predicción, *-dikthiǒn'*, sf. prediction.
predilección, *-lěkthiǒn'*, sf. predilection.
predilecto, ta, *-lěk'tǒ*, a. darling, favourite.
predio, *prě'diǒ*, sm. landed property; farm; - rústico, piece of cultivated ground; - urbano, town- *or* country-house. [minate, to prevail; to command.
predominar, *prědǒminǎr'*, v. a. to predo-
predominio, *-dǒmē'niǒ*, sm. predominant power, superiority.
preeminencia, *-ēminěn'thiǎ*, sf. pre-eminence, superiority of power.
preeminente, *-něn'tě*, a. pre-eminent, superior. [existence.
preexistencia, *-ěksistěn'thiǎ*, sf. pre-
preexistente, *-těn'tě*, p. & a. pre-existent.
preexistir, *-tīr'*, v. n. to pre-exist, to exist before.
prefacio, *-fǎ'thiǒ*, sm. preface.
prefecto, *-fěk'tǒ*, sm. prefect.
prefectura, *-fěktǒ'rǎ*, sf. prefecture.
preferencia, *-fěrěn'thiǎ*, sf. preference.
preferible, *-fěrǐ'blě*, a. preferable.
preferir, *-fěrǐr'*, v. a. to prefer.
prefijar, *-fǐhǎr'*, v. a. to prefix, to fix beforehand.
pregón, *prěgǒn'*, sm. publication made in public places by the common crier, hue and cry. [public places.
pregonar, *-gǒnǎr'*, v. a. to proclaim in
pregonero, *-nǒ'rǒ*, sm. common crier; -, ra, a. publishing.
pregunta, *-gǔn'tǎ*, sf. question; inquiry.
preguntar, *-tǎr'*, v. a. to question, to demand; to inquire. [tive person.
preguntón, ona, *-tǒn'*, sm. & f. inquisi-
prelacía, *-lǎthě'ǎ*, sf. prelacy.
prelada, *prělǎ'dǎ*, sf. abbess.
prelado, *-dǒ*, sm. prelate. [nary.
preliminar, *-lǐmǐnǎr'*, a. & sm. prelimi-
preludio, *-lǒ'diǒ*, sm. prelude.
prematuro, ra, *-mǎtǒ'rǒ*, a. premature, precocious. [ditation, forethought.
premeditación, *-měditǎthiǒn'*, sf. preme-
premeditar, *-tǎr'*, v. a. to premeditate, to think out. [munerate.
premiar, *prěmǐǎr'*, v. a. to reward, to re-
premio, *prě'miǒ*, sm. reward, recompense; premium.
premisa, *prěmǐs'ǎ*, sf. premise.
premura, *-mǒ'rǎ*, sf. narrowness, pressure, haste, hurry.
prenda, *prěn'dǎ*, sf. pledge; sweetheart; person *or* thing dearly loved; -s, pl. accomplishments, talents.
prendar, *-dǎr'*, v. a. to pledge; to ingratiate oneself; -se, to take a fancy to oneself.

prender, *prěndǎr'*, v. a. to seize, to catch, to lay hold of; to imprison; -, v. n. to take root; -se, to adorn oneself.
prendería, *-děrǐ'ǎ*, sf. pawnbroker's shop; frippery. [dawdler, slow-coach.
prendero, *prěndě'rǒ*, sm. pawnbroker;
prendido, *-dǐ'dǒ*, sm. attire of women; pattern for bone-lace. [capture.
prendimiento, *-dimiěn'tǒ*, sm. seizure;
prensa, *prěn'sǎ*, sf. press. [stuff).
prensado, *-sǎ'dǒ*, sm. lustre, gloss (of
prensadura, *-dǒ'rǎ*, sf. pressing, pressure.
prensar, *prěnsǎr'*, v. a. to press.
prensista, *-sĭs'tǎ*, sm. pressman in a printing-office.
preñado, da, *prěnyǎ'dǒ*, a. full, pregnant; big with child; -, sm. pregnancy.
preñez, *prěnyěth'*, sf. pregnancy.
preocupación, *prěǒkǔpǎthiǒn'*, sf. preoccupation. [another; to preoccupy.
preocupar, *-pǎr'*, v. a. to occupy before
preparación, *-pǎrǎthiǒn'*, sf. preparation.
preparar, *-pǎrǎr'*, v. a. to prepare; -se, to be prepared.
preparativo, va, *-tǐ'vǒ*, a. preparative, qualifying; -, sm. preparative.
preparatorio, ria, *-tǒ'riǒ*, a. preparatory. [ponderance.
preponderancia, *-pǒnděrǎn'thiǎ*, sf. pre-
preponderar, *-dǎr'*, v. n. to preponderate, to prevail. [position.
preposición, *-pǒsǐthiǒn'*, sf. (gr.) pre-
prepucio, *prěpǒ'thiǒ*, sm. prepuce, foreskin. [privilege.
prerrogativa, *-rǒgǎtǐ'vǎ*, sf. prerogative,
presa, *prě'sǎ*, sf. capture, seizure; carcass of a fowl; dike, dam, mole; -s, pl. tusks, fangs, claws. [forebode.
presagiar, *prěsǎ'hiǎr'*, v. a. to presage, to
presagio, *prěsǎ'hiǒ*, sm. presage.
presbiterado, *presbǐtěrǎ'dǒ*, **presbiterato**, *-rǎ'tǒ*, sm. priesthood.
presbiteral, *-rǎl'*, a. sacerdotal.
presbiterio, *-tě'riǒ*, sm. sanctuary.
presbítero, *presbě'těrǒ*, sm. priest, clergyman. [foreknowledge.
presciencia, *-thiěn'thiǎ*, sf. prescience,
prescindir, *prěsthǐndǐr'*, v. a. to prescind, to cut off; to abstract.
prescribir, *prěskrǐbǐr'*, v. a. to prescribe.
prescripción, *-skrǐpthiǒn'*, sf. prescription.
prescriptible, *-skrǐp'tǐble*, a. prescriptible.
prescripto, ta, *-skrǐp'tǒ*, a. & p. prescribed.
presea, *prěsě'ǎ*, sf. jewel. [existence.
presencia, *prěsěn'thiǎ*, sf. presence, co-
presenciar, *-thiǎr'*, v. n. to assist, to be present.
presentación, *-tǎthiǒn'*, sf. presentation.
presentar, *-tǎr'*, v. a. to present; -se, to present oneself. [present.
presente, *prěsěn'tě*, sm. present, gift; -, a.
presentemente, *-měn'tě*, ad. presently, now. [sentiment.
presentimiento, *-sěntǐmiěn'tǒ*, sm. pre-
presentir, *-sěnǐr'*, v. a. to have a presentiment. [tion.
preservación, *-sěrvǎthiǒn'*, sf. preserva-

preservador, ra, –*vădŏr'*, sm. preserver.

preservar, –*văr'*, v. a. to preserve, to defend from evil.

preservativo, –*tĕ'vŏ*, sm. preservative.

presidencia, *presĕden'thĭă*, sf. presidentship; presidency.

presidente, –*dĕn'tĕ*, sm. president.

presidiario, –*dĭă'rĭŏ*, sm. criminal condemned to hard labour or banishment in a garrison.

presidio, *presĕ'dĭŏ*, sm. penitentiary, garrison of soldiers; Bridewell, house of correction in London.

presidir, *presĭdĭr'*, v. a. to preside.

presilla, *presĭl'yă*, sf. small string; loop in clothes.

presión, *presĭŏn'*, sf. pressure, pressing.

preso, sa, *prĕ'sŏ*, sm. & f. prisoner.

prestamero, *prestămĕ'rŏ*, sm. incumbent of an ecclesiastical sinecure.   [der.

prestamista, –*mĭs'tă*, sm. borrower, lender.

préstamo, *prĕs'tămŏ*, sm. loan.

prestar, *prestăr'*, v. a. to lend.

preste, *prĕs'tĕ*, sm. priest who celebrates high mass.   [speed.

presteza, *prestĕ'thă*, sf. quickness, haste.

prestigiador, *prestĭ'kĭădŏr'*, sm. cheat, juggler, impostor.   [ture.

prestigio, *prestĕ'hĭŏ*, sm. prestige; imposto, ta, *prĕs'tŏ*, a. quick, prompt,

presto, ta, *prĕs'tŏ*, a. quick, prompt, ready; –, ad. soon, quickly.

presumible, *presŭmĕ'blĕ*, a. presumable.

presumido, da, –*sŭmĕ'dŏ*, a. presumptuous, arrogant.   [jecture.

presumir, –*sŭmĭr'*, v. a. to presume, to conjecture; conceit.

presunción, –*sŭnhĭŏn'*, sf. presumption, conjecture; conceit.

presuntivo, va, –*tĕ'vŏ*, a. presumptive.

presuntuoso, sa, –*tŭŏ'sŏ*, a. presumptuous.   [pose.

presuponer, –*sŭpŏnĕr'*, v. a. to presuppose.

presupuesto, –*pŭĕs'tŏ*, sm. motive, pretext, pretence; presumed cost; budget.

presuroso, sa, –*sŭrŏ'sŏ*, a. hasty, prompt, quick; nimble.   [of a horse.

pretal, *pretăl'*, sm. poitrel, breast-leather

pretender, –*tendĕr'*, v. a. to pretend, to claim; to try, to attempt.

pretendiente, –*dĭĕn'tĕ*, a. pretender.

pretensión, –*sĭŏn'*, sf. pretension.

pretérito, ta, *pretĕ'rĭtŏ*, a. preterite, past.

pretextar, –*tĕkstăr'*, v. a. to find a pretext or pretence.

pretexto, –*tĕks'tŏ*, sm. pretext, pretence.

pretil, *pretĭl'*, sm. battlement, breast-work.

pretina, *pretĕ'nă*, sf. girdle, waistband;

pretor, *pretŏr'*, sm. pretor.   [belt.

pretorial, –*tŏrĭăl'*, **pretoriano, na,** *pretŏrĭă'nŏ*, a. pretorian.

pretorio, *pretŏ'rĭŏ*, sm. Pretorium.

pretura, –*tŏ'ră*, sf. pretorship.

prevalecer, –*vălĕthĕr'*, v. n. to prevail; to outshine; to take root.   [cation.

prevaricación, –*vărĭkăthĭŏn'*, sf. prevarication.

prevaricar, –*kăr'*, v. a. to prevaricate; to fail in one's duty.

prevención, –*venthĭŏn'*, sf. disposition,

preparation; supply of provisions; foresight; prevention; (mil.) police-guard.

prevenido, da, –*venĕ'dŏ*, a. prepared, provided; plentiful, abundan.; provident, careful, cautious, foreseeing, forecasting.

prevenir, –*venĭr'*, v. a. to prepare; to foresee, to foreknow; to prevent; to advise; –se, to be prepared; to be predisposed.

preventivo, va, –*tĕ'vŏ*, a. preventive.

prever, *prevĕr'*, v. a. to foresee, to forecast.

previo, via, *prĕ'vĭŏ*, a. previous.

previsión, *prevĭsĭŏn'*, sf. foresight, prevision, forecast.

previsor, ra, –*vĭsŏr'*, a. foreseer.

priesa, *prĭĕ'să*, sf. haste, speed, hurry.

prieto, ta, *prĭĕ'tŏ*, a. blackish; narrowminded; indigent.

prima, *prĕ'mă*, sf. the first three hours of the day; prime; treble; female cousin.

primacía, *prĭmăthĕ'ă*, sf. priority; primateship, primacy.

primado, –*mă'dŏ*, sm. primeness; primate.

primavera, –*vĕ'ră*, sf. spring (the season).

primeramente, *prĭmĕrămĕn'tĕ*, ad. in the first place, mainly.

primeriza, *prĭmerĕ'thă*, sf. woman who has borne her first child.

primero, ra, *prĭmĕ'rŏ*, a. first, prior, former; –, ad. first, rather, sooner.

primicia, *prĭmĕ'thĭă*, sf. first-fruits.

primitivo, va, *prĭmĭtĕ'vŏ*, a. primitive, original.

primo, ma, *prĕ'mŏ*, a. first; –, sm. cousin.

primogénito, ta, *prĭmŏ'hĕ'nĭtŏ*, a. & sm. sf. first-born; firstling.   [geniture.

primogenitura, –*'hĕnĭtŏ'ră*, sf. primogeniture.

primor, *prĭmŏr'*, sm. beauty; dexterity, ability; [fine, excellent; handsome.

primoroso, sa, –*rŏ'sŏ*, a. neat, elegant.

princesa, *prĭnthĕs'ă*, sf. princess.

principado, –*thĭpă'dŏ*, sm. princedom.

principal, –*thĭpăl'*, a. principal, chief.

príncipe, *prĭn'thĭpĕ*, sm. prince.

principiante, –*thĭpĭăn'tĕ*, sm. beginner, learner.   [to begin.

principiar, –*thĭpĭăr'*, v. a. to commence.

principio, *prĭnthĕ'pĭŏ*, sm. beginning, commencement; principle.

pringada, –*gă'dă*, sf. slice of toasted bread steeped in gravy.

pringar, –*găr'*, v. a. to baste; to grease; to take a share in; to stain one's reputation; –se, to embezzle, to misappropriate, to defraud.   [–, sm. grease-stain.

pringón, ona, –*gŏn'*, a. dirty, greasy;

pringoso, sa, –*gŏ'sŏ*, a. greasy, fat.

pringue, *prĭn'gĕ*, sm. & f. grease, lard.

prior, *prĭŏr'*, sm. prior; –, a. prior, previous.

priora, *prĭŏ'ră*, sf. prioress.   [ceding.

prioral, *prĭŏrăl'*, a. belonging to a prior.

priorato, –*ră'tŏ*, sm. priorship.

prioridad, –*rĭdăd'*, sf. priority.   [hood.

prioste, *prĭŏs'tĕ*, sm. steward of a brother-

prisa, *prĕ'să*, sf. celerity, promptness.

prisión, *prĭsĭŏn'*, sf. seizure, capture; prison; prey.

prisionero, –*nĕ'rŏ*, sm. prisoner.

prisma, *pris'ma*, sm. prism.

privación, *privath'ion'*, sf. privation, want.

privada, *—vā'dä*, sf. filth or dirt thrown into the street. [—, sm. favourite.

privado, da, *—vā'dĕ*, a. private; particular;

privanza, *—vän'thä*, sf. familiar intercourse.

privar, *—vär'*, v. a. to deprive; to prohibit; —se, to deprive oneself.

privative, va, *—tĕ'vŏ*, a. private, one's own; particular, peculiar.

privilegiar, *privĭl̆ĕ'hĕär'*, v. a. to privilege.

privilegio, *—lĕ'hĭŏ*, sm. privilege.

pro, *prŏ*, sm. & f. profit, benefit, advantage; buena —, much good may it do you.

proa, *prŏ'ä*, sf. (mar.) prow.

probabilidad, *prŏäbĭlĭdäd'*, sf. probability, likelihood.

probable, *prŏbä'blĕ*, a. probable, likely.

probado, da, *prŏbä'dŏ*, a. proved, tried.

probadura, *—bädŏ'rä*, sf. trial.

probanza, *prŏbän'thä*, sf. proof, evidence.

probar, *—bär'*, v. a. to try; to prove; to taste; —, v. n. to suit, to agree.

probatorio, ria, *—tŏ'rĭŏ*, a. probatory.

probidad, *prŏbĭdäd'*, sf. probity.

problema, *prŏblĕ'mä*, sm. problem.

problemático, ca, *—blĕmä'tĭkŏ*, a. problematical.

probóscide, *prŏbŏs'thĭdĕ*, sm. proboscis.

procacidad, *—käthĭdäd'*, sf. impudence, petulance. [forward.

procaz, *prŏkäth'*, a. impudent, petulant,

procedencia, *—thĕdĕn'thĭä*, sm. derivation.

proceder, *—thĕdĕr'*, sm. procedure; —, v. n. to proceed, to go on; to issue; to prosecute any design. [ing; legal procedure.

procedimiento, *—dĭmĭĕn'tŏ*, sm. proceeding.

proceloso, sa, *—thĕlŏ'sŏ*, a. tempestuous, stormy. [persons.

próceres, *prŏ'thĕrĕs*, sm. pl. the topping

procesado, *prŏthĕsä'dŏ*, a. prolix and circumstantial (of legal papers).

procesar, *—thĕsär'*, v. a. to inform against, to prosecute.

procesión, *—thĕsĭŏn'*, sf. procession.

proceso, *prŏthĕ'sŏ*, sm. process, law-suit.

proclama, *prŏklä'mä*, sf. proclamation, publication. [tion; acclamation.

proclamación, *—mäthĭŏn'*, sf. proclama-

proclamar, *—mär'*, v. a. to proclaim.

procónsul, *—kŏn'sŭl*, sm. proconsul.

proconsulado, *—sŭlä'dŏ*, sm. proconsulship.

proconsular, *—kŏnsŭlär'*, a. proconsular.

procreación, *—krĕäthĭŏn'*, sf. procreation, generation. [generate.

procrear, *—krĕär'*, v. a. to procreate, to

procuración, *—kŭräthĭŏn'*, sf. power of attorney; procurement.

procurador, *—dŏr'*, sm. procurer; attorney; proctor. [fice; proctorship.

procuraduría, *—dŭrĕ'ä*, sf. attorney's of-

procurar, *—rär'*, v. a. to solicit; to act as an attorney.

prodigalidad, *—dĭgälĭdäd'*, sf. prodigality; plenty, abundance.

prodigar, *—gär'*, v. a. to waste, to lavish.

prodigio, *prŏdĭ'h'ĭŏ*, sm. prodigy, monster.

prodigioso, sa, *—dĭ'hĭŏ'sŏ*, a. prodigious, monstrous; exquisite, excellent.

pródigo, ga, *prŏ'dĭgŏ*, a. prodigal.

producción, *prŏdŭkthĭŏn'*, sf. production.

producible, *—dŭthĕ'blĕ*, a. producible.

producir, *—thĭr'*, v. a. to produce; (law) to produce as evidence.

productivo, va, *—dŭktĕ'vŏ*, a. productive.

producto, *prŏdŭk'tŏ*, sm. product.

proemio, *prŏĕ'mĭŏ*, sm. preface, introduction. [bravery.

proeza, *prŏĕ'thä*, sf. prowess, valour.

profanación, *—fänäthĭŏn'*, sf. profanation.

profanar, *—fänär'*, v. a. to profane.

profano, na, *prŏfä'nŏ*, a. profane.

profecía, *—fĕthĕ'ä*, sf. prophecy.

profesar, *—fĕsär'*, v. a. to profess, to declare openly; to take the vows; to take the veil.

profesión, *—fĕsĭŏn'*, sf. profession.

profeso, sa, *—fĕ'sŏ*, a. professed.

profesor, *—fĕsŏr'*, sm. professor.

profeta, *prŏfĕ'tä*, sm. prophet.

profético, ca, *—tĭkŏ*, a. prophetic.

profetisa, *—fĕtĕ'sä*, sf. prophetess.

profetizar, *—tĭthär'*, v. a. to prophesy.

prófugo, ga, *prŏ'fŭgŏ*, a. fugitive.

profundidad, *—fŭndĭdäd'*, sf. profundity, profoundness; depth; grandeur.

profundizar, *—fŭndĭthär'*, v. a. to profound or to deepen; to penetrate.

profundo, da, *prŏfŭn'dŏ*, a. profound.

profusamente, *—fŭsämĕn'tĕ*, ad. profusely.

profusión, *—fŭsĭŏn'*, sf. profusion, prodigality. [generation, off-spring, issue.

progenie, *prŏhĕ'nĭĕ*, sf. progeny, race,

progenitor, *—'hĕnĭtŏr'*, sm. progenitor, ancestor, forefather.

progenitura, *—'hĕnĭtŏ'rä*, sf. progeny; primogeniture.

programa, *—grä'mä*, sm. programme.

progresar, *—grĕsär'*, v. n. to progress.

progresión, *—grĕsĭŏn'*, sf. progression.

progresivo, va, *—sĕ'vŏ*, a. progressive.

progreso, *prŏgrĕ'sŏ*, sm. progress.

prohibición, *—hĭbĭthĭŏn'*, sf. prohibition, forbiddance. [bid, to hinder.

prohibir, *—hĭbĭr'*, v. n. to prohibit, to for-

prohibitivo, va, *—hĭbĭtĕ'vŏ*, a. prohibitory. [tion.

prohijamiento, *—hĭ'hämĭĕn'tŏ*, sm. adop-

prohijar, *—hĭ'här'*, v. a. to adopt (a son).

prohombre, *—ŏm'brĕ*, sm. topping man.

prójimo, *prŏ'h'ĭmŏ*, sm. fellow-creature; neighbour. [race.

prole, *prŏ'lĕ*, sf. issue, offspring, progeny,

proletario, ria, *prŏlĕtä'rĭŏ*, a. proletarian.

prolijidad, *—lĭhĭdäd'*, sf. prolixity; minute attention to trifles.

prolijo, ja, *prŏlĕ'hŏ*, a. prolix, tedious.

prólogo, *prŏ'lŏgŏ*, sm. prologue. [gation.

prolongación, *prŏlŏngäthĭŏn'*, sf. prolon-

prolongar, *—gär'*, v. a. to prolong.

promediar, *—mĕ'dĭär'*, v. a. to share.

equally; —, v. n. to interpose in a friendly
manner.   [offering.
promesa, *prŏmĕs'ă,* sf. promise; pious
prometer, *—mĕtĕr',* v. a. to promise, to
asseverate, to assure; **-se,** v. r. to flatter
oneself.   [bidding.
prometido, *—tē'dŏ,* sm. promise; out-
prominencia, *—mĭnĕn'thĭă,* sf. protuberance, knob.   [ting out.
prominente, *—nĕn'tĕ,* a. prominent, jut-
promiscuo, cua, *—mĭs'kŭŏ,* a. promiscuous, confusedly mingled; ambiguous.
promisión, *—mĭsĭŏn',* sf. promise.
promoción, *—mŏthĭŏn',* sf. promotion.
promontorio, *—mŏntŏ'rĭŏ,* sm. promontory, cape.   [warder.
promotor, *—mŏtŏr',* sm. promoter, for-
promover, *—mŏvĕr',* v. a. to promote, to
advance.   [mulgation.
promulgación, *—mŭlgăthĭŏn',* sf. pro-
promulgador, *—dŏr',* sm. publisher, pro-
mulgator.   [to publish.
promulgar, *—găr',* v. a. to promulgate,
pronombre, *—nŏm'brĕ,* sm. pronoun.
pronosticación, *—nŏstĭkăthĭŏn',* sf. prognostication.   [teller, prognosticator.
pronosticádor, ra, *—dŏr',* sm. & f. fore-
pronosticar, *—kăr',* v. a. to prognosticate, to predict, to foretell, to conjecture. .
pronóstico, *prŏnŏs'tĭkŏ,* sm. prognostic,
prediction; omen, foretoken; almanac
published by astrologers.   [promptness.
prontitud, *prŏntĭ'tŭd,* sf. promptitude.
pronto, ta, *prŏn'tŏ,* a. prompt, ready; —,
ad. promptly; **-,** sm. promptitude.
prontuario, *—tŭă'rĭŏ,* sm. memorandum-
book.   [nunciation.
pronunciación, *—nŭnthĭăthĭŏn',* sf. pro-
pronunciamiento, *—thĭămĭĕn'tŏ,* sm.
(law) publication, insurrection, sedition.
pronunciar, *—thĭăr',* v. a. to pronounce;
-se, to rebel.   [tion; extension.
propagación, *—păgăthĭŏn',* sf. propaga-
propagador, ra, *—dŏr',* sm. & f. pro-
pagator.
propaganda, *—găn'dă,* sf. college at Rome,
consisting of cardinals peculiarly charged
with propagating the Roman catholic faith.
propagar, *—păgăr',* v. a. to propagate;
to dilate, to increase.   [divulge.
propalar, *—pălăr',* v. a. to publish, to
propasar, *—păsăr',* v. a. to go beyond, to
exceed.
propender, *—pĕndĕr',* v. n. to incline.
propensión, *—pĕnsĭŏn',* sf. propensity, inclination.   [clined.
propenso, sa, *prŏpĕn'să,* a. prone, in-
propiciación, *—pĭthĭăthĭŏn',* sf. propitiation, tatonement.
propiciar, *—pĭthĭăr',* v. a. to propitiate.
propiciatorio, ria, *—thĭătŏ'rĭŏ,* a. & sm.
propitiatory.
propicio, cia, *prŏpĕ'thĭŏ,* a. propitious.
propiedad, *—pĭĕdăd',* sf. dominion, possession; right of property; propriety.
propietario, ria, *—tă'rĭŏ,* a. & sm. proprietor; **-s,** pl. proprietary.

propina, *prŏpĕ'nă,* sf. present, salary, pay;
fees of office.
propinar, *—pĭnăr',* v. a. to invite to drink.
propincuidad, *—pĭnkŭĭdăd',* sf. propinquity.   [tiguous.
propincuo, cua, *prŏpĭn'kŭŏ,* a. near, con-
propio, pia, *'prŏ'pĭŏ,* a. proper; —, sm.
peculiar quality; **-s,** s. pl. lands, estates.
proponer, *—pŏnĕr',* v. a. to propose.
proporción, *—pŏrthĭŏn',* sf. proportion;
symmetry.
proporcionado, da, *—thĭŏnă'dŏ,* a. pro-
portionate, fit, comfortable.
proporcional, *—thĭŏnăl',* a. proportional.
proporcionar, *—thĭŏnăr',* v. a. to proportion; to adjust, to adapt.
proposición, *—pŏsĭthĭŏn',* sf. proposition.
propósito, *prŏpŏ'sĭtŏ,* sm. purpose; á —,
for the purpose; **de —,** on purpose, purposely; **fuera de —,** untimely, not to the
purpose.   [representation.
propuesta, *prŏpŭĕs'tă,* sf. proposal, offer;
prorrata, *prŏrră'tă,* sf. quota.
prorratear, *—rătĕăr',* v. a. to divide a
quantity into certain shares.
prorrateo, *—rătĕ'ŏ,* sm. distribution.
prórroga, *prŏr'rŏgă,* sf. prolongation.
prorrogable, *—rŏgă'blĕ,* a. capable of
being prorogued.
prorrogar, *—rŏgăr',* v. a. to prorogue.
prorrumpir, *—rŭmpĭr',* v. n. to break
forth, to burst forth.
prosa, *prŏ'să,* sf. prose.
prosador, *prŏsădŏr',* sm. sarcastic speaker.
prosaico, ca, *prŏsă'ĭkŏ,* a. prosaic.
prosapia, *prŏsă'pĭă,* sf. race, generation.
proscenio, *prŏsthĕ'nĭŏ,* sm. proscenium.
proscribir, *—skrĭbĭr',* v. a. to proscribe,
to outlaw.   [tion.
proscripción, *—skrĕpthĭŏn',* sf. proscrip-
proscripto, *—skrĭp'tŏ,* sm. outlaw.
prosecución, *—sĕkŭthĭŏn',* sf. prosecution,
pursuit.
proseguible, *—sĕgĕ'blĕ,* a. pursuable.
proseguir, *—sĕgĭr',* v. a. to pursue, to
prosecute.
prosélito, *prŏsĕ'lĭtŏ,* sm. proselyte.
prosodia, *prŏsŏ'dĭă,* sf. prosody.
prosopopeya, *—sŏpŏpĕ'yă,* sf. proso-
popœia, personification; splendour,
pageantry.
prospecto, *prŏspĕk'tŏ,* sm. prospectus.
prosperar, *prŏspĕrăr',* v. a. to make
happy; to favour; —, v. n. to prosper, to
thrive.
prosperidad, *—rĭdăd',* sf. prosperity.
próspero, ra, *prŏs'pĕrŏ,* a. prosperous.
prostitución, *prŏstĭtăthĭŏn',* sf. prostitution.
prostituir, *—tĭtŭĭr',* v. a. to prostitute.
prostituta, *—tĭtŭ'tă,* sf. prostitute, woman
of the town.
protección, *prŏtĕkthĭŏn',* sf. protection.
protector, *—tŏr',* sm. protector.
proteger, *—tĕ'hĕr',* v. a. to protect.
protervia, *prŏtĕr'vĭă,* sf. insolence.

protervo, va, –*vŏ,* a. stubborn, peevish, arrogant, insolent.

protesta, –*tĕś'tă,* sf. (law) protest.

protestación, –*tăthŏn',* sf. protestation.

protestante, –*tăn'tĕ,* sm. Protestant.

protestar, –*tăr',* v. a. to protest; to make public declaration of faith.

protoalbéitar, *prŏtŏălbĕ'tăr,* sm. chief veterinary surgeon.

protoalbeiterato, –*ălbĕtĕră'tŏ,* sm. tribunal for examining veterinary surgeons previously to licensing them to practise.

protocolar, –*kŏlăr',* **protocolizar,** –*kŏlĭthăr',* v. a. to place in the protocol.

protocolo, –*kŏ'lŏ,* sm. protocol. [tyr.

protomártir, –*măr'tĭr,* sm. the first martyr.

protomedicato, –*mĕdĭkă'tŏ,* sm. college of king's physicians, where students of medicine are examined and licensed.

protomédico, –*mĕd'ĭkŏ,* sm. first physician (to the king). [notary.

protonotario, –*nŏtă'rĕŏ,* sm. protoprototype, –*tĕ'pŏ,* sm. prototype.

prototipo, –*tĕ'pŏ,* sm. prototype.

provecho, *prŏvĕtsh'ŏ,* sm. profit.

provechoso, sa, –*tshŏ'sŏ,* a. profitable.

provecto, ta, –*vĕk'tŏ,* a. advanced in years or learning.

proveedor, ra, –*vĕĕdŏr',* sm.&f. purveyor.

proveeduría, –*dĕrĕ'ă,* sf. store-house where provisions are kept and distributed; office of a purveyor.

proveer, –*vĕĕr',* v. a. to provide; to provision; to confer an employment; to decree; –se, to ease the body.

proveído, –*vĕĭ'dŏ,* sm. judgment, sentence, decree. [ing.

proveimiento, –*mĕĕn'tŏ,* sm. provision.

provenir, –*vĕnĭr',* v. n. to arise, to proceed; to issue.

proverbial, –*vĕrbĭăl',* a. proverbial.

proverbio, *prŏvĕr'bĭŏ,* sm. proverb; –s, pl. Book of Proverbs.

providencia, *prŏvĭdĕn'thĭă,* s. providence; foresight; divine providence. [tial.

providencial, –*dĕnthĭăl',* a, providencial, –*thĭăr',* v. a. to ordain, to command.

providenciar, –*thĭăr',* v. a. to ordain, to command.

próvido, da, *prŏ'vĭdŏ,* a. provident.

provincia, *prŏvĭn'thĭă,* sf. province.

provincial, –*thĭăl',* a. & sm. provincial; pasquinade, libel. [a provincial.

provincialato, –*thĭălă'tŏ,* sm. office of a provincial.

provinciano, na, –*thĭă'nŏ,* a. & sm. & f. native of Biscay. [visions; provender.

provisión, *prŏvĭsĭŏn',* sf. store of provisional, –*năl',* a. provisional.

provisional, –*năl',* a. provisional.

provisionalmente, –*mĕn'tĕ,* ad. provisionally. [vider; vicar-general.

provisor, ora, *prŏvĭsŏr',* sm. & f. provocación, –*vŏkăthĭŏn',* sf. provocation.

provocación, –*vŏkăthĭŏn',* sf. provocation.

provocador, ora, –*dŏr',* sm. & f. provoker. [cite.

provocar, –*kăr',* v. a. to provoke, to excite.

provocativo, va, –*tĕ'vŏ,* a. provocative; quarrelsome. [kindred by birth.

proximidad, *prŏksĭmĭdăd',* sf. proximity.

próximo, ma, *prŏk'sĭmŏ,* a. next, nearest.

proyección, *prŏyĕkthĭŏn',* sf. projection.

proyectar, –*yĕktăr',* v. a. to project, to scheme.

proyecto, *prŏyĕk'tŏ,* sm. project. [dom.

prudencia, *prŭdĕn'thĭă,* sf. prudence, wis-prudente, *prŭdĕn'tĕ,* a. prudent.

prudente, *prŭdĕn'tĕ,* a. prudent.

prueba, *prŭĕ'bă,* sf. proof, reason, argument; token; experiment, essay, attempt; relish, taste.

prurito, *prŭrĭ'tŏ,* sm. prurience, itching.

pu, pŏ, sf. excrements of children; ¡–! ¡fy! exclamation of disgust at a bad smell.

púa, *pŏ'ă,* sf. sharp point, prickle; shoot of a tree engrafted in another; weaver's reed; mental pain; sly person.

pubertad, *pŭbĕrtăd',* sf. puberty. [tion.

publicación, *pŭblĭkăthĭŏn',* sf. publicapublicano, –*kă'nŏ,* sm. publican.

publicano, –*kă'nŏ,* sm. publican.

publicar, –*kăr',* v. a. to publish, to proclaim. [cation.

publicata, –*kă'tă,* sf. certificate of publipublicidad, –*thĭdăd',* sf. publicity; en

publicidad, –*thĭdăd',* sf. publicity; en –, publicly.

público, ca, *pŏ'blĭkŏ,* a. sm. public.

pucia, *pŏ'thĭă,* sf. chemist's jar, gallipot.

puchada, *pŏtshă'dă,* sf. poultice.

puchero, *pŏtshĕ'rŏ,* sm. glazed earthen pot; meat boiled in an earthen pot; grimace which precedes crying.

puches, *pŏtsh'ĕs,* sm. pl. pap, meal-pap.

pudicicia, *pŭdĭthĕ'thĭă,* sf. pudicity, chastity, chasteness.

púdico, ca, *pŏ'dĭkŏ,* a. chaste, pure.

pudiente, *pŭdĭĕn'tĕ,* a. rich, opulent.

pudingo, *pŭdĭn'gŏ,* sm. pudding.

pudor, *pŭdŏr',* sm. bashfulness, shamefacedness.

pudrición, *pŭdrĭthĭŏn',* sf. rottenness.

pudridero, –*dd'rŏ,* sm. rotting-place.

pudrimiento, –*mĕĕn'tŏ,* sm. rottenness.

pudrir, *pŭdrĭr',* v. a. to make putrid; –, v. n. to rot, to be rotten.

pueblo, *pŭĕ'blŏ,* sm. town, village; population; populace. [bridge.

puente, *pŭĕn'tĕ,* sm. & f. bridge; (mus.)

puerca, *pŭĕr'kă,* sf. sow, female pig.

puerco, ca, *pŭĕr'kŏ,* a. nasty, filthy, dirty; rude, coarse; –, sm. hog; – espin, porcupine.

puericia, *pŭĕrĕ'thĭă,* sf. boyhood.

pueril, *pŭĕrĭl',* a. boyish, childish.

puerilidad, –*lĭdăd',* sf. puerility, boyishness.

puerro, *pŭĕr'rŏ,* sm. leek. [ness.

puerta, *pŭĕr'tă,* sf. door, doorway, gateway; duty paid at the entrance of the gates in towns; – trasera, back-door.

puerto, *pŭĕr'tŏ,* sm. port, harbour, haven; narrow pass, defile. [then.

pues, *pŭĕś,* ad. then, therefore; ¡–! well,

puesto, *pŭĕś'tŏ,* sm. place; particular spot; retail-shop; post, employment; barracks; stand, bushes to conceal sportsmen; put; –, ad. because; – que, – caso, although.

¡puf! *pŭf,* fy! exclamation of disgust at a bad smell.

pugilato, *pŭ'hĭlă'tŏ,* sm. pugilism.

pugna, *pŭg'nă,* sf. combat, battle.

pugnar, pŭgnăr′, v. n. to fight, to combat; to solicit earnestly.. [sale.

puja, pŭ′h′ă, sf. outbidding at a public

pujante, —′hăn′tă, a. powerful, strong, robust, stout, strapping.

pujanza, —′hăn′thă, sf. power, strength.

pujar, pŭ′hăr′, v. a. to outbid. [tool).

pujavante, pŭ′hăvăn′tă, sm. parer(farrier's

pujo, pŭ′h′ŏ, sm. tenesmus; violent desire.

pulcritud, pŭl′krĭtŭd′, sf. beauty.

pulcro,cra, pŭl′krŏ a.beautiful;affectedly nice in dress.

pulga, pŭl′gă, sf. flea; **tener malas —s,** to be easily piqued; to be ill-tempered.

pulgada, —gă′dă, sf. inch.

pulgar, pŭlgăr′, sm. thumb. [tobacco).

pulgarada, —ră′dă, sf. fillip; pinch (of

pulgón, pŭlgŏn′, sm. vine-fretter, vine-

pulgoso, sa, —gŏ′sŏ, a. pulicose. [grub.

pulguera, —gă′ră, sf. place abounding with fleas; (bot.) flea-wort. [instrument).

pulicán, pŭlĭkăn′, sm. pelican (surgical

pulidez, pŭlĭdĕth′, sf. neatness.

pulido, da, pŭlĭ′dŏ, a. neat, nice.

pulidor, pŭlĭdŏr′, sm. polisher; instrument used for polishing and burnishing.

pulimento, —mĕn′tŏ, sm. polish, glossiness.

pulir, pŭlĭr′, v. a. to polish, to burnish; to put the last touches to; **—se,** to adorn oneself; to become polished.

pulmón, pŭlmŏn′, sm. lungs. [lungs.

pulmonía, —nĕ′ă, sf. inflammation of the

púlpito, pŭl′pĭtŏ, sm. pulpit.

pulpo, pŭl′pŏ, sm. cuttle-fish; polypus.

pulposo, sa, —pŏ′sŏ, a. pulpous.

pulsación, pŭlsăthĭŏn′, sf. pulsation.

pulsar, pŭlsăr′, v. a. to touch; to feel the pulse; to explore, to try; —, v. n. to pulse.

pulsera, pŭlsĕ′ră, sf. bandage applied to the vein or artery of a sick person; **—s,** pl. bracelets.

pulso, pŭl′sŏ, sm. pulse; firmness or steadiness of the hand; attention, care.

pulular, pŭlŭlăr′, v. n. to pullulate.

pulverización, pŭlvĕrĭthăthĭŏn′, sf. pulverization.

pulverizar, —thăr′, v. a. to pulverize.

pulla, pŭl′yă, sf. smart repartee; obscene expression.

pundonor, pŭndŏnŏr′, sm. point of honour.

pundonoroso, sa, —rŏ′sŏ, a. having a nice sense of honour, punctilious.

pungir, pŭn′hĭr′, v. a. to punch, to prick.

punición, pŭnĭthĭŏn′, sf. punishment.

punta, pŭn′tă, sf. point. [chastisement.

puntada, —tă′dă, sf. stitch made with a needle and thread.

puntal, pŭntăl′, sm. prop, stay, buttress.

puntapié, pŭntăpĭĕ′, sm. kick.

puntear, pŭntĕăr′, v. a. to play the guitar; to point out; to stitch; —, v. n. (mar.) to tack. [glass.

puntel, pŭntĕl′, sm. iron tube for blowing

puntería, —tĕr′ĕ′ă, sf. aiming of (fire-arms).

puntero, pŭntĕ′rŏ, sm. fescue; —, ra, a. aiming well (with fire-arms). [pointed.

puntiagudo, da, pŭntĭăgŭ′dŏ, a. sharp,

puntilla, —tĭl′yă, sf. narrow lace-edging; **de —s,** on tiptoe.

puntillazo, —yă′thŏ, sm. kick.

puntillo, pŭntĭl′yŏ, sm. punctilio, trifling, despicable thing.

punto, pŭn′tŏ, sm. point; end, design; point of honour; aim, sight; stitch; mesh of a net; **al —,** instantly.

puntuación, —tŭăthĭŏn′, sf. punctuation.

puntual, pŭntŭăl′, a. punctual, exact.

puntualidad, —tĭdăd′, sf. punctuality; certainty. [mind or memory; to accomplish.

puntualizar, —lĭthăr′, v. a. to fix on the

puntuar, pŭntŭăr′, v. a. to punctuate, to point. [compunction.

punzada, —thă′dă, sf. prick, sting; pain;

punzador, ora, —thădŏr′, sm. & f. pricker.

punzadura, —dŭ′ră, sf. puncture, prick.

punzar, pŭnthăr′, v. a. to punch, to prick.

punzón, —thŏn′, sm. punch. [to sting.

puñada, pŭnyă′dă, sf. cuff, blow with the

puñado, —dŏ, sm. handful. [fist.

puñal, pŭnyăl′, sm. poniard, dagger.

puñalada, pŭnyălă′dă, sf. stab.

puñetazo, pŭnyĕtă′thŏ, sm. blow with the closed fist. [band; hand-ruffle; hilt.

puño, pŭn′yŏ, sm. fist; handful; wristband.

pupila, pŭpĭ′lă, sf. eye-ball, pupil; orphan girl. [house.

pupilaje, —lă′h′ĕ, sm. pupilage; boarding-

pupilar, —lăr′, a. pupilary.

pupilo, pŭpĭ′lŏ, sm. pupil; scholar.

pureza, pŭrĕ′thă, sf. purity, chastity.

purga, pŭr′gă, sf. purging-draught.

purgación, —găthĭŏn′, sf. purgation.

purgante, —găn′tĕ, sm. purgative.

purgar, —găr′, v. a. to purge, to purify; to atone, to expiate. [purging.

purgativo, va, —gătĭ′vŏ, a. purgative.

purgatorio, —tŏ′rĭŏ, sm. purgatory.

purificación, pŭrĭfĭkăthĭŏn′, sf. purification. [purificatory.

purificador, ora, —dŏr′, sm. & f. purifier;

purificar, —kăr′, v. a. to purify; **—se,** to be churched after lying-in.

purismo, pŭrĭs′mŏ, sm. purism, affectation of purity in verbal delivery.

purista, pŭrĭs′tă, sm. purist.

puritano, na, pŭrĭtă′nŏ, a. puritanical; —, sm. & f. Puritan.

puro, ra, pŏ′rŏ, a. pure, unmingled, mere; genuine; chaste, incorrupt.

púrpura, pŭr′pŭră, sf. purple-shell.

purpurado, —ră′dŏ, sm. cardinal.

purpurar, —răr′, v.a. to colour with purple.

purpurear, —rĕăr′, v. n. to grow purple.

purpúreo, rea, pŭrpŏ′rĕŏ, a. purple.

purulento, ta, pŭrŭlĕn′tŏ, a. purulent.

pus, pŭs′, sm. pus, matter, gleet.

pusilánime, pŭsĭlă′nĭmĕ,a. pusillanimous, faint-hearted. [lanimity.

pusilanimidad, —ănĭmĭdăd′, sf. pusil-

pústula, pŭs′tŭlă, sf. pustule, pimple.

putativo, va, pŭtătĭ′vŏ, a. putative, supposed. [tion.

putrefacción, pŭtrĕfăkthĭŏn′, sf. putrefac-

pútrido, da, pŏ′trĭdŏ, a. putrid, rotten.

Q.

que, kĕ, that; who; which; what.
quebrada, kĕbră′dă, sf. broken, uneven ground.
quebradero, —dĕ′rŏ, sm. breaker; — de cabeza, that which molests and importunes.
quebradizo, za, —dĕ′thŏ, a. brittle, flexible.
quebrado, kĕbră′dŏ, sm. (ar.) fraction.
quebradura, —dŏ′ră, sf. fracture; rupture, hernia. [ture, rupture, bursting.
quebrantadura, kĕbrăntădŏ′ră, sf. fracquebrantamiento, —mĕĕn′tŏ, sm. fracture, rupture; breaking out of prison; weariness, fatigue; violation of the law.
quebrantar, —tăr′, v. a. to break, to crack, to burst; to pound, to grind; to violate; to fatigue; to weaken.
quebranto, kĕbrăn′tŏ, sm. weakness, lassitude; great loss, severe damage.
quebrar, kĕbrăr′, v. a. to break, to transgress a law, to violate; —, v. n. to fail; —se, to break into pieces, to be ruptured.
quechemarín, kĕtshĕmărín′, sm. (mar.) lugger. [too.
queda, kĕ′dă, sf. resting-time; (mil.) tatquedar, kĕdăr′, v. a. to stay; to be wanting; —se, to falter, to stop short.
quedito, kĕdĕ′tŏ, ad. softly, gently.
quedo, da, kĕ′dŏ, a. quiet, still; —, ad. softly, gently.
quehacer, kĕăthĕr′, sm. business.
queja, kĕ′hă, sf. complaint.
quejarse, —′ărsĕ, v. r. to complain of.
quejido, —′hĕ′dŏ, sm. complaint [ous.
quejoso, sa, —′hŏ′sŏ, a. plaintful, querulquejumbroso, sa, —′hŭmbrŏ′sŏ, a. complaining, plaintive. [fire.
quema, kĕ′mă, sf. burning, combustion, fire.
quemador, ra, kĕmădŏr′, sm. & f. incendiary; burner. [fire, burn.
quemadura, —dŏ′ră, sf. mark made by
quemar, —măr′, v. a. to burn; to kindle; —, v. n. to be too hot; —se, to be parched with heat; to burn oneself.
quemazón, —thŏn′, sf. burn; [tation.
querella, kĕrĕl′yă, sf. complaint, lamenquerellarse, —yăr′sĕ, v. r. to lament, to complain; to lodge a complaint in a court of justice.
querelloso, sa, —yŏ′sŏ, a. querulous.
querer, kĕrĕr′, v. a. to wish, to desire; to will; —, sm. will, desire.
querido, da, kĕrĕ′dŏ, a. dear, beloved; —, sm. & f. darling, fondling, minion, lover; — mío ó —da mía, my dear, my love, my darling.
querubín, kĕrŏŏbĕn′, sm. cherub.
quesera, kĕsĕ′ră, sf. dairy.
quesero, kĕsĕ′rŏ, sm. cheesemonger.
queso, kĕ′sŏ, sm. cheese.
quicial, kĕthĕăl′, sf. side-post; jamb.
quicio, kĕ′thĕŏ, sm. hook, hinge (of a door).
quidam, kĕ′dăm, sm. someone, a certain person.

quiebra, kĕĕ′bră, sf. crack, fracture; bankruptcy.
quiebro, kĕĕ′brŏ, sm. (mus.) trill; inclination of the body. [other.
quien, kĕĕn′, pn. who, which; one or the
quienquiera, —kĕĕ′ră, a. whosoever, whatever.
quieto, ta, kĕĕ′tŏ, a. quiet, still, peaceable.
quietud, kĕĕtŏŏd′, sf. quietness, peace, tranquillity, calmness.
quijada, kĕ′hă′dă, sf. jaw, jaw-bone.
quijotada, kĕ′hŏtă′dă, sf. quixotic action.
quijote, kĕ′hŏ′tĕ, sm. cuish; a man who engages in quixotic enterprises.
quijotería, —tĕrĕ′ă, sf. quixotism, quixotry.
quijotesco, ca, —tĕs′kŏ, a. quixotic.
quilatar, kĕlătăr′, v. a. to assay.
quilate, kĕlă′tĕ, sm. carat.
quilificar, kĕlĕfĕkăr′, v. a. to chylify.
quilla, kĕl′yă, sf. keel.
quilma, kĕl′mă, sf. large back, sack.
quilo, kĕ′lŏ, sm. (med.) chyle.
quiloso, sa, kĕlŏ′sŏ, a. chylous.
quimera, kĕmĕ′ră, sf. dispute, quarrel.
quimérico, ca, kĕmĕ′rĕkŏ, a. chimerical, fantastic. [brawler.
quimerista, kĕmĕrĭs′tă, sm. wrangler,
química, kĕ′mĭkă, sf. chemistry.
químico, kĕ′mĭkŏ, sm. chemist; —, ca, a. chemical.
quina, kĕ′nă, sf. Peruvian bark.
quincalla, kĭnkăl′yă, sf. hard-ware.
quince, kĭn′thĕ, a. & sm. fifteen; fifteenth.
quinceno, na, —thĕ′nŏ, a. fifteenth.
Quincuagésima, —kŏŏă′hĕ′sĭmă, sf. Quinquagesima. [years.
quindenio, —dĕ′nĭŏ, sm. period of fifteen
quinientos, tas, kĭnĭĕn′tŏs, a. five hundred.
quinquina, —kĕ′nă, sf. quinine.
quinquonal, —kĕnăl′, a. quinquennial.
quinquenio, —kĕ′nĭŏ, sm. space of five years.
quinquillería, —kĭlyĕrĕ′ă, sf. hard-ware.
quinquillero, —kĭlyĕ′rŏ, sm. hawker, pedlar, hard-ware man.
quinta, kĭn′tă, sf. country-seat, country-house; levy, drafting of soldiers; quint (mus. and piquet).
quintaesencia, —ĕ′sĕn′thĕă, sf. quintessence.
quintal, kĭntăl′, sm. quintal, hundred-weight. [fiye; to levy, to draft soldiers.
quintar, kĭntăr′, v. a. to draw one out of
quintería, —tĕrĕ′ă, sf. farm; grange.
quintero, —tĕ′rŏ, sm. farmer; servant who takes care of a farm. [of five verses.
quintilla, —tĭl′yă, sf. metrical composition
quinto, kĭn′tŏ, sm. fifth; share of a pasture-ground; drafted soldier; —, ta, a. fifth.
quíntuplo, pla, kĭn′tŏŏplŏ, a. quintuple, fivefold.
quiñón, kĭnyŏn′, sm. dividend.
quiñonero, —yŏnĕ′rŏ, sm. part-owner.
quirite, kĕrĕ′tĕ, sm. Roman citizen.
quiromancia, kĕrŏmăn′thĕă, sf. chiromancy.
quirúrgico, ca, kĕrŏŏr′hĭkŏ, a. surgical.
quirurgo, kĕrŏŏr′gŏ, sm. surgeon.

quisicosa, *kĭsĭkŏ′sǎ,* sf. riddle; obscure question.   [trifling dispute.

quisquilla, *kĭskĭl′yǎ,* sf. ridiculous nicety;

quisquilloso, sa, *–yŏ′sŏ,* a. nice, difficult, touchy, peevish, irritable.

quisto, ta, *kĭs′tŏ,* p. & a. only used with **bien** and **mal; bien –,** well received, generally beloved; **mal –,** ill received, hated.   [away with you!

¡quita! ** *kĭ′tǎ,* God forbid! **¡– de ahí!

quitamanchas, *kĭtǎmǎn′tshǎs,* sm. scourer of clothes.

quitapellijos, *–pĕlĭ′yŏs,* sm. wheedler.

quitapesares, *–pĕsǎ′rĕs,* sm. & f. comfort, consolation.

quitapón, *–pŏn′,* sm. ornament for the head-stall of draught-mules.

quitar, *kĭtǎr′,* v. a. to take away, to remove; to fetch away; to redeem a pledge; to abrogate, to annul; to free from an obligation; to parry (in fencing); **–se,** to abstain; to get rid of.

quitasol, *kĭtǎsŏl′,* sm. parasol.

quita y pon, (de), *kĭtǎ ĕ pŏn′,* ad. that can be put on or off, as one likes.

quite, *kĕ′tĕ,* sm. obstacle, impediment.

quito, ta, *kĕ′tŏ,* a. free from an obligation, exempt.   [haps.

quizá, *kĭthǎ′,* **quizás,** *kĭthǎs′,* ad. per-

R.

rabadán, *rǎbǎdǎn′,* sm. head-shepherd.

rabadilla, *–dĭl′yǎ,* sf. rump, croup.

rabanero, ra, *–nǎ′rŏ,* sm. & f. seller of radishes.

rabaniza, *–nĭ′thǎ,* sf. radish-seed.

rábano, *rǎ′bǎnŏ,* sm. radish.

rabia, *rǎ′bĭǎ,* sf. rage, fury.

rabiar, *rǎbĭǎr′,* v. n. to be furious, to rage.

rabicorto, ta, *–kŏr′tŏ,* a. short-tailed.

rabieta, *rǎbĭĕ′tǎ,* sf. touchiness, petulance, bad temper.

rabilargo, ga, *–lǎr′gŏ,* a. long-tailed.

rabino, *rǎbĕ′nŏ,* sm. rabbi, rabbin.

rabioso, sa, *rǎbĭŏ′sŏ,* a. rabid; furious.

rabisalsera, *–sǎlsĕ′rǎ,* a. petulant, saucy, impudent (applied to women).

rabo, *rǎ′bŏ,* sm. tail.

rabón, ona, *rǎbŏn′,* a. docked, short-tailed.

rabosear, *rǎbŏsĕǎr′,* v. a. to spatter.

rabotear, *–tĕǎr′,* v.a. to cut or crop the tail.

rabudo, da, *rǎbŏ′dŏ,* a. long-tailed.

racimo, *rǎthĕ′mŏ,* sm. bunch of grapes.

racimoso, sa, *rǎthĭmŏ′sŏ,* a. grape-bearing.

raciocinar, *rǎthĭŏthĭnǎr′,* v. n. to reason, to argue, to ratiocinate.   [ment.

raciocinio, *–thĕ′nĭŏ,* sm. reasoning; argu-

ración, *rǎthĭŏn′,* sf. ration; prebend so called in Spanish cathedrals.

racional, *–nǎl′,* a. rational; reasonable.

racionalidad, *–nǎlĭdǎd′,* sf. rationality.

racionero, *–nǎ′rŏ,* sm. prebendary.

rada, *rǎ′dǎ,* sf. anchoring-ground for ships at some distance from shore, roadstead.

radiacion, *rǎdĭǎthĭŏn′,* sf. radiation.

radiante, *rǎdĭǎn′tĕ,* a. radiant.

radiar, *rǎdĭǎr′,* v. n. (poet.) to radiate.

radicación, *rǎdĭkǎthĭŏn′,* sf. taking root; becoming rooted (of a habit).

radical, *–kǎl′,* a. radical.

radicarse, *–kǎr′sĕ,* v. r. to take root.

radio, *rǎ′dĭŏ,* sm. radius; ray.

radiómetro, *rǎdĭŏ′mĕtrŏ,* sm. forestaff.

radioso, sa, *rǎdĭŏ′sŏ,* a. radiant.

raedera, *rǎĕdĕ′rǎ,* sf. scraper, raker.

raedura, *–dŏ′rǎ,* sf. erasure; scrapings.

raer, *rǎĕr′,* v. a. to scrape, to grate; to erase.

ráfaga, *rǎ′fǎgǎ,* sf. violent squall of wind.

raído, da, *rǎĕ′dŏ,* a. scraped; worn out; impudent.

raíz, *rǎĕth′,* sf. root; base, basis; origin; **bienes raíces,** pl. landed property.

raja, *rǎ′hǎ,* sf. splinter, chip of wood; chink, fissure; coarse cloth.

rajabroqueles, *–brŏkĕ′lĕs,* sm. braggart, boasting fellow, bravado.

rajar, *rǎ′hǎr′,* v. a. to split, to chop, to cleave; (fig. & fam.) to boast.

ralea, *rǎlĕ′ǎ,* sf. race, breed; species.

ralear, *rǎlĕǎr′,* v. n. to thin.

raleza, *rǎlĕ′thǎ,* sf. thinness; rarity.

ralo, la, *rǎ′lŏ,* a. thin, rare.

ralladura, *rǎlyǎdŏ′rǎ,* sf. mark left by the grater; small particles taken off by grating.

rallar, *rǎlyǎr′,* v. a. to grate; to importune.

rallo, *rǎl′yŏ,* sm. grater.

rama, *rǎ′mǎ,* sf. branch (of a tree, of a family); printer's chase, form.

ramadán, *–dǎn′,* sm. Mohammedan Lent.

ramaje, *rǎmǎ′hĕ,* sm. ramage; flowering branches designed in cloth.

ramal, *rǎmǎl′,* sm. halter.   [in a rock.

rambla, *rǎm′blǎ,* sf. sandy place; cavern

ramera, *rǎmǎ′rǎ,* sf. whore, prostitute.

ramificación, *rǎmĭfĭkǎthĭŏn′,* sf. ramification.

ramificarse, *–fĭkǎr′sĕ,* v. r. to ramify.

ramillete, *rǎmĭlyĕ′tĕ,* sm. nosegay.

ramilletero, *–yĕtĕ′rŏ,* sm. vase with artificial flowers for ornamenting altars.

ramo, *rǎ′mŏ,* sm. branch of a tree.

ramonear, *–nĕǎr′,* v. n. to cut off the branches of trees.

ramoso, sa, *rǎmŏ′sŏ,* a. branchy.

rampante, *rǎmpǎn′tĕ,* a. rampant.

rampojo, *–pŏ′hŏ,* sm. rape.

rampollo, *–pŏl′yŏ,* sm. shoot, sprig, sucker.

rana, *rǎ′nǎ,* sf. frog.

rancio, cia, *rǎn′thĭŏ,* a. rank, rancid.

ranchear, *rǎntshĕǎr′,* v. a. to build huts.

ranchero, *–tshĕ′rŏ,* sm. steward of a mess.

rancho, *rǎn′tshŏ,* sm. mess; mess-room.

ranúnculo, *rǎnŭn′kŭlŏ,* sm. (bot.) crowfoot.   [childish action.

rapacería, *rǎpǎthĕrĕ′ǎ,* sf. puerility;

rapacidad, *–thĭdǎd′,* sf. rapacity.

rapadura, *–dŏ′rǎ,* sf. shaving; baldness.

rapar, *rǎpǎr′,* v. a. to shave; to plunder.

rapaz, za, *rǎpǎth′,* a. rapacious, **–, za,** sm. & f. young boy or girl.   [speech.

rapazada, *–thǎ′dǎ,* sf. childish action or

rape, *rǎ′pĕ,* sm. shaving.

rapé, *rắpā̆,* sm. rappee.
rapidez, *rắpĭdĕth',* sf. rapidity.
rápido, da, *rắpĭdŏ,* a. rapid, swift.
rapiña, *rắpín'yā̆,* sf. rapine, robbery.
rapiñar, *-yār',* v. a. to plunder.
raposa, *rắpŏ'sā̆,* sf. female fox; cunning, deceitful person.
raposería, *-sĕr'ĕ'ā̆,* sf. trick, wile, cunning.
raposo, *rắpŏ'sŏ,* sm. male fox.
rapto, *rắp'tŏ,* sm. rapine; ecstasy, rapture; ravishment.
raptor, *rắptŏr',* sm. ravisher.
raqueta, *rắkĕ'tā̆,* sf. racket, battledoor.
raquítico, ca, *rắkĭ'tĭkā̆,* a. rickety.
raquitis, *rắkĭ'tĭs,* sf. rickets.
rareza, *rắrĕ'thā̆,* sf. rarity, rareness.
raridad, *rắrĭdắd',* sf. rarity.
raro, ra, *rắ'rŏ,* a. rare, scarce, extraordinary; —, ad. rarely.
ras, *rắs,* sm. level, even surface.
rasadura, *rắsắdŏ'rā̆,* sf. levelling with a strickle (in measuring grain).
rasar, *rắsắr',* v. a. to strike off with a strickle, or level a measure of grain.
rascador, *rắskắdŏr',* sm. scraper; diamond head-pin. [scraping or rasping.
rascadura, *-dŏ'rā̆,* sf. act of scratching.
rascar, *rắskĕr',* v. a. to scratch, to scrape.
rasero, *rắsĕ'rŏ,* sm. strickle.
rasgar, *rắsgắr',* v. a. to tear, to rend.
rasgo, *rắs'gŏ,* sm. dash, stroke; grand or magnanimous action.
rasgón, *rắsgŏn',* sm. rent, rag, tatter.
rasguear, *rắsgĕắr',* v. n. to form bold strokes with the pen; (mus.) to play arpeggios.
rasgueo, *rắsgā̆'ŏ,* sm. arpeggio. [scrape.
rasguñar, *-gŭnyắr',* v. a. to scratch, to
rasguño, *-gắn'yŏ,* sm. scratch.
raso, *rā̆'sŏ,* sm. satin; glade; —, sa, a. plain; flat; al —, in the open air.
raspa, *rắs'pā̆,* sf. beard of an ear of corn; back-bone of fish; stalk of grapes; rasp.
raspadera, *-dŏ'rā̆,* sf. raker.
raspador, *-dŏr',* sm. rasp.
raspadura, *-dŏ'rā̆,* sf. filing, scraping; filings. [stea
raspar, *rắspắr',* v. a. to scrape, to ra... to
raspear, *rắspĕắr',* v. n. to splutter (of pens).
rastra, *rắs'trā̆,* sf. sledge. [a whip.
rastrallar, *-trắl'yắr',* v. n. to crack with
rastrear, *-trĕắr',* v. a. to trace; to inquire into; —, v. n. to skim along close to the ground (of birds).
rastrero, ra, *-trā̆'rŏ,* a. creeping; low, humble, cringing, reptile; —, sm. inspector of a slaughterhouse.
rastrillador, ora, *-trĭlyắdŏr',* sm. & f. hackler, flax-dresser, raker.
rastrillar, *-yắr',* v. a. to hackle, to dress flax; to rake.
rastrillo, *rắstrĭl'yŏ,* sm. hackle; flax-comb, portcullis; hammer of a gun-lock; rake. [house; sign, token.
rastro, *rắs'trŏ,* sm. track; sledge; slaughter-
rastrojera, *-'hā̆'rā̆,* sf. stubble-ground.
rastrojo, *rắstrŏ'h'ŏ,* sm. stubble.

rasurar, *rắsŭrắr',* v. a. to shave.
rata, *rắ'tā̆,* sf. she-mouse; rat.
ratafia, *rắtắfĭā̆,* sf. ratafia (liquor).
ratear, *rắtĕắr',* v. a. to filch, to commit petty thefts; v. n. to creep.
ratería, *-rĕ'ā̆,* sf. larceny, petty theft.
ratero, ra, *rắtĕ'rŏ,* a. creeping, mean, vile.
ratificación, *rắtĭfĭkắthĭŏn',* sf. ratification. [of.
ratificar, *-kắr',* v. a. to ratify, to approve
ratina, *rắtĭ'nā̆,* sf. ratteen.
rato, *rắ'tŏ,* sm. mouse; moment; á...-s perdidos, in leisure-time.
ratón, *rắtŏn',* sm. mouse.
ratonar, *-nắr',* v. a. to gnaw (of animals).
ratonera, *-nĕ'rā̆,* sf. mouse-trap; wall where rats breed.
raudal, *rắŭdắl',* sm. torrent.
raya, *rắ'yā̆,* sf. stroke; line; frontier; ray, roach (fish). [arms).
rayado, da, *rắyắ'dŏ,* a. rifled (of fire-
rayano, na, *rắyắ'nŏ,* a. neighbouring, contiguous. [gate; to rifle.
rayar, *rắyắr',* v. a. to draw lines; to varie-
rayo, *rắ'yŏ,* sm. ray, beam of light; radius.
rayoso, sa, *rắyŏ'sŏ,* a. radiating, striped.
raza, *rắ'thā̆,* sf. race, lineage; quality.
razón, *rắthŏn',* sf. reason; ratiocination; reasonableness; account, calculation.
razonable, *-nā̆'blĕ,* a. reasonable.
razonado, da, *-nā̆'dŏ,* a. rational, prudent. [ing, discourse.
razonamiento, *-nắmĭĕn'tŏ,* sm. reason-
razonar, *-nắr',* v. n. to reason, to discourse; to talk.
reacción, *rĕắkthĭŏn',* sf. reaction.
reagravar, *rĕắgrắvắr',* v. a. to aggravate anew. [camp; real (a Spanish coin).
real, *rĕắl',* a. real, actual; royal; —, sm.
reales, *rĕắl'thā̆,* sm. embossment; flash; lustre, splendour.
realengo, ga, *-lĕn'gŏ,* a. royal, kingly.
realidad, *-lĭdắd',* sf. reality; sincerity.
realista, *-lĭs'tā̆,* sm. royalist.
realizar, *-lĭthắr',* v. a. to realize.
realzar, *rĕắlthắr',* v. a. to raise, to elevate; to emboss; to heighten.
reanimar, *-ănĭmắr',* v. a. to cheer, to encourage, to reanimate. [resume.
reasumir, *-ăsŭmĭr',* v. a. to retake, to
reata, *rĕắ'tŏ,* sf. collar, leash; string of horses; leading mule; (fig.) submission to the opinion of others.
reato, *rĕắ'tŏ,* sm. obligation of atonement for a sin which is unabsolved.
rebaja, *rĕbắ'hā̆,* sf. abatement, deduction.
rebajar, *-bă'hắr',* v. a. to abate, to lessen, to diminish.
rebalsa, *-bắl'sā̆,* sf. pool, puddle.
rebalsar, *-bắlsắr',* v. a. to dam a stream.
rebanada, *-bắnắ'dā̆,* sf. slice. [of cattle.
rebaño, *-bắn'yŏ,* sm. flock of sheep, herd
rebatir, *-bắtĭr',* v. a. to resist; to parry, to ward off; to refute; to repress.
rebato, *-bắ'tŏ,* sm. unexpected attack, surprise; alarm. [rebel; to resist.
rebelarse, *-bĕlắr'sĕ,* v. r. to revolt; to

rebelde, –bĕl'dĕ, sm. rebel; –, a.rebellious.

rebeldía, –dĕ'ă, sf. rebelliousness, contumaciousness, disobedience; (law) contumacy; en –, by default.

rebelion, rĕbĕlŏn', sf. rebellion, revolt.

rebenque, –bĕn'kĕ, sm. cat-o'-nine-tails.

rebollar, –bŏlyăr', sm. underwood.

rebollo, –bŏl'yŏ, sm. trunk of a tree.

rebolludo, da, –bŏlyṳ'dŏ, a. thick-set.

rebosadura, –bŏsădŏ'ră, sf. overflow.

rebosar, –bŏsăr', v. a. to run over, to overflow; to abound.

rebotar, –bŏtăr', v. a. to clinch the point of a spike or nail; to repel; –, v. n. to rebound.   [second mission.

rebote, rĕbŏ'tĕ, sm. rebound; de –, on a rebotica, –tĭkă, sf. back-room behind an apothecary's shop; cistern.

reboso, rĕbŏ'thŏ, sm. muffling of oneself up; (fig.) pretext; cloak.   [move.

rebullir, –bṳlyĭr', v. n. to stir, to begin to

reburujar, –bằrṳ'hăr', v. a. to wrap up, to pack up in bundles.

reburujón, –'hŏn', sm. bundle wrapped up carelessly and without order.

rebusca, rĕbṳs'kă sf. research; refuge, remains.   [researcher.

rebuscador, ora, –dŏr', sm. & f. gleaner;

rebuscar, rĕbṳskăr' v. a. to glean the remains of grapes left by the vintagers; to search, to inquire.

rebuznar, –bṳthnăr', v. n. to bray.

rebuzno, –bṳth'nŏ, sm. braying of an ass.

recabar, –kăbăr', v.a. to obtain by entreaty.

recado, –kă'dŏ, sm. message; gift; compliments sent to an absent person.

recaer, –kăĕr', v. n. to fall back.

recaída, –kă'ĕ'dă, sf. relapse.

recalcar, –kălkăr', v. n. to squeeze; to stuff; –se, to utter repeatedly; to lean back in a chair.

recalcitrar, –kălthĭtrăr', v. n. to kick; to wince; to be recalcitrant.

recalentamiento, –kălĕntămĭĕn'tŏ, sm. incandescence.

recalentar, –kălĕntăr', v. a. to heat again.

recalzar, –kălthăr', v. a. to pounce, to prick the outlines of a design on paper; to underwall.   [raised work.

recamar, –kămăr', v. a. to embroider with

recámara, rĕkă'mără, sf. wardrobe; chamber of a gun.

recantón, –kăntŏn', sm. corner-stone.

recapacitar, –kăpăthĭtăr', v. a. to call to recollection.   [capitulation.

recapitulación, –kăpĭtṳlăthŏn', sf. recapitular, –kăpĭtṳlăr', v. a. to recapitulate.

recargar, –kărgăr', v. a. to recharge; to charge again; to remand to prison on a new charge.

recargo, rĕkăr'gŏ, sm. new charge or accusation; increase of a fever.

recatado, da, –kătă'dŏ, a. prudent, circumspect, modest.

recatar, –kătăr', v. a. to conceal carefully; –se, to take care.

recato, rĕkă'tŏ, sm. prudence, circumspection; modesty; bashfulness.

recaudación, –kăṳdăthŏn', sf. recovery of debts; collector's office.

recaudador, rĕkăṳdădŏr', sm.tax-gatherer.

recaudar, –dăr', v. a. to gather; to obtain.   [a second time.

recavar, –kăvăr', v. a. to dig the ground

recelar, –thĕlăr', v. a. to fear, to suspect, to misdoubt.   [trust.

recelo, –thĕ'lŏ, sm. dread, suspicion, mis-

receloso, sa, –thĕlŏ'sŏ, a. mistrustful, shy.

recentadura, –thĕntădŏ'ră, sf. leaven preserved for the kneading and raising of bread.

recental, –thĕntăl', a. sucking (of lambs).

recepción, –thĕpthŏn', sf. reception; acceptation.   [refuge, asylum.

receptáculo, –thĕptă'kṳlŏ, sm. receptacle;

receptor, –thĕptŏr', sm. receiver, treasurer; investigating official.

receptoría, –tŏrĕ'ă, sf. receiver's or treasurer's office.   [account, list.

receta, –thĕ'tă, sf. recipe; prescription;

recetar, –thĕtăr', v. a. to prescribe medicines.

recetario, rĕthăă'rĭŏ, sm. register of the prescriptions made by a physician; apothecary's file.

recibidor, –thĭbĭdŏr', sm. receiver.

recibimiento, –mĭĕn'tŏ, sm. reception, receipt; antechamber.

recibir, –thĭbĭr', v. a. to accept, to receive; to let in; to go to meet; –se, to be admitted.

recibo, –thĕ'bŏ, sm. receipt, acquittance.

recién, –thĕn', ad. recently, lately.

reciente, –thĕn'tĕ, ad. recent, new, fresh; modern.

recinto, –thĭn'tŏ, sm. precinct; district.

recio, cia, rĕ'thĭŏ, a. stout, strong, robust; coarse, thick; rude; arduous, rigid; –, ad. strongly, stoutly; hablar –, to talk loud.

récipe, rĕ'thĭpĕ, sm. prescription of a physician; (fig. & fam.) displeasure, disgust.

recipiente, –thĭpĭĕn'tĕ, sm. (chem.) recipient.   [procity.

reciprocidad, –thĭprŏthĭdăd', sf. reci-

recíproco, ca, –thĕ'prŏkŏ, a. reciprocal, mutual.

recisión, –thĭsĭŏn', sf. abscission.

recitación, –thĭtăĭhŏn', sf. recitation.

recitar, –thĭtăr', v. a. to recite.

recitativo, va, –thĭtătĭ'vŏ, a. recitative.

reclamación, –klămăthŏn', sf. reclamation; remonstrance.

reclamar, –klămăr', v. a. to decoy birds with a call or whistle; to reclaim.

reclamo, –klă'mŏ, sm. decoy-bird; a bird trained to decoy others; call; an instrument for calling; allurement; reclamation; catch-word (in printing).

reclinación, –klĭnăthŏn', sf. reclining.

reclinar, –klĭnăr', v. a. & n. to recline, to lean back.

reclinatorio, –klĭnătŏ'rĭŏ, sm. couch.

recluir, –klṳĭr', v. a. to shut up.

reclusión, –klṳsŏn', sf. reclusion; reces

recluta, –klō´tā, sf. recruiting; –, sm. recruit.   [ficer.

reclutador, –klātādōr´, sm. recruiting-officer.

reclutar, –klūtār´, v. a. to recruit.

recobrar, –kōbrār´, v. a. to recover; –se, to recover from sickness; to recollect.

recobro, –kō´brō, sm. recovery.

recocer, –kōthēr´, v. a. to boil again; –se, to consume oneself with rage.

recocido, da, –kōthē´dō, a. skilful, clever.

recodar, –kōdār´, v. n. to lean th elbow upon anything   [out.

recodo, –kō´dō, sm. corner or angle jutting

recogedero, –kō´hā´dʼrō, sm. meeting-place, rendezvous; collecting instrument.

recogedor, –kō´hēdōr´, sm. harbourer, shelterer; gatherer; scraper (instrument).

recoger, –kō´hēr´, v. n. to retake, to take back; to gather; to shelter; to compile; to ask charity; –se, to take shelter or refuge; to retire to rest; to withdraw from the world.   [cluded; stout.

recogido, da, –kō´hē´dō, a. retired, secluded.

recogimiento, –´hīmiēn´tō, sm. collection, retreat, shelter; abstraction from all worldly concerns.   [recollection.

recolección, –kōlēkthiōn´, sf. summary.

recoleto, ta, –kōlē´tō, sm. & f. Recollet (friar).

recomendación, –kōmēndāthiōn´. sf. recommendation.   [to recommend.

recomendar, –kōmēndār´, v. a. to charge;

recompensa, –kōmpēn´sā, sf. compensation; recompense, reward.

recompensar, –kōmpēnsār´, v. a. to recompense, to reward.   [compose.

recomponer, –kōmpōnēr´, v. a. to re-

reconcentrar, –kōnthēntrār´, v. a. to concentre; to dissemble.   [conciliation.

reconciliación, –kōnthīliāthiōn´, sf. re-

reconciliar, –kōnthīliār´, v. a. to reconcile; –se, to make one's peace for slight offences.   [secret; concealed.

recóndito, ta, –kōn´dītō, a. recondite,

reconocedor, ra, –kōnōthēdōr´, sm. & f. examiner, reviser.

reconocer, –kōnōthēr´, v. a. to examine closely; to acknowledge favours received; to consider; (mil.) to reconnoitre; –se, to know oneself; to repent.   [ful.

reconocido, da, –kōnōthī´dō, a. grate-

reconocimiento, –thīmiēn´tō, sm. recognition; acknowledgment; gratitude; confession; submission; inquiry.

reconquista, –kōnkīs´tā, sf. reconquest.

reconquistar, –kōnkīstār´, v. a. to reconquer.   [cover from sickness.

reconvalecer, –kōnvālēthēr´, v. n. to re-

reconvención, –kōnvēnthiōn´, sf. recrimination.   [to recriminate.

reconvenir, –kōnvēnīr´, v. a. to retort,

recopilación, –kōpīlāthiōn´, sf. summary, abridgment.

recopilador, –kōpīlādōr´, sm. compiler.

recopilar, –kōpīlār´, v. a. to compile.

recordación, –kēkōrdāthiōn´, sf. remembrance, memory, memento.

recordar, –kōrdār´, v. a. to remind; – v. n. to awake from sleep; to call to mind.   [peruse; to mend, to repair.

recorrer, –kōrrēr´, v. a. to run over, to

recortar, –kōrtār´, v. a. to cut away, to pare off.

recorte, rēkōr´tē, sm. outline; shred.

recoser, –kōsēr´, v. a. to sew again.

recostar, –kōstār´, v. a. to lean against, to recline; –se, to go to rest.

recreación, –krēāthiōn´, sf. recreation, amusement.   [to recreate.

recrear, –krēār´, v. a. to amuse, to delight,

recreativo, va, –krēātē´vō, a. recreative, diverting.

recreo, rēkrē´ō, sm. rec eation.

recriminacion, –krimi āthiōn´, sf. recrimination.   [minate.

recriminar, –krīmīnār´, v. a. to recri-

rectángulo, la, rēktān´gūlō, a. rectangular; –, sm. rectangle.   [fication.

rectificación, –rēktīfīkāthiōn´, sf. recti-

rectificar, –fīkār´, v. a. to rectify.

rectilíneo, nea, rēktīlī´nēō, a. rectilinear.

rectitud, –tūd´, sf. straightness; rectitude; justness, honesty; exactitude.

recto, ta, rēk´tō, a. straight, right; just, honest.

rector, ra, rēktōr´, sm. & f. superior of a community or establishment; rector (of a university); curate, rector.

rectorado, –rā´dō, sm. rectorship.

rectoral, –rāl´, a. rectorial.

rectoría, –rē´ā, sf. rectory, curacy; rectorship.   [burden.

recua, rā´kā, sf. droye of beasts of

recudimiento, rēkūdīmiēn´tō, sm. power vested in a person to gather rents or taxes.

recuento, –kūēn´tō, sm. inventory.

recuerdo, –kūēr´dō, sm. remembrance, memory.   [descent

recuesto, –kūēs´tō, sm. declivity, gradual

reculada, –kūlā´dā, sf. falling astern of a ship; recoil.   [recoil.

recular, –kūlār´, v. n. to fall back, to

reculones, –kūlō´nēs, ā–, ad. backwards.

recuperable, –kūpērā´blē, a. recoverable.

recuperación, –rāthiōn´, sf. recovery.

recuperar, –pērār´, v. a. to recover; –se, to recover from sickness.

recurrir, –kūrrīr´, v. a. to recur.

recurso, –kūr´sō, sm. recourse.

recusación, –kūsāthiōn´, sf. refusal; recusation.   [to admit.

recusar, –kūsār´, v. a. to refuse; to refuse

rechazamiento, –tshāthāmiēn´tō, sm. repulsion.   [pulse; to contradict.

rechazar, –tshāthār´, v. a. to repel, to re-

rechazo, –tshā´thō, sm. rebound.

rechifla, –tshē´flā, sf. mockery, derision.

rechiflar, –tshīflār´, v. a. to mock, to laugh.

rechinamiento, –tshīnamiēn´tō, sm. creaking of a machine; gnashing of teeth.

rechinar, –tshīnār´, v. n. to gnash the teeth.

rechino, –tshē´nō, sm. creaking.

rechoncho, cha, –tshōn´tshō, a. chubby

red, rā´d, sf. net; grate through which fish

or bread are sold; snare, wile, fraud; silk coif. [office.

redacción, *redākthiŏn'*, sf. editing; editor's

redactar, *–dāktăr'*, v. a. to edit a news-

redactor, *–tŏr'*, sm. editor. [paper.

redaño, *–dăn'yŏ*, sm. caul, omentum.

redargüir, *–dargüĭr'*, v. a. to retort, to re-

redecilla, *–dĕthĭl'yă*, sf. hair-net. [ply.

rededor, *–dĕdŏr'*, sm. environs; **al –,** round about.

redención, *–dĕnthiŏn'*, sf. redemption; ransom; assistance, support.

redentor, ra, *–tŏr'*, sm. & f. redeemer.

redil, *rĕdĭl'*, sm. sheep-fold, sheep-cot.

redimible, *–dĭmĕ'blĕ*, a. redeemable.

redimir, *–dĭmĭr'*, v. a. to redeem, to ran-som; to succour.

redingote, *–dĭngŏ'tĕ*, sm. riding-coat.

rédito, *rĕ'dĭtŏ*, sm. revenue, rent. [rent.

redituar, *–dĭtŭăr'*, v. a. to yield profit; to

redoblado, da, *–dŏblā'dŏ*, a. redoubled; stout and thick. [rivet.

redoblar, *–dŏblăr'*, v. a. to redouble; to

redoble, *rĕdŏ'blĕ*, sm. doubling, repeti-tion; (mus.) octave; (mil.) roll of a drum.

redoma, *–dŏ'mă*, sf. phial.

redondear, *–dŏndĕăr'*, v. a. to round; **–se,** to extricate oneself from a difficulty.

redondel, *–dŏndĕl'*, sm. round cloak; circle. [lar form.

redondez, *–dŏndĕth'*, sf. roundness, circu-

redondilla, *–dŏndĭl'yă*, sf. roundel, roundelay.

redondo, da, *rĕdŏn'dŏ*, a. round.

redopelo, *–dŏpĕ'lŏ*, sm. scuffle, affray; **al –,** against all rule and reason; **traer á –,** to vex, to drag about contemptuously.

reducción, *–dŭkthiŏn'*, sf. reduction; mu-tation; dissolution, liquefaction; ex-change, change of money. [vertible.

reducible, *–dŭthĕ'blĕ*, a. reducible, con-

reducir, *–dŭthĭr'*, v. a. to reduce; to ex-change; to convert; **–se,** to cut down one's expenses, to economise.

reducto, *rĕdŭk'tŏ*, sm. (mil.) redoubt.

redundancia, *–dŭndăn'thiă*, sf. super-fluity, redundance, excess.

redundante, *–tĕ*, a. overflowing.

redundar, *–dŭndăr'*, v. n. to overflow, to be redundant; to contribute. [ing.

reedificación, *–ĕdĭfĭkāthiŏn'*, sf. rebuild-

reedificar, *–ĕdĭfĭkăr'*, v. a. to rebuild.

reeleccion, *–ĕlĕkthiŏn'*, sf. re-election.

reelegir, *–ĕlĕ'hĭr'*, v. a. to re-elect, to elect again. [money advanced; to reimburse.

reembolsar, *–ĕmbŏlsăr'*, v. a. to recover

reembolso, *–ĕmbŏl'sŏ*, sm. reimburse-ment; **contra –,** by reimbursement.

reemplazar, *–ĕmplăthăr'*, v. a. to replace, to restore. [substitute in the militia.

reemplazo, *–ĕmplă'thŏ*, sm. replacing; substitute in the militia.

reencuentro, *–ĕnkŭĕn'trŏ*, sm. rencounter.

reenganchar, *–ĕngăntshăr'*, v. a. (mil.) to re-enlist; **–se,** to enlist again.

reengendrar, *–ĕn'hĕndrăr'*, v. a. to re-generate, to reproduce. [freshment.

refacción, *–făkthiŏn'*, sf. refection, re-

refajo, *rĕfă'h'ŏ*, sm. short petticoat worn by mountaineers.

refectorio, *–fĕktŏ'riŏ*, sm. refectory.

referencia, *–fĕrĕn'thiă*, sf. reference.

referendario, *–fĕrĕndă'riŏ*, sm. junior barrister.

referir, *–fĕrĭr'*, v. a. to refer, to relate, to report; **–se,** to refer to, to relate to.

refinadera, *–fĭnădĕ'ră*, sf. refiner (a long cylindrical stone). [artful.

refinado, da, *–fĭnā'dŏ*, a. refined; subtle,

refinador, *–dŏr'*, sm. refiner.

refinadura, *dŏ'ră*, sf. refining.

refinar, *–fĭnăr'*, v. a. to refine.

refitolero, *–fĭtŏlĕ'rŏ*, a. surveyor of the refectory.

reflectar, *–flĕktăr'*, v. n. to reflect (light).

reflejar, *–flĕ'hăr'*, v. n. to reflect the rays

reflejo, *rĕflĕ'h'ŏ*, sm. reflection. [of light.

reflexión, *–flĕkthiŏn'*, sf. reflexion; medi-tation, reflection. [to meditate.

reflexionar, *–flĕkthiŏnăr'*, v. n. to reflect,

reflexivo, va, *–flĕkthĕ'vŏ*, a. reflexive; re-flective. [again.

reflorecer, *–flŏrĕthĕr'*, v. n. to blossom

refluir, *–flŭĭr'*, v. n. to flow back, to reflow. [flujo **y –,** the tides.

reflujo, *rĕflŭ'h'ŏ*, sm. reflux, ebb-tide;

refocilación, *–fŏthĭlāthiŏn'*, sf. restora-tion, refection. [to revive.

refocilar, *–fŏthĭlăr'*, v. a. to strengthen,

reforma, *rĕfŏr'mă*, sf. reform; correction; dismissal from office. [reform.

reformación, *–măthiŏn'*, sf. reformation.

reformado, *–mă'dŏ*, sm. reformed officer.

reformar, *–măr'*, v. a. to reform, to correct, to restore; **–se,** to mend, to have one's manners reformed *or* corrected; to be prudent and moderate in speech and conduct.

reforzada, *–fŏrthā'dă*, sf. narrow taper.

reforzado, da, *–dŏ*, a. extra thick and strong at the breech (of fire-arms).

reforzar, *–fŏrthăr'*, v. a. to strengthen, to fortify; **–se,** to be strengthened and recovered.

refracción, *–frăkthiŏn'*, sf. refraction.

refractario, ria, *–tă'riŏ*, a. refractory.

refrán, *rĕfrăn'*, sm. proverb.

refregar, *–frĕgăr'*, v. a. to rub one thing against another.

refregón, *–frĕgŏn'*, sm. friction, rubbing of one thing against another.

refrenamiento, *–frĕnămiĕn'tŏ*, sm. curb, refraining.

refrenar, *–frĕnăr'*, v. a. to refrain.

refrendación, *–frĕndāthiŏn'*, sf. counter-signing.

refrendar, *–frĕndăr'*, v. a. to countersign.

refrendario, *–frĕndă'riŏ*, sm. officer ap-pointed to countersign edicts, ordinances, or other public acts. [ture.

refrendata, *–frĕndă'tă*, sf. counter-signa-

refrescar, *–frĕskăr'*, v. a. to refresh; **–,** v. n. to cool; to take the air.

refresco, *rĕfrĕs'kŏ*, sm. refreshment.

refriega, *–frĭĕ'gă*, sf. affray, skirmish, encounter, fray.

refrigerar, *-frĭ'hĕrăr'*, v. a. to cool, to refresh, to comfort, to refrigerate.

refrigerio, *-'hĕ'rĭŏ*, sm. refrigeration, refreshment; consolation, comfort.

refuerzo, *-fŭĕr'thŏ*, sm. reinforcement.

refugiar, *-fŭ'hĭăr'*, v. a. to shelter; -se, to take refuge.

refugio, *refŭ'hĭŏ*, sm. refuge, asylum.

refulgente, *-fŭl'hĕn'tĕ*, a. refulgent.

refundición, *-fŭndĭthĭŏn'*, sf. act of casting metals anew.

refundir, *-fŭndĭr'*, v. a. to melt metal again; -, v. n. to convert to.

refunfuñadura, *-fŭnfŭnyădōō'ră*, sf. growling, grumbling. [to grumble.

refunfuñar, *-yăr'*, v. n. to snarl, to growl, to grumble.

refutación, *-fŭtăhĭŏn'*, sf. refutation.

refutar, *-fŭtăr'*, v. a. to refute.

regadera, *-gădā'ră*, sf. watering-pot.

regadio, dia, *regă'dĭŏ*, a. irrigated, watered.

regadizo, za, *-dē'thŏ*, a. that can be irrigated or watered.

regadura, *-dōō'ră*, sf. irrigation, watering.

regalado, da, *-lă'dŏ*, a. convenient, pleasant, delicate, dainty.

regalar, *-lăr'*, v. a. to regale; to refresh; to caress; -se, to feast; to regale oneself.

regalía, *-lĕ'ă*, s. sf. regalia; privilege.

regaliza, *-lē'thă*, sf. licorice.

regalo, *regă'lŏ*, sm. present, gift, largess; regalement.

regalón, ona, *-lŏn'*, a. delicate; pampered.

regañar, *-gănyăr'*, v. n. to growl, to grumble; to quarrel.

regaño, *regăn'yŏ*, sm. sourness of countenance; sternness of look.

regañón, ona, *-yŏn'*, a. snarling, growling, grumbling; troublesome.

regar, *regăr'*, v. a. to water, to irrigate.

regata, *regă'tă*, sf. irrigating-ditch; regatta.

regatear, *-gătĕăr'*, v. n. to use evasions; -, v. a. to haggle, to higgle.

regateo, *-gătĕ'ŏ*, sm. act of haggling or bartering. [ona, a. retailing.

regatón, *-gătŏn'*, sm. socket, ferrule; -,

regazo, *-gă'thŏ*, sm. lap of a woman.

regencia, *rĕ'hĕn'thĭă*, sf. regency; regentship. [generation.

regeneración, *rĕ'hĕnĕrăhĭŏn'*, sf. regenerar, *-'hĕnĕrăr'*, v. a. to regenerate.

regenta, *rĕ'hĕn'tă*, sf. wife of a regent.

regentar, *-tăr'*, v. a. to rule; to govern.

regente, *rĕ'hĕn'tĕ*, sm. regent; manager (in printing-offices).

regiamente, *rĕ'hĭămĕn'tĕ*, ad. royally.

regidor, *rĕ'hĭdŏr'*, sm. alderman; governor, prefect. [ment; (gr) rules of verbs.

régimen, *rā'hĭmĕn*, sm. regimen, management.

regimiento, *-mĭĕn'tŏ*, sm administration, government; regimen, diet; magistracy of a city; municipality; (mil.) regiment.

regio, gia, *rā'hĭŏ*, a. royal, kingly.

región, *rĕ'hĭŏn'*, sf. region, tract of country.

regir, *rĕ'hĭr'*, v. a. to rule, to govern, to direct. [controller.

registrador, *rĕ'hĭstrădŏr'*, sm. registrar.

registrar, *-trăr'*, v. a. to survey, to inspect; to examine; to record, to enter in a register; -se, to be registered.

registro, *rĕ'hĭs'trŏ*, sm. examining; enrolling office; register.

regla, *rā'glă*, sf. rule, ruler. [perate.

reglado, da, *reglă'dŏ*, a. regulated, temperate.

reglamento, *-mĕn'tŏ*, sm. regulation; by-law. [to regulate; -se, to reform.

reglar, *reglăr'*, a. regular; -, v. a. to rule;

reglón, *reglŏn'*, sm. level (used by masons).

regocijar, *regŏthĭhăr'*, v. a. to rejoice.

regocijo, *-thĭ'h'ŏ*, sm. joy, pleasure, merriment, rejoicing.

regodearse, *-dĕăr'sĕ*, v. r. to be merry, to be delighted; to dally, to trifle, to play the fool; to joke, to jest. [sion.

regodeo, *-dĕ'ŏ*, sm. joy, merriment, diversion.

regojo, *regŏ'h'ŏ*, sm. crumb or piece of bread left on the table after meals.

regoldar, *-gŏldăr'*, v. n. to belch.

regolfar, *-gŏlfăr'*, v. n. to flow back.

regona, *regŏ'nă*, sf. irrigation-works, pl.

regordete, *-gŏrdā'tĕ*, a. chubby, plump.

regresar, *-grĕsăr'*, v. n. to return to a place, to regress.

regreso, *regrĕs'ŏ*, sm. return, regression.

regüeldo, *-gŭĕl'dŏ*, sm. eructation, belch.

reguera, *-gā'ră*, sf. canal for watering lands or plants.

reguero, *-gā'rŏ*, sm. small rivulet; trickling line of spilt liquid; drain, gutter.

regulación, *-gŭlăthĭŏn'*, sf. regulation; comparison, computation.

regulador, ra, *-dŏr'*, sm. & f. regulator.

regular, *-lăr'*, v. a. to regulate, to adjust; -, a. regular; ordinary.

regularidad, *-lărĭdăd'*, sf. regularity.

rehabilitación, *-ăbĭlĭtăthĭŏn'*, sf. rehabilitation.

rehabilitar, *-tăr'*, v. a. to rehabilitate.

rehacer, *-ăthĕr'*, v. a. to repair, to make again; -se, to regain strength and vigour; (mil.) to rally. [broad-shouldered.

rehecho, cha, *rĕĕth'ŏ*, a. remade; squat,

rehén, *rĕĕn'*, sm. hostage.

rehilete, *-ĭlā'tĕ*, sm. shuttle-cock bearded with feathers.

rehogar, *-ŏgăr'*, v. a. to roast.

rehusar, *-ŭsăr'*, v. a. to refuse, to decline.

reimpresión, *-ĭmprĕsĭŏn'*, sf.reimpression.

reimprimir, *-ĭmprĭmĭr'*, v.a. to reimprint.

reina, *rĕĕ'nă*, sf. queen.

reinado, *rĕĭnă'dŏ*, sm. reign.

reinar, *rĕĭnăr'*, v. a. to reign, to govern.

reincidencia, *-ĭnthĭdĕn'thĭă*, sf. reiteration, relapse. [back.

reincidir, *-dĭr'*, v. n. to relapse, to fall

reino, *rĕĕ'nŏ*, sm. kingdom, reign.

reintegración, *-ĭntĕgrăthĭŏn'*, sf. reintegration, restoration.

reintegrar, *-tĕgrăr'*, v. a. to reintegrate, to restore; -se, to be reinstated or restored.

reintegro, *-tĕ'grŏ*, sm. reintegration.

reir, *rĕĕr'*, v. n. to laugh. [reiteration.

reiteración, *-lĕĕrăthĭŏn'*, sf. repetition,

reiterar, –tĕrār', v. a. to reiterate, to repeat. [ing.

reja, rĕh'ä, sf. plough-share; lattice, grat-

rejalgar, –'hälgär', sm. (chem.) realgar.

rejilla, –'hïl'yä, sf. small lattice in confessionals. [sting of an insect.

rejo, rĕh'ŏ, sm. pointed iron bar or spike;

rejón, rĕhŏn', sm. dagger, poniard; spear used by bull-fighters; short broad knife with a sharp point.

rejonazo, –nä'thŏ, sm. dagger-thrust.

rejonear, –'hŏnār', v. a. to spear bulls.

rejuela, –'hüä'lä, sf. foot-stove, warming-pan. [young again, to be rejuvenated.

rejuvenecer, –'hüvĕnĕthār', v. n. to grow

relación, –läthïŏn', sf. relation; report; account; romance; distant relation.

relacionar, –när', v. a. to relate.

relajación, –lä'häthïŏn', sf. relaxation; remission; laxity; commutation of a vow; delivery of an offender by the ecclesiastical judge to a criminal court of justice, in cases of murder; hernia.

relajar, –lä'här', v. a. to relax, to slacken; –se, to be relaxed; to labour under a hernia.

relamer, –lämār', v. a. to lick again; –se, to lick one's lips; to relish; to paint oneself to excess. [nice in dress.

relamido, da, –lämē'dŏ, a. affected, over-

relámpago, rĕläm'pägŏ, sm. flash of lightning. [flash.

relampaguear, –gār', v. n. to lighten, to

relapso, sa, rĕläp'sŏ, a. relapsed.

relatar, –lätār', v. a. to relate.

relativo, va, –lätē'vŏ, a. relative.

relato, rĕlä'tŏ, sm. recital.

relator, –lätŏr', sm. relater, narrator; (law) reporter.

relatoria, –tŏrē'ä, sf. office of a reporter of judicial causes in a court of justice.

releer, rĕlĕēr', v. a. to read again.

relegación, –lĕgäthïŏn', sf. relegation, exile. [to exile.

relegar, –gär', v. a. to relegate, to banish;

relente, rĕlĕn'tĕ, sm. evening-dew.

relentecer, –tĕthār', v. n. to be damp with dew.

relevación, –lĕväthïŏn', sf. relevation; alleviation, relief; remission, pardon.

relevante, –vän'tĕ, a. excellent, great, eminent.

relevar, –vār', v. a. to emboss, to work in relief; to exonerate, to disburden; to relieve from a burden or charge; to assist, to succour; to forgive, to pardon; to exalt, to aggrandize; (pict.) to paint an object to appear as if rising; to relieve (of soldiers.

relevo, rĕlĕ'vŏ, sm. (mil.) relief.

relicario, –lïkä'rïŏ, sm. reliquary.

relieve, rĕlïĕ'vĕ, sm. relievo.

religión, rĕlïhïŏn', sf. religion.

religionario, –nä'rïŏ, sm. & f. religionist; Reformist, Calvinist.

religiosidad, –sïdäd', sf. religiousness.

religioso, sa, –hïŏ'sŏ, a. religious, pious.

relinchar, –lïntchär', v. n. to neigh.

relincho, rĕlïn'tchŏ, sm. neigh, neighing.

reliquia, rĕlï'kïä, sf. residue, remains; saintly relic.

reloj, rĕlŏh', sm. clock, watch.

relojería, –lŏ'hĕrē'ä, sf. watch-making.

relojero, –'hĕ'rŏ, sm. watch-maker.

relucir, –lüthïr', v. n. to shine, to glitter; to excel, to be brilliant. [shine.

relumbrar, –lümbrär', v. n. to sparkle, to

relumbrón, –brŏn', sm. lustre.

rellenar, –lyĕnär', v. a. to fill again.

relleno, –lyĕ'nŏ, sm. forced meat; –, na, a. satiated.

remachar, –mätchär', v. a. to rivet.

remansarse, –mänsär'sĕ, v. r. to obstruct the course of a stream.

remanso, rĕmän'sŏ, sm. stagnant water;

remar, rĕmär', v. n. to row. [tardiness.

rematadamente, –mätädämĕn'tĕ, ad. entirely, totally. [terly ruined.

rematado, da, –tä'dŏ, a. totally lost, ut-

rematar, –mätär', v. a. to terminate, to finish; to adjudge to the best bidder; –, v. n. to be at an end; –se, to be utterly ruined. [or best bid.

remate, rĕmä'tĕ, sm. end, conclusion; last

remedar, –mĕdär', v. a. to copy, to imitate, to mimic.

remediable, –dïä'blĕ, a. remediable.

remediador, ra, –dïädŏr', sm. & f. helper; curer.

remediar, –dïär', v. a. to remedy; to assist, to help; to free from danger.

remedio, rĕmĕ'dïŏ, sm. remedy, reparation; help; amendment, correction; resource; refuge.

remedo, rĕmĕ'dŏ, sm. imitation, copy.

remendar, rĕmĕn'där', v. a. to patch, to mend; to correct.

remendón, –dŏn', sm. botcher, cobbler.

remero, rĕmĕ'rŏ, sm. rower, oarsman.

remesa, rĕmĕ'sä, sf. sending of goods; remittance of money.

remiendo, rĕmïĕn'dŏ, sm. patch, clout.

remilgarse, rĕmïlgär'sĕ, v. r. to be affectedly nice or grave. [gravity.

remilgo, rĕmïl'gŏ, sm. affected nicety or

reminiscencia, rĕmïnïsthĕn'thïä, sf. reminiscence, recollection. [tious.

remirado, da, rĕmïrä'dŏ, a. prudent, cau-

remirar, rĕmïrär', v. a. to revise, to review; –se, to do very carefully; to consider.

remisible, rĕmïsē'blĕ, a. remissible.

remisión, –sïŏn', sf. act of sending back; remission, forgiveness. [indolent.

remiso, sa, rĕmï'sŏ, a. remiss, careless,

remitir, –mïtïr', v. a. to remit, to transmit; to pardon a fault; to suspend, to put off; –, v. n., –se, to slacken.

remo, rĕ'mŏ, sm. oar; long and hard labour; –s, pl. limbs (of a person); legs (of an animal). [motion.

remoción, rĕmŏthïŏn', sf. removal, re-

remojadero, –'hädĕ'rŏ, sm. steeping-tub.

remojar, –'här', v. a. to steep; – la palabra, to go and drink liquor.

remojo, rĕmŏ'h'ŏ, sm. steeping, soaking.

remolacha, –mŏlätch'ä, sf. beet-root.

remolcar, —mõlkãr', v. a. (mar.) to tow.
remolinar, —mõlĩnãr', v. n. to spin round;
—se, to collect together tumultuously (of
a crowd). [pool.
remolino, —lẽ'nõ, sm. whirlwind; whirl-
remolón, ona, —lõn', a. soft, lazy; —, sm.
upper tusk of a wild boar.
remolonearse, —lõnẽãr'sõ, v. r. to refuse,
to tarry, to delay.
remolque, rẽmõl'kẽ, sm. towing a ship.
remonta, rẽmõn'tã, sf. (mil.) remount,
supply of cavalry-horses.
remontar, —tãr', v. a. to frighten away;
to remount cavalry; to repair saddles;
—se, to tower, to soar.
remontista, —tĩs'tã, sm. commissioner
for the purchase of cavalry-horses.
remordedor, ra, —mõrdẽdõr', a. causing
regret, disquieting, discomposing.
remorder, —dẽr', v. a. to cause remorse;
—se, to manifest or express concern.
remordimiento, —dĩmẽn'tõ, sm. remorse.
remoto, ta, rẽmõ'tõ, a. remote, distant, far.
remover, —mõvẽr', v. a. to remove; to
excite an animal; to dismiss.
removimiento, —vĩmẽn'tõ, sm. removal;
restlessness.
remozar, —mõthãr', v. a. to rejuvenate.
rempujar, rẽmpũhãr', v. a. to push or
shove a person out of his place. [thrust.
rempujón, —hõn', sm. impulse, push,
remuneración, rẽmũnẽrãthẽõn', sf. remuneration, recompense. [munerator.
remunerador, ra, —dõr', sm. & f. re-
remunerar, —rãr', v. a. to reward, to
remunerate. [to be new-born.
renacer, —nãthẽr', v. n. to be born again;
renacimiento, —thĩmẽn'tõ, sm. regeneration; new birth.
renacuajo, —kũãh'õ, sm. hop o' my
rencilla, rẽnthĩl'yã, sf. slight grudge re-
maining after a quarrel. [quarrelsome.
rencilloso, sa, —yõ'sõ, a. peevish,
rencor, rẽnkõr', sm. rancour, grudge.
rencoroso, sa, —rõ'sõ, a. rancorous.
rendición, rẽndĩthẽõn', sf. rendition; profit.
rendidamente, —dĩdãmẽn'tẽ, ad. humbly.
rendija, rẽndĩh'ã, sf. crevice, crack, cleft.
rendimiento, —dĩmẽn'tõ, sm. rendition;
weariness, submission; humbling compliance; rent, income.
rendir, rẽndĩr', v. a. to subject, to subdue;
to surrender; —se, to be tired out.
renegado, rẽnẽgã'dõ, sm. apostate; wicked
person.
renegar, —gãr', v. a. to deny, to disown;
to detest, to abhor; —, v. n. to apostatize;
to blaspheme, to curse.
renglón, rẽnglõn', sm. written or printed
line; part of one's income; —ones, pl.
writings. [or blasphemy.
reniego, rẽnĩẽ'gõ, sm. kind of execution
renitencia, —tẽn'thĩã, sf. resistance, opposition, stubbornness.
renitente, —tẽn'tẽ, a. refractory, repugnant.
renombrado, da, —nõmbrã'dõ, a. renowned.
renombre, rẽnõm'brẽ, sm. surname.

renovación, —nõvãthẽõn', sf. renovation,
renewal. [to reform.
renovar, —nõvãr', v. a. to renew, to renovate,
renquear, rẽnkẽãr', v. n. to limp, to halt.
renta, rẽn'tã, sf. rent, income.
rentero, rẽntẽ'rõ, sm. renter, farmer.
rentilla, rẽntĩl'yã, sf. game at cards.
renuevo, rẽnũẽ'võ, sm. sprout, shoot.
renuncia, —nũn'thĩã, sf. renunciation,
resignation. [be renounced.
renunciable, —thĩã'blẽ, a. that which can
renunciar, —thĩãr', v. a. to renounce, to
resign. [whom anything is resigned.
renunciatario, —thĩã'rĩõ, sm. he to
renuncio, rẽnũn'thĩõ, sm. renounce (at
cards). [at odds.
reñido, da, rẽnyĩ'dõ, a. at variance,
reñir, rẽnyĩr', v. a. & n. to wrangle, to
quarrel; to scold, to chide.
reo, rẽ'õ, sm. offender, criminal.
reojo, rẽõ'hõ, sm. mirar de —, to look
at furtively.
repanchigarse, —pãnthĩgãr'sẽ, repan-
tigarse, —pãntĩgãr'sẽ, v. r. to stretch
oneself out in a chair. [diable.
reparable, —pãrã'blẽ, a. reparable, reme-
reparación, —pãrãthẽõn', sf. reparation,
repair. [a horse.
reparada, —pãrã'dã, sf. sudden bound of
reparar, —pãrãr', v. a. to repair; to consider, to observe; to give heed; —, v. n.
to parry; to pass (at cards).
reparativo, va, —tẽ'võ, a. reparative.
reparo, rẽpã'rõ, sm. repair, reparation;
notice; consideration; difficulty; cataplasm.
reparón, ona, —põn', a. too cautious.
repartición, —pãrtĩthẽõn', sf. distribution.
repartidor, —dõr', sm. & f. distributer;
assessor of taxes.
repartimiento, —mẽn'tõ, sm. distribution;
assessment of taxes.
repartir, —pãrtĩr', v. a. to distribute.
repasadora, —pãsãdõ'rã, sf. wool-comber.
repasar, —pãsãr', v. n. to repass; to revise.
repasata, —pãsã'tã, sf. reprehension, cen-
repaso, rẽpã'sõ, sm. revision. [sure.
repechar, —pẽtshãr', v. a. & n. to ascend
a declivity.
repecho, rẽpẽtsh'õ, sm. declivity, slope.
repeladura, —pẽlãdõ'rã, sf. second
shearing. [one's hair.
repelar, —pẽlãr', v. a. to tear out some-
repeler, —pẽlẽr', v. a. to repel; to refute,
to reject.
repelón, —lõn', sm. tearing of hair; á
—ones, by degrees, little by little; de —,
by the way; in haste.
repente, —pẽn'tẽ, de —, ad. suddenly, on
a sudden; off-hand.
repentino, na, —tẽ'nõ, a. sudden, unforeseen. [tempore verses.
repentista, —tĩs'tã, sm. maker of ex-
repentón, —tõn', sm. unexpected event
or incident. [tion.
repercusión, —pẽrkũsẽõn', sf. reverbera-
repercutir, —kũtĩr', v. n. to reverberate.
repertorio, —tõ'rĩõ, sm. repertory, index.

repetición, *–pĕtĭthĭŏn',* sf. repetition; (unus.) repeat.

repetidor, ra, *–dŏr',* sm. & f. repeater.

repetir, *–pĕtīr',* v. a. to repeat.

repicar, *–pĭkăr',* v. a. to chime, to ring a merry peal; to count ninety before the other player counts one (at piquet); —se, to pique oneself on.

repique, *rĕpī'kĕ,* sm. chime; counting of ninety before the other player has counted one (at piquet).

repiquetear, *–tĕăr',* v. a. to ring a merry peal on festive occasions; —se, to bicker, to wrangle.

repisa, *rĕpī'să,* sf. pedestal or stand.

replegar, *rĕplĕ'găr,* v. a. to redouble; (mil.) to wheel round the wing of an army; —se, (mil.) to fall back.

repleto, ta, *–plĕ'tŏ,* a. replete, very full.

réplica, *rĕ'plĭkă,* sf. reply, answer; repartee.

replicar, *rĕplĭkăr',* v. n. to reply. [arguer.

replicón, ona, *–kŏn',* sm. & f. constant

repollo, *rĕpŏl'yŏ,* sm. white cabbage; head of lettuce; cabbage-head.

repolludo, da, *–yŏ̆'dŏ,* a. cabbage-headed; round-headed.

reponer, *–pŏnĕr',* v. a. to replace; to re-store a suit at law to its primitive state; —se, to recover lost health or property.

reportado, da, *–pŏrtă'dŏ,* a. moderate, temperate.

reportar, *–tăr',* v. a. to refrain; to obtain, to reach; to attain, to carry, to bring.

reportorio, *–tŏ'rĭŏ,* sm. repertory; al-manac. [settled (wine).

reposado, da, *–pŏsă'dŏ,* a. quiet, peaceful.

reposar, *–pŏsăr',* v. n. to rest, to repose.

reposición, *–pŏsĭthĭŏn',* sf. restoring of a suit at law to its primitive state.

reposo, *rĕpŏ'sŏ,* sm. rest, repose.

repostería, *–pŏstĕrē'ă,* sf. repository in the royal palaces of Spain.

repostero, *–tĕ'rŏ,* sm. principal officer of the repostería. [to blame.

reprender, *–prĕndĕr',* v. a. to reprehend.

reprensible, *–sĕ'blĕ,* a. reprehensible.

reprensión, *–sĭŏn',* sf. reprehension, blame, blemish, reproach.

represa, *rĕprē'să,* sf. stoppage, retention.

represalia, *–să'lĭă,* sf. reprisal, reprise.

represar, *–săr',* v. a. to stop, to retain, to repress. [able.

representable, *–sĕntă'blĕ,* a. represent-

representación, *–tăthĭŏn',* sf. representation; authority.

representante, *–tăn'tĕ,* sm. & f. repre-sentative, player, understudy (stage).

representar, *–tăr',* v. a. to represent; to play on the stage. [sentative.

representativo, va, *–tătĕ'vŏ,* a. repre-

represión, *–prĕsĭŏn',* sf. repression.

reprimenda, *–prĭmĕn'dă,* sf. reprimand.

reprimir, *–prĭmīr',* v. a. to repress, to re-frain, to contain.

reprobable, *–prŏbă'blĕ,* a. reprehensible.

reprobación, *–thĭŏn',* sf. reprobation, reproof. [demn, to upbraid.

reprobar, *–băr',* v. a. to reject, to con-

réprobo, ba, *rĕ'prŏbŏ,* a. reprobate.

reprochar, *rĕprŏtshăr',* v. a. to reproach.

reproducción, *–prŏdŭkthĭŏn',* sf. repro-duction.

reproducir, *–thīr',* v. a. to reproduce.

reptil, *rĕptĭl',* sm. reptile.

república, *rĕpŭ'blĭkă,* sf. republic.

republicano, na, *–kă'nŏ,* a. & sm. & f. republican.

repudiar, *–pŭdĭăr',* v. a. to repudiate.

repudio, *rĕpŭ'dĭŏ,* sm. repudiation.

repuesto, *–pŭĕs'tŏ,* sm. store laid up against the future. [repugnance.

repugnancia, *–pŭgnăn'thĭă,* sf. reluctance,

repugnante, *–tĕ,* a. repugnant.

repugnar, *–pŭgnăr',* v. a. to oppose, to act with reluctance. [cast a seam.

repulgar, *–pŭlgăr',* v. a. to hem; to over-

repulgo, *rĕpŭl'gŏ,* sm. hem.

repulsa, *rĕpŭl'să,* sf. refusal. [to refuse.

repulsar, *–săr',* v. a. to reject, to decline,

repulsión, *–sĭŏn',* sf. repulsion.

reputación, *–pŭtăthĭŏn',* sf. reputation, renown.

reputar, *–tăr',* v. a. to repute, to estimate.

requebrar, *–kĕbrăr',* v. a. to break to pieces; to woo, to court.

requerimiento, *–kĕrĭmĭĕn'tŏ,* sm. request, requisition; intimation.

requerir, *–kĕrīr',* v. a. to intimate, to notify; to request, to require, to need.

requesón, *–kĕsŏn',* sm. cheese-curds.

requiebro, *–kĭĕ'brŏ,* sm. endearing ex-pression; trill, quaver. [clarinet.

requinto, *rĕkĭn'tŏ,* sm. tithe of a tithe;

requisa, *rĕkĭ'să,* sf. night and morning visit of a gaoler to his prisoners.

requisito, *–kĭsī'tŏ,* sm. requisite.

requisitorio, ria, *–tŏ'rĭŏ,* a. examinatory, requisitory; —, sm. (law) request, petition.

res, res, sf. head of cattle.

resabiar, *rĕsăbĭăr',* v. a. to contract evil habits; —se, to become vicious; to grumble.

resabio, *–să'bĭŏ,* sm. unpleasant taste left on the palate; vicious habit, bad custom.

resaca, *–să'kă,* sf. surge, surf.

resalado, da, *–să'lă'dŏ,* a. very graceful.

resaltar, *–săltăr',* v. n. to rebound; to jut out; to be evident.

resarcimiento, *–sărthĭmĭĕn'tŏ,* sm. com-pensation, reparation.

resarcir, *–sărthīr',* v. a. to compensate, to make amends. [place or road.

resbaladero, *rĕsbălădă'rŏ,* sm. slippery

resbaladizo, za, *–dē'thŏ,* sm. & f. slip-pery, glib. [backsliding.

resbaladura, *–dŏ'ră,* sf. slippery track;

resbalar, *–bălăr',* v. n. & r. to slip, to slide.

resbalón, *–bălŏn',* sm. slip, sliding.

rescatar, *–kătăr',* v. a. to ransom, to rescate, *rĕskă'tĕ,* sm. ransom. [redeem.

rescindir, *–thĭndīr',* v. a. to rescind, to annul. [tion.

rescisión, *–thĭsĭŏn',* sf. rescission, revoca-

rescoldo, *–kŏl'dŏ,* sm. embers, cinders.

rescripto, *–skrĭp'tŏ,* sm. rescript.

resecar, *–sĕkăr',* v. a. to dry again.

resellar, —sĕlyăr′, v. a. to coin again.
resello, —sĕl′yŏ, sm. recoinage.
resentimiento, —sĕntĭmĭĕn′tŏ, sm. resentment. [way; to resent.
resentirse, —tĕr′sĕ, v. r. to begin to give
reseña, —sĕn′yă, sf. review; muster; signal.
reseñar, —yăr′, v. a. to describe from appearance.
reserva, —sĕr′vă, sf. reserve; reservation.
reservado, da, —vă′dŏ, a. reserved, cautious, circumspect.
reservar, —văr′, v. a. to reserve; —se, to preserve oneself; to act with circumspection.
resfriado, —frĭă′dŏ, sm. cold, rheum.
resfriar, —frĭăr′, v. n. to begin to be cold; —se, to catch cold.
resguardar, —gŭărdăr′, v. a. to preserve, to defend; —se, to be on one's guard.
resguardo, —gŭăr′dŏ, sm. guard, security, safety; body of custom-house officers.
residencia, —sĭdĕn′thĭă, sf. residence.
residenciar, —thĭăr′, v. a. to call a public officer to account for his administration.
residente, —dĕn′tĕ, p. & a. residing; —, sm. resident [to assist personally.
residir, —sĭdĭr′, v. n. to reside, to dwell;
residuo, —sĕ′dŭŏ, sm. residue, remainder.
resignación, —sĭgnăthĭŏn′, sf. resignation.
resignadamente, —dămĕn′tĕ, ad. resignedly.
resignar, —năr′, v. a. —se, to resign.
resina, —sĕ′nă, sf. resin; rosin.
resinoso, sa, —sĭnŏ′sŏ, a. resinous.
resisa, —sĕ′să, sf. extra collection of taxes.
resisar, —sĭsăr′, v. r. to diminish any measures or things which have already been taxed. [opposition.
resistencia, —sĭstĕn′thĭă, sf. resistance.
resistero, —sĭstĕ′rŏ, sm. heat produced by the reflexion of the sun's rays.
resistir, —sĭstĭr′, v. n. & a. to resist, to oppose; to gainsay.
resma, rĕs′mă, sf. ream (of paper).
resollar, —sŏlyăr′, v. n. to respire; to talk; to take breath.
resolución, —sŏlŭthĭŏn′, sf. resolution, boldness; decision; activity.
resolutivo, va, —tĭ′vŏ, a. (med.) resolutive; analytical.
resolver, —vĕr′, v. a. to resolve, to decide; to analyze; —se, to resolve, to determine.
resonar, —sŏnăr′, v. n. to resound.
resoplar, —sŏplăr′, v. n. to snore; to snort; to huff. [breathing.
resoplido, —sŏplĕ′dŏ, sm. continued audible
rescate, —sĕr′tĕ, sm. spring (elastic body).
respaldar, —spăldăr′, v. a. to endorse; —se, to recline against a chair or bench; —, sm. back (of seats).
respaldo, —spăl′dŏ, sm. back; endorsement; back of a seat.
respectivo, va, —spĕktĕ′vŏ, a. respective.
respecto, —spĕk′tŏ, sm. relation, respect; á —, al —, relatively, respectively.
respetable, —spĕtă′blĕ, a. respectable.

respetar, —spĕtăr′, v. a. to respect; to revere. [sideration; homage.
respeto, —spĕ′tŏ, sm. respect, regard, consideration; homage.
respetoso, sa, —tŏ′sŏ, a. respectable; respectful.
respetuoso, sa, —tŭŏ′sŏ, a. respectful.
réspice, rĕs′pĭthĕ, sm. short reply.
respigar, —spĭgăr′, v. a. to glean.
respigón, —spĭgŏn′, sm. hag-nail; sty on the eyelid. [wince.
respingar, —spĭngăr′, v. n. to kick, to wince.
respingo, —spĭn′gŏ, sm. kick, yerk.
respiración, —spĭrăthĭŏn′, sf. respiration, breathing. [hole; rest, repose.
respiradero, —dĕ′rŏ, sm. vent, breathing-hole.
respirar, —răr′, v. n. to respire, to breathe.
resplandecer, —splăndĕthĕr′, v. n. to emit rays of light; to glisten. [splendent.
resplandeciente, —thĭĕn′tĕ, p. & a. resplendent.
resplandor, —dŏr′, sm. splendour, brilliancy.
responder, —spŏndĕr′, v. a. & n. to answer; to re-echo; to correspond; to be responsible for. [reply.
respondón, ona, —dŏn′, a. ever ready to reply.
responsable, —să′blĕ, a. responsible, accountable, answerable. [sibility.
responsabilidad, —bĭlĭdăd′, sf. responsibility.
responso, —spŏn′sŏ, sm. response for the dead.
responsorio, —sŏr′ĭŏ, sm. response.
respuesta, —pŭĕs′tă, sf. answer, reply.
resquicio, —kĕ′thĭŏ, sm. aperture between the jamb and leaf of a door; crack, cleft; subterfuge, evasion.
resta, rĕs′tă, sf. rest, residue, remainder.
restablecer, —stăblĕthĕr′, v. a. to re-establish; —se, to recover from a disease, &c.
restablecimiento, —thĭmĭĕn′tŏ, sm. reestablishment.
restallar, —stălyăr′, v. n. to smack, to click.
restañar, —stănyăr′, v. a. to stanch, to stop blood.
restar, rĕstăr′, v. a. to subtract; —, v. n. to be left, to rest. [tion.
restauración, —stăŭrăthĭŏn′, sf. restoration.
restaurar, —stăŭrăr′, v. a. to restore.
restitución, —stĭtŭthĭŏn′, sf. restitution.
restituir, —tŭĭr′, v. a. to restore; —se, to return.
resto, rĕs′tŏ, sm. remainder, rest. [return.
restricción, —strĭkthĭŏn′, sf. restriction, limitation.
restringir, —strĭn′hĭr′, v. a. to restrain, to restrict, to limit. [tion.
restriñimiento, —yĭmĭĕn′tŏ, sm. restriction.
restriñir, —yĭr′, v. a. to make costive; to restrain. [to revive; to renew.
resucitar, —sŭthĭtăr′, v. a. to resuscitate,
resudar, —sŭdăr′, v. n. to perspire, to transpire. [shortness of breath.
resuello, —sŭĕl′yŏ, sm. breath, breathing;
resuelto, ta, —sŭĕl′tŏ, a. resolute, determined, prompt. [sequence.
resultado, —sŭltă′dŏ, sm. result, consequence.
resultar, —sŭltăr′, v. n. to result.
resumen, rĕsŏ′mĕn, sm. summary, recapitulation. [marily.
resumidamente, —sŭmĭdămĕn′tĕ, ad. summarily.

resumir, *-mîr'*, v. a. to abridge; to re-
　sume. 　　　　　　　[tion, revival.
resurrección, *-sûrrékthîōn'*, sf. resurrec-
retablo, *-tǎ'blô*, sm. picture drawn on a
　board; splendid altars-ornament.
retocar, *-tǎkǎr'*, v. a. to hit a ball twice
　at billiards. 　　　　　　　　[piece.
retaco, *-tǎ'kô*, sm. short, light fowling-
retador, *-tǎdôr'*, sm. challenger.
retaguardia, *-gǎǎr'dǐǎ*, sf. rear-guard.
retahila, *-ǎ'lǎ*, sf. file, range, series.
retal, *rêtǎl'*, sm. remnant.
retar, *rêtǎr'*, v. a. to challenge, to call out.
retardar, *-ǐǎrdǎr'*, v. a. to retard, to delay.
retardo, *-tǎr'dô*, sm. delay, procrastina-
　tion.
retazo, *-tǎ'thô*, sm. remnant; cutting.
retejar, *-tê'hǎr'*, v. a. to repair the roof
　of a house.
retejo, *-tê'h'ô*, sm. repair of a roof.
retén, *-tên'*, sm. store, stock, reserve.
retención, *-thîôn'*, sf. retention. 　[back.
retener, *-tênêr'*, v. a. to retain, to keep
retentar, *-têntǎr'*, v. a. to threaten with
　a relapse of a former disorder. 　[dence.
retentiva, *-tê'vǎ*, sf. circumspection, pru-
reticencia, *-tthên'thǐǎ*, sf. reticence.
retina, *-tê'nǎ*, sf. retina.
retintín, *-tîntîn'*, sm. tingling sound; af-
　fected tone of voice.
retiñir, *-tînyîr'*, v. n. to tingle, to resound.
retirada, *-tǐrǎ'dǎ*, sf. (mil.) retreat.
retirar, *-tǐrǎr'*, v. a. to withdraw, to
　retire; to print the back of a sheet; *-se*,
　to retire, to retreat.
retiro, *-tê'rô*, sm. retreat, retirement.
reto, *rê'tô*, sm. challenge; threat, menace.
retocar, *-tôkǎr'*, v. a. to retouch a paint-
　ing; to mend; to finish any work com-
　pletely.
retoñar, *-tônyǎr'*, v. n. to sprout again.
retoño, *-tôn'yô*, sm. after-math.
retoque, *-tô'kê*, sm. finishing stroke; re-
　touching.
retorcer, *-tôrthêr'*, v. a. to twist; to retort.
retorcimiento, *-thîmîên'tô*, sm. twisting,
　contortion.
retórica, *-tô'rîkǎ*, sf. rhetoric.
retórico, ca, *-rîkô*, a. rhetorical; *-*, sm.
　rhetorician.
retornar, *-tôrnǎr'*, v. a. to return, to turn,
　to twist; *-*, v. n. to return.
retorno, *-tôr'nô*, sm. return; barter, ex-
retorta, *-tôr'tǎ*, sf. retort. 　　　[change.
retortero, *-tê'rô*, sm. twirl, rotation;
　andar al *-*, to hover about.
retortijón, *-tî'hôn'*, sm. twisting; *- de*
　tripas, gripes.
retozar, *-tôthǎr'*, v. n. to frisk, to skip;
　to play the fool; *-*, v. a. to tickle; to
　amuse.
retozo, *-tô'thô*, sm. lascivious gaiety.
retozón, ona, *-tôthôn'*, a. wanton, romping.
retracción, *-trǎkthîôn'*, sf. retraction.
retractación, *-tǎthîôn'*, sf. retractation,
　recantation.
retractar, *-tǎr'*, v. a. to retract, to unsay.
retracto, *-trǎk'tô*, sm. (law) retraction.

retraer, *-trǎêr'*, v. a. to draw back; to
　dissuade; *-se*, to take refuge; to flee.
retranca, *-trǎn'kǎ*, sf. large crupper.
retrasar, *-trǎsǎr'*, v. a. to defer, to put
　off; *-*, v. n. to retrograde, to fall off.
retraso, *-trǎs'ô*, sm. lateness; (rail.) el
　tren ha tenido *-*, the train is overdue
　or late.
retratar, *-trǎtǎr'*, v. a. to portray.
retratista, *-tîs'tǎ*, sm. portrait-painter.
retrato, *-trǎ'tô*, sm. portrait, effigy.
retreta, *-trê'tǎ*, sf. (mil.) retreat, tattoo.
retrete, *-trê'tê*, sm. closet; water-closet.
retribución, *-trǐbûthîôn'*, sf. retribution.
retribuir, *-bêr'*, v. a. to repay.
retroacción, *-trôǎkthîôn'*, sf. retroaction.
retroactivo, va, *-ǎktǐ'vô*, a. retroactive.
retroceder, *-thêdêr'*, v. n. to go back-
　ward, to fly back.
retrocesión, *-tshêsîôn'*, sf. retrocession.
retrogradar, *-grǎdǎr'*, v. n. to retrograde.
retrógrado, da, *rêtrô'grǎdô*, a. retrograde.
retrucar, *-trǔkǎr'*, v. n. to screw back
　(at billiards). 　　　　　　[upon words.
retruécano, *-trǔê'kǎnô*, sm. pun, play
retruque, *-trô'kê*, sm. screw-back, can-
　noning back of a ball at billiards; over-
　bid at cards. 　　　　　　　　[jingle.
retumbar, *-tǔmbǎr'*, v. n. to resound, to
retumbo, *-tǔm'bô*, sm. resonance, echo.
reuma, *rê'ûmǎ*, sf. rheum.
reumático, ca, *rêûmǎ'tǐkô*, a. rheumatic.
reumatismo, *-tîs'mô*, sm. rheumatism.
reunión, *-ûnîôn'*, sf. reunion, meeting.
reunir, *-ûnîr'*, v. a. to reunite, to unite.
revalidación, *-vǎlǐdǎtîôn'*, sf. confirma-
　tion, ratification.
revalidar, *-dǎr'*, v. a. to ratify, to con-
　firm; *-se*, to be admitted to a higher
　post or class.
revelación, *-vêlǎthîôn'*, sf. revelation.
revelar, *-lǎr'*, v. a. to reveal.
revendedor, *-vêndêdôr'*, sm. retailer,
　huckster.
revendedora, *-dô'rǎ*, sf. hucksteress.
revender, *-dêr'*, v. a. to retail.
revenirse, *-vênǐr'sê*, v. r. to be pricked,
　to grow sour (of wine and conserves).
reventadero, *-tǎdê'rô*, sm. rough, un-
　even ground; laborious work.
reventar, *-tǎr'*, v. n. to burst, to crack;
　to toil, to drudge; *-*, v. a. to molest, to
　harass.
rever, *-vêr'*, v. a. to review, to revise.
reverberación, *-vêrbêrǎthîôn'*, sf. re-
　verberation.
reverberar, *-rǎr'*, v. a. to reverberate.
reverdecer, *-vêrdêthêr'*, v. n. to grow
　green again. 　　　　　[respect, veneration.
reverencia, *-vêrên'thǐǎ*, sf. reverence,
reverenciar, *-thǐǎr'*, v. a. to venerate,
　to revere.
reverendas, *-rên'dǎs*, sf. pl. dimissory
　letters; qualities worthy of reverence.
reverendo, da, *-dô*, a. reverend.
reverente, *-tê*, a. respectful, reverent.
reversión, *-vêrsîôn'*, sf. reversion, return.
reverso, *-vêr'sô*, sm. reverse.

revés, —vés', sm. back-side; disappointment, misadventure.

revesado, da, —sá dó, a. obstinate; difficult, entangled, perplexed, obscure.

revesino, —sé nó, sm. game at cards.

revestir, —vestir', v. a. to dress, to put on clerical robes.

revisar, —visar', v. a. to revise, to review.

revisión, —visión', sf. revision.

revisor, —sor', sm. reviser, corrector.

revista, —vis tá, sf. review, revision.

revistar, —vistar', v. a. to revise a suit at law; to review troops.

revocable, —voká blé, a. revocable.

revocación, —káshión', sf. revocation.

revocadura, —dó rá, sf. rough-cast.

revocar, —kar', v. a. to revoke.

revocatorio, ria, —kató rió, a. revoking, annulling.

revolcadero, —volkadé ró, sm. wallow.

revolcarse, —kar sé, v. r. to wallow.

revolotear, —volteár', v. n. to flutter.

revoloteo, —lóté ó, sm. fluttering.

revoltillo, —vóltil yó, sm. confusion, disorder.   [ditious.

revoltoso, sa, —tó só, a. turbulent, sedition.

revolución, —volúshión', sf. revolution; disturbance, sedition.   [disturber.

revolvedor, ra, —vedor', sm. & f. revolter.

revolver, —ver', v. a. to return; to revolve; —se, to move to and fro; to change (of the weather).

revólver, —vól ver', sm. revolver, m.

revoque, —vó ké, sm. brick-work; rough-cast.   [volution, revolt.

revuelta, —vuél tá, sf. second turn; revoy, re é, sm. king; king (in cards or chess).

reyerta, reyér tá, sf. dispute.

rezagar, —thagár', v. a. & n. to leave behind; to defer; to remain behind.

rezago, réthá gó, sm. remainder, residue.

rezar, réthar', v. a. to pray, to say one's prayers.

rezo, ré thó, sm. prayer; divine office.

rezumarse, réthúmar sé, v. r. to ooze, to run gently, to leak.

ria, ré á, sf. mouth of a river.

riada, riá dá, sf. inundation, overflow.

ribazo, ribá thó, sm. hillock, ridge.

ribera, —bé rá, sf. shore, strand.

ribereño, ña, —beréñ yó, a. belonging to the sea-shore or bank of a river.

ribete, —bé té, sm. trimming; seam, border.

ribetear, —beteár', v. a. to hem, to border.

ricacho, cha, —kátsh ó, a. very rich.

rico, ca, ré kó, a. noble, rich; delicious.

ricohombre, —óm' bré, ricohome, —ó mé, sm. grandee.   [ridicule.

ridículez, —díkúlésth', sf. ridiculous action;

ridiculizar, —líthar', v. a. to ridicule.

ridículo, la, —dé kúló, a. ridiculous.

riego, ré gó, sm. irrigation.

rienda, rién dá, sf. rein of a bridle; á—suelta, loose-reined, swiftly.

riesgo, riés gó, sm. danger, risk.   [tery.

rifa, ré fá, sf. scuffle, dispute; raffle, lottery.

rifar, rifar', v. a. to raffle.

rigidez, ríhídésth', sf. rigidity.   [severe.

rígido, da, ré hídó, a. rigid, rigorous,

rigor, rigor', sm. rigour, rigor.

riguroso, sa, —gúró só, a. rigorous.

rija, ríh á, sf. lachrymal fistula; quarrel,

rima, ré má, sf. rhyme.   [scuffle, dispute.

rimar, rimar', v. a. & n. to investigate; to rhyme.

rimero, —mé ró, sm. collection of things placed regularly one over another.

rincón, rínkón', sm. inside corner.

rinconada, —ná dá, sf. corner formed by two houses, streets, &c.

rinconera, —né rá, sf. small triangular table placed in a corner.

ringlera, rínglé rá, sf. row, file.

ringorango, —góráng' gó, sm. flourish with a pen; extravagant nicety in dress.

rinoceronte, rínotherón' té, sm. rhinoceros.

riña, rín yá, sf. quarrel, dispute.

riñón, rínyón', sm. kidney.

río, ré ó, sm. river, stream.

riolada, riólá dá, sf. assemblage of many things at one time.

riqueza, ríké thá, sf. riches, wealth.

risa, ré sá, sf. laugh, laughter.

risada, —sá dá, sf. horse-laugh.

risco, rís kó, sm. steep rock.

riscoso, sa, —kó só, a. steep and rocky.

risible, rísé blé, a. risible, laughable.

ristra, rís trá, sf. string of onions; row, file.

ristre, —tré, sm. socket for a lance.

risueño, na, rísúén yó, a. smiling.

rítmico, ca, rít mékó, a. rhythmical.

ritmo, rít mó, sm. rhythm.

rito, ré tó, sm. rite, ceremony.

ritual, ritúál', a. & sm. ritual.

rival, rivál', sm. rival, competitor.

rivalidad, —dád', sf. rivalry.   [with.

rivalizar, —líthar', v. a. to rival, to vie

rizar, ríthár', v. a. to curl hair; to plait.

rizo, ré thó, sm. curl, frizzle; crimping; cut velvet; —s, pl. short pieces of braided cordage.

ro, ró, word used to lull children to sleep.

robador, ra, róbádór', sm. & f. robber.

robar, —bar', v. a. to rob, to plunder; to abduct a woman.

roble, ró blé, sm. oak-tree.

robledal, —dál', sm. oak-grove.

robo, ró bó, sm. robbery, theft.

roborar, —rar', v. a. to corroborate, to give strength.

robre, ró bré, sm. rubber (at whist).

robustez, —bústéth', sf. robustness.

robusto, ta, —bés tó a. robust, vigorous.

roca, ró ká, sf. rock, cliff; hard substance; —s, pl. precipice.

rocalla, —kál yá, sf. pieces of rock-crystal.

roce, ró thé, sm. familiarity; friction.

rociada, —thiá dá, sf. aspersion, sprinkling; dew-drops; malicious censure.

rociador, —dór', sm. instrument for sprinkling cloth.

rociar, —thiar', v. a. to sprinkle; to scatter about; —, v. n. to fall (of dew).

rocín, -thĭn', sm. hack; heavy, stupid person.

rocinal, -nāl', a. belonging to a hack.

rocinante, -nān'tĕ, sm. miserable hack.

rocío, rŏthē'ŏ, sm. dew.

rodada, -dā'dā, sf. rut, track of a wheel.

rodadura, -dŏ'rā, sf. act of rolling.

rodaja, -dā'hā, sf. rowel of a spur; jagging-iron used by pastry-cooks.

rodaje, -dā'hē, sm. wheelworks.

rodapié, -dāpiē', sm. fringe round the foot of a bedstead. [of a key.

rodaplancha, -plān'tshā, sf. main ward

rodar, rŏdār', v. a. to roll.

rodear, -dĕār', v. n. to encompass; to go a round-about way; —, v. a. to wrap up, to circle; to compass.

rodela, -dā'lā, sf. shield, target.

rodeo, -dā'ŏ, sm. act of going round; circuitous way; delay; subterfuge.

rodete, -dā'tĕ, sm. large wheel, formed of many pieces; bolster; splinter-bar; ward of a key. [sisting of many pieces.

rodezno, -dĕth'nŏ, sm. large wheel, consisting

rodilla, -dīl'yā, sf. knee; rubber, clout; de -s, on one's knees. [knee.

rodillazo, -yā'thŏ, sm. push with the knee.

rodillo, -dīl'yŏ, sm. roller.

rodo, rŏ'dŏ, sm. rolling-stone.

rodrigar, -drĭgār', v. a. to prop up vines.

rodrigón, -gŏn', sm. prop for vines.

roedor, ra, rŏĕdŏr', sm. & f. gnawer; de-roedura, -dŏ'rā, sf. gnawing. [tractor.

roer, rŏĕr', v. n. to gnaw, to corrode.

rogación, -gāthŏn', sf. petition, supplication; -ones, pl. Rogation days.

rogar, -gār', v. a. to entreat; to pray.

rogativa, -tē'vā, sf. supplication, prayer.

rojez, rŏ'hĕth', sf. redness.

rojizo, za, -hē'thŏ, a. reddish.

rojo, ja, rŏ'h'ŏ, a. red; ruddy.

rol, rŏl, sm. list, roll, catalogue.

rollizo, za, rŏlyē'thŏ, a. plump, robust, chopping.

rollo, rŏl'yŏ, sm. roll; spiral.

romadizo, rŏmādē'thŏ, sm. catarrh.

romana, rŏmā'nā, sf. steelyard.

romanar, -nār', v. a. to weigh with a steelyard. [language; romance.

romance, rŏmān'thĕ, sm. common Spanish

romancero, ra, -thā'rŏ, a. romancing; —, sm. collection of romances or ballads; -romancer.

romancista, -thĭs'tā, sm. author who writes in the vulgar Spanish language; surgeon practiser.

romano, na, rŏmā'nŏ, a. Roman.

rombo, rŏm'bŏ, sm. rhomb.

romboide, -bŏē'dĕ, sm. rhomboid.

romería, rŏmĕrē'ā, sf. pilgrimage.

romero, rŏmā'rŏ, sm. (bot.) rosemary.

romo, ma, rŏ'mŏ, a. blunt; flat-nosed.

romper, rŏmpĕr', v. a. & n. to break, to dash, to fracture; to break up land; to pierce; to begin.

rompimiento, -pĭmĭĕn'tŏ, sm. rupture; crack, cleft; first ploughing of land.

ron, rŏn, sm. rum.

ronca, rŏn'kā, sf. menace; boast, brag.

roncar, -kār', v. n. to snore; to make a harsh noise; to roar; to threaten, to boast, to brag. [evasions.

rondear, -thĕār', v. n. to defer, to use

roncería, -thĕrē'ā, sf. laziness, tardiness; flattery.

roncero, ra, -thā'rŏ, a. snarling, growling, flattering; slow, tardy (applied to the sailing of a ship).

ronco, ca, rŏn'kŏ, a. hoarse; husky; coarse.

roncón, -kŏn', sm. drone of a bag-pipe.

roncha, rŏn'tshā, sf. wheal, pustule.

ronda, rŏn'dā, sf. night-patrol. [guard.

rondador, -dādŏr', sm. watchman, night-rondar, -dār', v. a. & n. to patrol; to take walks by night about the streets; to go

rondel, -dĕl', sm. roundelay. [round.

rondín, -dĭn', sm. rounds of an officer visiting sentinels.

ronquear, -kĕār', v. n. to be hoarse.

ronquera, -kē'rā, sf. hoarseness.

ronquido, -kē'dŏ, sm. snore; rough, harsh

ronzal, -thāl', sm. halter. [sound.

ronzar, -thār', v. a. to chew, to munch, to grind.

roña, rŏn'yā, sf. scab, mange; craft, fraud, cunning; nastiness, filth. [gardliness.

roñería, -yĕrē'ā, sf. craft, cunning; nig-roñoso, sa, -yŏ'sŏ, a. scabby.

ropa, rŏ'pā, sf. cloth; stuff; clothing, wearing-apparel; robe.

ropaje, rŏpā'hĕ, sm. clothing, drapery.

ropavejería, -vĕhĕrē'ā, sf. frippery.

ropavejero, -'hā'rŏ, sm. fripperer; old-clothes-man. [clothes-shop; wardrobe.

ropería, rŏpĕrē'ā, sf. trade in old clothes;

ropero, rŏpā'rŏ, sm. clothes-merchant.

ropón, rŏpŏn', sm. wide, loose gown worn over the rest of the clothes.

roque, rŏ'kĕ, sm. rook (at chess).

roquete, rŏkā'tĕ, sm. roquet.

ros, rŏs, sm. (mil.) Spanish shako.

rosa, rŏ'sā, sf. rose; red spot appearing in any part of the body. [rosy.

rosado, da, rŏsā'dŏ, a. crimsoned, flushed;

rosal, -sāl', sm. rose-bush, rosier.

rosario, -sā'rĭŏ, sm. rosary.

rosca, rŏs'kā, sf. screw; any thing round and spiral; sea-rusk (kind of biscuit).

roseta, rŏsā'tā, sf. rosette. [tecture).

rosetón, -sĕtŏn', sm. carved rose (archi-rosicler, rŏsĭklĕr', sm. bright rose colour.

rosoli, rŏsŏ'lĭ, sm. rossolis.

rosquilla, rŏskĭl'yā, sf. sweet spiral-shaped cake.

rostro, rŏs'trŏ, sm. feature, human face.

rota, rŏ'tā, sf. rout, defeat; ecclesiastical court in some Catholic countries.

rotación, rŏtāthŏn', sf. rotation.

roto, ta, rŏ'tŏ, a. broken, destroyed; leaky; debauched. [pan.

rótula, rŏ'tŭlā, sf. whirlbone of the knee-rotular, rŏtŭlār', v. a. to inscribe, to label.

rótulo, rŏ'tŭlŏ, sm. inscription put on books and papers, label; printed bill posted up in public places.

rotura, rŏtŏ'rā, sf. rupture, crack, cleft.

roya, *rŏ'yā,* sf. rust, corn-blight; (bot.) madder.

rozadura, *rŏthădŏ'rā,* sf. graze, scratch.

rozagante, *–gán'tĕ,* a. trailing, sweeping (of gowns); splendid.

rozar, *–thár',* v. a. to stub up; to nibble the grass; to scrape; to touch slightly; to cut each other; to falter, to stammer.

roznar, *rŏthnár',* v. a. to chew, to nibble; to bray.

roznido, *–nĕ'dŏ,* sm. noise made by the teeth in eating, smacking of the lips; braying of an ass. [weeding.

rozo, *rŏ'thŏ,* sm. chip of wood; stubbing,

rubí, *rubĕ',* sm. ruby.

rubia, *rŏ'bĭā,* sf. (bot.) madder.

rubicundo, da, *rŭbĭkŭn'dŏ,* a. reddish, rubicund. [sm. red gurnard.

rubio, bia, *rŏ'bĭŏ,* a. reddish, ruddy;

rublo, *rŏ'blŏ,* sm. rouble.

rubor, *rŭbŏr',* sm. blush; bashfulness.

rúbrica, *rŏ'brĭkā,* sf. bloodstone; red mark; flourish at the end of a signature; rubric.

rubricar, *rŭbrĭkár',* v. a. to mark with a red colour; to sign with one's peculiar flourish; to subscribe, sign and seal a writing.

rucio, cia, *rŏ'thĭŏ,* a. light gray; gray-haired; – rodado, dappled-grey (of horses). [horses].

ruda, *rŏ'dā,* sf. rue.

rudeza, *rŭdā'thā,* sf. roughness, rudeness; stupidity.

rudimento, *rŭdĭmĕn'tŏ,* sm. principle; beginning; –s, pl. rudiments. [stupid.

rudo, da, *rŏ'dŏ,* a. rude, rough, coarse;

rueca, *rŭā'kā,* sf. distaff. [sun-fish.

rueda, *rŭā'dā,* sf. wheel; circle; crown;

ruedo, *rŭā'dŏ,* sm. rotation; circuit; border, selvage; round mat to sit upon.

ruego, *rŭā'gŏ,* sm. request, prayer, petition, entreaty, supplication.

rufián, *rŭfĭán',* sm. pimp, pander.

rufo, fa, *rŏ'fŏ,* a. red-haired; frizzed, curled. [the vapours, pl.

rugido, *rŭ'hĕ'dŏ,* sm. roaring of a lion;

rugir, *rŭ'hĭr',* v. n. to roar, to bellow; to rumble. [crack.

rugoso, sa, *rŭgŏ'sŏ,* a. wrinkled. [crack.

ruibarbo, *rŭĭbár'bŏ,* sm. rhubarb.

ruido, *rŭĭ'dŏ,* sm. noise. [loud.

ruidoso, sa, *rŭĭdŏ'sŏ,* a. noisy, clamorous,

ruin, *rŭĭn',* a. mean, vile, despicable; wicked; avaricious.

ruina, *rŭĭ'nā,* sf. ruin, downfall, destruction; –, pl. ruins of an edifice.

ruindad, *rŭĭndád',* sf. meanness, baseness, avarice. [destructive.

ruinoso, sa, *rŭĭnŏ'sŏ,* a. worthless, ruinous,

ruiseñor, *rŭĭsĕnyŏr',* sm. nightingale.

rumbo, *rŭm'bŏ,* sm. point of the compass; road, route, way; pomp, ostentation.

rumboso, sa, *rŭmbŏ'sŏ,* a. pompous, liberal.

rumiar, *rŭmĭár',* v. a. to ruminate.

rumión, ona, *rŭmĭŏn',* a. ruminating much; (fig.) harping on a subject.

rumor, *rŭmŏr',* sm. rumour, report.

runrún, *rŭnrŭn',* sm. rumour, report.

ruptura, *rŭptŏ'rā,* sf. rupture.

rural, *rŭrál',* a. rural. [coarseness.

rusticidad, *rŭstĭthĭdád',* sf. rusticity;

rústico, ca, *rŭs'tĭkŏ,* a. rustic; –, sm. peasant.

ruta, *rŏ'tā,* sf. route, itinerary.

rutilar, *rŭtĭlár',* v. n. (poet.) to radiate, to shine. [from custom.

rutina, *rŭtĕ'nā,* sf. routine, habit formed

rutinero, *rŭtĭnā'rŏ,* a. of routine.

S.

sábado, *sā'bādŏ,* sm. Saturday; sabbath.

sábana, *sā'bānā,* sf. sheet; altar-cloth.

sabandija, *sābăndĭ'hā,* sf. grub, beetle, insect.

sabañón, *sābănyŏn',* sm. chilblain.

sabatina, *sābātĕ'nā,* sf. divine service on Saturday; literary exercise performed by students on Saturday evening.

sabedor, ora, *sābĕdŏr',* sm. & f. well-informed person.

saber, *sābĕr',* v. a. to know; to experience; –, v. imp. to have a taste of; –, sm. learning, knowledge. [formed.

sabido, da, *sābĕ'dŏ,* a. learned, well informed

sabiduría, *sābĭdŭrĕ'ā,* sf. learning, knowledge, wisdom; notice.

sabiendas, *sābĭĕn'dās, &–,* ad. knowingly.

sabina, *sābĕ'nā,* sf. (bot.) savin, sabine.

sabio, bia, *sā'bĭŏ,* a. sage, wise; –, sm. & f. sage, a wise person.

sabiondez, *sābĭŏndĕth',* sf. sciolism.

sabiondo, da, *sābĭŏn'dŏ,* a. sciolist.

sablazo, *sāblā'thŏ,* sm. sabre-cut.

sable, *sā'blĕ,* sm. sabre, cutlass.

sabor, *sābŏr',* sm. relish, taste, savour.

saborear, *sābŏrĕár',* v. a. to give a taste or zest; to engage one's affections; –se, to swallow slowly and with great enjoyment; to be pleased.

saboyana, *sābŏyā'nā,* sf. wide petticoat.

sabroso, sa, *sābrŏ'sŏ,* a. savoury; palatable; salted, saltish. [hound.

sabueso, *sābŭā'sŏ,* sm. blood-hound; lime-

saca, *sā'kā,* sf. exportation; sack.

sacabala, *–bā'lā,* sf. bullet-drawer (used by surgeons).

sacabocado(s), *–bŏkā'dŏ(s),* sm. puncheon.

sacabotas, *–bŏ'tās,* sf. boot-jack.

sacabuche, *–bŭtsh'ĕ,* sf. sackbut.

sacacorchos, *–kŏr'tshŏs,* sm. cork-screw.

sacadinero(s), *–dĭnā'rŏ(s),* sm. catch-penny; tinsel finery.

sacadura, *–dŏ'rā,* sf. sloping cut by which tailors make clothes fit better.

sacaliña, *–lĭn'yā,* sf. knack of tricking a person out of something with art and craft. [of clothes.

sacamanchas, *–măn'tshās,* sm. scourer

sacamuelas, *–mŭā'lās,* sm. tooth-drawer, dentist. [at cards.]

sacanete, *–nā'tĕ,* sm. lansquenet (game

sacapotras, *–pŏ'trās,* sm. nickname for a bad surgeon.

sacar, *săkăr',* v. a. to draw out; to except; to pull out; to draw lots; to bowl (at
sacatón, *-tón',* sm. cork-screw. [play).
sacatrapos, *-trä'pŏs,* sm. worm of a ramrod.
sacerdocio, *săthĕrdŏ'thĭŏ,* sm. priesthood.
sacerdotal, *-dŏtäl',* a. sacerdotal.
sacerdote, *-dŏ'tĕ,* sm. priest, clergyman.
sacerdotisa, *-dŏtĭ'ä,* sf. priestess. [play.
saciar, *săthĭăr',* v. a. to satiate.|
saciedad, *săthĭĕdäd',* sf. satiety.
saco, *să'kŏ,* sm. sack; sagum.
sacramental, *săkrămĕntäl',* a. sacramental.
sacramentar, *-mĕntär',* v. a. to administer the sacraments.
sacramento, *-mĕn'tŏ,* sm. sacrament.
sacrificadero, *săkrĭfĭkădĕ'rŏ,* sm. place of sacrifice.
sacrificar, *-kär',* v. a. to sacrifice; —se, to devote oneself to religion.
sacrificio, *-fĭ'thĭŏ,* sm. sacrifice.
sacrilegio, *-lĕ'hĭŏ,* sm. sacrilege.
sacrilego, ga, *săkrĕ'lĕgŏ,* a. sacrilegious.
sacristán, *săkrĭstän',* sm. sacristan, sexton.
sacristana, *-tä'nä,* sf. nun sacristan.
sacristanía, *-tänĕ'ä,* sf. office of a sexton.
sacristía, *-tĕ'ä,* sf. sacristy, vestry.
sacro, cra, *să'krŏ,* a. holy, sacred.
sacrosanto, ta, *-săn'tŏ,* a. very holy.
sacudida, *săkŭdĭ'dä,* sf. shake, jerk.
sacudidura, *-dŭdŏ'rä,* sf. dusting, cleaning. [off.
sacudimiento, *-dĭmĭĕn'tŏ,* sm. shaking
sacudir, *-dĭr',* v. a. to shake, to jerk; to dart; to beat, to chastise with blows; —se, to reject with disdain.
saeta, *săĕ'tä,* sf. arrow, dart.
saetar, *săĕtär',* v. a. to wound with an arrow.
saetazo, *săĕtä'thŏ,* a. arrow-wound.
saetín, *săĕtĭn',* sm. mill-trough; peg, pin, tack; satin.
sáfico, ca, *să'fĭkŏ,* a. (poet.) sapphic.
sagacidad, *săgăthĭdäd',* sf. sagacity.
sagaz, *săgäth',* a. sagacious.
Sagitario, *să'hĭtä'rĭŏ,* **Sagittarius,** *să'hĭtä'rĭŭs,* sm. Archer (sign of the zodiac).
sagrado, da, *săgrä'dŏ,* a. sacred, consecrated; —, sm. asylum.
sagrario, *săgrä'rĭŏ,* sm. place in a church wherein consecrated things are deposited; cibary. [smoke, to fume.
sahumar, *săŭmär',* v. a. to perfume; to
saín, *săĭn',* sm. grease or fat of an animal; dirt on clothes. [delicate bit.
sainete, *-nĕ'tĕ,* sm. farce; flavour, relish;
sajadura, *săhădŏ'rä,* sf. scarification.
sajar, *săhär',* v. a. to scarify.
sal, *säl,* sf. salt.
sala, *să'lä,* sf. hall, saloon; council-room, session-room; guest-chamber.
saladero, *-dĕ'rŏ,* sm. salting-place; salting-tub. [tious.
salado, da, *sălä'dŏ,* a. salted; witty, facetious.
saladura, *-dŏ'rä,* sf. salting; saltness.
salamandra, *-măn'drä,* sf. salamander.
salar, *sălär',* v. a. to salt.

salario, *-rĭŏ,* sm. salary.
salazón, *săläthŏn',* sf. seasoning, salting.
salcochar, *sălkŏtshär',* v. a. to dress meat, leaving it half raw and without salt.
salchicha, *sältshĭtshä,* sf. sausage.
salchichería, *-tshĕrĕ'ä,* sf. shop in which sausages are sold. [of sausages.
salchichero, *-tshĕ'rŏ,* a. maker or seller
saledizo, za, *sălĕdĭ'thŏ,* a. salient.
salero, *sălĕ'rŏ,* sm. salt-cellar.
saleroso, *sălĕrŏ'sŏ,* a. graceful.
salida, *sălĭ'dä,* sf. outgoing; outlet; issue, result; (mil.) sally; —, a. in heat (of a bitch). [mine.
salina, *sălĭ'nä,* sf. salt-pit, salt-work, salt-
salinero, *sălĭnĕ'rŏ,* sm. salter; salt-maker.
salino, na, *sălĭ'nŏ,* a. saline.
salir, *sălĭr',* v. n. ir. to go out of a place; to depart, to set out; to appear; to issue from; to cost; —se, to drop, to leak.
salitrado, da, *sălĭträ'dŏ* a. impregnated with saltpetre.
salitral, *-träl',* sm. saltpetre-works.
salitre, *sălĭ'trĕ,* sm. saltpetre.
salitrería, *sălĭtrĕrĕ'ä,* sf. saltpetre-work.
salitrero, *-trä'rŏ,* sm. saltpetre-refiner.
salitroso, sa, *-trŏ'sŏ,* a. nitrous.
saliva, *sălĭ'vä,* sf. saliva.
salivar, *sălĭvär',* v. n. to spit, to salivate.
salivoso, sa, *-vŏ'sŏ,* a. salivous.
salmear, *sălmĕär',* **salmodiar,** *-mŏdĭär',* v. a. to sing psalms.
salmista, *-mĭs'tä,* sm. psalmist.
salmo, *săl'mŏ,* sm. psalm.
salmodia, *sălmŏ'dĭä,* sf. psalmody.
salmón, *sălmŏn',* sm. salmon. [salmon.
salmonado, da, *-nä'dŏ,* a. tasting like
salmonete, *-nĕ'tĕ,* sm. red-mullet.
salmuera, *sălmŭä'rä,* sf. brine.
salobre, *sălŏ'brĕ,* a. brackish, saltish.
salomar, *sălŏmär',* v. n. (mar.) to sing out.
salón, *sălŏn',* sm. saloon.
salpicar, *sălpĭkär',* v. a. to bespatter.
salpicón, *-pĭkŏn',* sm. salmagundy.
salpimentar, *-pĭmĕn'tär',* v. a. to season with pepper and salt. [salt and pepper.
salpimienta, *-pĭmĕn'tä,* sf. mixture of
salpresar, *-prĕsär',* v. a. to salt.
salpullido, *-pŭlyĭdŏ,* sm. (med.) eruption, rash.
salpullir, *-pŭlyĭr',* v. a. to break out in pustules or pimples on the skin.
salsa, *săl'sä,* sf. sauce.
salsera, *sălsĕ'rä,* sf. saucer. [colours.
salserilla, *-sĕrĭ'yä,* sf. small cup for
salsero, *-sĕ'rŏ,* sm. (bot.) Spanish thyme.
saltabancos, *săltäbän'kŏs,* sm. saltinbanco, mountebank.
saltadero, *-tädĕ'rŏ,* sm. leaping-place; artificial fountain, jet.
saltado, da, *-tä'dŏ,* a. prominent, jutting.
saltador, *-tädŏr',* sm. jumper, leaper.
saltar, *-tär',* v. n. to leap, to jump; to be irritated or agitated.
saltarín, ina, *-tärĭn',* sm. & f. dancer; restless young rake.
saltatriz, *-tätrĭth',* sf. female rope-dancer.
salteador, *-tĕädŏr',* sm. highwayman.

saltear, –těăr', v. a. to rob on the highway.
salterio, –tě'rĭŏ, sm. Psalter.
salto, săl'tŏ, sm. leap, jump.
saltón, sălŏn', sm. grasshopper; –, ona, a. hopping or leaping much.
salubre, sălŏ'brě, a. healthful.
salubridad, sălŏbrĭdăd', sf. healthfulness.
salud, sălŭd', sf. health, sound state of the body. [some.
saludable, –dă'blě, a. salubrious, whole-
saludador, –dă'dŏr, sm. greeter; quack.
saludar, –dăr', v. a. to greet, to salute.
saludo, sălŏ'dŏ, sm. (mil.) salute.
salutación, sălŏtăthĭŏn', sf. salutation, greeting; exordium. [arms.
salva, săl'vă, sf. (mil.) salute with fire-
salvación, –văthĭŏn', sf. salvation.
salvado, –vă'dŏ, sm. bran.
Salvador, –dŏr', sm. Saviour.
salvaguardia, –găr'dĭă, sm. safeguard.
salvaje, sălvă'h'ě, a. savage. [manners.
salvajería, –herĭ'ă, sf. rusticity, uncouth
salvamiento, –mĭěn'tŏ, sm. safety; salvation; asylum. [escape from danger.
salvar, sălvăr', v. a. to save; –se, to
¡ salve! săl'vě, God bless you!
salvia, săl'vĭă, sf. (bot.) sage.
salvilla, –vĭl'yă, sf. salver. [excepting.
salvo, va, săl'vŏ, a. saved; –, ad. saving.
salvoconducto, –kŏndŏk'tŏ, sm. safe-conduct.
sallar, săl'yăr, v. a. to weed.
sallo, săl'yŏ, sm. hoe.
sambenito, sămběnĭ'tŏ, sm. garment, with a yellow cross at back and front, worn by penitents of the Inquisition; note of infamy.
san, săn, a. saint.
sanable, sănă'blě, a. curable, healable.
sanalotodo, –lŏtŏ'dŏ, sm. panacea, general remedy. [ably.
sanamente, –měn'tě, ad. naturally; agree-
sanar, sănăr', v. a. & n. to heal.
sanción, sănthĭŏn', sf. sanction.
sancionar, –thĭŏnăr', v. a. to sanction.
sandalia, –dă'lĭă, sf. sandal.
sándalo, săn'dălŏ, sm. bergamot-mint; sandal-wood.
sandez, –děth', sf. folly, stupidity.
sandio, dia, săn'dĭŏ, a. foolish, nonsensical.
saneamiento, săněămĭěn'tŏ, sm. surety, bail. [demnify.
sanear, săněăr', v. a. to give bail; to in-
sanedrín, –drĭn', sm. sanhedrim.
sangradera, săngrădě'ră, sf. lancet.
sangrador, –dŏr', sm. blood-letter.
sangradura, –dŏ'ră, sf. bleeding.
sangrar, săngrăr', v. a. & n. to bleed; –se, to be bled.
sangre, săn'grě, sf. blood; á – fria, in cool blood; á – y fuego, without mercy.
sangría, –grĭ'ă, sf. bleeding; wound, incision.
sangriento, ta, –grĭěn'tŏ, a. bloody, stained with blood, gory; blood-thirsty.
sanguijuela, –gĭhŏ'lă, sf. leech; sharper.
sanguinaria, –gĭnă'rĭă, sf. knot-grass; sanguine (a stone). [cruel, bloody.
sanguinario, ria, –rĭŏ, a. sanguinary,

sanguíneo, nea, –gĭ'ně-ŏ, a. sanguine; sanguineous. [sacramental element.
sanguis, săngĭs', sm. blood of Christ, as
sanidad, sănĭdăd', sf. soundness, health.
sanjuanista, –hŏănĭs'tă, sm. knight of the order of St. John of Jerusalem.
sano, na, să'nŏ, a. sound, sane.
Santabárbara, săntăbăr'bără, sf. (mar.) powder-magazine. [tuary.
santasantórum, –săntŏ'rŭm, sm. sanc-
santaguista, săntăgĭs'tă, sm. knight of St. James. [ling of an eye.
santiamén, –ăměn', sm. moment, twink-
santidad, –dăd', sf. sanctity.
santificación, –fĭkăthĭŏn', sf. sanctification.
santificador, –fĭkădŏr', sf. sanctifier.
santificar, –fĭkăr', v. a. to sanctify; to justify.
santiguador, ra, –gădŏr', sm. & f. one who cures by making the sign of the cross.
santiguar, –gădr', v. a. to make the sign of the cross over a sick person; to chastise, to punish. [moniousness.
santimonia, –mŏ'nĭă, sf. sanctity; sancti-
santo, ta, săn'tŏ, a. & sm. saint, holy; sacred; image of a saint; (mil.) watch-word. [monk.
santón, săntŏn', sm. hypocrite; Moorish
santoral, –tŏrăl', sm. lives of the saints; church-choir book, hymn-book.
santuario, –tŏă'rĭŏ, sm. sanctuary.
santurrón, ona, –tŭrrŏn', sm. & f. & a. hypocrite pretending holiness.
santurronería, –něrĭ'ă, sf. hypocrisy.
saña, săn'yă, sf. anger, passion.
sañudo, da, sănyŏ'dŏ, a. furious, enraged.
sapo, să'pŏ, sm. large toad.
saporífero, ra, –rě'fěrŏ, a. saporific.
saque, să'kě, sm. striking out the ball.
saqueador, ra, săkěădŏr', sm. & f. ransacker, freebooter. [plunder.
saquear, săkěăr', v. a. to ransack, to
saqueo, săkě'ŏ, sm. pillage, freebooting.
sarampión, sărămpĭŏn', sm. measles, pl.
sarao, sără'ŏ, sm. ball, dance.
sarcasmo, sărkăs'mŏ, sm. sarcasm.
sarcástico, ca, –kăs'tĭkŏ, a. sarcastic.
sarcófago, –kŏ'făgŏ, sm. sarcophagus.
sardina, –dĭ'nă, sf. sardine, anchovy.
sardinero, ra, –dĭně'rŏ, sm. & f. dealer in anchovies; –, a. belonging to anchovies.
sardio, săr'dĭŏ, sardo, –dŏ, sm. sardine (a stone). [cious stone).
sardónice, –dŏ'nĭthě, sf. sardonyx (pre-
sarga, săr'gă, sf. serge.
sargento, –hěn'tŏ, sm. serjeant.
sarmiento, –mĭěn'tŏ, sm. vine shoot.
sarna, săr'nă, sf. itch; mange; (fig.) envy.
sarnoso, sa, –nŏ'sŏ, a. itchy, scabby, mangy. [rescence.
sarpullido, –pŭlyĭ'dŏ, sm. flea-bite; efflo-
sarpullir, –pŭlyĭr', v. n. to be flea-bitten; –se, to be full of flea-bites.
sarracina, –răthĭ'nă, sf. tumultuous contest between a number of persons.

sarria, *sắr'rĭ̆ă,* sf. wide net made of ropes, in which straw is carried.

sarro, *sắr'rŏ,* sm. incrustation of the tongue in violent fevers; foulness of the teeth; sediment which adheres to vessels.

sarroso, sa, *-rŏ'sŏ,* a. incrusted.

sarta, *sắr'tă,* sf. string of beads, pearls, &c.; string, row.

sartén, *sărtĕn',* sf. frying-pan, saucepan.

sartenada, *-nä'dă,* sf. saucepan-full.

sartenazo, *-nä'thŏ,* sm. blow with a frying-pan; heavy blow.

sastre, *săs'trĕ,* sm. tailor.

sastrería, *-rē'ă,* sf. tailor's shop.

Satanás, *sătănäs',* sm. Satan.

satélite, *săt̆ē'lĭt̆ē,* sm. bailiff, constable; satellite.

sátira, *să'tĭră,* sf. satire.

satírico, ca, *-tē'rĭkŏ,* a. satirical.

satirizar, *-tĭrĭthär',* v. a. to satirize.

sátiro, *să'tĭrŏ,* sm. satyr.

satisfacción, *sătĭsfăkthĭŏn',* sf. satisfaction; presumption; confidence.

satisfacer, *-făthĕr',* v. a. to satisfy; to atone; **-se,** to satisfy oneself; to vindicate oneself.

satisfactorio, ria, *-făktŏ'rĭŏ,* a. satisfactory.

satisfecho, cha, *-fĕtshŏ,* a. satisfied.

sátrapa, *să'trăpă,* sm. satrap; sly, crafty fellow.

saturación, *sătŭrăthĭŏn',* sf. (chem.) saturation.

saturnal, *sătŭrnäl',* a. saturnalian.

Saturno, *sătŭr'nŏ,* sm. Saturn; (chem.) lead.

sauce, *să'ŭthĕ,* sm. (bot.) willow.

saúco, *săŏ'kŏ,* sf. (bot.) elder.

sanquillo, *sănkĭl'yŏ,* sm. (bot.) dwarf-elder.

savia, *să'vĭă,* sf. sap.

saya, *să'yă,* sf. skirt; ancient tunic or gown worn by men.

sayal, *săyäl',* sm. sackcloth.

sayalete, *-lă'tĕ,* sm. thin or light stuff.

sayo, *să'yŏ,* sm. large wide coat without buttons; any loose coat or dress.

sayón, *săyŏn',* sm. corpulent, ill-looking fellow.

sayuelo, *săyŭĕ'lŏ,* sm. small jacket, little frock.

sazón, *săthŏn',* sf. maturity; season, taste, flavour; opportunity; **en –,** seasonably, opportunely; maturely, seasonably.

sazonadamente, *-nădămĕn'tĕ,* ad. maturely, seasonably.

sazonado, da, *-nä'dŏ,* a. witty.

sazonar, *-năr',* v. a. to season; to mature; **-se,** to ripen.

se, *sĕ,* pn. (reflexive pronoun).

sebo, *sä'bŏ,* sm. suet; (fig.) large capital, great fortune.

seboso, sa, *sĕbŏ'sŏ,* a. fat, greasy.

seca, *sĕ'kă,* sf. drought, dry weather; inflammation and swelling in the glands.

secadera, *-dă'ră,* sm. place where fruit is dried.

secamente, *-mĕn'tĕ,* ad. drily, briefly.

secano, *sĕkä'nŏ,* sm. dry, arable land which is not irrigated.

secansa, *sĕkän'să,* sf. game at cards.

secante, *-kän'tĕ,* sm. drying-oil used for painting; **–,** sf. (geom.) secant.

secar, *-kär',* v. a. to dry; **-se,** to grow dry; to become meagre; to decay.

sección, *sĕkthĭŏn',* sf. section.

seco, ca, *sĕ'kŏ,* a. dry; not rainy; arid, sapless; meagre; barren.

secreta, *sĕkrä'tă,* sf. privy, water-closet; **-s,** pl. private orisons said in a low voice by the priest at the beginning of the mass.

secretaria, *sĕkrĕtă'rĭă,* sf. secretary's wife; lady's secretary or amanuensis.

secretaria, *-tär̆ĭ'ă,* sf. secretaryship.

secretario, *-tä'rĭŏ,* sm. confidant; secretary. **[–,** sm. secrecy.

secreto, ta, *sĕkrä'tŏ,* a. secret; hidden;

secta, *sĕk'tă,* sf. sect; doctrine.

sectario, ria, *-tä'rĭŏ,* a. & sm. & f. sectarian, sectary.

secuaz, *sĕkŭäth',* a. sectary.

secuela, *-kŭä'lă,* sf. sequel, continuation.

secuencia, *-kŭĕn'thĭă,* sf. sequence in prose or verse said in mass after the epistles.

secuestrar, *-kŭĕsträr',* v. a. to sequestrate.

secuestro, *-kŭĕs'trŏ,* sm. sequestration.

secular, *sĕkŭlär',* a. secular; laical.

secularización, *-rĭthăthĭŏn',* sf. secularization.

secularizar, *-thär',* v. a. to secularize.

secundario, ria, *sĕkŭndä'rĭŏ,* a. secondary.

secura, *sĕkŏ'ră,* sf. dryness. **[dary.**

sed, *sĕd,* sf. thirst; eagerness.

seda, *sä'dă,* sf. silk; silk-stuff.

sedal, *sĕdäl',* sm. fishing-line; seton.

sede, *sä'dĕ,* sf. see, seat of episcopal power. **[or silver.**

sedear, *sĕdĕär',* v. a. to clean jewels, gold.

sedentario, ria, *-dĕntä'rĭŏ,* a. sedentary.

sedería, *-dĕr̆ē'ă,* sf. silk, silk-stuff; silk-mercer's shop.

sedero, *-dä'rŏ,* sm. silk-mercer.

sedición, *-dĭthĭŏn',* sf. sedition, mutiny.

sedicioso, sa, *-thĭŏ'sŏ,* a. seditious, mutinous. **[desirous.**

sediento, ta, *-dĭĕn'tŏ,* a. thirsty; eagerly

seducción, *-dŭkthĭŏn',* sf. seduction.

seducir, *-dŭthĭr',* v. a. to seduce.

seductivo, va, *-dăktē'vŏ,* a. seductive.

seductor, *-tŏr',* sm. seducer.

segadera, *sĕgădä'ră,* sf. reaping-hook.

segador, ra, *-dŏr',* sm. & f. reaper, harvester. **[harvest.**

segar, *sĕgär',* v. a. to reap, to mow, to

seglar, *sĕglär',* a. worldly; secular.

segmento, *sĕgmĕn'tŏ,* sm. segment.

segregación, *sĕgrĕgăthĭŏn',* sf. segregation, separation. **[apart.**

segregar, *-gär',* v. a. to separate, to set

seguida, *sĕgē'dă,* sf. following; succession; **de –,** successively.

seguidilla, *-dĭl'yă,* sf. merry Spanish tune and dance; **-s,** pl. diarrhœa.

seguido, da, *sĕgē'dŏ,* a. continued, successive, followed.

seguidor, ra, *-dŏr',* sm. & f. follower; ruled paper for teaching to write straight.

seguimiento, *-mĭĕn'tŏ,* sm. pursuit.

seguir, *sĕgīr',* v. a. to follow, to pursue; **-se,** to ensue; to succeed.

según, *-gŭn',* pr. according to.

segundar, -gŭndắr', v. a. to second; —, v. n. to be second.

segundario, ria, -dắ'rĭŏ, a. secondary.

segundo, da, -gŭn'dŏ, a. second; —, sm. second (of time). [family.

segundón, -dŏn', sm. second son of a family.

segur, -gŭr', sf. axe, large hatchet.

seguridad, -rĭdắd', sf. security, surety, certainty, safety.

seguro, ra, -gŏ'rŏ, a. secure, sure, certain; firm, constant; —, sm. leave, license; insurance of ships; safe-conduct.

seis, sĕ'ĭs, a. six, sixth; —, sm. six.

seiscientos, tas, -thĭĕn'tŏs, a. six hundred.

selección, sĕlĕk'thĭŏn', sf. selection, choice.

selecto, ta, -lĕk'tŏ, a. select, choice.

selva, sĕl'vă, sf. forest.

sellador, sĕlyădŏr', sm. sealer.

selladura, -dŏ'ră, sf. sealing.

sellar, -yăr', v. a. to seal; to finish.

sello, sĕl'yŏ, sm. seal; stamp-office; — de franqueo, postage-stamp.

semana, sĕmă'nă, sf. week.

semanal, -năl', a. weekly.

semanario, ria, -nă'rĭŏ, sm. weekly work.

semblante, sĕmblăn'tĕ, sm. face; countenance. [pared for sowing.

sembradío, día, -brădĕ'ŏ, a. fit or presembrado, -bră'dŏ, sm. corn-field.

sembrador, -dŏr', sm. sower, seedsman.

sembradura, -dŏ'ră, sf. sowing.

sembrar, -brăr', v. a. to sow.

semejante, sĕmĕhăn'tĕ, a. similar, like.

semejanza, -hăn'thă, sf. resemblance, likeness.

semejar, -hăr', v. n. to resemble.

semen, sĕ'mĕn, sm. semen, animal seed.

sementera, sĕmĕntĕ'ră, sf. sowing; land sown with seed.

semi, sĕ'mĭ, sm. (in comp.) half.

semibreve, -bră'vĕ, (mus.) semibreve.

semicircular, -thĭrkŭlăr', a. semicircular.

semicírculo, -thĭr'kŭlŏ, sm. semicircle.

semicorchea, -kŏrtshă'ă, sf. (mus.) semiquaver.

semidioses, -dĭŏs', sm. demigod.

semidoble, -dŏ'blĕ, a. semidouble (of Catholic church-feasts).

semidocto, -dŏk'tŏ, sm. sciolist.

semifusa, -fŭ'să, sf. (mus.) double demisemilla, sĕmĭl'yă, sf. seed. [semiquaver.

semillero, -yĕ'rŏ, sm. seed-plot.

seminario, sĕmĭnă'rĭŏ, sm. seminary; origin, course.

seminarista, -nărĭs'tă, sm. scholar who boards and is instructed in a seminary.

semínima, sĕmĕ'nĭmă, sf. (mus.) crotchet.

semiplena, sĕmĭplă'nă, sf. (law) imperfect proof, half-proof.

semitono, -tŏ'nŏ, sm. (mus.) semitone.

semivocal, -vŏkăl', a. semivowel.

sémola, sĕ'mŏlă, sf. groats, grits.

sempiterna, sĕmpĭtĕr'nă, sf. serge-cloth.

sempiterno, na, -tĕr'nŏ, a. everlasting, sempiternal.

senado, sĕnă'dŏ, sm. senate. [of a senate.

senadoconsulto, -kŏnsŭl'tŏ, sm. decree

senador, sĕnădŏr', sm. senator.

senatorio, ria, -tŏ'rĭŏ, a. senatorial.

sencillez, sĕnthĭlyĕth', sf. slightness; simplicity; silliness. [silly; harmless.

sencillo, lla, -thĭl'yŏ, a. simple; light;

senda, sĕn'dă, sf. **sendero,** -dĕ'rŏ, sm. path, footpath.

senescal, sĕnĕskăl', sm. seneschal.

seno, sĕ'nŏ, sm. breast, bosom; lap; womb; hole, cavity; sinus; asylum, refuge. [sing.

sensación, sĕnsăthĭŏn', sf. sensation, feel-

sensato, ta, -să'tŏ, a. judicious, reasonable.

sensibilidad, -sĭbĭlĭdăd', sf. sensibility.

sensible, -sĕ'blĕ, a. sensible; sensitive; causing pain.

sensitiva, -sĭtĭ'vă, sf. sensitive plant.

sensitivo, va, -tĭ'vŏ, a. sensitive; sensible.

sensual, sĕnsăl', a. sensive; sensual, lewd. [desire.

sensualidad, -lĭdăd', sf. sensuality; carnal

sentado, da, sĕntă'dŏ, a. sedate, judicious.

sentar, -tăr', v. a. to fit, to set up; to seat; —se, to sit down.

sentencia, -tĕn'thĭă, sf. sentence; opinion.

sentenciar, -thĭăr', v. a. to sentence, to pass judgment; to give one's opinion.

sentencioso, sa, -thĭŏ'sŏ, a. sententious.

sentido, sĕntĭ'dŏ, sm. sense; reason; signification; meaning; —, a. sensible, feeling.

sentimental, -mĕntăl', a. sentimental.

sentimiento, -mĭĕn'tŏ, sm. sentiment; grief; chink; resentment; judgment, opinion. [well.

sentina, sĕntĭ'nă, sf. sink, drain; (mar.)

sentir, sĕntĭr', v. a. to feel; to hear, to perceive; to suffer; to grieve, to mourn; to judge, to think; to foresee; —se, to find oneself; to be moved, to feel pain; to crack (of walls, &c.). [(mil.) password.

seña, sĕn'yă, sf. sign, mark, token; signal;

señal, sĕnyăl', sf. sign, signature, token; landmark; footstep; earnest-money.

señaladamente, -lădămĕn'tĕ, ad. especially; namely. [brated, noble.

señalado, da, -lă'dŏ, a. famous, cele-

señalamiento, -lămĭĕn'tŏ, sm. assignation.

señalar, -lăr', v. a. to stamp, to mark; to sign decrees; to signalize; —se, to distinguish oneself, to excel.

Señor, sĕnyŏr', sm. Lord; Sir; sacrament of the Eucharist; master; governor.

Señora, -yŏ'ră, sf. lady; mistress; gentlewoman.

señorear, -rĕăr', v. a. to master, to domineer; to govern one's passions; —se, to affect a peculiar gravity in one's deportment. [his title is given.

Señoría, -rĕ'ă, sf. lordship; person to whom

señoril, -rĭl', a. lordly. [in action.

señorío, -rĕ'ŏ, sm. seigniory; self-control

señuelo, -yăĕ'lŏ, sm. lure, enticement.

separable, sĕpŏră'blĕ, a. separable.

separación, -răthĭŏn', sf. separation.

separar, -răr', v. a. to separate; —se, to separate, to be disunited; to withdraw.

14*

septentrión, *sĕptĕntrĭón'*, sm. septentrion, north. [northern.]
septentrional, *-trĭónăl'*, a. septentrional.
septiembre, *sĕptĭĕm'brĕ*, sm. September.
séptimo, ma, *sĕp'tĭmŏ*, a. seventh.
sepulcral, *sĕpŭlkrăl'*, a. sepulchral.
sepulcro, *-pŭl'krŏ*, sm. sepulchre, grave, tomb; Santo —, Holy Sepulchre.
sepultar, *-pŭltăr'*, v.a. to bury, to inter.
sepultura, *-tŏ'rā*, sf. sepulture, interment.
sepulturero, *-tŭrā'rŏ*, sm. grave-digger, sexton.
sequedad, *sĕkĕdăd'*, sf. aridity, dryness.
sequía, *sĕkĭ'ā*, sf. dryness; thirst; drought.
séquito, *sĕ'kĭtŏ*, sm. retinue, suite; public applause.
ser, *sĕr'*, v.n. to be; to exist; to fall out; to be useful, to serve; —, sm. being.
sera, *sā'rā*, sf. large pannier.
seráfico, ca, *sĕrā'fĭkŏ*, a. seraphic.
serafín, *sĕrăfín'*, sm. seraph.
serenar, *sĕrĕnăr'*, v.a. & n. to clear up; to settle, to grow clear; to pacify, to tranquillize; to be serene.
serenata, *-nā'tā*, sf. (mus.) serenade.
sereni, *-nĭ'*, sm. (mar.) yawl, light boat.
serenidad, *-nĭdăd'*, sf. serenity.
sereno, *-rā'nŏ*, sm. evening-dew; night-watch; —, na, a. serene, calm, quiet.
serie, *sā'rĭĕ*, sf. series.
seriedad, *sĕrĭĕdăd'*, sf. seriousness; sternness of mien; sincerity.
serijo, *-rĭ'hŏ*, serillo, *-rĭl'yŏ*, sm. small basket made of palm leaves.
serio, ria, *sā'rĭŏ*, a. serious; severe.
sermón, *sĕrmón'*, sm. sermon.
sermonear, *-nĕăr'*, v.a. to lecture, to reprimand, [carry figs, raisins, &c.]
serón, *sĕrón'*, sm. large pannier used to
serosidad, *sĕrŏsĭdăd'*, sf. serosity.
seroso, sa, *-rŏ'sŏ*, a. serous. [a serpent.]
serpentear, *sĕrpĕntĕăr'*, v.n. to move like
serpentina, *-ĭ'nā*, sf. cock of a gun-lock; culverin. [strument.]
serpentón, *-tón'*, sm. serpent (musical instrument)
serpiente, *-pĭĕn'tĕ*, sf. serpent.
sérpol, *sĕr'pŏl*, sm. (bot.) wild thyme.
serrador, *sĕrrādŏr'*, sm. sawyer.
serraduras, *-dŏ'rās*, sf. pl. saw-dust.
serrallo, *-rāl'yŏ*, sm. seraglio.
serranía, *-rānĕ'ā*, sf. range of mountains, mountainous country.
serrano, na, *-rā'nŏ*, sm. &f. mountaineer.
serrar, *-rār'*, v.a. to saw.
serrín, *-rín'*, sm. saw-dust.
serrucho, *-rŭtsh'ŏ*, sm. hand-saw with a small handle.
servible, *-vĕ'blĕ*, a. fit for service.
servicial, *-vĭthĭăl'*, a. obsequious, serviceable; —, sm, clyster.
servicio, *-vĕ'thĭŏ*, sm. service; attendance; good-turn; divine service; sum of money voluntarily offered to the king; utility; close-stool; service for the table.
servidero, ra, *-vĭdā'rŏ*, a. serviceable.
servidor, *-dŏr'*, sm. servant, waiter.
servidora, *-dŏ'rā*, sf. maid-servant.

servidumbre, *-dŭm'brĕ*, sf. attendance, servitude; slavery; servility; privy, commode.
servil, *sĕrvĭl'*, a. servile. [mon-sewer.]
servilleta, *-lyĕ'tā*, sf. napkin.
servir, *sĕrvĭr'*, v.a. to serve; to pay voluntarily a sum of money to the king; to wait at table; —se, to deign, to please; to make use of.
sesada, *sĕsā'dā*, sf. fried brains.
sesenta, *sĕsĕn'tā*, sm. sixty; —, a. sixtieth.
sesentón, ona, *-tón'*, sm. person over sixty years of age.
sesera, *sĕsā'rā*, sf. brain-pan; brain.
sesgadura, *sĕsgādŏ'rā*, sf. slope, sloping.
sesgar, *-gār'*, v.a. to slope, to cut slantwise.
sesgo, *sĕs'gŏ*, sm. slope; —, ga, a. sloping, oblique; grave; al —, obliquely.
sesión, *sĕsĭón'*, sf. session; conference.
seso, *sĕ'sŏ*, sm. brain. [dinner.]
sestear, *sĕstĕăr'*, v.n. to take a nap after
sesudo, da, *sĕsŏ'dŏ*, a. judicious, discreet, prudent.
seta, *sĕ'tā*, sf. brittle; fungus (in general).
setecientos, tas, *sĕtĕthĭĕn'tŏs*, a. seven
setena, *sĕtā'nā*, sf. seven. [hundred.]
setenario, ria, *-tĕnā'rĭŏ*, a. septenary.
setenta, *-tĕn'tā*, a. seventy.
setentón, ona, *-tón'*, a. turned of seventy.
setentrión, *-trĭón'*, a. septentrional.
setiembre, *sĕtĭĕm'brĕ*, sm. September.
sétimo, ma, *sĕ'tĭmŏ*, a. seventh.
seto, *sĕ'tŏ*, sm. fence, enclosure, hedge.
setuagenario, ria, *sĕtwāhĕnā'rĭŏ*, a. seventy years old.
setuagésimo, ma, *-hā'sĭmŏ*, setuplo, pla, *sĕtŭ'plŏ*, a. sevenfold.
seudo, *sĕ'ŭdŏ*, sm. pseudo, false.
severidad, *sĕvĕrĭdăd'*, sf. severity; punctuality, exactness.
severo, ra, *sĕvā'rŏ*, a. severe, rigorous; grave, serious; punctual, exact.
sexagenario, ria, *sĕksāhĕnā'rĭŏ*, a. sixty years old.
sexagésimo, ma, *-hā'sĭmŏ*, a. sixtieth.
sexenio, *sĕksā'nĭŏ*, sm. space of six years.
sexo, *sĕk'sŏ*, sm. sex.
sexta, *sĕks'tā*, sf. sequence of six cards at piquet; sixth (minor canonical hour after tierce). [containing canonical decrees.]
sexto, ta, *sĕks'tŏ*, a. sixth; —, sm. book
si, *sĭ*, sm. (mus.) B, seventh note of the gamut; —, c. if, when.
sí, *sĭ'*, ad. yes, without doubt; indeed; —, pn. himself; de por, apart; de —, spontaneously. [luxurious.]
sibarítico, ca, *sĭbārĭ'tĭkŏ*, a. sybaritical.
sibila, *sĭbĭ'lā*, sf. prophetess; sibyl.
sicomoro, *sĭkŏmŏ'rŏ*, sm. (bot.) sycamore.
sidra, *sĭ'drā*, sf. cider.
siega, *sĭĕ'gā*, sf. harvest, mowing.
siembra, *sĭĕm'brā*, sf. seed-time.
siempre, *sĭĕm'prĕ*, ad. always; — jamás, for ever and ever.
siempreviva, *-vĕvā'*, sf. (bot.) immortelle.
sien, *sĭĕn'*, sf. temple (of the head).
sierpe, *sĭĕr'pĕ*, sf. serpent.
sierra, *sĭĕr'rā*, sf. saw; range of mountains.

siervo, va, *siĕr'vŏ*, sm. & f. serf, slave; servant (by courtesy).

siesta, *siĕs'tă*, sf. siesta, after-dinner nap.

siete, *siĕ'tĕ*, a. & sm. seven.

sietemesino, na, *—mĕsē'nŏ*, a. born seven months after conception.

sigilo, *sĭ-hŭ'lŏ*, sm. seal; secret.

sigiloso, sa, *—lŏ'sŏ*, a. reserved; silent.

siglo, *sē'glŏ*, sm. century.

signar, *sĭgnăr'*, v. a. to sign, to seal; —se, to make the sign of the cross.

signatura, *—tŏ'ră*, sf. sign, mark; signature (in printing); [cation.

significación, *sĭgnĕfĭkăthĭŏn'*, sf. signifi-

significado, *—fĭkă'dŏ*, sm. signification.

significar, *—fĭkăr'*, v. a. to signify.

significativo, va, *—fĭkătē'vŏ*, a. significant.

signo, *sĭg'nŏ*, sm. sign, mark. [cant.

siguiente, *sĭgĭĕn'tĕ*, a. following, successive, sequent. [position.

sílaba, *sĭ'lăbă*, sf. syllable; metrical composilabario, *—bă'rĭŏ*, sm. primer.

silabear, *—bĕăr'*, v. a. to spell.

silbar, *sĭlbăr'*, v. a. to hiss; —, v. n. to whistle.

silbato, *sĭlbă'tŏ*, sm. whistle.

silbido, *sĭlbĭ'dŏ*, silbo, *sĭl'bŏ*, sm. hiss, whistling. [silence! hush!

silencio, *sĭlĕn'thĭŏ*, sm. silence; !—!

silencioso, sa, *—thĭŏ'sŏ*, a. silent.

silo, *sē'lŏ*, sm. subterranean granary for wheat.

silogismo, *sĭlŏ'hĭs'mŏ*, sm. syllogism.

silogizar, *sĭlŏ'hĭthăr'*, v. a. to reason, to argue.

silvestre, *sĭlvĕs'trĕ*, a. wild, uncultivated; savage.

silla, *sĭl'yă*, sf. chair; see; saddle; seat; — de manos, sedan-chair; — poltrona, elbow chair; do — á —, face to face.

sillar, *sĭlyăr'*, sm. square hewn stone.

sillería, *—yĕrē'ă*, sf. set of chairs; saddler's shop; stalls about the choir of a church; building of hewn stone.

sillero, *sĭlyĕ'rŏ*, sm. saddler; chair-maker.

silleta, *sĭlyĕ'tă*, sf. close-stool. [maker.

silletero, *—yĕtĕ'rŏ*, sm. chairman; chair-

sillico, *sĭlyē'kŏ*, sm. basin of a close-stool.

sillón, *sĭlyŏn'*, sm. large arm-chair; side-saddle for ladies.

sima, *sē'mă*, sf. deep and dark cavern.

simbólico, ca, *sĭmbŏ'lĭkŏ*, a. symbolical.

simbolizar, *sĭmbŏlĭthăr'*, v. n. to symbolize.

símbolo, *sĭm'bŏlŏ*, sm. symbol; device.

simetría, *sĭmĕtrē'ă*, sf. symmetry.

simétrico, ca, *sĭmĕ'trĭkŏ*, a. symmetrical.

simia, *sē'mĭă*, sf. she-ape.

simiente, *—mĭĕn'tĕ*, sf. seed. [lar, like.

simil, *sē'mĭl*, sm. resemblance; —, a. simi-

similitud, *sĭmĭlĭtŭd'*, sf. similitude.

similor, *sĭmĭlŏr'*, sm. pinchbeck.

simio, *sē'mĭŏ*, sm. male ape, monkey.

simón, *sĭmŏn'*, sm. & f. hackney coachman in Madrid.

simonía, *sĭmŏnē'ă*, sf. simony. [simony.

simoníaco, ca, *—nē'ăkŏ*, sm. & f. guilty of

simpatía, *sĭmpătē'ă*, sf. sympathy.

simpático, ca, *sĭmpă'tĭkŏ*, a. sympathetic.

simple, *sĭm'plĕ*, a. single, simple, silly; insipid; —, sm. simple (medicinal plant).

simpleza, *sĭmplĕ'thă*, sf. simpleness, silliness; rusticity.

simplicidad, *sĭmplĭthĭdăd'*, sf. simplicity.

simplificar, *—fĭkăr'*, v. a. to simplify, to make simple.

simulación, *sĭmŭlăthĭŏn'*, sf. simulation.

simulacro, *—lă'krŏ*, sm. simulachrum, idol.

simuladamente, *—lădămĕn'tĕ*, ad. deceptively, hypocritically.

simular, *—lăr'*, v. a. to simulate.

simultaneidad, *sĭmŭltănĕĭdăd'*, sf. simultaneity. [neous.

simultáneo, nea, *—tă'nĕŏ*, a. simulta-

sin, *sĭn*, pr. without, besides.

sinagoga, *sĭnăgŏ'gă*, sf. synagogue.

sincerar, *sĭnthĕrăr'*, v. a. to exculpate, to justify.

sinceridad, *—thĕrĭdăd'*, sf. sincerity.

sincero, ra, *sĭnthĕ'rŏ*, a. sincere, ingenuous, honest.

síncopa, *sĭn'kŏpă*, sf. (gr. mus.) syncope.

sincopar, *—kŏpăr'*, v. a. to syncopate.

síncope, *sĭn'kŏpĕ*, sf. (med.) syncope, fainting fit.

sindicado, *—dĭkă'dŏ*, sm. syndicate.

sindicar, *—dĭkăr'*, v. a. to lodge an information; to accuse.

síndico, *sĭn'dĭkŏ*, sm. syndic.

sinfonía, *sĭnfŏnē'ă*, sf. symphony.

singular, *—gŭlăr'*, a. singular; particular.

singularidad, *—lărĭdăd'*, sf. singularity.

singularizar, *—lărĭthăr'*, v. a. to distinguish; to singularize; —se, to distinguish oneself; to be singular.

siniestra, *sĭnĭĕs'tră*, sf. left hand.

siniestro, tra, *—trŏ*, a. left, sinister; unhappy; —, sm. depravity; evil habit.

sino, *sē'nŏ*, c. if not; but, except; besides; only.

sinodal, *sĭnŏdăl'*, a. synodic, synodal, —; sm. examiner of curates and confessors.

sínodo, *sē'nŏdŏ*, sm. synod; conjunction of the heavenly bodies.

sinónimo, ma, *sĭnŏ'nĭmŏ*, a. synonymous.

sinónomo, ma, *—nŏmŏ*, a. synonymous.

sinrazón, *—răthŏn'*, sf. injustice.

sinsabor, *—săbŏr'*, sm. displeasure, disgust.

sintaxis, *—tăk'sĭs*, sf. syntax.

síntesis, *sĭn'tĕsĭs*, sf. synthesis.

sintético, ca, *—tĕ'tĭkŏ*, a. synthetical.

síntoma, *sĭn'tŏmă*, sm. symptom.

sinuosidad, *sĭnŭŏsĭdăd'*, sf. sinuosity.

sinuoso, sa, *sĭnŭŏ'sŏ*, a. sinuous.

siquiera, *sĭkĭĕ'ră*, c. at least; though, although.

sirena, *sĭrĕ'nă*, sf. syren. [although.

sirga, *sĭr'gă*, sf. tow-rope, tow-line.

sirgar, *sĭrgăr'*, v. a. to tow a vessel.

sirte, *sĭr'tĕ*, sf. moving sand-bank.

sirvienta, *—vĭĕn'tă*, sf. female servant, serving-maid, maid-servant.

sirviente, *—tĕ*, sm. & f. a servant.

sisa, *sē'să*, sf. petty theft; clippings which tailors steal in cutting clothes; assize; excise. [cock.

sisón, *sĭsŏn'*, sm. filcher, pilferer; moor-

sistema, *sĭstā′mă,* sm. system. [matic.
sistemático, ca, *sĭstēmä′tĭkŏ,* a. syste-
sitiador, *sĭtĭädŏr′,* sm. besieger.
sitiar, *sĭtĭär′,* v. a. to besiege.
sitio, *sē′tĭŏ,* sm. place; situation (of a town, &c.); (mil.) siege, blockade.
sito, ta, *sē′tŏ,* a. situated.
situación, *sĭtŭäthĭŏn′,* sf. situation.
situado, *sĭtŭä′dŏ,* sm. allowance.
situar, *sĭtŭär′,* v. a. to place, to situate; to assign a fund; —se, to be established in place or business; to station oneself.
so, *sŏ,* pr. under; below (used in composi-tion, it occasionally diminishes the import of the verb; ¡—¡ used to stop horses or cattle.
soba, *sŏ′bă,* sf. making soft; beating.
sobaco, *sŏbä′kŏ,* sm. arm-pit, arm-hole.
sobadura, *sŏbä′dŏ′ră,* sf. kneading, rubbing.
sobajar, *—hăr′,* v. a. to scrub, to rub hard.
sobar, *sŏbär′,* v. a. to handle, to soften; to pummel, to beat, to whip; to scrub, to rub hard; to rumple clothes.
sobarba, *—bär′bă,* sf. nose-band.
sobarbada, *—bärbä′dă,* sf. chuck under the chin; jerk; (fig.) reprimand, scolding.
soberanía, *sŏbĕränē′ă,* sf. sovereignty; pride, haughtiness.
soberano, na, *—rä′nŏ,* a. & sm. sovereign.
soberbia, *—bĕr′bĭă,* sf. pride, haughtiness; presumption.
soberbio, bia, *—bĭŏ,* a. proud, haughty.
sobina, *sŏbē′nă,* sf. wooden pin or peg.
sobón, *sŏbŏn′,* sm. lazy fellow.
sobornador, ra, *—bŏrnädŏr′,* sm. & f. suborner, briber.
sobornar, *—när′,* v. a. to suborn, to bribe.
soborno, *sŏbŏr′nŏ,* sm. subornation, bribe.
sobra, *sŏ′bră,* sf. overplus, surplus, excess; offence; de —, over and above.
sobradamente, *sŏbrädämĕn′tĕ,* ad. super-abundantly.
sobradillo, *—dēl′yŏ,* sm. small granary; penthouse; shelter over a balcony.
sobrante, *—brän′tĕ,* sm. residue, super-fluity, surplus.
sobrar, *—brär′,* v. n. to have more than is necessary; to be more than enough; to remain, to be left.
sobre, *sŏ′brĕ,* pr. above, over; super; moreover; a little more; —, sm. direction and cover of a letter. [superabundance.
sobreabundancia, *—äbŭndän′thĭă,* sf.
sobreabundar, *—äbŭndär′,* v. n. to super-abound. [treble.
sobreagudo, *—äg̃ŏ′dŏ,* sm. (mus.) highest
sobrealzar, *—älthär′,* v. a. to praise, to extol.
sobreasar, *—äsär′,* v. a. to roast again.
sobrecama, *—kä′mă,* sf. coverlet, quilt.
sobrecaña, *—kän′yă,* sf. tumour in a horse's leg.
sobrecarga, *—kär′gă,* sf. additional bundle thrown over a load; surcharge, over-burden.
sobrecargar, *—kärgär′,* v. a. to overload; to sew the whole night long.
sobrecargo, *—kär′gŏ,* sm. supercargo.

sobreceja, *—thĕ′h′ă,* sf. part of the fore-head over the eye-brows. [nyŏ, sm. frown.
sobrecejo, *—thĕ′h′ŏ,* sobreceño, *—thĕn′-*
sobrecoger, *—kŏ′hĕr′,* v. a. to surprise.
sobrecubierta, *—kŭbĭĕr′tă,* sf. double cover. [mentioned.
sobredicho, cha, *—dētsh′ŏ,* a. above-
sobrediente, *—dĭĕn′tĕ,* sm. gag-tooth, projecting tooth. [palliate, to exculpate.
sobredorar, *—dŏrär′,* v. a. to overgild; to
sobrehueso, *—hĕ′sŏ,* sm. morbid swelling on the bones or joints; trouble, encum-brance. [human.
sobrehumano, na, *—ämä′nŏ,* a. super-
sobrellevar, *—lyĕvär′,* v. a. to ease, to alleviate; to suffer, to tolerate.
sobremanera, *—mänĕ′ră,* ad. excessively.
sobremesa, *—mĕs′ă,* sf. table-cover; des-sert; de —, immediately after dinner.
sobrenadar, *—nädär′,* v. a. to swim on the surface, to float.
sobrenatural, *—nätŭräl′,* a. supernatural.
sobrenaturalmente, *—mĕn′tĕ,* ad. super-naturally. [nickname.
sobrenombre, *—nŏm′brĕ,* sm. surname;
sobrentender, *sŏbrĕntĕndĕr′,* v. a. to under-stand. [augmentation of pay.
sobrepaga, *sŏbrĕpä′gă,* sf. increase or
sobreparto, *—pär′tŏ,* sm. time of lying-in.
sobrepelliz, *—pĕlyĭth′,* sf. surplice.
sobrepeso, *—pä′sŏ,* sm. overweight.
sobrepié, *—pĭä′,* sm. osseous tumour at the top of horses' hoofs.
sobreplan, *—plän′,* sm. (mar.) rider.
sobreponer, *—pŏnĕr′,* v. a. to put one thing over or on another; —se, to put oneself out of reach of, to shew oneself superior to.
sobreprecio, *—prä′thĭŏ,* sm. extra price.
sobrepujanza, *—pŭ′hän′thă,* sf. excessive strength. [surpass, to excel.
sobrepujar, *—pŭ′här′,* v. a. to exceed, to
sobrerropa, *—rŏ′pă,* sf. long robe.
sobresaliente, *—sälĭĕn′tĕ,* a. (mil.) com-manding a picket; —, sm. substitute.
sobresalir, *—sälĭr′,* v. a. to exceed in height, to surpass.
sobresaltar, *—sältär′,* v. a. to make an unexpected attack; to frighten.
sobresalto, *—säl′tŏ,* sm. sudden assault; sudden dread. [letter.
sobrescrito, *—skrē′tŏ,* sm. address of a
sobreseer, *—sĕĕr′,* v. n. to supersede; to overrule. [sion, suspension.
sobreseimiento, *—sĕĭmĭĕn′tŏ,* sm. omis-
sobresello, *—sĕl′yŏ,* sm. double seal.
sobrestante, *—stän′tĕ,* sm. overseer; fore-man. [one's pay or allowance.
sobresueldo, *—sŭĕl′dŏ,* sm. addition to
sobretodo, *—tŏ′dŏ,* sm. surtout, great-coat.
sobrevenir, *—vĕnĭr′,* v. n. to happen, to come unexpectedly; to supervene.
sobrevivir, *—vĭvĭr′,* v. n. to survive.
sobriedad, *sŏbrĭĕdäd′,* sf. sobriety.
sobrina, *sŏbrē′nă,* sf. niece.
sobrino, *—nŏ,* sm. nephew.
sobrio, ria, *sŏ′brĭŏ,* a. sober, frugal.

socaliña, sŏkălĭn´yă, sf. extortion, cheating. [cunning.

socaliñar, -lĭnyăr´, v. a. to extort by cunning.

socarrar, sŏkărrăr´, v. a. to half-roast.

socarrón, ona, -rŏn´, a. cunning, sly, crafty. [ning, artfulness.

socarronería, -nĕrĭă, sf. craft, cunning.

socavar, -kăvăr´, v. a. to undermine.

sociabilidad, sŏthĕăbĭlĭdăd´, sf. sociableness.

sociable, -thĭă´blĕ, a. sociable. [ness.

social, sŏthĭăl´, a. social.

sociedad, sŏthĭĕdăd´, sf. society.

socio, sŏ´thĭŏ, sm. associate, companion.

socolor, -kŏlŏr´, sm. pretext, pretence.

socorredor, ra, sŏkŏrrĕdŏr´, sm. & f. succourer, helper.

socorrer, -kŏrrĕr´, v. a. to succour.

socorrido, da, -rĭ dŏ, a. furnished, supplied.

socorro, sŏkŏr´rŏ, sm. succour, help; part of a salary or allowance advanced or paid beforehand.

sochantre, -tshăn´trĕ, sm. sub-chanter.

sodomía, sŏdŏmĭ´ă, sf. sodomy.

sodomita, -mĭ´tă, sm. sodomite.

soez, sŏĕth´, a. mean, vile, lousy.

sofisma, sŏfĭs´mă, sm. sophism.

sofista, fĭs´tă, sm. sophister.

sofistería, -tĕrĭă, sf. sophistry.

sofisticar, -tĭkăr´, v. a. to sophisticate.

sofístico, ca, sŏfĭs´tĭkŏ, a. sophistical.

sofocar, sŏfŏkăr´, v. a. to suffocate.

sofrenada, -frĕnă´dă, sf. sudden check given to a horse with the bridle; severe reprimand.

sofrenar, -frĕnăr´, v. a. to check a horse by a violent pull of the bridle; to reprimand severely. [for shame!

soga, sŏ´gă, sf. rope of bass-wood; ¡-! fy!

soguería, sŏgĕrĭ´ă, sf. rope-walk, rope-making. [yard.

soguero, -gĕ´rŏ, sm. rope-maker.

sojuzgador, sŏhŭthgădŏr´, sm.conqueror, subduer. [subdue.

sojuzgar, -hŭthgăr´, v. a. to conquer, to

sol, sŏl, sm. sun; (mus.) sol.

solamente, -lămĕn´tĕ, ad. only, solely.

solana, sŏlă´nă, sf. sunny place; open gallery for taking the sun.

solano, -nŏ, sm. easterly wind.

solapa, sŏlă´pă, sf. lappet; pretence, pretext. [artful.

solapado, da, -pă´dŏ, a. cunning, crafty,

solapar, -păr´, v. a. to button one's coat across; to hide under a false pretence.

solar, sŏlăr´, sm. building-lot; real estate; ancestral mansion of a noble family; -, a. solar; -, v. a. to floor a room; to sole shoes or boots.

solariego, ga, -rĭĕ´gŏ, a. belonging to the ancestral mansion of a noble family.

solaz, sŏlăth´, sm. solace, consolation; á -, pleasantly, agreeably.

solazar, -thăr´, v. a. to solace, to comfort.

solazo, sŏlă´thŏ, sm. scorching sun.

soldada, sŏldă´dă, sf. wages.

soldadesca, -dĕs´kă, sf. soldiery.

soldadesco, ca, -kŏ, a. soldierly, soldierlike.

soldado, sŏldă´dŏ, sm. soldier; - raso, common soldier, private.

soldador, -dŏr´, sm. solderer; soldering-iron. [correction.

soldadura, -dŏ´ră, sf. soldering; solder; to correct.

soldar, sŏldăr´, v. a. to solder; to mend,

solecismo, sŏlĕthĭs´mŏ, sm. solecism.

soledad, -lĕdăd´, sf. solitude; solitariness; lonely place; desert.

solemne, -lĕm´nĕ, a. solemn; celebrated; grand, high; gay, cheerful.

solemnidad, -nĭdăd´, sf. solemnity.

solemnizar, -nĭthăr´, v. a. to solemnize, to praise.

soler, sŏlĕr´, v. n. to be accustomed.

soleta, sŏlĕ´tă, sf. linen sole put into stockings.

solfa, sŏl´fă, sf. (mus.) gamut; solmization; accordance, harmony; sound flogging.

solfeador, -fĕădŏr´, sm. songster; music-master; dealer of blows.

solfear, -făr´, v. n. (mus.) to solfa.

solfeo, -fĕ´ŏ, sm. solfeggio.

solfista, -fĭs´tă, sm. & f. skilful musician.

solicitación, sŏlĭthĭtăthĭŏn´, sf. solicitation.

solicitar, -tăr´, v. a. to solicit.

solícito, ta, sŏlĭ´thĭtŏ, a. solicitous.

solicitud, -thĭtŭd´, sf. solicitude.

solidar, -dăr´, v. a. to consolidate.

solideo, -dĕ´ŏ, sm. calotte.

solidez, -dĕth´, sf. solidity.

sólido, da, sŏ´lĭdŏ, a. solid.

soliloquio, sŏlĭlŏ´kĭŏ, sm. soliloquy, monologue.

solimán, -măn´, sm. (chem.) corrosive sublimate.

solio, sŏ´lĭŏ, sm. throne.

solitaria, -tă´rĭă, sf. solitaire.

solitario, ria, -rĭŏ, a. solitary; -, sm. hermit.

solo, sŏ´lŏ, sm. (mus.) solo; -, la, a. alone, single; á solas, alone, unaided; á sus solas, quite alone; sólo, ad. only.

solomillo, sŏlŏmĭl´yŏ, solomo, sŏlŏ´mŏ, sm. loin, chine.

solsticio, sŏlstĭ´thĭŏ, sm. solstice.

soltar, sŏltăr´, v. a. to untie, to loosen; to set at liberty; -se, to get loose; to lose all decency and modesty. [woman.

soltera, -tĕ´ră, sf. spinster, unmarried

soltería, -tĕrĭ´ă, sf. celibacy.

soltero, sŏltĕ´rŏ, sm. bachelor, unmarried man; -, a. unmarried.

soltura, -tŭ´ră, sf. liberation; release; agility, activity.

soluble, sŏlŭ´blĕ, a. soluble; solvable.

solución, sŏlŭthĭŏn´, sf. solution; catastrophe of a drama.

solutivo, va, -tĭ´vŏ, a. solutive.

solvente, sŏlvĕn´tĕ, a. dissolvent; solvent.

sollo, sŏl´yŏ, sm. common pike.

sollozar, -thăr´, v. a. to sob.

sollozo, sŏlyŏ´thŏ, sm. sob.

somanta, sŏmăn´tă, sf. beating, severe chastisement.

somatén, sŏmătĕn´, sm. armed corps destined for the defence of a city or province; one who serves in such a corps.

sombra, sŏm´bră, sf. shade, shadow.

sombraje, _–brä'hě,_ sm. hut covered with branches.

sombrear, _–brěăr',_ v. a. to shade.

sombrerazo, _–brěră'thǒ,_ sm. large hat; slap with a hat. [butter-bur.

sombrerera, _–rǎ'ră,_ sf. hat-box; (bot.)

sombrerería, _–rěrě'ă,_ sf. hat-factory; hat-shop. [maker.

sombrerero, _–rǎ'rǒ,_ sm. hatter, hat-

sombrerillo _–ril'yǒ,_ sm. (bot.) navel-wort.

sombrero, _sŏmbră'rǒ,_ sm. hat.

sombrío, bría, _sŏmbrě'ǒ,_ a. shady, darksome, gloomy.

someter, _sŏmětěr',_ v. a. to submit; to subdue; **–se,** to humble oneself; to submit. [sion.

sometimiento, _–tǐmēěn'tǒ,_ sm. submis-

somnolencia, _sŏmnŏlěn'thǐă,_ sf. sleepiness, drowsiness. [cloth; rudeness.

somonte, _sŏmŏn'tě,_ sm. shaggy part of

somorgujar, _sŏmŏrgŭ'hăr',_ v. a. to dive.

son, _sŏn,_ sm. sound, report; **á –,** at the sound of. [generally reported.

sonado, da, _–nǎ'dǒ,_ a. celebrated; famous;

sonaja, _–nǎ'ẋă,_ sf. timbrel (musical instrument).

sonajero, _–hǎ'rǒ,_ sm. small timbrel.

sonámbulo, _sŏnám'bŭlǒ,_ a. & sm. sleep-walking; somnambulist.

sonar, _sŏnăr',_ v. a. to play upon a musical instrument; **–,** v. n. to sound; **–se,** to blow one's nose.

sonata, _–nă'tă,_ sf. (mus.) sonata.

sonda, _sŏn'dă,_ sf. sounding; catheter.

sondable, _–dǎ'blě,_ a. that may be sounded.

sond(e)ar, _–d(ě)ăr',_ v. a. (mar.) to sound.

sonecillo, _sŏněthǐl'yǒ,_ sm. short little tune.

soneto, _sŏnă'tǒ,_ sm. sonnet.

sonido, _sŏnǐ'dǒ,_ sm. sound.

sonoro, ra, _sŏnǒ'rǒ,_ a. sonorous.

sonreírse, _sŏnrěǐr'sě,_ v. r. to smile.

sonrisa, _–rě'să,_ sf. smile.

sonroj(e)ar, _–rǒ'h(ě)ăr',_ v. a. to make one blush with shame.

sonrojo, _–rǒ'h'ǒ,_ sm. blush; offensive word which causes a blush.

sonros(e)ar, _–rǒs(ě)ăr',_ v. a. to dye a rose colour; **–se,** to blush.

sonroseo, _–rǒsǎ'ǒ,_ sm. blush. [wheedler.

sonsacador, ra, _–săkădǒr',_ sm. & f.

sonsacamiento, _–săkămēěn'tǒ,_ sm. wheedling, extortion. [out of a person.

sonsacar, _–săkăr',_ v. a. to pump a secret

sonsonete, _–sǒnǎ'tě,_ sm. tapping noise; scornful, derisive tone.

soñador, ra, _sǒnyădǒr',_ sm. & f. dreamer.

soñar, _sŏnyăr',_ v. a. to dream.

soñoliento, ta, _sǒnyǒlěn'tǒ,_ a. sleepy, drowsy; causing sleep; dull, lazy.

sopa, _sǒ'pă,_ sf. sop; soup.

sopalanda, _–lăn'dă,_ sf. ragged clothes worn by poor students.

sopapo, _–pă'pǒ,_ sm. slap given with the hand; sucker of a pump.

sopera, _–pǎ'ră,_ sf. soup-dish.

sopero, _–pǎ'rǒ,_ sm. soup-plate.

sopetear, _–pětěăr',_ v. a. to steep bread in sauce; to abuse with foul language.

sopetón, _–tǒn',_ sm. hard box on the ears; **de –,** suddenly. [spruce.

soplado, da, _sǒplă'dǒ,_ a. over-nice and

soplamocos, _–mǒ'kǒs,_ sm. slap in the face.

soplar, _sǒplăr',_ v. n. & a. to blow; to blow bellows; to steal in an artful manner; to suggest; to inspire; to tipple, to drink much; to accuse, to denounce any one; **–se,** to dress in style.

soplete, _sǒplǎ'tě,_ sm. blowing-pipe.

soplo, _sǒ'plǒ,_ sm. blowing; puff of wind; advice given secretly; instant, moment.

soplón, ona, _sǒplǒn',_ sm. & f. tale-bearer.

soponcio, _sǒpǒn'thǐǒ,_ sm. grief arising from disappointment.

sopor, _sǒpǒr',_ sm. drowsiness, sleepiness.

soporífero, ra, _–rǐ'fěrǒ,_ a. soporific, soporiferous.

soporoso, sa, _–rǒ'sǒ,_ a. soporiferous.

soportable, _sǒpǒrtă'blě,_ a. tolerable, supportable. [portable.

soportal, _–tăl',_ sm. portico.

soportar, _–tăr',_ v. a. to suffer, to tolerate; to support.

sor, _sǒr,_ sister (used only to nuns).

sorber, _–běr',_ v. a. to sip, to suck; to absorb, to swallow; to imbibe.

sorbete, _–bě'tě,_ sm. sherbet.

sorbo, _sǒr'bǒ,_ sm. sipping; a little; small quantity of anything.

sordera, _sǒrdǎ'ră,_ sf. deafness, surdity.

sordidez, _–dǐděth',_ sf. sordidness, nastiness, covetousness. [dirty; licentious.

sórdido, da, _sǒr'dǐdǒ,_ a. sordid; nasty,

sordina, _–dǐ'nă,_ sf. damper.

sordo, da, _sǒr'dǒ,_ a. deaf; silent, quiet; secret. [slowness.

sorna, _sǒr'nă,_ sf. sluggishness, laziness,

sornavirón, _–vǐrǒn',_ sm. sudden stroke with the back of the open hand.

sorprender, _–prěnděr',_ v. a. to surprise, to fall upon unexpectedly.

sorpresa, _–prě'să,_ sf. surprise.

sorteador, _–těădǒr',_ sm. one who casts lots; dexterous bull-fighter.

sortear, _–těăr',_ v. n. to draw or cast lots; to fight bulls with skill and dexterity.

sorteo, _sǒrtǎ'ǒ,_ sm. act of casting or drawing lots.

sortija, _–tǐ'h'ă,_ sf. ring; hoop; buckle.

sortilegio, _–tǐlě'h'ǐǒ,_ sm. sortilege, sorcery.

sosegado, da, _sǒsěgă'dǒ,_ a. quiet, peaceful.

sosegar, _–găr',_ v. a. to appease, to calm; **–,** v. n. to rest, to repose; to be calm or composed.

sosería, _–sěrě'ă,_ sf. insipidity.

sosiego, _–sǐǎ'gǒ,_ sm. tranquillity, calmness, heart's ease. [thing obliquely.

soslayar, _–slăyăr',_ v. a. to do or place a

soslayo, _–slă'yǒ,_ ad. obliquely; **al ó de –,** askew, sideways.

soso, sa, _sǒ'sǒ,_ a. insipid, tasteless.

sospecha, _sǒspěch'ă,_ sf. suspicion, mistrust.

sospechar, _–těhăr',_ v. a. to suspect.

sospechoso, sa, _–ǐshǒ'sǒ,_ a. suspicious, mistrustful.

sostén, *sŏstĕn',* sm. support; steadiness of a ship in pursuing her course.

sostener, *–tĕner',* v. a. to sustain, to maintain; **–se,** to support or maintain oneself.

sostenido, *–tĕnĕ'dŏ,* sm. (mus.) sharp.

sostenimiento, *–mĭen'tŏ,* sm. sustenance.

sota, *sŏ'tă,* sf. knave (at cards). [bing.

sotana, *sŏtă'nă,* sf. cassock; flogging, drub-

sotanilla, *–nĭl'yă,* sf. college gown.

sótano, *sŏ'tănŏ,* sm. cellar under ground.

sotavento, *–vĕn'tŏ,* sm. (mar.) leeward, lee.

sotechado, *sŏtĕchă'dŏ,* sm. roofed or covered place. [growth.

soto, *sŏ'tŏ,* sm. grove, thicket; under-

su, *sŏ,* pn. his, her, its, one's; sus, theirs.

suave, *sŏă'vĕ,* a. smooth, soft, delicate; gentle, mild, meek. [ness; suavity.

suavidad, *–vĭdă',* sf. softness, sweet-

suavizar, *–vĭthăr',* v. a. to soften.

subalterno, na, *sŏbăltĕr'nŏ,* a. subaltern, inferior. [under-tenant.

subarrendador, ra, *–ărrĕndădŏr',* sm. & f.

subarrendar, *–ărrĕndăr',* v. a. to sub-rent.

subarriendo, *–ărrĭen'dŏ,* sm. sub-lease.

subasta, *–ăs'tă,* **subastación,** *–ăstă-thĭon',* sf. judicial auction, open sale.

subastar, *–ăstăr',* v. a. to sell by auction.

subdelegación, *–dĕlĕgăthĭon',* sf. sub-delegation, substitution.

subdelegado, *–dĕlĕgă'dŏ,* sm. subdelegate.

subdelegar, *–dĕlĕgăr',* v. a. to subdelegate.

subdiaconado, *–dĭăkŏnă'dŏ,* **subdiaconato,** *–nă'tŏ,* sm. subdeaconship.

subdiácono, *–dĭă'kŏnŏ,* sm. subdeacon.

súbdito, ta, *sŏb'dĭtŏ,* a. subject.

subdividir, *sŏbdĭvĭdĭr',* v. a. to subdivide.

subdivisión, *–dĭvĭsĭon',* sf. subdivision.

subida, *sŏbĭ'dă,* sf. mounting; ascent, ac-clivity, rise; enhancement, augmentation of value or price.

subido, da, *–bĭ'dŏ,* a. deep-coloured; very fine, very excellent.

subir, *sŏbĭr',* v. n. to mount, to ascend, to climb; to increase, to swell; to enter leaves (of silk-worms, in making their cocoons); to rise in dignity, fortune, &c.; **–,** v. a. to ascend; to go up; to enhance.

súbito, ta, *sŏ'bĭtŏ,* a. sudden, hasty, un-foreseen. [junctive.

subjuntivo, *sŏbhŭntĭ'vŏ,* sm. (gr.) sub-

sublevación, *–lĕvăthĭon',* sf. sedition, revolt. [bellion; to rise in rebellion.

sublevar, *–lĕvăr',* v. a. to excite a re-

sublimado, *sŏblĭmă'dŏ,* sm. sublimate.

sublime, *sŏblĭ'mĕ,* a. sublime.

sublimidad, *sŏblĭmĭdă',* sf. sublimity.

subordinación, *–ŏrdĭnăthĭon',* sf. sub-ordination.

subordinar, *–ŏrdĭnăr',* v. a. to sub-ordinate.

subrepción, *–rĕpthĭon',* sf. hidden action, underhand business; subreption.

subrepticio, cia, *–tĭ'thĭŏ,* a. surrep-titious; done in a clandestine manner.

subrogación, *–rŏgăthĭon',* sf. surroga-tion, subrogation, substitution.

subrogar, *–rŏgăr',* v. a. to surrogate, to subrogate. [mend, to repair.

subsanar, *–sănăr',* v. a. to excuse; to

subsidio, *–sĕ'dĭŏ,* sm. subsidy, aid.

subsistencia, *–sĭstĕn'thĭă,* sf. subsistence; permanence, stability.

subsistir, *–sĭstĭr',* v. n. to subsist.

substancia, *–stăn'thĭă,* sf. substance.

substancial, *–stănthĭăl',* a. substantial.

substancialmente, *–mĕn'tĕ,* ad. sub-stantially. [to aver, to verify.

substanciar, *–stănthĭăr',* v. a. to abridge;

substancioso, sa, *–thĭŏ'sŏ,* a. substan-tial, nutritive, nutritious. [tion.

substracción, *–străkthĭon',* sf. subtrac-

substraer, *–străĕr',* v. n. to subtract; **–se,** to retire, to withdraw. [tenant.

subteniente, *–tĕnĭen'tĕ,* sm. sub-lieu-

subterfugio, *sŏbtĕrfŏ'hĭŏ,* sf. subterfuge, shift. [terraneous; **–,** sm. subterrane.

subterráneo, nea, *sŏbtĕrră'nĕŏ,* a. sub-

subvenir, *–vĕnĭr',* v. a. to aid, to suc-cour. [overthrow.

subversión, *–vĕrsĭon',* sf. subversion.

subversivo, va, *–vĕrsĕ'vŏ,* a. subversive.

subvertir, *–vĕrtĭr',* v. a. to subvert, to destroy, to ruin.

subyugar, *–yŏgăr',* v. a. to subdue, to subjugate. [herit.

suceder, *sŭthĕdĕr',* v. n. to succeed, to in-

sucesión, *sŭthĕsĭon',* sf. succession; issue, offspring; hereditary succession.

sucesivo, va, *–sĕ'vŏ,* a. successive.

suceso, *sŭthĕ'sŏ,* sm. success. [heir.

sucesor, *–sŏr',* sm. successor, succeeder;

suciedad, *sŭthĭĕdă',* sf. nastiness, filthi-ness, dirt, mire.

sucinto, ta, *–hĭn'tŏ,* a. succinct, concise.

sucio, cia, *sŏ'thĭŏ,* a. dirty, nasty, filthy; obscene; dishonest. [juicy.

suculento, ta, *sŭkŭlĕn'tŏ,* a. succulent,

sucumbir, *–kŭmbĭr',* v. n. to succumb.

sud, *sŭd,* sm. south; south wind.

sudar, *sŭdăr',* v. a. to sweat; to give with repugnance.

sudario, *–dă'rĭŏ,* sm. sweat-cloth.

sudeste, *sŭdĕs'tĕ,* sm. south-east.

sudoeste, *–dŏĕs'tĕ,* sm. south-west.

sudor, *sŭdŏr',* sm. sweat. [sweat.

sudoriento, ta, *–rĭen'tŏ,* a. moist with

sudorífico, ca, *–rĭfĭkŏ,* a. sudorific.

sudoso, sa, *–dŏ'sŏ,* a. sweaty.

suegra, *sŭĕ'gră,* sf. mother-in-law.

suegro, *–grŏ,* sm. father-in-law.

suela, *sŭĕ'lă,* sf. sole of the shoe; sole leather.

sueldo, *sŭĕl'dŏ,* sm. ancient Roman coin; sou (French halfpenny); wages, salary.

suelo, *sŭĕ'lŏ,* sm. soil, surface; sole; district.

suelta, *sŭĕl'tă,* sf. loosening, loose; tethers; hobbles; **dar –,** to liberate for a short time.

suelto, ta, *sŭĕl'tŏ,* a. loose; expeditious, swift; **–,** sm. loose piece of metal found near mines.

sueño, *sŭĕn'yŏ,* sm. sleep; vision, dream.

suero, *sŭå'rŏ*, sm. whey.
suerte, *sŭår'tĕ*, sf. chance, lot, fortune, good-luck, hap-hazard; kind, sort; species; manner.
suficiencia, *sŭfĭthĕn'thĕå*, sf. sufficiency; á —, sufficiently, enough. [capable.
suficiente, *-thĕn'tĕ*, a. sufficient; fit,
sufocación, *sŭfŏkåthĭón'*, sf. suffocating.
sufocar, *-kår'*, v. a. to suffocate, to choke; to quench.
sufragáneo, *sŭfrågå'nĕŏ*, sm. suffragan; —, ea, a. belonging to a suffragan.
sufragar, *-frågår'*, v. a. to aid, to assist.
sufragio, *sŭfrå'hĭŏ*, sm. vote, suffrage; aid, assistance.
sufrible, *sŭfrē'blĕ*, a. sufferable.
sufrido, da, *sŭfrē'dŏ*, a. long suffering, patient. [patience.
sufrimiento, *-mĭĕn'tŏ*, sm. sufferance,
sufrir, *sŭfrēr'*, v. a. to suffer, to bear with patience; to permit.
sugerir, *sŭ'hĕrēr'*, v. a. to suggest.
sugestión, *-'hĕstĭón'*, sf. suggestion.
suicida, *sŭĭthē'då*, sm. suicide, self-murderer.
suicidio, *-thē'dĭŏ*, sm. suicide, self-murder.
sujeción, *sŭ'hĕthĭón'*, sf. subjection; argument. [ject.
sujetar, *-'hĕtår'*, v. a. to subdue; to subsujeto, ta, *sŭ'hĕ'tŏ*, a. subject, liable, exposed; —, sm. subject; matter under discussion.
sulfúreo, rea, *sŭlfŏ'rĕŏ*, a. sulphureous.
sulfúrico, *-rĭkŏ*, a. sulphuric.
sultán, *sŭltån'*, sm. sultan.
sultana, *-tå'nå*, sf. sultana, sultaness.
suma, *sŭ'må*, sf. sum; substance.
sumar, *-mår'*, v. a. to add, to sum up; —, v. n. to cast up accounts.
sumario, ria, *-må'rĭŏ*, a. summary; —, sm. compendium, summary.
sumergir, *-mĕr'hēr'*, v. a. to submerge.
sumersión, *-mĕrsĭón'*, sf. submersion, immersion.
sumidero, *-mĭdĕ'rŏ*, sm. sewer, drain.
sumiller, *-mĭlyĕr'*, sm. chief of several offices in the king's household; — de corps, Lord Chamberlain.
suministración, *-mĭnĭstråthĭón'*, sf. supply, furnishing.
suministrador, ra, *-trådŏr'*, sm. & f. provider. [furnish.
suministrar, *-trår'*, v. a. to supply, to sumir, *sŭmēr'*, v. a. to take, to receive the chalice at mass; —se, to sink under ground; to be sunken (of one's features).
sumisión, *-mĭsĭón'*, sf. submission.
sumiso, sa, *-mē'sŏ*, a. submissive, humble.
sumo, ma, *sŭ'mŏ*, a. highest, greatest; á lo —, at most; to the highest pitch.
súmulas, *sŏ'mŭlås*, sf. pl. synopsis of the first elements of logic.
sumulístico, ca, *sŭmŭlēs'tĭkŏ*, a. belonging to summaries of logic. [ness.
suntuosidad, *sŭntŭŏsĭdåd'*, sf. sumptuoussuntuoso, sa, *-tŭŏ'sŏ*, a. sumptuous.
supeditación, *sŭpĕdĭtåthĭón'*, sf. trampling under foot.

supeditar, *-tår'*, v. a. to trample under foot.
superable, *sŭpĕrå'blĕ*, a. superable, conquerable. [superabundance.
superabundancia, *-åbŭndån'thĭå*, sf.
superabundar, *-åbŭndår'*, v. n. to superabound.
superar, *sŭpĕrår'*, v. a. to surpass.
superchería, *sŭpĕrchĕrē'å*, sf. deceit, fraud. [smattering.
superficial, *-fĭthĭål'*, a. superficial;
superficie, *-fē'thĭĕ*, sf. superficies, surface.
superfino, na, *-fē'nŏ*, a. superfine.
superfluidad, *-flŭĭdåd'*, sf. superfluity.
superfluo, ua, *sŭpĕr'flŭŏ*, a. superfluous, unnecessary. [superintendence.
superintendencia, *-ĭntĕndĕn'thĭå*, sf.
superintendente, *-dĕn'tĕ*, sm. superintendent, intendant.
superior, *sŭpĕrĭór'*, a. superior; upper (in geography); —, sm. superior.
superioridad, *-rĭdåd'*, sf. superiority.
superlativo, va, *sŭpĕrlåtē'vŏ*, a. & sm. (gr.) superlative. [supernumerary.
supernumerario, ria, *-nŭmĕrå'rĭŏ*, a.
superstición, *-stĭthĭón'*, sf. superstition.
supersticioso, sa, *-stĭthĭŏ'sŏ*, a. superstitious.
supino, na, *sŭpē'nŏ*, a. supine, on one's back; —, sm. (gr.) supine.
suplantación, *sŭplåntåthĭón'*, sf. supplanting. [with a document.
suplantar, *-tår'*, v. a. to falsify or tamper
suplefaltas, *sŭplĕfål'tås*, sm. substitute.
suplemento, *-mĕn'tŏ*, sm. supplement.
súplica, *sŏ'plĭkå*, sf. petition, request, supplication. [plicant.
suplicante, *sŭplĭkån'tĕ*, a. & sm. supsuplicar, *-kår'*, v. a. to supplicate; to make a humble reply to a superior; to petition against a sentence. [rogatory.
suplicatorio, *-tŏ'rĭŏ*, sf. (law) letters suplicio, *sŭplē'thĭŏ*, sm. capital punishment.
suplir, *sŭplēr'*, v. a. to supply; to serve instead of, to perform another's functions; to disguise. [surmise.
suponer, *-pŏnĕr'*, v. a. to suppose; to grant authority.
suposición, *-pŏsĭthĭón'*, sf. supposition; authority.
supremo, ma, *sŭprĕ'mŏ*, a. supreme.
supresión, *-prĕsĭón'*, sf. suppression.
suprimir, *sŭprĭmēr'*, v. a. to suppress.
supuesto, *-pŭĕs'tŏ*, sm. supposition; —, ta, a. supposititious, supposed; — que, allowing that, granting that.
supuración, *-råthĭón'*, sf. suppuration.
supurar, *-pŭrår'*, v. a. to suppurate.
supurativo, va, *-råtē'vŏ*, a. promoting suppuration.
sur, *sŭr*, sm. south; south wind.
surcador, *-kådŏr'*, sm. ploughman.
surcar, *-kår'*, v. a. to furrow.
surco, *sŭr'kŏ*, sm. furrow.
surgidero, *-hĭdĕ'rŏ*, sm. anchoring-place.
surgir, *-hēr'*, v. a. to anchor; to surge.
surtido, *-tē'dŏ*, sm. assortment, supply.

surtidor, ra, –tĭdŏr´, sm. & f. purveyor, caterer; water-spout. [to provide.

surtir, sûrtĭr´, v. a. to supply, to furnish.

susceptible, sŭsthĕptĕ´blĕ, a. susceptible.

suscitar, –thĭtăr´, v. a. to excite, to stir up.

suscribir, sŭskrĭbĭr´, v. a. to subscribe.

suscripción, –skrĭpthĭŏn´, sf. subscription; signature. [scriber.

suscriptor, ra, –skrĭptŏr´, sm. & f. subscriber.

susodicho, cha, sŭsŏdĭtsh´ă, a. fore-mentioned, aforesaid.

suspender, –pĕndĕr´, v. a. to suspend.

suspensión, –pĕnsĭŏn´, sf. suspension.

suspensivo, va, –sĕ´vŏ, a. suspensive.

suspenso, sa, –pĕn´sŏ, a. suspended, unfinished. [& f. suspensory.

suspensorio, ria, –pĕnsŏ´rĭŏ, a. & sm.

suspicacia, sŭspĭkă´thĭă, sf. suspiciousness, jealousy.

suspicaz, –kăth´, a. suspicious, jealous.

suspirar, –spĭrăr´, v. n. to sigh.

suspiro, sŭspĕ´rŏ, sm. sigh; sugar sweetmeat. [jectives, &c. as substantives.

sustantivar, sŭstăntĭvăr´, v. a. to use adjectives, &c. as substantives.

sustantivo, va, –tĕ´vŏ, a. & sm. (gr.) substantive, noun.

sustentación, –tĕntăthĭŏn´, sf. sustentation, support. [support, to nourish.

sustentar, –tĕntăr´, v. a. to sustain; to

sustento, –tĕn´tŏ, sm. food, sustenance.

sustitución, –tĭtŭthĭŏn´, sf. substitution.

sustituir, –tĭtŭĭr´, v. a. to substitute.

sustituto, –tĭtŭ´tŏ, a. & sm. substitute.

susto, sŭs´tŏ, sm. fright, sudden terror.

susurrar, sŭsŭrrăr´, v. n. to whisper, to divulge a secret; to murmur (of streams); –se, to be whispered about.

susurro, sŭsŭrrŏ, sm. whisper, murmur.

sutil, sŭ´tĭl, a. subtile; subtle.

sutileza, sŭtĭlĕthă, sf. subtlety.

sutilizar, –tĭlĭzăr´, v. a. to subtilize; to polish; to discuss profoundly.

suyo, ya, sŭ´yŏ, a. his, hers, theirs, one's; his, her, its own, one's own or their own; de –, spontaneously; –s, sm. pl. their own, near friends, relations, acquaintances, servants.

T.

taba, tă´bă, sf. bone of the knee-pan; small bone. [snuff.

tabaco, tăbă´kŏ, sm. tobacco; – de polvo,

tábano, tă´bănŏ, sm. hornet.

tabaola, tăbăŏ´lă, sf. noise, shouting.

tabaquera, –kĕ´ră, sf. snuff-box.

tabaquero, –kĕ´rŏ, sm. tobacconist.

tabardillo, tăbărdĭl´yŏ, sm. burning fever.

taberna, tăbĕr´nă, sf. tavern.

tabernáculo, –nă´kŭlŏ, sm. tabernacle.

tabernero, –nĕ´rŏ, sm. tavern-keeper.

tabicar, tăbĭkăr´, v. a. to wall up. [wall.

tabique, tăbĕ´kĕ, sm. thin wall; partition-

tabla, tă´blă, sf. board; table; butcher's block; index of a book; bed of earth in a garden; –s, pl. tables containing the Decalogue; backgammon-board.

tablado, tăblă´dŏ, sm. scaffold, stage; frame of a bedstead; (mar.) platform.

tablajería, –hĕrĕ´ă, sf. gaming, gambling.

tablajero, –hă´rŏ, sm. gamester; butcher.

tablazo, –lă´thŏ, sm. blow with a board; arm of the sea or of a river.

tablazón, –thŏn´, sf. boarding, planking, decks and sheathing of a ship.

tablero, tăblĕ´rŏ, sm. planed board; chess-board; draft-board; gambling-house; stock of a crossbow; tailor's shop-board.

tableta, –blĕ´tă, sf. tablet; cracknel.

tabletear, –blĕtĕăr´, v. n. to move boards noisily.

tablilla, –blĭl´yă, sf. list of persons excommunicated exhibited in churches; tablet of chocolate; – de mesón, sign of an inn.

tabuco, tăbŏ´kŏ, sm. hut, small apartment.

taburete, –bŭră´tĕ, sm. chair without arms.

taburón, –rŏn´, sm. shark (fish).

tacañería, tăkănyĕrĕ´ă, sf. malicious cunning; niggardliness.

tacaño, ña, –kăn´yŏ, a. artful, knavish; stingy, sordid.

tácito, ta, tă´thĭtŏ, a. tacit, silent; implied.

taciturno, na, tăthĭtŭr´nŏ, a. tacit, silent; melancholy. [rammer; billiard-cue.

taco, tă´kŏ, sm. stopper, stopple; wad;

tacón, tăkŏn´, sm. heel-piece. [heels.

taconear, –nĕăr´, v. n. to walk on one's

taconeo, –nĕ´ŏ, sm. clatter of the heels in walking. [dancing.

táctica, tăk´tĭkă, sf. tactics.

tacto, tăk´tŏ, sm. touch, feeling; tact.

tacha, tătsh´ă, sf. fault, defect; small nail.

tachar, tătshăr´, v. a. to find fault with; to reprehend; to blot, to efface.

tachonar, tătshŏnăr´, v. a. to ornament with lace trimming; to stud with gilt-headed nails.

tachuela, tătshŭĕ´lă, sf. tack, nail.

tafanario, tăfănă´rĭŏ, sm. breeches, posterior, backside.

tafetán, tăfĕtăn´, sm. taffety.

táfilete, tăfĭlĕ´tĕ, sm. Morocco leather.

tahalí, tăălĕ´, sm. shoulder-belt.

tahona, tăŏ´nă, sf. horse-mill; crushing-mill; bakehouse. [mill.

tahonero, tăŏnă´rŏ, sm. miller of a horse-

tahur, tăŭr´, sm. gambler, gamester.

tahurería, –rĕrĕ´ă, sf. gaming-house; fraudulent gambling. [crafty.

taimado, da, tăĭmă´dŏ, a. sly, cunning,

taja, tă´hă, sf. cut, incision; dissection; tally. [ness.

tajada, tă´hĕ´dă, sf. slice; (fam.) hoarse-

tajadera, –dĕ´ră, sf. chopping-knife.

tajador, ra, –dŏr´, sm. & f. chopper, cutter; chopping-block; trencher.

tajadura, –dŏ´ră, sf. cut, notch; section.

tajaplumas, –plŏ´măs, sm. pen-knife.

tajar, tă´hăr´, v. a. to cut, to chop; to hew; to cut a quill.

tajo, tă´hŏ, sm. cut, incision; cutting of a quill with a pen-knife; chopping-block.

tajuela, *tā´hãd´lã,* sf., **tajuelo,** *–lõ,* sm. low stool with four feet.

tal, *tãl,* a. such; con –, provided that; no hay –, no such thing.

tala, *tã´lã,* sf. felling of trees.

talabera, *–bã´rã,* sf. kind of crockery.

talador, ra, *–dõr´,* sm. & f. destroyer.

taladrar, *–drãr´,* v. a. to bore, to pierce.

taladro, *tãlã´drõ,* sm. borer, gimblet, auger.

tálamo, *tã´lãmõ,* sm. bride-chamber; bridal bed.

talanquera, *tãlãnkã´rã,* sf. parapet, breast-work.

talante, *tãlãn´tõ,* sm. manner of performance; appearance, aspect; will, pleasure.

talar, *tãlãr´,* v. a. to fell trees; to desolate, to havoc; –, a. trailing, down to the heels (of clothes); –, sm. wing on the heels (of Mercury).

taloo, *tãl´kõ,* sm. talk.   [heel of Mercury.

talega, *tãlã´gã,* sf. bag; bagful.

talego, *–gõ,* sm. gunny-sack; clumsy, awkward fellow.

taleguilla, *tãlãgīl´yã,* sf. small bag.

talento, *tãlãn´tõ,* sm. talent.

talión, *tãliõn´,* sf. retaliation, requital.

talismán, *tãlismãn´,* sm. talisman.

talón, *tãlõn´,* sm. heel; heel-piece of a shoe; (rail.) luggage-ticket; receipt; (am.) duplicate-check.

talonear, *–nãr´,* v. n. to walk fast.

talla, *tãl´yã,* sf. raised work; sculpture; stature, size; measure of any thing; hand, draw, turn (at cards); media –, half-relief.   [graved.

tallado, da, *tãlyã´dõ,* a. cut, carved, en-

tallador, *–dõr´,* sm. engraver.

tallar, *tãlyãr´,* v. a. to cut, to chop; to carve in wood; to engrave; –, sm. forest of wood fit for cutting.   [waist.

talle, *tãl´yõ,* sm. shape, size, proportion;

taller, *tãlyõr´,* sm. workshop, laboratory.

tallista, *–yīs´tã,* sm. wood-carver, engraver.

tallo, *tãl´yõ,* sm. shoot, sprout.

talludo, da, *–yõ´dõ,* a. thick-stalked.

tamañito, *tãmãnyī´tõ,* a. fearful, intimidated.

tamaño, *tãmãn´yõ,* sm. size, shape, bulk; – ña, a. showing the size, shape or bulk of anything.

tamarindo, *tãmãrīn´dõ,* sm. tamarind-tree.

tamarisco, *–rīs´kõ,* **tamariz,** *–rīth´,* sm. tamarisk-shrub.   [ger, to waver.

tambalear, –se, *tãmbãlããr´,* v. n. to stagger.

tambaleo, *–bãlã´õ,* sm. staggering, reeling.

también, *tãmbiãn´,* c. & ad. also, likewise; as well.

tambor, *tãmbõr´,* sm. drum; drummer; iron cylinder; small inclosure as a screen to the gates of a fortress; –mayor, (mil.) drum-major.

tamboril, *–bõrīl´,* sm. tabour, tabor.

tamborilada, *–bõrīlã´dã,* sf., **tamborilazo,** *–lã´thõ,* sm. blow or fall on one's posterior.   [plane or level types.

tamborilear, –rīlãr´, v. n. to tabour; to

tamborilero, *–lã´rõ,* sm. tabourer.

tamborilete, *–lã´tõ,* sm. planer (in printing).

tamborítero, *–tã´rõ,* sm. tabourer. [ing).

tamiz, *tãmīth´,* sm. fine sieve.

tamo, *tã´mõ,* sm. fluff which falls from woollen or linen in weaving; corn-dust; dust under beds or behind furniture.

tamorlán, *tãmõrlãn´,* sm. Tartar emperor.

tampoco, *tãmpõ´kõ,* ad. neither, not either.

tan, *tãn,* sm. sound of the tabour; –, ad. so, so much, as well, as much.

tanda, *tãn´dã,* sf. turn; rotation; task; gang; number of persons employed in a work; en –, number of lashes.

tanganillas, *tãngãnīl´yãs,* ad. waveringly.

tanganillo, *–nīl´yõ,* sm. small prop or stay.   [bone used at hob.

tángano, *tãn´gãnõ,* sm. hob (boys' game);

tangente, *tãn´hõn´tõ,* sf. (geom.) tangent

tangible, *–hõ´blõ,* a. tangible.

tantarantán, *–tãrãntãn´,* sm. roll of a drum; sounding blow.

tantear, *–tãr´,* v. a. to measure, to proportion; to mark the game with counters; to consider; to examine; –se, to redeem a barony or lordship.

tanteo, *tãntã´õ,* sm. computation, calculation; playing-counters; valuation.

tanto, *tãn´tõ,* sm. certain sum or quantity; copy of a writing; –, ta, a. so much, as much; very great; –, ad. so, in such a manner; a long time.

tañedor, ra, *tãnyãdõr´,* sm. & f. player on a musical instrument.

tañer, *tãnyõr´,* v. imp. to concern.

tañido, *tãnyī´dõ,* sm. tune; sound; clink.

tapa, *tã´pã,* sf. lid, cover; – de los sesos, top of the skull.

tapadera, *–dã´rã,* sf. lid of a pot, cover.

tapadero, *–dã´rõ,* sm. large stopper.

tapadillo, *–dīl´yõ,* sm. covercle; covered register in an organ-pipe.

tapadura, *–dã´rã,* sf. act of covering.

tapafunda, *–fūn´dã,* sf. holster-cover.

tapar, *tãpãr´,* v. a. to stop up, to cover; to conceal, to hide.

tapatán, *–tãn´,* **taparatapán,** *–rãtãpãn´,* sm. word indicating the sound of a drum.

tapete, *tãpã´tõ,* sm. small floor-carpet.

tapia, *tã´piã,* sf. mud-wall.   [walls.

tapial, *tãpiãl´,* sm. mould for making mud-

tapiar, *tãpiãr´,* v. a. to brick up with a mud-wall; to stop up a passage.

tapicería, *tãpīthãrã´ã,* sf. tapestry.

tapicero, *–thã´rõ,* sm. tapestry-maker.

tapiz, *tãpīth´,* sm. tapestry.   [pestry.

tapizar, *tãpīthãr´,* v. a. to hang with ta-

tapón, *tãpõn´,* sm. cork, plug, bung.

tapujarse, *tãpã´hãr´sõ,* v. r. to muffle oneself up.   [writing.

taquigrafía, *tãkīgrãfī´ã,* sf. short-hand

taquígrafo, *tãkī´grãfõ,* sm. short-hand writer.

tara, *tã´rã,* sf. tare.

taracea, *–thã´ã,* sf. marquetry, checker-work.

taracear, *–thãr´,* v. a. to make inlaid work;

taragallo, *–gãl´yõ,* sm. clog, piece of wood suspended from the neck of beasts.

tarambana, *tãrãmbã´nã,* sm. & f. giddy person of little stability or judgment.

tarantela, _tărăntă'lă_, sf. tarantella, Neapolitan peasant dance; its tune.
tarántula, _tărăn'tŭlă_, sf. tarantula.
tararira, _tărără'ră_, sf. noisy mirth.
tarasca, _tărăs'kă_, sf. figure of a serpent borne in processions, indicating the triumph of Christ over the devil; ugly, ill-natured woman. [answer.
tarascada, _kă'dă_, sf. bite; pert, harsh
taravilla, _tărăvîl'yă_, sf. mill-clack; wooden latch; prattler, tattler.
tarazón, _-thŏn'_, sm. large slice, especially of fish.
tardanza, _tărdăn'thă_, sf. slowness, delay.
tardar, _-dăr'_, v. n. to delay, to put off, to tarry. [late.
tarde, _tăr'dă_, sf. afternoon; evening; —, ad.
tardepiache, _-pîătsh'ă_, ad. very late.
tardío, dia, _tărdî'ŏ_, a. late; slow, tardy.
tardo, da, _tăr'dŏ_, a. a sluggish, tardy.
tarea, _tără'ă_, sf. task.
tarifa, _tărî'tă_, sf. tariff. [tariff.
tarifar, _-tăr'_, v. a. to tariff, to set up a
tarima, _tărî'mă_, sf. window-ledge; step.
tarjeta, _tărhĕ'tă_, sf. visiting-card; card; — postal, post-card.
tarreñas, _tărrĕn'yăs_, sf. pl. rattle.
tarro, _tăr'rŏ_, sm. glazed earthen pan.
tarta, _tăr'tă_, sf. tart; pan for baking tarts.
tartalear, _tărtălăăr'_, v. n. to reel, to stagger; to be perplexed. [to stammer.
tartamudear, _-mŏdăăr'_, v. n. to stutter,
tartamudo, da, _-mŏ'dŏ_, a. stammering.
tartana, _tărtă'nă_, sf. tartan.
Tártaro, _tăr'tărŏ_, sm. Tartar; (poet.) hell.
tartera, _tărtă'ră_, sf. baking-pan (for tarts).
tarugo, _tărŏ'gŏ_, sm. wooden peg or pin.
tasa, _tăs'ă_, sf. rate, assize; measure, rule; valuation. [praisement.
tasación, _tăsăthŏn'_, sf. valuation, appraiser.
tasador, _-dŏr'_, sm. appraiser.
tasar, _tăsăr'_, v. a. to appraise, to value.
tascar, _tăskăr'_, v. a. to break flax or hemp; to nibble grass; to champ the bit.
tasco, _tăs'kŏ_, sm. refuse of flax or hemp; toppings of hemp.
tasto, _tăs'tŏ_, sm. nasty taste.
tatarabuelo, _tătără̆bŭĕ'lŏ_, sm. great-great-grandfather. [grandson.
tataranieto, _-nîĕ'tŏ_, sm. great-great-tatel ta'tĕ, take care! beware!
taumaturgo, _tăŭmătŭr'gŏ_, sm. miracle-worker. [zodiac).
Tauro, _tă'ŭrŏ_, sm. Taurus (sign of the
tautología, _tăŭtŏlŏ'hî'ă_, sf. tautology.
taza, _tă'thă_, sf. cup; basin of a fountain; (fig. & fam.) buttocks, breech.
taxmia, _tăthmî'ă_, sf. share of tithes.
te, _tă_, sm. (bot.) tea.
te, _tĕ_, pn. thee.
tea, _tĕ'ă_, sf. candle-wood; torch.
teatral, _tĕătrăl'_, a. theatrical.
teatro, _tĕă'trŏ_, sm. theatre, playhouse.
tecla, _tĕk'lă_, sf. key of an organ or piano-forte.
teclado, _tĕklă'dŏ_, sm. key-board.
técnico, ca, _tĕk'nîkŏ_, a. technical.
techo, _tĕtsh'ŏ_, sm. roof; dwelling-house.

techumbre, _-ŭm'brĕ_, sf. upper roof, ceiling. [ing.
Tedéum, _tĕdă'ŭm_, sm. Te Deum.
tedio, _tĕ'dîŏ_, sm. disgust, dislike, abhorrence.
teja, _tĕ'hă_, sf. roof-tile. [rence.
tejado, _tĕhă'dŏ_, sm. roof covered with tiles. [tile.
tejar, _tĕhăr'_, sm. tile-works; —, v. a. to
tejedor, _tĕhĕdŏr'_, sm. weaver.
tejedura, _-dŏ'ră_, sf. texture, weaving; woven stuff. [cleverness; restlessness.
tejemaneje, _-mănĕ'hĕ_, sm. artfulness,
tejer, _tĕhĕr'_, v. a. to weave. [kiln.
tejera, _-hă'ră_, tejería, _-hĕrĕ'ă_, sf. tile-
tejero, _-hă'rŏ_, sm. tile-maker.
tejido, _-hî'dŏ_, sm. texture, web.
tejo, _tĕ'hŏ_, sm. quoit; yew-tree.
tejón, _tĕhŏn'_, sm. badger.
tela, _tĕ'lă_, sf. cloth; woven stuff.
telar, _tĕlăr'_, sm. loom.
telaraña, _-răn'yă_, sf. cobweb.
telefonio, _tĕlĕfŏ'rî'ŏ_, sm. telephon.
telegráfico, ca, _-gră'fîkŏ_, a. telegraphic.
telégrafo, _tĕlă'grăfŏ_, sm. telegraph.
telescopio, _tĕlĕskŏ'pîŏ_, sm. telescope.
telón, _tĕlŏn'_, sm. drop-scene in a playhouse
tema, _tă'mă_, sm. theme; —, sf. hobby.
temblar, _tĕmblăr'_, v. n. to tremble.
tembleque, _-blĕ'kĕ_, sm. diamond pin, plume, or other ornament for ladies' head-dresses.
temblón, ona, _-blŏn'_, a. tremulous.
temblor, _-blŏr'_, sm. trembling.
temer, _tĕmĕr'_, v. a. to fear, to doubt.
temerario, ria, _-ră'rîŏ_, a. rash, temerarious. [prudence.
temeridad, _-rîdăd'_, sf. temerity, immense.
temeroso, sa, _-rŏ'sŏ_, a. timid, timorous.
temible, _tĕmĕ'blĕ_, a. dreadful, terrible.
temor, _-mŏr'_, sm. dread, fear.
tímpano, _tĕm'pănŏ_, sm. tympanum.
temperamento, _-pĕrămĕn'tŏ_, sm. temperament.
temperar, _-pĕrăr'_, v. a. to temperate.
temperatura, _-pĕrătŏ'ră_, sf. temperature.
tempestad, _-pĕstăd'_, sf. tempest, storm; violent commotion.
tempestuoso, sa, _-tŏŏ'sŏ_, a. tempestuous, stormy. [perately, moderately.
templadamente, _-plădămĕn'tĕ_, ad. tem-
templado, da, _-plă'dŏ_, a. temperate, tempered.
templador, _-dŏr'_, sm. & f. tuning-key.
templanza, _-plăn'thă_, sf. temperance, moderation; temperature.
templar, _-plăr'_ v. a. to temper, to moderate, to cool; to tune; —se, to be moderate.
templario, _-plă'rîŏ_, sm. templar.
temple, _tĕm'plĕ_, sm. temperature; temper, temperament; harmonious accordance of musical instruments; al —, painted in distemper.
templo, _tĕm'plŏ_, sm. temple. [distemper.
Témpora, _tĕm'pŏră_, sf. Ember-days.
temporada, _-ră'dă_, sf. certain space of time, epoch, period.
temporal, _-răl'_, a. temporary, temporal; —, sm. season; tempest, storm.

temporalidad, _–lĭdăd′_, sf. temporality.
temporalizar, _–lĭthăr′_, v. a. to make temporary what should be everlasting.
temprano, na, _–prā′nŏ_, a. early, anticipated; _–_, ad. very early, prematurely.
tenacillas, _tĕnăthĭl′yăs_, sf. pl. small tongs.
tenacidad, _–thĭdăd′_, sf. tenacity; obstinacy.
tenada, _tĕnā′dă_, sf. sheepfold.
tenaz, _–năth′_, a. tenacious; stubborn.
tenaza, _tĕnā′thă_, sf. tongs, pincers.
tenazada, _–thā′dă_, sf. grip with pincers or tongs; act of biting strongly.
tenazmente, _–mĕn′tĕ_, ad. tenaciously; obstinately.
tenca, _tĕn′kă_, sf. tench.
ten con ten, _tĕn kŏn tĕn′_, sm. moderation, temperance; _–_, ad. equally.
tendedero, _–dĕdā′rŏ_, sm. drying-lines.
tendedor, _–dōr′_, sm. stretcher.
tendencia, _–dĕn′thĭă_, sf. stretching; tendency.
tender, _–dĕr′_, v. a. to stretch out, to expand, to extend; _–se_, to stretch oneself at full length out.
tender, _tĕn′dĕr_, sm. (rail.) tender.
tendero, ra, _dā′rŏ_, sm. & f. haberdasher.
tendido, _–dĕ′dŏ_, sm. row of seats for the spectators at a bull-fight.
tendinoso, sa, _–nŏ′sŏ_, a sinewy, gristly.
tendón, _–dŏn′_, sm. tendon, sinew.
tenebrario, _–lĕnĕbrā′rĭŏ_, sm. large candle-stick with a triangular branch, holding 15 candles (in Roman Catholic churches).
tenebroso, sa, _–brō′sŏ_, a. dark, obscure.
tenedor, _–dōr′_, sm. holder, keeper, tenant; fork.
tenencia, _tĕnĕn′thĭă_, sf. possession; lieutenancy.
tener, _tĕnĕr′_, v. a. to take, to hold, to possess; to have; _–se_, to take care not to fall; to stop, to halt; to resist; to adhere.
tenería, _–rā′ă_, sf. tan-yard.
teniente, _tĕnĭĕn′tĕ_, sm. lieutenant.
tenor, _tĕnŏr′_, sm. tenour; (mus.) tenor.
tensión, _tĕnsĭŏn′_, sf. tension.
tentación, _–tăthĭŏn′_, sf. temptation.
tentador, ra, _–dŏr′_, sm. & f. tempter.
tentar, _–tăr′_, v. a. to touch; to try; to grope; to tempt; to attempt; to tent.
tentativa, _–tē′vă_, sf. attempt, trial.
tente bonete, _tĕn′tĕ bŏnā′tĕ_, ad. abundantly.
tenue, _tā′nŏĕ_, a. thin, tenuous, slender.
tenuidad, _tĕnŭĭdăd′_, sf. slenderness, weakness; trifle.
teñidura, _tĕnyĭdŏ′ră_, sf. dyeing.
teñir, _–yĭr′_, v. a. to tinge, to dye.
teologal, _tĕŏlŏgăl′_, a. theological.
teología, _–lŏ′hă_, sf. theology, divinity.
teológico, ca, _–lŏ′hĭkŏ_, a. theological.
teólogo, _tĕŏ′lŏgŏ_, sm. theologian, divine.
teorema, _tĕŏrā′mă_, sf. theorem.
teoría, _tĕŏrē′ă_, teórica, _tĕŏ′rĭkă_, sf. theory.
teórico, ca, _tĕŏ′rĭkŏ_, a. theoretical.
tercena, _tĕrthā′nă_, sf. wholesale tobacco warehouse.
tercenista, _–thĕnĭs′tă_, sm. keeper of a wholesale tobacco warehouse.
tercería, _–thĕrē′ă_, sf. mediation, arbitration; depositary.

tercero, _–thā′rŏ_, sm. third person; pimp; mediator.
tercerola, _–thĕrŏ′lă_, sf. short carbine; tierce, terce.
terceto, _–thā′tŏ_, sm. terzarima, tiercet; (mus.) trio.
tercia, _tĕr′thĭă_, sf. third; canonical hour falling at three o'clock; series of three falling at three o'clock.
terciado, _–thā′dŏ_, sm. cutlass.
terciana, _–thā′nă_, sf. tertian-fever.
tercianario, ria, _–nā′rĭŏ_, sm. & f. person suffering from tertian-fever.
terciar, _–thĭăr′_, v. a. to put on sideways; to divide into three parts; to plough the third time; _–_, v. n. to mediate.
terciario, _–thĭā′rŏ_, sm. Spanish foot-soldier (16th and 17th centuries).
tercio, oia, _tĕr′thĭŏ_, a. third; _–_, sm. third part; half a load; Spanish regiment (in the 16th century); hacer bueno _–_, to do good to.
terciopelado, _–pĕlā′dŏ_, sf. velveteen; _–_, a. velvety.
terciopelero, _–pĕlā′rŏ_, sm. velvet-weaver.
terciopelo, _–pā′lŏ_, sm. velvet.
terco, ca, _tĕr′kŏ_, a. pertinacious, obstinate; hard as marble.
tergiversación, _–hĕversăthĭŏn′_, sf. tergiversation, evasion.
tergiversar, _–săr′_, v. a. to tergiversate.
teriaca, _tĕrĭă′kă_, sf. treacle.
tericia, _tĕrē′thĭă_, sf. jaundice.
terliz, _tĕrlĭth′_, sm. tick, twilled stuff for termal, _–māl′_, a. thermal.
termas, _tĕr′măs_, sf. pl. thermal-waters, pl.
terminacho, _–mĭnătsh′ŏ_, sm. rude word or phrase.
terminación, _–năthĭŏn′_, sf. termination; conclusion; last syllable of a word.
terminante, _–năn′tĕ_, a. decisive.
terminar, _–năr′_, v. a. to terminate.
terminativo, va, _–nătē′vŏ_, a. terminative.
término, _tĕr′mĭnŏ_, sm. term; end; boundary; limit.
terminote, _–nŏ′tĕ_, sm. vulgar or affected expression.
termómetro, _–mŏ′mĕtrŏ_, sm. thermometer.
terna, _tĕr′nă_, sf. ternary number.
ternero, ra, _–nā′rŏ_, sm. & f. calf; veal; heifer.
ternera, _–nā′thă_, sf. softness, delicacy, tenderness.
ternilla, _–nĭl′yă_, sf. gristle.
ternilloso, sa, _–yŏ′sŏ_, a. gristly, cartilaginous.
terno, _tĕr′nŏ_, sf. ternary number; ornaments for celebrating high-mass.
ternura, _–nŏ′ră_, sf. tenderness.
terquedad, _–kĕdăd′_, terquería, _–kĕrē′ă_, terqueza, _–kĕ′thă_, sf. stubbornness, obstinacy.
terrado, _tĕrrā′dŏ_, sm. terrace.
terraja, _–rā′hă_, sf. screw-plate.
terraplén, _–plĕn′_, sm. horizontal surface of a rampart; terrace, platform.
terraplenar, _–plĕnăr′_, v. a. to make a platform or terrace.
terraza, _tĕrrā′thă_, sf. glazed jar with two handles.
terremoto, _tĕrrĕmŏ′tŏ_, sm. earthquake.
terrenal, _–năl′_, a. terrestrial, earthly.
terreno, na, _tĕrrā′nŏ_, a. earthly, terrestrial; _–_, sm. land, ground, field.
terrestre, _tĕrrĕs′trĕ_, a. terrestrial.

terribilidad, *térrĭbĭldăd*, sf. roughness, ferocity. [ferocious.
terrible, *térrĭb/ĕ*, a. terrible, dreadful;
territorial, *térrĭtŏrĭál*, a. territorial.
territorio, *–tŏ'rĭŏ*, sm. territory.
terrón, *térrŏn*, sm. clod of earth, glebe; lump; —ones, pl. landed property.
terror, *térrŏr*, sm. terror, dread.
terrorismo, *–rĭs'mŏ*, sm. terrorism.
terrorista, *–rĭs'tă*, sm. & f. terrorist.
tersar, *térsăr*, v. a. to smooth.
terso, sa, *tér'sŏ*, a. smooth, glossy.
tersura, *–sŏ'ră*, sf. smoothness, purity.
tertulia, *–tŭ'lĕă*, sf. club, assembly, circle.
tertuliano, *–ĭtă'nŏ*, sm. member of a club.
tesauro, *tĕsă'ŭrŏ*, sm. polyglot dictionary.
tesis, *tă'sĭs*, sf. thesis.
tesón, *tĕsŏn*, sm. tenacity, firmness.
tesorería, *–sŏrĕrĕ'ă*, sf. treasury.
tesorero, *–ră'rŏ*, sm. treasurer.
tesoro, *–sŏ'rŏ*, sm. treasure; exchequer.
testa, *tĕs'tă*, sf. forehead; front, face.
testado, da, *–tă'dŏ*, a. leaving a will.
testador, *–dŏr*, sm. testator.
testadora, *–dŏ'ră*, sf. testatrix.
testadura, *–dŏ'ră*, sf. erasure.
testamentaria, *–mĕntă'rĕă*, sf. testamentary execution.
testamentario, *–mĕntă'rĭŏ*, sm. executor of a will; —, ria, a. testamentary.
testamento, *–mĕn'tŏ*, sm. will, testament. [will]; to bequeath; to scratch out.
testar, *tĕstăr*, v. a. & n. to make one's
testarudo, da, *–rŏ'dŏ*, a. obstinate, wrong-headed. [seat of a carriage.
testera, *–tă'ră*, sf. front of anything; back
testerada, *–ĭ'ă'dă*, sf. blow with the head; stubbornness. [genitals.
testículo, *–tĕ'kŭlŏ*, sm. testicle; –s, pl.
testificación, *–tĭfĭkăthŏn'*, sf. attestation.
testificar, *–kăr'*, v. a. to attest, to witness.
testificativo, va, *–kătĕ'vŏ*, a. that which testifies.
testigo, *–tĕ'gŏ*, sm. witness, deponent.
testimonial, *–tĭmŏnĭál'*, a. testimonial; –es, sf. pl. testimonials, pl.
testimoniar, *–mŏnĭăr'*, v. a. to attest, to bear witness.
testimonio, *–mŏ'nĭŏ*, sm. testimony; instrument legalized by a notary.
testuz, *–tŭth'*, sm. back of the head, poll.
tesura, *tĕsŏ'ră*, sf. stiffness, firmness; affected gravity.
teta, *tă'tă*, sf. dug, teat.
tetar, *tĕtăr'*, v. a. to suckle, to give suck.
tetera, *–tă'ră*, sf. tea-pot, tea-kettle.
tetilla, *–tĭ'yă*, sf. small teat.
tetrarca, *–trăr'kă*, sm. tetrarch. [surly.
tétrico, ca, *tă'trĭkŏ*, a. gloomy, sullen,
tetuda, *–tŏ'dă*, a. having large teats or nipples; –, sf. oblong olive. [type.
texto, *tĕks'tŏ*, sm. text; a certain size of
textual, *–tŭăl'*, a. textual.
textualista, *–tŭ'tă*, sm. he who adheres to the text. [hue.
tes, *tĕth*, sf. shining surface; complexion,
ti, *tĭ*, sm. & f. oblique case of tú.

tía, *tĭ'ă*, sf. aunt; good old woman.
tiara, *tĭă'ră*, sf. tiara.
tibieza, *–bĭă'thă*, sf. lukewarmness.
tibio, bia, *tĕ'bĭŏ*, a. lukewarm, careless.
tiburón, *tĭbŭrŏn'*, sm. shark.
tiempo, *tĭĕm'pŏ*, sm. time; term; occasion, opportunity; season.
tienda, *tĭĕn'dă*, sf. tent; awning; tilt; shop.
tienta, *tĭĕn'tă*, sf. probe (for surgeons).
tiento, *–tŏ*, sm. touch; circumspection; á –, gropingly.
tierno, na, *tĭĕr'nŏ*, a. tender.
tierra, *tĭĕr'ră*, sf. earth; land, ground; native country.
tieso, sa, *tĭă'sŏ*, a. stiff, hard, firm; robust; valiant; stubborn. [pot.
tiesto, *tĭĕs'tŏ*, sm. potsherd; large earthen
tigre, *tĕ'grĕ*, sm. tiger. [woodcatcher.
tijeras, *tĭ'hă'răs*, sf. scissors; drift-
tijeretada, *–hĕrĕtă'dă*, sf. cut with scissors, clip.
tijeretas, *–rĕ'tăs*, sf. pl. tendrils.
tijeretear, *–tĕăr'*, v. a. to cut with scissors; to dispose of other people's affairs at one's pleasure. [stigmatize.
tildar, *tĭldăr'*, v. a. to blot; to brand, to
tilde, *tĭl'dĕ*, sf. dot over a letter; iota, tittle; very small thing.
tilla, *tĭl'yă*, sf. midship, gangway.
tilo, *tĕ'lŏ*, sm. linden-tree, lime-tree.
timbal, *tĭmbăl'*, sm. kettle-drum.
timbalero, *–lă'rŏ*, sm. kettle-drummer.
timbre, *tĭm'brĕ*, sm. crest of a coat of arms.
timidez, *tĭmĭdĕth'*, sf. timidity.
tímido, da, *tĕ'mĭdŏ*, a. timid, cowardly.
timón, *–mŏn'*, sm. helm, rudder.
timorato, ta, *–mŏră'tŏ*, a. full of the fear of God.
tímpano, *tĭm'pănŏ*, sm. kettle-drum; tympanum; tympan of a printing-press.
tina, *tĕ'nă*, sf. dyer's copper.
tinaja, *tĭnă'h'ă*, sf. large earthen jar.
tinajero, *–hă'rŏ*, sm. water-jar maker.
tinajón, *–'hŏn'*, sm. small tub, kit.
tinelo, *–nă'lŏ*, sm. servants' dining-room.
tinglado, *tĭnglă'dŏ*, sm. shed, cart-house.
tiniebla, *–mĕ'blă*, sf. darkness, obscurity; –s, pl. utter darkness.
tino, *tĕ'nŏ*, sm. skill in discovering things by feel; judgment, prudence.
tinta, *tĭn'tă*, sf. tint, hue; ink.
tinte, *–tĕ*, sm. tint, dye.
tintero, *–tă'rŏ*, sm. inkhorn, inkstand.
tinto, ta, *tĭn'tŏ*, a. deep-coloured (of wine).
tintorería, *–rĕrĕ'ă*, sf. dyer's shop.
tintorero, *–ră'rŏ*, sm. dyer.
tintura, *–tŏ'ră*, sf. tincture. [tincture.
tinturar, *–tŭrăr'*, v. a. to tinge, to dye, to
tiña, *tĭn'yă*, sf. scab. [niggardly.
tiñoso, sa, *tĭnyŏ'sŏ*, a. scabby, scurvy;
tío, *tĕ'ŏ*, sm. uncle; good old man.
tiple, *tĕ'plĕ*, sm. (mus.) treble; one who sings treble; small guitar.
tipo, *tĕ'pŏ*, sm. type.
tipografía, *tĭpŏgră'fĕă*, sf. typography.
tipográfico, ca, *–gră'fĭkŏ*, a. typographical.
tipógrafo, *tĭpŏ'grăfŏ*, sm. printer.

tira, *tĭ´rä,* sf. long and narrow stripe; **-s,** pl. clerks' fees in appeal causes.

tirabraguero, *-brägä´rŏ,* sm. truss.

tirabuzón, *-bäthŏn´,* sm. cork-screw.

tirada, *tĭrä´dä,* sf. cast, throw; distance from one place to another.

tirador, ra, *-dŏr´,* sm. & f. thrower; drawer; pressman; **— de oro,** gold-wire drawer.

tirana, *tĭrä´nä,* sf. female tyrant.

tiranía, *-nĭ´ä,* sf. tyranny.

tiránico, ca, *tĭrä´nĭkŏ,* a. tyrannical.

tiranizar, *-nĭthär´,* v. a. to tyrannize.

tirano, na, *tĭrä´nŏ,* a. tyrannical; **—,** sm. tyrant.

tirante, *tĭrän´tĕ,* sm. joist which runs across a beam; trace; gear; brace of a drum; **—,** a. taut, extended, drawn.

tirantez, *-tĕth´,* sf. span; tautness.

tirapié, *-pĭĕ´,* sm. stirrups, pl.; strap.

tirar, *tĭrär´,* v. a. to throw, to cast; to pull; to draw; to fire off; to persuade; to draw metal into slender threads; to tend, to aim at.

tiritaña, *tĭrĭtän´yä,* sf. thin woollen cloth; thing of little value.

tiritar, *-tär´,* v. n. to shiver.

tiritona, *-tŏ´nä,* sf. shiver, shaking with cold.

tiro, *tĭ´rŏ,* sm. cast, throw, shot; prank, imposition; set of coach-horses; trace (of harness); **-s,** pl. sword-belts; **errar el —,** to miss (at shooting).

tirón, *tĭrŏn´,* sm. pull, haul, tug.

tirotear, *-tĕär´,* v. n. to shoot at random.

tiroteo, *-tĕ´ŏ,* sm. random-shooting, sharp-shooting.

tirria, *tĭr´rĭä,* sf. antipathy.

tirso, *tĭr´sŏ,* sm. thyrse, wand covered with ivy-leaves, used in sacrifices to Bacchus.

tisana, *tĭsä´nä,* sf. ptisan (a medical drink).

tísico, ca, *tĭ´sĭkŏ,* a. phthisical.

tisis, *tĭ´sĭs,* sf. phthisis.

tisú, *tĭsū´,* sm. tissue.

títere, *tĭ´tĕrĕ,* sm. puppet; ridiculous little fellow.

titiritaina, *tĭtĭrĭtä´ĭnä,* sf. noisy sport.

titiritero, *-tĕ´rŏ,* sm. puppet-player.

tito, *tĭ´tŏ,* sm. chick-pea; close-stool.

titubear, *tĭtŭbĕär´,* v. n. to threaten ruin; to stammer; to vacillate, to hesitate.

titubeo, *-bĕ´ŏ,* sm. vacillation.

titular, *-lär´,* v. a. to title; **—,** v. n. to obtain a title; pretence, under pretext.

título, *tĭ´tŭlŏ,* sm. title; name; **á —,** on tixnar, *tĭhnär´,* v. a. to smut; to tarnish.

tizne, *tĭth´nĕ,* sm. soot, smut of coal.

tiznón, *-nŏn´,* sm. spot, stain.

tizo, *tĭ´thŏ,* sm. half-burnt charcoal.

tizón, *tĭthŏn´,* sm. half-burnt wood.

Tizona, *-thŏ´nä,* sf. sword (of the Cid Ruy Diaz).

tizonada, *-thŏnä´dä,* sf. tizoñazo, *-nä´thŏ,* sm. stroke with burning charred wood; (fam.) hell-fire. charcoal.

tizonera, *-nĕ´rä,* sf. heap of ill-burnt to I tŏ, word used to call a dog; oh!

toalla, *tŏäl´yä,* sf. towel; **- rusa,** rough towel.

tobillo, *-bĭl´yŏ,* sm. ankle.

toca, *tŏ´kä,* sf. hood; a thin stuff.

tocado, *tŏkä´dŏ,* sm. head-dress, head-gear.

tocador, *-dŏr´,* sm. one who touches; toilet, toilet-table; tact; inspiration.

tocamiento, *-mĭĕn´tŏ,* sm. touch, contact.

tocante (á), *-kän´tĕ,* pr. concerning, relating to.

tocar, *-kär´,* v. a. to touch; to attain with the hand: (mus.) to play on; to ring a bell; to try metals on a touch-stone; to test; **—,** v. n. to belong; to concern; to be a duty or obligation; to import; to fall to one's share; **-se,** to put on one's hat.

tocayo, ya, *-kä´yŏ,* a. name-sake.

tocinero, *-thĭnĕ´rŏ,* sm. porkman.

tocino, *-thĭ´nŏ,* sm. bacon, salt pork; hog's lard; **hoja de —,** flitch. still.

todavía, *-dävĕ´ä,* ad. nevertheless; yet.

todo, da, *tŏ´dŏ,* a. all, entire; **—,** sm. whole.

todopoderoso, *-pŏdĕrŏ´sŏ,* a. almighty.

toesa, *tŏĕ´sä,* sf. toise, fathom (French measure).

toga, *tŏ´gä,* sf. toga; superior judgeship.

togado, da, *tŏgä´dŏ,* a. gowned.

Toisón, *tŏĭsŏn´,* sm. order of the Golden Fleece.

tolano, *-lä´nŏ,* sm. tumour in horses' gums; **-s,** pl. short hair on the neck.

toldillo, *tŏldĭl´yŏ,* sm. covered sedan-chair.

toldo, *tŏl´dŏ,* sm. awning; penthouse.

tolerable, *tŏlĕrä´blĕ,* a. tolerable supportable. indulgence.

tolerancia, *-rän´thĭä,* sf. tolerance, indulgence.

tolerante, *-rän´tĕ,* a. tolerant.

tolerar, *-rär´,* v. n. to tolerate, to suffer.

tolondro, *tŏlŏn´drŏ,* tolondrón, *-drŏn´,* sm. contusion arising from a blow; **—,** ona, a. giddy, hare-brained.

tolva, *tŏl´vä,* sf. mill-hopper. at once.

toma, *tŏ´mä,* sf. portion of any thing taken.

tomar, *tŏmär´,* v. a. to take, to seize, to grasp; to understand, to interpret, to perceive; **á cuestas,** to take upon oneself; **-se,** to get rusty, to rust.

tomate, *-mä´tĕ,* sm. (bot.) tomato.

tomatera, *-tĕ´rä,* sf. tomato-plant.

tomillar, *-mĭl´yär,* sm. bed of thyme.

tomillo, *-mĭl´yŏ,* sm. (bot.) thyme.

tomo, *tŏ´mŏ,* sm. bulk; tome; volume.

ton, *tŏn,* sm. tone; **sin - ni son,** without rhyme or reason.

tonada, *-nä´dä,* sf. tune, melody.

tonadilla, *-dĭl´yä,* sf. interlude of music; short tune.

tonel, *tŏnĕl´,* sm. cask, barrel.

tonelada, *-lä´dä,* sf. tun; collection of casks in a ship; (mar.) tonnage-duty.

tonelería, *-lĕrĕ´ä,* sf. cooper's trade; cooper's workshop.

tonelero, *-lĕ´rŏ,* sm. cooper, hooper.

tonelete, *-lĕ´tĕ,* sm. little barrel.

tónico, ca, *tŏ´nĭkŏ,* a. tonic, strengthening.

tono, *tŏ´nŏ,* sm. tone.

tonsura, *tŏnsŭ´rä,* sf. tonsure.

tonsurar, *-sŭrär´,* v. a. to give the tonsure.

tontada, *-tä´dä,* sf. nonsense. to.

tontear, *-tĕär´,* v. n. to talk nonsense, to act foolishly.

tontería, *-tĕrĕ´ä,* sf. foolery, nonsense.

tontillo, *-tĭl'yŏ*, sm. farthingale.
tonto, ta, *tŏn'tŏ*, a. stupid, foolish.
topacio, *tŏpä'thĭŏ*, sm. topaz.
topar, *tŏpär'*, v. a. to run or strike against.
tope, *tŏ'pĕ*, sm. butt, rub; scuffle; -s, pl. (rail.) buffers.
topera, *tŏpā'rä*, sf. mole-hole.
topetada, *-pĕtä'dä*, sf. butt (by a horned
topetar, *-tär'*, v. a. to butt. [animal).
topetón, *-tŏn'*, sm. collision, encounter,
tópico, ca, *tŏ'pĭkŏ*, a. topical. [blow.
topinera, *tŏpĭnā'rä*, sf. mole-hill.
topo, *tŏ'pŏ*, sm. mole, molewarp; stumbler.
topografía, *tŏpŏgräfĕ'ä*, sf. topography.
topográfico, ca, *-grä'fĭkŏ*, a. topo-
graphical.
toque, *tŏ'kĕ*, sm. touch; bell-ringing; crisis.
torada, *tŏrä'dä*, sf. drove of bulls.
torbellino, *tŏrbĕlyē'nŏ*, sm. whirlwind;
lively, boisterous, restless person.
torcaz, *-käth'*, a., paloma -, ring-dove,
wood-pigeon.
torcecuello, *-thĕkŭĕl'yŏ*, sm. wry-neck.
torcedor, ra, *-thēdŏr'*, sm. & f. twister
(spindle); anything causing displeasure.
torcedura, *-dŏ'rä*, sf. twisting; light,
paltry wine.
torcer, *-thēr'*, v. a. to twist, to double, to
curve, to distort; to refute an argument;
-se, to change a resolution.
torcida, *-thĕ'dä*, sf. wick.
torcidillo, *-dĭl'yŏ*, sm. twisted silk.
torcido, da, *-thĕ'dŏ*, a. oblique, tortuous.
torcimiento, *-mĭĕn'tŏ*, sm. bending, deflection; circumlocution. [prints.
tórculo, *tŏr'kŭlŏ*, sm. rolling press for
tordo, *tŏr'dŏ*, sm. thrush, throstle; -, da,
-a. speckled black and white. [horseback.
toreador, *tŏrĕädŏr'*, sm. bull-fighter on
torear, *-rār'*, v. n. to fight bulls.
toreo, *-rā'ŏ*, sm. bull-fighting.
torero, *-rā'rŏ*, sm. bull-fighter on foot.
toril, *-rĭl'*, sm. place where bulls are shut
up until brought out.
torillo, *-rĭl'yŏ*, sm. little or young bull.
tormenta, *tŏrmĕn'tä*, sf. storm, tempest.
tormento, *-tŏ*, sm. torment, pain, anguish;
torture; tedious affliction. [wedding.
tornaboda, *tŏrnäbŏ'dä*, sf. day after a
tornaguía, *-gĕ'ä*, sf. debenture.
tornar, *-när'*, v. a. & n. to return; to
restore; to repeat.
tornasol, *-sŏl'*, sm. (bot.) turnsol.
tornasolado, *-sŏlä'dŏ*, a. changing colours;
chatoyant (of silk-stuff).
torneador, *-ädŏr'*, sm. turner.
tornear, *-nār'*, v. a. & n. to turn (on a
lathe); to turn; to tilt at tournaments.
torneo, *-nā'ŏ*, sm. tournament. [nery.
tornero, *-nā'rä*, sf. door-keeper of a nun-
tornero, *-rŏ*, sm. turner.
tornillo, *-nĭl'yŏ*, sm. male screw.
torniscón, *-nĭskŏn'*, sm. slap in the face.
torno, *tŏr'nŏ*, sm. wheel; revolution.
toro, *tŏ'rŏ*, sm. bull.
toronja, *tŏrŏn'hä*, sf. thick-peeled orange.
toronjil, *tŏrŏn'hĕl'*, sm. (bot.) balm.

torozón, *-rŏthŏn'*, sm. gripes (among
animals).
torpe, *tŏr'pĕ*, a. dull, heavy; torpid; stupid;
unchaste, obscene; infamous.
torpeza, *-pĕ'thä*, sf. heaviness, dulness;
torpor; obscenity; stupidity. [church.
torre, *tŏr'rĕ*, sf. tower; turret; steeple of a
torrejón, *-hŏn'*, sm. ill-shaped turret.
torrente, *-rĕn'tĕ*, sm. torrent.
torreznada, *-rĕthnä'dä*, sf. plentiful dish
of rashers.
torrezno, *-rĕth'nŏ*, sm. rasher. [hot.
tórrido, da, *tŏr'rĭdŏ*, a. torrid, parched,
torrija, *-rē'hä*, sf. slice of bread, fried in
white wine, eggs, and butter or oil.
torta, *tŏr'tä*, sf. tart.
tortada, *-tä'dä*, sf. meat-pie.
tortera, *-tā'rä*, sf. pan for baking tarts.
tortilla, *-tĭl'yä*, sf. omelet, pancake.
tórtola, *tŏr'tŏlä*, sf. turtle-dove.
tortuga, *-tŏ'gä*, sf. tortoise. [cuitous.
tortuoso, sa, *-tŭŏ'sŏ*, a. tortuous, cir-
tortura, *-tŏ'rä*, sf. tortuosity, flexure;
rack, torture.
torvo, va, *tŏr'vŏ*, a. stern, grim, torvid.
torzal, *-thäl'*, sm. cord, twist.
tos, *tŏs*, sf. cough. [grossly.
toscamente, *-kämĕn'tĕ*, ad. coarsely,
tosco, ca, *tŏs'kŏ*, a. coarse, ill-bred, clumsy.
toser, *tŏsēr'*, v. n. to cough. [tree).
tósigo, *tŏ'sĭgŏ*, sm. poison (from the yew-
tostada, *tŏstä'dä*, sf. slice of toasted bread.
tostado, da, *-dŏ*, a. parched, sun-burnt;
light-yellow, light-brown. [toasting-fork.
tostador, ra, *-dŏr'*, sm. & f. toaster;
tostar, *-tär'*, v. a. to toast, to roast.
total, *tŏtäl'*, sm. whole, totality; -, a
total, entire.
totalidad, *-lĭdäd'*, sf. totality.
traba, *trä'bä*, sf. obstacle, impediment;
trammel, fetter.
trabacuenta, *-kŭĕn'tä*, sf. error, mistake;
dispute, controversy.
trabajador, ra, *-hädŏr'*, sm. & f. labourer, painstaker.
trabajar, *-här'*, v. a. to work, to labour.
trabajo, *-bä'hŏ*, sm. work, labour, toil;
difficulty; -s, pl. troubles. [ful.
trabajoso, sa, *-hŏ'sŏ*, a. laborious; pain-
trabar, *-bär'*, v. a. to join, to unite; to
dispute, to quarrel; to take hold of; to
fetter, to shackle; to set the teeth of a saw.
trabazón, *-thŏn'*, sf. juncture, union.
trabilla, *-bĭl'yä*, sf. stitch dropped in
knitting; strap (of trowsers). [mistake.
trabucación, *-bŭkäthŏn'*, sf. confusion,
trabucar, *-bŭkär'*, v. a. to derange, to
confound; -se, to mistake.
trabucazo, *-kä'thŏ*, sm. shot with a blunderbuss; sudden fright.
trabuco, *-kŏ*, sm. catapult; blunderbuss.
tradición, *-dĭthŏn'*, sf. tradition.
traducción, *-dŭkthŏn'*, sf. version, translation.
traducir, *-dŭthēr'*, v. a. to translate.
traductor, *-dŭktŏr'*, sm. translator.
traer, *trāēr'*, v. a. to bring, to carry, to
attract; to persuade; -se, to be dressed

in style; to have a graceful *or* ungainly deportment. [ful management of affairs.

tráfago, *trä fäg̃o̱,* sm. traffic, trade; care-

traficación, *-fïkäthïŏn',* sf. traffic, trade.

traficante, *-kän' tĕ,* sm. merchant, dealer.

traficar, *-kär',* v. n. to traffic, to commerce, to do business, to deal (in).

tráfico, *trä fïkŏ,* sm. traffic, trade.

tragadero, *-gädä'rŏ,* sm. œsophagus, gullet; gulph, abyss; **tener buenos –s ó buenas tragaderas,** to be very credulous. [gobbler.

tragador, ra, *-dŏr',* sm. & f. glutton,

tragaldabas, *-gäldä' bäs,* sm. gluton.

tragaleguas, *-gälä' gäs,* sm. great walker.

tragalux, *-lŭth',* sm. sky-light.

tragantada, *-gäntä' dä,* sf. large draught of liquor. [–, a. gluttonous.

tragantón, ona, *-tŏn',* sm. & f. glutton;

tragar, *trä hä' dĕ,* v. a. to swallow, to glut; to swallow up; **-se,** to dissemble.

tragedia, *trä hä' dĕä,* sf. tragedy.

trágico, ca, *trä' hïkŏ,* a. tragic, tragical.

trago, *trä gŏ,* sm. draught of liquor; adversity, misfortune; **á –s,** by degrees.

tragón, ona, *-gŏn',* a. gluttonous.

traición, *träïthïŏn',* sf. treason.

traidor, *-dŏr',* sm. traitor; **–, ra,** a. treacherous.

trailla, *träï' yä,* sf. leash, lash.

traillar, *-yär',* v. a. to level the ground.

traje, *trä'h'ĕ,* sm. complete dress of a woman; costume; fashion, mode.

trajinar, *-'hïnär',* v. a. to convey.

trajinero, *-'hïnä'rŏ,* sm. waggoner.

trama, *trä' mä,* sf. plot, complot.

tramador, ra, *-dŏr',* sm. & f. plotter; artful contriver. [machinate.

tramar, *-mär',* v. a. to weave; to plot, to

trámite, *trä' mïtĕ,* sm. path; (law) procedure.

tramo, *trä' mŏ,* sm. piece, morsel; piece of ground separated from another; flight of stairs. [vanity, pride.

tramontana, *-mŏntä' nä,* sf. north wind;

tramontano, na, *-nŏ,* a. transmontane.

tramontar, *-tär',* v. n. to cross the mountains; **–,** v. a. to assist, to relieve; **-se,** to fly, to escape.

tramoya, *-mŏ' yä,* sf. scene, theatrical decoration; craft, wile, artful trick.

tramoyista, *-yïs' tä,* sm. scene-painter; swindler, diddler, humbug.

trampa, *träm' pä,* sf. trap, snare; trap-door; fraud; debt fraudulently contracted.

trampantojo, *-päntŏ'h'ŏ,* sm. trick played before one's eyes.

trampear, *-pĕär',* v. n. & a. to swindle out of one's money; to impose upon, to deceive.

trampista, *-pïs' tä,* sm. cheat, impostor, swindler, sharper, fourbe. [ling.

tramposo, sa, *-pŏ' sŏ,* a. deceitful, swind-

tramvía, *-vï' ä,* sm. tram-way.

tranca, *trän' kä,* sf. cross-bar, cross-beam.

trancar, *-kär',* v. a. to barricade.

trancazo, *-kä' thŏ,* sm. blow with a bar.

trance, *trän' thĕ,* sm. danger; last stage of life; sale of a debtor's property.

tranco, *trän' kŏ,* sm. long step *or* stride.

tranchete, *-tshä' tĕ,* sm. shoemaker's heel-knife. [repose, heart's ease.

tranquilidad, *-kïlïdäd',* sf. tranquillity;

tranquilizar, *-kïlïthär',* v. a. to tranquilize, to calm. [quiet.

tranquilo, la, *-kï' lŏ,* a. tranquil, calm,

transacción, *tränsäkthïŏn',* sf. accommodation, adjustment. [to copy.

transcribir, *-skrïbïr',* v. a. to transcribe, ¡ **tránseat!** *träns' ĕät,* let it pass!

transeunte, *tränsĕŭn' tĕ,* a. transitory; **–,** sm. passenger. [defer.

transferir, *-fĕrïr',* v. a. to transfer; to

transfigurable, *-fïgŭrä' blĕ,* a. changeable.

transfiguración, *-fïgŭräthïŏn',* sf. transformation, transfiguration.

transfigurarse, *-fïgŭrär' sĕ,* v. r. to be transfigured; to be metamorphosed.

transfixión, *-fïksïŏn',* sf. transfixing.

transflorear, *-flŏrĕär',* v. a. to enamel.

transformación, *-fŏrmäthïŏn',* sf. transformation.

transformar, *-fŏrmär',* v. a. to transform; **-se,** to change one's sentiments *or* manners. [sm. deserter, fugitive.

tránsfuga, *träns' fŭgä,* **tránsfugo,** *-fŭgŏ,*

transfundir, *-fŭndïr',* v. a. to transfuse; to communicate.

transfusión, *-fŭsïŏn',* sf. transfusion.

transgresión, *-grĕsïŏn',* sf. transgression.

transgresor, *-grĕsŏr',* sm. transgressor, law-breaker.

transición, *-sïthïŏn',* sf. transition.

transido, da, *-sï' dŏ,* a. worn out with anguish; avaricious. [differences.

transigir, *-sï'hïr',* v. a. to accommodate

transitar, *-sïtär',* v. n. to travel, to pass by a place.

transitivo, ya, *-sïtï' vŏ,* a. transitive.

tránsito, *trän' sïtŏ,* sm. passage; transition; road, way; change, removal; death of holy *or* virtuous persons.

transitorio, ria, *-sïtŏ' rïŏ,* a. transitory.

translación, *-läthïŏn',* sf. translation.

transmarino, na, *-märĕ'nŏ,* a. transmarine. [migration.

transmigración, *-mïgräthïŏn',* sf. trans-

transmigrar, *-mïgrär',* v. a. to transmigrate.

transmitir, *-mïtïr',* v. a. to transmit.

transmutable, *-mŭtä' blĕ,* a. transmutable, changeable. [tation.

transmutación, *-mŭtäthïŏn',* sf. transmu-

transmutar, *-mŭtär',* v. a. to transmute.

transparentarse, *-pärĕntär' sĕ,* v. r. to be transparent; to shine through.

transparente, *-pärĕn' tĕ,* a. transparent.

transpiración, *tränspïräthïŏn',* sf. transpiration.

transpirar, *-spïrär',* v. a. to transpire.

transportación, *tränspŏrtäthïŏn',* sf., **transportamiento,** *-mïĕn' tŏ,* sm. transportation.

transportar, *-pŏrtär',* v. a. to transport, to convey; **-se,** to be in a transport.

transporte, -pōr'tā, sm. transport, conveyance; transport-ship.

transposición, -pōstthōn', sf. transposition, transposal.

transubstanciación, trănsŭbstănthiā-thōn', sf. transubstantiation.

transubstancial, -sŭbstănthiăr, a. converted into another substance.

transubstanciar, -sŭbstănthiăr, v. a. to transubstantiate. [lateral.

transversal, -vērsăr, a. transverse; col-

tranzadera, trănthădā'rā, sf. knot of plaited cords or ribbons. [to defraud.

trapacear, trăpāthēăr, v. n. to deceive,

trapacería, -rē'ā, sf. fraud, deceit.

trapacero, ra, -thā'rō, a. deceitful.

trapacista, -this'tā, sm. impostor, cheat.

trapajo, trăpā'hō, sm. rag, tatter.

trapajoso, sa, -'hō'sō, a. ragged, tattered.

trápala, trā'pălā, sf. stamping with the feet; bawling; babbler; garrulity.

trapalear, -lēăr, v. n. to babble.

trapalón, ona, -lōn', a. loquacious.

trapería, -pēr'ā, sf. frippery, rag-fair; woollen-draper's shop.

trapero, ra, -pā'rō, sm. & f. dealer in rags.

trapisonda, -pisōn'dā, sf. bustle, noise, confusion.

trapo, trā'pō, sm. rag, tatter.

traquear, trākēăr, v. n. to crack; -, v. a. to shake, to agitate.

traqueo, -kā'ō, sm. noise of artificial fireworks; shaking; moving to and fro.

tras, trăs, pr. after, behind; -, sm. breach, bottom; blow attended with noise; -, bang, bang.

trascartarse, -kārtăr'sē, v. r. to remain (of a card which, had it come sooner, would have won the game).

trascartón, -kārtōn', sm. drawing of a winning card after the game is lost.

trascendencia, -thēndēn'thiā, sf. transcendency; penetration. [dent.

trascendental, -thēndēntăr, a. transcen-

trascender, -thēndēr', v. a. to go beyond; to rise above; -, v. n. to emit a strong smell. [to cross a mountain.

trascolar, -kōlăr, v. a. (med.) to strain;

trascordarse, -kōrdăr'sē, v. r. to forget.

trascoro, -kō'rō, sm. space of a church at the back of the choir.

trascurso, -kūr'sō, sm. course of time.

trasegar, -sēgăr, v. a. to overset; to decant.

trasera, trăsā'rā, sf. back-part; croup.

trasero, ra, -rō, a. hind, hinder; -, sm. buttock. [restless, noisy boy.

trasgo, trăs'gō, sm. hobgoblin; lively,

trashojar, -ō'hăr, v. a. to turn over the leaves, to skim a book.

trashumar, -ŭmăr, v. a. to drive sheep to or from the common pasture-ground or the mountains in spring and autumn.

trasiego, -siā'gō, sm. removal; decanting of liquors.

trasladar, -lădăr, v. a. to transport; to translate; to transcribe, to copy.

traslado, -lă'dō, sm. copy; image; resemblance. [parent; to conjecture.

traslucirse, -lŭthir'sē, v. r. to be trans-

traslumbrarse, -lŭmbrăr'sē, v. r. to be dazzled with excessive light; to vanish.

trasluz, -lŭth', sm. light which passes through a transparent body; transverse light.

trasmallo, -măl'yō, sm. trammel.

trasnochar, -nōtshăr', v. n. to watch, to sit up a whole night.

traspapelarse, -păpēlăr'sē, v. r. to be mislaid among other papers.

traspasar, -păsăr', v. n. to pass over; -, v. a. to remove, to transport; to transfix, to transpierce; to return, to repass; to exceed the proper bounds; to trespass; to transfer. [pass.

traspaso, -păs'ō, sm. conveyance; tres-

traspié, -piē', sm. trip; slip, stumble.

trasplantar, -plăntăr, v. a. to transplant.

trasplante, -plăn'tē, sm. transplantation.

trasponer, -pōnēr', v. a. to remove, to transport; to take a circuitous road in order to get out of sight; to conceal; -se, to be drowsy.

traspuesta, -pŭēs'tā, sf. transport; hiding-place in a wood; flight.

traspuesto, ta, -tō, a. & p. transported.

traspunte, -pŭn'tē, sm. prompter.

trasquilador, -kilădōr, sm. shearer.

trasquiladura, -kilădō'rā, sf. shearing.

trasquilar, -kilăr, v. a. to shear sheep; to clip. [hair badly cut.

trasquilón, -kilōn', sm. cut of the shears.

traste, trăs'tē, sm. fret of a guitar.

trasteado, -iā'dō, sm. number of frets round a guitar's handle. [fellow.

trasteador, ra, -iādōr', sm. & f. noisy

trastear, -iāăr', v. a. to put frets round the handle of a guitar; to move furniture.

trastejador, -tē'hădōr', sm. tiler.

trastejar, -tē'hăr', v. a. to cover with tiles.

trastera, trăstā'rā, sf. lumber-room.

trastería, -tēr'ā, sf. heap of lumber; ridiculous or foolish action.

trastienda, -tiēn'dā, sf. back-room behind a shop; prudence, forecast. [person.

trasto, trăs'tō, sm. furniture; useless

trastornador, -tōrnădōr', sm. & f. disturber, turbulent person.

trastornar, -tōrnăr', v. a. to overthrow, to overturn; to perplex the mind.

trastorno, -tōr'nō, sm. overthrow.

trastrocar, -trōkăr', v. a. to invert the order of things. [spire.

trasudar, -sŭdăr', v. a. to sweat, to per-

trasudor, -sŭdōr', sm. gentle sweat.

trasvenarse, -vēnăr'sē, v. r. to be spilled or lost by shedding.

tratable, trătă'blē, a. tractable; compliant.

tratado, -iā'dō, sm. treaty, convention; treatise. [style of address.

tratamiento, -miēn'tō, sm. treatment;

tratante, -tăn'tē, sm. dealer in provisions.

tratar, -tăr', v. a. to treat on a subject; to traffic, to trade; to use, to treat; to be careful to attain an object; —se, to entertain a friendly intercourse; to live well or ill.

trato, *trä´tõ*, sm. treatment; manner, address; trade, traffic; conversation.

través, *trävés´*, sm. bias; traverse of a fortress; de ó al —, across, athwart.

travesaño, *–sän´yõ*, sm. cross-timber; transom. [transverse, across.

travesero, *–sä´rõ*, sm. transom; —, ra, a.

travesía, *–sä´ä*, sf. transverse position or manner; trajectory; (mar.) side-wind.

travestido, da, *–vēstĩ´dõ*, a. disguised.

travesura, *–sõ´rä*, sf. running to and fro in a restless manner; penetration, lively fancy; wickedness, knavery.

travieso, sa, *träviõ´sõ*, a. restless, uneasy, fidgety; turbulent; lively; debauched.

traza, *trä´thä*, sf. first sketch; trace, outline; project; manner; means; appearance. [ject; to trace.

trazar, *–thär´*, v. a. to plan out; to project.

trazo, *trä´thõ*, sm. sketch, plan, design.

trébedes, *trä´bēdēs*, sf. pl. trevet, tripod.

trébol, *trä´bõl*, sm. trefoil, clover.

trece, *trä´thē*, a. thirteen; thirteenth.

trecho, *trētsh´õ*, sm. space, distance of time or place; á –s, at intervals.

trecientos, tas, *trēthiēn´tõs*, a. three hundred. [hostilities.

tregua, *trā´güä*, sf. truce, cessation of

treinta, *trā´ĩntä*, a. thirty.

treinteno, na, *trāĩntä´nõ*, a. thirtieth.

tremendo, da, *–mēn´dõ*, a. terrible, formidable; awful, grand.

trementina, *–mēntĩ´nä*, sf. turpentine.

tremés, *trēmēs´*, **tremesino**, na, *–sĩ´nõ*, a. three months old. [colours; to wave.

tremolar, *–mõlär´*, v. a. to hoist the

tremolina, *–lä´nä*, sf. rustling of the wind; bustle, confused noise. [bling.

trémulo, la, *trä´mũlõ*, a. tremulous, trem-

tren, *trēn*, sm. train, retinue; show, ostentation; (rail.) train; – ordinario, – ómnibus, parliamentary train, slow train; –correo, –de gran velocidad, fast or express train, mail-train; – de mercancías, goods train, luggage-train; – ascendente, up-train; – descendente, down-train. [band.

trencilla, *–thĩl´yä*, sm. gold or silver hat-

trenos, *trä´nõs*, sm. pl. lamentation.

trenza, *trēn´thõ*, sf. braided hair, plaited silk.

trenzado, *–thä´dõ*, sm. braided hair.

trenzar, *–thär´*, v. a. to braid the hair.

trepar, *trēpär´*, v. n. to climb, to crawl.

tres, *trēs*, a. & s. three. [wile.

treta, *trä´tä*, sf. thrust in fencing; trick.

triaca, *trä´kä*, sf. theriaca, treacle.

triangular, *triängũlär´*, a. triangular.

triángulo, *triän´gũlõ*, sm. triangle.

tribu, *trĩ´bũ*, sm. & f. tribe.

tribulación, *–läthiõn´*, sf. tribulation, affliction.

tribuna, *–bõ´nä*, sf. tribune. [justice.

tribunal, *–bũnäl´*, sm. tribunal, court of

tribunali (pro –), *–nä´li*, ad. in public courts; in a decisive tone.

tribuno, *–bõ´nõ*, sm. tribune.

tributar, *–bũtär´*, v. a. to pay tribute; to contribute to; to pay homage and respect.

tributario, ria, *–tä´riõ*, a. tributary.

tributo, *–bõ´tõ*, sm. tribute.

tricolor, *trĩkõlõr´*, a. tricoloured.

tricorne, *–kõr´nē*, a. three-horned.

tridente, *–dēn´tē*, a. three-pronged; –, sm.

trienal, *triēnäl´*, a. triennial. [trident.

trienio, *triē´niõ*, sm. space of three years.

trigaza, *–gä´thä*, sf. short straw.

trigésimo, ma, *–hä´sĩmõ*, a. thirtieth.

trigo, *trē´gõ*, sm. wheat; –de las Indias, maize.

trigueño, ña, *trĩgēn´yõ*, a. swarthy.

triguero, ra, *–gä´rõ*, a. growing among wheat; –, sm. winnowing-sieve, screen; corn-merchant.

trilingüe, *–lĩn´güē*, a. talking three, or relating to three languages.

trillado, da, *trĩlyä´dõ*, a. beaten; trite, stale, hackneyed; camino –, common

trillador, *–dõr´*, sm. thrasher. [routine.

trilladura, *–dõ´rä*, sf. act of thrashing.

trillar, *–yär´*, v. a. to thrash.

trillo, *trĩl´yõ*, sm. flail. [months.

trimestre, *trĩmēs´trē*, sm. space of three

trinado, *–nä´dõ*, sm. trill, quaver.

trinar, *–när´*, v. n. to trill, to quaver.

trincar, *trĩnkär´*, v. a. to break into small pieces; (mar.) to keep close to the wind; to fasten the rope-ends. [knife.

trinchante, *–tshän´tē*, sm. carver; carving-

trinchar, *–tshär´*, v. a. to carve, to divide meat; to decide with an air of authority.

trinchera, *–tshä´rä*, sf. trench, entrench-

trinchero, *–tshä´rõ*, sm. trencher. [ment.

trinchete, *–tshä´tē*, sm. paring-knife.

Trinidad, *trĩnĩdäd´*, sf. Trinity.

trinitaria, *–tä´riä*, sf. three-coloured violet, heart's ease.

trino, na, *trĩ´nõ*, a. containing three distinct things; –, sm. trill. [quet; tennis.

trinquete, *trĩnkä´tē*, sm. foremast; trin-

trío, *trē´õ*, sm. (mus.) trio.

tripa, *trē´pä*, sf. gut, tripe, intestine; belly of a vessel; core.

tripe, *trē´pē*, sm. shag.

tripería, *trĩpärĩ´ä*, sf. tripe-market, tripery.

tripero, *–pä´rõ*, tripicallero, ra, *–pĩkälyä´rõ*, sm. & f. tripe-man.

triple, *trē´plē*, a. triple, treble.

triplicar, *trĩplĩkär´*, v. a. to treble.

triplo, la, *trē´plõ*, a. treble, triplicate.

trípode, *trē´põdē*, sm. tripod, trivet.

triptongo, *trĩptõn´gõ*, sm. triphthong.

tripudo, da, *–põ´dõ*, a. big-bellied.

tripulación, *–pũläthiõn´*, sf. crew of a ship. [out.

tripular, *–lär´*, v. n. to man ships; to fit

triquitraque, *trĩkĩträ´kē*, sm. clack, clatter, clashing.

tris, *trĩs*, sm. noise made by the breaking of glass; trice, instant; estar en un –, to be on the point of.

trisagio, *–sä´hiõ*, sm. trisagion; holy, holy, holy is the Lord.

triscar, *trĭskär'*, v. n. to make a noise with the feet; to frisk about.

trisílabo, ba, *–sĭ'läbŏ*, a. trisyllabic.

triste, *trĭs'tĕ*, a. sad, mournful, melancholy. [ing.

tristeza, *–tĕ'thä*, sf. melancholy, mourntritono, *trĭtŏ'nŏ*, sm. musical interval of three tones.

trituración, *–tŭräthĭŏn'*, sf. pulverization.

triturar, *–tŭrär'*, v. a. to reduce to powder, to grind, to pound.

triunfal, *trĭŭnfäl'* a. triumphal.

triunfar, *–fär'*, v. n. to triumph; to trump at cards. [(at cards.)

triunfo, *trĭŭn'fŏ*, sm. triumph; trump

triunvirato, *–vĭrä'tŏ*, sm. triumvirate.

triunviro, *–vĕ'rŏ*, sm. triumvir.

trivial, *trĭvĭäl'*, a. frequented, beaten; vulgar, trivial.

trivialidad, *–lĭdäd'*, sf. vulgarity.

triza, *trĕ'thä*, sf. mite; cord, rope.

trobador, *trŏbädŏr'*, sm. troubadour.

trocable, *–kä'blĕ*, a. changeable.

trocar, *–kär'*, v. a. to exchange, to barter; –se, to be changed or reformed.

trochemoche, *trŏtshĕmŏ'tshĕ*, (á –), ad. helter-skelter.

trofeo, *trŏfĕ'ŏ*, sm. trophy.

troj, *trŏ'h*, troje, *trŏ'h'ĕ*, sf. granary, fruit-loft. [large top.

trompa, *trŏm'pä*, sf. trumpet; proboscis;

trompada, *–pä'dä*, sf. blow with the nose or trunk. [adverse accident.

trompazo, *–pä'thŏ*, sm. heavy blow;

trompeta, *–pä'tä*, sf. trumpet; –, sm. trumpeter. [trumpet

trompetear, *–tĕär'*, v. n. to sound the

trompetero, *–tĕ'rŏ*, sm. trumpeter; trumpet-maker.

trompetilla, *–tĭl'yä*, sf. small trumpet; speaking-trumpet.

trompicar, *–pĭkär'*, v. n. & a. to stumble frequently; to trip, to occasion stumbling.

trompicón, *–kŏn'*, sm. stumbling.

trompo, *trŏm'pŏ*, sm. whipping-top.

tronada, *trŏnä'dä*, sf. thunder-storm.

tronar, *–när'*, v. n. to thunder.

troncar, *trŏnkär'*, v. a. to truncate, to mutilate. [stock.

tronco, *trŏn'kŏ*, sm. trunk; log of wood;

tronchar, *–tshär'*, v. a. to cut off at the stalk. [stalk.

troncho, *trŏn'tshŏ*, sm. sprig, stem or

tronchudo, da, *–tshŏ'dŏ*, a. having a long stem or stalk.

tronera, *trŏnĕ'rä*, sm. embrasure of a battery; loop-hole; dormer; hare-brained person; pocket of a billiard-table.

trono, *trŏ'nŏ*, sm. throne; –s, pl. seventh choir of angels.

tronzar, *trŏnthär'*, v. a. to shatter, to break into pieces; to plait, to fold.

tropa, *trŏ'pä*, sf. troop.

tropel, *trŏpĕl'*, sm. confused noise; hurry, bustle, confusion, heap of things; crowd: de –, in a tumultuous and confused manner.

tropelía, *–lĕ'ä*, sf. precipitation, hurry, confusion, vexation, oppression.

tropezadero, *–thädĕ'rŏ*, sm. any stumbling or slippery place.

tropezar, *–thär'*, v. n. to stumble; to be detained or obstructed; to meet accidentally; to cut the feet in walking (horses).

tropezón, ona, *–thŏn'*, a. stumbling; á –ones, impeded and obstructed; –, sm. tripping. [tropical.

trópico, *trŏ'pĭkŏ*, sm. tropic; –, ca, a.

tropiezo, *trŏpĭĕ'thŏ*, sm. stumble, trip; obstacle; slip, fault; quarrel; dispute.

tropo, *trŏ'pŏ*, sm. trope.

troquel, *trŏkĕl'*, sm. solid piece of steel, in which a hollow figure is engraved.

trotador, ra, *trŏtädŏr'*, sm. & f. trotter.

trotar, *trŏtär'*, v. n. to trot.

trote, *trŏ'tĕ*, sm. trot; á –, in haste.

trovador, ra, *trŏvädŏr'*, sm. & f. troubadour.

trovar, *–vär'*, v. a. to versify; to parody.

troxo, *trŏ'thŏ*, sm. piece cut off; (rail.) section of a line.

trucar, *trŭkär'*, v. n. to lead (at cards.)

truco, *trŏ'kŏ*, sm. skilful push at trucks; –s, pl. trucks, pl.

trucha, *trŭtsh'ä*, sf. trout; crane.

truchuela, *–tshŭĕ'lä*, sf. small cod-fish.

trueno, *trŭĕ'nŏ*, sm. thunder-clap.

trueque, *trŭĕ'kĕ*, sm. exchange, truck, barter. [barter.

truhán, *trŭän'*, a. buffoon.

truhanear, *–nĕär'*, v. n. to play the buffoon.

truhanería, *–nĕrĕ'ä*, sf. buffoonery.

truhanesco, ca, *–nĕs'kŏ*, a. belonging to a buffoon. [a buffoon.

trujal, *trŭ'häl'*, sm. oil-mill.

truncado, da, *trŭnkä'dŏ*, a. truncated.

truncamiento, *–mĭĕn'tŏ*, sm. truncation.

truncar, *–kär'*, v. a. to truncate, to maim.

truque, *trŭ'kĕ*, sm. a game at cards.

truquero, *–kĕ'rŏ*, sm. keeper of a truck-table.

tu, *tŏ*, a. thy, thine.

tú, *tŏ*, pn. thou.

tuáutem, *tŏä'ŭtĕm*, sm. principal person.

tubo, *tŏ'bŏ*, sm. tube. [essential point.

tuerca, *tŏĕr'kä*, sf. female screw.

tuerto, ta, *tŏĕr'tŏ*, a. one-eyed; squint-eyed; –, sm. wrong, injury.

tuétano, *tŏĕ'tänŏ*, sm. marrow. [smell.

tufarada, *tŏfärä'dä*, sf. strong scent or

tufo, *tŏ'fŏ*, sm. warm vapour arising from the earth; offensive smell; ear-lock.

tulipán, *tŏlĭpän'*, sm. tulip.

tullido, da, *tŏlyĕ'dŏ*, a. crippled, maimed.

tullimiento, *–mĭĕn'tŏ*, sm. maiming.

tullir, *–yĭr'*, v. n. to drop excrement (of birds); –se, to be crippled or maimed.

tumba, *tŏm'bä*, sf. tomb; roof of a coach; tumble.

tumbaga, *–bä'gä*, sf. pinchbeck, tomback.

tumbar, *–bär'*, v. a. to tumble (to throw down); –, v. n. to tumble (to fall down); –se, to lie down to sleep. [ing.

tumor, *tŏmŏr'*, sm. tumour, morbid swell-

túmulo, *tŏ'mŭlŏ*, sm. tomb, sepulchral monument.

tumulto, *tŏmŭl'tŏ*, sm. tumult, uproar.

tumultoso, sa, –tŏŏ´sŏ, a. tumultuous.
tuna, tō´nä, sf. Indian fig; idle life.
tunante, tänän´tĕ, a. & p. cunning; leading a licentious life; –, sm. rake, lazy loiterer.
tunar, –när´, v. n. to lead a licentious life; to loiter. [severe chastisement.
tunda, tän´dä, sf. (act of shearing cloth;
tundidor, –dïdŏr´, sm. shearer of cloth.
tundir, –dïr´, v. a. to shear; to cudgel, [to flog.
túnica, tō´nïkä, sf. tunic. [to flog.
tuno, tō´nŏ, sm. truant, rake.
tupé, tŭpĕ´, sm. toupet, foretop.
tupir, tŭpïr´, v. a. to press close; –se, to stuff oneself with eating and drinking.
turba, tŭr´bä, sf. crowd; turf, sod.
turbación, –thïŏn´, sf. perturbation, confusion, trouble, disorder.
turbador, ra, –dŏr´, sm. & f. disturber.
turbante, –bän´tĕ, sm. turban.
turbar, –bär´, v. a. to disturb, to trouble.
turbio, bia, tŭr´bïŏ, a. muddy, troubled.
turbión, –bïŏn´, sm. heavy shower of rain; hurricane. [disturbance.
turbulencia, –bälĕn´thïä, sf. turbulence.
turbulento, ta, –lĕn´tŏ, a. turbid, muddy; turbulent.
turnar, tŭrnär´, v. n. to alternate.
turno, tŭr´nŏ, sm. turn; vicissitude.
turquesa, tŭrkĕs´ä, sf. turquoise.
turquí, tŭrkï´, a. of a deep blue colour.
turrar, tŭrrär´, v. a. to toast, to roast.
turrón, tŭrrŏn´, sm. nougat (almond cake).
turrenero, –nä´rŏ, sm. nougat-maker or seller. [head.
turumbón, –rŭmbŏn´, sm. contusion on the
tus, tŭs, word used for calling dogs.
tuteamiento, tŭtĕämĕn´tŏ, sm. thouing.
tutear, –tĕär´, v. a. to thou.
tutela, –tĕ´lä, sf. guardianship, tutelage.
tutelar, –tĕlär´, a. tutelar, tutelary.
tutor, –tŏr´, sm. guardian, tutor.
tutora, –tŏ´rä, sf. tutoress.
tutoría, –tŏrï´ä, sf. tutelage.
tuyo, ya, tŭ´yŏ, a. thine; –s, pl. friends and relations of the party addressed.

U.

U, c. or (instead of ó, when the following word begins with an o); ¡–! ah! alas!
ubre, ŏ´brĕ, sf. dug, teat, udder.
ufanamente, ŭfänämĕn´tĕ, ad. ostentatiously, boastfully.
ufanarse, –när´sĕ, v. r. to boast.
ufanía, –nï´ä, sf. haughtiness.
ufano, na, ŏfä´nŏ, a. haughty, arrogant;
ujier, ŭ´hïĕr´, sm. usher. [gay, cheerful.
úlcera, ŭl´thĕrä, sf. ulcer.
ulceración, –räthïŏn´, sf. ulceration.
ulcerar, –rär´, v. n. to ulcerate.
ulceroso, sa, –rŏ´sŏ, a. ulcerous. [ther.
ulterior, ŭltĕrïŏr´, a. ulterior, farther, fur-
ultimátum, –tïmä´täm, sm. ultimatum.
último, ma, ŭl´tïmŏ, a. last, hindmost.
ultrajador, ra, –trä´hädŏr´, sm. & f. one who outrages or insults.

ultrajar, –´här´, v. a. to outrage; to despise, to depreciate; to abuse.
ultraje, –trä´hĕ, sm. outrage.
ultramar, –trämär´, a. & sm. ultramarine.
ultramarino, na, –märï´nŏ, a. ultramarine, oversea. [montane.
ultramontano, na, –mŏntä´nŏ, a. ultra-
umbilical, ŭmbïlïkäl´, a. umbilical.
umbral, –bräl´, sm. threshold; architrave; beginning, rudiment.
un (m, a. one (for uno).
unánime, –ä´nïmĕ, a. unanimous.
unanimidad, –mïdäd´, sf. unanimity.
unción, ŭnthïŏn´, sf. unction; extreme or last unction; –ones, pl. course of salvanoiz, –thïr´, v. a. to yoke. [tion.
undécimo, ma, –dä´thïmŏ, a. eleventh.
undísono, na, –dï´sŏnŏ, a. billowy.
undoso, sa, –dŏ´sŏ, a. wavy, rising in waves. [king, sovereign.
ungido, –hï´dŏ, sm. anointed of the Lord,
ungir, –hïr´, v. a. to anoint.
ungüento, –gŭĕn´tŏ, sm. unguent; ointment. [simply.
únicamente, ŭ´nïkämĕn´tĕ, ad. only,
único, ca, ŭ´nïkŏ, a. singular, unique.
unicornio, –kŏr´nïŏ, sm. unicorn.
unidad, –däd´, sf. unity; conformity, union. [animously.
unidamente, –dämĕn´tĕ, ad. jointly, un-
uniformar, –förmär´, v. a. to make uniform. [(mil.) uniform, regimentals.
uniforme, –för´mĕ, a. uniform; –, sm.
uniformidad, –mïdäd´, sf. uniformity.
unigénito, –hä´nïtŏ, a. only-begotten.
unión, ŭnïŏn´, sf. union.
unir, ŭnïr´, v. a. to join, to unite; to mingle, to bind, to tie; –se, to associate.
unísono, na, ŭnï´sŏnŏ, a. unison.
unitivo, va, –tï´vŏ, a. unitive.
universal, –vĕrsäl´, a. universal.
universalidad, –lïdäd´, sf. universality.
universidad, –sïdäd´, sf. university; university.
universo, –vĕr´sŏ, sm. universe.
uno, (na, sm. one; –, na, a. one; sole, only; –á otro, one another; –&–, one by one; á una, jointly, together.
untar, ŭntär´, v. a. to anoint; to grease; –se, to be greased with unctuous matter.
unto, ŭn´tŏ, sm. grease; fat of animals.
untuoso, sa, –tŏŏ´sŏ, a. unctuous, greasy.
untura, –tŏ´rä, sf. unction; unguent.
uña, ŭn´yä, sf. nail; hoof; claw, talon; pointed hook of instruments.
uñada, –yä´dä, uñarada, –yärä´dä, sf. scratch with the nail.
uñero, –yä´rŏ, sm. whitlow.
uñeta, –yä´tä, sf. sculptor's gouge; nail-claw; chuck-farthing (boys' game).
¡upa! ŭ´pä, up! up! (to make children get up from the ground).
upar, ŭpär´, v. n. to endeavour to get up.
urbanidad, ŭrbänïdäd´, sf. urbanity, politeness.
urbano, na, –bä´nŏ, a. polite, well-bred.
urdidor, ra, –dïdŏr´, sm. & f. warper; warping-mill.

urdidura, -dŏˈrä, sf. warping.

urdiembre, -dēmˈbrĕ, urdimbre, -dīmˈbrĕ, sf. chain, warp.

urdir, -dēˈr, v. a. to warp; to contrive.

urgencia, -hĕnˈthä, sf. urgency, pressure of difficulty, need, necessity.

urgentemente, -tēmēnˈtĕ, ad. urgently.

urgir, -hēr, v. n. to be urgent.

urinario, ria, ṳrēnäˈrēŏ, a. urinary.

urna, ṳrˈnä, sf. urn; glass-case in which small statues or images are kept.

urraca, ṳrräˈkä, sf. magpie.

usado, da, ṳsäˈdŏ, a. used; experienced.

usagre, ṳsäˈgrĕ, sm. milk-scab, kind of breaking out in the faces of children.

usanza, ṳsänˈthä, sf. usage, use, custom.

usar, ṳsäˈr, v. a. to use, to make use of; to accustom; -se, to be in use, to be wont. [Your Lordship.

Usía, ṳsēˈä (= Vuestra Señoría), sf.

uso, ṳˈsŏ, sm. use, service; custom; mode.

Usted, ṳstēdˈ, sm. & f. you (contraction of **Vuestra Merced**.)

usuario, ria, ṳsṳäˈrēŏ, a. (law) having only the use of a thing.

usufructo, -frṳkˈtŏ, sm. usufruct.

usufructuar, -frṳktṳäˈr, v. a. to enjoy the usufruct of any thing; to render productive. [the usufruct of any thing.

usufructuario, ria, -tṳäˈrēŏ, a. possessing

usura, ṳsṳˈrä, sf. usury.

usurario, ria, -räˈrēŏ, a. belonging to usury.

usurero, -rēˈrŏ, sm. usurer. [usury.

usurpación, ṳsṳrpäthēŏnˈ, sf. usurpation.

usurpador, ra, -dŏrˈ, sm. & f. usurper.

usurpar, -pärˈ, v. a. to usurp.

utensilio, ṳtēnsēˈlēŏ, sm. utensil.

uterino, na, ṳtērēˈnŏ, a. uterine.

útero, ṳˈtērŏ, sm. uterus, womb.

útil, ṳˈtēl, a. useful, profitable; -, sm.

utilidad, -lēdädˈ, sf. utility. [ntility.

utilizar, -lēthärˈ, v. a. to make useful; to be useful; to yield profit; -se, to take advantage of.

ut supra, ṳt sṳˈprä, ad. as above.

uva, ṳˈvä, sf. grape; barberry.

V.

vaca, väˈkä, sf. cow; beef.

vacaciones, -thēŏˈnēs, sf. pl. holidays.

vacada, -käˈdä, sf. drove of cows.

vacante, -känˈtĕ, a. vacant; -, sf. vacancy.

vacar, -kärˈ, v. n. to be vacant.

vaciadero, -thēädēˈrŏ, sm. drain, sink.

vaciador, -ädŏrˈ, sm. moulder.

vaciar, -thēärˈ, v. a. to empty, to clear; to mould; -, v. n. to fall, to decrease (of waters); -se, to be spilt, to be emptied.

vacilación, -thēläthēŏnˈ, sf. vacillation; irresolution.

vacilar, -lärˈ, v. n. to vacillate.

vacío, cia, väthēˈŏ, a. void, empty; unoccupied; concave; vain; presumptuous; unemployed; -, sm. vacuum; concavity.

vacuna, -kŏˈnä, sf. cow-pox, vaccine virus.

vacunar, -kṳnärˈ, v. a. to vaccinate.

vacuno, na, väkŏˈnŏ, a. belonging to black cattle.

vade, väˈdĕ, sm. satchel.

vadeable, -dēäˈblĕ, a. fordable.

vadear, -dēärˈ, v. a. to wade, to ford.

vado, väˈdŏ, sm. ford.

vagabundo, da, -gäbṳnˈdŏ, a. vagabond.

vagamundear, -mṳndēärˈ, v. a. to rove or loiter about.

vagamundo, da, -mṳnˈdŏ, a. vagabond.

vagancia, -gänˈthä, sf. vagrancy.

vagar, -gärˈ, v. n. to rove or loiter about; to be loose and irregular; -, sm. leisure; slowness. [vulsive sob.

vagido, -hēˈdŏ, sm. cry of a child; convago, ga, väˈgŏ, a. vagrant; restless; vague; -, sm. vagabond; en -, in vain; unsteadily.

vagón, -gŏnˈ, sm. (rail.) waggon; - cama, sleeping-car; - cuadra, cattle-van; - freno, brake-van; - jaula, latticed waggon; - de mercancías, goods van; - de borde alto ó bajo, truck.

vaguear, -gēärˈ, v. n. to rove, to loiter.

vahído, väˈēdŏ, sm. vertigo, giddiness.

vaho, väˈŏ, sm. steam, vapour.

vaina, väˈēnä, sf. scabbard of a sword; knife-case; pod, husk. [person.

vainazas, -näˈthäs, sm. humdrum, dull

vainilla, -nēˈlyä, sf. (bot.) vanilla.

vaivén, -vēnˈ, sm. fluctuation, vacillation, instability; giddiness; risk, danger.

vajilla, -hēˈlyä, sf. table-service.

vale, väˈlĕ, sm. farewell; promissory note, I.O.U.; note of pardon given to schoolboys by the master. [binding.

valedero, ra, -dēˈrŏ, a. valid, efficacious,

valentía, -lēntēˈä, sf. valour, courage; brag, boast; public place where mended old shoes are sold in Madrid.

valentón, -tŏnˈ, sm. braggadocio, hector.

valentonada, -näˈdä, sf. brag, boast.

valer, väˈlēr, v. n. to be valuable, to be deserving; to be marketable; to prevail; to avail; to serve as an asylum; to be valid; to have power, to be worth; to yield; to produce; to amount to; to have influence; to be equivalent to; to be current; -, v. a. to protect, to favour; -se, to employ, to make use of; to have recourse to. [strong, powerful.

valeroso, sa, -rŏˈsŏ, a. valiant, brave;

valetudinario, ria, -tēdēnäˈrēŏ, a. valetudinarian, sickly. [party.

valía, -lēˈä, sf. valuation; credit, favour;

validación, -lēdäthēŏnˈ, sf. validity.

validar, -därˈ, v. a. to give validity.

validez, -dēthˈ, sf. validity, stability.

valido, väˈlēdŏ, sm. favourite.

válido, da, väˈlēdŏ, a. valid; obligatory.

valiente, -lēēnˈtĕ, a. robust, vigorous; valiant, brave; boasting.

valimiento, -mēēnˈtŏ, sm. use, utility, advantage; contribution; favour, protection, support.

valisa, -lēˈthä, sf. beacon.

valona, välŏˈnä, sf. tucker; cape, pelerine.

valor, *vălŏr',* sm. value, price; validity; force; power; courage, valour.

valor(e)ar, *—r(ĕ)ăr',* v. a. to value.

valuación, *—lăăthŏn',* sf. valuation.

valuar, *—lăăr',* v. a. to value, to appraise.

valla, *văl'yă,* sf. intrenchment; barricade.

vallado, *—yă'dŏ,* sm. enclosure with stakes or palisades.

valle, *văl'yĕ,* sm. dale, valley.

vampiro, *vămpē'rŏ,* sm. vampire.

vanagloria, *vănăglŏ'rĕă,* sf. vainglory.

vanagloriarse, *—glŏrĕăr'sĕ,* v. r. to be vainglorious, to boast of.   [glorious.

vanaglorioso, sa, *—glŏrĕŏ'sŏ,* a. vain-

vandalismo, *văndălĭs'mŏ,* sm. vandalism.

vandalo, la, *—dă'lŏ,* sm. & a. vandal.

vanguardia, *—găr'dĭă,* sf. vanguard, van.

vanidad, *vănĭdăd',* sf. vanity; ostentation; futility; flirtation; illusion, phantom.

vanidoso, sa, *—dŏ'sŏ,* a. vain, showy; haughty, self-conceited.

vano, na, *vă'nŏ,* a. vain; useless; frivolous; arrogant; futile; **en —,** in vain.

vapor, *văpŏr',* sm. vapour, steam; breath.

vaporoso, sa, *—rŏ'sŏ,* a. vaporous.

vapular, *—pŭlăr',* v. a. to whip, to flog.

vaquerizo, za, *—kĕrē'thŏ,* a. relating to cows; **—,** sm. cow-herd.

vaquero, *—kă'rŏ,* sm. cow-herd; **—, ra,** a. belonging to cow-herds.

vaqueta, *—kă'tă,* sf. sole-leather; ramrod.

vara, *vă'ră,* sf. rod; pole, staff; verge; yard (measure); **- alta,** sway, high hand; **-s,** pl. shafts of a coach, pl.   [person.

varal, *—răl',* sm. long pole; tall, slender

varapalo, *—răpă'lŏ,* sm. long perch; blow with a pole; trouble, vexation.

varar, *—răr',* v. a. to launch a new-built ship; **—,** v. n. to be stranded.

varchilla, *vărtshĭl'yă,* sf. measure of grain, containing the third part of a fanega.

vardasca, *—dăs'kă,* sf. a thin twig.

vardascazo, *—dăthŏ,* sm. stroke with a switch.   [by the yard.

vareaje, *vărĕă'hĕ,* sm. selling or measuring

varear, *—rĕăr',* v. a. to knock the fruit off trees with a pole; to goad a bull; to measure or sell by the yard; **-se,** to grow thin or lean.

vareta, *—rĕ'tă,* sf. lime-twig for catching birds; stripe in any kind of stuff different in colour from the ground; **irse de —,** to suffer from diarrhoea.

variable, *—rĭă'blĕ,* a. variable, changeable.

variación, *—rĭăthŏn',* sf. variation.

variado, da, *—rĭă'dŏ,* a. variegated.

variar, *—rĭăr',* v. a. to change; **—,** v. n. to vary.   [stancy.

variedad, *—rĭĕdăd',* sf. variety; incon-

varilla, *—rĭl'yă,* sf. small rod; curtain-rod; spindle, pivot; **-s,** pl. jaw-bones; rib of a fan.

vario, ria, *vă'rĭŏ,* a. various, different; vague; variegated; **-s,** pl. some.

varon, *—rŏn',* sm. man, male human being; man of respectability.   [cendants.

varonia, *—nĕ'ă,* sf. male issue; male des-

varonil, *—nĭl',* a. male, masculine; manful.

vasallaje, *văsăllyă'hĕ,* sm. vassalage.

vasallo, *—săl'yŏ,* sm. vassal, liegeman.

vasar, *—săr',* sm. buffet on which glasses or vessels are put.

vascuence, *văskŭĕn'thĕ,* sm. Biscay dialect.

vasija, *—sē'hă,* sf. vessel (in which liquors are kept).

vaso, *vă'sŏ,* sm. vessel; vase. [are kept).

vástago, *văs'tăgŏ,* sm. bud, shoot.

vasto, ta, *—tŏ,* a. vast, huge. [diviner.

vaticinador, *vătĭthĭnădŏr',* sm. prophet, diviner.

vaticinar, *—thĭnăr',* v. a. to divine, to foretell.

vaticinio, *—thĭ'nĭŏ,* sm. divination.

vecindad, *vĕthĭndăd',* sf. inhabitants of a place; neighbourhood.

vecindario, *—dă'rĭŏ,* sm. number of inhabitants of a place.

vecino, na, *—thē'nŏ,* a. neighbouring; near; **—,** sm. neighbour, inhabitant.

veda, *vă'dă,* sf. prohibition. [to impede.

vedar, *vĕdăr',* v. a. to prohibit, to forbid;

vedija, *—dē'hă,* sf. entangled lock of wool; flake; tuft of entangled hair, matted hair.

veedor, *vĕĕdŏr',* sm. overseer, inspector.

veeduría, *—dŏrē'ă,* sf. inspector's office.

vega, *vă'gă,* sf. fruitful plain.

vegetación, *vĕ'hĕtăthŏn',* sf. vegetation.

vegetal, *—tăl',* a. vegetable.

vegetar, *—tăr',* v. n. to vegetate. [force.

vehemencia, *vĕĕmĕn'thĭă,* sf. vehemence.

vehemente, *—mĕn'tĕ,* a. vehement, violent.

vehículo, *vĕĕ'kŭlŏ,* sm. vehicle.

veinte, *vă'ĭntĕ,* a. & sm. twenty.

veintena, *—tă'nă,* sf. twentieth part; score.

veinteno, na, *—tă'nŏ,* a. twentieth.

vejación, *vĕ'hăthŏn',* sf. vexation, molestation; oppression, cumber.

vejamen, *—hă'mĕn,* sm. taunt. [censure.

vejar, *—hăr',* v. a. to vex, to molest; to

vejestorio, *—hĕstŏ'rĭŏ,* sm. old trumpery; petulant old man.

vejete, *—hă'tĕ,* sm. ridiculous old man; actor of an old man.

vejez, *—hĕth',* sf. old age.

vejiga, *—hē'gă,* sf. bladder; blister.

vejigatorio, *—gătŏ'rĭŏ,* sm. blistering-plaster; **—, ria,** a. raising blisters.

vela, *vă'lă,* sf. watch; watchfulness; night-guard; candle; a horse's ear; sail; ship; **hacerse á la —,** to set sail.

velación, *vĕlăthŏn',* sf. watching; **-ones,** pl. nuptial benedictions, pl.

velador, *—dŏr',* sm. watchman; careful observer; large wooden candlestick.

velaje, *—lă'hĕ,* sm. sails, pl.; sailwork.

velamen, *—lă'mĕn,* sm. set of sails.

velar, *—lăr',* v. n. to watch; to wake; to be attentive; (mar.) to appear; **—,** v. a. to guard, to watch; to marry.

veleidad, *—lĕĭdăd',* sf. lowest degree of desire; feeble will; inconstancy.

veleidoso, sa, *—dŏ'sŏ,* a. inconstant, fickle.

velero, ra, *—lă'rŏ,* a. swift sailing.

veleta, *—lĕ'tă,* sf. weather-cock.

velo, *vă'lŏ,* sm. veil; pretext.

velocidad, *vĕlŏthĭdăd',* sf. velocity.

velón, *vĕlŏn',* sm. oil-lamp.

velonero, —nā′rŏ, sm.-lamp-maker.

veloz(mente), velŏth′(měn′tĕ), a. (& ad.) swift(ly). [downy hair.

vello, vel′yŏ, sm. down; gossamer; short

vellón, velyŏn′, sm. fleece; lock of wool; copper coin of the province of Castile.

vellorí, velyŏrī′, sm. second-rate cloth.

velloso, sa, —yŏ sŏ, a. downy, cottony.

velludo, da, —yŏ dŏ, a. shaggy, woolly.

vena, vā′nā, sf. vein, blood-vessel.

venablo, venā′blŏ, sm. javelin.

venado, —nā′dŏ, sm. deer; venison.

venal, —nāl′, a. belonging to the veins; saleable; mercenary.

venalidad, —lĭdād′, sf. venality.

venático, ca, venā′tĭkŏ, a. a little mad.

venatorio, ria, —tŏ′rĭŏ, a. used in hunting.

vencedor, —venthēdŏr′, sm. & f. conqueror, victor, foiler.

vencejo, —thĕ′hŏ, sm. martinet (bird).

vencer, —thēr′, v. a. to conquer, to vanquish; —se, to govern one's desires and passions. [able.

vencible, —thĕ′blĕ, a. vincible, conquerable.

vencido, da, —thĭ′dŏ, a. to be paid afterwards, due. [ing down.

vencimiento, —mĭen′tŏ, sm. victory; bending down.

venda, ven′dā, sf. bandage; fillet; diadem.

vendaje, —dā′hĕ, sm. brokerage; bandage, dressing of wounds. [wink.

vendar, —dār′, v. a. to bandage; to hood-

vendaval, —dăvăl′, sm. a strong south-by-west wind.

vendedor, ra, —dēdŏr′, sm. & f. seller.

vender, vēndēr′, v. a. to sell.

vendible, —dē′blĕ, a. saleable, vendible.

vendimia, —dē′mĭā, sf. vintage.

vendimiador, ra, —dĭmĭādŏr′, sm. & f. vintager. [vintage.

vendimiar, —mĭār′, v. a. to gather the

veneno, vēnē′nŏ, sm. poison, venom.

venenoso, sa, vēnēnŏ′sŏ, a. venomous, poisonous.

venera, —nā′rā, sf. porcelain shell; badge worn by the knights of military orders.

venerable, —nēră′blĕ, a. venerable.

veneración, —thĭŏn′, sf. veneration, worship. [ship.

venerar, —rār′, v. a. to venerate, to worship.

venéreo, rea, —nā′rĕŏ, a. venereal.

venero, —nā′rŏ, sm. vein of metal in a mine; source of water. [geance.

venganza, —gan′thā, sf. revenge, vengeance.

vengar, —gār′, v. a. to revenge, to avenge; —se, to be revenged on.

vengativo, va, —tĭ′vŏ, a. revengeful.

venia, vā′nĭā, sf. pardon; leave, permission; bow.

venial, vēnĭāl′, a. venial. [sion; bow.

venida, vēnĭ′dā, sf. arrival; return; overflow of a river. [pl. posterity.

venidero, ra, —dā′rŏ, a. future; —s, sm.

venir, vēnīr′, v. n. to come, to arrive; to follow, to succeed; to spring from; —se, to ferment.

venoso, sa, —nŏ′sŏ, a. veiny, veined.

venta, ven′tā, sf. sale; poor inn on roads.

ventaja, —tā′hā, sf. advantage.

ventajoso, sa, —hŏ′sŏ, a. advantageous.

ventana, —tā′nā, sf. window; window-shutter; nostril; [dows in a building.

ventanaje, —nā′hĕ, sm. number of windows in a building.

ventanazo, —nā′thŏ, sm. banging off a window. [from the window.

ventanear, —nĕār′, v. n. to gaze repeatedly

ventarrón, —rŏn′, sm. violent wind.

ventear, —tĕār′, v. a. to smell, to scent; to investigate, to examine; to expose to the air; to be filled with wind; to break wind. [side inn.

ventero, —tā′rŏ, sm. & f. keeper of a road-

ventilación, —tĭlăthĭŏn′, sf. ventilation; discussion. [to discuss.

ventilar, —tĭlār′, v. a. to ventilate; to fan;

ventisca, —tĭs′kā, sf. ventisco, —kŏ, sm. snow-storm. [drifts (snow).

ventiscar, —kār′, v. n. to drift, to lie in

ventisquero, —tĭskā′rŏ, sm. snow-drift; —s, pl. glaciers. [ness.

ventolera, —tŏlā′rā, sf. gust; pride, loftiness.

ventor, —tŏr′, sm. setter. [house.

ventorrillo, —tŏrrī′yŏ, sm. roadside pot-

ventosa, —tŏ′sā, sf. cupping-glass.

ventosear, —tŏsĕār′, v. n. to break wind.

ventosidad, —sĭdād′, sf. flatulency.

ventoso, sa, —tŏ′sŏ, a. windy; flatulent.

ventrículo, —trĭ′kŭlŏ, sm. ventricle.

ventrílocuo, —trē′lŏkŭŏ, sm. ventriloquist.

ventrudo, da, —trŏ′dŏ, a. big-bellied.

ventura, —tŏ′rā, sf. luck, favourable chance, fortune; por —, by chance.

venturilla, —tŏrē′yā, sf. good luck.

venturina, —tŏrē′nā, sf. precious stone of a yellowish brown colour.

venturoso, sa, —rŏ′sŏ, a. lucky, fortunate, happy.

Venus, vā′nŭs, sf. evening-star.

ver, vēr′, v. a. to see, to look; to observe; to visit; —se, to be seen; to be conspicuous; to find oneself; to have a bone to pick with someone; —, sm. sense of the sight; appearance.

veracidad, vērăthĭdād′, sf. veracity.

veran(e)ar, —rān(ĕ)ār′, v. n. to pass the summer season.

verano, —rā′nŏ, sm. summer season.

veras, vā′rās, sf. pl. truth, sincerity; de —, in truth, really.

veraz, vērăth′, a. veracious.

verbal, vērbăl′, a. verbal.

verbena, —bā′nā, sf. (bot.) vervain.

verbigracia, —bĭgră′thĭă, ad. for example.

verbo, vēr′bŏ, sm. word, term; (gr.) verb.

verbosidad, —sĭdād′, sf. verbosity.

verboso, sa, —bŏ′sŏ, a. verbose.

verdacho, —dātsh′ŏ, sm. green chalk.

verdad, verdād′, sf. truth, veracity, reality; certain existence of things; — de Perogrullo, notorious truth. [in fact.

verdaderamente, —dĕrămĕn′tĕ, ad. truly.

verdadero, ra, —dā′rŏ, a. true, real; sincere.

verde, vēr′dĕ, sm. & a. green. [sincere.

verdear, verdĕār′, **verd—er,** —dĕhēr′, v. n. to grow green.

verdecillo, —dĕthĭl′yŏ, sm. green-finch.

verdegay, —gā′ĭ, sm. parrot-green.

verdín, verdīn′, sm. verdure.

verdinegro, gra, *–nā'grŏ,* a. of a deep green colour.

verdolaga, *verdŏlā'gā,* sf. purslain.

verdor, *verdŏr',* sm. verdure; vigour; youth; **–es,** pl. age of vigour.

verdoso, sa, *–dŏ'sŏ,* a. greenish, greeny.

verdugo, ga, *–dŏ'gŏ,* sm. young shoot of a tree; hangman; very cruel person.

verduguillo, *–dăgĭl'yŏ,* sm. small, narrow razor; long, narrow sword.

verdulero, *–lā'rŏ,* sf. green-grocer.

verdura, *–dŏ'rā,* sf. verdure; vegetables, garden-stuff; vigour.

vereda, *verā'dā,* sf. path; circular order sent to several towns or places.

veredero, *verĕdā'rŏ,* sm. messenger sent with orders or despatches. [(mar.) yard.

verga, *ver'gā,* sf. cord of the crossbow;

vergajo, *–gā'hŏ.* sm. pizzle.

vergonzante, *–gŏnthăn'tĕ,* a. bashful, shamefaced. [fulness; confusion.

vergüenza, *–găĕn'thā,* sf. shame; bashfulness; confusion.

vericueto, *verĭkŭā'tŏ,* sm. rough road.

verídico, ca, *verĭ'dĭkŏ,* a. veridical, truthful, worthy of faith.

verificación, *–fĭkāthĭŏn',* sf. verification.

verificar, *–fĭkār',* v. a. to verify; **–se,** to be verified, to turn out true.

verificativo, va, *–fĭkātĭ'vŏ,* a. tending to prove. [lar.

verisímil, *–sĕ'mĭl,* a. probable, verisimilar.

verisimilitud, *–sĭmĭlĭtŭd',* sf. probability, likelihood. [bably.

verisímilmente, *–sĭmĭlmĕn'tĕ,* ad. probably.

verja, *ver'hā,* sf. grate, lattice.

verjel, *ver'hĕl',* sm. orchard; (fig.) thing agreeable to the sight.

vermejo, *vermĕ'hŏ,* a. vermeil.

vermellón, *mĕlyŏn',* sm. vermilion.

vermífugo, *–mĕ'fŭgŏ,* a. & sm. vermifuge. [grubs.

verminoso, sa, *–mĭnŏ'sŏ,* a. full of

verónica, *verŏ'nĭkā,* sf. (bot.) speedwell.

verosímil, *verŏsĕ'mĭl,* a. verisimilar.

verosimilitud, *–sĭmĭlĭtŭd',* sf. verisimilar.

verraco, *verrā'kŏ,* sm. boar. [lity.

verraquear, *–kā‹r',* v. n. to grunt like a boar. [boar in rutting time.

verriondo, da, *–rĭŏn'dŏ,* a. foaming like a

verruga, *–rŏ'gā,* sf. wart, pimple.

verrugoso, sa, *–rŭgŏ'sŏ,* a. warty.

versado, a, *–sā'dŏ,* a. versed.

versal, *–săl',* a. capital (of letters).

versar, *–săr',* v. n. **–se,** to be versed; to grow skilful.

versátil, *–sā'tĭl,* a. versatile.

versículo, *–sē'kŭlŏ,* sm. versicle; verse of a chapter. [tion.

versificación, *–sĭfĭkāthĭŏn',* sf. versificación.

versificador, *–fĭkādŏr',* sm. versifier.

versificar, *–fĭkār',* v. a. to versify.

versión, *versĭŏn',* sf. translation, version.

verso, *ver'sŏ,* sm. verse.

vértebra, *ver'tĕbrā,* sf. vertebre.

vertedero, *–tĕd'rŏ,* sm. sewer, drain.

vertedor, ra, *–dŏr',* sm. & f. nightman; conduit, sewer; (mar.) scoop. [empty.

verter, *vertĕr',* v. a. to spill, to shed; to

vertical, *–tĭkāl',* a. vertical.

vértice, *ver'tĭtĕ,* sm. vertex, zenith; crown of the head.

vertiente, *–tĭĕn'tĕ,* sm. waterfall, cascade.

vertiginoso, sa, *–tĭ'hĭnŏ'sŏ,* a. giddy.

vértigo, *ver'tĭgŏ,* sm. giddiness, vertigo.

Véspero, *vĕs'pĕrŏ,* sm. Vesper (evening-star).

vespertino, na, *–tĕ'nŏ,* a. vespertine.

vestíbulo, *vĕstĕ'bŭlŏ,* sm. vestibule, lobby.

vestido, *vĕstĕ'dŏ,* sm. dress, suit of clothes.

vestidura, *–dŏ'rā,* sf. dress, wearing-apparel; robe of distinction.

vestigio, *vĕstĕ'hĭŏ,* sm. vestige, footstep.

vestiglo, *–glŏ,* sm. horrid monster.

vestir, *vestĭr',* v. a. to clothe, to dress; to accoutre; to adorn; to cloak, to disguise.

vestuario, *–tŭā'rĭŏ,* sm. clothes; uniform; vestry; green-room; vestiary.

veta, *vā'tā,* sf. vein (in mines, wood &c.); stripe of a different colour in cloth.

vetado, da, *vĕtā'dŏ,* a. striped, veined.

veterano, na, *vĕtĕrā'nŏ,* a. experienced, long practised; **–,** sm. veteran, old soldier.

vez, *vĕth,* sf. turn, return; **cada –,** each time; **una –,** once; **á veces,** sometimes, by turns.

vía, *vĕ'ā,* sf. way, road, route, mode, manner, method; (rail.) railway, line.

viajar, *vĭā'hār',* v. n. to travel.

viaje, *vĭā'hĕ,* sm. journey, voyage, travel.

viajero, *–hā'rŏ,* sm. traveller.

viático, *vĭā'tĭkŏ,* sm. viaticum.

víbora, *vĕ'bŏrā,* sf. viper.

viborezno, *vĭbŏrĕth'nŏ,* sm. young viper.

vibración, *vĭbrāthĭŏn',* sf. vibration.

vibrar, *vĭbrār',* v. a. to vibrate, to brandish; to throw, to dart; **–,** v. n. to vibrate.

vicaría, *vĭkārĕ'ā,* sf. vicarship; vicarage.

vicariato, *–tŏ'rĭā,* sm. vicarage.

vicario, *vĭkā'rĭŏ,* sm. vicar; **–, ria,** a.

vice, *vĕ'thĕ,* (in comp.) vice.. [vicarial.

vicealmiranta, *–ălmĭrăn'tā,* sf. the galley next in order to that of the admiral.

vicealmirante, *–tĕ,* sm. vice-admiral.

viceconsulado, *–kŏnsŭlā'dŏ,* sm. vice-consulate.

viciar, *vĭthĕăr',* v. n. to vitiate, to corrupt; to annul; to deprave; **–se,** to become vitiated; to deliver oneself up to vice.

vicio, *vĕ'thĭŏ,* sm. vice.

vicioso, sa, *vĭthĭŏ'sŏ,* a. vicious.

vicisitud, *vĭthĭsĭtŭd',* sf. vicissitude.

víctima, *vĭk'tĭmā,* sf. victim; sacrifice.

victor, *vĭktŏr',* sm. shout, acclamation.

victorear, *–rĕăr',* v. a. to shout, to huzza.

victoria, *–tŏ'rĭā,* sf. victory.

victorioso, sa, *–rĭŏ'sŏ,* a. victorious.

vid, *vĭd,* sf. (bot.) vine.

vida, *vĕ'dā,* sf. life. [ware, crockery.

vidriado, *vĭdrĭā'dŏ,* sm. glazed earthenware.

vidriar, *–rĭăr',* v. a. to glaze earthenware.

vidriera, *–rĭā'rā,* sf. glass case.

vidriería, *–rĭĕrĕ'ā,* sf. glazier's shop; glass-house.

vidriero, *–drĭā'rŏ,* sm. glazier. [house.

vidrio, *vĕ'drĭŏ,* sm. glass.

vidrioso, sa, *vĭdrĭŏ'sŏ,* a. glassy, brittle; slippery; very delicate.

viejo,ja, viĕh'ŏ,a. old; ancient, antiquated.
viento, viĕn'tŏ, sm. wind; air.
vientre, viĕn'trĕ, sm. belly.
viernes, viĕr'nĕs, sm. Friday; — Santo, Good-Friday. [of timber].
viga, vĕ'gā, sf. beam (large and long piece
vigente, vĭ'hĕn'tĕ, a. in force.
vigésimo, ma, vĭ'hā'sĭmŏ, a. twentieth.
vigía, vĭ'hĕ'ā, sf. (mar.) look-out; —, sm. watchman. [watchfulness.
vigilancia, vĭ'hĭlān'thĕā, sf. vigilance,
vigilante, –lān'tĕ, a. watchful, vigilant.
vigilar, –lār', v. n. to watch over.
vigilia, vĭ'hĕ'lĭā, sf. nocturnal study; vigil; watch.
vigor, vĭgŏr', sm. vigour, strength.
vigoroso, sa, –rŏ'sŏ, a. vigorous.
vihuela, vĭŭĕ'lā, sf. guitar.
vihuelista, –lĭs'tā, sm. guitar-player.
vil, vĭl, a. mean, sordid, low; worthless; infamous; ungrateful. [abjectness.
vileza, vĭlā'thā, sf. meanness, lowness;
vilipendiar, vĭlĭpĕndĭār', v. a. to contemn, to revile. [dain.
vilipendio, –pĕn'dĭŏ, sm. contempt, dis-
vilmente, vĭlmĕn'tĕ, ad. vilely; abjectly.
vilordo, da, vĭlŏr'dŏ, a. lazy, heavy.
vilorta, vĭlŏr'tā, sf. ring made of twisted willow; cricket (in Old Castile).
villa, vĭl'yā, sf. town which enjoys peculiar privileges by charter; its magistracy.
Villadiego, –dĕĕ'gŏ, sm., tomar las de —, to run away.
villancico, vĭlyānthĕ'kŏ, sm. Christmas carol; hackneyed answers, pl.
villanesco, ca, –nĕs'kŏ, a. rustic.
villanía, –nĕ'ā, sf. lowness of birth; villany; indecorous word or act.
villano, na, –yā'nŏ, a. rustic, clownish; villanous; –, sm. villain; rustic.
villorín, –yŏrĭn', sm. second-rate cloth.
villorio, –yŏ'rĭŏ, sm. miserable little hamlet.
vinagre, vĭnā'grĕ, sm. vinegar. [let.
vinagrera, –grā'rā, sf. vinegar-cruet.
vinagrero, –grā'rŏ, sm. vinegar-merchant.
vinajera, –hā'rā, sf. vinegar-cruet; flagon.
vinariego, –rĭĕ'gŏ, sm. vintager.
vinatería, –tĕrĕ'ā, sf. vintry; wine-trade.
vinatero, –tā'rŏ, sm. vintner. [entailed.
vinculable, vĭnkŭlā'blĕ, a. that may be
vinculación, –lāthĭŏn', sf. entail.
vincular, –lār', v. a. to entail an estate; to perpetuate. [entail.
vínculo, vĭn'kŭlŏ, sm. tie, link, chain;
vindicación, vĭndĭkāthĭŏn', sf. revenge.
vindicar, –kār', v. a. to revenge.
vindicativo, va, –kātĕ'vŏ, a. vindictive.
vindicta, vĭndĭk'tā, sf. vengeance.
vino, vĕ'nŏ, sm. wine; – tinto, red wine; – del reino, home-grown wine.
vinolento, ta, vĭnŏlĕn'tŏ, a. inebriated.
vinoso, sa, vĭnŏ'sŏ, a. vinous, vinose.
viña, vĭn'yā, sf. vineyard.
viñador, vĭnyādŏr', sm. wine-grower.
viñedo, vĭnyā'dŏ, sm. vine-clad hills, pl.
viñero, –nā'rŏ, sm. wine-grower, vine-
viñeta, –yā'tā, sf. vignette. [dresser.
violación, vĭŏlāthĭŏn', sf. violation.

violado, da, –lā'dŏ, a. violet-coloured; violated. [profaner.
violador, ra, –lādŏr', sm. & f. violator;
violar, –lār', v. a. to violate; to ravish; to profane a church.
violencia, –lĕn'thĭā, sf. violence.
violentar, –tār', v. a. to enforce by violent means. [absurd.
violento, ta, –lĕn'tŏ, a. violent, forced;
violeta, –vĭŏlā'tā, sf. (bot.) violet,
violín, vĭŏlĭn', sm. violin, fiddle.
violinista, –nĭs'tā, sm. comma.
violón, vĭŏlŏn', sm. bass-viol.
violoncelo, –thĕ'lŏ, sm. violoncello.
viperino, na, vĭpĕrĕ'nŏ, a. viperine.
vira, vĭ'rā, sf. welt of a shoe.
virada, vĭrā'dā, sf. (mar.) tacking.
virar, vĭrār', v. a. to tack.
virgen, vĭr'hĕn, sm. & f. virgin.
virginal, –hĭnāl', a. virginal.
virginidad, –hĭnĭdād', sf. virginity, maidenhood.
Virgo, vĭr'gŏ, sf. Virgo (sign of the zodiac).
virguilla, vĭrgŭĭl'yā, sf. comma.
viril, vĭrĭl', sm. clear and transparent glass; monstrance; –, a. virile, manly. [vigour.
virilidad, –lĭdād', sf. virility, manhood;
virolento, ta, vĭrŏlĕn'tŏ, a. diseased with the small-pox; pock-pitted.
virote, vĭrŏ'tĕ, sm. dart, arrow; showy, vain loiterer; conceited person.
virreinato, vĭrrĕĭnā'tŏ, sm. viceroyship.
virrey, –rā'ĭ, sm. viceroy.
virtual, vĭrtūāl', a. virtual.
virtud, vĭrtūd', sf. virtue; efficacy, force; vigour, courage; –es, pl. the fifth of the nine celestial choirs.
virtuoso, sa, –tūŏ'sŏ, a. virtuous.
viruela, vĭrūā'lā, sf. small-pox.
virulencia, –lĕn'thĭā, sf. virulence.
virulento, ta, –lĕn'tŏ, a. virulent.
viruta, vĭrū'tā, sf. cuttings, pl.
visaje, vĭsā'h'ĕ, sm. grimace; visage.
víscera, vĭs'thĕrā, sf. vital organ.
viscosidad, vĭskŏsĭdād', sf. viscosity.
viscoso, sa, –kŏ'sŏ, a. viscous, glutinous.
visera, vĭsā'rā, sf. visor.
visible, vĭsē'blĕ, a. visible; apparent.
visión, vĭsĭŏn', sf. sight, vision; frightful, ugly or ridiculous person; phantom.
visionario, ria, –nā'rĭŏ, a. visionary.
visir, vĭsĭr', sm. vizier.
visita, vĭsē'tā, sf. visit.
visitación, vĭsĭtāthĭŏn', sf. visitation.
visitador, ra, –dŏr', sm. & f. visitor; surveyor. [be on visiting terms, to visit.
visitar, vĭsĭtār', v. a. to visit; –se, to
vislumbrar, vĭslŭmbrār', v. a. to catch a glimpse; to perceive indistinctly; to know imperfectly, to conjecture.
vislumbre, –lŭm'brĕ, sf. glimmering light, conjecture; imperfect knowledge; slight resemblance. [apparent likeness.
viso, vĕ'sŏ, sm. prospect; lustre; pretext;
víspera, vĭs'pĕrā, sf. evening before; evening before a festival; –s, pl. vespers.
vist, vĭst, sm. whist (juego de naipes de origen inglés).

vista, *vĭs′tă,* sf. sight, view; eye; appearance; prospect; intention, purpose; (law) − **de un pleito,** day of trial; −, sm. employment of a custom-house officer; −s, pl. presents made to a bride by a bridegroom the day preceding the nuptials; windows, pl.

vistazo, *vĭstă′thŏ,* sm. glance.

vistillas, *vĭstĭl′yăs,* sf. pl. height affording an extensive prospect.

visto, *vĭs′tŏ,* − **que,** c. considering that.

vistoso, sa, *vĭstŏ′sŏ,* a. beautiful, delightful.
　　　　　　　　　　　　　　　　[sight.

visual, *vĭsŭăl′,* a. visual, belonging to the

vital, *vĭtăl′,* a. vital.

vitalicio, cia, *vĭtălĭ′thĭŏ,* a. during life.

vitalidad, *vĭtălĭdăd′,* sf. vitality.

vitela, *vĭtĕ′lă,* sf. calf; vellum, calf-skin.

¡ vítor ! *vĕ′tŏr,* long life!
　　　　　　　　　　　　　　　　[plaud.

vitorear, *vĭtŏrĕăr′,* v. a. to shout, to applaud.

vitrificar, *vĭtrĭfĭkăr′,* v. a. to change into

vitriolo, *vĭtrĕ′ŏlŏ,* sm. vitriol.
　　　　　　　　　　　　　　　　[glass.

vitualla, *vĭtŭăl′yă,* sf. victuals, pl.

vituallado, da, −*yă′dŏ,* a. victualled.

vituperable, *vĭtŭpĕră′blĕ,* a. blameable.

vituperación, −*thĭŏn′,* sf. blame.

vituperador, ra, −*dŏr′,* sm. & f. blamer.

vituperar, *vĭtŭpĕrăr′,* v. a. to blame.

vituperio, −*pĕ′rĭŏ,* sm. blame; infamy.

viuda, *vĭŭ′dă,* sf. widow; dowager.

viudedad, *vĭŭdĕdăd′,* sf. widowhood; dowry.

viudez, *vĭŭdĕth′,* sf. widowhood.

viudo, *vĭŭ′dŏ,* sm. widower; −, a. applied to pairing birds.
　　　　　　　　　　　　　　　　[liness.

vivacidad, *vĭvăthĭdăd′,* sf. vivacity, liveliness.

vivamente, −*mĕn′tĕ,* ad. lively; to the life.

vivandero, *vĭvăndĕ′rŏ,* sm. (mil.) sutler.

vivaque, *vĭvă′kĕ,* **vivac, vivák,** sm. (mil.) bivouac.

vivaquear, −*kĕăr′,* v. n. (mil.) to bivouac.

vivar, *vĭvăr′,* sm. warren; vivary.

vivaracho, cha, −*rătsh′ŏ,* a. lively, smart, sprightly.

vivera, *vĭvĕ′ră,* sf. **vivero,** −*rŏ,* sm. warren; fish-pond; vivary.

víveres, *vĕ′vĕrĕs,* sm. pl. provisions, pl.

viveza, *vĭvĕ′thă,* sf. liveliness; strong resemblance.

vividero, ra, *vĭvĭdĕ′rŏ,* a. habitable.

vividor, ra, −*dŏr′,* a. thrifty manager.

vivienda, −*ĕn′dă,* sf. dwelling-house.

vivificación, −*fĭkăthĭŏn′,* sf. vivification.

vivificador, ra, −*dŏr′,* sm. & f. one who vivifies, animates or enlivens; −, a. vivifying, animating.

vivificar, −*kăr′,* v. a. to vivify, to enliven.

vivificativo, va, −*kătĭ′vŏ,* a. animating, comforting.

vivíparo, ra, *vĭvĕ′părŏ,* a. viviparous, − sm. viviparous.

vivir, *vĭvĭr′,* v. n. to live; to last.

vivo, va, *vĕ′vŏ,* a. living; lively; **al −,** to the life.
　　　　　　　　　　　　　　　　[ship.

vizcondado, *vĭthkŏndă′dŏ,* sm. viscount-

vizconde, −*kŏn′dĕ,* sm. viscount.

vizcondesa, −*kŏndĕs′ă,* sf. viscountess.

vocablo, *vŏkă′blŏ,* sm. word, term, diction.

vocabulario, −*bŭlă′rĭŏ,* sm. vocabulary; (fig.) a mine of science.

vocación, −*thĭŏn′,* sf. vocation.

vocal, *vŏkăl′,* sf. vowel; −, sm. voter; − a. vocal, oral.

vocativo, va, −*tĕ′vŏ,* sm. (gr.) vocative.

voceador, *vŏthĕădŏr′,* sm. vociferator.

vocear, −*thĕăr′,* v. n. to cry, to scream, to bawl, to shriek.

vocería, −*rĕ′ă,* sf. vociferation.

vociferación, *vŏthĭfĕrăthĭŏn′,* sf. vociferation; praise.
　　　　　　　　　　　　　　　　[bragger.

vociferador, ra, −*dŏr′,* sm. & f. boaster.

vociferar, −*răr′,* v. n. to bawl, to proclaim in a loud voice.

vocinglería, *vŏthĭnglĕrĕ′ă,* sf. clamour, outcry; loquacity.
　　　　　　　　　　　　　　　　[prattling.

vocinglero, ra, −*glĕ′rŏ,* a. brawling.

volador, ra, *vŏlădŏr′,* a. flying; running fast; −, sm. flying-fish.

volandas, *vŏlăn′dăs,* **en −,** ad. in the air.

volandera, −*dĕ′ră,* sf. runner (in oil-mills); movable ledge on a type-galley.

volandero, ra, −*dĕ′rŏ,* a. volatile; casual; unsettled.
　　　　　　　　　　　　　　　　[air.

volandillas, −*dĭl′yăs,* **en −,** ad. in the

volante, −*lăn′tĕ,* sm. screen put before a candle; shuttle-cock; livery-servant, footman.

volar, −*lăr′,* v. n. to fly; to pass or to move swiftly; to execute with great promptitude and facility; − v. a. to rouse game; to blow up, to discharge a mine; to irritate.

volatería, −*tĕrĕ′ă,* sf. fowling; fowls, pl.

volátil, −*lă′tĭl,* a. volatile; flying.

volatilizar, −*tĭlĭthăr′,* v. a. to volatilize.

volatín, −*tĭn′,* sm. rope-dancer.

volcán, *vŏlkăn′,* sm. volcano.

volcánico, −*kă′nĭkŏ,* a. volcanic.

volcar, −*kăr′,* v. a. to overset, to turn up; to make giddy; to tire out one's patience.

volear, *vŏlĕăr′,* v. n. to throw up in the air.

voleo, *vŏlĕ′ŏ,* sm. volley; step in a Spanish dance.
　　　　　　　　　　　　　　　　[inconstant.

voltario, ria, *vŏltă′rĭŏ,* a. fickle, variable.

volteador, −*tĕădŏr′,* sm. tumbler.

voltear, −*tĕăr′,* v. a. to whirl, to overset; −, v. n. to tumble.

voltereta, −*rĕ′tă,* **volteta,** −*tĕ′tă,* sf. light tumble in the air; turning up of a trump (at cards).

volubilidad, *vŏlŭbĭlĭdăd′,* sf. volubility.

voluble, *vŏlŏ′blĕ,* a. inconstant, fickle.

volumen, −*mĕn,* sm. volume; size.

voluminoso, sa, −*mĭnŏ′sŏ,* a. voluminous.

voluntad, *vŏlŭntăd′,* sf. will.
　　　　　　　　　　　　　　　　[ous.

voluntario, ria, −*tă′rĭŏ,* a. voluntary; −, sm. volunteer.
　　　　　　　　　　　　　　　　[tuous.

voluptuoso, sa, *vŏlŭptŭŏ′sŏ,* a. volup-

volver, *vŏlvĕr′,* v. a. & n. to return; to restore, to repay; to turn; to send back a present; to change a thing from one place to another; −se, to turn sour; to turn towards; to retract an opinion.

vómica, *vŏ′mĭkă,* sf. (med.) vomica.

vómico, ca, _mĭkŏ, a. causing vomiting,
vomitar, _tār', v.a. to vomit. [emetic.
vomitivo, va, _tĭ vŏ, a. & sm. emetic.
vómito, vŏ'mĭtŏ, sm. vomiting.
vomitón, ona, _tŏn', a. often throwing up
  milk from the stomach (of a sucking child).
vomitona, _tŏ'nă, sf. violent vomiting
  after eating heartily.
voracidad, vŏrăthĭdăd', sf. voracity.
voraz(mente), vŏrăth'(mĕn'tĕ), a. (& ad.)
vos, vŏs, pn. you, ye. [voracious(ly).
vosotros, tras, vŏsŏ'trŏs, pn. pl. you, ye.
votación, vŏtăthĭŏn', sf. voting.
votador, ra, _dŏr', sm. & f. vower; voter.
votar, vŏtăr', v.n. to vow; to vote.
votivo, va, _tĭ vŏ, a. votive.
voto, vŏ'tŏ, sm. vow; vote; opinion, advice; wish; supplication to God; execration.
voz, vŏth, sf. voice; outcry; word, term.
Vuecelencia, vŭĕthĕlĕn'thĭă, sf. contraction
  of Vuestra Excelencia, Your Excel-
vuelco, vŭĕl'kŏ, sm. overturning. [lency.
vuelo, vŭĕ'lŏ, sm. flight; wing; part of a
  building which projects beyond the wall;
  width of clothes; ruffle, frill; space flown
  through at once; elevation in discoursing;
  á –, al –, flying, expeditiously.
vuelta, vŭĕl'tă, sf. turn; circuit; return;
  petition; ruffle; excursion.
Vuesamerced, vŭĕsămĕrthĕd', sf. Your
  Worship, Your Honour (contraction of
  Vuestra Merced).
Vueseñoría, _sĕnyŏrĕ'ă, sf. My Lady
  (contraction of Vuestra Señoría).
vuestro, tra, vŭĕs'trŏ, pn. your, yours.
vulgacho, vŭlgătsh'ŏ, sm. mob, populace.
vulgar, vŭlgăr', a. vulgar, common.
vulgaridad, _rĭdăd', sf. vulgarity; vul-
vulgata, vŭlgă'tă, sf. vulgate. [garism.
vulgo, vŭl'gŏ, sm. populace, mob.
vulneración, vŭlnĕrăthĭŏn', sf. wounding.
vulnerar, _răr', v.a. to injure the character or reputation.
vulnerario, ria, _rā'rĭŏ, a. vulnerary.
vulto, vŭl'tŏ, sm. volume; bulk; face.

X.

xarro, ksăr'rŏ, sm. hawler. [helpless.
xaurado, da, ksăŭră'dŏ, a. abandoned,
xilografía, ksĭlŏgră'fĭă, sf. xylography.
xilógrafo, ksĭlŏ'grăfŏ, sm. xylographer.
xinglar, ksĭnglăr', v.n. to cry joyfully.

Y.

y, ĭ, c. and.
ya, yă, ad. already; presently; immediately; finally; – que, since, seeing
  that; – si, when, while, if; ¡ – ! exclamation on being brought to recollect a thing.
yacer, yăthĕr', v.n. to lie, to lie down.
ya(o)te, yă(k)'tĕ, sm. (mar.) yacht.

yámbico, ca, yăm'bĭkŏ, a. iambic.
yambo, _bŏ, sm. iambic foot (∪ –).
yedra, yĕ'dră, sf. ivy; – terrestre,
yegua, yĕ'gŭă, sf. mare. [ground-ivy.
yeguada, _gŭă'dă, sf. stud.
yeguar, yĕgŭăr', a. belonging to a mare.
yegüero, _gŭĕ'rŏ, sm. keeper of breeding
  mares. [mares.
yelmo, yĕl'mŏ, sm. helmet, helm.
yelo, yĕ'lŏ, sm. frost; ice.
yema, yĕ'mă, sf. bud, gem; yolk; – del
  dedo, tip of the finger.
yendo allá, yĕn'dŏ ălyă', a. thitherward.
yerba, yĕr'bă, sf. herb; – buena, mint;
  –s, pl. greens, vegetables, pl. [waste.
yermar, _măr', v.a. to depopulate, to lay
yermo, yĕr'mŏ, sm. desert, wilderness; –
  ma, a. waste, desert.
yerno, yĕr'nŏ, sm. son-in-law.
yerro, yĕr'rŏ, sm. error, mistake, fault.
yerto, ta, yĕr'tŏ, a. stiff, inflexible; rigid.
yesal, yĕsăl', yesar, _săr', sm. gypsum-
yesca, yĕs'kă, sf. spunk, tinder. [pit.
yesera, yĕs'ră, sf. kiln where gypsum is
  calcined.
yesería, _sĕr'ă, sf. building constructed
  with gypsum. [of gypsum.
yesero, _sĕ'rŏ, sm. preparer or seller
yesizo, _sĕ'thŏ, a. gypseous. [of Paris.
yeso, yĕ'sŏ, sm. gypsum; – mate, plaster
yesón, yĕsŏn', sm. fragment of gypsum already used in building.
yesquero, yĕskĕ'rŏ, sm. tinder-box.
yo, ĭ'ŏ, pn. I; – mismo, I myself.
yugada, yŭgă'dă, sf. yoke of land.
yugo, yŭ'gŏ, sm. yoke.
yunque, yŭn'kĕ, sm. anvil; constancy.
yunta, yŭn'tă, sf. couple, pair, yoke.
yusera, yŭsĕ'ră, sf. bedder, under mill-
  stone in oil-mills.

Z.

¡za! thă, word used to frighten dogs.
zabordar, thăbŏrdăr', v.n. (mar.) to get
  ashore, to be stranded. [agitate.
zabucar, _bŭkăr', v.a. to shake, to
zabullidura, _bŭlyĭdŏ'ră, sf. submersion,
  ducking.
zabullir, _bŭlyĭr', v.a. to plunge, to immerge; –se, to plunge suddenly under
  water; to lie concealed.
zacatín, _kătĭn', sm. clothes market.
zafar, _făr', v.a. to adorn, to embellish;
  to lighten a ship; –se, to escape; to
  avoid; to free oneself from trouble.
zafarancho, _fărăn'tshŏ, sm. (mar.) clearing for action; hacer –, (mar.) to clear.
zafiedad, _fĭĕdăd', sf. clownishness, rusticity, awkwardness.
zafio, fia, thă'fĭŏ, a. clownish, coarse.
zafir, _fĭr', zafiro, _fĭ'rŏ, sm. sapphire.
zaga, thă'gă, sf. load packed at the back
  of a carriage; –, sm. last player at a
  game of cards; –, ad. behind.
zagal, _găl', sm. out-rider; swain.

zagala, _gä'lä_, sf. shepherdess, lass, girl.

zagalejo, _gälä'h'ŏ_, sm. under-petticoat.

zaguán, _gwän'_, sm. porch, hall.

zaheridor, ra, _ērīdŏr'_, sm. & f. censurer.

zaherimiento, _mīēn'tŏ_, sm. censure, blame.　　　　　　[braid.

zaherir, _ērĭr'_, v. a. to reproach; to up-

zahones, _ŏ'nēs_, sm. pl. overalls, pl.

zahorí, _ŏrī'_, sm. vulgar impostor pretending to see hidden things, although in the bowels of the earth.

zahurda, _ūr'dä_, sf. hogsty; dirty hole.

zaino, na, _thä'ĭnŏ_, a. of a chestnut colour; vicious (applied to animals); treacherous, wicked; **mirar de ó á lo —**, to look sideways.

zalagarda, _lägär'dä_, sf. ambuscade, ambush; trap, snare; surprise; vulgar noise.

zalamería, _lämērī'ä_, sf. flattery.

zalamero, ra, _mā'rŏ_, sm. & f. wheedler.

zalea, _thälā'ä_, sf. undressed sheepskin.

zalear, _lēär'_, v. a. to move any thing with care from one place to another.

zamacuco, _mäkū'kŏ_, sm. dunce, doit.

zamarra, _mär'rä_, sf. dress made of undressed sheepskins.

zamarro, _rŏ_, sm. shepherd's coat made of sheepskins; sheep or lambskin; stupid person.

zambo, ba, _thäm'bŏ_, a. bandy-legged.

zambomba, _bŏm'bä_, sf. rural drum.

zambombo, _bŏ_, sm. clown, lubber.

zambra, _thäm'brä_, sf. Moorish festival attended with dancing and music; noisy

zambucar, _būkär'_, v. a. to hide.　[mirth.

zambullida, _būlyĭt'dä_, sf. dipping, submersion.　　　　　　[into water, to dive.

zambullirse, _būlyĭr'sē_, v. r. to plunge

zampar, _pär'_, v. a. to devour eagerly; **—se**, to thrust oneself suddenly into any place.　　　　　　[clown, rustic.

zampatortas, _pätŏr'täs_, sm. glutton;

zampear, _pēär'_, v. a. to stake, to prop.

zampoña, _pŏn'yä_, sf. shawm; inmate of a workhouse.　　　　　　[dive.

zampuzar, _pūthär'_, v. a. to plunge, to

zampuzo, _pō'thŏ_, sm. submersion.

zanahoria, _thänäŏ'rĭä_, sf. (bot.) carrot.

zanca, _thän'kä_, sf. shank of a fowl; long

zancada, _kä'dä_, sf. stride.　　　[shank.

zancadilla, _dĭl'yä_, sf. trip; trick.

zancajear, _hēär'_, v. a. to run about the streets bespattering the legs with dirt.

zancajo, _kä'h'ŏ_, sm. heel-bone.

zancajoso, sa, _kä'hŏ'sŏ_, a. bandy-legged.

zancarrón, _rŏn'_, sm. heel-bone.

zanco, _thän'kŏ_, sm. stilt.

zancudo, da, _kū'dä_, a. long-shanked.

zangandongo, _gändŏn'gŏ_, sm. idler; dolt.　　　　　　[ness.

zanganear, _gänēär'_, v. n. to live in idle-

zángano, _thän'gänŏ_, sm. drone; idler, sponger.　　　　　　[a guitar.

zangarrear, _gärrēär'_, v. n. to scrape on

zangarullón, _gärŭlyŏn'_, sm. tall, lazy lad.　[a violent yet ridiculous manner.

zangolotear, _gŏlŏtēär'_, v. r. to move in

zangoloteo, _lŏtā'ŏ_, sm. violent yet ridiculous waddling; wagging movement.

zanguayo, _gwä'yŏ_, sm. tall idler that pretends to be ill or silly.

zanja, _thän'hä_, sf. ditch, trench.

zanjar, _här'_, v. a. to open ditches; to lay a foundation.　[much and fast.

zanquear, _kēär'_, v. n. to waddle, to walk.

zanquilargo, ga, _kĭlär'gŏ_, a. long-shanked.

zapa, _thä'pä_, sf. spade; **caminar á la —** (mil.) to advance by sap or mine.

zapador, _dŏr'_, sm. (mil.) sapper.

zapar, _pär'_, v. n. to sap, to mine.

zaparrastrar, _rästrär'_, v. n. to trail, to drag along on the ground.

zaparrastroso, sa, _rästrŏ'sŏ_, a. dirty, from trailing along on the ground.

zaparrazo, _rä'thŏ_, sm. violent fall, attended with great noise; sudden calamity.

zapata, _pä'tä_, sf. piece of sole-leather put on the hinge of a door to prevent its creaking.　　　　　　[shoe.

zapatazo, _tä'thŏ_, sm. blow with a

zapatear, _tēär'_, v. a. to strike with the shoe; to beat time with the sole of the shoe; **—se**, to resist in debating.

zapatera, _tä'rä_, sf. shoemaker's wife; olive spoiled in the pickle.

zapatería, _tērē'ä_, sf. trade of a shoemaker; shoemaker's shop.

zapatero, _tä'rŏ_, sm. shoemaker; **— de viejo**, cobbler.

zapatilla, _tĭl'yä_, sf. pump(shoe); piece of shamois put behind the lock of a gun or pistol.

zapatillero, _tĭlyä'rŏ_, sm. shoemaker who makes pumps and children's shoes.

zapato, _pä'tŏ_, sm. shoe.

¡zape! _thä'pē_, word used to frighten cats away; God forbid!

zaque, _thä'kē_, sm. wine-bag; tippler.

zar, _thär_, sm. czar.　　　　　　[(dance).

zarabanda, _thärä'bän'dä_, sf. saraband

zaragüelles, _güēl'yēs_, sm. pl. wide breeches; overalls, pl.

zaramullo, _mūl'yŏ_, sm. busybody.

zaranda, _thärän'dä_, sf. frame for sifting sand.

zarandajas, _dä'h'äs_, sf. pl. trifles, pl.

zarandar, _där'_, v. a. to winnow corn.

zarandillo, _dĭl'yŏ_, sm. frisker.

zaratán, _thärätän'_, sm. cancer in the breast.

zarcillo, _thärthĭl'yŏ_, sm. ear-ring; tendril.

zarja, _thär'hä_, sf. reel.

zarpa, _pä_, sf. dirt on clothes; claw.

zarpar, _pär'_, v. a. to weigh anchor.

zarpazo, _pä'thŏ_, sm. sound or thud of a body falling on the ground.　[malion.

zarrapastrón, _räpästrŏn'_, sm. tatterde-

zarrapastroso, sa, _pästrŏ'sŏ_, a. ragged.

zarza, _thär'thä_, sf. common bramble.

zarzal, _thärthäl'_, sm. briery.　　　[bush.

zarzamora, _thämŏ'rä_, sf. blackberry-

zarzaparrilla, _pärĭl'yä_, sf. (bot.) sarsa-

zarzo, _thär'thŏ_, sm. hurdle.　　　[parilla.

zarzoso, sa, _thŏ'sŏ_, a. briery.

] zas, zas ! *thăs'*, flap ! slap! [upstart.
zascandil, *–kăndĭl'*, sm. crafty swindler;
zequí, *thĕkĭ'*, sm. zechin (Arabic gold coin). [with blows.
zipizape, *thĭpĭthă'pĕ*, sm. noisy scuffle
] zis, zas ! *this thăs*, flap! slap!
zizaña, *thĭthăn'yă*, sf. (bot.) darnel; disagreement; any thing injurious.
zizañar, *–yăr'* v. a. to sow discord.
zizañero, *–yă'rŏ*, sm. makebate.
zócalo, *thŏ'kălŏ*, sm. socle.
zoclo, *thŏ'klŏ*, sm. wooden shoe; golosh.
zodiaco, *thŏdĭ'ăkŏ*, sm. zodiac.
zona, *thŏ'nă*, sf. zone; girdle.
zonzo, za, *thŏn'thŏ*, a. insipid, tasteless.
zoología, *thŏŏlŏ·hĕ'ă*, sf. zoology.
zopenco, ca, *thŏpĕn'kŏ*, a. doltish, very stupid.
zopo, pa, *thŏ'pŏ*, a. lame, maimed; –, sm. clumsy, stupid fellow.
zoquete, *thŏkĕ'tĕ*, sm. block; morsel of bread; blockhead.
zorra, *thŏr'ră*, sf. fox; prostitute, strumpet.
zorrastrón, ona, *–răstrŏn'*, sm. & f. cunning, roguish person.
zorrera, *–ră'ră*, sf. fox-hole.
zorrería, *–rĕrĕ'ă*, sf. artfulness of a fox; cunning, craft. [fellow.
zorro, *thŏr'rŏ*, sm. male fox; cunning
zorronglón, ona, *–rŏnglŏn'*, a. slow, [heavy, lazy.
zorzal, *thŏrthăl'*, sm. thrush. [heavy, lazy.
zote, *thŏ'tĕ*, sm. stupid, lazy person.
zozobra, *thŏthŏ'bră*, sf. uneasiness, anxiety.
zozobrar, *–brăr'*, v. n. to be weatherbeaten; to be in great danger; to be afflicted; (mar.) to founder.
zueco, *thwĕ'kŏ*, sm. wooden shoe; golosh.
zullarse, *thŭlyăr'sĕ*, v. r. to break wind.
zullón, *thŭlyŏn'*, sm. flatulence.
zumacar, *thŭmăkăr'*, v. a. to tan with sumach.
zumaque, *thŭmă'kĕ*, sm. sumach-tree.

zumba, *thŭm'bă*, sf. large bell, used by carriers; facetious raillery.
zumbar, *–băr'*, v. n. to resound, to hum; –se, to jest, to joke. [sound.
zumbido, *–bĭ'dŏ*, sm. humming, buzzing
zumbón, ona, *–bŏn'*, a. waggish.
zumo, *thŏ'mŏ*, sm. sap, juice; – de cepas ó parras, juice of the grape, wine.
zumoso, sa, *thŭmŏ'sŏ*, a. juicy, succulent.
zupia, *thŏ'pĭă*, sf. wine which is turned; liquor with a bad taste; refuse. [darning.
zurcidura, *thŭrthĭdŏ'ră*, sf. fine-drawing;
zurcir, *–thĭr'*, v. a. to darn, to fine-draw; to join, to unite; to hatch lies.
zurdo, da, *thŭr'dŏ*, a. left; left-handed.
zurra, *thŭr'ră*, sf. currying leathers; flogging, drubbing; drudgery. [currier.
zurrador, *–rădŏr'*, sm. leather-dresser,
zurrapa, *–ră'pă*, sf. lees, dregs; anything vile or despicable. [and dregs.
zurraposo, sa, *–pŏ'sŏ*, a. full of lees
zurrar, *–răr'*, v. a. to curry; to chastise with a whip; –se, to have a sudden call of nature; to dirty oneself. [tops.
zurriaga, *–rĭă'gă*, sf. thong; whip for
zurriagar, *–găr'*, v. a. to flog, to whip.
zurriagazo, *–gă'thŏ*, sm. severe lash with a whip; unfortunate calamity.
zurriago, *–rĭă'gŏ*, sm. whip for inflicting punishment [ging; noisy quarrel.
zurribanda, *–băn'dă*, sf. repeated flog-
zurriburri, *–bŭr'rĭ*, sm. ragamuffin.
zurrido, *thŭrrĭ'dŏ*, sm. humming, buzzing; confused noise. [tinkle.
zurrir, *–rĭr'*, v. n. to hum, to buzz, to
zurrón, *–rŏn'*, sm. shepherd's pouch; husks of grain.
zurruscarse, *–răskăr'sĕ*, v. r. to experience a sudden call of nature; to dirty oneself.
zurrusco, *–rŭs'kŏ*, sm. overtoasted slice of bread.
zutano, na, *thŭtă'nŏ*, a. such a one; – y fulano, such and such a one, so and so.

Nombres geográficos los más importantes, que no se corresponden en ambas lenguas.

Abisinia, *ăbĭsĕ'nĭă*, f. Abyssinia.

Adriático, *ădrĭă'tĭkŏ*, m. Adriatic, Adriatic Sea.

africano, a, *ăfrĭkă'nŏ*, m. & f. & a. African.

albanés, a, *ălbănĕs'*, m. & f. & a. Albanian.

alemán, a, *ălĕman'*, m. & f. & a. German. [many.

Alemania, *—nĭă*, f. Germany.

alpecienses, *ălpĕthĭĕn'sĕs*, m. pl. alpines.

Alpes, *ăl'pĕs*, m. pl. Alps.

alpino, a, *ălpĕ'nŏ*, a. alpine.

Alsacia, *ălsă'thĭă*, f. Alsace.

alsaciano, a, *—thĭă'nŏ*, m. & f. & a. Alsatian.

Amberes, *ămbĕ'rĕs*, m. Antwerp.

americano, a, *ămĕrĭkă'nŏ*, m. & f. & a. American.

Andalucía, *ăndălŭthĕ'ă*, f. Andalusia.

andaluz, a, *ăndălŭth'*, m. & f. & a. Andalusian.

Anseáticas, *ănsĕă'tĭkăs*, f. pl. Hanse Towns.

Apeninos, *ăpĕnĕ'nŏs*, m. pl. Apennines.

Apulia, *ăpŭl'yă*, f. Apulia.

Aquisgrán, *ăkĭsgrăn'*, sm. Aix la Chapelle.

árabe, *ă'răbĕ*, m. & f., arábico, *ără'bĭkŏ*, a. Arab.

aragonés, a, *ărăgŏnĕs'*, m. & f. & a. Aragonese.

Archipiélago, *ărtshĭpĭĕ'lăgŏ*, m. Archipelago.

Argel, *ăr'hĕl'*, m. Algiers.

armónico, a, armenio, a, *ărmĕ'nĭ(k)ŏ*, m. & f. & a. Armenian.

asiano, a, *ăsĭă'nŏ*, asiático, a, *—tĭkŏ*, m. & f. & a. Asiatic. [Athens.

Atenas, *ătĕ'năs*, f. pl. Athens.

ateniés, a, *ătĕnĭĕs'*, ateniense, *—tĕn'sĕ*, m. & f. & a. Athenian.

Atlántico, *ătlan'tĭkŏ*, m. Atlantic. [Augsburg.

Ausburgo, *ăŭsbŭr'gŏ*, m.

australasino, a, *ăŭstrălă'sĕ'nŏ*, m. & f. & a. Australian.

austriaco, a, *ăŭstrĭă'kŏ*, m. & f. & a. Austrian.

Báltico, *băl'tĭkŏ*, m. Baltic Sea. [Barbadoes.

Barbadas, *bărbă'dăs*, f. pl.

Basilea, *băsĭlĕ'ă*, f. Basle.

bátavo, a, *bă'tăvŏ*, m. & f. & a. Batavian.

bavario, a, *băvă'rĭŏ*, bávaro, a, *bă'vărŏ*, m. & f. & a. Bavarian. [varia.

Baviera, *băvĭĕ'ră*, f. Bavaria.

Belen, *bĕlĕn'*, m. Bethlehem.

belga, *bĕl'gă*, m. & f., bélgico, a, *—'hĭkŏ*, a. Belgian.

Bélgica, *—'hĭkă*, f. Belgium.

Bengala, *bĕngă'lă*, f. Bengala. [bary.

Berbería, *bĕrbĕrĕ'ă*, f. Barbary.

Beocia, *bĕŏ'thĭă*, f. Bœotia.

beociano, a, *—thĭă'nŏ*, m. & f. & a. Bœotian.

berlinés, a, *bĕrlĭnĕs'*, m. & f. & a. Berlinian.

Bizancio, *bĭthăn'thĭŏ*, m. Byzantium.

bohémico, a, *bŏĕ'mĭkŏ*, a., bohemo, a, *—mŏ*, m. & f. Bohemian. [gundy.

Borgoña, *bŏrgŏn'yă*, f. Burgundy.

borgoñés, a, *bŏrgŏnyĕs'*, m. & f. & a. Burgundian.

Bósforo, *bŏs'fŏrŏ*, m. Bosphorus.

Brasil, *brăsĭl'*, m. Brazil.

brasileño, a, *—lĕn'yŏ*, m. & f. & a. Brazilian.

Bretaña, *brĕtăn'yă*, f. Britany; Gran —, Great Britain.

breton, a, *brĕtŏn'*, m. & f. & a. British; Briton.

Brunsvick, *brŭns'vĭk*, m. Brunswick. [Brussels.

Bruselas, *brŭsĕ'lăs*, f. pl. Brussels.

búlgaro, a, *bŭl'gărŏ*, m. & f. & a. Bulgarian.

Burdeos, *bŭrdĕ'ŏs*, m. Bordeaux.

Cachemir, *kătshĕmĭr'*, m. Cashmere.

Cádiz, *kă'dĭth*, f. Cadiz.

Cafrería, *kăfrĕrĕ'ă*, f. Caffraria.

calabrés, a, *kălăbrĕs'*, m. & f. & a. Calabrian.

Caldea, *kăldă'ă*, f. Chaldea.

Calés, *kălĕs'*, m. Calais.

calmuco, *kălmĭ'kŏ*, m. Calmuck.

Cambrigia, *kămprĭ'h'ĭă*, Cambrije, *—brĭ'h'ĕ*, f. Cambridge. [Campeachy.

Campeche, *kămpĕtsh'ĕ*, f. Campeachy.

Canarias, *kănă'rĭăs*, f. pl. Canaries, Canary-Islands.

candiote, *kăndĭŏ'tĕ*, m. & f. & a. Candian.

Cantórberi, *kăntŏr'bĕrĭ*, f. Canterbury. [rinthia.

Carintia, *kărĭn'tĭă*, f. Carinthia.

Carpetanos, *kărpĕtă'nŏs*, m. pl. Carpathians. [Sea.

Caspio, *kăs'pĭŏ*, m. Caspian.

castellano, a, *kăstĕlyă'nŏ*, m. & f. & a. Castilian.

Castilla, *kăstĭl'yă*, f. Castile.

catalán, a, *kătălăn'*, m. & f. & a. Catalonian.

Cataluña, *kătălŭn'yă*, f. Catalonia. [casus.

Cáucaso, *kăŭ'kăsŏ*, m. Caucasus.

Ceilán, *thĕĭlăn'*, m. Ceylon.

Cerdeña, *thĕrdĕn'yă*, f. Sardinia. [f. Champagne.

Champaña, *tshămpăn'yă*, f. Champagne.

chino, a, *tshĕ'nŏ*, m. & f. & a. Chinese.

Chipre, *tshĕ'prĕ*, m. Cyprus.

Circasia, *thĭrkă'sĭă*, f. Circassia.

circasiano, a, *—sĭă'nŏ*, m. & f. & a. Circassian.

Colonia, *kŏlŏ'nĭă*, f. Cologne.

Constantinopla, *kŏnstăntĭnŏ'plă*, f. Constantinople. [sica.

Copenaga, *kŏpĕnă'gă*, f. Copenhagen.

Córcega, *kŏr'thĕgă*, f. Corsica.

Corfú, *kŏrfŭ'*, m. Corfu.

Corinto, kŏrĭn'tŏ, m. Corinth. [Cornwall.
Cornualla, kŏrnŭăl'yă, f.
corsés, a, kŏrsĕs', corso, a, kŏr'sŏ, m. & f. & a. Corsican. [sack.
cosaco, kŏsă'kŏ, m. Cos-
Cracovia, krăkŏ'vĭă, f. Cracow.
cretense, krĕtĕn'sĕ, crético, a, krĕ'tĭkŏ, m. & f. & a. Cretan. [tia.
Croacia, krŏă'thĭă, f. Croa-
croato, a, –tŏ, m. & f. & a. Croatian. [Corland.
Curlandia, kŭrlăn'dĭă, f.

Dalmacia, dălmă'thĭă, f. Dalmatia.
dalmático, a, dălmăt'ĭkŏ, m. & f. & a. Dalmatian.
Damasco, dămăs'kŏ, m. Damascus.
danés, a, dănĕs', m. & f. & a. Dane; Danish.
Danubio, dănŏ'bĭŏ, m. Danube.
Delfinado, dĕlfĭnă'dŏ, m. Dauphinate, Dauphiny.
Delfos, dĕl'fŏs, f. Delphos.
Dinamarca, dĭnămăr'kă, f. Denmark. [Danish.
dinamarqués, a, –kĕs', a.
Dovres, dŏ'vrĕs, m. Dover.
Dresde, drĕs'dĕ, f. Dresden.
Dunquerque, dŭnkĕr'kĕ, m. Dunkirk.
Duvre, dŭ'vrĕ, m. Dover.

Edimburgo, ĕdĭmbŭr'gŏ, m. Edinburgh.
Efeso, ĕ'fĕsŏ, m. Ephesus.
egipiaco, a, ĕ'hĭpĭă'kŏ, egipciano, a, –thĭă'nŏ, egipcio, a, ĕ'hĭp'thĭŏ, m. & f. & a. Egyptian.
Egipto, ĕ'hĭp'tŏ, m. Egypt.
Epiro, ĕpĭ'rŏ, m. Epirus.
Escafusa, ĕskăfŭ'să, f. Schaffhausen.
Escalda, ĕskăl'dă, m. Scheld.
Escandinavia, ĕskăndĭnă'vĭă, f. Scandinavia.
Esclavonia, ĕsklăvŏ'nĭă, f. Sclavonia.
esclavón, a, ĕsklăvŏn', esclavonio, a, –vŏ'nĭŏ, m. & f. & a. Sclavonian.
escocés, a, ĕskŏthĕs', m. & f. & a. Scotsman, Scotch-woman; Scotch, Scottish.
Escocia, ĕskŏ'thĭă, f. Scot-land. [Smyrna.
Esmirna, ĕsmĭr'nă, f.
España, ĕspăn'yă, f. Spain.
español, a, ĕspănyŏl', m. & f. & a. Spaniard; Spanish.
Esparta, ĕspăr'tă, f. Sparta.

espartano, –tă'nŏ, m. & f. & a. Spartan.
esquimales, ĕskĭmă'lĕs, m. pl. Esquimaux.
Estiria, ĕstĭ'rĭă, f. Stiria.
estiriano, a, –rĭă'nŏ, m. & f. & a. Stirian.
Estocolmo, ĕstŏkŏl'mŏ, m. Stockholm.
Estrasburgo, ĕstrăsbŭr'gŏ, m. Strasburg.
Europa, ĕŭrŏ'pă, f. Europe.
europeo, a, ĕŭrŏpĕ'ŏ, m. & f. & a. European.

Fenicia, fĕnĭ'thĭă, f. Phe-nicia. [a, Phenician.
fenicio, a, –thĭ'ŏ, m. & f. &
finlandés, a, fĭnlăndĕs', m. & f. & a. Finlander.
Finlandia, –lăn'dĭă, f. Finland.
flamenco, a, flămĕn'kŏ, m. & f. & a.Fleming; Flemish.
Flándes, flăn'dĕs, f. Flan-ders. [Flushing.
Flesinga, flĕsĭn'gă, f.
Florencia, flŏrĕn'thĭă, f. Florence.
florentín, a, –tĭn', m. & f. & a. Florentine.
francés, a, frănthĕs', m. & f. & a. Frenchman, French-woman; French; los franceses, the French (s. pl.).
Francfort del Mein, frănk'fŏrt dĕl mĕĭn, m. Frankfort on the Main.
Francoforte, frănkŏfŏr'tĕ, m. Frankfort. [Friburg.
Friburgo, frĭbŭr'gŏ, m.
Frisia, frĕ'sĭă, f. Friesland.
frisón, a, frĭsŏn', m. & f. & a. Frieslander.

Gáles, gă'lĕs, m. Wales.
galés, a, gălĕs', m. & f. & a. Welsh, Gælic.
Galia, gă'lĭă, f. Gaul.
Galicia, gălĭth'ĭă, f. Galicia.
gálico, a, gă'lĭkŏ, m. & f. & a. Gaul.
Galilea, gălĭlĕ'ă, f. Galilee.
Ganges, găn'hĕs, m. Ganges.
Gante, găn'tĕ, m. Ghent.
Gascuña, găskŭn'yă, f. Gascony. [Germany.
Germania, hĕrmă'nĭă, f.
Génova, hĕ'nŏvă, f. Genoa.
genovés, a, –vĕs', m. & f. & a. Genoese. [neva.
Ginebra, hĭnĕ'bră, f. Ge-
ginebrés, a, hĕnĕbrĕs', m. & f. & a. Genevese.
Grecia, grĕ'thĭă, f. Greece.

griego, a, grĭĕ'gŏ, m. & f. & a. Greek. [Grisons,
Grisones, grĭsŏ'nĕs, m. pl.
groenlandés, a, grŏĕn-lăndĕs', m. & f. & a. Green-lander. [Greenland.
Groenlandia, –lăn'dĭă, f.
Groninga, grŏnĭn'gă, f. Groningen. [Guelderland.
Guéldres, gĕl'drĕs, m.

Habana, ăbă'nă, f. Havan-nah. [Hamburg.
Hamburgo, ămbŭr'gŏ, m.
Haya, ă'yă, f. Hague.
Helvecia, ĕlvĕ'thĭă, f. Hel-vetia. [Hessian.
hesés, a, ĕsĕs', m. & f. & a.
Hesia, ĕs'ĭă, f. Hesse.
Holanda, ŏlăn'dă, f. Hol-land.
holandés, a, –dĕs', m. & f. & a. Hollander, Dutch-man, Dutchwoman; Dutch.
húngaro, a, ŭn'gărŏ, m. & f. & a. Hungarian. [gary.
Hungría, ŭngrĕ'ă, f. Hun-

Iliria, ĭlĕ'rĭă, f. Illyria.
Indias, ĭn'dĭăs, f. pl. Indies;
— orientales, East-In-dies; — occidentales, West-Indies. [a. Indian.
indio, a, ĭn'dĭŏ, m. & f. &
Inglaterra, ĭnglătĕr'ră, f. England.
inglés, a, ĭnglĕs', m. & f. & a. Englishman, English-woman; English; los ingleses, the English (s. pl.).
irlandés, a, ĭrlăndĕs', m. & f. & a. Irishman, Irish-woman; Irish. [land.
Islanda, ĭslăn'dă, f. Ice-
islandés, a, –dĕs', m. & f. & a. Icelander.
Italia, ĭtă'lĭă, f. Italy.
italiano, a, –lĭă'nŏ, m. & f. & a. Italian.

Japón, hăpŏn', m. Japan.
japonés, a, –nĕs', m. & f. & a. Japanese.
Jerusalén, hĕrŭsălĕn', m. Jerusalem. [Jutland.
Jutlandia, hŭtlăn'dĭă, f.

laconio, a, lăkŏ'nĭŏ, m. & f. & a. Lacedæmonian.
lapón, a, lăpŏn', m. & f. & a. Laplander. [land.
Laponia, lăpŏ'nĭă, f. Lap-
León, lĕŏn', m. Lyons.
Líbano, lĕ'bănŏ, m. Leba-non.
Lieja, lĭĕ'hă, f. Liege.

Spanish and English.

16

Lila, *lĭ'lä,* f. Lisle.
Liorna, *lĭŏr'nä,* f. Leghorn.
Lipsia, *lĭp'sĭä,* f. Leipsic.
Lisboa, *lĭsbŏ'ä,* f. Lisbon.
Lituania, *lĭtŭä'nĭä,* f. Lithuania.
lituánico, a, *-nĭkŏ,* **lituaniense,** *-nĭen'sĕ,* m. & f. & a. Lithuanian.
livoniano, a, *lĭvŏnĭä'nŏ,* m. & f. & a. Livonian.
Lombardía, *lŏmbärdĕ'ä,* f. Lombardy.
lombárdico, a, *-bär'dĭkŏ,* a., **lombardo,** *-bär'dŏ,* m. & f. & a. Lombard.
Londres, *lŏn'drĕs,* m. London.
londrés, a, *lŏndrĕs',* m. & f. & a. Londonian.
Lorena, *lŏrĕ'nä,* f. Lorraine.
Lucemburgo, *lŭthĕmbŭr'gŏ,* **Lujemburgo,** *lŭ'hĕmbŭr'gŏ,* m. Luxemburg.
Lusacia, *lŭsä'thĭä,* f. Lusatia. [& f. & a. Lusatian.
lusaciano, a, *-thĭä'nŏ,* m.

macedónico, a, *mäthĕdŏ'nĭkŏ,* m. & f. & a. Macedonian. [deira.
Madera, *mädĕ'rä,* f. **Madrileño,** a, *mädrĭlĕn'yŏ,* m. & f. & a. inhabitant of Madrid; from Madrid.
Maguncia, *mägŭn'thĭä,* f. Mentz.
Malina, *mälĕ'nä,* f. Malines.
maltés, a, *mältĕs',* m. & f. & a. Maltese. [jorca.
Mallorca, *mälyŏr'kä,* f. Majorca.
Marruecos, *märrŭĕ'kŏs,* m. pl. Morocco. [Marseilles.
Marsella, *märsĕl'yä,* f.
Meca, *mĕ'kä,* f. Mecca.
Mediterráneo, *mĕdĭtĕrrä'nĕŏ,* m. Mediterranean.
mejicano, a, *mĕ'hĭkä'nŏ,* m. & f. & a. Mexican.
Méjico, *mĕ'hĭkŏ,* m. Mexico.
Menorca, *mĕnŏr'kä,* f. Minorca. [sina.
Mesina, *mĕsĭ'nä,* f. Messina.
Milano, *mĭlä'nŏ,* f. Milan.
Molucas, *mŏlŭk'äs,* f. pl. Moluccas.
moravo, a, *mŏrä'vŏ,* m. & f. & a. Moravian.
moro, a, *mŏ'rŏ,* m. & f. & a. Moor; Moorish.
Mosa, *mŏ'sä,* m. Meuse.
Moscovia, *mŏskŏ'vĭä,* f. Moscovy.
Moscu, *mŏs'kŭ,* f. Moscow.
Mosela, *mŏsĕ'lä,* m. Moselle.
mulato, a, *mŭlä'tŏ,* m. & f. & a. Mulatto, Mulattress.

Munich, *mänĭk',* m. Munich.
Nápoles, *nä'pŏlĕs,* m. Naples.
napolitano, a, *näpŏlĭtä'nŏ,* m. & f. & a. Neapolitan.
Neucastel, *nĕäkästĕl',* m. Neufchatel, Neuchatel.
Nilo, *nĕ'lŏ,* m. Nile. [guen.
Nimega, *nĭmä'gä,* f. Nimeguen.
Niza, *nĕ'thä,* f. Nice.
Normandía, *nŏrmändĕ'ä,* f. Normandy.
normando, a, *-män'dŏ,* **normánico,** a, *-mä'nĭkŏ,* m. & f. & a. Norman.
Noruega, *nŏrŭĕ'gä,* f. Norway. [& a. Norwegian.
noruego, a, *-gŏ,* m. & f.
nubio, a, *nŏ'bĭŏ,* m. & f. & a. Nubian. [f. New-York.
Nueva-York, *nŭ'ĕvä yŏr'k,* **Nuremberga,** *nŭrĕmbĕr'gä,* f. Nuremberg.

Olimpo, *ŏlĭm'pŏ,* m. Olympus. [Orkneys.
Orcadas, *ŏrkä'däs,* f. pl.
Ostende, *ŏstĕn'dĕ,* f. Ostend.
Pacífico, *päthĕ'fĭkŏ,* m. Pacific. [m. Palatinate.
Palatinado, *pälätĭnä'dŏ,* **Palestina,** *pälĕstĕ'nä,* f. Palestine.
parisiense, *pärĭsĭĕn'sĕ,* m. & f. & a. Parisian.
Parnaso, *pärnäs'ŏ,* m. Parnassus. [m. Petersburg.
Pedroburgo, *pĕdrŏbŭr'gŏ,* **Peloponeso,** *pĕlŏpŏnä'sŏ,* m. Peloponnesus.
persa, *pĕr'sä,* m. & f., **persiano,** a, *-stä'nŏ,* a. Persian.
Perú, *pĕrŏ',* m. Peru.
Piamonte, *pĭämŏn'tĕ,* m. Piedmont.
piamontés, a, *-tĕs',* m. & f. & a. Piedmontese.
Pirineos, *pĭrĭnĕ'ŏs,* m. pl. Pyrenees.
polaco, a, *pŏlä'kŏ,* m. & f. & a. Pole; Polish.
Polonia, *pŏlŏ'nĭä,* f. Poland.
Ponto, *pŏn'tŏ,* m. Pontus.
portugués, a, *pŏrtŭgĕs',* m. & f. & a. Portuguese.
Praga, *prä'gä,* f. Prague.
Provenza, *prŏvĕn'thä,* f. Provence.
Prusia, *prŭs'ĭä,* f. Prussia.
prusiano, a, *-stä'nŏ,* m. & f. & a. Prussian.
Puente Euxino, *pŭĕn'tĕ ĕŭksĕ'nŏ,* m. Euxine-Sea.

Puerta, *pŭĕr'tä,* f. Ottoman Empire.
Pulla, *pŭl'yä,* f. Apulia.
Ratisbona, *rätĭsbŏ'nä,* f. Ratisbon. [venna.
Ravena, *rävĕ'nä,* f. Ra- **Rin, Rhin,** *rĭn,* m. Rhine.
Ródano, *rŏ'dänŏ,* m. Rhone.
Rodas, *rŏ'däs,* f. pl. Rhodes.
Roma, *rŏ'mä,* f. Roma.
Romania, *rŏmä'nĭä,* f. Roumania. [f. & a. Roman.
romano, a, *rŏmä'nŏ,* m. &
Rusia, *rŭs'ĭä,* f. Russia.
rusiano, a, *-stä'nŏ,* m. & f. & a. Russian.
Saboya, *säbŏ'yä,* f. Savoy.
saboyano, a, *-yä'nŏ,* m. & f. & a. Savoyard.
sajón, a, *sä'hŏn',* **sajono,** a, *sä'hŏ'nŏ,* m. & f. & a. Saxon. [Saxony.
Sajonia, *sä'hŏ'nĭä,* f. **samoyedo,** *sämŏyĕ'dŏ,* m. Samoied. [a. Sardinian.
sardo, a, *sär'dŏ,* m. & f. &
Sena, *sĕ'nä,* m. Seine.
siberiano, a, *sĭbĕrĭä'nŏ,* m. & f. & a. Siberian.
Sicilia, *sĭthĕ'lĭä,* f. Sicily.
siciliano, a, *-lĭä'nŏ,* m. & f. & a. Sicilian.
silesio, a, *sĭlĕ'sĭŏ,* m. & f. & a. Silesian.
Suecia, *sŭĕ'thĭä,* f. Sweden.
sueco, a, *-kŏ,* m. & f. & a. Swede; Swedish.
Suiza, *sŭĭ'thä,* f. Switzerland. [Swiss.
suizo, a, *-thŏ,* m. & f. & a.
Sun, *sŭn,* m. the Sound.
Tajo, *tä'hŏ,* m. Tagus.
Támesis, *tä'mĕsĭs,* m. Thames. [tary.
Tartaria, *tärtä'rĭä,* f. Tar- **tártaro,** a, *tär'tärŏ,* m. & f. & a. Tartar.
Termópilas, *tĕrmŏ'pĭläs,* f. pl. Thermopylae.
Terranova, *tĕrränŏ'vä,* f. Newfoundland. [suly.
Tesalia, *tĕsä'lĭä,* f. Thes- **Tesalónica,** *-lŏ'nĭkä,* f. Thessalonica.
tésalo, a, *tĕs'älŏ,* m. & f. & a. Thessalian.
tirolés, a, *tĭrŏlĕs',* m. & f. & a. Tirolese.
Tolón, *tŏlŏn',* m. Toulon.
Tolosa, *tŏlŏ'sä,* f. Toulouse.
Toscana, *tŏskä'nä,* f. Tuscany.
Tracia, *trä'thĭä,* f. Thracia.
Transilvania, *tränsĭlvä'nĭä,* f. Transylvania.

Trento, *trĕn'tŏ*, m. Trent.
Tréveris, *trĕ'vĕrĭs*, m. Triers.
Troya, *trŏ'yă*, f. Troy.
Troyano, a, *trŏyă'nŏ*, m. & f. & a. Trojan.
Túnez, *tŏ'nĕth*, f. Tunis.
turco, a, *tŭr'kŏ*, m. & f. & a. Turk; Turkish.
Turingia, *tŭrĭn'hĭă*, f. Thuringia.
turingio, a, *–nĭŏ*, m. & f. & a. Thuringian.

Turquía, *tŭrkĕ'ă*, f. Turkey.
Utreque, *ŭtrĕ'kĕ*, f. Utrecht.
valaco, a, *vălă'kŏ*, m. & f. & a. Wallachian.
Valaquia, *vălă'kĭă*, f. Wallachia.
Varsovia, *vărsŏ'vĭă*, f. Warsaw.
Venecia, *vĕnĕ'thĭă*, f. Venice.
veneciano, a, *vĕnĕthĭă'nŏ*, m. & f. & a. Venetian.

Versalles, *vĕrsăl'yĕz*, m. Versailles.
Vesuvio, *vĕsŏ'vĭŏ*, m. Vesuvius.
Viena, *vĭĕ'nă*, f. Vienna.
vienés, a, *–nĕs'*, m. & f. & a. Viennese.
Vincenas, *vĭnthĕ'năs*, f. pl. Vincennes.
Virtembergo, *vĭrtĕmbĕr'gŏ*, m. Wurtemberg.
Zelandia, *thĕlăn'dĭă*, f. Zealand.
Zurico, *thŭr'kŏ*, m. Zurico.

Nombres de Bautismo los más comunes, que no se corresponden en ambas lenguas.

Abrahán, *ăbrăăn'*, Abraham.
Adán, *ădăn'*, Adam.
Adelaida, *ădĕlă'dă*, Adelaide.
Adolfo, *ădŏl'fŏ*, Adolphus.
Agustín, *ăgŭstĭn'*, Austin.
Alejandro, *ălĕ'hăn'drŏ*, Alexander. [sus.
Alfonso, *ălfŏn'sŏ*, Alphonso.
Ambrosio, *ămbrŏ'sĭŏ*, Ambrose.
Amalia, *ămă'lĭă*, Amelia.
Amata, *ămă'tă*, Amy.
Ana, *ă'nă*, Ann.
Andreo, *ăndrĕ'ŏ*, **Andrés**, *ăndrĕs'*, Andrew.
Anita, *ănĕ'tă*, Nan, Nancy, Jean, Janet.
Antonio, *ăntŏ'nĭŏ*, Anthony.
Augusto, *ăŭgŭs'tŏ*, Augustus.

Bártolo, *băr'tŏlŏ*, **Bartolomé**, *–mĕ'*, **Bartolomeo**, *–mĕŏ*, Bartholomew.
Beatriz, *bĕătrĭth'*, Beatrice.
Beltrán, *bĕltrăn'*, Bertram.
Benjaminito, *bĕn'hămĭnĕ'tŏ*, Ben. [Bennet.
Benito, *bĕnĕ'tŏ*, Benedict.
Bianca, *bĭăn'kă*, Blanche.
Brígida, *brĭ'hĭdă*, Bridget.
Brigidita, *–dĕ'tă*, Biddy.

Carlos, *kăr'lŏs*, Charles.
Carlota, *kărlŏ'tă*, Charlotte.
Carolina, *kărŏlĕ'nă*, Caroline, Cary.
Catalina, *kătălĕ'nă*, Catharine, Kate. [Cissy.
Cecilia, *thĕthĭ'lĭă*, Cecily.
Constancia, *kŏnstăn'thĭă*, Constance. [stantine.
Constantino, *–tĕ'nŏ*, Constantine.
Cristo, *krĭs'tŏ*, Christ.
Cristóbal, *krĭstŏ'băl*, Christopher.

Chombo, *tshŏm'bŏ*, **Jerónimo**, *hĕrŏ'nĭmŏ*, Jerome.

Diego, *dĭĕ'gŏ*, James.
Dorotea, *dŏrŏtĕ'ă*, Dorothy.
Doroteita, *–tĕĭ'tă*, Dolly.

Eduardo, *ĕdŭăr'dŏ*, Edward. [nor.
Elena, *ĕlĕ'nă*, Ellen, Eleanor.
Emilia, *ĕmĭ'lĭă*, Emily.
Enrique, *ĕnrĕ'kĕ*, Henry.
Enriqueta, *–kĕ'tă*, Harriet.
Enriquito, *–kĕ'tŏ*, Harry, Hal.
Esteban, *ĕstĕ'băn*, Stephan.
Ester, *ĕstĕr'*, Esther.
Eugenio, *ĕŭhĕ'nĭŏ*, Eugene.
Eva, *ĕ'vă*, Eve.

Faquita, *făkĕ'tă*, Fanny.
Federizo, *fĕdĕrĭ'kŏ*, Frederick.
Felipe, *fĕlĭ'pĕ*, Philip.
Fernando, *fĕrnăn'dŏ*, Ferdinand. [Frances.
Francisca, *frănthĭs'kă*, **Francisco**, *–kŏ*, Francis, Frank.

Gaspar, *găspăr'*, Jasper.
Geofredo, *hĕŏfrĕ'dŏ*, Geoffrey, Jeffrey.
Gertrudis, *hĕrtrŏ'dĭs*, **Tula**, *tŭ'lă*, Gertrud, Gerty.
Gofredo, **Godofredo**, *gŏ(dŏ)frĕ'dŏ*, Godfrey.
Gregorio, *grĕgŏ'rĭŏ*, Gregory. [ter.
Gualterio, *gŭăltĕ'rĭŏ*, Walter.
Guido, *gĕ'dŏ*, Guy.
Guillelma, *gĭlyĕl'mă*, Wilhelmine.
Guillelmo, **Guillermo**, *gĭlyĕl'mŏ*, *–yĕr'mŏ*, William, Will, Willy, Bill, Billy. [vus.
Gustavo, *gŭstă'vŏ*, Gustavus.

Hedwigia, *ĕdwĭ'h'ĭă*, Edwiga.
Helena, *ĕlĕ'nă*, Helen.
Hilario, *ĭlă'rĭŏ*, Hilary.

16*

Hugo, *ŏ'gŏ*, Hugh.
Hunfredo, *ŭnfrŏ'dŏ*, Humphrey.

Ignacio, *ĭgnă'thĭŏ*, Ignacio. — Inés, *ĭnĕs'*, Agnes. [tius.
Isabel, *ĭsăbĕl'*, Elizabeth, Eliza, Lizzie.
Isabelita, *—lĭ'tă*, Bess, Betsy, Betty.

Jaime, *'hă'ĭmĕ*, James, Jem, Jemmy.
Jorge, *'hŏr'hĕ*, George.
José, *'hŏsĕ'*, Joseph.
Juan, *'hŏăn'*, John.
Juana, *—nă*, Jane.
Juanita, *—ĭ'tă*, Jenny.
Juanito, *—ĭ'tŏ*, Johnny, Jack.
Juliana, *'hŭlĭă'nă*, Julian.
Julio, *'hŏ'lĭŏ*, Julius.

Leonor, *lĕŏnŏr'*, Eleanor.
Liseta, *lĭsĕ'tă*, Lizzie.
Lucas, *lŏ'kăs*, Luke.
Lucía, *lŏthĭ'ă*, Lucy.
Luis, *lŭĭs'*, Lewis.
Luisa, *lŭĭ'să*, Louisa.

Magdalena, *măgdălĕ'nă*, Magdalen, Maud.
Manuel, *mănŭĕl'*, Emanuel.
Marcos, *măr'kŏs*, Mark.
Margarita, *mărgărĭ'tă*, Margaret, Madge, Margery, Peggy.
María, *mărĭ'ă*, Mary.
Mariquita, *mărĭkĭ'tă*, Maruja, *mărŭ'h'ă*, Moll, Molly. [Mat.
Mateo, *mătĕ'ŏ*, Matthew.
Mauricio, *mădrĭ'thĭŏ*, Morris.
Miguel, *mĭgĕl'*, Michael.

Nicolas, *nĭkŏlăs'*, Nicholas.

Pablo, *pă'blŏ*, Paul.
Patricio, *pătrĭ'thĭŏ*, Patrick, Paddy.
Pedro, *pă'drŏ*, Peter.
Pepe, *pĕ'pĕ*, **Pepillo,** *—pĭ'yŏ*, Joe.

Ramón, *rămŏn'*, Raymund.
Reinaldo, *rĕĭnăl'dŏ*, Reynald. [Dicky.
Ricardito, *rĭkărdĭ'tŏ*, Dick,

Ricardo, *rĭkăr'dŏ*, Richard.
Roberto, *rŏbĕr'tŏ*, Robert, Bob, Robin.
Rogerio, *rŏ'hă'rĭŏ*, Roger.
Rodolfo, Rodulfo, *rŏdŭl'fŏ*, Ralph.
Roldán, *rŏldăn'*, **Rolando,** *rŏlăn'dŏ*, Rowland.

Sabedeo, *săbĕdĕ'ŏ*, Zebedee.
Salomón, *sălŏmŏn'*, Solomon. [Sam.
Samuel, *sămŭĕl'*, Samuel.
Sara, *să'ră*, Sarah, Sally.
Sofía, *sŏfĭ'ă*, Sophia, Sophy.
Susana, *sŭsă'nă*, Susan, Sue, Suky.

Teresa, *tĕrĕ'să*, Theresa.
Timóteo, *tĭmŏ'tĕŏ*, Timothy. [Tom.
Tomás, *tŏmăs'*, Thomas,

Valentino, *vălĕntĭ'nŏ*, Valentine.

Zacarías, *thăkărĭ'ăs*, Zachary.

Abreviaturas
que más comunmente se usan en castellano.

Las palabras precedidas de asterisco han de llevar una raya, tilde ó rasgo encima, y á veces debajo, puesto á la larga, cruzando los trazos altos ó bajos de las letras.

A., Alteza; Aprobado (en examen).
a, área.
(a), *alias*.
(a), arroba.
(a)(a), arrobas.
A. A., Autores; Altezas.
ab., abad.
ab.l, abril.
Abs. gen., Absolución general.
A. C. ó A. de C., Año de Cristo.
*admón, administración.
adm.or, administrador.
af.mo, afectísimo.
af.to, afecto.
Ag.n, Agustín.
ag.to, agosto.
alc.de, alcalde.
Alej.o, Alejandro.
Alf.o, Alfonso.
Al.o, Alonso.
Á L. R. P. de V. M., A los reales pies de Vuestra Majestad.
Álv.o, Álvaro.
am.o, amigo.
*ana, antífona.
anac., anacoreta.
Ant.o, Antonio.
ap., aparte; apóstol.
ap.a, ap.o ó *aplica, aplicó, apostólica, apostólico.
apóst., apóstol.
art. ó art.o, artículo.
*arz. ó arzbpo., arzobispo.
Aud.a, Audiencia.

B., Beato; Bueno (en examen).
Bar.mé, Bartolomé.
Bern.o, Bernardo.
B. L. M. ó b. l. m., besa la mano.
B. L. P. ó b. l. p., beso los pies.
B.mo P.e, Beatísimo Padre.
B. p., Bendición papal.
Br. ó br., bachiller.

c.a, c.ía ó *comp., compañía.
c. ó cap., capítulo.

cap.n, capitán.
capp.n, capellán.
Card.l, Cardenal.
C. de J., Compañía de Jesús.
cénts., céntimos.
cf., conf. ó confr., confesor; confirma (en documentos antiguos).
cg., centigramo, centigramos.
cl., centilitro, centilitros.
Clem.te, Clemente.
*cllo, cuartillo.
cm., centímetro, centímetros.
C. M. B. ó m. b., cuyas manos beso.
col. ó col.a, columna; colonia.
comis., comisario.
cons.o, consejo.
Const., Constitución.
const., constitucional.
conv.te, conveniente.
corr.te, corriente.
C. P. B. ó c. p. b., cuyos pies beso.
cps., compañeros.
crec.te, creciente.
cs., cuartos; céntimos.

D. ó D.n, Don.
D.a, Doña.
D.D., doctores.
Dg., decagramo, decagramos.
*dha, dho, dhas, dhos, dicha, dicho, dichas, dichos.
dic.e, 10e ó 10bre, diciembre.
Dl., decalitro, decalitros.
dl., decilitro, decilitros.
Dm., decámetro.
dm., decímetro, decímetros; decigramo, decigramos.
Doct., D.r ó dr., doctor.
docum.to, documento.
D. O. M., *Deo Optimo Maximo*.
Dom.o, Domingo.
dom.o, domingo.
*dra, dro, dras, dros, derecha, derecho, derechas, derechos.
dup.do, duplicado.

E., este (oriente).

ec.ca, ec.co, eclesiástica, eclesiástico.
E. M., Estado Mayor.
Em.a, Eminencia.
E. M. G., Estado Mayor General.
Em.mo ó * Emmo, Eminentísimo.
ENE, estenordeste.
en.o, enero.
E. P. D., En paz descanse.
E. P. M., En propia mano.
ermit., ermitaño.
esc.o, escudo.
escrit.a, escritura.
* escrnia, escribanía.
* escrno, escribano.
escs, escudos.
ESE, estesudeste.
etc. ó &a.., etcétera.
Eug.o, Eugenio.
Evang.o, Evangelio.
Evang.ta, Evangelista.
Exc.a, Excelencia.
Exc.ma, Exc.mo ó * Excma, Excmo,
Excelentísima, Excelentísimo.

F., Fulano.
F.co ó Franc.o, Francisco.
F. de T., Fulano de Tal.
feb.o, febrero.
Fern.do, Fernando.
* fha, fho, fecha, fecho.
f.o ó fol., folio.
Fr., Fray; Frey.
* Frns ó * Fz, Fernandez.
fund., fundador.

G., gracia.
g., gramo, gramos.
g.de ó * gue, guarde.
Gen.l, general (dignidad).
G.o, Gonzalo.
gob.o, gobierno.
gob.r, gobernador.
* Gonz, González.
* gral, general.
Greg.o, Gregorio.
Guill.o, Guillermo.

hect., hectárea, hectáreas.
Hg., hectogramo, hectogramos.
Hl., hectolitro, hectolitros.
Hm., hectómetro, hectómetros.
hol., holandesa.

ib., *ibidem.*
id., *idem.*
i. e., *id est* (esto es).
* igl.a, iglesia.
Ign.o, Ignacio.
Ildef.o, Ildefonso.
Il.e, Ilustre.
Il.ma, Il.mo ó * Illma, Ilmo, Ilustrísima, Ilustrísimo.
Indulg. plen. ó I P., Indulgencia ple-
naria.
in p. inf., *in pártibus infidélium.*
inq.r, inquisidor.
intend.te, intendente.
It., *item.*

* izq.a, izq.o ó izq.da, izq.do, izquierda,
izquierdo.

Jac.to, Jacinto.
J. C., Jesucristo.
Jerón.o, Jerónimo.
* Jhs, Jesús.
J.o, Ju.o (ant.), Juan.
* Jph, José.
juev., jueves.
Jul.n, Julián.

kg., kilogramo, kilogramos.
kl., kilolitro, kilolitros.
km., kilómetro, kilómetros.

L., L.do ó l.do, Licenciado.
l., ley; libro; litro, litros.
* lbs, libras.
lín., línea.
Lor.zo, Lorenzo.
L. S., *Locus sigilli* (lugar del sello).
lun., lunes.

M., Madre (religiosa); Majestad; Merced;
Maestro; Mediano (en examen).
m., minuto, minutos; metro, metros; mañana.
Man.l, Manuel.
M.a, María.
Marg.ta, Margarita.
mart., martes.
márts ó mrs, mártires.
may.mo, mayordomo.
M.e, Madre (religiosa).
meng., menguante.
mg., miligramo, miligramos.
miérc., miércoles.
Mig.l, Miguel.
milés.s, milésimas.
min.o, ministro.
Mm., miriámetro, miriámetros.
mm., milímetro, milímetros.
monast.o, monasterio.
Mons., Monseñor.
M. P. S., Muy Poderoso Señor.
Mr, Monsieur; Míster.
mr, mártir.
mrd, merced.
* Mrn, Martín.
* Mrnz, Martínez.
* Mro, Maestro.
mrs, maravedises; mártires.
M. S., manuscrito.
m.s a.s, muchos años.
M. SS., manuscritos.

N., norte; Notablemente aprovechado (en
examen).
n., noche.
N.a S.a, Nuestra Señora.
N. B., *Notabene.*
NE, nordeste.
NNE, nornordeste.
NNO, nornoroeste.
NO, noroeste.
n.o, número (1. primero, 2. segundo etc.).
nov.e, 9e ó 9bre, noviembre.
Nov. Recop., Novísima Recopilación.

N. Recop., Nueva Recopilación.
` ira, nro, nras, nros, ntra, ntro, ntras, ntros, nuestra, nuestro, nuestras, nuestros.
núm. ó núm.o, núms ó núm.s, número, números.
N. S., Nuestro Señor.
N. S. J. C., Nuestro Señor Jesucristo.

O, oeste.
ob. ú * obpo, obispo.
oct.e, 8e ú 8bre, octubre.
ONO, oestenoroeste.
onz., onza.
*** orn,** orden.
OSO, oessudoeste.

P., Papa; Padre; Pregunta.
P. A., Por ausencia; Por autorización.
p.a, para.
pág., págs, página, páginas.
Part., Partida.
Patr., Patriarca.
*** pbro ó presb., presbítero.**
P. D., Posdata.
P.e, Padre.
p. ej., por ejemplo.
penit., penitente.
perg. ó pno, pergamino.
Pf., Pfs, peso fuerte, pesos fuertes.
P. M., Padre Maestro.
P. O., Por orden.
P.o, Pedro.
p.o, pero.
p0/o, por ciento.
P. P., Porte pagado; Por poder.
*** p.p.do,** próximo pasado.
p.r, por.
*** pral,** principal.
priv., privilegio.
proc., procesión.
prof., profeta.
pról., prólogo.
*** pror,** procurador.
prov.a, provincia.
prov.or, provisor.
P. S., *Post scriptum* (posdata).
P. S. M., Por su mandato.
ps, pesos.
pta, pasta.
ptas, pesetas.
p.te, parte.

Q. B. S. M. ó q. b. s. m., que besa su mano.
Q. B. S. P. ó q. b. s. p., que besa sus piés.
Q. D. G. ó q. D. g., que Dios guarde.
q.e, que.
q. e. g. e., que en gloria esté.

R., Reverendo; Reverencia; Respuesta; Reprobado (en examen).
R), Responde ó respuesta (en libros de rezo).
Raf.l, Rafael.
R.bí, Recibí.
R. D., Real Decreto.
Rde M. ó R. M., Reverenda Madre.
Rdo P. ó R. P., Reverendo Padre.
R.e, Récipe.

R. I. P., *Requiescat in pace* (en paz descanse).
r.l, real (moneda).
R.l, Real (del Rey).
*** Rmrz,** Ramírez.
R. O., Real Orden.
R. S., Real Servicio.
rs ó r.s, reales (moneda).
R.s, Reales (del rey).
rúst., rústica.

S., San ó Santo; sur; Sobresaliente (en examen).
S.a, Señora.
S. A., Su Alteza.
sáb., sábado.
S. A. I., Su Alteza Imperial.
S. A. R., Su Alteza Real.
S. A. S., Su Alteza Serenísima.
Sb.n, Sebastián.
S. C. ó s. c., su casa.
S. C. M., Sacra, Católica Majestad.
S. C. C. R. M., Sacra, Cesárea, Católica Real Majestad.
S. D., Se despide.
S. D. M., Su Divina Majestad.
SE, sudeste.
secret.a, secretaría.
s. e. ú o., salvo error ú omisión.
sept.e, 7e ó 7bre, septiembre.
Ser.ma, Ser.mo ó * Serma, Sermo, Serenísima, Serenísimo.
serv.o, servicio.
serv.or, servidor.
set.e, setiembre.
sig.te, siguiente.
S. M., Su Majestad.
S. M. A., Su Majestad Apostólica.
S. M. B., Su Majestad Británica.
S. M. C., Su Majestad Católica.
S. M. F., Su Majestad Fidelísima.
S. M. I., Su Majestad Imperial.
S.n, San.
S. N., Servicio Nacional.
SO, sudoeste.
*** Sor,** Señor.
*** Sores,** Señores.
*** spre,** siempre.
S.r ó Sr, Señor.
*** Sra, Sras,** Señora, Señoras.
Sres ó S.res, Señores.
*** Sría,** Secretaría.
s.ria, s.rio ó * sria, srio, secretaría, secretario.
S. R. M., Su Real Majestad.
Srta ó * Srta, Señorita.
S. S., Su Santidad.
S. S.a, Su Señoría.
SS. AA., Sus Altezas.
SSE, sudsudeste.
SS. MM., Sus Majestades.
SS.mo, Santísimo.
SS.mo P., Santísimo Padre.
SS.no, escribano.
SSO, sudsudoeste.
S. S. S., su seguro servidor.
Sta, Santa.
Sto, Santo.
sup., suplica.

supert.te, superintendente.
supl.te, suplente.

t., tarde.
ten.te, teniente.
test.mto, testamento.
test.o, testigo.
tít. ó tít.o, título.
t.o ó tom., tomo.
✻ tpo, tiempo.
trib.l, tribunal.

U. ó Ud, Usted.
Uds, Ustedes.

V., Usted; Venerable; Véase.
V. ó Vers.o, Versículo.
V.a, Vigilia.
V. A., Vuestra Alteza.
V. A. R., Vuestra Alteza Real.
V. B.d, Vuestra Beatitud.
V. E., Vuestra Excelencia ó Vuecencia.
vg., verbigracia; virgen.
v. g. ó v. gr., verbigracia.

vgs, vírgenes.
Vict.a, Victoria.
Vic.te, Vicente.
vier., viernes.
virg., virgs, virgen, vírgenes.
V. M., Vuestra Majestad.
Vm. ó Vmd, Vuestra Merced ó Usted.
vn, vellón.
V.o B.o, Visto bueno.
vol., volumen; voluntad.
vols, volúmenes.
V. O. T., Venerable Orden Tercera.
V. P., Vuestra Paternidad.
V. R., Vuestra Reverencia.
✻ vra, vro, vras, vros, vuestra, vuestro, vuestras, vuestros.
V. S., Vueseñoría ó Usía.
V. S. I., Vueseñoría, ó Usía, Ilustrísima.
v.ta, v.to, vuelta, vuelto.
V. V., Ustedes.

x.mo, diezmo.
✻ xpiano, xptiano, cristiano.[1]
✻ Xpo, Xpto, Cristo.[1]
✻ Xptóbal, Cristóbal.[1]

1) Los dos primeros caracteres de estas cinco últimas abreviaturas son las letras griegas χ (ji) y ϱ (rho).

Monedas, Pesos y Medidas españolas.
(Spanish Currency, Weights and Measures).

Since 1871, Spain has adopted the metric system.
The Spanish measures vary more or less in the different provinces of the
kingdom.

Monedas (Currency).

Standard coin: la peseta = 100 céntimos.
Gold coins: pieces of 5, 10, 25 y 100 pesetas.
    la onza = 80 pesetas.
    la media onza = 40 pesetas.
    el doblón de oro = 20 pesetas.
Silver coins: el real = 25 céntimos.
    dos reales = 50 céntimos.
    cuatro reales = 100 céntimos = peseta.
    dos pesetas = 200 céntimos.
    el duro = 20 reales = 5 pesetas.
    el escudo = 2,50 pesetas.
    la peseta columnaria = 1,25 pesetas.
Copper coins: pieces of 1, 2, 5 céntimos
    (vulg. perro chico), and of 10 céntimos
    (vulg. perro grande).
Paper-money: Bank of Spain notes for 25,
50, 100, 500 and 1000 pesetas.

Pesos (Weights).

Kilogramo = 1000 gramos.
Hectogramo = 100 gramos.
Decagramo = 10 gramos.
Quintal métrico = 100 kilogramos.
Libra = 4 cuarterones = 16 onzas = 460
    gramos.
Cuarterón = 4 onzas = 115 gramos.
Onza = 16 adarmes = 287 decigramos.
Tomín = 6 centigramos.
Arroba = 4 cuartillas = 25 libras = 11,502
    kilogramos.   [kilogramos.
Cuartilla = 1/4 arroba = 6,25 libras = 2,875
Quintal = 4 arrobas = 46 kilogramos.

Medidas longitudinales (Linear Measure).

Standard: metro.
Pie = 1/3 vara = 12 pulgadas = 278 decímetros.

Medidas longitudinales (Linear Measure).

Pulgada = 1/12 pie = 12 líneas = 25 milí-
metros.
Línea = 1/12 pulgada = 12 puntos = 2
milímetros.
Vara = 4 palmos = 3 pies = 36 pulgadas
= 834 decímetros.
Braza = 1,672 metro.
Legua de posta = 3,894 kilómetros.
Milla = 1/3 legua = 1,298 kilómetro.

Medidas para áridos (Dry Measure).

Litro = 1 decímetro cubo.
Fanega = 12 celemines = 55,5 litros.
Celemín = 4 cuartillos = 4,625 litros.
Cuartillo = 1/4 celemín = 1,156litros.
Cahiz = 12 fanegas = 6,66 hectolitros.

Medidas para líquidos (Liquid Measure).

Moyo = 16 cántaras = 2,58 hectolitros.
Cántara = 4 cuartillas = 16,133 litros.
Cuartilla = 2 azumbres = 4,039 litros.
Azumbre = 4 cuartillos = 2,016 litros.
Cuartillo = 5,04 decilitros.

Medidas agrarias (Square Measure).

Área = 100 metros cuadrados.
Hectárea = 100 áreas = 10,000 metros cua-
    drados.
Centiárea = 1 metro cuadrado.
Fanega de tierra = 576 estadales = 64,6 áreas.
Estadal = 1,19 deciáreas.
Aranzada = 400 estadales = 44,8 áreas.
Caballería = 60 fanegas = 3,8758 hectáreas.

Medidas cúbicas (Cubic Measure).

Estéreo = 1 metro cúbico.
Decastéreo = 10 metros cúbicos.
Decistéreo = 1/10 metro cúbico.

Irregular Verbs[1]).

Infinitivo.	Presente del Indicativo.	Pretérito perfecto.	Futuro.	Imperativo.	Participio.
abastecer	conjugated	as	nacer		
aborrecer	conjugated	as	nacer		
abrir					abierto
absolver	yo absuelvo, tú absuelves, él absuelve, ellos absuelven			absuelve tú, absuelva él, absuelvan ellos	absuelto
acertar	yo acierto, tú aciertas, él acierta, ellos aciertan			acierta tú, acierte él, acierten ellos	
acordar	conjugated	as	acostar		
acostar	yo acuesto, tú acuestas, él acuesta, ellos acuestan			acuesta tú, acueste él, acuesten ellos	
acrecentar	conjugated	as	acertar		
adestrar	conjugated	as	acertar		
adherir	conjugated	as	sentir		
adquirir	conjugated	as	sentir		
advertir	conjugated	as	sentir		
agorar	conjugated	as	acostar		
alentar	conjugated	as	acertar		
almorzar	conjugated	as	acostar		
amolar	conjugated	as	acostar		
andar	v. Ir.	yo anduve, tu anduviste &c.	yo iré &c. (v. Ir.)		
apacentar	conjugated	as	acertar		
aportar	conjugated	as	acostar		
apostar	conjugated	as	acostar		
apretar	conjugated	as	acertar		
aprobar	conjugated	as	acostar		
argüir	yo arguyo, tú arguyes, él arguye, ellos arguyen			arguye tú &c.	
arrendar	conjugated	as	acertar		
arrepentirse	conjugated	as	sentir		
ascender	yo asciendo, tú asciendes, él asciende, ellos ascienden			asciende tú, ascienda él, asciendan ellos	
asentar	conjugated	as	acertar		
asestar	conjugated	as	acertar		
asir	yo asgo			asga él, asgan ellos	
asolar	conjugated	as	acostar		
atender	conjugated	as	ascender		
aterrar	conjugated	as	acertar		
atestar	conjugated	as	acertar		
atravesar	conjugated	as	acertar		
atribuir	conjugated	as	argüir		
aventar	conjugated	as	acertar		
avergonzar	conjugated	as	acostar		
bendecir[2])	yo bendigo, tú bendices, él bendice, ellos bendicen	yo bendije, tú bendijiste &c.	yo bendeciré, tú bendecirás &c.	bendice tú, bendiga él, bendigan ellos	bendido (bendecido)

1) The persons *not* given in the tables, as well as the tenses in the columns of which a blank is left, are conjugated *regularly*. — 2) Gerundio: bendiciendo.

Infinitivo.	Presente del Indicativo.	Pretérito perfecto.	Futuro.	Imperativo.	Participio.
bregar	conjugated	as	acertar		
caber	yo quepo	yo cupe, tú cupiste &c.	yo cabré, tú cabrás &c.	quepa él, quepan ellos	
caer	yo caigo	él cayó, ellos cayeron		caiga él, caigamos nosotros, caigan ellos	
calentar	conjugated	as	acertar		
cegar	conjugated	as	acertar		
ceñir	conjugated	as	pedir		
cerner	conjugated	as	ascender		
cerrar	conjugated	as	acertar		
cimentar	conjugated	as	acertar		
cocer	conjugated	as	absolver		
colar	conjugated	as	acostar		
colegir	conjugated	as	pedir		
colgar	conjugated	as	acostar		
comenzar	conjugated	as	acertar		
compeler					compulso [(compelido)
competir	conjugated	as	pedir		
concebir	conjugated	as	pedir		
concertar	conjugated	as	acertar		
concluir	conjugated	as	argüir		concluso (concluido)
condoler	conjugated	as	absolver		
conducir	yo conduzco	yo conduje, tú condujiste &c.		conduzca él, conduzcamos nosotros, conduzcan ellos	
conferir	conjugated	as	sentir		
confesar	conjugated	as	acertar		
confundir					confuso (confundido)
conmover	conjugated	as	absolver		
conocer	conjugated	as	nacer		
consolar	conjugated	as	acostar		
constituir	conjugated	as	argüir		
constreñir	conjugated	as	pedir		
contar	conjugated	as	acostar		
cortener	conjugated	as	tener		
contradecir	conjugated	as	bendecir.		
contribuir	conjugated	as	argüir		
controvertir	conjugated	as	sentir		
convencer					convicto (convencido)
convertir	conjugated	as	sentir		
costar	conjugated	as	acostar		
crecer	conjugated	as	nacer		
cubrir					cubierto
dar	yo doy	yo dí, tú diste, él dió &c.			
decentar	conjugated	as	acertar		
decir 1)	yo digo, tú dices, él dice, ellos dicen	yo dije, tú dijiste &c.	yo diré, tú dirás &c.	di tú, diga él, digamos nosotros, digan ellos	dicho
deducir	conjugated	as	conducir		
defender	conjugated	as	ascender		
deferir	conjugated	as	sentir		
degollar	conjugated	as	acostar		
demoler	conjugated	as	absolver		
derrengar	conjugated	as	acertar		
derretir	conjugated	as	pedir		
derrocar	conjugated	as	acostar		
desasir	conjugated	as	asir		
descollar	conjugated	as	acostar		
descontar	conjugated	as	acostar		
desdecir	conjugated	as	bendecir		

1) Gerundio: diciendo.

Infinitivo.	Presente del Indicativo.	Pretérito perfecto.	Futuro.	Imperativo.	Participio.
desleir	conjugated	as	pedir		
desmembrar	conjugated	as	acertar		
desmentir	conjugated	as	sentir		
desolar	conjugated	as	acostar		
despedir	conjugated	as	pedir		
despernar	conjugated	as	acertar		
despertar					despierto (des-[pertado)
desterrar	conjugated	as	acertar		
destruir	conjugated	as	argüir		
detener	conjugated	as	tener		
dezmar	conjugated	as	acertar		
diferir	conjugated	as	sentir		
digerir	conjugated	as	sentir		
discernir	conjugated	as	sentir		
disolver	conjugated	as	absolver		
distribuir	conjugated	as	argüir		
divertir	conjugated	as	sentir		
doler	conjugated	as	absolver		
dormir 1)	yo duermo, tú duermes él duerme, ellos duermen	él durmió, ellos durmieron		duerme tú, duerma él, durmamos nosotros, duerman ellos	
elegir	conjugated	as	pedir		electo(elegido)
empedrar	conjugated	as	acertar		
empezar ·	conjugated	as	acertar		
emporcar	conjugated	as	acostar		
encarecer	conjugated	as	nacer		
encender	conjugated	as	ascender		
encerrar	conjugated	as	acertar		
encomendar	conjugated	as	acertar		
encontrar	conjugated	as	acostar		
encordar	conjugated	as	acostar		
engreirse	conjugated	as	pedir		
engrosar	conjugated	as	acostar		
enjugar					enjuto (enju-[gado)
enmendar	conjugated	as	acertar		
entender	conjugated	as	ascender		
enterrar	conjugated	as	acertar		
envestir	conjugated	as	pedir		
errar	conjugated	as	acertar		
escarmentar	conjugated	as	acertar		
escribir					escrito
esforzar	conjugated	as	acostar		
estar	yo estoy	yo estuve, tú estuviste &c.			
estregar	conjugated	as	acertar		
excluir	conjugated	as	argüir		excluso (ex-[cluído)
expedir	conjugated	as	pedir		
expeler					expulso(expe-[lido)
exponer	conjugated	as	poner		
expresar					expreso (ex-[presado)
extender	conjugated	as	ascender		
extinguir					extinto(extin-[guido)
extraer	conjugated	as	traer		
fijar					fijo (fijado)
florecer	conjugated	as	nacer		
fluir	conjugated	as	argüir		
forzar	conjugated	as	acostar		
fregar ·	conjugated	as	acertar		
freir	conjugated	as	pedir		
gemir	conjugated	as	pedir		
gobernar	conjugated	as	acertar		
guarnecer	conjugated	as	nacer		

1) Gerundio: durmiendo.

Infinitivo.	Presente del Indicativo.	Pretérito perfecto.	Futuro.	Imperativo.	Participio.
haber 1)	yo he, tú has, él ha, nosotros hemos, vosotros habéis,	yo hube, tú hubiste, él hubo &c.	yo habré, tú habrás &c.	haya él, hayamos nosotros, hayan ellos	habido
hacer	yo hago [ellos han	yo hice, tú hiciste, él hizo &c.	yo haré, tú harás &c.	haz tú, haga él, hagamos nosotros, hagan ellos	hecho
hartar					harto (hartado)
heder	conjugated	as	ascender		
helar	conjugated	as	acertar		
henchir	conjugated	as	pedir		
hender	conjugated	as	ascender		
herir	conjugated	as	sentir		
herrar	conjugated	as	acertar		
hervir	conjugated	as	sentir		
holgar	conjugated	as	acostar		
hollar	conjugated	as	acostar		
huir	conjugated	as	argüir		
imbuir	conjugated	as	argüir		
incluir	conjugated	as	argüir		[cluido) incluso (in-
incurrir					incurso (incu-rrido)
inducir	conjugated	as	conducir		
inferir	conjugated	as	sentir		
ingerir	conjugated	as	sentir		ingerto (inge-
inquirir	conjugated	as	sentir		rido)
insertar					inserto (inser-
instituir	conjugated	as	argüir		tado)
instruir	conjugated	as	argüir		
introducir	conjugated	as	conducir		
invernar	conjugated	as	acertar		[vertido)
invertir	conjugated	as	sentir		inverso (in-
ir 2)	yo voy, tú vas, él va, nosotros vamos, vosotros vais, ellos van	yo fui, tú fuiste, él fué &c.	yo iré, tú irás &c.	ve tú, vaya él, vayamos (vamos) nosotros, id vosotros, vayan ellos	
jugar	conjugated	as	acostar		
juntar					junto (jun-tado)
lucir	conjugated	as	nacer		
llover	conjugated	as	absolver		[decido)
maldecir	conjugated	as	bendecir		maldito (mal-
manifestar	conjugated	as	acertar		manifiesto
mantener	conjugated	as	tener		[(manifestado)
marchitar					marchito
medir	conjugated	as	pedir		[(marchitado)
mentar	conjugated	as	acertar		
mentir	conjugated	as	sentir		
merendar	conjugated	as	acertar		
moler	conjugated	as	absolver		
morder	conjugated	as	absolver		
morir	conjugated	as	dormir		muerto
mostrar	conjugated	as	acostar		
mover	conjugated	as	absolver		
nacer	yo nazco			nazca él, nazcan ellos	
negar	conjugated	as	acertar		
nevar	conjugated	as	acertar		
obscurecer	conjugated	as	nacer		
obstruir	conjugated	as	argüir		

1) Pres. del Subj.: yo haya &c. Imperf. del Ind.: yo había &c.; Imperf. del Subj.: yo hubiese &c. Condic. del Ind.: yo habría &c.; Cond. del Subj.: yo hubiera &c. Fut. del Subj.: yo hubiere &c. Gerundio: habiendo. — 2) Pres. del Subj.: yo vaya &c. Imperf. del Ind.: yo iba &c.; Imperf. del Subj.: yo fuese &c. Condic. del Indic.: yo iría &c.; Condic. del Subj.: yo fuera &c. Fut. del Subj.: yo fuere &c. Gerundio: yendo.

Infinitivo.	Presente del Indicativo.	Pretérito perfecto.	Futuro.	Imperativo.	Participio.
ofrecer	conjugated	as	nacer		
oír 1)	yo oigo, tú oyes &c.	yo oí, tú oiste, él oyó, ellos oyéron		oiga él, oigamos nosotros, oigan ellos	
oler	conjugated	as	absolver		[do]
omitir					omiso (omiti-
oprimir					opreso (opri-
pacer	conjugated	as	nacer		[mido]
parecer	conjugated	as	nacer		
pensar	conjugated	as	acertar		
pedir 2)	yo pido, tú pides, él pide, ellos piden	él pidió, ellos pidieron		pide tú, pida él, pidamos nosotros, pidan ellos	
perder	conjugated	as	ascender		
perfeccionar					perfecto (per-
placer, v.def.3)	me (te, le) place	me &c. plugo			[feccionado]
plegar	conjugated	as	acertar		
poblar	conjugated	as	acostar		
poder 4)	yo puedo, tú puedes, él puede, ellos pueden	yo pude, tú pudiste &c.	yo podré, tú podrás &c.		
podrir	yo pudro, tú pudres, él pudre, ellos pudren	yo pudrí, tú pudriste &c.	yo pudriré, tú pudrirás &c.	pudre tú, pudra él, pudramos nosotros, pudran ellos	pudrido
poner	yo pongo	yo puse, tú pusiste &c.	yo pondré, tú pondrás &c.	pon tú, ponga él, pongamos nosotros, pongan ellos	
preferir	conjugated	as	sentir		[do]
prender					preso (prendi-
prescribir					prescrito (pre-
probar	conjugated	as	acostar		[scribido]
producir	conjugated	as	conducir		
prostituir	conjugated	as	argüir		
proveer					provisto (pro-
quebrar	conjugated	as	acertar		[veído)
querer	yo quiero, tú quieres, él quiere, ellos quieren	yo quise, tú quisiste &c.	yo querré, tú querrás &c.	quiere tú, quiera él, quieran ellos	
recluir	conjugated	as	argüir		recluso (reclu-
recomendar	conjugated	as	acertar		[ido]
reconocer	conjugated	as	nacer		
recordar	conjugated	as	acostar		
reducir	conjugated	as	conducir		
referir	conjugated	as	sentir		
regir	conjugated	as	pedir		
reír	conjugated	as	pedir		
renacer	conjugated	as	nacer		
rendir	conjugated	as	pedir		
renovar	conjugated	as	acostar		
reñir	conjugated	as	pedir		
reprobar	conjugated	as	acostar		
resentirse	conjugated	as	sentir		
retentar	conjugated	as	acertar		
retorcer	conjugated	as	absolver		
retribuir	conjugated	as	argüir		
reventar	conjugated	as	acertar		
revolcarse	conjugated	as	acostar		
rodar	conjugated	as	acostar		
romper					roto (rompido)

1) Gerundio: oyendo. — 2) Gerundio: pidiendo. — 3) Pres. del Subj.: plegue ó plazga (á Dios). Imperf. del Subj.: pluguiese (á Dios). Fut. del Subj.: si me plugiere &c. Condic. del Subj.: pluguiera (á Dios). — 4) Gerundio: pudiendo.

Infinitivo.	Presente del Indicativo.	Pretérito perfecto.	Futuro.	Imperativo.	Participio.
saber	yo sé(Pres.delSubj yo sepa &c.)	yo supe, tú supiste &c.	yo sabré, tú sabrás &c.	sepa él, sepan ellos	
salir	yo salgo		yo saldré, tú saldrás &c.	sal tú, salga él, salgamos nosotros, salgan ellos	
segar	conjugated	as	acertar		
seguir	conjugated	as	pedir		
sembrar	conjugated	as	acertar		
sentar	conjugated	as	acertar		
sentir	yo siento, tú sientes, él siente, ellos sienten	él sintió, ellos sintieron		siente tú, sienta él, sientan ellos	
ser 1)	yo soy, tú eres, él es, nosotros somos, vosotros sois, ellos son	yo fui,tú fuiste, él fué &c.	yo sere, tú serás &c.	se tú, sea él, seamos nosotros, sean ellos	sido
serrar	conjugated.	as	acertar		
servir	conjugated	as	pedir.		
soldar	conjugated	as	acostar		
soler	conjugated	as	absolver		
soltar	conjugated	as	acostar		solto (soltado)
sonar	conjugated	as	acostar		
soñar	conjugated	as	acostar		
sostener	conjugated	as	tener		
substituir	conjugated	as	argüir		
sugerir	conjugated	as	sentir		
suprimir					supreso(suprimido)
temblar	conjugated	as	acertar		
tender	conjugated	as	ascender		
tener	yo tengo, tú tienes, él tiene, ellos tienen	yo tuve, tú tuviste &c.	yo tendré, tú tendrás &c.	ten tú, tenga él, tengamos nosotros, tengan ellos	
tentar.	conjugated	as	acertar		
teñir	conjugated	as	pedir		
torcer	conjugated	as	absolver		
tostar	conjugated	as	acostar		
traducir	conjugated	as	conducir		
traer	yo traigo	yo traje, tu trajiste &c.			
tronar	conjugated	as	acostar		
trasferir	conjugated	as	sentir		
tropezar	conjugated	as	acertar		
valer	yo valgo		yo valdré, tú valdrás &c.	valga el, valgamos nosotros, valgan ellos	
venir 2)	yo vengo,tú vienes, él viene, ellos vienen	yo vine, tú viniste &c.	yo vendré, tú vendrás &c.	ven tú, venga él, vengan ellos	
ver					
verter	conjugated	as	ascender		visto
vestir	conjugated	as	pedir		
volar	conjugated	as	acostar		
volcar	conjugated	as	acostar		
volver	conjugated	as	absolver		vuelto
yacer, v. def.3)	(yago) él yace, ellos yacen				

1) Pres. del Subj.: yo sea &c. Imperf. del Ind.: yo era &c., nosotros éramos; Imperf. del Subj.: yo fuese &c. Condic. del Ind.: yo sería &c.; Condic. del Subj.: yo fuera &c. Futuro del Subj.: yo fuere &c. Gerundio: siendo. — 2) Gerundio: viniendo. — 3) Imperf.: él yacia, ellos yacian.

A LIST OF POPULAR WORDS
ENGLISH–SPANISH

accelerator, s. acelerador, m.
aerial, s. antena, f.
aeroplane, s. aeroplano, avión, m.
aileron, s. alerón, m.
air brake, s. freno neumático
air brush, s. pulverizador de aire comprimido
air compressor, s. compresor de aire
air-cooled, a. enfriado por aire
aircraft, s. máquina o máquinas de volar
air drill, s. taladro neumático
airdrome, s. aeródromo, m., campo de aviación
air fleet, s. flotilla de aeroplanos
air furnace, s. horno de tiro natural; horno de calentar aire
airman, s. aviador, aeronauta, m.
airport, s. paradero o estación para aeroplanos   [ventilación
air shaft, s. respiradero, pozo de
airship, s. aeronave, dirigible, f.
air-speed indicator, s. indicador de algebra, s. álgebra, f.   [velocidad
altimeter, s. altímetro, m.
ammeter, s. amperímetro, m.
amperage, s. amperaje, m.
ampere, s. amperio, m.
amphibian, s. anfibio, a., aeroplano de tierra y agua
antenna, s. antena (radio) f.
automobile, s. automóvil, m.
aviation, s. aviación, f.
aviator, s. aviador, m.

biplane, s. biplano, m.
broadcast (radio), perifonear, v. a.
broadcasting (radio), s. perifonía, f., radiodifusión; a. emisor, difusor, radiodifusor
bumper (auto), s. parachoques, m.

cam shaft, s. engranaje del eje de carburetor, s. carburador, m. [levas
chassis, s. chasis, m.
condenser, s. condensador, m.
connecting rod, s. biela, f.
crank shaft, s. cigüeñal, m.

detector (elec.), s. detector, m.

elevator, s. ascensor, elevador, m.
exhaust fan, s. ventilador aspirador

film play, s. drama cinematográfico
fuselage, s. fuselaje, m.

garage, s. garaje, m.
gasoline, s. gasolina, f.
generator (elec.), s. generador, dí-
glider, s. deslizador, m.   [namo, m.

hangar (aer.), s. hangar, m.
headlight, s. linterna delantera, f.
hook-up (radio), s. circuito, m.
hydroplane, s. hidroplano, hidroavión, m.

kilowatt, s. kilovatio, m.

loudspeaker, s. altoparlante, m.

magneto, s. magneto, m.   [ción, f.
merger, s. combinación, consolida-
mileage, s. kilometraje, m.
monoplane, s. monoplano, m.
moratorium, s. moratoria, f.
motorcycle, s. motocicleta, f.

neon, s. neón, m.

parachute, s. paracaídas, m.
power plant (auto), s. motor y sus accesorios

radiator, s. calorífero, (auto) radiador, m.
radio, s. radiocomunicación, f.
radiobroadcast, v. a. y v. n. perifonear, difundir por radiotransmisión
radiogram, s. radiograma, m.
radiotelephone, s. radioteléfono, m.
radium (chem.), s. radio, m.

seaplane, s. hidroavión, m.
soviet, s. sóviet, m.
sparkplug, s. bujía, f.
steering wheel (auto), s. volante de dirección
street-car, s. (coche de) tranvía, m.

tail light, s. farol trasero, m.
tank car, s. vagón tanque, m.
television, s. televisión, m.
tennis, s. tenis, m.   [tractor
tractor, s. tractor; m., automóvil
trade-mark, s. marca de fábrica, f.

windshield, s. parabrisa, m.
windshield wiper, s. limpiavidrios para el parabrisa
wireless, s. radiocomunicación, f.

256

ENGLISH AND SPANISH.

A.

a, á, art. un, uno, una; —, pr. á, al, en.
aback, *ăbăk',* ad. detrás, atrás; (mar.) en facha; **to be taken —,** ser consternado.
abacus, *ă'băkŭs,* s. tabla aritmética, f.; ábaco, tablero de un capitel, m.
abaft, *ăbăft',* ad. (mar.) á ó en popa.
abandon, *ăbăn'dŭn,* v. a. abandonar, dejar.
abandonment, *—mĕnt,* s. abandonamiento, abandono, m.; desamparo, m.
abase, *ăbās',* v.a. abatir, humillar, envilecer.
abasement, *—mĕnt,* s. abatimiento, m.; humillación, f.; confusión, sonrojar.
abash, *ăbăsh',* v. a. avergonzar, causar
abashment, *—mĕnt,* s. confusión, vergüenza, f.; rubor, m., consternación, f.
abate, *ăbāt',* v. a. minorar, disminuir, rebajar; —, v. n. disminuirse.
abatement, *—mĕnt,* s. rebaja, diminución, f.
abature, *ăbā'tjŭr,* s. pista, huella, f.
abb, *ăb,* s. urdi(e)mbre, f.
abbacy, *ă'băsĕ,* s. abadía, f.
abbess, *ă'bĕs,* s. abadesa, f.
abb(e)y, *ă'bĕ,* s. abadía, f.
abbot, *ă'bŭt,* s. abad, m.; abadía, f.
abbotship, *—ship,* s. dignidad de abad, f.;
abbreviate, *ăbrē'vēāt,* v. a. abreviar, acortar, compendiar; ción, f.
abbreviation, *ăbrēvēā'shŭn,* s. abreviación.
abdicate, *ăb'dĭkāt,* v. a. abdicar, renunciar.
abdication, *ăbdĭkā'shŭn,* s. abdicación, renuncia, f.; vientre, m.
abdomen, *ăbdō'mĕn,* s. abdomen, bajo
abdominal, *ăbdŏ'mĭnăl,* a. abdominal.
abduct, *ăbdŭkt',* v. a. abducir; desviar, apartar, separar una cosa de otra.
abductor, *—ŭr,* s. músculo abductor, m.
abecedarian, *ăbēsēdā'rēăn,* s. maestro de primeras letras, m.
abed, *ăbĕd',* ad. en (la) cama.
aberrance (-cy), *ăbĕr'răns(ĕ),* **aberration,** *ăbĕrrā'shŭn,* s. error, desvío, m.; aberración, f.; viado.
aberrant, *—rănt,* p. & a. errante, extraviado.
abet, *ăbĕt',* v. a. favorecer, patrocinar, sostener; excitar, animar. ff.
abetment, *—mĕnt,* s. apoyo, m.; instigación,
abetter, abettor, *—tŭr,* s. fautor, m.; instigador, m.
abeyance, *ăbā'ăns,* s. (law) expectativa, f.
abhor, *ăbhŭr',* v. a. aborrecer, detestar.
abhorrence (-cy), *—ĕns(ĕ),* s. aborrecimiento, odio, m.

abhorrent, *—rĕnt,* a. horrorizado; contrario.
abide, *ăbīd',* v. n. habitar, morar; continuar; —, v. a. soportar, sufrir, defender, sostener.
abigail, *ă'bĭgăl,* s. camarera, f.; mujer muy parlanchina, f.
ability, *ăbĭl'ĭtĕ,* s. potencia, habilidad, capacidad, aptitud, f.; **abilities,** pl., talento, m.; bienes, medios, m. pl.
abintestate, *ăbĭntĕs'tăt,* a. ab intestato, sin testamento.
abject, *ăb'jĕkt,* a. vil, despreciable, bajo.
abjection, *ăbjĕk'shŭn,* **abjectness,** *ăb'jĕktnĕs,* s. bajeza, vileza, f. [mente.
abjectly, *ăb'jĕktlĭ,* ad. vilmente, baja
abjuration, *ăbjŭrā'shŭn,* s. abjuración, f.
abjure, *ăbjŭr',* v. a. abjurar; renunciar.
ablactate, *ăblăk'tăt,* v. a. destetar.
ablactation, *ăblăktā'shŭn,* s. destete, m.
ablation, *ăblā'shŭn,* s. ablación, extirpación, f.
ablative, *ăb'lătĭv,* s. (gr.) ablativo, m.
ablaze, *ăblāz',* a. en llamas.
able, *ā'bl,* a. fuerte, capaz, hábil; rico; **to be —,** poder. [rose.
able-bodied, *—bŏdĕd,* a. robusto, vigoroso.
ablegate, *ăb'lĕgāt,* v. a. enviar ó dar empleo á alguno en país extranjero; diputar.
ablegation, *ăblĕgā'shŭn,* s. misión, f.
ablocate, *ăb'lŏkāt,* v. a. dar en arriendo.
ablocation, *ăblŏkā'shŭn,* s. alquilamiento, arriendo, m.
ablution, *ăblū'shŭn,* s. ablución, f.
ably, *ā'blĕ,* ad. con habilidad.
abnegate, *ăb'nĕgāt,* v. a. negar, renunciar.
abnegation, *ăbnĕgā'shŭn,* s. abnegación, resignación, f.
abnormal, *ăbnŏr'măl,* a. irregular, deforme; fuera del modo acostumbrado.
abnormity, *ăbnŏr'mĭtĕ,* s. irregularidad, deformidad, f.
aboard, *ăbōrd',* ad. abordo; **to fall — of a ship,** abordar un navío. [f.
abode, *ăbōd',* s. domicilio, m., habitación,
abolish, *ăbŏl'ĭsh,* v. a. abolir, anular, destruir ó dar fin á alguna cosa; revocar.
abolishment, *—mĕnt,* **abolition,** *ăbŏlĭsh'ăn,* s. abolición, anulación, f.
abominable, *ăbŏm'ĭnăbl,* a. abominable, detestable; **-bly,** ad. abominablemente.
abominableness, *—nĕs,* s. calidad de lo que es abominable, f.; odiosidad, f.

abominate, *ăbŏm'mĕnăt,* v. a. abominar, detestar.   [nación, detestación, f.

abomination, *ăbŏmmĕnā'shăn,* s. abomi-

aboriginal, *ăbŏrĭj'ĭrăl,* a. lo que pertenece á los habitadores primitivos de algún país.

aborigines, *ăbŏrĭj'ĕnēz,* s. pl. aborigenes, primeros habitantes de un país, m. pl.

abort, *ăbŏrt',* v. n. abortar, malparir. [m.

abortion, *ăbŏr'shăn,* s. aborto, malparto.

abortive, *ăbŏr'tĭv,* a. abortivo; intempestivo; intempestivamente.

r̂bortment, *ăbŏrt'mĕnt,* s. aborto, m.

ăbound, *ăbŏŭnd',* v. n. abundar; **to —
with,** abundar de.

ăbout, *ăbŏŭt',* pr. cerca de, por ahí, hacia;
acerca, tocante á. **I carry no money
— me,** no traigo dinero; —, ad. en contorno,
aquí y allá; **to be — to,** estar para; **to
go —,** andar acá y acullá; **to go — a
thing,** emprender alguna cosa; **all —,** en
todo lugar.

ăbove, *ăbŭv',* pr. encima, sobre, superior,
más alto (en cuanto á situación, dignidad,
&c.); —, ad. arriba; **— all,** sobre todo, principalmente; **— mentioned,** ya mencio-
nado.

abrade, *ăbrād',* v. a. raer.   [lo

abrasion, *ăbrā'zhŭn,* s. raspadura, f.;
que se quita de la superficie raspando.

abreast, *ăbrĕst',* ad. de costado.

abridge, *ăbrĭj',* v. a. abreviar, compendiar; acortar.

abridgment, *—mĕnt,* s. compendio, m.

abroach, *ăbrōtsh',* ad. para derramarse;
to set —, barrenar.

abroad, *ăbrōd',* ad. fuera de casa ó del
país; en todas partes ó dirección; **to go —,**
salir; **to set —,** divulgar, publicar.

abrogate, *ăb'rŏgāt,* v. a. abrogar, anular.

abrogation, *ăbrŏgā'shăn,* s. abrogación,
anulación, f.

abrupt, *ăbrŭpt',* a. quebrado, desigual;
precipitado, repentino; bronco, rudo; **—ly,**
ad. precipitadamente; bruscamente.

abruption, *ăbrŭp'shăn,* s. separación re-
pentina y violenta, rotura, f.

abruptness, *ăbrŭpt'nĕs,* s. precipitación,
inconsideración, f.; descortesía, f.   [f.

abscess, *ăb'sĕs,* s. absceso, m., apostema.

abscind, *ăbsĭnd',* v. a. cortar, tajar,
trinchar.

abscission, *ăbsĭsh'ŭn,* s. cortadura, f.

abscond, *ăbskŏnd',* v. n. esconderse; huirse.

absconder, *—ăr,* s. la persona que se
esconde; desertor, m.

absence, *ăb'sĕns,* s. ausencia, f.; distracción, f.; negligencia, f.

absent, *ăb'sĕnt,* a. ausente; fuera de sí;
distraído; —, *ăbsĕnt',* v. a. ausentarse.

absentee, *ăbsĕntē',* s. el que está ausente
de su empleo &c.

absenter, *ăbsĕnt'ăr,* s. el que abandona
su obligación ú oficio.

absinth, *ăbsĭnth',* s. ajenjo, m.

absolute, *ăb'sŏlăt,* a. absoluto; catego-
rico; positivo; arbitrario; **—ly,** ad. absolutamente.

absoluteness, *—nĕs,* s. independencia, f.;
despotismo, poder absoluto, m.

absolution, *ăbsŏlū'shăn,* s. absolución, f.

absolutism, *ăb'sŏlătĭzm,* s. absolutismo,
m.

absolutist, *ăb'sŏlătĭst,* s. absolutista, m.

absolutory, *ăbsŏl'ŭtără,* a. absolutorio.

absolve, *ăbzŏlv',* v. a. absolver, dispensar, exentar.   [nante.

absonant, *ăb'sŏnănt,* a. absurdo; diso-

absorb, *ăbsŏrb',* v. a. absorber.   [cina).

absorbent, *—ĕnt,* a. & s. absorbente (medi-

absorption, *ăbsŏrp'shăn,* s. absorción, f.

abstain, *ăbstān',* v. n. abstenerse, privarse.

abstemious, *ăbstē'mĕŭs,* a. abstemio, sobrio, moderado; **—ly,** ad. moderadamente.

abstemiousness, *—nĕs,* s. sobriedad,
templanza, abstinencia, f.

abstention, *ăbstĕn'shăn,* s. detención, f.

absterge, *ăbstĕrj',* v. a. absterger, limpiar.

abstergent, *—ĕnt,* a. abstersivo, lo que
sirve para purificar, abstergente.

abstersion, *ăbstĕr'shăn,* s. abstersión,
purificación, f.   [templanza, f.

abstinence, *ăb'stĭnĕns,* s. abstinencia, f.;

abstinent, *ăb'stĭnĕnt,* a. abstinente, sobrio;
—ly, ad. abstinentemente.

abstract, *ăbstrăkt',* v. a. abstraer; compendiar; —, *ăb'străkt,* a. abstracto; —, s.
extracto, m.; sumario, m.; **in the —,** de
un modo abstracto.

abstracted, *ăbstrăkt'ĕd,* a. separado; abstraído; **—ly,** ad. abstractamente.

abstracter, *ăbstrăkt'ăr,* s. compendiador,
extractor, m.

abstraction, *ăbstrăk'shăn,* s. abstracción,
f.; distracción, f.; destilación, f.

abstractive, *ăbstrăkt'ĭv,* a. abstractivo.

abstractly, *—lĕ,* ad. en abstracto.

abstruse, *ăbstrōs',* a. abstruso, recondito,
obscuro; **—ly,** ad. obscuramente.

abstruseness, *—nĕs,* s. obscuridad, dificultad, f.; misterio, m.

absurd, *ăbsŭrd',* a. absurdo, repugnante
á la razón; **—ly,** ad. absurdamente.

absurdity, *—ĭtĕ,* s. absurdidad, f.

abundance, *ăbŭn'dăns,* s. abundancia,
copia, f.

abundant, *—dănt,* a. abundante; **—ly,** ad.
abundantemente, en copia.

abuse, *ăbūz',* v. a. abusar; engañar; ultrajar, violar; —, *ăbūs',* s. abuso, engaño,
m.; corruptela, seducción, f.; injuria,
afrenta, f.

abusive, *ăbū'sĭv,* a. abusivo, injurioso;
—ly, ad. abusivamente.

abusiveness, *—nĕs,* s. palabras injuriosas,
f. pl.; propensión á injuriar á otro, f.

abut, *ăbŭt',* v. n. terminar, confinar.

abutment, *—mĕnt,* s. confín, límite, m.

abuttals, *—tălz,* s. pl. confines, m. pl.

abysmal, *ăbĭs'măl,* a. abismal, insondable.

abyss, *ăbĭs',* s. abismo, m.; golfo, m.; in-
acacia, *ăkā'shĕă,* s. acacia, f.   [fierno, m.

academic(al), *ăkădĕm'ĭk(ăl),* a. académico.

academician, *ăkădĕmĭsh'ăn,* s. academist,
ăkā'dĕmĭst, s académico, el individuo
de alguna academia, m.   [universidad, f.

academy, *ăkād'dĕmĕ,* s. academia, f.;

accede, *ăksēd',* v. n. acceder, convenir en
alguna cosa, asentir.

accedence, ăk'sēdēns, s. asenso, m.
accelerate, ăksĕl'lūrāt, v. a. acelerar.
acceleration, ăksĕllŭrā'shŭn, s. aceleración, priesa, f., apremio, m.
accelerative, ăksĕl'lŭrātiv, accelera-tory, ăksĕl'lŭrātŭrĕ, a. acelerativo.
accent, ăk'sĕnt, s. acento, m., modulación, f., tono. m.; (poet.) lenguaje, m.; —, ăk-sĕnt', v. a. acentuar, colocar los acentos; (poet.) articular.
accentuate, ăksĕn'tjūāt, v. a. acentuar.
accentuation, ăksĕntjūā'shŭn, s. acen-tuación, f. [recibir cariñosamente.
accept, ăksĕpt', v. a. aceptar;. admitir;
acceptable, —ăbl, a. aceptable, grato, digno de aceptación.
acceptableness, —nĕs, acceptability, ăksĕptăbil'itĕ, s. aceptabilidad, f.
acceptably, —ĕ, ad. gustosamente, grata-mente.
acceptance, —tăns, acceptation, ăksĕp-tā'shŭn, s. aceptación, recepción, f.; re-cibimiento, m.; acepción, f.
acception, —shŭn, s. sentido ó significado en que se toma alguna cosa, m.
access, ăksĕs', s. acceso, m.; entrada, f.; aumento, acceso periódico (de alguna en-fermedad), m. [mente.
accessarily, ăk'sĕssărĕlĕ, ad. accessoria-
accessariness, ăk'sĕssărĕnĕs, s. complici-dad, f.; participación, f.
accessary, ăk'sĕssărĕ, s. cómplice, m.; —, a. accesorio; eventual, casual.
accessible, ăksĕs'sibl, a. accesible.
accession, ăksĕsh'ŭn, s. aumento, acre-centamiento, m.; advenimiento, m.; ac-ceso, m.
accessory, ăk'sĕssŏrĕ, a. accesorio; confe-derado. [tos de la gramática, m.
accidence, ăk'sĕdĕns, s. libro de rudimen-
accident, ăk'sĕdĕnt, s. accidente, m., casualidad, f.; suceso imprevisto, lance (funesto), m.
accidental, ăksĕdĕn'tăl, a. casual, contin-gente; —ly, ad. accidentalmente.
acclaim, ăkklām', v. a. aclamar, aplaudir.
acclamation, ăkklămā'shŭn, s. aclama-ción, f.; aplauso, m.
acclimatise, ăkklī'mătīz, v. a. aclimatar.
acclivity, ăkkliv'itĕ, s. cuesta, rampa, subida, ladera, f. [declive.
acclivous, ăkklī'vŭs, a. lo que sube en
accommodable, ăkkŏm'mŏdăbl, a. acomo-dable, acomodadizo.
accommodate, —mŏdāt, v. a. acomo-dar, ajustar; —, v. n. conformarse; —, a. acomodado; apto; —ly, ad. cómodamente, convenientemente. [vicial.
accommodating, ăkkŏm'mŏdāting, a. ser-
accommodation, —dā'shŭn, s. comodidad, conveniencia, adaptación, f.; ajuste, m.; conciliación, f. [forma, f.
accommodation-bill, —bĭl, s. letra pro
accompaniment, ăkkŭm'pănĕmĕnt, s. (mus.) acompañamiento, m.
accompanist, —pănĭst, s. (mus.) acom-pañador, acompañante, m.
accompany, —pănĕ, v. a. acompañar.
accomplice, ăkkŏm'plĭs, s. cómplice, m.

accomplish, ăkkŏm'plĭsh, v. a. efectuar, completar; cumplir; adornar.
accomplished, —d, a. perfecto, completo, elegante, consumado.
accomplishment, —mĕnt, s. cumplimiento entero de alguna cosa, m.; perfección, f.; —s, pl. talentos, conocimientos, m. pl.
accord, ăkkŏrd', s. acuerdo, convenio, m.; armonía, f.; simetría, f.; with one —, uná-nimemente; of one's own —, espontánea-mente; —, v. a. ajustar; —, v. n. acordar; convenir una cosa con otra.
accordance, —ăns, s. conformidad, f.; acuerdo, m. [veniente.
accordant, —ănt, a. acorde, conforme, con-
according, —ĭng, pr. según, conforme; — as, según que, como; —ly, ad. en confor-midad, de consiguiente, en efecto. [m.
accordion, ăkkŏr'dĭŏn, s. acordeón,
accost, ăkkŏst', v. a. saludar á uno yendo hacia él; trabar conversación. [tero, m.
accoucheur, ăkkōōshūr', s. comadrón, par-
account, ăkkŏŭnt', s. cuenta, f., cálculo, m.; caso, m.; estimación, f.; aprecio, m.; narrativa de alguna cosa, f.; motivo, m.; on no —, de ninguna manera; por ningún título; on — of, por motivo de; to call to —, pedir cuenta; to turn to —, hacer provechoso; —, v. a. tener, reputar; con-tar, computar. [ponsabilidad, f.
accountability, ăkkŏŭntăbil'itĕ, s. res-
accountable, —ăbl, a. responsable.
accountant, —ănt, s. contador, m.; arit-mético, m. [m.
account-book, —bŭk, s. libro de cuentas.
accoutre, ăkkōō'tŭr, v. a. equipar, vestir.
accoutrement, —mĕnt, s. atavío, apresto, m.; vestidura, f.; ornamento, m. [cinar.
accredit, ăkkrĕd'it, v. a. acreditar, patro-
accrue, ăkkrōō', v. n. resultar, provenir.
accumulate, ăkkū'mŭlāt, v. a. acumular; amontonar; —, v. n. crecer.
accumulation, ăkkūmŭlā'shŭn, s. acumu-lación, f.; amontonamiento, m. [tivo.
accumulative, ăkkū'mŭlātiv, a. acumula-
accuracy, ăk'kŭrăsĕ, s. exactitud, diligen-cia, f., esmero, m.
accurate, ăk'kŭrăt, a. exacto, puntual; —ly, ad. exactamente.
accurateness, —nĕs, s. exactitud, puntua-lidad, precisión, f.
accursed, ăkkŭrsd', a. maldito, malde-cido; execrable; excomulgado; fatal; — be I; mal haya!
accusation, ăkkūză'shŭn, s. acusación, f.
accusative, ăkkū'zătiv, s. (gr.) acusativo.
accusatory, —zătŏrĕ, a. acusatorio. [m.
accuse, ăkkūz', v. a. acusar; culpar.
accuser, —ăr, s. acusador, m.; denuncia-dor, m. [usar.
accustom, ăkkŭs'tŭm, v. a. acostumbrar,
accustomarily, —ărĕlĕ, ad. de costumbre, comúnmente, ordinariamente.
accustomary, —ărĕ, a. acostumbrado, usual, ordinario. [brado, habitual.
accustomed, ăkkŭs'tŭmd, a. acostum-
ace, ăs, s. as; atomo, m.; migaja, partí-cula, f.; within an — of, casi, casi; pos poco no . . .

4

acerbity, *ăsĕr′bĭtĕ,* s. amargura, severidad, aspereza, dureza, acerbidad, f.

acetate, *ă′sĕtăt,* s. (chem.) acetato, m.

acetous, *ăsĕ′tŭs,* a. acetoso. [doler.

ache, *ăk,* s. dolor continuo, mal, m.; —, v. n.

achieve, *ătshĕv′,* v. a. ejecutar, perfeccionar; ganar, obtener, acabar.

achievement, *—mĕnt,* s. ejecución, f.; acción heroica, f.; hazaña, f.

achiever, *—ăr,* s. hacedor, el que ejecuta, gana ó consigue. [f.

aching, *ă′kĭng,* s. dolor, m.; incomodidad, f.

achromatic, *ăkrŏmăt′ĭk,* a. (opt.) acromático.

acid, *ăs′ĭd,* a. ácido, agrio, acedo.

acidify, *ăssĭd′ĭfĭ,* v. a. (chem.) acidificar.

acidity, *—ĭtĕ,* s. agrura, acedia, acidez, acritud, f.

acidulae, *—ĭd,* s. pl. acídulas, f. pl.

acidulate, *—ădĭt,* v. a. acidular; —d **drops,** pl. bombones de limón, m. pl.

acknowledge, *ăknŏl′lĕj,* v. a. reconocer, confesar. [decido.

acknowledging, *—ĭng,* a. reconocido, agradecido.

acknowledgment, *—mĕnt,* s. reconocimiento, m.; gratitud, f.; concesión, f.

acme, *ăk′mĕ,* s. crisis, f.; cima, f.; cenit, apogeo, m.

acolyte, *ăk′ŏlĭt,* s. acólito, m.

aconite, *ăk′ŏnĭt,* s. (bot.) acónito, m.

acorn, *ă′kŏrn,* s. bellota, f.

acoustics, *ăkŏŭs′tĭks,* s. acústica, f.

acquaint, *ăkkwănt′,* v. a. informar, advertir, avisar.

acquaintance, *—ăns,* s. conocimiento, f.; familiaridad, f.; conocido, m.

acquiesce, *ăkkwĭĕs′,* v. n. someterse, consentir, asentir. [niento, m.

acquiescence, *—sĕns,* s. asenso, consentimiento.

acquiescent, *—sĕnt,* a. deferente.

acquirable, *ăkkwī′răbl,* a. adquirible, asequible.

acquire, *ăkkwīr′,* v. a. adquirir, ganar, aprender. [adquirida, f.

acquirement, *—mĕnt,* s. adquisición, cosa adquirida, f.

acquisition, *ăkkwĭzĭsh′ŭn,* s. adquisición, obtención, f. [absolver.

acquit, *ăkkwĭt′,* v. a. libertar, descargar, acquittal.

acquittal, *—mĕnt,* acquittal, —tăl, s. absolución, f.; pago, pagamento, descargo, m. [cibo, finiquito, descargo, m.

acquittance, *—tăns,* s. carta de pago, f., recibo.

acre, *ă′kĕr,* s. acre, m. (medida de tierra en Inglaterra que tiene 4840 varas cuadradas.)

acrid, *ă′krĭd,* a. acre, mordaz. [das).

acridity, *ăkrĭd′ĭtĕ,* s. acidez, f. [sivo.

acrimonious, *ăkrĭmŏ′nĕŭs,* a. acre; corrosivo.

acrimony, *ăk′krĭmŏnĕ,* **acrity,** *ă′krĭtĕ,* s. acrimonia, acritud, f.

across, *ăkrŏs′,* ad. de través, de una parte á otra; **to come —,** sobrevenir algún impedimento ú obstáculo.

acrostic, *ăkrŏs′tĭk,* s. poema acróstico, m.

act, *ăkt,* v. a. representar; obrar; —, v. n. hacer; —, s. acto, hecho, m.; acción, f.; efecto, m.; jornada (de una comedia), f.; —s, pl. actas, f. pl.; —s **of the apostles,** Actos, m. pl. [f.

acting, *—ĭng,* s. acción, f.; representación,

action, *ăk′shŭn,* s. acción, operación, f.; batalla, f.; gesticulación, f.; proceso, m.; —s, pl. fondos públicos, m. pl.

actionable, *—ăbl,* a. acusable; punible.

actionary, *—ărĕ,* s. accionista, m.

action-taking, *—tăkĭng,* a. litigioso, contencioso.

active, *ăk′tĭv,* a. activo; eficaz, ocupado; ágil; —ly, ad. activamente, ágilmente, eficazmente.

activeness, *—nĕs,* **activity,** *ăktĭv′ĭtĕ,* s. agilidad, actividad, f.; prontitud, f.; vivacidad, f. [(en los teatros) m.

actor, *ăk′tăr,* s. agente, m.; cómico, actor

actress, *ăk′trĕs,* s. comedianta, actriz, f.

actual, *ăk′tjŭăl,* a. actual; cierto, real; efectivo; —ly, ad. en efecto, realmente.

actuality, *ăktjŭăl′ĭtĕ,* s. actualidad, f.

actuary, *ăk′tjŭărĕ,* s. secretario, m.; registrador, m. [facción.

actuate, *ăk′tjŭăt,* v. a. excitar; poner en

aculeate, *ăkŭ′lĕăt,* a. punzante, puntiagudo, agudo.

acumen, *ăkŭ′mĕn,* s. punta aguzada, f.; agudeza, perspicacia, penetración, f.

acuminate, *ăkŭ′mĕnăt,* v. a. aguzar, afilar; —, v. n. terminar en punta.

acute, *ăkŭt′,* a. agudo; ingenioso; — accent, s. acento agudo, m.; —angle, s. ángulo agudo, m.; —ly, ad. con agudeza.

acuteness, *—nĕs,* s. agudeza, f.; perspicacia, sagacidad, f.

adage, *ă′dăj,* s. proverbio, m. [titud, f.

adagio, *ădă′jĕō,* (mus.) s. adagio, m.; lentitud.

adamant, *ă′dămănt,* s. diamante, m.

adamantine, *ădămăn′tĭn,* a. diamantino (poet.) impenetrable.

adapt, *ădăpt′,* v. a. adaptar, acomodar una cosa á otra; ajustar.

adaptability, *ădăptăbĭl′ĭtĕ,* s. facilidad de adaptarse, f.

adaptable, *ădăpt′ăbl,* a. adaptable.

adaptation, *ădăptă′shŭn,* adaptación, f.

add, *ăd,* v. a. aumentar; juntar; **to — up,** sumar.

addendum, *ădden′dŭm,* s. suplemento, m.

adder, *ăd′dăr,* s. culebra, f.; víbora, f.

addible, *ăd′dĕbl,* a. aumentable; sumable.

addict, *ăddĭkt′,* v. a. dedicar; **to — one's self,** entregarse á.

addictedness, *—ĕdnĕs,* **addiction,** *ăddĭk′shŭn,* s. inclinación, propensión, dedicación, f.; devoción, afición, f.; obsequio, m.

addition, *ăddĭsh′ăn,* s. adición, f. [m.

additional, *—ăl,* a. adicional; —ly, ad. en ó por adición.

addle, *ăd′dl,* a. vacío, vano, infecundo, estéril; —, v. a. hacer estéril.

addle-headed, *—hĕdĕd,* -pated, -pă′tĕd, a. totalmente inepto para alguna cosa.

address, *ăddrĕs′,* v. a. hablar, interceder ó rogar; dirigir; —, s. petición, f.; memorial, m.; dedicatoria, f.; destreza, f.

adduce, *ăddŭs′,* v. a. alegar, aducir. [f.

ademption, *ădĕm′shŭn,* s. (law) privación.

adept, *ădĕpt′,* s. adepto, sabio, m.; alquimista, m.; —, a. adepto.

adequacy, *ă′dĕkwăsĕ,* s. suficiencia, f.; proporcionalidad, f.

adequate, *ắ'dĕkwắt*, a. adecuado, proporcionado; suficiente; –ly, ad. adecuadamente. [ción exacta, f.

adequateness,–*nĕs*,s.adecuación, propor

adhere, *ădhēr'*, v. n. adherir; aficionarse.

adherence, –*ēns*, s. viscosidad, f.; adherencia, f.

adherent, –*ĕnt*, a. pegajoso; tenaz; adherente; –, s. adherente, partidario, m.

adhesion, *ădhē'shắn*, s. adhesión, f.

adhesive, –*sīv*, a. pegajoso, tenaz.

adhesiveness, –*nĕs*, s. adhesividad, f.

adieu, *ădū'*, ad. á Dios; –, s. despedida, f.

adipose, *ăd'ēpōs*, a. adiposo.

adit, *ắ'dĭt*, s. conducto subterráneo, m.; entrada de una mina, f.

adjacency, *ădjā'sĕnsĕ*, adjacence, –*sĕns*, s. contigüidad, vecindad, f. [tiguo.

adjacent, *ădjā'sĕnt*, a. adyacente, con

adjectival, *ădjĕk'tĭvặl*, a. adjetivado; –ly, ad. adjetivamente.

adjective, *ăd'jĕktĭv*, s. adjetivo, m.; –ly, ad. como adjetivo. [estar contiguo.

adjoin, *ădjŏin'*, v. a. juntar; unir; –, v. n.

adjourn, *ădjŭrn'* v. a. diferir, remitir.

adjournment, –*mĕnt*, s. prorroga, f.

adjudge, *ădjŭdj'*, adjudicate, *ădjū'dĭkắt*, v. a. adjudicar; condenar; decretar.

adjunct, *ăd'jŭnkt*, s. adjunto, m.

adjuration, *ădjūrā'shắn*, s. conjuro, m.; juramento, m.

adjure, *ădjūr'*, v. a. juramentar; conjurar.

adjust, *ădjŭst'*, v. a. ajustar, acomodar.

adjuster, –*ŭr*, s. aforador, m.; mediador, m.

adjustment, –*mĕnt*, s. ajustamiento, arreglo, m. [f.

adjutancy, *ăd'jŭtănsĕ*, s. (mil.) ayudantía.

adjutant, *ăd'jŭtănt*, s. (mil.) ayudante, ayudante, m.

adjute, *ădjūt'*, v. a. ayudar. [m.

admeasurement, *ădmĕzh'ŭrmĕnt*, s. reparto judicial, m.

administer, *ădmĭn'ĭstŭr*, v. a. administrar; gobernar; contribuir; to — an oath, prestar juramento.

administration, *ădmĭnĭstrā'shắn*, s. administración, f.; gobierno, m.

administrative, *ădmĭn'ĭstrātĭv*, a. administrativo. [nistrador, m.

administrator, *ădmĭnĭstrā'tŭr*, s. admi

admirability, *ădmĕrăbĭl'tĭ*, s. excelencia de alguna cosa, f.

admirable, –*bl*, a. admirable; –bly, ad. admirablemente, á maravilla.

admiral, *ăd'mĕrắl*, s. almirante, m.; almiranta (nave), f.

admiralship, –*shĭp*, s. almirantía, f.

admiralty, –*tĭ*, s. almirantazgo, m.

admiration, *ădmĕrā'shắn*, s. admiración, f.; maravilla, f.

admire, *ădmīr'*, v. a. admirar; amar; –, v. n. admirarse de alguna cosa. [m.

admirer, –*ŭr*, s. admirador, m.; amante,

admiringly, *ădmī'rĭnglĕ*, ad. con admiración.

admissible, *ădmĭs'sĕbl*, a. admisible.

admission, *ădmĭsh'ŭn*, s. admisión, recepción, entrada, f.

admit, *ădmĭt'*, v. a. admitir. dar entrada; recibir, conceder, permitir.

admittance, –*tắns*, s. entrada, admisión, f.

admittedly, –*tĕdlĕ*, a. permisivamente.

admixture, *ădmĭks'tjŭr*, s. mistura, mezcla, f. [reprender.

admonish, *ădmŏn'nĭsh*, v. a. amonestar,

admonishment, –*mĕnt*, admonition, *ădmŏnĭsh'ŭn*, s. amonestación, f.; consejo, aviso, m. [nesta, exhortatorio.

admonitory, *ădmŏn'nĭtŭrĕ*, a. lo que amo

adolescence (–cy), *ădŏlĕs'sĕns(ĕ)*, s. adolescencia, f. [m.; fatiga, f.

adolescent, –*nĕs*, s. excelencia, f.

adorably, –*ĕ*, ad. de un modo adorable.

adoration, *ădŏrā'shắn*, s. adoración, f.

adore, *ădōr'*, v. a. adorar. [nos, adornar.

adorn, *ădŏrn'*, v. a. hermosear con ador

adornment, –*mĕnt*, s. adorno, atavio, m.

adrift, *ădrĭft'*, ad. flotando, á merced de las olas; á la ventura.

adroit, *ădrŏit'*, a. diestro, hábil, mañoso.

adroitness, –*nĕs*, s. destreza, f.

adulation, *ădūlā'shắn*, s. adulación, lisonja, zalamería, f.

adulatory, *ắ'dūlătŭrĕ*, a. lisonjero.

adult, *ădŭlt'*, a. adulto; –, s. adulto, m.; adulta, f.

adulterate, –*ărăt*, v. a. adulterar, corromper, falcificar; –, a. adulterado, falsificado. [corrupción, f.

adulteration, –*ārā'shắn*, s. adulteración.

adulterer, –*ărŭr*, s. adultero, m.

adulteress, –*ărĕs*, s. adultera, f.

adulterine, –*ărīn*, adulterous, –*ărăs*, a. adulterino; espurio.

adultery, –*ărĕ*, s. adulterio, m.

advance, *ădvắns'*, v. a. avanzar; promover; pagar adelantado; –, v. n. hacer progreso; –, s. avance, m.; paga adelantada, f.

advancement, –*mĕnt*, s. adelantamiento, m.; progreso, m.; promoción, f.

advantage, *ădvắn'tắj*, s. ventaja, superioridad, f.; provecho, m.; lucro, m.; ocasión favorable, f.; to take — of, sacar provecho de; –, v. a. ganar; remunerar; promover. [ventajoso.

advantage-ground, –*grŏŭnd*, s. puesto

advantageous, *ădvăntắ'jŭs*, a. ventajoso, útil; –ly, ad. ventajosamente.

advantageousness, –*nĕs*, s.ventaja,utilidad, f. [Adviento, m.

advent, *ăd'vĕnt*, s. venjda, f.; Advent, s.

adventitious, *ădvĕntĭsh'ŭs*, a. adventicio.

adventure, *ădvĕn'tjŭr*, s. aventura, casualidad, f.; riesgo, m.; at all –s, al acaso; –, v. n. osar, emprender; –, v. a. aventurar.

adventurer, –*ŭr*, s. aventurero, m.

adventuresome, –*sŭm*, adventurous, *ădvĕn'tjŭrŭs*, a. intrépido; atrevido; valeroso; –ly, ad. arriesgadamente.

adventuress, –*ĕs*, s. aventurera, f.

adverb, *ăd'vĕrb*, s. adverbio, m.

adverbial, *ădvĕr'bĕl*, a. adverbial; –ly, ad. adverbialmente. [migo, m.

adversary, *ăd'vĕrsắrĕ*, a. adversario, ene

alga, *ál'gă*, s. alga (planta que se cría en el mar), f.
algebra, *ál'jĕbră*, s. álgebra, f.
algebraic(al), *áljĕbrá'ĭk(ăl)*, a. algebraico.
algebraist, —*ĭst*, s. algebrista, m.
alias, *ā'lĭăs*, ad. de otra manera.
alibi, *ál'ĭbĕ*, s. (law) coartada, f.
alien, *āl'yĕn*, a. & s. extraño; forastero(m.).
alienable, —*ăbl*, a. enajenable.
alienate, —*āt*, v. a. enajenar.
alienation, *ălyĕnā'shăn*, s. enajenación, f.; — of mind, devaneo, m.
alight, *ălīt'*, v. n. descender; apearse; —, a. encendido; ardiente, lo que arde.
alike, *ălīk'*, a. semejante, igual; —, ad. igualmente.
aliment, *ál'ĭmĕnt*, s. alimento, m.
alimental, *ălĭmĕn'tăl*, alimentary,—*tărĕ*, a. alimentoso, nutritivo.
alimentation, *ălĭmĕntā'shăn*, s. alimentación, f.
alimony, *ál'ĭmănĕ*, s. alimentos, m. pl.
aliquot part, *ál'ĭkwŏt pärt*, s. parte alícuota, f.
alive, *ălīv'*, a. vivo, viviente; activo.
alkali, *ál'kălĕ*, s. álcali, m.
alkaline, *ál'kălĕn*, a. alcalino.
all, *ăl*, a. todo; —, ad. enteramente; ~ at once, — of a sudden, de repente; — the same, absolutamente lo mismo; — the better, tanto mejor; not at —, no por cierto; once for —, una vez por todas, una buena y enmendarse; una que valga mil; —, s. todo, m.
allay, *ălā'*, v. a. aliviar, apaciguar.
allayment, —*mĕnt*, s. alivio, desahogo,m.; aligación, f.; disculpa, f.; cita,f.
allegation, *ălĕgā'shăn*, s. alegación, f.
allege, *ălĕj'*, v. a. alegar; declarar.
allegiance, *ălĕ'jăns*, s. lealtad, fidelidad, f.
allegorical, *ălĕgó'rĭkăl*, a. alegórico; —ly, ad. alegóricamente.
allegorise, *ál'lĕgŏrīz*, v. a. alegorizar.
allegory, *ál'lĕgŏrĕ*, s. alegoría, f.
allegro, *ălĕ'grŏ*, s. (mus.) alegro, m.
alleviate, *ălĕ'vĕāt*, v. a. aliviar, aligerar.
alleviation, *ălĕvĕā'shăn*, s. alivio, m.; mitigación, f.
alley, *ál'lĕ*, s. paseo de árboles, m.; calle-juela, f.
all-hallowmas, *ălhál'lŏmăs*, all-hallow-tide, —*tīd*, s. tiempo cercano al día de todos los santos, m.
alliance, *ăllī'ăns*, s. alianza,f.; parentela, f.
allied, *ălīd'*, a. aliado, confederado.
alligate, *ál'lĕgāt*, v. a. ligar, afianzar una cosa á otra.
alligation, *ăllĕgā'shăn*, s. regla de aleación, f.
alligator, —*ăr*, s. aligador, m.
allitteration, *ăllĭtĕrā'shăn*, s. alliteración.
allocation, *ăllŏkā'shăn*, s. añadidura, f.
allocution, *ăllŏkū'shăn*, s. alocución, f.
allodium, *ăllŏ'dĕăm*, s. alodio, m.
allopathy, *ăl'lŏpăthĕ*, s. alopatía, f.
allot, *ăllŏt'*, v. a. distribuir por suerte; asignar.
allotment, —*mĕnt*, s. asignación,f.; repartimiento, m.
allow, *ăllŏu'*, v. a. conceder, aprobar; permitir; dar, pagar.
allowable, —*ăbl*, a. admisible, permitido.
allowance, —*ăns*, s. concesión, f.; licencia, f.; (mar.) ración, f., alimentos, m. pl.

alloy, *ăllŏy'*, v. a. ligar, mezclar un metal con otro; quilatar oro; —, s. liga, mezcla,f.; quilate, m. [f. pl. (pimienta, clavos &c.).
allspice, *ál'spīs*, s. especerías, especias,
allude, *ăllūd'*, v. a. aludir.
allure, *ăllūr'*, v. a. alucinar, cebar.
alluring, —*rĭng*, s. poder de halagar, m.; —ly, ad. seductoramente.
alluringness, —*nĕs*, allurement, *ăllūr'mĕnt*, s. halago, cebo, aliciente, atractivo,
allusion, *ăllū'zhăn*, s. alusión, f. [m.
allusive, —*sĭv*, a. alusivo; —ly, ad. de un modo alusivo.
alluvial, —*vĭăl*, a. aluvial.
alluvion, —*vĕăn*, s. aluvión, f.; terreno, m.
ally, *ăllī'*, s. aliado, m.; pariente, m. (& f.); —, v. a. hacer alianza.
alwise, *ál'wĭs*, a. omniscio.
almanac, *ál'mănăk*, s. almanaque, m. [f.
almightiness, *ălmī'tĭnĕs*, s. omnipotencia, f.
almighty, —*tĕ*, a. omnipotente, todopoderoso. [agallas de la garganta, f. pl.
almond, *ä'mănd*, s. almendra, f.; —s, pl.
almond-milk, —*mĭlk*, s. almendrada, f.
almond-tree, —*trĕ*, s. almendro, m.
almoner, *ál'mănăr*, s. limosnero, m.
almonry, —*rĕ*, s. hospicio para pobres,m.
almost, *ál'mŏst*, ad. casi, cerca de.
alms, *ämz*, s. limosna, f.
alms-house, —*hŏus*, s. hospicio para pobres, m.
alms-people, —*pĕpl*, s. hospicianos, m.pl.
alnage, *ál'nŏj*, s. medición por anas, f.
aloe, *á'lŏ*, s. áloe, lináloe, m.
aloft, *ălŏft'*, pr. arriba, sobre.
alone, *ălŏn'*, a. solo; —, ad. solamente, sólo; to let —, dejar en paz.
along, *ălŏng'*, ad. á lo largo; adelante; junto con; (mar.) al costado; —side, al lado.
aloof, *ălŏof'*, ad. lejos, de lejos, á lo largo.
aloud, *ălŏud'*, a. con voz fuerte, recio.
alphabet, *ál'făbĕt*, s. alfabeto, m.
alphabetical, *ălfăbĕt'ĭkăl*, a. alfabético; —ly, ad. alfabéticamente.
alpine, *ál'pĭn*, a. alpino. [antes de ahora.
already, *álrĕ'dĕ*, ad. ya, á la hora de esta.
also, *ál'sŏ*, ad. también, igualmente, además.
altar, *ál'tăr*, s. altar, m.
altar-piece, —*pĕs*, s. retablo, m.
alter, *ál'tăr*, v. a. alterar, mudar.
alterable, —*ăbl*, a. alterable, mudable; —bly,ad. de una manera mudable.
alteration, *áltără'shăn*, s. alteración, f.
alterative, *ál'tărătĭv*, a. alterativo. [f.
altercate, *ál'tărkāt*, v. n. trabarse de palabras.
altercation, *áltărkā'shăn*, s. altercación, f.
alternate, *áltĕr'năt*, a. alternativo, recíproco; —, v. a. alternar, variar; —ly, ad. alternativamente. [f.
alternation, *áltĕrnā'shăn*, s. alternación, f.
alternative, *áltĕr'nătĭv*, s. alternativa, f.; —, a. alternativo; —ly, ad. alternativamente. [obstante, bien que.
although, altho', *ál'thŏ'*, c. aunque, no
altitude, *ál'tĕtūd*, s. altitud, altura, f.
altogether, *áltŏgĕth'ăr*, ad. del todo.

agency, *d'jĕnsĕ,* s. agencia, f.
agent, *d'jĕnt,* a. operativo; —, s. agente; asistente, m. [merar; —, v. n. ovillarse.
agglomerate, *ăgglŏm'mĕrăt,* v. a. aglomerar.
agglomeration, *ăgglŏmmĕrd'shăn,* s. aglomeración, f.
agglutinate, *ăgglū'tĕnăt,* v.a. conglutinar, unir. [elevar.
aggrandize, *ăg'grăndlz,* v.a. engrandecer;
aggrandizement, *—mĕnt,* s. engrandecimiento, m. [agerar.
aggravate, *ăg'grăvăt,* v. a. agravar; exaggerar.
aggravation, *ăggrăvā'shăn,* s. agravación, f. [unión, f.; —, v. a. agregar; reunir.
aggregate, *ăg'grĕyăt,* s. agregado, m.;
aggregation, *ăggrĕgā'shăn,* s. agregación, f.
aggress, *ăggrĕs',* v. n. acometer. [ción, f.
aggress, —, **aggression,** *—shăn,* s. agresión, ofensa, f.; asalto, m.
aggressive, *—sĭv,* a. ofensivo.
aggressor, *—săr,* s. agresor, m.
aggrieve, *ăggrēv',* v. a. injuriar, gravar, dañar; apesadumbrar; —, v. n. lamentar.
aggroup, *ăggrōp',* v. a. agrupar.
aghast, *ăgăst',* a. horrorizado.
agile, *ă'jĭl,* a. ágil, vivo; diestro.
agility, *ăjĭl'tĕ,* s. agilidad, f.; destreza, f.
agitate, *ă'jĕtăt,* v. a. agitar; discutir.
agitation, *ăjĕtā'shăn,* s. agitación, f.; perturbación, f.
agitator, *—tăr,* s. agitador, incitador, m.
agnail, *ăg'năl,* s. uñero, panadizo, m.
agnate, *ăg'năt,* s. agnado, m.; agnada, f.
agnation, *ăgnā'shăn,* s. agnación, f.
ago, *ăgō',* ad. pasado, largo tiempo; después; **how long—?** ¿cuánto ha? [desear.
agog, *ăgŏg',* ad. con deseo; **to set—,** hacer
agoing, *ăgō'ĭng,* ad. en acción, en movimiento; dispuesto á.
agonising, *ăgŏnīs'ĭng,* a. agonizando.
agony, *ă'gŏnĕ,* s. agonía, f.; angustia extrema, f.
agrarian, *ăgrā'rĕăn,* a. agrario.
agree, *ăgrē',* v. n. concordar, convenir.
agreeable, *—ăbl,* a. conveniente, agradable; amable; **—bly,** ad. agradablemente; **—with,** según, conforme á.
agreeableness, *—ăblnĕs,* s. conformidad, f.; amabilidad, gracia, f.
agreed, *ăgrēd',* a. establecido, convenido; **—! ad.** ¡de acuerdo! [formidad, unión, f.
agreement, *—mĕnt,* s. concordia, f.; conformidad, unión, f.
agricultural, *ăgrĭkŭl'tūrăl,* a. agrario.
agriculture, *—tjŭr,* s. agricultura, f.
agriculturist, *—ĭst,* s. agricultor, m. [f.
agrimony, *ă'grĭmŭnĕ,* s. (bot.) agrimonia,
aground, *ăgrŏnd',* ad. (mar.) barado, encallado. [tente, f.
ague, *ă'gū,* s. fiebre, calentura interminitente, f.
aguish, *ă'gŭĭsh,* a. febril.
ah! ¡ah! ¡ay!
ahead, *ăhĕd',* ad. más allá, delante de otro; (mar.) por la proa.
ahoy! *ăhŏğ',* (mar.) ¡ohé! ¡ahupa!
ahull, *ăhŭl',* ad. (mar.) á palo seco.
aid, *ăd,* v. a. ayudar, socorrer; —, s. ayuda, f.; auxilio, socorro, m.
aide-de-camp, *—dĕkăn(g),* s. (mil.) ayudante de campo, m.

aider, *—ăr,* s. auxiliador, m.; **—and abetter,** (law) cómplice, m.
ail, *āl,* v. a. afligir, molestar; **what—s you?** ¿qué le duele á U.?
ailing, *—ĭng,* a. doliente, valetudinario.
ailment, *—mĕnt,* s. dolencia, indisposición, f.
aim, *ăm,* v. a. apuntar, dirigir el tiro con el ojo; aspirar á; intentar; —, s. desiguio, m.; mira, f.; puntería, f.; blanco, m.
aimless, *—lĕs,* a. sin desigulo, sin objeto.
ain't, *ănt,* ad. no es, no hay.
air, *ăr,* s. aire, m.; aire de música; semblante, m.; —, v. a. airear; secar; ventilar.
air-balloon, *—băllōn,* s. globo aerostático, m. [nado de aire, m.
air-cushion, *—kŭshŭn,* s. cojinete relleno de aire, m.
air-gun, *—găn,* s. escopeta de viento, f.
air-hole, *—hŏl,* s. respiradero, m.
airiness, *—ĕnĕs,* s. ventilación, f.
airing, *—ĭng,* s. caminata, f. [cado.
airless, *—lĕs,* a. falto de ventilación, sofocado.
air-pump, *—pămp,* s. máquina neumática, f. [m.
air-shaft, *—shăft,* s. respiradero de mina, f.
air-tight, *—tīt,* a. herméticamente cerrado.
air-trap, *—trăp,* s. ventilador, m.
air-vessel, *—vĕssl,* s. recipiente, m.
airy, *—ĕ,* a. aéreo.
aisle, *īl,* s. nave de una iglesia, f.
ajar, *ăjăr',* a. entreabierto.
akimbo, *ăkĭm'bŏ,* a. corvo.
akin, *ăkĭn',* a. consanguíneo, emparentado.
alabaster, *ăl'ăbăstăr,* s. alabastro, m.; —, a. alabastrino. [ción de dolor ó lástima).
alack-(a-day!) *ălăk'(dăd),* ¡ay! (exclamación de dolor ó lástima).
alacrity, *ălă'krĭtĕ,* s. alegría, f.; buen humor, m. [v. a. alarmar; inquietar.
alarm, *ălărm',* s. alarma, f.; rebato, m.;
alarm-bell, *—bĕll,* s. campana de rebato, f.
alarmist, *—ĭst,* s. alarmista, m.
alarm-post, *—pŏst,* s. puesto de aviso, m.
alarm-watch, *—wŏtsh,* s. reloj despertador, m. [dor, m.
alarum, *ălā'răm,* s. alarma, f. [dor, m.
alas, *ălăs',* ¡ay! [los ojos), m.
albe(e), *ălb',* s. alba, f.
albeit, *ălbē'ĭt,* c. aunque. [los ojos), m.
albugo, *ălbū'gŏ,* s. albugo (enfermedad de los ojos), m.
album, *ăl'băm,* s. album, m.
alchemical, *ălkĕm'mĕkăl,* a. alquímico.
alchemist, *ăl'kĕmĭst,* s. alquimista, m.
alchemy, *ăl'kĕmĕ,* s. alquimia, f.
alcohol, *ăl'kŏhŏl,* s. alcohol, espíritu rectificado de vino, m.
alcoholic, *ălkŏhŏl'ĭk,* a. alcohólico.
alcove, *ăl'kŭv,* s. alcoba, f.
alder, *ăl'dăr,* s. aliso (árbol), m. [nicipal).
alderman, *—măn,* s. regidor, m. (oficial municipal).
ale, *āl,* s. cerveza, f.
a-lee, *ălĕ',* ad. (mar.) á sotavento.
alehouse, *ăl'hŏŭs,* s. cervecería, taberna, f.
alehouse-keeper, *—kēpăr,* s. cervecero, m.
alembic, *ălĕm'bĭk,* s. alambique, m. [m.
alert, *ălĕrt',* a. vigilante; vivo.
alertness, *—nĕs,* s. cuidado, m.; vigilancia, viveza ó lo largo, actividad, f.
ale-silver, *ăl'sĭlvăr,* s. derecho impuesto sobre la cerveza, m.
ale-stake, *—stăk,* s. muestra de taberna, f.
ale-wife, *—wĭf,* s. cervecera, f.

adversative, ădvĕr'sătĭv, a. adversativo, contrario. [ad. al contrario.
adverse, ăd'vĕrs, a. adverso, contrario; -ly,
adversity, ădvĕr'stē, s. adversidad, calamidad, f.; infortunio, m. [atentamente.
advert, ădvĕrt', v. n. advertir, considerar
advertence, -ĕns, s. atención, f.
advertise, ădvĕrtīz', v. a. avisar, advertir.
advertisement, ădvĕr'tĭsment, s. aviso, m.
advertising, ădvĕrtī'zĭng, s. anuncio, m.
advice, ădvīs', s. consejo, m.; aviso, m.
advice-boat, -bōt, s. (mar.) embarcación de aviso, f. [conveniencia, f.
advisability, ădvīzăbĭl'ĭtē, s. prudencia,
advisable, -zăbl, a. prudente, conveniente.
advise, ădvīz', v. a. aconsejar; avisar; -,
v. n. considerar, deliberar. [sadamente.
advisedly, -dlē, ad. prudentemente, avi-
advisedness, -dnĕs, s. prudencia, f.
advocacy, ăd'vŏkăsē, s. vindicación, defensa, apología, f.
advocate, ăd'vŏkăt, s. abogado, m.; protector, m.; -, v. a. defender.
advocateship, -shĭp, s. abogacía, f.
advowee, ădvŏŭē', s. patrono, m.
advowson, ădvŏŭ'sŭn, s. patronato, pa-
adze, ădz, s. azuela, f. [tronazgo, m.
ægis, ē'jĭs, s. egida, f., escudo, m.
æon, ē'ŏn, s. era, f.; eternidad, f.
æra, ē'ră, s. era, época, data fija, f.
aerial, āē'rĭăl, a. aéreo, puesto en el aire.
aerolite, ā'rŏlīt, s. aerolito m.
aerometer, āărŏ'mĕtăr, s. aerómetro, m.
aeronaut, ā'rŏnăt, s. aeronauta, m.
aerostat, ā'rŏstăt, s. globo aerostático, m.
aerostatics, ărŏstăt'ĭks, **aerostation**, āărŏstā'shăn, s. aerostación, f.
æruginous, ērŏ'jĭnăs, a. herrumbroso.
afar, ăfăr', ad. lejos, distante; from -, de algún lugar distante.
affability, ăffăbĭl'ĭtē, s. afabilidad, urbanidad, dulzura, f.
affable, ăf'făbl, a. afable, complaciente; -bly, -blē, ad. afablemente.
affair, ăffăr', s. asunto, m.; negocio, m.; (mil.) acción, f.
affect, ăffĕkt', v. a. conmover; afectar.
affectation, -ā'shăn, s. afectación, f.; pasión, f.
affected, -ĕd, p. & a. afectado, lleno de afectación; inclinado; -ly, ad. con afectación.
affectingly, -ĭnglē, ad. con afecto.
affection, ăffĕk'shăn, s. afección, f.; amor, m.; afición, f. [-ly, ad. cariñosamente.
affectionate, -ĕt, a. afectuoso, benévolo;
affectionateness, -nĕs, s. afecto, m.; benevolencia, f.
affiance, ăffī'ăns, s. confianza, f.; -, v. a. contraer esponsales; inspirar confianza.
affidavit, ăffĭdā'vĭt, s. declaración jurada, f.
affiliate, ăffĭl'ĭăt, v. a. ahijar.
affiliation, ăffĭlĭā'shăn, s. adopción, f. [f.
affinity, ăffĭn'nĭtē, s. afinidad, atracción,
affirm, ăffĕrm', v. a. afirmar, declarar, confirmar, ratificar, aprobar.
affirmation, -ā'shăn, s. afirmación, f.
affirmative, -tĭv, a. afirmativo; -ly, ad. afirmativamente.

affix, ăffĭks', v. a. anexar, añadir, fijar; -, ăf'fĭks, s. (gr.) afijo, m.
afflict, ăfflĭkt', v. a. afligir; atormentar.
affliction, ăfflĭk'shăn, s. aflicción, f.; dolor, m.
afflictive, -tĭv, a. aflictivo, penoso.
affluence, ăf'flūĕns, s. copia, abundancia, f.
affluent, ăf'flūĕnt, a. afluente, opulento.
afflux, ăf'flŭks, s. confluencia, afluencia, f.
afford, ăffōrd', v. a. dar; proveer; producir.
affray, ăffrā', s. asalto, m.; tumulto, m.
affright, ăffrīt', v. a. espantar; -, s. espanto, m.
affront, ăffrŭnt', s. afrenta, injuria, f.; -, v. a. afrentar, insultar, ultrajar.
affrontive, -tĭv, a. injurioso.
afield, ăfēld', ad. en el campo.
afire, ăfīr', ad. en llamas.
aflame, ăflām', ad. en llamas. [del suelo.
aflat, ăflăt', ad. ras con la tierra, á nivel
afloat, ăflōt', ad. flotante, á flote.
afoot, ăfŭt', ad. á pie.
afore, ăfōr', pr. antes; -, ad. primero.
afraid, ăfrād', a. espantado, tímido; I am -, temo.
afresh, ăfrĕsh', ad. de nuevo, otra vez.
aft, ăft, ad. (mar.) á popa.
after, ăf'tăr, pr. después; detrás; según; -, ad. en seguida de; - all, en fin, en suma.
after-ages, -ājĭz, s. pl. tiempos venideros, siglos venideros, m. pl.
after-birth, -bĕrth, s. secundinas, f. pl.
after-cost, -kŏst, s. gastos extraordinarios, m. pl.
after-crop, -krŏp, s. segunda cosecha, f.
after-days, -dāz, s. pl. tiempo venidero, m. [m.
after-game, -gām, s. juego de desquite,
afterglow, -glō, s. reflejo del sol poniente en el hielo, m.
after-hours, -ŏŭrz, s. pl. tiempo subsiguiente á una acción, m.
after-life, -līf, s. vida venidera, f.
aftermath, -măth, s. retoño, m., segunda hierba, f.
afternoon, -nōn, s. tarde, f.
after-pains, -pānz, s. pl. dolores de sobreparto, m. pl.
after-part, -părt, s. parte posterior, f.
after-piece, -pēs, s. farsa, f.; intermedio, m. [escote, m.
after-reckoning, -rĕkkning, s. sobrerreparto, m.
after-taste, -tāst, s. resabio, m.
after-thought, -thăt, s. reflexión fuera de tiempo, f.
afterward, -wărd, **afterwards**, -wărds, ad. después, en seguida.
after-wit, -wĭt, s. entendimiento tardío, m.; sabiduría, f.
again, ăgĕn', ad. otra vez; - and -, muchas veces; as much -, otra vez tanto.
against, -st', pr. contra; enfrente; - the grain, á contrapelo; de mala gana.
agape, ăgăp', s. ágape, m.
agate, ăgăt', s. ágata, f. (piedra preciosa).
age, āj', s. edad, f.; siglo, m.; vejez, f.; under -, menor; -, v. a. envejecer.
aged, -ĕd, a. viejo, anciano; -ly, ad. á manera de viejo.

alum, *ăl'lŭm,* s. alumbre, m. [minio, m.
aluminium, *ălŭmĭn'nĭŭm,* s. (chem.) alu-
aluminous, *ălŭ'mĭnŭs,* a. aluminoso.
alum-salt, *ăl'lŭmsălt,* s. sal mineral, f.
always, *ăl'wăz,* ad. siempre, constantemente, en todo tiempo, sin cesar.
amain, *ămăn',* ad. con vehemencia, vigorosamente. [diferentes metales, f.
amalgam(a), *ămăl'găm(ă),* s. mezcla de
amalgamate, *-ăt,* v. a. & n. amalgamar.
amalgamation, *ămălgămă'shŭn,* s. amalgamación, f. [secretario, m.
amanuensis, *ămănŭĕn'sĭs,* s. amanuense,
amaranth, *ăm'ărănth,* s. (bot.) amaranto,
m. [f.
amaryllis, *ămărĭl'lĭs,* s. (bot.) amarilis.
amass, *ămăss',* v. a. acumular, amontonar.
amateur, *ămătûr',* s. aficionado, m.
amativeness, *ăm'ătĭvnĕs,* s. amatividad, f.
amatory, *ăm'ătŭrrĕ,* a. amatorio; erótico.
amaze, *ămăz',* v. a. espantar; sorprender.
amazedly, *-ĕdlĕ,* ad. fuera de sí.
amazement, *-mĕnt,* s. espanto, pasmo, m.
amazing, *ămă'zĭng,* a. extraño, pasmoso;
-ly, ad. pasmosamente.
amazon, *ăm'ăzŭn,* s. amazona, f.
ambassador, *ămbăs'sădŭr,* s. embajador,
m. [f.
ambassadress, *-sădrĕs,* s. embajadora.
amber, *ăm'bŭr,* s. ámbar, m.; **-,** a. ambarino.
ambidextrous, *ămbĕdĕk'strŭs,* a. ambi-
ambient, *ăm'bĭĕnt,* a. ambiente. [dextro.
ambiguity, *ămbĕgŭ'ĕtĕ,* s. ambigüedad,
duda, f.; equívoco, m.
ambiguous, *ămbĭg'gŭs,* a. ambiguo; **-ly,**
ad. ambiguamente. [cia, f.
ambit, *ăm'bĭt,* s. circuito, m.; circunferen-
ambition, *ămbĭsh'ŭn,* s. ambición, f.
ambitious, *-ŭs,* a. ambicioso; **-ly,** ad.
ambiciosamente.
amble, *ăm'bl,* s. paso de andadura del caballo, m.; **-,** v. n. amblar. [andadura, f.
ambler, *-ŭr,* s. caballo que anda paso de
ambrosial, *ămbrō'zhĭl,* a. delicioso.
ambry, *ăm'brĕ,* s. armario, m.; despensa, f.
ambs-ace, *ămz'ăs,* s. parejas de ases en
algunos juegos, f. pl. [de campaña, m.
ambulance, *ăm'bŭlăns,* s. (mil.) hospital
ambuscade, *ămbŭskăd',* s. emboscada, celada, f.; sorpresa,
f.; to lie in **-,** estar emboscado.
ambush, *ăm'bŭsh,* v. a. emboscar.
ameliorate, *ămĕl'yŏrăt,* v. a. mejorar.
amelioration, *ămĕlyŏră'shŭn,* s. mejoramiento, m.
amenable, *ămē'năbl,* a. responsable.
amend, *ămĕnd',* v. a. enmendar; **-,** v. n.
enmendarse, reformarse, restablecerse.
amendable, *-ăbl,* a. reparable, corregible.
amendment, *-mĕnt,* s. enmienda, reforma, f. [f.
amends, *-z,* s.recompensa, compensación,
amenity, *ămĕn'nĕtĕ,* s. amenidad, f.
amerce, *ămĕrs',* v. a. multar.
amercement, *-mĕnt,* s. multa, f.
amethyst, *ăm'ĕthĭst,* s. amatista, f.
amiability, *ămĕăbĭl'ĭtĕ,* s. amabilidad, f.
amiable, *ā'mĕăbl,* a. amable, amigable.
amiableness, *-nĕs,* s. amabilidad, gracia, f.

amiably, *-ĕ,* ad. amablemente.
amianthus, *ămĕăn'thŭs,* s. amianto, m.
amicable, *ăm'mĕkăbl,* a. amigable, amistoso;
-bly, ad. amigablemente.
amice, *ăm'mĭs,* s. amito, m., ornamento
sagrado.
amid(st), *ămĭd'(st)* pr. entre, en medio de.
amiss, *ămĭss',* ad. culpablemente, errada-
mente. [mente, mal.
amity, *ăm'mĕtĕ,* s. amistad, f.
ammonia, *ămmō'nĕă,* s. amoníaco, m.
ammunition, *ămmŭnĭsh'ŭn,* s. munición,
f. [general, m.
amnesty, *ăm'nĕstĕ,* s. amnistía, f.; olvido
among(st), *ămăng'(st),* pr. entre, mezclado
con, en medio de. [amorosamente.
amorous, *ăm'mŏrŭs,* a. amoroso; **-ly,** ad.
amorousness, *-nĕs,* s. cariño, m.; calidad
de ser amoroso, f.
amorphous, *ămŏr'fŭs,* a. informe.
amount, *ămŏwnt',* s. importe, m.; **-,** v. n.
montar, importar, subir, ascender.
amour, *ămŏr',* s. intriga de amor, f.
amphibian, *ămfĭb'ĕăn,* s. anfibio, m.
amphibious, *ămfĭb'ĕŭs,* a. anfibio. [m.
amphitheatre, *ămfĭthē'ătŭr,* s. anfiteatro,
ample, *ăm'pl,* a. amplio, largo.
ampleness, *-nĕs,* s. amplitud, abundancia, f. [plificación, f.; extensión, f.
amplification, *ămplĕfĭkă'shŭn,* s. am-
amplify, *ăm'plĕfĭ,* v. a. ampliar, extender; **-,** v. n. extenderse.
amplitude, *ăm'plĭtăd,* s. amplitud, extensión, f.; abundancia, f. [samente.
amply, *ăm'plĕ,* ad. ampliamente, copio-
amputate, *ăm'pŭtăt,* v. a. amputar.
amputation, *ămpŭtă'shŭn,* s. amputación,
f.; cortamiento, m.
amuck, *ămŭk',* ad. furiosamente.
amulet, *ăm'ŭlĕt,* s. amuleto, m.
amuse, *ămăz',* v. a. entretener, divertir.
amusement, *-mĕnt,* s. diversión, f., pasatiempo, entretenimiento, m.
amusing, *ămă'zĭng,* **amusive,** *-ĭv,* a.
divertido; **-ly,** ad. entretenidamente.
an, *ăn,* art. un, uno, una. [anabaptistas, f.
anabaptism, *ănăbăp'tĭzm,* s. herejía de los
anabaptist, *ănăbăp'tĭst,* s. anabaptista,
m. [mo, m.
anachronism, *ănăk'rŏnĭzm,* s. anacronis-
anæmia, *ănē'mĕă,* s. anemia, f.
anæmic, *ănē'mĭk,* a. anémico.
analogical, *ănălŏj'ĕkăl,* a. analógico;
-ly, ad. analógicamente.
analogous, *ănă'lŏgŭs,* a. análogo.
analogy, *ănă'lŏjĕ,* s. analogía, conformi-
analysis, *ănă'lĕsĭs,* s. análisis, f. [dad, f.
analyse, *ă'nălĭz,* v. a. analizar.
analyst, *ă'nălĭst,* s. analizador, m.
analytical, *ănălĭt'ĕkăl,* a. analítico; **-ly,**
ad. analíticamente. [confuso.
anarchic(al), *ănăr'kĭk(ăl),* a. anárquico,
anarchy, *ă'nărkĕ,* s. anarquía, f.
anathema, *ănă'thĕmă,* s. anatema, m. & f.,
excomunión, f.
anathematize, *-tĭz,* v. a. anatematizar.
anatomical, *ănătŏm'ĕkăl,* a. anatómico;
-ly, ad. anatómicamente.
anatomist, *ănă'tŏmĭst,* s. anatomista, m.
anatomize, *-tŏmĭz,* v. a. anatomizar.

anatomy, *-tŏmĕ,* s. anatomía, f.

ancestor, *ăn'sĕstŭr,* s. abuelo, m.; **-s,** pl. antepasados, m, pl.

ancestral, *ăn'sĕstrăl,* a. hereditario.

ancestry, *ăn'sĕstrĕ,* s. linaje de antepasados, m.; raza, alcurnia, f.

anchor, *ăng'kŭr,* s. ancla, áncora, f.; **-,** v. n. ancorar, echar las anclas.

anchorage, *-dj,* s. anciaje, m.

anchorite, *ăng'kŏrīt,* s. anacoreta, m.

anchovy, *ăntshō'vĕ,* s. anchova, f.

ancient, *ăn'shŭnt,* a. antiguo; **-ly,** ad. antiguamente.

ancientness, *-nĕs,* s. antigüedad, f.

ancientry, *-rĕ,* s. antigüedad de linaje, f.

and, *ănd,* c, y, ç; aun. [hierro, m.

andiron, *ănd'īŭrn,* s, morillo, caballete de

anecdotal, *ănĕkdō'tăl,* a. anecdótico.

anecdote, *ăn'ĕkdōt,* s. anécdota, f.

anemone, *ănĕm'ōnĕ,* s. (bot) anémona, f.

anent, *ănĕnt',* pr. contra.

anew, *ănū',* ad. de nuevo, nuevamente.

angel, *ān'jĕl,* s. ángel, m.

angelic(al), *ănjĕl'ĭk(ăl),* a, angélico.

anger, *ăng'gŭr,* s. ira, cólera, f.; **-,** v. a. enojar, irritar, encolerizar.

angle, *ăng'gl,* s. ángulo, m.; caña de pescar, f.; **-,** v. a. pescar con caña; halagar.

angled, *-d,* a. anguloso.

angler, *-ŭr,* s, pescador de caña, m.

anglicism, *ăng'glĭsĭzm,* s. anglicismo, m.

angling-line, *ăng'glĭng līn,* s, sedal, m.

angling-rod, *-rŏd,* s. caña de pescar, f.

angrily, *ăn'grĕlĕ,* ad. coléricamente, con **angry,** *ăng'grĕ,* a, colérico, irritado. [ira.

anguish, *ăng'gwĭsh,* s. ansia, pena, angustia, f.

angular, *ăng'gŭlăr,* a. angular.

angularity, *ăngŭlăr'ĭtĕ,* s. forma angular, f.

anigh, *ănĭ,* pr. cerca. [lar, f.

anight(s), *ănīt'(s),* ad. de noche, todas las **anil,** *ăn'nĭl,* s. añil, m. [noches.

animadversion, *ănĕmădvĕr'shŭn,* s. animadversión, f.; advertencia, f.; reprensión, f. [observar; censurar; reprochar.

animadvert, *ănĕmădvĕrt',* v.n.considerar,

animal, *ăn'ĕmăl,* s. & a, animal (m.).

animalcule, *ănĕmăl'kŭl,* s, animalejo, m.

animality, *ănĕmăl'ĕtĕ,* s, vida animal, f.

animate, *ăn'ĕmāt,* v. a. animar; **-,** a. viviente, animado.

animation, *ănĕmā'shŭn,* s. animación, f.

animosity, *ănĕmŏs'ĕtĕ,* s. animosidad, f.

animus, *ăn'ĕmŭs,* s. voluntad, f.; intención, f.

anise, *ăn'ĭs,* s, anís, m. [ción, f.

aniseed, *ăn'ĭsēd,* s. simiente de anís, f.

ankle, *ăng'kl,* s. maléolo, m.; **--bone,** hueso del tobillo, m.

annals, *ăn'nălz,* s. anales, m. pl.

anneal, *ănnēl',* v. a. templar el vidrio.

annex, *ănnĕks',* v. a. anejar; **-,** s. anejo, m.

annexation, *-d'shăn,* s. anexión, f.

annihilable, *ănnī'hĕlăbl,* a. aniquilable.

annihilate, *ănnī'hĕlāt,* v. a. aniquilar.

annihilation, *ănnĭhĕlā'shăn,* s. aniquilación, f. [rio, m.; **-,** a. anual.

anniversary, *ănnĕvĕr'sărĕ,* s. aniversa-

aniotate, *ăn'nŏtāt,* v. n. anotar.

annotation, *-d'shăn,* s. anotación, f.

announce, *ănnŏŭns',* v. a. anunciar, publicar. [aviso, anuncio, m.

announcement, *-mĕnt,* s. advertencia, f.

annoy, *ănnŏĕ',* v. a. molestar, hacer mal.

annoyance, *-ăns,* s. molestia, f.

annoying, *ănnŏĕ'ĭng,* a. enfadoso, molesto, fastidioso, importuno.

annual, *ăn'nŭăl,* a. anual; **-ly,** ad. anualmente, de año en año.

annuitant, *ănnū'ĕtănt,* s. proprietario de renta vitalicia, m.

annuity, *ănnū'ĕtĕ,* s. renta vitalicia, f.

annul, *ănnŭl',* v. a. anular, aniquilar.

annular, *ăn'nŭlăr,* a. anular.

annulet, *ăn'nŭlĕt,* s. anillejo, m.

annulment, *ănnŭl'mĕnt,* s. anulación, f.

annunciate, *ănnŭn'shĕāt,* v. a. anunciar.

annunciation, *ănnŭnshĕā'shŭn,* s. anunciación, f.

anodyne, *ăn'ōdĭn,* a. (med.) anodino.

anoint, *ănŏĭnt',* v. a. untar, ungir; (vulg.) apalear á uno.

anomalous, *ănŏm'mălŭs,* á. anómalo, irregular; **-ly,** ad. irregularmente.

anomaly, *ănŏm'mălĕ,* s, anomalía, irregularidad, f.

anon, *ănŏn',* ad. presto, al instante, inmediatamente; ever and **-,** bien á menudo.

anonymous, *ănŏn'nĕmŭs,* a. anónimo; **-ly,** ad. anónimamente. [**-,** uno á otro.

another, *ănŭ'thŭr,* a. otro, diferente; one

answer, *ăn'sŭr,* a. responder, replicar; corresponder; **-,** v. n. surtir efecto; **-,** s. respuesta, réplica, f.

answerable, *-ăbl,* a. responsable; conforme. [dad, f.; correspondencia, f.

answerableness, *-nĕs,* s. responsabilidad, f.

ant, *ănt,* s, hormiga, f.

antagonism, *ăntă'gŏnĭzm,* s.antagonismo, m., rivalidad, f.

antagonist, *-gŏnĭst,* s. antagonista, m.

antarctic, *ăntărk'tĭk,* a. antártico.

ant-bear, *ănt'băr,* **ant-eater,** *-ētŭr,* s. oso hormiguero, m. [f.

antecedence, *ăntĕsē'dĕns,* s. precedencia, f.

antecedent, *ăntĕsē'dĕnt,* a. antecedente; **-s,** s. pl. antecedentes, m. pl. [mara, f.

antechamber, *ăntĕtshăm'băr,* s. anteca-

antedate, *ăn'tĕdāt,* v, a. antedatar.

antediluvian, *ăntĕdĭlū'vĕăn,* a. antediluviano.

antelope, *ăn'tĕlŏp,* s. cabra líbica, f.

antemeridian, *ăntĕmĕrĭd'ĕăn,* a. antes de mediodía. [gunos insectos, f. pl.

antennae, *ăntĕn'nē,* s, pl. antenas de al-

antepenultimate, *ăntĕpĕnŭl'tĕmăt,* s. antepenúltima, f. [dente.

anterior, *ăntē'rĕŭr,* a, anterior, prece-

anteriority, *ăntĕrĕŏr'ĕtĕ,* s. anterioridad, precedencia, f.

anthem, *ăn'thĕm,* s. antífona, f.

anther, *ăn'thĕr,* s. (bot.) antera, f.

ant-hill, *ănt'hĭl,* s. hormiguero, m.

anthology, *ănthŏl'ōjĕ,* s. antología, f.

Anthony's fire, *ăn'tŏnēsĭr,* s. (med.) fuego de San Antonio, m.

anthracite, *ăn'thrăsīt,* s. antracita, f.

anthropology, *ănthrŏpŏl'ōjĕ,* s. antropología, f.

antic, ăn'tĭk, a. grotesco; —, s. bufón, m.
Antichrist, ăn'tĭkrĭst, s. Anticristo, m.
anticipate, ăntĭs'ĭpāt, v. a. anticipar, prevenir; [ción, f.
anticipation, ăntĭsĭpā'shŭn, s. anticipa-
anticipatory, ăntĭs'ĭpătărĕ, anticipant, -sĕpănt, a. anticipante. [neno, m.
antidote, ăn'tĭdōt, s. antídoto, contrave-
antimacassar, ăntĭmăkăs'sŭr, s. funda de reclinatorio de un sofá, f.
antimony, ăn'tĭmŏnĕ, s. antimonio, m.
antipathy, ăntĭ'păthĕ, s. antipatía, f.
antipodes, ăn'tĭpōdz, s.pl. antipodas, m.pl.
antiquary, ăn'tĭkwŭrĕ, s. anticuario, m.
antiquated, ăn'tĭkwātĕd, a. anticuado.
antique, ăntĭk', a. antiguo; —, s. anti-gualla, f. [ancianidad, f.
antiquity, ăntĭ'kwĕtĕ, s. antigüedad, f.;
antiseptic, ăntĭsĕp'tĭk, a. antiséptico.
antithesis, ăntĭ'thĕsĭs, s. antítesis, contra-riedad, f.
antitype, ăn'tĭtīp, s. antitipo, m.
antler, ănt'lŭr, s. mogotes del ciervo, m.pl.
anvil, ăn'vĭl, s. yunque, m.; bigornia, f.
anxiety, ăngzī'ĕtĕ, s. ansiedad, ansia, f.; afán, m. [ansiosamente.
anxious, ăngk'shŭs, a. ansioso; —ly, ad.
any, ĕn'nĕ, a. & pn. cualquier, cualquiera, alguno, alguna, todo; —body, alguno, cualquiera; —how, de cualquier modo que sea; —more, más; —thing, algo; —where, en cualquier lugar.
apace, ăpās', ad. apriesa, con presteza ó prontitud.
apart, ăpărt', ad. aparte, separadamente.
apartment, —mĕnt, s. cuarto, m.
apathetic, ăpăthĕt'ĭk, a. apático.
apathy, ăp'ăthĕ, s. apatía, f.
ape, āp, s. mono (also fig.), m.; —, v. a. contrahacer, imitar. [mar.) á pique.
apeak, ăpēk', ad. perpendicularmente
aperient, ăpē'rĭĕnt, a. (med.) aperitivo.
aperture, ăp'ĕrtūr, s. abertura, f.
apery, ăp'ărĕ, s. monería, f.
apex, ā'pĕks, s. ápice, colmo, m.; cima, f.
aphorism, ăf'ŏrĭzm, s. aforismo, m.; máxi-ma, f.
aphoristical, ăfŏrĭs'tĭkăl, a. aforístico.
apiary, ā'pĕărĕ, s. colmena, f.
apiece, ăpēs', ad. por cabeza, por persona.
apish, ā'pĭsh, a. gestero, mímico, monero; —ly, ad. afectadamente.
apishness, —nĕs, s. monada, f.
Apocalypse, ăpŏk'ălĕps, s. Apocalipsis, f.
apocrypha, ăpŏ'krĕfă, s. pl. libros apó-crifos, m. pl. [nónico.
apocryphal, —krĕfăl, a. apócrifo, no ca-
apodictic, ăpŏdĭk'tĭk, a. apodíctico.
apologetical, ăpŏlŏjĕt'ĭkăl, a. apologético.
apologise, ăpŏl'lōjīz, v. a. apologizar, de-fender, disculpar, excusar.
apologist, —lōjĭst, s. apologista, m.
apology, —lŏjĕ, s. apología, defensa, f.
apophthegm, ăp'ŏthĕm, s. apotegma. m.
apoplectic(al), ăpŏplĕk'tĭk(ăl), a. apoplé-tico.
apoplexy, ăp'ŏplĕksĕ, s. apoplejía, f.
apostasy, ăpŏs'tăsĕ, s. apostasía, f.

apostate, ăpŏs'tāt, s. apóstata, m.
apostatise, —tātīz, v. n. apostatar.
apostle, ăpŏs'sl, s. apóstol, m.
apostleship, —shĭp, s. apostolado. m.
apostolic(al), ăpŏstŏl'ĭk(ăl), a. apostólico.
apostrophe, ăpŏs'trŏfĕ, s. apóstrofe, f.; (gr.) apóstrofo, m.
apostrophise, —trŏfīz, v. a. apostrofar.
apothecary, ăpŏth'ĕkărĕ, s. boticario, m.; —'s shop, s. botica, f. [cación, f.
apotheosis, ăpŏthē'ōsĭs, s. apoteosis, deifi-
appal, ăppăl', v. a. espantar, aterrar.
appanage, ăp'pănĕj, s. heredamiento, m.; infantazgo, m. [tren, m.
apparatus, ăppără'tŭs, s. aparato, aparejo,
apparel, ăppăr'rĕl, s. traje, vestido, m.; —, v. a. vestir, trajear; adornar.
apparent, ăppăr'rĕnt, a. evidente, aparente; —ly, ad. claramente. [sión, f.
apparition, ăppărĭsh'ăn, s. aparición, vi-
apparitor, ăppăr'rĕtŭr, s. ujier, m.; al-guacil (de corona ó de la curia eclesiás-tica), m.
appeal, ăppēl', v. n. apelar, recurrir á un tribunal superior; llamar por testigo; —, s. (law) apelación, f. [ser evidente.
appear, ăppēr', v. n. aparecer, manifestar;
appearance, —ăns, s. apariencia, probabili-dad, f.; first-, primer paso en un negocio &c., m. [conciliable.
appeasable, ăppē'zăbl, a. aplacable, re-
appease, ăppēz', v. a. aplacar, reconciliar.
appellant, ăppĕl'lănt, s. (law) apelante, m. [ción, f.
appellation, ăppĕllā'shŭn, s. (law) apela-
appellative, ăppĕl'lătĭv, s. (gr.) apelativo, m [mado, m.
appellee, ăppĕllē', s. (law) apelado, inti-
append, ăppĕnd', v. a. anejar.
appendage, —dj, s. cosa accesoria, f.
appendix, —ĭks, s. apéndice, m. [f.
appertain, ăppĕrtān', v.n. pertenecer, tocar
appetence, ăp'pĕtĕns, s. concupiscencia, f.
appetise, ăp'pĕtīz, v. a. excitar el apetito.
appetising, ăp'pĕtīzĭng, a. apetitivo.
appetite, ăp'pĕtĭt, s. apetito, m.
applaud, ăpplăd', v. a. aplaudir; alabar, palmear; aclamar.
applauder, —ŭr, s. aclamador, m.
applause, ăpplăz', s. aplauso, m.
apple, ăp'pl, s. manzana, f.; pupila del ojo, f.; —of discord, manzana de la dis-cordia. [m.; in—order, en sumo orden.
apple-pie, —pī, s. pastelillo de manzanas,
apple-tree, —trē, s. manzano, m.
appliance, ăpplī'ăns, s. aplicación, f.; re-curso, m.
applicability, ăpplĭkăbĭl'ĕtĕ, s. aptitud, f.
applicable, ăp'plĭkăbl, a. aplicable, apto; conforme; —bly, ad. de un modo apli-cable.
applicant, ăp'plĭkănt, s. aspirante, m.
application, ăpplĭkā'shŭn, s. aplicación, f.
apply, ăpplī', v. a. aplicar, acomodar; v. n. dirigirse á, recurrir á. [nar, decretar.
appoint, ăppŏint', v. a. señalar, determi-
appointee, —ē, s. funcionario, m.
appointment, —mĕnt, s. estipulación, f.; decreto, mandato, m.; sueldo, m.

apportion, *ăppŏr'shăn,* v.a. proporcionar.

apportionment, *-mĕnt,* s. repartición, f.

appose, *ăppŏz',* v.a. cuestionar, examinar.

apposite, *ăp'pŏzīt,* a. adaptado; propio;
—ly, ad. convenientemente, á propósito.

appositeness, *-nĕs,* s. adaptación, f.;
propiedad, f.; atributo, m.

apposition, *ăppŏzīsh'ăn,* s. aposición, f.

appraise, *ăpprāz',* v.a. apreciar; tasar;
estimar.   [mación, f.

appraisement, *-mĕnt,* s. aprecio, m., esti-

appraiser, *-ŭr,* s. apreciador, tasador, m.

appreciable, *ăpprē shĕăbl,* a. apreciable.

appreciate, *ăpprē shĕăt,* v. a. apreciar,
estimar, valuar.   [m.; tasa, f.

appreciation, *ăpprēshĕā'shăn,* s. aprecio,

appreciative, *-tīv,* a. apreciativo.

apprehend, *ăpprēhĕnd',* v. a. aprehender,
prender; concebir, comprender; temer.

apprehension, *ăpprēhĕn'shăn,* s. aprehensión, f.; recelo, m.; presa, captura, f.

apprehensive, *-sīv,* a. aprehensivo,
tímido; perspicaz.

apprentice, *ăpprĕn'tīs,* s. aprendiz, m.;
—, v. a. poner á alguno de aprendiz.

apprenticeship, *-shīp,* s. aprendizaje, m.

apprise, *ăpprīz',* v.a. informar, instruir.

approach, *ăpprōtsh',* v. a. (& n.) aproxi-
mar(se); —, s. acceso, m.

approachable, *-ăbl,* a. accesible. [ción, f.

approbation, *ăpprŏbā'shăn* s. aproba-

approbatory, *ăp'prŏbătŭrē,* a. aprobativo.

appropriate, *ăpprō'prĕāt,* v. a. apropiar,
adaptar; —, a. apropiado, particular, peculiar.   [bación.

approvable, *ăpprō'văbl,* a. digno de apro-

approval, *-văl,* s. aprobación, f.

approve, *ăpprōv',* v. a. aprobar.

approver, *-ŭr,* s. aprobador, m.

approximate, *ăpprŏk'sēmāt,* v. a. (& n.)
acercar(se); —, a. aproximativo.

approximation, *ăpprŏksēmā'shăn,* s.
aproximación, f.   [mativo.

approximative, *ăpprŏk'sēmātīv,* a. aproxi-

appurtenance, *ăppŭr'tēnăns,* s. (law)
dependencia, pertenencia, f.

apricot, *ā'prīkŏt,* s. albaricoque, m.

April, *ā'prīl,* s. abril, m.   [de cañón, f.

apron, *ā'pŭrn,* s. delantal, m.; plomada

apsidal, *ăp'sīdăl,* a. perteneciente al ápside.

apsis, *ăp'sīs,* s. ápside.   [mente.

apt, *ăpt,* a. apto, idóneo; —ly, ad. apta-

aptitude, *ăp'tītūd,* **aptness,** *ăpt'nēs,* s.
aptitud, f.; disposición natural, f.

aqua fortis, *ăk'kwŏfŏrtĭs,* s. agua fuerte, f.

Aquarius, *ăkwā'rēŭs,* s. Acuario, m. (signo
del zodiaco).

aquatic, *ăkwăt'īk,* a. acuático, acuátil.

aqueduct, *ăk'kwēdŭkt,* s. acueducto. m.

aqueus, *ā'kwēŭs,* s. acuoso.

aquiline, *ăk'kwīlīn,* a. aguileño.

arabesque, *ăr'răbĕsk,* s. arabesco, m.

arable, *ăr'ăbl,* a. labrantío.

arbalist, *ăr'bălīst,* s. ballesta, f.

arbiter, *ăr'bītŭr,* s. arbitrador, árbitro, m.

arbitrament, *ărbī'trămĕnt,* s. arbitrio, m.

arbitrarily, *ăr'bītrărīlē,* ad. arbitraria-
mente.   [tismo, m.

arbitrariness, *ăr'bītrărīnĕs,* s. despo-

---

arbitrary, *-rē,* a. arbitrario, despótico.

arbitrate, *ăr'bītrāt,* v. a. arbitrar, juzgar
como árbitro.

arbitration, *ărbītrā'shăn,* **arbitrement,**
ărbī'trēmĕnt, s. arbitramento, arbitrio, m.

arbitrator, *ăr'bītrātŭr,* s. arbitrador, árbitro, m.

arborescent, *ărbŏrēs'sĕnt,* a. arborescente.

arbour, *ăr'bŭr,* s. emparrado, m.; enramada,

arbute, *ăr'būt,* s. (bot.) fresal, m.   [f.

arcade, *ărkād',* s. arcada, bóveda, f.

arcanum, *ărkā'năm,* s. arcano, m.

arch, *ărtsh,* s. arco (de círculo, de puente
&c.), m.; —, v. a. cubrir con arcos; —, a.
principal, insigne; grande; infame: artero,
bellaco; (se usa en composición como
aumentativo).   [lógico.

archæological, *ărkăŏlŏj'īkăl,* a. arqueo-

archæology, *ărkăŏl'ŏjē,* s. arqueología, f.

archaic, *ărkā'īk,* a. arcaico.

archangel, *ărkăn'jĕl,* s. arcángel, m.

archbishop, *ărtshbīsh'ăp,* s. arzobispo, m.

archbishopric, *-rīk,* s. arzobispado, m.

archduchess, *ărtshdŭt'shĕs,* s. archiduquesa, f.

archduke, *-dūk',* s. archiduque, m.

archdukedom, *-dăm,* s. archiducado, m.

archer, *ărtsh'ŭr,* s. arquero, m.

archery, *-ē,* s. arte de tirar con arco y
flecha, m.

archiepiscopacy, *ărkēĕpīs'kŏpăsē,* s. dignidad de arzobispo, f.

architect, *ăr'kītĕkt,* s. arquitecto, m.

architectural, *ărkītĕk'tūrăl,* a. lo perteneciente á la arquitectura.   [f.

architecture, *ăr'kītĕktŭr,* s. arquitectura.

archives, *ăr'kīvz,* s. pl. archivos, m. pl.

archivist, *ăr'kīvīst,* s. archivero, m.

archly, *ărtsh'lē,* ad. jocosamente; sútilmente; con ingenio.

archness, *-nĕs,* s. astucia, malignidad, f.;
travesura maula, f.

archpriest, *-prēst,* s. arcipreste, m.

archway, *-wā,* s. arcada, bóveda, f.

arctic, *ărk'tīk,* a. ártico, septentrional.

ardency, *ăr'dĕnsē,* s. ardor, ardour, ŭr'dŭr, s. ardor, m.; vehemencia, f.; pasión, f.

ardent, *ăr'dĕnt,* a. ardiente; apasionado;
—ly, ad. con pasión.

arduous, *ăr'dŭŭs,* a. arduo; laborioso;
area, *ā'rēă,* s. área, f.; espacio, m. [difícil.

arenaceous, *ărēnā'shŭs,* a. arenoso.

areometer, *ărēŏm'mĕtŭr,* s. areómetro, m.

argentiferous, *ărjĕntīf'fĕrŭs,* a. argentí-
fero, argil, ăr'jīl, s. arcilla, f.   [fero.

argillaceous, *ărjīllā'shŭs,* a. arcilloso.

argue, *ăr'gū,* v. n. disputar, discurrir; —,
v. a. probar con argumentos; acusar.

argument, *ăr'gūmĕnt,* s. argumento, m.,
controversia, f.   [mentación, f.

argumentation, *ărgūmĕntā'shăn,* s. argu-

argumentative, *ărgūmĕn'tătīv,* a. lo que
contiene argumento, argumentoso.

argus-oyed, *ăr'gŭs īd,* a. que tiene vista
de lince.

arid, *ăr'rīd,* a. árido, seco, estéril.

aridity, *ărīd'ītē,* s. sequedad, f.

Aries, *ā'rēz,* s. Aries, m. (signo del zodíaco).

aright, *ărīt'*, ad. rectamente, justamente, bien; **to set —**, rectificar.

arise, *ărīz'* s. n. levantarse; nacer. pro-

aristocracy, *ărĭstŏ'krăsĕ*, s. aristocracia, f.

aristocrat, *ărĭs'tŏkrăt*, s. aristócrata,

aristocratic, *ărĭstŏkrăt'ĭk*, a. aristocrá- tico; **-ally**, ad. aristocráticamente.

arithmetic, *ărĭth'mĕtĭk*, s. aritmética, f.

arithmetical, *-mĕt'ĭkăl*, a. aritmético; **-ly**, ad. aritméticamente.

arithmetician, *ărĭthmĕtĭsh'ăn*, s. arit- mético, m.   [arca del testamento.

ark, *ărk*, s. arca, f.; **- of the covenant**,

arm, *ărm*, s. brazo, m.; rama del árbol, f.; poder, m.; arma, f.; -, v.a. (& n.) armar(se).

armament, *ăr'măměnt*, s. (mar.) arma- mento de navíos, m.; (mil.) armamento.

arm-chair, *ărm'tshâr*, s. silla de brazos, f.

armful, *-fŭl*, s. brazada, f.

arm-hole, *-hōl*, s. sobaco, m.

armistice, *ăr'mĭstĭs*, s. armisticio, m.

armlet, *ărm'lĕt*, s. brazuelo, m.; brazalete, m.; guardabrazo de la armadura, m.   [m.

armorial, *ărmŏr'rĕăl*, s. libro de blasones,

armour, *ăr'mŭr*, s. armadura, f.

armour-bearer, *-bârĕr*, s. escudero, m.

armoury, *ăr'mŭrĕ*, s. armería, f.; insignias genealógicas, f. pl.

arm-pit, *ărm'pĭt*, s. sobaco, m.

army, *ăr'mĕ*, s. ejército, m.; tropas, f. pl.

aroma, *ărō'mă*, s. aroma, m.

aromatic(al), *ărŏmăt'ĭk(ăl)*, a. aromático.

aromatize, *ărō'mătīz*, v. n. aromatizar.

around, *ărŏŭnd'*, pr. en, cerca; —, ad. al rededor.   [sublevar.

arouse, *ărŏŭz'*, v. a. despertar; excitar;

arquebuse, *ăr'kĕbŭs*, s. arcabuz, m.

arrack, *ăr'răk*, s. aguardiente de arroz, m.

arraign, *ărrān'*, v. a. citar, delatar en justicia; acusar.   [proceso criminal, m.

arraignment, *-měnt*, s. acusación, f.;

arrange, *ărrānj'*, v. a. colocar, poner en orden.   [orden, arreglo, m.

arrangement, *-měnt*, s. colocación, f.;

arrant, *ăr'rănt*, a. malo, perverso; infame; **-ly**, ad. corruptamente, vergonzosamente.

arras, *ăr'răs*, s. tapicerías tejidas, f. pl.

array, *ărrā'*, s. adorno, vestido, m.; orden de batalla, f.; colocación de los jurados, f.; -, v. a. colocar; vestir, adornar; co- locar los jurados.   [atraso, m.

arrear, *ărrēr'*, s. resto de una deuda, m.;

arrest, *ărrěst'*, s. prisión, f.; arresto, m.; —, v. a. arrestar, embargar las cosas.

arrival, *ărrī'văl*, s. arribo, m.; llegada, venida, f.

arrive, *ărrīv'*, v. n. arribar; conseguir.

arrogance, *ăr'rŏgăns*, s. arrogancia, pre- sunción, f.

arrogant, *ăr'rŏgănt*, a. arrogante, presun- tuoso; **-ly**, ad. arrogantemente.

arrogate, *ăr'rŏgăt*, v. a. arrogarse, presu- mir de sí.

arrogation, *ărrŏgă'shŏn*, s. arrogación, f.

arrow, *ăr'rō*, s. flecha, saeta, f.

arsenal, *ăr'sěnăl*, s. (mil.) arsenal, m.; (mar.) atarazana, armería, f.

arsenic, *ăr'sěnĭk*, s. arsénico, m.

arson, *ăr'sŭn*, s. fuego incendiario, delito de incendiar, m.   [ciencia, f.

art, *ărt*, s. arte, m & f., industria, f.;

arterial, *ărtē'rĕăl*, n. arterial, arterioso.

artesian well, *ărtē'shăn wěll*, s. pozo ar-

artery, *ăr'tŭrĕ*, s. arteria, f.   [tesiano, m.

artful, *ărt'fŭl*, a. artificioso; diestro, **-ly**, ad. artificiosamente, diestramente.   [f.

artfulness, *-fŭlněs*, s. astucia, habilidad,

artichoke, *ăr'tĕtshŏk*, s. alcachofa, f.

article, *ăr'tĭkl*, s. artículo, m.; -, v. n. capitular, contratar mutuamente.

articulate, *ărtĭk'kŭlăt*, a. articulado, claro, distinto, **-ly**, ad. distintamente. -, v. a. articular, pronunciar distintamente.

articulation, *ărtĭkŭlă'shŏn*, s. articula- ción, f.; (bot.) nudo en las plantas, m.

artifice, *ăr'tĕfĭs*, s. artificio, fraude, m.

artificer, *ărtĭf'fĭsĕr*, s. artesano, m.

artificial, *ărtĕfĭsh'ăl*, a. artificial; artifi- cioso; **-ly**, ad. artificialmente; artificiosa- mente.   [cia, f.; destreza, f.

artificiality, *ărtĕfĭshĕăl'ĭtĕ*, s. arte, astu-

artillery, *ărtĭl'lŭrĕ*, s. artillería, f.

artillery-man, *-măn*, s. artillero, m.   [m.

artillery-practice, *-prăktĭs*, s. cañoneo,

artisan, *ăr'tĕzăn*, s. artista, artesano, m.

artist, *ăr'tĭst*, s. artista, m.

artistic, *ărtĭs'tĭk*, a. artístico.

artless, *ărt'lěs*, a. sencillo, simple; **-ly**, ad. sencillamente, naturalmente.

artlessness, *-něs*, s. sencillez, f.

as, *ăs*, c. como; mientras; también; **visto que, pues que**; **- for**, **- to**, en cuanto á.

asbestos, *ăsběs'tŭs*, s. asbesto, amianto, m.

ascend, *ăsěnd'*, v. n. ascender, subir.

ascendant, *-ănt*, s. ascendiente, m.; -, a. superior, predominante.

ascendency, *-ěnsĕ*, s. influjo, poder, m.

ascension, *ăsěn'shŏn*, s. ascensión, f.

ascent, *ăsěnt'*, s. subida, f.; eminencia, f.; altura, f.   [establecer; reglar el precio.

ascertain, *ăsěrtān'*, v. a. asegurar, fijar,

ascetic, *ăsět'ĭk*, a. ascético; -, s. asceta, m.   [adjudicar.

ascribe, *ăskrīb'*, v. a. adscribir; atribuir;

ash, *ăsh*, s. (bot.) fresno, m.; **-es, -z**, pl. ceniza, f.; reliquias de un cadáver, f. pl.

ashamed, *ăshāmd'*, a. avergonzado.

ash-coloured, *ăsh'kŭllŭrd*, a. ceniciento.

ashen, *ăsh'n*, a. hecho de fresno.

ash-hole, *ăsh'-hōl*, **--pan**, **--pĭt**, s. cenicero, cenizal, m.

ashore, *ăshōr'*, ad. en tierra, á tierra; **to get —**, desembarcar.   [coles de ceniza, m.

Ash-Wednesday, *ăsh'wěndzdā*, s. miér- coles de ceniza, m.

ashy, *ăsh'ĕ*, a. cenizoso, ceniciento.

aside, *ăsīd'*, ad. al lado, á parte.

ask, *ăsk*, v. a. pedir, rogar, interrogar; **to - out**, convidar.

askance, *ăskăns'*, **askant**, *ăskănt'*, ad. al sesgo, oblicuamente.   [con desdén.

askew, *ăskū'*, ad. al lado; de lado; de través;

aslant, *ăslănt'*, ad. oblicuamente.

asleep, *ăslēp'*, a. dormido; **to fall —**, dor- asp, *ăsp*, s. áspid, m.   [mirse.

asparagus, *ăspăr'răgŭs*, s. espárrago, m.

aspect, *ăs'pěkt*, s. aspecto, m; vista, f.; aire, m.; semblante, m.

aspen(-tree), *ăs'pĕn(trē)*, s. álamo temblón, m., —, a. de álamo temblón.

asperity, *ăspĕr'ĭtĭ*, s. aspereza, rudeza, f.

asperse, *ăspĕrs'*, v.a. calumniar, infamar.

aspersion, *ăspŭr'shăn*, s. aspersión, f.; defamación, calumnia, f.

asphalt, *ăs'fălt*, s. asfalto, m.

asphyxia, *ăsfĭk'sĕă*, s. (med.) asfixia, f.

asphyxiate, *ăsfĭk'sĕăt*, v.a. asfixiar.

aspirant, *ăspĭ'rănt*, s. aspirante, m.

aspirate, *ăs'pĕrăt*, v.a. aspirar, pronunciar con aspiración; —, s. sonido aspirado, m.

aspiration, *ăspĕrā'shăn*, s. aspiración, f.

aspire, *ăspīr'*, v.n. aspirar, desear.

asquint, *ăskwĭnt'*, ad. de través.   [ff.

ass, *ăss*, s. borrico, asno, m.; she —, borrica,

assail, *ăssāl'*, v.a. asaltar, atacar.

assailable, *-ăbl*, a. lo que puede ser asaltado.   [tador, agresor, m.

assailant, *-ănt*, assailer, *-ŭr*, s. asaltador, agresor, m.

assassin, *ăssăs'ĭn*, s. asesino, matador, m.

assassinate, *-āt*, v.a. asesinar, matar.

assassination, *ăssăssĭnā'shăn*, s. asesinato, m.   [—, v.a. acometer, asaltar.

assault, *ăssălt'*, s. asalto, m.; insulto, m.;

assay, *ăssā'*, s. ensayo, f.; prueba, f.; experimento, m.; —, v.a. tentar; probar.

assayer, *-ŭr*, s. ensayador, m.   [ensayar.

assemblage, *ăssĕm'blĭj*, s. agregado, m.; multitud, f.   [—, v.n. arrogarse.

assemble, *-bl*, v.a. congregar, convocar;

assembly, *-blĭ*, s. asamblea, junta, f.; congreso, m.

assent, *ăssĕnt'*, s. asenso, m.; aprobación, f.; —, v.n. asentir, aprobar.

assert, *ăssĕrt'*, v.a. sostener, mantener; afirmar; asegurar.

assertion, *ăssĕr'shăn*, s. aserción, f.

assertive, *ăssŭr'tĭv*, a. perentorio.

assess, *ăssĕs'*, v.a. amillarar.

assessable, *-ăbl*, a. el que puede ser amillarado.   [m.; catastro, m.

assessment, *-mĕnt*, s. amillaramiento,

assets, *ăssĕts'*, s. pl. bienes de un difunto, m. pl.   [v.a. aseverar, afirmar.

assever, *ăssĕv'ŭr*, asseverate, *-ărăt*,

asseveration, *ăssĕvĕrā'shăn*, s. aseveración, afirmación, f.

assiduity, *ăssĭdū'ĭtĭ*, s. asiduidad, aplicación, f.; constancia, f.

assiduous, *ăssĭd'ŭăs*, a. asiduo, aplicado; -ly, ad. constantemente; diligentemente.

assign, *ăssīn'*, v.a. asignar; disputar; transferir algún derecho á otro.

assignable, *-ăbl*, a. asignable.

assignation, *ăssĭgnā'shăn*, s. asignación, f.; cesión, f.; cita, f.

assignee, *ăssĭnē'*, s. síndico, apoderado, m.; cesionario, m.

assignment, *ăssĭn'mĕnt*, s. asignación, f.; cesión, f.; señalamiento, m.   [asemejar.

assimilate, *ăssĭm'ĭlăt*, v.a. asimilar.

assimilation, *ăssĭmĭlā'shăn*, s. asimilación, f.   [rrer.

assist, *ăssĭst'*, v.a. asistir, ayudar, socorrer.

assistance, *-ăns*, s. asistencia, f.; socorro, m.   [m.

assistant, *-ănt*, s. asistente, ayudante,

assize, *ăssīz'*, s. tribunal que entiende en los asuntos criminales, m.; tasa del pan, f.

associate, *ăssō'shēăt*, v.a. asociar, acompañar; frecuentar -, a. asociado, —, s. socio, compañero, m).

association, *ăssōshēā'shăn*, s. asociación, unión, sociedad, f.

assonance, *ăs'sŏnăns*, s. asonancia, f.

assort, *ăssŏrt'*, v.a. clasificar, adecuar.

assortment, *-mĕnt*, s. surtido, m.

assuage, *ăswāj'* v.a. mitigar, suavizar; —, v.n. disminuir, apaciguarse.   [f.

assuagement, *-mĕnt*, s.mitigación, calma, f.

assume, *ăssūm'*, v.a. arrogar, apropiar, presumir; —, v.n. arrogarse.

assumption, *ăssăm'shăn*, s. presunción, f.; postulado, m.; Assumption, s. Asunción de la bienaventurada Virgen María, f.

assurance, *ăshō'răns*, s. seguridad, certeza, f.; fianza, f.

assure, *ăshōr'*, v.a. asegurar, afirmar.

assuredly, *-ĕdlĭ*, ad. ciertamente, sin astorisk, *ăs'tĕrĭsk*, s. asterisco, m. [duda.

astern, *ăstĕrn'*, ad. (mar.) por la popa.

asthma, *ăst'mă*, s. asma, f.

asthmatic, *ăstmăt'ĭk*, a. asmático.

astir, *ăstŭr'*, ad. agitado, en turbación.

astonish, *ăstŏn'ĭsh*, v.a. pasmar, sorprender.   [-ly, ad.asombrosamente.

astonishing, *ăstŏn'ĭshĭng*, a. asombroso;

astonishment, *-mĕnt*, s. espanto, pasmo, asombro, m.; sorpresa, f.

astound, *ăstōnd'*, v.a. consternar, aterrar, pasmar, conturbar.

astounding, *-ĭng*, a. consternativo.

astraddle, *ăstrăd'dl*, ad. á horcajadas.

astral, *ăs'trăl*, a. astral, de los astros.

astray, *ăstrā'*, ad. extraviado, descaminado; to lead —, desviar, seducir.

astriction, *ăstrĭk'shăn*, s. astricción, f.

astride, *ăstrīd'*, ad. á horcajadas.

astringent, *ăstrĭn'jĕnt*, a. astringente.

astrolabe, *ăs'trōlăb*, s. astrolabio, m.

astrologer, *ăstrŏl'ōjŭr*, s. astrólogo.

astrological, *ăstrŏlŏj'ĭkăl*, s. astrológico.

astrology, *ăstrŏl'ōjē*, astrología, f.   [m.

astronomer, *ăstrŏn'ōmŭr*, s. astrónomo,

astronomical, *ăstrŏnŏm'ĭkăl*, a. astronómico.

astronomy, *ăstrŏn'ōmĕ*, s. astronomía, f.

astute, *ăstūt'*, a. astuto; aleve.   [parte.

asunder, *ăsŭn'dŭr*, ad. separadamente, á

asylum, *ăsī'lăm*, s. asilo, refugio, m.

at, *ăt*, pr. á, en; — once, al instante, de un golpe; — all, generalmente, — all events, á todo trance; — first, en el principio; — large, ampliamente, á larga; á la inclemencia; — last, por último; his honour is — stake, le va en ello de su honor.

atheism, *ā'thĕĭzm*, s. ateísmo, m.

atheist, *ā'thĕĭst*, s. ateísta, ateo, m.

atheistic(al), *āthĕĭst'ĭk(ăl)*, a. impío.

athirst, *ăthŭrst'*, ad. sediento, con gana

athlete, *ăth'lēt*, s. atleta, m. [de beber.

athletic, *ăthlĕt'ĭk*, a. atlético, vigoroso.

athwart, *ăthwărt'*, pr. al través.

atilt, *ătĭlt'*, ad. en ademán de dar una estocada, f.   [cada,

atlas, *ăt'lăs*, s. atlas; atlante, m.

atmosphere, ăt' mŏsfĕr, s. atmósfera, f.
atmospherical, ătmŏsfĕr'ĭkăl, a. atmos-
atom, ā'tŭm, s. átomo, m.   [férico.
atomic(al), ătŏn'ĭk(ăl), a. atómico.
atone, ătōn', v. a. expiar, aplacar.
atonement, —mĕnt, s. expiación, propiciación, f.
atop, ătŏp', ad. encima, en la punta ó
parte superior de alguna cosa.
atrabilious, ătrăbĭl'ĕăs, a. atrabiliario,
melancólico.
atrocious, ătrō'shŭs, a. atroz; enorme,
odioso; —ly, ad. atrozmente.   [dad, f.
atrocity, ătrŏs'ĕtĭ, s. atrocidad, enormi-
atrophy, ā'trŏfĕ, s. (med.) atrofia, f.
attach, ăttătsh', v. a. prender, pillar, asir,
coger; ganar, adquirir, atraer á sí.
attaché, ăttăshā', s. agregado á alguna
legación, m.
attachment, ăttătsh'mĕnt, s. adherencia,
f.; afecto, m.; secuestro, m.   [ataque, m.
attack, ăttăk', v. a. atacar, acometer; —s.
attain, ăttān', v. a. ganar, conseguir, ob-
attainable, —ăbl, a. asequible.   [tener.
attainder, —dĕr, s. imputación de algún
delito, tacha, deshonra, infamia, f.
attainment, —mĕnt, s. logro, m.; consecución de lo que se pretende, f.; —s, pl. conocimientos, m. pl.
attaint, —t', v. a. convencer de algún delito;
corromper, viciar, manchar; —s. mácula,
f.; auto jurídico, m.
attar, ăt'tăr, s. aceite rosado ó de rosas, m.
attempt, ăttĕmt', v. a. tentar; probar, experimentar; —s. empresa, f.; experimento
(peligroso), m.; tentativa, f.
attend, ăttĕnd', v. a. servir, asistir, acompañar; —v. n. prestar atención; considerar.
attendance, —ăns, s. corte, f.; tren, séquito, m.; servicio, m.; cuidado, m.   [m.
attendant, —ănt, s. sirviente, m.; cortejo,
attention, ăttĕn'shŭn, s. atención, f.; cuidado, m.   [—ly, ad. con atención.
attentive, —tĭv, a. atento; cuidadoso;
attenuate, ăttĕn'ūăt, v. a. atenuar, disminuir.   [f.
attenuation, ăttĕnūā'shŭn, s. atenuación, f.
attest, ăttĕst', v. a. atestiguar.
attestation, —ā'shŭn, s. atestación, f.; testimonio, m.
attic, ăt'tĭk, s. desván, m.; guardilla, f.;
—, a. ático, juicioso, picante (aplícase al
estilo).   [nar, ataviar.
attire, ăttĭr', s. atavío, m.; —, v. a. ador-
attitude, ăt'tĕtŭd, s. actitud, postura, f.
attitudinarian, ăttĕtŭdĭnā'rĭăn, s. asentador, m.   [actitud.
attitudinise, ăttĕtŭ'dĭnīz, v. n. tomar cierta
attorney, ăttŭr'nĕ, s. procurador, poderhabiente, m.; —general, fiscal, m.
attract, ăttrăkt', v. a. atraer, persuadir.
attraction, ăttrăk'shŭn, s. atracción, f.;
atractivo, m.
attractive, —tĭv, a. atractivo, halagüeño;
—ly, ad. por atracción.
attributable, ăttrĭb'ŭtăbl, a. imputable.
attribute, ăttrĭb'ŭt, v. a. atribuir, imputar; —, s. ăt'trĕbŭt, atributo, m.

attribution, ăttrĭbū'shŭn, s. atributo, m.;
reputación, f.   [atrición, f.
attrition, ăttrĭsh'ŭn, s. trituración, f.;
attune, ăttūn', v. a. acordar; armonizar.
auburn, ā'bŭrn, a. moreno, castaño.   [f.
auction, āk'shŭn, s. venta pública, subasta,
auctioneer, —ĕr', s. corredor de almoneda,
vendutero, m.   [—ly, ad. atrevidamente.
audacious, ădā'shŭs, a. audaz, temerario;
audacity, ădăs'ĕtĭ, s. audacia, osadía, f.
audible, ā'dĕbl, a. perceptible al oído;
—ly, ad. de modo que se pueda oir, alto.
audience, ā'dĕĕns, s. audiencia, f.; auditorio, m.
audit, ā'dĭt, s. remate de una cuenta, m.;
—, v. a. rematar una cuenta, examinar.
auditor, ā'dĕtŏr, s. oidor, m.   [tivo.
auditory, —ĕ, s. auditorio, m.; —, a. audi-
auger, ā'gŭr, s. barrena, f.
aught, āt, pn. algo, alguna cosa.
augment, āgmĕnt', v. a. aumentar, acrecentar, —, v. n. crecer   [f.; aumento, m.
augmentation, —ā'shŭn, s. aumentación,
augur, ā'gŭr, v. n. augurar, adivinar por
conjeturas.
augury, ā'gŭrĕ, s. agüero, presagio, m.
August, ā'gŭst, s. agosto, m. (mes).
august, āgŭst', a. augusto; majestuoso.
augustness, —nĕs, s. grandeza, f.
aulic, ā'lĭk, a. aulico.
aunt, ānt, s. tía, f.
aureola, ārĕ'ŏlă, s. auréola, f.
auricular, ărĭk'ŭlăr, aural, ā'răl, a.
dicho al oído; lo que se sabe por tradición; —ly, ad. al oído; secretamente.
auriferous, ărĭf'ĕrŭs, a. aurífero.
aurora, ārō'ră, s. aurora, f.; — borealis,
aurora boreal, f.
auscultation, ăskŭltā'shŭn, s. ausculta-
ción, f.   [tección, f.
auspices, ā'spĭsĕz, s. pl. auspicio, m.; pro-
auspicious, ăspĭsh'ŭs, a. próspero, favorable; propicio, —ly, ad. prósperamente.
austere, ăstēr', a. austero, severo, rígido;
—ly, ad. austeramente.   [ficación, f.
austerity, ăstĕr'ĕtĭ, s. austeridad; morti-
austral, ās'trăl, a. austral, austrino.
authentic(al), ăthĕn'tĭk(ăl), a. auténtico;
—ly, ad. auténticamente.
authenticate, —ăt, v. a. autenticar.
authenticity, ăthĕntĭs'ĕtĭ, s. autenticidad, f.
author, ā'thŭr, s. autor, m.; escritor, m.
authoress, —ĕs, s. autora, escritora, f.
authorisation, ăthŏrĕzā'shŭn, s. autorización, f.
authorise, ā'thŏrīz, v. a. autorizar.
authoritative, ăthŏr'ĕtătĭv, a. autoritativo; —ly, ad. autoritativamente, con autoridad.   [apariencia autoritativa, f.
authoritativeness, —nĕs, s. presunción, f.;
authority, ăthŏr'ĕtĭ, s. autoridad, f.
authorship, ā'thŭrshĭp, s. calidad de autor.
autocracy, ātŏk'răsĕ, s. autocracia, f. [f.
autocrat, ā'tŏkrăt, s. autócrata, m.   [tico.
autocratic(al), ātŏkrăt'ĭk(ăl), a. autocrá-
autograph, ā'tŏgrăf, s. autógrafo, m.
autography, ātŏg'răfĕ, s. autografía, f.
automatic, ātŏmăt'ĭk, a. automático.

automaton, ảtŏ́mȧtŏn, s. automato, m.
autonomy, ȧtŏ́n'ŏmĕ, s. autonomía, f.
autopsy, ȧ'tŏpsĕ, s. autopsia, f.
autumn, ȧ'tŭm, s. otoño, m.
autumnal, ȧtŭm'nȧl, a. otoñal.
auxiliary, ȧgzĭl'yȧrĕ, a. auxiliar, asistente.
auxiliaries, -z, s. pl. tropas auxiliares, f. pl.
avail, ȧvȧl', v. a. aprovechar; —, v. n. servir, ser ventajoso; —, s. provecho, m.; ventaja, f.
available, -ȧbl, a. útil, ventajoso.
avalanche, ȧv'ḋlȧntsh, s. alud, lurte, m.
avarice, ȧv'ȧrĭs, s. avaricia, f.
avaricious, ȧvȧrĭsh'ŭs, a. avaro; —ly, ad. avaramente.
avaunt, ȧvȧnt'! ¡fuera! ¡quita!
avenge, ȧvĕnj', v. a. vengarse, castigar.
avenue, ȧv'ĕnū, s. calle de árboles, f.; avenida, f.
aver, ȧvĕr', a. v. afirmar, verificar, declarar.
average, ȧv'ĕrḋj, v. a. tomar un término medio; —, s. precio medio, m.; (mar.) avería, f.   [—ly, ad. con repugnancia.
averse, ȧvĕrs', a. contrario, repugnante;
aversion, ȧvĕr'shŭn, aversation, ȧvĕrsḋ'shŭn, s. aversión, f., disgusto, m.
avert, ȧvĕrt', v. a. desviar, apartar.
aviary, ȧ'vĕȧrĕ, s. pajarera, f.
avidity, ȧvĭd'ĭtĕ, s. codicia, avidez, f.
avocation, ȧvŏkȧ'shŭn, s. ocupación, f.; estorbo, m.   [(law) anular.
avoid, ȧvŏĭd', v. a. evitar, escapar, huir;
avoidable, -ȧbl, a. evitable.   [fuga, f.
avoidance, -ȧns, s. vacación, f.; evitación,
avoirdupois, ȧvŭrdŭpŏĭz', a. peso inglés de diez y seis onzas, m.   [sostener.
avouch, ȧvŏtsh', v. a. afirmar, justificar,
avow, ȧvŏ́', v. a. confesar, declarar.
avowal, -ȧl, s. declaración justificativa, confesión, f.   [abiertamente.
avowedly, -ĕdlĕ, ad. declaradamente,
await, ȧwȧt', v. a. aguardar; —, v. n. estar.
awake, ȧwȧk', v. a. & n. despertar; dejar de dormir; —, a. despierto.
awaken, -n, v. n. despertar.
awaking, -ĭng, s. despertamiento, m.
award, ȧwȧrd', v. a. juzgar, sentenciar; —, v. n. determinar; —, s. sentencia, decisión, f.   [dado! ¡mira!
aware, ȧwȧr', a. cauto, vigilante; —! ¡cuidado!
away, ȧwȧ', ad. ausente, fuera; —! ¡fuera, quita de ahí, marcha! far and —, de mucho, con mucho.
awe, ḋ, s. miedo, temor reverencial, m.; —, v. a. infundir miedo ó temor reverencial.
awful, -fŭl, a. tremendo; funesto; horroroso; —ly, ad. con respeto y veneración.
awfulness, -nĕs, s. veneración, f.; horror, m.
awhile, ȧhwĭl', ad. un rato, algún tiempo.
awkward, ȧk'wȧrd, a. tosco, inculto, rudo, poco diestro; —ly, ad. groseramente, toscamente.   [poca habilidad, f.
awkwardness, -nĕs, s. tosquedad, grosería,
awl, ȧl, s. lesna, f.
awning, ȧ'nĭng, s. (mar.) toldo (para guardarse del sol), m.   [al través, m.
awry, ȧrĭ', ad. oblicuamente, torcidamente,
axe, ȧks, s. segur, f.; hacha, f.

axiom, ȧk'sĭŭm (ȧk'shŭm), s. axioma, m.
axis, ȧk'sĭs, s. eje, m.
axle(-tree), ȧk'sl(trĕ), s. eje de una rueda,
ay, ȧĭ, ad. sí; —! ¡ay de mí!   [m.
azalea, ȧzȧlĕ'ḋ, s. (bot.) azalea, f.   [leo, m.
azure, ȧ'zhŭr, a. azulado; —, s. color cerú-

B

baa, bȧ, s. balido, m.; —, v. n. balar.
babble, bȧb'bl, v. n. charlar, parlotear; —, babbling, -ĭng, s. charla, cháchara, f., flujo de hablar, m.
babbler, -ȧr, s. charlador, charlatán, m.
babe, bȧb, baby, bȧ'bĕ, s. niño pequeño, nene, m.; infante, m.   [grande.
baboon, bȧbŏn', s. cinocéfalo, m., mono
babyhood, bȧ'bĕhŭd, s. niñez, f.
babyish, -ĭsh, a. piñero; pueril.
baby-linen, -lĭnĕn, s. envoltura de una criatura recién nacida, f.
bacchanalian, bȧkkȧnȧ'lĕȧn, a. disipado, licencioso, disoluto.   [m.
bachelor, bȧtsh'ĕlȧr, s. soltero, m.; bachiller,
bachelorship, -shĭp, s. soltería, f.; bachillerato, m.
back, bȧk, s. dorso, m.; revés de la mano, m.; recazo, m.; —, ad. atrás, detrás; otra ó segunda vez; — of, detrás; a few years —, algunos años ha; —, v. a. montar á caballo; sostener, apoyar, favorecer.
backbite, -bĭt, v. a. hablar mal del que está ausente; difamar.
backbiter, -bĭtȧr, s. detractor, m.
back-board, -bȯrd, s. respaldo de bote, m.
backbone, -bȯn, s. hueso dorsal, espinazo,
backdoor, -dȯr, s. puerta trasera, f.   [m.
backer, -ȧr, s. partidario, m.
backfriend, -frĕnd, s. amigo falso, m.
backgammon, -gȧm'mŭn, s. juego de chaquete ó tablas, m.
background, -grȯnd, s. fondo, m.; hondo (de una perspectiva, &c.), m.
back-number, -nŭmbȧr, s. número atrasado de algún periódico, m.   [sada, f.
back-payment, -pȧmĕnt, s. paga atrasada, f.
back-sight, -sĭt, s. mira (de una escopeta), f.   [versar.
backslide, -slĭd, v. n. apostatar; tergiversar.
backstairs, -stȧrs, s. pl. escalera secreta, f.
backward, -wȧrd, a. opuesto, enemigo; tardo, lento; —, -s, -ly, ad. preposteramente; con repugnancia.
backwardness, -wȧrdnĕs, s. torpeza, tardanza, f.; repugnancia, f.
backwoods, -wŭdz, s. pl. bosques del
bacon, bȧ'kn, s. tocino, m.   [Misuri, m. pl.
bad, bȧd, a. mal, malo; perverso; infeliz; dañoso; indispuesto; —ly, ad. malamente.
badge, bȧj, s. señal, f.; símbolo, m.; divisa, f.; —, v. a. divisar.
badger, -ȧr, s. tejón, m.; —, v. a. fatigar; cansar, atormentar.   [f.
badness, bȧd'nĕs, s. maldad, mala calidad,
baffle, bȧf'fl, v. a. eludir; confundir, hundir; acosar.   [v. a. entalegar.
bag, bȧg, s. saco, m.; talega, f., bolsa, f.; —,

baggage, *băg'gĕj*, s. bagaje, equipaje, m.

bagging, *băg'ging*, s. tela basta, f.

bagman, *băg'măn*, s. comisionista viajante de una casa de comercio, m.

bagnio, *băn'yō*, s. estufa, f.; burdel, m.

bagpipe, *băg'pĭp*, s. gaita, f.

bail, *bāl*, s. fianza, caución (juratoria),f.; fiador, m.; –, v. a. caucionar, fiar.

bailable, *–ābl*, a. caucionable.

bailee, *–ē'*, s. (law) depositario, m.

bailiff, *bā'lĭf*, s. alguacil, m.; mayordomo, bailío, m. [m.

bait, *bāt*, v. a. cebar; azuzar; atraer; –, v. n. tomar un refrigerio; –, s. cebo, m.; anzuelo, m.; refrigerio, m.

baize, *bāz*, s. bayeta, f.

bake, *bāk*, v. a. cocer en horno. [dería, f.

bakehouse, *–hŏŭs*, bakery, *–rĭ*, s. pana-

baker, *–ŭr*, s. hornero, panadero, m.; –'s dozen, trece piezas.

balance, *băl'lăns*, s. balanza, f.; equilibrio, m.; volante de reloj, m.; saldo de una cuenta, m.; to lose one's –, caerse, dar en tierra; –, v. a. pesar en balanza; contrapesar; saldar; considerar, examinar; –, v. n. dudar, fluctuar.

balance-sheet, *–shēt*, s. bilance, m.

balancing-pole, *băl'lănsĭngpōl*, s. balan-

balcony, *băl'kŏnĕ*, s. balcón, m. [cín, m.

bald, *băld*, a. calvo; desabrido.

baldness, *–nĕs*, s. calvez, f.; desnudez, f.

bale, *bāl*, s. bala, f.; fardo de mercaderías, m.; –, v. a. embalar; tirar el agua del bote.

baleful, *–fŭl*, a. triste, funesto; –ly, ad. tristemente; miseramente.

balk, *băk*, s. viga, f.; contratiempo, m.; agravio, perjuicio, m.; –, v. a. frustrar; faltar á la palabra; pasar, omitir. [m.

ball, *băl*, s. bola, f.; pelota, f.; bala, f.; baile.

ballad, *băl'lăd*, s. balada ó balata, f.

ballad-singer, *–sĭngŭr*, s. jacarero, m.

ballast, *băl'lăst*, s. lastre, m.; –, v. a.lastrar.

ballet, *băl'lĕt*, s. baileto, m.

balloon, *băllōn'*, s. globo, m.; máquina aerostática, f.

ballot, *băl'lŏt*, s. bolilla para votar f.; escrutinio, m.; –, v. n. votar con balotas.

balm, *băm*, balsam, *băl'săm*, s. bálsamo, m.; –, v. a. untar con bálsamo; suavizar.

balmy, *–ĭ*, balsamic, *bălsăm'ĭk*, a. bal-sámico; fragante; lo que mitiga y suaviza.

baluster, *băl'lŭstŭr*, s. balaustre, m.

balustrade, *băllŭstrād'*, s. balaustrada, f.

bamboo, *bămbō'*, s. bambou, f.

bamboozle, *bămbō'zl*, v.a. (vulg.) engañar; cansar, burlar.

ban, *băn*, s. bando, anuncio, m.; excomunión, f.; proclama, f.; –, v. a. excomulgar; maldecir.

band, *bănd*, s. venda, faja, unión, f.; cuadrilla, f.; banda (de soldados), f.; orquesta, capilla, f.; –, v. a. unir, juntar; vendar.

bandage, *–dj*, s. venda, faja, f.; vendaje, m.; –, v. a. vendar, fajar. [sombrerera, f.

bandbox, *–bŏks*, s. caja para cintas, f.; bandit, *băn'dĭt*, s. bandido, m.

band-master, *bănd'măstŭr*, s. (mus.) maestro de capilla, m.

bandy, *băn'dĭ*, v. n. pelotear; discutir.

bandy-legged, *–lĕggĕd*, a. patizambo.

bane, *băn*, s. veneno, m.; ruina, f.; rat's–, arsénico, m.; –, v. a. envenenar.

baneful, *–fŭl*, a. venenoso, destructivo.

bang, *băng*, s. puñada, f.; golpe, m.; –, v. a. dar puñadas, sacudir; cerrar con violencia. [las indias, m.

bangle, *băng'gl*, s. brazalete delgado de banish, *băn'nĭsh*, v. a. desterrar, echar fuera, proscribir, expatriar.

banishment, *–mĕnt*, s. destierro, m.

banjo, *băn'jō*, s. banjo, m., guitarra de los negros.

bank, *băngk*, s. orilla (de río), f.; montón de tierra, m.; banco, m.; dique, m.; escollo, m.; –, v. a. poner dinero en un banco; detener el agua con diques.

banker, *–ŭr*, s. banquero, cambista, m.

bank-note, *–nŏt*, s. billete de banco, m.

bankrupt, *–rŭpt*, a. insolvente; –, s. fallido, quebrado, m. [bra, f.

bankruptcy, *–rŭptsĕ*, s. bancarrota, quiebanner, *băn'nŭr*, s. bandera, f.; estandarte, m.

banneret, *–nŭrĕt*, s. ricohombre de pendón y caldera, m.; bandereta, f.

bannister, *–nĭstŭr*, s. balaustre, m.

banquet, *băng'kwĕt*, s. banquete, m.; –, v. a. banquetear.

bantam, *băn'tăm*, s. bantama, f. (ave).

banter, *băn'tŭr*, v. a. zumbar; divertirse á costa de alguno; –, s. zumba, burla, f.

bantling, *bănt'lĭng*, s. chicuelo, m.; chicuela, f.

baptise, *băp'tĭz*, v. a. bautizar.

baptism, *băp'tĭzm*, s. bautismo, m.

baptismal, *băptĭz'măl*, a. bautismal.

baptistery, *băp'tĭstŭrĕ*, s. bautisterio, m.

bar, *băr*, s. barra, f.; tranca, f.; obstáculo, m.; (law) estrados, m. pl.; aparador, m.; –, v. a. cerrar con barras; impedir; prohibir; excluir.

barb, *bărb*, s. barba, f.; caballo de Berbería, m.; –, v. a. hacer la barba; guarnecer á un caballo con barda; armar flechas con lengüetas. [m.; –, s. bárbaro, cruel.

barbarian, *bărbā'rĭăn*, s. hombre bárbaro,

barbarism, *băr'bărĭzm*, s. (gr.) barba-rismo, m.; crueldad, f. [humanidad, f.

barbarity, *bărbăr'ĭtĕ*, s. barbaridad, in-

barbarous, *băr'bărŭs*, a. bárbaro, cruel; –ly, ad. bárbaramente, cruelmente.

barber, *băr'bŭr*, s. barbero, m.

bard, *bărd*, s. bardo, m.; poeta, m.

bare, *băr*, a. desnudo, descubierto; simple; público; pobre; puro; –, v. a. desnudar, descubrir, priyar. [muy flaca, f.

barebone, *–bŏn*, s. esqueleto, m.; persona barefaced, *–făsd*, a. desvergonzado, impudente. [patos.

barefoot(ed), *–fŭt(ĕd)*, a. descalzo, sin za-

bareheaded, *–hĕdĕd*, a. descubierto, con la cabeza al aire. [nas,

barelegged, *–lĕggĕd*, a. con las pier-

barely, *–lĕ*, ad. apenas, solamente; pobremente.

bareness, *–nĕs*, s. desnudez, f.; pobreza,f.

bargain, *băr'gĭn*, s. contrato, pacto, m.; compra ó venta, f.; a –! 'tis a –! ¡sea! –, v. n. pactar; negociar.

barge, bárj, s. falúa, chalupa, f.

bargeman, —mān, bargee, bärjē, s. barquero, m.

bar-iron, bär'tärn, s. hierro en barras, m.

baritone, băr'ĭ tōn, s. (mus.) baritono, m.

bark, bärk, s. corteza; ladra, f. (del perro); —, v. a. descortezar; —, v. n. ladrar.

barley, bär'lĭ, s. cebada, f.

barmaid, băr'mād, s. moza de taberna, f.

barn, bärn, s. granero, henil, pajar, m.

barnacles, băr'näklz, s. pl. acial, m.

barn-floor, bärn'flōr, s. era, f.; pajar, m.

barometer, bărŏ'mĕtär, s. barómetro, m.

baron, băr'rŭn, s. barón, m.; juez de la baronage, —ĝj, s. baronía, f. [tesorería, m.

baroness, —ĕs, s. baronesa, f.

baronet, —ĕt, s. título de honor inferior al de barón y superior al de caballero, m.

baronial, bărŏ'nĭdl, a. de barón.

barony, băr'răne, s. baronía, f.

barrack, băr'răk, s. cuartel, m.

barratry, băr'rātrĕ, s. baratería, f.; engaño, [m.

barrel, băr'rĕl, s. barril, m.; cañón de escopeta, m.; cilindro, m.; —, v. a. embarrilar.

barrelled, —d, a. (of fire-arms) con ... cañones; (of roads) encorvado.

barrel-organ, —ŏr'găn, s. gaita, f.; organillo de cilindro, m.

barren, băr'rĕn, a. estéril, infructuoso; —ly, ad. infructuosamente, sin fruto.

barrenness, —nĕs, s. esterilidad, infecundidad, f.; falta de ingenio, f.; tibieza, f.

barricade, băr'ĭkād, s. barricada, f.; estacada, f.; barrera, f.; —, v. a. cerrar con barreras, empalizar; atrincherar. [m.

barrier, băr'rĭär, s. barrera, f.; obstáculo, barring, băr'rĭng, ad. excepto, fuera de.

barrister, băr'rĭstär, s. abogado, m.

bar-room, băr'rōm, s. taberna, f.

barrow, băr'rō, s. angarillas, f. pl.; puerco, barter, băr'tär, v. n. baratar, traficar; —, v. a. cambiar, trocar.

basaltes, băsäl'tĕz, s. basalto, m.

base, bās, s. fondo, m.; basa, f.; pedestal, m.; contrabajo, m.; —, v. a. apoyar; —, a. bajo, vil; —ly, ad. bajamente.

baseless, —lĕs, a. sin fondo ó base.

basement, —mĕnt, s. basamento, m.

baseness, —nĕs, s. bajeza, vileza, f.; ilegitimidad de nacimiento, f.; mezquinería, f.

bashaw, băshā', s. bajá, m.

bashful, băsh'fŭl, a. vergonzoso, modesto, tímido; —ly, ad. vergonzosamente.

basilisk, băz'zĭlĭsk, s. basilisco, m.

basin, băs'sn, s. jofaina, bacía, f.

basis, băs'sĭs, s. base, f.; fundamento, m.

bask, băsk, v. n. ponerse á tomar el sol.

basket, băs'kĕt, s. cesta, canasta, f.

bass, băss, s. estera, f.; —, băs, (mus.) contrabajo, m.

bassoon, băssōn', s. bajón, m.

bass-viol, băss'ī'ōl, s. viola, f.

bass-voice, băs'vŏĭs, s. bajo cantante, m.

bastard, băs'tärd, s. & a. bastardo (m.).

bastardy, —ĕ, s. bastardía, f.

baste, băst, v. a. dar golpes con un bastón; pringar la carne en el asador; hilvanar.

bastinado, băstĭnā'ō, s. bastonada, f.; —, v. a. dar golpes con un bastón.

basting, băs'tĭng, s. hilván, m.; apuleamiento, m., paliza, f.

bastion, băs'yŏn, s. (mil.) bastión, m.

bat, băt, s. garrote, m.; murciélago, m.

batch, bătsh, s. cochura, hornada, f.

bate, băt, v. a. minorar; bajar el precio, bat-fowling, băt'fōwlĭng, s. caza de pájaros

bath, băth, s. baño, m. [por la noche, f.

bathe, băth, v. a. (& n.) bañar(se). [m.

bathing-gown, bā'thĭnggōōn, s. peinador, bath-keeper, băth'kēpär, s. bañero, m.

bathos, bā'thŏs, s. estilo bajo en la poesía, m.

bath-tub, băth'tŭb, s. baño, m. (la cuba).

battalion, băttăl'yăn, s. (mil.) batallón, m.

batten, băt'tn, s. astilla, f.; —, v. a. cebar; —, v. n. engordar.

batter, băt'tär, v. a. apalear; batir, cañonear; demoler; —, s. batido, m.

battering-ram, —ĭngrăm, s. (mil.) ariete, battery, —ĕ, s. batería, f. [m.

battle, băt'tl, s. combate, m.; batalla, f.; —, v. n. batallar, combatir.

battle-array, —ărră, s. orden de batalla, f.

battledore, —dŏr, s. raqueta, f.

battlement, —mĕnt, s. muralla almenada, f.

bauble, bā'bl, s. chuchería, cosa de poca importancia, pero pulida y delicada, f.

bawl, băl, v. n. gritar, vocear; ladrar.

bay, bā, s. puerto donde se abrigan las embarcaciones, m.; bahía, f.; laurel, lauro, m.; —, v. n. ladrar; balar; —, a. bayo.

bayonet, bā'ŏnĕt, s. bayoneta, f.; —, v. a. traspasar con la bayoneta.

bay-window, bā'wĭndō, s. ventana salebe, bē, v. n. ser; estar. [diza, f.

beach, bētsh, s. costa, ribera, orilla, f.; cabo, m.; —, v. a. (mar.) encallar.

beacon, bēk'n, s. valiza, almenara, f.

bead, bĕd, s. cuenta, f.; —s, s. pl. rosario, m.

beadle, bē'dl, s. macero, m.; bedel (en las universidades), m.; alguacil, ministril, m. (en los tribunales).

beagle, bē'gl, s. sabueso, m.

beak, bēk, s. pico; espolón de navío, m.

beaker, —är, s. taza con pico, f.

beam, bēm, s. lanza de coche, f.; rayo de luz, m.; volante, m.; brazos de balanza, m. pl.; —, v. n. emitir rayos, brillar. [m.

bean, bēn, s. haba, f.; French —, faséolo, bear, băr, v. a. llevar alguna cosa como carga; sostener, apoyar; soportar; producir; parir; —, v. n. sufrir (algún dolor); pasar á algún paraje.

bear, —, s. oso, m.; she —, osa, f.

bearable, —ăbl, a. soportable.

board, bōrd, s. barba, f.; arista de espiga, f.; —, v. a. insultar á uno.

bearded, —ĕd, a. barbado.

beardless, —lĕs, a. desbarbado, joven.

bearer, băr'är, s. portador, m.; árbol fructífero, m.

bearing, bā'rĭng, s. situación, f.; modo de portarse en lo exterior, m.; dolor, m.

beast, bēst, s. bestia, f.; hombre brutal, m.; — of burden, acémila, f.

beastliness, —lĭnĕs, s. bestialidad, brutalidad, f. [mente.

beastly, —lĕ, a. bestial, brutal; —, ad. brutalbeat, bēt, v. a. golpear; batir; tocar (un tambor); pisar; abatir; —, v. n. pulsar, palpitar; —, s. golpe, m.; pulsación, f.

beatific, *băătĭf ĭk*, a. beatífico.

beatify, *băă tĭfī*, v. a. beatificar, santificar.

beating, *bēt ĭng*, s. paliza, zurra, f.; pulsación, f.

beatitude, *băăt ĭtŭd*, s. beatitud, felicidad, f.

beau, *bō*, s. petimetre, currutaco, m.

beauteous, *bū tĭŭs*, a. bello, hermoso.

beautiful, *bū tĭfŭl*, a. hermoso, bello; **-ly**, ad. con belleza ó perfección.

beautify, *bū tĭfī*, v. a. hermosear; embellecer; adornar; —, v. n. hermosearse.

beauty, *bū tĭ*, s. hermosura, belleza, f. **--spot**, s. lunar, m.

beaver, *bē vŭr*, s. castor, m.; sombrero de pelo de castor, m.

becalm, *bĕkăm'*, v. a. serenar, calmar alguna tempestad; sosegar.

because, *bĭkăz'*, c. porque, á causa de.

beck, *bĕk*, s. seña, indicación muda, f.

beckon, *-kn*, v. n. hacer seña con la cabeza, ó la mano.

become, *bĭkŭm'*, v. a. convenir; estar bien; —, v. n. hacerse, convertirse, venir á parar.

becoming, *bĭkŭm'ĭng*, a. decente, conveniente; **-ly**, ad. decentemente.

becomingness, *-nĕs*, s. decencia, elegancia, propiedad, f.

bed, *bĕd*, s. cama, f.; —, v. a. meter en la cama, acostar.

bedaub, *bĕdăb'*, v. a. salpicar; ensuciar.

bed-chamber, *bĕd'tshămbŭr*, s. dormitorio, m.

bed-clothes, *-klōz*, s. pl. cobertores, mantas ó colchas, pl.

bedding, *-ĭng*, s. ropa de cama, f.

bedecked, *bĕdĕk'd*, a. adornado.

bedew, *bĕdū'*, v. a. rociar; regar.

bedim, *bĕdĭm'*, v. a. obscurecer.

bedizen, *bĕdī'zn*, v. a. ataviar; perifollar.

bedlam, *bĕd'lăm*, s. manicomio, m.

bedlamite, *-īt*, s. loco, orate, m.

bed-post, *bĕd'pōst*, s. pilar de cama, m.

bedraggle, *bĕdrăg'gl*, v. a. vulg. enlodar.

bedridden, *bĕd'rĭdn*, a. postrado en cama (sea por vejez ó enfermedad).

bedstead, *-stĕd*, s. armazón de cama, f.

bed-time, *-tĭm*, s. hora de irse á la cama, f.

bee, *bē*, s. abeja, f.

beech, *bētsh*, s. haya, f.

beechen, *-n*, a. de haya.

beech-nut, *-nŭt*, s. hayuco, m.

beef, *bēf*, s. buey (toro ó vaca), m.; **beeves**, *bēvz*, pl. ganado vacuno, m.

beef-eater, *-ĕtŭr*, s. alabardero real, m.

beef-fork, *-fŏrk*, s. tenedor de cocina, m.

beef-steak, *-stāk*, s. lonja de carne de buey, f.

beef-tea, *-tē*, s. caldo, m.

bee-hive, *bē'hĭv*, s. colmena, f.

bee-line, *-lĭn*, s. línea recta, f. (floja, f.

beer, *bēr*, s. cerveza, f.; **small**, — cerveza floja, f.

beeswax, *bēz'wăks*, s. cera, f.

beet, *bēt*, s. acelga, f.

beetle, *-l*, s. escarabajo, m.; pisón, m.

beet-root, *-rōt*, s. betarraga, f. (venir.

befall, *bĭfăl'*, v. n. suceder, acontecer, sobrevenir.

befit, *bĕfĭt'*, v. a. convenir, acomodarse á.

befool, *bĭfūl'*, v. a. infatuar.

before, *bĭfōr'*, ad. & pr. más adelante; delante, enfrente; ante, antes de.

beforehand, *-hănd*, ad. de antemano, anticipadamente.   (tiempo atrás.

beforetime, *-tĭm*, ad. en tiempo pasado,

befoul, *bĕfŏul'*, v. a. ensuciar, emporcar.

befriend, *bĕfrĕnd'*, v. a. favorecer, proteger, amparar.

beg, *bĕg*, v. a. mendigar, rogar; suplicar; suponer; —, v. n. vivir de limosna.

beget, *bĕgĕt'*, v. a. engendrar.   (pobrecer.

beggar, *bĕg'gŭr*, s. mendigo, m.; —, v. a. em-

beggarliness, *-lĭnĕs*, s. mezquindad, pobreza, miseria, f.

beggarly, *-lĭ*, a. pobre, miserable; —, ad. mezquinamente, pobremente.

beggary, *-ĭ*, s. mendicidad, mendiguez, f.

begin, *bĭgĭn'*, v. a. & n. comenzar, principiar.

beginner, *-nŭr*, s. principiante, m.; novicio, m.   (—s, pl. rudimentos, m. pl.

beginning, *-nĭng*, s. principio, origen, m.;

begone, *bĕgŏn'*! ¡fuera, apártate de ahí!

begrime, *bĕgrĭm'*, v. a. encenagar, ennegrecer, embarrar, manchar.

begrudge, *bĕgrŭj'*, v. a. envidiar.

beguile, *bĕgĭl'*, v. a. engañar.

behalf, *bĕhăf'*, s. favor, patrocinio, m.; consideración, f.   (bien ó mal.

behave, *bĕhăv'*, v. n. comportarse, portarse

behaviour, *bĕhăv'yŭr*, s. conducta, f.; modo de portarse, m.   (cabeza.

behead, *bĕhĕd'*, v. a. decapitar, cortar la

behest, *bĕhĕst'*, s. mandato, precepto, m.

behind, *bĕhĭnd'*, pr. detrás; atrás; inferior á; —, ad. atrasadamente; fuera de la vista

behindhand, *-hănd*, ad. con atraso.

behold, *bĕhōld'*, v. a. ver, contemplar, observar; —! ¡he aquí! ¡ved ahí!

beholden, *-n*, a. obligado (por gratitud).

behoof, *bĕhōf'*, s. provecho, m.; utilidad, ventaja, f.   (ó necesario.

behove, *bĕhōv'*, v. n. importar, ser útil

being, *bē ĭng*, s. existencia, f.; estado, m.; ente, m.; persona (que existe), f.; —, c. ya que, puesto que.   (das.

belabour, *bĕlā'bŭr*, v. n. apalear, dar puña-

belated, *bĕlā'tĕd*, a. trasnochado.

belch, *bĕlsh*, v. n. eructar, vomitar; —, s. eructo, m.; eructación, f.

beldam, *bĕl'dăm*, s. vejezuela, f.; bruja, f.

beleaguer, *bĕlē'gŭr*, v. a. sitiar, bloquear.

belfry, *bĕl'frĭ*, s. campanario, m.

belie, *bĕlī'*, v. a. contrahacer; desmentir, calumniar.   (f.; credo, m.

belief, *bĕlēf'*, s. fe, creencia, f.; opinión,

believable, *bĕlē'văbl*, a. creíble.

believe, *bĕlēv'*, v. a. creer; —, v. n. pensar, imaginar.   (m.

believer, *-ŭr*, s. creyente, fiel, cristiano,

bell, *bĕl*, s. campana, f.: to bear the —, ser el primero; —, v. n. crecer una planta en figura de campana; gritar (como los ciervos).

bellicose, *bĕl'lĭkōs*, a. belicoso.

belligerent, *bĕllĭj'ărĕnt*, a. beligerante.

bellman, *bĕl'măn*, s. pregonero, m.

bellow, *bĕl'lō*, v. n. bramar; rugir; vociferar; —, s. bramido, m.

bellows, *bĕl'lōz* (vulg. *bĕl'lŭs*), s. fuelle, m.

bell-pull, *bĕl'pŭl*, **bell-rope**, *-rōp*, s. conductor de una campanilla, m.

bell-ringer, -ríngŭr, s. campanero, m.

belly, bĕl'lĭ, s. vientre, m.; panza, f.

bellyful, -fūl, s. panzada, f.; hartura, f.

belong, bĕlóng', v. n. pertenecer, tocar á, concernir.

belongings, -ĭngs, s. pl. calidades, f. pl.

beloved, bĕlŭvd', a. querido, amado.

below, bĕlō', ad. &'pr. debajo, inferior; [abajo.

belt, bĕlt, s. cinturón, cinto, m.

bemoan, bĕmōn', v. a. deplorar, lamentar.

bench, bĕnsh s. banco, m.; King's —, tribunal principal de justicia, m.; una prisión

bencher, -ŭr, s. asesor, m. [de Londres.

bend, bĕnd, v. a. encorvar, inclinar, plegar; hacer una reverencia; —, v. n. encorvarse, inclinarse; —, s. comba, encorvadura, f.

beneath, bĕnéth', ad. & pr. debajo, abajo; de lo más hondo. [f.

benediction, bĕnĕdĭk'shŭn, s. bendición.

benefaction, bĕnĕfăk'shŭn, s. beneficio, m.; gracia, f.

benefactor, -tŭr, s. bienhechor, m.

benefactress, -trĕs, s. bienhechora, f.

benefice, bĕn'rĕfĭs, s. beneficio, m.; beneficio eclesiástico.

beneficence, bĕnĕf'ĭsĕns, s. beneficencia, liberalidad, f. [benéficamente.

beneficent, -ĭsĕnt, a. benéfico; -ly, ad.

beneficial, bĕnĕfĭsh'ăl, a. beneficioso, provechoso, útil; -ly, ad. provechosamente, ventajosamente.

beneficiary, -ărĭ, s. beneficiario, m.

benefit, bĕn'nĕfĭt, s. beneficio, m.; utilidad, f.; provecho, m.; —, v. a. beneficiar; —, v. n. utilizarse; prevalerse.

benefit-night, -nīt, s. representación dramática al beneficio de un actor ó de una actriz, f.

benevolence, bĕnĕv'ōlĕns, s. benevolencia, f.; donativo gratuito, m.

benevolent, -ōlĕnt, a. benévolo.

benighted, bĕnīt'ĕd, (p. & j a. anochecido.

benign, bĕnīn', a. benigno; afable; liberal; -ly, ad. benignamente.

benignant, bĕnĭg'nănt, a. bondadoso,

benignity, -nĭtĕ, s. benignidad, bondad, dulzura, f.

bent, bĕnt, s. encorvadura, f.; inclinación.

benumb, bĕnŭm', v. a. entorpecer. [f.

benzine, bĕn'zēn, s. (chem.) benzina, f.

benzoin, bĕn'zŏĭn, s. benjuí, m. [camente.

bepraise, bĕprāz', v. a. lisonjear hiperbóli-

bequeath, bĕkwēth', v. a. legar en testa-

bequeather, -ŭr, s. testador, m. [mento.

bequest, bĕkwĕst', s. legado, m.

bereave, bĕrēv', v. a. despojar, privar.

bereavement, -mĕnt, s. despojo, m.

berlin, bĕr'lĭn, s. berlina, f. (coche).

berry, bĕr'rĕ, s. baya, f. [navío, m.

berth, bŭrth, s. (mar.) alojamiento de un

beseech, bĕsēch', v. a. suplicar, implorar, conjurar, rogar.

beseem, bĕsēm', v. n. convenir, parecer bien.

beseeming, -ĭng, s. gracia, decencia, f.

beset, bĕsĕt', v. a. sitiar; cercar; perseguir.

besetting, -ĭng, a. habitual.

beside(s), bĕsīd(s)', pr. al lado de; excepto; sobre; fuera de; —, ad. por otra parte, aun.

besiege, bĕsēj', v. a. sitiar, bloquear.

besmear, bĕsmēr', v. a. salpicar, ensuciar.

besot, bĕsŏt', v. a. infatuar; embrutecer.

bespatter, bĕspăt'tŭr, v. a. manchar con porquería; disfamar. [alguna cosa.

bespeak, bĕspēk', v. a. ordenar, apalabrar

besprinkle, bĕsprĭng'kl, v. a. rociar, esparcir sobre. [lo mejor.

best, bĕst, a. mejor; —, ad. más bien; —, s.

bestial, bĕst'yăl, a. bestial, brutal; -ly, ad. bestialmente. [brutalidad, f.

bestiality, bĕstyăl'ĭtĕ, s. bestialidad,

bestir, bĕstŭr', v. n. removerse, intrigar.

bestow, bĕstō' v. a. dar, conferir; otorgar; dar en matrimonio; regalar.

bestowal, -ăl, s. donativo, m.

bestrew, bĕstrō', v. a. esparcir ó derramar sobre; polvorear, salpicar.

bet, bĕt, s. apuesta, f.; —, v. a. apostar.

betake, bĕtāk', v. a. recurrir, acudir; one's self to, aplicarse.

bethink, bĕthĭnk', v. a. recordar algo; —, v. n. considerar, pensar.

betide, bĕtīd', v. n. acaecer, suceder.

betoken, bĕtō'kn, v. a. anunciar; denotar.

betime(s), bĕtīm(z)', ad. con tiempo, en sazón; pronto. [gar algún secreto.

betray, bĕtrā', v. a. hacer traición; divul-

betrayal, -ăl, s. traición, f.

betroth, bĕtrŏth', v. a. contraer esponsales.

betrothal, -ăl, s. esponsales, m. pl.

better, bĕt'tŭr, a. & ad. mejor; mejor, más bien; so much the —, tanto mejor; —s, s. pl. superiores, m. pl.; —, v. a. mejorar, reformar.

bettor, bĕt'tŭr, s. apostador, m.

between, bĕtwēn', betwixt, bĕtwĭkst' pr. entre, en medio de; —whiles, (vulg.) á ratos, mientras tanto.

bevel, bĕv'ĕl, s. cartabón, m.; —, v. a. cortar un ángulo al sesgo. [m.

beverage, bĕv'ŭrăj, s. bebida, f.; trago,

bevy, bĕv'ĭ, s. bandada (de aves), f.

bewail, bĕwāl', v. a. lamentar, deplorar.

beware, bĕwār', v. n. guardarse.

bewilder, bĕwĭl'dŭr, v. a. descaminar; embarazar; pasmar; —, v. n. extraviarse.

bewilderment, -mĕnt, s. extravío, m.; embarazo, m.

bewitch, bĕwĭtsh', v. a. encantar, hechizar.

bewitchingly, -ĭnglĕ, ad. halagüeñamente. [slante, fuera de.

beyond, bĕyŏnd', pr. más allá, más ade-

bezel, bĕz'ĕl, s. chatón, m.

bezoar, bĕz'zŏr, s. bezar, m.

bias, bī'ăs, s. propensión, inclinación, f.; sesgo, m.; objeto, fin, m.; —, v. a. inclinar; preocupar; ganar.

bib, bĭb, s. babador, m.

bibber, -bŭr, s. bebedor, borrachón, m.

Bible, bī'bl, s. Biblia (la sagrada escritura), f.

biblical, bĭb'lĭkăl, a. bíblico. [f.

bibliography, bĭblŏg'răfĭ, s. bibliografía,

bicker, bĭk'kŭr, v. n. escaramucear, reñir, disputar.

bickern, -n, s. pico de bigornia, m.

bid, bĭd, v. a. convidar; mandar, ordenar; ofrecer; — adieu to, despedirse.

bidding, -dĭng, s. orden, f., mandato, m.; ofrecimiento, m.

bide, *bíd*, v. a. sufrir, aguantar; —, v. n.
biennial, *bïän'niäl*, a. bienal. [residir.
bier, *bér*, s. féretro, ataúd, m.
biffin, *bïf'fïn*, s. manzana cocida en el
horno, f. [puntas ó dientes.
bifurcated, *bïfür'kätëd*, a. dividido en dos
big, *bïg*, a. grande, lleno; inflado.
bigamist, *bïg'ämïst*, s. bígamo, m.
bigamy, *bïg'ämë*, s. bigamia, f.
bight, *bït*, s. bahía, f. [bulto, m.
bigness, *bïg'nës*, s. grandeza, f.; tamaño,
bigot, *bïg'öt*, s. beatón, m.; hipócrita, m.
bigoted, —*ëd*, a. santurrón, beatón; —ly,
ad. como un santurrón.
bilander, *bïl'ändër*, s. balandra, f.
bilberry, *bïl'bërrë*, s. arándano, f.; —es, s. pl.
bilbo, *bïl'bö*, s. estoque, m.; —es, s. pl.
cepo con grillos, m.
bile, *bïl*, bilis, f.; cólera, f. [hacer agua.
bilge, *bïlj*, s. pantoque, m.; —, v. a. (mar.)
bilious, *bïl'yüs*, a. bilioso.
bilk, *bïlk*, v. a. engañar, defraudar.
bill, *bïll*, s. pico de ave, m.; honcejo, m.;
papel, billete, m.; cédula, f.; cuenta, f.;
— of exchange, letra de cambio, f.;
doctor's —, receta de médico, f.; — of lading, conocimiento, m.; — of fare, minuta
ó lista de una comida, f.; —s, pl. letras de
cambio, cartas de pago, f. pl.; —s-pay-
able, s. letras pagaderas; —s-receiv-
able, s. letras aceptables; —, v. n. arrullar, acariciar. [dor, m.
bill-broker, —*brökär*, s. agiotador, corre-
billet, *bïl'lët*, s. billete, s. zoquete de
leña, m.; —, v. a. alojar soldados.
billiard-ball, *bïl'yärdböl*, s. billa, f.
billiard-pocket, —*pökkït*, s. bolsa en las
mesas de billar, f.
billiards, —*z*, s. billar, m.
billiard-table, —*täbl*, s. mesa de billar, f.
Billingsgate, *bïl'lïngsgät*, s. pescadería
en Londres, f.; lenguaje bajo, m.
billion, *bïl'yün*, s. millón de millones, m.
billow, *bïl'ö*, s. ola grande, f.
billowy, —*ë* a. hinchado como las olas.
bill-poster, *bïll'pöstär*, bill-sticker,
—*stïkkär*, s. fijacarteles, m.
bin, *bïn*, s. artesón, cofre, m.; armario, m.;
despensa, f.
bind, *bïnd*, v. a. atar; unir; encuadernar;
obligar, constreñir; impedir; poner á uno
á servir; —, v. n. ser obligatorio.
binder, —*är*, s. encuadernador, m.
binding, —*ïng*, s. venda, faja, f.
binnacle, *bïn'äkl*, s. (mar.) bitácora, f.
binocular, *bïnök'ülär*, a. (opt.) binocular.
biographer, *bïög'räfër*, s. biógrafo, m.
biographical, *bïögräf'ïkäl*, a. biográfico.
biography, *bïög'räfë*, s. biografía, f.
biped, *bï'pëd*, s. bípede, m.
birch, *bürtsh*, s. abedul, m.; —, v. a. varear.
birchen, —*n*, a. de abedul.
bird, *bürd*, s. ave, f.; pájaro, m.; —, v. n.
cazar ó coger pájaros.
bird-lime, —*lïm*, s. liga, f. [jaro, m.
bird's eye-view, —*s'ï vü*, s. vista de pá-
birth, *bürth*, s. nacimiento, m.; origen, m.;
parto, m.; puesto, m.; alojamiento de un
navío, m.

birth-day, —*dä*, s. cumpleaños, m.
birth-place, —*pläs*, s. suelo nativo, m.
birth-right, —*rït*, s. derechos de nacimiento, m. pl.; primogenitura. f.
biscuit, *bïs'kït*, s. bizcocho, m.
bisect, *bïsëkt'*, v. a. dividir en dos partes.
bishop, *bïsh'öp*, s. obispo, m.
bishopric, —*rïk*, s. obispado, m.
bismuth, *bïz'müth*, s. bismuto, m.
bison, *bï'zön*, s. bisonte, m.
bit, *bït*, s. bocado, m.; pedacito, m.; — of a
bridle, bocado del freno, m.; — of a key,
paletón de llave, m.; —, v. a. enfrenar.
bitch, *bïtsh*, s. perra, f.; (fig.) zorra, f.
bite, *bït*, v. a. morder; punzar, picar; satirizar; engañar; — the dust, morder
la tierra, morir; —, s. mordedura, f.; engañador, impostor, ladrón, m.
bitter, *bït'tär*, a. amargo, áspero; mordaz, satírico; penoso; —ly, ad. amarga-
mente; con pena; severamente.
bittern, —*n*, s. alcaraván, bitor, m.
bitterness, —*nës*, s. amargor, m.; rencor,
m.; pena, f.; dolor, m.
bitumen, *bïtü'mën*, s. betún, m.
bituminous, —*mïnüs*, a. bituminoso.
bivouac, *bïv'äk*, s. (mil.) vivac, vivaque,
m.; —, v. n. vivaquear.
bizarre, *bïzär'*, a. raro, extravagante.
blab, *bläb*, v. a. parlar, charlar, divulgar;
—, v. n. chismear; —, s. chismoso, soplón, m.
black, *bläk*, a. negro, obscuro; tétrico,
malvado; funesto; —, s. color negro, m.;
—, v. a. teñir de negro, negrecer; limpiar
(las botas).
blackamoor, —*ämör*, s. negro, m.
black-art, —*ärt*, s. nigromancia, f.
black-ball, —*böl*, v. a. excluir á uno vo-
tando con una bolita negra. [sano).
black-beetle, —*bëtl*, s. farinal, m. (gu-
blackberry, —*bërrë*, s. zarzamora, f.
blackbird, —*bürd*, s. merla, f. [f.
black-board, —*börd*, s. tabla, plancha,
black-book, —*bük*, s. libro de nigromancia, m.; (mil.) lista de castigos, f. [m.
black-cattle, —*kättl*, s. ganado vacuno,
black-draught, —*dräft*, s. infusión de
sene, f. [grecer.
blacken, —*n*, v. a. teñir de negro; enne-
blackfriar, —*frï'är*, s. dominicano, m.
blackguard, —*gärd*, s. hombre soez, galopín, m.
black-lead, —*lëd*, s. lápiz-plomo, m.
blackleg, —*lëg*, s. bribón, m.
black-letter, —*lëttär*, s. letra gótica, f.
blackmail, —*mäl*, s. tributo ó rescate que
los viajeros pagan á los salteadores, m.
blackness, —*nës*, s. negrura, f.
black-pudding, —*püddïng*, s. morcilla, f.
black-sheep, —*shëp*, s. oveja sarnosa, f.
blacksmith, —*smïth*, s. herrero, m.
black-thorn, —*thörn*, s. endrino, m.
bladder, *bläd'där*, s. vejiga, f.
blade, *blädd*, s. brizna, f.; hoja, f.; pala (de
remo), f.; jaquetón, m.
blamable, *blä'mäbl*, a. culpable; vituperable; —bly ad. culpablemente.
blame, *bläm*, v. a. vituperar; —, s. culpa,
vituperación, imputación, f.

blameless, -lĕs, a. inocente, irreprensible, puro; -ly, ad. inocentemente.

blanch, blănsh, v. a. blanquear; mondar, pelar; hacer pálido. [cible.

bland, blănd, a. blando, suave, dulce, apacible.

blandishment, -ĭshmĕnt, s. halago, m.; zalamería, f.; caricia, f.

blank, blăngk, a. blanco; pálido; (poet.) sin rima; confuso; -, s. blanco, m.; carta blanca, f. [quilla, f. (especie de pera).

blanket, -ĕt, s. cubierta de cama; blanblaspheme, blăsfēm', v. a. blasfemar, jurar, decir blasfemias.

blasphemous, blăs'fĕmŭs, a. blasfematorio; -ly, ad. blasfemamente.

blasphemy, blăs'fĕmĕ, s. blasfemia, f.

blast, blăst, s. soplo de aire, m.; influjo de astro maligno, m.; anublo, m.; -, v. a. marchitar, secar; arruinar; infamar; volar por medio de pólvora.

blast-furnace, -fŭrnăs, s. horno soplante.

blatant, blā'tănt, a. vocinglero.

blaze, blāz, s. llama, f.; rumor, m.; estrella, f.; -, v. n. encenderse en llama; brillar, resplandecer; -, v. a. inflamar; divulgar.

blazon, blā'zn, v. a. blasonar; decorar; brillar. [publicar.

blazonry, -rĕ, s. blasón, m.

bleach, blētsh, v. a. blanquear al sol; -, v. n. blanquear. [belado.

bleak, blēk, a. pálido, descolorido; frío, bleakness, -nĕs, s. frialdad, f.; palidez, f.

blear(-eyed), blēr'(īd), a. lagañoso.

blearedness, -ĕdnĕs, s. lagaña, f.

bleat, blēt, s. balido, m.; -, v. n. balar.

bleed, blēd, v. n. sacar sangre; -, v. a. sangrar.

bleeding, -ĭng, s. sangría, f. [sangrar.

blemish, blĕm'ĭsh, v. a. manchar; ensuciar; infamar; -, s. tacha, f.; deshonra, infamia, f. [brarse.

blench, blĕnsh, v. a. obstar; -, v. n. asombiend, blĕnd, v. a. mezclar, confundir.

bless, blĕs, v. a. bendecir, alabar; - me! ¡buen Dios! [santidad, beatitud, f.

blessedness, -ĕdnĕs, s. felicidad, f.

blessing, -sĭng, s. bendición, f.; favores del cielo, m. pl.

blight, blīt, s. tizón, m.; pulgón, m.; alheña, f.; -, v. a. anieblar las mieses.

blind, blīnd, a. ciego; oculto; obscuro; - alley, s. callejón sin salida, m.; -, v. a. cegar; deslumbrar; -, s. velo, m.; (Venetian -) persiana, f.

blindfold, -fōld, v. a. vendar los ojos; -, a. con los ojos vendados.

blindly, -lĕ, ad. ciegamente, á ciegas.

blindman's-buff, -mănbŭff, s. gallina ciega, f. (un juego). [f.

blindness, -nĕs, s. ceguedad; alucinación.

blind-side, -sīd, s. el flaco de alguna persona, f.

blind-worm, -wŭrm, s. cecilia, f.

blink, blĭngk, v. n. guiñar, cerrar los ojos; echar llama; -, s. ojeada, f.

blinker, -ăr, s. antojera, f.

bliss, blĭs, s. felicidad (eterna), f.

blissful, -fŭl, a. feliz en sumo grado; beato, bienaventurado; -ly, ad. felizmente. [dad, f.

blissfulness, -fŭlnĕs, s. suprema felici-

blister, blĭs'tăr, s. vejiga, ampolla, f.; vejigatorio, m.; -, v. n. ampollarse; -, v. a. aplicar un vejigatorio.

blithe, blĭth, a. alegre, contento, gozoso.

blizzard, blĭz'zărd, s. (am.) huracán, m.

bloat, blōt, v. a. hinchar; -, v. n. entumecerse; -, a. hinchado, turgente.

bloatedness, -ĕdnĕs, s. turgencia, f.

bloater, -ăr, s. arenque ahumado, m.

block, blŏk, s. zoquete, m.; horma (de sombrero), f.; tajo de cocina, m.; obstáculo, m.; - (up), v. a. bloquear.

blockade, -kād', s. bloqueo, m.; -, v. a. bloquear. [m.

blockhead, -hĕd, s. bruto, necio, zópenco.

blockship, -shĭp, s. barco costeño, m.

block-system, -sĭstĕm, s. (rail.) sistema de cobertura de una vía, m.

block-up, -ŭp, s. embarazo, m.

blond, blŏnd, a. blonda, f.

blood, blŭd, s. sangre, f.; linaje, parentesco, m.; ira, cólera, f.; -, v. a. ensangrentar; exasperar.

blood-guiltiness, -gŭltĭnĕs, s. homicidio, asesinato, m.

blood-hound, -hŏŭnd, s. sabueso, m.

bloodily, -tĕ, ad. cruelmente, inhumanamente.

bloodiness, -nĕs, s. (fig.) crueldad, f.

bloodless, -lĕs, a. exangüe; sin efusión de sangre; muerto. [botomista, m.

blood-letter, -lĕttăr, s. sangrador, flebloodletting, -lĕttĭng, s. sangría, f.

bloodshed, -shĕd, s. efusión de sangre, f.; matanza, f.

bloodshot, -shŏt, a. ensangrentado.

blood-sucker, -sŭkkăr, s. sanguijuela, f.; (fig.) desollador, m.

blood-vessel, -vĕssĕl, s. vena, f.; canal de la sangre, m.

bloody, -ĕ, a. sangriento, ensangrentado; cruel; -flux, s. disentería, f.; --minded, a. sanguinario.

bloom, blōm, s. flor, f.; (also fig.); -, v. n. florecer.

blossom, blŏs'sŭm, s. flor, f.

blot, blŏt, v. a. manchar (lo escrito); cancelar; denigrar; -, s. canceladura; mancha, f.

blotch, blŏtsh, s. roncha, f.

blotting-case, blŏt'tĭngkās, -pad, -păd, s. papelera, f.

blotting-paper, -pāpăr, s. papel de secar, m.; teleta, f.

blouse, blŏŭs, s. blusa, f., sobretodo de tela, en forma de camisa.

blow, blō, v. n. soplar; sonar; florecer; -, v. a. soplar; inflar; calentar algo con el aliento; to - up, volar(se) por medio de pólvora; -, s. golpe, m.

blow-pipe, -pĭp, s. soplete, m.

blubber, blŭb'băr, s. grasa de ballena, f.; -, v. n. & a. llorar hasta hincharse los carrillos. [gües, m. pl.

bluchers, blō'tshărz, s. pl. botines, borce-bludgeon, blŭd'ăn, s. cachiporra, f.; palocorto, m.

blue, blōō, a. azul; -, v. a. teñir de azul.

blue-bottle, -bŏttl, s. (bot.) campanilla, f.; coronida, f. (mosca).

blue-devils, *-dĕvls,* blues, *blūz,* s. pl. mal de bazo, m.; hipocondría, f.

blue-eyed, *-īd,* a. ojizarco.

blueness, *-nĕs,* s. color azul, m.

blue-peter, *-pētĕr,* s. (mar.) pabellón de partida, m. [f.

blue-stocking, *-stŏkkĭng,* s. mujer docta.

bluff, *blŭf,* a. rústico; rudo; —, v. a. vendar los ojos.

bluffness, *-nĕs,* s. asperidad, rusticidad, f.

bluish, *blū'ĭsh,* a. azulado.

blunder, *blŭn'dĕr,* s. desatino, m.; error craso, m.; atolondramiento, m.; —, v. a. & n. confundir; desatinar. [corta).

blunderbuss, *-bŭs,* s. trabuco, m. (escopeta

blunt, *blŭnt,* a. obtuso; lerdo; bronco; grosero; —, v. a. embotar; enervar; calmar (un dolor). [obtusamente.

bluntly, *-lĭ,* ad. sin artificio; claramente.

bluntness, *-nĕs,* s. embotadura, grosería f.

blur, *blŭr,* s. mancha, f.; —, v. a. manchar; desamar. [y á locas.

blurt(out), *blŭrt(ŏut'),* v. a. hablar á tontas

blush, *blŭsh,* s. rubor, m.; sonrojo, m.; —, v. n. ponerse colorado (de vergüenza).

bluster, *blŭs'tĕr,* s. ruido, tumulto, m.; jactancia, f.; —, v. n. hacer ruido tempestuoso.

blusterous, *-ŭs,* a. tumultuoso, tempestuoso; violento.

boa, *bŏā,* s. boa, f. (serpiente); pelerina, f. (vestido de mujeres).

boar, *bōr,* s. verraco, m.; **wild** —, jabalí, m.

board, *bōrd,* s. tabla, f.; mesa, f.; tribunal, consejo, m.; (mar.) puente, m.; —, v. a. abordar; entablar; —, v. n. estar á pupilaje; tomar pupilos.

boarder, *-ĕr,* s. pensionista, pupilo, m.

boarding-house, *-ĭnghŏūs,* s. casa de pupilos, f.; casa de huéspedes.

boarding-school, *-ĭngskōl,* s. casa-pensión, f.

board-wages, *-wā'jĕz,* s. ración en dinero que se da á los criados para mantenerse, f.

boast, *bōst,* v. n. jactarse; —, s. jactancia, f.; ostentación, f.

boastful, *-fŭl,* a. jactancioso.

boat, *bōt,* s. bote, m.; barca, chalupa, f.

boathook, *-hŏk,* s. (mar.) cloque, bichero.

boatman, *-mĭn,* s. barquero, m. [m.

boating, *bōt'ĭng,* s. barcaje, m.; paseo en barquilla, m.; regata, f.

boatswain, *bōt'sn,* s. contramaestre, m.

bob, *bŏb,* s. pingajo, m.; pendiente de oreja, m.; pulla, chufleta, f.; (cant) chelín, m.; —, v. a. apalear; engañar; —, v. n. bambolear.

bobbin, *bŏb'ĭn,* s. canilla, broca, f.

bobtail, *-tāl,* s. rabón, m.; cola cortada, f.

bode, *bōd,* v. a. presagiar, pronosticar.

bodice, *bŏd'ĭs,* s. corsé, m.; cotilla, f.

bodied, *bŏd'ĭd,* a. corpóreo.

bodiless, *bŏd'ĭlĕs,* a. incorpóreo.

bodiliness, *bŏd'ĭlĭnĕs,* a. corporeidad.

bodily, *bŏd'ĭlĭ,* a. & ad. corpóreo; corporalmente. [aguja de jareta, f.

bodkin, *bŏd'kĭn,* s. punzón de sastre, m.

body, *bŏd'ĭ,* s. cuerpo, m.; individuo, m.; gremio, m.; **any** —, cualquier; **every** —, cada uno.

body-clothes, *-klōz,* s. pl. caparazón, m.

body-colour, *-kŭllŭr,* s. primera mano de color, f. [corpe, f.

body-guard, *-gārd,* s. (mil.) guardia de corps.

body-snatcher, *-snātchĕr,* s. resureccionista, m. (en Inglaterra).

bog, *bŏg,* s. pantano, m.

bogey, *-ĭ,* s. duende, m. [cear.

boggle, *-gl,* v. n. titubear, vacilar, balancear.

boggy, *-gĭ,* a. pantanoso, palustre.

bogus, *bō'gŭs,* a. postizo.

bohea, *bŏhē',* s. te negro de la China.

boil, *bŏĭl,* v. n. hervir; bullir; hervirle á uno la sangre; —, v. a. cocer; —, s. furúnculo, m.

boiler, *-ĕr,* s. marmita, f.; caldero, m.

boisterous, *bŏĭs'tŭrŭs,* a. borrascoso, tempestuoso; violento; **-ly,** ad. tumultuosamente, furiosamente.

bold, *bōld,* a. ardiente, valiente; audaz; temerario; impudente; **-ly,** ad. descaradamente. [osadía, f.

boldness, *-nĕs,* s. intrepidez, f.; valentía, f.;

bole, *bōl,* s. tronco, m.; bolo, m.; medida de grano de seis fanegas, f.

bolster, *bōl'stĕr,* s. travesero, m.; cabezal, m.; —, v. a. recostar la cabeza en el travesero; apoyar.

bolt, *bōlt,* s. dardo, m.; flecha, f.; cerrojo, m.; —, v. a. cerrar con cerrojo, examinar, amarrar con grillos; cribar.

bolter, *-ĕr,* s. cedazo, m. [colar, m.

bolting-cloth, *-ĭngklŏth,* s. tamiz para colar.

bolting-house, *-ĭnghŏūs,* s. cernedero.

bolus, *bō'lŭs,* s. bola, bolilla, f. [m.

bomb, *bŏm,* s. (mil.) bomba, f.

bombard, *-bārd,* v. a. bombardear.

bombardier, *-bārdēr',* s. bombardero, m.

bombardment, *-bārd'mĕnt,* s. bombardeo, m.

bombast, *bŭm'bāst,* s. hinchazón, f. [m.

bombastic, *bŭmbāst'ĭk,* a. pomposo, hinchado, ampuloso.

bond, *bŏnd,* s. ligadura, f.; vínculo, m.; vale, m.; obligación, f.; —, v. a. poner en depósito. [f.

bondage, *-āj,* s. esclavitud, servidumbre, f.

bond-holder, *-hōldĕr,* s. tenedor de unos vales, m. [almacén de la aduana, m.

bonding-warehouse, *-ĭngwārhŏūs,* s.

bond(s)man, *-mĭn,* s. esclavo, siervo, m.; (law) fiador, m.

bone, *bōn,* s. hueso, m.; —, v. a. desosar.

bonelace, *-lĕs,* s. encaje de hilo, m.

boneless, *-lĕs,* a. sin huesos; desosado.

bonesetter, *-sĕttĕr,* s. algebrista, m.

bonfire, *bŏn'fĭr,* s. fuego de regocijo, m.

bonnet, *bŏn'nĕt,* s. gorra, f.; bonete, m.

bonny, *bŏn'nĭ,* a. bonito, galán, gentil.

bonus, *bō'nŭs,* s. cuota, prima, f.

bony, *bō'nĭ,* a. osudo.

booby, *bō'bĭ,* s. zote, hombre bobo, m.

book, *bŭk,* s. libro, m.; **to bring** —, v. a. pedir cuenta; asentar en un libro.

book-binder, *-bĭndĕr,* s. encuadernador de libros.

book-case, *-kās,* s. armario para libros, m.

book-keeper, *-kēpĕr,* s. tenedor de libros, m. [libros, f.

book-keeping, *-kēpĭng,* s. teneduría de

book-making, —*mák*i*ng*, s. apuesta en las corridas de caballos, f.

book-marker, —*márkür*, s. registro de un libro, m.

book-post, —*póst*, s., by —, bajo faja.

book-seller, —*sélür*, s. librero, m.

book-worm, —*wûrm*, s. polilla que roe los libros, f.; hombre del todo aficionado á los libros, m.

boom, *bóm*, s. (mar.) botalón, m.; cadena para cerrar un puerto, f.; —, v. n. zumbar.

boon, *bón*, s. presente, regalo, m.; favor, m.; gracia, f.; —, a. alegre, festivo; generoso.

boor, *bór*, s. patán, villano, m.

boorish, —*ish*, a. rústico, agreste; —ly, ad. rústicamente. [sería, f.

boorishness, —*ishnés*, s. rusticidad, grosería.

boot, *bót*, s. ganancia, f.; provecho, m.; bota, f.; to —, ad. además.

booted, —*ed*, a. calzado con botas.

booth, *bóth*, s. barraca, cabaña, f.

boot-jack, *bót'jäk*, s. sacabotas, m.

bootless, —*lés*, a. inútil, sin provecho, vano.

boot-tree, —*tré*, s. ensanchador, m.

boots, —*s*, s. limpiabotas, m.

booty, —*tí*, s. botín, m.; presa, f.; saqueo, m.

booze, *bóz*, v. n. emborracharse.

borax, *bó'rāks*, s. borraj, m.

border, *bór'dür*, s. orilla, f.; borde, m.; margen, f.; frontera, f.; —, v. n. confinar —, v. a. ribetear; limitar.

borderer, —*ür*, s. confinante, m.

bore, *bór*, v. a. taladrar; barrenar; fastidiar; —, s. taladro, m.; calibre, m.; hombre enfadoso, m.

boreal, *bó'rél*, a. septentrional, boreal.

Boreas, *bó'réäs*, s. viento del septentrión, m.

boredom, *bór'däm*, s. incomodidad, f.

born, *bórn*, a. nacido; destinado.

borough, *bór'ró*, s. villa, f.; burgo, m.

borrow, *bór'ró*, v. a. tomar fiado; pedir prestado.

borrower, —*ür*, s. prestamista, m.

boscage, *bós'kāj*, s. boscaje, m.; arboleda, f.

bosh, *bósh*, s. galimatías, m.

bosom, *bó'zäm*, s. seno, pecho, m.; amor, m.; cariño, m.; — of a shirt, guirindola, f.; —, v. a. guardar en el pecho.

bosom-friend, —*frénd*, s. amigo íntimo, m.

boss, *bós*, s. clavo, m.; jiba, joroba, f.; — bós, (am.) patrón, maestro, m.

botanic(al), *bótän'ik(äl)*, a. botánico.

botanise, *bót'änīz*, v. a. herborizar.

botanist, *bót'änist*, s. botánico, m.

botany, *bót'äni*, s. botánica, f.

botch, *bótsh*, s. remiendo, m.; roncha, f.; úlcera, f.; —, v. a. remendar; chapuzar.

botcher, —*ür*, s. sastre remendón, m.

both, *bóth*, a. ambos, entrambos; ambas, entrambas; —, c. tanto como.

bother, *bór'thür*, v. a. aturrullar; confundir; —, s. terquería, terqueza, terquedad, f.

bottle, *bó'tl*, s. botella, f.; gavilla de heno, f.; —, v. a. embotellar.

bottle-holder, —*hóldür*, s. partidario, m.; segundo (en duelo), m.

bottom, *bó'täm*, s. fondo, m.; fundamento, m.; valle, m.; buque, m.; fin, designio, m.; —, a. inferior, de debajo; —, v. a. ovillar,

devanar un ovillo —, v. n. apoyarse; — upwards, ad. lo de arriba abajo.

bottomless, —*lés*, a. insondable; excesivo; impenetrable.

bottomry, —*rí*, s. (mar.) casco y quilla, m.

bough, *bóu*, s. brazo del árbol; ramo, m.

bounce, *bóuns*, v. n. arremeter, brincar; jactarse; —, s. golpazo, brinco, m.; bravata, f.

bouncer, —*ür*, s. fanfarrón, m.; mentira, f.

bound, *bóund*, s. límite, m.; salto, m.; repercusión, f.; —, v. a. confinar, limitar; destinar; obligar; reprimir; —, v. n. resaltar; —, a. destinado. [f.

boundary, *bóun'däré*, límite, m.; frontera, f.

bounden, *bóun'dn*, a. obligado; obligatorio.

boundless, —*lés*, a. ilimitado, infinito.

bounteous, *bóun'téüs*, bountiful, *bóun'téfül*, a. liberal, generoso, bienhechor —ly, ad. generosamente, liberalmente.

bounty, —*tí*, s. liberalidad, bondad, f.

bouquet, *bó'ká*, s. ramillete de flores, m.

bourn, *bórn*, s. distrito, m.; confín, m.

bout, *bóut*, s. vez, f.; experimento, rato, m.

bovine, *bó'vīn*, a. bovino.

bow, *bóu*, v. a. encorvar, doblar, oprimir; —, v. n. encorvarse; hacer reverencia; —, s. reverencia, inclinación, f. [f.; nudo, m.

bow, *bó*, s. arco, m.; arco de violín; corbata, f.

bowels, *bóu'élz*, s. pl. intestinos, m. pl.; entrañas, f. pl.; ternura, compasión, f.

bower, *bóu'ür*, s. enramada de jardín; bóveda, f.; aposento retirado, m.

bowie-knife, *bó'énf*, s. puñal, largo y ancho, m. [á las bochas.

bowl, *ból*, s. taza; bola, f.; —, v. n. jugar

bowlder, *ból'dür*, s. guijarro, m.

bowline, *ból'lín*, s. (mar.) bolina, f.

bowling-green, *ból'ínggrén*, s. bolingrín, m.; boleo, plano para jugar á las bochas, m. [m.

bowsprit, *bó'sprit*, s. (mar.) bauprés.

bowstring, —*string*, s. cuerda del arco, f.

bow-window, —*windó*, s. ventana arqueada, f.

box, *bóks*, s. boj (árbol), m.; caja, cajita, f.; palco de teatro, m.; — on the ear, bofetada, f.; —, v. a. meter alguna cosa en una caja; apuñetear; —, v. n. combatir á puñadas.

boxen, —*n*, a. hecho de boj.

boxer, —*ür*, s. púgil, m.

boxing-day, —*ingdá*, —night, —*nít*, s. el segundo día de Navidad.

box-keeper, *bóks'képür*, s. portero de los palcos, m. (en el teatro).

box-maker, —*mákür*, s. cofrero, m.

box-seat, —*sét*, s. pescante, m.

boy, *bói*, s. muchacho, m.; niño, m.; criado, lacayo, m.

boycot, —*kót*, v. a. desacreditar, echar fuera; —, s. terrorismo que consiste en declarar por desechado á los propietarios de tierras en Irlanda, m.

boyhood, —*húd*, s. muchachez, f.

boyish, —*ish*, a. pueril; frívolo; —ly, ad. puerilmente. [muchachería, f.

boyishness, —*ishnés*, s. puerilidad,

brace, *brás*, s. abrazadera, f.; sopanda de coche, f.; par, m.; -s, pl. tirantes para sostener los pantalones, m. pl.; -, v. a. ligar, amarrar; (mar.) bracear.

bracelet, *-lět*, s. brazalete, m.

bracken, *brák' kn*, s. (bot.) helecho, m.

bracket, *brák' kět*, s. puntal, m.; listón, m.; to — with, v. a. unir, ligar.

brackish, *brák' ish*, a. salobre.

bracing, *brás' ing*, a. confortante.

brad, *brád*, s. tachuela, punta, f.

brad-awl, *-ál*, s. lesna, f.

brag, *brág*, s. jactancia, f.; -, v. n. jactarse, fanfarronear.   [m.

braggadocio, *-gád' shě̌*, s. fanfarrón.

braggart, *-gárt*, a. & s. jactancioso; fanfarrón, m.

braid, *bréd*, s. trenza, f.; -, v. a. trenzar.

brain, *brán*, s. cerebro, m.; seso, juicio, m.; -, v. a. descerebrar, matar á uno.

brain-fever, *-fěvăr*, s. cerebritis, f.

brainless, *-lěs*, a. tonto, insensato.

brain-pan, *-pán*, s. cráneo, m.

brain-sick, *-sĭk*, a. frenético.

brake, *brák*, s. helechal, m.; agramadera, f.; amasadera, f.; palanca, f.; (rail.) freno, m.   [frenos, m.

brakesman, *brá' ksmăn*, s. (rail.) guarda-

brake-van, *brák' ván*, s. (rail.) vagón-freno, m.

bramble, *brám' bl*, s. zarza, espina, f.

bran, *brán*, s. salvado, m.

branch, *bránch*, s. ramo, m.; rama, f.; -, v. a. (& n.) ramificar(se).

branch-house, *-hŏŭs*, s. comandita, f.

branch-line, *-lin*, s. (rail.) empalme, ramal, m., hijuela de ferrocarril, f.

brand, *bránd*, s. tizón, m.; nota de infamia, f.; -, v. a. marcar con un hierro ardiendo; infamar.

brandish, *-ish*, v. a. blandir, ondear.

bran(d)new, *-nú*, a. flamante.

brandy, *brán' dě*, s. aguardiente, m.

brangle, *bráng' gl*, s. quimera, disputa, f.; -, v. a. reñir, disputar.

brass, *brás*, s. bronce, m.; desvergüenza, f.; red -, tumbaga, f.

brass-founder, *-fŏŭndăr*, s. fundidor de bronce, m.

brat, *brát*, s. rapaz; chulo, m.

bravado, *brávă' dŏ*, s. baladronada, f.

brave, *bráv*, a. bravo, valiente, atrevido; -, v. a. bravear; -, s. bravo, m.; -ly, ad. bravamente.

bravery, *-ărě*, s. valor, m.; magnificencia, f.; bravata, f.

brawl, *brál*, s. quimera, disputa, camorra, f.; -, v. n. alborotar; vocinglear.   [f.

brawn, *brán*, s. pulpa, f.; carne de verraco.

brawny, *-ě*, a. carnoso, musculoso.

bray, *brá*, v. a. triturar; -, v. n. rebuznar; -, s. rebuzno (del asno), m.; ruido bronco, m.   [broncear.

braze, *bráz*, v. a. soldar con latón.

brazen, *-n*, a. de bronce; desvergonzado; impudente; -, v. n. hacerse descarado.

brazier, *brá' zhär*, s. latonero, m.; brasero, m.   [lolación, f.

breach, *brětsh*, s. rotura, f.; brecha, f.;

bread, *brěd*, s. pan, m. (fig.) sustento, m.; brown -, pan moreno.

breadstuffs, *-stǔfz*, s. pl. granos, m. pl.

breadth, *brědth*, s. anchura, f.

break, *brák*, v. n. romper; vencer; quebrantar; violar; domar; arruinar; interrumpir; -, v. n. romperse; reventarse algún tumor; separarse; (com.) quebrar; to - out, abrirse salida; derramarse, desaguar; -, s. rotura, abertura, f.; interrupción, f.; - of day, despuntar del día, m., aurora, f.

breakdown, *-dŏŭn*, s. descalabro, m.

breakfast, *brěk' fást*, s. almuerzo, desayuno, m.; -, v. n. almorzar.

breaking, *brák' ing*, s. rompimiento, m.; principio de las vacaciones en las escuelas, m.; fractura, f.   [picio, m.

breakneck, *-něk*, s. derrumbadero, precipicio, m.

breakwater, *-wátăr*, s. muelle, m.

breast, *brěst*, s. pecho, seno, m.; tetas, f. pl.; corazón, m.; -, v. a. acometer; resistir; -, v. n. brincar (los caballos).

breast-bone, *-bŏn*, s. esternón, m.

breast-high, *-hi*, a. alto hasta el pecho.

breast-plate, *-plát*, s. peto, m.; pectoral, m.; coraza, f.

breast-work, *-wärk*, s. parapeto, m.

breath, *brěth*, s. aliento, m., respiración, f.; soplo de aire, m.; momento, m.

breathe, *brěth*, v. a. & n. respirar; exhalar; to - after, desear, ansiar.

breathing, *-ing*, s. aspiración, f.; respiración, f.; aliento, m.   [poso, m.

breathing-time, *-tim*, s. descanso, reposo, m.

breathless, *brěth' lěs*, a. falto de aliento; desalentado.   [cañón ó fusil, f.

breech, *brěch*, s. trasero, m.; culata de cañón ó fusil, f.

breeches, *-ěz*, s. pl. calzones, f. pl.

breed, *brěd*, s. casta, raza, f.; -, v. a. procrear, engendrar; producir; educar; -, v. n. parir; multiplicarse.

breeder, *-ăr*, s. criador, m.; yegua de cría ó vientre, f.   [cación, f.

breeding, *-ing*, s. crianza, f.; buena educación, f.

breeze, *brěz*, s. brisa, f.; tábano, m.

breezy, *brě' ze*, a. refrescado con brisas.

brethren, *brěth' rěn*, s. pl. (de *brother*) hermanos, m. pl. (en estilo grave).

brevet, *brěv' ět*, s. despacho, título, m.

breviary, *brě' vărě*, s. epítome, compendio, m.; breviario, m.

brevity, *brěv' tě*, s. brevedad, concisión, f.

brew, *brŏ*, v. a. tramar, maquinar, mezclar; -, v. n. hacer cerveza; -, s. calderada de cerveza, f.

brewer, *-ăr*, s. cervecero, m.

brewery, *-ărě*, s. cervecería, f.

briar, brier, *bri' ăr*, s. zarza, f., espino, m.

bribe, *brib*, s. cohecho, soborno, m.; -, v. a. cohechar, corromper, sobornar.

bribery, *-ărě*, s. cohecho, soborno, m.

brick, *brĭk*, s. ladrillo, m.; ladrillo de pan; hombre alegre, m.; -, v. a. enladrillar.

brick-bat, *-bát*, s. pedazo de ladrillo, m.

brick-layer, *-lăăr*, s. albañil, m.

bridal, *bri' dăl*, a. nupcial; -, s. boda, f.

bride, *brid*, s. novia, f.

bridegroom, *-grŏm*, s. novio, m.

bridesmaid, *-s'mdd*, s. madrina de boda, f.

bridge, *brĭj*, s. puente, m. & f.; caballete de la nariz, m.; puente de violín, m.; to — (over), v. a. construir un puente.

bridle, *brī'dl*, s. brida, f., freno, m.; —, v. a. embridar; reprimir, refrenar.

brief, *brĕf*, a. breve, conciso, sucinto; —, s. compendio, m.; breve, m.

briefly, *-lĭ*, ad. brevemente, en pocas palabras.

brig, *brĭg*, **brigantine**, *-ǎntēn*, s. (mar.) bergantín, m.

brigade, *brĭgád'*, s. (mil.) brigada, f.

brigadier, *-ēr'*, s. (mil.) general de brigada, m.

brigand, *brĭg'ǎnd*, s. bandido, m.

bright, *brīt*, a. claro, luciente, brillante; *-ly*, ad. espléndidamente.

brighten, *-n*, v. a. pulir, dar lustre; ilustrar; —, v. n. aclarar.

brightness, *-nĕs*, s. esplendor, m., brillantez, f.; agudeza, f.; claridad, f.

brilliancy, *brĭl'yǎnsĕ*, s. brillantez, f.

brilliant, *brĭl'yǎnt*, a. brilliante; *-ly*, ad. espléndidamente; —, s. brillante (diamante abrillantado), m.

brim, *brĭm*, s. borde extremo, m.; orilla, f.; —, v. a. llenar hasta el borde; —, v. n. estar lleno.

brimful, *-fŭl*, a. lleno hasta el borde.

brimstone, *-stōn*, s. azufre, m.

brindled, *brĭn'dld*, a. abigarrado.

brine, *brīn*, s. salmuera, f.; (fig.) lágrimas, f. pl.

bring, *brĭng*, v. a. llevar, traer; conducir; inducir, persuadir; **to — about**, efectuar; **to — forth**, producir; parir; **to — up**, educar; [borde, m.

brink, *brĭngk*, s. orilla, f.; margen, m. & f.,

briny, *brī'nĕ*, s. salado.

brisk, *brĭsk*, a. vivo, alegre, jovial; fresco.

brisket, *-ĕt*, s. pecho (de un animal), m.

briskly, *-lĭ*, ad. vigorosamente; alegremente; vivamente.

briskness, *-nĕs*, s. vivacidad, alegría, f.

bristle, *brĭs'sl*, s. cerda, seta, f.; —, v. n. erizarse.

bristly, *brĭs'slĕ*, a. cerdoso, lleno de cerdas.

brittle, *brĭt'tl*, a. quebradizo, frágil.

brittleness, *-nĕs*, s. fragilidad, f.

broach, *brōtsh*, s. asador, m.; —, v. a. espetar; divulgar; propagar mentiras, barrenar.

broad, *brǒd*, a. ancho; abierto; grosero; **at — noon**, al medio día.   [f. pl.

broadbeans, *-bĕns*, s. pl. habas de laguna,

broadcloth, *-klŏth*, s. paño fino, m.

broaden, *-n*, v. n. ensancharse.

broadly, *-lĭ*, ad. anchamente.

broadness, *-nĕs*, s. ancho, m.; anchura, f.; grosería, f.   [m.; andanada, f.

broadside, *-sĭd*, s. costado de navío,

broadsword, *-sŏrd*, s. espada ancha, f.; alfanje, m.   [lo ancho.

broadwise, *-wīs*, ad. á lo ancho, por

brocade, *brōkád'*, s. brocado, m.

brogue, *brōg*, s. abarca, f.; idioma corrompido, m.

broider, *brŏt'dēr*, v. a. bordar.

broil, *brŏtl*, s. tumulto, m.; riña, f.; —, v. a. asar (carne); —, v. n. padecer calor.

broken, *brō'kn*, p. roto, interrumpido; **— english**, inglés mal articulado, m.; **—meat**, carne cortada, f.; **— week**, s. una semana que tiene días de fiesta, f.

broker, *brō'kēr*, s. corredor, m.; chamarillero, chamarilero, chalán, m.

brokerage, *-dj*, s. corretaje, m.

bronchial, *brŏng'kĕál*, a. bronquial.

bronchitis, *brŏngkī'tĭs*, s. bronquitis, f.

bronze, *brŏnz*, s. bronce, m.; —, v. a. broncear.   [adornar con joyas.

brooch, *brōtsh*, s. broche, m.; —, v. a.

brood, *brōd*, v. n. cobijar; pensar alguna cosa con cuidado; madurar; —, s. raza, f.; nidada, f.

brood-hen, *-hĕn*, s. empolladora, f.

brook, *brōk*, s. arroyo, m.; —, v. n. sufrir, tolerar.   [hiniesta, f.

broom, *brōm*, s. hiniesta, f.; escoba de

broom-stick, *-stĭk*, s. palo de escoba, m.

broth, *brŏth*, s. caldo, m.

brothel, *brŏth'ĕl*, s. burdel, m.

brother, *brŭth'ēr*, s. hermano, m.

brotherhood, *-hŭd*, s. hermandad, f.; fraternidad, f.

brother-in-law, *-ĭnlá*, s. cuñado, m.

brotherly, *-lĭ*, a. & ad. fraternal; fraternalmente.

Brougham, *brō'ăm*, s. coche cerrado que anda en cuatro ruedas, m.

brow, *brŏd*, s. ceja, f.; frente, f.; cima, f.

browbeat, *-bĕt*, v. a. mirar con ceño.

brown, *brŏŭn*, a. bruno, moreno; **to be in a — study**, estar melancólico; **— paper**, s. papel de estraza, m.; **—sugar**, s. azúcar terciado, m.; —, s. color moreno, m.; —, v. a. volver moreno ó bruno.

browse, *brŏŭz*, v. a. ramonear; —, v. n. pacer la hierba; —, s. (bot.) pimpollos, renuevos, vástagos, m. pl.

bruin, *brū'n*, s. oso, m.

bruise, *brŭz*, v. a. magullar, machacar, abollar, majar; pulverizar; —, s. magulladura, contusión, f.

bruit, *brŏt*, v. a. echar voz, dar fama.

brunt, *brănt*, s. choque, m.; esfuerzo, m.; desastre, m.

brush, *brăsh*, s. bruza, f.; escobilla, f.; asalto, m.; combate, m.; —, v. a. acepillar; **to — off**, huir; —, v. n. mover apresuradamente; pasar ligeramente.

brushwood, *-wŭd*, s. breñal, zarzal, m.

brushy, *-ĕ*, a. cerdoso; velludo.   [mente.

brutal, *brū'tăl*, a. brutal; *-ly*, ad. brutal-

brutality, *brŏtál'tĭ*, s. brutalidad, f.

brutalize, *brō'tălĭz*, v. a. (& n.) embrutecer(se).   [irracional.

brute, *brŏt*, s. bruto, m.; —, a. feroz, bestial;

brutish, *brō'tĭsh*, a. brutal, bestial; feroz; *-ly*, ad. brutalmente.

bubble, *băb'bl*, s. burbuja, f.; bagatela, f.; engañifa, f.; —, v. n. burbujear, bullir; [cano), m.   —, v. a. engañar.

buccanier, *băkkănēr'*, s. corsario (americano), m.

buck, *băk*, s. gamo, m.; macho (de algunos animales), m.; lejía, f.

bucket, *-ĕt*, s. cubo, pozal, m.

buckle, -l, s. hebilla, f.; -, v. a. hebillar; afianzar; -, v. n. encorvarse.
buckler, -lâr, s. escudo, m.; adarga, f.
buckram, -râm, s. bocací, m. [tido, m.
buckskin, -skín, s. cuero de gamo cur-
buckwheat, -hwêt, s. trigo negro, m.
bucolic, bûkôl'ík, a. bucólico.
bud, bûd, s. pimpollo, botón, m.; -, v. a. & n. inocular; abotonar. [m.
budding-knife, -dïng nîf, s. injertador,
budge, bûj, v. n. moverse, menearse.
budget, bûj'êt, s. presupuesto de los gastos del Estado, m.; mochila, f.
buff, bûf, s. ante, m.; búfalo, m.; color de amarillo ligero, m.; -, a. de ante; -s, s. pl. correaje de un soldado, m.
buffalo, bûf'âlô, s. búfalo, m.
buffer(-head), bûf'fâr(hêd), s. (rail.) acol-chado de la fricción, m. [topes, m. pl.
buffers, bûf'fârz, s. pl. (rail.) parachoques,
buffet, bûf'fêt, s. puñada, f.; aparador, m.; -, v. n. combatir á puñadas.
buffoon, bûffôn', s. bufón, chocarrero, m.
buffoonery, -ârî, s. bufonada, bufonería,
bug, bûg, s. chinche, f. [f.
bugbear, -bâr, s. espantajo, coco, m.
buggy, -gî, a. chinchero.
buglehorn), bû'gl(hôrn), s. trompa de buhl, bûl, s. taracea, f. [caza, f.
build, bûld, v. a. edificar; construir; -, v.n. fiarse. [obras, m.
builder, -âr, s. arquitecto, m.; maestro de
building, -ïng, s. fábrica, f.; edificio, m.; construcción, f.
bulb, bûlb, s. bulbo, m.; cebolla, f.
bulbous, -ûs, a. bulboso.
bulge, bûlj, v. n. hacer agua; combarse.
bulk, bûlk, s. masa, f.; volumen, m.; gro-sura, f.; mayor parte, f.; capacidad de un buque, f.; in -, en grueso. [tud, f.
bulkiness, -înês, s. bulto,m.; masa,magni-
bulky, -ê, a. macizo, grueso, grande.
bull, bûl, s. toro, m.; descuido, m., bula, f.; breve pontificio, m.; dicho absurdo, m.
bull-baiting, -bâting, s. combate de toros y perros, m.
bull-dog, -dôg, s. perro de presa, m.
bullet, bûl'lêt, s. bala, f.
bull-finch, bûl'fïntsh, s. pinzón real, m.
bullion, bûl'yûn, s. oro ó plata en barras.
bullock, bûl'lûk, s. novillo capado, m.
bully, bûl'lê, s. espadachín, m.; -, v. n. fanfarronear.
bulrush, bûl'rûsh, s. junco, m.
bulwark, bûl'wûrk, s. baluarte, m.; -, v. a. fortificar con baluartes.
bumble-bee, bûm'blbê, s. abejarrón, abejón, abejorro, zángaro, m.
bumboat, -bôt, s. bote vivandero, m.
bump, bûmp, s. hinchazón, f.; jiba, f.; bollo, m.; barriga, f.; -, v. a. estrellarse.
bumper, -âr, s. copa, f.; vaso lleno, m.
bumpkin, -kîn, s. patán, m.; villano, m.
bumptious, bûm'shûs, a. presumido.
bun, bûn, s. cañamiza, f.
bunch, bûnsh, s. tumor, m.; jiba, f.; nudo, m.; -, v. n. formar corcova.
bunch-backed, -bâkd, a. jorobado.
bunchy, -ê, a. racimoso; jiboso.

bundle, bûn'dl, s. atado, furdillo, m., haz, m.(de leña &c.); paquete, m.; rollo, m.; -, v. a. atar, hacer un lío.
bung, bûng, s.tapón, m.; -, v. a. atarugar.
bungalow, bûng'gâlô, s. quinta de piso bajo en las Indias, f. [licores), f.
bung-hole, -hôl, s. boca (para envasar
bungle, bûng'gl, v.a. chapucear, chafallar; -, v. n. hacer algo chabacanamente; -, s. yerro, m.; obra mal hecha, f.
bun(n)ion, bûn'yûn, s. juanete, m., callo-sidad que se forma en los pies.
bunting, bûn'tïng, s. lanilla para ban-deras, f. [boyar.
buoy, bûê, s. (mar.) boya, f.; -, v. a.
buoyancy, -ânsê, s. fluctuación, f.
buoyant, -ânt, a. boyante.
bur, bûr, s. (bot.) bardana, f.
burden, bûr'dn, s. carga, f.; estrambote, m.; -, v. a. cargar; embarazar.
burdensome, -sûm, a. gravoso, molesto, incómodo.
burdock, bûr'dôk,.s. bardana (planta), f.
bureau, bû'rô, s. armario, m.; escritorio,
bureaucrat, -krât, s. burócrata, m. [m.
burgess, bûr'jês, s. ciudadano, m.
burgher, bûr'gâr, s. ciudadano, vecino,m.
burglar, bûr'glâr, s. salteador de noche en poblado, m. [de una casa, m.
burglary, -ê, s. asalto y robo nocturno
burgomaster, bûr'gômâstâr, s. burgo-maestre, m. [quias, f. pl.
burial, bêr'êal, s. enterramiento, m.; exe-
burial-place, -plâs, s. cimenterio, m.
burlesque, bûrlêsk', s. & a. lengua burles-ca, f.; burlesco, m.; -, v. a. burlar, zumbar.
burly, bûr'lê, a. voluminoso, turbulento.
burn, bûrn, v. a. quemar, abrasar ó herir, incendiar; -, v. n. arder; -, s. quema-dura, f.
burner, -âr, s. quemador, m.; mechero, m.
burning-glass, -ïngglâs, s. espejo ó vi-drio ustorio, m. [-, v. n. tomar lustre.
burnish, bûr'nïsh, v.a. bruñir, dar lustre;
burnisher, -âr, s. bruñidor, m.
burr, bûr, s. lóbulo de la oreja, m.; (bot.) bardana, f.
burrow, bûr'rô, s. conejera, f.; -, v. n. esconderse en la conejera.
bursar, bûr'sâr, s. tesorero, m.
burse, bûrs, s. bolsa, lonja, f.
burst, bûrst, v. n. reventar; abrirse; to -into tears, prorrumpir en lágrimas; to -with laughing, descoyuntarse de risa; -, s. reventón, m.; rebosadura, f. [der.
bury, bêr'ê, v. a. enterrar, sepultar; escon-
burying-ground, -ïnggrônd, s. cimen-terio, m.
bus, bûs, s. ómnibus, m.
busby, bûs'bê, s. gorra de húsar, f.
bush, bûsh, s. arbusto, espinal, m.; cola de zorra, f.
bushel, -êl, s. fanega, f. [lanudo.
bushy, -ê, s. espeso, lleno de arbustos;
busily, bïz'ïlê, ad. solícitamente, diligente-mente, apresuradamente.
business, bïz'nês, s. empleo, m.; ocupa-ción, f.; negocio, m.

busk, *băsk*, s, ballena de corsé, f. [m.
buskin, *băs'kĭn*, s. borceguí, m.; coturno,
buss, *băs*, s. beso, m.; (mar.) neura, f.
bust, *băst*, s. busto, m.
bustard, *băs'tărd*, s. abutarda, f.
bustle, *băs'sl*, v. n. hacer ruido; entremeterse; —, s. baraúnda, f.; ruido, m.
busy, *bĭz'ĕ*, a. ocupado; entremetido; —,
v. a. ocupar.
busybody, —*bŏddĕ*, s. entremetido, m.
but, *băt*, c. excepto, menos; pero; solamente.
butcher, *băt'shŭr*, s. carnicero, m.; —, v. a.
matar atrozmente.
butcherly, —*lĕ*, a. sanguinario, cruel.
butcher's shop, —s *shŏp*, s. tienda del
butchery, —*ĕ*, s. matadero, m. [carnicero, f.
butler, *băt'lăr*, s. despensero, m.
butt, *bătt*, s. terrero, m.; blanco, hito, m.;
bota, f.; —, v. a. topar.
butter, *băt'tăr*, s. manteca, f.; —, v. a.
batir la leche; untar con manteca; doblar
las puestas (en el juego).
butter-cup, —*kăp*, s. (bot.) amargón,
diente de león, m.
butterfly, —*fl*, s, mariposa, f.
butter-milk, —*mĭlk*, s. suero de manteca, m.
buttery, —*ĕ*, s. despensa, f.; —, a. manteCOSO. [charros, m. pl.
buttock, *băt'tŏk*, s. anca, f.; (mar.) cubutton, *băt'n*, s. botón, m.; —, v. a. abobutton-hole, —*hŏl*, s. ojal, m. [tonar.
button-hook, —*hŏk*, s. abotonador, m.
buttress, *băt'trĕs*, s. estribo, m.; apoyo,
m.; —, v. a. estribar.
buxom, *băk'săm*, a. obediente; vivo, alegre, jovial; —ly, ad. jovialmente; amobuy, *bĭ*, v. a. comprar. [rosamente.
buzz, *băz*, s. susurro, soplo, m.; —, v. n.
zumbar; cuchuchear.
buzzard, *băz'zărd*, s. modrego, buaro, m.
by, *bĭ*, pr. por; á, en; de; cerca, al lado
de; — and —, de aquí á poco, ahora; —
the —, de paso; — much, con mucho; —
all means, cueste lo que cueste.
bygone, —*gŏn*, a. pasado.
by-lane, —*lăn*, s. contracalle, f.
by-law, —*lâ*, s. ley local, f.
by-name, —*năm*, s. apodo, m.
by-path, —*păth*, s. atajo, m., trocha, f.
by-place, —*plăs*, s. lugar oculto, m.
by-road, —*rŏd*, s. camino descarriado, m.
bystander, —*stăndăr*, s. mirador, m.;
uno que está presente, m.
by-street, —*strĕt*, s. calle extraviada, f.
by-word, —*wŭrd*, s. proverbio, refrán, m.

C.

cab, *kăb*, s. coche de plaza, m.
cabalistic, *kăbăls'tĭk*, a. cabalístico.
cabbage, *kăb'băj*, s. berza, col, f.; —, v. a.
hurtar retazos. [menca, f.
cabbage-lettuce, —*lĕttĭs*, s. lechuga flacabin, *kăb'ĭn*, s. cabaña, cámara de navío, f.; —, v. a. & n. encerrar en cabaña;
vivir en cabaña. [capitán, m.
cabin-boy, —*bŏĕ*, s. paje de la cámara del

cabinet, *kăb'ĭnĕt*, s. gabinete, m.; escritorio, m. [ministros, m.
cabinet-council, —*kŏŭnsĭl*, s. consejo de
cabinet-maker, —*măkăr*, s. ebanista, m.
cable, *kā'bl*, s. (mar.) cable, m.; —'s
length, medida de 120 brazas, f. [m.
cabman, *kăb'măn*, s. calesero, m.; simón,
caboose, *kăbŏŏz*, s. (mar.) cocina, f.
cabstand, *kăb'stănd*, s. punto de los
coches de plaza, m.
cache, *kăsh*, s. (am.) silo, m.
cackle, *kăk'kl*, v. n. cacarear ó graznar;
—, s. cacareo, m.; charla, f. [m.
cackler, —*ăr*, s cacareador, m.; parlanchín.
cad, *kăd*, s. cochero, m.
cadaverous, *kăddŭ'ărŭs*, a. cadavérico.
caddy, *kăd'dĕ*, s. caja para el te, f.
cade, *kăd*, s. barril, m.; banasta, f.
cadence, *kā'dĕns*, s. (mus.) cadencia, f.
cadet, *kădĕt*, s. cadete, m.; hermano menor, m. [enjaular.
cage, *kăj*, s. jaula, f.; prisión, f.; —, v. a.
cairn, *kărn*, s. galgal, m.
cajole, *kăjŏl*, v. a. lisonjear, adular.
cajolery, —*ărĕ*, s. adulación, lisonja, f.;
zalamería, f.
cake, *kăk*, s. bollo, m.; tortita, f.; —, v. n.
endurecerse (como el pan en el horno).
calamitous, *kălăm'ĭtŭs*, a. calamitoso.
calamity, —*ĭtĕ*, s. calamidad, miseria, f.
calcareous, *kălkă'rĕŭs*, a. calcáreo.
calcine, *kăl'sĭn*, v. a. calcinar.
calculable, *kăl'kŭlăbl*, a. calculable.
calculate, —*kŭlăt*, v. a. calcular, contar.
calculation, *kălkŭlă'shăn*, s. calculación,
f.; cálculo, m.
calculus, *kăl'kŭlŭs*, s. cálculo, m.
caldron, *kăl'drŏn*, s. caldera, f.
calendar, *kăl'ĕndăr*, s. calendario, almanaque, m. [sar con calandria.
calender, —*ĕndăr*, s. calandria, f.; —, v. a. prencalf, *kăf*, s. ternero, m.; ternera, f.; carne
de ternero, f.
calibre, *kăl'ĭbăr*, s. calibre, m.
calico, *kăl'ĕkŏ*, s. calicó, m.
caligraphy, *kălĭg'răfĕ*, s. caligrafía, f.
calisthenics, *kălĭsthĕn'ĭks*, s. pl. ejercicios gimnásticos, m. pl.
calk, *kăk*, v. a. (mar.) calafatear un navío.
call, *kăl*, v. a. llamar, nombrar; convocar;
citar; apelar; to — for, preguntar por alguno, ir á buscarle; to — attention, llamar la atención; to — names, injuriar;
to — upon, visitar; —, s. llamada, f.; instancia, f.; invitación, f ; urgencia, f.;
vocación, f.; profesión, f.; empleo, m.;
(mar.) pito, m.
call-boy, —*bŏĕ*, s. mozo, sirviente, m.
caller, —*ăr*, s. visitador, m.
calligraphy, *kălĭg'răfĕ*, s. caligrafía, f.
calling, *kăl'lĭng*, s. profesión, vocación, f.
callosity, *kăllŏs'ĭtĕ*, s. callosidad, dureza
de la especie del callo, f. [sensible.
callous, *kăl'lŭs*, a. calloso; endurecido; insensible.
callow, *kăl'lŏ*, a. pelado, desplumado.
calm, *kăm*, s. calma, tranquilidad, f.; —, a.
quieto, tranquilo; —, v. a. calmar; aplacar, aquietar; —ly, ad. tranquilamente,
quieta y sosegadamente.

calmness, _nĕs_, s. tranquilidad, calma, f.
calomel, _kăl'ŏmĕl_, s. calomel, m.
caloric, _kălŏr'ĭk_, s. calórico, m.
calumet, _kăl'ŭmĕt_, s. cañutillo de una pipa de fumar, m.
calumniation, _kălŭmnĕă'shăn_, calumny, _kăl'ŭmnĕ_, s. calumnia, f.
calumniate, _kălăm'nĕăt_, v. a. calumniar.
calumnious, _nĕŭs_, a. calumnioso.
Calvary, _kăl'vărĕ_, s. calvario, m.
calve, _kăv_, v. n. parir, producir la vaca.
Calvinist, _kăl'vĭnĭst_, s. calvinista, m.
cambric, _kăm'brĭk_, s. batista, f.
camel, _kăm'ĕl_, s. camello, m.
camelopard, _kămĕl'ŏpărd_, s. camellopar-
cameo, _kăm'ĕŏ_, s. camafeo, m. [dal, m.
camera, _kăm'ĕră_, s. aparato para foto-grafiar, m.
camlet, _kăm'lĕt_, s. camelote, m.
camomile, _kăm'ŏmĭl_, s. manzanilla, f.
camp, _kămp_, s. (mil.) campo, m.; —, v. n. acampar.
campaign, _kămpān'_, s. campaña, f.; —, v.n. servir en campaña.
campaigner, _—ŭr_, s. campeador, m.
camp-follower, _kămp'fŏl'lŭr_, s. (mil.) mozo de campaña, m.
camping-out, _kămpĭng'ŏŭt_, s. (am.) dor-mir á campo raso, m.
camphor, _kăm'fŭr_, s. alcanfor, m.
camp-meeting, _kămp'mētĭng_, s. oficio divino de campaña, m.
camp-stool, _—stōl_, s. silla de tijera, f.
can, _kăn_, v. n. ir. poder; —, s. jarro, m.
canal, _kănăl'_, s. estanque, m.; canal, m.
canary-bird, _kănē'rŭbărd_, s. canario, m.
cancel, _kăn'sĕl_, v. a. cancelar, borrar; anular, invalidar. [m.
cancer, _kăn'sŭr_, s. cangrejo, m.; cáncer, Cancer, —, s. Cáncer, m. (signo del zodiaco).
cancerous, _—ŭs_, a. canceroso.
candid, _kăn'dĭd_, a. cándido, sencillo, inge-nuo, sincero; —ly, ad. cándidamente, fran-camente. [pretendiente, m.
candidate, _kăn'dĕdăt_, s. candidato, m.;
candied, _kăn'dĭd_, a. bañado de azúcar.
candle, _kăn'dl_, s. candela, f.; vela, f.
candle-light, _—lĭt_, s. luz de candela, f.
Candlemas, _—măs_, s. Candelaria, f.
candle-snuffers, _—snŭf'ŭrz_, s. despabila-deras, f. pl. [branched —, araña, f.
candlestick, _—stĭk_, s. candelero, m.;
candle-waster, _—wăstŭr_, s. ladrón (en la vela), m.; gastador, m.
cando(u)r, _kăn'dŭr_, s. candor, m.; sin-ceridad, ingenuidad, f. [m. pl.
candy, _kăn'dĕ_, v. a. confitar; —, s. confites
cane, _kăn_, s. caña, f.; bastón, m.; —, v. n. apalear con un bastón ó caña.
cane-bottom(ed) chair, _—bŏttăm(d) tshăr_, s. silla de caña, f.
cane-mill, _—mĭl_, s. fábrica de azúcar, f.
canicular, _kănĭk'ŭlŭr_, a. perteneciente á la canícula.
canine, _kănĭn'_, a. canino, perruno.
caning, _kăn'ĭng_, s. aporreo, m.
canister, _kăn'ĭstŭr_, s. canastillo, m.; vasija (para tener te, tabaco, &c.), f.
canister-shot, _—shŏt_, s. metralla, f.

canker, _kăng'kŭr_, s. gangrena, f.; cáncer, m.; —, v. a. roer, corromper; —, v. n. co-rromperse, roerse. [tropófago, m.
cannibal, _kăn'nĭbăl_, s. caníbal, m.; an-cannibalism, _—ĭsm_, s. canibalismo, m.
cannie, _kăn'nĕ_, a. cuerdo, discreto.
cannon, _kăn'năn_, s. cañón, m.
cannonade, _—ād'_, s. cañoneo, m.; —, v. a. cañonear.
cannon-ball, _—băl_, s. bala de artillería, f.
cannonier, _—ŭr'_, s. cañonero, artillero, m.
canoe, _kănō'_, s. canoa, f.
canon, _kăn'ăn_, s. canon, m.; regla, f.; —law, derecho canónico.
canoness, _—ĕs_, s. canonesa, f.
canonical, _kănŏn'ĭkăl_, a. canónico; —s, s. pl. vestidos clericales, m. pl.
canonization, _kănŏnĕzā'shăn_, s. canoniza-ción, f.
canonize, _kăn'ŏnĭz_, v. a. canonizar.
canonry, _kăn'ănrĕ_, s. canonicato, m.
canopy, _kăn'ŏpĕ_, s. dosel, pabellón, m.
cant, _kănt_, s. jerigonza, f.; almoneda pú-blica, f.; —, v. n. hablar en jerigonza.
cantaloupe, _kăn'tălŭp_, s. cantalú, m. (melón).
cantankerous, _kăntăng'kŭrŭz_, a. áspero, fastidioso.
canteen, _kăntēn'_, s. cantina, f.
canter, _kănt'ŭr_, s. hipócrita, f.; galope corto, m. [das, f. pl.
cantharides, _kănthăr'ĭdz_, s. pl. cantári-canticle, _kăn'tĭkl_, s. cántico, salmo, m.
canton, _kăn'tŏn_, s. cantón, m.; —, v. a. acantonar. [m.
cantonment, _—mĕnt_, s. acantonamiento,
canvas, _kăn'văs_, s. cañamazo, m.; el acto de solicitar votos (parar lograr algún destino); —, v. a. escudriñar, examinar; controvertir; —, v. n. solicitar votos; pre-tender.
canvasser, _—sŭr_, s. solicitador, m.
caoutchouc, _kō'tshŭk_, s. cautchuc, m., goma elástica, f.
cap, _kăp_, s. gorra, f.; birreta, f.; reverencia hecha con la gorra, f.; —, v. a. cubrir la cabeza. [titud, inteligencia, f.
capability, _kăpăbĭl'ĭtĕ_, s. capacidad, ap-capable, _kā'păbl_, a. capaz, idóneo. [vasto.
capacious, _kăpā'shŭs_, a. capaz; espacioso,
capacitate, _kăpăs'ĕtāt_, v. a. hacer capaz.
capacity, _kăpăs'ĭtĕ_, s. capacidad, f.; in-teligencia, habilidad, f.; calidad, f.
caparison, _kăpăr'ĕsăn_, s. caparazón, m.; —, v. a. enjaezar un caballo.
cape, _kăp_, s. cabo, promontorio, m.
caper, _kā'pŭr_, s. cabriola, f.; alcaparra, f.; corsario, m.; to cut a —, cabriolar; —, v. n. hacer cabriolas.
capillary, _kăp'ĭlărĕ_, a. capilar.
capital, _kăp'ĭtăl_, a. capital, excelente; principal; —, s. capitel, m.; capital, f. (la ciudad principal); capital, fondo, m.; mayúscula, f.; —ly, ad. superiormente, admirablemente, capitalmente; con pena de muerte.
capitalize, _—ĭz_, v. a. capitalizar.
capitalist, _—ĭst_, s. capitalista, m.
capitation, _kăpĕtā'shăn_, s. capitación, f.

Capitol, kăp'ĕtŏl, s. Capitolio, m.
capitulary, kăp'tŭlărĕ, s. capitular (individuo de algún capítulo), m.
capitulate, —tŭlāt, v. n. (mil.) capitular.
capitulation, kăptŭlā'shŭn, s. capitulación, f.
capon, kā'pn, s. capón (pollo castrado), m.
capote, kăpōt', s. capote, levitón, m.
caprice, kăprēs', s. capricho, m.; extravagancia, f.   [—ly, ad. caprichosamente.
capricious, kăprĭsh'ŭs, a. caprichoso;
capricorn, kăp'rĭkŏrn, s. capricornio, m.
Capricorn, —, s. Capricornio, m. (signo del zodíaco).   [zozobrar.
capsize, kăpsīz', v. a. (mar.) trabucar,
capstan, kăp'stăn, s. (mar.) cabrestante, m.
capsule, kăp'sŭl, s. cápsula, f.
captain, kăp'tĭn, s. capitán, m.; — of foot, capitán de infantería, m.   [capitanía, f.
captaincy, —sĕ, captainship, —shĭp, s.
caption, kăp'shŭn, s. presa, captura, f.
captious, kăp'shŭs, a. sofístico, insidioso, engañoso, caviloso; —ly, ad. cavilosamente.
captiousness, —nĕs, s. cavilación, trapacería, f.; engaño, fraude, m.   [clavizar.
captivate, kăp'tĕvāt, v. a. cautivar; esclavizar.
captivation, kăptĕvā'shŭn, s. atractivo, m.
captive, kăp'tĭv, s. cautivo, esclavo, m.
captivity, kăptĭv'ĭtĕ, s. cautividad, esclavitud, f., cautiverio, m.
captor, kăp'tŭr, s. apresador, pirata, m.
capture, kăp'tŭr, s. captura, f.; presa, f.; —, v. a. apresar, capturar.   [capucha, f.
capuchin, kăpŭshĕn', s. capuchino, m.
car, kăr, s. carreta, f.; carro, m.
carabine, kăr'bĭn, s. carabina, f.
carabinier, kărbĭnēr', s. carabinero, m.
caracole, kăr'ăkŏl, s. vuelta que hace el caballo de una ó dos pistas, f.
caramel, kăr'ămĕl, s. caramelo, m.
caravan, kărăvăn', s. caravana, f.
caravansary, —sărĕ, s. caravanera, f.
caraway, kăr'ăwā, s. (bot.) alcaravea, f.
carbolic acid, kărbŏl'ĭk ăs'sĭd, s. ácido carbólico, m.
carbon, kăr'bŏn, s. carbón dulce, m.
carboniferous, kărbŏnĭf'ĕrŭs, a. carbonífero.
carbonize, kăr'bŏnīz, v. a. carbonizar.
carbuncle, kărbŭng'kl, s. carbúnculo, rubí, m.; carbunco, tumor maligno, m.
carcass, kăr'kăs, s. (mil.) carcasa, f.; cadáver, m.
card, kărd, s. naipe, m.; carta, f.; cardencha, f.; pack of —s, baraja de naipes, f.; —, v. a. cardar lana.
card-board, —bŏrd, s. cartón, m.
cardiac, kăr'dĕăk, a. cardíaco.
cardinal, kăr'dĕnăl, s. cardinal, principal; —, s. cardenal, m.
card-table, kărd'tābl, s. mesa para jugar, f.
care, kăr, s. cuidado, m.; solicitud, f.; —, v. n. cuidar, tener cuidado ó pena, inquietarse; estimar, apreciar; what — I? ¿á mí qué me importa?
careen, kărēn', v. a. carenar.
career, kărēr', s. carrera, f.; curso, m.; —, v. n. correr á carrera tendida.

careful, kăr'fŭl, a. cuidadoso, ansioso, diligente, prudente; —ly ad. cuidadosamente.
carefulness, —nĕs, s. cuidado, m., cautela, atención, diligencia, f.
careless, kăr'lĕs, a. descuidado, negligente; indolente; —ly, ad. descuidadamente.
carelessness, —nĕs, s. negligencia, indiferencia, f.   [ciar, alhagar.
caress, kărĕs', s. caricia, f.; —, v. a. acariciar,
caressing, —sĭng, a. cariñoso; —ly, ad. con cariño.
cargo, kăr'gō, s. cargamento de navío, m.
caricature, kăr'ĕkătūr, s. caricatura, f.; —, v. a. hacer caricaturas, ridiculizar.
caricaturist, kărĕkătū'rĭst, s. el que hace caricaturas.
caries, kăr'rēz, s. caries, m.
cark, kărk, v. a. rascar, arañar; to — and care, tener cuidado.
carman, kăr'măn, s. carretero, m.
Carmelite, kăr'mĕlīt, s. carmelita, m.
carminative, kăr'mĭn ătĭv, a. carminante, carminativo.
carmine, kăr'mĭn, s. carmín, m.
carnage, kăr'nĕj, s. carnicería, matanza, f.
carnal, kăr'năl, a. carnal; sensual; —ly, ad. carnalmente.   [sualidad, f.
carnality, kărnăl'ĭtĕ, s. carnalidad, sencarnation, kărnā'shŭn, s. encarnación, f.; clavel, m. (flor).
carnival, kăr'nĭvăl, s. carnaval, m.
carnivorous, kărnĭv'ŏrŭs, a. carnívoro.
carol, kăr'ŏl, s. villancico, m., canción de alegría ó piedad, f.; —, v. a. celebrar con villancicos.
carotic, kărŏt'ĭk, a. comatoso; — state, s. sueño letárgico, m.
carotid, kărŏt'ĭd, a. carotídeo; — artery, s. carótida, f.
carousal, kărŏz'ăl, s. cachiboda, f.
carouse, kărŏz', v. a. beber excesivamente.
carp, kărp, s. carpa, f.; —, v. n. censurar, criticar, reprobar.
carpenter, kăr'pĕntăr, s. carpintero, m.; —'s bench, banco de carpintero, m.
carpentry, kăr'pĕntrĕ, s. carpintería, f.
carper, kăr'pŭr, s. criticón, censurador, m.
carpet, kăr'pĕt, s. tapete de mesa, m.; tapiz, m.; —, v. n. cubrir con alfombras.
carpet-bag, —băg, s. baulillo de viandante, m.
carpeting, —ĭng, s. tapiz en piezas, m.
carpet-knight, —nīt, s. caballerete, m.
carping, kăr'pĭng, a. capcioso, caviloso; —ly, ad. malignamente.
carriage, kăr'rĭj, s. porte, talante, m.; coche, m., carroza, f.; vehículo, m.; carga, f.; cureña de cañón, f.; a — and four, carroza con cuatro caballos, f.
carriage-free (—paid), —frē(pād), a. franco de porte.
carriage-house, —hŏs, s. cochera, f.
carrier, kăr'rēăr, s. portador, carretero, m.
carrier-pigeon, —pĭj'ăn, s. paloma correo ó mensajera, f.
carrion, kăr'rĕăn, s. carroña, f.
carronade, kăr'rŏnād, s. carronada, f.
carrot, kăr'rŏt, s. chirivía, f.
carroty, —ĕ, a. pelirrojo.

carry, kăr'ré, v. a. llevar, conducir; lograr; —, v. n. portarse; to – the day, quedar victorioso; to – it high, afectar grandeza; to – on, conducir.

carry-all, –ál, s. ómnibus, m.

carrying-business, –íngbíznés, s. negocio de expedición, m.

cart, kărt, s. carro, m.; carreta, f.; —, v. a. & n. carretear; usar carretas ó carros.

cartage, –dj, carting, –íng, s. carretaje, m.

cartel, kăr'tél, s. cartel, m. [m.

carter, kărt'ür, s. carretero, m.

cart-horse, kărt'hórs, s. caballo de tiro, m.; caballo de coche.

Carthusian, kărthú'zhíán, s. cartujo (monje), m. [nilla, f.

cartilage, kăr'tilăj, s. cartilago, m.; ternilla, f.

cart-load, kărt'lód, s. carretada, f.

cartoon, kărtón', s. cartón, m.

cartouch, kărtósh', cartridge, kăr'-tríj, s. cartucho, m.; ball—, cartucho con bala; blank —, cartucho sin bala.

cartridge-box, kăr'tríjbóks, s. cartuchera, f. [tero de prieto, m.

cartwright, kărt'rít, s. carretero, carpintero, carv, v. a. cincelar; trinchar; grabar; —, v. n. esculpir. [m.

carver, –ür, s. escultor, m.; trinchante, carving, kărv'íng, s. escultura, f.

carving-knife, –níf, s. cuchillo grande de mesa, m.

case, kăs, s. estado, m.; situación, f.; caso, m.; estuche, m.; vaina, f.; in –, si acaso.

case-hardened, –hárdnd, a. acerado.

case-knife, –níf, s. cuchillo grande de cocina, m.

casemate, –mát, s. (mil.) casamata, m.

casement, –mént, s. puerta ventana, f.

case-shot, –shót, s. balas encajonadas, f. pl. [—, v. a. cobrar dineros.

cash, kăsh, s. dinero contante, m.; caja, f.;

cashier, kăsh'ér, s. cajero, m.; —, v. a. privar á uno de su empleo.

cashmire, kăsh'mér, s. cachemira, f.

casing, kă'síng, s. forro, m., cubierta, f.

cask, kăsk, s. barril, tonel, m.; —, v. a. entonelar, [poner en cajita.

casket, –ét, s. cajita para joyas, f.; —, v. a.

cassation, kăssá'shún, s. (law) casación, f.; court of –, tribunal que anula ó confirma las sentencias de los tribunales inferiores, m.

cassock, kăs'sók, s. sotana, f.

cassowary, kăs'sówaré, s. casoar, m.

cast, kăst, v. a. tirar, lanzar; ganar; modelar; imponer una pena; to – an account, ajustar una cuenta; to – lots, echar suertes; —, v. n. maquinar alguna cosa; —, s. tiro, golpe, m.; forma, f.; aire, m.; echamiento, m.; apariencia exterior, f.; (of the eyes) ojeada, f. [f. pl.

castanets, kăs'tănéts, s. pl. castañetas.

castaway, kăst'áwá, s. réprobo, m.

cast-down, –dón, a. humillado.

caste, kăst, s. casta, corporación, f.

castellan, kăs'tellăn, s. castellano, m.

caster, kăst'ür, s. calculador, m.; pimentero, m.; tirador, m.; adivino, m.; ruecita, f.

castigate, kăs'tégát, v. a. castigar.

castigation, kăstégá'shún, s. castigo, m.; pena, f.

casting-voice(-vote), kăst'íngvóís(vót), s. voto decisivo, m.

castings, –z, s.pl. obras de fundición, f.pl.

cast-iron, kăst'írn, s. hierro colado, m.

castle, kăs'sl, s. castillo, m.; fortaleza, f.; —, v. a. to – one's king, enrocar (en el juego de ajedrez).

castled, –d, a. fortificado con castillo.

castor, kăs'tŭr, s. castor, m.; sombrero fino hecho del pelo de castor, m.

castoreum, kăstŏr'éŭm, s. castóreo, m.

castor-oil, kăs'tăról, s. aceite de ricino ó de palmacristi, m.

castration, kăstrá'shŭn, s. capadura, f.

cast steel, kăst'stél, s. acero fundido, m.

casual, kăzh'dăl, a. casual, fortuito; –ly, ad. casualmente, fortuitamente.

casualty, –té, s. casualidad, f.; acaso, accidente, m.

casuist, kăzh'ŭst, s. casuista, m.

casuistical, kăzhúst'íkăl, a. casuístico,

cat, kăt, s. gato, m.; gata, f.; – o' nine tails, s. (mar.) azote con nueve cordeles, m.; –'s paw (mar.), soplo, m.; (fig.) engañado. m. [vio, m.

cataclysm, kă'tăklízm, s. cataclismo, diluvio, m.

catacombs, kă'tăkómz, s. pl. catacumbas, f. pl.

catalepsy, kă'tălépsé, s. catalepsis, f.

catalogue, kă'tălóg, s. catálogo, m.

catamount, kăt'ámónt, s. gato montaraz, m.

cataplasm, kă'tăplăsm, s. cataplasma, f.

catapult, kă'tăpúlt, s. catapulta, f.

cataract, kă'tărăkt, s. cascada, f.; catarata, f.; to couch the –, operar la catarata, f.

catarrh, kătăr', s. catarro, m.; reuma, f.

catarrhal, –rál, a. catarral.

catastrophe, kătá'strófé, s. catástrofe, f.

cat-call, kăt'kál, s. silbido,m.; reclamo,m.

catch, kătsh, v. a. coger, agarrar, asir; atrapar; pillar; sorprender; —, v. n. pegarse, ser contagioso; to – cold, resfriarse; to – fire, encenderse; —, s. presa, f.; captura, f.; idea, f.; (mus.) repetición, f.; provecho, m.; trampa, f. [m.

catcher, –ür, s. cogedor, m.; engañador,

catching, –íng, a. contagioso.

catchword, –würd, s. reclamo, m.

catechise, kăt'ékíz, v.a. catequizar, examinar.

catechism, kăt'ékízm, s. catecismo, m.

catechist, kăt'ékíst, s. catequista, m.

categorical, kătégór'íkăl, a. categórico; –ly, ad. categóricamente.

category, kăt'égóré, s. categoría, f.

cater, kă'tür, v. n. abastecer, proveer.

caterer, –ür, s. proveedor, abastecedor, m.

caterpillar, kăt'ürpíllăr, s. oruga, f.

caterwaul, kăt'ürwál, v. n. maullar; cencerrear; —, s. maullido, maullo, m.; cencerrada, f.

cat-gut, kăt'gŭt, s. cuerda de violón, f.

cathedral, kăthé'drăl, s. catedral, f.

cat-hole, kăt'hól, s. gatera, f.

catholic, *kăth'ŏlĭk*, a. & s. católico (m.).

catholicism, *kăthŏl'ĕsĭzm*, s. catolicismo, m.   [les), f.

catkin, *kăt'kĭn*, s. candeda (de los árbo-

cattle, *kăt'tl*, s. ganado, m.; black —, ganado vacuno, m.

cattle-plague, *-plāg*, s. epizootia, f.

cattle-show, *-shō*, s. exposición de ganados, f.   [s, (rail.) vagón cuadra, m.

cattle-van, *-văn*, cattle-box, *-bŏks*,

caucus, *kă'kŭs*, s. (am.) junta electoral, f.

caul, *kăl*, s. cofia, redecilla, f.

cauliflower, *kŏl'ĭflōŭr*, s. coliflor, f.

cause, *kăz*, s. causa, f.; razón, f.; motivo, m.; proceso, m.; —, v. a. causar, hacer.

causeless, *-lĕs*, a. infundado, sin razón.

causeway, *-wā*, s. arrecife, m.

caustic, *kăs'tĭk*, a. & s. cáustico (m.); lunar —, s. piedra infernal, f.

cauterise, *kă'tărĭz*, v. a. cauterizar.

caution, *kă'shŭn*, s. prudencia, precaución, f.; aviso, m.; —, v. a. avisar; amonestar; advertir.

cautionary, *-ărĭ*, a. dado á fianzas.

cautious, *kă'shŭs*, a. prudente, circunspecto, cauto.   [gata, cabalgada, f.

cavalcade, *kăv'ălkād, kăvălkăd'*, s. cabal-

cavalier, *kăvălēr'*, s. jinete, m.; caballero,

cavalry, *kăv'ălrē*, s. caballería, f.   [m.

cave, *kāv*, s. caverna, f.; bodega, f.

caveat, *kā'vēăt*, s. aviso, m.; advertencia, f.; (law) notificación, f.

cavern, *kăv'ărn*, s. caverna, f.; bodega, f.

cavernous, *-ŭs*, a. cavernoso.

caviar, *kăv'ĭar*, s. cabial, m.

cavil, *kăv'ĭl*, s. cavilación, sofistería, f.; —, v. n. cavilar; criticar.

caviller, *-lŭr*, s. sofista, enredador, m.

cavity, *kăv'ĭtē*, s. hueco, m.

caw, *kă*, v. n. graznar, crascitar.

cease, *sēs*, v. a. parar, suspender; —, v. n. desistir.   [-ly, ad. perpetuamente.

ceaseless, *-lĕs*, a. incesante, continuo;

cedar, *sē'dăr*, s. cedro, m.

cede, *sēd*, v. a. ceder, transferir.

ceil, *sēl*, v. a. techar.   [habitación, m.

ceiling, *-ĭng*, s. techo ó cielo raso de una

celebrate, *sĕl'ĕbrāt*, v. a. celebrar; elogiar.

celebration, *sĕlĕbră'shŭn*, s. celebración, f.; alabanza, f.

celebrity, *sĕlĕb'rĭtē*, s. celebridad, fama, f.

celerity, *sĕlĕr'ĭtē*, s. celeridad, velocidad, f.

celery, *sĕl'ĕrē*, s. apio, m.

celestial, *sĕlĕs'tyăl*, a. celeste, divino; —, s. celícola, m.

celibacy, *sĕl'ĭbăsē*, s. celibato, m., sol-

celibate, *sĕl'ĭbăt*, s. soltero; soltera.

cell, *sĕl*, s. celdilla, f.; alvéolo, m.: cueva,

cellar, *-lŭr*, s. sótano, m.; bodega, f.   [f.

cellarage, *-lărĕj*, s. cueva, f.

cellaret, *-lărĕt*, s. cantina, frasquera, f.

cellarist, *-lărĭst*, s. cillereio, m.

cellular, *-lŭlăr*, a. celular.

cellule, *-lūl*, s. celdita, f.

cellulose, *-lŭlōs*, s. (chem.) celulosa, f.

cement, *sĕmĕnt'*, s. argamasa, f.; cimento; (fig.) vínculo, m.; —, v. a. pegar con cimento; —, v. n. unirse.

cemetery, *sĕm'ĕtărē*, s. cimenterio, m.

cenotaph, *sĕn'ŏtăf*, s. cenotafio, m.

censer, *sĕn'sŭr*, s. incensario, m.

censor, *sĕn'sŏr*, s. censor, m.; crítico, n

censorious, *sĕnsō'rĕŭs*, a. severo, crítico; —ly, ad. severamente.

censorship, *sĕn'sŏrshĭp*, s. censura, f. (oficio).   [sura.

censurable, *sĕn'shŭrăbl*, a. digno de censura.

censure, *sĕn'shŭr*, s. censura, reprensión, f.; —, v. a. censurar, reprender; criticar.

census, *sĕn'sŭs*, s. censo, empadronamiento.

cent, *sĕnt*, s. ciento, m.   [m.

centenarian, *sĕntĕnă'rĭăn*, s. centenario, m.; centenaria, f.   [centenario.

centenary, *sĕn'tĕnărĕ*, s. centena, f.; —, a.

centennial, *sĕntĕn'nĭăl*, a. centenario.

centimeter, *sĕntĭm'ĕtăr*, s. centímetro, m.

centipede, *sĕn'tĕpĕd*, s. escolopendra, f.

central, *sĕn'trăl*, a. central; —ly, ad. centralmente, en el centro.

centralize, *-ĭz*, v. a. centralizar.

centre, *sĕn'tŭr*, s. centro, m.; —, v. a. colocar en un centro; reconcentrar; —, v. n. colocarse en el centro; reconcentrarse.

centrifugal, *sĕntrĭf'ŭgăl*, a. centrífugo.

centripetal, *sĕntrĭp'ĕtăl*, a. centrípeto.

centuple, *sĕn'tŭpl*, a. céntuplo; —, v. a. centuplicar.

century, *sĕn'tŭrĕ*, s. centuria, f.; siglo, m.

cereals, *sĕr'ēălz*, s. pl. cereales, f. pl.

cerecloth, *sĕr'klŏth*, cerement, *-mĕnt*, s. encerado, hule, m.

ceremonial, *sĕrĕmō'nĭăl*, a. & s. ceremonial, m.; rito externo, m.

ceremonious, *sĕrĕmō'nĭŭs*, a. ceremonioso; —ly, ad. ceremoniosamente.

ceremony, *sĕr'ĕmŏnĕ*, s. ceremonia, fórmulas exteriores, f. pl.

certain, *sŭr'tĭn*, a. cierto, evidente; seguro; —ly, ad. ciertamente, sin duda.

certainty, *-tĕ*, certitude, *sŭr'tĕtŭd*, s. certeza, f.; seguridad, f.

certificate, *sŭrtĭf'ĕkăt*, s. certificado, testimonio, m.   [cado, m.

certification, *sŭrtĭfĕkā'shŭn*, s. certificertify, *sŭr'tĭfĕ*, v. a. certificar, afirmar.

cerulean, *sĕrū'lĕăn*, a. cerúleo, azulado.

cerumen, *sĕrū'mĕn*, s. cera de los oídos, f.

cesarean section, — operation, *sĕză'rĕăn sĕk'shŭn* ú *ŏpĕră'shŭn*, s. (med.) operación cesárea, f.

cessation, *sĕssā'shŭn*, s. cesación, f.; — of arms, suspensión de armas, f.

cession, *sĕsh'ŭn*, s. cesión, f.   [m.

cesspool, *sĕs'pōl*, s. cloaca, f.; sumidero,

chafe, *tshāf*, v. a. frotar, enojar, irritar; —, v. n. acalorarse; —, s. cólera, f.; ardor,

chafer, *-ăr*, s. escarabajo, m.   [m.

chaff, *tshăf*, s. zurrón, hollejo, m.; paja menuda, f.; (fig.) paja.

chaff-cutter, *-kŭttăr*, s. tajador, m.

chaffer, *-făr*, v. n. regatear, baratear.

chaffinch, *-fĭntsh*, s. pinzón, m.

chagrin, *shăgrēn'*, s. zapa, f.

chain, *tshān*, s. cadena, f.; serie, sucesión, f.; —s, pl. esclavitud, f.; —, v. a. encadenar, atar con cadena.   [m.

chain-bridge, *-brĭj*, s. puente colgante,

chain-gang, _-gång_, s. gavilla de malhechores encadenados juntos, f.

chain-shot, _-shŏt_, s. balas encadenadas, f. pl. [m.; -, v. a. llevar en triunfo.

chair, _tshār_, s. silla, f.; asiento portátil.

chair-bottomer, _-bŏttămăr_, s.sillero,m.

chair-man, _-măn_, s. presidente, m.; silletero, m. [coche, m.

chaise, _shās_, s. silla volante, f.; calesín,

chalice, _tshăl'ĭz_, s. cáliz, m.

chalk, _tshăk_, s. greda, f.; marga, f.; French -, espuma de mar, f.; -, v. a. dibujar con yeso; bosquejar, lapizar.

chalk-pit, _-pĭt_, s. gredera, f.; marguera,

chalky, _-ĕ_, a. gredoso. [f.

challenge, _tshăl'lĕnj_, s. desafío, cartel, m.; pretensión, f.; recusación, f.; -, v. a. desafiar; provocar; reclamar; (mil.)llamar ¿quién vive?

challenger, _-ŭr_, s. desafiador, m.

chalybeate, _kălĭb'ŭĕt_, a. ferruginoso.

chamber, _tshăm'băr_, s. cámara, f.; aposento, m.; (mil.) cámara de mina.

chamber-counsel, _-kŏŭnsĕl_, s. jurisconsulto, m.

chamberlain, _-lăn_, s. camarero, m.

chamberlainship, _-lănshĭp_, s.camarería.

chamber-maid, _-măd_, s. moza de cámara.

chamber-pot, _-pŏt_, s. orinal, m. [f.

chameleon, _kămē'lĕan_, s. camaleón, m.

chamois-leather, _shăm'wăĭthăr_, s. gamuza, f. [- up, devorar.

champ, _tshămp_, v. a. morder, mascar; to

champagne, _shămpān'_, s. vino de Champaña, m. [nura, f.

champaign, _shăm'păn_, s. campiña, llanura, f.

champion, _tshăm'pĭon_, s. campeón, m.; -, v. a. desafiar, retar.

championship, _-shĭp_, s. campeonaje, m.

chance, _tshăns_, s. ventura, suerte, f.; acaso, m.; riesgo, m.; by -, por acaso; -, v. n. acaecer, acontecer. [la iglesia).

chancel, _tshăn'sĕl_, s. presbiterio, m. (en

chancellor, _-ĭr_, s. cancelario, m.; lord high -, ministro de justicia, gran canciller, m. [f.

chancellorship, _-ŭrshĭp_, s. cancillería.

chancery, _tshăn'sŭrē_, s. chancillería, f.

chancre, _shăng'kŭr_, s. úlcera venérea, f.; cáncer, m. [f.; candelero, m.

chandelier, _shăndĕlēr'_, s. araña de luces,

chandler, _tshănd'lăr_, s. cerero, m.; lonjista, m.; regatón, m.

change, _tshănj_, v. a. cambiar; trasmutar; -, v. n. variar, alterarse; -, s. mudanza, variedad, f.; vicisitud, f.; cambio, m.; -, a. fortuito.

changeable, _-ăbl_, changeful, _-fŭl_, a. variable, inconstante; mudable.

changeableness, _-ăblnĕs_, s. mutabilidad, inconstancia, f.

changeless, _-lĕs_, a. constante, inmutable.

changeling, _-lĭng_, s. niño cambiado (por otro), hijo supuesto, m.; veleidoso, m.; inconstante, m.

channel, _tshăn'nĕl_, s. canal, álveo, m.; -, v. a. acanalar, estriar.

chant, _tshănt_, s. canto (llano), m.; -, v. a. cantar.

English and Spanish.

chanticleer, _-ĭklĕr'_, s. gallo, m.; cantor sonoro, m.

chantry, _-rĕ_, s. chantría, f.

chaos, _kā'ŏs_, s. caos, m.; confusión, f.

chaotic, _kăŏt'ĭk_, a. confuso.

chap, _tshăp_, v. n. rajarse, henderse; -, s. hendrija, rendija, f.; mandíbula, f.

chape, _tshăp_, s. chapa de cinturón, f.; charnela de hebilla, f.

chapel, _tshăp'ĕl_, s. capilla, f.

chap-fallen, _tshăp'făln_, a. boquihundido.

chapiter, _tshăp'ĕtŭr_, s. capitel, m.

chaplain, _tshăp'lĭn_, s. capellán, m.; limosnero, m. [m.

chaplet, _tshăp'lĕt_, s. guirnalda, f.; rosario,

chapman, _tshăp'măn_, s. comprador, m.; vendedor, m.; traficante, m. [m.

chapter, _tshăp'tŭr_, s. capítulo, m.; cabildo,

char, _tshār_, v. a. hacer carbón de leña; -, v. n. trabajar á jornal; -, s. (trabajo á) jornal, m.

character, _kăr'ăktŭr_, s. carácter, m.; señal, f.; forma de la letra, f.; calidad, f.; -, v. a. esculpir, grabar.

characteristic(al), _kărăktŭrĭst'ĭk(ăl)_, a. característico; -ally, ad. característicamente. [zar, imprimir.

characterize, _kăr'ăktŭrīz_, v. a. caracteri-

characterless, _kăr'ăktŭrlĕs_, a. sin carácter.

charade, _shărăd'_, s. charada, f.

charcoal, _tshār'kōl_, s. carbón de leña, m.

charcoal-pencil, _-pĕn'sĭl_, s. carboncillo para bosquejar, m.

charge, _tshārj_, v. a. encargar, comisionar; cargar; acusar, imputar; -, s. cargo, cuidado, m.; mandato, m.; acusación, f.; (mil.) ataque, m.; depósito, m.; carga, f.

chargeable, _-ăbl_, a. dispendioso; imputable. [caballo de guerra, m.

charger, _-ŭr_, s. fuente, f., plato grande, m.;

chariness, _tshăr'ĭnĕs_, s. circunspección, cordura, f. [militar, m.

chariot, _tshăr'ĕŏt_, s. faetonte, m.; carro

charioteer, _-ēr'_, s. cochero, m.

charitable, _tshăr'ĭtăbl_, a. caritativo; benigno, clemente; -bly, ad. caritativamente.

charitableness, _-nĕs_, s. caridad, f.

charity, _tshăr'ĭtē_, s. caridad, benevolencia, f.; limosna, f. [f.

charity-school, _-skōl_, s. escuela gratuita,

charlatan, _shăr'lătăn_, s. charlatán, m.

charlatanry, _-rĕ_, s. charlatanería, f.

Charles's-Wain, _tshărlz'ĕzwān_, s. Osa Mayor, f. [amarillo, m.

charlock, _tshār'lŏk_, s. alhacena, f.; alhelí

charm, _tshārm_, s. encanto, m.; atractivo, m.; -, v. a. encantar, embelesar, atraer.

charmingly, _-ĭnglĕ_, ad. agradablemente, deleitosamente.

charnel-house, _tshăr'nĕlhŏŭs_, s. carnero, m.

chart, _tshārt_, s. carta de navegar, f. [m.

charter, _tshăr'tŭr_, s. letra patente, f.; privilegio, m.; -, v. a. fletar un buque.

charter-party, _-pārtĕ_, s. (mar.) contrato de fletamento, m. [f.

char-woman, _tshăr'wŭmăn_, s. jornalera,

chary, _tshā'rĕ_, a. circunspecto; frugal.

chase, *tshās*, v. a. cazar; perseguir; cincelar; —, s. caza, f.

chasing, *tshās'ing*, s. cinceladura, f.

chasm, *kāzm*, s. hendidura, f.; vacío, m.

chaste, *tshāst*, a. casto; puro; honesto; púdico.

chasten, *tschās'n*, v. a. corregir, castigar.

chastisement, *tshās'tizmēnt*, s. castigo, m. [mar, corregir.

chastise, *tshāstīz'*, v. a. castigar, reformar

chastity, *tshās'tītē*, s. castidad, pureza, f.

chat, *tshāt*, v. n. charlar; —, s. charla, cháchara, f.; garrulidad, f.; astilla, f.

chattel, —*tl*, s. bienes muebles, m. pl.

chatter, —*tār*, v. n. cotorrear; rechinar; charlar; —, s. chirrido, m.; charla, f.

chatter-box, —*tărbŏks*, chatterer, —*tărār*, s. parlero, hablador, gárrulo, m.

chatty, —*tē*, a. locuaz, parlanchín.

chaw, *tshã*, v. a. mascar, masticar.

cheap, *tshēp*, a. barato; -ly, ad. á poco precio.

cheapen, —*n*, v. a. regatear; abaratar.

cheapness, —*nēs*, s. baratura, f.; bajo precio, m.

cheat, *tshēt*, v. a. engañar, defraudar; trampear; —, s. trampa, f.; fraude, engaño, m.; trampista, m.

check, *tshēk*, v. a. reprimir, refrenar; regañar; registrar; —, s. restricción, f.; freno, m.; represión, f.; jaque, m.; pagaré, m.

checker, —*ār*, v. a. taracear.

checker-board, —*bŏrd*, s. tablero de ajedrez, m.

checker-work, —*wārk*, s. taracea, f.

check-mate, *tshēk'māt*, s. mate, m.

cheek, *tshēk*, s. carrillo, m.; mejilla f.; (fam.) desvergüenza, f.; atrevimiento, m.; — by jowl, cara á cara.

cheek-bone, —*bōn*, s. hueso del carrillo, m.

cheer, *tshēr*, s. banquete, m.; alegría, f.; aplauso, m.; buen humor, m.; vigor, m.; —, v. a. animar, alentar; —, v. n. alegrarse.

cheerful, —*fūl*, a. alegre, vivo, jovial; -ly, ad. alegremente.

cheerfulness, —*fūlnēs*, cheeriness, —*ēnēs*, s. alegría, f.; buen humor, júbilo, m.

cheerings, —*ings*, s. pl. aplauso, m.

cheerless, —*lēs*, a. triste, melancólico.

cheese, *tshēs*, s. queso, m.

cheese-dairy, —*dārē*, s. quesera, f.

cheese-hopper, —*hŏppār*, s. arador, m.

cheese-monger, —*mŭngār*, s. quesero, el que hace ó vende queso, m. [queso, f.

cheese-paring, —*pāring*, s. raedura de

chemical, *kĕm'ĭkāl*, a. químico.

chemist, *kĕm'ĭst*, s. químico, m.

chemistry, —*rē*, s. química, f.

cherish, *tshĕr-ĭsh*, v. a. mantener, fomentar, proteger. [cigarro).

cheroot, *shārŏt'*, s. manilla, f. (especie de

cherry, *tshĕr'rē*, s. cereza, f.; —, a. bermejo.

cherry-stone, —*stōn*, s. cuesco de cereza.

cherry-tree, —*trē*, s. cerezo, m. [m.

cherub, *tshĕr'ŭb*, s. querubín, m.

chess, *tshēs*, s. juego del ajedrez, m.

chess-board, —*bŏrd*, s. tablero (para jugar al ajedrez). m.

chess-man, —*mān*, s. pieza de ajedrez, f.

chest, *tshēst*, s. pecho, m.; arca, f.; — of drawers, cómoda, f.

chestnut, —*nūt*, s. castaña, f.; color de castaña, m.

chestnut-tree, —*nūttrē*, s. castaño, m.

chetah, *tshē'tā*, s. lobo-tigre, m.

cheval-glass, *shĕvăl' glăs*, s. espejo que gira, m.

chew, *tshō*, v. a. mascar, masticar; rumiar, meditar, reflexionar.

chicane, *shĕkān'*, s. cavilación, trampa, f.; —, v. n. cavilar, sofisticar.

chicaner, —*ār*, s. sofista, trampista, m.

chicanery, —*ārē*, s. sofistería, quisquilla, f.

chick(en), *tshĭk(ĕn)*, s. polluelo, m.; (fig.) joven, m. & f.

chicken-hearted, —*knhārtĕd*, a. cobarde, tímido, gallina. [f. pl.

chicken-pox, —*knpŏks*, s. viruelas locas,

chick-pea, —*vē*, s. garbanzo, m.

chicoory, *tshĭk'ŏrē*, s. achicoria, f.

chide, *tshīd*, v. a. reprobar, regañar; —, v. n. reñir, alborotar.

chider, —*ār*, s. regañón, m.

chief, *tshēf*, a. principal, capital; -ly, ad. principalmente; —, s. jefe, principal, m.

chieftain, —*tĭn*, s. jefe, comandante, m.

chilblain, *tshĭl'blān*, s. sabañón, m.

child, *tshīld*, s. infante, m.; hijo, m.; hija, f.; from a —, desde niño; with —, preñada, embarazada.

child-bed, —*bĕd*, s. sobreparto, m.

childhood, —*hŭd*, s. infancia, niñez, f.

childish, —*īsh*, a. frívolo, pueril; -ly, ad. puerilmente.

childishness, —*ĭshnĕs*, s. puerilidad, f.

childless, —*lĕs*, a. sin hijos.

childlike, —*līk*, a. pueril. [m. pl.

children, *tshĭl' drĕn*, s. pl. de *child*, niños,

chill, *tshĭl*, a. frío, friolero; —, s. frío, m.; —, v. a. enfriar; helar. [f.

chilliness, —*lĭnĕs*, s. calofrío, m.; tiritona,

chilly, —*lē*, a. friolero, friolento.

chime, *tshīm*, s. armonía, f.; clave, m.; —, v. n. sonar con armonía; concordar.

chimera, *kēmē'rā*, s. quimera, f.

chimerical, *kēmēr'ĭkāl*, a. quimérico; -ly, ad. quiméricamente.

chimney, *tshĭm'nē*, s. chimenea, f.

chimney-corner, —*kŏrnār*, s. rincón de chimenea, m.

chimney-doctor, —*dŏk'tūr*, s. fumista, f.

chimney-piece, —*pēs*, s. dintel que adorna la chimenea, m. [chimeneas, m.

chimney-sweeper, —*swēpār*, s. limpia-

chin, *tshĭn*, s. barba, f. [loza de China, f.

china(-ware), *tshī'nā(wār)*, s. porcelana,

chine, *tshīn*, s. espinazo, m.; solomo, m.

chink, *tshĭnk*, s. grieta, hendedura, f.; —, v. n. henderse; resonar.

chints, *tshĭnts*, s. zaraza, f.

chip, *tshĭp*, v. a. desmenuzar picar; —, v. n. reventarse; —, s. brizna, astilla, f.; raspaduras de la corteza del pan, f. pl.

chirographer, *kīrŏg'rāfār*, s. quirógrafo, m.; quirografario, m.

chirography, —*rāfē*, s. quirografía, f.

chiromancy, *kī'rōmănsē*, s. quiromancia, f.

chiropodist, *kĭrŏp'ŏdĭst*, s. pedicuro, m.

chirp, *tshŭrp*, v. n. chirriar, gorjear; —, s. gorjeo, chirrido, m.

chirping, *-ĭng*, s. canto de las aves, m.

chisel, *tshĭz'ĕl*, s. escoplo, cincel, m.; —, v. a. escoplear, cincelar, grabar.

chit, *tshĭt*, s. niño, m.; tallo (del grano), m.

chit-chat, *-tshăt*, s. charla, parlería, f.

chitterlings, *-tŭrlĭngz*, s. embuchado de tripas, m.

chivalrous, *shĭv'ălrŭs*, chivalric, *-rĭk*, a. caballeresco.

chivalry, *shĭv'ălrĕ*, s. caballería, f.; ha-

chives, *tshĭvz*, s. pl. cebolleta, f. [zaña,f.

chloral, *klōr'ăl*, s. (chem.) cloral, m.

chloroform, *klōr'ŏfŏrm*, s. cloroformo, m.

chlorosis, *klōrō'sĭs*, s. (med.) clorosis, f.

chock-full, choke-full, *tshŏk'fŭl*, a. de bote en bote, completamente lleno.

chocolate, *tshŏ'kŏlăt*, s. chocolate, m.

chocolate-drop, *-drŏp*, s. pastilla de chocolate, f.

chocolate-pot, *-pŏt*, s. chocolatera, f.

chocolate-stick, *-stĭk*, s. molinillo, m.

choice, *tshŏĭs*, s. elección, preferencia, f.; selecto, m.; —, a. selecto, exquisito, excelente; -ly, ad. escogidamente, primorosamente.

choiceless, *-lĕs*, a. sin poder elegir.

choiceness, *-nĕs*, s. delicadeza f.; discernimiento, m.

choir, *kwīr*, s. coro, m.

choke, *tshōk*, v. a. sufocar; oprimir; tapar.

choker, *-ŭr*, s. (fam.) cravata, f.

choky, *tshō'kĕ*, a. sufocante.

choler, *kŏl'ŭr*, s. cólera,f.; bilis, f.; ira, f.

cholera, *kŏl'lără*, s. cólera, m.

choleric, *kŏl'ărĭk*, a. colérico.

choose, *tshōz*, v. a. escoger, elegir; —, v. n. tener facultad para elegir.

chop, *tshŏp*, v. a. tajar, cortar; picar; —, v. n. girar, mudar; trocar; —, s. tajada de carne, f.; costilla de ternera, f.; raja, f.; -s, pl. (vulg.) quijadas, f. pl.

chopper, *-pŭr*, s. cuchillo de carnicero, m.

chopping-block, *-pĭngblŏk*, s. tajo de cocina, m.

chopping-knife, *-pĭngnĭf*, s. machete, m.

choral, *kō'răl*, a. coral.

chord, *kŏrd*, s. cuerda, f.; —, v. a. encordar.

chorist, *kō'rĭst*, chorister, *kŏr'ĭstŭr*, s.

chorus, *kō'rŭs*, s. coro, m. [corista, m.

chouse, *tshŏŭs*, v. a. engañar, engatusar.

chrism, *krĭzm*, s. crisma, m. & f.

Christ, *krīst*, s. Jesucristo, m.

christen, *krĭs'n*, v. a. cristianar, bautizar.

christendom, *-dăm*, s. cristianismo, m.; cristiandad, f.

christening, *-ĭng*, s. bautismo, m.

Christian, *krĭst'yăn*, a. & s. cristiano (m.); -name, nombre de bautismo, m.

christianise, *krĭst'yănĭz*, v. a. cristianizar.

Christianity, *krĭstyăn'ĭtĕ*, s. cristianismo, m.; cristiandad, f. [mente.

christianly, *krĭst'yănlĕ*, ad. cristiana-

Christmas, *krĭs'măs*, s. Natividad, f.

Christmas-box, *-bŏks*, s. aguinaldo, m.

Christmas-eve, *-ĕv*, s. víspera de Natividad, f.

chromatic, *krōmăt'ĭk*, a. cromático.

chromo, *krō'mō*, chromolithography, *-lĭth'ŏgrăfĕ*, s. cromolitografía, f.

chronic(al), *krŏn'ĭk(ăl)*, a. crónico.

chronicle, *-ĭkl*, s. crónica, f.; —, v. a. formar una crónica.

chronicler, *-ŭr*, s. cronista, m.

chronological, *krŏnŏlŏj'ĭkăl*, a. cronológico; -ly, ad. cronológicamente.

chronology, *krŏnŏl'ŏjĕ*, s. cronología, f.

chronometer, *krŏnŏm'ĕtŭr*, s. cronómetro, m.

chrysalis, *krĭs'ălĭs*, s. crisálida, f. [m.

chub, *tshŭb*, s. gobio, m. (pez).

chubby, *-bĕ*, a. gordo, cariancho.

chuck, *tshŭk*, v. n. cloquear; —, v. a. dar una sobarbada; —, s. cloqueo, m.; sobarbada, f. [v. n. reírse á carcajadas.

chuckle, *-kl*, v. a. cloquear, acariciar; —

chum, *tshŭm*, s. compañero de cuarto (entre estudiantes), m. [tronco, m.

chump, *-p*, chunk, *tshŭngk*, s. tajo,

church, *tshŭrtsh*, s. iglesia, f.; —, v. a. ir á misa; —, v. n. ejecutar las ceremonias de la purificación con alguna mujer recién parida.

church-ale, *-ăl*, s. fiesta del lugar, f.

churching, *-ĭng*, s. ceremonia de la purificación, f.

church-law, *-lă*, s. derecho canónico, m.

churchman, *-măn*, s. sacerdote, eclesiástico, m. [de la iglesia, m.

church-warden, *-wărdn*, s. mayordomo

churchyard, *-yărd*, s. cimenterio, m.

churl, *tshŭrl*, s. patán, rústico, m.

churlish, *-ĭsh*, a. rústico, grosero; tacaño; -ly, ad. rudamente, brutalmente.

churn, *tshŭrn*, s. mantequera, f.; —, v. a. mazar, batir la leche para hacer manteca.

churn-staff, *-stăf*, s. batidera, f.

cicatrice, *sĭk'ătrĭs*, s. cicatriz, f.

cider, *sī'dŭr*, s. sidra, f.

cigar, *sĕgăr'*, s. cigarro, m. [m.

cigar-divan, *-dĭvăn*, s. salón para fumar,

cigarette, *sĕg'ărĕt*, s. cigarrito, m.

cigar-holder, *-hōldăr*, cigar-tip, *-tĭp*, s. boquilla, f.; portacigarros, m.

cimeter, *sĭm'ĕtŭr*, s. cimitarra, f.

cincture, *sĭngk'tshŏr*, s. cinto, ceñidor, m., cinta, pretinilla, f.

cinder, *sĭn'dŭr*, s. ceniza gruesa y caliente.

cinnabar, *sĭn'năbăr*, s. cinabrio, m.

cinnamon, *sĭn'nămŏn*, s. canela, f.

cipher, *sī'fŭr*, s. cifra, f.; —, v. n. numerar, calcular.

circle, *sŭr'kl*, s. círculo, m.; corrillo, m.; asamblea, f.; —, v. a. circundar; cercar, ceñir; —, v. n. circular.

circlet, *-klĕt*, s. círculo pequeño, m.

circuit, *-kĭt*, s. circuito, m.; recinto, m.

circuitous, *sŭrkū'ĭtŭs*, a. circular.

circular, *sŭr'kŭlăr*, a. circular, redondo; —, s. carta circular, f. [al rededor.

circulate, *-kŭlăt*, v. n. circular; moverse

circulating-library, *-kŭlătĭnglībrărĕ*, s. gabinete de lectura, m.

circulation, *sŭrkŭlă'shŭn*, s. circulación, f.

circumcise, *sŭr'kŭmsīz*, v. a. circuncidar.

circumcision, *sŭrkŭmsĭzh'ŭn*, s. circuncisión, f. [ferencia, f.; circuito, m.

circumference, *sŭrkŭm'fĕrĕns*, s. circun-

circumflex, –flĕks, s. acento circunflejo, m.
circumjacent, –já' sĕnt, a. convecino, contiguo.
circumlocution, –lŏkä' shăn, s. circunlocución, f.
circumlocutory, –lŏk' ütărĕ, a. con perifrasis.
circumnavigate, –năv' ĕgāt, v. a. navegar.
circumnavigation, –năvĕgā' shăn, s. circumnavegación, f.
circumscribe, –skrīb', v. a. circunscribir.
circumscription, –skrĭp' shăn, s. circunscripción, f.
circumspect, săr' kŭmspĕkt, a. circunspecto, prudente, reservado; –, v. a. examinar con atención.
circumspection, –spĕk' shăn, s. circunspección, prudencia, f.
circumstance, –stăns, s. circunstancia, condición, f.; incidente, m.
circumstanced, –stănsd, a. en condición, circunstanciado.
circumstantial, –stăn' shăl, a. accidental; accesorio; –ly, ad. circunstanciadamente, exactamente.
circumstantiate, –stăn' shiăt, v. a. circunstanciar, detallar.
circumvent, –vĕnt, v. a. circumvenir.
circumvention, –vĕn' shăn, s. engaño, m.; trampa, f.; embrollo, m.
circus, săr' kŭs, s. circo, m.
cistern, sĭs' tŭrn, s. cisterna, f.
citadel, sĭt' ădĕl, s. ciudadela, fortaleza, f.
citation, sĭtā' shăn, s. citación, cita, f.
cite, sĭt, v. a. citar (á juicio); alegar; referirse á.
citizen, sĭt' ĭzĕn, s. ciudadano, m.
citizenship, –shĭp, s. ciudadanía, f.
citron, sĭt' rŏn, s. cidra, f.
citron-tree, –trē, s. cidro, m.
cittern, sĭt' tŭrn, cithern, sĭth' ŭrn, s. cítara, f.
city, sĭt' ĕ, s. ciudad, f.
civet, sĭv' ĕt, s. gato de algalia, m.; algalia, f.
civic, sĭv' ĭk, a. cívico.
civil, sĭv' ĭl, a. civil, cortés; –ly, ad. civilmente.
civilian, sĕvĭl' yăn, s. paisano, m.; jurisconsulto.
civilisation, sĭvĭlĭzā' shăn, s. civilización, f.
civilise, sĭv' ĭlĭz, v. a. civilizar.
civility, sĕvĭl' ĭtĕ, s. civilidad, urbanidad, cortesía, f.
clack, klăk, s. ruido continuo, estrépito, m.; cítola de molino, f.; –, v. n. cencerrear.
clad, klăd, v. a. vestido, cubierto.
claim, klām, v. a. pedir en juicio, reclamar, pretender como cosa debida; –, s. pretensión, f.; derecho, m. [dador, m.
claimant, –ănt, s. reclamante, m.; demandador.
clam, klăm, v. a. empastar, pegar.
clamber, –băr, v. n. gatear, trepar.
clamminess, –mĭnĕs, s. viscosidad, f.
clammy, –mĕ, a. viscoso, tenaz.
clamorous, klăm' ărŭs, a. clamoroso, tumultuoso, estrepitoso; –ly, ad. clamorosamente. [v. n. vociferar, gritar.
clamour, klăm' ŭr, s. clamor, grito, m.; –,
clamp, klămp, s. empalmadura; laña, f.; –, v. a. empalmar.
clan, klăn, s. familia, tribu, raza, f.
clandestine, klăndĕs' tĭn, a. clandestino, oculto; –ly, a. clandestinamente.

clang, klăng, s. rechino, sonido desapacible, m.; –, v. n. rechinar.
clangorous, –gŭrŭs, a. ruidoso.
clangour, –găr, s. rechinamiento, m.
clank, klăngk, v. n. chillar; –, s. chischás, retintín, m.
clap, klăp, v. a. batir; aplicar; palmear; –, s. estrépito, m.; golpe, m.; trueno, m.; palmoteo, m.
clapper, –păr, s. palmoteador, m.; badajo de campana, m.; cítola de molino, f.; llamador (de una puerta), m.
clapping, –pĭng, s. palmada, f.; aplauso, palmoteo, m. [engañabobos, m.
clap-trap, –trăp, s. lance de teatro, m.
clare-obscure, klărŏbskŭr', s. claroscuro, m.
claret, klă' rĕt, s. clarete, m. (vino).
clarification, klărĭfĕkā' shăn, s. clarificación, f.
clarify, klăr' ĕfĭ, v. a. clarificar, aclarar; –, v. n. ponerse claro.
clarinet, klă' rĕnĕt, s. clarinete, m.
clarion, klăr' ĕŏn, s. clarín, m.
clash, klăsh, v. n. rechinar, encontrarse; contradecir; –, s. rechino, crujido, m.; estrépito, m.; disputa, f.; choque, m.
clasp, klăsp, s. broche, m.; hebilla, f.; abrazo, m.; –, v. a. abrochar; abrazar.
clasp-knife, –nĭf, s. navaja, f.
class, klăs, s. clase, f.; orden, f.; –, v. a. clasificar, coordinar. [clásico, m.
classic(al), –sĭk(ăl), a. clásico; –, s. autor
classification, –sĭfĕkā' shăn, s. clasificación, f.
classify, –sĭfĭ, v. a. clasificar. [ción, f.
clatter, klăt' tăr, v. n. resonar; hacer ruido; –, s. ruido, fracaso, m. [estipulación, f.
clause, klăz, s. cláusula, f.; artículo, m.
claustral, klăs' trăl, a. claustral.
clavicle, klăv' ĭkl, s. clavícula, f.
claw, klă, s. garra, f.; garfa, f.; –, v. a. desgarrar, arañar; lisonjear.
clawed, –d', a. armado de garras.
clay, klā, s. arcilla, f.
clayey, –ĕ, clayish, –ĭsh, a. arcilloso.
clay-pit, –pĭt, s. barrizal, m.
clean, klēn, a. limpio; casto; –, ad. enteramente; –, v. a. limpiar.
cleanliness, –lĭnĕs, s. limpieza, f.; curiosidad en el vestir, f.
cleanly, –lĕ, a. limpio; puro, delicado; –, ad. primorosamente, aseadamente.
cleanness, –nĕs, s. limpieza, f.; pureza, f.
cleanse, klĕnz, v. a. limpiar, purificar; purgar.
clear, klĕr, a. claro; neto; diáfano; sereno; evidente; inocente; –, ad. claramente; enteramente; –, v. a. clarificar, aclarar; justificar, absolver; to – accounts, liquidar cuentas; –, v. n. aclararse.
clearage, –rāj, s. despejo, m.
clearance, –ăns, s. albalá de pago y finiquito, m. & f.
clearly, –lĕ, ad. claramente, evidentemente.
clearness, –nĕs, s. claridad, transparencia, f.; esplendor, m.; perspicacia, f.; sinceridad, f. [cioso.
clear-sighted, –sītĕd, a. perspicaz, jui-
clearstarch, –stărtsh, v. a. almidonar.

Cleave, *klĕv*, v. a. & n. hender; partir; dividir; pegarse.

cleaver, *-ăr*, s. cuchillo de carnicero, m.

cleft, *klĕft*, s. hendedura, abertura, f.

clematis, *klĕm'ătĭs*, s. clemátita, f.

clemency, *klĕm'ĕnsĕ*, s. clemencia, f.

clement, *klĕm'ĕnt*, a. clemente, benigno.

clenched, *klĕnshă*, a. cerrado (dícese de la mano ó del puño).

clergy, *klŭr'jĕ*, s. clero, m.

clergyman, *-măn*, s. eclesiástico, m.; little —, aprendiz de un deshollinador, m.

clerical, *klĕr'ĭkăl*, a. clerical, eclesiástico.

clerk, *klărk*, s. eclesiástico, clérigo, m.; estudiante, m.; amanuense, escribiente, m.; – of a parish, sacristán, m.

clerkship, *-shĭp*, s. educación literaria, f.; empleo de clérigo ó escribiente, m.

clever, *klĕv'ăr*, a. diestro, hábil, mañoso; propio; –ly, ad. diestramente, hábilmente. [f.

cleverness, *-nĕs*, s. destreza, habilidad, f.

clew, *klū*, s. ovillo de hilo, m.; – (up), v. a. (mar.) cargar las velas.

click, *klĭk*, v. n. retiñir.

client, *klī'ĕnt*, s. cliente, m. [f.

cliff, *klĭff*, s. peñasco, m.; roca escarpada,

climacteric, *klĭmăk'tărĭk*, a. climactérico. [tura, f.

climate, *klī'măt*, s. clima, m.; temperatura, f.

climatic, *klī'mă'tĭk*, a. climatérico.

climax, *klī'măks*, s. clímax, m.

climb, *klīm*, v. a. escalar, trepar; –, v. n. subir.

clinch, *klĭnsh*, v. a. empuñar, cerrar el puño; remachar un clavo; –, s. pulla; f.; equívoco, m.

clincher, *-ăr*, s. laña, f.

cling, *klĭng*, v. n. colgar, adherirse, pegarse.

clinic(al), *klĭn'ĭk(ăl)*, a. clínico.

clink, *klĭngk*, v. a. hacer resonar; –, v. n. retiñir, resonar; –, s. retintín, m.

clinker, *-ăr*, s. cagaferro, m.; ladrillo refractor, m. [timar.

clip, *klĭp*, v. a. abrazar; cortar á raíz; esca-

clipper, *-pŭr*, s. cercenador de monedas, m.; (mar.) navío velero, m.

clippings, *-pĭngz*, s. pl. tundizno, m.

clique, *klĕk*, s. gatería, f.

cloak, *klōk*, s. capa, f.; pretexto, m.; –, v. n. encapotar; paliar.

cloak-room, *-rōm*, s. (rail.) factoría, f., equipajes, mpl. [it? ¿qué hora es?

clock, *klŏk*, s. reloj, m.; what o'clock is

clock-dial, *-dĭăl*, s. muestra de un reloj.

clock-maker, *-măkăr*, s. relojero, m. [f.

clock-work, *-wŭrk*, s. mecanismo de un reloj, m.; –, a. sumamente exacto y puntual. [m.; –, v. n. coagularse.

clod, *klŏd*, s. terrón, m.; césped, m.; zoquete,

clog, *klŏg*, s. obstáculo, m.; galocha, f.; –, v. a. cargar, embarazar; –, v. n. coagularse; unirse. [culo, m.

clogginess, *-gĭnĕs*, s. embarazo, obstá-

cloister, *klŏĭs'tŭr*, s. claustro, monasterio, m.

close, *klōz*, v. a. cerrar; concluir, terminar; –, v. n. cerrarse, unirse; convenirse; –, s. cercado, m.; fin, m.; conclusión, f.; –, a.

cerrado; preso; estrecho, angosto; ajustado; secreto; avaro; retirado; obscuro; denso; reservado; – fight, s. viva pelea, f.; –, ad. de cerca; – by, muy arrimado; junto. [tado.

close-fisted, *-fĭstĕd*, a. mezquino, apre-

closely, *-lĕ*, ad. estrechamente; secretamente. [reclusión, f.

closeness, *-nĕs*, s. estrechez, espesura,

closet, *-ĕt*, s. retrete, m.; gabinete, m.; –, v. a. encerrar en un retrete ó gabinete.

closure, *klō'zhŭr*, s. cerradura, f.; conclusión, f. [v. n. engrumecerse.

clot, *klŏt*, s. grumo, m.; zoquete, m.; –,

cloth, *klŏth*, s. paño, m.; mantel, m.; vestido, m.; lienzo, m.

clothe, *klōth*, v. a. vestir, cubrir.

clothes, *klōthz*, s. pl. vestidura, f.; ropaje, m.; ropa de cama, f.; suit of –, s. vestido completo, m.; bed—, cobertores, m. pl.

clothes-basket, *-băskĕt*, s. cesta grande, f.

clothes-horse, *-hōrs*, s. enjugador, m.

clothes-peg, *-pĕg*, s. percha, f.

clothes-press, *-prĕs*, s. guardarropa, f.

clothier, *klōth'ĭăr*, s. pañero, m.

clothing, *-ĭng*, s. vestidos, m. pl.

cloud, *klŏŭd*, s. nube, f.; nublado, m.; manchita, f.; (fig.) adversidad, f.; –, v. a. anublar; obscurecer; –, v. n. anublarse; obscurecerse.

cloudily, *-lĭ*, ad. obscuramente.

cloudiness, *-nĕs*, s. nublosidad, f.; obscuridad, f.

cloudless, *-lĕs*, a. sin nubes, claro, sereno.

cloudy, *-ĕ*, a. nublado, nubloso; obscuro; sombrío, melancólico.

clout, *klŏŭt*, s. rodilla, f.; remiendo, m.; –, v. a. remendar; chapucear.

clove, *klōv*, s. clavo, m. (flor.)

clover, *-ăr*, s. trébol, m.; to live in –, vivir lujosamente. [m.

clown, *klŏŭn*, s. patán, rústico, m.; payaso,

clownish, *-ĭsh*, a. rústico; grosero; –ly, ad. toscamente, groseramente.

cloy, *klŏĭ*, v. a. saciar, hartar; clavar.

club, *klŭb*, s. clava, cachiporra, f.; escote, m.; club, m.; –, v. n. contribuir; unirse.

club-law, *-lă*, s. la ley del más fuerte, f.

clue, *klū*, s. ovillo de hilo, m.; seña, idea, guía, norma, f., vestigio, indicio, apoyo, m.

clump, *klŭmp*, s. trozo sin forma; bosquecillo, m.

clump-soles, *-sōlz*, s. pl. suelas dobladas, f. pl. [ramente.

clumsily, *klŭm'zĭlĭ*, ad. zafiamente, grose-

clumsiness, *klŭm'zĭnĕs*, s. zafiedad, rustiquez, grosería, f. [arte.

clumsy, *klŭm'zĭ*, a. tosco, pesado; sin

cluster, *klŭs'tăr*, s. racimo, m.; manada, f.; pelotón, m.; –, v. a. agrupar; –, v. n. arracimarse.

clutch, *klŭtsh*, s. garra, f.; presa, f.; –, v. a. empuñar.

coach, *kŏtsh*, s. coche, m.; carroza, f.; –, (up) v. a. infundir, inculcar.

coach-box, *-bŏks*, s. pescante de coche, m.

coach-hire, *-hĭr*, s. alquiler de coche, m.

coach-house, *-hŏŭs*, s. cochera, f.

coachman, *-măn*, s. cochero, m.

coaction, *kŏăk'shăn,* s. coacción, necesidad, fuerza, f.;   [pañero, m.

coadjutor, *kŏădjŏ'tŭr,* s. coadjutor, compañero, m.

coagulate, *kŏăg'dŭlt,* s. a. coagular, cuajar, condensar lo que es líquido; —, v. n. coagularse, cuajarse, espesarse.

coagulation, *kŏăgŭlă'shŭn,* s. coagulación, f.

coal, *kōl,* s. carbón de piedra, m. [ción, f.

coalesce, *kŏălĕs',* v. n. juntarse, incorporarse.

coalescence, *-sĕns,* s. coalescencia, f.

coal-heaver, *kōl'hĕvŭr,* s. mozo de barco de carbonero, m.

coal-hole, *-hōl,* s. carbonera, f.

coalition, *kŏălĭsh'ŭn,* s. coalición, confederación, f.

coal-mine, *kōl'mĭn,* **coal-pit,** *-pĭt,* s. mina de carbón, carbonería, f.

coarse, *kōrs,* a. basto, rústico, grosero; —ly, ad. groseramente.   [f.

coarseness, *-nĕs,* s. tosquedad, grosería, f.

coast, *kōst,* s. costa, f.; —, v. n. costear.

coaster, *-ŭr,* s. piloto, m.; buque costacoasting,** *-ĭng,* s. cabotaje, m. [nero, m.

coat, *kōt,* s. casaca, f.; frac, m.; hábito, m.; —aya, f.; — of mail, — of arms, cota de malla, f.; —, v. a. cubrir, vestir.

coating, *-ĭng,* s. revestimiento, m.

coax, *kōks,* v. a. lisonjear, acariciar.

coaxer, *-ŭr,* s. adulador, mimador, m.

cob, *kŏb,* s. gaviota, f.; mazorca de maíz, f.; caballo doble, m.   [(zapatos).

cobble, *-bl,* v. a. chapucear; remendar

cobbler, *-blŭr,* s. chapucero, m.

cobweb, *-wĕb,* s. telaraña, f.; (fig.) trama, f.

cochineal, *kŏtsh'ĕnēl,* s. cochinilla, f.

cock, *kŏk,* s. gallo, m.; macho, m.; giraldilla, f.; llave, f.; montoncillo de heno, m.; pie de gato de escopeta, m.; gnómon de reloj de sol, m.; armadura de sombrero, f.; aguja de romana, f.; at half —, desamartillado (escopeta); at full —, amartillado, montado (escopeta); —, v. a. armar el sombrero; amartillar, montar una escopeta; amontonar heno.

cockade, *-kād',* s. cucarda, f.

cock-a-doodle-doo, *-ădōōdlădŏ,* s. canto del gallo, m.

cockatoo, *-dtŏ',* s. cacatoy, m.

cockatrice, *kŏk'ătrĭs,* s. basilisco, m.

cock-chafer, *-tshăf'ŭr,* s. saltón, m. (insecto.)

cock-crow, *-krŏ,* s. canto del gallo, m.

cocker, *-ŭr,* v. a. acariciar.

cockerel, *-ŭrĕl,* s. gallipollo, m.

cocket, *-ĕt,* s. sello de la aduana, m.; albalá de pago, m. & f.   [gallos, f.

cock-fight(ing), *-fīt(ĭng),* s. riña de

cockle, *-kl,* s. caracol de mar, m.; (bot.) zizaña, f.; —, v. a. arrugar; doblar; —, v. n. plegarse, doblarse.

cock-loft, *-lŏft,* s. desván, zaquizamí, m.

cockney, *-nĕ,* s. pazguato de Londres, m.; hombre afeminado, m...

cockpit, *-pĭt,* s. reñidero de gallos, m.; (mar.) entarimado del sollado, m.

cock's comb, *kŏks'kōm,* s. cresta de gallo, f.; (fig.) currutaco, m.   [trón de bote, m.

cockswain, coxwain, *kŏk'sn,* s. pa-

cocoa, *kŏ'kŏ,* s. coco, m.; cacao, m.

cocoon, *kŏkŏn',* s. capullo del gusano de seda, m.   [(bot.) vaina, f.

cod, *kŏd,* s. bacalao, m.; merluza, f.; **coddle,** *-dl,* v. a. medio cocer; acariciar; afeminar.

code, *kŏd,* s. código, m.

codicil, *kŏd'ĭsĭl,* s. (law) codicilo, m.

codify, *kŏ'dĭfĭ,* v. a. hacer un código. [f.

codling, *kŏd'lĭng,* s. manzana medio cocida,

cod-liver oil, *kŏd'lĭvŭrŏĭl,* s. aceite de merluza, m.   [m.

coefficient, *kŏĕffĭsh'ĕnt,* s. coeficiente,

coequal, *kŏ'ēkwŏl,* a. igual.

coerce, *kŏŭrs',* v. a. contener, refrenar; restringir.

coercion, *kŏŭr'shŭn,* s. coerción, opresión,

coercive, *kŏŭr'sĭv,* a. coercitivo.   [(m.).

coeval, *kŏĕ'văl,* a. s. coevo; contemporáneo

coexistence, *kŏĕgzĭs'tĕns,* s. coexistencia

coffee, *kŏf'fē,* s. café, m.

coffee-berry, *-bĕrrĕ,* s. fruto del café, m.

coffee-house, *-hŏŭs,* s. café, m.

coffee-pot, *-pŏt,* s. cafetera, f.

coffee-set, *-sĕt,* s. servicio para el café,

coffee-tree, *-trē,* s. cafeto, m.   [m.

coffer, *kŏf'fŭr,* s. cofre, m.; caja, f.

coffin, *kŏf'fĭn,* s. féretro, ataúd, m.; —, v. a. meter en un ataúd.

cog, *kŏg,* s. diente (de rueda), m.; —, v. a. adular, lisonjear; to — a die, cargar un dado (con plomo).

cogency, *kŏ'jĕnsĕ,* s. fuerza, urgencia, f.

cogent, *kŏ'jĕnt,* a. convincente, urgente; —ly, ad. de un modo convincente.

cogitate, *kŏj'ĭtăt,* v. n. pensar, meditar.

cogitation, *kŏjĕtă'shŭn,* s. meditación, f.

cognate, *kŏg'năt,* a. cognado.

cognation, *kŏgnă'shŭn,* s. cognación, f.

cognition, *kŏgnĭsh'ŭn,* s. conocimiento, m.; convicción, f.

cognizance, *kŏg'nĭzăns,* s. conocimiento, m.; divisa, f.; competencia, f.

cognizant, *kŏg'nĭzănt,* a. informado; (law) competente.

cog-wheel, *kŏg'hwēl,* s. rueda dentada, f.

cohabit, *kŏhăb'ĭt,* v. n. cohabitar.

cohabitation, *-ă'shŭn,* s. cohabitación, f.

coheir, *kŏăr',* s. coheredero, m.

coheiress, *-ĕs,* s. coheredera, f.

cohere, *kŏhēr',* v. n. pegarse; unirse; convenir, conformarse.   [f.

coherence, *-ĕns,* s. coherencia, conexión,

coherent, *-ĕnt,* a. coherente; consiguiente

cohesion, *kŏhē'zhŭn,* s. coherencia, f.

cohesive, *kŏhē'sĭv,* a. coherente.

coif, *kŏĭf,* s. cofia, redecilla, f.

coil, *kŏĭl,* v. a. recoger; to — a cable, (mar.) adujar un cable; —, s. barafunda, f.; fracaso, m.; (mar.) adujada, f.

coin, *kŏĭn,* s. rincón, m.; moneda acuñada, f.; dinero, m.; —, v. a. acuñar moneda; falsificar; inventar.

coinage, *-dj,* s. acuñación, f., braceaje, m.; falsificación, f.; invención, f.

coincide, *kŏĭnsĭd',* v. n. coincidir, concurrir, convenir.   [f.

coincidence, *kŏĭn'sĭdĕns,* s. coincidencia,

coincident, *kŏĭn'sĭdĕnt,* a. coincidente.

coiner, *kŏin'ûr*, s. acuñador de moneda, monedero falso, m.; inventor, m.
coke, *kŏk*, s. cok, m.
colander, *kŭl'ândâr*, s. coladera, f.; colador, pasador, m.
cold, *kŏld*, a. frío; indiferente, insensible; reservado; -ly, ad. fríamente; indiferentemente; -, s. frío, m.; frialdad, f.
cold-blooded, *-blâdĕd*, a. impasible.
coldness, *-nĕs*, s. frialdad, f.; indiferencia, insensibilidad, apatía, f.
cole-wort, *kŏl'wûrt*, s. berza verde, f.
colic, *kŏl'ĭk*, s. cólico, m.
collaborate, *kŏlăb'ŏrăt*, v. a. cooperar.
collaboration, *kŏllăbŏrā'shân*, s. cooperación, f.
collapse, *kŏllăps'*, v. n. descaecer; -, s. hundimiento, f. (med.) colapso, m.
collar, *kŏl'lâr*, s. collar, m.; collera, f.; -, v. a. agarrar á uno de los cabezones; arrollar.
collar-bone, *-bōn*, s. clavícula, f.
collate, *kŏllăt'*, v. a. comparar, confrontar.
collateral, *kŏllăt'ŭrăl*, a. colateral; indirecto; -ly, ad. colateralmente; indirectamente; -, s. colación, f.
collation, *kŏllā'shân*, s. colación; colección, f.
colleague, *kŏl'lĕg*, s. colega, compañero, m.
collect, *kŏllĕkt'*, v. a. recoger, colegir; -, *kŏl'lĕkt*, s. colecta, f.; compilación, f.
collection, *kŏllĕk'shân*, s. colección, f.
collective, *kŏllĕk'tĭv*, a. colectivo, congregado; -ly, ad. colectivamente.
college, *kŏl'lĕj*, s. colegio, m.; colegio, m.
collegian, *kŏllē'jân*, s. miembro de un colegio.
collegiate, *kŏllē'jât*, a. colegiado.
collide, *kŏllīd'*, v. n. colidir.
collier, *kŏl'yûr*, s. carbonero, m.; barco carbonero.
colliery, *-ĕ*, s. carbonera, f.; carbonero, m.
collision, *kŏllĭzh'ân*, s. colisión, f.; ludimiento, m.; carne, f.
collop, *kŏl'lŏp*, s. tajada (pequeña de carne).
colloquial, *kŏllō'kwâl*, a. dialogal; íntimo; -ly, ad. familiarmente.
colloquialism, *-ĭzm*, s. lengua usual, f.
colloquy, *kŏl'lōkwĕ*, s. coloquio, m.; conversación, plática, f.
collusion, *kŏllū'zhân*, s. colusión, f.
collusive, *kŏllū'sĭv*, a. colusorio; -ly, ad. colusoriamente.
colon, *kŏ'lŏn*, s. colon perfecto, m.; (:).
colonel, *kûr'nĕl*, s. (mil.) coronel, m.
colonelcy, *-sĕ*, s. coronelía, f.
colonial, *kŏlō'nĭăl*, a. colonial.
colonise, *kŏl'ŏnīz*, v. a. colonizar.
colonist, *-ŏnĭst*, s. colono.
colony, *-ŏnĕ*, s. colonia, f.
colophony, *-ŏfōnĕ*, s. colofonia, f.
colossal, *kŏlŏs'sâl*, a. colosal.
colossus, *-sŭs*, s. coloso, m.
colour, *kŭl'ûr*, s. color, m.; pretexto, m.; -s, pl. bandera, f.; -, v. a. colorar; paliar; -, v. n. ponerse colorado.
colourable, *-ăbl*, a. especioso, plausible.
colourably, *-ăblĕ*, ad. plausiblemente.
colour-blind, *-blīnd*, a. que tiene daltonismo.
colouring, *-ĭng*, s. colorido, m.
colourist, *-ĭst*, s. colorista, m.

colourless, *-lĕs*, a. descolorido, sin color.
colt, *kŏlt*, s. potro, m.; mozuelo sin juicio.
colter, *-ûr*, s. reja de arado, f. [m.
columbine, *kŏl'ŭmbĭn*, s. (bot.) aguileña, f.; -, a. violado.
column, *kŏl'ŭm*, s. columna, f.
columnar, *kŏlŭm'nâr*, a. columnario.
coma, *kŏ'mă*, s. coma, letargo, m.
comatose, *kŏ'mătŏs*, a. comatosa, f.
comb, *kŏm*, s. peine, m; almohaza, f.; -, v. a. peinar; almohazar; cardar la lana.
combat, *kŭm'băt*, s. combate, m.; batalla, f.; single -, duelo, m.; -, v. n. combatir; -, v. a. resistir.
combatant, *-ânt*, s. combatiente, m.
combative, *kŭm'bătĭv*, a. quisquilloso.
comber, *kŏm'ûr*, s. cardador, m.
combination, *kŏmbĭnā'shân*, s. combinación, coordinación, f.; unirse.
combine, *-bīn'*, v. a. combinar; -, v. n.
combing-cloth, *kŏm'ĭngklŏth*, s. peinador, m.; bustible, m.
combustible, *kŏmbŭs'tĭbl*, a. & s. combustion, *-bŭs'tyân*, s. combustión, f.; incendio, m.
come, *kŭm*, v.n. venir; acontecer; proceder; -! ¡sus! ¡ánimo! [mico, m.
comedian, *kŏmē'dĭân*, s. comediante, cómico, m.
comedy, *kŏm'ĕdĕ*, s. comedia, f. [m.
comeliness, *kŭm'lĭnĕs*, s. gracia, f.; garbo, m.
comely, *kŭm'lĕ*, a. garboso, decente; -, ad. decentemente.
comestible, *kŏmĕs'tĭbl*, a. comestible.
comet, *kŏm'ĕt*, s. cometa, f.
comfit, *kŭm'fĭt*, s. confite, m.
comfort, *kŭm'fûrt*, s. confortación, f.; ayuda, f.; consuelo, m.; comodidad, f.; -, v. a. confortar; alentar, consolar.
comfortable, *-ăbl*, a. cómodo, consolatorio. [agrado, m.; comodidad, f.
comfortableness, *-ăblnĕs*, s. consuelo, comfortably, *-ăblĕ*, ad. agradablemente, cómodamente. [de, f.
comforter, *-ûr*, s. consolador, m.; bufan-
comfortless, *-lĕs*, a. desconsolado; desagradable. [-ly, ad. cómicamente.
comic(al), *kŏm'ĭk(ăl)*, a. cómico, burlesco; comicalness, *-ălnĕs*, s. facecia, f.; gracejo, chiste, m. [-, a. venidero, viniente.
coming, *kŭm'ĭng*, s. venida, llegada, f.;
comma, *kŏm'mă*, s. (gr.) coma, f.
command, *kŏmmănd'*, v. a. comandar, ordenar; -, v. n. gobernar; -, s. orden, f., comando, m.
commander, *-ûr*, s. comandante, m.
commandment, *-mĕnt*, s. mandato, precepto, m. [conmemorar; celebrar.
commemorate, *kŏmmĕm'mŏrăt*, v. a.
commemoration, *-mĕmŏrā'shân*, s. conmemoración, f.
commence, *-mĕns'*, v. a. & n. comenzar.
commencement, *-mĕnt*, s. principio, m.
commend, *-mĕnd'*, v. a. encomendar; alabar; enviar.
commendable, *-ăbl*, a. recomendable.
commendably, *-ăblĕ*, ad. loablemente.
commendation, *-d'shân*, s. recomendación, f. [comendatorio.
commendatory, *kŏmmĕn'dătûrĕ*, a. re-

commensurability, *kŏmmĕnsŭrăbŭl'ĭté,* s. conmensurabilidad, f. [mensurable.

commensurable, *–mĕn'sŭrăbl,* a. conmensurate, *–mĕn'sŭrăt,* v. a. conmensurar; *–,* a. conmensurativo, proporcionado.

comment, *kŏm'mĕnt,* s. comento, m.; glosa, f.; *–,* v. a. comentar, glosar.

commentary, *–tărĕ,* s. comentario, m.; interpretación, f.

commentator, *–tă'tŭr,* s. comentador, m.

commerce, *kŏm'mŭrs,* s. comercio, tráfico, trato, negocio, m.

commercial, *–mŭr'shăl,* a. comercial; **– directory,** s. almanaque de negocio. m.

comminatory, *–mĭn'ătărĕ,* a. conminatorio, conminatiyo. [clar.)s.

commingle, *–mĭng'gl,* v. a. (& n.) mezcommiserate, *–mĭz'ărăt,* v. a. compadecer, tener compasión.

commiseration, *–mĭzŭră'shŭn,* s. conmiseración, piedad, f.

commissariat, *–mĭssă'rĭăt,* s. comisaría, f.; comisariato, m. [m.

commissary, *kŏm'mĭssărĕ,* s. comisario.

commission, *kŏmmĭsh'ŭn,* s. comisión, f.; patente, f.; *–,* v. a. comisionar; encargar, apoderar. [gado, m.

commissioner, *–ăr,* s. comisionado, delecommit, *kŏmmĭt',* v. a. cometer; depositar; encargar. [s. auto de prisión, m.

commitment, *–mĕnt,* s. committal, *–tăl,*

committee, *–tĕ,* s. comité, m.

commodious, *kŏmmŏ'dĭŭs,* a. cómodo, conveniente; *–,* ad. cómodamente.

commodity, *–mŏd'ĭtĕ,* s. ventaja, utilidad, f.; provecho, m.; comodidad, f.; mercaderías, f. pl. [escuadra, m.

commodore, *kŏm'mŏdŏr,* s. (mar.) jefe de

common, *kŏm'mŏn,* a. común; bajo; **in –,** comunmente; **– prayer,** s. liturgia de la Iglesia anglicana, f.; *–,* s. pastos comunales, m. pl.

commonage, *–ăj,* s. derecho de pastar ganados en algún común, m.

commonalty, *–ăltĕ,* s. populacho, m.; sociedad, comunidad, f. [municipal.

common-council, *–kŏŭnsĭl,* s. concejo

commoner, *–ăr,* s. plebeyo, m.; miembro de la cámara baja (en Inglaterra), m. [f.

common-hall, *–hăl,* s. casa consistorial,

common-law, *–lă,* s. ley municipal, f.; costumbre que tiene fuerza de ley, f.

commonly, *–lĕ,* ad. comunmente, frecuentemente. [cuencia, f.

commonness, *–nĕs,* s. comunidad, f.; fre-

common-place, *–plăs,* s. lugares comunes, m. pl.; *–,* a. trivial.

commons, *–z,* s. pl. pueblo bajo, m.; cámara baja (en Inglaterra), f.

commonwealth, *–wĕlth,* s. república, f.

commotion, *kŏmmŏ'shŭn,* s. tumulto, m.; perturbación del ánimo, f.

commune, *–mŭn',* v. a. conversar, conferir.

communicable, *–mŭ'nĕkăbl,* a. comunicable, impartible. [cante, m.

communicant, *–mŭ'nĕkănt,* s. comunicommunicate, *–mŭ'nĕkăt,* v. a. comunicar, participar; *–,* v. n. comunicarse.

communication, *–mŭnĭkă'shŭn,* s. comunicación, f.; participación, f.; comercio, m.

communicative, *–mŭ'nĕkătĭv,* a. comunicativo. [comunicativo, m.

communicativeness, *–nĕs,* s. carácter

communion, *kŏmmŭn'yŭn,* s. comunidad, f.; comunión, f.

communist, *kŏm'mŭnĭst,* s. comunista, m.

community, *–mŭ'nĭtĕ,* s. comunidad, f.; república, f.

commutable, *–mŭ'tăbl,* a. conmutable, cambiable. [conmutación, f.

commutation, *–mŭtă'shŭn,* s. mudanza, f.;

commute, *–mŭt',* v. a. conmutar.

compact, *–păkt',* a. compacto, sólido, denso; *–,* kŏm'păkt, s. pacto, convenio, m.; **–ly,** *kŏmpăkt'lĕ,* ad. estrechamente; en pocas palabras.

compactness, *–nĕs,* s. solidez, densidad, f.

companion, *kŏmpăn'yŭn,* s. compañero, socio, compinche, m.

companionable, *–ăbl,* a. sociable.

companionship, *–shĭp,* s. sociedad, compañía, f.

company, *kŭm'pănĕ,* s. compañía, sociedad, f.; compañía de comercio.

comparable, *kŏm'părăbl,* a. comparable.

comparative, *kŏmpăr'ătĭv,* a. comparativo; **– degree,** s. (gr.) comparativo, m.; **–ly,** ad. comparativamente.

compare, *–păr',* v. a. comparar, colacionar; *–,* s. comparación, f.; semejanza, f.

comparison, *–păr'ĭsŭn,* s. comparación, f.; símil, m. [miento, m.

compartment, *–părt'mĕnt,* s. compartimiento, m.

compass, *kŭm'păs,* s. circuito, alcance, m.; circunferencia, f.; compás de la voz, m.; compás; *–,* v. a. circundar; conseguir; acabar. [tica, f.

compass-card, *–kărd,* s. (mar.) rosa náu-

compasses, *–ĭz,* s. pl. compás, m.

compassion, *kŏmpăsh'ŭn,* s. compasión, piedad, f. [alguno; *–,* a. compasivo.

compassionate, *–ăt,* v. a. compadecer á

compatibility, *kŏmpătĕbĭl'ĭtĕ,* s. compatibilidad, f.

compatible, *–păt'ĕbl,* a. compatible.

compatriot, *–pă'trĭŭt,* s. compatriota, m.

compeer, *–pēr',* s. compañero, colega, m.

compel, *–pĕl',* v. a. compeler, obligar, constreñir. [tome, m.

compend, *kŏm'pĕnd,* s. compendio, epí-

compendious, *kŏmpĕn'dĭŭs,* a. compendioso, sucinto; **–ly,** ad. compendiosamente.

compensate, *–pĕn'săt,* v. a. compensar.

compensation, *–pĕnsă'shŭn,* s. compensación, f.; resarcimiento, m.

compete, *–pēt',* v. n. concurrir, competir.

competence, *kŏm'pĕtĕns,* s. competencia, f.; suficiencia, f.

competent, *–pĕtĕnt,* a. competente, bastante; **–ly,** ad. competentemente.

competition, *kŏmpĕtĭsh'ŭn,* s. competencia, f.; concurrencia, f.

competitive, *–pĕt'ĭtĭv,* a. que compete. [m.

competitor, *–pĕt'ĭtŭr,* s. competidor, rival,

compilation, *–pĭlă'shŭn,* s. compilación,

compile, *–pīl',* v. a. compilar. [f.

complacence, –plá'sĕns, s. complacencia, deferencia, f. [cortés.

complacent, –plá'sĕnt, a. complaciente,

complain, –plān', v. n. quejarse, lamentarse, lastimarse, dolerse.

complaint, –t', s. queja, pena, f.; lamento, llanto, quejido, m. [dad, f.

complaisance, kŏmplăzăns', s. oficiosi-

complaisant, kŏmplăzănt', a. oficioso.

complement, kŏm'plĕment, s. complemento, m.

complete, kŏmplēt', a. completo, perfecto; –ly, ad. completamente; –, v. a. completar, acabar. [colmo, m.

completion, –plē'shăn, s. complemento,

complex, kŏm'plĕks, a. complexo, compuesto. [m.; complexión, f.; tez, f.

complexion, kŏmplĕk'shăn, s. complexo,

complexioned, –d, a. complexionado.

complexity, –plĕk'sĭtĭ, s. complexo, m.

compliance, –plī'ăns, s. complacencia, sumisión, condescendencia, f. [cioso.

compliant, –plī'ănt, a. complaciente, ofi-

complicate, kŏm'plĭkāt, v. a. complicar.

complication, kŏmplĭkā'shăn, s. complicación, f.

complier, –plī'ăr, s. consentidor, m.

compliment, kŏm'plĭment, s. cumplimiento, m.; –, v. a. cumplimentar; hacer ceremonias. [plimentero, ceremonioso.

complimentary, kŏmplĭmĕn'tără, a. cum-

compline, kŏm'plĭn, s. completas, f. pl. (vísperas). [cender, conformarse.

comply, kŏmplī', v. n. cumplir; condes-

component, –pō'nĕnt, s. componente.

comport, –pōrt', v. a. & n. sufrir; comportarse. [concertar, reglar, ordenar.

compose, –pōz', v. a. componer; sosegar;

composed, –d, a. compuesto, moderato; –ly, ad. tranquilamente, serenamente.

composer, –ăr, s. autor, m.; compositor, m.; cajista, m. [ponedor, m.

composing-stick, –pōz'ĭng stĭk, s. com-

composition, –pŏzĭ'shăn, s. composición, f.; compuesto; acomodamiento, m.

compositor, –pŏz'ĭtăr, s. cajista, m.

compost, kŏm'pŏst, s. abono, estiércol, m.

composure, kŏmpō'zhăr, s. composición, f.; tranquilidad, sangre fría, f.

compound, –pŏŭnd', v. a. componer, combinar; –, v. n. concertarse; ajustar; –, a. & s. compuesto, (m.).

comprehend, –prēhĕnd', v. a. comprender, contener; entender.

comprehensible, –prēhĕn'sĭbl, a. comprensible; –ly, ad. comprensiblemente.

comprehension, –shăn, s. comprensión, f.; inteligencia, f.

comprehensive, –sĭv, a. comprensivo, corto; –ly, ad. comprensivamente.

comprehensiveness, –nĕs, s. concisión, precisión, f.

compress, kŏmprĕs', v. a. comprimir, estrechar; –, kŏm'prĕs, s. cabezal, m.

compression, –prĕsh'ăn, s. compresión, f.

comprise, –prīz', v. a. comprender, incluir. [m.; –, v. a. comprometer.

compromise, kŏm'prŏmĭz, s. compromiso,

compulsion, kŏmpŭl'shăn, s. compulsión, f.; apremio, m.

compulsive, –pŭl'sĭv, compulsory, –pŭl'sără, a. compulsivo; –ly, ad. por fuerza. [ción, contrición, f.

compunction, –pŭngk'shăn, s. compun-

computable, –pū'tăbl, a. computable, calculable. [cuenta hecha, f.

computation, –pūtā'shăn, s. computación,

compute, –pū', v. a. computar, calcular.

comrade, kŏm'răd, s. camarada, compañero, m. [estudiar, reflexionar.

con, kŏn, pr. contra; –, v. a. meditar,

concatenation, kŏnkătĕnā'shăn, s. encadenamiento, m.; serie, f.

concave, kŏn'kăv, a. cóncavo.

concavity, kŏnkăv'ĭtĭ, s. concavidad, f.

conceal, kŏnsēl', v. a. ocultar, esconder.

concealment, –mĕnt, s. ocultación, f.; encubrimiento, m.

concede, –sēd', v. a. conceder, asentir.

conceit, –sēt', s. concepción, f.; capricho, m.; pensamiento, m.; presunción, f.; –, v. n. imaginar, creer.

conceited, –ĕd, a. afectado, vano, presumido; –ly, ad. fantásticamente.

conceivable, kŏnsē'văbl, a. concebible, inteligible.

conceive, –sēv', v. a. concebir, comprender; –, v. n. imaginar, pensar.

concentrate, –sĕn'trāt, v. a. concentrar.

concentration, –sĕntrā'shăn, s. concentración, f.

concentric(al), –sĕn'trĭk(ăl), a. concéntrico. [sentimiento, m.

conception, –sĕp'shăn, s. concepción, f.;

concern, –sărn', v. a. concernir, importar, pertenecer; –, s. negocio, m.; interés, m.; importancia, consecuencia, f.; afecto, m.

concerning, –ĭng, pr. tocante á.

concert, kŏn'sărt, s. concierto, m.; convenio, m.; –, kŏnsărt', v. a. (& n.) concertar(se). [privilegio, m.

concession, kŏnsĕsh'ăn, s. concesión, f.

conch, kŏngk, s. concha, f.

conciliate, kŏnsĭl'ĭāt, v. a. conciliar; atraer.

conciliation, –sĭlĭā'shăn, s. conciliación, f.

conciliator, –sĭl'ĭātăr, s. conciliador, m.

conciliatory, –ĕ, a. conciliativo.

concise, kŏnsīs', a. conciso, sucinto; –ly, ad. concisamente. [nismo, m.

conciseness, –nĕs, s. concisión, f.; laco-

conclude, kŏnklūd', v. a. concluir; decidir; determinar.

conclusion, –klū'zhăn, s. conclusión, determinación, f.; fin, m.

conclusive, –klū'sĭv, a. decisivo, conclusivo; –ly, a. concluyentemente. [durar.

concoct, –kŏkt', v. a. cocer, digerir; ma-

concoction, –kŏk'shăn, s. digestión, f.; cocción, maduración, f.

concomitant, –kŏm'ĭtănt, a. concomitante; –, s. compañero, m.

concord, kŏng'kŏrd, s. concordia, armonía, f.; buena inteligencia, f. [cia, f.

concordance, –kŏn'kŏrdăns, s. concordan-

concordant, –dănt, a. concordante, conforme. [venio, m.

concordat, –dăt, s. concordato, m.; con-

concourse, *kŏng' kŏrs*, s. concurso, m.; multitud, f., gentío, m.

concrete, *kŏng' krēt*, s. concreto, m.; -, *kŏngkrēt'*, v. n. concretar. [agregado, m.

concretion, *kŏnkrē' shŭn*, s. concreción, f.

concubinage, *-kū' bĭndj*, s. concubinato, m.

concubine, *kŏng' kūbĭn*, s. concubina, f.

concupiscence, *kŏnkū' pĭssĕns*, s. concupiscencia, codicia, f.

concur, *-kŭr'*, v. n. concurrir; juntarse.

concurrence, *-rĕns*, s. concurrencia, f.; unión, f.; asistencia, f.

concussion, *kŏnkŭsh'ŭn*, s. concusión, f.

condemn, *-dĕm'*, v. a. condenar; desaprobar; vituperar. [ción.

condemnation, *-nā' shŭn*, s. condenación, f.

condemnatory, *kŏndĕm' nătŭrĕ*, a. condenatorio. [sación, f.

condensation, *kŏndĕnsā' shŭn*, s. condensación, f.

condense, *-dĕns'*, v. a. condensar.

condescend, *-dĕsĕnd'*, v. n. condescender; consentir. [cendencia, f.

condescension, *-dĕsĕn' shŭn*, s. condescendign, *-dĭn'*, a. condigno, merecido.

condiment, *kŏn' dĭmĕnt*, s. condimento, m.; salsa, f.

condition, *kŏndĭsh'ŭn*, s. situación, condición, calidad, f.; estado, m.; esfera, f.

conditional, *-ăl*, a. condicional, hipotético; -ly, ad. condicionalmente.

conditioned, *-d*, a. hecho de natura.

condole, *kŏndōl'*, v. a. lamentar (con otro); -, v. n. condolerse.

condolence, *-ĕns*, s. compasión, lástima, f.

condonation, *kŏndōnā' shŭn*, s. pardón, m.

condone, *-dōn'*, v. a. perdonar.

conduce, *-dūs'*, v. a. conducir, concurrir.

conducive, *-dū' sĭv*, a. conducente, oportuno.

conduct, *kŏn' dŭkt*, s. conducta, f.; manejo, proceder, m.; conducción (de tropas), f.; -, *kŏndŭkt'*, v. a. conducir, guiar.

conduction, *kŏndŭk' shŭn*, s. conducta, conducción, f.

conductor, *-dŭkt' ŭr*, s. conductor, m.; guía, director, m.; conductor de electricidad. [m.

conduit, *kŏn' dĭt*, s. conducto, m.; caño, cone, *kōn*, s. cono, m.

confabulate, *kŏnfăb' ŭlāt*, v. n. platicar.

confection, *kŏnfĕk' shŭn*, s. confitura, f.; confección, f.

confectioner, *-ŭr*, s. confitero, m.

confederacy, *kŏnfĕd' ŭrăsĕ*, s. confederación, f.

confederate, *-fĕd' ŭrāt*, v.n. confederarse; -, a. & s. confederado (m.).

confer, *-fŭr'*, v. n. conferenciar; -, v. a. conferir, comparar.

conference, *kŏn' fŭrĕns*, s. conferencia, f.

confess, *kŏnfĕs'*, v. a. (& n.) confesar(se).

confessedly, *-fĕs' sĕdlĕ*, ad. conocidamente, infaliblemente.

confession, *-fĕsh'ŭn*, s. confesión, f.

confessional, *-ăl*, s. confesionario, m.

confessor, *-fĕs' ŭr*, s. confesor, m.

confidant, *kŏn' fĭdănt(kŏnfĭdănt')*, s. confidente, amigo íntimo, m.

confide, *kŏnfĭd'*, v. a. & n. confiar; fiarse.

confidence, *kŏn' fĭdĕns*, s. confianza, seguridad, f.

confident, *kŏn' fĭdĕnt*, a. cierto, seguro; confiado; atrevido; -, s. confidente, m.

confidential, *kŏnfĭdĕn' shăl*, a. confidencial. [figuración, f.

configuration, *-fĭgŭrā' shŭn*, s. configuración, f.

confine, *kŏn' fĭn*, s. confín, límite, m.; -, *kŏnfĭn'*, v. a. limitar; aprisionar; -, v. n. confinar. [estreñimiento, m.

confinement, *kŏnfĭn' mĕnt*, s. prisión, f.

confirm, *kŏnfŭrm'*, v. a. confirmar; ratificar. [ratificación, f.; prueba, f.

confirmation, *-d' shŭn*, s. confirmación, f.;

confirmative, *kŏnfŭrm' ătĭv*, confirmatory, *kŏnfŭrm' ătŭrĕ*, a. confirmativo.

confiscate, *kŏnfĭs' kāt*, v. a. confiscar. [f.

confiscation, *-fĭskā' shŭn*, s. confiscación, f.

conflagration, *-flăgrā' shŭn*, s. conflagración, f., incendio general, m.

conflict, *kŏn' flĭkt*, s. conflicto, m.; combate, m.; pelea, f.; -, *kŏnflĭkt'*, v. a. contender; combatir. [concurso, m.

confluence, *kŏn' flōĕns*, s. confluencia, f.;

confluent, *kŏn' flōĕnt*, a. confluente.

conform, *kŏnfŭrm'*, v. a. (& n.) conformar(se).

conformable, *-ăbl*, a. conforme, semejante; -bly, ad. conformemente.

conformation, *-d' shŭn*, s. conformación, f.

conformity, *-ĭtĕ*, s. conformidad, conveniencia, f. [fundir; destruir.

confound, *kŏnfōŭnd'*, v. a. turbar, confront, *-frŏnt'*, v. a. afrontar; confrontar; comparar.

confuse, *-fūz'*, v.a. confundir; desordenar.

confusedly, *-ĕdlĕ*, ad. confusamente.

confusion, *kŏnfū' zhŭn*, s. confusión, f.; perturbación, f.; desorden, m.

confute, *-fūt'*, v. a. confutar, refutar.

congeal, *-jēl'*, v. a. & (& n.) helar, congelar(se).

congelation, *-jĕlā' shŭn*, s. congelación, f.

congenial, *-jē' nĭăl*, a. congenial.

congeniality, *-jĕnĭăl' ĭtĕ*, s. semejanza de conger, *kŏng' gŭr*, s. congrio, m. [genio, f.

congestion, *kŏnjĕs' tshŭn*, s. congestión, f.; formación de una masa, acumulación, f.

conglomerate, *-glŏm' ĕrāt*, v. a. conglomerar, aglomerar; -, a. aglomerado.

conglomeration, *-glŏmŭrā' shŭn*, s. aglomeración, f. [lar, felicitar.

congratulate, *-grăt' ŭlāt*, v. a. congratular.

congratulation, *-grătŭlā' shŭn*, s. congratulación, f. [tulatorio.

congratulatory, *-grăt' ŭlătŭrĕ*, a. congregate, *kŏng' grĕgāt*, v. a. congregar, reunir. [gación, reunión, f.

congregation, *kŏnggrĕgā' shŭn*, s. congregación, f.

congress, *kŏng' grĕs*, s. congreso, m.; conferencia, f.

congruity, *kŏngrŏ' ĭtĕ*, s. congruencia, f.

congruous, *kŏn' grŏŭs*, a. idóneo, congruo, apto; -ly, ad. oportunamente.

conic(al), *kŏn' ĭk(ăl)*, a. cónico; -ally, ad. en forma cónica.

coniferous, *kŏnĭf' ĕrŭs*, a. (bot.) conífero.

conjectural, *kŏnjĕk' tŭrăl*, a. conjetural; -ly, ad. conjeturalmente.

conjecture, —jĕk'tŭr, s. conjetura, apariencia, f.; —, v. a. conjeturar; pronosticar.

conjoin, —jŏĭn' v. a. juntar; asociar; —, v. n. unirse, ligarse.

conjoint, —t, a. asociado, confederado.

conjugal, kŏn'jŭgăl, a. conyugal, matrimonial; —ly, ad. conyugalmente.

conjugate, kŏn'jŭgăt, v. a. (gr.) conjugar.

conjugation, kŏnjŭgā'shăn, s. conjugación, f. [f.; unión, f.

conjunction, —jŭnk'shăn, s. conjunción,

conjunctive, —jŭnk'tĭv, a. conjunto; conjuntivo. [ocasión, f.; tiempo crítico, m.

conjuncture, —jŭnk'tŭr, s. coyuntura, f.;

conjuration, —jŭrā'shăn, s. súplica ardiente, f.; conspiración, f.

conjure, —jŭr', v. a. rogar, pedir con instancia; —, kŏn'jŭr, v. n. conjurar, exorcizar; encantar; hechizar.

conjurer, kŏn'jŭrŭr, s. conjurador, encantador, m.

connate, —nāt, a. innato. [lazar.

connect, kŏnnĕkt', v. a. juntar, unir, en-

connexion, —nĕk'shăn, s. conexión, f.

connivance, —nī'văns, s. conivencia, f.

connive, —nīv', v. n. guiñar el ojo; tolerar.

connoisseur, kŏnĭssŭr' (kŏn'ĭssŭr), s. conocedor, m. [trimonial.

connubial, kŏnnū'bĭăl, a. conyugal ma-

conquer, kŏng'kŭr, v. a. conquistar; vencer. [dor, m.

conqueror, —ŭr, s. vencedor, conquista-

conquest, kŏng'kwĕst, s. conquista, f.

consanguineous, kŏnsănggwĭn'ĭŭs, a. consanguíneo.

consanguinity, —sănggwĭn'ĭtĭ, s. consanguinidad, f. [escrúpulo, m.

conscience, kŏn'shĕns, s. conciencia, f.;

conscientious, kŏnshĕn'shŭs, a. concienzudo, escrupuloso; —ly, ad. según conciencia. [cido; —ly, ad. á sabiendas.

conscious, kŏn'shŭs, a. sabedor, conven-

conscript, kŏn'skrĭpt, a. conscripto.

conscription, kŏnskrĭp'shăn, s. asiento en algún registro, m.; reclutamiento, m.

consecrate, kŏn'sĕkrāt, v. a. consagrar; dedicar. [ción, f.

consecration, kŏnsĕkrā'shăn, s. consagra-

consecutive, —sĕk'ŭtĭv, a. consecutivo; —ly, ad. consecutivamente.

consent, —sĕnt', s. consentimiento, asenso, m.; aprobación, f.; —, v. n. consentir; aprobar. [cia, f.; importancia, f.

consequence, kŏn'sĕkwĕns, s. consecuen-

consequent, —sĕkwĕnt,a. consecutivo, concluyente; —ly, ad. consiguientemente.

consequential, kŏnsĕkwĕn'shăl, a. presumido. [ción, f.

conservation, —sĕrvā'shăn, s. conserva-

conservative, —sĕr'vătĭv, a. conservativo.

conservator, —sĕrvā'tŭr, s. conservador, m.; defensor, m. [vatorio (m.).

conservatory, —sĕr'vătŭrē, a. & s. conser-

consider, —sĭd'ŭr, v. a. considerar, examinar; —, v. n. pensar, deliberar.

considerable, —ăbl, a. considerable; importante; —bly, ad. considerablemente.

considerate, —ăt, a. considerado, prudente, discreto; —ly, ad. juiciosamente; prudentemente.

consideration, —d'shăn, s. consideración, f.; deliberación, f.; importancia, f.; valor, mérito, m.

considering, —ĭng, c. en atención á; —that, á causa de; visto que, en razón á.

consign, kŏnsīn', v. a. consignar.

consignee, —ē', s. agente, m.

consignment, —mĕnt, s. consignación, f.

consist, kŏnsĭst', v. n. consistir; acordarse. [f.

consistence(cy), —ĕns(sē), s. consistencia,

consistent, —ĕnt, a. consistente; conveniente, conforme; sólido, estable; —ly, ad. consistentemente.

consistory, kŏnsĭs'tŭrē, s. consistorio, m.

consolable, —sō'lăbl, a. consolable.

consolation, —sŏlā'shăn, s. consolación, f.; consuelo, m.

consolatory, —sŏl'ătŭrē, a. consolatorio.

console, —sōl', v. a. consolar; —, kŏn'sōl, s. cartela, f. [solidar(se).

consolidate, —sŏl'ĭdāt, v. a. (& n.) con-

consolidation, —sŏlĭdā'shăn, s. consolidación, f. [dos), m. pl.

consols, kŏn'sōls, s. pl. consolidados (fon-

consonance, kŏn'sŏnăns, s. consonancia, f.; armonía, f.

consonant, kŏn'sŏnănt, a. consonante, conforme; —, s. (gr.) consonante, f.

consort, kŏn'sŏrt, s. consorte, socio, m.; esposo, m.; esposa, f.; —, kŏnsŏrt', v. n. asociarse.

conspicuous, kŏnspĭk'ŭŭs, a. conspícuo, aparente; notable; —ly, ad. claramente, insignemente.

conspiracy, —spĭr'ăsē, s. conspiración, f.

conspirator, —spĭr'ātŭr, s. conspirador, m.

conspire, —spīr', v. n. conspirar, maquinar.

constable, kŏn'stăbl, s. condestable, m.

constabulary, kŏnstăb'ŭlŭrē, s. policía, f.

constancy, kŏn'stănsē, s. constancia, f.; perseverancia, persistencia, f.

constant, kŏn'stănt, a. constante; perseverante; —ly, ad. constantemente.

constellation, kŏnstĕllā'shăn, s. constelación, f.; conjunto de circunstancias, m.

consternation, —stĕrnā'shăn, s. consternación, f.; terror, m.

constipate, kŏn'stĭpāt, v. a. espesar, condensar; obstruir.

constituency, kŏnstĭt'ŭĕnsē, s. junta electoral, f. [—, a. constituyente.

constituent, —ĕnt, s. constitutivo, m.;

constitute, kŏn'stĭtŭt, v. a. constituir; establecer; diputar.

constitution, kŏnstĭtū'shăn, s. constitución, f.; estado, m.; temperamento, m.

constitutional, —ăl, a. constitucional, legal. [restringir.

constrain, —strān', v. a. constreñir, forzar;

constrainable, —ăbl, a. constreñible.

constrainedly, —ĕdlē, ad. por fuerza.

constraint, —t', s. constreñimiento, m.; fuerza, violencia, f. [char.

constrict, kŏnstrĭkt', v. a. constreñir, estre-

constringent, *kŏnstrĭn'jĕnt*, a. constrictivo. [ficar.

construct, *-străkt'*, v. a. construir, edificar.

construction, *-străk'shăn*, s. construcción, f.; interpretación, f.

construe, *-strō'*, v. a. construir; interpretar.

consul, *kŏn'sŭl*, s. cónsul, m. [pretar.

consular, *kŏn'sŭlăr*, a. consular.

consulate, *kŏn'sŭlăt*, consulship, *kŏn'sŭlshĭp*, s. consulado, m. [aconsejar(se).

consult, *kŏnsŭlt'*, v. a. & n. consultar(se);

consultation, *-sŭltă'shăn*, s. consulta, deliberación, f. [destruible.

consumable, *-sū'măbl*, a. consumible.

consume, *-sūm'*, v. a. consumir; disipar; —, v. n. consumirse. [quiano, m.

consumer, *-ŭr*, s. consumidor, parroquiano, m.

consummate, *kŏn'sŭmmăt*, v. a. consumar, acabar, perfeccionar; —, *kŏnsŭm'măt*, a. cumplido, consumado.

consummation, *kŏnsŭmmă'shăn*, s. consumación, perfección, f.

consumption, *-sŭm'shăn*, s. consunción, f.; disipación, f.; tisis, f. [tísico, ético.

consumptive, *-sŭm'tĭv*, a. consuntivo;

contact, *kŏn'tăkt*, s. contacto, tocamiento, m. [infición, infección, f.

contagion, *kŏntă'jŭn*, s. contagio, m.;

contagious, *-tă'jŭs*, a. contagioso.

contain, *-tān'*, v. a. contener, comprender; caber; reprimir, refrenar.

contaminate, *-tăm'ĭnăt*, v. a. contaminar; corromper; —, a. contaminado, corrompido. [minación, f.

contamination, *-tămĭnă'shăn*, s. contaminación, f.

contemn, *-tĕm'*, v. a. despreciar, menospreciar, desestimar; desdeñar.

contemplate, *kŏntĕm'plăt* (*kŏn'tĕmplăt*), v. a. contemplar. [plación, f.

contemplation, *-tĕmplă'shăn*, s. contemplación, f.

contemplative, *-tĕm'plătĭv*, a. contemplativo; -ly, ad. con atención y estudio.

contemporaneous, *-tĕmpŏră'nĭŭs*, contemporary, *kŏntĕm'pŏrărĕ*, a. contemporáneo.

contempt, *-tĕmt'*, s. desprecio, desdén, m.

contemptible, *-tĭbl*, a. despreciable, vil; -bly, ad. vilmente.

contemptuous, *-tĕm'tŭŭs*, a. desdeñoso, insolente; -ly, ad. con desdén.

contend, *-tĕnd'*, v. n. contender, disputar, afirmar.

content, *-tĕnt'*, a. contento, satisfecho; —, v. a. contentar, satisfacer; —, s. contento, m.; satisfacción, f.; -s, pl. contenido, m.; tabla de materias, f.

contentedly, *-ĕdlĕ*, ad. de un modo satisfecho; con paciencia.

contentedness, *-ĕdnĕs*, s. contento, m., satisfacción, f. [altercación, f.

contention, *kŏntĕn'shăn*, s. contención,

contentious, *-tĕn'shŭs*, a. contencioso, litigioso; -ly, ad. contenciosamente.

contentment, *-tĕnt'mĕnt*, s. contentamiento, placer, m.

contest, *-tĕst'*, v. a. contestar, disputar, litigar; —, *kŏn'tĕst*, s. disputa, contestación, altercación, f.

contestant, *kŏntĕs'tănt*, a. contestante.

context, *kŏn'tĕkst*, s. contexto, m.; contextura, f. [tejido, m.

contexture, *kŏntĕks'tŭr*, s. contextura, f.

contiguity, *-tĭgū'tĕ*, s. contigüidad, f.

contiguous, *-tĭg'ŭŭs*, a. contiguo, vecino.

continence(cy), *kŏn'tĭnĕns(ĕ)*, s. continencia, f.; castidad, f.

continent, *kŏn'tĭnĕnt*, a. continente; -ly, ad. castamente; —, s. continente, m.

continental, *kŏntĭnĕn'tăl*, a. continental.

contingency, *-tĭn'jĕnsĕ*, s. contingencia, f.; acontecimiento, m.; eventualidad, f.

contingent, *-tĭn'jĕnt*, s. contingente, m.; cuota, f.; —, a. contingente, casual; -ly, ad. casualmente. [continuamente.

continual, *-tĭn'ŭăl*, a. continuo; -ly, ad.

continuance, *-tĭn'ŭăns*, s. continuación, permanencia, f.; duración, f.

continuation, *-tĭnŭă'shăn*, s. continuación, serie, f.

continue, *-tĭn'ū*, v. a. continuar; —, v. n. durar, perseverar, persistir.

continuedly, *-ĕdlĕ*, ad. continuadamente.

continuity, *kŏntĭnū'tĕ*, s. continuidad, f.

continuous, *-tĭn'ŭŭs*, a. continuo, unido.

contort, *-tŏrt'*, v. a. torcer.

contortion, *-tŏr'shăn*, s. contorsión, f.

contour, *-tŏr'*, s. contorno, m.

contraband, *kŏn'trăbănd*, s. contrabando, m.; —, a. prohibido, ilegal.

contrabandist, *-ĭst*, s. contrabandista, m.

contract, *kŏntrăkt'*, v. a. contraer; abreviar; contratar; —, v. n. contraerse; —, *kŏn'trăkt*, s. contrato, pacto, m.

contraction, *kŏntrăk'shăn*, s. contracción, f.; abreviatura, f.

contractor, *-trăk'tŭr*, s. contratante, m.

contradict, *-trădĭkt'*, v. a. contradecir.

contradiction, *-dĭk'shăn*, s. contradicción, oposición, f.

contradictoriness, *-dĭk'tŭrĭnĕs*, s. oposición en sumo grado, f. [torio.

contradictory, *-dĭk'tŭrĕ*, a. contradictorio.

contrariety, *-rĭ'ĕtĕ*, contrariness, *kŏn'trărĭnĕs*, s. contrariedad, oposición, f.

contrary, *kŏn'trărĕ*, a. contrario, opuesto; —, s. contrario, m.; on the —, al contrario.

contrast, *kŏn'trăst*, s. contraste, m.; oposición, f.; —, *kŏntrăst'*, v. a. contrastar, oponer. [vención, f.

contravention, *kŏntrăvĕn'shăn*, s. contra-

contributary, *-trĭb'ŭtărĕ*, a. contributario.

contribute, *-trĭb'ūt*, v. a. contribuir, ayudar. [ción, f.; tributo, m.

contribution, *-trĭbū'shăn*, s. contribución, f.

contributor, *-trĭb'ŭtăr*, s. contribuidor, m.

contributory, *-ĕ*, contributive, *-trĭb'ŭtĭv*, a. contribuyente; tributario.

contrite, *kŏn'trīt*, a. contrito, arrepentido.

contrition, *kŏntrĭsh'ăn*, s. penitencia, contrición, f. [invención, f.; concepto, m.

contrivance, *-trĭ'văns*, s. designio, m.;

contrive, *-trīv'*, v. a. inventar, trazar, maquinar; manejar; combinar.

control, *kŏntrōl'*, s. contrarregistro, m.; inspección, f.; —, v. a. restringir; gobernar; refutar; registrar; criticar. [m.

controller, *-lăr*, s. contralor, registrador,

controversial, _kŏntrŏvăr' shăl,_ a. polémico, f. [f.
controversy, _kŏn' trŏvărsĕ,_ s. controversia.
controvert, _kŏn' trŏvărt,_ v.a. controvertir, disputar.
contumacious, _kŏntŭmă' shŭs,_ a. contumaz; -ly, ad. contumazmente.
contumacy, _kŏn' tŭmăsĕ,_ s. contumacia, resistencia, f.
contumelious, _kŏntŭmē' lĭŭs,_ a. contumelioso, injurioso; -ly, ad. contumeliosamente. [juria, f.
contumely, _kŏn' tŭmĕlĕ,_ s. contumelia, in-
contusion, _kŏntŭ' zhŭn,_ s. contusión, f., magullamiento, m.
conundrum, _kŏnŭn' drŭm,_ s. pulla, f.
convalescence, _kŏnvălĕs' sĕns,_ s. convalecencia, f.
convalescent, _-sĕnt,_ a. convaleciente.
convene, _kŏnvēn',_ v.a. convocar; juntar, unir; -, v. n. convenir, juntarse.
convenience, _-vē' nĭĕns,_ s. conveniencia, comodidad, conformidad, f.
convenient, _-vē' nĭĕnt,_ a. conveniente, apto, cómodo, propio; -ly, ad. cómodamente, oportunamente. [monasterio, m.
convent, _kŏn' vĕnt,_ s. convento, claustro,
conventicle, _kŏnvĕn' tĭkl,_ s. conventículo, m.
convention, _-vĕn' shŭn,_ s. convención, f.; contrato, tratado, m. [pulado.
conventional, _-ăl,_ a. convencional, estipulado.
conventual, _kŏnvĕn' tŭăl,_ a. conventual.
converge, _-vĕrj',_ v. n. convergir.
convergence, _-vĕr' jĕns,_ s. convergencia, f.
convergent, _-vĕr' jĕnt,_ a. convergente.
conversable, _-vĕr' săbl,_ a. conversable, sociable. [timo.
conversant, _-vĕr' sănt,_ a. versado en; íntimo.
conversation, _-vĕrsă' shŭn,_ s. conversación, familiaridad, f. [divertido, m.
conversationalist, _-ălĭst,_ s. hombre
converse, _-vĕrs',_ v. n. conversar; platicar; -, _kŏn' vĕrs,_ s. conversación, plática, f.; familiaridad, f.; comercio, m.
conversely, _kŏnvĕrs' lĕ,_ ad. mutuamente, recíprocamente. [transmutación, f.
conversion, _-vĕr' shŭn,_ s. conversión, f.
convert, _-vĕrt',_ v. a. (& n.) convertir(se); -, _kŏn' vĕrt,_ s. converso, convertido, m.
convertible, _kŏnvĕr' tĭbl,_ a. convertible, transmutable.
convex, _kŏn' vĕks,_ a. convexo.
convexity, _kŏnvĕk' sĭtĕ,_ s. convexidad, f.
convey, _-vā',_ v. a. transportar; transmitir, trasferir, transferir.
conveyance, _-ăns,_ s. transporte, m.; conducción, f.; escritura de traspaso, f.
conveyancer, _-ănsăr,_ s. notario, m.
convict, _kŏnvĭkt',_ v. a. convencer, probar un delito; -, _kŏn' vĭkt,_ s. convicto, m.
conviction, _-vĭk' shŭn,_ s. convicción, f.; refutación, f.
convince, _-vĭns',_ v. a. convencer, poner en evidencia. [modo convincente.
convincingly, _-vĭn' sĭnglĕ,_ ad. de un
convivial, _-vĭ' vĭăl,_ a. sociable; hospitalario.
conviviality, _-ĭtĕ,_ s. sociabilidad, f.

convocation, _kŏnvŏkă' shŭn,_ s. convocación, f.; sínodo, m.
convoke, _-vōk',_ v. a. convocar, reunir.
convolvulus, _-vŏl' vŭlŭs,_ s. (bot.) albohol, m., bigorda, f.
convoy, _-vŏĭ',_ v. a. convoyar; -, _kŏn' vŏĭ,_ s. convoy, m.; conserva, f.; escolta, f.
convulse, _-vŭls',_ v. a. conmover, trastornar. [conmoción, f.; tumulto, m.
convulsion, _-vŭl' shŭn,_ s. convulsión, f.;
convulsive, _-vŭl' sĭv,_ a. convulsivo; -ly, ad. convulsivamente.
cony, _kō' nĕ,_ s. conejo, m.
coo, _kō,_ v. n. arrullar. [halago, m.
cooing, _kō' ĭng,_ s. arrullo de palomas, m.;
cook, _kŏk,_ s. cocinero, m.; cocinera, f.; -, v. a. aderezar las viandas; -, v. n. cocinar; guisar.
cookery, _-ărĕ,_ s. arte culinaria, f.
cool, _kŏl,_ a. fresco; indiferente; -, s. frescura, f.; -, v. a. enfriar, refrescar, atemperar. [frigerante, m.
cooler, _-ăr,_ s. enfriadera, f.; (med.) recoolly, _-lĕ,_ ad. frescamente; indiferentemente. [frescura, f.
coolness, _-nĕs,_ s. fresco, m.; frialdad, f.
coom, _kŏm,_ s. unto de coche, m.
coop, _kŏp,_ s. caponera, f.; redil, m.; -, v. a. enjaular, encarcelar.
cooper, _-ăr,_ s. cubero, tonelero, m.
cooperate, _kŏŏp' ărăt,_ v. n. cooperar.
cooperation, _kŏŏpără' shŭn,_ s. cooperación, f. [cooperante.
cooperative, _kŏŏp' ărătĭv,_ a. cooperativo;
coordination, _kŏŏrdĭnă' shŭn,_ s. coordinación, elección, f. [socio, m.
copartner, _kŏpărt' năr,_ s. compañero,
cope, _kŏp,_ s. capa pluvial, f.; cualquier cobertura, f.; -, v. n. competir, lidiar con
copier, _kŏp' ĭăr,_ s. copista, m. [otro.
coping, _kō' pĭng,_ s. cumbre de edificio, f.
copious, _kō' pĭŭs,_ a. copioso, abundante; -ly, ad. en abundancia.
copiousness, _-nĕs,_ s. abundancia, copia, f.
copper, _kŏp' păr,_ s. cobre, m.; calderón, m.; moneda de cobre, f.
copperas, _-ăs,_ s. caparrosa, f.
copper-plate, _-plăt,_ s. lámina de cobre, f.; estampa, f.
coppersmith, _-smĭth,_ s. calderero, m. [f.
copper-work, _-wŭrk,_ s. fábrica de cobre,
coppery, _-ĕ,_ a. cobrizo. [bajo, m.
coppice, _kŏp' pĭs,_ copse, _kŏps,_ s. monte
copy, _kŏp' ĕ,_ s. copia, f.; original, m.; ejemplar de algún libro, m.; -, v. a. copiar; imitar.
copy-book, _-bŭk,_ s. copiador de cartas (libro), m. [nero, m.
copying-clerk, _-ĭngklărk,_ s. expedicionario, m. [fica-machine, _-ĭngmăshĕn,_ s. pantó-
copyist, _-ĭst,_ s. copista, m. [grafo, m.
copyright, _-rĭt,_ s. propiedad de una obra literaria, f.; derechos de autor, m. pl.
coquet, _kŏkĕt',_ v. n. cocar, cortejar.
coquetry, _kō' kĕtrĕ,_ s. coquetería, f.
coquettish, _kŏkĕt' tĭsh,_ a. pisaverde, coquettish, _kŏr' ăl,_ s. coral, m. [queta.
coralline, _-ĭn,_ s. coralina, f.

cord, *kŏrd*, s. cuerda, f.; cordel, m.; montón de leña, m.; –, v. a. encordelar.

cordage, *kŏr'dáj*, s. cordaje, m.

cordial, *kŏr'diál*, a. cordial, de corazón, amistoso; –ly, ad. cordialmente; –, s. remedio confortativo, m.

cordiality, *kŏrdiăl'tiĕ*, s. cordialidad, f.

corduroy, *kŏrdŭrŏĕ'*, s. terciopelo cruzado, m.

core, *kŏr*, s. cuesco, m.; interior, centro, corazón, m.; pus, m.; materia, f.

cork, *kŏrk*, s. alcornoque, m.; corcho, m.; –, v. a. tapar botellas con corchos.

cork-screw, *–skrŏ*, s. tirabuzón, m.

corky, *–ĕ*, a. de corcho. [glotón, m.

cormorant, *kŏr'mŏránt*, s. corvejón, m.;

corn, *kŏrn*, s. grano, m.; callo, m.; –, v. a. salar; granular.

corn-cob, *–kŏb*, s. (am.) mazorca, f.

cornelian, *kŏrnĕ'liăn*, (tree), s. cornejo, m.; (stone), cornerina, f.

corner, *kŏr'nŭr*, s. ángulo, m.; rincón, m.; extremidad, f.; remate, m.

corner-house, *–hŏŭs*, s. casa esquina, f.

corner-stone, *–stŏn*, s. piedra angular, f.; mocheta, f. [darte, m.

cornet, *kŏr'nĕt*, s. corneta, f.; portaestan-

cornetcy, *–sĕ*, s. grado de portaestandarte, m. [de granos, f.

corn-exchange, *kŏrn'ĕkstshánj*, s. lonja

corn-field, *–fĕld*, s. sembrado, m.

corn-flower, *–flŏŭr*, s. azulejo, aciano, m.

cornice, *kŏr'nĭs*, s. cornisa, f. [m.

corn-rose, *kŏrn'rŏs*, s. ababa, amapola, f.

corn-salad, *–sálád*, s. macha, valerianilla, f.

corny, *kŏr'nĕ*, a. lo que produce ó contiene grano; de pan llevar; calloso.

corollary, *kŏr'ŏllárĕ*, s. corolario, m.

coronation, *kŏrŏná'shăn*, s. coronación, f.

coroner, *kŏr'ŏnŭr*, s. oficial que hace la inspección jurídica de los cadáveres, m.

coronet, *kŏr'ŏnĕt*, s. corona pequeña, f.

corporal, *kŏr'pŏrál*, s. caporal, m.; –, a. corpóreo; material; –ly, ad. corporalmente.

corporate, *kŏr'pŏrát*, a. formado en cuerpo ó en comunidad. [ción, f.; gremio, m.

corporation, *kŏrpŏrá'shăn*, s. corpora-

corporeal, *kŏrpŏ'riál*, a. corpóreo.

corps, *kŏr*, s. cuerpo de ejército, m.; regimiento, m.

corpse, *kŏrps*, s. cadáver, m. [lencia, f.

corpulence(cy), *kŏr'pŭlĕns(sĕ)*, s. corpu-

corpulent, *kŏr'pŭlĕnt*, a. corpulento, gordo.

Corpus-Christi-Day, *kŏr'pŭskrĭstidá*, s. día de Corpus, m. [m.

corpuscle, *kŏr'pŭskl*, corpúsculo, átomo,

correct, *kŏrrĕkt'*, v. a. corregir, reprender, castigar; enmendar, amonestar; –, a. correcto, revisto; –ly, ad. correctamente.

correction, *kŏrrĕk'shăn*, s. corrección, f.; castigo, m.; enmienda, f.; censura, f.

corrective, *kŏrrĕk'tĭv*, a. correctivo; –, s. correctivo, m.; restricción, f.

correctness, *kŏrrĕkt'nĕs*, s. exactitud, f.

correlative, *kŏrrĕl'átĭv*, a. correlativo.

correspond, *kŏrrĕspŏnd'*, v. n. corresponder; corresponderse.

correspondence, *–ĕns*, s. correspondencia, f.; inteligencia, f.

correspondent, *–ĕnt*, a. correspondiente, conforme; –, s. corresponsal, m.

corrigible, *kŏr'rĭjĭbl*, a. corregible.

corroborate, *kŏrrŏb'ŏrát*, v. a. corroborar.

corroboration, *kŏrrŏbŏrá'shăn*, s. corroboración, f. [borativo.

corroborative, *kŏrrŏb'ŏrátĭv*, a. corro-

corrode, *kŏrrŏd'*, v. a. corroer.

corrosion, *kŏrrŏ'zhăn*, s. corrosión, f.

corrosive, *kŏrrŏ'sĭv*, a. & s. corrosivo (m.).

corrupt, *kŏrrŭpt'*, v. a. corromper; sobornar; infectar; –, v. n. corromperse, pudrirse; –, a. corrompido; depravado.

corruptible, *–ĭbl*, a. corruptible.

corruption, *kŏrrŭp'shăn*, s. corrupción, f.; depravación, f.; alteración, f.; pus, m.

corruptive, *–tĭv*, a. corruptivo.

corruptness, *–nĕs*, s. corruptela, corrupción, f. [forbante, m.

corsair, *kŏr'sár*, s. corsario, pirata, m.;

corset, *kŏr'sĕt*, s. corsé, corpiño, m.

coruscation, *kŏrŭská'shăn*, s. resplandor, m. [beta, f.

corvette, *kŏrvĕt'*, *kŏr'vĕt*, s. (mar.) cor-

cosily, *kŏ'silĕ*, ad. cómodamente, con facilidad.

cosmetic, *kŏzmĕt'ĭk*, a. & s. cosmético (m.).

cosmopolitan, *kŏzmŏpŏl'ĭtán*, cosmo-polite, *kŏzmŏp'ŏlĭt*, a. & s. cosmopolita (m.),

cosset, *kŏs'sĕt*, v. a. mimar.

cost, *kŏst*, s. coste, precio, m.; expensas, f. pl.; –, v. n. costar. [gŭr, s. frutero, m.

coster, *kŏs'tŭr*, coster-monger, *–măn'-* [gŭr, s. frutero, m.

costive, *kŏs'tĭv*, a. restriñente.

costiveness, *–nĕs*, s. constipación, f.

costliness, *kŏst'lĭnĕs*, s. suntuosidad, f.

costly, *kŏst'lĕ*, a. costoso, suntuoso, caro; espléndido, suntuoso.

costume, *kŏstúm'*, s. traje, m.

cosy, *kŏ'sĕ*, a. cómodo.

cot, *kŏt*, s. cabaña, f.; barquillo, m.

cotillion, *kŏtĭl'yăn*, s. cotillón, m.

cotrustee, *kŏtrăstĕ'*, s. curador, m.

cottage, *kŏt'tĭj*, s. cabaña, casucha, f.

cottager, *kŏt'tĭjŭr*, s. aldeano, lugareño, m.

cotton, *kŏt'tn*, s. algodón, m.; cotonía, f.; –, v. n. cubrirse de pelusa; acordarse.

cotton-mill, *–mĭl*, s. hilandería de algodón, [f.

cotton-tree, *–trĕ*, s. algodonero, m.

cotton-wool, *–wŭl*, s. algodón basto, m.

couch, *kŏŭtsh*, v. n. echarse; agobiarse; –, v. a. acostar; extender; esconder; bajar (los ojos); (in writing) componer; –, s. cama, f.; lecho, m.; canapé, m.

cough, *kŏf*, s. tos, f.; –, v. n. toser.

councillor, *kŏŭn'sĭlŭr*, s. concejal, individuo del concejo, m.

council, *kŏŭn'sĭl*, s. concilio, consejo, m.; sínodo, m. [consejo, f.

council-board, *–bŏrd*, s. reunión del

counsel, *kŏŭn'sĕl*, s. consejo, aviso, m.; abogado, m. [gado, m.

counsellor, *–lŭr*, s. consejero, m.; abo-

count, *kŏŭnt*, v. a. contar, numerar; calcular, reputar; –, s. cuenta, f.; cálculo, m.; conde, m.

countenance, *kŏun'tĕnăns*, s. rostro, m.; aspecto, m.; (buena ó mala) cara, f.; protección, f.; favor, m.; aire, m.; –, v. a. proteger, favorecer.

counter, *kŏun'tŭr*, s. contador, m.; ficha, f.; –, ad. contra, al contrario, al revés.

counteract, *–ăkt*, v.a. contrariar, impedir, estorbar; frustrar.

counteraction, *–ăk'shăn*, s. oposición, f.

counterbalance, *–băl'ăns*, v. a. contrapesar; igualar, compensar; –, *–bălăns'*, s. contrapeso, m.

counterfeit, *–fĭt*, v.a. contrahacer, imitar, falsear ; –, s. contrahacedor, impostor, m.; falsificación, f.; *–ă*, a. falsificado; fingido.

counterfeiter, *–fĭtăr*, s. contrahacedor, falsario, m.; – of coin, monedero falso, m.

counter-foil, *–fŏĭl*, s. contramarca, f.

counterjumper, *–jŭmpăr*, s. hortera, m.

countermand, *–mănd'*, v. a. contramandar; revocar.

counterpane, *–pān*, s. colcha de cama, f.; cobertor, m. [diente, f.

counterpart, *–părt*, s. parte correspondiente

counterplot, *–plŏt*, s. contratreta, f.

counterpoise, *–pŏĭz*, v.a. contrapesar; –, *kŏun'tŭrpŏĭz*, s. contrapeso, m.

counterscarp, *–skărp*, s. contraescarpa, f.

countersign, *–sĭn*, v. a. refrendar ; firmar un decreto. [trarrestar.

countervail, *–vāl*, v. a. contrapesar, con-

countess, *kŏun'tĕs*, s. condesa, f.

counting-house, *kŏun'tĕnghŏus*, s. despacho, escritorio, m.

countless, *kŏun'tlĕs*, a. innumerable.

countrified, *kŭn'trĭfĭd*, a. rústico ; tosco, rudo.

country, *kŭn'trĕ*, s. país, f.; campo, m.; región, f.; patria, f.; –, a. rústico; campestre, rural.

country-dance, *–dăns*, s. contradanza, f.

country-house, *–hŏus*, s. casa de campo, granja, f. [patriota, m.

countryman, *–măn*, s. paisano, m.; compatriota, m.

country-squire, *–skwīr*, s. caballero de provincia, hidalgo de aldea, m.

county, *kŏun'tĕ*, s. condado, m.

couple, *kŭp'l*, s. par, m.; lazo, m.; –, v. a. unir, parear; casar ; –, v. n. juntarse carnalmente.

couplet, *kŭp'lĕt*, s. copla, f.; par, m.

couplings, *kŭp'lĭngz*, s. pl. (rail.) locomotoras acopladas, f. pl.

courage, *kŭr'ĭj*, s. coraje, valor, f.

courageous, *kŭr'ĭjŭs*, a. corajudo, valeroso; *–ly*, ad. valerosamente. [preso, m.

courier, *kŭr'tŭr*, s. correo, mensajero, m.

course, *kōrs*, s. curso, m.; carrera, f.; camino, m.; ruta, f.; viaje de comidas, m.; curso, m.; método, m.; entrada, f.; servicio, m.; regularidad, orden, f.; *–s*, pl. menstruación, f.; –, v. a. & n. cazar; correr; of –, por supuesto, sin duda.

courser, *–ŭr*, s. corcel, corredor, m.

court, *kōrt*, s. corte, f.; palacio, m.; tribunal de justicia, m.; cortejo, m.; patio, m.; –, v. a. cortejar ; solicitar, adular.

court-day, *–dā*, s. día de besamanos, m.

court-dresser, *–drĕssŭr*, s. lisonjeador, m.

courteous, *kŭr'tyŭs*, a. cortés ; benévolo; *–ly*, ad. cortésmente.

courter, *kōr'tŭr*, s. cortejador, amante, m.

courtesan, *kŭr'tĕzăn*, s. cortesana, f.

courtesy, *kŭr'tĕsĕ*, s. cortesía, f.; benignidad, f.; –, v. n. hacer la reverencia.

court-house, *kōrt'hŏus*, s. foro, tribunal, m. [m.; cortejo, m.

courtier, *kōrt'yĕr*, s. cortesano, palaciego,

courtliness, *kōrt'lĭnĕs*, s. cortesía, urbanidad, política, f.; elegancia, f.

courtly, *–lĕ*, a. cortesano, elegante.

court-martial, *–mărshăl*, s. (mil.) corte marcial, f.; consejo militar, m. [m.

court-plaster, *–plăstăr*, s. tafetán inglés,

courtship, *–shĭp*, s. cortejo, m.; galan-

court-yard, *–yărd*, s. patio, m. [tería, f.

cousin, *kŭz'n*, s. primo, m.; prima, f.; first –, primo hermano, m. [pícaro, m.

cove, *kōv*, s. (mar.) ensenada, caleta, f.;

covenant, *kŭv'ĕnănt*, s. contrato, m.; convención, f.; –, v. n. pactar, estipular.

cover, *kŭv'ăr*, s. cubierta, f.; abrigo, m.; pretexto, m.; under open –, bajo faja; –, v. a. cubrir; tapar; ocultar; proteger; paliar, honestar.

covering, *–ĭng*, s. ropa, f.; vestido, m.

coverlet, *–lĕt* coverlid, *–lĭd*, s. colcha, f.

covert, *–t*, s. cubierto, m.; refugio, m.; –, a. cubierto; oculto, secreto; *–ly*, ad. secretamente.

coverture, *–tŭr*, s. abrigo, refugio, m.

covet, *kŭv'ĕt*, v.a. codiciar, desear con ansia.

covetous, *–ŭs*, a. avariento, sórdido; *–ly*, ad. codiciosamente. [mezquindad, f.

covetousness, *–ŭsnĕs*, s. codicia, avaricia,

covey, *kŭv'ĕ*, s. nidada, pollada, f.

cow, *kŏu*, s. vaca, f.; –, v. a. acobardar, intimidar.

coward, *–ărd*, s. cobarde, medroso, m.

cowardice, *–ărdĭs*, s. cobardía, timidez, f.

cowardly, *–ărdlĕ*, a. & ad. cobarde; pusilánime; cobardemente.

cower, *–ăr*, v. n. agacharse.

cow-herd, *–hĕrd*, s. vaquero, m.

cow-house, *–hŏus*, s. boyera, f.

cowl, *kŏul*, s. capuz, m.

cowslip, *kŏu'slĭp*, s. prímula, primavera, f.

coxcomb, *kŏks'kōm*, s. petimetre, m.

coy, *kŏĭ*, a. recatado, modesto ; esquivo; *–ly*, ad. con esquivez.

coyness, *–nĕs*, s. esquivez, modestia, f.

coz, *kŭz*, s. (fam.) primo, m.; prima, f.

cozen, *–n*, v. a. engañar, defraudar.

cozenage, *–n'dj*, s. engaño, m.; trampa, f.

crab, *krăb*, s. cangrejo, m.; manzana silvestre, f.

crab-apple, *–ăp'pl*, s. manzana silvestre, f.; crab-apple-tree, *–trĕ*, s. manzano silvestre, m.

crabbed, *–bĕd*, a. áspero, austero, bronco, tosco; *–ly*, ad. de mal humor; ásperamente.

crabbedness, *–bĕdnĕs*, s. aspereza, rigideza, f.; austeridad, f.; dificultad, f.

crack, *krăk*, s. crujido, m.; hendedura, quebraja, f.; fanfarrón, m.; –, v. a. hender, rajar; romper; –, v. n. reventar; jactarse; –, a. raro, fino. [estúpido.

crack-brained, *–brănd*, a. alocado,

cracker, -ŭr, s. fanfarrón, m.; pastillita de chocolate, f.; cohete, m.
crackle, -kl, v. n. crujir, chillar.
crackling, -lĭng, s. estallido, crujido, m.
cracknel, -nĕl, s. hojuela, f. [cuna.
cradle, krā'dl, s. cuna, f.; —, v. a. mecer la
craft, krăft, s. arte, m.; artificio, m.; astucia,
craftily, -tĭlĕ, ad. astutamente. [f.
craftiness, -ĭnĕs, s. astucia, estratagema, f.
craftsman, -s'măn, s. artífice, artesano, m.
crafty, -ĕ, a. astuto, artificioso.
crag, krăg, s. despeñadero, m.; nuca, f.
cragged, -gĕd, a. escabroso, áspero.
cragginess, -gĭnĕs, s. escabrosidad, aspereza, f.
craggy, -gĕ, a. escabroso, áspero.
cram, krăm, v. a. embutir; engordar; empujar; —, y. n. atracarse de comida.
cramp, krămp, s. calambre, m.; laña, f.; —, v. a. lañar; constreñir. [ga, f. (pez)
cramp-fish, -fĭsh, s. torpedo, m., tremiel-
cramp-iron, -ĭrn, s. laña, f.
cranberry, krăn'bĕrrĕ, s. arandilla, f.
crane, krăn, s. grulla, f.; grúa, f.; pescante, m.; sifón, m.; —, v. a. guindar.
crank, krăngk, s. manecilla, f.; sinuosidad, f.; —, a. sano, alegre; vigoroso.
crannied, krăn'nĕd, a. hendido.
cranny, krăn'nĕ, s. grieta, hendedura, f.
crape, krăp, s. crespón, m.
crash, krăsh, v. n. estallar, rechinar; —, s. estallido, fracaso, m.
crass, krăs, a. craso, grueso, basto, tosco, grosero. [lozas.
crate, krăt, s. cesta grande para embalar
crater, krā'tŭr, s. cráter, m.; boca de volcán.
cravat, krăvăt', s. corbata, f. [f.
crave, krăv, v. a. rogar, suplicar. [m.
craven, -n, s. gallo vencido, m.; cobarde,
craving, krā'vĭng, a. insaciable, pedigüeño; —, s. deseo ardiente, m.
craw, krā, s. buche de ave, m. [m.
crawfish, -fĭsh, s. cangrejo de agua dulce,
crawl, krāl, v. n. arrastrar; to — with, hormiguear.
crayfish, krā'fĭsh, s. cangrejo de río, m.
crayon, krā'ŏn, s. lápiz, m.
craze, krăz, v. a., quebrantar; romper. [f.
craziness, krā'zĭnĕs, s. debilidad, f.; locura,
crazy, krā'zĕ, a. decrépito; caduco; fatuo.
creak, krēk, v. n. crujir, estallar. [simple.
cream, krēm, s. crema, f.; —, v. a. desnatar; —, v. n. criar nata.
creamy, -ĕ, a. lleno de crema.
crease, krēs, s. pliegue, m.; —, v. a. plegar.
create, krēāt', v. a. crear; causar. [ción, f.
creation, krēā'shŭn, s. creación, f.; elec-
creative, krēā'tĭv, a. creativo.
creator, krēā'tŭr, s. criador, m.
creature, krē'tĭŭr, s. criatura, f.
credence, krē'dĕns, s. creencia, fe, f.; renombre, m. [credenciales, f. pl.
credentials, krēdĕn'shŭls, s. pl. cartas
credibility, krēdĭbĭl'ĭtĕ, s. credibilidad, f.
credible, krēd'ĭbl, a. creíble; -bly, ad. creíblemente; según se cree.
credit, krēd'ĭt, s. crédito, m.; creencia, f.; reputación, f.; autoridad, f.; —, v. a. creer, fiar, acreditar.

creditable, -ăbl, a. estimable, honorífico; -bly, ad. honorablemente.
creditableness, -ăblnĕs, s. reputación, estimación, f.
creditor, -ŭr, s. acreedor, m.
credulity, krēdŭ'lĭtĕ, s. credulidad, f.
credulous, krēd'ŭlŭs, a. crédulo; -ly, ad.
creed, krēd, s. credo, m. [con credulidad.
creek, krēk, s. bahía pequeña, f.; (am.) arroyo, m. [placer trepador.
creep, krēp, v. n. arrastrar, serpear; com-
creeper, -ŭr, s. solano trepador; reptil, m.
creep-hole, -hōl, s. huronera, f.; subterfugio, m.; escapatoria, f. [res.
cremate, krēmāt', v. a. incinerar cadáve-
cremation, krēmā'shŭn, s. cremación, f.
crenellated, krēn'ĕlltĕd, a. dentado.
crescent, krēs'sĕnt, a. creciente; —, s. creciente, f. (fase de la luna).
cress, krĕs, s. lepidio, mastuerzo, m. [m.
crest, krĕst, s. cresta, f.; copete, m.; orgullo,
crested, -ĕd, a. crestado. [de espíritu.
crest-fallen, -fŭlln, a. acobardado, abatido
cretaceous, krētā'shŭs, a. cretáceo.
crevice, krĕv'ĭs, s. raja, hendedura, f.
crew, krō, s. banda, tropa, f.; (mar.) tripulación, f.
crewel, -ŭl, s. ovillo de estambre, m.
crib, krĭb, s. pesebre, m.; casucha, f.
crick, krĭk, s. chirrido, m.
cricket, -ĕt, s. grillo, m.; bilorta, f. (juego).
crier, krī'ŭr, s. pregonero, m.
crime, krĭm, s. crimen, m.; culpa, f.
criminal, krĭm'ĭndl, a. criminal, reo; -ly, ad. criminalmente; —, s. reo convicto, m.
criminality, krĭmĭndl'ĭtĕ, s. criminalidad, f.
criminate, krĭm'ĭndt, v. a. acriminar.
crimination, krĭmĭnā'shŭn, s. criminación, f.
crimp, krĭmp, s. comisionista, m.; (mil.) enganchador, m.; —, v. a. rizar, encrespar.
crimson, krĭm'zn, a. & s. carmesí (m.)
cringe, krĭnj, s. bajeza, f.; —, v. n. incensar, adular con bajeza. [a. serpentear.
crinkle, krĭng'kl, s. sinuosidad, f.; —, v.
crinoline, krĭn'ŏlĭn, s. crinolina, f.
cripple, krĭp'l, s. & a. estropeado (m.); —, v. a. derrengar, estropear.
crisis, krī'sĭs, s. crisis, f.; esfuerzo, m.
crisp, krĭsp, a. crespo; —, v. a. crespar, rizar.
crispness, -nĕs, s. encrespadura, f.
criterion, krītē'rĭŏn, s. criterio, m.
critic, krĭt'ĭk, s. crítico, m.; crítica, f.
critic(al), -(ăl), a. crítico; exacto; delicado; -ally, ad. exactamente, rigurosamente.
criticise, krĭt'ĭsĭz, v. a. criticar, censurar.
criticism, krĭt'ĭszm, s. crítica, f.
croak, krōk, v. n. graznar, crocitar.
crockery, krŏk'ŭrĕ, s. loza, f.; vasijas de barro, f.; vidriado, m.
crocodile, krŏk'ŏdĭl, s. cocodrilo, m.
crone, krōn, s. anciana, vieja, f.
crony, krō'nĕ, s. amigo (ó conocido) antiguo, m.
crook, krŏk, s. gancho, m.; artificio, m.; —, v. a. encorvar, torcer; pervertir.

crooked, krŭk'ĕd, a. torcido, corvo; perverso; —ly, ad. torcidamente; de mala gana.

croon, krōn, v. n. zumbir; arrullar.

crop, krŏp, s. buche de ave, m.; caballo desorejado, m.; corbacho, m.; cosecha, f.; —, v. a. segar las mieses; pacer la hierba; cortar las orejas.

croquet, krŏkā', s. juego de pelota cerrado y de poca extensión para el boleo, m.

crosier, krō'zhŭr, s. cayado pastoral de obispo, m.

cross, krŏs, s. cruz, f.; carga, f.; trabajo, m.; pena, aflicción, f.; tormento, m.; —, a. contrario, opuesto, atravesado; mal humorado; —, pr. al través; —, v. a. atravesar, cruzar; to — over, traspasar.

cross-bar, —bär, s. —beam, —bēm, s. travesaño, m.

cross-breed, —brēd, s. raza cruzada, f.

cross-examine, —ĕgzăm'ĭn, v. a. preguntar á un testigo.

cross-grained, —grānd, a. perverso, inhumorado.

crossing, —sĭng, cross-line, —lĭn, s. (rail.) cruzamiento de dos vías, m.

crossing-sweeper, —swēpŭr, s. barrendero de las encrucijadas, m.

crossly, —lĭ, ad. contrariamente, desgraciadamente.

crossness, —nĕs, s. espíritu de contradicción, m.; malicia, travesía, f.

cross-purpose, —pŭrpŭs, s. disposición contraria, f.; contradicción, f.

cross-road, —rōd, s. (rail.) paso á nivel, m.; camino de travesía, m.

cross-way, —wā, s. camino de travesía, m.

crotch, krŏtsh, s. gancho, corchete, m.

crotchet, —ĕt, s. corchea, f.; capricho, m.; corchete, m.

crouch, krŏtsh, v. n. agacharse, bajarse.

croup, krŏp, s. obispillo, m.; grupa (de caballo), f.; coqueluche, m.

crow, krŏ, s. cuervo, m.; barra, f.; canto del gallo, m.; —, v. n. cantar el gallo.

crowd, krŏd, s. tropel, m.; turba, muchedumbre, f.; —, v. a. amontonar; to — sail, hacer fuerza de vela; —, v. n. estrecharse.

crown, krŏn, s. corona, f.; guirnalda de flores, f.; moneda de plata del valor de cinco chelines, f.; complemento, colmo, m.; —, v. a. coronar; recompensar; dar cima; cubrir el peón que ha llegado á ser dama.

crown-glass, —glās, s. vidrio fino, m.

crown-lands, —lănds, s. pl. dominios de la corona, m. pl.

crown-prince, —prĭns, s. príncipe real, m.

crucial, krŏ'shĭăl, a. en forma de cruz, crucial.

crucible, krŏ'sĭbl, s. crisol, m.

crucifix, krŏ'sĭfĭks, s. crucifijo, m.

crucify, krŏ'sĭfī, v. a. crucificar; atormentar. [fecto; —ly, ad. crudamente.

crude, krŏd, a. crudo, indigesto, imperfecto; —ly, ad. crudamente.

crudity, krŏ'dĭtĕ, s. crudeza, f.; indigestión, f. [cruelmente.

cruel, krŏ'ĕl, a. cruel, inhumano; —ly, ad.

cruelty, —tĕ, s. crueldad, f.

cruet, krŏ'ĕt, s. vinagrera, f.

cruet-stand, —stănd, s. angarillas, f. pl.

English and Spanish.

cruise, krōz, s. jícara, f.; (mar.) corso, m.; —, v. n. (mar.) andar en corso. [m.

cruiser, krŏz'ŭr, s. crucero, m.; corsario, m.

crumb, krŭm, s. miga, f.

crumble, —bl, v. a. desmigajar, desmenuzar; —, v. n. desmigajarse.

crummy, —mĕ, a. blando, tierno.

crumple, krŭm'pl, v. a. arrugar.

crusade, krŏsād', s. cruzada, f.

crush, krŭsh, v. a. apretar, oprimir; amilanar; —, s. choque, m.

crushing-mill, —ĭngmĭl, s. bocarte, m.

crust, krŭst, s. costra, f.; corteza, f.; —, v. a. (& n.) encostrar(se). [chado.

crustaceous, —d'shŭs, a. crustáceo; concrustily, —tĕ, ad. enojadamente, broncamente. [f.; mal genio, m.

crustiness, —tnĕs, s. dureza de la costra, f.

crusty, —tĕ, a. costroso; bronco, áspero.

crutch, krŭtsh, s. muleta, f.

cry, krī, v. a. & n. gritar; pregonar; exclamar; llorar; —, s. grito, m.; lloro, m.; clamor, m. [nea), f.

crypt, krĭpt, s. cripta (bóveda subterránea, f.

crystal, krĭs'tăl, s. cristal, m.

crystalline, —lĭn, a. cristalino; transparente. [talización, f.

crystallisation, krĭstălīzā'shŭn, s. cristalización, f.

crystallise, krĭs'tălīz, v. a. (& n.) cristalizar(se). [(la cosa ó zorra).

cub, kŭb, s. cachorro, m.; —, v. n. parir.

cube, kŭb, s. cubo, m.

cubic(al), kŭ'bĭk(ăl), a. cúbico.

cubiform, kŭ'bĭfŏrm, a. cúbico.

cubit, kŭ'bĭt, s. codo, m. (medida).

cuckoo, kŭk'ŏ, s. cuclillo, cuco, m.

cucumber, kŭ'kŭmbŭr, s. cohombro, pepino, m.

cud, kŭd, s. panza, f., primer estómago de los rumiantes; pasto contenido en la panza, m.; to chew the —, rumiar; fig. reflexionar.

cuddle, —l, v. n. agacharse, agazaparse.

cuddy, kŭd'dĕ, s. camarote de proa, m. (mar.)

cudgel, kŭd'jĕl, s. garrote, palo, m.; —, v. a. apalear.

cudgelling, —lĭng, s. bastonada, f.

cue, kŭ, s. cola, f.; apunte de comedia, m.; humor, m.; taco (de billar), m.

cuff, kŭf, s. puñada, f.; vuelta de manga de vestido, f.

cuirass, kwĭrăs', s. coraza, f.

cuirassier, —sēr', s. coracero, m.

culinary, kŭ'lĭnărĕ, a. culinario, de la cocina. [f.

cull, kŭl, v. a. escoger, elegir.

culminate, kŭl'mĭnāt, v. n. culminar. [f.

culpability, kŭlpăbĭl'ĭtĕ, s. culpabilidad, f.

culpable, kŭl'păbl, a. culpable, criminal; —bly, ad. culpablemente, criminalmente, por la vía criminal.

culprit, kŭl'prĭt, s. reo acusado, m.

cultivate, kŭl'tĭvāt, v. n. cultivar, mejorar; perfeccionar. [f.; cultivo, m.

cultivation, kŭltĭvā'shŭn, s. cultivación, f.

culture, kŭl'tjŭr, s. cultura, f.

culverin, kŭl'vŭrĭn, s. (mil.) culebrina, f.

cumber, kŭm'bŭr, v. a. embarazar, embrollar.

4

cumbersome, *–săm,* **cumbrous,** *kăm'brŭs,* a. engorroso, pesado, confuso.
cumulative, *kămŭld'tiv,* a. cumulativo.
cunning, *kăn'ning,* a. experto; artificioso, astuto; intrigante; *–ly,* ad. astutamente; expertamente; *–,* s. astucia, sutileza, f.
cup, *kŭp,* s. copa, taza, jícara, f.; (bot.) cáliz, m.; **– and ball,** boliche, m.; *–,* v. a. aplicar ventosas.
cupboard, *–bŏrd,* s. armario, m.
cupidity, *kŭpid'tiĕ,* s. concupiscencia, f.
cupola, *kŭ'pŏlă,* s. cúpola, f.
cupping-glass, *kŭp'pinglăs,* s. ventosa, f.
cup-shot, *kŭp'shŏt,* a. embriagado.
cur, *kŭr,* s. perro de mala ralea, m.; vicurable.
curable, *kŭ'răbl,* a. curable. [llano, m.
curacy, *kŭ'răsĕ,* s. tenencia, f.; vicariato, m. [párroco, m.
curate, *kŭ'răt,* s. teniente de cura, m.;
curative, *kŭ'rătiv,* a. curativo. [m.
curator, *kŭrd'tŭr,* s. curador, m.; guardián,
curb, *kŭrb,* s. barbada, f.; freno, m.; restricción, f.; *–,* v. a. refrenar, contener, moderar. [coagular.
curd, *kŭrd,* s. cuajada, f.; *–,* v. a. cuajar,
curdle, *–l,* v. a. (& n.) cuajar(se), coagular(se).
cure, *kŭr,* s. cura, f.; remedio, m.; *–,* v. a. curar, sanar; **to –skins,** curar con sal las pieles. [chimenea, m.
curfew, *kŭr'fŭ,* s. guardafuego, tapador de
curing, *kŭ'ring,* s. curación, f.
curiosity, *kŭriŏs'tiĕ,* s. curiosidad, f.; rareza, f.
curious, *kŭ'riŭs,* a. curioso, exacto, delicado; exquisito; *–ly,* ad. curiosamente, elegantemente.
curl, *kŭrl,* s. rizo de pelo, m.; tortuosidad, f.; *–,* v. a. encrespar el pelo; ondear; *–,* v. n. rizarse.
curling-iron, *–ingirn,* s., **curling-tongs,** *–ingtŏngz,* s. pl. encrespador, m.
curling-paper, *–ingpdpŭr,* s. papel á propósito para hacer los rizos, m.
curly, *kŭr'lĕ,* a. rizado. [tacaño, m.
curmudgeon, *kŭrmŭj'ŭn,* s. hombre
currant, *kŭr'rănt,* s. grosella, f.; uva de Corinto, f.; **rough –,** grosella espinosa, f.
currency, *kŭr'rĕnsĕ,* s. circulación, f.; valor corriente de alguna cosa, m.; duración, f.
current, *kŭr'rĕnt,* a. corriente, común; *–,* s. curso, progreso, m., marcha, f.; corriente, f., fluido (eléctrico), m.; **alternant –,** corriente eléctrica inversa. [moda.
currently, *–lĕ,* ad. corrientemente; á la
currier, *kŭr'riŭr,* s. curtidor, m.
currish, *kŭr'rish,* a. perruno, brutal, regañón; *–ly,* ad. brutalmente.
curry, *kŭr'rĕ,* v. a. zurrar; almohazar; *–,* s. especeria anglo-india, compuesta de varios ingredientes, f.
currycomb, *–kŏm,* s. almohaza, f.
curse, *kŭrs,* v. a. maldecir; *–,* v. n. imprecar; blasfemar; *–,* s. maldición, f.; imprecación, f. [minablemente.
cursedly, *–ĕdlĕ,* ad. miserablemente, abo-

cursive, *kŭr'siv,* a. cursivo.
cursorily, *kŭr'sŏrilĕ,* ad. precipitadamente, de paso. [siderado.
cursory, *kŭr'sŏrĕ,* a. precipitado, inconsiderado.
court, *kŭrt,* a. sucinto.
curtail, *kŭrtăl',* v. a. cortar; mutilar.
curtain, *kŭr'tĭn,* s. cortina, f.; telón en los teatros, m.; *–,* v. a. proveer con cortinas.
curtain-lecture, *–lĕktjŭr,* s. reconvención conyugal, f. [f.
curtain-rod, *–rŏd,* s. varilla de cortinaje.
curtsy, *kŭrt'sĕ,* s. saludo á una mujer, m.
curvated, *kŭr'ydtĕd,* a. corvo, encorvado.
curvature, *kŭr'vdtŭr,* s. curvatura, f.
curve, *kŭrv,* v. a. encorvar; *–,* a. corvo, torcido; *–,* s. corva, combadura, f.
curvet, *kŭr'vĕt,* s. corveta, f.; *–,* v. n. corcovear; saltar de alegria. [f.
cushion, *kŭsh'ŭn,* s. cojín, m., almohada,
cusp, *kŭsp,* s. cuerno de la luna, m.
custard, *kŭs'tărd,* s. natillas, f. pl.
custodian, *kŭstŏ'diăn,* s. custodio, m.
custody, *kŭs'tŏdĕ,* s. custodia, f.; prisión, f.
custom, *kŭs'tŭm,* s. costumbre, f., uso, m.; despacho, m.; derechos de aduana, m. pl. [nariamente.
customarily, *–ărilĕ,* ad. comunmente, ordi-
customary, *–ărĕ,* a. usual, acostumbrado, ordinario.
customer, *–ăr,* s. parroquiano, m.
custom-free, *–frĕ,* a. exento de derechos.
custom-house, *–hŏŭs,* s. aduana, f.
custom-house duty, *–dū'tĭ,* s. derechos de aduana, m. pl. [aduanero, m.
custom-house officer, *–ŏf'tsŭr,* s.
cut, *kŭt,* v. a. cortar; separar; herir; dividir; alzar los naipes; **to – short,** interrumpir, cortar la palabra; **to – capers,** cabriolar; **to – teeth,** nacerle los dientes (á un niño); *–,* v. n. traspasar; cruzarse; *–,* s. cortadura, f.; estampa, f.; grabado, m.; hechura, figura, f.; lonja, f.; herida, f.; **– and dry,** a. pronto.
cut-away, *–ăwā,* s. frac, m.
cuticle, *kū'tikl,* s. epidermis, f.; lapa, f.
cutlass, *kŭt'lăs,* s. espada ancha, f.; alcutler, *kŭt'lŭr,* s. cuchillero, m. [fanje, f.
cutlery, *–ĕ,* s. cuchillería, f.
cutlet, *kŭt'lĕt,* s. costilla asada de carnero, f.
cutter, *kŭt'tŭr,* s. cortador, m.; (mar.) cúter, m.
cut-throat, *kŭt'thrŏt,* s. asesino, m.
cutting, *kŭt'ting,* s. cortadura, f.; incisión, f.; alce de naipes, m.; trinchado, m.
cutting-nippers, *–nippărz,* s. pl. pinzas, tenacillas, f. pl. [del timón, m.
cutwater, *kŭt'wătŭr,* s. (mar.) azafrán
cycle, *st'kl,* s. ciclo, m.
cyclopædia, *siklŏpē'dĭă,* s. enciclopedia, f.
cygnet, *sig'nĕt,* s. pollo del cisne, m. [m.
cylinder, *sil'indŭr,* s. cilindro, m.; rollo,
cylindric(al), *sĭlin'drik(ăl),* a. cilíndrico.
cymbal, *sim'băl,* s. címbalo, m.
cynic(al), *sin'ik(ăl),* a. cínico; obsceno; *–,* s. cínico, m. (filósofo).
Cynosure, *sĭ'nŏshŭr,* s. Cinosura, f.
cypress, *sĭ'prĕs,* s. ciprés, m.
czar, *zăr,* s. Zar, m.
czarina, *zărĕ'nă,* s. Zarina, f.

D.

dab, *dăb*, v. a. rociar; empapar; —, s. pedazo pequeño, m.; salpicadura, f.; golpe blando, m.; barbada, f. (pez).
dabble, *-bl*, v. a. rociar, salpicar; —, v. n. chapotear.
dabbler, *-blăr*, s. chisgaravís, m.
dace, *dăs*, s. albur, gobio, yáculo, m. (pez).
dad(dy), *dăd'(dě)*, s. papá, m. [cudo, m.
daddy-longlegs, *-dělŏnglěgs*, s. zancaffodil, *dăf'fŏdĭl*, s. narciso, m.
daffodil, *dăf'fŏdĭl*, s. narciso, m.
dagger, *dăg'găr*, s. puñal, m.
daily, *dā'lĕ*, a. diario, cotidiano; —, ad. diariamente, cada día.
daintily, *dān'tĭlĕ*, ad. delicadamente.
daintiness, *dān'tĭnĕs*, s. elegancia, f.; delicadeza, f. [s. bocado exquisito, m.
dainty, *dān'tĕ*, a. delicado; elegante; —,
dairy, *dā'rĕ*, s. lechería, quesera, f.
dairy-maid, *-măd*, s. lechera, manteca, quera, f.
daisy, *dā'sĕ*, s. margarita, maya, f.
dale, *dāl*, s. cañada, f.; valle, m.
dalliance, *dăl'lĭăns*, s. diversión, f.; juguete, m.; dilación, f.
dally, *dăl'lĕ*, v. n. juguetear, divertirse; burlarse; tardar; —, v. a. dilatar, suspender; hacer pasar el tiempo con gusto.
dam, *dăm*, s. madre, f. (en los animales); dique, m.; azud, presa, f.; —, v. a. representar; tapar.
damage, *dăm'ĕj*, s. daño, detrimento, m.; resarcimiento de daño, m.; —, v. a. dañar.
damageable, *-bl*, a. perjudicial; nocivo.
damask, *dăm'ăsk*, s. damasco, m.; —, a. de damasco; —, v. a. adamascar.
damaskeen, *-ēn*, v. a. ataujiar.
dame, *dām*, s. dama, señora, f.
damn, *dăm*, v. a. condenar; silbar.
damnable, *-năbl*, a. condenable; -bly, ad. de un modo condenable; horriblemente, detestablemente.
damnation, *-nā'shăn*, s. condenación, f.
damp, *dămp*, a. húmedo; triste, abatido; —, s. aire húmedo, m.; aflicción, f.; —, v. a. humedecer; desanimar; abatir.
dampen, *-n*, v. a. humedecer.
damper, *-ăr*, s. sordina, f.; apagador, m.; tarasca, m.
dampness, *-něs*, s. humedad, f.
damsel, *dăm'zěl*, s. damisela, señorita, f.
damson, *dăm'zn*, s. damascena, f. (ciruela).
dance, *dăns*, s. danza, f.; baile, m.; —, v. n. bailar; **to — attendance**, servir con prontitud y atención.
dancer, *-ăr*, s. danzarín, bailarín, m.
dancing-master, *dăns'ĭngmăstăr*, s. maestro de baile ó danza, m.
dandle, *dăn'dl*, v. a. mecer; halagar; acariciar.
dandruff, *dăn'drŭf*, s. caspa, f. [ciar.
dandy, *dăn'dĕ*, s. petimetre, currutaco, m.
danger, *dăn'jăr*, s. peligro, riesgo, m.
dangerous, *-ăs*, a. peligroso; -ly, ad. peligrosamente. [estar colgado en el aire.
dangle, *dăng'gl*, v. n. temblar, fluctuar;
dangler, *-ăr*, s. Juan de las damas, m.

dank, *dăngk*, a. húmedo.
dapper, *dăp'păr*, a. activo, vivaz, despierto.
dapple, *dăp'pl*, v. a. abigarrar; —, a. vareteado; rayado; **—grey horse**, s. caballo tordo, m.
dare, *dār*, v. n. osar, atreverse, arriesgarse; —, v. a. desafiar, provocar.
daring, *dăr'ĭng*, s. osadía, f.; —, a. osado, temerario; emprendedor; -ly, ad. atrevidamente, osadamente.
dark, *dărk*, a. obscuro; opaco; ciego; ignorante; -ly, ad. obscuramente, secretamente; —, s. obscuridad, f.; ignorancia, f.
darken, *-n*, v. a. (& n.) obscurecer(se).
dark-lantern, *-lăn'tărn*, s. lanterna sorda, f. [blas, f. pl.
darkness, *-něs*, s. obscuridad, f.; tinie**darksome**, *-sŭm*, a. obscuro, opaco, sombrío. [m.; —, a. querido, amado.
darling, *dăr'lĭng*, s. predilecto, favorito,
darn, *dărn*, v. a. zurcir.
darnel, *dăr'něl*, s. zizaña, f. [dora, f.
darner, *dăr'năr*, s. zurcidor, m.; zurcidart, *dărt*, s. dardo, m.; —, v. a. lanzar, tirar; —, v. n. volar como dardo.
dart, *dărt*, s. dardo, m.; —, v. a. lanzar, tirar; —, v. n. volar como dardo.
dash, *dăsh*, v. a. arrojar, chocar, romper; salpicar; borrar; confundir; —, v. n. saltar, zambullirse en el agua de golpe; —, s. colisión, f.; choque, m.; golpe, m.; **— of a pen**, rasgo de pluma, m.; **at one —**, de un golpe.
dash-board, *-bŏrd*, s. paralodo, m.
dashing, *-ĭng*, a. vistoso, brillante.
dastard, *dăs'tărd*, s. collón, m.
dastardly, *-lĕ*, a. cobarde, tímido.
date, *dāt*, s. data, fecha, f.; conclusión, f.; (bot.) dátil, m.; —, v. a. datar.
dative, *dā'tĭv*, s. dativo, m.; —, a. dado, dativo. [manchar, ensuciar.
daub, *dăb*, v. a. pintorrear; untar; paliar;
dauber, *-ăr*, s. pintor tosco, m.
daughter, *dă'tăr*, s. hija, f.; **—in-law**, nuera, f.
daunt, *dănt*, v. a. intimidar, espantar.
dauntless, *-lĕs*, a. intrépido, arrojado.
Dauphin, *dă'fĭn*, s. delfín, m. (de Francia).
davenport, *dăv'ĕnpŏrt*, s. papelera para [señoras, f.
daw, *dă*, s. corneja, f.
dawdle, *dă'dl*, v. n. gastar tiempo.
dawdler, *-ăr*, s. bausán, bodoque, m.
dawn, *dăn*, s. alba, f.; albor, m.; —, v. n. amanecer.
day, *dā*, s. día, m.; luz, f.; **by —**, de día; **— by —**, de día en día; **-s**, pl. tiempo, m.; vida, f. [nista, m.
day-boarder, *-bŏrdăr*, s. semipensio**day-book**, *-bŭk*, s. diario, m.
day-break, *-brăk*, s. alba, f.
day-labourer, *-lāvărăr*, s. jornalero, m.
day-light, *-lĭt*, s. luz del día, luz natural, f.
day-scholar, *-skŏlăr*, s. externo, m.
day-spring, *-sprĭng*, s. alba, f.
day-star, *-stăr*, s. lucero del alba, m.
daytime, *-tĭm*, s. tiempo del día, m.
dazed, *dăz'd*, a. achacoso.
dazzle, *dăz'zl*, **daze**, *dăz*, v. a. deslumbrar, ofuscar.
deacon, *dē'kn*, s. diácono, m.

4 *

dead, *dĕd*, a. muerto; flojo, entorpecido; vacío, inútil, triste; apagado, sin espíritu; despoblado; evaporado; marchito; devuelto (hablando de cartas); **– bargain**, s. precio muy bajo, m.; **– water**, s. agua muerta, f.; **– wood**, s. leña seca, f.; **– silence**, s. silencio profundo, m.; **the –**, pl. los finados.

dead-drunk, *–drŭngk*, a. hecho un cuero.

deaden, *–n*, v. a. amortecer.

deadhead, *–hĕd*, s. cero, hombre que vale para nada, m.; (am.) plaza supuesta, f.

dead-heat, *–hĕt*, s. corrida indecisa, f.

dead-house, *–hŏŭs*, s. sitio público en donde se exponen los cadáveres encontrados, m.

deadly, *–lĕ*, a. mortal; terrible, implacable; **–**, ad. mortalmente.   [f.

dead-march, *–mārtsh*, marcha fúnebre.

deadness, *–nĕs*, s. flojedad, inercia, f.; amortiguamiento, m.   [m.

dead-nettle, *–nĕt'tl*, s. cáñamo bastardo.

deaf, *dĕf*, a. sordo; estéril.

deafen, *–n*, v. a. ensordar; causar sordera.   [ción á oir, f.

deafness, *–nĕs*, s. sordera, f.; desinclina-

deal, *dēl*, s. parte, f.; cantidad, f.; madera de pino, f.; **a great –**, mucho; **a good –**, bastante; **–**, v. a. distribuir; dar; **–**, v. n. traficar, repartir; **to – with**, tratar con; contender con.

dealer, *–ār*, s. mercader, traficante, m.; el que da las cartas en el juego de naipes.

dealing, *–ing*, s. conducta, f.; trato, m.; tráfico, comercio, m.

dean, *dēn*, s. dean, m.

deanery, *–ārē*, s. deanato, m.

dear, *dēr*, a. predilecto, amado; caro, costoso; **–ly**, ad. caramente, tiernamente.

dearness, *–nĕs*, s. cariño, amor, m.; carestía, f.

dearth, *dārth*, s. carestía, f.; esterilidad, f.

death, *dĕth*, s. muerte, f.   [f.; agonía, f.

death-bed, *–bĕd*, s. cama del moribundo,

death-bell, *–bĕl*, s. toque de agonía, m.

death-blow, *–blō*, s. golpe mortal, m.

death-dealing, *–dēl'ing*, a. mortífero.

deathlike, *–līk*, a. quedo; letárgico.

death-penalty, *–pĕnđlē*, s. pena de muerte, f.

death-throe, *–thrō*, s. agonía, f.

death-warrant, *–wŏrrănt*, s. sentencia de muerte, f.

death-watch, *–wŏtsh*, s. grillo, m.

debar, *dēbār'*, v. a. excluir, no admitir.

debarkation, *dēbārkā'shăn*, s. desembarco, m.

debase, *dēbās'*, v. a. humillar, envilecer; falsificar.   [envilecimiento, m.

debasement, *–mĕnt*, s. abatimiento, m.;

debatable, *dēbāt'ābl*, a. disputable.

debate, *dēbāt'*, s. debate, m.; riña, disputa, f.; **–**, v. a. discutir; examinar; **–**, v. n. deliberar; disputar.

debater, *–ār*, s. controversista, m.

debauch, *dēbātsh'*, s. vida disoluta, f.; exceso, m.; **–**, v. a. & n. corromper; hacer excesos.   [disolución, f.

debauchery, *–ārē*, s. desarreglo, m.;

debenture, *dēbĕn'tūr*, s. vale, m.; drawback, m.

debilitate, *dēbil'ĭtāt*, v. a. debilitar, enervar.   [f.

debility, *dēbil'ĭtē*, s. debilidad, languidez,

debit, *dĕb'ĭt*, s. debe, m.; **–**, v. a. (com.) adeudar, cargar en una cuenta.

debouch, *dēbōsh'*, v. n. (mil.) desfilar; desembocar un río.

debt, *dĕt*, s. deuda, f.; débito, m.; obligación, f.; **to run into –s**, adeudar(se).

debtor, *–tūr*, s. deudor, m.

decade, *dĕk'ād*, s. década, f.

decadence, *dĕkā'dĕns*, s. decadencia, f.

Decalogue, *dĕk'ŏlŏg*, s. Decálogo, m.

decamp, *dēkămp'*, v. n. (mil.) decampar, levantar el campo; escapar.

decampment, *–mĕnt*, s. (mil.) levantamiento de un campamento, m.

decant, *dēkănt'*, v. a. decantar; trasegar.

decanter, *–ār*, s. garrafa, f.

decapitate, *dēkăp'ĭtāt*, v. a. decapitar, degollar.   [ción, f.

decapitation, *dēkăpĭtā'shăn*, s. decapita-

decay, *dēkā'*, v. n. decaer, descaecer, declinar; degenerar; **–**, s. descaecimiento, m.; decadencia, declinación, disminución, f.

decease, *dēsēs'*, s. muerte, f.   [postura, f.

deceit, *dēsēt'*, s. engaño, fraude, m., im-

deceitful, *–fŭl*, a. fraudulento, engañoso; falaz; **–ly**, ad. fraudulentamente, falsamente.

deceive, *dēsēv'*, v. a. engañar, defraudar.

December, *dēsĕm'bŭr*, s. diciembre, m.

decency, *dē'sĕnsĭ*, s. decencia, f.; modestia,

decennial, *dēsĕn'nĭăl*, a. decenal.   [f.

decent, *dē'sĕnt*, a. decente, razonable; propio, conveniente; **–ly**, ad. decentemente.

deception, *dēsĕp'shăn*, s. decepción, impostura, f.; engaño, m.

deceptive, *dēsĕp'tĭv*, a. falso, engañoso.

decide, *dēsīd'*, v. a. & n. decidir, determinar, resolver, juzgar.

decidedly, *–ĕdlĭ*, ad. determinadamente.

decidence, *dĕsĭ'dĕns*, s. (bot.) caída de las hojas, f.

decider, *–ār*, s. árbitro, juez, m.

deciduous, *dĕsĭ'dŭs*, a. perecedero; (bot.) decedente.

decimal, *dĕs'ĭmăl*, a. decimal.

decimate, *dĕs'ĭmāt*, v. a. diezmar.

decimation, *dĕsĭmā'shăn*, s. diezmo, m.

decipher, *dēsī'fŭr*, v. a. descifrar.

decision, *dēsĭ'ăn*, s. decisión, determinación, resolución, f.   [decisivamente.

decisive, *dēsī'sĭv*, a. decisivo; **–ly**, ad.

deck, *dĕk*, s. (mar.) bordo, m.; cubierta, f.; **–**, v. a. adornar.

deck-hand, *–hănd*, s. marinero de río, m.

declaim, *dēklām'*, v. n. declamar, perorar.

declamation, *dĕklămā'shăn*, s. declamación, arenga, f.   [torio.

declamatory, *dēklăm'ătārē*, a. declama-

declaration, *dēklărā'shăn*, s. declaración, publicación, f.; explicación, f.

declare, *dēklār'*, v. a. declarar, manifestar.

declension, *dēklĕn'shăn*, s. declinación, f.; declivio, m.

declination, *dĕklĭnä´shŭn,* s. declinación,
f.; decremento, m.

decline, *dĕklīn´,* v. a. (gr.) declinar; huir,
evitar; —, v. n. decaer, desmejorar; inclinarse; —, s. declinación, decadencia, f.;
consunción, f.

declivity, *dĕklĭv´tĭ,* s. declividad, f.;
pendiente (de algún terreno), m. & f.

declivous, *dĕklī´vŭs,* a. en declive, pendiente.   [(med.) cocimiento, m.

decoction, *dĕkŏk´shŭn,* s. cocción, f.;

decompose, *dĕkŏmpōz´,* v. a. descomponer.   [composición, f.

decomposition, *dĕkŏmpŏzĭsh´ŭn,* s. des-

decorate, *dĕk´ōrāt,* v. a. decorar, adornar.

decoration, *dĕkŏrä´shŭn,* s. decoración, f.

decorative, *dĕk´ōrätĭv,* a. decorativo.

decorator, *dĕk´ōrätŭr,* s. adornista, m.;
guarnecedor, m.; tapicero, m.; el sujeto
en general de los negocios y dependencias
de alguna casa; intendente de las decora-
ciones de un teatro, m.

decorous, *dĕk´ōrŭs,* a. decente, decoroso;
—ly, ad. decorosamente.

decorum, *dĕkō´rŭm,* s. decoro, garbo, m.;
decencia, f.; conveniencia, f.

decoy, *dĕkŏĕ´,* v. a. atraer (algún pájaro);
embaucar, engañar; —, s. seducción, f.;
cazadero con señuelo, m.   [m.

decoy-bird, —*bŭrd,* s. pájaro de reclamo.

decrease, *dĕkrēs´,* v. a. disminuir, minoo-
rar; —, s. decremento; descaecimiento, m.
diminución, f.   [v. a. decretar; ordenar.

decree, *dĕkrē´,* s. decreto, edicto, m.; —;

decrepit, *dĕkrĕp´ĭt,* a. decrépito.   [m.

decrial, *dĕkrī´ăl,* s. gritería, f.; insulto,

decrier, *dĕkrī´ŭr,* s. difamador, m.

decry, *dĕkrī´,* v. a. desacreditar, censurar
públicamente; disfamar.

decuple, *dĕk´ŭpl,* v. a. multiplicar por
diez; —, a. décuplo.   [grar.

dedicate, *dĕd´ĭkāt,* v. a. dedicar; consa-

dedication, *dĕdĭkä´shŭn,* s. dedicación, f.;
dedicatoria, f.

dedicatory, *dĕd´ĭkätŭre,* a. dedicatorio.

deduce, *dĕdūs´,* v. a. deducir; concluir,
inferir.

deduct, *dĕdŭkt´,* v. a. deducir, sustraer.

deduction, *dĕdŭk´shŭn,* s. deducción, f.;
consecuencia, f.; descuento, m.

deductively, —*tĭvlĕ,* ad. por ilación ó
consecuencia.

deed, *dēd,* s. acción, f.; hecho, m.; hazaña,
f.; instrumento auténtico, m.

deem, *dēm,* v. n. juzgar, pensar, estimar.

deep, *dēp,* a. profundo; sagaz; artificioso;
grave; obscuro; taciturno; —, s. el piélago,
la mar.   [cer.

deepen, —*n,* v. a. profundizar; obscure-

deep-laid, —*lād,* a. profundo, infernal.

deeply, —*lĕ,* ad. profundamente; astutamente; tristemente; obscuramente.

deepness, —*nĕs,* s. profundidad, f.

deer, *dēr,* s. ciervo, venado, m.

deface, *dĕfās´,* v. a. borrar, destruir; desfigurar, afear.

defacement, —*mĕnt,* s. desfiguración, f.

defalcate, *dĕfäl´kāt,* v. a. desfalcar, deducir.

defamation, *dĕfämä´shŭn,* s. difamación,
calumnia, f.   [difamatorio.

defamatory, *dĕfäm´ätŭrĕ,* a. calumnioso.

defame, *dĕfām´,* v. a. disfamar; calumniar.

default, *dĕfält´,* s. culpa, f.; delito, m.;
defecto, m.; falta, f.; —, v. a. & n. faltar,
ofender.

defaulter, —*ŭr,* s. (law) contumaz, m.

defeat, *dĕfēt´,* s. derrota, f.; vencimiento,
m.; —, v. a. derrotar; frustrar.

defect, *dĕfĕkt´,* s. defecto, m.; falta, f.

defection, *dĕfĕk´shŭn,* s. defección, f.

defective, —*tĭv,* a. defectivo, imperfecto.

defence, *dĕfĕns´,* s. defensa, f.; protección,
f., amparo, m.   [tente.

defenceless, —*lĕs,* a. indefenso; impo-

defend, *dĕfĕnd´,* v. a. defender; proteger;
prohibir.   [mandado, m.

defendant, —*ănt,* s. defensor, m.; reo de-

defensive, —*sĭv,* a. defensivo; —ly, a.
de un modo defensivo; —, s. estado de
defensa, m.   [v. n. diferir.

defer, *dĕfŭr´,* v. a. diferir, retardar; —;

deference, *dĕf´ŭrĕns,* s. deferencia, f.;
respeto, m.; consideración, f.

deferential, *dĕfŭrĕn´shŭl,* a. respetoso.

defiance, *dĕfī´ăns,* s. desafío, cartel, m.

defiant, —*t,* a. desconfiado.

deficiency, *dĕfĭsh´ĕns,* s. defecto, m.;
imperfección, f. falta, f.; insolvencia, f.

deficient, *dĕfĭsh´ĕnt,* a. deficiente.

deficit, *dĕf´ĭsĭt,* s. déficit, descubierto, m.

defile, *dĕfīl´,* s. desfiladero, m.; —, v. a.
ensuciar.   [minable.

definable, *dĕfī´năbl,* a. definible; deter-

define, *dĕfīn´,* v. a. definir; limitar; determinar; —, v. n. decidir, juzgar.

definite, *dĕf´ĭnĭt,* a. definido, exacto,
preciso, limitado, cierto.

definition, *dĕfĭnĭsh´ŭn,* s. definición, f.

definitive, *dĕfĭn´ĭtĭv,* a. definitivo; —ly,
ad. definitivamente.

deflect, *dĕflĕkt´,* v. n. desviarse; ladearse.

deflection, *dĕflĕk´shŭn,* s. desvío, rodeo,
m.   [florar, estuprar.

deflour, deflower, *dĕflŏŭr´,* v. a. des-

defoliation, *dĕfōlĭä´shŭn,* s. caída de las
hojas, m.   [figurar.

deform, *dĕfŏrm´,* v. a. desformar, des-

deformity, *dĕfŏrm´ĭtĕ,* s. deformidad, f.

defraud, *dĕfräd´,* v. a. defraudar; frustrar.

defray, *dĕfrā´,* v. a. costear.

deft, *dĕft,* a. despierto, despejado, diestro;
—ly, ad. con ingenio y viveza.

defunct, *dĕfŭngkt´,* a. difunto, muerto;
—, s. difunto, m.   [deñar, negar.

defy, *dĕfī´,* v. a. desafiar; despreciar; des-

degeneracy, *dĕjĕn´ŭräsĕ,* s. degeneración,
bajeza, depravación, f.

degenerate, *dĕjĕn´ŭrāt,* v. n. degenerar;
—, a. degenerado.   [ción, f.

degeneration, *dĕjĕnŭrä´shŭn,* s. degenera-

degradation, *dĕgrädä´shŭn,* s. degradación, f.; degeneración, f.

degrade, *dĕgräd´,* v. a. degradar; deshonrar, envilecer.

degree, *dēgrē'*, s. grado, m.; rango, m.; condición, f.; **by —s,** gradualmente.
deification, *dē‘ĭfĭkā'shŭn*, s. apoteosis, f.
deify, *dē'ĭfĭ*, v. a. deificar; divinizar.
deign, *dān*, v. n. dignarse.
deism, *dē'ĭzm*, s. deismo, m.
deist, *dē'ĭst*, s. deista, m.
deity, *dē'ĭtĭ*, s. deidad, divinidad, f.
deject, *dējĕkt'*, v. a. abatir, desanimar.
dejection, *dējĕk'shŭn*, s. tristeza, aflicción, f.; (med.) cámara, f.
delay, *dēlā'*, v. a. diferir; retardar; —, s. dilación, f.; retardo, m.
delectable, *dēlĕk'tăbl*, a. deleitoso; **-bly,** ad. deleitosamente; con gusto.
delegate, *dĕl'ēgāt*, v. a. delegar, diputar; —, s. delegado, diputado, m.
delegation, *dĕlēgā'shŭn*, s. delegación, diputación, comisión, f.
delf(t), *dĕlf*, s. loza vidriada, f.
deliberate, *dēlĭb'ērāt*, v. a. deliberar, considerar; —, a. cauto; avisado; **-ly,** ad. deliberadamente.
deliberateness, *—nĕs*, **deliberation,** *dēlĭbērā'shŭn*, s. deliberación, circunspección, f., miramiento, m.
deliberative, *dēlĭb'ērātĭv*, a. deliberativo.
delicacy, *dĕl'ĭkăsĭ*, s. delicadeza, f.; tenuidad, f.
delicate, *dĕl'ĭkăt*, a. delicado; exquisito; afeminado; —, ad. delicadamente; afeminadamente.
delicious, *dēlĭsh'ŭs*, a. delicioso; exquisito; **-ly,** ad. deliciosamente. [m.
deliciousness, *—nĕs*, s. delicia, f.; gusto,
delight, *dēlīt'*, s. delicia, f.; placer, gozo, encanto, m.; —, v. a. (& n.) deleitar(se).
delightful, *—fŭl*, a. delicioso; deleitable; **-ly,** ad. deliciosamente. [miento, m.
delimitation, *dēlĭmĭtā'shŭn*, s. amojonamiento, m.
delineate, *dēlĭn'ēāt*, v. a. delinear, diseñar.
delineation, *dēlĭnēā'shŭn*, s. delineación, f.; delineamento, m. [culpa, f.
delinquency, *dēlĭn'gkwĕnsĭ*, s. delito, m.;
delinquent, *—kwĕnt*, s. delincuente, m.
delirious, *dēlĭr'ĭŭs*, a. delirante, desvariado; **-bly,** [riado.
delirium, *—rĭŭm*, s. delirio, m.
deliver, *dēlĭv'ĕr*, v. a. dar; rendir; libertar; recitar, relatar; partear.
deliverance, *—ăns*, s. libramiento, m.
delivery, *—ărĭ*, s. entrega, f.; libramiento, m.; parto, m.
dell, *dĕl*, s. valle hondo, m.; hondonada, f.
delude, *dēlūd'*, v. a. engañar.
deluge, *dĕl'ūj*, s. inundación, f.; diluvio, m.; —, v. a. diluviar. [sión, f.
delusion, *dēlū'zhŭn*, s. engaño, m.; ilusión, f.
delusive, *—sĭv*, a. engañoso, falaz.
delve, *dĕlv*, s. foso, m.; hoyo, m.; mina, f.
demagogue, *dĕm'ăgŏg*, s. demagogo, m.
demand, *dēmănd'*, s. demanda, f.; petición jurídica (de una deuda), f.; venta continuada, f.; —, v. a. demandar, reclamar.
demarcate, *dēmărkāt'*, v. a. amojonar.
demarcation, *dēmărkā'shŭn*, s. demarcación, f.; límite, m.
demean, *dēmēn'*, v. n. portarse.
demeanour, *—ŭr*, s. porte, el modo de gobernarse ó portarse en la conducta.

demented, *dēmĕn'tĕd*, a. demente, loco.
demerit, *dēmĕr'ĭt*, v. a. desmerecer.
demesnes, *dēmēns'*, s. pl. posesión de bienes raíces, f. [mento; —, s. muerte, f.
demise, *dēmĭz'*, v. a. legar, dejar en testamento.
demisemiquaver, *dē'mĭsĕmĭkwāvŭr*, s. (mus.) semicorchea, f.
demission, *dēmĭsh'ŭn*, s. aflojamiento, m.
democracy, *dēmŏk'răsē*, s. democracia, f.
democrat, *dēm'ŏkrăt*, s. demócrata, m.
democratic(al), *dēmŏkrăt'ĭk(ăl)*, a. democrático; [nar; arrasar.
demolish, *dēmŏl'ĭsh*, v. a. demoler, arruinar.
demolition, *dēmŏlĭsh'ăn*, s. demolición, f.
demon, *dē'mŏn*, s. demonio, diablo, m.
demoniac, *dēmō'nĭăk*, a. demoniaco; endemoniado; —, s. energúmeno, m.
demonstrable, *dēmŏn'străbl*, a. demostrable; **-bly,** ad. demostrablemente, ostensiblemente.
demonstrate, *dēmŏn'strāt*, v. a. demostrar, probar. [mostración, f.
demonstration, *dēmŏnstrā'shŭn*, s. demostrativo; **-ly,** ad. demostrativamente.
demonstrative, *dēmŏn'strătĭv*, a. demostrativo; **-ly,** ad. demostrativamente.
demoralization, *dēmŏrălĭzā'shŭn*, s. desmoralización, f.
demoralize, *dēmŏr'ălĭz*, v. a. desmoralizar.
demur, *dēmŭr'*, v. n. objetar; suspender; vacilar, fluctuar; —, v. a. dudar; —, s. duda, f.
demure, *dēmŭr'*, a. reservado; decente; grave, serio; **-ly,** ad. modestamente.
demureness, *—nĕs*, s. seriedad, gravedad de aspecto, f. [prorroga, f.
demurrer, *dēmŭr'rŭr*, s. (law) demora, f.
den, *dĕn*, s. caverna, f.; antro, m.
deniable, *dēnī'ăbl*, a. negable, recusable.
denial, *dēnī'ăl*, s. denegación, repulsa, f.
denizen, *dĕn'ĭzn*, s. extranjero naturalizado, m.; —, v. a. naturalizar.
denominate, *dēnŏm'ĭnāt*, v. a. denominar, nombrar.
denomination, *dēnŏmĭnā'shŭn*, s. denominación, f.; título, nombre, apelativo, m. [nominador, m.
denominator, *dēnŏm'ĭnătŭr*, s. (ar.) denote, m.
denote, *dēnōt'*, v. a. denotar, indicar.
denounce, *dēnŏuns'*, v. a. denunciar; promulgar; declarar.
dense, *dĕns*, a. denso, espeso.
density, *dĕn'sĭtĭ*, s. densidad, solidez, f.
dent, *dĕnt*, s. muesca, f.; —, v. a. abollar.
dental, *—ăl*, a. dental; —, s. letra dental, f.
dentifrice, *dĕn'tĭfrĭs*, s. dentífrico, m.
dentist, *dĕn'tĭst*, s. dentista, m.
dentistry, *—rĭ*, s. arte del dentista, m.
denudation, *dēnŭdā'shŭn*, s. despojo de ropa, m.
denude, *dēnūd'*, v. a. desnudar, despojar.
denunciate, *dēnŭn'sĭāt*, v. a. denunciar, delatar. [ciación, f.; publicación, f.
denunciation, *dēnŭnsĭā'shŭn*, s. denuncia, f.
deny, *dēnī'*, v. a. negar, rehusar; renunciar; abjurar.
deodorize, *dēō'dŭrĭz*, v. a. desinficionar.
depart, *dēpărt'*, v. n. partir(se); morir; desistir. [trito, m.
department, *—mĕnt'*, s. departamento, dis-

departure, -úr, s. partida, f.; abandono, m.

depend, dĕpĕnd', v. n. depender, estar dependiente; — on ó upon, confiar.

dependant, -ánt, dependent, -ént, a. & s. dependiente (m.).

dependence(cy), -ĕns(sĕ), s. dependencia, f.; confianza, f.; foreign —, colonia, f.

depict, dĕpíkt', v. a. pintar, retratar; describir. [f.

depilation, dĕpĭlá'shăn, s. caída del pelo,

depletion, dĕplé'shăn, s. (med.) deplección, f.

deplorable, dĕplŏ'rábl, a. deplorable, lamentable; -bly, ad. deplorablemente.

deplore, dĕplŏ'r', v. a. deplorar, lamentar.

deploy, dĕplŏĭ', v. a. (mil.) desplegar.

deponent, dĕpŏ'nĕnt, s. (law) testigo, m.

depopulate, dĕpŏp'ŭlát, v. a. despoblar, devastar. [ción, f.; devastación, f.

depopulation, dĕpŏpŭlá'shăn, s. despoblación, f.; destierro, m.

deportation, dĕpŏrtá'shăn, s. deportación, f.; destierro, m.

deportment, dĕpŏrt'mĕnt, s. conducta, f.; porte, manejo, m. [testificar.

depose, dĕpŏ'z', v. a. deponer; destronar;

deposit, dĕpŏz'ĭt, v. a. depositar; —, s. depósito, m.

deposition, dĕpŏzĭsh'ăn, s. deposición, f.; testimonio, m.; destitución, f.

depository, dĕpŏz'ĭtŏrĭ, s. depositaría, f.

deprave, dĕprá'v', v. a. depravar, corromper.

depraved, dĕprá'vd', a. depravado.

depravity, dĕprá'vĭtĭ, s. depravación, f.

deprecate, dĕp'rĕkát, v. a. suplicar con instancia, deprecar.

deprecation, dĕprĕká'shăn, s. súplica para conjurar los males, f. [suplicante.

deprecatory, dĕp'rĕkătŏrĭ, s. deprecativo.

depreciate, dĕprĕ'shĭát, v. a. rebajar el precio; despreciar, deprimir.

depreciation, dĕprĕshĭá'shăn, s. descrédito, m.; desestimación, f. [quear.

depredate, dĕp'rĕdát, v. a. depredar, saquear.

depredation, dĕprĕdá'shăn, s. depredación, f.; pillaje, m.

depress, dĕprĕs', v. a. deprimir, humillar.

depressed, dĕprĕs'd', a. desgraciado.

depression, dĕprĕsh'ăn, s. depresión, f.; abatimiento, m. [pérdida, f.

deprivation, dĕprĭvá'shăn, s. privación, f.

deprive, dĕprĭ'v', v. a. privar, despojar.

depth, dĕpth, s. hondura, profundidad, f.; abismo, m.; (fig.) rigor, m.; obscuridad, f.

deputation, dĕpŭtá'shăn, s. diputación, f.

depute, dĕpŭ't', v. a. diputar, delegar.

deputy, dĕp'ŭtĭ, s. diputado, delegado, m.

derange, dĕránj', v. a. desarreglar, desordenar. [orden, m.

derangement, -mĕnt, s. desarreglo, desorden, m.

derelict, dĕr'ĕlĭkt, a. (mar.) abandonado en alta mar.

dereliction, dĕrĕlĭk'shăn, s. desamparo, abandono, m.; (law) dejación de bienes, f.

deride, dĕrĭ'd', v. a. burlar, mofar.

derision, dĕrĭzh'ăn, s. irrisión, mofa, f.; escarnio, m.; burla, chulada, f.

derisive, dĕrĭ'sĭv, a. irrisorio. [cible.

derivable, dĕrĭ'vábl, a. derivable, dedu-

derivation, dĕrĭvá'shăn, s. derivación, f.

derive, dĕrĭ'v', v. a. (& n.) derivar(se); descender, proceder.

derogate, dĕr'ŏgát, v. n. derogar.

derogation, dĕrŏgá'shăn, s. derogación, f.

derogatory, dĕrŏg'ătŏrĭ, a. derogatorio.

derrick, dĕr'rĭk, s. máquina para levantar pesos, f.

dervish, dĕr'vĭsh, s. derviche, m.

descant, dĕs'kánt, v. n. discantar; discurrir; —, s. (mus.) discante, m.

descend, dĕsĕnd', v. n. descender.

descendent, -ĕnt, a. descendiente.

descent, dĕsĕnt', s. descenso, m.; pendiente, m.; invasión, f.; descendencia, posteridad, f.

describe, dĕskrĭ'b', v. a. describir, delinear. [f.

description, dĕskrĭp'shăn, s. descripción.

descriptive, dĕskrĭp'tĭv, a. descriptivo.

descry, dĕskrĭ', v. a. espiar; observar; describir.

desecrate, dĕs'ĕkrát, v. a. profanar.

desecration, dĕsĕkrá'shăn, s. profanación, f. [—, a. desierto, solitario.

desert, dĕz'ărt, s. desierto, m.; soledad, f.;

desert, dĕzărt', v. a. abandonar; desertar; —, s. mérito, m. [m.

deserter, dĕzăr'tăr, s. desertor, tránsfuga.

desertion, dĕzăr'shăn, s. deserción, f.

deserve, dĕzărv', v. a. merecer; ser digno.

deservedly, -ĕdlĭ, ad. merecidamente, dignamente.

deserving, dĕzăr'vĭng, a. meritorio.

deshabille, dĕzăbĭl', s. paños menores, m. pl. [se desea, m.; lo que falta.

desiderata, dĕsĭdărá'tăm, s. objeto que

design, dĕzĭn', v. a. designar, proyectar; tramar; diseñar; —, s. designio, intento, m.; empresa, f.; diseño, m.

designate, dĕz'ĭgnát, v. a. apuntar, señalar; distinguir. [f.

designation, dĕzĭgná'shăn, s. designación.

designatory, dĕz'ĭgnătŏrĭ, a. designativo.

designedly, dĕzĭ'nĕdlĭ, ad. de propósito, de intento.

designing, dĕzĭn'ĭng, a. insidioso, astuto.

desirability, dĕzĭrábĭl'ĭtĭ, s. apetencia, ansia, f.

desirable, dĕzĭ'rábl, a. deseable.

desire, dĕzĭ'r', s. deseo, m.; apetencia, f.; —, v. a. desear, apetecer.

desirous, dĕzĭ'rŭs, a. deseoso, ansioso; -ly, ad. ansiosamente.

desist, dĕzĭst', v. n. desistir.

desk, dĕsk, s. escritorio, m., papelera, f.; bufete, m.; atril (de coro), m.

desolate, dĕs'ŏlát, v. a. desolar; devastar; —, a. desolado; solitario.

desolation, dĕsŏlá'shăn, s. desolación, ruina, destrucción, f. [v. n. desesperar.

despair, dĕspá'r', s. desesperación, f.; —,

despairingly, -ĭnglĭ, ad. desesperadamente. [despacho, m.; expreso, m.

despatch, dĕspátsh', v. a. despachar; —, s.

despatch-boat, -bŏt, s. (mar.) aviso, m.

despatch-box, -bŏks, s. escritorio portátil, m. [vido, m.

desperado, dĕspĕrá'dŏ, s. hombre atre-

desperate, dĕs'pẽrăt, a. desesperado;
furioso; **-ly,** ad. desesperadamente, furiosamente; sumamente. [ción, f.
desperation, dĕspẽră'shăn, s. desespera-
despicable, dĕs'pĭkăbl, a. despreciable,
bajo; **-bly,** ad. despreciablemente.
despise, dĕspīz', v.a. despreciar; desdeñar.
despite, dĕspīt', s. despecho, m.; despique,
m.; malicia, f.; **in — of,** á despecho de.
despoil, dĕspŏil', v. a. despojar; privar.
despond, dĕspŏnd', v. n. desconfiar, aba-
tirse; desesperar. [abatimiento, m.
despondency, —ĕnsĕ, s. desesperación, f.;
despot, dĕs'pŏt, s. déspota, m.
despotic(al), dĕspŏt'ĭk(ăl), a. despótico,
absoluto; **-ally,** ad. despóticamente.
despotism, dĕs'pŏtĭzm, s. despotismo, m.
dessert, dĕzzẽrt', s. postres, m. pl. [f.
destination, dĕstĭnā'shăn, s. destinación,
destine, dĕs'tĭn, v. a. destinar, señalar.
destiny, dĕs'tĭnĕ, s. destino, hado, m.;
suerte, f. [nado, privado.
destitute, dĕs'tĭtŭt, a. destituído, abando-
destitution, dĕstĭtŭ'shăn, s. destitución,
privación, f.; abandono, m.
destroy, dĕstrŏi', v. a. destruir, arruinar.
destruction, dĕstrŭk'shăn, s. destrucción,
ruina, f.
destructive, dĕstrŭk'tĭv, a. destructivo,
ruinoso; **-ly,** ad. destructivamente.
desultoriness, dĕs'ŭltŏrĭnĕs, s. instabilidad, falta de método, f.
desultory, dĕs'ŭltŏrĕ, a. irregular, inconstante, sin método.
detach, dĕtătsh', v. a. (mil.) destacar.
detachment, —mĕnt, s. (mil.) destacamento, m.
detail, dĕtāl', s. detalle, m.; (am.) recluta,
f.; **in —,** al por menor; **—,** v. a. detallar;
referir por menor. [pedir.
detain, dĕtān', v. a. retener, detener; im-
detect, dĕtĕkt', v. a. descubrir, revelar.
detector, —ẽr, s. descubridor, m.; delator, m.
detection, dĕtĕk'shăn, s. descubrimiento,
m.; revelación, f. [secreta, m.
detective, dĕtĕk'tĭv, s. oficial de policía
detention, dĕtĕn'shăn, s. detención, retención, f.; cautividad, f.; cautiverio, m.
deter, dĕtẽr', v. a. desanimar; disuadir.
deterge, dĕtẽrj', v. a. deterger, limpiar,
bañar una llaga.
deteriorate, dĕtē'rĭŏrāt, v. a. deteriorar.
deterioration, dĕtērĭŏră'shăn, s. deterioración, f. [nable.
determinable, dĕtẽr'mĭnăbl, a. determi-
determinate, dĕtẽr'mĭnăt, a. determinado,
decidido; **-ly,** ad. determinadamente.
determination, dĕtẽrmĭnā'shăn, s. determinación, f.; decisión, f.
determine, dĕtẽr'mĭn, v. a. determinar,
decidir; **—,** v. n. terminar, concluir.
detest, dĕtĕst', v. a. detestar, aborrecer.
detestable, —ăbl, a. detestable, abominable;
-bly, ad. detestablemente.
detestation, dĕtĕstā'shăn, s. detestación,
f.; aborrecimiento, m.
dethrone, dĕthrōn', v. a. destronar. [m.
dethronement, —mĕnt, s. destronamiento,
detonate, dĕ'tŏnāt, v. n. (chem.) detonar.

detonation, dĕtŏnā'shăn, s. detonación, f.
detract, dĕtrăkt', v.a. detractar; dismiuuir.
detraction, dĕtrăk'shăn, s. detracción, f.
detriment, dĕt'rĭmĕnt, s. detrimento, daño,
perjuicio, m.
detrimental, dĕtrĭmĕn'tăl, a. perjudicial.
deuce, dūs, s. dos (en los juegos), m.;
diantre, m.
devastate, dĕv'ăstăt, v. a. devastar; robar.
devastation, dĕvăstā'shăn, s. devastación,
ruina, f. [arrollar.
develop, dĕvĕl'ŏp, v. a. desenvolver; des-
development, dĕvĕl'ŏpmĕnt, s. desarro-
deviate, dĕ'vĭăt, v. n. desviarse. [llo, m.
deviation, dĕvĭā'shăn, s. desvío, m.; devia-
ción, f.
device, dĕvīs', s. proyecto, expediente, m.;
invención, f.; divisa, f.
devil, dĕv'l, s. diablo, demonio, m.
devilish, —ĭsh, a. diabólico; **-ly,** ad. diabólicamente.
devilkin, —kĭn, s. diablillo, m.
devilment, —mĕnt, s. diablería, f.
devilry, —rĕ, s. diablura, f.; maleficio, m.
devious, dĕ'vĭăs, a. desviado; errante.
devise, dĕvīz', v.a. trazar; inventar; idear;
legar; **—,** s. legado, m., donación testa-
deviser, —ẽr, s. inventor, m. [mentaria, f.
devisor, dĕvī'sẽr, s. testador, m.
devoid, dĕvŏid', a. vacío; privado.
devolve, dĕvŏlv', v. a. rodar abajo; tras-
mitir, transmitir, m.
devote, dĕvōt', v. a. dedicar; consagrar.
devotedness, —ĕdnĕs, s. devoción, f.
devotee, dĕv'ŏtē, s. santurrón, m.
devotion, dĕvō'shăn, s. devoción, f.; oración, f.; rezo, m.; afición, f.
devotional, —ăl, a. devoto, religioso.
devour, dĕvŏur', v. a. devorar; echar á
perder.
devout, dĕvŏut', a. devoto, piadoso; **-ly,**
ad. devotamente.
dew, dū, s. rocío, m.; **—,** v. a. rociar.
dewlap, —lăp, s. papada del buey, f.
dew-worm, —wŭrm, s. lombriz, f.
dowy, —ĕ, a. rociado.
dexterity, dĕkstĕr'ĭtĕ, s. destreza, f.
dexterous, dĕks'tẽrăs, a. diestro, hábil;
-ly, ad. diestramente.
diabetes, dĭăbē'tēz, s. diabetes, m.
diabolic(al), dĭăbŏl'ĭk(ăl), a. diabólico;
-ally, ad. diabólicamente.
diadem, dī'ădĕm, s. diadema, m. & f.
diagnosis, dĭăgnō'sĭs, s. (med.) diagnosis, f.
diagnostic, dĭăgnŏs'tĭk, s. diagnóstico;
-s, pl. diagnóstica, f. [diagonalmente.
diagonal, dĭă'gŏnăl, s. diagonal; **-ly,** ad.
diagram, dī'ăgrăm, s. diagrama, m.
dial, dī'ăl, s. reloj de sol, m.; cuadrante, m.
dialect, dī'ălĕkt, s. dialecto, m.
dialogue, dī'ălŏg, s. diálogo, m.
diameter, dīăm'ĕtẽr, s. diámetro, m.
diametrical, dīămĕt'rĭkăl, a. diametral;
-ly, ad. diametralmente.
diamond, dī'ămănd, s. diamante, m.; (at
cards) oros, m.pl.; **— cut into angles,**
diamante abrillantado, brillante, m.
diamond-cutter, —kŭttẽr, s. diamantista,
m.

diamond-letter, –lĕttär, s. corpus cuatro, m.   [–, v. a. matizar; adamascar.
diaper, dī′päär, s. lienzo adamascado, m.;
diapason, dīăpā′zŏn, s. (mus.)diapasón, m.
diaphragm, dī′äfräm, s. diafragma, m.
diarrhœa, dīärrē′ä, s. diarrea, f.
diary, dī′ärĭ, s. diario, m.
dibble, dīb′l, v. a. plantar con plantador.
dice, dīs, s. pl. dados, m. pl.
dice-box, –bŏks, s. cubilete de dados, m.
dickens, dīk′nz, s. (vulg.) diablo, m.
dictate, dīk′tät, v.a. dictar; –, s. dictamen, m.; lección, f.
dictation, dīktā′shän, s. dictado, m.
dictatorial, dīktătō′rĭäl, a. autoritativo; magistral.   [f.; dictatura, f.
dictatorship, dīktā′tärshĭp, s. dictadura,
diction, dīk′shän, s. dicción, f.; estilo, m.
dictionary, –ärĭ, s. diccionario, m.
didactic(al), dīdäk′tĭk(ăl), a. didáctico.
diddle, dīd′l, v. n. vacilar; anadear.
die, dī, v. n. morir, expirar; evaporarse; desvanecerse; marchitarse.
die, dī, s. dado, m.; cuño, m.; (fig.) suerte,f.
diet, dī′ĕt, s. dieta, f.; régimen, m.; asamblea, f.; –, v. a. alimentar; –, v. n. estar á dieta.   [cinal, f.
dietary, –ärĭ, a. dietético; –, s. dieta medi-
differ, dĭf′fär, v. n. diferenciarse; contradecir.   [f.
difference, –ĕns, s. diferencia, disparidad,
different, –ĕnt, a. diferente; desemejante; –ly, ad. diferentemente.   [renciar.
differentiate, dĭffärĕn′shĭät, v. a. dife-
difficult, dĭf′fĭkŭlt, a. difícil, áspero; –ly, ad. difícilmente.   [m.; duda, f.
difficulty, –ĕ, s. dificultad, f.; obstáculo,
diffidence, dĭf′fĭdĕns, s. difidencia, f.
diffident, dĭf′fĭdĕnt, a. desconfiado; –ly, ad. desconfiadamente.
diffraction, dĭffräk′shän, s. (opt.) difracción de los rayos luminosos, f.
diffuse, dĭffūz′, v. a. difundir, esparcir; –,a. difundido, esparcido; prolijo; –ly,ad. copiosamente.   [dad,f.; esparcimiento, m.
diffusion, dĭffū′zhän, s. difusión, prolijidad,f.
diffusive, dĭffū′sĭv, a. diffusivo; prolijo.
dig, dĭg, v. a. cavar, ahondar, azadonar; –, s. empujo, m.
digest, dĭjĕst′, v. a. digerir, ordenar; rumiar; –, v. n. supurar; –, s. (law) digesto, m.; –of the case, resumen del pleito, m.
digestible, –ĭbl, a. digerible.
digestion, dĭjĕst′tän, s. digestión, f.
digestive, dĭjĕs′tĭv, s. medicamento digestivo.   [tivo, m.
digger, dĭg′gär, s. cavador, m.
digit, dĭj′ĭt, s. dígito (medida longitudinal),
dignified, dĭg′nĭfĭd, a. altivo.   [m.
dignify, dĭg′nĭfĭ, v. a. exaltar, elevar.
dignitary, dĭg′nĭtärĭ, s. dignitario, m.
dignity, dĭg′nĭtĭ, s. dignidad, f.; rango, m.; aire noble, m.
digress, dĭgrĕs′, v. n. hacer digresión.
digression, dĭgrĕsh′än, s. digresión, f.; desvío, m.   [lijo.
digressive, dĭgrĕs′sĭv, a. digresivo, prodike, dĭk, s. dique, canal, m.

dilapidated, dĭläp′ĭdātĕd, a. malgastado.
dilapidation, dĭlăpĭdā′shän, s. dilapidación, f.; ruina, f.
dilate, dĭlāt′, v. a. (& n.) dilatar(se), extender(se).
dilatory, dĭl′ätärĭ, a. tardo, dilatorio.
dilemma, dĭlĕm′mä, s. dilema, m.
diligence, dĭl′ĭjĕns, s. diligencia, f.; exactitud, f.   [–ly, ad. diligentemente.
diligent, dĭl′ĭjĕnt, a. diligente, asiduo;
dilly-dally, dĭl′lĭdăl′lĕ, v. n. entretenerse con patarraias.
dilucid, dĭlū′sĭd, a. lúcido, claro.
diluent, dĭl′ūĕnt, a. diluente.
dilution, dĭlū′shän, s. dilución, f.
diluvial, dĭlū′vĭäl, a. diluviano.
dim, dĭm, a. turbio de vista, lerdo; obscuro; –, v. a. ofuscar, obscurecer; eclipsar.
dimension, dĭmĕn′shän, s. dimensión, medida, extensión, f.
diminish, dĭmĭn′ĭsh, v. a. (& n.) decrecer, disminuir(se).   [f.; descrédito, m.
diminution, dĭmĭnū′shän, s. disminución,
diminutive, dĭmĭn′ūtĭv, s. & a. diminutivo; –ly, ad. diminutivamente.
dimissory, dĭmĭs′särĕ, a. dimisorio.
dimity, dĭm′ĭtĭ, s. fustán, bombasí, m.
dimly, dĭm′lĕ, ad. obscuramente.
dimness, dĭm′nĕs, s. ofuscamiento, m.; estupidez, f.
dimple, dĭm′pl, s.hoyuelo de la mejilla,m.
din, dĭn, s. ruido violento, alboroto, m.; –, v. a. atolondrar.
dine, dĭn, v. a. dar de comer; –, v.n. comer.
diner-out, –ärŏŭt, s. el que toma la comida en el mesón, m.; mogollón, m.
dingy, dĭn′jĕ, a. moreno, obscuro.
dining-hall, dī′nĭnghäl, dining-room, –rŏm, s. comedor, m.; refectorio, m.
dinner, dĭn′när, s. comida, f.
dinner-time, –tĭm, s. hora de comer, f.
dinner-waggon, –wäggŏn,s. (fam.)marmitón, m.   [de.
dint, dĭnt, s. golpe, m.; by–of, en fuerza
diocese, dī′ōsĕs, s. diócesis, diócesi, f.
diorama, dīōrā′mä, s. diorama, m.
dip, dĭp, v. a. remojar, sumergir; repasar ligeramente; –, v.n. sumergirse; penetrar; –, s. (of the horizon) depresión, f.; (of the needle) inclinación, f.; plumada de tinta, f.; inmersión, f.
diphtheria, dĭfthē′rĭä, s. difteritis, f.
diphthong, dĭp′thŏng, s. diptongo, m.
diploma, dĭplō′mä, s. diploma, m.; letra patente, f.
diplomacy, dĭplō′măsĕ, s. diplomática, f.
diplomatic, dĭplōmăt′ĭk, a. diplomático; –s, s. pl. diplomacia, f.   [tico, m.
diplomat(ist), dĭplō′măt(ĭst), s. diplomádipsomania, dĭpsōmā′nĭä,s.dipsomanía,f.
dire, dīr, a. horrendo; cruel.
direct, dĭrĕkt′ a. directo, derecho; claro; –, v. a. dirigir, enderezar; reglar, ordenar.
direction, dĭrĕk′shän, s. dirección, f.; instrucción, f.; mandado, m.
directly, dĭrĕkt′lĕ, ad. directamente, inmediatamente.
director, dĭrĕk′tär, s. director, m.
directory, –ĕ, s. directorio, m.

dirge, *dörj*, s. canción lúgubre, f.

dirigent, *dir'ijent*, s. dirigente, director, m.

dirt, *dört*, s. lodo, m.; porquería, f.; —, v. a. ensuciar, emporcar.

dirtily, *-tli*, ad. puercamente; vilmente.

dirtiness, *-tnès*, s. suciedad, f.; bajeza, f.

dirty, *-ö*, a. puerco, sucio; vil, bajo.

disability, *disäbil'tè*, s. impotencia, f.; inhabilidad, incapacidad, f.

disable, *disä'bl*, v. a. hacer incapaz; (mar.) desaparejar un navío.

disablement, *-mènt*, s. (law) impedimento legal, m.; (mar.) desaparejo de una nave de resultas de algún combate, m.

disabuse, *disäbúz'*, v. a. desengañar.

disaccustom, *disäkküs'tüm*, v. a. desacostumbrar.　[desconocer.

disacknowledge, *disäknöl'èj*, v. a. negar.

disadvantage, *disädvän'täj*, s. desventaja, f.; daño, m.; —, v. a. dañar, perjudicar.

disadvantageous, *disädvänté'jüs*, a. desventajoso; -ly, ad. desventajosamente.

disaffect, *disäffèkt'*, v. a. descontentar; indisponer.　[m.; desamor, m.

disaffection, *disäffèk'shün*, s. desafecto, m.

disagree, *disägrè'*, v. n. desconvenir, discordar.

disagreeable, *-èbl*, a. desagradable, contrario; -bly, ad. desagradablemente.

disagreeableness, *-nès*, s. desavenencia, f.; contradicción, f.

disagreement, *-mènt*, s. diferencia, f.; discordia, f.　[n. negar, prohibir.

disallow, *disällö'*, v. a. desaprobar; -, v.

disappear, *disäpper'*, v. n. desaparecer; ausentarse.　[m.

disappearance, *-äns*, s. desaparecimiento, f.

disappoint, *disäppöint'*, v. a. frustrar, faltar á la palabra; engañar.

disappointment, *-mènt*, s. chasco, m.; contratiempo, m.

disapprobation, *disäpprobä'shün*, dis-approval, *disäppro'väl*, s. desaprobación, censura, f.

disapprove, *disäpprö'v*, v. a. desaprobar.

disarm, *disärm'*, v. a. desarmar, privar de armas.　[armamiento, m.

disarmament, *disärm'ämènt*, s. desarray, *disärrä'*, s. desarreglo, m.; —, v. a. desnudar; desarreglar.

disaster, *disäs'tär*, s. desastre, m.; infortunio, m.

disastrous, *disäs'trüs*, a. desastroso, infeliz; calamitoso, -ly, ad. desastradamente.　[cer.

disavow, *disävö'*, v. a. negar; desconocer.

disavowal, *-äl*, s. denegación, f.

disband, *disbänd'*, v. a. descartar, despedir.　[confianza, f.

disbelief, *disbèléf'*, s. incredulidad, desconfianza, f.

disbelieve, *disbèlèv'*, v. a. descreer, desconfiar.　[m.

disbeliever, *-är*, s. descreído, incrédulo, m.

disburden, *disbür'dn*, v. a. descargar.

disburse, *disbürs'*, v. a. desembolsar, pagar.

disbursement, *-mènt*, s. desembolso, m.

disc, disk, *disk*, s. disco, tejo, m.; (rail.) disco de señales.

discard, *diskärd'*, v. a. descartar, licenciar.

---

discern, *diszärn'*, v. a. discernir, percibir, distinguir.

discernible, *-ibl*, a. perceptible; sensible.

discerning, *-ïng*, a. juicioso, perspicaz; -ly, ad. juiciosamente.

discharge, *distshärj'*, v. a. descargar, pagar (una deuda); dispensar; ejecutar, cumplir; descartar; —, v. n. descargarse; despedir; cumplir con su obligación; —, s. descarga, f.; descargo, m.; finiquito, m.; dimisión, f.; absolución, f.

disciple, *dissï'pl*, discípulo, m.

disciplinarian, *dissïplïnä'rïän*, a. disciplinario; —, s. dómine, m.; presbiteriano, m.

discipline, *dis'sïplïn*, s. disciplina, f.; enseñanza, f.; ciencia, f.; rigor, m.; —, v. a. disciplinar, instruir.

disclaim, *disklä'm*, v. a. negar, renunciar.

disclaimer, *-är*, s. denegación, f.

disclose, *disklö'z*, v. n. descubrir; revelar.

disclosure, *disklö'zhär*, s. descubrimiento, m.; revelación, f.

discoloration, *diskülärä'shün*, s. descoloramiento, m.; tinte, m.

discolour, *disküll'är*, v. a. descolorar.

discomfit, *disküm'fït*, v. a. derrotar, vencer, deshacer.　[miento, m.

discomfiture, *-s*, s. derrota, f.; vencimiento, m.

discomfort, *disküm'fürt*, s. desconsuelo m.; aflicción, f.　[dar, molestar.

discommode, *diskömmö'd*, v. a. incomodar.

discompose, *disköm'pö'z*, v. a. descomponer; desordenar; turbar.

discomposure, *disköm'pö'zhär*, s. descomposición, f.; confusión, f.

disconcert, *disköns'ürt'*, v. a. desconcertar, confundir, turbar.

disconnect, *diskön'nèkt'*, v. a. desunir, unión, f.

disconnection, *diskön'nèk'shün*, s. desunión, f.

disconsolate, *diskön'söl't*, a. inconsolable; -ly, ad. desconsoladamente.

discontent, *diskön'tènt'*, s. descontento, m.; —, a. malcontento; —, v. a. descontentar.

discontinuation, *diskön'tïnüä'shün*, s. descontinuación, cesación, interrupción, f.

discontinue, *diskön'tïn'ü*, v. n. descontinuar, interrumpir; cesar.

discord, *dis'körd*, discordance, *diskör'däns*, s. discordia, f.; discordancia, disensión, f.

discordant, *diskör'dänt*, a. discorde; incongruo; -ly, ad. con discordancia.

discount, *diskö'ünt*, s. descuento, m.; rebaja, f.; —, *diskö'ünt'*, v. a. descontar.

discountenance, *diskö'ün'tènäns*, v. a. aturdir, inmutar; desaprobar.

discourage, *diskür'ïj*, v. a. desalentar, desanimar.　[m.

discouragement, *-mènt*, s. desaliento, m.

discourse, *diskörs'*, s. discurso, m.; tratado, m.; —, v. n. conversar, discurrir, tratar (de).

discursive, *diskör'sïv*, a. discursivo.

discourteous, *disk'ürt'yüs*, a. descortés, grosero; -ly, ad. descortésmente.

discourtesy, *disk'ür'tèsè*, s. descortesía, grosería, f.　[llar; manifestar.

discover, *disk'üv'är*, v. a. descubrir; reve-

discoverable, –_ăbl_, a. descubrible.

discovery, –_ĕ_, s. descubrimiento, m.; revelación, f.

discredit, _dĭskrĕd'ĭt_, s. discrédito, deshonor, m.; –, v. a. desacreditar, deshonrar.

discreditable, –_ăbl_, a. ignominioso.

discreet, _dĭskrēt'_, a.discreto; circunspecto; –ly, ad. discretamente.

discrepancy, _dĭskrĕp'ănsĕ_, s. discrepancia, diferencia, f.

discretion, _dĭskrĕsh'ŭn_, s. discreción, f.

discretionary, –_ărĕ_, a. ilimitado.

discriminate, _dĭskrĭm'ĭnăt_, v. a. distinguir; señalar; –ly, ad. distintamente

discrimination, _dĭskrĭmĭnā'shŭn_, s. distinción, f.; distintivo, m.

discursive, _dĭskŭr'sĭv_, a. inconstante; discursivo; –ly, ad. de un modo argu-

discuss, _dĭskŭs'_, v. a. discutir. [mentoso.

discussion, _dĭskŭsh'ŭn_, s. discusión, f.

disdain, _dĭsdān'_, v. a. desdeñar, despreciar; –, s. desdén, desprecio, m.

disdainful, –_fŭl_, a. desdeñoso; –ly, ad. desdeñosamente.

disease, _dĭzēz'_, s. mal, m.; enfermedad, f.

diseased, –_d'_, a. enfermo.

disembarcation, _dĭsĕmbărkā'shăn_, s. (mil.) desembarco de tropas.

disembark, _dĭsĕmbărk'_ v. a. & n. desembarcar.

disembarrass, _dĭsĕmbăr'răs_, disencumber, _dĭsĕnkŭm'băr_, v. a. desembarazar. [lizado.

disembodied, _dĭsĕmbŏd'ĭd_, a. inmaterial

disembogue, _dĭsĕmbŏg'_, v. n. desembocar.

disenchant, _dĭsĕntshănt'_, v. a. desencantar. [m.

disenchantment, –_mĕnt_, s. desencanto.

disencumbrance, _dĭsĕnkŭm'brăns_, s. desembarazo, m.

disengage, _dĭsĕngāj'_, v. a. desenredar, librar; –, v. n. libertarse de desembarazarse. [dar, separar; desembarazar.

disentangle, _dĭsĕntăng'gl_, v. a. desenredar

disentanglement, –_mĕnt_, s.desenredo, m.

disentomb, _dĭsĕntōm'_, v. a. exhumar.

disestablish, _dĭsĕstăb'lĭsh_, v. a. expeler, desalojar.

disfavour, _dĭsfā'văr_, v. a. desfavorecer; –, s. disfavor, disgusto, m.

disfiguration, _dĭsfĭgūrā'shăn_, disfigurement, _dĭsfĭg'ŭrmĕnt_, s. deformidad, f.

disfigure, _dĭsfĭg'ăr_, v. a. desfigurar, afear. [franquicias.

disfranchise, _dĭsfrăn'tshĭz_, v. a. quitar

disgorge, _dĭsgŏrj'_, v. a. vomitar.

disgrace, _dĭsgrās'_, s. deshonra, f.; desgracia, f.; disfavor, m.; –, v. a. deshonrar; hacer caer en desgracia.

disgraceful, –_fŭl_, a. deshonroso, ignominioso; –ly, ad. vergonzosamente.

disguise, _dĭsgīz'_, v. a. disfrazar, enmascarar; simular; –, s. disfraz, m.; máscara, f.

disgust, _dĭsgŭst'_, s. disgusto, m.; aversión, f.; –, v. a. disgustar.

dish, _dĭsh_, s. fuente, f., plato, m.; taza, f.; –, v. a. servir la vianda en fuente; to – up, servir la comida.

dish-clout, –_klŏŭt_, s. rodilla, f.

dishearten, _dĭshăr'tn_, v. a. desalentar, decorazonar.

dishevel, _dĭshĕv'l_, v. a. desgreñar.

dishonest, _dĭsŏn'ĕst_, a. deshonesto; ignominioso; –ly, ad. deshonestamente. [f.

dishonesty, –_ĕ_, deshonestidad, impureza,

dishonour, _dĭsŏn'ăr_, s. deshonra, ignominia, f.; –, v. a. deshonrar, infamar.

dishonourable, –_ăbl_, a. deshonroso, afrentoso,indecoroso; –bly,ad.ignominiosamente. [dor, m.

dish-warmer, _dĭsh'wărmăr_, s. escalfa-

dish-water, –_wătăr_, s. lavacías, f. pl.

disillusion, _dĭsĭllū'shŭn_, s. desengaño, m.

disinclination, _dĭsĭnklĭnā'shăn_, s. desafecto, m., aversión, f.

disincline, _dĭsĭnklīn'_, v. a. desinclinar.

disinfect, _dĭsĭnfĕkt'_, v. a. desinficionar.

disingenuous, _dĭsĭnjĕn'ŭăs_, a. falso, disimulado.

disinherit, _dĭsĭnhĕr'ĭt_, v. a. desheredar.

disinter, _dĭsĭntăr'_, v. a. desenterrar.

disinterested, _dĭzĭn'tărĕstĕd_, a. desinteresado; –ly, ad. desinteresadamente.

disinterestedness, –_nĕs_, s.desinterés,m.

disinterment, _dĭsĭntăr'mĕnt_, s. desenterramiento, m.

disjoint, _dĭsjŏĭnt'_, v. a. dislocar, desmembrar; –, v. n. desmembrarse.

dislike, _dĭslīk'_, s. aversión, f. ; disgusto, m.; –, v. a. disgustar; desaprobar.

dislocate, _dĭs'lŏkăt_, v. a. dislocar, descoyuntar. [f.; descoyuntamiento, m.

dislocation, _dĭslŏkā'shăn_, s. dislocación,

dislodge, _dĭslŏj'_, v. a. & n. desalojar.

disloyal, _dĭslŏĭ'ăl_, a. desleal; infiel; –ly, ad. deslealmente. [dad, perfidia, f.

disloyalty, –_ăltĕ_, s. deslealtad, infideli-

dismal, _dĭz'măl_, a. triste, funesto; horrendo; –s, s. pl. hipocondría, f.

dismantle, _dĭsmăn'tl_, v. a. (mil.) desmantelar (una plaza); (mar.) desaparejar.

dismast, _dĭsmăst'_, v. a. desarbolar (un navío). [–, v. a. & n. desmayar(se).

dismay, _dĭsmā'_, s. desmayo, m.; terror,m.;

dismember, _dĭsmĕm'băr_, v. a. desmembrar, despedazar. [descartar.

dismiss, _dĭsmĭs'_, v. a. despedir; echar;

dismissal, –_ăl_, dismission, _dĭsmĭsh'ăn_, despedida, f.; dimisión, f.

dismount, _dĭsmŏŭnt'_, v. a. desmontar, apearse del caballo; –, v. n. desmontar, descender. [dicencia, f.

disobedience, _dĭsŏbē'dĭĕns_, s. desobe-

disobedient, _dĭsŏbē'dĭĕnt_, a. desobediente.

disobey, _dĭsŏbā'_, v. a. desobedecer.

disobliging, _dĭsŏblī'jĭng_, a. desagradable.

disorder, _dĭsŏr'dăr_, s. desorden, m.; confusión, f.; indisposición, f.; –, v. a. desordenar, confundir, perturbar.

disorderly, –_lĕ_, a. desarreglado, confuso; ad. desordenadamente; ilegalmente.

disorganization, _dĭsŏrgănĭzā'shăn_, s. desorganización, f. [zar.

disorganize, _dĭsŏr'gănĭz_, v. a. desorgani-

disown, _dĭsŏn'_, v. a. negar, desconocer, renunciar.

disparage, _dĭspăr'ăj_, v. a. envilecer, mofar, desdorar.

disparagement, —*mĕnt*, s. desdoro, m.; casamiento desigual, m.; censura, f.; desprecio, m.; insulto, m.

disparity, *dĭspăr'ĭtē*, s. disparidad, f.

dispassionate, *dĭspăsh'ănăt*, a. sereno, desapasignado; templado.

dispel, *dĭspĕl'*, y. a. expeler.

dispensary, *dĭspĕn'sărē*, s. dispensario, m.   [ción, f.; dispensa, f.

dispensation, *dĭspĕnsă'shăn*, s. distribu-

dispensatory, *dĭspĕn'sătŭrē*, s. farma-copea, f.   [tribuir.

dispense, *dĭspĕns'*, v. a. dispensar; dis-

disperse, *dĭspŭrs'*, v. a. esparcir, dispar; distribuir.   [separación, f.

dispersion, *dĭspŭr'shăn*, s. dispersión, f.

dispirit, *dĭspĭr'ĭt*, v. a. desalentar, desani-mar.   [nar.

displace, *dĭsplās'*, v. a. dislocar, desorde-

displant, *dĭsplănt'*, v. a. trasplantar.

display, *dĭsplā'*, v. a. desplegar; explicar; exponer; ostentar; —s. ostentación, f.; despliegue, m.   [gustar; ofender.

displease, *dĭsplēz'*, v. a. desplacer, dis-

displeasure, *dĭsplĕzh'ŭr*, s. desplacer, dis-gusto, m.; indignación, f.

disport, *dĭspōrt'*, v. a. juguetear; —, v. n. divertirse.

disposal, *dĭspō'zăl*, s. disposición, f.

dispose, *dĭspōz'*, v. a. disponer, dar; arreglar; —, v. n. vender; transferir.

disposed, —*d*, a. (& p.) dispuesto, in-clinado, — *of*, vendido.

disposition, *dĭspŏzĭsh'ăn*, s. disposición, f.; orden, m.; índole, f.; inclinación, f.

dispossess, *dĭspŏzĕs'*, v. a. desposeer.

dispraise, *dĭsprāz'*, v. a. vituperar.

disproportion, *dĭsprŏpōr'shăn*, s. des-proporción, f.   [nado.

disproportionate, —*ăt*, a. desproporcio-

disprove, *dĭsprōv'*, v. a. confutar; des-aprobar.   [testable.

disputable, *dĭspū'tăbl*, a. disputable, con-

disputant, *dĭs'pŭtănt*, s. disputador, m.

disputation, *dĭspŭtă'shăn*, s. disputa, controversia, f.   [quisquilloso.

disputatious, *dĭspŭtā'shŭs*, a. disputador.

dispute, *dĭspūt'*, s. disputa, controversia, f.; —, v. a. & n. disputar, controvertir, argüir.   [inhabilidad, f.

disqualification, *dĭskwŏlĭfĭkă'shăn*, s.

disqualify, *dĭskwŏl'ĭfĭ*, v. n. hacer inhábil.

disquiet, *dĭskwī'ĕt*, s. inquietud, pertur-bación, f.; —, v. a. inquietar, turbar.

disquietude, —*ūd*, s. inquietud, f.

disquisition, *dĭskwĭzĭsh'ăn*, s. disquisi-ción, f.; examen, m.

disregard, *dĭsrēgärd'*, v. a. desatender, desdeñar; —, s. desatención, f.; desdén, m.

disregardful, —*fŭl*, a. desatento, negli-gente; —*ly*, ad. desatentamente.

disrelish, *dĭsrĕl'ĭsh*, s. disgusto, tedio, hastío, m.; —, v. a. desaprobar; tener tedio.   [de la memoria.

disremember, *dĭsrēmĕm'băr*, v. a. irse

disrepair, *dĭsrēpār'*, s. destrozo, m.

disreputable, *dĭsrĕp'ŭtăbl*, a. deshonroso; —*bly*, ad. deshonrosamente.

disrespect, *dĭsrēspĕkt'*, s. irreverencia, f.

disrespectful, —*fŭl*, a. irreverente, des-cortés; —*ly*, ad. irreverentemente.

disrobe, *dĭsrōb'*, v. a. desnudar, despojar.

disruption, *dĭsrŭp'shăn*, s. rompimiento, m.; fractura, f.   [contento, disgusto, m.

dissatisfaction, *dĭssătĭsfăk'shăn*, s. des-

dissatisfy, *dĭssăt'ĭsfĭ*, v. a. descontentar, desagradar.

dissect, *dĭssĕkt'*, v. a. disecar.

dissecting-room, —*ĭngrōm*, s. sala de anatomía, f.

dissection, *dĭssĕk'shăn*, s. disección, ana-tomía, f.; examen minucioso, m.

dissemble, *dĭssĕm'bl*, v. a. disimular; —, v. n. hacer el papel de hipócrita.

disseminate, *dĭssĕm'ĭnāt*, v. a. diseminar, sembrar, esparcir.   [cordia, f.

dissension, *dĭssĕn'shăn*, s. disensión, dis-

dissent, *dĭssĕnt'*, v. n. disentir, diferen-ciarse; —, s. disensión, contrariedad de opinión, f.   [formista, m.

dissenter, —*ŭr*, s. disidente, m.; no con-

dissentient, *dĭssĕn'shĭĕnt*, a. discrepante.

dissertation, *dĭssŭrtă'shăn*, s. diserta-ción, f.   [separar.

dissever, *dĭssĕv'ŭr*, v. a. partir, dividir.

dissimilar, *dĭssĭm'ĭlăr*, a. desemejante, heterogéneo.   [neidad, f.

dissimilarity, *dĭssĭmĭlăr'ĭtē*, s. heteroge-

dissimulate, *dĭssĭm'ūlāt*, v. a. disimular.

dissimulation, *dĭssĭmūlă'shăn*, s. disi-mulación, f.

dissipate, *dĭs'sĭpāt*, v. a. disipar.

dissipation, *dĭssĭpă'shăn*, s. disipación, f.; dispersión, f.

dissociate, *dĭssō'shĭāt*, v. a. disociar.

dissoluble, *dĭs'sŏlūbl*, a. disoluble.

dissolute, *dĭs'sŏlūt*, a. disoluto, libertino.

dissolution, *dĭssŏlū'shăn*, s. disolución, f.; muerte, f.   [disolverse, derretirse.

dissolve, *dĭzzŏlv'*, v. a. disolver; —, v. n.

dissolving scenes, *dĭzzŏl'vĭngsĕns*, dis-solving views, —*vūz*, s. pl. cromotro-pos, m. pl.   [desconcierto, m.

dissonance, *dĭs'sŏnăns*, s. disonancia, f.;

dissonant, *dĭs'sŏnănt*, a. disonante; dis-cordante; diferente.

dissuade, *dĭsswād'*, v. a. disuadir.

dissuasion, *dĭsswă'shăn*, s. disuasión, f.

dissuasive, *dĭsswā'sĭv*, a. disuasivo.

dissyllable, *dĭssĭl'lăbl*, a. disílabo.

distaff, *dĭs'tăf*, s. rueca, f.

distance, *dĭs'tăns*, s. distancia, f.; respeto, m.; esquivez, f.; at a —, de lejos; out of —, fuera de vista; —, v. a. apartar; sobre-pasar; espaciar.

distant, *dĭs'tănt*, a. distante; esquivo.

distaste, *dĭstāst'*, s. hastío, disgusto, tedio, m.   [dable; chocante; maligno.

distasteful, —*fŭl*, a. desabrido, desagra-

distemper, *dĭstĕm'păr*, s. indisposición, enfermedad, f.; desasosiego, m.; desorden tumultuoso, m.; —, v. a. perturbar; causar una enfermedad.

distend, *dĭstĕnd'*, v. a. extender, ensanchar.

distension, *dĭstĕn'shăn*, s. dilatación, f.

distich, *dĭs'tĭk*, s. dístico, m.   [chura, f.

distil, *dĭstĭl'*, v. a. & n. destilar; gotear.

distillation, —*lă'shăn*, s. destilación, f.

distillery, -lărĕ, s. destilatorio, m.
distinct, dĭstĭngkt', a. distinto, diferente, diverso; claro, formal; -ly, ad. distintamente. [diferencia, f.
distinction, dĭstĭngk'shŭn, s. distinción, f.
distinctive, dĭstĭngk'tĭv, a. distintivo; -ly, ad. distintamente, claramente.
distinctness, dĭstĭngkt'nĕs, s. distinción, claridad, f. [guir; discernir.
distinguish, dĭstĭng'gwĭsh, v. a. distinguishable, -ăbl, a. distinguible, notable.
distort, dĭstôrt', v. a. retorcer; desviar.
distortion, dĭstôr'shŭn, s. contorsión, f.; torcimiento, m.
distract, dĭstrăkt', v. a. distraer; separar; perturbar. [ad. locamente.
distracted, -ĕd, a. loco, perturbado; -ly,
distraction, dĭstrăk'shŭn, s. distracción, f.; confusión, f.; frenesí, m. [trar.
distrain, dĭstrān', v. a. embargar, secuestrar
distraint, dĭstrānt', s. (law) secuestro, m.
distress, dĭstrĕs', s. secuestro, m.; calamidad, miseria, f.; -, v. a. secuestrar; angustiar, congojar. [turbativo.
distressing, dĭstrĕs'ĭng, a. penoso, conturbativo
distribute, dĭstrĭb'ūt, v. a. distribuir, dividir, repartir. [f.
distribution, dĭstrĭbū'shŭn, s. distribución, f.
district, dĭs'trĭkt, s. distrito, m.; región, f.; jurisdicción, f.
distrust, dĭstrŭst', v. a. desconfiar; -, s. desconfianza, sospecha, f.
distrustful, -fŭl, a. desconfiado; sospechoso; -ly, ad. desconfiadamente.
disturb, dĭstŭrb', v. a. perturbar, estorbar.
disturbance, -ăns, s. disturbio, m.; confusión, f.; tumulto, m. [día, f.
disunion, dĭsū'nĭŭn, s. desunión, discordia
disunite, dĭsūnīt', v. a. (& n.) desunir(se), separar(se).
disuse, dĭsūs', s. desuso, m.; -, v. a. desusar, desacostumbrar, cesar.
ditch, dĭtsh, s. zanja, f.; foso, m.; -, v. a. abrir zanjas ó fosos.
ditty, dĭt'ĭ, s. canción, jácara, f.
diuretic, dĭūrĕt'ĭk, a. (med.) diurético.
diurnal, dĭŭr'năl, a. diurno, cotidiano; -, s. diario, jornal, m.
dive, dĭv, v. n. sumergirse; bucear.
diver, -ŭr, s. buzo, m.; colimbo, m. (ave); cortabolsas, m.
diverge, dĭvŭrj', v. n. divergir(se).
divergence, -ĕns, s. divergencia, f.
divergent, -ĕnt, a. divergente. [m. pl.
divers, dĭ'vŭrz, a. varios, diversos, muchos,
diverse, dĭ'vŭrs, a. diverso, diferente; variado; -ly, ad. diversamente.
diversion, dĭvŭr'shŭn, s. diversión, f.; pasatiempo, m. [riegación, f.
diversity, dĭvŭr'sĭtĭ, s. diversidad, f.; variedad
divert, dĭvŭrt', v. a. desviar; divertir; recrear. [despojar.
divest, dĭvĕst', v. a. desnudar; privar,
divestiture, dĭvĕs'tĭtūr, s. desarropamiento, m.
divide, dĭvīd', v. a. dividir, distribuir; desunir; -, v. n. desunirse, dividirse.
dividend, dĭ'vĭdĕnd, s. dividendo, m.

divider, dĭvī'dŭr, s. (ar.) divisor, m.; distribuidor, m.
divination, dĭvĭnā'shŭn, s. divinación, f.
divine, dĭvīn', a. divino, sublime, excelente; -, s. teólogo, m.; -, v. a. adivinar; -, v. n. presentir.
divinely, -lĕ, ad. divinamente.
diving-bell, dĭv'ĭngbĕl, s. campana de buzo, f. [natoria, f.
diving-rod, dĭv'ĭngrŏd, s. vara divinity, dĭvĭn'ĭtĭ, s. divinidad, f.; deidad, f.; teología, f. [f.
divisibility, dĭvĭzĭbĭl'ĭtĭ, s. divisibilidad,
divisible, dĭvĭz'ĭbl, a. divisible.
division, dĭvĭzh'ŭn, s. (ar.) división, f.; desunión, f.
divisor, dĭvī'zŭr, s. (ar.) divisor, m.
divorce, dĭvôrs', s. divorcio, m.; -, v. a. divorciar.
divulge, dĭvŭlj', v. a. divulgar, publicar.
dizziness, dĭz'zĭnĕs, s. vértigo, m.; ligereza, f.
dizzy, dĭz'zĕ, a. vertiginoso; ligero.
do, dō, v. a. hacer, ejecutar, obrar; finalizar; despachar; dejar algún empeño; cocer; -, v. n. comportarse; estar; - [de gracia] [apacible.
docible, dŏs'ĭbl, docile, dŏs'ĭl, a. dócil,
docility, dŏsĭl'ĭtĭ, s. docilidad, f.
dock, dŏk, s. bardana, f.; lampazo, m.; trozo, m.; (rail.) dock, m.; (mar.) dique, m.; atarazana, f.; -, v. a. descolar; cortar. [-, v. a. rotular.
docket, -ĕt, s. rótulo, m.; extracto, m.;
dockyard, -yârd, s. (mar.) astillero, m.
doctor, dŏk'tŭr, s. doctor, m.; médico, m.; -, v. a. medicinar.
doctoress, -ĕs, s. doctora, f. [mático,
doctrinal, dŏk'trĭnăl, a. doctrinal, dog-
doctrine, dŏk'trĭn, s. doctrina, erudición, f.; ciencia, f. [precepto, m.
document, dŏk'ūmĕnt, s. documento, m.;
documentary, dŏkūmĕn'tărĕ, a. documental.
dodge, dŏj, v. a. trampear, entrampar.
dodger, -ŭr, s. trampista, m.
doe, dō, s. gama, f.; --rabbit, coneja, f.
dog, dŏg, s. perro, m.; -, v. a. cazar con perros; espiar.
dog-cheap, -tshēp, a. muy barato.
dog-days, -dāz, s. pl. días caniculares, m. pl. [m.
doge, dŏj, s. dux (de Venecia y Génova),
dog-fish, dŏg'fĭsh, s. tiburón, m.
dogged, dŏg'gĕd, a. ceñudo, intratable, áspero, brutal; -ly, ad. con ceño.
doggedness, -nĕs, s. ceño, m.; mohina, bronquedad, f. [de versos).
doggerel, dŏg'grĕl, a. vil, bajo (hablando
dog-hole, dŏg'hōl, dog-kennel, -kĕnnĕl, s. perrera, f.
dog-latin, -lătĭn, s. latín bárbaro, m.
dogmatic(al), dŏgmăt'ĭk(ăl), a. dogmático; -ly, ad. dogmáticamente.
dog-rose, dŏg'rōs, s. rosa silvestre, f.
dog's-ear, -s ēr, s. pliegue en los ángulos de la hoja de un libro, m.
Dog-star, -stăr, s. Sirio, m.; canícula, f.

doings, *dŏ'ĭngs,* s. pl. hechos, m. pl.; acciones, f. pl.; eventos, m. pl.

doldrums, *dŏl'drŭms,* s. pl. mal humor, m.; vientos bonancibles del Ecuador, m. pl. (mar.)

dole, *dōl,* s. distribución, f.; porción, f.; limosna, f.; —, v. a. repartir, distribuir.

doleful, *–fŭl,* a. doloroso, lúgubre, triste.

doll, *dŏll,* s. muñeca, f.

dollar, *dŏl'lăr,* s. escudo americano, m.; peso, m. (moneda de España).

dollman, *dŏl'măn,* s. dolimán, m.

dolomite, *dŏl'ŏmĭt,* s. dolomita, f. (min.)

dolour, *dŏ'lŭr,* s. dolor, pesar, m., dolencia, f.

dolphin, *dŏl'fĭn,* s. delfín, m. [cia, f.

dolt, *dŏlt,* s. hombre bobo, m.

domain, *dŏmān',* s. dominio, m.

dome, *dōm,* s. cúpula, f.

domestic, *dŏmĕs'tĭk,* a. doméstico, intestino.

domesticate, *–āt,* v. a. domesticar.

domestication, *dŏmĕstĭkā'shŭn,* s. domesticación, f.

domesticity, *dŏmĕstĭс'ĭtĭ,* s. domesticidad, f.

domicile, *dŏm'ĭsĭl,* s. domicilio, m.

domiciliary, *dŏmĭsĭl'ĭărĭ,* a. domiciliario; – visit, *vĭzĭt,* s. (law) visita judicial de la habitación de alguno como indagación, f.

dominate, *dŏm'ĭnāt,* v. n. dominar, predominar. [f.; imperio, m.

domination, *dŏmĭnā'shŭn,* s. dominación, f.

domineer, *dŏmĭnēr',* v. n. dominar, señorear.

dominie, *dŏm'ĭnĭ,* s. (vulg.) cura, m.

dominion, *dŏmĭn'yăn,* s. dominio, territorio, m.; soberanía, f.

domino, *dŏm'ĭnō,* s. dominó, m., traje de máscara; –es, pl. dominó (juego).

don, *dŏn,* v. a. meter el vestido.

donate, *dōnāt',* v. a. donar.

donation, *dōnā'shŭn,* s. donación, f.

done, *dŭn,* p. & a. hecho; cocido, asado.

donkey, *dŏng'kĕ,* s. asno, borrico, m.; ––engine, *ĕnjĭn,* s. secunda máquina de los vapores, f.

donor, *dō'nŏr,* s. donador, m. [m.

doodle, *dō'dl,* s. (vulg.) haragán, holgazán, m.

doom, *dōm,* s. sentencia, f.; condena, f.; suerte, f.; –, v. a. sentenciar, juzgar, condenar. [sal, m.

doomsday, *–s'dā,* s. día del juicio universal.

door, *dŏr,* s. puerta, f.; within –s, en casa.

door-keeper, *–kēpăr,* s. portero, m.

door-plate, *–plāt,* s. planchuela, f.

door-way, *–wā,* s. portada, f.

dormant, *dŏr'mănt,* a. durmiente; secreto.

dormer-window, *dŏr'mărwĭndō,* s. lumbrera, f.

dormitory, *dŏr'mĭtărĭ,* s. dormitorio, m.

dormouse, *dŏr'mŏus,* s. lirón, m.

dorsal, *dŏr'săl,* a. dorsal.

dose, *dōs,* s. dosis, porción, f.; –, v. a. disponer la dosis de un remedio.

dot, *dŏt,* s. tilde, m.; –, v. a. tildar.

dotage, *dō'tĭj,* s. chochera, chochez, f.; cariño excesivo, m.

dotard, *dō'tărd,* s. viejo que chochea, m.

dotation, *dōtā'shŭn,* s. dotación, f.

dote, *dōt,* v. n. chochear.

dotingly, *dō'tĭnglă,* ad. con cariño excesivo.

double, *dŭb'l,* a. doble, duplicado; falso; –, v. a. doblar; plegar; disimular; –, s. duplo, m.; engaño, m.; artificio, m.

double-chin, *–tshĭn,* s. papada, f.

double-dealing, *–dēlĭng,* s. duplicidad, f.

double-edged, *–ĕjd,* a. con dos filas.

double-entry, *–ĕntrĕ,* s. (com.) partida doble, f.

double-faced, *–fāsd,* a. disimulado.

double-lock, *–lōk,* v. a. echar segunda vuelta á la llave. [doblado.

double-quick, *–kwĭk,* a. (mil.) á paso redoblado.

doublet, *dŭb'lĕt,* s. justillo, m.

double-tongued, *–tăngd,* a. falso.

doubloon, *dŭblōn',* s. doblón, m.

doubly, *dŭb'lĕ,* ad. doblemente.

doubt, *dŏut,* s. duda, sospecha, f.; –, v. a. & n. dudar; sospechar.

doubtful, *–fŭl,* a. dudoso, dudable; incierto; –ly, ad. dudosamente. [sin duda.

doubtless, *–lĕs,* a. indubitable; –ly, ad.

dough, *dō,* s. masa, f.

doughty, *dŏu'tĭ,* a. bravo, valeroso.

douse, *dŏus,* v. a. (& n.) zabullir(se).

dove, *dŭv,* s. paloma, f. [palomar, m.

dove-cot, *–kŏt,* s. dove-house, *–hŏus,* s.

dovelike, *–lĭk,* a. columbino, inocente.

dove-tail, *–tāl,* s. cola de milano, f.

dowager, *dŏu'ăjăr,* s. viuda de calidad que goza viudedad de su marido, f.

dowdy, *dŏu'dĕ,* s. mujer desaliñada, f.

dower, *dŏu'ăr,* s. dote, viudedad, f.; dotación, f.

dowered, *–d,* a. dotado. [ción, f.

down, *dŏun,* s. plumón, m.; flojel, m.; –, pr. abajo; en el suelo; to sit –, sentarse; upside –, lo de arriba abajo; up and –, acá y acullá. [bajo.

downcast, *–kăst,* a. apesadumbrado, cabizbajo.

downfall, *–făl,* s. ruina, decadencia, f.

down-hill, *–hĭl,* s. declivio, m.

downright, *–rīt,* a. patente, manifiesto; –, ad. á plomo.

down-train, *–trān,* s. (rail.) tren descendente, m., el que desde la capital marcha en dirección de otro punto lejano.

downward, *–wărd,* a. inclinado; cabizbajo, triste; –(s), ad. hacia abajo.

downy, *–ĕ,* a. velloso; suave. [dormitar.

doze, *dōz,* s. atontar, entorpecer; –, v. n.

dozen, *dŭz'n,* s. docena, f.

doziness, *dō'zĭnĕs,* s. somnolencia, f.

dozy, *dō'zĕ,* a. soñoliento.

drab, *drăb,* s. paño castaño, m.; mujercilla, f.; –, a. de color entre gris y moreno.

drachm, *drăm,* s. dracma, f.

draft, *drăft,* s. dibujo, m.; letra de cambio, f.; –, v. a. dibujar; (mil.) destacar.

drag, *drăg,* v. a. arrastrar; tirar con fuerza; –, v. n. arrastrar por el suelo; –, s. carretilla, f.; instrumento con garfio ó gancho, m.

draggle, *–gl,* v. a. emporcar alguna cosa arrastrandola por el suelo; –, v. n. ensuciarse alguna cosa por llevarla arrastrando.

drag-net, *–nĕt,* s. red barredera, f.

dragoman, *drā'gŏmăn,* s. dragomán, m.

dragon, _drăg'ŏn,_ s. dragón, m.
dragon-fly, _-flî,_ s. libélula, f.
dragoon, _drăgŏn',_ s. (mil.) dragón, m.
drain, _drăn,_ v. a. desaguar; secar; —, s. desaguadero, m.; (mar.) colador, m.
drainage, _-dj,_ s. desagüe, m.; derramamiento, m.
drake, _drăk,_ s. ánade macho, m.
dram, _drăm,_ s. dracma, f.; porción de licor que se bebe de una vez, f.; —, v. n. beber aguardiente.
drama, _drä'mä,_ s. drama, m.
dramatic(al), _drămăt'ĭk(ăl),_ a. dramático; **-ally,** ad. dramáticamente.
dramatist, _drăm'ătĭst,_ s. dramático, m.
dramatize, _drăm'ătĭz,_ v. a. dramatizar.
drape, _drăp,_ v. a. trapear.
draper, _-ăr,_ s. pañero, m.
drapery, _-ĕ,_ s. manufactura de paños, f.; ropaje, m.
drastic, _drăs'tĭk,_ a. (med.) drástico.
draught, _drăft,_ s. trago, m.; porción de cualquier licor que se bebe de una vez, f.; bebida medicinal, f.; dibujo, m.; letra de cambio, f.; libranza, f.
draught-board, _-bŏrd,_ s. tablero, m.
draught-horse, _-hŏrs,_ s. caballo de tiro, m. [m.
draughts, _-s,_ s. pl. juego de las damas,
draughty, _drăf'tĕ,_ a. expuesto al aire colado.
draw, _drä,_ v. a. tirar, traer; atraer; arrastrar; dibujar; librar una letra de cambio; **to — nigh,** acercarse; —, v. n. tirar; encogerse; moverse.
drawback, _-băk,_ s. draubac, m., restitución de los derechos al tiempo de exportar los géneros.
draw-bridge, _-brĭj,_ s. puente levadizo.
drawer, _-ăr,_ s. aguador, m.; mozo de taberna, m.; gaveta, f.; **-s,** pl. calzoncillos.
drawing, _-ĭng,_ s. dibujo, m. [m. pl.
drawing-board, _-ĭngbŏrd,_ s. tabla para dibujar, f.
drawing-room, _-ĭngrŏm,_ s. sala de palacio, f.; sala principal de alguna casa, f.; recepción en la corte, f.
drawl, _drăl,_ v. n. hablar con pesadez.
draw-well, _-wĕl,_ s. pozo hondo, m.
dray-(cart, _drä'(kărt),_ s. carromato, m.
dray-man, _-măn,_ s. carromatero, m.
dread, _drĕd,_ s. miedo, terror, espanto, m.; —, a. terrible; —, v. a. & n. espantar; temer.
dreadful, _-fŭl,_ a. terrible, espantoso; **-ly,** ad. terriblemente.
dream, _drēm,_ s. sueño, m.; fantasía, f.; —, v. n. soñar; imaginar. [m.
dreaminess, _drē'mĭnĕs,_ s. sopor, letargo.
dreamy, _-ĕ,_ a. quimérico, fabuloso.
drearily, _drē'rĭlĕ,_ ad. espantosamente, tristemente.
dreary, _drē'rĕ,_ a. espantoso, triste.
dredge, _drĕj,_ v. a. (mar.) rastrear con el rezón.
dredger, _-ăr,_ s. pescador de ostras, m.
dredging-machine, _drĕj'ĭngmăshĕn,_ s. máquina para limpiar un río, estanque &c., f.
dregs, _drĕgs,_ s. pl. heces, f.; morralla, f.

drench, _drĕnsh,_ v. a. empapar, humedecer; abrevar; —, s. bebida purgante (para ciertos animales), f.
dress, _drĕs,_ v. a. vestir, ataviar; curar las heridas; almohazar; ajustar; cocinar; podar las vides; —, v. n. vestirse; —, s. vestido, m.; atavío, tocado, m.
dresser, _-săr,_ s. mozo de cámara, m.; mesa de cocina, f.; aparador, m.
dressing, _-sĭng,_ s. curación, f.; adorno, m.; cultivo de tierra labrantía, m.
dressing-gown, _-sĭnggŏŭn,_ s. peinador, m.; bata, f. [tocador, m.
dressing-room, _-sĭngrŏm,_ s. gabinete-
dressing-table, _-sĭngtăbl,_ s. tocador, m.
dressy, _-sĕ,_ a. aficionado á ataviarse.
dribble, _drĭb'bl,_ v. n. hacer caer gota á gota; —, v. n. gotear.
dribblet, _drĭb'lĕt,_ s. deuda pequeña, f.
drift, _drĭft,_ s. impulso, m.; tempestad, f.; montón, m.; objeto de discurso, m.; designio, m.; manejo, m.; (mar.) deriva, f.; **— of ice,** hielo flotante, m.; **— of sand,** arena movediza, f.; **— of snow,** nevada con ventisca, f.; —, v. a. impeler; amontonar; —, v. n. formar en montones.
drift-wood, _-wŭd,_ s. leña acarreada por el agua, f.
drill, _drĭl,_ s. taladro, m.; terraja, f.; (mil.) instrucción de reclutas, f.; —, v. a. taladrar; (mil.) disciplinar reclutas.
drink, _drĭngk,_ v. a. & n. beber, embeber, absorber; embriagarse; —, s. bebida, f.
drinkable, _-ăbl,_ a. potable.
drinking-bout, _-ĭngbŏŭt,_ s. borrachera, f.
drip, _drĭp,_ v. a. despedir algún líquido á gotas; —, v. n. gotear, destilar; —, s. gotilla, f.
dripping, _-pĭng,_ s. pringue, m. & f.
dripping-pan, _-pĭngpăn,_ s. grasera, f.
drive, _drĭv,_ v. a. & n. impeler; guiar, conducir (algún carruaje); llevar, torzar á; reducir á; andar en coche; **to — at,** tener puesta la mira en; —, s. paseo en coche, m.
drivel, _drĭv'l,_ s. baba, f.; —, v. n. babear.
driver, _drĭv'ăr,_ s. empujador, m.; cochero, m.; carretero, m.; boyero &c., m.; (am.) inspector de esclavos, m.
drizzle, _drĭz'l,_ v. n. gotear; lloviznar. [f.
drizzling-rain, _drĭz'lĭngrăn,_ s. llovizna,
droll, _drŏl,_ a. jocoso, facecioso; gracioso; —, s. bufón, m.; **-y,** ad. jocosamente.
drollery, _-ărĕ,_ s. bufonería, bufonada, farsa, f.
dromedary, _drăm'ĕdărĕ,_ s. dromedario, m.; (cant) ladrón desmañado, m.
drone, _drŏn,_ s. zángano de colmena, m.; haragán, m.; —, v. n. zanganear; dar un sonido sordo. [sumirse; desfallecer.
droop, _drŏp,_ v. n. descaecer; penar, con-
drooping, _-ĭng,_ a. lánguido.
drop, _drŏp,_ s. gota, f.; pendiente con diamantes pequeños, m.; by **-s,** gota á gota; **:—,** v. a. destilar; soltar; cesar; dejar; —, v. n. gotear; morir de repente; desvanecerse; sobrevenir.
drops, _drŏps,_ s. (rail.) plano inclinado, m.
drop-scene, _drŏp'sĕn,_ s. telón de foro, m.
dropsical, _-sĭkăl,_ a. hidrópico.

dropsy, _sĕ, s. hidropesía, f.
dross, dròs, s. escoria de metales, f.; hez, f.
drought, dròйt, s. seca, f.; sequedad, f.; sed, f.
drove, dròv, s. manada, f.; hato, m.; muchedumbre de gente, f.
drover, _àr, s. ganadero, m.
drown, dròйn, v. a. anegar; eumergir; —, v. n. anegarse. [lentamente.
drowsily, dròй'zĭlĕ, ad. soñolientamente;
drowsiness, dròй'zĭnĕs, s. somnolencia, pereza, indolencia, f.
drowsy, dròй'zĕ, a. soñoliento; estúpido.
drub, dròb, s. golpe, m., puñada, f.; —, v. a. apalear, sacudir.
drudge, dròj, v. n. afanarse; —, s. ganapán, m.; yunque, esclavo, m.
drudgery, _àrĕ, s. trabajo vil, m.
drudgingly, _ĭnglĕ, ad. trabajosamente.
drug, dròg, s. droga, f.; frusleria, f.; —, v. a. sazonar ó mezclar con drogas.
drugget, _gĕt, s. droguete, m.
druggist, _gĭst, s. droguero, m.
drum, dròm, s. tambor, m.; tímpano (del oído), m.; —, v. n. tocar el tambor; (am.) atraer parroquianos. [m.
drum-head, _hĕd, s. parche del tambor,
drum-major, _mājàr, s. tambor mayor, m.
drummer, _màr, s. tambor, m.; (am.) el que atrae parroquianos.
drumming, _mĭnĕ, s. toque del tambor, m.
drum-stick, _stĭk, s. palillo de tambor, m.
drunk, dròngk, a. borracho, ebrio, embriagado. [el que bebe mucho.
drunkard, _àrd, s. borrachón, cuero, m.;
drunken, _n, a. ebrio. [borrachera, f.
drunkenness, _n'nĕs, s. embriaguez, f.;
dry, drĭ, a. árido, seco; sediento; frío; insípido; —, v. a. secar; enjugar; —, v. n. secarse, enjugarse.
dry-goods, _gйds, s. pl. géneros que se venden al una ó al corte, m. pl. [m.
drying-lines, _ĭnglĭnz, s. pl. tendedero,
dryly, _lĕ, ad. secamente, fríamente; estérilmente. [estilo, f.
dryness, _nĕs, s. sequedad, f.; aridez de
drynurse, _màrs, s. ama que alimenta á un niño sin darle de mamar, f.; —, v. a. criar á un niño sin darle de mamar.
dry-rot, _ròt, s. podre, m. & f., podredumbre, f. [pies secos.
dry-shod, _shòd, a. á pie enjuto, con los
dual, dй'àl, s. binario, m.
dub, dòb, v. n. armar á alguno caballero.
dubious, dй'bĭàs, a. dudoso; —ly, ad. dudosamente. [dosamente.
ducal, dй'kàl, a. ducal.
ducat, dйk'àt, s. ducado, m.
duchess, dйtsh'ĕs, s. duquesa, f.
duchy, dйtsh'ĕ, s. ducado, m.
duck, dòk, s. ánade, m. & f.; tela para velas, f.; mona, querida, f. (voz de cariño); —, v. n. (& n.) zabullir(se).
duckling, _lĭnĕ, s. anadeja, f.
duckweed, _wĕd, s. lenteja acuática, f.
ductile, dйk'tĭl, a. dúctil, flexible; tratable.
ductility, dйktĭl'ĭtĕ, s. ductilidad, f.; docilidad, f.
dudgeon, dйj'òn, s. ojeriza, malicia, f.
duds, dйds, s. pl. atavío, m.

due, dй, a. debido, apto; —, ad. exactamente; —, s. derecho, m.; tributo, impuesto, m. [en duelo.
duel, dй'ĕl, s. duelo, m.; —, v. n. combatir
duellist, _lĭst, s. duelista, m.
duet, dй'ĕt, s. (mus.) dúo, m.
duffer, dйf'fàr, s. (vulg.) ropavejero, m.;
dug, dйg, s. teta, f. [embustero, m.
dug-out, _dйt, s. (am.) piragua, f.
duke, dйk, s. duque, m.
dukedom, _dàm, s. ducado, m.
dulcimer, dйl'sĭmàr, s. (mus.) tímpano, m.
dull, dйl, a. lerdo, estúpido; insípido; obtuso; tosco; triste, murrio; opaco; — of hearing, algo sordo; —, v. a. entontecer; obstruir; contristar; ofuscar; —y, ad. estúpidamente; lentamente.
dullard, _làrd, s. estólido, m.
dulness, _nĕs, s. estupidez, torpeza, f.; somnolencia, f.; pereza, f.; pesadez, f.
duly, dй'lĕ, ad. debidamente; puntualmente.
dumb, dàm, a. mudo; —ly, ad. sin chistar.
dumb-bell, _bĕl, s. halterio, m.
dumbfound, _fòйnd, v. a. confundir; enmudecer.
dumbness, _nĕs, s. mudez, f.; silencio, m.
dumb-show, _shò, s. pantomimo, m.
dumb-waiter, _wàtàr, s. mesita giratoria, mesa de servicio, f.
dummy, dàm'mĕ, s. (vulg.) mudo, m.; espantajo, m.; maniquí, m.
dump, dàmp, s. murria, tristeza, f.
dumpling, _lĭnĕ, s. bola de pasta, f.
dumpy, _ĕ, a. gordo, rollizo.
dun, dàn, a. bruno; sombrío; —, s. acreedor importuno, m.; —, v. a. pedir un acreedor á su deudor con importunidad.
dunce, dàns, s. zote, zopenco, m.
dune, dàn, s. mégano, m., duna, f.
dung, dàng, s. estiércol, m.; —, v. a. estercolar.
dungeon, dàn'jàn, s. calabozo, m.
dung-hill, dàng'hĭl, s. estercolero, m.
duodécimo, dйòdĕs'ĭmò, s. libro en dozavo, m. [embaucar.
dupe, dйp, s. bobo, m.; —, v. a. engañar,
duplicate, dй'plĭkàt, s. duplicado, m.; copia, f.; —check, tshĕk, s. (rail.) talón, m.
duplicity, dйplĭs'ĭtĕ, s. doblez, duplicidad, f. [f.
durability, dйràbĭl'ĭtĕ, s. dura, duración, f.
durable, dй'ràbl, a. durable, duradero; —bly, ad. duraderamente.
durance, dй'ràns, s. cautividad, f.
duration, dйrà'shàn, s. duración, f.
during, dй'rĭng, pr. mientras, durante el tiempo que.
dusk, dàsk, a. obscurecido, fusco; —, s. color fusco, m.; crepúsculo, m.; —, v. a. obscurecer; —, v. n. hacerse noche.
duskily, dàsk'ĭlĕ, ad. obscuramente.
duskiness, _ĭnĕs, s. principio de la obscuridad, f.
dusky, dàsk'ĕ, a. obscuro. [curidad, m.
dust, dàst, s. polvo, m.; —, v. a. despolvorear; llenar de polvo.
dust-cart, _kàrt, s. carro de basura, m.
duster, _àr, s. rodilla, f.
dustman, _màn, s. basurero, m.

dust-shot, *–shŏt,* s. cendra, escoria de plomo, f.

dusty, *–ĕ,* a. polvoriento.

dutch courage, *dätsh kŭr'ĕj,* s. valor fingido, m.

duteous, *dū'tĕŭs,* a. fiel, leal.

dutiful, *dū'tĭfŭl,* a. obediente, sumiso; respetoso; **–ly,** ad. obedientemente, respetosamente.

dutifulness, *–nĕs,* s. obediencia, f.; respeto, homenaje, m.

duty, *dū'tĕ,* s. deber, m.; obligación, f.; respeto, homenaje, m.; (mil.) facción, f.; aduana, f., derechos de aduanas, m. pl.

dwarf, *dwärf,* s. enano, m.; enana, f.; **–,** v. a. impedir que alguna cosa llegue á su tamaño natural.

dwarfish, *–ĭsh,* a. enano, pequeño.

dwell, *dwĕl,* v. n. habitar, morar; dilatarse.

dwelling, *–lĭng,* s. habitación, f.; domicilio, m. [nuirse: degenerar; consumirse.

dwindle, *dwĭn'dl,* v. n. mermar, dismi-

dye, *dī,* v. a. teñir; **–,** s. tinte, m.

dyer, *–ŭr,* s. tintorero, m.

dye(e)ing, *–ĭng,* s. tintorería, f.; tintura, f.

dye-works, *–wärks,* s. pl. taller del tintorero, m. [bundo; **–,** s. muerte, f.

dying, *–ĭng,* p. & a. agonizante, moribundo; **–,** s. muerte, f.

dynamics, *dīnäm'ĭks,* s. dinámica, f.

dynamite, *dīn'ămĭt,* s. dinamita, f.

dynamiter, *–tŭr,* s. dinamitista, m.

dynamo, *dīnăm'ō,* s. dínamo, m., máquina generatriz de las corrientes eléctricas, f.

dynasty, *dīn'ăstĕ,* s. dinastía, f.

dysentery, *dĭs'ĕntŭrĕ,* s. disentería, f.

dyspepsia, *dĭspĕp'sĭä,* s. (med.) dispepsia, f.

dyspeptic, *dĭspĕp'tĭk* a. dispéptico. [f.

E.

each, *ĕtsh,* pn. cualquiera; cada uno; **– other,** unos á otros, mutuamente.

eager, *ē'gŭr,* a. deseoso; fogoso; ardiente, vehemente; **–ly,** ad. vehementemente, ardientemente. [hemencia, f.; ardor, m.

eagerness, *–nĕs,* s. ansia, f.; anhelo, m.; vehemencia, f.; ardor, m.

eagle, *ē'gl,* s. águila; moneda de oro (= 10 dollars), f.

eagle-eyed, *–īd,* a. de vista lince.

eaglet, *ē'glĕt,* s. aguilucho, m.

ear, *ēr,* s. oreja, f.; oído, m.; asa, f.; espiga, f.; by **–,** de oreja; **–,** v. n. espigar.

ear-ache, *–āk,* s. dolor de oídos, m.

earl, *ŭrl,* s. conde, m.

ear-lap, *ēr'läp,* s. punta de la oreja, f.

earldom, *ŭrl'dŭm,* s. condado, m.

earliness, *ŭr'lĭnĕs,* s. precocidad, f.; presteza, prontitud, f. [prano.

early, *ŭr'lĕ,* a. temprano, presto; **–,** ad. temprano.

earn, *ŭrn,* v. a. ganar, obtener, conseguir.

earnest, *ŭr'nĕst,* a. ardiente, fervoroso, serio, importante; **–,** s. seriedad, f.; estrena, f.; señal, f.; esperanza, f.; prueba, f.; in good **–,** de buena fe, ; **–ly,** ad. seriamente; ansiosamente.

earnest-money, *–mŭnĕ,* s. caparra, f.

earnestness, *–nĕs,* s. ansia, f.; ardor, celo, m.; seriedad, vehemencia, f.

ear-ring, *ēr'rĭng,* s. zarcillo, pendiente, m.

earth, *ŭrth,* s. tierra, f.; terrestre, m.; **–,** v. a. enterrar; **–,** v. n. retirarse debajo de tierra.

earth-born, *–bŏrn,* a. de bajo nacimiento; terrestre.

earthen, *–n,* a. terreno; hecho de tierra.

earthenware, *–nwăr,* s. loza de barro, f.

earthiness, *–ĭnĕs,* s. terrenidad; grosería, f.

earthliness, *–lĭnĕs,* s. vanidad mundana, f.

earthly, *–lĕ,* a. terrestre, mundano; sensual.

earthquake, *–kwāk,* s. terremoto, m.

earthwork, *–wärk,* s. (mil.) fuerte de tierra, m.

earth-worm, *–wŭrm,* s. lombriz, f.

ear-trumpet, *ēr'trŭmpĕt,* s. trompetilla, f.

ear-wig, *–wĭg,* s. soplón, m. [m.

ear-witness, *–wĭtnĕs,* s. testigo de oídos, m.

ease, *ēz,* s. quietud, f.; reposo, ocio, m.; comodidad, f.; facilidad, f.; at **–,** con desahogo; **–,** v. a. aliviar; mitigar.

easel, *ē'zl,* s. caballete (de los pintores), m.

easement, *ēz'mĕnt,* s. alivio, apoyo, m.; ventaja, f.

easily, *ē'zĭlĕ,* ad. fácilmente; quietamente.

easiness, *ē'zĭnĕs,* s. condescendencia, f.

east, *ēst,* s. oriente, f.; este, m.

Easter, *–tŭr,* s. Pascua de resurrección, f.; **– Eve,** Sábado santo, m.

easterly, *–tŭrlĕ,* eastern, *–tŭrn,* a. oriental.

eastward, *–wărd,* ad. hacia el oriente.

easy, *ē'zĕ,* a. fácil; cortés, sociable; cómodo, pronto; libre; tranquilo, aliviado; **– going,** inalterable, sereno.

eat, *ēt,* v. a. comer; roer; **–,** v. n. alimentarse.

eatable, *–äbl,* a. comestible; **–s,** s. pl. víveres, m. pl. [tible, f.

eatableness, *–nĕs,* s. calidad de lo comestible, f.

eating-house, *–ĭnghŏŭs,* s. bodegón, m.;

eaves, *ēvz,* s. pl. socarrén, m. [hostería, f.

eaves-drop, *–drŏp,* v. a. escuchar á la ventana lo que se habla dentro de la casa.

ebb, *ĕb,* s. menguante, f.; decremento, m.; **–,** v. n. menguar; decaer, disminuir.

ebon, *ĕb'ŏn,* a. de ébano; negro.

ebony, *ĕb'ŏnĕ,* s. ébano, m.; **to deal in –,** comerciar en negros. [mentación, f.

ebullition, *ĕbŭlĭsh'ŭn,* s. ebullición, fermentación, f.

eccentric(al), *ĕksĕn'trĭk(äl),* a. excéntrico.

eccentricity, *ĕksĕntrĭs'ĭtĕ,* s. excentricidad, f. [tico, m.

ecclesiastic, *ĕkklēzĭäs'tĭk,* a. & s. eclesiástico, m.

echo, *ĕk'ō,* s. eco, m.; **–,** v. n. resonar; **–,** v. a. repercutir (la voz).

eclectic, *ĕklĕk'tĭk,* a. ecléctico.

eclipse, *ĕklĭps',* s. eclipse, m.; **–,** v. a. eclipsar.

ecliptic, *ĕklĭp'tĭk,* s. eclíptica, f.

economic(al), *ĕkŏnŏm'ĭk(äl),* a. económico, frugal, parco, moderado.

economist, *ĕkŏn'ŏmĭst,* s. economista, m.

economise, *ĕkŏn'ŏmīz,* v. a. economizar.

economy, *ĕkŏn'ŏmĕ,* s. economía, f.; frugalidad, f.

ecstasy, *ĕk'stăsĕ,* s. éxtasi, éxtasis, m.

ecstatic(al), *ĕkstät'ĭk(äl),* a. extático; **–ally,** ad. en éxtasis.

eddy, *ĕd'dĕ,* s. reflujo de agua, m.; remolino, m.; **–,** v. n. remolinar.

edge, *ĕj,* s. filo, m.; punta, f.; esquina, f.; margen, m. & f.; acrimonia, f.; —, v. a. afilar, ribetear; introducir; —, v. n. oponerse.

edge-tool, *-tōl,* s. herramienta cortante, f.

edge-ways, *-wāz,* ad. de filo, de lado.

edging, *ĕj'ing,* s. orla, orilla, f.

edible, *ĕd'ĭbl,* a. comedero, comestible.

edict, *ĕ'dĭkt,* s. edicto, mandato, m.   [f.

edification, *ĕdĭfĭkā'shŭn,* s. edificación, f.

edifice, *ĕd'ĭfĭs,* s. edificio, m.; fábrica, f.

edify, *ĕd'ĭfĭ,* v.a. edificar; fabricar; instruir.

edit, *ĕd'ĭt,* v. a. publicar alguna obra ajena ó ser su editor.   [ción, f.; impresión, f.

edition, *ĕdĭsh'ŭn,* s. edición, f.; publica-

editor, *ĕd'ĭtŭr,* s. editor, m.

editorial, *ĕdĭtō'rĭäl,* a. editorial.

educate, *ĕd'ŭkāt,* v. a. educar; enseñar.

education, *ĕdŭkā'shŭn,* s. educación, f.

eel, *ēl,* s. anguila, f.   [crianza, f.

eel-pout, *-pōut,* s. lamprea de río, f.

eerie, *ē'rē,* a. aduendado.

efface, *ĕffās'* v. a. borrar, destruir.

effect, *ĕffĕkt'* s. efecto, m.; realidad, f.; —s, s. pl. efectos, bienes, m. pl.; —, v. a. efectuar, ejecutar.

effective, *-tĭv,* a. eficaz; efectivo; real; —ly, ad. efectivamente, en efecto; —s, s. pl. gente de guerra, f.

effectual, *ĕffĕk'tŭäl,* a. eficiente, eficaz; —ly, ad. eficazmente.   [f.

effeminacy, *ĕffĕm'ĭnäsĕ,* s. afeminación, f.

effeminate, *-mĭnāt,* v. a. afeminar, debilitar; —, v. n. afeminarse, enervarse; —, a. afeminado; —ly, ad. con afeminación.

effervesce, *ĕffŭrvĕs',* v. n. hervir, fermentar.   [hervor, m.

effervescence, *-sĕns,* s. efervescencia, f.

effete, *ĕffēt',* a. estéril.   [ad. eficazmente.

efficacious, *ĕffĭkā'shŭs,* a. eficaz; —ly,

efficacy, *ĕf'ĭkäsĕ,* s. eficacia, f.   [tud, f.

efficiency, *ĕffĭsh'ĕnsĕ,* s. eficiencia, vir-

efficient, *ĕffĭsh'ĕnt,* a. eficaz   [m.

effigy, *ĕf'ĭjĕ,* s. efigie, imagen, f. retrato,

efflorescence, *ĕfflōrĕs'ĕns,* s. eflorescencia, f.; excrecencia, f.   [nación, f.

effluvium, *ĕfflō'vĭäm,* s. efluvio, m.; ema-

effort, *ĕf'fŏrt,* s. esfuerzo, empeño, m.

effrontery, *ĕffrŭn'tärĕ,* s. descaro, m.; impudencia, desvergüenza, f.   [m.

effulgence, *ĕffŭl'jĕns,* s. esplendor, fulgor,

effulgent, *-jĕnt,* a. resplandeciente.

effusion, *ĕffū'zhŭn,* s. efusión, f.; flujo de palabras, m.

eft, *ĕft,* s. lagartija, f.

egg, *ĕg,* s. huevo, m.; **to - on,** v. a. airar.

egg-cup, *-kŭp,* s. huevera, f.

egg-flip, *-flĭp,* **--nog,** *-nŏg,* s. leche de gallina, f.

egg-shell, *-shĕl,* s. cáscara de huevo, f.

eglantine, *ĕg'läntĭn,* s. agabanzo, m.

ego(t)ism, *ĕg'ō(t)ĭzm,* s. egoísmo, m.

ego(t)ist, *ĕg'ō(t)ĭst,* s. egoísta, m.

ego(t)istical, *ĕgō(t)ĭs'tĭkäl,* a. egoístico.

egregious, *ĕgrē'jŭs,* a. egregio, famoso, excelente; —ly, ad. egregiamente.

egress, *ĕ'grĕs,* **egression,** *ĕgrĕsh'ŭn,* s. salida, f.

eiderdown, *ĕ'därdŏŭn,* s. edredón, m.; emplumado, cubrepiés, m.

eight, *āt,* a. ocho; **pieces of —,** s. pl. escudos de España, m. pl.

eighteen, *ā'tēn,* a. diez y ocho.

eighteenth, *-th,* a. décimoctavo.

eighth, *āth,* a. octavo; —ly, ad. en el octavo lugar.

eightieth, *ā'tĭĕth,* a. octogésimo.

eighty, *ā'tĭ,* a. ochenta.

either, *ē'thŭr,* pn. cualquiera, uno de dos; —, c. ó, sea, ya.   [pedir.

ejaculate, *ĕjäk'ŭlāt,* v. a. arrojar, des-

ejaculation, *ĕjäkŭlā'shŭn,* s. ejaculatoria,

eject, *ĕjĕkt',* v. a. expeler, desechar.   [f.

ejection, *ĕjĕk'shŭn,* s. expulsión, f.; (med.) evacuación, f.   [hacer crecer.

eke, *ēk,* v.a. aumentar; alargar; prolongar.

elaborate, *ĕläb'ŏrāt,* v. a. elaborar; —, a. elaborado, primoroso; —ly, ad. cuidadosamente.

elapse, *ĕläps',* v. n. pasar, correr (el tiempo).   [cursivo.

elastic(al), *ĕläs'tĭk(äl),* a. elástico; reper-

elasticity, *ĕlästĭs'ĭtĕ,* s. elasticidad, f.

elate, *ĕlāt',* a. altivo, orgulloso; —, v. a. ensoberbecer; exaltar, elevar.

elation, *ĕlā'shŭn,* s. altivez, soberbia, f.

elbow, *ĕl'bō,* s. codo; —, v. a. codear; —, v. n. formar recodos.

elbow-chair, *-tghār,* s. silla de brazos, f.

elbow-room, *-rōm,* s. anchura, f.; espacio suficiente, m.; (fig.) libertad, latitud, f.

eld, *ĕld,* s. los ancianos.   [mayor.

elder, *ĕl'dŭr,* saúco, m. (árbol); —, a.

elderly, *-lĕ,* a. de edad ya madura.

elders, *-z,* s. pl. ancianos, antepasados, m. pl.   [genitura, f.

eldership, *-shĭp,* s. ancianidad, f.; primo-

eldest, *ĕl'dĕst,* a. el, la ó lo más anciano.

eldritch, *ĕl'drĭtsh,* a. aduendado.

elect, *ĕlĕkt',* v. a. elegir; —, a. elegido, escogido.

election, *ĕlĕk'shŭn,* s. elección, f.

electioneering, *-ēr'ĭng,* s. maniobras secretas en la elección de parlamentario, m.

elective, *ĕlĕk'tĭv,* a. electivo; - attraction, afinidad química, f.; —ly, ad. electivamente.

elector, *ĕlĕk'tŭr,* s. elector, m.

electoral, *-tŭräl,* a. electoral.

electorate, *-tŏrāt,* s. electorado, m.

electric(al), *-trĭk(äl),* a. eléctrico.

electrician, *ĕlĕktrĭsh'än,* s. persona versada en la electricidad, f.

electricity, *ĕlĕktrĭs'ĭtĕ,* s. electricidad, f.

electrify, *ĕlĕk'trĭfĭ,* v. a. electrizar.

electro-gilding, *-trōgĭldĭng,* **--plating,** *-plātĭng,* s. doradura galvánica, f.

electrolize, *-lĭz,* v. a. descomponer por electricidad.

electuary, *ĕlĕk'tŭärĕ,* s. electuario, m.

eleemosinary, *ĕlēmŏz'ĭnärĕ,* a. pobre que vive de limosna, m.

elegance, *ĕl'ĕgäns,* s. elegancia, f.

elegant, *ĕl'ĕgänt,* a. elegante, delicado; —ly, ad. elegantemente.

elegiac(al), *ĕlĕjĭ'ăk(ăl)*, a. elegiaco.

elegy, *ĕl'ĕjĕ*, s. elegía, f.

element, *ĕl'ĕmĕnt*, s. elemento, m.; fundamento, m.

elemental, *ĕlĕmĕn'tăl*, elementary, *-tărĕ*, a. elemental, simple, inicial.

elephant, *ĕl'ĕfănt*, s. elefante, m.

elephantine, *ĕlĕfăn'tīn*, a. inmenso.

elevate, *ĕl'ĕvăt*, v. a. elevar, alzar, exaltar.

elevation, *ĕlĕvā'shŭn*, s. elevación, f.; altura, f.; alteza (de pensamientos), f.

eleven, *ĕlĕv'n*, a. once.

eleventh, *-th*, a. onceno, undécimo.

elf, *ĕlf*, s. duende, m.; —, v. a. enmarañar el pelo.

elfin, *-ĭn*, a. lo perteneciente á duendes.

elicit, *ĕlĭs'ĭt*, v. a. ejecutar lo ideado; sacar de; atraer

eligibility, *ĕlĭjĭbĭl'ĭtĕ*, s. elegibilidad, f.

eligible, *ĕl'ĭjĭbl*, a. elegible; deseable.

eliminate, *ĕlĭm'ĭnăt*, v. a. eliminar, descartar.

elk, *ĕlk*, s. alce, m.

ell, *ĕl*, s. ana, f.

ellipse, *ĕllĭps'*, s. (gr.) elipsis, f.; (geom.)

elliptic(al), *-ĭk(ăl)*, a. elíptico. [elipse,f.

elm, *ĕlm*, s. olmo, m. [habla.

elocution, *ĕlŏkū'shŭn*, s. elocución, f.;

elocutionist, *-ĭst*, s. profesor de declamación, m.

elongate, *ĕlŏn'găt*, v. a. alargar, apartar, alejar; —, v. n. alejarse, desviarse.

elope, *ĕlōp'*, v. n. escapar, huir, evadirse.

elopement, *-mĕnt*, s. fuga, huída, evasión, f.

eloquence, *ĕl'ŏkwĕns*, s. elocuencia, f.

eloquent, *ĕl'ŏkwĕnt*, a. elocuente; —ly, ad. elocuentemente.

else, *ĕls*, pn. otro; —, c. de otro modo ó manera; sino.

elsewhere, *-hwăr*, ad. en otra parte.

elucidate, *ĕlū'sĭdăt*, v. a. dilucidar, explicar.

elucidation, *ĕlūsĭdā'shŭn*, s. elucidación, explicación, f.

elude, *ĕlūd'*, v. a. eludir, evitar.

elusion, *ĕlū'zhŭn*, s. escapatoria, f.; fraude, artificio, m.

elusive, *-zĭv*, elusory, *-sŭrĕ*, a. artificioso, falaz.

emaciate, *ĕmāsh'ĭăt*, v. a. extenuar, adelgazar; —, v. n enflaquecer.

emaciation, *ĕmāshĭā'shŭn*, s. emaciación, f.; enflaquecimiento, m.

emanate (from), *ĕm'ănăt*, v. n. emanar.

emanation, *ĕmănā'shŭn*, s. emanación, f.; origen, m. [dar libertad.

emancipate, *ĕmăn'sĭpăt*, v. a. emancipar;

emancipation, *ĕmănsĭpā'shŭn*, s. emancipación, f.

embalm, *ĕmbăm'*, v. a. embalsamar.

embank, *ĕmbăngk'*, v. a. terraplenar.

embankment, *-mĕnt*, s. allanamiento de algún terreno añadiéndole yezones &c. m.; encajonamiento, m. [de buques), m.

embargo, *ĕmbăr'gō*, s. embargo (detención

embark, *ĕmbărk'*, v. a. embarcar.

embarkation, *ĕmbărkā'shŭn*, s. embarcación, f. [redar.

embarrass, *ĕmbăr'răs*, v.a. embarazar, en-

embarrassment, *-mĕnt*, s. embarazo, enredo, m.

embassy, *ĕm'băssĕ*, s. embajada, f.

embattle, *ĕmbăt'l*, v. a. formar en orden de batalla. [nar.

embellish, *ĕmbĕl'lĭsh*, v.a.hermosear,ador-

embellishment, *-mĕnt*, s. adorno, m.

ember-days, *ĕm'bărdăz*, s.pl. Témpora, f.

embers, *ĕm'bŭrz*, s. pl. rescoldo, m.

embezzle, *ĕmbĕz'l*, v. a. apropiarse alguna cosa ilícitamente; malgastar.

embezzlement, *-mĕnt*, s. hurto, m.

embitter, *ĕmbĭt'ŭr*, v. a. hacer amargo.

emblazon, *ĕmblā'zn*, v. a. blasonar. [m.

emblem, *ĕm'blĕm*, s. emblema, s.; esmalte,

emblematic(al), *ĕmblĕmăt'ĭk(ăl)*, a. emblemático, simbólico; [ción, f.

embodiment, *ĕmbŏd'ĭmĕnt*, s. incorpora-

embody, *ĕmbŏd'ĕ*, v. a. incorporar.

embolden, *ĕmbŏl'dn*, v. a. animar.

emboss, *ĕmbŏs'*, v. a. formar alguna cosa en relieve. [—, s. abrazo, m.

embrace, *ĕmbrās'*, v. a. abrazar; contener;

embrasure, *ĕmbrā'shŭr*, s. tronera, f.

embrocation, *ĕmbrŏkā'shŭn*, s. (med.) embrocación, f.

embroider, *ĕmbrŏĭ'dŭr*, v. a. bordar.

embroidery, *-ĕ*, s. bordado, m.; bordadura, f. [fundir.

embroil, *ĕmbrŏĭl'*, v. a. embrollar; con-

embryo, *ĕm'brĭŏ*, s. embrión, m.

emendation, *ĕmĕndā'shŭn*, s. enmienda, corrección, f.

emerald, *ĕm'ĕrăld*, s. esmeralda, f.

emerge, *ĕmĕrj'*, v. n. salir, proceder.

emergency, *-ĕnsĕ*, s. emersión, f.; emergencia; necesidad urgente, f.

emery, *ĕm'ŭrĕ*, s. esmeril, m.

emetic, *ĕmĕt'ĭk*, s. emético, vomitivo, m.

emigrant, *ĕm'ĭgrănt*, s. emigrado, m.

emigrate, *ĕm'ĭgrăt*, v. n. emigrar.

emigration, *ĕmĭgrā'shŭn*, s. emigración, f.

eminence, *ĕm'ĭnĕns*, s. altura, sumidad, f.; eminencia, excelencia, f.

eminent, *ĕm'ĭnĕnt*, a. eminente, elevado; distinguido; —ly, ad. eminentemente.

omissary, *ĕm'ĭssărĕ*, s. emisario, m.; espía,

emission, *ĕmĭsh'ăn*, s. emisión, f. [m.

emit, *ĕmĭt'*, v. a. emitir, echar de sí; arrojar, despedir.

emmet, *ĕm'mĕt*, s. hormiga, f.

emollient, *ĕmŏl'lĭĕnt*, a. emoliente; —, s. emolientes (medicamentos), m. pl.

emolument, *ĕmŏl'ŭmĕnt*, s. emolumento, provecho, m. [conmoción, f.

emotion, *ĕmŏ'shŭn*, s. agitación del ánimo,

emotional, *ĕmŏ'shŭnăl*, a. concitativo.

emperor, *ĕm'pĕrŭr*, s. emperador, m.

emphasis, *ĕm'făsĭs*, s. énfasis, m. & f.

emphasise, *ĕm'făsĭz*, v. a. hablar con énfasis.

emphatic(al), *ĕmfăt'ĭk(ăl)*, a. enfático; —ally, ad. enfáticamente.

empire, *ĕm'pīr*, s. imperio, m.

empiric, *ĕmpĭr'ĭk*, s. empírico, medicastro, m.; —al, a. empírico; —ally, ad. como un empírico.

5*

employ, *ĕmplŏī'*, v. a. emplear, ocupar; —, s. empleo, m.; ocupación, f.; oficio público, m. [m.

employer, *ĕmplŏī'ẽr*, s. amo, dueño,

employment, *—mĕnt,* s. empleo, m.; ocupación, f.

emporium, *ĕmpŏ'rĭăm,* s. emporio, m.

empower, *ĕmpŏū'ẽr,* v. a. autorizar, dar poder.

empress, *ĕm'prĕs,* s. emperatriz, f.

emptiness, *ĕm'tĭnĕs,* s. vaciedad, f.; vacuo, m.; futilidad, f.

empty, *ĕm'tĕ,* a. vacío; vano; ignorante; —, v. a. vaciar, evacuar.

empyrean, *ĕmpĭrē'ăn,* a. empíreo, celestial.

emulate, *ĕm'ŭlāt,* v. a. emular, competir; imitar.

emulation, *ĕmŭlā'shŭn,* s. emulación, f.; rivalidad, f.

emulgent, *ĕmŭl'jĕnt,* a. emulgente.

emulous, *ĕm'ŭlŭs,* a. émulo; —ly, ad. á competencia.

emulsion, *ĕmŭl'shŭn,* s. emulsión, f.

enable, *ĕnā'bl,* v. n. habilitar; poner en estado de.

enact, *ĕnăkt',* v. a. establecer, decretar.

enactment, *—mĕnt,* s. decreto, dictamen, m.

enamel, *ĕnăm'ĕl,* s. esmalte, m.; —, v. a. esmaltar.

enamour, *ĕnăm'ŭr,* v. a. enamorar.

encage, *ĕnkāj',* v. a. enjaular, encerrar.

encamp, *ĕnkămp',* v. n. acamparse.

encampment, *—mĕnt,* s. campamento, m.

encase, *ĕnkās',* v. a. encajar, encajonar.

encaustic, *ĕnkäs'tĭk,* a. encáustico; —painting, s. pintura encáustica, f.

enchain, *ĕntshān',* v. a. encadenar.

enchant, *ĕntshănt',* v. a. encantar.

enchantingly, *—ĭnglĕ,* ad. de un modo deleitoso.

enchantment, *—mĕnt,* s. encanto, m.

enchantress, *—rĕs,* s. encantadora, f.

encircle, *ĕnsŭr'kl,* v. a. cercar, circundar.

enclose, *ĕnklōz',* v. a. cercar, circunvalar, circundar; incluir. [cercado, m.

enclosure, *ĕnklō'zhŭr,* s. cercamiento, m.

encomium, *ĕnkō'mĭŭm,* s. encomio, elogio, m. [cercar; circuir.

encompass, *ĕnkăm'păs,* v. a. circundar;

encore, *ängkŏr',* ad. otra vez, de nuevo; —, v. a. pedir que un actor repita segunda vez lo que ha cantado.

encounter, *ĕnkŏūn'tŭr,* s. encuentro, m.; duelo, m.; pelea, f.; —, v. a. encontrar; —, v. n. encontrarse; combatir.

encourage, *ĕnkŭr'ĕj,* v. a. animar, alentar.

encouragement, *—mĕnt,* s. estímulo, patrocinio, m. [zar gradualmente.

encroach, *ĕnkrōtsh',* v. a. usurpar, avanzar.

encroachment, *—mĕnt,* s. usurpación, intrusión, f.

encrusted, *ĕnkrŭst'ĕd,* a. incrustado.

encumber, *ĕnkŭm'bŭr,* v. n. embarazar, cargar. [pedimento, m.

encumbrance, *—brăns,* s. embarazo, impedimento, m.

encyclical, *ĕnsĭk'lĭkăl,* a. encíclico, circular.

end, *ĕnd,* s. fin, m.; extremidad, f.; término, m.; resolución, f.; intento, m.; to the — that, para que; to no —, en vano; on —, en pie, de pie; —, v. a. matar; concluir, fenecer; —, v. n. acabarse, terminarse. [gar.

endanger, *ĕndān'jŭr,* v. a. peligrar, arriesgar.

endear, *ĕndēr',* v. a. encarecer.

endearment, *—mĕnt,* s. encarecimiento, m.

endeavour, *ĕndĕv'ŭr,* v. n. esforzarse; intentar; —, v. n. tentar; —, s. esfuerzo, m.

endemic(al), *ĕndĕm'ĭk(ăl),* a. endémico.

ending, *ĕnd'ĭng,* s. conclusión, cesación, f.; muerte, f.

endive, *ĕn'dĭv,* s. (bot.) endibia, f.

endless, *ĕnd'lĕs,* a. infinito, perpetuo; —ly, ad. sin fin, perpetuamente.

endorse, *ĕndŏrs',* v. a. endosar una letra de cambio.

endorsee, *ĕndŏrsē',* s. endosatario, m.

endorsement, *—mĕnt,* s. endoso, m. [m.

endorser, *—ŭr,* s. endosador, endosante,

endow, *ĕndŏū',* v. a. dotar á una mujer.

endowment, *—mĕnt,* s. dote, dotación, f.

endurable, *ĕndū'răbl,* a. sufrible, tolerable.

endurance, *—răns,* s. duración, f.; paciencia, f.; sufrimiento, m. [v. n. durar.

endure, *ĕndūr',* v. a. sufrir, soportar; —,

endways, *ĕnd'wāz,* **endwise,** *—wīz,* ad. de punta, derecho. [m.; diablo, m.

enemy, *ĕn'ĕmĕ,* s. enemigo, antagonista,

energetic, *ĕnŭrjĕt'ĭk,* a. enérgico, vigoroso.

energy, *ĕn'ŭrjĕ,* s. energía, fuerza, f.

enervate, *ĕnŭr'vāt,* v. a. enervar, debilitar, quitar las fuerzas.

enfeeble, *ĕnfē'bl,* v. a. debilitar, enervar.

enfilade, *ĕnfĭlād',* s. hila, hilera, f.; —, v. a. (mil.) enfilar. [rodear.

enfold, *ĕnfōld',* v. a. envolver, arrollar.

enforce, *ĕnfŏrs',* v. a. esforzar; violentar; compeler.

enforcement, *—mĕnt,* s. compulsión, coacción, f., fuerza, f.; sanción, f.; aprieto, m.

enfranchise, *ĕnfrăn'tshĭz,* v. a. franquear; naturalizar.

engage, *ĕngāj',* v. a. empeñar, obligar; halagar; ocupar; —, v. n. pelear, empeñarse.

engagement, *—mĕnt,* s. empeño, m.; combate, m.; pelea, f.; obligación, f.

engagingly, *—ĭnglĕ,* ad. de un modo halagüeño.

engender, *ĕnjĕn'dŭr,* v. a. engendrar; producir; —, v. n. producirse.

engine, *ĕn'jĭn,* s. ingenio, m.; máquina, f.; locomotora, f.; instrumento, m.

engine-driver, *—drĭvŭr,* s. conductor de una locomotora, m. [nista, m.

engineer, *—ēr',* s. ingeniero, m.; maquinista, m.

engineering, *—ĭng,* s. arte del ingeniero, f. [tallar.

engrave, *ĕngrāv',* v. a. grabar; esculpir;

engraving, *ĕngrā'vĭng,* s. grabado, m.; estampa, f. [monopolizar.

engross, *ĕngrōs',* v. n. engordar, engrosar;

engulf, *ĕngŭlf',* v. a. engolfar; engullir.

enhance, *ĕnhäns',* v. a. encarecer, levantar en alto; agravar.

enigma, ĕnĭg'mă, s. enigma, m.

enigmatical, ĕnĭgmăt'ĭkăl, a. enigmático; **-ly,** ad. enigmáticamente.

enjoin, ĕnjŏĭn', v. a. ordenar, prescribir; advertir.

enjoy, ĕnjŏĭ', v. a. gozar; poseer; **-,** v. n. vivir felizmente.

enjoyment, -mĕnt, s. goce, disfrute, m.; placer, m., fruición, f.

enlarge, ĕnlărj', v. a. engrandecer, dilatar, extender; desaprisionar; **-,** v. n. extenderse, dilatarse.

enlargement, -mĕnt, s. aumento, m., ampliación, f. soltura, f. [nar; instruir.

enlighten, ĕntlī'tn, v. a. alumbrar; ilumi-

enlightenment, -mĕnt, s. luces, f. pl.

enlist, ĕnlĭst', v. a. alistar.

enlistment, -mĕnt, s. alistamiento, m.

enliven, ĕnlīv'n, v. a. animar; avivar; alegrar; [de improviso.

enmesh, ĕnmĕsh', v. a. coger con arte ó

enmity, ĕn'mĭtĕ, s. enemistad, f.; odio, m.

ennoble, ĕnnō'bl, v. a. ennoblecer.

enormity, ĕnŏr'mĭtĕ, s. enormidad, f.; atrocidad, f. [enormemente.

enormous, -mŭs, a. enorme; **-ly,** ad.

enough, ĕnŭf', ad. bastantemente; basta; **-,** s. bastante, m.

enounce, ĕnŏuns', v. a. declarar.

enquire, ĕnkwīr', v. a. informarse, tomar informes, averiguar, inquirir.

enquiry, ĕnkwī'rĕ, s. indagación, f.

enrage, ĕnrăj', v. a. enfurecer, irritar.

enrapture, ĕnrăp'tŭr, v. a. arrebatar, entusiasmar; encantar.

enrich, ĕnrĭtsh', v. a. enriquecer; adornar.

enrichment, -mĕnt, s. enriquecimiento, m.

enrol, ĕnrŏl', v. a. registrar; arrollar.

ensconce, ĕnskŏns', v. a. (mil.) resguardar con un fortín. [reliquia.

enshrine, ĕnshrīn', v. a. guardar para

ensign, ĕn'sīn, s. (mil.) bandera, f.; abanderado, m.; (mar.) alférez, m. [m.

ensign-bearer, -bărĕr, s. abanderado.

enslave, ĕnslāv', v. a. esclavizar, cautivar.

ensnare, ĕnsnăr', v. a. entrampar; engañar.

ensue, ĕnsū', v. n. seguirse; suceder.

entablature, ĕntăb'lătŭr, s. entablamento, m. [m.; **-,** v. a. vincular.

entail, ĕntāl', s. (law) vínculo, mayorazgo,

entangle, ĕntăng'gl, v. a. enmarañar, embrollar, embarazar. [m.

entanglement, -mĕnt, s. enredo, embarazo,

enter, ĕn'tăr, v. a. entrar; admitir; registrar; empezar; **-,** v. n. entrar; empeñarse en algo; emprender, aventurar.

enterprise, -prīz, s. empresa, f.

entertain, -tăn', v. a. conversar; tratar; hospedar; mantener; entretener.

entertainer, -tăn'ăr, s. huésped, m.

entertainment, -tăn'mĕnt, s. conversación, f.; festejo, m.; mantenimiento, m.; entretenimiento, pasatiempo, m.

enthral, ĕnthrăl', v. a. oprimir, esclavizar.

enthralling, -ĭng, a. opresivo.

enthrone, ĕnthrōn', v. a. entronizar.

enthusiasm, ĕnthū'zĭăsm, s. entusiasmo, m.

enthusiast, -zĭăst, s. entusiasta, m. [m.

enthusiastic(al), ĕnthūzĭăs'tĭk(ăl), a. entusiasmado. [tar, inducir.

entice, ĕntīs', v. a. halagar, acariciar, exci-

entire, ĕntīr', a. entero, cumplido, completo, perfecto; **-ly,** ad. enteramente.

entirety, -tē, s. entereza, integridad, f.

entitle, ĕntī'tl, v. a. intitular; conferir algún derecho.

entity, ĕn'tĭtĕ, s. entidad, existencia, f.

entomb, ĕntōm', v. a. sepultar. [logo, m.

entomologist, ĕntŏmŏl'ŏgĭst, s. entomó-

entomology, -ŏjĕ, s. entomología, f.

entrails, ĕn'trălz, s. pl. entrañas, f. pl.

entrance, ĕn'trăns, s. entrada, f.; admisión, f.; principio, m. [torcer.

entrance-hall, -hăl, s. pórtico, vestíbulo.

entrance-money, -mŭnĕ, s. entrada, f.

entrap, ĕntrăp' v. a. entrampar; enredar; engañar.

entreat, ĕntrēt', v. a. rogar, suplicar. [f.

entreaty, -ĕ, s. petición, súplica, instancia,

entrust, ĕntrŭst', v. a. confiar.

entry, ĕn'trĕ, s. entrada, f. [torcer.

entwine, ĕntwīn', v. a. entrelazar, enroscar,

enumerate, ĕnū'mĕrāt, v. a. enumerar, numerar, contar una á una. [ción, f.

enumeration, ĕnŭmĕrā'shŭn, s. enumera-

enunciate, ĕnŭn'sĭāt, v. a. enunciar, declarar. [ción, f.

enunciation, ĕnŭnsĭā'shŭn, s. enuncia-

envelop, ĕnvĕl'ŏp, v. a. envolver, aforrar.

envelope, ĕnvĕlŏp', s. envolvedero, m.; cubierta, f. [sigar.

envenom, ĕnvĕn'ŏm, v. a. envenenar, atosigar.

enviable, ĕn'vĭăbl, a. envidiable.

envious, ĕn'vĭŭs, a. envidioso; **-ly,** ad. envidiosamente. [contornos, m. pl.

environs, ĕnvī'rŏnz, s. pl. vecindad, f.;

envoy, ĕn'vŏĭ, s. enviado, m.; mensajero, m.

envy, ĕn'vĕ, s. envidia, malicia, f.; **-,** v. a. envidiar.

epaulet, ĕp'ălĕt, s. (mil.) charretera, f.

ephemeral, ĕfĕm'ĕrăl, a. efímero, efímero.

epic, ĕp'ĭk, a. épico.

Epicure, ĕp'ĭkūr, s. hombre voluptuoso, m.

epicurean, ĕpĭkŭrē'ăn, a. epicúreo.

epidemic(al), ĕpĭdĕm'ĭk(ăl), a. epidémico; **-,** s. epidemia, f.

epigram, ĕp'ĭgrăm, s. epigrama, m. & f.

epigrammatic, ĕpĭgrămmăt'ĭk, a. epigramático.

epilepsy, ĕp'ĭlĕpsĕ, s. epilepsia, f.

epileptic(al), ĕpĭlĕp'tĭk(ăl), a. epiléptico.

epilogue, ĕp'ĭlŏg, s. epílogo, m.

Epiphany, ĕpĭf'ănĕ, s. Epifanía, f.

episcopacy, ĕpĭs'kŏpăsĕ, s. episcopado, m.

episcopal, ĕpĭs'kŏpăl, a. episcopal.

episcopalian, ĕpĭskŏpā'lĭăn, a. anglicano.

episode, ĕp'ĭsŏd, s. episodio, m. [m.

epistle, ĕpĭs'l, s. epístola, f.

epistolary, ĕpĭs'tŏlărĕ, a. epistolar.

epitaph, ĕp'ĭtăf, s. epitafio, m.

epithet, ĕp'ĭthĕt, s. epíteto, m. [m.

epitome, ĕpĭt'ŏmĕ, s. epítome, compendio,

epitomize, ĕpĭt'ŏmīz, v. a. epitomar, abreviar. [viar.

epoch, ĕp'ŏk, s. época, f.

equable, ĕk'wăbl, a. uniforme; **-bly,** ad. uniformemente.

equal, *e'kwŏl,* a. igual; justo; semejante; imparcial; —, s. igualdad, f.; compañero, m.; —, v. a. igualar; compensar.

equalisation, *ēkwŏlĭsā'shŭn,* s. igualamiento, m.

equalise, *ē̆a,* v. a. igualar. [dad, f.

equality, *ē̆kwŏl'tĭ,* s. igualdad, uniformidad, f.

equally, *e'kwŏllĕ,* ad. igualmente. [f.

equanimity, *ēkwănĭm'tĭ,* s. ecuanimidad, f.

equation, *ēkwā'shŭn,* s. ecuación, f.

equator, *ēkwā'tŭr,* s. ecuador, m.

equatorial, *ēkwătō'rĭăl,* a. ecuatorial, ecuatorio. [m.; establo, m.

equerry, *ēk'wĕrrĕ,* s. caballerizo del rey,

equestrian, *ēkwĕs'trĭăn,* a. ecuestre; — performer, s. diestro en caballos, m.

equilateral, *ēkwĭlăt'ĕrăl,* a. equilátero.

equilibrist, *ēkwĭl'ĭbrĭst,* s. equilibrista, m.

equilibrium, *ēkwĭlĭb'rĭăm,* s. equilibrio,

equine, *e'kwĭn,* a. caballar. [m.

equinoctial, *ēkwĭnŏk'shăl,* a. equinoccial.

equinox, *e'kwĭnŏks,* s. equinoccio, m.

equip, *ēkwĭp',* v. a. equipar, pertrechar; aprestar un navío. [carroza, f.

equipage, *ēk'wĭpăj,* s. equipaje, tren, m.

equipment, *ēkwĭp'mĕnt,* s. equipaje, m.; apresto, m.

equipoise, *e'kwĭpŏĕz,* s. equilibrio, m.

equitable, *ēk'wĭtăbl,* a. equitativo, imparcial; -bly, ad. equitativamente.

equity, *ēk'wĭtĭ,* s. equidad, justicia, imparcialidad, f. [lente (m.).

equivalent, *ēkwĭv'ălĕnt,* a. & s. equivalente.

equivocal, *—ōkăl,* a. equívoco, ambiguo; -ly, ad. equivocadamente, ambiguamente.

equivocate, *—ōkāt,* v. a. equivocar, usar equívocos. [m.; anfibología, f.

equivocation, *ēkwĭvōkā'shŭn,* s. equívoco,

era, *e'rā,* s. era, data determinada, f.

eradicate, *ērăd'ĭkāt,* v. a. desarraigar, extirpar. [f.

eradication, *ērădĭkā'shŭn,* s. extirpación, f.

erase, *ērās',* v. a. cancelar, rayar.

eraser, *—ŭr,* s. raspador, m.; rascador, m.

erasure, *ērā'shŭr,* s. rascadura, f.

ere, *ār,* ad. antes, más, pronto, antes que.

erect, *ērĕkt',* v. a. erigir; establecer; —, a. derecho, levantado hacia arriba.

erection, *ērĕk'shŭn,* s. establecimiento, m.

ermine, *ŭr'mĭn,* s. armiño, m.

erotic, *ērŏt'ĭk,* a. erótico.

err, *ŭr,* v. n. vagar, errar; desviarse.

errand, *ĕr'rănd,* s. recado, mensaje, m.

errand-boy, *—bŏĕ,* s. mozo de mandados, m.

errant, *ĕr'rănt,* a. errante; vagabundo.

errantry, *—rĕ,* s. vida errante, f.; caballería andante, f.

errata, *ărrā'tă,* s. pl. fe de erratas, f.

erratic, *ărrăt'ĭk,* a. errático, errante; irre**erring,** *ŭr'rĭng,* a. errado, errante. [gular.

erroneous, *ărrō'nĭŭs,* a. erróneo; falso; -ly, ad. erróneamente. [errada, f.

error, *ŭr'rŭr,* s. error, yerro, m.; dirección

eructation, *ērŭktā'shŭn,* s. eructación, f.;

erudite, *ĕr'ŏdĭt,* a. erudito. [eructo, m.

erudition, *ērŏdĭsh'ŭn,* s. erudición, f.; doctrina, f.

eruption, *ērŭp'shŭn,* s. erupción, f.; excursión hostil, f.

erysipelas, *ērĭsĭp'ĕlăs,* s. erisipela, f.

escalade, *ēskălād',* s. escalada, f.

escape, *ēskāp',* v. a. evitar; escapar; —, v. n. evadirse, salvarse; —, s. escapada, huída, fuga, f.; inadvertencia, f.; to make one's —, poner pies en polvorosa. [m.

escarpment, *ēskărp'mĕnt,* s. (mil.) escarpe,

eschalot, *ēshălŏt',* s. (bot.) chalote, m.

escheat, *ĕstshēt',* s. desherencia, f.; provecho inesperado, m.; —, v. n. caer en devolución, devolverse.

eschew, *ĕstshŏ',* v. a. huir, evitar, evadir.

escort, *ĕs'kŏrt,* s. escolta, f.; —, *ĕskŏrt',* v. a. escoltar, convoyar. [medero, (m.)

esculant, *ĕs'kŭlĕnt,* a. & s. comestible; co**escutcheon,** *ēskŭtsh'ŭn,* s. escudo, m.

esoteric, *ĕsōtĕr'ĭk,* a. esotérico.

especial, *ēspĕsh'ăl,* a. especial; -ly, ad. especialmente.

espial, *ēspī'ăl,* s. espionage, *ĕs'pĭŏnăj,* s. espionaje, m. [f.

esplanade, *ēsplănād',* s. (mil.) esplanada,

espousals, *ēspŏŭ'zăls,* s. pl. esponsales, m. pl.

espouse, *ēspŏŭz',* v. a. desposar. [brir.

espy, *ēspī',* v. a. espiar; percibir; descu**Esquire,** *ēskwīr',* s. Señor, m. (título).

essay, *ĕssā',* v. a. ensayar, tentar, probar; —, *ĕs'sā,* s. conato, ensayo, m.; tentativa, f.; prueba, experiencia, f.

essayist, *ĕs'sāĭst,* s. tratadista, m.

essence, *ĕs'sĕns,* s. esencia, f.; perfume, m.

essential, *ĕssĕn'shăl,* a. esencia, f.; —, a. esencial, substancial, principal; -ly, ad. esencialmente. [dar, fijar; confirmar.

establish, *ēstăb'lĭsh,* v. a. establecer, fun**establishment,** *—mĕnt,* s. establecimiento, m.; estatuto, m.; fundación, f.; institución, f. [hacienda, f.; bienes, m. pl.

estate, *ēstāt',* s. estado, m.; rango, m.;

esteem, *ēstēm',* v. a. estimar, apreciar; pensar; —, s. estima, f.; consideración, f.

esthetic(al), *ēsthĕt'ĭk(ăl),* a. estético; -s, s. pl. estética, f.

estimable, *ĕs'tĭmăbl,* a. estimable.

estimate, *ĕs'tĭmāt,* v. a. estimar, apreciar, tasar. [valuación, f.; opinión, f.

estimation, *ĕstĭmā'shŭn,* s. estimación, f.

estrange, *ēstrănj',* v. a. extrañar, apartar, enajenar.

estrangement, *—mĕnt,* s. enajenamiento, m.; extrañeza, distancia, f.

estuary, *ĕs'tŭărĕ,* s. estuario, brazo de mar, m.; desembocadura de lago ó río, f.

etch, *ĕtsh,* v. a. grabar al agua fuerte.

etching, *—ĭng,* s. grabado al agua fuerte, m.

eternal, *ētĕr'năl,* a. eterno, perpetuo, inmortal; -ly, ad. eternamente.

eternity, *ētŭr'nĭtĕ,* s. eternidad, f.

ether, *e'thŭr,* s. éter, m.

ethereal, *ēthē'rĕăl,* a. etéreo, celeste.

etherealise, *—ĭz,* v. a. eterificar.

ethic(al), *ĕth'ĭk(ăl),* a. ético; -ly, ad. má ralmente; -s, s. pl. ética, f.

etymological, *ĕtĭmŏlŏj'ĭkăl*, a. etimológico. [m.
etymologist, *ĕtĭmŏl'ŏjĕst*, s. etimologista.
etymology, *ĕtĭmŏl'ŏjĕ*, s. etimología, f.
Eucharist, *d'kărĕst*, s. Eucaristía, f.
eulogise, *d'lŏjĭz*, v. a. elogiar.
eulogy, *d'lŏjĕ*, s. elogio, encomio, m.; alabanza, f.
eunuch, *d'nŭk*, s. eunuco, m. [banza, f.
euphemism, *d'fĕmĭzm*, s. eufemismo, m.
euphony, *d'fŏnĕ*, s. eufonía, f.
evacuate, *ĕvăk'ŭăt*, v. a. evacuar. [f.
evacuation, *ĕvăkŭā'shŭn*, s. evacuación.
evade, *ĕvād'*, v. a. evadir, escapar, evitar.
evanescent, *ĕvănĕs'ĕnt*, a. fugitivo; imperceptible.
evangelic(al), *ĕvănjĕl'ĭk(ăl)*, a. evangélico; -ally, ad. evangélicamente.
evangelist, *ĕvăn'jĕlĭst*, s. evangelista, m.
evaporate, *ĕvăp'ŏrāt*, v. a. despedir vapores; —, v. n. evaporarse; disiparse.
evaporation, *ĕvăpŏrā'shŭn*, s. evaporación, f. [fugio, m.
evasion, *ĕvā'shŭn*, s. evasión, f.; escape, refugio, m.
evasive, *ĕvā'sĭv*, a. evasivo; sofístico; -ly, ad. sofísticamente.
eve, *ĕv*, s. tardecita, f.; vigilia, víspera, f.
even, *ĕ'vn*, a. llano, igual; par, semejante; —, ad. aun; aun cuando, supuesto que; no obstante; — as, como; — now, ahora mismo; — on, derechamente; — so, lo mismo, de veras; — or odd, pares ó nones; —, v. a. igualar, allanar.
even-handed, *-hăndĕd*, a. imparcial, equitativo.
evening, *-ĭng*, s. tardecita, f.
evenly, *-lĕ*, ad. igualmente, llanamente.
evenness, *-nĕs*, s. igualdad, f.; uniformidad, f.; llanura, f.; imparcialidadf, f.
event, *ĕvĕnt'*, s. evento, acontecimiento, m.; éxito, m.
eventful, *-fŭl*, a. lleno de acontecimientos.
eventual, *ĕvĕn'tŭăl*, a. eventual, fortuito; -ly, ad. por acaso.
eventuality, *-tŭăl'ĭtĕ*, s. enventualidad, f.
ever, *ĕv'ŭr*, ad. siempre; for — and —, siempre jamás, eternamente; — since, después; — and anon, de cuando en cuando.
evergreen, *-grēn*, a. siempre verde; —, s. siempreviva (planta), f. [nidad, f.
everlasting, *-lăst'ĭng*, a. eterno; —, eternidad, f.
evermore, *-mŏr*, ad. eternamente, para siempre jamás.
every, *-ĕ*, a. cada uno ó cada una; — where, en ó por todas partes; -thing, todo; -one, -body, cada uno, cada una.
evict, *ĕvĭkt'*, v. a. despojar jurídicamente.
eviction, *ĕvĭk'shŭn*, s. evicción, f., despojo jurídico, m.
evidence, *ĕv'ĭdĕns*, s. evidencia, f.; testimonio, m., prueba, f.; —, v. a. evidenciar.
evident, *ĕv'ĭdĕnt*, a. evidente; patente, manifiesto; -ly, ad. evidentemente.
evil, *ĕ'vĭl*, a. malo, depravado, pernicioso; dañoso; —, s. maldad, f.; daño, m.; calamidad, f.
evil-doer, *-dŏŭr*, s. malhechor, m.
evilly, *-lĕ*, ad. malamente.

evil-minded, *-mĭndĕd*, a. malicioso, mal intencionado.
evil-speaking, *-spēkĭng*, s. maledicencia, murmuración, calumnia, f.
evince, *ĕvĭns'*, v. a. probar, justificar, demostrar.
evocation, *ĕvŏkā'shŭn*, s. evocación, f.
evoke, *ĕvŏk'*, v. a. evocar.
evolution, *ĕvŏlū'shŭn*, s. desplegadura, f.; evolución, f.
evolve, *ĕvŏlv'*, v. a. & n. desenvolver; desplegarse; extraer.
ewe, *ū*, s. oveja, f. (hembra del carnero).
ewer, *-ŭr*, s. palancana ó palangana, f.
exacerbate, *ĕksăb'ŭr bāt*, v. a. exasperar.
exact, *ĕgzăkt'*, a. exacto, puntual; cuidadoso; —, v. a. exigir. [sión, f.
exaction, *ĕgzăk'shŭn*, s. exacción, extorsión, f.
exactly, *ĕgzăkt'lĕ*, a. exactamente, puntualmente. [exactitud, f.
exactness, *-nĕs*, exactitude, -titud, s.
exaggerate, *ĕgzăj'ărāt*, v. a. exagerar.
exaggeration, *ĕgzăjărā'shŭn*, s. exageración, f. [bar; realzar.
exalt, *ĕgzălt'*, v. a. exaltar, elevar; alaexaltation, *-tā'shŭn*, s. exaltación, elevación, f. [m.
examination, *ĕgzămĭnā'shŭn*, s. examen, f.
examine, *ĕgzăm'ĭn*, v. a. examinar; escudriñar. [plo, m.
example, *ĕgzăm'pl*, s. ejemplar, m.; ejemexasperate, *ĕgzăs'părāt*, v. a. exasperar, irritar, enojar, provocar; agravar, amargar. [peración, irritación, f.
exasperation, *ĕgzăspărā'shŭn*, s. exasexcavate, *ĕks'kăvāt*, v. a. excavar, ahondar. [f.; cavidad, f.; excava, f.
excavation, *ĕkskăvā'shŭn*, s. excavación, —, v. n. excederse.
exceed, *ĕksēd'*, v. a. exceder; sobrepujar; —, v. n. excederse.
exceeding, *-ĭng*, a. excesivo; -ly, ad. extremamente, en sumo grado.
excel, *ĕksĕl'*, v. a. sobresalir, exceder.
excellence, *ĕk'sĕllĕns*, s. excelencia, f.; preeminencia, f. [tulo), f.
Excellency, *ĕk'sĕllĕnsĕ*, s. Excelencia (título), f.
excellent, *ĕk'sĕllĕnt*, a. excelente; -ly, ad. excelentemente.
except, *ĕksĕpt'*, v. a. exceptuar, excluir; —, v. n. recusar; -(ing), pr. excepto, á excepción de. [clusión, f.
exception, *ĕksĕp'shŭn*, s. excepción, f.
exceptionable, *-ăbl*, a. recusable, expuesto á reparos y contradicciones.
exceptional, *-ăl*, a. excepcional.
excerpt, *ĕksŭrpt'*, v. a. extraer.
excess, *ĕksĕs'*, s. exceso, m.; intemperancia, f. [cesivamente.
excessive, *-sĭv*, a. excesivo; -ly, ad. exexchange, *ĕkstshānj'*, v. a. cambiar; trocar, permutar; —, s. cambio, m.; bolsa, lonja, f.
exchangeable, *-ăbl*, a. cambiable.
exchequer, *ĕkstshĕk'ŭr*, s. fisco, m.; tesorería, f.
exchequer-bill, *-bĭl*, exchequer-bond, *-bŏnd*, s. vale real, m.

excise, *ĕksīz'*, s. sisa, f.

exciseman, *-măn*, s. sisero, m.   [f.

excitability, *ĕksĭtăbĭl'ĭtĕ*, s. excitabilidad,

excitable, *ĕksī'tăbl*, a. excitable.

excite, *ĕksīt'*, v. a. excitar; estimular.

excitement, *-mĕnt*, s. estímulo, incita-
miento, m.   [mucho.

exclaim, *ĕksklām'*, v. n. exclamar, clamar

exclamation, *-klămā'shŭn*, s. exclamación, f.; clamor, m.   [torio.

exclamatory, *ĕksklăm'ătŭrĕ*, a. exclama-

exclude, *ĕksklūd'*, v. a. excluir; exceptuar.

exclusion, *-klū'shŭn*, s. exclusión, ex-
clusiva, excepción, f.

exclusive, *-klū'sĭv*, a. exclusivo; -ly,
ad. exclusivamente.   [excomulgar.

excommunicate, *ĕkskŏmmū'nĭkāt*, v. a.

excommunication, *-kā'shŭn*, s. excomunión, f.   [f.

excoriation, *ĕkskōrĭā'shŭn*, s. excoriación.

excrement, *ĕks'krĕmĕnt*, s. excremento,
. m., materias fecales, f. pl.   [cia, f.

excrescence, *ĕkskrĕs'sĕns*, s. excrescen-

excruciating, *ĕkskrū'shĭātĭng*, a. atroz,
enorme, grave.   [justificar.

exculpate, *ĕkskŭl'pāt*, v. a. disculpar;

exculpation, *-pā'shŭn*, s. disculpa, f.

exculpatory, *-pătŭrĕ*, a. justificativo.

excursion, *ĕkskŭr'shŭn*, s. excursión, f.;
digresión, f.   [siones.

excursionist, *-ĭst*, s. el que hace excur-

excusable, *ĕkskū'zăbl*, a. excusable.

excuse, *ĕkskūz'*, v. a. excusar; perdonar;
-, s. excusa, f.   [testable.

execrable, *ĕks'ĕkrăbl*, a. execrable, de-

execrably, *-ĕ*, ad. execrablemente.

execrate, *-krāt*, v. a. execrar, maldecir.

execration, *-krā'shŭn*, s. execración,
maldición, f.   [ciar.

execute, *ĕks'ĕkūt*, v. a. ejecutar; ajusti-

execution, *-kū'shŭn*, s. ejecución, f.

executioner, *-ŭr*, s. ejecutor, m.; verdugo, m.

executive, *ĕgzĕk'ŭtĭv*, a. ejecutivo.

executor, *-ŭtŭr*, s. testamentario, m.

executrix, *-ŭtrĭks*, s. (law) albacea, eje-
cutora testamentaria, f.

exemplar, *ĕgzĕm'plăr*, s. ejemplar, original, modelo, m.

exemplary, *ĕgzĕmplărĕ*, a. ejemplar.

exemplify, *ĕgzĕm'plĭfī*, v. a. ejemplificar.

exempt, *ĕgzĕmpt'*, a. exento, libre por privilegio.   [quicia, f.

exemption, *ĕgzĕm'shŭn*, s. exención, fran-

exercise, *ĕk'sŭrsīz*, s. ejercicio, m.; ensayo, m.; tarea, f.; práctica, f.; -, v. n.
hacer ejercicio; -, v. a. ejercitar; atarear.

exert, *ĕgzŭrt'*, v. a. emplear; to - one's
self, esforzarse.

exertion, *ĕgzŭr'shŭn*, s. esfuerzo, m.

exfoliate, *ĕksfō'lĭāt*, v. n. exfoliarse.

exfoliation, *ĕksfōlĭā'shŭn*, s. exfoliación, f.

exhalation, *ĕgzhălā'shŭn*, s. exhalación,
f.; vapor, m.

exhale, *ĕgzhāl'*, v. a. exhalar.

exhaust, *ĕgzhăst'*, v. a. apurar, agotar.

exhaustion, *ĕgzhăs'tyŭn*, s. agotamiento,
m., extenuación, f.

exhaustive, *-ĭv*, a. agotable.

exhibit, *ĕgzhĭb'ĭt*, v. a. exhibir; mostrar;
-, s. (law) memorial, libelo, m.

exhibition, *ĕgzhĭbĭsh'ăn*, s. exhibición,
presentación, f.; beca, f.; espectáculo, m.

exhibitioner, *-ŭr*, s. beca, f., colegial
prebendado, m.   [público, m.

exhibitor, *ĕgzhĭb'ĭtŭr*, s. ostentador en

exhilarate, *ĕgzhĭl'ărāt*, v. a. alegrar,
causar alegría.

exhilaration, *-rā'shŭn*, s. alegría, f.;
buen humor, regocijo, m.

exhort, *ĕgzhōrt'*, v. a. exhortar, excitar.

exhortation, *-tā'shŭn*, s. exhortación, f.

exhume, *ĕks hūm'*, v. a. exhumar, desen-
terrar.   [dad, urgencia, f.

exigency, *ĕks'ĭjĕnsĕ*, s. exigencia, necesi-

exile, *ĕg'zīl*, s. destierro, m.; -, v. a.
desterrar, deportar.

exist, *ĕgzĭst'*, v. n. existir.

existence, *-ĕns*, s. existencia, f.

existent, *-ĕnt*, a. existente.

existing, *-ĭng*, a. actual, presente.

exit, *ĕks'ĭt*, s. partida, salida, f.; éxito, m.

exonerate, *ĕgzŏn'ărāt*, v. a. exonerar,
descargar.

exoneration, *-rā'shŭn*, s. exoneración, f.

exorbitance, *ĕgzŏr'bĭtăns*, s. exorbitancia,
enormidad, f.   [cesivo.

exorbitant, *-bĭtănt*, a. exorbitante, ex-

exorcise, *ĕks'ŏrsīz*, v. a. exorcizar, conjurar.

exorcism, *ĕks'ŏrsĭzm*, s. exorcismo, m.

exordium, *ĕgzŏr'dĭŭm*, s. exordio, m.

exotic, *ĕgzŏt'ĭk*, a. exótico, extranjero; -,
s. planta exótica, f.

expand, *ĕkspănd'*, v. a. extender, dilatar.

expanse, *ĕkspăns'*, s. extensión de lugar, f.

expansion, *-shŭn*, s. expansión, f.

expansive, *-sĭv*, a. expansivo.

expatiate, *ĕkspā'shĭāt*, v. n. espaciarse.

expatriate, *-trĭāt*, v. a. expatriar.

expect, *ĕkspĕkt'*, v. a. esperar, aguardar.

expectance, *-ăns*, expectancy, *-ĕ*, s.
expectación, esperanza, f.

expectant, *-ănt*, s. esperador, m.

expectation, *-tā'shŭn*, s. expectación,
expectativa, f.   [torar.

expectorate, *ĕkspĕk'tŭrāt*, v. a. expec-

expectoration, *-rā'shŭn*, s. expectoración, f.   [conveniencia, oportunidad, f.

expediency, *ĕkspē'dĭĕnsĕ*, s. propiedad, f.

expedient, *-dĭĕnt*, a. oportuno, conveniente; -, s. expediente, medio, m.; -ly,
ad. convenientemente.   [dir.

expedite, *ĕks'pĕdīt*, v. a. acelerar; expe-

expedition, *-dĭsh'ăn*, s. expedición,
priesa, f.   [-ly, ad. prontamente.

expeditious, *-ŭs*, a. pronto, expedito;

expel, *ĕkspĕl'*, v. a. expeler, desterrar.

expend, *ĕkspĕnd'*, v. a. expender; desembolsar.   [sembolso, m.

expenditure, *ĕkspĕn'dĭtŭr*, s. gasto, des-

expense, *ĕkspĕns'*, s. expensas, f. pl.;
coste, m.

expensive, *ĕkspĕn'sĭv*, a. pródigo; costoso; -ly, ad. costosamente.

experience, *ĕkspē'rĭĕns*, s. experiencia, f.;
práctica, f.; -, v. a. experimentar.

experiment, *ĕkspĕr'ĭmĕnt*, s. experimento,
m.; -, v. a. experimentar.

experimental, ĕkspĕrĭmĕn'tăl, a. experimental; -ly, ad. experimentalmente.

expert, ĕkspŭrt', a. experto, práctico, diestro; -ly, ad. diestramente.

expertness, -nĕs, s. maña, destreza, habilidad, f. [daño.

expiate, ĕks'pĭăt, v. a. expiar; reparar un

expiation, ĕkspĭă'shăn, s. expiación, f.

expiatory, -tŭrĕ, a. expiatorio.

expiration, ĕkspĭră'shăn, s. expiración, f.; muerte, f.; vapor, vaho, m.

expire, ĕkspīr', v. n. expirar.

explain, ĕksplān', v. a. explanar, explicar.

explanation, ĕksplănă'shăn, s. explanación, explicación, f.

explanatory, ĕksplăn'ătŭrĕ, a. explicativo.

expletive, ĕks'plĕtĭv, a. expletivo.

explicable, ĕks'plĭkăbl, a. explicable. [f.

explication, ĕksplĭkă'shăn, s. explicación,

explicit, ĕksplĭs'ĭt, a. explícito; -ly, ad. explícitamente.

explode, ĕksplōd', v. a. & n. disparar con estallido; reprobar; condenar.

exploit, ĕksplŏĭt', s. hazaña, f.; hecho heroico, m. [ción, f.; examen, m.

exploration, ĕksplŏră'shăn, s. exploración,

explore, ĕksplŏr', v. a. explorar, examinar; sondear.

explosion, ĕksplō'zhăn, s. explosión, f.

explosive, -sĭv, a, explosivo; – cotton, s. piróxilo, m. [m.

exponent, ĕkspō'nĕnt, s. (ar.) exponente,

export, ĕkspŏrt', v. a. exportar.

export, ĕks'pŏrt, exportation, ĕkspŏrtă'shăn, s. exportación, f.

expose, ĕkspōz', v. a. exponer; mostrar; descubrir; poner en peligro.

exposition, ĕkspŏzĭsh'ăn, s. exposición; f.; interpretación, f. [contender.

expostulate, ĕkspŏs'tŭlāt, v. n. debatir,

expostulation, ĕkspŏstŭlā'shăn, s. debate, m.; disputa, f.

exposure, ĕkspō'zhŭr, s. situación peligrosa, f.; exposición, f. [pretar.

expound, ĕkspōund', v. a. exponer; inter-

express, ĕksprĕs', v. a. exprimir; representar; –, a. expreso, claro; á propósito; –, s. expreso, correo, m.; (rail.) tren expreso, m.

expression, ĕksprĕsh'ăn, s. expresión, f.; locución, f.; animación del rostro, f.

expressionless, -lĕs, a. sin expresión (cara). [expresivamente.

expressive, -sĭv, a. expresivo; -ly, ad.

expressly, -lĕ, ad. expresamente.

expropriate, ĕksprō'prĭăt, v. a. expropiar (por causa de utilidad pública).

expropriation, ĕksprōprĭă'shăn, s. (law) expropiación, f.

expulsion, ĕkspŭl'shăn, s. expulsión, f.

expunge, ĕkspŭnj', v. a. borrar, cancelar.

expargate, ĕkspŭr'găt, v. a. expurgar.

expurgation, -gă'shăn, s. purificación, f.; expurgo, m.

exquisite, ĕks'kwĭzĭt, a. exquisito, perfecto, excelente; -ly, ad. exquisitamente.

exquisiteness, -nĕs, s. primor, m., excelencia, f.

extant, ĕks'tănt, s. estante, existente.

extemporaneous, ĕkstĕmpŏră'nĭăs, extemporary, ĕkstĕm'pŏrărĕ, a. extemporáneo, improviso. [in promptu.

extempore, ĕkstĕm'pŏrĕ, ad. de improviso,

extemporize, -pŏrīz, v. n. improvisar.

extend, ĕkstĕnd', v. a. extender; amplificar; –, v. n. extenderse.

extension, ĕkstĕn'shăn, s. extensión, f.

extensive, -sĭv, a. extenso, dilatado; -ly, ad. extensivamente.

extent, ĕkstĕnt', s. extensión, f.

extenuate, ĕkstĕn'ŭāt, v. a. extenuar, disminuir, atenuar. [mitigación, f.

extenuation, -ă'shăn, s. extenuación, f.;

exterior, ĕkstē'rĭŭr, a. & s. exterior (m.).

exteriority, ĕkstērĭŏr'ĭtĕ, s. exterioridad, f. [nar; extirpar.

exterminate, ĕkstŭr'mĭnăt, v. a. exterminar, destruir; desarraigar.

extermination, -nă'shăn, s. exterminación, extirpación, f.

external, ĕkstŭr'năl, a. externo; -ly, ad. exteriormente; -s, s. pl. exterior, m.

extinct, ĕkstĭngkt', a. extinto; abolido.

extinction, ĕkstĭngk'shăn, s. extinción, f.; abolición, f. [guir; suprimir.

extinguish, ĕkstĭng'gwĭsh, v. a. extin-

extinguisher, -ŭr, s. matacandelas, m.

extirpate, ĕkstŭr'păt, v. a. extirpar.

extirpation, -pă'shăn, s. extirpación, f.; exterminio, m. [zar, exaltar.

extol, ĕkstŏl', v. a. alabar, magnificar, al-

extort, ĕkstŏrt', v. a. sacar por fuerza; adquirir por violencia.

extortion, ĕkstŏr'shăn, s. extorsión, f.

extortionate, -ăt, a. violento.

extortioner, -ŭr, s. exactor, m.

extra, ĕks'tră, ad. extra; –, –special, s. suplemento extraordinario de un periódico, m.

extract, ĕkstrăkt', v. a. extraer; extractar; –, ĕks'trăkt, s. extracto m.; compendio, m.

extraction, ĕkstrăk'shăn, s. extracción, f.; descendencia, f. [dición, f.

extradition, ĕkstrădĭsh'ăn, s. (law) extradición, f.

extraneous, ĕkstrā'nĭăs, a. extraño, exótico. [extraordinariamente.

extraordinarily, -dĭnărĭlĕ, ad.

extraordinary, -dĭnărĕ, a. extraordinario.

extravagance, ĕkstrăv'ăgăns, s. extravagancia, f.; gastos excesivos, m. pl.

extravagant, -ăgănt, a. extravagante, singular, exorbitante; pródigo; -ly, ad. extravagantemente.

extreme, ĕkstrēm', a. extremo, supremo; último; –, s. extremo, m.; -ly, ad. extremamente.

extremity, ĕkstrĕm'ĭtĕ, s. extremidad, f.

extricate, ĕks'trĭkăt, v. a. desembarazar, desenredar. [zo, desempeño, m.

extrication, ĕkstrĭkă'shăn, s. desembarazo,

extrinsic(al), ĕkstrĭn'sĭk(ăl), a. extrínseco, exterior. [tuberancia, f.

exuberance, ĕkstă'bŭrăns, s. (med.) pro-

exuberance, ĕgzŭ'bŭrăns, s. exuberancia, suma abundancia, f.

exuberant, -bŭrănt, a. exuberante, abundantísimo; -ly, ad. abundantemente.

exude, ĕksūd', v. n. transpirar. [triunfar.

exult, ĕgzŭlt', v. a. exultar, regocijarse,

exultation, *-tă'shăn*, s. exultación, f.; regocijo, m.

eye, *ī*, s. ojo, m.; corcheta, f.; (bot.) yema, f., botón, m.; —, v. a. ojear, contemplar, observar.

eye-ball, *-băl*, s. niña del ojo, f.

eye-brow, *-brŏă*, s. ceja, f.   [ocular, f.

eye-glass, *-glăs*, s. anteojo, m.; lente

eye-lash, *-lăsh*, s. pestaña, f.

eyeless, *-lĕs*, a. ciego; sin ojos.

eyelet, *-lĕt*, s. resquicio, m.; ojete, m.

eye-lid, *-lĭd*, s. párpado, m.   [vista, f.

eye-sight, *-sīt*, s. potencia visiva, f.;

eye-sore, *-sŏr*, s. mal de ojos, m.

eye-tooth, *-tŏth*, s. colmillo, m.

eye-wash, *-wŏsh*, s. colirio, m.

eye-witness, *-wĭtnĕs*, s. testigo ocular, m.

eyry, eyrie, *ā'rĕ*, s. nido de ave de rapiña, m.

F.

fable, *fā'bl*, s. fábula, f.; ficción, f.

fabric, *făb'rĭk*, s. fábrica, f.; edificio, m.; manufactura, f.; tejido, m.

fabricate, *-rĭkāt*, v. a. fabricar, edificar.

fabrication, *-kā'shăn*, s. fabricación, f.

fabulous, *făb'ŭlăs*, a. fabuloso; -ly, ad. fabulosamente.

face, *fās*, s. cara, faz, f.; haz, f.; superficie, f.; fachada, f.; frente, f.; aspecto, m.; apariencia, f.; atrevimiento, m.: in my —, á mi presencia; —, v. a. encararse; hacer frente; volver un naipe.

face-ache, *-āk*, s. nevralgia facial, f.

faced, *-d*, a. con cara (in comp.).

facet, *făs'ĕt*, s. faceta, f.

facetious, *fāsē'shăs*, a. chistoso, alegre, gracioso; -ly, ad. chistosamente.

facial, *fā'shĭăl*, a. facial.

facile, *făs'ĭl*, a. fácil, afable.

facilitate, *fāsĭl'ĭtāt*, v. a. facilitar.

facility, *-ĭtĕ*, s. facilidad, ligereza, f.; afabilidad, f.   [frente.

facing, *fā'sĭng*, s. paramento, m.; —, pr. en

fac-simile, *făksĭm'ĭlĕ*, s. facsímile, m.

fact, *făkt*, s. hecho, m.; realidad, f.; in —, con ó en efecto; in the —, en el acto.

faction, *făk'shăn*, s. facción, f.; disensión, f.

factionist, *-ĭst*, s. faccioso, inquieto, m.

factious, *făk'shăs*, a. faccioso; -ly, ad. sediciosamente.   [m.

factiousness, *-nĕs*, s. espíritu de facción,

factitious, *făktĭsh'ăs*, a. facticio.

factor, *făk'tăr*, s. factor (agente), m.; (ar.)

factory, *-ĕ*, s. factoría, f.   [factor.

factotum, *făktŏ'tăm*, s. criado que hace de todo, m.   [privilegio, m.

faculty, *făk'ăltĕ*, s. facultad, f.; poder, fad, *făd*, s. fruslería, niñería, f.

fade, *fād*, v. n. decaer, marchitarse, fallecer.

fag, *făg*, s. trabajador, m.; esclavo, m.; nudo en el paño, m.; —, v. n. desmayarse.

fag-end, *-ĕnd*, s. cadillos, m. pl.

fagot, *făg'ŏt*, s. haz, m., gavilla de leña, f.

fail, *fāl*, v. a. & n. omitir, abandonar; descuidar; faltar; perecer; perderse; —, s. desgracia, f.; omisión, f.

failing, *-ĭng*, s. falta, f.; defecto, m.

failure, *-ăr*, s. falta, f.; culpa, f.; descuido, m.; quiebra, bancarrota, f.

fain, *fān*, a. obligado, estrechado; —, ad. de buena gana.

faint, *fānt*, v. n. desmayarse, debilitarse; —, s. deliquio, m.; —, a. lánguido; cobarde; -ly, ad. desmayadamente, débilmente.

faint-hearted, *-hărtĕd*, a. cobarde, medroso, pusilánime; -ly, ad. medrosamente.

faintness, *-nĕs*, s. languidez, flaqueza, f.; timidez, f.

fair, *fār*, a. hermoso, bello; blanco; rubio; claro, sereno; favorable; recto, justo; franco; —, ad. cortésmente; con buena armonía; —, s. feria, f.; belleza, f.

fairing, *-ĭng*, s. ferias, f. pl.

fairly, *-lĕ*, ad. bellamente; agradablemente, ingenuamente.   [f.; candor, m.

fairness, *-nĕs*, s. hermosura, f.; honradez,

fair-spoken, *-spŏkn*, a. bien hablado, cortés.

fairy, *-ĕ*, s. duende, m.; bruja, encantadora, f.; —, a. lo que pertenece á los duendes.

faith, *fāth*, s. fe, f.; dogma de fe, m.; fidelidad, sinceridad, f.   [mente.

faithful, *-fŭl*, a. fiel, leal; -ly, ad. fielmente.

faithfulness, *-nĕs*, s. fidelidad, lealtad, f.

faithless, *-lĕs*, a. infiel, pérfido, desleal.

falchion, *făl'shăn*, s. cimitarra, f. (espada corta).

falcon, *fă'kn*, s. halcón, m.

falconer, *-ăr*, s. halconero, m.

falconry, *-rĕ*, s. halconería, f.

fall, *făl*, v. n. caer(se); perder el poder; disminuir, decrecer en precio; to - asleep, dormirse; to - short, faltar, chasquear; to - sick, enfermar; to - in love, enamorarse; to - off, desaparecer, disolverse; separarse; apostatar; to - out, reñir, disputar; acaecer, acontecer; to - upon, atacar, asaltar; —, s. caída, f.; declive, m.; catarata, f.

fallacious, *fălā'shăs*, a. falaz, fraudulento; -ly, ad. falazmente.   [engaño, m.

fallacy, *făl'ăsĕ*, s. falacia, sofistería, f.;

fallibility, *fălĭbĭl'ĭtĕ*, s. falibilidad, f.

fallible, *făl'ĭbl*, a. falible.   [lepsia, f.

falling-sickness, *făl'ĭngknĕs*, s. epilepsia, f.

fallow, *făl'ŏ*, a. flavo; - deer, s. corzo, m.; corza, f.   [terreno, f.

fallowness, *-nĕs*, s. esterilidad de algún terreno, f.

false, *făls*, a. falso, pérfido; -ly, ad. falsamente; pérfidamente.

falsehood, *-hŭd*, falseness, *-nĕs*, s. falsedad, f.; perfidia, f.

falsify, *făl'sĭfī*, v. a. falsificar.

falsity, *-sĭtĕ*, s. falsedad, mentira, f.

falter, *făl'tăr*, v. n. tartamudear; faltar.

faltering, *-ĭng*, s. debilidad, f.; defecto, m.; -ly, ad. balbuciente, tartamudo; con lengua tropezosa.

fame, *fām*, s. fama, f.; renombre, m.

famed, *-d*, a. célebrado, famoso.

familiar, *fămĭl'yăr*, a. familiar; casero; -ly, ad. familiarmente; —, s. amigo íntimo, m.

familiarity, *famīliăr'ĭtĕ,* s. familiaridad, f.

familiarize, *famĭl'yărĭz,* v.a. familiarizar.

family, *făm'ĭlĕ,* s. familia, f.; linaje, m.; clase, especie, f.

famine, *făm'ĭn,* s. hambre, f.; carestía, f.

famish, *-ĭsh,* v. a. hambrear; —, v. n. morirse de hambre. [sad. famosamente.

famous, *fā'mŭs,* a. famoso, afamado; —ly, ad.

fan, *făn,* s. abanico, m.; aventador, m.; —, v. a. abanicar; aventar.

fanatic, *fănăt'ĭk,* a. & s. fanático (m.).

fanaticism, *-ĭsĭzm,* s. fanatismo, m.

fanciful, *făn'sĭfŭl,* a. imaginativo, caprichoso; —ly, ad. caprichosamente.

fancifulness, *-nĕs,* s. antojo, capricho, m.

fancy, *făn'sĕ,* s. fantasía, imaginación, f.; capricho, m.; —, v. a. imaginar; amar; —, v. n. apasionarse, figurarse; fantasear.

fancy-articles, *-ărtĭkls,* fancy-goods, *-gŭds,* s. pl. novedades, modas, f. pl.

fancy-ball, *-băl,* s. baile de máscaras, m.

fancy-fair, *-făr,* s. bazar, m.

fancy-sick, *-sĭk,* a. enfermo imaginario.

fanfare, *făn'făr,* s. (mus.) charanga, f.

fang, *făng,* s. colmillo, m.; garra, uña, f.

fanged, *-d,* a. colmilludo.

fantastic(al), *făntăst'ĭk(ăl),* a. fantástico; caprichoso; —ally, ad. fantásticamente.

fantasticalness, *-dĭnĕs,* s. fantasía, f.; capricho, m.

fantasy, *făn'tăsĕ,* s. fantasía, f.

far, *făr,* ad. lejos, á una gran distancia; —, a. lejano, distante, remoto; — and away, con mucho, de mucho; — off, distante. [lejano.

farce, *fărs,* s. farsa, f.

farcical, *făr'sĭkăl,* a. burlesco.

farcy, *făr'sĕ,* s. lamparones, m. pl.

fardel, *făr'dĕl,* s. fardel, fardillo, m.

fare, *făr,* s. comida, f.; viajero, m.; pasaje, m.; —, v. n. viajar; encontrarse.

farewell, *-wĕl',* s. despedida, f.; —! ad. ¡á Dios! ¡siga U. bueno! [farináceo.

farinaceous, *fărĭnā'shŭs,* a. harinoso.

farm, *fărm,* s. tierra arrendada, f.; alquería f.; —, v. a. arrendar; tomar en arriendo; cultivar.

farmer, *-ăr,* s. arrendatario de tierra labrantía, m.; labrador, m.

farming, *-ĭng,* s. agricultura, f.

farm-yard, *-yărd,* s. corral, m.

farrago, *fărā'gō,* s. fárrago, m.; broza, f.

farrier, *făr'yăr,* s. herrador, m.

farriery, *-ĕ,* s. albeitería f.

farrow, *făr'rō,* s. lechigada de puercos, f.; —, v. a. parir la puerca.

far-seeing, *făr'sēĭng,* a. perspicaz.

farther, *făr'thăr,* ad. más lejos; más adelante; —, a. más lejos, ulterior.

farthest, *făr'thĕst,* ad. lo más lejos; lo más tarde; á lo más. [m.; ardite, m.

farthing, *făr'thĭng,* s. cuarto de penique, m.

fascinate, *făs'sĭnāt,* v.a. fascinar, encantar.

fascination, *-nā'shŭn,* s. fascinación, f.; encanto, m.

fascine, *făssēn',* s. fagina, haz, f.

fashion, *făsh'ŭn,* s. forma, figura, f.; moda, f.; uso, m.; condición (de nacimiento), f.;

people of —, gente de tono, f.; —, v. a. formar, amoldar.

fashionable, *-ăbl,* a. hecho á la moda; elegante; the — world, el gran mundo; —bly, ad. á ó según la moda.

fashionableness, *-nĕs,* s. moda, elegancia, f.

fast, *făst,* v. n. ayunar; —, s. ayuno, m.; —, a. firme, estable; veloz, pronto; —, ad. firmemente; estrechamente; de priesa; á menudo.

fast-day, *-dā,* s. día de ayuno, m.

fasten, *făs'n,* v.a. afirmar, asegurar, atar; fijar; —, v. n. fijarse, establecerse.

faster, *făst'ăr,* s. ayunador, m.

fastidious, *făstĭd'ĕŭs,* a. fastidioso, desdeñoso; —ly, ad. fastidiosamente.

fastness, *făst'nĕs,* s. prontitud, f.; firmeza, f.; fortaleza, f. [grasa, f.

fat, *făt,* a. gordo, pingüe; —, s. gordo, m.;

fatal, *fā'tăl,* a. fatal; funesto; —ly, ad.

fatalist, *-ĭst,* s. fatalista, m. [fatalmente.

fatality, *fătăl'ĭtĕ,* s. fatalidad, predestinación, f. [Parcas, f. pl.

fate, *făt,* s. hado, destino, m.; —s, pl. (poet.)

fated, *-ĕd,* a. lo que está decretado por los

fateful, *-fŭl,* a. fatídico. [hados,

father, *fā'thăr,* s. padre, m.

fatherhood, *-hŭd,* s. paternidad, f.

father-in-law, *-ĭnlā,* s. suegro, m.

fatherland, *-lănd,* s. patria, f.

fatherless, *-lĕs,* a. huérfano de padre.

fatherly, *-lĕ,* a. (& ad.) paternal(mente).

fathom, *făth'ŭm,* s. braza (medida), f.; —, v. a. abrazar; sondar; penetrar.

fathomless, *-lĕs,* a. insondable. [cansar.

fatigue, *fătēg',* s. fatiga, f.; —, v. a. fatigar,

fatigue-party, *-părtĕ,* s. (mil.) servicio, m.; función, f.

fatling, *făt'lĭng,* s. cebón, m.

fatness, *făt'nĕs,* s. gordura, pingüosidad, f.

fatten, *făt'n,* v. a. cebar, engordar; —, v. n. engrosarse.

fattening, *-ĭng,* s. cebadura, f.

fatty, *făt'tĕ,* a. untoso, craso, pingüe.

fatuity, *fătū'ĭtĕ,* s. fatuidad, simpleza, f.

fatuous, *făt'dŭs,* a. fatuo, tonto, imbécil.

fault, *fălt,* s. falta, culpa, f.; delito, m.; defecto, m.

fault-finder, *-fĭndăr,* s. censurador, m.

faultily, *-ĭlĕ,* ad. defectuosamente. [m.

faultiness, *-ĭnĕs,* s. culpa, f.; defecto, m.

faultless, *-lĕs,* a. perfecto, cumplido.

faulty, *-ĕ,* a. culpable, defectuoso.

faun, *făn,* s. fauno, m.

favour, *fā'văr,* s. favor, beneficio, m.; patrocinio, m.; blandura, f.; with (o under) your —, con licencia ó permiso de U.; —, v. a. favorecer, proteger.

favourable, *-ăbl,* a. favorable, propicio; —bly, ad. favorablemente.

favoured, *-d,* a. favorecido. [cido.

favourite, *-ĭt,* s. favorito, m.; —, a. favore-

fawn, *făn,* s. cervato, m.; —, v. n. parir la cierva; adular servilmente.

fawningly, *-ĭnglĕ,* ad. lisonjeramente, con adulación servil. [con otra.

fay, *fā,* v. n. cuadrar, venir bien una cosa

fealty, *fĭ'ăltĭ,* s. homenaje, m.; fidelidad, lealtad, f.   [miedo, m.
fear, *fēr,* v. a. espantar; —, v. n. temer; —, s.
fearful, *-fŭl,* a. medroso, temeroso; tímido; —ly, ad. medrosamente, temerosamente.
fearless, *-lĕs,* a. intrépido, atrevido; —ly, ad. sin miedo.
fearlessness, *-nĕs,* s. intrepidez, f.
feasibility, *fēzĭbĭl'ĭtĭ,* s. posibilidad, f.
feasible, *fē'zĭbl,* a. factible, hacedero.
feast, *fēst,* s. banquete, festín, m.; fiesta, f.; —, v. a. festejar, regalar; —, v. n. comer opíparamente.
feaster, *-ŭr,* s. goloso, m.; anfitrión, m.
feat, *fēt,* s. hecho, m.; acción, hazaña, f.
feather, *fĕth'ŭr,* s. pluma, f.; (fig.) bagatela, f.; —, v. a. emplumar; enriquecer.
feather-bed, *-bĕd,* s. plumón, m.; colchra, f.   [plumita.
feathery, *-ĭ,* a. plumado; ligero como una pluma, f.
feature, *fē'tŭr,* s. rostro, m.; facción del rostro, f.; forma, f.
febrile, *fēb'rĭl,* a. febril.
February, *fĕb'rōărĭ,* s. febrero, m.
fecula, *fĕk'ŭlă,* s. fécula, f.
fecund, *fĕk'ănd,* a. fecundo, fértil.
fecundity, *fēkŭn'dĭtĭ,* s. fecundidad, fertilidad, f.; abundancia, f.
federal, *fĕd'ĕrăl,* a. federal.
federalist, *-ĭst,* s. federalista, m.
federate, *fĕd'ŭrăt,* a. confederado, m.
federation, *-d'shŭn,* s. confederación, f.
fee, *fē,* s. feudo, m.; paga, gratificación, f.; salario, m.; —, v. a. pagar; premiar; sobornar.   [bornar.
feeble, *fē'bl,* a. flaco, débil.   [bornar.
feebleness, *-nĕs,* s. debilidad, f.
feebly, *-blĭ,* ad. débilmente.
feed, *fēd,* v. n. pacer; nutrir; alimentar; —, v. n. nutrirse; engordar; —, s. alimento, m.; pasto, m.
feeder, *-ŭr,* s. el que da de comer, m.; glotón, m.; babadero, m.; tolva de molino, f.
feeding-bottle, *-ĭngbŏtl,* s. bebedero, m.
feel, *fēl,* v. a. sentir; palpar; —, v. n. tener sensibilidad; —, s. tacto, sentido, m.   [f.
feeler, *-ŭr,* s. antenas, f. pl.; (fig.) tentativa, f.
feeling, *-ĭng,* s. tacto, m.; sensibilidad, f.
feelingly, *-ĭnglĭ,* ad. sensiblemente.   [f.
feet, *fēt,* s. pl. (de foot) (mil.) infantería,
feign, *fān,* v. a. inventar, fingir; disimular; —, v. n. referir falsedades imaginadas.
feignedly, *-ĕdlĭ,* ad. fingidamente.
feint, *fānt,* s. ficción, f.; finta, f.
felicitate, *fēlĭs'ĭtăt,* v. a. felicitar; congratularse (con otro).   [gratulación, f.
felicitation, *-tā'shŭn,* s. felicitación, congratulación, f.
felicitous, *fēlĭs'ĭtŭs,* a. feliz, dichoso.
felicity, *-tĭ,* s. felicidad, dicha, f.
feline, *fē'lĭn,* a. gatuno.
fell, *fĕl,* a. cruel, bárbaro; —, s. cuero, m.; piel, f.; pellejo, m.; —, v. a. matar las reses; cortar árboles.
fellow, *fĕl'lō,* s. compañero, camarada, m.; socio de algún colegio, m.   [m.
fellow-citizen, *-sĭtzn,* s. concludadano.
fellow-creature, *-krētŭr,* s. prójimo, m.
fellow-feeling, *-fēlĭng,* s. simpatía, f.
fellow-prisoner, *-prĭz'ŏnŭr,* s. compañero de prisión, m.

fellowship, *-shĭp,* s. compañía, sociedad, f.; beca, (en un colegio) f.
fellow-soldier, *-sōl'jŭr,* s. conmilitón, m.
fellow-student, *-stūdĕnt,* s. condiscípulo, m.   [de infortunio, m.
fellow-sufferer, *-sŭffŭrŭr,* s. compañero
fellow-traveller, *-trăvĕllŭr,* s. compañero de viaje, m.
felly, *fĕl'lĭ,* s. pina de una rueda, f.
felon, *fĕl'ŏn,* s. reo de un delito capital, m.; —, a. cruel, traidor.
felonious, *fēlō'nĭŭs,* a. traidor, pérfido; —ly, ad. traidoramente.
felony, *fĕl'ŏnĭ,* s. felonía, f.
felt, *fĕlt,* s. fieltro, m.; pellejo, m.
felucca, *fēlŭk'kă,* s. faluca, f.
female, *fē'māl,* s. hembra, f.; —, a. femenino.   [tierno; afeminado, amujerado.
feminine, *fĕm'ĭnĭn,* a. femenino; femenil, f.
fen, *fĕn,* s. marjal, pantano, m.
fence, *fĕns,* s. cerca, palizada, f.; defensa, f.; —, v. a. cercar; defender, preservar; —, v. n. esgrimir.   [cercado.
fenceless, *-lĕs,* a. abierto, lo que no está
fencing, *fĕn'sĭng,* s. esgrima, f.
fencing-master, *-măstŭr,* s. maestro de armas, m.   [defenderse.
fend, *fĕnd,* v. a. parar; rechazar; —, v. n.
fender, *-ŭr,* s. barandilla que se pone delante del hogar, f.
fennel, *fĕn'nĕl,* s. (bot.) hinojo, m.
ferment, *fŭr'mĕnt,* s. fermento m.; —, fŭrmĕnt', v. a. o n. hacer fermentar; fermentar.
fermentation, *fŭrmĕn'shŭn,* s. fermentación, f.   [tación, f.
fern, *fŭrn,* s. (bot.) helecho, m. [tación, f.
fernery, *-ărĭ,* s. helechar, m.
ferocious, *fērō'shŭs,* a. feroz; fiero; —ly, ad. ferozmente.
ferocity, *fērŏs'ĭtĭ,* s. ferocidad, fiereza, f.
ferret, *fĕr'rĕt,* s. hurón, m.; —, v. a. huronear; to — out, descubrir, echar fuera.
ferreter, *-ŭr,* s. (fig.) espía, m.
ferruginous, *fĕrrō'jĭnŭs,* a. ferruginoso.
ferrule, *fĕr'rŭl,* s. birola, f.
ferry, *fĕr'rĭ,* s. barca de transporte, f.; —, v. a. llevar en barca.
ferry-man, *-măn,* s. barquero, m.
fertile, *fŭr'tĭl,* a. fértil, fecundo.
fertilise, *fŭrt'ĭlīz,* v. a. fertilizar.   [f.
fertility, *fŭrtĭl'ĭtĭ,* s. fertilidad, fecundidad,
ferule, *fĕr'ŭl,* s. férula, palmeta, f.
fervency, *fŭr'vĕnsĭ,* s. fervor, celo, m.
fervent, *fŭr'vĕnt,* a. ferviente; fervoroso; —ly, ad. con fervor.
fervid, *fŭr'vĭd,* a. ardiente, vehemente.
fervour, *fŭr'vŭr,* s. fervor, ardor, m.
fescue, *fĕs'kū,* s. puntero, m.
festal, *fĕs'tăl,* festive, fĕs'tĭv, a. festivo.
fester, *fĕs'tŭr,* v. n. enconarse, inflamarse.
festival, *fĕs'tĭvăl,* a. festivo; —, s. día festivo, m.
festivity, *fĕstĭv'ĭtĭ,* s. festividad, f. [near.
festoon, *fĕstōn',* s. festón, m.; —, v. a. festo-
fetch, *fĕtsh,* v. a. ir á traer algo; producir; llevar; arrebatar; —, s. estratagema, f.; artificio, ardid, m.
fetid, *fĕt'ĭd,* a. fétido, hediondo.
fetidness, *-nĕs,* s. fetor, m.

fetlock, *fĕt'lŏk*, s. cerneja, f.
fetter, *fĕt'tŭr* v. a. atar con cadenas.
fetters, –z, s. pl. grillos, m. pl.
feud, *fūd*, s. riña, contienda, f.; feudo, m.
feudal, –ăl, a. feudal.
feudalism, –ĭtizm, s. feudalismo, m.
feudatory, –ătŭrě, s. feudatario, m.
fever, *fē'vŭr*, s. fiebre, f.; yellow –, vómito [negro, m.
feverish, –ĭsh, a. febricitante.
few, *fū*, a. poco; a –, algunos; – and far between. lo que ocurre rara vez.
fewer, –ŭr, a. menor; –, ad. menos.
fewness, –nĕs, s. poquedad, f.; corto número, m.
fiat, *fī'ăt*, s. mandato absoluto, m.
fib, *fĭb*, s. mentira, f.; –, v. n. mentir.
fibre, *fī'bŭr*, s. fibra, hebra, f.
fibrin, –brĭn, s. fibrina, f.
fibrous, –brŭs, a. fibroso, f. [dable, ligero.
fickle, *fĭk'l*, a. voluble, inconstante, mu-
fickleness, –nĕs, s. volubilidad, incon-stancia, f. [f.
fiction, *fĭk'shŭn*, s. ficción, f.; invención
fictitious, *fĭktĭsh'ŭs*, a. ficticio; fingido; –ly, ad. fingidamente.
fiddle, *fĭd'l*, s. violin, m.; –, v. n. tocar el violín; chocarrear.
fiddler, –ŭr, s. violinista, m.
fiddlesticks! –stĭks, s. pl. ¡ niní naná! m.
fiddle-string, –strĭng, s. cuerda de vio-lín, f.
fidelity, *fĭdĕl'ĭtĕ*, s. fidelidad, lealtad, f.
fidget, *fĭj'ĕt*, v. n. (vulg.) contonearse; –, s. agitación inquieta, f.; hombre azogado, azogue, m.
fidgety, –ĕ, a. (fam.) inquieto, impaciente.
fie, *fī*, ¡vaya!
fief, *fēf*, s. feudo, m.
field, *fēld*, s. campo, m.; campaña, f.; espa-cio, m.; to take the –, (mil.) salir á cam-paña, m. [paña.
field-book, –bŭk, s. catastro, m.
field-day, –dā, s. (mil.) día de la revista, m.
fieldfare, –fŭr, s. zorzal, m. (pájaro).
field-marshal, –mărshăl, s. feldmariscal, m.; general en jefe de un ejército, m.
field-mouse, –mŏŭs, s. turón, m.
field-officer, –ŏf'ĭsŭr, s. (mil.) oficial del estado mayor, m. [paña, f.
field-piece, –pēs, s. artillería de cam-
field-practice, –prăktĭs, s. (mil.) manio-bras grandes, f. pl.
field-sports, –spōrts, s. pl. entretenimien-tos de la caza, m. pl.
field-work, –wŭrk, s. (mil.) fortín, m.; –, s. pl. (mil.) obras de campaña, f. pl.
fiend, *fēnd*, s. enemigo, m.; demonio, m.
fiendish, –ĭsh, a. demoníaco.
fierce, *fērs*, a. fiero, feroz; cruel, furioso; –ly, ad. furiosamente.
fierceness, –nĕs, s. a. fiereza, ferocidad, f.
fieriness, *fī'ărĭnĕs*, s. ardor, m.; fogosi-dad, f.
fiery, *fī'ărĕ*, a. ígneo; fogoso, colérico.
fife, *fīf*, s. pífano, m.
fifteen, *fĭf'tēn*, a. quince.
fifteenth, –th, a. décimoquinto. [lugar.
fifth, *fĭfth*, s. quinto; –ly, ad. en quinto
fiftieth, *fĭf'tĭĕth*, a. quincuagésimo.

fifty, *fĭf'tĕ*, a. cincuenta.
fig, *fĭg*, s. higo, m.; (fig.) bagatela, f.
fight, *fīt*, v. a. & n. reñir; batallar; com-batir; –, s. batalla, f.; combate, m.; pelea,
fig-leaf, *fĭg'lēf*, s. hoja de higuera, f. [f.
fig-pecker, –pĕkkŭr, s. becafigo, m.
fig-tree, –trē, s. higuera, f.
figurative, *fĭg'ŭrătĭv*, a. figurativo; –ly, ad. figuradamente.
figure, *fĭg'ŭr*, s. figura, forma, hechura, f.; imagen, f.; cifra, f.; –, v. a. figurar.
figure-head, –hĕd, s. (mar.) león, m., figura de proa, f. [fibra, f.
filament, *fĭl'ămĕnt*, s. filamento, m.;
filbert, *fĭl'bŭrt*, s. avellana de cáscara
filch, *fĭltsh*, v. n. ratear. [delgada, f.
filcher, –ŭr, s. ratero, ladroncillo, m.
file, *fīl*, hilo, m.; lista, f.; (mil.) fila, hi-lera, f.; lima, f.; –, v. a. enhilar; limar; pulir; to – off, (mil.) desfilar. [f.
file-cutter, –kŭttŭr, s. picador de limas,
filial, *fĭl'ĭăl*, a. de hijo, filial.
filibuster, *fĭlĭbŭs'tŭr*, s. pirata, filibustero,
filigree, *fĭl'ĭgrē*, s. filigrana, f. [m.
filings, *fī'lĭngz*, s. pl. l'maduras, f. pl.
fill, *fĭl*, v. a. llenar, henchir; hartar; –, v. n. hartarse; –, s. hartura, abundan-cia, f. [nera, f.
fillet, *fĭl'lĕt*, s. venda, faja, f.; tapa de ter-
fillip, *fĭl'ĭp*, s. papirote, m.
filly, *fĭl'lĕ*, s. potranca, f.
film, *fĭlm*, s. película, membrana, f.
filter, *fĭl'tŭr*, s. filtro, m.; –, v. a. filtrar.
filth(iness), *fĭlth'(ĭnĕs)*, s. inmundicia, por-quería, f.; fango, lodo, m.
filthily, –ĭlĕ, ad. puercamente.
filthy, –ĕ, a. sucio, puerco.
filtration, *fĭltrā'shăn*, s. filtración, f.
fin, *fĭn*, s. aleta, f. (de pez). [mente.
final, *fī'năl*, a. final, último; –ly, ad. final-
finance, *fĭnăns'*, s. renta, f.
financial, *fĭnăn'shăl*, a. rentístico.
financier, *fĭnănsēr'*, s. rentista, hacendista,
finch, *fĭnsh*, s. pinzón, m. [m.
find, *fīnd*, v. a. hallar, descubrir; proveer; to – one's self, hallarse, estar; –, s. hallazgo, m.
fine, *fīn*, a. fino; agudo, cortante; claro, trasparente; delicado; astuto; diestro; ga-lán, lindo; elegante; bello; bien criado; –, s. multa, f.; in –, finalmente, por fin; –, v. a. afinar, refinar; multar.
fine-draw, –drā, v. a. zurcir.
finely, –lĕ, ad. con elegancia. [mosura, f.
fineness, –nĕs, s. fineza, delicadeza, her-
finery, –ărĕ, s. adorno, atavío, m.
fine-spun, –spŭn, a. (fig.) ingeniosamente ideado. [manosear; manejar.
finger, *fĭng'gŭr*, s. dedo, m.; –, v. a. tocar,
finger-board, –bōrd, s. teclado, m.; teclas,
finger-glass, –glăs, s. enjuague, m. [f. pl.
fingering, –ĭng, s. tecleo, m.; modo de tocar un instrumento de música, m.
finger-post, –pōst, s. columna miliaria, f.
finger-stall, –stăl, s. dedal, m.
finical, *fĭn'ĭkăl*, a. afectado.
finish, *fĭn'ĭsh*, v. a. acabar, terminar, con finite, *fī'nĭt*, a. finito. [cluir.

finny, *fĭn'nĕ*, a. armado de aletas.

fir (-tree), *fŭr'trē*, s. abeto, m.

fire, *fīr*, s. fuego, m.; incendio, m.; –, v. a. quemar, inflamar; –, v. n. encenderse; (mil.) tirar, hacer fuego. [f. pl.

fire-arms, *–ärms*, s. pl. armas de fuego.

fire-ball, *–bŏll*, s. granada real ó de mano, f.; meteoro, meteoro, m. [rio, m.

fire-brand, *–brănd*, s. tizón, m.; incendiario.

fire-brigade, *–brĭgād*, s. bomberos, m. pl.

fire-damp, *–dămp*, s. aire inflamable, m.

fire-eater, *–ētâr*, s. fanfarrón, m.

fire-engine, *–ĕnjĭn*, s. bomba de apagar los incendios.

fire-escape, *–ĕskāp*, s. aparato de salvamento para incendios, m.

fire-fly, *–flī*, s. luciérnaga, f.

fire-man, *–măn*, s. bombero, m.; (rail.) fuellero, m.

fire-place, *–plās*, s. hogar, fogón, m.

fire-policy, *–pŏlĭsē*, s. carta de seguro contra los incendios, f.

fire-proof, *–prŏf*, a. apiro, macizo.

fire-screen, *–skrēn*, s. pantalla de chimenea, f.

fire-shovel, *–shŭvl*, s. paleta, f.; badil.

fire-side, *–sīd*, s. fogón de chimenea, m.

fire-water, *–wätâr*, s. aguardiente, m.

fire-wood, *–wŭd*, s. leña para la lumbre, f.

firing, *fī'rĭng*, s. leña, f.; (mil.) descarga, f.

firkin, *fŭr'kĭn*, s. cuarterola, f. (medida inglesa = ¼ barrel).

firm, *fŭrm*, a. firme, estable, constante; –, s. (com.) razón, firma, f.; –ly, ad. firmemente.

firmament, *fŭr'mâmĕnt*, s. firmamento, m.

firmness, *–nĕs*, s. firmeza, f.; constancia, f.

first, *fŭrst*, a. primero; –, ad. primeramente; at –, al principio, m.; –ly, ad. en primer lugar.

firstling, *–lĭng*, s. primogénito, m.

fisc, *fĭsk*, s. fisco, m., la Hacienda pública.

fiscal, *fĭs'kăl*, a. fiscal.

fish, *fĭsh*, s. pez, m.; –, v. n. pescar.

fish-bone, *–bŏn*, s. cepina, f. [nca, m.

fish-day, *–dā*, s. día de abstinencia de carne.

fisher, *–âr*, **fisherman**, *–ärmân*, s. pescador, m.

fishery, *–ârē*, s. pesca, f.; pesquera, f.

fish-hook, *–hŏk*, s. anzuelo, m.

fishing, *–ĭng*, s. pesca, f.

fishing-line, *–ĭnglĭn*, s. sedal, m.

fishing-rod, *–ĭngrŏd*, s. caña de pescar, f.

fish-market, *–märkĕt*, s. pescadería, f.

fish-monger, *–mŭnggâr*, s. pescadero, f.

fish-pond, *–pŏnd*, s. estanque de peces, m.

fish-wife, *–wīf*, s. pescadera, f.

fishy, *–ĕ*, a. abundante de pescado.

fissure, *fĭsh'âr*, s. grieta, hendedura, f.

fist, *fĭst*, s. puño, m.

fistula, *fĭs'tūlă*, s. fístula, fístola, f.

fit, *fĭt*, s. paroxismo, m.; convulsión, f.; capricho, m.; ataque repentino de algún mal ó de alguna pasión de ánimo, m.; –, a. apto, idóneo, capaz; cómodo; justo; –, v. a. ajustar, acomodar, adaptar; to – out, proveer; –, v. n. convenir.

fitful, *–fŭl*, a. alternado con paroxismos.

fitly, *–lĕ*, ad. aptamente, justamente.

fitness, *–nĕs*, s. aptitud, conveniencia, f.; proporción, f.; oportunidad, f.

fitting, *–tĭng*, a. conveniente, idóneo, justo; –, s. conveniencia, f.; –s, pl. guarnición, f.

five, *fīv*, a. cinco. [f.

fiver, *fī'vâr*, s. billete de cinco libras ester-

fives, *–z*, s. pl. juego de pelota, m. [lín, m.

fix, *fĭks*, v. a. fijar, establecer; –, v. n. fijarse, determinarse.

fixedly, *–ĕdlĕ*, ad. fijamente, ciertamente.

fixedness, *–ĕdnĕs*, **fixity**, *–ĭtĕ*, s. firmeza, f.; constancia, f.

fixings, *–ĭngz*, s. pl. equipajes, m. pl.; pertrechos, m. pl.; ajuar, m.

fixture, *–târ*, s. mueble fijo de una casa, f.

fizz(le), *fĭz'(l)*, v. n. silbar. [m.

flabby, *flăb'bĕ*, a. blando, flojo, lacio.

flaccid, *flăk'sĭd*, a. flojo, flaco; flácido.

flag, *flăg*, s. bandera, f.; (mar.) pabellón, m.; (bot.) gladiolo, m.; –, v. a. (with stones) ensolar; –, v. n. pender; debilitarse.

flagellate, *flăj'ĕllāt*, v. a. azotar. [tarse.

flageolet, *flăj'ŏlĕt*, s. flajolé, m. [vado.

flagitious, *flăjĭsh'ŭs*, a. facineroso, malvado.

flag-man, *flăg'măn*, s. (rail.) guardavía, m.

flag-officer, *–ŏffĭsâr*, s. (mar.) jefe de una escuadra, m.

flagon, *flăg'ŏn*, s. frasco, m. [midad, f.

flagrancy, *flăg'grănsĕ*, s. escándalo, m.; enormidad, f.

flagrant, *–grănt*, a. flagrante; notorio.

flag-ship, *flăg'shĭp*, s. navío almirante, m.

flag-staff, *–stăf*, s. asta del pabellón, m.

flail, *flāl*, s. mayal, m.

flake, *flāk*, s. copo, m.; lámina, f.; (of fire), centella, f.; (of ice), carámbano, m.; –, v. n. romperse en láminas.

flaky, *flā'kĕ*, a. vedijoso; roto en pequeñas laminillas. [m.; –, v. n. arder; brillar.

flame, *flām*, s. llama, f.; fuego (del amor).

flaming, *flā'mĭng*, a. inflamado, compuesto de llamas.

flange, *flănj*, s. listón, bocel, m.

flank, *flănk*, s. ijada, f.; (mil.) flanco, m.; –, v. a. atacar el flanco; flanquear.

flannel, *flăn'nĕl*, s. franela, flanela, f.

flap, *flăp*, s. falda, faldilla, f.; válvula, f.; oreja (de los zapatos), f.; golpe ligero, m.; –, v. a. mosquear; –, v. n. aletear. [f.

flare, *flār*, v. n. lucir, brillar; –, s. llama.

flash, *flăsh*, s. relámpago, m.; llamarada, f.; borbollón, m.; – of wit, agudeza, f.; rasgo, m.; –, v. a. despedir agua á borbollones; –, v. n. relampaguear, brillar; –, a. falso, contrahecho.

flashy, *–ĕ*, a. superficial; insulso, desabrido.

flask, *flăsk*, s. frasco, m.; botella, f.

flat, *flăt*, a. llano, p ano; insípido; –, s. llanura, f.; plano, m.; (mar.) bajío, m.; (mus.) bemol, m.; –ly, ad. horizontalmente; llanamente, enteramente; de plano, de nivel; francamente.

flatness, *–nĕs*, s. llanura, f.; insipidez, f.

flatten, *–n*, v. a. allanar; abatir; –, v. n. aplanarse; atontarse. [allanador, m.

flatter, *flăt'târ*, v. a. adular, lisonjear; –, s.

flattery, *–ĕ*, s. adulación, lisonja, f. [m.

flatting-mill, *flăt'tĭngmĭl*, s. laminador,

flatulence, *flăt'ŭlĕns*, s. (med.) flatulencia, f. [yano, fútil, frívolo, caduco.
flatulent, *-lĕnt*, a. flatulento; hinchado,
flatwise, *-wīz*, ad. de llano. [f.
flaunt, *flånt*, v. n. pavonearse; —, s. borla,
flavour, *flā'vŭr*, s. sainete, perfume, m.; —, v. a. dar un olor suave.
flavourless, *-lĕs*, a. desabrido, soso.
flaw, *flå*, s. resquebradura, hendedura, f.; falta, tacha, f.; ráfaga, f.; —, v. a. rajar,
flawless, *-lĕs*, a. sin defecto. [hender.
flax, *flåks*, s. lino, m.; to dress —, rastrillar lino.
flaxen, *-n*, flaxy, *-ĭ*, a. de lino; blondo.
flay, *flā*, v. a. desollar, descortezar.
flea, *flĕ*, s. pulga, f.
flea-bite, *-bīt*, s. picadura de pulga, f.
fledge, *flĕj*, v. a. dar alas ó plumas.
flee, *flĕ*, v. n. escapar; huir.
fleece, *flĕs*, s. vellón, m.; —, v. a. esquilar; desnudar, despojar.
fleecy, *flĕ'sĕ*, a. lanudo. [ligero.
fleet, *flĕt*, s. flota, f.; —, a. veloz, acelerado,
fleeting, *-ĭng*, a. pasajero, fugitivo.
fleetness, *-nĕs*, s. velocidad, ligereza, f.
flesh, *flĕsh*, s. carne, f.; —, v. a. hartar, saciar. [m.
flesh-broth, *-brŏth*, s. caldo (de carne),
flesh-brush, *-brŭsh*, s. cepillo de dar friegas, m.
fleshiness, *-ĭnĕs*, s. gordura extremada, f.
fleshings, *-ĭngz*, s. pl. fajos, m. pl.
fleshless, *-lĕs*, a. flaco; descarnado.
fleshy, *-ĭ*, a. carnoso, pulposo.
flexibility, *flĕkstbĭl'ĭtĕ*, s. flexibilidad, f.
flexible, *flĕks'ĭbl*, flexile, *-ĭl*, a. flexible.
flexion, *flĕk'shŭn*, s. flexión, corvadura, f.
flick, *flĭk*, v. a. robar, hurtar con ligereza.
flicker, *flĭk'ŭr*, v. a. aletear; fluctuar.
flier, *flī'ŭr*, s. fugitivo, m.; volante de unas máquinas, m.
flight, *flīt*, s. huida, fuga, f.; vuelo, m.; bandada (de pájaros); f.; (fig.) elevación, f.
flighty, *-ĭ*, a. veloz, inconstante.
flimsiness, *flĭm'zĭnĕs*, s. textura débil y
flimsy, *-zĭ*, a. débil; fútil. [ligera, f.
flinch, *flĭnsh*, v. n. echarse con la carga, desistir, faltar; retirarse.
fling, *flĭng*, v. a. lanzar, echar; —, v. n. brincar, resentirse; —, s. tiro, m.; burla,
flint, *flĭnt*, s. pedernal, m. [chufleta, f.
flint-glass, *-glås*, s. cristal de piedra, m.
flinty, *-ĭ*, a. roqueño; pedregoso; inexorable.
flip, *flĭp*, v. a. arrojar, lanzar.
flippancy, *-pånsĕ*, s. volubilidad, f.; petulancia, f.; impertinencia, f.
flippant, *-pånt*, a. ligero, veloz; petulante, locuaz.
flirt, *flŭrt*, v. a. arrojar, lanzar; —, v. n. mofar; coquetear; —, s. coqueta, f.
flirtation, *flŭrtā'shŭn*, s. coquetería, f.
flit, *flĭt*, v. n. volar, huir; aletear.
flitch, *flĭtsh*, s. hoja de tocino, f.
float, *flōt*, v. a. inundar; —, v. n. flotar; fluctuar; —, s. cosa que flota, f.
floating-bridge, *-brĭj*, s. pontón, m.

floating-capital, *-kăp'ĭtăl*, s. capital en circulación, m.
floating-debt, *-dĕt*, s. deuda flotante, f.
flock, *flŏk*, s. manada, f.; rebaño, m.; gentío, m.; vedija de lana, f.; —, v. n. congregarse.
floe, *flō*, s. carámbano, m.
flog, *flŏg*, v. a. azotar.
flogging, *-gĭng*, s. tunda, zurra, f.
flood, *flŭd*, s. diluvio, m.; inundación, f.; flujo, m.; —, v. a. inundar.
floor, *flōr*, s. pavimento, suelo, piso, m.; piso de una casa; —, v. a. solar.
flooring, *-ĭng*, s. estrado, m.; ensamblaje de madera para suelos, m.
floral, *flō'rål*, a. floral.
florescence, *flōrĕs'sĕns*, s. florescencia, f.
florid, *flŏr'ĭd*, a. florido.
florin, *flŏr'ĭn*, s. florín, m.
florist, *flŏr'ĭst*, s. florista, m.
floss-silk, *flŏs'sĭlk*, s. filadiz, m.
flossy, *-sĕ*, a. blando como la seda.
flotilla, *flŏtĭl'lå*, s. (mar.) flotilla, f.
flounce, *flŏûns*, s. farfalá, m.; —, v. a. guarnecer con falbalás; —, v. n. revolcarse en agua ó cieno.
flounder, *flŏûn'dŭr*, s. acedía, platija (pez de mar), f.; —, v. n. patear, brincar.
flour, *flŏûr*, s. harina, f.
flourish, *flŭr'ĭsh*, v. a. exornar con flores retóricas; adornar; vibrar (una espada); —, v. n. florecer; gozar de prosperidad; jactarse; escribir haciendo lazos con la pluma; amplificar; (mus.) preludiar, florear; —, s. belleza, f.; floreo de palabras, m.; lazo, m.; (mus.) floreo, preludio, m. [mofa, burla, f.
flout, *flŏût*, v. a. mofar, burlarse; —, s.
flow, *flō*, v. n. fluir, manar; crecer la marea; ondear; —, s. creciente de la marea, f.; abundancia, f.; flujo, m.
flower, *flŏû'ŭr*, s. flor, f.; harina, f.; (fig.) lo mejor; —, v. a. & n. florear; florecer.
flower-bed, *-bĕd*, s. cuadro (en un jardín), m.
flower-girl, *-gŭrl*, s. florera, f.
floweret, *-ĕt*, s. florecilla, florecita, f.
flower-pot, *-pŏt*, s. tiesto de flores, m.
flowery, *-ĕ*, a. florido.
flower-show, *-shō*, s. exposición de flores, f. [suspenso.
fluctuate, *flŭk'tūåt*, v. n. fluctuar; estar
fluctuation, *flŭktūå'shŭn*, s. fluctuación, f.
flue, *flō*, s. humero, m.; pelusa, f. [f.
fluency, *-ĕnsĕ*, s. fluidez, f.; volubilidad, f.
fluent, *-ĕnt*, a. fluido; fluente; fácil; -ly, ad. con facundia.
fluid, *-ĭd*, a. & s. fluido (m.).
fluidity, *flōĭd'ĭtĕ*, s. fluidez, f.
fluke, *flōk*, s. lengüeta de áncora, f.; acedía, f. (pez).
flummery, *flŭm'årĕ*, s. gachas de harina de avena, f. pl.; lisonja grosera, f. [m.
flunkey, *flŭng'kĕ*, s. lacayo, m.; estafero,
flurry, *flŭr'rĕ*, s. ráfaga, f.; priesa, agitación, f.; —, v. a. confundir; alarmar.
flush, *flŭsh*, v. a. sonrojar; exaltar; —, v. n. fluir con violencia; ponerse colorado; —, s. flujo rápido, m.; (at cards) flux, m.

rubor suelto, m.; —, a. fresco, robusto, opulento; próligo.

fluster, *flŭs'tar*, v. a. confundir, atropellar. [estriar.

flute, *flōt*, s. flauta, f.; estría, f.; —, v. a.

flutist, *-ĭst*, s. flautista, m.

flutter, *flŭt'tar*, v. a. turbar, desordenar; —, v. n. revolotear; estar en agitación; —, s. confusión, f.; agitación, f.; undulación, f. [disentería, f.

flux, *flŭks*, s. flujo, m.; concurso, m.;

fly, *flī*, v. a. & n. volar; pasar ligeramente; saltar, reventar; huir, escapar; —, s. mosca, f.; volante, m.; diligencia, f. (coche); Spanish —, cantárida, f.

fly-blow, *-blō*, s. cresa, f.

fly-catcher, *-kătshar*, s. papamoscas, m.

fly-fish, *-fĭsh*, v. a. pescar con moscas.

fly-flap, *-flăp*, s. mosqueador, m.

flying-fish, *flī'ĭngfĭsh*, s. volador, pez volante, m.

fly-man, *-măn*, s. calesero, m.

foal, *fōl*, s. potro, m., potra, f.; buche, m.; —, v. a. parir una yegua.

foam, *fōm*, s. espuma, f.; —, v. n. espumar.

foamy, *-ĭ*, a. espumoso. [m.

fob, *fŏb*, s. faltriquera pequeña, f.; engaño,

focus, *fō'kŭs*, s. foco, m., el punto céntrico.

fodder, *fŏd'dar*, s. forraje, m.

foe, *fō*, s. adversario, enemigo, m.

fog, *fŏg*, s. niebla, f.

fogey, *fō'gĕ*, s. patán, zompo, m.

foggy, *fŏg'gĕ*, a. nebuloso, brumoso.

foible, *fōĭ'bl*, s. debilidad, parte flaca, f.

foil, *fōĭl*, v. a. vencer; frustrar; —, s. desventaja, desgracia, f.; chasco, m.; hoja (de estaño), f.; florete, m.

foist, *fōĭst*, v. a. insertar (subrepticiamente).

fold, *fōld*, s. redil, aprisco, m.; plegadura, f.; hoja de una puerta, f.; —, v. a. apriscar el ganado; plegar.

folder, *-ar*, s. plegador, m., plegadera, f.

folding, *-ĭng*, s. plegadura, f.

folding-bed, *-ĭngbĕd*, s. catre de tijera ó de campaña, m.

folding-chair, *-ĭngtshār*, s. silla de tijera, f. [f.

folding-door, *-ĭngdōr*, s. media puerta,

folding-screen, *-ĭngskrēn*, s. biombo,

foliage, *fō'lĭăj*, s. follaje, m. [m.

foliation, *fōlĭă'shăn*, s. (bot.) foliación, f.; azogamiento de los espejos, m.

folio, *fō'lĭō*, s. infolio,-libro en folio, m.

folk, *fōk*, s. gente, f., mundo, m.

follow, *fŏl'lō*, v. a. seguir; acompañar; imitar; —, v. n. seguirse, resultar, provenir.

follower, *-ar*, s. seguidor, m.; imitador, m.; secuaz, partidario, m.; adherente, m.; compañero, m.

folly, *fŏl'lĕ*, s. extravagancia, bobería, f.

foment, *fōmĕnt'*, v. a. fomentar; proteger.

fomentation, *-ā'shăn*, s. fomentación, f.; fomento, m.

fond, *fŏnd*, a. loco, enamorado (por), apasionado, demasiado indulgente; **-ly,** ad. locamente, cariñosamente.

fondle, *-l*, v. a. mimar, hacer caricias.

fondling, *-lĭng*, s. favorito, niño mimado, m. [pasión loca, f.; indulgencia, f.

fondness, *-nĕs*, s. debilidad, f.; terneza,

font, *fŏnt*, s. pila bautismal, f.

food, *fōd*, s. alimento, m.; comida, f.

fool, *fōl*, s. loco, tonto, m.; bufón, m.; —, v. a. engañar; infatuar; —, v. n. tontear.

foolery, *-ar̆ĕ*, s. tontería, bobería, f.

foolhardiness, *-hārdĭnĕs*, s. temeridad, locura, f.

foolhardy, *-hārdĕ*, a. temerario.

foolish, *-ĭsh*, a. bobo, tonto; **-ly,** ad. bobamente, sin juicio.

foolscap, *-s'kăp*, s. papel grifón, m.

foot, *fŭt*, s. pie, m.; base, f.; infantería, f.; estado, m.; sistema, m.; paso, m.; **—by—,** paso entre paso; **on ó by —,** á pie; —, v. n. bailar, saltar, brincar; ir á pie; —, v. a. patear, pisotear; rechazar con el pie; remontar botas. [los pies, m.

foot-ball, *-băl*, s. balón para jugar con

foot-bath, *-băth*, s. pediluvio, m.

foot-board, *-bōrd*, s. estribo, m.

foot-bridge, *-brĭj*, s. puentecilla, f.

foot-guards, *-gārds*, s. pl. guardias del rey que sirven á pie, f. pl. [el pie, m.

foot-hold, *-hōld*, s. espacio en que cabe

footing, *-ĭng*, s. base, f.; piso, paso, m.; estado, m.; condición, f.; fundamento, m.

foot-lights, *-lĭtz*, s. pl. lámparas del proscenio, f. pl. [infantería, m.

footman, *-măn*, s. lacayo, m.; soldado de

foot-muff, *-mŭf*, s. folgo, m.

foot-note, *-nōt*, s. anotación debajo de un escrito, f.

foot-pace, *-pās*, s. paso lento ó corto, m.

foot-pad, *-păd*, s. salteador á pie, m.

foot-path, *-păth*, s. senda, f.

foot-pavement, *-pāvment*, s. acera, f.

foot-post, *-pōst*, s. peatón, m.

foot-print, *-prĭnt*, s. huella, pisada, f.

foot-step, *-stĕp*, s. vestigio, m.; huella, f.

foot-stool, *-stōl*, s. escabelo, m.

foot-warmer, *-wărmar*, s. estufilla, f.

foot-way, *-wā*, s. sendero, m.

fop, *fŏp*, s. petimetre, pisaverde, m.

foppery, *-pĕrĕ*, s. tontería, f.; afectación (en el vestirse), f.

foppish, *-pĭsh*, vanidoso; afectado.

for, *fōr*, pr. por, á causa de; para; á pesar de; —, c. porque, para que; por cuanto; **as — me,** tocante á mí; **— as much,** respecto á; por lo tocante á; **what — ?** á qué? á qué fin? para qué?

forage, *fōr'ăj*, s. forraje, m.; —, v. a. forrajear; saquear.

forager, *-ar*, s. forrajero, m.

forbear, *fōrbār'*, v. n. cesar, detenerse, abstenerse; —, v. a. omitir; soportar.

forbearance, *-ăns*, s. paciencia, indulgencia, f.

forbid, *fōrbĭd'*, v. a. prohibir, vedar; impedir; **God — !** ¡Dios no quiera!

force, *fōrs*, s. fuerza, f.; poder, vigor, m.; violencia, f.; necesidad, f.; **-s,** pl. tropas, f. pl.; —, v. a. forzar, violentar; esforzar; constreñir; —, v. n. esforzarse. [fuerza.

forcedly, *-ĕdlĕ*, ad. forzosamente, por

forced march, *fôrs'd mártsh*, s. (mil.) marcha forzada, f.　[de comadrón, f.
forceps, *fôr'séps*, s. fórceps, m., tenaza
forcible, *fôr'sibl*, a. fuerte, eficaz, poderoso, prevaleciente; **–bly**, ad. fuertemente, forzadamente.　[dero, m.
forcing-house, *fôr'sínghôus*, s. invernadero, m.
ford, *fôrd*, s. vado, m.; –, v. a. vadear.
fordable, *–ûbl*, a. vadeable.
fore, *fôr*, a. anterior; –, ad. delante, antes.
forebode, *–bôd'*, v. n. pronosticar, presagiar.
forecast, *–kâst'*, v. n. proyectar, prever; conjeturar de antemano; –, *fôr'kâst*, s. previsión, f.; proyecto, m.　[el paso.
foreclose, *–klôz'*, v. a. excluir; impedir
foreclosure, *–klô'shûr*, s. exclusión, f.; impedimento, m.
foredoom, *–dôm'*, v. a. predestinar.
forefather, *–fáther*, s. abuelo, antecesor, m.
forefend, *–fénd'*, v. a. prohibir, vedar.
forefinger, *–fínggûr*, s. índice, m.　[der.
forego, *–gô'*, v. a. ceder, abandonar; preceder.
foregone, *–gôn'*, a. pasado; anticipado.
foreground, *–grôûnd*, s. delantera, f.
forehead, *–héd*, s. frente, f.; insolencia, f.
foreign, *fôr'ín*, a. extranjero; extraño.
foreigner, *–ûr*, s. extranjero, forastero, m.　[f.
foreknowledge, *fôrnôl'éj*, s. presciencia, f.
foreland, *–lând*, s. cabo, promontorio, m.
forelock, *–lôk*, s. melena, f., copete, m.
foreman, *–mân*, s. presidente del jurado, m.; primer mancebo en las tiendas ó talleres, m.　[quete, m.
foremast, *–mâst*, s. (mar.) palo de trinquete, m.
forementioned, *–mén'shûnd*, a. ya citado, arriba citado.
foremost, *–môst*, a. delantero.
forenoon, *–nôn*, s. mañana, f.
forensic, *fôrén'sîk*, a. forense.
forepart, *fôr'pârt*, s. delantera, f.
forerunner, *–rûnnûr*, s. precursor, m.; predecesor, m.
foresail, *–sâl*, s. (mar.) vela de trinquete, m.
foresee, *–sê'*, v. a. prever.　[f.
foreshadow, *–shâd'ô*, v. a. pronosticar; simbolizar.
foreshorten, *–shôr'tn*, v. a. recortar.　[f.
foresight, *–sît*, s. previsión, f.; presciencia, f.
forest, *fôr'ést*, s. bosque, m.; selva, f.
forestall, *fôrstâl'*, v. a. anticipar; preocupar, prevenir; monopolizar.
forester, *fôr'éstûr*, s. guardabosque, m.
foretaste, *fôrtâst'*, v. a. tener presciencia; catar ó gustar antes que; –, *fôr'tâst*, s. goce anticipado, m.
foretell, *fôrtél'*, v. a. predecir, profetizar.
foreteller, *–lûr*, s. profeta, m.
forethought, *fôr'thât*, s. providencia, f.; premeditación, f.
fore-top, *–tôp*, s. tupé, m.　[mano.
forewarn, *–wârn'*, v. a. prevenir de antemano.
forfeit, *fôr'fît*, s. multa, f.; confiscación, f.; confiscado, m.; –, v. a. confiscar; perder; pagar una multa.　[f.
forfeiture, *–ûr*, s. confiscación, f.; multa,

forge, *fôrj*, s. fragua, f.; fábrica de metales, f.; –, v. a. forjar; contrahacer; inventar.
forger, *–ûr*, s. forjador, m.; falsario, m.
forgery, *–ûrê*, s. falsificación, f.; forjadura, f.
forget, *fôrgét'*, v. a. olvidar; descuidar.
forgetful, *–fûl*, a. olvidadizo; descuidado.
forgetfulness, *–fûlnés*, s. olvido, m.; negligencia, f.　[silla, f.
forget-me-not, *–ménôt*, s. (bot.) velloforgive, *fôrgív'*, v, a. perdonar, remitir.
forgiveness, *–nés*, s. perdón, m.; remisión, f.
fork, *fôrk*, s. tenedor, m.; horca, f.; –, v. n. bifurcarse; –, v. a. ahorquillar.
forked, *–êd*, **forky,** *–ê*, a. horcado.
forlorn, *fôrlôrn'*, a. abandonado, perdido; **– hope,** (mil.) centinela perdida, f.
forlornness, *–nés*, s. miseria, f.; soledad, f.; abandono, desamparo, m.
form, *fôrm*, s. forma, f.; modelo, m.; modo, m.; formalidad, f.; método, m.; banco, m.; molde, m. –, v. a. formar.
formal, *fôr'mâl*, a. formal, metódico; ceremonioso; **–ly**, ad. formalmente.
formality, *fôrmâl'îtê*, s. formalidad, f.; ceremonia, f.
formation, *fôrmâ'shûn*, s. formación, f.
former, *fôr'mûr*, a. precedente; anterior, pasado; **–ly**, ad. antiguamente, en tiempos pasados.　[terrible.
formidable, *fôr'mîdâbl*, a. formidable, temible.
formula, *fôr'mûlâ*, s. fórmula, f.
formulary, *fôr'mûlârê*, s. formulario, m.
formulate, *fôr'mûlât*, v. a. formular, articular.
forsake, *fôrsâk'*, v. a. dejar, abandonar.
forsooth, *fôrsôth'*, ad. en verdad, ciertamente.　[juramento; perjurar.
forswear, *–swâr'*, v. a. renunciar con
fort, *fôrt*, s. castillo, m.; fortaleza, f.
forth, *fôrth*, ad. en adelante; fuera; hasta lo último; **and so –,** y así de lo demás, et cetera.　[parecer.
forthcoming, *–kûming*, a. pronto á comparecer.
forthwith, *–with'*, a. inmediatamente, sin tardanza.
fortieth, *fôr'tîéth*, s. cuadragésimo, m.
fortification, *fôrtîfîkâ'shûn*, s. fortificación, f.
fortify, *fôr'tîfî*, v. a. fortificar; corroborar.
fortitude, *fôr'tîtûd*, s. fortaleza, f.; valor, m.
fortnight, *fôr'nît*, s. quince días, m. pl.; dos semanas, f. pl.; **–ly**, a. & ad. cada quince días.
fortress, *fôr'trés*, s. (mil.) fortaleza, f.
fortuitous, *fôrtû'îtûs*, a. impensado; casual; **–ly**, ad. fortuitamente.
fortunate, *fôr'tûnât*, a. afortunado; **–ly**, ad. felizmente.
fortune, *fôr'tjûn*, s. fortuna, suerte, f.; estado, m.; condición, f.; bienes de fortuna, m. pl.; hacienda, dote, f.
fortune-hunter, *–hûntûr*, s. aventurero, m.; el que va en busca de esposa rica.
fortune-teller, *–téllûr*, s. sortílego, adivino, m.
forty, *fôr'tî*, a. cuarenta.　[vino, m.

forward, *fŏr'wărd,* a. apresurado; presumido; anterior; pronto, activo, dispuesto; —, ad. adelante, más allá; —ly, ad. apresuradamente; atrevidamente; —, v. a. acelerar; promover, patrocinar.

forwarder, —*ăr,* s. promotor, m.; (am.) comisionista, m.

forwardness, —*nĕs,* s. prontitud, f.; progreso, m.; precocidad, f.; audacia, f.

forwards, —*z,* ad. adelante.

foss, *fŏs,* s. foso, m., zanca, f.

fossil, *fŏs'sĭl,* a. & s. fósil (m.).

foster, *fŏs'tăr,* v. a. criar, nutrir.

foster-brother, —*brŭdhăr,* s. hermano de leche, m.

foster-child, —*tshĭld,* s. alumno, m.

foster-father, —*făthăr,* s. el que cría y enseña á un hijo ajeno, m. [f.

foster-mother, —*mŭthăr,* s. ama de leche,

foster-son, —*sŭn,* s. hijo de leche, m.

foul, *fŏul,* a. sucio, puerco; impuro, detestable; — copy, s. borrador, m.; —ly, ad. suciamente; ilegítimamente; — v. a. ensuciar. [dad, f.

foulness, —*nĕs,* s. porquería, f.; deformi-

found, *fŏund,* v. a. fundar, establecer; edificar; fundir. [fundamento, m.

foundation, *fŏundă'shăn,* s. fundación, f.;

foundationer, —*ăr,* s. bolsero, m.

foundation-stone, —*stōn,* s. piedra fundamental, f.

founder, *fŏund'ăr,* s. fundador, m.; fundidor, m.; —, v. n. (mar.) irse á pique.

foundery, —*ĭ,* s. fundería, f.

foundling, *fŏund'lĭng,* s. niño expósito, m.

fount, *fŏunt,* fountain, —*ĕn,* s. fuente, f.; —s, pl. artificio de una fuente, m. [m.

fountain-head, —*inhĕd,* s. origen de fuente,

four, *fōr,* a. cuatro.

fourfold, —*fōld,* a. cuádruplo.

four-footed, —*fŭtĕd,* a. cuadrúpedo.

fourscore, —*skōr,* a. ochenta.

fourteen, —*tēn,* a. catorce.

fourteenth, —*tēnth,* a. décimocuarto.

fourth, *fōrth,* a. cuarto; —ly, ad. en cuarto

fowl, *fŏul,* s. ave, f.; volatería, f. [lugar.

fowler, —*ăr,* s. pajarero, m.

fowling, —*ĭng,* s. cetrería, caza de aves, f.

fowling-piece, —*pēs,* s. escopeta de pajarero, f.

fox, *fŏks,* s. zorra, f.; (fig.) zorro, m.

fox-glove, —*glŭn,* s. (bot.) dedalera, f.

fraction, *frăk'shăn,* s. fracción, f.

fractional, —*ăl,* a. fraccionario.

fractious, *frăk'shăs,* a. regañón, enojadizo.

fracture, *frăk'tăr,* s. fractura, f.; —, v. a. fracturar, romper.

fragile, *frăj'ĭl,* a. frágil; débil.

fragility, *frăjĭl'ĭtĭ,* s. fragilidad, f.; debilidad, flaqueza, f.

fragment, *frăg'mĕnt,* s. fragmento, m.

fragmentary, —*tărĭ,* a. fragmentario.

fragrance, *frā'grăns,* s. fragancia, f.

fragrant, *frā'grănt,* a. fragrante, oloroso; —ly, ad. con fragancia.

frail, *frāl,* a. frágil, débil.

frailty, —*tĭ,* s. fragilidad, f.; debilidad, f.

frame, *frām,* s. fábrica, f.; marco, cerco, m.; bastidor, m.; telar, m.; cuadro de vidriera, m.; estructura, f.; sistema, m.; organización, orden, disposición, f.; figura, forma, f., cuerpo, m.; forjadura, f.; —, v. a. fabricar, componer, construir, formar; ajustar; idear; poner en bastidor; forjar.

frame-work, —*wărk,* s. labor hecha en el bastidor ó telar, f.; armazón, f.

franchise, *frăn'tshĭz,* s. franquicia, inmunidad, f.; privilegio, m.

frank, *frăngk,* a. franco, liberal; —, s. carta franca, f.; franco, m. (moneda); —, v. a. franquear una carta.

frankincense, —*ĭnsĕns,* s. incienso, m.

frankly, —*lĭ,* ad. francamente. [dad, f.

frankness, —*nĕs,* s. franqueza, ingenuidad,

frantic, *frăn'tĭk,* a. frenético, furioso.

fraternal, *frătăr'năl,* a., —ly, ad. fraternal(mente).

fraternity, *frătăr'nĭtĭ,* s. fraternidad, f.

fraternize, *frăt'ărnĭz,* v. n. hermanarse.

fratricide, *frăt'rĭsĭd,* s. fratricidio, m.; fratricida, m.

fraud, *frŏd,* s. fraude, engaño, m. [f.

fraudulence, *frŏ'dŭlĕns,* s. fraudulencia,

fraudulent, *frŏ'dŭlĕnt,* a. fraudulento; —ly, ad. fraudulentamente.

fraught, *frŏt,* a. cargado, lleno.

fray, *frā,* s. riña, disputa, querella, f.; —, v. a. estregar; espantar.

freak, *frēk,* s. fantasía, f.; capricho, m.

freckle, *frĕk'l,* s. peca, f.

freckled, —*d,* a. pecoso.

free, *frē,* a. libre; liberal; franco, ingenuo; exento, dispensado, privilegiado; —, v. a. libertar; librar; eximir. [m.

freebooter, —*bŏtăr,* s. filibustero, forbante,

freedman, —*d'măn,* s. esclavo manumiso, m. [dad, f.

freedom, —*dŭm,* s. libertad, f.; inmunidad,

free-hearted, —*hărtĕd,* a. liberal, generoso.

freehold, —*hōld,* s. feudo franco, m.

freely, —*lĭ,* ad. libremente; espontáneamente; liberalmente. [dadano, m.

freeman, —*măn,* s. hombre libre, m.; ciu-

freemason, —*măsn,* s. francmasón, m. [f.

freemasonry, —*măsnrĭ,* s. francmasonería,

freeness, —*nĕs,* s. libertad, f.; sinceridad, f.; liberalidad, f.

free-school, —*skŏl,* s. escuela gratuita, f.

free-spoken, —*spōkn,* a. dicho sin reserva.

free-thinker, —*thĭngkăr,* s. libertino, m.

free-thinking, —*thĭnking,* s. incredulidad, f.

free-trade, —*trăd,* s. libre cambio, m.

free-will, —*wĭl,* s. libre albedrío, m.; voluntariedad, f. [gelar.

freeze, *frēz,* v. n. helar(se); —, v. a. con-

freight, *frăt,* s. carga, f.; flete, m.; —, v. a. (mar.) fletar; cargar.

freighter, —*ăr,* s. fletador, m.

frenchify, *frĕnsh'ĭfĭ,* v. a. afrancesarse.

frenzied, *frĕn'zĭd,* a. loco, delirante.

frenzy, *frĕn'zĭ,* s. frenesí, m.; locura, f.

frequency, *frē'kwĕnsĭ,* s. frecuencia, f.; multitud, f.

frequent, *frē'kwĕnt,* a. —ly, ad. frecuente(mente); —, *frĕkwĕnt',* v. a. frecuentar.

frequentative, *frēkwĕn'tătĭv,* a. frecuentativo. [m.

frequenter, *frēkwĕnt'ar,* s. frecuentador,

fresco, *frĕs'kō,* s. pintura al fresco, f.

fresh, *frĕsh,* a. fresco; nuevo, reciente; **– water,** s. agua dulce, f.

freshen, *–n,* v. a. (& n.) refrescar(se).

freshet, *–ĕt,* s. arroyo de agua dulce, m.

freshly, *–lĕ,* ad. frescamente; reciente-

freshman, *–măn,* s. novicio, m. [mente.

freshness, *–nĕs,* s. frescura, f.; fresco, m.

freshwater, *–wătăr,* s. (mar.) fig. zapatero, marinero inexperimentado, m.

fret, *frĕt,* s. (mar.) estrecho, m.; enojo, m.; **–,** v. a. frotar; corroer; cincelar; irritar; agitar, enojar; **–,** v. n. agitarse, enojarse.

fretful, *–fūl,* a. enojadizo, colérico; **–ly,** ad. de mala gana. [humor, m.

fretfulness, *–fūlnĕs,* s. mal genio, mal

fret-saw, *–sâ,* s. serrucho, m.

fretting, *–tĭng,* s. agitación, f.

friability, *frĭăbĭl'ĭtĕ,* s. friabilidad, f.

friable, *frĭ'ăbl,* a. friable, desmenuzable.

friar, *frĭ'ăr,* s. fraile, m.; **–'s lantern,** s. fuego fatuo, m.

friary, *–ĕ,* s. convento de frailes, m.

Friday, *frĭ'dâ,* s. viernes, m.; **good –,** Viernes Santo, m. [pl. parientes, m. pl.

friend, *frĕnd,* s. amigo, m.; amiga, f.;

friendless, *–lĕs,* a. sin amigos.

friendliness, *–lĭnĕs,* s. amistad, benevolencia, bondad, f.

friendly, *–lĕ,* a. amigable, amistoso.

friendship, *–shĭp,* s. amistad, f.

frieze, *frēz,* s. friso, m.

frigate, *frĭg'āt,* s. (mar.) fragata, f.

fright, *frīt,* s. espanto, terror, m.

frighten, *–n,* v. a. espantar.

frightful, *–fūl,* a. espantoso, horrible; **–ly,** ad. espantosamente, terriblemente.

frigid, *frĭj'ĭd,* a. frío, frígido; **–ly,** ad. friamente. [rencia, f.; impotencia, f.

frigidity, *frĭjĭd'ĭtĕ,* s. frialdad, f.; indiferill, *frĭl,* s. escote, vuelo, m.

fringe, *frĭnj,* s. franja, f.; **–,** v. a. guarnecer con franjas. [vieja, f.

frippery, *frĭp'părĕ,* s. ropavejería, f.; ropa

frisk, *frĭsk,* v. n. saltar, cabriolar; **–,** s. gambeta, f.; brinco, m.

frisky, *–ĕ,* a. alegre, placentero.

frith, *frĭth,* s. estrecho, brazo de mar, m.

fritter, *frĭt'tăr,* s. fritilla, f.; **–,** v. a. tajar carne; desmenuzar.

frivolity, *frĭvŏl'ĭtĕ,* s. frivolidad, f.

frivolous, *frĭv'ŏlŭs,* a. frívolo, vano; **–ly,** ad. frivolamente, sin substancia.

frizz(le), *frĭz'(l),* v. a. frisar; rizar.

fro, *frō,* ad. atrás; **to go to and –,** ir y venir. [sayo, m.; túnica, f.

frock, *frŏk,* s. blusa, f.; bata de niño, f.;

frog, *frŏg,* s. rana, f.

frolic(k), *frŏl'ĭk,* a. alegre, vivo; **–,** s. fantasía, f.; capricho, m.; **–,** v. n. loquear. juguetear, triscar.

frolicsome, *–săm,* a. juguetón, travieso.

from, *frŏm,* pr. de; después; desde.

frond, *frŏnd,* s. rama verde, f.

front, *frŭnt,* s. frente, f.; frontispicio, m.; **–,** v. a. hacer frente.

frontal, *–tăl,* s. frontero, m.; venda, f.

frontier, *frŏn'tĕr,* s. frontera, f.

frontispiece, *frŏn'tĭspĕs,* s. frontispicio, m.; frontis grabado de un libro, m.

frontlet, *frŭnt'lĕt,* s. frontal, m.; venda para la frente, f.

frost, *frŏst,* s. helada, f.; hielo, m.

frost-bitten, *–bĭtn,* a. helado, quemado del hielo.

frosty, *–ĕ,* a. helado, frío como el hielo.

froth, *frŏth,* s. espuma (de algún líquido), f.; **–,** v. n. espumar.

frothy, *–ĕ,* a. espumoso; frívolo, vano.

froward, *frō'wărd,* a. incorregible; impertinente; **–ly,** ad. insolentemente.

frowardness, *–nĕs,* s. mal genio, m.; petulancia, f. [ceño, m.; enojo, m.

frown, *frŏŭn,* v. a. mirar con ceño; **–,** s.

frozen, *frō'zn,* a. helado.

frugal, *frō'găl,* a. frugal; económico; sobrio; **–ly,** ad. frugalmente. [ción, f.

frugality, *frŏgăl'ĭtĕ,* s. frugalidad, moderafruit, *frŏt,* s. fruto, m.; producto, m.

fruiterer, *–ărăr,* s. frutero, m.

fruitful, *–fūl,* a. fructífero; fértil; provechoso, útil; **–ly,** ad. con fertilidad.

fruitfulness, *–fūlnĕs,* s. fertilidad, f.

fruitless, *–lĕs,* a. estéril; inútil; **–ly,** ad. vanamente, inútilmente.

fruit-tree, *–trē,* s. frutal, m.

frump, *frŭmp,* s. vieja cotorrera, f.

frustrate, *frŭs'trāt,* v. a. frustrar; anular.

frustration, *frŭstrā'shŭn,* s. contratiempo, chasco, m.

fry, *frī,* s. freza, f.; fritura, f.; enjambre, m.; montón, m.; hígado, m.; **–,** v. a. freir.

frying-pan, *–ĭngpăn,* s. sartén, f.

fuchsia, *fū'shĭă,* s. (bot.) fuchsia, f.

fuddle, *fŭd'l,* v. a. (& n.) emborrachar(se).

fudge, *fŭj,* ¡quita de ahí!, ¡vete allá!

fuel, *fū'ĕl,* s. combustible, m.

fugitive, *fū'jĭtĭv,* a. & s. fugitivo (m.).

fugue, *fūg,* s. (mus.) fuga, f.

fulcrum, *fŭl'krŭm,* s. apoyo de palanca ó alzaprima, m.

fulfil, *fŭlfĭl',* v. a. colmar; cumplir.

fulfilment, *–mĕnt,* s. cumplimiento, m.

full, *fūl,* a. lleno, repleto, completo; todo; perfecto; **–,** s. total, m.; complemento, m.; **–,** ad. enteramente, del todo; **–,** v. a. batanar el paño.

full-blown, *–blōn,* a. desplegado completamente (hablando de las flores).

full-cock, *–kŏk,* a. montado, amartillado (dícese de una escopeta).

full-compass, *–kămpăs,* a. (mus.) con siete octavas. [m.

full-cry, *–krī,* s. grito agudo y penetrante,

full-dress, *–drĕs,* s. vestido de gala, m.

fuller, *–lăr,* s. batanero, m. [f.

full-length, *–lĕngth,* s. grandeza natural,

fulling-mill, *–ĭngmĭl,* s. batán, m.

full-moon, *–mōn,* s. plenilunio, m.; luna llena, f. [pliamente.

fully, *–ĕ,* ad. llenamente, enteramente, am-

fulminant, *fŭl'mĭnănt,* a. fulminante.

fulminate, *fŭl'mĭnāt,* v. a. & n. fulminar.

fulmination, *fŭlmĭnā'shŭn,* s. fulminación, f.

6*

fulness, fůl'nĕs, s. plenitud, llenura, abundancia, f.

fulsome, fůl'sŭm, a. rancio; impuro.

fumble, făm'bl, v. a. & n. tartamudear; chapucear, muchachear; andar á tientas.

fume, fům, s. humo, vapor, m.; cólera, f.; vanidad, f.; —, v. a. ahumar; —, v. n. humear, exhalar; encolerizarse. [mar.

fumigate, fů'mĭgāt, v. a. perfumar, sahu-

fumigation, fůmĭgā'shŭn, s. sahumerio, m., fumigación, f. [toria, f.

fumigator, fů'mĭgātŭr, s. máquina fumiga-

fun, fŭn, s. chanza, burla, f. [pleo, m.

function, fŭngk'shŭn, s. función, f.; em-

functionary, —ärē, s. empleado, m.

fund, fŭnd, s. fondo, m.; fondos públicos, m. pl.; —, v. a. poner dinero en los fondos públicos.

fundament, —ămĕnt, s. fundamento, m.

fundamental, —ămĕn'tăl, a. fundamental; —ly, ad. fundamentalmente.

funeral, fů'nĕrăl, s. funeral, m.; —,

funereal, fůnē'rĭăl, n. funeral, fúnebre.

fungosity, fănggŏs'ĭtē, s. fungosidad, f.

fungous, făng'gŭs, a. fungoso; esponjoso.

fungus, —, s. hongo, m.; seta, f.

funk, făngk, s. (vulg.) hedor, m.

funnel, fŭn'nĕl, s. embudo, m.; cañón (de chimenea), m.

funny, fŭn'nē, a. burlesco, bufón.

fur, fŭr, s. forro de pieles, m.; pelo, m.; —, v. a. aforrar con pieles.

furbelow, fŭr'bĕlō, s. falbalá, m.

furbish, fŭr'bĭsh, v. a. acicalar, pulir.

furious, fů'rĭăs, a. furioso, frenético; —ly, ad. con furia. [las velas.

furl, fŭrl, v. a. desdoblar; (mar.) aferrar

furlong, fŭr'lŏng, s. estadio, m. (octava parte de una milla). [miso, m.

furlough, fŭr'lō, s. (mil.) licencia, f.; per-

furnace, fŭr'nās, s. borno, m.; hornaza, f.

furnish, fŭr'nĭsh, v. a. suplir, proveer; equipar; (a house) amueblar una casa.

furnisher, —ŭr, s. proveedor, m.

furniture, fŭr'nĭtūr, s. ajuar, m.; aparejo, m. [chero de alhajas (&c.), m.

furniture-broker, —brōkŭr, s. cambala-

furrier, fŭr'rĭŭr, s. peletero, m.

furrow, fŭr'rō, s. surco, m.; —, v. a. surcar; estriar. [pieles.

furry, fŭr'rē, a. hecho ó guarnecido de

further, fŭr'thŭr, a. ulterior, más distante; —, ad. más lejos, más allá; aun; además de eso; —, v. a. adelantar, promover, ayudar.

furtherance, —ăns, s. adelantamiento, m.; progreso, m.; ayuda, asistencia, f.

furthermore, —mōr, ad. además.

furthest, fŭr'thĕst, ad. lo más lejos, lo más remoto. [ad. furtivamente.

furtive, fŭr'tĭv, a. furtivo; secreto; —ly,

fury, fů'rē, s. furor, m.; furia, f.; ira, f.

furze, fŭrz, s. (bot.) tojo, m.

fuse, fůz, v. a. & n. fundir; derretirse.

fusee, —ē', s. huso, m.; fusil, m.; espoleta, f.

fusible, fů'zĭbl, a. fusible, fundible.

fusilier, fůzĭlēr', s. fusilero, m.

fusion, fů'shŭn, s. fusión, licuación, f.

fuss, fŭs, s. (vulg.) alboroto, tumulto, m.

fussy, fŭs'ē, a. jactancioso; [sonante, m.

fustian, fŭs'tăn, s. fustán, m.; estilo alti-

fustiness, fŭs'tĭnĕs, s. enmohecimiento, m.;

fusty, fŭs'tē, a. mohoso. [hedor, m.

futile, fů'tĭl, a. fútil, frívolo.

futility, fůtĭl'ĭtē, s. futilidad, vanidad, f.

future, fů'tūr, a. futuro; —, s. lo futuro, el tiempo venidero. [venideros, m. pl.

futurity, fůtū'rĭtē, s. futuro, m.; sucesos

fy, fī! ¡vaya! — **for shame,** ¡qué vergüenza!

G.

gab, găb, s. (fam.) locuacidad, f.

gabble, —bl, v. n. charlar, parlotear; —, s. algarabía, f.

gable-end, gā'blĕnd, s. socarrén, alero, m.

gaby, gā'bē, s. papanatas, m.

gad, găd, v. n. tunar, corretear, andorrear.

gad-fly, —flī, s. tábano, m.

gaff, găf, s. (mar.) cangreja, f.

gag, găg, s. mordaza, f.; —, v. a. tapar la boca con mordaza.

gage, gāj, s. prenda, f.

gaiety, gā'ĕtē, s. alegría, f.

gaily, gā'lē, ad. alegremente.

gain, gān, s. ganancia, f.; interés, provecho, m.; —, v. a. ganar; conseguir; —, v. n. enriquecerse; prevalecer, obtener

gainer, —ŭr, s. ganador, m. [influjo.

gainings, —ĭngz, s. pl. ganancia, f.; provecho, m. [tuoso.

gainless, —lĕs, a. desventajoso, infruc-

gainsay, —sā, v. a. contradecir; negar; contrariar.

gait, gāt, s. marcha, f.; porte, m.

gaiter, —ŭr, s. polaina, f.; botín, m.

galaxy, găl'ăksē, s. galaxia, vía láctea, f.

gale, gāl, s. (mar.) viento fresco, m.

galiot, găl'ĭŏt, s. (mar.) galeota, f.

gall, găl, s. hiel, f.; rencor, odio, m.; —, v. a. desollar; acibarar.

gallant, găl'ănt, a. galante, elegante; valeroso; —ly, ad. galantemente; bravamente; —, s. galán, cortejo, m. [f.

gallantry, —rē, s. galantería, f.; bravura,

galleon, găl'lĕŏn, s. (mar.) galeón, m.

gallery, găl'lărē, s. galería, f.; corredor, m.

galley, găl'lē, s. (mar.) galera, f.

galley-slave, —slāv, s. galeote, m.

gallinaceous, gălĭnā'shŭs, a. gallináceo.

gallipot, găl'lĭpŏt, s. orza, f.

gall-nut, găl'nŭt, s. agalla, f.

gallon, găl'lŏn, s. galón m.(medida). [pear.

gallop, găl'lŭp, s. galope, m.; —, v. n. galo-

galloshes, gălŏsh'ĕz, s. pl. chanclos, m.

gallows, găl'lōz, s. horca, f. [cos, m. pl.

galvanic, gălvăn'ĭk, a. galvánico.

galvanise, găl'vănĭz, v. a. galvanizar.

galvanism, găl'vănĭzm, s. galvanismo, m.

gambit, găm'bĭt, s. gambit, gambís, m. (jugada de ajedrez).

gamble, găm'bl, v. n. jugar con exceso.

gambler, —ŭr, s. tahur, garitero, fullero, m.

gambling-house, -blĭnghŏŭs, s. garito, m.; casa de juego, f. [gamba, f.

gamboge, gămbŏj', s. gomaguta, guta-

gambol, găm'bŏl, s. cabriola, f.; —, v. n. brincar, saltar.

game, găm, s. juego, m.; pasatiempo, m.; burla, f.; caza, f.; —, v. n. jugar. [dor, f.

game-bag, -băg, s. mochila de un caza-

game-cock, -kŏk, s. gallo de riña, m.

game-keeper, -kēpẽr, s. guarda de coto, m.

gamesome, -sŭm, a. juguetón, retozón; -ly, ad. alegremente.

gamester, -stẽr, tahur, jugador, m.

gaming, gā'mĭng, s. juego, m. [duria, f.

gammon, găm'mŭn, s. jamón, m.; habla-

gamut, găm'ŭt, s. (mus.) gama, f.

gander, găn'dẽr, s. ánsar, ganso, m.

gang, găng, s. cuadrilla, banda, f.

gangrene, găng'grēn, s. gangrena, f.

gangway, -wā, s. pasamano de un navío, m.

gaol, jāl, s. cárcel, prisión, f. [portalón, m.

gaoler, -ẽr, s. carcelero, m.

gap, găp, s. boquete, m.; brecha, f.

gape, găp, v. n. bostezar, boquear; ansiar, hendirse: estar con la boca abierta.

gaping, gā'pĭng, s. bostezo, m.

garb, gărb, s. vestidura, f.; traje, m.; apariencia exterior, f.

garbage, -ĭj, s. tripas, f. pl.

garble, găr'bl, v. a. entresacar; garbillar.

garden, găr'dn, s. huerto, m.; jardín, m.; —, v. n. cultivar un jardín ó un huerto.

garden-engine, -engĭn, garden-hose, -hōs, s. regadera, f.

gardener, -ẽr, s. jardinero, m.; jardinera, f.

gardening, -ĭng, s. jardinería, f.

gargle, găr'gl, v. a. & n. gargarizar; —, s. gargarismo, m.

gargoyle, găr'gŏĭl, s. gárgola, f.

garish, găr'ĭsh, a. pomposo, ostentoso.

garland, găr'lănd, s. guirnalda, f.

garlic, găr'lĭk, s. (bot.) ajo, m.

garment, găr'mĕnt, s. vestidura, f.

garner, găr'nẽr, s. granero, m.

garnet, găr'nĕt, s. granate, m.; (mar.) candeletón, m.

garnish, găr'nĭsh, v. a. guarnecer, ador-nar; —, s. guarnición, f.; adorno, m.

garret, găr'rĕt, s. guardilla, f.; desván, m.

garrison, găr'rĭsn, s. (mil.) guarnición, f.; —, v. a. (mil.) guarnecer.

garrote, găr'ŏt, v. a. estrangular.

garroter, -ẽr, s. estrangulador, m.

garrulity, găr'rŏlĭtĭ, s. garrulidad, locua-cidad, charladuría, f. [charlador.

garrulous, găr'rŏlŭs, a. gárrulo, locuaz, garter, găr'tẽr, s. cenojil, m.; jarretera, f.

gas, găs, s. gas, m.

gasalier, -lēr', s. candil de gas, m.

gas-burner, -bũrnẽr, s. mechero de gas, m.

gaseous, gā'zĭŭs, a. gaseoso. [m.

gash, găsh, s. cuchillada, f.; cicatriz, f.; —, v. a. dar una cuchillada.

gas-holder, găs'hōldẽr, gasometer, găsŏm'ĕtẽr, s. gasómetro, m.

gas-jets, -jĕts, s. pl. gasíferos, m. pl.

gas-lighting, -lītĭng, s. alumbramiento de gas, m.

gasp, găsp, v. n. boquear; anhelar; —, s. respiración difícil, f.

gastric, găs'trĭk, a. gástrico. [mico.

gastronomic, găstrŏnŏm'ĭk, a. gastronó-

gas-works, găs'wũrks, s. pl. fábrica de gas, f.

gate, găt, s. puerta, f.; puerta de cercado.

gate-way, -wā, s. puerta cochera, f.

gather, găth'ẽr, v. a. recoger, amontonar; fruncir; inferir; arrugar, plegar; —, v. n. condensarse, aumentarse, juntarse; su-purar. [lecta, f.

gathering, -ĭng, s. acumulación, f.; co-

gaudily, gâ'dĭlĭ, ad. ostentósamente, fasto-samepte. [ción, f.

gaudiness, gâ'dĭnĕs, s. pompa, f.; ostenta-

gaudy, -ĕ, a. fastoso; pomposo; —, s. fiesta, f.; festín, m.

gauge, gâj, s. aforo, m.; —, v. a. aforar.

gauger, -ẽr, s. aforador, m.

gaunt, gânt, a. & s. flaco, delgado (m.).

gauntlet, gânt'lĕt, s. guantelete, m.; manc-gauze, gâz, s. gasa, f. [pla, f.

gawky, gâ'kĕ, a. bobo, tonto, rudo.

gay, gā, a. gayo, alegre. [mirada, f.

gaze, gāz, v. n. contemplar, considerar; —, s.

gazelle, găzĕl', s. gacela, f.

gazer, gā'zẽr, s. mirón, m.

gazette, găzĕt', s. gaceta, f.

gazetteer, găzĕttēr', s. gacetero, m.; dic-cionario geográfico, m.

gear, gēr, s. atavío, m.; vestido, m.; apa-rejo, m.; tirantes, m. pl.

gelatin(e), jĕl'ătĭn, s. jaletina, jalea, f.

gelatinous, jĕlăt'ĭnŭs, a. gelatinoso.

geld, gĕld, v. a. castrar, capar.

gelding, -ĭng, s. caballo capón, m.

gem, jĕm, s. joya, f.; yema, f.; —, v. n. ador-nar con piedras preciosas; —, v. n. abotonar.

Gemini, jĕm'ĭnē, s. Géminis, m. (signo del gender, jĕn'dẽr, s. género, m. [zodíaco].

genealogical, jĕnĕālŏj'ĭkăl, a. genealógico.

genealogy, jĕnĕăl'ōjĕ, s. genealogía, f.

general, jĕn'ẽrăl, a. general, común, usual; in —, por lo común; -ly, ad. general-mente; —, s. general, m.; generala, f.

generalisation, jĕnĕrălīzā'shŭn, s. gene-ralización, f.

generalise, jĕn'ẽrălīz, v. a. generalizar.

generality, jĕnĕrăl'ĭtĕ, s. generalidad, mayor parte, f. [m.

generalship, jĕn'ẽrălshĭp, s. generalato,

generate, jĕn'ẽrāt, v. a. engendrar; pro-ducir; causar.

generation, -rā'shŭn, s. generación, f.

generator, -tẽr, s. engendrador, m.

generic, jĕnĕr'ĭk, a. genérico. [ralidad, f.

generosity, jĕnĕrŏs'ĭtĕ, s. generosidad, libe-

generous, jĕn'ẽrŭs, a. generoso; -ly, ad. magnánimamente. [f.

genet, jĕn'ĕt, s. jaca de España, f.; jineta,

genial, jē'nĭăl, a. genial, natural; alegre; -ly, ad. genialmente. [gría, f.

geniality, jēnĭăl'ĭtĕ, s. ingenuidad, f.; ale-

genitive, jĕn'ĭtĭv, s. genitivo, m.

genius, jē'nĭŭs, s. genio, m.

genteel, jĕntēl', a. gentil, lindo, galán, elegante; -ly, ad. gentilmente.

gentian, *jĕn'sиăn,* s. (bot.) genciana, f.
gentile, *jĕn'til,* s. gentil, pagano, m.
gentility, *jĕntil'ĭtĕ,* s. gentileza, f.; gentilidad, f.; nobleza de sangre, f.
gentle, *jĕn'tl,* a. suave, dócil, manso, moderado; benigno.   f.
gentlefolks, —*fōkz,* s. pl. gente bien nacida.
gentleman, —*măn,* s. gentilhombre, caballero, m.   [urbano.
gentlemanlike, —*mănlĭk,* a. caballeroso,
gentleness, —*nĕs,* s. dulzura, suavidad de carácter, f.; nobleza, f.
gentlewoman, —*wŭmăn,* a. señora, dama, f.
gently, *jĕn'tlĕ,* ad. gentilmente.   [m. pl.
gentry, *jĕn'trĕ,* s. ciudadanos distinguidos.
genuflexion, *jĕnŭflĕk'shăn,* s. genuflexión, f.   puramente, naturalmente.
genuine, *jĕn'ŭĭ,* a. genuino, puro; -ly,
genuiness, —*nĕs,* s. pureza, f.
genus, *jē'nŭs,* s. género, m.
geographer, *jĕŏg'răfăr,* s. geógrafo, m.
geographical, *jĕŏgrăf'ĭkăl,* a. geográfico.
geography, *jĕŏg'răfĕ,* s. geografía, f.
geological, *jĕŏlŏj'ĭkăl,* a. geológico.
geologist, *jĕŏl'ŏjĭst,* s. geólogo, m.
geology, *jĕŏl'ŏjĕ,* s. geología, f.   [trico.
geometric(al), *jĕŏmĕt'rĭk(ăl),* a. geomé-
geometrician, *jĕŏmĕtrĭsh'ăn,* s. geómetra.
geometry, *jĕŏm'ĕtrĕ,* s. geometría, f.   [m.
geranium, *jĕrā'nĭăm,* s. (bot.) geranio, m.
germ, *jŭrm,* s. (bot.) germen, m.
german, *jŭr'măn,* a. alemán; pariente.
germinal, *jŭr'mĭnăl,* a. germinativo.
germinate, *jŭr'mĭnāt,* v. n. brotar.
gesticulate, *jĕstĭk'ŭlāt,* v. n. gesticular.
gesticulation, —*lā'shăn,* s. gesticulación, f.
gesture, *jĕs'tŭr,* s. gesto, movimiento expresivo, m.
get, *gĕt,* v. a. granjear, ganar; conseguir, obtener, alcanzar; coger; agarrar, robar; persuadir; —, v. n. alcanzar; llegar, venir; hacerse, ponerse; prevalecer; introducirse; **to — by heart,** aprender de memoria; **to — the better,** salir vencedor, sobrepujar; **to — with child,** poner encinta á una mujer.
getter-up, —*tărŭp,* s. promotor, m.   [m.
gewgaw, *gū'gŭ,* s. chuchería, f.; miriñaque,
Geyser, *gī'sŭr,* s. Géiser, m.; fuente caliente en Islandia, f.   [davérica, f.
ghastliness, *găst'lĭnĕs,* s. palidez, cara ca-
ghastly, —*lĭ,* a. pálido, espantoso.   [m.
gherkin, *gŭr'kĭn,* s. pepinillo, cohombrillo,
ghost, *gōst,* s. alma racional, f.; espectro,
ghostly, —*lĭ,* a. espiritual.   [m.
giant, *jī'ănt,* s. gigante, m.
giantess, —*ĕs,* s. giganta, f.
gibberish, *gĭb'bărĭsh,* s. jerigonza, f.
gibbet, *jĭb'bĭt,* s. horca, f.; —, v. a. ahorcar.
gibe, *jīb,* v. n. escarnecer, burlarse, mofar; —, s. mofa, burla, f.   [(de aves), m. pl.
giblets, *jĭb'lĭts,* s. pl. despojos y menudillos
giddily, *gĭd'dĭlĕ,* ad. con vértigos; descuidadamente.   [tancia, f.
giddiness, —*dĭnĕs,* s. vértigo, m.; inconstancia, f.
giddy, —*dĕ,* a. vertiginoso; inconstante.
gift, *gĭft,* s. don, m.; dádiva, f.; talento, m.

gig, *gĭg,* s. tílburi, calesín, m.; trompo, m. perínola, f.; esquife, m.   [gigantesco.
gigantic(al), *jīgăn'tĭk(ăl),* a. gigante,
giggle, *gĭg'gl,* v. n. fisgarse sonriéndose.
gild, *gĭld,* v. a. dorar.
gilding, —*ĭng,* gilt, *gĭlt,* s. doradura, f.
gill, *jĭl,* s. cuarta parte de pinta, f.; hiedra terrestre, f.; torrentera, f.; —s, pl. barbas del gallo, f. pl.; agallas de los peces, f. pl.
gillyflower, —*tflŏŭr,* s. (bot.) alelí, m.
gimcrack, *jĭm'krăk,* s. carraca, f.
gimlet, *jĭm'lĕt,* s. barrena pequeña, f.
gimp, *gĭmp,* s. encaje de hilo ó seda, m.
gin, *jĭn,* s. trampa, f.; cabria, f.; aguardiente de nebrina, m.
ginger, —*jăr,* s. jengibre, m.
gingerbread, —*brĕd,* s. pan de jengibre, m.
gipsy, *jĭp'sĕ,* s. gitano, m.
giraffe, *jĭrăf',* s. jirafa, f.   [farse.
gird, *gŭrd,* v. a. ceñir; cercar; —, v. n. mo-
girder, —*dr,* s. cuartón, m.
girdle, —*l,* s. cinturón, m.; —, v. a. ceñir.
girl, *gŭrl,* s. muchacha, doncellita, f.
girlhood, —*hŭd,* s. doncellez, soltería, f.
girlish, —*ĭsh,* a. juvenil.
girth, *gŭrth,* s. cincha, f.; circunferencia, f.
gist, *jĭst,* s. punto principal de una acusación, f.
give, *gĭv,* v. a. & n. dar, donar; conceder; renunciar; abandonar; pronunciar; aplicarse, dedicarse.
gizzard, *gĭz'zărd,* s. molleja, f.
glacial, *glā'shăl,* a. glacial.   [m.
glacier, *glā'shǔr (glăsē'),* s. ventisquero,
glad, *glăd,* a. alegre, contento, agradable;
I am — to see, me alegro de; -ly, alegremente.
gladden, —*n,* v. a. alegrar, recrear.
glade, *glād,* s. cañada, f.; (am.) nevisca, f.
gladiator, *glădiā'tăr,* s. gladiator, m.
gladness, *glăd'nĕs,* s. alegría, f.
gladsome, —*săm,* a. alegre, contento.
glair, *glār,* s. claro de huevo, m.
glamour, *glăm'ăr,* s. ilusión óptica, f.
glance, *glăns,* s. vislumbre, f.; relámpago, m.; ojeada, f.; —, v. a. lanzar miradas; raspar; pasar ligeramente; —, v. n. centellar; hojear.
gland, *glănd,* s. glándula, f.
glanders, *glănd'ărz,* s. muermo, m.
glare, *glār,* s. deslumbramiento, m.; mirada feroz y penetrante, f.; —, v. n. relumbrar, brillar; echar miradas de indignación.
glaring, —*ĭng,* a. deslumbrante; manifiesto; que clama al cielo.
glass, *glăs,* s. vidrio, m.; telescopio, m.; vaso para beber, m.; espejo, m.; reloj de arena, m.; barómetro, m.; —es, pl. anteojo, m.; —, a. vítreo.   [vidrio, m.
glass-blower, —*blŏăr,* s. soplador de
glass-door, —*dŏr,* s. puerta con vidrieras, f.
glass-work, —*wŭrk,* s. fábrica de vidrio ó cristales, f.
glassy, —*ĕ,* a. vítreo, cristalino, vidrioso.
glaze, *glāz,* v. a. vidriar; embarnizar.
glazier, *glā'zhăr,* s. vidriero, m.
glazing, —*ĭng,* s. conjunto de vidrios, m.
gleam, *glēm,* s. relámpago, rayo, m.; —, v. n. relampaguear, brillar.

glean, *glén*, v. a. espigar; recoger.

glebe, *gléb*, s. gleba, f.; terrón, m.

glee, *glí*, s. alegría, f.; gozo, m.; jovialidad, f.; canción jovial, f.

gleeful, *fúl*, a. alegre, gozoso.

gleet, *glít*, s. gonorrea, f.; pudre, m.

glen, *glén*, s. valle, m.; llanura, f.

glib, *glíb*, a. liso, resbaladizo; -ly, ad. corrientemente, volublemente.

glide, *glíd*, v.n. resbalar; pasar ligeramente.

glim, *glím*, s. farol de ronda, m.; linterna sorda, f. [vislumbrarse.

glimmer, *már*, s. vislumbre, f.; -, v. n.

glimpse, *glímps*, s. vislumbre, f.; relámpago, m.; ojeada, f.; -, v. a. (am.) descubrir, percibir. [lucir, brillar.

glisten, *glís'n*, glitter, *glít'tár*, v. n. relucir, brillar.

gloaming, *glóm'ing*, s. crepúsculo, m.

gloat, *glót*, v. n. ojear con admiración.

globe, *glób*, s. globo, m.; esfera, f.

globular, *glób'dlár*, a. globoso.

globule, *glób'úl*, s. glóbulo, m.

gloom, *glóm*, gloominess, *inés*, s. obscuridad, f.; melancolía, tristeza, f.; -ly, ad. obscuramente; tristemente.

gloomy, *é*, a. sombrío, obscuro; cubierto de nubes; triste, melancólico.

glorification, *glórífká'shän*, s. glorificación, alabanza, f.

glorify, *glór'ífi*, v. a. glorificar, celebrar.

glorious, *glór'rús*, a. glorioso, ilustre; -ly, ad. gloriosamente.

glory, *glór'ré*, s. gloria, fama, celebridad, f.; aureola, f.; -, v. n. gloriarse, jactarse.

gloss, *glós*, s. glosa, f.; escolio, m., lustre, m.; -, v. a. glosar, interpretar; notar;

glossary, *áré*, s. glosario, m. [barnizar.

glosser, *ár*, s. comentador, m.

glossy, *sé*, a. lustroso, brillante.

glove, *gláv*, s. guante, m.

glover, *ár*, s. guantero, m.

glow, *gló*, v. n. arder; inflamarse; relucir; -, s. color vivo, m.; viveza de color, f.; vehemencia de una pasión, f.

glower, *gló'ár*, v. n. mirar con ceño.

glow-worm, *wúrm*, s. luciérnaga, f.

gloze, *glóz*, v. n. adular, lisonjear.

glue, *glú*, s. cola, f.; visco, m., -, v. a. encolar, pegar.

gluey, *é*, a. viscoso, pegajoso.

glum, *glám*, a. tétrico, triste.

glut, *glát*, v. a. engullir, tragar, devorar; saciar; -, s. hartura, abundancia, f.

gluten, *glú'tén*, s. gluten, m.

glutinous, *glú'tínús*, a. glutinoso, viscoso.

glutton, *glút'n*, s. glotón, tragón, m.

gluttony, *é*, s. glotonería, f.

glycerine, *glís'árín*, s. glicerina, f.

gnarled, *nár'ld*, a. nudoso. [dientes.

gnash, *násh*, v. a. & n. chocar; crujir los

gnat, *nát*, s. mosquito, m.

gnaw, *ná*, v. a. roer; mordicar.

gnome, *nóm*, s. gnomo, m.

go, *gó*, v. n. ir, irse, andar, caminar; partir(se), marchar; huir; pasar; – to ¡vamos!, ¡á ello!

goad, *gód*, s. aguijada, aljada, f.; -, v. a. aguijar; estimular, incitar.

goal, *gól*, s. meta, f.; fin, m. [m.

goat, *gót*, s. cabra, cliva, f.; he—, cabrón,

goat-herd, *hérd*, s. cabrero, m.

gobble, *gób'bl*, v. a. engullir, tragar; -, v. n. gorgorear como los gallipavos.

gobbler, *ár*, s. glotón, m.

go-between, *gó'bétwén*, s. mediador, m.; entremetido, m.

goblet, *gób'lét*, s. copa, f. [duende, m.

goblin, *gób'lín*, s. espíritu ambulante,

God, *gód*, s. Dios, m. [m.

god-child, *tshíld*, s. ahijado, hijo de pila,

god-daughter, *ddtár*, s. ahijada, hija

goddess, *dés*, s. diosa, f. [de pila, f.

god-father, *fáthár*, s. padrino, m.

godhead, *héd*, s. deidad, divinidad, f.

godless, *lés*, a. infiel, impío, sin Dios.

godlike, *lík*, a. divino. [ateo.

godliness, *línés*, s. piedad, devoción, santidad, f.

godly, *lé*, a. piadoso, devoto, religioso; recto, justificado; -, ad. piadosamente, justamente.

god-mother, *máthár*, s. madrina, f.

god-son, *sán*, s. ahijado, m.

goer, *gó'ár*, s. andador, paseante, m.

goggle, *góg'gl*, v. n. volver los ojos.

goggle-eyed, *íd*, a. bisojo, bizco.

going, *gó'ing*, s. paso, m.; andadura, f.; partida, f.; progreso, m.

gold, *góld*, s. oro, m. [batihoja, m.

gold-beater, *bétár*, s. batidor de oro,

gold-bound, *bóúnd*, a. guarnecido de oro.

golden, *n*, a. áureo, de oro; excelente; – rule, s. (ar.) regla de tres, f.

gold-fish, *físh*, s. dorado, m.

gold-leaf, *léf*, s. hoja de oro batido, f.

goldsmith, *smith*, s. orífice, m.

golf, *gólf*, s. juego de pelota escocés, m.

golosh, *gólósh'*, s. galocho, m.

gondolier, *gándólér'*, s. gondolero, m.

gone, *gón*, a. ido; perdido, pasado; gastado; muerto.

gong, *góng*, s. atabal chino, m.

good, *gúd*, a. bueno, benévolo, cariñoso; conveniente, apto; -, ad. bien; -, s. bien, m. prosperidad, ventaja, f.; -s, pl. bienes muebles, m. pl.; mercaderías, f. pl.

good-bye, *bí'* ! ¡á Dios!

goodies, *íz*, s. pl. golosinas, f. pl.

goodliness, *línés*, s. hermosura, elegancia, gracia, f.

goodly, *lé*, a. hermoso, espléndido; alegre.

good-nature, *ná'júr*, s. bondad, f.

good-natured, *ná'júrd*, a. bondadoso.

goodness, *nés*, s. bondad, f.

goodwill, *wíl*, s. benevolencia, bondad, f.

goose, *gós*, s. ganso, m.; oca, f.; plancha de sastre, f.

gooseberry, *bérré*, s. uva espina, f.

goose-step, *stép*, s. (mil.) desfilada, f.

gopher, *gó'fár*, s. turón, m.

gore, *gór*, s. sangre cuajada, f.; -, v. a. punzar con puñal; herir un animal con sus cuernos á otro.

gorge, *górj*, s. gorja, garganta, f.; -, v. a. engullir, tragar.

gorgeous, *gór′jĕås,* a. primoroso, brillante, vistoso; **-ly,** ad. con esplendor y magnificencia.

gorget, *gór′jĕt,* s. gola, f.

Gorgon, *gór′gŏn,* s. Gorgona, f.

gormandize, *gór′măndīz,* v. n. glotonear.

gormandizer, *-ŭr,* s. golosazo, m.

gory, *gó′rĕ,* a. cubierto de sangre grumosa.

goshawk, *gós′hǎk,* s. azor, halcón palumbario, m.

gosling, *gŏz′lĭng,* s. gansarón, m.

gospel, *gŏs′pĕl,* s, evangelio, m.

gossamer, *gŏs′ămăr,* s. vello, m.; pelusa (de frutas), f.

gossip, *gŏs′sĭp,* s. compadre, m.; comadre, f.; charla, f.; **-,** v. n. charlar.

gothic, *gŏth′ĭk,* a. gótico.

gouge, *gŏj,* s. gubia, f.; escoplo, m.

gourd, *gŏrd,* s. (bot.) calabaza, f.

gout, *gŏŭt,* s. gota, f. (enfermedad).

gouty, *-ĕ,* a. gotoso.

govern, *gŭv′ărn,* v. a. gobernar, dirigir, regir.

governable, *-ĭbl,* a. dócil, manejable.

governess, *-ĕs,* s. gobernadora, f.

government, *-mĕnt,* s. gobierno, m.; administración pública, f.

governor, *-ŭr,* s. gobernador, m.

gown, *gŏŭn,* s. talar, m.; toga, f.; vestido de mujer, m.; bata, f.; camiseta, f.

gownsman, *-s′măn,* s. estudiante de alguna universidad, m.

grabble, *grăb′bl,* **grab,** *grăb,* v. a. tentar, palpar.

grace, *grās,* s. gracia, f.; favor, m.; merced, f.; perdón, m.; gracias, f. pl.; to say **-,** bendecir la mesa; **-,** v. a. adornar; agraciar.

Grace, -, s. Alteza (título), f.

graceful, *grās′fŭl,* a. gracioso, primoroso; **-ly,** ad. elegantemente, con gracia.

graceless, *-lĕs,* a. desagraciado; réprobo, malvado.

gracious, *grā′shăs,* a. gracioso; favorable; **-ly,** ad. graciosamente.

graciousness, *-nĕs,* s. gracia, bondad, f.

gradation, *grădā′shăn,* s. graduación, f.

grade, *grād,* s. grado, m.

gradient, *grād′ĭĕnt,* s. (rail.) pendiente y contrapendiente, m. & f.; **falling -,** (rail.) declive, m.

gradual, *grăd′ŭăl,* a. gradual; **-ly,** ad. gradualmente.

graduate, *grăd′ŭăt,* v. a. graduar; adelantar.

graduation, *grădŭă′shăn,* s. graduación, f.

graft, *grăft,* s. injerto, m.; **-,** v. a. injertar, ingerir.

grafting-knife, *-ĭngnĭf,* s. ingeridor, m.

grain, *grān,* s. grano, m.; semilla, f.; grana, f.; disposición, índole, f.; **-s,** pl. orujo, burujo, m.; **against the -,** contra pelo; con repugnancia.

grained, *-d′,* a. granado; áspero; teñido en grano.

gram, *grăm,* s. gramo, m. (peso).

grammar, *grăm′măr,* s. gramática, f. [m.

grammarian, *grămmā′rĭăn,* s. gramático, m.

grammatic(al), *grămmăt′ĭk(ăl),* a. **-ally,** ad. gramatical(mente).

grampus, *grăm′păs,* s. marsopa, f. (pez).

granary, *grăn′ărĕ,* s. granero, m.

grand, *grănd,* a. grande, ilustre.

grandchild, *-tchīld,* s. nieto, m.; nieta, f.

granddaughter, *-dătŭr,* s. nieta, f.; **great -,** biznieta, f.

grandee, *-ē′,* s. grande (de España), m.

grandeur, *grănd′yŭr,* s. grandeza, f.; pompa, f. [-, bisabuelo, m.

grandfather, *-făthăr,* s. abuelo, m.; **great -,** bisabuelo, m.

grandiloquent, *grăndĭl′ŏkwĕnt,* a. grandílocuo.

grandiose, *grănd′ĭōs,* a. grandioso.

grandly, *grănd′lĕ,* ad. grandemente, sublimemente. [great -, bisabuela, f.

grandmother, *-mŭthăr,* s. abuela, f.; **great -,** bisabuela, f.

grand-sire, *-sīr,* s. abuelo, m.

grandson, *-săn,* s. nieto, m.; **great -,** biznieto, m.

grange, *grănj,* s. granja, f. [biznieto, m.

granite, *grăn′ĭt,* s. granito, m.

grant, *grănt,* v. a. conceder; **to take for -ed,** presuponer; **-,** s. concesión, f.

granulate, *grăn′ŭlāt,* v. a. granular.

granule, *grăn′ŭl,* s. granillo, m.

grape, *grāp,* s. uva, f.; **bunch of -s,** racimo de uvas, m.

grape-shot, *-shŏt,* s. (mil.) metralla, f.

grape-stone, *-stōn,* s. granuja, f.

graphic(al), *grăf′ĭk(ăl),* a. gráfico; pintoresco; **-ally,** ad. gráficamente.

grapnel, *grăp′nĕl,* s. (mar.) arpeo, m.

grapple, *grăp′pl,* v. a. (& n.) agarrar(se); **-s,** s. arpeo, m.

grasp, *grăsp,* v. a. empuñar, asir, agarrar; **-,** v. n. esforzarse á agarrar; **-,** s. puño, puñado, m.; poder, m.

grass, *grăs,* s. hierba, f.; herbaje, m.

grass-hopper, *-hŏppăr,* s. cigarrón, m.

grass-plot, *-plŏt,* s. césped, m.

grass-widow, *-wĭdō,* s. (am.) mujer cuyo marido está ausente, f.

grassy, *-sĕ,* a. herboso.

grate, *grāt,* s. reja, verja, rejilla, f.; **-,** v. a. rallar; rechinar (los dientes); enrejar; ofender. [ad. agradecidamente.

grateful, *-fŭl,* a. grato, agradecido; **-ly,** ad. agradecidamente.

gratefulness, *-fŭlnĕs,* s. gratitud, f.

grater, *-ăr,* s. rallo, m. [ción, f.

gratification, *grătĭfĭkā′shăn,* s. gratificación, f.

gratify, *grăt′ĭfī,* v. a. contentar; gratificar.

grating, *grā′tĭng,* s. rejado, m.; **-,** a. áspero; ofensivo.

gratis, *grā′tĭs,* ad. gratis, de balde.

gratitude, *grăt′ĭtŭd,* s. gratitud, f.

gratuitous, *grătŭ′ĭtăs,* a. gratuito, voluntario; **-ly,** ad. gratuitamente.

gratuity, *grătŭ′ĭtĕ,* s. gratificación, recompensa, f.

gratulate, *grăt′ŭlāt,* v. a. congratular.

gratulation, *grătŭlā′shăn,* s. congratulación, f.

grave, *grāv,* s. sepultura, f.; **-,** v. a. grabar, esculpir; **-,** a. grave, serio; **-ly,** ad. con gravedad, seriamente.

grave-clothes, *-klōthz,* s. pl. mortaja, f.

grave-digger, *-dĭggăr,* s. sepulturero, m.

gravel, *grăv′ĕl,* s. cascajo, m.; mal de piedra, m.; **-,** v. a. cubrir con cascajo; embarazar.

graveless, *grāv′lĕs,* a. insepulto.

gravelly, *grăv′ĕllĕ,* a. arenisco, cascajoso.

gravel-pit, *grăv′ĕlpĭt,* s. arenaria, f.

gravel-walk,–*wâk*, s. camino empedrado,
graven, *grâ'vn*, a. grabado. [m.
graver, *grâ'vûr*, s. grabador, m.; buril, m.
grave-stone, *grâv'stôn*, s. piedra sepulcral, f.
gravitate, *grâv'itât*, v. n. gravitar. [f.
gravitation, *grâvitâ'shûn*, s. gravitación.
gravity, *grâv'itê*, s. gravedad, f. [f.
gravy, *grâ'vê*, s. jugo de la carne, f.; salsa,
gray, *grâ*, a. gris; cano ; –, s. gris, m.
gray-beard, –*bêrd*, s. barbicano, m.
grayish, –*ish*, a. pardusco; entrecano.
grayling, –*ling*, s. tímalo, m. (pez).
grayness, –*nês*, s. color gris, m.
graze, *grâz*, v. a. pastorear; tocar ligeramente; –, v. n. rozar; pacer.
grazier, *grâ'zhûr*, s. ganadero, m.
grease, *grês*, s. grasa, f.; –, v. a. untar.
greasiness, –*ines*, s. grasa, f., pringue,
m. & f.; porquería, f.
greasy, –*ê*, a. grasiento, craso, gordo.
great, *grât*, a. gran, grande; principal;
ilustre; noble, magnánimo; –ly, ad. muy,
mucho; grandemente.
great-coat, –*kôt*, s. sobretodo, m.
greatness, –*nês*, s. grandeza, f.; dignidad,
f.; poder, m.; magnanimidad, f.
greedily, *grê'dili*, ad. vorazmente, ansiosamente.
greediness, *grê'dinês*, greed, *grêd*, s.
voracidad, f.; gula, f.; codicia, f.
greedy, *grê'dê*, a. voraz, hambriento ; ansioso, deseoso; insaciable.
Greek, *grêk*, s. griego (idioma), m.
green, *grên*, a. verde, fresco, reciente; no
maduro; –, s. verde, m.; llanura verde,
f.; –s, pl. verduras, f. pl.
greenback, –*bâk*, s. rana de zarzal, f.;
–s, pl. (am.) papel moneda, m.
green-gage, –*gâj*, s. ciruela verdal, f.
green-grocer, –*grôsûr*, s. verdulero, m.
green-horn, –*hôrn*, s. (vulg.) joven sin
experiencia, m.
green-house, –*hôûs*, s. invernáculo, m.
greenish, –*ish*, a. verdoso.
greenness, –*nês*, s. verdín, verdor, vigor,
m.; frescura, falta de experiencia, f.; novedad, f. [descanso, m. (en los teatros).
green-room, –*rôm*, s. hogar, salón de
green-sickness, –*siknês*, s. opilación,
clorosis, f. [frutas y verduras, m.
green-stall, –*stâl*, s. puesto para vender
green-sward, –*swârd*, s. césped, m.
green-wood, –*wûd*, s. bosque verde, m.
green-yard, –*yârd*, s. leñera, f.
greet, *grêt*, v. a. saludar, congratular; –,
v. n. encontrarse y saludarse.
greeting, –*ing*, s. salutación, f.
gregarious, *grêgâ'rûs*, a. gregal.
grenade, *grênâd'*, s. (mil.) granada, f.
grenadier, *grênâdêr'*, s. granadero, m.
grey, *grâ*, a. gris, pardo.
greyhound, –*hôûnd*, s. galgo, m.
gridiron, *grid'îrn*, s. parrillas, f. pl.
grief, *grêf*, s. dolor, m.; aflicción, pena, f.
grievance, *grê'vâns*, s. pesar, m.; molestia, f.; agravio, m.; injusticia, f.; perjuicio, m. [afligirse; llorar.
grieve, *grêv*, v. a. agraviar, afligir; –, v. n.

grievous, *grê'ûs*, a. doloroso; enorme,
atroz; –ly, ad. penosamente; cruelmente.
griffin, *grif'fin*, s. grifo, m. [rrero, m.
grig, *grig*, s. anguila pequeña, f.; chaparrill, *gril*, v. a. asar en parrillas.
grim, *grim*, a. feo; horrendo; ceñudo.
grimace, *grimâs'*, s. visaje, m.; mueca, f.
grimalkin, *grimâl'kin*, s. gatazo, m.
grime, *grim*, s. porquería, f.; –, v. a. ensuciar. [m.
grimness, *grim'nês*, s. grima, f.; horror,
grimy, *grî'mê*, a. ensuciado.
grin, *grin*, s. mueca, f.; rechino de los
dientes, m.; –, v.n. hacer visajes; rechinar
los dientes.
grind, *grind*, v. a. moler; pulverizar;
afilar; estregar; mascar; rechinar los
dientes; (– students) preparar.
grinder, –*ûr*, s. molinero, m.; molinillo,
m.; amolador, m.; preparador, m.; muela,
piedra molar, f. [f.
grindstone, –*stôn*, s. piedra amoladera,
grip, *grip*, v. a. desaguar; –, s. caz, m.
gripe, *grip*, v. a. asir, empuñar; dar
cólico; –, v. n. padecer cólico; –, s.
toma, f.; presa, f.; opresión, f.; tenedor,
m.; –s, pl. dolor cólico, m.
griper, –*ûr*, s. usurero, m.
griskin, *gris'kin*, s. costilla de tocino, f.
grisly, *griz'lê*, grisled, –*ld*, a. horroroso.
grist, *grist*, s. molienda, f.; provisión, f.
gristle, *gris'l*, s. tendón, nervio, m.
gristly, *gris'lê*, a. tendinoso, nervioso.
grit, *grit*, s. moyuelo, m.; avena mondada
y medio molida, f.; arena, f.
gritty, *grit'tê*, a. arenoso.
grizzle, *griz'l*, s. gris, m.
grizzled, –*d*, grizzly, *griz'lê*, a. mezclado
con gris, pardusco. [gemido, suspiro, m.
groan, *grôn*, v. n. gemir, suspirar; –, s.
groat, *grôt*, s. moneda del valor de cuatro
peniques, f.; –s, pl. avena mondada y
medio molida, f.
grocer, *grô'sûr*, s. especiero, abacero, m.
grocery, –*ê*, s. especería, abacería, f.
grog, *grôg*, s. grog, ponche, m.
groggy, –*gê*, a. medio borracho.
groin, *grôin*, s. ingle, f.
groom, *grôm*, s. establero, m.; criado, m.;
novio, m.; –, v. a. cuidar los caballos.
groomsman, –*smân*, s. padrino, m., el
que conduce al novio.
groove, *grôv*, s. cavidad profunda, f.;
muesca, f.; –, v. a. acanalar.
grope, *grôp*, v. a. & n. tentar, buscar á
obscuras; andar á tientas.
gross, *grôs*, a. grueso, corpulento, espeso;
grosero; estúpido; –ly, ad. groseramente;
en bruto; –, s. grueso, m.; todo, m.
grossness, –*nês*, s. rudeza, grosería, f.
grot(to), *grôt'(tô)*, s. gruta, f.
grotesque, *grôtêsk'*, a. grotesco.
ground, *grôûnd*, s. tierra, f., país, m.;
terreno, suelo, pavimento, m.; fundamento, m.; razón fundamental, f.; campo
(de batalla), m.; fondo, m.; –s, pl. hez,
f.; poso, m.; –, v. a. establecer; (mar.)
varar.

ground-floor, ... s. entresuelo, m.
ground-ivy, —*ivy,* s. hiedra terrestre, f.
groundless, —*lês,* a. infundado; —ly, ad. sin fundamento, sin razón ó motivo.
groundlessness, —*lêsnês,* s. falta de razón ó fundamento, f.
ground-plot, —*plót,* s. solar, terreno, m.; (fig.) fundamento, m.   [raíz, f.
ground-rent, —*rênt,* s. renta de un bien
groundsel, —*sêl,* s. hierba caña, f.
ground-work, —*wûrk,* s. plan, fundamento, m.
group, *grôp,* s. grupo, m.; —, v. a. agrupar.
grouse, *grôûs,* s. gallina silvestre, f.
grout, *grôût,* s. harina basta, f.; liez, f.; borras, f. pl.
grove, *grôv,* s. arboleda, f.; boscaje, m.
grovel, *grôv'l,* v. n. serpear; bajarse.
grow, *grô,* v. a. cultivar; —, v. n. crecer, aumentarse; nacer; vegetar; adelantar; hacerse, ponerse ó volverse; — up, crecer.
grower, —*ûr,* s. arrendador, m.
growl, *grôûl,* v. n. regañar, gruñir, rezongar; —, s. gruñido, m.
growth, *grôth,* s. vegetación, f.; crecimiento, m.; producto, m.; aumento, m.; progreso, adelanto, m.
grub, *grûb,* s. hombre pequeño, m.; gorgojo, m.; —, v. a. desarraigar; desmontar, rozar.
grudge, *grûj,* s. rencor, odio, m.; envidia, f.; —, v. a. & n. envidiar; repugnar.
grudgingly, *grûj'inglê,* ad. con repugnancia, de mala gana.
gruel, *grô'êl,* s. harina de avena mondada, f.   [ásperamente.
gruff, *grûf,* a. ceñudo, grosero; —ly, ad.
gruffness, —*nês,* s. aspereza, severidad, f.
grumble, *grûm'bl,* v. n. gruñir; murmurar.
grumpy, —*pê,* a. regañón.   [rar.
Grundy, Mrs. —, *mis'trîs grûn'dê,* s. moralista mimosa, f.
grunt, *grûnt,* v. n. gruñir; gemir.
guarantee, *gàrântê',* s. garante, fiador, m.; garantía, f.; —, v. a. garantir.
guaranty, —, *gàr'ântê,* s. garante, m.; garantía, f.
guard, *gârd,* s. guarda, guardia, f.; (rail.) conductor, m.; —, v. a. guardar; defender; —, v. n. guardarse; prevenirse.
guarded, —*êd,* a. mesurado, circunspecto.
guard-house, —*hôûs,* **guard-room,** —*rôm,* s. (mil.) cuerpo de guardia, m.
guardian, *gâr'diân,* s. tutor, m.; curador, m.; guardián (prelado), m.; —, a. tutelar.
guardianship, —*shîp,* s. tutela, f.; guardianía, f.
guard-ship, *gârd'shîp,* s. navío de guardia
gudgeon, *gûj'ân,* s. gobio, m. (pez); bobo, m.
guerdon, *gâr'dn,* s. galardón, m.
guess, *gês,* v. a. & n. conjeturar; adivinar; —, s. conjetura, f.   [forastero, m.
guest, *gêst,* s. huésped, convidado, m.;
guffaw, *gûfà',* s. carcajada, f.   [ción, f.
guidance, *gî'dâns,* s. gobierno, m.; dirección, f.
guide, *gîd,* v. a. guiar, dirigir; —, s. guía, m.
guide-book, —*bûk,* s. itinerario, m.
guild, *gîld,* s. gremio, m.; corporación, f.

guild-hall, —*hôl,* s. casa consistorial, f.
guile, *gîl,* s. engaño, fraude, m.
guileful, —*fûl,* a. engañoso, impostor.
guileless, —*lês,* a. cándido, sincero.
guillotine, *gîl'ôtên,* s. guillotina, f.; —, v. a. guillotinar.
guilt, *gîlt,* s. delito, m.; culpa, f.
guiltless, —*lês,* a. inocente, libre de culpa.
guilty, —*ê,* a. reo, culpable.
guinea, *gîn'ê,* s. guinea, f. (moneda).   [f.
guinea-hen, —*hên,* s. gallinaza de Indias
guise, *gîz,* s. modo, m.; manera, f.; práctica, f.
guitar, *gîtâr',* s. guitarra, f.   [tica, f.
gulch, *gûltsh,* s. glotón, m.
gulf, *gûlf,* s. golfo, m.; abismo, m.
gull, *gûl,* s. gaviota, f.; engaño, m.; bobo, m.; impostor, m.; —, v. a. engañar.
gullet, —*lêt,* s. gaznate, m.; gola, f.
gullibility, —*lîbîl'îtê,* s. credulidad, f.
gullible, —*lîbl,* a. crédulo.
gully, —*lê,* v. n. fluir murmurando.
gully-hole, —*hôl,* s. sumidero, albañal, m.
gulp, *gûlp,* s. trago, m.; —, v. n. engullir, tragar.   [engomar.
gum, *gûm,* s. goma, f.; encía, f.; —, v. a.
gummy, —*mê,* a. gomoso.   [f.; juicio, m.
gumption, *gûm'shûn,* s. (fam.) inteligencia,
gum-tree, *gûm'trê,* s. árbol gomífero, m.
gun, *gûn,* s. arma de fuego, f.; cañón, m.
gun-boat, —*bôt,* s. cañonera, f.
gun-carriage, —*kârrîj,* s. afuste, m.
gun-metal, —*mêtâl,* s. bronce de cañones, f.
gunnel, —*nêl,* t. (mar.) borda, f.   [m.
gunner, —*nûr* artillero, m.
gunnery, —*nûrê,* s. artillería, f.
gunpowder, —*pôdûr,* s. pólvora, f.
gun-room, —*rôm,* s. (mar.) Santabárbara, f.
gun-shot, —*shôt,* s. tiro de escopeta, m.; alcance de unas armas, m.   [m.
gunsmith, —*smîth,* s. arcabucero, armero,
gun-stock, —*stôk,* s. caja de escopeta, f.
gurgle, *gûr'gl,* v. n. salir con ruido.
gush, *gûsh,* v. n. brotar; chorrear; —, s. chorro, m.
gushing, —*îng,* a. superabundante.
gusset, *gûs'sêt,* s. cuadrado, m.
gust, *gûst,* s. gusto, m.; soplo de aire, m.
gusty, —*ê,* a. tempestuoso.
gut, *gût,* s. intestino, m.; glotonería, f.; —, v. a. desventrar, destripar.
gutter, —*tûr,* s. gotera, f.; —, v. a. & n. acanalar; caer en gotas.
guttural, —*tûrâl,* a. gutural.
guy, *gî,* s. (mar.) retenida, f.; Juan de las Viñas, m.   [glotonería.
guzzle, *gûz'zl,* v. a. & n. beber ó comer con
gymnasium, *jîmnâ'zîûm,* s. gimnasio, m.
gymnast, *jîm'nâst,* s. gimnasta, m.
gymnastic(al), *jîmnâs'tîk(âl),* a. gimnástico; —s, s. gimnástica, f.
gyrate, *jîrât',* v. n. girar.

H.

haberdasher, *hàb'ûrdâshûr,* s. tendero, m.
haberdashery, —*ê,* s. mercería, f.   [m.
habiliment, *hàbîl'îment,* s. vestido, m.; compostura, f.

habilitate, -tāt, v. a. habilitar.
habit, hăb'ĭt, s. hábito, vestido, m.; uso, m., costumbre, f.; complexión, f.
habitable, -ăbl, a. habitable.
habitation, hăbĭtā'shăn, s. habitación, f.; domicilio, m. [habitualmente.
habitual, hăbĭt'ůăl, a. habitual; -ly, ad.
habituate, -āt, v. a. habituar, acostumbrarse.
habitude, hăb'ĭtůd, s. costumbre. f.
hack, hăk, s. caballo de alquiler, rocín, m.; muesca, f.; -, v. a. tajar, cortar; hablar mal una lengua. [f.; -, v. a. rastrillar.
hackle, -l, s. rastrillo, m.; seda cruda,
hackney, -nē, s. caballo de alquiler, m.; -, a. alquilado.
hackneyed, -nēd, a. trillado, trivial.
haddock, hăd'dŏk, s. egrefín, gado, m. (pez).
haft, hăft, s. mango, m.; asa, f.; -, v. a. poner mango á alguna cosa.
hag, hăg, s. bruja, hechicera, f.
haggard, -gărd, a. feroz, huraño.
haggle, -gl, v. a. cortar en tajadas; -, v.n.
haggler, -glăr, s. regatón, m. [regatear.
ha-ha, hă hă, s. salto de lobo, m.
hail, hăl, s. granizo, m.; saludo, m.; -, v. a. saludar; (mar.) venir á la voz; -, v. imp. granizar; -, ¡salve! [m.
hail-fellow, -fĕllō, s. compañero íntimo.
hail-stone, -stōn, s. piedra de granizo, f.
hair, hăr, s. pelo; (of the head) cabello, m. [m.; casi nada, f.
hair-breadth, -brĕdth, s. ancho de un pelo,
hair-cloth, -klŏth, s. cilicio, m.
hair-dresser, -drĕssăr, s. peluquero.
hairless, -lĕs, a. calvo. [peinador, m.
hair-pin, -pĭn, s. alfiler para afianzar los cabellos, m.
hair-powder, -pŏddăr, s. polvos de peinar ó para el pelo, m. pl.
hair-sieve, -sĭv, s. tamiz para colar, m.
hair-splitting, -splĭtĭng, s.quisquilla,f.
hairy, -ĕ, a. peludo, velludo, cabelludo.
halberd, hăl'bărd, s alabarda, f.
halberdier, -ĭr, s. alabardero, m.
halcyon, hăl'sĭăn, a. quieto, tranquilo; -, s. alción, alción, m. (ave).
halo, hăl a. sano, vigoroso; ileso.
half, hăf, s. mitad, f.; -, a. medio.
half-blood, -blŭd, s. medio hermano, m.; media hermana, f. [mestizo.
half-bred, -brĕd, half-caste, -kăst, a.
half-caste, -kăst, s. casta cruzada, f.
half-cock, -kŏk, a. desmontado (escopeta).
half-moon, -mōn, s. semilunio, m.
half-penny, hă'pĕnnĕ, s. medio penique, m.
halfway, hăf wă, ad. á medio camino.
hall, hăl, s. vestíbulo, m.; salón, colegio, m.
halliards, hăl'yărdz, s. pl. (mar.) driza, f.
halloo, hăllō', ¡hola!, ¡ea! -, v. n. azuzar (á los perros en la caza); llamar á uno gritando.
hallow, hăl'lō, v. a. consagrar, santificar.
hallucination, hăllūsĭnā'shăn, s. alucinación, f.
halo, hăl'lō, s. halón, m. [ción, f.
halt, hălt, v. n. cojear; parar; dudar; -, s. cojera, f.; parada, f.; alto, m.
halter, -ăr, s. soga, f.; cuerda, f.
halve, hăv, v. a. partir en dos mitades.

ham, hăm, s. corva, f.; jamón, m.
hamlet, hăm'lĕt, s. villorro, m.
hammer, hăm'măr, s. martillo, m.; serpentín de fusil, m.; subasta, f.; -, v. a. martillar; forjar; -, v. n. trabajar.
hammer-cloth, -klŏth, s. paño del pescante de un coche, m.
hammock, hăm'mŏk, s. hamaca, f.
hamper, hăm'păr, s. cuévano, m.; -, v. a. embarazar; entrampar.
hamstring, hăm'strĭng, s. tendón de la corva, m.; -, v. a. desjarretar.
hand, hănd, s. mano, f.; palmo, m. (medida); carácter de escritura, m.; poder, m.; talento, m.; (mar.) marinero, m.; obrero, m.; mano de un reloj; at -, á la mano, al lado; - in -, de acuerdo; -, v. a. alargar; guiar por la mano; echar la mano; manejar.
hand-barrow, -bărrō, s. angarillas, f.pl.
hand-bell, -bĕl, s. campanilla, f.
hand-bill, -bĭl, s. cartel, m.
hand-book, -bŭk, s. manual, m.
hand-cuff, -kăf, s. manilla, f.
handed, -ĕd, a. transmitido, pasado de uno á otro.
handful, -fŭl, s. manojo, puñado, m.
hand-gallop, -găllăp, s. galope corto, m.
handicap, -dĭkăp, s. carrera ciega con caballos de peso igualado, f.
handicapper, -păr, s. arbitrador en las carreras ciegas, m. [f.
handicraft, hăn'dĭkrăft, s. arte mecánica.
handicraftsman, -s'măn, s. artesano, m.
handily, hăn'dĭlĕ, ad. mañosamente.
handiness, hăn'dĭnĕs, s. maña, habilidad, f. [f.
handiwork, hăn'dĭwărk, s. obra manual.
handkerchief, hăn'kărtshĭf, s. pañuelo, m. [manija, f.; -, v. a. manejar, tratar.
handle, hăn'dl, s. mango, puño, m.; asa, f.
handling, hăn'dlĭng, s. manejo, m.; toque,
hand-mill, -mĭl, s. molinillo, m. [m.
hand-rail, -rāl, s. guardalado, m.
handsel, hăn'sĕl, s. estreno, m.; -, v. a. estrenar alguna cosa.
handsome, hăn'săm, a. hermoso, bello, gentil; -ly, ad. hermosamente, primorosamente.
hand-spike, hănd'spĭk, s. palanca, f.
hand-writing, -rītĭng, s. carácter de escritura, m.
handy, hăn'dĕ, a. manual; diestro, mañoso.
hang, hăng, v. a. colgar, suspender; ahorcar; entapizar; -, v. n. colgar; ser ahorcado; pegarse; quedarse suspenso; depender. [f.
hanger, -ăr, s. alfanje, m.; espada ancha,
hanger-on, -ăr ŏn, s. dependiente, m.; mogollón, m.
hangings, -ĭngz, s. pl. tapicería, f.
hangman, -măn, s. verdugo, m.
hank, hăngk, s. madeja de hilo, f.
hanker, -ăr, v. n. ansiar, apetecer.
hansom, hăn'săm, s. cabriolé, m.
hap-hazard, hăp'hăzărd, s. accidente, [rado.
hapless, -lĕs, a. desgraciado, desventu-
haply, -lĕ, ad. por casualidad.

happen, —*pn*, v. n. acontecer, acaecer.

happily, —*ptli*, ad. felizmente.

happiness, —*ptnes*, s. felicidad, dicha, f.

happy, —*pe*, a. feliz, bienaventurado.

harangue, *hárâng'*, s. arenga, f.; —, v. n. arengar.   [matar de cansancio.

harass, *hár'âs*, v. a. cansar, fatigar; —out,

harbinger, *hár'binjur*, s. precursor, m.

harbour, *hár'bûr*, s. albergue, m.; puerto, m.; asilo, m.; —, v. a. albergar; hospedar; —, v. n. tomar albergue.

hard, *hárd*, a. duro, firme; difícil; penoso; cruel, severo, rígido; —of hearing, medio sordo; —, ad. cerca, á la mano; difícilmente; —by, muy cerca.

harden, —*n*, v. a. (& n.) endurecer(se).

hard-hearted, —*hárted*, a. duro de corazón, insensible.   [valor, m.

hardihood, *hár'dihûd*, s. atrevimiento,

hardiness, *hár'dines*, s. fatiga, f.; intrepidez, f.; atrevimiento.

hardly, *hárd'li*, ad. apenas; severamente.

hardness, —*nés*, s. dureza, f.; dificultad, f.; inhumanidad, f.; severidad, f.

hardship, —*shtp*, s. injuria, opresión, f.; injusticia, f.; penalidad, f.; trabajo, m.; molestia, fatiga, f.

hardware, —*wâr*, s. quincallería, f.

hardy, *hár'dé*, a. atrevido, bravo, intrépido; fuerte, robusto.

hare, *hâr*, s. liebre, f.   [follada, f.

harebell, —*bél*, s. campánula rotundifolia, f.

hare-brained, —*brând*, a. aturdido, atolondrado.

hare-lipped, —*ltpped*, a. labihendido.

hark, *hárk*, i.[the!, ¡oye!, ¡mira!   [m.

harlequin, *hár'lêkwtn*, s. arlequín, bufón,

harlot, *hár'lât*, s. puta, meretriz, f.

harm, *hárm*, s. mal, daño, m.; desgracia, f.; perjuicio, m.; —, v. a. dañar, injuriar, ofender.   [—ly, ad. dañosamente.

harmful, —*fôl*, a. dañoso; perjudicial;

harmless, —*lés*, a. sencillo, inocente; —ly, ad. inocentemente; sin daño.

harmonic(al), *hármón'tk(âl)*, a. armónico.

harmonious, *hármó'néûs*, a. armonioso; —ly, ad. armoniosamente.

harmonise, *hár'móntz*, v. a. ajustar, concertar; —, v. n. convenir, corresponder.

harmony, *hár'móné*, s. armonía, f.

harness, *hár'nés*, s. arreos de un caballo, m. pl.; —, v. a. enjaezar.

harp, *hárp*, s. arpa, f.; —, v. a. & n. tocar el arpa; machacar.

harpist, —*tst*, s. arpista, m.

harpoon, *hárpón'*, s. arpón, m.

harpsichord, *hárp'sîkôrd*, s. clavicordio, harpy, *hár'pé*, s. arpía, f.   [m.

harridan, *hár'rîdân*, s. rocín, m.

harrier, *hár'rîâr*, s. galgo, m.

harrow, *hár'ró*, s. grada, f.; rastro, m.; —, v. a. gradar.

harry, *hár'ré*, v. a. tormentar.

harsh, *hársh*, a. áspero, agrio, rígido, duro, austero; —ly, ad. ásperamente, severamente.   [deza, austeridad, severidad, f.

harshness, —*nés*, s. aspereza, dureza, rubart, *hárt*, s. ciervo, m.

harum-scarum, *hár'rûm skâ'rûm*, ad. cochite hervite.

harvest, *hár'vêst*, s. cosecha, f.; agosto, m.; —, v. a. recoger las mieses.

harvester, —*âr*, s. agostero, m.

harvest-home, —*hóm*, s. fiesta al acabar la siega, f.

hash, *hâsh*, s. jigote, m.; —, v. a. picar.

hasp, *hâsp*, s. aldaba de candado, f.; broche, m.; —, v. a. abrochar; cerrar con aldaba.

hassock, *hâs'sôk*, s. cojín de paja, n.

haste, *hâst*, s. priesa, f.; presteza, f.; to be in —, estar de priesa.

hasten, *hâs'n*, v. a. acelerar, apresurar; —, v. n. estar de priesa.   [airadamente.

hastily, *hâs'tili*, ad. precipitadamente;

hastiness, *hâs'tînes*, s. precipitación, f.

hasty, *hâs'té*, a. pronto, apresurado; colérico; temprano.

hasty-pudding, —*pâdding*, s. papilla hecha con leche y harina, f.

hat, *hât*, s. sombrero, m.; —s off! ¡quítense el sombrero!

hat-band, —*bând*, s. cinta del sombrero, f.

hat-box, —*bôks*, hat-case, —*kâs*, s. sombrerera, f.

hatch, *hâtsh*, v. a. criar pollos; empollar; tramar; —, s. pollada, nidada, f.; media puerta, f.   [f.

hatchet, —*êt*, s. destral, m.; hacha pequeña,

hatchment, —*mênt*, s. escudo fúnebre, m.

hatchway, —*wâ*, s. (mar.) escotilla, f.

hate, *hât*, s. odio, aborrecimiento, m.; —, v. a. odiar, detestar.

hateful, —*fôl*, a. odioso, detestable; —ly, ad. detestablemente, con tirria.

hatred, *hâ'trêd*, s. odio, aborrecimiento, m.

hatter, *hât'târ*, s. sombrerero, m.

haughtily, *hâ'tili*, ad. fieramente, orgullosamente.   [vez, f.

haughtiness, *hâ'tînes*, s. orgullo, m.; altihaughty, *hâ'té*, a. altanero, altivo, orgulloso.   [m.

haul, *hâl*, v. a. tirar, halar; —, s. estirón,

haunch, *hânsh*, s. anca, f.

haunt, *hânt*, v. a. frecuentar, rondar; —, s. guarida, f.; costumbre, f.

hautboy, *hó'bôí*, s. (mus.) oboe, m.

have, *hâv*, v. a. ir, haber, tener; poseer; to—rather, querer más, preferir.   [m.

haven, *hâ'vn*, s. puerto, m.; abrigo, asilo,

havoc, *hâv'ôk*, s. estrago, m.; ruina, f.

haw, *hâ*, s. cañada, cerca, f.; —, v. n. tartamudear.

hawk, *hâk*, s. halcón, m.; —, v. n. cazar con halcón; llevar y vender mercaderías por las calles.   [buhonero, m.

hawker, —*âr*, s. mercanchista, mercachifle,

hawser, *hâ'sâr*, s. (mar.) guríln, m.; (mar.) remolque, m.

haw-thorn, *hâ'thôrn*, s. espino blanco, m.

hay, *hâ*, s. heno, m.

hay-cock, —*kôk*, s. pila de heno, f.

hay-loft, —*lôft*, s. henil, m.

hay-making, —*mâking*, s. henaje, m.

hay-rick, —*rîk*, hay-stack, —*stâk*, s. niara, f.

hazard, *há'ŭrd*, s. acaso, accidente, m.; riesgo, m.; juego de azar á los dados, m.; —, v. a. arriesgar; aventurar.

hazardous, *—ŭs*, a. arriesgado, peligroso; —ly, ad. peligrosamente.

haze, *ház*, s. niebla, f.

hazel, *há'zĕl*, s. avellano, m.

hazel(ly), *—(lĕ)*, a. castaño.

hazel-nut, *—nŭt*, s. avellana, f.

hazy, *há'zĕ*, a. anieblado; obscuro.

he, *hĕ*, pn. él.

head, *hĕd*, s. cabeza, f.; jefe, m.; juicio, m.; talento, m.; título (de un libro), m.; puño (de bastón), m.; fuente, f.; nacimiento de un río, m.; cabeza de jabalí, f.; —, v. a. gobernar, dirigir; degollar; podar los árboles.

head-acho, *—ăk*, s. dolor de cabeza, m.

head-dress, *—drĕs*, s. cofia, f.; tocado, m.

headiness, *—ĭnĕs*, s. precipitación, obstinación, f.

head-land, *—lănd*, s. promontorio, m.

headless, *—lĕs*, a. inconsiderado.

headlong, *—lŏng*, a. & ad. temerario, inconsiderado; temerariamente; precipitadamente.

head-master, *—măstŭr*, s. profesor de las clases superiores, m.

headmost, *—mŏst*, a. primero.

head-piece, *—pĕs*, s. casco, yelmo, m.; entendimiento, m. [cuartel general, m.

head-quarters, *—kwŏrtŭrz*, s. (mil.)

headship, *—shĭp*, s. primado, m.; autoridad, f. [m.

headsman, *—z'măn*, s. degollador, verdugo,

headstall, *—stál*, s. cabezada del freno, testera, f. [zudo, obstinado.

headstrong, *—strŏng*, a. testarudo, cabezudo.

head-way, *—wá*, s. buen éxito, m.

heady, *—ĕ*, a. temerario; obstinado; violento.

heal, *hĕl*, v. a. & n. curar; sanar. [lento.

health, *hĕlth*, s. salud, sanidad, f.; brindis.

healthiness, *—ĭnĕs*, s. sanidad, f. [dio, m.

healthy, *—ĕ*, a. sano; sanativo.

heap, *hĕp*, s. montón, m.; turba, f.; —, v. a. amontonar, acumular.

hear, *hĕr*, v. a. oir; entender; obedecer; —, v. n. oir; escuchar.

hearer, *—ŭr*, s. oyente, oidor, m.

hearing, *—ĭng*, s. oído, m.; audiencia, f.

hearken, *hár'kn*, v. n. escuchar, atender.

hearsay, *hĕr'sá*, s. rumor, m.; fama, f.

hearse, *hŭrs*, s. ataúd, féretro, m.

heart, *hárt*, s. corazón, m.; interior, centro, m.; ánimo, valor, m.; amor, m.; by —, de memoria; with all my —, con toda mi alma. [—, s. congoja, f.

heart-breaking, *—brák'ĭng*, a. congojoso;

heart-burning, *—bŭrning*, s. cardialgía, f.

heart-felt, *—fĕlt*, a. sentido en el fondo del corazón.

hearth, *hárth*, s. hogar, fogón, m.

heartily, *hár'tĭlĕ*, ad. sinceramente, cordialmente. [ceridad, f.

heartiness, *hár'tĭnĕs*, s. cordialidad, sinceridad.

heartless, *—lĕs*, a. tímido; inclemente; —ly, ad. tímidamente. [m.; trinitaria, f.

heart's-ease, *—s'ĕz*, s. (bot.) pensamiento,

heart-sick, *—sĭk*, a. dolorido, afligido.

heart-whole, *—hól*, a. que tiene aun libre su corazón.

hearty, *—ĕ*, a. sincero; sano; vigoroso.

heat, *hĕt*, s. ardor, calor, m., vehemencia, f.; animosidad, f.; —, v. a. calentar, encender.

heater, *—ŭr*, s. escalfador, m. [cender.

heath, *hĕth*, heather, *hĕth'ŭr*, s. (bot.) brezo, m.; brezal, matorral, m.

heathen, *hĕ'thn*, s. gentil, pagano, m.; —ish, a. gentílico; salvaje; —ishly, ad. á la manera de los paganos.

heathenism, *—ĭzm*, s. paganismo, m.

heave, *hĕv*, v. a. alzar; elevar; hincharse; (mar.) birar para proa; —, v. n. palpitar; respirar trabajosamente; tener náuseas; —, s. esfuerzo para levantarse, m.; suspiro de congoja, m.

heaven, *hĕv'n*, s. cielo, m.; firmamento, m.

heavenly, *—ly*, a. & ad. celeste, divino; divinamente.

heavily, *hĕv'ĭlĕ*, ad. pesadamente.

heaviness, *hĕv'ĭnĕs*, s. pesadez, f.; aflicción, f.; opresión, f.

heavy, *hĕv'ĕ*, a. grave, pesado; opresivo, penoso, molesto; triste; tardo, soñoliento.

hebrew, *hĕ'brŏ*, s. hebreo, judío, m.

hecatomb, *hĕk'ătŏm*, s. hecatomba, f.

hectic(al), *hĕk'tĭk(ăl)*, a. hético.

hector, *hĕk'tŭr*, s. matasiete, fanfarrón, m.; —, v. n. baladronear, bravear.

hedge, *hĕj*, s. seto, m.; —, v. a. cercar con seto.

hedge-hog, *—hŏg*, s. erizo, m. [un seto.

hedger, *—ŭr*, s. cercador, m.

hedge-row, *—rŏ*, s. serie de árboles en los cercados, f.

heed, *hĕd*, v. a. atender, observar; —, s. cuidado, m.; atención, precaución, f.

heedful, *—fŭl*, a. vigilante, atento; circunspecto; —ly, ad. cautelosamente.

heedless, *—lĕs*, a. descuidado, negligente; —ly, ad. negligentemente.

heel, *hĕl*, s. talón, m.; to take to one's —s, apretar los talones, huir; —, v. a. taconear. [mahometanos.

Hegira, *hĕjĭ'rá*, s. egira, f., era de los

heifer, *hĕf'ŭr*, s. becerra, vaquilla, ternera, f. [f.; sublimidad, f.

height, *hĭt*, s. altura, elevación, sumidad, f.; sublimidad, f.

heighten, *—n*, v. a. realzar; adelantar; mejorar; exaltar.

heinous, *há'nŭs*, a. atroz, odioso; —ly, ad. atrozmente, horriblemente.

heir, *dr*, s. heredero, m.; — apparent, heredero forzoso, m.

heirdom, *—dŭm*, s. herencia, heredad, f.

heirloom, *—lŏm*, s. vínculo de bienes

heiress, *—ĕs*, s. heredera, f. [muebles, m.

heliograph, *hĕ'lĭŏgráf*, s. heliografía, f.

hell, *hĕl*, s. infierno, m.

hell-bred, *—brĕd*, a. producido en los infiernos.

hell-cat, *—kăt*, s. bruja, f. [fiernos.

hellenism, *hĕl'lĕnĭzm*, s. helenismo, m.

hellenist, *hĕl'lĕnĭst*, s. helenista, m.

hell-hound, *hĕl'hŏŭnd*, s. Cerbero, m.; pícaro, m. [ad. diabólicamente.

hellish, *hĕl'ĭsh*, a. infernal, malvado; —ly,

helm, *hělm*, s. (mar.) timón, gobernalle.
helmet, *-ět*, s. yelmo, m.   [m.
help, *hělp*, v. a. (& n.) ayudar, asistir, socorrer; servir á la mesa; aliviar, remediar, reparar; evitar; I cannot – it, no puedo remediarlo; no puedo dejarlo de hacer; –, s. ayuda, f.; socorro, remedio, m.
helper, *-ẽr*, helpmate, *-mǎt*, helpmeet, *-mẽt*, s. auxiliador, socorredor, m.; esposa, f.
helpful, *-fůl*, a. útil; saludable.
helpless, *-lěs*, a. abandonado; irremediable; *-ly*, ad. irremediablemente, sin recurso.   [trochemoche, en desorden.
helter-skelter, *hěl'těrskěl'tẽr*, ad. á helve, *hělv*, s. mango, m.; astil de hacha, m.
hem, *hěm*, s. ribete, m.; –, v. a. ribetear; repulgar; –! ¡ho! ¡he!   [¡he!
hemisphere, *hěm'ĭsfēr*, s. hemisferio, m.
hemlock, *hěm'lŏk*, s. cicuta, f.
hemorrhage, *hěm'ŏrrǎj*, s. hemorragia, f.
hemorrhoids, *hěm'ŏrrŏidz*, s. pl. hemorroides.   [des, m. pl.
hemp, *hěmp*, s. cáñamo, m.
hempen, *-n*, a. cᵈᵉ ñameño.
hen, *hěn*, s. gallina, f.
hence, *hěns*, ad. de aquí; por esto.
henceforth, *-forth*, henceforward, *-for'wǎrd*, ad. de aquí en adelante; en lo venidero; para siempre.   [s. gallinero, m.
hen-coop, *hěn'kōp*, hen-house, *-hŏůs*, hen-pecked, *-pěkt*, a. marición, m.
hen-roost, *-rŏst*, s. gallinero, m.
her, *hẽr*, pn. su, ella, de ella, ó ella.
herald, *hẽr'ǎld*, s. heraldo, m.
heraldic, *hěrǎl'dĭk*, a. heráldico.
heraldry, *hẽr'ǎldrĭ*, s. heráldica, f.
herb, *hẽrb*, s. yerba, f.; *-s*, pl. legumbre, hortaliza, f.
herbaceous, *hẽrbā'shŭs*, a. herbáceo.
herbage, *hẽr'bǎj*, s. herbaje, m.
herbalist, *-ĭst*, s. herbolario, m.
herbivorous, *hẽrbĭv'ŏrŭs*, a. herbívoro.
herd, *hẽrd*, s. hato, rebaño, m.; manada, f.; grey, f.; –, v. n. ir en hatos; asociarse.
herdsman, *-ᵄmǎn*, s. guarda de ganado, m.
here, *hẽr*, ad. aquí, acá.   [dor.
hereabout(s), *-bŏůt'(z)*, ad. aquí al rededor.
hereafter, *-ǎf'tẽr*, ad. en el tiempo venidero, en lo futuro; –, s. estado venidero,
hereby, *-bī'*, ad. por esto.   [m.
hereditary, *hěrěd'ĭtǎrĭ*, a. hereditario.
heredity, *-ĭtĭ*, s. derecho de sucesión, f.
herefrom, *-frŏm'*, ad. de aquí.
herein, *-ĭn'*, ad. en esto, aquí dentro.
hereof, *-ŏf'*, ad. de esto, de aquí.
heresy, *hě'rěsĭ*, s. herejía, f.   [tico.
heretic, *hě'rětĭk*, s. hereje, m.; –, a. herético, *hěrět'ĭk*, s. hereje, m.; –, a. hereto, *hẽrtō'*, ad. á esto, para esto.
heretofore, *hẽrtōfōr'*, ad. antes, en tiempos pasados.
hereupon, *-ŭpŏn'*, ad. sobre esto.
herewith, *-wĭth'*, ad. con esto.
heritance, *hẽr'ĭtǎns*, s. herencia, f.
hermetic(al), *hẽrmět'ĭk(ǎl)*, a. hermético; *-ly*, ad. herméticamente.
hermit, *hẽr'mĭt*, s. ermitaño, eremita, m.
hermitage, *hẽr'mĭtǎj*, s. ermita, f.
hernia, *hẽr'nĭǎ*, s. hernia, rotura, f.

hero, *hē'rō*, s. héroe, m.   [heroicamente.
heroic(al), *hěrō'ĭk(ǎl)*, a. heroico; *-ally*, ad.
heroine, *hě'rōĭn*, s. heroína, f.
heroism, *hě'rōĭzm*, s. heroísmo m.
heron, *hě'rŏn*, s. garza, f.   [zas, m.
heronry, *-rĭ*, s. lugar para criar las garherring, *hě'rĭng*, s. arenque, m.
hers, *hẽrz*, pn. suyo, de ella.
herself, *hẽrsělf'*, pn. ella misma.
hesitate, *hěz'ĭtǎt*, v. a. dudar; tardar.
hesitation, *hězĭtā'shŏn*, s. hesitación, duda, irresolución, f.
heterodox, *hět'ěrŏdŏks*, a. heterodoxo.
heterogeneous, *hětěrōjē'nĭŭs*, a. heterogeneo.
hew, *hū*, v. a. leñar; tajar; cortar, picar.
hewer, *-ẽr*, s. leñador, m.
hey, *hā*, ¡he!   [¡ hei
heyday, *-dā*, s. alegría, f.; gozo, m.; – ¡
hiatus, *hĭā'tŭs*, s. abertura, hendedura, f.; (gr.) hiato, m.
hibernate, *hĭbẽr'nǎt*, v. n. invernar.
hiccough, *hĭk'ŭp*, s. hipo, m.; –, v. n. tener hipo.
hickory, *hĭk'ŏrĭ*, s. noguera americana, f.
hide, *hĭd*, v. a. esconder; (vulg.) apalear; –, s. cuero, m.; piel, f.   [riblemente.
hideous, *hĭd'ĭŭs*, a. horrible; *-ly*, ad. horhiding-place, *hī'dĭngplǎs*, s. escondite, escondrijo, m.
hierarchy, *hī'ẽrǎrkĭ*, s. jerarquía, f.
hieroglyphic, *hīẽrōglĭf'ĭk*, a. & s. jeroglífico, m.
higgle, *hĭg'l*, v. n. regatear.
higgledy-piggledy, *-dĭglĭg'ldĭ*, ad. (vulg.) contusamente.
higgler, *-ẽr*, s. revendedor, m.
high, *hī*, a. alto, elevado; arduo; altivo; noble, ilustre; sublime; violento; solemne; caro.
high-altar, *-ǎl'tẽr*, s. altar mayor, m.
high-born, *-bŏrn*, a. noble, ilustre por nacimiento.   [color.
high-coloured, *-kŭl'ŭrd*, a. subido de high-flown, *-flŏn*, a. altivo, orgulloso.
highland, *-lǎnd*, s. tierras montañosas, f.
highlander, *-lǎndẽr*, s. montañés, m.   [pl.
highly, *-lĭ*, ad. altamente; en sumo grado; arrogantemente; ambiciosamente.   [nimo.
high-minded, *-mĭnděd*, a. fiero, magnáhighness, *-něs*, s. altura, f.; alteza, f.
high-water, *-wǎtẽr*, s. marea alta, f.
highway, *-wǎ*, s. camino real, m.
highwayman, *-wǎmǎn*, s. salteador de caminos, m.
hilarious, *hĭlā'rĭŭs*, a. alegre.
hilarity, *hĭlǎr'ĭtĭ*, s. alegría, f.; regocijo, m.
hill, *hĭl*, s. collado, m.   [m.
hillock, *-lŏk*, s. colina, f.; otero, m.
hilly, *-lĭ*, a. montañoso.
hilt, *hĭlt*, s. puño de espada, m.
him, *hĭm*, pn. le, á él.
himself, *-sělf'*, pn. á él mismo.
hind, *hĭnd*, a. trasero, posterior; –, s. cierva, f. (hembra del ciervo); criado, m.; patán, m.
hinder, *hĭn'dẽr*, v. a. impedir, embarazar.
hinder, *hīn'dẽr*, a. trasero.
hind(e)rance, *hĭn'd(ẽ)rǎns*, s. impedimento, obstáculo, m.

hind(er)most, *hīnd'(ẽr)mōst,* a. postrero.

hind-quarter, *–kwȧrtẽr,* s. pie trasero, m.

hinge, *hīnj,* s. charnela, bisagra, f.; razón principal, f.; –, v. a. engoznar.

hint, *hīnt,* s. seña, f.; sugestión, insinuación, f.; luz, f.; aviso, m.; –, v. a. apuntar, insinuar; sugerir; hacer señas.

hip, *hīp,* cadera, f.

hip-bath, *–bȧth,* s. baño inglés, m. [m.

hippodrome, *hīp'pōdrōm,* s. hipódromo,

hippopotamus, *hīppōpŏt'ãmŭs,* s. hipopótamo, m. [quiler, m.; salario, m.

hire, *hīr,* v. a. alquilar; arrendar; –, s. alquiler, m.; salario, m.

hireling, *–līng,* s. jornalero, m.; hombre mercenario, m.; –, a. mercenario, venal.

hirsute, *hãrsūt',* a. hirsuto, velludo, áspero.

his, *hĭs,* pn. su, suyo, de él.

hiss, *hĭs,* v. a. & n. silbar.

hist, *hĭst,* ¡chito! ó ¡chitón!

historian, *hĭstō'rãn,* s. historiador, m.

historic(al), *hĭstōr'ĭk(ãl),* a. histórico; –ally, ad. históricamente.

history, *hĭs'tõrē,* s. historia, narración, f.

histrionic, *hĭstrĭŏn'ĭk,* a. estudiado, gestero.

hit, *hĭt,* v. a. golpear; atinar; –, v. n. acaecer, acontecer (felizmente); salir bien; encontrar(se); –, s. golpe, m.; suerte feliz, f.; alcance, m.

hitch, *hĭtsh,* v. n. menearse; engancharse; –, s. impedimento, m.; (mar.) vuelta de cabo, f.

hither, *hĭth'ẽr,* ad. acá; á este fin; –, a. citerior; –to, hasta ahora, hasta aquí.

hive, *hīv,* s. colmena, f.; –, v. a. enjambrar; –, v. n. vivir muchos en un mismo [lugar.

hoar, *hōr,* a. blanco, cano.

hoard, *hōrd,* s. montón, m.; tesoro escondido, m.; –, v. a. atesorar, acumular.

hoar-frost, *hōr'frŏst,* s. escarcha, f.

hoariness, *hō'rĭnĕs,* s. blancura, f.; canas de viejo, f. pl. [mente.

hoarse, *hōrs,* a. ronco; –ly, ad. roncamente.

hoarseness, *–nĕs,* s. ronquera, carraspera, f.

hoary, *hō'rē,* a. blanquecino, cano, [f.

hoax, *hōks,* s. burla, f.; petardo, m.; –, v. a. engañar, burlar.

hob, *hŏb,* s. patán, m.

hobble, *–bl,* v. n. cojear; –, v. a. enredar; –, s. dificultad, f.; cojera, f.

hobby, *–bē,* s. caballico, m.; zoquete, m.

hobby-horse, *–bēhŏrs,* s. objeto predilecto, m.; caballico en que corren los niños, m.

hobgoblin, *–gŏb'lĭn,* s. duende, m. [m.

hobnail, *–nāl,* s. clavo de herradura, m.

hob-nob, *–nŏb,* v. n. hermanarse con otro.

Hobson's choice, *–sŭns tshŏĭs,* s. alternativa entre eso ó nada, f.

hock, *hŏk,* s. vino añejo del Rin, m.; jarrete, m.; –(le), v. a. desjarretar.

hockey, *hŏk'ē,* s. juego de pelota inglés

hocus, *hō'kŭs,* v. a. engañar. [m.

hocus-pocus, *–pōkŭs,* s. pasapasa, f.

hodge-podge, *hŏj'pŏj,* s. almodrote, m.

hodman, *hŏd'mãn,* s. peón de albañil, m.

hoe, *hō,* s. azada, f.; –, v a. cavar la tierra con azada.

hog, *hŏg,* s. cerdo, puerco, m.

hoggish, *–gĭsh,* a. porcuno; –ly, ad. puercamente; vorazmente. [m.

hogshead, *–z'hĕd,* s. oxoft (barril grande),

hoiden, hoyden, *hŏĭd'n,* s. payo, m.; paya,

hoist, *hŏĭst,* v. a. alzar; (mar.) izar. [f.

hold, *hōld,* v. a. tener, asir; detener; sostener; mantener; juzgar, reputar; poseer; continuar, proseguir; contener; celebrar; apostar; –, v. n. valer; mantenerse; durar; abstenerse; adherirse á depender; ¡tente! ¡para! éstate quieto; –, s. presa, f.; mango, m.; asa, f.; prisión, f.; custodia, f.; (mar.) bodega, f.; apoyo, m.; poder, f.

holdfast, *–fȧst,* s. grapa, laña, f. [m.

holding, *–ĭng,* s. tenencia, posesión, f.; influencia, f. [m.

hole, *hōl,* s. agujero, m.; cueva, f.; hoyo,

holiday, *hŏl'ĭdā,* s. día de fiesta, m.; aniversario, m.; –s, pl. vacaciones, f. pl.

holiness, *hō'lĭnĕs,* s. santidad, f.

hollow, *hŏl'lō,* a. hueco; disimulado; –, s. cavidad, caverna, f.; –, v. a. excavar, ahuecar. [ción, f.

hollowness, *–nĕs,* s. cavidad, f.; simulación, f.

holly, *hŏl'lē,* s. (bot.) acebo, m.

holly-hock, *–hŏk,* s. malva hortense, f.

holocaust, *hŏl'ōkȧst,* s. holocausto, m.

holster, *hōl'stẽr,* s. funda de pistola, f.

holy, *hō'lē,* a. santo, pío; consagrado.

holy-water, *–wȧtẽr,* s. agua bendita, f.

holy-week, *–wĕk,* s. semana santa, f.

homage, *hŏm'āj,* s. homenaje, m.; –, v. a. reverenciar.

home, *hōm,* s. casa propia, morada, f.; patria, f.; domicilio, m.; –ly, ad. á su propia casa; á su país.

home-bred, *–brĕd,* a. nativo; casero.

home-keeping, *–kēpĭng,* a. apoltronado en su casa.

homeless, *–lĕs,* a. sin casa ni hogar.

homeliness, *–lĭnĕs,* s. simpleza, f.; grosería, f. [sería, f.

homely, *–lē,* a. casero, grosero.

home-made, *–mȧd,* a. hecho en casa.

home-rule, *–rōl,* s. proyecto de ley acerca de la autonomía de Irlanda, m.

home-ruler, *–ãr,* s. individuo del partido irlandés que quiere la autonomía por su propio país. [isla, m.

home-sick, *–sĭk,* a. nostálgico.

home-sickness, *–sĭknĕs,* s. mal del país, m., nostalgia, f. [basto.

home-spun, *–spŭn,* a. casero; grosero,

homeward, *–wãrd,* a. hacia casa, hacia su país.

homicidal, *hŏmĭsī'dãl,* a. homicida.

homicide, *hŏm'ĭsīd,* s. homicidio, m.; homicida, m.

homily, *hŏm'ĭlē,* s. homilía, f.

homœopathist, *hŏmēŏpȧth'ĭst,* s. homeopatista, m. [patía, f.

homœopathy, *hŏmēŏp'ãthē,* s. homeopatía, f.

homogeneous, *hŏmōjē'nĭŭs,* a. homogéneo.

hone, *hōn,* s. piedra amoladera, f. [géneo.

honest, *ŏn'ĕst,* a. honesto; justo; casto; –ly, ad. honestamente.

honesty, *–ē,* s. honestidad, justicia, f.

honey, *hŭn'ē,* s. miel, f.; dulzura, f.; my –, querida mía, f.

honey-comb, *–kōm,* s. panal, m.

honey-dew, —dū, s. rocío dulce, m.
honeymoon, —mūn, s. luna de miel, f., primer mes de casados, m. [selva, f.
honey-suckle, —sŭkl, s. (bot.) madreselva, f.
honied, hŭn'id, a. dulce, meloso, enmelado.
honorary, ŏn'ŭrāri, a. honorario.
honour, ŏn'ŭr, s. honra, f.; honor, m.; —, v. a. honrar; hacer honor á una letra de cambio.
honourable, —ăbl, a. honorable; ilustre.
honourably, —ăbli, ad. honorablemente.
hood, hŭd, s. caperuza, f.; capirote (de graduados), m.; capucha (de religioso), f.; —, v. a. cubrir con caperuza delante de los ojos. [la gallina ciega, m.
hoodman-blind, —mănblĭnd, s. juego de
hoodwink, —wĭnk, v. a. vendar á uno los ojos; engañar. [m.
hoof, hŏf, s. casco de las bestias caballares.
hoof-bound, —bŏŭnd, a. estrecho de cascos.
hook, hŏk, s. gancho, m.; anzuelo, m.; by — or crook, de un modo ú otro; —, v. a. enganchar.
hooked, —d, a. enganchado, encorvado.
hook-nosed, —nŏsd, s. cariaguileño.
hoop, hŏp, s. cerco de barril, m.; tontillo, m.; —, v. a. cercar; —, v. n. gritar.
hooper, —ŭr, s. tonelero, m. [silva, f.
hooping-cough, —ĭngkŏf, s. tos convulsiva.
hoopoo, hŏ'pŏ, s. abubilla, f. (ave).
hoot, hŏt, v. n. gritar; —, s. grito, m.
hop, hŏp, s. (bot.) lúpulo, m.; salto, m.; to —(beer), v. a. echar lúpulo en la cerveza; —, v. n. saltar, brincar.
hope, hŏp, s. esperanza, f.; —, v. n. esperar.
hopeful, —fŭl, a. lleno de buenas calidades; esperanzado; —ly, ad. con esperanza.
hopefulness, —fŭlnĕs, s. buena esperanza, f. [sin esperanza.
hopeless, —lĕs, a. desesperado; —ly, ad.
hop-garden, —hŏp'gärdn, s. plantío de lúpulos, m. [(en los molinos).
hopper, hŏp'pŭr, s. saltador, m.; tolva, f.
hop-pole, hŏp'pŏl, s. estaca de hoblón, f.
horary, hŏ'rări, a. horario.
horde, hŏrd, s. horda, f.
horizon, hŏr'zŭn, s. horizonte, m.
horizontal, hŏrĭzŏn'tăl, a. horizontal; —ly, ad. horizontalmente.
horn, hŏrn, s. cuerno, m.; corneta de monte, f.
horn-beetle, —bĕtl, s. escarabajo, m.
horn-blower, —blŏŭr, s. trompetero, m.
horned, —d, a. cornudo. [bocinero, m.
hornet, hŏr'nĕt, s. tábano, m.; abejón, m.
horn-owl, hŏrn'ŏŭl, s. buho cornudo, m.
horn-pipe, —pĭp, s. gaita, f.
horny, —ĕ, a. hecho de cuerno; calloso.
horrible, hŏr'rĭbl, a. horrible, terrible.
horribly, —ĕ, ad. horriblemente; enormemente.
horrid, hŏr'rĭd, a. húrrido, horrible.
horrific, hŏrrĭf'ĭk, a. horrífico; horroroso.
horror, hŏr'rŭr, s. horror, terror, m.
horse, hŏrs, s. caballo, m.; caballería, f.; caballete, m.; —, v. a. cabalgar.
horseback, —băk, ad. on —, á caballo.
horse-block, —blŏk, s. montadero, m.

horse-breaker, —brākŭr, s. picador ó domador de caballos, m.
horse-chesnut, —tshĕsnŭt, s. castaño de Indias, m. [ballo, f.
horse-cloth, —klŏth, s. mantilla de caballo, f.
horse-fly, —flĭ, s. moscarda, f., moscardón, m. [á caballo, f. pl.
horse-guards, —gärds, s. pl. guardias de
horse-hair, —hār, s. crin de caballo, f.
horse-laugh, —läf, s. carcajada, f.
horse-leech, —lètsh, s. sanguijuela, f.; albeitar, m.
horseman, —măn, s. jinete, m. [f.
horsemanship, —mănshĭp, s. equitación, f.
horseplay, —plā, s. chanza pesada, f.
horsepond, —pŏnd, s. vado, m.; vadera, f.
horse-race, —rās, s. carrera ó corrida de caballos, f. [m.
horse-radish, —rădĭsh, s. rábano silvestre,
horse-shoe, —shŏ, s. herradura de caballo, f. [f.; —, v. a. azotar.
horsewhip, —hwĭp, s. látigo, m.; fusta, f.
horsewoman, —wŭmăn, s. caballera, f.
horticulture, hŏrtĭkal'tŭr, s. horticultura, jardinería, f. [dinero, m.
horticulturist, —tŭrĭst, s. hortelano, jardinero, m.
hose, hŏz, s. bragas, f. pl.; calzones, m. pl.
hosier, hŏ'zhŭr, s. bonctero, m.
hosiery, —ĕ, s. bonetería, f.
hospitable, hŏs'pĭtăbl, a. hospital.
hospitably, —ĕ, ad. con hospitalidad.
hospital, hŏs'pĭtăl, s. hospital, m.
hospitality, hŏspĭtăl'ĭtĕ, s. hospitalidad, f.
host, hŏst, s. huésped, m.; mesonero, m.; ejército, m.; hostia, f.
hostage, hŏs'tăj, s. rehén, m.
hostess, hŏst'ĕs, s. posadera, mesonera, f.
hostile, hŏs'tĭl, a. hostil.
hostility, hŏstĭl'ĭtĕ, s. hostilidad, f.
hot, hŏt, a. cálido, ardiente; fervoroso; violento. [estufas), m.
hot-bed, —bĕd, s. era, f.; invernadero (con
hotch-potch, hŏtsh'pŏtsh, s. almodrote, m.
hotel, hŏtĕl', s. posada, fonda, f.
hot-house, hŏt'hŏŭs, s. estufa, f.
hotly, —lĕ, ad. con calor; violentamente.
hotspur, —spŭr, s. colérico, exaltado, m.
hough, hŏk, s. jarrete, m.; —, v. a. desjarretar.
hound, hŏŭnd, s. sabueso, m. [jarretar.
hour, ŏŭr, s. hora, f. [(mar.) ampolleta, f.
hour-glass, —glăs, s. reloj de arena, m.
hour-hand, —hănd, s. mano del reloj que señala las horas, f.
hourly, —lĕ, ad. á cada hora.
hour-plate, —plāt, s. muestra de reloj, f.
house, hŏŭs, s. casa, f.; familia, f.; linaje, m.; cámara (del parlamento), f.; —, v. a. & n. albergar; residir.
house-breaker, —brākŭr, s. ladrón que fuerza las puertas de una casa para robarla, m.
house-dog, —dŏg, s. mastín, m.
household, —hŏld, s. familia, f.; manejo doméstico, m.; —bread, pan casero ó bazo, m. [padre de familia, m.
householder, —hŏldŭr, s. amo de casa,
housekeeper, —kēpŭr, s. amo de casa, jefe de familia, m.; ama de llaves, f.

housekeeping, –*kēpĭng,* s. gobierno doméstico, m.

houseless, –*lĕs,* a. sin habitación ó sin casa.

house-maid, –*mād,* s. criada de casa, f.

house-warming, –*wārming,* s. convite que se da al tiempo de estrenar una casa nueva, m.

housewife, –*wĭf,* s. ama de una casa, f.; ama de gobierno, mujer económica, f.; –, *hăz'zĭf,* bolsillo de señora, m. [f.

housewifery, –*rĕ,* s. economía doméstica.

housing, *hăz'ĭng,* s. almacenaje, m.; –s, pl. gualdrapa, f.

hovel, *hŏv'ĕl,* s. choza, cabaña, f.

hover, *hŏv'ăr,* v. n. colgar; dudar; rondar.

how, *hŏŭ,* ad. como, cuanto; – do you do? ¿cómo le va á U.? – so? ¿por qué? ¿cómo así?

how(so)ever, –(*sŏ)ĕv'ăr,* ad. como quiera, como quiera que sea; aunque; no obstante.

howitzer, *hŏd'ĭtsăr,* s. (mil.) obús, m. (mortero para arrojar granadas).

howl, *hŏŭl,* v. n. aullar; –, s. aullo, m.

hubbub, *hŭb'bŭb,* s. (vulg.) grito, ruido, m.; alboroto, tumulto, m.

huckaback, *hŭk'băk,* s. alemanisco, m.

huckle, *hŭk'kl,* s. codera, f.

huckster, *hŭk'stăr,* s. revendedor, m.

huddle, *hŭd'dl,* v. a. tapujar, confundir; –, s. confusión, barahúnda, f.

hue, *hū,* s. color, m.; tez del rostro, f.; matiz, m.; – and cry, alarma que se da contra un criminal, f.

huff, *hŭf,* s. arrebato, m.; cólera, f.; –, v. a. bufar, bravear; –, v. n. patear de enfado.

huffish, –*fĭsh,* a. arrogante, insolente; –ly, ad. con arrogancia, insolentemente.

hug, *hŭg,* v. a. abrazar, acariciar; –, s. abrazo apretado, m.

huge, *hūj,* a. vasto, enorme; –ly, ad. inmensamente. [mesurada, f.

hugeness, –*nĕs,* s. grandeza enorme ó desmesurada.

hulk, *hŭlk,* s. (mar.) casco de la embarcación, m.; armatoste, m. [buque, m.

hull, *hŭl,* s. cáscara, f.; (mar.) casco de un buque, m.

hum, *hŭm,* v. n. zumbar, susurrar; murmurar; –, s. zumbido, m.; chasco, m.; –!

human, *hū'măn,* a. humano. [¡ya!

humane, *hūmān',* a. humano; benigno; –ly, ad. humanamente.

humanise, *hū'mănĭz,* v. a. humanizar.

humanist, *hū'mănĭst,* s. humanista, m.

humanity, *hūmăn'ĭtĕ,* s. humanidad, f.

humankind, *hū'mănkĭnd,* s. el género ó linaje humano.

humanly, –*lĕ,* ad. humanamente.

humble, *hŭm'bl,* a. humilde, modesto; –, v. a. humillar, postrar.

humble-bee, –*bē,* s. zángano, m.

humbleness, –*nĕs,* s. humildad, f.

humbly, *hŭm'blĕ,* ad. con humildad.

humbug, *hŭm'bŭg,* s. engaño, m.; trampa, f.; –, v. a. engañar, chasquear.

humdrum, *hŭm'drŭm,* a. lerdo, estúpido; monótono.

humid, *hū'mĭd,* a. húmedo, algo mojado.

humidity, *hūmĭd'ĭtĕ,* s. humedad, f.

humiliate, *hūmĭl'ĭāt,* v. a. humillar.

humiliation, *hūmĭlĭā'shăn,* s. humillación, mortificación, f.

humility, *hūmĭl'ĭtĕ,* s. humildad, f.

humming-bird, *hŭm'mĭngbŭrd,* s. guainambí, colibrí, m. (pajarito).

humming-top, –*tŏp,* s. trompo, peón, m.

humorist, *hū'mŭrĭst,* s. hombre caprichoso ó fantástico, m.; bufón, m.

humorous, *hū'mŭrăs,* a. caprichoso, chistoso, placentero; –ly, ad. de buen humor; caprichosamente. [prichoso.

humorsome, *hū'mŭrsŭm,* a. petulante, caprichoso.

humour, *hū'măr,* s. humor, m.; humorada, fantasía, f.; capricho, m.; –, v. a. complacer, dar gusto; ejecutar lo que á uno se le manda.

hump, *hŭmp,* s. jiba, joroba, f.

humpbacked, –*băkd,* a. jorobado, jiboso.

hunch, *hŭnsh,* s. puñada, f.; codazo, m.; jiba, f.; –backed, a. jorobado, jiboso.

hundred, *hŭn'drĕd,* a. ciento; –, s. centenar, m.; un ciento.

hundredfold, –*fōld,* a. céntuplo.

hundredth, –*th,* a. centésimo.

hundred-weight, –*wăt,* s. quintal, m.

hung-beef, *hŭng'bēf,* s. carne ahumada, f.

hunger, *hŭng'găr,* s. hambre, f.; –, v. n. hambrear. [mente.

hungrily, *hŭng'grĭlĕ,* ad. hambrienta.

hungry, *hŭng'grĕ,* a. hambriento; voraz.

hunk, *hŭngk,* s. pedazo grande, m.

hunks, –*s,* s. hombre sórdido, m.

hunt, *hŭnt,* v. a. montear, cazar; perseguir; buscar; –, v. n. andar á caza; –, s. caza, f.

hunter, –*ăr,* s. cazador, m.; caballo de caza, m.; perro de monte, perro braco, m.

hunting, –*ĭng,* s. montería, caza, f. [f.

hunting-box, –*ĭngbŏks,* s. casa de campo.

hunting-crop, –*krŏp,* s. corbacho, m.

hunting-horn, –*ĭnghŏrn,* s. corneta de caza, f. [caza, m.

hunting-watch, –*ĭngwŏtsh,* s. reloj de caza, m.

huntress, –*rĕs,* s. cazadora, f.

huntsman, –*smăn,* s. cazador, montero, m.

hurdle, *hŭr'dl,* s. zarzo, m. [rana, f.

hurdy-gurdy, *hŭr'dĭgŭrdĕ,* s. gaita zamorana.

hurl, *hŭrl,* v. a. tirar con violencia; arrojar.

hurly-burly, *hŭr'lĭbŭr'lĕ,* s. alboroto, m.; confusión, babilonia, f.

hurricane, *hŭr'rĭkăn,* s. huracán, m.

hurry, *hŭr'rĕ,* v. a. acelerar, apresurar, precipitar; –, v. n. atropellarse, apresurarse; –, s. precipitación, f.; confusión, f.

hurt, *hŭrt,* v. a. dañar; herir; ofender; –, s. mal, daño, perjuicio, m.; golpe, m.; herida, f. [–ly, ad. dañosamente.

hurtful, –*fŭl,* a. dañoso, nocivo; injurioso.

hurtfulness, –*nĕs,* s. lo nocivo de una cosa.

husband, *hŭz'bănd,* s. marido, m.; labrador, m.; ship's –, armador de navío, m.; –, v. a. gobernar con economía; labrar la tierra. [m.

husbandman, –*măn,* s. labrador, viñador.

husbandry, –*rĕ,* s. agricultura, f.; economía, f.

hush! *hŭsh,* ¡chitón! ¡silencio! –, v. a. aquietar; acallar; –, v. n. estar quieto.

hush-money, –*mănĕ,* s. cohecho que se da á alguno para que calle, m.

husk, *hŏsk,* s. cáscara, f.; pellejo, m.; –, v. a. descascarar, mondar.

huskiness, *–nĕs,* s. ronquedad, f.

husky, *–ĕ,* a. lleno de cáscaras; ronco.

hussar, *hŏzzăr',* s. húsar, m. (soldado de á caballo).

hussy, *hŏz'zĕ,* s. mujercilla, f. [caballo).

hustings, *hŏs'tĭngz,* s. tribuna para las elecciones, f. [con fuerza.

hustle, *hŏz'l,* v. a. escaramuzar; empujar

hut, *hŭt,* s. cabaña, barraca, f.

hutch, *hŏtsh,* s. arca, f.; cofre, m.; madriguera de conejos, m.

hyacinth, *hī'sĭnth,* s. jacinto, m. [f.

hydrant, *hī'drănt,* s. llave de un encañado.

hydraulic(al), *hī́drâ'lĭk(ăl),* a. hidráulico; –s, s. pl. hidráulica, f.

hydrophobia, *hī́drŏfō'bĭă,* s. hidrofobia, f.

hydrostatics, *hī́drōstăt'ĭks,* s. pl. hidroyena, *hī́'nă,* s. hiena, f. [stática, f.

hygiene, *hī'jĭĕn,* s. higiene, f.

hymen, *hī'mĕn,* s. himeneo, m.

hymeneal, *hĭmĭnē'ăl,* a. nupcial.

hymn, *hĭm,* s. himno, m. [ageración, f.

hyperbole, *hīpŭr'bōlĕ,* s. hipérbole, m.; exhyperbolic(al),** *hīpŭrbŏl'ĭk(ăl),* a. hiperbólico; –ally, ad. hiperbólicamente.

hypercritic, *hīpŭrkrĭt'ĭk,* s. rigorista, crítico austero, m.

hyphen, *hī'fĕn,* s. (gr.) división, f.

hypochondria, *hīpōkŏndrī'ă,* s. hipocondría, f. [porcondriaco (m.).

hypochondriac, *hīpōkŏn'drĭăk,* a. & s. hi-

hypocrisy, *hīpŏk'rĭsĕ,* s. hipocresía, f.

hypocrite, *hĭp'ōkrĭt,* s. hipócrita, m.

hypocritic(al), *hĭpŏkrĭt'ĭk(ăl),* a. hipócrita, disimulado.

hypothesis, *hīpŏth'ĕsĭs,* s. hipótesis, f.

hypothetic(al), *hīpōthĕt'ĭk(ăl),* a. hipotético; –ly, ad. condicionalmente.

hyssop, *hĭs'sŭp,* s. hisopo, m.

hysteric(al), *hĭstĕr'ĭk(ăl),* a. histérico.

hysterics, *hĭstĕr'ĭks,* s. pl. paroxismo histérico, m.

I.

I, ĭ, pp. yo.

ice, *ĭs,* hielo, m.; –, v. a. helar.

ice-bound, *–bōŭnd,* a. rodeado de hielos.

ice-box, *–bŏks,* **ice-cellar,** *–sĕllăr,* **ice-house,** *–hŏŭs,* **ice-safe,** *–săf,* s. nevecicle,** *ĭ'sĭkl,* s. cerrión, m. [ría, f.

iciness, *ĭ'sĭnĕs,* s. congelación, f.; congelamiento, m.

iconoclast, *īkŏn'ŏklăst,* s. iconoclasta, m.

icy, *ĭ'sĕ,* a. helado; frío.

idea, *īdē'ă,* s. idea, imagen mental, f.

ideal, *–ăl,* a. ideal, intelectual; –ly, ad. idealmente.

identic(al), *īdĕn'tĭk(ăl),* a. idéntico.

identify, *–tĭfĭ,* v. a. identificar.

identity, *–tĭtĕ,* s. identidad, f.

idiocy, *ĭd'ĭŏsĕ,* s. idiotismo, m.

idiom, *ĭd'ĭŭm,* s. idioma, m.

idiomatic(al), *ĭdĭōmăt'ĭk(ăl),* a. peculiar á alguna lengua.

idiosyncrasy, *ĭdĭōsĭng'krăsĕ,* s. idiosincrasia, f.

idiot, *ĭd'ĭŏt,* s. idiota, necio, m.

idiotic(al), *ĭdĭŏt'ĭk(ăl),* a. tonto, bobo.

idle, *ĭ'dl,* a. ocioso, perezoso, desocupado, holgazán; inútil, vano, frívolo; –, v. n. holgazanear; estar ocioso.

idleness, *–nĕs,* s. ociosidad, pereza, negligencia, f.; frivolidad, f. [{

idler, *ĭ'dlŭr,* s. holgazán, hombre poltrón, m.

idly, *ĭ'dlĕ,* ad. ociosamente; vanamente.

idol, *ĭ'dŏl,* s. ídolo, m.; imagen, f.

idolater, *ĭdŏl'ătŭr,* s. idólatra, m.

idolatrous, *–trŭs,* a. idolátrico.

idolatry, *–trĕ,* s. idolatría, f.

idolise, *ĭ'dŏlĭs,* v. a. idolatrar.

idyl, *ĭ'dĭl,* s. idilio, m.

idyllic, *īdĭl'ĭk,* a. idílico. [sino.

if, *ĭf,* c. si; aunque, supuesto que: – not,

igneous, *ĭg'nĕŭs,* a. ígneo, de fuego. [m.

ignis-fatuus, *ĭg'nĭsfăt'ŭŭs,* s. fuego fatuo,

ignite, *ĭgnīt',* v. a. encender, abrasar.

ignition, *ĭgnĭsh'ŭn,* s. (chem.) ignición, m.

ignoble, *ĭgnō'bl,* a. innoble; bajo.

ignobly, *–ĕ,* ad. vilmente, bajamente.

ignominious, *ĭgnōmĭn'ĭŭs,* a. ignominioso; –ly, ad. ignominiosamente. [famia, f.

ignominy, *ĭg'nōmĭnĕ,* s. ignominia, inignoramus,** *ĭgnōrā'mŭs,* s. ignorante, tonto,

ignorance, *ĭg'nōrăns,* s. ignoran ia, f. [m.

ignorant, *ĭg'nōrănt,* a. ignorante; –ly, ad. ignorantemente.

ignore, *ĭgnōr',* v. a. ignorar.

ill, *ĭl,* a. malo, enfermo, doliente; –, s. mal, infortunio, m.; –, ad. mal, malamente.

illegal, *ĭllē'găl,* a. –ly, ad. ilegal(mente).

illegality, *ĭllēgăl'ĭtĕ,* s. ilegalidad, f.

illegible, *ĭllĕj'ĭbl,* a. ilegible.

illegibly, *–ĕ,* ad. de un modo ilegible. [f.

illegitimacy, *ĭllĕjĭt'ĭmăsĕ,* s. ilegitimidad,

illegitimate, *ĭllĕjĭt'ĭmăt,* a. ilegítimo; –ly, ad. ilegítimamente. [teo.

ill-favoured, *ĭl'fā'vŭrd,* a. mal carado;

illiberal, *ĭllĭb'ĕrăl,* a. innoble; mezquino; –ly, ad. sin libertad; mezquinamente.

illiberality, *ĭllĭbărăl'ĭtĕ,* s. cortedad de ánimo, f.; tacañería, f.

illicit, *ĭllĭs'ĭt,* a. ilícito.

illimitable, *ĭllĭm'ĭtăbl,* a. ilimitado.

illiterate, *ĭllĭt'ărăt,* a. indocto, iliterato.

illness, *ĭl'nĕs,* s. enfermedad, f.; maldad, f.

illogical, *ĭllŏj'ĭkăl,* a. no conforme á las reglas de la lógica. [hecho.

ill-shaped, *ĭl'shăpt,* a. disforme; mal

ill-timed, *ĭl'tīmd,* a. intempestivo, á deshora. [tratar.

ill-treat, *ĭl'trēt,* **ill-use,** *–ūz,* v. a. maltratar.

illuminate, *ĭllū'mĭnăt,* v. a. iluminar.

illumination, *ĭllūmĭnā'shŭn,* s. iluminación, f.

illumine, *ĭllū'mĭn,* v. a. iluminar.

illusion, *ĭllū'zhŭn,* s. ilusión, f.

illusive, *ĭllū'sĭv,* **illusory,** *ĭllū'sŭrĕ,* a. ilusivo, ilusorio.

illustrate, *ĭllŭs'trāt,* v. a. ilustrar; explicar.

illustration, *ĭllŭstrā'shŭn,* s. ilustración, f.; elucidación, f.

illustrative, *ĭllŭs'trătĭv,* a. explicativo.

illustriors, *ĭllŭs'trĭŭs*, a. ilustre, insigne, célebre; **-ly**, ad. ilustremente.

ill-will, *ĭl'wĭl*, s. malquerencia, f.

image, *ĭm'ĭj*, s. imagen, estatua, f.; **-**, v. a. imaginar.

imagery, *ĭm'ĭj'ŭrĕ*, s. imagen, pintura, f.; vuelos de la fantasía, m. pl.   [cebible.

imaginable, *ĭmăj'ĭnăbl*, a. imaginable, con-

imaginary, *ĭmăj'ĭnărĕ*, a. imaginario.

imagination, *ĭmăjĭnā'shŭn*, s. imaginación, f.; idea fantástica, f.

imaginative, *ĭmăj'ĭnătĭv*, a. imaginativo.

imagine, *ĭmăj'ĭn*, v. a. imaginar; idear, inventar.

imbecile, *ĭm'bĕsĭl* a. imbécil, necio.

imbecility, *ĭmbĕsĭl'ĭtĕ*, s. imbecilidad, mentecatez, f. idiotismo, m.

imbedded, *ĭmbĕd'ĕd*, a. incrustado.

imbibe, *ĭmbīb'*, v. a. embeber; chupar.

imbroglio, *ĭmbrō'lĭō*, s. embrollo, m.; maraña, f.

imbrue, *ĭmbrō'*, v. a. remojar.

imbue, *ĭmbū'*, v. a. imbuir, infundir.

imbursement, *ĭmbŭrs'mĕnt*, s. pagamento.

imitable, *ĭm'ĭtăbl*, a. imitable.   [m.

imitate, *ĭm'ĭtāt*, v. a. imitar, copiar.   [f.

imitation, *ĭmĭtā'shŭn*, s. imitación, copia.

imitative, *ĭm'ĭtătĭv*, a. imitativo, imitado.

immaculate, *ĭmmăk'ŭlāt*, a. inmaculado, puro.   [poco importante.

material, *ĭmmătē'rĭăl*, a. inmaterial;

imature, *ĭmmătūr'*, a. inmaduro.

immeasurable, *ĭmmĕzh'ŭrăbl*, a. inmensurable, inmenso.   [inmensurablemente.

immeasurably, *-ē*, ad. inmensamente.

immediate, *ĭmmē'dĭăt*, a. inmediato; **-ly**, ad. inmediatamente.

immemorial, *ĭmmēmō'rĭăl*, a. inmemorial.

immense, *ĭmmĕns'*, a. inmenso; vasto; **-ly**, ad. inmensamente.   [dumbre, f.

immensity, *-sĭtĕ*, s. inmensidad, muche-

immerge, *ĭmmŭrj'*, immerse, *ĭmmŭrs'*, v. a. sumergir, zambullir.

immersion, *ĭmmŭr'shŭn*, s. inmersión, f.

immigrant, *ĭm'mĭgrănt*, s. inmigrante, m.

imminent, *ĭm'mĭnĕnt*, a. inminente.

immobile, *ĭmmō'bĭl*, a. inmovil.   [f.

immobility, *ĭmmōbĭl'ĭtĕ*, s. inmovilidad.

immoderate, *ĭmmŏd'ŭrăt*, a. inmoderado, excesivo; **-ly**, ad. inmoderadamente.

immodest, *ĭmmŏd'ĕst*, a. inmodesto; **-ly**, ad. inmodestamente.

immodesty, *-ē*, s. inmodestia, f.

immolate, *ĭm'mōlāt*, v. a. inmolar, sacrificar.   [f.

immolation, *ĭmmōlā'shŭn*, s. inmolación.

immoral, *ĭmmŏr'ăl*, a. inmoral, depravado.

immorality, *ĭmmŏrăl'ĭtĕ*, s. pravedad, corrupción de costumbres, f.   [(mente).

immortal, *ĭmmŏr'tăl*, a. **-ly**, ad. inmortal-

immortalise, *ĭmmŏr'tălĭz*, v. a. inmortalizar, eternizar.   [dad, f.

immortality, *ĭmmŏrtăl'ĭtĕ*, s. inmortali-

immovable, *ĭmmōō'băbl*, a. inmoble; inmovible; **-s**, s. pl. bienes raíces, m. pl.

immovably, *-ē*, a. inmoblemente.

immunity, *ĭmmū'nĭtĕ*, s. inmunidad, franquicia, f. privilegio, m.

immure, *ĭmmūr'*, v. a. emparedar.

immutability, *ĭmmūtăbĭl'ĭtĕ*, s. inmutabilidad, f.

immutable, *ĭmmū'tăbl*, a. inmutable.

immutably, *-ē*, ad. inmutablemente.

imp, *ĭmp*, s. diablillo, duende, m.; injerto, m.; vástago, m.

impact, *ĭm'păkt*, s. impulso, m.

impair, *ĭmpār'*, v. a. empeorar, deteriorar; disminuir.

impale, *ĭmpāl'*, v. a. empalar á un reo.

impalpable, *ĭmpăl'păbl*, a. impalpable.

impannel, *ĭmpăn'nĕl*, v. a. (law) inscribir á los jurados según la lista.

impart, *ĭmpărt'*, v. a. comunicar, dar parte.

impartial, *ĭmpăr'shăl*, a. **-ly**, ad. imparcial(mente).   [dad, f.

impartiality, *ĭmpărshăl'ĭtĕ*, s. imparciali-

impassable, *ĭmpăs'săbl*, a. intransitable, impracticable.   [bilidad, f.

impassibility, *ĭmpăssĭbĭl'ĭtĕ*, s. impasi-

impassion, *ĭmpăsh'ŭn*, v. a. mover las pasiones.

impassive, *ĭmpăs'sĭv*, a. impasible.

impatience, *ĭmpā'shĕns*, s. impaciencia, f.

impatient, *ĭmpā'shĕnt*, a. **-ly**, ad. impaciente(mente).

impeach, *ĭmpētsh'*, v. a. acusar, denunciar.

impeachable, *-ăbl*, a. delatable.   [f.

impeachment, *-mĕnt*, s. acusación pública.

impecunious, *ĭmpēkū'nĭŭs*, a. indigente.

impede, *ĭmpēd'*, v. a. impedir, embarazar.

impediment, *ĭmpĕd'ĭmĕnt*, s. impedimento, obstáculo, m.

impel, *ĭmpĕl'*, v. a. impeler.

impend, *ĭmpĕnd'*, v. n. amenazar, aproximarse un peligro &c.

impenetrability, *ĭmpĕnĕtrăbĭl'ĭtĕ*, s. impenetrabilidad, f.   [trable.

impenetrable, *ĭmpĕn'ĕtrăbl*, a. impene-

impenetrably, *-ē*, ad. impenetrablemente.

impenitence, *ĭmpĕn'ĭtĕns*, s. impenitencia, f.   [**-ly**, ad. sin penitencia;

impenitent, *ĭmpĕn'ĭtĕnt*, a. impenitente;

imperative, *ĭmpĕr'ătĭv*, a. imperativo; **-ly**, ad. imperativamente.   [ceptible.

imperceptible, *ĭmpŭrsĕp'tĭbl*, a. imper-

imperceptibly, *-ē*, ad. imperceptiblemente.

imperfect, *ĭmpŭr'fĕkt*, a. imperfecto, defectuoso; **-ly**, ad. imperfectamente; **-**, s. (gr.) pretérito imperfecto, m.

imperfection, *ĭmpŭrfĕk'shŭn*, s. imperfección, f. defecto, m.

imperial, *ĭmpē'rĭăl*, a. imperial; **-**, s. imperial, cielo, m.; mostacho, m.

imperialists, *-ĭsts*, s. pl. tropas del antiguo emperador de Alemania, f. pl.

imperil, *ĭmpĕr'ĭl*, v. a. arriesgar.

imperious, *ĭmpē'rĭŭs*, a. imperioso; arrogante; **-ly**, ad. imperiosamente, arrogantemente.   [tible; eterno.

imperishable, *ĭmpĕr'ĭshăbl*, a. indestruc-

impermeable, *ĭmpŭr'mĭbl*, a. impermeable.   [personal(mente).

impersonal, *ĭmpŭr'sŏnăl*, a. **-ly**, ad. im-

impersonate, *ĭmpŭr'sŏnāt*, v. a. personalizar.   [sentación (de un actor), f.

impersonation, *ĭmpŭrsŏnā'shŭn*, s. repre-

7 *

impertinence, _impŭr' tĭnĕns_, s. impertinencia, f.; descaro, m.

impertinent, _impŭr' tĭnĕnt_, a. impertinente; -ly, ad. impertinentemente; fuera de propósito.

imperturbable, _impŭrtŭrb' ăbl_, a. imperturbable; -bly, ad. sin perturbación.

impervious, _impŭr' vĭŭs_, a. impenetrable.

impetuosity, _impĕtdŏs' ĭtĭ_, s. impetuosidad, f., ímpetu, m. [ad. impetuosamente.

impetuous, _impĕt' dŭs_, a. impetuoso; -ly,

impetus, _ĭm' pĕtŭs_, s. ímpetu, m. [f.

impiety, _impī' tĭ_, s. impiedad, irreligión,

impinge (on), _impĭnj' (ŏn)_, v. a. tener influjo en. [-ly, ad. impíamente.

impious, _ĭm' pĭŭs_, a. impío, irreligioso;

implacable, _impld' kăbl_, a. implacable, irreconciliable. [irreconciliablemente.

implacably, _-bĭ_, ad. implacablemente,

implant, _implănt'_, v. a. plantar; injertar; imprimir. [f.; utensilio, m.; mueble, m.

implement, _ĭm' plĕmĕnt_, s. herramienta,

implicate, _ĭm' plĭkăt_, v. a. implicar, envolver. [f.

implication, _implĭkā' shŭn_, s. implicación.

implicit, _implĭs' ĭt_, a. implícito; -ly, ad. implícitamente.

implore, _implōr'_, v. a. implorar, suplicar.

imply, _implī'_, v. a. implicar; comprender.

impolite, _impŏlīt'_, a. descortés, impolítico.

impoliteness, _-nĕs_, s. falta de cortesía, f.

impolitic(al), _impŏl' ĭtĭk, impŏlĭt' ĭkăl_, a. imprudente; impolítico.

import, _impōrt'_, v. a. importar; significar; —, _ĭm' pōrt_, s. importancia, f.; importe, m.; sentido, m.; significación, f.; -duty, derechos de entrada, m. pl.

importance, _impōr' tăns_, s. importancia, f.

important, _-tănt_, a. importante.

importation, _impōrtā' shŭn_, s. importación, f. [géneros extranjeros, m.

importer, _impōr' tŭr_, s. introductor de

importunate, _impōr' tănĕt_, a. importuno; -ly, ad. importunamente.

importune, _impōrtūn'_, v. a. importunar.

importunity, _-tĭ_, s. importunidad, f.

impose, _impōz'_, v. a. imponer; engañar.

imposing, _-ĭng_, a. imponente, que infunde respeto.

imposition, _impŏzĭsh' ŭn_, s. imposición, carga, f.; impostura, f. [bilidad, f.

impossibility, _impŏssĭbĭl' ĭtĭ_, s. imposi-

impossible, _impŏs' sĭbl_, a. imposible.

impost, _ĭm' pōst_, s. impuesto, tributo, m.

impostor, _impŏs' tŭr_, s. impostor, m.

imposture, _-tŭr_, s. impostura, f.; engaño, m. [capacidad, f.

impotence, _ĭm' pŏtĕns_, s. impotencia; in-

impotent, _ĭm' pŏtĕnt_, a. impotente; incapaz; -ly, ad. sin poder. [rralar.

impound, _impŏŭnd'_, v. a. encerrar, aco-

impoverish, _impŏv' ŭrĭsh_, v. a. empobrecer.

impoverishment, _-mĕnt_, s. empobrecimiento, m. [imposibilidad, f.

impracticability, _imprăktĭkăbĭl' ĭtĭ_, s.

impracticable, _imprăk' tĭkăbl_, a. impracticable, imposible.

imprecate, _ĭm' prĕkăt_, v. a. maldecir.

imprecation, _imprĕkā' shăn_, s. imprecación, maldición, f.

impregnable, _imprĕg' năbl_, a. inexpugnable. [pregnar.

impregnate, _-năt_, v. a. empreñar; im-

impregnation, _imprĕgnā' shŭn_, s. fecundación, f.; impregnación, f.

impress, _imprĕs'_, v. a. imprimir, estampar; hacer una leva; —, _ĭm' prĕs_, s. impresión, f.; empresa, f.; divisa, f.

impressible, _imprĕs' sĭbl_, a. impressionable, _-shănăbl_, a. impresionable.

impression, _imprĕsh' ŭn_, s. impresión, f.; edición, f.

impressive, _imprĕs' sĭv_, a. penetrante; impresionable; -ly, ad. de un modo eficaz.

imprint, _imprĭnt'_, v. a. imprimir; estampar.

imprison, _imprĭz' n_, v. a. aprisionar.

imprisonment, _-mĕnt_, s. prisión, f.; encierro, m. [babilidad, f.

improbability, _imprŏbăbĭl' ĭtĭ_, s. impro-

improbable, _imprŏb' ăbl_, a. improbable.

improbably, _-ĭ_, ad. improbablemente.

improbity, _imprŏb' ĭtĭ_, s. falta de probidad, f. [mente.

impromptu, _imprŏm' tŭ_, a. extemporánea-

improper, _imprŏp' ŭr_, a. impropio, indecente; -ly, ad. impropiamente.

impropriety, _imprŏprī' ĭtĭ_, s. impropiedad, incongruencia, f.

improve, _improov'_, v. a. & n. mejorar, perfeccionar; mejorar; hacer progresos.

improvement, _-mĕnt_, s. progreso, mejoramiento, m. [cia, falta de previsión, f.

improvidence, _imprŏv' tdĕns_, s. impruden-

improvident, _-ĭdĕnt_, a. imprόvido; -ly, ad. imprόvidamente.

improvise, _imprŏvīz'_, v. a. improvisar.

imprudence, _imprŏo' dĕns_, s. imprudencia, f.

imprudent, _-dĕnt_, a. imprudente; -ly, ad. imprudentemente.

impudence, _ĭm' pūdĕns_, s. impudencia, f.

impudent, _ĭm' pūdĕnt_, a. impudente; -ly, ad. desvergonzadamente; impúdicamente.

impugn, _impŭn'_, v. a. impugnar.

impulse, _ĭm' pŭls_, **impulsion**, _impŭl' shŭn_, s. impulsión, f.; impulso, m.

impulsive, _impŭl' sĭv_, a. impulsivo.

impunity, _impū' nĭtĭ_, s. impunidad, f.

impure, _impūr'_, a. impuro; impúdico, sucio; -ly, ad. impuramente. [pureza, f.

impurity, _impū' rĭtĭ_, s. impuridad, im-

imputation, _impŭtā' shŭn_, s. imputación, f.

impute, _impūt'_, v. a. imputar. [f.

in, _ĭn_, pr. á, en, por, á, de, mientras, bajo, con, para. [pacidad, f.

inability, _inăbĭl' ĭtĭ_, s. inhabilidad, inca-

inaccessible, _inăksĕs' sĭbl_, a. inaccesible.

inaccuracy, _inăk' kŭrăsĭ_, s. incuria, negligencia, f.; incorrección, f.

inaccurate, _inăk' kŭrăt_, a. inexacto.

inaction, _inăk' shăn_, s. inacción, holgazanería, f.

inactive, _inăk' tĭv_, a. flojo, perezoso, negligente. [día, f.

inactivity, _inăktĭv' ĭtĭ_, s. ociosidad, desi-

inadequate, _inăd' ĕkwăt_, a. inadecuado, defectuoso; imperfecto, insuficiente.

inadmissible, *inădmis'sibl,* a. inadmisible. [f.

inadvertence, *-vŭr'tĕns,* s. inadvertencia.

inadvertently, *-vŭr'tĕntli,* ad. inadvertidamente. [inalienable.

inalienable, *ināl'yĕnābl,* a. inajenable.

inanimate, *inăn'ĭmāt* a. inánime, inanimado.

inanition, *inănĭsh'ăn,* s. inanición, f.

inanity, *inăn'ĭtĭ,* s. vacuidad, f.; nulidad, f.

inapplicable, *inăp'plĭkăbl,* a. inaplicable.

inapposite, *inăp'pŏzĭt,* a. mal puesto, mal colocado. [apreciable, inestimable.

inappreciable, *inăpprē'shĭăbl,* a. inapreciable.

inappropriate, *inăpprō'prĭăt,* a. impropio.

inaptitude, *inăp'tĭtūd,* s. ineptitud, f.

inarticulate, *inărtik'ŭlăt,* a. inarticulado; -ly, ad. indistintamente. [que.

inasmuch, *inăzmŭtsh',* ad. visto ó puesto

inattention, *inăttĕn'shun,* s. desatención, f.; descuido, [dado.

inattentive, *-tĭv,* a. desatento, descuidado. [dado.

inaudible, *inā'dĭbl,* a. inaudible, lo que no se puede oir.

inaugural, *inā'gŭrăl,* a. inaugural.

inaugurate, *inā'gŭrāt,* v. a. inaugurar.

inauguration, *ināgŭrā'shun,* s. inauguración, f.

inauspicious, *inăspĭsh'ŭs,* a. malaventurado; -ly, ad. desgraciadamente.

inborn, *in'bŏrn,* inbred, *in'brĕd,* a. innato, insito. [lable.

incalculable, *inkăl'kŭlăbl,* a. incalculable.

incandescent, *inkăndĕs'sĕnt,* a. incandescente; -light, s. luz eléctrica incandescente, f. [miento, m.

incantation, *inkăntā'shun,* s. encantamiento, m.

incapability, *inkāpăbĭl'ĭtĭ,* s. incapacidad, f.

incapable, *inkā'păbl,* a. incapaz, inhábil.

incapacitate, *inkăpăs'ĭtāt,* v. a. inhabilitar.

incapacity, *-tĭ,* s. incapacidad, f.

incarcerate, *inkăr'sĕrāt,* v. a. encarcelar, aprisionar.

incarnate, *inkăr'năt,* a. encarnado.

incarnation, *inkărnā'shun,* s. encarnación, encarnadura, f.

incase, *inkās',* v. a. encajar, incluir.

incautious, *inkā'shus,* a. incauto; -ly, ad. incautamente.

incendiary, *insĕn'dĭărĭ,* s. incendiario, m.

incense, *in'sĕns,* s. incienso, m.; —, *insĕns'* v. a. exasperar, irritar, provocar.

incentive, *insĕn'tĭv,* s. estímulo, m.

inception, *insĕp'shun,* s. principio, m.

incertitude, *insŭr'tĭtūd,* s. incertidumbre, f.

incessant, *insĕs'sănt,* a. incesante, constante; -ly, ad. continuamente.

incest, *in'sĕst,* s. incesto, m.

incestuous, *insĕs'tūūs,* a. incestuoso.

inch, *insh,* s. pulgada, f. (duodécima parte de un pié); —by, _, palmo á palmo.

incidence, *in'sĭdĕns,* s. incidencia, f.; accidente, m.

incident, *in'sĭdĕnt,* a. incidente; dependiente; —, s. incidente, m.

incidental, *insĭdĕn'tăl,* a. accidental, casual; —, ad. incidentemente.

incipient, *insĭp'ĭĕnt,* a. incipiente.

incise, *insĭz',* v. a. tajar, cortar, grabar.

incision, *insĭzh'ăn,* s. incisión, f.

incisive, *insĭ'sĭv,* a. incisivo, incisorio.

incisor, *-zŭr,* s. incisivos, m. pl.

incite, *insĭt',* v. a. incitar, estimular.

incivility, *insĭvĭl'ĭtĭ,* s. incivilidad, descortesía, f. [severidad, f.

inclemency, *inklĕm'ĕnsĭ,* s. inclemencia,

inclement, *-ĕnt,* a. inclemente, verso.

inclination, *inklĭnā'shun,* s. inclinación, propensión, f.; declive, m.

incline, *inklĭn',* v. a. & n. inclinar(se).

include, *inklōd',* v. a. incluir, comprender.

inclusive, *inklō'sĭv,* a. inclusivo; -ly, ad. inclusivamente.

incognito, *inkŏg'nĭtō,* ad. de incógnito.

incoherence, *inkōhē'rĕns,* s. incoherencia, f.

incoherent, *-rĕnt,* a. incoherente, inconsecuente; -ly, ad. incongruamente.

incombustible, *inkŏmbŭs'tĭbl,* a. incombustible. [anual, m.

income, *in'kŭm,* s. renta, f.; beneficio

incommensurable, *inkŏmmen'shŭrăbl,* a. inconmensurable.

incommode, *inkŏmmōd',* v. a. incomodar.

incommodious, *inkŏmmō'dĭŭs,* a. incómodo; molesto. [parable, excelente.

incomparable, *inkŏm'părăbl,* a. incomparably, -ĭ, ad. incomparablemente. [compatibilidad, f.

incompatibility, *inkŏmpătĭbĭl'ĭtĭ,* s. incompatible, *inkŏmpăt'ĭbl,* a. incompatible, opuesto. [petencia, f.

incompetency, *inkŏm'pĕtĕnsĭ,* s. incompetent, *-pĕtĕnt,* a., ad. incompetente(mente). [falto, imperfecto.

incomplete, *inkŏmplēt',* a. incompleto.

incomprehensibility, *inkŏmprĕhĕnsĭbĭl'ĭtĭ,* s. incomprehensibilidad, f.

incomprehensible, *inkŏmprĕhĕn'sĭbl,* a. incomprehensible.

inconceivable, *inkŏnsē'văbl,* a. incomprehensible, inconcebible.

inconclusive, *-klō'sĭv,* a. no concluyente; —, ad. sin conclusión. [incongruidad, f.

incongruity, *-grō'ĭtĭ,* s. incongruencia.

incongruous, *inkŏn'grŭŭs,* s. incongruo; -ly, ad. incongruamente.

inconsequent, *inkŏn'sēkwĕnt,* a. inconsecuente. [frivolo, poco considerable.

inconsiderable, *inkŏnsĭd'ĕrăbl,* a. inconsiderate, *-sĭd'ŭrăt,* a. inconsiderado; -ly, ad. inconsideradamente.

inconsistency, *-sĭs'tĕnsĭ,* s. incompatibilidad, incongruencia, f.

inconsistent, *-sĭs'tĕnt,* a. inconsistente; -ly, ad. incongruamente.

inconsolable, *-sō'lăbl,* a. inconsolable.

inconstancy, *inkŏn'stănsĭ,* s. inconstancia, f. [dable.

inconstant, *-stănt,* a. inconstante, mudable. [incontestable, incontrastable. [mente.

incontestable, *inkŏntĕs'tăbl,* a. incontestable, incontrastable. [mente.

incontestably, *-ĭ,* ad. incontestable-

incontinence, *ĭnkŏn'tĭnĕns,* s. incontinencia, f.   [ad. incontinentemente.

incontinent, *-tĭnĕnt,* a. incontinente; **-ly,**

incontrovertible, *ĭnkŏntrŏvŭr'tĭbl,* a. incontrovertible.

inconvenience, *ĭnkŏnvē'nĭĕns,* s. inconveniencia, incomodidad, f.; —, v. a. incomodar.

inconvenient, *-nĭĕnt,* a. incómodo, inconveniente; **-ly,** ad. incómodamente.

inconvertible, *-vŭr'tĭbl,* a. inconvertible.

incorporate, *ĭnkŏr'pŏrāt,* v. a. (& n.) incorporar(se); —, a. incorporado.

incorporation, *-rā'shŭn,* s. incorporación, f.

incorporeal, *ĭnkŏrpŏ'rĭăl,* a. incorpóreo, incorporal.   [ad. de un modo incorrecto.

incorrect, *ĭnkŏrrĕkt',* a. incorrecto; **-ly,**

incorrigible, *ĭnkŏr'rĭjĭbl,* a. incorregible.

incorrupt, *ĭnkŏrrŭpt'* a. incorrupto.

incorruptibility, *-rŭptĭbĭl'ĭtĕ,* s. incorruptibilidad, f.

incorruptible, *-rŭp'tĭbl,* a. incorruptible.

increase, *ĭnkrēs',* v. a. acrecentar, aumentar; —, v. n. crecer, tomar aumento; —, *ĭn'krēs,* s. aumento, acrecentamiento, m.

incredibility, *ĭnkrĕdĭbĭl'ĭtĕ,* s. incredibilidad, f.

incredible, *ĭnkrĕd'ĭbl,* a. increíble.

incredibly, *-ĭ,* a. increíblemente.   [f.

incredulity, *ĭnkrĕdū'lĭtĕ,* s. incredulidad,

incredulous, *ĭnkrĕd'ūlŭs,* a. incrédulo.

increment, *ĭn'krĕmĕnt,* s. incremento, m.

incriminate, *ĭnkrĭm'ĭnāt,* v. a. acriminar, acusar de algún crimen.

incrust, *ĭnkrŭst',* v. a. incrustar.

incubate, *ĭn'kūbāt,* v. n. empollar.

incubator, *ĭn'kūbātŭr,* s. horno para empollar, m.

incubus, *ĭn'kūbŭs,* s. íncubo, m.

inculcate, *ĭnkŭl'kāt,* v. a. inculcar.

inculpate, *ĭnkŭl'pāt,* v. a. inculpar.

incumbency, *ĭnkŭm'bĕnsē,* s. posesión de un beneficio eclesiástico, f.

incumbent, *ĭnkŭm'bĕnt,* a. echado; obligatorio; —, s. beneficiado, m.

incur, *ĭnkŭr',* v. a. incurrir; ocurrir.

incurability, *ĭnkŭrăbĭl'ĭtĕ,* s. incurabilidad, f., estado incurable, m.

incurable, *ĭnkū'răbl,* a. incurable.

incurably, *-ĭ,* ad. de un modo incurable.

incursion, *ĭnkŭr'shŭn,* s. incursión, invasión, f.   [peñado.

indebted, *ĭndĕt'ĕd,* a. endeudado, empeñado.

indecency, *ĭndē'sĕnsē,* s. indecencia, mala crianza, f.   ad. indecentemente.

indecent, *ĭndē'sĕnt,* a. indecente; **-ly,**

indecision, *ĭndēsĭzh'ŭn,* s. irresolución, f.

indecisive, *ĭndēsī'sĭv,* a. indeciso.

indecorous, *ĭndēkō'rŭs,* a. indecoroso, indecente.   [veras.

indeed, *ĭndēd',* ad. verdaderamente, de

indefatigable, *ĭndēfăt'ĭgăbl,* a. infatigable.

indefinite, *ĭndĕf'ĭnĭt,* a. indefinido, indeterminado; **-ly,** ad. indefinidamente.

indelible, *ĭndĕl'ĭbl,* a. indeleble.

indelicacy, *ĭndĕl'ĭkăsĕ,* s. falta de delicadeza, grosería, indecencia, f.

indelicate, *ĭndĕl'ĭkāt,* a. poco delicado.

indemnification, *ĭndĕmnĭfĭkā'shŭn,* s. indemnización, f.; resarcimiento de daño, m.

indemnify, *ĭndĕm'nĭfĭ,* v. a. indemnizar.

indemnity, *-nĭtĕ,* s. indemnidad, f.

indent, *ĭndĕnt',* v. a. dentar.   [tada, f.

indentation, *-tā'shŭn,* s. recortadura dentada, f.

indenture, *ĭndĕn'tŭr,* s. contrato de un aprendiz, m.   [dencia, f.

independence, *ĭndēpĕn'dĕns,* s. independencia, f.   [—, a. independiente;

independent, *-dĕnt* a. independiente; **-ly,** ad. independientemente.

indescribable, *ĭndēskrī'băbl,* a. indescribible, indescriptible.

indestructible, *ĭndēstrŭk'tĭbl,* a. indestructible.

indeterminate, *ĭndētŭr'mĭnāt,* a. indeterminado; **-ly,** ad. indeterminadamente.

index, *ĭn'dĕks,* s. indicio, m.; índice, m., tabla de un libro, f.; manecilla de reloj, f.

India-man, *ĭn'dĭămăn,* s. nave índica, f.

India-rubber, *-rŭbbŭr* s. goma elástica, f.   [verano tardío, m.

indian-summer, *ĭn'dĭănsŭmmŭr,* s.(am.)

indicate, *ĭn'dĭkāt,* v. a. indicar.

indication, *ĭndĭkā'shŭn,* s. indicación, f.; indicio, m.; señal, f.   [cativo (m.)

indicative, *ĭn'dĭkātĭv,* a. & s. (gr.) indicativo,

indicator, *ĭn'dĭkātŭr,* s. indicador, apuntador, m.

indictment, *ĭndīt'mĕnt,* s. acusación ante el jurado, f.   [imparcialidad, f.

indifference, *ĭndĭf'fŭrĕns,* s. indiferencia,

indifferent, *-fŭrĕnt,* a. indiferente; **-ly,** ad. indiferentemente.   [breza, f.

indigence, *ĭn'dĭjĕns,* s. indigencia, pobreza, f.

indigenous, *ĭndĭj'ĕnŭs,* a. indígena.

indigent, *ĭn'dĭjĕnt,* a. indigente, pobre.

indigestible, *ĭndĭjĕs'tĭbl,* a. indigestible.

indigestion, *-tshŭn,* s. indigestión, f.

indignant, *ĭndĭg'nănt,* a. airado.

indignation, *ĭndĭgnā'shŭn,* s. indignación, f.; desprecho, m.

indignity, *ĭndĭg'nĭtĕ,* s. indignidad, f.

indigo, *ĭn'dĭgō,* s. añil, m.

indirect, *ĭndĭrĕkt',* a. indirecto; **-ly,** ad. indirectamente.

indiscreet, *ĭndĭskrēt',* a. indiscreto, inconsiderado; **-ly,** ad. indiscretamente.

indiscretion, *ĭndĭskrĕsh'ŭn,* s. indiscreción, imprudencia, inconsideración, f.

indiscriminate, *ĭndĭskrĭm'ĭnăt,* a. indistinto; **-ly,** ad. sin distinción.   [pensable.

indispensable, *ĭndĭspĕn'săbl,* a. indispensably,** *-ĭ,* ad. indispensablemente.

indispose, *ĭndĭspōz',* v. a. indisponer.

indisposed, *-d'* a. indispuesto, achacoso,

indisposition, *ĭndĭspŏzĭsh'ŭn,* s. indisposición, f.; mala gana, f.   [table.

indisputable, *ĭndĭspūt'ăbl,* a. indisputable; **indisputably,** *-ĭ,* ad. indisputablemente.

indissoluble, *ĭndĭs'sōlŭbl,* a. indisoluble.

indistinct, *ĭndĭstĭngkt',* a. indistinto, confuso; **-ly,** ad. indistintamente.

indistinguishable, *ĭndĭstĭng'gwĭshăbl,* a. indistinguible.

indite, *ĭndīt'*, v. a. redactar.
individual, *ĭndĭvĭd'ūăl*, a. individual, individuo; **-ly,** ad. individualmente; **—,** s. individuo, m. [dualidad, f.
individuality, *ĭndĭvĭdūăl'ĭtĭ*, s. indivi-
indivisible, *ĭndĭvĭz'ĭbl*, ad. indivisible; **-bly,** ad. indivisiblemente.
indocil, *ĭndŏs'ĭl*, a. indócil, cerril.
indocility, *ĭndŏsĭl'ĭtĭ*, s. indocilidad, pertinacia, f. [f.
indolence, *ĭn'dŏlĕns*, s. indolencia, pereza,
indolent, *ĭn'dŏlĕnt*, a. indolente; **-ly,** a. con negligencia.
indomitable, *ĭndŏm'ĭtăbl*, a. indomable.
indorse, *ĭndŏrs'*, v. a. endosar una letra, vale, ú otro documento.
indubitable, *ĭndū'bĭtăbl*, a. indubitable.
indubitably, **-ĭ,** ad. indubitablemente.
induce, *ĭndūs'*, v. a. inducir, persuadir; causar. [tivo, m.
inducement, *—mĕnt*, s. inducimiento, mo-
induction, *ĭndŭk'shŭn*, s. inducción, deducción, f.; ilación, f.
inductive, *—tĭv*, a. inductivo; ilativo.
indue, *ĭndū'*, v. a. vestir; dotar; proveer.
indulge, *ĭndŭlj'*, v. a. & n. favorecer; conceder; ser indulgente.
indulgence, *—ĕns*, s. indulgencia, f.
indulgent, *—ĕnt*, a. indulgente; **-ly,** ad. de un modo indulgente.
induration, *ĭndūrā'shŭn*, s. endurecimiento, m.; dureza de corazón, f.
industrial, *ĭndŭs'trĭăl*, a. industrial.
industrious, *ĭndŭs'trĭŭs*, a. industrioso; laborioso; **-ly,** ad. industriosamente.
industry, *ĭn'dŭstrĭ*, s. industria, f.
inebriate, *ĭnē'brĭāt*, v. a. embriagar.
inebriation, *ĭnēbrĭā'shŭn*, **inebriety,** *ĭnēbrī'ĕtĭ*, s. embriaguez, f.
ineffable, *ĭnĕf'ăbl*, a. inefable.
ineffective, *ĭnĕffĕk'tĭv*, **ineffectual,** *—tūăl*, a. ineficaz; **-ly,** ad. sin efecto.
inefficacious, *ĭnĕffĭkā'shŭs*, a. ineficaz.
inefficacy, *ĭnĕf'ĭsh'ĕnsĭ*, s. ineficacia, f.
inefficient, *ĭnĕffĭsh'ĕnt*, a. ineficaz.
inelegant, *ĭnĕl'ĕgănt*, a. inelegante; sin pulimento. [excluye elección, f.
ineligible, *ĭnĕl'ĭjĭbl*, s. calidad que
ineptitude, *ĭnĕp'tĭtūd*, s. ineptitud, f.
inequality, *ĭnēkwŏl'ĭtĭ*, s. desigualdad, disparidad, diferencia, f.
inert, *ĭnŭrt'*, a. inerte, perezoso; **-ly,** ad. indolentemente.
inertness, *—nĕs*, inercia, f. [inapreciable.
inestimable, *ĭnĕs'tĭmăbl*, a. inestimable,
inevitable, *ĭnĕv'ĭtăbl*, a. inevitable.
inexcusable, *ĭnĕkskū'zăbl*, a. inexcusable.
inexcusably, **-ĭ,** ad, inexcusablemente.
inexhaustible, *ĭnĕgzhăs'tĭbl*, a. inexhausto, inagotable. [flexible, duro.
inexorable, *ĭnĕks'ŏrăbl*, a. inexorable, in-
inexpediency, *ĭnĕkspē'dĭĕnsĭ*, s. inconveniencia, falta de oportunidad, f.
inexpedient, *—dĭĕnt*, a. impropio.
inexpensive, *ĭnĕkspĕn'sĭv*, a. de poco gasto. [encia, impericia, f.
inexperience, *ĭnĕkspē'rĭĕns*, s. inexperi-

inexpert, *ĭnĕkspŭrt'*, a. inexperto.
inexpiable, *ĭnĕks'pĭăbl*, a. inexpiable.
inexplicable, *—plĭkăbl*, a. inexplicable.
inexpressible, *—prĕs'ĭbl*, a. indecible; **—,** s. pl. pantalones, m. pl.
inexpressibly, **-ĭ,** ad. de una manera indecible.
inextricable, *ĭnĕks'trĭkăbl*, a. intrincado; [enmarañado.
infallibility, *ĭnfălĭbĭl'ĭtĭ*, s. infalibilidad,
infallible, *ĭnfăl'ĭbl*, a. infalible. [f.
infallibly, **-ĭ,** ad, infaliblemente.
infamous, *ĭn'fămŭs*, a. vil, infame; **-ly,** ad. infamemente.
infamy, **-fămĭ,** s. infamia, f.
infancy, *—fănsĭ*, s. infancia, f.
infant, *—fănt*, s. infante, m.; niño, m.
infanta, *ĭnfăn'tă*, s. infanta, f.
infanticide, *ĭnfăn'tĭsīd*, s. infanticidio, m.; infanticida, m. & f. [pueril, infantil.
infantile, *ĭn'făntĭl*, **infantine,** *—tĭn*, a.
infantry, *—făntrĭ*, s. infantería, f. [bobar.
infatuate, *ĭnfăt'ūāt*, v. a. infatuar, em-
infatuation, *—tūā'shŭn*, s. infatuación, f.
infect, *ĭnfĕkt'*, v. a. infectar.
infection, *ĭnfĕk'shŭn*, s. infección, f.
infectious, *—shŭs*, a. infecto, inficionado; **-ly,** ad. por infección.
infer, *ĭnfŭr'*, v. a. inferir. [f.
inference, *ĭn'fĕrĕns*, s. inferencia, ilación,
inferior, *ĭnfē'rĭŭr*, a. inferior; **—,** s. oficial subordinado, m.
inferiority, *ĭnfērĭŏr'ĭtĭ*, s. inferioridad, f.
infernal, *ĭnfŭr'năl*, a. infernal; **-stone,** s. piedra infernal, f.
infest, *ĭnfĕst'*, v. a. infestar, incomodar.
infidel, *ĭn'fĭdĕl*, s. infiel, pagano, m.
infidelity, *ĭnfĭdĕl'ĭtĭ*, s. infidelidad, f.; perfidia, f. [**-ly,** ad. infinitamente.
infinite, *ĭn'fĭnīt*, a. infinito, innumerable;
infinitive, *ĭnfĭn'ĭtĭv*, s. infinitivo, m.
infirm, *ĭnfŭrm'*, a. enfermo, débil.
infirmary, *—ărĭ*, s. enfermería, f. [f.
infirmity, *—ĭtĭ*, s. fragilidad, enfermedad,
inflame, *ĭnflām'*, v. a. (& n.) inflamar(se).
inflammable, *ĭnflăm'măbl*, a. inflamable.
inflammation, *—mā'shŭn*, s. inflamación, f.
inflammatory, *—mătŭrĭ*, a. inflamatorio.
inflate, *ĭnflāt'*, v. a. inflar, hinchar.
inflation, *ĭnflā'shŭn*, s. inflación, f.; hinchazón, f.; acumulación excesiva de oro ó plata, f. [modulación de la voz, f.
inflection, *ĭnflĕk'shŭn*, s. inflexión, f.
inflexibility, *ĭnflĕksĭbĭl'ĭtĭ*, s. inflexibilidad, f. [flexible.
inflexible, *ĭnflĕks'ĭbl*, a. inmoble, in-
inflexibly, **-ĭ,** ad. inflexiblemente.
inflict, *ĭnflĭkt'*, v. a. castigar; imponer penas corporales. [pena corporal, f.
infliction, *ĭnflĭk'shŭn*, s. imposición de una
influence, *ĭn'flūĕns*, s. influencia, f.; **—,** v. a. influir.
influential, *ĭnflūĕn'shăl*, a. influente.
influenza, *—ză*, s. influenza, gripa, f.
influx, *ĭn'flŭks*, s. influjo, m.; infusión, f.
inform, *ĭnfŏrm'*, v. a. informar, enseñar.
informal, *—ăl*, a. informal; irregular.
informality, *—ăl'ĭtĭ*, s. informalidad, f.

informant, ĭnfŏr'mănt, s. denunciador, acusador, m. [instrucción, f.

information, —mā'shŭn, s. información, f.

infraction, ĭnfrăk'shŭn, s. infracción, f.

infrangible, ĭnfrăn'jĭbl, a. infrangible.

infrequent, ĭnfrē'kwĕnt, a. raro, insólito; —ly, ad. raramente.

infringe, ĭnfrĭnj', v. a. violar (una ley ó pacto), contravenir á. [m.

infringer, —ŭr, s. violador, contraventor,

infuriate, ĭnfū'rĭăt, v. a. irritar, provocar, enfurecer.

infuse, ĭnfūz', v. a. infundir. [ción, f.

infusion, ĭnfū'zhŭn, s. infusión, f.; inspir-

ingathering, ĭngăth'ŭrĭng, s. cosecha, f.

ingenious, ĭnjē'nĭŭs, a. ingenioso; —ly, ad. ingeniosamente.

ingenuity, ĭnjĕnū'ĭtĭ, s. ingeniosidad, f.; ingenuidad, f.; destreza, f.

ingenuous, ĭnjĕn'ūŭs, a. ingenuo, sincero; —ly, ad. ingenuamente.

ingle, ĭng'gl, s. chimenea, f.

inglorious, ĭnglō'rĭŭs, a. ignominioso, vergonzoso; —ly, ad. ignominiosamente.

ingot, ĭn'gŏt, s. barra de metal (sin labrar).

ingraft, ĭngrăft', v. a. injertar. [f.

ingrained, ĭngrānd', a. inveterado.

ingrate, ĭngrāt', a. ingrato.

ingratiate, ĭngrā'shĭăt, v. n. insinuarse; congraciarse.

ingratitude, ĭngrăt'ĭtūd, s. ingratitud, f.

ingredient, ĭngrē'dĭĕnt, s. ingrediente, m.

ingress, ĭn'grĕs, s. entrada, f.

ingulf, ĭngŭlf', v. a. engolfar, tragar, sumir.

inhabit, ĭnhăb'ĭt, v. n. & n. habitar; vivir, residir.

inhabitable, —ăbl, a. habitable. [m.

inhabitant, —ănt, s. habitador, habitante,

inhale, ĭnhāl', v. a. inspirar.

inharmonious, ĭnhărmō'nĭŭs, a. disonante, discordante.

inherent, ĭnhē'rĕnt, a. inherente.

inherit, ĭnhĕr'ĭt, v. a. heredar.

inheritance, —ăns, s. herencia, f.

inheritor, —ŭr, s. heredero, m.

inhospitable, ĭnhŏs'pĭtăbl, a. inhospitable, inhospedable. [lidad, f.

inhospitality, ĭnhŏspĭtăl'ĭtĭ, s. inhospita-

inhuman, ĭnhū'măn, a. inhumano, cruel; —ly, ad. inhumanamente. [crueldad, f.

inhumanity, ĭnhūmăn'ĭtĭ, s. inhumanidad,

inhume, ĭnhūm', v. a. enterrar, sepultar.

inimical, ĭnĭm'ĭkăl, a. enemigo.

inimitable, ĭnĭm'ĭtăbl, a. inimitable.

iniquitous, ĭnĭk'wĭtŭs, a. inicuo, injusto.

iniquity, ĭnĭk'wĭtĭ, s. iniquidad, injusticia, f. [cial, f.

initial, ĭnĭsh'ăl, a. inicial; —s, letra ini-

initiate, ĭnĭsh'ĭăt, v. a. principiar, iniciar.

initiation, ĭnĭshĭā'shŭn, s. principio, m.; iniciación, f.

inject, ĭnjĕkt', v. a. inyectar.

injection, ĭnjĕk'shŭn, s. inyección, f.

injudicious, ĭnjūdĭsh'ŭs, a. poco juicioso; —ly, ad. sin juicio. [cepto, m.

injunction, ĭnjŭngk'shŭn, s. mandato, pre-

injure, ĭn'jūr, v. a. injuriar, ofender.

injurious, ĭnjū'rĭŭs, a. injurioso, injusto; —ly, ad. injuriosamente. [daño, m.

injury, ĭn'jūrĭ, s. injuria, afrenta, f.;

injustice, ĭnjŭs'tĭs, s. injusticia, f.; agravio, m. [tinta.

ink, ĭngk, s. tinta, f.; —, v. a. linear con

ink-horn, —hŏrn, s. tintero (de faltriquera).

inkling, —lĭng, s. aviso secreto, m. [m.

ink-stand, —stănd, s. tintero, m.

inky, —ĭ, a. de tinta; semejante á la tinta.

inlaid, ĭnlād', a. ataraceado.

inland, ĭn'lănd, a. interior; —, ĭnlănd', ad. dentro de un país.

inlay, ĭnlā', v. a. ataracear; —, ĭn'lā, s. [ataracea, f.

inlet, ĭn'lĕt, s. entrada, f.

inmate, ĭn'māt, s. inquilino, m.

inmost, ĭn'mōst, a. íntimo.

inn, ĭn, s. posada, f.; mesón, m.

innate, ĭnnāt', a. innato, natural, insito.

inner, ĭn'nŭr, a. interior.

innermost, —mōst, a. íntimo.

inning, ĭn'nĭng, s. mano en los naipes, f.; —s, pl. tierras aluviales cerradas con diques, f. pl. [nero, m.

inn-keeper, ĭnn'kēpŭr, s. posadero, meso-

innocence, ĭn'nŏsĕns, s. inocencia, f.

innocent, —nŏsĕnt, a. inocente; —ly, ad. inocentemente.

innocuous, ĭnnŏk'ūŭs, a. innocuo, inocente; —ly, ad. inocentemente.

innovate, ĭn'nŏvāt, v. a. innovar.

innovation, ĭnnŏvā'shŭn, s. innovación, f.

innoxious, ĭnnŏk'shŭs, a. inocente; no nocivo; —ly, ad. sin hacer daño.

innuendo, ĭnnŭĕn'dŏ, s. indirecta, insinuación, f. [rrable.

innumerable, ĭnnū'mŭrăbl, a. innume-

inoculate, ĭnŏk'ūlăt, v. a. inocular; injertar. [f.

inoculation, ĭnŏkūlā'shŭn, s. inoculación,

inoffensive, ĭnŏffĕn'sĭv, a. pacífico; inofensivo. [niente, no oportuno.

inopportune, ĭnŏppŏrtūn', a. inconve-

inordinate, ĭnŏr'dĭnăt, a. desordenado; —ly, ad. desordenadamente. [nico.

inorganic(al), ĭnŏrgăn'ĭk(ăl), a. inorgá-

inquest, ĭn'kwĕst, s. pesquisa, f.

inquire, ĭnkwīr', v. a. preguntar alguna cosa; —, v. n. inquirir, examinar.

inquiry, ĭnkwī'rĭ, s. interrogación, f.; pesquisa, f. [escudriñamiento, m.

inquisition, ĭnkwĭzĭsh'ŭn, s. inquisición, f.;

inquisitive, ĭnkwĭz'ĭtĭv, a. curioso; —ly, ad. inquisitivamente. [inquisidor, m.

inquisitor, —ĭtŭr, s. juez pesquisidor, m.;

inroad, ĭn'rŏd, s. incursión, invasión, f.

insane, ĭnsān', a. insano, loco, demente.

insanity, ĭnsăn'ĭtĭ, s. insania, f.; locura, f.

insatiable, ĭnsā'shĭăbl, a. insaciable, inhartable; deseoso.

inscribe, ĭnskrīb', v. a. inscribir; dedicar.

inscription, ĭnskrĭp'shŭn, s. inscripción; dedicación, f.

inscrutable, ĭnskrō'tăbl, a. inescrutable.

insect, ĭn'sĕkt, s. insecto, m. [guro.

insecure, ĭnsĕkūr', a. desconfiado; no se-

insecurity, ĭnsĕkū'rĭtĭ, s. peligro, riesgo, m.

insensate, ĭnsĕn'sāt, a. insensato. [in-

insense, *insēns'*, v. a. enojar á uno.
insensibility, *insensibil'tié*, s. insensibilidad, f.; estupidez, f.
insensible, *insēn'sibl*, a, insensible; imperceptible.
insensibly, *—é*, ad. insensiblemente.
inseparable, *insep'árabl*, a. inseparable.
inseparably, *—é*, ad. inseparablemente.
insert, *insúrt'*, v. a. insertar, ingerir una cosa en otra.
insertion, *insúr'shán*, s. inserción, f.
inside, *in'síd*, s. interior, m.; *—,* ad. adentro, dentro.
insidious, *insíd'iús*, a. insidioso; *—ly,* ad. insidiosamente.
insight, *in'sít*, s. conocimiento profundo, m.
insignia, *insíg'niá*, s. pl. insignias, f. pl.; estandartes, m. pl.
insignificance, *insígnif'ikáns*, s. insignificación, f.; nulidad, f.
insignificant, *—kánt*, ad. insignificativo, frívolo; *—ly,* ad. sin significación.
insincere, *insinsēr'*, a. poco sincero.
insincerity, *—sér'tié*, s. disimulación, f.
insinuate, *insín'úát*, v. a. insinuar.
insinuation, *insinúá'shán*, s. insinuación, f.
insipid, *insíp'id*, a. insípido; insulso; *—ly,* ad. insulsamente.
insipidity, *insipid'tié*, s. insipidez, insulsez, f.
insist, *insíst'*, v. n. insistir, persistir.
insistence, *—áns,* s. insistencia, f.
insolence, *in'sóléns*, s. insolencia, f.
insolent, *in'sólént*, a. insolente; *—ly,* ad. insolentemente.
insoluble, *insól'úbl*, a. insoluble; indisoluble.
insolvency, *insól'vénsé*, s. insolvencia, f.
insolvent, *insól'vént*, a. insolvente.
insomuch, *insómútsh'*, c. de manera que.
inspect, *inspékt'*, v. a. reconocer, examinar, inspeccionar.
inspection, *inspék'shán*, s. inspección, f.
inspector, *—tár*, s. inspector, superintendente, m.
inspiration, *inspirá'shán*, s. inspiración, f.
inspire, *inspír'*, v. a. inspirar (el aire); inspirar, sugerir.
inspirit, *inspir'it*, v. a. alentar, animar.
instability, *instábil'tié*, s. instabilidad, inconstancia, f.
instal, *instál'*, v. a. instalar.
installation, *instálá'shán*, s. instalación, f.
instalment, *instál'mént*, s. instalación, f.; pago parcial, m.
instance, *in'stáns*, s. instancia, f.; solicitación, f.; ejemplo, documento, m.; prueba, f.; for *—,* por ejemplo; *—,* v. n. alegar ejemplos.
instant, *in'stánt*, a. instante, urgente; *—ly,* ad. en un instante; *—,* s. instante, momento, m.
instantaneous, *instántá'niús*, a. instantáneo; *—ly,* ad. instantáneamente.
instead, (of), *instéd'*, pr. por, en lugar de, en vez de.
instep, *in'stép*, s. empeine del pie, m.
instigate, *in'stigát*, v. a. instigar, mover.
instigation, *instigá'shán*, s. instigación, sugestión, provocación á hacer daño, f.
instil, *instíl'*, v. a. insinuar, instilar.

instinct, *in'stingkt*, s. instinto, m.; *—,* a. vivo, despabilado.
instinctive, *instingk'tiv*, a. instintivo; *—ly,* ad. por instinto.
institute, *in'stitút*, v. a. instituir, establecer; *—,* s. instituto, m.; principio, m.
institution, *—tú'shán*, s. institución, f.
instruct, *instrúkt'*, v. a. instruir, enseñar.
instruction, *instrúk'shán*, s. instrucción, enseñanza, f.
instructive, *instrúk'tiv*, a. instructivo.
instructor, *—tár*, s. instructor, m.
instrument, *in'strómént*, s. instrumento; contrato, m.
instrumental, *—mén'tál*, a. instrumental.
insubordinate, *insúbór'dinát*, a. insubordinado.
insubordination, *—ná'shán*, s. insubordinación, f.
insufferable, *insúf'fúrábl*, a. insufrible, insoportable.
insufferably, *—é*, ad. insoportablemente, insufriblemente.
insufficiency, *insúffish'énsé*, s. insuficiencia, f.
insufficient, *—ént*, a. insuficiente; *—ly,* ad. insuficientemente.
insular, *in'súlár*, a. insular, isleño.
insulate, *in'súlát*, v. a. aislar (las corrientes eléctricas).
insult, *insúlt'*, v. a. insultar; *—,* *in'súlt*, s. insulto, m.
insulter, *insúl'tár*, s. insultador, m.
insultingly, *—ínglé*, ad. con insolencia.
insuperable, *insú'púrábl*, a. insuperable.
insuperably, *—é*, ad. invenciblemente.
insupportable, *insúppór'tábl*, a. insoportable, inaguantable.
insupportably, *—é*, ad. intolerablemente, insoportablemente.
insurance, *inshō'ráns*, s. (com.) seguro, m.; seguridad, f.
insure, *inshōr'*, v. a. asegurar.
insurgent, *insúr'jént*, s. insurgente, rebelde, m.
insurmountable, *insúrmóūn'tábl*, a. insuperable.
insurrection, *insúrrék'shán*, s. insurrección, sedición, f.
insurrectionary, *—shúnáré*, a. insurreccionario.
intact, *intákt'*, a. salvo, sano, entero.
intaker, *in'tákár*, s. recaudador, m.
integral, *in'tégrál*, a. íntegro; (chem.) integrante, f.; *—,* s. todo, m.
integrity, *intég'ritié*, s. integridad; pureza, f.
intellect, *in'téllékt*, s. entendimiento, m.
intellectual, *intéllék'túál*, a. intelectual, mental.
intelligence, *intél'léjéns*, s. inteligencia, f.; conocimiento, m.; correspondencia, f.; nueva, f.; concierto, m.
intelligencer, *—jénsár*, s. novelero, m.
intelligent, *—léjént*, a. inteligente.
intelligible, *—léjibl*, a. inteligible.
intelligibly, *—é*, ad. inteligiblemente.
intemperance, *intém'púráns*, s. intemperancia, f.
intemperate, *—púrát*, a. destemplado, inmoderado; *—ly,* ad. destempladamente, inmoderadamente.
intend, *inténd'*, v. a. intentar.
intendant, *—ánt*, s. intendente, m.
intense, *inténs'*, a. intenso; vehemente; *—ly,* ad. intensamente.

intensity, -ĭtĭ, s. intensidad, f.; exceso, m.

intent, ĭntĕnt´, s. atento, cuidadoso; -ly, ad. con aplicación; -, s. intento, designio, m. [signio.

intention, ĭntĕn´shŭn, s. intención, f.; de-intentional, -ăl, a. intencional; -ly, ad. de intento.

inter, ĭntŭr´, v. a. enterrar, soterrar.

intercede, ĭntŭrsēd´, v. n. interceder, mediar. [pedir.

intercept, -sĕpt´, v. a. interceptar; in-intercession, -sĕsh´ŭn, s. intercesión, mediación, f. [diador, m.

intercessor, -sĕs´ŭr, s. intercesor, me-interchange, ĭn´tŭrtshānj, v. a. alternar, trocar; -, s. comercio, m.; permuta de géneros, f. [comunicación, f.

intercourse, ĭn´tŭrkōrs, s. comercio, m.;

interdict, ĭn´tŭrdĭkt, s. entredicho, m.; -, ĭntŭrdĭkt´, v. a. interdecir; entredecir.

interdiction, ĭntŭrdĭk´shŭn, s. interdicción, prohibición, f.

interest, ĭn´tŭrĕst, v. a. interesar; empeñar; -, s. interés, provecho, m.; influjo, empeño, m.; compound -, interés de interés. [mezclarse.

interfere, ĭntŭrfēr´, v. n. entremeterse, interference, -ĕns, s. interposición, mediación, f. [entre tanto; en el ínterin.

interim, ĭn´tŭrĭm, s. intermedio, m.; ad -, interior, ĭntē´rĭŭr, a. interior, interno.

interjection, ĭntŭrjĕk´shŭn, s. (gr.) interjección, f.

interlace, -lās´, v. a. entretejer.

interlard, -lärd´, v. a. mechar.

interleave, -lēv´, v. a. interpolar hojas blancas entre las impresas de un libro.

interline, -līn´, v. a. interlinear.

interlocution, -lōkū´shŭn, s. interlocución, f.

interlocutor, -lōk´ŭter, s. interlocutor, m.

interlope, -lōp´, v. n. entremeterse; traficar sin licencia. [bandista, m.

interloper, -lō´pŭr, s. entremetido; cont.a-intermarriage, -măr´rĕj, s. doble casamiento entre dos familias, m.

intermarry, -măr´rē, v. n. unirse por un doble casamiento.

intermediate, mĕ´dĭăt, a. intermedio.

interment, ĭntŭr´mĕnt, s. entierro, m.; sepultura, f. [nable, ilimitado.

interminable, ĭntŭr´mĭnăbl, a. intermi-intermingle, ĭntŭrmĭng´gl, v. a. & n. entremezclar; mezclarse. [interrupción, f.

intermission, -mĭsh´ŭn, s. intermisión, f.

intermit, -mĭt´; v. a. intermitir; -, v. n. descontinuar, cesar. [ternamente.

internal, ĭntŭr´ndl, a. interno; -ly, ad. in-international, ĭntŭrnă´shŭnl, a. internacional. [ción, f.

interpellation, -pĕllā´shŭn, s. interpela-interpolate, ĭntŭr´pōldt, v. a. interpolar.

interpolation, -pōlā´shŭn, s. interpolación, f.

interpose, -pōz´, v. a. interponer, entreponer; -, v. n. interponerse.

interposer, -ŭr, s. mediador, m. [ción, f.

interposition, -pōsĭsh´ŏn, s. interposi-

interpret, ĭntŭr´prĕt, v. a. interpretar.

interpretation, ĭntŭrprĕtā´shŭn, s. interpretación, f.

interpreter, ĭntŭr´prĕtŭr, s. intérprete, m.

interregnum, ĭntŭrrĕg´năm, s. interregno, m. [examinar.

interrogate, ĭntŭr´rōgāt, v. a. interrogar, interrogation, ĭntŭrrōgā´shŭn, s. interrogación, pregunta, f.

interrogative, -rŏg´dtĭv, interrogatory, -rŏg´dtŏrĕ, a. interrogativo.

interrupt, -rŭpt´, v. a. interrumpir.

interruptedly, -ĕdlĕ, ad. con interrupción.

interruption, -rŭp´shŭn, s. interrupción, f. [v. n. intersecarse.

intersect, ĭntŭrsĕkt´, v. a. entrecortar; -, intersection, -sĕk´shŭn, s. intersección, f. [cosa entre otras.

intersperse, -spŭrs´, v. a. esparcir una interstice, ĭn´tŭrstĭs, (ĭntŭr´stĭs), s. intersticio, intervalo, m.

intertwine, ĭntŭrtwīn´, v. a. entretejer.

interval, ĭn´tŭrvăl, s. intervalo, m.

intervene, ĭntŭrvēn´, v. n. intervenir; ocurrir. [interposición, f.

intervention, -vĕn´shŭn, s. intervención, interview, ĭn´tŭrvū, s. entrevista, f.; -, v. a. pescudar á los políticos (dícese de periodistas).

interviewer, -ŭr, s. periodista que va pescudando á los hombres de Estado, m.

interweave, ĭntŭrwēv´, v. a. entretejer, enlazar.

intestate, ĭntĕs´tāt, a. intestado.

intestinal, -tĭnăl, a. intestinal.

intestine, -tĭn, a. intestino, doméstico; -s, s. pl. intestinos, m. pl.

inthral, ĭnthrăl´, v. a. esclavizar.

inthralment, -mĕnt, s. esclavitud, f.

intimacy, ĭn´tĭmăsĕ, s. intimidad, confianza, f.

intimate, ĭn´tĭmăt, s. amigo íntimo, m.; -, s. íntimo, familiar; -ly, ad. íntimamente; -, ĭn´tĭmāt, v. a. insinuar, dar á entender. [directa.

intimation, -mă´shŭn, s. insinuación, in-intimidate, ĭntĭm´ĭdāt, v. a. intimidar.

into, ĭn´tŏ, pr. en, dentro, adentro.

intolerable, ĭntŏl´ărăbl, a. intolerable.

intolerably, -ĕ, ad. intolerablemente.

intolerance, -ărăns, s. intolerancia, f.

intolerant, -ărănt, a. intolerante.

intonation, ĭntŏnā´shŭn, s. entonación, f.

intoxicate, ĭntŏks´ĭkāt, v. a. embriagar.

intoxication, -kā´shŭn, s. embriaguez, f.

intractable, ĭntrăk´tăbl, a. intratable.

intransitive, ĭntrăn´sĭtĭv, a. (gr.) intransitivo. [v. n. usurpar, invadir.

intrench, ĭntrĕnsh´, v. a. atrincherar; -, intrepid, ĭntrĕp´ĭd, a. arrojado; intrépido; -ly, ad. intrépidamente.

intrepidity, ĭntrĕpĭd´ĭtĭ, s. intrepidez, f.

intricacy, ĭn´trĭkăsĕ, s. embrollo, embarazo, m.; dificultad, f.

intricate, ĭn´trĭkăt, a. intricado, complicado; -ly, ad. intricadamente.

intrigue, ĭntrēg´, s. intriga, f.; -, v. n. intrigar.

intrinsic(al), *intrin'sik(ál),* a. intrínseco, interno; **-ally,** ad. intrínsecamente.
introduce, *intródús',* v. a. introducir. [f.
introduction, *-dûk'shûn,* s. introducción.
introductive, *-dûk'tiv,* **introductory,** *-dûk'tûrë,* a. previo, preliminar.
introspection, *-spëk'shûn,* s. examen interior, m. [ducirse.
intrude, *intrôd',* v. n. entremeterse, intro-
intruder, *-ûr,* s. intruso, entremetido, m.
intrusion, *intrô'shûn,* s. intrusión, f.; entremetimiento, m.
intrust, *intrûst',* v. a. confiar.
intuition, *intúish'ûn,* s. intuición, f.
intuitive, *intú'itiv,* a. evidente; intuitivo.
inundate, *inûn'dât,* v. a. inundar.
inundation, *inûndá'shûn,* s. inundación, f.
inure, *inûr',* v. a. acostumbrar, habituar.
inurement, *-mënt,* s. hábito, m., costumbre,
inutility, *inútil'tië,* s. inutilidad, f. [f.
invade, *invâd',* v. a. invadir, asaltar.
invader, *-ûr,* s. usurpador, invasor, m.
invalid, *invál'id,* a. inválido, nulo; **-,** *invâlëd',* s. inválido, m.
invalidate, *-idât,* v. a. invalidar, anular.
invalidity, *invâlid'itië,* s. invalidación, nulidad, f.; debilidad, f.
invaluable, *invál'úâbl,* a. inapreciable.
invariable, *invá'riâbl,* a. invariable.
invariably, *-ë,* ad. invariablemente.
invasion, *invá'zhûn,* s. invasión, f.
invective, *invëk'tiv,* s. invectiva, f.
inveigh, *invâ',* v. n. escribir ó decir invectivas.
inveigle, *invë'gl,* v. a. seducir, persuadir.
invent, *invënt',* v. a. inventar.
invention, *invën'shûn,* s. invención, f.
inventive, *-tiv,* a. inventivo. [m.
inventor, *-tûr,* s. inventor, m.; forjador,
inventory, *in'vëntûrë,* s. inventario, m.
inverse, *invûrs',* a. inverso, trastornado.
inversion, *invûr'shûn,* s. inversión, f.
invert, *invûrt',* v. a. invertir, trastrocar.
invest, *invëst',* v. a. investir.
investigate, *invës'tigât,* v. a. investigar.
investigation, *invëstigá'shûn,* s. investigación, pesquisa, f.
investiture, *invës'titûr,* s. investidura, f.
investment, *invëst'mënt,* s. vestido, m., vestidura, f.
inveterate, *invët'ërât,* a. inveterado.
invidious, *invid'iûs,* a. envidioso; **-ly,** ad. envidiosamente. [vigor.
invigorate, *invig'ûrât,* v. a. vigorar, dar
invincible, *invin'sibl,* a. invencible.
invincibly, *-ë,* ad. invenciblemente.
inviolable, *invi'ôlâbl,* a. inviolable; invulnerable.
inviolate, *invi'ôlât,* a. ileso.
invisibility, *invizibil'itië,* s. invisibilidad, f.
invisible, *inviz'ibl,* a. invisible.
invisibly, *-ë,* ad. invisiblemente.
invitation, *invitá'shûn,* s. convite, m.
invite, *invit',* v. a. convidar.
invocation, *invôká'shûn,* s. invocación, f. (la acción de invocar y la fórmula con que se invoca).
invoice, *in'vôis,* s. (com.) factura, f.

invoke, *invôk',* v. a. invocar.
involuntarily, *invôl'ûntârilë,* ad. involuntariamente.
involuntary, *-ântârë,* a. involuntario.
involve, *invôlv',* v. a. envolver, implicar.
invulnerable, *invûl'nërâbl,* a. invulnerable.
inward, *in'wârd,* a. interior; interno; **-, -s, -ly,** ad. interiormente; internamente, hacia dentro.
iodine, *i'ôdin,* s. (chem.) iodo, m.
I. O. U. (I owe you), *i ô yû,* vale, m.
irascible, *irâs'ibl,* a. irascible.
irate, *irât,* irful, *ir'fûl,* a. irato, iracundo
ire, *ir,* s. ira, iracundia, f.
iridescent, *iridës'ënt,* a. iridescente.
iris, *i'ris,* s. arco iris, m.
irksome, *ûrk'sûm,* a. tedioso, fastidioso.
iron, *i'rn,* s. hierro, m.; **-,** a. férreo; **-,** v. a. aplanchar; poner en grillos.
iron-dust, *-dûst,* s. limadura de hierro, f
ironic(al), *irôn'ik(âl),* a. irónico; **-ly,** ad con ironía.
ironing, *i'rning,* s. planchado, m.
iron-monger, *i'rnmûngûr,* s. traficante de hierro, m.
iron(-)mould, *-môld,* s. robín, m.
iron-ware, *-wâr,* s. ferretería, f.; quincallería, f. [herrería, f.
iron-work, *-wûrk,* s. herraje, m.; **-s,** pl.
irony, *i'rônë,* s. ironía, f.
irradiate, *irrâ'diât,* v. a. irradiar, brillar.
irrational, *irrâsh'ûnâl,* a. irracional.
irreclaimable, *irrëklâm'âbl,* a. incorregible. [liable, implacable.
irreconcilable, *-kônsil'âbl,* s. irreconciliable, incurable.
irrecoverable, *-kûv'ûrâbl,* a. irrecuperable; irremediable. [tizable (deuda).
irredeemable, *irrëdëm'âbl,* a. no amortizable (deuda).
irrefragable, *irrëf'râgâbl,* a. irrefragable.
irregular, *irrëg'úlâr,* a. **-ly,** ad. irregular(mente). [f.
irregularity, *-gûlâr'itië,* s. irregularidad,
irrelevant, *irrël'ëvânt,* a. no aplicable; lo que no prueba nada; no concluyente.
irreligion, *irrëlij'ûn,* s. irreligión, impiedad, f. [irreligiosamente.
irreligious, *-ûs,* a. irreligioso; **-ly,** ad.
irremediable, *irrëmë'diâbl,* a. irremediable.
irreparable, *irrëp'ârâbl,* a. irreparable.
irreproachable, *irrëprôtsh'âbl,* a. irreprensible.
irresistible, *-zist'ibl,* a. irresistible.
irresolute, *irrëz'ôlút,* a. irresoluto; **-ly,** ad. irresolutamente.
irresolution, *-lú'shûn,* s. irresolución, f.
irrespective, *-spëk'tiv,* a. inconsiderado.
irresponsible, *-spôn'sibl,* a. no responsable. [irreparable.
irretrievable, *-trë'vâbl,* a. irrecuperable,
irretrievably, *-ë,* ad. irreparablemente.
irreverence, *irrëv'ërëns,* s. irreverencia, f.
irreverent, *-ûrënt,* a. irreverente; **-ly,** ad. irreverentemente.
irrevocable, *irrëv'ôkâbl,* a. irrevocable
irrigate, *ir'rigât,* v. a. regar, mojar.
irrigation, *-gá'shûn,* s. regamiento, m.
irritability, *irritâbil'itië,* s. irritabilidad, f

irritable, *ír'ri̯tăbl*, a. irritable.   [m.
irritant, *ír'ri̯dănt*, s. (med.) estimulante,
irruption, *irrŭp'shŭn*, s. irrupción, entrada forzada, f.
isinglass, *í'zingglăs*, s. cola de pescado, f.
Islamism, *ís'lămĭzm*, s. islamismo, m.
island, *í'lănd*, s. isla, f.
islander, *-ăr*, s. isleño, m.
isle, *íl*, **islet,** *í'lĕt*, s. islote, m., isleta, f.
isolate, *í'sŏlăt*, v. a. aislar.
issue, *ísh'shŭ*, s. salida, f.; evento, m.; resulta, f.; fin, término, m.; cauterio, m.; prole, progenie, f.; —, v. n. salir; prorrumpir, brotar; venir, proceder; provenir; —, v. a. echar; expedir, despachar; publicar; emitir.
isthmus, *íst'mŭs*, s. istmo, m.
it, *ĭt*, pn. él, ella, ello, lo, la, le.
italic, *ĭtăl'ĭk*, s. letra cursiva, f.
itch, *ĭtsh*, s. sarna, f.; picazón, f.; prurito, m.; —, v. n. picar.   [s. artículo, m.
item, *í'tĕm*, ad. ítem, otro sí, aun más; —,
iteration, *ĭtŭrā'shŭn*, s. reiteración, f.
itinerant, *ĭtín'ă̯rănt*, a. ambulante, errante.
itinerary, *-ă̯rărĕ*, s. itinerario, m.
its, *ĭts*, pn. su, suyo.   [mismo.
itself, *ĭtsĕlf'*, pn. el mismo, la misma, lo
ivory, *í'vŏrĕ*, s. marfil, m.
ivy, *í'vĕ*, s. hiedra, f.

J.

jabber, *jăb'băr*, v. n. charlar, farfullar.
jabberer, *-ăr*, s. farfullador, parlanchín, m.
jack, *jăk*, s. sacabotas, m.; martinete, m.; torno de asador, m.; jarro de cuero encerado, m.; cota de malla, f.; boliche, m.; macho, m.; burro, m.; lucio, m.; —o'-lantern, fuego fatuo, m.; **to be — of all trades,** meterse en todo.
jackal, *-ăl*, s. adiva, f., adive, m.
jackanapes, *-ănăps*, s. pisaverde, mequetrefe, m.
jack-ass, *-ăs*, s. garañón, burro, m.
jack-boots, *-bŏts*, s. pl. botas grandes y fuertes, f. pl.
jack-daw, *-dă*, s. grajo, m.
jacket, *-ĕt*, s. chaqueta, jaqueta, f.
jade, *jăd*, s. rocín, m.; —, v. a. cansar.
jag, *jăg*, s. diente de sierra, m.; mella, f.; —, v. a. dentar.
jagged, *-gĕd*, a. desigual, dentado.
jaguar, *jăg'dăr*, s. jaguar, m.
jail, *jăl*, s. cárcel, f.
jail-bird, *-bărd*, s. preso, m.
jailer, *-ăr*, s. carcelero, m.
jam, *jăm*, s. conserva, f.; mermelada de frutas, f.; —, v. a. acuñar estrechamente.
jamb, *jăm*, s. quicial, m.
jangle, *jăng'gl*, v. n. reñir, altercar.
janitor, *jăn'ĭtăr*, s. ujier, portero, m.
Janizary, *jăn'ĭzărĕ*, s. jenízaro, m.
jant, *jănt*, s. pina de la rueda, f.
January, *jăn'dărĕ*, s. enero, m.   [rolar.
Japan, *jăpăn'*, s. charol, m.; —, v. a. charolista; m.
japanner, *-năr*, s. charolista, m.
jar, *jăr*, v. n. chocar; (mus.) discordar;

reñir; —, s. jarro, m.; **tinaja,** f.; riña, f.; sonido desapacible, m.
jargon, *jăr'gŏn*, s. jerga, jerigonza, f.
jasper, *jăs'păr*, s. jaspe, m.
jaundice, *jăn'dĭs*, s. ictericia, f.
jaundiced, *-d*, a. ictérico.
jaunt, *jănt*, s. excursión, f.
jaunty, *-ĕ*, a. alegre, festivo.
jaw, *jă*, s. quijada, f.; boca, f.
jay, *jă*, s. picaza, urraca, marica, f. (ave).
jealous, *jĕl'ŭs*, a. celoso; envidioso.
jealousy, *-ĕ*, s. celos, m. pl.
jeer, *jĕr*, v. n. befar, mofar, escarnecer; —, s. befa, mofa, burla, f.
Jehu, *jĕ'hŭ*, s. cochero arrojado, m.
jelly, *jĕl'lĕ*, s. jalea, gelatina, f.
jelly-broth, *-brŏth*, s. consumado, m.
jelly-fish, *-fĭsh*, s. aguamar, m.; medusa, f.
jeopard(ise), *jĕp'ărd(ĭz)*, v. a. arriesgar, poner en riesgo.   [dar latigazos, azotar.
jerk, *jărk*, s. sacudida, sobarbada, f.; —, v. a.
jessamine, *jĕs'ămĭn*, s. jazmín, m.
jest, *jĕst*, s. chanza, burla, f.
jester, *-ăr*, s. mofador, bufón, m.
jestingly, *-ĭnglĕ*, ad. de burlas.
Jesuit, *jĕz'ŭĭt*, s. jesuíta, m.; **—'s bark,** quina, cascarilla, f.
jesuitic(al), *jĕzŭĭt'ĭk(ăl)*, a. jesuítico.
jet, *jĕt*, s. azabache, m.; surtidor, m.
jetty, *-tĕ*, a. hecho de azabache; —, s. muelle, m.
Jew, *jŭ*, s. judío, m.   [muelle, m.
jewel, *-ĕl*, s. joya, f.
jeweller, *-lăr*, s. joyero, m.
jewelry, *-rĕ*, s. joyería, f.
Jewess, *jŭ'ĕs*, s. judía, f.
jewish, *-ĭsh*, a. judaico, judío.
jewry, *-rĕ*, s. judería, f.
Jews'harp, *jŭz'hărp*, s. birimbao, m.
jib, *jĭb*, s. (mar.) maraguto, foque, m.
jig, *jĭg*, s. baile alegre, m.
jilt, *jĭlt*, s. coqueta, f.; —, v. n. coquetear.
jingle, *jĭng'gl*, v. n. retiñir, resonar; —, s. retintín, resonido, m.
job, *jŏb*, s. friolera, f.; destajo, m.; engaña, f.; cucaña, f.; —, v. a. & n. dar una mojada; cambalachar.
jobation, *jŏbā'shŭn*, s. paulina, f.
jobber, *jŏb'băr*, s. agiotista, m.; destajero, m.; usurero, m.
jobbing, *-bĭng*, s. infundios, m. pl.
job-master, *-măstăr*, s. alquilador de caballos, m.
jockey, *jŏk'ĕ*, s. jinete, chalán, m.; persona apasionada por los caballos, f.; engañabobos, m.; —, v. a. trampear, engañar.
jocose, *jŏkŏs'*, a. jocoso, burlesco; **-ly,** ad. jocosamente.
jocosity, *jŏkŏs'ĭtĕ*, s. jocosidad, chanza, f.
jocular, *jŏk'ŭlăr*, **jocund,** *-ănd*, a. jocoso, alegre.
jog, *jŏg*, v. a. empujar; dar un golpe suave; —, v. n. bambolearse; andar á saltos; —, s. empellón, m.; traqueo, m.   [tina, f.
jog-trot, *-trŏt*, s. trote de perro, m.; rutina, f.
John Bull, *jŏn băl'*, s. apodo de los ingleses.   [juntarse, asociarse.
join, *jŏĭn*, v. a. juntar, unir; —, v. n. unirse,
joiner, *-ăr*, s. carpintero de taller, m.

Joinery, *-ăré,* s. carpintería, f.

Joint, *jŏint,* s. coyuntura, articulación, f.; charnela, f.; cuarto, m.; nudo (de una planta), m.; —, a. unido; participante; **— heir,** s. coheredero, m.; —, v. a. juntar; descuartizar.

Jointly, *-lé,* ad. juntamente.

Joint-stock-company, *-stŏk kăm' păné,* s. (com.) sociedad por acciones, f.

Jointure, *jŏin' tûr,* s. viudedad, f.

Joist, *jŏist,* s. viga de bovedilla ó suelo, f.

Joke, *jŏk,* s. chanza, burla, f.; —, v. n. chancear.

Jollity, *jŏl' tié,* s. alegría, f.; regocijo, m.

Jolly, *jŏl' lé,* a. alegre, gallardo.

Jolly-boat, *-bōt,* s. botequín, m.

Jolt, *jŏlt,* v. a. traquear, sacudir; —, s. traqueo, m.

Jonathan, Brother, *— brŏth' ăr jŏn' ăthăn,* s. apodo de los americanos del norte.

Jostle, *jŏs' l,* v. rempujar.

Jot, *jŏt,* s. jota, f.; punto, m.

Journal, *jûr' năl,* s. jornal, diario, m.

Journalism, *-izm,* s. periodismo, m.

Journalist, *-ĭst,* s. periodista, m.

Journey, *jûr' né,* s. jornada, f.; viaje, m.; —, v. a. viajar.

Journeyman, *-măn,* s. jornalero, m.

Journey-work, *-wûrk,* s. jornal, m.

Joust, *jŭst* (*jŏst*), s. torneo, m.; justa, f.; —, v. n. justar. [con jovialidad.

Jovial, *jŏ' vĭăl,* a. jovial, alegre; **-ly,** ad.

Joviality, *jŏvĭăl' tié,* s. jovialidad, f.

Joy, *jŏi,* s. alegría, f.; júbilo, m.; **to give or wish —,** congratular.

Joyful, *-fŭl,* **joyous,** *-ŭs,* s. alegre, gozoso; **-ly,** ad. alegremente.

Joyless, *-lĕs,* a. triste, sin alegría.

Jubilant, *jŏ' bĭlănt,* a. lleno de júbilo.

Jubilation, *-lā' shăn,* s. júbilo, regocijo,

Jubilee, *jŏ' bĭlé,* s. jubileo, m. [m.

Judaism, *jŏ' dăĭzm,* s. judaísmo, m.

Judge, *jŭj,* s. juez, m.; —, v. n. juzgar; inferir. [opinión, decisión, f.

Judgment, *-mĕnt,* s. juicio, m.; sentir, m.;

Judicature, *jŏ' dĭkătûr,* s. judicatura, f.

Judicial, *jŏdĭsh' ăl,* a. **-ly,** ad. judicial- (mente). [-ly, ad. juiciosamente.

Judicious, *jŏdĭsh' ăs,* a. juicioso, prudente;

Jug, *jŭg,* s. jarro, m.

Juggle, *-gl,* s. juego de manos, m.; —, v. n. hacer juegos de manos.

Juggler, *-glăr,* s. juglar, m.

Juice, *jŏs,* s. zumo, jugo, m.; suco, m.

Juicy, *-é,* a. jugoso.

July, *jŏlī',* s. julio, m. (mes).

Jumble, *jăm' bl,* v. a. mezclar confusamente; —, s. mezcla, confusión, f.

Jump, *jămp,* v. n. saltar, brincar; convenir, concordar; —, s. salto, m.

Junction, *jŭngk' shăn,* s. junta, unión, f.

Juncture, *-tûr,* s. juntura, coyuntura, f.

June, *jŏn,* s. junio, m. (mes).

Jungle, *jăn' gl,* s. matorral, m.

Junior, *jŏ' nĭŭr,* a. más joven.

Juniper, *jŏ' nĭpŭr,* s. (bot.) enebro, m.

Junket, *jăng' kĕt,* s. dulce seco; convite familiar, m.; —, v. n. dar un convite en secreto. [asamblea, f.; reunión, f.

Junta, *jăn' tă,* **junto,** *jăn' tŏ,* s. junta,

Juridic(al), *jŏrĭd' ĭk(ăl),* a. jurídico, judicial; **-ly,** ad. jurídicamente.

Jurisdiction, *jŏrĭsdĭk' shăn,* s. jurisdicción, f. [dencia, f.

Jurisprudence, *-prŏ' dĕns,* s. jurispru-

Jurist, *jŏ' rĭst,* s. jurista, m. [rado, m.

Juror, *jŏ' rŭr,* **juryman,** *jŏ' rĭmăn,* s. ju-

Jury, *jŏ' ré,* s. junta de jurados, f.; jurado, m.

Just, *jăst,* a. justo, honrado, virtuoso; —, ad. justamente, exactamente; **— as,** como; **— now,** ahora mismo.

Justice, *jăs' tĭs,* s. justicia, f.; juez, m.; —, v. a. administrar justicia.

Justifiable, *jăstĭf' ăbl,* a. conforme á razón, según justicia.

Justifiably, *-é,* ad. con justicia y rectitud.

Justification, *jăstĭfĭkā' shăn,* s. justificación, f.; defensa, f.

Justify, *jăs' tĭfĭ,* v. a. justificar.

Justle, *jăs' l,* v. a. & n. rempujar; chocar.

Justly, *jăst' lé,* ad. justamente; exactamente. [tud, f.

Justness, *-nĕs,* s. justicia, equidad, exacti-

Jut, *jăt,* v. n. chocar en algo cuando se va corriendo; **to — out,** sobresalir.

Jute, *jŏt,* s. jute, m.

Juvenile, *jŏ' vĕnĭl,* a. juvenil.

Juxtaposition, *jăkstăpŏzĭsh' ăn,* s. yuxtaposición, f.

K

Kale, *kăl,* s. col, berza, f. [pio, m.

Kaleidoscope, *kălī' dŏskŏp,* s. kaleidosco-

Kangaroo, *kăng' gărŏ,* s. canguro, m.

Keel, *kĕl,* s. (mar.) quilla, f.

Keen, *kĕn,* a. afilado, agudo; penetrante, sútil, vivo; vehemente; satírico, picante; **-ly,** ad. agudamente; sútilmente; agriamente. [spicacia, f.; aspereza, f.

Keenness, *-nĕs,* s. agudeza, sutileza, per-

Keen-sighted, *-sītĕd,* a. perspicaz.

Keep, *kĕp,* v. a. tener, mantener, retener; preservar, guardar; proteger; detener; conservar; reservar; sostener; observar; solemnizar; —, v. n. perseverar; soler; mantenerse; quedar; vivir, residir; tener cuidado; —, s. torre, f.; guardia, f.; sustentación, f. [prison, carcelero, f.

Keeper, *-ăr,* s. guardián, m.; **— of a**

Keeping, *-ĭng,* s. custodia, f.; guarda, f.

Keepsake, *-sāk,* s. dádiva en memoria, f.

Keg, *kĕg,* s. barrica, f. [f.; regalo, m.

Ken, *kĕn,* s. vista, f. [rrera, f.

Kennel, *-nĕl,* s. perrera, f.; jauría, f.; zo-

Kerb-stone, *kŭrb' stŏn,* s. brocal de pozo, m.; guardacantón, m.

Kerchief, *kŭr' tshĭf,* s. pañuelo, m.

Kernel, *kŭr' nĕl,* s. almendra, pepita, f.; meollo, m.

Ketch, *kĕtsh,* s. quaiche, queche, m.

Kettle, *kĕt' tl,* s. caldera, f.

kettle-drum, -drăm. s. timbal, atabal, m.
key, kĕ, s. llave, f.; (mus.) clave, f.; tecla, f.
key-board, -bŏrd. s. teclado de órgano, m.
key-hole, -hŏl, s. agujero de la llave, m.
key-note, -nŏt, s. (mus.) tónica, f.
key-ring, -rĭng, s. colgajo de llaves, m.
key-stone, -stŏn, s. llave de un arco ó bóveda, f. [-, s. puntapié, m.; patada, f.
kick, kĭk, v. a. acocear; -, v. n. patear;
kickshaw, -shă, s. patarada, fruslería.
kid, kĭd, s. cabrito, m. [bagatela, f.
kidnap, -năp, v. a. robar niños ú hombres.
kidney, -nĕ, s. riñón, m.; (fig.) especie, f.
kilderkin, kĭl'dărkĭn, s. medio barril, m.
kill, kĭl, v. a. matar, asesinar.
kiln, kĭl, s. horno, m. [horno.
kiln-dry, -drĭ, v. a. secar ó quemar en
kilt, kĭlt, s. saya de los escoceses serranos, f.
kimbo, kĭm'bŏ, a. encorvado, torcido; to set one's arms a -, ponerse en asas.
kin, kĭn, s. parentesco, m.; afinidad, f.; next of -, pariente próximo, m.
kind, kĭnd, a. benévolo, benigno, afable, cariñoso; -, s. género, m.; especie, naturaleza, manera, f.; calidad, f.
kindle, kĭn'dl, v. a. & n. encender; arder.
kindliness, kĭnd'lĭnĕs, s. benevolencia, f.
kindly, -lĕ, a. blando, suave, tratable; -, ad. benignamente. [beneficio, m.
kindness, -nĕs, s. benevolencia, f.; favor,
kindred, kĭn'drĕd, s. parentesco, m.; parentela, casta, f.; -, a. emparentado.
king, kĭng, s. rey, m.
kingdom, -dŭm, s. reino, m. [m. (ave).
king-fisher, -fĭshăr, s. martín pescador, m.
kinglike, -lĭk, kingly, -lĕ, a. real; regio; -, ad. como de rey.
king's evil, -s'ĕvl, s. escrófula, f.
kinsfolk, kĭnz'fŏk, s. parientes, m. pl.
kinship, kĭn'shĭp, s. parentela, f.
kinsman, kĭnz'măn, s. pariente, m.
kinswoman, -wŭmăn, s. parienta, f.
kirtle, kăr'tl, s. sobretodo, m.
kiss, kĭs, s. beso, ósculo, m.; -, v. a. besar.
kissing, -ĭng, s. beso, m.; - of hand, besamano, m. [m.
kissing-crust, -ĭngkrŭst, s. beso del pan.
kit, kĭt, s. botellón, m.; violín pequeño, m.; vasija para salmón, f., colodra, f.
kitchen, kĭtsh'ĕn, s. cocina, f. [cocina, f.
kitchen-dresser, -drĕssăr, s. mesa de
kitchen-garden, -gărdn, s. huerta, f.
kitchen-maid, -măd, s. cocinera, f.
kitchen-range, -rănj, s. cocina inglesa, f.
kite, kĭt, s. milano, m.; cometa, birlocha, f.
kitten, kĭt'tn, s. gatillo, m.; -, v. n. parir (la gata). [f.
knack, năk, s. chuchería, f.; maña, destreza,
knacker, -ăr, s. cordelero, suguero, m.
knapsack, năp'săk, s. mochila, f.
knave, năv, s. bribón, pícaro, m.; (at cards) sota, f.
knavery, -ărĕ, s. picardía, bribonada, f.
knavish, nă'vĭsh, a. fraudulento, m., pícaro, m.; -ly, ad. pícaramente.
knead, nĕd, v. a. amasar.
kneading-trough, -ĭngtrŏf, s. amasadera, f.

knee, nĕ, s. rodilla, f.; (mar.) curva, f.; ángulo, m.
kneed, -d, a. lo que tiene rodillas.
knee-deep, -dĕp, a. metido ó subido hasta las rodillas.
kneel, nĕl, v. n. arrodillarse.
knee-pan, nĕ'păn, s. rótula, f.
knell, nĕl, s. clamoreo, m.
knickerbockers, nĭk'ărbŏk'ărz, s. pl. calzones de cazador, m. pl. [juguete, m.
knick-knacks, nĭk'năks, s. pl. bujería, f.;
knife, nĭf, s. cuchillo, m.
knight, nĭt, s. caballero, m.; -, v. a. crear á uno caballero. [dante, m.
knight-errant, -ĕrrănt, s. caballero andante.
knighthood, -hŭd, s. caballería, f. (dignidad de caballero). [llero.
knightly, -lĕ, a. propio ó digno de caballero.
knit, nĭt, v. a. & n. enlazar; atar, unir; trabajar á punto de aguja; to - the brows, fruncir las cejas.
knitter, -tăr, s. calcetero, mediero, m.
knitting-needle, -tĭngnĕdl, s. aguja de hacer media, f.
knob, nŏb, s. bulto, m.; nudo en la madera, m., botón de las flores, m.
knobby, -bĕ, a. lleno de nudos.
knock, nŏk, v. a. & n. chochar; golpear, tocar; pagar; to - down, derribar; -, s. golpe, m.; llamada, f.
knocker, -ăr, s. llamador, m.; aldaba, f.
knoll, nŏl, s. cima de una colina, f.
knot, nŏt, s. nudo, m.; lazo, m.; maraña, f.; dificultad, f., confederación, f.; -, v. a. enredar, juntar; -, v. n. hechar nudos las plantas.
knotty, -lĕ, a. nudoso; dificultoso.
knout, nŏŭt, s. knut, m.; bastonada rusa, f.
know, nŏ, v. a. & n. conocer, saber; tener noticia de.
knowing, -ĭng, a. instruído, inteligente, entendido; -ly, ad. hábilmente; á sabiendas; á propósito.
knowledge, nŏl'ĕj, s. conocimiento, f., ciencia, f., inteligencia, habilidad, f.
knuckle, nŭk'l, s. nudillo, m.; jarrete de ternero, m.

L.

la, lă, ¡he aquí!, ¡ved aquí!
label, lă'bĕl, s. esquela, f.; marbete, m.; rótulo, m., -, v. a. rotular ó señalar alguna cosa con un rótulo.
labial, lă'bĭăl, a. labial.
laboratory, lăb'ŏrătărĕ, s. laboratorio, m.
laborious, lăbŏ'rĭŭs, a. laborioso; difícil; -ly, ad. laboriosamente.
labour, lă'băr, s. trabajo, m.; labor, f.; fatiga, f.; to be in -, estar de parto; -, v. a. trabajar; afanarse; estar con dolores de parto. [dor, m.
labourer, -ăr, s. labrador, m.; trabajador.
labyrinth, lăb'rĭnth, s. laberinto, m.
lac, lăk, s. laca, goma laca, f.
lace, lăs, s. lazo, cordón, m.; encaje, m.; randa, f.; galón, m.; -, v. a. abrochar, encordonar; galonear.

lacerate, *lăs'ẽrăt*, v. a. lacerar, rasgar.
lachrymose, *lăk'rĭmōs*, a. lloroso.
lack, *lăk*, v. a. & n. carecer, necesitar; faltar algo; —, s. falta, f.; menester, m.
lackey, *lăk'ĕ*, s. lacayo, m.
laconic(al), *lăkŏn'ĭk(ăl)*, a. lacónico.
lacquer, *lăk'ẽr*, s. laca, f.
lad, *lăd*, s. mozo, muchacho, m.
ladder, *lăd'dẽr*, s. escala ó escalera portátil, f.
lade, *lăd*, v. a. cargar.
lading, *lā'dĭng*, s. carga, f.; cargamento, m.
ladle, *lā'dl*, s. cucharón, m.   [m.
ladleful, *-fŭl*, s. cucharada, f.
lady, *lā'dĕ*, s. señora, señorita, dama, f.
lady-bird, *-bẽrd*, s. vaquilla de Dios (insecto), f.   [de nuestra Señora, m.
Lady-day, *-dā*, s. día de la Anunciación
lady-killer, *-kĭllẽr*, s. favorito de las mujeres, m.
ladylike, *-lĭk*, a. afeminado; elegante.
lady-love, *-lŭv*, s. dama, querida, f.
ladyship, *-shĭp*, s. señoría, f.   [atrás.
lag, *lăg*, v. n. moverse lentamente; quedarse
laggard, *-gŭrd*, lagger, *-gẽr*, s. haragán, holgazán, m.
lagoon, *lăgŏn'*, s. laguna, f.
lair, *lār*, s. cubil, m.; pastura, f.
laity, *lā'ĭtĕ*, s. estado seglar, m.
lake, *lăk*, s. lago, m.; laguna, f.
lamb, *lăm*, s. cordero, m.; —, v. n. parir corderos.
lambent, *lăm'bĕnt*, a. centelleante.
lambkin, *-kĭn*, s. corderito, m.
lame, *lăm*, a. lisiado, estropeado; imperfecto; —ly, ad. con cojera; imperfectamente; —, v. a. lisiar, estropear.
lameness, *-nĕs*, s. cojera, f.; imperfección, f.; estado de una persona estropeada, m.
lament, *lămĕnt'*, v. a. (& n.) lamentar(se); —, s. lamento, m.   [deplorable.
lamentable, *lăm'ĕntăbl*, a. lamentable,
lamentation, *lămĕntā'shŭn*, s. lamentación
lamp, *lămp*, s. lámpara, f.   [ción, f.
lamp-black, *-blăk*, s. negro de humo, m.
lampoon, *lămpŏn'*, s. sátira, f.; libelo, m.; —, v. a. escribir sátiras.
lamp-post, *lămp'pōst*, s. candelabro, m.
lamprey, *lăm'prĕ*, s. lamprea, f. (pez).
lance, *lăns*, s. lanza, f.; —, v. a. dar un lancetazo; hacer una operación quirúrgica con lanceta.
lancer, *-ẽr*, s. (mil.) lancero, m.
lancet, *lăn'sĕt*, s. lanceta, f.
land, *lănd*, s. país, m.; región, f.; territorio, m.; tierra, f.; —, v. a. & n. desembarcar; saltar en tierra.
landau, *lăndō'*, s. landó, m. (coche).
landed, *lănd'ĕd*, a. hacendado.
land-forces, *-fōrsĕz*, s. pl. tropas de tierra, f. pl.
land-holder, *-hōldẽr*, s. hacendado, m.
landing, *-ĭng*, s. desembarco, m.
landing(-place), *-ĭng(plās)*, s. desembarcadero, m.   [nera, posadera, f.
landlady, *-lādĕ*, s. propietaria, f.; mesolandlord, *-lōrd*, s. propietario, m.; huésped, posadero, m.   [m.
land-lubber, *-lŭbbẽr*, s. marinero de río.

land-mark, *-mărk*, s. mojón, m.; marca, f.
landscape, *-skāp*, s. paisaje, m.
land-slip, *-slĭp*, s. hundimiento, desplomamiento de un terreno, m.   [m.
land-tax, *-tăks*, s. tributo sobre tierras,
landward, *-wărd*, ad. hacia la tierra.
lane, *lăn*, s. callejuela, f.   [guaje, m.
language, *lăng'gwĭj*, s. lengua, f.; lenguid, *lăng'gwĭd*, a. lánguido, débil; —ly, ad. lánguidamente, débilmente.
languish, *-gwĭsh*, v. n. entristecerse, afligirse.
languor, *-gwŭr*, s. languidez, f.   [girse.
lank(y), *lăngk(ĕ)*, a. alto y delgado.   [m.
lansquenet, *lăn'skĕnĕt*, s. soldado de á pie,
lantern, *lăn'tẽrn*, s. linterna, f.; farol, m.; dark —, linterna sorda, f.
lap, *lăp*, s. faltas, f. pl.; regazo, m.; —, v. a. arrollar, envolver; lamer.
lap-dog, *-dŏg*, s. perro de faldas, m.
lapidary, *lăp'ĭdārĕ*, s. lapidario, m.
lappet, *lăp'pĕt*, s. falda, f.
lapse, *lăps*, s. caída, f.; falta ligera, f.; traslación de derecho ó dominio, f.; lapso, m.; —, v. n. escurrir, manar; deslizarse.
lapwing, *lăp'wĭng*, s. avefría, f.
larboard, *lăr'bōrd*, s. (mar.) babor, m. (lado izquierdo del navío).
larceny, *lăr'sĕnĕ*, s. ratería, f.
larch, *lărtsh*, s. alerce, lárice, m. (árbol).
lard, *lărd*, s. lardo, tocino gordo, m.; —, v. a. mechar.
larder, *-ẽr*, s. despensa, f.
larding-pin, *-ĭngpĭn*, s. mechera, f.
large, *lărj*, a. amplio, vasto; large, liberal; at —, á lo largo; —ly, ad. largamente, copiosamente, liberalmente.
largeness, *-nĕs*, s. grandor, m.; anchura, amplitud, f.
largess, *lăr'jĕs*, s. liberalidad, f.
lark, *lărk*, s. alondra, f.
larva, *lăr'vă*, s. larva, oruga, f.
lascivious, *lăssĭv'ĭŭs*, a. lascivo; —ly, ad. lascivamente.
lash, *lăsh*, s. latigazo, m.; punta del látigo, f.; pihuela, f.; sarcasmo, m.; —, v. a. dar latigazos; atar; satirizar.
lass, *lăs*, s. doncella, moza, f.
lassitude, *lăs'ĭtŭd*, s. lasitud, fatiga, f.
last, *lăst*, a. último, postrero, pasado; at —, últimamente; al fin, —ly, ad. la última vez; al fin; finalmente; —, s. horma de zapatero, f.; (mar.) carga de un navío, f.; —, v. n. durar.
lasting, *-ĭng*, a. duradero, permanente; —ly, ad. perpetuamente; —, s. lastén, m. (tela).   [a. cerrar con aldaba.
latch, *lătsh*, s. aldaba de puerta, f.; —, v.
latch-key, *-kĕ*, s. llave maestra, f.
late, *lāt*, a. tardío; tardo, lento; difunto; (rail.) the train is ten minutes, — el tren ha sufrido retraso de diez minutos; —, ad. tarde; of —, de poco tiempo acá; —ly, ad. poco ha, recientemente.
lateness, *-nĕs*, s. tiempo avanzado, m.
latent, *lā'tĕnt*, a. escondido, oculto.
lateral, *lăt'ẽrăl*, a.; —ly, ad. lateral(mente).
lath, *lăth*, s. lata, f., listón, m.; —, v. a. poner latas en las techumbres.
lathe, *lăth*, s. torno, m.

lather, *láth'ár*, s. jabonaduras, f. pl.; —, v. a. & n. bañar con espuma de jabón;

latten, *lát'tn*, s. latón, m. [espumar.

latter, *lát'tár*, a. posterior, último; -ly, ad. últimamente, recientemente.

lattice, *lát'tis*, s. celosía, f.; —, v. a. enrejar.

laudable, *lâd'ábl*, a. laudable, loable.

laudably, —*é*, ad. laudablemente, loablemente.

laugh, *láf*, v. n. reir; —, s. risa, risada, f.

laughable, —*ábl*, a. risible. [risa.

laughingly, *-inglé*, ad. alegremente, con

laughing-stock, *-ingstók*, s. hazmerreir, m.

laughter, *-tár*, s. risa, risada, f.

launch, *lánsh*, v. a. (& n.) lanzar(se); —, s. (mar.) lancha, f.

laundress, *lán'drés*, s. lavandera, f.

laundry, *lán'dré*, s. lavadero, m.

laureate, *lâ'réát*, a. laureado.

laurel, *lôr'él*, s. laurel guindo ó regio, m.

laurelled, —*d*, a. laureado.

lava, *lâ'vá*, s. lava, f.

lavender, *láv'éndár*, s. (bot.) espliego, m., lavándula, f.

lavish, *láv'ish*, a. pródigo; -ly, ad. pródigamente; —, v. a. disipar.

law, *lâ*, s. ley, f.; derecho, m.; litigio judicial, m.; jurisprudencia, f.

lawful, —*fûl*, a. legal; legítimo; -ly, ad. legalmente.

law-giver, —*givár*, s. legislador, m.

lawless, —*lés*, a. ilegal; anárquico.

lawlessness, —*nés*, s. anarquía, f.

law-maker, —*mákár*, s. legislador, m.

lawn, *lân*, s. prado, m.; linón, m.

law-suit, *lâ'sût*, s. proceso, lite, m.

lawyer, *lâ'yár*, s. abogado, jurisperito, m.

lax, *láks*, a. laxo, flojo.

laxity, *-tié*, s. laxitud, flojedad, f.

lay, *lâ*, v. a. poner, colocar, extender; calmar, sosegar; imputar; apostar; exhibir; to — claim, reclamar; pretender; —, v. n. aovar, poner huevos las aves; tramar.

layer, —*ár*, s. lecho, m.; cama, f.; pimpollo, m.; gallina que pone, f.

layman, —*mán*, s. lego, seglar, m.; maniquí, f. [estúpido.

lazaretto, *lázáret'tó*, lazar-house, *lá'zárhôûs*, s. lazareto, f.

lazily, *lá'zilé*, ad. perezosamente; lentamente.

laziness, *-zinés*, s. pereza, f.

lazy, *-zé*, a. perezoso, tardo, pesado.

lea, *lé*, s. prado, m., pradera, f.

lead, *léd*, s. plomo, m.; —s, pl. techo emplomado, m.; —, *léd*, v. a. conducir, guiar; gobernar; emplomar; —, v. n. mandar en jefe; ser mano (en el juego de naipes); —, s. conducta; (at cards) mano, f.

leaden, *léd'n*, s. hecho de plomo; pesado.

leader, *léd'ár*, s. guía, conductor, m.; jefe, general, m.

leading, —*ing*, a. principal; capital; -article, s. artículo de fondo de una gaceta, m.; -hand, s. el que juega primero en las partidas de naipes; -horse, s. caballo de silla, m. [res, m. pl.; traílla, f.

leading-strings, —*stringz*, s. pl. andado-

leaf, *léf*, s. hoja, f.; hoja de un libro; hoja de puerta.

leafy, —*é*, a. frondoso, hojudo.

league, *lég*, s. liga, alianza, f.; legua, f.; —, v. n. confederarse.

leaguer, —*ár*, s. confederado, m.

leak, *lék*, s. (mar.) vía de agua, f.; —, v. n. (mar.) hacer agua.

leakage, —*áj*, s. derrame, m., merma, f.

leaky, —*é*, a. roto, agujereado.

lean, *lén*, v. a. & n. ladear, inclinar, apoyarse; —, a. magro. [f.

leanings, —*ingz*, s. ladeo, m.; inclinación,

leanness, —*nés*, s. magrura, f.

leap, *lép*, v. n. saltar, brincar; salir con ímpetu; palpitar; —, s. salto, m.

leap-year, —*yér*, s. año bisiesto ó intercalar, m. [aprender.

learn, *lûrn*, v. a. & n. instruir, enseñar;

learned, —*d*, a. docto; the —, s. pl. literatos, m. pl.; -ly, ad. doctamente.

learner, —*ár*, s. tirón, m.; escolar, m.; aprendiz, m. [erudición, f.

learning, —*ing*, s. literatura, ciencia,

lease, *lés*, s. arriendo, m.; —, v. a. arrendar.

leasehold, —*hôld*, s. arriendo, m.

leash, *lésh*, s. pihuela, correa, f.; —, v. a. atar con correa.

least, *lést*, a. mínimo; -ly, ad. lo menos; at —, á lo menos; not in the —, ni en lo más mínimo.

leather, *léth'ár*, s. cuero, pellejo, m.

leathern, —*n*, a. (hecho) de cuero.

leathery, —*é*, a. correoso.

leave, *lév*, s. licencia, f.; permiso, m.; despedida, f.; to take —, despedirse; —, v. a. & n. dejar, abandonar; ceder; cesar.

leaven, *lév'vn*, s. levadura, f.; fermento, m.; —, v. a. fermentar. [relieves, m. pl.

leavings, —*vingz*, s. pl. sobras, f. pl.;

lection, *lék'shún*, s. lección, lectura, f.

lecture, *lek'tár (lék'tshúr)*, s. lectura, leyenda, f.; corrección, f.; reprensión, f.; —, v. a. enseñar; censurar.

lecturer, —*ár*, s. lector, instructor, m.

ledge, *léj*, s. capa, tonga, f.; borde, m.

ledger, *léj'ár*, s. (com.) libro mayor, m.

led-horse, *léd'hôrs*, s. caballo de mano, m. [ventado.

lee, *lé*, s. (mar.) sotavento, m.; —, a. sota-

leech, *létsh*, s. sanguijuela, f.; médico, m.

leek, *lék*, s. (bot.) puerro, m.

leer, *lér*, s. ojeada, f.; —, v. n. ojear al través. [poso, m.

lees, *léz*, s. pl. heces, f. pl.; sedimento,

lee-side, *lé'síd*, s. (mar.) banda de sotavento, f.

leeward, —*wárd*, a. (mar.) sotavento.

left, *léft*, a. siniestro, izquierdo; on the —, á la izquierda.

left-handed, —*hándéd*, a. zurdo; morga-

leg, *lég*, s. pierna, f.; pie. m. [nático.

legacy, *lég'ásé*, s. legado, m.; manda, f.

legal, *lé'gál*, a. legal, legítimo; -ly, ad. legalmente. [dad, f.

legality, *légál'té*, s. legalidad, legitimi-

legalize, *lé'gáliz*, v. a. legalizar, autorizar.

legate, *lég'át*, s. legado, diputado, m.

legatee, *lĕgắtī'*, s. legatario, f.
legation, *lĕgã'shŭn*, s. legación, embajada, f.
legend, *lĕj'ĕnd*, s. leyenda, legenda, f.
legendary, *-ărĭ*, a. fabuloso, quijotesco.
legerdemain, *lĕj'ărdĕmān*, s. juego de manos, m. [italiano, m.
leghorn, *lĕg'hŏrn*, s. sombrero de paja
legible, *lĕj'ĭbl*, a. legible, que puede leerse.
legibly, *-ĕ*, ad. legiblemente.
legion, *lĕ'jŭn*, s. legión, f.
legislate, *lĕj'ĭslāt*, v. a. legislar.
legislation, *lĕjĭslā'shŭn*, s. legislación, f.
legislative, *-ĭtĭv*, a. legislativo.
legislator, *-tăr*, s. legislador, m.
legislature, *lĕj'ĭslātŭr*, s. legislatura, f.
legitimacy, *lĭjĭt'ĭmăsĭ*, s. legitimidad, f.
legitimate, *-ĭmāt*, a. legítimo; -ly, ad. legítimamente; -, v. a. legitimar.
leisure, *lĕ'zhŭr*, s. desocupación, f.; ocio, m.; comodidad, f.; at -, leisurely, ad. cómodamente, con sosiego.
lemon, *lĕm'ŏn*, s. limón, m.
lemonade, *-ād*, s. limonada, f.
lemon-tree, *-trē*, s. limonero, m.
lend, *lĕnd*, v. a. prestar.
length, *lĕngth*, s. longitud, f.; duración, f.; distancia, f.; at -, finalmente.
lengthen, *-n*, v. a. alargar; -, v. n. alargarse, dilatarse.
lengthy, *-ĕ*, a. largo; fastidioso.
leniency, *lē'nĭensĕ*, s. benignidad, f. [(m).
lenient, *lĕ'nĭent*, a. & s. leniente; lenitivo.
lenitive, *lĕn'ĭtĭv*, a. & s. lenitivo, (m.).
lenity, *lĕn'ĭtĕ*, s. lenidad, benignidad, f.
lens, *lĕns*, s. lente, m. & f. (vidrio convexo).
lent, *lĕnt*, s. cuaresma, f.
lentil, *lĕn'tĭl*, s. lenteja, f.
leonine, *lĕ'ŏnīn*, a. leonino.
leopard, *lĕp'ărd*, s. leopardo, m.
leper, *lĕp'ăr*, s. leproso, m.
leprosy, *lĕp'rŏsĕ*, s. lepra, f.
leprous, *lĕp'rŭs*, a. leproso.
less, *lĕs*, a. menor; -, ad. menos.
lessee, *lĕssē'*, s. arrendatario, m.
lessen, *lĕs'sn*, v. a. minorar, disminuir; -, v. n. disminuirse.
lesser, *-săr*, a. más pequeño [sión, f.
lesson, *lĕs'sn*, s. lección, f.; fraterna, reprensión.
lessor, *lĕs'ăr*, s. arrendador, m.
lest, *lĕst*, c. para que no, de miedo que.
let, *lĕt*, v. a. dejar, permitir; arrendar; impedir.
lethal, *lĕ'thăl*, a. letal.
lethargic(al), *lĕthăr'jĭk(ăl)*, a. letárgico.
lethargy, *lĕth'ărjĕ*, s. letargo, m.
letter, *lĕt'tăr*, s. letra, f.; carta, f.
letter-box, *-bŏks*, s. buzón para las cartas, m.
letter-case, *-kās*, s. cartera, f.
lettered, *-d*, a. letrado, docto.
letter-press, *-prĕs*, s. impresión, obra impresa, f.
lettuce, *lĕt'tĭs*, s. lechuga, f.
levant, *lĕvănt'*, s. levante, oriente, m.
levee, *lĕv'ē*, s. tiempo de levantarse por la mañana, m.: corte, f.; besamanos, m.
level, *lĕv'ĕl*, a. llano, igual; nivelado; allanado; -, s. llanura, f.; plano, m.; nivel, m.; -, v. a. allanar; nivelar.
lever, *lĕ'văr*, s. palanca, f.
leverage, *lĕv'ărăj*, s. momento estático, m.

leveret, *lĕv'ĕrĕt*, s. lebratillo, m.
levite, *lĕ'vīt*, s. levita, m.
levity, *lĕv'ĭtĕ*, s. levedad, ligereza, f.; inconstancia, veledad, f. [hacer leva.
levy, *lĕv'ĕ*, s. leva (de tropas), f.; -, v. a.
lewd, *lūd*, a. lascivo, disoluto.
lewdness, *-nĕs*, s. lascivia, disolución, f.
lexicographer, *lĕksĭkŏg'răfăr*, s. lexicógrafo, m.
lexicon, *lĕks'ĭkŏn*, s. diccionario, m.
liability, *lĭăbĭl'ĭtĕ*, s. responsabilidad, f.
liable, *lī'ăbl*, a. sujeto, expuesto á; responsable.
liar, *lī'ăr*, s. embustero, m.
libation, *lĭbā'shŭn*, s. libación, f.
libel, *lī'bĕl*, s. libelo, m.; -, v. a. difamar.
libeller, *-ăr*, s. libelista, f.
libellous, *-lŭs*, a. difamatorio.
liberal, *lĭb'ărăl*, a. liberal, generoso; -ly, ad. liberalmente. [rosidad, f.
liberality, *lĭbărăl'ĭtĕ*, s. liberalidad, generosidad, f.
liberate, *lĭb'ărāt*, v. a. libertar.
liberation, *lĭbără'shŭn*, s. liberación, f.
libertine, *lĭb'ărtĭn*, s. libertino, m.; -, a. disoluto. [m.
liberty, *lĭb'ărtĕ*, s. libertad, f.; privilegio,
Libra, *lī'bră*, s. Libra, f. (signo del zodíaco).
librarian, *lībrā'rĭăn*, s. bibliotecario, m.
library, *lī'brărĕ*, s. librería, f.; biblioteca, f.
licence, *lī'sĕns*, s. licencia, f.; permiso, m.
licentious, *lĭsĕn'shŭs*, a. licencioso; -ly, ad. licenciosamente.
lichen, *lī'kĕn*, *(lĭtsh'ĕn)*, s. (bot.) liquen, m.
lick, *lĭk*, v. a. lamer, chupar; (vulg.) golpear.
licking, *-ĭng*, s. paliza, f. [pear.
lid, *lĭd*, s. tapa, f.; párpado, m.
lie, *lī*, s. mentira, f.; -, v. n. ir. mentir; echarse; reposar, acostarse; yacer.
lief, *lēf*, ad. de buena gana.
liege, *lēj*, a. ligio; súbdito. [m.
lien, *lī'ĕn*, *(lĕn)*, s. derecho de retención.
lieu, *lū*, s. lugar, m.; in-of, en vez de.
lieutenancy, *lĕftĕn'ănsĕ*, s. lugartenencia, f.
lieutenant, *-ănt*, s. lugarteniente, m. [f.
life, *līf*, s. vida, f.; conducta, f.; vivacidad, f.; mundo, m.; high-, el gran mundo; for-, por toda la vida; to the -, al natural.
life-belt, *-bĕlt*, s. ceñidor para nadar, m.
life-guard, *-gărd*, s. guardia de corps, f.
lifeless, *-lĕs*, a. muerto, inanimado; sin vivacidad. [de la vida, m.
life-office, *-ŏffĭs*, s. oficio de aseguración
life-preserver, *-prĕzărvăr*, s. macana, f.
life-size, *-sīz*, s. grandeza natural, f.
life-time, *-tīm*, s. duración de la vida, f.
lift, *lĭft*, v. a. alzar, elevar, levantar; hurtar, robar; -, s. esfuerzo para levantar alguna cosa pesada, m.; alzamiento, m.; alza, f.; ayuda, f.; ascensor (hidráulico), m.; at one -, de un golpe; to give one a -, ayudar á uno.
ligament, *lĭg'ăment*, ligature, *lĭg'ătŭr*, s. ligamento, m.; ligadura, f.
light, *līt*, s. luz, f.; claridad, f.; conocimiento, m.; día, m.; -, a. ligero, leve, fácil; frívolo; superficial; ágil; inconstante; claro; blondo; -, v. a. encender; alumbrar; -, v. n. hallar, encontrar; desmontarse; desembarcar.

lighten, –n, v. n. relampaguear ; –, v. a. iluminar , aligerar.

lighter. –ûr, s. (mar.) alijador, m. [m.

lighterman, –ûrmûn, s.(mar.) lanchonero,

light-hearted, –hûrtĕd, a. ligero, inconsiderado.   [m.

light-house, –hôŭs, s. (mar.) faro, fanal,

lighting, –ĭng, s. iluminación, f.

lightly, –lĕ, ad. ligeramente; fácilmente, alegremente.   [velocidad, f.

lightness, –nĕs, s. ligereza, f.; agilidad,

lightning, –nĭng, s. relámpago, m.

lightning-rod, –nĭngrŏd, s. pararrayos, m.

lights, –z, s. pl. bofes, m. pl.   [alegre.

lightsome, –sŭm, a. luminoso, claro;

ligneous, lĭg'nĕŭs, a. leñoso.

like, lĭk, a. semejante; igual; verosímil; –, s. semejante, m.; semejanza, f.; –, ad. como, del mismo modo que; –, v. a. & n. querer, amar; gustar, agradar alguna cosa; as you – it, como quisiere.

likelihood, –lĭhŭd, s. apariencia, f.; probabilidad, f.   [probablemente.

likely, –lĕ, a. probable, verosímil; –, ad.

liken, –n, v. a. asemejar; comparar.

likeness, –nĕs, s. semejanza, f.; igualdad, f.; retrato fiel, m.

likewise, –wĭs, ad. también; igualmente.

liking, lĭ'kĭng, s. robustez, f.; gusto, agrado,

lilac, lĭ'lăk, s. lila, f.; lilas, m.   [m.

lily, lĭl'ĕ, s. lirio, m.; – of the valley, lirio de los valles.

limb, lĭm, s. miembro, m.   [avantrén, m.

limber, –bŭr, a. manejable, flexible; –, s.

lime, lĭm, s. cal, f.; liga, f.; lima, f. (especie de limón); (–tree), tilo, m.; –, v. a. untar con liga.

lime-stone, –stŏn, s. piedra de cal, f. [f.

lime-pit, –pĭt, s. cantera de piedra caliza,

limit, lĭm'ĭt, s. límite, término, m.; –, v. a. restringir.   [restricción, f.

limitation, lĭmĭtā'shŭn, s. limitación, f.;

limitless, lĭm'ĭtlĕs, a. inmenso.

limn, lĭm, v. a. pintar; dibujar; retratar.

limner, –nŭr, s. pintor, m.; retratista, m.

limp, lĭmp, v. n. cojear; –, s. cojera, f.; –, a. débil, flaco.   [parente.

limpid, lĭm'pĭd, a. limpio, claro, trans-

linch-pin, lĭnsh'pĭn, s. pezonera, f.

linden-(tree), lĭn'dn(trē), s. tilo, m.

line, lĭn, s. línea, f.; (mil.) línea de batalla, f.; raya, f.; esquicio, contorno, m.; ecuador, m.; ferrocarril, m.; vía, f.; renglón, m.; verso, m.; linaje, m.; cordón (muy delgado), m.; –, v. a. forrar; revestir.

lineage, lĭn'ĕăj, s. linaje, m.; descendencia, f.   [recta.

lineal, lĭn'ĕăl, a. lineal; –ly, ad. en línea

lineament, lĭn'ĕămĕnt, s. lineamentos, m.

linear, lĭn'ĕăr, a. lineal.   [m. pl.

line-keeper, lĭn'kēpŭr, s. (rail.) guardavía, guardabarreras, m.

line-keeper's lodge, –s lŏj, s. (rail.) casilla de guarda, f.   [de lienzo.

linen, lĭn'ĕn, s. lienzo, lino, m.; –, a. hecho

linen-draper, –drăpŭr, s. lencero, m.

linger, lĭng'gŭr, v. n. consumirse, penar; tardar.

lingering, –ĭng, s. tardanza, dilación, f.; –ly, ad. lentamente; lánguidamente.

linguist, lĭng'gwĭst, s. lingüista, m.

liniment, lĭn'ĭmĕnt, s. linimento, m.

lining, lĭ'nĭng, s. forro, m.

link, lĭngk, s. anillo de cadena, m.; cadena, f., (mar.) hacha de viento, f.; –, v. a. juntar; encadenar.

link-boy, –bŏĕ, s. paje de hacha, m.

linnet, lĭn'nĕt, s. pardillo, m.

linseed, lĭn'sēd, s. linaza, f.

linsey-woolsey, lĭn'zĭwŭl'zĕ, s. tejido de lana grosero y con mezcla de hilo, m.

lint, lĭnt, s. lino, m.; hilas, f. pl.

lintel, lĭn'tĕl, s. dintel, tranquero, m.

lion, lĭ'ŏn, s. león, m.

lioness, –nĕs, s. leona, f.   [á la moda.

lionize, lĭ'ŏnĭz, v. a. poner á uno el hombre

lip, lĭp, s. labio, borde, m.

liquefy, lĭk'wĕfĭ, v. a. licuar, liquidar; –, v. n. liquidarse.

liqueur, lĭkŭr', s. aguardiente, m.

liquid, lĭk'wĭd, a. líquido; –, s. licor, m.

liquidate, lĭk'wĭdāt, v. a. liquidar.   [f.

liquidation, lĭkwĭdā'shŭn, s. liquidación,

liquor, lĭk'ŭr, s. licor, m.

liquorice, –ĭs, s. orozuz, m., regaliza, f.

lisp, lĭsp, v. n. tartamudear, cecear; –, s. tartamudeo, ceceo, m.

list, lĭst, s. lista, f.; gana, f.; voluntad, f.; cenefa, f.; –, v. n. querer, desear; –, v. a. registrar; (mil.) alistar.

listen, lĭs'n, v. n. escuchar, atender.

listless, lĭst'lĕs, a. indiferente, descuidado; –ly, ad. negligentemente.

listlessness, –nĕs, s. descuido, m.

litany, lĭt'ănĭ, s. letanía, f.

literal, lĭt'ĕrăl, a. –ly, ad. literal(mente).

literary, lĭt'ĕrărĕ, a. literario.

literature, lĭt'ĕrātŭr, s. literatura, f.

lithe, lĭth, a. flexible, manejable.

lithograph, lĭth'ŏgrăf, s. litografía, f.; –, v. a. litografiar.

lithographer, lĭthŏg'răfŭr, s. litógrafo, m.

lithography, –răfĕ, s. litografía, f.

litigant, lĭt'ĭgănt, s. litigante, m.

litigate, –ĭgāt, v. a. litigar, pleitear.

litigation, lĭtĭgā'shŭn, s. litigio, m.

litigious, lĭtĭj'ŭs, a. litigioso.

litter, lĭt'tŭr, s. litera, cama portátil, f.; lechigada, ventregada, f.; –, v. a. parir los animales; desordenar.

little, lĭt'tl, a. pequeño, poco; by – and –, poco á poco; –, s. poco, m.; parte pe-

littleness, –nĕs, s. pequeñez, f. [queña, f.

liturgy, lĭt'ŭrjĭ, s. liturgia, f.

live, lĭv, v. n. vivir; mantenerse; habitar; –, lĭv, a. vivo.   [cia, f.

livelihood, lĭv'lĭhŭd, s. vida, f.; subsisten-

liveliness, –lĭnĕs, s. vivacidad, f.

lively, –lĕ, a. vivo, brioso; gallardo.

liver, lĭv'ŭr, s. viviente, m.; hígado, m.

livery, –ĕ, s. librea, f.; the Livery, cuerpo de ciudadanos de Londres, m.

livid, lĭv'ĭd, a. lívido; cárdeno.

living, lĭv'ĭng, s. modo de vivir, m.; subsistencia, f.; –, a. vivo.

lizard, lĭz'ărd, s. lagarto, m.

lo, _lô,_ ¡he aquí!, ¡ved aquí!

load, _lôd,_ v. a. cargar; —, s. carga, f. [f.

loadstar, lodestar, _-stär,_ s. estrella polar.

loadstone, _-stôn,_ s. imán, m. [azúcar, m.

loaf, _lôf,_ s. pan, m.; (of sugar) pilón de

loafer, _-âr,_ s. holgazán, gandul, m.

loam, _lôm,_ s. marga, f.

loan, _lôn,_ s. préstamo, empréstito, m.

loathe, _lôth,_ v. a. aborrecer; tener hastío; —, v. n. fastidiar.

loathing, _-îng,_ s. disgusto, m., aversión, f.

loathly, _-lê,_ loathsome, _lôth'säm,_ a. detestable, fastidioso.

lobby, _lôb'bê,_ s. vestíbulo, m.

lobe, _lôb,_ s. lóbulo, m.

lobster, _lôb'stär,_ s. langosta, f.

local, _lô'käl,_ a. local.

locality, _lôkäl'itê,_ s. localidad, f.

localize, _lô'kälîz,_ v. a. localizar.

loch, _lôk,_ s. lago, m. (en Escocia).

lock, _lôk,_ s. cerradura, cerraja, f.; llave (de arma de fuego), f.; cerca, f.; vedija de lana, f.; —, v. a. cerrar; estar una cosa cerrada; to — one out, cerrar la puerta á uno para que no entre.

locker, _lôk'är,_ s. armario, m. [dallón, m.

locket, _-êt,_ s. broche, corchete, m.; me-

lock-jaw, _-jä,_ s. trismo, m.

lock-out, _-öut,_ s. cesación del trabajo, f.

locksmith, _-smith,_ s. cerrajero, m.

locomotion, _lôkômô'shän,_ s. locomoción, f.

locomotive, _lôkômô'tiv,_ a. movible; —, s. locomotora, f.

locust, _lô'käst,_ s. langosta, f.

lodge, _lôj,_ s. casa de guarda en el bosque, f.; casita pequeña, f.; —, v. a. alojar; fijar en la memoria; —, v. n. residir, habitar.

lodger, _-är,_ s. huésped, inquilino, m.

lodging, _lôj'îng,_ s. yáciga, f.; —s, pl. casa, habitación, f.

lodging-house, _-hôus,_ s. posada, f.

loft, _lôft,_ s. piso, m.; desván, m.

loftiness, _-înês,_ s. altura, f.; sublimidad, f.; soberbia, f.

lofty, _-ê,_ a. alto; sublime; altivo.

log, _lôg,_ s. leño, trozo de árbol, m.; (mar.) barquilla, f. [gación, m.

log-book, _-bûk,_ s. (mar.) diario de navi-

loggerhead, _-gärhêd,_ s. zote, m.

logic, _lôj'îk,_ s. lógica, f.

logical, _-äl,_ a. lógico.

logician, _lôjîsh'än,_ s. lógico, m.

log-line, _lôg'lîn,_ s. (mar.) corredera, f.

logwood, _-wûd,_ s. palo de Campeche, m.

loin, _lôîn,_ lomo, m.; —s, pl. lomos, m. pl.

loiter, _lôî'tär,_ v. n. haraganear.

loiterer, _-är,_ s. haragán, holgazán, m.

loll, _lôl,_ v. a. tender; —, v. n. apoyarse, recostarse. [solitario; solo.

lone(ly), _lôn'(lê),_ lonesome, _lôn'säm,_ a.

loneliness, _-lînês,_ s. soledad, f.]

long, _lông,_ a. largo; —, ad. á una gran distancia; mucho; —, v. n. desear con vehemencia, anhelar.

longevity, _lônjêv'îtê,_ s. longevidad, duración larga de la vida. [helo, m.

longing, _lông'îng,_ s. deseo vehemente, an-

longitude, _lôn'jîtûd,_ s. longitud, f. [nal.

longitudinal, _lônjîtû'dînäl,_ a. longitudi-

loo, _lô,_ s. especie de juego de naipes.

look, _lûk,_ v. a. & n. mirar, considerar, pensar, contemplar, esperar; parecer; tener traza de; buscar; —, s. aspecto, m.; mirada, f.

looking-glass, _-înggläs,_ s. espejo, m.

look-out, _-öut,_ s. (mil.) centinela, f.; (mar.) vigía, f. [mar.

loom, _lôm,_ s. telar, m.; —, v. n. (mar.) aso-

loop, _lôp,_ s. ojal, m.; presilla, f. [f.

loop-hole, _-hôl,_ s. tronera, f.; escapatoria.

loose, _lôs,_ a. suelto, desatado; flojo; suelto de vientre; vago, relajado; disoluto; desenredado; descuidado; —ly, ad. sueltamente; —, loosen, _-n,_ v. a. aflojar, laxar, desliar. [f.; flujo de vientre, m.

looseness, _-nês,_ s. flojedad, f.; relajación,

loot, _lôt,_ v. a. saquear.

loo-table, _lô'tâbl,_ s. velador, m.

lop, _lôp,_ v. a. desmochar.

lop-eared, _-êrd,_ a. con las orejas caídas.

lop-sided, _-sîdêd,_ a. (vulg.) ladeado, sesgado. [dor.

loquacious, _lôkwâ'shäs,_ a. locuaz, charla-

loquacity, _lôkwäs'itê,_ s. locuacidad, charla, garrulidad, f.

Lord, _lôrd,_ s. señor, m.; Dios, m.; amo, dueño, m.; Lord, m.; Mayor, Corregidor de Londres, m.; —, v. n. señorear, dominar. [f.; orgullo, m.

lordliness, _-lînês,_ s. señorío, m.; altivez,

lordling, _-lîng,_ s. lord pequeño, m.

lordly, _-lê,_ a. señoril; orgulloso, imperioso; —, ad. imperiosamente, altivamente.

Lordship, _-shîp,_ s. Excelencia, Señoría, f.

lore, _lôr,_ s. lección, doctrina, instrucción, f.

lose, _lôz,_ v. a. perder; disipar, malgastar; —, v. n. perderse, decaer.

loss, _lôs,_ s. pérdida, f.; daño, m.; to be at a —, desatinar. [porción, f.

lot, _lôt,_ s. suerte, f.; lote, m.; cuota, f.;

loth, _lôth,_ a. repugnante, disgustado.

lotion, _lô'shän,_ s. loción, ablución, f.

lottery, _lôt'tärê,_ s. lotería, rifa, f.

loud, _lôud,_ a. ruidoso, alto; clamoroso; —ly, ad. altamente. [m.

loudness, _-nês,_ s. tono elevado, m.; ruido,

lounge, _lôunj,_ v. n. haraganear.

louse, _lôus_ (pl. lice), s. piojo, m.

lousy, _lôu'zê,_ a. piojoso; miserable, vil.

lout, _lôut,_ s. patán, rústico, zafio, m.

loutish, _-ish,_ a. rústico, tosco.

lovable, _lûv'äbl,_ a. amable.

love, _lûv,_ s. amor, cariño, m.; galanteo, m.; to fall in —, enamorarse; —, v. a. amar; gustar. [amorosa, f.

love-letter, _-lêttär,_ s. esquela, carta

loveliness, _-lînês,_ s. amabilidad, f., agrado, m.; belleza, f.

lovely, _-lê,_ a. amable, hermoso.

lover, _-är,_ s. amante, galán, cortejo, m.

love-sick, _-sîk,_ a. enamorado; herido de [afectuosamente.

loving, _-îng,_ p. & a. aficionado; —ly, ad.

loving-kindness, _-kindnês,_ s. gracia, f., afecto, m.

low, _lô,_ a. bajo, pequeño; hondo; abatido; vil; —, ad. á precio bajo; vilmente.

8*

low, lō, v. n. mugir.

lower, lō'ŭr, a. más bajo; —, v. a. abajar, humillar; disminuir; —, v.n. disminuirse; encapotarse.

lowering, lōā'ŭring, a. sombrío.

lowermost, lō'ŭrmōst, **lowest**, lō'ĕst, a. más bajo, ínfimo.

lowing, lō'ing, s. mugido, m.

lowland, —lānd, s. tierra baja, f. [f.

lowliness, —linĕs, s. bajeza, f.; humildad,

lowly, —li, a. humilde; vil; —, ad. humildemente; vilmente.

lowness, —nĕs, s. bajeza, f.

lowry, —rĕ, s. (rail.) lorri, truck, m.

low-water, —wātŭr, s. baja mar, f.

loyal, lŏi'ăl, a. leal, fiel; —ly, ad. lealmente.

loyalty, —tĕ, s. lealdad, f.; fidelidad, f.

lozenge, lŏz'ĕnj, s. rombo, m.; pastilla de boca, f.

lubber, lŭb'bŭr, s. bobo, m.; bigardo, m.

lubberly, —li, a. perezoso, bigardo.

lubricate, lō'brĭkāt, v. a. untar con materias crasas.

lucid, lō'sĭd, a. luciente, luminoso.

lucidity, lōsĭd'ĭtĕ, s. esplendor, resplandor, m.   [pajuela química, f.

Lucifer, lō'sĭfŭr, s.Lucero, m.; —(-match),

luck, lŭk, s. acaso, m.; fortuna, f.

luckily, —lĕ, ad. por fortuna, afortunadamente.

luckless, —lĕs, a. infeliz, desventurado.

lucky, —ĕ, a. afortunado, feliz, venturoso.

lucrative, lō'krātĭv, a. lucrativo.

lucre, lō'kŭr. s. lucro, m.; ganancia, f.

lucubration, lōkŭbrā'shŭn, s. lucubración, f.   [burlescamente.

ludicrous, lō'dĭkrŭs, a. burlesco; —ly, ad.

luff, lŭf, v. a. (mar.) ceñir el viento.

lug, lŭg, v. n. tirar; (mar.) halar.

luggage, lŭg'gdj, s. baggage, m.; (rail.) bulto, equipaje, m.; **small—**, (rail.) bultos á la mano, m. pl

luggage-office, —ŏffĭs, s. (rail.) factoría, f.; equipajes, m. pl.   [m.

luggage-ticket, —tĭkkĕt, s. (rail.) talón,

luggage-train, —trān, s. (rail.) tren de mercancías, m.

luggage-van, lŭg'văn, **luggage-waggon**, —wăgŏn, s. (rail.) vagón completo, vagón de mercancías, m.

lugger, lŭg'gŭr, s. lugre, m.

lugubrious, lōgū'brĭŭs, a. lúgubre, triste.

lukewarm, lōk'wărm, a. tibio; —ly, ad. tibiamente.   [tar.

lull, lŭl, v. a. arrullar; adormecer; aquietar.

lullaby, —lăbĭ, s. arrullo, m.

lumbago, lŭmbā'gō, s. lumbago, m.

lumber-room, lŭm'bŭrrōm, s. trastera, f.

luminary, lō'mĭnărĕ, s. luminar, m.; lumbrera, f.   [ciente.

luminous, —nŭs, a. luminoso, resplandeciente.

lump, lŭmp, s. masa informe, f.; **by the —**, por grueso ó por junto; —, v. a. tomar alguna cosa por junto ó por mayor.

lunacy, lō'năsĕ, s. locura, f., frenesí, m.

lunar, —ŭr, a. lunar, **— caustic**, s. nitrato de plata, m.   [tástico.

lunatic, —nătĭk, a. lunático, frenético; fán-

lunch, lănsh, **luncheon**, lănsh'ŭn, s. merienda, f.

lunette, lŭnĕt', s. (mil.)media luna, f.

lung, lăng, **lungs**, lăngz, pl. pulmones, m. pl.

lurch, lŭrtsh, s. abandono, m. [m. pl.

lure, lōr, s. señuelo, m., añagaza, f.; cebo, m.; —, v. a. atraer, inducir.

lurk, lŭrk, v. n. espiar, ponerse en acecho.

lurking-place, —ĭngplăs, s. escondrijo, m.; guarida, f.

luscious, lŭsh'ăs, a. dulzazo; delicioso.

lust, lŭst, s. lujuria, sensualidad, f.; concupiscencia, f. —, v. n. lujuriar.

lustful, —fŭl, a. lujurioso, voluptuoso; —ly, ad. lujuriosamente.

lustily, lŭs'tĭlĕ, ad. vigorosamente.

lustiness, —tĭnĕs, s. vigor, m.; robustez, f.

lustre, —tŭr, s. lustre, m.; brillantez, f.

lustring, —trĭng, s. lustrina, f. (tela).

lusty, —tĕ, a. fuerte, vigoroso.

lute, lōt, s. laúd, m.; luten, m.

Lutheran, lō'thĕrăn, s. luterano, m.

luxuriance, lŭgzŭ'rĭăns, s. exuberancia, superabundancia, f.   [abundante.

luxuriant, —rĭănt, a. exuberante, super-

luxuriate, —rĭāt, v. n. crecer con exuberancia.   [te, —ly, ad. voluptuosamente.

luxurious, —rĭŭs, a. lujurioso; exuberan-

luxury, lŭks'ŭrĕ, s. lujuria, voluptuosidad, f.; exuberancia, f.

lyceum, līsē'ŭm, s. liceo, m.

lye(-washing), lī('wŏshĭng), s. lejía, f.

lying, lī'ing, s. acto de mentir, m.; mentira, f.

lying-in, —ĭn, s. parto, m.   [tira, f.

lymph, lĭmf, s. linfa, f.

lymphatic, lĭmfăt'ĭk, a. linfático.

lynch, lĭntsh, v. a. ajusticiar al reo en el acto el populacho (am.).

lynx, lĭngks, s. lince, m.

lyre, lĭr, s. lira, f.

lyric(al), lĭr'ĭk(ăl), a. lírico.

M.

macadamize, măkăd'ămĭz, v. a. empedrar un camino al estilo de MacAdam.

macaroni, măkărō'nĕ, s. macarrones, m.pl.

macaroon, măkărōn', s. almendrado, m.

mace, măs, s. maza, f.; macis, f.

macerate, măs'ărāt, v.a. macerar; mortificar el cuerpo.

machinate, măk'ĭnāt, v. n. maquinar.

machination, măkĭnā'shŭn, s. maquinación, trama, f.

machine, măshēn', s. máquina, f.

machinery, —ărē, s. maquinaria, mecánica, f.

machinist, —ĭst, s. maquinista, m.

mackerel, măk'ărĕl, s. escombro, m. (pez).

mackintosh, măk'ĭntŏsh, s. sobretodo impermeable, m.   [sato.

mad, măd, a. loco, furioso, rabioso, insen-

madam, măd'ăm, s. madama, señora, f.

mad-cap, măd'kăp, s. locarias, orate, m.

madden, —dn, v. a. enloquecer.

madder, —dŭr, s. (bot.) rubia, f.

mad-house, –*hŏds*, s. casa de locos, f.

madly,–*lĕ* ad. furiosamente; como un loco.

madman, –*măn*, s. loco, maniático, m.

madness, –*nĕs*, g. locura, manía, f.; furor, m. (mar.) Santabárbara, f.

magazine, *măgăzēn'*, s. almacén, m.

maggot, *măg'gŏt*, s. gusano, m.; capricho, m.

magic, *măj'ĭk*, s. magia negra, f.; –, a. mágico; –ally, ad. mágicamente.

magician, *măjĭsh'ăn*, s. mago, nigromante, m.

magisterial, *măjĭstĕ'rĭăl*, a. magistral; imperioso; –ly, ad. magistralmente.

magistracy, *măj'ĭstrăsĭ*, s. magistratura, f.

magistrate, –*ĭstrăt*, s. magistrado, m.

magnanimity, *măgnănĭm'ĭtĕ*, s. magnanimidad, f.

magnanimous, *măgnăn'ĭmŭs*, a. magnánimo; –ly ad. magnánimamente.

magnet, *măg'nĕt*, s. imán, m., piedra imán, f.

magnetic(al), *măgnĕt'ĭk(ăl)*, a. magnético.

magnetism, *măg'nĕtĭzm*, s. magnetismo, m.

magnificence, *măgnĭf'ĭsĕns*, s. magnificencia, f.

magnificent, –*ĭsĕnt*, a. magnífico; –ly, ad. pomposamente.

magnify, *măg'nĭfī*, v. a. magnificar; exaltar, exagerar.

magnitude, –*nĭtŭd*, s. magnitud, grandeza, f.

magpie, *măg'pī*, s. urraca, picaza, f.

mahogany, *măhŏg'ănĕ*, s. caoba, caobana, f.

maid(en), *mād'('n)*, s. doncella, joven, f.; moza, criada, f.

maiden, –*n*, a. virgíneo, virginal; nuevo, intacto.

maidenhood, –*hŏd*, s. doncellez, virginidad, f.

maidenly, –*lĭ*, a. virginal, púdico.

maiden-speech, –*spētsh*, s. primer discurso de un diputado en el parlamento, m.

mail, *māl*, a. cota de malla, f.; mala, balija, f.

mail-coach, –*kōtsh*, s. diligencia, f.

mail-train, –*trān*, s. (rail.) tren correo, m.

maim, *mām*, v. a. mutilar; estropear; –, s. mutilación, f.

main, *mān*, a. principal; esencial; –, s. grueso, m.; océano, m., alta mar, f.; fuerza, f.; in the –, en general.

mainland, –*lănd*, s. continente, m.

main-line, –*līn*, s. (rail.) línea principal, f., tronco, m. [todo.

mainly, –*lĭ*, ad. principalmente, sobre main-mast, –*măst*, s. palo mayor de un navío, m. [sostener.

maintain, *māntān'*, v. a. & n. mantener;

maintenance, *mān'tĕnăns*, s. mantenimiento, m.; protección, f.; sustento, m.

maize, *māz*, s. maíz, trigo de las Indias ó de la Turquía, m.

majestic(al), *măjĕs'tĭk(ăl)*, a. majestuoso; grande; –ally ad. majestuosamente.

majesty, *măj'ĕstĕ*, s. majestad, f.

major, *mā'jŭr*, a. mayor; –, s. (mil.) sargento mayor, m.; primera proposición de un silogismo, f.

majority, *măjŏr'ĭtĕ*, s. mayoría, f.; pluralidad, f.; (mil.) sargentía mayor, f.

make, *māk*, v. a. hacer, crear, producir; formar, fabricar; ejecutar; obligar, forzar; –, v. n. hacerse; ir, encaminarse; –, s. hechura, forma, figura, f.

make-believe, –*bĕlēv*, s. disimulo, m.; pretexto, m. [dor, m.

makepeace, –*pēs*, s. pacificador, conciliamakeshift, –*shĭft*, s. expediente, m.; lo pésimo. [peso, m.

make-weight, –*wāt*, s. complemento de making, –*ĭng*, s. composición, f.; estructura, hechura, f.

malady, *măl'ădĕ*, s. enfermedad, f.

malapert, *măl'ăpărt*, a. desvergonzado.

malaria, *măl'ă'rĭă*, s. aire infecto, m.

malcontent, *măl'kŏntĕnt*, a. & s. malcontento (m.).

male, *māl*, a. masculino; –, s. macho, m.

malediction, *mălĕdĭk'shŭn*, s. maldición, f.

malefactor, –*făk'tŭr*, s. malhechor, m.

maleficent, –*f'ĭsĕnt*, a. maléfico, maligno.

malevolence, *mălĕv'ŏlĕns*, s. malevolencia, f. [malignamente.

malevolent, –*ŏlĕnt*, a. malévolo; –ly, ad.

malice, *măl'ĭs*, s. malicia, f.

malicious, *mălĭsh'ŭs*, a. malicioso; –ly, ad. maliciosamente.

malign, *mălīn'*, a. maligno; contagioso; –, v. a. envidiar; dañar.

malignant, *mălĭg'nănt*, a. maligno; –ly, ad. malignamente.

malignity, –*nĭtĕ*, s. malignidad, f.

malleable, *măl'ĕăbl*, a. maleable.

mallet, *măl'lĕt*, s. mazo, m.

mallows, *măl'lōz*, s. (bot.) malva, f.

malmsey, *măm'zĕ*, s. malvasía, f.

malpractice, *mălprăk'tĭs*, s. malversación, f.; maltrato, m. [la cerveza, f.

malt, *mălt*, s. cebada preparada para hacer

maltreat, *măltrēt'*, v. a. maltratar.

maltster, *mălt'stŭr*, s. obrero que prepara la cebada para hacer cerveza, m.

mam(ma), *măm(mă')*, s. mamá, f.

man, *măn*, s. hombre, m.; marido, m.; criado, m.; peón, m.; –of war, navío de guerra, m.; – to –, el uno como el otro, –, v. a. (mar.) tripular, armar.

manacle, *măn'ăkl*, s. manilla, f.; –s, pl. esposas, f. pl.; –, v. a. maniatar.

manage, *măn'dj*, v. a. & n. manejar, gobernar, administrar; tomar sus disposiciones.

manageable, –*ăbl*, a. manejable; dócil, tratable. [ministración; conducta, f.

management, –*mĕnt*, s. manejo, m.; administración, f.

manager, –*ŭr*, s. administrador, director, m.; hombre económico, m. [sión, f.

mandate, *măn'dăt*, s. mandato, m., comimandatory, *măn'dătŭrĕ*, a. mandatorio, m.

mandrake, *măn'drăk*, s. (bot.) mandrágora, f.

mane, *măn*, s. crines del caballo, f. pl.

man-eater, *măn'ētŭr*, s. caribe, antropófago, m. [valerosamente.

manful, –*fŭl*, a. bravo, valiente; –ly, ad.

mange, *mănj*, s. roña, sarna perruna, f.

manger, *măn'jŭr*, s. pesebre, m.

mangle, *măng'gl*, s. calandria, f.; –, v. a. pasar por la calandria, mutilar.

mangy, *măn'jĕ*, a. sarnoso.   [m.
manhood, *măn'hŭd*, s. edad viril, f.; valor,
mania, *mā'nĭá*, s. manía, f.   [maniaco.
maniac(al), *mă'nĭák(ăl)*, a. maniático,
manifest, *măn'ĭfĕst*, a. manifiesto, patente;
   —, s. manifiesto, m.; —, v. a. manifestar.
manifestation, *mănĭfĕstā'shŭn*, s. manifestación, f.
manifold, *măn'ĭfŏld*, a. muchos, varios.
manikin, *măn'ĭkĭn*, s. hombrecillo, m.
manipulate, *mănĭp'ŭlāt*, v. a. manejar.
manipulation, *mănĭpŭlā'shŭn*, s. manipulación, f.   [humano, m.
mankind, *măn'kĭnd*, s. género ó linaje
manlike, *măn'lĭk*, a. varonil.
manliness, *măn'lĭnĕs*, s. valentía, f.; valor, m.
manly, *măn'lĕ*, a. varonil, valeroso.
man-midwife, *—mĭdwĭf*, s. comadrón,
   partero, m.
manner, *măn'nŭr*, s. manera, f.; modo,
   m.; forma, f.; método, m.; maña, f.; hábito, m.; moda, f.; especie, f.; —s, pl. mo-
   dales, m. pl.; urbanidad, crianza, f.
manœuvre, *mănŏ'vŭr*, s. maniobra, f.; —,
   v. n. maniobrar.
manor, *măn'ŭr*, s. señorío, m.; feudo, m.
manorial, *mănō'rĭăl*, a. señorial.
mansion, *măn'shŭn*, s. mansión, morada,
   residencia, f.   [(sin premeditación), m.
manslaughter, *măn'slátŭr*, s. homicidio
mantle, *măn'tl*, s. campana de chimenea, f.
mantle-piece, *—pēs*, s. repisa de chimenea,
manual, *măn'ŭăl*, a. & s. manual (m.).   [f.
manufactory, *mănŭfăk'tŭrĕ*, s. fábrica,
   manufactura, f.
manufacture, *—tŭr*, s. manufactura, f.;
   artefacto, m.; —, v. a. fabricar, manufacturar.
manufacturer, *—ŭr*, s. fabricante, m.
manumission, *mănŭmĭsh'ŭn*, s. manu-
   misión, f.
manure, *mănŭr'*, s. abono, m.; estiércol,
   m.; fiemo, m.; —, v. a. abonar, estercolar,
   cultivar.   [m.
manuscript, *măn'ŭskrĭpt*, s. manuscrito,
many, *mĕn'ĕ*, a. muchos, muchas; — a
   time, muchas veces; how —? ¿cuántos?
   as — as, tantos como.
map, *măp*, s. mapa, f. (carta geográfica);
   —, v. a. delinear mapas.
maple, *mā'pl*, s. arce, m. (plátano falso).
mar, *măr*, v. a. dañar, corromper.
marauder, *mără'dŭr*, s. merodeador, m.
marble, *măr'bl*, s. mármol, m.; bolilla de
   mármol, f.; —, a. marmóreo; —, v. a. jaspear.
March, *mărtsh*, s. marzo, m. (mes).
march, —, s. marcha, f.; —, v. n. marchar,
   caminar.   [f.
marchioness, *măr'tshŏnĕs*, s. marquesa,
mare, *măr*, s. yegua, f.
margin, *măr'jĭn*, s. margen, m. & f., borde,
   m., orilla, f.; —, v. a. marginar.
marginal, *—ăl*, a. marginal.
marigold, *măr'ĭgŏld*, s. (bot.) caléndula, f.
marine, *mărēn'*, a. marino; —, s. marina,
   f., soldado de marina, m.
mariner, *măr'ĭnŭr*, s. marinero, m.
marital, *măr'ĭtăl*, a. marital.
maritime, *măr'ĭtĭm*, a. marítimo, naval.

marjoram, *măr'jŏrăm*, s. mejorana, f.
mar-joy, *măr'jŏĭ*, s. derramasolaces, m.
mark, *mărk*, s. marca, f.; señal, nota, f.;
   blanco, m.; —, v. a. marcar; —, v. n. advertir.   [compra, f.
market, *măr'kĕt*, s. mercado, m.; venta,
marketable, *—ăbl*, a. común, corriente.
marksman, *mărks'măn*, s. tirador, m.
marl, *mărl*, s. marga, f.; —, v. a. margar.
marl-pit, *—pĭt*, s. marguera, f.
marly, *—lĕ*, a. margoso.
marmalade, *măr'mălăd*, s. mermelada, f.
marmoset, *măr'mŏzĕt*, s. mico pequeño, m.
marmot, *măr'mŏt*, s. marmota, f.
maroon, *mărōn'*, s. castaña, f.
mar-plot, *măr'plŏt*, s. travieso, m.
marquee, *mărkvē'*, s. marquesina, f.
marquess, *măr'kvĕs*, s. marqués, f.
marquetry, *—kĕtrĕ*, s. marquetería, atara-
marquis, *—kvĭs*, s. marqués, m.   [cea, f.
marquisate, *—kvĭzăt*, s. marquesado, m.
marriage, *măr'rĭj*, s. maridaje, m.; matrimonio, m.; casamiento, m.
marriageable, *—ăbl*, a. casadero, núbil.
marriage-articles, *—ăr'tĭkls*, s. pl., —
   settlement, *—sĕt'tlmĕnt*, s. contrato matrimonial, m.
married, *măr'rĭd*, a. casado, conyugal.
marrow, *măr'rŏ*, s. meollo, m.; médula, f.
marry, *măr'rĕ*, v. n. casar(se).
marsh, *mărsh*, s. pantano, m., laguna, f.
marshal, *măr'shăl*, s. mariscal, m.
marshy, *măr'shĕ*, a. pantanoso.
mart, *mărt*, s. emporio, m.; comercio, m.
marten, *măr'tĕn*, s. marta, f.   [feria, f.
martial, *măr'shăl*, a. marcial, guerrero;
   — law, s. derecho militar, m.   [tin, m.
Martinmas, *măr'tĭnmăs*, s. día de S. Mar-
martyr, *măr'tŭr*, s. mártir, m.
martyrdom, *—dŏm*, s. martirio, m.
marvel, *măr'vĕl*, s. maravilla, f.; —, v. n.
   maravillar(se).   [maravillosamente.
marvellous, *—lŭs*, a. maravilloso; -ly, ad.
masculine, *măs'kŭlĭn*, a. masculino, varonil   [v. a. amasar; mezclar.
mash, *măsh*, s. mezcla, f.; fárrago, m.; —,
mask, *măsk*, s. máscara, f.; pretexto, color,
   m.; —, v. a. enmascarar; disimular, ocultar; —, v. n. andar enmascarado.
masker, *—ŭr*, s. el ó la que se enmascara.
mason, *mā'sn*, s. albañil, m.
masonry, *—rĕ*, s. albañilería, f.
masquerade, *măskĕrăd'*, s. mascarada, f.
masquerader, *—ŭr*, s. máscara, m. & f.
mass, *măs*, s. masa, f.; misa, f.; montón, m.
massacre, *măs'săkŭr*, s. carnicería, matanza, f.; —, v. a. matar atrozmente, hacer
   una carnicería.
massive, *măs'sĭv*, a. macizo, sólido.
mast, *măst*, s. árbol de navío, palo, m.;
   fabuco, m.; —, v. a. arbolar un palo.
master, *măs'tŭr*, s. amo, dueño, m.;
   maestro, m.; señor, m.; señorito, m.; (mar.)
   maestre, patrón, m.; —, v. a. domar, domeñar; gobernar, dominar.
master-hand, *—hănd*, s. mano maestra,
   maestría, f.
masterly, *—lĕ*, a. imperioso, despótico; —
   ad. con maestría.

master-piece, –pḗs, s. obra ó pieza maestra, f.
master-stroke, –strŏk, master-touch,
 –tŭtsh, s. golpe de maestro ó diestro, m.
mastery, –ḗ, s. superioridad, maestría, f.
masticate, mǎs'tĭkāt, v. a. mascar, mas-
mastiff, mǎs'tĭf, s. mastín, m.   [car.
mat, mǎt, s. estera, esterilla, f.; (mar.) pa-
 lleta, f.; –, v. a. esterar.
match, mǎtsh, s. mecha, pajuela, f.; fósforo, m.; partido, m.; contrincante, m.;
 pareja, f.; casamiento, m.; combate, m.;
 –, v. a. igualar; aparear; casar; –, v. n.
 hermanarse.
match-box, –bŏks, s. cajita de fósforos, f.
matchless, –lḗs, a. incomparable, sin par.
match-maker, –mākŭr, s. casamentero, m.
mate, mǎt, s. consorte, m.; compañero, m.;
 compañera, f.; (mar.) piloto, m.; –, v. a.
 desposar; igualar;   [(mente).
material, mǎtḗ'rĭǎl, a. –ly, ad. material
materialism, –ĭzm, s. materialismo, m.
maternal, mǎtŭr'nǎl, a. maternal, materno.
maternity, –nĭtḗ, s. maternidad, f.
mathematic(al), mǎthḗmǎt'ĭk(ǎl), a. matemático; –ly, ad. matemáticamente.
mathematician, mǎthḗmǎtĭsh'ǎn, s. matemático, m.   [máticas, f. pl.
mathematics, mǎthḗmǎt'ĭks, s. pl. mate-
matins, mǎt'ĭnz, s. pl. maitines, m. pl.
matricide, mǎt'rĭsīd, s. matricidio, m.;
 matricida, m.
matriculate, mǎtrĭk'ūlāt, v. a. matricular.
matriculation, mǎtrĭkūlā'shǎn, s. matri-
 culación, f.   [nial, marital.
matrimonial, mǎtrĭmō'nĭǎl, a. matrimo-
matrimony, mǎt'rĭmŏnē, s. matrimonio,
 casamiento, m.
matron, mā'trŏn, s. matrona, f.   [grave.
matronly, –lḗ, a. como matrona, seria,
matter, mǎt'tŭr, s. materia, substancia material, f.; asunto, objeto, m.; cuestión, importancia, f.; it is no –, no importa;
 what is the –? ¿ de qué se trata? a –
 of fact, un hecho; –, v. n. importar.
mattings, mǎt'tĭngs, s. pl. esteras, f. pl.
mattock, –tŏk, s. azadón de peto, m.
mattress, –trĕs, s. colchón, m.
mature, mǎtūr', a. maduro; juicioso; –,
 v. a. madurar.
maturity, mǎtū'rĭtḗ, s. madurez, f.
maul, mǎl, v. a. apalear, maltratar á golpes.
maul-stick, –stĭk, s. tiento, m.
Maundy-Thursday, mǎn'dāthŭrz'dā, s.
 Jueves Santo, m.
mausoleum, mǎsōlē'ŭm, s. mausoleo, m.
maw, mǎ, s. cuajar, m.; molleja de las
 aves, f.   [bundo.
mawkish, –kĭsh, a. fastidioso, nausea-
may, mā, v. n. ir. poder; – be, acaso, quizá.
May, –, s. mayo, m. (mes).
May-day, –dā, s. día primero de mayo, m.
May-pole, –pōl, s. mayo (árbol), m.
mayor, mā'ŭr, s. corregidor, m.
mayoralty, –ǎltē, s. corregimiento, m.
mayoress, –ĕs, s. corregidora, f.
maze, mǎz, s. laberinto, m.; perplejidad, f.
mazy, mā'zē, a. confuso, embrollado.

me, mḗ, pn. me.
mead, mḗd, s. aguamiel, f.
meadow, mḗd'ō, s. pradería, f.; prado, m.
meagre, mḗ'gŭr, a. magro; flaco; –ly, ad.
 pobremente, estérilmente.   [f.
meagreness, –nḗs, s. flaqueza, f.; escasez,
meal, mḗl, s. comida, f.; harina, f.
mealy, –ḗ, a. harinoso.
mean, mḗn, s. bajo, vil, despreciable; abatido; mediocre; in the –time, –while,
 ínterin, mientras tanto; –, s. medio, m.;
 expediente, m.; –s, pl. medios, m. pl.;
 caudal, m.; –, v. a. & n. significar; hacer
 intención, pensar.   [tortuoso, m.
meander, mḗǎn'dŭr, s. laberinto, camino
meaning, mḗn'ĭng, s. intención, f.; inteligencia, f.; sentido, significado, m.
meanly, mḗn'lḗ, ad. mediocremente; pobremente; vilmente.
meanness, –nḗs, s. bajeza, f.; pobreza, f.;
 mezquindad, f.; mediocridad, f.
measles, mḗ'zlz, s. pl. sarampión, f.
measurable, mḗzh'ŭrǎbl, a. mensurable.
measure, mḗzh'ŭr, s. medida, f.; (mus.)
 compás, m.; –, v. a. medir; ajustar.
measurement, –mḗnt, s. medición, f.
measurer, –ŭr, s. medidor, m.
meat, mḗt, s. carne, f.; vianda, f.
mechanic, mḗkǎn'ĭk, s. mecánico, m.
mechanical, –ǎl, a. mecánico; servil, bajo;
 –ly, ad. mecánicamente.
mechanician, mḗkǎnĭsh'ǎn, mechanist,
 mḗk'ǎnĭst, s. mecánico, maquinista, m.
mechanics, mḗkǎn'ĭks, s. pl. mecánica, f.
mechanism, mḗk'ǎnĭzm, s. mecanismo, m.
medal, mḗd'ǎl, s. medalla, f.; moneda an-
 tigua, f.
medallion, mḗdǎl'yǔn, s. medallón, m.
meddle, mḗd'l, v. n. entremeterse.
meddler, –ŭr, s. entremetido, m.
mediate, mḗ'dĭāt, v. n. mediar.
mediation, mḗdĭā'shǎn, s. mediación, interposición, f.
medical, mḗd'ĭkǎl, a. médico.   [m.
medicament, –ĭkǎmĕnt, s. medicamento,
medicate, –ĭkāt, v. a. medicinar.
medicinal, mḗdĭs'ĭnǎl, a. medicinal.
medicine, mḗd'ĭsĭn, s. medicina, f.; medicamento, m.   [f.
mediocrity, mḗdĭŏk'rĭtḗ, s. mediocridad,
meditate, mḗd'ĭtāt, v. a. meditar, idear.
meditation, mḗdĭtā'shǎn, s. meditación, f.
meditative, mḗd'ĭtātĭv, a. meditativo, contemplativo.   [terráneo.
mediterranean, mḗdĭtĕrrā'nḗǎn, a. medi-
medium, mḗ'dĭǔm, s. medio, m.; expediente, m.; moderación, f.
medlar, mḗd'lǔr, s. níspero, m.; níspola, f.
medley, mḗd'lḗ, s. miscelánea, mezcla, m.
meek, mḗk, a. mego, apacible; dulce; –ly,
 ad. suavemente.
meekness, –nḗs, s. suavidad, f.; modestia,
 f.; dulzura, f.   [f.
meerschaum, mḗr'shǒǔm, s. piedra loca,
meet, mḗt, v. a. encontrar; convocar; –,
 v. n. encontrarse; juntarse; –, a. idóneo,
 propio.
meeting, –ĭng, s. asamblea, f.; congreso,
 m., entrevista, f.; conventículo, m

melancholy, *mĕl'ăngkŏlĕ,* s. melancolía, f.; —, a. melancólico.
mellifluous, *mĕllĭf'lŭăs,* a. melifluo.
mellow, *mĕl'lŏ,* a. maduro, meloso; tierno; —, v. a. (& n.) madurar(se).
mellowness, *—nĕs,* s. madurez, f.
melodious, *mĕlŏ'dĭăs,* a. melodioso -ly, ad. melodiosamente.
melody, *mĕl'ŏdĕ,* s. melodía, f.
melon, *mĕl'ŏn,* s. melón, m.
melt, *mĕlt,* v a. derretir, fundir; liquidar; enternecer, —, v. n. derretirse, liquidarse.
member, *mĕm'bŭr,* s. miembro, m.; parte, f., individuo, m.
membrane, *mĕm'brăn,* s. membrana, f.
memento, *mĕmĕn'tŏ,* s. memento, m.
memoir, *mĕm'wŭr,* s. memoria, relación, narrativa, f.   [memorando.
memorable, *mĕm'ŏrăbl,* a. memorable, memorably, *-lĕ,* ad. memorablemente.
memorandum, *mĕmŏrăn'dăm,* memorándum, m.   [morial, m.
memorial, *mĕmŏ'rĭăl,* s. memoria, f.; memory, *mĕm'ŏrĕ,* s. memoria, f.; recuerdo, m.   [amenazar.
menace, *mĕn'ăs,* s. amenaza, f.; —, v. a.
menagery, *mĕnăzh'ŭrĕ,* s. casa de fieras ó animales raros, f.
mend, *mĕnd,* v. a. reparar, remendar, retocar; mejorar, corregir.
mendacious, *mĕndā'shăs,* a. mendoso.
mendacity, *mĕndăs'ĭtĕ,* s. falsedad, mentira, f.
mendicancy, *mĕn'dĭkănsĕ,* mendicity, *mĕndĭs'ĭtĕ,* s. mendiguez, mendicidad, f.
mendicant, *-dĭkănt,* a. & s. mendicante
mendicate, *-dĭkăt,* v. a. mendigar. [(m.).
menial, *mĕ'nĭăl,* a. servil, doméstico.
menstruation, *mĕnstrŭā'shăn,* s. menstruo, m.   [f.
mensuration, *mĕnsŭrā'shăn,* s. medición.
mental, *mĕn'tăl,* a. mental, intelectual; -ly, ad. mentalmente, intelectualmente.
mention, *mĕn'shăn,* s. mención, f.; —, v. a. mencionar.
Mentor, *mĕn'tŏr,* s. ayo, guía, m.
mephitic(al), *mĕfĭt'ĭk(ăl),* a. mefítico.
mercantile, *mŭr'kăntĭl,* a. mercantil.
mercenary, *mŭr'sănărĕ,* a. & s. mercenario (m.).
mercer, *mŭr'sŭr,* s. mercero, sedero, m.
mercery, *-ĕ,* s. mercería, sedería, f.   [f.
merchandise, *mŭr'tshăndĭz,* s. mercancía.
merchant, *mŭr'tshănt,* s. comerciante, m.
merchantman, *-măn,* s. navío mercantil, m.   [-ly, ad. misericordiosamente.
merciful, *mŭr'sĭfŭl,* a. misericordioso;
merciless, *-lĕs,* a. duro de corazón, inhumano; -ly, ad. cruelmente.
mercurial, *mŭrkū'rĭăl,* a. vivo, activo; mercurial.
mercury, *mŭr'kŭrĕ,* s. mercurio, m.
mercy, *mŭr'sĕ,* s. misericordia, piedad, f.; perdón, m.   [mente; puramente.
mere, *mēr,* a. mero, puro; -ly, ad. simple-
meretricious, *mĕrĕtrĭsh'ăs,* a. meretricio.
merge, *mŭrj,* v. a. sumergir.   [cio.
meridian, *mĕrĭd'ĭăn,* s. mediodía, m.; meridiano, m.

meridional, *-ĭŏnăl,* a. meridional.
merit, *mĕr'ĭt,* s. mérito, m.; —, v a. merecer.
meritorious, *mĕrĭtŏ'rĭăs,* a. meritorio; -ly, ad. meritoriamente.
mermaid, *mŭr'măd,* s. sirena, f.
merrily, *mĕr'rĭlĕ,* ad. alegremente.
merriment, *mĕr'rĭmĕnt,* s. diversión, f.; regocijo, m.
merry, *mĕr'rĕ,* a. alegre, jovial, festivo.
Merry-Andrew, *-ăn'drŏ,* s. bufón, [chulo, m.
mesh, *mĕsh,* s. malla, f.
Mesmerism, *mĕs'mărĭzm,* s. mesmerismo, m.   [ción, f.
mess, *mĕs,* s. plato, m.; rancho, m.; por-
message, *-sdj,* s. mensaje, m.
messenger, *-sĕnjŭr,* s. mensajero, m.
mess-mate, *-măt,* s. comensal, m.
messuage, *-swdj,* s. mensje, ajuar de casa, m.; habitación, f.   [espíritu, m.
metal, *mĕt'ăl,* s. metal, m.; (fig.) coraje,
metallic(al), *mĕtăl'ĭk(ăl),* a. metálico.
metallurgy, *mĕt'ăllŭrjĕ,* s. metalurgia, f.
metamorphose, *mĕtămŏr'fŏs,* v a. transformar.   [morfosis, f.
metamorphosis, *mĕtămŏr'fŏsĭs,* s. meta-
metaphor, *mĕt'ăfŏr,* s. metáfora, f.
metaphoric(al), *mĕtăfŏr'ĭk(ăl),* a. metafórico.   [sico; -ly, ad. metafísicamente.
metaphysic(al), *mĕtăfĭz'ĭk(ăl),* a. metafí-
metaphysics, *-ĭks,* s. pl. metafísica, f.
mete, *mĕt,* v. a. medir.
meteor, *mĕ'tĕŭr,* s. meteoro, meteoro, m.
meteorological, *mĕtĕŏrŏlŏj'ĭkăl,* a. meteorológico.   [gía, f.
meteorology, *mĕtĕŏrŏl'ŏjĕ,* s. meteorolo-
meter, *mĕ'tŭr,* s. medidor, m.
methinks, *mĕthĭnks',* v. imp. me parece, creo, pienso.
method, *mĕth'ŏd,* s. método, m.
methodic(al), *mĕthŏd'ĭk(ăl),* a. metódico; -ly, ad. metódicamente.
methodist, *mĕth'ŏdĭst,* m. metodista, m.
metre, *mĕ'tŭr,* s. metro, m.
metrical, *mĕt'rĭkăl,* a. métrico.
metropolis, *mĕtrŏp'ŏlĭs,* s. metrópoli, f.
metropolitan, *mĕtrŏpŏl'ĭtăn,* s. metropolitano, m.   [m.
mettle, *mĕt'l,* s. brío, valor, coraje, ardor,
mettled, *-d,* mettlesome, *-săm,* a. brioso, vivo, ardiente.
mew, *mū,* s. jaula, f.; gaviota, f.; caballeriza, f.; —, v. a. enjaular; —, v. n. maullar (como el gato).   [m.
microscope, *mĭ'krŏskŏp,* s. microscopio,
microscopic(al), *mĭkrŏskŏp'ĭk(ăl),* m. mimid, *mĭd,* a. medio.   [croscópico.
mid-course, *-kŏrs,* s. media carrera, f.; medio camino, m.
mid-day, *-dā,* s. mediodía, m.
middle, *-dl,* a. medio, intermedio; mediocre; —, s. medio, centro, m.
middling, *-dlĭng,* a. mediano, mediocre.
midland, *-lănd,* a. mediterráneo.
midnight, *-nĭt,* s. media noche, f.   [f.
midshipman, *-shĭpmăn,* s. guardia marina,
midst, *mĭdst,* s. medio, centro, m.
midsummer, *mĭd'sămmŭr,* s. solsticio estival, m.; rigor del estío, m.

midway, *—wá,* s. medio camino, m.; —, ad. á medio camino.

midwife, *—wíf,* s. comadre, partera, f.

midwifery, *—wífré,* s. obstetricia, f.

mien, *mén,* s. semblante, m.

might, *mít,* s. poder, m , fuerza, f.; — and main, suma fuerza, f. [mente.

mightily, *—ílí,* ad. poderosamente, suma-

mightiness, *—ínés,* s. poder, m ; potencia,

mighty, *—í,* a. fuerte, potente. [f.

mignonette, *mín'yónét,* s. (bot.) reseda, f.

migrate, *mí'grát,* v n. emigrar

migration, *mígrá'shán,* s. emigración, f.

migratory, *mí'grátúré,* a. migratorio.

milch, *mílsh,* a. lactífero.

mild, *míld,* a. indulgente, blando, dulce, apacible, suave, moderado, **—ly,** ad. suave-mente, con blandura.

mildew, *míl'dú,* s. tizón, tizoncillo, m.

mildness, *míld'nés,* s. clemencia, dulzura,

mile, *míl,* s. milla, f. [f.

mileage, *—dj,* s. indemnidad kilométrica,

mile-stone, *—stón,* s. mijero, m. [f.

milfoil, *míl'fóíl,* s (bot) milenrama, f.

militant, *míl'ítánt,* a. militante.

military, *míl'ítúré,* a. & s. militar (m.).

militate, *míl'ítát,* v n. militar.

militia, *mílísh'á,* s. milicia, f.

milk, *mílk,* s. leche, f.; —, v. a. ordeñar

milk-maid, *—mád,* s. lechera, f.

milk-sop, *—sóp,* s. marica, f.

milky, *—í,* a. lácteo, lactífero; lechal; — way, s. galaxia, vía láctea, f.

mill, *míl,* s. molino, m.; —, v. a. moler; batir con el molinillo; estampar.

mill-dam, *—dám,* s. esclusa de molino, f.

millennium, *míllén'níúm,* s. espacio de mil años, m.

miller, *míl'úr,* s. molinero, m.

millet, *míl'ít,* s. (bot.) mijo, m.

milliner, *míl'ínúr,* s. modista, m. & f.

millinery, *—í,* s. modas, f. pl. [vulgo, m.

million, *míl'yán,* s. millón, m.; the —,

millionth, *—th,* a. millonésimo.

mill-stone, *—stón,* s. muela, f.

mime, *mím,* s. mimo, bufón, m.

mimic, *mím'ík,* v. a. imitar, contrahacer; —(al), a. burlesco.

mimicry, *—ré,* s. mímica, f.; bufonería, f.

mince, *míns,* v. a. picar la carne; —, v. n. hablar con afectación; andar muy poco á poco afectadamente. [afectación.

mincingly, *mín'síngle,* ad. á pedacitos; con

mind, *mínd,* s. mente, f.; entendimiento, m.; gusto, afecto, m.; voluntad, intención, f.; pensamiento, m.; opinión, f.; ánimo, m.; —, v. a. notar, observar, considerar; pensar; —, v. n. inclinarse; estar dispuesto.

minded, *—éd,* a. inclinado, dispuesto.

mindful, *—fúl,* a. atento, diligente; **—ly,** ad. atentamente.

mindless, *—lés,* a. descuidado, negligente.

mine, *mín,* pn. mío, mía, mi; —, s. mina; —, v. n. minar, cavar.

miner, *—úr,* s. minador, m.

mineral, *mín'ú rál,* a. & s. mineral (m.).

mineralogy, *mínúrá'ōjé,* s. mineralogía, f.

mingle, *míng'gl,* v. a. mezclar.

miniature, *mín'túr,* s. miniatura, f.

minim, *mín'ím,* s. (mus.) mínima, f.

minimise, *mín'ímíz,* v. a. reducir á un mínimum.

minimum, *mín'ímūm,* s. mínimum, m.

minion, *mín'yán,* s. favorito, m.

minister, *mín'ístúr,* s. ministro, m.; —, v. a. ministrar; servir; suministrar; pro-veer; socorrer.

ministerial, *mínístê'ríál,* a. ministerial.

ministration, *mínístrá'shán,* s. agencia, f.; ministerio, m.

ministry, *mín'ístré,* s. ministerio, m.

minnow, *mín'nó,* s. vario, m. (pez).

minor, *mí'núr,* a. menor, pequeño; infe-rior; —, s. menor (de edad), m. [ría, f.

minority, *mínó'rítí,* s. minoridad, f.; mino-

minster, *mín'stúr,* s. iglesia catedral, f.

minstrel, *mín'strél,* s. ministril, m.

mint, *mínt,* s. (bot.) menta, f.; ceca, casa de moneda, f.; —, v. a. acuñar.

mintage, *—dj,* s. derechos de cuño, m. pl.

minuet, *mín'ét,* s. minuete, minué, m.

minus, *mí'nús,* ad. menos.

minute, *mínút',* a. menudo, pequeño; **—ly,** ad. exactamente.

minute, *mín'ít,* s. minuto, m.; momento, instante, m.; minuta, f.

minute-book, *—búk,* s. libro de minutas, m.

minuteness, *mínút'nés,* s. minucia, pe-queñez, f.

minutiae, *mínú'shíé,* s. pl. minucias, f. pl.

minx, *míngks,* s. moza atrevida y libre, f.

miracle, *mír'ákl,* s. milagro, m.; mara-villa, f. [**—ly,** ad. maravillosamente.

miraculous, *mírák'úlús,* a. milagroso;

mirage, *mí'ráj (mírázh'),* s. espejismo, m.

miro, *mír,* s. fango, limo, m. [pañado.

mirky, *múr'kí,* a. sombrío; turbio; em-

mirror, *mí'rúr,* s. espejo, m.

mirth, *múrth,* s. alegría, f.; regocijo, m.

mirthful, *—fúl,* a. alegre, jovial.

miry, *mí'ré,* a. cenagoso, lodoso.

misadventure, *mísádvén'túr,* s. desven-tura, f.; infortunio, m.

misalliance, *—állí'áns,* s. mal matrimo-nio, m. [m.

misanthrope, *mís'ánthróp,* s. misántropo,

misanthropy, *mísán'thrópé,* s. misan-tropía, f. [aplicación, f.

misapplication, *—ápplíká'shán,* s. mala

misapply, *—áplí',* v. a. usar de alguna cosa impropiamente.

misapprehend, *—áppréhénd',* v. a. en-tender mal. [error, yerro, m.

misapprehension, *—ápprêhén'shán,* s.

misbehave, *—béhâv',* v. n. portarse mal.

misbehaviour, *—béháv'yúr,* s. mala con-ducta, f. [heterodoxia, f.

misbelief, *—bélêf',* s. opinión falsa, f.;

misbeliever, *—bélê'vúr,* s. incrédulo, m.

miscalculate, *—kál'kúlát,* v. a. calcular mal.

miscarriage, *—kár'rij,* s. éxito infeliz de alguna empresa, m.; mala conducta, f.; aborto, m. [grarse; abortar.

miscarry, *—kár'ré,* v. n. frustrarse, malo-

miscellaneous, *missellă'nĕăs*, a. mez-
cladio. [miscelánea, f.
miscellany, *missel'lănĕ (mĭs sĕllănĕ)*, s.
mischance, *mĭstshăns'*, s. desventura, f.;
infortunio, mal suceso, m. [m.
mischief, -*tshĭf*, s. mal, daño, infortunio,
mischief-maker, -*măkăr*, s. derramasolaces, destripamerjendas, m.
mischievous, -*tshĭvăs*, a. dañoso, malicioso, malévolo; -ly, ad. malignamente.
misconceive, -*kŏnsĕv'*, v. a. concebir una
idea falsa. [cación, f.
misconception, -*kŏnsĕp'shăn*, s. equivo-
misconduct, -*kŏn'dăkt*, s. mala conducta,
f.; -, -*kŏndăkt'*, v. a. portarse mal.
misconstruction, -*kŏnstrăk'shăn*,s. mala
construcción, interpretación siniestra, f.
misconstrue, -*kŏn'strŏ*, v. a. interpretar
mal. [m.; malvado, malhechor, m.
miscreant, *mĭs'krĕănt*, s. infiel, incrédulo,
misdeed, *mĭsdĕd'*, s. mal hecho, delito, m.
misdemeanour, -*demĕn'ăr*, s. mala conducta, f.
misdirect, -*dĭrĕkt'*, v. a. dirigir errada-
misdoubt, -*dŏăt'*, v. a. recelar, sospechar.
miser, *mĭ'zăr*, s. hombre tacaño y avariento, m. [pobre; mezquino.
miserable, *mĭz'ărăbl*, a. miserable, infeliz;
miserably, -*ĕ*, ad. miserablemente; avaramente.
miserly, *mĭ'zărlĕ*, a. mezquino, tacaño.
misery, *mĭz'ărĕ*, s. miseria, f.; infortunio,
m. [que cae mal, f.
misfit, *mĭsfĭt'*, s. condición de un vestido
misfortune, *mĭsfŏr'tăn*, s. infortunio, m.;
calamidad, f. [cer temer.
misgive, -*gĭv'*, v. a. llenar de dudas; ha-
misgiving, -*gĭv'ĭng*, s. recelo, m.; duda,
f.; presentimiento, m.
misgovern, -*găv'ărn*, v. a. gobernar mal.
misguide, -*gĭd'*, v. a. guiar mal. [m.
mishap, -*hăp'*, s. desventura, f.; desastre,
misinform, -*ĭnfŏrm'*, v. a. informar mal.
misinterpret, -*ĭntăr'prĕt*, v. a. interpretar mal.
misjudge, -*jăj'*, v. n. juzgar mal.
mislay, -*lĕ'*, v. a. colocar mal, extraviar.
mislead, -*lĕd'*, v. a. extraviar, descaminar; seducir.
mismanage, -*măn'dj*, v. a. manejar mal.
mismanagement, -*mĕnt*, s. mala administración, f.; desarreglo, m.
misname, -*năm'*, v. a. dar un nombre falso.
misnomer, -*nŏ'măr*, s. nombre ó título
falso, m.
misogynist, *mĭsŏg'ĭnĭst*, s. misógino, m.
misplace, -*plăs'*, v. a. colocar mal; sacar
algo de su quicio.
misprint, -*prĭnt'*, v. a. imprimir mal; -,
s. errata de un libro, f.
misrepresent, -*rĕprĕzĕnt'*, v. a. representar mal. [tación falsa, f.
misrepresentation,-*tă'shăn*,s. represen-
misrule, *mĭsrŏl'*, s. tumulto, m.; confusión, f.
Miss, *mĭs*, s. señorita, f.; pérdida, falta, f.;
-, v. a. errar, perder; omitir; -, v. n.
frustrarse; faltar.

missal, *mĭs'ăl*, s. misal, m. [gurar.
misshape, *mĭsshăp'*, v. a. deformar, desfi-
missile, *mĭs'sĭl*, s. proyectil, m.
missing, *mĭs'sĭng*, a. lo que falta; perdido.
mission, *mĭsh'ăn*, s. misión, comisión, f.
missionary, -*ărĕ*, s. misionero, m.
missive, *mĭs'sĭv*, s. carta misiva, f.; -, a.
mist, *mĭst*, s. niebla, f. [misivo.
mistake, *mĭstăk'*, v. a. equivocar; -, v.
n. equivocarse, engañarse; to be mis-
taken, haberse equivocado; -, s. equivocación, f.; yerro, engaño, m.
Mister, *mĭs'tăr*, s. Señor (título), m.
mistiness, *mĭs'tĭnĕs*, s. nebulosidad, f.
mistletoe, *mĭs'ltŏ*, s. (bot.) muérdago, m.;
liga, f. [-, (mĭs'tŭs), señora, doña, f.
mistress, *mĭs'trĕs*, s. ama,f.; concubina,f.;
mistrust, *mĭstrăst'*, v. a. desconfiar, sospechar; -, s. desconfianza, sospecha, f.
mistrustful, -*făl*, a. desconfiado, sos-
misty, *mĭs'tĕ*, a. nebuloso. [pechoso.
misunderstand, *mĭsăndărstănd'*, v. a.
entender mal una cosa.
misusage, -*ă'zdj*, s. abuso, m. [algo.
misuse, -*ăs'*, v. a. maltratar; abusar de
mite, *mĭt*, s. crèsa, f.; pizca, f.
mitigate, *mĭt'ĭgăt*, v. a. mitigar, calmar.
mitigation, *mĭtĭgă'shăn*, s. mitigación, f.;
mitre, *mĭ'tăr*, s. mitra, f. [alivio, m.
mittens, *mĭt'ns*, s. pl. mitones, m. pl.
mix, *mĭks*, v. a. mezclar. [mezcla, f.
mixture, *mĭks'tjăr*, s. mistura, mixtura,
mizzen, *mĭz'n*, s. (mar.) mesana, f.
mizzle, *mĭz'l*, v. n. mollizuar, lloviznar.
moan, *mŏn*, s. lamento, gemido, m.; -, v.
a. lamentar, gemir; -, v. n. afligirse.
moanful, -*făl*, a. -ly, ad. lamentable
(mente). [canales de agua.
moat, *mŏt*, s. mota, f.; -, v. a. rodear con
mob, *mŏb*, s. populacho, m., canalla, f.; -,
v. a. tumultuar.
mobilise, *mŏb'ĭlĭz*, v. a. (mil.) movilizar.
mobility, *mŏbĭl'ĭtĕ*, s. movilidad,f.; (vulg.)
populacho, m. [de los indianos, m.
moccasin, *mŏ'kăssn*, s. zapato rampión
mock, *mŏk*, v. a. mofar, burlar; -, s. mofa,
burla, f.; -, a. ficticio, falso.
mockery, -*ărĕ*, s. mofa, burla, zumba, f.
mocking-bird, -*ĭngbărd*, s. burlón, m.
(ave). [nera, f.; costumbre, f.
mode, *mŏd*, s. modo, m.; forma, f.; ma-
model, *mŏd'ĕl*, s. modelo, m.; -, v. a.
modelar.
modeller, -*ăr*, s. trazador, dibujador, m.
moderate, *mŏd'ărăt*, a. moderado; mediocre; -ly, ad. moderadamente; -, v. a.
moderar. [f.
moderation, *mŏdără'shăn*, s. moderación,
modern, *mŏd'ărn*, a. moderno, reciente.
modernize, *mŏd'ărnĭz*, v. a. modernizar.
modest, *mŏd'ĕst*, a. modesto; -ly, ad.
modestamente.
modesty, -*ĕ*, s. modestia, decencia, f.
modification, *mŏdĭfĭkă'shăn*, s. modifica-
modify, *mŏd'ĭfĭ*, v. a. modificar. [ción,f.
modulate, *mŏd'ŭlăt*, v. a. modular.
modulation, *mŏdŭlă'shăn*, s. (mus.) modulación, f.

mohair, *mō'hār*, s. tela hecha de pelo de

moiety, *mōi'ĕti*, s. mitad, f.   [camello, f.

moist, *mōist*, a. húmedo, mojado.

moisten, *mōi'sn*, y. a. humedecer.

moisture, *mōis'tŭr*, s. humedad, f.; jugo, m.   [nuelas, f. pl.

molar, *mō'lăr*, a. molar : — teeth, s. pl.

molasses, *mŏlăs'sēz*, s. pl. melaza, f.

mole, *mōl*, s. moln, f.; muelle, dique, m.;

mole-hill, *-hil*, s. topinera, f.   [topo, m.

molest, *mōlĕst'*, v. a. molestar, atormentar.

molestation, *mŏlĕstā'shŭn*, s. molestia, f.; enfado, m.

mollify, *mŏl'lifī*, v. a. ablandar..

mollusk, *mŏl'lŭsk*, s. molusco, m.

molten, *mōl'tn*, a. derretido ; the — calf, el becerro de fundición. (Exod. 32, 8.)

moment, *mō'mĕnt*, s. momento, m.; importancia, f.

momentarily, *-ărĭlĭ*, ad. á cada momento.

momentary, *-ărĭ*, a. momentáneo.

momentous, *mŏmĕn'tŭs*, a. importante.

momentum, *-tŭm*, s. fuerza de impulsión de un cuerpo, f.

monarch, *mŏn'ărk*, s. monarca, m.

monarchic(al), *mŏnărk'ĭk(ăl)*, a. monárquico.

monarchy, *mŏn'ărkĭ*, s. monarquía, f.

monastery, *mŏn'ăstŭrĭ*, s. monasterio, m.

monastic(al), *mŏnăs'tĭk(ăl)*, a. monástico.

Monday, *mŭn'dā*, s. lunes, m.

monetary, *mŏn'ĕtŭrĭ*, a. monetario.

money, *mŭn'ĕ*, s. moneda, f.; dinero, m.; ready —, in hand, dinero contante.

moneyed, monied, —*ĕd*, a. adinerado, rico.

monger, *mŭng'gŭr*, s. tratante, traficante, m.

mongrel, *mŏng'grĕl*, a. & s. mestizo (m.)

monition, *mŏnĭsh'ŭn*, s. amonestación, f.

monitor, *mŏn'ĭtŭr*, s. admonitor, m.; (mar.) monitor, m.

monitory, *mŏn'ĭtŭrĭ*, a. monitorio.

monk, *mŭngk*, s. monje, m.   [ñada, f.

monkery, *-ărĭ*, s. vida monástica, f.; frai-

monkey, *-ĕ*, s. mono, m.

monkish, *-ĭsh*, a. monástico.   [níaco.

monomaniac, *mŏnŏmā'nĭăk*, s. monoma-

monopolist, *mŏnŏp'ŏlĭst*, s. monopolista,

monopolize, *-līz*, v.a. monopolizar. [m.

monopoly, *-lĭ*, s. monopolio, m.

monosyllabic, *mŏnŏsĭllăb'ĭk*, a. mono-silabo.

monosyllable, *-sĭl'lăbl*, s. monosílabo, m.

monotonous, *mŏnŏt'ŏnŭs*, a. monótono.

monotony, *-ŏnĭ*, s. monotonía, f.

monsoon, *mŏnsŏn'*, s. (mar.) monzón, m.

monster, *mŏn'stŭr*, s. monstruo, m.

monstrosity, *mŏnstrŏs'ĭtĭ*, s. monstruosidad, f.   [ad. monstruosamente.

monstrous, *mŏn'strŭs*, a. monstruoso; —ly,

month, *mŭnth*, s. mes, m.

monthly, *-lĭ*, a. (& ad.) mensual(mente).

monument, *mŏn'ūmĕnt*, s. monumento, m.

monumental, *mŏnūmĕn'tăl*, a. hecho en memoria.   [pricho, m.

mood, *mōd*, s. (gr.) modo, m.; humor, ca-

moodiness, *-ĭnĕs*, s. capricho, m.; extra-

moody, *-ĕ*, a. caprichoso.   [vagancia, f.

moon, *mōn*, s. luna, f.

moon-beam, *-bēm*, s. rayos lunares, m.pl.

moon-light, *-līt*, s. luz de la luna, f.

moon-shine, *-shīn*, s. claridad de la luna, f.; (fig.) ilusión, f.

moon-struck, *-strŭk*, a. lunático, loco.

moor, *mōr*, s. pantano, marjal, m.; moro, negro, m.; —, v. a. (mar) amarrar.

moot, *mōt*, v. a. debatir materias de ley.

mop, *mŏp*, s. estropajo, m.; —, v. a. aljofifar.   [estar triste.

mope, *mōp*, v. n. dormitar, entontecerse,

moral, *mŏr'ăl*, a. —ly, ad. moral(mente); —, s. moralidad, f.; —s, s. pl. costumbres, f. pl., usanza general, f.

moralise, *mŏr'ălīz*, v. a. & n. moralizar.

moralist, *-ĭst*, s. moralista, m.

morality, *mŏrăl'ĭtĭ*, s. ética, moralidad, f.

morass, *mŏrăs'*, s. lavajo, pantano, m.

morbid, *mŏr'bĭd*, a. enfermo, morboso.

more, *mōr*, s. & ad. más; never —, nunca más, jamás; once —, otra vez; — and —, más y más ó cada vez más; so much the —, cuanto más.   [también.

moreover, *mŏrō'vŭr*, ad. además, —, c.

morning, *mŏr'nĭng*, (poet.) morn, *mŏrn*, s. mañana, f.; good —, buenos días, m.pl.

morning-gown, *-gōn*, s. bata, f.

morning-star, *-stăr*, s. lucero de la mañana, m.   [marroquí, m.

morocco(-leather), *mŏrŏk'kō (lĕthŭr)*, s.

morose, *mŏrōs'*, a. moroso ; cubezudo; —ly, ad. morosamente.

morrow, *mŏr'rō*, s. mañana, f.

morse, *mŏrs*, s. manatí,m., vaca marina,f.

morsel, *mŏr'sĕl*, s. bocado, m.

mortal, *mŏr'tăl*, a. mortal ; humano; —ly, ad. mortalmente ; —, s. mortal, m. (el hombre ó la mujer)

mortality, *mŏrtăl'ĭtĭ*, s. mortalidad, f.

mortar, *mŏr'tăr*, s. mortero, m.

mortgage, *mŏr'gāj*, s. hipoteca, f.; —, v.a. hipotecar.

mortgagee, *-ĕ*, s. acreedor hipotecario, m.

mortgager, *-ăr*, s. deudor hipotecario, m.

mortification, *mŏrtĭfĭkā'shŭn*, s. mortificación, f.; gangrena, f.

mortify, *mŏr'tĭfī*, v. a. (& n.) mortificar(se).

mortmain, *mŏrt'mān*, s. mano muerta, f.

mortuary, *mŏr'tūărĭ*, a. funeral.

mosaic, *mŏzā'ĭk*, s. obra mosaica, f.; —, a.

mosque, *mŏsk*, s. mezquita, f.   [mosaico.

mosquito, *mŏskē'tō*, s. mosquito, m.

moss, *mŏs*, s. (bot.) musgo, m.; moho, m.

mossy, *-ĕ*, a. mohoso.

most, *mōst*, a. los, las ó lo más; —, ad. sumamente, en sumo grado; —, s: los más; mayor número, m.; mayor valor,m.; at —, á lo más; —ly, ad. por lo común.

mote, *mōt*, s. mota, f.; átomo, m.

moth, *mŏth*, s. polilla, f.

mother, *mŭth'ŭr*, s. madre, f.; —of pearl, madreperla, f.

motherhood, *-hŭd*, s. maternidad, f.

mother-in-law, *-ĭnlă*, s. suegra, f.

motherless, *-lĕs*, a. sin madre.

motherly, *-lĭ*, a. maternal, materno.

mothy, *mŏth'ĕ*, a. apolillado.

motion, *mō'shŭn,* s. movimiento, m., moción, f.; proposición, f.; —, v. a. proponer.

motionless, *—lĕs,* a. inmoble, inmóvil.

motive, *mō'tiv,* a. & s. razón, f.; motivo, (m.). [garrado, gayado, barajado.

motley, *mŏt'lĕ,* mottled, *mŏt'tld,* a. abigotto, *mŏt'tō,* s. mote, m.; divisa, f.

mould, *mōld,* s. moho, m.; tierra, f.; suelo, m.; molde, m.; matriz, f.; —, v. a. enmohecer, moldar; formar; —, v. n. enmohecerse. [n.) convertir(se) en polvo.

moulder, *—ŭr,* s. moldeador, m.; —, v. a. (&

mouldiness, *—ĭnĕs,* s. moho, m.

moulding, *—ĭng,* s. molduras, f. pl., cornisamiento, m.

mouldy, *—ĕ,* a. mohoso, lleno de moho.

moult, *mōlt,* v. n. mudar, estar de muda las aves. [m.

mound, *mŏŭnd,* s. terraplén, baluarte, dique,

mount, *mŏŭnt,* s. monte, m.; montaña, f.; —, v. a. subir, levantar. [f., monte, m.

mountain, *mŏŭn'tĭn,* s. montaña, sierra,

mountaineer, *—ēr',* s. montañés, m.

mountainous, *—ŭs,* a. montañoso.

mountebank, *mŏŭn'tĕbăngk,* s. saltimbanco, charlatán, m.

mourn, *mōrn,* v. a. deplorar; —, v. n. lamentar; llevar luto.

mourner, *—ŭr,* s. lamentador, m.; llorón, m. [mente.

mournful, *—fŭl,* a. triste; —ly, ad. tristemourning, *—ĭng,* s. lamento, m.; luto, m.

mourningly, *—ĭnglĕ,* ad. tristemente.

mouse, *mŏŭs,* s. (mice, pl.) ratón, m.

moustache, *mŭstăsh',* s. bigotes, m. pl.

mouth, *mŏŭth,* s. boca, f.; entrada, f.; embocadura, f.; —, *mŏŭth,* v. a. & n. mascar; hablar á gritos.

mouthful, *mŏŭth'fŭl,* s. bocado, m.

mouth-piece, *—pēs,* s. boquilla de un instrumento de música, f.

move, *mōv,* v. a. mover; proponer; excitar; persuadir; mover á piedad; —, v. n. moverse, menearse; andar; marchar un ejército; —, s. movimiento, m.; movimiento (en el juego de ajedrez).

moveable, *—ŭbl,* a. movible, movedizo; —s, s. pl. muebles, m. pl. [moción, f.

movement, *—mĕnt,* s. movimiento, m.;

mover, *—ŭr,* s. motor, m.

moving, *—ĭng,* s. movimiento, m.; —, a. patético, persuasivo; —ly, ad. patéticamow, *mō,* v. a. guadañar; segar. [mente.

mower, *—ŭr,* s. guadañero, m.

much, *mŭtsh,* a. & ad. mucho; con mucho.

mucilage, *mŭ'sĭlăj,* s. mucílago, m.

mucous, *mŭ'kŭs,* a. mocoso, viscoso.

mud, *mŭd,* s. fango, limo, m.

muddle, *—dl,* v. a. enturbiar; embriagar.

muddy, *—dĕ,* a. cenagoso; turbio.

mud-wall, *—wăl,* s. tapia, f.

muff, *mŭf,* s. manguito, f.

muffle, *—l,* v. a. embozar; envolver.

mug, *mŭg,* s. cubilete, m.

muggy, *—gĕ,* a. húmedo. [morera, f.

mulberry, *mŭl'bĕrrĕ,* s. mora, f.; —tree, s. mora, f.

mulct, *mŭlkt,* v. a. multar; —, s. multa, f.

mule, *mŭl,* s. mulo, m.; mula, f.

mule-driver, *—drivŭr,* muleteer, *mŭlĕtēr',* s. mulero, m. [quier licor.

mull, *mŭl,* v. a. entibiar, calentar cualmullet, *mŭl'lĕt,* s. múgil, sargo, m. (pez).

multifarious, *mŭltĭfā'rĕŭs,* a. vario, diferente. [múltiplo, m.

multiple, *mŭl'tĭpl,* a. multíplice; —, s.

multiplicand, *mŭltĭplĭkănd',* s. (ar.) multiplicando, m.

multiplication, *mŭltĭplĭkā'shŭn,* s. multiplicación, f.; —table, tabla de multiplicar, f. [dor, m.

multiplicator, *—tŭr,* s. (ar.) multiplica-

multiplicity, *mŭltĭplĭs'ĭtĕ,* s. multiplicidad, f.

multiply, *mŭl'tĭplĕ,* v. a. multiplicar.

multitude, *mŭl'tĭtŭd,* s. multitud, f.; vulgo, m. [roso.

multitudinous, *mŭltĭtū'dĭnŭs,* a. nume-

mum, *mŭm,* ¡chito!, ¡silencio!

mumble, *mŭm'bl,* v. a. barbotar; —, v. n. gruñir, mormullar.

mummer, *mŭm'mŭr,* s. máscara, m. & f.

mummery, *—mărĕ,* s. momería, f.

mummy, *—mĕ,* s. momia, f.

mumps, *mŭmps,* s. pl. murria, f.; angina, f.

munch, *mŭntsh,* v. a. masticar á bocados grandes.

mundane, *mŭn'dān,* a. mundano.

municipal, *mŭnĭs'ĭpŭl,* a. municipal.

municipality, *mŭnĭsĭpăl'ĭtĕ,* s. municipalidad, f. [liberalidad, f.

munificence, *mŭnĭf'ĭsĕns,* s. munificencia,

munificent, *—sĕnt,* a. munífico, liberal.

muniment, *mū'nĭmĕnt,* s. (law) título, documento, m.

muniment-house, *—hŏŭs,* s. archivo, m.

munition, *mŭnĭsh'ŭn,* s. pl. municiones, f. pl. [corona mural, f.

mural, *mū'rŭl,* a. mural; —crown, s.

murder, *mŭr'dŭr,* s. asesinato, homicidio, m.; —, v. a. asesinar, cometer homicidio.

murderer, *—ŭr,* s. asesino, m.

murderess, *—ĕs,* s. matadora, f.

murderous, *—ŭs,* a. sanguinario, cruel.

murky, *mŭr'kĕ,* a. obscuro, lóbrego.

murmur, *mŭr'mŭr,* s. murmullo, murmurio, m.; —, v. n. murmurar.

murmuringly, *—ĭnglĕ,* ad. con murmullo.

murrain, *mŭr'rān,* s. morriña, f.

muscle, *mŭs'l,* s. músculo, m.

muscular, *mŭs'kŭlŭr,* a. muscular.

muse, *mūz,* s. musa, f.; meditación profunda, f.; —, v. r. meditar; pensar profundamente.

museum, *mūzē'ŭm,* s. museo, m.

mushroom, *mŭsh'rŏm,* s. (bot.) seta, f.

music, *mū'zĭk,* s. música, f.

musical, *—ăl,* a. musical; melodioso; —ly, ad. con armonía.

music-hall, *—hăl,* s. sala de concierto, f.

musician, *mūzĭsh'ăn,* s. músico, m.

musing, *mū'zĭng,* s. meditación, f.

musk, *mŭsk,* s. musco, m.

musket, *mŭs'kĕt,* s. mosquete, m.

musketeer, *—ēr',* s. mosquetero, m.

musketry, *—rĕ,* s. mosquetería, f.

musky, *mŭs'kĕ,* a. almizcleño.

muslin, *mŭz'lĭn,* s. muselina, f.

mussel, *mŭs'ĕl,* s. marisco, m.

must, *mŭst,* v. imp. & def. estar obligado; ser menester, ser necesario, convenir.

mustard, *mŭs'tŭrd,* s. mostaza, f. [f.

mustard-seed, *—sēd,* s. simiente de jenabe.

muster, *mŭs'tŭr,* v. a. pasar revista de tropa; agregar; —, s. (mil.) revista, f.

musty, *mŭs'tĭ,* a. mohoso, añejo.

mutability, *mūtăbĭl'ĭtĭ,* s. mutabilidad, inconstancia, f. [mutación, f.

mutation, *mūtā'shŭn,* s. mudanza, f.

mute, *mūt,* a. mudo, silencioso; **—ly,** ad. mudamente, sin chistar.

mutilate, *mū'tĭlāt,* v. a. mutilar.

mutilation, *mūtĭlā'shŭn,* s. mutilación, f.

mutineer, *mūtĭnēr',* s. amotinador, sedicioso, m. [amotinadamente.

mutinous, *mū'tĭnŭs,* a. sedicioso; **—ly,** ad.

mutiny, *mū'tĭnĭ,* s. motín, tumulto, m.; —, v. n. amotinarse, rebelarse.

mutter, *mŭt'tŭr,* v. a. & n. murmurar, musitar; —, s. murmuración, f.

mutton, *mŭt'n,* s. carnero, m.

mutual, *mū'tūăl,* a. mutuo, mutual, recíproco; **—ly,** ad. mutuamente, recíprocamente.

muzzle, *mŭz'l,* s. bozal, frenillo, m.; hocico, m.; jeta, f.; —, v. a. embozar.

my, *mī,* pn. mi, mis, mía; mío, mía; míos, mías.

myriad, *mĭr'ĭăd,* s. miriada, f.; gran número, m.

myrrh, *mŭr,* s. mirra, f. [mero, m.

myrtle, *mŭrt'l,* s. mirto, arrayán, m.

myself, *mĭsĕlf',* pn. yo mismo.

mysterious, *mĭstē'rĭŭs,* a. misterioso; **—ly,** ad. misteriosamente.

mystery, *mĭs'tŭrĭ,* s. misterio, m.

mystic(al), *mĭs'tĭk(ăl),* a. místico; **—ally,** ad. místicamente. [m.; burla, f.

mystification, *mĭstĭfĭkā'shŭn,* s. chasco.

mystify, *mĭs'tĭfī,* v. a. chasquear, burlar.

myth, *mĭth,* s. fábula mitológica, f.

mythologic(al), *mĭthŏlŏj'ĭk(ăl),* a. mitológico.

mythology, *mĭthŏl'ŏjē,* s. mitología, f.

N.

nab, *năb,* v. a. atrapar, apiolar.

nag, *năg,* s. haca, jaca, f. [—, v. a. clavar.

nail, *nāl,* s. uña, f.; garra, f.; clavo, m.; **—ailery,** *—ŭrē,* s. fábrica de clavos, f.

naked, *nā'kĕd,* a. desnudo; evidente; puro, simple; **—ly,** ad. desnudamente; claramente, patentemente. [f.

nakedness, *—nĕs,* s. desnudez, f.; claridad, f.; —, v. n. nombrar; mencionar.

name, *nām,* s. nombre, m.; fama, reputación, f.; —, v. n. nombrar; mencionar.

nameless, *—lĕs,* a. anónimo.

namely, *—lĕ,* ad. particularmente; á saber.

namesake, *—sāk,* s. tocayo, colombroño.

nankeen, *năngkēn',* s. mahón, m. [m.

nap, *năp,* s. sueño ligero, m.; lanilla, f.

nape, *nāp,* s. nuca, f.

naphtha, *năp'thă,* s. nafta, f.

napkin, *năp'kĭn,* s. servilleta, f.

narcissus, *nărsĭs'sŭs,* s. (bot.) narciso, m.

narcotic(al), *nărkŏt'ĭk(ăl),* a. narcótico.

narrate, *năr'rāt,* v. a. narrar, relatar.

narration, *nărrā'shŭn,* s. narración, relación de alguna cosa, f.

narrative, *năr'rătĭv,* a. narrativo.

narrow, *năr'rō,* a. angosto, estrecho; avariento; próximo; escrupuloso; **—ly,** ad. estrechamente; —, v. a. estrechar; limitar.

narrowness, *—nĕs,* s. angostura, estrechez.

nasal, *nā'săl,* a. nasal. [f.; pobreza.

nascent, *năs'sĕnt,* a. naciente.

nastily, *năs'tĭlĕ,* ad. suciamente.

nastiness, *năs'tĭnĕs,* s. porquería, obscenidad, f. [sórdido.

nasty, *năs'tĭ,* a. sucio, puerco; obsceno;

natal, *nā'tăl,* a. nativo; natal.

nation, *nā'shŭn,* s. nación, f. [(mente).

national, *năsh'ŭnăl,* a. **—ly,** ad. nacional.

nationalise, *năsh'ŭnălīz,* v. a. hacer nacional. [f.

nationality, *năshŭnăl'ĭtĭ,* s. nacionalidad, f.

native, *nā'tĭv,* a. nativo; —, s. natural, m.

nativity, *nătĭv'ĭtĭ,* s. nacimiento, m.; origen, m.; horóscopo, m.

natural, *năt'ŭrăl,* a. natural; sencillo; ilegítimo; **—ly,** ad. naturalmente; —, s. (mus.) becuadro, m.

naturalist, *—ĭst,* s. naturalista, m.

naturalise, *năt'ŭrălīz,* v. a. naturalizar.

nature, *nā'tŭr* (*nā'tshŭr*), s. naturaleza, f.; índole, f. [verso, indigno.

naught, *nŏt,* s. nada, f.; —, a. malo, perverso.

naughtily, *—tĭlē,* ad. malvadamente.

naughtiness, *—tĭnĕs,* s. maldad, malignidad, f. [dad, f.

naughty, *—ē,* a. malo, malvado.

nausea, *nŏ'shĭă,* s. náusea, gana de vomitar, f. [sear, tener disgusto.

nauseate, *—shāt,* v. a. dar disgusto; nausear.

nauseous, *nŏ'shŭs,* a. fastidioso; **—ly,** ad. con náusea. [náutico, naval.

nautic(al), *nŏ'tĭk(ăl),* a. naval, *nā'văl,* a.

nave, *nāv,* s. cubo, m.; nave (de la iglesia).

navel, *nā'vl,* s. ombligo, m. [f.

navigable, *năv'ĭgăbl,* a. navegable.

navigate, *năv'ĭgāt,* v. n. navegar. [f.

navigation, *năvĭgā'shŭn,* s. navegación, f.

navvy, *năv'vē,* s. quebrantaterrones, m.

navy, *nā'vē,* s. marina, f.; armada, f.

nay, *nā,* ad. no; y aun, aun más.

near, *nēr,* pr. cerca de, junto á; —, ad. casi; cerca, cerca de; —, a. cercano, próximo, inmediato; allegado. [mente.

nearly, *—lē,* ad. á poca distancia; estrechamente.

nearness, *—nĕs,* s. proximidad, f.; mezquindad, f.

near-sighted, *nēr'sītĕd,* a. miope.

neat, *nēt,* a. hermoso, pulido; puro, neto; **—ly,** ad. elegantemente; —, s. ganado vacuno, m.

neatness, *—nĕs,* s. pulidez, elegancia, f

nebulous, *nĕb'ŭlŭs,* a. nebuloso.

necessaries, *nĕs'ĕsărĭz,* s. pl. necesario, m.

necessarily, *nĕs'ĕsărĭlĕ,* ad. necesariamente.

necessary, *nĕs'ĕsărĭ,* a. necesario.

necessitate, *nĕsĕs'tĭtāt,* v. a. necesitar.

necessitous, *—tŭs,* a. indigente, pobre.

necessity, *-ĭtĭ,* s. necesidad. f.

neck, *nĕk,* s. cuello, m.; **-of land,** lengua de tierra entre dos mares, f.

neckerchief, *-ărtshĭf,* s. corbata, f.; pañuelo de cuello, m.

necklace, *-lās,* s. collar, m. [f.

necromancy, *nĕk'rŏmănsĭ,* s. necromancia.

nectar, *nĕk'tăr,* s. néctar, m.

need, *nēd,* s. necesidad, f.; pobreza, f.; **-,** v. a. & n. pedir; necesitar.

needful, *-fŭl,* a. necesario, indispensable; **-ly,** ad. necesariamente. [f.

neediness, *-ĭnĕs,* s. indigencia, pobreza.

needle, *nē'dl,* s. aguja, f. [m.

needle-case, *-kās,* s. alfiletero, palillero.

needless, *nēd'lĕs,* a. superfluo, inútil.

needle-work, *nē'dlwŭrk,* s. costura, f.; bordado de aguja, m., obra de punto, m.

needs, *nēdz,* ad. necesariamente. [pobre.

needy, *nē'dĭ,* a. indigente, necesitado.

nefarious, *nĕfā'rĭŭs,* a. nefario.

negation, *nĕgā'shŭn,* s. negación, f.

negative, *nĕg'ătĭv,* a. negativo; **-ly,** ad. negativamente; **-,** s. negativa, f.

neglect, *nĕglĕkt',* v. a. descuidar, desatender; **-,** s. negligencia, f. [descuido, f.

negligence, *nĕg'lĭjĕns,* s. negligencia, f.

negligent, *nĕg'lĭjĕnt,* a. negligente, descuidado; **-ly,** ad. negligentemente.

negotiable, *nĕgō'shĭăbl,* a. negociable.

negotiate, *nĕgō'shĭāt,* v. n. negociar, comerciar. [ción, f.; negocio, m.

negotiation, *nĕgōshĭā'shŭn,* s. negociación, f.

negress, *nē'grĕs,* s. negra, f.

negro, *nē'grō,* s. negro, etíope, m. [m.

neigh, *nā,* v. n. relinchar; **-,** s. relincho.

neighbour, *nā'bŭr,* s. vecino, m.; **-,** v. a. confinar. [vecindario, m.

neighbourhood, *-hŭd,* s. vecindad, f.

neighbourly, *-lĭ,* a. sociable.

neither, *nē'thăr* c. ni; **-,** pn. ninguno, ni uno ni otro.

neophyte, *nē'ŏfĭt,* s. neófito, novicio, m.

nephew, *nĕv'ū,* s. sobrino, m.

nepotism, *nĕp'ŏtĭzm,* s. nepotismo, m.

nerve, *nŭrv,* s. nervio, m.; vigor, m.

nerveless, *-lĕs,* a. enervado, débil.

nervous, *năr'vŭs,* a. nervoso; nervudo.

nest, *nĕst,* s. nido, m.; nidada, f.

nestle, *nĕs'l,* v. a. anidarse.

nestling, *nĕs'tlĭng,* s. pollo, m.

net, *nĕt,* s. red, f.

nether, *nĕth'ŭr,* a. inferior, más bajo.

netting, *nĕt'tĭng,* s. mallado, m.

nettle, *nĕt'tl,* s. ortiga, f.; **-,** v. a. picar como ortiga; irritar. [(gr.) neutro.

neuter, *nū'tăr,* a. neutral, indiferente; **-,**

neutral, *nū'trăl,* a. neutral; **-ly,** ad. neutralmente.

neutrality, *nūtrăl'ĭtĭ,* s. neutralidad, f.

neutralize, *nū'trălīz,* v. a. neutralizar.

never, *nĕv'ăr,* ad. nunca, jamás; **- mind,** no importa; **- a whit,** ni una pizca.

nevertheless, *-thĕlĕs,* ad. no obstante que.

new, *nū,* a. nuevo, fresco, reciente; **-ly,** ad. nuevamente.

new-comer, *-kŭmăr,* s. recién llegado, m.

new-fangled, *-făngld,* a. inventado por [novedad.

newness, *-nĕs,* s. novedad, f.

news, *nūz,* s. pl. novedad, nuevas, f. pl.

news-monger, *-mŭngŭr,* s. novelero, m.

newspaper, *-pāpŭr,* s. gaceta, f.

next, *nĕkst,* a. próximo; **the - day,** el día siguiente; **-,** ad. luego, inmediatamente después.

nib, *nĭb,* s. pico, m.; punta, f. [después.

nibble, *-bl,* v. a. picar; **-,** v. n. mordiscar; criticar.

nice, *nĭs,* a. delicado, exacto, solícito; circunspecto; tierno; fino; elegante; escrupuloso; **-ly,** ad. primorosamente.

niceness, *-nĕs,* **nicety,** *-ĭtĭ,* s. exactitud, f.; esmero, m.; delicadeza, f.; niceties, m.

niche, *nĭtsh,* s. nicho, m. [pl. golosina, f.

nick, *nĭk,* s. punto crítico, m.; ocasión oportuna, f.; **- old -,** el diablo; **-,** v. a. dar en el hito; llegar á tiempo.

nickel, *nĭk'kl,* s. níquel, m.

nickname, *-nām,* s. mote, apodo, m.; **-,** v. a. poner apodos.

niece, *nēs,* s. sobrina, f.

niggard, *nĭg'gărd,* s. hombre avaro y mezquino, m. [seria, f.

niggardliness, *-lĭnĕs,* s. tacañería, f.

niggardly, *-lĭ,* a. avaro, sórdido; **-,** ad. tacañamente, miserablemente.

nigger, *nĭg'gŭr,* s. negro, m. **-s,** pl. recortadores de piezas de moneda, m. pl.

nigh, *nī,* pr. cerca, no lejos; **-,** ad. cerca, inmediato; **-,** a. cercano; **-ly,** ad. cercanamente. [good - buenas noches.

night, *nīt,* s. noche, f.; **by -,** de noche;

night-fall, *-făl,* s. anochecer, m.

nightingale, *-ĭngāl,* s. ruiseñor, m.

night-light, *-līt,* s. vela de noche, f.; lamparillas para luz, f. pl.

nightly, *-lĭ,* ad. por las noches, todas las noches; **-,** a. nocturno.

night-mare, *-mār,* s. pesadilla, f. [f.

night-shade, *-shăd,* s. (bot.) hierbamora.

nihilist, *nī'hĭlĭst,* s. nihilista, m.

nimble, *nĭm'bl,* a. ligero, activo, listo, ágil.

nimbly, *-ĭ,* ad. ágilmente.

nimbus, *nĭm'bŭs,* s. auréola, f.

nine, *nīn,* a. nueve.

nine-pins, *-pĭnz,* s. juego de bolos, m.

nineteen, *-tēn,* a. diez y nueve.

nineteenth, *-tēnth,* a. décimonono.

ninetieth, *-tĭĕth,* a. nonagésimo.

ninety, *-tĭ,* a. noventa.

ninny, *nĭn'nĭ,* s. badulaque, bobo, m.

ninth, *nĭnth,* a. nono, noveno; **-ly,** ad. en nono lugar.

nip, *nĭp,* v. a. arañar, rasguñar; morder.

nippers, *-pŭrz,* s. pl. alicates, m. pl.

nipping, *-pĭng,* a. sensible (frío).

nipple, *-pl,* s. pezón, m.

nit, *nĭt,* s. liendre, f.

nitre, *nī'tŭr,* s. nitro, m.

no, *nō,* ad. no; **-,** a. ningún, ninguno.

nobility, *nōbĭl'ĭtĭ,* s. nobleza, f.

noble, *nō'bl,* a. noble; insigne; generoso; **-,** s. noble, m.

nobleman, *-măn,* s. noble, m.

nobleness, *-nĕs,* s. nobleza, f.

nobly, *nō'blĭ,* ad. noblemente.

nobody, *nō'bŏdĭ,* s. nadie, ninguna persona, f. [turno,

nocturnal, *nŏktŭr'năl,* a. nocturnal, noc-

nod, *nŏd,* s. cabeceo, m.; señal, f.; —, v. n. cabecear; amodorrarse.

node, *nŏd,* s. nudo, m.; nodo, tumor, m.

noise, *nŏiz,* s. ruido, estruendo, m.; rumor, m.; —, v. a. divulgar alguna noticia.

noiseless, *—lĕs,* a. atentado, sin ruido.

noisily, *—lĭ,* ad, con ruido.

noisiness, *—ĭnĕs,* s. estrépito, ruido, tumulto, alboroto, m. [asqueroso.

noisome, *nŏi'săm,* a. nocivo, malsano;

noisy, *nŏi'zĭ,* a. ruidoso, turbulento.

nomadic, *nŏmăd'ĭk,* a. á modo de nómadas. [clatura, f.

nomenclature, *nŏmĕnklā'tūr,* s. nomenclatura, f.

nominal, *nŏm'ĭnăl,* a. -ly, ad. nominal- (mente).

nominate, *nŏm'ĭnāt,* v. a. nombrar. [f.

nomination, *nŏmĭnā'shăn,* s. nominación, f.

nominative, *nŏm'ĭnătĭv,* s. (gr.) nominativo, m. [f.

non-age, *nŏn'āj,* s. minoridad, menoredad, f.

non-attendance, *nŏnătĕn'dăns,* s. falta de asistencia, f.

non-descript, *—dĕskrĭpt',* a. no descrito.

none, *năn,* a. nadie, ninguno.

nonentity, *nŏnĕn'ĭtĭ,* s. nada, falta de existencia, f. [falta de ejecución, f.

non-performance, *nŏnpărfŏrm'ăns,* s.

nonplus, *nŏn'plŭs,* s. embarazo, m.; perplejidad, f.; —, v. a. confundir, embarazar.

non-resistance, *nŏnrĕzĭs'tăns,* s. obediencia pasiva, f. [m.

nonsense, *nŏn'sĕns,* s. disparate, absurdo,

nonsensical, *nŏnsĕn'sĭkăl,* a. absurdo.

nonsuit, *nŏn'sūt,* s. desistimiento de un proceso, m.; —, v. a. absolver de la instancia. [—s, pl. (am.) fideos, m. pl.

noodle, *nŏŏ'dl,* s. simplón, mentecato, m.;

nook, *nŏk,* s. rincón, ángulo, m.

noon, *nōn,* s. mediodía, m.

noontide, *—tĭd,* s. tiempo del mediodía, m.

noose, *nōz,* s. lazo corredizo, m.; —, v. a. [enlazar.

nor, *nŏr,* c, ni.

normal, *nŏr'măl,* a. normal. [nal.

north, *nŏrth,* s. norte, m.; —, a. septentrio-

northerly, *nŏr'thŭrlĭ,* **northern,** *nŏr'thărn,* a. septentrional.

north-pole, *nŏrth'pōl,* s. polo ártico, m.

northward(s), *—wărd(z),* ad. hacia el norte.

nose, *nōz,* s. nariz, f.; olfato, m.; sagacidad, f.

nose-bag, *—băg,* s. morral, m. [dad, f.

nosegay, *—gā,* s. ramillete, m.

nostril, *nŏs'trĭl,* s. ventana de la nariz, f.

nostrum, *nŏs'trăm,* s. arcano, m.

not, *nŏt,* ad. no.

notable, *nŏ'tăbl,* a. notable; memorable.

notably, *—ĭ,* ad. notablemente.

notary, *nŏ'tărĭ,* s. notario, m. [muescas.

notch, *nŏtsh,* s. muesca, f.; —, v. a. hacer

note, *nŏt,* s. nota, marca, f.; señal, f.; aprecio, m.; billete, m.; consecuencia, f.; noticia, f.; indirecta, f.; —, v. a. notar, marcar; observar.

note-book, *—bŭk,* s. librito de apuntes, m.

noted, *—ĕd,* a. afamado, célebre.

nothing, *năth'ĭng,* s. nada, f.; **good for —,** lo que sirve para nada.

notice, *nŏ'tĭs,* s. noticia, f.; aviso, m.; —, v. a. observar.

noticeable, *—ăbl,* a. notable, reparable.

notification, *nŏtĭfĭkā'shăn,* s. notificación, f.

notify, *nŏ'tĭfī,* v. a. notificar. [f.

notion, *nŏ'shăn,* s. noción, f.; opinión, f.; idea, f.

notoriety, *nŏtŏrī'ĕtĭ,* s. notoriedad, f.

notorious, *nŏtŏ'rĭŭs,* a. notorio; -ly, ad. notoriamente. [obstante, aunque.

notwithstanding, *nŏtwĭthstănd'ĭng,* c. no

nought, *nŏt,* s. nada, f.

noun, *nŏŭn,* s. (gr.) nombre, sustantivo, m.

nourish, *nŭr'ĭsh,* v. a. nutrir, alimentar.

nourishment, *—mĕnt,* s. nutrimiento, alimento, m.

novel, *nŏv'ĕl,* s. novela, f. [mento, m.

novelist, *—ĭst,* s. novelador, m.

novelty, *—tĭ,* s. novedad, f.

November, *nŏvĕm'băr,* s. noviembre, m.

novice, *nŏv'ĭs,* s. novicio, m.

noviciate, *nŏvĭsh'ĭāt,* s. noviciado, m.

now, *nŏŭ,* ad. ahora, en el tiempo presente; **— and then,** de cuando en cuando.

nowadays, *—dādz,* ad. al presente.

nowhere, *nŏ'hwăr,* ad. en ninguna parte.

nowise, *nŏ'wīz,* ad. de ningún modo.

noxious, *nŏk'shŭs,* a. nocivo, dañoso; -ly, ad. ad. perniciosamente.

nucleus, *nū'klĕŭs,* s. núcleo, m.

nude, *nūd,* a. desnudo, en carnes, en cueros, sin vestido; (law) nulo.

nudge, *nŭj,* v. a. dar del codo á uno para avisarle secretamente.

nudity, *nū'dĭtĭ,* s. desnudez, f.

nugatory, *nū'gătŭrĭ,* a. nugatorio, frívolo.

nuisance, *nū'săns,* s. daño, perjuicio, m.; incomodidad, f.

null, *nŭl,* a. nulo, inválido.

nullify, *nŭl'ĭfī,* v. a. anular, invalidar.

nullity, *nŭl'ĭtĭs,* s. nulidad, f. [pecer.

numb, *năm,* a. entorpecido; —, v. a. entor-

number, *năm'băr,* s. número, m., cantidad, f.; —, v. a. numerar. [mero.

numberless, *—lĕs,* a. innumerable, sin nú-

numbness, *năm'nĕs,* s. torpor, m.

numeral, *nū'mĕrăl,* a. numeral. [f.

numeration, *nūmĕrā'shăn,* s. numeración,

numerator, *nū'mĕrātŏr,* s. (ar.) numerador, m.

numerical, *nūmĕr'ĭkăl,* a. numérico.

numerous, *nū'mĕrŭs,* a. numeroso.

numismatics, *nūmĭsmăt'ĭks,* s. pl. numismática, f.

numskull, *năm'skŭl,* s. zote, m.

nun, *năn,* s. monja, religiosa, f. [m.

nunnery, *năn'nărĭ,* s. convento de monjas,

nuptial, *nŭp'shăl,* a. nupcial; **-s,** pl. nupcias, f. pl.

nurse, *nŭrs,* s. ama de cria, f.; enfermera, —, v. a. criar criaturas; alimentar.

nursery, *—ărĭ,* s. crianza, f.; plantel, m.

nursling, *nŭrs'lĭng,* s. niño de teta, m.

nurture, *nŭr'tŭr,* v. a. criar, educar.

nut, *nŭt,* s. nuez, f. [ces, m.

nut-crackers, *—krăkărz,* s. pl. cascanue-

nut-gall, *—gŏl,* s. agalla de monte, f.

nutmeg, *—mĕg,* s. quez moscada, f.

nutriment, *nū'trĭmĕnt,* s. nutrimento, alimento, m. [trimiento, m.

nutrition, *nūtrĭsh'ăn,* s. nutrición, f.; nu-

nutritious, nútrísh'ás, nutritive, nú'trītŭv, a. nutritivo, nutricio.
nut-shell, nŭt'shĕl, s. cáscara de nuez, f.
nut-tree, –trē, s. avellano, m.
nymph, nĭmf, s. ninfa, f.

O.

oaf, ōf, s. idiota, zoquete, m.
oak, ōk, s. roble, m.
oak-apple, –ăppl, s. agalla, f.
oaken, –n, a. (hecho) de roble.
oakum, ō'kŭm, s. (mar.) estopa, f.
oar, ōr, s. remo, m.
oarsman, ōrz'măn, s. remero, m.
oasis, ōā'sĭs, s. oasis, f.
oat, ōt, s. avena, f.
oath, ōth, s. juramento, m.
obduracy, ŏb'dŭrāsē, s. endurecimiento, m.; dureza de corazón, f.
obdurate, ŏb'dŭrāt, a. endurecido, duro; –ly, ad. tercamente, ásperamente.
obedience, ŏbē'dīĕns, s. obediencia, f.
obedient, ŏbē'dīĕnt, a. –ly, ad. obediente(mente).
obeisance, ŏbā'săns, s. cortesía, reverencia, f.
obelisk, ŏb'ēlĭsk, s. obelisco, m.
obese, ŏbēs', a. obeso, gordo.
obesity, ŏbē'sĭtē, s. obesidad, crasitud, f.
obey, ŏbā', v. a. obedecer.
obituary, ŏbĭt'ūārē, s. necrología, f.
object, ŏb'jĕkt, s. objeto, m.; –, ŏbjĕkt', v. a. objetar.
objection, ŏbjĕk'shŭn, s. oposición, objeción, f.; réplica, f.
objectionable, –ăbl, a. capaz de objeción.
objective, ŏbjĕk'tĭv, a. objetivo. [f.
oblation, ŏblā'shŭn, s. oblación, ofrenda, f.
obligation, ŏblĭgā'shŭn, s. obligación, f.
obligatory, ŏb'lĭgătŭrē, a. obligatorio.
oblige, ŏblīj', v. a. obligar; complacer, favorecer. [cortesmente.
obliging, ŏblī'jĭng, a. servicial; –ly, ad.
oblique, ŏblēk', a. oblicuo; indirecto; –ly, ad. oblicuamente.
obliquity, ŏblĭk'wĭtē, s. oblicuidad, f.
obliterate, ŏblĭt'ārăt, v. a. borrar.
oblivion, ŏblĭv'ĕăn, s. olvido, m.
oblivious, –ĭăs, a. olvidadizo.
oblong, ŏb'lŏng, a. oblongo.
obloquy, ŏb'lōkwē, s. maledicencia, f.; deshonra, f. [pable.
obnoxious, ŏbnŏk'shăs, a. sujeto; culpable.
obscene, ŏbsēn', a. obsceno, impúdico.
obscenity, ŏbsēn'ĭtē, s. obscenidad, f.
obscure, ŏbskūr', a. obscuro; –ly, ad. obscuramente; –, v. a. obscurecer.
obscurity, ŏbskū'rĭtē, s. obscuridad, f.
obsequies, ŏb'sēkwĭz, s. pl. exequias, honras funerales, f. pl.
obsequious, ŏbsē'kwĭăs, a. obsequioso; –ly, ad. obsequiosamente. [spicuo.
observable, ŏbzŭr'văbl, a. notable, conspicuo.
observance, –văns, s. observancia, f.; reverencia, f. [tuoso.
observant, –vănt, a. observante, respe-

observation, ŏbzŭrvā'shŭn, s. observación, f. [rio, m.
observatory, ŏbzŭr'vătŭrē, s. observatorio, m.
observe, ŏbzŭrv', v. a. observar, mirar; –, v. n. ser circunspecto.
observer, –ŭr, s. observador, m.
observingly, ŏbzŭr'vĭnglē, ad. cuidadosamente, atentamente.
obsolete, ŏb'sōlĕt, a. obsoleto.
obstacle, ŏb'stăkl, s. obstáculo, m.
obstinacy, ŏb'stĭnăsē, s. obstinación, f.
obstinate, ŏb'stĭnăt, a. obstinado; –ly, ad. obstinadamente.
obstreperous, ŏbstrĕp'ărŭs, a. estrepitoso, turbulento. [pedir.
obstruct, ŏbstrŭkt', v. a. obstruir; impedir.
obstruction, ŏbstrŭk'shŭn, s. obstrucción, f.; impedimento, m.; obstrucción de los debates parlamentarios.
obtain, ŏbtān', v. a. obtener, adquirir; –, v. n. estar establecido.
obtainable, –ăbl, a. asequible. [lencia.
obtrude, ŏbtrōd', v. a. introducir con violencia.
obtrusive, ŏbtrō'sĭv, a. intruso, importuno. [torpe.
obtuse, ŏbtūs', a. obtuso, sin punta; lerdo, torpe.
obviate, ŏb'vĭăt, v. a. obviar, evitar.
obvious, ŏb'vĭăs, a. obvio, evidente; –ly, ad. patentemente.
occasion, ŏkkā'zhăn, s. ocasión, ocurrencia, f.; tiempo oportuno, m.; –, v. a. ocasionar, causar. [ad. ocasionalmente.
occasional, –ăl, a. ocasional, casual; –ly,
occident, ŏk'sĭdĕnt, s. occidente, m.
occidental, ŏksĭdĕn'tăl, a. occidental.
occult, ŏkkŭlt', a. oculto, escondido.
occupancy, ŏk'kăpănsē, s. toma de posesión, f.
occupant, ŏk'kăpănt, occupier, ŏk'kŭpīăr, s. ocupador, m.; poseedor, m.; inquilino, m. [f.; empleo, m.
occupation, ŏkkăpā'shŭn, s. ocupación, f.
occupy, ŏk'kŭpī, v. a. ocupar, emplear.
occur, ŏkkŭr', v. n. ocurrir; encontrarse.
occurrence, –rĕns, s. ocurrencia, f.; incidente, m.
ocean, ō'shăn, s. océano, m.; alta mar, f.
oceanic, ōshĕăn'ĭk, a. oceánico; inmenso.
ochre, ō'kŭr, s. ocra, f.
octave, ŏk'tăv, s. octava, f. [octavo.
octavo, ŏktā'vō, s. libro en octavo, m.; –, a.
October, ŏktō'băr, s. octubre, m.
ocular, ŏk'ŭlăr, a. ocular.
oculist, ŏk'ŭlĭst, s. oculista, m.
odd, ŏd, a. impar; particular; extravagante; extraño; tonto; –ly, ad. extrañamente. [dad, rareza, f.
oddity, –dĭtē, s. singularidad, particularidad, f.
oddness, –nĕs, s. disparidad, desigualdad, f.; singularidad, f.
odds, –z, s. diferencia, disparidad, f.; ventaja, superioridad, f. [mente.
odious, ō'dĭăs, a. odioso; –ly, ad. odiosamente.
odium, ō'dĭăm, s. odiosidad, f.; odio, m.
odorous, ō'dărŭs, a. odorífero.
odour, ō'dăr, s. olor, m.; fragancia, f.
of, ŏv, pr. de; tocante; según.
off, ŏf, ad. lejos, á distancia; –hand, de repente; –! ¡fuera!, ¡abajo!

offal, *ŏf′făl*, s. sobras, f. pl.; desecho, m.

offence, *ŏffĕns′*, s. ofensa, f.; injuria, f.

offend, *ŏffĕnd′*, v. a. ofender, irritar; injuriar; —, v. n. pecar.

offender, *—ăr*, s. delincuente, ofensor, m.

offensive, *ŏffĕn′sĭv*, a. ofensivo; injurioso; **—ly**, ad. ofensivamente.

offer, *ŏf′făr*, v. a. ofrecer; inmolar; atentar; —, v. n. ofrecerse; —, s. oferta, f.

offering, *—ĭng*, s. sacrificio, m.; oferta, f.

offertory, *—tărĭ*, s. ofertorio, m. [cio, m.

office, *ŏf′fĭs*, s. oficio, empleo, m.; servicio, m.

officer, *—ăr*, s. oficial, empleado, m.

official, *ŏffĭsh′ăl*, a. oficial; **—ly**, ad. de oficio; —, s. empleado, m.

officiate, *—āt*, v. a. hacer alguna cosa de oficio; —, v. n. oficiar. [ciosamente.

officious, *—ŭs*, a. oficioso; **—ly**, ad. oficiosamente.

offing, *ŏf′ĭng*, s. pleamar, f.

offscouring, *ŏf′skŏŭrĭng*, s. basura, f.; lavaduras, f. pl.

offset, *—sĕt*, s. pimpollo, m.

offspring, *—sprĭng*, s. prole, f.; linaje, m.; descendencia, f. [ad. muchas veces.

oft, *ŏft*, **often**, *ŏf′n*, **oftentimes**, *—tīmz*, ad. muchas veces.

ogle, *ō′gl*, v. a. mirar al soslayo; guiñar.

ogre, *ō′gr*, s. ogro, m. [aceitar.

oil, *ŏĭl*, s. aceite, m.; óleo, m.; —, v. a.

oil-cloth, *—klŏth*, s. encerado, hule, m.

oil-colour, *—kŭlăr*, s. color preparado con aceite.

oilman, *—măn*, s. aceitero, m. [aceite, m.

oil-painting, *—pāntĭng*, s. pintura al óleo, f. [rado, hule, m.

oil-silk, *—sĭlk*, **oil-skin**, *—skĭn*, s. encerado, hule, m.

oily, *—ĭ*, a. aceitoso, oleaginoso.

ointment, *ŏĭnt′mĕnt*, s. ungüento, m.

old, *ōld*, **olden**, *ōl′dn*, a. viejo; antiguo; of —, antiguamente.

oleaginous, *ōlĕăj′ĭnŭs*, a. oleaginoso.

oleander, *ōlăn′dăr*, s. adelfa, f.; baladre, f.

olfactory, *ŏlfăk′tărĭ*, s. olfatorio, [m.

olive, *ŏl′ĭv*, s. olivo, m.; oliva, f.

olive-grove, *—grōv*, s. olivar, m.

olive-oil, *—ŏĭl*, s. aceite de olivas, m.

olive-tree, *—trĭ*, s. olivo, m.

omelet, *ŏm′lĕt*, s. tortilla de huevos, f.

omen, *ō′mĕn*, s. agüero, presagio, m.

omened, *—d*, a. fatídico, augural.

ominous, *ŏm′ĭnŭs*, a. ominoso; **—ly**, ad. ominosamente. [cuido, m.

omission, *ŏmĭsh′ăn*, s. omisión, f.; descuido, m.

omit, *ŏmĭt′*, v. a. omitir.

omnibus, *ŏm′nĭbŭs*, s. ómnibus, m.

omnipotence, *ŏmnĭp′ōtĕns*, s. omnipotencia, f. [dopoderoso.

omnipotent, *—tĕnt*, a. omnipotente, todopoderoso.

omniscience, *ŏmnĭsh′ĭĕns*, s. omnisciencia, f.

on, *ŏn*, pr. sobre, encima, en; de; á; —; ad. adelante, sin cesar; — ! ¡vamos! ¡adelante!

once, *wŭns*, ad. una vez; — for all, una vez por todas; at —, a un golpe; all at —, de una vez, de seguida; — more, más todavía, otra vez. [uno por uno.

one, *wŭn*, a. un, uno; — by —, uno á uno.

onerous, *ŏn′ărŭs*, a. oneroso, molesto.

oneself, *wŭnsĕlf′*, pn. sí mismo.

onion, *ŭn′yŭn*, s. cebolla, f.

only, *ōn′lĭ*, a. único, solo; —, ad. solamente.

onset, *ŏn′sĕt*, **onslaught**, *ŏn′slăt*, s. primer ímpetu, m.; ataque, m.

onward(s), *ŏn′wărd(z)*, ad. adelante.

ooze, *ōz*, s. fango, m.; —, v. n. manar ó correr algún líquido suavemente.

opacity, *ŏpăs′ĭtĭ*, s. opacidad, f.

opal, *ō′păl*, s. ópalo, m.

opaque, *ōpāk′*, a. opaco.

open, *ō′pn*, a. abierto; patente, evidente; sincero, franco; **—ly**, ad. con franqueza; —, v. a. (& n.) abrir(se); descubrir(se).

open-handed, *—hăndĕd*, a. dadivoso, liberal. [sencillo.

open-hearted, *—hărtĕd*, a. franco, sincero, sencillo.

opening, *—ĭng*, s. abertura, f.; (com.) salida, f.; principio, m. [sinceridad, f.

openness, *—nĕs*, s. claridad, f.; franqueza, f.; sinceridad, f.

open-work, *—wărk*, s. obra á claros, f.

opera, *ŏp′ără*, s. ópera, f.

opera-glass, *—glăs*, s. anteojo de ópera, m.

opera-hat, *—hăt*, s. clac, m.

operate, *ŏp′ărāt*, v. n. obrar, operar.

operatical, *ŏpărăt′ĭkăl*, a. de ópera.

operation, *ŏpărā′shăn*, s. operación, f.; efecto, m.

operative, *ŏp′ărătĭv*, a. operativo.

operator, *ŏp′ărātăr*, s. operario, m.; (med.) operador, m.

ophthalmy, *ŏf′thălmĭ*, s. oftalmía, f.

opiate, *ō′pĭāt*, s. opiata, f.

opine, *ōpīn′*, v. n. opinar, juzgar.

opinion, *ōpĭn′yŭn*, s. opinión, f.; juicio, m.

opinionative, *—ătĭv*, a. obstinado, pertinaz. [arguyente, m.

opponent, *ŏppō′nĕnt*, s. antagonista, m.; arguyente, m.

opportune, *ŏppŏrtūn′*, a. oportuno; **—ly**, ad. oportunamente. [f.

opportunity, *—ĭtĭ*, s. oportunidad, sazón, f.

oppose, *ŏppōz′*, v. n. oponer(se).

opposite, *ŏp′pŏsĭt*, a. fronterizo, opuesto; contrario; **—ly**, ad. enfrente; —, s. antagonista, adversario, m.

opposition, *ŏppŏzĭsh′ăn*, s. oposición, f.; resistencia, f.; impedimento, m.

oppress, *ŏpprĕs′*, v. a. oprimir. [ción, f.

oppression, *ŏpprĕsh′ăn*, s. opresión, vejación, f.

oppressive, *ŏpprĕs′sĭv*, a. opresivo, cruel.

oppressor, *ŏpprĕs′săr*, s. opresor, m.

opprobrious, *ŏpprō′brĭŭs*, a. oprobioso, ignominioso. [oprobio, m.

opprobrium, *—brĭăm*, s. ignominia, f.; oprobio, m.

optic(al), *ŏp′tĭk(ăl)*, a. óptico; **—s**, s. pl. óptica, f.

optician, *ŏptĭsh′ăn*, s. óptico, m.

optimist, *ŏp′tĭmĭst*, s. optimista, m.

option, *ŏp′shăn*, s. opción, f.; deseo, m. [f.

optional, *—ăl*, a. facultativo.

opulence, *ŏp′ŭlĕns*, s. opulencia, riqueza, f.

opulent, *ŏp′ŭlĕnt*, a. opulento; **—ly**, ad. opulentamente.

or, *ŏr*, ó; ú.

oracle, *ŏr′ăkl*, s. oráculo, m.

oracular, *ŏrăk′ŭlăr*, a. obscuro, ambiguo.

oral, *ō′răl*, a. oral, vocal; **—ly**, ad. verbalmente, de palabra.

orange, *ŏr′ĕnj*, s. naranja, f.

orange-tree, *—trĭ*, s. naranjo, m.

oration, ŏrā´shŏn, s. oración, arenga, f.

orator, ŏr´ātŏr, s. orador, m.　　　[ric.

oratorio(al), ŏrătŏ´rĭŏ(ăl), a. retórico, orato-

oratory, ŏr´ătŏrĕ, s. oratoria, f.; oratorio, m.; elocuencia, arte oratoria, f.

orb, ŏrb, s. orbe, m.; esfera, f.; globo, m.

orbit, ŏr´bĭt, s. órbita, f.

orchard, ŏ´tshărd, s. pomar, verjel, m.

orchestra, ŏr´kĕstrā, s. orquesta, f.

ordain, ŏrdān´, v. a. ordenar; establecer.

ordeal, ŏr´dēăl, s. ordalía, f.

order, ŏr´dĕr, s. orden, m. & f.; regla, f.; mandato, m.; serie, clase, f.; —, v. a. or- denar, arreglar; mandar. [disposición, f.

ordering, -ĭng, s. manejo, m.; dirección,

orderly, -lĕ, a. ordenado, regular.

ordinance, ŏr´dĭnăns, s. ordenanza, f.

ordinarily, ŏr´dĭnărĭlĕ, ad. ordinaria- mente.　　　[dinario, m.; hostería, f.

ordinary, ŏr´dĭnărĕ, a. ordinario; —, s. or-

ordination, ŏrdĭnā´shŏn, s. ordenación, f.

ordnance, ŏrd´năns, s. artillería, f., caño- ore, ŏr, s. mineral, m.　　　[nes, m. pl.

organ, ŏr´găn, s. órgano, m.

organic(al), ŏrgăn´ĭk(ăl), a. orgánico.

organisation, ŏrgănĭzā´shŏn, s. organi- zación, f.

organise, ŏr´gănĭz, v. a. organizar.

organism, ŏr´gănĭzm, s. organismo, m.

organist, ŏr´gănĭst, s. organista, m.

organ-pipe, ŏr´gănpīp, s. fístula de ór- gano, f.　　　[gano, m.

organ-stop, -stŏp, s. registro de un ór-

oriental, ŏrĭĕn´tăl, a. oriental.

orifice, ŏr´ĭfĭs, s. orificio, m.

origin, ŏr´ĭjĭn, s. origen, principio, m.

original, ŏrĭj´ĭnăl, a. original, primitivo; -ly, ad. originalmente.

originality, ŏrĭjĭnăl´ĭtĕ, s. originalidad, f.

originate, ŏrĭj´ĭnāt, v. a. (& n.) originar(se).

orison, ŏr´ĭzŏn, s. oración, f.; rezo, m.

ormolu, ŏr´mŏlū, s. oro molido, m.

ornament, ŏr´nămĕnt, s. ornamento, m.; —, v. a. ornamentar, adornar.　　[adorno.

ornamental, -mĕn´tăl, a. lo que sirve de

ornate, ŏr´nāt, a. adornado, ataviado.

orphan, ŏr´făn, a. & s. huérfano (m.).

orphanage, -āj, s. orfandad, f.

orphan-asylum, -ăsīlŭm, s. casa de huérfanos, f.; orfanotrofio, m.

orthodox, ŏr´thŏdŏks, a. ortodoxo.

orthodoxy, -ĕ, s. ortodoxia, f.

orthographical, ŏrthŏgră´fĭkăl, a. ortográ- fico; -ly, ad. ortográficamente.

orthography, ŏrthŏg´răfĕ, s. ortografía, f.

oscillate, ŏs´sĭlāt, v. n. oscilar, vibrar.

oscillation, ŏssĭllā´shŏn, s. oscilación, vibración, f.

osier, ŏ´zhĕr, s. (bot.) mimbrera, f.

osprey, ŏs´prā, s. águila marina, f.

ossification, ŏssĭfĭkā´shŏn, s. osificación, f.

ossify, ŏs´sĭfĭ, v. a. & n. osificar(se).　[f.

ostensible, ŏstĕn´sĭbl, a. ostensible, mani- festable.

ostensibly, -sĭblĕ, ad. ostensiblemente.

ostentation, ŏstĕntā´shŏn, s. ostentación, f.

ostentatious, -shŭs, a. ostentoso, fas- tuoso; -ly, ad. pomposamente.

ostler, ŏs´lĕr, s. mozo de caballos, m.

ostracise, ŏs´trăsĭz, v. a. desterrar por medio del ostracismo.

ostrich, ŏs´trĭtsh, s. avestruz, m.

other, ŭth´ĕr, pn. otro.　　　[otra parte.

otherwise, -wĭz, ad. de otra manera, por

otter, ŏt´tĕr, s. nutra, nutria, f.

ottoman, ŏt´tŏmăn, s. otomana, f.; sofá, m.

ought, ăt, v. imp. & def. deber, ser menes-

ounce, ŏŭns, s. onza, f.　　　[ter.

our, ŏŭr, ours, ŏŭrz, pn. nuestro, nuestra, nuestros, nuestras.　・　　　[mos.

ourselves, -sĕlvz, pn. pl. nosotros mis-

oust, ŏŭst, v. a. quitar; desposeer.

out, ŏŭt, ad. fuera, afuera; —, v. a. expeler.

outbid, -bĭd´, v. a. pujar.　　　[desposeer.

outbreak, ŏŭt´brāk, s. erupción, f.

outburst, -bŭrst´, s. explosión, f.

outcast, ŏŭt´kăst, a. desechado; desterra- do, expulso.　　　[venta pública, f.

outcry, -krī, s. clamor, m.; gritería, f.;

outdo, -dŏ´, v. a. exceder á otro, sobre-

outer, ŏŭt´ĕr, a. exterior.　　　[pujar.

outermost, -mŏst, a. extremo; lo más exterior.

outfit, ŏŭt´fĭt, s. vestidos, m. pl.; ropa, f.

outfitter, -fĭttŭr, s. confeccionador, m.

outgoing, -gŏĭng, s. salida, f.; -s, pl. gasto, m.　　　[en vegetación.

outgrow, -grŏ´, v. a. sobrecrecer; exceder

outhouse, ŏŭt´hŏŭs, s. dependencia de una casa, f.

outlandish, -lănd´ĭsh, a. extranjero.

outlast, -lăst´, v. a. exceder en duración.

outlaw, ŏŭt´lă, s. proscripto, m.; bandido, m.; —, v. a. proscribir.

outlawry, -lărĕ, s. proscripción, f.

outlay, -lā, s. despensa, f., gastos, m. pl.

outlet, -lĕt, s. salida, f.　　　[m.

outline, -līn, s. contorno, m.; bosquejo,

outlive, -lĭv´, v. a. sobrevivir.

outlying, -lĭĭng, a. distante de, lejos de.

outnumber, -nŭm´bĕr, v. a. exceder en número.

out of doors, ŏŭt´ŏvdŏrs, ad. fuera de casa.

outpost, ŏŭt´pŏst, s. puesto avanzado, m.

outrage, -rāj, s. ultraje, m.; -, v. a. ultrajar.

outrageous, -rā´jŭs, a. ultrajoso; atroz; -ly, ad. injuriosamente; enormemente.

outrider, -rīdŭr, s. palafrenero, m.

outright, -rīt, ad. cumplidamente, luego.

outrun, -rŭn´, v. a. correr más que otro.

outset, ŏŭt´sĕt, s. principio, m.

outshine, -shīn´, v. a. exceder en brillan- tez, eclipsar.　　　[m.; apariencia, f.

outside, ŏŭt´sīd, s. superficie, f.; exterior,

outsiders, -ărz, s. pl. público, m.

outskirt, -skŭrt, s. parte exterior, f.; suburbio, m.　　　　[alargar.

outstretch, -strĕtsh´, v. a. extenderse,

outstrip, -strĭp´, v. a. dejar atrás; sobre- pujar.

outwall, ŏŭt´wăl, s. antemural, m.

outward, -wărd, a. exterior, externo; -ly, ad. fuera; exteriormente.

outweigh, -wā´, v. a. preponderar.

outwit, -wĭt´, v. a. engañar á uno á fuerza de tretas.

outworks, *ôŭt'wŭrkz*, s. pl. (mil.) obras avanzadas, f. pl

oval, *ô'vȧl*, s. óvalo, m.; –, a. oval.

ovary, *ô'vȧrȧ*, s. ovario, m.

ovation, *ôvā'shȧn*, s. ovación, f.

oven, *ŭv'n*, s. horno, m.

over, *ô'vȧr*, pr. sobre, encima; **all** –, por todos lados; –, ad. más, demás, **– again**, otra vez, **– against**, enfrente, **– and –**, repetidas veces.

overall, –*ăl'*, s. sobretodo, m.

overawe,–*ă'*, v. a. tener á freno; imponer respeto.   [rur; –, s. preponderancia, f.

overbalance, –*băl'ȧns*, v. a. preponderar.

overbear, –*băr'*, v. a. sujetar, oprimir.

overbearing, –*băr'ing*, a. ultrajoso, despótico.   [bordo, al mar.

overboard, –*bôrd*, ad. (mar.) encima del

overburden, –*bŭr'dn*, v. a. sobrecargar.

overcast, –*kȧst'*, v. a. anublar, obscurecer; repulgar, valuar demasiado.

overcharge, –*tshärj'*, v. a. sobrecargar; poner alguna cosa á precio muy subido.

overcloud, –*kloŭd'*, v. a. cubrir de nubes.

overcome, –*kŭm'*, v. a. vencer; superar.

over-confident, *kŏn'fĭdent*, a. demasiado atrevido.   [sario.

overdo, –*dô'*, v. n. hacer más de lo nece-

overdrafts, –*drȧfts*, s.pl. adelantos, m. pl.

overdress, –*drĕs'*, v. a. engalanar con exceso.   [todo, hastío.

overeat, –*ĕt'*, v. n. tupirse.   [exceso.

overflow, –*flô'*, v. a. & n. inundar; salir de madre; rebosar; –, *ô'vĕrflô*, s. inundación, f.; superabundancia, f.

overfond, –*fŏnd'*, a. el que quiere ó gusta demasiado de alguna cosa.

overgrow, –*grô'*, v. n. crecer demasiado.

overgrowth, *ô'vĕrgrôth*, s. vegetación exuberante, f.

overhang, *ôvĕrhăng'*, v. a. estar colgando sobre alguna cosa; salir algo fuera del nivel de un edificio.   [lo alto.

overhead, –*hĕd'*, ad. sobre la cabeza, en

overhear, –*hĕr'*, v. a. oír algo por casualidad.   [lidad.

overheat, –*hĕt'*, v. a. acalorar.

overjoyed, –*jôĭd'*, a. muy gozoso.

overlay, –*lā'*, v. a. abrumar.

overlook, –*lŏk'*, v. a. mirar desde lo alto; examinar; rever; repasar, pasar por alto, tolerar; descuidar; desdeñar.

overmuch, –*mŭtsh'*, a. demasiado.   [omitir.

overpass, –*pȧs'*, v. a. pasar por alto;

overplus, *ô'vĕrplŭs*, s. sobrante, m.

overpower, *ôvĕrpoŭ'ȧr*, v. a. predominar, oprimir.

overrate, *ôvĕrrāt'*, v. a. apreciar ó valuar alguna cosa en más de lo que vale.

overreach, –*rētsh'*, v. a. sobresalir, exceder en altura; engañar.   [con exceso.

override, –*rīd'*, v. a. fatigar un caballo

overrule, –*rōl'*, v. a. predominar, dominar.

overrun, –*rŭn'*, v. n. hacer correrías; cubrir enteramente; inundar; infestar; repasar; –, v. n. rebosar.   [omitir.

oversee, –*sĕ'*, v. a. inspeccionar; pasar.

overseer, –*ȧr*, s. superintendente, m.

overset, –*sĕt'*, v. a. volcar; trastornar; –, v. n. volcarse, caerse.   [obscurecer.

overshadow, –*shăd'ô*, v. a. asombrar,

overshoe, *ô'vȧrshô*, s. galocha, f.

overshoot, *ôvȧrshôt'*, v. a. tirar más allá del blanco; –, v. n. pasar de raya.

oversight, *ô'vȧrsīt*, s. yerro, m.; equivocación, f.   [siado.

oversleep, *ôvȧrslēp'*, v. n. dormir demasiado.

overspread, –*sprĕd'*, v. a. desparramar.

overstate, –*stāt'*, v. n. exagerar.   [cubrir.

overstep, –*stĕp'*, v. a. pasar más allá

overt, *ô'vȧrt*, a. abierto, público; –**ly**, ad. abiertamente.   [en el hecho.

overtake, *ôvȧrtāk'*, v. a. alcanzar; coger

overtax, –*tăks'*, v. a. oprimir con tributos.

overthrow, –*thrô'*, v. a. trastornar; demoler; destruir; –, *ô'vȧrthrô*, s. trastorno, m.; ruina, derrota, f.

overture, *ô'vȧrtȧr*, s. abertura, f.; (mus.) obertura, f.   [tornar.

overturn, *ôvȧrtŭrn'*, v. a. subvertir, trastornar.

overweening, –*wĕn'ing*, a. presuntuoso.

overweight, *ô'vȧrwĕt*, s. preponderancia, f.; exceso en el peso, m.

overwhelm, *ôvȧrhwĕlm'*, v. a. abrumar; oprimir; sumergir.   [siado.

overwork, –*wȧrk'*, v. a. trabajar demasiado.

oviparous, *ôvĭp'ȧrŭs*, a. ovíparo.

owe, *ô*, v. a. deber, tener deudas; estar obligado.   [causa de.

owing, *ô'ing*, a. que es debido; **– to**, por

owl, *oŭl*, **owlet**, –*ĕt*, s. lechuza, f.

own, *ôn*, a. propio; **my** –, mío, mía; –, v. a. reconocer, poseer, confesar.

owner, –*ȧr*, s.dueño, propietario, m.; **– of a ship**, naviero, m.   [piedad, f.

ownership, –*ȧrshĭp*, s. dominio, m.; propiedad, f.

ox, *ŏks*, s. buey, m.; –, pl. **oxen**, ganado vacuno, s.

oxidize, *ŏks'ĭdĭz*, v. a. oxidar.

oxygen, *ŏks'ĭjĕn*, s. oxígeno, m.

oyster, *ôĭs'tȧr*, s. ostra, f.

P.

pace, *pās*, s. paso, m.; –, v. a. medir á pasos; –, v. n. pasear.   [dura, m.

pacer, –*ȧr*, s. caballo de paso de andadura, m.

pacific(al), *pȧsĭf'ĭk(ȧl)*, a. pacífico.

pacification, *pȧsĭfĭkā'shȧn*, s. pacificación, f.

pacify, –*pȧs'ĭfĭ*, v. a. pacificar.   [ción, f.

pack, *păk*, s. lío, fardo, m.; baraja de naipes, f.; muta, perrada, f.; cuadrilla, f.; –, v. a. enfardelar, embalar; empaquetar; empandillar el naipe.

package, –*ȧj*, s. fardo, m.; embalaje, m.

pack-cloth, –*klŏth*, s. arpillera, f.

packet, –*ĕt*, s. paquete, m.

packet-boat, –*bôt*, s. paquebote, m.

pack-horse, –*hôrs*, s. caballo de carga, m.

packing, –*ing*, s. embalaje, m.   [gulta, f.

pack-thread, –*thrĕd*, s. bramante, m.

pad, *păd*, s. senda, f.; haca, f.; salteador de caminos á pie, m.; silla de montar baja y blanda, f.; –, v. a. acolchar con algodón.

paddle, –*dl*, v. n. remar; chapotear; –, s. canalete, m. (especie de remo).

9*

paddock, —ŏk, s. escuerzo, sapo, m.; par-
padlock, —lŏk, s. candado, m.   [que, m.
pagan, pā'găn, a. & s. pagano (m.).
paganism, —ĭzm, s. paganismo, m.
page, pāj, s. página, f.; paje, m.; —, v. a.
  foliar.   [m.
pageant, pāj'ĕnt, s. espectáculo público,
pageantry, —rĕ, s. fasto, m.; pompa, f.
pail, pāl, s. colodra, f.; cubo, pozal, m.
pain, pān, s. pena, f.; castigo, m.; dolor,
  m.; —, v. a. afligir.
painful, —fŭl, a. dolorido; penoso; —ly,
  ad. dolorosamente, con pena.
painless, —lĕs, a. sin pena; sin dolor.
painstaking, pānz'tākĭng, a. laborioso,
  incansado.
paint, pānt, v. a. & n. pintar; afeitarse.
painter, —ŭr, s. pintor, m.
painting, —ĭng, s. pintura, f.
pair, pār, s. par, m.; —, v. a. (& n.) parear
palace, pāl'ăs, s. palacio, m.   [(se).
palatable, pāl'ătăbl, a. sabroso.
palate, pāl'ăt, s. paladar, m.; gusto, m.
palatial, pălā'schăl, a. palatino.
palatinate, pălăt'ĭnăt, s. palatinado, m.
palatine, pāl'ătĭn, a. palatino.
palaver, pălā'vŭr, s. charla, f.; fruslería,
  f.; zalamería, f.; —, v. n. & n. congraciarse
  con zalamerías; charlar.
pale, pāl, a. pálido; claro; —, s. palidez,
  f.; palizada, f.; —, v. a. empalizar.
paleness, —nĕs, s. palidez, f.
palfrey, pāl'frĕ, s. palafrén, m.
paling, pā'lĭng, **palisade,** pālĭsād', s.
  estacada, palizada, f.
pall, pāl, s. paño de tumba, m.; palio de
  arzobispo, m.; —, v. n. desvanecerse, —,
  v. a. evaporar; condecorar con palio.
pallet, pāl'lĕt, s. camilla, cama pequeña
palliate, pāl'lĭăt, v. a. paliar.   [y pobre.
palliation, pāllĭā'shŭn, s. paliación, f.
palliative, pāl'lĭătĭv, a. & s. paliativo(m.).
pallid, pāl'lĭd, a. pálido.
pallor, pāl'ŭr, s. palidez, f.
palm, pām, s. (bot.) palma, f.; victoria, f.;
  palma (de la mano); —, v. a. escamotar;
  manosear.
palmated, pālmā'tĕd, s. palmeado.
palmistry, pāl'mĭstrĕ, s. quiromancia, f.
Palm-Sunday, pām'sŭndā, s. domingo
  de ramos, m.
palpable, pāl'păbl, a. palpable; evidente.
palpably, —ĕ, ad. palpablemente; clara-
palpitate, pāl'pĭtāt, v. n. palpitar.   [mente.
palpitation, —ā'shŭn, s. palpitación, f.
palsied, pāl'zĕd, s. paralítico.
palsy, pāl'zĕ, s. parálisis, perlesía, f.
paltry, pāl'trĕ, a. vil, mezquino.
pamper, pām'pŭr, v. a. atracar, engordar.
pamphlet, pām'flĕt, s. folleto, librejo, m.
pamphleteer, —ŭr', s. folletista, m.
pan, pān, s. cazucia, f.
panacea, pănăsē'ă, s. panacea, f.
pancake, pān'kāk, s. buñuelo, m.
pander, pān'dŭr, s. alcahuete, m.; —, v. a.
  alcahuetear.
pane, pān, s. cuadro de vidrio, m.

panegyric, pănĕjĭr'ĭk, s. panegírico, m.
panel, pān'ĕl, s. entrepaño, m.; (law)
  lista de jurados, f.
pang, păng, s. angustia, congoja, f.
panic, pān'ĭk, a. & s. pánico; terror pánico
pannier, pān'nŭr, s. cuévano, m.   [(m.).
panoply, pān'ŏplĕ, s. panoplia, f.
pansy, pān'sĕ, s. (bot.) trinitaria, f.
pant, pănt, v. n. palpitar; jadear; **to—for**
  or after, suspirar por.
pantaloon, păntălōn', s. Pantalón, bufón,
  m., —s, pl. pantalones, m. pl.   [f.
pantechnicon, păntĕk'nĭkŏn, s. trastera.
panther, pān'thŭr, s. pantera, f.
pantomime, pān'tŏmĭm, s. pantomimo,
  m.; pantomima, f.
pantry, pān'trĕ, s. despensa, f.; oficio en
  una casa principal, m.
pap, păp, s. pezón, m.; papa, papilla, f.;
  carne (de la fruta), f.
papacy, pā'păsĕ, s. papado, m.
papal, pā'păl, a. papal.
paper, pā'pŭr, s. papel, m.; jornal, m.;
  —s, pl. escrituras, f. pl.; (com.) fondos,
  m. pl.; —, a. de papel; —, v. a. entapizar
  con papel.   [papel moneda, m.
paper-credit, —krĕdĭt, (—currency), s.
paper-weight, —wāt, s. sujetapapeles, m.
papist, pā'pĭst, s. papista, m.
pappy, pāp'pĕ, a. mollar, jugoso.
par, pār, s. equivalencia, f.; igualdad, f.;
  at —, (com.) á la par.
parable, pār'ăbl, s. parábola, f.
parade, părād', s. ostentación, pompa, f.;
  (mil.) parada, f.; —, v. a. & n. formar
  parada, pasear; hacer gala.
paradise, pār'ădĭs, s. paraíso.   [paradojo.
paradoxical, părădŏks'ĭkăl, a. paradójico,
paragon, pār'ăgŏn, s. modelo perfecto, m.
paragraph, pār'ăgraf, s. párrafo, m.
parallel, pār'ăllĕl, a. paralelo; —, s. línea
  paralela, f.; —, v. a. paralelizar; parango-
paralyse, pār'ălĭz, v. a. paralizar.   [nar.
paralysis, părăl'ĭsĭs, s. parálisis, f.
paralytic(al), părălĭt'ĭk(ăl), a. paralítico.
paramount, pār'ămŏŭnt, a. supremo,
  superior; —, s. jefe, superior, m.
paramour, pār'ămŏŭr, s. cortejo, m.
parasite, pār'ăsĭt, s. gorrista, m.   [Jero.
parasitic, părăsĭt'ĭk, a. adulatorio, lison-
parasol, pār'ăsŏl, s. parasol, quitasol, m.
parboil, pār'bŏĭl, v. a. medio cocer.
parcel, pār'sĕl, s. paquete, m.; porción,
  cantidad, f.; equipajes, bultos, m. pl.;
  —'s post, —zpōst, m. diligencia, f.; —'s
  delivery office, —z dĕlŭ'ŭrĕ ŏffĭs, s.
  entrega de equipajes, f.; —, v. a. partir.
parch, pārtsh, v. a. tostar.   [dividir.
parchment, —mĕnt, s. pergamino, m.
pardon, pār'dn, s. perdón, m.; —, v. a. per-
pardonable, —ăbl, a. perdonable.   [donar.
pare, pār, v. a. recortar.
parent, pā'rĕnt, s. padre, m.; madre, f.
parentage, —tāj, s. parentela, f.; extracción, f.
parental, pārĕn'tăl, a. paternal.   [m.
parenthesis, părĕn'thĕsĭs, s. paréntesis,

parish, *pär'ish*, s. parroquia, f.; —, a. parroquial.

parishioner, *pär'ish'ănŭr*, s. parroquiano.

park, *pärk*, s. parque, m.; —, v. a. cerrar un coto. [entretenimiento, m.

parlance, *pär'lăns*, s. conversación, f.;

parley, *pär'lĕ*, s. conferencia, plática, f.

parliament, *pär'liměnt*, s. parlamento, m.

parliamentary, *—liměnt'ărĕ*, a. parlamentario; — train, s. (rail.) tren ordinario, tren ómnibus, m. [recibimiento, f.

parlour, *pär'lŭr*, s. parlatorio, m., sala de

parochial, *părō'kiăl*, a. parroquial.

parody, *pär'ŏdĕ*, s. parodia, f.; —, v. a. parodiar. [m.

paroquet, *pär'ŏkĕt*, s. papagayo pequeño,

parricide, *pär'risĭd*, s. parricidio, m.; parricida, m.

parrot, *pär'rŏt*, s. papagayo, m.

parry, *pär'rĕ*, v. n. parrar, rechazar.

parse, *pärs*, v. a. (gr.) construir.

parsimonious, *pärsĭmō'niŭs*, a. económico, moderado en sus gastos; —ly, ad. con parsimonia.

parsimony, *pär'sĭmŏnĕ*, s. parsimonia, f.

parsley, *pär'slĕ*, s. (bot.) perejil, m.

parsnip, *pär'snĭp*, s. (bot.) chirivía, f.

parson, *pär'sn*, s. párroco, m.

parsonage, *—dj*, s. beneficio, curado, m.

part, *pärt*, s. parte, f., partido, m.; oficio, m.; papel (de un actor), m.; obligación, f.; —s, pl. partes, f. pl. paraje, distrito, m.; —, v. a. partir, separar, desunir; —, v. n. partirse, separarse; —ly, ad. en parte. [tomar parte en.

partake, *pärtāk'*, v. a. & n. participar;

partaker, *—ŭr*, s. participante, m.

partial, *pär'shăl*, a. —ly, ad. parcial-(mente)

partiality, *pärshăl'itĕ*, s. parcialidad, f.

participant, *pärtis'ipănt*, a. participante, partícipe.

participate, *—pāt*, v. a. participar.

participation, *pä'tisipā'shŭn*, s. participación, f. [m.

participle, *pär'tisĭpl*, s. (gr.) participio,

particle, *pär'tĭkl*, s. partícula, f.

particular, *pärtĭk'ŭlăr*, a. particular, singular; —ly, ad. particularmente. —, s. particular, m., particularidad, f.

particularise, *pärtĭk'ŭlărĭz*, s. particularizar. [laridad, circunstancia, f.

particularity, *pärtĭkŭlăr'itĕ*, s. particu-

parting, *pärt'ing*, s. separación, partida, f., raya (en los cabellos), f.

partisan, *pär'tizăn*, s. partidario, m.

partition, *pärtish'ăn*, s. partición, separación, f.; —, v. a. partir, dividir en varias partes. [f.

partition-wall, *—wăl*, s. pared medianera,

partner, *pärt'nŭr*, s. socio, compañero, m [de comercio, f.

partnership, *—shĭp*, s. compañía, sociedad

partridge, *pär'trĭj*, s. perdiz, f.

party, *pär'tĕ*, s. partido, m.; parte, f.; función, f.; (mil.) partida, f.

party-coloured, *—kŭlŭrd*, a. abigarrado.

party-man, *—măn*, s. partidario, m.

party-wall, *—wăl*, s. pared medianera, f.

paschal, *päs'kăl*, a. pascual.

pass, *päs*, v. a. pasar; traspasar; transferir; —, v. n. pasar, ocurrir; —, s. pasillo, m.; paso, camino, m.; pase, m.; estado, m.; condición, f., estocada, f.

passable, *—săbl*, a. pasadero, transitable.

passage, *—sdj*, s. pasaje, m.; travesía, f.; pasadizo, m.; acontecimiento, m.

passenger, *—sĕnjŭr*, s. pasajero, m.

passer-by, *—sŭrbī*, s. el que pasa.

passing, *—sing*, a. sobresaliente, eminente; —, ad. eminentemente. [á muerto, f.

passing-bell, *—bĕl*, s. campana que toca

passion, *päsh'ăn*, s. pasión, f.; amor, m.; celo, ardor, m.

passionate, *—ât*, a. apasionado; colérico; —ly, ad. apasionadamente; ardientemente.

passion-flower, *—flŏŭr*, s. pasionaria, f.

Passion-week, *—wĕk*, s. semana de Pasión, f. [mente.

passive, *päs'ĭv*, a. pasivo; —ly, ad. pasiva-

pass-key, *päs'kĕ*, s. llave maestra, f.

Passover, *päs'ŏvŭr*, s. Pascua, f.

passport, *—pŏrt*, s. pasaporte, m.

pass-word, *—wŭrd*, s. (mil.) pase de la palabra, m.

past, *päst*, a. pasado; gastado; —, s. (gr.) pretérito, m.; —, pr. más; fuera.

paste, *päst*, s. pasta, f.; engrudo, m.; —, v. a. engrudar.

pasteboard, *—bŏrd*, s. cartón fuerte, m.

pastel, *päs'tĕl*, s. hierba pastel, f.; glasto, m.

pastern, *päs'tŭrn*, s. cuartilla del caballo, f. [versión, f.

pastime, *päs'tĭm*, s. pasatiempo, m.; di-

pastor, *päs'tŭr*, s. pastor, m.

pastoral, *—ăl*, a. pastoril; pastoral.

pastry, *päs'trĕ*, s. pastelería, f.

pasturage, *päs'tŭrdj*, s. pasturaje, m.

pasture, *päs'tŭr*, s. pastura, f.; —, v. a. pastar, apacentar; —, v. n. pastar, pacer.

pasty, *päs'tĕ*, s. pastel, borrón, m.

pat, *pät*, a. apto, conveniente, propio; —, s. golpecillo, m.; —, v. a. dar golpecillos.

patch, *pätsh*, s. remiendo, m.; lunar, m.; —, v. a. remendar; adornar el rostro con lunares. [f., chapucería, f.

patch-work, *—wŭrk*, s. obra de retacitos.

pate, *pät*, s. (fam.) cabeza, f.

paten, *pät'ĕn*, s. patena de cáliz, f.

patent, *pă'tĕnt*, s. —, patente; privilegiado; —, a. patente, f.; —, v. a. privilegiar.

patentee, *—ē*, s. el que posee un privilegio de invención. [lizado, m.

patent-leather, *—lĕăthŭr*, s. cuero embar-

paternal, *pătŭr'năl*, a. paternal.

paternity, *pătŭr'nitĕ*, s. paternidad, f.

path, *päth*, s. senda, f.

pathetic(al), *păthĕt'ĭk(ăl)*, a. patético; —ally, ad. patéticamente. [table.

pathless, *päth'lĕs*, a. sin senda, intransi-

pathological, *păthŏlŏj'ĭkăl*, a. patológico.

pathology, *păthŏl'ŏjĕ*, s. patología, f.

patience, *pā'shĕns*, s. paciencia, f.

patient, *—shĕnt*, a. paciente, sufrido; —ly, ad. con paciencia. —, s. enfermo, m.

patriarch, *pā'trārk*, s. patriarca, m.
patrimony, *păt'rĭmŏnĕ*, s. patrimonio, m.
patriot, *pā'trĭŏt*, s. patriota, m.
patriotic, *pătrĭŏt'ĭk*, a. patriótico.   [m.
patriotism, *pā'trĭŏtĭzm*, s. patriotismo,
patrol, *pătrŏl'*, s. patrulla, f.; —, v. n. pa-
    trullar.
patron, *pā'trŏn*, s. patrón, protector, m.
patronage, *-āj*, s. patrocinio, m.; patro-
    nato, patronazgo, m.
patroness, *pā'trŏnĕs*, s. patrona, f.
patronise, *pā'trŏnīz*, v. a. patrocinar,
    proteger.   [lumna, f.
patten, *păt'tĕn*, s. galocha, f.; base de co-
patter, *păt'tăr*, v. n. patalear, patear.
pattern, *-n*, s. modelo, f.; ejemplar, m.
patty, *păt'tĕ*, s. pastelillo, m.   [tidad, f.
paucity, *pā'sĭtĕ*, s. poquedad, pequeña can-
paunch, *pänsh*, s. panza, f.; vientre, m.
pauper, *pā'păr*, s. pobre, m.
pauperism, *-ĭzm*, s. pauperismo, m.
pause, *păz*, s. pausa, f.; —, v. a. pausar;
    deliberar.   [dosar.
pave, *păv*, v. a. empedrar; enlosar, embal-
pavement, *-mĕnt*, s. pavimento, empe-
    drado de calle, m.
pavilion, *păvĭl'yŏn*, s. (mar.) pabellón,
    (tienda), m.; pabellón (bandera).   [losa, f.
paving-stone, *pā'vĭngstōn*, s. ladrillo, m.
paw, *pā*, s. garra, f.; —, v. a. herir con el
    pie delantero.· manosear alguna cosa con
    poca maña.   [empeñar.
pawn, *pän*, s. prenda, f.; peón, m.; —, v. a.
pawn-broker, *-brōkăr*, s. prendero, m.
pay, *pā*, v. a. pagar; sufrir por; —, s.
    paga, f.; salario, m.
payable, *-ĭbl*, a. pagadero.
pay-day, *-dā*, s. día de paga, m.   [m.
payee, *-ē'*, s. portador de una libranza,
pay-master, *-măstăr*, s. pagador, m.
payment, *-mĕnt*, s. paga, f.; pagamento,
    pago, m.
pea, *pē*, s. (pease, pl.) guisante, m.
peace, *pēs*, s. paz, f.; —¡ ¡paz! ¡silencio!
peaceable, *-ĭbl*, peaceful, *-fŭl*, a. tran-
    quilo, pacífico.
peach, *pētsh*, s. melocotón, durazno, m.
peach-tree, *-trē*, s. melocotonero, m.
peacock, *pē'kŏk*, s. pavón, pavo real, m.
peahen, *-hĕn*, s. pava real, f.
peak, *pēk*, s. cima, f.
peal, *pēl*, s. campaneo, m.; estruendo, m.;
    —, v. a. & n. hacer resonar; devolver el
    eco los sonidos.
pear, *pār*, s. pera, f.
pearl, *părl*, s. perla, f.; catarata en el ojo,
pearled, *-d*, a. guarnecido de perlas.   [f.
pearly, *-ĕ*, a. lo que tiene perlas ó es
    semejante á ellas.
pear-tree, *pār'trē*, s. peral, m.
peasant, *pĕz'ănt*, s. labriego, patán, m.
pea-shooter, *pē'shōtăr*, s. cerbatana, f.
peat, *pēt*, s. turba, f.; césped de tierra, m.
pebble, *pĕb'bl*, s. guija, f.; guijarro, m.
pebbly, *pĕb'blĕ*, a. guijarroso.
peccadillo, *pĕkkădĭl'lō*, s. pecadillo, m.
peck, *pĕk*, s. picotazo, m.; celemín, m. (me-
    dida de granos); —, v. a. picotear; picar.

pectoral, *pĕk'tŏrăl*, a. pectoral; —, s.
    medicamento pectoral, m.
peculate, *pĕk'ŭlāt*, v. n. robar al público.
peculation, *pĕkŭlā'shŭn*, s. peculado, m.
peculiar, *pĕkū'lĭăr*, a. peculiar, particu-
    lar, singular; -ly, ad. peculiarmente.
peculiarity, *pĕkŭlĭăr'ĭtĕ*, s. particulari-
    dad, singularidad, f.
pecuniary, *pĕkū'nĭărĕ*, a. pecuniario.
pedagogue, *pĕd'ăgŏg*, s. pedagogo, m.,
    pedante, m.   [órganos, m. pl.
pedal, *pĕ'dăl* (*pĕd'ăl*), s. pedales de los
pedant, *pĕd'ănt*, s. pedante, m.
pedantic(al), *pĕdănt'ĭk(ăl)*, s. pedantesco
pedantry, *pĕd'ăntrĕ*, s. pedantería, f.
peddle, *pĕd'dl*, v. n. ocuparse en frioleras.
peddling, *pĕd'dlĭng*, a. fútil, frívolo.
pedestal, *pĕd'ĕstăl*, s. pedestal, m.
pedestrian, *pĕdĕs'trĭăn*, s. andador, peón,
    m.; —, a. pedestre.
pedigree, *pĕd'ĭgrē*, s. genealogía, f.
pediment, *pĕd'ĭmĕnt*, s. frontis, m.
pedlar, *pĕd'lăr*, s. buhonero, m.
peel, *pēl*, v. a. descortezar: —, s. corteza,
    f.; pellejo (de frutas), m.; pala de horno, f.
peep, *pēp*, v. n. asomar; atisbar; piar los
    pollos; —, s. asomo, m.; alba, f.; ojeada,
peep-hole, *-hōl*, s. atisbadero, m.   [f.
peer, *pēr*, s. compañero, m.; Par, m.
    (grande de Inglaterra).
peerage, *-āj*, s. dignidad de Par, f.
peeress, *-ĕs*, s. mujer de un Par, f.; señora
    noble, f.
peerless, *-lĕs*, a. incomparable.
peevish, *pēv'ĭsh*, a. regañón, bronco;
    enojadizo; -ly, ad. con impertinencia.
peevishness, *-nĕs*, s. mal humor, m.
peg, *pĕg*, s. clavija, espita, f.; —, v. a. cla-
pelf, *pĕlf*, s. riquezas, f. pl.   [var.
pelican, *pĕl'ĭkăn*, s. pelícano, m.
pelisse, *pĕlĭs'*, s. ropón, m.
pell, *pĕl*, s. pellejo, cuero, m.
pellet, *pĕl'lĕt*, s. pelotilla, f.
pellicle, *pĕl'lĭkl*, s. película, f.
pell-mell, *pĕlmĕl'*, ad. á trochemoche.
pelt, *pĕlt*, s. pellejo, cuero, m., pelta, f.
pen, *pĕn*, s. pluma, f.; caponera, f.; —, v. a.
    enjaular, encerrar; escribir.
penal, *pē'năl*, a. penal.   [multa, f.
penalty, *pĕn'ăltĕ*, s. pena, f., castigo, m.;
penance, *pĕn'ăns*, s. penitencia, f.
pence, *pĕns*, s. pl. de penny.
pencil, *pĕn'sĭl*, s. pincel, m.; lápiz, m.;
    —, v. a. pintar; escribir con lápiz.
pencil-case, *-kās*, s. lapicero, m.
pendant, *pĕn'dănt*, s. pendiente, m.; (mar.)
    gallardete, m.
pendent, *-dĕnt*, a. pendiente.
pending, *-dĭng*, a. pendiente, indeciso.
pendulum, *-dŭlăm*, s. péndulo, m.
penetrate, *pĕn'ĕtrāt*, v. a. & n. penetrar.
penetration, *pĕnĕtrā'shŭn*, s. penetra-
    ción, sagacidad, f.   [m.
pen-holder, *pĕn'hōldăr*, s. portapluma, m.
peninsula, *pĕnĭn'sŭlă*, s. península, f.
penitence, *pĕn'ĭtĕns*, s. penitencia, f.

penitent, *-tĕnt,* a. & s. penitente (m.);
-ly, ad. con arrepentimiento.

penitential, *pĕnĭtĕn'shăl,* a. penitencial.

penitentiary, *-shărĕ,* s. penitenciario, m.

pen-knife, *pĕn'nĭf,* s. cortaplumas, m.

penman, *-măn,* s. pendolista, m.; autor,
escritor, m. 			[fesión de escritor, f.

penmanship, *-shĭp,* s. caligrafía, f.; pro-

pennant, *pĕn'nănt,* pennon, *pĕn'nŏn,* s.
(mar.) flámula, banderola, f.

penniless, *pĕn'nĭlĕs,* a. falto de dinero.

penny, *pĕn'nĕ,* s. penique, m.; dinero, m.

penny-a-liner, *-ălĭnăr,* s. gacetista que
recibe un penique por cada línea, m.

penny-post, *-pōst,* s. correo interior, m.

pennyweight, *-wăt,* s. peso de 20 granos
tory, m.

penny-wise, *-wĭz.* a. económico de manera falsa, - and pound-foolish, ganador en los gastos menores, gastador en
los mayores. 			[nique, m.

penny-worth, *-wŭrth,* s. valor de un pe-

pension, *pĕn'shŭn,* s. pensión, f.; -, v. a.
dar alguna pensión.

pensionary, *-ărĕ,* **pensioner,** *-ăr,* s.
pensionista, pensionado, m.

pensive, *pĕn'sĭv,* a. pensativo; -ly, ad.
melancólicamente.

Pentecost, *pĕn'tĕkŏst,* s. Pentecostés, m.

penthouse, *pĕnt'hŏŭs,* s. cobertizo, tejadillo, m.

penultimate, *pĕnŭl'tĭmăt,* a. penúltimo.

penurious, *pĕnū'rĭŭs,* a. tacaño, avaro.

penury, *pĕn'ūrĕ,* s. penuria, carestía, f.

peony, *pĕ'ŏnĕ,* s. peonía, f.

people, *pē'pl,* s. pueblo, m.; nación, f.;
vulgo, m.; gente, f.; -, v. a. poblar.

pepper, *pĕp'păr,* s. pimienta, f.; -, v. a.
sazonar con pimienta; golpear.

pepper-box, *-bŏks,* s. pimentero, m.

pepper-corn, *-kŏrn,* s. semilla de pi-
per, *păr,* pr. por. 			[mienta, f.

peradventure, *-ădrĕn'tūr,* ad. por acaso.

perambulate, *-ăm'bŭlāt,* v. a. transitar,
recorrer algún territorio. 		[para niños, m.

perambulator, *-ăm'bŭlātăr,* s. cochecito

perceivable, *-sē'văbl,* a. perceptible.

perceive, *-sēv',* v. a. percibir, comprender.

percentage, *-sĕn'dĕ,* s. tasa del por
ciento, f. 			[bilidad, f.

perceptibility, *-sĕptĭbĭl'ĭtĕ,* s. percepti-

perceptible, *-sĕp'tĭbl,* a. perceptible.

perceptibly, *-ĕ,* ad. perceptiblemente.

perception, *-sĕp'shŭn,* s. percepción, idea,
noción, f. 			[perchar.

perch, *pŭrtsh,* s. pértica, f.; -, v. a. em-

perchance, *pŭrtshăns',* ad. acaso, quizá.

percolate, *păr'kŏlāt,* v. a. colar; filtrar.

percussion, *pŭrkŭsh'ŭn,* s. percusión, f.;
golpe, m.

percussion-cap, *-kăp,* s. pistón, m.

perdition, *pŭrdĭsh'ŭn,* s. pérdida, ruina, f.

peregrination, *pĕrĕgrĭnā'shŭn,* s. pere-
grinación, f. 		[mente, definitivamente.

peremptorily, *pĕr'ĕmtŏrĭlĕ,* ad. perentoria-

peremptoriness, *-ĕmtŏrĭnĕs,* s. decisión
absoluta, f.

peremptory, *-ĕmtŭrĕ,* a. perentorio; decisivo.

perennial, *-ĕn'nĭăl,* a. perenne; perpetuo.

perfect, *-fĕkt,* a. perfecto, acabado, puro;
-ly, ad. perfectamente; -, v. a. perficio-
nar, acabar.

perfection, *pŭrfĕk'shŭn,* s. perfección, f.

perfidious, *-fĭd'yŭs,* a. pérfido, desleal;
-ly, ad. pérfidamente.

perfidy, *-fĭdĕ,* s. perfidia, f.

perforate, *-fŏrāt,* v. a. horadar.

perforation, *-fŏrā'shŭn,* s. perforación, f.

perforce, *-fŏrs',* ad. forzosamente.

perform, *pŭrfŏrm',* v.a.ejecutar; efectuar;
-, v. n. representar, hacer papel.

performance, *-ăns,* s. ejecución, f.; cumplimiento, m.; obra, f.; representación
teatral, función, f.

performer, *-ăr,* s. ejecutor, m.; actor, m.

perfume, *păr'fŭm,* s. perfume, m.; fragrancia, f.; -, *pŭrfūm',* v. a. perfumar.

perfumer, *-ăr,* s. perfumero, perfumista, m.

perfunctory, *pŭrfŭngk'tŭrĕ,* a. descuidado, superficial, negligente.

perhaps, *-hăps',* ad. quizá, quizás.

peril, *pĕr'ĭl,* s. peligro, riesgo, m.

perilous, *-ŭs,* a. peligroso, -ly, ad. peligrosamente.

period, *pĕ'rĭŏd,* s. período, m.

periodic(al), *pĕrĭŏd'ĭk(ăl),* a. periódico;
-ly, ad. periódicamente, -, s. jornal
periódico, m. 			[peripatético (m).

peripatetic(al), *pĕrĭpătĕt'ĭk(ăl),* a. & s.

periphrase, *pĕ'rĭfrăz,* s. perífrasis, circunlocución, f.

perish, *pĕr'ĭsh,* v. n. perecer.

perishable, *-ăbl,* a. perecedero.

peristyle, *pĕr'ĭstĭl,* s. peristilo, m.

periwig, *pĕr'ĭwĭg,* s. peluca, f.

periwinkle, *pĕr'ĭwĭngkl,* s. caracol marino, m.; (bot.) vincapervinca, f.

perjure, *pŭr'jŭr,* v. a. perjurar.

perjury, *-ĕ,* s. perjurio, m.

perk, *pŭrk,* v. n. pavonearse. 		[f.

permanence, *pŭr'mănĕns,* s. permanencia,

permanent, *-mănĕnt,* a. -ly, ad. perma-
nente(mente).

permeate, *-mĕāt,* v. a. penetrar, atravesar.

permissible, *-mĭs'ĭbl,* a. lícito, permiso.

permission, *-mĭsh'ŭn,* s. permisión, licencia, f.

permissive, *-mĭs'ĭv,* a. admisible.

permit, *-mĭt',* v. a. permitir; -, *păr'mĭt,*
s. guía, f.; permiso, m. 			[f.

permutation, *-mūtā'shŭn,* s. permutación,

pernicious, *-nĭsh'ŭs,* a. pernicioso; perjudicial, -ly, ad. perniciosamente.

peroration, *pĕrŏrā'shŭn,* s. peroración, f.

perpendicular, *pŭrpĕndĭk'ŭlăr,* a. -ly,
ad. perpendicular(mente); -, s. línea per-
pendicular, f. 		[meter algún delito.

perpetrate, *-pĕtrāt,* v. a. perpetrar, co-

perpetration, *-pĕtrā'shŭn,* s. perpetra-
ción, f. 			[perpetuamente.

perpetual, *-pĕt'ūăl,* a. perpetuo, -ly, ad.

perpetuate, *-pĕt'ūāt,* v. a. perpetuar, eternizar.

perpetuation, *-pĕtŭá'shŭn,* s. perpetuación, f.

perpetuity, *-pĕtū'ĭtĕ,* s. perpetuidad, f.

perplex, *-plĕks',* v. a. confundir, embrollar.

perplexity, *-plĕks'ĭtĕ,* s. perplejidad, f.

perquisite, *-kwĭzĭt,* s. percance, emolumento, gaje, m.

perry, *pĕr'rĕ,* s. cidra de peras, f.

persecute, *pŭr'sĕkŭt,* v. a. perseguir, importunar.

persecution, *-sĕkŭ'shŭn,* s. persecución, f.

perseverance, *-sĕvē'rāns,* s. perseverancia, f.

persevere, *pŭrsĕvē',* v. n. perseverar.

perseveringly, *-ĭnglĕ,* ad. con perseverancia.

persist, *pŭrsĭst',* v. n. persistir.

persistency, *-ēnsĕ,* s. persistencia, f.

persistent, *-ēnt,* a. persistente.

person, *pŭr'sŏn,* s. persona, f.

personage, *-dj,* s. personaje, m.

personal, *-ăl,* a. -ly, ad. personal(mente); –estate, –goods, bienes muebles, m. pl.

personality, *-ăl'ĭtĕ,* s. personalidad, f.

personalty, *-ăltĕ,* s. (law) bienes muebles, m. pl.

personate, *-ăt,* v. a. representar. [m. pl.

personation, *-ā'shŭn,* s. disfraz, m.

personification, *-ĭfĭkă'shŭn,* s. prosopopeya, f.

personify, *-ĭfĭ,* v. a. personificar.

perspective, *pŭrspĕk'tĭv,* s. perspectiva, f.; –, a. perspectivo.

perspicacious, *-spĭkă'shŭs,* a. perspicaz.

perspicacity, *-spĭkăs'ĭtĕ,* a. perspicacia, f.

perspicuity, *-spĭkū'ĭtĕ,* s. perspicuidad, f.

perspiration, *-spīrā'shŭn,* s. transpiración, f.

perspire, *-pīr',* v. n. transpirar.

persuade, *-swād',* v. a. persuadir.

persuasion, *-swā'shŭn,* s. persuasión, f.

persuasive, *-swā'sĭv,* a. persuasivo; -ly, ad. de un modo persuasivo.

pert, *pŭrt,* a. listo, vivo; petulante.

pertain, *pŭrtān',* v. n. pertenecer.

pertinacious, *-tĭnā'shŭs,* a. pertinaz, obstinado; -ly, ad. pertinazmente.

pertinacity, *-tĭnăs'ĭtĕ,* s. pertinacia, f.

pertinence, *pŭr'tĭnēns,* s. conexión, relación de una cosa con otra, f.

pertinent, *-tĭnēnt,* a. pertinente; perteneciente; -ly, ad. oportunamente.

pertness, *pŭrt'nĕs,* s. impertinencia, f.; vivacidad, f.

perturb, *pŭrtŭrb',* v. a. perturbar.

perturbation, *-tŭrbā'shŭn,* s. perturbación, agitación de ánimo, f.

peruke, *pĕrōk',* s. peluca, f.

perusal, *pĕrō'zăl,* s. lectura, lección, f.

peruse, *pĕrōz',* v. a. leer; examinar atentamente.

peruser, *-ŭr,* s. lector, m.; revisor, m.

Peruvian-bark, *pĕrō'vĭănbărk,* s. quina, f.

pervade, *pŭrvād',* v. a. atravesar, penetrar.

perverse, *-vŭrs',* a. perverso, depravado; -ly, ad. perversamente.

perversion, *-vŭr'shŭn,* s. perversión, f.

perversity, *-vŭr'sĭtĕ,* s. perversidad, f.

pervert, *-vŭrt',* v. a. pervertir, corromper.

pervious, *pŭr'vĭŭs,* a. penetrable; penetrante.

pessimist, *pĕs'sĭmĭst,* s. pesimista, m.

pest, *pĕst,* s. peste, pestilencia, f.

pester, *pĕs'tŭr,* v. a. molestar, cansar.

pest-house, *pĕst'hŏŭs,* s. lazareto, m.

pestilence, *pĕs'tĭlēns,* s. pestilencia, f.

pestilent, *pĕs'tĭlēnt,* **pestilential,** *pĕstĭlēn'shăl,* a. pestilente, pestilencial.

pestle, *pĕs'l,* s. mano de almirez, f.; majadero de mortero, m.; –, v. a. mimar.

pet, *pĕt,* s. enojo, enfado, m.; favorito, m.; petal, *pĕt'ăl,* s. (bot.) pétalo, m.

petard, *pĕtārd',* s. petardo, m.

petition, *pĕtĭsh'ŭn,* s. memorial, m.; representación, petición, súplica, f.; –, v. a. suplicar; requerir en justicia.

petitioner, *-ŭr,* s. suplicante, m.

petrel, *pĕt'rĕl,* s. petrel, m., procelaria, f. (ave).

petrification, *pĕtrĭfĭkă'shŭn,* s. petrificación, f.

petrify, *pĕt'rĭfĭ,* –y, a. & n. petrificar.

petroleum, *pĕtrō'lĕăm,* s. petróleo, m.

petticoat, *pĕt'tĭkōt,* s. guardapiés, zagalejo, m., basquiña, f. [guardilla, m.

pettifogger, *pĕt'tĭfŏggŭr,* s. abogado de pettifogging,* *-fŏg'gĭng,* s. embrollos de los malos abogados, m. pl.

pettiness, *-nĕs,* s. pequeñez, f.

pettish, *pĕt'tĭsh,* a. caprichudo, regañón.

pettitoes, *pĕt'tĭtōz,* s. pl (vulg.) los pies.

petty, *pĕt'tĕ,* a. pequeño, corto.

petulance, *pĕt'ŭlăns,* s. petulancia, f.

petulant, *pĕt'ŭlănt,* a. petulante; -ly, ad. con petulancia.

pew, *pū,* s. banco cerrado de iglesia, m.

pewter, *pū'tŭr,* s. peltre, m.

phaeton, *fā'ĕtŏn,* s. factón, faetonte, m.

phalanx, *făl'ăngks,* s. falange, f.

phantasm, *făn'tăzm,* **phantom,** *făn'tŏm,* s. fantasma, f.

phare, *făr,* s. faro, m.

pharisaic(al), *fărĭsā'ĭk(ăl),* a. farisaico.

pharisee, *făr'ĭsĕ,* s. fariseo, m.

pharmaceutic(al), *fărmăsū'tĭk(ăl),* a. farmacéutico. [copea, f.

pharmacopœia, *fărmăkŏpē'ă,* s. farmacopharmacy,** *făr'măsĕ,* s. farmacia, f.

phase, *fās,* **phasis,** *fā'sĭs,* s. fase, f.

pheasant, *fĕz'ănt,* s. faisán, m.

phenomenal, *fĕnŏm'ĕnăl,* a. prominente.

phenomenon, *fĕnŏm'ĕnŏn,* s. fenómeno, m.

phial, *fī'ăl,* s. redomilla, f. [lantrópico.

philanthropic(al), *fĭlănthrŏp'ĭk(ăl),* a. fiphilanthropist,** *fĭlăn'thrŏpĭst,* s. filántropo, m.

philanthropy, *-thrŏpĕ,* s. filantropía, f.

philological, *fĭlŏlŏj'ĭkăl,* a. filológico.

philologist, *fĭlŏl'ŏjĭst,* s. filólogo, m.

philology, *fĭlŏl'ŏjĕ,* s. filología, m.

philosopher, *fĭlŏs'ŏfŭr,* s. filósofo, m.; natural –, físico, m.

philosophic(al), *fĭlŏsŏf'ĭk(ăl),* a. filosófico; -ally, ad. filosóficamente.

philosophise, *fĭlŏs'ŏfĭz,* v. n. filosofar.

philosophy, *fĭlŏs'ŏfĕ,* s. filosofía, f.; natural –, física, f.

philter, *fĭl'tŭr*, s. filtro, m.

phiz, *fĭz*, s. (vulg.) facha, cara, f.

phlegm, *flĕm*, s. flema, f. [tico.

phlegmatic(al), *flĕgmăt'ĭk(ăl)*, a. flemá-

phosphoric, *fŏsfōr'ĭk*, a. fosfórico.

phosphorus, *fŏs'fŭrŭs*, s. fósforo, m.

photograph, *fō'tōgrăf*, s. fotografía, f.;
—, v. a. fotografiar. [m.

photographer, *fōtŏg'răfŭr*, s. fotógrafo,

photographic(al), *fōtōgrăf'ĭk(ăl)*, a. foto-
gráfico.

photography, *fōtŏg'răfé*, s. fotografía, f.

phrase, *frās*, s. frase, f.; estilo, m.; —, v. a.
nombrar; expresar. [m.

phraseology, *frāzēŏl'ōjē*, s. libro de frases.

phrenology, *frēnŏl'ōjē*, s. frenología, f.

phthisis, *tĭz'ĭs*, s. tisis, f.

physic, *fĭz'ĭk*, s. medicina, f., medicamento, m.; —s, s. pl. física, f.; —, v. a.
medicamentar. [mente.

physical, *—l*, a. físico; —ly, ad física-

physician, *fĭzĭsh'ăn*, s. médico, m.

physiognomist, *fĭzĭŏg'nōmĭst*, s. fisonomista, fisónomo, m. [f.

physiognomy, *fĭzĭŏg'nōmē*, s. fisonomía,

physiological, *fĭzĭŏlŏj'ĭkăl*, a. fisiológico.

physiologist, *fĭzĭŏl'ōjĭst*, s. fisiologista,
fisiólogo, m.

physiology, *fĭzĭŏl'ōjē*, s. fisiología, f.

pianist, *pĭăn'ĭst*, s. pianista, m. & f.

piano, *pĭă'nō*, s. piano-forte, m.

piaster, *pĭăs'tŭr*, s. escudo, m. (moneda
italiana); peso, m. (moneda española).

picaroon, *pĭkărōn'*, s. picarón, m.; ladrón, m.

pick, *pĭk*, v. a. escoger, elegir; recoger,
mondar, limpiar; —, v. n. mascullar,
roer; —, s. pico, m.; lo escogido.

pick-axe, *—ăks*, s. pico, m.

pickerel, *—ĕrĕl*, s. sollito, m. (pez).

picket, *—ĕt*, s. (mil.) piquete, m. [bechar.

pickle, *—l*, s. salmuera, f.; —, v. a. esca-

picklock, *—lŏk*, s. ganzúa, f.

pickpocket, *—pŏkĕt*, pickpurse, *—pŭrs*,
s. cortabolsas, m. [se paga entre muchos, f.

picnic, *pĭk'nĭk*, s. comida, merienda, que

pictorial, *pĭktō'rĭăl*, a. pictórico.

picture, *pĭk'tŭr* (*pĭk'tshŭr*), s. pintura,
f.; retrato, m.; —, v. a. pintar; figurar.

picturesque, *—ĕsk'*, a. pintoresco.

pie, *pĭ*, s. pastel, m.; marica, f. [colores.

piebald, *—bōld*, a. manchado de varios

piece, *pēs*, s. pedazo, m.; pieza, obra, f.;
cañón ó fusil, m.; a—, cada uno; —, v. a.
remendar. [dividido.

piecemeal, *—mēl*, ad. en pedazos; —, a.

pied, *pĭd*, a. variegado, manchado.

pier, *pēr*, s. estribo de puente, m.; muelle,
m. [ladrar; excitar.

pierce, *pērs*, v. a. penetrar, agujerear, ta-

piercingly, *—ĭnglé*, ad. agudamente.

pier-glass, *pēr'glăs*, s. trumó, m.

pier-table, *—tābl*, s. repisa, f.

piety, *pĭ'ĕtĕ*, s. piedad, devoción, f.

pig, *pĭg*, s. cochinillo, lechón, m.; lingote,
m.; —, v. n. parir la puerca.

pigeon, *pĭj'ŭn*, s. palomo, m.; paloma, f.

pigeon-hole, *—hōl*, s. mechinal, m.; casilla para guardar cartas, f.

pigeon-house, *—hŏŭs*, s. palomar, m.

pig-headed, *pĭg'hĕdĕd*, a. estúpido.

pigment, *—mĕnt*, s. pigmento, m.; afeite, m.

pigmy, *—mĕ*, s. pigmeo, m.

pig-sty, *—stĭ*, s. zahurda, f.

pike, *pĭk*, s. lucio, m.; pica, f.

pilaster, *pĭlăs'tŭr*, s. pilastra, f.

pile, *pĭl*, s. estaca, f.; pila, f.; montón, m.;
pira, f.; edificio grande y macizo, m.;
pelo, m.; pelillo (en las telas de lana), m.;
—s, pl. almorranas, f. pl.; —, v. a. amontonar, apilar.

pilfer, *pĭl'fŭr*, v. a. ratear.

pilgrim, *pĭl'grĭm*, s. peregrino, romero, m.

pilgrimage, *—dj*, s. peregrinación, f.

pill, *pĭl*, s. púdora, f.

pillage, *—lĭdj*, s. pillaje, botín, saqueo, m.;
—, v. a. pillar, hurtar.

pillar, *pĭl'lŭr*, s. pilar, m.

pillion, *—yŭn*, s. jalma, enjalma, f.

pillory, *—lŭrē*, s. argolla, f.; cepo, m.; —,
v. a. empicotar, poner á un malhechor á
la vergüenza en alguna picota ó argolla.

pillow, *pĭl'lō*, s. almohada, f.

pillow-case, *—kds*, s. funda, f.

pilot, *pĭ'lŏt*, s. piloto, m.; —, v. a. guiar un
navío en su navegación.

pilotage, *—dj*, s. pilotaje, m.

pimp, *pĭmp*, s. alcahuete, m.

pimpernel, *pĭm'pŭrnĕl*, s. pimpinela, f.

pimple, *pĭm'pl*, s. postilla, pupa, buba, f.

pimpled, *—d*, a. engranujado.

pin, *pĭn*, s. alfiler, m.; cavilla, f.; —, v. a.
prender con alfileres; fijar con clavija.

pinafore, *—āfōr*, s. delantal, m.

pin-case, *—kds*, s. alfiletero, m. [pl.

pincers, *pĭn'sŭrs*, s. pinzas, tenazuelas, f.

pinch, *pĭnsh*, v. a. pellizcar, apretar con
pinzas; estrechar á alguno persiguiéndole;
—, v. n. ser frugal, excusar gastos; —, s.
pellizco, m.; pulgarada, f.; aprieto, m.

pinch-beck, *—bĕk*, s. crisocalco, m.

pin-cushion, *pĭn'kŭshŭn*, s. acerico, m.

pine, *pĭn*, s. (bot.) pino, m.; —, v. n. estar
lánguido; ansiar alguna cosa.

pine-apple, *—ăppl*, s. ananas, piña, f.

pinion, *pĭn'yŭn*, s. piñón, m.; ala, f.; —,
v. a. atar las alas; maniatar.

pink, *pĭngk*, s. (bot.) clavel, m.; (mar.)
pingüe, m.; —, a. rojizo; pequeño.

pin-money, *pĭn'mŭnē*, s. alfileres, m. pl.

pinnace, *pĭn'nās*, s. (mar.) pinaza, f.

pinnacle, *pĭn'năkl*, s. pináculo, chapitel, m.

pint, *pĭnt*, s. pinta, f. (medida de líquidos).

pioneer, *pĭōnēr'*, s. (mil.) zapador, m.

pious, *pĭ'ŭs*, a. pío, devoto; —ly, ad. piadosamente. [aves.

pip, *pĭp*, s. pepita, f.; —, v. n. piar ciertas

pipe, *pĭp*, s. tubo, cañón, conducto, caño,
m.; pipa para fumar, f.; churumbela, f.;
—, v. n. tocar la flauta; graznar.

pipe-clay, *—klā*, s. arcilla refractaria, f.

piper, *—ŭr*, s. flautero, flautista, m.

piping, *—ĭng*, a. enfermizo; hirviente.

pipkin, *pĭp'kĭn*, s. pucherito, m.

pippin, *pĭp'pĭn*, s. (bot.) esperiega, f.

piquancy, pĭ'kŭnsĭ, s. picante, m.; acrimonia, f. [ad. agriamente.

piquant, -kănt, a. punzante, picante; -ly,

pique, pēk, s. pique, m.; desazón, f.; ojeriza, f.; pundonor, m.; -, v.a. picar; irritar.

piquet, pĕkĕt', s. juego de los cientos, m.

piracy, pī'răsĭ, s. piratería, f.

pirate, pī'răt, s. pirata, forbante, m.; -, v. n. & a. piratear; robar.

piratical, pĭrăt'ĭkăl, a. pirático.

Pisces, pĭs'sēz, s. Piscis, m. (signo del

pish! pĭsh, [quita allá! [zodíaco).

pistachio, pĭstă'shĭō, s. (bot.) alfónsigo,

pistol, pĭs'tŏl, s. pistolete, m. [pistacho, m.

pistol-shot, -shŏt, s. pistoletazo, m.

piston, pĭs'tŏn, s. émbolo, m.

pit, pĭt, s. hoyo, m.; sepultura, f.; patio, m.; -, v. n. azuzar á uno para que riña. [f.

pit-a-pat, -ăpăt, s. palpitación de corazón,

pitch, pĭtsh, s. pez, f.; cima, f.; grado de elevación, m.; -, v. a. fijar, plantar; colocar, ordenar; tirar, arrojar; embrear; obscurecer; -, v. n. caerse alguna cosa hacia abajo; caer de cabeza; escoger.

pitch-dark, -dărk, a. negro como la pez.

pitcher, -ăr, s. cántaro, m. [pasón, m.

pitchfork, -fŏrk, s. horca, f.; (mus.) diapiteous, pĭt'ĕŭs, a. lastimoso; compasivo, tierno; miserable; -ly, ad. lastimosa-

pitfall, pĭt'făl, s. trampa, f. [mente.

pith, pĭth, s. meollo, m.; médula, f.; energía, f.

pithily, pĭth'ĭlĭ, ad. vigorosamente. [gía, f.

pithy, -ĭ, a. enérgico; meduloso.

pitiable, pĭt'ĭăbl, a. lastimoso.

pitiful, pĭt'ĭfăl, a. lastimoso, compasivo; -ly, ad. lastimosamente. [misericordia, f.

pitifulness, -nĕs, s. compasión, piedad,

pitiless, pĭt'ĭlĕs, a. desapiadado, cruel; -ly, ad. cruelmente. [porcioncilla, f.

pittance, pĭt'tăns, s. pitanza, ración, f.;

pitted, pĭt'ĕd, a. cavado, picado,

pity, pĭt'ĭ, s. piedad, compasión, f.; -, v. a. compadecer; -, v. n. lastimarse.

pivot, pĭv'ŏt, s. espigón, quicio, m.

pix, pĭks, s. píxide, f.

placable, plă'kăbl, a. aplacable.

placard, plăk'ărd, s. placarte, m.

place, plās, s. lugar, sitio, m.; (mil.) plaza, fortaleza, f.; rango, empleo, m.; -, v. a. colocar; poner dinero á ganancias.

placid, plăs'ĭd, a. plácido, quieto; -ly, ad. apaciblemente.

plagiarism, plā'jărĭzm, s. plagio, m.

plagiarist, -jărĭst, plagiary, -jărĭ, s. plagiario, m.

plague, plāg, s. peste, plaga, f.; -, v. a. atormentar; infestar, apestar.

plaguily, plā'gĭlĭ, ad. molestamente.

plaice, plās, s. platija, f. (pez).

plaid, plăd, s. capa suelta de sarga listada que usan los montañeses de Escocia, m.

plain, plān, a. liso, llano, abierto; sincero; puro, simple, común; claro, evidente, distinto; -ly, ad. llanamente; claramente; -, s. llano, m.; llanada, f.

plain-dealing, -dēlĭng, s. buena fe, f.

plainness, -nĕs, s. llanura, igualdad f.; sinceridad, f.; claridad, f.

plain-speaking, -spēkĭng, a. franco.

plaint, plānt, s. queja, f.; lamento, m.

plaintiff, plān'tĭf, s. (law) demandador, m.

plaintive, -tĭv, a. lamentoso, lastimoso; -ly, ad. de un modo lastimoso.

plait, plāt, s. pliegue, m.; trenza, f.; -, v. a. plegar; trenzar; rizar; tejer.

plan, plăn, s. plano, m.; delineación (de un edificio), f.; -, v. a. proyectar.

plane, plān, s. plano; cepillo, m.; -, v. a. allanar; acepillar.

planet, plăn'ĕt, s. planeta, m.

planetary, plăn'ĕtărĭ, a. planetario.

plane-tree, plān'trē, s. plátano, m.

plank, plăngk, s. tablón; (mar) tablaje, m.; -, v. a. entablar.

plant, plănt, s. planta, f.; planta (asiento del pie); -, v. a. plantar.

plantain, plăn'tăn, s. (bot.) llantén, m.

plantation, plăntă'shŭn, s. plantación, f.; colonia, f. [m.

planter, plănt'ăr, s. plantador, m.; colono,

plant-louse, -lŏŭs, s. pulgón, m.

plash, plăsh, s. charquillo, lagunajo, m.

plaster, plăs'tăr, s. yeso, m.; emplasto, m.; -, v. a. enyesar; emplastar.

plastic(al), plăs'tĭk(ăl), a. plástico.

plat, plăt, s. pedazo de tierra, m.; cintilla de paja, f.; estera, f.; -, v. a. entretejer.

plate, plăt, s. plancha ó lámina de metal, f.; plata labrada, f.; vajilla, f.; plato, m.; -, v. a. planchear; batir hoja. [vía, m.

plate-layer, -lăăr, s. (rail.) asentador de

platform, plăt'fŏrm, s. plataforma, f.

platinum, plăt'ĭnŭm, s. platina, f.

platoon, plătŏŏn', s. (mil.) pelotón, m. [m.

platter, plăt'ăr, s. fuente, f., plato grande,

plaudit, plă'dĭt, s. aplauso, m. [dad, f.

plausibility, plăzĭbĭl'ĭtĭ, s. plausibilidad, f.

plausible, plă'zĭbl, a. plausible.

plausibly, -ĭ, ad. plausiblemente.

play, plā, s. juego, m.; representación dramática, f.; -, v. a. & n. jugar; juguetear; burlarse; representar; (mus) tocar. [m.

play-bill, -bĭl, s. programa de espectáculo,

player, -ăr, s. jugador, m.; comediante, actor, m.; tocador, m.

play-fellow, -fĕllō, play-mate, -măt, s. camarada, m.

playful, -făl, a. juguetón, travieso; -ly, ad. juguetonamente, retozando.

playfulness, -nĕs, s. jovialidad, f.

play-house, -hŏŭs, s. teatro, m.

plaything, -thĭng, s. juguete, m.

play-wright, -rĭt, s. poeta dramático, m.

plea, plē, s. defensa, f.; excusa, f.; pretexto, socolor, efugio, m. [gar.

plead, plēd, v. a. defender en juicio, alepleadable, -ăbl, a. pleiteable.

pleader, -ăr, s. abogado, m.; defensor, m.

pleading, -ĭng, s. acto de abogar, m.

pleasant, plĕz'ănt, a. agradable; placentero, alegre; -ly, ad. alegremente; placenteramente. [recreo, m.

pleasantness, -nĕs, s. alegría, f.; placer,

pleasantry, -rĭ, s. chocarrería, chanza, f.

please, plēz, v. a. agradar, contar, complacer. [tero.

pleasing, plēz'ĭng, a. agradable, placen-

pleasurable, *plĕzh'ŭrăbl,* a. deleitante, divertido, alegre; [arbitrio, m.

pleasure, *plĕzh'ŭr,* s. gusto, placer, m.;

pleasure-ground, *-grŏŭnd,* s. parque de recreo, jardín, m. [plebeyo (m.).

plebeian, *plèbē'ăn,* a. & s. vulgar, bajo;

pledge, *plĕj,* s. prenda, f.; fianza, f.; —, v. a. empeñar, dar fianzas.

plenary, *plē'nărē,* a. plenario, entero.

plenipotentiary, *plĕnĭpōtĕn'shĭărĕ,* s. & a. plenipotenciario (m.). [dancia, f.

plenitude, *plĕn'ĭtŭd,* s. plenitud, abun-

plenteous, *plĕn'tŭs,* **plentiful,** *plĕn'tĭfŭl,* a. copioso, abundante; —ly, ad. con abundancia.

plenty, *plĕn'tē,* s. copia, abundancia, f.

plethora, *plĕth'ōră,* s. plétora, replecíón, f.

plethoric, *plĕthŏr'ĭk,* a. pletórico, repleto.

pleurisy, *plŏ'rĭsē,* s. pleuresía, f. [dócil.

pliable, *plī'ăbl,* **pliant,** *-ănt,* a. flexible,

pliancy, *-ănsē,* s. flexibilidad, f.

plight, *plīt,* v. a. empeñar; —, s. estado, m.; condición, f. [trearse.

plod, *plŏd,* v. n. afanarse mucho, aje-

plodding, *-ĭng,* s. trabajo improbo, m.

plot, *plŏt,* s. pedazo pequeño de terreno, m.; plano, m.; conspiración, trama, f.; estratagema, f.; —, v. a. & n. trazar; conspirar; tramar.

plotter, *-tŭr,* s. conspirador, m.

plough, *plŏŭ,* s. arado, m.; —, v. a. arar, labrar la tierra.

plough-boy, *-bŏĭ,* s. arador, m.

plough-share, *-shăr,* s. reja de arado, f.

plover, *plŏ'vŭr,* s. frailecillo, m. (ave).

pluck, *plŭk,* v. a. tirar con fuerza; arrancar; desplumar; —s. asadura, f.; arranque, tirón, m.

plucky, *-ē,* a. guapo, gallardo. [rugar.

plug, *plŭg,* s. tapón, tarugo, m.; —, v. a. atapar.

plum, *plŭm,* s. ciruela, f.

plumage, *plŏm'dj,* s. plumaje, m.

plumb, *plŭm,* s. plomada, f.; —, ad. á plomo; —, v. a. aplomar.

plumbago, *plŭmbā'gō,* s. lápiz plomo, m.

plumber, *plŭm'ŭr,* s. plomero, m.

plumb-line, *-lĭn,* s. cuerda de plomada, f.; nivel, m.

plume, *plŏm,* s. pluma, f.; plumaje, penacho, m.; —, v. a. desplumar; adornar con plumas.

plummet, *plŭm'mĕt,* s. plomada, f.

plump, *plŭmp,* a. gordo, rollizo; —, ad. de repente; —, v. a. & n. hinchar, caer á plomo.

plumpness, *-nĕs,* s. gordura, corpulencia, obesidad, f. [m.

plum-pudding, *plŭm'pŭddĭng,* s. pudín,

plum-tree, *-trē,* s. ciruelo, m.

plunder, *plŭn'dŭr,* v. a. saquear, pillar, robar; —, s. pillaje, botín, m.; (am.) bagaje, m. [cipitarse.

plunge, *plŭnj,* v. a. & n. sumergir(se), pre-

plunger, *-ŭr,* s. buzo, somorgujador, m.

plural, *plŏ'răl,* a. & s. plural (m.).

plurality, *plŏrăl'ĭtē,* s. pluralidad, f.

plush, *plŭsh,* s. tripe, m. (tela felpada).

ply, *plī,* v. a. trabajar con ahinco; importunar, solicitar; —, v. n. afanarse; aplicarse; (mar.) barloventear.

pneumatic(al), *nŭmăt'ĭk(ăl),* a. neumático.

pneumonia, *nŭmō'nĭă,* s. neumonía, f.

poach, *pōtsh,* v. a. medio cocer (huevos); —, v. n. cazar en vedado.

poacher, *-ŭr,* s. cazador furtivo, m.

pock, *pŏk,* s. viruela, pústula, f.

pocket, *pŏk'ĕt,* s. bolsillo, m.; faltriquera, f.; —, v. a. embolsar; **to — an affront,** tragarse una injuria.

pocket-book, *-bŭk,* s. librito de memoria, m.; cartera, f. [gastos menudos, m.

pocket-money, *-mănē,* s. dinero para los

pod, *pŏd,* s. vaina, f.

poem, *pō'ĕm,* s. poema, m.

poesy, *pō'ĕsē,* s. poesía, f.

poet, *pō'ĕt,* s. poeta, m.

poetaster, *pō'ĕtăs'tŭr,* s. poetastro, m.

poetess, *pō'ĕtĕs,* s. poetisa, f.

poetic(al), *pōĕt'ĭk(ăl),* a. poético; —ly, ad. poéticamente.

poetics, *pōĕt'ĭks,* s. poética, f.

poetise, *pō'ĕtīz,* v. n. poetizar.

poetry, *pō'ĕtrē,* s. poesía, f.

poignancy, *pŏĭ'nănsē,* s. picante, m.; acrimonia, f.

poignant, *-nănt,* a. picante; punzante; satírico; —ly, ad. con satirización.

point, *pŏĭnt,* s. punta, f.; punto, m.; promontorio, m.; puntillo, m.; estado, m.; —, v. a. apuntar; aguzar; puntuar.

point-blank, *-blăngk,* ad. directamente.

pointed, *-ĕd,* a. puntiagudo; epigramático; —ly, ad. sútilmente.

pointer, *-ŭr,* s. apuntador, m.; perro de punta y vuelta, m.

pointless, *-lĕs,* a. obtuso, sin punta.

pointsman, *-s'măn,* s. (rail.) guardaaguja, m.; —'s lodge, s. garita, f.

poise, *pŏĭz,* s. peso, m.; equilibrio, m.; —, v. a. pesar, equilibrar.

poison, *-n,* s. veneno, m.; —, v. a. envenenar, atosigar. [rruptor, m.

poisoner, *-nŭr,* s. envenenador, m.; co-

poisonous, *-nŭs,* a. venenoso.

poke, *pōk,* s. barjuleta, bolsa, f.; —, v. a. andar á tientas; hurgar la lumbre.

poker, *-ŭr,* s. hurgón, m.; (am.) coco, m.

polar, *pō'lăr,* a. polar.

pole, *pōl,* s. polo, m.; (mar.) palo, m.; pértiga, f.; lanza de coche, f.; percha, f.

pole-axe, *-ăks,* s. hachuela de mano, f.

pole-cat, *-kăt,* s. gato montés, m.

polemic, *pōlĕm'ĭk,* a. & s. polémico (m.); controversista (m.); —s, s. pl. polémica, f.

pole-star, *-stăr,* s. Cinosura, f.

police, *pōlēs',* s. policía, f. [m.

police-court, *-kōrt,* s. tribunal de policía,

policeman, *-măn,* s. oficial de policía, m.

policy, *pŏl'ĭsē,* s. política de estado, f.; astucia, f.

polish, *pŏl'ĭsh,* v. a. pulir, alisar; limar; —, v. n. recibir pulimento; —, s. pulimento, m.

polished, *-d,* a. elegante, pulido.

polite, *pōlīt',* a. pulido, cortés; —ly, ad. urbanamente.

politeness, *-nĕs,* s. cortesía, f.

politic, *pŏl'ĭtĭk,* a. político, astuto.

political, *polít'ikâl,* a. político; **-ly,** ad. según reglas de política.

politician, *polítish'ân,* s. político, m.

politics, *pól'ítiks,* s. pl. política, f.

poll, *pól,* s. cabeza, f.; lista de los que votan en alguna elección, f.; voto, m.; **—,** v. a. descabezar; desmochar; **—,** v. n. dar voto en las elecciones.

pollard, *pól'lârd,* s. árbol desmochado, m.

pollen, *pól'lĕn,* s. (bot.) polen, m.

poll-tax, *pól'tâks,* s. capitación, f.

pollute, *póllút',* v. a. ensuciar; corromper.

polluter, *—ûr,* s. corruptor, m.

pollution, *póllú'shân,* s. polución, contaminación, f.

poltroon, *póltrón',* s. collón, m.

polygamist, *políg'âmist,* s. polígamo, m.

polygamy, *—âmĭ,* s. poligamia, f.

polyglot, *pól'ĭglŏt,* a. & s. polígloto (m.).

polygon, *pól'ĭgŏn,* s. polígono, m.

polypus, *pól'ĭpûs,* s. pólipo, m.

polysyllable, *pól'ĭs'ĭlâbl,* s. polisílabo, m.

polytechnic, *pólĭtĕk'nĭk,* a. politécnico.

pomade, *pómâd',* | **pomatum,** *pómâ'tûm,* s. pomada, f. [nado, m.; granada, f.

pomegranate, *pûm'grânât,* s. (bot.) granado, m.

pommel, *pŏm'mĕl,* s. pomo de espada, m.; **—,** v. a. cascar.

pomp, *pŏmp,* s. pompa, f.; esplendor, m.

pomposity, *pŏmpŏs'ĭtĭ,* s. ostentación, f.; énfasis, m. & f. [pomposamente.

pompous, *pŏm'pûs,* a. pomposo; **-ly,** ad.

pond, *pŏnd,* s. estanque de agua, m.

ponder, *pŏn'dûr,* v. a. ponderar, considerar.

ponderous, *—ûs,* a. ponderoso, pesado; **-ly,** ad. pesadamente. [herir con puñal.

poniard, *pŏn'yârd,* s. puñal, m.; **—,** v. a.

pontiff, *pŏn'tĭf,* s. pontífice, papa, m.

pontifical, *pŏntĭf'ĭkâl,* a. & s. pontifical (libro) (m.). [m.

pontificate, *—ĭkât,* s. pontificado, papado, m.

pontoon, *pŏntón',* s. pontón, m.

pony, *pó'nĭ,* s. haca, f.; jaco, m.

poodle, *pó'dl,* s. perro de aguas, m.

pool, *pól,* s. charco, m.; lago, m.

poop, *póp,* s. (mar.) popa, f.; toldilla, f.

poor, *pór,* a. pobre; humilde; de poco valor; estéril; **-ly,** ad. pobremente; **the —,** s. los pobres, m. pl. [m.

poor-box, *—bŏks,* s. tronco de los pobres.

poor-house, *—hŏūs,* s. casa de caridad, f.

poor-law, *—lâ,* s. ley de asistencia pública.

poorness, *—nĕs,* s. pobreza, f. [f.

poor-rate, *—rât,* s. contribución al provecho de los pobres, f.

pop, *pŏp,* s. chasquido, m.; **—,** v. a. & n. entrar ó salir de sopetón; meter alguna cosa repentinamente.

Pope, *pŏp,* s. papa, m.

Popedom, *—dŏm,* s. papado, m.

popery, *—ûrĭ,* s. papismo, m.

pop-gun, *pŏp'gûn,* s. escopetilla con que juegan los muchachos, f. [verde, m.

popinjay, *—ĭnĭjâ,* s. papagayo, m.; pisa-

popish, *pó'pĭsh,* a. papal, romano; **-ly,** ad. á la manera de los papistas.

poplar, *pŏp'lâr,* s. álamo temblón, m.

poplin, *—lĭn,* s. popelina, moselina de lana y seda, f. [pola, f.

poppy, *—pĕ,* s. (bot.) adormidera, amapola, f.

populace, *—ûlâs,* s. populacho, m.

popular, *—ûlâr,* a. **-ly,** ad. popular(mente).

popularity, *pŏpûlâr'ĭtĕ,* s. popularidad, f.

popularize, *pŏp'ûlârĭz,* v. a. popularizar.

populate, *—ûlât,* v. n. poblar.

population, *pŏpûlâ'shân,* s. población, f.

populous, *pŏp'ûlûs,* a. populoso.

populousness, *—nĕs,* s. abundancia de habitantes, f. [loza fina, f.

porcelain, *pŏrs'lân,* s. porcelana, china,

porch, *pŏrtsh,* s. pórtico, vestíbulo, m.

porcupine, *pŏr'kûpĭn,* s. puerco espín, m.

pore, *pór,* s. poro, m.

pork, *pŏrk,* s. carne de puerco, f.

porker, *—ûr,* s. porcino, cochino, f.

porosity, *pŏrŏs'ĭtĕ,* s. porosidad, f.

porous, *pó'rûs,* a. poroso.

porphyry, *pŏr'fĭrē,* s. pórfido, m.

porpoise, *—pûs,* s. puerco marino, m.

porridge, *—rĭj,* s. potaje, m.; sopa, f.

porringer, *—rĭnjâr,* s. escudilla, f.

port, *pŏrt,* s. puerto, m.; (mar.) babor, m.; vino de Oporto, m.

portable, *—âbl,* a. portátil.

portal, *—âl,* s. portal, m.; portada, f.

portend, *pŏrtĕnd',* v. a. pronosticar.

portent, *pŏrtĕnt',* s. portento, prodigio, m.

portentous, *—ûs,* a. portentoso.

porter, *pŏrt'ûr,* s. portero, m.; mozo, m.; cerveza fuerte (en Londres), f.

porterage, *—âj,* s. porte, m. [m.

portfire, *pŏrt'fĭr,* s. lanzafuego, botafuego,

portfolio, *pŏrtfó'lĭó,* s. cartera, f.

portico, *pŏr'tĭkó,* s. pórtico, portal, m.

portion, *pŏr'shûn,* s. porción, parte, f.; dote, m. & f.; **—,** v. a. partir, dividir; dotar. [m.

portliness, *pŏrt'lĭnĕs,* s. porte majestuoso,

portly, *pŏrt'lĕ,* a. majestuoso; rollizo. [u.

portmanteau, *pŏrtmân'tó,* s. portamanteo,

portrait(ure), *pŏr'trât(ûr),* s. retrato, m.

portray, *pŏr'trâ,* v. a. retratar.

portrayer, *—ûr,* s. retratista, m.

pose, *póz,* v. a. parar; confundir; preguntar, interrogar. [que confunde.

poser, *—ûr,* s. examinador, m.; pregunta

position, *pózĭsh'ân,* s. posición, situación, f.; proposición, f.

positive, *pŏz'ĭtĭv,* a. positivo, real, verdadero; **-ly,** ad. positivamente; ciertamente; perentoriamente.

positiveness, *—nĕs,* s. carácter positivo, m.; realidad, f.; determinación, f.; obstinación, f.

posse, *pós'sĕ,* s. la fuerza armada.

possess, *pŏzzĕs',* v. a. poseer; gozar.

possession, *pŏzzĕsh'ân,* s. posesión, f.

possessive, *pŏzzĕss'ĭv,* a. posesivo.

posset, *pós'sĕt,* s. suero, m., agua de leche, f. [f.

possibility, *pŏssĭbĭl'ĭtĕ,* s. posibilidad, f.

possible, *pós'sĭbl,* a. posible; **-ly,** ad. quizá, quizás.

post, *póst,* s. posta, estafeta, f.; correo, m.; puesto, m.; empleo, m.; poste, m.;

—, v. a. apostar; —, v. n. 'r en posta, correr la posta.

postage, —dj, s. porte de carta, m.

postage-stamp, —stămp, s. sello, sello de correo ó de franqueo, m.

post-boy, —bŏť, s. postillón, m.

post-captain, —kăptín, s. capitán de navío, m.

post-card, —kărd, s. tarjeta postal, f.

post-chaise, —shās, s. silla de posta, f.

posterior, pŏstḗ rĭŭr, a. posterior, trasero.

posterity, pŏstḗr tĭé, s. posteridad, f.

postern, pŏsť ŭrn, s. postigo, m.; poterna, f

post-haste, —hāst, ad. á rienda suelta.

posthumous, pŏsť ŭmŭs, a. póstumo.

postilion, pŏsťľ yŭn, s. postillón, m.

posting, pŏsť ĭng, s. viaje con el correo, m. [rural —, peatón, m.

postman, —mŭn, s. cartero, m.; correo, m.;

post-mark, —mărk, s. timbre de posta, m.

post-master, —măstŭr, s. administrador de correos, m.

post-office, —ŏfĭs, s. administración de correos, f.; a letter under address "Post-office", carta en lista de correos. [rreos, f.

post-paid, —pād, a. franco. [rreos.

postpone, pŏstpōn', v. a. diferir, suspender; posponer.

postscript, pŏsť skrĭpt, s. posdata, f.

posture, pŏs' tŭr (pŏs' tshŭr), s. postura, f.; positura, f.

p sy, pŏ' zĕ, s. mote, m.; ramillete de flores, m.

pot, pŏt, s. marmita, f.; olla, f.; —, v. a. preservar en marmitas.

potable, pō' tăbl, a. potable.

potash, pŏť ăsh, s. potasa, f.

potation, pŏtā' shŭn, s. trago, m.

potato, pŏtā' tō, s. patata, f.

pot-bellied, pŏť bĕllĭd, a. panzudo.

pot-boy, —bŏť, s. mozo de cervecero, m.

potent, pŏ' tĕnt, a. potente, poderoso, eficaz.

potentate, pŏ' tĕntăt, s. potentado, m.

potential, pŏtĕn' shăl, a. potencial, poderoso.

pot-hanger, pŏť hăngŭr, s. llares, m. pl.

pother, pŏtʹʾ ŭr, s. baraúnda, f.; alboroto, bullicio, m.

pot-herb, pŏť hĕrb, s. hortaliza, f.

pot-hook, —hŏk, s. asa de caldera, f.

pot-house, —hŏŭs, s. ventorrillo, m.

potion, pŏ' shŭn, s. poción, bebida medicinal, f. [f.

pot-luck, pŏť lŭk, s. comida ordinaria,

potter, pŏť tŭr, s. alfarero, m.; —'s ware, pottery, —ĕ, s. alfar, m. [vidriado, m.

pouch, pŏŭtsh, s. bolsillo, m.; faltriquera, f. [m.

poulterer, pŏľ tŭrŭr, s. pollero, gallinero,

poultice, pōl' tĭs, s. cataplasma, f.

poultry, pŏľ tră, s. aves caseras, f. pl.

poultry-yard, —yărd, s. corral donde se crían las aves caseras, m.

pounce, pŏŭns, s. garra, f.; grasilla, f.; cisquero, m.; —, v. a. apomazar.

pound, pŏŭnd, s. libra, f.; libra esterlina, f.; corral de concejo, m.; —, v. a. machacar.

pounder, —ŭr, s. pera de á libra, f.; cañón

de á tantas libras de bala, m.; mano de almirez, f.; embargador de bestias, m.

pour, pŏr, v. a. echar ó vaciar líquidos de una parte en otra; arrojar alguna cosa continuadamente; —, v. n. fluir con rapidez; llover á cántaros.

pout, pŏŭt, v. n. ponerse ceñudo.

poverty, pŏv' ŭrtĕ, s. pobreza, f.

powder, pŏŭ' dŭr, s. polvo, m.; pólvora, f.; —, v. a. pulverizar; salar.

powder-chest, —tshĕst, s. pl. (mar.) caja de fuego, fpl. [pólvora, m.

powder-horn, —hŏrn, s. frasco para

powdery, —ĕ, a. polvoriento.

power, pŏŭ' ŭr, s. poder, m.; potestad, f.; imperio, m.; potencia, f.; autoridad, f.; fuerzas militares, f. pl.

powerful, —fŭl, a. poderoso; —ly, ad. poderosamente, con mucha fuerza.

powerless, —lĕs, a. impotente.

pox, pŏks, s. viruelas, f. pl.; chicken—, viruelas locas, f. pl.; cow—, vacuna, f.

practicability, prăktĭkăbĭľ tĕ, s. posibilidad de hacer una cosa, f. [hacedero.

practicable, prăk' tĭkăbl, a. practicable;

practically, —ĕ, ad. posiblemente.

practical, prăk' tĭkăl, a. práctico; —ly, ad. prácticamente.

practice, prăk' tĭs, s. práctica, f.; uso, m., costumbre, f.; —s, pl. intrigas, f. pl.

practise, —, v. a. & n. practicar, ejercer.

practitioner, prăktĭsh' ŭnŭr, s. práctico (médico), m.

pragmatic(al), prăgmăt' ĭk(ăl), a. pragmático; entremetido; —ally, ad. impertinentemente.

prairie, prā' rĕ, s. pradería, f.

praise, prāz, s. fama, f.; renombre, m.; alabanza, f.; —, v. a. celebrar, alabar.

praiseworthy, —wŭrthĕ, a. digno de alabanza.

prance, prăns, v. n. cabriolar. [banza.

prank, prăngk, s. travesura, extravagancia, f.

prate, prāt, v. a. charlar; —, s. charla, f.

prattle, prăt' tl, v. n. charlar; —, s. parlería, charla, f.

pray, prā, v. a. & n. suplicar, rogar; orar.

prayer, —ŭr, s. oración, súplica, f.; Lord's —, oración dominical, f.; Padre nuestro, m.

prayer-book, —bŭk, s. libro de devociones,

preach, —prētsh, v. a. & n. predicar. [m,

preacher, —ŭr, s. predicador, m.

preaching, —ĭng, s. predicación, f.

preamble, prēăm' bl, s. preámbulo, m.

prebend, prĕb' ĕnd, s. prebenda, f.

prebendary, —ărĕ, s. prebendado, m.

precarious, prēkā' rĭŭs, a. precario, incierto; —ly, ad. precariamente.

precariousness, —nĕs, s. incertidumbre, f.

precaution, prēkā' shŭn, s. precaución, f.

precautionary, —ărĕ, a. preventivo.

precede, prēsēd' v. a. anteceder, preceder.

precedence, —sĕ' dĕns, s. precedencia, f.

precedent, —sĕ' dĕnt, a. & s. precedente (m).

precentor, —sĕn' tŭr, s. chantre, m.

precept, prē' sĕpt, s. precepto, m.

preceptor, prēsĕp' tŭr, s. preceptor, m.

precinct, prē' sĭngkt, s. límite, lindero, m.

precious, *presh'ŭs*, a. precioso; -ly, ad. preciosamente.

preciousness, -*nĕs*, s. preciosidad, f.

precipice, *prē'sĭpĭs*, s. precipicio, m.

precipitate, *prĕsĭp'ĭtāt*, v. a. & n. precipitar(se); -, a. precipitado, m.; -ly, ad. precipitadamente; -, s. precipitado, m.

precipitation, -*sĭptītā'shŭn*, s. precipitación, inconsideración, f.

precipitous, -*sĭp'ĭtŭs*, a. precipitoso.

precise, -*sīs'*, s. preciso, exacto; -ly, ad. precisamente, exactamente.

precision, -*sĭzh'ŭn*, s. precisión, limitación exacta, f.

preclude, -*klūd'*, v. a. prevenir, impedir.

precocious, -*kō'shŭs*, a. precoz, temprano, prematuro.

precocity, -*kŏs'ĭtĕ*, s. precocidad, f.

preconceive, prēkŏnsēv', v. a. opinar ó imaginar con antelación, [ocupación, f.

preconception, -*kŏnsĕp'shŭn*, s. preocupación, f.

preconcert, -*kŏnsŭrt'*, v. a. concertar, convenir ó estipular de antemano.

precursor, prēkŭr'sŭr, s. precursor, m.

predatory, prēd'ātŭrē, a. rapaz, voraz.

predecessor, prēdĕsĕs'sŭr, s. predecesor, antecesor, m. [destinación, f.

predestination, prēdĕstīnā'shŭn, s. predestine, -dĕs'tĭn, v. a. predestinar.

predicament, -dĭk'ămĕnt, s. predicamento, m.; categoría, f.

predicate, prēd'ĭkāt, v. a. afirmar; -, s. predicado, m. [f.

predication, prēdĭkā'shŭn, s. afirmación.

predict, prēdĭkt', v. a. predecir.

prediction, -dĭk'shŭn, s. predicción, f.

predictor, -dĭk'tŭr, s. adivino, m.

predilection, prēdĭlĕk'shŭn, s. predilección, f.

predispose, -dĭspōz', v. a. predisponer.

predisposition, -dĭspōzĭsh'ŭn, s. predisposición, f. [nio, m.

predominance, prēdŏm'ĭnāns, s. predominio.

predominant, -ĭnănt, a. predominante.

predominate, -ĭnāt, v. a. predominar.

pre-eminence, prēĕm'ĭnĕns, s. preeminencia, f.

pre-eminent, -ĭnĕnt, s. preeminente.

pre-emption, -ĕm'shŭn, s. compra de antemano, f. [peño anterior, m.

pre-engagement, -ĕngāj'mĕnt, s. empeño anterior, m.

pre-existence, -ĕgzĭs'tĕns, s. preexistencia, f. [hacer un prólogo á un libro.

preface, prĕf'ās, s. prefación, f.; -, v. a.

prefatory, prĕf'ātŭrē, a. preliminar.

prefect, prē'fĕkt, s. prefecto, m.

prefecture, -fĕktŭr, s. prefectura, f.

prefer, prēfŭr', v. a. preferir, proponer en público; exhibir.

preferable, prĕf'ŭrăbl, a. preferible.

preference, -ŭrĕns, s. preferencia, f.

preferment, prĕfŭr'mĕnt, s. promoción, f.; preferencia, f. [s. (gr.) prefijo, m.

prefix, prēfĭks', v. a. prefijar; -, prē'fĭks,

pregnancy, prĕg'nănsē, s. preñez, f.

pregnant, -nănt, a. preñada; fértil.

prejudge, prējŭj', v. a. juzgar provisionalmente.

prejudice, prĕj'ŭdĭs, s. perjuicio, daño, m.; -, v. a. perjudicar, hacer daño.

prejudicial, -dĭsh'ăl, a. perjudicial, dañoso.

prelacy, prĕl'ăsē, s. prelacía, f. [ñoso.

prelate, -ăt, s. prelado, m.

preliminary, prēlĭm'ĭnărē, a. preliminar.

prelude, prĕl'ŭd, s. preludio, m.; -, prēlŭd', v. a. (mus.) florear.

premature, prēmātūr', a. prematuro; -ly, ad. anticipadamente.

prematureness, -nĕs, s. madurez ó sazón anticipada, f. [meditación, f.

premeditation, prēmĕdĭtā'shŭn, s. premeditación, f.

premier, prēm'ĭŭr, s. primer ministro, m.

premise, prĕm'ĭs, v. a. exponer premisas.

premises, prĕm'ĭsĕz, s. pl. premisas, f. pl.; predio rústico, m.

premium, prē'mĭŭm, s. premio, m.; remuneración, f.; prima, f. [tivo.

premonitory, prēmŏn'ĭtŭrē, a. preventivo.

preoccupation, prēŏkkŭpā'shŭn, s. anticipación de la adquisición, f.; preocupación (del ánimo), f.

preparation, prēpărā'shŭn, s. preparación, f.; cosa preparada, f. [rio.

preparatory, prēpăr'ătŭrē, a. preparatorio.

prepare, -pār, v. a. (& n.) preparar(se).

prepay, prēpā', v. a. franquear una carta.

prepense, prēpĕns', a. (law) premeditado.

preponderance, prēpŏn'dŭrăns, s. preponderancia, f. [derar.

preponderate, -dŭrāt, v. a. & n. preponderar.

preposition, prēpŏzĭsh'ŭn, s. preposición, f.

prepossessing, prēpŏzĕs'ĭng, s. atractivo. [ción, f.; prevención, f.

prepossession, -pŏzĕsh'ŭn, s. preocupación, f.

preposterous, prēpŏs'tŭrŭs, a. prepóstero; absurdo; -ly, ad. al revés, sin razón. [f.

prerogative, prērŏg'ătĭv, s. prerrogativa, f.

presage, prē'sāj, s. presagio, pronóstico, m.; -, prēsāj', v. a. presagiar.

prescience, prē'shĭĕns, s. presciencia, f.

prescient, -shĭĕnt, a. profético.

prescribe, prēskrīb', v. a. & n. prescribir, ordenar; recetar.

prescription, -skrĭp'shŭn, s. prescripción, f.; receta medicinal, f. [m.

presence, prĕz'ĕns, s. presencia, f.; talle.

presence-chamber, -tshāmbŭr, pres- ence-room, -rōm, s. sala de recibimiento, f.

present, prĕz'ĕnt, s. presente, regalo, m.; -, a. presente; -ly, ad. al presente; -, prēzĕnt', v. a. ofrecer, presentar; regalar; (am.) acusar. [coroso.

presentable, prēzĕnt'ăbl, a. decente, decoroso.

presentation, prēzĕntā'shŭn, s. presentación, f. [regalado, m.

presentation-copy, -kŏpē, s. ejemplar regalado, m.

presentiment, prēsĕn'tĭmĕnt, s. presentimiento, m. [ción, f.

presentment, prēzĕnt'mĕnt, s. presentación, f.

preservation, prēzŭrvā'shŭn, s. preservación, f. [in.

preservative, -zŭr'vătĭv, s. preservativo.

preserve, –zúrv', v. a. preservar, conservar; hacer conservas de frutas; –, s. conserva, confitura, f.

preside, présíd', v. n. presidir; dirigir.

presidency, préz'ídénse, s. presidencia, f.

president, –dént, s. presidente, m.

press, prés, v. a. aprensar, apretar; oprimir, angustiar; compeler; importunar; estrechar; hacer levas; –, v. n. apresurarse; agolparse la gente al rededor de una persona ó cosa; –, s. prensa, turba, f.; armario, m. [matrícula, f.

press-gang, –gáng, s. (mar.) ronda de

pressing, –íng, p. & a. –ly, ad. urgente-(mente). [sión, f.; opresión, f.

pressure, présh'úr, s. prensadura, f.; pre-

presumable, prézúm'ábl, a. presumible.

presume, prézúm', v.n. presumir, suponer.

presumption, prézúm'shún, s. presunción, f. [–ly, ad. presuntuosamente.

presumptuous, –túús, a. presuntuoso;

presuppose, présúppóz', v.a. presuponer.

presupposition, présúppózísh'ún, s. presuposición, f. [sión, f.

pretence, préténs', s. pretexto, m.; preten-

pretend, –ténd', v. a. & n. pretender; presumir.

pretender, –úr, s. pretendiente, m.

pretendingly, –ínglé, ad. presuntuosamente.

pretension, –shún, s. pretensión, f.

preterite, prét'érít, s. pretérito, m.

preternatural, prétúrnát'úrál, s. sobrenatural.

pretext, prétékst', s. pretexto, socolor, m.

prettily, prít'tílé, ad. bonitamente; agradablemente. [f.

prettiness, –tínés, s. lindeza, f.; belleza,

pretty, –té, a. lindo, bien parecido; hermoso; –, ad. algo, un poco. [minar.

prevail, prévál', v. n. prevalecer, predo-

prevailing, –íng, a. dominante (uso, costumbre). [superioridad, f.

prevalence, prév'áléns, s. predominio, m.;

prevalent, –lént, a. predominante, eficaz.

prevaricate, prévár'íkát, v.n. prevaricar; transgredir. [ción, transgresión, f.

prevarication, –ká'shún, s. prevaricación, f.

prevent, prévént', v. a. prevenir; impedir.

prevention, –vén'shún, s. prevención, preocupación, f. [servativo, m.

preventive, –tív, a. preventivo; –, s. pre-

previous, prév'úús, a. previo; antecedente; –ly, ad. de antemano.

prey, prá, s. botín, m.; rapiña, f.; –, v. a. rapiñar, pillar, robar.

price, prís, s. precio, m.; premio, m.

priceless, –lés, a. inapreciable.

prick, prík, v. a. punzar, picar; apuntar; excitar, estimar; poner en música una canción; –, s. puntura, f.; picadura, f.; punzada, f.; pista, f. [f.

pricking, –íng, s. picadura, f.; punzada, f.

prickle, –l, s. pincho, m.; espina, f.

prickly, –lé, a. espinoso.

pride, príd, s. orgullo, m.; vanidad, f.; jactancia, f.; –, v. n. jactarse.

priest, prést, s. sacerdote, presbítero, m.

priestess, –és, s. sacerdotisa, f.

priesthood, –húd, s. clerecía, f.; sacerdocio, m.

priestly, –lé, a. sacerdotal. [docio, m.

priest-ridden, –ríddn, a. gobernado por sacerdotes. [verde, m.

prig, príg, v. p. hurtar, ratear; –, s. pisa-

priggish, –gísh, a. afectado.

prim, prím, a. perpuesto, afectado.

primacy, prí'másé, s. primacía, f.

primarily, prí'márílé, ad. primariamente, sobre todo. [primero.

primary, prí'máré, a. primario, principal, primero.

primate, prí'mát, s. primado, m.

prime, prím, s. madrugada, alba, f.; (fig.) flor, nata, f.; primavera, f.; principio, m.; –, a. primero; primoroso, excelente; –, v. a. cebar; imprimir. [f.

primer, prím'úr, a. cartilla para los niños.

primeval, prímé'vál, a. primitivo.

priming, prí'míng, s. cebo, m.; imprimación, f. [primitivamente.

primitive, prím'ítív, a.primitivo; –ly, ad.

primness, prím'nés, s. afectación, f.

primogeniture, prímójén'itúr, s. primogenitura, f.

primrose, prím'róz, s. (bot.) prímula, f.

prince, príns, s. príncipe, soberano, m.

princedom, –dóm, s. principado, m.

princely, –lé, a. semejante ó correspondiente á un príncipe; –, ad. como un príncipe. [príncipe.

princess, –és, s. princesa, f.

principal, prín'sípál, a. –ly, ad. principal(mente); –, s. principal, jefe, m.; capital, m. [m.

principality, prínsípál'íté, s. principado,

principle, prín'sípl, s. principio, m.; causa primitiva, f.; fundamento, motivo, m.

print, prínt, v. a. estampar, imprimir; –, s. impresión, estampa, edición, f.; impreso, m.; out of –, vendido, agotado (libros).

printer, –úr, s. impresor, m.; indianero, m.; –'s reader, corrector, m.

printing-house, –íng hóús, **printing-office,** –ófís, s. imprenta, f.

prior, prí'úr, a. anterior, precedente; –, s. prior (prelado), m.

prioress, –és, s. priora, f.

priority, príór'íté, s. prioridad, f.

priory, prí'óré, s. priorato, m.

prism, prízm, s. prisma, m.

prison, príz'n, s. prisión, cárcel, f.

prisoner, –úr, s. prisionero, m.

pristine, prís'tín, a. prístino, antiguo.

privacy, prí'vásé, s. secreto, m.; retiro, m.

private, prí'vát, a. secreto, privado; particular; **– soldier,** s. soldado raso, m.; –ly, ad. en secreto, en particular.

privateer, –váér', s. corsario, m.

privation, prívá'shún, s. privación, f.

privilege, prív'ítéj, s. privilegio, m.; –, v. a. privilegiar.

privily, prív'ílé, a. secretamente.

privity, prív'íté, s. confianza, f.; consentimiento, m.

privy, prív'é, a. privado, secreto; confidente; –, s. secreta, letrina, f.

prize, *priz*, s. premio, m.; precio, m.; presa, f.; —, v. a. apreciar, valuar.

pro, *pró*, pr. para. [verisimilitud, f.

probability, *prŏbǎbǐ'tǐ*, s. probabilidad,

probable, *prŏb'ǎbl*, a. probable, verisímil; —bly, ad. probablemente.

probate, *prŏ'bǎt*, s. verificación de los testamentos, f. [men, m.; noviciado, m.

probation, —*bǎ'shǎn*, s. prueba, f., exa-

probationary, —*dré*, a. probatorio.

probationer, —*ǎr*, s. novicio, m.

probe, *prŏb*, s. (med.) tienta, f.; —, v. a. tentar (alguna herida). [f.

probity, *prŏb'ǐtǐ*, s. probidad, sinceridad,

problem, *prŏb'lěm*, s. problema, m.

problematical, *prŏblěmǎt'ǐkǎl*, a. problemático; —ly, ad. problemáticamente.

proboscis, *prŏbŏs'sǐs*, s. probóscide, m.

procedure, *prŏsēd'ǔr*, s. procedimiento, m.; progreso, proceso, m.

proceed, *prŏsēd'*, v. n. proceder; provenir; portarse; originarse; —s, *prŏ'sēdz*, s. pl. producto, m.; rédito, m.; gross —s, producto íntegro; net —s, producto neto.

proceeding, —*ǐng*, s. procedimiento, m.; proceso, m.; conducta f. [m.

process, *prŏ'sĕs*, s. proceso, m.; progreso,

procession, —*sĕsh'ǎn*, s. procesión, f.

proclaim, *prŏklǎm'*, v. a. proclamar, promulgar; publicar.

proclamation, *prŏklǎmǎ'shǎn*, s. proclamación, f.; decreto, bando, m.

proclivity, *prŏklǐv'ǐtǐ*, s. propensión, inclinación, f.

proconsul, *prŏkŏn'sǔl*, s. procónsul, m.

procrastinate, *prŏkrǎs'tǐnǎt*, v. a. diferir, retardar. [ción, tardanza, f.

procrastination, —*krǎstǐnǎ'shǎn*, s. dilatación

procrastinator, —*krǎstǐnǎ'tǎr*, s. pelmazo, m. [escolástico, m.

proctor, *prŏk'tǎr*, s. procurador, m.; juez

proctorship, —*shǐp*, s. procuraduría, f.

procurable, *prŏkǎ'rǎbl*, a. asequible.

procuration, *prŏkǔrǎ'shǎn*, s. procuración, f.

procurator, —*ǎ'tǎr*, s. procurador, m.

procure, *prŏkǔr'*, v. a. procurar.

procurement, —*mĕnt*, s. procuración, f.

procurer, —*ǎr*, s. entremetido, m.

prodigal, *prŏd'ǐgǎl*, a. pródigo; —ly, ad. pródigamente; —, s. disipador, m. [f.

prodigality, *prŏdǐgǎl'ǐtǐ*, s. prodigalidad,

prodigious, *prŏdǐj'ǎs*, a. prodigioso; —ly, ad. prodigiosamente.

prodigy, *prŏd'ǐjě*, s. prodigio, m.

produce, *prŏdūs'*, v. a. producir, criar; causar; —, *prŏd'ǎs*, s. producto, m.

producer, *prŏdū'sǎr*, s. producente, m.

product, *prŏd'ǎkt*, s. producto, m.; obra, f.; efecto, m. [f.; producto, m.

production, *prŏdǎk'shǎn*, s. producción,

productive, *prŏdǎk'tǐv*, a. productivo.

productiveness, —*nĕs*, s. producibilidad, f.

profanation, *prŏfǎnǎ'shǎn*, s. profanación, f. [fanamente; —, v. a. profanar.

profane, *prŏfǎn'*, a. profano; —ly, ad. pro-

profess, *prŏfěs'*, v. a. profesar; ejercer; declarar.

professedly, —*ĕdlě*, ad. declaradamente; públicamente.

profession, *prŏfĕsh'ǎn*, s. profesión, f.

professional, —*ǎl*, a. lo que tiene relación con una profesión particular.

professor, *prŏfĕs'ǎr*, s. profesor, catedrático, m. [f.

professorship, —*shǐp*, s. profesorado, m.; cátedra, f. [—, s. oferta, f.

proffer, *prŏf'fǎr*, v. a. proponer, ofrecer;

proficiency, *prŏfǐsh'ĕnsě*, s. aprovechamiento, m.

proficient, —*ĕnt*, a. proficiente, adelantado. [tado.

profile, *prŏ'fǐl*, s. perfil, m.

profit, *prŏf'ǐt*, s. ganancia, f.; provecho, m.; ventaja, f.; —, v. a. & n. aprovechar, servir, ser útil; adelantar; aprovecharse.

profitable, —*ǎbl*, a. provechoso, ventajoso; —bly, ad. provechosamente.

profitableness, —*bǐnĕs*, s. ganancia, f.; provecho, m.

profitless, —*lĕs*, a. inútil, sin provecho.

profligacy, *prŏf'lǐgǎsě*, s. perversidad, disolución, f.; desarreglo, m.

profligate, *prŏf'lǐgǎt*, a. licencioso, perdido; —ly, ad. disolutamente.

profound, *prŏfŏwnd'*, a. profundo; —ly, ad. profundamente.

profundity, —*fǔnd'ǐtǐ*, s. profundidad, f.

profuse, *prŏfūs'*, a. profuso, pródigo; —ly, ad. profusamente. [abundancia, f.

profusion, —*fū'zhǎn*, s. prodigalidad, f.;

progenitor, *prŏjĕn'ǐtǔr*, s. progenitor, m.

progeny, *prŏj'ĕně*, s. progenie, casta, f.

prognostic, *prŏgnŏs'tǐk*, s. pronóstico, m.

prognosticate, —*ǐtkǎt*, v. a. pronosticar.

prognostication, —*ǐtkǎ'shǎn*, s. pronosticación, f.; pronóstico, m.

programme, *prŏ'grǎm*, s. programa, m.

progress, *prŏ'grĕs*, s. progreso, m.; viaje, curso, m.; —, *prŏgrĕs'*, v. n. hacer progresos. [adelantamiento, m.

progression, *prŏgrĕsh'ǎn*, s. progresión, f.;

progressive, *prŏgrĕs'sǐv*, a. progresivo; —ly, ad. progresivamente. [impedir.

prohibit, *prŏhǐb'ǐt*, v. a. prohibir, vedar;

prohibition, *prŏhǐbǐsh'ǎn*, s. prohibición, f.; auto prohibitorio, m.

prohibitory, *prŏhǐb'ǐtǎrě*, a. prohibitivo.

project, *prŏjĕkt'*, v. a. proyectar, trazar; —, *prŏj'ĕkt*, s. proyecto, m.

projectile, *prŏjĕk'tǐl*, s. proyectil, m.

projection, —*shǎn*, s. proyección, f.; proyectura, f.

projector, —*tǎr*, s. proyectista, m.

proletarian, *prŏlĕtǎ'rǐǎn*, a. proletario, vulgar. [cundo.

prolific(al), *prŏlǐf'ǐk(ǎl)*, a. prolífico, fe-

prolix, *prŏ'lǐks*, a. prolijo, difuso.

prolixity, *prŏlǐks'ǐtǐ*, s. prolijidad, f.

prologue, *prŏ'lǒg*, s. prólogo, m.

prolong, *prŏlŏng'*, v. a. prolongar; diferir. [dilatación, f.

prolongation, —*gǎ'shǎn*, s. prolongación.

promenade, *prŏm'ĕnǎd*, v. n. pasearse; —, *prŏmĕnǎd'*, s. paseo, m. [f.

prominence, *prŏm'ǐnĕns*, s. prominencia,

prominent,–*ĭnĕnt,* a. prominente, saledizo.

promiscuous, *prŏmĭs´kūŭs,* a. promiscuo; **–ly,** ad. promiscuamente. [prometer.

promise, *prŏm´ĭs,* s. promesa, f.; –, v. a.

promissory, –*ĭssŭrĕ,* a. promisorio. [m.

promontory, *prŏm´ŏntŭrĕ,* s. promontorio.

promote, *prŏmōt´,* v. a. promover.

promoter, –*ŭr,* s. promotor, promovedor, m.; **– of a joint-stock-company,** fulbustero de banco, m.

promotion, *prŏmō´shŭn,* s. promoción, f.

prompt, *prŏmt,* a. pronto; constante; **–ly,** ad. prontamente; –, v. a. sugerir, insinuar; apuntar (en el teatro).

prompter, –*ŭr,* s. apuntador de teatro, m.

promptitude, –*ĭtūd,* **promptness,** –*nĕs,* s. prontitud, presteza, f. [publicar.

promulgate, *prŏmŭl´gāt,* v. a. promulgar,

promulgation, –*mŭlgā´shŭn,* s. promulgación, f.

prone, *prōn,* a. prono, inclinado.

proneness, –*nĕs,* s. inclinación, propensión, f. [labrador, m. pl.

prong, *prŏng,* s. dientes de una horca de

pronominal, *prŏnŏm´ĭnăl,* a. pronominal.

pronoun, *prŏ´nŏŭn,* s. pronombre, m.

pronounce, *prŏnŏŭns´,* v. a. pronunciar; recitar. [nunciación, f.

pronunciation, *prŏnŭnsĭā´shŭn,* s. pronunciación, f.

proof, *prŏf,* s. prueba, f.; –, a. impenetrable; de prueba.

proof-sheets, –*shēts,* s. pl. pruebas, primeras muestras de la composición tipográfica, f. pl.

prop, *prŏp,* v. a. sostener; apuntalar; –, s. apoyo, puntal m.; sostén, m. [f.

propaganda, *prŏpăgăn´dă,* s. propaganda,

propagate, *prŏp´ăgāt,* v. a. (& n.) propagar(se). [ción, f.

propagation, *prŏpăgā´shŭn,* s. propagación, f.

propel, *prŏpĕl´,* v. a. impeler.

propeller, –*ŭr,* s. navío á hélice, m.

propensity, *prŏpĕn´sĭtĕ,* s. propensión, tendencia, f.

proper, *prŏp´ŭr,* a. propio; conveniente; exacto; bien parecido; **–ly,** ad. propiamente, justamente.

property, –*tĕ,* s. propiedad, calidad, f.

prophecy, *prŏf´ĕsĕ,* s. profecía, f.

prophesy, *prŏf´ĕsī,* v. a. profetizar; predicar. [dicar.

prophet, *prŏf´ĕt,* s. profeta, m.

prophetess, –*ĕs,* s. profetisa, f.

prophetic(al), *prŏfĕt´ĭk(ăl),* a. profético; **–ally,** ad. proféticamente.

propinquity, *prŏpĭng´kwĭtĕ,* s. propincuidad, proximidad, f.; parentesco, m.

propitiate, *prŏpĭsh´ĭāt,* v. n. propiciar.

propitiation, *prŏpĭshĭā´shŭn,* s. propiciación, acción agradable á Dios, f.

propitiatory, –*tĭătŭrĕ,* a. propiciatorio.

propitious, –*ŭs,* a. propicio, favorable; **–ly,** ad. propiciamente.

proportion, –*tĕ,* s. proporción, f.; simetría, f.; –, v. n. proporcionar.

proportionable, –*ăbl* **proportional,** –*ăl,* a. proporcional, proporcionable.

proposal, *prŏpōz´ăl,* s. propuesta, proposición, f.; oferta, f.

propose, *prŏpōz´,* v. a. proponer.

proposition, *prŏpŏzĭsh´ŭn,* s. proposición, propuesta, f. [sentar una proposición.

propound, *prŏpŏŭnd´,* v. a. proponer;

proprietary, *prŏprī´ĕtărĕ,* a. propio.

proprietor, –*ĕtŭr,* s. propietario, m.

proprietress, –*ĕtrĕs,* s. propietaria, f.

propriety, –*tĭĕ,* s. propiedad, f. [ción, f.

prorogation, *prŏrŏgā´shŭn,* s. prorrogación, f.

prorogue, *prŏrōg´,* v. a. prorrogar.

prosaic, *prŏzā´ĭk,* a. prosaico, en prosa.

proscenium, *prŏsē´nĭŭm,* s. proscenio, m.

proscribe, *prŏskrīb´,* v. a. proscribir.

proscription, *prŏskrĭp´shŭn,* s. proscripción, f.

prose, *prōz,* s. prosa, f. [ción, f.

prosecute, *prŏs´ĕkūt,* v. a. proseguir.

prosecution, –*kū´shŭn,* s. prosecución, f.; seguimiento de una causa criminal, m.

prosecutor, –*kŭtŭr,* s. acusador, m.

proselyte, *prŏs´ĕlīt,* s. prosélito, m.

prosody, *prŏs´ŏdĕ,* s. prosodia, f.

prospect, *prŏs´pĕkt,* s. perspectiva, f.; esperanza, f. [lejos; prévido.

prospective, *prŏspĕk´tĭv,* a. lo que mira de

prospectus, *prŏspĕk´tŭs,* s. prospecto, m.

prosper, *prŏs´pŭr,* v. a. & n. prosperar.

prosperity, *prŏspăr´ĭtĕ,* s. prosperidad, f.

prosperous, *prŏs´părŭs,* a. próspero, feliz; **–ly,** ad. prósperamente. [s. prostituta, f.

prostitute, *prŏs´tĭtūt,* v. a. prostituir; –,

prostitution, –*tū´shŭn,* s. prostitución, f.

prostrate, *prŏs´trāt,* a. prosternado; –, v. a. postrar.

prostration, *prŏstrā´shŭn,* s. postración, f.

protect, *prŏtĕkt´,* v. a. proteger; amparar.

protection, *prŏtĕk´shŭn,* s. protección, f.

protective, –*tĭv,* a. protectorio.

protector, –*tŭr,* s. protector, patrono, m.

protest, *prŏtĕst´,* v. n. protestar; –, *prŏ´tĕst,* s. protesta, f., protesto, m.

protestant, *prŏt´ĕstănt,* s. protestante, m.

protestantism, –*ĭzm,* s. protestantismo, m.

protestation, *prŏtĕstā´shŭn,* s. protestación, f.; protesta, f.

protocol, *prŏ´tŏkŏl,* s. protocolo, m.

prototype, *prŏ´tŏtīp,* s. prototipo, m.

protract, *prŏtrăkt´,* v. a. prolongar, dilatar. [ción, dilatación, f.

protraction, *prŏtrăk´shŭn,* s. prolongación, f.

protrude, *prŏtrōd´,* v. a. empujar; impeler; –, v. n. empujarse. [rancia, f.

protuberance, *prŏtū´bŭrăns,* s. protuberancia, f.

protuberant, –*bŭrănt,* a. prominente, saliente. [ad. soberbiamente.

proud, *prŏŭd,* a. soberbio, orgulloso; **–ly,**

prove, *prŏv,* v. a. probar, justificar; experimentar; –, v. n. resultar; salir (bien ó mal).

provender, *prŏv´ĕndŭr,* s. forraje, m.

proverb, *prŏv´ărb,* s. proverbio, m.

proverbial, *prŏvăr´bĭăl,* a. **–ly,** ad. proverbial(mente).

provide, *prŏvīd´,* v. a. proveer.

provided, –*ĕd* (– that), c. con tal que.

providence, *prŏv´ĭdĕns,* s. providencia, f.; economía, f.

provident, *prŏv´ĭdĕnt,* a. prévido; providente; **–ly,** ad. prévidamente.

10

providential, prŏvĭdĕn'shăl, a. -ly, ad. providencial(mente).

province, prŏv'ĭns, s. provincia, f.; obligación particular, f. [(m.).

provincial, prŏvĭn'shăl, a. & s. provincial

provision, prŏvĭzh'ŭn, s. provisión, f.; precaución, f. [(mente).

provisional, -ăl, a. -ly, ad. provisional-

proviso, prŏvī'zō, s. estipulación, f.

provisory, prŏvī'zŭrĕ, a. provisorio.

provocation, prŏvōkă'shŭn, s. provocación, f.; apelación, f.

provoke, prŏvōk', v. a. provocar; apelar.

provokingly, -ĭnglĕ, ad. de un modo provocativo.

provost, prŏv'ŏst, s. preboste, m.

prow, prŏů, s. (mar.) proa, f.

prowess, -ĕs, s. proeza, valentía, f.

prowl, prŏůl, v. n. andar en busca de pillaje; rondar, vagar; rastrear.

prowler, -ŭr, s. ladrón, estafador, m.

proximate, prŏks'ĭmăt, a. próximo; -ly, ad. próximamente.

proximity, prŏksĭm'ĭtĕ, s. proximidad, f.

proxy, prŏks'ĕ, s. procuración, f.; procura-

prude, prŏd, s. mojigata, f. [dor, m.

prudence, -ĕns, s. prudencia, f.

prudent, -ĕnt, a. prudente, circunspecto; -ly, ad. con juicio.

prudential, prŏdĕn'shăl, a. juicioso.

prudentials, -z, s. pl. máximas de prudencia, f. [gatez, f.

prudery, prŏd'ārĕ, s. gazmoñería, moji-

prudish, prŏd'ĭsh, a. gazmoño, mojigato.

prune, prŏn, v. a. podar; escamondar los árboles; -, s. ciruela pasa, f.

prunello, prŏnĕl'lō, s. ciruelita, f.; carro de oro, m. (tela de lana).

pruning-hook, prŏn'ĭnghŏk, pruning-knife, -nīf, s. podadera, f. [rito, m.

pruriency, prŏ'rĭĕnsĕ, s. comezón, f.; pru-

prurient, -rĭĕnt, a. lo que padece prurito.

prussic acid, prŭs'sĭk ăs'sĭd, s. ácido prúsico, m.

pry, prī, v. n. espiar, acechar. [azul, m.

psalm, săm, s. salmo, m. [m.

psalter, săl'tŭr, s. salterio, libro de salmos,

pseudonym, sū'dōnĭm, s. seudónimo, m.

pshaw! shă, ¡vaya!; ¡fuera!; ¡quita!; ¡malhaya!. [¡lógico.

psychologic(al), sīkŏlŏj'ĭk(ăl), a. sico-

psychology, sīkŏl'ŏjĕ, s. sicología, f.

puberty, pū'bŭrtĕ, s. pubertad, f.

public, pŭb'lĭk, a. público; común; notorio; -ly, ad. públicamente; -, s. público, m.

publican, -ăn, s. publicano, m.; tabernero, m. [f.; edición, f.

publication, pŭblĭkă'shŭn, s. publicación,

publicist, pŭb'lĭsĭst, s. publicista, m.

publicity, pŭblĭs'ĭtĕ, s. publicidad, f.

publish, pŭb'lĭsh, v. a. publicar.

publisher, -ŭr, s. publicador, editor, m.

pucker, pŭk'ŭr, v. a. arrugar, hacer pliegues. [morcilla, f.

pudding, pŭd'ĭng, s. pudín, pudingo, m.;

puddle, pŭd'dl, s. lodazal, cenagal, m.; -, v. a. enlodar; enturbiar el agua con lodo.

pudenda, pŭdĕn'dă, s. partes vergonzosas, f. pl.

pudicity, pūdĭs'ĭtĕ, s. pudor, recato, m.

pudor, pū'dŏr, s. pudor, m.; modestia, f.

puerile, pū'ărĭl, a. pueril.

puff, pŭf, s. bufido, soplo, m.; bajín, m.; borla para empolvar, f.; rizado, m.; reclamo, m., -, v. a. hinchar; soplar; ensoberbecer; -, v. n. inflarse; bufar; resoplar.

puffiness, -ĭnĕs, s. hinchazón, f. [soplar.

puffing, -ĭng, s. reclamo, m.

puff-paste, -păst, s. hojaldre, m.

puffy, -ĕ, a. hinchado, entumecido.

pug, pŭg, s. perrillo fino, m.

pugilism, pū'jĭlĭzm, s. pugilato, m.

pugilist, pū'jĭlĭst, s. pugil, m.

pugnacious, pŭgnă'shŭs, a. pugnaz; -ly, ad. con valor. [f.

pug-nose, pŭg'nōz, s. nariz roma ó chata.

puisne, pū'nĕ, a. inferior; pequeño; segundón. [m.

puling, pū'lĭng, s. gemido, m.; plamiento,

pull, pŭl, v. a. tirar; coger; rasgar, desgarrar; to-off, arrancar; -, s. tirón, m.; sacudida, f.

pull-back, -băk, s. obstáculo, m.

pullet, -lĕt, s. polla, f.

pulley, pŭl'ĕ, s. polea, garrucha, f.

pulmonary, pŭl'mŏnărĕ, pulmonic(al), pŭlmŏn'ĭk(ăl), a. pulmoníaco.

pulp, pŭlp, s. pulpa, f.

pulpit, pŭl'pĭt, s. púlpito, m.

pulpy, pŭlp'ĕ, a. pulposo.

pulsate, pŭl'săt, v. n. pulsar, latir.

pulsation, pŭlsă'shŭn, s. pulsación, f.

pulse, pŭls, s. pulso, m.; legumbres, f. pl.

pulverization, pŭlvŭrĭză'shŭn, s. pulverización, f.

pulverize, pŭl'vŭrĭz, v. a. pulverizar.

pumice, pū'mĭs, s. piedra pómez, f.

pump, pŭmp, s. bomba, f.; escarpín, m.; -, v. a. dar á la bomba; sondear; sonsacar.

pumpkin, pŭm'kĭn, s. calabaza, f.

pump-room, -rōm, s. pabellón para beber termas, m.

pun, pŭn, s. equívoco, chiste, m.; -, v. n. jugar del vocablo, decir equívocos.

punch, pŭnsh, s. punzón, m.; ponche, m. (bebida); arlequín, m.

puncheon, -ŭn, s. punzón, m.; cuño, m.; medida de veinte arrobas, f. [fón, m.

punchinello, -ĭnĕl'lō, s. polichinela, bu-

punctilio, pŭngktĭl'ĭō, s. puntillo, m.

punctilious, -ŭs, a. puntoso.

punctual, pŭngk'tŭăl, a. puntual, exacto; -ly, ad. puntualmente. [tualidad, f.

punctuality, -tŭăl'ĭtĕ, s. exactitud, pun-

punctuate, -tŭăt, v. n. puntuar.

punctuation, -tŭă'shŭn, s. puntuación, f.

puncture, -tŭr, s. puntura, f.

pungency, pŭn'jĕnsĕ, s. acrimonia, f.; picante, m.

pungent, -jĕnt, a. picante, acre, mordaz.

punic, pū'nĭk, a. púnico, pérfido.

puniness, pū'nĭnĕs, s. pequeñez, f.

punish, pŭn'ĭsh, v. a. castigar, penar.

punishable, -ăbl, a. punible.

punishment, -mĕnt, s. castigo, m.; pena, f.

punster, pŭns'tŭr, s. truhán, m.; dichero, m.

punt, *pŭnt*, v. a. apuntar, parar (poner el dinero á las cartas); —, s. barco llano, m.

punter, -*ŭr*, s. apuntador, m. (en el juego de faraón).

puny, *pū'ně*, a. joven, pequeño; inferior.

pup, *pŭp*, s. cachorrillo, m.; —, v. n. parir la perra. [discípulo, m.

pupil, *pū'pĭl*, s. pupila, f.; pupilo, m.;

pupilage, -*dj*, s. pupilaje, m.

pupillary, -*ărě*, a. pupilar.

puppet, *pŭp'pĕt*, s. títere, muñeco, m.

puppet-show, -*shō*, s. representación de títeres, f.

puppy, *pŭp'pě*, s. perrillo, trasto, m.

puppyism, -*ĭzm*, s. fatuidad, f.

purblind, *pŭr'blīnd*, a. miope, cegato.

purchase, *pŭr'tshās*, v. a. comprar; mercar; —, s. compra, f.; adquisición, f.

purchaser, -*ŭr*, s. comprador, m.

pure, *pūr*, a. puro; -ly, ad. puramente.

purgation, *pŭrgā'shŭn*, purging, *pŭrj'ing*, s. purgación, f.

purgative, *pŭr'gătĭv*, a. purgativo.

purgatory, *pŭr'gătŭrě*, s. purgatorio, m.

purge, *pŭrj*, v. a. purgar. [ción, f.

purification, *pŭrĭfĭkā'shŭn*, s. purificación, purify, *pū'rĭfī*, v. a. (& n.) purificar(se).

purist, *pū'rĭst*, s. purista, m.

puritan, *pū'rĭtăn*, s. puritano, m.

purity, *pū'rĭtě*, s. pureza, f.

purl, *pŭrl*, s. cerveza de ajenjos, f.; murmullo, m.; —, v. n. murmurar.

purlieu, *pŭr'lū*, s. comarca, f.

purloin, *pŭrlōĭn'*, v. a. hurtar, robar.

purple, *pŭr'pl*, a. purpúreo; —, s. púrpura, f.; -s, s. pl. (med.) tabardillo pintado, m.; —, v. a. purpurear.

purplish, -*plĭsh*, a. purpurino.

purport, *pŭr'pōrt*, s. designio, m.; contenido, m.; —, v. a. significar, designar.

purpose, *pŭr'pŭs*, s. intención, f.; designio, proyecto, m.; to the —, al propósito; to no —, inútilmente; on —, de propósito; —, v. n. proponer. [son contentos.

purr, *pŭr*, v. n. roncar los gatos cuando

purse, *pŭrs*, s. bolsa, f.; —, v. a. embolsar.

purse-proud, -*prŏŭd*, a. plutocrático.

purslain, *pŭrs'lān*, s. (bot.) verdolaga, f.

pursuance, *pŭrsū'ăns*, s. prosecución, f.

pursuant, -*ănt*, a. hecho en consecuencia de. . . . [acosar; continuar.

pursue, *pŭrsū'*, v. a. & n. perseguir; seguir,

pursuit, *pŭrsūt'*, s. perseguimiento, m.;

pursy, *pŭrs'ě*, a. asmático. [ocupación, f.

purulence, *pū'rŏlěns*, s. purulencia, f.

purulent, -*lěnt*, a. purulento.

purvey, *pŭrvā'*, v. a. & n. proveer; procurar. [sión, f.

purveyance, -*ăns*, s. abasto m.; provisión, f.

purveyor, -*ŭr*, s. abastecedor, f.

push, *pŭsh*, v. a. empujar; estrechar, apretar; —, v. n. hacer esfuerzos; —, s. impulso, m.; empujón, m.; momento crítico, m.; esfuerzo, m.; asalto, m.

pushing, -*ĭng*, a. emprendedor.

pusillanimity, *pŭsĭllănĭm'ĭtě*, s. pusilanimidad, f. [lánime.

pusillanimous, *pŭsĭllăn'ĭmŭs*, a. pusi-

puss, *pŭs*, s. miz, m. (voz de cariño para pustule, *pŭs'tūl*, s. pústula, f. [el gato).

put, *pŭt*, v. a. poner, colocar; proponer; imponer, obligar; —, v. n. brotar, germinar.

putative, *pū'tătĭv*, a. putativo, reputado,

put-off, *pŭt'ŏf*, s. retardo, m.; dilatación,

put-on, -*ŏn*, s. engaño, m. [f.

putrefaction, *pūtrěfăk'shŭn*, s. putrefacción.

putrefy, *pū'trěfī*, v. n. pudrirse. [ción, f.

putrescence, *pūtrěs'sěns*, s. pudrición, f.

putrescent, -*sěnt*, putrid, *pū'trĭd*, a. podrido, pútrido. [ción, f.

putridness, -*něs*, s. podredumbre, pudri-

putty, *pŭt'tě*, s. almáciga, f.

puzzle, *pŭz'zl*, s. embarazo, m.; perplejidad, f.; —, v. a. embrollar; —, v. n. confundirse.

pyramid, *pĭr'ămĭd*, s. pirámide, f.

pyramidal, *pĭrăm'ĭdăl*, a. piramidal.

pyre, *pīr*, s. pira, hoguera, f. [tecnica, f.

pyrotechnics, *pĭrōtěk'nĭks*, s. pl. pirotpython, *pīth'ŏn*, s. pitón atigrado, m.

pythoness, *pĭ'thŏněs*, s. pitonisa, f.

pyx, *pĭks*, s. píxide, copón, m.

Q.

quack, *kwăk*, v. n. graznar (como un pato); —, s. charlatán, m.

quackery, -*ŭrě*, s. charlatanería, f.

quadragésima, *kwŏdrăjěs'ĭmă*, s. cuadragésima, f. [m.

quadrangle, *kwŏd'răngl*, s. cuadrángulo,

quadrant, -*rănt*, s. cuarto, m.; cuadrante, m.; (mar.) octante, m.

quadrennial, *kwŏdrěn'nĭăl*, a. cuadrienal.

quadrilateral, *kwŏdrĭlăt'ěrăl*, a. cuadrilátero.

quadrille, *kădrĭl'*, s. contradanza, f.

quadroon, *kwŏdrōōn'*, s. cuarterón, m.

quadruped, *kwŏd'rūpěd*, s. cuadrúpedo, m.

quadruple, *kwŏd'rūpl*, a. cuádruplo.

quaff, *kwăf*, v. a. beber á grandes tragos; —, v. n. beber demasiado.

quaffer, -*ŭr*, s. borracho, m.

quagmire, *kwăg'mīr*, s. tremedal, m.

quail, *kwāl*, s. codorniz, f.

quaint, *kwānt*, a. nimiamente exacto; pulido; exquisito; -ly, ad. pulidamente.

quaintness, -*něs*, s. elegancia, f.; delicadeza, f.

quake, *kwāk*, v. n. temblar; tiritar.

quaker, -*ŭr*, s. cuáscaro, m. (sectario).

qualification, *kwŏlĭfĭkā'shŭn*, s. calificación, f.; prendas, f. pl.

qualify, *kwŏl'ĭfī*, v. a. calificar; modificar; (am.) afirmar con juramento; templar.

qualitative, *kwŏl'ĭtătĭv*, a. cualitativo.

quality, *kwŏl'ĭtě*, s. calidad, f.

qualm, *kwăm*, s. deliquio, desmayo, m.

qualmish, -*ĭsh*, a. desfallecido, lánguido.

quandary, *kwŏndā'rě*, s. incertidumbre, duda, f. [tivo.

quantitative, *kwŏn'tĭtătĭv*, a. cuantita-

quantity, *kwŏn'tĭtě*, s. cantidad, f.

quantum, *kwŏn'tăm*, s. tanto, m.

quarantine, *kwŏr'ăntēn*, s. cuarentena, f.

10*

quarrel, *kwŏr'rĕl,* s. quimera, riña, contienda, f.; —, v. n. reñir, disputar.

quarreller, *-lŭr,* s. quimerista, m.

quarrelsome, *-sŭm,* a. pendenciero, quimerista, f. [merista.

quarry, *kwŏr'rĕ,* s. cantera, f. [merista.

quarryman, *-măn,* s. cavador de cantera, m. [cientos); media azumbre, f.

quart, *kwărt,* s. cuarta, f. (en el juego de los cientos); media azumbre, f.

quartan, *kwăr'tăn,* s. cuartana, f.

quarter, *-tŭr,* s. cuarto, m.; cuarta parte, f.; cuartel, m.; barriada, f.; —of an hour, un cuarto de hora; —, v. a. cuartear; acuartelar.

quarter-deck, *-dĕk,* s. (mar.) alcázar, m.

quarterly, *-lĕ,* a. lo que se hace cada tres meses; —, ad. una vez cada trimestre.

quartern, *-tărn,* s. cuarta parte de un cuartillo, f.

quartet, *kwărtĕt',* s. (mus.) cuarteto, f.

quarto, *kwŏr'tŏ,* s. libro en cuarto, m.

quartz, *kwărts,* s. (min.) cuarzo, m.

quash, *kwŏsh,* v. a. fracasar; cascar; anular, abrogar. [v. n. gorgoritear, trinar.

quaver, *kwā'vŭr,* s. (mus.) corchea, f.; —, v. n. gorgoritear, trinar.

quay, *kĕ,* s. muelle, m.

quean, *kwēn,* s. mujercilla, f.

queasiness, *kwē'zĭnĕs,* s. hastío, m.

queasy, *kwē'zĕ,* a. nauseabundo; fastidioso.

queen, *kwēn,* s. reina, f.; dama, f. (en el juego de damas y en el ajedrez). [reina.

queen-like, *-lĭk,* **queenly,** *-lĕ,* a. á lo reina.

queer, *kwēr,* a. estraño; ridículo; **-ly,** ad. ridículamente.

queerness, *-nĕs,* s. rareza, ridiculez, f.

quell, *kwĕl,* v. a. subyugar, postrar, avasallar.

quench, *kwĕnsh,* v. a. apagar; extinguir.

querist, *kwē'rĭst,* s. inquisidor, preguntador, m. [quejosamente.

querulous, *kwĕr'ŭlŭs,* a. quejoso; **-ly,** ad. quejosamente.

querulousness, *-nĕs,* s. la disposición ó costumbre de quejarse.

query, *kwē'rĕ,* s. cuestión, pregunta, f.; —, v. a. preguntar. [busca, f.

quest, *kwĕst,* s. pesquisa, inquisición; busca, f.

question, *kwĕst'yŭn,* s. cuestión, f.; disquisición, f.; asunto, m.; duda, f.; cuestión de tormento; —, v. a. cuestionar, preguntar; —, v. n. dudar, desconfiar.

questionable, *-ăbl,* a. cuestionable, dudoso. [dor, f.

questioner, *-ŭr,* s. inquiridor, preguntador, f.

questor, *kwĕst'ŭr,* s. cuestor, m.

quibble, *kwĭk'bl,* s. juguete de vocablo, m.; —, v. n. jugar del vocablo, decir equívocos.

quick, *kwĭk,* a. vivo, viviente; veloz; ligero, pronto; ágil, ardiente, penetrante; **-ly,** ad. con presteza; —, s. carne viva, f.

quicken, *-n,* v. a. vivificar; acelerar; animar. [mar.

quick-lime, *-lĭm,* s. cal viva, f. [mar.

quickness, *-nĕs,* s. presteza, f.; actividad, f.; viveza, penetración, f.

quick-sand, *-sănd,* s. arena movediza, f.

quickset, *-sĕt,* s. plantón, m.; **—hedge,** seto vivo, m.

quick-sighted, *-sītĕd,* a. perspicaz. [m.

quick-silver, *-sĭlvŭr,* s. azogue, mercurio, f.

quick-silvered, *-sĭlvŭrd,* a. azogado.

quick-witted, *-wĭttĕd,* a. agudo, perspicaz.

quid, *kwĭd,* s. pedazo de tabaco que mascan los marineros, m. [f.

quiddity, *-ĭtĕ,* s. cavilación, trampa legal, f.

quidnunc, *-nŭngk,* s. fanfarrón, m.

quiescent, *kwĭĕs'sĕnt,* a. quieto, descansado. [**-ly,** ad. quietamente.

quiet, *kwī'ĕt,* a. quedo, quieto, tranquilo; **-ly,** ad. quietamente.

quietism, *-ĭzm,* s. tranquilidad de ánimo, f.

quietness, *-nĕs,* **quietude,** *-ŭd,* s. quietud, tranquilidad, f.

quietus, *kwī'ētŭs,* s. finiquito, m.; muerte, f.

quill, *kwĭl,* s. pluma (para escribir), f.; canilla, f.

quill-driver, *-drīvŭr,* s. cagatinta, m.

quilt, *kwĭlt,* s. colcha, f. [brillo, m.

quince, *kwĭns,* s. (bot.) membrillero, membrillo, m.

quincunx, *kwĭng'kŭngks,* s. quincunce, f.

quinine, *kwĭn'ĭn,* s. quinina, f. [m.

quinquennial, *kwĭnkwĕn'nĭăl,* a. lo que dura un quinquerio ó sucede una vez en cinco años.

quinsy, *kwĭn'zĕ,* s. esquinancia, f.

quint, *kwĭnt,* s. quinta, f. (en algunos juegos de naipes).

quintal, *kwĭn'tăl,* s. quintal, m. [cia, f.

quintessence, *kwĭntĕs'sĕns,* s. quinta esencia, f.

quintet, *kwĭntĕt',* s. (mus.) quinteto, m.

quintuple, *kwĭn'tŭpl,* a. quíntuplo.

quip, *kwĭp,* s. indirecta, f.; —, v. a. echar pullas. [pullas.

quire, *kwīr,* s. mano de papel, f. [pullas.

quirk, *kwŭrk,* s. pulla, f.; sutileza, f.

quit, *kwĭt,* v. a. descargar; desempeñar; absolver; —, a. libre, descargado.

quite, *kwĭt,* ad. totalmente, enteramente, absolutamente.

quits, *kwĭts,* ¡en paz! [peño, m.

quittance, *kwĭt'ĭtns,* s. finiquito, desempeño, m.

quiver, *kwĭv'ŭr,* s. aljaba, f.; —, v. n. temblar; —, a. armado con aljaba.

quixotic, *kwĭksŏt'ĭk,* a. quijotesco.

quiz, *kwĭz,* v. a. burlar, chulear.

quizzing-glass, *kwĭz'ĭnggls,* s. anteojo de puño, m.; lágrima jocosa, f.

quoit, *k(w)ŏĭt,* s. tejo, m.

quondam, *kwŏn'dăm,* a. antiguo.

quorum, *kwŏr'ŭm,* s. número competente [de jueces, m.

quota, *kwŏ'tă,* s. cuota, f. [de jueces, m.

quotation, *kwŏtā'shŭn,* s. citación, cita, f.

quote, *kwŏt,* v. a. citar. [— he, él dijo.

quoth, *kwăth (kwŏth),* v. imp. — I, dije yo;

quotidian, *kwŏtĭd'ĭăn,* s. calentura cotidiana, f.

quotient, *kwŏ'shĕnt,* s. cociente, m.

R.

rabbet, *răb'bĕt,* s. ranura, f.

rabbi, *răb'bĕ,* s. rabí, rabino, m.

rabbit, *răb'bĭt,* s. conejo, m.

rabble, *răb'bl,* s. gentuza, canalluza, f.

rabid, *răb'ĭd,* a. rabioso, furioso.

race, *răs,* s. raza, casta, f.; carrera, f.; sabor rancio del vino, m.; —, v. n. correr con mucha ligereza.

racer, –ŭr, s. caballo de carrera, m.

raciness, rā'sĭnĕs, s. calidad rancia del vino, f. [carrera ciega, f.

racing, rās'ĭng, s. corrida de caballos,

rack, rāk, s. tormento. m.; rueca, f.; morillos de asador, m. pl.; pesebre, m.; –, v. n. atormentar; trasegar. [queta, f.

racket, –ĕt, s. baraúnda, confusión, f.; raqueta, f.

rack-rent, –rĕnt, s. arriendo exorbitante,

racy, rā'sĕ, a. rancio, espirituoso. [m.

radiance, rā'dĭăns, s. brillo, esplendor, m.

radiant, –dĭănt, a. radiante, brillante.

radiate, –dĭāt, v. n. echar rayos, centellear.

radiation, rādĭā'shŭn, s. irradiación, f.

radical, rā'dĭkăl, a. –ly, ad. radical(mente).

radicalism, –ĭzm, s. radicalismo, m.

radish, rā'dĭsh, s. rábano, m.

radius, rā'dĭŭs, s. radio, semidiámetro, m.

raffle, rā'fl, s. rifa, f. (juego); –, v. n. rifar.

raft, rāft, s. balsa, almadía, f.; jangada, f.

rafter, –ŭr, s. cabrio, m.; viga, f.

rag, rāg, s. trapo, andrajo, girón, m.

ragamuffin, –ămŭf'fĭn, s. andrajo, mendigo, pordiosero, m.; bribón, m.

rage, rāj, s. rabia, f.; furor, m.; –, v. n. rabiar; encolerizarse.

rag-gatherer, rāg'găthŭrŭr, (—man, —picker) s. trapero, m.

ragged, rāg'gĕd, a. andrajoso.

raging, rāj'ĭng, s. furia, rabia, f.; –ly, ad.

raid, rād, s. invasión, f. [rabiosamente.

raider, –ŭr, s. merodeador, m.

rail, rāl, s. baranda, barrera, f.; balaustrada, f.; (rail.) rail, carril de los caminos de hierro, m.; –, v. a. cercar con balaustradas; –, v. n. injuriar de palabra. [m.

railer, –ŭr, s. maldiciente, murmurador,

raillery, rāl'ŭrĕ, s. chocarrería, burla, f.

railroad, rāl'rōd, railway, –wā, s. ferrocarril, m.

raiment, rā'mĕnt, s. ropa, f.; vestido, m.

rain, rān, s. lluvia, f.; –, v. n. llover.

rainbow, –bō, s. arco iris, arco celeste, m.

rain-water, –wătŭr, s. agua llovediza, f.

rainy, –ĕ, a. lluvioso.

raise, rāz, v. a. levantar, alzar; fabricar, edificar; engrandecer, elevar; excitar, causar.

raisin, rā'zn, s. pasa, f. (uva seca). [sar.

rake, rāk, s. rastro, rastrillo, m.; tunante, hombre perdulario, m.; –, v. a. rastrillar; raer; rebuscar.

rakish, rāk'ĭsh, a. libertino, disoluto.

rally, rāl'lĕ, v. a. (mil.) reunir; ridiculizar; –, v. n. reunirse; burlarse de alguno.

ram, rām, s. morueco, m.; ariete, m.; –, v. a. impeler con violencia.

ramble, rām'bl, v. n. vagar; callejear; –, s. correría, f.

rambler, –ŭr, s. vagabundo, callejero, m.

ramification, rāmĭfĭkā'shŭn, s. ramificación, f.

ramify, rām'ĭfĭ, v. n. ramificarse.

rammer, rām'mŭr, s. maza, f.; baqueta de escopeta, f.

rampant, rām'pănt, a. exuberante.

rampart, rām'pärt, s. plataforma, f.; terraplén, m.; (mil.) muralla, f. [dor, m.

ramrod, rām'rŏd, s. baqueta, f.; atacador,

ramshackle, rām'shăkl, a. en ruina.

rancid, rān'sĭd, a. rancio.

rancidity, rānsĭd'ĭtĕ, s. rancidez, f.

rancour, rāng'kŭr, s. rencor, m.

random, rān'dŏm, s. ventura, casualidad, f.; at –, á trochemoche.

range, rānj, v. a. colocar, ordenar; cerner; –, v. n. vagar; –, s. clase, f.; orden, m.; hilera, f.; correría, f.; línea de un tiro de artillería, f.; reja de cocina, f.; lanza de coche, f.

rank, rāngk, a. exuberante; rancio; fétido, –, s. fila, hilera, clase, f.; grado de dignidad, m.

rankle, –l, v. n. enconarse, inflamarse.

rankness, –nĕs, s. exuberancia, f.; olor ó gusto rancio, m.; fuerza, f., vigor, m.

ransack, rān'săk, v. a. saquear, pillar.

ransom, rān'sŭm, v. a. saquear, pillar.

rant, rānt, v. n. decir disparates.

ranter, –ŭr, s. declamador, m.

rap, rāp, v. a. & n. dar un golpe vivo y repentino; arrebatar; –, s. golpe ligero y vivo, m. [con rapacidad.

rapacious, răpā'shŭs, a. rapaz; –ly, ad.

rapacity, răpăs'ĭtĕ, s. rapacidad, f.

rape, rāp, s. fuerza, f.; estupro, m.; (bot.) nabo silvestre, m. [mente.

rapid, rāp'ĭd, a. rápido; –ly, ad. rápida-

rapidity, răpĭd'ĭtĕ, s. rapidez, f.

rapier, rā'pĭŭr, s. espadín, m.

rapine, rāp'ĭn, s. rapiña, f.

rapper, rāp'pŭr, s. llamador ó aldabón de puerta, m.; mentira grosera, f.

rapt, rāpt, a. encantado, enajenado.

rapture, rāp'tshŭr, s. rapto, m.; éxtasis, m.

rapturous, –ŭs, a. maravilloso.

rare, rār, a. raro, extraordinario; ralo; –ly, ad. raramente. [dinuevo, m.

rareshow, rā'rĕshō, s. mundinovi, mun-

rarefaction, rārĕfăk'shŭn, s. rarefacción, f.

rarefy, rā'rĕfĭ, v. a. rarificar.

rarity, rā'rĭtĕ, s. raridad, rareza, f.

rascal, rās'kăl, s. pícaro, bribón, m.

rascality, răskăl'ĭtĕ, s. pillada, f.

rascallion, răskăl'yŭn, s. villano, m.

rash, rāsh, a. precipitado, temerario; –ly, ad. temerariamente; –, s. roncha, f.

rasher, –ŭr, s. torrezno, m.

rashness, –nĕs, s. temeridad, f., arrojo, m.

rasp, rāsp, s. raspador, m.; –, v. a. raspar; escofinar. [frambueso, f.

raspberry, –bĕrĕ, s. frambuesa, f.; —bush,

rat, rāt, s. rata, f.

rate, rāt, s. tasa, f.; precio, valor, m.; grado, m.; manera, f.; –, v. a. tasar, apreciar; reñir á uno. [bien; antes.

rather, rāth'ŭr, ad. de mejor gana; más

ratification, rātĭfĭkā'shŭn, s. ratificación, f.

ratify, rāt'ĭfĭ, v. a. ratificar. [ción, f.

ratio, rā'shĭō, s. razón, f. [porción, f.

ration, rā'shŭn, s. (mil.) ración, f.; pro-

rational, răsh'ŭnăl, a. racional; razonable; –ly, ad. racionalmente. [natural, f.

rationality, răshŭnăl'ĭtĕ, s. razón, luz

rat's-bane, rāts'bān, s. arsénico, m.

rattan, rătăn', s. (bot.) rotén, m.

ratteen, *rătteñ*, s. ratina (tela de lana), f.

rattle, *răt'tl*, v. a. & n. hacer ruido; regatiar; zumbar, zurrir; to - in the throat, resollar con fuerza agonizando; -, s. sonido rechino; sonajero, m. [bel, f.

rattle-snake, *snăk*, s. culebra de cascabel, f.

ravage, *răv'dj*, v. a. saquear; pillar; asolar; -, s. saqueo, m.

rave, *răp*, v. n. delirar; enfurecerse.

ravel, *răv'l*, v. a. embrollar; -, v. n. enraven, *rá'vn*, s. cuervo, m. [redarse.

ravenous, *-ŭs*, a. -ly, ad. voraz(mente).

ravine, *răvēn'*, s. barranca, f.

raving, *răv'ĭng*, a furioso, frenético; -ly, ad. como un loco furioso.

ravish, *răv'ĭsh*, v. a. estuprar; arrebatar.

ravisher, *-ŭr*, s. estuprador, forzador, m.

ravishingly, *-ĭnglē*, ad. de un modo encantador. [m.

ravishment, *-mĕnt*, s. rapto, m.; éxtasis,

raw, *rá*, a. crudo; puro; nuevo; novato, m.

raw-boned, *-bōnd*, a. huesudo; magro.

rawness, *-nĕs*, s. crudeza, f.; falta de experiencia, f.

ray, *rá*, s. rayo de luz, m.; raya, f. (pez).

rayless, *-lĕs*, a. sin brillo, apagado.

raze, *rāz*, v. a. arrasar, extirpar; borrar.

razor, *rá'zŭr*, s. navaja de barbero, m.

reach, *rētsh*, v. a. alcanzar; llegar hasta; -, v. n. extenderse, llegar; alcanzar, penetrar; esforzarse, -, s. alcance, poder, m.; capacidad, f.; astucia, f.

react, *rēăkt'*, v. a. rechazar; obrar recíprocamente.

reaction, *rēăk'shăn*, s. reacción, f.

read, *rēd*, v. a. leer; enseñar en público; -, v. n. estudiar; saber; -, *rĕd*, a. literado, [erudito.

readable, *-ăbl*, a. legible.

reader, *-ŭr*, s. lector, m. [gana.

readily, *rĕd'ĭlē*, ad. prontamente; de buena

readiness, *rĕd'ĭnĕs*, s. facilidad, f.; vivacidad del ingenio, f.; voluntad, gana, f.; prontitud, f.

reading, *rĕd'ĭng*, s. lectura, f.

reading-room, *-rōm*, s. gabinete de lectura, m.

re-adjust, *rēădjŭst'*, v. a. recomponer.

ready, *rĕd'ē*, a. listo, pronto; inclinado; fácil; ligero; -, ad. prontamente, presto.

real, *rē'ăl*, a. real, verdadero, efectivo; inmoble; -ly, ad. realmente.

reality, *rēăl'ĭtē*, s. realidad, entidad, f.

realization, *rĕălĭzá'shăn*, s. realización, f.

realize, *rē'ălĭz*, v. a. realizar. [f.

realm, *rĕlm*, s. reino, m.

ream, *rēm*, s. resma, f.

re-animate, *rēăn'ĭmāt*, v. a. reanimar.

reap, *rēp*, v. a. segar.

reaper, *-ŭr*, s. segador, m.

reaping-hook, *-ĭnghŏk*, s. hoz, f.

re-appear, *rēăppēr'*, v. n. parecer de nuevo. [f.; -, v. n. levantar, alzar.

rear, *rēr*, s. retaguardia, f.; última clase,

re-ascend, *rēăssĕnd'*, v. a. & n. subir otra vez. [& n. razonar, raciocinar.

reason, *rē'zn*, s. razón, f.; causa, f.; -, v. a.

reasonable, *-ăbl* a. razonable.

reasonableness, *-nĕs*, s. razón, f.; racionalidad, f.

reasonably, *-ē*, ad. razonablemente.

reasoner, *-ŭr*, s. razonador, m.

reasoning, *-ĭng*, s. raciocinio, m.

re-assure, *rēăshōr'*, v. a. volver á asegurar; (com.) dar un nuevo seguro.

rebel, *rĕb'ĕl*, s. rebelde. m.; -, *rĕbĕl'*, v. n. rebelarse.

rebellion, *rĕbĕl'yăn*, s. rebelión, f.

rebellious, *-yŭs*, a. rebelde. [repercutir.

rebound, *rĕbŏŭnd'*, v. a. & n. rechazar;

rebuff, *rĕbŭf'*, s. repercusión, f.; -, v. a. rechazar.

rebuild, *rēbĭld'*, v. a. reedificar.

rebuke, *rĕbŭk'*, v. a. reprender, regañar; -, s. reprensión, f.

rebus, *rē'bŭs*, s. pl. equivoquillos, m. pl.

rebut, *rĕbŭt'*, v. n. repercutir.

recalcitrant, *rĕkăl'sĭtrănt*, a. recalcitrante. [ción. f.

recall, *rĕkăl'*, v. a. revocar; -, s. revoca-

recant, *rĕkănt'*, v. a. retractarse, desdecirse.

recantation, *-á'shăn*, s. retractación, f.

recapitulate, *rēkăpĭt'ŭlāt*, v. a. recapitular.

recapitulation, *rēkăpĭtŭlá'shăn*, s. recapitulación, f. [navío, f.

recapture, *rēkăp'tŭr*, s. represa de un

recede, *rēsēd'*, v. n. retroceder; desistir.

receipt, *rēsēt'*, s. recibo, m.; receta, f.; (rail.) talón, m.; -, s. pl. abastos, m. pl.

receivable, *rēsēv'ăbl*, a. recibidero, misible.

receive, *rēsēv'*, v. a. recibir; aceptar, admitir. [-ly, ad. recientemente.

recent, *rē'sĕnt*, a. reciente, nuevo; fresco;

receptacle, *rēsĕp'tăkl*, s. receptáculo, m.

reception, *rēsĕp'shăn*, s. acogida, f.

recess, *rēsĕs'*, s. retiro, m.; fondo, m.

recession, *rēsĕsh'ăn*, s. retirada, f.

recipe, *rĕs'ĭpē*, s. receta de médico, f.

recipient, *rēsĭp'ĭĕnt*, s. recipiente. m.

reciprocal, *rēsĭp'rōkăl*, a. recíproco; -ly, ad. recíprocamente.

reciprocate, *-rōkāt*, v. n. reciprocar. [f.

reciprocity, *rĕsĭprŏs'ĭtē*, s. reciprocidad,

recital, *rēsī'tăl*, recitation, *rĕsĭtá'shăn*, s. recitación, f. [m.

recitative, *rĕsĭtătēv'*, s. (mus.) recitativo,

recite, *rēsīt'*, v. a. recitar; referir, relatar.

reck, *rĕk*, v. a. & n. cuidar.

reckless, *-lĕs*, a. descuidado, omiso; -ly, ad. con descuido.

reckon, *rĕk'n*, v. a. contar, numerar; -, v. n. computar, calcular. [f.

reckoning, *-ĭng*, s. cuenta, f.; calculación,

reclaim, *rēklām'*, v. a. reformar, corregir; reclamar.

reclaimable, *-ăbl*, a. redimible.

recline, *rēklīn'*, v. a. & n. reclinar; reposar.

recluse, *rēklōz'*, a. recluso, retirado; -, s. persona retirada del mundo, f.

reclusion, *rēklō'zhăn*, s. reclusión, f.

recognisance, *rēkŏg'nĭzăns*, s. reconocimiento; m.; obligación, f.

recognise, *rĕk'ŏgnīz*, v. a. reconocer.

recognition, *rēkŏgnĭsh'ŭn*, s. reconocimiento; recuerdo, m.

recoil, *rēkŏĭl'*, v. n. recular.

recollect, rĕkŏllĕkt', v. a. acordarse; recobrarse. [m.; reminiscencia, f.
recollection, rĕkŏllĕk'shăn, s. recuerdo,
recommence, rĕkŏmmĕns', v. a. empezar de nuevo. [dar.
recommend, rĕkŏmmĕnd', v. a. recomendación,
recommendation, –dā'shăn, s. recomendación, f. [datorio.
recommendatory, –ātŭrĕ, a. recomendatorio.
recompense, rĕk'ŏmpĕns, s. recompensa, f.; –, v. a. recompensar.
recompose, rĕkŏmpōz', v. a. volver á componer; tranquilizar de nuevo.
reconcilable, rĕkŏnsī'lăbl, a. reconciliable.
reconcile, rĕk'ŏnsīl, v. a. reconciliar.
reconciliation, rĕkŏnsīlĭā'shăn, s. reconciliación, f. [vado.
recondite, rĕk'ŏndīt, a. recondito, reservado.
reconnoitre, rĕkŏnnŏi'tŭr, v. a. (mil.) reconocer. [de nuevo.
reconsider, rĕkŏnsīd'ŭr, v. a. considerar reconstruct, rĕkŏnstrŭkt', v. a. reedificar
record, rĕkŏrd', v. a. registrar; protocolar; –, rĕk'ŏrd, s. registro, archivo, m.; –s, pl. anales, m. pl.
recorder, rĕkŏrd'ŭr, s. registrador, archivero, m. [de nuevo.
recount, rĕkŏwnt', v. a. referir; contar
recourse, rĕkŏrs', s. recurso, retorno, m.
recover, rĕkŭv'ŭr, v. a. recobrar; reparar; restablecer; –, v. n. convalecer, restablecerse; to – one's self, volver en sí.
recoverable, –ăbl, a. recuperable. [m.
recovery, –ĭ, s. convalecencia, f.; recobro, recreant, rĕk'rēănt, a. & s. cobarde, m.; apóstata, m. [divertir.
recreate, rĕk'rēāt, v. a. recrear, deleitar, recreation, rĕkrēā'shăn, s. recreación, f.
recreative, rĕk'rēātĭv, s. recreativo, m.
recriminate, rĕkrĭm'ĭnāt, v. a. & v. n. recriminar, acusar al acusador. [minación, f.
recrimination, rĕkrĭmĭnā'shăn, s. recriminación, f.
recruit, rĕkrŏt', v. a. reclutar; to – one's self, restablecerse; –, s. (mil.) recluta, m.
recruiting, –ĭng, s. recluta, f.
rectangle, rĕk'tănggl, s. rectángulo, m.
rectangular, rĕktăng'gŭlăr, a. rectangular.
rectification, rĕktĭfĭkā'shăn, s. rectificación, f. [ción, f.
rectify, rĕk'tĭfĭ, v. a. rectificar. [ción, f.
rectilinear, rĕktĭlĭn'ēăr, a. rectilíneo.
rectitude, rĕk'tĭtŭd, s. rectitud, derechura, f. [jefe, m.
rector, rĕk'tŭr, s. rector, m.; párroco, m.;
rectorship, –shĭp, s. rectorado, m.
rectory, –ĭ, s. rectoría, f. [clinado.
recumbent, rĕkŭm'bĕnt, a. recostado, reclinado.
recuperative, rĕkŭ'părătĭv, a. recuperativo.
recur, rĕkŭr', v. n. recurrir. [tivo.
recurrence, –rĕns, s. retorno, m.; vuelta, recurrent, rĕk'ŭrĕnt, a. periódico. [f.
recusant, rĕk'ŭzănt, s. nonconformista, m.
red, rĕd, a. rojo; rubio; –, s. rojez, f.
red-breast, –brĕst, s. pitirrojo, m.
redcoat, –kōt, s. soldado inglés, m.
redden, –n, v. a. teñir de color rojo; –, v. n. ponerse colorado.
reddish, –ĭsh, a. rojizo.
redeem, rĕdēm', v. a. redimir, rescatar.

redeemable, –ăbl, a. redimible.
redeemer, –ŭr, s. redentor, m.
redemption, rĕdĕm'shăn, s. redención, f.
redhanded, rĕd'hăndĕd, a. en fragante, en el acto.
redhot, –hŏt, a. candente, ardiente.
red-lead, –lĕd, s. minio, bermellón, m.
red-letter day, –lĕttŭrdā, s. día colendo,
redness, –nĕs, s. rojez, bermejura, f. [m.
redolence, –rĕd'ōlĕns, s. fragancia, f.
redolent, rĕd'ōlĕnt, a. fragante, fragante, oloroso.
redouble, rĕdŭb'l, v. a. (& n.) redoblar(se).
redoubt, rĕdŏŭt', s. (mil.) reducto, m.
redoubtable, –ăbl, a. formidable, terrible.
redound, rĕdŏŭnd', v. n. resaltar, rebotar; redundar.
redress, rĕdrĕs', v. a. enderezar; corregir; reformar; rectificar; –, s. reforma, corrección, f.
redresser, –ŭr, s. reformador, m.
red-tapist, rĕd'tăpĭst, s. burócrata, m.
reduce, rĕdūs', v. a. reducir; disminuir; sujetar.
reducible, rĕdū'sĭbl, a. reducible.
reduction, rĕdŭk'shăn, s. reducción, f.
reductively, –tĭvlĭ, ad. por reducción.
redundancy, rĕdŭn'dănsĕ, s. redundancia, f. [fluo.
redundant, –dănt, a. redundante, superfluo.
reduplicate, rĕdū'plĭkāt, v. a. reduplicar.
reduplication, rĕdūplĭkā'shăn, s. reduplicación, f.
re-echo, rĕēk'ō, v. n. resonar el eco.
reed, rĕd, s. caña, f.; flecha, f.
reedy, –ĭ, a. lleno de cañas.
reef, rĕf, v. a. (mar.) tomar rizos á las velas.
reek, rĕk, s. humo, vapor, m.; –, v. n. humear; vahear.
reel, rĕl, s. aspa, devanadera, f.; un baile, m.; –, v. a. aspar; –, v. n. vacilar al andar.
re-election, rĕēlĕk'shăn, s. reelección, f.
re-engage, rĕēngāj', v. a. empeñar de nuevo. [vado, m.
re-engagement, –mĕnt, s. empeño renovado.
re-enter, rĕĕn'tŭr, v. a. volver á entrar.
re-establish, rĕĕstăb'lĭsh, v. a. restablecer, volver á establecer una cosa.
re-establishment, –mĕnt, s. restablecimiento, m.; restauración, f.
refection, rĕfĕk'shăn, s. refección, f.
refectory, rĕfĕk'tŭrĕ, s. refectorio, m.
refer, rĕfŭr', v. a. & n. referir, remitir; referirse.
referee, rĕfŭrē', s. arbitrador, árbitro, m.; (com.) en caso necesario á . . . .
reference, rĕf'ŭrĕns, s. referencia, relación, f. [v. n. purificarse.
refine, rĕfīn', v. a. refinar, purificar; –,
refinement, –mĕnt, s. refinación, f.; refinadura, f.; elegancia afectada, f.
refinery, –ŭrĕ, s. refinadura, f.
refit, rĕfĭt', v. a. reparar; (mar.) embonar.
reflect, rĕflĕkt', v. a. & n. reflejar, repercutir; reflectar; reflexionar; recaer, refluir en. [tación, f.
reflection, rĕflĕk'shăn, s. reflexión, meditación, f.
reflective, –tĭv, a. reflexivo.

reflector, *-tặr*, s. telescopio de reflexión.

reflex, *rĕ'flĕks*, a. reflejo.　　　[m.

reform, *rĕfórm'*, v. s. (& n.) v. a. reformar(se).　　　[*shŭn*, s. reformación. f.

reform, *rĕfórm'*, reformation, *rĕfórm'ẽr*, s. reformador, m.

reformer, *rĕfórm'ẽr*, s. reformador, m.

reformist, *rĕf'ŏrmĭst*, s. religioso reformado. m.

refract, *rĕfrăkt'*, v. a. refringir.

refraction, *rĕfrăk'shŭn*, s. refracción. f.

refractoriness, *-tŭrĭnĕs*, s. obstinación, terqueza, f.　　　[tinado.

refractory, *-tŭrĕ*, a. refractario, obstinado.

refrain, *rĕfrăn'*, v. a. refrenar, reprimir.

refresh, *rĕfrĕsh'*, v. a. refrigerar. [rio, m.

refreshment, *-mĕnt*, s. refresco, refrigerefreshment-bar, *-bǎr*, s. pabellón en la calle para beber. m.

refrigerator, *rĕfrĭj'ŭrātŭr*, s. enfriadera.

refuge, *rĕf'dj*, s. refugio, asilo, m.　　[f.

refugee, *rĕfūjĕ'*, s. refugiado, m.

refund, *rĕfŭnd'*, v. a. restituir; volver á pagar.　　　[f.

refusal, *rĕfū'zŭl*, s. repulsa, denegación.

refuse, *rĕfūz'*, v. a. rehusar, repulsar; *-s, rĕf'ŭs*, desecho, m., zupia, sobra, f.

refutation, *rĕfŭtăsh'ŭn*, s. refutación, f.

refute, *rĕfūt'*, v. a. refutar.

regain, *rĕgăn'*, v. a. recobrar, recuperar.

regal, *rĕ'gŭl*, a. real.

regale, *rĕgăl'*, v. a. regalar.

regalia, *rĕgā'lĭă*, s. insignias, f. pl.

regard, *rĕgărd'*, v. a. estimar; considerar; *-s*, consideración, f.; respeto, m.　[mente.

regardful, *-fŭl*, a. atento; *-ly*, ad. atentaregarding, *-ĭng*, pr. concerniente á.

regardless, *-lĕs*, a. descuidado, negligente; desacatado.

regatta, *rĕgăt'tă*, s. regata. f.　　　[m.

regency, *rĕ'jĕnsĕ*, s. regencia, f.; gobierno.

regenerate, *rĕjĕn'ŭrăt*, v. a. regenerar; *-*, a. regenerado.　　　[ción, f.

regeneration, *rĕjĕnŭră'shŭn*, s. regeneraregent, *rĕ'jĕnt*, s. regente, m.　　[dio, m.

regicide, *rĕj'ĭsĭd*, s. regicida, m.; regiciregimen, *rĕj'ĭmĕn*, s. régimen, m.; dieta, f.

regiment, *-t*, s. regimiento, m.　　　[m.

regimental, *rĕjĭmĕn'tălz*, s.pl. uniforme.

region, *rĕ'jŭn*, s. región, f.; distrito, m.

register, *rĕj'ĭstŭr*, s. registro, m.; *-*, v. a. registrar, encabezar, empadronar; *-ed* letter, s. carta certificada. f.

registrar, *rĕj'ĭstrăr*, s. registrador, m.

registration, *rĕjĭstră'shŭn*, s. registro, m.; empadronamiento, m.

registry, *rĕj'ĭstrĕ*, s. asiento, registro, m.

regressive, *rĕgrĕs'sĭv*, a. retrógrado.

regret, *rĕgrĕt'*, s. arrepentimiento, m.; *-*, v. a. sentir pena ó dolor.

regretful, *-fŭl*, a. pesaroso.

regular, *rĕg'ŭlăr*, a. regular; ordinario; *-ly*, ad. regularmente; *-*, s. regular, m.

regularity, *rĕgŭlăr'ĭtĕ*, s. regularidad, f.

regulate, *rĕg'ŭlăt*, v. a. regular, ordenar.

regulation, *rĕgŭlă'shŭn*, s. regulación, f.; arreglo, m.　　　[registro de reloj,

regulator, *rĕg'ŭlătŭr*, s. regulador, m.;

regulus, *rĕg'ŭlŭs*, s. régulo, m.

rehabilitate, *rĕhăbĭl'ĭtăt*, v. a. rehabilitar.

rehabilitation, *rĕhăbĭlĭtă'shŭn*, s. rehabilitación, f.

rehearsal, *rĕhŭrs'ăl*, s. repetición, f.; relación, f.; prueba, f. (de una pieza de teatro).

rehearse, *rĕhŭrs'*, v. a. repetir, recitar.

reign, *rān*, s. reinado, reino, m.; *-*, v. n. reinar, prevalecer.

reimburse, *rĕĭmbŭrs'*, v. a. reembolsar.

reimbursement, *-mĕnt*, s. reembolso, m.

rein, *rān*, s. rienda, f.; *-*, v. a. refrenar.

reindeer, *-dĕr*, s. reno, rangífero, m.

re-insert, *rĕĭnsŭrt'*, v. a. insertar de nuevo.

re-instate, *rĕĭnstăt'*, v. a. instalar de nuevo; restablecer.　　　[gurar; refirmar.

re-insure, *rĕĭnshŏr'*, v. a. (com.) reasere-issue, *rĕĭsh'shŭ*, s. nueva edición, f.

reiterate, *rĕ·ĭt'ŭrăt*, v. a. reiterar.

reiteration, *rĕĭtŭră'shŭn*, s. reiteración, repetición, f.

reject, *rĕjĕkt'*, v. a. rechazar, rebatir.

rejection, *rĕjĕk'shŭn*, s. desecho, m.

rejoice, *rĕjŏĭs'*, v. a. (& n.) regocijar(se).

rejoicing, *-ĭng*, s. regocijo, m.

rejoin, *rĕjŏĭn'*, v. n. volver á juntarse; *-*, v. a. replicar.

rejoinder, *-dŭr*, s. contrarréplica, f.

relapse, *rĕlăps'*, v. n. recaer; *-*, s. reincidencia, f.

relate, *rĕlăt'*, v. a. & n. relatar, referirse

related, *-ĕd*, a. emparentado.

relater, *-ŭr*, s. relator, m.

relation, *rĕlă'shŭn*, s. relación, f.; parentesco, m.; pariente, m.

relationship, *-shĭp*, s. parentesco, m.

relative, *rĕl'ătĭv*, a. relativo; *-ly*, ad. relativamente; *-*, s. pariente, m.

relax, *rĕlăks'*, v. a. & n. relajar, aflojar.

relaxation, *rĕlăksă'shŭn*, s. relajación, f.

relay, *rĕlă'*, s. parada ó posta, f.

release, *rĕlĕs'*, v. a. soltar, libertar; relejar; *-*, s. soltura, f.; descargo, m.

relegate, *rĕl'ĕgăt*, v. a. desterrar, relegar.

relegation, *rĕlĕgăsh'ŭn*, s. relegación, f.; destierro, m.

relent, *rĕlĕnt'*, v. n. relentecer, ablandarse.

relentless, *-lĕs*, a. empedernido, inflexible.

relevant, *rĕl'ĕvănt*, a. lo que alivia ó auxilia.　　　[fiar.

reliable, *rĕlī'ăbl*, a. en quien se puede

reliance, *rĕlī'ăns*, s. confianza, f.

relic, *rĕl'ĭk*, s. reliquia, f.

relict, *rĕl'ĭkt*, s. viuda, f.　　　[suelo, m.

relief, *rĕlēf'*, s. relieve, m.; alivio, consuelo, m.

relieve, *rĕlēv'*, v. a. aliviar, consolar; socorrer.　　　[limosnero, m.

relieving-officer, *rĕlēv'ĭng ŏf'ĭsŭr*, s.

religion, *rĕlĭj'ŭn*, s. religión, f.

religious, *rĕlĭj'ŭs*, a. religioso; *-ly*, ad. religiosamente.

religiousness, *-nĕs*, s. religiosidad, f.

relinquish, *rĕlĭng'kwĭsh*, v. a. abandonar, dejar.

relinquishment, *-mĕnt*, s. abandono, m.

reliquary, *rĕl'ĭkwărĕ*, s. relicario, m.

relish, rĕl'ĭsh, s. sainete, sabor, m.; gusto, deleite, m.; —, v. a. tener buen gusto; gustar, agradar.

reluctance, rĕlăk'tăns, s. repugnancia, f.

reluctant, -tănt, a. repugnante.

rely, rĕlī', v. n. confiar en; contar con.

remain, rĕmān', v. n. quedar, restar, permanecer, durar.

remainder, -dăr, s. resto, residuo, m.

remains, rĕmāns', s. pl. restos, residuos, m. pl., sobras, f. pl.

remand, rĕmānd', v. a. enviar á alguno al paraje donde había estado antes.

remark, rĕmărk', s. observación, nota, f.; —, v. a. notar, observar.

remarkable, -ăbl, a. notable, interesante.

remarkably, -ăblĭ, ad. notablemente.

remediable, rĕmē'dĭăbl, a. remediable.

remedial, rĕmē'dĭăl, a. curativo.

remedy, rĕm'ĕdĭ, s. remedio, medicamento, m.; —, v. a. remediar. [mentar; recordar.

remember, rĕmĕm'băr, v. a. acordarse, remembrance, rĕmĕm'brăns, s. memoria, f.; recuerdo, m.

remind, rĕmīnd', v. a. acordar, recordar.

reminiscence, rĕmĭnĭs'ŭns, s. reminiscencia, f.

remiss, rĕmĭs', a. remiso, flojo, perezoso, negligente; -ly, ad. negligentemente.

remissible, -ĭbl, a. remisible, perdonable.

remission, rĕmĭsh'ŭn, s. remisión, f.; perdón, m. [lencia, f.

remissness, rĕmĭs'nĕs, s. incuria, indoremit, rĕmĭt', v. a. & n. remitir, perdonar; disminuir; debilitarse.

remittance, -tăns, s. remesa, f.

remnant, rĕm'nănt, s. resto, residuo, m.

remodel, rĕmŏd'ĕl, v. a. reformar.

remonstrance, rĕmŏn'străns, s. súplica motivada, f. [tar á lo vivo.

remonstrate, rĕmŏn'strāt, v. n. represenremorse, rĕmŏrs', s. remordimiento, m.; compunción, f. [mordimientos.

remorseless, -lĕs, a. insensible á los reremote, rĕmōt', a. remoto, lejano; -ly, ad. remotamente, lejos. [tancia, f.

remoteness, -nĕs, s. alejamiento, m.; distremount, rĕmōunt', v. a. & n. remontar; volver á subir.

removable, rĕmōv'ăbl, a. amovible. [f.

removal, rĕmōv'ăl, s. remoción, deposición, remove, rĕmōv', v. a. remover, alejar; deponer del empleo; —, v. n. mudarse; —, s. cambio de puesto, m.; partida, f.

remunerate, rĕmū'nĕrāt, v. a. remunerar.

remuneration, rĕmūnĕrā'shăn, s. remuneración, f. [ratorio.

remunerative, rĕmū'nŭrātĭv, a. remunerencounter, rĕnkŏun'tăr, s. encuentro, m.; (mil.) refriega, f. [rasgar.

rend, rĕnd, v. a. lacerar, hacer pedazos, render, rĕn'dăr, v. a. volver, restituir; traducir; rendir.

rendezvous, rĕn'dĕvō, s. cita, f.; lugar señalado para encontrarse, m. [m.

renegade, rĕn'ĕgăd, s. renegado, apóstata, renew, rĕnū', v. a. renovar, restablecer.

renewal, -ăl, s. renovación, f.

rennet, rĕn'nĕt, s. cuajo, m.

renounce, rĕnŏŭns', v. a. renunciar.

renovate, rĕn'ōvāt, v. a. renovar.

renovation, rĕnŏvā'shăn, s. renovación, f.

renown, rĕnŏun', s. renombre, m.; celebrirenowned, -d, a. célebre. [dad, f.

rent, rĕnt, s. renta, f.; arrendamiento, m.; alquiler, m.; rasgón, m.; cisma, f.; —, v. a. arrendar, alquilar.

rental, -ăl, s. lista de arriendos, f.

renter, -ăr, s. rentero, arrendador, m.

renunciation, rĕnŭnsĭā'shăn, s. renuncia, renunciación, f.

reopen, rĕō'pn, v. a. abrir de nuevo.

reorganization, rĕōrgănĭzā'shăn, s. reorganización, f.

reorganize, rĕōr'gănĭz, v. a. reorganizar.

repair, rĕpār', v. a. reparar; resarcir; —, v. n. ir; —, s. reparo, m.

reparable, rĕp'ărăbl, a. reparable.

reparation, rĕpără'shăn, s. reparación, f.

repartee, rĕpărtē', s. réplica aguda ó picante, f.

repast, rĕpăst', s. comida, colación, f.

repay, rĕpā', v. a. volver á pagar, restituir.

repayment, -mĕnt, s. pago, m.

repeal, rĕpēl', v. a. abrogar, revocar; —, s. revocación, anulación, f.

repealable, -ăbl, a. capaz de ser abrogado.

repeat, rĕpēt', v. a. repetir.

repeatedly, -ĕdlĭ, ad. repetidamente.

repeater, -ăr, s. reloj de repetición, m.

repel, rĕpĕl', v. a. repeler, rechazar.

repent, rĕpĕnt', v. n. arrepentirse.

repentance, -ăns, s. arrepentimiento, m.

repentant, -ănt, a. arrepentido.

repeople, rĕpē'pl, v. a. poblar de nuevo.

repertory, rĕp'ărtŭrĭ, s. repertorio, m.

repetition, rĕpĕtĭsh'ŭn, s. repetición, reiteración, f.

repine, rĕpīn', v. n. afligirse, arrepentirse.

repining, -ĭng, s. pesar, m.

replace, rĕplās', v. a. reemplazar; reponer.

replant, rĕplănt', v. a. trasplantar. [m.

replantation, rĕplăntā'shăn, s. trasplante, replenish, rĕplĕn'ĭsh, v. a. llenar, surtir.

replete, rĕplēt', a. repleto, lleno.

repletion, rĕplē'shăn, s. repleción, plenitud, f. [v. a. replicar.

reply, rĕplī', s. réplica, respuesta, f.; —, report, rĕpōrt', v. a. referir, contar; dar cuenta; —, s. voz, f.; rumor, m.; fama, f.; relación, f. [m.

reporter, -ăr, s. relator, m.; estenógrafo, repose, rĕpōz', v. a. fiar, confiar; —, v. n. reposar; fiarse de; —, s. reposo, m.

reposite, rĕpōz'ĭt, v. a. depositar.

repository, rĕpōz'ĭtŭrĭ, s. depósito, m.

repossess, rĕpŏzĕs', v. a. recuperar lo perdido.

reprehend, rĕprĕhĕnd', v. a. reprender.

reprehensible, rĕprĕhĕn'sĭbl, a. reprensible. [sión, fraterna, f.

reprehension, rĕprĕhĕnsh'ŭn, s. reprenrepresent, rĕprĕzĕnt', v. a. representar.

representation, rĕprĕzĕntā'shăn, s. representación, f.

representative, rĕpˈrĕzĕntˈătĭv, a. representativo ; —, s. representante, m.

repress, rĕprĕsˈ, v. a. reprimir, domar.

repression, rĕprĕshˈŭn, s. represión, f.

repressive, rĕprĕsˈsĭv, a. represivo.

reprieve, rĕprēvˈ, v. a. suspender una ejecución; dar espera; —, s. dilación, f. (de algún castigo).

reprimand, repˈrĭmănd, v. a. reprender, corregir; —, s. reprensión, f.; reprimenda, f.

reprint, rēprĭntˈ, v. a. reimprimir.

reprisal, rĕprīˈzăl, s. represalia, f.

reproach, rĕprōˈăsh, s. improperio, oprobio, m.; —, v. a. improperar; vituperar.

reproachful, —fŭl, a. ignominioso; —ly, ad. ignominiosamente.

reprobate, repˈrōbāt, v. a. reprobar; —, s. réprobo, malvado, m.

reprobation, repˈrōbāˈshŭn, s. reprobación, f.

reproduce, repˈrōdūsˈ, v. a. reproducir.

reproduction, repˈrōdŭkˈshŭn, s. reproducción, f.

reproof, rĕprōfˈ, s. reprensión, f.

reprove, rĕprōvˈ, v. a. censurar; improperar.

reptile, repˈtĭl, s. reptil, m.

republic, rĕpŭbˈlĭk, s. república, f.

republican, —ăn, a. & s. republicano (m.).

republicanism, —ănĭzm, s. republicanismo.

repudiate, rĕpūˈdĭăt, v. a. repudiar.

repugnance, rĕpŭgˈnăns, s. repugnancia, desgana, f. (de muy mala gana.

repugnant, —nănt, a. repugnante; —ly, ad.

repulse, rĕpŭlsˈ, v. a. repulsar, desechar; —, s. repulsa, f.; rechazo, m. (pulsa, f.

repulsion, rĕpŭlˈshŭn, s. repulsión, repulsive, rĕpŭlˈsĭv, a. repulsivo.

repurchase, rĕpŭrˈtshăs, v. a. recomprar.

reputable, repˈūtăbl, a. honroso.

reputably, —ĕ, ad. honrosamente.

reputation, repˈūtāˈshŭn, s. reputación, f.

repute, rĕpūtˈ, v. a. reputar.

request, rĕkwĕstˈ, s. petición, súplica, f.; —, v. a. rogar, suplicar.

require, rĕkwīrˈ, v. a. requerir, demandar.

requirement, —mĕnt, s. requisito, m.; exigencia, f. (pensable; —, s. requisito, m.

requisite, rekˈwĭzĭt, a. necesario, indispensable; —, s. requisito, m.

requisition, rekˈwĭzĭshˈŭn, s. pedimento, m.; petición, demanda, f. (pensa, f.

requital, rĕkwīˈtăl, s. retorno, m.; recompensa, f.

requite, rĕkwītˈ, v. a. recompensar.

rescind, rĕsĭndˈ, v. a. rescindir, abrogar.

rescript, rēˈskrĭpt, s. rescripto, edicto, m.

rescue, resˈkū, v. a. librar, rescatar; —, s. libramiento, recobro, m. (m.

research, rĕsŭrtshˈ, s. escudriñamiento, f.

reseat, rĕsētˈ, v. a. asentar de nuevo. (f.

resemblance, rĕzĕmˈblăns, s. semejanza, f.

resemble, rĕzĕmˈbl, v. n. asemejarse.

resent, rĕzĕntˈ, v. a. resentirse. (agravio.

resenter, —ŭr, s. el que se resiente de un

resentful, —fŭl, a. resentido; vengativo; —ly, ad. con resentimiento.

resentment, —mĕnt, s. resentimiento, m.

reservation, rĕzŭrvāˈshŭn, s. reservación, reserva, f.; restricción mental, f.

reserve, rĕzŭrvˈ, v. a. reservar; —, s. reserva, f.

reservedly, —ĕdlĕ, ad. con reserva.

reset, rĕsĕtˈ, v. a. recibir géneros hurtados.

reside, rĕzīdˈ, v. n. residir, morar.

residence, rĕzˈĭdĕns, s. residencia, morada, f.

resident, rezˈĭdĕnt, a. residente. (da, f.

residuary, rĕzīdˈūărĕ, a. sobrado; — legatee, s. (law) legatario universal, m.

residue, rĕzˈĭdū, s. residuo, resto, m.

residuum, rĕzīdˈūŭm, s. (chem.) residuo, m.

resign, rĕzīnˈ, v. a. & n. resignar, renunciar, ceder, resignarse, rendirse. (f.

resignation, rĕzĭgnāˈshŭn, s. resignación, f.

resin, rĕzˈĭn, s. resina, f.

resinous, —ŭs, a. resinoso.

resist, rĕzĭstˈ, v. a. resistir, oponerse.

resistance, —ăns, s. resistencia, f.

resolute, rĕzˈōlūt, a. resuelto; —ly, ad. resueltamente.

resolution, rĕzōlūˈshŭn, s. resolución, f.

resolve, rĕzōlvˈ, v. a. & n. resolver(se).

resonance, rĕzˈōnăns, s. resonancia, f.

resonant, rĕzˈōnănt, a. resonante.

resort, rĕzōrtˈ, v. n. recurrir, frecuentar; —, s. concurso, m.; resorte, m.

resound, rĕzōŭndˈ, v. n. resonar.

resource, rĕsōrsˈ, s. recurso, m.; expediente, m.

respect, rĕspĕktˈ, s. respecto, m.; respeto, m.; motivo, m.; —, pl. enhorabuena, f.; —, v. a. apreciar; respetar; venerar.

respectability, rĕspĕktăbĭlˈĭtĕ, s. consideración, f., carácter respetable, m.

respectable, rĕspĕktˈăbl, a. respetable; considerable; —bly, ad. notablemente.

respectful, —fŭl, a. respetuoso; —ly, ad. respetuosamente.

respecting, —ĭng, pr. con respecto á.

respective, —ĭv, a. respectivo, relativo; —ly, ad. respectivamente.

respirator, rĕsˈpĭrātŭr, s. respirador, m.

respiratory, rĕspˈrătŭrĕ, a. respirable.

respite, rĕsˈpĭt, s. suspensión, f.; respiro, m.; —, v. a. suspender, diferir.

resplendence, rĕsplĕnˈdĕns, s. resplandor, brillo, m.

resplendent, —dĕnt, a. resplandeciente.

respond, rĕspŏndˈ, v. a. responder; corresponder.

respondent, —ĕnt, s. (law) defensor, m.

response, rĕspŏnsˈ, s. respuesta, réplica, f.

responsibility, rĕspŏnsĭbĭlˈĭtĕ, s. responsabilidad, f.

responsible, rĕspŏnˈsĭbl, a. responsable.

responsive, —sĭv, a. conforme.

rest, rĕst, s. reposo, m.; sueño, m.; quietud, f.; (mus.) pausa, f.; resto, residuo, m.; —, v. a. poner á descansar; apoyar; —, v. n. dormir, reposar. (m.

resting-place, —ĭngplās, s. descansadero, m.

restitution, rĕstĭtūˈshŭn, s. restitución, f.

restive, rĕsˈtĭv, a. repropio; obstinado.

restless, rĕstˈlĕs, a. insomne; inquieto.

restoration, rĕstōrāˈshŭn, s. restauración, f.

restorative, rĕstōrˈătĭv, a. restaurativo; —, s. medicamento restaurativo, m.

restore, rĕstōrˈ, v. a. restaurar, restituir.

restrain, rĕstrán', v.a. restringir, restriñir.

restraint, —t, s. refrenamiento, constreñimiento, m.

restrict, rĕstríkt', v. a. restringir, limitar.

restriction, rĕstrík'shŭn, s. restricción, f.

restrictive, rĕstríkt'iv, a. restricto.

result, rĕzŭlt', v. n. resultar; —, s. resulta, f. [nuevo.

resume, rĕzúm', v.a. resumir; empezar de nuevo.

resumption, rĕzŭm'shŭn, s. reasunción, f.

resurrection, rĕsŭrrĕk'shŭn, s. resurrección, f.; —pie, s. fajardo, m.

resurrectionist, —ist, s. resurrectionista, m. (en Inglaterra, el que desentierra los muertos para vender sus cadáveres á los disectores).

resuscitate, rĕsŭs'sitát, v. a. resucitar.

retail, rĕtil', v. a. revender, regatonear; —, s. venta por menor, f.

retain, rĕtán', v. a. retener, guardar.

retainer, —ŭr, s. adherente, partidario, m.; —s, pl. comitiva, f.; seguito, m.

retake, rĕták', v. a. volver á tomar.

retaliate, rĕtál'iát, v. a. talionar.

retaliation, rĕtáliá'shŭn, s. talión, m.

retard, rĕtárd', v. a. retardar.

retardation, —á'shŭn, s. retardación, f.

retch, rĕtsh', v. n. esforzarse á vomitar.

retention, rĕtĕnsh'ŭn, s. retención, f.

retentive, rĕtĕn'tiv, a. retentivo.

reticence, rĕt'isĕns, s. reticencia, f.

reticle, rĕt'ikl, s. redecilla, f. [mujeres].

reticule, rĕt'ikŭl, s. saquita f. (entre las mujeres).

retina, rĕt'iná, s. reticula, f. (del ojo).

retine, rĕt'iné, s. retina, f. (túnica del ojo).

retire, rĕtír', v. a. (& n.) retirar(se).

retired, —d, a. apartado, retirado. [m.

retirement, —mĕnt, s. retiro, retiramiento, m.

retort, rĕtórt', v. a. redargüir, retorcer (un argumento); —, s. redargución, f.; (chem.) retorta, f.

retouch, rĕtŭtsh', v. a. retocar.

retrace, rĕtrás', v. a. volver á trazar.

retract, rĕtrákt', v. a. retraer; retractar.

retreat, rĕtrét', s. retirada, f.; —, v. n. retirarse.

retrench, rĕtrĕnsh', v. a. cercenar; (mil.) atrincherar; —, v. n. cercenar sus gastos.

retrenchment, —mĕnt, s. atrincheramiento, m.; trinchera, f.

retribution, rĕtribú'shŭn, s. retribución, recompensa, f. [reparable.

retrievable, rĕtrév'ŭbl, a. recuperable.

retrieve, rĕtrév', v. a. recuperar, recobrar.

retriever, —ŭr, s. sabueso, m.

retrograde, rĕ'trógrád, a. retrógrado; —, v. n. retrogradar. [gradación, f.

retrogression, rĕtrógrĕsh'ŭn, s. retrogradación, f.

retrospect, rĕ'tróspĕkt, retrospection, rĕtróspĕk'shŭn, s. reflexión de las cosas pasadas, f.

retrospective, —spĕk'tiv, a. retrospectivo.

return, rĕtŭrn', v. a. retribuir; restituir; volver; —, s. retorno, m.; vuelta, f.; recompensa, retribución, f.; vicisitud, f.; recaída, f.

reunion, rĕŭn'yŭn, s. reunión, f.

reunite, rĕŭnít', v. a (& n.) reunir(se).

reveal, rĕvél', v. a. revelar.

revel, rĕv'ĕl, v. n. andar en borracheras; —, s. borrachera, f. [divina, f.

revelation, rĕvĕlá'shŭn, s. revelación divina, f.

reveller, rĕv'ĕlŭr, s. vividor, novillero, m.

revelry, rĕv'ĕlrĕ, s. borrachera, f.

revenge, rĕvĕnj', v. a. vengar; —, s. venganza, f. [con venganza.

revengeful, —fŭl, a. vengativo; —ly, ad. con venganza.

revenue, rĕv'ĕnú, s. renta, f.; rédito, m.

reverberate, rĕvŭr'bŭrát, v. a. & n. reverberar; resonar, retumbar.

reverberation, rĕvŭrbŭrá'shŭn, s. rechazo, m.; reverberación, f.

revere, rĕvér', v. a. reverenciar, venerar.

reverence, rĕv'ĕrĕns, s. reverencia, f.; —, v. a. reverenciar.

reverend, rĕv'ĕrĕnd, a. reverendo; venerable; —, s. abad, m.; pastor, m.

reverent, rĕv'ĕrĕnt, reverential, rĕvĕrĕn'shŭl, a. reverencial, respetuoso; —ly, ed. reverencialmente.

reversal, rĕvŭr'sŭl, s. revocación de una sentencia, f.

reverse, rĕvŭrs', v. a. trastrocar; abolir; —, s. vicisitud, f.; contrario, m.; reverso, m. (de una moneda).

reversible, —ibl, a. revocable.

reversion, rĕvŭr'shŭn, s. futura, f.; reversión, f.

reversionary, —árĕ, a. reversible.

revert, rĕvŭrt', v. a. & n. trastrocar; volverse atrás.

revertible, —ibl, a. reversible.

revictual, rĕvĭt'l, v. a. volver á proveer de víveres. [—, s. revista, f.; reseña, f.

review, rĕvú', v. a. rever; (mil.) revistar.

reviewer, —ŭr, s. revisor, m.; redactor de una revista.

revile, rĕvíl', v. a. ultrajar; disfamar.

revise, rĕvíz', v. a. rever; —, s. revista, f.; segunda prueba de un pliego, f.

reviser, —ŭr, s. revisor, m.

revision, rĕvĭzh'ŭn, s. revisión, f.

revisit, rĕvĭz'it, v. a. volver á visitar.

revival, rĕvĭ'vŭl, s. restauración, f.

revive, rĕvív', v. a. avivar; restablecer; —, v. n. revivir, m.

reviver, —ŭr, s. vivificador, m.

revocable, rĕv'ókŭbl, a. revocable.

revocation, rĕvókŭ'shŭn, s. revocación, f.

revoke, rĕvók', v. a. revocar, anular.

revolt, rĕvólt', v. n. rebelarse; —, s. rebelión, f.

revolting, —ing, a. escandaloso.

revolution, rĕvólú'shŭn, s. revolución, f.

revolutionary, —árĕ, a. revolucionario.

revolutionist, —ist, s. revolucionario, m.

revolve, rĕvólv', v. a. revolver; meditar; —, v. n. girar.

revolver, —ŭr, s. revolvedor, m. (pistola).

revolving, —ing, a. periódico.

revulsion, rĕvŭl'shŭn, s. (med.) revulsión, f. [recompensar.

reward, rĕwárd', s. recompensa, f.; —, v. a. recompensar.

rewarder, —ŭr, s. remunerador, m.

rhapsody, ráp'sódá, s. rapsodia, f.

rhetoric, rĕt'órĭk, s. retórica, f.

rhetorical, rĕtór'ikŭl, a. retórico.

rhetorician, *rětŏrĭsh'ăn*, s. retórico, m.
rheum, *rōm*, s. reuma, m.
rheumatic, *rŏmăt'ĭk*, a. reumático.
rheumatism, *rŏ'mătĭzm*, s. reumatismo, [m.
rhinoceros, *rĭnŏs'ărŏs*, s. rinoceronte, m.
rhomb, *rŏm*, s. rombo, m.
rhomboid, *–bŏĭd*, s. romboide, m.
rhubarb, *rŏ'bârb*, s. ruibarbo, m.
rhyme, *rĭm*, s. rima, f.; poema, m.; –, v. n. rimar.
rhym(st)er, *–(st)ŭr*, s. versista, m.
rhythm, *rĭthm*, s. ritmo, m.
rhythmical, *rĭth'mĭkăl*, a. rítmico.
rib, *rĭb*, s. costilla, f.
ribald, *rĭb'ăld*, s. hombre lascivo, m.
ribaldry, *–rĭ*, s. lenguaje obsceno, m.
ribband, *rĭb'ănd*, ribbon, *–ŏn*, s. listón,
rice, *rĭs*, s. arroz, m.   [m., cinta, f.
rich, *rĭtsh*, a. rico; opulento; abundante;
  –ly, ad. ricamente.
riches, *–ĕz*, s. pl. riqueza, f.
richness, *–nĕs*, s. riqueza, f.; abundancia,
rick, *rĭk*, s. niara, pila de cereal, f.   [f.
rickets, *–ĕts*, s. raquitis, f.
rickety, *–ĕtĭ*, a. raquítico.   [franco.
rid, *rĭd*, v. a. librar, desembarazar; –, a.
riddance, *–dăns*, s. libramiento, m.; za-
fada, f.   [cribar.
riddle, *–dl*, s. enigma, m.; criba, f.; –, v.a.
ride, *rĭd*, v. n. cabalgar; andar en coche;
  –, s. paseo á caballo ó en coche, m.
rider, *–ŭr*, s. caballero, cabalgador, m.
ridge, *rĭj*, s. espinazo, lomo, m.; cumbre,
f.; –, v. a. formar lomos ó surcos.
ridicule, *rĭd'ĭkŭl*, s. ridiculez, f.; ridículo,
m.; –, v. a. ridiculizar.
ridiculous, *rĭdĭk'ŭlŭs*, a. ridiculoso; –ly,
ad. ridiculamente.
ridiculousness, *–nĕs*, s. calidad ridícula,
riding, *rĭ'dĭng*, s. acción de andar á caballo ó en coche, f.; paseo á caballo ó en
coche, m.   [zona, m.
riding-habit, *–hăbĭt*, s. traje de ama-
riding-hood, *–hŭd*, s. capirote, gabán, m.
riding-school, *–skŏl*, s. picadero, m.
rife, *rĭf*, a. común, frecuente.   [m.
riff-raff, *rĭf'răf*, s. desecho, desperdicio,
rifle, *rĭ'fl*, v. a. robar, pillar; estriar,
rayar; –, s. carabina rayada, f.
rifle-man, *–măn*, s. escopetero, m.
rig, *rĭg*, v. a. ataviar; (mar.) aparejar; –,
s. burla, f.
rigging, *–ĭng*, s. (mar.) aparejo, m.
right, *rĭt*, a. derecho, recto; justo; honesto;
– l bien l, l bueno! –ly, ad. rectamente,
justamente; –, s. justicia, f.; razón, f.;
derecho, m.; mano derecha, f.; –, v. a.
hacer justicia.
righteous, *rĭt'yŭs*, a. justo, honrado; –ly,
ad. justamente.   [radez, f.
righteousness, *–nĕs*, s. equidad, f.; hon-
rigid, *rĭj'ĭd*, a. rígido; austero, severo;
  –ly, ad. con rigidez.
rigidity, *rĭjĭd'ĭtĭ*, s. rigidez, austeridad, f.
rigmarole, *rĭg'mărŏl*, s. galimatías, m.
rigorous, *rĭg'ărŭs*, a. rigoroso; –ly, ad.
rigorosamente.
rigour, *rĭg'ŭr*, s. rigor, m.; severidad, f.

rill, *rĭl*, s. riachuelo, m.
rim, *rĭm*, s. margen, m. & f.; orilla, f.
rime, *rĭm*, s. escarcha, f.
rimy, *rĭ'mĭ*, a. nebuloso, húmedo.
rind, *rĭnd*, s. corteza, f.; hollejo, m.
ring, *rĭng*, s. círculo, cerco, m.; anillo, m.;
campaneo, m.; –, v. a. sonar; –, v. n.
retiñir, retumbar; to – the bell, tirar de
la campanilla.
ringer, *–ŭr*, s. campanero, m.
ring-finger, *–fĭnggŭr*, s. dedo anular, m.
ringleader, *–lēdŭr*, s. cabeza de partido
ringlet, *–lĕt*, s. anillejo, m.   [ó bando, f.
ring-worm, *–wŭrm*, s. (med.) tiña favosa,
rinse, *rĭns*, v. a. lavar, limpiar.   [f.
riot, *rĭ'ŏt*, s. tumulto, bullicio, m.; borrachera, f.; –, v. n. andar en borracheras;
causar alborotos.   [m.
rioter, *–ŭr*, s. hombre disoluto ó sedicioso,
riotous, *–ŭs*, a. bullicioso, sedicioso; disoluto; –ly, ad. disolutamente.
rip, *rĭp*, v. a. rasgar, lacerar; descoser.
ripe, *rĭp*, a. maduro, sazonado; –ly, ad.
maduramente.
ripen, *–n*, v. a. & n. madurar.
ripeness, *–nĕs*, s. madurez, f.
ripple, *rĭp'pl*, v. n. manar ó hervir el
agua á borbotones.   [á borbollones, m.
rippling, *rĭp'lĭng*, s. movimiento del agua
rise, *rĭz*, v. n. levantarse; nacer, salir (hablando de los astros); rebelarse; ascender;
hincharse; elevarse; resucitar; –, s. levantamiento, m.; elevación, f.; subida, f.;
salida (del sol), f.; causa, f.
risible, *rĭz'ĭbl*, a. risible.
rising, *rĭz'ĭng*, s. salida del sol, f.; fin de
una junta ó sesión, m.   [riesgar.
risk, *rĭsk*, s. riesgo, peligro, m.; –, v. a. ar-
risky, *–ĭ*, a. (am.) peligroso.
rite, *rĭt*, s. rito, m.
ritual, *rĭt'ŭăl*, a. & s. ritual (m.).
rival, *rĭ'văl*, s. émulo; –, s. rival, m.; –,
v. a. competir, emular.
rivalry, *–rĭ*, s. rivalidad, f.
rive, *rĭv*, v. a. (& n.) hender(se).
river, *rĭv'ŭr*, s. río, m.   [machar, roblar,
rivet, *rĭv'ĕt*, s. remache, m.; –, v. a. re-
rivulet, *rĭv'ŭlĕt*, s. riachuelo, m.
roach, *rŏtsh*, s. raya, f.; as sound as a
  –, en perfecta salud.
road, *rŏd*, s. camino real, m.
roadstead, *–stĕd*, s. (mar.) rada, f.
roadster, *–stŭr*, s. (mar.) buque anclado
en la rada, m.; caballo de viaje, m.
roam, *rŏm*, v. a. (& n.) corretear; tunar.
roan, *rŏn*, a. roano, ruano.
roar, *rŏr*, v. n. rugir; aullar; bramar; –,
s. rugido, m.; bramido, truendo, m.; mu-
roast, *rŏst*, v. a. asar; tostar.   [gido, m.
roastbeef, *–bēf*, s. asado de vaca, m.
roaster, *–ŭr*, s. asador, m.
rob, *rŏb*, v. a. robar, hurtar.
robber, *–bŭr*, s. robador, ladrón, m.
robbery, *–bărĭ*, s. robo, m.
robe, *rŏb*, s. manto, m.; toga, f.; –, v. a.
vestir de gala.   [s. petirrojo, m.
robin(-redbreast), *rŏb'ĭn(redbrĕst)*, s
robust, *rŏbŭst'*, a. robusto.

robustness, –nĕs, s. robustez, f.
rock, rŏk, s. roca, f.; escollo, m.; rueca, f.; –, v. a. mecer; arrullar; (am.) apedrear; –, v. n. bambolear.
rock-crystal, –krĭstăl, s. cuarzo, m.
rocker, –ŭr, s. cunera, f.
rocket, –ĕt, s. roquete, m.
rock-oil, –ŏĭl, s. petróleo, m.
rock-salt, –sălt, s. sal gema, f.
rock-work, –wŭrk, s. grotesco, m.
rocky, –ĕ, a. peñascoso.
rod, rŏd, s. varilla, verga, caña, f.
rodents, rŏ'dĕnts, s. pl. roedores, m. pl.
rodomontade, rŏdŏmŏntăd', s. fanfarria, f.
roe, rŏ, s. corzo, m.; hueva, f.
roebuck, –bŭk, s. corzo, m.
rogation, rŏgă'shŭn, s. rogaciones, f. pl.
rogue, rŏg, s. bribón, pícaro, villano, m.
roguery, rŏ'gŭrĕ, s. picardía, f.
roguish, rŏ'gĭsh, a. pícaro.
roister, rŏĭs'tŭr, v.n. bravear, fanfarronear.
roll, rŏl, v. a. rodar; volver; arrollar; –, v. n. rodar; girar; –, s. rodadura, f.; rollo, m.; lista, f.; catálogo, m.; rasero, m.; roleo, m.; voluta, f.; bollo, m.; panecillo, m.
roller, –ŭr, s. rodillo, cilindro, m.
rollicking, rŏl'lĭkĭng, a. ruidoso.
rolling-pin, rŏl'ĭngpĭn, s. rodillo de pastelero, m.
romance, rŏmăns', s. romance, m.; ficción, f.; cuento, m.; fábula, f.
romancist, rŏmăn'sĭst, s. romancero, m.
romantic(al), –tĭk(ăl), a. quijotesco.
romish, rŏ'mĭsh, a. romano.
romp, rŏmp, s. muchacha retozona, f.; –, v. n. retozar.
rood, rŏd, s. pértiga para medir, f.
roof, rŏf, s. tejado, m.; paladar, m.; imperial de un coche, f.; –, v. a. techar.
roofing, –ĭng, s. techado, tejo de bóveda, m.
rook, rŏk, s. corneja de pico blanco, f.; roque, m. (en el juego de ajedrez); trampista, m.; –, v. n. trampear.
rookery, –ŭrĕ, s. árboles donde hacen sus nidos muchas cornejas, m. pl.; lugar sospechoso, m.; cámara, f.
room, rŏm, s. lugar, espacio, m.; aposento, m.
roominess, –ĭnĕs, s. espaciosidad, capacidad, f.
roomy, –ĕ, a. espacioso.
roost, rŏst, s. pértiga del gallinero, f.; –, v. n. dormir las aves en una pértiga.
root, rŏt, s. raíz, f.; origen, m.; –, v. a. & n. (– out) desarraigar; arraigar.
rooted, –ĕd, a. inveterado.
rope, rŏp, s. cuerda, f.; cordel, m.; –, v. n. hacer hebras.
rope-dancer, –dănsŭr, s. volatín, bailarín de cuerda, m.
rope-maker, –măkŭr, s. cordelero, m.
rope-walk, –wăk, **rope-yard,** –yărd, s. cordelería, f.
rosary, rŏ'zărĕ, s. rosario, m.
rose, rŏz, s. rosa, f.
roseate, rŏ'zĕăt, a. róseo.
rose-bed, –bĕd, s. campo de rosales, m.
rose-bud, –bŭd, s. capullo de rosa, m.
rosemary, –mărĕ, s. (bot.) romero, m.
rose-tree, –trĕ, s. rosal, m.
rosette, rŏzĕt', s. roseta, f.
rosewood, –wŭd, s. palo de rosa, m.

rosin, rŏz'ĭn, s. trementina, f.
rosiness, rŏ'zĭnĕs, s. color róseo, m.
rosy, rŏ'zĕ, a. róseo.
rot, rŏt, v. n. pudrirse; –, s. morriña, f.; putrefacción, f.
rotate, rŏ'tăt, v. a. & n. girar.
rotation, rŏtă'shŭn, s. rotación, f.
rotatory, rŏ'tătŭrĕ, a. lo que rueda.
rote, rŏt, s. uso, m.; práctica, f.
rotgut, rŏt'gŭt, s. (vulg.) mala cerveza, f.
rotten, rŏt'n, a. podrido, corrompido.
rottenness, –nĕs, s. podredumbre, putrefacción, f.
rotund, rŏtŭnd', a. rotundo, redondo, circular, esférico.
rotundity, –tĭ, s. rotundidad, redondez, f.
rouble, rŏ'bl, s. rublo, m.
rouge, rŏzh, s. arrebol, colorete, m.
rough, rŭf, a. áspero, tosco; bronco, bruto, brusco; tempestuoso; –ly, ad. rudamente.
rough-cast, –kăst, v. a. bosquejar una figura ó cuadro; –, s. modelo en bruto, m.
rough-draw, –dr̃, v. a. bosquejar.
roughen, –n, v. a. poner áspero.
rough-hew, –hŭ, v. a. formar el modelo tosco de alguna cosa.
roughness, –nĕs, s. aspereza, f.; rudeza, tosquedad, f.; tempestad, f.; bruto.
roughwork, –wŭrk, v. a. trabajar en bruto.
round, rŏnd, a. redondo; cabal; franco, sincero; –, s. círculo, m.; redondez, f.; vuelta, f.; giro, m.; escalón, m.; (mil.) ronda, f.; andanada de cañones, f.; descarga, f.; –, ad. redondamente; por todos lados; –ly, ad. redondamente; francamente; –, v. a. cercar, rodear; redondear.
roundabout, –ăbŏt, a. amplio; indirecto, vago; –, s. (am.) jubón, m.
roundelay, rŏn'dĕlă, s. coplas que se cantan en rueda, f. pl.; sivo, m.
roundhand, rŏnd'hănd, s. carácter cursivo, m.
roundly, –lĕ, ad. redondamente; francamente.
roundness, –nĕs, s. redondez, f.; mente.
rouse, rŏz, v. a. despertar; excitar.
rout, rŏut, s. rota, derrota, f.; –, v. a. derrotar.
route, rŏt, s. ruta, f.; camino, m.
rove, rŏv, v. n. vagar, vaguear.
rover, –ŭr, s. vagamundo, m.; pirata, m.
row, rŏu, (rŏ), s. camorra, f.; zipizape, m.
row, rŏ, s. hilera, fila, f.; –, v. a. & n. (mar.) remar, bogar.
rowdy, rŏu'ĭdĕ, s. (am.) alborotador, bullanguero, m.
rowel, rŏu'ĕl, s. estrella de espuela, f.
rower, rŏ'ŭr, s. remero, m.; ceras, f. pl.
row-locks, rŏ'lŏkz, s. pl. (mar.) chumacera, f.
royal, rŏī'ăl, a. real; regio; –ly, ad. regiamente.
royalist, –ĭst, s. realista, m.; mente.
royalty, –tĕ, s. realeza, dignidad real, f.; navío real, m.; honorarios que paga el editor al autor por cada ejemplar vendido de su obra, m. pl.; **royalties,** pl. regalías, f. pl.; insignias de la corona, f. pl.
rub, rŭb, v. a. estregar, fregar, frotar; raspar; –, s. frotamiento, m.; (fig.) embarazo, m.; dificultad, f.
rubber, –bŭr, s. estropajo, m.; escofina, f.
rubber-ball, –băl, s. goma elástica, f.
rubbish, rŭb'bĭsh, s. escombro, m.; ruinas, f. pl.; andrajos, m. pl.
rubicund, rŏ'bĭkŭnd, a. rubicundo.

rubric, *rōō̆brĭk*, s. rúbrica, f.
ruby, *rō̆bĕ*, s. rubí, m.
rudder, *rŭd'dŭr*, s. timón, m. [cendida,f.
ruddiness, *rŭd'dĭnĕs*, s. tez lustrosa y encendida, f.
ruddy, *rŭd'dĕ*, a. colorado, rubio.
rude, *rōd*, a. rudo, brutal, rústico, grosero; tosco; -ly, ad. rudamente, groseramente.
rudeness, *-nĕs*, s. descortesía, f.; rudeza, insolencia, f.
rudiment, *rōō̆dĭmĕnt*, s. rudimentos, m. pl.
rue, *rō*, v. n. compadecerse; -, s. (bot.) ruda, f.
rueful, *-fŭl*, a. lamentable, triste.
ruff, *rŭf*, s. lechuguilla, f. [-, a. brutal.
ruffian, *-fĭän*, s. malhechor, bandolero, m.;
ruffianly, *-lĕ*, a. malvado, perverso.
ruffle, *rŭf'fl*, v. a. desordenar, desazonar; rizar; -, s. vuelo de las mangas de mujer, m.; tumulto, m.
rug, *rŭg*, s. paño burdo, m.; frazada, f.
rugged, *-gĕd*, a. áspero, tosco; brutal; peludo.
ruin, *rōō̆ĭn*, s. ruina, f.; perdición, f.; escombros, m. pl.; -, v.a. arruinar; destruir.
ruinous, *-ŭs*, a. ruinoso; -ly, ad. ruinosamente.
rule, *rōl*, s. mando, m.; regla, f.; regularidad, f.; -, v. a. & n. gobernar; reglar, arreglar, dirigir
ruler, *-ŭr*, s. gobernador, m.; regla, f.
rum, *rŭm*, s. ron, m.; -, a. (vulg.) raro.
rumble, *-bl*, v. n. crujir, rugir. [singular.
ruminate, *rōō̆mĭnāt*, v. a. rumiar. [-
rumination, *rōmĭnā'shŭn*, s. meditación, -, s. rumiar.
rummage, *rŭm'mādj*, v. a. trastornar; -, s. tumulto.
rummer, *rŭm'mŭr*, s. vaso para beber, m.
rumour, *rōō̆mŭr*, s. rumor, m.; -, v. a. divulgar alguna noticia.
rump, *rŭmp*, s. obispillo de ave, m.
rumple, *rŭm'pl*, s. arruga, f.
run, *rŭn*, v. a. arrojar con violencia; traspasar; to – the risk, aventurar, arriesgar; -, v. n. correr; fluir, manar; pasar rápidamente; proceder; -, s. corrida, carrera, f.; curso, m.; serie, f.; moda, f.; ataque, m.
runaway, *-ŭwā*, s. fugitivo, desertor, m.
run(d)let, *rŭn(d)'lĕt*, s. barrilejo, m.
rung, *rŭng*, s. escalón, peldaño, m. (de escalera de mano). [mensajero, m.
runner, *rŭn'nŭr*, s. corredor, m.; correo,
running, *rŭn'nĭng*, s. carrera, corrida, f.; curso, m.
running-ice, *-īs*, s. hielo movedizo, m.
rupture, *rŭp'tshŭr*, s. rotura, f.; hernia, quebradura, f.; -, v. a. reventar, romper.
rural, *rōō̆răl*, a. rural, campestre, rústico.
ruse, *rōz*, s. astucia, maña, artería, f.
rush, *rŭsh*, s. junco, m.; (fig.) bledo, ardite, m.; ímpetu, m.; -, v. n. abalanzarse, tirarse. [noche, f.
rush-light, *-līt*, s. vela ó lamparilla de
rusk, *rŭsk*, s. galleta, f.
russet, *rŭs'sĕt*, a. bermejizo.
Russia-leather, *rŭsh'ä lĕthŭr*, s. cuero de Moscovia, m. [v. n. enmohecerse.
rust, *rŭst*, s. herrumbre, f.; robín, m.; -,

rustic(al), *rŭs'tĭk(ăl)*, a. rústico; -, s. patán, rústico, m.
rusticate, *-āt*, v. n. vivir en el campo; -, v. a. desterrar al campo. [pestre, f.
rustication, *rŭstĭkā'shŭn*, s. vida campestre, f.
rusticity, *rŭstĭs'ĭtĕ*, s. rusticidad, f.
rustiness, *rŭs'tĭnĕs*, s. herrumbre, f.
rustle, *rŭs'l*, v. n. crujir, rechinar. [m.
rustling, *rŭs'lĭng*, s. estruendo, m.; crujido,
rusty, *rŭs'tĕ*, a. oriniento, mohoso; rancio.
rut, *rŭt*, v. n. bramar los venados y ciervos cuando están en celo; -, s. brama, f.; carril, m. [-ly, ad. inhumanamente.
ruthless, *rōth'lĕs*, a. cruel, insensible;
rye, *rī*, s. (bot.) centeno, m.

S.

sabbath, *săb'băth*, s. sábado, m.
sable, *sā'bl*, s. cebellina, f. [con sable.
sabre, *sā'bŭr*, s. sable, m.; -, v. a. matar
sacerdotal, *săsŭrdō'tăl*, a. sacerdotal.
sack, *săk*, s. saco, m.; vino dulce de Canarias, m.; -, v. a. meter en sacos, saquear. [Eucaristía, f.
sacrament, *săk'rămĕnt*, s. sacramento, m.;
sacramental, *săkrămĕnt'ăl*, a. -ly, ad. sacramental(mente).
sacred, *săk'krĕd*, a. sagrado, sacro; inviolable; -ly, ad. sagradamente, inviolable.
sacredness, *-nĕs*, s. santidad, f. [mente.
sacrifice, *săk'rĭfīz*, s. sacrificio, m. -, v. a. & n. sacrificar. [los sacrificios.
sacrificial, *săkrĭfĭsh'ăl*, a. perteneciente á
sacrilege, *săk'rĭlĕj*, s. sacrilegio, m.
sacrilegious, *săkrĭlē'jŭs*, a. sacrílego.
sad, *săd*, a. triste, melancólico; infausto, obscuro; -ly, ad. tristemente.
sadden, *-n*, v. a. entristecer.
saddle, *săd'l*, s. silla, f.; -, v. a. ensillar.
saddle-bag, *-băg*, s. saco para dinero, m.
saddle-cloth, *-klŏth*, s. mantilla de silla, f.
saddle-horse, *-hŏrs*, s. caballo de montar,
saddler, *-ŭr*, s. sillero, m. [m.
sadlery, *-ŭrĕ*, s. guarnicionería, f.
sadness, *săd'nĕs*, s. tristeza, f.; aspecto tétrico, m.
safe, *săf*, a. seguro; -ly, ad. á salvo; - and sound, sano y salvo; -, s. despensa, f. [ducto, m.
safe-conduct, *-kŏn'dŭkt*, s. salvoconducto.
safe-guard, *-gärd*, s. salvaguardia, f.
safety, *-tĕ*, s. seguridad, f.; salvamento, f.
saffron, *săf'rŏn*, s. azafrán, m.
sagacious, *săgā'shŭs*, a. sagaz, sutil; -ly, ad. sagazmente. [f.
sagacity, *săgăs'ĭtĕ*, s. sagacidad, astucia,
sage, *sādj*, s. (bot.) salvia, f.; sabio, m.; -, a. sabio; -ly, ad. sabiamente.
Sagittarian, *săjĭtā'rĭăn*, s. Sagitario, m. (signo del zodíaco).
sago, *sā'gō*, s. (bot.) zagú, m.
sail, *săl*, s. vela, f.; -, v. n. dar á la vela,
sailer, *-ŭr*, s. navío, buque, m. [navegar.
sailing, *-ĭng*, s. navegación, f.

sailor, -ăr, s. marinero, m.

saint, sănt, s. santo, m., santa, f.

saint, sănt, sainted, -ĕd, saintly, -lĭ, a. santo; saintly, ad. santamente.

sake, săk, s. causa, razón, f.; for God's -, por amor de Dios.

salad, săl'ăd, s. ensalada, f.

salad-bowl, -bōl, s. ensaladera, f.

salad-oil, -ŏil, s. aceite de olivas, m.

salamander, săl'ămăndăr, s. salamandra, f.

salary, săl'ărĭ, s. salario, m. [f.

sale, săl, s. venta, f.

saleable, săl'ăbl, a. vendible.

sale-goods, -gŭdz, s. pl. mercancías para vender, f. pl

salesman, -z'măn, s. ropero, m.

salient, săl'lĭĕnt, a. saliente, saledizo.

saline, sălĭn', a. salino.

saliva, săl'ĭvă, s. saliva, f.

sallow, săl'lō, a. cetrino, pálido.

sally, săl'lĭ, s. (mil.) salida, surtida, f.; -, v. n. salir.

salmon, săm'ŏn, s. salmón, m.

salmon-trout, -trŏŭt, s. trucha salmonada, f.

saloon, săl'ŏŏn', s. salón, m. [nada, f.

salt, sălt, s. sal, f., (fig.) sabor, m.; agudeza, f., -, a. salado, -, v. a. salar.

salt-cellar, -sĕllăr, s. salero, m. (en la mesa).

salter, -ăr, s. salinero, m.

salting-tub, -ĭngtŭb, s. saladero, m.

saltness, -nĕs, s. saladura, f.

saltpetre, -pētŭr, s. nitro, salitre, m.

salt-works, -wŭrks, s. pl. salina, f.

salubrious, sălŏŏ'brĭŭs, a. salubre, saludable.

salubrity, sălŏŏ'brĭtĭ, s. salubridad, f.

salutary, săl'ŭtărĭ, a. salubre, salutífero.

salutation, sălŭtā'shăn, s. salutación, f.

salute, sălŏŏt', v. a. saludar; -, s. salutación, f. [salvamento, m.

salvage, săl'vāj, s. (mar.) s. derecho de salvación, f.

salvation, sălvā'shăn, s. salvación, f.

salve, săv, s. emplasto, ungüento, m.

salver, săl'văr, s. salvilla, bandeja, f.

salvo, săl'vō, s. reservación, excusa, f.

same, săm, a. mismo, idéntico.

sameness, -nĕs, s. identidad, f.

sample, săm'pl, s. muestra, f.; ejemplo, m., -, v. a. ejemplificar. [delo, m.

sampler, -ăr, s. muestra, f.; dechado, mo-

sanctificator, săngktĭfĭkā'shăn, s. santificación, f., cousagración, f.

sanctify, săngk'tĭfĭ, v. a. santificar.

sanctimonious, săngktĭmō'nĭŭs, a. semejante á santo. [santidad, f.

sanctimony, săngk'tĭmŏnĭ, s. santimonia, f.

sanction, săngk'shăn, s. sanción, f.; -, v. a. sancionar.

sanctity, săngk'tĭtĭ, s. santidad, f.

sanctuary, săngk'tŭārĭ, s. santuario, m.; asilo, m.

sand, sănd, s. arena, f.; -, v. a. enarenar.

sandal, săn'dăl, s. sandalia, f.

sand-bags, sănd'băgs, s. pl. (mil.) sacos de tierra, m. pl. [salvadera, f.

sand-box, -bŏks, s. banco de arena, m.

sanded, -ĕd, a. arenoso.

sand-pit, -pĭt, s. arenal, m.

sandstone, -stōn, s. piedra arenisca, f.

sandy, -ĭ, a. arenoso, arenisco.

sane, săn, a. sano.

sanguinary, săng'gwĭnărĭ, a. sanguinario.

sanguine, săng'gwĭn, a. sanguíneo. [f.

sanguineness, -nĕs, s. anhelo, m.; ansia,

sanguineous, sănggwĭn'ĕŭs, a. sanguino; sanguíneo. [món, m.

sanity, săn'ĭtĭ, s. juicio sano, sentido co-

sap, săp, s. savia, f.; (mil.) zapa, f.; -, v. a. zapar.

sapient, sā'pĭĕnt, a. sabio, cuerdo.

sapling, săp'lĭng, s. renuevo, m.

sapper, -pŭr, s. (mil.) zapador, m.

sapphire, săf'ĭăr, s. zafir, zafiro, m.

sarcasm, săr'kăzm, s. sarcasmo, m.

sarcastic(al), sărkăs'tĭk(ăl), a. mordaz, cáustico; -ally, ad. mordazmente. [m.

sarcenet, sărs'nĕt, s. tafetán de Florencia,

sarcophagus, sărkŏf'ăgŭs, s. sarcófago, sepulcro, m.

sardine, săr'dĭn, s. sardina, f.

sash, săsh, s. cíngulo, m., cinta, f.

sash-window, -wĭndō, s. ventana ó vidriera corrediza, f.

Satan, săt'ăn, s. Sátanas, m.

satanic(al), sătăn'ĭk(ăl), a. diabólico.

satchel, sătsh'ĕl, s. recado, quillo, m.

satellite, săt'ĕllĭt, s. satélite, m. [hartar.

satiate, sā'shĭăt, sate, săt, v. a. saciar,

satiety, săt'ĭĭtĭ, s. saciedad, hartura, f.

satin, săt'ĭn, s. raso, m.

satinet, -ĕt, s. rasete, m.

satire, săt'ĭr, s. sátira, f.

satiric(al), sătĭr'ĭk(ăl), a. satírico; -ly, ad. satíricamente.

satirist, săt'ĭrĭst, s. autor satírico, m.

satirize, săt'ĭrĭz, v. a. satirizar [f.

satisfaction, sătĭsfăk'shăn, s. satisfacción,

satisfactorily, -tărĭlĭ, ad. satisfactoriamente.

satisfactory, -tărĭ, a. satisfactorio.

satisfy, săt'ĭsfĭ, v. a. satisfacer.

satrap, să'trăp, s. sátrapa, m.

saturate, săt'ŭrăt, v. a. saturar

saturday, săt'ŭrdā, s. sábado, m.

saturnine, săt'ŭrnĭn, a. saturnino, melancólico.

satyr, săt'ŭr, s. sátiro, m.

sauce, săs, s. salsa, f., (am.) legumbre, f., -, v. a. condimentar.

saucepan, -păn, s. cazo para estofar, m.

saucer, -ăr, s. salsera, f.; platillo, m.

saucily, săl'sĭlĭ, ad. desvergonzadamente.

sauciness, -sĭnĕs, s. insolencia, impudencia, f.

saucy, săl'sĭ, a. insolente.

saunter, săn'tăr, v. n. callejear, corretear.

sausage, să'săj, s. salchicha, f.

savage, săv'ăj, a. salvaje, bárbaro; -ly, ad. bárbaramente; -, s. salvaje, m.

savageness, -nĕs, s. salvajería, f.; crueldad, f.

savagery, -ărĭ, s. yermo, m.; crueldad, f.

savannah, săvăn'nă, s. sábana, f.

save, săv, v. a. salvar; economizar; conservar; ad. salvo, excepto.

save-all, -ăl, s. cañón de candelero, m.

saveloy, *săv'ĕlŏĩ*, s. chorizo, m. [m.

saver, *sā'vẽr*, s. libertador, m.; ahorrador,

saving, *sā'vĩng*, a. frugal, económico; —, pr. fuera de, excepto; —ly, ad. económicamente, parcamente; —, s. salvamiento, m.; —s, pl. ahorro, m., economía, f.

Saviour, *sā'vĩẽr*, s. Redentor, m.

savour, *sā'vẽr*, s. olor, m.; sabor, m.; —, v. a. gustar, saborear. [grancia, f.

savouriness, *-ĩnẽs*, s. paladar, m.; frasavoury, *-ẽ*, a. sabroso.

saw, *sā*, s. sierra, f.; —, v. a. serrar.

saw-dust, *-dŏst*, s. aserraduras, f. pl.

saw-fish, *-fĩsh*, s. priste, m.

saw-mill, *-mĩl*, s. molino de aserrar, m.

saw-pit, *-pĩt*, s. fosa de los serraderos de

sawyer, *-yẽr*, s. aserrador, m. [largo, f.

say, *sā*, v. a. decir, hablar; —, s. habla, f.

saying, *-ĩng*, s. dicho, proverbio, m.

scab, *skăb*, s. roña, f.; roñoso, m.

scabbard, *-bărd*, s. vaina de espada, f.; cobertura, f.

scabbiness, *-bĩnẽs*, s. estado roñoso, m.

scabby, *-bĕ*, scabious, *skā'bĩũs*, a. sarnoso. [m.

scaffold, *skăf'fōld*, s. tablado, m.; cadalso,

scaffolding, *-ĩng*, s. construcción de tablados ó andamios, f.

scald, *skāld*, v. a. escaldar; —, s. tiña, f.

scale, *skāl*, s. balanza, f.; escama, f.; escala, f.; gama, f.; laminita, f.; pair of —s, peso de cruz, m.; —, v. a. a. escalar; descostrarse.

scales, *skālz*, s. pl. Libra, f. (signo del zodíaco). [de sitio, f.

scaling-ladder, *skā'lĩnglāddẽr*, s. escala

scallion, *skăl'yũn*, s. ascalonia, cebolleta, f. [festonear.

scallop, *skălŏp*, s. peine, m.; —, v. a.

scalp, *skălp*, s. cráneo, m.; —, v. a. levantar los tegumentos que cubren el cráneo.

scamp, *skămp*, s. bribón, ladrón, m.

scamper, *-ẽr*, v. n. escapar, huir.

scan, *skăn*, v. a. escudriñar; medir las sílabas de un verso. [f.

scandal, *-dăl*, s. escándalo, m., infamia,

scandalize, *-dălĩz*, v. a. escandalizar.

scandalous, *-dălũs*, a. escandaloso; —ly, ad. escandalosamente. [sórdido.

scant, *skănt*, scanty, *-ĕ*, a. escaso, parco,

scantily, *skănt'ĩlĕ*, ad. escasamente, estrechamente.

scantiness, *skănt'ĩnẽs*, s. estrechez, escasez, f. [f.

scantling, *skănt'lĩng*, s. cantidad pequeña.

scape-goat, *skāp'gōt*, s. chivo emisario,

scape-grace, *-grās*, s. pícaro, m. [m.

scar, *skăr*, s. cicatriz, f.; —, v. a. hacer alguna cicatriz.

scarce, *skărs*, a. raro; —ly, ad. apenas.

scarcity, *skărs'ĩtĕ*, s. escasez, f.; raridad, f.

scare, *skār*, v. a. espantar.

scarecrow, *-krō*, s. espantajo, m.

scarf, *skărf*, s. trena, f.

scarify, *skăr'ĩfĩ*, v. a. sajar.

scarlatina, *skărlătĩ'nă*, s. escarlatina, f.

scarlet, *skăr'lĕt*, s. escarlata, f.; —, a. de color de escarlata ó grana.

scarp, *skărp*, s. escarpa, f.

scat, *skăt*, s. chaparrón, m.

scatter, *skăt'tẽr*, v. a. esparcir; disipar.

scavenger, *skăv'ẽnjẽr*, s. basurero, m.

scene, *sẽn*, s. escena, f. [teatro), f.

scenery, *-ũrẽ*, s. vista; f.; decoración (de

scenic(al), *sẽn'ĩk(ăl)*, a. escénico.

scent, *sẽnt*, s. olfato, m.; olor, m.; rastro, m.; —, v. a. oler. [de olor, m.

scent-bottle, *-bŏttl*, s. frasquito con agua

scentless, *-lẽs*, a. sin olfato; inodoro.

sceptic, *skĕp'tĭk*, s. escéptico, m.

sceptic(al), *-tĭk(ăl)*, a. escéptico.

scepticism, *-tĭsẽm*, s. escepticismo, m.

sceptre, *sĕp'tẽr*, s. cetro, m.

schedule, *shĕd'ūl*, *(sĕd'jūl)*, s. esquela, f.; cédula, f.

scheme, *skẽm*, s. proyecto, designio, m.; plan, modelo, m.; —, v. a. proyectar.

schemer, *-ẽr*, s. proyectista, invencionero,

schism, *sĭzm*, s. cisma, m. & f. [m.

schismatic(al), *sĭzmăt'ĭk(ăl)*, s. cismático, m. [literato, m.

scholar, *skŏl'ẽr*, s. escolar, estudiante, m.;

scholarship, *-shĭp*, s. ciencia, f.; educación literaria, f.

scholastic, *skŏlăs'tĭk*, a. escolástico.

school, *skōl*, s. escuela, f.; —, v. a. enseñar.

school-boy, *-bŏĩ*, s. niño de escuela, m.

schooling, *-ĩng*, s. instrucción, f.

school-master, *-măstẽr*, s. maestro de escuela, m. [de niños ó niñas, f.

school-mistress, *-mĭstrĕs*, s. maestra

schooner, *skōn'ẽr*, s. (mar.) goleta, f.

sciatica, *sīăt'ĭkă*, s. ciática, f.

science, *sĩ'ẽns*, s. ciencia, f.

scientific(al), *sĩĕntĭf'ĭk(ăl)*, a. científico; —ally, ad. científicamente.

scimitar, *sĭm'ĭtăr*, s. cimitarra, f.

scintillate, *sĩn'tĭllāt*, v. n. chispear, centellar. [m.

scintillation, *sĩntĭllā'shũn*, s. chispazo,

sciolist, *sĩ'ŏlĭst*, s. semisabio, m. [m.

scion, *sĩ'ŏn*, s. verduguillo, m.; vástago,

scission, *sĭzh'ũn*, s. separación, partición,

scissors, *sĭz'ẽrz*, s. pl. tijeras, f. pl. [f.

scoff, *skŏf*, v. n. mofarse, burlarse; —, s. mofa, burla, f.

scoffer, *-fẽr*, s. mofador, m. [nio.

scoffingly, *-fĩnglĕ*, ad. con mofa y escar-

scold, *skōld*, v. a. & n. regañar, reñir, refunfuñar; —, s. regañona, f.

sconce, *skŏns*, s. cornucopia, f.

scoop, *skōp*, s. cucharón; (naʊ.) achicador, m.; —, v. a. cavar, socavar.

scope, *skōp*, s. objeto, intento, designio, blanco, espacio, m.; libertad, f.

scorbutic, *skŏrbū'tĭk*, a. escorbútico.

scorch, *skŏrtsh*, v. a. quemar por encima; tostar; —, v. n. quemarse, secarse.

score, *skōr*, s. muesca, canalita, f.; consideración, f.; cuenta, f.; escote, m.; razón, f.; motivo, m.; veintena, f.; —, v. a. sentar alguna deuda; imputar; señalar con una línea.

scoria, *skō'rĭă*, s. escoria, hez, f.

scorn, *skŏrn*, v. a. & n. despreciar; mofar, —, s. desdén, menosprecio, m.

scorner, *-ẽr*, s. desdeñador, m. [desdén.

scornful, *-fũl*, a. desdeñoso; —ly, ad. con

scorpion, *skŏr'pĭŭn*, s. escorpión, m.
Scorpion, —, s. Escorpión, m. (signo del
scot, *skŏt*, s. escote, m. [zodíaco).
scotch, *skŏtsh*, s. cortadura, incisión, f.;
—, v. a. escoplear. [m.
scoundrel, *skŏŭn'drĕl*, s. belitre, pícaro,
scoundrelly, —*lĭ*, a. ruin, de pícaro.
scour, *skŏŭr*, v. a. fregar, estregar; limpiar; —, v. n. corretear.
scourge, *skŭrj*, s. azote, m.; castigo, m.;
—, v. a. azotar, castigar.
scout, *skŏŭt*, s. (mil.) batidor de la campaña, m.; centinela avanzada, f.; espía,
m.; —, v. n. reconocer secretamente los
movimientos del enemigo.
scowl, *skŏŭl*, v. n. mirar con ceño; —, s.
ceño, semblante ceñudo, m.
scowlingly, —*ĭnglĭ*, ad. con ceño.
scragginess, *skrăg'gĭnĕs*, s. flaqueza,
extenuación, f.; aspereza, f.
scraggy, *skrăg'gĕ*, a. áspero; macilento.
scramble, *skrăm'bl*, v. n. arrapar; trepar;
disputar; —, s. disputa, f.; juego de muchachos, m. [pedacito, m.
scrap, *skrăp*, s. migaja, f.; sobras, f. pl.;
scrape, *skrāp*, v. a. & n. raer, raspar;
arañar; tocar mal un instrumento; —, s.
embarazo, m.; dificultad, f.
scraper, —*ăr*, s. rascador, f.; aprendiz
de violín, m.
scratch, *skrătsh*, v. a. rascar, raspar;
raer, garrapatear; —, s. rascadura, f.
scrawl, *skrăl*, v. a. & n. garrapatear; —, s.
garabatos, m. pl.
scream, *skrēm*, screech, *skrētsh*, v. n.
chillar, dar alaridos; —, s. chillido, grito,
alarido m.
screech-owl, —*ŏl*, s. zumaya, f.
screen, *skrēn*, s. biombo, m.; mámpara,
f.; abanico de chimenea, m.; harnero, m.;
—, v. a. abrigar, esconder; cribar, cerner.
screw, *skrŏ*, s. tornillo, m.; female —,
tuerca, f.; —, v. a. torcer con tornillo;
forzar, apretar, estrechar.
screw-driver, —*drĭvăr*, s. destornillador,
screw-nut, —*nŭt*, s. tuerca, f. [m.
screw-steamer, —*stēmăr*, s. navío á
hélice, m. [escrito de poco mérito, m.
scribble, *skrĭb'bl*, v. a. escarabajear; —, s.
scribe, *skrĭb*, s. escritor, m.; escriba, m.
scrimmage, *skrĭm'mădj*, s. turbamulta, f.
scrip, *skrĭp*, s. bolsa, taleguilla, f.; cédula,
scriptural, *skrĭp'tŭrăl*, a. bíblico. [f.
Scripture, *skrĭp'tŭr(skrĭp'tshŭr)*, s.Escri-
tura sagrada, f. [público, m.
scrivener, *skrĭv'ĕnăr*, s. escribano,notario
scrofula, *skrŏf'ŭlă*, s. escrófula, f.
scrofulous, *skrŏf'ŭlŭs*, a.escrofuloso. [m.
scroll, *skrŏl*, s. rollo (de papel ó pergamino),
scrub, *skrŭb*, v. a. estregar con un estropajo; —, s. belitre, m.; estropajo, m.
scruple, *skrŏ'pl*, s. escrúpulo, m.; —, v. n.
escrupulizar, tener duda. [sidad, f.
scrupolosity, *skrŏpŏlŏs'ĭtĕ*, s. escrupulo-
scrupulous, *skrŏ'pŭlŭs*, a. escrupuloso;
—ly, ad. escrupulosamente.
scrutinize, *skrŏ'tĭnĭz*, v. a. escudriñar,
examinar.

scrutiny, *skrŏ'tĭnĕ*, s. escrutinio, examen,
soud, *skŭd*, v. n. huirse, escaparse. [m.
scuffle, *skŭf'fl*, s. quimera, riña, f.; —, v. n.
reñir, pelear.
scull, *skŭl*, s. cráneo, m.; barquillo, m.
scullery, —*lărĕ*, s. espetera, f.; fregadero,
m. [gona, f.
scullion, *skŭl'yŭn*, s. marmitón, m.; fre-
sculptor, *skŭlp'tăr*, s. escultor, m.
sculpture, *skŭlp'tăr (skŭlp'tshŭr)*, s.
escultura, f.; —, v. a. esculpir.
scum, *skŭm*, s. nata, f.; espuma, f.; escoria, f.; —, v. a. espumar.
scurf, *skŭrf*, s. tiña, f.; costra de una
herida, f. [nada, f.
scurrility, *skŭrrĭl'ĭtĕ*, s. bufonería, bufo-
scurrilous, *skŭr'rĭlŭs*, a. vil, bajo; injurioso; —ly, ad. injuriosamente.
scurvily, *skŭrv'ĭlĕ*, ad. vilmente.
scurviness, *skŭr'vĭnĕs*, s. ruindad, f.
malignidad, f.
scurvy, *skŭr'vĕ*, s. escorbuto, m.; —, a. escorbútico; vil, despreciable. [m.
scutcheon, *skŭtsh'ŭn*, s. escudo de armas,
scuttle, *skŭt'tl*, s. banasta, f.; —, v. n.
apretar á correr.
scythe, *sĭth*, s. guadaña, f. [f.
sea, *sĕ*, s. mar, m. & f.; heavy —, oleada
seaboard, —*bōrd*, s. (mar.) mar adentro,
al largo.
sea-breeze, —*brēz*, s. viento de mar, m.
sea-coast, —*kōst*, s. costa marítima, f.
sea-fight, —*fĭt*, s. combate naval, m.
sea-green, —*grēn*, a. verdemar.
sea-gull, —*gŭl*, s. gaviota, f.
sea-horse, —*hŏrs*, s. morso, m.
seal, *sēl*, s. sello, m.; —, v. a. sellar.
sealing-wax, —*ĭngwăks*, s. lacre, m.
seam, *sēm*, s. costura, f.; cicatriz, f.; —, v. a.
seaman, *sē'măn*, s. marinero, m. [coser.
seamanship, —*shĭp*, s. pericia en la navegación, m.
seamstress, *sēm'strĕs*, s. costurera, f.
seamy, *sēm'ĕ*, a. lo que tiene costuras.
sea-piece, *sē'pēs*, s. pintura marítima, f.
sea-port, —*pŏrt*, s. puerto de mar, m.
sear, *sēr*, v. a. cauterizar.
search, *sŭrtsh*, v. a. examinar; escudriñar;
inquirir, tentar; investigar, buscar; —, s.
pesquisa, f.; busca, f.; buscada, f.
search-light, —*lĭt*, s. reflector eléctrico, m.
sea-shore, *sē'shŏr*, s. ribera, f., litoral, m.
sea-sick, —*sĭk*, a. mareado. [mareo, m.
sea-sickness, —*sĭknĕs*, s. mareamiento,
sea-side, —*sĭd*, s. orilla ó ribera del mar, m.
season, *sē'zn*, s. estación, f.; tiempo oportuno, m.; sazón, f.; —, v. a. sazonar; imbuir; —, v. n. sazonarse.
seasonable, —*ăbl*, a.oportuno, á propósito.
seasonably, —*ăblĕ*, ad. en sazón.
seasoning, —*ĭng*, s. condimento, m.
season-ticket, —*tĭkĕt*, s. (rail.) abono de
pasaje, m.
seat, *sēt*, s. silla, morada, f.; domicilio, m.;
situación, f.; —, v. a. situar; colocar;
asentar.
sea-term, *sē'tĕrm*, s. término naval, m.
seaward, —*wărd*, a. del litoral; —, sea-
wards, hacia el mar.

sea-weed, *—wĕd*, s. alga marina, f.
sea-worthy, *—wŭrthĕ*, a. á propósito para
     [navegar.
secant, *sē′kănt*, s. secante, f.
secede, *sēsēd′*, v. n. apartarse, separarse.
secession, *sēsĕsh′ŭn*, s. apartamiento, m.;
     separación, f.
seclude, *sēklūd′*, v. a. apartar, excluir.
seclusion, *sēklū′zhŭn*, s. separación, f.;
     exclusión, f.
second, *sĕk′ŭnd*, a. segundo; **-ly**, ad. en
     segundo lugar; **—**, s. padrino, m.; defensor,
     m.; segundo, m.; (mus.) segunda, f.; **—**,
     v. a. ayudar; segundar.
secondary, *—ărĕ*, a. secundario.
secondhand, *—hănd*, s. segunda mano, f.
     (en las compras).
secrecy, *sē′krĕsĕ*, s. secreto, silencio cul-
     dadoso, m.   [ad. secretamente.
secret, *sē′krĕt*, a. & s. secreto (m.); **-ly**,
secretary, *sĕk′rĕtărĕ*, s. secretario, m.
secretaryship, *—shĭp*, s. secretaría, f.
secrete, *sēkrēt′*, v. a. esconder; (med.)
     secretar.
secretion, *sēkrē′shŭn*, s. secreción, f.
secretive, *sēkrē′tĭv*, a. misterioso.
sect, *sĕkt*, s. secta, f.   [s. sectario, m.
sectarian, *sĕktā′rĭăn*, sectary, *sĕk′tărĕ*,
section, *sĕk′shŭn*, s. sección, f.
sector, *sĕk′tŭr*, s. sector, m.
secular, *sĕk′dlăr*, a. secular, seglar.
secularity, *sĕkŭlăr′tĭĕ*, s. apego á las
     cosas mundanas, m.
secularize, *sĕk′dlărĭz*, v. a. secularizar.
secure, *sēkūr′*, a. seguro; salvo; **-ly**, ad.
     seguramente; **—**, v. a. asegurar; salvar.
security, *sēkūr′tĭĕ*, s. seguridad, f.; de-
     fensa, f.; confianza, f.; fianza, f.
sedan, *sēdăn′*, s. silla de manos, f.
sedate, *sēdāt′*, a. sosegado, tranquilo;
     -ly, ad. tranquilamente.
sedateness, *—nĕs*, s. tranquilidad, f.
sedative, *sĕd′ătĭv*, a. sedativo.
sedentary, *sĕd′ĕntărĕ*, a. sedentario.
sederunt, *sĕdē′rŭnt*, s. (law)estrados, m. pl.
sedge, *sĕj*, s. (bot.) lirio espadañal, m.
sediment, *sĕd′ĭmĕnt*, s. sedimento, m.;
     hez, f.; poso, m.
sedition, *sēdĭsh′ŭn*, s. sedición, f.; tumulto,
     alboroto, motín, m.; revuelta, f.
seditious, *sēdĭsh′ŭs*, a. sedicioso; **-ly**, ad.
     sediciosamente.
seditiousness, *—nĕs*, s. turbulencia, f.
seduce, *sēdūs′*, v. a. seducir; engañar.
seducer, *—ŭr*, s. seductor, m.
seduction, *sēdŭk′shŭn*, s. seducción, f.
seductive, *sēdŭk′tĭv*, a. seductivo.
sedulous, *sĕd′ŭlŭs*, a. asiduo; **-ly**, ad.
     diligentemente.
see, *sē*, v. a. & n. ver, observar, descubrir;
     advertir; conocer, juzgar; comprender;
     —, ¡mira! **—**, s. silla episcopal, f.
seed, *sēd*, s. semilla, simiente, f.; **—**, v. n.
     granar.
seedling, *—lĭng*, s. planta de semillero, f.
seed-plot, *—plŏt*, s. semillero, plantel, m.
seedsman, *—z′măn*, s. tratante en semi-
     llas, m.
seed-time, *—tĭm*, s. sementera, siembra, f.

seedy, *—ĕ*, a. granado, lleno de granos.
seeing, *sē′ĭng*, s. vista, f.; acto de ver
     m.; **—** that, visto que.
seek, *sēk*, v. a. & n. buscar; pretender.
seem, *sēm*, v. n. parecer, semejarse.
seeming, *—ĭng*, s. apariencia, f.; **-ly**, ad.
     al parecer.
seemliness, *—lĭnĕs*, s. decencia, f.
seemly, *—lĕ*, a. decente, propio.
seer, *sē′ŭr*, s. profeta, m.   [lancear.
seesaw, *sē′să*, s. vaivén, m.; **—**, v. n. ba-
seethe, *sēth*, v. n. hervir, bullir.
seether, *—ŭr*, s. caldera, marmita, f.
segment, *sĕg′mĕnt*, s. segmento de un cír-
     culo, m.   [(bienes ó efectos).
seize, *sēz*, v. a. asir, agarrar; secuestrar
seizure, *sē′zhŭr*, s. captura, f.; secuestro, m.
seldom, *sĕl′dŭm*, ad. raramente, rara vez.
select, *sēlĕkt′*, v. a. elegir, escoger; **—**, a.
     selecto, escogido.
selection, *sēlĕk′shŭn*, s. selección, f.
self, *sĕlf*, pr. mismo, propio.
self-command, *—kŏmmănd*, s. imperio
     sobre sí mismo, m.
self-conceit, *—kŏnsēt′*, s. presunción, f.
self-confident, *—kŏnfĭdĕnt*, a. que tiene
     confianza en sí mismo.   [f.
self-defence, *—dēfĕns*, s. defensa propia.
self-denial, *—dēnĭăl*, s. abnegación de sí
     mismo, f.
self-evident, *—ĕvĭdĕnt*, a. natural.   [m.
self-interest, *—ĭntĕrĕst*, s. propio interés,
selfish, *—ĭsh*, a. **-ly**, ad. interesadamente.
selfishness, *—ĭshnĕs*, s. egoísmo, m.
self-possession, *—pŏzzĕsh′ŭn*, s. sangre
     fría, tranquilidad de ánimo, f.
self-respect, *—rĕspĕkt*, s. estima de sí
     mismo, f.   [lo mismo exactamente.
self-same, *—sām*, a. idéntico, el mismo ó
self-seeking, *—sēkĭng*, a. egoístico.
self-styled, *—stĭld*, a. titulado.
self-taught, *—tăt*, a. autodidacto.
self-willed, *—wĭld*, a. obstinado.
sell, *sĕl*, v. a. & n. vender; traficar; **—**, s.
seller, *—lŭr*, s. vendedor, m. [engaño, m.
selling-off, *—lĭng ŏf*, s. venta pública, f.
selvage, *sĕl′văj*, s. orilla del paño, f.
semblance, *sĕm′blăns*, s. semejanza, apa-
     riencia, f.   [f.
semibreve, *sĕm′ĭbrĕv*, s. (mus.) semibreve,
semicircle, *—sŭrkl*, s. semicírculo, m.
semicircular, *—sŭr′kŭldr*, a. semicircular.
semicolon, *—kō′lŏn*, s. punto y coma, m.
seminary, *sĕm′ĭnărĕ*, s. seminario, m.
semiquaver, *sĕm′ĭkwāvŭr*, s. (mus.) semi-
     corchea, f.
semitone, *—tōn*, s. (mus.) semitono, m.
sempstress, *sĕm′strĕs*, s. costurera, f.
senate, *sĕn′ăt*, s. senado, m.
senate-house, *—hŏŭs*, s. senado, m.; casa
     de ayuntamiento, m.
senator, *sĕn′ătŭr*, s. senador, m.
senatorial, *sĕnātō′rĭăl*, a. senatorio.
send, *sĕnd*, v. a. enviar, despachar, man-
     dar; enviar; producir.
sender, *—ŭr*, s. comisionista, m.
seneschal, *sĕn′ĕshăl*, s. senescal, m.
senile, *sē′nĭl*, a. senil.

senility, *sĕnĭl'ĭtĕ,* s. senectud; vejez, f.
senior, *sēn'yŭr,* s. anciano, m.
seniority, *sēnĭŏr'ĭtĕ,* s. antigüedad, ancianidad, f.
senna, *sĕn'nä,* s. (bot.) sen ó sena, f.
sennight, *sĕn'nĭt,* s. ocho días, m. pl.; semana, f.
sensation, *sĕnsā'shŭn,* s. sensación, f.
senso, *sĕns,* s. sentido, m.; entendimiento, m.; razón, f., juicio, m.; sentimiento, m.
senseless, *—lĕs,* a. insensible; insensato; **—ly,** ad. insensatamente.
senselessness, *—lĕsnĕs,* s. tontería, insensibilidad, f.
sensibility, *sĕnsĭbĭl'ĭtĕ,* s. sensibilidad, f.
sensible, *sĕn'sĭbl,* a. sensible, sensitivo; juicioso.
sensibly, *—blĕ,* ad. sensiblemente.
sensitive, *sĕn'sĭtĭv.* a. sensitivo; —, s. (bot.) sensitiva, f. **—ly,** ad. sensual(mente)
sensual, *sĕn'shŭäl,* **sensuous,** *—shŭŭs,* a.
sensualist, *—ĭst,* s. persona sensual, f.
sensuality, *sĕnshŭäl'ĭtĕ,* s. sensualidad, f.
sentence, *sĕn'tĕns,* s. sentencia, f.; —, v. a. sentenciar, condenar.
sententious, *sĕntĕn'shŭs,* a. sentencioso; **—ly,** ad. sentenciosamente.
sentient, *sĕn'shĕnt,* a. sensitivo.
sentiment, *sĕn'tĭmĕnt,* s. sentimiento, m.; opinión, f.
sentimental, *sĕntĭmĕn'täl,* a. sentimental.
sentinel, *sĕn'tĭnĕl,* **sentry,** *sĕn'trĕ,* s. centinela, f. [f.
sentry-box, *—bŏks,* s. garita de centinela,
separable, *sĕp'äräbl,* a. separable.
separate, *sĕp'ärät,* v. a. (& n.) separar(se); —, a. separado; **—ly,** ad. separadamente.
separation, *sĕpärä'shŭn,* s. separación, f.
sepoy, *sē'pŏĕ,* s. soldado natural de las Indias orientales, m.
September, *sĕptĕm'bŭr,* s. setiembre, m.
septennial, *sĕptĕn'nĭäl,* a. sieteñal.
septuagenarian, *sĕptŭäjĕnä'rĭän,* s. septuagenario, m. [nebre.
sepulchral, *sĕpŭl'kräl,* a. sepulcral, fúnebre.
sepulchre, *sĕp'ŭlkŭr,* s. sepulcro, m.
sepulture, *sĕp'ŭltŭr,* s. sepultura, f.
sequel, *sē'kwĕl,* s. secuela, consecuencia, f.
sequence, *sē'kwĕns,* s. serie, continuación, f.
sequester, *sĕkwĕs'tŭr,* **sequestrate,** *sĕkwĕs'trät,* v. a. secuestrar. [cuestro, m.
sequestration, *sĕkwĕsträ'shŭn,* s. seraglio,* *sĕräl'yō,* s. seralio, m.
seraph, *sĕr'äf,* s. serafín, m.
serenade, *sĕrĕnäd',* s. serenata, f.; —, v. a. dar serenatas. [mente.
serene, *sĕrēn',* a. sereno; **—ly,** ad. serenaserenity,* *sĕrĕn'ĭtĕ,* s. serenidad, f.
serf, *sŭrf,* s. siervo, esclavo, m.
serge, *sŭrj,* s. sarga, f. (tela de lana fina).
sergeant, serjeant, *sär'jĕnt,* s. sargento, m.; alguacil, m.; abogado de primera clase, m.
serial, *sē'rĭäl,* a. que sale á luz en series; —, s. publicación en cuadernos periódicos, f.
series, *sē'rĭz,* s. serie, f.
serious, *sē'rĭŭs,* a. serio, grave; **—ly,** ad. seriamente.

sermon, *sĕr'mŏn,* s. sermón, f.; oración evangélica, f.
sermonise, *—īz,* v. a. sermonear.
serous, *sē'rŭs,* a. seroso, acuoso.
serpent, *sŭr'pĕnt,* s. serpiente, sierpe, f.
serpentine, *—īn,* a. serpentino; —, a. (chem.) serpentina, f.
serrated, *sĕr'rätĕd,* a. serratiforme.
serum, *sē'rŭm,* s. suero, m.
servant, *sŭr'vänt,* s. criado, m.; criada, f.
servant-girl, *—gŭrl,* **servant-maid,** *—mäd,* s. criada, f.
serve, *sŭrv,* v. a. & n. servir; asistir (á la mesa); ser á propósito; **to—a warrant,** ejecutar un auto de prisión.
service, *sŭr'vĭs,* s. servicio, m.; servidumbre, utilidad, f.; culto divino, m.; acomodo, m.
serviceable, *—äbl,* a. servicial; oficioso.
servile, *sŭr'vĭl,* a. vil; —, ad. servil(mente).
servility, *sŭrvĭl'ĭtĕ,* s. bajeza, vileza de ánimo, f. [vitud, f.
servitude, *sŭr'vĭtŭd,* s. servidumbre, esclavitud, f.
session, *sĕsh'ŭn,* s. junta, f.; sesión, f.
set, *sĕt,* v. a. poner, colocar, fijar; establecer, determinar; parar (en el juego); —, v. n. ponerse (el sol ó los astros); cuajarse; aplicarse; —, s. juego, conjunto de buenas cartas, m.; servicio (de plata), m.; conjunto ó agregado de muchas cosas, m.; cuadrilla, bandada, f.; —, a. puesto, fijo.
set-off, *—ŏf,* s. adorno, m.; guarnición, f.
set-out, *—ŏut,* s. festejo, m.
settee, *—tē,* s. canapé pequeño, m.
setter, *—tŭr,* s. perro de muestra, m.; espín, m.; el que compone música.
setter-on, *—tŭr ŏn,* s. instigador, m.
setting, *—tĭng,* s. establecimiento, m.; **— of the sun,** puesta del sol, f.
settle, *sĕt'l,* v. a. colocar, fijar, afirmar; arreglar; calmar; —, v. n. reposarse; establecerse; sosegarse; —, s. asiento, m.
settlement, *—mĕnt,* s. establecimiento, m.; domicilio, m.; contrato, m.; empleo, m.; poso, m.; colonia, f.
settler, *—ŭr,* s. colono, m.
set-to, *sĕt tō',* s. riña, f.; combate, m.
seven, *sĕv'n,* a. siete.
sevenfold, *—fōld,* a. séptuplo.
seventeen, *—tēn,* a. diez y siete.
seventeenth, *—tēnth,* a. décimoséptimo.
seventh, *—th,* a. séptimo; **—ly,** ad. en séptimo lugar.
seventieth, *—tĭĕth,* a. septuagésimo.
seventy, *—tĕ,* a. setenta.
sever, *sĕv'ŭr,* v. a. & n. separar.
several, *—äl,* a. diversos, muchos; particular; **—ly,** ad. separadamente.
severance, *—äns,* s. separación, f.
severe, *sĕvēr',* a. severo, riguroso, áspero, duro; **—ly,** ad. severamente.
severity, *sĕvĕr'ĭtĕ,* s. severidad, f. [que.
sew, *sō,* v. a. & n. coser; desaguar un estanque.
sewer, *sŭ'ŭr,* s. albañal, m.; —, *sō'ŭr,* costurera, f.
sewerage, *sŭ'ŭräj,* s. construcción de albañales, f.; agua de sumidero, f.
sex, *sĕks,* s. sexo, m.

11 *

sexennial, *seks'en'nïl,* a. lo que dura ó acontece en seis años.

sextant, *seks'tänt,* s. sextante, m.

sexton, *seks'tŭn,* s. sepulturero, m.

sextuple, *seks'tûpl,* a. séxtuplo.

sexual, *seks'ûĭl,* a. sexual. [namente.

shabbily, *shăb'bïlĕ,* ad. vilmente, mezquinamente.

shabbiness, *shăb'bïnĕs,* s. vileza, bajeza, miseria, f. [pado; tacaño.

shabby, *shăb'bĕ,* a. vil, bajo; desharrapado; tacaño.

shackle, *shăk'l,* v. a. encadenar; —s, s. pl.

shad, *shăd,* s. alosa, f. [grillos, m. pl.

shade, *shād,* s. sombra, obscuridad, f.; matiz, m.; sombrilla, f.; —, v. a. asombrar; abrigar; proteger. [umbría, f.

shadiness, *shā'dïnĕs,* s. sombraje, m.;

shadow, *shăd'ō,* s. sombra, f.; protección, f.

shadowy, *—ĕ,* a umbroso; obscuro; quimérico.

shady, *shā'dĕ,* a. opaco, obscuro, sombrío.

shaft, *shăft,* s. flecha, saeta, f.; fuste de columna, m.; lanza de los coches, f.

shag, *shăg,* s. pelo áspero y lanudo, m.; felpa, f.

shagged, *—gĕd,* **shaggy,** *—gĕ,* a. afelpado.

shagreen, *shăgrēn',* s. zapa, lija, f.

shake, *shāk,* v. a. sacudir; agitar; —, v. n. vacilar; temblar; **to — hands,** darse las manos mutuamente en señal de amistad; —, s. concusión, sacudida, f.; vibración, f.

shaking, *shā'kïng,* a. sacudimiento; tembloroso, f.

shaky, *shā'kĕ,* a. titubeante. [blor, m.

shall, *shăl,* v. n. def. deber.

shallop, *shăl'lŏp,* s. (mar.) chalupa, f.

shallow, *shăl'lō,* a. somero, superficial; trivial; —, s. bajío, m. (banco de arena).

shallowness, *—nĕs,* s. poca profundidad, f.; necedad, f.

sham, *shăm,* v. a. engañar, chasquear; —, s. socolor, m.; fingimiento, m.; impostura, f.; —, a. fingido, disimulado.

shambles, *shăm'bls,* s. pl. carnicería, f.

shambling, *shăm'blïng,* a. lo que se mueve toscamente.

shame, *shām,* s. vergüenza, f.; deshonra, f.; —, v. a. avergonzar, deshonrar. [roso.

shamefaced, *—fāsd,* a. vergonzoso, pudoroso; —ly, ad. ignominiosamente.

shameful, *—fŭl,* a. vergonzoso; deshonroso; —ly, ad. ignominiosamente.

shameless, *—lĕs,* a. desvergonzado; **—ly,** ad. desvergonzadamente. [impudencia, f.

shamelessness, *—lĕsnĕs,* s. desvergüenza,

shamois, *shăm'ŏĕ,* s. gamuza, f.

shampoo, *shămpō',* v. a. dar las friegas.

shampooing, *—ïng,* s. friega, f.; friegas, pl.

shamrock, *shăm'rŏk,* s. trébol, m.

shank, *shăngk,* s. pierna, f.; asta, f.; asta de ancla; cañón de pipa, m.

shanty, *shăn'tĕ,* s. cabaña, f.

shape, *shāp,* v. a. & n. formar; proporcionar; concebir; —, s. forma, figura, f.; molde, m. [delo, m.

shapeless, *—lĕs,* a. informe.

shapely, *—lĕ,* a. bien hecho.

share, *shār,* s. parte, porción, f.; (com.) acción, f.; reja del arado, f.; —, v. a. & n. repartir; participar. [m.

shareholder, *—hōldĕr,* s.(com.) accionista,

sharer, *—ŭr,* s. partícipe, m.

shark, *shărk,* s. tiburón, m.; petardista, m.

sharp, *shărp,* a. agudo, aguzado; astuto; perspicaz; penetrante; acre, mordaz, severo, rígido; vivo, violente; —, s. (mus.) becuadro, m.

sharpen, *—n,* v. a. afilar, aguzar.

sharper, *—ŭr,* s. petardista, estafador, m.

sharply, *—lĕ,* ad. con filo; severamente, agudamente; ingeniosamente.

sharpness, *—nĕs,* s. agudeza, f.; sutileza, perspicacia, f.; acrimonia, f.

shatter, *shăt'tŭr,* v. a. destrozar, estrellar; —, v. n. hacerse pedazos; —, s. pedazo, m.

shave, *shāv,* v. a. rasurar; raspar; rozar; (fig.) escatimar.

shaver, *—ŭr,* s. barbero, m.; usurero, m.

shaving, *—ïng,* s. raedura, f.; rasura, f.

shawl, *shăl,* s. chal, m.

she, *shē,* pn. ella.

sheaf, *shēf,* s. gavilla, f.; —, v. a. agavillar.

shear, *shēr,* v. a. atusar; tundir; —s, s. pl. tijeras grandes, f. pl.

sheath, *shēth,* s. vaina, f.; —, *shēth,* v. a. envainar; (mar.) aforrar el fondo de un navío.

shed, *shĕd,* v. a. verter, derramar; esparcir; —, s. sotechado, tejadillo, m.; cabaña, f.

sheen, *shēn,* s. resplandor, m.

sheep, *shēp,* s. oveja, f.; carnero, m.; papanatas, m. [redil, m.

sheep-cot, *—kŏt,* **sheep-fold,** *—fōld,* s.

sheepish, *—ïsh,* a. vergonzoso; tímido.

sheepishness, *—ïshnĕs,* s. timidez, cortedad de genio, f. [ojeada modesta, f.

sheep's-eye, *—z ī,* s. mirada al soslayo, f.;

sheepskin, *—skïn,* s. piel de carnero, m.

sheep-walk, *—wăk,* s. dehesa, f.; carneril, pasto de ovejas, m.

sheer, *shēr,* a. puro, claro, sin mezcla; —, ad. de un golpe; —, v. n. alargarse, escaparse.

sheet, *shēt,* s. sábana, f.; pliego de papel, m.; (mar.) escota, f.; **book in —s,** libro no encuadernado, m. [de un navío, f.

sheet-anchor, *—ăngkŭr,* s. áncora mayor

sheeting, *—ïng,* s. tela para sábanas, f.

sheet-iron, *—ïrn,* s. plancha de hierro batido, f. [gueamiento, m.

sheet-lightning, *—lïtnïng,* s. relampa-

shelf, *shĕlf,* s. anaquel, m.; (mar.) arrecife, m.; escollera, f.; **on the —,** desecho.

shell, *shĕl,* s. cáscara, f.; silicua, f.; concha, f.; corteza, f.; —, v. a. descascarar, descortezar; —, v. n. descascararse.

shelter, *shĕl'tŭr,* s. guarida, f.; amparo abrigo, m.; asilo, refugio, m.; —, v. a. guarecer, abrigar; acoger.

shelterless, *—lĕs,* a. sin asilo. [conar.

shelve, *shĕlv,* v. a. echar á un lado, arrin-

shelving, *shĕl'vïng,* a. inclinado en declive; —, s. lleno de escollos. [clive.

shelvy, *—ĕ,* a. lleno de escollos.

shepherd, *shĕp'ŭrd,* s. pastor, m.; zagal, m.

shepherdess, *—ĕs,* s. pastora, f.; zagala, f.

sherbet, *shŭr'bĕt,* s. sorbete, m.

sheriff, *shĕr'ĭf,* s. jerif, m.

sherry, *shĕr'rĕ,* s. vino de Jerez, m.

shield, *shēld,* s. escudo, m.; patrocinio, a.; —, v. a. defender.

shift, *shĭft,* v. n. cambiarse; mudarse el vestido; ingeniarse; trampear; —, v. a. mudar, cambiar; transportar; —, s. último recurso, m.; artificio, m.; astucia, f.; efugio, m.; camisa de mujer, f.

shifter, *-ār,* s. tramoyista, m.

shillelagh, *shĭlĕ'lä,* s. macana, f.

shilling, *shĭl'lĭng,* s. chelin, m.

shin(-bone), *shĭn('bōn),* s. espinilla, f.

shine, *shĭn,* v. n. lucir, brillar, resplandecer. [herpes, m. & f. pl.

shingle, *shĭng'gl,* s. ripia, f.; —s, pl. (med.)

shining, *shĭ'nĭng,* a. resplandeciente; —, s. esplendor, m.

shiny, *shĭn'ĕ,* a. brillante, luciente.

ship, *shĭp,* s. nave, f.; bajel, navío, buque, m.; —, v. a. embarcar. [on —, á bordo.

ship-board, *-bōrd,* s. tablón de navío, m.;

ship-boy, *-bŏĭ,* s. grumete, m.

ship-building, *-bĭldĭng,* s. arquitectura naval, f.

shipmate, *-mĕt,* s. (mar.) ayudante, m.

shipment, *-mĕnt,* s. cargazón, f.

ship-owner, *-ōnŭr,* s. naviero, m.

shipwreck, *-rĕk,* s. naufragio, m.

shire, *shĭr* (in comp. *shŭr*), s. condado (de Inglaterra), m.

shirt, *shŭrt,* s. camisa de hombre, f. [f.

shirting, *-ĭng,* s. indiana para camisas.

shiver, *shĭv'ŭr,* s. cacho, pedazo, fragmento, m.; —, v. n. tiritar de frío; —, v. a. estrellar. [plor, m.

shivering, *-ĭng,* s. horripilación, f.; tem-

shoal, *shōl,* s. multitud, muchedumbre, f.; bajío, m.; —, a. lleno de bajíos; —, v. n. atroparse; estar lleno de bajíos.

shoaly, *-ĕ,* a. lleno de bajíos.

shock, *shŏk,* s. choque, encuentro, m.; combate, m.; ofensa, f.; hacina, f.; —, v. a. sacudir; ofender.

shoddy, *shŏd'dĕ,* s. caedura, f.

shoe, *shō,* s. zapato, m.; herradura de caballo, f.; —, v. a. calzar; herrar un caballo.

shoe-black, *-blăk,* **shoe-boy,** *-bŏĭ,* s. limpiabotas, m.

shoeing, *-ĭng,* s. acto de herrar, m.

shoeing-horn, *-ĭnghōrn,* s. calzador, m.

shoelace, *-lăs,* s. correa de zapato, f.

shoemaker, *-mākŭr,* s. zapatero, m. [m.

shoe-string, *-strĭng,* s. lazo de zapato.

shoot, *shōt,* v. a. tirar, arrojar, lanzar, disparar; —, v. n. brotar, germinar; sobresalir; lanzarse; —, s. tiro, m.; vástago, m.

shooter, *-ŭr,* s. tirador, m. [tiro, m.

shooting, *-ĭng,* s. caza con escopeta, f.;

shop, *shŏp,* s. tienda, f.; taller, m.

shop-bill, *-bĭl,* s. señal, f.

shop-front, *-frŏnt,* s. escaparate, m. [m.

shop-keeper, *-kēpŭr,* s. tendero, mercader,

shop-lifter, *-lĭftŭr,* s. ladrón de tiendas, m.

shop-man, *-măn,* s. hortera, mancebo de tienda, m. [tienda, m.

shop-walker, *-wŏkŭr,* s. celador de

shop-woman, *-wŭmăn,* s. tendera, f.

shore, *shōr,* s. costa, ribera, playa, f.

short, *shŏrt,* a. corto, breve, sucinto, conciso; **-ly,** ad. brevemente; presto; en pocas palabras.

shortcoming, *-kŭmĭng,* s. insuficiencia, f.; déficit, m.

shorten, *-n,* v. a. acortar; abreviar.

shorthand, *-hănd,* s. taquigrafía, estenografía, f.

shorthand-writer, *-hăndrītŭr,* s. taquígrafo, estenógrafo, m. [f.

shortness, *-nĕs,* s. cortedad, f.; brevedad,

short-sighted, *-sītĕd,* a. corto de vista.

short-sightedness, *-sītĕdnĕs,* s. cortedad de vista, f.

shot, *shŏt,* s. tiro, m.; alcance, m.; perdigones, m. pl.; escote, m.

shoulder, *shōl'dŭr,* s. hombro, m.; brazuelo, m.; —, v. a. cargar al hombro.

shout, *shŏŭt,* v. n. dar vivas, aclamar; reprobar con gritos; —, s. aclamación, gritería, f.

shouting, *-ĭng,* s. gritos de alegría, m. pl.

shove, *shŭv,* v. a. & n. empujar; impeler; —, s. empujón, m.

shovel, *shŭv'l,* s. pala, f.; —, v. a. traspalar

show, *shō,* v. a. mostrar; descubrir; manifestar; probar; enseñar, explicar; —, v. n. parecer; —, s. espectáculo, m.; muestra, f.; exposición, parada, f.

shower, *shŏŭ'ŭr,* s. nubada, f.; llovizna, f.; (fig.) abundancia, f.; —, v. n. llover.

showery, *-ĕ,* a. lluvioso.

showful, *shŏ'fŭl,* s. moneda falsa, f.

showy, *shŏ'ĕ,* a. ostentoso, suntuoso.

shred, *shrĕd,* s. cacho, pedazo pequeño, m.; —, v. a. picar. [musgaño, m.

shrew, *shrŏ,* s. mujer de mal genio, f.;

shrewd, *shrŏd,* a. astuto; maligno; **-ly,** ad. astutamente.

shrewdness, *-nĕs,* s. astucia, f.

shrewish, *shrŏ'ĭsh,* a. regañón; **-ly,** ad. con mal humor. [musaraña, f.

shrewmouse, *-mŏŭs,* s. musgaño, m.

shriek, *shrĕk,* v. n. chillar; —, s. chillido, m.

shrill, *shrĭl,* a. agudo, penetrante. [m.

shrillness, *-nĕs,* s. aspereza del sonido ó de la voz, f. [hombrecillo, m.

shrimp, *shrĭmp,* s. camarón, m.; enano,

shrine, *shrĭn,* s. relicario, m.

shrink, *shrĭngk,* v. n. encogerse; angostarse, acortarse. [—, v. a. arrugar;

shrivel, *shrĭv'l,* v. n. arrugarse, encogerse;

shroud, *shrŏŭd,* s. cubierta, f.; mortaja, f.; **-s,** pl. (mar.) obenques, m. pl.; —, v. a. cubrir, defender; amortajar; proteger; —, v. n. guarecerse, refugiarse.

shrovetide, *shrŏv'tĭd,* s. martes de carnaval, m.

shrub, *shrŭb,* s. arbusto, m. [m.

shrubbery, *-bŭrĕ,* s. plantío de arbustos,

shrug, *shrŭg,* v. a. encogerse de hombros; —, s. encogimiento de hombros, m.

shudder, *shŭd'ŭr,* v. n. estremecerse, despeluzarse; —, s. despeluzamiento, temblor, m.

shuffle, *shŭf'l,* v. a. & n. poner en confusión, desordenar; barajar los naipes; trampear; tergiversar; hacer esfuerzos; —, s. barajadura, f.; treta, f.

shuffling, *shŭf'lĭng,* s. tramoya, f.

shun, *shŭn,* v. a. huir, evitar.

shunt, *shŭnt*, s. (rail.) bifurcación, f., cambio de vía, m.

shut, *shŭt*, v. a. cerrar, encerrar.

shutter, *tŭr*, s. postigo de ventana, m.

shuttle, *tl*, s. lanzadera, f. [m.

shuttle-cock, *tkŏk*, s. volante, rehilete, m.

shy, *shī*, a. tímido; reservado; vergonzoso, contenido; —ly, ad. tímidamente.

shyness, *nĕs*, s. timidez, f.

sibyl, *sĭb'ĭl*, s. sibila, profetisa, f.

sick, *sĭk*, a. malo, enfermo; disgustado.

sicken, *n*, v. a. enfermar; —, v. n. caer enfermo.

sickle, *sĭk'kl*, s. hoz, f.

sickliness, *lĭnĕs*, s. indisposición habitual.

sickly, *lĕ*, a. enfermizo. [tual.

sickness, *nĕs*, s. enfermedad, f.

side, *sīd*, s. lado, m.; costado, m.; facción, f.; partido, m.; —, a. lateral; oblicuo; —, v. a. unirse con alguno. [f.

sideboard, *bōrd*, s. aparador, m.; alacena, f.

sideface, *fās*, s. cabeza en perfil, f.

sidelong, *lŏng*, a. lateral; —ly, ad. de lado. [m. pl.

side-scene, *sēn*, s. bastidores de un teatro, m. pl.

sideways, *wās*, ad. de lado, al través.

siding, *sī'dĭng*, s. toma de partido, f.; (rail.) aguja, f. [de lado.

sidle, *sī'dl*, v. n. estar echado de lado, ir de lado.

siege, *sēj*, s. (mil.) sitio, m.

sieve, *sĭv*, s. tamiz, m.; criba, f.; cribo, m.

sift, *sĭft*, v. a. cerner; cribar; examinar, investigar.

siftings, *ĭngz*, s. pl. granzas, f. pl.

sigh, *sī*, v. n. suspirar, gemir; —, s. suspiro, m.

sight, *sīt*, s. vista, f.; mira, f. [m.

sightless, *lĕs*, a. ciego.

sightly, *lĕ*, a. vistoso, hermoso.

sight-seeing, *sēĭng*, s. curiosidad, f.

sign, *sīn*, s. señal, f., indicio, m.; tablilla, f.; signo, m.; firma, f.; seña, f.; —, v. a. señalar; hacer señas. [insigne, señalado.

signal, *sĭg'năl*, s. señal, f., aviso, m.; —, a. señalar.

signalize, *īz*, v. a. señalar.

signal-light, *līt*, s. (rail.) farol, m. (de mano ó de disco).

signal-man, *măn*, s. (rail.) guardavía, m.

signature, *sĭg'nătūr*, s. marca, f.; seña, f.; signatura, f.

signet, *sĭg'nĕt*, s. sello (del rey), m. [f.

significance, *sĭgnĭf'ĭkăns*, s. importancia, f.

significant, *sĭgnĭf'ĭkănt*, a. significante.

signification, *sĭgnĭfĭkā'shŭn*, s. significación, f.; sentido, m. [tener energía.

signify, *sĭg'nĭfī*, v. a. significar; —, v. n.

sign-post, *sīn'pōst*, s. pilar de anuncio, m.

silence, *sī'lĕns*, s. silencio, m.; —, v. a. imponer silencio. [ciosamente.

silent, *sī'lĕnt*, a. silencioso; —ly, ad. silenciosamente.

silex, *sī'lĕks*, s. guijarro, m.

silk, *sĭlk*, s. seda, f.

silken, *n*, a. hecho de seda; sedeño.

silkiness, *ĭnĕs*, s. blandura, molicie, f.

silk-man, *măn*, s. mercader de seda, m.

silk-pod, *pŏd*, s. capullo del gusano de seda, m.

silk-worm, *wŭrm*, s. gusano de seda, m.

silky, *ĕ*, a. hecho de seda; sedeño.

sill, *sĭl*, s. umbral de puerta, m.

sillily, *sĭl'ĭlĕ*, ad. tontamente.

silliness, *sĭl'lĭnĕs*, s. simpleza, bobería, tontería, necedad, f.

silly, *sĭl'lĕ*, a. tonto, mentecato, imbécil.

silver, *sĭl'vŭr*, s. plata, f.; —, a. de plata; —, v. a. platear. [platero, m.

silverer, *dr*, s. silversmith, *smĭth*, a.

silvery, *ĕ*, a. plateado.

similar, *sĭm'ĭlŭr*, a. similar; semejante; —ly, ad. similitudinariamente.

similarity, *sĭmĭlăr'ĭtĕ*, similitude, *sĭmĭl'ĭtūd*, s. semejanza, f.

simile, *sĭm'ĭlĕ*, s. semejanza, similitud, f.

simmer, *sĭm'mŭr*, v. n. hervir á fuego lento.

simony, *sĭm'ŏnĕ*, s. simonía, f. [risa, f.

simper, *sĭm'pŭr*, v. n. sonreirse; —, s. sonrisa, f.

simple, *sĭm'pl*, a. simple, puro, sencillo.

simpleness, *nĕs*, s. simplicidad, f.

simpleton, *tŏn*, s. simplón, simplonazo, m.

simplicity, *sĭmplĭs'ĭtĕ*, s. simplicidad, f.; simpleza, f. [plificación, f.

simplification, *sĭmplĭfĭkā'shŭn*, s. simplificación, f.

simplify, *sĭm'plĭfī*, v. a. simplificar.

simply, *sĭm'plĕ*, ad. simplemente.

simulate, *sĭm'ūlāt*, v. a. simular, fingir.

simulation, *sĭmūlā'shŭn*, s. simulación, f.

simultaneous, *sĭmŭltā'nĕŭs*, a. simultáneo. [faltar.

sin, *sĭn*, s. pecado, m.; —, v. n. pecar.

since, *sĭns*, ad. ya que; desde que; pues que; —, pr. desde, después.

sincere, *sĭnsēr'*, a. sencillo; sincero; —ly, ad. sinceramente; — yours (ending to a letter), de U., S.S.S. (su segurísimo servidor); quedo de U. su ato y S.S. (su atento y seguro servidor).

sincerity, *sĭnsĕr'ĭtĕ*, s. sinceridad, f.

sinecure, *sī'nĕkūr*, s. sueldo sin empleo, m.

sinew, *sĭn'ū*, s. tendón, m.; nervio, m.

sinewy, *ĕ*, a. nervoso, robusto.

sinful, *sĭn'fŭl*, a. pecaminoso, malvado; —ly, ad. malvadamente.

sinfulness, *nĕs*, s. corrupción, f.

sing, *sĭng*, v. n. & a. cantar; gorjear los pájaros; (poet.) celebrar.

singe, *sĭnj*, v. a. chamuscar.

singer, *sĭng'ŭr*, s. cantor, m.; cantora, f.

singing, *sĭng'ĭng*, s. canto, m.

single, *sĭng'gl*, a. sencillo, simple, solo; soltero, soltera; —, v. a. singularizar; separar.

singleness, *nĕs*, s. sencillez, sinceridad, f.

singly, *sĭng'glĕ*, ad. separadamente.

singular, *sĭng'gŭlŭr*, a. singular, peculiar; —ly, ad. singularmente. [f.

singularity, *sĭnggŭlăr'ĭtĕ*, s. singularidad, f.

sinister, *sĭn'ĭstŭr*, a. siniestro, izquierdo; viciado; infeliz, funesto.

sink, *sĭngk*, v. n. hundirse; sumergirse; bajarse; penetrar; arruinarse, decaer; —, v. a. hundir, echar á lo hondo; deprimir, destruir; —, s. alcantarilla, f.; sentina, f.

sinking-fund, *ĭngfŭnd*, s. caja de amortización, f.

sinner, *sĭn'nŭr*, s. pecador, m.; pecadora, f.

sin-offering, *sĭn'ŏffŭrĭng*, s. sacrificio propiciatorio, m.

sinuosity, *sĭnūŏs'ĭtĕ*, s. sinuosidad, f.

sinuous, *sĭn'ŭŭs,* a. sinuoso.

sinus, *sī'nŭs,* s. seno, m.; bahía, f.

sip, *sĭp,* v. a. beborrotear, echar sorbitos; —, s. sorbo, m.

siphon, *sī'fŏn,* s. sifón, m.

sippet, *sĭp'pĕt,* s. rebanada de pan, tostada, f.

Sir, *sŭr,* s. Señor, m.

sire, *sīr,* s. caballero, m.; (poet.) padre, m.

siren, *sī'rĕn,* s. sirena, f.

sirloin, *sŭr'lŏĭn,* s. lomo de buey ó vaca, m.

sister, *sĭs'tŭr,* s. hermana, f.; religiosa, f.

sister-in-law, *–ĭnlă,* s. cuñada, f.

sisterhood, *–hŭd,* s. hermandad, f.

sisterly, *–lĕ,* a. con hermandad.

sit, *sĭt,* v. n. sentarse; estar situado.

site, *sīt,* s. sitio, m.; situación, f.

sitting, *sĭt'tĭng,* s. sesión, junta, f.; sentada, f.

situate, *sĭt'ŭăt,* a. situado.

situation, *sĭtŭā'shăn,* s. situación, f.

six, *sĭks,* a. seis.

sixpence, *–pĕns,* s. seis peniques (medio chelín), m. pl.

sixteen, *–tēn,* a. diez y seis.

sixteenth, *–tēnth,* a. décimosexto.

sixth, *–th,* a. sexto; —ly, ad. en sexto lugar.

sixtieth, *–tĭĕth,* a. sexagésimo.

sixty, *–tĕ,* a. sesenta.

size, *sīz,* s. tamaño, talle, m.; calibre, m.; dimensión, f.; estatura, f.; condición, f.; cola de retazo, f.; —, v. a. encolar.

sized, *–d,* a. lo que pertenece al tamaño ó grandor de las cosas.

skate, *skāt,* s. patín, m.; —, v. n. correr sobre el hielo con patines.

skating, *–ĭng,* s. el ejercicio de correr patines sobre el hielo.

skating-rink, *–rĭngk,* s. camino trillado para patinar, m.

skein, *skān,* s. madeja, f.

skeleton, *skĕl'ĕtŏn,* s. esqueleto, m.

skeleton-key, *–kĕ,* s. llave maestra, f.

sketch, *skĕtsh,* s. esbozo, m.; esquicio, m.; —, v. a. esquiciar, bosquejar.

skew, *skū,* a. oblicuo.

skewer, *–ŭr,* s. aguja de lardear, f.; espetón, m.; —, v. a. espetar.

skid, *skĭd,* s. arrastradera de un carruaje, f.; —, v. a. enrayar.

skiff, *skĭf,* s. esquife, m.

skilful, *skĭl'fŭl,* a. práctico, diestro; —ly, ad. diestramente.

skilfulness, *–nĕs,* s. destreza, f.

skill, *skĭl,* s. destreza, arte, pericia, f.

skilled, *–lĕd,* a. práctico, instruido.

skillet, *–lĕt,* s. marmita pequeña, f.

skim, *skĭm,* v. a. espumar; tratar superficialmente; —, s. espuma, f.

skimmer, *–mŭr,* s. espumadera, f.

skin, *skĭn,* s. cutis, m. & f.; —, v. a. desollar.

skinned, *–d,* a. desollado.

skinner, *–nŭr,* s. pellejero, m.; peletero, m.

skinny, *–nĕ,* a. flaco, macilento.

skip, *skĭp,* v. n. saltar, brincar; —, v. a. pasar, omitir; —, s. salto, brinco, m.

skirmish, *skŭr'mĭsh,* s. escaramuza, f.; —, v. n. escaramuzar.

skirmisher, *–ŭr,* s. escaramuzador, m.

skirt, *skŭrt,* s. falda, orla, f.; —, v. a. orillar.

skit, *skĭt,* s. burla, zumba, f.

skittish, *skĭt'tĭsh,* a. espantadizo, retozón; terco; inconstante; —ly, ad. caprichosamente.

skittle, *skĭt'tl,* s. bolo, m.

skulk, *skŭlk,* v. n. escuchar, acechar.

skull, *skŭl,* s. cráneo, m.

skull-cap, *–kăp,* s. gorro, m.

sky, *skī,* s. cielo, firmamento, m.

sky-light, *–lĭt,* s. claraboya, f.

sky-rocket, *–rŏkĕt,* s. cohete, m.

slab, *slăb,* s. losa, f.

slabber, *–bŭr,* v. n. babear; ensuciar.

slack, *slăk,* a. flojo, perezoso, negligente, lento.

slack(en), *–(n),* v. a. & n. aflojar; ablandar; entibiarse; decaer; relajar; aliviar.

slackness, *–nĕs,* s. flojedad, remisión, f.; descuido, m.

slag, *slăg,* s. escoria, f.

slake, *slāk,* v. a. extinguir.

slam, *slăm,* s. capote, m. (en los juegos de naipes); —, v. a. dar capote; empujar con violencia.

slander, *slăn'dŭr,* v. a. calumniar, infamar; —, s. calumnia, f.

slanderer, *–dŭrŭr,* s. calumniador, maldiciente, m.

slanderous, *–dŭrŭs,* a. calumnioso; —ly, ad. calumniosamente.

slang, *slăng,* s. jerigonza, f.

slant, *slănt,* v. n. pender oblicuamente.

slanting, *–ĭng,* a. sesgado, oblicuo.

slap, *slăp,* s. manotada, f.; (on the face), bofetada, f.; —, ad. de sopetón; —, v. a. golpear, dar una bofetada.

slash, *slăsh,* v. a. acuchillar; —, s. cuchillada, f.

slate, *slāt,* s. pizarra, f.; —, v. a. empizarrar.

slate-pencil, *–pĕnsĭl,* s. lápiz de pizarra, m.

slater, *–ŭr,* s. pizarrero, m.

slating, *slā'tĭng,* s. techo de pizarras, m.

slattern, *slăt'tŭrn,* s. mujer desaliñada, f.

slatternly, *–lĕ,* ad. desaliñadamente.

slaughter, *slă'tŭr,* s. carnicería, matanza, f.; —, v. a. matar atrozmente; matar en la carnicería.

slaughter-house, *–hŏŭs,* s. rastro, matadero, m.

slaughterer, *–ŭr,* s. matador, asesino, m.

slave, *slāv,* s. esclavo, m.; esclava, f.; —, v. n. trabajar como esclavo.

slaver, *–ŭr,* s. negrero, m. (navío).

slaver, *slāv'ŭr,* s. baba, f.; —, v. n. babosear.

slavery, *slā'vŭrĕ,* s. esclavitud, f.

slavish, *slā'vĭsh,* a. servil, humilde; —ly, ad. servilmente.

slavishness, *–nĕs,* s. bajeza, servidumbre, f.

slay, *slā,* v. a. matar, quitar la vida.

slayer, *–ŭr,* s. matador, m.

sled, *slĕd,* **sledge,** *slĕj,* **sleigh,** *slā,* s. rastra, narria, f.; trineo, m.

sledge-hammer, *slĕj'hămmŭr,* s. macho, m.

sleek, *slēk,* a. liso, bruñido; —, v. a. alisar, pulir.

sleep, *slēp,* v. n. dormir; —, s. sueño, m.

sleeper, *–ŭr,* s. zángano, m.; travesaño, m.

sleepily, *–lĕ,* ad. con somnolencia ó torpeza.

sleepiness, *–ĭnĕs,* s. adormecimiento, m.

sleeping-room, *–ĭngrŏm,* s. dormitorio, m.

sleepless, *–lĕs,* a. desvelado.

sleep-walking, *–wăkĭng,* s. sonambulismo, m.

sleepy, *–ĕ,* a. soñoliento.

sleet, *slēt,* s. aguanieve, f.; —, v. n. caer aguanieve.

sleeve, *slēv,* s. manga, f.

sleight, slīt, s. astucia, maña, f.

slender, slĕn'dẽr, a. delgado, sútil, débil, pequeño, escaso; -ly, ad. delgadamente.

slenderness, -nĕs, s. delgadez, f.; tenuidad, f.; pequeñez, f. [f.; -, v. a. rebanar.

slice, slīs, s. rebanada, longa, f.; espátula, f.

slide, slīd, v. n. resbalar, deslizarse; correr por encima del hielo; -, s. resbalón, m.; resbaladero, m.; corredera, f.

sliding, slīd'ĭng, s. deslizamiento, m.

slight, slīt, a. ligero, leve, pequeño; -, s. desculdo, m.; -, v. a. despreciar.

slightingly, -ĭnglĭ, ad. con desprecio.

slightly, -lĭ, ligeramente. [gencia, f.

slightness, -nĕs, s. debilidad, f.; negligencia

slim, slĭm, a. delgado, sútil.

slime, slīm, s. lodo, m.; substancia viscosa,

sliminess, slī'mĭnĕs, s. viscosidad, f. [f.

slimy, slī'mĕ, a. viscoso, pegajoso.

sling, slĭng, s. honda, f.; hondazo, m.; -, v. a. tirar con honda.

slink, slĭngk, v. n. escaparse; esconderse.

slip, slĭp, v. n. resbalar; escapar, huirse; -, v. a. meter ó introducir secretamente; dejar; -, s. resbalón, m.; tropiezo, m.; escapada, f.

slipper, -pẽr, s. chinela, f. [diza, f.

slipperiness, -pẽrĭnĕs, s. calidad resbaladiza

slippery, -pẽrĕ, a. resbaladizo.

slip-shod, -shŏd, a. en chancletas.

slip-slop, -slŏp, s. aguachirle, f.

slit, slĭt, v. a. rajar, hender; -, s. raja, hendedura, f.

slobber, slŏb'bẽr, s. baba, f.

sloe, slō, s. endrina, f.

sloop, slōp, s. (mar.) balandra, f.

slop, slŏp, s. aguachirle, f.; lodazal, m.; -s, pl. greguescos, m. pl.

slope, slōp, s. sesgo, m.; declivio, m.; escarpa, f.; -, v. a. sesgar.

sloping, slō'pĭng, a. oblicuo; declive.

slop-pail, slŏp'pāl, s. cubeta, f.

sloppy, slŏp'pĕ, a. lodoso.

sloth, slōth, s. pereza, f.; perezoso, m. (animal de América).

slothful, -fŭl, a. perezoso.

slouch, slŏuch, v. a. & n. estar cabizbajo (como un patán); bambolearse pesadamente.

slough, slŏŭ, s. lodazal, m.; -, slŭf, pellejo de serpiente, m.; escara, f. (de una herida).

sloughy, slŏŭ'ĕ, a. lodoso.

sloven, slŭv'ĕn, s. hombre desaliñado, m.

slovenliness, -lĭnĕs, s. desaliño, m.; porquería, f.

slovenly, -lĭ, a. desaliñado, puerco, sucio.

slow, slō, a. tardío, lento, torpe, perezoso; -ly ad. lentamente. [dez, f.

slowness, -nĕs, s. lentitud, tardanza, pesadez

slow-worm, -wŭrm, s. cecilia, f.

slug, slŭg, s. holgazán, zángano, m.; babosa, f.; pedazo de metal, m.

sluggard, -gẽrd, s. haragán, holgazán, m.

sluggish, -gĭsh, a. perezoso; lento; -ly, ad. perezosamente.

sluggishness, -nĕs, s. pereza, f.

sluice, slōs, s. compuerta, f.; -, v. a. soltar la compuerta de un canal etc.

slum, slŭm, s. garito, m.; callejuela, f.; (vulg.) carta, f. [sueño ligero, m.

slumber, slŭm'bẽr, v. n. dormitar; -, s.

slur, slŭr, v. a. ensuciar; pasar ligeramente; -, s. (mus.) ligado, m.

slush, slŭsh, s. lodo, barro, cieno, m.

slut, slŭt, mujer sucia, f.

sly, slī, a. astuto; -ly, ad. astutamente.

slyness, -nĕs, s. astucia, maña, f.

smack, smăk, s. sabor, gusto, m.; beso fuerte (que se oye), m.; chasquido de látigo, m.; -, v. n. saber; besar con ruido.

small, smăl, a. pequeño, menudo; -, s. parte estrecha de cualquiera cosa, f.

smallish, -ĭsh, a. algo pequeño.

smallness, -nĕs, s. pequeñez, f.

small-pox, -pŏks, s. viruelas, f. pl.

small-talk, -tăk, s. charla, prosa, f.

smalt, smălt, s. esmalte, m.

smart, smărt, s. escozor, m.; -, a. punzante, agudo, agrio; ingenioso; mordaz; doloroso; -, v. n. escocer.

smartly, -lĭ, ad. agudamente, vivamente.

smartness, -nĕs, s. agudeza, viveza, sutileza, f. [-, s. fracaso, m.

smash, smăsh, v. a. romper, quebrantar;

smatterer, smăt'ẽrẽr, s. erudito á la violeta, m. [superficial, m.

smattering, smăt'tẽrĭng, s. conocimiento

smear, smēr, v. a. untar; emporcar.

smell, smĕl, v. a. & n. oler; percibir; -, s. olfato, m.; olor, m.; hediondez, f.

smelling-bottle, -ĭngbŏttl, s. pomito de olor, m. [v. a. fundir (el metal).

smelt, smĕlt, s. esprementue de mar, m.; -,

smelter, -ẽr, s. fundidor, m.

smile, smīl, v. n. sonreirse; -, s. sonrisa, f.

smirk, smẽrk, v. n. sonreirse.

smite, smīt, v. a. herir, golpear.

smith, smĭth, s. forjador de metales, m.

smithery, -ẽrĕ, **smithy,** -ĕ, s. herrería, f.

smock, smŏk, s. camisa de mujer, f.

smock-frock, -frŏk, s. blusa, f.

smoke, smŏk, s. humo, m.; vapor, m.; -, v. a. & n. ahumar; humear; fumar (tobacco).

smoke-consumer, -kŏnsūmẽr, s. locomotora fumívora, f. [humo.

smoke-dry, -drī, v. a. ahumar, secar al

smokeless, -lĕs, a. sin humo.

smoker, -ẽr, s. fumador, m.

smoky, smŏ'kĕ, a. humeante; humoso.

smooth, smŏŏth, a. liso, pulido, llano, suave; afable; -, s. (am.) pradería, f.; -, v. a. allanar; alisar; lisonjear. [dura, f.

smoothly, -lĭ, ad. llanamente; con blandura

smoothness, -nĕs, s. lisura; llanura; suavidad, f. [mir; -, s. humareda, f.

smother, smŭth'ẽr, v. a. sufocar; suprimir

smoulder, smŏl'dẽr, v. n. acclocarse; arder debajo la ceniza. [graba, mugre, f.

smudge, smŭj, v. a. ahogar, asfixiar; -, s.

smug, smŭg, a. atildado, nimiamente compuesto. [matutear.

smuggle, -gl, v. a. hacer el contrabando,

smuggler, -glẽr, s. contrabandista, m.

smuggling, -glĭng, s. contrabando, m.

smut, smŭt, s. tiznón, m.; suciedad, f.; -, v. a. tiznar; ensuciar.

smuttily, -tĭlĕ, ad. suciamente.   [dad, f.
smuttiness, -ĭtnĕs, s. tizne, m.; obsceni-
smutty, -tĕ,a.tiznado; anieblado; obsceno.
snack, snăk, s. parte, porción, f.
snaffle, snăf'fl, s. brida con muserola, f.
snag, snăg, s. dentadura, f.; corcova, f.;
   nudo en la madera, m.
snail, snāl, s. caracol, m.
snake, snāk, s. culebra, f.
snaky, snā'kĕ, a. serpentino.
snap, snăp, v. a. & n. romper; agarrar;
   morder; insultar; (one's fingers) castañetear; —, s. estallido, m.   [m.
snapdragon, -drăgŏn, s. (bot.) antirrino,
snappers, -părz, s. pl. castañetas, f. pl.
snappish, -pĭsh, a. mordaz; regañon.
   -ly, ad. agriamente.   [el trato, m.
snappishness, -pĭshnĕs, s. despego en
snare, snăr, s. lazo, m.; trampa, f.
snarl, snărl, v. n. regañar, gruñir.
snarler, -ăr, s. regañon, m.
snast, snăst, s. pábilo de una vela, m.
snatch, snătsh, v. a. arrebatar; agarrar;
   —, s. arrebatamiento, m.; arrebatiña, f.;
   bocado, m.   [servil, m.
sneak, snēk, v. n. arrastrar; —, s. hombre
sneer, snēr, v. n. hablar con desprecio;
   fisgarse; —, s. fisga, f.
sneeringly, -ĭnglĕ, ad. con desprecio.

sneeze, snēz, v. n. estornudar.   [arriba.
sniff, snĭf, v. n. resollar con fuerza hacia
snigger, snĭg'găr, v. n. reir á menudo.
snip, snĭp, v. a. tijeretear; —, s. tijeretada,
   f., pedazo pequeño, m.; porción, f.
snipe, snĭp, s. agachadiza, f.; zopenco, m.
snivel, snĭv'l, s. moquita, f.; —, v. n. mo-
sniveller, -ăr, s. lloraduelos, m.   [quear.
snob, snŏb, s. medrado, m.; galopin, m.
snobbish, -bĭsh, a. á manera de medrado.
snood, snōd, s. peripuesto; liso.
snooze, snōz, s. sueño ligero, m.
snore, snōr, v. n. roncar; —, s. ronquido, m.
snort, snŏrt, v. n. resoplar (bufar como
   un caballo fogoso).   [fante, f.
snout, snŏŭt, s. hocico, m.; trompa de ele-
snow, snō, s. nieve, f.; —, v. n. nevar.
snow-ball, -băl, s. pelota de nieve, f.
snow-drop, -drŏp, s. (bot.) campanilla
snow-slip, -slĭp, s. alud, m.   [blanca, f.
snowy, -ĕ, a. nevoso; nevado.
snub, snŭb, v. a. reprender, regañar.
snub-nosed, -nōzd, a. romo.
snuff, snŭf, s. moco de candela, m.; pábilo,
   m.; tabaco de polvo, m.; —, v. a. atraer en
   la nariz con el aliento; despabilar; oler.
snuff-box, -bŏks, s. tabaquera, f.
snuffers, -ărz, s. pl. despabiladeras, f. pl.
snuffle, -fl, v. n. ganguear, hablar gangoso.
snuff-taker, -tăkăr, s. tabaquista, m.
snug, snŭg, a. abrigado; conveniente;
   cómodo, agradable, grato.
so, sō, ad. así; tal; de modo que; and —
   forth, y así de lo demás.
soak, sōk, v. n. & a. remojarse; calarse;
   empapar, remojar.
soaker, -ăr, s. beberrón, m.
soap, sōp, s. jabón, m.; —, v. a. jabonar.

soap-ball, -băl, s. bola de jabón, f.
soap-boiler, -bŏĭlăr, s. jabonero, m.
soap-bubble, -bŭbl, s.ampolla de jabón,f.
soap-suds, -sŭdz, s. jabonaduras, f. pl.
soapy, -ĕ, a. jabonoso.
soar, sōr, v. n. remontarse, sublimarse.
soaring, -ĭng, s. vuelo muy alto, m.
sob, sŏb, s. sollozo, m.; —, v. n. sollozar.
sober, sō'băr, a. sobrio; serio; -ly, ad.
   sobriamente; juiciosamente.
sobriety, sōbrī'ĕtĕ, s. sobriedad, f.; seriedad, sangre fría, f.
sociability, sōshăbĭl'ĭtĕ, s. sociabilidad, f.
sociable, sō'shăbl, a. sociable, comuni-
   sociably, -ĕ, ad. sociablemente.   [cativo.
social, sō'shăl, a. social, sociable; -ly, ad.
   sociablemente.
society, sōsī'ĕtĕ, s. sociedad, f.; compañia,
sock, sŏk, s. escarpín, m.; zueco, m.   [f.
socket, -ĕt, s. cañón del candelero, m.;
   cuenca del ojo, f.; alvéolo de un diente, m.
socle, sō'kl, s. zócalo, plinto, m.
sod, sŏd, s. césped, m.; turba, f.
soda, sō'dă, s. sosa, f.
soever, sōĕv'ăr, c. que sea.
sofa, sō'fă, s. sofá, m.
soft, sŏft, a. blando, mole, suavecito; benigno, tierno; jugoso; afeminado; -ly,
   ad. suavemente; paso á paso.   [necer.
soften, sŏf'n, v.a.ablandar, mitigar; enter-
soft-hearted, sŏft'hărtĕd, a. compasivo.
softness, sŏft'nĕs, s. blandura, dulzura, f.
soft-spoken, -spōkn, a. afable.
soil, sŏĭl, v. a. ensuciar, emporcar; —, s.
   mancha, porquería, f.; terreno, m.; estiércol, m.   [morada, f.; residencia, f.
sojourn, sō'jŭrn, v. n. residir, morar; —, s.
solace, sŏl'ds, v. a. solazar, consolar; —, s.
solar, sō'lăr, a. solar.   [s. consuelo, m.
sold, sōld, s. sueldo estipendio, m.   [f.
solder, sōl'dăr, v.a. soldar; —, s.soldadura,
soldier, sōl'jăr, s. soldado, m.   [dadesco.
soldierlike, -lĭk, soldierly, -lĕ, a. sol-
soldiery, -ĕ, s. soldadesca, f.
sole, sōl, s. planta del pie, f.; suela del zapato, f.; —, a. único, solo; —, v. a. solar.
solecism, sŏl'ĕsĭzm, s. (gr.) solecismo, m.
solemn, sŏl'ĕm, a. -ly, ad.solemne(mente).
solemnity, sŏlĕm'nĭtĕ, s. solemnidad, f.
solemnization, sŏlĕmnĭzā'shŭn, s. solem-
   nización, f.
solemnize, sŏl'ĕmnīz, v. a. solemnizar.
solicit, sŏlĭs'ĭt, v. a. solicitar; implorar.
solicitation, sŏlĭsĭtā'shŭn, s. solicitación,
   f.   [tador, m.
solicitor, sŏlĭs'ĭtăr, s. procurador, solici-
solicitous, sŏlĭs'ĭtŭs, a. solícito, diligente;
   -ly, ad. solícitamente.
solicitude, sŏlĭs'ĭtŭd, s. solicitud, f.
solid, sŏl'ĭd, a. sólido, compacto; -ly, ad.
   sólidamente.
solidify, sŏlĭd'ĭfī, v. a. solidificar.
solidity, sŏlĭd'ĭtĕ, s. solidez, f.   [solas.
soliloquize, sŏlĭl'ŏkwĭz, v. n. hablar á
soliloquy, sŏlĭl'ŏkwĕ, s. soliloquio, m.
solitaire, sŏlĭtăr', s. solitario, m., grueso
   diamante.
solitarily, sŏl'ĭtărĭlĕ, ad. solitariamente.

solitariness, *sŏl'ĭtărĭnĕs,* s. soledad, f.; retiro, m.

solitary, *sŏl'ĭtărĕ,* a. solitario, retirado; —, s. ermitaño, m.

solitude, *sŏl'ĭtŭd,* s. soledad, f.; vida solitaria, f.

solo, *sō'lō,* s. (mus.) solo, m.

solstice, *sŏl'stĭs,* s. solsticio, m.

soluble, *sŏl'ŭbĭ,* a. soluble.

solution, *sōlō'shŭn,* s. solución, f.

solve, *sŏlv,* v. a. solver, disolver.

solvency, *sŏl'vĕnsĕ,* s. solvencia, f.

solvent, *—vĕnt,* a. & solvente.

some, *sŭm,* a. algo de, un poco, algún, alguno, alguna, unos, pocos, ciertos.

somebody, *—bŏdĕ,* s. alguien, m.

somehow, *—hŏŭ,* ad. de algún modo.

somerset, *sŭm'ŭrsĕt,* **somersault,** *—sălt,* s. salto mortal, m.

something, *sŭm'thĭng,* s. alguna cosa, algo; —, ad. algún tanto. [guamente.

sometime, *—tīm,* ad. en algún tiempo, antiguamente.

sometimes, *—tīmz,* ad. algunas veces.

somewhat, *—whŏt,* s. alguna cosa, algo; —, ad. algún tanto, un poco. [lugar.

somewhere, *—hwŏr,* ad. en cualquier lugar.

somnambulism, *sŏmnăm'bŭlĭzm,* s. somnambulismo, m. [bulo, m.

somnambulist, *sŏmnăm'bŭlĭst,* s. sonámbulo, m.

somnolence, *sŏm'nŏlĕns,* s. somnolencia, f.

somnolent, *—lĕnt,* a. somnolente.

son, *sŭn,* s. hijo, m.

sonata, *sŏnä'tă,* s. (mus.) sonata, f.

song, *sŏng,* s. canción, f.; old—, cantinela, f.

songster, *—stŭr,* s. cantor, m. [f.

songstress, *—strĕs,* s. cantatriz, f.

son-in-law, *—ĭnlä,* s. yerno, m.

sonnet, *sŏn'nĕt,* s. soneto, m.

sonorous, *sŏnō'rŭs,* a. sonoro; —ly, ad. sonoramente. [que.

soon, *sŏn,* ad. presto, pronto; as — as, luego que.

sooner, *—ŭr,* ad. más pronto, primero que.

soonest, *—ĕst,* ad. cuanto antes.

soot, *sŭt,* s. hollín, m. [daderamente.

sooth, *sŏth,* s. verdad, f.; in good —, verdaderamente.

soothe, *sŏth,* v. a. adular; calmar.

soothsayer, *sŏth'săŭr,* s. adivino, m.

sooty, *sŭt'ĕ,* a. holliniento, fuliginoso.

sop, *sŏp,* s. sopa, f.

sophism, *sŏf'ĭzm,* s. sofisma, m.

sophist, *sŏf'ĭst,* s. sofista.

sophistic(al), *sŏfĭs'tĭk(ăl),* a. sofístico.

sophisticate, *sŏfĭs'tĭkăt,* v. a. sofisticar; falsificar.

sophistry, *sŏf'ĭstrĕ,* s. sofistería, f.

soporific, *sŏpŏrĭf'ĭk,* a. soporífero.

sorcerer, *sŏr'sŭrŭr,* s. hechicero, m.

sorceress, *sŏr'sŭrĕs,* s. hechicera, f.

sorcery, *sŏr'sŭrĕ,* s. hechizo, encanto, m.

sordid, *sŏr'dĭd,* a. sórdido, sucio; avariento; —ly, ad. codiciosamente. [dad, f.

sordidness, *—nĕs,* s. sordidez, mezquindad, f.

sore, *sŏr,* s. llaga, úlcera, f.; —, a. doloroso, penoso; —ly, ad. penosamente.

soreness, *—nĕs,* s. dolencia, f.; mal, m.

sorrel, *sŏr'ĕl,* s. (bot.) acedera, f.; —, a. alazán rojo. [mente.

sorrily, *sŏr'rĭlĕ,* ad. malamente, pobremente.

sorrow, *sŏr'rō,* s. pesar, m.; tristeza, f.; —, v. n. entristecerse

sorrowful, *—fŭl,* a. pesaroso, afligido; —ly, ad. con aflicción. [for it, lo siento.

sorry, *sŏr'rĕ,* a. triste, afligido; I am —

sort, *sŏrt,* s. suerte, f.; género, m.; especie, f.; calidad, f.; manera, f.; —, v. a. separar en distintas clases; escoger, elegir.

sot, *sŏt,* s. zote, m. [pemente.

sottish, *—tĭsh,* a. torpe, rudo; —ly, ad. torpemente.

soul, *sŏl,* s. alma, f.; esencia, f.; persona, f.

soul-bell, *—bĕl,* s. toque á agonía, m.

sound, *sŏŭnd,* a. sano; entero; puro; firme; —ly, ad. sanamente, vigorosamente; —, s. tienta, sonda, f.; sonido, ruido, m.; —, v. a. sondar; tocar; celebrar —, v. n. sonar, resonar.

sound(ing)-board, *—(ĭng) bŏrd,* s. diapasón, m.; sombrero de púlpito, m.

sounding-lead, *—ĭnglĕd,* s. escandallo, m.

sounding-line, *—ĭnglīn,* s. sondalesa, f.

soundings, *—z,* s. pl. (mar.) sondeo, m.; (mar.) surgidero profundo, m. [lidez, f.

soundness, *—nĕs,* s. sanidad, f.; fuerza, solidez, f.

soup, *sŏp,* s. sopa, f.

sour, *sŏŭr,* a. agrio, ácido; áspero; —ly, ad. agriamente; —, v. a. & n. agriar, acedar; agriarse. [m.

source, *sŏrs,* s. manantial, m.; principio, m.

sourness, *sŏŭr'nĕs,* s. acedía, agrura, f.; acrimonia, f.

souse, *sŏŭs,* s. salmuera, f.; —, ad. (vulg.) zas, con violencia; —, v. a. escabechar; chapuzar

south, *sŏŭth,* s. mediodía, sud, sur, m.

southerly, *sŭ'thŭrlĕ,* **southern,** *sŭth'ŭrn,* a. meridional [sudoeste.

southernmost, *—ŭrnmŏst,* a. sur cuarta al sudoeste.

southward, *sŏŭthwărd,* ad. hacia el mediodía

southwester, *sŏŭthwĕst'ŭr,* s. (mar.) viento de sudoeste, m.; sombrero grande de los marineros, m.

sovereign, *sŏv'ŭrĭn,* a. & s. soberano (m.).

sovereignly, *—lĕ,* ad. soberanamente.

sovereignty, *—tĕ,* s. soberanía, f.

sow, *sŏŭ,* s. puerca, marrana, f.

sow, *sō,* v. a. sembrar; esparcir.

sowing-time, *—ĭngtīm,* s. sementera, siembra, f.

space, *spăs,* s. espacio, m.; intersticio, m.

spacious, *spă'shŭs,* a. espacioso, amplio; —ly, ad. con bastante espacio.

spaciousness, *—nĕs,* s. espaciosidad, f.

spade, *spăd,* s. laya, azada, f.; espadas, f. pl. (en los naipes). [palmos.

span, *spăn,* s. palmo, m.; —, v. a. medir á

spangle, *spăng'gl,* s. lentejuela, f.; —, v. a. adornar con lentejuelas.

spaniel, *spăn'yĕl,* s. sabueso, m.

Spanish fly, *spăn'ĭsh flī,* s. cantárida, f.

Spanishleather, *—lĕth'ŭr,* s. cordobán, m.

spar, *spăr,* s. espato, m.; —, v. n. fingir un combate á puñadas.

spare, *spăr,* v. a. & n. ahorrar, economizar; perdonar; vivir con economía; —, a. escaso, económico; —ly, ad. escasamente; —ly built, a. magro.

sparing, *spă'rĭng,* a. escaso, raro, económico; —ly, ad. parcamente, frugalmente.

sparingness, *-nĕs*, s. economía, f

spark, *spárk*, s. chispa, f.; (poet.) centella, f.; pisaverde, m.   [chispear; espumar.

sparkle, *-l*, s. centella, chispa, f.; —, v. n.

sparrow, *spár'ró*, s. gorrión, pardal, m.

sparrow-hawk, *-hák*, s. hembra del gavilán, f.   [tenuemente.

sparse, *spárs*, a. delgado, tenue; —ly, ad

spasm, *spázm*, s. espasmo, m.

spasmodic, *spázmód'ĭk*, a. espasmódico.

spatter, *spát'tár*, v. a. salpicar, manchar

spatterdashes, *-dáshĕz*, s. pl. polainas.

spatula, *spát'ŭlă*, s. espátula, f.   [f. pl.

spavin, *spáv'ĭn*, s. esparaván, m.

spawn, *spán*, s. freza, f.; —, v. a. & n. desovar; engendrar.

spawner, *-ár*, s. hembra en los peces, f.

spawning, *-ĭng*, s. freza, f.

speak, *spék*, v. a. & n. hablar; decir; arengar; conversar; pronunciar.

speaker, *-ár*, s. el que habla; orador, m.

speaking-trumpet, *-ĭng trǔmpĕt*, s. bocina, f.   [herir con lanza.

spear, *spér*, s. lanza, f.; arpón, m.; —, v. a.

special, *spésh'ăl*, a. especial, particular; —ly, ad. especialmente.   [cialidad, f.

specialty, *-tĕ*, speciality, *-ĭtĕ*, s. espe-

specie, *spésh'ĕ*, s. dinero contante, m.

species, *spé'shéz*, s. especie, f.

specific(al), *spésĭf'ĭk(ăl)*, a. específico; —, s. específico, m.

specifically, *-ăllĕ*, ad. en especie.

specification, *spésĭfĭkă'shăn*, s. especificación, f.

specify, *spés'ĭfĭ*, v. a. especificar.

specimen, *spés'ĭmĕn*, s. muestra, f.; prueba, f.   [—ly, ad. especiosamente.

specious, *spé'shăs*, a. especioso, hermoso;

speck(le), *spék(l)*, s. mácula, tacha, f.; —, v. a. abigarrar, manchar.

spectacle, *spék'tăkl*, s. espectáculo, m.; —s, pl. anteojos, m. pl.

spectator, *spéktá'tár*, s. espectador, m.

spectral, *spék'trăl*, a. aduendado; espectométrico; — analysis, s. análisis del espectro solar, f.

spectre, *spék'tár*, s. espectro, m.

speculate, *spék'ŭlăt*, v. n. especular; reflexionar.

speculation, *spékŭlă'shăn*, s. especulación, f.; especulativa, f.; meditación, f.

speculative, *spék'ŭlătĭv*, a. especulativo, teórico.

speculum, *spék'ŭlăm*, s. espejo, m.

speech, *spétsh*, s. habla, m.; arenga, f.; conversación, f.

speechify, *-ĭfĭ*, v. n. arengar.

speechless, *-lĕs*, a. mudo.

speed, *spéd*, s. priesa, f.; celeridad, f.; suceso, m.; —, v. a. apresurar; despachar; ayudar; —, v. n. darse priesa; salir bien.

speedily, *-ĭlĕ*, ad. aceleradamente, de priesa.   [precipitación, f.

speediness, *-ĭnĕs*, s. celeridad, prontitud,

speedy, *-ĕ*, a. veloz, pronto, diligente.

spell, *spél*, s. hechizo, encanto, m.; —, v. a. & n. escribir correctamente; deletrear; hechizar, encantar.

spelling-book, *-ĭng bák*, s. silabario, m.

spelter, *spél'tár*, s. zinc, m.

spend, *spénd*, v. a. gastar; disipar; consumir; —, v. n. hacer gastos; consumirse.

spendthrift, *-thrĭft*, s. pródigo, m.

spent, *spént*, a. alcanzado de fuerzas.

sperm, *spárm*, s. esperma, f.

spermaceti, *spármăsé'tĕ*, s. espermaceti, m.

spew, *spú*, v. n. (vulg.) vomitar.

sphere, *sfér*, s. esfera, f.

spheric(al), *sfér'ĭk(ăl)*, a. esférico; —ly, ad. en forma esférica.   [a. especiar.

spice, *spĭs*, s. especia, f., migaja, f.; —, v.

spick-and-span, *spĭk'ánd spán'*, a. flamante.

spicy, *spĭ'sĕ*, a. aromático.

spider, *spĭ'dár*, s. araña, f.

spigot, *spĭg'ŏt*, s. llave de fuente, f.

spike, *spĭk*, s. espiga de grano, f.; espigón, m.; —, v. n. clavar con espigones.

spill, *spĭl*, v a. derramar, verter; —, s. clavija, espiga, f.

spin, *spĭn*, v. a. hilar; alargar, prolongar; —, v. n. hilar; correr hilo á hilo.

spinach, spinage, *spĭn'áj*, s. espinaca, f.

spinal, *spĭ'năl*, a. espinal.

spindle, *spĭn'dl*, s. huso, m.; quicio. m.

spindle-legged, *-légged*, --shanked, *-shánkd*, a. zanquivano.

spine, *spĭn*, s. espinazo, m. espina, f.

spinet, *spĭn'nĕt*, s. (mus.) espineta, f.

spinner, *spĭn'nár*, s. hilador, m.; hilandera, f.

spinney, *spĭn'né*, s. maleza, f. dera, f.

spinning-jenny, *spĭn'nĭng jénné*, s. máquina de hilar, f.   [m.

spinning-wheel, *-hwél*, s. torno de hilar,

spinster, *spĭn'stár*, s. hilandera, f.; doncella, soltera, f.   [de espiral.

spiral, *spĭ'răl*, a. espiral -ly, ad. en figura

spire, *spĭr*, s. espira, f.; pirámide, m.; aguja, f. (de una torre).

spirit, *spĭr'ĭt*, s. aliento, m.; espíritu, m.; ánimo, valor, m.; brío, m.; humor, m.; fantasma, m.; —, v. a. incitar, animar; to – away, quitar secretamente.

spirited, *-ĕd*, a. vivo, brioso; -ly, ad. con espíritu.

spirit-lamp, *-lámp*, s. velón ó quinqué alimentado con alcohol, m.

spiritless, *-lĕs*, a. abatido, sin espíritu.

spiritual, *-ăl*, a. -ly, ad. espiritual (mente).

spiritualist, *-ălĭst*, s. espiritualista, m.

spirituality, *spĭrĭtŭál'ĭtĕ*, s. espiritualidad, inmaterialidad, f.

spirituous, *spĭr'ĭtŭăs*, a. espirit(u)oso.

spirt, *spárt*, v. a. & n. arrojar un líquido en un chorro; jeringar.   [tar; escupir.

spit, *spĭt*, s. asador, m.; —, v. a. & n. espe-

spite, *spĭt*, s. rencor, m., malevolencia, f.; in – of, á pesar de, á despecho; —, v. a. dar pesar.

spiteful, *-fŭl*, a. rencoroso, malicioso; -ly, ad. malignamente, con tirria.   [m.

spitefulness, *-fŭlnĕs*, s. malicia, f., rencor,

spitfire, *spĭt'fĭr*, s. locarias, m.

spittle, *spĭt'tl*, s. saliva, f.; esputo, m.

spittoon, *spĭttón'*, s. escupidera, f.

splash, *splásh*, v. a. salpicar, enlodar.

splash-board, –*bŏrd,* s. mantelete, m.

splay, *splā,* v. a. despaldar á un caballo.

splay-footed, –*fŭted,* a. patiestevado.

spleen, *splēn,* s. bazo, m.; esplín, m.

splendid, *splĕn'dĭd,* a. espléndido, magnífico; –**ly,** ad. espléndidamente.

splendour, *splĕn'dŭr,* s. esplendor, m.; pompa, f.

splenetic(al), *splĕnĕt'ĭk(ăl),* a. atrabiliario.

splice, *splīs,* v. a. (mar.) empalmar, empletar.   [zales, m. pl.

splint, *splĭnt,* s. astilla, f.; –s, pl. brasplinter, *splĭn'tŭr,* s. cacho, m.; astilla, f.; brisna, f.; –, v. a. (& n.) hender(se).

split, *splĭt,* v. a. hender, rajar; –, v. n. henderse.

spoil, *spŏĭl,* v. a. pillar, robar; despojar; arruinar; –, v. n. corromperse, dañarse; –, s. despojo, botín, m.; ruina, f.

spoiler, –*ŭr,* s. corruptor, robador, m.

spoke, *spōk,* s. rayo de la rueda, m.

spokesman, *spōks'măn,* s. interlocutor, m.

spoliate, *spō'lĭāt,* v. a. robar, pillar.

spoliation, *spōlĭā'shŭn,* s. despojo, m.; espoliación de bienes, f.

sponge, *spŭnj,* s. esponja, f.; –, v. a. limpiar con esponja; –, v. n. meterse de mogollón.

sponge-bath, –*băth,* s. baño inglés, m.

sponger, –*ŭr,* s. pegote, mogollón, m.

sponginess, *spŭnj'ĭnĕs,* s. calidad esponjosa, f.

sponging-house, *spŭnj'ĭnghŏŭs,* s. casa á adonde llevan á los deudores insolventes antes de ponerlos en la cárcel, f.

spongy, *spŭnj'ĕ,* a. esponjoso.

sponsor, *spŏn'sŭr,* s. fiador, m.; padrino, m.; madrina, f.   [dad, voluntariedad, f.

spontaneity, *spŏntănē'ĭtĕ,* s. espontaneidad, f.

spontaneous, *spŏntā'nĕŭs,* a. espontáneo; –**ly,** ad. espontáneamente.

spool, *spōl,* s. canilla, broca, f.

spoon, *spōn,* s. cuchara, f.

spoonful, –*fŭl,* s. cucharada, f.

sporadic(al), *spŏrăd'ĭk(ăl),* a. esporádico.

sport, *spōrt,* s. juego, retozo, m.; juguete, divertimiento, recreo, pasatiempo, m.; –, v. a. divertirse; –, v. n. chancear, juguetear.

sportive, –*ĭv,* a. festivo, juguetón. [tear.

sportiveness, –*ĭvnĕs,* s. festividad, holganza, f.   [á la pesca &c., m.

sportsman, –*s'măn,* s. aficionado á la caza,

spot, *spŏt,* s. mancha, f.; borrón, m.; sitio, lugar, m.; –, v. a. abigarrar; manchar.

spotless, –*lĕs,* a. limpio, inmaculado.

spotted, –*tĕd,* **spotty,** –*tĕ,* a. lleno de manchas, sucio.   [matrimonial, nupcial.

spousal, *spŏŭ'zăl,* s. nupcias, f. pl.; –, a.

spouse, *spŏŭz,* s. esposo, m.; esposa, f.

spout, *spŏŭt,* v. a. & n. arrojar agua con mucho ímpetu; borbotar; chorrear; estar de hocico; –, s. llave de fuente, f.; gárgola, f.; bomba marina, f.   [locación, f.

sprain, *sprān,* a. descoyuntar; –, s. dis-

sprat, *sprăt,* s. meleta, nuesa, f. (pez).

sprawl, *sprăl,* v. n. bregar; revolcarse.

spray, *sprā,* s. leña menuda, f.; vástago, m.; espuma de la mar, f.

spread, *sprĕd,* v. a. extender, desplegar; esparcir, divulgar; –, v. n. extenderse, desplegarse; –, s. extensión, dilatación, f.

spree, *sprē,* s. fiesta, f., festín, m.

sprig, *sprĭg,* s. ramito, m.   [cidad, f.

sprightliness, *sprīt'lĭnĕs,* s. alegría, viva-

sprightly, *sprīt'lĕ,* a. alegre, despierto, vivaracho.

spring, *sprĭng,* v. n. brotar, arrojar; nacer, provenir; dimanar, originarse; saltar, brincar; –, v. a. ojear la caza; hacer volar; –, s. primavera, f.; elasticidad, f.; muelle, resorte, m.; salto, m.; manantial, m.; hendidura, f.

springe, *sprĭnj,* s. lazo de cazador, m.

springiness, *sprĭng'ĭnĕs,* s. elasticidad, f.

spring-tide, *sprĭng'tĭd,* s. marea viva, f.

spring-water, –*wătŭr,* s. agua de fuente.

springy, *sprĭng'ĕ,* a. elástico.   [f.

sprinkle, *sprĭng'kl,* v. a. rociar; hisopear; salpimentar.

sprinkling, –*ĭng,* s. viso, tinte, m.; brizna, f.

sprite, *sprīt,* s. espíritu, m.; fantasma, f.

sprout, *sprŏŭt,* s. vástago, renuevo, m.; –s, s. pl. bretones, m. pl.; –, v. n. brosar.

spruce, *sprŏŭs,* a. pulido, gentil; –**ly,** ad. bellamente, lindamente; –, v. n. vestirse con afectación.   [f.

spruceness, –*nĕs,* s. lindeza, hermosura, f.

spume, *spŭm,* s. espuma, f.; –, v. n. espumar.

spur, *spŭr,* s. espuela, f.; espolón (del gallo), m.; estímulo, m.; –, v. a. espolear; estimular.   [trahecho; supuesto; bastardo.

spurious, *spū'rĭŭs,* a. espurio, falso; con-

spurn, *spŭrn,* v. a. acocear; despreciar.

sputter, *spŭt'tŭr,* v. n. escupir con frecuencia; babosear; barbotar.

sputterer, –*ŭr,* s. faramallero, m.

spy, *spī,* s. espía, m.; –, v. a. & n. espiar, columbrar.

spy-glass, –*glăs,* s. anteojo de larga vista.

squab, *skwŏb,* a. implume; cachigordo, regordete; –, s. canapé, m.; cojín, m.; pichón, m.   [riña, disputa, f.

squabble, –*bl,* v. n. reñir, disputar; –, s.

squabbler, –*blŭr,* s. pendenciero, m.

squad, *skwŏd,* s. escuadra de soldados, f.

squadron, –*rŏn,* s. (mil.) escuadrón, m.

squalid, *skwŏl'ĭd,* a. sucio, puerco.

squall, *skwăl,* s. fugada, f.; chubasco, m.; –, v. n. chillar.

squally, –*ĕ,* a. borrascoso.

squalor, *skwŏl'ŭr,* s. porquería, suciedad, f.

squander, *skwŏn'dŭr,* v. a. malgastar, disipar.

square, *skwăr,* a. cuadrado, cuadrángulo; exacto; cabal; –, s. cuadro, m.; plaza, f.; escuadra, f.; –, v. a. cuadrar; ajustar, arreglar; –, v. n. ajustarse.

squareness, –*nĕs,* s. cuadratura, f.

squash, *skwŏsh,* v. a. aplastar.

squat, *skwŏt,* v. n. agacharse; –, a. agachado; rechoncho.   [m.

squatter, –*tŭr,* s. (am.) colono usurpador,

squaw, *skwă,* s. hembra de un indiano, f.

squeak, *skwēk,* v. n. plañir, chillar; –, s. grito, plañido, m.

squeal, *skwēl,* v. n. plañir, gritar.

squeamish, *skwēm'ĭsh,* a. fastidioso; demasiado delicado.

squeeze, *skwēz,* v. a. apretar, comprimir; estrechar; —, s. compresión, f.

squib, *skwĭb,* s. cohete, m.

squint, *skwĭnt,* a. ojizaino; bizco; —, v. n. bizquear. (de cortesía.)

Squire, *skwīr,* s. Caballero, m. (tratamiento

squirrel, *skwĕr'rĭl,* s. ardilla, f.

squirt, *skwĕrt,* v. a. jeringar; —, s. jeringa, f.; chorro, m.; (am.) pisaverde, m.

stab, *stăb,* v. a. matar á puñaladas; —, s. puñalada, f. [f.

stability, *stăbĭl'ĭtē,* s. estabilidad, solidez,

stable, *stā'bl,* s. establo, m.; —, v. a. poner en el establo; —, a. estable.

stabling, *stā'blĭng,* s. caballerizas, f. pl.

stack, *stăk,* s. niara, f.; —, v. a. hacinar.

staff, *stăf,* s. báculo, palo, m.; apoyo, m.; (mil.) estado mayor, m.

stag, *stăg,* s. ciervo, m.

stage, *stāj,* s. tablado, m.; teatro, m.; parada, f.; escalón, m. [perimentado.

stager, *stā'jĕr,* s. cómico, m.; hombre experimentado.

stagger, *stăg'gĕr,* v. n. vacilar, titubear; estar incierto; —, v. a. asustar; hacer vacilar. [nă'shŭn, s. estagnación, f.

stagnancy, *stăg'nănsē,* **stagnation,** *stăg-* **stagnant,** *stăg'nănt,* a. estancado.

stagnate, *—nāt,* v. n. estancarse.

staid, *stād,* a. grave, serio.

staidness, *—nĕs,* s. gravedad, f.

stain, *stān,* v. a. manchar; empañar la reputación; —, s. mancha, f.; deshonra, f.

stainer, *—ĕr,* s. tintorero, m.

stainless, *lĕs,* a. limpio; inmaculado.

stair, *stār,* s. escalón, m.; —s, pl. escalera,

staircase, *—kās,* s. escalera, f. [f.

stake, *stāk,* s. estaca, f.; posta, f. (en el juego); —, v. a. estacar; poner en el juego.

stale, *stāl,* a. añejo, viejo, rancio; —, s. orina, f.; —, v. n. orinar.

staleness, *—nĕs,* s. vejez, f.; rancidez, f.

stalk, *stăk,* v. n. andar con paso majestuoso; —, s. paso orgulloso, m.; tallo, pie, tronco, m.; troncho, m. (de ciertas hortalizas).

stalking-horse, *—ĭnghŏrs,* s. caballo verdadero ó figurado que sirve á los cazadores para ocultarse y cazar, m.; máscara, f.; disfraz, m.

stall, *stăl,* s. pesebre, m.; tienda portátil, f.; tabanco, m.; silla, f. (de coro); butaca en el teatro, f.; —, v. a. meter en el establo.

stallion, *stăl'yŭn,* s. caballo padre, m.

stalwart, *—wărt,* a. robusto, vigoroso.

stamen, *stăm'ĕn,* s. estambre, m.; fundamento, m. [m. pl.

stamina, *stăm'ĭnă,* s. pl. (bot.) estambres,

stammer, *stăm'mĕr,* v. n. tartamudear.

stammerer, *—ĕr,* s. tartamudo, m.

stamp, *stămp,* v. a. patear; moler, majar; estampar, imprimir; acuñar; andar con mucha pesadez; —, s. cuño, m.; sello, m.; impresión, f.; estampa, f. [pánico, m.

stampede, *stămpēd',* s. (am.) susto, terror

stanch, *stănsh,* v. a. (& n.) estancar(se); —, a. sano; firme, seguro, zeloso.

stand, *stănd,* v. n. estar en pie ó derecho; sostenerse; resistir; permanecer; pararse; hacer alto, estar situado; hallarse; erizarse el pelo; —, v. a. sostener, defender; —, s. puesto, sitio, m.; posición, situación, f.; parada, f.; embarazo, m.; estado, m. (fijo); velador para poner la luz, m.; estante, vasar, m.

standard, *—ărd,* s. estandarte, m.; modelo, m.; precio ordinario, m.; norma, f.

standing, *—ĭng,* a. permanente, fijado, establecido; estancado; —, s. duración, f.; posición, f.; puesto, m.

stand-still, *—stĭl,* s. pausa, f.; alto, m.

staple, *stā'pl,* s. emporio de comercio, m.; escala de depósito, f.; cerradero, m.; —, a. ajustado, establecido.

star, *stăr,* s. estrella, f.; asterisco, m.

starboard, *—bōrd,* s. estribor, m. [donar.

starch, *stărtsh,* s. almidón, m.; —, v. a. almidonar.

stare, *stăr,* v. a. clavar la vista; —, s. mirada fija, f.

staringly, *stăr'ĭnglē,* ad. brillantemente.

stark, *stărk,* a. fuerte, áspero; puro; —, ad. del todo.

starless, *stăr'lĕs,* a. sin estrellas.

starling, *stăr'lĭng,* s. estornino, m.; esquina del estribo de un puente, f.

starred, *stărd,* **starry,** *stăr'rē,* a. estrellado.

start, *stărt,* v. n. sobrecogerse, sobresaltarse, estremecerse; levantarse de repente; salir los caballos en las carreras; —, v. a. sobrecoger; suscitar; descubrir; —, s. sobresalto, m.; ímpetu, m.; paso primero, m.

starter, *—ĕr,* s. el oficial que da la salida en las carreras; hombre pavorido, m.

starting-point, *—ĭngpŏĭnt,* s. poste de salida, m. (en las carreras).

startle, *stăr'tl,* v. n. sobresaltarse, estremecerse de repente; —, s. espanto, susto repentino, m. [bre, inanición, f.

starvation, *stărvā'shŭn,* s. muerte de hambre.

starve, *stărv,* v. n. perecer de hambre. [m.

starveling, *—ĭng,* s. hombre hambriento,

state, *stāt,* s. estado, m.; condición, f.; Estado (político); pompa, grandeza, f.; —, v. a. ajustar, arreglar. [f.

stateliness, *—lĭnĕs,* s. grandeza, pompa,

stately, *—lē,* a. augusto, majestuoso.

statement, *—mĕnt,* s. relación, cuenta, f.

statesman, *—s'măn,* s. estadista, político,

statesmanship, *—shĭp,* s. política, f. [m.

statics, *stăt'ĭks,* s. estática, f.

station, *stā'shŭn,* s. estación, f.; empleo, puesto, m.; situación, postura, f.; grado, m.; condición, f.; (rail.) estación; **intermediate —,** estación auxiliar de señales; —, v. a. apostar.

stationary, *—ărē,* a. estacionario, fijo.

stationer, *—ĕr,* s. librero-papelero, m.

stationery, *—ărē,* s. toda especie de papel y demás cosas necesarias para escribir, f.

statist, *stă'tĭst,* s. estadista, m.

statistic(al), *stătĭs'tĭk(ăl),* a. estadístico.

statistics, *stătĭs'tĭks,* s. pl. estadística, f.

statuary, *stăt'ŭărē,* s. estatuario, escultor,

statue, *stăt'ŭ,* s. estatua, f. [m.

stature, *stăt'ŭr*, s. estatura, talla, f. |m.
statute, *stăt'ŭt*, s. estatuto, m.; reglamento,
stave, *stāv*, v. a. descabezar algun barril;
  —s, s. pl. duelas de barril, f. pl.
stay, *stā*, s. estancia, mansión, f.; —s, s. pl.
  corsé, justillo, m.; —, v. n. quedarse,
  estarse; tardar, detenerse; aguardarse, es-
  perarse; —, v. a. detener; contener; apoyar.
stead, *stěd*, s. lugar, sitio, paraje, m.
steadfast, *—făst*, a. firme, estable, sólido;
  —ly, ad. firmemente, con constancia.
steadfastness, *—făstnĕs*, s. firmeza, constancia, f.   [mente.
steadily, *—ĭlĕ*, ad. firmemente; invariable-
steadiness, *—ĭnĕs*, s. firmeza, estabilidad, f.   [firme.
steady, *—ĕ*, a. firme, fijo; —, v. a. hacer
steak, *stāk*, s. tajada de carne cocida ó
  asada, f.
steal, *stēl*, v. a. & n. hurtar, robar; introducirse clandestinamente; escapar sin ser
  visto.   [dillas.
stealth, *stělth*, s. hurto, m.; by—, á hurta-
stealthily, *—ĭlĕ*, ad. furtivamente.
stealthy, *—ĕ*, a. furtivo.
steam, *stēm*, s. vapor, m.; —, v. n. vahear;
  to — it, viajar ó navegar á vapor.
steam-bath, *—băth*, s. baño de vapor, m.
steam-boiler, *—bŏilŭr*, s. caldera de una
  máquina de vapor, f.
steam-carriage, *—kărrĭj*, s. (rail.) locomotora, f.; (rail.) vagón, m.   [vapor, f.
steam-engine, *—ĕnjĭn*, s. máquina de
steamer, *stēm'ŭr*, **steam-boat,** *—bŏt*,
  steam-vossel, *—vĕsl*, s. vapor, buque
  de vapor, m.
steed, *stēd*, s. caballo de regalo, m.
steel, *stēl*, s. acero, m.; eslabón, m.; —,
  v. a. acerar; fortalecer, endurecer.
steelyard, *—yărd*, s. romana, f.
steep, *stēp*, a. escarpado; —, s. precipicio,
  m.; —, v. a. empapar.
steeple, *—l*, s. torre, f.; campanario, m.
steeple-chase, *—tshās*, s. carrera ciega, f.
steepness, *—nĕs*, s. precipicio, m.; escarpa,
  f.   [nar.
steer, *stēr*, s. novillo, m.; —, v. a. gober-
steerage, *—ĕj*, s. gobierno, m.; (mar.) antecámara de un navío, f.
steerage-way, *—wā*, s. (mar.) estela, f.
stellar, *stĕl'lăr*, a. estrellado.
stem, *stěm*, s. vástago, tallo, m.; estirpe,
  f.; (mar.) branque, m.; —, v. a. cortar la
stench, *stěnsh*, s. hedor, m.   [corriente.
stencil, *stěn'sĭl*, s. patrón, dechado, m.
stenographer, *stěnŏg'răfŭr*, s. estenógrafo, m.
stenographic(al), *stěnŏgrăf'ĭk(ăl)*, a.
  estenográfico.   [f.
stenography, *stěnŏg'răfĕ*, s. estenografía,
step, *stěp*, s. paso, escalón, m.; huella, f.;
  —, v. n. dar un paso; andar.
step-brother, *—brŭthŭr*, s. medio hermano,
step-daughter, *—dătŭr*, s. hijastra, f. |m.
step-father, *—făthŭr*, s. padrastro, m.
step-mother, *—mŭthŭr*, s. madrastra, f.
stepping-stone, *—pĭngstōn*, s. pasadera, f.
step-sister, *—sĭstŭr*, s. media hermana, f.

step-son, *—sŭn*, s. hijastro, m.
stereotype, *stěr'ĕŏtĭp*, s. estereotipía, f.;
  —, v. a. estereotipar.
sterile, *stěr'ĭl*, a. estéril.
sterility, *stěrĭl'ĭtĕ*, s. esterilidad, f.
sterling, *stŭr'lĭng*, a. esterlín, genuino,
  verdadero; —, s. moneda esterlina, f.
stern, *stŭrn*, a. austero, rígido, severo;
  —, s. (mar.) popa, f.; —ly, ad. austeramente.
stertorous, *stŭr'tŏrŭs*, a. roncador.
stethoscope, *stěth'ŏskŏp*, s. (med.) este-
  toscopio, m.   [m.
stevedore, *stĕ'vĕdŏr*, s. (mar.) estivador,
stew, *stū*, v. a. estofar; —, s. estufa, f.
steward, *—ŭrd*, s. mayordomo, m.; (mar.)
  despensero, m.
stewardship, *—shĭp*, s. mayordomía, f.
stew-pan, *—păn*, s. cazuela, f.
stick, *stĭk*, s. palo, palillo, bastón, m.;
  vara, f.; —, v. a. pegar, hincar; picar,
  punzar; —, v. n. pegarse; detenerse; perseverar; dudar.
stickiness, *—ĭnĕs*, s. viscosidad, f.
stickle, *—l*, v. n. tomar partido; disputar.
stickler, *—lŭr*, s. padrino en un duelo,
  m.; partidario, m.
sticky, *—ĕ*, a. viscoso, tenaz.
stiff, *stĭf*, a. tieso; duro, torpe; rígido;
  obstinado; —ly, ad. obstinadamente.
stiffen, *stĭf'n*, v. a. atiesar, endurecer; —,
  v. n. endurecerse.   [tuerto, m.
stiff-neck, *—něk*, s. torticoli, m.; cabiz-
stiffness, *—nĕs*, s. tesura, rigidez, f.; obstina-
stifle, *stĭf'l*, v. a. sufocar.   [ción, f.
stigma, *stĭg'mă*, s. nota de infamia, f.
stigmatize, *—tīz*, v. a. infamar, manchar.
stile, *stīl*, s. portillo con escalones, m. (para
  pasar un cercado á otro); gnomon, m.;
  estilo, m.
stiletto, *stĭlĕt'tŏ*, s. verduguillo, m.
still, *stĭl*, v. a. aquietar, aplacar; destilar;
  —, a. silencioso, tranquilo; —, s. silencio,
  m.; alambique, m.; —, ad. todavía; siempre, hasta ahora; no obstante.
still-born, *—bŏrn*, a. nacido muerto.
stillness, *—nĕs*, s. calma, quietud, f.
stilts, *stĭlts*, s. pl. zancos, m. pl.
stimulant, *stĭm'ŭlănt*, s. estimulante, m.
stimulate, *—lāt*, v. a. estimular, aguijonear.
stimulation, *stĭmŭlā'shŭn*, s. estímulo,
  m.; estimulación, f.
stimulative, *stĭm'ŭlātĭv*, a. estimulante.
stimulus, *—lŭs*, s. estímulo, m.
sting, *stĭng*, v. a. picar ó morder (un insecto); —, s. aguijón, m.; punzada, picadura, picada, f.; remordimiento de conciencia, m.
stingily, *stĭn'jĭlĕ*, ad. avaramente.   [f.
stinginess, *—nĕs*, s. tacañería, avaricia,
stinging-nettle, *stĭng'ĭngnětl*, s. ortiga, f.
stingy, *stĭn'jĕ*, a. mezquino, tacaño, avaro.
stink, *stĭngk*, v. n. heder; —, s. hedor, m.
stint, *stĭnt*, v. a. limitar; —, s. límite, m.;
  restricción, f.   [salario, m.
stipend, *stĭ'pěnd*, s. estipendio, m.; sueldo,
stipendiary, *stĭpěn'dĕărĕ*, a. estipendiario.
stipulate, *stĭp'ŭlāt*, v. n. estipular.

stipulation, *stĭpŭlá'shŭn,* s. estipulación, f.; contrato mutuo, m.
stir, *stŭr,* v. a. remover; agitar; incitar; —, v. n. moverse; —, s. tumulto, m.; turbulencia, f.
stirrer, *-rŭr,* s. instigador, m.
stirrup, *stĭr'rŭp,* s. estribo, m.
stirrup-leather, *-lĕthŭr,* s. ación, f.
stitch, *stĭtsh,* v. a. coser; —, s. puntada, f.
stoat, *stōt,* s. comadreja, f. [f.; punto, m.
stuck, *stŏk,* s. tronco, m.; injerto, m.; zoquete, estólido, m.; mango, m.; corbatín, m.; estirpe, f., linaje, m.; capital, principal, m.; fondo, m.; –s, pl. acciones en los fondos públicos, f. pl.; —, v. a. proveer, abastecer.
stockade, *stŏkkăd',* s. palizada, f.; estocada, f.
stock-fish, *stŏk'fĭsh,* s. bacalao seco, m.
stock-holder, *-hōldŭr,* s. accionista, m.
stocking, *-ĭng,* s. media, f.
stock-jobber, *-jŏbbŭr,* s. agiotador, m.
stock-still, *-stĭl,* a. inmoble, inmóvil.
stoic, *stō'ĭk,* s. estoico, m. [mente.
stoical, *-ăl,* a. estoico; –ly, ad. estoica-
stoicism, *stō'ĭsĭzm,* s. estoicismo, m.
stoker, *stō'kŭr,* s. fuellero, m.
stole, *stōl,* s. estola, f.
stomach, *stŭm'ŭk,* s. estómago, m.; apetito, m.; –, v. n. enojarse.
stomacher, *-ŭr,* s. peto, m.
stomachic(al), *stŏmăk'ĭk(ăl),* a. estomáctico; –, s. medicamento estomacal, m.
stone, *stōn,* s. piedra, f.; cálculo, cuesco, m.; pepita, f.; testículo, m.; hueso de fruta, m.; peso de catorce libras, m.; –, a. de piedra; –, v. a. apedrear; quitar los huesos de las frutas; empedrar; trabajar de albañilería.
stone-blind, *-blīnd,* a. enteramente ciego.
stone-cutter, *-kŭttŭr,* s. picapedrero, m.
stone-dead, *-dĕd,* a. muerto.
stone-fruit, *-frōt,* s. fruta de hueso, f.
stone-horse, *-hōrs,* s. caballo entero, m.
stone-pit, *-pĭt,* s. cantera, f.
stone-ware, *-wăr,* s. loza de piedra, f.
stoning, *stōn'ĭng,* s. apedreamiento, m.
stony, *-ē,* a. de piedra, pétreo; duro.
stool, *stōl,* s. banquillo, taburete, m.; cámara, evacuación, f.
stoop, *stōp,* v. n. encorvarse, inclinarse; bajarse; –, s. inclinación hacia abajo, f.; abatimiento, m. [hacia abajo.
stoopingly, *-ĭnglē,* ad. con inclinación
stop, *stŏp,* v. a. detener, parar, diferir; tapar; –, v. n. pararse, hacer alto; –, s. pausa, f.; obstáculo, m.
stoppage, *-pdj,* **stopping,** *-pĭng,* s. obstrucción, f.; impedimiento, m.; (rail.) alto, f.
stopple, *-pl,* s. tapón, m. [m.
stop-watch, *-wŏtsh,* s. reloj que da los segundos, m. [almacenaje, m.
storage, *stō'rdj,* s. almacenamiento, m.;
store, *stōr,* s. abundancia, f.; provisión, f.; almacén, m.; –, v. a. surtir, proveer, abastecer. [m.
store-keeper, *-kēpŭr,* s. guardaalmacén,
storey, *stō'rē,* s. piso de una casa, f.

storied, *stō'rĭd,* a. historiado; (of houses) [con pisos.
stork, *stŏrk,* s. cigüeña, f.
storm, *stŏrm,* s. tempestad, borrasca, f.; asalto, m.; –, v. a. tomar por asalto; –, v. n. tempestar.
stormily, *-ĭlē,* a. violentamente.
stormy, *-ē,* a. tempestuoso; violento.
story, *stō'rē,* s. historia, f.; fábula, f.; piso, m. (de una casa).
stout, *stŏt,* a. robusto, corpulento, vigoroso; terco; –ly, ad. valientemente; obstinadamente; –, s. cerveza fuerte, f.
stoutness, *-nĕs,* s. valor, m.; fuerza, f.; corpulencia, f.
stove, *stōv,* s. estufa, f. [estivar.
stow, *stō,* v. a. ordenar, colocar; (mar.)
stowage, *-dj,* s. almacenaje, m.; (mar.) arrumaje, m.
straggle, *străg'gl,* v. n. vagar.
straggler, *-ŭr,* s. soldado rezagado; vagamundo, m. [luego; directamente.
straight, *strāt,* a. derecho; estrecho; –, ad.
straighten, *-n,* v. a. enderezar.
straightforward, *-fōr'wŭrd,* a. derecho; franco; leal. [chura, f.
straightforwardness, *-nĕs,* s. derechura, f.
straightway, *strāt'wā,* ad. inmediatamente, luego.
strain, *strān,* v. a. colar, filtrar; apretar (á uno contra sí); forzar, violentar; –, v. n. esforzarse; –, s. retorcimiento, m.; raza, f.; linaje, m.; estilo, m.; sonido, m.; armonía, f.
strainer, *-ŭr,* s. colador, m.; coladera, f.
strait, *strāt,* a. estrecho, angosto; íntimo; rígido, exacto; escaso; –ly, ad. estrechamente; –, s. estrecho, m.; aprieto, peligro, m.; penuria, f.
straiten, *-n,* v. a. acortar, estrechar.
straitness, *-nĕs,* s. estrechez, f.; penuria, f.; severidad, f. [& n. (mar.) encallar.
strand, *strănd,* s. costa, playa, f.; –, v. a.
strange, *strānj,* a. extranjero; extraño; –ly, ad. extrañamente, extraordinariamente. [trañeza, f.
strangeness, *-nĕs,* s. extranjería, f.; ex-
stranger, *-ŭr,* s. extranjero, m.
strangle, *străng'gl,* v. a. ahogar.
strangulation, *strănggŭlā'shŭn,* s. ahogamiento, m. [tirante de bota, m.
strap, *străp,* s. correa, tira de cuero, f.;
strapping, *-pĭng,* a. abultado, corpulento.
stratagem, *străt'ăjĕm,* s. estratagema, f.; astucia, f.
strategic, *strătē'jĭk,* a. estratégico, m.
strategy, *străt'ăjē,* s. estrategia, f.
stratum, *strā'tŭm,* s. lecho, m.; bancal, m.
straw, *strā,* s. paja, m.; bagatela, f.
straw-bed, *-bĕd,* s. jergón, m.
strawberry, *-bĕrrē,* s. fresa, f.
strawberry-tree, *bĕrrĭtrē,* s. madroño, m.
straw-cutter, *-kŭttŭr,* s. tajador, m. (máquina).
stray, *strā,* v. n. extraviarse; perder el camino; –, s. descarriamiento, m.; –, a. extraviado.
streak, *strēk,* s. raya, lista, f.; –, v. a. rayar.
stream, *strēm,* s. arroyo, río, torrente, m.; –, v. n. correr; echar rayos.

streamer, -ăr, s. (mar.) flámula, f.

streamlet, -lĕt, s. arroyo, arroyuelo, m.

street, strĕt, s. calle, f.

strength, strĕngth, s. fuerza, robustez, f.; vigor, m.; fortaleza, f.

strengthen, -n, v. a. fortificar; corroborar.

strenuous, strĕn'ŭŭs, a. estrenuo, valeroso; ágil; -ly, ad. acérrimamente; valerosamente. [m.; vigor, m.

strenuousness, -nĕs, s. valor, esfuerzo,

stress, strĕs, s. fuerza, f.; peso, m.; importancia, f.; acento, m.; — syllable, s. sílaba acentuada, f.

stretch, strĕtsh, v. a. & n. extender, alargar; estirar; extenderse; esforzarse; —, s. extensión, f.; esfuerzo, m.; estirón, m.

stretcher, -ăr, s. cualquier cosa que sirve para alargar ó estirar á otra, f.

strew, strŏ, v. a. esparcir; sembrar.

striated, strĭ ātĕd, a. estriado.

strict, strĭkt, a. estricto, estrecho; exácto, riguroso, severo; -ly, ad. exactamente, con severidad. [dad, f.

strictness, -nĕs, s. exactitud, f.; severi-

stricture, strĭk'tŭr, s. sello, m.; marca, f.; contracción, f.

stride, strĭd, s. tranco, m.; —, v. n. atrancar.

strife, strĭf, s. contienda, disputa, f.

strike, strĭk, v. a. & n. golpear; herir; castigar; tocar; amedrentar; chocar; sonar; cesar de trabajar; —, s. rasero, m.; cesación de trabajadores, huelga, f.

striking, strī'kĭng, a. lo que sorprende; -ly, ad. de un modo sorprendente.

string, strĭng, s. cordón, m.; hilo, m.; cuerda, f.; hilera, f.; fibra, f.; —, v. a. encordar; enhilar; estirar.

stringent, strĭn'jĕnt, a. astringente.

stringy, strĭng'ĕ, a. fibroso. [tira, f.

strip, strĭp, v. a. desnudar, despojar; —, s.

stripe, strĭp, s. raya, lista, f.; azote, m.; —, v. a. rayar. [bete, m.

stripling, strĭp'lĭng, s. mozuelo, mozalbete, m.

strive, strĭv, v. n. esforzarse; empeñarse; disputar, contender; oponerse.

stroke, strŏk, s. golpe, m.; toque (en la pintura), m.; sonido (del reloj), m.; plumada, f.; —, v. a. acariciar.

stroll, strŏl, v. n. tunar, vagar.

strong, strŏng, a. fuerte, vigoroso, robusto; poderoso; violento; -ly, ad. fuertemente, con violencia.

strong-box, -bŏks, s. cofre fuerte, m.

stronghold, -hŏld, s. plaza fuerte, f.

strop, strŏp, s. cuero á navajas, suavizador, m.

strophe, strŏf'ĕ, s. estrofa, f. [dor, m.

structure, strŭk'tŭr, (strŭk'tshŭr), s. estructura, f.; edificio, m.

struggle, strŭg'gl, v. n. esforzarse; luchar; agitarse. [tienda, lucha, f.

struggling, strŭg'lĭng, s. esfuerzo, m.; contienda, lucha, f.

strum, strŭm, v. a. (mus.) tocar malísimamente.

strumpet, strŭm'pĕt, s. ramera, puta, f.

strut, strŭt, v. n. pavonearse; —, s. constoneo, m.

stub, stŭb, s. tronco, m. [toneo, m.

stubble, -bl, s. rastrojo, m.

stubborn, -bŭrn, a. obstinado, testarudo; -ly, ad. obstinadamente.

stubbornness, -bŭrnnĕs, s. obstinación, pertinacia, f.

stubby, -bĕ, a. cachigordete; gordo.

stucco, stŭk'kŏ, s. estuco, m.

stud, stŭd, s. estaca, f.; tachón, m.; —, v. a. tachonar.

student, stŭ'dĕnt, s. estudiante, m.

stud-horse, stŭd'hŏrs, s. caballo entero, m.

studied, stŭd'ĭd, a. docto, leído, versado.

studio, stŭd'ĭŏ, s. estudio de un artista, m.

studious, stŭd'ĭŭs, a. estudioso; diligente; -ly, ad. estudiosamente, diligentemente.

study, stŭd'ĕ, s. estudio, m.; aplicación, f.; meditación profunda, f.; —, v. a. estudiar; observar; —, v. n. estudiar; aplicarse.

stuff, stŭf, s. materia, f.; material, m.; jarope, m.; estofa, f.; — | bagatela!, | niñería! ; —, v. a. henchir, llenar; —, v. n. atracarse; tragar.

stuffing, -ĭng, s. relleno, m.

stuffy, -fĕ, a. audaz, resuelto.

stultify, stŭl'tĭfĭ, v. a. bobear, atontar.

stumble, stŭm'bl, v. n. tropezar; —, s. traspié, tropiezo, m.

stumbling-block, stŭm'blĭngblŏk, s. tropezadero, m.; piedra de escándalo, f.

stump, stŭmp, s. tronco, m.; tocón, m.; —, v. a. esfumar.

stun, stŭn, v. a. aturdir, ensordecer.

stunner, -nŭr, s. cualquier cosa que sorprende, f.

stunt, -t, v. a. no dejar crecer. [prende, f.

stupefaction, stŭpĕfăk'shŭn, s. aturdimiento, estupor, m.

stupefy, stŭ'pĕfĭ, v. a. atontar, atolondrar.

stupendous, stŭpĕn'dŭs, a. estupendo, maravilloso. [pidamente.

stupid, stŭ'pĭd, a. estúpido; -ly, ad. estúpidamente, estupidez, f.

stupidity, stŭpĭd'ĭtĕ, s. estupidez, f.

stupor, stŭ'pŏr, s. estupor, m.

sturdily, stŭr'dĭlĕ, ad. insolentemente; obstinadamente. [f.; obstinación, f.

sturdiness, stŭr'dĭnĕs, s. fuerza, fortaleza,

sturdy, stŭr'dĕ, a. fuerte, tieso, robusto; bronco, insolente.

sturgeon, stŭr'jŏn, s. esturión, m.

stutter, stŭt'tŭr, v. n. tartamudear.

sty, stĭ, s. zahurda, f.; pocilga, f.

stye, —, s. orzuelo, m.

style, stĭl, s. estilo, m.; título, m.; gnomon, m.; modo, m.; —, v. a. intitular; nombrar. [galancete.

stylish, stĭl'ĭsh, a. elegante, en buen estilo;

suave, swäv, a. suave; -ly, ad. suavemente.

suavity, swäv'ĭtĕ, s. suavidad, dulzura, f.

subaltern, săb'ăltŭrn, a. subalterno.

subdivide, -dĭvĭd', v. a. subdividir.

subdivision, -dĭvĭzh'ŭn, s. subdivisión, f.

subdual, -dŭ'ăl, s. sujeción, f.

subdue, -dŭ', v. a. sojuzgar, sujetar; conquistar; mortificar.

subject, săb'jĕkt, a. sujeto; sometido á; —, s. sujeto, m.; -, săbjĕkt', v. a. sujetar; exponer.

subjection, -jĕk'shŭn, s. sujeción, f.

subjoin, -jŏĭn', v. a. sobreañadir.

subjugate, -jŭgāt', v. a. sojuzgar, sujetar.

subjugation, -jŭgā'shŭn, s. sujeción, f.

subjunctive, –jăngk'tĭv, s. subjuntivo.
sublet, sŭblĕt', v. a. subarrendar. [m.
sublimate, –lĭmăt, s. sublimado, m.; –,
v. a. sublimar.
sublime, –lĭm', a. sublime, excelso; –ly,
ad. de un modo sublime; –, s. sublime, m.
sublimity, –lĭm'ĭtĭ, s. sublimidad, f.
sublunar(y), –lō'năr(ĭ), a. sublunar; terrestre.
submarine, –mărēn', a. submarino.
submerge, –mŭrj', v. a. sumergir.
submersion, –mŭr'shăn, s. sumersión, f.
submission, –mĭsh'ăn, s. sumisión, f.
submissive, –mĭs'ĭv, a. sumiso, obsequioso; –ly, ad. con sumisión.
submissiveness, –nĕs, s. obsequio, m.;
sumisión, f.
submit, sŭbmĭt', v. a. (& n.) someter(se).
sub-officer, –ŏf'ĭsŭr, s. sargento, m.
subordinate, –ŏr'dĭnăt, a. subordinado,
inferior; –, v. a. subordinar. [nación, f.
subordination, –ŏrdĭnă'shăn, s. subordi-
suborn, –ŏrn', v. a. sobornar, cohechar.
subornation, –ŏrnă'shăn, s. soborno, m.
subpoena, –pē'nă, s. comparendo, m.
subscribe, –skrĭb', v. a. & n. suscribir,
certificar con su firma; consentir.
subscriber, –ăr, s. subscriptor, m.
subscription, sŭbskrĭp'shăn, s. suscripción, f. [siguiente(mente)
subsequent, sŭb'sĕkwĕnt, a. –ly, ad. sub-
subserve, –sŭrv', v. a. servir, estar subordinado.
subserviency, –sŭr'vĭĕnsĭ, s. servicio,
m.; utilidad, f.; concurso, m.; ayuda, f.
subservient, –sŭr'vĭĕnt, a. subordinado;
útil. [fondo.
subside, –sĭd', v. n. sumergirse, irse al
subsidence, –sĭ'dĕns, s. derrumbamiento,
subsidiary, –sĭd'ĭărĭ, a. subsidiario. [m.
subsidize, sŭb'sĭdĭz, v. a. dar subsidios.
subsidy, –sĭdĭ, s. subsidio, socorro, m.
subsist, sŭbsĭst', v. n. subsistir; existir.
subsistence, –sĭs'tĕns, s. existencia, f.;
subsistencia, f. [dad, f.; esencia, f.
substance, sŭb'stăns, s. substancia, f.; enti-
substantial, sŭbstăn'shăl, a. substancial;
real, material; substancioso; fuerte; –ly,
ad. substancialmente.
substantiality, –stănshĭăl'ĭtĭ, s. existencia, material, f.; solidez, f. [existir.
substantiate, –stăn'shĭăt, v. a. hacer
substantive, sŭb'stăntĭv, s. sustantivo, m.
substitute, –stĭtŭt, v. a. sustituir.
substitution, sŭbstĭtū'shăn, s. sustitución,
substratum, –strā'tăm, s. lecho, m. [f.
subterfuge, sŭb'tŭrfŭj, s. subterfugio, m.;
evasión, f. [neo.
subterranean, sŭbtĕrrā'nĕăn, a. subterrá-
subtile, sŭb'tĭl (sŭt'l), a. sútil, delicado,
tenue; penetrante, agudo; –ly, ad. sutil-
mente.
subtility, sŭbtĭl'ĭtĭ, s. sutilidad, f. [ción, f.
subtilization, –tĭlĭză'shăn, s. sutiliza-
subtilize, sŭb'tĭlĭz, v. a. sutilizar.
subtle, sŭt'l, a. sútil, astuto.
subtlety, –tĕ, s. sutileza, astucia, f.
subtly, sŭt'lĭ, ad. sútilmente.

subtract, sŭbtrăkt', v. a. (ar.) sustraer.
suburb, sŭb'ŭrb, s. suburbio, m.
suburban, sŭbŭr'băn, a. suburbano.
subversion, –vŭr'shăn, s. subversión, f.
subversive, –vŭr'sĭv, a. subversivo.
subvert, –vŭrt', v. a. subvertir, destruir.
subway, sŭb'wă, s. túnel, m.
succeed, sŭksēd', v. n. & a. suceder,
seguir; conseguir, lograr, tener suceso.
success, sŭksĕs', s. suceso, éxito, m.
successful, –fŭl, a. próspero, dichoso;
–ly, ad. prósperamente.
succession, sŭksĕsh'ŭn, s. sucesión, f.;
descendencia, f.; herencia, f.
successive, sŭksĕs'sĭv, a. sucesivo; –ly,
ad. sucesivamente.
successor, sŭksĕs'sŭr, s. sucesor, m.
succinct, sŭksĭngkt', a. sucinto, compendioso; –ly, ad. con brevedad.
succour, sŭk'kŭr, v. a. socorrer, ayudar;
–, s. socorro, m.; ayuda, asistencia, f.
succulence, sŭk'kŭlĕns, s. jugosidad, f.
succulent, sŭk'kŭlĕnt, a. suculento, jugoso.
succumb, sŭkkŭm', v. n. sucumbir.
such, sŭtsh, pn. tal, semejante; –as, el
que, los que, las que, lo que.
suck, sŭk, v. a. & n. chupar; mamar.
sucking-pig, –ĭngpĭg, s. lechoncillo, m.
suckle, –l, v. a. amamantar.
suckling, –lĭng, s. mamantón, m.
suction, sŭk'shăn, s. (med.) succión, f.
sudden, sŭd'dn, a. repentino, no prevenido; –ly, ad. de repente, súbitamente.
suddenness, –nĕs, s. precipitación, f.
sudorific, sŭdŏrĭf'ĭk, a. & s. sudorífico(m.)
suds, sŭdz, s. lejía de agua y jabón, f.
sue, sū, v. a. & n. poner por justicia; supli-
suet, sū'ĕt, s. sebo, m. [car.
suffer, sŭf'fŭr, v. a. & n. sufrir, padecer;
tolerar, permitir.
sufferable, –dŏl, a. sufrible, soportable.
sufferance, –ăns, s. sufrimiento, m.;
tolerancia, f.
suffering, –ĭng, s. pena, f.; dolor, m.
suffice, sŭffĭs', v. n. bastar, ser suficiente.
sufficiency, sŭffĭsh'ĕnsĭ, s. suficiencia, f.;
capacidad, f. [ad. bastante.
sufficient, sŭffĭsh'ĕnt, a. suficiente; –ly,
suffocate, sŭf'fŏkăt, v. a. sufocar.
suffocation, sŭffŏkă'shăn, s. sufocación, f.
suffragan, sŭf'frăgăn, s. sufragáneo, m.
suffrage, sŭf'frăj, s. sufragio, voto, m.
suffuse, sŭffŭz', v. a. difundir, derramar.
suffusion, sŭffū'zhăn, s.(med.) sufusión, f.
sugar, shŭg'ăr, s. azúcar, m.; –, v. a.
azucarar.
sugar-basin, –băsn, s. azucarero, m.
sugar-cane, –kăn, s. caña de azúcar, f.
sugar-loaf, –lŏf, s. pan de azúcar, m.
sugar-plum, –plăm, s. confite, m.
sugary, –ĭ, a. azucarado.
suggest, sŭjjĕst' (sŭdjĕst'), v. n. sugerir.
suggestion, sŭjjĕs'tshăn, s. sugestión, f.
suicidal, sŭĭsĭ'dăl, a. de suicida.
suicide, sū'ĭsĭd, s. suicidio, m.; suicida, m.
suit, sūt, s. vestido (entero), m.; galanteo,
m.; petición, f.; pleito, m.; surtido, m.;

—, v. a. & n. adaptar; surtir; ajustarse, acomodarse.

suitable, *—ăbl,* a. conforme, conveniente.

suitableness, *—ăblnĕs,* s. conformidad, conveniencia, f.

suitably, *—ăblĕ,* ad. según, conforme.

suite, *swēt,* s. serie, f.; tren, m., comitiva, f.   [cortejo, m.: pleiteante, m.

suitor, *sūt'ŭr,* s. suplicante, m.; amante,

sulkiness, *sŭl'kĭnĕs,* s. mal humor, m.

sulky, *sŭl'kĕ,* a. regañón, vinagre; terco.

sullen, *sŭl'lĕn,* a. malcontento; intratable; —ly, ad. de mal humor; tercamente.

sullenness, *—nĕs,* s. mal humor, m.; obstinación, pertinacia, terquedad, f.

sully, *sŭl'lĕ,* v. a. manchar, ensuciar.

sulphur, *sŭl'fŭr,* s. azufre, m.

sulphurous, *—ăs,* a. sulfúreo, azufroso.

sultan, *sŭl'tăn,* s. sultán, m.

sultana, *sŭltă'nă,* s. sultana, f.

sultriness, *sŭl'trĭnĕs,* s. bochorno, m.

sultry, *sŭl'trĕ,* a. caluroso; sufocante.

sum, *sŭm,* s. suma, f.; —, v. a. sumar; recopilar.

summarily, *—mărĭlĕ,* ad. sumariamente.

summary, *—mărĕ,* a. & s. sumario (m.).

summer, *sŭm'mŭr,* s. verano, estío, m.

summer-house, *—hŏŭs,* s. glorieta de jardín, f.

summit, *sŭm'mĭt,* s. ápice, m.; cima, f.

summon, *sŭm'măn,* v. a. citar, requerir por auto de juez; convocar, convidar; (mil.) intimar la rendición.

summoner, *—nŭr,* s. convidador, m.

summons, *—z,* s. citación, f.; requerimiento,

sumptuary, *sŭm'tŭŭrĕ,* s. suntuario.   [m.

sumptuous, *sŭm'tŭŭs,* a. suntuoso; —ly, ad. suntuosamente.

sumptuousness, *—nĕs,* s. suntuosidad, f.

sun, *sŭn,* s. sol, m.

sun-beam, *—bēm,* s. rayo del sol, m.

sun-burnt, *—bŭrnt,* a. tostado por el sol,

Sunday, *—dă,* s. domingo, m.   [asoleado.

sunder, *—dŭr,* v. a. separar, apartar.

sun-dial, *—dĭăl,* s. reloj de sol, cuadrante, m.

sundry, *—drĕ,* a. varios, muchos, diversos.

sunflower, *—flŏŭr,* s. girasol, m.

sun-glass, *—glăs,* s. espejo ustorio; m.

sunless, *—lĕs,* a. sin sol; sin luz.

sun-light, *—lĭt,* s. luz del sol, f.

sunny, *—nĕ,* a. semejante al sol; asoleado; brillante.

sun-rise, *—rĭz,* **sun-rising,** *—rĭzĭng,* s. salida del sol, f., nacer del sol, m.

sunset, *—sĕt,* s. puesta del sol, f.

sun-shade, *—shăd,* s. quitasol, m.

sun-shine, *—shĭn,* s. solana, f.; claridad, del sol, f.   [el sol.

sunshiny, *—shĭnĕ,* a. resplandeciente como

sun-stroke, *—strŏk,* s. insolación, f.

sup, *sŭp,* v. a. sorber, beber á sorbos; —, v. n. cenar; —, s. sorbo, m.

super, *sū'pŭr,* s. comparsa, m. & f.

superabound, *sŭpŭrăbŏŏnd',* v. n. superabundar.   [abundancia, f.; lo superfluo.

superabundance, *—ăbŭn'dăns,* s. super-

superabundant, *—ăbŭn'dănt,* a. —ly, ad. superabundante(mente).

superadd, *—ădd',* v. a. sobreañadir.

superaddition, *—ădĭsh'ŭn,* s. sobreañadidura, f.   [pensionado.

superannuated, *—ăn'nūătĕd,* a. añejado;

superannuation, *—ănnŭă'shŭn,* s. pensión, jubilación, f.; retiro, m.

superb, *sūpŭrb',* a. soberbio; —ly, ad. soberbiamente.   [cargo, m.

supercargo, *sūpŭrkăr'gŏ,* s. (mar.) sobre-

supercilious, *—sĭl'ĭăs,* a. arrogante, altanero; —ly, ad. con altivez.   [erogación, f.

supererogation, *—ĕrŏgă'shŭn,* s. super-

supererogatory, *—ĕrŏg'ătŭrĕ,* a. supererogatorio.   [ficial(mente).

superficial, *—fĭsh'ăl,* a. —ly, ad. super-

superficies, *—fĭsh'ĭēz,* s. superficie, f.

superfine, *—fĭn',* a. superfino.

superfluity, *—flŏ'ĭtĕ,* s. superfluidad, f.

superfluous, *sūpŭr'flŭăs,* a. superfluo.

superhuman, *sūpŭrhū'măn,* a. sobrehumano.   [vigilar.

superintend, *—ĭntĕnd',* v. a. inspeccionar,

superintendence, *—ĕns,* s. superintendencia, f.   [dente, m.

superintendent, *—ĕnt,* s. superinten-

superior, *sūpē'rĭŭr,* a. & s. superior (m.).

superiority, *sūpĕrĭŏr'ĭtĕ,* s. superioridad, f.

superlative, *sūpŭr'lătĭv,* a. & s. superlativo, m.; —ly, ad. superlativamente, en sumo grado.   [natural.

supernatural, *sūpŭrnăt'ŭrăl,* a. sobre-

supernumerary, *—nū'mŭrĕrĕ,* a. supernumerario.

superscribe, *—skrĭb',* v. a. sobreescribir.

superscription, *—skrĭp'shŭn,* s. sobreescrito, m.   [invalidar.

supersede, *—sēd',* v. a. sobreseer; diferir;

superstition, *—stĭsh'ăn,* s. superstición, f.

superstitious, *—stĭsh'ăs,* a. supersticioso; —ly, ad. supersticiosamente.

superstructure, *—strŭk'tshŭr,* s. edificio levantado sobre otra fábrica, m.

supervene, *—vēn',* v. n. sobrevenir.

supervise, *—vĭz',* v. a. inspeccionar, revistar.   [cia, f.

supervision, *—vĭzh'ŭn,* s. superintenden-

supervisor, *—vĭ'zŭr,* s. superintendente, m.   [ad. descuidadamente.

supine, *sŭpĭn',* a. supino; negligente; —ly,

supineness, *—nĕs,* s. negligencia, f.

supper, *sŭp'pŭr,* s. cena, f.; Lord's institución de la Eucaristía, f.

supperless, *—lĕs,* a. sin haber cenado.

supplant, *sŭpplănt',* v. a. suplantar.

supple, *sŭp'pl,* a. flexible, manejable; blando; —, v. a. hacer flexible.   [m.

supplement, *sŭp'plĕmĕnt,* s. suplemento,

supplemental, *sŭpplĕmĕn'tăl,* **supplementary,** *sŭpplĕmĕn'tărĕ,* a. adicional.

suppleness, *sŭp'plnĕs,* s. flexibilidad, f.

suppli(c)ant, *sŭp'plĭ(k)ănt,* s. suplicante,

supplicate, *sŭp'plĭkăt,* v. a. suplicar.   [m.

supplication, *sŭpplĭkă'shŭn,* s. súplica, suplicación, f.

supplicatory, *săp'plĭkătŭrĕ,* a. lo que suplica.

supply, *sŭpplĭ',* v. a. suplir, completar; surdir; —, s. socorro, refuerzo, m.

support, *sŭppōrt',* v. a. sostener; soportar, asist...

supportable, *—ăbl,* a. soportable.

supporter, *—ăr,* s. sustentáculo, m.; apoyo, m.; protector, m.

suppose, *sŭppōz',* v. a. suponer.

supposition, *sŭppōzĭsh'ŭn,* s. suposición.

supposititious, *sŭppŏzĭtĭsh'ŭs,* a. supuesto, falso, fingido.

suppress, *sŭpprĕs',* v. a. suprimir.

suppression, *sŭpprĕsh'ŭn,* s. supresión, f.

suppurate, *sŭp'pŭrăt,* v. n. supurar.

suppuration, *sŭppŭrā'shŭn,* s. supuración, f.

supremacy, *sŭprĕm'ăsĕ,* s. supremacía, f.

supreme, *sŭprēm',* a. supremo; **-ly,** ad. supremamente.

surcease, *sŭrsēs',* s. cesación, parada, f.

surcharge, *sŭrtshārj',* v. a. sobrecargar.

surcingle, *sŭrsĭng'gl,* s. sobrecincha, f.

surcoat, *sŭr'kōt,* s. sobretodo, gabán, m.

sure, *shōr,* a. seguro, cierto; firme; estable; **to be —,** sin duda; ya se ve; **-ly,** ad. ciertamente, seguramente, sin duda.

sureness, *—nĕs,* s. certeza, seguridad, f.

surety, *—tĕ,* s. seguridad, f.; fiador, m.

surf, *sŭrf,* s. (mar.) resaca, f.

surface, *sŭr'făs,* s. superficie, sobrefaz, f.

surfeit, *sŭr'fĭt,* v. a. & n. hartar, saciar; ahitarse, saciarse; —, s. ahito, empacho, m.; indigestión, f.

surge, *sŭrj,* s. ola, onda, f.; —, v. n. embravecerse el mar.

surgeon, *sŭr'jŭn,* s. cirujano, m.

surgery, *sŭr'jŭrĕ,* s. cirujía, f.

surgical, *sŭr'jĭkăl,* a. quirúrgico.

surlily, *sŭr'lĭlĕ,* ad. con mal humor.

surliness, *sŭr'lĭnĕs,* s. mal humor, m.

surly, *sŭr'lĕ,* a. áspero de genio.

surmise, *sŭrmīz',* v. a. sospechar; —, s. sospecha, f.

surmount, *sŭrmōŭnt',* v. a. sobrepujar.

surmountable, *—ăbl,* a. superable.

surname, *sŭr'nām,* s. apellido, sobrenombre, m.; —, *sŭrnām',* v. a. apellidar.

surpass, *sŭrpăs',* v. a. sobresalir, sobrepujar, exceder, aventajar.

surpassing, *—ĭng,* a. sobresaliente.

surplice, *sŭr'plĭs,* s. sobrepelliz, m.

surplus(age), *sŭr'plŭs(ădj),* s. sobrante, m.

surprise, *sŭrprīz',* v. a. sorprender; —, s. sorpresa, f.

surprising, *sŭrprī'zĭng,* a. maravilloso.

surrender, *sŭrrĕn'dŭr,* v. a. & n. rendir; ceder; rendirse; —, s. rendición, f.

surreptitious, *sŭrrĕptĭsh'ŭs,* a. subrepticio; **-ly,** ad. subrepticiamente.

surrogate, *sŭr'rōgăt,* v. a. subrogar; —, s. subrogado, m.

surround, *sŭrrōŭnd',* v. a. circundar, cercar, rodear.

survey, *sŭrvā',* v. a. inspeccionar, examinar; apear; —, *sŭr'vā,* s. inspección, f.; apeo (de tierras), m.

surveyor, *—ŭr,* s. sobrestante, m.; agri-

surveyorship, *—shĭp,* s. empleo de sobrestante, m.

survive, *sŭrvīv',* v. n. sobrevivir.

survivor, *sŭrvī'vŭr,* s. sobreviviente, m.

susceptibility, *sŭssĕptĭbĭl'ĭtĕ,* s. susceptibilidad, f.

susceptible, *sŭssĕp'tĭbl,* a. susceptible.

suspect, *sŭspĕkt',* v. a. & n. sospechar.

suspend, *sŭspĕnd',* v. a. suspender.

suspense, *sŭspĕns',* s. suspensión, f.; detención, f.; incertidumbre, f.

suspension, *sŭspĕn'shŭn,* s. suspensión, f.; **— of arms,** tregua, f.

suspension-bridge, *—brĭj,* s. puente colgante ó colgado, m.

suspensor(y), *sŭspĕn'sŭr(ĕ),* s. braguero, m.

suspicion, *sŭspĭsh'ŭn,* s. sospecha, f.

suspicious, *sŭspĭsh'ŭs,* a. suspicaz; **-ly,** ad. sospechosamente.

suspiciousness, *—nĕs,* s. suspicacia, f.

sustain, *sŭstăn',* v. a. sostener, sustentar, mantener; apoyar; sufrir.

sustainable, *—ăbl,* a. sustentable.

sustainer, *—ŭr,* s. apoyo, sostén, m.

sustenance, *sŭs'tĕnăns,* s. sostenimiento, sustento, m.

sutler, *sŭt'lŭr,* s. vivandero, m.

sutling-booth, *sŭt'lĭngbōth,* s. cantina, f.

suture, *sū'tŭr,* s. sutura, costura, f.

swab, *swŏb,* s. lampazo, m.

swaddle, *swŏd'dl,* v. a. fajar.

swaddling-clothes, *—ĭngklōthz,* s. pl. pañales, m. pl.

swagger, *swăg'gŭr,* v. n. baladronear.

swaggerer, *—ŭr,* s. fanfarrón, baladrón, m.

swain, *swăn,* s. zagal, joven aldeano, pastorcillo, m.

swallow, *swŏl'lō,* s. golondrina, f.; gula, f.; —, v. a. tragar, engullir.

swamp, *swŏmp,* s. pantano, m.

swampy, *—ĕ,* a. pantanoso.

swan, *swŏn,* s. cisne, m.

swanskin, *—skĭn,* s. moletón, m.

swap, *swŏp,* v. a. cambalachear.

sward, *swărd,* s. césped, m.

swarm, *swărm,* s. enjambre, m.; gentío, m.; hormiguero, m.; —, v. n. enjambrar; hormiguear de gente; abundar.

swart, *swărt,* **swarthy,** *swărth'ĕ,* a. atezado.

swarthiness, *swărth'ĭnĕs,* s. tez morena, f.

swash-buckler, *swŏsh'bŭklŭr,* s. fanfarrón, m.

swath, *swŏth,* s. tranco, m.

swathe, *swăth,* v. a. fajar; —, s. faja, f.

sway, *swă,* v. a. empuñar; dominar, gobernar; —, v. n. ladearse, inclinarse; tener influjo; —, s. bamboneo, m.; poder, imperio, influjo, m.

swear, *swăr,* v. a. & n. jurar; hacer jurar.

sweat, *swĕt,* s. sudor, m.; —, v. n. sudar; trabajar con fatiga.

sweep, *swēp,* v. a. & n. barrer; arrebatar; deshollinar; pasar ó tocar ligeramente; oscilar; —, s. barredura, f.; vuelta, f.; giro, m.; —, s. pl. duras, f. pl.

sweeping, *—ĭng,* a. rápido; **-s,** pl. barreduras.

sweep-stakes, *—stăks,* s. pl. el que gana todo cuanto se apuesta ó se juega,

12*

sweet, *swĕt,* a. dulce, grato, gustoso; suave; oloroso; melodioso; hermoso; amable; —, s. ad. dulcemente, suavemente; —, s. dulzura, f.; querida, f.   [f. pl.

sweet-bread,—*brĕd,* s. mellejas de ternera.

sweeten, —*n,* v. a. endulzar; suavizar; aplacar; perfumar.

sweetener, —*nŭr,* s. calmante, m.

sweetheart, —*hārt,* s. galanteador, m.; querida, f.   [m. pl.

sweetmeats, —*mĕtz,* s. pl. dulces secos.

sweetness, —*nĕs,* s. dulzura, suavidad, f.

sweet-scented, —*sĕntĕd,* a. perfumado.

sweet-william, —*wĭlyăm,* s. (bot.) dianto, clavel, m.

swell, *swĕl,* v. n. hincharse; ensoberbecerse; embravecerse; —, v. a. hinchar, inflar, agravar; —, s. hinchazón, f.; bulto, m.; petimetre, m.; mar de leva, m.; —, a. á la moda.

swelling, —*ĭng,* s. hinchazón, f., tumor, m.

swelter, *swĕl'tŭr,* v. a, & n. ahogar(se) de calor.

swerve, *gwŭrv,* v. n. vagar; desviarse.

swift, *swĭft,* a. veloz, ligero, rápido; —, s. vencejo, m.

swiftly, —*lĕ,* ad. velozmente.

swiftness, —*nĕs,* s. velocidad, rapidez, f.

swill, *swĭl,* v. a. beber con exceso; —, s. bazofia, f.

swim, *swĭm,* v. n. nadar; abundar en; ser vertiginoso; —, v. a. pasar á nado; —, s. nadadera de pez, f.

swimming, —*mĭng,* s. natación, f.; vértigo, m.; —ly, ad. lisamente, sin dificultad.

swindle, *swĭn'dl,* v. a. petardear, estafar.

swindler, —*dr,* s. petardista, trampista, m.

swine, *swĭn,* s. puerco, cochino, m.

swine-herd, —*hārd,* s. porquero, m.

swing, *swĭng,* v. n. balancear, columpiarse; vibrar; agitarse; —, v. a. vibrar; —, s. vibración, f.; balanceo, m.; columpio, m.

swing-door, —*dor,* s. puerta con un peso colgante, f.

swinging, —*ĭng,* a. (vulg.) grande, monstruoso; —ly, ad. monstruosamente.

swinish, *swĭ'nĭsh,* a. porcuno, cochino, grosero.

swirl, *swŭrl,* s. hacer remolinos el agua.

switch, *swĭtsh,* s. varilla, f.; (rail.) aguja, f.; —, v. a. varear.   [baladero, f.

switchback railway, —*băk rāĭwă,* s. res-

switchman, —*măn,* s. (rail.) guardaaguja.

swivel, *swĭ'vl,* s. alacrán, m.   [m.

swoon, *swŏn,* v. n. desmayarse; —, s. desmayo, deliquio, pasmo, m.

swoop, *swŏp,* v. a. coger, agarrar; —, s. acto de echarse una ave de rapiña sobre su presa, m.; at one —, de un golpe.

sword, *sŏrd,* s. espada, f.

sword-arm, —*ārm,* s. brazo derecho, m.

sword-cutler, —*kŭtlăr,* s. espadero, m.

sword-fish, —*fĭsh,* s. pez espada, f.   [m.

swordsman, —*z'măn,* s. guerrero, soldado,

sybaritic, *sĭb ărĭt'ĭk,* a. sibarítico.

sycamore, *sĭk'ămŏr,* s. sicomoro, m. (árbol).

sycophant, *sĭk'ŏfănt,* s. sicofante, m.

syllabic(al), *sĭllăb'ĭk(ăl),* a. silábico.

syllable, *sĭl'lăbl,* s. sílaba, f.   [m.

syllabus, *sĭl'lăbŭs,* s. extracto, resumen,

syllogism, *sĭl'lŏjĭzm,* s. silogismo, m.

sylph, *sĭlf,* s. silfio, m.; sílfida, f.

symbol, *sĭm'bŏl,* s. símbolo, m.

symbolic(al), *sĭmbŏl'ĭk(ăl),* a. simbólico.

symbolise, *sĭm'bŏlĭz,* v. a. simbolizar.

symmetrical, *sĭmmĕt'rĭkăl,* a. simétrico; —ly, ad. con simetría.

symmetry, *sĭm'mĕtrĕ,* s. simetría, f.

sympathetic(al), *sĭmpăthĕt'ĭk(ăl),* a. simpático; —ally, ad. simpáticamente.

sympathize, *sĭm'păthĭz,* v. n. compadecerse.

sympathy, *sĭm'păthĕ,* s. simpatía, f.

symphony, *sĭm'fŏnĕ,* s. sinfonía, f.

symptom, *sĭm'tăm,* s. síntoma, m.

synagogue, *sĭn'ăgŏg,* s. sinagoga, f.

synchronism, *sĭn'krŏnĭzm,* s. sincronismo, m.   [nismo, m.

syndic, *sĭn'dĭk,* s. síndico, m.

syndicate, *sĭn'dĭkăt,* s. sindicato, m.

synod, *sĭn'ŏd,* s. sínodo, m.

synonyme, *sĭn'ŏnĭm,* s. sinónimo, m.

synonymous, *sĭnŏn'ĭmŭs,* a. sinónimo; —ly, ad. con sinonimia.   [rio, m.

synopsis, *sĭnŏp'sĭs,* s. sinopsis, f.; suma-

synoptical, *sĭnŏp'tĭkăl,* a. sinóptico.

syntax, *sĭn'tăks,* s. sintaxis, f.

synthesis, *sĭn'thĕsĭs,* s. síntesis, f.

syringe, *sĭr'ĭnj,* s. jeringa, lavativa, f.; —, v. a. jeringar.

system, *sĭs'tĕm,* s. sistema, m.

systematic(al), *sĭstĕmăt'ĭk(ăl),* a. sistemático; —ally, ad. sistemáticamente.

T.

tabby, *tăb'bĕ,* s. tabí, m.

tabernacle, *tăb'ărnăkl,* s. tabernáculo, m.

tablature, *tăb'lătŭr,* s. pentagrama, m.

table, *tā'bl,* s. mesa, f.; tabla, f.; —, v. a. apuntar en forma sinóptica; poner sobre la mesa; d'hôte, mesa redonda.

table-cloth, —*klŏth,* s. mantel, m.

table-spoon, —*spŏn,* s. cuchara para comer, f.

table-land, —*lănd,* s. meseta, f.   [f.

tablet, *tăb'lĕt,* s. tableta, f.; plancha (grabada ó pintada), f.

tahoo, *tăbŏ',* v. a. interdecir.

tabular, *tăb'ŭlăr,* a. reducido á índices.

tacit, *tăs'ĭt,* a. tácito; —ly, ad. tácitamente.

taciturn, *tăs'ĭtŭrn,* a. taciturno, callado.

taciturnity, *tăsĭtŭrn'ĭtĕ,* s. taciturnidad, f.

tack, *tăk,* s. tachuela, f.; bordo, m.; —, v. a. atar; pegar; —, v. n. virar.

tackle, —*kl,* s. todo género de instrumentos ó aparejos, m.; (mar.) cordaje, m., jarcia, f.

tact, *tăkt,* s. tacto, m.   [f.

tactician, *tăktĭsh'ăn,* s. táctico, m.

tactics, *tăk'tĭks,* s. pl. táctica, f.

tadpole, *tăd'pŏl,* s. ranilla, f.; sapillo, m.

taffeta, *tăf'ĕtă,* s. tafetán, m.

tag, *tăg,* s. herrete, m.; —, v. n. herretear.

tagrag, —*răg,* s. canalla, f.

tail, *tăl,* s. cola, f., rabo, m.

tailor, *tāl'ăr,* s. sastre, m.

taint, *tānt,* v. a. tinturar, manchar; inficionar; viciar; —, s. mácula, mancha, f.

taintless, *–lĕs,* a. incorrupto, incontaminado, sin tacha.

take, *tāk,* v. a. tomar, coger, asir; recibir; aceptar; hurtar, pillar; prender; admitir; entender; —, v. n. encaminarse, dirigirse; salir bien, efectuarse una cosa; arraigarse; prender el fuego; —, s. toma, f.; presa, f.

take-in, *–ĭn',* s. engaño, m.

take-off, *–ŏf',* s. caricatura, f.

taker, *–ăr,* s. tomador, m.

taking, *tā'kĭng,* a. agradable, manso; —, s. presa, f.; secuestro, m.

tale, *tāl,* s. cuento, m.; fábula, f.

tale-bearer, *–bā'răr,* s. soplón, f.

talent, *tāl'ĕnt,* s. talento, m.; capacidad, f.

talented, *–ĕd,* a. talentoso.

talisman, *tăl'ĭsmăn,* s. talismán, m.

talk, *tāk,* v. n. hablar, conversar; charlar; —, s. plática, habla, f.; charla, f.; fama, f.

talkative, *tāk'ătĭv,* a. gárrulo, locuaz.

talkativeness, *–nĕs,* s. locuacidad, f.

tall, *tāl,* a. alto, elevado; robusto.

tallness, *–nĕs,* s. talle, cuerpo, m.

tallow, *tāl'lō,* s. sebo, m.; –, v. a. ensebar.

tallowy, *–ē,* a. seboso.

tally, *tāl'lē,* v. a. ajustar; tarjar.

talon, *tāl'ŏn,* s. garra del ave de rapiña, f.

tamable, *tā'măbl,* a. domable.

tamarind, *tăm'ărĭnd,* s. tamarindo, m.

tamarisk, *tăm'ărĭsk,* s. tamarisco, m.

tambourine, *tămbŭrēn',* s. tamboril, m.

tame, *tām,* a. amansado, domado, domesticado; abatido; sumiso; –ly, ad. mansamente; bajamente; —, v. a. domar, domesticar.

tameness, *–nĕs,* s. domesticidad, f.; sumisión, f.; carácter apocado, m.

tamper, *tăm'păr,* v. n. jaroparse.

tan, *tăn,* v. a. curtir, zurrar; —, s. casca, f.

tandem, *tăn'dĕm,* ad. á lo largo; **to drive** —, conducir un coche con caballo de guía.

tangent, *tăn'jĕnt,* s. tangente, f.

tangible, *tăn'jĭbl,* a. tangible.

tangle, *tăng'gl,* v. a. enredar, embrollar.

tank, *tăngk,* s. cisterna, f.; aljibe, m.

tankard, *tăng'kărd,* s. cántaro con tapa.

tanner, *tăn'năr,* s. curtidor, m. [dera, m.

tantalize, *tăn'tălĭz,* v. a. atormentar á alguno mostrándole placeres que no puede alcanzar.

tantamount, *tănt'ămŏŭnt,* a. equivalente.

tantivy, *tăn'tĭvē,* ad. á rienda suelta, á tan-yard, *tăn'yărd,* s. tenería, f. [escape.

tap, *tăp,* v. a. tocar ligeramente; barrenar; extraer el jugo de un árbol por incisión; sacar agua del cuerpo humano; —, s. palmada suave, f.; toque ligero, m.; espita, f.

tape, *tăp,* s. cinta, f.; galón, m.; —s, pl. tiras de papel del telégrafo que contienen los telegramas, f. pl. [v.n. rematar en punta.

taper, *–ăr,* s. cirio, m.; –, a. cónico; –, tapestry, *tăp'ĕstrē,* s. tapiz, m.; tapicería, f.

tape-worm, *tāp'wŭrm,* s. tenia, f. [f.

tap-house, *tăp'hŏŭs,* s. taberna, f.

tar, *tăr,* s. brea, f.; (vulg.) marinero, m.; –, v. a. embrear.

tardily, *tăr'dĭlē,* ad. lentamente.

tardiness, *tăr'dĭnĕs,* s. lentitud, tardanza, f.

tardy, *tăr'dē,* a. tardo, lento. [f.

tare, *tăr,* s. (bot.) zizaña, f.; tara, f.

target, *tăr'gĕt,* s. rodela, f.; blanco, m.

tariff, *tăr'ĭf,* s. tarifa, f. [(para tirar).

tarlatan, *tăr'lătăn,* s. tarlatana, f.

tarn, *tărn,* s. aguazal, m., laguna, f.

tarnish, *tăr'nĭsh,* v. a. (& n.) deslustrar(se).

tarpaulin, *tărpă'lĭn,* s. tela embreada, f.

tarragon, *tăr'răgŏn,* s. (bot.) estragón, m.

tarry, *tăr'rē,* v. n. tardar, pararse; –, *tăr'rē,* a. embreado. [mente.

tart, *tărt,* a. acedo, acre; –ly, ad. agriamente.

tart, *tărt,* **tartlet,** *–lĕt,* s. tarta, torta, f.

tartar, *tăr'tăr,* s. tártaro, m.

tartness, *tărt'nĕs,* s. agrura, acedia, f.

task, *tăsk,* s. tarea, f.; –, v. a. atarear.

tassel, *tăs'sl,* s. registro de un libro, m.; borlita, f.; –s, pl. capotas, f. pl.

taste, *tāst,* s. gustadura, f.; gusto, m.; sabor, m.; saboreo, m.; ensayo, m.; –, v. a. & n. gustar; probar; experimentar; agradar; tener sabor. [samente.

tasteful, *–fŭl,* a. sabroso; –ly, ad. sabrosamente.

tasteless, *–lĕs,* a. insípido, sin sabor.

taster, *–ăr,* s. catador, m.

tastily, *–tĭlē,* ad. con gusto.

tasty, *tăst'ē,* a. hecho ó expresado con gusto.

tatter, *tăt'tăr,* s. andrajo, arrapiezo, m.

tatterdemalion, *–dĕmăl'yŭn,* s. pobre andrajoso, m.

Tattersall, *–săl,* s. grandes caballerizas en Londres en donde se venden caballos de corrida, f. pl. [charla, f.

tattle, *tăt'tl,* v. n. charlar, parlotear; –, s.

tattoo, *tăttō',* s. (mil.) retreta, queda, f.; picadura y pintura del cuerpo, f.; –, v. a. pintarse el cuerpo los salvajes.

taunt, *tănt,* v. a. mofar; ridiculizar; dar chanza; –, s. mofa, buria, chanza, f.

tauntingly, *–tĭnglē,* ad. con mofa.

Taurus, *tă'rŭs,* s. Tauro, m. (signo del **taut,** *tăt,* a. tieso, terco. [zodíaco).

tautological, *tătŏlŏj'ĭkăl,* a. tautológico.

tautology, *tătŏl'ōjē,* s. tautología, f.

tavern, *tăv'ărn,* s. taberna, f.

tavern-keeper, *–kēpăr,* s. tabernero, m.

taw, *tă,* v. a. ablandar pieles; –, s. bolita de mármol, f.

tawdriness, *tă'drĭnĕs,* s. oropel, m.

tawdry, *tă'drē,* a. jarifo, vistoso, chabacano.

tawer, *tă'ăr,* s. curtidor (con alumbre), m.

tawny, *tă'nē,* a. curtido, moreno.

tax, *tăks,* s. impuesto, m.; contribución, f.; –, v. a. imponer tributos; acusar.

taxable, *–ăbl,* a. sujeto á impuestos.

taxation, *–ă'shăn,* s. imposición de impuestos, f. [impuestos, m.

tax-gatherer, *–găthărăr,* s. colector de impuestos, m.

taxing-master, *–ĭngmăstăr,* s. tasador, m.

tea, *tē,* s. te, m.

teach, *tētsh,* v. a. enseñar, instruir; –, v. n. tener por oficio la enseñanza pública ó particular.

teachable, _ábl_, a. dócil.

teacher, _ár_, s. preceptor, enseñador, m.

tea-garden, _gárdn_, s. café cantante, m.

teak, _tēk_, s. teca, f. (árbol).

tea-kettle, _tē kĕtl_, s. tetera, f.

teal, _tēl_, s. cerceta, zarcela, f.

team, _tēm_, s. tiro de caballos, m.

teamster, _stūr_, s. galerero, m.

tear, _tār_, v. a. despedazar, lacerar; ras-
tear, _tĕr_, s. lágrima, f.; gota, f.   [gañar.

tearful, _tār fŭl_, a. lloroso; —ly, ad. con

tearless, _lĕs_, a. sin lágrimas.   [lloro.

tease, _tēz_, v. a. cardar (lana ó lino); im-
teasel, _tē zl_, s. capota, f.   [portunar.

tea-service, _tē sŭrvĭs_, tea-set, _sĕt_,
tea-things, _thĭngz_, s. pl. servicio para

teat, _tēt_, s. ubre, teta, f.   [el te, m.

techiness, _tĕtsh ĭnĕs_, s. caprichos, m. pl.

technical, _tĕk nĭkál_, a. técnico.

technicalities, _tĕknĭkál ĭtĭz_, s. pl. términos técnicos, m. pl.

technology, _tĕknŏl ŏjĕ_, s. tecnología, f.

techy, _tĕtsh é_, a. caprichoso.

tedious, _tē dĭŭs_, a. tedioso, fastidioso;
—ly, ad. fastidiosamente.

tediousness, _nĕs_, tedium, _tē dĭŭm_, s.
tedio, fastidio, m.

teem, _tēm_, v. a. & n. parir; estar en cinta.

teens, _tēnz_, s. pl. años desde 13 hasta 20
años.   [dentecer.

teeth, _tēth_, s. pl. de tooth; —, v. n. en-

teetotal, _tētō tál_, a. moderado, sobrio.

teetotaller, _ŭr_, s. hombre sobrio, m.

teetotalism, _ĭzm_, s. sobriedad, f.

teetotally, _lĕ_, ad. (am.) totalmente.

teetotum, _tōtŭm_, s. perinela, f.

telegram, _tĕl ĕgrăm_, s. telegrama, m.

telegraph, _tĕl ĕgráf_, s. telégrafo, m.

telegraphic, _tĕlĕgráf ĭk_, a. telegráfico.

telegraphy, _tĕlĕg ráfĕ_, s. telegrafía, f.

telephone, _tĕl ĕfōn_, s. teléfono, m.

telescope, _tĕl ĕskōp_, s. telescopio, m.

telescopic(al), _tĕlĕskŏp ĭk(ál)_, a. teles-
cópico.   [numerar, relevar.

tell, _tĕl_, v. a. & n. decir; informar, contar,

teller, _lŭr_, s. relator, m.; computista, f.

telling, _ĭng_, a. que hace impresión.

tell-tale, _tĕl_, s. soplón, m.

temerity, _tĕmĕr ĭtĕ_, s. temeridad, f.

temper, _tĕm pŭr_, v. a. templar, moderar;
s'emperar; —, s. temperamento, m.   [m.

temperament, _ámĕnt_, s. temperamento,

temperance, _áns_, s. templanza, moderación, f.

temperate, _át_, a. templado, moderado,
sobrio; —ly, ad. templadamente. [perie, f.

temperature, _átŭr_, s. temperatura, tem-

tempered, _d_, a. templado, acondicionado.

tempest, _tĕm pĕst_, s. tempestad, f.

tempestuous, _tĕmpĕs tūŭs_, a. tempestuoso,
proceloso.   [m.

templar, _tĕm plŭr_, s. estudiante de leyes,

temple, _tĕmpl_, s. templo, m.; sien, f.

temporal, _tĕm pŏrál_, a. —ly, ad. temporal-
(mente).   [mente.

temporarily, _tĕm pŏrărĭlĕ_, ad. temporal-

temporary, _tĕm pŏrărĕ_, a. temporario.

temporise, _tĕm pŏrīz_, v. n. temporizar.

tempt, _tĕmt_, v. a. tentar; provocar.

temptation, _tĕm tāshŭn_, s. tentación, f.

ten, _tĕn_, a. diez.

tenable, _tĕn ábl_, a. defendible.   [(mente).

tenacious, _tĕnā shŭs_, a. —ly, ad. tenaz-

tenacity, _tĕnăs ĭtĕ_, s. tenacidad, f.; porfía,

tenancy, _tĕn ánsĕ_, s. tenencia, f.   [f.

tenant, _tĕn ánt_, s. arrendador, inquilino,
m.; —, v. n. arrendar.

tenantless, _lĕs_, a. sin inquilinos.

tenantry, _rĕ_, s. arriendo, m.; conjunto
de los arrendatarios, m.

tench, _tĕnsh_, s. tenca, f. (pez).

tend, _tĕnd_, v. a. guardar, velar; —, v. n.
tirar, dirigirse.

tendency, _tĕnd ĕnsĕ_, s. tendencia, f.

tender, _tĕn dŭr_, a. tierno, delicado; sensible; —ly, ad. tiernamente; —, s. oferta,
f., patache, m.; (rail.) tender de una locomotora, m.; —, y. a. ofrecer; estimar.

tenderness, _nĕs_, s. terneza, delicadeza, f.

tendon, _tĕn dŏn_, s. tendón, m.

tendril, _tĕn drĭl_, s. zarcillo, m.

tenement, _tĕn ĕment_, s. tenencia, f.

tenet, _tĕn ĕt_, s. dogma, m.; aserción, f.

tenfold, _tĕn fōld_, a. décuplo.

tennis, _tĕn nĭs_, s. raqueta, f. (juego).

tennis-court, _kōrt_, s. sitio en que se
juega la raqueta, f.   [m.; substancia, f.

tenor, _tĕn ŏr_, s.(mus.) tenor, m.; contenido

tense, _tĕns_, a. tieso, tenso; —, s. (gr.)
tiempo, m.

tension, _tĕn shŭn_, s. tensión, tirantez, f.

tent, _tĕnt_, s. (mil.) tienda de campaña, f.;
—, v. n. alojarse en tienda.

tentacle, _tĕn tăkl_, s. tentáculo, m.

tentative, _tĕn tătĭv_, a. de ensayo, de
prueba; —ly, ad. como prueba.

tenter, _ŭr_, s. rama, f.

tenter-hook, _hōk_, s. clavija de rama, f.

tenth, _tĕnth_, a. décimo; —ly, ad. en décimo lugar.

tenuity, _tĕnū ĭtĕ_, s. tenuidad, f.

tenure, _tĕn ŭr_, s. tenencia, f.

tepid, _tĕp ĭd_, a. tibio.   [versación, f.

tergiversation, _tărjĭvŭrsā shŭn_, s. tergi-

term, _tŭrm_, s. término, confín, m.; dicción,
f.; vocablo, m.; condición, estipulación,
f.; —, v. a. nombrar, llamar.

termagant, _tŭr măgănt_, s. diabla, f.

terminate, _tŭr mĭnāt_, v. a. & n. terminar,
limitar.   [conclusión, f.

termination, _tŭrmĭnā shŭn_, s. terminación,

terminus, _tŭr mĭnŭs_, s. (rail.) última estación de ferrocarril, f.

terrace, _tĕr rás_, s. terrado, m.; terraplén,
m.; —, v. a. terraplenar.

terrestrial, _tĕrrĕs trĭál_, a. terrestre, terreno.

terrible, _tĕr rĭbl_, a. terrible.

terribly, _lĕ_, ad. terriblemente.

terrier, _tĕr rĭŭr_, s. zorrero, m.

terrific, _tĕrrĭf ĭk_, a. terrífico.

terrify, _tĕr rĭfī_, v. a. aterrar, espantar.

territorial, _tĕrrĭtō rĭál_, a. territorial. [m.

territory, _tĕr rĭtŏrĕ_, s. territorio, distrito,

terror, _tĕr rŏr_, s. terror, pavor, m.

terrorist, _ĭst_, s. terrorista, m.   [pulidez.

terse, _tŭrs_, a. terso, pulido; —ly, ad. con

terseness, *-nès,* s. elegancia, f.
tertian, *tûr'shûn,* s. terciana, f. [logía).
tertiary, *tûr'shíârè,* a. terciario (en geo
tesselate, *tès'sèlát,* v. a. taracear.
test, *tèst,* s. copela, f.; piedra de toque, f.;
prueba, f.
testaceous, *tèstá'shûs,* a. testáceo.
testament, *tès'tâmènt,* s. testamento, m.
testamentary, *tèstâmént'ârè,* a. testamen
testator, *tèstá'tûr,* s. testador, m. [tario.
testatrix, *tèstá'trìks,* s. testadora, f.
tester, *tès'tûr,* s. cielo de cama, m.
testicles, *tès'tìklz,* s. pl. testículos, m. pl.
testifier, *tès'tìfíâr,* s. testificante, m.
testify, *tès'tìfí,* v. a. testificar, atestiguar.
testily, *tès'tìlè,* ad. con morosidad.
testimonial, *tèstìmó'nìâl,* s. atestación, f.
testimony, *tès'tìmûnè,* s. testimonio, m.
testiness, *tès'tìnès,* s. mal humor, m.
testy, *tès'tè,* a. tétrico.
tether, *tèth'ûr,* s. traba, f.; maniota, f.
text, *tèkst,* s. texto, m. [gordo, m.
text-hand, *-hând,* s. carácter de letra muy
textile, *tèks'tìl,* a. hilable.
textual, *tèks'tûâl,* a. textual.
texture, *tèks'tûr,* s. textura, f.; tejido, m.
than, *thân,* ad. que, de. [cias.
thank, *thângk,* v. a. agradecer, dar gra
thankful, *-fûl,* a. grato, agradecido; -ly,
ad. con gratitud.
thankfulness, *-fûlnès,* s. gratitud, f.
thankless, *-lès,* a. ingrato.
thank-offering, *-ôffûring,* s. ofrecimiento
en acción de gracias, m.
thanks, *-s,* s. pl. gracias, f. pl.
thanks-giving, *-s'gìving,* s. acción de
gracias, f.; -Day, día de dar gracias en los
Estados Unidos.
that, *thât,* pn. aquel, aquello, aquella;
que; este; —, c. porque; para que; **so** —,
de modo que. [v. a. techar con paja.
thatch, *thâtch,* s. techo de paja, m.; —,
thaw, *thâ,* s. deshielo, m.; —, v. n. deshelarse.
the, *thè,* (thè), art. el, la, lo; los, las.
theatre, *thè'âtûr,* s. teatro, m.
theatrical, *thèât'rìkâl,* a. teatral; -ly, ad.
según las reglas del teatro.
thee, *thè,* pn. te, á ti.
theft, *thèft,* s. hurto, m.
their, *thâr,* pn. su, suyo, suya; de ellos, de
ellas; -s, el suyo, la suya, los suyos, las
suyas; de ellos, de ellas.
theism, *thè'ìzm,* s. teísmo, deísmo, m.
theist, *thè'ìst,* s. teísta, deísta, m.
them, *thèm,* pn. los, las, les; ellos, ellas;
á aquellos, á aquellas.
theme, *thèm,* s. tema, m.
themselves, *thèmsèlvz',* pn. pl. ellos mismos, ellas mismas; sí mismos.
then, *thèn,* ad. entonces, después; en tal
caso; **now and** —, de cuando en cuando.
thence, *thèns,* ad. desde allí, de ahí, por eso.
thenceforth, *-fôrth,* ad. desde entonces.
theocracy, *thèôk'râsè,* s. teocracia, f.
theocratic(al), *thèôkrât'ìk(âl),* a. teocrático.
theologic(al), *thèôlôj'ìk(âl),* a. teológico.

theologian, *thèôlô'jìân,* s. teólogo, m.
theology, *thèôl'ôjè,* s. teología, f.
theorem, *thè'ôrèm,* s. teorema, m.
theoretic(al), *thèôrèt'ìk(âl),* a. teórico; -ly,
ad. teóricamente.
theorise, *thè'ôrìz,* v. a. teorizar.
theorist, *thè'ôrìst,* s. teórico, m.
theory, *thè'ôrè,* s. teoría, f. [f.
therapeutics, *thèrâpú'tìks,* s. terapéutica,
there, *thâr,* ad. allí, allá; [acerca de.
thereabout(s), *thâr'âbôût(s),* ad. por ahí,
thereafter, *thârâf'tûr,* ad. después; según.
thereat, *-ât',* ad. por eso, á causa de eso;
allá. [eso.
thereby, *-bì',* ad. con eso; por medio de
therefore, *thâr'fôr,* ad. por esto, por esta
razón; á consecuencia de eso.
therefrom, *thârfrôm',* ad. de allí, de allá;
de eso, de aquello.
therein(to), *-ìn'(tô'),* ad. en aquello, en
eso; dentro de aquello. [ello.
thereof, *-ôf',* ad. de esto, de aquello, de
thereon, *-ôn',* ad. en eso, sobre eso.
thereunder, *-ûn'dûr,* ad. debajo de eso.
there(un)to, *-(ûn)tô',* a. á eso, á ello.
thereupon, *-âpôn',* ad. en consecuencia
de eso. [llo; luego, inmediatamente.
therewith, *-wìth',* ad. con eso ó con aque
therewithal, *-wìthâl',* ad. además, á más.
thermal waters, *thûr'mâl wâtûrz,* s. pl.
termas, f. pl. [metro, m.
thermometer, *thûrmôm'ètûr,* s. termó
these, *thèz,* pn. pl. estos, estas.
thesis, *thè'sìs,* s. tesis, f.
they, *thâ,* pn. pl. ellos, ellas.
thick, *thìk,* a. espeso, denso, turbio; grueso;
frecuente; grosero; **to speak** —, hablar
con media lengua; —, s. grueso, m.; -ly,
ad. frecuentemente, continuadamente.
thicken, *-n,* v. a. & n. espesar, condensar;
condensarse.
thicket, *-èt,* s. espesura de un bosque, f.
thick-head(ed), *-hèd(èd),* a. estúpido.
thickness, *-nès,* s. espesura, densidad, f.;
grosería, f. [rechoncho.
thick-set, *-sèt,* a. plantado muy espeso;
thief, *thèf,* s. ladrón, m.; moco de una luz, m.
thief-catcher, *-kâtshûr,* s. alguacil, m.
thieve, *thèv,* v. n. hurtar, robar.
thievish, *thèv'ìsh,* a. inclinado á hurtar;
-ly, ad. como ladrón.
thievishness, *-nès,* s. ladronicio, m.
thigh, *thì,* s. muslo, m.
thill, *thìl,* s. vara de un carro, f.
thiller, *-ûr,* thill-horse, *-hôrs,* s. caballo de varas, m.
thimble, *thìmbl,* s. dedal, m.
thin, *thìn,* a. delgado, delicado, sútil, flaco;
claro; ralo; —, v. a. enrarecer, atenuar;
adelgazar; aclarar.
thine, *thìn,* pn. tuyo, tuya, tuyos, tuyas.
thing, *thìng,* s. cosa, f.; criatura, f.
think, *thìngk,* v. a. & n. pensar, imaginar,
meditar, considerar; creer, juzgar.
thinker, *-ûr,* s. pensador, m.
thinking, *-ìng,* s. pensamiento, m.; juicio,
m.; opinión, f. [número.
thinly, *thìn'lè,* ad. delgadamente; en corto

thinness, —nĕs, s. tenuidad, delgadez, raleza, f.   [—ly, ad. en tercer lugar.
third, thȧrd, a. tercero; —, s. tercio, m.;
thirst, thȧrst, s. sed, f.; —, v. n. tener ó padecer sed.
thirstily, —ĭlĕ, a. con anhelo.
thirsty, —ĕ, a. sediento.
thirteen, thȧr'tĕn, a. trece.
thirteenth, —th, a. décimotercio.
thirtieth, thȧr'tĭĕth, a. trigésimo.
thirty, thȧr'tĕ, a. treinta.
this, thĭs, pn. este, esta, esto; aqueste, aquesta, aquesto.
thistle, thĭs'l, s. cardo silvestre, m.
thither, thĭth'ȧr, ad. allá, á aquel lugar.
thong, thȯng, s. correa, correhuela, f.
thorn, thȯrn, s. espino, m.; espina, f.
thorny, —ĕ, a. espinoso; arduo.
thorough, thȧr'ȯ, pr. por, por medio; —, a. entero, cabal, perfecto; —, ad. enteramente, cabalmente.
thoroughbred, —brĕd, a. de sangre, de casta (hablando de caballos).
thoroughfare, —fȧr, s. paso, tránsito, m.
thorough-paced, —pȧst, a. cabal, perfecto.
those, thȯz, pn. pl. aquellos, aquellas.
thou, thȯŭ, pn. tú.   [que, como sí.
though, thȯ, c. aunque, no obstante; como
thought, thȧt, s. pensamiento, juicio, m.; opinión, f.; cuidado, m.
thoughtful, —fŭl, a. pensativo, meditabundo; —ly, ad. de un modo muy pensativo.   [profunda, f.
thoughtfulness, —fŭlnĕs, s. meditación
thoughtless, —lĕs, a. descuidado; insensato; —ly, ad. descuidadamente, sin reflexión.   [inadvertencia, f.
thoughtlessness, —lĕsnĕs, s. descuido, m.;
thousand, thȯŭ'zȧnd, a. mil.
thousandfold, —fȯld, a. mil veces otro tanto.
thousandth, —th, a. milésimo.
thraldom, thrȧl'dȧm, s. esclavitud, f.
thrall, thrȧl, s. esclavo, m.; esclava, f.
thrash, thrȧsh, v. a. trillar (grano); golpear; —, v. n. trabajar.
thrasher, —ȧr, s. trillador, m.
thrashing-floor, —ĭngflȯr, s. era, f.
thread, thrĕd, s. hilo, m.; —, v. a. enhebrar; atravesar.
threadbare, —bȧr, a. raído, muy usado.
threat, thrĕt, s. amenaza, f.
threaten, —n, v. a. amenazar.
threatening, —nĭng, s. amenaza, f.; —ly, ad. con amenazas.
three, thrĕ, a. tres.
three-cornered, —kȯrnȧrd, a. triangular.
threefold, —fȯld, a. tríplice, triplo.
three-master, —mȧstȧr, s. (mar.) buque de tres palos, m.
threshold, thrĕsh'ȯld, s. umbral, m.
thrice, thrĭs, ad. tres veces.
thrift, thrĭft, s. ganancia, utilidad, f.; economía, frugalidad, f.
thriftily, —ĭlĕ, ad. frugalmente.   [monía, f.
thriftiness, —ĭnĕs, s. frugalidad, parsithriftless, —lĕs, a. manirroto, pródigo.
thrifty, —ĕ, a. frugal, económico.
thrill, thrĭl, v. a. taladrar, horadar; —, v. n. estremecer(se); —, s. estremecimiento, m.

thrive, thrĭv, v. n. prosperar, adelantar, aprovechar.
thrivingly, thrĭ'vĭnglĕ, ad. prósperamente
throat, thrȯt, s. garganta, f.
throat-band, —bȧnd, s. ahogadero, m.
throb, thrȯb, v. n. palpitar; —, s. palpitación, f.   [agonía, f.
throe, thrȯ, s. dolores de parto, m. pl.;
throne, thrȯn, s. trono, m.
throng, thrȯng, s. tropel de gente, m.; —, v. a. & n. venir de tropel; estrujar á uno la concurrencia muy numerosa y apiñada de gente.   [—, v. a. ahogar.
throttle, thrȯt'tl, s. gaznate, garguero, m.;
through, thrȯ, pr. de medio á medio; por medio de; — and —, de un lado á otro.
throughout, —ȯŭt, pr. por todo; —, ad. en todas partes.
throw, thrȯ, v. a. & n. echar(se), arrojar(se), tirar, lanzar; —, s. tiro, m.; golpe, m.
thrum, thrŭm, v. a. rascar las cuerdas de un instrumento.
thrush, thrŭsh, s. tordo, m. (ave).
thrust, thrŭst, v. a. & n. empujar, impeler; estrechar; entremeterse, introducirse; —, s. estocada, f.; puñalada, f.; lanzada, f.
thud, thŭd, s. estrépito, m.; ráfaga, f.
thumb, thŭm, s. pulgar, m.; —, v. a. manosear con poca destreza; emporcar con los dedos.
thumbscrew, —skrȯ, s. pulgueras, f. pl.
thump, thŭmp, s. porrazo, golpe, m.; —, v. a. aporrear, apuñetear.
thumping, —ĭng, a. grueso, pesado.
thunder, thŭn'dȧr, s. trueno, m.; —, v. a. & n. tronar; atronar; fulminar.
thunder-bolt, —bȯlt, s. rayo, m.
thunder-clap, —klȧp, s. tronada, tempestad de truenos, f.
thunder-storm, —stȯrm, s. temporal, m.
Thursday, thȧrz'dȧ, s. jueves, m.
thus, thŭs, ad. así, de este modo.
thwack, thwȧk, v. a. aporrear, apuñear.
thwart, thwȧrt, v. a. cruzar, atravesar; contradecir; —, s. banco de remero, m.
thy, thĭ, pn. tu, tus.
thyme, tĭm, s. (bot.) tomillo, m.
thyself, thĭsĕlf, pn. ti mismo.
tiara, tĭȧ'rȧ, s. tiara, f.
tick, tĭk, s. crédito, m.; garrapata (insecto), f.; funda de almohada, f.   [billete, m.
ticket, —ĕt, s. boleta, f.; cédula, f.; (rail.)
ticket-collector, —kȯllĕktȧr, ticketholder, —hȯldȧr, s. (rail.) expendedor de billetes, m.
ticket-office, —ȯffĭs, s.(rail.) despacho, m.
ticket-porter, —pȯrtȧr, s. (rail.) encomendero, comisionista, m.
ticking, tĭk'ĭng, s. terliz, m.; tic-tac, m.
tickle, tĭk'l, v. a. hacer cosquillas á alguno; —, v. n. tener cosquillas.
tickling, —ĭjng, s. cosquillas, f. pl.
ticklish, —lĭsh, a. cosquilloso.
ticklishness, —lĭshnĕs, s. propiedad de ser cosquilloso, f.
tidal, tĭ'dȧl, a. (mar.) de la marea.
tide, tĭd, s. tiempo, m.; estación, f.; marea, f.; —, v. n. (mar.) andar con la marea.

tide-waiter, _–wāt'ăr,_ s. aduanero en el litoral, m.

tidily, _tīd'ĭlĭ,_ ad. mañosamente. [aseo, m.

tidiness, _tīd'ĭnĕs,_ s. maña, prontitud, f.;

tidings, _tī'dĭngz,_ s. pl. nuevas, noticias, f.

tidy, _tīd'ĭ,_ a. airoso, aseado; diestro. [pl.

tie, _tī,_ v. a. anudar, atar; –, s. nudo, m.; atadura, f.; lazo, m.

tier, _–ăr,_ s. fila, hilera, f.

tiff, _tĭf,_ s. bebida, f.; pique, disgusto, m.

tiffany, _tĭf'fănĭ,_ s. tafetán sencillo, m.

tiger, _tī'găr,_ s. tigre, m.; lacayo, m.

tight, _tīt,_ a. tirante, tieso, tenso; aseado.

tighten, _–n,_ v. a. tirar, estirar.

tightly, _–lĭ,_ ad. bien apretado; con aseo.

tightness, _–nĕs,_ s. tensión, tirantez, f.

tigress, _tī'grĕs,_ s. tigra, f.

tile, _tīl,_ s. teja, f.; – v. a. tejar.

tiling, _–ĭng,_ s. tejado, m.

till, _tĭl,_ pr. & c. hasta que, hasta; –, s. cajón, m.; gaveta, f.; –, v. a. cultivar, labrar.

tillage, _–lădj,_ s. labranza, f. [del timón, f.

tiller, _–lăr,_ s. agricultor, m.; (mar.) caña

tilling, _–lĭng,_ s. labranza, f.

tilt, _tĭlt,_ s. tienda, cubierta, f.; justa, f.; torneo, m.; –, v. a. entoldar; apuntar la lanza; empinar; –, v. n. justar.

tilth, _tĭlth,_ s. labranza, f.

timber, _tĭm'băr,_ s. madera de construcción, f.; vigas maestras, f. pl.; –, v. a. enmaderar.

timber-work, _–wărk,_ s. maderaje, m.

timber-yard, _–yărd,_ s. astillero, m.

timbrel, _tĭm'brĕl,_ s. pandero, m.

time, _tĭm,_ s. tiempo; (mus.) compás, m.; **in –,** á tiempo; **from – to –,** de cuando en cuando; –, v. a. adaptar al tiempo.

time-keeper, _–kēpăr,_ s. reloj astronómico,

timeliness, _–lĭnĕs,_ s. oportunidad, f. [m.

timely, _–lĭ,_ ad. con tiempo; á propósito; –, a. oportuno.

time-piece, _–pēs,_ s. reloj astronómico, m.

time-server, _–sărvăr,_ s. (fig.) veleta, f.

time-serving, _–sărvĭng,_ s. servilismo, m.

time-worn, _–wŏrn,_ a. usado, deslustrado.

timid, _tĭm'ĭd,_ a. tímido, temeroso; **–ly,** ad. con timidez.

timidity, _tĭmĭd'ĭtĭ,_ s. timidez, f.

timorous, _tĭm'ărŭs,_ a. temeroso; **–ly,** ad. temerosamente.

tin, _tĭn,_ s. estaño, m.; –, v. a. estañar.

tincture, _tĭngk'tăr,_ s. tintura, f.; tinte, m.; –, v. a. teñir, tinturar.

tinder, _tĭn'dăr,_ s. yesca, f.

tinge, _tĭnj,_ v. a. tinturar, teñir.

tingle, _tĭng'gl,_ v. n. zumbar los oídos; latir, punzar. [m.; latido, m.

tingling, _tĭng'glĭng,_ s. zumbido de oídos.

tinker, _tĭngk'ăr,_ s. latonero, m.; calderero remendón, m. [los oídos.

tinkle, _tĭng'kl,_ v. a. & n. cencerrear; zumbar, [m.

tinman, _tĭn'măn,_ s. hojalatero, m.

tinmine, _tĭn'mīn,_ s. minero de estaño, m.

tinplate, _tĭn'plāt,_ s. hoja de lata, f.

tinsel, _tĭn'sĕl,_ s. brocadillo, m.; oropel, m.; s. tinte, m.; –, v. a. teñir.

tintack, _tĭn'tăk,_ s. tachuela de estaño, f.

tiny, a. (vulg.) pequeño, chico.

tip, _tĭp,_ s. punta, extremidad, f.; –, v. a. herretear; golpear ligeramente.

tippet, _–pĕt,_ s. palatina, f.

tipple, _–pl,_ v. n. beber con exceso; –, s. bebida, f. [f.

tipsiness, _–sĭnĕs,_ s. pequeña embriaguez,

tipstaff, _–stăf,_ s. alguacil de vara, m.

tipsy, _–sĭ,_ a. borrachuelo, entre dos vinos.

tiptoe, _–tō,_ s. punta del pie, f.

tiptop, _–tŏp,_ a. excelente, el ó lo mejor; –, s. cumbre, f. [dencia, f.

tirade, _tĭrād',_ s. invectiva, f.; (mus.) ca-

tire, _tīr,_ s. fila, hilera, f.; atavío, m.; –, v. a. cansar, fatigar; –, v. n. cansarse; fastidiarse.

tiresome, _tīr'sŭm,_ a. tedioso, molesto.

tiresomeness, _–nĕs,_ s. tedio, fastidio, m.

tiring-room, _tī'rĭngrŏm,_ s. vestuario, m.

tissue, _tĭsh'ū,_ s. tisú, f.; –, v. a. entretejer.

tit, _tĭt,_ s. haca, f.; paro, m.; **– for tat,** ad. taz á taz.

titbit, _–bĭt,_ s. bocado regalado, m.

tithe, _tĭth,_ s. diezmo, m.

titillate, _tĭt'ĭlāt,_ v. n. titilar.

title, _tī'tl,_ s. título, m.; –, v. a. titular.

title-deed, _–dēd,_ s. derecho de propiedad, m. [m.

title-page, _–pādj,_ s. frontispicio de un libro,

titmouse, _tĭt'mŏŭs,_ s. paro, m. (pájaro).

titter, _tĭt'tăr,_ v. n. sonreírse; –, s. sonrisa

tittle, _tĭt'tl,_ s. tilde, m.; mínima, f. [f.

tittle-tattle, _–tăt'tl,_ s. charla, f.

titular(y), _tĭt'ŭlăr(ĭ),_ a. titular.

to, _tō (tŏ),_ pr. á, al, á la, á los, á las; para; por; de; hasta; en; con; que; delante de un verbo, indica sólo el infinitivo y no se traduce.

toad, _tōd,_ s. sapo, escuerzo, m. [traduce.

toad-stool, _–stŏl,_ s. (bot.) hongovejín, m.

toady, _–ĭ,_ v. n. andar de gorra.

toadyism, _–ĭzm,_ s. servilismo, m.

toast, _tōst,_ v. a. tostar; brindar; –, s. tostada, f.; brindis, m.

toaster, _–ăr,_ s. parrillas, f. pl.

tobacco, _tŏbăk'kō,_ s. tabaco, m.

tobacco-box, _–bŏks,_ s. tabaquera, f.

tobacconist, _–nĭst,_ s. tabaquero, m.

tobacco-pouch, _–pŏŭtsh,_ s. petaca, f.

tocsin, _tŏk'sĭn,_ s. campana á rebato, f.

to-day, _tŏdā',_ ad. hoy.

toddle, _tŏd'dl,_ v. n. trotar.

toddy, _tŏd'dĭ,_ s. grog, m.

toe, _tō,_ s. dedo del pie, m.

together, _tŏgĕth'ăr,_ ad. juntamente, en compañía de otro; al mismo tiempo.

toggery, _tŏg'gărĭ,_ s. fruslería, f.; ropavejería, f.

toil, _tŏĭl,_ v. n. fatigarse, trabajar mucho; afanarse; –, s. trabajo, m.; fatiga, f.; afán, m.

toilet, _tŏĭl'ĕt,_ s. tocador, m. [m.

toilsome, _tŏĭl'sŭm,_ a. trabajoso; fatigoso.

token, _tō'kn,_ s. señal, f.; memoria, f.; recuerdo, m.

tolerable, _tŏl'ărăbl,_ a. tolerable; mediocre.

tolerably, _–ĭ,_ ad. tolerablemente, así así.

tolerance, _tŏl'ărăns,_ **toleration,** _tŏlără-shŭn,_ s. tolerancia, f.

tolerant, _tŏl'ărănt,_ a. tolerante.

tolerate, _tŏl'ărāt,_ v. a. tolerar.

toll, *tōl*, s. peaje, m.; —, v. a. tocar una campana. [m.

toll-gatherer, *gōthårăr*, s. portazguero,

tomahawk, *tŏm'dhåk*, s. hacha de armas ź de los indios americanos, f.

tomato, *tŏmå'tŏ*, s. tomate, m.

tomb, *tŏm*, s. tumba, f.; sepulcro, m.

tomboy, *tŏm'bŏĭ*, s. villano, m.; doncella pizpireta y respingona, f. [cral, f.

tomb-stone, *tŏm'stŏn*, s. piedra sepul-

tom-cat, *tŏm'kåt*, s. gato entero, m.

tomfoolery, *tŏmfŏl'ărĕ*, s. pataratas, frioleras, f. pl.

to-morrow, *tŏmŏr'rŏ*, ad. mañana.

tomtit, *tŏm'tĭt*, s. paro, m. (pájaro).

ton, *tŭn*, s. tonelada, f.

tone, *tŏn*, s. tono de la voz, m.; acento, m.

tongs, *tŏngz*, s. pl. tenaza, f.

tongue, *tŭng*, s. lengua, f.; habla, f.; bahía, f.; (of a balance) lengua en el peso: to hold the —, callar.

tongueless, *—lĕs*, a. mudo.

tonic, *tŏn'ĭk*, a. (med.) tónico.

to-night, *tŏnīt'*, ad. esta tarde.

tonnage, *tŭn'dj*, s. porte de un buque, m.

tonsil, *tŏn'sĭl*, s. agallas, f. pl.

tonsure, *tŏn'shår*, s. tonsura, f.

too, *tŏ*, ad. demasiado; así mismo, aun.

tool, *tŏl*, s. herramienta, f.; utensilio, m.

tooth, *tŏth*, s. diente, m.; gusto, m.; —, v. a. dentar; encajar unos dientes en otros.

tooth-ache, *—åk*, s. dolor de muelas, m.

toothless, *—lĕs*, a. desdentado.

toothpick, *—pĭk*, s. mondadientes, m.

toothpowder, *—pŏŭdăr*, s. dentrífico, m.

toothsome, *—săm*, a. sabroso; comedero.

top, *tŏp*, s. cima, cumbre, f.; último grado, m.; tupé, m.; trompo, m.; (mar.) cofa, f.; —, v. a. & n. elevarse por encima; sobrepujar, exceder; cubrir el mango, el cabo; descabezar los árboles.

topaz, *tŏ'păz*, s. topacio, m.

toper, *tŏ'păr*, s. borrachón, bebedor, m.

topic, *tŏp'ĭk*, s. principio general, m.; remedio tópico, m.

topmost, *tŏp'mŏst*, a. lo más alto.

topographic(al), *tŏpŏgrăf'ĭk(ăl)*, a. topográfico.

topography, *tŏpŏg'răfĕ*, s. topografía, f.

topple, *tŏp'pl*, v. n. vulcarse.

topsy-turvy, *tŏp'sĭ tŭr'vĕ*, ad. al revés.

torch, *tŏrtsh*, s. antorcha, hacha, f.

torch-bearer, *—bărăr*, s. hachero, m.

torch-light, *—līt*, s. luz de antorcha, f.; --procession, procesión con antorchas,f.

torment, *tŏr'mĕnt'*, v. a. atormentar; *tŏr'mĕnt*, s. tormento, m. [cán, m.

tornado, *tŏrnå'dŏ*, s. turbonada, f.; hura-

torpedo, *tŏrpē'dŏ*, s. tremielga, f. (pez).

torpid, *tŏr'pĭd*, a. entorpecido. [m.

torpor, *tŏr'pŏr*, s. entorpecimiento, estupor,

torrent, *tŏr'rĕnt*, s. torrente, m.

torrid, *tŏr'rĭd*, a. tórrido, tostado.

tortoise, *tŏr'tĭs*, s. tortuga, f. [f.

tortoise-shell, *—shĕl*, s. concha de tortuga,

tortuous, *tŏr'tŭăs*, a. tortuoso, sinuoso.

torture, *tŏr'tŭr*, s. tortura, f.; —, v. a. atormentar.

Tory, *tŏ'rĕ*, s. tory, m. (partido conservativo de Inglaterra).

toss, *tŏs*, v. a. tirar, lanzar, arrojar; agitar, sacudir; (in a blanket) mantear; —, s. sacudida, f.; cabezada, f. [mente.

total, *tŏ'tăl*, a. total, entero; —ly, ad. total

totality, *tŏtăl'ĭtĕ*, s. totalidad, f.

totter, *tŏt'tŭr*, v. n. bambolear; vacilar.

touch, *tŭtsh*, v. a. & n. tocar, palpar; —, s. tocamiento, m.; contacto, m.; tacto, m.; toque, m.; prueba, f.

touch-hole, *—hŏl*, s. fogón, m.

touchiness, *—ĭnĕs*, s. susceptibilidad, f.

touching, *—ĭng*, a. patético, conmovedor; —, pr. por lo que toca á. [rial, m.

touch-me-not, *—mĕnŏt*, s. (bot.) mercu-

touch-stone, *—stŏn*, s. piedra de toque, f.

touch-wood, *—wŭd*, s. yesca, f.

touchy, *—ĕ*, a. cosquilloso, vidrioso.

tough, *tŭf*, a. correoso; tieso; viscoso.

toughen, *—n*, v. n. hacerse correosa alguna cosa. [dad, f.; tesura, f.

toughness, *—nĕs*, s. tenacidad, f.; viscosi-

tour, *tŏr*, s. viaje, m.; peregrinación, f. [m.

tourist, *—ĭst*, s.viajero,m.; escritor de viajes.

tournament, *—nåmĕnt*, s.torneo,m.; justa,f.

tout, *tŏt*, s. el todo; trasero, m.; otero, m.

tow, *tŏ*, s. estopa, f.; remolque, m.; —, v. a. (mar.) remolcar, atoar.

towage, *—dj*, s. (mar.) remolque, atoaje.

toward(s), *tŏ'ård(z)*, pr. & ad. hacia, con dirección á; cerca de, con respecto á.

towel, *tŏŭ'ĕl*, s. toalla, f.

towel-horse, *—hŏrs*, s. enjugador, m.

tower, *tŏŭ'ăr*, s. torre, m.; ciudadela, f.; —, v. n. remontarse; elevarse á una altura

town, *tŏŭn*, s. ciudad, f. [desmesurada.

town-councillor, *—kŏŭnsĭllăr*, s. concejal, concejil, m.

town-crier, *—krīăr*, s. pregonero, m.

town-hall, *—hŏl*, town-house, *—hŏŭs*, s. casa consistorial, f. [dad, f.

townsfolk, *—zfŏk*, s. pl. gente de la ciu-

township, *—shĭp*, s. ayuntamiento, m.

townsman, *—zmăn*, s. concivdadano, m.

toy, *tŏĭ*, s. chuchería, f.; miriñaque, juguete, m.; —, v. n. jugar, divertirse.

trace, *trăs*, s. huella, pisada, f.; —, v. a. trazar, delinear.

track, *trăk*, s. vestigio, m.; huella, f.; rodada, f.; estola, f.; —, v. a. rastrear.

trackless, *—lĕs*, a. lo que no presenta vestigio de que hayan andado por encima.

tract, *trăkt*, s. trecho, m.; región, comarca, f.; serie, f.; tratado, m.

tractable, *trăk'tăbl*, a. tratable, afable.

tractableness, *—nĕs*, s. afabilidad, docili-

tractably, *—ĕ*, ad. dócilmente. [dad, f.

traction, *trăk'shăn*, s. acarreo, m.

trade, *trăd*, s. comercio, tráfico, m.; negocio, trato, m.; ocupación, f.; —, v. n. merciar, traficar. [navío mercante.

trader, *—ăr*, s. comerciante, trafican

tradesman, *—zmăn*, s. tendero, me m. [los artes

trades-union, *—z'ŭnyăn*, s. aso

trade-winds, *—wĭnds*, s. pl. zón, m.

trading, *trå'dĭng*, s. comerci

tradition, *trădĭsh'ăn,* s. tradición, f.
traditional, *-ăl,* a. tradicional; *-ly,* ad. por tradición. [niar; acusar; propagar.
traduce, *trădūs',* v. a. vituperar; calumtraffic, *trăf'fĭk,* s. tráfico, m.; mercaderías, f. pl.; *-,* v. n. traficar, comerciar.
trafficker, *-ăr,* s. traficante, comerciante, negociante, mercader, m.
tragedian, *trăjē'dĭăn,* s. actor trágico, m.
tragedy, *trăj'ĕdĕ,* s. tragedia, f.
tragic(al), *trăj'ĭk(ăl),* a. trágico; *-ally,* ad. trágicamente. [dad, f.
tragicalness, *-ălnĕs,* s. tristeza, calamitragicomedy, *trăjĭkŏm'ĕdĕ,* s. tragicomedia, f. [cómico.
tragi-comical, *trăjĭkŏm'ĭkăl,* a. tragitrail, *trāl,* v. a. & n. rastrear; arrastrar; *-,* s. rastro, m.; pisada, f.; cola, f.
train, *trān,* v. a. arrastrar, amaestrar, enseñar, criar, adiestrar; disciplinar; *-,* s. estratagema, f., engaño, m.; serie, f.; séquito, tren, m.; cebo, m.; (rail.) tren.
train-bands, *-băndz,* s. pl. milicias, f. pl.
trainer, *-ăr,* s. maestro, enseñador, m.
training, *-ĭng,* s. educación, disciplina, f.
train-oil, *-ŏĭl,* s. aceite de ballena, m.
trait, *trā,* s. rasgo de carácter, m.
traitor, *trā'tŭr,* s. traidor, m.
traitorous, *-ŭs,* a. pérfido, traidor; *-ly,* ad. traidoramente.
traitress, *trā'trĕs,* s. traidora, f.
trammel, *trăm'mĕl,* s. trasmallo, m.; *-,* v. a. coger, interceptar. [en el suelo, f.
tramp, *trămp,* s. vagabundo, m.; patada
trample, *trămp'l,* v. n. pisar muy fuerte.
trampling, *trămp'lĭng,* s. pataleo, m.
tram-way, *-wā,* s. tranvía, m.
trance, *trăns,* s. rapto, m.; éxtasi, m.
tranquil, *trăn'kwĭl,* a. tranquilo; *-ly,* ad. tranquilamente. [f.
tranquillity, *trănkwĭl'ĭtĕ,* s. tranquilidad,
tranquillize, *trăn'kwĭlĭz,* v. a. tranquilizar.
transact, *trănsăkt',* v. a. negociar; transigir.
transaction, *-ăk'shăn,* s. transacción, f.; negociación, f.; *-s,* pl. memorias, f. pl.
transactor, *-ăk'tŭr,* s. negociador, m.
transatlantic, *-ătlăn'tĭk,* a. transatlántico.
transcend, *trănsĕnd',* v. a. trascender, pasar; exceder.
transcendency, *-ĕnsĕ,* s. excelencia, f.
transcendent, *-sĕn'dĕnt,* a. sobresaliente; *-ly,* ad. excelentemente.
transcribe, *-skrĭb',* v. a. trascribir, copiar.
transcriber, *-ăr,* s. copiante, m.
transcript, *trăn'skrĭpt,* s. trasunto, m.
transcription, *trănskrĭp'shăn,* s. traslado, m.; copia, f. [una iglesia, f.
transept, *trăn'sĕpt,* s. nave transversal de
transfer, *trănsfŭr',* v. a. transferir, transportar; *-,* *trăns'fŭr,* s. cesión, f.
transferable, *-fŭr'ăbl,* a. transferible.
transfiguration, *trănsfĭgūră'shăn,* s. transfiguración, f.
transfigure, *-fĭg'ŭr,* v. a. transformar.
transfix, *-fĭks',* v. a. traspasar.
transform, *-fŏrm',* v. a. (& n.) transformar(se) [mación, f.
transformation, *-fŏrmă'shăn,* s. transfor-

transgress, *-grĕs',* v. a. & n. transgredir, violar. [f.
transgression, *-grĕsh'ăn,* s. transgresión,
transgressor, *-grĕs'ăr,* s. transgresor, m.
transient, *trăn'shĕnt,* a. pasajero, transitorio; *-ly,* ad. de un modo transitorio.
transit, *trăns'ĭt,* s. tránsito, m.
transition, *trănzĭsh'ăn,* s. tránsito, m.; transición, f. [uno á otro.
transitional, *-ăl,* a. que se transfiere de
transitive, *trăns'ĭtĭv,* a. transitivo.
transitoriness, *-ĭtŭrĭnĕs,* s. brevedad, f.
transitory, *-ĭtŭrĕ,* a. transitorio.
translate, *trănslāt',* v. a. trasladar, traducir. [traducción, f.
translation, *-lā'shăn,* s. translación, f.;
translator, *-lā'tŭr,* s. traductor, m.
translucent, *-lō'sĕnt,* a. trasluciente, diáfano.
transmarine, *-mărēn',* a. trasmarino.
transmigration, *-mĭgrā'shăn,* a. transmigración, f. [f.
transmission, *-mĭsh'ăn,* s. transmisión,
transmit, *-mĭt',* v. a. transmitir.
transmutation, *-mŭtā'shăn,* s. transmutación, f.
transom, *trăn'sŏm,* s. travesaño, m.
transparency, *trănspā'rĕnsĕ,* s. transparencia, f. [diáfano.
transparent, *-pā'rĕnt,* a. transparente, f.
transpire, *trănspīr',* v. a. transpirar.
transplant, *trănsplănt',* v. a. trasplantar.
transplantation, *-plăntā'shăn,* s. trasplantación, f., trasplante, m.
transport, *trănspŏrt',* v. a. transportar; deportar, *-,* *trăns'pŏrt,* s. transportación, f.; (mar.) transporte, m.; criminal condenado á la deportación, m.
transportation, *-pŏrtā'shăn,* s. transportación, f., transportamiento, m.
transporting, *-pŏr'tĭng,* a. embelesador.
transpose, *-pōz',* v. a. transponer.
transposition, *-pŏzĭsh'ăn,* s. transposición, f. [shăn, s. transsubstanciación, f.
transubstantiation, *trănsŭbstănshĭā'*
transverse, *trănsvŭrs',* a. transverso; *-ly,* ad. transversalmente.
trap, *trăp,* s. trampa, f.; *-,* v. n. hacer caer en la trampa. [escotillón, f.
trap-door, *-dŏr,* s. puerta disimulada, f.;
trapeze, *trăpēz',* s. trapecio, m.
trapper, *-pŭr,* s. (am.) cazador de animales pelíferos, m.
trappings, *-pĭngz,* s. pl. jaeces, m. pl.
trash, *trăsh,* s. heces, f. pl., desecho, m.; zupia, f. [valor.
trashy, *-ĕ,* a. vil, despreciable, de ningún
travail, *trăv'ĕl,* s. dolores de parto, m.
travel, *trăv'ĕl,* v. n. viajar; *-,* s. viaje, m.
traveller, *-ăr,* s. viajante, viajero, m.
travelling, *-ĭng,* s. viajes, m. pl.
traverse, *trăv'ărs,* v. a. atravesar, cruzar.
travesty, *trăv'ĕstĕ,* s. disfraz, m.; *-,* a. disfrazado; *-,* v. a. disfrazar.
trawl, *trāl,* v. n. pescar con red rastrera.
tray, *trā,* s. salvilla, batea, f.; artesa, f.

treacherous, trĕtsh'ărŭs, a. traidor, pérfido; -ly, ad. traidoramente.

treachery, trĕtsh'ărĕ, s. perfidia, deslealtad, traición, f.

treacle, trē'kl, s. triaca, f.

tread, trĕd, v. a. & n. pisar, hollar, apretar con el pie; pisotear; patalear; caminar con majestad; —, s. pisa, f.; pisada, f.; galladura, f.

treadle, -l, s. cárcola, f.; galladura, f.

treason, trē'zn, s. traición, f.; high —, delito de lesa majestad, f.   [á traición.

treasonable, -ăbl, a. traidor; -bly, ad.

treasure, trĕsh'ŭr, s. tesoro, m.; —, v. a.

treasurer, -ŭr, s. tesorero, m.   [atesorar.

treasurership, -ărshĭp, s. tesorería, f. (empleo).

treasury, -ĕ, s. tesorería, f. (oficina).

treat, trēt, v. a. & n. tratar; regalar; —, s. trato, banquete, festín, m.

treatise, -ĭz, s. tratado, m.

treatment, -mĕnt, s. trato, m.

treaty, -ĕ, s. tratado, m.

treble, trĕb'l, a. triplice; —, v. a. & n. triplicar(se); —, s. (mus.) tiple, m.

trebly, trĕb'lĭ, ad. triplicadamente.

tree, trĕ, s. árbol, m.; cepo, m., asta, f.

trefoil, trĕ'fŏĭl, s. trébol, m.

trellis, trĕl'lĭs, s. enrejado, m.

tremble, trĕm'bl, v. n. temblar.

trembling, -blĭng, s. temor, m.; trino, m.

tremblingly, -lĕ, ad. trémulamente.

tremendous, trĕmĕn'dŭs, a. tremendo; -ly, ad. de un modo tremendo.

tremor, trĕm'ŏr, s. tremor, temblor, m.

tremulous, trĕm'ŭlŭs, a. trémulo.

tremulousness, -lŭsnĕs, s. temblor, m.; —, s. foso, m.; (mil.) trinchera, f.

trench, trĕnsh, v. a. cortar; atrincherar;

trenchant, trĕn'shănt, a. afilado, cortante.

trencher, trĕnsh'ŭr, s. trinchero, m.; mesa.

trencher-man, -ărmăn, s. comedor, m. [f.

trepan, trĕpăn', s. trépano, m.; —, v. a. trepanar.

trespass, trĕs'păs, v. a. quebrantar, transpasar, violar; —, s. transgresión, violación.

trespasser, -ŭr, s. transgresor, m.   [f.

tress, trĕs, s. trenza, f.; rizo de pelo, m.

trestle, trĕs'sl, s. armazón de la mesa, f.; caballete de serrador, m.

trial, trī'ăl, s. prueba, f.; ensayo, m.; examen (judicial), m.

triangle, trī'ăngl, s. triángulo, m.

triangular, trĭăng'gŭlăr, a. triangular.

tribal, trĕ'băl, a. perteneciente á una tribu.

tribe, trĭb, s. tribu, m. (& f.); raza, casta, f.

tribulation, trĭbŭlā'shăn, s. tribulación, f.

tribunal, trĭbū'năl, s. tribunal, m.

tribune, trĭb'ăn, s. tribuno, m.; tribuna, f.

tributary, trĕb'ătărĕ, a. & s. tributario (m.).

tribute, trĕb'ăt, s. tributo, m.

trice, trĭs, s. momento, tris, m.

trick, trĭk, s. engaño, fraude, m.; superchería, astucia, f.; burla, f.; maña, f.; baza, f. (en el juego de naipes); —, v. a. engañar; ataviar; hacer juegos de manos.

trickery, -ărĕ, s. engaño, dolo, m.

trickster, -stŭr, s. engañador, m.

trickle, -l, v. n. gotear.

tricky, -ĕ, a. astuto, artificioso.

trident, trī'dĕnt, s. tridente, m. (cetro).

triennial, trĭĕn'nĭăl, a. trienal.

trifle, trī'fl, s. bagatela, niñería, f.; —, v. n. bobear; chancear, juguetear.

trifler, -ŭr, s. necio, m.; tararira, m.

trifling, trī'flĭng, a. frívolo, inútil; -ly, ad. frívolmente, sin consecuencia.

trigger, trĭg'gŭr, s. gatillo de escopeta (ó pistola), m.; pararruedas, m.   [metría, f.

trigonometry, trĭgŏnŏm'ĕtrĕ, s. trigonometría, f.

trilateral, trĭlăt'ărăl, a. trilátero.

trill, trĭl, s. trino, m.; —, v. a. trinar.

trim, trĭm, a. compuesto, ataviado; —, v. a. aparejar, preparar; acomodar; adornar; podar; (mar.) rasurar; orientar (las velas); —, v. n. balancear, vacilar; —, s. atavío, adorno, aderezo, m.

trimly, -lĕ, ad. lindamente, con primor.

trimming, -mĭng, s. guarnición de vestido.

Trinity, trĭn'ĭtĕ, s. Trinidad, f.   [f.

trinket, trĭng'kĕt, s. joya, alhaja, f.; adorno, m.; bujería, f.; juguetes, m.

trio, trĕ'ŏ, s. (mus.) trío, m.

trip, trĭp, v. a. hacer caer á uno echándole la zancadilla; —, v. n. tropezar; resbalar; hacer un viaje corto; —, s. zancadilla, f.; resbalón, m.; viaje corto, m.

tripartite, trĭpăr'tĭt, a. tripartito.

tripe, trĭp, s. tripa, f.; intestino, m.

triple, trĭp'l, a. triplice, triplo; —, v. a. triplicar.   [pl. trigemelos, m. pl.

triplet, trĭp'lĕt, s. (poet.) tercerilla, f.; -s,

tripod, trĕ'pŏd, s. trípode, m.

tripping, trĭp'pĭng, a. veloz, ligero, ágil; —, s. baile ligero, m.; tropiezo, m.; -ly, ad. velozmente.

trireme, trĕ'rēm, s. trirreme, m.

trisect, trĭsĕkt', v. a. tripartir.   [f.

trisyllable, trĭsĭl'ăbl, s. palabra trisilábica,

trite, trĭt, a. trivial; usado; -ly, ad. vulgarmente.

triteness, -nĕs, s. trivialidad, f.

triturate, trĭt'ŭrăt, v. a. triturar.

triumph, trĕ'ŭmf, s. triunfo, m.; —, v. n. triunfar.

triumphal, trĭŭm'făl, a. triunfal.

triumphant, trĭŭm'fănt, a. triunfante; victorioso; -ly, ad. en triunfo.

triumvirate, trĭŭm'vĭrăt, s. triumvirato, m.   [trivialmente.

trivial, trĕv'ĭăl, a. trivial, vulgar; -ly, ad.

triviality, trĭvĭăl'ĭtĕ, s. trivialidad, f.

troat, trŏt, v. n. bramar.   [andorrear.

troll, trŏl, v. a. voltear; —, v. n. girar;

trolley, trŏl'lĕ, s. (rail.) lorri, truck, m.

trollop, trŏl'lŏp, s. gorrona, f.

troop, trŏp, s. tropa, f.; cuadrilla, turba, f.; —, v. n. atroparse.

trooper, -ŭr, s. soldado á caballo, m.

trophy, trŏ'fĕ, s. trofeo, m.; (poet.) triunfo, m.

tropics, trŏp'ĕks, s. pl. trópico, m.   [m.

tropical, -ăl, a. trópico.

trot, trŏt, s. trote, m.; —, v. n. trotar.

trotter, -tŭr, s. caballo trotón, m.

trouble, trŭb'l, v. a. disturbar; afligir,

—, s. turbación, f.; disturbio, m.; inquietud, f.; aflicción, pena, f.; congoja, f.

troublesome, *-sŭm*, a. penoso, fatigoso; importuno. [dad, molestia, f.

troublesomeness, *-sŭmnĕs*, s. incomodi-

troublous, *trŭb'lŭs*, a. turbulento, confuso.

trough, *trŏf*, s. artesa, gamella, f.; dornajo, m. [talones, m.

trousering, *trŏŭ'zŭrĭng*, s. paño para pan-

trousers, *trŏŭ'zŭrz*, s. pl. calzones largos,

trout, *trŏŭt*, s. trucha, f. (pez). [m. pl.

trowel, *trŏ'ĕl*, s. trulla, llana, f. [(m.).

truant, *trŏ'ănt*, a. & s. holgazán, haragán

truce, *trŏs*, s. tregua, suspensión de armas, f.

truck, *trŭk*, v. n. trocar, cambiar; —, s. cambio, trueque, m.; rueda de cureña, f.; (rail.) truck, lorri, m. [cita, f.

truckle, *-l*, v. n. someterse; —, s. ruede-

truckle-bed, *-bĕd*, s. carriola, f.

truck-system, *trŭk'sĭstĕm*, s. paga de los obreros en especie, en ser, f. [f.

truculence, *trŭk'dŭlĕns*, s. fiereza, crueldad,

truculent, *-lĕnt*, a. truculento, cruel.

trudge, *trŭj*, v. n. andar con afán; afanarse. [exacto.

true, *trŏ*, a. verdadero, cierto; sincero;

true-born, *-bŏrn*, a. legítimo.

true-bred, *-brĕd*, a. de casta legítima.

true-hearted, *-härtĕd*, a. leal, sincero, franco, fiel.

true-love, *-lŭv*, a. (bot.) uva de oso, f.

truffle, *trŭf'l*, s. criadilla de tierra, f.

truism, *trŏ'ĭzm*, s. verdad indubitable, f.

truly, *trŏ'lĕ*, ad. en verdad; sinceramente.

trump, *trŭmp*, s. trompeta, f.; triunfo (en el juego de naipes), m.; —, v. a. ganar con el triunfo; to — up, forjar; inventar.

trumpery, *-ŭrĕ*, s. hojarasca, f.; bujería, baratija, f. [trompetear; divulgar.

trumpet, *trŭm'pĕt*, s. trompeta, f.; —, v. a.

trumpeter, *-ŭr*, s. trompetero, m.

truncate, *trŭng'kāt*, v. a. truncar; troncar.

truncheon, *trŭn'shŭn*, s. cachiporra, f.

trundle, *trŭn'dl*, s. rueda baja, f.; carreta de ruedas bajas, f.; rodillo, m., —, v. a. rodar. [trompa, f.

trunk, *trŭngk*, s. tronco, baúl, cofre, m.;

trunk-line, *-lĭn*, **trunk-road**, *-rŏd*, (rail.) tronco, m., línea principal, f.

trunk-maker, *-mākŭr*, s. cofrero, m.

trunnion, *trŭn'yŭn*, s. muñón, m.

truss, *trŭs*, s. braguero, m.; haz, f.; atado, m.; —, v. a. empaquetar; arremangar.

trust, *trŭst*, s. confianza, f.; cargo, depósito, m.; crédito, m.; asociación comercial para monopolizar la venta de algún género, f.; —, v. a. & n. confiar; encargar y fiar; confiarse, fiarse; dar crédito; esperar. [m.

trustee, *trŭstē*, s. fideicomisario, curador,

trustful, *trŭst'fŭl*, a. fiel; confiado.

trustily, *-ĭlĕ*, a. fielmente.

trustiness, *-ĭnĕs*, s. fidelidad, probidad, f.

trustworthy, *-wŭrthē*, a. digno de confianza. [fianza.

trusty, *-ĕ*, a. fiel, leal; seguro. [fianza.

truth, *trŏth*, s. verdad, f.; fidelidad, f.; realidad, f.; in —, en verdad.

truthful, *-fŭl*, a. verídico.

truthfulness, *-fŭlnĕs*, s. veracidad, f.

try, *trī*, v. a. & n. examinar, ensayar, probar; experimentar; tentar; intentar; juzgar; purificar, refinar.

trying, *-ĭng*, a. crítico; penoso; cruel.

tub, *tŭb*, s. cubo, m.; tina de madera, f.

tube, *tūb*, s. tubo, cañón, cañuto, m.

tubercle, *tū'bŭrkl*, s. (med.) tubérculo, m.

tuberose, *tū'bŭrōz*, s. (bot.) tuberosa, f.

tubular, *tū'bŭlăr*, a. tubular.

tuck, *tŭk*, s. estoque, m.; alforza, f.; pliegue; m.; —, v. a. arremangar, recoger.

tucker, *-ŭr*, s. gargantilla, f.

Tuesday, *tūz'dā*, s. martes, m.

tuft, *tŭft*, s. borla, f.; penacho, m.; mazorca de flores, &c., f.; grupo, m.; moño, m.

tufted, *-ĕd*, a. frondoso, velludo. [m.

tug, *tŭg*, v. a. tirar con fuerza; arrancar; —, v. n. esforzarse; —, s. tirada, f.; esfuerzo, m.; (mar.) remolcador, m.

tuition, *tŭĭsh'ăn*, s. tutoría, tutela, f.

tulip, *tū'lĭp*, s. tulipa, f.; tulipán, m.

tumble, *tăm'bl*, v. n. caer, hundirse, voltear; revolcarse; —, v. a. revolver; rodar; volcar; —, s. caída, f.; vuelco, m.

tumbler, *-ăr*, s. volteador, m.; vaso (sin pie) para beber, m.

tumbrel, *tăm'brĕl*, s. (mil.) caja de municiones, f.; chirrión, m.

tumbril, *tăm'brĭl*, s. pesebre hecho de esteras de mimbre, m.

tumefy, *tū'mĕfĭ*, v. a. hacer entumecerse.

tumor, *tū'mĕr*, s. tumor, m., hinchazón, f.

tumult, *tū'mŭlt*, s. tumulto, m.

tumultuous, *tămŭl'tŭŭs*, a. tumultuoso; **-ly**, ad. tumultuariamente. [fiada, f.

tun, *tŭn*, s. tonel, m.; (fam.) cuero, m.; tone-

tune, *tūn*, s. tono, m.; armonía, f.; aria, f.; humor, m.; —, v. a. templar un instrumento músico. [dioso.

tuneful, *-fŭl*, a. armonioso, acorde, melo-

tuneless, *-lĕs*, a. disonante.

tunic, *tū'nĭk*, s. túnica, f. [quilla tónica, f.

tuning-fork, *tū'nĭngfŏrk*, s. (mus.) hor-

tunnel, *tăn'nĕl*, s. cañón de chimenea, m.; túnel, m.; —, v. a. hacer una cosa en forma de embudo. [f.

tunnelling, *-ĭng*, s. abertura de un túnel,

tunny, *tăn'nĕ*, s. atún, m. (pez).

turban, *tŭr'băn*, s. turbante, m.

turbid, *tŭr'bĭd*, a. turbio, cenagoso.

turbot, *tŭr'bŏt*, s. rodaballo, rombo, m. (pez). [confusión, f.

turbulence, *tŭr'bŭlĕns*, s. turbulencia,

turbulent, *tŭr'bŭlĕnt*, a. turbulento, tumultuoso; **-ly**, ad. tumultuariamente.

tureen, *tŭrēn'*, s. sopera, f.

turf, *tŭrf*, s. césped, m.; turba, f.; hipódromo, m., corrida de caballos, f.; —, v. a. cubrir con céspedes.

turgid, *tŭr'jĭd*, a. túmido, inflado.

turkey, *tŭr'kĕ*, s. pavo, m.; pava, f.

turmoil, *tŭr'mŏĭl*, s. disturbio, m.; barahúnda, f.

turn, *tŭrn*, v. a. volver, trocar; verter, traducir; cambiar; tornear; —, v. n. volver,

girar, rodar; voltear; dar vueltas; volverse
á, mudarse, transformarse; volver casaca;
—, s. vuelta, f.; giro, m.; rodeo, m.; turno,
m.; vez, f.; procedimiento, modo de portarse, m.; inclinación, f.; servicio, m.;
forma, figura, hechura, f.

turncoat, —*kōt*, s. desertor, renegado, m.

turncock, —*kŏk,* s. fontanero, m.

turner, —*dr,* s. torneador, tornero, m.

turning, —*ĭng,* s. vuelta, f.; rodeo, m.

turning-in, —*ĭng ĭn,* s. pliegue, m.

turning-lathe, —*ĭng lǎth,* s. torno, m.

turnip, *tŭr'nĭp,* s. (bot.) nabo, m.

turnkey, *tŭrn'kĕ,* s. demandadero de una
cárcel, m.

turn-off, *tŭrn'ŏff,* s. encrucijada, f.

turn-out, —*ŏŭt,* s. cesación del trabajo,
f.; (rail.) aguja, f.; coche y demás aparejo,
m.; producto limpio ó neto, m.

turnpike, —*pĭk,* s. molinete, m.; barrera,
f.

turn-plate, —*plāt,* **turn-rail,** —*rāl,*
turn-table, —*tābl,* s. (rail.) plataforma
giratoria, tornavía, f.

turnscrew, —*skrŏ,* s. destornillador, m.

turnspit, —*spĭt,* s. galopín de cocina que
da vueltas al asador de mano, m.

turnstile, —*stĭl,* s. molinete, m.'

turpentine, *tŭr'pĕntĭn,* s. trementina, f.

turpitude, *tŭr'pĭtŭd,* s. torpeza, infamia,
f.

turquoise, *tŭrkŏĭz,* s. turquesa, f.

turret, *tŭr'rĕt,* s. torrecilla, f.

turreted, —*ĕd,* a. armado con torrecillas.

turtle, *tŭr'tl,* s. tórtola, f.; tortuga de mar,
f.

turtle-dove, —*dŭv,* s. tórtola, f.

tush! *tŭsh,* tut! *tŭt,* ¡ tararira !

tusk, *tŭsk,* s. colmillo, m.

tusked, —*ĕd,* a. colmilludo.

tassle, *tǎs'sl,* s. alboroto, m.; grita, f.

tutelage, *tū'tĕldj,* s. tutela, tutoría, f.

tutelar, *tū'tĕlâr,* a. tutelar.

tutor, *tū'târ,* s. tutor, m.; preceptor, m.;
—, v. a. enseñar, instruir; señorear.

tutoress, —*ĕs,* s. tutriz, aya, f.

twaddle, *twŏd'dl,* v. n. charlar.

twain, *twān,* a. dos.

twang, *twăng,* v. a. & n. producir un sonido
agudo; restallar; —, s. ganguéo, m.; sonido
agudo, m.

tweezers, *twē'zĕrz,* s. pl. tenacillas, f. pl.

twelfth, *twĕlfth,* a. duodécimo.

Twelfth-day, —*dā,* **Twelfth-night,**
—*nĭt,* s. día de reyes, m.; Epifanía, f.

twelve, *twĕlv,* a. doce.   [meses].

twelvemonth,—*mŭnth,* s. año, m. (doce
meses).

twentieth, *twĕn'tĭĕth,* a. vigésimo.

twenty, *twĕn'tĕ,* a. veinte.

twice, *twĭs,* ad. dos veces; al doble.

twig, *twĭg,* s. vareta, varilla, f.; vástago,
m.

twilight, *twĭ'lĭt,* s. crepúsculo, m.   [m.

twill, *twĭl,* s. crucero, m.

twin, *twĭn,* s. gemelo, m.

twine, *twĭn,* v. a. torcer; enroscar; —, v. n.
entrelazarse; caracolear; —, s. guita, f.;
abrazo, m.

twinge, *twĭnj,* v. a. punzar, pellizcar; —,
s. dolor agudo ó punzante, m.

twinkle, *twĭng'kl,* v. n. centellear; parpadear.

twinkling, *twĭng'klĭng,* s. vislumbre, f.;
guiñada, f.; pestañeo, m.

twirl, *twŭrl,* v. a. voltear; —, s. rotación, f.

twist, *twĭst,* v. a. & n. torcer, retorcer; entretejer; retortijarse; —, s. trenza, f.; cordón, m., hilo de algodón, m.; torcedura,
f.

twit, *twĭt,* v. a. regañar.

twitch, *twĭtsh,* v. a. pellizcar; —, s. pellizco, m.   [jeo, m.

twitter, *twĭt'târ,* v. n. gorjear; —, s. gor-

two, *tō,* a. dos.   [ad. al doble.

twofold, —*fōld,* a. doble, duplicado; —,

tympan(um), *tĭm'pân(ŭm),* s. tímpano, m.

type, *tĭp,* s. tipo, m.; letra, f.

typhoid, *tĭ'fŏĭd,* a. tifoideo.

typhus, *tĭ'fŭs,* s. tifo, m.

typic(al), *tĭp'ĭk(ăl),* a. típico; —ly, ad.
simbólicamente.

typographer, *tĭpŏg'râfâr,* s. tipógrafo, m.

typographic(al), *tĭpŏgrăf'ĭk(ăl),* a. tipográfico.

typography, *tĭpŏg'râfĭ,* s. tipografía, f.

tyrannic(al), *tĭrăn'nĭk(ăl),* a. tiránico;
—ly, ad. tiránicamente.

tyrannise, *tĭr'ănĭz,* v. a. tiranizar.

tyranny, *tĭr'dnĕ,* s. tiranía, f.; crueldad, f.

tyrant, *tĭ'rănt,* s. tirano, m.

tyro, *tĭ'rō,* s. tirón, bisoño, m.

U.

ubiquitous, *ŭbĭk'wĭtŭs,* a. ubicuo.

ubiquity, *ŭbĭk'wĭtĕ,* s. ubicuidad, f.

udder, *ĕd'dâr,* s. ubre, f.   [f.

ugliness, *ŭg'lĭnĕs,* s. fealdad, deformidad,

ugly, *ŭg'lĭ,* a. feo, disforme.

ulcer, *ŭl'sâr,* s. úlcera, f.

ulcerate, —*dt,* v. a. ulcerar.

ulceration, *ŭlsârā'shŭn,* s. ulceración, f.

ulterior, *ŭltē'rĭâr,* a. ulterior.

ultimate, *ŭl'tĭmdt,* a. último; —ly, ad.
últimamente.

ultimatum, *ŭltĭmā'tŭm,* s. ultimátum, m.;
última condición irrevocable, f.

ultramarine, *ŭltrâmârēn',* s. ultramar,
m.; —, a. ultramarino.   [tano.

ultramontane, —*mŏn'tān,* a. ultramon-

umber, *ŭm'bâr,* s. tierra de sombras, f.

umbrage, *ŭm'brâj,* s. sombra, f.; umbría,
f.; pretexto, m.; take —, tener sospecha.

umbrageous, *ŭmbrā'jŭs,* a. sombrío,
umbrío, sombroso.   [m.

umbrella, *ŭmbrĕl'lâ,* s. parasol, quitasol,

umpire, *ŭm'pĭr,* s. árbitro, m.

unabashed, *ŭnâbăsh't,* v. a. descocado.

unabated, *ŭnâbā'tĕd,* a. no disminuído;

unable, *ŭnā'bl,* a. incapaz.   [cabal.

unaccommodating, *ŭnâkkŏm'mŏdātĭng,*
a. inconveniente.   [sin acompañamiento.

unaccompanied, *ŭnâkkŭm'pânĭd,* a. solo,

unaccomplished, *ŭnâkkŏm'plĭsht,* a. incompleto, no acabado.

unaccountable, *ŭnâkkŏŭnt'âbl,* a. inexplicable, extraño.

unaccountably, —*ĭ,* ad. extrañamente.

unaccustomed, *ănăkkŭs'tŭmd*, a. desacostumbrado, desusado.

unacknowledged, *ănăknŏl'ějd*, a. desconocido; negado, [cido; ignorado.

unacquainted, *ănăkkwănt'ĕd*, a. desconoudorned, *ănădŏrnd'*, a. sin adorno.

unadulterated, *ănădŭl'tărātĕd*, a. genuino, puro; sin mezcla.

unaffected, *ănăffĕkt'ĕd*, a. sincero, sin afectación; -ly, ad. naturalmente.

unaided, *ănăd'ĕd*, a. sin ayuda.

unaltered, *ănăl'tărd*, a. invariado.

unambitious, *ănămbish'ŭs*, a. no ambicioso. [f.

unanimity, *ănănim'itĕ*, s. unanimidad.

unanimous, *ănăn'imŭs*, a. unánime; -ly, ad. unánimemente.

unanswerable, *ănăn'sŭrăbl*, a. incontrovertible, incontestable.

unanswered, *ănăn'sŭrd*, a. no respondido.

unapproachable, *ănăpprōtsh'ăbl*, a. inaccesible.

unarmed, *ănărmd'*, a. inerme, desarmado.

unasked, *ănăskt'*, a. no llamado, no convidado. [ser asaltado.

unassailable, *ănăssăl'ăbl*, a. incapaz de

unassisted, *ănăssist'ĕd*, a. sin socorro, sin auxilio, sin ayuda.

unassuming, *ănăssūm'ing*, a. nada presuntuoso, modesto. [disponible.

unattached, *ănătătsht'*, a. independiente;

unattainable, *ănăttăn'ăbl*, a. inasequible.

unattempted, *ănăttĕm'tĕd*, a. no experimentado; no intentado.

unattended, *ănăttĕnd'ĕd*, a. sin comitiva.

unavailing, *ănăvăl'ing*, a. inútil, vano, infructuoso.

unavoidable, *ănăvōĭd'ăbl*, a. inevitable.

unavoidably, *-ĕ*, ad. inevitablemente.

unaware, *ănăwăr'*, a. desatento.

unawares, *-z*, ad. inadvertidamente; de improviso.

unbar, *ănbăr'*, v. a. desatrancar.

unbearable, *ănbăr'ăbl*, a. intolerable.

unbecoming, *ănbĕkŭm'ing*, a. indecente, indecoroso; -ly, ad. indecentemente.

unbelief, *ănbĕlēf'*, s. incredulidad, f.

unbeliever, *ănbĕlēv'ŭr*, s. incrédulo, infiel, m.

unbend, *ănbĕnd'*, v. a. aflojar. [fiel, m.

unbending, *-ing*, a. inflexible.

unbiassed, *ănbī'ăst*, a. exento de preocupaciones. [pontáneo.

unbidden, *ănbĭd'dn*, a. no convidado; espontáneo.

unbind, *ănbīnd'*, v. a. desatar.

unbleached, *ănblētsht'*, a. no blanqueado.

unblemished, *ănblĕm'isht*, a. sin mancha, sin tacha, irreprensible.

unblest, *ănblĕst'*, a. maldito; desgraciado.

unblushing, *ănblŭsh'ing*, a. impudente.

unbolt, *ănbōlt'*, v. a. desatrancar.

unborn, *ănbŏrn'*, a. que no ha nacido aun.

unbosom, *ănbŏz'ŭm*, v. a. abrir su pecho á alguno. [desatado.

unbound, *ănbŏŭnd'*, a. rio encuadernado.

unbounded, *-ĕd*, a. infinito; ilimitado; -ly, ad. ilimitadamente.

unbred, *ănbrĕd'*, a. descortés, impolítico.

unbridle, *ănbrī'dl*, v. a. desenfrenar; -d, a. desenfrenado, licencioso.

unbroken, *ănbrō'kn*, a. indómito; entero.

unbuckle, *ănbŭk'kl*, v. a. deshebillar.

unburden, *ănbŭr'dn*, v. a. descargar, aliunburied, *ănbĕr'ĕd*, a. insepulto. [viar.

unbutton, *ănbŭt'tn*, v. a. desabotonar.

uncalled for, *ănkăld' fŏr*, a. de por su propia voluntad.

uncared for, *ănkărd' fŏr*, a. descuidado.

unceasing, *ănsēs'ing*, a. sin cesar, continuo.

uncertain, *ănsŭrt'ĕn*, a. incierto, dudoso.

uncertainty, *-tĕ*, s. incertidumbre, f.

unchangeable, *ăntshănj'ăbl*, a. inmutable. [dad, f.

unchangeableness, *-nĕs*, s. inmutabili-

unchangeably, *-ĕ*, ad. inmutablemente.

unchanged, *ăntshănjd'*, a. no alterado.

unchanging, *ăntshănj'ing*, a. inalterable, inmutable. [tivo, duro.

uncharitable, *ăntshăr'ĭtăbl*, a. nada cari-

uncharitableness, *-nĕs*, s. falta de caridad, dureza, f.

unchecked, *ăntshĕkt'*, a. desenfrenado.

unchristian, *ănkrĭst'yăn*, a. indigno de un cristiano.

uncivil, *ănsĭv'il*, a. grosero, descortés.

uncivilized, *-īzd*, a. tosco, salvaje, no civilizado.

unclad, *ănklăd'*, a. sin vestido, desnudo.

unclaimed, *ănklāmd'*, a. sin reclamación.

uncle, *ăng'kl*, s. tío; (cant) prendero, m.

unclean, *ănklēn'*, a. inmundo, puerco, sucio. [-nĕs, s. suciedad, f.; impureza, f.

uncleanness, *-nĕs*, s. uncleanliness.

unclose, *ănklōz'*, v. a. abrir; descubrir, revelar. [sereno.

unclouded, *ănklŏŭd'ĕd*, a. libre de nubes.

uncock, *ănkŏk'*, v. a. desarmar una escopeta.

uncoil, *ănkŏĭl'*, v. a. desarrollar.

uncombed, *ănkōmd'*, a. no peinado.

uncomely, *ănkŭm'lĕ*, a. indecente; feo; desagradable.

uncomfortable, *ănkŭm'fŭrtăbl*, a. desconsolado; desagradable, descómodo.

uncomfortableness, *-nĕs*, s. descomodidad, f.; desconsuelo, m.

uncomfortably, *-ĕ*, ad. desconsoladamente; incómodamente; tristemente.

uncommon, *ănkŏm'mŏn*, a. raro, extraordinario; -ly, ad. extraordinariamente; raramente.

uncommonness, *-nĕs*, s. raridad, f.

uncompromising, *ănkŏm'prŏmīzing*, a. irreconciliable. [descuido, m.

unconcern, *ănkŏnsŭrn'*, s. indiferencia, f.

unconcerned, *-d*, a. indiferente; -ly, ad. con indiferencia. [condiciones, absoluto.

unconditional, *ănkŏndĭsh'ăndl*, a. sin

unconfined, *ănkŏnfīnd'*, a. libre, ilimitado.

unconfirmed, *ănkŏnfŭrmd'*, a. irresoluto, sin resolución, indeciso.

unconnected, *ănkŏnnĕk'tĕd*, a. inconexo.

unconquerable, *ănkŏng'kŭrăbl*, a. invencible, insuperable.

unconscionable, *ănkŏn'shăndbl*, a. desrazonable; -bly, ad. sin razón.

unconscious,_ănkŏn'shŭs,_ a. inconciente; —ly, ad. sin conocimiento ó conciencia de las cosas. [luntario.

unconstrained,_ănkŏnstrānd'_, a. libre, voluntario.

uncontrolled,_ănkŏntrōld'_, a. desenfrenado, irresistible. [vincente.

unconvincing,_ănkŏnvĭn'sĭng_, a. no convincente.

uncork,_ănkŏrk'_, v. a. destapar.

uncorrected,_ănkŏrrĕk'tĕd_, a. incorrecto, no corregido. [íntegro.

uncorrupted,_ănkŏrrŭp'tĕd_, a. incorrupto, íntegro.

uncouple,_ănkŭp'l_, v. a. desatraillar.

uncouth,_ănkōth'_, a. extraño; grosero; —ly, ad. groseramente.

uncouthness,_—nĕs_, s. extrañeza, rareza, f.

uncover,_ănkŭv'ŭr_, v. a. descubrir.

uncrown,_ănkrŏŭn'_, v. a. destronar.

unction,_ăngk'shŭn_, s. unción, f.

unctuous,_ăngk'tŭŭs_, a. untuoso.

uncultivated,_ănkŭl'tĭvātĕd_, a. inculto.

uncurl,_ănkŭrl'_, v. a. desenrizar el pelo.

uncut,_ănkŭt'_, a. no cortado, entero.

undamaged,_ăndăm'ĭjd_, a. ileso, libre de daño.

undaunted,_ăndănt'ĕd_, a. intrépido.

undeceive,_ăndēsēv'_, v. a. desengañar.

undecided,_ăndēsī'dĕd_, a. indeciso.

undefiled,_ăndēfīld'_, a. impoluto, puro.

undeniable,_ăndēnī'ăbl_, a. innegable, incontestable; —bly, ad. indubitablemente.

under,_ăn'dŭr_, pr. &. ad. debajo, inferior á; soto; menos que.

underbid,_—bĭd'_, v. a. ofrecer por alguna cosa menos de lo que vale.

under-clerk,_—klŭrk_, s. sotosecretario, m.

underclothing,_—klōthĭng_, s. vestido de debajo, m.

undercut,_—kŭt_, s. solomo, m. [debajo, m.

underdone,_—dŭn'_, a. poco cocido.

undergo,_—gō'_, v. a. sufrir; sostener.

undergraduate,_—grăd'ŭāt_, s. estudiante que no ha recibido ningún grado, m.

underground,_—grŏŭnd_, s. soterráneo, m.

undergrowth,_—grōth_, s. soto, monte tallar, m. [—, a. secreto, clandestino.

underhand,_—hănd'_, ad. clandestinamente.

underlet,_—lĕt'_, v. a. subarrendar.

underlie,_—lī'_, v. n. estar debajo.

underline,_—lĭn'_, v. a. rayar las palabras.

underling,_—lĭng_, s. agente inferior, m.; hombre vil, m.

undermine,_—mīn'_, v. a. minar. [brevil, m.

undermost,_—mōst_, a. ínfimo.

underneath,_—nēth_, ad. debajo.

under-part,_—pärt_, s. parte inferior, f.

underrate,_—rāt'_, v. a. despreciar.

under-secretary,_—sĕkrĕtărĭ_, s. subsecretario, m. [(que otro).

undersell,_—sĕl'_, v. a. vender por menos

understand,_—stănd'_, v. a. entender, comprender.

understanding,_—stănd'ĭng_, s. entendimiento, m.; inteligencia, f.; conocimiento, m.; correspondencia, f.; —, a. inteligente, perito. [ponder.

undertake,_—tāk'_, v. a. & n. emprender, responder.

undertaker,_—tāk'ŭr_, s. empresario, m.; asentista, m. [peño, m.

undertaking,_—tāk'ĭng_, s. empresa, f.; empeño, m.

undertone,_—tōn_, s. ton bajo, m.

undervalue,_—văl'ū_, v. a. despreciar; apreciar en menos. [m.

undervaluer,_—văl'ūŭr_, s. menospreciador.

underwood,_—wŭd_, s. monte bajo, m.

underwork,_—wŭrk'_, v. a. suplantar; —, ăn'dŭrwŭrk, s. menudencias, f. pl.

underwrite,_—rīt'_, v. a. suscribir; asegurar contra los riesgos del mar.

undeserved,_ăndēzŭrvd'_, a. no merecido; —ly, ad. sin habérlo merecido.

undeserving,_ăndēzŭr'vĭng_, a. indigno de.

undesigned,_ăndēzīnd'_, a. involuntario, hecho sin intención. [cillo.

undesigning,_ăndēzīn'ĭng_, a. sincero, sencillo.

undesirable,_ăndēzī'răbl_, a. lo que no es deseable. [minado, indeciso.

undetermined,_ăndētŭr'mĭnd_, a. indeterminado, indeciso.

undeviating,_ăndēvĭātĭng_, a. regular, firme, estable.

undigested,_ăndĭjes'tĕd_, a. indigesto.

undiminished,_ăndĭmĭn'ĭsht_, a. entero, no disminuido.

undiscerning,_ăndĭszŭrn'ĭng_, a. falto de discernimiento. [plinado.

undisciplined,_ăndĭs'ĭplĭnd_, a. indisciplinado.

undisguised,_ăndĭsgīzd'_, a. sin disfraz, cándido, sincero.

undismayed,_ăndĭsmād'_, a. intrépido.

undisputed,_ăndĭspū'tĕd_, a. incontestable.

undisturbed,_ăndĭstŭrbd'_, a. quieto, tranquilo.

undivided,_ăndĭvī'dĕd_, a. indiviso, entero.

undo,_ăndō'_, v. a. deshacer, desatar.

undoubted,_ăndŏŭt'ĕd_, a. indubitado, evidente; —ly, ad. indubitablemente.

undress,_ăndrĕs'_, v. a. desnudar; —, ăn'drĕs, s. paños menores, m. pl., ropa de casa, f.

undried,_ăndrīd'_, a. mojado. [casa, f.

undue,_ăndū'_, a. indebido; injusto.

undulate,_ăn'dŭlāt_, v. n. ondear. [f.

undulation,_ăndŭlā'shŭn_, s. undulación, f.

unduly,_ăndū'lĭ_, ad. indebidamente; ilícitamente.

undutiful,_ăndū'tĭfŭl_, a. desobediente; —ly, ad. inobedientemente. [falta de respeto, f.

undutifulness,_—nĕs_, s. desobediencia, f.;

undying,_ăndī'ĭng_, a. inmortal.

unearth,_ănŭrth'_, v. a. desenterrar.

unearthly,_—lĭ_, a. celeste.

uneasily,_ănē'zĭlĭ_, ad. inquietamente, incómodamente. [incómodo.

uneasy,_ănē'zĭ_, a. inquieto, desasosegado.

unedifying,_ănĕd'ĭfĭĭng_, a. lo que no edifica con su ejemplo. [ocioso.

unemployed,_ănĕmplōīd'_, a. desocupado.

unenlightened,_ănĕnlī'nd_, a. no iluminado. [notono, insípido.

unentertaining,_ănĕntŭrtā'nĭng_, a.

unenviable,_ănĕn'vĭăbl_, a. lo que no debe envidiarse. [(mente).

unequal,_ănē'kwŏl_, a. —ly, ad. desigual.

unequalled,_—d_, a. incomparable.

unerring,_ănŭr'rĭng_, a. —ly, ad. infalible (mente).

uneven,_ănē'vn_, a. desigual; barrancoso; impar; —ly, ad. desigualmente.

unevenness,_—nĕs_, s. desigualdad,

unexampled, ănĕgzăm′pld, a. sin ejemplo, único. [irreprensible; irrecusable.
unexceptionable, ănĕksĕp′shănăbl, a.
unexpected, ănĕkspĕk′tĕd, a. inesperado; inopinado; **-ly,** ad. de repente; inopinadamente.
unexpectedness, –nĕs, s. repentón, m.
unexplored, ănĕksplōrd′, a. ignorado, no descubierto.
unfading, ănfā′dĭng, a. inmarcesible.
unfailing, ănfā′lĭng, a. infalible, seguro.
unfair, ănfār′, a. doble, falso; injusto; **-ly,** ad. injustamente.
unfaithful, ănfāth′fŭl, a. infiel, pérfido.
unfaithfulness, –nĕs, s. infidelidad, perfidia, f. [rado.
unfaltering, ănfăl′tŭrĭng, a. firme, asegu-
unfamiliar, ănfămĭl′yăr, a. desacostumbrado, poco común.
unfashionable, ănfăsh′ănăbl, a. opuesto á la moda; **-bly,** ad. contra la moda.
unfasten, ănfăs′n, v. a. desatar, soltar, aflojar. [dable, impenetrable.
unfathomable, ănfăth′ămăbl, a. inson-
unfavourable, ănfā′vărăbl, a. no favorable. [poco favorable.
unfavourably, –lĭ, ad. de una manera
unfed, ănfĕd′, a. falto de alimento.
unfeeling, ănfēl′ĭng, a. insensible, duro de corazón.
unfeigned, ănfānd′, a. verdadero, genuino; **-ly,** ad. sinceramente.
unfelt, ănfĕlt′, a. no sentido.
unfilial, ănfĭl′ĭăl, a. indigno de un hijo.
unfinished, ănfĭn′ĭsht, a. imperfecto, no acabado.
unfit, ănfĭt′, a. desconveniente, inepto, incapaz; **-ly,** ad. impropiamente; **–,** v. a. inhabilitar. [dad, f.
unfitness, –nĕs, s. ineptitud, f.; impropie-
unfitting, –tĭng, a. desconvenible. [dar.
unfix, ănfĭks′, v. a. soltar, aflojar; liqui-
unfixed, –ĕd, a. errante, vacilante.
unfledged, ănflĕjd′, a. implume.
unfold, ănfōld′, v. a. desplegar; revelar; desencerrar.
unforeseen, ănfōrsēn′, a. imprevisto.
unforgiving, ănfōrgĭv′ĭng, a. implacable.
unfortunate, ănfōr′tănĕt, a. desafortunado, infeliz; **-ly,** ad. por desgracia, infelizmente. [mento.
unfounded, ănfŏănd′ĕd, a. sin funda-
unframed, ănfrāmd′, a. sin forma ó figura.
unfrequent, ănfrē′kwĕnt, a. raro, nada frecuente; **-ly,** ad. raramente.
unfrequented, ănfrĕkwĕnt′ĕd, a. nada frecuentado. [benevolencia, f.
unfriendliness, ănfrĕnd′lĭnĕs, s. falta de
unfriendly, ănfrĕnd′lĭ, a. nada afable.
unfruitful, ănfrŏt′fŭl, a. estéril; infructuoso. [fecundidad, f., infructuosidad, f.
unfruitfulness, –nĕs, s. esterilidad, in-
unfurl, ănfŭrl′, v. a. desplegar, extender.
unfurnished, ănfŭr′nĭsht, a. sin muebles; desprovisto.
ungainly, ăngān′lĭ, a. zafio, desmañado.
ungenerous, ănjĕn′ărŭs, a. ignoble, bajo.

ungentlemanly, ănjĕn′tlmănlĭ, a. indigno de un hombre bien criado.
unglazed, ănglāzd′, a. que no tiene vidrieras; que está sin vidriar.
ungodliness, ăngŏd′lĭnĕs, s. impiedad, f.
ungodly, ăngŏd′lĭ, a. impío.
ungovernable, ăngŭv′ărnăbl, a. indomable, ingobernable.
ungoverned, ăngŭv′ărnd, a. desgobernado, desenfrenado.
ungrammatical, ăngrămmăt′ĭkăl, a. contrario á las reglas de la gramática.
ungrateful, ăngrāt′fŭl, a. ingrato; desagradable, **-ly,** ad. ingratamente.
ungratefulness, –nĕs, s. ingratitud, f.
ungrounded, ăngrŏănd′ĕd, a. infundado.
ungrudgingly, ăngrŭj′ĭnglĕ, ad. de buena gana. [defensa; negligente.
unguarded, ăngărd′ĕd, a. sin guarda ó
unhallowed, ănhăl′lōd, a. profano.
unhand, ănhănd′, v. a. soltar las manos.
unhandsome, –săm, a. feo, falto de gracia; **-ly,** ad. sin gracia; feamente.
unhandy, ănhănd′ĕ, a. desmañado.
unhappily, ănhăp′pĭlĕ, ad. infelizmente.
unhappiness, ănhăp′pĭnĕs, s. infelicidad,
unhappy, ănhăp′pĕ, a. infeliz. [f.
unharmed, ănhārmd′, a. ileso, sano y salvo.
unhealthiness, ănhĕlth′ĭnĕs, s. insalubridad, f.; falta de salud, f.
unhealthy, ănhĕlth′ĕ, a. enfermizo.
unheard (of), ănhĕrd′ (ŏf), a. inaudito, extraño, sin ejemplo. [preciado.
unheeded, ănhēd′ĕd, a. no atendido, des-
unheedful, ănhēd′fŭl, **unheeding,** ănhēd′ĭng, a. negligente; distraído.
unhinge, ănhĭnj′, v. a. desquiciar; desordenar.
unholy, ănhōl′ĕ, a. profano, impío.
unhonoured, ănŏn′ărd, a. despreciado, no venerado.
unhook, ănhŏk′, v. a. desganchar.
unhoped (for), ănhōpd′ (fŏr), a. inesperado.
unhorse, ănhŏrs′, v. a. botar de la silla al jinete.
unhurt, ănhŭrt′, a. ileso.
unicorn, ū′nĭkŏrn, s. unicornio, m.
uniform, ū′nĭfŏrm, a. **-ly,** ad. uniforme (mente); **–,** s. uniforme, m.
uniformity, ūnĭfŏr′mĭtĕ, s. uniformidad, f.
unimaginable, ănĭmăj′ĭnăbl, a. inimaginable. [no alterado.
unimpaired, ănĭmpārd′, a. no disminuído,
unimpeachable, ănĭmpētsh′ăbl, a. incontestable. [portante.
unimportant, ănĭmpŏr′tănt, a. nada im-
uninformed, ănĭnfŏrmd′, a. ignorante.
uninhabitable, ănĭnhăb′ĭtăbl, a. uninhabitable. [desierto.
uninhabited, ănĭnhăb′ĭtĕd, a. inhabitado,
uninjured, ănĭn′jărd, a. ileso, no dañado.
uninstructed, ănĭnstrŭk′tĕd, a. ignorante, sin educación. [es instructivo.
uninstructive, ănĭnstrŭk′tĭv, a. lo que no
unintelligible, ănĭntĕl′lĭjĭbl, a. ininteligible. [teligible.
unintelligibly, –lĕ, a. de un modo inin-

unintentional, ănĭntĕn'shănăl, a. lo que se hace sin intención.   [sado.
uninterested, ănĭn'tărĕstĕd, a. desintere-
uninteresting, ănĭn'tărĕstĭng, a. poco interesante.
uninterrupted, ănĭntărrŭp'tĕd, a. sin interrupción, continuo; —ly, ad. continuamente.
uninvited, ănĭnvī'tĕd, a. no convidado.
union, ūn'yŭn (ūn'yăn), s. unión, f.
unionist, ūn'yănĭst, s. unitario, m.
unique, yūn'ēk, a. único, uno, singular.
unison, ūn'ĭsăn, s. unisonancia, f.; unisón, unit, ū'nĭt, s. unidad, f.   [m.
unitarian, ūnĭtā'rĭăn, s. unitario, m.
unite, ūnīt', v. a. & n. unir(se), juntarse.
unitedly, ūnī'tĕdlĕ, ad. unidamente, de acuerdo.   [formidad, f.
unity, ū'nĭtĕ, s. unidad, concordia, con-
universal, ūnĭvăr'săl, a. —ly, ad. universal(mente).   [lidad, f.
universality, ūnĭvărsăl'ĭtĕ, s. universa-
universe, ū'nĭvărs, s, universo, m.
university, ūnĭvăr'sĭtĕ, s. universidad, f.
unjust, ŭnjŭst', a. injusto; —ly, ad. injustamente.
unjustifiable, ŭnjŭs'tĭfīăbl, a. indisculpable; —bly, ad. inexcusablemente.
unkempt, ŭnkĕmt', a. (fig.) tosco, impolítico.
unkind, ŭnkīnd', a. nada cortés; —ly, a. & ad poco favorable; ásperamente.
unkindness, —nĕs, s. desafecto, m.; malignidad, f.
unknowingly, ŭnnō'ĭnglĕ, ad. sin saberlo.
unknown, ŭnnōn', a. incógnito.   [lazar.
unlace, ŭnlās', v. a. desabrochar; desen-
unlawful, ŭnlô'făl, a. ilegítimo, ilícito; —ly, ad. ilegítimamente.
unlawfulness, —nĕs, s. ilegalidad, f.
unlearn, ŭnlŭrn', v. a. desaprender.
unlearned, —ĕd, a. indocto.
unleavened, ŭnlĕv'nd, a. ázimo.
unless, ŭnlĕs', c. á menos que, si no.
unlettered, ŭnlĕt'tŭrd, a. iliterato.
unlicensed, ŭnlī'sĕnst, a. sin licencia.
unlike, ŭnlīk', unlikely, —lĕ, a. diferente, disímil; improbable; inverosímil; —ly, ad. improbablemente.   [f.
unlikelihood, —līhŭd, s. inverisimilitud.
unlimited, ŭnlĭm'ĭtĕd, á. ilimitado; —ly, ad. ilimitadamente.
unload, ŭnlōd', v. a. descargar.   [dura.
unlock, ŭnlŏk', v. a. abrir alguna cerra-
unlooked (for), ŭnlŏkt' (fŏr), a. inopinado.
unloose, ŭnlŏs', v. a. desatar.   [mente.
unluckily, ŭnlŭk'ĭlĕ, ad. desafortunada-
unlucky, ŭntăk'ĕ, a. desafortunado; si-
unmake, ŭnmāk', v. a. deshacer.   [niestro.
unman, ŭnmăn', v. a. afeminar; castrar, capar; desarmar.   [jable, intratable.
unmanageable, ŭnmăn' djăbl, a. inmane-
unmanly, ŭnmăn'lĕ, a. inhumano; afeminado.   [tal, grosero.
unmannered, ŭnmăn'nŭrd, a. rudo, bru-
unmannerliness, ŭnmăn'nărlĭnĕs, s. mala crianza, descortesía, f.
unmannerly, ŭnmăn'nărlĕ, a. malcriado, descortés.

unmarried, ŭnmăr'rĭd, a. soltero; soltera.
unmarry, ŭnmăr'rĕ, v. a. divorciar, descasar.
unmask, ŭnmăsk', v. a. quitar la máscara.
unmeaning, ŭnmēn'ĭng, a. insignificativo.
unmentionable, ŭnmĕn'shănăbl, a. que no se puede mencionar.
unmerited, ŭnmĕr'ĭtĕd, a. desmerecido.
unmindful, ŭnmīnd'fŭl, a. olvidadizo, negligente.   [—bly, ad. con evidencia.
unmistakable, ŭnmĭstāk'ăbl, a. evidente;
unmoved, ŭnmŏvd', a. inmoto, firme.
unnatural, ŭnnăt'ŭrăl, a. contrario á las leyes de la naturaleza; —ly, ad. contra la naturaleza.   [cesidad; inútilmente.
unnecessarily, ŭnnĕs'sĕsărĭlĕ, ad. sin ne-
unnecessary, ŭnnĕs'sĕsărĕ, a. inútil, no necesario.   [con sus vecinos; descortés.
unneighbourly, ŭnnā'bărlĕ, a. poco atento
unnerve, ŭnnărv', v. a. enervar.
unnoticed, ŭnnō'tĭst, a. no observado.
unnumbered, ŭnnăm'bŭrd, a. innumerable.
unobserved, ŭnŏbzărvd', a. no observado.
unobtainable, ŭnŏbtān'ăbl, a. lo que no puede obtenerse.
unobtrusive, ŭnŏbtrŏ'sĭv, a. modesto.
unoccupied, ŭnŏk'kŭpīd, a. desocupado.
unoffending, ŭnŏffĕnd'ĭng, a. sencillo, inocente.
unorthodox, ŭnŏr'thŏdŏks, a. heterodoxo.
unpack, ŭnpăk', v. a. desempaquetar; desenvolver.
unpaid, ŭnpād', a. no pagado.
unpalatable, ŭnpăl'ătăbl, a. desabrido.
unparalleled, ŭnpăr'ăllĕld, a. sin paralelo; sin par.   [sible.
unpardonable, ŭnpăr'dănăbl, a. irremi-
unpardonably, —ĕ, ad. sin perdón.
unparliamentary, ŭnpărlĭmĕn'tărĕ, a. contrario á las reglas del parlamento.
unpeople, ŭnpē'pl, v. a. despoblar.
unperceived, ŭnpărsēvd', a. no percibido.
unpitying, ŭnpĭt'ĭng, a. incompasivo.
unpleasant, ŭnplĕz'ănt, a. —ly, ad. desagradable(ment.).
unpleasantness, —nĕs, s. desagrado, m.
unpolished, ŭnpŏl'ĭsht, a. que no está pulido; rudo, grosero.   [maculado.
unpolluted, ŭnpŏllŭ'tĕd, a. impoluto, inmaculado.
unpopular, ŭnpŏp'ŭlăr, a. no popular.
unpractised, ŭnprăk'tĭst, a. inexperto, no versado.   [ejemplo.
unprecedented, ŭnprĕg'ĕdĕntĕd, a. sin
unprejudiced, ŭnprĕj'ŏdĭst, a. no preocupado.
unpremeditated, ŭnprĕmĕd'ĭtātĕd, a. inopinado; no premeditado, no pensado con anterioridad.
unprepared, ŭnprĕpārd', a. no preparado.
unpretending, ŭnprĕtĕnd'ĭng, a. el que no tiene pretensiones.
unprincipled, ŭnprĭn'sĭpld, a. el que no tiene principios.
unproductive, ŭnprŏdŭk'tĭv, a. estéril.
unprofitable, ŭnprŏf'ĭtăbl, a. inútil, vano, que para nada sirve.

unprofitableness, –nĕs, s. inutilidad, f.
unprofitably, –ĕ, ad. inútilmente, sin provecho. [no favorable.
unpropitious, ŭnprŏpĭsh'ŭs, a. infausto,
unprotected, ŭnprŏtĕkt'ĕd, a. desvalido, sin protección.
unprovided, ŭnprŏvī'dĕd, a. desprovisto.
unpublished, ŭnpŭb'lĭsht, a. secreto, oculto, no publicado; inédito.
unpunctual, ŭnpŭngk'tūăl, a. inexacto.
unpunished, ŭnpŭn'ĭsht, a. impune.
unquenchable, ŭnkwĕnsh'ăbl, a. inextinguible.
unquestionable, ŭnkwĕst'yŏnăbl, a. indubitable, indisputable; –bly, ad. sin duda, sin disputa.
unquestioned, ŭnkwĕst'yŏnd, a. incontestable, no preguntado.
unquiet, ŭnkwī'ĕt, a. inquieto, agitado.
unravel, ŭnrăv'l, v. a. desenredar; desbastar.
unread, ŭnrĕd', a. no leído; ignorante.
unready, –ĕ, a. desprevenido, no preparado; pesado.
unreal, ŭnrē'ăl, a. sin realidad.
unreasonable, ŭnrē'znăbl, a. desrazonable.
unreasonableness, –nĕs, s. sinrazón, f.
unreasonably, –ĕ, ad. irracionalmente.
unregarded, ŭnrĕgărd'ĕd, a. descuidado; despreciado. [inflexible.
unrelenting, ŭnrĕlĕnt'ĭng, a. incompasivo,
unremitting, ŭnrĕmĭt'ĭng, a. constante, incansable.
unrepentant, ŭnrĕpĕnt'ănt, unrepenting, ŭnrĕpĕnt'ĭng, a. impenitente.
unreserved, ŭnrĕzŭrvd', a. sin restricción; franco; –ly, ad. abiertamente. [cia.
unresisting, ŭnrĕzĭst'ĭng, a. sin resistencia.
unrestrained, ŭnrĕstrānd', a. desenfrenado; ilimitado.
unriddle, ŭnrĭd'dl, v. a. desatar un enigma.
unrighteous, ŭnrīt'yŭs, a. injusto; –ly, ad. inicuamente. [justicia, f.
unrighteousness, –nĕs, s. iniquidad, injusticia, f.
unripe(ned), ŭnrīp'(nd), a. inmaturo.
unripeness, –nĕs, s. falta de madurez, f.
unrivalled, ŭnrī'văld, a. sin rival, sin igual.
unroll, ŭnrōl', v. a. desarrollar. [igual.
unroof, ŭnrōf', v. a. destechar.
unruffle, ŭnrŭf'fl, v. n. calmar.
unruliness, ŭnrō'lĭnĕs, s. turbulencia, f.; desenfreno, m. [glado.
unruly, ŭnrō'lĕ, a. desenfrenado, desarreglado.
unsaddle, ŭnsăd'dl, v. a. desensillar.
unsafe, ŭnsāf', a. no seguro, peligroso; –ly, ad. peligrosamente.
unsaleable, ŭnsāl'ăbl, a. invendible.
unsatisfactory, ŭnsătĭsfăk'tūrĕ, a. lo que no satisface ó no convence. [harto.
unsatisfied, ŭnsăt'ĭsfīd, a. descontento; no
unsavouriness, ŭnsā'vŭrĭnĕs, s. insipidez, f. [sípido.
unsavoury, ŭnsā'vŭrĕ, a. desabrido, inschooled, ŭnskōld', a. indocto.
unscrew, ŭnskrō', v. a. desentornillar.
unseasonable, ŭnsē'znăbl, a. intempestivo, fuera de propósito. [m.
unseasonableness, –nĕs, s. despropósito,

unseasonably, –ĕ, ad. fuera de sazón.
unseat, ŭnsēt', v. a. tomar el asiento de otra persona. [f.
unseemliness, ŭnsēm'lĭnĕs, s. indecencia,
unseemly, ŭnsēm'lĕ, a. indecente. [visto.
unseen, ŭnsēn', a. invisible; que no se ha
unselfish, ŭnsĕlf'ĭsh, a. desinteresado.
unsettle, ŭnsĕt'tl, v. a. perturbar; hacer incierta alguna cosa.
unsettled, –d, a. voluble, inconstante, irresuelto; sin residencia fija. [moble.
unshaken, ŭnshā'kn, a. firme, estable, insheath, ŭnshēth', v. a. desenvainar.
unsheltered, ŭnshĕl'tŭrd, a. desvalido.
unship, ŭnshĭp', v. a. desembarcar.
unshod, ŭnshŏd', a. descalzo; desherrado.
unshorn, ŭnshŏrn', a. que no ha sido esquilado.
unshrinking, ŭnshrĭngk'ĭng, a. intrépido.
unsightliness, ŭnsīt'lĭnĕs, s. fealdad, deformidad, f. [vista.
unsightly, ŭnsīt'lĕ, a. desagradable á la
unskilful, ŭnskĭl'fŭl, a. inhábil, poco mañoso; –ly, ad. con poca maña.
unskilfulness, –nĕs, s. falta de maña, f.
unskilled, ŭnskĭld', a. inhábil.
unsociable, ŭnsō'shăbl, a. insociable, intratable, huraño.
unsold, ŭnsōld', a. no vendido.
unsoldierlike, ŭnsōl'jŭrlīk, unsoldierly, –lĕ, a. indigno de un soldado.
unsought, ŭnsăt', a. hallado sin buscarlo.
unsound, ŭnsōnd', a. falto de salud; erróneo; podrido. [de solidez, f.
unsoundness, –nĕs, s. heterodoxia, f.; falta
unsparing, ŭnspār'ĭng, a. liberal, generoso. [decible.
unspeakable, ŭnspēk'ăbl, a. inefable, inunspeakably, –ĕ, ad. indeciblemente.
unstable, ŭnstā'bl, a. instable, inconstante.
unsteadily, ŭnstĕd'ĭlĕ, ad. ligeramente, inconstantemente. [inconstancia, f.
unsteadiness, ŭnstĕd'ĭnĕs, s. ligereza,
unsteady, ŭnstĕd'ĕ, a. voluble, inconstante.
unstruck, ŭnstrŭk', a. impávido.
unstudied, ŭnstŭd'ĭd, a. no estudiado; no premeditado.
unsubdued, ŭnsŭbdūd', a. indomado.
unsubstantial, ŭnsŭbstăn'shăl, a. imaginario; impalpable.
unsuccessful, ŭnsŭksĕs'fŭl, a. infeliz, desafortunado; –ly, ad. infelizmente.
unsuitable, ŭnsūt'ăbl, a. desproporcionado, incongruente.
unsullied, ŭnsŭl'ĭd, a. inmaculado, puro.
untamable, ŭntā'măbl, a. indomable.
untamed, ŭntāmd', a. indómito, indomado, no domado.
untaught, ŭntăt', a. ignorante; novato.
unteachable, ŭntētsh'ăbl, a. incapaz de ser enseñado.
untenable, ŭntĕn'ăbl, a. insostenible.
untenanted, ŭntĕn'ăntĕd, a. desarrendado.
unthankful, ŭnthănk'fŭl, a. ingrato; –ly, ad. ingratamente.
unthankfulness, –nĕs, s. ingratitud, f.
unthinking, ŭnthĭngk'ĭng, a. descuidado, indiscreto.

13*

unthought(of), *ănthặt' (ŏf)*, a. impensado.

untidiness, *ănt' dĭnĕs*, s. desaliño, m.

untidy, *ănt' dĕ*, a. sucio.

untie, *ăntī'*, v. a. desatar, deshacer, soltar.

until, *ăntĭl'*, ad. hasta; hasta que.

untimely, *ăntīm' lĕ*, a. intempestivo, que no está en sazón; —ly, ad. intempestivamente.

untiring, *ăntīr' ĭng*, a. incansable.

unto, *ăn' tŏ*, pr. á, para en.

untold, *ăntōld'*, a. que no se ha referido, que no se ha dicho. [sido tocado.

untouched, *ăntŭtsht'*, a. intacto, que no ha

untoward, *ăntō' ărd*, a. testarudo, desmañado; siniestro, adverso; —ly, ad. indócilmente; con poca maña; fatalmente.

untravelled, *ăntrăv' ĕld*, a. no frecuentado de pasajeros.

untried, *ăntrīd'*, a. no ensayado ó probado.

untrod(den), *ăntrŏd' (n)*, a. lo que no ha sido pisado. [tranquilo.

untroubled, *ăntrŭb' ld*, a. no perturbado,

untrue, *ăntrō'*, a. falso; pérfido.

untruly, *ăntrō' lĕ*, ad. falsamente.

untrustworthy, *ăntrŭst' wŭrthĕ*, a. indigno de la confianza.

untruth, *ăntrŏth'*, s. falsedad, mentira, f.

untutored, *ăntū' tŭrd*, a. mal educado; no instruido. [sólito.

unused, *ănūzd'*, a. inusitado, no usado; in-

unusual, *ănū' zhūăl*, a. inusitado, raro; —ly, ad. inusitadamente, raramente.

unutterable, *ănŭt' tŭrăbl*, a. inefable.

unvaried, *ănvā' rĭd*, a. invariado.

unvarying, *ănvā' rĭng*, a. lo que no varía.

unveil, *ănvāl'*, v. n. quitar el velo, descubrir. [sado.

unversed, *ănvŭrst'*, a. inexperto, no ver-

unwarrantable, *ănwŏr' răntăbl*, a. indisculpable. [no asegurado.

unwarranted, *ănwŏr' răntĕd*, a. incierto,

unwary, *ănwā' rĕ*, a. incauto, imprudente.

unwelcome, *ănwĕl' kăm*, a. desagradable, importuno.

unwell, *ănwĕl'*, a. enfermizo, malo.

unwholesome, *ănhōl' săm*, a. malsano, insalubre.

unwieldy, *ănwēl' dĕ*, a. pesado.

unwilling, *ănwĭl' ĭng*, a. desinclinado; —ly, ad. de mala gana. [nancia, f.

unwillingness, *—nĕs*, s. mala gana, repug-

unwind, *ănwīnd'*, v. a. desenredar, desenmarañar.

unwise, *ănvīz'*, a. imprudente.

unwittingly, *ănwĭt' tĭnglĕ*, ad. sin saber.

unwonted, *ănwŏn' tĕd*, a. insólito.

unworthily, *ănwŭr' thĭlĕ*, ad. indignamente. [dad, bajeza, f.

unworthiness, *ănwŭr' thĭnĕs*, s. indigni-

unworthy, *ănwŭr' thĕ*, a. indigno; vil.

unyielding, *ănyēld' ĭng*, a. inflexible, reacio.

unyoke, *ănyōk'*, v. a. desuncir. [reacio.

up, *ăp*, ad. arriba, en lo alto; levantado; —, pr. hacia; hasta; — ! ¡arriba ! — and down, ad. acá y allá, arriba y abajo.

upbear, *—bār'*, v. a. sostener en alto.

upbraid, *—brād'*, v. a. echar en cara, vituperar. [convención.

upbraidingly, *—ĭnglĕ*, ad. por vía de re-

upheaval, *ăphē' văl*, s. alzamiento, m.

uphill, *—hĭl*, a. difícil, penoso; —, s. subida, f. [tener, apoyar, proteger.

uphold, *—hōld'*, v. n. levantar en alto; sostener, apoyar, proteger.

upholder, *—ăr*, s. fautor, m.; sustentáculo, apoyo, m.

upholsterer, *—hōl' stŭrăr*, s. tapicero, m.

upland, *ăp' lănd*, s. país montañoso, m.; —, a. alto, elevado.

uplift, *—lĭft'*, v. a. levantar en alto.

upon, *ăpŏn'*, pr. sobre, encima, á, por.

upper, *ăp' pŭr*, a. superior; más elevado.

upper-hand, (fig.) *—hănd*, s. superioridad, f. [premo; to be —, predominar.

uppermost, *—mōst*, a. lo más alto, supremo.

uppish, *ăp' pĭsh*, a. engreído, altivo.

upright, *ăp' rīt*, a. derecho, perpendicular, recto; puesto en pie; equitativo; —ly, ad. perpendicularmente; derechamente, rectamente; sinceramente.

uprightness, *—rītnĕs*, s. elevación perpendicular, f.; rectitud, probidad, f.

uproar, *ăp' rōr*, s. tumulto, alboroto, m.

uproot, *—rōt'*, v. a. desarraigar.

upset, *—sĕt'*, v. a. (vulg.) trastornar.

upshot, *ăp' shŏt*, s. remate, m.; fin, m.; conclusión, f. [abajo.

upside-down, *—sīddŏn*, ad. de arriba

upstart, *—stărt*, s. medrado, m.

upward, *—wărd*, a. lo que se dirige hacia arriba; —s, ad. hacia arriba.

uptrain, *ăp' trăn*, s. (rail.) tren ascendente, m., el que marcha al interior en dirección de la capital.

urban, *ŭr' băn*, a. urbano.

urbanity, *ŭrbăn' tĕ*, s. urbanidad, f.

urchin, *ŭr' tshĭn*, s. erizo, m.

urethra, *ŭrē' thră*, s. uretra, f.

urge, *ŭrj*, v. a. & n. incitar, hurgar; activar; irritar; urgir.

urgency, *—ĕnsĕ*, s. urgencia, f.

urgent, *—ĕnt*, a. urgente; —ly, ad. instantemente. [mente.

urinal, *ū' rĭnăl*, s. orinal, m.

urinary, *ū' rĭnărĕ*, a. urinario.

urine, *ū' rĭn*, s. orina, f.

urn, *ŭrn*, s. urna, f.

us, *ŭs*, pn. nos; nosotros.

usable, *ū' zăbl*, a. apto, hábil.

usage, *ū' zdj*, s. tratamiento, m.; uso, m.

usance, *ū' zăns*, s. uso, m.

use, *ūs*, s. uso, m.; servicio, m.; utilidad, práctica, f.; —, v. a. & n. usar, emplear, servirse; acostumbrar; tratar; practicar; soler.

useful, *—fŭl*, a. —ly, ad. útil(mente).

usefulness, *—fŭlnĕs*, s. utilidad, f.

useless, *—lĕs*, a. inútil; —ly, ad. inútilmente.

uselessness, *—lĕsnĕs*, s. inutilidad, f.

usher, *ăsh' ŭr*, s. ujier, m.; sotomaestro, m.; —, v. a. introducir; anunciar.

usual, *ū' zhŭăl*, a. usual, común, usado; —ly, ad. usualmente, ordinariamente.

usurer, *ū' zhŭrăr*, s. usurero, m.

usurious, *ūzhō' rĭŭs*, a. usurario.

usurp, *ūzŭrp'*, v. a. usurpar.

usurpation, *ūzŭrpā' shŭn*, s. usurpación, f.

usury, *ü'zhŭrĕ,* s. usura, f.
utensil, *üten'sil,* s. utensilio, m.
uterine, *ü'tĕrĭn,* a. uterino.
utilise, *ü'tĭlīz,* v. a. utilizar.
utility, *ütĭl'ĭtĕ,* s. utilidad, f.
utmost, *ŭt'mōst,* a. extremo, sumo; último.
utter, *ŭt'tŭr,* a. exterior; todo; extremo; entero; —, v. a. proferir; expresar; publicar. [presión, f.; venta, f.
utterance, *ŭt'tŭrăns,* s. prolación, habla, expresión, f.
utterly, *ŭt'tŭrlĕ,* ad. enteramente, del todo.
uvula, *ü'vülā,* s. gallillo, m.
uxorious, *ŭgzō'rĭŭs,* a. gurrumino; **—ly,** ad. con gurrumina.

V.

vacancy, *vā'kănsĕ,* s. vacío, m.; vacante, m.; vacación, f. [vacante.
vacant, *vā'kănt,* a. vacío; desocupado; [vacante.
vacate, *vākāt',* v. a. anular, invalidar.
vacation, *vākā'shūn,* s. vacación, f.
vaccinate, *vāk'sĭnāt,* v. a. vacunar.
vaccination, *vāksĭnā'shūn,* s. vacunación, f.
vacillate, *vās'ĭllāt,* v. n. vacilar. [f.
vacillation, *vāsĭllā'shūn,* s. vaivén, m.
vacuity, *vākū'ĭtĕ,* s. vacuidad, f.
vacuous, *vāk'ūūs,* a. vacío.
vacuum, *vāk'ūm,* s. vacuo, m.
vagabond, *vāg'ăbŏnd,* a. vagabundo; —, s. vagamundo, m. [vagancia, f.
vagary, *vāgā'rĕ,* s. capricho, m.; extravagancia, f.
vagrancy, *vā'grănsĕ,* s. tuna, f.
vagrant, *vā'grănt,* a. vagabundo.
vague, *vāg,* a. vago; **—ly,** ad. vagamente.
vails, *vālz,* s. pl. propina, f.
vain, *vān,* a. vano, inútil; vanidoso.
vainglorious, *vānglō'rĭŭs,* a. vanaglorioso.
vainglory, *vānglō'rĕ,* s. vanagloria, f.
vainly, *—lĕ,* ad. vanamente. [gada, f.
valance, *vāl'ăns,* s. cenefada de cama colvale,** *vāl,* s. (poet.) valle, m. [vale, m.
valediction, *vālĕdĭk'shūn,* s. despedida, f.
valedictory, *—tŏrĕ,* a. haciendo despedida.
valentine, *vāl'ĕntīn,* s. filipina, f., apuesta amorosa que hacen en Inglaterra, el día de 14 febrero, los jóvenes y las jóvenes entre sí.
valerian, *vālē'rĭăn,* s. (bot.) valeriana, f.
valet, *vāl'ĕt,* s. criado, m.
valetudinarian, *vālĕtūdĭnā'rĭăn,* a. valetudinario, enfermizo.
valiant, *vāl'yănt,* a. valiente, valeroso; **—ly,** ad. valientemente.
valid, *vāl'ĭd,* a. válido, fuerte.
validity, *vālĭd'ĭtĕ,* s. validación, fuerza, f.
valley, *vāl'lĕ,* s. valle, m. [con valor.
valorous, *vāl'ŏrŭs,* a. valeroso; **—ly,** ad.
valour, *vāl'ŭr,* s. valor, aliento, brío, esfuerzo, m.; fortaleza, f.
valuable, *vāl'ūābl,* a. precioso; **—s,** s. pl. cosas preciosas, f. pl.
valuation, *vālūā'shūn,* s. tasa, valuación, f.
value, *vāl'ū,* s. valor, precio, m.; —, v. a. valuar; estimar, apreciar.

valueless, *—lĕs,* a. que no vale nada.
valve, *vălv,* s. válvula, f.
vamose, *vāmōs' (vā'mōs),* v. n. (am.) escavamp,** *vāmp,* v. a. remendar. [parse.
vampire, *vām'pĭr,* s. vampiro, m.
van, *vān,* s. vanguardia, f.; abanico, m.; bieldo, m.
vandalism, *vān'dālĭzm,* s. vandalismo, m.
vane, *vān,* s. veleta, f.; (mar.) grímpola, f.
vanguard, *vān'gărd,* s. vanguardia, f.
vanilla, *vănĭl'lā,* s. vainilla, f. [aparecer.
vanish, *vān'ĭsh,* v. n. desvanecerse, desvanity,** *vān'ĭtĕ,* s. vanidad, f. [quistar.
vanquish, *văng'kwĭsh,* v. a. vencer, convanquisher,** *—ŭr,* s. vencedor, m,
vantage(-ground), *văn'tăjgrŏȗnd),* s. ventaja, f.; provecho, m.; oportunidad, f.; superioridad, f. [sípido.
vapid, *văp'ĭd,* a. exhalado, evaporado; invapidness,** *—nĕs,* s. insipidez, f.
vaporous, *văp'ŏrŭs,* a. vaporoso. [f.
vapour, *vā'pŭr,* s. vapor, m.; exhalación,
variable, *vā'rĭăbl,* a. variable.
variableness, *—nĕs,* s. instabilidad, inconstancia, f.
variably, *—ĕ,* ad. variablemente.
variance, *vā'rĭăns,* s. discordia, desavenencia, f. [danza, f.
variation, *vārĭā'shūn,* s. variación, muvaricose vein,** *vā'rĭkōs vān,* s. variz, f.
variegated, *vā'rĭĕgātĕd,* a. abigarrado.
variegation, *vārĭĕgā'shūn,* s. variedad de colores, f.
variety, *vārī'ĕtĕ,* s. variedad, f.
various, *vā'rĭŭs,* a. vario, diverso, diferente; **—ly,** ad. variamente. [barnizar.
varnish, *văr'nĭsh,* s. barniz, m.; —, v. a.
varnisher, *—ŭr,* s. embarnizador, m.
vary, *vā'rĕ,* v. a. & n. variar, diferenciar; cambiar, mudarse, discrepar.
vase, *vās,* s. vaso, m.
vassal, *văs'săl,* s. vasallo, m.
vassalage, *—āj,* s. vasallaje, m.
vast, *văst,* a. vasto; inmenso; **—ly,** ad. excesivamente.
vastness, *—nĕs,* s. vastedad, inmensidad, f.
vat, *văt,* s. tina, f.
vault, *vălt,* s. bóveda, f.; cueva, f.; caverna, f.; —, v. a. abovedar; —, v. n. voltear.
vaunt, *vānt,* v. n. jactarse, vanagloriarse.
vaunter, *—ŭr,* s. baladrón, fanfarrón, m.
veal, *vēl,* s. ternera, f.; ternero, m.
veer, *vēr,* v. n. (mar.) virar.
vegetable, *vĕj'ĕtābl,* a. vegetable; —, s. vegetal, m.; **—s,** s. pl. legumbre, f.
vegetable-garden, *—gărdn,* s. huerta, f.
vegetarian, *vĕjĕtā'rĭăn,* s. vegetariano, m.
vegetate, *vĕj'ĕtāt,* v. n. vegetar.
vegetation, *vĕjĕtā'shūn,* s. vegetación, f.
vegetative, *vĕj'ĕtātĭv,* a. vegetativo.
vehemence(cy), *vē'ĕmĕns(sĕ),* s. vehemencia, violencia, f.
vehement, *vē'ĕmĕnt,* a. vehemente, violento; **—ly,** ad. vehementemente, patéticamente.
vehicle, *vē'ĭkl,* s. vehículo, m.; carruaje, m.

veil, *vēl*, s. velo, m.; disfraz, m.; —, v. a. encubrir, ocultar.
vein, *vān*, s. vena, f.; cavidad, f.; inclinación del ingenio, f.; humor, m.
veined, -*d*, veiny, -*ē*, a. venoso; velado.
vellum, *vēl'ŭm*, s. vitela, f.
velocity, *vēlŏs'ĭtē*, s. velocidad, f.
velvet, *vēl'vĕt*, s. terciopelo, m.; —, a. hecho de terciopelo; terciopelado.
velveteen, *velvetēn'*, s. felpa, f., velludo.
velvet-pile, -*pĭl*, s. moqueta, f.   [m.
venal, *vē'nŭl*, a. venal, mercenario.
venality, *vēnăl'ĭtē*, s. venalidad, f.
vend, *vēnd*, v. a. vender por menor.
veneer, *vēnēr'*, v. a. taracear.
venerable, *vēn'ŭrŭbl*, a. venerable.
venerably, -*ē*, ad. venerablemente.
venerate, *vēn'ŭrāt*, v. a. venerar, honrar.
veneration, *vēnŭrā'shŭn*, s. veneración, f.
venereal, *vēnē'rēŭl*, a. venéreo.
vengeance, *vēn'jāns*, s. venganza, f.
venial, *vē'nĭŭl*, a. venial.
venison, *vēn'zn*, s. (carne de) venado, f.
venom, *vēn'ŏm*, s. veneno, m.
venomous, -*ŭs*, a. venenoso; -ly, ad. venenosamente.
venomousness, -*ŭsnĕs*, s. venenosidad, f.
vent, *vēnt*, s. respiradero, m.; salida, f.; venta, f.; —, v. a. dar salida; echar fuera; divulgar (un proyecto &c.); ventear.
vent-hole, -*hŏl*, s. respiradero, m.
ventilate, *vēn'tĭlāt*, v. a. ventilar; aventar; discutir.   [f.
ventilation, *vēntĭlā'shŭn*, s. ventilación, f.
ventricle, *vēn'trĭkl*, s. ventrículo, m.
ventriloquist, *vēntrĭl'ŏkwĭst*, s. ventrílocuo, m.
venture, *vēn'tŭr* (*vēn'tshŭr*), s. riesgo, m.; ventura, f.; at a —, á la aventura; —, v. n. osar, aventurarse; —, v. a. aventurar, arriesgar.
venturesome, *vēn'tŭrsŭm*, venturous, -*ŭs*, a. osado, atrevido; -ly, ad. osadamente.
venturousness, -*nĕs*, s. temeridad, f.
veracious, *vērā'shŭs*, a. veraz.
veracity, *vērăs'ĭtē*, s. veracidad, f.
verb, *vŭrb*, s. (gr.) verbo, m.
verbal, -*ŭl*, a. verbal, literal; -ly, ad. verbalmente.   [palabra.
verbatim, *vŭrbā'tĭm*, ad. palabra por verbose, *vŭrbōs'*, a. verboso.
verbosity, *vŭrbŏs'ĭtē*, s. verbosidad, f.
verdant, *vŭr'dŭnt*, a. verde.
verdict, *vŭr'dĭkt*, s. (law) veredicto, m.; dictamen, m.
verdigris, *vŭr'dĭgrēs*, s. cardenillo, verdín, f.
verdure, *vŭr'dūr*, s. verdura, f.   [m.
verge, *vŭrj*, s. vara, f.; maza, f.; borde, m.; margen, m. & f.; —, v. n. inclinarse ó doblarse hacia abajo.   [dral, n.
verger, -*ŭr*, s. pertiguero de una catedral, n.
verification, *vŭrĭfĭkā'shŭn*, s. verificación, f.
verify, *vĕr'ĭfī*, v. a. verificar.   [ción, f.
verily, *vĕr'ĭlē*, ad. en verdad.
verjuice, *vŭr'jōs*, s. agraz, m.
vermicelli, *vŭrmĭtshĕl'lē*, s.pl.fideos, m.pl.

vermicular, *vŭrmĭk'dŭr*, a. vermicular.
vermifuge, *vŭr'mĭfūj*, s. vermífugo, m.
vermilion, *vŭrmĭl'yŭn*, s. bermellón, m.; —, v. a. teñir de cinabrio.
vermin, *vŭr'mĭn*, s. bichos, m. pl.
vernacular, *vŭrnăk'ŭlŭr*, a. nativo.
vernal, *vŭr'nŭl*, a. vernal.
versatile, *vŭr'sătĭl*, a. versátil, voluble.
versatility, *vŭrsătĭl'ĭtē*, s. veleidad, f.
verse, *vŭrs*, s. verso, m.; versículo, m.
versed, -*d*, a. versado.
version, *vŭr'shŭn*, s. versión, traducción, f.
versus, *vŭr'sŭs*, pr. contra.
vertebra, *vŭr'tēbrŭ*, s. vértebra, f.
vertebral, *vŭr'tēbrŭl*, vertebrate, *vŭr'tēbrăt*, a. vertebral.
vertex, *vŭr'tĕks*, s. cenit, vértice, m.
vertical, *vŭr'tĭkŭl*, a.; -ly, ad. verticalmente.
vertigo, *vŭr'tĭgō*, s. vértigo, m.   [(mente).
very, *vĕr'ē*, a. verdadero; real; idéntico, mismo; —, ad. muy, mucho, sumamente.
vesicle, *vĕs'ĭkl*, s. vejiguela, f.
vespers, *vĕs'pŭrz*, s. pl. vísperas, f. pl.
vessel, *vĕs'sĕl*, s. vasija, f.; vaso, m.; buque, bajel, m.   [investir.
vest, *vĕst*, s. chaleco, m.; —, v. a. vestir.
vestal, *vĕs'tŭl*, s. vestal, f. (virgen).
vested, *vĕs'tĕd*, a. vestido, envestido.
vestige, *vĕs'tĭj*, s. vestigio, m.   [dura, f.
vestment, *vĕst'mĕnt*, s. vestido, m.; vestidura, f.
vestry, *vĕs'trē*, s. sacristía, f.; concejo abierto, m.   [vestidura, f.
vesture, *vĕs'tŭr* (*vĕst'tshŭr*), s. vestido, m.; vetch, *vĕtsh*, s. (bot.) alverjana, f.
veteran, *vĕt'ĕrăn*, a. & s. veterano (m.).
veterinary, *vĕt'ĕrĭnărē*, a. lo que pertenece
veto, *vē'tō*, s. veto, m.   [á la veterinaria.
vex, *vĕks*, v. a. vejar, molestar.
vexation, -*ĭshŭn*, s. vejación, molestia, f.
vexatious, -*ĭshŭs*, a. penoso, molesto, enfadoso; -ly, ad. penosamente.
viaduct, *vī'ădŭkt*, s. viaducto, m.
vial, *vī'ŭl*, s. redoma, ampolleta, f.
viand, *vī'ănd*, s. vianda, f.
viaticum, *vīăt'ĭkŭm*, a. viático, m.
vibrate, *vī'brāt*, v. a. vibrar.
vibration, *vībrā'shŭn*, s. vibración, f.
vicar, *vĭk'ŭr*, s. vicario, m.
vicarage, -*ăj*, s. vicaría, f.
vicarious, *vĭkā'rĭŭs*, a. sustituto.
vice, *vīs*, s. vicio, m.; culpa, f.; tornillo, m.; garra, f.; —, ad. (in comp.) vice.
viceroy, *vīs'rŏē*, s. virrey, m.   [dad, f.
vicinity, *vĭsĭn'ĭtē*, s. vecindad, proximidad, f.
vicious, *vĭsh'ŭs*, a. vicioso; -ly, ad. de una manera viciosa.
vicissitude, *vĭsĭs'ĭtūd*, s. vicisitud, f.
victim, *vĭk'tĭm*, s. víctima, f.
victimize, -*īz*, v. a. sacrificar.
victor, *vĭk'tŭr*, s. vencedor, m.
victorious, *vĭktō'rĭŭs*, a. victorioso; -ly, ad. victoriosamente.
victory, *vĭk'tŭrē*, s. victoria, f.   [m.
victual, *vĭt'l*, v. a. abastecer.
victualler, -*tŭr*, s. abastecedor, proveedor, m.
victuals, *vĭt'lz*, s. pl. vituallas, f. pl.
videlicet, *vēdĕl'ĭsĕt*, ad. á saber.

vie, *ví*, v. n. competir.
view, *vú*, s. vista, f.; perspectiva, f.; aspecto, m.; examen, m.; apariencia, f.; -, v. a. mirar, ver; examinar.
vigil, *víy'il*, s. vela, f.; vigilia, f.
vigilance, *-âns*, s. vigilancia, f.
vigilant, *-ânt*, a. vigilante, atento; **-ly**, ad. con vigilancia. [vigorosamente.
vigorous, *víg'âras*, a. vigoroso; **-ly**, ad.
vigour, *víg'âr*, s. vigor, m.; robustez, f.; energía, f.
vile, *vú*, a. vil, bajo; **-ly**, ad. vilmente.
vileness, *-nês*, s. vileza, bajeza, f.
vilify, *víl'ífí*, v. a. envilecer.
villa, *víl'á*, s. quinta, casa de campo, f.
village, *víl'ídj*, s. aldea, f.
villager, *-âr*, s. aldeano, m.
villainy, *víl'ânâ*, s. villanía, vileza, f.
villanous, *víl'ânâs*, a. bellaco, vil, ruín; villano; **-ly**, ad. vilmente.
vindicate, *vin'díkât*, v. a. vindicar, defender. [f.; justificación, f.
vindication, *vindíkd'shân*, s. vindicación,
vindictive, *vindík'tiv*, a. vengativo; **-ly**, ad. por medio de vindicación.
vine, *vin*, s. vid, f. [rrado, m.
vine-arbour, *-ârbâr*, s. parral, empa-
vine-branch, *-brânsh*, s. sarmiento, m.
vine-dresser, *-drêsâr*, s. viñador, m.
vine-estate, *-êstât*, s. viñedo, m.
vinegar, *vin'êgâr*, s. vinagre, m. [f.
vine-growing, *vin'gróing*, s. viticultura,
vine-stick, *-stik*, s. rodrigón, m.
vine-stock, *-stôk*, s. cepa, f.
vineyard, *vin'yârd*, s. viña, f.
vinous, *vin'âs*, a. vinoso.
vintage, *vin'tâj*, s. vendimia, f.
vintager, *-âr*, s. vendimiador, m.
vintner, *vint'nâr*, s. vinatero, m.
viol, *ví'ôl*, s. (mus.) viola, f.
violate, *ví'ôlât*, v. a. violar.
violation, *víôlá'shân*, s. violación, f.
violator, *ví'ôlâtâr*, s. violador, m.
violence, *ví'ôlêns*, s. violencia, f.
violent, *ví'ôlênt*, a. violento; **-ly**, ad. violentamente.
violet, *ví'ôlêt*, s. (bot.) violeta, f.
violin, *ví'ôlin*, s. (mus.) violín, m.
violinist, *-ist*, s. violinista, m.
violoncello, *víôlóntshêl'ló*, s. (mus.) violón, violoncello, m.
viper, *ví'pâr*, s. víbora, f.
viperine, *-in*, **viperous**, *-âs*, s. viperino.
virago, *víró'gô*, s. marimacho, m.
virgin, *vâr'jin*, s. virgen, f.; -, a. virginal.
virginal, *-âl*, s. g. virginal.
virginity, *vârjin'tiê*, s. virginidad, f.
Virgo, *vâr'gô*, s. Virgo, f. (signo del zo-
virile, *vir'il* (*vír'il*), a. viril. [díaco).
virility, *vírtl'itiê*, s. virilidad, f. [artes).
virtu, *vâr'tô*, s. gusto, m. (en las bellas
virtual, *vâr'tâl*, a. **-ly**, ad. virtual(mente).
virtue, *vâr'tâ*, s. virtud, f.
virtuous, *vâr'tâs*, a. virtuoso; **-ly**, ad. virtuosamente.
virulence, *vir'âlêns*, s. virulencia, f.
virulent, *vir'âlênt*, a. virulento; **-ly**, ad. malignamente.

virus, *ví'râs*, s. virus, m.
visage, *víz'âj*, s. rostro, m.; cara, f.
viscera, *vis'êrâ*, s. pl. intestinos, m. pl.
viscosity, *viskô'itiê*, s. viscosidad, f.
viscount, *ví'kônt*, s. vizconde, m.
viscountess, *-ês*, s. vizcondesa, f.
viscous, *vis'kâs*, a. viscoso, glutinoso.
visibility, *vizibíl'itiê*, s. visibilidad, f.
visible, *víz'ibl*, a. visible.
visibly, *-i*, ad. visiblemente.
vision, *vizh'ân*, s. visión, f., fantasma, m.
visionary, *-rê*, a. & s. visionario (m.).
visit, *víz'it*, v. a. (& n.) visitar(se); -, s. visita, f.
visitant, *-ânt*, s. visitador, m.
visitation, *-dshân*, s. visitación; visita, f.
visitor, *-âr*, s. visitador, m.
visor, *víz'âr*, s. visera, f.; máscara, f.
visored, *-d*, a. enmascarado, disfrazado.
vista, *vis'tâ*, s. vista, perspectiva, f.
vital, *ví'tâl*, a. vital; **-ly**, ad. vitalmente; **-s**, s. pl. partes vitales, f. pl.
vitality, *vitâl'itiê*, s. vitalidad, f.
vitiate, *vish'iât*, v. a. viciar, corromper.
vitiation, *vishiá'shân*, s. depravación, f.
vitreous, *vit'riâs*, a. vítreo, de vidrio.
vitrify, *vit'rifi*, v. a. (& n.) vitrificar(se).
vitriol, *vit'riôl*, s. vitriolo, m.
vituperate, *vitiú'pârât*, v. a. vituperar.
vivacious, *vivá'shâs*, a. vivaz, despejado.
vivacity, *vivâs'itiê*, s. vivacidad, f.
vivid, *viv'id*, a. vivo; **-ly**, ad. vivamente.
vividness, *-nês*, s. vivacidad, f.
vivification, *vivifikâ'shân*, s. vivificación,
vivify, *viv'ifi*, v. a. vivificar. [f.
viviparous, *vivip'ârâs*, a. vivíparo. [f.
vivisection, *vivisêk'shân*, s. vivisección,
vivisectionist, *-ist*, s. partidario de la vivisección, m.
vivisector, *-târ*, s. vivisector, m.
vixen, *viks'n*, s. zorra, raposa, f.; mujer vociglera, f.
vixenish, *-ish*, a. quimerista.
viz, *viz*, ad. á saber.
vizier, *víz'yâr*, s. visir, m. [m.
vocabulary, *vôkâb'ûlârê*, s. vocabulario,
vocal, *vô'kâl*, a. vocal. [tatriz, f.
vocalist, *vô'kâlist*, s. cantador, m.; can-
vocation, *vôkâ'shân*, s. vocación, f.; oficio, m.; carrera, profesión, f.
vocative, *vôk'âtiv*, s. vocativo, m.
vociferate, *vôsif'ârât*, v. n. vociferar.
vociferation, *vosifârâ'shân*, s. vocería, grita, f.
vociferous, *vôsif'ârâs*, a. vociglero, clamoroso; **-ly**, ad. de una manera clamorosa.
vogue, *vôg*, s. moda, f.; boga, f. [rosa.
voice, *vois*, s. voz, f.; sufragio, m.
void, *void*, a. vacío, desocupado, nulo; falto, privado; -, s. vacuo, m.; -, v. a. vaciar, desocupar.
volatile, *vôl'âtil*, a. volátil; voluble.
volatility, *vôlâtil'itiê*, s. volatilidad, f.
volcanic, *vôlkân'ik*, a. volcánico.
volcano, *vôlkâ'nô*, s. volcán, m.
volition, *vôlish'ân*, s. voluntad, f.

volley, *vŏl'lĕ*, s. descarga de armas de fuego, f.; salva, f.; rociada de insultos &c., f.
volt, *vŏlt*, s. vuelta, f. (entre jinetes).
volubility, *vŏlŭbĭl'ĭtĕ*, s. volubilidad, f.
voluble, *vŏl'ŭbl*, a. voluble; ligero, veloz.
volume, *vŏl'ŭm*, s. volumen, m.; libro, m. (encuadernado).
voluminous, *vŏlŭ'mĭnŭs*, a. voluminoso.
voluntarily, *vŏl'ŭntărĭlĕ*, ad. voluntariamente.   [(mus.) capricho, m.
voluntary, *vŏl'ŭntărĕ*, a. voluntario; —, s.
volunteer, *vŏlŭntĕr'*, s. (mil.) voluntario, m.; —, v. n. servir como voluntario.
voluptuary, *vŏlŭp'tŭărĕ*, s. hombre voluptuoso, m.
voluptuous, *vŏlŭp'tŭŭs*, a. voluptuoso; -ly, ad. voluptuosamente.
voluptuousness, *-nĕs*, s. sensualidad, f.
volute, *vŏlŭt'*, s. voluta, f. (roleo de columna).
vomica, *vŏm'ĭkă*, s. (med.) vómica, f.
vomit, *vŏm'ĭt*, v. a. vomitar; —, s. vómito, m.; vomitivo, m.   [(mente).
voracious, *vŏrā'shŭs*, a. -ly, ad. voraz-voracity, *vŏrăs'ĭtĕ*, s. voracidad, f.
vortex, *vŏr'tĕks*, s. remolino, torbellino, m.
votary, *vō'tărĕ*, s. el que ama apasionadamente alguna cosa.
vote, *vōt*, s. voto, sufragio, m.; —, v. a. votar.
voter, *-ăr*, s. votante, m.   [votar.
votive, *vō'tĭv*, a. votivo.   [afirmar.
vouch, *vŏŭtsh*, v. a. atestiguar, certificar, s. testigo, m.; documento justificativo, m.   [dignarse.
vouchsafe, *-sāf'*, v. a. conceder; —, v. n.
vow, *vŏŭ*, s. voto, m.; —, v. a. & n. dedicar, consagrar; votar.
vowel, *-ĕl*, s. vocal, f.
voyage, *vŏ'ĭdj*, s. viaje por mar, m.; —, v. n. hacer un viaje por mar.
voyager, *vŏ'ĭdjăr*, s. navegador, m.
vulcano, *vŭlkā'nō*, s. volcán, m.
vulgar, *vŭl'găr*, a. -ly, ad. vulgar(mente); —, s. vulgo, populacho, m.
vulgarism, *-ĭzm*, s. palabrota, f.
vulgarity, *vŭlgăr'ĭtĕ*, s. vulgaridad, f.; bajeza, f.
vulgarize, *-ĭz*, v. a. vulgarizar.
vulnerable, *vŭl'nărăbl*, a. vulnerable.
vulnerary, *vŭl'nărărĕ*, a. vulnerario.
vulpine, *vŭl'pĭn*, a. zorruno, vulpino.
vulture, *vŭl'tŭr* (*văl'tshŭr*), s. buitre, m.
vying, *vī'ĭng*, s. emulación, f.

W.

wad, *wŏd*, s. atado de paja, m.; borra, f.; taco, m.; —, v. a. acolchar.
wadding, *-ĭng*, s. entretela, f.; taco, m.
waddle, *wŏd'dl*, v. n. anadear.
wade, *wād*, v. n. vadear.
wafer, *wā'făr*, s. hostia, f.; oblea, f.
waffle, *wŏf'fl*, s. hojuela, f.
waft, *wăft*, v. a. llevar por el aire ó por encima del agua; —, v. n. flotar; —, s. banderín, m.

wag, *wăg*, v. a. mover ligeramente; —, s. persona chocarrera, f.
wage, *wădj*, v. a. hacer guerra.
wager, *-ăr*, s. apuesta, f.; —, v. a. apostar.
wages, *-ĕz*, s. pl. salario, m.   [nada, f.
waggery, *wăg'găre*, s. chocarrería, bufo-
waggish, *wăg'gĭsh*, a. chocarrero.
waggishness, *-nĕs*, s. juguete, m.; chocarrería, f.
waggle, *wăg'gl*, v. n. anadear; menearse.
waggon, *wăg'gŏn*, s. carro grande para llevar géneros ó equipajes, m.; (rail.) vagón,
waggoner, *-ăr*, s. carretero, m.   [m.
wagtail, *wăg'tāl*, s. motolita, nevatilla, f.
waif, *wăf*, s. bienes mostrencos, m. pl.
wail, *wāl*, s. lamento, gemido, m.
wain, *wăn*, s. carruaje, m.
wainscot, *wăn'skŏt*, s. enmaderamiento de ensambladura, m.; —, v. a. entablar.
waist, *wăst*, s. cintura, f. (parte inferior del talle).   [m.
waistcoat, *wăst'kŏt* (*wĕs'kŏt*,) s. chaleco,
wait, *wăt*, v. a. & n. esperar, aguardar, asechar; quedarse; —, s. asechanza, celada, f.
waiter, *-ăr*, s. mozo de café, sirviente, m.
waiting, *-ĭng*, s. espera, f.; servicio, m.
waiting-maid, (—woman), *-ĭngmād*, (*wŭmăn*), s. doncella, f.
waits, *-s*, s. pl. murga, f.; músicos que tocan de noche por las calles en ciertas épocas del año y especialmente por Navidad.
waive, *wăv*, v. a. abandonar.
wake, *wăk*, v. n. velar; despertarse; —, v. a. despertar; —, s. vela, f.; vigilia, f.; (mar.) estela, f.
wakeful, *-fŭl*, a. vigilante; despierto.
wakefulness, *-nĕs*, s. vigilancia, f.; insomnia, f.
waken, *wā'kn*, v. a. (& n.) despertar(se).
waking, *-kĭng*, s. vela, f.
wale, *wăl*, s. (mar.) cinta, f.
walk, *wăk*, v. a. & n. pasear, ir; andar, caminar; —, s. paseo, m.; sitio para pasearse, m.
walker, *-ăr*, s. paseador, andador, m.
walking, *-ĭng*, s. paseo, m.
wall, *wăl*, s. pared, f.; muralla, f.; muro, m.; —, v. a. cercar con muros.
wall-creeper, *-krēpăr*, s. pico murario, m.
wallet, *wŏl'lĕt*, s. mochila, f.; morral de viandante, m.   [m.
wall-flower, *wăl'flŏăr*, s. (bot.) alelí doble,
wall-fruit, *-frŏt*, s. fruta de espalera, f.
wallow, *wŏl'lŏ*, v. n. encenagarse.
walnut, *wăl'nŭt*, s. nogal, m.; nuez, f.
walrus, *wăl'rŭs*, s. caballo marino, m.
waltz, *wăltz*, s. vals, m. (baile).
wan, *wŏn*, a. pálido.
wand, *wŏnd*, s. vara, f.; vara divinatoria.
wander, *wŏn'dăr*, v. a. & n. errar; vagar; wanderer, *-ăr*, s. vagamundo, m.   [rodar.
wandering, *-ĭng*, s. paseos, m. pl.; extravío, m.
wane, *wăn*, v. n. disminuir; decaer; —, s. decadencia, f.; (of the moon) menguante de la luna, f.

wanness, *wŏn'nĕs*, s. palidez, f.; languidez, f.

want, *wŏnt*, v. a. & n. haber menester; necesitar; faltar; —, s. necesidad, f.; indigencia, f.; falta, f.

wanting, *-ĭng*, a. falto, defectuoso.

wanton, *wŏn'tŏn*, a. lascivo, licencioso; juguetón; —, s. hombre ó mujer lasciva, —, v. n. retozar, juguetear. [mente.

wantonly, *-lĭ*, ad. lascivamente; alegre-

wantonness, *nĕs*, s. lascivia, impudicia, f.; juguete, m.; chanza, f.

war, *wăr*, s. guerra, f.; —, v. n. guerrear.

warble, *wăr'bl*, v. n. trinar; gorjear.

ward, *wărd*, v. a. guardar, defender; (off), evitar; —, s. guarda, defensa, f.; cuartel, m.; tutela, f.; pupilo, m.

warden, *-n*, s. custodio, guardián, m.; alcaide de una cárcel, m.; bedel, m.; gobernador, m.

warder, *-ăr*, s. guarda, guardia, f.

wardmote, *-mōt*, s. junta de barrio, f.

wardrobe, *-rōb*, s. guardarropa, f.

wardship, *-ship*, s. tutela, f.

ware, *wăr*, s. mercadería, f.

warehouse, *-hŏŭs*, s. almacén, m.

warehouse-keeper, *-hŏŭs kēpăr*,
warehouse-man, *-hŏŭsmăn*, s. guarda-almacén, almacenero, m. [dado, f.

warfare, *wăr'făr*, s. guerra, f.; vida del sol-

warily, *wăr'rĭlĭ*, ad. prudentemente. [f.

wariness, *wăr'ĭnĕs*, s. cautela, prudencia, f.

warlike, *wăr'lĭk*, a. guerrero, belicoso.

warlock, *-lŏk*, s. brujo, hechicero, m.

warm, *wărm*, a. cálido; caliente; furioso, celoso; —, v. a. calentar.

warming-pan, *-ĭngpăn*, s. calentador, m.

warmly, *-lĭ*, ad. con color, ardientemente.

warmth, *wărmth*, s. calor (moderado), m.; celo, m.

warn, *wŏrn*, v. a. avisar; advertir, precaver.

warp, *wărp*, s. urdimbre, f.; —, v. n. torcerse, alabearse; —, v. a. torcer; urdir.

warrant, *wŏr'rănt*, v. a. autorizar; privilegiar; garantir, asegurar; —, s. testimonio, m.; justificación, f.; decreto de prisión, m.; autorización, f. [ficable.

warrantable, *-ăbl*, a. abonable, justi-

warranter, *-ăr*, s. garante, fiador, m.

warranty, *-ĭ*, s. garantía, seguridad, f.

warren, *wŏr'rĕn*, s. conejero, m.

warrior, *wŏr'rĭăr*, s. guerrero, soldado, m.

wart, *wărt*, s. verruga, f.

warty, *-ĭ*, s. verrugoso.

wary, *wăr'rĕ*, a. cauto, prudente.

wash, *wŏsh*, v. a. lavar; bañar; —, v. n. lavarse; —, s. lavadura, f.; loción, ablución, f.; pantano, m.; bazofia, f. [dera, f.

washer-woman, *-ărwŭmăn*, s. lavan-

washhand-basin, *-hăndbăsn*, s. balangana, f.

wash-house, *-hŏŭs*, s. lavadero, m.

washing, *-ĭng*, s. lavadura, f.

washy, *-ĭ*, a. húmedo, mojado.

wasp, *wŏsp*, s. avispa, f.

waspish, *-ĭsh*, a. enojadizo, caprichudo.

wassail, *wŏs'sĕl*, s. orgía, orgía, f.

waste, *wăst*, v. a. disminuir; malgastar, disipar; destruir, arruinar, asolar; —, v. n. gastarse; —, s. desperdicio, m.; destrucción, f.; despilfarro, m.; baldío, m.

wasteful, *-fŭl*, a. destructivo; pródigo; —ly, ad. pródigamente.

wastefulness, *-fŭlnĕs*, s. prodigalidad, f.

waste-paper, *-pāpăr*, s. papel de desecho, m.

waster, *-ăr*, s. disipador, gastador, m.

watch, *wŏtsh*, s. desvelo, m.; vigilia, f.; vela, f.; centinela, f.; reloj de faltriquera, m.; —es, s. pl. desvelo, m.; —, v. a. & n. velar, guardar, custodiar; espiar, observar.

watcher, *-ăr*, s. observador, espía, m.

watch-fire, *-fīr*, s. fuego de bivac, m.

watchful, *-fŭl*, a. vigilante; —ly, ad. cuidadosamente.

watchfulness, *-fŭlnĕs*, s. vigilancia, f.

watch-light, *-lĭt*, s. farol, m.

watch-maker, *-mākăr*, s. relojero, m.

watch-man, *-măn*, s. sereno, m. [f.

watch-tower, *-tŏŭăr*, s. atalaya, garita,

watch-word, *-wărd*, s. (mil.) santo, m.; seña, f.

water, *wă'tăr*, s. agua, f.; marea, f.; —, v. a. regar, humedecer, mojar, bañar; —, v. n. chorrear agua.

waterage, *-āj*, s. barcaje, m.

water-closet, *-klŏzĕt*, s. común á la inglesa, m. [f. pl.

water-colours, *-kŭlărz*, s. pl. aguadas,

water-course, *-kŏrs*, s. corriente de las aguas, f. [m. pl.

water-cresses, *-krĕsĕs*, s. (bot.) berros,

water-cure, *-kŭr*, s. hidropatía, f.

water-dog, *-dŏg*, s. perro de aguas, m.

water-fall, *-fŭl*, s. cascada, f.

watering, *-ĭng*, s. riego, m.; abrevadura, f.; prensado, m. [m.

watering-place, *-ĭngplăs*, s. abrevadero,

watering-pot, *-ĭngpŏt*, s. regadera, f.

water-lily, *-lĭlĭ*, s. ninfea, f.

water-line, *-lĭn*, s. (mar.) línea) flotación, f.

water-man, *-măn*, s. barquero, m.

water-melon, *-mĕl'ŏn*, s. zandía, f.

water-shed, *-shĕd*, s. cumbre de las vertientes de las aguas, f. [marina, f.

water-spout, *-spŏŭt*, s. manga, bomba

water-tight, *-tĭt*, a. impermcable.

watery, *-ĭ*, a. acuoso, acueo.

wattle, *wŏt'tl*, s. zarco, m.; barbas de gallo, f. pl.; —, v. a. enzarcar. [fluctuar.

wave, *wăv*, s. ola, onda, f.; —, v. n. ondear;

waver, *wă'văr*, v. n. vacilar, balancear, estar suspenso. [solución, f.

wavering, *-ĭng*, a. inconstante; —, s. irre-

wavy, *wă'vĕ*, a. ondeado, undoso.

wax, *wăks*, s. cera, f.; —, v. a. encerar; —, v. n. crecer; hacerse.

waxen, *-n*, a. de cera.

wax-taper, *-tāpăr*, s. cerilla, f.

wax-work, *-wărk*, a. figura de cera, f.

waxy, *-ĭ*, a. ceroso.

way, *wă*, s. camino, m.; vía, f.; ruta, f.; modo, m.; expediente, m.; to give—, ceder; —s and means, s. pl. posibles, términos, m. pl.

wayfarer, —fâ'rûr, s. pasajero, viajador, m.
waylay, —lâ, v. n. insidiar.
wayside, —sîd. s. acera, f.
wayward, —wûrd, a. caprichoso, cabezudo.
we, wê, pn. nosotros, nosotras.
weak, wêk, a. —ly, ad. débil(mente.)
weaken, —n, v. a. debilitar.
weakling, —lîng, s. alfeñique, m.; persona muy delicada, f.
weakness, —nês, s. debilidad, f.; parte flaca de una persona, f.
weal, wêl, s. prosperidad, f.; bien, m.
wealth, wêlth, s. riqueza, f.; bienes, m. pl.
wealthily, —ílê, ad. ricamente, opulentamente.
wealthiness, —nês, s. opulencia, f.
wealthy, —ê, a. rico, opulento.
wean, wên, v. a. destetar.
weanling, —lîng, s. niño ó animal recién [destetado, m.
weapon, wêp'n, s. arma, f.
wear, wâr, v. a. gastar, consumir; usar, llevar; —, v. n. consumirse; —, s. uso, m.
wearable, —bbl, a. lo que se puede traer.
weariness, wêr'înês, s. cansancio, m.; fatiga, f.; enfado, m. [senfadosamente.
wearisome, wêr'îsûm, a. tedioso; —ly, ad.
weary, wêr'ê, v. a. cansar, fatigar: molestar; —, a. cansado, fatigado; tedioso.
weasel, wê'zll, s. comadreja, f.
weather, wêth'ûr, s. tiempo, m., temperatura, f.; tempestad, f.; —, v. a. doblar; (out), sufrir, superar. [la intemperie.
weather-beaten, —bêtn, a. endurecido á
weather-cock, —kôk, s. gallo de campanario, m., giraldilla, veleta, f.
weather-glass, —glâs, s. barómetro, m.
weatherwise, —wîz, s. vaticinador de las mudanzas del tiempo, m.
weave, wêv, v. a. tejer; trenzar.
weaver, —ûr, s. tejedor, m.
weaving, wêv'îng, s. tejido, m.
web, wêb, s. tela, f.; tejido, m.
webbed, —bd, a. lo que está unido por medio de una telilla.
wed, wêd, v. a. (& n.) casar(se).
wedding, —dîng, s. nupcias, f. pl.; casamiento, m. [—, v. a. acuñar; apretar.
wedge, wêj, s. cuña, f. (para partir leña);
wedlock, wêd'lôk, s. matrimonio, m.
Wednesday, wênz'dâ, s. miércoles, m.
wee, wê, a. pequeñito.
weed, wêd, s. mala hierba, f.; vestido de luto, m.; —, v. a. escardar.
weedy, —ê, a. lleno de malas hierbas.
week, wêk, s. semana, f.; to-morrow —, mañana en una semana; yesterday, —, ayer hace ocho días.
week-day, —dâ, s. día de trabajo, m.
weekly, —lê, a. semanal; —, ad. semanalmente, por semana.
weep, wêp, v. a. & n. llorar; lamentar.
weeping-willow, —îngwîllô, s. sauce de Babilonia, m.
weevil, wê'vl, s. gorgojo, m. (insecto).
weft, wêft, s. trama, f.; tejido, m. [siderar.
weigh, wâ, v. a. & n. pesar; examinar, consider.
weight, wât, s. peso, m.; pesadez, f.
weightily, —ílê, ad. pesadamente.

weightiness, —înês, s. ponderosidad, pesadez, f.; importancia, f.
weighty, —ê, a. ponderoso; importante.
weir, wêr, s. azud, pesquera, f.
welcome, wêl'kûm, a. recibido con agrado; — ! ¡bien venido! —, s. bienvenida, f.; —, v. a. dar la bienvenida á alguno.
weld, wêld, v. a. soldar el hierro. [tar, m.
welfare, wêl'fâr, s. prosperidad, f.; bienestar, m.
well, wêl, s. fuente, f.; manantial, m.; pozo (para sacar agua), m.; —, a. bueno, sano; —, ad. bien, felizmente; favorablemente; suficientemente; convenientemente; as—as, así como, también como, lo mismo que.
well-being, —bêîng, s. felicidad, prosperidad, f. [educado.
well-bred, —brêd, a. bien criado, bien
well-doing, —dôîng, s. beneficio, m.
well-met! —mêt, ¡bien hallado!
well-to-do, —tûdô, a. contento, gozoso.
well-wisher, —wîshûr, s. amigo, partidario, m.
welt, wêlt, s. ribete, m.; —, v. a. ribetear.
welter, —ûr, v. n. revolcarse en lodo.
wen, wên, s. lobanillo, m., lupia, f.
wench, wênsh, s. mozuela, cantonera, f.
wend, wênd, v. a. ir; rodear.
west, wêst, s. poniente, occidente, m.; —, a. occidental.
westerly, —ûrlê, **western,** —ûrn, a. occidental. [occidente.
westward, —wûrd, ad. á poniente, hacia poniente.
wet, wêt, a. húmedo, mojado; —, s. humedad, f.; —, v. a. mojar, humedecer.
wether, wêth'ûr, s. carnero llano, m.
wetness, wêt'nês, s. humedad, f.
wetnurse, wêt'nûrs, s. ama de leche, f.
whack, hwâk, v. a. aporrear; —, s. golpe, m.
whale, hwâl, s. ballena, f. [fin.
whale-bone, —bôn, s. ballena, f.
whaler, —ûr, s. pescador de ballena, m.
wharf, hwôrf, s. muelle, m.
wharfage, —âj, s. muellaje, m.
wharfinger, —înjûr, s. fiel de muelle, m.
what, hwôt, pn. que, el que, la que, lo que.
what(so)ever, —(sô)êv'ûr, pn. cualquier ó cualquiera cosa que, que sea.
wheat, hwêt, s. trigo, m.
wheaten, —n, a. hecho de trigo.
wheedle, hwêd'l, v. a. halagar, engañar con lisonjas.
wheel, hwêl, s. rueda, f.; —, v. a. (hacer) rodar; volver, girar; —, v. n. rodar.
wheel-barrow, —bârrô, s. carretón de una rueda, m.
wheeler, —ûr, **wheel-horse,** —hôrs, s. s. caballo de tronco, m.
wheel-wright, —rît, s. carpintero de prieto, m.
wheeze, hwêz, v. n. jadear.
whelm, hwêlm, v. a. cubrir; oprimir.
whelp, hwêlp, s. cachorro, m.; —, v. n. parir (la perra).
when, hwên, ad. cuando; mientras que.
whence, hwêns, ad. de donde; de quien.
whence(so)ever, —(sô)êv'ûr, ad. de donde quiera. [quiera que, siempre que.
when(so)ever, hwên(sô)êv'ûr, ad. cuando

where, *hwâr,* ad. donde; **any —,** en cualquier parte; **every —,** en todas partes.

whereabout(s), *–ăbŏŭt(s),* ad. hacia donde.

whereas, *–ăs',* ad. por cuanto, mientras que; pues que, ya que.

whereat, *–ăt',* ad. á lo cual.

whereby, *–bî',* ad. por lo cual, con lo cual, por donde, de que.　[cuyo motivo.

wherefore, *whârfôr,* ad. por lo que, por

wherefrom, *whârfrŏm',* ad. de donde.

wherein, *–în',* ad. en donde, en lo cual, en que.

whereinto, *–în'tŏ,* ad. dentro de lo que.

whereof, *–ŏf',* ad. de la cual, de que.

whereon, *–ŏn',* ad. sobre lo cual, sobre que.　[en cualquiera parte que.

wheresoever, *–sŏĕv'ûr,* ad. donde quiera.

where(un)to, *–(ŭn)tŏ',* ad. á lo que, á que.

wherever, *–ĕv'ûr,* ad. donde quiera que.

whereupon, *–ăpŏn',* ad. sobre que; entonces.　[con lo cual.

wherewith(al), *–wĭth(ăl)',* ad. con que.

wherry, *hwĕr'rĕ,* s. esquife, m.; barca, f.

whet, *hwĕt,* v. a. afilar, amolar; excitar.

whether, *hwĕth'ûr,* ad. si, sea, sea que; **—,** pn. cual, cual de los dos.

whetstone, *hwĕt'stōn,* s. aguzadera, f.

whey, *hwā,* s. suero, m.

which, *hwĭtsh,* pn. que, el cual, la cual, los cuales, las cuales.

which(so)ever, *–sŏ)ĕv'ûr,* pn. cualquiera.

whiff, *hwĭf,* s. vaharada, f.; bocanada de humo, fumada, f.　[terra, m.

Whig, *hwĭg,* s. partido liberal en Inglaterra.

while, *hwîl,* s. rato, m.; vez, f.; **a — ago,** rato ha.

while, *hwîl,* **whilst,** *hwîlst,* ad. mientras.

whim, *hwĭm,* s. antojo, capricho, m.

whimper, *–pûr,* v. n. sollozar, gemir.

whimsical, *–sĭkăl,* a. caprichoso, fantástico.　[quejido, lamento, m.

whine, *hwîn,* v. n. llorar, lamentar; **—,** s.

whinny, *hwĭn'nĕ,* v. n. relinchar los caballos.　[a. & n. azotar; andar de priesa.

whip, *hwĭp,* s. azote, m.; látigo, m.; **—,** v.

whip-hand, *–hănd,* s. ventaja, f.

whipper-in, *–pûr'ĭn,* s. cabo de hilera, m. (en el Parlamento de Londres).

whipple-tree, *–pl trē,* s. balancín, m. (de coche &c.).

whirl, *hwûrl,* v. a. & n. girar; hacer girar; mover(se) rápidamente; **—,** s. giro muy rápido, m.

whirligig, *hwûr'lĭgĭg,* s. peripola, f.

whirlpool, *–pŏl,* s. vórtice, m.

whirlwind, *–wĭnd,* s. torbellino, m.

whisk, *hwĭsk,* s. escobilla, f.; cepillo, m.

whisker, *–ûr,* s. mostacho, m.; patilla, f.

whisky, *–ĕ,* s. aguardiente de grano, m.; calesín, m.　[surrar.

whisper, *hwĭs'pûr,* v. n. cuchichear; su-

whispering, *–ĭng,* s. cuchicheo, m.; susurro, m.

whist, *hwĭst,* s. wist, m. (juego de naipes).

whistle, *hwĭs'sl,* v. a. & n. silbar; chiflar; **—,** s. silvo, silbido, m.

whit, *hwĭt,* s. algo, m.; **not a —,** nada.

white, *hwît,* a. blanco, pálido; cano; puro; **—,** s. color blanco, m.; clara del huevo, f.　[m., breca, f. (pez).

whitebait, *–băt,* s. albur, alburno, gobio,

white-lead, *–lĕd,* s. albayalde, m. (cal de plomo).

white-heat, *–hĕt,* s. incandescencia, f.

white-hot, *–hŏt,* a. incandescente.

whiten, *–n,* v. a. & n. blanquear; emblanquecerse.　[f.

whiteness, *–nĕs,* s. blancura, f.; palidez,

white-wash, *–wŏsh,* s. blanquete, m.; enlucimiento, m.; **—,** v. a. encalar; jalbegar.

whither, *hwĭth'ûr,* ad. adonde, donde.

whithersoever, *–sŏĕv'ûr,* ad. adonde quiera.　[(pez).

whiting, *hwî'tĭng,* s. albur, cadoce, m.

whitish, *hwî'tĭsh,* a. blanquizco, blanquecino.

whitlow, *hwĭt'lŏ,* s. panadizo, panarizo, m.

Whitsuntide, *hwĭt'sŭntîd,* s. Pentecostés, m., fiesta judaica y cristiana.

whittle, *hwĭt'tl,* v. a. cortar con navaja.

whiz, *hwĭz,* v. n. zumbar, silbar.

who, *hŏ,* pn. quien, que.

who(so)ever, *–(sŏ)ĕv'ûr,* pn. quienquiera que, cualquiera que.　[**—,** s. total, m.

whole, *hōl,* a. todo, total; sano, entero;

wholesale, *–săl,* s. venta por mayor, f.

wholesome, *–săm,* a. sano, saludable; **–ly,** ad. saludablemente.　[f.

wholesomeness, *–sămnĕs,* s. salubridad,

wholly, *hōl'lĕ,* ad. enteramente.

whom, *hŏm,* pn. acusativo de **who.**

whomsoever, *–sŏĕv'ûr,* pn. acusativo de **whosoever.**　[chear, gritar.

whoop, *hŏp,* s. gritería, f.; **—,** v. n. hu-

whooping-cough, *–ĭng kŏf,* s. pertusis, f.

whore, *hōr,* s. puta, f.

why, *hwî,* ad. porque.

wick, *wĭk,* s. torcida, f.; pábilo, m.

wicked, *wĭk'ĕd,* a. malvado, perverso; **–ly,** ad. malamente.　[nidad, f.

wickedness, *–nĕs,* s. perversidad, malig-

wicker, *wĭk'ûr,* s. mimbre, m.; **—,** a. tejido de mimbres.

wicket, *wĭk'ĕt,* s. postigo, m.; portezuela, f.

wide, *wîd,* a. ancho, vasto, remoto; **–ly,** ad. lejos; anchamente; **far and —,** por todos lados.

wide-awake, *–ăwăk,* a. despierto.

widen, *–n,* v. a. ensanchar, extender.

wideness, *–nĕs,* s. anchura, extensión, f.

widgeon, *wĭj'ŭn,* s. avucasta, avutarda, f.

widow, *wĭd'ō,* s. viuda, f.; **—,** v. a. privar á una mujer de su marido.

widower, *–ûr,* s. viudo, m.

widowhood, *–hŭd,* s. viudez, viudedad, f.

width, *wĭdth,* s. anchura, f.　[f.

wield, *wĕld,* v. a. manejar, empuñar.

wife, *wîf,* s. esposa, consorte, f.; mujer, f.

wifely, *–lĕ,* a. lo que conviene á una esposa.

wig, *wĭg,* s. peluca, f.

wig-block, *–blŏk,* s. cabeza de madera, f.

wight, *wît,* s. persona, criatura racional, f.

wig-maker, *wĭg'măkûr,* s. peluquero, m.

wigwam, *wĭg'wăm,* s. cabaña de los indios, f.　[salvaje; **—,** s. yermo, desierto, m.

wild, *wîld,* a. silvestre, feroz; desierto;

wilderness, *wĭl'dẽrnẽs,* s. desierto, m.
wildfire, *wīld'fīr,* s. fuego griego, m.; erisipela, f.
wilding, *wīld'ĭng,* s. manzana silvestre, f.
wildly, *wīld'lẽ,* ad. sin cultivo; desatinadamente.
wildness, *wīld'nẽs,* s. selvatiquez, f.; brutalidad, f.
wile, *wīl,* s. dolo, engaño, m.; astucia, f.
wilful, *wĭl'fŭl,* a. voluntarioso, temoso; -ly, ad. obstinadamente.
wilfulness, *-nẽs,* s. obstinación, f.
wiliness, *wĭl'ĭnẽs,* s. fraude, engaño, m.
will, *wĭl,* s. voluntad, f.; testamento, m.; -, v. a. querer, desear.
willing, *-lĭng,* a. inclinado, pronto; -ly, ad. de buena gana. buena gana, f.
willingness, *-lĭngnẽs,* s. buena voluntad,
willow, *wĭl'lõ,* s. sauce, m. (árbol.)
wily, *wĭl'lẽ,* a. astuto, insidioso.
wimble, *wĭm'bl,* s. berbiquí, m.
wimple, *wĭm'pl,* s. velo, m.; (mar.) gallardete, m. lograr.
win, *wĭn,* y a. ganar, conquistar; alcanzar
winoe, *wĭns,* v. n. cocear.
winch, *wĭnsh,* s. cigüeña de torno, f.
wind, *wĭnd,* s. viento, m.; aliento, m.; pedo, m.
wind, *wĭnd,* v. a. & n. soplar; dar vuelta; torcer; ventear; serpentear; mudar, cambiar; envolver; volverse, cambiarse.
winded, *wĭnd'ẽd,* a. desalentado.
winder, *wīn'dẽr,* s. argadillo, m.
windiness, *wĭn'dĭnẽs,* s. ventosidad, flatulencia, f.
winding, *wīnd'ĭng,* s. vuelta, revuelta, f.
winding-sheet, *-shẽt,* s. mortaja, f.
windlass, *wĭnd'lãs,* s. árgano, m.
wind-mill, *wĭnd'mĭl,* s. molino de viento,
window, *wĭn'dõ,* s. ventana, f. [m.
wind-pipe, *wĭnd'pĭp,* s. tráquea, f.
windward, *wĭnd'wãrd,* ad. (mar.) á barwindy, *wĭn'dẽ,* a. ventoso. [lovento.
wine, *wĭn,* s. vino, m.
wine-bibber, *-bĭbbãr,* s. borracho, m.
wine-press, *-prẽs,* s. prensa, f.; lagar, m.
wine-taster, *-tãstãr,* s. piloto, m.
wing, *wĭng,* s. ala, f., aventador, m.; -, v. a. dar alas; mover las alas.
winged, *-d,* a. alado.
wink, *wĭngk,* v. n. cerrar los ojos; guiñar; -, s. pestañeo, m.; guiño, m.
winner, *wĭn'nãr,* s. ganador, vencedor, m.
winning, *wĭn'nĭng,* s. ganancia, f.; lucro, m.; -, a. atractivo, encantador.
winnow, *wĭn'nõ,* v. a. aventar.
winsome, *wĭn'sãm,* a. alegre, jovial.
winter, *wĭn'tãr,* s. invierno, m.; -, v. n. invernar.
wintry, *wĭn'trẽ,* a. brumal, invernal.
wipe, *wĭp,* v. a. limpiar; borrar; -, s. limpiadura, f.; limpión, m.; pulla, f.
wire, *wĭr,* s. alambre, m.
wiredraw, *-drã,* v. a. tirar á hilo algunos metales; prolongar. [trigante, m.
wire-puller, *-pŭl'lãr,* s. tiritero, m.; in-
wire-pulling, *-pŭl'lĭng,* s. maquinaciones secretas, f. pl.
wiry, *wĭ'rẽ,* a. hecho de alambre.

wisdom, *wĭz'dãm,* s. sabiduría, prudencia, f. [juicio, f. pl.
wisdom-teeth, *-tẽth,* s. pl. muelas del
wise, *wĭz,* a. sabio, docto, juicioso, prudente; -, s. modo, m., manera, f.
wiseacre, *-dkãr,* s. necio, tonto, m.
wisely, *-lẽ,* ad. sabiamente, con prudencia
wish, *wĭsh,* v. a. desear, anhelar, ansiar; -, s. anhelo, deseo, m. [anhelo.
wishful, *-fŭl,* a. deseoso; -ly, ad. con
wisp, *wĭsp,* s. manojo de heno &c., m.
wistful, *wĭst'fŭl,* a. pensativo, atento; -ly, ad. atentamente.
wit, *wĭt,* s. entendimiento, ingenio, m.; to -, ad. es á saber.
witch, *wĭtsh,* s. bruja, hechicera, f.
witchcraft, *-krãft,* s. brujería, f.; sortilegio, m.
witchery, *-ãrẽ,* s. hechicería, f.
with, *wĭth,* pr. con; por, de, á. [también.
withal, *wĭthãl',* ad. además, á más de esto;
withdraw, *wĭthdrã',* v. a. quitar; privar; retirar; -, v. n. retirarse, apartarse.
withe, *wĭth,* s. mimbre, m.
wither, *wĭth'ãr,* v. n. marchitarse, secarse; -, v. a. marchitar. [dir, retener.
withhold, *wĭthhõld',* v. a. detener, impe-
withholder, *-ãr,* s. detentador, m.
within, *wĭthĭn',* pr. dentro, adentro; -, ad. interiormente; en casa.
without, *wĭthãt',* pr. sin, con falta de; fuera, afuera; -, ad. exteriormente; -, c. si no, sin que, á menos que.
withstand, *wĭthstãnd',* v. a. resistir.
withy, *wĭth'ẽ (wĭth'ẽ),* s. mimbre, m.
witless, *wĭt'lẽs,* a. necio, tonto, falto de ingenio.
witling, *wĭt'lĭng,* s. truhán, chocarrero, m.
witness, *wĭt'nẽs,* s. testimonio, m.; testigo, m.; -, v. a. atestiguar, testificar; -, v. n. servir de testigo.
witted, *wĭt'tẽd,* a. ingenioso.
wittily, *wĭt'tĭlẽ,* ad. ingeniosamente.
wittiness, *wĭt'tĭnẽs,* s. agudeza, f.; chiste, ingenioso, m.; viveza de ingenio, f. [sito.
wittingly, *wĭt'tĭnglẽ,* ad. adrede, de propó-
witty, *wĭt'tẽ,* a. ingenioso, agudo, chistoso.
wizard, *wĭz'ãrd,* s. brujo, hechicero, m.
woad, *wõd,* s. hierba pastel, gualda, f.
woe, *wõ,* s. dolor, m.; miseria, f.
woeful, *-fŭl,* a. triste, funesto; -ly, ad. tristemente.
wolf, *wŭlf,* s. lobo, m.; **she-**, loba, f.
wolfish, *-ĭsh,* a. lobero.
woman, *wŭm'ãn,* s. mujer, f.; **- of the town,** dama cortesana, f.
woman-hater, *-hãtãr,* s. aborrecedor de las mujeres, m. [m.
womanhood, *-hŭd,* s. estado de mujer,
womanish, *-ĭsh,* a. mujeril.
womankind, *-kĭnd,* s. mujeriego, m.
womanly, *-lẽ,* a. mujeril, mujeriego.
womb, *wõm,* s. útero, m.
wonder, *wŭn'dãr,* s. milagro, m.; maravilla, f.; -, v. n. maravillarse de.
wonderful, *-fŭl,* maravilloso; -ly, ad. maravillosamente.

wondrous — wrong   205

wondrous, *wŏn'drŭs*, a. maravilloso.
won't, *wŏnt*, abrev. de will not.
wont, *wŭnt*, s. uso, m., costumbre, f.
wonted, *—ĕd*, a. acostumbrado, usual.
woo, *wŏ*, v. a. cortejar, requerir de amores
wood, *wŭd*, s. bosque, m.; selva, f.; madera, f.; leña, f.
wood-bine, *—bīn*, s. (bot.) madreselva, f.
wood-cock, *—kŏk*, s. chocha, becada, f.
wood-cut, *—kŭt*, s. estampa de madera, f.
wood-cutter, *—kŭttŭr*, s. grabador en láminas de madera, xilógrafo, m.
wooded, *—ĕd*, a. arbolado.
wooden, *—n*, a. hecho de madera.
wood-land, *—lănd*, s. arbolado, m.
wood-louse, *—lŏŭs*, s. cucaracha, f.
woodman, *—măn*, s. cazador, m.; guardabosque. m.   [m.
wood-pecker, *—pĕkŭr*, s. picamaderos,
wooer, *wŏ'ŭr*, s. galanteador, m.
woof, *wŏf*, s. trama, f.; textura, f.
wool, *wŭl*, s. lana, f.
wool-gathering, *—găthŭrĭng*, a. his wits have gone —, tiene distracciones.
woolly, *—lĕ*, a. lanudo, lanoso.
word, *wŭrd*, s. palabra, voz, f.; —, v. a. expresar; componer en escritura; —, v. n. disputar, trabarse de palabras.
wordiness, *—nĕs*, s. verbosidad, f.
wordy, *—ĕ*, a. verboso.
work, *wŭrk*, v. n. trabajar; obrar; estar en movimiento ó en acción; fermentar; —, v. a. trabajar, labrar; fabricar, manufacturar; —, s. trabajo, m.; fábrica, f.; obra (de manos), f.; fatiga, f.
worker, *—ŭr*, s. trabajador, obrero, m.
work-house, *—hŏŭs*, s. fábrica, f.; obrador, taller, m.   [m.
working-day, *—ĭngdā*, s. día de trabajo,
workman, *—măn*, s. artífice, labrador, m.
workmanship, *—mănshĭp*, s. manufactura, f.; destreza del artífice, f.
workshop, *—shŏp*, s. taller, obrador, m.
work-woman, *—wŭmăn*, s. costurera, f.; obrera, f.
world, *wŭrld*, s. mundo, m.; universo, m.; modo de vida, m.; gente, f.; gentío, m.; cantidad, f.; —to-be, el otro mundo.
worldliness, *—nĕs*, s. vanidad mundana, f.; profanidad, f.; avaricia, f.
worldling, *—lĭng*, s. hombre mundano, m.
worldly, *—lĕ*, a. mundano, terreno.
worm, *wŭrm*, s. gusano, gorgojo, m.; (of a screw) rosca de tornillo, f.; —, v. n. trabajar ú obrar lentamente y debajo de mano; —, v. a. suplantar por medios secretos.   [llado.
worm-eaten, *—ĕtn*, a. carcomido, apoliworm-wood, *—wŭd*, s. (bot.) ajenjo, m.
worry, *wŭr'rĕ*, v. a. molestar, atormentar
worse, *wŭrs*, a. & ad. peor; de un modo más malo.
worship, *wŭr'shĭp*, s. culto, m.; adoración, f.; your—, Usía, f.; Vuestra Merced, f.; —, v. a. adorar, venerar.
worshipful, *—fŭl*, a. venerable.
worshipping, *—pĭng*, s. adoración, f.

worst, *wŭrst*, a. pésimo, malísimo, —, s. lo peor, lo más malo, m.; —, v. a. vencer,
worsted, *wŭr'stĕd*,s.estambre,m. [sujetar.
wort, *wŭrt*, s. hierba, f.; cerveza nueva, f.
worth, *wŭrth*, s. valor, precio, m.; mérito, m.; —, a. digno, benemérito; que vale.
worthily, *wŭr'thĭlĕ*, ad. dignamente, convenientemente.   [mérito, m.
worthiness, *wŭr'thĭnĕs*, s. dignidad, f.;
worthless, *wŭrth'lĕs*,a. indigno.
worthlessness, *—nĕs*, s. indignidad, vileza, f.   [s. varón ilustre, m.
worthy, *wŭr'thĕ*, a. digno, benemérito; —
would-be, *wŭd'bĕ*, a. titulado, llamado.
wound, *wŏŭnd*, s. herida, llaga, f.; —, v. a. herir, llagar.
wove(n), *wŏv('n*), a. semejante á la vitela.
wraith, *rāth*, s. fantasma, m.
wrangle, *răng'gl*, v. n. pelotear, reñir; —, s. pelotera, riña, f.   [m.
wrangler, *—ŭr*, s. pendenciero, disputador,
wrap, *răp*, v. a. arrollar; envolver.
wrapper, *—pŭr*, s. envolvedero, m.; ropa de casa, f.; chal pequeño, m.
wrath, *răth*, s. ira, rabia, cólera, f.
wrathful, *—fŭl*, a. furioso, irritado.
wreak, *rēk*, v. a. vengar; to — one's anger, descargar la cólera.
wreath, *rēth*, s. corona, guirnalda, f.; —, *rēth*, v. a. coronar; enroscar, torcer.
wreck, *rĕk*, s. naufragio, m.; destrucción, f.; navío naufragado, m.; —, v. a. & n. naufragar; arruinar; salir mal de algún negocio.
wren, *rĕn*, s. reyezuelo, m. (avecilla).
wrench, *rĕnsh*, v. a. arrancar; dislocar; torcer; —, s. torcedura del pie, f.; destornillador, m.   [arrebatar.
wrest, *rĕst*, v. a. arrancar, quitar á fuerza.
wrestle, *rĕs'l*, v. n. luchar; disputar.
wrestling, *rĕs'lĭng*, s. lucha, f.
wretch, *rĕtsh*, s. pobre infeliz, hombre muy miserable, m.; poor —! ¡pobre diablo!
wretched, *—ĕd*, a. infeliz, miserable; mezquino; -ly, ad. miserablemente.
wretchedness, *—ĕdnĕs*, s. miseria, f.; vileza, bajeza, f.
wriggle, *rĭg'gl*, v. n. menearse, agitarse.
wright, *rĭt*, s. artesano, obrero, m. [jar.
wring, *rĭng*, v. a. torcer; arrancar; estrujar.
wrinkle, *rĭng'kl*, s. arruga (de la cara, del paño), f.; —, v. a. arrugar.
wrist, *rĭst*, s. muñeca, f.
wrist-band, *—bănd*, s. puño de camisa, m.
writ, *rĭt*, s. escrito, m.; escritura, f.; orden,
write, *rīt*, v. a. escribir; componer. [f.
writer, *—ŭr*, s. escritor, autor, m.
writhe, *rĭth*, v. a. torcer; —, v. n. acongojarse.   [m.; manuscrito, m.
writing, *rī'tĭng*, s. escritura, f.; escrito,
writing-book, *—bŭk*, s. cuaderno, m.
writing-desk, *—dĕsk*, s. escritorio, m.
writing-master, *—măstŭr*, s. maestro de escribir, m.   [escribir, m.
writing-paper, *—pāpŭr*, s. papel para
wrong, *rŏng*, s. injuria, f.; injusticia, f.;

perjuicio, m.; error, m.; —, a. errado, falso; —, ad. mal, injustamente; al revés; —, v. a. agraviar, injuriar.

wrongful, –ful, a. injusto, inicuo; –ly, ad. injustamente.

wroth, rôth, a. encoleradizo.

wrought, rôt, a. hermoseado.

wry, rí, a. torcido, tuerto, no derecho.

wry-face, –fâs, s. mueca, f.

wry-neck, –něk, s. torcecuello, m. (ave).

X.

zebec, zě′běk, s. (mar.) jabeque, m.

Xmas, krís′mâs, s. Natividad, f.

xylography, zĭlŏg′râfĭ, s. arte de grabar en láminas de madera, f.

Y.

yacht, yŏt, s. (mar.) yacte, yac, m.

yam, yâm, s. (bot.) batata, f.

Yankee, yâng′kě, s. indígena de los Estados Unidos, m.

yard, yârd, s. corral, m.; yarda (medida), f.; (mar.) verga, f.   [m.

yarn, yârn, s. estambre, m.; hilo de lino,

yarrow, yâr′rô, s. (bot.) milhojas, f.

yawl, yŏl, s. (mar.) serení, m.

yawn, yân, v. n. bostezar.

yclept, ĕklěpt′, a. nombrado, llamado.

ye, yě, pn. vos.

yea, yâ, ad. sí, verdaderamente.

yean, yěn, v. n. parir la oveja.

year, yěr, s. año, m.

year-book, –bůk, s. anales, m. pl.

yearling, –lĭng, s. animal que tiene un año, m.   [todos los años.

yearly, –lĭ, a. anual; –, ad. anualmente.

yearn, yârn, v. n. compadecerse; afligirse interiormente.

yearning, –ĭng, s. compasión, f.

yeast, yěst, s. jiste, m.

yell, yěl, v. n. aullar; –, s. aullido, m.

yellow, yěl′lô, a. amarillo; –, s. color amarillo, m.

yellow-boy, –bŏĭ, s. (vulg.) guinea, f.

yellowish, –ĭsh, a. amarillento.

yellowness, –něs, s. amarillez, f.

yelp, yělp, y. n. latir, gañir.

yelping, –ĭng, s. gañido, m.

yeoman, yô′mân, s. hacendado, m.; ciertos guardias del rey de Inglaterra, m. pl.

yeomanry, –rě, s. conjunto de los hacendados de alguna provincia, m.; uno de los cuerpos de guardias del rey de Inglaterra.   [ballerías; –, s. embuje, m.

yerk, yûrk, v. a. golpear; cocear las caballerías, yes (vulg. yis), ad. sí.

yesterday, yěs′tûrdâ, ad. ayer.

yet, yět, c. sin embargo; pero; –, ad. además.

yew, yô, s. tejo, m. (árbol).   [más; aun.

yield, yēld, v. a. dar, producir; ceder, admitir; conceder; –, v. n. rendirse, someterse; asentir.

yielding, –ĭng, a. condescendiente.

yoke, yôk, s. yugo, m.; yunta, f.; –, v. a. uncir; sojuzgar.   [(árbol).

yoke-elm, –ělm, s. carpe, ojaranzo, m.

yolk, yôk, yelk, yělk, s. yema de huevo, f.

yon(der), yŏn(′dâr), ad. allí, allá.

yore, yôr, ad. tiempo hace, en los tiempos de entonces.

you, yô, pn. vosotros, U., Vd., Uds., Vds.

young, yûng, a. joven, mozo.

youngish, –gĭsh, a. mozuelo, jovencillo.

youngster, –stâr, s. jovencito, joven, m.

your(s), yôr(z), pn. vuestro, de U(ds).; sincerely –s, de U. S.S.S. (su seguro servidor).

yourself, –sělf′, Ud. mismo.   [celo.

youth, yôth, s. juventud, adolescencia, f.; joven, m.   [modo juvenil.

youthful, –ful, a. juvenil; –ly, ad. de un

youthfulness, –něs, s. juventud, f.

Z.

zany, zâ′ně, s. gracioso (de las comedias italianas), m.; bufón, m.

zeal, zěl, s. celo, m.; ardor, m.

zealot, zěl′ôt, s. celador, m.

zealotry, zěl′ôtrě, zealousness, –ûsněs, s. fanatismo, m.   [celo.

zealous, zěl′ûs, a. celoso; –ly, ad. con zenith, zěn′ĭth, s. zenit, cenit, m.

zephyr, zěf′âr, s. céfiro, m.

zero, zě′rô, s. zero, cero, m.   [na, f.

zest, zěst, s. luquete, m.; sainete, m.; biz-zigzag, zĭg′zâg, s. ese, f.; ziczag, m.

zinc, zĭngk, s. zinc, m. (metal).

zodiac, zô′dĭâk, s. zodíaco, m.

zone, zôn, s. banda, faja, f.; zona, f.

zoological, zôôlŏj′ĭkâl, a. zoológico.

zoologist, zôŏl′ôjĭst, s. zoólogo, m.

zoology, zôŏl′ôjě, s. zoología, f.

zoophyte, zô′ôfĭt, s. zoófito, m.

zounds, zôûnds, i [cáscaras!

List of the most remarkable geographical names, that differ in the two languages.

Abruzzi, ăbrŏt'sĕ, Abruzos, m. pl. [sínia, f.

Abyssinia, ăbĭssĭn'yd, Abisínia, f.

Adriatic, ādrĭăt'ĭk, s. (Mar) Adriático, m.

African, ăf'rĭkăn, s. & a. africano. [a. albanés.

Albanian, ălbā'nĭăn, s. &

Algiers, ăljērz', s, Argel, m.

Alpine, ăl'pĭn (ăl'pīn), a. alpino, a.; −s, s, pl. alpecienses, m. pl.

Alps, ălps, s, pl. Alpes, m. pl.

Alsace, ălsās', Alsacia, f.

Alsatian, ălsā'shĭăn, s. & a. alsaciano.

American, ămĕr'ĭkăn, s. & a. americano.

Andalusia, ăndălō'zhă, Andalucía, f.

Andalusian, ăndălō'zhăn, s. & a. andaluz.

Antwerp, ănt'wŭrp, Amberes, m.

Apennines, ăp'pĕnnĭnz, Apeninos, m. pl.

Apulia, ăpō'lĭă, Apulia, Pulla, f.

Arab, ăr'ăb, Arabian, ărā'bĭăn, s. & a. árabe, arábigo.

Arabia, ărā'bĭă, Arabia, f.

Aragonese, ărăgōnēs', s. & a. aragonés.

Archipelago, ărkĭpĕl'ăgō, Archipiélago, m.

Armenian, ărmē'nĭăn, s. & a. armenio, arménico.

Asia, ā'zhă (ā'shĭă), Asia, f.

Asiatic, ăzhĭăt'ĭk, s. & a. asiático, asiano.

Athenian, ăthē'nĭăn, s. & a. ateniense. [f. pl.

Athens, ā'thĕnz, Atenas, f.

Atlantic, ătlăn'tĭk, (Mar) Atlántico, m. [burgo, m.

Augsburg, ăgs'burg, Aus-

Australian, ăstrā'lĭăn, s. & a. australasino.

Austrian, ăs'trĭăn, s. & a. austriaço.

Baltic, băl'tĭk, Mar Báltico, m. [badas, f. pl.

Barbadoes, bărbā'dōz, Bar-

Barbary, bär'bărĭ, Berbería, f. [f.

Basle, bā'zĕl (băl), Basilea,

Batavian, bătā'vĭăn, s. & a. bátavo. [f.

Bavaria, băvā'rĭă, Baviera, f.

Bavarian, −m, s. & a. bavario, bávaro.

Belgian, bĕl'jĭăn, s. & a. belga, m.; bélgico, f.

Belgium, bĕl'jăm, Bélgica, f.

Bengal, bĕngăl', Bengala, f.

Bengalese, bĕngălēz', s. & a. bengalés.

Berlin, bār'lĭn (bŭrlĭn'), Berlín, m. [Belén, m.

Bethlehem, bĕth'lĕhĕm, Biscay, bĭs'kĕ, Vizcaya, f.

Black Forest, blăk fŏr'ĕst, Selva Negra, f.

Bœotia, bĕ'shĭă, Beocia, f.

Bœotian, −n, s. & a. beociano.

Bohemian, bŏhē'mĭăn, s. & a. bohemo, m.; bohémico.

Bordeaux, bŏr'dō, Burdeos, m. [foro, m.

Bosphorus, bŏs'fŏrŭs, Bós-

Brazil, brăzĭl', Brasil, m.

Brazilian, −ydn, s. & a. brasileño. [m.

Breton, brĕt'tŏn, s. bretón,

Britain, brĭt'ĕn, (Great-) Gran Bretaña, f.

Briton, brĭt'ŏn, s. bretón, m. & f.

Brittany, brĭt'ănĭ, Bretaña, f.

British, brĭt'ĭsh, a. bretón; − Channel, la Mancha. [Brunsvick, m.

Brunswic(k), brŭnz'wĭk,

Brussels, brŭs'sĕlz, Bruselas, f. pl.

Bulgarian, bŭlgā'rĭăn, s. & a. búlgaro.

Burgundian, bŭrgŭn'dĭăn, s. & a. borgoñón, borgoñés.

Burgundy, bŭr'gŭndĕ, Borgoña, f. [Bizancio, m.

Byzantium, bĭzăn'shĭăm,

Cadiz, kā'dĭz, Cádiz, f.

Caffraria, kăfrā'rĭă, Cafrería, f.

Calabrian, kălā'brĭăn, s. & a. calabrés.

Calais, kăl'ĕs, Calés, m.

Calmuck, kăl'mŏk', calmuco, m.

Cambridge, kăm'brĭj, Cambrije, Cambrigia, f.

Campeachy, kămpē'tshĕ, Campeche, f.

Canaries, kănā'rĭz, Canary-islands, Canarias, f. pl.

Candian, kăn'dĭăn, s. & s. candiote.

Canterbury, kăn'tŭrbĕrrĕ, Cantórberi, f. [riptia, f.

Carinthia, kărĭn'thĭă, Car-

Carpathians, kărpā'thĭănz, Montes Carpetanos, m. pl. [chemir, m.

Cashmere, kăshmēr', Ca-

Caspian Sea, kăs'pĭăn sĕ, (Mar) Caspio, m.

Castile, kăstēl', Castilla, f.

Castilian, kăstĭl'ydn, s. & a. castellano.

Catalonia, kătălō'nĭă, Cataluña, f. [talán.

Catalonian, −n, s. & a. ca-

Caucasus, kă'kăsŭs, Cáucaso, m.

Ceylon, sĕ'lŏn, Ceilán, m.

Chaldea, kăldē'ă, Caldea, f.

Champagne, shămpān', Champaña, f.

China, tshī'nă, China, f.

Chinese, tshĭnēz', s. & a. chino. [casia, f.

Circassia, sŭrkăs'shĭă, Cir-

Circassian, −sĭăn, s. & a. circasiano.

Cologne, kŏlōn', Colonia, f.

Constantinople, kŏnstăntīnō'pl, Constantinopla, f.

W
X
Y
Z

Copenhagen, kŏpĕnhā'gĕn, Copenaga, f.

Corfu, kŏrfŏ', Corfú, f.

Corinth, kŏr'ĭnth, Corinto, m. [nualla, f.

Cornwall, kŏrn'wŏl, Cornuailla, f.

Corsica, kŏr'sĭkā, Córcega, f. [corso.

Corsican, —n, s. &a. corsés,

Cossack, kŏs'sāk, cosaco, m. [landia, f.

Courland, kŏr'lānd, Curlandia, f.

Cracow, krā'kŏ, Cracovia, f.

Cretan, krē'tān, s. & a. cretense, m.; crético.

Crimea, krĭmē'ā, Crimea, f.

Croatia, krŏā'shĭā, Croacia, f. [a.

Croatian, —n, s. & a. croato,

Cyprus, sī'prŭs, Chipre, f.

Dalmatia, dālmā'shĭā, Dalmacia, f. [mático.

Dalmatian, —n, s. & a. dalmasco, m. [m. & f.

Damascus, dāmās'kŭs, Damasco, m.

Dane, dān, s. dinamarqués,

Danish, dā'nĭsh, a. danés, dinamarqués. [m.

Danube, dān'ŭb, Danubio, f.

Dauphinate, dō'fĭndt, Delfinado, m.

Dauphiny, dō'fĭné, Delfinado, m.

Delphos, dĕl'fŭs, Delfos, f.

Denmark, dĕn'mārk, Dinamarca, f. [Dovres, f.

Dover, dŏ'vŭr, Duvre, m.,

Dresden, drĕs'dn, Dresde, Dresda, f. [querque, m.

Dunkirk, dŭn'kŭrk, Dunkerque, m.

Dutch, dŭtsh, a. Dutchman, —mān, Dutchwoman, —wŏmān, s. holandés, m., holandesa, f.

East-Indies, ĕst ĭn'dĭz, Indias orientales, f. pl.

Edinburgh, ĕd'ĭnbŭrrŏ, Edimburgo, m.

Egypt, ē'ĭpt, Egipto, m.

Egyptian, ējĭp'shĭan, s. & a. egipciaco, egipciano, egipcio [terra, f.

England, ĭng'glānd, Inglaterra, f.

English, ĭng'glĭsh, a. inglés, s.; — Channel, la Mancha.

Englishman, —mān, Englishwoman, —wŭmān, inglés, m., inglesa, f.

Ephesus, ĕf'ēsŭs, Efeso, m.

Epiros, ĕpī'rŭs, Epiro, m.

Esquimaux, ĕs'kĭmŏ, esquimales, m. pl.

Europe, ū'rŏp, Europa, f.

European, ūrŏpē'ān, s. & a. europeo.

Euxine, ū'ksĭn, Mar Negro, Puente-Euxino, m.

Finland, fĭn'lānd, Finlandia, f. [landés.

Finlander, —ŭr, s. & a. finlandés.

Flanders, flān'dŭrz, Flandes, f. [flamenco.

Fleming, flĕm'ĭng, s. & a. Flemish, flĕm'ĭsh, a. flamenco [cia, f.

Florence, flŏr'ĕns, Florencia, f.

Florentine, flŏr'ĕntĭn, s. & a. florentín.

Flushing, flŭsh'ĭng, Flesinga, f.

France, frāns, Francia, f.

Frankfort, frānk'fŏrt, Francoforte, m.

French, frĕnsh, a. francés, a; the —, s. pl. los franceses.

Frenchman, —mān, s. Frenchwoman, —wŭmān, francés, m., francesa, f. [m.

Friburg, frĭ'bŭrg, Friburgo, f.

Friesland, frēz'lānd, Frisia, f. [frisón.

Frieslander, —ŭr, s. & a.

Frozen Ocean, frŏ'zn ŏ'shān, Mar Glacial, Mar Helado, m.

Gaelic, gā'lĭk, s. & a. galés.

Galicia, gālish'ĭā, Gali(t)cia, f.

Galilee, gā'rĭlē, Galilea, f.

Ganges, gān'jēz, Ganges, m. [cuña, f.

Gascony, gās'kŏné, Gascuña, f.

Gaul, gāl, s. & a. Galia, f.; gálico.

Geneva, jĕnĕ'vā, Ginebra, f.

Genevese, jĕnĕvēz', s. & a. ginebrés, ginebrino, a.

Genoa, jĕn'ŏā, Génova, f.

Genoese, jĕnŏēz', s. & a. genovés.

German, jŭr'mān, s. & a. alemán. [Germania, f.

Germany, —ĭ, Alemania, f.

Ghent, gĕnt, Gante, m.

Grecian, grē'shān, s. & a. griego.

Greece, grēs, Grecia, f.

Greek, grēk, s. & a. griego.

Greenland, grēn'lānd, Groenlandia, f.

Greenlander, —ŭr, s. & a. groenlandés.

Grisons, grē'sŏnz, Grisones, m. pl.

Groningen, grŏ'nĭngĕn, Groninga, f.

Guelderland, gĕl'dūrlānd, Gueldres, m.

Hague, hāg, Haya, f.

Hamburg, hām'bŭrg, Hamburgo, m.

Hanse Towns, hāns' tŏŭns, Ciudades Anseáticas, f. pl.

Havannah, hāvān'nā, Habana, f. [yecia, f.

Helvetia, hĕlvē'shĭā, Helvecia, f.

Hercynian Forest, hĕr'sĭn'yān fŏr'ĕst, Harz, härts, el bosque de Harz.

Hesse, hĕs, Hesia, f. [m.

Hessian, hĕsh'ān, s. & a. besés. [da, f.

Holland, hŏl'lānd, Holanda, f.

Hollander, —ŭr, holandés, m. [Hungria, f.

Hungaria, hānggā'rĭā, Hungría, f.

Hungarian, —n, s. & a. húngaro. [gría, f.

Hungary, hăng'gārĕ, Hungría, f.

Iceland, īs'lānd, Islandia, f.

Icelander, —ŭr, s. & a. islandés, m.; islándico.

Illyria, ĭllĭr'ĭā, Iliria, f.

Indian, ĭn'dĭān, s. & a. indiano; indio.

Indies, ĭn'dĭz, las Indias.

Ireland, ī'rlānd, Irlanda, f.

Irish, ī'rĭsh, a. irlandés.

Irishman, —mān, Irishwoman, —wŏmān, irlandés, m., irlandesa, f.

Italian, ĭtāl'tān, s. & a. italiano.

Italy, ĭt'ālĕ, Italia, f.

Japan, jāpān', Japón, m.

Japanese, jāpānēz', s. & a. japonés. [rusalén, m.

Jerusalem, jĕrŏ'sālĕm, Jerusalén, m.

Jutland, jŭt'lānd, Jutlandia, f.

Lacedæmonian, lāsĕdēmŏ'nĭān, s. & a. laconio.

Lapland, lāp'lānd, Laponia, f. [lapón.

Laplander, —ŭr, s. & a. lapón.

Lebanon, lĕb'ānŏn, Líbano, m. [f.

Leghorn, lĕg'ŏrn, Liorna, f.

Leipsic, līp'sĭk, Lipsia, f.

Liege, lĕj, Lieja, f.

Lisbon, lĭz'bŏn, Lisboa, f.

Lisle, lēl, Lila, f.

Lithuania, lĭthā'nĭā, Lituania, f.

Lithuanian, —n, s. & a. lituaniense, m.; lituáni(c)o.

Livonian, lĭvŏ'nĭān, s. & a. livoniano.

Lombard, lŏm'bārd, s. & a. lombardo, m.; lombárdico.

Lombardy, —ĕ, Lombardia, f. [m.

London, lŏn'dn, Londres, f.

Lorraine, lŏrrān', Lorena, f.

Low-Countries, *lō' kŭn-trĭz,* Países Bajos, m. pl.
Lusatia, *lūsd' shĭā,* Lusacia, f. [ciano.
Lusatian, *—n,* s. & a. lysa-
Luxemburg, *lŭks' ēmbŭrg,* Lucemburgo, Lujemburgo, m.
Lyons, *lī' ănz,* León, m.

Macedonian, *măsĕdō' nĭăn,* s. & a. macedónio, m.; ma-cedónico. [f.
Madeira, *mădī' rā,* Madera, f.
Mæse, *māz,* Mosa, f.
Majorca, *măjŏr' kā,* Mallorca, f.
Malines, *mălēn',* Malina, f.
Maltese, *măltēz',* s. & a. maltés. [sella, f.
Marseilles, *mărsālz',* Mar-
Mecca, *mĕk' kā,* Meca, f.
Mediterranean, *mĕdĭter-rā'nĭăn,* Mediterráneo, m.
Mentz, *mĕnts,* Maguncia, f.
Messina, *mĕssē' nā,* Mesina, f. [mejicano.
Mexican, *mĕks' ĭkăn,* s. & a.
Mexico, *mĕks' ĭkō,* Méjico, m.
Milan, *mǐl' ăn,* Milano, m.
Minorca, *mǐnŏr' kā,* Me-norca, f. [lucas, f. pl.
Moluccas, *mŏlŭk' kăz,* Mo-
Moor, *mōr,* s. **Moorish,** *-ĭsh,* a. moro.
Moravian, *mŏrā' vĭăn,* s. & a. moravo.
Morocco, *mŏrŏk' kō,* Mar-ruecos, m. pl.
Moscow, *mŏs' kō,* Moscú, f.
Moselle, *mŏzĕl',* Mosela, f.
Mulatto, *mŭlăt' ō,* mulato, m., **Mulattress,** *mŭlăt'-res,* mulata, f.
Munich, *mū' nĭk,* Monaco, Munich, m. [moscovita.
Muscovite, *mŏs' kŏvīt,* s. a.
Muscovy, *mŏs' kŏvē,* Mos-covia, f.

Naples, *nā' plz,* Nápoles, m.
Neapolitan, *nēăpŏl' ĭtăn,* s. & a. napolitano.
Netherlands, *nĕ' thär-lăndz,* Países Bajos, m. pl.
Neufchatel, *nūshātĕl',* Neucastel, m.
New-Foundland, *nū'-făndlănd,* Terranova, f.
New York, *nū yŏrk',* Nueva York, f.
Nice, *nēs,* Niza, f.
Nile, *nīl,* Nilo, m.
Nimeguen, *nĭmā' gĕn,* Ni-mega, f.
Norman, *nŏr' măn,* s. & a. normando, m.; normánico.

Normandy, *-dĕ,* Norman-dia, f.
North America, *nŏrth ămā' ĭkā,* América del Norte, f. [f.
Norway, *nŏr' wā,* Noruega,
Norwegian, *nŏrwē' jĭăn,* s. & a. noruego.
Nubian, *nū' bĭăn,* s. & a. nubio.
Nuremberg, *nū' rĕmbŭrg,* Nuremberga, f.

Olympus, *ŏlĭm' pŭs,* Olim-po, m. [f. pl.
Orkneys, *ŏrk' nĭz,* Orcadas,
Ostend, *ŏstĕnd',* Ostende, f.
Ottoman Empire, *ŏt' tō-măn ĕm' pīr,* la Puerta.

Pacific, *păsĭf' ĭk,* (Mar) Pacífico, m. [latinado, m.
Palatinate, *pălăt' ĭnăt,* Pa-
Palestine, *păl' ĕstīn,* Pa-lestina, f. [parisiense.
Parisian, *părĭs' ĭăn,* s. & a.
Parnassus, *părnăs' sŭs,* Parnaso, m.
Peloponnesus, *pĕlŏpŏnē'-sŭs,* Peloponeso, m.
Persian, *pĕr' shăn,* s. & a. persia, m.; persiano.
Peru, *pĕrō',* Perú, m.
Petersburg, *pē' tŭrzbŭrg,* Pedroburgo, m.
Phenicia, *fĕnē' shĭā,* Feni-cia, f. [nicio.
Phenician, *-n,* s. & a. fe-
Piedmont, *pēd' mŏnt,* Pia-monte, m.
Piedmontese, *pēdmŏntēz',* s. & a. piamontes.
Poland, *pō' lănd,* Polonia, f.
Pole, *pōl,* m., **Polish,** *pō'-lĭsh,* a. polaco.
Pontus, *pŏn' tŭs,* Ponto, m.
Portuguese, *pŏrtŭgēz',* s. & a. portugués.
Prague, *prăg,* Praga, f.
Provence, *prŏvăns',* Pro-venza, f. [f.
Prussia, *prŭs' shĭā,* Prusia,
Prussian, *prŭsh' ăn,* s. & a. prusiano.
Pyrenean Mountains, *pĭrĕnē' ăn mŏŭn' tĭnz,* **Pyr-enees,** *pĭr' ĕnēz,* Pirineos, m. pl.

Ratisbon, *răt' ĭzbŏn,* Ratis-bona, f. [vena, f.
Ravenna, *răvĕn' nā,* Ra-
Rhenish, *rĕn' ĭsh,* a. del Rin ó del Rhin.
Rhine, *rīn,* Rin ó Rhin, m.
Rhinelander, *-lăndăr,* ha-bitante del Rhin, m.

Rhodes, *rō' dĭz,* Rodas, f. pl.
Rhone, *rōn,* Ródano, m.
Roman, *rō' măn,* s. & a. ro-mano.
Rome, *rōm,* Roma, f.
Roumania, *rōmā' nĭā,* Ro-mania, f.
Russia, *răs' shĭā,* Rusia, f.
Russian, *răsh' ăn,* s. & a. ruso, m., rusiano.

Samoied, *săm' ō yĕd,* Samo-yedo, m. [desia, f.
Sardinia, *sărdĭn' ĭā,* Cer-
Sardinian, *-ĭăn,* s. & a. sardo.
Savoy, *săvŏĭ',* Saboya, f.
Savoyard, *-ärd',* s. sabo-yano, a, m. & f.
Saxon, *săks' ăn,* s. & a. sa-jón, m.; sajono, a.
Saxony, *-ŏnē,* Sajonia, f.
Scandinavia, *skăndĭnā'-vĭă,* Escandinavia, f.
Schaffhausen, *shăfhŏŭs'n,* Escafusa, f.
Scheldt, *skĕlt,* Escalda, f.
Solavonia, *sklăvō' nĭā,* Es-clavonia, f.
Sclavonian, *-n,* s. & a. es-clavón, m.; esclavonio.
Scotch, *skŏtsh,* a. escocés; **-man,** *-măn,* s. escocés, m.; **-woman,** *-wŭmăn,* s. escocesa, f. [cia, f.
Scotland, *skŏt' lănd,* Esco-
Scottish, *skŏt' ĭsh,* a. es-cocés.
Seine, *săn,* Sena, m.
Servian, *sĕr' vĭăn,* s. & a. servio.
Siberia, *sībē' rĭā,* Siberia, f.
Siberian, *-n,* s. & a. siberiano. [siciliano.
Sicilian, *sĭsĭl' ĭăn,* s. & a.
Sicily, *sĭs' ĭlĭ,* Sicilia, f.
Silesian, *sĭlē' zhĭăn,* s. & a. silesiano, m.; silesio.
Smyrna, *smĭr' nā,* Esmirna, f. [da, f.
Sound, *sŏŭnd,* Sunda, Son-
South Sea, *sŏŭth sē,* Mar Austral, m.
Spain, *spān,* España, f.
Spaniard, *spăn' yărd,* s. español, a, m. & f.
Spanish, *spăn' ĭsh,* a. es-pañol.
Sparta, *spär' tā,* Esparta, f.
Spartan, *-n,* s. & a. es-partano.
Stiria, *stĭr' ĭā,* Estiria, f.
Stirian, *-n,* s. & a. esti-riano. [colmo, m.
Stockholm, *stŏk' ŏlm,* Esto-
Strasburg, *străs' bŭrg,* Es-trasburgo, m. [gardo, m.
Stutgart, *stŭt' gärt,* Estu-

Suabia, swâ′bĭâ, Suabia, f.
Suabian, —n, s. & a. suabo.
Swede, swêd, s. sueco, m. & f.
Sweden, swê′dĕn, Suecia, f.
Swedish, swê′dĭsh, a. sueco.
Swiss, swĭs, s. & a. suizo.
Switzerland, swĭt′zŭr-lând, Suiza, f. [cusa, f.
Syracuse, sĭr′ăkŭs, Sira-

Tagus, tâ′gŭs, Tajo, m.
Tartar, tär′tŭr, s. & a. tártaro.
Tartary, tär′tărĭ, Tartaria, f.
Thames, tĕmz, Támesis, m.
Thermopylæ, thŭrmŏp′ĭlê, Termópilas, f. pl.
Thessalonica, thĕssălŏn′ĭkâ, Tesalónica, f.
Thessalian, thĕssâ′lĭân, s. & a. tesaliense, tesalo.
Thessaly, thĕs′sâlĭ, Tesalia, f.
Thracia, thrâ′shĭâ, Tracia, f.
Thuringia, thŭrĭn′jĭâ, Turingia, f.

Thuringian, —n, s. & a. turingiano, turingio.
Toulon, tōlŏn′, Tolón, m.
Toulouse, tōlōs′, Tolosa, f.
Transylvania, trânsĭlvâ′nĭâ, Transilvania, f.
Trent, trĕnt, Trento, m.
Treves, trêvz, Tréveris, m.
Trojan, trō′ân, s. & a. troyano, a.
Troy, trŏ̂, Troya, f.
Tunis, tŭ′nĭs, Túnez, m.
Turk, tŭrk, s. turco, a, m. & f.
Turkey, tŭr′kĕ, Turquía, f.
Turkish, —ĭsh, a. turco, a.
Tuscany, tŭs′kânĭ, Toscana, f.
Tyrol, tĭr′ōl, el Tirol.
Tyrolese, tĭrōlêz′, s. & a. tirolés.

the United States (of North America), thĕ ŭnî′tĕd stâts, Estados Unidos, m. pl.
Utrecht, ū′rĕkt, Utreque, m.

Venetian, vĕnê′shĭân, s. & a. veneciano.
Venice, vĕn′ĭs, Venecia, f.
Versailles, vĕrsâlz′, Versalles, m. [suyic, m.
Vesuvius, vĕsū′vĭŭs, Vesuvius, Ve-
Vienna, vĭĕn′nâ, Viena, f.
Viennese, vĭĕnnêz′, s. & a. vienés.
Vincennes, vĭnsĕnz′, Vincénas, f. pl.

Wales, wâlz, Gales, m.
Wallachia, wŏllâ′kĭâ, Valaquia, f. [valaquo.
Wallachian, —n, s. & a. valaco.
Warsaw, wŏr′sâ, Varsovia, f. [Vallés.
Welsh, wĕlsh, s. natural de Vallés.
West-Indies, wĕst ĭn′dĕz, Indias occidentales, f. pl.
Wurtemberg, wŭr′tĕmbärg, Vurtembergo, m.

Zealand, zê′lând, Zelanda, f.
Zurich, zū′rĭk, Zurico, m.

List of the most usual christian names, that differ in the two languages.

Abraham, â′brâhăm, Abrahán.
Adam, ăd′ăm, Adán. [da.
Adelaide, ăd′ĕllâd, Adelai-
Adolphus, ădŏl′fŭs, Adolfo.
Alexander, ălĕgzăn′dŭr, Alejandro. [so.
Alphonso, ălfŏn′zō, Alfonso.
Ambrose, ăm′brōz, Ambrosio.
Amelia, âmê′lĭâ, Amalia.
Amy, â′mĕ, Amata.
Andrew, ăn′drō, Andreo. [Andrés.
Ann, ăn, Ana.
Anthony, ăn′tŏnĕ, Antonio.
Augustus, âgŭs′tŭs, Augusto.
Austin, ăs′tĭn, Agustín.

Bartholomew, bärthŏl′ō-mâ, Bartolomé, Bartolomeo, Bártolo.

Beatrice, bê′âtrĭs, Beatriz.
Ben, bĕn, Benjamínito.
Benedict, bĕn′ĕdĭkt, Benito.
Bernard, bŭr′nărd, Bernardo.
Bertha, bŭr′thâ, Berta. [do.
Bertie, bŭr′tĕ, abreviatura de: Bertram, bŭr′trăm, Beltrán.
Bess, bĕs, Bessy, —ĭ, Betsey, bĕt′sĕ, Isabelita.
Biddy, bĭd′dĕ, Brigidita.
Bill, Billy, bĭl′(lĕ), abreviatura de: William.
Blanche, blânsh, Bianca.
Bob, Bobby, bŏb′(bĕ), abreviatura de: Robert.
Bridget, brĭt′jĕt, Brígida.

Carry, kăr′rĕ, abreviatura de: Caroline, Carolina.
Catherine, kă′thĕrĭn, Catalina.

Cecily, sĕs′ĭlĭ, Cecilia.
Charles, tshärlz, Carlos.
Charlotte, shär′lŏt, Carlota.
Christ, krĭst, Cristo. [lota.
Christopher, krĭs′tŏfŭr, Cristóbal.
Constance, kŏn′stâns, Constanza. [Constantino.
Constantine, kŏn′stântĭn,

Dan, dăn, abreviatura de: Daniel.
Dick, dĭk, Ricardito.
Doll, dŏl, Doroteíta.
Dorothy, dŏr′ŏthĕ, Dorotea.

Edward, ĕd′wŭrd, Eduardo.
Edwiga, ĕdwĕ′gâ, Hedvigia.
Effie, ĕf′ĕ, abreviatura de: Euphemia.
Eleanor, ĕl′ĕnŏr, Leonor.

Elizabeth, *ēlīz'ăbĕth*, Isabel. [bel.
Ellen, *ĕl'lĕn*, Elena.
Ellie, *ĕl'lĭ*, abreviatura de: Eleanor.
Emily, *ĕm'ĭlĭ*, Emilia.
Essie, *ĕs'sĭ*, abreviatura de: Esther, Ester.
Eugene, *ū jēn*, Eugenio.
Eva, *ē'vā*, **Eve**, *ĕv*, Eva.

Fanny, *făn'nĭ*, Faquita.
Ferdinand, *fŭr'dĭnănd*, Fernando. [cisca.
Frances, *frăn'sĕs*, Francisca.
Francis, *frăn'sĭs*, **Frank**, *frănk*, Francisco.
Frederica, *frĕdĕrĭk'ā*, Federica. [gerico.
Frederic(k), *frĕd'ĕrĭk*, Federico.

Geoffr(e)y, *jĕf'frĭ*, Geofredo.
George, *jōrj*, Jorge. [do.
Giles, *jīlz*, Julio.
Gillian, *jĭl'ĭăn*, Juliana.
Godfrey, *gŏd'frĭ*, Gofredo, Godofredo. [rio.
Gregory, *grĕg'ŏrĭ*, Gregorio.
Gustavus, *gŭstā'vŭs*, Gustavo.
Guy, *gī*, Guido.

Hal, *hăl*, Enriquito.
Hannah, *hăn'nā*, Ana.
Harriet, *hăr'ĭĕt*, Enriqueta.
Harry, *hăr'rĭ*, por: Henry.
Helen, *hĕl'lĕn*, Helena.
Henry, *hĕn'rĭ*, Enrique.
Hilary, *hĭl'ārĭ*, Hilario.
Hodge, *hŏj*, abreviatura de: Hugh, *hū*, Hugo. [Roger.
Humphrey, *hŭm'frĭ*, Hunfredo.

Ignatius, *ĭgnā'shŭs*, Ignacio.
Isabel, *ĭz'ābĕl*, Elizabeth.

Jack, *jăk*, por: John, Juanillo, Juanito.
James, *jāmz*, Diego, Jaime.
Jane, *jān*, Juana.
Jasper, *jās'pār*, Gaspar.
Jeffry, *jĕf'rĭ*, Geofredo.
Jemmy, *jĕm'mĭ*, abreviatura de: James.
Jenny, *jĕn'nĭ*, Juanita.
Jeremy, *jĕr'ĕmĭ*, Jeremías.
Jerry, *jĕr'rĭ*, abreviatura de Jeremy.
Jessie, *jĕs'sĭ*.

Jim, *jĭm*, abreviatura de: James.
Joan, *jōn* (*jō'ăn*), Juana.
Joe, *jō*, Pepe, Pepillo.
John, *jŏn*, Juan.
Johnny, *-nĭ*, Juanito.
Joseph, *jō'zĕf*, José, Pepe.

Kate, *kāt*, **Kit**, **Kitty**, *kĭt'(tĭ)*, abreviatura de: Catherine.
Kit, *kĭt*, abreviatura de Christopher.

Laurence, *lā'rĕns*, Lorenzo.
Lewis, *lū'ĭs*, Luis.
Lizzie, **Lizz(e)y**, *lĭz'zĭ*, Lizeta.
Lola, *lō'lā*, Dolores.
Loo, *lō*, abreviatura de: Louisa, *lō'ĕ zā*, Luisa.
Lucretia, *lōkrē'shĭā*, Lucrecia.
Lucy, *lō'sĭ*, Lucía.

Mabel, *mā'bĕl*.
Madeline, *măd' lĭn*, **Magdalen**, *măg'dālĕn*, Magdalena.
Madge, *măj*, **Margery**, *mār'jŭrĭ*, abreviatura de: Margaret. [Margarita.
Margaret, *mār'gărĕt*,
Mark, *mārk*, Marcos.
Martha, *mār'thā*, Marta.
Mary, *mā'rĭ*, María.
Mat, *măt*, abreviatura de: Matthew, *măt'thū*, Mateo.
Matilda, *mătĭl'dā*, Matilde.
Maud, *mŏd*, abreviatura de: Magdalen.
Meg, *mĕg*, abreviatura de: Margaret.
Michael, *mī'kĕl*, Miguel.
Moll, **Molly**, *mŏl'(lĭ)*, (por: Mary), Mariquita, Maruja.
Morris, *mŏr'rĭs*, Mauricio.

Nan, *năn*, abreviatura de Anna.
Nancy, *năn'sĭ*, Anita.
Ned, *nĕd*, abreviatura de Edward.
Nell, **Nelly**, *nĕl'(lĭ)*, abreviatura de: Eleanor.
Nick, *nĭk*, abreviatura de Nicholas, Nicolas.
Noll, *nŏl*, abreviatura de: Oliver, *ŏl'ĭvār*, Oliveros.

Patty, *păt'tĭ*, por: Matilda.
Paul, *pŏl*, Pablo. [da.
Peg, **Peggy**, *pĕg'(gĭ)*, por: Margaret.
Peter, *pē'tār*, Pedro.
Phil, *fĭl*, abreviatura de: Philip, *fĭl'ĭp*, Felipe.
Poll, **Polly**, *pŏl'(lĭ)*, Maruja.

Ralph, *rălf* (*rāf*), Rodolfo, Rodulfo.
Raymond, *rā'mŭnd*, Raimundo, Ramón.
Reynold, *rĕn'ŏld*, Reinaldo.
Richard, *rĭtsh'ārd*, Ricardo. [rŏ'bĕrt, Roberto.
Robin, *rŏb'ĭn*, por: Robert.
Roger, *rŏj'ŭr*, Rogerio.
Rose, *rōz*, **Rosie**, *rō'sĭ*, Rosa. [Rolando.
Rowland, *rō'lănd*, Roldán.

Sal, **Sally**, *săl'(lĭ)*, por: Sarah, Sara.
Sam, *săm*, abreviatura de: Samuel, Samuel.
Sandy, *săn'dĭ*, abreviatura de: Alexander.
Solomon, *sŏl'ŏmŏn*, Salomón. [sŏf'ĭ, Sofía.
Sophia, *sŏfī'ā*, **Sophy**,
Stephen, *stē'vĕn*, Esteban.
Susan, *sū'zăn*, **Susannah**, *sūzăn'nā*, Susana.

Ted, **Teddy**, *tĕd'(dĭ)*, por: Edward.
Theresa, *tĕrē'zā*, Teresa.
Tim, *tĭm*, abreviatura de: Timothy. [steo.
Timothy, *tĭm'ŏthĭ*, Timoteo.
Tobias, *tōbī'ās*, **Toby**, *tō'bĭ*, Tobías.
Tom, **Tommy**, *tŏm'(mĭ)*, por: Thomas, *tŏm'ās*, Tomás. [Anthony.
Tony, *tō'nĭ*, abreviatura de:

Valentine, *văl'ĕntīn*, Valentino.
Violet, *vī'ŏlĕt*, Vióleta.

Walter, *wŏl'tār*, Gualterio.
Will, *wĭl*, abreviatura de: William, *wĭl'yăm*, Guillelmo, Guillermo.

Zachary, *zăk'ārĭ*, Zacarías.

A List of the most usual Abbreviations in Writing and Printing.

A. B., *artium baccalaureus,* Bachelor of Arts = B.A.
A. B., able-bodied seaman.
Abp., Archbishop.
A. C., *ante Christum,* before Christ.
a/c., account.
A. D., *anno Domini,* in the year of our Lord.
A. D. C., aide-de-camp.
ad lib., ad libit., *ad libitum,* at pleasure.
Æ., ÆT., *ætatis,* aged.
A. G., adjutant-general.
a. m., *ante meridiem,* before noon.
A. M., *artium magister,* Master of Arts = M. A.
Anon., anonymous.
A. R. A., Associate of the Royal Academy.
A. S., AS, Anglo-Saxon.
A. V., Authorized Version.
avdp., avoirdupois.

b., born.
B. A., Bachelor of Arts.
Bart., Bt., Baronet.
B. C., before Christ.
B. C. L., Bachelor of Civil Law.
B. D., Bachelor of Divinity.
bd., bound (of books).
bds., boards (of books).
B. I., British India.
B. L., Bachelor of Law.
Bp., Bishop.
Bros., Brothers.
B. S. L., Botanical Society of London.

Cam., Camb., Cambridge.
Cantab., *Cantabrigiensis,* Cambridge student.
Cantuar., *Cantuariensis,* Canterbury student.
Cap., *caput,* chapter.
Caps., capitals, capital letters.
Capt., captain.
C. B., Companion of the Bath.
C. C. C., Corpus Christi College, Cambridge.
C. E., Civil Engineer.
cf., *confer,* compare.
C. G., Consul-General.
Ch. Ch., Christ Church, Oxford.
chap., chapter.
Chas., Charles.
C. I., Order of the Crown of India.
cif., cost; insurance.
C. J., Chief Justice.

cl., cloth (of books).
Co., Company; county.
Col., Colonel.
Coll., College.
coll., colloq., colloquial.
con., *contra,* against.
C. P. S., *custos privati sigilli,* Keeper of the Privy Seal.
crim. con., criminal conversation.
C. S. I., Companion of the Star of India.
C. T., Certificated Teacher.
cwt., hundredweight.

d., died; *denarius,* penny.
D. C. L., Doctor of Civil Law.
D. D., Doctor of Divinity.
dep., deputy.
dept., department.
D. G., *Dei gratia,* by the grace of God.
D. L., Deputy Lieutenant.
do., Do., ditto, the same.
doz., dozen.
Dr., Doctor.
D. V., *Deo volente,* God willing.
dwt., pennyweight.

E. C., East Central postal district of London.
Ed., editor.
E. E., errors excepted.
e. g., *exempli gratia,* for instance.
E. I., East India.
E. I. C., East India Company.
E. I. C. S., East India Company's Service.
E. long., eastern longitude.
E. N. E., east-north-east.
E. S. E., east-south-east.
Esq., Esqr., Esquire.
etc., &c., *et cetera,* and so on.
et seq., *et sequentes,* and the following.
ex., example; **exx.,** examples.
Exch., Exchequer.
E. & O. E., errors and omissions excepted.

F., Fellow; Fahrenheit; folio.
fo., fol., folio.
Fahr., Fahrenheit (thermometer).
F. A. S., Fellow of the Antiquarian Society.
F. B. S., Fellow of the Botanical Society.
fcp., fcap., foolscap.
F. D., *fidei defensor,* Defender of the Faith.
fec., *fecit,* he did it.
F. G. S., Fellow of the Geological Society.

s. v., *sub voce.*
S. W., south-west.

Thos., Thomas.
Tim., Timothy.
Trin., Trinity.

U. C., Upper Canada.
U. K., United Kingdom.
ult., ultimo.
U. S., United States.

V., Victoria.
v., *versus*, against; *vide*, see.
Va., Virginia.
V. A., Vice-Admiral; Apostolical Vicar.
V. C., Victoria Cross; Vice-Chancellor.
Ven., Venerable (title).
V. G., Vicar-General.
viz., *videlicet.*
vol., volume; vols., volumes.
V. P., Vice-President.
V. R., Victoria Regina.

V. S., Veterinary Surgeon.
Vt., Vermont.

W., west; western postal district.
W. C., Western Central postal district; water-closet.
W. I., West-Indies.
W. long., western longitude.
W. N. W., west-north-west.
Wp., Worship (title of a judge).
Wpful., Worshipful (title).
W. S., writer of the signet.
W. S. W., west-south-west.
wt., weight.

X., Xt., Christ.
Xmas., Christmas.

Y. C., Yacht-Club.
yd., yard; yds., yards.
yr., your; year; yrs., yours.

Z. G., Zoological Gardens.

British Currency, Weights and Measures.
(Monedas, Pesos y Medidas inglesas).

Currency (Monedas).

Sovereign (de oro), Pound Sterling (£) = 20 shillings = 240 pence = 25 pesetas.
Shilling (s.) (de plata) = 12 pence = 1,25 pesetas.
Penny (d.) (de cobre) = 4 farthings = 10,42 céntimos.
Guinea (de oro) = 21 shillings = 26,25 pesetas.
Crown (de plata) = 5 shillings = 6,25 pesetas.
Florin (de plata) = 2 shillings = 2,50 pesetas.
Papel-moneda: Billetes del Banco de Inglaterra, en series de 5, 10, 20, 50 and 100 pounds sterling.

Weights (Pesos).

Troy pound (lb.) = 12 ounces = 373,25 gramos.
Avoirdupoids pound, avdp. = 16 ounces = 454 gramos.
Ounce (oz.) = 16 drams = 28,33 gramos.
Dram = 1,77 gramos.
Hundredweight (cwt.) = 50,803 kilogramos.
Ton = 20 hundredweight = 1016 kilogramos.

Linear Measure (Medidas longitudinales).

Yard = 3 feet = 9,15 decímetros.
Foot = 12 inches = 3,05 decímetross.
Inch = 2,54 centímetros.
Ell = 1¼ yard = 1,144 metro.

Fathom = 2 yards = 1,83 metro.
Cable-length = 120 fathoms = 219,00 metros.
Furlong = 220 yards = 201,3 metros.
British Mile = 1760 yards = 1,609 kilómetros.
Sea-Mile = 1/60 0 = 1,855 kilómetros.

Dry Measure (Medidas para áridos).

Imperial Quarter = 8 bushels = 2,908 hectolitros.
Bushel = 36,35 litros.

Liquid Measure (Medidas para líquidos).

Imperial Gallon = 4,543 litros.
Imperial Quart = ¼ gallon = 1,136 litros.
Imperial Pint = ½ Quart = 0,568 litro.

Square Measure (Medidas agrarias).

Square Yard = 8,36 decímetros cuadrados.
Square Pole = 30¼ square yards = 25,29 metros cuadrados.
Acre of land = 160 square poles = 4840 square yards = 40,46 áreas.
30 acres = 12 hectáreas.
640 acres = 1 square mile = 259 hectáreas.

Cubic Measure (Medidas cúbicas).

Cubic yard = 27 cubic feet = 8,69 decímetros cúbicos. metros cúbicos.
Cubic foot = 144 cubic inches = 3,32 decímetros cúbicos.
Cubic inch = 2,66 centímetros cúbicos.